CONTEMPORARY
NOVELISTS

Contemporary Writers Series

Contemporary Dramatists
Contemporary Literary Critics
Contemporary Novelists
  (including short story writers)
Contemporary Poets
Contemporary World Writers

CONTEMPORARY NOVELISTS

SIXTH EDITION

PREFACE TO THE SIXTH EDITION
MALCOLM BRADBURY

EDITOR
SUSAN WINDISCH BROWN

DISCARDED

ST. JAMES PRESS
An ITP Information/Reference Group Company

I(T)P
Changing the Way the World Learns

NEW YORK • LONDON • BONN • BOSTON • DETROIT • MADRID
MELBOURNE • MEXICO CITY • PARIS • SINGAPORE • TOKYO
TORONTO • WASHINGTON • ALBANY NY • BELMONT CA • CINCINNATI OH

Susan Windisch Brown, *Editor*
Christine Ferran, John Taylor Howard, *Contributing Editors*

ST. JAMES PRESS STAFF

Michael J. Tyrkus, *Project Editor*

Margaret Mazurkiewicz, *Associate Editor*
Laura Standley Berger, Nicolet V. Elert, Miranda H. Ferrara, Janice Jorgensen, *Contributing Editors*

Peter M. Gareffa, *Managing Editor*

Mary Beth Trimper, *Production Director*
Shanna Heilveil, *Production Assistant*
Cynthia Baldwin, *Art Director*

Victoria B. Cariappa, *Research Manager*
Barbara McNeil, *Research Specialist*

∞™ This book is printed on acid-free paper that meets the minimum requirements of American National Standard for Information Sciences—Permanence Paper for Printed Library Materials, ANSI Z39.48-1984.

Library of Congress Catalog Card Number 95-36181
ISBN 1-55862-189-X
Printed in the United States of America

I(T)P™ Gale Research Inc., an International Thomson Publishing Company.
ITP logo is a trademark under license.

10 9 8 7 6 5 4 3 2 1

CONTENTS

PREFACE

If, as Mark Twain famously protested, the rumours of his death in the press were greatly exaggerated, so have been the endless and innumerable rumours of the death of the contemporary novel. Its demise has been announced so often the epitaphs would fill a very large cathedral, and they have continued to multiply in our own age of pluralism, postmodernism, and virtual reality. Among the most striking was Marshall McLuhan's prediction in the 1960s that the Gutenberg Galaxy had imploded, the age of print-based culture ended, in short, that new visual technologies meant the death of the book. The novel—the imaginative form that can surely be said to have begun with the appearance of Miguel de Cervantes' *Don Quixote* in 1605, flourished in the 18th century right across Europe, and described much of the western 19th century to itself—had been through more than one fundamental revolution when McLuhan made his prophecy. Not least there was the revolution of the Modern: with its new emphases on psychology, uncertainty, relativity, the fluidity of consciousness, and the infolding of time, the 20th century transformed the underlying formulae of the genre. "I have an idea that I will invent a new name for my books to supplant 'novel,'" Virginia Woolf wrote in her diary, responding to this, "A new —— by Virginia Woolf." But of all the prophecies of change McLuhan's was the most formidable, and the most dismal: not just the Death of the Novel, or the Death of the Author, but the demise of the technology on which it all depends: the Death of the Book.

The later 20th century has spent much of its time disproving the truth of McLuhan's assertion—or showing it to be true only in part. There is no doubt that the later twentieth century has seen a massive technological and image revolution—one that has changed the status and the nature of the novel, the role of writing, and the book. What the age of the new technologies has not done is dispense with the book altogether. In fact many, many more novels are now written, and a good many more are now published, than ever before in world history. They come from a far wider range of cultural sources and a much vaster span of the world—making the very task of listing and chronicling the most interesting and significant figures, in a volume like this one, ever more difficult. The new technologies have, of course, transformed the content of writing, the way in which writers write it (pen to word processor in a couple of literary generations), the scale of its distribution, the way in which it is promoted, purchased, and read (or, in the age of the audio-book, listened to). In the course of my own writing lifetime (I began to write fiction in the 1950s), the transformation has been massive. I grew up in what was still essentially a high literary culture, with an already established sense of the writer, the genre, the fictional tradition. What we have seen is the explosion of a postmodern pluri-culture in which all of these elements have been challenged. Traditions slide over borders, national cultures reach seamlessly one into another. The genres of narrative, newly teased and tested in the experimentalism of the 1960s (the French *nouveau roman,* American postmodern fiction, Latin American and Eastern European magical realism), have grown plural and fluid.

Postmodern culture has not to displaced or eliminated the novel, but rather the reverse. It has changed the fictional contract, shifted the ambience. On the one hand, there is the world of the multi-media: film and television, the CD-ROM and the VDU, the Internet and the Information Superhighway, the peripatetic writer and the world-aware reader. On the other, there is the whole rich history of narrative and genre, stored in the novels of the past and extended and developed into the novels of the present, gratifying the everlasting need—which has intensified rather than diminished in our plural and image-hungry world—for narrative, stories, myths, and dreams. The visual media have certainly not displaced the novel; it's reckoned, for instance, that three-quarters of our movies are based on novels, old or new. In turn funds of narrative and the riches of the novel's storytelling have been extended by the visual media, which have had a great impact on the writing of fiction. The crucial point is that, in an age rich in signs, images, and cultural commodities of every kind, not just the book but the genre of the novel has survived; indeed one striking feature of modern culture is the appetite for new, and old, fiction. And the novel's classic function—of exploring, at the hands of one distinctive author, the potential of its own form and of the kind of place the world has been and is now becoming—has survived and developed too.

Today it's more than 50 years since the Modernist novel ended. The last monumental work was surely James Joyce's *Finnegans Wake,* which appeared in February 1939, a few months before the outbreak of the Second World War in Europe. When, after 1945, the novel attempted to reconstruct itself, a large part of the new tradition laid down in the first part of the century had been broken. Modernism acquired a classic status; however, the novel of the world after the wake, the world of Cold War, the Holocaust, and nuclear anxiety, was largely founded on a sense of discontinuity from its inheritance, a different set of ideologies and perception. For this reason the general character of fiction after the Modern movement has been strangely hard to grasp and define. Many major writers appeared: Alesandr Sozenitsyn and Gunther Grass, Saul Bellow and Thomas Pynchon, Doris Lessing and William Golding, Samuel Beckett and Nathalie Sarraute, Italo Calvino and Umberto Eco, Patrick White and Chinua Achebe, Nadine Gordimer and Toni Morrison. But it would be hard to say what as novelists they shared stylistically in common—except for the clear conviction that the novel remained a powerful and commanding instrument of human expression. Though some postmodern writers in the West, like John Barth, playfully commented two decades back on "the literature of exhaustion," the tiredness of myths, the used-upness of stories, others continued to write of the harsh texture of history, the threat to human existence in the time of potential nuclear annihilation, or the oppressions of politics.

In fact the general impression that has been left, as the years have passed and the decades have rolled, is not so much of an era of exhaustion but of new plenitude. The changing shape of the late 20th century world—the collapse of European empires, the rise of America and Russia as superpowers, the oppression in Eastern Europe, the emergence of new nations into political and cultural confidence, the change in racial relations, the rise of feminism—transformed the whole sphere of history in which fictions were set. New cultures, new histories, new mythologies, new folklores made their way into the novel, and in a time of increased global interaction and migration many novels became what Salman Rushdie has called "migrants' tales." Some of our most interesting narratives, like John Barth's own, splendidly dealt with the playfulness of fiction, the tricksiness of its illusion. Meantime other writers elsewhere used the novel to confront the historical and political crises of the age: the shame of the gulags, the repression of Central and Eastern Europe, the magical process of constructing an imaginative history for Latin America or post-imperial India or Africa, the changing map of cultural origins (African American fiction, Native American fiction), the changing role of the genders—and the changed world that has just begun to shape and steer history after the coming down of the Berlin Wall in November 1989.

In the world after Modernism, most writers of fiction have been anxious about whether the novel still had a place in the sun, a fresh story to tell. One important part of the achievement of recent fiction has been to re-explore the textures, strategies, and genres of the novel itself; and what we can now see in recent fiction is an extended era of significant experiment—though much of it has remained unnamed or else very vaguely named (Postmodernism, Magical Realism, Dirty Realism, and so on). But no less important has been the continued power of our novelists to confront and explore our shifting human geography and our changing history. At the end of centuries—the place where we are now—the sense of narrative and history generally tends to accelerate. In such great transitions, fiction often becomes both retrospective and newly original. The genres generally go through a playful redefinition; the measure of the past and future is taken afresh. Our ideas of history and identity shift, our notions of race, culture, and gender transform, our notion of the familiar—as indeed, in the west, of the family itself—becomes less familiar. I have always believed that the strength of the novel lies in its power to tell us, with all the self-conscious trickery of a fiction, new stories that give us something of the measure of our historical situation, explore our conscience and our consciousness, and probe our sense of the past and the future.

Today the novel—a genre that particularly developed in Europe and America in the past two centuries—is practiced worldwide. It comes from many cultures, and many of the meeting places of cultures. Its settings and its mythic funds are wide, its languages many (though English plays a dominant role right across world fiction, and London and New York remain prime centers of publication), the genres are many and varied—from high literary fiction through to the historical romance, the crime story, horror, science fiction, and future fantasy. In the great shopping mall world of pluri-culture, these genres leak freely into one another—exactly as the various layers and categories of culture, from the avant garde to the populist, constantly interpenetrate one another. Writers no longer have the certainty of a clear tradition behind them. For most contemporary writers, the fictional situation now more resembles that celebrated in the 1860s by Henry James, when he remarked to a friend that American writers had become, unlike Europeans, the "heirs to all the ages": "we can deal freely with forms of civilization not our own, can pick and choose and assimilate and in short (aesthetically etc.) claim our property wherever we find it." In consequence, our writing is infinitely various, and so one of the values of a book like this lies in its range of entries, its width of record. It covers and details the life and the work of a great many of the best living practitioners of fiction in English over a number of different literary generations. It displays many different views of the practice and form of the novel in the invaluable comments made by writers on their own work. The scale and variety of its roll-call tells us that fiction is still a primary adventure of the imagination.

Around a hundred years ago, as the last century ended, Henry James reflected on "The Future of Fiction" in an essay of that title. "It has arrived, in truth, the novel, late at self-consciousness, but it has done its utmost ever since to make up for lost opportunities." It had also, he said, become "the most surprising example . . . of swift and extravagant growth, a development beyond the very measure of every early appearance. It is a form that had a fortune so little to have been foretold in its christening." In short, the fairies at the birth of the novel seemed to have had little notion of what it would grow into. The point James was making was that innumerable forms, genres, cultures, and types of story were making their way into the novel. A hundred years on, this stays true. The novel is many things: a form of truth, (a "bright book of life," as D.H. Lawrence put it) and a popular entertainment; a social record, and a remarkable fantasy; a political fable, and a self-destructing game of language. James wrote his words when literacy was expanding and the marketplace growing; we ourselves write in the age of computer-literacy and the shimmering world of the global village. But, for the time being at least, the lesson seems clear. The novel is still a surprising example of swift and extravagant growth, and at its best it remains about the finest, most discovering means we have of exploring ourselves, our times, our crises, and the changing atlas of our universe. The novelists here have charted a good part of the passage from the end of the Second World War to the coming of the third millennium, and they have, I believe, set the novel on course for another age of adventure into the virtual realities of the future.

—MALCOLM BRADBURY

EDITOR'S NOTE

The selection of writers included in this book is based on the recommendations of the advisers listed on page xii.

The entry for each writer consists of a biography, a complete list of separately published books, and a signed essay. In addition, entrants were invited to comment on their work.

Original British and United States editions of all books have been listed; other editions are listed only if they are first editions. All uncollected short stories published since the entrant's last collection, plus others mentioned by the entrant, have been listed; in those cases where an uncollected story was originally published in a magazine and later in an anthology, we have tended to list the anthology. As a rule all books written about the entrant are listed in the Critical Studies section; the reviews and essays listed have been recommended by the entrant.

We would like to thank the entrants and contributors for their patience and cooperation in helping us compile this book.

ADVISERS

Walter Allen
Bernard Bergonzi
Earle Birney
Elmer Borklund
Malcolm Bradbury
Richard Brown
Anthony Burgess
D.D.C. Chambers
Richard Corballis
Helen Daniel
Margaret Drabble
Dorothy Driver
Peter Ferran
Leslie A. Fiedler
Roy Fuller
James Gindin
D.C.R.A. Goonetilleke
Albert Guerard
James B. Hall
John Hawkes
Laurie Hergenhan
Susan Hill
A. Norman Jeffares
Bruce King
Jerome Klinkowitz
James Korges
Hermione Lee

John Lehmann
Harry Levin
David Lodge
David Madden
Harry T. Moore
J.E. Morpurgo
Stephen Murray-Smith
Shyamala A. Narayan
W.H. New
Cynthia Ozick
Desmond Pacey
Marge Piercy
Hal Porter
Anthony Powell
Arthur Ravenscroft
John M. Reilly
Kenneth Rexroth
H. Winston Rhodes
Alan Ross
Barney Rosset
Mark Schorer
Tony Tanner
Fay Weldon
Mark Williams
Michael Wood
George Woodcock

CONTRIBUTORS

Stephen Akey
Walter Allen
Patricia Altner
Richard Andersen
Susan Ang
Alvin Aubert
Jane S. Bakerman
John Clement Ball
William C. Bamberger
John Barnes
Ian A. Bell
Samuel I. Bellman
Bruce Bennett
Sally H. Bennett
Bernard Bergonzi
Reginald Berry
Marshall A. Best
William Bittner

William Borden
Elmer Borklund
Frederick Bowers
Malcolm Bradbury
M.E. Bradford
Peter Brigg
Juliette Bright
W.S. Broughton
Lloyd W. Brown
Richard Brown
Lynne Bryer
Harry Bucknall
Herbert C. Burke
Jackie Buxton
Mary Cadogan
Frank Campenni
Charles Caramello
Victoria Carchidi
Frederic I. Carpenter

Hayden Carruth
D.D.C. Chambers
Gerda Charles
Ann Charters
Tracy Chevalier
Shirley Chew
Paul Seiko Chihara
Laurie Clancy
Anderson Clark
Samuel Coale
Loretta Cobb
John Colmer
Tom Colonnese
Judy Cooke
Richard Corballis
John Cotton
Ralph J. Crane
Edmund Cusick
Hallvard Dahlie
Helen Daniel
Barrie Davies
Terence Dawson
Doreen D'Cruz
Leon de Kock
Peter Desy
Susie deVille
Peter Dickinson
R.H.W. Dillard
Dale K. Doepke
David Dowling
Paul A. Doyle
Deborah Duckworth
Klay Dyer
Ursula Edmands
Chester E. Eisinger
Geoffrey Elborn
James A. Emanuel
Michel Fabre
Mark A.R. Facknitz
Richard J. Fein
Brenda R. Ferguson
Peter Ferran
John W. Fiero
John J. Figueroa
M.J. Fitzgerald
Ruel E. Foster
Jill Franks
Anne French
Warren French
Melvin J. Friedman
Lucy Frost
John Fuegi
David Galloway
David Geherin
James Gindin
D.C.R.A. Goonetilleke
Lois Gordon
Pat Gordon-Smith
William Goyen
Marian Gracias
Colin Graham
Sinda Gregory

George Grella
Jessica Griffin
Albert Guerard
Prabhu S. Guptara
Laurie Schwartz Guttenberg
Jay L. Halio
James B. Hall
Joan Wylie Hall
Cherry A. Hankin
John Hanrahan
June Harris
James A. Hart
Sue Hart
Thomas Hastings
Heather B. Hayes
David M. Heaton
John Herbert
Katharine Hodgkin
Janis Butler Holm
Craig Hudziak
Van Ikin
Louis James
A. Norman Jeffares
David K. Jeffrey
Annibel Jenkins
Ron Jenkins
H.R.F. Keating
Margaret Keith
Wendy Robbins Keitner
Peter Kemp
Sandra Kemp
Burton Kendle
Liam Kennedy
Robert F. Kiernan
Bruce King
Nicola King
H. Gustav Klaus
Marcus Klein
Jerome Klinkowitz
Judith C. Kohl
Richard Kostelanetz
Mary M. Lay
Robert Lecker
Thomas LeClair
Chris Leigh
Barry Lewis
Peter Lewis
Stanley W. Lindberg
Bernth Lindfors
Jack Lindsay
Jennifer Livett
Devoney Looser
John Lucas
Robert E. Lynch
Gina Macdonald
Clinton Machann
Ed Madden
Veronica Makowsky
Irving Malin
Paul Marx
Roland Mathias
Brian E. Matthews

John McCormick
Frederick P.W. McDowell
Margaret B. McDowell
John McLeod
Ian McMechan
Kevin McNeilly
John Mepham
Patricia Merivale
Robert E. Mielke
D. Quentin Miller
Stephen Milnes
Naomi Mitchison
Radhika Mohanram
David Montrose
Gerald Moore
Harry T. Moore
Robert A. Morace
Anne Morddel
Robert K. Morris
Eric Muirhead
Heather Murray
Shyamala A. Narayan
W.H. New
Judie Newman
Leslie Norris
Maril Nowak
Robert Nye
Liam O'Brien
D.J. O'Hearn
John O'Leary
Bridget O'Toole
Desmond Pacey
Malcolm Page
Joseph Parisi
Marian Pehowski
Barbara M. Perkins
George Perkins
Frank T. Phipps
Marge Piercy
Jan Pilditch
Sanford Pinsker
Marco Portales
John Povey
Jeremy Poynting
Joanna Price
Lyn Pykett
Isabel Quigly
Arthur Ravenscroft
Sandra Ray
J.C. Reid
John M. Reilly
H. Winston Rhodes
Alan Riach
Karen Robertson
Marilyn Rose
S.A. Rowland
Trevor Royle
Louis D. Rubin, Jr.
Geoff Sadler

Hana Sambrook
David Sanders
Stewart Sanderson
William J. Schafer
Lynda D. Schrecengost
Alexander Scott
Clement Semmler
Linda Semple
Alan R. Shucard
David Shuttleton
Victoria A. Smallman
Angela Smith
Christopher Smith
Curtis C. Smith
Andy Solomon
Eric Solomon
Jane W. Stedman
Caroline Steemson
Carol Simpson Stern
James R. Stevens
Joan Stevens
Brian Stonehill
Victor Strandberg
J.R. Struthers
W.J. Stuckey
Maggi R. Sullivan
Judith Summers
John Sutherland
Arlene Sykes
Anna-Marie Taylor
Roy Thomas
Chris Tiffin
H.M. Tiffin
Philippa Toomey
Shirley Toulson
Nicolas Tredell
C.W. Truesdale
Richard Tuerk
Roland Turner
Susan O'Dell Underwood
Peter G.W. van de Kamp
Penny van Toorn
Aruna Vasudevan
Thomas A. Vogler
William Walsh
Val Warner
Diane Watson
Harold H. Watts
John A. Weigel
Perry D. Westbrook
Margaret Willy
Janet Wilson
Bill Witherup
George Woodcock
Tim Woods
Michael Woolf
Leopoldo Y. Yabes
Heather Zwicker

CONTEMPORARY
NOVELISTS

LIST OF ENTRANTS

Ahmad Abbas
Walter Abish
Peter Abrahams
Chinua Achebe
Kathy Acker
Peter Ackroyd
Alice Adams
Glenda Adams
Richard Adams
Renata Adler
Ama Ata Aidoo
Brian Aldiss
James Aldridge
Lisa Alther
T.M. Aluko
A. Alvarez
Elechi Amadi
Eric Ambler
Kingsley Amis
Martin Amis
Mulk Raj Anand
Rudolfo A. Anaya
Barbara Anderson
Jessica Anderson
I.N.C. Aniebo
Michael Anthony
Ayi Kwei Armah
Jeannette Armstrong
Thea Astley
Margaret Atwood
Louis Auchincloss
Paul Auster

Murray Bail
Paul Bailey
Beryl Bainbridge
Elliott Baker
Nicholson Baker
J.G. Ballard
Lynne Reid Banks
Russell Banks
John Banville
A.L. Barker
Pat Barker
Julian Barnes
Stan Barstow
John Barth
Frederick Barthelme
Jonathan Baumbach
Nina Bawden
Ann Beattie
Stephen Becker
Barry Beckham
Sybille Bedford
Madison Smartt Bell

Saul Bellow
David Benedictus
John Berger
Thomas Berger
Chaim Bermant
Doris Betts
Graham Billing
Rachel Billington
Maeve Binchy
Neil Bissoondath
Caroline Blackwood
Clark Blaise
Burt Blechman
Fred Bodsworth
Vance Bourjaily
John Bowen
Paul Bowles
William Boyd
Clare Boylan
T. Coraghessan Boyle
Malcolm Bradbury
Ray Bradbury
David Bradley
John Ed Bradley
Melvyn Bragg
Sasthi Brata
Errol Brathwaite
André Brink
Erna Brodber
Harold Brodkey
E.M. Broner
Christine Brooke-Rose
Anita Brookner
Brigid Brophy
George Mackay Brown
Rita Mae Brown
Rosellen Brown
Frederick Buechner
James Lee Burke
Alan Burns
William S. Burroughs
Janet Burroway
Frederick Busch
A.S. Byatt

Hortense Calisher
Philip Callow
Marion Campbell
Peter Carey
R.V. Cassill
Brian Castro
David Caute
Fred Chappell
Gerda Charles
Jerome Charyn

Upamanyu Chatterjee
Alan Cheuse
Shimmer Chinodya
Eleanor Clark
Arthur C. Clarke
Austin C. Clarke
Jon Cleary
William Cobb
Jonathan Coe
J.M. Coetzee
Leonard Cohen
Matt Cohen
Barry Cole
Isabel Colegate
Cyrus Colter
Richard Condon
Evan S. Connell, Jr.
David Cook
Lettice Cooper
William Cooper
Robert Coover
Jack Cope
Peter Cowan
Jim Crace
Harry Crews
Michael Crichton
Moira Crone
Ian Cross

David Dabydeen
Blanche d'Alpuget
O.R. Dathorne
Guy Davenport
Lionel Davidson
Robertson Davies
Liam Davison
Jennifer Dawson
Louis de Bernières
Ralph de Boissière
Len Deighton
Samuel R. Delany
Don DeLillo
Anita Desai
Boman Desai
G.V. Desani
Shashi Deshpande
Joan Didion
Stephen Dixon
E.L. Doctorow
J.P. Donleavy
Ellen Douglas
Roddy Doyle
Margaret Drabble
Robert Drewe
C.J. Driver
Allen Drury
Andre Dubus
Marilyn Duckworth
Alan Duff
Maureen Duffy
Elaine Dundy
Nell Dunn

John Gregory Dunne
Dorothy Dunnett
Geoffrey Dutton

William Eastlake
Cyprian Ekwensi
Stevan Eldred-Grigg
Stanley Elkin
Janice Elliott
Alice Thomas Ellis
Bret Easton Ellis
James Ellroy
David Ely
Buchi Emecheta
Isobel English
Louise Erdrich
Ahmed Essop

Zoë Fairbairns
Nuruddin Farah
Beverley Farmer
Howard Fast
Sebastian Faulks
Irvin Faust
Raymond Federman
Elaine Feinstein
Leslie A. Fiedler
Eva Figes
Timothy Findley
Tibor Fischer
Penelope Fitzgerald
Thomas Flanagan
Shelby Foote
Jesse Hill Ford
Richard Ford
Leon Forrest
Margaret Forster
Frederick Forsyth
David Foster
John Fowles
Janet Frame
Ronald Frame
Dick Francis
Michael Frayn
Nicolas Freeling
Gillian Freeman
Marilyn French
Bruce Jay Friedman

William Gaddis
Ernest J. Gaines
Mavis Gallant
Janice Galloway
Kenneth Gangemi
Helen Garner
George Garrett
William H. Gass
Maggie Gee
Maurice Gee
Martha Gellhorn
Zulfikar Ghose
Amitav Ghosh

Graeme Gibson
William Gibson
Ellen Gilchrist
Brendan Gill
Brian Glanville
Julian Gloag
Douglas Glover
Rumer Godden
Dave Godfrey
Gail Godwin
Herbert Gold
William Goldman
Nadine Gordimer
Giles Gordon
Mary Gordon
Robert Gover
Patricia Grace
Winston Graham
Shirley Ann Grau
Alasdair Gray
Stephen Richard Gray
Joanne Greenberg
John Grisham
Doris Grumbach
Albert Guerard
Romesh Gunesekera
Allan Gurganis

Arthur Hailey
Russell Haley
James B. Hall
Rodney Hall
Marion Halligan
Hammond Innes
Clifford Hanley
Barry Hannah
Ron Hansen
Elizabeth Hardwick
Frank Hardy
Mark Harris
Wilson Harris
Jim Harrison
Elizabeth Harrower
Nicholas Hasluck
Jon Hassler
Epeli Hau'ofa
Marianne Hauser
John Hawkes
Shirley Hazzard
Roy A.K. Heath
Robert Hellenga
Joseph Heller
David Helwig
Aidan Higgins
George V. Higgins
Carol Hill
Susan Hill
Noel Hilliard
Thomas Hinde
Barry Hines
Edward Hoagland
Russell Hoban

Jack Hodgins
Alice Hoffman
Desmond Hogan
Alan Hollinghurst
Hugh Hood
Christopher Hope
Janette Turner Hospital
Elizabeth Jane Howard
Maureen Howard
David Hughes
Keri Hulme
William Humphrey
Emyr Humphreys
Evan Hunter
Kristin Hunter

Michael Ignatieff
Witi Ihimaera
David Ireland
John Irving
Kazuo Ishiguro
Festus Iyayi

Dan Jacobson
Howard Jacobson
Kelvin Christopher James
P.D. James
Tama Janowitz
Robin Jenkins
Ruth Prawer Jhabvala
Charles Johnson
Denis Johnson
Diane Johnson
Jennifer Johnston
Elizabeth Jolley
Gayl Jones
Glyn Jones
Gwyn Jones
Madison Jones
Marion Patrick Jones
Mervyn Jones
Erica Jong
Neil Jordan
Arun Joshi
Gabriel Josipovici
Ward Just

Johanna Kaplan
Steve Katz
Molly Keane
Victor Kelleher
William Melvin Kelley
M.T. Kelly
James Kelman
Thomas Keneally
A.L. Kennedy
William Kennedy
Ken Kesey
Fiona Kidman
Benedict Kiely
Jamaica Kincaid
Francis King

Thomas King
Maxine Hong Kingston
W.P. Kinsella
John Knowles
Elizabeth Knox
C.J. Koch
Joy Kogawa
Bernard Kops
Richard Kostelanetz
Robert Kroetsch
Hanif Kureishi

George Lamming
Mary Lavin
John le Carré
SKY Lee
Ursula K. Le Guin
Alan Lelchuk
Elmore Leonard
Doris Lessing
Ira Levin
Norman Levine
Janet Lewis
Catherine Lim
Emanuel Litvinoff
Penelope Lively
David Lodge
Earl Lovelace
Jack Ludwig
Alison Lurie
Morris Lurie
Andrew Lytle

Robie Macauley
Bernard MacLaverty
David Madden
Norman Mailer
Clarence Major
Manohar Malgonkar
David Malouf
Jerre Mangione
Wolf Mankowitz
Hilary Mantel
Kamala Markandaya
Wallace Markfield
David Markson
Daphne Marlatt
Adam Mars-Jones
Owen Marshall
Paule Marshall
Bobbie Ann Mason
Allan Massie
Hilary Masters
Peter Mathers
Harry Mathews
Jack Matthews
Peter Matthiessen
Elizabeth Mavor
William Maxwell
Patrick McCabe
Cormac McCarthy
Sue McCauley

Joseph McElroy
Ian McEwan
John McGahern
Patrick McGrath
Thomas McGuane
Jay McInerney
Larry McMurtry
James A. McPherson
Candia McWilliam
Barbara Mertz
John Metcalf
Leonard Michaels
James A. Michener
O.E. Middleton
Stanley Middleton
Alex Miller
Steven Millhauser
Susan Minot
Mark Mirsky
Rohinton Mistry
Joseph Mitchell
Julian Mitchell
W.O. Mitchell
Naomi Mitchison
Timothy Mo
N. Scott Momaday
Paul Monette
Michael Moorcock
Brian Moore
Lorrie Moore
Frank Moorhouse
Wright Morris
Toni Morrison
John Mortimer
Penelope Mortimer
Nicholas Mosley
Es'kia Mphahlele
Mudrooroo
Bharati Mukherjee
John Munonye
Alice Munro
Iris Murdoch
Gerald Murnane

Chaman Nahal
V.S. Naipaul
R.K. Narayan
Gloria Naylor
Njabulo Ndebele
Jay Neugeboren
P.H. Newby
C.J. Newman
Charles Newman
Ngugi wa Thiong'o
Hugh Nissenson
Lawrence Norfolk
Robert Nye

Joyce Carol Oates
Edna O'Brien
Tim O'Brien
Julia O'Faolain

Ben Okri
Tillie Olsen
Michael Ondaatje
Vincent O'Sullivan
Cynthia Ozick

Grace Paley
Charles Palliser
Edith Pargeter
Orlando Patterson
Bill Pearson
Anne Perry
Kathrin Perutz
Jerzy Peterkiewicz
Harry Mark Petrakis
Ann Petry
Caryl Phillips
Jayne Anne Phillips
Marge Piercy
David Plante
James Plunkett
Frederik Pohl
Chaim Potok
Anthony Powell
J.F. Powers
Richard Powers
David Pownall
Terry Pratchett
Reynolds Price
V.S. Pritchett
David Profumo
E. Annie Proulx
James Purdy
Mario Puzo
Thomas Pynchon

Rajo Rao
Frederic Raphael
Simon Raven
Piers Paul Read
John Rechy
Ishmael Reed
Vic Reid
Ruth Rendell
Anne Rice
Tom Robbins
Michèle Roberts
Kim Stanley Robinson
Marilynne Robinson
Peter Robinson
Mary Robison
Daphne Rooke
Sinclair Ross
Judith Rossner
Leo Rosten
Henry Roth
Philip Roth
Bernice Rubens
Jane Rule
Michael Rumaker
Salman Rushdie
Joanna Russ

Nayantara Sahgal
Lisa St. Aubin de Teran
Garth St. Omer
J.D. Salinger
Andrew Salkey
May Sarton
Thomas Savage
Susan Fromberg Schaeffer
Budd Schulberg
I. Allan Sealy
Carolyn See
Hubert Selby, Jr.
Will Self
Olive Senior
Vikram Seth
Mary Lee Settle
Maurice Shadbolt
Tom Sharpe
Wilfrid Sheed
Carol Shields
Bapsi Sidhwa
Clancy Sigal
Leslie Marmon Silko
Alan Sillitoe
Robert Silverberg
Mona Simpson
Andrew Sinclair
Khushwant Singh
F. Sionil Jose
Carolyn Slaughter
Jane Smiley
Emma Smith
Iain Crichton Smith
Susan Sontag
Gilbert Sorrentino
Terry Southern
Wole Soyinka
Muriel Spark
Alan Spence
Colin Spencer
Elizabeth Spencer
C.K. Stead
John Steffler
Michael Stephens
Daniel Stern
Richard G. Stern
Robert Stone
David Storey
Randolph Stow
Francis Stuart
William Styron
Ronald Sukenick
Graham Swift

Amy Tan
Emma Tennant
Shashi Tharoor
Alexander Theroux
Paul Theroux
Audrey Thomas
D.M. Thomas
Colin Thubron

Gillian Tindall
Peter Tinniswood
Miriam Tlali
Barbara Trapido
Rose Tremain
William Trevor
Rachel Trickett
Niccoló Tucci
Frank Tuohy
George Turner
Amos Tutuola
Anne Tyler

Barry Unsworth
John Updike
Edward Upward
Leon Uris
Fred Urquhart

Laurens van der Post
Peter Vansittart
M.G. Vassanji
Gore Vidal
Noel Virtue
Kurt Vonnegut, Jr.

David Wagoner
Dan Wakefield
Alice Walker
Margaret Walker
Mildred Walker
Marina Warner
Keith Waterhouse
David Watmough
Ian Wedde

James Welch
Fay Weldon
Eudora Welty
Albert Wendt
Mary Wesley
Anthony C. West
Morris West
Paul West
William Wharton
Edmund White
John Edgar Wideman
Rudy Wiebe
Michael Wilding
John A. Williams
Connie Willis
A.N. Wilson
Colin Wilson
Sloan Wilson
Jeanette Winterson
Tim Winton
Larry Woiwode
Tom Wolfe
Tobias Wolff
Herman Wouk
Charles Wright
Rudolph Wurlitzer

James Yaffe
Helen Yglesias
Jose Yglesias
Al Young
Marguerite Young
Sol Yurick

Roger Zelazny

A

ABBAS, (Khwaja) Ahmad

Nationality: Indian. **Born:** Panipat, Punjab, 7 June 1914. **Education:** Hali Muslim High School; Aligarh Muslim University, B.A. 1933, LL.B. 1935. **Family:** Married Mujtabai Khatoon in 1942 (died 1958); one daughter. **Career:** Reporter and sub-editor, 1936-39, and editor of the Sunday edition and columnist, 1939-47, Bombay *Chronicle*. Since 1947 contributing columnist ("Last Page"), *Blitz* magazine, Bombay; since 1951 proprietor, Naya Sansar film production company, Bombay. Leader, Indian Film Delegation, U.S.S.R., 1954. **Awards:** *Hindustan Times* prize, 1950; President of India's gold medal, for film, 1964; Padma Shree, 1969; Haryana State Robe of Honour, 1969. **Address:** c/o Blitz Publications, Canada Building, 3rd Floor, D.N. Road, Bombay 400 001, India.

PUBLICATIONS

Novels

Tomorrow Is Ours! Bombay, Popular Book Depot, 1943; as *Divided Heart,* New Delhi, Paradise, 1968.
Defeat for Death: A Story Without Names. Baroda, Padmaja, 1944.
Blood and Stones. Bombay, Hind Kitabs, 1947.
Inqilab. Bombay, Jaico, 1955.
When Night Falls. New Delhi, Hind, 1968.
Mera Naam, Joker. New Delhi, Hind, 1970.
Maria. New Delhi, Hind, 1972.
Boy Meets Girl. New Delhi, Sterling, 1973.
Bobby. New Delhi, Sterling, 1973.
Distant Dream. New Delhi, Sterling, 1975.
The World Is My Village. New Delhi, Ajanta, 1983.

Short Stories

Not All Lies! Privately printed, 1945.
Rice and Other Stories. Bombay, Kutub, 1947.
Cages of Freedom and Other Stories. Bombay, Hind Kitabs, 1952.
One Thousand Nights on a Bed of Stones and Other Stories. Bombay, Jaico, 1957.
The Black Sun and Other Stories. Bombay, Jaico, 1963.
The Most Beautiful Woman in the World. New Delhi, Paradise, 1968.
The Walls of Glass. New Delhi, Himalaya, 1977.
Men and Women. New Delhi, NV, 1977.
The Thirteenth Victim. New Delhi, Amar Prakashan, 1986.

Plays

Zubeida (produced Bombay, 1944).
Invitation to Immortality. Bombay, Padma, 1944.
Lal Gulab Ki Wapsi (produced Bombay, 1964).
Barrister-at-Law: A Play about the Early Life of Mahatma Gandhi. New Delhi, Orient, 1977.

Screenplays: *Naya Sansar,* 1941; *Dr. Kotnis,* 1945; *Dharti Ke Lal,* 1946; *Awara,* 1951; *Anhonee,* 1951; *Rahi,* 1952; *Munna,* 1954; *Shri 420,* 1955; *Pardesi,* 1957; *Chardil Char Rahen,* 1959; *Shehar Aur Sapna,* 1963; *Hamara Gaar,* 1964; *Aasman Bahal,* 1966; *Bambai Raat Ki Bahon Mein,* 1968; *Saat Hindustani,* 1969; *Mera Naam, Joker,* 1970; *Do Boond Pani,* 1971; *Bobby,* 1973; *Achanak,* 1973; *Faaslah,* 1974.

Other

Outside India: The Adventures of a Roving Reporter. New Delhi, Hali, 1938.
Let India Fight for Freedom. Bombay, Sound Magazine, 1943.
An Indian Looks at America. Bombay, Thacker, 1943.
And One Did Not Come Back: The Story of the Congress Medical Mission to China. Bombay, Sound Magazine, 1944.
Report to Gandhiji, with N.G. Yog. Bombay, Hind Kitabs, 1944.
I Write as I Feel (selections from Bombay *Chronicle*). Bombay, Hind Kitabs, 1948.
Kashmir Fights for Freedom. Bombay, Kutub, 1948.
China Can Make It. Bombay, Bhatt, 1952.
In the Image of Mao Tse-tung. Bombay, People's Publishing House, 1953.
Face to Face with Khrushchev. New Delhi, Rajpal, 1960.
Till We Reach the Stars: The Story of Yuri Gagarin. London, Asia Publishing House, 1961; New York, Asia Publishing House, 1962.
Indira Ghandi: Return of the Red Rose. Bombay, Popular Prakashan, 1966.
That Woman: Her Seven Years in Power. New Delhi, Indian Book Company, 1973; revised edition, as *That Woman: Indira Gandhi's Ten Years in Power,* 1976.
Face to Face with Indira Gandhi, with R.K. Karanjia. New Delhi, Chetana, 1974.
Jawaharlal Nehru: Portrait of an Integrated Indian. New Delhi, National Council of Educational Research and Training, 1974.
I Am Not an Island: An Experiment in Autobiography. New Delhi, Vikas, and Columbia, South Asia Books, 1977.
The Mad, Mad, Mad World of Indian Films. New Delhi, Hind, 1977.
Four Friends. New Delhi, Arnold-Heinemann, 1977.
20th March 1977: A Day Like Any Other. New Delhi, Vikas, 1978.
Janata in a Jam? Bombay, Jaico, 1978.
The Naxalites. New Delhi, Lok, 1979.
Sarojini Naidu: An Introduction to a Fascinating Personality. Bombay, Bharatiya Vidya Bhavan, 1980.
Bread, Beauty and Revolution, Being a Chronological Selection from the Last Pages 1947 to 1981. New Delhi, Marwah, 1982.
Indira Gandhi: The Last Post. Bombay, Popular Prakashan, and London, Sangam, 1985.
Bombay, My Bombay! The Love Story of the City. New Delhi, Ajanta, 1987.

Translator, *I Cannot Die,* by Krishnan Chandar. Poona, Kutub, 1943(?).
Translator, *Shadows Speak,* by A.H. Sahir Ludhianvi. Bombay, P.P.H. Bookstall, 1958.

*

Critical Study: *The Novels of Khwaja Ahmad Abbas* by Ahmad Hasib, Delhi, Seema, 1987.

Ahmad Abbas comments:

(1991) Highbrow literary critics in India have sometimes sneeringly labeled my novels and short stories as "mere journalese." The fact that most of them are inspired by aspects of the contemporary historical reality, as sometimes chronicled in the press, is sufficient to put them beyond the pale of literary creation. I have no quarrel with the critics. Maybe I am an unredeemed journalist and reporter, masquerading as a writer of fiction. But I have always believed that while the inner life of man undoubtedly is, and should be, the primary concern of literature, this inner personal life impinges upon the life of the community—and of humanity—at every critical turning point of human experience. "No man is an island . . ." said John Donne, and one may add that even if he was, no island is free from the inroads of the sea, as no man is free from the impact of social forces and the life around him.

This interaction of the individual in society, both in its psychological and social complexity, is of particular interest to me as a writer. It has inspired, provoked, or colored most of what I have written.

Mirrored in my works are many fragments of our recent history—the war, the religious riots and the killings, the partition, the post-freedom years of disillusionment, of the new hopes engendered, and problems raised, by the industrialization and mechanization of agriculture. But I do hope I have also revealed glimpses of the "inner life" of my contemporaries, the people of a new India, in their moments of tenderness and passion, of frustration and exultation, as they evolve from the passive (but by no means ignoble) fatalism, so characteristic of the Indian peasant rooted in tradition, towards the hopeful dynamism, the remarkable adaptability and the willingness to change, which, paradoxically enough, is also an Indian characteristic.

If there is one thing that I have tried consistently to do in my novels and stories, it is to give the readers a little peep into the hearts and minds, the inner life, of my contemporaries and fellow Indians, to show that their life is being influenced and changed and reshaped by the historical and social forces that are greater than us and our "destiny."

*   *   *

Ahmad Abbas is one of the most popular Indian writers in English. He is, however, one of the least regarded of them from a scholarly point of view. This is due partly to the uneven quality of the large amount of material he has produced, and partly to the popular forms in which he works. His populist orientation is evident from the fact that he has chosen to write much of his work in English specifically because he wants to communicate with Indians from all linguistic backgrounds (according to the last census, India has over a thousand languages: Hindi and English are the two official languages, but Hindi, though used by 40 percent of the country, is the mother-tongue of only one region; English, though used by a far smaller number—only around ten per cent of the country—has the "advantage" of being equally foreign to all parts of the country! All educated Indians know English, but not all educated Indians know Hindi, despite considerable governmental pressure to learn the language). Indian intellectuals like to pride themselves on their secularism. Abbas has not been greatly helped by the fact that he comes from a Muslim background.

The forms in which Abbas has written include short stories, novels, plays, and Hindi-language filmscripts for the huge Indian film industry. Elite snobbishness toward Indian films—with their song-and-fight formulas and their pastiche of fabulous Indian (rather than realist Western) conventions—has no doubt helped to deprive Abbas of the right credentials to be taken seriously by literary scholars. Abbas's favorite genre, the short story, does not have an enthusiastic following among Indian literary critics either, and his use of English is not marked by that Oxbridge ease so beloved of some Indian critics; nor does he seem to have had the inclination to theorize about his linguistic experiments in the way of other writers, such as Mulk Raj Anand and Raja Rao. What Abbas has been trying to produce is genuinely home-grown work which speaks to the people. In a hierarchical country like India, it is not surprising that his work should, then, not speak to scholars and critics. If it is pastiche the people want, as in the Indian cinema, he is willing to work within the enormous constraints imposed by the conventions of Indian pastiche in order to get his message across.

The message is not easy to decipher, because he has been a Gandhian, is now better-known for his sympathy with the Soviet Union and, in an article published not long ago, he summed up his position as consisting in the almost Romantic words, "Bread, Beauty and Revolution." The first of Abbas's collections of short stories in English, *Not All Lies!*, typifies his output. It is primarily satirical, and attacks hypocrisy and the unscrupulously mercenary character of the middle classes. Several of the stories are sharply anti-British. But his anti-British sentiments are consequent upon his concern with the social and political issues facing the country. In this sense, Abbas has remained a Gandhian: all his work is rooted in a concern for India; patriotism and the unity and welfare of the country seem to be the driving force of all of his work. Abbas is an Indian even before he is a Gandhian. The different way in which he has at various times put his beliefs shows, not a change in fundamentals, but his view of what is of greatest concern to the country at that moment. No other English-language writer in the country uses its history so fully. No other writer knows so well the currents and moods of contemporary India. No one else speaks so effectively to them. He turned the script of his successful film *Saat Hindustani* (Seven Indians) into a novel, *Maria,* which features companions in an undercover operation who help liberate the Portuguese colony of Goa in 1961 and reunite it with India. After the success of the operation, six of them scatter to other parts of India. Seven years later, Maria is ill, and, feeling herself near death, sends telegrams to the others to ask them to see her one last time. Caught up in their own lives, it takes them some time to respond and, by the time they arrive, Maria is already dead. When they meet at the graveside, they are alienated from each other by the sorts of concerns and tensions that have fueled regionalist politics in India but, recalling their mutual affection in the past and their comradeship in the struggle to liberate Goa, they are brought to a reconciliation. *The Naxalites* is one of the few attempts by an Indian writer to explore the history, psychology, and relative success of the Maoist revolutionary movement which attracted some of the most intelligent and well-educated young Indians to its cadres and required extensive operations by the Indian Army before it was suppressed.

What saves Abbas's work from being merely propagandist is precisely his love for his subjects, for he loves them in their strengths as well as their weaknesses. Mulk Raj Anand once said that Abbas "grasps the weaknesses of his characters amid their strengths." That is Abbas's strength as a writer. His strength as an *Indian* writer is that he brings to India, similarly, "the only kind of love which can redeem its present wretchedness and stretch out to its unexplored future."

Abbas's first English-language novel, *Tomorrow Is Ours!* celebrates a 20-year-old heroine, Parvati. Beautiful and sharply conscious of social problems, she is forced to give up her medical studies because of the death of her mother. Becoming a dancer in a different part of the country, she falls in love with one of the regular patrons, Dr. Shrikant. Shrikant's rather conservative mother, Ramadevi, does not approve of Parvati. However, the couple get married in a civil ceremony, and Ramadevi needs to be almost at death's door from injury during the bombardment of Calcutta (the action is set during World War II) before she relents. This novel's bold opposition to caste prejudice was, at that time, fairly new in Indian literature. In creating a modern couple who ignore tradition and get away with it, and in making the conservative Ramadevi give up her beliefs in the face of circumstances, the novel was inverting the usual way in which such themes were handled. The anti-imperial and anti-fascist theme in the novel is subordinated to the story, and to the immediate problems faced by the characters.

Inqilab (Revolution) is a more ambitious novel which attempts to portray the whole history of the national movement. The novel took some seven years to write, for the idea for the novel came to Abbas after 8 August 1942, when the Indian National Congress passed its famous "Quit India" resolution. The novel's protagonist, Anwar, is a young Muslim intellectual committed to the nationalist struggle, and the novel plainly draws on Abbas's childhood in a traditional Muslim family, his student days at university, and his life as a journalist and as someone slowly drawn into the freedom struggle. However, key events in Anwar's life have been movingly reconstructed from history: the Amritsar massacre in 1919, the Salt March, the declaration of Independence, the proceedings of the Congress Working Party. When Anwar rebukes some Muslim separatists, his uncle reveals the family secret of Anwar's parentage to deflate him: Anwar is not in fact a Muslim but the illegitimate son of a Hindu. The novel concludes: "Could it be that he who by birth was neither a Hindu nor wholly a Muslim or, rather, who was both, an oddly symbolic Son of India, was in a peculiarly advantageous position to understand both the communities and to work for the synthesis that was already symbolized in his person." That clumsily multisyllabic ending is symptomatic of the points in Abbas's work where his literary judgment is subverted by his idealism.

Abbas's work has also been accused of being too political, too journalistic, too crowded, too crammed with incidental detail, too sweeping, too sentimental. But there is, in all his work, an attempt to contain and recreate the whole experience of modern India, an attempt undertaken by few others.

—Prabhu S. Guptara

ABISH, Walter

Nationality: American. **Born:** Vienna, Austria, 24 December 1931; became American citizen, 1960. **Family:** Married Cecile Gelb (i.e., the sculptor Cecile Abish). **Career:** Adjunct professor, Empire State College, New York, 1975; writer-in-residence, Wheaton College, Norton, Massachusetts, 1976; Visiting Butler Professor, State University of New York, Buffalo, 1977; lecturer in English and comparative literature, Columbia University, New York, 1979-86; visiting professor, Yale University, New Haven, Connecticut, 1985, Brown University, Providence, Rhode Island, 1986, and The Cooper Union, 1993, 1994. Since 1981 contributing editor, *Conjunctions Magazine*. Member of the Executive Board, PEN American Center, 1982-84; Board of Governors, New York Foundations for the Arts, 1990-93. **Awards:** New Jersey Council on the Arts fellowship, 1972; Rose Isabel Williams Foundation grant, 1974; Ingram Merrill Foundation grant, 1977; National Endowment for the Arts fellowship, 1980, 1985; PEN-Faulkner award, 1981; Guggenheim fellowship, 1981; Creative Artists Pubic Service grant, 1981; DAAD fellowship (Berlin), 1987; MacArthur fellowship, 1987; American Academy Award for Merit medal, for the novel, 1991; Lila Wallace-Reader's Digest fellowship, 1992-95. **Agent:** Candida Donadio, 121 West 27th Street, Suite 704, New York, New York 10011. **Address:** P.O. Box 485, Cooper Station, New York, New York 10276, U.S.A.

PUBLICATIONS

Novels

Alphabetical Africa. New York, New Directions, 1974.
How German Is It. New York, New Direction, 1980; Manchester, Carcanet, 1982.
Eclipse Fever. New York, Knopf, and London, Faber, 1993.

Short Stories

Minds Meet. New York, New Directions, 1975.
In the Future Perfect. New York, New Directions, 1977; London, Faber, 1984.
99: The New Meaning. Providence, Rhode Island, Burning Deck, 1990.

Uncollected Short Stories

"Auctioning Australia," in *Text-Sound Texts,* edited by Richard Kostelanetz. New York, Morrow, 1980.
"Alphabet of Revelations," in *New Directions 41.* New York, New Directions, 1980.
"The Idea of Switzerland," in *The Best American Short Stories 1981,* edited by Hortense Calisher and Shannon Ravenel. Boston, Houghton Mifflin, 1981.
"Happiness," in *New Directions 50.* New York, New Directions, 1986.
"Furniture of Desire," in *Granta* (Cambridge), Autumn 1989.
"The Coming Ice Age," in *Salmagundi* (Saratoga Springs, New York), Winter-Spring 1990.
"House on Fire," in *Antaeus* (New York), Spring-Autumn 1990.

Poetry

Duel Site. New York, Tibor de Nagy, 1970.

*

Critical Studies: "Through a Continent Darkly," in *Picked-Up Pieces* by John Updike, New York, Knopf, 1975, London, Deutsch, 1976; interview with Jerome Klinkowitz, in *Fiction International*

(Canton, New York), Fall 1975, and *The Life of Fiction,* Urbana, University of Illinois Press, 1977, "Walter Abish and the Surfaces of Life," in *Georgia Review* (Athens), Summer 1981, *The Self-Apparent Word,* Carbondale, Southern Illinois University Press, 1984, and *Structuring the Void,* Durham, North Carolina, Duke University Press, 1992, all by Klinkowitz; "Restrictive Fiction" by Kenneth Baker, in *New Directions 35,* New York, New Directions, 1977; "Self-Portrait," in *Individuals: Post Movement Art in America,* New York, Dutton, 1977, "The Fall of Summer," in *Conjunctions* (New York), 1984, and "Family," in *Antaeus* (New York), Spring 1984, all by Abish; "In So Many Words" by Irving Malin, in *Ontario Review* (Windsor), Winter 1978-79; "Present Imperfect" by Tony Tanner, in *Granta* (Cambridge), 1979; "The Writer-to-Be: An Impression of Living" by Abish, and "The Puzzle of Walter Abish" by Alain Arias-Misson, in *Sub-Stance 27* (Madison, Wisconsin), Winter 1980; interview with Sylvere Lotringer, in *Semiotext(e)* (New York), 1982; *Silverless Mirrors: Book, Self, and Postmodern American Fiction* by Charles Caramello, Tallahassee, Florida State University Press, 1983; "Walter Abish's Fictions: Perfect Unfamiliarity, Familiar Imperfections" by Richard Martin, in *Journal of American Studies 17* (Norwich), 1983; *The Novel in Motion* by Richard Pearce, Athens, Ohio University Press, 1983; *American Fictions 1940-1980* by Frederick Karl, New York, Harper, 1983; "Walter Abish: *How German Is It*" by Paul West, in *Sheer Fiction,* New Paltz, New York, McPherson, 1987; interview with Larry McCaffery, in *Alive and Writing,* Urbana, University of Illinois Press, 1987; *Postmodernist Fiction* by Brian McHale, New York, Methuen, 1987; "The New Novel and TV Culture: Reflections on Walter Abish's *How German Is It*" by Alain Arias-Misson, in *Fiction International* (San Diego), 1987; "Walter Abish and the Questioning of the Reader" by Christopher Butler, in *Facing Texts,* Durham, North Carolina, Duke University Press, 1988; "Walter Abish's *How German Is It: Representing the Postmodern,"* in *Contemporary Literature,* n.p., 1989; *Circus of the Mind in Motion* by Lance Olsen, Detroit, Wayne State University Press, 1990; "Walter Abish's *How German Is It:* Postmodernism and the Past" by Maarten van Delden, in *Salmagundi* (Saratoga Springs, New York), Winter-Spring 1990; "Walter Abish and the Topographies of Desire" by Jerry Varsave, in *Contingent Meanings,* Florida State University Press, 1990; "Comic Politics and Politics of the Comic" by Anthony Schirato, in *Critique: Studies in Contemporary Fiction,* Winter 1992.

*   *   *

Walter Abish—born in Vienna, raised in China, settled in Israel, and trained as a city planner, the occupation which first brought him to America and a job in New York City—began publishing fiction in 1970. His major work has appeared in the semi-annual anthologies produced by New Directions, the publisher who has also issued two of his three collections of short fiction and two novels. A master of the stiff-upper lip, self-consciously presentational prose style made famous by Donald Barthelme, Abish has devised his own techniques by which the language of his stories explores itself in search of the ironies of human communication and behaviour.

His first novel, *Alphabetical Africa,* is a *tour de force* demonstration of how words can refer to their own artificiality at the same time they operate as linguistic signifiers. The first chapter is titled "A," and every word therein begins with that letter ("Ages ago, Alex, Allen and Alva arrived at Antibes, and Alva allowing all, al-

lowing anyone, against Alex's admonition, against Allen's angry assertion: another African amusement," etc.). The second-chapter, "B," adds words beginning with the letter *B,* and so forth until the books expands to its full linguistic possibilities. Such a self-apparent structure makes the reader painfully aware of the words themselves, and of how an artificial discipline of language determines just what reality may transpire. For example, a character named Herman can't appear until chapter "H"; the first person narrator must keep his comments to himself until chapter "I"; and the characters cannot travel to Jedda until chapter "J." By chapter "Z" the full exercise of language may have lulled the reader into complacency. But the book is only half done, for the 27th chapter is titled "Z" once more, followed by "Y," "X," and so forth back through the now-contracting alphabet. Familiar persons, places, and things are lost at each receding chapter as the book's mimetic action literally effaces itself in one's hands, until at the end one is left with the solemn toiling at the minimally expressive letter A. Like breathing in and then breathing out, the reader has experienced the expansion and contraction, the life and death of a work of fiction. At no point can one suspend disbelief and sink into the pantomime of suspended disbelief, for at all times attention is riveted to the self-conscious making and unmaking of the physical book.

Minds Meet collects 12 of Abish's short fictions from the early 1970s. The title piece is based upon improvisation with the theme of human communication: "Taken Aback by the Message," "The Abandoned Message," "Abased by the Message," and so forth. Another story, "This Is Not a Film. This is a Precise Act of Disbelief," employs the semiology of contemporary American culture, whereby the needs of people are served by an assortment of surface details ("pure signifiers" as the structuralists would say). Abish's most characteristic style in these shorter pieces is to write sentences composed of radically different thoughts which collide at the caesura; readers are thus aware of content and linguistic form at the same time, and especially how syntax presupposed judgment—an irony Abish enjoys exploiting with his humour of sexual innuendo. By these collisions, the story moves forward; its real subject is nothing other than itself.

The stories of *In the Future Perfect* are distinguished by their mechanical structures which call attention to their component words. "Ardor/Awe/Atrocity" consists of block paragraphs headed by three superscripted words, their presence in the following sections numbered in alphabetical order. One is thus aware of the 78 key words which will be featured long before they pop up in the narrative; when they do, the reader should be more inclined to treat them as signifiers—as creatures of the writer's invention—than as signified in the outside world of associations. "In So Many Words" assembles the words of each paragraph in alphabetical order before those same terms are repeated in syntactic sense, making attention to the writer's artifice (and the words themselves) more pronounced. Even the apparently conventional stories in this volume, by virtue of their circular technique, return to key elements ("perfection," "repetition") which the author selects at the start of each section.

How German Is It, Abish's second novel, is disarmingly conventional. But only on the surface is it a simple story of a writer's return to "the new Germany." A story from *In the Future Perfect,* "The English Garden," is actually its prolegomena, and the epigraph from John Ashbery indicates Abish's deeper interests in the linguistically contrived nature of human behaviour: "Remnants of the old atrocity subsist, but they are converted into ingenious shifts in scenery, a sort of 'English Garden' effect, to give the required air of naturalness, pathos and hope."

Abish's practice of reading the world in terms of its surface details yields a phenomenology of action on the purely textual level that makes *How German Is It* less of a documentary account than a fictive exercise in examining the unyielding surface of topographical features, a strategy that conforms to Abish's own experience at the time, having never visited Germany yet "knowing" it by virtue of representations in the media. The imaginative act that results from matching biography with text, however, is examined in excerpts from one of the author's works in progress, a textual autobiography examining the status of "the writer-to-be." Here Abish revisits not just the locations of his childhood but texts and documents associated with it; maps, photographs, and diaries from the past imply a history, but in order to reconvert it into "his story" Abish must establish the writer's role in committing these details not into an externally necessary narrative but into items placed on the page's flat surface, from whence will be formed a fiction based on relationships among its own parts rather than to outside matters. That this same method can reinvent our reading of fiction is evident from *99: The New Meaning,* a collection of narratives composed by numbering sentences, mixing them up, then reprinting them in the scrambled order, or else by arranging first paragraphs from a great number of novels written by others into a sequence that form a narrative of their own quite apart from the original intentions; as always, the emphasis is on ordering within the surface action of the printed (and read) page rather than on points of external (or even previous) reference.

As Walter Abish's long awaited third novel, *Eclipse Fever* locates many of the author's familiar concerns in an apparently more recognizable world, that of contemporary Mexico. Yet because it is a world of postmodern aesthetic concerns being acted out within the limits of a still-powerful colonialism, Abish's Mexico equals his Germany as a place where surface typologies alternately reflect and contradict the history of what lies beneath their surfaces. The action is defined by distinctive characters who cross this landscape in various pursuits, including the American novelist Jurud who travels to Mexico for a meeting with his translator (and lover), Mercedes; Mercedes's husband, the critic Alejandro, who journeys to the countryside for dealings with possibly stolen pre-Columbian art; Preston, an American developer who would turn the Pyramid of the Sun into condominiums; and Jurud's daughter Bonny, who approaches Mexico from the opposite direction to witness a solar eclipse. Each character becomes an element in the other's narrative, with the novel itself thus forming a complex of interrelationships that comprises father/daughter, husband/wife, wife/lover, author/translator, author/critic, and so forth. The special appeal of these relationships is not only that they interweave but also that they do so in the context of present-day Mexico's position with regard to its Spanish colonial past and its proximity to American imperial self-interest. As a result, Abish once more demonstrates that social reality is an invention as arbitrary yet as determining as language itself.

—Jerome Klinkowitz

ABRAHAMS, Peter (Henry)

Nationality: South African. **Born:** Vrededorp, near Johannesburg, in 1919. **Education:** Church of England mission schools and colleges. **Family:** Married Daphne Elizabeth Miller; three children.

Career: Merchant seaman, 1939-41; then moved to England; regular contributor to the *Observer,* London, and the *Herald Tribune,* New York and Paris, 1952-64; editor, *West Indian Economist,* and controller, *West Indian News,* Jamaica, 1955-64; chairman, Radio Jamaica, Kingston, 1977-80. **Address:** Red Hills, St. Andrew, Jamaica.

PUBLICATIONS

Novels

Song of the City. London, Crisp, 1945.
Mine Boy. London, Crisp, 1946; New York, Knopf, 1955.
The Path of Thunder. New York, Harper, 1948; London, Faber, 1952.
Wild Conquest. New York, Harper, 1950; London, Faber, 1951.
A Wreath for Udomo. New York, Knopf, and London, Faber, 1956.
A Night of Their Own. New York, Knopf, and London, Faber, 1965.
This Island Now. London, Faber, 1966; New York, Knopf, 1967; revised edition, Faber, 1985.
The View from Coyaba. London, Faber, 1985.
The Fan. New York, Warner, 1995.

Short Stories

Dark Testament. London, Allen and Unwin, 1942.

Poetry

A Blackman Speaks of Freedom! Durban, Universal Printing Works, 1938(?).

Other

Return to Goli (reportage). London, Faber, 1953.
Tell Freedom: Memories of Africa. London, Faber, and New York, Knopf, 1954.
Jamaica: An Island Mosaic. London, Her Majesty's Stationery Office, 1957.
The World of Mankind, with others. New York, Golden Press, 1962.

*

Critical Studies: *Peter Abrahams* by Michael Wade, London, Evans, 1972; *The Writing of Peter Abrahams* by Kolawole Ogungbesan, London, Hodder and Stoughton, 1979; *The Novels of Peter Abrahams and the Rise of Nationalism in Africa* by Robert Ensor, Essen, Verlag Die Blaue Eule, 1992.

*   *   *

Peter Abrahams left South Africa in 1939, when he was only 20 years old, but the racial and political problems of that troubled land for many years continued to dominate his imagination. All but the last two of his eight novels have been set entirely or in part in South Africa, and even the exceptions, *This Island Now* and *The View from Coyaba,* deal with problems in plural societies in which there is great friction between blacks and whites. Abrahams has also written two autobiographical books, *Tell Freedom* and *Return to Goli,* both of which focus on his experiences as a mulatto in South Africa.

Abrahams's early novels were influenced by Marxist ideas so they tend to be concerned more with race and economics than with politics. *Song of the City* and *Mine Boy* tell of the consequences of urbanization and industrialization on the lives of young black workers who move from the country to the city. *Song of the City* takes place at the time of the second world war, *Mine Boy* against the backdrop of booming gold mines in Johannesburg. In both novels nonwhites are mistreated and oppressed by whites.

In his next novel, *The Path of Thunder,* Abrahams turns to the theme of interracial love, exploring its impact on a young Colored schoolteacher and an Afrikaner girl whose passionate affair ultimately ends in tragedy when the Afrikaner community discovers they are lovers. Two years later Abrahams moves in yet another direction, this time reconstructing the era of the Afrikaner migration or "Great Trek" in *Wild Conquest,* an historical novel in which he makes an effort to be fair to all the major ethnic groups in South Africa—Bantu, Boer and Briton.

After these early works, all of which were written in the 1940s, Abrahams's fiction becomes more political. *A Wreath for Udomo,* published just before Ghana attained its independence, is an attempt to predict what might happen when independent black African nations are confronted with the choice between the financial advantages of collaborating with the white regimes in southern Africa and the moral imperative of opposing them by actively supporting black liberation movements. *A Night of Their Own* carries the revolutionary theme further by detailing the adventures of an African underground agent involved in smuggling funds to an Indian resistance organization in South Africa. *This Island Now* tells of racial tensions and internal power struggles in a small, black-ruled Caribbean island-state, and *The View from Coyaba,* certainly his most ambitious historical novel, covers more than 150 years of black experience in tropical Africa, the Caribbean and the deep south of the United States. In each successive novel Abrahams moves further and further away from a depiction of South African social realities to the construction of hypothetical situations which afford greater elbow room. Even *A Night of Their Own,* though set in South Africa, has elements of fantasy and wishful thinking in it. Abrahams's increased independence on his imagination in these later novels may reflect how far out of touch he is with contemporary conditions in his native land.

Abrahams has always written in a simple, direct prose style which wavers between superior reportage and maudlin romanticizing. He is at his best when transcribing newsworthy events which have a basis in fact; his autobiographical and travel writings, for instance, are superb. However, he has a regrettable tendency to sentimentalize personal relationships between men and women, especially if they are of different races, as they so often are in his novels. His accounts of miscegenated love are nearly always literary disasters because they are bathed in lachrymose artificiality.

Yet when he writes of exciting happenings, such as spontaneous labor strikes, bloody frontier battles, underground resistance campaigns, or the highly-charged political debates at a Pan-African congress, Abrahams can carry the reader along swiftly and persuasively, building up a spell-binding momentum which is broken only when he veers from the external world of his characters into the internal world of their thoughts and dreams. Abrahams has not yet learned to write a decent interior monologue, and his novels would be more aesthetically satisfying if his heroes and heroines were less inclined to moments of moody introspection. His surface sketches are much more convincing than his psychological probings.

Because Abrahams was one of the first African writers to achieve international recognition, his works received a good deal of patronizing attention at first. European and American critics were all too eager to embrace him as a literary phenomenon—a nonwhite South African who could not only write but could actually write fairly well! Therefore, they wrote glowing reviews of his early novels, emphasizing their strong points and ignoring obvious flaws. Today, in the midst of an African literary awakening, Abrahams tends to be regarded with less enthusiasm, for his novels are recognized as far less interesting and accomplished than those produced in West Africa by such talented artists as Chinua Achebe, Wole Soyinka, and Ayi Kwei Armah. Abrahams has certainly carved a niche for himself in African literary history, but it is a small niche somewhere at the base of the monument, passionately but clumsily hewn.

—Bernth Lindfors

ACHEBE, Chinua

Nationality: Nigerian. **Born:** Albert Chinualumogu in Ogidi, 16 November 1930. **Education:** Government College, Umuahia, 1944-47; University College, Ibadan, 1948-53, B.A. (London) 1953. **Family:** Married Christiana Chinwe Okoli in 1961; two sons and two daughters. **Career:** Talks producer, Lagos, 1954-57, controller, Enugu, 1958-61, and director, Voice of Nigeria, Lagos, 1961-66, Nigerian Broadcasting Corporation; chairman, Citadel Books Ltd., Enugu, 1967. Senior research fellow, 1967-73, professor of English, 1973-81, and since 1984 professor emeritus, University of Nigeria, Nsukka. Visiting professor, 1972-75, and Fulbright Professor, 1987-88, University of Massachusetts, Amherst; visiting professor, University of Connecticut, Storrs, 1975-76; Regents' Lecturer, University of California, Los Angeles, 1984; Visiting Distinguished Professor of English, City College, New York, 1989. Visiting professor, Stanford University, 1990. Founding editor, Heinemann African Writers series, 1962-72 and since 1970 director, Heinemann Educational Books (Nigeria) Ltd., and Nwankwo-Ifejika Ltd. (later Nwamife), publishers, Enugu; since 1971 editor, *Okike: An African Journal of New Writing,* Nsukka; since 1983 governor, Newsconcern International Foundation, London; since 1984 founder and publisher, *Uwa Ndi Igbo: A Bilingual Journal of Igbo Life and Arts.* **Awards:** Margaret Wrong Memorial prize, 1959; Nigerian National trophy, 1960; Rockefeller fellowship, 1960; Unesco fellowship, 1963; Jock Campbell award (*New Statesman*), 1965; Commonwealth Poetry prize, 1973; Neil Gunn International fellowship, 1974; Lotus award for Afro-Asian writers, 1975; Nigerian National Merit award, 1979; Commonwealth Foundation award, 1984. Litt.D.: Dartmouth College, Hanover, New Hampshire, 1972; University of Southampton, 1975; University of Ife, 1978; University of Nigeria, 1981; University of Kent, Canterbury, 1982; University of Guelph, Ontario, 1984; Mount Allison University, Sackville, New Brunswick, 1984; Franklin Pierce College, Rindge, New Hampshire, 1985; University of Ibadan, 1989; Skidmore College, Saratoga Springs, New York, 1990; D. Univ.: University of Stirling, 1975; Open University, Milton Keynes, Buckinghamshire, 1989; LL.D.: University of Prince Edward Island, Charlottetown, 1976; D.H.L.: University of Massachusetts, 1977; Westfield College, London, 1989; Georgetown University,

Washington, D.C., 1990. Honorary Fellow, Modern Language Association (USA), 1975; member, Order of the Federal Republic of Nigeria, 1979; Honorary Member, American Academy, 1982; Fellow, Royal Society of Literature, 1983. **Member:** University of Lagos Council, 1966; chairman, Society of Nigerian Authors, 1966, and Association of Nigerian Authors, 1982-86; member, Anambra State Arts Council, 1977-79; Pro-Chancellor and Chairman of Council, Anambra State University of Technology, Enugu, 1986-88. Since 1981 member of the Executive Committee, Commonwealth Arts Organization, London; since 1983 member, International Social Prospects Academy, Geneva; since 1984 director, Okike Arts Center, Nsukka. Served on diplomatic missions for Biafra during Nigerian Civil War, 1967-69; deputy national president, People's Redemption Party, 1983. **Address:** P.O. Box 53, University of Nigeria, Nsukka, Anambra State, Nigeria.

PUBLICATIONS

Novels

Things Fall Apart. London, Heinemann, 1958; New York, McDowell Obolensky, 1959.
No Longer at Ease. London, Heinemann, 1960; New York, Obolensky, 1961.
Arrow of God. London, Heinemann, 1964; New York, Day, 1967.
A Man of the People. London, Heinemann, and New York, Day, 1966.
Anthills of the Savannah. London, Heinemann, 1987; New York, Doubleday, 1988.
The African Trilogy. London, Picador, 1988.

Short Stories

The Sacrificial Egg and Other Stories. Onitsha, Etudo, 1962.
Girls at War. London, Heinemann, 1972; New York, Doubleday, 1973.

Poetry

Beware, Soul-Brother and Other Poems. Enugu, Nwankwo-Ifejika, 1971; revised edition, Enugu, Nwamife, and London, Heinemann, 1972; revised edition, as *Christmas in Biafra and Other Poems,* New York, Doubleday, 1973.

Other (for children)

Chike and the River. London and New York, Cambridge University Press, 1966.
How the Leopard Got His Claws, with John Iroaganachi. Enugu, Nwamife, 1972; New York, Third Press, 1973.
The Flute. Enugu, Fourth Dimension, 1977.
The Drum. Enugu, Fourth Dimension, 1977.

Other

Morning Yet on Creation Day: Essays. London, Heinemann, and New York, Doubleday, 1975.
In Person: Achebe, Awoonor, and Soyinka at the University of Washington. Seattle, University of Washington African Studies Program, 1975.

The Trouble with Nigeria. Enugu, Fourth Dimension, 1983; London, Heinemann, 1984.
The World of the Ogbanje. Enugu, Fourth Dimension, 1986.
Hopes and Impediments: Selected Essays 1965-1987. London, Heinemann, 1988; New York, Doubleday, 1990.
The University and the Leadership Factor in Nigerian Politics. Enugu, ABIC, 1988.
A Tribute to James Baldwin. Amherst, University of Massachusetts Press, 1989.

Editor, *The Insider: Stories of War and Peace from Nigeria.* Enugu, Nwankwo-Ifejika, and Chatham, New Jersey, Chatham Booksellers, 1971.
Editor, with Jomo Kenyatta and Amos Tutuola, *Winds of Change: Modern Stories from Black Africa.* London, Longman, 1977.
Editor, with Dubem Okafor, *Don't Let Him Die: An Anthology of Memorial Poems for Christopher Okigbo.* Enugu, Fourth Dimension, 1978.
Editor with C.L. Innes, *African Short Stories.* London, Heinemann, 1985.
Editor, *Beyond Hunger in Africa: Conventional Wisdom and a Vision of Africa in 2057.* Nairobi, Heinemann Kenya, and London, Currey, 1990.

*

Bibliography: In *Africana Library Journal* (New York), Spring 1970; *Chinua Achebe: A Bibliography* by B.M. Okpu, Lagos, Libriservice, 1984; *Chinua Achebe* by C.L. Innes, Cambridge University Press, 1990.

Critical Studies: *The Novels of Chinua Achebe* by G.D. Killam, London, Heinemann, and New York, Africana, 1969, revised edition, as *The Writings of Chinua Achebe,* Heinemann, 1977; *Chinua Achebe* by Arthur Ravenscroft, London, Longman, 1969, revised edition, 1977; *Chinua Achebe* by David Carroll, New York, Twayne, 1970, revised edition, London, Macmillan, 1980, 1990; *Chinua Achebe* by Kate Turkington, London, Arnold, 1977; *Critical Perspectives on Chinua Achebe* edited by Bernth Lindfors and C.L. Innes, London, Heinemann, and Washington, D.C., Three Continents Press, 1978; *Achebe's World: The Historical and Cultural Context of the Novels of Chinua Achebe* by Robert M. Wren, Washington, D.C., Three Continents Press, 1980, London, Longman, 1981; *The Four Novels of Chinua Achebe: A Critical Study* by Benedict C. Njoku, Bern, Switzerland, Lang, 1984; *The Traditional Religion and Its Encounter with Christianity in Achebe's Novels* by E.M. Okoye, Bern, Switzerland, Lang, 1987; *Chinua Achebe* by C.L. Innes, Cambridge, Cambridge University Press, 1990; *Reading Chinua Achebe: Language and Ideology in Fiction* by Simon Gikandi, London, Currey, 1991; *Approaches to Teaching Achebe's "Things Fall Apart"* edited by Bernth Lindfors, New York, Modern Language Association of America, 1991; *Chinua Achebe: A Celebration* edited by Kirsten Holst Petersen and Anna Rutherford, Oxford, England, Heinemann, 1991; *Chinua Achebe: New Perspectives* by Umela Ojinmah, Ibadan, Spectrum, 1991; *Reading Chinua Achebe: Language and Ideology in Fiction* by Simon Gikandi, London, Currey, 1991; *Gods, Oracles and Divination* by Kalu Ogbaa, Trenton, N.J., Africa World Press, 1992; *Art, Rebellion and Redemption* by Romanus Okey Muonaka, New York, Lang, 1993; *South Asian Responses to Chinua Achebe* edited by Bernth Lindfors and Bala Kothandaraman, New Delhi, Prestige Books International, 1993.

Chinua Achebe comments:

I am a political writer. My politics is concerned with universal human communication across racial and cultural boundaries as a means of fostering respect for all people. Such respect can issue only from understanding. So my primary concern is with clearing the channels of communication in my own neighborhood by hacking away at the thickets that choke them.

Africa's meeting with Europe must be accounted a terrible disaster in this matter of human understanding and respect. The nature of the meeting precluded any warmth of friendship. First Europe was an enslaver; then a colonizer. In either role she had no need and made little effort to understand or appreciate Africa; indeed she easily convinced herself that there was nothing there to justify the effort. Today our world is still bedeviled by the consequences of that cataclysmic encounter.

I was born into the colonial era, grew up in the heady years of nationalist protest and witnessed Africa's resumption of independence. (It was not, however, the same Africa which originally lost her freedom that now retained it, but a different Africa created in the image of Europe—but that's another story.) So I have seen in my not very long lifetime three major eras in precipitate succession, leaving us somewhat dazed. My response as a writer has been to try to keep pace with these torrential changes. First I had to tell Europe that the arrogance on which she sought to excuse her pillage of Africa, i.e., that Africa was the Primordial Void, was sheer humbug; that Africa had a history, a religion, a civilization. We reconstructed this history and civilization and displayed it to challenge the stereotype and the cliché. Actually it was not to Europe alone that I spoke. I spoke also to that part of ourselves that had come to accept Europe's opinion of us. And I was not alone nor even the first.

But the gauntlet had barely left our hands when a new historic phase broke on us. Europe conceded independence to us and we promptly began to misuse it, or rather those leaders to whom we entrusted the wielding of our new power and opportunity did. So we got mad at them and came out brandishing novels of disenchantment. Actually we had all been duped. No independence was given—it was never given but taken, anyway. Europe had only made a tactical withdrawal on the political front and while we sang our anthem and unfurled our flag she was securing her iron grip behind us in the economic field. And our leaders in whose faces we hurled our disenchantment neither saw nor heard because they were not leaders at all but marionettes.

So the problem remains for Africa, for black people, for all deprived peoples and for the world. And so for the writer, for he is like the puppy in our proverb: that stagnant water in the potsherd is for none other but him. As long as one people sit on another and are deaf to their cry, so long will understanding and peace elude all of us.

*   *   *

Chinua Achebe established his reputation with *Things Fall Apart,* one of the first novels to be published in post-independence Africa. It was admired for many reasons, notably the tragic profundity of its theme and the insights it offered on traditional Ibo life. Western critics also approved of Achebe's acceptance of the formal conventions of the genre even while he proved that the English language could be modified to express the very different African cultural context. This book became both archetype and classic, and many budding authors have attempted to emulate Achebe without demonstrating his competence. *Things Fall Apart* has been translated into many languages and is an established text in schools. It has sustained extensive critical examination and yet its poignant story still retains its capacity to move the reader.

Achebe's declared intention was to provide evidence that traditional African life was not the primitive barbarism that was the common judgment of the colonialists. Set in the early period of the initial British intrusion into Nigeria, the novel shows a society which, if not perfect, had structure and dignity; where human relations had order and security. Into this world came the foreigner and "things fall apart." The title, taken from Yeats, makes a subtle comment on the theme, because it expresses some degree of inevitability rather than calculated cause. Perhaps neither side could foresee the consequences of actions which seemed entirely reasonable within their own context. Though setting straight the record, this is not an anti-colonialist novel in the simplistic sense. Achebe discerns a terrifying truth, that when powerful worlds clash, even the best of men are defeated and only the accommodators prosper. Okonkwo exemplifies all the virtues of his people, but he is too harsh and inflexible to tolerate the inescapable changes. His friend Obierika is a far weaker but more sensible person. He survives, like others who yield their honor and adapt, preferring prosperity at the cost of their heritage. While understanding that this is a reasonable decision, which in time created the society which Achebe inherits, he clearly indicates where honor rests. Okonwo is "the greatest man."

Three further novels form a tetralogy which covers Ibo history from the first arrival of the British to the violent coup of 1966. Though third to be published, it is *Arrow of God* which carries on the historical sequence. Its theme is similar to that of *Things Fall Apart.* Ezeulu, a distinguished village man, this time a high priest, finds himself in conflict with the now established British administration, a conflict activated as much by ignorance as malice. Angered by imprisonment and the failure of his people to assist him, Ezeulu imposes harsh penalties upon them. At last their misery is so acute they turn to the Christian missionaries who are preaching a less oppressive religion. With a terrible irony the priest's fierce battle to sustain the tribal god causes his destruction. Again there is the depiction of strength, admirable in itself, but too harsh to see the advantage and necessity of compromise. The man who most exemplifies traditional virtues, just like Okonkwo, brings about their destruction along with his own. In a further plot twist, Ezeulu sends his son to learn the ways of the white missionaries. He does not anticipate the conversion of the boy who then denies his heritage and begins to exemplify the cultural ambivalence and generational opposition which education inescapably brings.

The other two novels examine this dualistic situation. The revealing title of *No Longer at Ease* comes from T.S. Eliott. Obi, a bright, eager young man, is sent to England to study and returns to the luxury of the high Civil Service appointment previously reserved for the British. He is confident and optimistic, feeling he represents the hopes for a better Nigeria which will flourish under the direction of this new class of youthful, educated, and therefore honest and efficient administrators. In fact his position imposes peculiar strains. A salary, huge by village standards, proves insufficient to live the European life expected of him. His indifference, even scorn, of the values of his tradition, learned during his time in England, offends his people who had funded him. Obi is exposed as an alien and becomes uncomfortable and ineffective in both worlds. He drifts into taking bribes and is soon as corrupt as those he used to despise. He is an inept crook, however, and is charged and imprisoned. At one level this is a depressing tale. If someone as decent as Obi succumbs, can anyone succeed in improving conditions in Nigeria? The cynical colonial characters express only passing surprise, gloating to find their prejudice confirmed: "All Africans are corrupt." Achebe has something much deeper to communicate. Given this history and these conditions, how is it possible for even the idealist to maintain his integrity? In the final analysis when the struggle with the system destroys even the best, who shall be blamed? It is a contemporary application of the issue raised in the two historical novels.

The situation in *A Man of the People* is even more depressing. It reflects the terrible political deterioration which Nigeria has suffered since independence. "The Man," is Nanga, a brutally corrupt politician who nevertheless manages to remain both popular and successful. The novel examines this disastrous paradox. The term "man of the people" seems to indicate an admirable figure. Then, as Nanga's vile deeds are revealed, the reader reverses his judgment. How can a crook be "of the people?" In an ending of shattering pessimism, Achebe seems to accept that people as greedy and immoral as these deserve such a man who does nothing more than exploit their own similar values; envy not accusation motivates the voters. The dedicated intellectual, Odili, is drawn not as the hero come to redeem his people, but as an arrogant and incompetent fool. His ideas are far more remote from the people's than Nanga's. Corruption they understand, merely wishing to share in it; idealism seems absurd and irrelevant. Naively unpolitical Odili is defeated and in the dismal conclusion makes off with the funds committed to his election campaign, justifying his theft with typical intellectual rationalizations. The nation falls into chaotic violence.

Achebe's pessimism was prescient. Social cohesion in Nigeria disintegrated. When the disastrous civil war broke out he was a prominent participant on the Biafran side. These efforts so preoccupied him and induced so deep a discouragement that since 1966 his output has been slender. From the battle came some short stories which realistically depicted the sufferings—and the continuing corruption—within the cause to which he had dedicated himself with such idealism and hope. His most poignant comments on the war are in the poems of *Beware, Soul-Brother.*

In 1987 a new novel appeared. *Anthills of the Savannah* addresses the same themes. The decades of independence have brought only minimal reasons for hope. Ruling governments have oscillated between corrupt citizens and violent army generals. For the first time Achebe chooses to disguise the setting by inventing a fictional state, Kangan. The rulers and their practices are closely modeled on the actual atrocities of Amin's Uganda. This may be intended to universalize the African situation, or indicate that Achebe can no longer bear to contemplate directly the misery to which his own country has come. But there are some flickers of hope. Interestingly enough, it is the female characters who display strength and assurance through the corruption and violence.

Perhaps Achebe has begun to lose confidence in the generation which he has served. Nevertheless, his early quartet stands as a masterly achievement that will inform generations of readers of the disasters colonialism brought to Africa—sometimes with benign intentions. The tragic realization in the books of the human misery that results from massive social and economic change brings to the mind the Wessex novels of Hardy.

—John Povey

ACKER, Kathy

Nationality: American. **Born:** 1948. **Education:** Brandeis University, Waltham, Massachusetts; University of California, San Diego. **Career:** Has had a variety of jobs including filing clerk, secretary, stripper, and performer in live sex shows and pornographic films. Instructor, San Francisco Art Institute. **Awards:** Pushcart prize, 1979. **Address:** San Francisco Art Institute, 800 Chestnut, San Francisco, California 94133, U.S.A.

PUBLICATIONS

Novels

The Childlike Life of the Black Tarantula: Some Lives of Murderesses (as the Black Tarantula). New York, Vanishing Rotating Triangle Press, 1975.
Kathy Goes to Haiti. N.p., Rumour Publications, 1978; in *Young Lust,* London, Pandora Press, 1989.
The Adult Life of Toulouse Lautrec by Henri Toulouse Lautrec. New York, TVRT Press, 1978.
Great Expectations. San Francisco, Re/Search Productions, 1982.
Blood and Guts in High School. New York, Grove Press, 1984; as *Blood and Guts in High School Plus Two* (includes *Great Expectations, Pier Paolo Pasolini's My Life My Death*), London, Picador, 1984.
Hello I'm Erica Long. New York, Contact II, 1984.
Algeria. London, Aloes, 1985.
Don Quixote: Which Was a Dream. New York, Grove Press, and London, Paladin, 1986.
Empire of the Senseless. New York, Grove Press, and London, Picador, 1988.
Young Lust. London, Pandora, 1989.
In Memoriam to Identity. New York, Grove Press, and London, Pandora Press, 1990.
Portrait of an Eye: Three Novels. New York, Pantheon, 1992.
My Mother: Demonology. New York, Pantheon, 1993.

Short Stories

The Seven Cardinal Virtues, with others, illustrations by Grizelda Holderness, edited by Alison Fell. London, Serpent's Tail, 1990.

Uncollected Short Stories

"New York City in 1979," in *The Pushcart Prize 6,* edited by Bill Henderson. Wainscott, New York, Pushcart Press, 1981.
"Male," in *Between C and D,* edited by Joel Rose and Catherine Texier. New York, Penguin, 1988.
"On Violence," in *Review of Contemporary Fiction* (Elmwood Park, Illinois), Fall 1989.

Plays

The Birth of the Poet (libretto), music by Peter Gordon (produced New York, 1985).

Screenplay: *Variety,* 1985.

Poetry

I Dreamt I Was a Nymphomaniac: Imagining. N.p., Empty Elevator Shaft Poetry Press, 1974.

Other

Literal Madness. New York, Grove Weidenfeld, 1989.
Hannibal Lecter, My Father edited by Sylvere Lotringer. New York, Semiotext(e), 1991.

*   *   *

Kathy Acker's first recognition as a postmodern author was achieved in Europe during her five-year residence in London. With her move to New York, the publication in the United States of her earlier novels, and the widely-reviewed *In Memoriam to Identity,* she is now achieving critical attention in some of the more prestigious academic literary journals in North America. Although she is a prolific creator of fictions, ranging over the world and its various literatures for her materials, it is possible to identify a number of themes and situations that characterize all of her work. Most conspicuous of these on first encounter is a calculated attempt to shock and outrage the sensibilities of ordinary, complacent consumers of commercial fiction. "It's necessary to go to as many extremes as possible," she wrote in "New York City in 1979," in a line that can well serve as a motto for all her work.

With occasional exceptions, Acker's fictions are set in a modern transnational urban space, seen through a perspective that fixates on its most disgusting extremes and rubs the reader's nose in them with a novelistic Brechtian theatricality. An amoral world, in which good and evil are replaced by pleasure and pain, it provides a relentless focus on the senses and on sex, in all its permutations, as a joyless, compulsive act, almost a mechanical reflex, universally pursued without any hope for more than the most transitory gratification. This pursuit goes on in a world of violence and betrayal, with herpes, gonorrhea, syphilis, AIDS, alcoholism, drug addiction, insanity, paranoia (glossed with references to Freud), terrorism, bestiality, rape, and suicide (used as a verb) setting the stage. But in spite of the explicit and shocking sex, often described in minute detail and always with four-letter words, her work is not pornographic either in intention or effect. And in spite of the grim subject-matter and thematics, there is a recurrent strain of playfulness with form and language, and a persistent seriousness of philosophical intentions that suggests a background of frustrated idealism for her shock tactics.

Along with her assault on the conventional moral sensibilities of her readers comes a calculated flaunting of all the artistic literary rules and expectations that have evolved in traditional literature. Consistency in plot and setting, stable characters, plausibility, and all other requirements of conventional realistic fiction are abandoned. Ordinary meaning and coherence are left behind, as narrative stances shift with amazing rapidity through fragmented consciousness, identities are transformed or disintegrate, and authorial "authority" is discarded for an effect of narrative patchwork that refuses to coalesce. Acker is deliberately trying to find her place as a writer in a world where everything has already been written, where the inadequacy of any new mode of representation among the multitudes of prior representation is seemingly inevitable. Yet she refuses to accede to the power and priority of the already-written, attacking and reappropriating the literary canon in an aggressive

spirit of self-assertion, writing her own *Great Expectations,* her own *Don Quixote,* in defiance of the rules of literary property and propriety. And even here "expectations" are created only to be betrayed as we turn the page to find ourselves in another text, or another language (French, German, Latin, Arabic), or facing grafitti-scrawled paper walls instead of words in a typographic text.

All this is done in the kind of flat, affectless prose favoured by many postmodern stylists, punctuated by occasional mysterious haunting lyrical flights that escape the otherwise deadpan ironic pose. Whole chunks of other writers' prose are stolen and dropped verbatim into pastiche, and chunks of her own prose can be repeated, at seemingly random intervals, or at times in a sequence until the effect of a stuck record has been produced. Other kinds of repetition enable one to pick out significant patterns in the apparent chaos. There is a recurrent first-person position, occupied by a female, sometimes called Kathy Acker or variations of that name. Usually this "narrator" has or had a mother who is addicted to alcohol and other drugs, sells her body (to husband and other "clients"), engages in compulsive acquisition of consumer products, and eventually "suicides." This caricature of the female role in modern capitalist consumer society has typically mated with a father for Kathy who is ambivalently charming, loving and sexually exploitative. The incest taboo is broken in every conceivable combination, including siblings when present. The urban scene dominates, and whether it is New York, London, Paris or Rome it provides the same setting of frantic transnational restlessness, violence and squalor. There is a persistent fascination with non-caucasian males (Black, Haitian, Japanese, Arabic) who seem to combine the extremes of erotic desire and fear with a political ambivalence towards terrorism as an inevitable but horrible necessity of modern life. These males are usually presented as fantasies or cultural stereotypes rather than realistic depictions; but they are oxymoronically "real fantasies" or forms of cultural representation that suggest a sophisticated awareness of the contemporary discourse on "Orientalism" as founded by Edward Said, who wrote: "If the Arab occupies scope enough for attention, it is as a negative value. He is seen as the disrupter of Israel's and the West's existence." Another thematic situation that occurs repeatedly is the bonding of star-crossed pairs of lovers or companions, ranging from the sexually ambidextrous Thivai and Abhor in *Empire of the Senseless* through Don Quixote and her dog in *Don Quixote* to Propertius and Cynthia in *Great Expectations* and Rimbaud and Verlaine and Capitol and Quentin (Faulknerian incestuous siblings) in *In Memoriam to Identity,* along with too many others to enumerate here. All these relationships are marked by the hopeless impossibility of providing a "love" adequate to the desperate intensity of the relationship.

But perhaps the most persistent strain throughout all her work is its consistent self-reflexive concern with its own language and procedures, including frequent references to contemporary theorists and critical movements. I'll conclude with an "insert" (her term) from *Don Quixote* that gestures towards the Arabian connection in Cervantes while providing a condensed self-description of her own work:

> The Arab leaders are liars; lying is part of the Arab culture in the same way that truthtelling and honest speech're American. Unlike American and Western culture (generally), the Arabs (in their culture) have no (concept of) originality. That is, culture. They write new stories paint new pictures et cetera only by embellishing old stories pictures. . . . They write by cutting chunks out of all-ready

written texts and in other ways defacing traditions: changing important names into silly ones, making dirty jokes out of matters that should be of the utmost importance to us such as nuclear warfare. . . . A typical Arab text or painting contains neither characters nor narrative, for an Arab, believing such fictions're evil, worships nothingness.

The question Acker poses to herself and to her reader, is whether or not such writing can be an effective form of counter-cultural politics in the desired transformation of a contemporary world that the idealistic Quixotes find always in the control of the "enchanters" (whose ranks for Acker include the editors of the *Times Literary Supplement* as well as Nixon and Hobbes's Angel of Death). At this stage of Acker's career one might well wonder how her future work will deal with the inevitable irony, that the more successful she is in her "attack on the institutions of prison via language [which] would demand the use of a language or languages which aren't acceptable, which are forbidden," the more she has failed in her attempts to break the codes that prove flexible enough to accept her too as another product for our literary consumption.

—Thomas A. Vogler

ACKROYD, Peter

Nationality: British. **Born:** London, 5 October 1949. **Education:** St. Benedict's, Ealing, 1960-67; Clare College, Cambridge, 1968-71; Yale University, New Haven, Connecticut (Mellon fellow), 1971-73. **Career:** Literary editor, 1973-77, and joint managing editor, 1978-81, the *Spectator,* London. Since 1986 chief book reviewer, the *Times,* London. Lives in London. **Awards:** Maugham award, 1984; Whitbread award, for biography, 1985, for fiction, 1986; Royal Society of Literature Heinemann award, for non-fiction, 1985; *Guardian* Fiction prize, 1985. Fellow, Royal Society of Literature, 1984. H.D.L.: Exeter University, 1993. **Agent:** Anthony Sheil Associates, 43 Doughty Street, London WC1N 2LF, England.

PUBLICATIONS

Novels

The Great Fire of London. London, Hamish Hamilton, 1982; Chicago, University of Chicago Press, 1988.
The Last Testament of Oscar Wilde. London, Hamish Hamilton, and New York, Harper, 1983.
Hawksmoor. London, Hamish Hamilton, 1985; New York, Harper, 1986.
Chatterton. London, Hamish Hamilton, 1987; New York, Grove Press, 1988.
First Light. London, Hamish Hamilton, and New York, Grove Weidenfeld, 1989.
English Music. London, Hamish Hamilton, 1991; New York, Knopf, 1993.
The House of Doctor Dee. London, Hamish Hamilton, 1993.
Dan Lemo and the Limehouse Golem. London, Sinclair Stevenson, 1994; as *The Trial of Elizabeth Cree,* New York, Doubleday, 1995.
Blake. London, Sinclair Stevenson, 1995.

Uncollected Short Stories

"The Inheritance," in *London Tales,* edited by Julian Evans. London, Hamish Hamilton, 1983.
"Ringing in the Good News," in *The Times* (London), 24 December 1985.

Poetry

London Lickpenny. London, Ferry Press, 1973.
Country Life. London, Ferry Press, 1978.
The Diversions of Purley and Other Poems. London, Hamish Hamilton, 1987.

Other

Notes for a New Culture: An Essay on Modernism. London, Vision Press, and New York, Barnes and Noble, 1976.
Dressing Up: Transvestism and Drag: The History of an Obsession. London, Thames and Hudson, and New York, Simon and Schuster, 1979.
Ezra Pound and His World. London, Thames and Hudson, and New York, Scribner, 1981.
T.S. Eliot (biography). London, Hamish Hamilton, and New York, Simon and Schuster, 1984.
Dickens (biography). London, Sinclair Stevenson, and New York, Harper Collins, 1990.

Editor, *PEN New Fiction.* London, Quartet, 1984.
Editor, *The Picture of Dorian Gray,* by Oscar Wilde. London, Penguin, 1985.
Editor, *Dickens' London: An Imaginative Vision.* London, Headline, 1987.

*   *   *

By the time Peter Ackroyd published his first novel in 1982, he was already well known in the literary world as a poet, critic, literary theorist, and cultural historian. Since his début as a novelist he has further enhanced his reputation as a non-fiction writer, first with his award-winning biography of T.S. Eliot and more recently with his imaginatively daring biography of Charles Dickens. Before the appearance of his first novel, it seemed that his writing career was likely to develop in the fields of literary criticism and biography, but with five novels in quick succession between 1982 and 1989 he has established himself as one of the most gifted and imaginative English novelists to have emerged during the recent past. Critical opinion may differ about whether his strikingly original talent is taking the right direction, but there is no disagreement about his potential.

Ackroyd's polemical book, *Notes for a New Culture,* contains a relentless attack on the parochialism and impoverishment of contemporary English culture, especially literature and the academic literary establishment; he makes clear his intellectual allegiance to Continental (primarily French and German) models and theories descending from such figures as de Sade, Nietzsche, Mallarmé, and Husserl, in opposition to what he sees as the stultifying tradition of empiricism, positivism, and humanism still dominant in English artistic and intellectual life. He insists on the autonomy and formal absoluteness of language, on the way in which language constitutes meaning only within itself, and he therefore challenges the philosophical basis of orthodox realistic fiction, regarding its conventions as no longer having any validity for the modern writer. As might be expected, his five novels are not conventionally realistic, but his innovative approach to fiction has not led him into the cul-de-sacs of hyper-selfconscious experimentalism or navel-gazing phenomenology. On the contrary, all five books possess a strong narrative drive and are highly readable, demonstrating that he has not felt the need to reject storytelling in order to develop his own type of literary fiction. At the same time, the five novels are very different from each other: Ackroyd is a novelist who likes to try something new with every book.

There is an element of deception in the title of Ackroyd's novels, especially as the first four, *The Great Fire of London, The Last Testament of Oscar Wilde, Hawksmoor,* and *Chatterton* could be the titles of historical or biographical studies rather than works of fiction. The fire in *The Great Fire of London* is not that of 1666, an event referred to in *Hawksmoor,* but an apocalyptic fictional one that begins with the burning of a film set for a screen adaptation of *Little Dorrit.* As if to substantiate his theoretical point that writing emerges from other writing rather than from life, Ackroyd draws on Dickens's novel in many ways, thus emphasizing the fictionality of his own fictional world, however realistic it may appear in some respects. Indeed, Ackroyd's novel is centrally concerned with the perpetual human activity of creating fictions in life as well as in art. The short opening section of *The Great Fire of London,* "the story so far," outlines the plot of *Little Dorrit* and ends: "although it could not be described as a true story, certain events have certain consequences"—including, of course, the writing of Ackroyd's novel. Dickens's eponymous heroine and the novel itself feature prominently in the minds of many of Ackroyd's characters, including Spenser Spender (a filmmaker, with two poets' names who is determined to put the novel on the screen), Rowan Phillips (a Canadian homosexual and Cambridge don currently working on Dickens), and Audrey Skelton (a telephone operator who is possessed by the spirit of Little Dorrit during a séance). The setting of much of *Little Dorrit,* the Marshalsea Prison, also provides a link between the two novels because its site is visited by several of Ackroyd's characters. With its panorama of London in the 1980s from left-wing activists to gay bars, *The Great Fire of London* is at least as much a London novel as *Little Dorrit.* Ackroyd's narrative structure, in which several strands begin in parallel and gradually intertwine and coalesce, is itself derived from Dickens's methods and techniques, especially in his later novels such as *Little Dorrit.* By using one of the greatest of English novels as his point of departure, Ackroyd inevitably takes the risk of being unflatteringly compared with Dickens, but *The Great Fire of London* must be taken on its own terms, not Dickens's, and as such it is an exuberant, inventive, and accomplished piece of writing.

Ackroyd's second novel draws its inspiration not from a major mid-Victorian novel but from an important late Victorian writer. *The Last Testament of Oscar Wilde* is the testament that Wilde himself did not write but that Ackroyd has written for him in the form of a journal-cum-memoir covering that last few months of Wilde's life in Paris in 1900. The book therefore purports to be Wilde's autobiographical confessions in the tradition of such writing that connects St. Augustine with Rousseau and De Quincey. To write *The Last Testament of Oscar Wilde* Ackroyd must have steeped himself in Wilde's biography as well as his writing, and presumably could have written yet another study of the man and his work. Instead Ackroyd has chosen the freedom of fiction to enter imaginatively into Wilde's mind as he lives through his last weeks in France

and simultaneously offers an explanation of his famous rise and infamous fall. The obvious danger with a novel of this type, not only about an historical personage but written from his point of view, is that readers will be tempted to compare the "facts" with the fictional re-creation, but this would be to approach the novel in far too literal-minded a way. As a fictional character, Ackroyd's Wilde cannot be the historical Wilde: for all its "factual" content, *The Last Testament of Oscar Wilde* is primarily a work of the imagination about the relationship between the artist and the world and about the difference between fictional and historical truth.

The skill with which Ackroyd creates a style and tone of voice for his narrator and sustains it throughout *The Last Testament of Oscar Wilde* is a remarkable technical achievement, but it pales beside the ludic and verbal virtuosity of *Hawksmoor,* in which he plays far more elaborate games with fact and fiction, history and imagination. The title is the name of Sir Christopher Wren's most distinguished assistant, Nicholas Hawksmoor, the great architect responsible for some of London's finest churches (referred to in *The Great Fire of London*), but in the novel these churches are attributed to Nicholas Dyer while Hawksmoor himself is a modern Detective Chief Superintendent investigating a series of murders in the East End. Although *Hawksmoor* contains characters who belong to history, such as Wren and Vanbrugh, and draws heavily on various historical sources, it is not an historical novel in the usual sense; indeed, it radically subverts the conventions of historical fiction. In a concluding note Ackroyd states that "this version of history is my own invention" and that "any relation to real people, either living or dead, is entirely coincidental." The six odd-numbered chapters in a book in which numerology plays a significant part are set in the early 18th century and are narrated by Dyer in a contemporary idiom, complete with old spellings and the initial capitalization of many words. Although a builder of churches, Dyer is secretly a Satanist and devotee of black magic, as well as being an opponent of the new scientific empiricism of the Royal Society, and dedicates his buildings to the dark powers by ensuring a human sacrifice in connection with each one. The six even-numbered chapters, set about two and a half centuries later, provide a third-person narration of the bizarre and puzzling killings associated with the same churches and of Hawksmoor's attempt to track down the culprit. Ackroyd creates mystery and suspense, but unlike orthodox writers of crime and detection he does not provide a solution. Despite the time shift between the two narratives, they flow smoothly into each other and run strictly in parallel. The last words of the first chapter are also the first words of the second chapter, for example, and the name of Dyer's first sacrificial victim is the same as that of the first person murdered in the 20th-century narrative. Time dissolves so that the modern policeman is, in a sense, investigating crimes of the past. One of Ackroyd's central concerns is the human continuity associated with place, specifically the East End of London, in spite of all the changes wrought by the passage of time. *Hawksmoor* is as multi-layered as the archaeological heritage beneath the baroque churches built by Dyer, a gothic figure in a landscape of rationalism, enlightenment, and superficial optimism. The dazzling erudition and ingenuity of Ackroyd's third novel bring to mind such authors as Borges, Nabokov, Pynchon, and Eco without seeming derivative in the pejorative sense.

Like *The Last Testament of Oscar Wilde, Chatterton* fictionalises the last part of an important literary figure's life, but in other respects, especially its handling of time and form, this novel is much closer to *Hawksmoor,* and is equally rich in internal echoes and cross-references. Like Ackroyd himself, the "marvellous boy" Thomas Chatterton was a master of pastiche and "faking," and it is easy to understand why Ackroyd should have been attracted by the fictional, rather than the biographical, possibilities offered by this extraordinarily precocious 18th-century poet. Chatterton committed suicide in 1770 while still in his teens, and for his Romantic successors his bizarre and tragic death ensured his status as a martyr in the cause of Art and Poetry. At a time when there was a great revival of interest in the Middle Ages, Chatterton was one of several poets who adopted a medieval style and presented their literary pastiches not as "imitations" but as authentic poetry of the past which they had unearthed. Chatterton attributed his "Rowley" poems to a 15th-century monk. However only some sections of the novel are set in the 18th century, with Chatterton either speaking in his own voice or being described. Much of the novel concerns a modern and frequently comic quest by a young poet and a much older woman novelist to discover the truth about Chatterton's death. An 18th-century manuscript provides these literary detectives with clues suggesting that Chatterton's suicide was itself faked and that he survived under another name. Interwoven with the 18th-century and 20th-century narratives are sections set in Victorian England dealing with Henry Wallis's famous and highly romanticised painting of Chatterton's death (1856), for which the model was George Meredith, then himself a young poet. In this intricately structured novel about the reality of literature and art and the fictionality of reality, Ackroyd continues to explore the main themes of *Hawksmoor*, but the pervasive issues of plagiarism and faking focus particular attention on the ambiguity of art ("a lie that tells the truth") and its relationship with life, which is no less ambiguous.

Ackroyd's 1989 novel, *First Light,* is his longest and arguably his most ambitious, but after *Hawksmoor* and *Chatterton* it seems disappointing. This is not because *First Light* is any less readable then its two predecessors. Again there is a mystery to be investigated—an archaeological one—and this provides a strong narrative drive. The problem arises from the task Ackroyd sets himself—to resuscitate pastoral romance by writing a modern version of it. Iris Murdoch is another writer who has attempted to revivify pastoral and romance, and *First Light* is more Murdochian than Ackroyd's earlier novels, but both novelists experience considerable difficulty in reconciling pastoral conventions with the contemporary world without being fey. The excavation of a Neolithic passage grave in a rural backwater of the West Country—indeed of Hardy's Wessex—is what brings a fairly large and diverse cast of characters together in a lavishly textured story of intrigue, comedy, and pathos. A further dimension is added by the astronomical investigation of a giant star at a nearby observatory, which parallels the archaeological probe into the past. Literary allusions, especially to Hardy's fiction, abound in Ackroyd's imaginative exploration of time, history, space, and landscape, yet the total effect is more precious and etiolated than in the two city novels that preceded *First Light*.

Ackroyd has said that he is not interested in realism in the novel, and has further developed in his next two novels, *English Music* and *The House of Doctor Dee,* a genre in which fact and fiction are equally intertwined. This choice suggests that the traditional confines of fiction are inadequate to express what Ackroyd wants to say. In both novels Ackroyd has incorporated historically "dead" people, who talk to the living fictional characters with the purpose of giving meaning to some quest of his "living" characters. As a writer who particularly projects what he has to say through other voices, he has been likened to a ventriloquist, or a "polyquilivist." *The Music of England* refers to composed music, but also to landmarks in the whole of English literature, painting, and architecture.

The novel provides an idiosyncratic survey of these arts, brought together in a total harmony through the imagination of Timothy Harcombe, an old bachelor, who recalls his boyhood life in the early 1920s. At night in alternating chapters, Timothy in either sleep or dream or trance, talks to historical and fictional characters and interacts with them as real people. The historical figures represent an unbroken link in "the great tradition" in English artistic creativity. Blake, whose life Ackroyd is currently completing, for example, has him "write" a Song of Albion, naming English poets up to the end of the nineteenth century who have been conscious of this English heritage. Ackroyd's choice of those who defend the ancient springs is of course a subjective one, and few would include the very minor Ernest Dowson, nor really expect Blake (if he could have read him) to admire him at all.

Pastiche is again a strong feature in *The House of Doctor Dee,* set, like *English Music,* in Clerkenwell, London, where the area is at least as important as the characters. At times Ackroyd seems to have made it more so, letting the atmosphere of shady back streets block the light that would develop his characters more fully. The discovery by Matthew Palmer, a historical researcher, that a house he has inherited from his father once belonged to the Elizabethan astrologer, Dr John Dee, is only the loose framework of the novel. Yet the framework, as in all Ackroyd's novels, is not limited to a simple structure or time scale and depends on a cumulative effect of rapid change of scene, period, and minutiae of often apparently irrelevant detail for the total effect. It is the means for informing the reader, amongst much else, about Dr Dee, black magic, and Palmer's father, who it transpires had a sexual relationship with a transvestite. Matthew as a character hardly matters, but what he explores does.

Dan Lemo and the Limehouse Golem was publicised as a departure for Ackroyd and described by the publisher as "a groundbreaking commercial entertainment." If it is taken at face value as an imitation of the Victorian crime novel, it indeed succeeds very well, with its search for the perpetrator of horrifically detailed serial killings. Inexact clues point suspicion at all of the main characters, but deliberately Ackroyd provides no solution. Many of the characters are not what they seem to be and have double identities. Lambeth Lizzie, hanged for the murder of her husband, may or may not have been guilty, but she wore men's clothes, while the eponymous Dan Lemo, a rather repulsive music-hall artist, is a female impersonator. The whole question of reality and appearance is raised by the use of "golem" of the title, a "mythical creature able to dissolve in thin air" but which takes its identity by absorbing the souls of others. *Dan Lemo and the Limehouse Golem* is a wild theatrical extravaganza, but Ackroyd justifies his insistence that the reader question everything in it by quoting from Oscar Wilde's *The Truth of Masks:* "Truth is independent of facts always, inventing or selecting them at pleasure. The true dramatist shows us life under the condition of art, not art in the form of life."

—Peter Lewis, updated by Geoffrey Elborn

ADAMS, Alice (Boyd)

Nationality: American. **Born:** Fredericksburg, Virginia, 14 August 1926. **Education:** Radcliffe College, Cambridge, Massachusetts, A.B. 1946. **Family:** Married in 1946 (divorced 1958); one son. **Career:** Has worked as secretary, clerk, and bookkeeper; now full-time writer. Lives in San Francisco. **Awards:** National Endowment for the Arts grant, 1976; Guggenheim fellowship, 1978. **Address:** c/o Knopf Inc., 201 East 50th Street, New York, New York 10022, U.S.A.

PUBLICATIONS

Novels

Careless Love. New York, New American Library, 1966; as *The Fall of Daisy Duke,* London, Constable, 1967.
Families and Survivors. New York, Knopf, 1975; London, Constable, 1976.
Listening to Billie. New York, Knopf, and London, Constable, 1978.
Rich Rewards. New York, Knopf, 1980.
Superior Women. New York, Knopf, 1984; London, Heinemann, 1985.
Second Chances. New York, Knopf, and London, Methuen, 1988.
Caroline's Daughters. New York, Knopf, 1991.
Almost Perfect. New York, Knopf, 1993.

Short Stories

Beautiful Girl. New York, Knopf, 1979.
To See You Again. New York, Knopf, 1982.
Molly's Dog. Concord, New Hampshire, Ewert, 1983.
Return Trips. New York, Knopf, 1985; London, Heinemann, 1986.
After You've Gone. New York, Knopf, 1989.

Uncollected Short Stories

"Earthquake Damage," in *New Yorker,* 7 May 1990.
"The Last Lovely City," in *New Yorker,* 11 March 1991.

Other

Roses, Rhododendron: Two Flowers, Two Friends. Minneapolis, Redpath Press, 1987.
Mexico: Some Travels and Travelers There. New York and London, Prentice Hall, 1990.

*   *   *

Alice Adams, in her collections of short stories and her several novels, is an investigator of the plight (and the good fortunes) of American women: women living in a period extending from the early 1940s to the present. Adams's women have a variety of histories and follow many different careers—most of these careers are, however, more or less "creative." But the histories take place within certain limits: limits that can be easily experienced by a reading of Adams's short stories—*Beautiful Girl, To See You Again, Return Trips,* and *After You've Gone.* As both the stories and the novels suggest, the Adams world is peopled by women who have "made it." Some have "arrived" with practically no effort at all. These women have rich parents who, usually after some delay, die and leave a heroine with money to redecorate her house and do whatever else comes to her mind (and this usually involves getting rid of a husband and finding a new love). Occasionally, however, a heroine has to seek a job and is even a little hampered by the presence of a child or so.

Not unimportant in the fictions is the "space" in which the hero-ines seek self—knowledge and self-realization. Three geographical regions "count;" the women have often, like Adams herself, been brought up in the south, have completed their educations in the Boston area, and more often than not follow careers that take them to San Francisco.

Against such backgrounds are acted out the dramas that are Adams's preoccupations: the passing of "interesting" women through several decades, from a time when self-realization for women was looked at with suspicion to later eras when orgasms can be talked about over a cup of coffee or a glass of tea. But none of the Adams women suffers unduly from the social reprisals free lifestyles once stirred up. Instead, in ambiances where people are quite often "rich" (a recurrent word in the novels) women advance to meet new partners or retreat in order to meditate on the lovers they have left behind. Marriages are dissolved without much ado, and it is usually harder to say good-bye to a lover than to a husband. The novels in particular offer many examples of women measuring the value of what they have endured with this man or that one.

Although the Adams women are well-read, the chief intellectual resource the heroines draw on is a schematic version of Freudian analysis. Many a woman understands her present troubles by recalling her attachment to her father or her opposition to her mother. All heroines worth their salt can discover latent homosexuality in their female friendships, and women can pass a pleasant afternoon speculating about the "real" sexual orientation of men near to them.

This is a general description of Adams's work. Each of the novels mentioned below operates as a terrain of vigorous action, but not as an area of surprise and innovation. A quick passage through the novels supports this point.

The heroine of *Careless Love,* Daisy Duke, has rejected her husband (too weak) and her lover (too mundane), and is finally delighted with a lover who has some of the élan of Valentino. The tale is a presage of the later narratives. *Families and Survivors* is primarily the history of a privileged Southern girl, Louisa Calloway, who is surrounded by a typical Adams clientele: a Jewish psychiatrist, a failed novelist (he becomes an English professor), and female friends who aid Louisa as she scans her life and who expect the same service from her. In this novel, which covers thirty-odd years of Louisa's life, there are brief references to current events; these work quite well for a person who has lived through the period. Adams appears to count on such a reader. The pace, in this novel and others, varies. Years are dismissed in a paragraph, and then the novel slows down while Louisa attends a party or prepares a meal for a new lover.

Listening to Billie is, again, the selective life-history of a woman, Eliza Hamilton Quarles (and her half-sister Daria as well). The girls are daughters of a famous woman writer. Daria makes a marriage that ends after a couple of decades of "success." Eliza, in contrast, strikes out for herself boldly, after the early death of her husband. (Husbands frequently disappear in this way.) Her most successful love-affair unites her to a famous film-director; her most painful one entangles her with an epicene antiques dealer who (it turns out characteristically) was deeply attractive years before to Eliza's husband. Across these and other complexities Eliza passes with some success; she is aided by a vivid recollection of a night-club performance by Billie Holiday.

Rich Rewards is essentially the tale of a long wait. Daphne Matthiessen (a product of Wisconsin, for a change) has, early in her marriage, a brief relationship with a young Frenchman, Jean-Paul. This done, she returns to America with her husband, leaves him, becomes an interior decorator . . . and waits. Passing lovers help her endure her solitude. But all this dissolves in happiness when Jean-Paul comes to America to lecture. Twenty years have passed, but Jean-Paul says to Daphne, as she passes him: "Daphne."

Superior Women is fuller and more coherent than some of the other novels. In it, Adams goes into the lives of four schoolmates of the 1940s, and does so with a thoroughness that her previous glancing methods did not always permit. In this novel, at least, the chief characters are intimately connected with their own pasts and loves and with those of their friends. The four girls are, of course, still thoroughly creatures of Adams's particular vision in which women reckon the worth of their lives in terms of the various loves they have known. And, as in the other novels, this worth is analyzed in terms that Freudian psychiatry has made familiar. Indeed, *Superior Women* is a clear reminder of all that Adams has seen from coast to coast.

—Harold H. Watts

ADAMS, Glenda

Nationality: Australian. **Born:** Sydney, 1939. **Education:** University of Sydney, B.A. (honours) 1962; Columbia University, New York, M.S. 1965. **Family:** Has one daughter. **Career:** Writing Workshop instructor, Columbia University, New York, and Sarah Lawrence College; fiction writing teacher at University of Technology, Sydney; associate director, Teachers and Writers Collaborative, New York, 1973-76. **Awards:** Miles Franklin Literary award, 1987; *Age* Fiction Book of the Year, 1990; National Book Council award for fiction, 1991. **Member:** Australian Society of Authors; Australian Writers Guild. **Agent:** Goodman Associates, 500 West End Ave., New York, New York 10024 USA. **Address:** Department of English, Columbia University, New York, New York 10027, U.S.A.

PUBLICATIONS

Novels

Games of the Strong. Sydney, Angus and Robertson, 1982; New York, Cane Hill Press, 1989.
Dancing on Coral. New York, Viking, and Sydney and London, Angus and Robertson, 1988.
Longleg. Sydney, Angus and Robertson, 1990; New York, Cane Hill Press, 1992.

Short Stories

Lies and Stories. N.p., 1976.
The Hottest Night of the Year. Sydney, Angus and Robertson, 1979; New York, Cane Hill Press, 1989.

Plays

Television Play: *Pride*, 1993; *Wrath*, 1993.

*

Manuscript Collection: Australian Defense Force Academy, University of New South Wales, Canberra, Australia.

* * *

Born in Sydney, Glenda Adams left an Australia she found too restrictive in 1964 and lived in New York for many years before finally returning to her home country in what she sees as the completion of a personal odyssey. Her first collection of short pieces, written and published in various periodicals in the United States, was *Lies and Stories,* but *The Hottest Night of the Year,* which includes seven stories from the first collection together with more recent work, was the first book to establish her reputation. Most of the stories are written in the first person and concern vulnerable or alienated female protagonists, who fiercely insist nevertheless on retaining their individuality and independence. The first six stories seem to be set in Sydney (though the setting is not always named) and deal with the experience of childhood and adolescence. Running through them is a note of implicit protest against the mistreatment of women. This emerges clearly in "The Music Masters," with its bitterly misognynistic father, and is carried on in several stories about the early days of marriages in which husbands invariably dismiss and behave condescendingly toward their new wives. The later stories are more playful and whimsically self-conscious in form. "Twelfth Night, or The Passion," for instance, shows the narrator determinedly exercising her option to have an improbably happy ending, whereas "Reconstruction of an Event" ostentatiously flaunts its different narrative possibilities. The stories are written in a deceptively simple style and marked often by a bizarre kind of humour and almost surreal disconnectedness, qualities that will emerge in Adams's later fiction.

Games of the Strong is, in retrospect, Adams's least characteristic novel. Written in the genre of the dystopian novel (a surprisingly ubiquitous one in Australian fiction) it describes an impoverished police state; dissidents are expelled to "The Island," where they are left to die, where poverty is rampant, and where no one is to be trusted. Its heroine, Neila, is hardly political at all and is mostly concerned to discover the truth about her parents' deaths (allegedly in a car accident), but slowly she is drawn into resisting the injustices and inequalities she sees all around her. It is a world that is full of betrayals and one in which, although she insists constantly on her own weakness ("I have no valour," "I am a coward and did not want to get hurt"), Neila develops into another of Adams's sturdily independent female protagonists. Perhaps the most puzzling aspect of the novel is its allegorical intention or lack of it. There is only one reference to this world, a brief mention of David Oistrakh playing a Beethoven concerto, but there are several contemptuous observations on outside democratic powers that willingly tolerate the excesses of "The Complex."

Adams came into her own as a writer, however, with her two most recent novels. *Dancing on Coral,* which won the Miles Franklin Award for the best Australian novel of the year, is a very funny and witty novel, its style built around a sense of derangement, non sequiturs, and conversations not connecting or at cross purposes. Lark Watters (who had appeared briefly in one of Adams's early stories) grows up in Sydney during the 1960s and falls in love with Solomon Blank, but he wins a scholarship in America. Then she is attracted to an American named Tom Brown. She and Donna Bird, her rival for Tom's attentions, embark on a freighter bound for the United States, but en route Lark, tormented by her dominant companion, allows her to be left behind when the ship sails.

The novel is in part a satire on what the author sees as a decade of silliness. It is peopled by grotesques, like the German captain of the freighter and Lark's father, who is building a coffin for himself and who indulges in trivial pursuits, such as learning how to get around London and memorising all the stops on the air route from Sydney to London. Underneath the comedy the serious point is being made, through a letter that Lark's mother writes to her saying that her father has disappeared: "Too, before I left on my holiday he said to tell you, you have made your own way in this tricky world. You have done it all yourself. There has not been much help from us, I am aware." Bereft of both lover and husband at the end, Lark is finally free to be her own person.

Independence is also a theme of *Longleg,* Adams's most disturbing novel. William Badger is ten when the novel opens shortly after the war and is fearful that his mother—beautiful, young, and dissatisfied with the country she lives in and with everything else—will leave him, which she does. When she eventually returns she is a different woman, from whom William closes himself off. We see William then at various stages of his life and in various places as he grows through relationships with women as if to gain the security he has never had—with Meg Meese, who takes him cave exploring with her Trogs, Tillie Pepper and her group of radical activists, the Pan-European Barbarians; and Amanda, the married woman he falls in love with until finally he realizes the truth of what the most sympathetic of the Barbarians had said to him: "I think you can always recognize when you have to take a new path and when you should stay where you are." It is a brilliantly inventive novel and in its protagonist, William, Adams has created her most sympathetic character.

Certain types appear constantly in Glenda Adams's fiction: the vulnerable adolescent or young woman often just married; the older, sophisticated woman who is a threat to the bride; idiosyncratic or irresponsible parents. Her principal characters are questers seeking to find the identity so many people leave undiscovered; even the constant name-changing is a symbol of their uncertainty. Voyages dominate her two most recent novels, which are both very funny and at times poignant.

—Laurie Clancy

ADAMS, Richard (George)

Nationality: British. **Born:** Newbury, Berkshire, 9 May 1920. **Education:** Bradfield College, Berkshire, 1933-38; Worcester College, Oxford, 1938-39, 1946-48, B.A. in modern history 1948, M.A. 1953. **Military Service:** Served in the British Army, 1940-46. **Family:** Married Barbara Elizabeth Acland in 1949; two daughters. **Career:** Worked in the Ministry of Housing and Local Government, London, 1948-68; Assistant Secretary, Department of the Environment, London, 1968-74. Writer-in-residence, University of Florida, Gainesville, 1975, and Hollins College, Virginia, 1976. President, Royal Society for the Prevention of Cruelty to Animals, 1980-82 (resigned). Independent Conservative parliamentary candidate for Spelthorne, 1983. **Awards:** Library Association Carnegie medal, 1972; *Guardian* award, 1973. Fellow, Royal Society of Literature, 1975. **Agent:** David Higham Associates Ltd., 5-8 Lower John Street, London W1R 4HA. **Address:** 26 Church Street, Whitchurch, Hampshire RG28 7AR, England.

PUBLICATIONS

Novels

Watership Down. London, Collings, 1972; New York, Macmillan, 1974.
Shardik. London, Allen Lane-Collings, 1974; New York, Simon and Schuster, 1975.
The Plague Dogs. London, Allen Lane-Collings, 1977; New York, Knopf, 1978.
The Girl in a Swing. London, Allen Lane, and New York, Knopf, 1980.
Maia. London, Viking, 1984; New York, Knopf, 1985.
Traveller. New York, Knopf, 1988; London, Hutchinson, 1989.

Fiction (for children)

The Bureaucats. London, Viking Kestrel, 1985.

Poetry

The Tyger Voyage (for children). London, Cape, and New York, Knopf, 1976.
The Ship's Cat (for children). London, Cape, and New York, Knopf, 1977.
The Legend of Te Tuna. Los Angeles, Sylvester and Orphanos, 1982; London, Sidgwick and Jackson, 1986.

Other

Voyage Through the Antarctic, with Ronald Lockley. London, Allen Lane, 1982; New York, Knopf, 1983.
A Nature Diary. London, Viking, 1985; New York, Viking, 1986.
The Day Gone By: An Autobiography. London, Hutchinson, 1990; New York, Knopf, 1991.

Editor, *Occasional Poets: An Anthology.* London, Viking, 1986.

Other (for children)

Nature Through the Seasons, with Max Hooper. London, Kestrel, and New York, Simon and Schuster, 1975.
Nature Day and Night, with Max Hooper. London, Kestrel, and New York, Viking Press, 1978.
The Watership Down Film Picture Book. London, Allen Lane, and New York, Macmillan, 1978.
The Iron Wolf and Other Stories (folktales). London, Allen Lane, 1980; as *The Unbroken Web,* New York, Crown, 1980.
Editor, *Grimm's Fairy Tales.* London, Routledge, 1981.
Editor, *Richard Adams's Favourite Animal Stories.* London, Octopus, 1981.
Editor, *The Best of Ernest Thompson Seton.* London, Fontana, 1982.

*

Richard Adams comments:

(1991) I can only say, like Trollope, that I am an entertainer, and the essence of fiction is that the reader should wish to turn the page.

*   *   *

Originally published as a book for children, *Watership Down* made Richard Adams's name as a novelist by becoming one of the leading bestsellers of the 1970s. Set in the rabbit world of the English countryside, it is primarily an adventure story, original in conception, but with excellent natural descriptions and evocations of such human virtues as courage, loyalty, and modesty. The story begins when a peaceful rabbit warren in Berkshire is destroyed by a new housing development and a party of young bucks escape, thanks to the ability of one of their number, Fiver, to foresee the future. What follows is an odyssey to find a new home, during which the rabbits encounter many strange and terrifying adventures. Danger comes from human beings, poisoned fields, machines, and also from another group of rabbits led by the despotic General Woundwort. "In combat he was terrifying, fighting entirely to kill, indifferent to any wounds he received himself and closing with his adversaries until his weight overbore and exhausted them. Those who had no heart to oppose him were not long in the feeling that here was a leader indeed." Eventually, the rabbits achieve their goal but have to fight a fiercely contested battle to protect their new territory.

Adams, a senior civil servant when he wrote *Watership Down,* admitted that many parts of the novel were created as stories to please his children during long car journeys and that much of the factual information came from R.M. Lockley's study *The Private Life of the Rabbit,* but his work is very much a fictional unity. Some critics have suggested that *Watership Down* is an allegory on man's indifference to the natural life of his planet and, taken that way, it presents a grimly satirical view; but the novel is best seen as part of the fantastic strain in English literature, in line with the work of C.S. Lewis, J.R.R. Tolkien, and Kenneth Grahame.

In his second novel, *Shardik,* Adams shifted his center of literary influences to the adventure genre of H. Rider Haggard and John Buchan. The action and setting are timeless and the background imaginary—the Beklan empire which has been over-run, and its inhabitants, the Ortelgans, enslaved. When a large bear is driven from their forests, the Ortelgans take him to be an ancient bear-god called Shardik. With his help they are able to drive off their oppressors and are returned to power. Kelderek, "a simple foolish fellow," becomes king of the Ortelgans but idleness and luxury lures him into wickedness. Once again the country is threatened but is redeemed by Shardik's blood sacrifice. Although Adams centered most of his attention on the bear, the humans are real enough and his ability to create an imaginary world may be considered the novel's great strength. In parts overwritten—a trap for any adventure novel—*Shardik* is, nevertheless, a powerful statement about man's inhumanity to man.

Adams was more successful when he returned to the animal world in *The Plague Dogs,* which is, among other things, a hard-hitting attack on the world of animal research. Snitter, a thoroughbred terrier, and Rowf, a mongrel, escape from a government research station in the Lake District and the novel is an account of their adventures to keep out of man's way before they escape to the mystical Isle of Dog. As in *Watership Down,* Adams gives his animals human characteristics but they are not men in dogs' guise. When Snitter and Rowf decide to live off the land, for example, it is a fox who teaches them the necessary tricks and they have difficulty understanding his thick local dialect. When they are seen, men appear only as the enemy and the animals themselves have little understanding of their world.

Although he has also written adventure novels in the style of *Shardik,* Adams is at his happiest in the animal world. The Arcadian worlds of the rabbits' Berkshire and the dogs' Lake District are peopled by an organized society of idealized, largely peaceful animals, but this is not simple anthropomorphism. The animals might be able to speak and to rationalize like human beings but they have not lost their animal characteristics. The rabbits of *Watership Down* even have the remnants of an ancient rabbit language with its own words like *n-Frith* for noon and *hrududu* for tractor or any other man-made machine. It is his ability to create the rabbits and dogs as sensible and sensitive creatures and not as animals-in-man's-clothing or as lovable furry creatures which gives Adams his greatest strength as a novelist.

—Trevor Royle

ADLER, Renata

Nationality: American. **Born:** Milan, Italy, 19 October 1938. **Education:** Bryn Mawr College, Pennsylvania, A.B. 1959; the Sorbonne, Paris, D.D'E.S. 1961; Harvard University, Cambridge, Massachusetts, M.A. 1962; Yale University, New Haven, Connecticut, J.D. 1979. **Career:** Since 1962 writer and reporter, the *New Yorker.* Film critic, New York *Times,* 1968-69; member of the editorial board, *American Scholar,* Washington, D.C., 1968-73. Fellow, Trumbull College, Yale University, 1969-72. **Awards:** Guggenheim fellowship, 1973; O. Henry award, for short story, 1974; Hemingway Foundation award, 1977; American Academy award, 1979. LL.D.: Georgetown University, Washington, D.C., 1989. **Member:** American Academy, 1987. **Agent:** International Creative Management, 40 West 57th Street, New York, New York 10019. **Address:** Hattertown Road, Newtown, Connecticut 06470, U.S.A.

PUBLICATIONS

Novels

Speedboat. New York, Random House, 1976; London, Hamish Hamilton, 1977.
Pitch Dark. New York, Knopf, and London, Hamish Hamilton, 1983.

Uncollected Short Stories

"Collect Calls," in *New Yorker,* 24 October 1970.
"Downers and Séances," in *New Yorker,* 13 February 1971.
"Castling," in *New Yorker,* 30 December 1972.
"Brownstone," in *Prize Stories 1974,* edited by William Abrahams. New York, Doubleday, 1974.
"Agency," in *New Yorker,* 16 February 1976.
"Drowning Nanny and an Aces Fellow," in *Vogue* (New York), October 1976.

Other

A Year in the Dark: Journal of a Film Critic 1968-69. New York, Random House, 1969.
Toward a Radical Middle: Fourteen Pieces of Reporting and Criticism. New York, Random House, 1970.

*Reckless Disregard: Westmoreland v. C.B.S. et al., Sharon v.
   "Time."* New York, Knopf, 1986.
Politics and Media (essays). New York, St. Martin's Press, 1988.

* * *

What distinguishes the novels of Renata Adler is the very quality she discerned some years ago in the fiction of Nathalie Sarraute and Iris Murdoch: "What is extraordinary about each of these writers is her complete consistency, her strict attention to only that psychological level that she has chosen to study . . . each manages to convey more truth by means of her polygraph than we are getting from many writers of cataclysmic aspiration, the seismologists among contemporary novelists." In *Speedboat,* runner-up for the 1977 National Book Critics Circle award for fiction, and *Pitch Dark,* Adler has proven herself an adept practitioner of the polygraph style she shares with not only Sarraute and Murdoch but more especially with her West Coast counterpart Joan Didion, and a number of younger American women writers, including Mary Robison. Theirs is a fiction as bleak, as anonymous, and as disjunctive as the modern world in which they set their stories. Yet despite the brittle syntax and jagged surface of her novels, Adler has been highly critical of the apocalyptic posturing and "unearned nihilism" of many contemporary writers, artists, and composers, whose fashionably avant-garde experiments she has judged pretentious and even boring (as critical, one might say, as she is of the news media in her highly polemical and politically conservative journalistic book, *Reckless Disregard*). Adler prefers the "radical middle," a delicate balance of hope and risk, tradition and innovation, in which the possibility of gain must always be weighed against the remembrance of personal loss. It is this elusive state that Adler's female protagonists long to reach but invariably fail to attain.

As the title of her first novel suggests, Adler's is a fiction about motion as well as a fiction that is itself in motion. Her characters work but never accomplish anything important or even substantive; they travel but never reach any clear, final destination, any still point in the whirling universe of transatlantic flights, rented cars, and speedboats. Adler's syntax reflects her characters' sensibility, a kind of emotional jet lag: "Things have changed very much, several times, since I grew up, and like everyone else in New York except the intellectuals, I have led several lives and I still lead some of them." This is a fiction of juxtaposed elements structured on the basis of coordination rather than (as in conventional fiction) subordination; it is a prose in which positions are stated only to be qualified and finally either contradicted or cancelled altogether. Makeshift transitional phrases pretend to connect random events that do not so much define as overwhelm the novel's characters. Adrift in time and space, they suddenly appear and just as suddenly disappear, known to the reader (and, one suspects, to the narrator-protagonist as well) merely as names or generic epithets—Bill, Maggie, "the young construction worker," "the wife of the Italian mineral-water tycoon."

As narrator of her own story-in-the-making, *Speedboat*'s Jen Fain fares somewhat better. For the 35-year-old Fain, whose biography resembles Adler's in many ways and whose name suggests willingness and contentment as well as deception and artifice, storytelling is a psychological necessity, the means by which she attempts to order her life retrospectively, to transform what she now sees as discrete and disjunctive events into a seamless and sensible narrative: a life story. Unfortunately, the story she tells becomes not a means to this end but instead an endless labyrinth from which

she finds occasional release as the result of her ironic (often self-reflexively ironic) sensibility and, more importantly, her refusal to heed the drunken voice whose advice is "'Forget it. . . . What's it for? Throw it away.'"

The end of a love affair (not, as in a cataclysmic writer like Pynchon, the end of the world) is the event, the "it," which causes Fain to tell her story and in this way to bridge the sudden chasm that has opened before her. The end of another love affair serves a similar purpose in Adler's second novel. As in *Speedboat, Pitch Dark*'s narrator, Kate, prefers not to deal directly with her loss but instead to turn her and the reader's attention to what at first glance appear to be unrelated matters. However, what seems unrelated to the novel's minimal plot turns out to be central to the novel's overall minimalist effect, which, as in the poetic fiction of John Hawkes, depends much less on the sequence of events than on the pattern of images: the various islands, for example, which suggest to the reader Kate's lonely isolation or the "pitch dark" through which she travels both literally and metaphorically.

For Kate even more than for Jen, the problem of living without her lover merges with the problem of how to tell the story of this loss, a story which is at once personal and representative. Once upon a time, Adler has pointed out, there were daring stories of daring lives that ended interestingly and conclusively; now there are only questions and complications, false starts rather than new beginnings, repetitions rather than denouements. With good reason, Kate sees herself as a latter-day Scheherazade wondering whether she will be able to please her lover/reader and thus save herself for another day, for another story. Her storytelling is, therefore, like Jen's, as much a necessity as a choice, as is her decision to adopt Emily Dickinson's dictum and tell all the truth but tell it slant. For the reader this means having to travel through a narrative pitch dark of barely distinguishable characters and unassigned dialogue in a narrative in which the narrator refers to herself in both the first and third persons and in which Adler's minimalist story propels the reader ahead and simultaneously turns him or her back to the beginning, or, more accurately, to a beginning. Lines repeat, becoming refrains that echo Kate's confusion and despair: "Here I am, for the first time, and yet again, alone at last on Orcas Island." Adler's flat, colorless yet oddly poetical prose embodies her characters' bleak existence, but against that grim Beckettian vision Adler posits her narrators' efforts to work their way through to something better, to that viable "radical middle" ground between romantic affirmation and postmodern apocalypse, between the wholeness of conventional fiction and the dislocations of contemporary existence.

—Robert A. Morace

AIDOO, (Christina) Ama Ata

Nationality: Ghanaian. **Born:** Abeadzi Kiakor, Ghana, 1942. **Education:** University of Ghana, Legon, B.A. (honours) 1964; Stanford University, California. **Career:** Lecturer in English, University of Cape Coast, Ghana, 1970-82; Minister of Education, 1982-83; writer-in-residence, University of Richmond, Virginia, 1989; chair, African Regional Panel of the Commonwealth Writers' prize, 1990, 1991. **Awards:** Fulbright scholarship, 1988. **Address:** P.O. Box 4930, Harare, Zimbabwe.

PUBLICATIONS

Novels

Our Sister Killjoy; or, Reflections from a Black-Eyed Squint. London, Longman, 1977; New York, NOK, 1979.
Changes: A Love Story. London, Women's Press, 1991; New York, Feminist Press at the City University of New York, 1993.

Short Stories

No Sweetness Here. London, Longman, 1970; New York, Doubleday, 1971.
The Eagle and the Chickens and Other Stories. Engu, Nigeria, Tana Press, 1986.

Plays

The Dilemma of a Ghost (produced Legon, 1964; Pittsburgh, 1988). Accra, Longman, 1965; New York, Macmillan, 1971.
Anowa (produced London, 1991). London, Longman, and New York, Humanities Press, 1970.

Poetry

Someone Talking to Sometime. Harare, Zimbabwe, College Press, 1985.
Birds and Other Poems. Harare, Zimbabwe, College Press, 1987.
An Angry Letter in January and Other Poems. Coventry, England, Dangaroo Press, 1992.

Other

Dancing Out Doubts. Engu, Nigeria, NOK, 1982.

*

Critical Studies: *Ama Ata Aidoo: The Dilemma of a Ghost* (study guide) by Jane W. Grant, London, Logman, 1980; *The Art of Ama Ata Aidoo: Polylectics and Reading Against Neocolonialism* by Vincent O. Odamtten, Gainesville, University Press of Florida, 1994.

*   *   *

Christina Ama Ata Aidoo's greatest strength is her ability to mix humor and hope with the serious issues of gender and social conflict. Her protagonists are caught in situations that are beyond their power to change; however, these characters' resistance to traditional roles and beliefs make them vibrant within these prescribed roles. Ghanaian critic Vincent Odamtten warns against using the terms of the (Western) liberal humanist tradition to describe the roles of these women: "individuality" and "independence" do not do justice to the different needs of African woman, he cautions. Their need for community, he believes, is greater than Western women's, and what they seek are relationships of equality with their men, not the wherewithal to live without them. Although this view is itself biased by Odamtten's own cultural and gender identity, it does appropriately state that Aidoo's protagonists seek fulfillment within their existing relationships rather than trying to live without men's love.

Aidoo's keen sense of drama is conveyed in both dramatic scripts and novels through witty, realistic, idiomatic dialogue and through careful juxtaposition of scenes that tell a story in pictures. In both plays, *Anowa* and *The Dilemma of a Ghost,* there are two sets of doubles to the main characters, whose scenes parallel the themes of the main duo. Characters called "Boy" and "Girl" bicker, slap, and insult the representative of the opposite sex, just as their grown-up counterparts do. The second set of doubles is the grandparent pair. Each play illustrates a social problem through the viewpoints of three generations. Aidoo surprises expectations through *chiasmus*: the grandfather figure speaks for the female protagonist's point of view, while the grandmother upholds the traditional view.

The plays discuss the social problems of gender roles and capitalism imposed on an agrarian society. *The Dilemma of a Ghost* features a strong woman married to a weak man who becomes corrupted by his own greed. When he decides to own slaves, she loses her mind because her values and love have been corrupted beyond her capacity of acceptance. In the contemporary setting of *Anowa,* on the other hand, the strong female protagonist is an African American who marries into a Ghanaian family. Her pivotal argument with his society is her belief in her right to delay childbirth. A side issue, which would provide an element of hilarity onstage, is that she smokes and drinks. The real issue of the play, however, is the imbalance of the day-to-day marital relationship: caught between the strong wills of mother and wife, the husband doesn't know who he agrees with. He wants whatever is easiest, not being able to make his own moral choices.

While Aidoo's dramas would make exciting stage productions because of their idiom, color, and tension, the novels make more entertaining reading. *Our Sister Killjoy,* written in 1966, is a precursor to the 1991 novel, *Changes: A Love Story,* in the same way that the play *Dilemma* foresees *Anowa.* The first novel tells the story of a sixteen-year-old Ghanaian girl who travels to Germany and London on an international government program for youth. The titular character, Sissie, earns her negative epithet of "killjoy" because she doubts the motives behind government programs such as student loans and grants to study abroad. Instead of celebrating the opportunity to expand their horizons, she deplores the suffering of her black brothers and sisters who live at poverty level in cold, unfriendly London, while deluding themselves that they are privileged to enroll in white education factories. Sissie urges them to return to Africa, to apply their skills to its economy instead. Many of her most "successful" compatriots are willfully blind to the horror they have bought into: soul-destroying white capitalism.

Sissie's idealism is touching, but it is not her only moral quality. The scene in which she "loses her innocence" is forceful and makes her seem cynical beyond her years. In rejecting a young German woman's love, Sissie observes her own enjoyment in causing pain to another. The reader wants her to connect her own enjoyment of power to her political ideas about white supremacy, to realize that she could be as abusive of power as a white person, but she does not make the connection.

Changes is the more polished novel: both narrator and protagonist are more mature. The protagonist, Esi, illustrates that, although the modern Ghanaian woman can "emancipate" herself by divorce, and obtain both love and independence by becoming another man's second wife, it is not enough. Although Esi's new lover is considered progressive in his views because he wants to honor her freedom and equality, his social status as an African male with the right to have many wives and girlfriends makes him different from Esi. Entirely honest in portraying the conflict between the need for love and the need for independence, *Changes* suggests that one thing that will not change, even if social structures do, is women's need for loving attention. Aidoo's characters are wise about gender differences; they do not blame everything on "the system" but recognize fundamental differences between men and women.

—Jill Franks

ALDISS, Brian (Wilson)

Nationality: British. **Born:** East Dereham, Norfolk, 18 August 1925. **Education:** Framlingham College, Suffolk, 1936-39; West Buckland School, 1939-42. **Military Service:** Served in the Royal Corps of Signals in the Far East, 1943-47. **Family:** Married Margaret Manson in 1965 (second marriage); four children, two from previous marriage. **Career:** Bookseller, Oxford, 1947-56; literary editor, Oxford *Mail,* 1958-69; science-fiction editor, Penguin Books, London, 1961-64; art correspondent, *Guardian,* London, 1969-71. President, British Science Fiction Association, 1960-65; co-founder, 1972, and chair, 1976-78, John W. Campbell Memorial award; co-president, Eurocon Committee, 1975-79; chair, Society of Authors, London, 1978-79; member, Arts Council Literature Panel, 1978-80; president, World SF, 1982-84. Since 1975 vice-president, Stapledon Society; since 1977 founding trustee, World Science Fiction, Dublin; since 1983 vice-president, H.G. Wells Society; since 1988 vice-president, Society of Anglo-Chinese Understanding; since 1990 council member, Council for Posterity. Since 1991 managing director, Avernus Ltd. **Awards:** World Science Fiction Convention citation, 1959; Hugo award, 1962, 1987; Nebula award, 1965; Ditmar award (Australia), 1970; British Science Fiction Association award, 1972, 1982, 1986, and special award, 1974; Eurocon award, 1976; James Blish award, for non-fiction, 1977; Cometa d'Argento (Italy), 1977; Jules Verne prize, 1977; Pilgrim award, 1978; John W. Campbell Memorial award, 1983; International Association for the Fantastic in the Arts award, for scholarship, 1986; Eaton award, 1986; World SF President's award, 1988; Kafka award, 1991. Guest of Honour, World Science Fiction Convention, London, 1965, 1979. Fellow, Royal Society of Literature, 1990. **Agents:** Robin Straus, 229 East 79th St., New York, New York 10021, USA; Michael Shaw, Curtis Brown, Haymarket House, 28/29 Haymarket, London SW1Y 4SP, England. **Address:** Woodlands, Foxcombe Road, Boars Hill, Oxfordshire OX1 5DL, England.

Publications

Novels

The Brightfount Diaries. London, Faber, 1955.
Non-Stop. London, Faber, 1958; as *Starship,* New York, Criterion, 1959.
Vanguard from Alpha. New York, Ace, 1959; as *Equator* (includes "Segregation"), London, Digit, 1961.
Bow Down to Nul. New York, Ace, 1960; as *The Interpreter,* London, Digit, 1961.
The Male Response. New York, Galaxy, 1961; London, Dobson, 1963.
The Primal Urge. New York, Ballantine, 1961; London, Sphere, 1967.
The Long Afternoon of Earth. New York, New American Library, 1962; expanded edition, as *Hothouse,* London, Faber, 1962; Boston, Gregg Press, 1976.

The Dark Light Years. London, Faber, and New York, New American Library, 1964.
Greybeard. London, Faber, and New York, Harcourt Brace, 1964.
Earthworks. London, Faber, 1965; New York, Doubleday, 1966.
An Age. London, Faber, 1967; as *Cryptozoic!,* New York, Doubleday, 1968.
Report on Probability A. London, Faber, 1968; New York, Doubleday, 1969.
Barefoot in the Head. London, Faber, 1969; New York, Doubleday, 1970.
The Hand-Reared Boy. London, Weidenfeld and Nicolson, and New York, McCall, 1970.
A Soldier Erect; or, Further Adventures of the Hand-Reared Boy. London, Weidenfeld and Nicolson, and New York, Coward McCann, 1971.
Frankenstein Unbound. London, Cape, 1973; New York, Random House, 1974.
The Eighty-Minute Hour. London, Cape, and New York, Doubleday, 1974.
The Malacia Tapestry. London, Cape, 1976; New York, Harper, 1977.
Brothers of the Head. London, Pierrot, 1977; New York, Two Continents, 1978.
Enemies of the System. London, Cape, and New York, Harper, 1978.
A Rude Awakening. London, Weidenfeld and Nicholson, 1978; New York, Random House, 1979.
Brothers of the Head, and Where the Lines Converge. London, Panther, 1979.
Life in the West. London, Weidenfeld and Nicolson, 1980; New York, Carroll and Graf, 1990.
Moreau's Other Island. London, Cape, 1980; as *An Island Called Moreau,* New York, Simon and Schuster, 1981.
The Helliconia Trilogy. New York, Atheneum, 1985.
  Helliconia Spring. London, Cape, and New York, Atheneum 1982.
  Helliconia Summer. London, Cape, and New York, Atheneum, 1983.
  Helliconia Winter. London, Cape, and New York, Atheneum 1985.
The Horatio Stubbs Saga. London, Panther, 1985.
The Year Before Yesterday. New York, Watts, 1987; as *Cracken at Critical,* Worcester Park, Surrey, Kerosina, 1987.
Ruins. London, Hutchinson, 1987.
Forgotten Life. London, Gollancz, 1988; New York, Atheneum, 1989.
Dracula Unbound. London, Grafton, and New York, Harper Collins, 1991.
Remembrance Day. London, HarperCollins, and New York, St. Martin's Press, 1993.
Somewhere East of Life. London, HarperCollins, and New York, Carroll and Graf, 1994.

Short Stories

Space, Time, and Nathaniel: Presciences. London, Faber, 1957; abridged edition, as *No Time Like Tomorrow,* New York, New American Library, 1959.
The Canopy of Time. London, Faber, 1959; revised edition, as *Galaxies Like Grains of Sand,* New York, New American Library, 1960.
The Airs of Earth. London, Faber, 1963.
Starswarm. New York, New American Library, 1964; London, Panther, 1979.

Best Science Fiction Stories of Brian Aldiss. London, Faber, 1965; as *Who Can Replace a Man?* New York, Harcourt Brace, 1966; revised edition, Faber, 1971.

The Saliva Tree and Other Strange Growths. London, Faber, 1966.

Intangibles Inc. London, Faber, 1969.

A Brian Aldiss Omnibus 1-2. London, Sidgwick and Jackson, 2 vols., 1969-71.

Neanderthal Planet. New York, Avon, 1970.

The Moment of Eclipse. London, Faber, 1970; New York, Doubleday, 1972.

The Book of Brian Aldiss. New York, DAW, 1972; as *The Comic Inferno,* London, New English Library, 1973 .

Excommunication. London, Post Card Partnership, 1975.

Last Orders and Other Stories. London, Cape 1977; New York, Carroll and Graf, 1989.

New Arrivals, Old Encounters: Twelve Stories. London, Cape, 1979; New York, Harper, 1980.

Foreign Bodies. Singapore, Chopmen, 1981.

Seasons in Flight. London, Cape, 1984; New York, Atheneum, 1986.

The Magic of the Past. Worcester Park, Surrey, Kerosina, 1987.

Best Science Fiction Stories of Brian W. Aldiss (not same as 1965 book). London, Gollancz, 1988; as *Man in His Time,* New York, Atheneum, 1989.

A Romance of the Equator: Best Fantasy Stories. London, Gollancz, 1989; New York, Atheneum, 1990.

A Tupolev Too Far. London, HarperCollins, 1993; New York, St. Martin's Press, 1994.

Plays

Distant Encounters, adaptation of his own stories (produced London, 1978).

SF Blues (produced London, 1987).

Television Play: *Life* (*4 Minutes* series), 1986.

Poetry

Pile: Petals from St. Klaed's Computer. London, Cape, and New York, Holt Rinehart, 1979.

Farewell to a Child. Berkhamsted, Hertfordshire, Priapus, 1982.

At the Caligula Hotel. London, Sinclair Stevenson, 1995.

Other

Cities and Stones: A Traveller's Jugoslavia. London, Faber, 1966.

The Shape of Further Things: Speculations on Change. London, Faber, 1970; New York, Doubleday, 1971.

Billion Year Spree: A History of Science Fiction. London, Weidenfeld and Nicolson, and New York, Doubleday, 1973.

Science Fiction Art, illustrated by Chris Foss. New York, Bounty, 1975; London, Hart Davis, 1976.

Science Fiction as Science Fiction. Frome, Somerset, Bran's Head, 1978.

This World and Nearer Ones: Essays Exploring the Familiar. London, Weidenfeld and Nicolson, 1979; Kent, Ohio, Kent State University Press, 1981.

Science Fiction Quiz. London, Weidenfeld and Nicolson, 1983.

The Pale Shadow of Science (essays). Seattle, Serconia Press, 1985.

. . . And the Lurid Glare of the Comet (essays). Seattle, Serconia Press, 1986.

Trillion Year Spree: The History of Science Fiction, with David Wingrove. London, Gollancz, and New York, Atheneum, 1986.

Science Fiction Blues (selections), edited by Frank Hatherley. London, Avernus, 1988.

Bury My Heart at W.H. Smith's: A Writing Life. London, Hodder and Stoughton, 1990.

The Detached Retina. Liverpool, Liverpool University Press, 1995.

Editor, *Penguin Science Fiction.* London, Penguin, 1961; *More Penguin Science Fiction,* 1963; *Yet More Penguin Science Fiction,* 1964; 3 vols. collected as *The Penguin Science Fiction Omnibus,* 1973.

Editor, *Best Fantasy Stories.* London, Faber, 1962.

Editor, *Last and First Men,* by Olaf Stapledon. London, Penguin, 1963.

Editor, *Introducing SF.* London, Faber, 1964.

Editor, with Harry Harrison, *Nebula Award Stories 2.* New York, Doubleday, 1967; as *Nebula Award Stories 1967,* London, Gollancz, 1967.

Editor, with Harry Harrison, *All about Venus.* New York, Dell, 1968; enlarged edition, as *Farewell, Fantastic Venus,* London, Macdonald, 1968.

Editor, with Harry Harrison, *Best SF 1967* [to *1975*]. New York, Berkley and Putnam, 7 vols., and Indianapolis, Bobbs Merrill, 2 vols., 1968-75; as *The Year's Best Science Fiction 1-9,* London, Sphere, 8 vols., 1968-76, and London, Futura, 1 vol., 1976.

Editor, with Harry Harrison, *The Astounding-Analog Reader.* New York, Doubleday, 2 vols., 1972-73; London, Sphere, 2 vols., 1973.

Editor, *Space Opera.* London, Weidenfeld and Nicolson, 1974; New York, Doubleday, 1975.

Editor, *Space Odysseys.* London, Futura, 1974; New York, Doubleday, 1976.

Editor, with Harry Harrison, *SF Horizons* (reprint of magazine). New York, Arno Press, 1975.

Editor, with Harry Harrison, *Hell's Cartographers: Some Personal Histories of Science Fiction Writers.* London, Weidenfeld and Nicolson, and New York, Harper, 1975.

Editor, with Harry Harrison, *Decade: The 1940's, The 1950's, The 1960's.* London, Macmillan, 3 vols., 1975-77; *The 1940's* and *The 1950's,* New York, St. Martin's Press, 2 vols., 1978.

Editor, *Evil Earths.* London, Weidenfeld and Nicolson, 1975; New York, Avon, 1979.

Editor, *Galactic Empires.* London, Weidenfeld and Nicolson, 2 vols., 1976; New York, St. Martin's Press, 2 vols., 1977.

Editor, *Perilous Planets.* London, Weidenfeld and Nicolson, 1978; New York, Avon, 1980.

Editor, with others, *The Penguin Masterquiz Book.* London, Penguin, 1985.

Editor, with Sam J. Lundwall, *The Penguin World Omnibus of Science Fiction.* London, Penguin, 1986; New York, Penguin, 1987.

Editor, *My Madness: The Selected Writings of Anna Kavan.* London, Pan, 1990.

*

Bibliography: *Brian W. Aldiss: A Bibliography 1954-1984* by Margaret Aldiss, San Bernardino, California, Borgo Press, 1991.

Manuscript Collections: Bodleian Library, Oxford University; Dallas Public Library.

Critical Studies: "Generic Discontinuities in SF: Brian Aldiss' *Starship*" by Fredric Jameson, in *Science-Fiction Studies* (Terre Haute, Indiana), vol. 1, no. 2, 1973; *Aldiss Unbound: The Science Fiction of Brian W. Aldiss* by Richard Mathews, San Bernardino, California, Borgo Press, 1977; *Apertures: A Study of the Writings of Brian Aldiss* by Brian Griffin and David Wingrove, Westport, Connecticut, Greenwood Press, 1984; article by Aldiss in *Contemporary Authors Autobiography Series 2* edited by Adele Sarkissian, Detroit, Gale, 1985; *A Is for Brian: A 65th Birthday Present for Brian W. Aldiss from His Family, Friends, Colleagues, and Admirers* edited by Frank Hatherley, London, Avernus, 1990.

Brian Aldiss comments:

(1991) With *Somewhere East of Life,* I have completed the Squire Quartet, which opened with *Life in the West.* These novels cover a great extent of territory, from the United States to Singapore and Turkmenistan, from Stockholm to Sicily. Always my native county of Norfolk, East Anglia, serves as a sort of fulcrum. Family affairs are set against the slow decline of the West and the abrupt demise of the Soviet Union.

An idea of how much I might encompass was brought home to me while writing the three Helliconia novels in the early to mid-1980s: *Helliconia Spring, Helliconia Summer,* and *Helliconia Winter.* I have never experienced that great divide some people detect between science fiction and the ordinary contemporary novel; this probably reflects my reading and the company I keep.

I write every day and always have done—not invariably for publication. My SF presents a spectrum moving from extreme surreal situations in the early novels to events merely colored by an incipient future. By the time I wrote *Report on Probability A* and *Barefoot in the Head,* I had already moved away from the confines of genre fiction.

Happily, my contemporary novels have been about as successful as the more imaginative ones. Recent pleasures include having a volume of critical essays and a selection of my poems published. I'm now working on a large-scale autobiographical "thing"—an unlicked cub as yet—which will contain my experience of and meditations on war.

To be able to write is a slice of great golden fortune.

*   *   *

The great contribution Brian Aldiss has made to the art of science fiction is to help to raise it to the point where it is now accepted, by all but the chronically bigoted, as a literary form worthy of serious consideration. I suspect that this has much to do with the fact that Aldiss has always looked upon himself primarily as a novelist rather than as a writer of SF, and he has written several novels other than those on science-fiction themes.

His first full length science-fiction novel was *Non-Stop,* which was based on the almost classic SF theme of a giant space-ship adrift in space. As a piece of storytelling, it is first class, and it displays all the excellences that are to be found in his later work: the ability to establish by carefully selected detail a convincing atmosphere of place and time, and a logical development of situations so that even the most outlandish become acceptable to the reader. In *Hothouse,* for example, Aldiss creates a world dominated by vegetation where we can sense the continual and overwhelming growth, even breathe the vegetable air, and in *Greybeard* the experience of being in post-atomic Oxford is remarkably vivid. But in *Non-Stop,* while the exploration of the ship (once built by giants)

by Roy Complain and his companions has parallels with the sense of awe and wonder experienced by the Old English poets when they encountered the ruins of Roman cities, the space ship becomes a microcosm of Earth which, too, can be seen as a giant ship itself endlessly adrift in space, and the exploration develops into a search for destination and purpose.

A quality which informs Aldiss's work, and which should not be overlooked, is his sense of humor. In *Non-Stop* one aspect of this can be seen in his pursuit of the idea that in the future psychology will develop its own theology and superstitions and replace our present religions. It is a plausible thesis and at the same time an amusing one, and often Aldiss's humor helps to save his SF novels from the over-seriousness that has engulfed other practitioners in this genre. It has been responsible too for the excellent humorous novels. The logical consequences of the invention and universal use of an "Emotional Register" are used in *The Primal Urge* to create a fantastic and hilarious story.

Since the late 1960s Aldiss has striven to extend the boundaries of his art. In *Report on Probability A* he attempted the first SF anti-novel, a study in relative phenomena which proved a *tour de force,* and in *Barefoot in the Head* he produced another "first," where groups of poems and "pop-songs" reflect and comment on the preceding prose chapters. In a Europe reeling psychodelically from an attack by an Arab state with Psycho-Chemical Aerosol Bombs, Chateris, the hero of *Barefoot in the Head,* gradually absorbs the acid-head poison in the atmosphere to find himself a new Messiah. As social and thought patterns disintegrate so does the language, and Aldiss develops a stunning-punning prose reminiscent of the verbal pyrotechnics of Joyce's *Finnegans Wake.* At the same time he creates a nightmare world reflecting trends observable in the situation already with us.

Though not strictly within a discussion of Aldiss's novels, we should not overlook his collections of short stories, *Space, Time, and Nathaniel* and *The Canopy of Time,* of which he is justly proud. The Horatio Stubbs series constitutes a fictional autobiography covering the years from the 1930s to the 1960s, where through the sexual and spiritual development of Horatio are examined certain aspects of the poverty of English middle-class life. The first, *The Hand-Reared Boy,* begins with Horatio as a boy, his masturbatory fantasies and his first sexual encounters. The direct and extremely realistic style of the first part of this novel might not be to everyone's taste, but it flowers into a most beautifully controlled story of Horatio's first and hopeless love for an older woman. In the second novel, *A Solder Erect,* we find Horatio still hard at it in the army and serving in India and Burma where his sexual and social education is broadened. The coarse brutality of wartime soldiering in the Far East is accurately and brutally portrayed, but redeemed by humor and set in contrast with Horatio's growing awareness of values beyond the more immediately erotic, a theme continued and brought to conclusion in the third novel in the series, *A Rude Awakening,* where Horatio encounters the Dutch, Indian, Japanese, Chinese, and Indonesian forces in Sumatra and finds himself with two girls.

On the SF side, Aldiss's *Frankenstein Unbound* breaks new ground again. As a result of the indiscriminate use of nuclear weapons within the ambits of the Earth-Lunar system the infrastructure of space is seriously damaged to the point where time and space go "on the brink." The consequent "time shifts" find Joe Boderland suddenly transported to Switzerland in the year 1816 where he encounters not only Mary Shelley, the creator of Frankenstein, but Frankenstein himself in a world where reality itself is equally unstable and the dividing line between the real and the imagined world has become confused. In this situation Boderland finds himself unsure of his own role, and it is the discovery and fulfillment of his mission which constitutes the central theme of the narrative. It is a measure of Aldiss's powers as a novelist that he persuades the reader of the *reality* of this fantastic situation. The theme, I suspect, was suggested by his researches into the origins of science fiction which he undertook to produce his history of the genre, *Billion Year Spree* (and now *Trillion Year Spree*), and in which he makes a powerful case for Mary Shelley's *Frankenstein* as the first true SF novel.

More recent novels increase one's admiration for Aldiss's versatility and unflagging powers of invention. *Brothers of the Head,* the story of Siamese twin boys with a third dominant head which becomes increasingly demanding, is a brilliant if disturbing excursion into the macabre, while *The Malacia Tapestry* almost defies definition. Set in an age-old city state, riddled with rival philosophies, under the spell of magicians, and where change is forbidden, it presents the reader with a panorama of dukes, wealthy merchants, thespians, courtesans, spongers, and soldiers. What we are never sure of is whereabouts in the time scale we are. Is it a medieval town? Then just a glimpse of something tells us no. An alternative world? But never explicitly so. The way in which Aldiss makes this totally imaginary world a reality is remarkable, a superb example of how to induce the suspension of disbelief.

Given Aldiss's run of the gamut of fictional styles and structures it was almost inevitable that sooner or later he would attempt a saga. In *The Helliconia Trilogy* he does just that and in inventing an entire solar system with its own history, dynasties, religions, mythologies, and cultures it is one of epic proportions. While parallels with life on Planet Earth can be observed, the chief and fundamental difference is in the length of Helliconia's seasons. Centuries long the whole of life changes as the seasons wear on, dormant life forms emerge and dynasties rise and fall. At the heart of this, nevertheless, is the struggle between the Humans and the Phagors, and a stroke of genius is to have hovering in the background an Earth Observation Platform which is itself declining into disaster, thus adding a further perspective to this cosmic vision. The other remarkable aspect of Aldiss's invented universe is that it is not, as is so often the case in science fiction, an ideal world held up in criticism of our own. Helliconia's history is as messy, corrupt, illogical, and confused as Earth's. If there is a message it is in Helliconia's acceptance of and adjustment to its even harsher physical environment, while the Earth Platform's disaster is directly related to Earth's attempt to over-control its environment.

The books themselves, *Spring, Summer,* and *Winter,* are full of action and incident: picaresque journeys, hierarchical struggles, natural disasters, feats of endurance, bravery, loyalty and affection, and dynastic warfare which make them each, in an old-fashioned phrase, a gripping read. They are in addition a remarkable achievement.

Aldiss moved on from the massive achievement of Helliconia to yet another achievement. Back to Earth and the mainstream novel his *Forgotten Life* is another remarkable example of Aldiss's ability to assemble and organize a mass of material, in this case ranging over 50 years and three continents. In a sense the novel can be seen as a sort of intellectual whodunit, a cerebral voyage of discovery.

In the novel Clement Winter, who is married to a successful author of fantasy novels, comes into the possession of his brother Joseph's letters and diaries. In going through these in order to find and comprehend a pattern in his brother's life, Clement comes to

review and assess his own. Aldiss calls upon his own experiences in pre-war Suffolk, wartime Burma and Sumatra, and his life as a writer in Oxford.

The real stuff of autobiography comes in *Bury My Heart at W.H. Smith's.* This is, not surprisingly, a wide-ranging story, haunted by wartime experience in Burma. True to its title Aldiss's autobiography is marked by a lightness of touch, and a cheerful friendly modesty. The story it tells is an intriguing one.

—John Cotton

ALDRIDGE, (Harold Edward) James

Nationality: Australian. **Born:** White Hills, Victoria, 10 July 1918. **Education:** Swan Hill High School; London School of Economics. **Family:** Married Dina Mitchnik in 1942; two sons. **Career:** Writer, Melbourne *Herald* and *Sun,* 1937-38, and London *Daily Sketch* and *Sunday Dispatch,* 1939; European and Middle East war correspondent, Australian Newspaper Service and North American Newspaper Alliance, 1939-44; Tehran correspondent, *Time* and *Life,* 1944. **Awards:** Rhys Memorial prize, 1945; World Peace Council gold medal; International Organization of Journalists prize, 1967; Lenin Memorial Peace prize, 1972; Australian Children's Book Council Book of the Year award, 1985; *Guardian* award, for children's book, 1987. **Agent:** Curtis Brown, 162-168 Regent Street, London W1R 5TB, England.

PUBLICATIONS

Novels

Signed with Their Honour. London, Joseph, and Boston, Little Brown, 1942.
The Sea Eagle. London, Joseph, and Boston, Little Brown, 1944.
Of Many Men. London, Joseph, and Boston, Little Brown, 1946.
The Diplomat. London, Lane, 1949; Boston, Little Brown, 1950.
The Hunter. London, Lane, 1950; Boston, Little Brown, 1951.
Heroes of the Empty View. London, Lane, and New York, Knopf, 1954.
I Wish He Would Not Die. London, Bodley Head, 1957; New York, Doubleday, 1958.
The Last Exile. London, Hamish Hamilton, and New York, Doubleday, 1961.
A Captive in the Land. London, Hamish Hamilton, 1962; New York, Doubleday, 1963.
The Statesman's Game. London, Hamish Hamilton, and New York, Doubleday, 1966.
My Brother Tom. London, Hamish Hamilton, 1966; as *My Brother Tom: A Love Story,* Boston, Little Brown, 1967.
A Sporting Proposition. London, Joseph, and Boston, Little Brown, 1973; as *Ride a Wild Pony,* London, Penguin, 1976.
Mockery in Arms. London, Joseph, 1974; Boston, Little Brown, 1975.
The Untouchable Juli. London, Joseph, 1975; Boston, Little Brown, 1976.
One Last Glimpse. London, Joseph, and Boston, Little Brown, 1977.

Goodbye Un-America. London, Joseph, and Boston, Little Brown, 1979.
The True Story of Lola MacKellar. London, Viking, 1992.

Short Stories

Gold and Sand. London, Bodley Head, 1960.

Uncollected Short Stories

"Braver Time," in *Redbook* (New York), May 1967.
"The Unfinished Soldiers," in *Winter's Tales 15,* edited by A.D. Maclean. London, Macmillan, 1969; New York, St. Martin's Press, 1970.
"The Black Ghost of St. Helen," in *After Midnight Ghost Book,* edited by James Hale. London, Hutchinson, 1980.

Plays

The 49th State (produced London, 1947).
One Last Glimpse (produced Prague, 1981).

Television Plays: Scripts for *Robin Hood* series.

Other

Undersea Hunting for Inexperienced Englishmen. London, Allen and Unwin, 1955.
The Flying 19 (for children). London, Hamish Hamilton, 1966.
Living Egypt, photographs by Paul Strand. London, MacGibbon and Kee, and New York, Horizon Press, 1969.
Cairo: Biography of a City. Boston, Little Brown, 1969; London, Macmillan, 1970.
The Marvelous Mongolian (for children). Boston, Little Brown, and London, Macmillan, 1974.
The Broken Saddle (for children). London, MacRae, 1982; New York, Watts, 1983.
The True Story of Lilli Stubek (for children). South Yarra, Victoria, Hyland House, 1984; London, Penguin, 1986.
The True Story of Spit MacPhee (for children). Ringwood, Victoria, Viking, and London, Viking Kestrel, 1986.

*

Critical Studies: "The Necessity of Freedom: A Discussion of the Novels of James Aldridge," in *Overland* (Melbourne), November 1956; "It All Comes Out Like Blood: The Novels of James Aldridge," in *Australians* by John Hetherington, Melbourne, Cheshire, 1960; "Man of Action, Words in Action" by Eric Partridge, in *Meanjin* (Melbourne), 1961; "The Heroic Ordinary" by Evelyn Juers, in *Age Monthly Review* (Melbourne), February 1987; *Workers and Sufferers: Town v. Self in James Aldridge's St. Helen Novels,* London, Australian Studies Centre, 1987, and "My Brother Tom: My Other Self," in *Orana* (Sydney), February 1989, both by Michael Stone.

*   *   *

James Aldridge left Australia when quite a young man as a war correspondent; and this fact has largely determined the material and the angle of approach in his work. He went through the Greek campaign and wrote two books based directly on his experiences in it. Here his method was strongly affected by Hemingway; but the books were saved from being mere imitations by the genuine freshness and truth of his presentation. He was learning how to build a narrative full of stirring events and based on historical developments which he knew at first-hand, and at the same time to link the story with the personal problems and struggles of his protagonists. With his next book, a collection of stories, came a break from the Hemingway influence. What he had gained from his apprenticeship was now integrated in his own method and outlook. The tales showed how well he was able to grasp situations with very diverse settings and convincingly to define aspects of national character in a compact form. Still drawing on his wartime experiences as a correspondent, he wrote *The Diplomat,* an ambitious large-scale work, dealing with both the Soviet Union and the region of the Kurds in northern Mesopotamia. With much skill he explored the devious world of diplomacy in the postwar world, making the issues concrete by their basis in the difficult national question of the Kurds. Aldridge emerged as an important political novelist. He showed himself able to handle complicated political themes without losing touch with the essential human issues. The political aspects were removed from triviality or narrowness by being linked with the painful struggles of the protagonist to understand the world in which he found himself an actor. Thus what gave artistic validity to the work, beyond any particular conclusions reached in the search for truth, was the definition of that search itself.

In *The Hunter* Aldridge next refreshed himself by dropping all large themes and turning to Canada in a work more concerned with immediacies of experience; his theme was the world of the hunter, a direct relationship to nature; and he showed he could conjure up a dimension of sheer physical living. But it was perhaps significant that when he turned from the theme of contemporary history and politics, it was to the sphere of nature he looked, not to everyday life in some specific society. For good and bad his uprooting through the war had made him into a novelist of the large national conflicts of our age. His material has thus been born of his journalism, but in transforming it into fiction he has overcome the journalistic limitations and been able to penetrate to deep human issues. He sees the problem in terms of real people and has never been guilty of inventing puppets to represent national or political positions.

He now turns again to the Near East, in *Heroes of the Empty View, I Wish He Would Not Die,* and *The Last Exile,* not dealing with such a remote issue as that of the Kurds, but taking up the problems of the Arab world, with special reference to Egypt. He has been helped by having many direct connections and sources of information; but despite his sympathy for the Arabs he has not oversimplified issues or made his works into tracts for a particular point of view. The stories clarify things and deepen one's understanding of the human beings entangled in vast conflicts. In his latest works he has again taken up the question of the Soviet Union but with less force and artistic success than in *The Diplomat* or the books on the near East. It would be hard to point to any contemporary novelist who has dealt more directly with postwar political problems on the international plane with such success, uniting a warm sympathy for the persons he writes about, with, in the last resort, a true artistic detachment.

—Jack Lindsay

ALTHER, Lisa

Nationality: American. **Born:** Lisa Reed in Kingsport, Tennessee, 23 July 1944. **Education:** Wellesley College, Massachusetts, 1962-66, B.A. 1966. **Family:** Married Richard Alther in 1966; one daughter. **Career:** Editorial assistant, Atheneum Publishers, New York, 1966; staff writer, Garden Way Publishers, Charlotte, Vermont, 1969-72; visiting lecturer, St. Michael's College, Winooski, Vermont, 1980. Lives in Hinesburg, Vermont. **Address:** c/o Watkins-Loomis Inc., 133 E. 35th St., No.1, New York, New York 10016, U.S.A.

PUBLICATIONS

Novels

Kinflicks. New York, Knopf, and London, Chatto and Windus, 1976.
Original Sins. New York, Knopf, and London, Women's Press, 1981.
Other Women. New York, Knopf, 1984; London, Viking, 1985.
Bedrock. New York, Knopf, and London, Viking, 1990.
Five Minutes in Heaven. New York, Dutton, and London, Viking, 1995.

Uncollected Short Stories

"Encounter," in *McCall's* (New York), August 1976.
"The Art of Dying Well," in *A Collection of Classic Southern Humor,* edited by George William Koon. Atlanta, Peachtree, 1984.
"Termites," in *Homewords,* edited by Douglas Paschall. Knoxville, University of Tennessee Press, 1986.
"The Politics of Paradise," in *Louder than Words,* edited by William Shore. New York, Vintage, 1989.

Other

Non-Chemical Pest and Disease Control for the Home Orchard. Charlotte, Vermont, Garden Way, 1973.

*

Critical Studies: "Condemned to Survival: The Comic Unsuccessful Suicide" by Marilynn J. Smith, in *Comparative Literature Studies* (Urbana, Illinois), March 1980; "Alther and Dillard: The Appalachian Universe" by Frederick G. Waase, in *Appalachia/America: The Proceedings of the 1980 Appalachian Studies Conference* edited by Wilson Somerville, Johnson City, Tennessee, Appalachian Consortium Press, 1981; article in *Women Writers of the Contemporary South* edited by Peggy Whitman Prenshaw, Jackson, University Press of Mississippi, 1984.

*   *   *

Lisa Alther comments with shrewdness, insight—and a hefty measure of irony—upon American types, their trendy habits, and their dreams. Typical though they be, Alther's protagonists are, nevertheless, fully realized individuals who are sometimes despairing, prickly, dense, or self-destructive, but who are also unfailingly interesting folk, often surprisingly courageous survivors. These fac-

tors, along with Alther's keen sense of place, her clever manipulation of point of view, and her exploitation of various levels of comedy are the chief strengths of *Kinflicks, Original Sins,* and *Other Women.*

Alther's manipulation of point of view contributes to the sprawling effect of her bulky novels even as it helps control them. The picaresque *Kinflicks* alternates between third-person narration of the present moment as Ginny Babcock Bliss keeps vigil at her mother's deathbed, and first-person flashbacks which hilariously and satirically recount Ginny's penchant for redesigning herself to suit those who successively dominate her affections—parents, gum-chewing football hero, motorcycle hood, lesbian reformer, snow-mobile salesman, disturbed Viet vet, baby daughter. Ultimately, alone but rather more determined, she sets out to suit herself. The distancing effect of Ginny's memories facilitates the bald, raucous humor of the book for, in effect, Ginny is laughing at herself *with* her readers; the detachment of the third-person narrator in the alternate chapters legislates against melodrama or shallow sentimentality.

Though *Original Sins* is told in the third person, major sections allow readers to share the consciousness of five protagonists. Members of a huge extended family, sisters Emily and Sally Prince, brothers Jed and Raymond Tatro, and Donny Tatro are inseparable as children, but are later driven apart by circumstances of sex, social class, personal ambition, and race (Donny is black). A *Bildungsroman, Original Sins* depicts youngsters who believe they can do anything, becoming adults who often wonder if anything worthwhile can be done—but who don't stop trying. *Other Women,* a "delayed *Bildungsroman,*" also uses the third person throughout and shifts between the consciousness of its protagonists, Carolyn Kelley, a single mother whose lesbian relationship is dissolving, and her therapist, Hannah Burke. As Hannah counsels Carolyn toward acceptance of herself, adulthood, and responsibility, some of her own very old, deep wounds begin to heal, and the novel concludes with a note of genuine hope symbolized by the women's developing friendship. In *Other Women* and *Original Sins,* the availability of each protagonist's thought processes lends immediacy and realism as it arouses empathy. Readers may not fully endorse the protagonists' decisions, but they remain involved and concerned with the characters because their motivations are so clearly drawn. Suitably, the humor in these novels is quieter, developing more from quirks of personality and wry social comment than from the slapstick situations of *Kinflicks.*

Because both *Kinflicks* and *Original Sins* are set primarily in Tennessee, her home state, Alther has been dubbed a regionalist. She recognizes the influence of fellow southerner Flannery O'Connor upon her literary sensibilities and freely acknowledges the usefulness and attraction of the "ready-made social context" available to southerners writing about their area (see her article "Will the South Rise Again?," *New York Times Book Review,* 16 December 1979). It is equally important, however, to note that Alther's settings range across the eastern United States. Her assessment of college life on a New York City campus, her stringent portrayal of the power struggles among supposedly egalitarian Northern civil rights workers (*Original Sins*), her lovingly drawn Vermont landscapes in *Other Women*—as well as her acknowledgment that conducting a private life privately is just as difficult in any closed Northern community as it is in a southern one (*Kinflicks*)—attest to her understanding of several locales and make explicit the wide scope of her social commentary. In this way, Alther differs a bit from regionalists who imply rather than dramatize the larger applications of their social comment.

Considered by many to be a feminist writer, Alther focuses primarily upon contemporary American women, giving great attention to the limitations thrust upon them, but she also details their self-imposed restrictions and stresses the need for each to assume responsibility for her own life. In an interview with Andrew Feinberg (*Horizon,* May 1981), she comments, "People are assigned roles because of their external characteristics and then are forced to play them out . . . unless they are lucky enough to figure out what is going on and get out." The process of getting out, always painful, sometimes unsuccessful, is the motivational force in Alther's plots and functions as effectively for several male characters as it does for females. Alther's awareness that despite the deep social divisions which exist between many contemporary women and men, there are also shared problems—such as the constrictions of traditionalism, the desire to escape from parents' demands, the difficulties of assimilation into another cultural-geographic region—demonstrates the universality of feminist fiction just as her humor reveals that feminist writers can treat serious subjects without being deadly dull. By modifying critical categories, Lisa Alther produces novels incorporating strong plots and intriguing characterizations with effective social commentary.

—Jane S. Bakerman

ALUKO, T(imothy) M(ofolorunso)

Nationality: Nigerian. **Born:** Ilesha, 14 June 1918. **Education:** Primary schools in Ilesha, 1926-32; Government College, Ibadan, 1933-38; Yaba Higher College, 1939-42; University of London, 1946-50, B.Sc. in engineering and diploma in town planning 1950; University of Newcastle-upon-Tyne (Unesco fellow), 1968-69, M.Sc. in engineering 1969; University of Lagos, Ph.D. in public health engineering 1976. **Family:** Married Janet Adebisi Fajemisin in 1950; six children. **Career:** Engineer, Public Works Department, Lagos, 1943-46; executive engineer, Public Works Department, Ibadan and Lagos, 1950-56; town engineer, Lagos Town Council, 1956-60; director and permanent secretary, Ministry of Works and Transport, Western Nigeria, 1960-66; senior lecturer, University of Ibadan, 1966; Senior Research Fellow in Municipal Engineering, 1966-78, and Associate Professor of Public Health Engineering, 1978, University of Lagos; resident partner, Scott Wilson Kirkpatrick, consulting engineers and transportation planners, Lagos, 1979 until retired. Commissioner of finance, Government of Western Nigeria, 1971-73. Fellow, Institution of Civil Engineers, Institution of Municipal Engineers, and Nigerian Society of Engineers. O.B.E. (Officer, Order of the British Empire), 1963; O.O.N. (Officer, Order of the Niger), 1964. **Address:** 53 Ladipo Oluwote Road, Apapa, Lagos, Nigera.

Publications

Novels

One Man, One Wife. Lagos, Nigerian Printing and Publishing Company, 1959; London, Heinemann, 1967; New York, Humanities Press, 1968.
One Man, One Matchet. London, Heinemann, 1964; Mystic, Connecticut, Verrey, 1965.

Kinsman and Foreman. London, Heinemann, 1966; New York, Humanities Press, 1967.
Chief the Honourable Minister. London, Heinemann, 1970.
His Worshipful Majesty. London, Heinemann, 1973.
Wrong Ones in the Dock. London, Heinemann, 1982.
A State of Our Own. London, Macmillan, 1986.
Conduct Unbecoming. Ibadan, Nigeria, Heinemann, 1993.

Uncollected Short Story

"The New Engineer," in *African New Writing.* London, Lutterworth Press, 1947.

*

Critical Study: *Long Drums and Cannons* by Margaret Laurence, London, Macmillan, and New York, Praeger, 1968.

*   *   *

T.M. Aluko's *One Man, One Wife* was the first African novel in English to be published in Nigeria, and in following it up with seven more books Aluko became one of the more productive African novelists. Aluko is, however, a much underrated writer whose very intelligent comic sense has been out of tune with the serious-mindedness of West African fiction generally and has thus caused his work to be overlooked or summarily dismissed. In his first three novels he applies a wry, comic detachment to the stresses between modern and traditional life among the Yoruba people.

Most reviewers and commentators have seen this detachment as a complete lack of commitment in social problems, about which they believe all African writers should be committed, and one suspects that they have sometimes mistaken for Aluko's own the clichés, grandiloquences, and superficial attitudes which, with considerable linguistic sophistication, he mocks by embedding them even in authorial narration; for instance, this bemused reflection upon the Christian catechist Royasin's message on Christmas Day: "How could this same Baby have founded a religion nearly two thousand years old? And how could this same mysterious Baby rule all the world? The invitation to all the faithful to come to Bethlehem, the geographical location of which even the great Royasin could not tell. . . ." (*One Man, One Wife*). In this novel Aluko captures the very accents of various levels of English used in Yorubaland, as he satirizes with amused impartiality the foibles of both Christians and polygamists, of both followers of the new faith who retain a toehold in the old, like Elder Joshua, and the blindly committed converts, like Bible Jeremiah. The comedy is largely verbal and cerebral, the mode deadpan, like that of the silent film comedian, Buster Keaton, but it is never malicious, and even as satire it finds cause for celebration in the rich absurdities of human behavior.

One Man, One Matchet plays upon the differences between the unprincipled, rabble-rousing Benjamin Benjamin, who is no more than a spiv with the gift of the gab, and the newly appointed Nigerian-born administrators trying to do an honest job but suspected by the traditionalists because of their command of "the White Man's language." The purpose is not anti-Nationalist but exposure of the spurious and the absurd wearing Nationalist garb. *Kinsman and Foreman* explores the trials and embarrassments of an overseas-trained Nigerian engineer who is employed by the Public Works Department in his home town and finds that his relations expect him to use his official position for their private benefit. It is a book that bubbles with cross-cultural misunderstandings.

Perhaps as a result of meager critical attention, Aluko tries to swim in the mainstream of Nigerian writing with *Chief the Honourable Minister,* a novel which, somewhat in the manner of Achebe's *A Man of the People,* deals with post-Independence political developments in Nigeria. This more "serious" venture confirms that Aluko's real gift is a judicious response to the comic, though the presentation of the idealistic Alade Moses's transformation into a corrupt politician is very skillfully done; Moses is for ever putting off as untimely the decision to resign on principle as a Minister in the government, and always succeeds in finding good principles to justify his continuing in office.

With some success *His Worshipful Majesty* treats tragically the inability of an *oba* or traditional king to make the transition from autocratic rule to mere chairmanship of a local government council hemmed in by bureaucratic regulations. In the details of the story, however, there is a muted return to Aluko's earlier comic manner, and he does achieve an uneasy poise in modulating the comic with the tragic within the same novel.

With *Wrong Ones in the Dock* Aluko seems to have abandoned the comic. He returns to the social satire of *Chief the Honourable Minister* with an indignant attack upon the inept workings of the machinery of justice in Nigeria, the general tone of which is captured in this extract from the final paragraph of the novel:

> What the Judge handed down was judgment without justice. It was unfortunately all that he was competent to give in the circumstances of the cumbersome judicial system which he operated. . . . Real justice was impossible under a truth-inhibiting judicial system which had been imported from a foreign clime and which, in spite of over a century of nursing in the inhospitable soil of an indigenous society, has yet, in that society, to grow roots that will reach down to the ground water of true justice.

It is a solemnity that sits uneasily on Aluko's pen and makes his full and detailed court-room scenes, for instance, awkward and lumbering, despite some telling satirical touches, rather than deft exposures of absurdity, ineptitude, hypocrisy, immorality, and injustice.

—Arthur Ravenscroft

ALVAREZ, A(lfred)

Nationality: British. **Born:** London, 5 August 1929. **Education:** Oundle School, Northamptonshire; Corpus Christi College, Oxford (senior research scholar and research scholar of Goldsmiths' Company, 1952-53, 1954-55), B.A. 1952, M.A. 1956; Princeton University, New Jersey (Procter visiting fellow, 1953-54); Harvard University, Cambridge, Massachusetts (Rockefeller fellow, 1955); University of New Mexico, Albuquerque (D.H. Lawrence fellow, 1958). **Family:** Married 1) Ursula Barr in 1956 (marriage dissolved 1961), one son; 2) Anne Adams in 1966, one son and one daughter. **Career:** Gauss Lecturer, Princeton University, 1957-58; visiting professor, Brandeis University, Waltham, Massachusetts, 1960, and State University of New York, Buffalo, 1966. Poetry critic and poetry editor, the *Observer,* London, 1956-66; editor, *Journal of Education,* London, 1957; drama critic, *New Statesman,* London, 1958-60; advisory editor, Penguin Modern European Poets in Translation, 1965-75; presenter, *Voices* programme, Channel 4 television, 1982. Lives in London. **Awards:** Rockefeller fellowship, 1958; Vachel Lindsay prize (*Poetry,* Chicago), 1961. **Agent:** Aitken and Stone Ltd., 29 Fernshaw Road, London SW10 0TG, England; or, Wylie Aitken and Stone, 250 West 57th Street, New York, New York 10107, U.S.A.

PUBLICATIONS

Novels

Hers. London, Weidenfeld and Nicholson, 1974; New York, Random House, 1975.
Hunt. London, Macmillan, 1978; New York, Simon and Schuster, 1978.
Day of Atonement. London, Cape, 1991.

Uncollected Short Stories

"The Smile," in *Cosmopolitan* (New York), December 1970.
"Laughter," in *Winter's Tales 17,* edited by Caroline Hobhouse. London, Macmillan, 1971; New York, St. Martin's Press, 1972.
"Summertime," in *Daily Telegraph Magazine* (London), 16 July 1971.
"Night Out," in *New Yorker,* 4 September 1971.
"Veterans," in *The Times Saturday Review* (London), 24 January 1976.

Play

Screenplay: *The Anarchist,* 1969.

Poetry

(*Poems*). Oxford, Fantasy Press, 1952.
The End of It. Privately printed, 1958.
Twelve Poems. London, The Review, 1968.
Lost. London, Turret, 1968.
Penguin Modern Poets 18, with Roy Fuller and Anthony Thwaite. London, Penguin, 1970.
Apparition. St. Lucia, University of Queensland Press, 1971.
The Legacy. London, Poem-of-the-Month Club, 1972.
Autumn to Autumn and Selected Poems 1953-1976. London, Macmillan, 1978.

Other

The Shaping Spirit: Studies in Modern English and American Poets. London, Chatto and Windus, 1958; as *Stewards of Excellence: Studies in Modern English and American Poets,* New York, Scribner, 1958.
The School of Donne. London, Chatto and Windus, and New York, Pantheon, 1961.
Under Pressure: The Artist and Society: Eastern Europe and the U.S.A. London, Penguin, 1965.
Beyond All This Fiddle: Essays 1955-1967. London, Allen Lane, 1968; New York, Random House, 1969.
The Savage God: A Study of Suicide. London, Weidenfeld and Nicolson, 1971; New York, Random House, 1972.

Beckett. London, Fontana, and New York, Viking Press, 1973.

Life after Marriage: Scenes from Divorce. London, Macmillan, 1982; as *Life after Marriage: Love in an Age of Divorce,* New York, Simon and Schuster, 1982.

The Biggest Game in Town (on gambling). London, Deutsch, and Boston, Houghton Mifflin, 1983.

Offshore: A North Sea Journey. London, Hodder and Stoughton, and Boston, Houghton Mifflin, 1986.

Feeding the Rat: Profile of a Climber. London, Bloomsbury, 1988; New York, Atlantic Monthly Press, 1989.

Rainforest, with Charles Blackman. Melbourne, Macmillan, 1988.

Night: Night Life, Language, Sleep and Breath. London, Cape, and New York, Norton, 1995.

Editor, *The New Poetry: An Anthology.* London, Penguin, 1962; revised edition, 1966.

Editor, *The Faber Book of Modern European Poetry.* London, Faber, 1992.

*

Manuscript Collection: British Library, London.

Critical Study: Interview with Ian Hamilton, in *New Review* (London), March 1978.

*   *   *

Alvarez, a self-acclaimed ambitious literary man, has written in all the genres, but he remains best known for *The Savage God,* his critical meditation on suicide with its now famous chapter about Sylvia Plath. In *Beyond All This Fiddle* and *Beckett,* as well as his other books of literary criticism, he expresses his temper, comes to terms with his literary masters, reveals the breadth of his literary interests, and displays the subtlety of his mind. In his poetry and novels his passion for language and curiosity about the human condition find expression. His imaginative writings suffer from some of the faults typical of a literary-critic-turned-creative-writer: they are too much under the spell of his literary gods and lack the freedom of invention characteristic of the best writers. Nonetheless, he writes well and is always eminently readable.

At his best in his novels, he creates a scene or person with life-like vividness. All Alvarez's writings attest to his fascination with people, their double-voiced talk, their messy lives, their qualified answers to questions, and their hesitant explanations about themselves. In his novels, especially *Day of Atonement,* he presses language into the service of his psyche, creating a plot and characters that allow him to probe subjects that have long interested him— marriage, divorce, guilt, and atonement. In *Day of Atonement* he plays with matters of point of view, dividing the narrative voice between his two central protagonists, Joe and Judy Constantine. His last two novels are thrillers, but similar to a number of the best contemporary writers in this genre, Alvarez exploits his literary and artistic temperament in this genre. His books are full of passages that offer lyrical descriptions of the urban wasteland or the mood of a day. He likes to write about the erotic: faithful to the genre, he includes scenes of pornographic exploits as well as scenes of domestic sexual pleasures. The thrill of gambling and the world of deals, sleazy characters, tough thugs, and crooked and clean cops also fit easily within the frame of a psychologically oriented detective thriller in which he writes.

In *Life After Marriage: Love in an Age of Divorce,* he explores the subject of divorce. More fascinated by the people's lives who have experienced divorce than by the statistics and data he had gathered when researching his book, Alvarez chose to blend the voices of those with whom he spoke and the incidents that they narrated to create his own "re-creations" of the felt and lived experience of divorce. He opens the book with a frank description of his own failed wedding night and failed marriage to the granddaughter of his two idols, D.H. Lawrence and Freida. Picturing his wife as the "Dark Goddess, the Muse, the Great Passion, and Mark II," he married her after a seven-week courtship and awakened the morning after his nuptial night to find her complaining that he did not cut the crusts off the toast he had so dutifully brought to her. From there, the story continues downhill to its sorry end in divorce. In other chapters of the book, he uses the strategy of the recreated narrative to tell the story of how people live together, suffer each others' faults and obsessions, bear grudges, launch into self-justification for the masochistic lives they are leading, and live with their doubt and guilt and grief. He ultimately concludes the book coming down on the side of marriage, saying "It has to be worked for like everything else worth having, and paid for in grinding small change, by compromise and growing older." In Alvarez's novels, he takes his subject of divorce and marriage into another venue and finds a mode that permits him to tell other people's stories as well as parts of his own, albeit disguised.

His first novel, *Hers,* is the story of a middle-aged woman's affair with one of her husband's students, a man some twelve years her junior. Julie, the wife of German extraction with a painful past, is married to the stereotypical university professor of letters, an older man who married her to capture the youth he neglected for his books. Alvarez' gift for caricaturing academe is not as rich as Kingsley Amis's in *Lucky Jim,* nor does it have the genius of an Iris Murdoch or Joyce Carol Oates when they tackle this subject. Nonetheless, his portrait of the professor Charles is both entertaining and honest. When Charles discovers his wife's adultery, he cannot speak his own words and feelings, rather it is Othello's words that he utters, preventing him from knowing himself. Charles is unable to register an emotion without filtering it through the language of literary characters. At one point, he lectures his student who is also his wife's lover. He talks about morality and literature, Matthew Arnold, Tolstoy, the "New Critics," T.S. Eliot and David Hume rather than simply expressing his anger and outrage. Julie is a complicated woman. German, blond, youthful in appearance, fragile, and the mother of two children, she has taken an older husband to forget her past—the abuses at the hands of the Russians and the murder of her father by the Nazis. Once she becomes the mistress of her husband's student, she breaks down. Returning to a sanatorium in Germany, she comes to terms with herself in a fairly predictable way. The best scenes in the novels are those showing Charles's paranoia, venting his hostility on the young and making himself the prey of a motorcycle gang. In one of the most memorable parts of the novel, he violently retakes possession of his wife, making her share in the complicity of their mutual violence.

Hunt and *Day of Atonement* are written in the traditions of the thriller. In *Hunt* Alvarez captures the drab life of Conrad Jessup, a man dulled by his marriage and tedious job. Jessup's quest for excitement takes him to the gambling tables and then out into the park, late at night, where he discovers the body of a woman who has been assaulted. His discovery leads to his arrest on suspicion of murder. Once released, he cannot resist finding the woman and he becomes caught in her web of international espionage. The plot is slow and obvious. The best moments in the novel are the scenes at the poker table where Conrad's compulsive gambling is so convincingly portrayed that the reader vicariously experiences his excitement and disillusionment. The world of pubs, gambling clubs, and boutiques is presented in this novel and its successor, *Day of Atonement*. Alvarez knows how to write of this world. His sense of detail, the excitement, and the people is unerring. He is not as brilliant at depicting this world as Dostoyevsky, but he is very good indeed.

Day of Atonement is a kinder book than its predecessors. The marriage between Joe and Judy is a strong one, capable of weathering the day of judgment that befalls these two characters when their friend, Tommy Apple, dies in suspicious circumstances and they find themselves hounded by figures from the underworld of drug traffickers and the police force. The Constantines' friend and benefactor of sorts, Tommy Apple, is a man who lives on the fast-track, always on the take, scheming, womanizing, setting up deals—one of which costs him his life—but also extending gifts to his friends. Joe has had to repay one of these gifts by putting his photographic talents at the behest of Tommy. It is Joe's photoshots of a kinky threesome in the sands of Tunisia that has compromised his conscience and his relationship to his third wife, Judy, and drawn him into the web of intrigue that dominates the book. At one level, the book is a who-dunnit and why? At another, it is a rich exploration of friendship, love, guilt, and reparation. The portraits of the central figures are compelling. Alvarez understands his characters and their predicaments. He writes a dialogue that rings true and he reaches closure in his book in an unexpected way.

Alvarez is a writer one wants to read. He is interested in contemporary society and its institutions. He wants to write about uncomfortable subjects: suicide, religious prejudice, divorce, and crime. He has an appetite for life. He is a wordsmith and a literary type through and through. His novels reflect all these interests and talents and they do it in the manner of the thriller.

—Carol Simpson Stern

AMADI, Elechi

Nationality: Nigerian. **Born:** Aluu, 12 May 1934. **Education:** University College, Ibadan, 1955-59, B.Sc. in mathematics and physics 1959. **Military Service:** Served in the Nigerian Federal Army, 1963-66, 1968-69. **Family:** Married Dorah Ohale in 1957; eight children. **Career:** Government survey assistant, Calabar, 1953-55, and surveyor, Enugu, 1959-60; science teacher in mission schools, Oba and Ahoada, 1960-63; principal, Asa Grammar School, 1967; administrative officer, 1970-74, and permanent secretary, 1975-83, Government of Rivers State, Port Harcourt; writer-in-residence and Dean of the Faculty of Arts, College of Education, Port Harcourt, 1984-87; Commissioner of Education, 1987-89, and Commissioner of Lands and Housing, 1989-90, Rivers State. **Awards:** International Writers Program grant, University of Iowa, 1973; Rivers State Silver Jubilee Merit award, 1992. **Address:** Box 331, Port Harcourt, Nigeria.

PUBLICATIONS

Novels

The Concubine. London, Heinemann, 1966.

The Great Ponds. London, Heinemann, 1969; New York, Day, 1973.
The Slave. London, Heinemann, 1978.
Estrangement. London, Heinemann, 1986.

Plays

Isiburu (in verse: produced Port Harcourt, Nigeria, 1969). London, Heinemann, 1973.
Peppersoup (produced Port Harcourt, Nigeria, 1977). Included in *Peppersoup, and The Road to Ibadan*, 1977.
The Road to Ibadan (produced Port Harcourt, Nigeria, 1977). Included in *Peppersoup, and The Road to Ibadan*, 1977.
Peppersoup, and The Road to Ibadan. Ibadan, Onibonoje Press, 1977.
Dancer of Johannesburg (produced Port Harcourt, Nigeria, 1979).

Other

Sunset in Biafra: A Civil War Diary. London, Heinemann, 1973.
Ethics in Nigerian Culture. Ibadan and London, Heinemann, 1982.

Translator, with Obiajunwo Wali and Greensille Enyinda, *Okwukwo Eri* (hymnbook). Port Harcourt, Nigeria, CSS Printers, 1969.
Translator, *Okupkpe* (prayerbook). Port Harcourt, Nigeria, CSS Printers, 1969.

*

Critical Studies: *The Concubine: A Crictial View* by Alastair Niven, London, Collings, 1981; *Elechi Amadi: The Man and His Work* by Ebele Eko, Ibadan, Kraft, 1991; *Elechi Amadi at 55 (Poems, Short Stories and Papers)* edited by W. Feuser and Ebele Eko, Ibadan, Heinemann, 1994.

Elechi Amadi comments:

(1991) I like to think of myself as a painter or composer using words in the place of pictures and musical symbols. I consider commitment in fiction a prostitution of literature. The novelist should depict life as he sees it without consciously attempting to persuade the reader to take a particular viewpoint. Propaganda should be left to journalists.

In my ideal novel the reader should feel a sense of aesthetic satisfaction that he cannot quite explain—the same feeling he gets when he listens to a beautiful symphony. For those readers who insist on being taught, there are always things to learn from a faithful portrayal of life in a well-written novel.

*   *   *

From his first appearance as a novelist, with *The Concubine* in 1966, Elechi Amadi established himself as a unique figure in African fiction. He was not alone in attempting to convey the day-to-day texture of traditional, pre-colonial life in an African village (Chinua Achebe's *Things Fall Apart* had already done this, at least in its earlier pages), but he distinguished himself by not offering any explicit contrasts between that traditional world and the one that replaced it. Whereas *Things Fall Apart* and many other African novels are concerned, in part at least, with the coming of the white man and the effect of that coming, Amadi's novels have never adverted to alien influences at all. The action of any of his three novels could have taken place either five years or a century before the colonial intrusion upon the area; the dilemmas which confront and finally destroy his heroes or heroines derive entirely from the beliefs, practices, and events of their indigenous culture.

The Concubine was followed by The Great Ponds and The Slave. Although not thematically related, all three novels take place in what is recognizably the same Ikweore environment. The action of all three appears to turn upon the working out of a fate which falls upon the characters from without, but which it would be meaningless, in this traditional and godfearing environment, to call unjust. Iheoma, heroine of The Concubine, is powerless to avert her spiritual marriage to the sea-king, which prevents her having any successful human relationship. Her attraction thus becomes a fatal one, resulting in the deaths of all those who seek to free her from her condition. Likewise, the hero of The Slave leaves the shrine of Amadioha to which his late father was bound as an osu (cult-slave) and appears to have right on his side in arguing for his emancipation, since he was not actually conceived there. Nevertheless, his brief career in freedom has an obstinately circular form curving through initial success to a series of disasters which brings him, friendless and alone, back to the shrine he had so hopefully deserted.

Amadi maintains a nicely judged ambiguity about the meaning of these events, which must depend entirely upon the reader himself. The society of which he writes would have rejected, perhaps still rejects, any clear distinction between the natural and spiritual orders of existence. These interpenetrate to such an extent that man cannot demand the mastery of his fate through will alone. The highest he can aspire to is to know his fate and tune his soul to its acceptance. Tragedy springs as much from failure to do this, as from the nature of that fate itself.

—Gerald Moore

AMBLER, Eric

Pseudonym: Eliot Reed. **Nationality:** British. **Born:** London, 28 June 1909. **Education:** Colfe's Grammar School, London; University of London, 1925-28. **Military Service:** Served in the Royal Artillery, 1940-46; assistant director of army kinematography, 1944-46: lieutenant colonel; Bronze Star (USA). **Family:** Married 1) Louise Crombie in 1939 (divorced 1958); 2) the writer Joan Harrison in 1958. **Career:** Engineering apprentice, 1928; advertising copywriter, 1929-37; director of an advertising agency, 1937-38. Created Checkmate TV series, 1959. **Awards:** Crime Writers Association Gold Dagger award, 1959, 1962, 1967, 1972, Diamond Dagger award, 1986; Mystery Writers of America Edgar Allan Poe award, 1964, and Grand Master award, 1975; Svenska Deckarakademins Grand Master, 1975; Grand Prix de Littérature Policière, 1976; Veterans of the Office of Strategic Services Golden Dagger, 1989. Honorary D.Litt., City University, 1993. O.B.E. (Officer, Order of the British Empire), 1981. **Agent:** Campbell Thomson and McLaughlin Ltd., 31 Newington Green, London N16 9PU, England.

PUBLICATIONS

Novels

The Dark Frontier. London, Hodder and Stoughton, 1936; New York, Mysterious Press, 1990.

Uncommon Danger. London, Hodder and Stoughton, 1937; as Background to Danger, New York, Knopf, 1937.
Epitaph for a Spy. London, Hodder and Stoughton, 1938; New York, Knopf, 1952; revised edition, London, Hodder and Stoughton, 1966.
Cause for Alarm. London, Hodder and Stoughton, 1938; New York, Knopf, 1939.
The Mask of Dimitrios. London, Hodder and Stoughton, 1939; as A Coffin for Dimitrios, New York, Knopf, 1939.
Journey into Fear. London, Hodder and Stoughton, and New York, Knopf, 1940.
Judgment on Deltchev. London, Hodder and Stoughton, and New York, Knopf, 1951.
The Schirmer Inheritance. London, Heinemann, and New York, Knopf, 1953.
The Night-Comers. London, Heinemann, 1956; as State of Siege, New York, Knopf, 1956.
Passage of Arms. London, Heinemann, 1959; New York, Knopf, 1960.
The Light of Day. London, Heinemann, 1962; New York, Knopf, 1963; as Topkapi, New York, Bantam, 1964.
A Kind of Anger. London, Bodley Head, and New York, Atheneum, 1964.
Dirty Story. London, Bodley Head, and New York, Atheneum, 1967.
The Intercom Conspiracy. New York, Atheneum, 1969; London, Weidenfeld and Nicolson, 1970.
The Levanter. London, Weidenfeld and Nicolson, and New York, Atheneum, 1972.
Doctor Frigo. London, Weidenfeld and Nicolson, and New York, Atheneum, 1974.
Send No More Roses. London, Weidenfeld and Nicolson, 1977; as The Siege of the Villa Lipp, New York, Random House, 1977; London, Prior, 1978.
The Card of Time. London, Weidenfeld and Nicolson, and New York, Farrar Straus, 1981.

Novels as Eliot Reed (with Charles Rodda)

Skytip. New York, Doubleday, 1950; London, Hodder and Stoughton, 1951.
Tender to Danger. New York, Doubleday, 1951; as Tender to Moonlight, London, Hodder and Stoughton, 1952.
The Maras Affair. London, Collins, and New York, Doubleday, 1953.
Charter to Danger. London, Collins, 1954.
Passport to Panic. London, Collins, 1958.

Short Stories

Waiting for Orders. New York, Mysterious Press, 1991.

Plays

Screenplays: The Way Ahead, with Peter Ustinov, 1944; United States, 1945; The October Man, 1947; The Passionate Friends (One Woman's Story), 1949; Highly Dangerous, 1950; The Magic Box, 1951; Gigolo and Gigolette, in Encore, 1951; The Card (The Promoter), 1952; Rough Shoot (Shoot First), 1953; The Cruel Sea, 1953; Lease of Life, 1954; The Purple Plain, 1954; Yangtse Incident (Battle Hell), 1957; A Night to Remember, 1958; The Wreck of the Mary Deare, 1960; Love Hate Love, 1970.

Other

The Ability to Kill and Other Pieces. London, Bodley Head, 1963;
    New York, Mysterious Press, 1987.
Here Lies: An Autobiography. London, Weidenfeld and Nicolson,
    1985; New York, Farrar Straus, 1986.
The Story So Far: Memories and Other Fictions. London,
    Weidenfeld and Nicolson, 1994.

Editor, *To Catch a Spy: An Anthology of Favorite Spy Stories.* Lon-
    don, Bodley Head, 1964; New York, Atheneum, 1965.

*

Manuscript Collection: Mugar Memorial Library, Boston University.

Critical Studies: "Eric Ambler Issue" of *Hollins Critic* (Hollins
College, Virgina), February 1971; *Festbuch Uber Eric Ambler* (includes bibliography) edited by Gerd Haffmans, Zurich, Diogenes,
1979; *Eric Ambler* by Peter Lewis, New York, Continuum, 1990.

Eric Ambler comments:

(1991) I have found that every statement I have ever tried to
make on the subject of my work later seems either pretentious or
meaningless. Besides, I am an unreliable witness. When *Uber Eric
Ambler* was published on my 70th birthday I gave a number of
interviews to European journalists. One of them pointed out that I
had answered a standard question (where do you get your ideas?)
in two entirely different ways. Which answer was the right one? I
explained that I always tried to avoid giving an interviewer the same
answer as I had given his colleague so that each had something
exclusive. He was deeply shocked. Did I not distinguish between
truth and falsehood? I could have said, "Not when answering dull
or unanswerable questions." Instead, I mumbled something about
only trying to be helpful. It failed to satisfy him. I stood convicted
of frivolity.

*   *   *

It was Graham Greene's view that Eric Ambler is Britain's best
thriller writer and there are many reasons for supporting this judgment. The most important is Ambler's capacity for telling a story.
He wastes no words; his narrative is economical yet evocative; his
grasp of detail matches his control of suspense.

Uncommon Danger, his second novel, may seem dated in some
aspects of its political background but the plot depends upon the
supply of oil and so has a certain immediacy in the 1990's. The
main character, Kenton, a reporter, increases in stature as the plot
proceeds, its tempo quickening into a final Buchan-like chase.

Ambler's ability to vary the tempo of stories is subtle. He is a
master of reconstruction without boredom. This technique is one
of the reasons for the success of an early book, *The Mask of
Dimitrios,* where his character Latimer, a detective story writer, becomes obsessed with the mysterious life of a man called Dimitrios
whose supposed body he sees in a Turkish morgue. He decides to
find out something of the man's odd past, and discovers more and
more of his intrigues in many countries, his altering identity, his
capacity for murder, pimping, political assassination, drug trafficking, and double crossing. Latimer's own search unfolds slowly,
then follows his unwilling cooperation with a former associate and

victim of Dimitrios. Gradually the narration speeds up until Latimer
is confronted by the fact that Dimitrios is alive, and not only alive
but deadly dangerous. The reader is involved in Latimer's searching, in the gradual building up of a biography, in the factual details
which reveal the ruthless cleverness of this professional crook. The
narration gives us a clear picture of Latimer's thoughts and shows
him building up theories about Dimitrios as his knowledge of the
man's past increases. Not only does the tension of a search which
is progressing steadily despite the inevitable setbacks keep the
reader's attention clearly focused on the details of the story, but the
relationship between Latimer and the mysterious Mr. Peters also
heightens the intensity.

In *The Mask of Dimitrios* no sympathy is evoked for the successful, ruthless criminal, nor indeed for Mr. Peters, the unsuccessful one. There is some alteration of viewpoint in some of
Ambler's later novels. For instance, in *Dirty Story,* the main character, Arthur Simpson (he first appeared in *The Light of Day*), is
described in an Interpol dossier as interpreter, chauffeur, waiter,
pornographer, and guide. He is also a pimp, and the story begins
with his urgent need for a passport. His stormy interview with Her
Majesty's Vice-Consul in Athens leaves us no possibility for illusions about the man whose life, according to the Vice-Consul, is
nothing but a long dirty story. Driven by lack of money (with which
to buy a Panlibhoncan passport) into acting as a casting director of
blue films, he eventually becomes a mercenary in Central Africa.
He does not cover himself with credit but eventually escapes to
Tangier. One of Ambler's particular skills is a capacity to create
modern rogue literature. Morally we dispise his character, but such
is the power of the tense narration that we follow his adventures
with an interest which verges between sympathy, as things go hopelessly wrong, and a wry sense of the sheer comedy latent in Arthur
Simpson's incongruous, unscrupulous, and ridiculous nature.

Judgment on Deltchev reflects the passage of time. It is a novel
dealing with a repressive Eastern European state in which a hero
of the people is being tried for treason in a show trial, in which the
penalty is death. Foster, a western journalist, becomes involved with
the former leader's family and is forced to ponder whether Deltchev
is hero or villain. Murder, assassination, terror, and the complexities of conspiracy have become more sinister, and *The Schirmer
Inheritance* continues this tough strain as an American lawyer and
his interpreter Maria Kolin search for the heir to the Schirmer fortune. The trail leads from a sergeant in the dragoons of Ansbach
(who deserts from the rearguard protecting the Prussian army after
the battle of Eylau in 1806) through America and Germany to the
Greece in which a German unit, led by a sergeant, had been ambushed by the ELAS. They discover the sergeant in an exciting
quickening of the story, very characteristic of Ambler's technique,
for he has been occupied with gaining our confidence by steadily
involving us in the search, which he develops with skill, building
it up with details of the methods used to trace whether a man existed or not.

The whole unscrupulous world of espionage occupies some of
Ambler's attention. In *The Intercom Conspiracy* the protagonist is
Theodore Carter, editor of *Intercom,* a journal owned by a retired,
somewhat crackpot American general of anti-Communist views.
When the general dies the journal is bought by a mysterious Arnold
Bloch, who supplies material for the journal which offends west
and east alike. Various intelligence agencies become interested in
Carter's sources, and eventually, after being, in the space of a few
hours, snatched, interrogated under duress, roughed up, threatened,
burgled, and gassed, he runs. We know that two clever and un-

scrupulous colonels have gotten disgruntled with their role in their respective intelligence services; their plot to play off the major powers and cash in on the situation involves Carter as cats-paw—and, of course, Latimer, Ambler's author character, created much earlier, who is busily writing up the story. The inclusion of Latimer, and his disappearance at the beginning of the book, allows Ambler to tell the story at different levels and from different viewpoints. As usual the tension heightens, the pace speeds up, as the reader becomes sufficiently *au fait* with the complex linkage of events. The story is realistic; its portrayal of the cynicism, indeed the theatrically self-conscious seediness and secrecy of the world of military and political intelligence, is convincing in its detail. Ambler's characters have sufficient depth and individuality to match this superb handling of plot. Carter, the journalist, is given to drink; his marriage has broken up earlier; and he is "a man of undoubted ability who takes pleasure in misusing it." Again, the central character is no orthodox hero, and must be taken with blemishes and all; and the two colonels realize he will have dangerous moments. This is a calculated risk and he must take his chance. And take it he does in the respectable surroundings of Geneva.

Ambler has two kinds of story, the simple and the complex. In *The Night-Comers* he unfolds a simple story of an English consulting engineer who is unwillingly involved in a military coup d'état in an island near Indonesia. He is on his way home, staying for a few days in a friend's flat on the top of the local radio station when the revolution begins. His situation is complicated, indeed endangered by the presence of a Eurasian girl with whom he is having a brief affair when the rebels make this their headquarters. The government forces close in on the radio station, and the novel describes the fighting with skilled economy. Tension is built up, the waiting alternates with hope and despair. Again Ambler's realism keeps the story convincing. At one period, when the Englishman realizes that one of the insurgent's leaders is a government agent and that his own life and the girl's are in danger, he is compelled to repair a generator so that the rebel general can broadcast his program to the outside world. This sudden involvement with the mechanical problems of drying out a generator, damaged by water seeping into the power house after a bomb blast, gives the story an authenticity which is compelling. It adds an extra dimension to the simple narrative by, as it were, describing one aspect of the situation of the insurgents in some depth. The effect of the rising on the hapless spectators, the Englishman and the Eurasian girl, gives the story the necessary counterpointing, and again is used to involve the reader's sympathy, to sharpen and hold his attention.

For Ambler's ability to juggle with a complex plot there is *A Kind of Anger* where a newspaperman becomes involved in the search for a missing girl, the mistress of a murdered Iraqi colonel, a Kurdish conspirator. Here there are rival buyers for the colonel's papers, which the girl possesses, and which the newspaperman, lonely, neurotic, suicidal, eventually helps her to sell. Here the mixture of cross purposes is skillfully woven into the tapestry of the story. This is ingeniously done, and the suspense mounts steadily as the various motives are brought together. *Send No More Roses* is more complex still. In this story the central character, Paul Firman, is reminiscent of Dimitrios, though he is more subtle in his machinations. He agrees to an interview with Professor Krom who thinks he can force him into an exposure of his methods. This interview takes place in a villa on the French Riviera; the verbal fencing gives way to violence. The end is skillfully linked up with the beginning, as the unraveling continues. *The Card of Time* is a good example of how Ambler can hold the reader's attention by the characters'

conversations until the story erupts into action. Gradually the reasons emerge for the choice of Robert Halliday as a go-between in delicate negotiations between Nato and a Middle Eastern leader; they are subtle and complex but credible because the reader has been involved in their unfolding. While Ambler's plots require sex and violence there is no excess of them, and when they do arise there is a touch of inevitability about them which adds to the conviction his narration has already established in the reader's mind. He is indeed a skilled, professional writer of the highest order.

—A. Norman Jeffares

AMIS, (Sir) Kingsley (William)

Nationality: British. **Born:** Clapham, London, 16 April 1922. **Education:** Norbury College; City of London School, 1935-39; St. John's College, Oxford, 1941, 1945-49, B.A. 1948, M.A. **Military Service:** Served in the Royal Corps of Signals, 1942-45. **Family:** Married 1) Hilary Ann Bardwell in 1948 (marriage dissolved 1965), two sons, including Martin Amis *q.v.*, and one daughter; 2) Elizabeth Jane Howard, *q.v.*, in 1965 (divorced 1983). **Career:** Lecturer in English, University College, Swansea, 1949-61; fellow in English, Peterhouse, Cambridge, 1961-63. Visiting fellow in Creative Writing, Princeton University, New Jersey, 1958-59; visiting professor, Vanderbilt University, Nashville, Tennessee, 1967. Lives in London. **Awards:** Maugham award, 1955; *Yorkshire Post* award, 1974, 1984; John W. Campbell Memorial award, 1977; Booker prize, 1986. Honorary Fellow, St. John's College, 1976; University College, Swansea, 1985. C.B.E. (Commander, Order of the British Empire), 1981. Knighted, 1990. **Agent:** Jonathan Clowes Ltd., Iron Bridge House, Bridge Approach, London NW1 8BD, England.

PUBLICATIONS

Novels

Lucky Jim. London, Gollancz, and New York, Doubleday, 1954.
That Uncertain Feeling. London, Gollancz, 1955; New York, Harcourt Brace, 1956.
I Like It Here. London, Gollancz, and New York, Harcourt Brace, 1958.
Take a Girl Like You. London, Gollancz, 1960; New York, Harcourt Brace, 1961.
One Fat Englishman. London, Gollancz, 1963; New York, Harcourt Brace, 1964.
The Egyptologists, with Robert Conquest. London, Cape, 1965; New York, Random House, 1966.
The Anti-Death League. London, Gollancz, and New York, Harcourt Brace, 1966.
Colonel Sun: A James Bond Adventure (as Robert Markham). London, Cape, and New York, Harper, 1968.
I Want It Now. London, Cape, 1968; New York, Harcourt Brace, 1969.
The Green Man. London, Cape, 1969; New York, Harcourt Brace, 1970.
Girl, 20. London, Cape, 1971; New York, Harcourt Brace, 1972.
The Riverside Villas Murder. London, Cape, and New York, Harcourt Brace, 1973.
Ending Up. London, Cape, and New York, Harcourt Brace, 1974.
The Alteration. London, Cape, 1976; New York, Viking Press, 1977.

Jake's Thing. London, Hutchinson, 1978; New York, Viking Press, 1979.
Russian Hide-and-Seek: A Melodrama. London, Hutchinson, 1980.
Stanley and the Women. London, Hutchinson, 1984; New York, Summit, 1985.
The Old Devils. London, Hutchinson, 1986; New York, Summit, 1987.
The Crime of the Century. London, Dent, 1987; New York, Mysterious Press, 1989.
Difficulties with Girls. London, Hutchinson, 1988; New York, Summit, 1989.
The Folks That Live on the Hill. London, Hutchinson, and New York, Summit, 1990.
We Are All Guilty. London, Hutchinson, 1991.
The Russian Girl. London, Hutchinson, 1992.
You Can't Do Both. London, Hutchinson, 1994.

Short Stories

My Enemy's Enemy. London, Gollancz, 1962; New York, Harcourt Brace, 1963.
Penguin Modern Stories 11, with others. London, Penguin, 1972.
Dear Illusion. London, Covent Garden Press, 1972.
The Darkwater Hall Mystery. Edinburgh, Tragara Press, 1978.
Collected Short Stories. London, Hutchinson, 1980; revised edition, 1987.
Mr. Barrett's Secret and Other Stories. London, Hutchinson, 1993.

Plays

Radio Play: *Something Strange,* 1962.

Television Plays: *A Question about Hell,* 1964; *The Importance of Being Harry,* 1971; *Dr. Watson and the Darkwater Hall Mystery,* 1974; *See What You've Done (Softly, Softly* series), 1974; *We Are All Guilty (Against the Crowd* series), 1975.

Poetry

Bright November. London, Fortune Press, 1947.
A Frame of Mind. Reading, Berkshire, University of Reading School of Art, 1953.
(Poems). Oxford, Fantasy Press, 1954.
A Case of Samples: Poems 1946-1956. London, Gollancz, 1956; New York, Harcourt Brace, 1957.
The Evans Country. Oxford, Fantasy Press, 1962.
Penguin Modern Poets 2, with Dom Moraes and Peter Porter. London, Penguin, 1962.
A Look round the Estate: Poems 1957-1967. London, Cape, 1967; New York, Harcourt Brace, 1968.
Wasted, Kipling at Bateman's. London, Poem-of-the-Month Club, 1973.
Collected Poems 1944-1978. London, Hutchinson, 1979; New York, Viking Press, 1980.

Recordings: *Kingsley Amis Reading His Own Poems,* Listen, 1962; *Poems,* with Thomas Blackburn, Jupiter, 1962.

Other

Socialism and the Intellectuals. London, Fabian Society, 1957.
New Maps of Hell: A Survey of Science Fiction. New York, Harcourt Brace, 1960; London, Gollancz, 1961.

The James Bond Dossier. London, Cape, and New York, New American Library, 1965.
Lucky Jim's Politics. London, Conservative Political Centre, 1968.
What Became of Jane Austen? and Other Questions. London, Cape, 1970; New York, Harcourt Brace, 1971.
On Drink. London, Cape, 1972; New York, Harcourt Brace, 1973.
Rudyard Kipling and His World. London, Thames and Hudson, 1975; New York, Scribner, 1976.
An Arts Policy? London, Centre for Policy Studies, 1979.
Every Day Drinking. London, Hutchinson, 1983.
How's Your Glass? A Quizzical Look at Drinks and Drinking. London, Weidenfeld and Nicolson, 1984.
The Amis Collection: Selected Non-Fiction 1954-1990, edited by John McDermott. London, Hutchinson, 1990.
Memoirs. London, Hutchinson, 1991.

Editor, with James Michie, *Oxford Poetry 1949.* Oxford, Blackwell, 1949.
Editor, with Robert Conquest, *Spectrum [1-5]: A Science Fiction Anthology.* London, Gollancz, 5 vols., 1961-65; New York, Harcourt Brace, 5 vols., 1962-67.
Editor, *Selected Short Stories of G.K. Chesterton.* London, Faber, 1972.
Editor, *Tennyson.* London, Penguin, 1973.
Editor, *Harold's Years: Impressions from the New Statesman and the Spectator.* London, Quartet, 1977.
Editor, *The New Oxford Book of Light Verse.* London and New York, Oxford University Press, 1978.
Editor, *The Faber Popular Reciter.* London, Faber, 1978.
Editor, *The Golden Age of Science Fiction.* London, Hutchinson, 1981.
Editor, with James Cochrane, *The Great British Songbook.* London, Joseph, 1986.
Editor, *The Amis Anthology: A Personal Choice of English Verse.* London, Hutchinson, 1988.
Editor, *The Pleasure of Poetry.* London, Cassell, 1990.

*

Bibliography: *Kingsley Amis: A Checklist* by Jack Benoit Gohn, Kent, Ohio, Kent State University Press, 1976; *Kingsley Amis: A Reference Guide* by Dale Salwak, Boston, Hall, and London, Prior, 1978.

Manuscript Collection (Poetry): State University of New York, Buffalo.

Critical Studies: *Kingsley Amis* by Philip Gardner, Boston, Twayne, 1981; *Kingsley Amis* by Richard Bradford, London, Arnold, 1989; *Kingsley Amis: An English Moralist* by John McDermott, London, Macmillan, 1989; *Kingsley Amis in Life and Letters* edited by Dale Salwak, London, Macmillan, 1990.

Kingsley Amis comments:
(1972) Anything a novelist (or any other artist) says about his own work should be regarded with suspicion. It will depend, at least partly, on his mood, the reception of his latest book, whether the one he is working on at the moment is coming well or badly (actually my own always come well, i.e. slowly but—so far—surely). And a novelist is far from being his own best critic, if only because, as Christopher Isherwood once remarked (in effect),

no writer is aware of more than about two-thirds of what he is actually doing and saying. Nor should he be.

Well, anyhow: what I think I am doing is writing novels within the main English-language tradition. That is, trying to tell interesting, believable stories about understandable characters in a reasonably straightforward style: no tricks, no experimental foolery. As the tradition indicates, my subject is the relations between people, and I aim at the traditional wide range of effects: humor, pathos, irony, suspense, description, action, introspection. If I had to find a label for my novels, I should call them serio-comedies, though I like to venture now and again into a kind of genre fiction that has always interested me, and have written a straight espionage thriller, a mainstream novel with espionage and science-fiction elements, and a mainstream novel with a large ghost-story interest. One day I may tackle a straight science-fiction novel and a straight detective story.

What I do not think I am doing, despite what some critics have said, is making any kind of statement about "society." As a private citizen I am deeply interested in politics; as a novelist I merely use political material along with domestic, personal, sexual, farcical, social, and other material. The novelist must always try to get the reader to believe that his story and characters are very probable. To do this he must get his background right, or right as he sees it, which means he must try to describe his times; but this is not his prime object. That object is to portray human nature as it has always been, the permanent human passions of love, sorrow, ambition, fear, anger, frustration, joy, and the rest. No "commitment" for me, except to literature.

*   *   *

Kinglsey Amis's principal distinction, in all his novels and other writings, is the sharp comic texture of his prose. Full of mimicry, elaborate satire of ordinary experience (like the bad taste of food or the pains of waking up with a hangover), stock characters tagged by occupation (dentists' mistresses abound in the early fiction), pseudological analyses of experience, satire of contemporary fads and social attitudes, Amis's prose is generally funny. At times, in works like *The Anti-Death League* or *Girl, 20,* the prose is flatter and less referential, the list of grievances less ebullient, but farcical events and sharply observed improbabilities keep the tone and texture comic. And some of the later work, like *Jake's Thing,* displays a biting wit directed against contemporary sex therapy and other fashionable distortions of relationships between the sexes. In some of the later fiction, what was, in Amis, an initial attitude of iconoclasm, mocking pretensions to culture, tourist-like enthusiasms for foreign lands, or attempts by characters to transcend themselves, has come to sound like a perverse grumble. Particularly in novels like *One Fat Englishman* or *Girl, 20,* or the more recent *Ending Up,* the spirited and farcical antics of the protagonists, originally, as in *Lucky Jim,* self-protective, turn into a series of aggressive and hostile tricks. Amis sometimes shades the line between the persona of the plain Englishman, fooled by neither the old-fashioned nonsense of faith in official or religious verities nor the contemporary nonsense of various rebellious or international fads, and the persona of the curmudgeon (a persona his recent *Memoirs* has further elaborated).

Amis is a careful craftsman in a wide variety of literary forms. He has always demonstrated a strong interest in science fiction and the novel of espionage. He has written a ghost story (*The Green Man*), a whodunit (*The Riverside Villas Murder*), a novel dependent on the imaginative historical assumption, detailed in terms of

1976, that Martin Luther became Pope instead of founding a new religion (*The Alteration*), and a futuristic novel set 50 years hence in a Russia that has abandoned Marxism to return to autocratic Czarist control while retaining the exploitive and brutal qualities Amis sees as endemic to both regimes (*Russian Hide-and-Seek*). The novels set in the more familiar contemporary world are also constructed carefully. Frequently, thematic strands, embodied in different satirically symbolic characters, are gradually drawn together toward a climactic scene that involves almost everyone in the novel. These culminating scenes, like the drunken lecture in *Lucky Jim,* the party in *Take a Girl Like You,* or the therapy workshop weekend in *Jake's Thing,* often take place in public, emphasizing the resolution of the novel in terms that are publicly and socially visible. For Amis, the novel is a rational construction, and he has frequently demonstrated his respect for the traditional novels of the 18th century, both explicitly, as in the great admiration for Fielding shown in *I Like It Here,* and implicitly, as in all the parallels followed by an ironically reversed conclusion between Richardson's *Pamela* and Amis's *Take a Girl Like You.* Amis's rational constructions lampoon deviation, excessive complexity, or eccentricity, and they resolve mystery, either directly in a novel like *The Riverside Villas Murder* or metaphorically, in social and psychological terms, in a novel like *That Uncertain Feeling.* Amis's fictional structures are seldom openended, containing little of the thematic corollaries of the open-ended, of introspection, self-doubt, emotional turbulence, indecision, or romanticism.

In spite of all the journalistic declarations in the late 1950's about "Angry Young Men," a rebellion he supposedly led, Amis has never been or claimed to be an iconoclast about society. Rather, the novels, whatever the setting, demonstrate an acceptance, no matter how ironic or grudging, of the social status quo. Frequently, as in *One Fat Englishman* and *I Want It Now,* Amis begins by satirizing a character who pretends to be iconoclastic by showing the iconoclasm as merely modish opportunism. As the novel develops, in a characteristic switch, Amis depicts the opportunism as much like everyone else's, perhaps slightly less selfish and self-deluding than that of others. The energetic iconoclast often learns to adjust in contemporary society, earns the rewards of jobs and good women by sensibly squelching deviation or insistence on self and following the axioms audible around him. Often, in the early novels like *Lucky Jim, Take a Girl Like You,* and *I Want It Now,* the central character is helped materially by an aristocrat, a symbolic representative of the pinnacle of society who leans down, like a fairy-godfather, to reward the deserving. Committed social rebels, those who would transform society in terms of a new or resurrected vision, are either peripheral fools or nonexistent in Amis's fiction.

Amis's attitude toward the social adjustment he endorses has altered in the course of his fictional career. Initially, in *Lucky Jim* and *That Uncertain Feeling,* the value of adjustment was debatable, although the process inevitable for a talented young man. *That Uncertain Feeling,* Amis's least certain, least consoling novel, and one that seems to catch contemporary social references strikingly, even develops sympathy for the man who is unable to adjust and must retreat to the provincial society he came from. Later, in *I Like It Here* and *Take a Girl Like You,* questions about the value of adjustment become more a matter of superficial comedy and the worth of adjustment, like that of learning to order a meal, drive a car, or lose virginity, is taken for granted. In *I Want It Now* adjustment becomes a positive virtue contrasted to the selfish deviation of eccentrics who are eventually exposed; in *Girl, 20,* the most curmudgeonly novel, the eccentrics can despoil and destroy contemporary

London and can only be countered by a rigid adherence to a nonpermissive social code. In some recent fiction, like *Jake's Thing,* adjustment is somewhat gentler, the 60-year-old protagonist's recognition that, although the social forms of sex therapy and the new female consciousness are ludicrous (including the theory that Hamlet was really a woman in disguise), he has learned to modify somewhat and accept the uncomfortable consequences of the male chauvinism by which he has lived. In other recent examples, like *Stanley and the Women,* adjustment is more difficult, requiring the protagonist to accept and attempt to understand both his son's breakdown and his second wife's lies and emotional explosions, both forms of "madness" against which he tries to pose the solid though very limited certainties of his origins in the lower-middle class of South London. Stanley is less the authorial voice of a nastily misogynistic sexism he has been accused of being than the example of a sane, too simple man in retreat from the psychological and social complexities of the modern world he can no longer absorb. The emphasis on the rightness of adjustment or accommodation in Amis's fiction is stated negatively, casually. At the end of *Lucky Jim* Jim Dixon, less arid and phony as a teacher than are the other academics, is rewarded because "It's not that you've got the qualifications. . . . You haven't got the disqualifications, though, and that's much rarer;" at the end of *I Want it Now* the hero and heroine acknowledge that all they can do is help "each other not to be as bad as we would be on our own;" Jake, at the end of *Jake's Thing,* learns that the "loss of libido" that propelled his excursion into the ludicrous new psychological world to which he partially adjusted may have been physical in origin after all. In other words, Amis characteristically wraps his resolving accommodations in layers of irony.

Amis's forms, his attitudes, and his ironic resolutions work against any sympathetic presentation of depth or intensity in human emotions. For example, in many of the novels, especially the early ones, sexual encounters are almost always material for comedy. Potentially emotional love-making is interrupted by mosquitoes, wasps, a pseudological analysis of how to defend different parts of the anatomy, or a manual of sexual technique to demonstrate the protagonist's social skills. Often, the actual scene generating emotion is omitted or severely compressed; at other times, it is subservient to another irony, as in *The Green Man,* in which the protagonist has wanted most to be in bed with his wife and his mistress simultaneously and arranges it only to find that the two women shut him out entirely. A similar irony resolves the plot of *The Alteration,* in which the imaginary contemporary theocratic world (brilliantly depicted in sharply semi-anachronistic prose) propounds the central question of castrating an exceptionally talented young church singer. Just as the talented boy is about to escape, a sudden illness makes castration medically necessary. When, as in *I Want It Now* and *The Anti-Death League,* Amis tries to depict sexuality or love directly, the comedy disappears, the prose becomes flat and banal, and the scene is sentimental. Only occasionally does the implicit Puritanism surface from underneath the irony. In *The Riverside Villas Murder,* in which the resolution is ratiocinatively clever and all the ends neatly tied but the motivation sketchy and unconvincing, the murderer is the woman who sexually initiated the young narrator in a long and conventionally steamy scene. Here, uncharacteristically, the introduction of Eve, the sensual woman who imposes evil on the innocent boy, overwhelms the design of the novel.

Although less skillfully comic than many of his novels, *The Anti-Death League* (in which L.S. Caton, the rather slimy editor and lecturer who writes in green ink and appears in almost all the earlier novels, is finally killed off) is one of Amis's most interesting and illustrative. A group of characters at and near a military base recognize the prospect of death and confront the issues of survival in their political, occupational, personal, and psychological ramifications. But the lovers, facing the possible death of one, are simply silent, as if all talk, all human articulation, is futile or pretentiously silly. The other characters spin off into farce, tricks, or deliberate evasion in order to survive. Similarly, in *Ending Up,* in which five old people share Tupenny-Hapenny cottage, Bernard, the most intelligent of them, learns that he has only a few months to live. He indulges in a series of malicious tricks on the others, expresses his defiance of death in hostility, and begins a chain of events that kills all five. *Stanley and the Women* does not fully face or resolve all the difficult psychological material about families and relationships it so sharply and effectively introduces. Often, Amis's protagonists assume a comic belligerent pose, as if potential humanity and sensitivity are hiding behind the masks, the tricks, all the paraphernalia of the comic survival kit (one that includes the capacity for self-satire as well), and the professional sharpness and skill. When the pose slips or is discarded, the books are suddenly silent, as if nothing else is there and we can infer sensitivity only from its negation. For the most part, Amis's characteristic virtue, as well as his characteristic limitation, is his sense of distance, his capacity for seeing clearly a great deal of what is ludicrous and pretentious even at the price of omitting what is most profoundly or intensely human.

—James Gindin

AMIS, Martin (Louis)

Nationality: British. **Born:** Oxford, 25 August 1949; son of Kingsley Amis, *q.v.* **Education:** Exeter College, Oxford, B.A. (honors) in English 1971. **Family:** Married Antonia Phillips in 1984; two sons. **Career:** Editorial assistant, *Times Literary Supplement,* London, 1972-75; assistant literary editor, 1975-77, and literary editor, 1977-79, *New Statesman,* London. Since 1979 full-time writer. Lives in London. **Awards:** Maugham award, 1974. **Agent:** Peters Fraser and Dunlop, 503-504 The Chambers, Chelsea Harbour, Lots Road, London SW10 0XF, England.

PUBLICATIONS

Novels

The Rachel Papers. London, Cape, 1973; New York, Knopf, 1974.
Dead Babies. London, Cape, 1975; New York, Knopf, 1976; as *Dark Secrets,* St. Albans, Hertfordshire, Triad, 1977.
Success. London, Cape, 1978; New York, Harmony, 1987.
Other People: A Mystery Story. London, Cape, and New York, Viking Press, 1981.
Money: A Suicide Note. London, Cape, 1984; New York, Viking, 1985.
London Fields. London, Cape, 1989; New York, Harmony, 1990.
Time's Arrow; or, The Nature of the Offence. London, Cape, and New York, Harmony, 1991.
The Information. New York, Crown Publishing, 1995.

Short Stories

Einstein's Monsters: Five Stories. London, Cape, and New York, Harmony, 1987.

Plays

Screenplays: *Mixed Doubles,* 1979; *Saturn 3,* 1980.

Other

Invasion of the Space Invaders. London, Hutchinson, 1982.
The Moronic Inferno and Other Visits to America. London, Cape, 1986; New York, Viking, 1987.
Visiting Mrs Nabokov and Other Excursions. London, Cape, 1993; New York, Harmony, 1994.

*

Bibliography: *Bruce Chatwin, Martin Amis, Julian Barnes: A Bibliography of Their First Editions* by David Rees, London, Colophon Press, 1992.

Critical Studies: *Venus Envy* by Adam Mars-Jones, London, Chatto and Windus, 1990.

Theatrical Activities:
Actor: **Film**—*A High Wind in Jamaica,* 1965.

*   *   *

Now that Martin Amis has eight novels under his belt as well as the short stories, the critical essays on American literature and a whole stack of literary journalism, it is easier to see the importance of the works—not just of his influential personal presence on the literary scene—especially for their reflection of the 1980s and 1990s. Though the novels are not without their detractors and it has even been fashionable in some circles to adopt an almost patronizing tone towards their cleverness of language and form, the works have been highly praised and are now beginning to receive the kind of serious academic attention that they no doubt deserve as Amis matures into one of the top dozen or so living contemporary British writers whose work we would be poorer without. Amis can now command large and well-publicised advances. He received £90,000 for *London Fields* and debates about the £500,000 advance he negotiated for *The Information* filled the press and television arts shows in England and the United States for weeks. If anyone can manage to retain both commercial and critical success on this scale it is Amis. Not least among his achievements is his having imported some of the self-confidence and classless linguistic energy of the post-war American novel into the British scene, while at the same time retaining a satirical distance on the worst excesses of self-obsessed modernity. In Amis's satire even the most traditionally British reader can find implied moral values of a congenial type but, perhaps more importantly, Amis's ambivalences are brilliantly accurate and are precisely those of his time.

Published in 1973, when Amis himself was only 24, *The Rachel Papers* created, in Charles Highway, a new adolescent hero of sexual and intellectual initiation who manages both to get and to get over needing his "older woman" Rachel and to bounce his way

into Oxford. Highway is hardly the virtuous, working-class hero of 1950s and 1960s prototypes for the genre but is 100 per cent more sympathetic than the gilded Kensington lobotomies that surround him. The novel is made more interesting by the emerging literary and cultural self-consciousness of its protagonist as well as by Amis's deft play with the possibilities of genre.

Dead Babies, which followed in 1975, also played with genre, cleverly announcing itself as a Menippean satire. Two groups of characters—the repulsively self-indulgent upper-class English set of Quentin Villiers and his wife Celia, and the extremely drug-and-sex-crazed Americans—team up for a weekend orgy of self-destruction that is not quite *self*-destruction since it is hurried on by the manipulative malignity of the mysterious "Johnny" who turns out to be none other than an alter ego of one of the "Appleseed Rectory" ravers. This narrative trickery which allowed Amis the freedom to ask questions about good and evil, about psychology and identity, and about the rules of narrative writing, without being stuffy or discursive, became a trade mark in subsequent fictions.

Success and *Other People* both disappointed certain reviewers, though for different reasons: the former, perhaps, because of its entrapment in some of Amis's obsessions; the latter, perhaps, because it attempted to break away from these obsessions and into new ground. In *Success,* Gregory Riding is another resident in the vicinity of what Phillip Larkin called "fulfillment's desolate attic." He is more repellingly self-infatuated than Charles Highway, but—even despite his incestuous affair with his sister—less purely evil than Quentin Villiers. As the wheel of fortune turns, he loses his superhuman abilities with women and goes poetical and mad. Terry, his foster-brother and erstwhile dupe, conversely ends up top dog. The novel is written as a dialogue alternating the narratives of the foster-brothers and subtly contrasting their points of view.

The amnesiac displacement of Mary Swan's sensibility that colors the narrative of *Other People,* might be thought of as providing some sort of continuity with Gregory's ending of *Success.* This displaced sensibility provides an opaque window through which we see the world of the novel and its events. These include Mary's escape from the hospital, her stay with a group of tramps and with the alcoholic family of one of them, until this relative domestic security is broken up by the violent Jock and Trev. Mary moves on to a hostel and then to a job as a waitress and a place in a squat where she manages a brief relationship with Alan en route to the world of ordinary domesticity, of the "other people," that both fascinates and eludes her. From the world of these "other people," Prince, the apparently friendly policeman comes with hints of her previous identity as a sexually predatory girl called Amy Hide (Jekyll and . . . ? Hide and seek?) who may or may not have been murdered by a mysterious Mr. Wrong.

By the end Mary seems to have rediscovered her old self but only, perhaps, in the sense that she has died into a cyclical after-life or else returned from the death of the novel into her previous life. The novel's epilogue, in the voice of its intrusive narrator, further draws together hints that Prince may in fact be Mr. Wrong and that either or both may be identical with the narrator, who seems aggrieved at something Mary has done to him and to be ultimately responsible for her death-in-life. Much of this is deliberately left unresolved and was condemned as incomprehensible by some readers. *Other People* is consequently Amis's most underrated novel. It demands but also rewards much careful re-reading and, while it is not as funny as his other books, its concerns are close to the lucid center of his art.

The attempt to explore the relationship of narrator to the character and to establish a new and compelling metaphor or narratorial complicity becomes a central thread of *Money,* and also of Amis's 1989 work, *London Fields.* In *Money,* the narrator is a grotesque high-and-low-life film producer called John Self who jets backwards and forwards across the Atlantic trying to put together a deal between British writers and American film stars and financial backers. Meanwhile his precarious life falls apart as sexual, financial, and literary plots become entangled in a series of schemes of which Self turns out not to be the perpetrator, as he supposed, but the victim. That the British scriptwriter in question is called Martin Amis suggests that the author has drawn on his own experience of writing for the cinema and introduces some of the dazzling play with multiple and reflected selfhood's that distinguishes the novel's characterization. Self's educated English-raised lover adds to the conundrum since she is called Martina Twain.

For some readers the delight of *Money* is its complex plotting; for others it is its clever play with literary sub-texts like *Othello* and Orwell's *Animal Farm* and *1984.* Not least is the huge figure of Self, himself, for whom Amis invents a whole new dialect of mid-Atlantic English in which a hairstyle is a "rug rethink;" a dentist is a "gum-coach;" Othello is a "flash spade general;" women wear "omniscient underwear;" and pornography is a genre of life and not just of fiction: "if you're a pornographic person, then pornographic things happen to you." The scintillating language of *Money* may be understood as a carnivalized or comic tribute to the Chicago, urban "high style" of Saul Bellow that Amis has praised in *The Moronic Inferno.* Arguably Self is the first fictional victim of bovine encephalitis: "I must have some new cow disease that makes you wonder whether you're real all the time, that makes your life feel like a trick, an act, a joke." Unquestionably he is the 1980s to a T. *Money* confirms Amis's territory as the life of the mind in those places which Freud described as being beyond the pleasure principle, and which Self describes as "this state, seeing the difference between good and bad and choosing bad—or consenting to bad, okaying bad."

Keith Talent (no character called Keith can survive in an Amis novel unscathed), the protagonist of *London Fields,* is still more at home in a west London pub than Self and has an equally well-developed taste for the bad. The opening statement "Keith Talent was a bad guy . . ." offers an apparently incontrovertible condemnation of his horrible taste for playing darts, more horrible appetite for video pornography, and completely dreadful habit of saying "Cheers!" and "innit" on all occasions. But Keith, repulsive though he is, is to be upstaged in the novel, both by its postmodern *femme fatale* Nicola Six and by the grander evil of the narrator Samson Young, whom she lures into being the instrument of her planned self-destruction. In some ways *London Fields* is a recasting of some of the ideas in *Other People* according to the lessons learnt in writing *Money.* It has an undercurrent—new since Amis's post-nuclear stories *Einstein's Monsters*—of global crisis and eco-consciousness. We are invited to "imagine the atomic cloud as an inverted phallus and Nicola's loins as ground zero." Language glitters again and identity is a hall of mirrors and, like his darting surrogate, Amis is a master of the devastating finish.

The Jewish-American background of the narrator of *London Fields* (described in the novel's racy idiolect as a "four-wheel Sherman") may have anticipated the theme of *Time's Arrow,* whose title had been a provisional title for the previous book. Also remi-

niscent of the two previous books is Amis's determination to take on the most enormous of the social issues of the 20th century: here it is the Nazi Holocaust and its aftermath. *Time's Arrow* is Amis's most ambitious technical achievement to date and is, indeed, one of the most extraordinary narrative experiments in existence, almost unprecedented outside of the science fiction of Philip K. Dick. The novel is written in reverse time, tracing a typical American suburban scene of the present back to the concentration camp Auschwitz, where its narrator, Odilo Unverdorben, has been an official. Reading *Time's Arrow* can be an extremely disturbing experience. Some readers have complained that the cleverness and showiness of the time experiment detracts from the seriousness of the subject, but this need not be so. Read in the tradition of an experimental and historically traumatised novel like Kurt Vonnegut's *Slaughterhouse Five,* or else backed-up by the critiques of rationalist intellectual constructions provided by postmodernist theoreticians like Adorno, the disturbances created by the novel's form and by its horrendous subject matter hang nightmarishly together.

If *Time's Arrow* might have led us to expect a development away from the brilliant satire of the early novels towards a more sober and mature seriousness in Amis's work, then *The Information* must represent something of a disappointment. It is a book that euphorically condemns middle-age but which is surely itself written out of a deeply repressed fear of ageing and its disillusionments. Fast writers who peak as young as Amis must greet forty years like a Porsche greeting a forty miles per hour city centre speed limit. For others (like Dante or like Joyce) forty would seem to be the start of something that could not have been achieved before. In *The Information* Amis turns his gaze towards a kind of forty-year-old alter ego called Richard Tull—a novelist who is quite pathetically unsuccessful and who ekes out a modicum of literary income and of self-respect from the occasional review. For the most part, it must be said, Amis's reviewers took this chastening portrait of their craft in fairly good part.

Whilst Tull vegetates in the ruins of his ego and ambition, his arch rival Gwyn Barry strides from success to success. Only further disappointments greet Tull, and what the novel calls "the information" is his growing sense of vacuity and despair. Amis is quite relentlessly brilliant here, once again, on the compromises to and erosions of literary ambition that are brought on by domesticity and by the loss of a sentimentally cherished but unattainable ideal. Tull is, in some ways, the most fully fleshed, and the most convincing of all of Amis's postmodern grotesques, and he would quite probably have been the most congenial if the author had once relaxed and allowed him to peep out from beneath the high steel-capped heels of his satire. Neither he, nor the author, seem to contemplate for a moment the redeeming possibility that literary success is neither the only nor the absolute in human values—perhaps much in postmodern culture would lead us to the same conclusion. Since, at the time when it was written, British politicians were discussing the "fell-good" factor, it was, perhaps, a kind of political gesture for Amis to publish such an unashamedly "feel-crap" novel. It stands at any rate as a reading of its times.

Nothing about *The Information* suggests the slightest slackening of Amis's powers. There's not the hint of an imaginative mid-life crisis, nor is there either the promise of any sustainably new direction. Amis's own persona as the celebrity writer continues to step wittily in and out of the frame of the fictions he creates. Whilst those fictions continue to occupy and to expand the vital mid-Atlantic cultural space and whilst he continues to voice an authentic and ground-breaking postmodernity through narrative, which is postmodernism's most distrusted and most interrogated mode of thought, we can be confident that the absolutely fabulous Martin Amis will continue to disturb and to delight us and that he will thrive.

—Richard Brown

ANAND, Mulk Raj

Nationality: Indian. **Born:** Peshawar, 12 December 1905. **Education:** Khalsa College, Amritsar; Punjab University, 1921-24, B.A. (honours) 1924; University College, University of London, 1926-29, Ph.D.; Cambridge University, 1929-30; League of Nations School of Intellectual Cooperation, Geneva, 1930-32. **Family:** Married 1) Kathleen Van Gelder in 1939 (divorced 1948); 2) Shirin Vajifdar in 1950, one daughter. **Career:** Lecturer, School of Intellectual Cooperation, Summer 1930, and Workers Educational Association, London, intermittently 1932-45; has also taught at the universities of Punjab, Benares, and Rajasthan, Jaipur, 1948-66; Tagore Professor of Literature and Fine Art, University of Punjab, 1963-66; Visiting Professor, Institute of Advanced Studies, Simla, 1967-68. Fine Art Chairman, Lalit Kala Akademi (National Academy of Art), New Delhi, 1965-70. Since 1946 editor, *Marg* magazine, Bombay: editor and contributor, *Marg Encyclopedia of Art,* 136 vols., 1948-81; since 1946 director, Kutub Publishers, Bombay. Since 1970 President of the Lokayata Trust, for creating a community and cultural centre in Hauz Khas village, New Delhi. **Awards:** Leverhulme fellowship, 1940-42; World Peace Council prize, 1952; Padma Bhushan, India, 1968; Akademi prize, for *Morning Face,* 1970; Sahitya Academy award, 1974; Birla award; distinguished writer award, State Goverment of Maharashtra, India. D.Litt: University of Delhi, University of Patiala, University of Andhra, University of Benaras, and University of Kanpur. Fellow, Indian Academy of Letters. **Address:** 25 Cuffe Parade, Bombay 400 005, India.

PUBLICATIONS

Novels

Untouchable. London, Wishart, 1935; New York, New York Liberty Press, n.d.; revised edition, London, Bodley Head, 1970.
The Coolie. London, Lawrence and Wishart, 1936; as *Coolie,* London, Penguin, 1945; New York, Liberty Press, 1952; revised edition, London, Bodley Head, 1972.
Two Leaves and a Bud. London, Lawrence and Wishart, 1937; New York, Liberty Press, 1954.
The Village. London, Cape, 1939.
Lament on the Death of a Master of Arts. Lucknow, Naya Sansar, 1939.
Across the Black Waters. London, Cape, 1940.
The Sword and the Sickle. London, Cape, 1942.
The Big Heart. London, Hutchinson, 1945; revised edition, edited by Saros Cowasjee, New Delhi, Arnold-Heinemann, 1980.
Private Life of an Indian Prince. London, Hutchinson, 1949; revised edition, London, Bodley Head, 1970.
Seven Summers: The Story of an Indian Childhood. London, Hutchinson, 1951.

The Old Woman and the Cow. Bombay, Kutub, 1960; as *Gauri,* New Delhi, Orient, 1976; Liverpool, Lucas, 1987.
The Road. Bombay, Kutub, 1961; London, Oriental University Press, 1987.
Death of a Hero. Bombay, Kutub, 1963.
Morning Face. Bombay, Kutub, 1968; Liverpool, Lucas, and East Brunswick, New Jersey, Books from India, 1986.
Confession of a Lover. New Delhi, Arnold-Heinemann, 1976; Liverpool, Lucas, 1988.
The Bubble. New Delhi, Arnold-Heinemann, 1987; Liverpool, Lucas, 1988.

Short Stories

The Lost Child and Other Stories. London, J.A. Allen, 1934.
The Barber's Trade Union and Other Stories. London, Cape, 1944.
The Tractor and the Corn Goddess and Other Stories. Bombay, Thacker, 1947.
Reflections on the Golden Bed. Bombay, Current Book House, 1947.
The Power of Darkness and Other Stories. Bombay, Jaico, 1958.
Lajwanti and Other Stories. Bombay, Jaico, 1966.
Between Tears and Laughter. New Delhi, Sterling, 1973.
Selected Short Stories of Mulk Raj Anand, edited by M.K. Naik. New Delhi, Arnold-Heinemann, 1977.

Play

India Speaks (produced London, 1943).

Other

Persian Painting. London, Faber, 1930.
Curries and Other Indian Dishes. London, Harmsworth, 1932.
The Golden Breath: Studies in Five Poets of the New India. London, Murray, and New York, Dutton, 1933.
The Hindu View of Art. Bombay, Asia Publishing House, and London, Allen and Unwin, 1933; revised edition, Asia Publishing House, 1957.
Letters on India. London, Routledge, 1942.
Apology for Heroism: An Essay in Search of Faith. London, Drummond, 1946.
Homage to Tagore. Lahore, Sangam, 1946.
Indian Fairy Tales: Retold (for children). Bombay, Kutub, 1946.
On Education. Bombay, Hind Kitabs, 1947.
The Bride's Book of Beauty, with Krishna Hutheesing. Bombay, Kutub, 1947; as *The Book of Indian Beauty,* Rutland, Vermont, Tuttle, 1981.
The Story of India (for children). Bombay, Kutub, 1948.
The King-Emperor's English; or, The Role of the English Language in the Free India. Bombay, Hind Kitabs, 1948.
Lines Written to an Indian Air: Essays. Bombay, Nalanda, 1949.
The Indian Theatre. London, Dobson, 1950; New York, Roy, 1951.
The Story of Man (for children). New Delhi, Sikh Publishing House, 1952.
The Dancing Foot. New Delhi, Ministry of Information, 1957.
Kama Kala: Some Notes on the Philosophical Basis of Hindu Erotic Sculpture. London, Skilton, 1958; New York, Lyle Stuart, 1962.
India in Colour. Bombay, Taraporevala, London, Thames and Hudson, and New York, McGraw Hill, 1959.
More Indian Fairy Tales (for children). Bombay, Kutub, 1961.

Is There a Contemporary Indian Civilisation? Bombay, Asia Publishing House, 1963.

The Story of Chacha Nehru (for children). New Delhi, Rajpal, 1965.

The Third Eye: A Lecture on the Appreciation of Art. Patiala, University of Punjab, 1966.

The Humanism of M.K. Gandhi: Three Lectures. Chandigarh, University of Panjab, 1967(?).

The Volcano: Some Comments on the Development of Rabindranath Tagore's Aesthetic Theories. Baroda, Maharaja Sayajirao University, 1968.

Roots and Flowers: Two Lectures on the Metamorphosis of Technique and Content in the Indian-English Novel. Dharwar, Karnatak University, 1972.

Mora. New Delhi, National Book Trust, 1972.

Author to Critic: The Letters of Mulk Raj Anand, edited by Saros Cowasjee. Calcutta, Writers Workshop, 1973.

Album of Indian Paintings. New Delhi, National Book Trust, 1973.

Folk Tales of Punjab. New Delhi, Sterling, 1974.

Seven Little-Known Birds of the Inner Eye. Rutland, Vermont, Tuttle, 1978.

The Humanism of Jawaharlal Nehru. Calcutta, Visva-Bharati, 1978.

The Humanism of Rabindranath Tagore. Aurangabad, Marathwada University, 1979.

Maya of Mohenjo-Daro (for children). New Delhi, Children's Book Trust, n.d.

Conversations in Bloomsbury (reminiscences). New Delhi, Arnold-Heinemann, and London, Wildwood House, 1981.

Madhubani Painting. New Delhi, Ministry of Information and Broadcasting, 1984; Oxford, Oxford University Press, 1995.

Pilpali Sahab: Story of a Childhood under the Raj (autobiography). New Delhi, Arnold-Heinemann, 1985.

Poet-Painter: Paintings by Rabindranath Tagore. New Delhi, Abhinav, 1985.

Homage to Jamnalal Bajaj: A Pictorial Biography. Ahmedabad, Allied, 1988.

Amrita Sher Gill: An Essay in Interpretation. New Delhi, National Gallery of Modern Art, 1989.

Kama Yoga. New Delhi, Arnold, and Edinburgh, Aspect, n.d.

Chitralakshana (on Indian painting). New Delhi, National Book Trust, n.d.

Editor, *Marx and Engels on India.* Allahabad, Socialist Book Club, 1933.

Editor, with Iqbal Singh, *Indian Short Stories.* London, New India, 1947.

Editor, *Introduction to Indian Art,* by A.K. Coomaraswamy. Madras, Theosophical Publishing House, and Wheaton, Illinois, Theosophical Press, 1956.

Editor, *Experiments: Contemporary Indian Short Stories.* Agra, Kranchalson, 1968.

Editor, *Annals of Childhood.* Agra, Kranchalson, 1968.

Editor, *Grassroots.* Agra, Kranchalson, 1968(?).

Editor, *Tales from Tolstoy.* New Delhi, Arnold-Heine- mann, 1978.

Editor, with Lance Dane, *Kama Sutra of Vatsyayana* (from translation by Sir Richard Burton and F.F. Arbuthnot). New Delhi, Arnold-Heinemann, and Atlantic Highlands, New Jersey, Humanities Press, 1982.

Editor, with S. Balu Rao, *Panorama: An Anthology of Modern Indian Short Stories.* New Delhi, Sterling, 1986; London, Oriental University Press, 1987.

Editor, *Chacha Nehru.* New Delhi, Sterling, 1987.

Editor, *Aesop's Fables.* New Delhi, Sterling, 1987.

Editor, *The Historic Trial of Mahatma Gandhi.* New Delhi, National Council of Educational Research and Training, 1987.

Editor, *The Other Side of the Medal,* by Edward Thompson. New Delhi, Sterling, 1989.

Editor, *Sati: A Writeup of Raja Ram Mohan Roy about Burning of Widows Alive.* New Delhi, B.R. Publishing, 1989.

*

Bibliography: *Mulk Raj Anand: A Checklist* by Gillian Packham, Mysore, Centre for Commonwealth Literature and Research, 1983.

Critical Studies: *Mulk Raj Anand: A Critical Essay* by Jack Lindsay, Bombay, Hind Kitabs, 1948, revised edition, as *The Elephant and the Lotus,* Bombay, Kutub, 1954; "Mulk Raj Anand Issue" of *Contemporary Indian Literature* (New Delhi), 1965; *An Ideal of Man in Anand's Novels* by D. Riemenschneider, Bombay, Kutub, 1969; *Mulk Raj Anand: The Man and the Novelist* by Margaret Berry, Amsterdam, Oriental Press, 1971; *Mulk Raj Anand* by K.N. Sinha, New York, Twayne, 1972; *Mulk Raj Anand* by M.K. Naik, New Delhi, and London, Arnold-Heinemann, and New York, Humanities Press, 1973; *Anand: A Study of His Fiction in Humanist Perspective* by G.S. Gupta, Bareilly, Prakash, 1974; *So Many Freedoms: A Study of the Major Fiction of Mulk Raj Anand* by Saros Cowasjee, New Delhi and London, Oxford University Press, 1978; *Perspectives on Mulk Raj Anand* edited by K.K. Sharma, Atlantic Highlands, New Jersey, Humanities Press, 1978; *The Yoke of Pity: A Study in the Fictional Writings of Mulk Raj Anand* by Alastair Niven, New Delhi, Arnold-Heinemann, 1978; *The Sword and the Sickle: A Study of Mulk Raj Anand's Novels* by K.V. Suryanarayana Murti, Mysore, Geetha, 1983; *The Novels of Mulk Raj Anand: A Thematic Study* by Premila Paul, New Delhi, Sterling, 1983; *The Wisdom of the Heart: A Study of the Works of Mulk Raj Anand* by Marlene Fisher, New Delhi, Sterling, 1985; *Studies in Mulk Raj Anand* by P.K. Rajan, New Delhi, Arnold, 1986; *Mulk Raj Anand: A Home Appraisal* edited by Atma Ram, Hoshairpur, Punjab, Chaarvak, 1988; *The Language of Mulk Raj Anand, Raja Rao, and R.K. Narayan* by Reza Ahmad Nasimi, New Delhi, Capital, 1989; *Mulk Raj Anand: A Short Story Writer* by Vidhya Mohan Shethi, New Delhi, Ashish, n.d.

Mulk Raj Anand comments:

I began to write early—a kind of free verse in the Punjabi and Urdu languages, from the compulsion of the shock of the death of my cousin when she was nine years old. I wrote a letter to God telling him He didn't exist. Later, going through the dark night of another bereavement, when my aunt committed suicide because she was excommunicated for interdining with a Muslim woman, I wrote an elegy. Again, when I fell in love with a young Muslim girl, who was married off by arrangement, I wrote calf love verse. The poet-philosopher, Muhammad Iqbal, introduced me to the problems of the individual through his long poem "Secrets of the Self." Through him, I also read Nietzsche to confirm my rejection of God. After a short term in jail, my father, who was pro-British, punished my mother for my affiliations with the Gandhi Movement. I went to Europe and studied various philosophical systems and found that these comprehensive philosophies did not answer life's problems. I was beaten up for not blacklegging against workers in 1926, in the coal-miner's strike. I joined a Marxist worker's study circle with

Trade Unionist Alan Hutt, and met Palme-Dutt, John Strachey, T.S. Eliot, Herbert Read, Bonamy Dobrée, Harold Laski, Leonard Woolf. During that time I fell in love with a young Welsh girl painter, Irene, whose father was a biologist. For her I wrote a long confession about the break-up of my family, the British impact, and my later life. Nobody would publish the narrative. So I began to re-write portions, as allegories, short stories, and novels. On a tour with Irene, in Paris, Rome, Vienna, Berlin, Brussels, I discovered Rimbaud, Gide, and Joyce. My first attempt at a novel was revised in Gandhi's Sabarmati Ashram in Ahmedabad, but was turned down by 19 publishers in London. The 20th offered to publish it if E.M. Forster wrote a Preface. This the author of *A Passage to India* did.

Since the publication of this first novel, I have written continuously on the human situation in the lives of people of rejects, outcasts, peasants, lumpen, and other eccentrics, thrown up during the transition from the ancient orthodox Indian society to the self-conscious modernist secular democracy.

I believe that creating literature is the true medium of humanism as against systematic philosophies, because the wisdom of the heart encourages insights in all kinds of human beings who grow to self-consciousness through conflicts of desire, will, and mood. I am inclined to think that the highest aim of poetry and art is to integrate the individual into inner growth and outer adjustment. The broken bundle of mirrors of the human personality in our time can only become the enchanted mirror if the sensibility is touched in its utmost pain and sheer pleasure and tenderest moments. No rounded answers are possible. Only hunches, insights, and inspirations and the *karuna* that may come from understanding.

The novelist's task is that of an all-comprehending "God," who understands every part of his creation, through pity, compassion, or sympathy—which is the only kind of catharsis possible in art. The world is itself action of the still center. The struggle to relate the word and the deed in the life of men is part of the process of culture, through which illumination comes to human beings. The world of art is communication from one individual to another, or to the group through the need to connect. This may ultimately yield the slogan "love one another," if mankind is to survive (against its own inheritance of fear, hatred, and contempt, now intensified through money-power, or privileges, and large-scale violence of wars) into the 21st century, in any human form.

*   *   *

Mulk Raj Anand is the champion of the underdog. All his novels deal with the underprivileged sections of Indian society. He was the first Indian novelist to make an untouchable the hero of a novel. *Untouchable* describes one day in the life of 18-year-old Bakha, who is treated as dirt by all Hindus just because his profession is to clean latrines. Artistically it is the most perfect of Anand's earlier novels. The distinction of Anand's writing lies in capturing Bakha's work ethic — Bakha tackles his odious job with a conscientiousness that invests his movements with beauty. The next novel, *Coolie,* has a wider canvas and is more diffuse in structure. Munoo, a young orphan, works at a variety of odd jobs at Daulatpur, Bombay, and Simla till he dies aged 15 of tuberculosis brought on by undernourishment. Munoo is exploited not because of caste but because he is poor. *Two Leaves and a Bud* is about the plight of the laborers in a tea plantation in Assam; the novel fails because Anand's approach is too simplistic; the English owners are shown as unmitigated villains. Anand's next work was a trilogy with the

young Lal Singh as hero. *The Village* is an authentic picture of a typical Punjabi village, and shows the adolescent Lal Singh rebelling against the narrow superstitions of the villagers—he goes so far as to cut his hair, unthinkable for a Sikh. *Across the Black Waters* shows Lal as a soldier fighting in the trenches of Flanders in World War I; his contact with the French makes him realize that the white races too are human, and not demigods like the British in India. *The Sword and the Sickle* shows Lal engaged in revolutionary activities in India after eloping with the village landlord's daughter; it is not as well written as the earlier two volumes.

Anand is a prolific writer, and has written a large number of extremely varied short stories. They reveal his gift for humor, and deal in a lighter vein with the problems that engage him in his novels—the exploitation of the poor, the impact of industrialization, colonialism, and race relations. One of Anand's best novels, *The Big Heart,* deals with the traditional coppersmiths who feel threatened by mechanization. The large-hearted Ananta tries to weld them into a trade union; he tells them that it is not the machines but the owners who exploit them, but he dies in a scuffle before his ideals can be realized.

The Old Woman and the Cow (republished as *Gauri*) takes up the plight of another underprivileged section of society — women. The heroine, Gauri, is sold to an old money-lender by her own mother out of economic necessity. Gauri re-enacts the *Ramayana* myth of Sita by staying for some time in the house of the old banker, just as Sita had to stay with Ravana. Gauri is reunited with her husband Panchi just as Sita was reunited with Rama, and Panchi rejects her later, just as Rama rejected the pregnant Sita because of social pressures. At this point, Anand gives a new turn to the old myth: unlike Sita who bore her sufferings meekly, Gauri rejects her cowardly husband and goes on to build a new life for herself. The story is well conceived and the use of the myth original, but the writing is hurried and slipshod, the harangues on social justice not organic to the plot. *Private Life of an Indian Prince,* a study of a neurotic maharajah, is confused and disorganized; some critics, however, have defended the narrative as a true reflection of the hero's psyche, and consider it Anand's best novel.

Anand is now at work on an ambitious seven-volume autobiographical novel, *The Seven Ages of Man. Seven Summers,* published more than four decades ago, is a lyrical account of early childhood, primarily from the child's point of view. *Morning Face* describes the life of the protagonist, Krishan Chander Azad, up to the age of 15, and we get a vivid picture of the brutality that once passed for school-teaching. *Confessions of a Lover* deals with Krishan's undergraduate days at Khalsa College, Amritsar. The novel is not only a moving human document, it is an authentic account of life in the Punjab in the 1920's, and records the ferment caused by Gandhi's *satyagraha*. The fourth volume, *The Bubble,* covers the period 1925-29; it shows Krishan as a student in England, obtaining a Ph.D. degree. He falls in love with Irene Rhys, and pours out his feelings by writing a long novel (just as Anand did in real life). Most of Anand's works have a linear structure, but *The Bubble* departs from this convention. It is in the form of letters, diary entries, and excerpts from the novel Krishan is writing; it also includes numerous philosophical discussions. The life of an Indian student in England of the time, and particularly Krishan's loneliness, are impressively portrayed. But, like *Morning Face* and *Confessions of a Lover, The Bubble* is too long (600 pages). If only the "outpourings" had been sensitively edited, *The Bubble* would have been Anand's best work, and a triumph in terms of technique.

The forthcoming *And So He Plays His Part* is the fifth volume of *The Seven Ages of Man.* Anand observes in his "Afterwords" (*sic*), "As the forthcoming novel entitled *And So He Plays His Part* is seven novels in one, I have decided to issue it in parts, beginning with *Little Plays of Mahatma Gandhi,* as work in progress, symbolic of my departure from the accepted form." This "novel" is in the form of 15 scenes of a drama, framed by a long letter to Irene and a postscript to this letter, and shows the hero Krishan Chaner Azad living in Gandhi's ashram at Sabarmati, working on a novel with an untouchable as hero. All the characters, including historical figures like Gandhi and Subhas Chandra Bose, speak the same bad English, and the exclamation mark seems to be the only punctuation in their speeches. The innumerable mistakes of spelling and grammar (perhaps the printer is to blame) make it difficult for the reader to appreciate Anand's new perspective on Mahatma Gandhi.

Anand attempts to capture the ambiance of Punjabi life by literally translating words and phrases, but this device does not always succeed. Readers outside the Punjab may find it difficult to make anything of phrases like "there is no talk," and "May I be your sacrifice." However, Anand is successful in presenting a vivid picture of the Punjabi peasant and the problems of the poor. The range of his novels is impressive, covering not only the Punjab but life in towns like Bombay and Simla, the trenches of Flanders, and the tea gardens of Assam. His concern for the underdog does not take the form of communism — he is above all a humanist, and his humanism embraces all aspects of life, from contemporary slums to ancient Indian art and philosophy.

—Shyamala A. Narayan

ANAYA, Rudolfo A(lfonso)

Nationality: American. **Born:** Pastura, New Mexico, 30 October 1937. **Education:** Albuquerque High School, graduated 1956; Browning Business School, Albuquerque, 1956-58; University of New Mexico, Albuquerque, B.A. in literature 1963, M.A. in literature 1968, M.A. in guidance and counseling 1972. **Family:** Married Patricia Lawless in 1966. **Career:** Teacher, Albuquerque public schools, 1963-70. Director of Counseling, 1971-73, associate professor 1974-88, professor of English, 1988-93, and since 1993, professor emeritus, University of New Mexico. Lecturer, Universidad Anahuac, Mexico City, Summer 1974; teacher, New Mexico Writers Workshop, Albuquerque, summers 1977-79. Associate editor, *American Book Review,* New York, 1980-85. Since 1989 founding editor, *Blue Mesa Review,* Albuquerque. Vice-president, Coordinating Council of Literary Magazines, 1974-80. **Awards:** Quinto Sol prize, 1971; University of New Mexico Mesa Chicana award, 1977; City of Los Angeles award, 1977; New Mexico Governor's award, 1978, 1980; National Chicano Council on Higher Education fellowship, 1978; National Endowment for the Arts fellowship, 1979; Before Columbus Foundation award, 1980; Corporation for Public Broadcasting Script Development award, 1982; Kellogg Foundation fellowship, 1983; Mexican Medal of Friendship, 1986. D.H.L.: University of Albuquerque, 1981; Marycrest College, Davenport, Iowa, 1984. **Address:** 5324 Canada Vista N.W., Albuquerque, New Mexico 87120, U.S.A.

PUBLICATIONS

Novels

Bless Me, Ultima. Berkeley, California, Quinto Sol, 1972.
Heart of Aztlán. Berkeley, California, Justa, 1976.
Tortuga. Berkeley, California, Justa, 1979.
The Legend of La Llorona. Berkeley, California, Tonatiuh-Quinto Sol, 1984.
Lord of the Dawn: The Legend of Quetzalcoatl. Albuquerque, University of New Mexico Press, 1987.
Alburquerque. Albuquerque, University of New Mexico Press, 1992.
Zia Summer. New York, Warner, 1995.
Jalamanta: A Message from the Desert. New York, Warner, 1996.

Short Stories

The Silence of Llano. Berkeley, California, Tonatiuh-Quinto Sol, 1982.

Uncollected Short Stories

"The Captain," in *A Decade of Hispanic Literature.* Houston, Revista Chincano-Riqueña, 1982.
"The Road to Platero," in *Rocky Mountain* (St. James, Colorado), April 1982.
"The Village Which the Gods Painted Yellow," in *Nuestro,* January-February 1983.
"B. Traven Is Alive and Well in Cuernavaca," in *Cuentos Chicanos,* revised edition. Albuquerque, University of New Mexico Press, 1984.
"In Search of Epifano," in *Voces.* Albuquerque, El Norte-Academia, 1987.

Plays

The Season of La Llorona (produced Albuquerque, 1979).
Who Killed Don Jose? (produced Albuquerque, 1987).
The Farolitos of Christmas (produced Albuquerque, 1987). New York, Hyperion, 1995.

Screenplay (documentary): *Bilingualism: Promise for Tomorrow,* 1976.

Poetry

The Adventures of Juan Chicaspatas. Houston, Arte Publico Press, 1985.

Other

A Chicano in China. Albuquerque, University of New Mexico Press, 1986.
Flow of the River. Albuquerque, Hispanic Culture Foundation, 1988.
The Anaya Reader. New York, Warner, 1995.

Editor, with Jim Fisher, *Voices from the Rio Grande.* Albuquerque, Rio Grande Writers Association, 1976.
Editor, with Antonio Márquez, *Cuentos Chicanos.* Albuquerque, New America, 1980; revised edition, Albuquerque, University of New Mexico Press, 1984.

Editor, with Simon J. Ortiz, *A Ceremony of Brotherhood 1680-
1980*. Albuquerque, Academia, 1981.
Editor, *Voces: An Anthology of Nuevo Mexicano Writers.* Albuquer-
que, El Norte-Academia, 1987.
Editor, with Francisco A. Lomeli, *Atzlan: Essays on the Chicano
Homeland.* Albuquerque, El Norte-Academia, 1989.
Editor, *Tierra: Contemporary Short Fiction of New Mexico.* El
Paso, Texas, Cinco Puntos Press, 1989.

Translator, *Cuentos: Tales from the Hispanic Southwest, Based on
Stories Originally Collected by Juan B. Rael,* edited by José
Griego y Maestas. Santa Fe, Museum of New Mexico Press,
1980.

*

Manuscript Collection: Zimmerman Library, University of New
Mexico, Albuquerque.

Critical Studies: "Extensive/Intensive Dimensionality in Anaya's
Bless Me, Ultima" by Daniel Testa, in *Latin American Literary
Review* (Pittsburgh), Spring-Summer 1977; "Degradacion y
Regeneracion en *Bless Me, Ultima*" by Roberto Cantu, in *The Identification and Analysis of Chicano Literature* edited by Francisco
Jimenez, New York, Bilingual Press, 1979; *Chicano Authors: Inquiry by Interview* edited by Juan Bruce-Novoa, Austin, University of Texas Press, 1980; *The Magic of Words: Rudolfo A. Anaya
and His Writings* edited by Paul Vassallo, Albuquerque, University of New Mexico Press, 1982; article by Anaya, in *Contemporary Authors Autobiography Series 4* edited by Adele Sarkissian,
Detroit, Gale, 1986; *Rudolfo A. Anaya: Focus on Criticism* edited
by César A. González-T., La Jolla, California, Lalo Press, 1990
(includes bibliography by Teresa Márquez).

Rudolfo A. Anaya comments:

I was born and raised in the eastern llano, plains country, of
New Mexico. I spent my first 14 years in Santa Rosa, New Mexico,
a town bisected by the Pecos River and Highway 66. My ancestors were the men and women of the Rio Grande Valley of the
Albuquerque area who went east to settle the llano.

The llano was important for grazing sheep, and yet there were
along the Pecos river little farming communities. My mother's family comes from such a small Hispanic village, Puerto de Luna. The
most important elements of my childhood are the people of those
villages and the wide open plains, and the landscape.

In my first novel, *Bless Me, Ultima,* I used the people and the
environment of my childhood as elements of the story. Like my
protagonist, Antonio, my first language was Spanish. I was shaped
by the traditions and culture of the free-wheeling cow punchers
and sheep herders of the llano, a lifestyle my father knew well, and
was also initiated into the deeply religious, Catholic settled life of
the farmers of Puerto de Luna, my mother's side of the family.

The oral tradition played an important role in my life. I learned
about story from the cuentistas, the oral storytellers. It is a tradition one often loses when one moves into print, but its elements
are strong and as valuable today as they have been historically. I
want my literature to be accessible to my community, and I want it
to reflect the strands of history which define us.

Because the Mexican American community has existed within
the larger Anglo American society since the 19th century, and legally since 1848, our place in the history of this country is unique.

We have a long history in the southwest, in the western United
States. That history is generally not well known. Cultural identity
is important to us as a way to keep the values and traditions of our
forefathers intact.

In the 1960s the Mexican Americans created a social, political,
and artistic movement known as the Chicano Movement. As a
writer, I was an active participant in that movement. My second
novel, *Heart of Aztlán,* deals with themes in the Chicano Movement. The novel explores a return to Mexican mythology. Chicano
artists and writers like me returned to Mexican legends, mythology, and symbolism to create part of our Chicano expression.

When I was 16 I hurt my back and stayed a summer in a hospital. In *Tortuga,* I explored some of the consequences of that stay.
The hero of the story is a young man who must find some redemption in suffering. The mythopoeic forces which had influenced
my first two novels also are at work in the healing process which
the protagonist must undergo.

Western writers reflect their landscape. We cannot escape the bond
we have to our environment, the elements, especially water. As a
Chicano writer I am part of a community which for the first time in
our contemporary era has produced enough literary works to create a literary movement. Prior to the 1960s western literature was
written about us, but seldom by us. Now the world has a truer
insight into our world; the view is now from within as more and
more Chicano and Chicana writers explore their reality.

(1995) Recently my work has taken a turn, and I have written
my first murder mystery, *Zia Summer.* Although the form has certain requirements, often called the formula of a murder mystery, I
have found the genre an interesting way to communicate my ideas.
As an insider into Nuevo Mexicano (New Mexico) culture, I explore the cultural history of the region. I want my work to reflect
the values of those ancestors who have lived in the Rio Grande
Valley for so many centuries.

I am very interested in the spiritual values that are my inheritance, both from the Spanish/Mexican heritage and from the Native
American side. As a mestizo, a person born from these two broad
streams (or more correctly, from *many* inheritances), I want to create a synthesis, a worldview. I use the murder mystery genre as a
tale of contemporary adventure, but the story within is laden with
the cultural depth and richness that is our way of life. Ancestral
values are the substratum of my work, as they have always been. I
hope this new type of "adventure" fiction creates a mirror for our
contemporary journey, a point of discussion of our world view.

This turn in my writing has been most enjoyable. The page-
turning quality of the murder mystery allows me to have fun.
Yes, fun. A writer should enjoy his work in spite of the cost.
Each one of us suffers his own pain. But the new form also has
a serious intent. It still allows me the deeper exploration that is
part of my search for meaning.

An example of this continuing journey of knowledge is a novella called *Jalamant, the Prophet,* which I wrote in 1994. The continuing clarity of the worldview I was exploring in the murder mystery series became strong enough to require a coalescing in this
philosophical work.

So nothing is lost to the writer. There is a pattern, and the communication to the reader continues in new forms.

*   *   *

Rudolfo A. Anaya is best known for a trilogy of novels published during the 1970s. Although *Bless Me, Ultima; Heart of*

Aztlán; and *Tortuga* offer separate worlds with different characters, there are suggestions and allusions in the second and third novels which loosely connect the three works.

Bless Me, Ultima, a first-person narrative, details the childhood and coming of age of young Antonio Marez, a boy who grows up in the rural environs of Las Pasturas and Guadalupe, New Mexico in the late 1940s and early 1950s. Behind almost every experience and adventure Antonio undergoes there is Ultima, a "cuarandera" who comes to live with the Marez family at the start of the novel. She is a miracle-worker who heals the sick through her extensive knowledge of the herbs and remedies of the ancient New Mexico settlers. Guided by her unseen but pervasively felt presence, Antonio moves through a series of incidents which show him the greed, evil, and villainy of men. The novel is significant mainly because it introduces characters and a type of writing not seen before in Chicano literature.

Heart of Aztlán, despite winning the Before Columbus Foundation American Book award, fared less well than its predecessor. The main character is Clemente Chavez, a farmer who loses his land at the start of the narrative and is forced to move into a barrio in Albuquerque. In the city, the Chavez family see their teenage children lose themselves in drugs, sex, and violence. Prompted by a desire to preserve his family, Clemente undertakes a soul-searching quest for an identity and a role for himself and the Chicanos in the barrio. The writing here is noticeably more labored than in *Ultima.* The book ends with a Chicano march against the oppressive Santa Fe Railroad, an attempt to provide a fictive analogue to the Chicano consciousness-raising efforts of the 1970s.

In *Tortuga,* Anaya engagingly captures life in a sanitarium for terminally-ill teenagers. There is much ado in this labyrinthine ward in the desert, and the novel shows that Anaya is particularly adept at plausibly instilling life, vigor, and reasons to live into characters abandoned by society.

Anaya has also published work in other genres. For some time he has been interested in using the media to advance the interests of Spanish-speaking American citizens, and in 1976 he wrote a screenplay, *Bilingualism: Promise for Tomorrow,* which was produced as a documentary and aired on primetime television. He is a tireless promoter of Chicano and other ethnic literatures and has edited a number of anthologies.

The Adventures of Juan Chicaspatas is something of a departure: a 48-page mock-heroic epic poem which employs the same type of search motif used in *Heart of Aztlán.* Anaya's tone and attitude here are quite different from those in his earlier work. In *Heart of Aztlán,* he was seriously engaged in creating a language appropriate to rendering one character's quest for self-definition, but *Juan Chicaspatas* (literally, John Smallfeet) is written in the language of the "vatos locos," or crazy barrio Chicanos who jest at virtually everything. In passing, Anaya points out that there are "many-tribes of Chicanos," which, of course, suggests that there are different languages as well. The prime message of the 16th-century Aztlán goddess he depicts is: "Go and tell your people about Aztláan. Tell them I live. Tell them the españoles will come and a new people will be born. Tell them not to become like the tribes of the Anglos, and remind them not to honor King Arthur. Tell them their Eden and their Camelot are in Aztlán. Their covenant is with the earth of this world." Anaya's message has not changed, but now the appeal is made not to the more middle-class Chicanos as in the earlier work, but in a language that is closer to the work of Alurista and Sergio Elizondo, two other writers who take great relish in Chicano slang.

Anaya has written several books that are widely appreciated and is still young enough to write quite a few more wonderful tales.

—Marco Portales

ANDERSON, Barbara

Nationality: New Zealander. **Born:** Barbara Lillian Romaine, 14 April 1926. **Education:** Woodford House secondary school, 1939-43; University of Otago, Dunedin, 1944-46, B.A. 1946; Victoria University, Wellington, 1979-83, B.A. 1983. **Family:** Married Neil Anderson in 1951; two sons. **Career:** Science teacher, Samuel Marsden Collegiate School, Wellington, 1947, Hastings Girls' High School, 1961, and Queen Margaret's College, Wellington, 1964-67; medical laboratory technologist, public hospitals in Napier, 1948-51, and Wellington, 1972-78. **Awards:** Queen Elizabeth II Arts Council grant, 1988, 1991; Victoria University fellowship, 1991; Goodman Fielder Wattie award, for *Portrait of the Artist's Wife,* 1992. **Agent:** Caroline Dawnay, Peters Fraser and Dunlop, 503-504 The Chambers, Chelsea Harbour, Lots Road, London SW10 0XF. **Address:** 36 Beauchamp Street, Karori, Wellington, New Zealand.

PUBLICATIONS

Novel

Girls High. Wellington, Victoria University Press, 1990; London, Secker and Warburg, 1991.
Portrait of the Artist's Wife. Wellington, Victoria University Press, and London, Secker and Warburg, 1992; New York, Norton and Norton, 1993.
All the Nice Girls. Wellington, Victoria University Press, 1993; London, Cape, 1994.

Short Stories

I Think We Should Go into the Jungle. Wellington, Victoria University Press, 1989; London, Secker and Warburg, 1993.

Uncollected Short Stories

"The Peacocks," in *Landfall* (Christchurch), 1985.
"I Thought There'd Be a Couch," in *Vital Writing: New Zealand Stories and Poems, 1989-90.* N.p., Godwit Press, 1990.
"We Could Celebrate," in *Speaking with the Sun.* Sydney, Allen and Unwin, 1991.

Play

Gorillas (produced Wellington, 1990).

Radio Plays: *Eric,* 1983; *Impossible to Tell,* 1984; *Hotbed,* 1984; *Close Shave,* 1988; *The Couch,* 1988; *Backwards Glance,* 1990.

*   *   *

Barbara Anderson's book of short stories, *I Think We Should Go into the Jungle,* is an eclectic collection, demonstrating a variety of thematic interests that defy easy categorization. Her technique, however, is more easily definable. She often constructs her stories out of the tension of unlikely conjunctions and juxtapositions. The gaps found in the strange marriage of extraordinarily disparate ideas provide the reader with the space for creative intervention, which is a pre-requisite for the story's completion. In Anderson's view, the story is not entirely an authorial product. It is produced through the combined efforts of reader and writer.

Anderson's first story in *I Think We Should Go into the Jungle* signals the theoretical assumptions underlying her craft, especially her deconstruction of the writer's authority. Entitled "Discontinuous Lives," it opens with the chance meeting of a reader and writer at a funeral. Anderson seems to suggest that reader and writer may be in collusion against death. The making of imaginative worlds is a resistance against death, and it is an enterprise in which the writer invites the reader's participation. The reader in Anderson's story avoids the invitation as she tries to privilege closure over unresolved endings. The writer insists that her gaps provide imaginative space for the reader. This impasse is relieved by the sudden discovery that the reader and pseudonymous writer had shared a childhood, which each recollects as having been filled with the collaborative spinning of exotic tales. The story invites the conclusion that a similar complicity in narration is expected between reader and writer. Anderson thus undermines the notion that the author has exclusive ownership of the text. Apart from alluding to the superficial disruption in their lives, which has produced misrecognition between this reader and this writer, the title also refers to the surrender of the fertile imagination of childhood for the passive role of the uncreative reader. As the story amply demonstrates, the discontinuities in Anderson's stories demand the reader's intervention to turn what may be a cryptic utterance into a meaningful statement.

One consequence of the encroachment of Anderson's text upon the reader's space is that the author is able to avoid imposing a rigorous ideological agenda upon her work. Anderson modulates her sensitivity to the liabilities inherent in women's roles with an equal sense of the timeless continuum in which our lives are played out. This is not to suggest that she diminishes the force of the present or the personal, but rather that she balances it with the sense of spatial and temporal vastness that acts as a corrective to a narrow vision. In "Egypt is a Timeless Land," Anderson juxtaposes the successive stations of a woman's life, finally eventuating in nervous collapse, with Egypt, the place of successive civilizations with their widely differing world views. Anderson's version of Egypt functions as a symbol which displaces the personal and immediate for the timelessness identified in the simultaneity of historical time. The panoramic sweep, which takes in the Egypt of the Pharoahs, Mosaic, Christian and Islamic Egypt, suggests that inevitably our interpretations of neuroses derive from the prevalent ideology. Feminism may be the most recent of such ideologies. Anderson's story concludes with the powerfully suggestive image of a fisherman drawing in his nets. With Christ's words, "I will make you fishers of men," repeated by Anderson and resonating in our heads, we realize we are all caught in the nets of some powerful myth which rationalizes experience.

Anderson's ambivalences about our historically conditioned interpretations do not prevent her from inhabiting occasionally through her stories certain of our current myths. "The Girls" carries dis-

tinctly Freudian overtones as the daughters turn away, one by one, from their mother to their father, whose skill with the knife in which he tutors them is the source of his attraction. The knife is an obviously phallic symbol, and for a while the girls are like young men under their father's tutelage. Anderson, unlike Freud, does not condemn the girls to futile envy. In "Feeding the Sparrows," Anderson conceives a Christ figure, whose compassion for birds is taken to the point of absurdity. The story suggests that Christ's sacrifice may have been a similarly ridiculous act. In "Shanties," Anderson views contemporary heterosexuality as a kind of jungle where all decencies dissolve.

The last two stories of Anderson's first book anticipate the characters and locale of her second work, *Girls High.* The episodic variety of "School Story" anticipates the plural points of view of *Girls High.* Like the minimalist plotting of *Girls High,* "School Story" is held together by the rivalry of Miss Franklin and Miss Tamp. In the last story "Fast Post," Anderson inaugurates what will be a recurring theme in *Girls High,* namely, the proximity of sex and mortality.

In *Girls High,* Anderson has devised a work that falls between a collection of short stories and a novel. There is a fixed cast of characters, a unifying locale, the school, although not all the happenings occur in the school, and temporal progression from the first staff meeting of the year to the final event of the school year, Leavers' Play. Having paid her respects to certain nominal unities, Anderson trusts her work to the diverse consciousnesses inhabiting her book. The titles of all the stories, except the first and last, indicate that what we are witnessing is filtered through individual characters. For instance one title reads, "Miss Franklin remembers the smell of pepper" and another, "Mr. Marden thinks about Carmen" too. The syntax of the titles scarcely varies, consisting of subject, abstract verb, object. The emphasis on introspection allows Anderson to avoid spatial and temporal confinement as the memories and thoughts of her characters often travel well out of range of the school and the present. Anderson seems to be suggesting that the banality of the quotidian, which is often within immediate view, is a deceptive front that hides significant depths.

A penetrating dive into Anderson's universe reveals that sex invariably carries the taint of death, signaling its fallen status. Lovemaking and death are in closest proximity in the relationship of Sooze and Bryce. Sooze cannot forget that Bryce fondles her body with the same hands that had touched dead bodies in the morgue. For Mrs. Toon's daughter, sex seems to carry the penalty of brain damage, which condemns her to a living death. Carmen had experienced the destructive negation of her will through attempted rape. The book's climactic final story reiterates the theme that happy sex belongs to a lost Eden, when one of the girls suffers a miscarriage.

The stories in *Girls High* proceed as much through their gaps as through their revelations, like those in *I Think We Should Go into the Jungle.* One aspect of the discontinuities in *Girls High* is that character is not a fixed constant, but the discrepant outcome of the interplay of different points of view. Anderson's choice of play for the school leavers, *Mother Courage,* perhaps serves as a covert retrospective comment on how her characters are situated vis-à-vis the reader. The many angles trained on any particular character discourage identification and ensure, if not alienation, at least a dispassionate distance.

The minimalist but clumsy plot of *Girls High* confirms Anderson's discomfort with and incapacity for a too ready rationalization of life.

Such hesitancy to rely on hegemonic visions seems more compatible with the short story than the sustained narrative, which raises interesting questions about the future direction of Anderson's narrations.

—Doreen D'Cruz

ANDERSON, Jessica (Margaret)

Nationality: Australian. **Born:** Jessica Margaret Queale, Gayndah, Queensland, 25 September 1916. **Education:** State schools in Brisbane; Brisbane Technical College art school. **Family:** Married and divorced twice; one daughter from first marriage. Lives in Sydney. **Awards:** Miles Franklin award, 1979, 1981; New South Wales Premier's award, 1981; *The Age* Book of the Year award, 1987. **Agent:** Elaine Markson Literary Agency, 44 Greenwich Avenue, New York, New York 10011, U.S.A.

PUBLICATIONS

Novels

An Ordinary Lunacy. London, Macmillan, 1963; New York, Scribner, 1964.
The Last Man's Head. London, Macmillan, 1970.
The Commandant. London, Macmillan, and New York, St. Martin's Press, 1975.
Tirra Lirra by the River. Melbourne, Macmillan, 1978; London and New York, Penguin, 1984.
The Impersonators. Melbourne, Macmillan, 1980; as *The Only Daughter,* New York and London, Viking, 1985.
Taking Shelter. Ringwood, Victoria, New York, and London, Viking, 1990.

Short Stories

Stories from the Warm Zone and Sydney Stories. New York, Viking, 1987; London, Viking, 1988.

Plays

Radio Plays: *The American,* 1966, *The Aspern Papers,* 1967, and *Daisy Miller,* 1968, all from works by Henry James; *The Maid's Part,* 1967; *The Blackmail Caper,* 1972; *Quite Sweet, Really,* 1972; *Tirra Lirra by the River,* 1975; *The Last Man's Head,* from her own novel, 1983; *A Tale of Two Cities* (serial), from the novel by Dickens; *Outbreak of Love* (serial), from the novel by Martin Boyd.

*

Manuscript Collections: Mitchell Library, Sydney; Australian National Library, Canberra.

Critical Studies: "Tirra Lirra by the Brisbane River," in *Literature in Northern Queensland,* vol. 10, no. 1, 1981, and "A Rare Passion for Justice: Jessica Anderson's *The Last Man's Head,*" in *Quadrant* (Sydney), July 1988, both by Donat Gallagher; "The Expatriate Vision of Jessica Anderson," in *Meridian* (Melbourne), vol. 3, no. 1, 1984, and *Fabricating the Self: The Fictions of Jessica Anderson,* St. Lucia, University of Queensland Press, 1992, both by Elaine Barry; interview with Jennifer Ellison, in *Rooms of Their Own,* Ringwood, Victoria, Penguin, 1986, and with Candida Baker, in *Yacker 2,* Woollahra, New South Wales, Pan, 1987; "Jessica Anderson: Arrivals and Places" by Alrene Sykes, in *Southerly* (Sydney), March 1986; article by Gay Raines, in *Australian Studies* (Stirling, Scotland), no. 3, 1989.

Jessica Anderson comments:

The settings of my seven works of fiction relate neatly to the three places where I have spent my life: mostly Sydney, a substantial portion of Brisbane, and a dash of London.

Now that I intend to write no more fiction, I can appreciate the pleasure I had in writing those seven books, and discount the pain, by realising how disappointed I would be if I had failed to produce them. That is not to say that I am wholly satisfied, but that I worked to my full capacity, and am pleased to have had this chance of deploying my imagination, observation, and experience.

* * *

In one of the more quietly startling moments of Jessica Anderson's *Tirra Lirra by the River,* Nora, the elderly narrator/protagonist, tells us almost off-handedly that in middle age she tried to commit suicide. One reason for the attempt was the failure of a face-lift operation, and she links this with the horrifying revelations coming out of post-war Germany: " . . . if I leap to explain that the weakness resulting from six bronchial winters, and the approach of menopause, left me morbidly defenceless against the post-war revelations of the German camps, it is because I am ashamed to admit that in the same breath as that vast horror, I can speak of the loss of my looks." Jessica Anderson's novels do not tackle broad social, political or historical issues head-on, but always the large event, the major issue, is in the background, while her characters move in a world where small personal experiences, experiences which are as nothing on a world scale, profoundly influence them.

Tirra Lirra by the River is one of three novels by Anderson which begins with a woman arriving in Australia from "overseas." In *The Commandant* the woman is 17-year-old Frances, arriving from Ireland in the 1830s to live with her sister and brother-in-law, Captain Patrick Logan, the commandant of the title, who is remembered in Australian history as a fanatical and brutal disciplinarian, loathed by the convicts under his charge in the penal settlement at Moreton Bay. Frances has initially the traditional role of innocent observer, until events make her unwillingly responsible for a young convict receiving 50 lashes—thus drawing her into "the system." In *Tirra Lirra by the River* and *The Impersonators,* however, the role of one-who-arrives is more complex, as both elderly Nora (*Tirra Lirra*) and middle-aged Sylvia (*The Impersonators*) are Australians returning home after many years of absence in Europe, bearing the accretions and conflicts of two cultures. The arrivals in these three books provide a promising opening, with their inherent possibilities of movement and change, but they also provide a direct entry into several of Anderson's major themes. (Her two earlier novels, *An Ordinary Lunacy* and *The Last Man's Head,* open with smaller but portentous visits.) Anderson is fascinated by the tug between the old culture (Europe) and the new (Australia).

In her novels, arrival is always part of a longer journey, an inner journey as well as a physical one, and thus relates to the getting of wisdom and our conflicting desires for flight and sanctuary. To arrive at an unfamiliar place normally sharpens our awareness of environment, and descriptions of place—particularly of houses, and the harbour and gardens of Sydney, shown as being deeply part of the consciousness of the women characters in particular—are among the strengths of Anderson's more recent novels.

Tirra Lirra by the River, the most highly regarded of Anderson's novels, has in fact been written in three forms: as a short story, as a radio play, and finally as a prize-winning novel. By no means overtly feminist, it has been praised by feminist critics as showing the difficulties of women's lives from the point of view of a woman born early in the century. As the title suggests, the novel has links with Tennyson's poem, "The Lady of Shallott." In the poem, the Lady, generally accepted as artist or perhaps anima, lives secluded in a tower on an island, weaving her magic web and watching the world indirectly through a mirror. When she hears Lancelot pass by, singing, she looks down for the first time on the "real" world; the mirror cracks, the web flies out the window, and the lady, dying, floats in her boat down to Camelot. Nora relates to the Lady in a quite complex way, which has at its base the idea of her as artist seeing the world indirectly, through the mirror of a culture (European) not her own. The process begins when she is a child, and a flaw in the glass of a window transforms as she looks through it ordinary sticks, stones, bits of grass, into the magic landscape, with rivulets, castles, lakes, of her story books; enchanted, she fails even to see the "real river" near her home. After a failed marriage, she goes to London, working there for many years making theatre costumes; finally, she returns to Australia, and, like the Lady of the poem, faces the "real:" for her, suppressed memories, mistaken beliefs, a real river instead of the river running down to Camelot, and the discovery that embroidered hangings she made before she left Australia are the most promising things she ever did. Like the Lady, she becomes very sick, but unlike the Lady, recovers, and the novel ends with her globe of memory (one of the recurrent images of the book) in full spin, with no dark sides hidden. The book is not as simplistic as this thematic sketch probably suggests; Anderson habitually tests and qualifies her themes, and in *Tirra Lirra* Nora's spiritual/physical journey is counterbalanced by the lives of other women, who are partly defined, though not judged, by the journeys they make—or do not make.

In *The Impersonators,* a more diffuse and less successful book than *Tirra Lirra,* the debate sparked by the return of Sylvia after nearly 20 years is one that was current until the 1970s but has less cogency for Australians today: essentially it is a debate between what is seen as the cultural richness of Europe and the raw discontinuity of Australia, and whether there is a moral imperative for Australians who have been abroad to centres where culture is more securely consolidated to "come home and use what they've learned." In the end Sylvia, like Nora accepting what for her is "real," recognises that she has been yearning over "other people's rituals," and decides to stay in Sydney with her lover. An equally important theme is signalled by the title of the book: in materialistic, fractured Sydney of 1977, most of the characters are in some sense impersonators, living part of their lives behind protective masks. Jessica Anderson's portrait is sharp-eyed, unsentimental, but compassionate rather than satiric.

—Alrene Sykes

ANIEBO, I(feanyichukwu) N(dubuisi) C(hikezie)

Nationality: Nigerian. **Born:** Nigeria in 1939. **Education:** Government College, Umuahia; University of California, Los Angeles, B.A., C.Phil., M.A. **Military Service:** Joined the Nigerian Army in 1959: attended cadet schools in Ghana and England; officer in the United Nations peace-keeping force in the Congo; at Command and General Staff College, Fort Leavenworth, Kansas; fought on the Biafran side in the Nigerian civil war; discharged from army, 1971. **Career:** Currently, Senior Lecturer in English, University of Port Harcourt. **Address:** Department of English, University of Port Harcourt, P.M.B. 5523, Port Harcourt, Rivers State, Nigeria.

PUBLICATIONS

Novels

The Anonymity of Sacrifice. London, Heinemann, 1974.
The Journey Within. London, Heinemann, 1978.

Short Stories

Of Wives, Talismans and the Dead. London, Heinemann, 1983.

Uncollected Short Stories

"The Jealous Goddess," in *Spear* (Lagos), October 1963.
"My Mother," in *Sunday Times* (Lagos), 22 December 1963.
"The Ring," in *Nigeria Magazine* (Lagos), December 1964.
"The Peacemakers," in *Nigeria Magazine* (Lagos), December 1965.
"Shadows," in *Black Orpheus 20* (Lagos), 1966.
"Mirage," in *Nigeria Magazine* (Lagos), March 1966.
"The Outing," in *Happy Home and Family Life* (Lagos), May 1972.
"Happy Survival, Brother," in *Ufahamu* (Los Angeles), vol. 7, no. 3, 1977.

*   *   *

Since 1963 I.N.C. Aniebo has been the author of a steady succession of short stories written for various periodical publications, a selection of them at last appearing as *Of Wives, Talismans and the Dead* in 1983. Most of them deal with the problems of Igbo people in Eastern Nigeria trying to cope with the transition from rural to urban living and with other pressures of accelerating social change, including that most hectic of such changes, war itself. The commonest experience in Aniebo's fiction is the bewilderment that results from lack of trust in other people and lack of faith in the efficacy of the gods, whether traditional African or imported Christian. He often plunges his characters into some variety of spiritual emptiness or near-despair after they have been betrayed by those closest to them in childhood, adolescence, work, or marriage. The acrid taste of defeat is perhaps Aniebo's most distinctive contribution to West African literature in English—his ability to record convincingly instances of human strength wilting and shriveling, usually as the indirect outcome of large social processes. If Aluko's writing captures the comedy of Nigerian life acclimatizing itself to the modern world, and Achebe's the tragedy of it within an historical perspective, and Soyinka's the human spirit refusing to be broken by it, then what Aniebo records is the intense pain that afflicts people when social change halts, trips, nonpluses, or defeats them.

In the story "Dilemma," the priestess addresses her wayward son: "The earth has never changed. The winds still continue to blow, the rains to fall, and men to be born and die. Only little things that don't matter change. Don't say because things change, you'll stop believing in God and believe in the Devil." Her words pronounce the traditional wisdom that many Nigerians today mock, or cannot accept, or covet, when it appears in others, or deliberately reject for the pursuit of personal ambition and the acquisition of consumer goods. Aniebo, however, presents such evaporation of faith not as an ordinary clash-of-cultures matter but as the heavy price that Nigerians pay for entry into the modern world. While it is more pervasive in large towns, like Port Harcourt in the novel *The Journey Within,* it characterizes also the stories in *Of Wives, Talismans and the Dead,* most of which are set in rural Igbo villages. Thus, in the privacy of their tender incestuous love, widowed father and devoted daughter and only surviving child, in "Maruma," find the true fulfillment of giving to another, but when her pregnancy makes their love public, their having broken a powerful social taboo destroys first their relationship and then themselves and their line. Yet, years later, their ruined, crumbling compound is symmetrically matched at the other end of the village by another as desolate, whose respectable and fecund owners had committed no "abomination." This even-handed "leveling" at the end of the story is the author's explicit comment, and it makes one wonder whether the dark views of the human condition that many of Aniebo's characters express aren't also his own, as in the war story, "In the Front Line:" "The war had proved that no matter what one did or worshipped one died all the same, and more often than not like a rat." Similarly, in the thoughts of Cristian Okoro in *The Journey Within:* " . . . his family had fought for survival, always getting up after a fall, always continuing to fight after a defeat. So, was life merely a getting-up after a fall?"

Aniebo's first published book, *The Anonymity of Sacrifice,* is a novel about the bitterness of successive Biafran "falls" during the Nigerian Civil War. It is a collection of very vivid, rapidly sketched illustrations of, admittedly, some heroic improvisations against great odds, but chiefly of betrayals, misunderstandings, personal defeats, frustration, and distrust, with the estrangement of the two major characters, and their pointless deaths, inadequately exploited novelistically. While the details of the narrative do indeed convey disillusion and corruption, there is little sense of their being worked into a firm design, and the title promises more significance than the book delivers.

The second novel, *The Journey Within,* is altogether more relaxed in execution, but again more ambitious in the endeavor than in the realization. It is centered upon the stories of two marriages, one traditional, the other Christian. In probing, to some depth, the joys, sorrows tensions, struggles, love, and hatred that are generated between husband and wife, Aniebo is clearly arguing that marriage (whatever its kind) is a very thorny experience. Unfortunately, by making the two marriages progressively less distinctive, he throws away the opportunity to break his larger theme with finer shades and more delicate ironies. Yet the novel is full of sardonic instances of human folly, as individuals seek their own fulfillments in an urban environment of free and selfish enterprise. While there is much mature observation of love and sexuality, some of the scenes between lovers are rendered with more mere titillation than the tone of the narration elsewhere strives after.

The collection of short stories is certainly the most successful of Aniebo's books, for under the pressure of brevity and pithiness, his particular gift, the rapid but accurate sketching of a scene without having to sustain its implications across a large design, is revealed as professional and complete in its own right. In the novels his transitions from one emotion to another are often incongruous, but in the stories he can move without inhibition or oddity across a gamut of emotions—anger at the exploitation of dockers in "Rats and Rabbits," self-confidence without moral crutches in "Godevil" (intentionally ambiguous as "Go devil" or "God evil"?), self-gratification in "Moment of Decision," the horror of murder within the family in "The Quiet Man" and "A Hero's Welcome," and, rarely, the consolation of faith in "Four Dimensions." The bleakness of Aniebo's vision is tempered, in his best writing, by a wry ironic sense that does not exclude muted compassion.

—Arthur Ravenscroft

ANTHONY, Michael

Nationality: Trinidadian. **Born:** Mayaro, 10 February 1932. **Education:** Mayaro Roman Catholic School; Junior Technical College, San Fernando, Trinidad. **Family:** Married Yvette Francesca in 1958; two sons and two daughters. **Career:** Lived in England, 1954-68; journalist, Reuters news agency, London, 1964-68; lived in Brazil, 1968-70; assistant editor, Texaco Trinidad, Pointe-à-Pierre, 1970-72. Since 1972 researcher, National Cultural Council (now Ministry of Culture), Port-of-Spain; broadcast historical radio programs, 1975-1989; University of Richmond, VA, teacher of creative writing, 1992. **Address:** 99 Long Circular Road, St. James, Port-of-Spain, Trinidad.

PUBLICATIONS

Novels

The Games Were Coming. London, Deutsch, 1963; Boston, Houghton Mifflin, 1968.
The Year in San Fernando. London, Deutsch, 1965.
Green Days by the River. Boston, Houghton Mifflin, and London, Deutsch, 1967.
Streets of Conflict. London, Deutsch, 1976.
All That Glitters. London, Deutsch, 1981.
Bright Road to El Dorado. Walton-on-Thames, Surrey, Nelson, 1982.
The Becket Factor. London, Collins, 1990.

Short Stories

Sandra Street and Other Stories. London, Heinemann, 1973.
Cricket in the Road and Other Stories. London, Deutsch, 1973.
Folk Tales and Fantasies. Port-of-Spain, Columbus, 1976.
The Chieftain's Carnival and Other Stories. London, Longman, 1993.

Other

Glimpses of Trinidad and Tobago, with a Glance at the West Indies. Port-of-Spain, Columbus, 1974.

Profile Trinidad: A Historical Survey from the Discovery to 1900. London, Macmillan, 1975.

The Making of Port-of-Spain 1757-1939. Port-of-Spain, Key Caribbean, 1978.

First in Trinidad. Port-of-Spain, Circle Press, 1985.

Heroes of the People of Trinidad and Tobago. Port-of-Spain, Circle Press, 1986.

The History of Aviation in Trinidad and Tobago 1913-1962. Port-of-Spain, Paria, 1987.

A Better and Brighter Day. Port-of-Spain, Circle Press, 1987.

Towns and Villages of Trinidad and Tobago. Port-of-Spain, Circle Press, 1988.

Parade of the Carnivals of Trinidad 1839-1989. Port-of-Spain, Circle Press, 1989.

The Golden Quest: The Four Voyages of Christopher Columbus. London, Macmillan Caribbean, 1992.

Editor, with Andrew Carr, *David Frost Introduces Trinidad and Tobago.* London, Deutsch, 1975.

*

Critical Studies: In *London Magazine,* April 1967; "Novels of Childhood" in *The West Indian Novel and Its Background* by Kenneth Ramchand, London, Faber, and New York, Barnes and Noble, 1970; *Green Days by the River* by Linda Flynn and Sally West, Oxford, Heinemann Educational, 1989.

Michael Anthony comments:

I see myself principally as a storyteller. In other words, I am not aware that I have any message. I think both the past life and the fascination of landscape play a most important part in my work.

My infancy has been very important in my literary development and so far almost everything I have written—certainly my novels—are very autobiographical.

It is strange that I have never had the desire to write about England, although I spent 14 years there. To some people, judging from my writing alone, I have never been out of Trinidad. And this is true in some sort of way.

I feel a certain deep attachment to Trinidad and I want to write about it in such a way that I will give a faithful picture of life here. But when I am writing a story I am not aware that I want to do anything else but tell the story.

*   *   *

Michael Anthony's most successful novels are set in southern Trinidad, deal with the experiences of childhood and youth, and are simple in structure. Where Anthony steps outside that framework, as he does in *Streets of Conflict,* and attempts explicit social comment, the results are disastrous. Yet it would be absurd to conclude, as some critics have done, that Anthony has nothing to say, and that his books are merely charming but naive semi-autobiographical remembrances of childhood.

His first novel, *The Games Were Coming,* subtly explores the need for a balance between restraint and joyful abandon. In a society where order has been a colonial imposition and the anarchic spirit of fete embraced as the only true guarantee of freedom, these are important issues. Anthony contrasts the cycling championships, for which the novel's hero, Leon, is training with self-denying discipline, and the approach of carnival which is associated with "fe-

ver," "chaos," and "release." Leon becomes so obsessed by the need for restraint that he neglects his girl friend, Sylvia, and nearly loses her. She in turn suffers for failing to know herself. She prides herself on being cool, controlled, and pure, but is embarrassed by indelicate thoughts which spring unbidden to her mind. She disapproves of carnival, but is willing to "jump-on" at night when no-one will see. She ignores these promptings of sexual energy and as a result is swept away by her feelings and Leon's neglect into the calculating arms of her middle-aged employer. Anthony suggests a resolution of these forces first in the character of Leon's younger brother, Dolphus, who is attracted equally to the Games and to carnival, and second by a subtle pattern of imagery which hints at the complementary of these events, so that the "madness and wildness" of jouvert morning is shown as the energy which is disciplined into the "richness and splendor" of Grand Carnival.

The Year in San Fernando is also much more than a sensitive novel about growing up. Although Anthony scrupulously adheres to the unfolding perceptions of 12-year-old Francis, from puzzled naiveté towards the growth of sympathetic understanding, what he creates in the novel is a richly textured and moving portrayal of the growth and disappearance in time of what is human. Set against the passage of the seasons is Francis's relationship with Mrs. Chandles, the old woman for whom he is brought as a companion from his impoverished village home in return for his board and schooling. Initially, she is all dominant will, a self-contained, bitter old lady who treats Francis as a virtual slave. He, when the year begins, is cowed and passive, scarcely more than a bundle of sensations. As the year passes, he observes Mrs. Chandles's spirit and flesh wilt in the drought of crop-season and comes to understand the reasons for her ill-temper. At the same time, Francis's self is growing powerfully as he begins to acknowledge his feelings, both positive and negative. There is a brief season of rain when Mrs. Chandles is released from her pain and the two meet as open and giving personalities. But then as Francis continues his growth to personhood, the personality of Mrs. Chandles disintegrates as she begins to die. Yet there is more for Francis to learn than his part in the cycle of life and death, and this is contained in a puzzling comment Mrs. Chandles makes. Throughout the dry season he has painstakingly tended her shriveling flowers and oiled and massaged her protesting limbs. She comments on his "willing mind" and bemuses him by telling him that she "connected willingness of mind with sacredness." It is through this "sacredness" that Francis redeems his year in San Fernando from time.

None of Anthony's other novels quite achieves the same degree of understated but unflawed art. *Green Days by the River* evokes another passage from adolescent freedom to adult responsibility in the countryside around Mayaro in prose of great beauty. But the novel seems to escape from Anthony's control, in a way which is interesting but damaging to its coherence, in the central relationship between Shellie, the youth, and Mr. Gidharee the Indian farmer who lures him into marriage with his daughter. Here the meeting is complicated by its Trinidadian ethnic resonances. In portraying Gidharee as a creolised Jekyll who charms Shellie into his confidence, and an Indian Hyde who sets his dogs to savage him as a warning about what will happen if he fails to marry his daughter, Anthony unavoidably appears to be making a veiled statement about ethnic relations. Two kinds of irony tangle. One is the dramatic irony that Shellie fails to see the twig being limed to catch him, the other is the irony of Shellie's racial innocence when so much of Gidharee's behavior adds up to a Creole stereotype of the Indian as an economic threat. The second irony leads to inconsistencies in the portrayal of Shellie, who is bright and sensitive in all respects except in his dealings with Gidharee, where he appears spineless and impercipient. It is hard to know in a somewhat evasive novel quite what Anthony intended.

Anthony's one attempt to deal with broader social issues, in *Streets of Conflict*, is an outright failure. It is an inept performance, inconsistent and shallow in characterization, broken-backed in plot and embarrassingly naive in its portrayal of society and politics in Brazil.

All That Glitters is at least a partial return to excellence. In some respects it can be seen as a return to familiar territory, to the growing awareness of young Horace Lumpers of the complications of the adult world around him, of the jealousies and deceptions provoked by the return of his sophisticated Aunty Roomeen to the village of Mayaro. In a more intense way than in any earlier novel, Anthony focuses on a child's attempt to discern whether people are being sincere or false. Words such as trickster, genuine, hypocrite, acting, feigned, frankoment, and pretensive act as leitmotifs in the text and Horace has to learn that being adult means wearing different faces. This play on truth and falsity is linked through the novel's two complementary mottoes ("Gold Is Where You Find It" and "All That Glitters") to Anthony's most conscious exploration of the nature of his art. The distinction is caught in the contrast between Horace's joy in discovering through writing what he thinks and feels, when he writes about the golden day with the fishermen or the sordid saga of the stolen golden chain, and the way that the adult clichés which his teacher Myra uses embalm experience. Nevertheless, for all her circumlocutions, she recognizes the child's magical directness, and it is her advice, "Make it colorful and vivid—and true" which both Horace and Michael Anthony follow.

—Jeremy Poynting

ARMAH, Ayi Kwei

Nationality: Ghanaian. **Born:** Takoradi in 1938. **Education:** Achimota College, Accra; Groton School, Massachusetts; Harvard University, Cambridge, Massachusetts, A.B. in social studies; Columbia University, New York. **Career:** Translator, *Révolution Africaine* magazine, Algiers; scriptwriter for Ghana Television; English teacher, Navrongo School, Ghana, 1966; editor, *Jeune Afrique* magazine, Paris, 1967-68; teacher at Teacher's College, Dar es Salaam, and universities of Massachusetts, Amherst, Lesotho, and Wisconsin, Madison. **Address:** c/o Heinemann Educational, Ighodaro Road, Jericho PMB 5205, Ibadan, Oyo State, Nigeria.

Publications

Novels

The Beautyful Ones Are Not Yet Born. Boston, Houghton Mifflin, 1968; London, Heinemann, 1969.
Fragments. Boston, Houghton Mifflin, 1970; London, Heinemann, 1975.
Why Are We So Blest? New York, Doubleday, 1972; London, Heinemann, 1975.
Two Thousand Seasons. Nairobi, East African Publishing House, 1973; London, Heinemann, 1979; Chicago, Third World Press, 1980.

The Healers. Nairobi, East African Publishing House, 1978; London, Heinemann, 1979.

Uncollected Short Stories

"A Short Story," in *New African* (London), December 1965.
"Yaw Manu's Charm," in *Atlantic* (Boston), May 1968.
"The Offal Kind," in *Harper's* (New York), January 1969.
"Doctor Kamikaze," in *Mother Jones* (San Francisco), October 1989.

*

Critical Studies: *The Novels of Ayi Kwei Armah: A Study in Polemical Fiction* by Robert Fraser, London, Heinemann, 1980; *Ayi Kwei Armah's Africa: The Sources of His Fiction* by Derek Wright, London, Zell, 1989; *Resistance in Postcolonial African Fiction* by Neil Lazarus, New Haven, Yale University Press, 1990; *Critical Perspectives on Ayi Kwei Armah* edited by Derek Wright, Washington D.C., Three Continents, 1992; *The Novels of Ayi Kwei Armah* by K. Damodar Rao, New Delhi, Prestige, 1993.

*   *   *

Ayi Kwei Armah's masterly control over language forces his reader to suspend his disbelief, however reluctant he may be to do so. The comic or horrific distortion of what is nearly recognizable reality in the first three novels has extraordinary imaginative power.

The title of the first novel refers to an inscription which the central character, known only as "the man," sees on a bus. By implication it refers back to the Teacher's story of Plato's cave, where the one man who escapes from the cave and returns to tell his fellow sufferers of the beautiful world outside is thought to be mad by those in the "reassuring chains." The man is anonymous because he is regarded as mad in his society, modern Accra. His family suffers from his refusal to take bribes in his position as a railway clerk, and his honesty is incomprehensible to "the loved ones." His former friend, Koomson, has become a Minister through corruption, and, though the regime of which he is a part falls, an equally corrupt one takes its place. The fusion of styles in *The Beautyful Ones* can be seen in the first few pages, which give a realistic account of a bus journey but also introduce the controlling symbol in the novel, that of money as decay, or excrement. The bus conductor smells a cedi note and finds it has "a very old smell, very strong, and so very rotten that the stench itself of it came with a curious, satisfying pleasure." This anticipates the comic and horrible way in which Koomson has to escape the new regime, by wriggling through a latrine. The depravity of the society is suggested by the manner in which a young man confesses he has made money in a lottery "in the embarrassed way of a young girl confessing love;" if he escaped from his society the man would only mirror his broken pencil sharpener, whose handle "sped round and round with the futile freedom of a thing connected to nothing else."

Armah's ability to invest apparently insignificant objects or scenes with meanings is clear in *Fragments*. Early in the novel there is a detailed account of the destruction of a mad dog by a man with a gross sexual deformity, while the little boy who loves the dog looks on helplessly. It is so vivid that it prepares the reader for the destruction of the central character, Baako, who returns to Ghana from New York wanting to write film scripts because "Film gets to everyone." He finds that his society wants material evidence of his "been-to" status. The new element in this novel is represented by Naana, Baako's blind grandmother, who is the voice of the traditional culture. Traditional ceremonies, such as Baako's baby nephew's outdooring, have lost their spiritual significance and become an opportunity for ostentation and avarice; the plot suggests that Naana's fears for the baby as the victim of this irreligious display are justified, for he dies in the course of it. The fragments of the title seem to be the members of the new society, placed within the opening and closing sections of the novel which express Naana's sense of meaningful community. The only other hopeful element is the growing love between Baako and the sensitive Puerto Rican, Juana.

Why Are We So Blest? is a more fragmented novel than *Fragments,* jumping between three narrators with no obvious narrative line, though we eventually discover that Solo, a failed revolutionary, is using the notebooks of Aimée, a white American, and Modin, a Ghanaian, intercut with his own text. The savage irony of the title is sustained throughout the novel, which lacks the cynical comedy of the two previous works and is much more overt in its distortion of reality. All the white women in the novel prey on the black men: Modin, a student who drops out of Harvard to go to Laccryville in North Africa as a would-be revolutionary, is used primarily by Aimée, who epitomizes the sexual sickness of all the white women. She is frigid when she meets Modin, and uses him as an object to stimulate her sexual fantasies of intercourse with a black servant. Modin's attempt to liberate her into a fuller sensitivity destroys him. The horrific scene, in which Aimée is raped and Modin castrated by white men, fully enacts Aimée's fantasy. She is sexually aroused and kisses Modin's bleeding penis, asking him to say that he loves her. Solo sees Modin as an African who does not know "how deep the destruction has eaten into himself, hoping to achieve a healing juncture with his destroyed people."

Armah's most recent novels are historical. *Two Thousand Seasons* is written in a new style, in its repetitiveness and long leisurely sentences suggesting that it is folk myth: "With what shall the utterers' tongue stricken with goodness, riven silent with the quiet force of beauty, with which mention shall the tongue of the utterers begin a song of praise whose perfect singers have yet to come?" Its narrator is not identified, though he participates in the action. The violation of his people's way of life by Arab and then European invaders is depicted powerfully but the ideal of "the way, our way" remains nebulous. *The Healers* is stylistically much more vigorous, and is set at a precise time in the past, during the Second Asante War. The idea of "inspiration" is gradually defined in the course of the novel as being a healing and creative force which can only work slowly, and Armah perhaps sees himself as one of those prophesied by Damfo in the novel, "healers wherever our people are scattered, able to bring us together again."

—Angela Smith

ARMSTRONG, Jeannette

Nationality: Canadian (Okanagan). **Born:** Penticton (Okanagan) Indian Reservation, British Columbia, Canada, 1948. **Education:** Okanagan College; University of Victoria, British Columbia, Canada, B.F.A. **Career:** Since 1989 director, En'owkin School of International Writing, Okanagan, British Columbia.

PUBLICATIONS

Novels

Slash. Penticton, British Columbia, Theytus, 1987.

Poetry

Breathtracks. Penticton, British Columbia, Theytus, 1991.

Other

Enwhisteetkwa; Walk in Water (for children). Penticton, British Columbia, Theytus, 1982.
Neekna and Chemai (for children), illustrated by Barbara Marchand. Penticton, British Columbia, Theytus, 1984.
The Native Creative Process: A Collaborative Discourse, with Douglas Cardinal. Penticton, British Columbia, Theytus, 1992.
We Get Our Living Like Milk from the Land: Okanagan Tribal History Book. Penticton, British Columbia, Theytus, 1993.

*   *   *

Along with Maria Campbell's *Halfbreed* (1973) and Beatrice Culleton's *In Search of April Raintree* (1983), Jeannette Armstrong's *Slash* established a place for writing by Canadian native women. Armstrong's text foregrounds key issues in the struggle for native self-expression, exploring the social and psychological pressures on young native people searching for a functional sense of community and self. Armstrong wants to discover how native people can confront what she calls their "postcolonial" situation, the double bind resulting from existence under the dominant white culture. How, Armstrong asks, can her protagonist, Slash, learn to cope with the pressures to conform to standards and values that are not exactly his own? How can he maintain a native identity when so much of his world tells him that it is not worthwhile? *Slash* explores the process of rebuilding native self-worth.

Armstrong's novel is a bildungsroman, a fictional autobiography tracing the growth of a single central figure, in this case the title character. The book begins with a brief "Prologue" in which Slash, an Okanagan man, looks back over his life; he says that he will trace his own progress from childhood innocence, through compulsively destructive adolescence, to a mature state of relative understanding. The novel's four long chapters begin with "The Awakening," in which a youthful Slash first comes to realize that being "Indian" in Canadian society means not fitting into the privileged white mainstream culture. In "Trying It On" and "Mixing It Up," he recounts his various experiences as an activist, a prisoner, a protester, a healer, a vagrant, and a community member. Slash tries on various roles and identities, shifting restlessly from place to place, focusing on his own inability to come to terms with what it means to be a native person. His three names suggest multiple senses of self: "Tommy," an Anglo-Celtic Christian name, indicates both family bond—his parents call him Tommy—and the assimilative force of the dominant Canadian culture; "Slash," a nickname he earns in a drug-related brawl in the city, represents his angry, urbanized, cynical, warrior self; and an undisclosed Okanagan name, which Slash tells us is given ceremonially to every one of his people after birth, suggests—because it remains unstated—the unrealized potential of his native identity.

The novel is also a picaresque, a traveler's tale, since its narrative consists of a loosely knit series of events involving numerous characters, many of whom do not recur in the rest of the text. For most of his tale, Slash passes from situation to situation, unsure of his position and unwilling to come to rest, although he maintains at various points in the novel a tenuous connection to family and to his tribal home in the Okanagan region of British Columbia. These two middle chapters, like Slash's own life, are largely unstructured and directionless; episodic rather than coherently plotted, they tend to wander away from preordained forms. The final chapter, "We Are a People," draws those loose threads together as Slash tries to make sense of his unsettled life. Armstrong reaffirms the collective identities of native people as distinct from any legal or constitutional definitions of culture based on nonnative ideals. Despite suffering and recurrent disillusionment, and despite the fact that the struggle for native self-determination continues, Slash seems to discover a point of balance for himself, resting on a confident sense of indigenous values, on a sense of place and meaning that comes from traditional native understandings of land and life.

Slash is somewhat polemical in its style; that is, Armstrong (who is deeply involved herself in native education) wants to use her fiction to make strong, clear political statements about native issues, and she tends to draw rigorous distinctions between what she sees as positive and negative—usually native and nonnative respectively. Much of the dialogue involves extended expositions about such problems as assimilation, land claims, civil disobedience, treaty negotiation, and constitutional reform. The novel in a sense acts as a discussion aid for young native people, offering Slash's hard-won personal success as an example of what perseverance and dedication can bring about in his readers' lives. "I guess," Slash writes, "that was the point of this whole trip: to educate." *Slash* confronts the personal and social problems that young natives face and offers hope for improvement through education and self-discovery. The text moves forward from frustration and anger through activism to self-affirmation, but this path is not so neatly drawn or simple. *Slash* engages the welter of events and ideologies in contemporary history and projects a vital, current role for native people in that history, a role played out in the narrative by Slash himself.

—Kevin McNeilly

ASTLEY, Thea

Nationality: Australian. **Born:** Thea Beatrice May Astley in Brisbane, Queensland, 25 August 1925. **Education:** The University of Queensland, Brisbane, 1943-47, B.A. 1947. **Family:** Married Edmund John Gregson in 1948; one son. **Career:** English teacher in Queensland, 1944-48, and in New South Wales, 1948-67; senior tutor, then fellow in English, Macquarie University, Sydney, 1968-85. Lives near Sydney. **Awards:** Commonwealth Literary Fund fellowship, 1961, 1964; Miles Franklin award, 1963, 1966, 1973; Moomba award, 1965; *The Age* Book of the Year award, 1975; Patrick White award, 1989. **Agent:** Elise Goodman, Goodman Associates, 500 West End Avenue, New York, New York 10024, U.S.A.

PUBLICATIONS

Novels

Girl with a Monkey. Sydney, Angus and Robertson, 1958; New York, Penguin, 1987.

A Descant for Gossips. Sydney and London, Angus and Robertson, 1960.

The Well-Dressed Explorer. Sydney and London, Angus and Robertson, 1962; New York, Penguin, 1988.

The Slow Natives. Sydney, Angus and Robertson, 1965; London, Angus and Robertson, 1966; New York, Evans, 1967.

A Boat Load of Home Folk. Sydney and London, Angus and Robertson, 1968; New York, Penguin, 1983.

The Acolyte. Sydney and London, Angus and Robertson, 1972; in *Two by Astley,* New York, Putnam, 1988.

A Kindness Cup. Melbourne, Nelson, 1974; in *Two by Astley,* New York, Putnam, 1988.

An Item from the Late News. St. Lucia, University of Queensland Press, 1982; New York, Penguin, 1984.

Beachmasters. Ringwood, Victoria, Penguin, 1985; New York, Viking, 1986.

It's Raining in Mango: Pictures from a Family Album. New York, Putnam, 1987; London, Viking, 1988.

Two by Astley [includes *A Kindness Cup*]. New York, Putnam, 1988.

Reaching Tin River. New York, Putnam, 1990.

Coda. New York, Putnam, 1994; London, Secker and Warburg, 1995.

Short Stories

Hunting the Wild Pineapple. Melbourne, Nelson, 1979; New York, Putnam, 1991.

Vanishing Points. New York, Putnam, 1992; London, Minerva, 1995.

Uncollected Short Stories

"Cubby," in *Coast to Coast.* Sydney, Angus and Robertson, 1961.

"The Scenery Never Changes," in *Coast to Coast.* Sydney, Angus and Robertson, 1963.

"Journey to Olympus," in *Coast to Coast.* Sydney, Angus and Robertson, 1965.

"Seeing Mrs. Landers," in *Festival and Other Stories,* edited by Brian Buckley and Jim Hamilton. Melbourne, Wren, 1974; Newton Abbot, Devon, David and Charles, 1975.

Other

Editor, *Coast to Coast 1969-1970.* Sydney, Angus and Robertson, 1971.

*

Thea Astley comments:

(1972) My main interest (and has been through my five published and current unpublished novels) is the misfit. Not the spectacular outsider, but the seedy little non-grandiose non-fitter who lives in his own mini-hell. Years ago I was impressed at eighteen or so by *Diary of a Nobody,* delighted by the quality Grossmith gave to the non-achiever and the sympathy which he dealt out. My five published novels have always been, despite the failure of reviewers to see it, a plea for charity—in the Pauline sense, of course—to be accorded to those not ruthless enough or grand enough to be gigantic tragic figures, but which, in their own way, record the same *via crucis.*

*   *   *

Towards the end of Thea Astley's fifth novel (*A Boat Load of Home Folk*) a hurricane descends upon Port Lena and rages violently while the problems and personal crises of the various characters draw towards some sort of resolution. The hurricane as a destructive natural phenomenon is slightly unusual in the imaginative world of Astley, but, as a symbol, it is not at all unfamiliar. For her characters seem to move perpetually in the artificially calm eye of the universe's innate anarchy: a symbolic storm encloses, yet also by its very existence and threatening nature, divides them. Moving in this constantly endangered pseudo-equilibrium, they brush often the edges of disaster, succumb to it occasionally, make what order they can with the opportunities that offer.

The impending, eager-to-consume anarchy of Astley's world is manifested variously: it can materialise as the chaos of the emotional life, that destroys identity, reduces "to a spineless receptivity" (*Girl with a Monkey*); it may take the form of spiritual annihilation by human viciousness exquisitely applied and cravenly veiled (*A Descant for Gossips*); or act through the confusing yet endlessly fascinating impulses of the uncomprehended self (*The Well-Dressed Explorer*); or emerge as that fatal disjunction from an intolerable world, experienced by those who, like "the wandering islands" of A.D. Hope's poem, ply "the long isolation of the heart" (*The Slow Natives*). Anarchy of a kind crowds in upon Astley's characters and they have few resources with which to resist it.

Because the action is caught, as it were, in the eye of the symbolic storm, her novels, especially the earlier ones, seem at times highly, even excessively, deliberated: characters move in a real enough world, yet often with fleetingly dream-like deliberateness, islands of intense self-consciousness seeking, in assertive almost desperate avowals of identity, bastions against encroaching chaos. Thus Elsie in *Girl with a Monkey*, is "caught static in a complete island of twenty-four hours"—a metaphor which continually reinforces a sense of extreme deliberation in action and thought. When she hears, at Mass "as through walls of water," it is an apt and summary image for the action of the whole book; similarly, Mrs. Crozier is pictured as moving "Almost epileptically . . . pruning as she went the ambient roses. . . ." In *A Descant for Gossips* the tragic relationship between Helen, Miller, and Vinny is captured, with momentary statuesqueness at its very inception, as "a dangerous montage," while at the end of the book, Vinny, coming to her crucial decision, is described as seeing everything with "an amazing clarity . . . the grass stood in millions of separate blades, green and sharp . . ." This has that quality of the dream that is not blurred and vague but horrifically more real than real. Again, George Brewster, hero of *The Well-Dressed Explorer*, builds his life on fantasy views of himself and dies in a "dream-streaked sleep" in which that life is paraded, insanely truncated, yet paradoxically illuminating and immensely moving. A similar quality is discoverable, though it is admittedly less obvious amidst a growing complexity, in the remaining two books.

This deliberation, even if it is occasionally overdone, is no mere quirk of "style," it is a quality, a condition, in the characters' lives and an element in the Astley universe. And it is necessary, indeed indispensable, if the people are to affirm identity and a concept of order in the face of a chaos of evil, sordidness, deadly triviality, and cavernous loneliness.

It is difficult to determine what real weapons her characters have in this essentially rearguard action against a universe morally and spiritually anarchic. Perhaps love, but that is plagued by infidelity, impediment, or possessiveness; perhaps the child's innocence, but in this world, that innocence, followed out, brings Vinny Lalor and

Keith Leverson to tragedy or near tragedy; perhaps religion. Thea Astley is certainly preoccupied with Catholic experience and upbringing, with Catholicism as an influence on personality and intellect and with the guilt and neurosis traditionally associated with Catholic sexual morality. But religion is not much comfort in the eye of the storm: it is at best irrelevant, at worst grotesque. Indeed grotesquerie and corruption become inseparable from Catholicism in Astley's vision, even if she suggests, in a way reminiscent of Greene, a road to sanctity through intimate knowledge of sin. A deeply personal conflict between religious commitment and revulsion against unhealthy inhibition and veiled corruption seems to be involved. It may be that in *A Boat Load of Home Folk,* where almost excessive sordidness and grotesqueness seem to suggest something like purgation, this conflict has reached a resolution.

Following that novel, Astley published *The Acolyte*—a brilliant, complex portrayal of the egocentric artist who enslaves and preys upon everyone around him, the more exquisitely and ruthlessly because he is blind. Like Brewster, but with much greater sophistication and intent, he creates chaos everywhere. *The Acolyte,* together with *A Kindness Cup*—a tense, remorseless study of fear and guilt which won *The Age* Book of the Year award—marks one of the peaks of Astley's continuing achievements in the novel form.

After Astley retired from her position at Macquarie University in Sydney she returned to North Queensland. With greater leisure and remote from interruptions in her tropical eyrie, she turned her attention to short stories, reflecting her new surroundings and perspective in a collection entitled *Hunting The Wild Pineapple.* These witty, engaging but sometimes savagely pungent stories are told in a characteristically dense, sometimes staccato style which never slips into tortuousness. The wounded and the misfits are all there; life is as uncontrollable as always. But the occasional straining for effect of earlier books is replaced by a marvellous confidence and control as a now middle-aged, quizzical Keith Leverson (of *The Slow Natives*) casts a tolerant eye over life in an ambiguous, tropical "Eden."

Several books have followed in quick succession. *An Item from the Late News* depicts events in the unlovely township of "Allbut"—classic Astley country where tensions, violence, and corrosive resentments stirred up by an eccentric anti-nuclear protester wait poised for the trigger that will release them. *Beachmasters* looks outward into the Pacific where a brief, unsuccessful revolution on a small island stands as that haunting hurricane presence that decides the fates of so many of Astley's struggling, vulnerably human characters.

Astley's work, now a major and substantial presence in contemporary Australian literature, still receives less attention than it merits from professional critics. But this does not alter the fact that she is one of the most significant and innovative of Australian writers.

—Brian E. Matthews

ATWOOD, Margaret (Eleanor)

Nationality: Canadian. **Born:** Ottawa, Ontario, 18 November 1939. **Education:** Victoria College, University of Toronto, 1957-61, B.A. 1961; Radcliffe College, Cambridge, Massachusetts, A.M. 1962; Harvard University, Cambridge, Massachusetts 1962-63, 1965-67. **Family:** Married; one daughter. **Career:** Lecturer in English, University of British Columbia, Vancouver, 1964-65; instructor in English, Sir George Williams University, Montreal, 1967-68; teacher of creative writing, University of Alberta, Edmonton, 1969-70; assistant professor of English, York University, Toronto, 1971-72. Editor and member of board of directors, House of Anansi Press, Toronto, 1971-73. Writer-in-residence, University of Toronto, 1972-73, University of Alabama, Tuscaloosa, 1985, Macquarie University, North Ryde, New South Wales, 1987, and Trinity University, San Antonio, Texas, 1989; Berg Visiting Professor of English, New York University, 1986. President, Writers Union of Canada, 1981-82, and PEN Canadian Centre, 1984-86. **Awards:** E.J. Pratt medal, 1961; President's medal, University of Western Ontario, 1965; Governor-General's award, 1966, 1986; Centennial Commission prize, 1967; Union League Civic and Arts Foundation prize, 1969, and Bess Hogkin prize, 1974 (*Poetry,* Chicago); City of Toronto award, 1976, 1989; St. Lawrence award, 1978; Radcliffe medal, 1980; Molson award, 1981; Guggenheim fellowship, 1981; Welsh Arts Council International Writers prize, 1982; Ida Nudel Humanitarian award, 1986; Toronto Arts award, 1986; Los Angeles *Times* Book award, 1986; Arthur C. Clarke Science-Fiction award, for novel, 1987; Humanist of the Year award, 1987; National Magazine award, for journalism, 1988; Harvard University Centennial medal, 1990; Trillium award, for *Wilderness Tips,* 1992, for *The Robber Bride,* 1994; Commonwealth Writer's prize, 1994, Sunday Times award for literary excellence, 1994, both for *The Robber Bride.* Chevalier dans L'Ordre des arts et des lettres, 1994. D.Litt.: Trent University, Peterborough, Ontario, 1973; Concordia University, Montreal, 1980; Smith College, Northampton, Massachusetts, 1982; University of Toronto, 1983; Mount Holyoke College, South Hadley, Massachusetts, 1985; University of Waterloo, Ontario, 1985; University of Guelph, Ontario, 1985; Victoria College, 1987; University of Leeds, 1994; LL.D.: Queen's University, Kingston, Ontario, 1974. Companion, Order of Canada, 1981. Fellow, Royal Society of Canada, 1987; Honorary Member, American Academy of Arts and Sciences, 1988. **Agent:** Phoebe Larmore, 228 Main Street, Venice, California 90291, U.S.A. **Address:** c/o Oxford University Press, 70 Wynford Drive, Don Mills, Ontario M3C 1J9, Canada.

Publications

Novels

The Edible Woman. Toronto, McClelland and Stewart, and London, Deutsch, 1969; Boston, Little Brown, 1970.
Surfacing. Toronto, McClelland and Stewart, 1972; London, Deutsch, and New York, Simon and Schuster, 1973.
Lady Oracle. Toronto, McClelland and Stewart, and New York, Simon and Schuster, 1976; London, Deutsch, 1977.
Life Before Man. Toronto, McClelland and Stewart, 1979; New York, Simon and Schuster, and London, Cape, 1980.
Bodily Harm. Toronto, McClelland and Stewart, 1981; New York, Simon and Schuster, and London, Cape, 1982.
The Handmaid's Tale. Toronto, McClelland and Stewart, 1985; Boston, Houghton Mifflin, and London, Cape, 1986.
Cat's Eye. Toronto, McClelland and Stewart, 1988; New York, Doubleday, and London, Bloomsbury, 1989.
The Robber Bride. Toronto, McClelland and Stewart, New York, Doubleday, and London, Bloomsbury, 1993.

Short Stories

Dancing Girls and Other Stories. Toronto, McClelland and Stewart, 1977; New York, Simon and Schuster, and London, Cape, 1982.

Encounters with the Element Man. Concord, New Hampshire, Ewert, 1982.
Murder in the Dark: Short Fictions and Prose Poems. Toronto, Coach House Press, 1983; London, Cape, 1984.
Bluebeard's Egg and Other Stories. Toronto, McClelland and Stewart, 1983; Boston, Houghton Mifflin, 1986; London, Cape, 1987.
Unearthing Suite. Toronto, Grand Union Press, 1983.
Hurricane Hazel and Other Stories. Helsinki, Eurographica, 1986.
Wilderness Tips. Toronto, McClelland and Stewart, New York, Doubleday, and London, Bloomsbury, 1991.
Good Bones. Toronto, Coach House Press, 1992; London, Bloomsbury, 1993; New York, Doubleday, 1994.

Uncollected Short Stories

"When It Happens," in *The Editors' Choice 1,* edited by George E. Murphy, Jr. New York, Bantam, 1985.
"Theology," in *Harper's* (New York), September 1988.
"Kat," in *New Yorker,* 5 March 1990.
"Weight," in *Vogue* (New York), August 1990.
"Hack Wednesday," in *New Yorker,* 17 September 1990.

Plays

Radio Plays: *The Trumpets of Summer,* 1964.

Television Plays: *The Servant Girl,* 1974; *Snowbird,* 1981; *Heaven on Earth,* with Peter Pearson, 1986.

Poetry

Double Persephone. Toronto, Hawskhead Press, 1961.
The Circle Game (single poem). Bloomfield Hills, Michigan, Cranbrook Academy of Art, 1964.
Talismans for Children. Bloomfield Hills, Michigan, Cranbrook Academy of Art, 1965.
Kaleidoscopes: Baroque. Bloomfield Hills, Michigan, Cranbrook Academy of Art, 1965.
Speeches for Doctor Frankenstein. Bloomfield Hills, Michigan, Cranbrook Academy of Art, 1966.
The Circle Game (collection). Toronto, Contact Press, 1966.
Expeditions. Bloomfield Hills, Michigan, Cranbrook Academy of Art, 1966.
The Animals in That County. Toronto, Oxford University Press, 1968; Boston, Little Brown, 1969.
Who Was in the Garden. Santa Barbara, California, Unicorn, 1969.
Five Modern Canadian Poets, with others, edited by Eli Mandel. Toronto, Holt Rinehart, 1970.
The Journals of Susanna Moodie. Toronto, Oxford University Press, 1970.
Oratorio for Sasquatch, Man and Two Androids: Poems for Voices. Toronto, Canadian Broadcasting Corporation, 1970.
Procedures for Underground. Toronto, Oxford University Press, and Boston, Little Brown, 1970.
Power Politics. Toronto, Anansi, 1971; New York, Harper, 1973.
You Are Happy. Toronto, Oxford University Press, and New York, Harper, 1974.
Selected Poems. Toronto, Oxford University Press, 1976; New York, Simon and Schuster, 1978.
Marsh, Hawk. Toronto, Dreadnaught, 1977.

Two-Headed Poems. Toronto, Oxford University Press, 1978; New York, Simon and Schuster, 1981.

True Stories. Toronto, Oxford University Press, 1981; New York, Simon and Schuster, and London, Cape, 1982.

Notes Towards a Poem That Can Never Be Written. Toronto, Salamander Press, 1981.

Snake Poems. Toronto, Salamander Press, 1983.

Interlunar. Toronto, Oxford University Press, 1984; London, Cape, 1988.

Selected Poems 2: Poems Selected and New 1976-1986. Toronto, Oxford University Press, 1986; Boston, Houghton Mifflin, 1987.

Selected Poems 1966-1984. Toronto, Oxford University Press, 1990.

Poems 1965-1975. London, Virago Press, 1991.

Morning in the Burned House. Toronto, McClelland and Stewart, Boston, Houghton Mifflin, and London, Virago, 1995.

Other (for children)

Up in the Tree. Toronto, McClelland and Stewart, 1978.

Anna's Pet, with Joyce Barkhouse. Toronto, Lorimer, 1980.

For the Birds. Toronto, Douglas and McIntyre, 1990.

Other

Survival: A Thematic Guide to Canadian Literature. Toronto, Anansi, 1972.

Days of the Rebels 1815-1840. Toronto, Natural Science of Canada, 1977.

Second Words: Selected Critical Prose. Toronto, Anansi, 1982; Boston, Beacon Press, 1984.

Margaret Atwood: Conversations, edited by Earl G. Ingersoll. Princeton, New Jersey, Ontario Review Press, 1990.

Editor, *The New Oxford Book of Canadian Verse in English.* Toronto, New York, and Oxford, Oxford University Press, 1982.

Editor, with Robert Weaver, *The Oxford Book of Canadian Short Stories in English.* Toronto, Oxford, and New York, Oxford Univeristy Press, 1986.

Editor, *The Canlit Food Book: From Pen to Palate: A Collection of Tasty Literary Fare.* Toronto, Totem, 1987.

Editor, with Shannon Ravenel, *The Best American Short Stories 1989.* Boston, Houghton Mifflin, 1989.

Editor, *Barbed Lyres.* Toronto, Key Porter, 1990.

*

Bibliography: "Margaret Atwood: An Annotated Bibliography" (prose and poetry) by Alan J. Horne, in *The Annotated Bibliography of Canada's Major Authors 1-2* edited by Robert Lecker and Jack David, Downsview, Ontario, ECW Press, 2 vols., 1979-80.

Manuscript Collection: Fisher Library, University of Toronto.

Critical Studies: *Margaret Atwood: A Symposium* edited by Linda Sandler, Victoria, British Columbia, University of Victoria, 1977; *A Violent Duality* by Sherrill E. Grace, Montreal, Véhicule Press, 1979, and *Margaret Atwood: Language, Text, and System* edited by Grace and Lorraine Weir, Vancouver, University of British Columbia Press, 1983; *The Art of Margaret Atwood: Essays in Criticism* edited by Arnold E. Davidson and Cathy N. Davidson, Toronto, Anansi, 1981; *Margaret Atwood* by Jerome H. Rosenberg, Boston,

Twayne, 1984; *Margaret Atwood: A Feminist Poetics* by Frank Davey, Vancouver, Talonbooks, 1984; *Margaret Atwood* by Barbara Hill Rigney, London, Macmillan, 1987; *Margaret Atwood: Reflection and Reality* by Beatrice Mendez-Egle, Edinburg, Texas, Pan American University, 1987; *Critical Essays on Margaret Atwood* edited by Judith McCombs, Boston, Hall, 1988; *Margaret Atwood: Vision and Forms* edited by Kathryn van Spanckeren and Jan Garden Castro, Carbondale, Southern Illinois University Press, 1988.

*　　*　　*

In interviews, Margaret Atwood has often commented that when she started writing in the late 1950s and early 1960s, "Canadian literature" was considered a contradiction in terms. Arguably, as a novelist, poet, critic, and literary/political activist, Atwood has done more to put Canada on the literary map than any other author. While Atwood is an accomplished poet—and the interconnections between her poetry, short fiction and her longer works are both rich and complex—it is primarily as a novelist that she has gained an international reputation. Her first novel, *The Edible Woman,* establishes a preoccupation that remains central in all her subsequent fiction: power politics, and in particular, sexual politics. Excavating their layered histories and formative childhood experiences, Atwood explores and exposes the unequal power relations that shape and inhibit the lives of her female protagonists. Novel by novel, she extends the scope and the complexity of this examination in an astute commentary on North American social and cultural politics and an unflinching recognition of our all too human capacity to both inflict and sustain harm. Although Atwood refuses any designations that may pigeonhole her as a writer, her work is clearly feminist and distinctively Canadian.

While Atwood's first three novels are quite different in form and tone—anti-comedy, mythic quest, and Gothic spoof—they are united by their focus on the individual effects of a society that encourages women to collude in their own objectification. The three protagonists: Marian in *The Edible Woman,* the significantly unnamed narrator in *Surfacing,* and Joan Foster in *Lady Oracle,* all experience (or witness) the transformations demanded by gendered social norms, with their illusory promise of a happily ever after. Atwood's heroines, however, are not the stuff of which fairy tales or costume gothics are made. Thus, *The Edible Woman* traces the ambivalent responses of Marian MacAlpin (who, ironically, works for a market research firm), to her upcoming marriage to a young rising lawyer. Here, Atwood links the economy of a consumer society with women's place in the economy of the marriage market, for Marian's engagement to Peter marks her transition from subject consumer to object consumed as she becomes entrapped by his conventional expectations of regulation femininity. As Peter, the epitome of a shrink-wrapped husband-to-be, starts subjecting Marian to his ideal wife makeover, Marian experiences an increasing sense of her self as an object, an alienation that is textually signalled by the movement from first to third-person narration. While she generally acquiesces to Peter's demands, her unconscious rejection of this process is played out quite literally in terms of consumption: Marian's body begins to refuse food. This rejection begins with steak, but as the wedding day approaches her rebellion escalates in a symbolic identification with any edible object. Finally, she flees her own engagement party before she is trapped forever in the menacing photographic frame of Peter's desires. Her return to subject status is marked by the baking of an edible woman; presenting this cake surrogate to her shocked fiancé, she rejects both his marriage proposal and his objectifying construction of her. Eating the cake herself, she moves from consumed victim to autonomous consumer.

Atwood's second novel develops many of the thematic concerns of her poetry in evocative prose. Like *The Edible Woman, Surfacing* presents a woman disabled by the consequences of her "marital" experience, but the protagonist's journey from psychic and emotional paralysis to unified agency has a powerful mythic dimension that the earlier novel lacks. With three companions, the narrator returns to the landscape of her childhood—a remote cabin on a lake in Northern Quebec—to search for her missing father. She is ambivalent about revisiting the scene of her past because it reminds her of a more immediate event, the loss of her child in a recent divorce. It is an experience that has left her anaesthetised, cut off from her emotions by a form of mind/body split, and her memories are so painful that she represses them in wilful amnesia. The quest in search of her father, however, triggers a quest of self-discovery, as the narrator's history refuses to remain submerged; she is haunted by memories of her parents, a marriage that never was, and her complicity in the abortion of her child. Eventually, she is forced to confront her spectres when a dive below the lake surface becomes a symbolic dive into her own unconscious. Abandoning her manipulative companions, she ritualistically sheds all vestiges of a language and culture that has led her into self-betrayal and murder. Alone on the island, she undergoes a shamanistic cleansing madness, ultimately surfacing with a newfound sense of self. The novel's conclusion resonates with Atwood's contemporaneous thematic guide to Canadian literature, *Survival.* Poised to return to the world that she has left, the narrator's vision leaves her with a resolution that speaks to her experience as both a Canadian and as a woman: "This above all, to refuse to be a victim."

Lady Oracle comes as something of a light relief as Atwood's concerns with metamorphosis and identity are given a comic spin. With a protagonist whose many incarnations give new meaning to "a.k.a.," Atwood parodies the conventions of romance and of the gothic in an exploration of the damaging effects of mass-produced fantasies for women. Joan Foster is the ultimate escape artist whose identity is made up of a number of different personae. Ostensibly, she is Joan Foster, self-effacing wife of an ineffectually radical husband, but she is also Joan Foster, celebrated author of a volume of feminist poetry. Secretly, she is Louisa K. Delacourt, author of some fifteen costume gothics. Lurking in the background is a freakish circus clown figure, the Fat Lady, a lingering self-conception from her years as an overweight, unloved child. When, under threat of blackmail, Joan's various lives are in danger of converging, she fakes her own drowning and flees to Italy. These personae, however, continue to surface as she completes her latest Harlequinesque offering, *Stalked By Love,* in an ironic and unconscious identification with her heroine's predicament. For all its droll comedy—Atwood even includes parodic autobiographical asides—*Lady Oracle,* like *The Edible Woman,* contains a serious message. Although Joan's recognition of her situation is debatable, the novel demonstrates the debilitating consequences for women of the beauty myth and the conventional romance plot.

Life Before Man is Atwood's bleakest exploration of relations between the sexes and her most atypical novel to date. Although popular with readers, it has been less well-received by critics, partly because of its uncharacteristic pessimism. Set in a claustrophic one-mile radius of metropolitan Toronto, the novel is dominated by a central symbolic locale, the dinosaur exhibit at the Royal Ontario Museum. Atwood's specimens are emotionally isolated characters involved in a love triangle: Elizabeth, whose icy self-control is a product of a dreadful childhood; Nate, her indecisive, politically disillusioned husband; and Lesje, a dreamy palaeontologist who becomes Nate's lover. Covering a precisely dated two-year span and structured by the alternating perceptions of the participants in this banal *ménage à trois, Life Before Man* traces the frustrated interactions of characters who cannot connect. Events in the novel are unrelentingly quotidian; even the dramatic suicide of Elizabeth's lover occurs before the story opens. Lesje's obsession with prehistory focuses the novel's exploration of time and extinction, and the age of the dinosaurs provides a metaphysical conceit for the eyeblink of human existence in cosmic terms. Perhaps, Atwood implies, we are only in the middle of a lengthy evolutionary process; certainly, the changes undergone by the three protagonists are minimal at best. Since they are products of social milieu that is all too recognizable as our own, "life before man" suggests that at this historical moment ours is a condition that is not yet fully human.

Challenged about the apparent hopelessness of *Life Before Man,* Atwood asserts the writer's responsibility to bear witness to the world around her. Moving her examination of power politics into an international arena, Atwood's next two novels, *Bodily Harm* and *The Handmaid's Tale,* translate this commitment into a moral imperative. Here, Atwood outlines the interconnected nature of various oppressions, for the protagonists' personal circumstances are literally or symbolically associated with systemic abuses of power. Initially, both Rennie Wilford in *Bodily Harm* and Offred in *The Handmaid's Tale* are complacently assured of their own political neutrality, in the mistaken belief that violence happens elsewhere to other people. They quickly learn, however, that immunity is a political myth. Rennie becomes embroiled in the after-effects of British and American foreign policy, while Offred exists in a chilling aggregate of historical and contemporary events pushed to their logical extreme: a totalitarian theocracy whose seeds lie in America's Puritan history. Both take up the challenge of documenting their experiences, bearing witness to the brutal realities of the worlds they inhabit. The novels are saved from didacticism, however, by their narrative strength and the ironic observations of the protagonists, who demonstrate that history, especially personal history, is never reducible to simplistic black and white categorizations.

Bodily Harm's protagonist is a journalist of sorts, but her work centres on surfaces rather than depths: Rennie writes trivial lifestyle pieces for city magazines. Her own insulated lifestyle, however, is disrupted by a malignant tumour. After a mastectomy and subsequent abandonment by her lover—a more sinister version of Peter in *The Edible Woman*—she flees to a Caribbean island attempting to escape her feelings of violation and a life that has become too horrifically real. Structured associatively, rather than chronologically, *Bodily Harm* demonstrates Atwood's talent for mining the multilayered possiblilities of metaphorical language as she links sexism with imperialism, cancer of the female body with cancer of the body politic. The fragmented narrative echoes Rennie' own sense of dismemberment. Like the narrator in *Surfacing,* she is alienated from the body that has betrayed her, a divorce that symbolically complements her inability to connect with others. Thus, she refuses to engage with the political situation in her island getaway, preferring instead to remain a professional tourist. When the island is shaken by a political coup, however, Rennie is dragged unwillingly into the thick of it. Witnessing the brutal torture of a defenceless prisoner and the equally viscious beating of her friend and cellmate, Lora, Rennie starts making some personal and political connections. Finally, she realizes the illusory nature of her belief in her own political exemption and of the pressing need for massive involvement. Clearly, Atwood's own involvement with Amnesty International marks this novel, for Rennie's projected response to the Canadian officials who release her and request her silence is a telling resolution: "In any case she is a subversive. She was not one once but now she is. A reporter. She will pick her time; then she will report."

The Handmaid's Tale—Atwood's first sustained prose foray into speculative fiction—struck many as a radical departure, but it is merely a versatile variation in her ongoing exploration of the intersections of sex and power. It is also the novel that best exemplifies her understanding of the political, a term that she defines as "who's allowed to do what to whom, who gets what from whom, who gets away with it and how." Revisioning Orwell's *1984* in feminist terms, Atwood creates the Republic of Gilead, a dystopian projection extrapolated from current trends. Although some critics derided its plausibility, the path of American affairs since the novel's publication makes *The Handmaid's Tale* read like prophetic realism. In Atwood's not-too-distant patriarchal future, New England has been taken over by right-wing Christian fundamentalists whose family values involve the state-enforced reduction of women to economic and biological functions, justified by selective readings of the Old Testament. As one of the few fertile women in a polluted world, the protagonist's role is that of a surrogate mother; she is a handmaid, ritually impregnated by the paternalistic Commander whose name she bears. Offred's "now" is partially explained by the memories that both pain and sustain her in a series of flashbacks to a past very similar to our own present. Then, Offred's chosen absence from history offered freedom; in Gilead this imposed absence constitutes historical erasure. Thus, her account documents her struggle to maintain her identity in a society that refuses to acknowledge it. Prohibited from access to pens or books, Offred's precocious command of language proves central to her self-preservation. And of course Offred is constructing and preserving her identity through the fragmented story that she relates, thus her text is strewn with postmodern allusions to the role of the reader in that process. As a subversive reporter on experience, Offred's plea for an audience becomes all the more pressing in the light of the ironic historical notes that conclude the novel.

With *Cat's Eye* and *The Robber Bride,* Atwood returns to the Toronto setting of her earlier work to explore the vicissitudes of female friendships. In many ways, *Cat's Eye* is also a return to the territory covered in *Surfacing,* not only in its autobiographical echoes, but also in its exploration of time and memory. Both present an artist protagonist reluctant to examine her personal and historical depths, who eventually wrestles with her inner demons in a psychic exorcism, but *Cat's Eye*'s complexities are more subtle and more fully realized. The novel is retrospective both in form and content. A retrospective exhibition brings a grudging Elaine Risley back to the city of her childhood in a return that initiates an imaginative narrative retrospective of her own supposedly forgotten past. A child of the 1940s and 1950s, (like Atwood), her reflections render the Toronto scene in every minute detail; thus, *Cat's Eye* functions not only as memoir, but also as a social document of postwar Canadian culture. The dramatic centre of the novel lies in Elaine's childhood experience of victimization at the hands of her three best friends and in her ambivalent feelings about the chief agent of her feminine indoctrination and torment, Cordelia. As Atwood presents it, the world of little girls is not marked by sugar and spice but rather by the same power politics that characterize adult life. Artis-

tic insight is offered, however, in the paintings that are the key to Elaine's unresolved anxieties and ultimately her attempt to master her past in a visionary blend of revenge and forgiveness, love and loss. *Cat's Eye* is perhaps Atwood's most profound achievement for here she, like her protagonist, transforms the scattered details of a life into a unified work of art.

If *Cat's Eye* ventures into the uncharted terrain of malicious little girls, then Atwood's most recent novel, *The Robber Bride,* plumbs the depths of female sexual competitiveness. Here, Atwood braids the contrasting histories and perceptions of three battle-scarred "veterans"—Charis, Tony and Roz—whose weaknesses are exploited by a machiavellian seductress. In a comic gender inversion of Grimm's tale, the titular villain is Zenia, a protean *femme fatale* who invades the protagonists' lives only to make off with the booty—their men. Indeed, warfare is the dominant motif, for Zenia's sexual terrorism is played out against a backdrop of past and present military conflict. As in *Bodily Harm,* the personal and the political are intricately intermingled. *The Robber Bride* also develops Atwood's characteristic concern with formative influences and female identity: Zenia, like Cordelia in *Cat's Eye,* functions not only as an atagonist, but also as a *Doppelgänger* for each of the characters. Although each woman's point of view is symmetrically apportioned, it is Tony—the text's literal and figurative historian—whose perspective frames the novel. Musing on the ambiguous promise of History's explanatory power and its relation to the inexplicability of Zenia, it is she who wonders whether the evil that Zenia represents may not also be a part of us. With Tony's concluding question, Atwood reiterates the central tenet of her moral vision: our human potential to be both a victim and victimizer and our responsibility to be neither.

—Jackie Buxton

AUCHINCLOSS, Louis (Stanton)

Nationality: American. **Born:** Lawrence, New York, 27 September 1917. **Education:** Groton School, Massachusetts, graduated 1935; Yale University, New Haven, Connecticut, 1935-38; University of Virginia Law School, Charlottesville, LL.B. 1941; admitted to the New York bar, 1941. **Military Service:** Served in the United States Naval Reserve, 1941-45: Lieutenant. **Family:** Married Adele Lawrence in 1957; three sons. **Career:** Associate lawyer, Sullivan and Cromwell, New York, 1941-51; associate, 1954-58, and partner, 1958-86, Hawkins Delafield and Wood, New York. Since 1966 president of the Museum of the City of New York. Trustee, Josiah Macy Jr. Foundation, New York; former member of the Executive Committee, Association of the Bar of New York City. **Awards:** New York State Governor's award, 1985. D.Litt.: New York University, 1974; Pace College, New York, 1979; University of the South, Sewanee, Tennessee, 1986. **Member:** American Academy. **Agent:** Curtis Brown, 10 Astor Place, New York, New York 10003. **Address:** 1111 Park Avenue, New York, New York 10128, U.S.A.

PUBLICATIONS

Novels

The Indifferent Children (as Andrew Lee). New York, Prentice Hall, 1947.

Sybil. Boston, Houghton Mifflin, 1951; London, Gollancz, 1952.

A Law for the Lion. Boston, Houghton Mifflin, and London, Gollancz, 1953.

The Great World and Timothy Colt. Boston, Houghton Mifflin, 1956; London, Gollancz, 1957.

Venus in Sparta. Boston, Houghton Mifflin, and London, Gollancz, 1958.

Pursuit of the Prodigal. Boston, Houghton Mifflin, 1959; London, Gollancz, 1960.

The House of Five Talents. Boston, Houghton Mifflin, 1960; London, Gollancz, 1961.

Portrait in Brownstone. Boston, Houghton Mifflin, and London, Gollancz, 1962.

The Rector of Justin. Boston, Houghton Mifflin, 1964; London, Gollancz, 1965.

The Embezzler. Boston, Houghton Mifflin, and London, Gollancz 1966.

A World of Profit. Boston, Houghton Mifflin, 1968; London, Gollancz, 1969.

I Come as a Thief. Boston, Houghton Mifflin, 1972; London, Weidenfeld and Nicolson, 1973.

The Partners. Boston, Houghton Mifflin, and London, Weidenfeld and Nicolson, 1974.

The Winthrop Covenant. Boston, Houghton Mifflin, and London, Weidenfeld and Nicolson, 1976.

The Dark Lady. Boston, Houghton Mifflin, and London, Weidenfeld and Nicolson, 1977.

The Country Cousin. Boston, Houghton Mifflin, and London, Weidenfeld and Nicolson, 1978.

The House of the Prophet. Boston, Houghton Mifflin, and London, Weidenfeld and Nicolson, 1980.

The Cat and the King. Boston, Houghton Mifflin, and London, Weidenfeld and Nicolson, 1981.

Watchfires. Boston, Houghton Mifflin, and London, Weidenfeld and Nicolson, 1982.

Exit Lady Masham. Boston, Houghton Mifflin, 1983; London, Weidenfeld and Nicolson, 1984.

The Book Class. Boston, Houghton Mifflin, and London, Weidenfeld and Nicolson, 1984.

Honorable Men. Boston, Houghton Mifflin, 1985; London, Weidenfeld and Nicolson, 1986.

Diary of a Yuppie. Boston, Houghton Mifflin, 1986; London, Weidenfeld and Nicolson, 1987.

The Golden Calves. Boston, Houghton Mifflin, 1988; London, Weidenfeld and Nicolson, 1989.

Fellow Passengers: A Novel in Portraits. Boston, Houghton Mifflin, 1989; London, Constable, 1990.

The Lady of Situations. Boston, Houghton Mifflin, 1990; London, Constable, 1991.

Tales of Yesteryear. Boston, Houghton Mifflin, 1994.

Short Stories

The Injustice Collectors. Boston, Houghton Mifflin, 1950; London, Gollancz, 1951.

The Romantic Egoists: A Reflection in Eight Minutes. Boston, Houghton Mifflin, and London, Gollancz, 1954.

Powers of Attorney. Boston, Houghton Mifflin, and London, Gollancz, 1963.

Tales of Manhattan. Boston, Houghton Mifflin, and London, Gollancz, 1967.

Second Chance. Boston, Houghton Mifflin, 1970; London, Gollancz, 1971.

Narcissa and Other Fables. Boston, Houghton Mifflin, 1983.

Skinny Island: More Tales of Manhattan. Boston, Houghton Mifflin, 1987; London, Weidenfeld and Nicolson, 1988.

False Gods. Boston, Houghton Mifflin, 1992; London, Constable, 1993.

Three Lives. Boston, Houghton Mifflin, 1993; London, Constable, 1994.

The Collected Short Stories of Louis Auchincloss. Boston, Houghton Mifflin, 1994.

Play

The Club Bedroom (produced New York, 1967).

Other

Edith Wharton. Minneapolis, University of Minnesota Press, 1961.

Reflections of a Jacobite. Boston, Houghton Mifflin, 1961; London, Gollancz, 1962.

Ellen Glasgow. Minneapolis, University of Minnesota Press, 1964.

Pioneers and Caretakers: A Study of 9 American Women Novelists. Minneapolis, University of Minnesota Press, 1965; London, Oxford University Press, 1966.

Motiveless Malignity (on Shakespeare). Boston, Houghton Mifflin, 1969; London, Gollancz, 1970.

Henry Adams. Minneapolis, University of Minnesota Press, 1971.

Edith Wharton: A Woman in Her Time. New York, Viking Press, 1971; London, Joseph, 1972.

Richelieu. New York, Viking Press, 1972; London, Joseph, 1973.

A Writer's Capital (autobiography). Minneapolis, University of Minnesota Press, 1974.

Reading Henry James. Minneapolis, University of Minnesota Press, 1975.

Persons of Consequence: Queen Victoria and Her Circle. New York, Random House, and London, Weidenfeld and Nicolson, 1979.

Life, Law, and Letters: Essays and Sketches. Boston, Houghton Mifflin, 1979; London, Weidenfeld and Nicolson, 1980.

Three "Perfect Novels" and What They Have in Common. Bloomfield Hills, Michigan, Bruccoli Clark, 1981.

Unseen Versailles. New York, Doubleday, 1981.

False Dawn: Women in the Age of the Sun King. New York, Doubleday, 1984.

The Vanderbilt Era: Profiles of a Gilded Age. New York, Scribner, 1989.

J.P. Morgan: The Financier as Collector. New York, Abrams, 1990.

Love Without Wings: Some Friendships in Literature and Politics. Boston, Houghton Mifflin, 1991.

Deborah Turbeville's Newport Remembered: A Photographic Portrait of a Gilded Past. New York, Abrams, 1994.

The Style's the Man: Reflections on Proust, Fitzgerald, Wharton, Vidal, and Others. New York, Scribner, 1994.

Editor, *An Edith Wharton Reader.* New York, Scribner, 1965.

Editor, *The Warden, and Barchester Towers,* by Trollope. Boston, Houghton Mifflin, 1966.

Editor, *Fables of Wit and Elegance.* New York, Scribner, 1975.

Editor, *Maverick in Mauve: The Diary of a Turn-of-the-Century Aristocrat,* by Florence Adele Sloane. New York, Doubleday, 1983.

Editor, *The Hone and Strong Diaries of Old Manhattan.* New York, Abbeville Press, 1989.

*

Bibliography: *Louis Auchincloss and His Critics: A Bibliographical Record* by Jackson R. Bryer, Boston, Hall, 1977.

Manuscript Collection: University of Virginia, Charlottesville.

Critical Studies: *The Novel of Manners in America* by James W. Tuttleton, Chapel Hill, University of North Carolina Press, 1972; *Louis Auchincloss* by Christopher C. Dahl, New York, Ungar, 1986; *Louis Auchincloss: The Growth of a Novelist* by Vincent Piket, Nijmegen, Netherlands, European University Press, 1989, New York, St. Martin's Press, and London, Macmillan, 1991; *Louis Auchincloss: A Writer's Life* by Carol W. Gelderman, New York, Crown, 1993.

Louis Auchincloss comments:

(1972) I do not think in general that authors are very illuminating on their own work, but in view of the harshness of recent (1970) reviewers, I should like to quote from a letter of Edith Wharton in my collection. It was written when she was 63, ten years older than I now am, but the mood is relevant. She is speaking of critics who have disliked her last novel: "You will wonder that the priestess of the life of reason should take such things to heart, and I wonder too. I never have minded before, but as my work reaches its close, I feel so sure that it is either nothing or far more than they know. And I wonder, a little desolately, which." Mrs. Wharton's work was far from its close, and I hope mine may be!

*   *   *

Louis Auchincloss is among the few dedicated novelists of manners at work in contemporary America. He is a successor to Edith Wharton as a chronicler of the New York aristocracy. In this role he necessarily imbues his novels with an elegiac tone as he observes the passing beauties of the city and the fading power of the white Anglo-Saxon Protestants of old family and old money who can no longer sustain their position of dominance in the society or their aristocratic ideals. His principal subject is thus the manners and morals, the money and marriages, the families and houses, the schools and games, the language and arts of the New York aristocracy as he traces its rise, observes its present crisis, and meditates its possible fall and disappearance. The point of vantage from which he often observes the aristocracy is that of the lawyer who serves and frequently belongs to this class.

The idea of good family stands in an uneasy relation to money in Auchincloss's fiction. Auchincloss dramatizes the dilemma of the American aristocracy by showing that it is necessary to possess money to belong to this class but fatal to one's standing within the class to pursue money. People who have connections with those who are still in trade cannot themselves fully qualify as gentlemen, as the opportunistic Mr. Dale in *The Great World and Timothy Colt* shows. On the other hand, Auchincloss is clearly critical of those aristocrats like Bertie Millinder or Percy Prime who do nothing constructive and are engaged simply in the spending of money. Auchincloss recognizes that the family is the most important of aristocratic institutions and that its place in its class is guaranteed by the conservation of its resources. This task of preserving the

family wealth falls to the lawyers, and his fiction is rich in the complexities, both moral and financial, of fiduciary responsibility; *Venus in Sparta* is a novel in point. The paradox that Auchincloss reveals but does not seem sufficiently to exploit is that the conservative impulse of the aristocracy, which emphasizes the past, is concerned ultimately with posterity, which of course emphasizes the future.

Auchincloss does, however, fully exploit the conflict between the marriage arranged for the good of the family, often by strong women, and romantic or sexual impulses that are destructive of purely social goals, as *Portrait in Brownstone* illustrates. Sex and love are enemies to the organicism of conservative societies, in which the will of the individual is vested in the whole. Auchincloss observes the workings of this organic notion in the structure of family and marriage as well as in institutions like the school and the club where a consensus judgment about value and behavior is formulated and handed down. Such institutions preserve a way of life and protect those who live by it from those on the outside who do not. *The Rector of Justin* is the most obvious of Auchincloss's novels to deal with an institution, or with a man as an institution, that performs this function.

Auchincloss's fiction does more than present us with a mere record of the institutions that support the American aristocracy. The dramatic interest in his novels and whatever larger importance may be accorded them lies in his recognition that the entire class is in jeopardy and that individual aristocrats are often failures. The closed, unitary life of the aristocracy is sometimes threatened by outsiders—Jews, for example, as in *The Dark Lady* and *The House of the Prophet*—who must be repelled or at worst absorbed. Sometimes Auchincloss sees problems arising within the context of aristocracy itself, as when individual will or desire comes in conflict with the organicism; perhaps Rees Parmalee, in *Pursuit of the Prodigal,* makes the most significant rebellion of all Auchincloss's characters, but he is rejecting a decadent aristocracy and not aristocracy itself. Auchincloss is severely critical of the idea of the gentleman when it is corrupted by allegiance to superficial qualities, like Guy Prime's capacity to hold his liquor or to behave with virile cordiality in *The Embezzler.* But the real failures are those aristocrats who suffer, as so many of Auchincloss's male characters do, from a sense of inadequacy and insecurity that leads them to self-destructiveness. They are not strong and tough-fibered, as so many of the women are; they seem too fastidious and over-civilized, and they are failing the idea of society and their class. In this way, and in others, Auchincloss regretfully chronicles the passing of the aristocracy, which cannot sustain its own ideals in the contemporary world: *A World of Profit* is the most explicit recognition of this failure.

Auchincloss has made his record of the New York aristocracy in a style which is clear and simple, occasionally elegant and brilliant, and sometimes self-consciously allusive. He has a gift for comedy of manners, which he has not sufficiently cultivated, and a fine model in Oscar Wilde. Other influences upon him include Edith Wharton, in ways already mentioned; Henry James, from whom he learned the manipulation of point of view, and the faculty of endowing things, art objects for example, with meaning; and St. Simon, a memorialist who did for the French court what Auchincloss wishes to do for Knickerbocker New York. Yet among his faults as a novelist, especially evident because of the particular genre he has chosen, is a failure to give the reader a richness of detail; he does well with home furnishings but is far less successful with the details of institutions. Furthermore, he sometimes loses control of his novels and permits action to overwhelm theme. The most serious criticism to be made of his work is that while he does indeed pose moral dilemmas for his characters, he too easily resolves their problems for them. He does not sufficiently convey a sense of the bitter cost of honesty or courage or moral superiority, a continuing difficulty for him, as *The Country Cousin* demonstrates.

This same ethical conflict is seen in *Three Lives,* which, like Gertrude Stein's work of the same title, consists of three novellas disclosing the lives of three characters from the same stratum of society. Being Auchincloss rather than Stein, his characters are three New Yorkers born to wealth around the turn of the century. In *Tales of Yesteryear,* we see as well an assortment of characters of wealth and privilege who suffer a hardening of the heart as a result of their station in society. In several tales, members of the older generation look back over their lives with quiet regret, suggesting that wealth and power do not bring contentment. From this collection come some of the stories in Auchincloss's fiftieth book, *The Collected Stories of Louis Auchincloss.* Here readers find a full range of Auchincloss, from one of his earliest stories, the perfectly composed "Maud," to his most recent "They That Have the Power to Hurt."

He has given us, on balance, a full enough record of upper-class life in New York, but he has fallen short of the most penetrating and meaningful kinds of social insight that the best of the novelists of manners offer.

—Chester E. Eisinger, updated by Sandra Ray

AUSTER, Paul

Nationality: American. **Born:** Newark, New Jersey, 3 February 1947. **Education:** Columbia University, New York, B.A. 1969, M.A. 1970. **Family:** Married 1) Lydia Davis in 1974; 2) Siri Hustvedt in 1981; two children. **Career:** Has had a variety of jobs, including merchant seaman, census taker, and tutor; creative writing teacher, Princeton University, New Jersey, 1986-90. **Awards:** Ingram Merrill Foundation grant, for poetry, 1975, 1982; PEN Translation Center grant, 1977; National Endowment for the Arts fellowship for poetry, 1979, and for creative writing, 1985. **Address:** c/o Viking, 375 Hudson Street, New York, New York 10014, U.S.A.

PUBLICATIONS

Novels

Squeeze Play (as Paul Benjamin). London, Alpha-Omega, 1982; New York, Avon, 1984.
The New York Trilogy. London, Faber, 1987; New York, Penguin, 1990.
    City of Glass. Los Angeles, Sun and Moon Press, 1985.
    Ghosts. Los Angeles, Sun and Moon Press, 1986.
    The Locked Room. Los Angeles, Sun and Moon Press, 1987.
In the Country of Last Things. New York, Viking, 1987; London, Faber, 1988.
Moon Palace. New York, Viking, 1989; London, Faber, 1990.
The Music of Chance. New York, Viking, 1990; London, Faber, 1991.
Leviathan. New York, Viking, and London, Faber, 1992.
Mr. Vertigo. New York, Viking, and London, Faber, 1994.

Uncollected Short Story

"Auggie Wren's Christmas Story," in *New York Times,* 25 December 1990.

Play

Eclipse (produced New York, 1977).

Poetry

Unearth: Poems 1970-72. Weston, Connecticut, Living Hand, 1974.
Wall Writing: Poems 1971-75. Berkeley, California, Figures, 1976.
Fragments from Cold. New York, Parenthèse, 1977.
Facing the Music. New York, Station Hill, 1980.
Disappearances. New York, Overlook Press, 1988.

Other

White Spaces. New York, Station Hill, 1980.
The Art of Hunger and Other Essays. London, Menard Press, 1982.
The Invention of Solitude. New York, Sun, 1982; London, Faber, 1988.
Ground Work: Selected Poems and Essays 1970-1979. London, Faber, 1990.
Smoke and Blue in the Face: Two Films. New York, Hyperion, 1995.

Editor, *The Random House Book of Twentieth-Century French Poetry.* London, Random House, 1982; New York, Vintage, 1984.
Editor and translator, *The Notebooks of Joseph Joubert: A Selection.* San Francisco, North Point Press, 1983.

Translator, *A Little Anthology of Surrealist Poems.* New York, Siamese Banana Press, 1972.
Translator, *Fits and Starts: Selected Poems of Jacques Dupin.* Weston, Connecticut, Living Hand, 1974.
Translator, with Lydia Davis, *Arabs and Israelis: A Dialogue,* by Saul Friedlander and Mahmoud Hussein. New York, Holmes and Meier, 1975.
Translator, *The Uninhabited: Selected Poems of André de Bouchet.* Weston, Connecticut, Living Hand, 1976.
Translator, with Lydia Davis, *Jean-Paul Sartre: Life Situations.* New York, Pantheon, 1977; as *Sartre in the Seventies: Interviews and Essays,* London, Deutsch, 1978.
Translator, with Lydia Davis, *China: The People's Republic 1949-76,* by Jean Chesneaux. New York, Pantheon, 1979.
Translator, with Françoise Le Barbier and Marie-Claire Bergère, *China from the 1911 Revolution to Liberation.* New York, Pantheon, 1979.
Translator, *A Tomb for Anatole,* by Stéphane Mallarmé. San Francisco, North Point Press, 1983.
Translator, *Vicious Circles,* by Maurice Blanchot. New York, Station Hill, 1985.
Translator, *On the High Wire,* by Philippe Petit. New York, Random House, 1985.
Translator, with Margit Rowell, *Joan Miró: Selected Writings.* Boston, Hall, 1986.

*   *   *

Paul Auster has frequently been called a "postmodern" novelist, partly because, one suspects, critics don't know what else to call a writer whose works include metaphysical detective stories, an anti-utopian fantasy, an extravagant *Bildungsroman,* and an ambiguous parable of fate and chance. To the extent that the term denotes an ironic stance towards language and its uses, Auster is indeed postmodern. Without surrendering this irony or foregoing the advantage of self-conscious narration, Auster has moved to a greater expansiveness of form and content. His more recent novels have not been embarrassed to ask big questions about the possibility of self-knowledge and personal redemption and they have conceded to the reader the pleasures, not unmediated, of character and story.

Such pleasures are rather scant in *The New York Trilogy,* the epistemological mystery novels that established Auster's reputation. What entertainment they provide is almost wholly cerebral: the delectation of intellectual puzzles that have little or no relation to a reality beyond the texts themselves. *City of Glass,* the first volume, is about a mystery novelist named Quinn whose attempt to live the life of the kind of hardened gumshoe he writes about ends in a tragic muddle. Not the least of the novel's ontological jokes is that the detective Quinn is mistaken for is named Paul Auster. Auster himself, or a simulacrum of him, appears in a scene in which the increasingly desperate Quinn goes to him for advice. Interrupted while composing an essay on the vanishing narrators of *Don Quixote,* Auster is unable to help; he's a writer, not a private investigator. This Paul Auster, however, is not the author of *City of Glass.* The "actual" author, it turns out, is a former friend of Auster's who heard the story from him and is convinced that Auster has "behaved badly throughout."

Ghosts extends the paradoxes about identity and fictive creation into a world of Beckett-like abstraction and austerity. White hires Blue to watch Black who does little but write and watch back: "Little does Blue know, of course, that the case will go on for years." Not even violence can finally break this stasis, and as the narrator says at the end, "we know nothing."

A reader may get the feeling that *The New York Trilogy* is too clever for its own good, that Auster engages knotty intellectual issues partly to evade more troubling emotional ones. *The Locked Room,* the concluding volume, is nothing if not clever, yet it reveals a new openness in Auster's sensibility. The Paul Auster-like narrator is a young writer of promise whose life is taken over by the appearance, or disappearance, of his *doppelgänger* Fanshawe, his best friend from his youth. Fanshawe is presumed dead but has left his manuscripts in the care of the narrator, who sees them through publication and to a literary acclaim far surpassing that of his own work. As Fanshawe's appointed biographer, the narrator discovers, in his obsessive investigation into the mystery of his friend's life, as much about himself as about Fanshawe, for the lines separating their two identities are, of course, convergent. *The Locked Room* may be no more than a game, but the stakes, which do not preclude the anguish that attends existential doubts about one's identity, are considerably higher than those in *City of Glass* and *Ghosts.*

The presence of a controlling author is no longer insisted upon in *In the Country of Last Things,* a nightmarish tale of total social breakdown in an unnamed city-state that could be New York some years in the future. This does not mean that Auster has resolved his doubts about the problematic relationship of language to real-

ity. The narrator, a young woman named Anna Blume comes to the city in search of a lost brother only to be trapped in its round of violence, despair, and physical and spiritual poverty, keeps a journal (the text of the novel) full of reflections on the inadequacy of words to describe a world where people scavenge viciously for garbage or plot their own suicides. Yet Anna, her lover and her two remaining friends retain their decency if not their dignity. The truly lost, Auster suggests, may be those who have given up on language itself.

Language acquires a renewed immediacy and momentum in *Moon Palace,* Auster's most entertaining novel, and his best. Its immensely complicated plot concerns the adventures of Marco Stanley Fogg, an orphan in the best Dickensian tradition, whose modest inheritance runs out in his senior year at Columbia University, consigning him, for reasons obscure even to himself, to a season of homelessness and near starvation in Central Park. Just before the weather turns cold he is rescued by his former college roommate and a young Chinese woman who becomes the love of his life. Soon thereafter he takes a job as an amanuensis to an eccentric and irascible old cripple whose wild stories of his youth as a painter and subsequent adventures in the old west Marco faithfully transcribes. Finally Marco meets up with the old man's abandoned son, now a middle-aged and obese professor of history at a succession of second-rate colleges. In the end Marco loses everything: father, father-figure, his loving girlfriend and their child, and yet his excruciating education has not been wasted. The novel ends with Marco watching the moon rise from a California beach and thinking, "This is where I start . . . this is where my life begins."

Auster's accustomed self-referentiality and playing up of literary patterns and allusions once again reveal the artifice that underlies any fictive representation of reality, but the emphasis in *Moon Palace* is on the reality, not the artifice. The more improbable the events described, the more bizarre the cast of characters, the more we believe. Marco wonders if old Thomas Effing's outlandish reminiscences can possibly be true, but they're as true as they need to be: true to Effing's private wounds and world, true to the chaotic social reality of America in the 20th century, true to the novel's themes of personal loss and recovery, of the endless invention of the self.

What *The Music of Chance* is "about" is rather less clear. As fluidly written as *Moon Palace,* it begins as a fairly straightforward account of the squandering of a family inheritance by a 35-year-old ex-fireman named Jim Nashe and shifts, about half-way through, into a Kafka-like parable in which Nashe and a young gambler named Jack Pozzi are entrapped on the estate of a pair of rich and sinister eccentrics and forced to build a huge wall from the rubble of a castle disassembled and shipped overseas from Ireland. Nashe grows in moral stature as his difficulties increase, but the chances that determine his fate are ordained by the author who ends the novel with a fatal car crash that is at once wholly arbitrary and perfectly logical. Although Auster's intelligence, humor, and inventiveness are evident throughout, the novel's realist and allegorical tendencies tend to work against each other. *The Music of Chance* remains rather opaque, but it also demonstrates Auster's engagement with issues much larger than those that concerned the hermetic fabulist of *The New York Trilogy.*

—Stephen Akey

B

BAIL, Murray

Nationality: Australian. **Born:** Adelaide, South Australia, 22 September 1941. **Education:** Norwood Technical High School, Adelaide. **Family:** Married Margaret Wordsworth in 1965. **Career:** Lived in India, 1968-70, and in England and Europe, 1970-74. Member of the Council, Australian National Gallery, Canberra, 1976-81. **Awards:** *The Age* Book of the Year award, 1980; National Book Council award, 1980; Victorian Premier's award, 1988. **Address:** c/o Faber and Faber, Inc., 50 Cross St., Winchester, Massachusetts 01890, U.S.A.

PUBLICATIONS

Novels

Homesickness. Melbourne, Macmillan, 1980; London, Faber, 1986.
Holden's Performance. London, Faber, 1987.

Short Stories

Contemporary Portraits and Other Stories. St. Lucia, University of Queensland Press, 1975; as *The Drover's Wife,* London, Faber, 1986.

Uncollected Short Stories

"Healing," in *New Yorker,* 16 April 1979.
"Home Ownership," In *Winter's Tales 27,* edited by Edward Leeson. London, Macmillan, 1981; New York, St. Martin's Press, 1982.

Other

Ian Fairweather. Sydney, Bay, 1981.
Longhand: A Writer's Notebook. Fitzroy, Victoria, McPhee Gribble, 1989.

Editor, *The Faber Book of Contemporary Australian Short Stories.* London, Faber, 1988.

*   *   *

Murray Bail was, with Peter Carey and Frank Moorhouse, one of the chief innovators in the tradition of the Australian short story during the early and mid-1970s. Since then he has gone on to establish a reputation as a distinctive and original novelist as well. Bail's first book was a collection of short stories, *Contemporary Portraits and Other Stories,* in which the first of many tricks is that there is no story called "Contemporary Portraits." His interest in the relationship between language and reality is present in all the stories and especially in "Zoellner's Definition" and the final story, "A, B, C, D, E, F, G, H, I, J, K, L, M, N, O, P, Q, R, S, T, U, V, W, X, Y, Z." The opening and longest story, "Heubler," concerns a man who decides to "photographically document . . . the existence of everyone alive." The best known story is "The Drover's Wife" in which Bail takes Henry Lawson's classic tale and rewrites it. His version is a monologue by the deserted drover himself, based on the famous painting by Russell Drysdale. The story "Portrait of Electricity" contains the embryo out of which Bail's first novel *Homesickness* grows. A great man is defined in terms of the various examples and evidence of his existence contained in a museum devoted to him, these beginning with an ashtray and culminating in an example of his excrement. It displays the same strange mixture of surrealist fantasy and broad satire of Australian life that characterizes all of Bail's work.

The motif of the museum is taken up in *Homesickness,* a funny, inventive, intelligent novel, one so original in conception and dense and compressed in execution that it is hard to do justice to. It reveals what Bail's second novel *Holden's Performance* confirms—that his obsession is with mythologizing what he sees as so far an unmythologized and therefore unpossessed country. One of the characters, Louisa Hoffman, says, "Even before we travel we're wandering in circles. There isn't much we understand. I should say, there isn't much we believe in. We have rather empty feelings. I think we even find love difficult. And when we travel we demand even the confusions to be simple." The novel is a dramatization of that insight. A group of travelers from Australia set out on a tour of the world. As they do so they shift about and continually form new groups, new liaisons. At the same time they encounter a series of museums, each of which seems a kind of paradigm of the culture which it is designed to commemorate.

The museum in Quito, Ecuador, for instance, is a Museum of Handicrafts. Many of the artifacts are British anachronisms, symbolic of the occupation of the country in the 19th century. In New York they see a re-enacted mugging in Central Park. In London there is a Museum of Lost and Found Objects: "The collection of lost luggage alone offered a valuable insight into changing attitudes, the gradual democratization of travel." There are many internal and self-referential jokes, witty aphorisms, characters with significant names. One joke concerns a little African boy whose name is Oxford University Press and who, when he grows up, wants to be a tourist. Throughout all the wit and inventiveness emerge Bail's abiding concerns, which are strikingly consistent in his three works of fiction. His interest in nationality is but part of his larger interest in identity, which is central to the novel's motifs of tourism, museums, homesickness ("They could hear Sasha being homesick in the basin") and national differences: at one stage the party go into a series of clichés about national identity that goes on for three pages. And in turn concern with identity merges into concern with language and the relationship between language and experience.

Holden's Performance is again an attempt to mythologize and therefore possess Australia. As the controlling metaphor for the previous novel was that of Australians circling the world looking for themselves and their home, so in this it is the most famous car Australia has produced: the title refers to both "Australia's own car" and the protagonist, Holden Shadbolt. The book covers his career from his birth in 1932 to the mid-1960s when he departs for America. The motif of the car is carried skillfully through to the final page of the novel, which is a summary of Holden himself:

Shadbolt, Holden.
Age 34.
Single.
Uncomplicated (relatively, in a sense).
Ability to idle all day. Slight overheating.
Stand for hours in the sun. No complaints.
Can go all day on a meat pie.
Strong body.
Style: *model Australian, no frills.*
Colour: *light tan. Khaki eyes.*
Leanings left or right: *nil.*
Size nines.
Smoking: *beginning.*
Other comments: *responsive to instructions in all weathers, all conditions. Predictable, matter-of-fact.*

Bail makes it clear in all sorts of ways that in documenting Holden he is documenting Australia from the 1930s and before that to the mid-1960s and the conclusion of the reign of the Prime Minister R.G. Amen.

At one point in the narrative we are told of Hoadley, ambassador to Egypt, that "More than most ambassadors it seems he had this obsession for building bridges—between men and city, city and country, words and action, the imagination and fact." The same is true of the author. The preoccupation with language itself is deeply evident. Bail says at one point that there is a "solidarity of words and objects" and this is one thing he tries to show. Holden literally eats words—newsprint. "What did Holden's early growth consist of? Words, words: a flawed grey-and-white view of the world." His health suffers as a result of the many errors in the newspaper he digests. *Holden's Performance* is a brilliantly inventive work, though rather less sure of its direction than Bail's first novel.

—Laurie Clancy

BAILEY, Paul

Nationality: British. **Born:** Peter Harry Bailey in Battersea, London, 16 February 1937. **Education:** Sir Walter St. John's School, London, 1948-53; Central School of Speech and Drama, London, 1953-56. **Career:** Actor, 1956-63. Literary Fellow, University of Newcastle-upon-Tyne and University of Durham, 1972-74; visiting lecturer, North Dakota State University, Fargo, 1977-79. **Awards:** Maugham award, 1968; Arts Council award, 1968; Authors' Club award, 1970; E.M. Forster Award (U.S.A.), 1974; Bicentennial Arts fellowship, 1976; Orwell Memorial prize, for essay, 1978. Fellow, Royal Society of Literature, 1982. **Address:** 79 Davisville Road, London W12 9SH, England.

Publications

Novels

At the Jerusalem. London, Cape, and New York, Atheneum, 1967.
Trespasses. London, Cape, 1970; New York, Harper, 1971.
A Distant Likeness. London, Cape, 1973.
Peter Smart's Confessions. London, Cape, 1977.

Old Soldiers. London, Cape, 1980.
Gabriel's Lament. London, Cape, 1986; New York, Viking, 1987.
Sugar Cane. London, Bloomsbury, 1993.

Plays

A Worthy Guest (produced Newcastle-upon-Tyne, 1973; London, 1974).
Alice (produced Newcastle-upon-Tyne, 1975).
Crime and Punishment, adaptation of a novel by Dostoevsky (produced Manchester, 1978).

Radio Play: *At Cousin Harry's,* 1964.

Television Play: *We Think the World of You,* with Tristram Powell, 1980.

Other

An English Madam: The Life and Work of Cynthia Payne. London, Cape, 1982.
An Immaculate Mistake: Scenes from Childhood and Beyond (autobiography). London, Bloomsbury, 1990; New York, Dutton, 1992.

*

Theatrical Activities:
Actor: **Plays**—roles in *The Sport of My Mad Mother* by Ann Jellicoe, London, 1958; *Epitaph for George Dillon* by John Osborne and Anthony Creighton, London, 1958; and other plays.

Paul Bailey comments:
(1991) I write novels for many reasons, some of which I have probably never consciously thought of. I don't like absolute moral judgments, the "placing" of people into types—I'm both delighted and appalled by the mysteriousness of my fellow creatures. I enjoy "being" other people when I write, and the novels I admire most respect the uniqueness of other human beings. I like to think I show my characters respect and that I don't sit in judgment on them. This is what, in my small way, I am striving for—to capture, in a shaped and controlled form, something of the mystery of life. I am writing, too, to expand and stimulate my own mind. I hope I will have the courage to be more ambitious, bolder and braver in my search for the ultimately unknowable, with each book I write.

*   *   *

Paul Bailey's first novel, *At the Jerusalem,* has been rightly acknowledged as one of the outstanding literary debuts of the 1960's in England, and among the reasons why it attracted attention when it appeared was that it departed so markedly from our usual expectations of first novels—autobiographies in thin disguise. What came as a surprise was to find a first novel by a young man in his twenties about old age and its attendant tribulations. Yet Bailey's achievement did not, of course, lie in merely writing about the elderly and their problems, but in doing so with such sympathetic understanding and sensitivity while maintaining sufficient detachment and objectivity to avoid any trace of sentimentality. There is no falsification, no whimsy, none of that awkwardness and emotional uncertainty that tend to afflict writers when dealing with the old. Bailey's depiction of an old people's home, the Jerusalem of the title, and especially of the central character, Mrs. Gadny, whose fairly rapid decline after entering the home is charted, carries complete conviction. Quiet and unpretentious as *At the Jerusalem* is, it is also an extraordinary feat of the imagination.

In retrospect, we can now see that *At the Jerusalem* introduced many of the themes and preoccupations which have come to be integral components of the Bailey world: isolation, suffering, death, suicide, old age, the pain of loss, psychological collapse, role-playing in an attempt to bear or ward off reality. If *At the Jerusalem* is mainly a study of disintegration—Mrs. Gadny's fate is to be taken to a mental hospital—Bailey's second novel, *Trespasses,* partly set in a mental hospital, is about an attempt at reintegration after personal breakdown and fragmentation. Surprisingly for a Bailey novel, *Trespasses* ends on a note of muted optimism, but much of the book is pervaded by anguish, leading to suicide in the case of one character and mental collapse in the case of another. Technically, *Trespasses* is much more adventurous work than the fairly orthodox and straightforward *At the Jerusalem.* Some sections of the novel are collages of short, fragmented monologues, appropriate enough for the subject but demanding considerable concentration and imaginative involvement on the part of the reader, who has to construct the total picture from the pieces like a jig-saw puzzle. This intricate cross-cutting between different minds is a most economical way of revealing characters and events; narrated in a conventional way, the novel would be very much longer and far less intense than it is, and the technique justifies itself as the pieces finally cohere into a highly organized pattern.

Bailey's pursuit of poetic concentration, a concomitant of his increasing technical sophistication and artistic discipline, is taken a stage further in his third novel, *A Distant Likeness.* Like *Trespasses,* the novel is fragmented and elliptical so that the reader again has to work hard to piece the information together. Bailey is almost as sparing of words as Webern was of musical notes. The book, about a policeman in charge of a murder investigation, is another study in disintegration, resulting in this case from the policeman's inner contradictions. Many critics have felt the "distant likeness" to be between the policeman and the murderer, but the sentence from Simone Weil's *Notebooks* that provides the novel with its title, "Privation is a distant likeness of death," is perhaps the key to the interpretation of this complex book. Bailey's subject is privation, and it appears in various forms. *A Distant Likeness* has been compared to *Crime and Punishment,* but Bailey's novel is not so much like Dostoevsky as a distillation of a super-refined Dostoevskian essence. The extreme compression can be likened to T.S. Eliot's miniaturization of epic form in *The Waste Land,* a parallel that suggests itself because of similarities between the imagery of the two works.

After the minimalist austerity and purity, as well as human bleakness, of *A Distant Likeness,* Bailey altered course somewhat, producing a much more relaxed novel in a comic, even picaresque, vein, *Peter Smart's Confessions.* Here the Dickensian side of his talent, evident but not prominent in his earlier books, is given freer rein, although he maintains his usual technical and stylistic control, never wasting words. *Peter Smart's Confessions* is a kind of *Bildungsroman,* dealing with the development of a sensitive and artistic boy surrounded by philistinism and other forms of paralyzing opposition. Yet much of the interest lies in the gallery of eccentrics and extraordinary characters with whom Peter comes into contact rather than in Peter himself. The later stages of the novel are more desultory and less subtle than the brilliant first half, but the novel as a whole opened up new possibilities for Bailey.

Old Soldiers is his most completely satisfying novel since *At the Jerusalem,* and is also about old age, the two main characters being men in their seventies with unforgettable memories of World War I—hence the title. Technically, the novel is not as "difficult" as *Trespasses* or *A Distant Likeness,* but it resembles them in its brevity, imagistic density, and dependence on suggestion rather than statement. As usual, much is left unsaid. Bailey's treatment of the two very different men, who are nevertheless drawn together after their paths cross, again reveals one of his central concerns as a novelist to be the essential isolation of human beings, the way in which everyone lives and dies alone. He exposes the vulnerable core at the heart of all individuals, the strategies by which people try to disguise their vulnerability and protect themselves from the daily assault of reality, including the inevitability of death. This marks him as a descendant of Conrad, a novelist he greatly admires. Yet if Bailey peels away the deceptions and self-deceptions, the masks and pretenses, by which his characters live, he does so with enormous sympathy for their predicament. Bailey respects the uniqueness of individuals, and possesses the true novelist's fascination with people of every description.

Since *Old Soldiers* in 1980, Bailey has undertaken a great deal of literary journalism and broadcasting, become an important advocate of Italian literature, and written a couple of non-fiction books, but has published only two novels, *Gabriel's Lament* and *Sugar Cane.* This is by far his longest work of fiction and encompasses over 40 years of English life, from the early years of World War II on. The lament of the title is Gabriel Harvey's belated expression of grief at the age of 40 when, in the closing stages of the novel, he discovers the truth about his mother's disappearance nearly 30 years earlier in 1950. What Gabriel learns in Minnesota when he opens a strange bequest from his father, a box of letters, is that his mother Amy had committed suicide within a few weeks of leaving home, supposedly to take an extended holiday. Although Gabriel has become a religious scholar and successful author, much of his life—his adolescence and adulthood—has been profoundly affected by Amy's mysterious absence as well as by the overbearing presence of his outrageously eccentric father, Oswald, one of Bailey's most brilliant creations and a comic character of Dickensian stature. Thirty-five years older than his wife, Oswald, whose lifestyle is transformed by an unexpected financial windfall, eventually reaches the Shavian age of 94. In one sense, the story of his life that Gabriel unfolds is one of loneliness and perplexity, but it is also hilariously funny at times because of Oswald's unpredictable behavior and speech. Oswald may make Gabriel suffer, but he simultaneously makes the reader laugh. Bailey achieves a delicate synthesis of the tragic and the comic in *Gabriel's Lament,* which like his other novels succeeds in widening our sympathies and extending our imaginations.

—Peter Lewis

BAINBRIDGE, Beryl (Margaret)

Nationality: British. **Born:** Liverpool, 21 November 1934. **Education:** Merchant Taylors' School, Liverpool; ballet school in Tring, Hertfordshire. **Family:** Married Austin Davies in 1954 (divorced 1959); one son and two daughters. **Career:** Actress with repertory theaters in Liverpool, Windsor, Salisbury, London, and Dundee,

1949-60; cellar woman in a bottle factory, London, 1970; clerk, Gerald Duckworth Ltd., publishers, London, 1961-73. Presenter, *Forever England* television series, 1986. Since 1987 weekly columnist, London *Evening Standard*. **Awards:** *Guardian* Fiction prize, 1974; Whitbread award, 1977. D. Litt.: University of Liverpool, 1986. Fellow, Royal Society of Literature, 1978. **Address:** 42 Albert Street, London NW1 7NU, England.

PUBLICATIONS

Novels

A Weekend with Claude. London, Hutchinson, 1967; revised edition, London, Duckworth, 1981; New York, Braziller, 1982.
Another Part of the Wood. London, Hutchinson, 1968; revised edition, London, Duckworth, 1979; New York, Braziller, 1980.
Harriet Said. London, Duckworth, 1972; New York, Braziller, 1973.
The Dressmaker. London, Duckworth, 1973; as *The Secret Glass,* New York, Braziller, 1974.
The Bottle Factory Outing. London, Duckworth, 1974; New York, Braziller, 1975.
Sweet William. London, Duckworth, 1975; New York, Braziller, 1976.
A Quiet Life. London, Duckworth, 1976; New York, Braziller, 1977.
Injury Time. London, Duckworth, 1977; New York, Braziller, 1978.
Young Adolf. London, Duckworth, 1978; New York, Braziller, 1979.
Winter Garden. London, Duckworth, 1980; New York, Braziller, 1981.
Watson's Apology. London, Duckworth, 1984; New York, McGraw Hill, 1985.
Filthy Lucre. London, Duckworth, 1986.
An Awfully Big Adventure. London, Duckworth, 1989; New York, Harper Collins, 1991.
The Birthday Boys. London, Duckworth, 1991; New York, Carrol and Graf, 1994.

Short Stories

Mum and Mr. Armitage: Selected Stories. London, Duckworth, 1985; New York, McGraw Hill, 1987.

Plays

Screenplay: *Sweet William,* 1980.

Television Plays: *Tiptoe Through the Tulips,* 1976; *Blue Skies from Now On,* 1977; *The Warrior's Return* (*The Velvet Glove* series), 1977; *Words Fail Me,* 1979; *The Journal of Bridget Hitler,* with Philip Saville, 1981; *Somewhere More Central,* 1981; *Evensong* (*Unnatural Causes* series), 1986.

Other

English Journey; or, The Road to Milton Keynes. London, Duckworth, and New York, Braziller, 1984.
Forever England: North and South. London, Duckworth, 1987.
Something Happened Yesterday. London, Duckworth, 1994.

Editor, *New Stories 6.* London, Hutchinson, 1981.

*

Beryl Bainbridge comments:

(1976) As a novelist I am committing to paper, for my own satisfaction, episodes that I have lived through. If I had had a camera forever ready with a film I might not have needed to write. I am not very good at fiction. . . . It is always me and the experiences I have had. In my last three novels I have used the device of accidental death because I feel that a book has to have a strong narrative line. One's own life, whilst being lived, seems to have no obvious plot and is therefore without tension.

I think writing is a very indulgent pastime and I would probably do it even if nobody ever read anything.

I write about the sort of childhood I had, my parents, the landscape I grew up in: my writing is an attempt to record the past. I am of the firm belief that everybody could write books and I never understand why they don't. After all, everyone speaks. Once the grammar has been learnt it is simply talking on paper and in time learning what not to say.

*   *   *

With the exception of *Sweet William* and *Winter Garden,* all Beryl Bainbridge's novels are centered on a death or act of violence. Her novels are also overshadowed by generalized violence, usually World War II. *The Dressmaker* evokes the Liverpudlian home front during the war, and *An Awfully Big Adventure* that city's postwar seediness. The title story and others in *Mum and Mr. Armitage* are set in the immediate postwar period. So is *A Quiet Life,* with German prisoners-of-war waiting to be repatriated, and *Harriet Said* slightly later, amid vivid memories of Italian prisoners-of-war. In *A Weekend with Claude,* the old Jewess may not forget the concentration camps, which in a sinisterly different way obsess the "Commandant" of the camping site in the earlier version of *Another Part of the Wood.* Since *Young Adolf* takes off from the possibility that Hitler may have lived in Liverpool in 1909, the book's very conception foreshadows the Holocaust and the war. *Winter Garden* is set against the Cold War. *Injury Time* draws on a background of terrorism and armed crime in contemporary London, while another London novel, *The Bottle Factory Outing,* relies for its effect on the build-up of a violently foreboding atmosphere in and around the bottle factory, without any political cause. *Watson's Apology* examines a clergyman's murder of his wife; it is based on an actual case of 1871. Bainbridge's novels in fact work largely by the build-up of violent atmosphere, drawn from both external circumstances and the characters themselves; this typically erupts in a death, albeit apparently accidental.

In *A Weekend with Claude* the central act of violence is a shooting, innocuous in its effect whatever its intention. Like her second novel, *Another Part of the Wood,* which Bainbridge also later rewrote, it lacks the taut spareness which distinguishes her work from *Harriet Said* on.

The questions of responsibility which her novels often beg so stylishly are twofold in *Harriet Said;* not only is the killing accidental, but it is done by a 13-year-old. On one level, the book is an amusing portrayal by a girl of her friend's sexuality and unnatural "wisdom": "We both tried very hard to give our parents love, and security, but they were too demanding." In *The Dressmaker* a young girl's pathetic first love for an American G.I. unfolds toward death against the stark symbolism of the work of the dressmaker, who "dreamed she was following mother down a country garden, severing with sharp scissors the heads of roses." Through the more flamboyant black comedy of *The Bottle Factory Outing* flickers the rare lyricism that as elsewhere in Bainbridge's work is a measure of her Joycean acceptance of her characters. This lyrical quality derives from the setting; the garden in *A Weekend with Claude* has become Windsor Great Park in the later novel. But the death precludes total acceptance.

In *Sweet William* a girl living in a London bedsit falls disastrously in love with the Don Juan of the title, a philandering playwright who moves nonchalantly among the human wreckage he creates. Outstanding here is the portrait of the girl's mother; it was in reaction against her vicious pettiness that the daughter was vulnerable to William. *A Quiet Life* takes an archetypal nuclear family to focus devastatingly again on what children become in reaction to their parents and, as is hinted, in turn cause any children they have to react against. Bainbridge begins several novels with a Chapter 0, implying what is to come, and here as brother and sister meet 15 years later, she both begins and ends with this device—as in *An Awfully Big Adventure*.

Injury Time describes the unorthodox dinner party of a middle-aged quartet, accidentally taken as hostages in a siege, to the special embarrassment of a married man dining *chez* his mistress. Beneath the black comedy, and as molded by formative early experiences, the meaner and more generous impulses of the two main characters come through, in all their ambivalence.

Young Adolf is Bainbridge's most ambitious book, with the tension deriving from our knowledge of what is to come, historically. Against this appalling factual scenario, details like the brown shirt made for the penniless Adolf by his sister-in-law—so that "he needn't sit wrapped in a blanket while his other one was in the wash"—are intensely black comedy.

Winter Garden hilariously follows an accident-prone civil servant masquerading as an artist in order to accompany his mistress in a delegation to the Soviet Union. In *Watson's Apology* Bainbridge traces a 26-year-old marriage to suggest how Rev. Watson came to murder his wife. Contemporary documents are used in a narrative remarkable for its authentic reconstruction of Victorian London, culminating in moving impressions of the aged Watson.

Whether *Filthy Lucre* written by Bainbridge in 1946, aged 11, represents publishers' "book-making" or another Daisy Ashford depends on individual taste. Several short stories in *Mum and Mr. Armitage* touch on the generation gap. Like many novelists, with stories Bainbridge takes risks not ventured in novels, for instance the surreal "The Man Who Blew Away" and "Beggars Would Ride." The setting of a *Peter Pan* production in "Clap Hands, Here Comes Charlie" is extended in *An Awfully Big Adventure*. 16-year-old assistant stage manager Stella understands nothing of the doomed homosexual loves surrounding her and virtually nothing of the equally doomed heterosexual loves, yet she is the catalyst for Bainbridge's inevitable act of violence.

Even in Bainbridge's earlier novels, the mandatory act of violence often seemed superfluous; this immensely gifted novelist's use of the device has now become formulaic.

—Val Warner

BAKER, Elliott

Nationality: American. **Born:** Buffalo, New York, 15 December 1922. **Education:** Indiana University, Bloomington, B.S. 1944.

Military Service: Served in the United States Army Infantry, 1943-46. **Career:** Writer for television programs *U.S. Steel Hour* and *Robert Montgomery Show;* script supervisor, *Zero One* series, BBC Television, London. **Address:** c/o Viking, 375 Hudson Street, New York, New York 10014, U.S.A.

PUBLICATIONS

Novels

A Fine Madness. New York, Putnam, and London, Joseph, 1964.
The Penny Wars. New York, Putnam, 1968; London, Joseph, 1969.
Pocock and Pitt. New York, Putnam, 1971; London, Joseph, 1972.
Klynt's Law. New York, Harcourt Brace, and London, Joseph, 1976.
And We Were Young. New York, Times, 1979; London, Joseph, 1980.
Unhealthful Air. New York, Viking, 1988.

Short Stories

Unrequited Loves. New York, Putnam, and London, Joseph, 1974.

Plays

The Deliquent, The Hipster, and *The Square* (broadcast, 1959). Published in *The Delinquent, The Hipster, The Square, and the Sandpile Series,* edited by Alva I. Cox, Jr., St. Louis, Bethany Press, 1962.

Screenplays: *A Fine Madness,* 1966; *Luv,* 1967; *Viva Max,* 1970.

Radio Plays: *The Delinquent, The Hipster,* and *The Square,* 1959.

Television Plays: *The Right Thing,* 1956 (U.K); *Crisis in Coroma* (*U.S. Steel Hour*), 1957; *The Entertainer,* from play by John Osborne, 1976; *Malibu,* from novel by William Murray, 1983; *Lace,* 1984, and *Lace II,* 1985, from novel by Shirley Conran.

*

Manuscript Collection: Indiana University, Bloomington.

*   *   *

Elliott Baker's first novels, *A Fine Madness* and *The Penny Wars,* demonstrate a diversity of ideas and themes but focus on moral and psychological growth and the life of the imagination. They are comic views of modern America informed by an underlying sense of tragedy or tragic potential. Baker's later works continue to present this tension.

A Fine Madness depicts the triumph of an artist, a kind of American Gulley Jimson, over the forces of conformity and death-in-life. Samson Shillitoe, a working-class hero, a Blakean poet driven by powerful artistic and sexual urges, is pursued and seized by a group of psychiatric experimenters. He is analyzed, institutionalized, and lobotomized but emerges whole, sane, and uncastrated, his creative (and procreative) energies intact. Baker uses his inside knowledge of modern psychotherapy to show the artist at war with a mechanical world and the mechanized minds of clinical psychology. Shillitoe is obsessed by imagination, driven by forces beyond his control.

He is amoral, anti-social, unconcerned with "adjustment" or mental health. The psychologists view him only as a specimen, a sample of neurosis or psychosis. Shillitoe's view triumphs: he conceives and produces an epic-sized poem and his common-law wife conceives his child. Life and creation vanquish death and destruction.

In *The Penny Wars* Baker creates a nostalgic vision of adolescence on the eve of World War II. Tyler Bishop, another rebel, grows up in 1939 in squalor and confusion of values. An unreconstructed liberal, Tyler worries about the Nazis while America's smugness and isolationism seem invincible, worries about his budding sexuality, worries about the world he will inherit. Himself a WASP, he stands up for Jews and Negroes, fights bigotry and ignorance—and loses. Through a series of social confrontations, Tyler begins to find his way toward a self-sufficient individualism.

Unrequited Loves, a set of related novellas, documents the youth (1939-45) of a persona named "Elliott Baker," especially initiations into love and sex. Each story is a comic odyssey wherein the young man discovers the battles and truces in the war between men and women. It is Baker's most genial and optimistic book, focusing the nostalgia of *The Penny Wars* on our national pastimes—love, war, baseball, growing up.

Pocock and Pitt is a satirical exploration of identity and childhood in the modern world. Wendell Pocock, American middle-class victim of repeated heart attacks, becomes Winston Pitt, British worker in an organ bank. A pawn in an international espionage duel, he discovers genuine love and redemption after exhausting the cold consolations of history and philosophy. The novel develops the slapstick mediations of *A Fine Madness* and widens Baker's scope to the state of the whole modern world.

Klynt's Law is a *tour de force* in combining genres—a satirical "college novel," a thriller of Las Vegas criminal shenanigans, a study of parapsychology and gambling compulsions. In it, Tobias Klynt (a.k.a. Kleinmann), an archetypal *klutz,* breaks with his shrewish wife, his university career, and the straight world to put the paranormal talents of four students to work on roulette wheels. They have evolved the perfect "system" to beat Las Vegas but fail to understand that gambling is not for winners. The irony is alternately black and farcical, and, as in all good gambling stories, winners are losers.

The same is true in *And We Were Young,* which traces four ex-rifle-squad members in the red-scare years after World War II. A tangle of coincidences—or synchronistic ironies—brings them together in New York City, where each betrays his youthful desires and beliefs in the enveloping glaciers of the Cold War. The book extends Baker's picture of the generation that grew up with World War II, begun in *The Penny Wars* and *Unrequited Loves,* and develops his vision of our society as it changed radically in a new internationalist world.

In *Unhealthful Air* Baker updates F. Scott Fitzgerald's Pat Hobby stories, by way of Damon Runyon. The novel follows the adventures of a devious, cynical Hollywood scriptwriter and gambler, Corey Burdick, who becomes entangled with a horserace-fixing syndicate, an Ozark nymphet, and her brutal husband. The book deals wittily with movie-TV *clichés* and the way our lives imitate the "art" of the movies. At one point, Burdick wonders in exasperation, "Was there any act of man that hadn't already appeared on the motion picture screen?" Using his native wit, Burdick manages to survive the "unhealthful air" of Los Angeles—and even to prosper.

—William J. Schafer

BAKER, Nicholson

Nationality: American. **Born:** New York, 7 January 1957. **Education:** Eastman School of Music, 1974-75; Haverford College, B.A. 1980. **Family:** Married Margaret Bretano in 1985; one daughter. **Career:** Has held various jobs, including oil analyst, word processor, and technical writer. **Agent:** Melanie Jackson Agency, 250 West 57th St., Suite 1119, New York, New York 10107, U.S.A.

Publications

Novels

The Mezzanine. New York, Weidenfeld and Nicholson, 1988.
Room Temperature. New York, Grove Weidenfeld, and London, Granta, 1990.
Vox. New York, Random House, 1992; London, Puls, 1993.
The Fermata. New York, Random House, 1994; London, Chatto and Windus, 1995.
Size of Thoughts. London, Chatto and Windus, 1995.

Other

U and I: A True Story. New York, Random House, and London, Granta, 1991.

*   *   *

In *U and I: A True Story,* Nicholson Baker describes his "lasting literary influences? Um—*The Tailor of Gloucester,* Harold Nicolson, Richard Pryor, Seuss's *If I Ran the Circus,* Edmund Burke, Nabokov, Boswell, Tintin, Iris Murdoch, Hopkins, Michael Polanyi, Henry and William James, John Candy, *you,* know, the usual crowd." The influences his reviewers see include "Abish, Barth, Borges, Bove, Calvino, Friedman, Joyce, Lem, O'Brien (Flann, not Tim or Edna), Perec, Ponge, Proust, Robbe-Grillet, Sterne, Tati, and Trow—never Updike."

Mentioned in neither list is William Gass, whose combination of mandarin phenomenology and erotic sensuality is echoed in all Baker's work. There is the same "pristine focus" and "baroque vocabulary." In the same book, Baker describes his aesthetic: "to capture pieces of mental life as truly as possible, as they unfold, with all the surrounding forces of circumstance that bear on the blastula of understanding allowed to intrude to the extent that they give a more accurate picture." Pictures, not stories; indeed: "The only thing I like are the clogs. . . . I wanted my first novel to be a veritable infarct of narrative cloggers; the trick being to feel your way through each clog by blowing it up until its obstructiveness finally revealed not blank mass but unlooked-for seepage-points of passage." (Baker's segue into a musing on blocked sewers).

"Passage" provides whatever narrative drive there is in his scientific devotion to the mind's weavings through the quotidian world. According to Robert Plunket, writing in the New York Times Book Review in 1989, Baker devotes himself to exploring "that part of the mind that processes the triviality of daily events that seem to have no importance but end up occupying so much of our existence." As a result, one reviewer felt he "was seeing the world I live in for the first time—as trite as that may sound."

As Baker puts it in his first novel, *The Mezzanine,* "What I wanted here was tribology: detailed knowledge of the interaction between the surfaces inflicting the wear and the surfaces receiving it." In that novel, the hero Howie spends an uneventful lunch hour buying shoelaces and eating a hot dog. What Howie observes of his equally worn laces—"it made the variables of private life seem suddenly graspable and law-abiding."—could also be said of Baker's technique. Whether it is a record player arm, a doorknob, a straw, or a shoelace, his disquisitions make one feel that the private life matters, can have logic, and even beauty. Sometimes his examinations have the aridity of a consumer magazine report, but mostly Baker surprises and charms with images which are both ingenious metaphors for the emotional subject, and exact in their own right. *The Mezzanine* also has extensive footnotes. Baker defends this self-reflexive typographic ploy because "digression . . . is sometimes the only way to be thorough . . . it doesn't end with the book; restatement and self-disagreement and the enveloping sea of referenced authorities all continue."

In *Room Temperature* of 1990, Mike feeds his baby girl during twenty minutes, during which he ruminates on everything from his breathing, to picking his nose, to the comma (those American books which "fail to stay pliantly allusive in their comprehensiveness and show little sensitivity to the civilizing power of the comma")—the baby is, of course, the father's "comma." Being a father reminds him of his own father, inspiring a glorious scene where the two help each other to handstand to the accompaniment of Stravinsky's *Rite of Spring*. Typically, the apparent digression eventually ties in to a patterned leitmotif—in this case, peanut butter jars.

The hero-worshipping narrator of *U and I* is not quite redeemed by his self-irony. He is, in short, a bit of a bore; indeed, he admits that such confessional writing as this "depends to an unusual extent on whether you like me." While it may be difficult to "like" a persona which "is at once self-abasing and self-advertising," according to *Times Literary Supplement* critic Peter Kemp in 1992, read as semiotics or phenomenology, Baker's text has self-reflexive appeal, whether describing his own "disappointment at the pallor a once-pressing idea finally assumes on my page," or complaining of the difficulty of writing novels because "all minds, dumb and smart alike, do such a poor job of impanating their doings in linear sentences."

Discussing Updike's language, the narrator confesses his fear of simple nouns, those "toxic words" which require the setting of

> a clunkier and uglier and more conspicuously Victorian vocabulary around it, full of "nearlys" and "indeeds" and "evens" and "himselfs"—terms of near but not perfect transparency . . . so that you can *use* the language freely, without being transfixed into a mute and foolish nounage by the sacredness of the words you learned first.

This attentiveness to style and its ability to illuminate our daily lives gives Baker's novels a Jamesian sense of resonant meaning exhaustively wrung from the quotidian.

In *Vox* two mature, consenting adults, one from an eastern and one from a western city, chat by phone "in the famous fiber-optical 'back room'" because "it's holier or more reverent than simple voyeurism." The two eagerly imagine a scene where a couple watch an erotic movie sitting beneath a blanket and each masturbates to climax without touching the other. By contrast, their own subsequent climaxes are anti-climaxes; in fact the whole book favors sensual dalliance across the tiny and textural over the larger rhythms of sexual excitation. Perhaps this is Baker's point: real enjoyment (especially for an aging middle class cowering before AIDS) comes

from the delight each caller manifestly feels in his or her own verbal ingenuity and wit. The male caller, for instance, considers

> an orgasm in an intelligent woman . . . you feel the alternative opportunity cost of her orgasm, you feel the force of all the other perceptive things she could be thinking at that moment and is not thinking because she is coming, and they enrich it.

The narrator of *The Fermata* of 1994 has discovered a technique for doing in fact what Baker's previous texts do willfully in fiction; that is, he freezes Wordsworthian spots of time so that they, or more precisely those on the bodies of women in the vicinity, can be examined minutely. The device gives the text its typical baroque lassitude, but the hero, despite protesting: "My curiosity has more love and tolerance in it than other men's does," comes across as smug, and his eroticism as unpleasantly voyeuristic. When he uses a "timefold" while driving on the freeway to leap into a passing car and replace the woman driver's tape with his own recording of his own pornographic novel (which the reader has just read), the "plot" is reduced to an adolescent male fantasy. Nevertheless, *The Fermata* contains some exquisite aperçus such as a discourse on the shared features of the fourth finger and the inner thigh, the intricacies of different male and female sounds of making water, or "the color of those older Tercels and Civics . . . whose paint had consequently oxidized into states of frescoesque, unsaturated beauty, like M&Ms sucked for a minute and spit back out into the palm for study."

If I had to predict the subject of Baker's next novel, I would guess something to do with the Internet. There is already in his work (especially in *Vox* and *The Fermata*) the solipsistic, masturbatory quality associated with hours spent late at night surfing the net. Only when he frames his perceptions with a personal history, relishing the tendency of memories "to screw up your fragmentary historiography with violas of lost emotion," do Baker's meditations cohere beyond the random delights of a medieval emblem book, with which Baker shares much in spirit and technique.

—David Dowling

BALLARD, J(ames) G(raham)

Nationality: British. **Born:** Shanghai, China, 15 November 1930. **Education:** Leys School, Cambridge; King's College, Cambridge. **Military Service:** Served in the Royal Air Force. **Family:** Married Helen Mary Matthews in 1954 (died 1964); one son and two daughters. **Awards:** *Guardian* Fiction prize, 1984; James Tait Black Memorial prize, 1985. **Agent:** Margaret Hanbury, 27 Walcot Square, London SE11 4UB. **Address:** 36 Old Charlton Road, Shepperton, Middlesex TW17 8AT, England.

PUBLICATIONS

Novels

The Wind from Nowhere. New York, Berkley, 1962; London, Penguin, 1967.
The Drowned World. New York, Berkley, 1962; London, Gollancz, 1963.

The Burning World. New York, Berkley, 1964; revised edition, as
  The Drought, London, Cape, 1965.
The Crystal World. London, Cape, and New York, Farrar Straus,
  1966.
Crash. London, Cape, and New York, Farrar Straus, 1973.
Concrete Island. London, Cape, and New York, Farrar Straus,
  1974.
High-Rise. London, Cape, 1975; New York, Holt Rinehart, 1977.
The Unlimited Dream Company. London, Cape, and New York,
  Holt Rinehart, 1979.
Hello America. London, Cape, 1981.
Empire of the Sun. London, Gollancz, and New York, Simon and
  Schuster, 1984.
The Day of Creation. London, Gollancz, 1987; New York, Farrar
  Straus, 1988.
Running Wild. London, Hutchinson, 1988; New York, Farrar Straus,
  1989.
The Kindness of Women. London, Harper Collins, 1991.

Short Stories

The Voices of Time and Other Stories. New York, Berkley, 1962;
  London, Orion, 1992.
Billenium and Other Stories. New York, Berkley, 1962.
The Four-Dimensional Nightmare. London, Gollancz, 1963.
Passport to Eternity and Other Stories. New York, Berkley, 1963.
Terminal Beach. London, Gollancz, 1964; abridged edition, New
  York, Berkley, 1964.
The Impossible Man and Other Stories. New York, Berkley, 1966.
The Disaster Area. London, Cape, 1967.
The Day of Forever. London, Panther, 1967.
The Overloaded Man. London, Panther, 1967.
Why I Want to Fuck Ronald Reagan. Brighton, Unicorn Bookshop,
  1968.
The Atrocity Exhibition. London, Cape, 1970; as *Love and Napalm:
  Export USA,* New York, Grove Press, 1972.
Chronopolis and Other Stories. New York, Putnam, 1971.
Vermilion Sands. New York, Berkley, 1971; London, Cape, 1973.
Low-Flying Aircraft and Other Stories. London, Cape, 1976.
The Best of J.G. Ballard. London, Futura, 1977.
The Best Short Stories of J.G. Ballard. New York, Holt Rinehart,
  1978.
The Venus Hunters. London, Panther, 1980.
News from the Sun. London, Interzone, 1982.
Myths of the Near Future. London, Cape, 1982.
Memories of the Space Age. Sauk City, Wisconsin, Arkham House,
  1988.
War Fever. London, Collins, 1990; New York, Farrar Straus, 1991.

*

Bibliography: *J.G. Ballard: A Primary and Secondary Bibliography* by David Pringle, Boston, Hall, 1984.

Critical Studies: *J.G. Ballard: The First Twenty Years* edited by James Goddard and David Pringle, Hayes, Middlesex, Bran's Head, 1976; *Re Search: J.G. Ballard* edited by Vale, San Francisco, Re Search, 1984; *J.G. Ballard* by Peter Brigg, San Bernardino, California, Borgo Press, 1985; *Out of the Night and into the Dream: A Thematic Study of the Fiction of J.G. Ballard,* New York, Greenwood Press, 1991.

J.G. Ballard comments:

I believe that science fiction is the authentic literature of the 20th century, the only fiction to respond imaginatively to the transforming nature of science and technology. I believe that the true domain of science fiction is that zone I have termed inner space, rather than outer space, and that the present, rather than the future, is now the period of greatest moral urgency for the writer. In my own fiction I have tried to achieve these aims.

*   *   *

As in the case of his acknowledged partial inspiration Graham Greene, J.G. Ballard seems to divide his distinguished canon into novels and "entertainments:" serious, challenging prose that makes new demands on us as readers, and breezier productions that serve as aesthetic holding actions. In the former category, one would find in chronological order *The Drowned World, The Crystal World, The Atrocity Exhibition, Crash, The Unlimited Dream Company, Empire of the Sun, The Day of Creation* and *The Kindness of Women.* Ballard's "entertainments" include *The Wind from Nowhere, The Drought,* the short story cycle *Vermilion Sands, Concrete Island, High-Rise, Hello America,* and *Running Wild.* Ballard's voluminous short fiction could profitably be divided along similar lines, with far greater debate concerning what works best. Ballard's own selection of his best fiction is very reliable: sympathetic readers of Ballard will share his enthusiasm for "The Voices of Time" and "The Terminal Beach." Nonetheless, he has consistently produced rewarding short prose since the last exhaustive anthology, most of which has been collected in *Low-Flying Aircraft, The Venus Hunters, Myths of the Near Future,* and *War Fever.*

This bare listing does not get at the delightful, harsh truth that easy, accessible Ballard is apt to strike the casual reader as more than a bit outré on first glance. One has to absorb 200 pages of erotic car crash fantasies (*Crash*) to curl up cozily with a novel that begins with its protagonist devouring a dog in a housing complex reduced to savagery (*High-Rise*). Any Ballard work is intimidating to the uninitiated, and one might do well to start reading an "entertainment" before venturing into the major canon. What one will find upon perusing that canon is its creator's brilliant, grasping imagination, his densely ironic voice, and a genuine moral vision.

Empire of the Sun provides the kindest entry into the major canon. This novel is both boy-book, a work written for adults about childhood, and war memoir. Jim, the protagonist, has received inevitable comparisons with his author. Both were interred in Japanese prisoner-of-war camps in China during World War II; Ballard admits these related events were his own in the foreword. *Empire of the Sun* as a result allows the credulous to "solve" the case of J.G. Ballard. The young author's separation from his parents, radical dislocation, and struggle for survival produce the traumatic scene of the Ballardian text: a world of flat affect where setting predominates over character and action (unless a generic formula is being ruthlessly parodied), a landscape littered with aircraft fuselages, automobiles, miasmas, and tarmac, all aching to burn under the silent, bone-revealing glare of the Nagasaki explosion Jim witnesses in the ontological climax of the novel: "the light was a premonition of his death, the sight of his small soul joining the larger soul of the dying world." Thus begins the death-in-life of Jim Ballard.

This youth, our mythic construction of the ideal Ballard-author, grows up to become a science-fiction writer: the world he experienced did not match the conventions of 19th-century fiction, so he turned to visions of the future, reading pulp magazines while an airman in Canada. W. Warren Wager in *Terminal Visions* offers us a helpful paradigm for reading Ballard's science fiction and experimental canon through time. Ballard, roughly, has moved from an obsession with feminized natural landscape in the quartet of so-called disaster novels (the world imperiled by the four elements, approximately), through an obsession with homoeroticized technological artifacts (*The Atrocity Exhibition* through *High-Rise*), to an achieved polymorphous perversity (*The Unlimited Dream Company*). Only after this long therapeutic journey could he return to the traumatic scene Vonnegut had to work up to *Slaughterhouse-Five*. He is cured; he need never write again, certainly not science fiction. One could also use Ballard's own statements to posit his work as progressing while usefully regressing from more distant future worlds to our present world of apartment complexes and flyovers, and ultimately to his Shanghai past. *Empire of the Sun* gives the critic marvelous ammunition for familiarizing an unsettling fictional presence. That flat affect Ballard shares with kindred maverick William S. Burroughs can be traced to the Japanese camps, even as Burroughs owes his style, ostensibly, more to the neurophysiological effects of heroin than to a Swiftian spirit.

Such reductive remarks could have passed for an accurate assessment of Ballard's work until he returned to the fantastic after *Empire of the Sun* with *The Day of Creation* and *Running Wild*. But even before these publications one was suspicious about this narrative of the career. Something is lost in the neatness of it all; most notably, the inescapable belatedness of the recent mainstream work. We read it in the light of the science fiction and experimental writing: the cramped cubicles of Lunghau C. A. C. irresistibly invoke the locales of "Billenium" and *High-Rise*. Ballard values the fabulative powers of science fiction too greatly to allow his summating work to stand outside them. The ultimate joke on the reader may be that *Empire of the Sun* is history revealed as the ultimate science fiction text, especially as Ballard writes either. As Gould remarks in "Low-Flying Aircraft," "The ultimate dystopia is the inside of one's own head." *Empire of the Sun* is an immense and real achievement, but only partially enlightening as a key to the canon. Other, less reductive structures can be suggested to illuminate Ballard's strategies.

One of the most helpful perspectives for enjoying Ballard can be located in Roland Barthes's explication of bourgeois myth. Myth is a secondary order of signification, a higher code of accepted meaning. The image of an oak tree in an insurance company advertisement, by a theft of the sign, becomes a signifier of longevity, dependability, etc. The artist has two strategies for attacking the conventional accretions of myth: she or he, according to Barthes, can either restore to physical objects their uncanniness and historicity or create a third order of signification by looking behind the myth for its concealed signification.

A fairly plausible case can be made that Ballard has always attacked conventional signification, progressing from Barthes's first strategy to an increasing use of his second strategy. The early novels restore to things their non-mythic materiality: especially the heightened elemental powers in the quartet, but also the technological flotsam and jetsam being blown about or floating by. The crystallization process in *The Crystal World* provides an almost perfect allegory of the defamiliarization of bourgeois nature.

But Ballard has been honing his skills at discovering the third order of signification (which Barthes infelicitously terms "Bouvard and Pécucheity" in honor of Flaubert's ironic skills) since *The Wind from Nowhere*. One of the few nice things one can say about this

work—produced in two short weeks, it remains Ballard's worst novel—is that it knows at all points that it's formulaic junk, a parody of the "cozy catastrophe" John Wyndham school of disaster writing. Its successor, *The Drowned World,* is playing similar games with its transparent allusiveness, but there is far greater interest in the code behind the code of disaster fiction. For Ballard and his protagonist Kerans, disaster is concealed psychic opportunity. In the clearly indicated "happy" ending of the work, Kerans embraces the destructive principle, the cathonic, by heading south into greater heat. As in most later Ballard, such self-destruction is always a symbolic invitation to transformation, a relentless reiteration that the old order is dying and a new one is coming up—and such a transformation won't look like liberal reform. (How puzzling that Marxists ever dismissed Ballard as neo-colonial or reactionary given such a recurrent stance of critical realism; post-Marxists Jean Baudrillard and Frederic Jameson have since redressed the misreading.) In Foucault's terminology, we are in a shifting episteme: writers like Ballard and Burroughs have their ears pressed closest to the rails, listening to the eschatological murmur. Such, after all, is the requisite stance for a survivor. Ballard reveals in *Empire of the Sun* that "a code within a code" always intrigued Jim. He would always watch bridge games for this reason; later, such skills would keep him alive.

In *The Atrocity Exhibition,* Ballard's talents as a reader of bourgeois myth emerge strikingly. The book dissects some of the psychoanalytic significance behind the overdetermination of 1960s culture: television coverage of the Vietnam war, the assassination of John F. Kennedy, Marilyn Monroe, the automobile, cancer victims all converge in a terrifying psychedelic hellbroth of image, redeemed, like *Naked Lunch,* only by its abiding ironic humor, its Swiftian critical distance, and its undeniable prophecy. The obsessional accuracy of this series of "condensed novels" has aged remarkably well, as a chapter title like "Why I Want to Fuck Ronald Reagan" indicates.

For some readers, *Crash* is even rougher going, a semiological anatomy of the automobile accident that exchanges breadth (in *The Atrocity Exhibition*) for depth of analysis. As in the later *Empire of the Sun,* Ballard toys with the reader by giving the narrator his own name. Ballard the character's quest for "the keys to a new sexuality born from a perverse technology" horrifies, delights, and enlightens. At his best, Ballard's imagination risks the unimaginable, even as his clunky, chunky prose—with its transparent allusions and similes, its hard-boiled rhythms, and its vague redundancies—acquires a paradoxical grace all its own: a bombed-out, flat affect poetry that perfectly ensnares our era. His sinister replication of medical school textbook argot in this second phase assures us Ballard has a good ear; he knows exactly what effects he's achieving in this minatory technological pornography.

Ballard's recent polymorphous phase has given us some of his finest writing, in *The Unlimited Dream Company, Empire of the Sun,* and *The Kindness of Women* (and his funniest in the overlooked *Hello America*). Lately, his quest for ultimate reality has passed through autobiographical incident to the ultimate contemporary reality: television. It remains an interesting question who's influencing whom: Ballard or Baudrillard, the cool rhetoric of "hyperreality," the triumphant televisual simulacrum. One suspects Ballard is the influence here, since Baudrillard has written on *Crash,* while Ballard seems uninterested in theory when interviewed. Be that as it may, I have been alluding to many postmodern theorists here because Ballard's practice so overtly complements their observations. Since at least *The Atrocity Exhibition* and short stories like "Motel Architecture" and "The Intensive Care Unit" in *Myths of the Near Future,* Ballard has been interested in the alternate gestalt of televisual reality. In his latest work, the simulational triumphs completely over the real. In *The Day of Creation,* a fantastic river appears in Africa, created out of the embodied wish fantasies of Mallory, the main character. He alternately wishes to destroy and preserve his creation, to drift down it and to explore its source. It is what Deleuze and Guattari would deem a "smooth space," a zone of easy movement and free play that comes suspiciously to resemble the world inside our VCRs. One character, Senger, carries a broken camera and "films" an "imaginary documentary." When they drift rapidly downstream, the scenery looks like "a reversed playback." As Senger explains to Mallory, "Television doesn't tell lies, it makes up a new truth. . . . Sooner or later, everything turns into television." Baudrillard couldn't have said it better.

By the time we get to *Running Wild,* a tale of videotaped violence and suburban mayhem that looks like a children's book but is definitely not for little Jill or Johnny, Ballard can revise reality through his simulations, as when the narrator compares some of the deadly children's journals to "*Pride and Prejudice* with its missing pornographic passages restored." The tone throughout all of Ballard, finely honed in the most recent books, is the creepy funny both/and double register of postmodernism, the mood of any Jack Nicholson or Dennis Hopper performance. Is Ballard writing satire? Social criticism? Whimsy? Yes.

The Kindness of Women is his most remarkable achievement along these thematic lines. This novel-autobiography hybrid is a sequel to *Empire of the Sun* and a virtual retrospective gallery exhibition of all the major phases discussed above: for example, the chapter called "The Exhibition" returns to the interests of *Crash;* the first three chapters rework *Empire of the Sun.* This book, if not his most accessible, is nonetheless the most thorough introduction available to Ballard's fictional project. And it offers a powerful culmination of his meditations on media and simulation. The climax of the book is his participation in Stephen Spielberg's filming of *Empire of the Sun.* Ironically, Spielberg chose to film the British section of Shanghai in Sunningdale, a residential area fifteen minutes away by car from Shepperton (a distant suburb of London where Ballard has lived for the last 35 years). As Ballard notes in his annotations to the *Re/Search* magazine reissue of *The Atrocity Exhibition,* "I can almost believe that I came to Shepperton 30 years ago knowing unconsciously that one day I would write a novel about my wartime experiences in Shanghai, and that it might well be filmed in these studios. Deep assignments run through all our lives; there are no coincidences." *The Kindness of Women* unifies all of Ballard's lifelong obsessions and enables him to return full circle to his childhood, now made more real as Hollywood film: "All the powers of modern film had come together for this therapeutic exercise." Echoing Samuel Beckett's wish to leave "a stain upon the silence," Ballard sees his true immortality as a blurred image in the film, which is all that remained of his cameo appearance after final editing: "this seemed just, like the faint blur which was all that any of us left across time and space."

One story in his latest short fiction collection *War Fever* also deserves mention in this regard, the hilarious "Secret History of World War 3." It zanily prophesies a change in the Constitution enabling Ronald Reagan to serve a third term in the nineties. His fading health comes to dominate the national consciousness so much that his vital signs scroll across all channels, his bowel movements deserve special news bulletins, and a brief nuclear exchange goes unnoticed by distracted viewers. Ballard was obviously thinking of Reagan's polyp operation, but the story eerily anticipates the ultimate media spectacle of the O.J. Simpson trial.

Ballard will undoubtedly continue to grow along the amazing and original course he has charted. Much of his supposed classism and racism seems unfounded; his use of formulaic heroines, though perodic and appropriate for his gender-bound, extreme loners, has drawn greater and more justified criticism from feminists. Recent stories like "Having a Wonderful Time" and "The Smile" and the character of Noon in *The Day of Creation* adumbrate his own interest in correcting these misperceptions. Thematically, he will continue to gesture towards a problematic social transformation, hoping for its arrival but uncertain of its shape, wishing for it to resemble the community in his utopian *Vermilion Sands,* but, ever the survivor, willing to settle for anything shy of Eniwetok. As long as we avoid choosing the latter (and perhaps for a bit on the day after if we do not manage that), Ballard will continue to interest us as our bravest explorer of the psychic contours of post-nuclear humanity, the fabulist chronicler of our overlooked median strips. Somehow this maverick presence has become one of the most important and distinguished writers of English prose working today. His metaphors will haunt any reader; he dares to articulate what only the most obscure regions of our animal brain contemplate: desires for nuclear apocalypse, for incestuous sex, for participating in auto wrecks. "Deep assignments run through all our lives; there are no coincidences."

—Robert E. Mielke

BANKS, Lynne Reid

Nationality: British. **Born:** London, 31 July 1929. **Education:** Schools in Canada; Queen's Secretarial School, London, 1945-46; Italia Centre Stage School, London, 1946; Royal Academy of Dramatic Art, London, 1947-49. **Family:** Married Chaim Stephenson in 1965; three sons. **Career:** Actress in British repertory companies, 1949-54; secretary to the writer Wolf Mankowitz, 1954; interviewer, reporter, and scriptwriter, Independent Television News, London, 1955-62; English teacher, Kibbutz Yasur School and Na'aman High School, Israel, 1963-71. **Awards:** Yorkshire Arts Association award, 1977. **Agent:** Watson Little Ltd., 12 Egbert Street, London NW1 8LJ, England.

PUBLICATIONS

Novels

The L-Shaped Room. London, Chatto and Windus, 1960; New York, Simon and Schuster, 1961.
An End to Running. London, Chatto and Windus, 1962; as *House of Hope,* New York, Simon and Schuster, 1962.
Children at the Gate. London, Chatto and Windus, and New York, Simon and Schuster, 1968.
The Backward Shadow. London, Chatto and Windus, and New York, Simon and Schuster, 1970.
Two Is Lonely. London, Chatto and Windus, and New York, Simon and Schuster, 1974.

Dark Quartet: The Story of the Brontës. London, Weidenfeld and Nicholson, 1976; New York, Delacorte Press, 1977.
Path to the Silent Country: Charlotte Brontë's Years of Fame. London, Weidenfeld and Nicolson, 1977; New York, Delacorte Press, 1978.
Defy the Wilderness. London, Chatto and Windus, 1981.
The Warning Bell. London, Hamish Hamilton, 1984; New York, St. Martin's Press, 1987.
Casualties. London, Hamish Hamilton, 1986; New York, St. Martin's Press, 1987.

Fiction (for children)

One More River. London, Vallentine Mitchell, and New York, Simon and Schuster, 1973.
Sarah and After: The Matriarchs. London, Bodley Head, and New York, Doubleday, 1975.
The Adventures of King Midas. London, Dent, 1976.
The Farthest-Away Mountain. London, Abelard Schuman, 1976; New York, Doubleday, 1977.
My Darling Villain. London, Bodley Head, and New York, Harper, 1977.
I, Houdini: The Autobiography of a Self-Educated Hamster. London, Dent, 1978; New York, Doubleday, 1988.
The Indian in the Cupboard. London, Dent, 1980; New York, Doubleday, 1981.
The Writing on the Wall. London, Chatto and Windus, 1981; New York, Harper, 1982.
Maura's Angel. London, Dent, 1984.
The Fairy Rebel. London, Dent, 1985; New York, Doubleday, 1988.
Return of the Indian. London, Dent, 1986; New York, Doubleday, 1987.
Melusine. London, Hamish Hamilton, 1988; New York, Harper, 1989.
The Secret of the Indian. London, Collins, and New York, Doubleday, 1989.

Plays

It Never Rains (televised 1954; produced Keighley, Yorkshire, 1954). London, Deane, 1954.
Miss Pringle Plays Portia, with Victor Maddern. London, Deane, 1955.
The Killer Dies Twice. London, Deane, 1956.
All in a Row. London, Deane, and Boston, Baker, 1956.
The Unborn (produced London, 1962).
Already It's Tomorrow (televised 1962). London, French, 1962.
The Gift (produced London, 1965).

Radio Plays: *The Stowaway,* 1967; *Lame Duck,* 1978; *Purely from Principle,* 1984.

Television Plays: *It Never Rains,* 1954; *Already It's Tomorrow,* 1962; *The Wednesday Caller,* 1963; *Last Word on Julie,* 1964; *The Eye of the Beholder* (*She* series), 1977.

Other

The Kibbutz: Some Personal Reflections (address). London, Anglo-Israel Association, 1972.
Letters to My Israeli Sons: The Story of Jewish Survival. London, W.H. Allen, 1979; New York, Watts, 1980.

Torn Country: An Oral History of the Israeli War of Independence. New York, Watts, 1982.

*

Manuscript Collection: Boston University.

Theatrical Activities:
Actress: **Radio**—*Purely from Principle,* 1984.

*   *   *

Lynne Reid Banks acquired sudden literary fame with her first novel, *The L-Shaped Room.* Despite her considerable output of fiction since then, she has remained best known for that one book. This may be partly because of Bryan Forbe's film, which starred Leslie Caron as Jane, the heroine waiting for the birth of her illegitimate child in a Fulham bedsit. The novel shows Jane coming to know the range of sleazy, eccentric, and ordinary characters in the house, and learning to be at peace with her plight. *The L-Shaped Room* was regarded as highly daring in its time, and though that frisson has worn off by now, the book is still notable for its originality and its compassionate observation of people. It can be faulted on construction: the room never acquires the dominant place it is clearly meant to have because there is too much happening outside it that engages our attention, and some of the other characters are tantalizingly sketchy. Jane's lover is a writer, Toby Cohen, and he remains a cameo of a type of person who was then considered fashionable. However, these faults are insignificant, because the story grips us. We care about the girl's dilemma, we worry about the future of the baby. One critic pointed out that the best things in this novel remind us of Orwell's *Down and Out in Paris and London;* the worst remind us of *Rebecca of Sunnybrook Farm.*

The Backward Shadow was the sequel to *The L-Shaped Room.* This has Jane enjoying motherhood and temporary isolation in a country cottage not far from London. Though she still loves Toby, she has decided not to burden him with responsibility for herself as this will interfere with his writing. Jane's nobility is rewarded by Toby's falling for a nymphet, and the story really becomes concerned with Jane's relationship with Dotty and Henry, partners in a boutique. Jane's friendship with them also collapses, because of her lack of confidence in herself and her occasional guardedness. The novel examines love and friendship, and the necessity of knowing when to offer your presence and when to withdraw it, when to express need of other people and when to leave it unexpressed. Jane is a thoroughly good sort of person, endearingly ready to discuss her feelings and her emotional development with the reader. However, her lack of irony, malice, and humor contribute to making the book somewhat duller than it might have been if Jane had not been the narrator.

The final novel in the trilogy about Jane, *Two Is Lonely,* has Jane still unmarried and finding it increasingly difficult to handle her son David who is now eight. Obsessed with his need for a father, he asks questions constantly, cannot sleep at night, and suffers from nightmares. Finally, he runs away from home and disappears. The focus of the novel is on Jane's relationships with men in the past and in the present, for she has continued her search for a mate. Banks believes that a woman is superior to a man in many ways, but does need a man (just as a man needs a woman). Jane is being wooed by a handsome widower, a rich and successful architect; however, she still dreams of Toby who has emigrated to Israel, but whose marriage is foundering. The architect wisely encourages Jane to look Toby up, and she goes to Israel with John, the black friend from *The L-Shaped Room.* Jane eventually finds Toby, but ends up rejecting him when he fails to make love to her. Jane returns to London when she hears of her son's disappearance; she discovers that another flame, Terry, has indulged in a face-lift and dye-job, so she rejects him too, leaving the field finally clear for the architect. Though a postscript hints at the continuation of the saga, Banks has not written one so far.

The strengths and weaknesses of the trilogy typify Banks's strengths and weaknesses in general: one always feels that her heart is in the right place, and she commands a fine economy in evoking scenes—especially those that involve the emotions. However, she has never mastered the architectonics of fiction, and her language veers from the over-rich to the monotonous. Her chief drawback, however, is that she treats in a curiously old fashioned way the paradoxes of being a woman who is both thoroughly modern and yet sensitive to questions of truth, morality, and commitment. But it is also true that Banks negotiated the journey from outrageous amorality to seeing its problems far more quickly and less spectacularly than Germaine Greer.

However, such preoccupations are not prominent in all of Banks's novels. For she went to Israel and found both a cause and a husband in that country. Though she, her husband, and her children eventually settled in Britain again, they decided to leave Israel for pragmatic considerations of making a living, and Banks has written several books in praise of Israel, for children, teenagers, and adults. The best known of the books is *Defy the Wilderness,* in which a woman writer is researching a book on contemporary right-wing Israel, hoping to make it a fairly objective account. However, as one critic put it, "her liberal principles are overwhelmed by a rogue-male Attila of Zionism for whom she falls." The intensifying need of the Jews to distinguish between those who are for Israel and those who are against it tears her irrevocably away from her insipid family life back home in England. Discursive, weighty, and frankly committed, the book failed to arouse any enthusiasm among critics, though it has been as popular with the public as any of her other works.

Bank's principal fault in the eyes of critics has been the ultimate sin of earnestness; there is nothing so damning as being described in the fashionable periodicals as a "bore." Banks is not a great novelist, but she does offer effective satire, the illuminating detail, and pithy dialogue. It is her misfortune that the gatekeepers of culture themselves typify the values with which she initially sympathized and on which she has now turned her back. She continues to defy them with her 1984 weapon, *The Warning Bell,* a frank exploration of what fashionable people find to be the most terrifying of timebombs, conscience.

—Prabhu S. Guptara

BANKS, Russell (Earl)

Nationality: American. **Born:** Newton, Massachusetts, 29 March 1940. **Education:** Colgate University, Hamilton, New York, 1958; University of North Carolina, Chapel Hill, 1964-67, A.B. 1967 (Phi Beta Kappa). **Family:** Married 1) Darlene Bennett in 1960 (divorced

1962), one daughter; 2) Mary Gunst in 1962 (divorced 1977), three daughters; 3) Kathy Walton in 1982 (divorced 1988); 4) Chase Twichell in 1989. **Career:** Mannequin dresser, Montgomery Ward, Lakeland, Florida, 1960-61; plumber, New Hampshire, 1962-64; publisher and editor, Lillabulero Press, and co-editor, *Lillabulero* magazine, Chapel Hill, North Carolina, and Northwood Narrows, New Hampshire, 1966-75; instructor, Emerson College, Boston, 1968 and 1971, University of New Hampshire, Durham, 1968-75, and New England College, Henniker, New Hampshire, 1975 and 1977-81. Since 1981 has taught at New York University and Princeton University, New Jersey. Lives in Princeton. **Awards:** Woodrow Wilson fellowship, 1968; St. Lawrence award, 1975; Guggenheim fellowship, 1976; National Endowment for the Arts grant, 1977, 1982; Merrill Foundation award, 1983; Dos Passos prize, 1985; American Academy award, 1986. **Agent:** Ellen Levine Literary Agency, 432 Park Avenue South, Suite 1205, New York, New York 10016. **Address:** c/o Ellen Levine Literary Agency, Suite 1801, 15 E. 26th Street, New York, New York 10010, U.S.A.

PUBLICATIONS

Novels

Family Life. New York, Avon, 1975.
Hamilton Stark. Boston, Houghton Mifflin, 1978.
The Book of Jamaica. Boston, Houghton Mifflin, 1980.
The Relation of My Imprisonment. Washington, D.C., Sun and Moon Press, 1983.
Continental Drift. New York, Harper, and London, Hamish Hamilton, 1985.
Affliction. New York, Harper, 1989; London, Picador, 1990.
The Sweet Hereafter: A Novel. New York, HarperCollins, 1991; London, Picador, 1992.

Short Stories

Searching for Survivors. New York, Fiction Collective, 1975.
The New World. Urbana, University of Illinois Press, 1978.
Trailerpark. Boston, Houghton Mifflin, 1981.
Success Stories. New York, Harper, and London, Hamish Hamilton, 1986.

Uncollected Short Stories

"Indisposed," in *Prime Number,* edited by Ann Lowry Weir. Urbana, University of Illinois Press, 1988.
"The Travel Writer," in *Antioch Review* (Yellow Springs, Ohio), Summer 1989.
"Xmas," in *Antaeus* (New York), Spring-Autumn 1990.

Poetry

15 Poems, with William Matthews and Newton Smith. Chapel Hill, North Carolina, Lillabulero Press, 1967.
30/6. New York, The Quest, 1969.
Waiting to Freeze. Northwood Narrows, New Hampshire, Lillabulero Press, 1969.
Snow: Meditations of a Cautious Man in Winter. Hanover, New Hampshire, Granite, 1974.

Other

Editor, with Michael Ondaatje and David Young, *Brushes with Greatness: An Anthology of Chance Encounters with Greatness.* Toronto, Coach House Press, 1989.

*   *   *

Russell Banks's novels and stories are various, ranging from the problematic intricacies of postmodernism of his early work to the semi-realism of his latest. However, though his techniques and forms vary, his work shows a remarkable thematic progress from an often convoluted questioning of the human predicament in the early novels to a lucid answering in *Continental Drift.* Banks early on experimented with a number of styles, forms, and types—fable, "relation," tale, parable, mannered avant-garde, stories-within-stories, realistic narrative. But always he has been primarily interested in the human predicament and modern man's place within and outside his traditions. His settings range from New England to Haiti, and places in between.

Family Life, Banks's first novel, is a self-conscious fabulistic romance that takes place in an imaginary kingdom and concerns the fates of King Egress, Queen Naomi Ruth, and their sons Orgone, Egress, Jr., and Dread. The novel is seriously marred by obscure literary references and jokes and nearly impenetrable passages of allusion alternating with farcical scenes. The "relevance" of the novel appears to be something on the order that we fight nameless wars in nameless countries, that we are misplaced and displaced persons searching for identity.

Hamilton Stark is told from an avant-garde point of view—shifting, multi-faceted, and fragmented, with long philosophical monologues, radical time shifts, psychological digressions, and tales-within-tales, often put together, again, self-consciously and often not convincingly. The real strength of the novel, and it is considerable, derives chiefly from the several points of view from which Stark is viewed by a number of the other characters. There is no definitive attempt to piece together these fragments, for that is, indeed, the theme of the novel—that there is no defining "self" mediating among the various understandings that would guarantee a static, comforting identity.

The Book of Jamaica concerns a novelist and professor from New England (Banks is a professor at Princeton who spent 18 months in Jamaica) who receives a grant to study the Jamaica Maroons, whose forebears were escaped African slaves who in the 17th and 18th centuries took to the mountains to fight the British. The main character is a liberal, guilt-ridden because of his identification with the wealthy, racist islanders and other whites. The narrator, on his own journey into the heart of darkness, is afflicted with the modern, overly analytical mind, suffers from alienation and loneliness, and attempts to find among the Maroons a self unburdened by 20th-century culture and tradition and to refashion himself both as a social creature and "natural" man. The narrator becomes "Johnny" among the Maroons, a name they give to friendly whites. He is assumed into Otherness, a kind of forgetfulness necessary to eliminate old cultural prejudices and the shackling of character and personality by the intellectual life that obscures elementary experience.

The Relation of My Imprisonment is told in the form of a "relation," a form popular with 17th-century Puritans; it is a first hand account of an imprisoned man's deviance from religious orthodoxy and is embellished by Scripture and sermon. The unnamed pris-oner, a builder of coffins, has been sentenced to 12 years for illegally plying his trade as coffin maker; he is a heretic. The book's larger theme involves the persecution of Puritan Dissenters in England, but its real concern is contemporary man's imprisonment, his fragmentation and consequent loss of self. The prison itself is a metaphor for the modern situation. While the ostensible form is old, the style and language are postmodernist, and the tale is told "expressly for the living."

Continental Drift, undoubtedly Banks's best novel, is also his most approachable. For the first time in the novel form (he has written more conventionally in his short fiction) his narrative is straightforward and the style unadorned and lucid; it is Banks's apparent break with postmodernism, and in this work he finds the full flowering of his talent. Bob Dubois is a $137.44-a-week 30-year-old oil-burner repairman in Catamount, New Hampshire who suddenly sees into his awful predicament: "He loves his wife and children. He has a girlfriend. He hates his life." He vows to start over, packs up his family and leaves for Florida to work for his brother in a liquor store. Dubois's story is alternated with and parallel to another, that of Vanise Dorsinville, an impoverished Haitian and her son and nephew who leave their country for the promise of America. Both main characters are united by the novel's central concern, the drifting quality of life in America in the last half of the 20th century and how individual life everywhere is as determined as are the tectonic plates of continents, by movements imperceptible to those affected by them. From a more distant perspective than that allowed to men living through the drift, the planet is seen "as an organic cell," a metaphor for human life and the futility of escape from constant motion. At the heart of the novel is a great sympathy for the characters, not hope for the transformation of this life: "Books get written—novels, stories and poems stuffed with particulars that try to tell us what the world is, as if our knowledge of people like Bob Dubois and Vanise and Claude Dorsinville will set people like them free. It will not. Knowledge of the facts of Bob's life changes nothing in the world. Our celebrating his life and grieving over his failure will."

—Peter Desy

BANVILLE, John

Nationality: Irish. **Born:** Wexford, 8 December 1945. **Education:** Christian Brothers School, and St. Peter's College, both Wexford. **Family:** Married Janet Dunham in 1969; two sons. **Career:** Copy editor, *Irish Press,* Dublin, 1970-83. Since 1989 literary editor, *Irish Times,* Dublin. **Awards:** Allied Irish Banks prize, 1973; Arts Council of Ireland Macaulay fellowship, 1973; Irish-American Foundation award, 1976; James Tait Black Memorial prize, 1977; *Guardian* Fiction prize 1981; Guinness Peat Aviation award, 1989. **Agent:** Sheil Land Ltd., 43 Doughty Street, London WC1N 2LF, England.

<small>PUBLICATIONS</small>

Novels

Nightspawn. London, Secker and Warburg, and New York, Norton, 1971.

Birchwood. London, Secker and Warburg, and New York, Norton, 1973.
Doctor Copernicus. London, Secker and Warburg, and New York, Norton, 1976.
Kepler. London, Secker and Warburg, 1981; Boston, Godine, 1983.
The Newton Letter: An Interlude. London, Secker and Warburg, 1982; Boston, Godine, 1987.
Mefisto. London, Secker and Warburg, 1986; Boston, Godine, 1989.
The Book of Evidence. London, Secker and Warburg, 1989; New York, Scribner, 1990.
Ghosts. London, Secker and Warburg, and New York, Scribner, 1993.
Athena. London, Secker and Warburg, and New York, Scribner, 1995.

Short Stories

Long Lankin. London, Secker and Warburg, 1970.

Uncollected Short Stories

"The Party," in *Kilkenny Magazine,* Spring-Summer 1966.
"Mr. Mallin's Quest" and "Nativity," in *Transatlantic Review* (London), Autumn-Winter 1970-71.
"Into the Wood," in *Esquire* (New York), March 1972.
"De rerum natura," in *Transatlantic Review 50* (London), 1975.
"Rondo," in *Transatlantic Review 60* (London), 1977

Plays

Screenplay: *Reflections,* 1984; *The Broken Jug (After Kleist),* 1994.

*

Manuscript Collection: Trinity College, Dublin.

Critical Studies: "John Banville Issue" of *Irish University Review* (Dublin), Spring 1981; *John Banville: A Critical Introduction* by Rudiger Imhof, Dublin, Wolfhound Press, 1989, Chester Springs, Pennsylvania, Dufour, 1990.

* * *

John Banville writes about writing. His characters are marionettes, entangled in self-reflexive explorations of the relationship between creation and reality. Banville's fiction is full of borrowings, from Marvell to Sir Arthur Eddington, yet it is saved from intellectualism and narcissism by its disciplined structure and Nabokovian narrative voice, deliberately uneasy and emotionally strained.

Its third-person narrative distinguishes *Long Lankin* from Banville's later books. Like *Dubliners,* this debut collection presents different stages in the lives of Irish characters in sets of episodic stories dealing with childhood, adolescence, and adulthood respectively. "The Possessed," a novella, is added as a coda. Each story centres on two dispossessed characters who frustrate each other's initial sense of freedom and end up in a state of arrest, wholly unable to fathom the "whatness of things." Ominously prominent background noises and shadows continually hint at Long Lankin, the leper from the old English ballad, whose cure depended on a ritual murder. He materializes in the novella as Ben White and radically upsets the tenor, chronology, and fictional level of the book. White's transformation into "Black Fang" intermediates his appearance in two preceding stories: in "Summer Voices" as a boy, bullied by his sister and fascinated with death; and in "Island" as an

unproductive writer who stares at Delos and is accused of murder by his demanding girlfriend. In "The Possessed," Ben demands a blood-sacrifice for creative freedom, metaphorically kills his sister by severing their—almost incestuous—ties, and lifts himself to the status of implied author, unleashing a savagery that reflects the author's urge to finish off the book.

Nightspawn is a sequel to "The Possessed" and exploits the metafictional effects of coalescing hero, narrator, and writer. Ben imitates Yeats, Prufrock, and Shelley, and in the best *nouveau roman* tradition he soon becomes a pawn in his own cliché thriller. His Greek island gets crowded with his stock characters who emotionally involve White beyond his narrative control and are to blame for the novel's doubles, double plots, and obscurity. Eager to get to "the real meat," but checked by "the conventions," White becomes the first of Banville's Beckettian heroes who must go on, or perish in silence and who are doomed at the end to return to the first sentence.

In *Birchwood,* Banville refutes many of his fabulations. Gabriel Godkin, the narrator, is once again autocratic and conditioned by his own narrative. His genre is the Irish big house with all its familiar trappings and stock characters. There are slapstick humour and morbid fun: Granny Godkin finds her end in the summerhouse by spontaneous combustion. Intermingled with the big house is the external world of romance, Prospero's circus, which Gabriel joins on his quest for a sister who is in fact an imaginative character created to deprive him of his inheritance by the aunt who proves to be his mother. Gabriel's anachronistic narrative is determined by his "search for time misplaced;" like the antics of Birchwood's grandfather clock, it transcends boundaries of time as deftly as Proust's *Recherches.* But the book's shifting frames of reference are firmly fixed in its philosophical observation that the expression of the memories of things is at best a two-dimensional mirror-image in which much is consistently reversed.

In his classical tetralogy, Banville translates his fascination for the relationship between creation and reality into eminent scientists' quests for truth. He even appends bibliographies with references to works on theoretical physics. In *Doctor Copernicus,* Duke Albrecht claims that he and Copernicus are "the makers of . . . supreme fictions." And indeed, Coppernigk is time and again likened to Wallace Stevens in order to show how science is art and how art cannot express truth, but only embody it. Coppernigk's quest leads from conceptualization to cognition, a unification with his anti-self, his syphilitic brother Andreas who repeats verbatim Eddington's "We *are* the truth." Although the book recreates the cruelty and stench of the Renaissance, it is not an historical novel. Copernicus is a protégé of a writer's consciousness which is informed by Einstein, Kierkegaard, Wittgenstein, Max Planck, Yeats, and Stevens—who are all quoted in a pandemonium of opposing philosophical contentions. Banville feels free to introduce a madcap, manic depressive paranoid called Rheticus, who claims responsibility for Copernicus's *De Revolutionibus,* lies like mad, lays bare the irrational undertones of the book and provides a delightfully comic interlude. Ultimately *Doctor Copernicus* is another metafiction; all characters may be figments of Copernicus's own mind; and he, in turn, acts and thinks as part of the literary creation. Every book of the novel is a closed entity, revolving within itself and resolving in a restatement of the first paragraph, with the very last sentence being a return to the very first. The narrative reads like a fugue, but despite its insistence on form it is immensely realistic in its depiction of a nightmarish era, where total chaos is just around the corner.

The structure of *Kepler* is a reflection of the hero's belief that "in the beginning is the shape." The five chapters are shaped like the polygons that Kepler envisaged within the intervals of the six planetary orbits; the sections acrostically spell out the names of famous scientists, and the shifts of time in each section reflect Kepler's discovery that the planets move in ellipses. In his Quixotic quest for a truthful order, Kepler the man becomes conditioned by the entropy that Kepler the scientist creates, with a paradoxical anti-hero as the result.

At the basis of *The Newton Letter* lies von Hofmannsthal's *Ein Brief;* the Nabokovian first sentence aptly reads "Words fail me, Clio." The epistolary form grants the narrator more autonomy than any of Banville's protagonists and emphasizes his treacherous subjectivity. The novel is the satire of the tetralogy and details the consequences of immersing an historian with a Newtonian mechanistic view in the common world of the big house, where Goethe's humanity reigns supreme. The hero is constantly baffled and blinded, misinterprets the inhabitants of Ferns and is Banville's most convincing example that truth is perhaps inhuman.

The Book of Evidence and *Athena* exploit even further than Banville's previous work the fragile span between reality and the need to believe and live in illusion. The first person narrative of Frederick Montgomery in *The Book of Evidence* is a confessional monologue of an art expert awaiting trial for murdering a young female servant, who caught him stealing a Dutch masterpiece, *A Portrait of a Woman with Gloves*, from a friend. He killed her simply because she was in the way. Montgomery, a gentleman and non-criminal type, has to make sense of his crimes, to discover the impulse that drove him to them. Articulately written, Montgomery's recollections of his past include scenes of viewing life from within, through windows, as if he had been imprisoned all his life. This feature continues when he appears in *Athena*. Montogmery, out of prison, changes his name to Morrow, but becomes no less self-obsessed. Banville's imaginative description of the Portrait of a Woman with Gloves, as seen by Montgomery, goes beyond what is on the canvas. Montgomery is able to brilliantly invent details of the life and circumstances of a long-dead woman in the portrait, but of the living woman he killed, he realises later, he cannot be forgiven because "I never imagined her vividly enough, that I never made her be there sufficiently, that I did not make her live. I could kill her because for me she was not alive." *Athena* develops Montgomery/Morrow's difficulties of identity in a scenario that is a fantastic play of words and images. Figures from *The Book of Evidence* recur, but slightly altered, and even the one solid character, described with a blend of humour and pathos, Morrow's dying aunt, is a fraud. Acting as a kind of subliminal commentary, paintings are described and analysed to reflect on Morrow's psyche and his pursuit of love via an imagined recreation of the murdered servant. In *The Book of Evidence* Montgomery declared that his task was to bring her back to life and that he would from then on be "living for two;" he later remarks in *Athena* "She had been mine for a time . . . from the start that was supposed to be my task: to give her life." Gombrich notes of Belli's *Pygmalion* "that his quest was 'for forms more perfect and more ideal than reality,'" which pinpoints Morrow's obsession and his tragic dual state of mind. Banville's handling of this extremely complex theme is faultless, for his great ability is to project us into the psychotic world of Montgomery/Morrow, and to share his confusion without question.

—Peter G.W. van de Kamp, updated by Geoffrey Elborn

BARCLAY, Bill. *See* **MOORCOCK, Michael.**

BARKER, A(udrey) L(ilian)

Nationality: British. **Born:** St. Paul's Cray, Kent, 13 April 1918. **Education:** Schools in Beckenham, Kent, and Wallington, Surrey. **Career:** Worked for Amalgamated Press, London, 1936; reader, Cresset Press, London, 1947; secretary and sub-editor, BBC, London, 1949-78. Member of the Executive Committee, English PEN, 1981-85. **Awards:** Atlantic award, 1946; Maugham award, 1947; Cheltenham Festival award, 1963; Arts Council award, 1970; South East Arts award, 1981; Society of Authors travelling scholarship, 1988. Fellow, Royal Society of Literature, 1970. **Agent:** Jennifer Kavanagh, 44 Langham Street, London W1N 5RC, England. **Address:** 103 Harrow Road, Carshalton, Surrey SM5 3QF, England.

PUBLICATIONS

Novels

Apology for a Hero. London, Hogarth Press, and New York, Scribner, 1950.
A Case Examined. London, Hogarth Press, 1965.
The Middling: Chapters in the Life of Ellie Toms. London, Hogarth Press, 1967.
John Brown's Body. London, Hogarth Press, 1969.
A Source of Embarrassment. London, Hogarth Press, 1974.
A Heavy Feather. London, Hogarth Press, 1978; New York, Braziller, 1979.
Relative Successes. London, Chatto and Windus, 1984.
The Gooseboy. London, Hutchinson, 1987.
The Woman Who Talked to Herself. London, Hutchinson, 1989.
Zeph. London, Hutchinson, 1992.

Short Stories

Innocents: Variations on a Theme. London, Hogarth Press, 1947; New York, Scribner, 1948.
Novelette with Other Stories. London, Hogarth Press, and New York, Scribner, 1951.
The Joy-Ride and After. London, Hogarth Press, 1963; New York, Scribner, 1964.
Lost upon the Roundabouts. London, Hogarth Press, 1964.
Penguin Modern Stories 8, with others. London, Penguin, 1971.
Femina Real. London, Hogarth Press, 1971.
Life Stories. London, Chatto and Windus, 1981.
No Word of Love. London, Chatto and Windus, 1985.
Any Excuse for a Party: Selected Stories. London, Hutchinson, 1991.

Play

Television Play: *Pringle,* 1958.

* * *

The theme of A.L. Barker's work is the ambivalence of love and the dangers of egoism. She examines those relationships which exist between victor and victim, he who eats and he who is eaten. This material is handled lightly and skilfully; she has the satirist's ability to select detail, placing her characters socially as well as psychologically. Her territory covers childhood, the worlds of the outcast and the ill and the impoverished lives of the lonely. She is close to the English tradition of the comic novel and like Angus Wilson, a major writer in this genre, she often indulges in caricature.

Many of her short stories reveal a fondness for the macabre, introducing elements of horror into seeming calm. Her first collection, *Innocents,* begins with a study of a boy testing his courage in swimming; he becomes involved in a scene of adult violence that is far more dangerous to him than the tree-roots in his river. Innocence in these stories is seen as inexperience, as the blinkered vision of the mad and as the selfishness of the egoist. *Lost upon the Roundabouts* is a further exploration of these ideas and contains two very fine short stories, "Miss Eagle" and "Someone at the Door."

The central characters in Barker's novels are parasites, dependent on other people for a sense of their own identity. For Ellie in *The Middling* love means "turning another person into a colony of myself." Charles Candy, the central character of *Apology for a Hero,* loves his wife Wynne "because she could give him himself." After Wynne's death he acquires a housekeeper and finds that "when he was with her he felt located." He meets death on a reckless voyage, persuaded that sea-trading will, at last, show him the real Mr. Candy.

The egoist in *A Case Examined* is Rose Antrobus, the chairman of a charity committee with the power to allocate money either to a destitute family or to the church hassock fund. Rose has always insulated herself against suffering. She remembers a childhood friend, Solange, whom she credits with the understanding of despair: Solange provokes violence, she feels, by her own wickedness. This fantasy is shattered by a visit to Paris and a meeting with the real Solange, whose account of Nazi persecution shakes Rose into compassion. A bridge has been made between the worlds of the two women, between the petty and the tragic, and the committee decision is altered accordingly.

Femina Real is an entertaining set of portraits, nine studies of the female character. In many of the situations an apparent vulnerability hides an underlying strength. A frail woman dominates those around her: adolescence vanquishes middle-age; a ten-year-old cripple turns the tables on the man holding her prisoner. As always, Barker's clear prose style matches the accuracy of her observations. Hers is a talent to be treasured.

—Judy Cooke

BARKER, Pat(ricia)

Nationality: British. **Born:** Thornaby-on-Tees, England, 1943. **Education:** LSE, B.Sc.1965. **Family:** Married David B. Barker in 1978; two children. **Career:** Has taught further education. **Awards:** Fawcett prize, for *Union Street.* **Agent:** Curtis Brown Associates, 162-168 Regent Street, London W1R 5TA, England.

PUBLICATIONS

Novels

Union Street. London, Virago, 1982; New York, Putnam, 1983.
Blow Your House Down. London, Virago, and New York, Putnam, 1984.
The Century's Daughter. London, Virago, and New York, Putnam, 1986.
The Man Who Wasn't There. London, Virago, 1989; New York, Ballantine, 1990.
Regeneration. London, Viking, 1991; New York, Dutton, 1992.
The Eye in the Door. London, Viking, 1993; New York, Dutton, 1994.

*

Film Adaptation: *Stanley and Iris,* from the novel *Union Street.*

* * *

Union Street was Pat Barker's first novel, and at once marked her as a powerful voice in objective realism. She had tried writing middle-class fiction but was encouraged by Angela Carter to write of her own working-class roots. Set in an unnamed northern England industrial town, *Union Street* consists of seven interlinked stories, each named after a working-class woman. These form a graphic account, in their own idiom, of women whose lives are circumscribed by poverty and violence. The first chapter, which is the longest, describes a childhood typically shared by the older characters and accounts for their attitudes as adults. Kelly Brown, an intelligent 11-year-old, is hardly cared for by her mother, who has been abandoned by her husband. Playing truant, Kelly roams the streets at night, and on one such occasion she is raped. This she conceals from her mother but, determined not to be defeated, is even more strongly compelled to wander alone. Barker treats Brown entirely sympathetically, so that when she vandalizes a middle-class house and her own school, the reader feels compassion rather than disgust at her actions. She encounters an old woman in a park who has chosen to abandon her house to avoid being put in an old people's home. The woman will die in the cold, and this understanding of the cruelty of life in the extreme encourages Kelly to return to her mother. The speech patterns of the characters are authentic northern English working-class, and the story of *Union Street* reveals bigotry caused by ignorance, overt racism, unwanted pregnancies, and a close society united and also torn apart by appalling social conditions. Running like a thread through all the chapters is the strong Iris King, whose capable way of organizing her own life while helping others provides hope in misery. The novel, which is cyclical, ends with the story of Alice Brown, a confused, senile woman who believes the workhouse still exists and has saved against the indignity of a pauper's funeral. In doing so she is half starved, and even after a severe stroke she refuses to go to a home. Knowing she will be forcibly moved and not allowed to end her days in her own house, she decides to die in the open. She is the woman Kelly met at the beginning of the novel, and Alice's reflections of her own past emphasize the unchanging patterns of life. Barker's skill was confirmed by her *Blow Your House Down,* a fictional reconstruction of prostitution and a Yorkshire Ripper prototype. More successful was *The Century's Daughter,* which covers a period of 80 years and has a large cast of characters, some of whom might have strayed from *Union Street*. In a sense a fictional history of the century, the most poignant section is about the sufferings of men in the trenches of World War I and the effect their deaths have on their families. It was a subject that has fascinated Barker, for she has made it very much her own in a projected trilogy about the Great War. *Regeneration* and *The Eye in the Door,* have been published, with the third, *The Ghost Road,* due in 1995. The fictional treatment of World War I was the domain of the male writer until Susan Hill broke new ground with *Strange Meeting*. Barker's two novels use a mixture of fiction and facts, which were accurately researched, about W. H. Rivers, an army doctor, and his shell-shocked patients at the Craiglockhart War Hospital in Edinburgh. The patients have to be cured before they are sent back to the front, probably to be killed. These include Wilfred Owen and Siegfried Sassoon, who figure as characters, and William Prior, a completely fictional creation who occurs in both novels. *Regeneration*—the regeneration of nerves, that is—examines in microscopic detail the horrific mental disorders caused by trench warfare. Much of the historical detail is already familiar, but Barker gives it a new perspective by providing a background to the soldier's lives to highlight their solitariness in war and at home. Prior is a key figure, for his mental disturbance is exacerbated by his past relationship with his violent father; his reversion as an adult to his childhood ways of escape by "changing" to another personality is a persistent feature of *Regeneration* and *The Eye in the Door.* Originally working-class but now an army officer, he is what the middle and upper classes snobbishly label as a "temporary gentleman." He is, however, acceptable for sex, and the second novel opens with a gay sex scene between him and an upper-class officer, whose hidebound class consciousness will gradually be eroded. Barker challenges attitudes toward pacifism, sexuality, and feminism by fictionally expanding on the facts of a genuine cause célèbre of a female pacifist wrongly imprisoned on trumped-up evidence she was plotting to kill Lloyd George. Fictionally called Beattie Roper, she tests Prior's loyalties, for he is supposed to question her as an intelligence officer. Also happening to be her lifelong friend, he is in the moral dilemma of wanting to prove evidence against an agent provocateur to help her but has his own beliefs as a nonpacifist. The third element of *The Eye in the Door* is the effort of a lunatic to expose homosexuals, his libel on an actress implying she is a lesbian, and his efforts to nail an M.P. for the same crime. All the characters feel watched, by conscience or under suspicion, and the "eye in the door" is the glass in a cell through which the inmate is constantly scrutinized. Although there is inevitable duplication between the first two novels, the publication of *The Ghost Road* will likely consolidate the trilogy as an extraordinary achievement.

—Geoffrey Elborn

BARNES, Julian (Patrick)

Pseudonym: Dan Kavanagh. **Nationality:** British. **Born:** Leicester, 19 January 1946. **Education:** City of London School, 1957-64; Magdalen College, Oxford, 1964-68, B.A. (honours) in modern languages 1968; also studied law. **Family:** Married Pat Kavanagh in 1979. **Career:** Editorial assistant, *Oxford English Dictionary* supplement, 1969-72; contributing editor, *New Review,* London, 1977-78; assistant literary editor, 1977-79, and television critic, 1977-81, *New Statesman,* London; deputy literary editor, *Sunday Times,* London, 1980-82; television critic, the *Observer,* London, 1982-86; London correspondent, *The New Yorker,* 1990-94. Lives in London. **Awards:** Somerset Maugham award, 1981; Faber Memorial prize, 1985; Médicis Essai prize (France), 1986; American Academy award 1986; Gutenberg prize (France), 1987; Premio Grinzane Cavour (Italy), 1988; Prix Fémina (France), 1992; Shakespeare prize (Hamburg), 1993. Chevalier de l'Ordre des Arts et des Lettres, 1988. **Agent:** Peters Fraser and Dunlop, 503-504 The Chambers, Chelsea Harbour, Lots Road, London SW10 0XF, England.

PUBLICATIONS

Novels

Metroland. London, Cape, 1980; New York, St. Martin's Press, 1981.
Before She Met Me. London, Cape, 1982; New York, McGraw Hill, 1986.
Flaubert's Parrot. London, Cape, 1984; New York, Knopf, 1985.
Staring at the Sun. London, Cape, 1986; New York, Knopf, 1987.
A History of the World in 10[up]1[xup]/[dn]2[xup] Chapters. London, Cape, and New York, Knopf, 1989.
Talking It Over. London, Cape, and New York, Knopf, 1991.
The Porcupine. London, Cape, and New York, Knopf, 1992.

Novels as Dan Kavanagh

Duffy. London, Cape, 1980; New York, Pantheon, 1986.
Fiddle City. London, Cape, 1981; New York, Pantheon, 1986.
Putting the Boot In. London, Cape, 1985.
Going to the Dogs. London, Viking, and New York, Pantheon, 1987.

Uncollected Short Stories

"The 50p Santa" (as Dan Kavanagh), in *Time Out* (London), 19 December 1985–1 January 1986.
"One of a Kind," in *The Penguin Book of Modern British Short Stories,* edited by Malcolm Bradbury. London and New York, Viking, 1987.
"Shipwreck," in *The New Yorker,* 12 June 1989.

Other

Letters from London. London, Picador, and New York, Vintage, 1995.

Translator, *The Truth about Dogs,* by Volker Kriegel. London, Bloomsbury, 1988.

*   *   *

The much-quoted glowing tribute paid to Julian Barnes by Carlos Fuentes has given him the reputation—by no means entirely undeserved—of being the most literary, the most intellectual and above all the most international of Britain's younger novelists. France—its locations, language, and literature—all figure largely in most of his books; Barnes's fluency is regularly praised. It may be to Italian contemporaries like Eco and Calvino, as well as to the

South Americans, that his most successful experiments in literary form can be most closely compared, but along with such international strains there is something very English deeply interfused in his work.

His first novel, *Metroland,* owes much to the language and traditions of English poetry. Philip Larkin (himself later to praise Barnes) is quoted on occasions and his steady, empirical temperament and suburban stoicism, as well as the atmosphere of his two often-neglected novels *Jill* and *A Girl in Winter* can be sensed behind the narrative. The plot, in which the young Englishman Christopher Lloyd visits France during *les évènements* of 1968 and has a brief affair with a French girl, carries a distant echo of the epic of English selfhood: Wordsworth's *The Prelude.* The novel immediately demonstrates Barnes's aptitudes as both meticulous stylist and careful recorder of closely observed detail. Its three balanced scenes are equally vivid and imaginative: the adolescent pranks of clever schoolboys Chris and his friend Toni; Chris's belated and intelligently unsentimentalised sexual initiation in Paris; and the suburban idyll of Chris's subsequent marriage, to which Toni's rather phoney iconoclasm is compared. The values may seem anti-extremist to the point of being smug, but the scenes are very convincing.

Graham Hendrick in *Before She Met Me* ditches the safe, non-sexual first wife for a faster, younger model (Ann) who suits him better at first, but her previous life as a minor, sexy film actress soon becomes the subject of his obsessive fascination. A typical Barnes protagonist, Hendrick is rather academic in temperament (he might be Lloyd 10 years on) and catalogues Ann's past life and celluloid loves meticulously until the supposed trail leads him back to the brash novelist host Jack Lupton at whose house he has first met her. This fact finally makes Hendrick lose his cool and leads him to the carefully planned murder and suicide he has devised in order to punish her.

Both of the early novels are good but neither gives such free range to Barnes's real obsession of literature—or to such terrific effect—as *Flaubert's Parrot.* In a year in which novels as successful as J.G. Ballard's *Empire of the Sun,* David Lodge's *Small World,* Martin Amis's *Money,* and Christine Brooke-Rose's *Amalgamemnon* all appeared, *Flaubert's Parrot,* which is part novel and part something else, clearly stood out. Universally praised, it combines the semi-academic protagonist Geoffrey Braithwaite and his interest in the complexities of marital love with a brilliant, well-informed, creative exploration of the French writer's life and work, which ultimately questions the philosophical nature of all history and knowledge. It is one of very few novels written in England whose inventiveness in form has kept pace with what has been such an intellectually lively period in literary theory and criticism. Perhaps it pleases so much because it uses essentially literary ideas to account for—or to demonstrate the impossibility of accounting for—life. It is an oasis of ideas and invention but by no means only abstract or intellectual, since it is grounded in and gains great weight from the reader's eventual realisation that Braithwaite, no less than Flaubert's Félicité, is a *"coeur simple"* who has *"comme tout le monde son histoire de l'amour."* Like Flaubert's Charles Bovary he is a cuckold with a stoical temperament and, as in Flaubert, adulterous love is put in the sobering context of death.

Barnes's other identity as crime writer Dan Kavanagh (complete with mildly racist fictional biography) was the worst kept literary secret of the last decade, casually announced in the cult literary magazine *Quarto* and then blown wide open when "Kavanagh" appeared on a front cover portrait in the *London Review of Books.* The first two novels featuring his bi-sexual ex-cop Duffy (*Duffy,* and *Fiddle City*) were very good fun, with the Soho sex clubs of the former and the airport smuggling of the latter providing vivid low-life detail. The books were as successful in their way as *Metroland* was in its. But by the time of *Putting the Boot In* and *Going to the Dogs,* with *Flaubert's Parrot* as the new yardstick, the joke and the material have been wearing a little thin. In the contemporary fiction scene a successful high-brow novel may well outsell a supposedly "popular" crime thriller, so profit alone is not sufficient motive. The Duffy novels helped give Barnes some street-credibility and may also have served to keep his desire to be sensational out of the mainstream fiction.

Structurally, like *Metroland, Staring at the Sun* is a triptych. The boldness of its form, its long time-perspectives and its compelling central metaphor (of a pilot who, by an accident of flying, experiences sunrise twice) make it another accomplished novel of ideas. It shows three moments in the life of Jean Sergeant: as a naive 17-year-old during World War II entering a sexually-closeted marriage; as a mother in her mid-fifties in 1984, who takes off on a trip to explore the wonders and wisdoms of the world; and finally as a widow on the eve of her 100th birthday in the 21st century, when all the answers to life's questions (at least the questions to which answers are possible) are stored on the General Purposes Computer on a programme that (depending on your degree of credulity or scepticism) is called either The Absolute Truth or TAT.

On the borders between fiction and history H.G. Wells produced a classic of Edwardian optimism in *A Short History of the World* which William Golding disturbingly exposed according to the lights of post-war scepticism in *The Inheritors.* Barnes's *A History of the World in 10[up]1[xup]/[dn]2[xup] Chapters* confronts history with postmodern theories of representation to produce the most successful yet of his novels of ideas. Its 10 chapters, each a tour de force, describe a succession of critical moments from our culture and history where nothing less is at stake than survival. Noah's Ark from the point of view of the woodworm and then in subsequent searches for the historical record of Ararat; a semi-academic Barnes protagonist lecturing on a Mediterranean cruise but caught up in a terrorist hi-jack; a girl who may be inventing her story to protect herself from emotional trauma; Gericault's *Raft of the Medusa,* first imagined as history and then brilliantly analysed as art, all lead up to a curiously empty achieved heaven at the end of survival's quest, in which Leicester City Football Club nauseatingly win the F.A. Cup year after year. Simultaneously playful and serious and packed with suggestive detail, the book gives us a world that is imagined through the postmodern concept of "fabulation," a world in which everything is subtly related to everything else by metaphor and analogy rather than by causal succession, a world comprehensible in terms of the "primal metaphor" of sea voyage and survival. Its lush parenthetical celebration of love links English poetry and postmodernism since, to return to Larkin's "almost" truth: "what will survive of us is love."

That yawning 1970s word "relationships" comes to mind with the latest novel but Barnes quickly preempts any desire to label it as "Play for Today stuff" or "a bit of a disappointment." *Talking It Over* is an effortlessly structured sequence of monologues which tells of the love triangle of the three principle speakers: boring banker Stuart; unpredictable TEFL teacher Oliver; and the rather simple-minded social-work-trained picture restorer Gillian, who comes between them. At first Stuart's schoolboy friendship for Oliver is hardly threatened by his love for and marriage to Gillian but love soon triangulates and transfers and Stuart gets left out in the cold. Though both men vigorously deny it, the male-bonding is obviously a powerful undercurrent, but love itself ("a system for getting someone to call you darling after sex" Stuart cynically concludes), the inevitability of repeated patterns, and the wonderful tendency of language (gestured at in the title) to turn something into something else are the smoothly handled themes. *Talking It Over* deftly absorbs some well-documented trends in the sociology of contemporary love: frankly capitalist and commercial metaphors; the intensification of romantic affection at a time when marriage frequently breaks up; background details of telephone pornography and AIDS. It returns to many of the things Barnes has done successfully in the earlier novels and does them better still, though one wonders why he didn't have a go at writing it as a play.

The Porcupine, a novella, and Barnes's seventh work of fiction written under his own name, appeared in 1992 as a very timely response to the political upheavals that occurred in the former Eastern Bloc countries. Whilst Romania made the biggest headlines of the day, Barnes took Bulgaria as his subject and produced an economical and convincing portrait of a society in the crisis of ideological revolution. Several aspects of *The Porcupine,* such as its length, its meticulous descriptive pace, its Eastern European setting, its hints of Kafka, and the tenor of its concern with issues of gender as well as those of politics suggest a new parallelism of approach with the work of his contemporary Ian McEwan. Indeed at first sight the novel suggests a clear continuation from neither the celebrated experimental mode of Barnes's earlier work nor the more personal sides of it.

However, it does perhaps bring into the foreground a theme that is central in different ways to each of the previous novels and that we may gloss as an attempt to evaluate competing claims to the truth in a postmodern cultural environment where all unitary claims are to be questioned. The two competing claims to truth in this situation are those of Stoyo Petkanov, the old party man and leader of the country for the past 33 years who now has to defend the whole of the past Communist regime and its ideals in the face of the new drive toward capitalism and its spokesman, the new Prosecutor General, Piotr Solinsky. Petkanov is the ready-made villain of the piece, but Barnes lets us in on his point of view, so that by the end of the trial we are warmed to him as a man of a certain kind of integrity and achievement. We are left in no doubt that, in the real world, politics is stronger than justice and that the best location for justice—poetic justice in its original sense—may lie in the balance and dialogue of the novel itself.

With this novel Barnes undoubtedly extends his fictional range but leaves his readers hungry for a return to and a development from the richer and more metafictional strain of his most successful works to date.

—Richard Brown

BARSTOW, Stan(ley)

Nationality: British. **Born:** Horbury, Yorkshire, 28 June 1928. **Education:** Ossett Grammar School. **Family:** Married Constance Mary Kershaw in 1951; one son and one daughter. **Career:** Draftsman and sales executive in the engineering industry, 1944-62. Lives in Hawath, West Yorkshire. **Awards:** Writers Guild award, 1974; Royal Television Society award, 1975. M.A.: Open University, Milton Keynes, Buckinghamshire, 1982. Honorary Fellow, Bretton Hall College, Wakefield Yorkshire, 1985. **Agent:** Lemon Unna and Durbridge Ltd., 24 Pottery Lane, London W11 4LZ, England.

PUBLICATIONS

Novels

A Kind of Loving: The Vic Brown Trilogy. London, Joseph, 1981.
   A Kind of Loving. London, Joseph, 1960; New York, Doubleday, 1961.
   The Watchers on the Shore. London, Joseph, 1966; New York, Doubleday, 1967.
   The Right True End. London, Joseph, 1976.
Ask Me Tomorrow. London, Joseph, 1962.
Joby. London, Joseph, 1964.
A Raging Calm. London, Joseph, 1968; as *The Hidden Part,* New York, Coward McCann, 1969.
A Brother's Tale. London, Joseph, 1980.
Just You Wait and See. London, Joseph, 1986.
B-Movie. London, Joseph, 1987.
Give Us This Day. London, Joseph, 1989.
Next of Kin. London, Joseph, 1991.

Short Stories

The Desperadoes. London, Joseph, 1961.
The Human Element and Other Stories, edited by Marilyn Davies. London, Longman, 1969.
A Season with Eros. London, Joseph, 1971.
A Casual Acquaintance and Other Stories, edited by Marilyn Davies. London, Longman, 1976.
The Glad Eye and Other Stories. London, Joseph, 1984.

Plays

Ask Me Tomorrow, with Alfred Bradley, adaptation of the novel by Barstow (produced Sheffield, 1964). London, French, 1966.
A Kind of Loving, with Alfred Bradley, adaptation of the novel by Barstow (broadcast 1964; produced Sheffield, 1965). London, Blackie, 1970.
An Enemy of the People, adaptation of a play by Ibsen (produced Harrogate, Yorkshire, 1969). London, Calder, 1977.
Listen for the Trains, Love, music by Alex Glasgow (produced Sheffield, 1970).
Stringer's Last Stand, with Alfred Bradley (produced York, 1971).
We Could Always Fit a Sidecar (broadcast 1974). Published in *Out of the Air: Five Plays for Radio,* edited by Alfred Bradley, London, Blackie, 1977.
Joby, adaptation of his own novel (televised 1975). London, Blackie, 1977.
The Human Element, and Albert's Part (televised 1977). London, Blackie, 1984.

Radio Plays: *A Kind of Loving,* from his own novel, 1964; *The Desperadoes,* from his own story, 1965; *The Watchers on the Shore,* from his own novel, 1971; *We Could Always Fit a Sidecar,* 1974; *The Right True End,* from his own novel, 1978; *The Apples of Paradise,* 1988; *Foreign Parts,* 1990.

Television Plays: *The Human Element*, 1964; *The Pity of It All*, 1965; *A World Inside* (documentary), with John Gibson, 1966; *A Family at War* (1 episode), 1970; *Mind You, I Live Here* (documentary), with John Gibson, 1971; *A Raging Calm*, from his own novel, 1974; *South Riding*, from the novel by Winifred Holtby, 1974; *Joby*, from his own novel, 1975; *The Cost of Loving*, 1977; *The Human Element*, 1977; *Albert's Part*, 1977; *Travellers*, 1978; *A Kind of Loving*, from his own novels, 1981; *A Brother's Tale*, from his own novel, 1983; *The Man Who Cried*, from the novel by Catherine Cookson, 1993.

Other

Editor, *Through the Green Woods: An Anthology of Contemporary Writing about Youth and Children*. Leeds, E.J. Arnold, 1968.

*

Stan Barstow comments:

Came to prominence about the same time as several other novelists from North of England working-class backgrounds, viz. John Braine, Alan Sillitoe, David Storey, Keith Waterhouse, and saw with satisfaction, and occasional irritation, the gains made in the opening up of the regions and the "elevation" of the people into fit subjects for fictional portrayal absorbed into the popular cultures of the cinema and TV drama series and comedy shows. Still, living in the provinces and using mainly regional settings, consider myself non-metropolitan oriented. The publication of some of my work in the U.S. and its translation into several European languages reassures me that I have not resisted the neurotic trendiness of much metropolitan culture for the sake of mere provincial narrowness; and the knowledge that some of the finest novels in the language are "regional" leads me to the belief that to hoe one's own row diligently, thus seeking out the universal in the particular, brings more worthwhile satisfactions than the frantic pursuit of a largely phoney jet-age internationalism.

(1995) As I review this comment in 1995, reading flourishes, yet the mainstream literary novel has a harder time than ever in the world of the "celebrity" novel, where fortunes are regularly made by doing badly what others have spent their working lives trying to do well.

*   *   *

It is never easy for the author of a best-selling first novel to come to terms with its success. All too often, publishers demand a sequel, or at the very least another novel written in the same vein, in an attempt to recreate the formula. Stan Barstow is one of the few novelists who has managed to keep intact the mold of their first success and then to have built upon it. Following the appearance of *A Kind of Loving* in 1960, he created a trilogy around Vic Brown, the driven central character who finds himself struggling against the odds in a tough and no-nonsense world. Written at the tail-end of the 1950s, when Britain was entering its first sustained period of postwar prosperity, it is very much a novel of its times. It also reflected a sense of proletarian evangelism: it was as if Barstow was desperate to write about real lives and real events, things normally ignored by the literary world at the time. Although the background was supplied by the potentially grim northern town of Cressley, this was not a joyless fortress but a living place whose inhabitants had created a close-knit community. In many ways too, Cressley was a metaphor for what was happening at the time, as

its population seemed to be unaware of the shift that was slowly eroding their existences. Vic is told this in terms that could be said to be prophetic: "But we're all living in a fool's paradise, that all. A fool's paradise, Vic. Full employment and business booming? It just isn't possible, lad. Don't say I didn't warn you when the crash comes."

Barstow's ability to grasp the moment and record it in fictional terms is typical of the way in which he attacks a novel. Tom Simpkins, caught up in a love affair in *A Raging Calm*, is aware of the possibilities that lie outside his own existence and wants to enjoy them but is also painfully aware of the inhibitions that have helped to shape his life and to give meaning to his sense of morality. (Here it is worth acknowledging that Barstow is particularly responsive to all the complexities for romantic and physical love and does not shirk from attempting to understand the motives for adultery, broken affairs, divorce and unhappiness.) With his ability to allow the narrative to unfold through the development of his main characters, it is little wonder that *A Raging Calm* was later transformed into an equally successful television play.

That Barstow was content to remain within the confines of a world which he knew best—the West Riding of Yorkshire—and with characters whom he understood—the working class of northern England—has been made abundantly clear by his later output. His trilogy of novels about the Palmer family during World War II is a good example—*Just You Wait and See, Give Us This Day*, and *Next of Kin*. The setting of the small Yorkshire town of Daker, another close-knit community of millhands and colliers, is a resonant background for a wide range of ordinary people who find themselves caught up, willy-nilly, in the maelstrom of war. By far the most notable of these is Ella, a mature 23-year-old who comes to prominence in *Give Us This Day*—the anxieties and hardships she has to face give the meaning to the book's title. A young war bride, she discovers that marriage means having to cope with the absence of her husband Walter as she struggles to make a home which they can enjoy once the war is over. Without ever descending into sentimentality, Barstow carefully recreates the tender embarrassment that invades their lives when they meet, and one of the novel's highlights is a firmly constructed set-piece scene in which Walter comes home on leave and the young couple have to rediscover one another all over again.

Mature and single-minded beyond her years, Ella is the still presence at the novel's center, and around her the other characters act almost like a chorus to record the desperate events of a world—their world, in the town of Daker—that has been plunged into war. One of the most memorable moments in the novel is Barstow's description of a mass air-raid on Sheffield that Ella and her mother witness from a train. "None of the pain and loss in her life had prepared her for the vast faceless malice of last night; for sitting in that train while the sky lit up, the bombs fell, the ground shook beneath her. And all the time, behind, in the middle of it, people they knew, whom they had only just left behind."

In its successor, *Next of Kin*, an older Ella has to struggle even harder to preserve her independence and to adjust to the privations of being a war widow. Although she revives a relationship with a former lover, Howard Strickland, he remains a shadowy figure who only brings new pressures into her life. As in the previous two novels, a key feature is Barstow's unerring ability to bring alive the atmosphere of life in a northern provincial town. A born storyteller, Barstow also underscores all his writing with a genuine love for the characters he has created.

—Trevor Royle

BARTH, John (Simmons)

Nationality: American. **Born:** Cambridge, Maryland, 27 May 1930. **Education:** The Juilliard School of Music, New York; Johns Hopkins University, Baltimore, A.B. 1951, M.A. 1952. **Family:** Married 1) Ann Strickland in 1950 (divorced 1969), one daughter and two sons; 2) Shelly Rosenberg in 1970. **Career:** Junior instructor in English, Johns Hopkins University, 1951-53; instructor, 1953-56, assistant professor, 1957-60, and associate professor of English, 1960-65, Pennsylvania State University, University Park; professor of English, 1965-71, and Butler Professor, 1971-73, State University of New York, Buffalo. Since 1973 Centennial Professor of English and Creative Writing, Johns Hopkins University; now emeritus. **Awards:** Brandeis University Creative Arts award, 1965; Rockefeller grant, 1965; American Academy grant, 1966; National Book award, 1973. Litt. D.: University of Maryland, College Park, 1969. **Member:** American Academy, 1977, and American Academy of Arts and Sciences, 1977. **Agent:** Wylie Aitken and Stone, 250 West 57th Street, New York, New York 10107. **Address:** c/o Writing Seminars, Johns Hopkins University, Baltimore, Maryland 21218, U.S.A.

PUBLICATIONS

Novels

The Floating Opera. New York, Appleton Century Crofts, 1956; revised edition, New York, Doubleday, 1967; London, Secker and Warburg, 1968.
The End of the Road. New York, Doubleday, 1958; London, Secker and Warburg, 1962; revised edition, Doubleday, 1967.
The Sot-Weed Factor. New York, Doubleday, 1960; London, Secker and Warburg, 1961; revised edition, Doubleday, 1967.
Giles Goat-Boy; or, The Revised New Syllabus. New York, Doubleday, 1966; London, Secker and Warburg, 1967.
Letters. New York, Putnam, 1979; London, Secker and Warburg, 1980.
Sabbatical: A Romance. New York, Putnam, and London, Secker and Warburg, 1982.
The Tidewater Tales: A Novel. New York, Putnam, 1987; London, Methuen, 1988.
The Last Voyage of Somebody the Sailor. Boston, Little Brown, 1991.
Once Upon a Time: A Floating Opera. Boston, Little Brown, 1994.

Short Stories

Lost in the Funhouse: Fiction for Print, Tape, Live Voice. New York, Doubleday, 1968; London, Secker and Warburg, 1969.
Chimera. New York, Random House, 1972; London, Deutsch, 1974.
Todd Andrews to the Author. Northridge, California, Lord John Press, 1979.

Other

The Literature of Exhaustion, and The Literature of Replenishment (essays). Northridge, California, Lord John Press, 1982.
The Friday Book: Essays and Other Nonfiction. New York, Putnam, 1984.

Don't Count on It: A Note on the Number of the 1001 Nights. Northridge, California, Lord John Press, 1984.
Further Fridays: Essays, Lectures, and Other Nonfiction, 1984-1994. Boston, Little Brown, 1995.

*

Bibliography: *John Barth: A Descriptive Primary and Annotated Secondary Bibliography* by Josephy Weixlmann, New York, Garland, 1976; *John Barth: An Annotated Bibliography* by Richard Allan Vine, Metuchen, New Jersey, Scarecrow Press, 1977; *John Barth, Jerzy Kosinski, and Thomas Pynchon: A Reference Guide* by Thomas P. Walsh and Cameron Northouse, Boston, Hall, 1977.

Manuscript Collection: Library of Congress, Washington, D.C.

Critical Studies: *John Barth* by Gerhard Joseph, Minneapolis, University of Minnesota Press, 1970; *John Barth: The Comic Sublimity of Paradox* by Jac Tharpe, Carbondale, Southern Illinois University Press, 1974; *The Literature of Exhaustion: Borges, Nabokov, and Barth* by John O. Stark, Durham, North Carolina, Duke University Press, 1974; *John Barth: An Introduction* by David Morrell, University Park, Pennsylvania State University Press, 1976; *Critical Essays on John Barth* edited by Joseph J. Waldmeir, Boston, Hall, 1980; *Passionate Virtuosity: The Fiction of John Barth* by Charles B. Harris, Urbana, University of Illinois Press, 1983; *John Barth* by Heide Ziegler, London, Methuen, 1987; *Understanding John Barth* by Stan Fogel and Gordon Slethaug, Columbia, University of South Carolina Press, 1990; *A Reader's Guide to John Barth* by Zack Bowen, Westport, Connecticut, Greenwood Press, 1994.

*   *   *

John Barth is often called one of the most important American novelists of the twentieth century. He combines the kind of experimentation associated with postmodernist writing with a mastery of the skills demanded of the traditional novelist. A progression toward postmodernism may be traced in his works from the more traditional treatments of his earlier books—*The Floating Opera, The End of the Road,* and *The Sot-Weed Factor*—to the wild experimentation that characterizes such works as *Giles Goat-Boy, Chimera, Letters,* and especially *Lost in the Funhouse.* In *Sabbatical,* he returns to the more traditional kind of narrative, with the added postmodernist twist that the novel itself is supposed to be the work produced by the two central characters in it. In *The Tidewater Tales,* too, the novel is supposed to be the work of one of the central characters. In fact, *The Tidewater Tales* combines many of the elements of postmodern fiction, including an awareness of itself as fiction, with the strong story line associated with more traditional novels. Barth's works after *Tidewater Tales—The Last Voyage of Somebody the Sailor* and *Once Upon a Time*—also involve many elements of postmodernist fiction, especially *Once Upon a Time,* in which the narrator constantly reminds the reader that the work is a piece of fiction.

Although Barth denies that he engages in experimentation for its own sake, the stories in *Lost in the Funhouse* give that appearance. Subtitled *Fiction for Print, Tape, Live Voice,* the work marks Barth's embrace of the world of the postmodern in which fiction and reality, and fictitious characters and the authors that produce them, become indistinguishable and in which consistent suspension of disbelief becomes almost impossible. Barth's insistence that some of the stories in this "series," as he calls it, were not composed "expressly for print" and thus "make no sense unless heard in live or recorded voices" is questionable, since they are in print and presumably the author did compose them in written form. Nonetheless, they show Barth's versatility with various fictional forms. Still, even if Barth really intended a story like "Echo," the eighth in the series, only for live or recorded voice, it is difficult to determine whether it is profound or merely full of gimmickry.

Barth calls *Letters* "an old time epistolary novel," yet it is anything but old-fashioned. In this monumental work, the author himself becomes a fictitious character with whom his "fictitious drolls and dreamers," many of whom are drawn from Barth's earlier works, correspond concerning their often funny yet sometimes horrifying problems. The letters they exchange gradually reveal the convoluted plot that involves abduction, possible incest, and suicide. That postmodernism may have reached a dead end in this book is something Barth himself seems to have recognized with his return to a more traditional form in *Sabbatical,* a novel with an easily summarizable plot involving clearly defined characters. *The Tidewater Tales,* too, has a very strong story line, yet like *Letters,* it has some characters familiar from other works by Barth, including the "real" authors of *Sabbatical.* It also includes a thinly disguised version of Barth himself, called Djean, familiar from *Chimera,* as well as many characters from other pieces of literature, including Ulysses and Nausicaa (also known as the Dmitrikakises), Don Quixote (called Donald Quicksoat), and Scheherazade, who is more closely modeled on the Scheherazade of Barth's *Chimera* than on the heroine of the *Arabian Nights.*

Along with Barth's movement from modernism to postmodernism may be traced a movement from what he calls "the literature of exhaustion" to what he calls "the literature of replenishment." The antiheroes of his earlier works—Todd Andrews, Jake Horner, and Ebenezer Cooke—give way to the genuinely heroic protagonist of *Giles Goat-Boy,* a book of epic dimensions containing a central figure and plot modeled largely on myths of various heroes, both pagan and Christian. This work may prove to be one of the most important pieces of literature of the twentieth century. The central character, Giles himself, may be lacking a human father (quite probably he was fathered by the computer that controls the world of the novel). As the book unfolds, he proceeds without hesitation to fulfill his typically heroic destiny to "*Pass All Fail All.*" Whatever victories he achieves are, of course, ambiguous, and his existence is left in doubt.

The part of the book involving the actual narrative of events in the life of George Giles is entitled "*R. N. S. The Revised New Syllabus of George Giles OUR GRAND TUTOR* Being the Autobiographical and Hortatory Tapes Read Out at New Tammany College to His Son *Giles (,) Stoker* By the West Campus Automatic Computer and by Him Prepared for the Furtherment of the Gilesian Curriculum." It contains a kind of comic, cosmic new testament, a collection of sacred-profane writings designed to guide future students in the university world in which the body of the novel is set. Narrating the life and adventures of George Giles, the goat-boy of the title, it recounts his intellectual, political, and sexual exploits. The introductory material to the "Revised New Syllabus," consisting of a "Publisher's Disclaimer," with notes from Editors A through D and written by "The Editor-in-Chief;" the "Cover-Letter to the Editors and Publisher," written by "This regenerate Seeker after

Answers, J. B.;" the "Posttape" as well as the "Postscript to the Posttape," again written by J. B.; and the "Footnote to the Postscript," written by "Ed.," are all part of this fiction.

From the paralysis of a Jacob Horner in *The End of the Road* to the action of a Giles is a long stride. Horner is paralyzed, he claims, because he suffers from "cosmopsis," "the cosmic view" in which "one is frozen like the bullfrog when the hunter's light strikes him full in the eyes, only with cosmopsis there is no hunter, and no quick hand to terminate the moment—there's only the light." An infinite number of possibilities leads to a paralyzing inability to choose any one. The same kind of cosmic view, however, causes no problem for George Giles, who, when unable to choose between existing possibilities, unhesitatingly creates his own, as he does when he first leaves the barn to seek his destiny in the outside world. Heroically, George realizes that he "had invented myself as I'd elected my name," and he accepts responsibility not only for himself but also for his world.

In *Sabbatical* and *The Tidewater Tales,* Barth draws heavily on the folklore of the Chesapeake Bay and the CIA. In the former, he writes of the end of a year-long sailing voyage taken by Fenwick, an ex-CIA agent, and Susan, a college professor, in order to decide what they will do with their lives. Their problem's resolution seems trite and unconvincing, but their path toward that resolution is interesting. Like *Chimera, Sabbatical* is a twentieth-century fairy tale, ending with the statement that the two central characters "lived/ Happily after, to the end/Of Fenwick and Susie. . . .*" The rhyme is completed in the footnote: "*Susan./Fenn." Obviously, in this work too it is often difficult to distinguish gimmickry and profundity. Sentimentality also pervades *The Tidewater Tales,* essentially the story of the ending of Peter Sagamore's writing block, as he and his pregnant wife travel the Chesapeake Bay on their sailboat named *Story.*

The Last Voyage of Somebody the Sailor is set partially and *Once Upon a Time* is set mostly on the Chesapeake Bay. Both are pieces of fantasy, the former loosely structured on the seven voyages of Sinbad the Sailor as told by Scheherazade in *1001 Arabian Nights.* Both are also structured, Barth claims in *Once Upon a Time,* on the hero quest, which he calls the Ur-myth. In fact, in *Once Upon a Time,* the narrator, who may also be the author, says that all of his works since *The Sot-Weed Factor* are variations on the Ur-myth, even though he claims not to have known about the myth when he wrote *The Sot-Weed Factor.*

Both *The Last Voyage of Somebody the Sailor* and *Once Upon a Time* draw largely on the author's life, so much so that the latter repeats many things from the former. The latter pretends to be autobiography masquerading as fiction, but it may be fiction masquerading as autobiography. At any rate, it recounts what its narrator claims both is and is not Barth's early life, his education, his two marriages, his teaching career, and the writing of his books and stories.

Barth then is one of the most important figures in twentieth-century American literature. He has consistently been at the forefront of literary experimentation, consequently producing works occasionally uneven and, as a result of his particular type of experimentation, occasionally too self-consciously witty. Still, he has produced some works that are now ranked and probably will continue to be ranked among the best of this century.

—Richard Tuerk

BARTHELME, Frederick

Nationality: American. **Born:** Houston, Texas, 10 October 1943; brother of the writer Donald Barthelme. **Education:** Tulane University, New Orleans, 1961-62; University of Houston, 1962-65, 1966-67; Johns Hopkins University, Baltimore (teaching fellow; Coleman Prose award, 1977), 1976-77, M.A. 1977. **Career:** Architectural draftsman, Jerome Oddo and Associates, and Kenneth E. Bentsen Associates, both Houston, 1965-66; exhibition organizer, St. Thomas University, Houston, 1966-67; assistant to director, Kornblee Gallery, New York, 1967-68; creative director, BMA Advertising, Houston, 1971-73; senior writer, GDL & W Advertising, Houston, 1973-76. Since 1977 professor of English, director of the Center for Writers, and editor of *Mississippi Review,* University of Southern Mississippi, Hattiesburg. Visual artist: exhibitions at galleries in Houston, Norman, Oklahoma, New York, Seattle, Vancouver, Buenos Aires, and Oberlin, Ohio, 1965-74. **Awards:** National Endowment for the Arts fellowship, 1979; University of Southern Mississippi research grant, 1980. **Address:** Box 5144, Hattiesburg, Mississippi 39406, U.S.A.

PUBLICATIONS

Novels

War and War. New York, Doubleday, 1971.
Second Marriage. New York, Simon and Schuster, 1984; London, Dent, 1985.
Tracer. New York, Simon and Schuster, 1985; London, Dent, 1986.
Two Against One. New York, Weidenfeld and Nicolson, 1988; London, Viking, 1989.
Natural Selection. New York, Viking, 1990.
The Brothers. New York, Viking, 1993.
Painted Desert. New York, Viking, 1995.

Short Stories

Rangoon. New York, Winter House, 1970.
Moon Deluxe. New York, Simon and Schuster, 1983; London, Penguin, 1984.
Chroma and Other Stories. New York, Simon and Schuster, 1987; London, Penguin, 1989.

Uncollected Short Stories

"Cooker," in *New Yorker,* 10 August 1987.
"Law of Averages," in *New Yorker,* 5 October 1987.
"Shopgirls," in *Esquire* (Japanese edition: Tokyo), August 1988.
"War with Japan," in *New Yorker,* 12 December 1988.
"Driver," in *New American Short Stories 2,* edited by Gloria Norris. New York, New American Library, 1989.
"With Ray and Judy," in *New Yorker,* 24 April 1989.
"Domestic," in *Fiction of the Eighties,* edited by Gibbons and Hahn, Chicago, TriQuarterly, 1990.
"The Philosophers," in *Boston Globe Magazine,* 22 July 1990.
"Margaret and Bud," in *New Yorker,* 15 May 1991.
"Jackpot," in *Frank Magazine,* 1992.
"Retreat," in *Epoch,* 1993.

*   *   *

Frederick Barthelme's early fiction—*Rangoon* and *War and War*—is self-consciously experimental, overly influenced (and greatly overshadowed) by the far more successful work of writers like his older brother Donald. It wasn't until more than a decade later, in the 17 stories that comprise *Moon Deluxe,* that he would begin writing the kind of fiction that would establish him as one of the most interesting of current American writers.

Barthelme's stories have the familiar look of the real world; they are meticulously detailed in such matters as the make and color of the cars the characters drive, the brand names of the products they buy, the names of the places where they live and the restaurants where they eat. On the other hand, they are eerily vague and indistinct about such matters as their location (the general setting is the Sun Belt states along the Gulf Coast), background information about the characters' jobs, their past, sometimes about their own names. Barthelme's fictional world is filled with real objects but empty of meaningful experience; his characters talk about things but seldom about things that matter.

The stories are typically narrated in present tense by men in their late thirties, either single or divorced, who live alone. Like Camus's Meursault, they report events in a detached, disengaged, almost affectless manner. (Several of the stories are told in second person, which distances the narrator even from himself.) Passive individuals, these men are watchers rather than doers; it is usually the women who are the aggressors, the men responding almost willy-nilly to their advances. These characters reveal so little of their real selves that they are virtually interchangeable from one story to another.

The emptiness of the characters' lives and the dead tone in which the tales are narrated combine to make a powerful statement about the loneliness that infects the lives of many who inhabit the modern shopping malls, fast food restaurants, and singles apartment complexes of contemporary suburban America. However, Barthelme avoids making his stories as bleak as his characters' lives by presenting incidents and dialogue with a decidedly comic touch. The stories also transmit a strong sense of expectation, an unsettling feeling that something dramatic is about to happen (it seldom does). In *Moon Deluxe* the dull and the routine seem charged with mystery.

Second Marriage is a brilliant comedy of contemporary social and sexual manners, rich in offbeat characters and wickedly funny dialogue. The novel tells the story of a man named Henry (no last name) whose ex-wife Clare moves in with him and his current wife Theo. The two women soon discover they like each other more than they like Henry, so they ask him to move out. The book records with wry humor his goofy experiences following his eviction by his wives.

Henry is in many ways a typical Barthelme character: decent but ineffectual, he finds himself pushed aside, a casualty of the sexual revolution; bewildered, he passes the time watching TV, vacuuming his apartment, cleaning the refrigerator, aimlessly reading magazine articles he doesn't understand. One activity that usually rouses him from his torpor is eating, a favorite pastime for all of Barthelme's characters. None of them especially savors food; going out to eat is simply something to do, a safe way of filling up time, though the fast food they routinely consume is as lacking in nutrition as the tentative relationships they stumble in and out of.

Martin, the narrator of *Tracer,* moves into the Florida motel-condo operated by his wife Alex's sister Dominica following the breakup of his marriage. He is soon sleeping with Dominica, which complicates matters when both Alex and Dominica's estranged husband Mel show up. Out of this tangled web of relationships Barthelme fashions another of his quirky comedies of modern life.

Tracer is rich in details, incidents, and dialogue which underscore Barthelme's favorite themes of displacement and failed connections. The central symbol of the novel is a P-38 Night Fighter plane which, like Martin, has come to rest on Dominica's property like a lost bird. The dialogue, composed largely of humorous yet pointless monologues, conversational non-sequiturs, and misunderstood statements, is as disconnected as the characters' lives. Even incidents (such as the bizarre episode involving a stranger who takes out a gun and inexplicably begins shooting at the P-38) seem to have become unglued from any sort of logical context.

Two Against One presents another familiar Barthelme triangle. Following a six-month separation, Elise returns to husband Edward on his 40th birthday with a novel suggestion: she wishes to invite her former lover Roscoe, whose wife has been killed in a traffic accident, to move in with the two of them. Sex isn't the motivating factor; some sort of connection is. Like the rest of Barthelme's aimless and confused heroes, Edward isn't sure what to do; he isn't entirely opposed to the idea, but he isn't sure he likes it either.

Like *Tracer, Two Against One* moves beyond the spare, elliptical quality of Barthelme's earlier fiction. The characters in this novel are also portrayed with more empathy, less scorn. They may not have any of the answers, but in contrast to many of their earlier counterparts, they are at least yearning for answers and taking tentative (albeit unorthodox) steps towards finding them.

The aimlessness that afflicts Barthelme's characters, and that is often the source of much of the humor in his books, takes on a decidedly darker hue in *Natural Selection*. Peter Wexler concludes he's not terribly happy in his marriage to second-wife Lily. Wandering the malls and haphazardly driving the freeways temporarily provides a comforting outlet for his uneasiness, as these activities commonly do for Barthelme's characters. But this time the resolution to his marital dilemma comes unexpectedly as a late-night drive on the freeway with his wife results in a fatal traffic accident in the final scene of the novel. The heartbreak that usually lurks just beneath the comic surface in Barthelme's novels surfaces with sudden impact at the end of *Natural Selection*.

Barthelme is a poet of the mundane who combines the satirist's knack for exposing the ridiculous in contemporary society with a photographer's ability to capture the quotidian details of everyday life. His fiction, situated somewhere between good-humored social satire and documentary realism, both captures the absurdity and celebrates the wonder of the ordinary.

—David Geherin

BAUMBACH, Jonathan

Nationality: American. **Born:** New York City, 5 July 1933. **Education:** Brooklyn College, New York, 1951-55, A.B. 1955; Columbia University, New York, 1955-56, M.F.A. 1956; Stanford University, California, 1958-61, Ph.D. 1961. **Military Service:** Served in the United States Army, 1956-58. **Family:** Married 1) Elinor Berkman in 1956 (divorced 1967), one son and one daughter; 2) Georgia A. Brown in 1968 (divorced 1990), two sons. **Career:** Instructor, Stanford University, 1958-60; instructor, 1961-62, and assistant professor, 1962-64, Ohio State University, Co-

lumbus; assistant professor, New York University, 1964-66. Associate professor, 1966-70, 1971-72, and since 1972 professor of English, Brooklyn College, City University of New York. Visiting professor, Tufts University, Medford, Massachusetts, 1970-71, and University of Washington, Seattle, 1978-79. Film critic, *Partisan Review,* New Brunswick, New Jersey, and Boston, 1974-83. Cofounder, 1974, co-director, 1974-78, and currently member of the Board of Directors, Fiction Collective, New York; chair, National Society of Film Critics, 1982-84. **Awards:** *New Republic* award, 1958; Yaddo grant, 1963, 1964, 1965; National Endowment for the Arts fellowship, 1967; Guggenheim fellowship, 1978; Ingram Merrill Foundation fellowship, 1983. **Agent:** Ellen Levine Literary Agency, 432 Park Avenue South, Suite 1205, New York, New York 10016. **Address:** 208 Marlborough Road, Brooklyn, New York 11226, U.S.A.

PUBLICATIONS

Novels

A Man to Conjure With. New York, Random House, 1965; London, Gollancz, 1966.
What Comes Next. New York, Harper, 1968.
Reruns. New York, Fiction Collective, 1974.
Babble. New York, Fiction Collective, 1976.
Chez Charlotte and Emily. New York, Fiction Collective, 1979.
My Father More or Less. New York, Fiction Collective, 1982.
Separate Hours. Boulder, Colorado, Fiction Collective 2, 1990.
Seven Wives: A Romance. Boulder, Colorado, Fiction Collective 2, 1994.

Short Stories

The Return of Service. Urbana, University of Illinois Press, 1979.
The Life and Times of Major Fiction. New York, Fiction Collective, 1987.

Uncollected Short Stories

"You Better Watch Out," in *Seems* (Sheboygan, Wisconsin), Fall 1978.
"Neglected Masterpieces III," in *Columbia* (New York), 1986.
"The History of Elegance," in *Columbia* (New York), April 1988.
"Low Light," in *Fiction International* (San Diego), Spring 1990.
"The Mother Murders," in *Witness* (Farmington Hills, Michigan) Summer-Fall 1990.
"The Man Who Invented the World," in *Film Comment* (New York), February 1991.
"Men at Lunch," in *Boulevard,* Fall 1991.
"Stills from Imaginary Movies," in *Film Comment,* May-June 1991.
"The Villa Mondare," in *Mississippi Review,* Spring 1992.
"The Reading," in *Boulevard,* Spring 1993.
"Outlaws," in *Georgetown Review,* Fall 1993.
"Bright Is Innocent," in *Iowa Review,* September 1994.
"His View of Her View of Him," in *Boulevard,* Spring 1995.

Play

The One-Eyed Man Is King (produced New York, 1956).

Other

The Landscape of Nightmare: Studies in the Contemporary American Novel. New York, New York University Press, 1965; London, Owen, 1966.

Editor, with Arthur Edelstein, *Moderns and Contemporaries: Nine Masters of the Short Story.* New York, Random House, 1968; revised edition, 1977.
Editor, *Writers as Teachers/Teachers as Writers.* New York, Holt Rinehart, 1970.
Editor, *Statements: New Fiction from the Fiction Collective.* New York, Braziller, 1975.
Editor, with Peter Spielberg, *Statements 2: New Fiction.* New York, Fiction Collective, 1977.

*

Manuscript Collection: Boston University Library.

Critical Study: *The Life of Fiction* by Jerome Klinkowitz, Urbana, University of Illinois Press, 1977; *Writing in a Film Age* edited by Keith Cohen, Boulder, University Press of Colorado.

Jonathan Baumbach comments:

Novels are an attempt to make sense out of experience and to make experience out of sense, to eschew the illusion of verisimilitude, to give form to what never existed, not to imitate life but to re-invent it out of language, to imagine the processes of the imagination, to imagine the imagining of the processes of the imagination, involved with cinema, dream, and memory, and the underground landscape of their conjunction.

No theory informs the work. It is what it comes to. My fiction is the illusion of itself.

*   *   *

A helpful preface to Jonathan Baumbach's fiction is his critical study, *The Landscape of Nightmare: Studies in the Contemporary American Novel.* Baumbach is representative of a new style of novelist (which includes Ronald Sukenick, Jerzy Kosinski, and William H. Gass), having earned a graduate degree before writing fiction himself. Baumbach's thesis, that "To live in this world, to live consciously in this world in which madness daily passes for sanity is a kind of madness in itself," describes a problem for literary art against which he poses his own fiction as solution. "Unable to believe in the surface (the *Life* magazine reality) of our world," he argues, "the best of the post-Second-World-War novelists have taken as their terrain the landscape of the psyche." Yet for that "landscape of nightmare" writers such as Bernard Malamud and William Styron were still using techniques more appropriate to social realism. In his own work Baumbach has striven to find a new style suitable for the innovative fiction he writes. As he emphasized to an interviewer in 1973, "I'm not just using the dream in the traditional sense, in the psychological sense where it's an almost compacted parable, with special symbols. I'm just trying to find another way of getting at reality. I mean, my sense is that the conventional novel, for me, anyway, is on its way to a dead end. And I'm trying to get at the way things are in a way that no one has ever seen them before."

Baumbach's first novel, *A Man to Conjure With,* synthesizes various trends outlined in his critical study. Much like William Styron's *Lie Down in Darkness,* Baumbach's work has a protagonist who moves simultaneously backward and forward in time, carefully orchestrating revelations of plot and character so that the present is gradually understood in a plausible and convincing way. As a result, the narrative is assembled as a psychological collage; only in the protagonist's final act do all the elements become clear. Baumbach's technical achievement has been to find a structural form which reflects this psychological state: a thoroughly spatial novel.

What Comes Next is a more tightly written exploration of this same structural theme. Again the situation is psychological: a young college student, beset by sexual and parental problems, is "flipping out," and Baumbach's novel expresses this confusion by its very form. Violence erupts on every page, though primarily as mental device, since it is usually sparked by newspaper headlines and fantasized incidents. The book organizes itself as a literal landscape of nightmare, as all reference points for the character's reality are located within his own disjointed perceptions. As far as temporal narrative, "what comes next" is created from the workings of his mind.

Baumbach's subsequent work has been even more strongly experimental. His third novel, *Reruns,* abandons plot and character entirely in favor of dream-like images from movies rerun page by page. *Babble,* a novel made up of several "baby stories" written through the mid-1970s, is more playful but no less daring in its technical achievement. In order to explore the workings of narrative, Baumbach records the stories his infant son allegedly tells him ("His second story is less fresh than the first, though of greater technical sophistication;" "The robot is after him again, this time disguised as a soda vending machine. 'You can't have any Coke,' the robot says, 'until you wash your face'"). Once more Baumbach has become the critic in order to fashion a new mode for fiction.

Technical resources for Baumbach's developing style of fiction are discussed in his introduction to *Writers as Teachers / Teachers as Writers.* Here, speaking as both a fiction writer and a literary critic, he reveals that in creative writing classes one can "talk to the real person, the secret outlaw hiding out in the 'good' student." This outlaw quality distinguishes the narrative artist, whose genius is to be in touch with himself or herself, with the personal voice inside that overcomes the "strategies of evasion" which in fact cover up the idiosyncratic qualities of expression (and therefore of beauty and insight). Such expression cannot be taught, but can only be developed in a context whereby the writer-to-be discovers his or her own talent. The strategies for doing this reflect Baumbach's own experiments in fiction: overcoming the fear of being foolish, learning that it is less important to understand something than appreciating how to live with it, and getting to know how to exist in a community with one's readers. In the process, one must fight against "years and years of systematic depersonalization to get at what's unique and alive." Consequently Baumbach and his contributors emphasize the importance of finding one's personal voice, a strategy that informs the more recent contributions to the fiction anthology Baumbach co-edited, *Moderns and Contemporaries,* the second edition of which features personally vocal stories by Grace Paley (also a contributor to the writing book) and Donald Barthelme.

Throughout the 1970s Baumbach continued to experiment with various structures for fiction, including the sub-genre parodies, movie mythologies, and dreamlike obsessions featured throughout his story collection *The Return of Service.* But it is his fifth novel, *Chez Charlotte and Emily,* which displays his greatest facility as a writer. Ostensibly the device by which a bored husband and wife communicate with each other (by proposing a narrative and then critiquing it), the novel is actually an excuse (à la *The Canterbury Tales*) for the telling of stories. Freed from the necessity of plausible context, Baumbach is able to spin out fantasies of shipwreck, sexual adventure, intrigue, and the complexity of human relationships—all as pure writing, justified by the arrangement of the couple's critical debate. Soon the two contexts, critical and fictional, merge—as they must, Baumbach would argue, for it is through works of the imagination that we preserve our consciousness of the world.

His sixth novel, *My Father More or Less,* experiments with forms of intertextuality to make this same point. Alternately narrated by Tom Terman and by a third-person narrator reflecting the actions of his father Lukas, the novel shows how Tom's visit to his father in London is shaped by the son's memory of his earlier abandonment, while the father's own coming to terms with his son, his mistress, and his employer becomes interwoven with the detective-story screenplay he's been working on. Lukas only superficially controls his film narrative, as its development toward the protagonist's death is impelled by the pressure of events unfolding in Terman's life. But these same events are enriched by the textual experience with his script. At times the writer's role takes over, as when Terman extricates himself from an unhappy situation by "writing himself a few lines of dialogue." For his part, Tom finds himself in a film script situation enhanced by the fact that actual movies have been shot on location in his father's house; but when events threaten, he is able to telephone his father for a rescue, much like a character calling upon the author for relief. That the father is creator of the son helps establish the naturalized quality of Baumbach's narrative. Although as experimentally intertextual as the most sophisticated literary experiments, *My Father More or Less* reads as accessibly as the most realistic fiction, indicating that Baumbach has found a useful device for bringing innovative fiction back within the literary mainstream.

Comfortable in his style that melds both tradition and innovation, Baumbach uses a range of familiar materials in the stories of *The Life and Times of Major Fiction* to show how fresh techniques for presentation are available to the writer who both knows the tricks of the trade and appreciates how readers will appreciate their use. His particular genius is displayed in "Mr. and Mrs. McFeely at Home and Away," based as it is on characters from a popular children's show who are, in their televised roles, the quintessence of familiarity, while their lives off-screen are shown as offering a challenge to the imagination, given that on TV the audience's imagining has been done for them. In similar manner, the challenge to write a story about basketball produces "How You Play the Game," an exercise in trying to make a narrative out of what is in essence merely a situation. The author, who is a character in his own story by virtue of having been asked in the first line to write it, struggles to make life as interesting as art, and succeeds only by following the most rudimentary role of fantasy: placing himself in the actual game.

A similar strategy informs *Separate Hours,* Baumbach's novel in which the long relationship of husband and wife becomes problematic for a novel, because its telling is complicated by the fact that each is a psychotherapist possessed of an entire battery of systems for just such interpretation. As in the basketball story, there are thus two streams to the narrative: action and interpretation. Problems result when one turns into the other. That each character wishes to be the narrator creates a dilemma for the reader in search of a story to be trusted. The dual nature of this and of all narrative is

Baumbach's continuing interest, evident in his experiments at combining photos and text as "stills from imaginary movies," sections of which have appeared as in progress.

—Jerome Klinkowitz

BAWDEN, Nina

Nationality: British. **Born:** Nina Mabey in London, 19 January 1925. **Education:** Ilford County High School; Somerville College, Oxford, B.A. 1946, M.A. 1951; Salzburg Seminar in American Studies, 1960. **Family:** Married 1) H.W. Bawden in 1946, two sons (one deceased); 2) the broadcast executive A.S. Kark in 1954, one daughter. **Career:** Assistant, Town and Country Planning Association, 1946-47; Justice of the Peace for Surrey, 1968-76. Regular reviewer, *Daily Telegraph,* London. **Awards:** *Guardian* award, for children's book, 1976; *Yorkshire Post* award, 1976. Fellow, Royal Society of Literature, 1970. CBE (Commander of the British Empire). **Member:** PEN Executive Committee, 1968-71; President, Society of Women Writers and Journalists. **Agent:** Curtis Brown, 162-168 Regent Street, London W1R 5TB. **Address:** 22 Noel Road, London N1 8HA, England; or, 19 Kapodistriou, Nauplion 21000, Greece.

PUBLICATIONS

Novels

Who Calls the Tune. London, Collins, 1953; as *Eyes of Green,* New York, Morrow, 1953.
The Odd Flamingo. London, Collins, 1954.
Change Here for Babylon. London, Collins, 1955.
The Solitary Child. London, Collins, 1956; New York, Lancer, 1966.
Devil by the Sea. London, Collins, 1957; Philadelphia, Lippincott, 1959; abridged edition (for children), London, Gollancz, and Lippincott, 1976.
Just Like a Lady. London, Longman, 1960; as *Glass Slippers Always Pinch,* Philadelphia, Lippincott, 1960.
In Honour Bound. London, Longman, 1961.
Tortoise by Candlelight. London, Longman, and New York, Harper, 1963.
Under the Skin. London, Longman, and New York, Harper, 1964.
A Little Love, A Little Learning. London, Longman, 1965; New York, Harper, 1966.
A Woman of My Age. London, Longman, and New York, Harper, 1967.
The Grain of Truth. London, Longman, and New York, Harper, 1968.
The Birds on the Trees. London, Longman, and New York, Harper, 1970.
Anna Apparent. London, Longman, and New York, Harper, 1972.
George Beneath a Paper Moon. London, Allen Lane, and New York, Harper, 1974; as *On the Edge,* London, Sphere, 1985.
Afternoon of a Good Woman. London, Macmillan, 1976; New York, Harper, 1977.
Familiar Passions. London, Macmillan, and New York, Morrow, 1979.

Walking Naked. London, Macmillan, 1981; New York, St. Martin's Press, 1982.

The Ice House. London, Macmillan, and New York, St. Martin's Press, 1983.

Circles of Deceit. London, Macmillan, and New York, St. Martin's Press, 1987.

Family Money. London, Gollancz, and New York, St. Martin's Press, 1991.

Fiction (for children)

The Secret Passage. London, Gollancz, 1963; as *The House of Secrets,* Philadelphia, Lippincott, 1964.

On the Run. London, Gollancz, 1964; as *Three on the Run,* Philadelphia, Lippincott, 1965.

The White Horse Gang. London, Gollancz, and Philadelphia, Lippincott, 1966.

The Witch's Daughter. London, Gollancz, and Philadelphia, Lippincott, 1966.

A Handful of Thieves. London, Gollancz, and Philadelphia, Lippincott, 1967.

The Runaway Summer. London, Gollancz, and Philadelphia, Lippincott, 1969.

Squib. London, Gollancz, and Philadelphia, Lippincott, 1971.

Carrie's War. London, Gollancz, and Philadelphia, Lippincott, 1973.

The Peppermint Pig. London, Gollancz, and Philadelphia, Lippincott, 1975.

Rebel on a Rock. London, Gollancz, and Philadelphia, Lippincott, 1978.

The Robbers. London, Gollancz, and New York, Lothrop, 1979.

Kept in the Dark. London, Gollancz, and New York, Lothrop, 1982.

The Finding. London, Gollancz, and New York, Lothrop, 1985.

Princess Alice. London, Deutsch, 1985.

Keeping Henry. London, Gollancz, 1988; as *Henry,* New York, Lothrop, 1988.

The Outside Child. London, Gollancz, and New York, Lothrop, 1989.

Humbug. London, Gollancz, and New York, Clarion Books, 1992.

The Real Plato Jones. London, Gollancz, 1993; New York, Clarion Books, 1994.

Other (for children)

William Tell. London, Cape, and New York, Lothrop, 1981.

St. Francis of Assisi. London, Cape, and New York, Lothrop, 1983.

In My Own Time. London, Virago Press, 1994; New York, Clarion Books, 1995.

*

Critical Study: Article by Gerda Seaman, in *British Novelists since 1960* edited by Jay L. Halio, Detroit, Gale, 1983.

Nina Bawden comments:

I find it difficult to comment on my adult novels. I suppose one could say that the later books, from *Just Like a Lady* onwards, are social comedies with modern themes and settings; the characters moral beings, hopefully engaged in living. People try so hard and fail so often, sometimes sadly, sometimes comically; I try to show how and why and to be accurate about relationships and motives. I have been called a "cryptomoralist with a mischievous sense of humor," and I like this description: it is certainly part of what I aim to be.

This quotation, from the *Christian Science Monitor,* though not the most flattering, might be useful:

> Nina Bawden is a writer of unusual precision who can depict human foibles with an almost embarrassing accuracy. Yet for all that she centres dead on target, there is always a note of compassion in her stories. The light thrown on her characters, clear though it is, is no harsh spotlight. It is a more diffuse beam that allows one to peer into the shadows and see causes even while it focuses on effects.

*   *   *

The world of the English middle classes is the focal point for most of Nina Bawden's fiction. In *The Birds on the Trees*—a key novel in her development—she observes life as she sees it, centering on an entirely believable middle-class family, with children who puzzle and dismay their parents, because these are the people she sees every day, and these are the children who interest and baffle her, too. She captures the capricious intensity of sibling love, rivalry, and loyalty; she is reluctant to pin blame and quick to display compassion; she is also logical enough to offer no easy solutions, but sufficiently warm-hearted to include realistic sprinklings of hope. Above all, she brings a sympathetic ear to the cadences of everyday speech, a virtue which heightens the intensity of the plot—a story of alienation and the betrayal by the pampered Toby of his vain self-righteous parents.

Her no-nonsense, no-holds-barred approach to contemporary social problems is taken a stage further in *Walking Naked,* a chillingly precise novel about people unable to come to grips with the worlds they inhabit. Laura is a novelist whose method of dealing with difficulties is to retreat into the realm of her imagination. These problems are induced by guilt—guilt about her parents, her first marriage, her son who is in jail, her friends, and her present husband. "I write because I am afraid of life," is her easy palliative to life's ills. Now life is taking its revenge. In the course of one fraught day Laura struggles to come to terms with what she has made of her life, to strip away the layers of anxiety which give her nightmares that her house is falling down about her ears, to avoid the self-deception which has made a mockery of her art, to walk naked and alone. The timescale gives the novel a sharp narrative vigor and the dialogue is always slyly intelligent and believable, but what gives *Walking Naked* its authority is Bawden's precise analysis of middle-class mores and the way in which they are brought to bear on a woman's life.

As in all her later fiction Bawden excels at revealing the tensions and hidden currents at work beneath the calm and humdrum exteriors of her characters. She is no mere moralist; rather, the matter of relationships is her main concern. In *The Ice House,* a caustic glance at the complexities of modern marriage, friendship, and loyalty, she examines the unlikely friendship of Daisy and Ruth who have been friends since their schooldays. As girls, Daisy was boisterous and extroverted; Ruth withdrawn and frightened, a victim of an overbearing father. Thirty years later Ruth has a successful career and, on the surface at least, has a happy marriage; Daisy, though, is less content. When a tragedy rocks the lives of the two women and their families, its repercussions force them out of uneasy self-deception into a new and painful reality which they both have to accept. *The Ice House* is an unusual and subtle novel about familiar themes—love, marriage, friendship, adultery—in which the emotional lives of the two female protagonists are viewed with a mixture of sympathy and disconcerting accuracy. No less tangled are their moral confusions and the task of unraveling them gives the novel its central narrative line. To her adult novels Bawden has brought psychological depth and a humorous focus on human moods, resignations and self-deceptions, tempered only by her powers of observation and discrimination.

Nina Bawden is one of the very few authors who will admit to making a conscious adjustment to writing for children. She has said: "I consider my books for children as important as my adult work, and in some ways more challenging." In all her children's novels childhood is seen with a special clarity and she has the gift of not only understanding childhood but also the childhoods of her own characters. *The Peppermint Pig,* for example, explores the reactions of a family of Edwardian children to their new and reduced circumstances and it is through their eyes that we see their reactions to the world around them. We can understand their hopes and fears, their relationships with each other and with the adult world: this is felt most clearly in a profound episode dealing with the inevitable death of Johnny, the children's pet pig. Bawden's secret is that her sympathy for the children never flags—she thereby retains her readers' sympathies, too.

—Trevor Royle

BEATTIE, Ann

Nationality: American. **Born:** Washington, D.C., 8 September 1947. **Education:** American University, Washington, D.C., B.A. 1969; University of Connecticut, Storrs, 1970-72, M.A. 1970. **Family:** Married 1) David Gates in 1973 (divorced), one son; 2) Lincoln Perry. **Career:** Visiting assistant professor, 1976-77, visiting writer, 1980, University of Virginia, Charlottesville; Briggs Copeland Lecturer in English, Harvard University, Cambridge, Massachusetts, 1977-78. **Awards:** Guggenheim fellowship, 1977; American University Distinguished Alumnae award, 1980; American Academy award, 1980; L.H.D., American University, 1983. Member of the American Academy and Institute of Arts and Letters since 1983. **Agent:** International Creative Management, 40 West 57th Street, New York, New York 10019, U.S.A. **Address:** c/o Random House, 201 East 50th Street, New York, New York 10022, U.S.A.

PUBLICATIONS

Novels

Chilly Scenes of Winter. New York, Doubleday, 1976.
Falling in Place. New York, Random House, 1980; London, Secker and Warburg, 1981.
Love Always. New York, Random House, and London, Michael Joseph, 1985.
Picturing Will. New York, Random House, and London, Cape, 1990; New York, Vintage, 1991.

Short Stories

Distortions. New York, Doubleday, 1976.
Secrets and Surprises. New York, Random House, 1978; London, Hamish Hamilton, 1979.
Jacklighting. Worcester, Massachusetts, Metacom Press, 1981.
The Burning House. New York, Random House, 1982; London, Secker and Warburg, 1983.
Where You'll Find Me and Other Stories. New York, Linden Press, 1986; London, Macmillan, 1987.
What Was Mine and Other Stories. New York, Random House, 1991.

Other

Spectacles (for children). New York, Workman, 1985.
Alex Katz (art criticism). New York, Abrams, 1987.
Americana, photographs by Bob Adelman. New York, Scribner, 1992.

Editor, with Shannon Ravenel, *The Best American Short Stories 1987.* Boston, Houghton Mifflin, 1987.

*

Theatrical Activities:
Actress: **Play**—Role in *The Hotel Play* by Wallace Shawn, New York, 1981.

*   *   *

Chilly Scenes of Winter and *Distortions* were published simultaneously, and, to Ann Beattie's consternation, she was quickly celebrated as the chronicler of the disillusioned 1960s counterculture. She was praised as an objective observer of the ennui and disillusion of the postlapsarian love children, the generation that turned on in the 1960s but totally dropped out in the 1970s. Of this Beattie said: "That's a horribly reductive approach. . . . What I've always hoped for is that somebody will then start talking more about the meat and bones of what I'm writing about," and one shares Beattie's sentiment. While it is true that many of her stories use the manners and jargon of the post-counterculture era as a backdrop—particularly its songs and culture heroes—these details function in much the same way as Raymond Carver's Pacific Northwest, or Donald Barthelme's New York City. They create a concrete setting from which larger human dilemmas may be extracted—in Beattie's case, the difficulties of adjusting to the modern world, the growing distance between one's youthful dreams and present responsibilities, and, most particularly, the fragility and difficulty of sustaining relationships and the despair of loneliness. What also persists in Beattie's fiction, at least until *Love Always,* is a focus on the common human decency and bonds of friendship that survive even the worst of times. Despite their personal circumstances, Beattie's men and women extend themselves to others.

Since the mid-1980s, Beattie has taken a more negative and less sympathetic or ironic and detached view toward the now-aging, careless, and smug inhabitants of Yuppieville. *Picturing Will,* while focusing on the problems of balancing career and parenthood, reveals entirely new concerns. As the title suggests, Beattie is not only interested in parenthood and children (here a boy named Will) but in the responsibilities incurred by human will, along with the contingencies determined by an impersonal fate.

Chilly Scenes of Winter, more than any of her subsequent works, details the dreams and values of the 1960s. It concerns a 27-year-old disaffected love-child, Charles, despairing over his girlfriend Laura's return to her husband. Instead of pursuing her, the helpless Charles busies himself with a cast of needy people—his childhood friend Sam, his suicidal mother, and ex-girlfriend Pamela (now experimenting with lesbianism), and his helplessly naive sister Susan. When he at last learns that Laura has left her husband he visits her, and they prepare to sail into the sunset.

Beattie treats the loss of optimism and first love as by-products of the 1960s youth culture. She also studies, through Charles and Sam, the aimlessness and ennui of the 1970s lost generation. "You could be happy . . . if you hadn't had your eyes opened in the sixties," is repeated throughout. Beattie retains a characteristic detachment—a balance between an objective (sometimes critical) and affectionate (sometimes mocking) portrait of the times. Charles, for example, is wistful toward the past. Everyone has died, he repeats—not just Janis Joplin and Brian Jones, but also Jim Morrison's widow, Amy Vanderbilt, Adele Davis, and maybe even Rod Stewart (about whom, of course, he is wrong). Elsewhere, the world-weary Charles and Sam lament that times have grown worse, because "women put their brassieres back on and want you to take them to Paul Newman movies." Beattie has a wonderful sense of humor.

The dreamer Charles, out of place in any time or locale, is afraid of the present; he is also obsessed with illness and death, and, like many others in the book, he longs to be a child again. But his earnestness, sympathy, and kind generosity are redemptive. Even so, the novel ends bitterly. Sam gets a new and ugly dog, "a terrible genetic mistake," as Charles observes, and one can't help thinking the same of his own reunion with Laura.

The stories in *Distortions* focus on the empty relationships of married and single couples, on the urgent need for companionship and definition that drives most people. Especially moving are the figures in "Dwarf House," "The Parking Lot," "A Platonic Relationship," "Snakes' Shoes," and "Vermont." Although these characters are only peripherally aware of their drab lives, the reader feels deeply for them. More fully portrayed are the characters in *Secrets and Surprises,* men and women once again trapped in unfulfilling jobs and personal relationships. A more affluent group, they are into gourmet cooking, jogging, health foods, weekends in the country, and the usual fare of the 1970s upper-middle-class mobile society. What they share is a deep sense of emptiness, although friendship and pets (particularly dogs) are once more their only comfort. Some of Beattie's most memorable evocations of loneliness and yearning are in the title story, "A Vintage Thunderbird," "A Reasonable Man," "Distant Music," and "The Lawn Party." Lines that summarize a lifetime—like one character's remark that people smile because they don't understand each other—underscore the collection. These people are trapped but they lack self-pity; they are lost but they still extend a hand.

An even more sophisticated society inhabits *The Burning House,* but it is the juxtaposition of loneliness and selflessness that continues to move the reader. Little occurs in the way of change, although there are occasional moments of muted insight; once again, the stories are evocations of mood, descriptive of states of being. There also remains very little trace of the 1960s past. Of particular interest is the title story and "Learning to Fall," where Beattie concretizes two characters' remarks: "What will happen can't be stopped," and "I'm sick of hearing how things might have been worse, when they might also have been better." "Girl Talk" is about two women, one young, unmarried, and pregnant, and the other, the unborn child's grandmother, who is many times married, wealthy, still beautiful but no longer capable of bearing children. It is about how "pain is relative." "The Cinderella Waltz," one of Beattie's most evocative stories, is about the complex of emotions exchanged between a mother and daughter and their estranged husband/father and his new male lover.

Falling in Place, Beattie's second novel, portrays the limited control one has over one's destiny and how life just seems to fall in place. Once again, Beattie measures the fragility of relationships, here focusing on the disintegration of a family and the guilt that falls to both parents and children. The book lacks a traditional plot; rather, Beattie shifts from character to character and then combines events from each chapter into brief italicized mood interludes. Set in Connecticut and New York in the summer of 1979, the novel focuses on the surrogate emotional relationships each member of the John Knapp family sets up. The climax revolves around the son's quasi-accidental shooting of his sister and how the family members finally face one another—things fall into place. Although the book ends with a positive resolution, like *Chilly Scenes of Winter,* it is bitter and the prognosis for future happiness is bleak.

Love Always, Beattie's third novel, marks a change in style and vision. Less detached, satiric, and sympathetic, her indictment of her materially successful, world-weary people is more pronounced. The book opens at a Vermont retreat, where the sophisticates of a trendy New York magazine, *Country Daze,* have gathered. Lucy Spenser, for example, under the pseudonym Cindi Coeur, writes both the letters and answers for a tongue-in-cheek Miss Lonelyhearts column. Lucy's niece, 14-year-old Nicole, who joins the group, is a TV actress who portrays an adolescent alcoholic on a popular soap opera. The brilliance of the novel results from Beattie's intertwining how the real-life Vermont group is defined not just by the bucolic fantasy of country life espoused by the magazine but also by the fantasies and grim truth of the Miss Lonelyhearts column, as well as the melodramatic, selfish, and sometimes cruel world of television and Hollywood soaps. The so-called real characters in the novel—infertile in every sense of the word—are as needy and blighted as any portrayed by the printed word or on screen. These characters also lack, one should note, the compassion and generosity that have characterized Beattie's earlier people.

The short stories in *Where You'll Find Me* are terse, minimalist profiles of Beattie's familiar 1960s and 1970s types, once again estranged from themselves and others. Now successful doctors, lawyers, and Indian chiefs, they have the money, possessions, and social respect that go along with their time, place, and economic efforts. But they suffer the losses that accompany people of their status and age, such as divorce, illness, and death. Beattie's focus is the enormous disparity between external success and inner emptiness. All the same, these figures retain our sympathy. "People and things never really get left behind," remarks one, very much aware that human connection remains possible.

Picturing Will confronts the next, logical question. Can one have it all: ambition, success, and a child? And if so, how does one deal with the probable eventualities of divorce, missing fathers, potential stepfathers, and, always of central concern, the young child? Will is the five- and six-year-old abandoned child of a scurrilous, selfish, and violent father. His mother, clearly the more caring parent, is torn between career and motherhood. It is her lover, Mel, who truly parents and completely loves Will. The novel is divided into three sections that reflect each family member's point of view: interwoven through these, in addition, is yet another commentary that functions as the authorial voice, in matters of true responsibility and a child's deepest needs. The commentary is, in fact, from Mel's diary.

If Beattie's earlier characters were passive products of a specific social, cultural, and political world, the figures here are personally responsible for their own lives, despite the vagaries of fate. But Beattie never loses her sense of humor. Mel, for example, remarks on the responsibilities of fatherhood: "Do everything right, all the time, and the child will prosper. It's as simple as that, except for fate, luck, heredity, chance, the astrological sign under which the child was born, his order of birth, his first encounter with evil, the girl who jilts him in spite of his excellent qualities."

The fragility of human relationships and their inevitable disintegration—between friends, spouses, children and parents—is once again Beattie's subject in *What Was Mine*. "You Know What," the ironic title of one story, could well characterize many of the others: characters speak on slightly tangential levels that are sufficiently askew to guarantee miscommunication. Mothers and fathers worry over children—whose lives justify worry—but the quality and definition of that worry is frequently inappropriate. In "Horatio's Trick," a 19-year-old college student criticizes his mother for being too intimidated by him to directly ask about his life. Beattie acknowledges the son's disturbance: "She was just sitting there, scared to death." The title piece tells of another son whose father died after World War II, and whose mother, true to the father's memory, lived with but never married "Uncle Herb." Ethan, the son, now a young man, loves Herb as a father, but they are forced to separate when the mother, "irrationally angry," decides she no longer wants him in the house. Herb tries to console the son with advice to listen to Billie Holiday's records, study Vermeer's paintings, and "look around" and "listen." He explains that "What to some people might seem the silliest sort of place might be, to those truly observant, a temporary substitute for heaven." One makes due with what one has at hand. The deep compassion in Beattie's portrayals of these necessary accommodations, along with her exquisite evocation of the emptiness and loneliness in both the self and world, continue to place her among the best fiction writers in America today. One is haunted by lines such as the following, exchanged between two 14-year-old boys: "We both suffered because we sensed that you had to *look* like John F. Kennedy in order to *be* John F. Kennedy."

—Lois Gordon

BECKER, Stephen (David)

Nationality: American. **Born:** Mount Vernon, New York, 31 March 1927. **Education:** Harvard University, Cambridge, Massachusetts, 1943-47, B.A. 1947; Yenching University, Peking, 1947-48. **Military Service:** Served in the United States Marine Corps, 1945. **Family:** Married Mary Elizabeth Freeburg in 1947; two sons and one daughter. **Career:** Instructor, Tsing Hua University, Peking, 1947-48; teaching fellow, Brandeis University, Waltham, Massachusetts, 1951-52; lecturer, University of Alaska, College, 1967, Bennington College, Vermont, 1971, 1977, 1978, University of Iowa, Iowa City, 1974, and Hollins College, Virginia, 1986. Since 1987 professor of English, University of Central Florida, Orlando. Editor, Western Printing Company, New York, 1955-56. **Awards:** Paul Harris fellowship, 1947; Guggenheim fellowship, 1954; Na-

tional Endowment for the Arts grant, for translation, 1984. **Agent:** Russell and Volkening Inc., 50 West 29th Street, New York, New York 10001. **Address:** 880 Benchwood Dr., Winter Spring, Florida 32708, U.S.A.

PUBLICATIONS

Novels

The Season of the Stranger. New York, Harper, and London, Hamish Hamilton, 1951.
Shanghai Incident (as Steve Dodge). New York, Fawcett, 1955; London, Fawcett, 1956.
Juice. New York, Simon and Schuster, 1958; London, Muller, 1959.
A Covenant with Death. New York, Atheneum, and London, Hamish Hamilton, 1965.
The Outcasts. New York, Atheneum, and London, Hamish Hamilton, 1967.
When the War Is Over. New York, Random House, 1969; London, Hamish Hamilton, 1970.
Dog Tags. New York, Random House, 1973; London, Barrie and Jenkins, 1974.
The Chinese Bandit. New York, Random House, 1975; London, Chatto and Windus, 1976.
The Last Mandarin. New York, Random House, and London, Chatto and Windus, 1979.
The Blue-Eyed Shan. New York, Random House, and London, Collins, 1982.
A Rendezvous in Haiti. New York, Norton, and London, Collins, 1987.

Uncollected Short Stories

"To Know the Country," in *Harper's* (New York), August 1951.
"The Town Mouse," in *The Best American Short Stories 1953,* edited by Martha Foley. Boston, Houghton Mifflin, 1953.
"A Baptism of Some Importance," in *Story.* New York, McKay, 1953.
"Monsieur Malfait," in *Harper's* (New York), June 1953.
"The New Encyclopaedist," in *The Year's Best SF 10,* edited by Judith Merril. New York, Delacorte Press, 1965.
"Rites of Passage," in *Florida Review* (Orlando) Autumn 1984.

Other

Comic Art in America: A Social History of the Funnies, the Political Cartoons, Magazine Humor, Sporting Cartoons, and Animated Cartoons. New York, Simon and Schuster, 1959.
Marshall Field III: A Biography. New York, Simon and Schuster, 1964.

Translator, *The Colors of the Day,* by Romain Gary. New York, Simon and Schuster, and London, Joseph, 1953.
Translator, *Mountains in the Desert,* by Louis Carl and Joseph Petit. New York, Doubleday, 1954; as *Tefedest,* London, Allen and Unwin, 1954.
Translator, *The Sacred Forest,* by Pierre-Dominique Gaisseau. New York, Knopf, 1954.
Translator, *Faraway,* by André Dhôtel. New York, Simon and Schuster, 1957.

Translator, *Someone Will Die Tonight in the Caribbean,* by René Puissesseau. New York, Knopf, 1958; London, W.H. Allen, 1959.

Translator, *The Last of the Just,* by André Schwarz-Bart. New York, Atheneum, and London, Secker and Warburg, 1961.

Translator, *The Town Beyond the Wall,* by Elie Wiesel. New York, Atheneum, 1964; London, Robson, 1975.

Translator, *The Conquerors,* by André Malraux. New York, Holt Rinehart, 1976.

Translator, *Diary of My Travels in America,* by Louis-Philippe. New York, Delacorte Press, 1977.

Translator, *Ana No,* by Agustín Gomez-Arcos. London, Secker and Warburg, 1980.

Translator, *The Forgotten,* by Elie Wiesel. New York, Schoken, 1995.

*

Critical Study: By Becker, in *Contemporary Authors Autobiography Series 1* edited by Dedria Bryfonski, Detroit, Gale, 1984.

*　　*　　*

Equally distinguished as a translator, a biographer, a commentator on the popular arts, and a novelist, Stephen Becker brings to his fiction a breadth of experience with world culture and human behavior which yields moral complexity and psychological verity in his work. Two major themes intertwine through his novels—the problems of justice and the necessity for self-knowledge and self-fulfillment.

Beginning most clearly with *Juice,* Becker concentrates on the moral and social complexities of law and justice, continuing this theme in *A Covenant with Death* and *When the War Is Over.* The problem Becker's protagonists face is to distinguish between the arbitrary and mechanical justice of the law and true human justice. The rigidity and absoluteness of law collide with human values—especially the need for expiation, mercy and compassion. The characters' dilemma is to choose between true justice and simple retribution and to use the mechanism of blind justice to solve difficult moral problems. Against this theme is developed another—an existential concept of the self, men struggling with themselves, with nature and with circumstances to become fully alive and functioning beings. This theme is isolated most clearly in *The Outcasts,* which describes a group of engineers building a bridge deep in a primeval jungle. There they must overcome the indifferent force of nature, their own weaknesses, their fears and prejudices.

In *Juice* the theme of human and mechanical justice arises when the central character, Joseph Harrison, kills a pedestrian in an auto accident. His friends and employer try to use the law and the power of money and position ("juice") to white-wash the occurrence, while Harrison demands an absolute judgment to redeem his error. The tensions between views of law and truth reshape Harrison's whole existence. In *A Covenant with Death* a young judge is confronted with a difficult decision in a murder case; through detective work, insights into motivation and a complete understanding of the limits of the law, Judge Lewis is able to render a humane verdict and still satisfy the meaning of law. The forces of procrustean and draconian legalism are averted through the judge's efforts, through an intense moral revaluation which ultimately changes the judge's own life. In this novel, humanity triumphs through the action of the law.

The tragedy of the law is exposed in *When the War Is Over,* Becker's most satisfying novel. It is the story of the last victim of the Civil War, a boy executed as a Confederate guerrilla long after hostilities had ceased. The moral struggle is embodied in Lt. Marius Catto, a young career officer caught between a genuine love of peace and justice and a natural inclination toward the arts of war. He works to prevent General Hooker from wreaking vengeance through law on the boy but fails and is left scarred and embittered by disillusionment. The novel, based on historical fact, is a brilliant reconstruction of the time and place and an intense scrutiny of moral and social values. It convincingly examines the mechanism of military order, social justice and our conflicting views of violence and law. The story uncovers basic contradictions in our organization of legal murder.

Dog Tags is another densely detailed chronicle of man at war and his ability to survive it humanly and intelligently. It focuses on Benjamin Beer, a Jew wounded in World War II and later interned in North Korea. His response to war is to become a skilled and humane doctor, as if in expiration for the universal crime of war. His life is a moral struggle for self-knowledge and understanding of man's limitless potentials; "You're worried about good and bad," he says, "well, I'm worried about good and evil." In his quest, Benjamin learns his own abilities and limitations and achieves peace and grace within himself.

The Chinese Bandit, The Last Mandarin, and *The Blue-Eyed Shan* are finely-wrought and highly atmospheric Asian tales which focus on the collision of Western adventurers with oriental culture. Each story details the effect of American mercenaries in search of action in China and Southeast Asia after World War II and develops the moral and social conflicts between the two cultures through tales of violence and individual struggles for survival. The landscape and social patterns of a changeless East are refracted through the sensibilities of self-sufficient and resourceful Americans who find themselves alone in the crowds of the orient.

In *A Rendezvous in Haiti,* Becker returns to the U.S. Marines as a focus for a romantic adventure. The novel follows a young Marine lieutenant, Robert McAllister, and his fiancée during a rebellion in Haiti in 1919. McAllister, a veteran of the brutality of World War I, must single-handedly rescue his fiancée from the rebels (and the romantic spell of a mysterious rebel chieftain), crossing the island and its dense jungles. The story, like Becker's earlier Conradian romances, is rich with authentic period details and feeling and also comments seriously on American political and cultural imperialism and adventurism.

Becker's examination of society's structure and limitations and his portrayal of men seeking "grace under pressure" is a significant contribution to contemporary fiction. The existential premises of the works—individuals finding meaning inside the arbitrary bounds of social order—reflect our acceptance of the civilization we have built.

—William J. Schafer

BECKHAM, Barry (Earl)

Nationality: American. **Born:** Philadelphia, Pennsylvania, 19 March 1944. **Education:** Brown University, Providence, Rhode Island, 1962-66, A.B. 1966; Columbia University Law School, New York. **Family:** Married 1) Betty Louise Hope in 1966 (divorced 1977), one son and one daughter; 2) Geraldine Lynne Palmer in 1979.

Career: Public relations consultant, 1966-67, and urban affairs associate, 1969-70, Chase Manhattan Bank, New York; public relations consultant, YMCA National Council, New York, 1967-68, and Western Electric Company, New York, 1968-69. Lecturer, 1970-72, assistant professor, 1972-78, since 1979 associate professor of English, and since 1980 director of Graduate Program in Creative Writing, Brown University. President, Beckham House Publishers, Hampton, Virginia. **Agent:** William Morris Agency, 1350 Avenue of the Americas, New York, New York 10019. **Address:** Department of English, Brown Station, Providence, Rhode Island 02912, U.S.A.

PUBLICATIONS

Novels

My Main Mother. New York, Walker, 1969; London, Wingate, 1970; as *Blues in the Night,* London, Tandem, 1974.
Runner Mack. New York, Morrow, 1972.
Double Drunk. Los Angeles, Holloway House, 1981.

Play

Garvey Lives! (produced Providence, Rhode Island, 1972).

Other

Editor, *The Black Student's Guide to Colleges.* New York, Dutton, 1982; revised edition, Providence, Rhode Island, Beckham House, 1984.
Editor, *The College Selection Workbook* (2nd edition). Providence, Rhode Island, Beckham House, 1987.

*

Manuscript Collection: Mugar Memorial Library, Boston University.

Critical Study: Interview with Sanford Pinsker, in *Black Images 3* (Toronto), Autumn 1974.

*   *   *

Barry Beckham's reputation rests modestly on two small novels published within the three-year period of 1969-72. Both are flawed and somewhat derivative, yet Beckham's talents suggest promising developments in fiction about black experience in America, a field which he thinks "has been inadequately treated for the most part." In both novels, Beckham moves decisively away from the ghetto novel of social protest and literary naturalism to the psychological effects of neglect and exploitation, portrayed in a blend of verbal impressionism and surrealism.

In *My Main Mother* Mitchell Mibbs tells his own story of how he came to murder his beautiful mother, Pearl, in their home in Chatsworth, Maine, where Mitch's grandparents were born. In this tragi-comic "confession of the soul," or "proclamation of my own emancipation," Mitchell plans an imaginary press release, a self-mocking and ironic outline-summary of Beckham's first novel: "A young black genius, sitting comfortably in an abandoned auto on the outskirts of town, announced today that he has killed his mother

for the best of all concerned. His testimony is a novel, profound manuscript of some eighty thousand words, listing various and sundry acts alleged to have prompted the macabre slaying. The acts have been arranged in narrative form, and the manuscript has been cited by leading authorities as extremely accomplished."

Perhaps the cruelest of mother Pearl's "various and sundry acts" is the exploitation and betrayal of old Mervin Pip, an honest, kindly uncle who services Mitch *in loco parentis* and is his one true friend. The title is therefore a triple play on the shaping environment: "main" refers to the geographical location, to Uncle Melvin and to Pearl, all of whom have made Mitchell what he is. Throughout, racial themes are both present and understated, while authentic portrayal of main characters, skillful use of point-of-view, and vivid imagery earn our attention. The title phrase is, of course, "black," and so are the idiom, characterizations, and occurrences of the novel without the stridency of naturalism or the "race novel." Present, nevertheless, are the props and concerns found in *Native Son* and *Black Boy,* the ur-works of modern black literary art: besides the title similarities, combined in this one work are Wright's dual depictions of the fatherless boy who murders a beautiful woman, the suppression of aspiration in a bright black boy, the hypocrisy of liberal or well-meaning whites, and the sense of entrapment, betrayal, and waste of youth.

Runner Mack is indebted to that other seminal and symbolic black novel, *Invisible Man* by Ralph Ellison. Beckham's Henry Adams, not a New England patrician but a poor Mississippi baseball player, comes to New York ostensibly for a baseball try-out ("this is the national past-time, they've got to be fair with me"), and then remains to be educated in the true national sport of "keeping this nigger running." Cheated by a midget manager of his fair chance in athletics (a prime source of upward mobility for American blacks), Henry tries the subtler game of American business, where he is given token opportunity in a dead-end job. In dreamlike sequences, he is hit by a Mack truck (before encountering "Runner Mack," the title character); a heedless Spanish building "super" steals his pajamas; Henry's wife is raped in his presence; a crippled corporation president delivers an inaudible Christmas speech; and a summons arrives requiring Henry to leave at once "to fight for my country." Like Ellison, Beckham casts his young innocent in a picaresque narrative reprise of black-American history, with emphasis on the absurdity of American rituals and the indecencies of American institutions.

Thus, the stage is set for the novel's second half, Henry's army adventures in a twin parody of war and revolution. Institutionalized racism is patriotically turned against "slopes" and "gooks" instead of blacks, so that even Henry may become both a racist and a good American. The Vietnam war is mysteriously transposed to the white Alaskan wilderness and since no "slopes" are ever found, the men slay seals and herds of Caribou, the ecological equivalent of defoliation. The young soldiers are terrified by the Pentagon mentality of Captain Nevins and the fierce, foul intensity of his need to kill. Then Henry encounters Runnington Mack, a cynical, honest black hipster, who becomes his mentor in a revolutionary plot to bomb the White House. "Runner" Mack, loose as a halfback and solid as a truck, stands in obvious contrast to the hysterical, murderous Captain Nevins, to the deformed baseball manager and corporation president and to the other obsessive, obscene whites whom Henry has had to follow. Swiftly, he learns from Mack of the hypocrisy of American leadership, the futility of reform in a death-directed culture, and the need for violent revolution. Henry Adams's "education" is poignantly completed when Runner Mack's thought-out plan fails abysmally because no one cares and Mack commits suicide in despair.

Although his main characters are believable in both novels, Beckham's characterizations sometimes divide humanity into wholly good or wholly despicable specimens, and nearly all white characters are negatively drawn. Despite this side-choosing, he elicits our sympathy for his good guys, such as Mitch, Henry, and Runner, and hostility toward Mitch's mother, her husband Julius, and assorted villains. His success at evoking reader empathy is largely attributable to Beckham's small-scale scenic method, whereby we see and feel the misery of a rustic old man lost in Harlem, the loneliness of a boy in a rusty, abandoned car in the woods, the isolation of a housewife deafened by television, the panic of a man running to a job interview. These and other carved images become slide-projections or backdrops in the larger enactments of black absurd theater.

—Frank Campenni

BEDFORD, Sybille

Nationality: British. **Born:** Sybille von Schoenebeck in Charlottenburg, Germany, 16 March 1911. **Education:** Privately in Italy, England, and France. **Family:** Married Walter Bedford in 1935. **Career:** Worked as a law reporter: covered the Auschwitz trial at Frankfurt for the *Observer,* London, and the *Saturday Evening Post,* Philadelphia, 1963-65, and the trial of Jack Ruby at Dallas for *Life,* New York, 1964. Vice-president, PEN, 1979. **Awards:** Society of Authors traveling scholarship, 1989. Fellow, Royal Society of Literature, 1964. O.B.E. (Officer, Order of British Empire), 1981. **Address:** c/o Greene and Heaton, 37 Goldhawk Rd., London W12 8Q0, England.

PUBLICATIONS

Novels

A Legacy. London, Weidenfeld and Nicolson, 1956; New York, Simon and Schuster, 1957.
A Favourite of the Gods. London, Collins, and New York, Simon and Schuster, 1963.
A Compass Error. London, Collins, 1968; New York, Knopf, 1969.
Jigsaw: An Unsentimental Education. London, Hamish Hamilton, and New York, Knopf, 1989.

Uncollected Short Stories

"Compassionata at Hyde Park Corner," in *23 Modern Stories.* New York, Knopf, 1963.
"Une vie de chateau," in *New Yorker,* 20 February 1989.

Other

A Visit to Don Otavio: A Mexican Journey. London, Gollancz, and New York, Harper, 1953; revised edition, New York, Atheneum, 1963; as *A Visit to Don Otavio: A Traveller's Tale from Mexico,* London, Collins, 1960.

The Best We Can Do: An Account of the Trial of John Bodkin Adams. London, Collins, 1958; as *The Trial of Dr. Adams,* New York, Simon and Schuster, 1959.
The Faces of Justice: A Traveller's Report. London, Collins, and New York, Simon and Schuster, 1961.
Aldous Huxley: A Biography. London, Chatto and Windus-Collins, 2 vols., 1973-74; New York, Knopf, 1 vol., 1974.
As It Was: Pleasures, Landscapes, and Justice. London, Sinclair Stevenson, 1990.

*

Critical Studies: By Evelyn Waugh, in *Spectator* (London), 13 April 1956; V.S. Pritchett, in *New Statesman* (London), 11 January 1963; P.N. Furbank, in *Encounter* (London), April 1964; Bernard Levin, in London *Daily Mail,* 12 September 1966; Constantine FitzGibbon, in *Irish Times* (Dublin), 19 October 1968; introductions to *A Favourite of the Gods* and *A Compass Error,* both London, Virago Press, 1984, and article in *London Magazine,* January 1991, all by Peter Vansittart; Robert O. Evans in *British Novelists since 1900* edited by Jack I. Biles, New York, AMS Press, 1987; David Leavitt in *Voice Literary Supplement,* June 1990; Gilbert Phelps in *Folio Quarterly* (London), Winter 1990; Anne Sebbaix in *Daily Telegraph,* 4 February 1995.

*   *   *

The stature of Sybille Bedford's first and still her finest novel, *A Legacy,* suggests Thomas Mann's *Buddenbrooks,* or the historical theme of Hermann Broch's *The Sleepwalkers.* All three writers are continental in their attention to the effects of historical event on the flow of family life and time. If Bedford lacks the philosophical dimension of Mann or the high and heavy seriousness of Broch, she possesses instead energy, gaiety, and a refreshing comic sense that seem unmistakably British.

What stays in the mind long after a reading of *A Legacy* is not the Prussia or Baden of 1810-1913 in which it is set, but characters, scenes, and individual sentences of fine prose. Bedford's best characters are improbable but memorable for her objective treatment of them. Johannes von Feldon once danced with a bear at a fair, became autistic from the brutality of his military academy, then a decorated, still autistic captain of cavalry. Julius von Felden, a central figure in the chronicle, is nominally Catholic, briefly a diplomat, member of the Jockey Club in Paris, collector of bibelots, and devoted to his monkey and two chimpanzees, whom he treats as human beings. He marries into the Merz family of Berlin, astonished that they are nominally Jewish rather than Catholic, but content to accept their over-stuffed largesse. The elder Merzes are wealthy philistines given to large, frequent meals, to generosity to their feckless offspring and their children, who acquire "the habit of being rich." The tragicomedy of the two families and their incompatible histories combine into a plot involving legacies, marriages, fornications, and displacements. The death of Julius's Merz wife, Melanie, a dim, determined girl, leads to his marriage to an Englishwoman, Caroline Trafford, a beautiful, fickle, interesting wife and, briefly, mother. The actual legacies are frittered away, and the figurative legacy of Caroline to Julius is a German house and a precocious daughter, who supposedly is narrator. The chronicle is mainly narrated in the third person.

A Favourite of the Gods, set in Italy, might appear to be a departure from *A Legacy,* but it is not. Often called "Jamesian" for its account of a wealthy American girl who marries a corrupt Roman minor aristocrat, it is James-like only in theme. The Italians here are caricatures, uttering "Già" and "Meno male," while Anna the American is such only by description. Over-filled with incident, the novel relates the education of Constanza, Anna's daughter, who is brought up in Edwardian England when Anna cannot stomach her husband's adultery. Again people eat and drink fabulously, fall in and out of loves and beds, while potted history is served in chunks: "Meanwhile, Mussolini marched on Rome." History here, as in the later *A Compass Error* and *Jigsaw,* is outlined, reported, but the characters do not actually live and have their fictional reality in that history. Constanza marries Simon Herbert, the author's least convincing character. A pacifist by conviction, he nevertheless is commissioned and sent to the trenches, emerging promptly with a convenient wound. A brilliant career follows, and an arranged divorce from Constanza permits his marriage to a press tycoon's daughter. Simon dies young. Constanza's daughter, Flavia, is born in 1914; after the war, Contanza moves from lover to lover but remains unmarried and at odds with Anna, the dowager-heroine. Wonderful episodes occur, but the novel suffers from a weak structure and a surfeit of raw matter.

Flavia is the narrator of *A Compass Error,* the structure of which is pure disaster. Left alone at 17 in Provence to swot for entrance to Oxford, Flavia engages in a lesbian affair and consumes some 53 pages of this brief novel to recapitulate in monologue to her lover the entire contents of *A Favourite of the Gods.* A psychologically improbable plot involving Constanza's last chance at marriage to a French intellectual unfolds. Flavia is again precocious, a great imbiber of claret, and intellectually ambitious as well as bisexual. Plot tends to falsify chronicle, which has its own twists and turns.

Jigsaw is a novel only by courtesy. Despite some novelistic touches, it is transparently personal memoir, as well as an explanation of the structural difficulties of the two preceding novels. We are back in the territory of *Legacy,* with the story of young Billi's (for Sybille) early years at Feldkirch with her father, the impoverished Julius, eating smoked mutton but drinking the rare clarets surviving from better days. Like Flavia, like Constanza, she moves as a young girl to London, then to Provence, and the dubious tutelage of her egotistical, beautiful, self-indulgent mother, who declines into poverty and drug addiction. Again the text is packed with incident, with essays on wine and politics, but now with actual historical figures: Aldous and Maria Huxley; Cyril Connolly, Roy Campbell, Ivy Compton-Burnett among them. Again a precocious girl aspires to university and fails, but a writer's career beckons (that distinguished career as travel writer and reporter which has also been Bedford's). Characters and entire episodes are lifted from the preceding narratives, but the story is frankly her own, with elements of confession and muted justification. Although eminently readable, the whole fails to do justice to splendid parts.

Bedford's affinity is perhaps not with Mann or Broch, but with Huxley and Compton-Burnett, whom she imitates, and with Molly Keane, who tells over and again the same story with elegant and delightful variations, comic turns with tragic overtones.

—John McCormick

BELL, Madison Smartt

Nationality: American. **Born:** Williamson County, Tennessee, 1 August 1957. **Education:** Princeton University, New Jersey, A.B. (summa cum laude) in English 1979; Hollins College, Virginia, M.A. 1981. **Family:** Married Elizabeth Spires in 1985; one daughter. **Career:** Writer-in-residence, Goucher College, Towson, Maryland, 1984-86, 1988-89; lecturer, YMHA Poetry Center, New York, 1984-86; visiting lecturer, University of Iowa Writers Workshop, Iowa City, 1987-88; lecturer, Johns Hopkins University Writing Seminars, Baltimore, Maryland, 1989-91. **Awards:** Lillian Smith award, 1989; Guggenheim fellowship, 1991; Maryland State Arts Council award, 1991; Howard Foundation fellowship, 1991; Robert Penn Warren award for the Fellowship of Southern Writers, 1995. **Agent:** Vivienne Schuster, John Farquharson Ltd., 162-168 Regent Street, London W1R 5TB, England; or, Jane Gelfman, John Farquharson Ltd., 250 West 57th Street, New York, New York 10107. **Address:** Department of English, Goucher College, Towson, Maryland 21204, U.S.A.

PUBLICATIONS

Novels

The Washington Square Ensemble. New York, Viking Press, and London, Deutsch, 1983.
Waiting for the End of the World. New York, Ticknor and Fields, and London, Chatto and Windus, 1985.
Straight Cut. New York, Ticknor and Fields, 1986; London, Chatto and Windus, 1987.
The Year of Silence. New York, Ticknor and Fields, and London, Chatto and Windus, 1987.
Soldier's Joy. New York, Ticknor and Fields, 1989.
Doctor Sleep. San Diego, Harcourt Brace, 1991.
Save Me, Joe Louis. San Diego, Harcourt Brace, 1993.
All Souls' Rising. New York, Pantheon, and London, Granta, 1995.

Short Stories

Zero db and Other Stories. New York, Ticknor and Fields, and London, Chatto and Windus, 1987.
Barking Man and Other Stories. New York, Ticknor and Fields, 1990.

Other

The History of the Owen Graduate School of Management. Nashville, Tennessee, Vanderbilt University, 1988.

*   *   *

Madison Smartt Bell's special province is the sensuousness of desperation, the aesthetic hideaways in which the disenchanted, disenfranchised, and dysfunctional seek refuge from storms raging in their own minds. That has been clear from his first novel, *The Washington Square Ensemble,* whose tangle of first-person narratives follows a gang of urban heroin dealers through a jungle of violence and sin.

The violence and frantic edge-running of Bell's novels invite comparison with the early novels of Robert Stone. Both writers probe the grimy underbelly of life and characters balanced precariously between suicide and murder. But as dark as Bell's tales may be, rays of affirmation seep in, unlike Stone's. For Stone's characters, the darkening world offers little chance to wrench from it a life. But for Bell's, the moral condition of the world is either static or cyclic rather than entropic. There are dusks, but there are also dawns. In that way, Bell's world may be truer than Stone's, and less soul-deadening.

Bell's characters are in quest of redemption and rebirth. They'll blow bullet holes in traditional moral tablets, as do Stone's, but they seem more eager to pick up a pen and write new ones than to cling to the pistol.

This quest appears in Bell's 1985 novel, *Waiting for the End of the World,* the story of a plot to detonate a nuclear device under New York. Larkin, an associate member of a cell led by the profoundly maladjusted psychiatrist Simon Rohnstock, has the unenviable position of human trigger for the weapon—a kind of guerrilla Valhalla entirely appropriate to Bell's message, for the author seems to suggest that only gestures of immense proportion can have any lasting impact in an age of mass lassitude.

Ultimately, collective will disintegrates as Rohnstock decides that this venture might be just the vehicle to propel him to para-political supremacy, and Larkin begins to doubt his own purpose. By this stage however, the focus has shifted towards the novel's other themes: Larkin has "adopted" Tommy, the child victim of vicious ritualistic abuse, and is being pursued by the boy's demented father—a dark avenging angel. Descending into the detritus of New York society, Bell unifies several quasi-religious sub-texts, blending a spate of spontaneous combustions, elements of Russian Orthodoxy, and a liberal dose of Satanism. The subsequent action takes on mystic overtones—Tommy's real name is revealed to be Gabriel, and he, previously mute, manifests visionary powers and a voice suitable to their expression. Larkin's own spectacular fate is just one of many impressive flashes of invention that litter a script which is both a convincing study of personal motivation and an accomplished semi-allegorical interpretation of late 20th-century malaise.

Straight Cut reveals a clear movement towards order. Bell follows the rivalry between Tracy Bateman and Kevin Carter, former friends and colleagues in an independent film-making company that has been their cover for drug smuggling. Kevin and Tracy represent two sides of the same nature, one scheming and manipulative, the other intuitive and unambiguous; platonically in love with each other and both in love with Tracy's estranged wife Lauren. The real interest of the book lies not in the high-tension plot twists, but in the duel between intellect and instinct, a tussle kept alive brilliantly by Bell's rapid scene shifting and neat line in tough-guy backchat.

The Year of Silence fuses multiple narrative perspectives, offering a series of individual reactions to Marian's death from an overdose. Friends, lovers, and nodding acquaintances are all struggling desperately to come to terms with a world bereft of her presence. In truth, only Gwen, Marian's cousin, has by the end of the book reached a compromise, and we leave her in the sanctuary of a white clapboard holiday home, preparing to restart her life. The loss of a "flair for transforming the tacky into something transcendent" is to be mourned, but whether it quite merits the indulgence of a whole book is questionable. Depending on your preference, Bell either offers a stunning essay on the idolization of vacuousness or fails to evoke sufficient sympathy for Marian for us to feel much moved by the bleatings of the bereaved.

If *The Year of Silence* lacks completeness, almost all of the pieces in *Zero db* are the finished article: polished, absorbing, and of a consistently high standard. This is Bell in virtuoso form, producing an utterly compelling range of voice and concern, and throwing off the shades of Faulkner and Poe which have coloured his previous technical and imaginative achievements. "Today Is a Good Day to Die" is a memorable highlight, and, happily, in "Triptych I" and "Triptych II" we are at last afforded a real insight, from an insider, into life on a Tennessee hog farm.

In *Soldier's Joy,* Thomas Laidlaw returns from Vietnam to his family's now-deserted farm outside Nashville. A loner, Laidlaw wants little more than peace, freedom to roam the landscape, and time to hone his considerable talents as a bluegrass banjo player. He's been half a world away dispensing and avoiding death.

Tennessee seems the ideal place to heal from a disorienting war. Bell's minutely observed description make Laidlaw's deliberate actions feel like Nick Adams returning to the Big Two-Hearted River, his farm an arcadian balm to his senses. Then comes Laidlaw's reunion with his black childhood friend and Vietnam comrade Rodney Redmon, and Laidlaw learns he has simply left one war zone for another. *Soldier's Joy* is a tale of life lived close to the bone. Once again Bell tenses his muscular grip on the feel and meaning of violence, wrenching a piece of literary art from a plot whose outline could sound like that of a television movie.

In *Doctor Sleep,* Bell weaves an arresting if uneven tapestry. Its several threads unfurl from three closely observed days and nights in the life of Adrian Strother. Four years earlier, Adrian had sworn off both heroin and New York City and moved to London. Now he works as a hypnotist, "a sort of psychological repairman," whose most interesting client, Eleanor Peavy, suffers multiple personalities: prim Miss Peavey by day, prostitute Nell by night.

She is the least of Adrian's problems. Wracked by insomnia, he walks London's streets where a serial killer brutally murders little girls. Mistaken for his friend Stuart (a born-again former addict now forming a heroin self-help center), Adrian is stalked by thugs and abducted by London's chief heroin distributor. When drug traffickers are not hunting him, he's hunting them under pressure from Scotland Yard. On free nights, he moonlights as a stage hypnotist at a burlesque club or works out at a tae kwon do studio and spars with his West Indian friend Terence after class in the dark.

Back in Adrian's flat, his pet boa constrictor is losing color and won't eat, and Adrian's neglected girlfriend Clara has left him for the fourth time. Nicole—the dazzling former call-girl Stuart battered and Adrian secretly married—is in London, maybe to pick up with Adrian again or maybe to ask him for a divorce. All the while, Adrian reflects obsessively on the Hermetic mysticism of Renaissance philosopher Giorano Bruno. Little wonder Adrian cannot sleep.

As far removed from the Tennessee hills, glacial pacing, and third-person restraint of *Soldier's Joy* as *Doctor Sleep* is, the two books feel strongly linked. Like returning soldier Thomas Laidlaw, Adrian seldom eats and never sleeps, has thematically important attachments to both his male friends and his animals, and is painfully reticent about his feelings. Most importantly, like Laidlaw just back from Vietnam, Adrian is a solitary figure in need of healing.

There is nothing new about that. Since his first novel, *The Washington Square Ensemble,* with its cluster of heroin dealers, Bell has always written with conspicuous sympathy for the alienated and the bruised. He searches for characters beaten down by a combination of life and poor choices, whose hearts (to paraphrase a line of Spires's) are a bit off-center, yet who desire affirmation. At some point, a moment flickers where new choice is possible, and they choose to move toward grace, often amid religious symbolism.

As the elements of *Doctor Sleep* bond artfully together—as Eleanor Peavey's pathology links to the vicious child murders which tie to the London drug lord who bears on Adrian's work with Scotland Yard and Adrian's need to face the truth which joins him in spirit to Eleanor Peavey—perhaps the most important element turns out to be Adrian's fasting snake. Adrian feels a Jungian connection to it and keeps it "in honor and acknowledgment of the snake in" himself. The boa constrictor will not eat for the same reason Adrian cannot sleep: he is undergoing a dramatic metamorphosis.

Bell may not always hid the symbolic seams where plot and philosophy join, he can oversensationalize an ending, and his fascination for characters from society's dingiest creases does put off some readers. But in *Doctor Sleep* he once again artfully blends perceptiveness, a deadpan mastery of the grotesque, and a startling profundity of mind.

Though Bell meanders between the beatific Appalachian rurality of his childhood, the decaying gothic grandeur of the New York that nursed from him his first novel, and foggy London, he is, in fact, a regional writer. His region is the misty border buffering purgatory from hell in the sootiest creases of contemporary society. In *Save Me, Joe Louis*, 23-year-old Macrae walks that border. He is AWOL from the army and living in New York's Hell's Kitchen. He hasn't enjoyed much of anything since his teen years in Tennessee when he was in love, without knowing it, with a spirited photographer named Lacy.

Petulant and lost, Macrae often takes "a wring fork in the crisscross trails of conversation" and blindly strews mines along his own path. He forms unfortunate attachments, one to a prostitute whose pimp decides to blow half her head off. Macrae's most dangerous alliance is with his increasingly unstable partner-in-crime Charlie, whose rationale—"Ain't nobody cares that much what you do"—faintly recalls Flannery O'Connor's Misfit. After they've made New York too hot for their comfort by forcing people to withdraw and turn over money from their ATMs, they head south to Baltimore where they add a third partner, a benign young black man named Porter, fresh off a jail term for a bar fight that turned inadvertently gory. The three hold up an armored bank truck, but police arrive, bullets fly, and the trio heads full speed for Macrae's father's farm outside of Nashville.

Were trigger-happy Charlie not with him, Macrae might at last feel he's returned from far east of Eden. There's the potential for a wholesome life in Tennessee. Adjacent to Macrae's land is the farm of Thomas Laidlaw, the hero of *Soldier's Joy*. Not only is Laidlaw there, still playing banjo with his bluegrass band and still with Adrienne Wells, but the beautiful Lacy has returned home from art school in Philadelphia. That she still loves Macrae is clear to everyone but him, who keeps stumbling aimlessly in restless confusion. After a robbery attempt which they botch even worse than the Baltimore fiasco, Macrae, Charlie, and Porter flee to the South Carolina coast. There it grows obvious that Macrae may have outlived his usefulness to Charlie, and that the book's final page won't be big enough to hold both of them.

In *Save Me, Joe Louis*, Bell once again invites us to care about characters who offer scarcely an inch of ground to build affection on. Yet once again, by combining subtle technique and native compassion, he succeeds, walking sympathetically among contemporary thieves and moral lepers with a charity that either converts or shames his readers.

—Ian McMechan, updated by Andy Solomon

BELLOW, Saul

Nationality: American. **Born:** Lachine, Quebec, Canada, 10 June 1915; grew up in Montreal; moved with his family to Chicago, 1924. **Education:** Tuley High School, Chicago, graduated 1933; University of Chicago, 1933-35; Northwestern University, Evanston, Illinois, 1935-37, B.S. (honors) in sociology and anthropology 1937; did graduate work in anthropology at University of Wisconsin, Madison, 1937. **Military Service:** Served in the United States Merchant Marine, 1944-45. **Family:** Married 1) Anita Goshkin in 1937 (divorced), one son; 2) Alexandra Tschacbasov in 1956 (divorced), one son; 3) Susan Glassman in 1961 (divorced), one son; 4) Alexandra Ionescu Tulcea in 1975 (divorced 1986); 5) Janis Freedman in 1989. **Career:** Teacher, Pestalozzi-Froebel Teachers College, Chicago, 1938-42; member of the editorial department, "Great Books" Project, *Encyclopaedia Britannica*, Chicago, 1943-44; freelance editor and reviewer, New York, 1945-46; instructor, 1946, and assistant professor of English, 1948-49, University of Minnesota, Minneapolis; visiting lecturer, New York University, 1950-52; Creative Writing Fellow, Princeton University, New Jersey, 1952-53; member of the English faculty, Bard College, Annandale-on-Hudson, New York, 1953-54; associate professor of English, University of Minnesota, 1954-59; visiting professor of English, University of Puerto Rico, Rio Piedras, 1961; Romanes Lecturer, 1990. Since 1962 professor and chairman, 1970-76, Committee on Social Thought, University of Chicago; now Gruiner Distinguished Services Professor. Co-editor, *The Noble Savage*, New York, then Cleveland, 1960-62. Fellow, Academy for Policy Study, 1966; fellow, Branford College, Yale University, New Haven, Connecticut. **Awards:** Guggenheim fellowship, 1948, 1955; American Academy grant, 1952, and gold medal, 1977; National Book award, 1954, 1965, 1971; Ford grant, 1959, 1960; Friends of Literature award, 1960; James L. Dow award, 1964; International Literary prize, 1965; Jewish Heritage award, 1968; Formentor prize, 1970; Nobel Prize for Literature, 1976; Pulitzer prize, 1976; Neil Gunn International fellowship, 1977; Brandeis University Creative Arts award, 1978; Malaparte award (Italy), 1984; Scanno award (Italy), 1988; National Book award, for lifetime achievement, 1990. D.Litt.: Northwestern University, 1962; Bard College, 1963; Litt.D.: New York University, 1970; Harvard University, Cambridge, Massachusetts, 1972; Yale University, 1972; McGill University, Montreal, 1973; Brandeis University, Waltham, Massachusetts, 1973; Hebrew Union College, Cincinnati, 1976; Trinity College, Dublin, 1976. Chevalier, 1968, and Commander, 1985, Order of Arts and Letters (France); Commander, Legion of Honor (France), 1983. **Member:** American Academy, 1970. **Agent:** Harriett Wasserman Literary Agency, 137 East 36th Street, New York, New York 10016. **Address:** Committee on Social Thought, University of Chicago, 1126 East 59th Street, Chicago, Illinois 60637, U.S.A.

PUBLICATIONS

Novels

Dangling Man. New York, Vanguard Press, 1944; London, Lehmann, 1946.
The Victim. New York, Vanguard Press, 1947; London, Lehmann, 1948.
The Adventures of Augie March. New York, Viking Press, 1953; London, Weidenfeld and Nicolson, 1954.

Henderson the Rain King. New York, Viking Press, and London, Weidenfeld and Nicolson, 1959.

Herzog. New York, Viking Press, 1964; London, Weidenfeld and Nicolson, 1965.

Mr. Sammler's Planet. New York, Viking Press, and London, Weidenfeld and Nicolson, 1970.

Humboldt's Gift. New York, Viking Press, and London, Secker and Warburg, 1975.

The Dean's December. New York, Harper, and London, Secker and Warburg, 1982.

More Die of Heartbreak. New York, Morrow, and London, Alison Press, 1987.

Short Stories

Seize the Day, with Three Short Stories and a One-Act Play (includes *The Wrecker*). New York, Viking Press, 1956; London, Weidenfeld and Nicolson, 1957.

Mosby's Memoirs and Other Stories. New York, Viking Press, 1968; London, Weidenfeld and Nicolson, 1969.

Him with His Foot in His Mouth and Other Stories. New York, Harper, and London, Secker and Warburg, 1984.

A Theft. New York and London, Penguin, 1989.

The Bellarosa Connection. New York and London, Penguin, 1989.

Something to Remember Me By: Three Tales. New York, Viking, and London, Penguin, 1991.

Uncollected Short Stories

"The Mexican General," in *Partisan Reader,* edited by William Phillips and Philip Rahv. New York, Dial Press, 1946.

"Dora," in *Harper's Bazaar* (New York), November 1949.

"A Sermon by Dr. Pep," in *The Best American Short Stories 1950,* edited by Martha Foley. Boston, Houghton Mifflin, 1950.

"The Trip to Galena," in *Partisan Review* (New York), November-December 1950.

"Address by Gooley MacDowell to the Hasbeens Club of Chicago," in *Nelson Algren's Book of Lonesome Monsters,* edited by Nelson Algren. New York, Lancer, 1962; London, Panther, 1964.

"The Old System," in *Playboy* (Chicago), January 1968.

"Burdens of a Lone Survivor," in *Esquire* (New York), December 1974.

Plays

The Wrecker (televised 1964). Included in *Seize the Day,* 1956.

Scenes from Humanitas: A Farce, in *Partisan Review* (New Brunswick, New Jersey), Summer 1962.

The Last Analysis (produced New York 1964; Derby, 1967). New York, Viking Press, 1965; London, Weidenfeld and Nicolson, 1966.

Under the Weather (includes *Out from Under, A Wen,* and *Orange Soufflé*) (produced Edinburgh and New York, 1966; as *The Bellow Plays,* produced London, 1966). *A Wen* published in *Esquire* (New York), January 1965; in *Traverse Plays,* edited by Jim Haynes, London, Penguin, 1966; *Orange Soufflé* published in *Traverse Plays,* 1966; in *Best Short Plays of the World Theatre 1968-1973,* edited by Stanley Richards, New York, Crown, 1973.

Television Play: *The Wrecker,* 1964.

Other

Dessins, by Jesse Reichek; text by Bellow and Christian Zervos. Paris, Editions Cahiers d'Art, 1960.

Recent American Fiction: A Lecture. Washington, D.C., Library of Congress, 1963.

Like You're Nobody: The Letters of Louis Gallo to Saul Bellow, 1961-62, Plus Oedipus-Schmoedipus, The Story That Started It All. New York, Dimensions Press, 1966.

Technology and the Frontiers of Knowledge, with others. New York, Doubleday, 1973.

The Portable Saul Bellow, edited by Gabriel Josipovici. New York, Viking Press, 1974; London, Penguin, 1977.

To Jerusalem and Back: A Personal Account. New York, Viking Press, and London, Secker and Warburg, 1976.

Nobel Lecture. Stockholm, United States Information Service, 1977.

Conversations with Saul Bellow, edited by Gloria L. Cronin and Ben Siegel. Jackson, University Press of Mississippi, 1994.

It All Adds Up: From the Dim Past to the Certain Future. New York, Viking, 1994.

Editor, *Great Jewish Short Stories.* New York, Dell, 1963; London, Vallentine Mitchell, 1971.

*

Bibliography: *Saul Bellow: A Comprehensive Bibliography* by B.A. Sokoloff and Mark E. Posner, Norwood, Pennsylvania, Norwood Editions, 1973; *Saul Bellow, His Works and His Critics: An Annotated International Bibliography* by Marianne Nault, New York, Garland, 1977; *Saul Bellow: A Bibliography of Secondary Sources* by F. Lercangée, Brussels, Center for American Studies, 1977; *Saul Bellow: A Reference Guide* by Robert G. Noreen, Boston, Hall, 1978; *Saul Bellow: An Annotated Bibliography* by Gloria L. Cronin, New York, Garland, 2nd edition, 1987.

Manuscript Collections: Regenstein Library, University of Chicago; University of Texas, Austin.

Critical Studies (selection): *Saul Bellow* by Tony Tanner, Edinburgh, Oliver and Boyd, 1965, New York, Barnes and Noble, 1967; *Saul Bellow* by Earl Rovit, Minneapolis, University of Minnesota Press, 1967, and *Saul Bellow: A Collection of Critical Essays* edited by Rovit, Englewood Cliffs, New Jersey, Prentice Hall, 1975; *Saul Bellow: A Critical Essay* by Robert Detweiler, Grand Rapids, Michigan, Eerdmans, 1967; *The Novels of Saul Bellow* by Keith Michael Opdahl, University Park, Pennsylvania State University Press, 1967; *Saul Bellow and the Critics* edited by Irving Malin, New York, New York University Press, and London, University of London Press, 1967, and *Saul Bellow's Fiction* by Malin, Carbondale, Southern Illinois University Press, 1969; *Saul Bellow: In Defense of Man* by John Jacob Clayton, Bloomington, Indiana University Press, 1968, revised edition, 1979; *Saul Bellow* by Robert R. Dutton, New York, Twayne, 1971, revised edition, 1982; *Saul Bellow* by Brigitte Scheer-Schäzler, New York, Ungar, 1973; *Saul Bellow's Enigmatic Laughter* by Sarah Blacher Cohen, Urbana, University of Illinois Press, 1974; *Whence the Power? The Artistry and Humanity of Saul Bellow* by M. Gilbert Porter, Columbia, University of Missouri Press, 1974; *Saul Bellow: The Problem of Affirmation* by Chirantan Kulshrestha, New Delhi and London, Arnold-Heinemann, 1978, Atlantic Highlands, New Jersey,

Humanities Press, 1979; *Critical Essays on Saul Bellow* edited by Stanley Trachtenberg, Boston, Hall, 1979; *Quest for the Human: An Exploration of Saul Bellow's Fiction* by Eusebio L. Rodrigues, Lewisburg, Pennsylvania, Bucknell University Press, 1981; *Saul Bellow* by Malcolm Bradbury, London, Methuen, 1983; *Saul Bellow's Moral Vision: A Critical Study of the Jewish Experience* by L.H. Goldman, New York, Irvington, 1983; *Saul Bellow: Vision and Revision* by Daniel Fuchs, Durham, North Carolina, Duke University Press, 1984; *Saul Bellow and History* by Judie Newman, New York, St. Martin's Press, and London, Macmillan, 1984; *A Sort of Columbus: The American Voyages of Saul Bellow's Fiction* by Jeanne Braham, Athens, University of Georgia Press, 1984; *On Bellow's Planet: Readings from the Dark Side,* Rutherford, New Jersey, Fairleigh Dickinson University Press, 1985, and *Herzog: The Limits of Ideas,* London, Maxwell Macmillan, 1990, both by Jonathan Wilson; *Saul Bellow* by Robert F. Kiernan, New York, Crossroad Continuum, 1988; *Saul Bellow and the Decline of Humanism* by Michael K. Glenday, London, Macmillan, 1990; *Saul Bellow: Against the Grain* by Ellen Pifer, University Park, Pennsylvania State University Press, 1990; *Saul Bellow: A Biography of the Imagination* by Ruth Miller, New York, St. Martin's Press, 1991; *Saul Bellow at Seventy-Five: A Collection of Critical Essays* edited by Gerhard Bach, Tubingen, Narr, 1991; *Saul Bellow* by Peter Hyland, New York, St. Martin's Press, 1992; *Saul Bellow: A Mosaic* compiled by Aharoni et al., New York, Lang, 1992; *Character and Narration in the Short Fiction of Saul Bellow* by Marianne M. Friedrich, New York, Lang, 1993; *Saul Bellow: The Feminine Mystique* by Tarlochan Singh Anand, Jalandhar, India, ABS, 1993; *Quest for Salvation in Saul Bellow's Novels* by Kyung-Ae Kim, Frankfurt am Main, Lang, 1994; *Saul Bellow and the Struggle at the Center* edited by Eugene Hollahan, New York, AMS Press, 1994.

*   *   *

Saul Bellow is the most distinguished novelist of the post war period in America. He is the most intellectual of American novelists, but one who, paradoxically, relies finally upon imagination and feeling; in the relatively late *Humboldt's Gift* he moves more surely than ever before toward intuition and mysticism, toward a nonrational epistemology. He may be the staunchest defender of the idea of the self in American fiction, but he frequently recognizes claims of brotherhood and love that limit the egoistic pursuit of the self. His fiction rests upon a conception of becoming or possibility, yet he recognizes the human initiative in creating and pursuing process is limited by powerful determinants beyond human control. Bellow is an optimist, despite the prevailing climate of pessimism and despair. His novels are built on these dichotomies and paradoxes and written in a language that is almost always vibrant and resourceful.

The evolution of Bellow's style is a key to the understanding of his fiction. He began, in *Dangling Man* and *The Victim,* with a tight conception of both language and structure, using Flaubert as his model. Both books are disciplined and spare; Bellow has said that he strove for a kind of correctness that would be acceptable to the Anglo-Saxon Protestant world that seemed to dominate American literature. But by the time he came to write *The Adventures of Augie March,* he had discovered rhetoric, he had gained confidence as a writer and as an American, and he had recognized the weakening of the WASP hold on literature in the United States. The result is that the language of this novel streams out of Bellow in a

fine, free flow; it is as larky as its protagonist and as various as the many levels of its discourse demand, ranging in its versatility from the talk of Jewish immigrants to the intercourse of University of Chicago intellectuals. As the language expanded, so did the book, and *Augie* is a sprawling, picaresque work in contrast to the carefully contained earlier novels. Succeeding novels show a curbing of rhetorical extravagance, but *Augie* established the essential mode of expression for the fiction Bellow has done since.

Bellow's taste for a vital and even eccentric language is related, first, to his conviction that words are a form of power, and second, to his hope that character can be preserved in contemporary fiction. With respect to the latter, he has made a considerable contribution by assembling in his novels a gallery of ill assorted oddballs, misfits, geniuses, and cranks, like Einhorn in *Augie,* or confidence men, like Dr. Tamkin in *Seize the Day.* Bellow commands Dickensian comic energies in the depiction of character, but he can also give us characters of size, power, subtlety, and cunning like Julius in *Humboldt's Gift,* who has the presence and imperious will of a Medici prince. The idea of character, furthermore, is associated with the survival of the self. Nothing is more important in Bellow's fiction, and Augie March, Henderson, and Tommy Wilhelm, among his protagonists, are all committed to the quest for identity and the salvation of the self. Bellow knows that, beginning in the 19th century, many forces, from Darwinism and Marxism to the Nazis and the logical positivists of the 20th century, have conspired to eliminate the self, and that writers like Joyce and Beckett have joined in this campaign. He believes, as he has said repeatedly in his fiction, that the main business of a man's life is to carry the burden of his personality or "to be the carrier of a load which was his own self," as he puts it in *Seize the Day.* By realizing the self, one asserts his humanity, that is, lays a claim to sharing in human suffering and joy, in the human destiny.

Realization of the self means surrender of the self. Bellow has always recognized this paradox, which he dramatizes nowhere more effectively than in *Henderson the Rain King.* Henderson begins as a man overwhelmed by the demands of his own ego. Neighbors, wives, children—nothing and nobody is permitted to stand in the way of his self gratification as he listens to an inner voice intoning, "I want! I want!" At the end of the book, his African experience has taught him that what men need is a right relation with the world of nature and with humanity as a whole. The guardianship he assumes of the lion cub and the little boy is an expression of love in both realms of being that signifies Henderson's surrender of the ego in order to realize the self through immersion in the order of nature and in the community of man. Similarly, Tommy Wilhelm in *Seize the Day* finds the consummation of his heart's need in the abandonment of self concern and the substitution of a generalized love for mankind.

Mr. Sammler's Planet, however, a novel of the 1970s, is far more critical of the idea of the self than any previous work. It is a book that documents Bellow's conviction that the conception of individualism or the self that we took first from Christianity and then from the Enlightenment has degenerated, in our time, into self-indulgence and license. But even in the face of this bitter revision of the optimistic history of the West, Bellow is unwilling to abandon in this novel the possibility that good may be found in human beings, and he persists in showing the need to pursue definition in one's life.

This hedged optimism in the face of his own pessimistic conclusions about the nature and fate of man is one of the most difficult situations that Bellow must confront in his fiction. Like Charlie

Citrine in *Humboldt,* Bellow wonders whether Americans have a theory of evil and speculates that the American experience is "uncorrected by the main history of human suffering." The evidence tells him that man is depraved. Observation shows that men tend to behave, in crisis, like rats in a sack, as H.G. Wells said. Reason crowds him to an acceptance of absurdity as the prime condition of man and the world. But Bellow simply refuses to credit what observation, reason, and ideas thrust before him. He knows that man is less than what the Golden Age promised us, but he refuses to believe that man is nothing. He is something, Bellow says, and saying it he performs an act of faith. He rests his conviction on his feelings, and like the Transcendentalists upon whom he calls so often in his fiction, he resorts to his intuition. *Herzog* is a clear-cut illustration of Bellow's rejection of pessimistic philosophies. Everyone believes that man is a sick animal, says the protagonist of this novel, but he himself refuses to acquiesce in this judgment or to accept such dark interpretations of human experience as are contained in Kierkegaardian despair and absurdity, Spengler's decline of the West, or Eliot's wasteland complex. Herzog is himself a victim in modern America, but he simply refuses to accept his fate. He refuses to accept the empirical evidence. Persisting in his quest for love, he comes at the end to a restoration of sanity and hope for the future.

As Bellow accepts the epistemological implications of feeling, he also accepts or indeed advocates openness to feeling as sentiment. *Dangling Man* contained a rejection of the stiff-lipped Hemingway code which demands the suppression of emotion, and in all subsequent work he tended to expand the role given to emotion. He believes in the power of feeling and thinks that the novel must show a sympathetic devotion to the life of someone else, that the reader, in other words, must be asked to respond with sympathetic devotion to the life of the characters. In this way, Bellow works toward human connection between author and reader, between reader and characters; these are the connections that will lead to understanding. This emphasis upon emotion in Bellow is to be traced, in part, to the influence of Wilhelm Reich, who related the liberation of the emotions to the struggle for life fulfillment, and in part to the influence of Hasidism, the Jewish creed in which the central proposition is that life is holy joy.

The emphasis upon the self, optimism, and feeling must be understood in relation to Bellow's attitude toward death. He believes that one cannot understand life until one comes to terms with death. He treats the theme everywhere in his fiction, but it is enough here to remark it in four of his books. In *Seize the Day,* Tommy Wilhelm is able to come fully into possession of life, to seize the day, only after he confronts death itself and undergoes a symbolic drowning. Death brings him to the recognition of the heart's ultimate need, which is love. Bellow is equally concerned with death in *Henderson the Rain King* but less successful with it. Henderson insists that we hate and fear death, but that there is nothing like it. He means that we all know we must face it and that we learn from facing it, as he learned from facing the lion, the meaning of life. In *Humboldt* Citrine says repeatedly that Whitman was right: the important question is the death question. One of the major attractions of Rudolf Steiner's anthroposophy for Citrine is that in death the soul will liberate itself from the body. *Mr. Sammler's Planet* is Bellow's most extensive treatment of death. It is an elegiac mediation, first, on the approaching death of Western culture, brought on by a new barbarism represented by those who surrendered traditional concepts of value. And it is, further, the story of a man who has come back from the dead, as it were, whose authority as a spokesman rests

upon his knowledge of death: he had dug what was supposed to be his own grave but had, by chance, crawled out of it; he had seen the Arab dead rotting at Gaza; he had himself killed a man. Throughout the novel he watches his friend and benefactor die. To have known death is to know the meaning of life and to know what it means to be a human being.

The Dean's December is a static novel in which the themes, substantial in themselves, lose some of their force because they have lost the urgency and novelty of initial revelation; we have heard them before from Bellow. The Dean is a humanistic journalist like Sammler attacking the violence and degeneracy of urban life and the collapse of standards, especially among the dirty, rebellious youth of the 1960s. Or the Dean is an academic like Herzog and must contend, like the latter, with a variety of "reality instructors," shrewd, hard, brutal, successful Chicago types who have contempt for the "moral excitement" that the Dean brings to his observation and assessment of American life. The novel is a meditation on death, as in so many previous Bellow fictions. Here it is death in Bucharest, an "Oppressive socialist wonderland" and in Chicago, and the protagonist is a man whose predilection is for philosophizing and whose tendency is toward an ill-controlled didacticism.

Him with His Foot in His Mouth, a collection of five pieces, recalls us to the boundless vitality and originality of the Jewish family members in *Augie,* an old Bellow subject that in this volume, like its other concerns, he makes new again. Here, as in "Cousins," the family center is an intellectual whose decision-making power affects nations, and the family ties expand to the cousinhood of mankind. In "What Kind of a Day Did You Have?" Bellow gives us perhaps the most compelling portrait of the intellectual in all his work thus far. Victor Wulpy, ill and living in the presence of death, staves off the end because "the excitement of thought . . . prevents[s] decay." He is the intellectual as a dying god, the descendant of Hercules, who addresses the ultimate questions about art and morality, sex and death, that define our humanity. Working in a full apprehension of the sense of an ending, of the impending moral and intellectual apocalypse (for which Chicago stands often as a symbol), Bellow has given us in this volume reason once more to regard him as the premier philosophical fiction writer of his time in America and as one in a select company of great writers in the 20th century.

Bellow's achievement is to have imposed upon the contending forces in his fiction—life and death, optimism and despair, reason and feeling, self and brotherhood—an idea of order. He has always known that the novelist begins at a great depth of distraction and disorder. Out of the chaos of experience and the tensions of conflicting claims, he has sought to create a coherent and compelling vision of experience. But it has been a tentative endeavor marked by a sad, sane, comic skepticism about the power of the artist or intellectual to affect the world in any way. Near the end of *Humboldt* Citrine says an extraordinary poetry is buried in America, "but none of the conventional means known to culture can even begin to extract it. . . . The agony is too deep, the disorder too big for art enterprises to be undertaken in the old way." The implication is not that we must, in despair, fall into silence, but that we must find another way to express delight and reveal beauty, to listen "in secret to the sound of truth that God puts into us," and achieve in the midst of disorder a framework of order willed by the artist.

—Chester E. Eisinger

BENEDICT, Peter. *See* **PARGETER, Edith (Mary).**

———

BENEDICTUS, David (Henry)

Nationality: British. **Born:** London, 16 September 1938. **Education:** Stone House, Broadstairs, Kent; Eton College, Berkshire; Balliol College, Oxford, B.A. in English 1959; University of Iowa, Iowa City. **Family:** Married Yvonne Daphne Antrobus in 1971; one son and one daughter. **Career:** Assistant trainee, BBC Radio, London, 1963-64; drama director, 1964-65, and story editor, *Wednesday Play* and *Festival* series, 1965, BBC Television, London; trainee director, Thames Television, Bristol, 1968-70; assistant director, Royal Shakespeare Company, London, 1970-71; Judith E. Wilson Visiting Fellow, and Fellow Commoner, Churchill College, Cambridge, 1981-82; commissioning editor, drama series and serials, Channel Four Television, London, 1984-86. Readings editor, 1989-90, and since 1991 editor: Readings, BBC Radio, London. Writer-in-residence, Central Library, Sutton, Surrey, 1975, Kibbutz Gezer, Israel, 1978, and Bitterne Library, Southampton, 1983-84. Antiques correspondent, London *Evening Standard,* 1977-80; director, Kingston Books. **Address:** 19 Oxford Road, Teddington, Middlesex TW11 0QA, England.

PUBLICATIONS

Novels

The Fourth of June. London, Blond, and New York, Dutton, 1962.
You're a Big Boy Now. London, Blond, 1963; New York, Dutton, 1964.
This Animal Is Mischievous. London, Blond, 1965; New York, New American Library, 1966.
Hump; or, Bone by Bone, Alive. London, Blond, 1967.
The Guru and the Golf Club. London, Blond, 1969.
A World of Windows. London, Weidenfeld and Nicholson, 1971.
The Rabbi's Wife. London, Blond and Briggs, and New York, Evans, 1976.
A Twentieth-Century Man. London, Blond and Briggs, 1978.
Whose Life Is It Anyway? (novelization of play). London, Weidenfeld and Nicolson, 1981.
Lloyd George (novelization of television series). London, Weidenfeld and Nicolson, 1981.
Who Killed the Prince Consort? London, Macmillan, 1982.
Local Hero (novelization of screenplay). London, Penguin, 1983.
Floating Down to Camelot. London, Macdonald, 1985.
Little Sir Nicholas (novelization of television series). London, BBC Publications, 1990.

Uncollected Short Stories

"Mother Love," in *Seventeen* (New York), September 1963.
"E-Type Charlie," in *Seventeen* (New York), September 1964.
"The Unworthiness of Caspar," in *Queen* (London), 1 September 1965.
"Eat Me!," in *Status* (New York), November 1968.

"Nose-Job," in *Pointer* (London), 1970.
"Dreamboat," in *Penthouse* (London), 1971.
"The Torture Chambers of the Mind," in *Men Only* (London), 1974.

Plays

The Fourth of June, adaptation of his own novel (produced London, 1964).
Angels (Over Your Grave) and Geese (Over Mine) (produced Edinburgh, 1967).
Dromedary, adaptation of his novel *Hump* (produced Newcastle-upon-Tyne, 1969).
The Happy Hypocrite, music by Tony Russell, adaptation of the work by Max Beerbohm (produced Bristol, 1969).
What a Way to Run a Revolution!, music by Guy Woolfenden (produced London, 1971).
Betjemania (also director: produced Richmond, Surrey, 1978).
The Golden Key (produced Cambridge, 1982).

Radio Play: *Fortune and the Fishmonger,* 1981.

Television Play: *Little Sir Nicholas* series, 1990.

Other

Junk! How and Where to Buy Beautiful Things for Next to Nothing. London, Macmillan, 1976.
The Antique Collector's Guide. London, Macmillan, 1980; New York, Atheneum, 1981.
The Essential Guide to London: The Best of Everything and Some of the Worst. London, Sphere, 1984; revised edition, as *The Absolutely Essential Guide to London,* 1986.
The Streets of London, photographs by Cressida Pemberton-Pigott. London, Thames Methuen, 1985.
Little Sir Nicholas (for children). London, BBC, 1990.
Odyssey of a Scientist: An Autobiography, with Hans Kalmus. London, Weidenfeld and Nicolson, 1991.
Sunny Intervals and Showers. London, Weidenfeld and Nicolson, 1992.

*

Theatrical Activities:
Director: **Play**—*Betjemania,* Richmond, Surrey, 1978.

David Benedictus comments:
   Given peace of mind, financial independence, and a modicum of luck, I may produce a novel to be proud of one day. But then, who wouldn't? In the meantime, I continue to rehearse in public.

*   *   *

   The range of David Benedictus's novels is very broad. Beginning as a penetrating social satirist in his first works—*The Fourth of June, You're a Big Boy Now, This Animal Is Mischievous*—he has become increasingly serious and experimental over the past decade. Throughout his fiction, Benedictus is concerned with British society's most rigid conventions of sexual and political behavior and with the many kinds of victims caused by the abrasions of caste and class. His caustic ironic vision is perhaps closer to that of Nathaniel West than that of Evelyn Waugh, to whom he has been compared.

Benedictus poses the stock characters of social comedy—bishops, clubmen, schoolmasters—against individuals often maimed, deranged, or outcast by society. A Kafkaesque quality of irony emerges in the novels. *Hump* is a dystopian fantasy about a humpback who loves his deformity in a world of increasing uniformity. *A World of Windows* is a dialectical drama between a voyeur and his wife, exploring the reciprocal madness of observed and observer. *The Guru and the Golf Club* poses a caricature of Eastern mysticism against a parallel caricature of British middle-class pretentions and aspirations.

The Rabbi's Wife and *A Twentieth-Century Man* are mordant and tragic investigations of our times through the refracting prism of Jewish experience. Each contrasts norms of British behavior with the catastrophes of the Holocaust and contemporary terrorism against Jews. In *The Rabbi's Wife* Palestinian terrorists separate a young mod rabbi and his wife, murdering children in a synagogue on the Day of Atonement. The terrorists, modern British Jews, and the indifferent mass of the population are detailed against the horrifying events of political diabolism. *A Twentieth-Century Man* establishes the same mordant ironies by juxtaposing scenes from the marriage of a Tory M.P. and his Dutch wife, whom he rescued from Bergen-Belsen in 1945. Bitter, disturbing comparisons arise between the destruction of the human spirit in the death camps and in contemporary urban civilization.

In *Who Killed the Prince Consort?* the answer to the title question is "practically everyone." The novel is a sly and highly comic satire on Victorian life and mores, focusing on the death of "dear Albert" and the internal politics of the royal family in 1861. The cast of characters includes Karl Marx, a young Sherlock Holmes, the royal physicians and servants, a 97-year-old Scots Pretender, and other parodic figures. Behind the bizarre satire is a serious investigation of hypocrisy, corruption, and mental aberration as the true basis of the Victorian ethos. In many ways, this is Benedictus's funniest work, full of quirky historical data and mock-tushery.

In recent years, Benedictus has worked with film scripts and "novelizations" of television series and films (Brian Clark's *Whose Life Is It Anyway?* and his own *Local Hero*), and he has created increasingly dramatic renderings in his fiction. The vision of his satire has covered our main cultural foibles and dissected the darker anatomy of British class and power.

Benedictus's forte in his fiction is the creation of vivid, complex characters that represent basic assumptions of our culture. His satire is Swiftian in intensity and in its distorted images of sexuality, violence, and brutality. Moving from the sublimated prison system of the quintessential British public school (Eton) to the torments of urban life, the death camps, and warfare by terrorism, Benedictus has compiled a sardonic catalogue of our century's ills. The collision between dead tradition and the anarchy of the present instant is Benedictus's entree into his characters.

These novels also demonstrate a measure of compassion for individuals trapped by the failures of our culture. Even when afflicted by bizarre sexual compulsions, failures of will and nerve, or base selfishness, many of his characters rise to small moments of love and heroism. If Benedictus's satire does not exempt many from its ironies, it also allows room for individuals' virtues. The survivors of our varied holocausts still struggle to live and love one another.

—William J. Schafer

BERGER, John (Peter)

Nationality: British. **Born:** Stoke Newington, London, 5 November 1926. **Education:** Central School of Art and the Chelsea School of Art, London. **Military Service:** Served in the Oxford and Buckinghamshire Infantry, 1944-46. **Family:** Married twice; three children. **Career:** Painter and drawing teacher, 1948-55; contributor, *Tribune* and *New Statesman,* both London, 1951-60; television narrator, *About Time,* 1985, and *Another Way of Telling,* 1989. Artist: exhibitions at Wildenstein, Redfern, and Leicester galleries, London, Denise Cade gallery, New York, 1994. **Awards:** Booker prize, 1972; *Guardian* Fiction prize, 1972; James Tait Black Memorial prize, 1973; New York Critics prize, for screenplay, 1976; George Orwell Memorial prize, 1977; Barcelona Film Festival Europa award, 1989; Lannan Foundation award, 1989; Australian State prize, 1989. **Address:** Quincy, Mieussy, 74440 Taninges, France.

PUBLICATIONS

Novels

A Painter of Our Time. London, Secker and Warburg, 1958; New York, Simon and Schuster, 1959.
The Foot of Clive. London, Methuen, 1962.
Corker's Freedom. London, Methuen, 1964; New York, Pantheon, 1993.
G. London, Weidenfeld and Nicolson, and New York, Viking Press, 1972.
Into Their Labours (trilogy in one volume). New York, Pantheon, 1991; London, Granta, 1992.
  Pig Earth (short stories). London, Writers and Readers, 1979; New York, Pantheon, 1980.
  Once in Europa (short stories). New York, Pantheon, 1987; Cambridge, Granta, 1989.
  Lilac and Flag: An Old Wives' Tale of a City. New York, Pantheon, 1990; Cambridge, Granta, 1991.
To the Wedding. New York, Pantheon, and London, Bloomsbury, 1995.

Plays

Jonas qui aura 25 ans en l'an 2000 (screenplay), with Alain Tanner. Lausanne, Cinémathèque Suisse, 1978; translated by Michael Palmer, as *Jonah Who Will Be 25 in the Year 2000,* Berkeley, California, North Atlantic, 1983.
A Question of Geography, with Nella Bielski (produced Marseille, 1984; Stratford-on-Avon, 1987; London, 1988). London, Faber, 1987.
Les Trois Chaleurs (produced Paris, 1985).
Boris, translated into Welsh by Rhiannon Ifans (produced Cardiff, 1985).
Goya's Last Portrait: The Painter Played Today, with Nella Bielski. London, Faber, 1989.

Screenplays, with Alain Tanner: *La Salamandre* (*The Salamander*), 1971, *Le Milieu du monde* (*The Middle of the World*), 1974, and *Jonas* (*Jonah Who Will Be 25 in the Year 2000*), 1976; *Play Me Something,* with Timothy Neat, 1989.

Poetry

Pages of the Wound: Poems, Photographs, Drawings by John Berger. London, Circle Press, 1994.

Other

Marcel Frishman, with George Besson. Oxford, Cassirer, 1958.

Permanent Red: Essays in Seeing. London, Methuen, 1960; as *Towards Reality,* New York, Knopf, 1962.

The Success and Failure of Picasso. London, Penguin, 1965; New York, Pantheon, 1980.

A Fortunate Man: The Story of a Country Doctor, photographs by Jean Mohr. London, Allen Lane, and New York, Holt Rinehart, 1967.

Art and Revolution: Ernst Neizvestny and the Role of the Artist in the U.S.S.R. London, Weidenfeld and Nicolson, and New York, Pantheon, 1969.

The Moment of Cubism and Other Essays. London, Weidenfeld and Nicolson, and New York, Pantheon, 1969.

The Look of Things, edited by Nikos Stangos. London, Penguin, 1972; New York, Viking Press, 1974.

Ways of Seeing, with others. London, BBC-Penguin, 1972; New York, Viking Press, 1973.

A Seventh Man: Migrant Workers in Europe, photographs by Jean Mohr. London, Penguin, and New York, Viking Press, 1975.

About Looking. London, Writers and Readers, and New York, Pantheon, 1980.

Another Way of Telling (on photography), with Jean Mohr. London, Writers and Readers, and New York, Pantheon, 1982.

And Our Faces, My Heart, Brief as Photos. London, Writers and Readers, and New York, Pantheon, 1984.

The White Bird, edited by Lloyd Spencer. London, Chatto and Windus, 1985; as *The Sense of Sight,* New York, Pantheon, 1986.

Keeping a Rendezvous. New York, Pantheon, 1991; London, Granta, 1992.

Translator, with Anya Bostock, *Poems on the Theatre,* by Bertolt Brecht. London, Scorpion Press, 1961; as *The Great Art of Living Together: Poems on the Theatre,* Bingley, Yorkshire, Granville Press, 1972.

Translator, with Anya Bostock, *Helene Weigel, Actress,* by Bertolt Brecht. Leipzig, Veb Edition, 1961.

Translator, with Anya Bostock, *Return to My Native Land,* by Aimé Césaire. London, Penguin, 1969.

Translator, with Lisa Appignanesi, *Oranges for the Son of Asher Levy,* by Nella Bielski. London, Writers and Readers, 1982.

Translator, with Jonathan Steffen, *After Arkadia: The Wickerwork Tram and The Barber's Head,* by Nella Bielski. London, Viking, 1991.

*

Critical Studies: *Seeing Berger: A Revaluation of Ways of Seeing* by Peter Fuller, London, Writers and Readers, 1980, revised edition as *Seeing Through Berger,* London, Claridge Press, 1988; *Ways of Telling: The Work of John Berger* by Geoff Dyer, London, Pluto, 1986.

*   *   *

From his 10 years as art critic for the *New Statesman* through to his present storytelling narratives of French peasant life, John Berger has been constantly experimenting with various perspectives, voices, and kinds of writing. But certain qualities remain constant in all of his mixed-genre writing: the seriousness of tone and attitude toward human life; the conviction that "seeing comes before words" (*Ways of Seeing*); the determination to show how the ways of the modern capitalist world distort and destroy lives and imaginations; the spirit of affirmation of, and faith and hope in, possibilities of the creative imagination and humans' capacity as social animals to recognize the roots of value and meaning and to bring about change. As an oppositional and interdisciplinary thinker, Berger sees writing as a social act and writes not only of any particular tradition, but out of his rational and humane Marxist convictions, mitigated somewhat over the years by broader philosophical investigations.

His first three novels are set in the London of the 1950s and 1960s. *A Painter of Our Time* uses the world of an émigré to explore the crossroads of culture and politics. It arose out of Berger's art critical essays of the 1950s and out of his experiences with people he knew in the art world, particularly certain émigré artists. The novel sets Hungarian painter and scientific socialist Janos Lavin's artistic and political ideals against modern London's cynical and opportunist art business, with which he must deal, and explores his isolation as an exile with no suitable context in which to work.

Berger "thought about [his next three novels] quite consciously in terms of British society" (interview with Diane Watson, May 1988). He maintains that bourgeois society "underdevelops" consciousness and life on an individual level, and empathy consistently informs his fictional portraits of those whose lives are most "underdeveloped," from his examination of those disabled by modern British society, to those ignored or dismissed by Marxism, such as the peasants about whom he now writes. In *The Foot of Clive* Berger departs permanently from the world of art in his fiction, and dramatizes the minutiae of the daily actions and the subconscious impulses of six men from across the class strata who are patients in a hospital ward. The lack of a collective dream and the void left by the society's destruction of a coherent heroic image informs the quality of life and relations in the ward, a microcosm of British society. Prevented from action, they lead a passive, static existence; all they can do is think, talk, and feed off their fears.

In *A Fortunate Man,* Berger's most moving work of non-fiction, he describes the situation of "wholesale cultural deprivation;" in *Corker's Freedom*—his most underrated novel—he *illuminates* the situation by examining the consequences of this deprivation for one particular individual, Corker, the owner of an employment agency and a self-proclaimed "traveler." Mainly by depicting the contours of Corker's self-consciousness, the novel traces several days in his awakening to what he feels to be his true potential and his struggle to liberate himself from his sister and from his society's expectations of him.

Berger's best known work of fiction, *G.,* closes out the phase of works written from inside the society of which he is most critical; it looks backwards to ideas and struggles of previous work and forwards to the solving of questions it raises about writing and to other possibilities of philosophical—mainly existential and phenomenological—and ideological perspective. This highly technically experimental novel grapples with the living of two kinds of time, historical and subjective, elucidates the workings of memory, and documents the historical preconditions that make a Don Juan possible:

the novel is set in the period between the late 19th century and the beginning of World War I. *G.* is grounded in *Ways of Seeing,* particularly in its consideration of sexual appetite and social roles as determined by political, historical, and cultural contexts. Its global resonance is brought about by the author's imaginative identification with not only particular individuals, but with a historical period of a continent, with a revolutionary class, and with women. The mysterious, cosmopolitan, Don Juan figure G. has brushes with all that is vital about his period in history, but is interested in engaging with nothing but moments of liberation through sexual passion.

Berger described his "thinking about narrative" as "having become tighter and more traditional" after *G.* ("The Screenwriter as Collaborator," interview in *Cineaste,* no. 10, 1980), and he turned his attention to a culture whose perspective predates that of progress and capitalism. Throughout the three-part project *Into Their Labours*—comprised of *Pig Earth, Once in Europa,* and *Lilac and Flag,* each of which addresses a different stage of this process—he acts as a witness to the disintegration of traditional French peasant work, perspective, and experience, and adopts a storytelling voice and narrative style. In storytelling, on which he is now concentrating, Berger has found a language that speaks of and from lived experience, in opposition to that which reflects and perpetuates the constraints and limitations of bourgeois society. He values the art of storytelling for its ability to situate people, individually and collectively, in history, and as a kind of narrative that feeds and answers to imaginative and metaphysical experience. This rich and lyrical trilogy contains some of his best writing so far, particularly in *Once in Europa,* a book of love stories that turn on the mystery and amplitude of intimacy.

Throughout Berger's evolution from one of Britain's best social realists to master storyteller his aim remains consistent: to point to possibilities of disalienation. And while his fiction moves increasingly in the direction of philosophical speculation and metaphysical rumination, it loses none of its political impact.

—Diane Watson

BERGER, Thomas (Louis)

Nationality: American. **Born:** Cincinnati, Ohio, 20 July 1924. **Education:** The University of Cincinnati, B.A. 1948; Columbia University, New York, 1950-51. **Military Service:** Served in the United States Army, 1943-46. **Family:** Married Jeanne Redpath in 1950. **Career:** Librarian, Rand School of Social Science, New York, 1948-51; staff member, *New York Times Index,* 1951-52; associate editor, *Popular Science Monthly,* New York, 1952-54; film critic, *Esquire,* New York, 1972-73; writer-in-residence, University of Kansas, Lawrence, 1974; Distinguished Visiting Professor, Southampton College, New York, 1975-76; visiting lecturer, Yale University, New Haven, Connecticut, 1981, 1982; Regents' Lecturer, University of California, Davis, 1982. **Awards:** Dial fellowship, 1962; Western Heritage award, 1965; Rosenthal award, 1965. Litt.D.: Long Island University, Greenvale, New York, 1986. **Agent:** Don Congdon Associates, 156 Fifth Avenue, Suite 625, New York, New York 10010, U.S.A.

PUBLICATIONS

Novels

Crazy in Berlin. New York, Scribner, 1958.
Reinhart in Love. New York, Scribner, 1962; London, Eyre and Spottiswoode, 1963.
Little Big Man. New York, Dial Press, 1964; London, Eyre and Spottiswoode, 1965.
Killing Time. New York, Dial Press, 1967; London Eyre and Spottiswoode, 1968.
Vital Parts. New York, Baron, 1970; London, Eyre and Spottiswoode, 1971.
Regiment of Women. New York, Simon and Schuster, 1973; London, Eyre Methuen, 1974.
Sneaky People. New York, Simon and Schuster, 1975; London, Methuen, 1980.
Who Is Teddy Villanova? New York, Delacorte Press, and London, Eyre Methuen, 1977.
Arthur Rex: A Legendary Novel. New York, Delacorte Press, 1978; London, Methuen, 1979.
Neighbors. New York, Delacorte Press, 1980; London, Methuen, 1981.
Reinhart's Women. New York, Delacorte Press, 1981; London, Methuen, 1982.
The Feud. New York, Delacorte Press, 1983; London, Methuen, 1984.
Nowhere. New York, Delacorte Press, 1985; London, Methuen, 1986.
Being Invisible. Boston, Little Brown, 1987; London, Methuen, 1988.
The Houseguest. Boston, Little Brown, 1988; London, Weidenfeld and Nicolson, 1989.
Changing the Past. Boston, Little Brown, 1989; London, Weidenfeld and Nicolson, 1990.
Orrie's Story. Boston, Little Brown, 1990.
Meeting Evil. Boston, Little Brown, 1992.
Robert Crews. New York, Morrow, 1994.

Short Stories

Granted Wishes. Northridge, California, Lord John Press, 1984.

Uncollected Short Stories

"Professor Hyde," in *Playboy* (Chicago), December 1961.
"A Monkey of His Own," in *Saturday Evening Post* (Philadelphia), 22 May 1965.
"Fatuous Fables," in *Penthouse* (London), March 1973.
"Envy," in *Oui* (Chicago), April 1975.
"The Achievement of Dr. Poon," in *American Review 25,* edited by Theodore Solotaroff. New York, Bantam, 1976.
"Tales of the Animal Crime Squad," in *Playboy* (Chicago), December 1980.
"The Methuselah Factor," in *Gentlemen's Quarterly* (New York), September 1984.
"Planet of the Losers," in *Playboy* (Chicago), November 1988.
"Gibberish," in *Playboy* (Chicago), December 1990.
"Personal Power," in *Playboy* (Chicago), December 1992.

Play

Other People (produced Stockbridge, Massachussetts, 1970).

*

Bibliography: "Thomas Berger: Primary and Secondary Works" by James Bense, in *Bulletin of Bibliography* 6(2), 1994.

Manuscript Collection: Boston University Library.

Critical Studies: "Bitter Comedy" by Richard Schickel, in *Commentary* (New York), July 1970; "Thomas Berger's *Little Big Man* as History" by Leo Oliva, in *Western American Literature* (Fort Collins, Colorado), vol. 8, nos. 1-2, 1973; "Thomas Berger's Elan" by Douglas Hughes, in *Confrontation* (New York), Spring-Summer 1976; "The Radical Americanist" by Brooks Landon, and "The Second Decade of *Little Big Man*" by Frederick Turner, both in *Nation* (New York), 20 August 1977; "Berger and Barth: The Comedy of Decomposition" by Stanley Trachtenberg, in *Comic Relief* edited by Sarah Blacher Cohen, Urbana, University of Illinois Press, 1978; "Thomas Berger Issue" (includes bibliography) of *Studies in American Humor* (San Marcos, Texas), Spring and Fall 1983; "Reinhart as Hero and Clown" by Gerald Weales, in *Hollins Critic* (Hollins College, Virginia), December 1983; "Laughter as Self-Defense in *Who Is Teddy Villanova?*," in *Studies in American Humor* (San Marcos, Texas), Spring 1986, and "A Murderous Clarity: A Reading of Thomas Berger's *Killing Time*," in *Philological Quarterly* (Iowa City), Winter 1989, both by Jon Wallace; *Thomas Berger* by Brooks Landon, Boston, Twayne, 1989.

Thomas Berger comments: I write to amuse and conceal myself.

*   *   *

Thomas Berger's novels exhibit an extraordinary comic sensibility, a satiric talent for wild caricature, and a concern for the quality of middle-class life in middle America. His novels chronicle the decline and fall of the Common Man in 20th-century America and meticulously detail the absurdities of our civilizations. Berger is one of the subtlest and most accurate parodists writing today, with a flawless sense of style and proportion that is charged with comic vitality.

His Reinhart saga (*Crazy in Berlin, Reinhart in Love, Vital Parts,* and *Reinhart's Women*) follows Carlo Reinhart from adolescence to middle age, detailing his career as a soldier in occupied Germany, a GI Bill student, and a failed wage-slave and decrepit father in the bewildering America of the 1980s. Reinhart epitomizes the failure of good intentions. A believer in the American Dream as purveyed in magazines, high-school classrooms, and advertisements, Carlo is a constant victim of deceit and fraud. Like the Good Soldier Schweik, Carlo takes the world at face value and assumes that appearance is reality; unlike Schweik, Carlo is guileless and incapable of hypocrisy, so he is perpetually victimized and disillusioned. The comedy arises in the gulf between Carlo's expectations and his experience.

In *Crazy in Berlin* Carlo is swept up in conspiracy, involved with spies and criminals dividing the spoils of the fallen Nazi state. A good-natured slob and summer soldier, Carlo survives, but he is driven to murder and madness, shattered not by war but by the lunacy of peace. The novel exudes the bitter ironies of sophisticated slap-stick comedy, similar to Preston Sturges's films. Carlo, a bewildered, optimistic average man, is driven mad by the Hobbesian nightmare of Occupied Germany.

The second novel, *Reinhart in Love,* continues the mock-heroic saga. Carlo returns to the purported normality of peace-time America to continue college on the GI Bill. Again he is duped,

exploited, and betrayed as Orlando himself, charged with cosmic love: *"Reinhart was in love with everything."* But as his boss tells him, the world is still a Hobbesian jungle, with every man's hand raised against his fellows: "life, real life, is exactly like the fighting, except in the latter you use guns and therefore don't destroy as many people." The novel ends with Carlo married by deception to a shrew, failed even at suicide and bereft of ideals and ambitions, ready to move upward and onward.

Vital Parts moves ahead 20 years to reveal Reinhart still married to his shrew and father to a fat, mooning daughter and a vicious ne'er-do-well son. He has failed at every capitalistic venture, lost his hair and youth, gained debts and a paunch. Again in suicidal despair, he becomes involved in a bizarre cryogenics scheme—to immortality via technology. He becomes the guinea pig in a scheme to freeze and revive a human being. Carlo feels he has little to choose between an absurd life, an absurd death, and a remote hope of immortality.

In *Reinhart's Women,* Carlo achieves a degree of peace with his wife and daughter, as he takes on a new role as a gourmet cook. Berger makes Carlo here less the ever-ready butt of slapstick and more the master of his destiny, as if Carlo were growing in later middle age into himself. The book's comedy is mellower and less acerbic than the view of corrupt post-World War II culture from which Berger began the saga.

In *Little Big Man* Berger also uses mock-heroic satire, here on the elaborate mythology of the Old West. A tale of cowboys and Indians told from *both* views, the novel describes the only white survivor of the Battle of the Little Big Horn—111-year-old Jack Crabb, victim of Indian attacks, Indian, Indian-fighter, gunfighter, gambler, con man, etc. The novel follows the "half-man, half-alligator" tradition of frontier humor, bursting with gigantic hyperbole. It is also a detailed, convincing picture of prairie life, both with the Cheyenne (the "Human Beings") and with the white settlers. The violence, squalor, and monotony of life in raw nature are as intensely realized as the farce. Jack Crabb is a frontier Carlo Reinhart, with the same insecurities, the same propensities for confusion and cowardice, the same common humanity.

Arthur Rex may be the finest redaction of the legend since Malory. It is a labor of love for pure story and style in which Berger's brilliant prose is honed like Excalibur itself. A straightforward rendering of the Arthurian material, the novel is a tribute to romance, adventure, and storytelling as the roots of our literature. Berger makes the characters come sharply alive in vigorous, dramatic scenes and retains the mixture of exuberance and nostalgia which defines the ancient cycle.

A theme inherent in Berger's work is that of metamorphosis—transformation, counterfeiting, deception, the shiftiness of reality. *Who Is Teddy Villanova?, Nowhere,* and *Neighbors* focus on this theme. Detective fiction and cold-war thrillers are parodied in the first two novels, which follow the hapless adventures of Russel Wren, an inept semi-pro detective who is constantly overwhelmed by violent events beyond his perception. *Who Is Teddy Villanova?* caricatures the conventions of the tough-guy detective novel, and *Nowhere* brilliantly combines the spy story and the utopian romance. An atmosphere of bizarre paranoia suffuses both installments of the Wren romance. In *Neighbors* the same mode is applied to suburban realities. Earl Keese, prone to hallucinations, is subjected to a series of emotional and mental assaults by a man and women who move in next door. The story turns on paradoxes and illusions, an increasingly grotesque feeling that things are never what they seem. In Berger's view, our culture has crashed through the looking glass, where absurdity rules all and everything turns by subtle and malicious irony into its opposite.

Sneaky People and *The Feud* also anatomize middle-class American life; both are set in the 1930s and deal with the peculiar conflation of acquisitiveness and sexuality which creates the ethos for the people-next-door culture described in *Neighbors*. A mixture of healthy cynicism and obvious nostalgia makes the narratives attractive as satires on the conventional American success story. *The Houseguest* extends the comedy of domestic paranoia that shaped *Sneaky People, Neighbors,* and *The Feud.* In his usual absurdist/surrealist manner, Berger constructs a Kafkaesque novel of invaded hospitality and territorial hostility.

Being Invisible and *Changing the Past* mine Berger's fantastic-speculative vein. Each is a cautionary tale about power—one on the old idea of the presumed powers of invisibility, the other a "three wishes" story of a man granted the power to relive his life. The novels are fables on the vanity of human wishes and the inevitability of over-reaching. Their comedy mirrors serious concerns with the ethics of power, the intractability of ego and the illusory nature of freedom and choice.

In *Orrie's Story* Berger retells the Orestes legend as a contemporary, post-Vietnam fiction. Less successfully than in the majestic *Arthur Rex,* he reinvents the past to illumine our complex present.

—William J. Schafer

BERMANT, Chaim (Icyk)

Nationality: British. **Born:** Breslev, Poland, 26 February 1929. **Education:** Queen's Park School, Glasgow, 1938-48; Glasgow Yeshiva (rabbinical college), 1949-51; Glasgow University, 1952-55, 1959-61, M.A. 1955, M.Litt. 1960; London School of Economics, 1955-57, M.Sc. 1957. **Family:** Married Judith Weil in 1962; two sons and two daughters. **Career:** Schoolmaster, 1955-57; economist, 1957-58; scriptwriter, Scottish Television, Glasgow, 1958-59, and Granada Television, London, 1959-60; features editor, *Jewish Chronicle,* London, 1964-66. **Awards:** Wingate award (*Jewish Chronicle*), for non-fiction, 1977. **Agent:** Gillon Aitken, Aitken and Stone Ltd., 29 Fernshaw Road, London SW10 0TG, England.

PUBLICATIONS

Novels

Jericho Sleep Alone. London, Chapman and Hall, 1964.
Berl Make Tea. London, Chapman and Hall, 1965.
Ben Preserve Us. London, Chapman and Hall, 1965; New York, Holt Rinehart, 1966.
Jericho Sleep Alone, and Berl Make Tea. New York, Holt Rinehart, 1966.
Diary of an Old Man. London, Chapman and Hall, 1966; New York, Holt Rinehart, 1967.
Swinging in the Rain. London, Hodder and Stoughton, 1967.
Here Endeth the Lesson. London, Eyre and Spottiswoode, 1969.
Now Dowager. London, Eyre and Spottiswoode, 1971.
Roses Are Blooming in Picardy. London, Eyre Methuen, 1972.

The Last Supper. London, Eyre Methuen, and New York, St. Martin's Press, 1973.
The Second Mrs. Whitberg. London, Allen and Unwin, and New York, St. Martin's Press, 1976.
The Squire of Bor Shachor. London, Allen and Unwin, and New York, St. Martin's Press, 1977.
Now Newman Was Old. London, Allen and Unwin, and New York, St. Martin's Press, 1978.
The Patriarch. London, Weidenfeld and Nicolson, and New York, St. Martin's Press, 1981.
The House of Women. London, Weidenfeld and Nicolson, and New York, St. Martin's Press, 1983.
Dancing Bear. London, Weidenfeld and Nicolson, 1984; New York, St. Martin's Press, 1985.
Titch. London, Weidenfeld and Nicolson, and New York, St. Martin's Press, 1987.
The Companion. London, Robson, 1987; New York, St. Martin's Press, 1988.

Plays

Television Plays: *Pews,* 1980; *The Party,* 1981; *The Mole,* 1982; *There's One Born Every Minute,* 1983.

Other

Israel. London, Thames and Hudson, and New York, Walker, 1967.
Troubled Eden: An Anatomy of British Jewry. London, Vallentine Mitchell, 1969; New York, Basic Books, 1970.
The Cousinhood: The Anglo-Jewish Gentry. London, Eyre and Spottiswoode, 1971; New York, Macmillan, 1972.
The Walled Garden: The Saga of Jewish Family Life and Tradition. London, Weidenfeld and Nicolson, 1974; New York, Macmillan, 1975.
Point of Arrival: A Study of London's East End. London, Eyre Methuen, 1975; as *London's East End: Point of Arrival,* New York, Macmillan, 1976.
Coming Home. London, Allen and Unwin, 1976.
The Jews. London, Weidenfeld and Nicolson, and New York, Times, 1977.
Ebla: An Archaeological Enigma, with Michael Weitzmann. London, Weidenfeld and Nicolson, and New York, Times, 1979.
Belshazzar: A Cat's Story for Humans. London, Allen and Unwin, 1979; New York, Avon, 1982.
On the Other Hand. London, Robson, 1982.
What's the Joke: A Study of Jewish Humour Through the Ages. London, Weidenfeld and Nicolson, 1986.
Lord Jakobovits: The Authorized Biography of the Chief Rabbi. London, Weidenfeld and Nicolson, 1990.
Murmurings of a Licensed Heretic. London, Halban, 1990.

Editor, with Murray Mindlin, *Explorations: An Annual on Jewish Themes.* London, Barrie and Rockliff, 1967; Chicago, Quadrangle, 1968.

*

Manuscript Collection: Mugar Memorial Library, Boston University.

Chaim Bermant comments: My characters are mainly Jewish, hapless but not helpless, beset by many small calamities which somehow never amount to an irreversible disaster and which certainly do not diminish their hope that even if the worst is not over the best is yet to come. The treatment is humorous, but the intention is serious.

*   *   *

Of Chaim Bermant's novels the one word consistently used by every reviewer is "funny." And so they are, with a crisp, snip-snap style based largely on wordplay and repetition, the one-line sentences tripping down the page in a way which makes the easiest of easy reading. Yet, although this accolade is almost the greatest a writer can receive today, one must look for other criteria when attempting judgment. However jokey and ephemeral the fashion of our time, the novel is still a serious art form and its most important task is still the creation of character.

By this standard, Bermant's first novel, *Jericho Sleep Alone,* is genuinely alive and kicking. Its hero is a young Jewish boy living with his Orthodox family and friends in Glasgow. So far, so autobiographical. His growing up, his uncertainty about himself, his bewilderment as to what makes personality, what qualities bring success, his infatuation with (inevitably) the "most popular girl" in his group (the best and most believable female character in the whole of his work)—all this is conveyed in a brisk, lively style. It is a most agreeable book, not sweet, not sour, but tart and fresh and truthful.

With *Berl Make Tea,* that well-known hazard, the second novel, the author, it must be said, doesn't quite make it. Berl is a squat philosophical little Jew, the eternal rubberball, taking all misfortunes and bouncing back every time. He (thankfully) loses his wife, loses his job, drifts from place to place encountering odd people and odd goings on. The characters are—as so often in this writer's work—line drawings rather than people; escapes from a sort of 19th-century, Yiddish, comic strip.

It is perhaps a pity that it was this book rather than *Jericho* which set the pattern for many of Bermant's subsequent novels (mostly written in the first person). *Ben Preserve Us:* the central character a young Rabbi in a Scottish town, eligible and, it is discovered, very rich but also Jewish-mother-ridden. *Swinging in the Rain:* central figure a rich chocolate manufacturer with business worries, a flighty daughter and an oafish son, and so on. (This author, apart from his archetypal Jewish parents, appears to be equally fascinated by the very rich and the oafs. They appear in practically every one of his novels).

Of the six or seven books of the "middle period," perhaps *Now Dowager,* though written in exactly the same style and tone as the rest, is probably the most enjoyable. The "I" character this time is a very rich, old Jewish widow trying to convert a non-Jewish girl to the faith. It is as wildly unbelievable as all his other books but is somehow more attractive and exhibits his abilities at their sparkling best. These abilities are a gift for endless but sometimes very amusing dialogue which, like salted biscuits or crisp celery, one can go on eating—or reading—forever; a real talent for economical, physical description; and powers of invention, shallow perhaps, but so quick and skillful and lively that the critical faculty invariably takes a holiday while actually reading. There is also very often a genuine touch of pathos. It is this last which gives the impression that if Bermant, instead of producing books which can be read in an hour and forgotten in 20 minutes (a fair example of Bermant's style of comment) were to forget what appears to have been an over-exposure to P.G. Wodehouse in his youth (since he has neither the ultimate

flair nor the meticulous sense of structure which underlies the great, classic comedy writers) he would be not only a much better novelist but also a true humorist rather than a jokester.

About midway in his career Bermant published a very slender book, hardly a novel, more a *conte,* entitled *Diary of an Old Man.* It is a simple account of one freezing, wintry month in the life of an old man living in one room. Yet, perhaps because of its very brevity, the author was able to give his tale the concentrated care really good fiction demands and the result was an imperfect but very moving little gem; imperfect because too often this author has a slapdash approach which leaves loose, contradictory bits of character and a handful of short ends lying around every novel.

The Last Supper is an ambitious attempt to break out of the snap, crackle and pop formula of his previous fiction. It is the story of the week's mourning which Jewish families observe when a close member—in this case the mother—dies. Again the milieu is that of a very rich, Anglo-Jewish, aristocratic family but this time the author has made a genuine try at distinguishing between his characters; brothers and sisters, aunts and uncles, in-laws. . . . During the week revelations are made, old scandals revived, subplots inserted. The book is a failure but the attempt is an honorable one, the characters emerging half-hewn as it were from the stone.

It is only fair to add that though up till now Bermant cannot be claimed as a novelist really to be reckoned with, he is an admirable and often brilliant journalist and also a respectable hard-backed sociologist, specializing in aspects of Anglo-Jewish life. Both *Troubled Eden* and *The Cousinhood,* a study of the rich, interwoven families of Jewish aristocracy in England, have been much praised—as have two other books, *Point of Arrival,* a history of the East End of London, and *The Walled Garden,* a study of Jewish family groupings and traditions.

As book succeeds book Bermant's writing grows ever more concerned with his abiding, not to say obsessive, interest in the English upper classes. This, since it still runs in harness with his equal obsession with his Jewishness, has produced at least two more volumes of slightly uneasy alliance. *Dancing Bear* is a novel about a young man brought up in a rich, Gentile family (or are they Gentile?) who is uncertain about his grandfather's origins (or was he his grandfather?) and sleeps with his aunt (or was she his mother?) and throughout is attempting to discover whether he is Jewish or not. Smallish sections of this book are very well done. Bermant is excellent, as always, on tiny vignettes of place: Germany, Egypt, Oxford, Arabia, to say nothing of America and Russia. On character he is occasionally both vivid and good. But the larger part is so convoluted, so dizzying with plot and maze that its smaller virtues are submerged.

It would be nice to find this improvement going onwards and upwards but the fact is that Bermant's talent for fiction seems to have reached a plateau.

The House of Women was written before *Dancing Bear* which seems to argue a slightly retrograde step. This one is again about an upper-middle-class family which hardly knows it's Jewish. There are a father, four daughters (the second, a clever, knowing girl named Ducks, is the narrator—a first-person mode which Bermant, in drag so to speak, carries off splendidly), and a son by a second marriage. Here, for almost the first time, nearly all of Bermant's more trying mannerisms, inversions, and tedious wordplay have disappeared. The tone, the dialogue, the development of real character are quite remarkably sustained.

But then comes *Titch,* one of his—as usual—crisp, readable efforts about a small young man with large ambitions which take him from provincial Jewry to the Polish army during World War II. *Titch* is Basic Bermant—so basic he could have written it in his sleep (Bermant, were he writing this, would have added "and probably did"), and goes down easily enough but it is unmemorable. *The Companion,* his last novel to date, is about Martha, a rich, elderly, waspish widow and Phyllis, her poor companion with a nice line in waspish behavior herself. The two women, living in biting proximity, sink together as the years go by into an equal squalor. What gives the book its distinction is the character of Phyllis (blood sister to the central character of *Diary of an Old Man*) who embodies much of this writer's specialty, a kind of perky heartlessness overlaying an essential sadness of situation. There is a somewhat improbably happy ending when, Martha dead, Phyllis finds herself a prince (even if he is called Stanley) and a glass slipper of perfect fit.

Two non-fiction books deserve mention. *Murmurings of a Licensed Heretic* is a near-perfect bedside book; a collection of short essays on every kind of subject but mainly Jewish, culled from every kind of journal over a period of 30 years: every one a gem, as fresh and entertaining as if written yesterday. For once the adjective "sparkling" is entirely apposite.

The other is a biography of Lord Jakobovits, soon to give up his post as chief Rabbi of Great Britain after a most distinguished tenure. Such biographies, especially of such a worthy and generally admirable man tend to be worthy in the other sense; in other words, dull. This book manages to maintain a quite remarkable readability and interest as well as making beautifully clear some of the many tangled skeins of Jewish politics and Jewish belief, the whole enlightened with much wit.

We still await a novel from Bermant as good of its kind as are his non-fiction books and his quite brilliant journalism.

—Gerda Charles

BETTS, Doris

Nationality: American. **Born:** Statesville, North Carolina, 4 June 1932. **Education:** Woman's College, Greensboro, North Carolina, 1950-53; University of North Carolina, Chapel Hill, 1954. **Family:** Married Lowry M. Betts in 1952; one daughter and two sons. **Career:** Journalist, *Statesville Daily Record,* 1950-51; *Chapel Hill Weekly and News Leader,* 1953-54; *Sanford Daily Herald,* 1956-57. Editorial staff, *N.C. Democrat,* 1961; editor, *Sanford News Leader,* 1962. Lecturer of creative writing, 1966-74, associate professor of English, 1974-78, professor of English, 1978-80, and since 1980 Alumni Distinguished Professor of English, University of North Carolina. Director, freshman-sophmore English, 1972-76; Fellows program, 1975-76; assistant dean, honors program, 1979-81; and faculty chair (elected), 1980-83, University of North Carolina. Visiting lecturer, Duke University, 1971; member of the board, 1979-81, and chair, 1981, Associated Writing Programs, National Endowment for the Arts. **Awards:** G.P. Putnam-U.N.C. Booklength Fiction prize, 1954; Sir Walter Raleigh Best Fiction by Carolinian award, 1957, for *Tall Houses in Winter,* 1965, for *Scarlet Thread;* Guggenheim fellowhsip, 1958; North Carolina Medal, 1975, for literature; Parker award, 1982-85, for literary achievement; John dos Passos award, 1983; American Academy of Arts and Letters Medal of Merit, 1989, for short story; Academy award,

for *Violet.* Honorary D.Litt., Greensboro College, 1987, and University of North Carolina, 1990; D.H.L., Erskine College, 1994. **Member:** National Humanities Center, 1993. **Agent:** Russell and Volkening, 50 West 29th Street, New York, New York 1001, USA. **Address:** c/o English Department, CB# 3520, University of North Carolina, Chapel Hill, North Carolina 27599-3520, USA.

PUBLICATIONS

Novels

Tall Houses in Winter. New York, Putnam, 1954; London, Gollancz, 1955.
The Scarlet Thread. New York, Harper, 1964.
The River to Pickle Beach. New York, Harper, 1972.
Heading West. New York, Knopf, 1981.
Souls Raised from the Dead. New York, Knopf, 1994.

Short Stories

The Gentle Insurrection. New York, Putnam, 1954.
The Astronomer and Other Stories. New York, Harper, 1966.
Beasts of the Southern Wild. New York, Harper, 1973.

*

Film Adaptation: V*iolet,* adaptation from her own short story *"The Ugliest Pilgrim."*

Manuscript Collection: Boston University, Boston.

Critical Study: *The Home Truth of Doris Betts,* Fayetteville, North Carolina, Methodist College Press, 1992.

*   *   *

Doris Betts's writing is deeply informed by her religious sensibility, not in a dogmatic or didactic sense but in the way of one who asks important questions about good and evil, life and death, and who finds meaning in the universe and in the ways people respond to it. The biblical story of Job's much-tried faith could be considered a touchstone for Betts, and her fiction concerns similar trials in the 20th-century South, particularly North Carolina. Her earliest work tends to probe these philosophical questions in a somewhat programmatic way, as in "Mr. Shawn and Father Scott" in her first collection of short stories, *The Gentle Insurrection.* But four decades later in her most recent novel, *Souls Raised From the Dead,* Betts's mature insights and highly developed techniques make her work incandescent with wisdom about the human condition.

In her second novel, *The Scarlet Thread,* Betts uses the experiences of the rapidly rising and dissolving Allen family of a North Carolina mill town to probe questions of human suffering. Through Thomas, the middle child, Betts explores the origins of evil. Thomas, from childhood on, exhibits anger and cruelty that culminate in the physical and mental abuse of his fragile wife, Nellie. One naturally wonders what made Thomas so, and one could respond that it was his belief that his siblings were "favored" both by life and their parents; his feelings of frustration and powerlessness were alleviated only through the power of cruelty. Betts, though, does not allow us to accept such a simplistic causal chain because

Thomas's childhood and family are at least as good, and probably better, than those of most people around him, particularly the "mill children" and even his own siblings. His sister, Esther, responds to a jilting by leaving town and founding a new life. His brother, David, an artist in a world of philistines, pulls himself out of a life of drift backed by his parents' money to accept the challenge of learning the art of stone carving. Betts seems to suggest that even though all meet adversity in one sense or another, it is the individual's response to it that reveals whatever happiness is possible.

Betts's third novel, *The River to Pickle Beach,* continues to engage the question of human suffering through the contrasting responses of a married couple, Jack and Bebe Sellars. Jack responds to life's uncertainties with reserve and caution. He learns, plans, and avoids as much as he can, but his anxieties about the future will not let him enjoy the present; when he and Bebe embark on a new life as managers of a small beach resort, his fear of the impending visit of the owner's retarded relations blocks his own exhilaration at their new venture. It also prevents him from sharing Bebe's pleasure in the world of ocean and beach since Bebe meets life with optimism and joy, despite such disappointments as her childlessness. Jack's old army buddy, Mickey McCane, however, uses his rough childhood as the son of a disappearing and whoring mother to justify his need for power through the sexual degradation of women. When Bebe rejects his advances, Mickey does not learn that his demeaning attitude bars him from any meaningful relations with women but instead seeks the phallic power of guns on the easy target of the physically and mentally defective visitors whom, he subconsciously fears, represent his real self.

Abduction by a criminal who calls himself Dwight Anderson is the trial for North Carolina librarian Nancy Finch in Betts's fourth novel, *Heading West.* What started as a kidnapping becomes an opportunity for Nancy to escape not only Dwight but her self-made bonds to her elderly mother, epileptic brother, and spoiled sister. Nancy chooses to "head west" with him, bypassing some possibilities of escape, since she seems to fear her trivialized servitude to her family more than this dangerous criminal; she is learning that all he can do is kill her quickly as opposed to the slow death her "normal" life has become. She tests herself through her grueling flight from Dwight in the Grand Canyon and emerges victorious; he plunges to his death in an attempt to make himself feel powerful by controlling her with taunts and threats. Throughout her captivity, Nancy has attempted to find out what made Dwight so manipulative, affectless, and dehumanized—essentially to confront the problem of evil—and she continues to investigate his background as she heads back east alone. She learns that he was the "bad twin" raised by a crazed and begging grandmother; his brother, however damaged, has remained law-abiding. Again, Betts suggests that it is not circumstances, but the response to them that makes the man or woman and that even the horrors of an abduction have the potential for good in one who can learn from them.

What many would regard as the ultimate horror or evil, the death of a child, is Betts's subject in her most recent novel, *Souls Raised from the Dead.* Over the course of the novel, lively, intelligent Mary Grace Thompson dies of chronic renal failure, and those around her are tested like Job. As she always has, Mary Grace's mother escapes into her narcissistic world of men, mobility, and beauty rituals. Her father, Frank, a policeman who has seen much evil and suffering, must come to terms with Mary's illness, an adversary that cannot be confronted and vanquished by physical force. Unlike Mary's mother, Frank overcomes his tendency to avoid emo-

tional situations in order to stand by Mary and to meet his commitments to life and work, friendships and family. His mother, Tacey, has always been a religious woman, but now her faith meets and surmounts, however tentatively, its ultimate challenge, surviving a grandchild who should have survived her. As this novel so painfully yet inspiringly suggests, for Betts we all have the potential to be "souls raised from the dead" no matter how life—and our situations in it—deny our circumstances.

—Veronica Makowsky

BILLING, Graham (John)

Nationality: New Zealander. **Born:** Dunedin, 12 January 1936. **Education:** Otago Boys High School, 1948-52; University of Otago, Dunedin, 1953-58; studied for Presbyterian ministry for 1 year. **Family:** Married 1) Atanui Ellison in 1959; 2) Diane Farmer in 1965, one daughter and one son; 3) Rowan Cunningham in 1978 (separated 1988). **Career:** Cadet officer, Shaw Saville Line, 1953-54; able seaman, Union Steam Ship Company, 1956; construction worker, 1956-58; junior reporter, later senior reporter, Dunedin *Evening Star,* 1958-62; information officer, New Zealand Antarctic Research Programme, Wellington and Ross Dependency, Antarctica, 1962-64; chief reporter, Radio New Zealand News, Christchurch, 1964-65; freelance writer, 1965-67, 1969-73, and 1975-76; broadcast media editor and columnist, *New Zealand Sunday Times,* Wellington, 1967-68; parliamentary correspondent, *New Zealand Truth,* 1968-69; lecturer in English, Mitchell College of Advanced Education, Bathurst, New South Wales, 1974-75; current affairs producer, Radio New Zealand, 1977. Writer-in-residence, University of Canterbury, Christchurch, 1985. **Awards:** Cowman Memorial prize, for journalism, 1962; New Zealand Literary Fund grant, 1965, 1983, 1984, and scholarship, 1971, 1981; University of Otago Robert Burns fellowship, 1973; Hubert Church Prose award, 1975. **Agent:** Elaine Markson Literary Agency, 44 Greenwich Avenue, New York, New York 10011, U.S.A.; or, Abner Stein, 10 Roland Gardens, London SW7 3PH, England. **Address:** 2/269 Fitzgerald Avenue, Christchurch, New Zealand.

PUBLICATIONS

Novels

Forbush and the Penguins. London, Hodder and Stoughton, 1965; New York, Holt Rinehart, 1966.
The Alpha Trip. Christchurch, Whitcombe and Tombs, and London, W.H. Allen, 1969.
Statues. London, Hodder and Stoughton, 1971.
The Slipway. New York, Viking Press, 1973; London, Quartet, 1974.
The Primal Therapy of Tom Purslane. Dunedin, Caveman Press, 1980.
The Chambered Nautilus. N.p., Canterbury University Press, 1993.

Plays

Radio Plays: *Forbush and the Penguins,* 1966; *Mervyn Gridfern versus the Baboons,* 1966; *The Slipway,* from his own novel, 1977.

Poetry

Changing Countries. Dunedin, Caveman Press, 1980.

Other

South: Man and Nature in Antarctica. Wellington, Reed, 1964; London, Hodder and Stoughton, 1969.
New Zealand, The Sunlit Land, photographs by R.J. Griffith. Wellington, Reed, 1966.
The New Zealanders, photographs by Robin Smith and Warren Jacobs. Auckland, Golden Press, 1975; revised edition, Christchurch, Kowhai, 1979.

Editor, *Wellington Town Plan: A Commentary on the District Planning Scheme 1967.* Wellington, Wellington City Council, 1967.

*

Manuscript Collection: Turnbull Library, Wellington.

Critical Studies: Interview with Richard Corballis, in *Landfall 135* (Christchurch), September 1980; article by Howard McNaughton, in *Landfall 139* (Christchurch), September 1981.

Graham Billing comments:

(1986) I am of the few New Zealanders who write about middle- and upper-middle-class people and intellectuals. Such subjects tend to be ignored here and I have always had to sell my novels in London or New York first rather than to the local industry. This has made me more determined to survive as an outsider in my own society and to be uncompromising in my choice of themes.

My first 16 years straddled World War II. They were privileged. My father was professor of economics at the world's most remote university—Otago at Dunedin. Until the post-war graduates flooded in from overseas it was more a family than a university. I didn't get educated, I grew. My mother's eccentricities and temperament affected me deeply. She taught me to sew and cook and made me learn the piano and elocution. I rebelled then but am now glad. My father countered by teaching me the rudiments of hunting, shooting, fishing, dog-handling, and sailing. It is out of such tensions that I create. But I lived in Paradise for a while, the only Worm being that I did slowly inherit my mother's manic-depressive condition. It would lead me into a deep search of my unconscious mind in middle life. I was not untouched either by her religious passions. Having fallen out with the patriarch God I turned in my early twenties to a contemplation of the Goddess sustained in turns by Robert Graves and C.G. Jung. These references abound in my writing. In my mid-life quest these ideas have been severely modified as I have found time to research original material instead of other writers' conclusions. People amaze me. I'm a slow thinker. Books come out whole mostly without need for revision. I still grieve that I didn't have the chance to work in a war. Antarctica was the closest thing and rather more dangerous then than it is now. I am watching myself with deep interest to see what happens next.

(1991) My writing concern of the 1990s is the war zone of drugs, alcohol, and the dysfunctional family.

*   *   *

Graham Billing's novels are remarkable for the intensity with which the central characters' inner lives are realized. He has no peer in New Zealand—and few world-wide—when it comes to evoking strong emotional and physical sensations.

He often has difficulty, however, in inventing a plot which can contain this rampant sensuousness. *The Primal Therapy of Tom Purslane* (published in 1980 but written as early as 1973) illustrates the problem very well. All that happens is that Purslane has a brief, unsatisfactory love affair which jeopardizes his marriage. It is not even clear just why the affair is unsatisfactory or what will become of the marriage. Billing seems scarcely interested in the story or the ancillary characters; it is Purslane's responses that fascinate him, and these are underlined by a cloying welter of symbols, symbolic episodes, dreams, and allusions.

The Primal Therapy of Tom Purslane is an extreme example—partly, no doubt, because Billing had the Romantics very much in mind (Hazlitt's *Liber Amoris* in particular) and therefore endeavored to "load every rift with ore." But *Statues* (which is Billing's own favorite among his novels to date) is another clear case of texture run wild and plot neglected. The other three novels are better balanced, but the same old problems recur to some extent. The plots seldom provide an adequate objective correlative to the central characters' responses, and nobody except the central character (who is always a man and always remarkably like Graham Billing) comes completely to life.

His first novel, *Forbush and the Penguins,* is still probably his best known—partly because it spawned a feature film and a radio play. Forbush goes to Antarctica to undertake a study of a penguin rookery at Cape Royds. Antarctica becomes for him a kind of laboratory—rather like Renaissance pastoral—where nature's extremes (the self-sacrificing love of the penguins and the violence of the predatory skuas and sea-leopards) are closely juxtaposed. This juxtaposition prompts him to reflect on the conflict between love and hate in his own experience, and he draws this conclusion from his observations and recollections:

> If all the penguins died and were eaten by all the sea-leopards, nothing would change. If no skua gull ever nested on the Cape again, nothing would change. Life is not an individual thing but a total thing, a volume like the sea. Therefore I am a victim. But if I know I am a victim I am a victim no longer. I am free.

This moral sounds rather too neat to be true, and its credibility is further undermined by the lack of any adequate background to Forbush's sense of himself as a victim. Billing's subsequent comments about the book have emphasized the "wounds" which Forbush's parents inflicted on him, but there is scarcely any sign of these in the published text. So although Forbush's present experiences (at Cape Royds) are well documented, the coverage of the past is too skimpy to justify his deeper reflections.

The Alpha Trip was written while Billing was working as an investigative journalist in Wellington. In the news at the time (1968-69) was a widely held suspicion that certain American communications bases in New Zealand were crucial links in America's nuclear strategy. The novel elaborates this idea and focuses on a Communist plot to destroy a base near Blenheim. But the plot itself is less important than the character at the center of it—Strachan, a New Zealand patriot who cannot accept the hegemony of either the Americans or the Communists. As usual Billing becomes so preoccupied with his protagonist that nobody else really comes to life. The two characters who suffer most from this neglect are Laetitia, who loves Strachan beyond the call of (Communist) duty but shows no real sign of the anxiety—danger even—that ought to result from this conflict, and Percival, the Communist super-mole, whose motives are dishonestly disguised early in the book. Still *The Alpha Trip* is a competent thriller as well as an eloquent plea for national self-awareness.

Billing's finest piece of fiction from the 1970s is *The Slipway,* a compelling study of the agonies and ecstasies, the deceptions and delusions of an alcoholic (Geoffrey Targett). The portrait is so powerful that one scarcely notices that there is a characteristic discrepancy between Geoffrey's predicament and the plot which is woven about it. Like many of Billing's characters, Geoffrey undergoes an intensely evoked descent into hell, and we expect him to emerge a changed man. But no; he goes straight back into a pub, as excruciatingly alcoholic and deluded as ever. (The problems Billing had with the book's structure are elaborated in the interview published in *Landfall 135.*)

The Chambered Nautilus, an ambitious novel on which Billing labored for more than a decade, looks like a determined attempt to refute the charge that he cannot construct plots. It deals not only with the relationship between a contemporary academic, his visionary Maori wife (Mareikura), her former husband, and various mutual friends, but also with the life and times of an early nineteenth-century missionary, who—in a distortion symptomatic of Billing's own—has become the central character of a book about whaling which the historian is writing. This grand design is quite beyond Billing's powers of construction, and the novel teeters on the brink of incoherence, redeemed by occasional purple passages and by the portrait of Mareikura, a character of greater substance than his earlier heroines.

Billing's novels have much in common besides the structural weaknesses and textual excellence discussed above. The descent-into-hell motif recurs frequently. And certain symbolic characters pop up again and again. For example, there is often an old salt-of-the-earth fellow (Collis in *Statues* and Chivers in *The Primal Therapy of Tom Purslane*) who embodies the normality from which the protagonist has departed. And there is generally a dog or some other animal who seems in some way to represent the protagonist's soul. Many of the protagonists have an important characteristic in common too. They are often artists—photographers for the most part. And when they are at their most creative they tend to see life in terms of circles. Likewise, as the *Landfall* interview indicates, Billing himself got the impulse to write both *Forbush and the Penguins* and *The Slipway* from an initial circular image (Forbush standing in a ring of stones; Geoffrey gazing at a radar-scope).

These recurrent circles are a symptom of the closed world inhabited by Billing's protagonists, who generally do not develop significantly or interact meaningfully with other characters. Billing tried to break the circle in *Statues* by dividing the narration between two characters—Bracken and his ex-wife Miriam—but the result is really just two closed circles instead of one. Likewise the promising "three-dimensional spiral" which constitutes the central symbol of *The Chambered Nautilus* ultimately provides no escape from the imprisoning circles. As one early reviewer put it, "the novel is not moving from the core of the nautilus spiral out into a wider understanding but inward towards the constriction of a meaningless vanishing-point."

—Richard Corballis

BILLINGTON, (Lady) Rachel (Mary)

Nationality: British. **Born:** Rachel Mary Pakenham, Oxford, 11 May 1942; daughter of the writers Lord Longford and Elizabeth Longford; sister of the writer Antonia Fraser. **Education:** University of London, B.A. (honors) in English 1963. **Family:** Married the film and theatre director Kevin Billington in 1967; two sons and two daughters. **Career:** Freelance writer; reviewer for *Financial Times* and *Evening Standard,* both London, and *New York Times;* columnist, *Sunday Telegraph,* London. **Agent:** David Higham Associates Ltd., 5-8 Lower John Street, London W1R 4HA, England. **Address:** The Court House, Poyntington, Nr. Sherborne, Dorset DT9 4LF, England.

PUBLICATIONS

Novels

All Things Nice. London, Heinemann, 1969.
The Big Dipper. London, Heinemann, 1970.
Lilacs Out of the Dead Land. London, Heinemann, 1971; New York, Saturday Review Press, 1972.
Cock Robin; or, A Fight for Male Survival. London, Heinemann, 1972.
Beautiful. London, Heinemann, and New York, Coward McCann, 1974.
A Painted Devil. London, Heinemann, and New York, Coward McCann, 1975.
A Woman's Age. London, Hamish Hamilton, 1979; New York, Summit, 1980.
Occasion of Sin. London, Hamish Hamilton, 1982; New York, Summit, 1983.
The Garish Day. London, Hamish Hamilton, 1985; New York, Morrow, 1986.
Loving Attitudes. London, Hamish Hamilton, and New York, Morrow, 1988.
Theo and Matilda. London, Macmillan, 1990; New York, HarperCollins, 1991.
Bodily Harm. London, Macmillan, 1993.

Uncollected Short Stories

"One Afternoon," in *Winter's Tales 1* (new series), edited by David Hughes. London, Constable, and New York, St. Martin's Press, 1985.
"The Photograph," in *Winter's Tales 2* (new series), edited by Robin Baird-Smith. London, Constable, and New York, St. Martin's Press, 1986.

Plays

Radio Plays: *Mrs. Bleasdale's Lodger,* 1976; *Mary, Mary,* 1977; *Sister, Sister,* 1978; *Have You Seen Guy Fawkes?,* 1979.

Television Plays: *Don't Be Silly,* 1979; *Life after Death,* 1981.

Other (for children)

Rosanna and the Wizard-Robot. London, Methuen, 1981.

The First Christmas. London, Collins Harvill, 1983; Wilton, Connecticut, Morehouse Barlow, 1987.

Star-Time. London, Methuen, 1984.

The First Easter. London, Constable, and Grand Rapids, Michigan, Eerdmans, 1987.

The First Miracles. London, Collins Harvill, 1990; Grand Rapids, Michigan, Eerdmans, 1991.

Other

The Great Umbilical, Mother Daughter Mother. London, Macmillan, 1994.

*   *   *

On a surface level the novels of Rachel Billington reflect the conventions of the upper-class comedy of manners. Her works are invariably set within an aristocratic milieu, their central characters a privileged churchgoing elite of country or London gentry, whose condescension towards the lower orders seems a natural response. Billington's books are distinguished by an adroit use of language, personalities revealed through conversations that display a keen, often caustic wit. Yet beneath the outward show of humor lurks a strong tendency to violence, which manifests itself in the conflicts of obsessional love.

In *All Things Nice* and *The Big Dipper* the wit and comedy predominate, these early novels emerging as vehicles for the author's stylistic skills. *Lilacs Out of the Dead Land* is both deeper and more dark. April, the younger daughter of moneyed parents, travels to Italy with her married lover. During their time together, she is forced to reassess their relationship in the context of her elder sister's death. The infatuation that draws her to the lover is slowly countered by the fear of being smothered by his love. As the tension builds inside her, events move swiftly to the cathartic act of violence. More complex and unsettling than its predecessors, *Lilacs Out of the Dead Land* shows considerable narrative skill, the author switching fluently from April's time with her lover to scenes with her parents, at the school where she teaches, and her last encounter with her sister. Dialogue fits the dovetailed scenes, each character perfectly matched by his or her patterns of speech. This novel is an early indication of the psychological depths that lie under the surface glitter of Billington's work.

Beautiful and *Cock Robin* are lighter, but accomplished creations, the elegant prose and polite behavior merely masking the pathological impulses deeper down. *Cock Robin* centers on the male narrator's passion for three girls at his university, all of them seemingly unattainable. The book follows the four of them in their careers, where the young man gradually emerges as the dominant figure, while the three goddesses prove to be tragic failures. The bitchy wit is in evidence, the story itself eminently credible, if marked by a heartless gloss. In *Beautiful,* obsessive passion again appears as a destructive force. Lucy, the flawless, amoral heroine of the novel, has thus far been able to shape the world in her image as it revolves around her. Alex, the discarded lover unwilling to let go, threatens to shatter that world and its fake stability: "Lucy prided herself on her understanding of the human psyche; with the unmentionable exception of Alex, no one had ever stepped out of the role in which she had cast them." Once more the course is set for a violent resolution. A light, tautly written work, with short terse scenes and skilful dialogue, *Beautiful* shows the author at her most assured, the hard sheen of the surface and the murky underlying depths in perfect balance.

A Painted Devil is altogether more sinister, revealing Billington's vision at its grimmest. Obsessional love is again the agent of destruction, embodied in Edward, the negative central character. A painter of genius, Edward draws unquestioning adoration from his wife and friends, while giving nothing in return. His cold, remote personality, its inhuman quality symbolized by his hatred of physical love, is subtly glimpsed in conversation and unuttered thoughts. In *A Painted Devil* the glittering crust of civilized behavior is thin indeed, the novel becoming increasingly horrific as one tragedy follows another. Cruellest of all Billington's works, it is nevertheless a memorable achievement.

A Woman's Age is a new departure, the comedy of manners forsaken for an epic novel spanning a period of 70 years. It focuses mainly on the figure of Violet Hesketh, who survives a difficult childhood and broken marriages to find a successful career in politics. A mammoth undertaking, the novel shows its author's ability to convey the essence of the passing years, but one cannot help feeling that it lacks the bite and conviction of some of her shorter works, and it is in the latter that her main strength as a writer lies.

With *Occasion of Sin* is another experiment, this time a contemporary retelling of Tolstoy's *Anna Karenina;* Billington's account of the lawyer's wife who falls for a computer software executive follows the original closely, both in characters and incidents, but avoids too slavish an interpretation, particularly in some of its solutions. A worthy variant of the classic novel, the depth of this novel's theme is matched by a highly effective use of language, with Billington's mastery of dialogue well to the fore. *The Garish Day* is an ambitious saga covering two generations of diplomats at the time of the British Raj. A similar epic approach is taken in *Theo and Matilda,* where the lovers of the title are explored in various incarnations, through Saxon, Tudor, and Victorian periods to the present day. Their adventures are set against the background of Abbeyfields, whose landscape changes with the centuries from monastery to manor house, lunatic asylum, mental hospital, and finally "des res." Billington handles her epic materials with style and conviction, and Theo and Matilda must be judged the most impressive of her large-scale works.

Loving Attitudes centers on the confrontation between the successful media professional Mary Tempest and her unacknowledged daughter, the product of a youthful love affair. Their unexpected meeting leads Mary to a reassessment of her marriage and family, and to a fresh exploration of that earlier love. The gradual unfolding of the tangle of relationships is accomplished neatly and without strain, the characters sensitively portrayed as they are forced to confront the consequences of their actions.

Bodily Harm, a more powerful, disturbing novel, opens with a brutal knife attack on a young woman by a total stranger in a London shop. The girl survives and her attacker is jailed, but the passage of time draws them inexorably back together. Their slow recovery and rehabilitation, the reasons behind the attack, and the eventual resolution are achieved with masterly skill, action presented from the alternating viewpoints of the two protagonists, the climactic scene approached with a sequence of brief snapshot images and incidents. *Bodily Harm* ranks with the finest of Billington's work and is clear proof of her ability to blend stylistic flair with increasingly complex themes.

—Geoff Sadler

BINCHY, Maeve

Nationality: Irish. **Born:** Dublin, 28 May 1940. **Education:** Holy Child Convent, Killiney, County Dublin; University College, Dublin, B.A. in education. **Family:** Married Gordon Snell in 1977. **Career:** History and French teacher, Pembroke School, Dublin, 1961-68. Since 1968 columnist, *Irish Times,* Dublin. **Agent:** Christine Green, 2 Barbon Close, London WC1N 3JX, England.

PUBLICATIONS

Novels

Light a Penny Candle. London, Century, 1982; New York, Viking, 1983.
Echoes. London, Century, 1985; New York, Viking, 1986.
Firefly Summer. London, Century, 1987; New York, Delacorte Press, 1988.
Circle of Friends. London, Century, 1990; New York, Delacorte Press, 1991.
The Copper Beach. London, Orion, 1992; New York, Delacorte Press, 1993.
The Glass Lake. London, Orion, 1994; New York, Delacorte Press, 1995.

Short Stories

Central Line. London, Quartet, 1978.
Victoria Line. London, Quartet, 1980.
Dublin 4. Dublin, Ward River Press, 1982; London, Century, 1983.
London Transports (includes *Central Line* and *Victoria Line*). London, Century, 1983; New York, Dell, 1986.
The Lilac Bus. Dublin, Ward River Press, 1984; London, Century, 1986; New York, Delacorte Press, 1992.
Silver Wedding. London, Century, 1988; New York, Delacorte Press, 1989.
Dublin People. Oxford, Oxford University Press, 1993.

Plays

End of Term (produced Dublin, 1976).
Half Promised Land (produced Dublin, 1979).

Television Plays: *Deeply Regretted By—,* 1976; *Echoes,* from her own novel, 1988; *The Lilac Bus,* from her own story, 1991.

Other

My First Book. Dublin, Irish Times, 1978.
Maeve's Diary. Dublin, Irish Times, 1979.
Dear Maeve: Writings from the "Irish Times." Dublin, Poolbeg Press, 1995.

*

Maeve Binchy comments:

I write novels and stories set within my own experience of time and place, but they are not autobiographical. They mainly touch on the emotions of women and the aspirations and hopes of young Irishwomen growing up in the relatively closed society of Ireland in the 1950s and 1960s.

*   *   *

Maeve Binchy's best-selling novels set in mid-century Ireland alternate in form between works that focus on one woman or a pair of friends and collections of interlocking stories organized in a posy or grand chain. This was a form she developed early in *The Lilac Bus,* a collection on a group of passengers who travel home from Dublin every weekend, and repeats in *The Copper Beach* and *Silver Wedding.* Binchy's work is marked by her understanding of the social and economic structure of small Irish county towns—the grid of shopkeepers, doctors, lawyers, and hotel keepers who serve and order the community under the omnipresent supervision of the church.

Binchy's work, though marketed as romances, by no means fits that category precisely. Binchy, a longstanding columnist for *The Irish Times,* presents a realistic picture of the lives of women ordered within the rigidities of Catholic orthodoxy that forbid divorce and abortion. In her work, women's survival is predicated on the creation of powerful, though informal, networks of alliance and friendships that survive the vicissitudes of pregnancy, forced marriage, and alcoholism.

Such sociological accuracy does not support the illusions of romance. Although Benny, the large, only daughter of over-protective shopkeepers, in *Circle of Friends,* does win the love of the handsome soccer hero of the university, she painfully discovers his insubstantiality. The romance pattern of other novels is complicated by Binchy's decision to pursue her heroines' lives after the altar. In *Echoes,* the heroine's triumphant marriage to the doctor's son is succeeded by a first year of domestic unhappiness, postpartum depression, and despair. In *Light a Penny Candle,* the heroine, safely married, in a quarrel pushes her husband down the stairs and kills him. In both novels, the promise of a safe haven in marriage is complicated by Binchy's clear insight into the painful restrictions of domesticity.

Although women's friendships, formed often at eight or ten, last through adolescent love, courtship, marriage, abortion, domestic violence, and encompass even murder, systems of political, religious, and social authority remain controlled by men. Binchy's heroines struggle against, but do not entirely triumph over these circumstances. Binchy is too aware of particular constraints on Irish women's lives to allow easy rewards. In *Echoes* the conventional Bildungsroman features an intelligent heroine Clare, aged ten, who enters an essay competition. We await the triumphant rise of the sweetshop owner's daughter. Yet the necessary boundaries around Clare's triumphs are suggested by the echoing story of the teacher who encourages her. Angela O'Hara was once a successful student. She, like Clare, won a scholarship, yet was inexorably pulled back to Castlebay by the domestic responsibilities for an ailing mother that devolve on an unmarried daughter in an Irish family. Add to that boundary of success for an intellectual woman, the unavailability of contraception, and Binchy has created a life for her heroine more realistically limited than the popular romance usually provides.

Light a Penny Candle traces the story of two women whose friendship began when Elizabeth arrived in a small Irish town as a wartime evacuee. The loyalty of the childhood friendship of Aisling and Elizabeth is deepened through the vicissitudes of feminine experience—an abortion in London, a lover who will never marry, an alcoholic husband, and an unconsummated marriage. The pattern of their lives is shaped by the men they marry, until, in a frightening, though not fully confronted moment, the Englishwoman, Elizabeth, pushes her husband down the stairs and kills him accidentally. The silence of her best friend over the manslaughter she has witnessed demonstrates the depth of female bonding. In *Light a Penny Candle,* Binchy suggests that this violent accident may be nurtured by the stifling restraints of bourgeois marriage. Elizabeth's mother dies in an insane asylum after a violent attack on her husband. Her mother's murder of her lover is the secret that isolates Leo from her friends in *The Copper Beach.*

Firefly Summer, combining the two forms, centers on the successful marriage of Kate and John Ryan, a marriage that survives the appalling, almost casual, accident that cripples Kate for life, and links that story with the varied responses in the village to the building of a luxury hotel in a Georgian mansion burned in the Troubles. Binchy is particularly clear about the restraints on economic change, the wariness of envy, the precautions against feuds, the aggression that flares in petty vandalism. These are the ties that restrict initiative, yet smooth social friction. The central characters survive, their lives shadowed by great losses. Binchy's willingness to acknowledge in her novels a sense of a world without purpose—"It was never meant to be like this. Pointless tragedy, and confusion everywhere"—creates a dense picture of Irish life in the 1950s and 1960s.

—Karen Robertson

BISSOONDATH, Neil

Nationality: Canadian (emigrated from Trinidad in 1973). **Born:** Devindra Bissoondath, Trinidad, West Indies, 19 April 1955. **Education:** York University, Toronto, B.A. in French 1977. **Career:** Teacher of English and French, Inlingua School of Languages, Toronto, 1977-80; teacher of English and French, Language Workshop, Toronto, 1980-85. **Awards:** McClelland and Stewart award for fiction, 1986, and National Magazine award, 1986, both for "Dancing." **Address:** c/o Macmillan of Canada, 39 Birch Ave., Toronto M4V 1E2, Canada.

PUBLICATIONS

Novels

A Casual Brutality. Toronto, Macmillan, 1988; New York, Potter, 1989.
The Innocence of Age. Toronto, Knopf, 1992.

Short Stories

Digging Up the Mountains. Toronto, Macmillan, 1985; New York, Viking, 1986.
On the Eve of Uncertain Tomorrows. Toronto, Dennys, and New York, Potter, 1990.

Other

Selling Illusions: The Cult of Multiculturalism in Canada. N.p., n.d.

*   *   *

Neil Bissoondath's writing takes readers into marginalized social and geographical territories, without ever moving far outside the conventions of literary realism. This combination of the exotic and the familiar has attracted a wide readership extending from North America to Europe, where his works have been translated into French and German.

Given his family history of double migration from India to Trinidad to Canada, it is not surprising that his narratives often focus on migrant experiences of displacement, uncertainty, isolation, cultural dislocation, and adaptation. These themes dominate many of the stories in *Digging Up the Mountains* and *On the Eve of Uncertain Tomorrows.* Of particular interest in such stories as "Christmas Lunch," "Veins Visible," "Security," and "The Power of Reason" is Bissoondath's alertness to the complexity of gender relations in multicultural contexts, and to differences between women's and men's respective experiences of migration and cultural adaptation.

Episodes of apparently random violence witnessed by Bissoondath in his early years in Trinidad find a place in his first novel *A Casual Brutality.* Narrated in the first person, the novel is a colonial Bildungsroman. The protagonist's inner journey towards maturity and understanding is bound up with a physical journey from a small Third World island to a metropolitan center of Western culture. Although the fictional island of Casaquemada resembles Trinidad in certain respects, Bissoondath's aim is not to recount a specific epoch in Trinidad's history, but rather to draw on episodes that took place in various West Indian countries. This desire to internationalize and universalize his stories, and to avoid analysis of specific historical episodes and political struggles, has attracted severe criticism from certain quarters.

Over time, Bissoondath's focus has shifted away from Trinidad toward his Canadian experiences and concerns. The title story of *On the Eve of Uncertain Tomorrows* penetrates the limbo world of a diverse group of fugitives from political violence and economic oppression who anxiously await the outcome of their applications for refugee status in Canada. "Uncertain Tomorrows" exposes the ethnocentricity of the legal criteria for granting refugee status, and the biases institutionalized in the court process. "The Power of Reason" emphasizes the gender-specificity of migrant experiences. Because equality of opportunity for women is often contingent upon their race and nation of origin, Canada's vertical mosaic has its own distinctive pink ghettos. Monica, an immigrant woman who cleans house for a white professional woman, has daughters who also work hard to take advantage of the opportunities gained through migration. Monica's sons, by contrast, either laze in front of the television or hang out on the street, mimicking the young Black American males they see on television. To Monica, her sons are complete strangers. The cultural gulf that opens up in many migrant families between the generations is compounded by a gap between gender roles.

Yet as *The Innocence of Age* suggests, migration is not a necessary prerequisite either to intergenerational conflict or to cultural alienation within the family. In Bissoondath's second novel, a father and son live in entirely different worlds, although both have always resided in Toronto. Except for the fact that its two main characters are Anglo-Canadian, and have no familial connection with another country, *The Innocence of Age* conforms in virtually every respect to the thematic and structural paradigms of "ethnic fiction." This would be a quintessential immigrant novel, were it not for the fact that its central characters are not immigrants. By writing an "ethnic novel" centering on people customarily perceived as "non-ethnic," Bissoondath effectively "ethnifies" Canada's dominant cultural group.

With each successive publication, it becomes increasingly clear that Bissoondath's novels and short stories occupy a place beside his interviews, newspaper and magazine articles, and his book on multiculturalism, *Selling Illusions: The Cult of Multiculturalism in Canada*—all contribute to the debate on Canadian multiculturalism. Irrespective of their geographical settings, which range from Trinidad to Europe and Japan as well as Canada, Bissoondath's works comment on the conditions under which the category of "multicultural writing" is constructed, and they critique the institutional circumstances under which "multicultural texts" are produced, interpreted, and evaluated. Bissoondath's literary practices and aesthetic values are entirely consistent with his critical stance on Canadian multiculturalism. By exploring what he sees as universal human themes, emotions, and experiences, Bissoondath endeavors to build and strengthen forms of mutual understanding and social cohesion that he would like to see asserted more strongly throughout Canadian society.

—Penny van Toorn

BLACKWOOD, Caroline (Maureen)

Nationality: British. **Born:** Lady Caroline Hamilton-Temple-Blackwood in Northern Ireland, 16 July 1931; daughter of the Marquis and Marchioness of Dufferin and Ava. **Education:** Attended a boarding school in England. **Family:** Married 1) the painter Lucian Freud (divorced); 2) Israel Citkovitz, three daughters (one deceased); 3) the poet Robert Lowell in 1972 (died 1977), one son. **Awards:** Higham award, 1976. **Address:** c/o Heinemann Ltd., 81 Fulham Rd., London SW3 6RB, England.

PUBLICATIONS

Novels

The Stepdaughter. London, Duckworth, 1976; New York, Scribner, 1977.
Great Granny Webster. London, Duckworth, and New York, Scribner, 1977.
The Fate of Mary Rose. London, Cape, and New York, Summit, 1981.
Corrigan. London, Heinemann, 1984; New York, Viking, 1985.

Short Stories

For All That I Found There (includes essays). London, Duckworth, 1973; New York, Braziller, 1974.
Goodnight Sweet Ladies. London, Heinemann, 1983.

Other

Darling, You Shouldn't Have Gone to So Much Trouble (cookbook), with Anna Haycraft. London, Cape, 1980.
On the Perimeter (on the Greenham Common nuclear protest). London, Heinemann, 1984; New York, Penguin, 1985.

In the Pink: Caroline Blackwood on Hunting. London, Bloomsbury, 1987.
The Last of the Duchess. New York, Pantheon, 1995.

*   *   *

Caroline Blackwood's first book, *For All That I Found There*, has a threefold division into "Fiction," "Fact," and "Ulster," which deals mostly with what seems to be autobiographical material. The rationale for the final section's form is given in the short story "The Interview" by the famous painter's widow, who criticizes a film about her husband as "a little too factual. . . . One should only ever be linked to the past through one's memory. Luckily memory is the most miserable, and unreliable, old muscle." It is perhaps the same rationale that underlies the "novel" form of *Great Granny Webster*, with its unnamed narrator and possibly autobiographical material.

Highlighting relationships in contemporary materialistic society, Blackwood's short stories were hard-hitting from the start. In her later collection, *Goodnight Sweet Ladies,* the title of each of the five stories is a female name or occupation. Whether written in the third or first person, in each story the central, rather unattractive figure (a woman, except in "Taft's Wife") is shown obsessively analyzing her predicament; after all, "Self-obsessed people can suffer just as much as unselfish ones." The "horrible fascination" of Blackwood's work lies in her inexorable probing of motivation, leavened by black humor. In the longest piece, "Angelica," an ex-actress imagines herself in love with a long-dead major in Brompton Cemetery in an attempt to recover from her abandonment by her young lover.

Blackwood is writing her own version of the novel of motivation as written by James, Proust, Anthony Powell—without their intricacy of social setting, and in black comedy. *The Stepdaughter* is told entirely in the form of letters to an imaginary friend from a woman who rarely leaves her claustrophobic Manhattan penthouse. She is, understandably, obsessed by the repulsive stepdaughter whom her ex-husband has foisted on her. The letters consist mainly of the woman's analysis of herself, her stepdaughter, and her ex-husband. The technique throws the focus of interest onto the woman, as we learn about her between the lines. This technique also allows Blackwood to manipulate dexterously the reader's sympathy as we respond to the woman's changing moods.

Great Granny Webster is, apparently, a loosely linked account of the selfish woman of the title, who by force of sheer longevity "had managed to be both the start of a line and the end of a line," and of the main characters in this line—the narrator's grandmother, once mistress of the decaying ancestral home in Ulster, but long in a mental hospital, her flighty Aunt Lavina, and her father, who died when she was nine—the blurred figure of the narrator's father is at the heart of the novel, doubly lost to her because he died before "the beginning of my memory's photography." The book's *pièce de résistance* is the final description of Great Granny Webster's funeral, actualizing the imagery of black and white running all through the book, one purpose of which is to blur certainties and whose first word is the "I" of the narrator and last word the "eye" of one of the narrated.

In *The Fate of Mary Rose,* by the brilliant structural device of making the narrator apparently the rapist and murderer of a child, although he does not remember this, Blackwood can deploy her extraordinary gift for minute analysis of motivation in a novel of suspense, beset by multiple ironies. She also probes the mass psychology in the Kent village after the killing. Though it grips like a thriller, through Blackwood's analysis of the narrator, his estranged, increasingly sick wife, and his friends among the London rich and talented, this novel transcends the form in a way comparable to John Fowles's *The Collector.*

Corrigan hinges on the same structural device as *The Fate of Mary Rose;* uncertainty is created in the reader's mind at the outset to engender mounting suspense—in this book regarding the honesty of the energetic wheelchair-bound charity fund-raiser, Corrigan, in his dealings with the naive widow Devina Blunt, whose sad, petty life he revolutionizes. Blackwood's characteristic unflinching and witty examination of the effects of Corrigan yet begs one basic question. Even if Corrigan turns out a con-man, Mrs. Blunt has emotionally still been given a good run for her money. But Corrigan has raised huge sums elsewhere for the supposed benefit of people who desperately need help; though Corrigan may be exonerated *vis-à-vis* Mrs. Blunt, this, the larger question, remains.

Recently, Blackwood's ironic style has reached a new pitch of *faux-naïf,* generally devastating, but occasionally inadequate, as sometimes in *On the Perimeter,* her account of the Greenham Common Peace Camps. Generally, Blackwood's wide-eyed, confrontational style is part of the honesty which often leads her to take as subject the uglier aspects of human relationships, while leaving open as many of the possibilities as one human being's perception can apprehend. Her voice is unique.

—Val Warner

BLAISE, Clark (Lee)

Nationality: Canadian. **Born:** Fargo, North Dakota, United States, 10 April 1940; became Canadian citizen, 1973. **Education:** Denison University, Granville, Ohio, 1957-61, A.B. 1961; University of Iowa, Iowa City, 1962-64, M.F.A. 1964. **Family:** Married Bharati Mukherjee, *q.v.,* in 1963; two sons. **Career:** Acting instructor, University of Wisconsin, Milwaukee, 1964-65; teaching fellow, University of Iowa, 1965-66; lecturer, 1966-67, assistant professor, 1967-69, associate professor, 1969-72, and professor of English, 1973-78, Sir George Williams University, later Concordia University, Montreal; professor of Humanities, York University, Toronto, 1978-80; Professor of English, Skidmore College, Saratoga Springs, New York, 1980-81, 1982-83. Visiting lecturer or writer-in-residence, University of Iowa, 1981-82, Saskatchewan School of the Arts, Saskatoon, Summer 1983, David Thompson University Centre, Nelson, British Columbia, Fall 1983, Emory University, Atlanta, 1985, Bennington College, Vermont, 1985, Columbia University, New York, Spring 1986, and New York State Writers Institute, Sarasota Springs, New York, summer 1994 and 1995; exchange professor, Meiji University, Japan, 1994. Currently, director of the International Writing Program, University of Iowa. **Awards:** University of Western Ontario President's medal, for short story, 1968; Great Lakes Colleges Association prize, 1973; Canada Council grant, 1973, 1977, and travel grant, 1985; St. Lawrence award, 1974; Fels award, for essay, 1975; *Asia Week* award, for non-fiction, 1977; *Books in Canada* prize, 1979; National Endowment for the Arts grant, 1981; Guggenheim grant, 1983. D.Litt.: Denison University, 1979. **Agent:** Janklow and Nesbit, 598 Madison Ave., New York, New York 10022. **Address:** 1021 Sheridan Avenue, Iowa City, Iowa 52240, U.S.A.

PUBLICATIONS

Novels

Lunar Attractions. New York, Doubleday, 1979.
Lusts. New York, Doubleday, 1983.

Short Stories

New Canadian Writing 1968, with Dave Godfrey and David Lewis Stein. Toronto, Clarke Irwin, 1969.
A North American Education. Toronto and New York, Doubleday, 1973.
Tribal Justice. Toronto and New York, Doubleday, 1974.
Personal Fictions, with others, edited by Michael Ondaatje. Toronto, Oxford Unversity Press, 1977.
Resident Alien. Toronto and New York, Penguin, 1986.
Man and His World. Erin, Ontario, Porcupine's Quill, 1992.

Play

Screenplay: *Days and Nights in Calcutta,* with Bharati Mukherjee, 1991.

Other

Days and Nights in Calcutta, with Bharati Mukherjee. New York, Doubleday, 1977; London, Penguin, 1986.
The Sorrow and the Terror: The Haunting Legacy of the Air India Tragedy, with Bharati Mukherjee. Toronto, Viking, 1987.
I Had a Father. New York, Addison-Wesley, 1993.

Editor, with John Metcalf, *Here and Now.* Ottawa, Oberon Press, 1977.
Editor, with John Metcalf, *78 [79, 80]: Best Canadian Stories.* Ottawa, Oberon Press, 3 vols., 1978-80.

*

Manuscript Collection: Calgary University Library, Alberta.

Critical Studies: *On the Line,* Downsview, Ontario, ECW Press, 1982, and *Another I: The Fiction of Clark Blaise,* ECW Press, 1988, both by Robert Lecker; article by Blaise in *Contemporary Authors Autobiography Series 3* edited by Adele Sarkissian, Detroit, Gale, 1986.

Clark Blaise comments:

(1981) My fiction is an exploration of threatened space; the space has been geographically and historically defined as French-Canada and French-America (New England), as well as extremely isolated areas of the deep South. Most of my fiction has been concerned with the effects of strong and contrasting parents, with the memory of Europe and of Canada, and the very oppressive reality, rendered minutely, of America. I am concerned with nightmare, terror, violence, sexual obsession, and the various artistic transformations of those drives. The tone of the work is not gothic or grotesque, however; I am devoted to the close observation of the real world, and to hold the gaze long enough to make the real world seem distorted. My work is also involved with the growth of the mind, the coming on of ideas about itself and the outside world. I would agree with critics who see my work as courting solipsism, and much of my own energy is devoted to finding ways out of the vastness of the first person pronoun.

*   *   *

Clark Blaise's short stories and novels are marked by their preoccupation with the tensions between a host of metaphorical extremes. Blaise is attracted to raw experience, spontaneous impulse, grotesque realism, uncultured thought: simultaneously, he is a polymath who needs reason, order, intellect, and learning in order to survive. For Blaise, these two worlds can never coincide; yet his fiction is driven by the strategies he employs in his attempt to *make* them coincide. The most obvious strategy involves doubling and superimposition. Blaise's characters are often two-sided, and their stories detail, through extended use of archetype and symbol, a profound desire to discover an integrated and authentic self. A list of the authors who influenced Blaise—including Pascal, Flaubert, Proust, Faulkner, and Céline—suggests that his work is philosophical, realistic, epic, eschatological, and existential. It is important to note this range, if only because Blaise has been viewed as a purely realistic writer involved with the tragic implications of his age. This perspective seems curious when one considers the extent to which Blaise's stories become self-conscious explorations of their own mode of articulation. Their ultimate reality is internal, psychological, personal, and self-reflective. To trace Blaise's growing preoccupation with this self-reflective mode is to describe the evolution of his fiction.

A North American Education, Blaise's first collection of linked short stories, is marked by the multi-leveled revelation of the fears, obsessions, and aesthetic values informing its three central narrators. In the final group of tales—"The Montreal Stories"—Norma Dyer begins to comment on the cosmopolitan milieu he inhabits from the removed and condescending perspective of an intellectual elitist who appears to be in full, if arrogant, control. But as the three stories comprising this section develop, panic sets in; the distanced third-person perspective of the opening eventually gives way to a revealingly fragmented first-person mode that details Dyer's personal and narrative collapse as he confesses that "I who live in dreams have suffered something real, and reality hurts like nothing in the world." In the "Keeler Stories" we hear the confessions of "a writer, a creator" who "would learn to satisfy himself with that." But here, as in the closing "Thibidault Stories," Blaise makes it clear that his narrators will never be satisfied with their creations, or with themselves. Yet they continue to deceive themselves in the belief that "anything dreamt had to become real, eventually."

The dreams shared by Blaise's narrators are always highly symbolic and archetypal in form, a conclusion supported by even the most cursory reading of Blaise's second short story collection, *Tribal Justice.* Here, in some of his richest and most evocative fiction, Blaise returns again and again to his narrators' meditations on their art. If there is a paradigmatic Blaise story—one that reveals the various tensions I have described—it is surely "Grids and Doglegs." It begins with its narrator recalling his interest in creativity, maps, education, history, archaeology, and cultural life; but no sooner is this interest articulated than it is ruthlessly undercut by hints of isolation and impending doom. Other stories—I think particularly of "Notes Beyond a History" and "At the Lake"—are framed by the same kind of divided opening, and by the same suggestion that the narrator who inhabits that opening is psychologically split.

Blaise's first two books established him as one of the finest short story writers in Canada at the very time he decided to explore a different genre. While *Lunar Attractions* proved that Blaise could master the novel form, it also demonstrated that his fundamental attraction to self-reflective writing remained central to his art. After all, *Lunar Attractions* is a semi-autobiographical account of a writer's development: David Greenwood insists on seeing himself in every aspect of his creation, so much so that his fiction becomes an intricate confession about his failure to get beyond himself. Yet *Lunar Attractions* is by no means purely solipsistic: it is a book about our times, about growing up in our times, and about the symbols and systems we use to explain our lives. Blaise has written that he wanted "to create the portrait of the authentically Jungian or even Freudian whole mind," which "sees every aspect of the natural and historical world being played out in its own imagination, and it literally creates the world that it sees."

These words suggest that for Blaise the writer can never be merely a recorder or even the interpreter of events. He must give form to experience and must be responsible to that form. The nature of this responsibility is the focus of Blaise's second and most recent novel—*Lusts.* Here the nature of writing is explored through Richard Durgin's struggle to understand the suicide of his wife, a successful poet who challenged Durgin's assumptions about the social and political implications of art.

If Rachel is Richard's "other self" then her death is doubly significant: it suggests that Blaise may have overcome the personal divisions that kept his successive narrators from becoming whole. Does this mean that he has found the integrated self he has sought throughout his work? A forthcoming volume of autobiographical essays may answer this question. But Blaise has written autobiography before—most notably in *Days and Nights in Calcutta*—only to return to the story of his personal and aesthetic search. The search is essential to his art, for the quality of his writing—its permutations, obsessions, and complex use of voice—is tragically dependent on Blaise's constant inability to find himself or his final story.

—Robert Lecker

BLECHMAN, Burt

Nationality: American. **Born:** Brooklyn, New York, 2 March 1927. **Education:** The University of Vermont, Burlington, B.A. 1949 (Phi Beta Kappa). **Career:** Formerly, instructor, New York University Medical School. **Awards:** Ingram Merrill Foundation award, 1965. **Address:** 200 Waverly Place, New York, New York 10014, U.S.A.

PUBLICATIONS

Novels

How Much? New York, Obolensky, 1961; London, Eyre and Spottiswoode, 1963.
The War of Camp Omongo. New York, Random House, 1963.
Stations. New York, Random House, 1963; London, Owen, 1966.
The Octopus Papers. New York, Horizon Press, 1965; London, Owen, 1966.

Maybe. Englewood Cliffs, New Jersey, Prentice Hall, and London, Owen, 1967.

*

Critical Studies: Article by Alfred Kazin in *The Great Ideas Today,* Chicago, Encyclopaedia Britannica, 1962; essay by Jacques Cabau in *L'Express* (Paris), December 1965; *The Jewish Writer in America* by Allen Guttman, New York, Oxford University Press, 1971.

*   *   *

For Armageddon is frightening only to those who fear progress.

(*Maybe*)

Though his first books, *How Much?* and *The War of Camp Omongo,* treated the same self-searching adolescents, ineffectual fathers, domineering mothers, and crass value systems as the work of other young Jewish novelists of the period, Burt Blechman focused on the total social picture rather than on a young male protagonist and created mothers whose comic vulgarity paradoxically earns them the compassion with which Blechman views all his characters (Mrs. Halpern's obsessive search for candlesticks in *How Much?* and boast of "Creative Shopping" during her brief appearance in *Omongo,* and Mrs. Levine's matching her quarter-carat ring against the three and two-and-one-half carat competition of the wealthier *Omongo* mothers). Just as these characters flesh out their caricature outlines, Blechman's entire fictional world transcends, without denying, the episodic structure and rapid pacing of the comic strip. *Stations,* which dramatizes the surrealistic world of a Catholic homosexual, was even stronger proof of Blechman's individuality, as were *The Octopus Papers* and *Maybe,* though all three books have stylistic and thematic parallels with his earlier novels.

Dramatizing their compulsions, Blechman's characters frantically fear and court the destruction that threatens either as individual confinement to perpetually shrinking spaces or as universal annihilation—"Little Normy Greenberg, the lousiest kid in the whole camp, paddling for all he was worth . . ." in a desperate attempt to triumph by the camp code he has always despised, achieves the goal he unconsciously sought: "The water was up to his ankles. Faster, Faster. His arms digging, digging, digging. A spade. A shovel. A grave" (*The War of Camp Omongo*). And the atmosphere of the novel tends to reinforce the belief of Eagle, the Indian caretaker, that his fellow Omongos are plotting the total slaughter of the white men who have usurped their land and who encourage catastrophe by the ritual war games they enact at the boys' camp.

In *How Much?* Jenny Stern's desire for independence in the home of her daughter and son-in-law, the Halperns, predictably traps her in a converted closet: "A drape, so Mama will think there's a window. We can even put a light behind so when she pulls the drape, open sesame, a little electric sun." Next Jenny inhabits the morgue, the cheapest room in Dr. Zatz's nursing home, where she must play dead during an inspector's visit. As the Halperns continually cry the title question in the face of bankruptcy, war, failure, and unresponsive auctioneers, "How much, dear God, how much does it cost to be happy?" they hasten the fate they profess to fear.

Myra Russell of *Maybe,* compulsively wasting money and time ("Maybe the biggest problem in life is how to spend it") while she calculates her shrinking future by her dwindling investments ironically resists her son's advice to move into a maisonette that has both a kitchenette and bathroomette, but is too small for a bedroomette. As the enemy's Tyranny Tests, countered by America's Freedom Tests, threaten to explode Myra's world, the newspapers stress the plight of the trapped Cave Girl. The two alternatives converge.

901, the homosexual voyeur of *Stations,* is driven by a conviction of the impending doom embodied in the vice-detective, Dom, to travel the Via Dolorosa of his confining subway "chapels" for what he believes to be the last time. His menacing universe, peopled by Madonna and Mother Superior, and filled with altars and confessionals, depends on a parody of Catholicism that combines elements of Genet with the science fiction-*cum*-paranoia of William Burroughs. Blechman employs a more general biblical parody in *How Much?, Maybe,* and in items like Steiner's commandments in *Omongo:* "Thou shalt have no other loyalties before me for I am the Lord Steiner who hath led thee from bondage in the land of thy parents. . . ." Though often brash and crude, Blechman's parody manages to ridicule both modern perversions of religious creeds and the original creeds themselves. Simultaneously, the parody laments a lost pattern of meaning that prevented or at least explained the chaos that perpetually waits to undo the universe. 901's abortive aspirations toward various careers parallel young Bernard Halpern's strivings in *How Much?* (Since Bernard appears in *The Octopus Papers* as B. Halpern, photographer, and in *Maybe* as B. Halpern, caricaturist, he apparently made a choice of a sort. His role as young Fat Stuff Halpern in *Omongo* reinforces the shared world view and tone of the books.)

The Octopus Papers, a collage of documents "selected, adapted, compiled, and annotated by Burt Blechman," is a literary hoax in the manner of *Gulliver's Travels* or *The Dunciad,* though the "Author's Apology" claims to be aping the style of Restoration Comedy. The book traces the history of Arsyn, an organization committed to the synthesis and marketing of the arts. Blechman has more tellingly satirized this tendency in *Omongo,* when a businessman attributed the widespread popularity of Van Gogh's "Sunflowers," in copies with simulated brushstrokes (cf. the "little electric sun" of Jenny's closet), to the artist's brilliant advertising ploy of self-mutilation. Moreover, the shadowy characterizations, thin texture, and surprisingly slow pace of *Octopus* make obtrusive Blechman's perpetual punning, as in the name of the trendsetting Newvoes, while this device seems venial amid the gusto and speed of the other books.

Pathetic little Norman Greenberg (*Omongo*), whose often hilarious obscenity helps define his loveless misery, epitomizes the combination of comic horror and pathos that is Blechman's major achievement. Similarly the humor in Jenny Stern's struggle against the senile amorousness of Mr. Lazar at the nursing home balances the compassionate responses she and her fellow inmates give to the news of their nurse's pregnancy, while they continue their litany of familiar complaints about their own children. What insures Blechman's status as a comic novelist, despite his often horrifying subject-matter is his complex parody, his word play that exposes an undercutting level of wit, his stylized handling of realistic dialogue, and ultimately, in Rabbi Yeslin's lament for his failure as a marriage broker, a prose that mocks an absurdity otherwise too painful to endure: "Nowadays, men wanted a special type, the kind you found late at night, alone in a delicatessen, waiting" (*The War of Camp Omongo*).

—Burton Kendle

BODSWORTH, (Charles) Fred(erick)

Nationality: Canadian. **Born:** Port Burwell, Ontario, 11 October 1918. **Education:** Port Burwell public and high schools. **Family:** Married Margaret Neville Banner in 1944; two daughters and one son. **Career:** Reporter, St. Thomas *Times-Journal,* Ontario, 1940-43; reporter and editor, Toronto *Daily Star* and *Weekly Star,* 1943-46; staff writer and editor, *Maclean's Magazine,* Toronto, 1947-55. Since 1955 freelance writer. Director and former president (1965-67), Federation of Ontario Naturalists: leader of worldwide ornithological tours. Since 1970 honorary director, Long Point Bird Observatory; chair of the Board of Trustees, James L. Baillie Memorial Fund for Ornithology, 1975-89; editor, Natural Science of Canada series, 1980-81. **Awards:** Doubleday Canadian Novel award, 1967. **Agent:** Curtis Brown, 10 Astor Place, New York, New York 10003, U.S.A. **Address:** 294 Beech Avenue, Toronto, Ontario M4E 3J2, Canada.

PUBLICATIONS

Novels

Last of the Curlews. Toronto and New York, Dodd Mead, 1955; London, Museum Press, 1956.
The Strange One. Toronto and New York, Dodd Mead, 1959; London, Longman, 1960.
The Atonement of Ashley Morden. Toronto and New York, Dodd Mead, 1964; as *Ashley Morden,* London, Longman, 1965.
The Sparrow's Fall. Toronto, McClelland and Stewart, New York, Doubleday, and London, Longman, 1967.

Other

The People's Health: Canada and WHO, with Brock Chisholm. Toronto, Canadian Association for Adult Education, 1949.
The Pacific Coast. Toronto, Natural Science of Canada, 1970.
Wilderness Canada, with others. Toronto, Clarke Irwin, 1970.

*

Critical Studies: Introduction by James Stevens to *Last of the Curlews,* Toronto, McClelland and Stewart, 1963; article in *The Oxford Companion to Canadian History and Literature* edited by Norah Story, Toronto, New York, and London, Oxford University Press, 1967; Don Gutteridge, in *Journal of Canadian Studies* (Peterborough, Ontario), August 1973; Olga Dey, in *Canadian Author and Bookman* (Toronto), Fall 1981; article in *A Reader's Guide to the Canadian Novel* by John Moss, Toronto, McClelland and Stewart, 1981.

Fred Bodsworth comments:

(1991) The major part of my work has been novels linking human and animal characters in a fiction format with strong natural history content and wilderness backgrounds. The nature storyteller who uses birds or mammals in fictional situations treads a narrow path if he wishes to be scientifically authentic and portray them as they really are. On the one hand, he has to personalize his animal as well as his human characters or he simply has no dramatic base for his story. Yet if the personalizing of animal characters goes too far and begins turning them into furry or feathered people—the nature writer's sin of anthropomorphism—the result is maudlin nonsense that is neither credible fable nor fiction. I enjoy the challenge of presenting wildlife characters as modern animal behavior studies are showing them to be—creatures dominated by instinct, but not enslaved by it, beings with intelligence very much sub-human in some areas yet fascinatingly superhuman in others. Out of the blending of human and animal stories comes the theme that I hope is inherent in all my books: that man is an inescapable part of all nature, that its welfare is his welfare, that to survive he cannot continue acting and regarding himself as a spectator looking on from somewhere outside.

*   *   *

Fred Bodsworth, writing in imaginative, uncomplicated prose, has used the Canadian Shield of pine-tree laden granite for the setting of his novels. He calls it "a benign land sometimes amiable, even indulgent, but at other times a land of perverse hostility." These sparsely Indian-populated lands provide a unique characteristic which distinguishes Canada from its gargantuan neighbor to the south. Bodsworth is then readily identifiable as a Canadian novelist.

The strength of his writing is the skillful portrayal of characters who are dependent upon the milieu and the forces within it. He is able to make his birds and humans unpredictable because of unforeseen but crucial subtleties in the environmental settings. Bodworth's naturalist and ornithological knowledge fosters such keen insight. Atook, a native hunter in *The Sparrow's Fall,* seems doomed because Christian myth interferes with his hunting prowess. But the will to survive, which resides in all his characters, eventually causes Atook to cast aside his alien beliefs and adjust to his natural surroundings.

Last of the Curlews is his most stimulating and moving novel. Bodsworth reveals the brutal and senseless slaughter of a bird that has not developed a fear of the earth's most irrational creature, man. In sensitive prose, the tiny bird becomes personalized but not human; thus he avoids sham. The theme of this novel has increased in importance since its writing because of the growing awareness of our threatened environment.

Although Bodsworth commits the occasional transgression by allowing his creatures to reason, it does not seriously detract from his animal characters.

In *The Strange One,* he adroitly interweaves the mating of an alien Hebridean Barra goose with a native Canada goose and the love of a young biologist for a Cree maiden, who has been socialized in the whiteman's world. Indian-white miscegenation is as old as Canada itself and this theme intertwined with the geese is unusual in Canadian literature. Bodsworth is the first to write about it. The parallel between man and bird in this novel clearly reveals the interrelationship of man with animal when Rory, the scientist, follows what appear to be almost instinctual feelings, disregards social convention and returns to the beautiful Cree, Kanina.

The Strange One and *The Atonement of Ashley Morden* involve what may be melodramatic relationships between men and birds, but the two themes are drawn together skillfully, and are quite effectively written. An underlying theme in both these novels, as well as the others, is the complicated, often contradictory behavior of men contrasted with the logical, conditioned instincts of animals and birds.

In the context of Canadian literature, Bodsworth is one of the leading traditional novelists.

—James R. Stevens

BOURJAILY, Vance (Nye)

Nationality: American. **Born:** Cleveland, Ohio, 17 September 1922. **Education:** Bowdoin College, Brunswick, Maine, B.A. 1947. **Military Service:** Served in the American Field Service, 1942-44, and in the United States Army, 1944-46. **Family:** Married Bettina Yensen in 1946; three children (one deceased). **Career:** Instructor at the Writers Workshop, 1957-58, and associate professor, 1960-64, 1966-67, 1971-72, University of Iowa, Iowa City; visiting professor, 1977-78, and professor, 1980-85, University of Arizona, Tucson. Member, United States Department of State mission to South America, 1959. Distinguished Visiting Professor, Oregon State University, Corvallis, Summer 1968. **Awards:** American Academy of Arts and Letters award, 1993. **Agent:** William Morris Agency, 1350 Avenue of the Americas, New York, New York 10019, U.S.A.

PUBLICATIONS

Novels

The End of My Life. New York, Scribner, 1947; London, W.H. Allen, 1963.
The Hound of Earth. New York, Scribner, 1955; London, Secker and Warburg, 1956.
The Violated. New York, Dial Press, 1958; London, W.H. Allen, 1962.
Confessions of a Spent Youth. New York, Dial Press, 1960; London, W.H. Allen, 1961.
The Man Who Knew Kennedy. New York, Dial Press, and London, W.H. Allen, 1967.
Brill among the Ruins. New York, Dial Press, 1970; London, W.H. Allen, 1971.
Now Playing in Canterbury. New York, Dial Press, 1976.
A Game Men Play. New York, Dial Press, 1980.
The Great Fake Book. New York, Weidenfeld and Nicolson, 1987.
Old Soldier. New York, Fine, 1990.

Uncollected Short Stories

"The Poozle Dreamers," in *Dial* (New York), Fall 1959.
"Fractional Man," in *New Yorker,* 6 August 1960.
"Goose Pits," in *New Yorker,* 25 November 1961.
"Varieties of Religious Experience," in *The Esquire Reader,* edited by Arnold Gingrich and others. New York, Dial Press, 1967.
"A Lover's Mask," in *Saturday Evening Post* (Philadelphia), 6 May 1967.
"The Amish Farmer," in *Great Esquire Fiction,* edited by L. Rust Hills. New York, Viking Press, 1983.
"The Duchess," in *Stand One,* edited by Michael Blackburn, Jon Silkin, and Lorna Tracy. London, Gollancz, 1984.

Play

$4000: An Opera in Five Scenes, music by Tom Turner (produced Iowa City, 1969). Published in *North American Review* (Cedar Falls, Iowa), Winter 1969.

Other

The Girl in the Abstract Bed (text for cartoons). New York, Tiber Press, 1954.
The Unnatural Enemy (on hunting). New York, Dial Press, 1963.
Country Matters: Collected Reports from the Fields and Streams of Iowa and Other Places. New York, Dial Press, 1973.
Fishing by Mail: The Outdoor Life of a Father and Son, with Philip Bourjaily. New York, Atlantic Monthly, 1993.

Editor, *Discovery 1-6.* New York, Pocket Books, 6 vols., 1953-55.

*

Manuscript Collection: Bowdoin College Library, Brunswick, Maine.

Critical Studies: *After the Lost Generation* by John W. Aldridge, New York, McGraw Hill, 1951, London, Vision Press, 1959; by Bourjaily in *Afterwords* edited by Thomas McCormack, New York, Harper, 1969; *The Shaken Realist* by John M. Muste, Baton Rouge, Louisiana State University Press, 1970.

*   *   *

Vance Bourjaily's first three novels trace the effects of World War II on his generation of Americans, people who were undergraduates at the time of Munich and Benny Goodman's rendition of "I Got It Bad and That Ain't Good." In the looser structure of his fourth book, *Confessions of a Spent Youth,* the war becomes one of several stages in the narrator's growing up, and Bourjaily attempts moods, situations, humor, and introspection that had not entered his more rigid earlier work. The novels that have followed this pivotal book have displayed a remarkable variety of subject and technique without gaining for Bourjaily the popularity or critical recognition that many have thought his due over the past 35 years.

The End of My Life recalls another slender novel of wartime ambulance service, Dos Passos's *One Man's Initiation—1917.* Skinner Galt, Bourjaily's hero, is another young man who believes in a few friends; any larger society or more complex idea repels him. He accounts for this emptiness by sifting through his slight reading and slighter experience to understand why he has "no principles, no truths, no ethics, no standards." *The Hound of Earth* is a parable of American responsibility for nuclear power, which describes the last days of the seven-year flight of an atomic scientist, who has left his work and family because these ties constantly remind him of the people he has helped to kill. In his reduced fugitive existence, he is run down by a "hound of earth," a nagging humanitarian impulse that makes him perform small acts of kindness to everyone he meets. *The Violated,* a far more ambitious novel, shows how four characters violate those whom they would love, and are, in turn, violated in the emptiness of their rapacious lives. The child of one of them (or perhaps two of them) plays the lead and directs other children in her own production of *Hamlet* before the parents, who sit as so many kings and queens stupefied or weary until when "frightened with false fire," a Claudius rises to end the show. This most sustained and complicated of Bourjaily's early plots thus ends with his first striking outburst of fictional invention.

Confessions of a Spent Youth is a retelling of *The End of My Life* that relieves the narrator, Quincy Quince, of the burden of philosophical exposition and allows him to reminisce easily about his young life; friendships, drinking, brushes with drugs, his loves, and his war service. The autobiographical element, admitted by Bourjaily, is clearest in Quincy's statement that "to recall is a pleasure," for these stories show the writer let loose with craft he had begun to tap with the children's play in *The Violated*.

In *The Man Who Knew Kennedy* Bourjaily examines the crises that overtake two friends in the months following the President's assassination. The connection between history and private lives is not altogether clear. Kennedy, according to the narrator, was killed by the psychotic force of someone writhing out of an abyss of frustration. A generation's illusions of invulnerability were smashed on impact. The gifted, graceful victim of this novel is, on the other hand, destroyed by his inexplicable ties to a woman as depraved as she is helpless. The man had traded on his talent instead of developing it, while the surviving friend realizes that he is the stronger of the two for such reasons as his "making necessary items out of wood—not fibreglass." *Brill among the Ruins* is Bourjaily's richest novel, and Brill, a middle-aged lawyer from a small town in southern Illinois, is his most fully realized character. He stands among two kinds of ruins, the hard bargain of his life and the archaeological sites of Oaxaca, developing on that line an understanding of himself that finally arrests his flight from responsibility. The accounts of digging are superb, surpassed only by the hunting scene where Brill alone "sculls" for ducks along the banks of the Mississippi before dawn.

A Game Men Play concerns yet another combat veteran, this one a poetic, reflective man trained as a killer and conditioned as a victim. *Is there anything at all that I can do?* he wires an old friend and tormentor upon learning of a family catastrophe. What he could or could not do to help is lost in the novel's (perhaps deliberate) loose ends, although the last glimpse of him in exile is utterly clear, recalling an incident decades before when he helped free the inmates of a German death camp and confronted their ragged warden: "'bitte . . .' He was the last man Chink killed in the Second World War. Chink did not stop to wonder if the man was asking for his life or for his death." If not Bourjaily's great novel, *A Game Men Play* is closer than the others to his summing up.

Bourjaily, always devoted to jazz, moved to New Orleans in the mid-1980s when he wrote widely-read articles and further sharpened the already distinctive language of his fiction. *Old Soldier,* a novella, celebrates a bond between brothers, the title character and his AIDS-ridden sibling, against a background of jazz argot and a few piped Highland melodies. *The Great Fake Book,* another story of a young man's search for his father, takes its title and particular inspiration from "Songs for Professional Musicians," which is explained to the hero, thus: "Now if you know you chords, you kin fake 'bout any song you'd ever want to play from just this one book here." Most of the narrative moves through sketches by the father bearing the titles of old standards, transitions aided by the son's notes. At its best, the novel is the "working book of magic spells" the father and son took their fake book to be.

—David Sanders

BOWEN, John (Griffith)

Nationality: British. **Born:** Calcutta, India, 5 November 1924. **Education:** Queen Elizabeth's Grammar School, Crediton, Devon; Pembroke College, Oxford (editor, *Isis*), 1948-51; St. Antony's College, Oxford (Frere Exhibitioner in Indian Studies), 1951-53, M.A. in modern history 1953; Ohio State University, Columbus, 1952-53. **Military Service:** Served in the Mahratha Light Infantry, 1943-47: Captain. **Career:** Assistant editor, *Sketch* magazine, London, 1953-56; copywriter, J. Walter Thompson Company, London, 1956-58; head of the copy department, S.T. Garland Advertising, London, 1958-60; script consultant, Associated Television, London, 1960-67; drama producer, Thames Television, London, 1978-79, London Weekend Television, 1981-83, and BBC, 1984. Since 1991 member of the board, Authors Licensing and Copyright Society. **Awards:** Society of Authors travelling scholarship, 1986. **Agent:** (fiction) Elaine Greene Ltd., 37 Goldhawk Road, London W12 8QQ; (theatre) Margaret Ramsay Ltd., 14-A Goodwin's Court, London WC2N 4LL. **Address:** Old Lodge Farm, Sugarswell Lane, Edgehill, Banbury, Oxfordshire OX15 6HP, England.

PUBLICATIONS

Novels

The Truth Will Not Help Us: Embroidery on an Historical Theme. London, Chatto and Windus, 1956.
After the Rain. London, Faber, 1958; New York, Ballantine, 1959.
The Centre of the Green. London, Faber, 1959; New York, McDowell Obolensky, 1960.
Storyboard. London, Faber, 1960.
The Birdcage. London, Faber, and New York, Harper, 1962.
A World Elsewhere. London, Faber, 1965; New York, Coward McCann, 1967.
Squeak: A Biography of NPA 1978A 203. London, Faber, 1983; New York, Viking, 1984.
The McGuffin. London, Hamish Hamilton, 1984; Boston, Atlantic Monthly Press, 1985.
The Girls: A Story of Village Life. London, Hamish Hamilton, 1986; New York, Atlantic Monthly Press, 1987.
Fighting Back. London, Hamish Hamilton, 1989.
The Precious Gift. London, Sinclair Stevenson, 1992.
No Retreat. London, Sinclair Stevenson, 1994.

Uncollected Short Stories

"Another Death in Venice," in *London Magazine,* June 1964.
"The Wardrobe Mistress," in *London Magazine,* January 1971.
"Barney," in *Mae West Is Dead,* edited by Adam Mars-Jones. London, Faber, 1983.
"The Rabbit in the Garden," in *Critical Quarterly* (Manchester), Summer 1987.

Plays

The Essay Prize, with A Holiday Abroad and The Candidate: Plays for Television. London, Faber, 1962.
I Love You, Mrs. Patterson (produced Cambridge and London, 1964). London, Evans, 1964.

The Corsican Brothers, based on the play by Dion Boucicault (televised 1965; revised version produced London, 1970). London, Methuen, 1970.

After the Rain, adaptation of his own novel (produced London, 1966; New York, 1967). London, Faber, 1967; New York, Random House, 1968; revised version, Faber, 1987.

The Fall and Redemption of Man (as *Fall and Redemption,* produced London, 1967; as *The Fall and Redemption of Man,* produced New York, 1974). London, Faber, 1968.

Silver Wedding (televised 1967; revised version, produced in *We Who Are about to . . .* , later called *Mixed Doubles,* London, 1969). London, Methuen, 1970.

Little Boxes (including *The Coffee Lace* and *Trevor*) (produced London, 1968; New York, 1969). London, Methuen, 1968; New York, French, 1970.

The Disorderly Women, adaptation of a play by Euripides (produced Manchester, 1969; London, 1970). London, Methuen, 1969.

The Waiting Room (produced London, 1970). London, French, 1970; New York, French, 1971.

Robin Redbreast (televised 1970; produced Guildford, Surrey, 1974). Published in *The Television Dramatist,* edited by Robert Muller, London, Elek, 1973.

Diversions (produced London, 1973). Excerpts published in *Play Nine,* edited by Robin Rook, London, Arnold, 1981.

Young Guy Seeks Part-Time Work (televised 1973; produced London, 1978).

Roger, in *Mixed Blessings* (produced Horsham, Sussex, 1973). Published in *London Magazine,* October-November 1976.

Florence Nightingale (as *Miss Nightingale,* televised 1974; revised version, as *Florence Nightingale,* produced Canterbury, 1975). London, French, 1976.

Heil Caesar!, adaptation of *Julius Caesar* by Shakespeare (televised 1974). London, BBC Publications, 1974; revised version (produced Birmingham 1974), London, French, 1975.

Which Way Are You Facing? (produced Bristol, 1976). Excerpts published in *Play Nine,* edited by Robin Rook, London, Arnold, 1981.

Singles (produced London, 1977).

Bondage (produced London, 1978).

The Inconstant Couple, adaptation of a play by Marivaux (produced Chichester, 1978).

Spot the Lady (produced Newcastle-upon-Tyne, 1981).

The Geordie Gentleman, adaptation of a play by Molière (produced Newcastle-upon-Tyne, 1987).

The Oak Tree Tea-Room Siege (produced Leicester, 1990).

Radio Plays: *Digby* (as Justin Blake, with Jeremy Bullmore), 1959; *Varieties of Love* (revised version of television play *The First Thing You Think Of*), 1968; *The False Diaghilev,* 1988.

Television Plays: created the *Garry Halliday* series; episodes in *Front Page Story, The Power Game, Wylde Alliance,* and *The Villains* series; *A Holiday Abroad,* 1960; *The Essay Prize,* 1960; *The Jackpot Question,* 1961; *The Candidate,* 1961; *Nuncle,* from the story by John Wain, 1962; *The Truth about Alan,* 1963; *A Case of Character,* 1964; *Mr. Fowlds,* 1965; *The Corsican Brothers,* 1965; *Finders Keepers,* 1967; *The Whole Truth,* 1967; *Silver Wedding,* 1967; *A Most Unfortunate Accident,* 1968; *Flotsam and Jetsam,* 1970; *Robin Redbreast,* 1970; *The Guardians* series (7 episodes), 1971; *A Woman Sobbing,* 1972; *The Emer-*

gency Channel, 1973; *Young Guy Seeks Part-Time Work,* 1973; *Miss Nightingale,* 1974; *Heil Caesar!,* 1974; *The Treasure of Abbot Thomas,* 1974; *The Snow Queen,* 1974; *A Juicy Case,* 1975; *Brief Encounter,* from the film by Noel Coward, 1976; *A Photograph,* 1977; *Rachel in Danger,* 1978; *A Dog's Ransom,* from the novel by Patricia Highsmith, 1978; *Games,* 1978; *The Ice House,* 1978; *The Letter of the Law,* 1979; *Dying Day,* 1980; *The Specialist,* 1980; *A Game for Two Players,* 1980; *Dark Secret,* 1981; *Honeymoon,* 1985.

Other (for children)

Pegasus. London, Faber, 1957; New York, A.S. Barnes, 1960.

The Mermaid and the Boy. London, Faber, 1958; New York, A.S. Barnes, 1960.

Garry Halliday and the Disappearing Diamonds [Ray of Death; Kidnapped Five; Sands of Time; Flying Foxes] (as Justin Blake, with Jeremy Bullmore). London, Faber, 5 vols., 1960-64.

*

Manuscript Collection: Mugar Memorial Library, Boston University; (television works) Temple University Library, Philadelphia.

Critical Studies: *Postwar British Fiction,* Berkeley, University of California Press, 1962, and "The Fable Breaks Down," in *Wisconsin Studies in Contemporary Literature* (Madison), vol. 8, no. 7, 1967, both by James Gindin.

Theatrical Activities:

Director: **Plays**—At the London Academy of Music and Dramatic Art since 1967; *The Disorderly Women,* Manchester, 1969, London, 1970; *Fall and Redemption,* Pitlochry, Scotland, 1969; *The Waiting Room,* London, 1970. Actor: **Plays**—In repertory in North Wales, summers 1950-51; Palace Theatre, Watford, Hertfordshire, 1965.

John Bowen comments:

I have always been interested in problems of form. Thus, in my first novel, *The Truth Will Not Help Us,* I wanted to try to tell a story of an historical occurrence of 1705 in Britain in terms of the political atmosphere and activities in the U.S.A. in 1953; in both these years political witch-hunting caused injustice and harm to innocent persons. My second novel, *After the Rain,* began as an attempt to do for science fiction what Michael Innes had done for the detective story: I failed in this attempt because I soon became more interested in the ideas with which I was dealing than in the form, and anyway made many scientific errors. My third novel was straightforwardly naturalistic, but in my fourth, *Storyboard,* I used an advertising agency as a symbol of a statement about public and private life, just as Zola used a department store in *Au Bonheur des Dames.* In my fifth novel, *The Birdcage,* I attempted to use a 19th-century manner—the objective detachment of Trollope, who presents his characters at some distance, displays and comments on them. In my sixth novel, *A World Elsewhere,* the hero, himself a wounded and needed politician, is writing a fiction about Philoctetes, the wounded archer, and until he has found his own reasons for returning to political life in London, cannot conclude his fiction, because he does not see why Philoctetes should allow himself to accompany Odysseus to Troy. In *Squeak,* the biography of a pigeon I once helped to rear, the story is told sometimes from Squeak's point of view, sometimes from that of her owners. In *The McGuffin* I tried to tell the story as the first-person narrative of one of the characters *inside* the kind of film Hitchcock might have made, the character himself being a reviewer of films. The same interest in different problems of form can be seen in my plays—the first Ibsenesque, the second borrowing from Brecht, Pirandello, and the Chinese theatre, the third a pair of linked one-acters, designed as two halves of the same coin, the fourth an attempt to rework the myth of *The Bacchae* as Sartre, Giraudoux, and Anouilh had used Greek myths, and to blend verse and prose, knockabout comedy, high tragedy, and Shavian argument. My full-length play *The Corsican Brothers* (an expansion of my earlier television play) has songs set within the play to music pirated from 19th-century composers, and I tried to make, from the melodramatic fantasies of Dumas and Dion Boucicault, a kind of Stendhalian statement about a society based on ideas of honour. In two of my television plays, *Miss Nightingale* and *The Emergency Channel*, I experimented with a narrative method that was associative, not lineal.

In this commentary, I am more confident in writing of form than of theme. One's themes are for the critics to set out neatly on a board: one is not always so clearly conscious of them oneself. There is a concern with archetypal patterns of behaviour (therefore with myth). There is a constant war between reasonable man and instinctive man. There is the pessimistic discovery that Bloomsbury values don't work, but that there seem to be no others worth holding. There is a statement of the need for Ibsen's "Life Lie" even when one knows it to be a lie, and Forster's "Only connect" becomes "Only accept" in my work. There is, particularly in *The McGuffin*, a concern with—and sorrow over—the ways in which human beings manipulate others of their kind.

I believe that novels and plays should tell a story, that the story is the mechanism by which one communicates one's view of life, and that no symbolism is worth anything unless it also works as an element in the story, since the final symbol is the story itself.

Inasmuch as the influences on one's style are usually those writers whom one has discovered in one's adolescence and early twenties, I might be said to have been influenced as a novelist by Dickens, Trollope, E.M. Forster, Virginia Woolf, E. Nesbit, P.G. Wodehouse, and Eveylyn Waugh—perhaps a little also by Hemingway and Faulkner. As a playwright, I have been influenced by Ibsen, Chekhov, Shaw, Pirandello, Anouilh, Giraudoux, and Noel Coward. Most of these names, I am sure, would be on any lists made by most of my contemporaries.

*   *   *

John Bowen has always been an intelligent and didactic novelist. His first novel, *The Truth Will Not Help Us,* uses a story of English seamen charged with piracy in a Scottish port in 1705 as a metaphor for the political evil of assuming guilt by rumor or association. *A World Elsewhere* uses the myth of Philoctetes as a parallel to complicated speculation about hypocrisy and engagement in contemporary political life. *The Birdcage* contains a long essay giving an account of the history and development of commercial television; a defense of advertising as not necessarily more corrupt than any other institution in urban, capitalistic society introduces *Storyboard.* Although Bowen's fictional lessons are invariably complex and thoughtful, the author's presence is always visible arranging, blocking out, and connecting the material. Myth is made pointedly and explicitly relevant; symbols, like the lovebirds in *The Birdcage* or the breaking of a bronze chrysanthemum at a funeral in

The Centre of the Green, sometimes seem attached heavy-handedly and literally. Bowen always acknowledges his own presence in his fiction, at times addressing the reader directly and becoming playful and intelligently skeptical about the complexities that prevent him from making any easy disposition of the characters and issues he has developed. The author is conspicuously articulate and instructive, but he does not attempt to play God; in fact, the danger of human substitutions for a non-existent or unknowable deity comprises part of the message of *After the Rain* and the skepticism underlying *The Birdcage* and *A World Elsewhere.*

Bowen's novels contain sharply memorable and effective scenes: the retired colonel expressing his style and his strength through his garden in *The Centre of the Green,* the nocturnal trip around Soho in which a character is beaten in *The Birdcage,* the picnic on a Greek island in *A World Elsewhere.* Often the best scenes involve a witty and comic treatment of dramatic conflict between two characters involved in close relationship, like the familial and sexual relationships in *The Centre of the Green* and *Storyboard,* the brilliantly handled quarrel between two contemporary London lovers who have lived together too long that takes place in the Piazza San Marco in *The Birdcage,* or the play with switching gender identities in *The McGuffin.* Bowen's comedy, however, no matter how strident initially, invariably turns into sympathy for his characters because they are unable to be more dignified or to match their own conceptions of a fuller humanity. This characteristic switch from satire to sympathy is emblematic of most of Bowen's fiction which works on reversals, on dramatically presented and thematically central violations of expected conclusions. The simple, muscle-flexing athlete, not the expected sensitive intellectual, finally defies and defeats the tyrant who would make himself God in *After the Rain.* Humanity and integrity appear in just those places most easily and generally thought the most corrupt in modern society in *Storyboard.* The family in which all members seem, superficially, most selfish and isolated can understand and respect each other in *The Centre of the Green.* This engagingly perverse positivism is often applied to social or political clichés, as in the forceful and complicated treatment of E.M. Forster's "Only connect" in *The Birdcage* or the ramifications on "politics is the art of the possible" developed in *A World Elsewhere.* Such clichés, in Bowen's fictional world, never honestly express the concerns or dilemmas of the characters who use them so glibly, although they may yet be partially true in ways the characters never intend and can seldom comprehend. The fact that people, in Bowen's novels, generally haven't a very good idea of what they're about is no warrant for denying their humanity or their capacity to invoke sympathy.

In the mid-1960s, Bowen turned to writing and producing plays for stage and television. Some of these, like adaptations of Euripides' *The Bacchae,* Shakespeare's *Julius Caesar,* and Dion Boucicault's *The Corsican Brothers,* compress the use of myth and symbol in dramatic confrontations, and suggest darker and more tragic versions of experience than do the novels. In the mid-1980s, after nearly 20 years away from novels, Bowen published two, *Squeak* and *The McGuffin.* Both depend on formal devices, dramatic fictional artifice: *Squeak* on the reconstruction of the knowable world through the carefully limited attention to a pigeon's perspective; *The McGuffin* on applying Alfred Hitchcock's term for the device in his films that triggered the action without itself being part of the plot to a more intricately locked version of menacing violations of expected identities. These novels function less as implicit social commentary than do some of Bowen's earlier ones, although, beneath the wit, they still convey humane and thoughtful lessons concerning the need to accept human deficiency and to respect forms of being, in oneself and in others, that one could not have initially imagined.

—James Gindin

BOWLES, Paul (Frederick)

Nationality: American. **Born:** New York City, 30 December 1910. **Education:** The University of Virginia, Charlottesville, 1928-29; studied music with Aaron Copland in New York and Berlin, 1930-32, and with Virgil Thomson in Paris, 1933-34. **Family:** Married Jane Sydney Auer (the writer Jane Bowles) in 1938 (died 1973). **Career:** Music critic, New York *Herald-Tribune*, 1942-46; also composer. Since 1947 has lived in Tangier. **Awards:** Guggenheim fellowship, 1941; American Academy award, 1950; Rockefeller grant, 1959; Translation Center grant, 1975; National Endowment for the Arts grant, 1977. **Agent:** William Morris Agency, 1350 Avenue of the Americas, New York, New York 10019, U.S.A. **Address:** 2117 Tanger Socco, Tangier, Morocco.

PUBLICATIONS

Novels

The Sheltering Sky. London, Lehmann, and New York, New Directions, 1949.
Let It Come Down. London, Lehmann, and New York, Random House, 1952.
The Spider's House. New York, Random House, 1955; London, Macdonald, 1957.
Up above the World. New York, Simon and Schuster, 1966; London, Owen, 1967.

Short Stories

The Delicate Prey and Other Stories. New York, Random House, 1950.
A Little Stone. London, Lehmann, 1950.
The Hours after Noon. London, Heinemann, 1959.
A Hundred Camels in the Courtyard. San Francisco, City Lights, 1962.
The Time of Friendship. New York, Holt Rinehart, 1967.
Pages from Cold Point and Other Stories. London, Owen, 1968.
Three Tales. New York, Hallman, 1975.
Things Gone and Things Still Here. Santa Barbara, California, Black Sparrow Press, 1977.
Collected Stories 1939-1976. Santa Barbara, California, Black Sparrow Press, 1979.
Midnight Mass and Other Stories. Santa Barbara, California, Black Sparrow Press, 1981; London, Owen, 1985.
Call at Corazón and Other Stories. London, Owen, 1988.
A Distant Episode: The Selected Stories. New York, Ecco Press, 1988.
Unwelcome Words. Bolinas, California, Tombouctou, 1988.
A Thousand Days for Mokhtor: Seven Stories. London, Owen, 1989.

Plays

Senso, with Tennessee Williams, in *Two Screenplays,* by Luigi Visconti. New York, Orion Press, 1970.

Screenplay: *Senso* (*The Wanton Countess,* English dialogue, with Tennessee Williams), 1949.

Poetry

Scenes. Los Angeles, Black Sparrow Press, 1968.
The Thicket of Spring: Poems 1926-1969. Los Angeles, Black Sparrow Press, 1972.
Next to Nothing. Kathmandu, Starstreams, 1976.
Next to Nothing: Collected Poems 1926-1977. Santa Barbara, California, Black Sparrow Press, 1981.

Other

Yallah (travel). Zurich, Manesse, 1956; New York, McDowell Obolensky, 1957.
Their Heads Are Green (travel). London, Owen, 1963; as *Their Heads Are Green and Their Hands Are Blue,* New York, Random House, 1963.
Without Stopping: An Autobiography. London, Owen, and New York, Putnam, 1972.
In the Red Room. Los Angeles, Sylvester and Orphanos, 1981.
Points in Time (on Morocco). London, Owen, 1982; New York, Ecco Press, 1984.
Two Years Beside the Strait: Tangier Journal 1987-1989. London, Owen, 1990; as *Days,* New York, Ecco Press, 1991.
Conversations with Paul Bowles, edited by Gena Dagel Caponi. Jackson, University Press of Mississippi, 1993.
Morocco, with photographs by Barry Brukoff. New York, Abrams, 1993.
Too Far from Home: The Selected Writings of Paul Bowles. Hopewell, New Jersey, Ecco Press, 1993.
In Touch: The Letters of Paul Bowles, edited by Jeffrey Miller. New York, Farrar Straus and Giroux, 1994.

Translator, *No Exit,* by Jean-Paul Sartre. New York, French, 1946.
Translator, *Lost Trail of the Sahara,* by Roger Frison-Roche. London, Hale, 1956; Englewood Cliffs, New Jersey, Prentice Hall, 1962.
Translator, *A Life Full of Holes,* by Driss ben Hamed Charhadi. New York, Grove Press, 1964; London, Weidenfeld and Nicolson, 1965.
Translator, *Love with a Few Hairs,* by Mohammed Mrabet. London, Owen, 1967; New York, Braziller, 1968.
Translator, *The Lemon,* by Mohammed Mrabet. London, Owen, 1969; New York, McGraw Hill, 1972.
Translator, *Mhashish,* by Mohammed Mrabet. San Francisco, City Lights, 1969; London, Owen, 1988.
Translator, *The Boy Who Set the Fire and Other Stories.* Los Angeles, Black Sparrow Press, 1974.
Translator, *For Bread Alone,* by Mohamed Choukri. London, Owen, 1974.
Translator, *Jean Genet in Tangier,* by Mohamed Choukri. New York, Ecco Press, 1974.
Translator, *The Oblivion Seekers,* by Isabelle Eberhardt. San Francisco, City Lights, 1975; London, Owen, 1988.

Translator, *Hadidan Aharam,* by Mohammed Mrabet. Los Angeles, Black Sparrow Press, 1975.

Translator, *Harmless Poisons, Blameless Sins,* by Mohammed Mrabet. Santa Barbara, California, Black Sparrow Press, 1976.

Translator, *Look and Move On,* by Mohammed Mrabet. Santa Barbara, California, Black Sparrow Press, 1976; London, Owen, 1989.

Translator, *The Big Mirror,* by Mohammed Mrabet. Santa Barbara, California, Black Sparrow Press, 1977; London, Owen, 1989.

Translator, *Five Eyes: Short Stories by Five Moroccans.* Santa Barbara, California, Black Sparrow Press, 1979.

Translator, *Tennessee Wiliams in Tangier,* by Mohamed Choukri. Santa Barbara, California, Cadmus, 1979.

Translator, *The Beach Café, and The Voice,* by Mohammed Mrabet. Santa Barbara, California, Black Sparrow Press, 1980.

Translator, *The Chest,* by Mohammed Mrabet. Bolinas, California, Tombouctou, 1983.

Translator, *She Woke Me Up So I Killed Her.* Tiburon, California, Cadmus, 1985.

Translator, *The Beggar's Knife,* by Rodrigo Rey Rosa. San Francisco, City Lights, 1985.

Translator, *Marriage with Papers,* by Mohammed Mrabet. Bolinas, California, Tombouctou, 1986.

Translator, *Look and Move On: An Autobiography,* by Mohammed Mrabet. Santa Rosa, California, Black Sparrow Press, 1989.

Translator, *Dust on Her Tongue,* by Rodrigo Rey Rosa. London, Owen, 1989.

Translator, *The Pelcari Project,* by Rodrigo Rey Rosa. London, Owen, 1991.

Published Music: *Tornado Blues* (chorus); *Music for a Farce* (chamber music); *Piano Sonatina; Huapango 1* and *2; Six Preludes for Piano; El Indio; El Bejuco; Sayula; La Cuelga; Sonata for Two Pianos; Night Waltz* (two pianos); *Songs: Heavenly Grass; Sugar in the Cane; Cabin; Lonesome Man; Letter to Freddy; The Years; Of All the Things I Love; A Little Closer, Please; David; In the Woods; Song of an Old Woman; Night Without Sleep; Two Skies; Que te falta?; Ya Llego; Once a Lady Was Here; Bluebell Mountain; Three; On a Quiet Conscience; El Carbonero; Baby, Baby; Selected Songs,* Santa Fe, Soundings Press, 1984.

Operas: *Denmark Vesey,* 1937; *The Wind Remains,* 1941.

Ballets: *Yankee Clipper,* 1937; *Pastorella,* 1941; *Sentimental Colloquy,* 1944; *Blue Roses,* 1957.

Incidental Music, for plays: *Horse Eats Hat,* 1936; *Dr. Faustus,* 1937; *My Heart's in the Highlands,* 1939; *Love's Old Sweet Song,* 1940; *Twelfth Night,* 1940; *Liberty Jones,* 1941; *Watch on the Rhine,* 1941; *South Pacific,* 1943; *Jacobowsky and the Colonel,* 1944; *The Glass Menagerie,* 1945; *Twilight Bar,* 1946; *On Whitman Avenue,* 1946; *The Dancer,* 1946; *Cyrano de Bergerac,* 1946; *Land's End,* 1946; *Summer and Smoke,* 1948; *In the Summer House,* 1953; *Edwin Booth,* 1958; *Sweet Bird of Youth,* 1959; *The Milk Train Doesn't Stop Here Anymore,* 1963; for films: *Roots in the Soil,* 1940; *Congo,* 1944.

Recordings: *The Wind Remains,* M.G.M.; *Café Sin Nombre,* New Music; *Sonata for Two Pianos,* Concert Hall; *Night Waltz,* Columbia; *Scènes d'Anabase,* Columbia; *Music for a Farce,* Columbia; *Song for My Sister,* Disc; *They Cannot Stop Death,* Disc; *Night Without Sleep,* Disc; *Sailor's Song,* Disc; *Rain Rots the Wood,* Disc; *Sonata for Flute and Piano,* Art of This Century; *Six Preludes,* Golden Crest; *Huapango 1* and *2,* New Music; *A Picnic Cantata,* lyrics by James Schuyler, Columbia, 1955; *El Bejuco* and *El Indio,* Art of This Century; *Blue Mountain Ballads,* Music Library; *Concerto for Two Pianos, Winds and Percussion,* Columbia; *Once a Lady Was Here, Song of an Old Person,* New World; *Six Latin American Pieces,* Etcetera, 1984; *Five Songs,* GSS, 1984; *Six Preludes, Eleven Songs,* 1989.

*

Bibliography: *Paul Bowles: A Descriptive Bibliography* by Jeffrey Miller, Santa Barbara, California, Black Sparrow Press, 1986.

Manuscript Collection: Humanities Research Center, University of Texas, Austin.

Critical Studies: "Paul Bowles and the Natural Man" by Oliver Evans, in *Recent American Fiction,* Boston, Houghton Mifflin, 1963; *Paul Bowles. The Illumination of North Africa* by Lawrence D. Stewart, Carbondale, Southern Illinois University Press, 1974; *Paul Bowles: Staticity and Terror* by Eric Mottram, London, Aloes, 1976; *The Fiction of Paul Bowles: The Soul Is the Weariest Part of the Body* by Hans Bertens, Amsterdam, Rodopi, and Atlantic Highlands, New Jersey, Humanities Press, 1979; "Paul Bowles Issue" of *Review of Contemporary Fiction,* vol. 2, no. 3, Elmwood Park, Illinois, 1982; *Paul Bowles: The Inner Geography* by Wayne Pounds, Bern, Switzerland, Lang, 1985; *A World Outside: The Fiction of Paul Bowles* by Richard F. Patteson, Austin, University of Texas Press, 1987; *An Invisible Spectator: A Biography of Paul Bowles* by Christopher Sawyer-Laucanno, London, Bloomsbury, 1989, New York, Ecco Press, 1990; *The Dream at the End of the World: Paul Bowles and the Literary Renegades in Tangier* by Michelle Green, New York, HarperCollins, 1991; *Paul Bowles: A Study of the Short Fiction* by Allen Hibbard, New York, Twayne, 1993; *Paul Bowles: Romantic Savage* by Gena Dagel Caponi, Carbondale, Southern Illinois University Press, 1994.

Paul Bowles comments:

All I can find of interest to say about my work is to mention the key role in the process of writing played by my subconscious. It knows far better than I what should be written and how it should sound in words.

*   *   *

Come on a vacation and wind up like this . . .
Up above the World

The recent news that Paul Bowles's works are among the most popular targets of bookstore thieves provides an ironic commentary on the power of his fiction and of his influence as a cult figure. For more than 40 years Bowles's novels and stories have focused on characters who, having freed themselves from the rote morality of western civilization, spectacularly defy traditional values through an obsession with sexual pleasure (*The Sheltering Sky*), theft and an apparently gratuitous murder (*Let It Come Down*), and father-son incest, desired if not practiced (*Pages from Cold Point*).

The motivation that transports these North Americans and Europeans to North Africa, Mexico, Central America, and Asia is presumably not the usual tourist desire for exotic scenery, food, and people. *The Sheltering Sky,* in fact, distinguishes between tourists with definite commitments to return home, and travelers without strict agendas. For Bowles's travelers, lush vegetation exists primarily to begin the process of decay and to generate impressive varieties of insect life, from the actual flies spreading a catalogue of dangerous diseases or making "their brief frantic love" on a dead man's lower lip to metaphorical "tiny yellow worms" of mango pulp that menace the eater.

Most often, as in the world of *The Sheltering Sky,* the traveler sees "a stony terrain too parched to shelter even the locusts," and feels "the sun's fierce attack," an image suggesting the universe of *The Stranger.* The sky protects "from what's behind," which is probably "Nothing, I suppose. Just darkness. Absolute night." But such precarious shelter offers little comfort. The "human landscape" is also, predictably, "cruelly lacking" in that sympathy which might reconcile travelers to the terrain. "The freshest air you'll ever smell," at least in the mountains, hardly compensates for "patches of fur in . . . rabbit stew," and "corpses" of weevils in soup: "They must have been in the noodles."

The travel impulse must therefore have different, deeper sources than those stimulating conventional tourists, motivations at best imperfectly understood by journeyers down the typical Bowles streets and roads that begin straightforwardly but, in nightmare fashion, curve and wind into "the interior" that Port Moresby seeks in *The Sheltering Sky.* This almost unconscious desire for the interior and the fascination with maps displayed by Port and by Dyar in *Let It Come Down,* among other Bowles protagonists, recalls Conrad's Marlow, similarly obsessed with undetailed maps of central Africa, the blankness of the maps suggesting unexplored depths within the traveler himself. Bowles's presentation of the theme also echoes similar material in Gide's *The Immoralist.* Bowles's autobiography, *Without Stopping,* mentions his youthful fascination with Gide's Lafcadio and the concept of the gratuitous act, a fascination that may have contributed to the matrix of forces shaping the archetypal Bowles character, who finds both terror and fulfillment in this interior.

The sudden revelation of the abyss behind the sheltering sky or within the individual ("At any moment the rip can occur, the edges fly back, and the giant maw will be revealed") may be destructive: Port apparently must die to allow his wife Kit to recognize and act out her authentic self, however terrifying the triumph. Or the revelation may produce a more conscious exaltation, as with Dyar, who, after a lifetime of doubts about his own existence and its acknowledgment by others, can boast that he has achieved "A place in the world, a definite status, a precise relationship with the rest of men. Even if it had to be one of open hostility, it was his, created by him." Such a heightened sense of self is a considerable accomplishment in a world that equates existence with the possession of a passport (the theft of Port's passport implies that his hold on existence is precarious). Dyar's self-definition inevitably suggests Meursault's epiphany at the climax of *The Stranger,* though Dyar's insight seems too abstract, too lacking in the sensuous immediacy that vivified Camus' hero.

Bowles's first two novels, *The Sheltering Sky* and *Let It Come Down,* and a handful of stories like "A Distant Episode," "Pages from Cold Point," and "The Delicate Prey" are his strongest works. *The Sheltering Sky* dramatizes a frightening quest for the buried self which forces both the central characters, and the reader, to re-

examine assumptions about morality and cultural norms, Port and Kit providing nicely shaded variations on the central theme. She is initially much less eager to travel, much less organized in her approach to Morocco than Port and, paradoxically, much more susceptible to the power of the new environment. Just as Bowles does not rely on conventions about the primitive versus the civilized, he does not sentimentalize the Moroccan terrain and its inhabitants—the clarity of the air exposes terrible truths about the land and its explorers. The relationship between drugs and vision does not, as in other Bowles works, make insight seem arbitrary and illusory. The novel convincingly presents the drugs as sources of freedom from the rational control that often is indistinguishable from arbitrary social mores. Port's death from typhoid may be in the tradition of Daisy Miller's succumbing to Roman Fever and the perils of European civilization, but Bowles goes beyond this metaphor for transcultural dangers to suggest that Port died not from the terrors of an unknown society, but from an incapacity to accept the terrors of existence itself.

The novel skillfully incorporates its existentialist themes into an adventure framework, a feat equaled by *Let It Come Down,* which wittily links Dyar's quest to his job in the "transit department" of a New York bank. Apparently impelled by tricks of time and opportunity into criminal activity, he explodes into a sense of his existence only after committing a murder. What separates this novel from most of Bowles's work, aside from some unsuccessful attempts at satire in some recent stories, is the wonderful comedy involving the large American lesbian writer Eunice Goode and her expatriate circle. For all her rebelliousness, Eunice is amusingly uneasy about the ethnicity of the Arab girl with whom she is infatuated and tries to pass her off as a Greek to avoid a social gaffe. Though many of the novel's episodes hint at roman-à-clef allusions that would heighten the enjoyment for insiders, they do not depend totally on this element, as do other Bowles stories. It is unfortunate that Bowles did not display his comic skills more frequently.

Up above the World devotes much space to the idea of freedom in a variety of contexts, from the apparently trivial ("The whole point is to be free. Not to have to make reservations ahead of time.") to the serious (" . . . free enough to be able to focus on God . . ."). The novel, following the adventures of a husband and wife from the United States as they journey through Central America, creates a feverish atmosphere of psychological and metaphysical danger, but then disappointingly reveals itself to be a rather conventional thriller with a villain who disastrously misreads the couple's actions. The result is neither a satisfactory thriller nor a serious treatment of the stimulating dangers of freedom.

The Spider's House ambitiously attempts to depict the reality of modern (mid-1950s) life in Fez and reveals both the French and the Moroccan radicals to be guilty of destroying the "purity" of traditional Moroccan culture, a theme developed in the fine early story "The Time of Friendship." The novel conveys the ambiguous richness of Muslim life through an adolescent protagonist, Amar. Bowles is scrupulous in depicting all facets of Amar's faith, including his belief that women are animals, a view only marginally altered by his acquaintance with a female "Nazarene." Such negative aspects of Amar's code raise questions about the obsession of an American writer Stenham, who views the boy as a personification of endangered Moroccan life (Amar plays the same role in the imagination of a revolutionary Moroccan leader). Amar's character threatens to crumble under this heavy symbolic burden, and his youth and background make less than credible the insight with which the novel credits him (a problem in other Bowles works that endow characters with a depth of awareness credible only in the author). Since the novel carefully excludes any sexual attraction between the man and the boy and does not present them as sufficiently charismatic exemplars of their respective cultures, some key motivation seems missing. Thus, Amar's final longing for a relation with Stenham weakens the novel's conclusion, however laudable Bowles's attempt to dramatize the vulnerable state of his beloved Morocco.

Bowles's strongest treatment of the theme of failed communication between cultures is "A Distant Episode," which rewards a language professor for "making a survey of variations in Maghrebi," with the violent loss of his tongue. Going considerably beyond conventional anti-academic satire, the story ironically suggests that the professor's mutilation and abasement to the status of mascot in a wandering Arab tribe may actually represent the transcendence of reason and ascendance to the status of "holy maniac." The story brilliantly balances its horror and irony.

Ultimately, Bowles's key achievement may be popularization of themes defined and developed by major writers like Conrad, Gide, Camus and, especially, Sartre, whose *No Exit* Bowles translated for its Broadway premiere. Bowles's characters frequently find themselves in small, imprisoning rooms which force them, with differing degrees of success, to confront their essential natures undistracted by the challenging terrains which initially attracted them. In an exciting variation on the theme, Kit is locked out of the house in which Port has just died and thus she must deal directly with the meaning of the sheltering sky. Bowles's fiction illuminates such existentialist themes with strong dramatic incidents, believable, often memorable, characters, and witty dialogue. His best work controls a complex tone that views physical and psychological horrors with detachment, yet never cancels out compassion for human vulnerability. These strengths explain Bowles's reputation among a devoted coterie.

—Burton Kendle

BOX, Edgar. *See* **VIDAL, Gore.**

BOYD, William

Nationality: British. **Born:** William Andrew Murray Boyd, Accra, Ghana, 7 March 1952. **Education:** Gordonstoun School, Elgin, Morayshire; University of Nice, France, diploma 1971; University of Glasgow, M.A. (honours) in English and philosophy 1975; Jesus College, Oxford, 1975-80. **Family:** Married Susan Anne Wilson in 1975. **Career:** Lecturer in English, St. Hilda's College, Oxford, 1980-83. Television critic, *New Statesman,* London, 1981-83. Lives in Chelsea, London. **Awards:** Whitbread award, 1981; Maugham award, 1982; Rhys Memorial prize, 1982; James Tait Black Memorial prize, 1990. Fellow, Royal Society of Literature, 1983; Sunday Express Book of the Year award, 1993. **Agent:** Lemon Unna and Durbridge Ltd., 24 Pottery Lane, London W11 4LZ, England.

PUBLICATIONS

Novels

A Good Man in Africa. London, Hamish Hamilton, 1981; New York, Morrow, 1982.
An Ice-Cream War. London, Hamish Hamilton, 1982; New York, Morrow, 1983.
Stars and Bars. London, Hamish Hamilton, 1984; New York, Morrow, 1985.
The New Confessions. London, Hamish Hamilton, 1987; New York, Morrow, 1988.
Brazzaville Beach. London, Sinclair Stevenson, 1990; New York, Morrow, 1991.
The Blue Afternoon. London, Sinclair Stevenson, 1993; New York, Knopf, 1995.

Short Stories

On the Yankee Station and Other Stories. London, Hamish Hamilton, 1981; New York, Morrow, 1984; revised edition, London, Penguin, 1988.
The Destiny of Nathalie "X". London, Sinclair Stevenson, 1995.

Plays

School Ties (includes the TV plays *Good and Bad at Games* and *Dutch Girls,* and an essay). London, Hamish Hamilton, 1985; New York, Morrow, 1986.
Care and Attention of Swimming Pools, and Not Yet Jayette (produced London, 1985).

Screenplays: *Stars and Bars,* 1988; *Aunt Julia and the Scriptwriter,* 1990; *Mr. Johnson,* 1990; *Chaplin,* 1992; *A Good Man in Africa,* 1994.

Radio Play: *On the Yankee Station,* from his own story, 1985; *Hommage to A.B.,* 1994.

Television Plays: *Good and Bad at Games,* 1983; *Dutch Girls,* 1985; *Scoop,* from the novel by Evelyn Waugh, 1987.

*   *   *

But for *An Ice-Cream War,* William Boyd would be firmly labelled an exponent of that familiar comic genre, the accident-prone hero novel, as practised by, among others, Kingsley Amis (*Lucky Jim*), Anthony Burgess (the Enderby series), and Tom Sharpe (the Wilt series). Both *A Good Man in Africa* and *Stars and Bars* feature protagonists—Morgan Leafy and Henderson Dores, respectively—entrusted with crucial assignments only to be hampered and finally thwarted by proliferating complications. Foreign locations enable Boyd to add occasional culture shock to their predicaments.

Morgan Leafy is a minor diplomat stationed in a provincial backwater in the "not-very-significant" West African nation of Kinjanja. For three years, his stupefying boredom has been palliated only by readily available alcohol and sex. Then, unexpectedly, his boss, Fanshawe, deputes him to cultivate, on behalf of H.M. Government, a local politician (Samuel Adekunle) who is a bigwig in the party set to win Kinjanja's forthcoming elections. At the same time, Morgan begins to court Priscilla, Fanshawe's attractive daughter.

Initially, the outlook seems promising: both Adekunle and Priscilla respond to Morgan's overtures. Subsequently, things deteriorate inexorably. Distractions and indignities dog him. Through a misunderstanding, he loses Priscilla to a hated underling. Then he finds himself being blackmailed by Adekunle. To secure his silence, Morgan must suborn an expatriate Scot, Dr. Murray, who is obstructing a lucrative swindle the politician hopes to transact. Unfortunately, Murray is a model of rectitude: Morgan's proposition only worsens matters. In the final pages, though, providence apparently rescues him.

Henderson Dores is an art expert who has recently left England to join the fledgling New York branch of Mulholland, Melhuish, a London auction house. Already he has become simultaneously involved with two alluring, imperious women: his former wife, Melissa, with whom he is discussing remarriage, and his mistress, Irene. Henderson's assignment entails travelling to the Deep South to talk Loomis Gage, a reclusive millionaire, into letting Mulholland, Melhuish handle the sale of his paintings: a coup that would "signal their arrival." Inconveniently, Bryant, Henderson's teenage stepdaughter-to-be, invites herself along, thereby jeopardising his plans to meet Irene while away. Then the Gage household proves to be chock-full of confusing and/or intimidating oddballs. Nevertheless, braving the violent opposition of Gage's elder son and assorted misadventures, Henderson brings matters to a successful conclusion. Gage, however, promptly suffers a fatal coronary, leaving him with only an unwitnessed oral agreement. Furthermore, Bryant announces her intention of eloping with Duane, the son of Gage's housekeeper. Abducting Bryant, Henderson decamps to New York. After further misadventures, the novel closes with him fleeing a vengeful Duane. By this time, Henderson has lost his job (perhaps temporarily) and both his women (probably permanently). The paintings, meanwhile, have been destroyed.

Stars and Bars contains various inventive comic flights, but several others seem decidedly routine, poking fun at soft targets like American speech, American cuisine (especially the downhome kind), radio "sermonettes," country and western music. Elsewhere, bedroom farce ensues when Henderson and Irene rendezvous at Atlanta's swishest hotel. *A Good Man in Africa* generally avoids such lapses into the familiar. In addition, the world created in *Stars and Bars* is distinctly cartoon-like: Henderson is a two-dimensional character whose pratfalls provide entertainment alone. Morgan's mishaps also arouse some sympathy: the reader discerns his real desperation as Adekunle turns the screw, his pricks of conscience at engaging, albeit unavailingly, in corruption.

At one stage in Julian Barnes's *Flaubert's Parrot* the narrator proposes that certain types of fiction be no longer written, including " . . . novels about small hitherto forgotten wars in distant parts of the British Empire, in the painstaking course of which we learn . . . that war is very nasty indeed." *An Ice-Cream War* is clearly one of the novels that has prompted this injunction: it is set mainly in East Africa during World War I, when the adjacent British and German colonies became a secondary battlefield. The description, though, is unjust: Boyd's point about the nature of war is a deeper one—he believes that literature has not only glossed over the bloodiness of war, but also its contingency.

Boyd's humour is altogether more grim here than in his other novels. Destiny is again antipathetic towards his characters, but the tricks of fate are now brutal rather than mischievous. An incongruous episode in *Stars and Bars* concerns Henderson's discovery that his father's death during World War II occurred when he was struck by a tin of pineapple chunks dropped from a supply plane.

In *An Ice-Cream War,* death and injury from comparably absurd causes are commonplace; accident rather than design is throughout the motive force behind events. One of the principal characters, Captain Gabriel Cobb, takes part in the sea-borne invasion of German East Africa, during which military order and discipline degenerate into chaos. Later, as an escaping POW, he is killed by German askaris who have misunderstood their commander's orders. In the novel's penultimate section, Gabriel's revenge-bent younger brother, Felix, tracks down the commander only to find that he has just died from influenza. Elsewhere, Felix and his brother-in-law are severely wounded in training botch-ups.

The action of the novel is witnessed through several centres of consciousness. The main ones—in addition to Gabriel and Felix—are (in Britain) Gabriel's wife, Charis, and (in Africa) an American planter, Temple Smith, whose martial activities are simply a means of continuing his quest to recover a prized farm machine confiscated by the Germans. *An Ice-Cream War* is easily Boyd's most substantial work, even if he rather overdoes the ironies and also perpetrates some false notes, notably the employment—decidedly old-hat—of a Scottish sergeant with an impenetrable accent.

The stories in *On the Yankee Station* do not represent Boyd at his best. Several might have been written for the glossy magazine market. The remainder feature some fine ideas, but they are developed perfunctorily and without the stylistic verve of the novels. "Next Boat from Douala" and "The Coup," however, are noteworthy for the presence of Morgan Leafy, while "Hardly Ever" deals with the public school world also explored in the screenplays of *School Ties.*

The New Confessions might be regarded as a forerunner of a type of self-examination, to be intensified in *Brazzaville Beach.* A fictitious, rumbustious "autobiography" of an outrageous Scotsman, John James Todd, presents a man, both "vile and contemptible" and "generous and selfless," with a self-deprecatory humour. Boyd's skill in sweeping rapidly through years and across continents matches a range of challenging situations that confront Todd, who eventually comes to terms with his life at age seventy.

Without any escape route of humour, *Brazzaville Beach* is the self-probing of Hope Clearwater, a woman trying to understand her life in England and Africa, burdened by incomprehensible tragic events. How much is she to blame, she asks? Firmly believing that "the unexamined life is not worth living," hers is one she insists has to be told honestly. The review is relayed in non-chronological episodes, between England, with the remembered life of her husband, his madness and suicide, and Africa, where she discovers that the chimpanzees she is to study are involved in a murderous war with each other. The novel operates as an allegory, for it is set within the Biafran war of 1963. Neither the death of her husband, the killings of the chimpanzees (some she was forced to shoot herself), or the human civil war could be avoided. Hope Clearwater's husband died because of a compulsive need to prove life by rigid mathematical formula, and his parallel figure in Africa nearly destroys Hope Clearwater because of his blindness to facts, which threaten to wreck a theory and his lifework. Simply being, Boyd argues, has rules, but they are not inflexible in a system that selects survivors. Hope's questioning, her "selections, willed and unwilled . . . of infinite alternatives and choices," resolve through flexible mathematics, as defined by Pascal. It does not matter if theories could be fully proved as long as they worked. "Intuition," Hope finally learns, rates "higher than vigorous proof."

—David Montrose, updated by Geoffrey Elborn

BOYLAN, Clare

Nationality: Irish. **Born:** Dublin, 1948. **Education:** Convent schools in Dublin. **Family:** Married Alan Wilkes in 1970. **Career:** editor, *Young Woman,* Dublin, 1969-71; staff feature writer, *Dublin Evening Press,* 1973-78; editor, *Image,* Dublin, 1981-84. Regular book reviewer and feature writer for *Sunday Times,* London, *Irish Times,* Dublin, *Evening Standard,* London, *New York Times, Los Angeles Times, The Guardian,* London, *Cosmopolitan, Vogue,* and *Good Housekeeping.* Lives in Kilbride, County Wicklow. **Awards:** Journalist of the Year award, 1973. **Agent:** Gill Coleridge, Rogers Coleridge and White Ltd., 20 Powis Mews, London W11 1JN, England.

PUBLICATIONS

Novels

Holy Pictures. London, Hamish Hamilton, and New York, Summit, 1983.
Last Resorts. London, Hamish Hamilton, 1984; New York, Summit, 1986.
Black Baby. London, Hamish Hamilton, 1988; New York, Doubleday, 1989.
Home Rule. London, Hamish Hamilton, 1993; as *11 Edward Street,* New York, Doubleday, 1994.

Short Stories

A Nail on the Head. London, Hamish Hamilton, 1983; New York, Penguin, 1985.
Concerning Virgins. London, Hamish Hamilton, 1989.
That Bad Woman. London, Little Brown, 1995.

Other

The Literary Companion to Cats. London, Sinclair Stevenson, 1994.

Editor, *The Agony and the God, Literary Essays.* London and New York, Penguin, 1994.

*

Clare Boylan comments:

My novels deal with the confrontative and revelatory nature of sexual relationships, the anarchy of innocence, and the difference between male and female morality. In my novels the random and exploitative nature of maternal love is a recurrent theme. Overall, there is the sense of a wonderful life in which the characters are not equipped to participate and the dark motifs are explored through humor and irony.

*   *   *

Clare Boylan chronicles the struggles of the personality under threat. Her novels and short stories describe the search of lonely individuals for love and freedom in a hostile environment, where acquiescence to its soul-destroying rules is tacitly assumed. Met by society's concerted pressures, her heroines' search is often vain, but sometimes one manages to find a chink in the world's armour, casting off the role that has been chosen for her.

In *Holy Pictures* it is the society of adults which dominates. To Nan and Mary, growing up in Dublin in 1925, the world of their elders is marked out by rules specifically designed to thwart the dreams and desires of the young, its unyielding rigidity typified by the old-fashioned corset produced by the workers in their father's factory. Nan, coming painfully and uncomprehendingly to adolescence in a strict convent school, is lured by the dream-world of the cinema with its promises of fame and beauty, finding a welcome glamour in the Jewish Schweitzer family, whose walls bear the cut-out pictures of the movie stars she worships at a distance. Inwardly Nan longs to escape from the drab, routine life which fate has allocated to her, glimpses of freedom coming to her in the brief moments of joy she finds, such as her dance as the fairy at a school concert: "She was a star, elevated as the lovely ladies of America who wore coatees of mink and ermine and walked on spirals of celestial stairs." Such dreams as she has, however—like Mary's money-making schemes—break down before the order of the adult world, met by a blind wall of indifference and rejection. Through the eyes of the teenage girls, Boylan reveals a grown-up universe appalling in its brutal, crass stupidity and pettiness, remarkable only for its ability to crush youthful ideals. To Nan and Mary, adulthood offers years of drudgery, and initiation into the more squalid activities of the human race. The author presents their rites of passage quietly, without sensationalism, deftly contrasting the innocence of her central characters against the flawed, often grotesque figures of their elders. Touches of humor lighten the story at times, notably with the comic servant Nellie and her amusing distortion of language. Such moments, however, only serve to emphasize the prevailing darkness of what is in essence a tragic work.

Holy Pictures is a skillfully achieved creation, Boylan's outwardly simple style concealing the depth of her insights. Visual imagery is subtly but continually used throughout the book—family photographs, pictures of film stars, the religious cards that give the novel its title and which Mary handles like talismans. Taken together, they provide a series of icons which serve as a focus for the dreams and longings of the characters. Unreal as the images themselves are, they are shown as calling out the purest qualities in those who worship them.

Last Resorts reverses the vision of *Holy Pictures,* its single-parent heroine dominated by her teenage children and their selfish needs. Foul-mouthed, crude, and unpleasant, the youngsters are exact counterparts of the adults in the previous novel, callously using their mother for their own convenience. Their tyranny is echoed by the brutal modernizing and milling tourists of a Greek island next to the one on which the family are holidaying. Harriet, the heroine of the book, is shown as essentially a conventional person who longs for the domesticity shorn from her by the desertion of her husband. "Contentment was more nourishing than joy. Being in love was not very peaceful." Snatching at happiness with a married lover who refuses to supply it, and thwarted when the needs of her children are compounded by the return of her husband and an additional set of demands, Harriet is forced to choose between the satisfaction of others and her own freedom. Boylan portrays her inner and outer struggles in a clear, restrained prose whose quietness occasionally startles the reader with a sharp, single-line image, as when Harriet visualizes the bare breasts of a woman as captive white rabbits. The reader comes to know the heroine gradually, encountering with her the monstrous dependence of her family, and the seeming reasonableness of their outrageous demands. Set in the present and in a more exotic location than *Holy Pictures, Last Resorts* nevertheless shows the exploration of a closely allied theme.

The stories of *A Nail on the Head* again pursue the search for love in all its forms. "The Wronged Woman" is a witty portrayal of the differing perceptions of a husband by his two wives, and in the generation clash of "Bad Natured Dog" the author displays considerable skill in showing the conflict of outward appearance and inner reality. The stories range from the frivolity of "Ears" to the bedroom tragedy of "Married," and the macabre atmosphere of "Mama" and "For Your Own Bad," both of which are peopled by grotesques akin to those of *Holy Pictures*. In each story the quiet, understated style stealthily creeps up on the reader, surprising and shocking by sudden twists of plot and startling revelations. Later writings display a continuing exploration of the novel and story forms, and with it a deepening psychological perception. *Black Baby* provides an unusual situation, where an African child formally adopted by a young Catholic girl years before, returns as an adult to seek out her now ageing "mother." The contrasting personalities of the large, assertive Dinah and the sad, withdrawn pensioner Alice, who at Dinah's prompting makes a late bid for her own independence, engage the interest and sympathy of the reader, although sadly the novel seems to fall away in its latter stages to an uncertain blurring of reality and dream. *Home Rule* returns to the familiar theme of a Dublin childhood in the 1890s, as experienced by Daisy Devlin and her siblings. Her struggle to escape from the grim city slums, out of the shadow of her ill-fated parents, only to fall in love with the handsome, feckless Cecil Cantwell, is movingly evoked. Boylan, as ever, blends humor and pathos with her own brand of atmospheric darkness. A similar quality is found in the stories of *Concerning Virgins,* where in a number of encounters various "innocents abroad" are forced into momentous decisions. The contents range from the wry wit of "Venice Saved," with its contrasting personal and cultural perceptions, to the nightmare adventures of two young girls in "The Picture House." Novels and stories alike show the same keen insights and a heightened, inspired use of language. Here, as elsewhere, Boylan avoids happy endings, her vision of life presented as a continuously absorbing, if unresolved, journey.

—Geoff Sadler

BOYLE, T. Coraghessan

Nationality: American. **Born:** 2 December 1948. **Education:** State University of New York, Potsdam, B.A. in English and history 1968; University of Iowa, Iowa City, M.F.A. in fiction 1974, Ph.D. in British literature 1977. **Family:** Married Karen Kvashay; one daughter and two sons. **Career:** Assistant professor, 1978-82, associate professor, 1982-86, and since 1986 professor of English, University of Southern California, Los Angeles. **Awards:** Coordinating Council of Literary Magazines award, 1977, for fiction; National Endowment for the Arts grant, St. Lawrence award, 1980, for *Descent of Man; Paris Review*'s Aga Khan prize, 1981, for fiction; *Paris Review,* John Train prize, 1984, for humor; Commonwealth Club of California, silver medal award, 1986, for *Greasy Lake,* gold medal, 1988, for *World's End;* Guggenheim fellowship,

1988; PEN/Faulkner Novel of the Year award, 1988, for *World's End;* O'Henry award, 1988, for "Sinking House," 1989, for "The Ape Lady in Retirement;" Prix Passion novel of the year, 1989, for *Water Music;* National Academy of Arts and Letters Howard D. Vursell memorial award, 1993, for prose excellence. D.H.L.: State University of New York, 1991. **Member:** Literature panel, National Endowment for the Arts, 1986-87. **Agent:** Georges Borchardt, 136 East 57th Street, New York, New York 10022, U.S.A.

PUBLICATIONS

Novels

Water Music. Boston, Little Brown, 1982; London, Gollancz, 1982.
Budding Prospects: A Pastoral. New York, Viking, and London, Gollancz, 1984.
World's End. New York, Viking, 1987; London, Macmillan, 1988.
East Is East. New York, Viking, 1990; London, Cape, 1991.
The Road to Wellville. New York, Viking, and London, Granta, 1993.
The Tortilla Curtain. New York, Viking, 1995.

Short Stories

The Descent of Man. Boston, Little Brown, 1979; London, Gollancz, 1980.
Greasy Lake and Other Stories. New York and Harmondsworth, Viking, 1985.
If the River Was Whiskey. New York, Viking, 1989.
The Collected Stories of T. Coraghessan Boyle. London, Granta, 1993.
Without a Hero. New York, Viking, and London, Granta, 1994.

*

Film Adaptations: *The Road to Wellville,* 1994.

*   *   *

A fictionist who delights in equal measures of the irreverent and the satiric, the ironical twist and the serious meditation, T. Coraghessan Boyle has been linked with writers such as Thomas Pychon and John Barth. What more accurately defines the arc of Boyle's career, however, is his persistent juggling of the mundane and the surreal. The result is not only stories filled with surprises; they are also balanced adroitly between the dazzle of invention and the systematic undercutting of the ordinary.

Boyle's earliest stories gave hints of longer, more ambitious novels to come. For example, "Heart of the Champion" (l975), focuses on popular TV canine/icon Lassie and her love affair with a sex-starved coyote; "A Women's Restaurant" concerns itself with a male protagonist's obsession with a women-only eatery. Seventeen of Boyle's stories from this period were collected in *The Descent of Man,* the title derived from a story about a woman's liaison with a chimpanzee who dotes on Nietzsche.

Water Music, his first novel, cobbles Mungo Park, the Scottish explorer, with a fictional counterpart named Red Rise. Their comic adventures in Africa are both informed by Park's actual expeditions of l795 and l805 and given a comic dimension by Rise's exploits as an irrepressible con man. What intrigued most critics, however, was the sheer verbal energy of Boyle's polysyllabic style. Here, in short, was a young, go-for-broke writer to reckon with.

Budding Prospects confirmed the suspicions that Boyle is a comic novelist potentially of the first rank. Felix Nasmyth, the novel's laconic protagonist, is a disillusioned teacher who finds himself entangled in a scheme to grow marijuana, and thus grow rich. For Nasmyth, the prospect of untold riches dances around his head like sugarplum fairies. The rub, alas, is that Nasmyth has a long track record as a quitter:

> I've always been a quitter. I quit the boy scouts, the glee club, the marching band. Gave up my paper route, turned my back on the church, stuffed the basketball team . . . I got married, separated, divorced. Quit smoking, quit jogging, quit eating red meat.

Ironically enough, the dope farm teaches the disillusioned teacher the lesson of hard work; and even when one of his associates, a fast-talking former CIA agent, skips off with the profits, it really doesn't matter. The money that had mattered so greatly at the beginning is no longer the center of Nasmyth's new, improved life.

Although Boyle continues to publish collections of short fiction (*Greasy Lake and Other Stories, If the River Was Whiskey,* and *Without a Hero*), the formula of bizarre action superimposed on seemingly normal settings has grown both predictable and limited. There is little doubt that Boyle has a way with the one-liner, much less that his short stories make for an engaging read. But, added together, they lack the heft one expects from a writer of his talent.

With *World's End,* however, the larger, more expansive canvas of the novel brought him the wide critical regard he apparently craves. Set in the Hudson River Valley of New York, *World's End* tells the interlocking tale of three families over ten generations. In a series of collisions, simultaneously literal and figurative, the past meets the present and historical mistakes are reenacted once again. An inescapable destiny thus shapes Boyle's most ambitious and aesthetically accomplished novel thus far. By contrast, *The Road to Wellville* has its comic way with an easier target: the health-food sanitarium run by cereal king John Harvey Kellogg. The high jinks that went on in Battle Creek, Michigan, during the early l900s become an extended analogy for present-day food fads. Flimflammers are, of course, an abiding subject in American humor, and *The Road to Wellville* is a worthy enough contribution to that tradition. One turns its pages laughing, which is more than one can say of the novel's film version.

Boyle has yet to settle down as a serious writer, but those who keep their eye on contemporary American literature's best prospects know his name and look forward to his next books with anticipation.

—Sanford Pinsker

————

BRADBURY, Edward P. *See* **MOORCOCK, Michael.**

————

BRADBURY, Malcolm (Stanley)

Nationality: British. **Born:** Sheffield, Yorkshire, 7 September 1932. **Education:** West Bridgford Grammar School, Nottingham, 1943-50; University College, Leicester, 1950-53, B.A. in English (1st class honours) 1953; Queen Mary College, University of London (research scholar), 1953-55, M.A. in English 1955; Indiana University, Bloomington (English-Speaking Union fellow), 1955-56; University of Manchester, 1956-58, Ph.D. in American Studies 1962; Yale University, New Haven, Connecticut (British Association for American Studies fellow), 1958-59. **Family:** Married Elizabeth Salt in 1959; two sons. **Career:** staff tutor in literature and drama, Department of Adult Education, University of Hull, Yorkshire, 1959-61; lecturer in English, University of Birmingham, 1961-65. Lecturer, 1957-67, senior lecturer, 1967-69, reader in English, 1969-70, professor of American studies, 1970-95, and since 1995 professor emeritus, University of East Anglia, Norwich. Visiting professor, University of California, Davis, 1966; visiting fellow, All Souls College, Oxford, 1969; visiting professor, University of Zurich, 1972; Fanny Hurst Professor, Washington University, St. Louis, 1982; Davis Professor, University of Queensland, Brisbane; and visiting professor, Griffith University, Nathan, Queensland, 1983, University of Birmingham, 1989, University of Hull, 1994. Series editor, Stratford-upon-Avon Studies, for Arnold publishers, London, 1971-84, and Contemporary Writers series for Methuen publishers, London. **Awards:** American Council of Learned Societies fellowship, 1965; Royal Society of Literature Heinemann award, 1976; Rockefeller fellowship, 1987; Emmy award, for television series, 1988; Monte Carlo Television Festival award, 1991. D.Litt.: University of Leicester, 1986; University of Birmingham, 1989; University of Hull, 1994. Fellow, Royal Society of Literature, 1973; Honorary Fellow, Queen Mary College, 1984. C.B.E. (Commander, Order of the British Empire), 1991. **Agent:** Curtis Brown, 4th Floor, Haymarket House, Haymarket, London SW1Y 4SP, England; or, 10 Astor Place, New York, New York 10003, U.S.A. **Address:** School of English and American Studies, University of East Anglia, Norwich, Norfolk NR4 7TJ, England.

PUBLICATIONS

Novels

Eating People Is Wrong. London, Secker and Warburg, 1959; New York, Knopf, 1960.
Stepping Westward. London, Secker and Warburg, 1965; Boston, Houghton Mifflin, 1966.
The History Man. London, Secker and Warburg, 1975; Boston, Houghton Mifflin, 1976.
Rates of Exchange. London, Secker and Warburg, and New York, Knopf, 1983.
Cuts: A Very Short Novel. London, Hutchinson, and New York, Harper, 1987.
Doctor Criminale. London, Secker and Warburg, and New York, Viking Penguin, 1993.

Short Stories

Who Do You Think You Are? Stories and Parodies. London, Secker and Warburg, 1976; augmented edition, London, Arena, 1984.

Plays

Between These Four Walls (revue), with David Lodge and James Duckett (produced Birmingham, 1963).

Slap in the Middle (revue), with others (produced Birmingham, 1965).

The After Dinner Game, with Christopher Bigsby (televised 1975). Included in *The After Dinner Game,* 1982.

Love on a Gunboat (televised 1977). Included in *The After Dinner Game,* 1982.

Standing In for Henry (televised 1980). Included in *The After Dinner Game,* 1982.

The Enigma, from the story by John Fowles (televised 1980). Included in *The After Dinner Game,* revised edition, 1989.

The After Dinner Game: Three Plays for Television. London, Arrow, 1982; revised edition (includes *The Enigma*), London, Arena, 1989.

Radio Plays: *Paris France* (documentary), 1960; *This Sporting Life,* with Elizabeth Bradbury, from the novel by David Storey, 1974; *Scenes from Provincial Life* and *Scenes from Married Life,* with Elizabeth Bradbury, from the novels by William Cooper, 1975-76; *Patterson,* with Christopher Bigsby, 1981; *Congress,* 1981; *See a Friend This Weekend,* 1985.

Television Plays: *The After Dinner Game,* with Christopher Bigsby, 1975; *Stones* (*The Mind Beyond* series), with Christopher Bigsby, 1976; *Love on a Gunboat,* 1977; *The Enigma,* from the story by John Fowles, 1980; *Standing In for Henry,* 1980; *Blott on the Landscape* series, from the novel by Tom Sharpe, 1985; *Porterhouse Blue* series, from the novel by Tom Sharpe, 1987; *Imaginary Friends* series, from the novel by Alison Lurie, 1987; *Anything More Would Be Greedy* series, 1989; *The Gravy Train* series, 1990; *The Green Man* series, from the novel by Kingsley Amis, 1990; *The Gravy Train Goes East* series, 1992; *Cold Comfort Farm,* from the novel by Stella Gibbons, 1995.

Poetry

Two Poets, with Allan Rodway. Nottingham, Byron Press, 1966.

Other

Phogey! How to Have Class in a Classless Society. London, Parrish, 1960.

All Dressed Up and Nowhere to Go: The Poor Man's Guide to the Affluent Society. London, Parrish, 1962.

Evelyn Waugh. Edinburgh, Oliver and Boyd, 1964.

What Is a Novel? London, Arnold, 1969.

The Social Context of Modern English Literature. Oxford, Blackwell, and New York, Schocken, 1971.

Possibilities: Essays on the State of the Novel. London, Oxford University Press, 1973.

The Outland Dart: American Writers and European Modernism (lecture). London, Oxford University Press, 1978.

All Dressed Up and Nowhere to Go (revised editions). London, Pavilion-Joseph, 1982.

The Expatriate Tradition in American Literature. Durham, British Association for American Studies, 1982.

Saul Bellow. London, Methuen, 1983.

The Modern American Novel. Oxford and New York, Oxford University Press, 1983; revised edition, 1991.

Why Come to Slaka? London, Secker and Warburg, 1986; New York, Penguin, 1988.

My Strange Quest for Mensonge: Structuralism's Hidden Hero. London, Deutsch, 1987; New York, Penguin, 1988.

No, Not Bloomsbury (essays). London, Deutsch, 1987; New York, Columbia University Press, 1988.

The Modern World: Ten Great Writers. London, Secker and Warburg, 1988; New York, Viking, 1989.

Unsent Letters: Irreverent Notes from a Literary Life. London, Deutsch, and New York, Viking, 1988.

From Puritanism to Postmodernism: The Story of American Literature, with Richard Ruland. London, Routledge, 1991.

The Modern British Novel. London, Secker and Warburg, 1994.

Dangerous Pilgrimages: Transatlantic Mythologies and the Novel. London, Secker and Warburg, 1995.

Editor, *Forster: A Collection of Critical Essays.* Englewood Cliffs, New Jersey, Prentice Hall, 1966.

Editor, *Pudd'nhead Wilson, and Those Extraordinary Twins,* by Mark Twain. London, Penguin, 1969.

Editor, *E.M. Forster: A Passage to India: A Casebook.* London, Macmillan, 1970.

Editor, with Eric Mottram, *U.S.A.,* in *The Penguin Companion to Literature 3.* London, Penguin, and New York, McGraw Hill, 1971.

Editor, with James McFarlane, *Modernism 1890-1930.* London, Penguin, 1976; Atlantic Highlands, New Jersey, Humanities Press, 1978.

Editor, *The Novel Today: Contemporary Writers on Modern Fiction.* Manchester, Manchester University Press, and Totowa, New Jersey, Rowman and Littlefield, 1977; revised edition, London, Fontana, 1990.

Editor, with Howard Temperley, *Introduction to American Studies.* London, Longman, 1981; revised edition, 1989.

Editor, *The Red Badge of Courage,* by Stephen Crane. London, Dent, 1983.

Editor, *The Penguin Book of Modern British Short Stories.* London, Viking, 1987; New York, Viking, 1988.

Editor, with others, *Unthank: An Anthology of Short Stories from the M.A. in Creative Writing at the University of East Anglia.* Norwich, University of East Anglia Centre for Creative and Performing Arts, 1989.

Editor, *The Sketch Book of Geoffrey Crayon, Gent,* by Washington Irving. London, Dent/Everyman, 1993.

Editor, *The Blithedale Romance,* by Nathaniel Hawthorne. London, Dent/Everyman, 1993.

Editor, *Present Laughter: An Anthology of Modern Comic Short Stories.* London, Weidenfeld and Nicolson, 1994.

Editor, *The Marble Faun,* by Nathaniel Hawthorne. London, Dent/Everyman, 1995.

Editor, *Class Work: An Anthology of 25 Years of Creative Writing at UEA.* London, Hodder and Stoughton, 1995.

*

Critical Studies: "Fictions of Academe" by George Watson, in *Encounter* (London), November 1978; "Images of Sociology and Sociologists in Fiction" by John Kramer, in *Contemporary Sociology* (Washington, D.C.), May 1979; "The Business of University Novels" by J.P. Kenyon, in *Encounter* (London), June 1980; "Malcolm Bradbury's *The History Man:* The Novelist as Reluctant Impresario" by Richard Todd, and interview with Todd, in *Dutch Quarterly Review* (Amsterdam), vol. 2, 1981-83; interviews in *The Radical Imagination and the Liberal Tradition* edited by Heide Ziegler and Christopher Bigsby, London, Junction, 1982, with Ronald Hayman, in *Books and Bookmen* (London), April 1983, with Alastair Morgan, in *Literary Review* (London), October 1983, and in *Novelists in Interview* by John Haffenden, London, Methuen, 1985; article by Melvin J. Friedman, in *British Novelists since 1960* edited by Jay L. Halio, Detroit, Gale, 1983; *The Dialogic Novels of Malcolm Bradbury and David Lodge* by Robert A. Morace, Carbondale, Southern Illinois University Press, 1989; article by Richard Todd, in *Post-War Literatures in English: A Lexicon of Contemporary Authors,* Bouhn Stafleu, Holland, 1994.

Malcolm Bradbury comments:

I suppose my fiction—six novels and a volume of short stories, as well as many television scripts and film screenplays, and three "television novels"—roughly follows the pattern, the styles and cultural and moral concerns, that have run through British fiction over the now five decades over which I've been writing. I began writing fiction in the 1950s when, in the period after the defeat of fascism, and in the aftermath of the Holocaust and the nuclear bomb, the novel in Britain moved back toward social and moral realism. In the wake of those events, there was also a strong concern with the problems affecting liberal and humanistic values. In fact if my books do possess one consistent theme (I believe they do), then that is their concern with the problems of liberalism, humanism, and general moral responsibility in the late 20th-century world.

In my earlier novels (*Eating People Is Wrong, Stepping Westward*), the central characters are concerned if confused moral agents, liberals not in the political but the moral sense, trying to do a reasonable amount of good in a difficult world, generally with comic, ironic or near-tragic results. I wrote *Eating People is Wrong* when I was 20 and was a university undergraduate, fascinated by the liberal universe of academic life, a place of often confused humanism and idealistic goodwill. I revised it a little later to make it more a retrospective general portrait of intellectual life in the British 1950s. With *Stepping Westward,* the result of several years in American universities as a graduate student, and about an American campus in the troubled years of anti-liberal sentiment that came from the witch-hunting of Senator McCarthy, I became interested in the different transatlantic meanings of liberalism, and I also began to explore my sense that humanism was in conflict with the hard realities of cold war politics and also with an age of materialist obsessions, self-seeking, and desire.

That theme is treated with a far harsher irony in *The History Man,* set in British academic life in the aftermath of the student revolutions of 1968. Its central character, Howard Kirk, is a radical sociologist who believes he is the spokesperson of a Marxist revolutionary process—history itself—that will still sweep away everything in its path; he tries to seduce his students and his colleagues into his bed and into the radical future. It is an ironic and a somewhat dark novel, as its liberal characters become incompetent in the face of inhumane theory and ideology. My next novel, *Rates of Exchange,* written at the beginning of the 1980s, is somewhat more hopeful. Dealing with various visits to Eastern European countries and my feeling that the rigid grid of the Marxist state was being increasingly undermined by the playfulness of language and the enduring power of the human imagination, it is set in an imaginary Eastern European state, Slaka, which is undergoing a language revolution. Its central character is a magical realist novelist, Katya

Princip, who uses fiction to break free of ideology—and who in a later incarnation (see further on) becomes president of the country after it finally throws off its Stalinism. Like a number of British novelists I had also by now become fascinated by the opportunities of television drama in Britain. My next book, *Cuts: A Very Short Novel,* deals with this. A comedy about the making of what proves an abortive television series in the monetarist years of Mrs Thatcher's 1980s, it is about cuts in two senses: the cuts to British services that happened in the New Conservative 1980s, and the filmic technique of cutting.

Since some of these books are set in or around universities, I have often been thought of as a "campus novelist," and described as a progenitor of what is now called "the university novel." This is true to a point: I was a first-generation university student fascinated by the strangeness of the academic and intellectual world, and so made it fictional country. I have also spent most of my adult life teaching in universities in a number of countries; I am a professor of American studies and a teacher of creative writing, though now part-time; I have written a good deal of literary criticism, and been influenced by it. So my first book is set in a British redbrick in the 1950s, when it was a place of social change; my second is set on American campus near the Rockies at the start of the 1960s when it seemed a place of liberation, my third is set in a British new university as the 1960s died and the 1970s began, and radical hopes were beginning to be replaced by hard economic realities. I see them more as books about their decades, their themes, ideas, emotions, hypocrisies, intellectual fashions, and preoccupations; a university environment means that I can write about historically self-conscious and self-critical characters, the types who most interest me. I most see myself as a comic novelist, mixing satirical and ironic social and intellectual observation with play and parody. If I started writing in a time when the British novel was both thematically and technically provincial, I have tried to break out of that and become a more cosmopolitan, international, and technically elaborate writer. In *Rates of Exchange,* for example, I sought to find not only a larger subject matter, the question of what ideology we seek to live by in the late 20th century, but also a different language; in fact much of the novel exploits the technique of using English spoken by non-native speakers as its tone of voice.

My books have thus changed considerably over the years (and will continue to do so), but so has British fiction, which during the later 1960s and 1970s grew far more cosmopolitan and technically varied. As writer and critic, I have been very interested in postmodern experiment and found many of my more recent influences abroad. From *The History Man* onward, my books became harsher in tone, more elaborate technically, and they challenge some of the traditional ideas of character, realism of presentation, and moral confidence with which British novels have so often been written. *Rates of Exchange* thus deals with the problem of the British writer who uses a language deeply changed by its modern role as a lingua franca, and a world where stories become less reassuring and more ambiguous. This probably makes some of my later works rather more ironic, parodic, and less companionable, though I also think it makes them better. During the 1980s, for various reasons, I also found myself using the form of what I think of as the "television novel," that is, novel-like forms and ideas written and produced as television series. I liked television's immediacy, its rich techniques, its fast narrative pace. *Anything More Would Be Greedy,* a six-part series for Anglia Television, is about a group of students growing older, richer, and ever more cynical in Mrs Thatcher's entrepreneurial Britain; while *The Gravy Train* and *The*

Gravy Train: The Economic Miracle (forthcoming) are both four-part drama series for Channel 4, dealing ironically with the European Community as it reaches toward the great late 20th century dream of European integration. The second series is once again about Slaka, after the fall of the Berlin Wall, and its attempts under President Katya Princip to join the mysterious entity of "Europe."

So my concerns and interests have widened. My sixth novel, *Doctor Criminale,* is a comedy about a tainted philosopher who has been a powerful intellectual influence during the Cold War period, and is now being seen as the philosopher of the Nineties. It's my attempt to deal with the great transformation that came with the end of the 45-year Cold War era, and to capture the climate as the new century, indeed a new millennium, approaches. I have continued to write regularly in a wide variety of media—books, television, film, and radio—and both in fiction and non-fiction, especially literary criticism and, increasingly, journalism. Having now retired from university teaching—mostly recently the teaching of creative writing—and working as a full-time writer, I am, though, returning ever more refreshed to the novel. I still think of it as my primary and essential form—an ever-changing form that inevitably alters a good deal in history for any writer who isn't chiefly concerned with perpetuating the popular genres or simply providing entertainment.

I view my books as works of comic and satirical observation, which amongst other things explore both the decades in which they're set, and the changing moods and modes of fiction. Socially they explore the moral 1950s, the radical 1960s, the cautious 1970s, the entrepreneurial 1980s, and now the nervous and increasingly cynical 1990s. In form they shift from moral comedy to harder irony, where the comic more nearly touches the tragic. I stay fascinated by fiction's fictionality, and regard all our forms of exploring knowledge as forms of fiction-making, which is one reason why I regard the novel as central. Since it acknowledges its fictionality, and often explores its own method and declares its own scepticism, it stays at best one of our chief ways of discovering and naming the world. At the same time it depends on a sense of truth, a feeling for reality, a response to the authentic experience of individual humanity. And, if my books are satirical explorations of current confusion, pain, and inauthenticity, they hardly (as some critics have said) betoken the end of humanism. In fact the novel belongs with the spirit of "liberalism," in the better sense of that word: the challenging of ideologies, intellectual fashions and inhuman systems or theories through sympathy and the imagination. Which is why I think the novel is always under challenge, but is far from dead.

*   *   *

Ever since the 1959 publication of his first novel, *Eating People Is Wrong,* Malcolm Bradbury has been regarded as an extremely witty satirist, lampooning topical phenomena and issues. He excels in group scenes: the cautiously wild and slap-stick university party that mixes faculty and students in *Eating People Is Wrong;* the American faculty committee meeting to choose a writer-in-residence that begins *Stepping Westward* and is ironically contrasted with the concluding one a year later; the department meeting that combines haggling over procedure, trivia, several forms of self-seeking, and genuine academic concerns in *The History Man;* the adult education class that was apparently cut from *Eating People Is Wrong* and, in revised form, printed in the collection of *Who Do You Think You Are?;* the guest lectures of and alcoholic lunches for the En-

glish linguist on a two-week tour of the country in "central Eastern Europe" that prides itself on "clean tractors" and a "reformed watercress industry" in *Rates of Exchange.* All these pieces bring people, representing various points of view on some current question of politics or communal definition, into sharp, comically outrageous conflict or misunderstanding.

Bradbury often castigates a whole contemporary milieu through scenes like the "with-it," consciously "existential" party, a license for free self-definition, arranged by the "new university" sociologist, Howard Kirk, in *The History Man.* Bradbury also exploits his talent for mimicry of current attitudes, modes of speech (like the variety of ways to mangle English in *Rates of Exchange*), and the style and themes of other writers. A long section of *Who Do You Think You Are?,* for example, contains astringent parodies of Snow, Amis, Murdoch, Braine, Sillitoe, and others, along with less biting and salient echoes of Angus Wilson and Lawrence Durrell. The use of Amis (with whose early work Bradbury's has often been compared) is particularly resonant. Like Amis, Bradbury sometimes includes characters from one fiction in another, like the free-loving psychologist, Flora Beniform, who is both Howard Kirk's uncommitted mistress in *The History Man* and a central character on the television panel concerning modern sexual mores satirized in the story "Who Do You Think You Are?" As an in-joke, Bradbury even appropriates the Amis character who doesn't appear, the fraudulent L.S. Caton used in a number of novels until Amis finally killed him off in *The Anti-Death League.* Bradbury makes him a professor, scheduled to visit Benedict Arnold University in the U.S. to give a lecture on the "angry young men," who never arrives. In spite of all the critical comparisons and interlocking references, Bradbury's satire is different from Amis's, Bradbury generally more concerned with issues and ideas, less implicitly committed to pragmatic success in the world or, until the recent *Rates of Exchange,* to mocking various forms of contemporary incompetence.

Much of Bradbury's fiction takes place within a university setting: the provincial red-brick during the 1950s in *Eating People Is Wrong,* the American university in the flat wilderness of the Plains states in *Stepping Westward,* the new south coast university in 1972 in *The History Man.* Yet, as Bradbury himself has rightly insisted, the applications of his fiction extend beyond the university, just as the implications of his moral treatments of contemporary experience are far from slapstick comedy. In *Stepping Westward* the Englishman, James Walker, who becomes writer-in-residence at the "moral supermarket" of the American university, begins with his own "decent modest radicalism" and tries to extend himself to assimilate more of the modern world, looking for "sense and design." The plot depends on Walker's public refusal to sign an American loyalty oath, part of his English "faith in unbelief," and the America he finds is one of "violence and meaninglessness and anarchy." In *The History Man* Howard Kirk, seen far less sympathetically than James Walker is, seeks "liberation" and "emancipation" in the new university for himself and others, ignoring or condescending to his old friend, Beamish, a rather bumbling locus of value in the novel, who claims "there is an inheritance of worthwhile life in this country." In this novel, written entirely in the rush of the present tense, Kirk chooses instead to redevelop the town, to lie, to manipulate others in the name of the "now" and the "new," and to ignore the voice of a young English teacher who sees her function as simply reading and talking about books. In both novels Bradbury's moral focus is clear and searching, although it sometimes seems slightly provincial. He attacks the self-seeking, the self-deceptive, and the meretricious, like a career academic named Froelich who becomes chairman in *Stepping Westward* and Kirk himself in *The History Man.* Yet some of Bradbury's work has more complexity and distance than outlining the moral framework might suggest. Sometimes, as in *The History Man,* which ends with Kirk's wife deliberately pushing her arm through the window, an act of self-destruction like that more ambivalently performed by Beamish at an earlier party, or in a short story entitled "A Very Hospitable Person," the satire seems brittle, almost cruel, in denying the central figures any humanity or self-doubt. At other times, as in an excellent story called "A Breakdown," about a student having a futile affair with a married man in Chesterfield who runs off to Spain to punish herself, or as in *Stepping Westward,* where James Walker recognizes that America has defeated him, that, in spite of all his morality, he could not really handle his own freedom to define himself, Bradbury's perspective is more sympathetic without diluting the moral concern. A prefatory note to *Rates of Exchange* characterizes the novel as "a paper fiction, offered for exchange" that illustrates "our duty to lie together, in the cause, of course, of truth." Beneath its comic texture of constant mutual misunderstanding and incompetence (sometimes overdone), Bradbury sensitively questions the comfortable assumption of virtue or truth in any of the various national, political, intellectual, or sexual languages that form systems of human exchange.

Bradbury's commitment to liberal humanism has always been tempered by a willingness to test its continuing viability against various cultural, political, and economic challenges. And nowhere is that willingness more clearly evident than in *Doctor Criminale.* This witty fiction about fashionable literary theory, as well as the fashion for literary theory, is also, appropriately enough, Bradbury's most self-consciously intertextual novel to date, drawing on an impressive array of literary precedents which include his own *Rates of Exchange, Cuts,* and two Gravytrain television series as well as his friend David Lodge's *Small World,* an updating of the campus novel for an age of the global campus. But in many respects the work *Doctor Criminale* draws on most is F. Scott Fitzgerald's "symbolist tragedy," *The Great Gatsby,* "about the struggle of the symbolic imagination to exist in lowered historical time, and about that symbol's inherent ambiguity, its wonder and its meretriciousness," as Bradbury wrote in *The Modern American Novel.*

Doctor Criminale is, of course, a comedy, not a tragedy, and its subject is theory's, not the symbol's, essential ambiguity. Bradbury's Nick Carraway is the hapless, anachronistlc Francis Jay, a verbal man and naive liberal humanist adrift in the visual culture of entrepreneurial England. And his Gatsby is a man no less able to inspire wonder in his admirers, the supercritic and celebrity thinker Bazlo Criminale. Criminale, the "text" Jay sets out to decode, proves a most elusive quarry. As mysterious as Eliot's famous MacCavity the Cat, he seems less a person than a floating signifier who exists largely as a collection of mutually exlusive interpretations, or signifieds. He is alternately a philosopher who has declared the end of philosophy and a master mystifier pulling books and articles out of his theoretical hat, perhaps a spy, though maybe a double agent, an ardent Communist or, what is just as likely, an ardent anti-Communist. Above all he is a version of the late Yale deconstructionist, Paul de Man, who posthumously became the subject of intense controversy following the discovery of articles he had written during the Nazi occupation. Like de Man, Criminale seems to be a man at best "flexible" and at worst "a moral disappointment." Bradbury's jokey magical mystery tour of the political, economic, and literary landscape at the end of the Cold War and on

the eve of the European Community, thus, does more than just delight; it also "problematizes" both fashionable theory and old-fashioned liberal humanism by having each "interrogate" the other. However, *Doctor Criminale* does more than illuminate their relative strengths and weaknesses; in examining theory in a specific historical context, Bradbury also examines many of the defining features of the culture in which theory has been so ardently promoted and just as strenuously resisted.

—James Gindin, updated by Robert A. Morace

BRADBURY, Ray(mond Douglas)

Nationality: American. **Born:** Waukegan, Illinois, 22 August 1920. **Education:** Los Angeles High School, graduated 1938. **Family:** Married Marguerite Susan McClure in 1947; four daughters. **Career:** Since 1943 full-time writer. President, Science-Fantasy Writers of America, 1951-53. Member of the Board of Directors, Screen Writers Guild of America, 1957-61. Lives in Los Angeles. **Awards:** O. Henry prize, 1947, 1948; Benjamin Franklin award, 1954; American Academy award, 1954; Boys' Clubs of America Junior Book award, 1956; Golden Eagle award, for screenplay, 1957; Ann Radcliffe award, 1965, 1971; Writers Guild award, 1974; Aviation and Space Writers award, for television documentary, 1979; Gandalf award, 1980. D.Litt.: Whittier College, California, 1979. **Agent:** Harold Matson Company, 276 Fifth Avenue, New York, New York 10001. **Address:** c/o Bantam, 666 Fifth Avenue, New York, New York 10103, U.S.A.

PUBLICATIONS

Novels

Fahrenheit 451. New York, Ballantine, 1953; London, Hart Davis, 1954.
Something Wicked This Way Comes. New York, Simon and Schuster, 1962; London, Hart Davis, 1963.
Death Is a Lonely Business. New York, Knopf, 1985; London, Grafton, 1986.
A Graveyard for Lunatics: Another Tale of Two Cities. New York, Knopf, and London, Grafton, 1990.
The Smile. Mankato, Minnesota, Creative Education, 1991.
Green Shadows, White Whale. New York, Knopf, and London, HarperCollins, 1992.

Short Stories

Dark Carnival. Sauk City, Wisconsin, Arkham House, 1947; abridged edition, London, Hamish Hamilton, 1948; abridged edition, as *The Small Assassin,* London, New English Library, 1962.
The Martian Chronicles. New York, Doubleday, 1950; as *The Silver Locusts,* London, Hart Davis, 1951.
The Illustrated Man. New York, Doubleday, 1951; London, Hart Davis, 1952.
The Golden Apples of the Sun. New York, Doubleday, and London, Hart Davis, 1953.

The October Country. New York, Ballantine, 1955; London, Hart Davis, 1956.

Dandelion Wine. New York, Doubleday, and London, Hart Davis, 1957.

A Medicine for Melancholy. New York, Doubleday, 1959.

The Day It Rained Forever. London, Hart Davis, 1959.

The Machineries of Joy. New York, Simon and Schuster, and London, Hart Davis, 1964.

The Vintage Bradbury. New York, Random House, 1965.

The Autumn People. New York, Ballantine, 1965.

Tomorrow Midnight. New York, Ballantine, 1966.

Twice Twenty Two (selection). New York, Doubleday, 1966.

I Sing the Body Electric! New York, Knopf, 1969; London, Hart Davis, 1970.

Bloch and Bradbury, with Robert Bloch. New York, Tower, 1969; as *Fever Dreams and Other Fantasies,* London, Sphere, 1970.

(Selected Stories), edited by Anthony Adams. London, Harrap, 1975.

Long after Midnight. New York, Knopf, 1976; London, Hart Davis MacGibbon, 1977.

The Best of Bradbury. New York, Bantam, 1976.

To Sing Strange Songs. Exeter, Devon, Wheaton, 1979.

The Stories of Ray Bradbury. New York, Knopf, and London, Granada, 1980.

The Last Circus, and The Electrocution. Northridge, California, Lord John Press, 1980.

Dinosaur Tales. New York, Bantam, 1983.

A Memory of Murder. New York, Dell, 1984.

The Toynbee Convector. New York, Knopf, 1988; London, Grafton, 1989.

Plays

The Meadow, in *Best One-Act Plays of 1947-48,* edited by Margaret Mayorga. New York, Dodd Mead, 1948.

The Anthem Sprinters and Other Antics (produced Los Angeles, 1968). New York, Dial Press, 1963.

The World of Ray Bradbury (produced Los Angeles, 1964; New York, 1965).

The Wonderful Ice-Cream Suit (produced Los Angeles, 1965; New York, 1987; musical version, music by Jose Feliciano, produced Pasadena, California, 1990). Included in *The Wonderful Ice-Cream Suit and Other Plays,* 1972.

The Day It Rained Forever, music by Bill Whitefield (produced Edinburgh, 1988). New York, French, 1966.

The Pedestrian. New York, French, 1966.

Christus Apollo, music by Jerry Goldsmith (produced Los Angeles, 1969).

The Wonderful Ice-Cream Suit and Other Plays (includes *The Veldt* and *To the Chicago Abyss*). New York, Bantam, 1972; London, Hart Davis, 1973.

The Veldt (produced London, 1980). Included in *The Wonderful Ice-Cream Suit and Other Plays,* 1972.

Leviathan 99 (produced Los Angeles, 1972).

Pillar of Fire and Other Plays for Today, Tomorrow, and Beyond Tomorrow (includes *Kaleidoscope* and *The Foghorn*). New York, Bantam, 1975.

The Foghorn (produced New York, 1977). Included in *Pillar of Fire and Other Plays,* 1975.

That Ghost, That Bride of Time: Excerpts from a Play-in-Progress. Glendale, California, Squires, 1976.

The Martian Chronicles, adaptation of his own stories (produced Los Angeles, 1977).

Fahrenheit 451, adaptation of his own novel (produced Los Angeles, 1979).

Dandelion Wine, adaptation of his own story (produced Los Angeles, 1980).

Forever and the Earth (radio play). Athens, Ohio, Croissant, 1984.

On Stage: A Chrestomathy of His Plays. New York, Primus, 1991.

Screenplays: *It Came from Outer Space,* with David Schwartz, 1952; *Moby-Dick,* with John Huston, 1956; *Icarus Montgolfier Wright,* with George C. Johnston, 1961; *Picasso Summer* (as Douglas Spaulding), with Edwin Booth, 1972.

Television Plays: *Shopping for Death,* 1956, *Design for Loving,* 1958, *Special Delivery,* 1959, *The Faith of Aaron Menefee,* 1962, and *The Life Work of Juan Diaz,* 1963 (all *Alfred Hitchcock Presents* series); *The Marked Bullet* (*Jane Wyman's Fireside Theater* series), 1956; *The Gift* (*Steve Canyon* series), 1958; *The Tunnel to Yesterday* (*Trouble Shooters* series), 1960; *I Sing the Body Electric!* (*Twilight Zone* series), 1962; *The Jail* (*Alcoa Premier* series), 1962; *The Groom* (*Curiosity Shop* series), 1971; *The Coffin,* from his own short story, 1988 (U.K.).

Poetry

Old Ahab's Friend, and Friend to Noah, Speaks His Piece: A Celebration. Glendale, California, Squires, 1971.

When Elephants Last in the Dooryard Bloomed: Celebrations for Almost Any Day in the Year. New York, Knopf, 1973; London, Hart Davis MacGibbon, 1975.

That Son of Richard III: A Birth Announcement. Privately printed, 1974.

Where Robot Mice and Robot Men Run round in Robot Towns: New Poems, Both Light and Dark. New York, Knopf, 1977; London, Hart Davis MacGibbon, 1979.

Twin Hieroglyphs That Swim the River Dust. Northridge, California, Lord John Press, 1978.

The Bike Repairman. Northridge, California, Lord John Press, 1978.

The Author Considers His Resources. Northridge, California, Lord John Press, 1979.

The Aqueduct. Glendale, California, Squires, 1979.

The Attic Where the Meadow Greens. Northridge, California, Lord John Press, 1980.

Imagine. Northridge, California, Lord John Press, 1981.

The Haunted Computer and the Android Pope. New York, Knopf, and London, Granada, 1981.

The Complete Poems of Ray Bradbury. New York, Ballantine, 1982.

Two Poems. Northridge, California, Lord John Press, 1982.

The Love Affair. Northridge, California, Lord John Press, 1983.

Other

Switch on the Night (for children). New York, Pantheon, and London, Hart Davis, 1955.

R Is for Rocket (for children). New York, Doubleday, 1962; London, Hart Davis, 1968.

S Is for Space (for children). New York, Doubleday, 1966; London, Hart Davis, 1968.

Teacher's Guide: Science Fiction, with Lewy Olfson. New York, Bantam, 1968.

The Halloween Tree (for children). New York, Knopf, 1972; London, Hart Davis MacGibbon, 1973.

Mars and the Mind of Man. New York, Harper, 1973.

Zen and the Art of Writing, and The Joy of Writing. Santa Barbara, California, Capra Press, 1973.

The Mummies of Guanajuato, photographs by Archie Lieberman. New York, Abrams, 1978.

Beyond 1984: Remembrance of Things Future. New York, Targ, 1979.

About Norman Corwin. Northridge, California, Santa Susana Press, 1979.

The Ghosts of Forever, illustrated by Aldo Sessa. New York, Rizzoli, 1981.

Los Angeles, photographs by West Light. Port Washington, New York, Skyline Press, 1984.

Orange County, photographs by Bill Ross and others. Port Washington, New York, Skyline Press, 1985.

The Art of Playboy (text by Bradbury). New York, van der Marck Editions, 1985.

Zen in the Art of Writing (essays). Santa Barbara, California, Capra Press, 1990.

Yestermorrow: Obvious Answers to Impossible Futures (essays). Santa Barbara, California, Capra Press, 1991.

Editor, *Timeless Stories for Today and Tomorrow.* New York, Bantam, 1952.

Editor, *The Circus of Dr. Lao and Other Improbable Stories.* New York, Bantam, 1956.

*

Manuscript Collection: Bowling Green State University, Ohio.

Critical Studies: Interview in *Show* (New York), December 1964; introduction by Gilbert Highet to *The Vintage Bradbury,* 1965; "The Revival of Fantasy" by Russell Kirk, in *Triumph* (Washington, D.C.), May 1968; "Ray Bradbury's *Dandelion Wine:* Themes, Sources, and Style" by Marvin E. Mengeling, in *English Journal* (Champaign, Illinois), October 1971; *The Ray Bradbury Companion* (includes bibliography) by William F. Nolan, Detroit, Gale, 1975; *The Drama of Ray Bradbury* by Benjamin P. Indick, Baltimore, T-K Graphics, 1977; *The Bradbury Chronicles* by George Edgar Slusser, San Bernardino, California, Borgo Press, 1977; *Ray Bradbury* (includes bibliography) edited by Joseph D. Olander and Martin H. Greenberg, New York, Taplinger, and Edinburgh, Harris, 1980; *Ray Bradbury* by Wayne L. Johnson, New York, Ungar, 1980; *Ray Bradbury and the Poetics of Reverie: Fantasy, Science Fiction, and the Reader* by William F. Toupence, Ann Arbor, Michigan, UMI Research Press, 1984; *Ray Bradbury* by David Mogen, Boston, Twayne, 1986.

Ray Bradbury comments:

I am not so much a science-fiction writer as I am a magician, an illusionist. From my beginnings as a boy conjurer I grew up frightening myself so as to frighten others so as to cure the midnight in our souls. I have grown into a writer of the History of Ideas, I guess you might say. Any idea, no matter how large or small, that is busy growing itself alive, starting from nowhere and at last dominating a town, a culture, or a world, is of interest. Man the problem solver is the writer of my tales. Science fiction becoming science fact. The machineries of our world putting away and keeping our facts for us so they can be used and learned from. Machines as humanist teachers. Ideas of men built into those machines in order to help us survive and survive well. That's my broad and fascinat-

ing field, in which I will wander for a lifetime, writing past science fictions one day, future ones another. And all of it a wonder and a lark and a great love. I can't imagine writing any other way.

*   *   *

Although he has written five novels, including *Something Wicked This Way Comes* and *Fahrenheit 451,* Ray Bradbury is primarily a writer of short stories. Ever the storyteller, Bradbury aims in each story at producing the horror, the surprise, or the single dominant effect of Poe, one of his principal mentors. Nonetheless, his short story collections—notably *The Martian Chronicles* and *Dandelion Wine*—have an overall meaning which exceeds the meaning of the parts. Although he often seems to write about disparate bits of experience, Bradbury does have an identifiable view of life.

"Here There Be Tygers" (*R Is for Rocket*) contains several of the elements of that view. Astronauts land on a previously unknown planet. One of them fears that there are dangers ("tygers") on the planet, and he wishes to kill whatever is alive and to exploit the remaining dead matter. He fulfills his own prophecy: the planet kills him. There *are* tygers on this pastoral world, but the other astronauts are drawn to them. The planet is not dead but alive, and when the astronauts dare to dream their favorite forbidden dreams into it, they awake to find them true. Bradbury follows Wordsworth, Coleridge, and Keats in believing that the childlike imagination can create a wonderful but also terrifying, and temporary, pleasure dome. All but one of the astronauts leave the strange Eden.

In *The Martian Chronicles,* the Eden is Mars. The ancient, delicate Martian civilization is destroyed by crass, polluting, materialistic American invaders. Bradbury the dystopian never entirely shuts out Bradbury the believer in fresh starts, however. "The Million Year Panic" concerns a family which escapes from nuclear war on Earth and uses the psychic energy or imaginative force of the dead Martians to make themselves into "Martians," capable of starting a new and more humane civilization.

The Illustrated Man and *Fahrenheit 451* continue the theme of the imagination threatened but ultimately triumphant. In "The Exiles" Poe, Bierce, and other writers of the fantastic and the macabre perish with their creations on Mars. Fahrenheit 451 is the temperature which the firemen of the future generate to burn all books. Both works point ways out, however. In *Fahrenheit 451* a rebel band memorizes books. "The Rocket," the last story in *The Illustrated Man,* concerns a junkman who makes a rocket ship out of tin cans, which creates for his children the illusion of going to Mars.

Thus Bradbury believes that the imagination may operate in humble and private places as well as in space, and that it is as important to make familiar things new as to make the new things of the space age familiar. *Dandelion Wine* grafts suggestions of horror and science-fiction machines onto "Green Town," Illinois (presumably a version of the Waukegan, Illinois, of Bradbury's childhood). A man who can remember the Civil War past becomes a "time machine" to the boys who listen to his stories. Electric cars, lawnmowers, and trolleys become as mysterious as spaceships. Each day of the summer of 1928 a flask of dandelion wine—a noble thing made from a common plant—is put away for winter use. Bradbury's short stories are flasks of this wine: each day, or each story, is a little different and must be tasted separately. No single flask of wine contains all the wonders and terrors of our kaleidoscopic world.

The stories of *A Medicine for Melancholy* and *The Machineries of Joy* use terror and delight to purge the reader of melancholy. In

"The Day It Rained Forever" 71-year-old Miss Hillgood, who has let her life pass by while she attended only to music, arrives at Joe Terle's Desert Hotel, where for years past there has been rain only one day of the year. When she begins to play, her music suddenly ceases to be sterile, and it magically causes a permanent end of the drought. To Bradbury, the unexpected can always happen. Life can always take a new turn precisely when and where you think of giving it up.

Both *The Machineries of Joy* and *I Sing the Body Electric!* contain Mars stories and others in the familiar Bradbury manner. But (particularly in the latter book) Bradbury experiments with replacing fantasy and plot twists with atmosphere, interior emotion, and character development. Too often the resulting stories lack the motivation and the logic which the fantastic never required. But Bradbury is a flexible and resourceful writer, and he may yet make successful use of the techniques of mainstream fiction.

Perhaps Bradbury's greatest value is as a social critic and a commentator on technology. Perceiving the madness of expansionist technology, Bradbury no longer shares the teenage boy's worship of the astronaut corps in "R Is for Rocket." But his Martians have a more advanced technology than Earth's, in many respects—their cities last, and Earthmen's do not. "Space travel has made children of us all," says the philosopher on the verso of *The Martian Chronicles*. The American astronauts are childish idiots, but space travel also makes possible the childlike wonder of the million-year-picnic. In "The End of the Beginning" (*A Medicine for Melancholy*) a man pauses from mowing his lawn to watch his son rocket into the twilight air to make the first space station. Bradbury suggests the unity of all technology: Ezkiel's wheel in the middle of the air, the wheeling space station and lawnmower, and the wheels in the man's watch. Moreover, life and technology are interrelated. The amoeba's climb from water to land prepared for man's climb from Earth. It is now a new age, but the man finishes mowing the lawn after watching the rocket launching. Bradbury is not against technology. He simply believes that man must look around and back at the same time he looks forward.

In the 1960s and 1970s Bradbury's career took an entirely new turn. Few of his recent stories are science fiction or fantasy. Instead, Bradbury now concentrates solely on what was always present in his writing, his compassion for likable but inadequate people struggling against the tragic ironies of life, and often being successful in ways they did not expect. "The Parrot Who Met Pappa" is about the theft of a parrot who knew Hemingway by a writer, Hemingway's contemporary, whose life is filled with jealousy of the great man. In "The Utterly Perfect Murder" Douglas returns to Green Town, Bradbury's fabled childhood world, to kill someone he hated as a child. But when Douglas finds this changed and almost pitiful person, his murderous feelings melt. "Have I Got a Chocolate Bar for You!" is the tale of a Catholic priest who saves an Irish Jew from the sin of chocolate addiction. His writing in the late 1970s and 1980s was chiefly stories for children, crime fiction, and poetry.

As we can tell from his essay "Zen and the Art of Writing," Bradbury is an ambitious writer with a theory behind what he is doing. He is trying to convey the zest that life can have in a less-than-ideal universe. Bradbury's early science fiction now seems dated, and the emotion in his more recent fiction is at times overdone, but Bradbury's compassion for his characters and for his readers deserves respect.

—Curtis C. Smith

BRADLEY, David (Henry, Jr.)

Nationality: American. **Born:** Bedford, Pennsylvania, 7 September 1950. **Education:** Bedford Area High School, graduated 1968; University of Pennsylvania, Philadelphia (Franklin scholar, Presidential scholar), 1968-72, B.A. (summa cum laude) in creative writing 1972; King's College, University of London (Thouron scholar), 1972-74, M.A. in area studies 1974. **Career:** Reader and assistant editor, J.B. Lippincott, publishers, Philadelphia, 1974-76; visiting lecturer in English, University of Pennsylvania, 1975. Visiting instructor, 1976-77, assistant professor, 1977-82, associate professor of English, 1982-89, and since 1989 professor of English, Temple University, Philadelphia. Editorial consultant, Lippincott, 1977-78, and Ace Science Fiction, New York, 1979; visiting lecturer, San Diego State University, 1980-81. Member of the Executive Board, PEN American Center, 1982-84. **Awards:** American Academy award, 1982; PEN-Faulkner award, 1982. **Agent:** Wendy Weil, Julian Bach Literary Agency, 747 Third Avenue, New York, New York 10017. **Address:** Department of English, Temple University, Philadelphia, Pennsylvania 19122, U.S.A.

PUBLICATIONS

Novels

South Street. New York, Grossman, 1975.
The Chaneysville Incident. New York, Harper, 1981; London, Serpent's Tail, 1986.
The Lodestar Project. New York, Pocket Books, 1986.

Uncollected Short Story

"197903042100 (Sunday)," in *Our Roots Grow Deeper than We Know,* edited by Lee Gutkind. Pittsburgh, University of Pittsburgh Press, 1985.

Play

Sweet Sixteen (produced Louisville, Kentucky, 1983).

Other

From Text to Performance in the Elizabethan Theatre: Preparing the Play for the Stage. Cambridge, Cambridge University Press, 1991.

*

David Bradley comments:

I believe a work of fiction ought to more or less speak for itself—certainly the author ought to keep his mouth shut about it; he's *had* his chance. On the other hand, I have noticed a few things about my own attitudes that might bear mentioning. Nothing so deliberate as a "what I am trying to do with my writing" statement (which I find pretentious and usually wrong), but just observations about what I tend to think is good. I am, first of all, an Aristotelian writer. Meaning that I believe in the Gospel as laid down in *The Poetics*. Plot is paramount, and I do not like *any*thing that does not have one. Second, I do not believe in a sharp distinction between fiction and non-fiction. Most of my writing is grounded in real places and people. I always find myself "adapting" reality to the writing, as one might "adapt" a novel for a film. Third, I do not believe in art for art's sake. Art *has* no sake; people do. A work of art that cannot be understood is a voice crying in the wilderness. Fourth, I demand a lot from readers. I do not write "easy" things; they require effort and emotional commitment from me—and they require the same from readers. I hope only that readers feel their time and sweat are well spent.

*   *   *

For David Bradley, place matters, and history haunts. If the Stephen Dedalus of James Joyce's *A Portrait of the Artist as a Young Man* tries desperately to fly over the nets of family, church, and state, Bradley speaks lyrically of those cords that bind him to his birthplace (the rural community of Bedford, Pennsylvania), to the black church in which he grew up, and to the family that nurtured his early interest in history, and in writing about that history. As put in "A Personal View from the Third Generation" (*New York Times Sunday Magazine*):

> For he [Bradley] realizes this is *his* church. Three generations of his family have occupied Mt. Pisgah's pulpit and worshipped in its pews. A plaque on the wall dedicates the 1960s redecoration to his grandmother. The Bible on the lectern was an offering by his father when his mother survived a dangerous illness. In the truest sense, he, not the denomination, owns Mt. Pisgah. And owes it.
>
> For, in a day when and a place where opportunities were restricted, Mt. Pisgah gave him the chance to speak, to lead, to learn the history of his people. When opportunities became available, it was the experience gained at Mt. Pisgah that equipped him to take advantage of them. But, after taking advantage of them, he abandoned the church that had nurtured him. He walked from Mt. Pisgah down into the Promised Land and never really looked back. Perhaps the time has come to turn around.

These are eloquent, confessional words. For Bradley has moved with astonishing speed from the raw, lusty talent that described the "street people" who hold forth on Philadelphia's *South Street* (published in 1975, when Bradley was only 24) to the sweep and ambition of *The Chaneysville Incident,* the novel that brought Bradley national recognition.

South Street is a novel anchored in the naturalism of "elephantine cockroaches and rats the size of cannon shells," but it is also a novel that reaches well beyond the geography of urban despair. Bradley's South Street poises itself at the border of Philadelphia's black ghetto, where it ties "the city's rivers like an iron bracelet or a wedding band, uniting the waters, sewer to sewer, before they meet at the city's edge." Place matters deeply, of course—in this case, the locus seems to be Lightnin' Ed's Bar—but it is the people, and Bradley's ear for their colorful language, that matters even more:

> Leo, the two-hundred-and-fifty-eight-pound owner-bartender-cashier-bouncer of Lightnin' Ed's Bar and Grill, looked up from the glass he was polishing to see a one-hundred-and-fifty-eight-pound white man walk into his bar. Leo's mouth fell open and he almost dropped the glass. One by one the faces along the bar turned to stare at the single pale face, shining in the dimness. "Yes, sir, cap'n," Leo said uneasily, "what can we be doin' for you?"
>
> George looked around nervously. "I, ah, had a little accident. I, ah, ran over a cat in the street, and I, uh, don't know what to do about it."
>
> "Whad he say?" a wino at the far end of the bar, who claimed to be hard of hearing, whispered loudly.
>
> The jukebox ran out and fell silent just as somebody yelled to him, "Paddy says he run over some cat out in the street." The sound echoed throughout the bar. Conversation died.
>
> "Goddamn!" said the wino.
>
> Leo leaned over the bar, letting his gigantic belly rest on the polished wood. "Yeah?" he said to George. "Didja kill him?"
>
> "Oh yes," George assured him. "I made certain of that."

Bradley is at his best when he moves inside the set pieces, the extended anecdotes, that give *South Street* its resonance. What might well have become yet another unrelenting grim account of sordid conditions and despairing lives transmogrifies itself into a high, more humane key. It was, in short, a novel that prompted reviewers to say "Keep your eye on Mr. Bradley." In this case, they were righter than they knew.

The Chaneysville Incident both widened and deepened the scope of Bradley's obvious talents. His postgraduate research in American history at the University of London sent him back, ironically enough, to a story he had heard in Bedford about 13 escaped slaves who asked to be killed rather than recaptured and about the 13 unmarked graves his mother once discovered.

The Chaneysville Incident tells this story from the perspective of John Washington, a black man who has bootstrapped himself from humble, rural origins to become a history professor at a Philadelphia university and who lives with Judith, a white psychologist. The question the book raises is simply, and perplexingly, how should a black man live in a world white men have made. The result is a thickly textured, multi-layered book, one that inextricably combines theory, historical research, and domestic tension. As Washington, the historian, puts it: "The key to the understanding of any society lies in the observation and analysis of the insignificant and the mundane. . . . If you doubt it [i.e. that America is a classed society], consider the sanitary facilities employed in America's three modes of public long-distance transportation: airplanes, trains, and buses."

Washington, however, not only discovers the historical truth of the "Chaneysville incident," but also that the truth is more complex, more riddling than he had imagined. If part of his character serves as Bradley's mouthpiece, part of him must, finally, be rejected by Bradley, the novelist. Luckily, it is the latter part that matters most, when one has recovered from the anger and whitey-baiting that gives this important novel much of its initial energy.

—Sanford Pinsker

BRADLEY, John Ed

Nationality: American. **Born:** Opelousas, Louisiana, 12 August 1958. **Education:** Louisiana State University, B.A. 1980. **Career:**

Staff writer, *Washington Post,* 1983-87; contributing writer, *Washington Post,* 1988-89. Since 1991 contributing editor, *Esquire;* since 1993 contributing writer, *Sports Illustrated.* **Agent:** Esther Newberg, International Creative Management, 40 West 57th St., New York, New York 10019, U.S.A.

PUBLICATIONS

Novels

Tupelo Nights. New York, Atlantic Monthly Press, and London, Bloomsbury, 1988.
The Best There Ever Was. New York, Atlantic Monthly Press, and London, Bloomsbury, 1990.
Love and Obits. New York, Holt, and London, Bloomsbury, 1992.
Smoke. New York, Holt, 1994.

*   *   *

John Ed Bradley's first novel establishes his niche in the tradition of southern Gothic writers. Emphasis on the grotesque, the macabre, and the excessive pull of environment is predominant. Much of the setting in *Tupelo Nights* features the local cemetery, where the hero's best friend is a gravedigger and where he meets Emma Groves, the love of his life. Emma goes every night to pray at the grave of her infant son. The cemetery motif is constant. John Girlie, the novel's antihero, works the graveyard shift at a pipeline company, and images of death haunt the book.

Girlie had been an all-America football player at Louisiana State University and had a promising offer to play professional football. Under his domineering mother's influence, however, he returns to his hometown and cannot until late in the novel extricate himself from his oedipal situation.

At times Bradley's plot flirts with melodrama, but this is more than overcome by his keen gift for dialogue and vivid descriptions that are often poetically lyrical. Bradley captures the atmosphere of time and place with persuasive authenticity, totally immersing the reader in the stifling environment and grimness of Girlie's small Louisiana town.

Harold Gravely, the main figure in *The Best There Ever Was,* is a college football coach in his sixties. Almost thirty years ago his team won the national championship. Since then Gravely's teams have had mostly losing seasons, and the students, alumni, and college officials want him to resign. Learning that he has lung cancer, he decides to forego any treatment in the hope that the situation generated by his condition will force the college administration to renew his contract so that he can coach one final year.

The figure of Coach Gravely is drawn with believable and persuasive strokes perfectly conveying his loud, egotistical, and overbearing temperament. As the Old Man, a term he favors, he is a memorable if unpleasant character. Bradley also cleverly uses comedy to satirize the coach and emphasize the grotesque aspects of the situation. The novel's weakness is that often the descriptions of Gravely and many of the episodes he is involved in become essentially repetitive. The book at times becomes too wordy; too much material is presented. Even after the coach is murdered, many additional pages are devoted to his widow; this leads to a feeble anticlimax.

Joseph Burke, in *Love and Obits,* is a newspaper reporter who has been demoted to writing obituaries. Divorced, Burke lives with his wheelchair-bound father. Although he and his father are on good terms, Joseph is presented as one of the melancholy, lonely men who walk about the city at night looking for something they never had or for something they have lost and will never find again.

Burke's father, Woody, takes on more cheerfulness and hope when he falls in love with his day care nurse; Burke himself becomes more positive when he attracts the attention of widow Laura Vannoy. Burke had written the obituary article about her prominent husband, so even love is entwined with death. At the book's end, Woody, in an epiphany of love, performs a Christ-like action of feeding his fisherman's catch to the poor.

Smoke is both a continuation of previous characteristics of Bradley's work and a worrisome development, which was present on occasion in the earlier books. Smoke is a small town in Louisiana where Jay Carnihan's goal is to kidnap Monster Mart's founder, billionaire Rayford Holly, and require him to apologize for forcing so many downtown stores in America out of business. Kidnapped on one of his nationwide inspection trips, Holly proves to be an exceedingly lovable, down-to-earth individual who even pitches in as a short order cook at the lunch counter of Carnihan's small store.

Again, Bradley demonstrates his gifted talent for recording dialogue and lively characterization, but the narrative becomes too far-fetched. There comes a point when a tall tale can become too tall, when a novel can sprawl to an excessive degree, and when even an admirable talent can be overwhelmed by too many episodes, too many words, too drawn out a plot, and an unconvincing conclusion. As in *The Best There Ever Was,* Bradley does not seem to know when to stop, and melodrama and sentimentality predominate. Even the theme of love over death, which was so effectively presented in *Love and Obits,* becomes mawkish and cloying in *Smoke.*

Bradley is a considerable talent in handling dialogue and characterization, but he must temper plot excesses and a tendency to over-elaborate a narrative.

—Paul A. Doyle

BRAGG, Melvyn

Nationality: British. **Born:** Carlisle, Cumberland, 6 October 1939. **Education:** Nelson-Thomlinson Grammar School, Wigton, Cumberland, 1950-58; Wadham College, Oxford, 1958-61, M.A. (honours) in modern history 1961. **Family:** Married 1) Marie-Elisabeth Roche in 1961 (died 1971), one daughter; 2) Catherine Mary Haste in 1973, one daughter and one son. **Career:** With BBC Television and Radio from 1961: general trainee, 1961-62; producer on *Monitor,* 1963; for BBC 2 editor on *New Release* (later *Review,* then *Arena*), *Writers World,* and *Take It or Leave It,* 1964-70; presenter, *In the Picture,* Tyne Tees Television, Newcastle-upon-Tyne, 1971, *Second House,* 1973-77, and *Read All About It,* 1976-77, BBC, London. Since 1978 editor and presenter, *South Bank Show;* Head of Arts, 1982-90; and since 1990 Controller of Arts, London Weekend Television; since 1988 presenter, *Start the Week,* BBC Radio 4. Chairman, Border Television, Carlisle. Since 1969 member, and chairman, 1977-80, Arts Council Literature Panel; president, Northern Arts, 1983-87, and National Campaign for the Arts since 1986. **Awards:** Writers Guild award, for screenplay, 1966; Rhys Memorial prize, 1968; Northern Arts Association prose award,

1970; Silver Pen award, 1970; Broadcasting Guild award, 1984; Ivor Novello award, for musical, 1985; BAFTA Dimbleby award, 1987. D.Litt.: University of Liverpool, 1986; University of Lancaster, 1990; D.Univ.: Open University, Milton Keynes, Buckinghamshire, 1988. Fellow, Royal Society of Literature, 1970, and Royal Television Society; Honorary Fellow, Lancashire Polytechnic; Domus Fellow, St. Catherine's College, Oxford, 1990. **Address:** 12 Hampstead Hill Gardens, London N.W.3., England.

PUBLICATIONS

Novels

For Want of a Nail. London, Secker and Warburg, and New York, Knopf, 1965.
The Second Inheritance. London, Secker and Warburg, 1966; New York, Knopf, 1967.
Without a City Wall. London, Secker and Warburg, 1968; New York, Knopf, 1969.
The Cumbrian Trilogy. London, Coronet, 1984.
    The Hired Man. London, Secker and Warburg, 1969; New York, Knopf, 1970.
    A Place in England. London, Secker and Warburg, 1970; New York, Knopf, 1971.
    Kingdom Come. London, Secker and Warburg, 1980.
The Nerve. London, Secker and Warburg, 1971.
The Hunt. London, Secker and Warburg, 1972.
Josh Lawton. London, Secker and Warburg, and New York, Knopf, 1972.
The Silken Net. London, Secker and Warburg, and New York, Knopf, 1974.
Autumn Manoeuvres. London, Secker and Warburg, 1978.
Love and Glory. London, Secker and Warburg, 1983.
The Maid of Buttermere. London, Hodder and Stoughton, and New York, Putnam, 1987.
A Time to Dance. London, Hodder and Stoughton, 1990; Boston, Little Brown, 1991.
Crystal Rooms. London, Hodder and Stoughton, 1992.

Fiction (for children)

A Christmas Child. London, Secker and Warburg, 1976.

Uncollected Short Story

"The Initiation," in *Winter's Tales 18,* edited by A.D. Maclean. London, Macmillan, and New York, St. Martin's Press, 1972.

Plays

Mardi Gras, music by Alan Blaikley and Ken Howard (produced London, 1976).
The Hired Man, adaptation of his own novel, music and lyrics by Howard Goodall (produced Southampton and London, 1984). London, French, 1986.

Screenplays: *Play Dirty,* with Lotte Colin, 1968; *Isadora* with Clive Exton and Margaret Drabble, 1969; *The Music Lovers,* 1970; *Jesus Christ Superstar,* with Norman Jewison, 1973; *The Seventh Seal,* 1993.

Radio Play: *Robin Hood,* 1971.

Television Plays: *The Debussy File,* with Ken Russell, 1965; *Charity Begins at Home,* 1970; *Zinotchka,* 1972; *Orion,* music by Ken Howard and Alan Blaikley, 1977; *Clouds of Glory,* with Ken Russell, 1978.

Other

Speak for England: An Essay on England 1900-1975. London, Secker and Warburg, 1976; revised edition, London, Coronet, 1978; as *Speak for England: An Oral History of England 1900-1975,* New York, Knopf, 1977.
Land of the Lakes. London, Secker and Warburg, 1983; New York, Norton, 1984.
Laurence Olivier. London, Hutchinson, 1984; New York, St. Martin's Press, 1985.
Rich: The Life of Richard Burton. London, Hodder and Stoughton, 1988; as *Richard Burton: A Life,* Boston, Little Brown, 1989.

Editor, *My Favourite Stories of Lakeland.* Guildford, Surrey, Lutterworth Press, 1981.
Editor, *Cumbria in Verse.* London, Secker and Warburg, 1984.

*

Melvyn Bragg comments:
(1972) The ways in which I came to write are sketched in the last chapters of *A Place in England:* they are made the notions of a fictional self—Douglas Tallentire.
Present ideas on fiction are represented in the novel *The Nerve* and in an essay "Class and the Novel" in *Times Literary Supplement* (London), 15 October 1971.

*   *   *

Melvyn Bragg began his writing career with two good novels about wasted human potential, *For Want of a Nail* and *The Second Inheritance.* But it was *Without a City Wall* which secured for him a deserved reputation as one of the best contemporary novelists. Theme and structure reinforce each other as Bragg traces, first, the awakening of passion in Richard Godwin, a self-imposed exile from the chaos of London, for Janice Beattie, a Cumberland girl of unusual intelligence and powerful ambition; and then the challenges that the life of consummated passion entails for both of them. The drama develops principally from Janice whose ambition and fastidiousness prove stronger than sexual passion or her sense of responsibility to others. Her passion for Richard contracts, while his for her continues to expand. Richard is driven to the brink of self-destruction, but recoils in time to force Janice to some kind of modus vivendi between the claims of his passion and the claims of her individuality. *The Silken Net* also develops the theme of sexual struggle. This book focuses on a restless intellectual, Rosemary Lewis, whose energy alienates her from life in the Cumberland village of Thurston. Her vigor is admirable but her egoism is destructive as she attempts to breed in her husband the same intensities that motivate her. The resulting conflict registers with less authority, however, than that developed in *Without a City Wall.*

The alternation of intensity and apathy in the passional life is again one subject explored in *The Hired Man.* Covering the years 1898 to 1920 in the life of John and Emily Tallentire, the novel articulates the nuances of their emotions. Communication between a man and a woman becomes a function of the body; and estrangement develops when perfect physical accord is broken. After Emily's death, at the age of 40, John is back where he was at the beginning, a man for casual hire on the great farms but now with all his zest gone. Bragg's artistry is at its best in his honest portrayal of the hard lives of agricultural laborers in the early 20th century. The protagonist of *A Place in England* is Joseph Tallentire, John's son. Bragg is less close to Joseph than to John; in fact, the most memorable pages of the novel feature the now patriarchal John. After much struggle Joseph is able to "be his own man" as owner of a public house; but his success is undercut by the disintegration of his marriage, a loss to him for which he cannot account.

Kingdom Come reveals much of the power found in *The Hired Man* and has much interest for the modern reader, as Bragg presents the contemporary generation of the Tallentire men. Lester, a con man and cousin, and Douglas, the son of Joseph and a writer of talent, lack the purposefulness and inner strength of their ancestors, though Harry, the adopted son who stays in Thurston, retains these qualities in large part. Douglas is the sympathetically presented protagonist who can neither be satisfied with the stern ancestral morality not get clear of the claims of responsibility which derive from it. His divided nature defeats him because it leads him to betray the woman he loves and whose real worth he realizes too late.

In two other novels Bragg has again had recourse to Cumberland and its people. In *Josh Lawton,* a moving parable, Lawton has overtones of a Biblical patriarch and suffers the predictable fate of those who are too good for this world. In *Autumn Manoeuvres* Bragg traces the destructive and self-destructive career of Gareth Johnson. His violent loathing of his stepfather and his own violent self-loathing are linked to the violence of his begetting (his mother had been gang raped in World War I). Is he the victim of fatality or is he his own victim? (more the second than the first, Bragg implies).

London figures more than Cumberland in *The Nerve* and *Love and Glory.* In *The Nerve* Bragg traces, in a first-person narrative, the stages in the mental breakdown of his protagonist, Ted. Power accrues when Ted, the narrator, actualizes some of his experiences of physical and mental pain, but the breakdown which is a "breakthrough" is not precisely characterized. In *Love and Glory* Bragg explores the various forms of love from self-serving passion to selfless devotion. The conflict centers on the relationship between Ian Grant, an actor of genius, and Caroline, his Scottish mistress, who loves him with greater devotion than he can reciprocate. The central character is a writer for television, Willie Armstrong, who is Grant's best friend. He comes to love Caroline to distraction but gives her up when she fails to respond to his advances and when he realizes the claims of his wife, Joanna, upon him. Willie thus gains in insight and understanding while Ian Grant retrogresses spiritually and becomes even more submerged in his egotism.

The immediacy of Bragg's Cumberland milieu is, at least superficially, the quality that impresses most in his fiction. As in Thomas Hardy and D.H. Lawrence, milieu is integrally fused with the fortunes and development of the characters. Like Hardy he has in unusual degree insight into human beings who confront the elemental realities of nature, and like Hardy's his people encounter problems difficult to resolve when they lose rapport with nature. Bragg's eye for detail, his compelling sense of drama, his penetration into the emotional and psychic life of his characters, his sense of the moral verities, and his supple and luminous prose have all contributed to his standing as a distinguished novelist.

—Frederick P.W. McDowell

BRATA, Sasthi

Nationality: British. **Born:** Sasthibrata Chakravarti in Calcutta, India, 16 July 1939. **Education:** Calcutta Boys School; Presidency College, Calcutta University. **Family:** Married Pamela Joyce Radcliffe (divorced). **Career:** Has worked in Europe as a lavatory attendant, kitchen porter, barman, air-conditioning engineer, and postman, and in New York as a freelance journalist; London columnist, *Statesman,* 1977-80. **Awards:** Arts Council grant, 1979. **Agent:** Barbara Lowenstein, 250 West 57th Street, Suite 701, New York, New York 10107, U.S.A. **Address:** 33 Savernake Road, London NW3 2JU, England.

PUBLICATIONS

Novels

Confessions of an Indian Woman Eater. London, Hutchinson, 1971; as *Confessions of an Indian Lover,* New Delhi, Sterling, 1973.
She and He. New Delhi, Orient, 1973.
The Sensuous Guru: The Making of a Mystic President. New Delhi, Sterling, 1980.

Short Stories

Encounter. New Delhi, Orient, 1978.

Poetry

Eleven Poems. New Delhi, Blue Moon, 1960.

Other

My God Died Young (autobiography). London, Hutchinson, and New York, Harper, 1968.
A Search for Home (autobiography). New Delhi, Orient, 1975.
Astride Two Worlds: Traitor to India. New Delhi, B.I. Publications, 1976; as *Traitor to India: A Search for Home,* London, Elek, 1976.
Labyrinths in the Lotus Land (on India). New York, Morrow, 1985.
India: The Perpetual Paradox. London, Tauris, 1986.

*

Sasthi Brata comments:

(1991) My first published book, *My God Died Young,* was a self-professed autobiography, written at the age of 28, before I had made any kind of a name for myself as a writer, or anything else. This led a good few publishers, readers, and finally critics to utter the exasperated cry: "What makes you think that the story of your life (woefully unlived-in up to that time) deserves to be told? Or that people will want to read it?" The answer to these questions was within the book itself, of course. But in a sense *all* of my writing, fiction, non-fiction, and journalism, has been an attempt to refute the assumptions lurking behind those superficially plausible and innocent-sounding queries. For they presume that only the heroic and the grand deserve artistic exploration and autobiographical treatment. While I believe, very firmly, that everyone, but everyone has *a* story to tell. The difference between the true artist and the pub bore is that the writer has a sure grasp over the instruments of his trade—words, sentences, paragraphs, syntax, metaphor, melody—and is then able to select, assemble, and present a somewhat more ordered and appetizing version of the world than the chaotic, often repetitive jumble of experiences from external reality which make up his raw material.

All my fiction has been supremely autobiographical. Even in those books which are listed as non-fiction on library shelves, I have used fictional devices, and equally freely introduced reportage techniques in books which profess to be novels. I should warn the prospective reader however not to deduce from this that every hero in every one of my novels is an exactly congruent picture of the man I am. In a review of the late Yukio Mishima's novels I wrote: "The obsessionally autobiographical writer may be an invisible man." For while he may not be telling lies, he is not necessarily telling the *truth* either, at least not of the kind the law courts would accept. Since he is an artist, he *has* used his imagination, but he has not necessarily let you into the secret of where the fictive imagination begins or where empirically verifiable reality ends.

There was a time when I used to be irked by attacks on the high sexual content in my writing. I am no longer. Few addicts of hardcore porn would find any of my books satisfactory. Prurient sensibilities, with a cavalier indifference to style and linguistic resonances, might equally be put off by their subject matter. Apologies to neither group.

I would call myself a "radical traditionalist" as a novelist, if only because to be a successful "experimental" writer, in the sense that Joyce and Borges are, requires a poetic sensibility I do not possess. It is easy to descend into the wholly bogus or deliberately pedantic in trying to achieve effects about which one is not totally sure. There are no rules in the use of language of course, but I would rather stick within certain wide but strictly defined limits, than stray into those unexplored territories where the arcane, obscure, or simply fraudulent vendors ply their wares. I believe that all my books can be read simply as good tales.

Labyrinths in the Lotus Land was my first commissioned work. I wrote it specifically for a Western audience. It was an ambitious attempt to inform a western reader, within the compass of a single book, everything that he or she might wish to know about the country, spanning the whole gamut of history, religion, art, politics, etc. Critics who complained about the apparent incongruity of introducing *personal* experiences into a book which purports to portray a picture of contemporary India were not aware of my long-held belief that by relating a particular incident or episode in a graphic and authentic manner, the universal is illuminated more poignantly than any amount of dry didactic scholarship can ever do.

*   *   *

Most of Sasthi Brata's books are written in the first person, and all his heroes seem to be modeled after the novelist himself. The hero is always a Bengali Brahmin, from a well-to-do family, who lives in Calcutta and studies physics at college. He leaves home in protest after the girl of his choice is married off to someone whom her parents have chosen. He drifts into a number of jobs, including journalism, and finally establishes himself comfortably in Hampstead. His chief hobby is haunting pubs. The narrator of his first novel, *Confessions of an Indian Woman Eater,* differs only in name from the narrator of the autobiographies *My God Died Young* and *Astride Two Worlds.* The physical characteristics remain the same, even if the hero is Zamir Ishmael of *She and He:* he is dark, of medium height, with dark eyes and an attractive smile; his suc-

cess with women is unlimited. Brata's books are quite readable; his style is racy and adequate for his purpose, which is generally limited to describing the exploits of his hero in bed. The exception is *Astride Two Worlds,* the second part of his autobiography, which touches upon many serious topics like racial discrimination in Britain, the involvement of the Indian government in the guerrilla activities of the Mukti Bahini in Bangladesh in 1971, and the growing disillusionment of the young with established politicians in India. A couple of chapters, written in the third person, serve to give a proper perspective to this autobiography.

Brata's best selling novel, *Confessions of an Indian Woman Eater,* begins where his first book, *My God Died Young,* an autobiography, let off: Amit Ray, like Sasthi Brata, runs away from his Calcutta home. Amit recounts his varied sexual experiences in a number of capitals—New Delhi, Rome, London, Paris, Copenhagen. He finally ends up in Hampstead with a steady job, and becomes a successful writer. For a certain readership the chief attraction of the book would lie in the step-by-step accounts of copulation, found almost every ten pages. The next novel, *She and He,* has a hero born of an Arab father and a French mother; he is at home in England and lands a good job because he can speak the language with the proper accent. He always talks about writing the "Great English Novel," but does nothing about it until one of his ex-girlfriends sends him an unfinished novel, having written her side of the story, with blank pages for the hero to fill in. The first person account of Zamir alternating with the third person narrative of Sally is an interesting stylistic innovation, but the hero's mindless drifting from bed to bed is ultimately boring.

The Sensuous Guru: The Making of a Mystic President, perhaps the most imaginative of Brata's works, recounts the rise of Ram Chukker (short for Ram Chakravarti, just as Sasthi Brata is the shortened form of Sasthibrata Chakravarti). Chukker initially sets himself up as a Guru in New York, and makes a good living. He writes a short autobiographical novel, *The Making of a Guru,* which outdoes the worst that America can produce in pornography. Through high-pressure promotion with the help of an influential literary agent Chukker wins the Pulitzer Prize, is nominated for the Nobel Prize, manages one for Peace, and is ultimately elected President of the United States.

Brata has also published a collection of stories; most of them are like his novels (some have appeared, with modifications, as chapters in his novels). One very good story is "Smiles among the Bric-a-Brac," about a young Oxford graduate from a rich English family, comfortably settling down to the girl and the job his parents have chosen for him, though he earlier loves the beautiful Nina Fernandez, of mixed parentage. The first person account, with the hero justifying the way he drops Nina, is a beautiful psychological study of the hero's lack of principles. It is significant that Robert Lomax, from an old English family, is very different from the usual Bengali hero. One feels that Brata could write better fiction, especially if he got rid of his autobiographical obsession.

—Shyamala A. Narayan

BRATHWAITE, Errol (Freeman)

Nationality: New Zealander. **Born:** Clive, Hawkes Bay, 3 April 1924. **Education:** Waipukurau District High School, 1929-37;

Timaru Boys' High School, 1938-39. **Military Service:** Served in the New Zealand Army in the City of Wellington's Own, 1942-43; Royal New Zealand Air Force, 1943-45, 1947-55; Royal New Zealand Signals, 1955-58. **Family:** Married Alison Irene Whyte in 1948; one son and one daughter. **Career:** Cadet, New Zealand Railways, 1940-42, 1945; farm trainee, Rehabilitation Department, King Country, 1946; copywriter, New Zealand Broadcasting Corporation, Christchurch, 1959-62, and Dobbs Wiggins McCann Erickson, Christchurch, 1962-66. Since 1969 copywriter and manager, 1971-73, Carlton Carruthers du Chateau, Christchurch. **Awards:** Otago *Daily Times* Centennial prize, 1961; New Zealand Award for Achievement, 1962. **Address:** 12 Fulton Avenue, Fendalton, Christchurch 1, New Zealand.

PUBLICATIONS

Novels

Fear in the Night. Christchurch, Caxton Press, 1959.
An Affair of Men. Auckland and London, Collins, 1961; New York, St. Martin's Press, 1964.
Long Way Home. Christchurch, Caxton Press, 1964.
The Flying Fish. Auckland and London, Collins, 1964; San Francisco, Tri-Ocean, 1969.
The Needle's Eye. Auckland and London, Collins, 1965; San Francisco, Tri-Ocean, 1969.
The Evil Day. Auckland and London, Collins, 1967; San Francisco, Tri-Ocean, 1969.
The Flame Box. Auckland, Collins, 1978.

Uncollected Short Story

"Williams and Christmas," in *New Zealand Weekly* (Auckland), 1968.

Plays

Radio Plays: *An Affair of Men,* 1962; *Long Way Home,* 1966; *The Needle's Eye,* 1969; *Marnot,* 1978; *Marnot and the Power Game,* 1979; *The Rehabilitation of Captain Marnot,* 1979; *Shape Up or Ship Out,* 1979; *Holes in the Air,* 1980.

Other

Morning Flight. Wellington, Commemoration Committee, 1970.
The Companion Guide to the North [South] Island of New Zealand. Auckland and London, Collins, 2 vols., 1970-72.
New Zealand and Its People. Wellington, New Zealand Government Printer, 1974.
The Beauty of New Zealand, photographs by Robin Smith. Auckland, Golden Press, 1974.
Historic New Zealand. Christchurch, Kowhai, 1979.
New Zealand. Christchurch, Kowhai, 1980.
Sixty Red Nightcaps and Other Curiosities of New Zealand History. Auckland, Bateman, 1980.
The Companion Guide to Westland. Auckland, Collins, 1981.
The Beauty of Waikato, Bay of Plenty, photographs by Warren Jacobs and Robin Smith. Christchurch, Kowhai, 1981.
Dunedin, photographs by Warren Jacobs. Christchurch, Kowhai, 1981.

The Beauty of New Zealand's North Island, photographs by Warren Jacobs and Robin Smith. Christchurch, Kowhai, 1982.
The Beauty of New Zealand's South Island, photographs by Warren Jacobs. Christchurch, Kowhai, 1982.
The Companion Guide to Otago, Southland, and Stewart Island. Auckland, Collins, 1982.
Just Looking: A View of New Zealand, illustrated by John Haycraft. Auckland, Bateman, 1982.
Beautiful New Zealand. Auckland, Bateman, 1985.
Pilot on the Run: The Epic Escape from Occupied France of Flight Sergeant L.S.M. (Chalky) White RNZAF. Auckland, Hutchinson, 1986.
Christchurch: North and Mid-Canterbury. Wellington, G.P. Books, 1988.
Portrait of New Zealand, photographs by Robin Smith and Warren Jacobs. Christchurch, Kowhai, 1988.
South Canterbury: Timura, Mt. Cook, and the Mackenzie Country, photographs by Roy Sinclair. Wellington, G.P. Books, 1989.

*

Errol Brathwaite comments:

It is difficult for me to comment on my own novels, since I never write with any other end in view than to tell a good story.

I regard life as a constant battle between good and evil, albeit a highly complex warfare, since both sides in any given encounter have within them leanings towards both good and evil. I strive to make my characters positive, though not necessarily strong—never clean-cut good or evil, though tending infinitely more strongly in one direction (usually towards good) than the other. I acknowledge the complexity of the battle by giving my creations multifaceted characters; and while I comment on life, I try to allow the commentary to grow as a by-product of observations and reportage. I do not deliberately attack attitudes or situations, but merely use them. To do otherwise would be to obtrude, to force myself and my opinions on the reader.

If I want a particular character to be a hero, I make him progress towards an obviously desirable goal somewhat in spite of himself, sometimes fortuitously and always with much stumbling and a modicum of obtuseness. I try to let the reader see the desirable objective, as it were from a height, observing the hero's ground-level side-tracking and stumbling progress. I do this in an attempt to involve the reader, which I regard as being a first principle of good entertainment.

I suppose that this is why war has so often been, if not the subject, then the setting of my novels. It is a pattern, in bold relief, of life itself. It is full of dramatic possibilities. It can face ordinary good/evil man with a rapid series of searing moral and other dilemmas.

I don't expect that I shall always write about war, but I regard conflict as being one of the two major dramatic themes, the other being the "Robinson Crusoe" situation, wherein man overcomes circumstance and bends it to his will.

What else is there to say? I believe that life itself is seldom tidy, and that its conclusion inevitably leaves a number of more or less untidy loose ends flapping around. I realize that in a novel there must be a rather greater degree of contrivance than in life, but I don't care to make my novels too unlifelike.

I suppose, to sum it all up, that I regard myself as an entertainer; a teller, as Kai Lung used to say, of imagined tales. I have, therefore, one source of material, which is human behavior, and three forms of presentation, which are drama, romance and comedy. Drama and comedy call for high, bold coloring techniques—the dash and splash of bright oils. Romance calls for water-color treatment, and I don't think that my brushwork is subtle enough. Therefore, I suppose that the highly dramatic will continue to be my chosen form, and that if there is any change, it will be to comedy.

*　　*　　*

In Errol Brathwaite's novels, the basic formula is that of men in a dangerous war-situation, submitted to physical and mental stress, which strips them down to basic responses and confronts them with moral dilemmas. His work represents an endeavor to add to the war-novel an extra dimension of moral significance and to highlight the complexity of circumstances which are usually treated in terms of mere physical endurance. His strength lies in his keen historical sense, his ability to tell exciting stories, his understanding of the psychology of fighting men (women make very rare appearances in his fiction) and his clean-cut, unfussy style. His weaknesses are seen in his tendency to view his characters at times as human beings, at others as representing abstract qualities, and his slightly mechanical organization of moments of tension. But he is one of the most readable of New Zealand novelists and at the same time sets his sights high.

His first two novels were *Fear in the Night* and *Long Way Home.* (Despite the publication date of *An Affair of Men,* 1961, it was written after *Long Way Home.*) Both come from the author's own aviation experience. In *Fear in the Night,* the crew of a bomber forced down in Japanese territory are under pressure to repair the plane before they are captured. Brathwaite's technical knowledge and his eye for detail combine with his skill in exploring the minds of his characters under the strain to create a convincing situation remarkable for its concentration of effect. *Long Way Home,* which deals with a search and rescue operation in New Zealand's Southern Alps, is similarly organized.

There is a real advance in *An Affair of Men.* This time the suspense story does not so much include the moral attitudes as dramatize them. Allied airmen who have crashed on the Pacific island Bougainville are pursued by the Japanese under Captain Itoh. His search is frustrated by a Christian-educated headman, Sedu, who insists on remaining neutral. The clash of wills and ideologies is handled with continual invention and boldness and is resolved in terms of the psychology and background of the antagonists. The drama reflects modern man's dilemma in his choice between two different sets of values, between peace and violence.

Brathwaite's trilogy, *The Flying Fish, The Needle's Eye,* and *The Evil Day,* follows the experiences of the fictional Major Williams in the Maori Wars of the 1860s and is the most ambitious treatment of this subject so far written. Again, it is not only the details of strategy and battles which engage Brathwaite and the various kinds of military sensibility which he analyzes, although these are treated with careful attention to historical fact, but the personal and moral problems posed by war itself. A further theme is the development of mutual understanding, paradoxically, between Maori and European through the wars and the question of where the real blame for the conflict lay. The characterization is firm and varied and Major Williams is one of the most completely realized characters in New Zealand fiction.

—J.C. Reid

BRINK, André (Philippus)

Nationality: South African. **Born:** Vrede, Orange Free State, 29 May 1935. **Education:** Lydenburg High School; Potchefstroom University, Transvaal, B.A. 1955, M.A. in English 1958, M.A. in Afrikaans and Dutch 1959; the Sorbonne, Paris, 1959-61. **Family:** Married 1) Estelle Naudé in 1959 (divorced), one son; 2) Salomi Louw in 1965 (divorced), one son; 3) Alta Miller in 1970 (divorced), one son and one daughter; 4) Marésa de Beer in 1990. **Career:** Lecturer, 1963-73, senior lecturer, 1974-75, associate professor, 1976-79, and professor, 1980-90, Department of Afrikaans and Dutch Literature, Rhodes University, Grahamstown. Since 1991 professor of English, University of Cape Town. Editor, *Sestiger* magazine, Pretoria, 1963-65; *Standpunte* magazine, Cape Town, 1986-87. President, Afrikaans Writers Guild, 1978-80. **Awards:** Geerligs prize, 1964; CNA award, 1965, 1979, 1983; South African Academy award, for translation, 1970; Médicis étranger prize (France), 1980; Martin Luther King Memorial prize (UK), 1980. D.Litt.: Rhodes University, 1975; University of the Witwatersrand, Johannesburg, 1985. Chevalier, Legion of Honour (France), 1982; Commander, Order of Arts and Letters (France), 1992. **Agent:** Ruth Liepman, Maienburgweg 23, Zurich, Switzerland. **Address:** Department of English, University of Cape Town, Private Bag, Rondebosch 7700, South Africa.

PUBLICATIONS

Novels

Die gebondenes. Johannesburg, Afrikaanse Pers, 1959.
Die eindelose weë. Cape Town, Tafelberg, 1960.
Lobola vir die lewe (Dowry for Life). Cape Town, Human & Rousseau, 1962.
Die ambassadeur. Cape Town, Human & Rousseau, 1963; as *The Ambassador,* Johannesburg, CNA, 1964; London, Faber, 1985; New York, Summit, 1986; as *File on a Diplomat,* London, Longman, 1967.
Orgie (Orgy). Cape Town, Malherbe, 1965.
Miskien nooit: 'n Somerspel. Cape Town, Human & Rousseau, 1967.
Kennis van die aand. Cape Town, Buren, 1973; as *Looking on Darkness,* London, W.H. Allen, 1974; New York, Morrow, 1975.
An Instant in the Wind. London, W.H. Allen, 1976; New York, Morrow, 1977.
Rumours of Rain. London, W.H. Allen, and New York, Morrow, 1978.
A Dry White Season. London, W.H. Allen, 1979; New York, Morrow, 1980.
A Chain of Voices. London, Faber, and New York, Morrow, 1982.
The Wall of the Plague. London, Faber, 1984; New York, Summit, 1985.
States of Emergency. London, Faber, 1988; New York, Summit, 1989.
An Act of Terror. London, Secker and Warburg, 1991.
The First Life of Adamastor. London, Secker and Warburg, and New York, Summit, 1993.
On the Contrary. London, Secker and Warburg, 1993; New York, Little Brown, 1994.

Short Stories and Novellas

Die meul teen die hang. Cape Town, Tafelberg, 1958.
Rooi, with others. Cape Town, Malherbe, 1965.
Oom Kootjie Emmer. Cape Town, Buren, 1973.
'n Emmertjie wyn: 'n versameling dopstories. Cape Town, Saayman & Weber, 1981.
Oom Kootjie Emmer en die nuwe bedeling: 'n stinkstorie. Johannesburg, Taurus, 1983.
Loopdoppies: Nog dopstories. Cape Town, Saayman & Weber, 1984.
Die Eerste lewe van Adamastor. Cape Town, Saayman & Weber, 1988.

Plays

Die band om ons harte (The Bond Around Our Hearts). Johannesburg, Afrikaanse Pers, 1959.
Caesar (in verse; produced Stellenbosch, Cape Province, 1965). Cape Town, Nasionale, 1961.
Die beskermengel en ander eenbedrywe (The Guardian Angel and Other One-Act Plays), with others. Cape Town, Tafelberg, 1962.
Bagasie (Baggage; includes *Die koffer, Die trommel, Die tas*) (produced Pretoria, 1965). Cape Town, Tafelberg, 1965.
Elders mooiweer en warm (Elsewhere Fair and Warm) (produced Bloemfontein, 1969). Cape Town, Malherbe, 1965.
Die verhoor (The Trial) (produced Pretoria, 1975). Cape Town, Human & Rousseau, 1970.
Die rebelle (The Rebels). Cape Town, Human & Rousseau, 1970.
Kinkels innie kabel (Knots in the Cable), adaptation of *Much Ado About Nothing* by Shakespeare. Cape Town, Buren, 1971.
Afrikaners is plesierig (Afrikaners Make Merry). Cape Town, Human & Rousseau, 1973.
Pavane (produced Pretoria, 1980). Cape Town, Human & Rousseau, 1974.
Bobaas van die Boendoe, adapted from Synge's *Playboy of the Western World* (produced Bloemfontein, 1974). Cape Town, Human & Rousseau, 1974.
Die Hamer van die hekse (The Hammer of the Witches). Cape Town, Tafelberg, 1976.
Toiings op die langpad (Toiings on the Long Road). Pretoria, Van Schaik, 1979.

Other

Die bende (The Gang; for children). Johannesburg, Afrikaanse Pers, 1961.
Platsak (Broke; for children). Johannesburg, Afrikaanse Pers, 1962.
Orde en chaos: 'n Studie oor Germanicus en die tragedies van Shakespeare (Order and Chaos: A Study of *Germanicus* and the Tragedies of Shakespeare). Cape Town, Nasionale, 1962.
Pot-pourri: Sketse uit Parys (Pot-pourri: Sketches from Paris). Cape Town, Human & Rousseau, 1962.
Die verhaal van Julius Caesar (for children). Cape Town, Human & Rousseau, 1963.
Sempre diritto: Italiaanse reisjoernaal (Sempre diritto: Italian Travel Journal). Johannesburg, Afrikaanse Pers, 1963.
Olé: Reisboek oor Spanje (Olé: A Travel Book on Spain). Cape Town, Human & Rousseau, 1965.
Aspekte van die nuwe prosa (Aspects of the New Fiction). Pretoria, Academica, 1967; revised edition, 1969, 1972, 1975.

Parys-Parys: Retoer (Paris-Paris: Return). Cape Town, Human & Rousseau, 1969.
Midi: Op reis deur Suid-Frankryk (Midi: Travelling Through the South of France). Cape Town, Human & Rousseau, 1969.
Fado: 'n reis deur Noord-Portugal (Fado: A Journey Through Northern Portugal). Cape Town, Human & Rousseau, 1970.
Die poësie van Breyten Breytenbach (The Poetry of Breyten Breytenbach). Pretoria, Academica, 1971.
Portret van die vrou as 'n meisie (Portrait of Woman as a Young Girl). Cape Town, Buren, 1973.
Aspekte van die nuwe drama (Aspects of the New Drama). Pretoria, Academica, 1974.
Brandewyn in Suid-Afrika. Cape Town, Buren, 1974; as *Brandy in South Africa,* 1974.
Dessertwyn in Suid-Afrika. Cape Town, Buren, 1974; as *Dessert Wine in South Africa,* 1974.
Die Klap van die meul (A Stroke from the Mill). Cape Town, Buren, 1974.
Die Wyn van bowe (The Wine from Up There). Cape Town, Buren, 1974.
Ik ben er geweest: Gesprekken in Zuid-Afrika (I've Been There: Conversations in South Africa), with others. Kampen, Kok, 1974.
Voorlopige rapport: Beskouings oor die Afrikaanse literatuur van sewentig (Preliminary Report: Views on Afrikaans Literature in the 1970s). Cape Town, Human & Rousseau, 1976; *Tweede voorlopige rapport* (Second Preliminary Report), 1980.
Jan Rabie se 21. Cape Town, Academica, 1977.
Why Literature?/Waarom literatur? Grahamstown, Rhodes University, 1980.
Heildronk uit Wynboer saamgestel deur AB ter viering van die blad se 50ste bestaansjaar. Cape Town, Tafelberg, 1981.
Die fees van die malles. Cape Town, Saayman & Weber, 1981.
Mapmakers: Writing in a State of Siege. London, Faber, 1983; as *Writing in a State of Siege,* New York, Summit, 1984.
Literatuur in die strydperk (Literature in the Arena). Cape Town, Human & Rousseau, 1985.

Editor, *Oggendlied: 'n bundel vir Uys Krige op sy verjaardag 4 Februarie 1977.* Cape Town, Human & Rousseau, 1977.
Editor, *Klein avontuur,* by Top Naeff. Pretoria, Academica, 1979.
Editor, with J.M. Coetzee, *A Land Apart: A South African Reader.* London, Faber, 1986; New York, Viking, 1987.

Translator, *Die brug oor die rivier Kwaï,* by Pierre Boulle. Cape Town, Tafelberg, 1962.
Translator, *Reisigers na die Groot Land,* by André Dhôtel. Cape Town, Tafelberg, 1962.
Translator, *Die wonderhande,* by Joseph Kessel. Cape Town, HAUM, 1962.
Translator, *Nuno, die visserseun,* by L.N. Lavolle. Cape Town, HAUM, 1962.
Translator, *Verhale uit Limousin,* by Léonce Bourliaguet. Cape Town, Human & Rousseau, 1963.
Translator, *Die slapende berg,* by Léonce Bourliaguet. Cape Town, Human & Rousseau, 1963.
Translator, *Land van die Farao's,* by Leonard Cottrell. Cape Town, Malherbe, 1963.
Translator, *Die bos van Kokelunde,* by Michel Rouzé. Cape Town, Malherbe, 1963.
Translator, *Moderato Cantabile,* by Marguerite Duras. Cape Town, HAUM, 1963.

Translator, *Die goue kruis,* by Paul-Jacques Bonzon. Cape Town, Malherbe, 1963.

Translator, *Land van die Twee Riviere,* by Leonard Cottrell. Cape Town, Malherbe, 1964.

Translator, *Volke van Afrika,* by C.M. Turnbull. Cape Town, Malherbe, 1964.

Translator, *Alice se avonture in Wonderland,* by Lewis Carroll. Cape Town, Human & Rousseau, 1965.

Translator, *Die mooiste verhale uit die Arabiese Nagte.* Cape Town, Human & Rousseau, 1966.

Translator, *Die avonture van Don Quixote,* retold by James Reeves. Cape Town, HAUM, 1966.

Translator, *Ek was Cicero,* by Elyesa Bazna. Johannesburg, Afrikaanse Pers, 1966.

Translator, *Koning Babar,* by Jean de Brunhoff. Cape Town, Human & Rousseau, 1966.

Translator, *Die Swerfling,* by Colette. Johannesburg, Afrikaanse Pers, 1966.

Translator, *Die vindingryke ridder, Don Quijote de la Mancha,* by Cervantes. Cape Town, Human & Rousseau, 1966.

Translator, *Speuder Maigret, Maigret en sy dooie, Maigret en die Lang Derm,* and *Maigret en die Spook,* by Simenon. Johannesburg, Afrikaanse Pers, 4 vols., 1966-69.

Translator, *Die mooiste sprokies van Moeder Gans,* by Charles Perrault. Cape Town, Human & Rousseau, 1967.

Translator, *Die eenspaaier,* by Ester Wier. Cape Town, Human & Rousseau, 1967.

Translator, *Die eendstert* (Brighton Rock), by Graham Greene. Johannesburg, Afrikaanse Pers, 1967.

Translator, *Mary Poppins in Kersieboomlaan,* by P.L. Travers. Cape Town, Malherbe, 1967.

Translator, *Die Leeu, die heks en die hangkas,* by C.S. Lewis. Cape Town, Human & Rousseau, 1967.

Translator, with others, *Die groot boek oor ons dieremaats.* Cape Town, Human & Rousseau, 1968.

Translator, with others, *Koning Arthur en sy ridders van die Ronde Tafel.* Cape Town, Human & Rousseau, 1968.

Translator, *Die Kinders van Groenkop,* by Lucy Boston. Cape Town, Human & Rousseau, 1968.

Translator, *Alice deur die spieël,* by Lewis Carroll. Cape Town, Human & Rousseau, 1968.

Translator, *Die Botsende rotse, Die Bul in die doolhoof, Die Horing van ivoor,* and *Die Kop van die gorgoon,* by Ian Serraillier. Cape Town, HAUM, 4 vols., 1968.

Translator, *Bontnek,* by Dhan Gopal Mukerji. Cape Town, HAUM, 1968.

Translator, *Die Draai van die skroef* (The Turn of the Screw), by Henry James. Johannesburg, Afrikaanse Pers, 1968.

Translator, *Die Gelukkige prins en ander sprokies,* by Oscar Wilde. Cape Town, Human & Rousseau, 1969.

Translator (into Afrikaans), *Richard III,* by Shakespeare. Cape Town, Human & Rousseau, 1969.

Translator, *Die Gestewelde kat,* by Charles Perrault. Cape Town, Human & Rousseau, 1969.

Translator, *Die groot golf,* by Pearl S. Buck. Cape Town, Human & Rousseau, 1969.

Translator, *Die Nagtegaal,* by H.C. Andersen. Cape Town, HAUM, 1969.

Translator, *Die Terroriste,* by Camus. Johannesburg, Dramatiese Artistieke en Letterkundige Organisasie, 1970.

Translator, *Eskoriaal,* by Michel De Ghelderode. Johannesburg, Dramatiese Artistieke en Letterkundige Organisasie, 1971.

Translator, *Ballerina,* by Nada ur ija-Prodanovi . Cape Town, Malherbe, 1972.

Translator, *Die Seemeeu* (The Seagull), by Chekhov. Cape Town, Human & Rousseau, 1972.

Translator, *Die Bobaas van die Boendoe* (The Playboy of the Western World), by Synge. Cape Town, Human & Rousseau, 1973.

Translator, *Jonathan Livingston Seemeeu,* by Richard Bach. Cape Town, Malherbe, 1973.

Translator, *Hedda Gabler,* by Ibsen. Cape Town, Human & Rousseau, 1974.

Translator, *Die Wind in die wilgers,* by Kenneth Grahame. Cape Town, Human & Rousseau, 1974.

Translator, *Die Tragedie van Romeo en Juliet,* by Shakespeare. Cape Town, Human & Rousseau, 1975.

Translator, *Die Tierbrigade,* and *Nuwe avontuur van die Tierbrigade,* by Claude Desailly. Cape Town, Tafelberg, 2 vols., 1978-79.

Translator, *Die Nagtegaal en die roos,* by Oscar Wilde. Cape Town, Human & Rousseau, 1980.

Translator, *Rot op reis,* by Kenneth Grahame. Cape Town, Human & Rousseau, 1981.

Translator, *Adam van die pad,* by Elizabeth Janet Gray. Cape Town, Human & Rousseau, 1981.

Translator, *Klein Duimpie,* by Charles Perrault. Cape Town, Human & Rousseau, 1983.

*

Manuscript Collections: University of the Orange Free State, Bloemfontein; National English Literary Museum, Grahamstown.

Critical Studies: *Donker Weerlig: Literêre opstelle oor die werk van André P. Brink* edited by Jan Senekal, Cape Town, Jutalit, 1988; "The Lives of Adamastor" by Anthony J. Hassall, in *International Literature in English* edited by Pobert L. Ross, London and Chicago, St. James Press, 1991.

André Brink comments:

My early work revealed the influence of existentialism (notably of Camus) and was largely a matter of technical exploration. Ever since a year-long stay in Paris in 1968 a deep awareness of the responsibility of the novelist towards his society has shaped my work: not in the sense of "using" the novel for propaganda purposes, which degrades literature, but as a profound evaluation of social and interpersonal relationships as they affect the individual: the individual doomed to solitude and to more or less futile attempts to break out of this spiritual "apartheid" by trying to touch others—which means that the sexual experience is of primary importance to my characters.

With the dismantling of apartheid there is a new freedom to broaden the scope of my writing and to explore the possibilities of an African magic realism.

*   *   *

André Brink is an Afrikaner dissident who has chosen to remain inside the South African apartheid society which he regards as morally insupportable. His powerful political and historical novels have been translated into 20 languages, while in South Africa he is regarded with a somewhat sceptical eye by writers and academics alike.

Brink is a prodigious, multi-talented literary figure. In addition to plays, travel writing, and critical work, he has written 16 novels and translated a great many works into Afrikaans. Formerly a professor of Afrikaans literature at Rhodes University, he now occupies a chair in English literature at the University of Cape Town. Despite three nominations for the Nobel Prize for literature, Brink is disliked by many Afrikaans writers and critics in South Africa, not so much (or not only) because of his outright moral opposition to apartheid, but for what is regarded as sentimentality and sensationalism in his writing. There is no doubt that Brink's writing is extremely uneven. His novels are almost always flawed in some respect, and they are often overwritten. Also, Brink has a singular penchant for placing gauche and inane statements in the mouths of his characters, while his rendition of sexual experience is often cliché-ridden and tasteless. Yet he has written some of the most powerful stories to emerge in recent South African writing, and he commands impressive narrative skills.

As an emerging Afrikaans novelist in the late 1950s and early 1960s, Brink almost singlehandedly modernised Afrikaans novel-writing. Arguably the most eclectic South African writer at the time, he knocked the conservative Afrikaans literary tradition out of complacency with themes and techniques drawn from writers like Camus, Beckett, Sartre, Nabokov, Henry Miller, Faulkner, Greene, and Durrell. In 1974, the Afrikaner establishment was hit by the sensational news that Brink's *Kennis van die aand,* later translated into English as *Looking on Darkness,* had been banned. The banning created a major division between the State and many of the country's Afrikaans writers, and introduced a new era of increasingly vocal dissidence from within the establishment. After a Supreme Court hearing and a further two appeals, the novel was finally unbanned in 1982, but given an age restriction which is impossible to enforce.

For Brink, expulsion from the laager was an important juncture. Capitalising on sudden international fame as South Africa's first Afrikaans writer to be banned under the country's comprehensive 1963 censorship legislation—usually reserved for girlie calendars, Communist publications, and morally and politically perverse writing in English—Brink translated *Kennis van die aand* into English and became, thenceforth, an international novelist writing in English. He has since produced nine weighty novels, roughly one every two years.

By his own admission Brink remains, in essence, an Afrikaner, but his recent novels are not "translated." Brink maintains that he produces the novels in both languages more or less simultaneously, starting out in Afrikaans, but completing the first "final" draft in English. However, Brink is far more idiomatic and comfortable in Afrikaans, and his English versions sometimes suffer from a certain rigidity of style.

Looking on Darkness is a compelling but uneven novel. As Nadine Gordimer has observed, it suffers from the "defiant exultation and relief" of Brink's first major cry of rebellion. The novel veers recklessly from profound historical reconstruction and metaphoric statement to the slushiest of sexual and emotional scenes. This book tells the story of Joseph Malan, a coloured man and a descendant of slaves who makes good as an actor after winning a grant to study at RADA in London, and who then comes home to launch a full-on cultural assault against apartheid. A passionate love affair with a white (British) woman develops, and Joseph is caught between the impossibility of love across the colour line, and the sinister manoeuvres of the Security Police against his theatre group. In a contrived and somewhat unconvincing denouement, Joseph

murders his lover, whereupon the Security Police half kill him in unspeakably brutal fashion. He is sentenced to death, and the narrative is written from the death cell on sheets of paper which (we are asked to believe) Joseph daily flushes down the toilet, so determined is he to escape the scrutiny of his gaolers.

Looking on Darkness sets the pattern for Brink's later novels in several important respects. There is an uncompromising engagement with issues of race and politics, an insistence on exposing the sinister, vicious, and hypocritical elements at the heart of the apartheid system, an ability to rediscover the present in terms of a rich and violent frontier history, and a persistent fictional exploration of sexual love as a framework for a higher form of enquiry into the state of modern existence, subject to the peculiar restraints of apartheid society.

In *An Instant in the Wind,* Brink's first "English" novel following *Looking on Darkness,* a runaway slave escorts an 18th-century Cape lady back to civilisation after her husband and their party come to grief in an expedition into the interior. The story is a rich investigation into pertinent South African themes, and has a strong romantic appeal, but the love story between the erstwhile slave and the fallen lady constantly verges on a kind of sentiment more appropriate to popular romance fiction.

However, Brink's best talents come to the fore powerfully in his next—arguably his best—novel, *Rumours of Rain.* Like its successor, *A Dry White Season,* the novel examines the moral options of a contemporary Afrikaner who is rooted to a potent nationalistic history, but who is vulnerable to the short-comings and hypocrisy of Afrikaner nationalism. *Rumours of Rain* achieves remarkable depth and complexity, and contains some of Brink's best characterisation.

The narrative inventiveness of *Rumours of Rain* and *A Dry White Season* is taken further in Brink's other *tour de force, A Chain of Voices.* This is a major novel which fictionalises a slave revolt in the early 19th century in the Cape. Brink gives each of his several characters a narrating voice, and out of the overlapping narratives a story of great force and interlocking complexity emerges. Brink's exceptional ability to re-animate the past—especially that of slavery in South Africa—enables him to establish the recurrent motifs of a frontier history in which South Africa remains confined.

True to form, Brink followed up this success with a work which is thoroughly mediocre. *The Wall of the Plague* is a particularly clumsy attempt at metaphorically associating the Black Death plague of medieval Europe with modern apartheid. The novel degenerates into a lengthy implied debate between three South African expatriates about the merits of exile as opposed to active engagement in the country itself, expressed in terms of black versus white sexual potency (there is a coloured girl in the middle) with a great deal of melodrama and sheer inanity thrown in.

However, Brink's 1988 novel, *States of Emergency,* shows outstanding novelistic deftness. The "story" consists of "notes" towards a love story set in violence-torn South Africa during the State of Emergency in the 1980s. The story skillfully interweaves public and political emergency with the private emergency of conducting an illicit love affair in the midst of ceaseless violence and upheaval. Despite its brilliance, the novel uneasily mixes metafictional self-consciousness with a series of unexamined illusions—principally the illusion that the novel one reads is not a novel at all but incomplete notes for a novel. In a project where every fictional device is brought to the surface for debate, it seems a massive sleight-of-hand—and contrary to the deconstructive spirit in which the writing takes place—not to examine this, the biggest fictional strategy of all.

States of Emergency is further complicated by the juxtaposition of Brink's actual divorce and his liaison with a young woman, and the metafictional "fabrication" of a similar story in the book: a love affair between a professor and a young colleague. The novel was embargoed for distribution in South Africa after its publication as part of a divorce settlement.

—Leon de Kock

BRODBER, Erna (May)

Nationality: Jamaican. **Born:** Woodside, St. Mary, Jamaica, 21 April 1940. **Education:** University College of the West Indies, London, 1960-63, B.A. (honours) in history 1963; University of Washington, Seattle, (Ford Foundation fellowship), 1967; University College of the West Indies, Kingston, M.Sc. in sociology 1968, Ph.D. in history 1985; University of Sussex, (Commonwealth fellowship), 1979. **Family:** One son. **Career:** Lecturer in sociology, University of the West Indies for seven years, research fellow and staff member, Institute of Social and Economic Research, University of the West Indies, 1972-83; associate professor, Randolph-Macon College (DuPont scholar). Visiting scholar, University of Michigan, Ann Arbor, 1973; visiting fellow, University of Sussex, 1981; visiting professor, Gettysburg College, Pennsylvania, Clark-Atlanta University, Georgia, and University of California, Santa Cruz. **Awards:** University of the West Indies postgraduate award, 1964; National Festival award, Jamaica Festival Commission, 1975; Commomwealth Writers Prize for Canada and the Americas, 1989; Fulbright fellowship, 1990. **Address:** Woodside, Pear Tree Grove, P.O. St. Mary/St. Catherine, Jamaica, West Indies.

PUBLICATIONS

Novels

Jane and Louisa Will Soon Come Home. London, New Beacon, 1980.
Myal. London, New Beacon, 1988.
Louisiana. London, New Beacon, 1994.

Play

Jane and Louisa Will Soon Come Home, adaptation of her own novel (produced, 1990).

Other

Abandonment of Children in Jamaica. Mona, Jamaica, Institute of Social and Economic Research, University of the West Indies, 1974.
Yards in the City of Kingston. Mona, Jamaica, Institute of Social and Economic Research, University of the West Indies, 1975.
Perceptions of Caribbean Women: Towards a Documentation of Stereotypes. Mona, Jamaica, Institute of Social and Economic Research, University of the West Indies, 1982.

Rural-Urban Migration and the Jamaican Child. Santiago, Chile, UNESCO, Regional Office for Education in Latin America and the Caribbean, 1986.

*

Manuscript Collection: University of the West Indies, Kingston.

Theatrical Activities:
Actor: **Radio**—*A Time to Remember,* for six years. **Play**—Role in *Eight O'Clock Jamaica Time.*

Erna Brobder comments:

My work, fiction and non-fiction, is devoted to helping Africans of the diaspora to understand themselves and hopefully to consequently undertake with more clarity the job of social (re)construction which we have to do. To better communicate with this target group, I use folk songs, etc., which are well known within the culture to make my points and to inform a group often far from archival data. I inject information which I think this group needs to have, and which I arrive at from my investigations, into my novels.

*   *   *

The time when Jean Rhys was the only female novelist included in surveys of Caribbean literature is over. Nowadays, women's writing dominates Caribbean literature, its flowering and status confirmed by the many anthologies devoted solely to Caribbean women writers and the steady proliferation of articles on, among others, Jamaica Kincaid, Michelle Cliff, Merle Hodge, Zee Edgell, and Erna Brodber.

Erna Brodber's generically adventurous *Jane and Louisa Will Soon Come Home* unites aesthetics and activism. As Nellie, the main character, searches for her voice and untangles her cultural identity, issues of class, race, gender, education, religion, social mobility, and Jamaica's relation to Africa, England, and the United States of America come to the fore. Incredibly, Brodber, a sociologist, states that her first novel, now considered a classic, "was not meant to find a public audience." It was meant for her students.

"Voices," the novel's first section, mirrors Nellie's psychological fragmentation and hints obliquely at the monumental struggle she (and we as readers) must undergo if psychic coherence and, by extension, social unity are to be achieved. The rapid juxtaposition of voices initially and deliberately confuses, yet this confusion testifies to the complexity of Jamaican society, whether in its days of slavery, emancipation, or independence, and illustrates the psychic and social disturbances that festered in the wake of the colonial emphasis on white European superiority and black African inferiority, a dichotomy that, once internalized, makes impossible demands on Jamaicans of African ancestry.

The relationship between William Whiting, a Jamaican-born white, and Tia Maria, a Jamaican-born black, functions as an archetype for the black-white relations that haunt society throughout the rest of the narrative. To improve her khaki children's social mobility, "Great grand Tia did everything to annihilate herself . . . her skin, her dress, her smell . . . the things she loved would prosper in inverse ratio to her disappearance." Repressing her culture and identifying with William's has disastrous consequences for Tia's descendants. Cultural disinheritance, Tia's legacy, estranges Nellie from her sense of self and society. Returning home, as the title suggests, allows Nellie to discover her cultural roots. This is not an idiosyncratic individual quest, but one essential for society as a whole if it is to move beyond the crippling paralysis Nellie embodies. Under Rasta-man Baba's tutelage, Nellie reclaims language and acknowledges and embraces all aspects of Jamaican experience: "I could no how wear my rightful Easter dress, sit in my granny's parlour, eat my cane nor walk in my beautiful garden unless I walked with them, the black and squat, the thin and wizened, all of them."

In terms of its form and themes, *Myal,* set in 1914-1919, a time of emergent black consciousness, bears many similarities to and duplicates the considerable achievement of *Jane and Louisa Will Soon Come Home,* thus consolidating Brodber's reputation as the most exciting novelist of the region. Both novels are wide ranging in allusiveness (the Bible, folk songs, Anancy tales, or literature), weave between past and present, shift easily within the diverse tiers of formal Jamaican English and the clipped rhythms of village and yard, and abridge the history of postemancipation Jamaica with astonishing brevity.

Psychological trauma is related to the historical trauma of colonization. Ella O'Grady-Langley, the mulatto main character, is ill, "tripped out in foreign." Foreign refers not only to her experience in the United States, where her white American husband Selwyn Langley exploited her stories for commercial gain, but to the alienating education she received in Jamaica. The European discourse—allegories and parables—she internalized as a child leaves her spiritless. Colonial education cultivates intellectual servitude and passivity, so that even in the postemancipation period freedom is curtailed because Jamaicans, as we see when Ella recites a Kipling poem, have internalized images and ideas that denigrate Africanness and blackness. Throughout the novel this process is called "spirit thievery."

There are two solutions to the problem of spirit thievery. Mass Cyrus, myal man and healer, uses traditional folk skills to cure Ella. Echoing the biblical account of creation, the healing process requires seven days to re-create Ella and restore harmony between her mind and body. Aside from this Afro-Jamaican remedy, another solution is critique and appropriation: read critically, refuse stereotypes, destroy old images, and create new home-grown ones in their place. Ella's decision to become a teacher marks the moment of her recovery and cultural repossession. By challenging "the printed word and the ideas it carries," Ella and her students can overcome the separation the colonial education system enforces between mind and body, mind and place. Brodber's description of herself as an "intellectual worker" applies to Ella also. "The half has never been told" is a frequent refrain in *Myal,* and Brodber, like so many Caribbean writers, tells the other half, boldly and beautifully.

—Stephen Milnes

BRODKEY, Harold (Roy)

Nationality: American. **Born:** Aaron Weintrub in Staunton, Illinois, 25 October 1930; adopted by Brodkey family. **Education:** Harvard University, Cambridge, Massachusetts, 1947-52, B.A. (cum laude) 1952. **Family:** Married 1) Joanna Brown in 1952 (divorced 1962), one daughter; 2) Ellen Schwamm in 1980. **Career:** Adjunct Associate Professor of English, Cornell University, Ithaca, New York, 1977-78, Spring 1979, and Fall 1981; writer-in-residence, City College, New York, 1987. Since 1987 staff writer, *New Yorker.* **Awards:** American Academy in Rome fellowship, 1959; Creative Artists Public Service grant, 1972; National Magazine award, 1974; Brandeis University Creative Arts award, 1975; Pushcart prize, 1975; O. Henry award, 1975, 1976; National Endowment for the Arts grant, 1984; Guggenheim fellowship, 1987. **Agent:** Deborah Karl, 52 W. Clinton Ave., Irvington, New York 10533. **Address:** The New Yorker, 25 West 43rd Street, New York, New York 10036, U.S.A.

PUBLICATIONS

Novel

The Runaway Soul. London, Cape, 1991.
Profane Friendship. New York, Farrar Straus, 1994.

Short Stories

First Love and Other Sorrows. New York, Dial Press, 1957; London, Hamish Hamilton, 1958.
Women and Angels. Philadelphia, Jewish Publication Society of America, 1985.
Stories in an Almost Classical Mode. New York, Knopf, 1988; as *The Abundant Dreamer,* London, Cape, 1989.

Uncollected Short Stories

"Spring Fugue," in *New Yorker,* 23 April 1990.
"What I Do for Money," in *New Yorker,* 18 October 1993.
"Religion," in *Glimmer Train Stories* (Portland), Spring 1995.

Poetry

A Poem about Testimony and Argument. New York, Jordan Davies, 1986.

*   *   *

Harold Brodkey's early published works are creditable if slender, although it was assumed—especially by awards committees—that his 1957 collection of nine short stories, *First Love and Other Sorrows,* forecast a luminous literary career.

The stories themselves were fresh, modest reprises of growing-up—puppy love to parenthood—not uncommon territory for a young writer. *First Love* assured Brodkey's welcome on college campuses where he has also read from his occasional later works. In the three decades since his story collection, however, Brodkey has produced only two novels, a few stories and a small scattering of poems and comment. Two stories were the 1975 and 1976 O. Henry first prize winners nonetheless. "His Son, in His Arms, in Light, Aloft," the 1976 selection, is a toddler-narrated reflection on a father-son relationship and is an obvious precursor of the recent sketch entitled "S.L."

Brodkey's creativity is said to be directed into a lengthy novel-in-progress, *A Party of Animals.* In recent years, two selections, "Lila" and "Ceil," were printed in the *New Yorker,* then were reprinted along with another segment, "Angel," collectively called *Women and Angels.* A fourth excerpt, "S.L.," has appeared in the *New Yorker.* Since these four pieces—character sketches of sorts—

are the only glimpses of what has been suggested is a life-work, they may not reliably define the novel to come. They little suggest a novel at all, except that they, again, cover a man's early years and are more or less set in the Jewish family milieu in a small Illinois town. Actually the excerpts have little to do with either being young or being Jewish; they may be autobiographical and therefore have much to do with being Brodkey. Whether that compels readers may depend on how they share the every-life-a-novel view which he presumably meant in a 1980 comment scoring those who feel "that our lives are perhaps not worth writing about."

A cyclonic tangle of recollections by Wiley Silenowicz about his Russian-Jewish birth-mother, Ceil, and his American Jewish adoptive-parents, Lila and S.L. Silenowicz compete with a one-hour appearance in the Harvard Yard by an Angel, who may be God or Truth or "Sheer Otherness."

Wiley was utterly egocentric even as a toddler with perfect recall of such trivia as shirt fabrics. His mean-spirited evaluations of his not one, but two Jewish mothers inevitably invites categorizing Brodkey's work in the Knock Mom school of fiction. It is also patronizingly Knock Dad in "S.L." and slides down the slippery (and obviously unfamiliar) slopes of philosophy into incomprehensibility in "Angel." If Wiley is too smart to Knock God in the quasi-interview that is "Angel," he again settles for patronizing as in "I suddenly wanted to be like It."

It is in narrative style that Brodkey insists on playing on all the keys at once. A cacophony of effects results. There is outrageous posturing and poetizing, eccentric syntax, arbitrary capitalization, italics and incremental repetition, heaped into overloaded sentences sagging under the weight of clause upon clause. This excess obscures the undeniable poetic gifts of language and rhythm that do manage to avoid inundation. A line like "The air, the masked rainlight, the wind pounding, hissing, pecking and pushing as if with a ruffled-feather breast—it is monstrous" suddenly soars out. Even the spontaneous burst of blabby, nervous S.L.'s compliment to baby Wiley, "You are really something; you are a bouquet on two legs—you know that?" is a delight. Yet, enamored of the sound of words, Brodkey too often tends to let meaning fall where it will, as in the aphoristic "Child flesh in its brevity and shine is witty."

Excessive shifts in time and point of view compound confusion. Wiley, hooked on interior monologue when knee-high, also narrates as himself at different ages, although in adult language. He even makes room for another voice to speak of him in the third person. Moreover, Wiley knows best what other characters mean despite what they say and interprets for the reader.

Brodkey has a way of melding narrative infelicities that does appear unique. The nuances of advertising copy join awkward syntax in " . . . no resistance emerges outward from me as my own statement from the auditoriums of awe that much of my personal consciousness is." Or here the sociological simplism pairs with a poor pun: "We have here a landscape of envy and emptiness—a place of temporary and embattled *comforts,* an American beauty (that which results from a meeting of what was here and a society of grand acquisitors)."

It is probably enough to say that when, or if, Brodkey chooses to complete *A Party of Animals* that will be time for a judgment on its entirety. As compulsive as a familiar exercise or as necessary as an exorcism—who but Brodkey would know?—the work completed may free him to go on to the great creativity long expected of him. Or, less likely, prove that Brodkey is already there.

—Marian Pehowski

BRONER, E(sther) M(asserman)

Nationality: American. **Born:** Detroit, Michigan, 8 July 1930. **Education:** Wayne State University, Detroit, B.A. 1950, M.A. 1962; The Union Institute, Cincinnati, Ohio, Ph.D. 1978. **Family:** Married Robert Broner; four children. **Career:** Member of the English Department, including professor of English, 1963-88, and since 1988 Professor Emerita, Wayne State University. Visiting professor, Haifa University, Israel, 1972 and 1975, Oberlin College, Ohio, 1979, University of California, Los Angeles, 1979, and Sarah Lawrence College, Bronxville, New York, 1982-87; visiting writer, New York University, Columbia University, and City College of New York. **Awards:** Bicentennial Playwriting prize, 1976; National Endowment for the Arts grant, 1979 and 1987; Wonder Woman award, 1983; Wayne State University Distinguished Alumna award, 1984. **Address:** 40 W. 22nd St., New York, New York 10010, U.S.A.

PUBLICATIONS

Novels

Her Mothers. New York, Holt Rinehart, 1975.
A Weave of Women. New York, Holt Rinehart, 1978.

Short Stories

Journal/Nocturnal and Seven Stories. New York, Harcourt Brace, 1968.
Ghost Stories. New York, Global City Books, 1995.

Uncollected Short Stories

"Remember, Daughter, Remember the Tale," in *Midstream* (New York), 1969.
"Traveler and His Telling," in *Commentary* (New York), September 1970.
"We Not Allowed," with Aryeh Seagull, in *Epoch* (Ithaca, New York), Fall 1971.
"A Saga of Great Men," in *Commentary* (New York), December 1971.
"Ken and Barbie," with Aryeh Seagull, in *Hot Apples* (Detroit), no. 2, 1973.
"Love and Ulpan in Jerusalem," in *National Jewish Monthly* (Washington, D.C.), March 1973.
"Hoorah, Hoorah, It's Tu B'Svat," in *Southern Humanities Review* (Auburn, Alabama), Summer 1973.
"The Galoot and the Substitute," in *Greensboro Review* (Greensboro, North Carolina), Spring 1974.
"Holiday," in *Nimrod* (Tulsa, Oklahoma), 1976.
"Is Fred Dead," in *Mother Jones* (San Francisco), January 1983.
"The Dancers," in *Ms.* (New York), November 1983.

Plays

Summer Is a Foreign Land (produced Detroit, 1967). Detroit, Wayne State University Press, 1966.
Colonel Higginson, with M. Zieve (produced Detroit, 1968).
The Body Parts of Margaret Fuller (produced Detroit and New York, 1976).

Letters to My Television Past (produced New York, 1985).

Television Play: *Wait Till I Swallow My Saliva,* 1968.

Other

The Telling: The Story of a Group of Jewish Women Who Journey to Spirituality through Community and Ceremony. San Francisco, HarperSanFrancisco, 1993.
Mournings and Mourning: A Kaddish Journal. San Francisco, HarperSanFrancisco, 1994.
The Women's Haggadah, with Naomi Nimrod. San Francisco, HarperSanFrancisco, 1994.

Editor, with Cathy N. Davidson, *The Lost Tradition: Mothers and Daughters in Literature.* New York, Ungar, 1981.

*

Critical Studies: "Of Holy Writing and Priestly Voices" by Nancy Jo Hoy, Summer 1983, and interview, Winter 1984, both in *Massachusetts Review* (Amherst); *On Being a Jewish Feminist* edited by Susannah Heschel, Schocken Press, 1983; "The Novels of E.M. Broner: A Study in Secular Feminism and Feminist Judaism" by Ann R. Shapiro, in *Jewish-American Journal* edited by Daniel Walden.

E.M. Broner comments:

(1986) I am not interested in the autobiographical in as much as that concerns the protagonist breathing against the mirror. I am not interested in love if it is an encapsulated event. I am interested in the epoch—in characters in landscape of time and politics. My characters are often peripheral, even, as in *A Weave of Women,* ultimately outlaws. Or, in a novel-in-progress on which I'm presently employed, street people. They may go on an uncharted journey, as in *Her Mothers,* a kind of Odyssey in which the maps have not been drawn as to the journeys of women to find one another and then themselves. That journey becomes mythic, biblical, literary, historical until they find their own names in the new alphabet of their lives.

I write about community, the establishment of union and communion. I write about small people overcoming their natures and doing large endeavors.

My earliest book was a sort of ethnic lyric—sentimental, traditional. But the traditional style of writing never interested me. By the second work, *Journal/Nocturnal,* a novella, I was already dividing my characters into columnar figures—thinking a domestic daily thought and a wild nocturnal thought on the same page, opposing sides.

My style in recent works has been more elegiac. I work with ritual and mystically, often using the Torah, Jewish legend upon which to build.

I believe there has to be a Woman's Torah and that our foremothers must be resuscitated, replaced in their heritage. I also have been working most recently on historical material and am looking for the voice that will be both present and past.

I am also a playwright, working with feminist themes, in *The Body Parts of Margaret Fuller,* or political hindsight in the one-act, *Letters to My Television Past.* I am involved, now, in the meeting of opposites—in their hard paths towards one another, in a new work, "The Olympics."

(1995) I have been a pioneer in the Jewish Feminist Movement, a theme in *Her Mothers* and *A Weave of Women,* and in my non-fiction, *The Telling,* in which I document the eighteen years of meetings by prominent New York women to perform alternative ceremonies, including a yearly Women's Passover. I co-authored *The Women's Haggadah,* with Naomi Nimrod, to put our foremothers back into their own history.

I conceive of fiction in which religion/magic and politics combine to make the novel, *The Repair Shop,* now in progress.

And I return to an earlier vision, in *A Weave of Women,* to do a filmscript which restates the autonomy, dignity, and ceremony of women who create magic in the magical city of Jerusalem.

*   *   *

E.M. Broner is an original novelist. Except for a short story or two and her novella *Journal/Nocturnal,* she has never worked in a realistic mode. Even her first published play, *Summer Is a Foreign Land* (she has written others produced in university and community theaters), includes a character who is both a doctor and the angel of death, and a grandmother with an inheritance of three magical wishes because she descended from a wonder-working Hassidic rabbi in Poland. The matter of that play is clear and pragmatic enough: assimilation, the loss of traditional values, the weakening of generational ties, family expectations in conflict with personal freedom, but the world of the play is one of ordinary marvels.

It is not entirely accurate to call *Journal/Nocturnal* realistic, although there are no wonder-working rabbis or angels of death to be found. The setting is an urban university; we have a double journal by a faculty wife who has been having an affair with a right-wing student of her husband's, during the years of the Vietnam war, the split in the nation reflected in the split in the psyche of the protagonist and in the journal itself. One journal, running down the left half of the page, contains what she is willing to cede to the world, the surface of realism; the other side is her secret emotional life, verging into madness and finally into an accident we cannot help but see as willful death.

Journal/Nocturnal and the other stories in that volume are interesting, even arresting, but *Her Mothers* represents a leap of mastery, breadth, emotional range and power. A strong narrative voice emerges, in this case the partially throttled, often uproarious, and extremely intelligent voice of Beatrix Palmer. The book begins with a datum, the 1944 high school yearbook page of photographs. Through the novel, a vaudeville routine runs.

> "Mother, I'm pregnant with a girl."
> "How old is she?"
> "Seventeen."
> "Then you're giving birth to me."

or

> "Mama, I'm giving birth to a baby girl."
> "What is she?"
> "Patient."
> "Then leave her in the hospital."

We have the dreadful misadventures of Beatrix's high school girl friends. We have the adventures of her elective foremothers, Margaret Fuller, Louisa May Alcott, Emily Dickinson, and Charlotte Forten, about whom Bea is writing a book. The other foremothers of her search for identity are the Biblical matriarchs, Sara, Rivka, Lea, and Rahel (Sarah, Rebecca, Leah, and Rachel, in the usual English versions), whose stories Broner retells.

Bea is in search of her lost and estranged daughter Lena, trying to place herself in history with a set of foremothers who lead to her and a daughter who will carry on from her. She wanders through history and through the world in search of her ancestors and progeny, in Detroit, Florida, California, sea to sea, in Israel, in dreams. She has an affair with a ghost on a Georgia sea island, where foremother Charlotte Forten taught former slaves. Finally her daughter comes to her and in a scene that takes place obliquely, they quarrel, Bea tries to return her to the salty womb of the sea, and they reach a bumpy and fragile reconciliation.

A Weave of Women is a novel about a group of women, friends in Israel who try to reclaim the female and lunar side of Judaism, to place themselves again in history and also in the holy cosmos that always underlies Broner's work, in an ancient stone house in Jerusalem across the street from a home for wayward girls. The book is full of rituals the women invent, rediscover, create together to celebrate the times, the seasons, the crises of women's lives.

The women are sharply individuated, yet seen as a collective. The highly imagistic, rhythmic, and often wry narrative voice carries us in and out of their diverse experiences. Many disasters befall. At a Purim celebration where Simah (Joy) is retelling the myth of Esther from a woman-centered viewpoint, her baby daughter is murdered by an Arab who thinks she is someone else. Tsipporah, one of the wayward girls whose name means bird, is unable to survive the lures of the underside of religious and criminal life in the old city and becomes a pigeon instead. Shula, a wayward girl rescued by the women and sent to art school, goes abroad to study and is raped and murdered in a closed train compartment and literally eaten alive. Others of the women find strength to change their lives and become politically and religiously potent.

Broner's world-view is thoroughly Judaic and religious, a living and sensuous and intelligent battle fought with her religion through all of her books with the intent of making Judaism extend justice to and become a home for women. The world created in her novels is very much the modern world, full of the threats, the perils, the problems of modern life, a life of jetting about, trying to get grants, single motherhood, racism, antisemitism, wars, and threats of global wars; yet it is also a world never merely natural. It is a world in which demons enter women who are frustrated and soured, and can be expelled by wise and caring friends. It is a world in which a tormented girl can become a pigeon. It is a world in which myths embody themselves for good or evil in men and women and walk the earth to be encountered and wrestled with.

The women of *A Weave of Women* are even more ambitious than Bea in *Her Mothers,* for they want not only to locate themselves and their daughters in history, but to re-experience the cosmos, to re-invent godhead and the law, to make a new heaven and a new earth. Broner is not a prolific writer, but, like some of the characters she invents, she is passionate, serious, and ambitious. Her concern with women's descent, foremothers, mothers and daughters, runs through her strongest work, along with a consciously priestly or rabbinical function of reinterpreting the law and ritual in the service of women's dignity. She is a writer in whom a passionate experimentation comes together with serious political and religious inquiry.

—Marge Piercy

152

BROOKE-ROSE, Christine

Nationality: British. **Born:** Geneva, Switzerland. **Education:** Somerville College, Oxford, 1946-49, B.A. in English, M.A. 1953; University College, London, 1950-54, B.A. in French, Ph.D. 1954. **Family:** Married Jerzy Peterkiewicz, *q.v.,* in 1948 (divorced 1975). **Career:** Freelance literary journalist, London, 1956-68; Maître de Conférences, 1969-75, and professeur, 1975-88, University of Paris VIII, Vincennes. **Awards:** Society of Authors traveling prize, 1965; James Tait Black Memorial prize, 1967; Arts Council translation prize, 1969. Litt.D.: University of East Anglia, Norwich, 1988. **Address:** c/o Cambridge University Press, P.O. Box 110, Cambridge CB2 3RL, England.

PUBLICATIONS

Novels

The Languages of Love. London, Secker and Warburg, 1957.
The Sycamore Tree. London, Secker and Warburg, 1958; New York, Norton, 1959.
The Dear Deceit. London, Secker and Warburg, 1960; New York, Doubleday, 1961.
The Middlemen: A Satire. London, Secker and Warburg, 1961.
Out. London, Joseph, 1964.
Such. London, Joseph, 1966.
Between. London, Joseph, 1968.
Thru. London, Hamish Hamilton, 1975.
Amalgamemnon. Manchester, Carcanet, 1984; Normal, Illinois, Dalkey Archive, 1994.
Xorandor. Manchester, Carcanet, 1986; New York, Avon, 1988.
Verbivore. Manchester, Carcanet, 1990.
Textermination. Manchester, Carcanet, and New York, New Directions, 1991.

Short Stories

Go When You See the Green Man Walking. London, Joseph, 1970.

Poetry

Gold. Aldington, Kent, Hand and Flower Press, 1955.

Other

A Grammar of Metaphor. London, Secker and Warburg, 1958.
A ZBC of Ezra Pound. London, Faber, 1971; Berkeley, University of California Press, 1976.
A Structural Analysis of Pound's Usura Canto: Jakobson's Method Extended and Applied to Free Verse. The Hague, Mouton, 1976.
A Rhetoric of the Unreal: Studies in Narrative and Structure, Especially of the Fantastic. Cambridge and New York, Cambridge University Press, 1981.
Stories, Theories and Things. Cambridge, Cambridge University Press, 1991.

Translator, *Children of Chaos,* by Juan Goytisolo. London, MacGibbon and Kee, 1958.

Translator, *Fertility and Survival: Population Problems from Malthus to Mao Tse Tung,* by Alfred Sauvy. New York, Criterion, 1960; London, Chatto and Windus, 1961.
Translator, *In the Labyrinth,* by Alain Robbe-Grillet. London, Calder and Boyars, 1968.

*

Critical Studies: "Christine Brooke-Rose" by Sarah Birch, in *Contemporary Fiction* (Oxford), 1994; Christine Brooke-Rose issue of *Review of Contemporary Fiction* (Elmwood Park, Illinois),1994.

Christine Brooke-Rose comments:
From *Out* onwards, experiments with language and forms of fiction.

*   *   *

Christine Brooke-Rose for many years taught American literature at the University of Paris, and this fact is important in considering the work of this cosmopolitan writer, whose later novels are much influenced by the French avant-garde of the late 1950s. Her early, biting satires are constructed in the usual manner of plot and character, but when she came to consider the work of such French writers as Robbe-Grillet, her style changed radically. She virtually discarded metaphor, and started to use language more as a concrete artifact than as a vehicle of communication and information.

In its least subtle forms, this manner of writing comes close to word games. At its best it pushes the reader into a new awareness of semantics and logical absurdities. The words are built up round a single theme, which acts as a prism for a multitude of facets. There is no plot in the conventional sense, and no character is sufficiently realized for the reader's emotions to become entangled. Even when Brooke-Rose treats of a global disaster, as she does in *Out* (the first novel of her new genre) she is careful to distance her reader, in this instance by the technical language of advanced science.

The next novel, *Such,* deals with a near-death experience, in which the central character, an astronomer called Larry (a deliberate echo of Lazarus) sees people in the same way as he had once seen the emerging and degenerating heavenly bodies. The protagonist of *Between* works as an interpreter from French to German, a circumstance that presents a natural occasion for the linguistic kaleidoscopes which are the meat of Brooke-Rose's cerebral work.

Thru is probably the most accessible, and certainly the funniest of these concrete novels. Here Brooke-Rose turns again to satire, taking for her target the faculty of a modern university, running courses in various aspects of linguistics, creative writing, and all sorts of fashionable sociological and feminist topics. The students' essays are matched against the discussions endlessly going on among the faculty members; and the triangular relationship that snakes its way through the work of the apprentice novelists is shadowed by the affairs taking place among the staff. The reader is not allowed to disentangle any of this too easily. Once again the main purpose of the novel is the exploration of language, and this is done even to the extent of discarding anything resembling conventional syntax in favor of pseudo-diagrams and concrete patterns. From time to time the reader is thrown a joke to ease the struggle for meaning. So a teaching method is defined as one in which "you peripatate along in ancient sunshine (known also as the peripatetic fallacy)." But anything as explicit as that is rare. The reader must

be prepared to approach these novels with the same sort of expectations that one brings to surrealist painting.

Although Brooke-Rose's work up to the mid-1970s was acclaimed by Angus Wilson, and Frank Kermode, she kept a nine-year silence after the publication of *Thru.* When *Amalgamemnon* finally appeared, the reader was once again plunged into the academic world, although in this instance there is a single protagonist, a woman teacher of literature and history, who becomes redundant. This character is as fluid as one would expect, and as her world and assumptions disintegrate around her in a collage of classical texts, radio weather forecasts, phone-ins only a little less awful than the real thing, anticipated conversations and the world of ancient myth and modern violence, we are presented with a kaleidoscope of wit and invention. Yet the play on words can pall. The joke of placing an initial "s" before almost every word beginning with "ex" struck me as sexasperating; but the skill with which Brooke-Rose can mimic voices and so create the cast which forms the background of this near-abstract novel is a source of admiration and pleasure.

With *Xorandor* the reader leaves academe for the world of science fiction in which the explosive development of the computer and the micro-chip (a marvelous opportunity for linguistic gymnastics) is combined with the urgent problem of nuclear waste disposal. The computer, which gives its name to the title, actually feeds off alpha-particles from fissile materials. Its story is told by two children, who dictate it to a word processor, which presents them with all kinds of linguistic experiences, except the vital one which comes from the communication between non-programmed, frequently irrational human beings.

—Shirley Toulson

BROOKNER, Anita

Nationality: British. **Born:** London, 16 July 1928. **Education:** James Allen's Girls' School; King's College, University of London; Courtauld Institute of Art, London, Ph.D. in art history. **Career:** Visiting lecturer, University of Reading, Berkshire, 1959-64; lecturer, 1964, and reader, 1977-88, Courtauld Institute of Art; Slade Professor, Cambridge University, 1967-68. Fellow, New Hall, Cambridge; fellow, King's College, 1990. **Awards:** Booker prize, 1984. C.B.E. (Commander, Order of the British Empire), 1990. **Address:** 68 Elm Park Gardens, London SW10 9PB, England.

PUBLICATIONS

Novels

A Start in Life. London, Cape, 1981; as *The Debut,* New York, Linden Press, 1981.
Providence. London, Cape, 1982; New York, Pantheon, 1984.
Look at Me. London, Cape, and New York, Pantheon, 1983.
Hotel du Lac. London, Cape, 1984; New York, Pantheon, 1985.
Family and Friends. London, Cape, and New York, Pantheon, 1985.
A Misalliance. London, Cape, 1986; as *The Misalliance,* New York, Pantheon, 1987.
A Friend from England. London, Cape, 1987; New York, Pantheon, 1988.

Latecomers. London, Cape, 1988; New York, Pantheon, 1989.
Lewis Percy. London, Cape, 1989; New York, Pantheon, 1990.
Brief Lives. London, Cape, 1990; New York, Random House, 1991.

Other

Watteau. London, Hamlyn, 1968.
The Genius of the Future: Studies in French Art Criticism: Diderot, Stendahl, Baudelaire, Zola, the Brothers Goncourt, Huysmans. London, Phaidon Press, 1971; Ithaca, New York, Cornell University Press, 1988.
Greuze: The Rise and Fall of an Eighteenth-Century Phenomenon. London, Elek, and Greenwich, Connecticut, New York Graphic Society, 1972.
Jacques-Louis David: A Personal Interpretation (lecture). London, Oxford University Press, 1974.
Jacques-Louis David. London, Chatto and Windus, 1980; New York, Harper, 1981; revised edition, Chatto and Windus, 1986; New York, Thames and Hudson, 1987.

Editor, *The Stories of Edith Wharton.* London, Simon and Schuster, 2 vols., 1988-89.

Translator, *Utrillo.* London, Oldbourne Press, 1960.
Translator, *The Fauves.* London, Oldbourne Press, 1962.
Translator, *Gauguin.* London, Oldbourne Press, 1963.

*   *   *

Anita Brookner, one of the most highly regarded contemporary British novelists, is a miniaturist. Her fictions are (usually) brief and exquisitely wrought—novellas rather than novels. Like Jane Austen she works on a little square of ivory rather than a broad canvas, and she has a similarly restricted social range. Her vision is, however, more somber than Austen's, and her muted tones and colors are designed to highlight the bleakness of ordinary life. The tone of her work is set in her first novel, *A Start in Life:* "'About suffering, they were never wrong, the Old Masters,' said Auden. But they were. Frequently. Death was usually heroic, old age serene and wise. And of course, the element of time, that was what was missing." Brookner's own element is time, and life in her novels is viewed as a long, slow, process of attrition, more or less passively endured.

Brookner's typical protagonist is a woman whose life slips by, shaped by the actions of others, as she herself watches and waits, imprisoned in darkened, often sumptuously furnished rooms. They are women whose lives are (like that of Ruth Weiss in Brookner's first novel) "ruined by literature," formed and deformed by the stories our culture tells to and about women. Ruth Weiss thinks that her life has been ruined by a "faulty moral education" which required that she should "ponder the careers of Anna Karenina and Emma Bovary" but "emulate" that of Little Dorrit; the real tragedy, of course, is that she should think (as so many of Brookner's heroines do) that life offers only a choice between these two extremes.

Brookner's women seem to be divided into those who watch, and those whose activities are watched, the over modest and those whose "immodesty . . . always wins concessions" (*A Misalliance*), or, as Edith the novelist-heroine of *Hotel du Lac* puts it, the tortoises and the hares. Edith writes romantic novels for "the tortoise market," Brookner makes the tortoises the center of novels which offer a critique of romance but, simultaneously, retain a profound attachment to it. Brookner's tortoises are relative creatures, defined by their relationship to others as mothers, daughters, sisters, and wives. However, they are often in the wrong relationship like Fay Langdon in *Brief Lives,* who laments of a friend, "she was more daughter than wife, whereas I had it in me to be more wife than daughter." Brookner's novels repeatedly focus on the way in which women's status as relative creatures results in their infantilization and dependence. Most of Brookner's heroines, like Blanche in *A Misalliance,* remain lonely but obedient children, and consequently find it difficult to take control of their own lives. They are almost always contrasted with women who attempt to gain control by displays of childish charm or temper.

The choice between marriage and the single life is one of Brookner's habitual concerns. Her novels are suffused with a desire for marriage and domesticity, and full of examples of the inadequacies, frustrations and petty tyrannies of actual marriages. She is particularly interested in the familial and cultural pressures which determine this choice, which is often made *for* rather than *by* the individual. Few of Brookner's characters achieve the clear-eyed perception of Fay Langdon (*Brief Lives*) that "There must be several things a woman can do other than think of love and marriage. The young, of course, know this, or they seem to nowadays. My generation was less realistic. It seems to me now that my own youth was passed in a dream, and that I only came to see the world as it was when it was already too late." It is in the nature of the Brookner world that all such perceptions (and not only those about the desirability or otherwise of marriage) if they come at all, come too late.

Although, in reviews and interviews, she has often been quite outspoken in her criticisms of feminists and feminism, Brookner's fiction habitually analyses sexual politics and explores the contradictions of marriage and romantic love in a way which many feminists would not find unsympathetic. She occasionally affirms the sustaining powers of "the company of women when any blow falls" (*Brief Lives*), but the main business of life in her novels is female-male relationships. The focus of the earlier novels, *A Start in Life, Providence,* and *Look at Me,* tends to be on the predicament of a young woman who fails to find the love she so desperately needs. These women seek in romantic love the gratification of emotional needs created by families which (in various ways and for different reasons) have denied them affection. These early novels are variations on the model of the *Bildungsroman* or apprenticeship novel, in which the heroines serve their apprenticeship for a life of disappointed hopes and lowered horizons. The intensity of their own need, their refinement of sensibility, the literary paradigms through which they view life, and, not least, those "chance throws of the dice that change lives" (*Latecomers*) conspire to frustrate their desires. Brookner returns to the pattern and preoccupations of these early novels in one of her most recent books, *Lewis Percy.* This time it is the eponymous hero who seeks domestic fulfillment, and whose life has been determined by an over-dependent relationship with his mother and an immersion in literature (ironically this self-effacing, morally scrupulous young man is writing a thesis on the unscrupulous, self-interested heroes of 19th-century French fiction). Interestingly, and in marked contrast to the bookish heroines, Lewis Percy is "rewarded" with a "happy" ending as he escapes from a loveless marriage to a possibly chaotic new life in America with the eccentric and demanding sister of his best friend.

Hotel du Lac and *A Friend from England* vary the pattern of the earlier novels by focusing on the differing responses of slightly older women who are in the process of relinquishing, or have relinquished, a relationship with a married man. Each of these novels employs subtle formal devices to probe the ambiguities and contradictions of the situations of its central female character. *Hotel du Lac* gradually brings together the developing story of the narrative present (told in the third person) with the story of the events which have brought Edith to the gloomy lakeside hotel (largely told in the first-person narrative of Edith's letters to her lover David—letters which are never sent). The reader thus shares in the character's emerging awareness of the nature of her predicament, but at the same time is granted a superior perspective on the sources of that predicament. In *A Friend from England* Rachel, the novel's Jamesian center of consciousness, has adopted the self-reliant, anti-romantic perspective that many a feminist would envy. However, the narrative that Brookner constructs on this occasion (indeed on most occasions) is designed to discomfort feminists and non-feminists alike. The price of Rachel's independence, it would appear, is to be the chorus rather than an actor in the drama of life. The moment of recognition comes in a dramatic reversal (which significantly for the water-phobic Rachel takes place in Venice), in which both character and reader share a typical Brookner epiphany: "To strike out and claim one's own life, to impose it on others, even to embrace a caprice, was, though monstrous, sometimes admirable . . . I would plough on to a game middle age . . . I . . . would be the audience, the reflector, the confidante, the baby-sitter. No-one would know the inner workings of my life."

Later novels, such as *A Misalliance* and *Brief Lives* weight up the meanings of a woman's life by exploring the present predicaments of older women through a retrospective on their past. This proves an excellent vehicle for Brookner's preoccupation with self-betrayal, the duplicity of others, and the betrayals of time. The defeats of time, and the painful survival of destroyed illusions are perhaps most feelingly portrayed in two novels which might be described as family chronicles: *Family and Friends* and *Latecomers.* The former quite brilliantly traces the contrasting stories of the members of the Dorn family by reading and projecting from a series of wedding photographs. *Latecomers,* a study of survivor-guilt, reviews the lives of the families of two Jewish friends—the melancholy Fibich and the epicurean Hartmann—through an emotional crisis in which Fibich comes to terms with his own (and perhaps the 20th century's) history. Each of these novels is a melancholy tale. There are no winners in the game of life as viewed by Brookner, there are only variously honorable ways of surviving defeat and disappointment.

—Lyn Pykett

BROPHY, Brigid (Antonia)

Nationality: British. **Born:** London, 12 June 1929. **Education:** St. Paul's Girls' School, London; St. Hugh's College, Oxford (Jubilee scholar), 1947-48. **Family:** Married Sir Michael Levey in 1954; one daughter. **Career:** Co-organiser, Writers Action Group, 1972-82; Executive Councillor, Writers Guild of Great Britain, 1975-78; vice-chairman, British Copyright Council, 1976-80. Since 1974 vice-president, Anti-Vivisection Society of Great Britain. Since 1984 has suffered from multiple sclerosis. **Awards:** Cheltenham Festival prize, 1954; *London Magazine* prize, 1962; Tony Godwin award, 1985. Fellow, Royal Society of Literature, 1973. **Address:** Fir Close, 2 Westgate, Louth, Lincolnshire LN11 9YH, England.

PUBLICATIONS

Novels

Hackenfeller's Ape. London, Hart Davis, 1953; New York, Random House, 1954.
The King of a Rainy Country. London, Secker and Warburg, 1956; New York, Knopf, 1957.
Flesh. London, Secker and Warburg, 1962; Cleveland, World, 1963.
The Finishing Touch. London, Secker and Warburg, 1963.
The Snow Ball. London, Secker and Warburg, 1964.
The Snow Ball, with The Finishing Touch. Cleveland, World, 1964.
In Transit. London, Macdonald, 1969; New York, Putnam, 1970.
The Adventures of God in His Search for the Black Girl: A Novel and Some Fables. London, Macmillan, 1973; Boston, Little Brown, 1974.
Palace Without Chairs: A Baroque Novel. London, Hamish Hamilton, and New York, Atheneum, 1978.

Short Stories

The Crown Princess and Other Stories. London, Collins, and New York, Viking Press, 1953.

Uncollected Short Stories

"Pilgrimage," in *Winter's Tales 3.* London, Macmillan, and New York, St. Martin's Press, 1957.
"De Bilbow," in *Shakespeare Stories,* edited by Giles Gordon. London, Hamish Hamilton, 1982.
"Singled Out," in *Short Story Monthly,* 1982.

Plays

The Waste-Disposal Unit (broadcast 1964). Published in *London Magazine,* April 1964; in *Best Short Plays of the World Theatre 1958-67,* New York, Crown, 1968.
The Burglar (produced London, 1967). London, Cape, and New York, Holt Rinehart, 1968.

Radio Play: *The Waste-Disposal Unit,* 1964.

Other

Black Ship to Hell. London, Secker and Warburg, and New York, Harcourt Brace, 1962.
Mozart the Dramatist: A New View of Mozart, His Operas, and His Age. London, Faber, and New York, Harcourt Brace, 1964; revised edition, London, Libris, and New York, Da Capo Press, 1988.
Don't Never Forget: Collected Views and Reviews. London, Cape, 1966; New York, Holt Rinehart, 1967.
Religious Education in State Schools. London, Fabian Society, 1967.
Fifty Works of English and American Literature We Could Do Without, with Michael Levey and Charles Osborne. London, Rapp and Carroll, 1967; New York, Stein and Day, 1968.
Black and White: A Portrait of Aubrey Beardsley. London, Cape, 1968; New York, Stein and Day, 1969.
The Longford Threat to Freedom. London, National Secular Society, 1972.

Prancing Novelist: A Defence of Fiction in the Form of a Critical Biography in Praise of Ronald Firbank. London, Macmillan, and New York, Barnes and Noble, 1973.

Beardsley and His World. London, Thames and Hudson, and New York, Crown, 1976.

Pussy Owl (for children). London, BBC Publications, 1976.

The Prince and the Wild Geese. London, Hamish Hamilton, and New York, St. Martin's Press, 1983.

A Guide to Public Lending Right. Aldershot, Hampshire, Gower, 1983.

Baroque-'n'-Roll and Other Essays. London, Hamish Hamilton, 1987.

Reads (essays). London, Sphere, 1989.

*

Manuscript Collection: Lilly Library, University of Indiana, Bloomington.

*   *   *

In the agreeably self-dramatizing preface to her play *The Burglar,* Brigid Brophy provides a definitive statement of her aims and methods as a critic and novelist. Like Shaw (whom she sees, along with Freud, as one of the "two mainstays of the twentieth century"), Brophy is an evolutionary vitalist, essentially optimistic despite a sharp eye for human failings and hypocrisies. And like Shaw she assumes the existence of a driving Life Force which strives to express itself in ever more competent and complex forms.

Art itself is a "function of the life instinct," which by its potent illusions brings us "into accord with reality" (unlike religion, which makes the mistake of taking its illusions as literal truths). The human race is a species "uniquely capable of imagination, rationality and moral choice," and therein lies man's justification and perilous responsibility. For Brophy, like Shaw once more, knows full well that our powers may be misused, that the human race is frighteningly capable of undoing what the Life Force has accomplished thus far. From Freud Brophy takes over the conception of life as a dynamic struggle between Eros, the binding and civilizing force, and Thanatos, the death instinct which seeks to destroy the work of Eros. Thus *Black Ship to Hell* has as its theme "man as a destructive and, more particularly, a self-destructive animal" and is in effect an encyclopedic investigation of the interrelationships of the two opposing principles in war, politics, art and religion. Brophy sees her work, finally, in the life-affirming tradition of Shaw and Freud: "I too am aiming to reform civilization." The necessary balance between Eros and Thanatos, the integration of work, love, and responsibility, gives Brophy the theme of her fiction: in the long run there may be reason to hope for civilization, but in the short run of individual lives there are failures as well as successes, an infinite fund of dramatic possibilities to be exploited.

Brophy's didacticism is apparent at once in her first collection of short stories, *The Crown Princess,* many of which are no more than fictionalized statements of a thesis or problem. But there is one story here, "Fordie," which unmistakably reveals a writer of remarkable power and intelligence. An intricate fable about the differences between the true creator and the self-seeking failure, "Fordie" belongs in the company of Henry James's great series of artist-parables. *Hackenfeller's Ape,* Brophy's first novel, is a disappointingly thin version of one of her persistent concerns, the treatment of animals "whom we have no right to maim, torture or kill."

Embedded here, however, is a dialogue between opposing forces which illustrates clearly the truth of Brophy's statement that all of her works are "baroque," that is, they all "proceed by contraposition; and in a reductive analysis the elements contraposited are always Eros and Thanatos." *The King of a Rainy Country,* a much more engaging novel, dramatizes the disordered forms Eros may assume in individual lives—in regressive, homoerotic relationships and more specifically in doomed, infantile quests for the "perfect moment." In this comic anti-romance the heroine learns at some painful cost that the static ideal is impossible: "you give from one person and take from another—give and take vitality, I mean. Nobody is a reservoir. It's just an exchange. It goes round in an endless cycle." *Flesh* continues to explore this vital give and take, dramatizing with splendid economy and wit the way in which love reclaims a diffident young man. Brophy avoids sentimentality, however, by indicating that in this particular relationship the cost of investigation has been high; the young man brought to life by Eros is now an object of both horror and desire for his wife; pain becomes a sinister bond in "a hostile and perhaps perverted situation."

The baroque method of construction is increasingly important in Brophy's later work, "deploying masses in such a way that each, as well as performing its own function, constitutes a funnel down which one gets a sharply unexpected view—ironic, tragic or comic." *The Snow Ball* is architectural with a vengeance: its complexity, Brophy boasts, "defies even my own intellectual analysis." But unfortunately the opposite is true: in this brittle, pretentious reworking of the Don Juan—Donna Anna theme (to which Brophy is addicted, seeing in the myth a paradigm of the human sexual emotions), only the contrived and quite obvious design engages the reader's attention. Man is not only *homo faber* and *homo artifax* for Brophy, but *homo Fabergé* as well, and hence her fascination with Beardsley, Firbank, and other aesthetes and dandies. *The Finishing Touch,* besides providing another example of Eros distorted, is an homage to Ronald Firbank, an imitative recreation of the very highest order.

In Transit is a radical departure from the quasi-naturalistic style of the earlier books. In "Fordie" the narrator had reflected that "perhaps the personality surrenders some of its philosophic right to be called a personality when the babbling to oneself, which is the mark of human identity, is halted. I would write a book on the subject, if anyone would attend to it." *In Transit* is that book, and a good deal more, anatomizing the layers of individual personality in a wild, punning Joycean flow of rhetoric which defies coherent description. The hero-heroine (we are hurled into a vortex where sexual differences are superficial) is "in transit," literally waiting to board a plane, but psychically in transit as well, pulled and pushed by a host of new energies. The secondary or simultaneous protagonist of *In Transit* is language itself, which is extended, inverted, parodied, and finally blown to bits by the onslaught of modern life. "I am," the psyche insists, but "communication is broken." In a sleight-of-hand finale, however, which is typical of Brophy's invincible optimism, the psyche is reintegrated "for Love of You"—the "You" being (apparently) the expectant interlocutor our consciousness by necessity posits and the eternal "you" of the audience, waiting for the voice of the artist to bring it back into accord with even the most disruptive modern reality.

The subtitle of *The Adventures of God in His Search for the Black Girl* is misleading. The first section of the book is made up of short fables, very much in the style of *The Crown Princess* and making many of the same points. The long title piece, however, is not really a novel at all, but a kind of philosophic dialogue in the manner of Lucian and Shaw. The chief character, God, is anxious to establish once and for all his "fictitious" nature as a being wholly created by man. The problems arise, he argues, when men take this fiction—or any of their other guiding fictions—as literal, historic truth. The issue here is a familiar one these days: all human beliefs and ideals are, like works of art, purely imaginative constructs. Some are benign, some are not. The implied goal, then, is to construct fictions which will be recognized as such and will still have the power to work for the benefit of mankind. The "Godifesto" is released in a dove-like shower over Rome, but in a wry epilogue Brophy seems to be suggesting that those receiving it will fail to understand what is at stake.

Palace Without Chairs is a novel of sorts, an extended if not entirely clear political allegory. The King and Queen of Evarchia and four of their five children kill themselves or disappear in a series of ludicrous accidents, and a military dictatorship promptly takes over; but the last of the royal children, Heather, a "pachydermous" lesbian, manages to reach London, where our final glimpse of her is an ambiguous one. Drunk in a small hotel bar and happily pursuing another ample lady, she still seems to her former governess (who may not be a reliable witness) to offer "some just cause for hope. . . . The very elements in her personality that most people condemned were . . . the sources of a vitality that should surmount both guilt and nostalgia." *Palace Without Chairs* is amusing enough at times but takes few risks and as a result is considerably less impressive than *In Transit*.

—Elmer Borklund

BROWN, George Mackay

Nationality: British. **Born:** Stromness, Orkney, Scotland, 17 October 1921. **Education:** Stromness Academy, 1926-40; Newbattle Abbey College, Dalkeith, Midlothian, 1951-52, 1956; Edinburgh University, 1956-60, 1962-64, B.A. (honors) in English 1960, M.A. **Awards:** Society of Authors travel award, 1968; Scottish Arts Council prize, 1969; Katherine Mansfield-Menton prize, 1971; James Tait Black Memorial prize, 1988. M.A.: Open University, Milton Keynes, Buckinghamshire, 1976; LL.D.: University of Dundee, 1977; D.Litt.: University of Glasgow, 1985. Fellow, Royal Society of Literature, 1977. O.B.E. (Officer, Order of the British Empire), 1974. **Address:** 3 Mayburn Court, Stromness, Orkney KW16 3DH, Scotland.

PUBLICATIONS

Novels

Greenvoe. London, Hogarth Press, and New York, Harcourt Brace, 1972.
Magnus. London, Hogarth Press, 1973.
Time in a Red Coat. London, Chatto and Windus, 1984; New York, Vanguard Press, 1985.
Vinland. London, Murray, 1992.
Beside the Ocean of Time. London, Murray, 1994.

Short Stories

A Calendar of Love. London, Hogarth Press, 1967; New York, Harcourt Brace, 1968.
A Time to Keep. London, Hogarth Press, 1969; New York, Harcourt Brace, 1970.
Hawkfall and Other Stories. London, Hogarth Press, 1974.
The Sun's Net. London, Hogarth Press, 1976.
Witch and Other Stories. London, Longman, 1977.
Andrina and Other Stories. London, Chatto and Windus, 1983.
Christmas Stories. Oxford, Perpetua Press, 1985.
The Hooded Fisherman. Pitlochry, Perthshire, Duval, 1985.
A Time to Keep and Other Stories. New York, Vanguard Press, 1987.
The Golden Bird: Two Orkney Stories. London, Murray, 1987.
The Masked Fisherman and Other Stories. London, Murray, 1989.

Plays

Witch (produced Edinburgh, 1969). Included in *A Calendar of Love,* 1967.
A Spell for Green Corn (broadcast 1967; produced Edinburgh, 1970). London, Hogarth Press, 1970.
The Loom of Light (produced Kirkwall, 1972). Included in *Three Plays,* 1984.
The Storm Watchers (produced Edinburgh, 1976).
The Martyrdom of St. Magnus (opera libretto), music by Peter Maxwell Davies, adaptation of his own novel (produced Kirkwall and London, 1977; Sante Fe, 1979). London, Boosey and Hawkes, 1977.
The Two Fiddlers (opera libretto), music by Peter Maxwell Davies, adaptation of his own story (produced London, 1978). London, Boosey and Hawkes, 1978.
The Well (produced at St. Magnus Festival, 1981). Included in *Three Plays,* 1984.
The Voyage of Saint Brandon (broadcast 1984). Included in *Three Plays,* 1984.
Three Plays. London, Chatto and Windus, 1984.
A Celebration for Magnus (son et lumière text), music by Peter Maxwell Davies (produced Kirkwall, Orkney, 1988). Nairn, Balnain, 1987.
Edwin Muir and the Labyrinth (produced Edinburgh, 1987).

Radio Plays: *A Spell for Green Corn,* 1967; *The Loom of Light,* 1967; *The Voyage of Saint Brandon,* 1984.

Television Plays: Three stories from *A Time to Keep,* 1969; *Orkney,* 1971; *Miss Barraclough,* 1977; *Four Orkney Plays for Schools,* 1978; *Andrina,* 1984.

Poetry

The Storm. Kirkwall, Orkney Herald Press, 1954.
Loaves and Fishes. London, Hogarth Press, 1959.
The Year of the Whale. London, Hogarth Press, 1965.
The Five Voyages of Arnor. Falkland, Fife, Duval, 1966.
Twelve Poems. Belfast, Festival, 1968.
Fishermen with Ploughs: A Poem Cycle. London, Hogarth Press, 1971.
Poems New and Selected. London, Hogarth Press, 1971; New York, Harcourt Brace, 1973.

Lifeboat and Other Poems. Crediton, Devon, Gilbertson, 1971.
Penguin Modern Poets 21, with Iain Crichton Smith and Norman MacCaig. London, Penguin, 1972.
Winterfold. London, Hogarth Press, 1976.
Selected Poems. London, Hogarth Press, 1977.
Voyages. London, Chatto and Windus, 1983.
Christmas Poems. Oxford, Perpetua Press, 1984.
Stone. Verona, Duval, 1987.
Two Poems for Kenna. Child Okeford, Dorset, Words Press, 1988.
Songs for St. Magnus Day. Oxford, Perpetua Press, 1988.
The Wreck of the Archangel. London, Murray, 1989.
Tryst on Egilsay. Wetherby, Yorkshire, Celtic Cross Press, 1989.
Selected Poems 1954-1983. London, Murray, 1991.
Forerdenhill. Germany, Babel, 1992.
The Lost Village. Yorkshire, Celtic Cross Press, 1993.

Other

Let's See the Orkney Islands. Fort William, Inverness, Thomson, 1948.
Stromness Official Guide. London, Burrow, 1956.
An Orkney Tapestry. London, Gollancz, 1969.
The Two Fiddlers (for children). London, Chatto and Windus, 1974.
Letters from Hamnavoe (essays). Edinburgh, Wright, 1975.
Edwin Muir: A Brief Memoir. West Linton, Peeblesshire, Castlelaw Press, 1975.
Pictures in the Cave (for children). London, Chatto and Windus, 1977.
Under Brinkie's Brae. Edinburgh, Wright, 1979.
Six Lives of Fankle the Cat (for children). London, Chatto and Windus, 1980.
Portrait of Orkney, photographs by Werner Forman. London, Hogarth Press, 1981; revised edition, photographs by Gunnie Moberg, and drawings by Evlend Brown, London, Murray, 1988.
Shorelines: Three Artists from Orkney (exhibition catalogue), with Tessa Jackson. Glasgow, Collins Gallery, 1985.
Keepers of the House (for children). London, Old Stile, 1986.
Letters to Gypsy. Nairn, Balnain, 1990.
Eureka! (for children). Nairn, Balnain, 1991.
Sea-King's Daughter. Nairn, Balnain, 1991.

Editor, *Selected Prose of Edwin Muir.* London, Murray, 1987.

*

Manuscript Collections: Scottish National Library, Edinburgh; Edinburgh University Library.

Critical Study: *George Mackay Brown* by Alan Bold, Edinburgh, Oliver and Boyd, and New York, Barnes and Noble, 1978; *La Narrativa de George Mackay Brown* by Valentia Poggi, Italy, Bologna University, 1985.

George Mackay Brown comments:

(1972) I find it very difficult to comment on my own work, except in some imaginary context. I have recently finished a short story called "Seal Skin" about a musician. He reads, in Dublin, an old Celtic manuscript, about "the intricate web of creation" that men are mindlessly exploiting and tearing; and he is much moved by it. The last paragraphs are as follows:

He [Magnus Olafson the musician] thought of the men who have thrown off all restraint and were beginning now to raven in the most secret and delicate and precious places of nature. They were the new priesthood; the world went down on its knees before every tawdry miracle—the phonograph, the motor car, the machine-gun, the wireless—that they held up in triumph. And the spoliation had hardly begun.

Was this then the task of the artist: to keep in repair the sacred web of creation—that cosmic harmony of God and beast and man and star and plant—in the name of humanity, against those who in the name of humanity are mindlessly and systematically destroying it?

If so, what had been taken from him was a necessary sacrifice.

*   *   *

The ancient and undulating landscape of the Orkney islands forms more than a backcloth to the work of George Mackay Brown: it provides motif upon motif for most of his novels and short stories, informing them with a sense of grandeur and venerable antiquity. Indeed, he demonstrates a wonderful ability to bring the past alive and to make the reader believe that a door has been opened into a new and enchanted world. In his introduction to a recent collection of short stories, *The Masked Fisherman and Other Stories,* Brown makes no attempt to disguise his continuing fascination with the past; on the contrary, he sees it as the main driving force and inspiration for just about everything that he writes. "The stuff of narrative lies thick everywhere, but in the past rather than in the present. Now the mind is too easily satisfied with the withering pages of newspapers, and with the fleeting shallow images of television serials." More than 20 years separate these stories from his first collection, *A Calendar of Love,* but it is easy to see the connection between the later story "The Tree and the Harp," with its triumphant message of the power of love and life over death, and the title story of the earlier collection.

One of Brown's favorite descriptions is "very ancient," and this phrase recurs again and again to build up a sense of timelessness in which chronology becomes increasingly unimportant. In his novel *Greenvoe* Brown views time as "not a conflagration; it is a slow grave sequence of grassblade, fish, apple, star, snowflake," and the natural symbolism is continued in the inevitable demise of the community of Greenvoe and the promise of its resurrection: "The sun rose. The stars were warm. They broke the bread." Although there is death in the novel, the death of the community, Brown uses the potent concept of renewal through the planting of seed both as a reminder of the island's heritage and as a reiteration of the doctrine of salvation through resurrection. Skarf, the Marxist fisherman, imagines the founding of the Orkney islands with strange visitors from the Mediterranean and Scandinavia bringing with them jars of seed to ensure their survival in a new life.

The descendants of those early invaders are the crofters and fishermen of Orkney who are the lifeblood of Brown's fiction. It is they who are the integral part of the circle of life and death and it is they who move inexorably in its rhythm of seedtime, birth, harvest, and death. Their participation and their knowledge of the historical intertwining of their present with their ancestors' past give a dignity to their lives and also prevents Brown's interest in them from sliding into sentimentality or nostalgia for the irretrievable past. In "The Life and Death of John Voe," a novella published in a single volume with *The Golden Bird,* Brown presents the familiar theme of a man being measured against his own life. Having wandered the world, Voe returns to Orkney and reaches a new understanding of the timeless heritage he has inherited from the people of the past.

The theme of renewal was also explored in *Hawkfall,* a collection of five related pieces which contemplate the survival of human characteristics in an Orkney family from the Bronze Age to the present day. Through the long sweep of history Brown traces both the story of his islands and the personal relationships that exist between succeeding generations of its people. The stories in *Hawkfall* are in the minor key, somber and suffused with ancient history, and it is fitting that the collection should end with "The Interrogator," a story that examines the impossible mystery of death. Exploring the enigma of life and death is also present in *The Sun's Net,* a collection of stories imbued with Brown's religious belief that each birth is the re-enactment of the nativity; in "A Winter's Tale" the ancient ritual of the sun king and the corn queen is contrasted with the simple birth of a child at a deserted croft. Children grow up to renew the community and in any season are blessed, but this child born at Christmas is seen by all, except the minister who has become blind to miracles, as a promise of the island's salvation.

Brown's fascination with the Christian theme of redemption finds its most vigorous form in his novel *Magnus* which tells the story of the 12th-century Earl of Orkney who was later sanctified for his martyrdom at the hands of his cousin Haakon. Equally beguiling is *Time in a Red Coat,* a densely packed novel which offers a moving parable on the stupidity of war. Set in an eastern kingdom, the novel is a kaleidoscope of images, stereotypes, and freakish landscapes, all described with Brown's customary inventiveness and economy of language. The atmosphere is timeless, yet fantasy and reality are mingled persuasively in evocations of past and present as they exist in the mind of a young girl charged with the mission of destroying the dragon of war before it engulfs the world in flames and death.

However, the central preoccupation in Brown's fiction remains Orkney, its history and traditions, the people who have contributed to its story and to its regeneration over many generations: these are the central strands with which Brown has woven a seamless literature, deceptively simple but universal in its appeal.

—Trevor Royle

BROWN, Rita Mae

Nationality: American. **Born:** Hanover, Pennsylvania, 28 November 1944. **Education:** University of Florida, Gainesville; New York University, B.A. 1968; New York School of Visual Arts, cinematography certificate 1968; Institute for Policy Studies, Washington, D.C., Ph.D. 1976. **Career:** Photo editor, Sterling Publishing Company, New York, 1969-70; lecturer in sociology, Federal City College, Washington, D.C., 1970-71. Since 1973 visiting member, faculty of feminist studies, Goddard College, Plainfield, Vermont. Founding member, Redstockings radical feminist group, New York, 1970s. **Awards:** New York Public Library Literary Lion award, 1986. **Agent:** Julian Bach Literary Agency, 747 Third Avenue, New York, New York 10017. **Address:** American Artists Inc., P.O. Box 4671, Charlottesville, Virginia 22905, U.S.A.

PUBLICATIONS

Novels

Rubyfruit Jungle. Plainfield, Vermont, Daughters, 1973; London, Corgi, 1978.
In Her Day. Plainfield, Vermont, Daughters, 1976.
Six of One. New York, Harper, 1978; London, W.H. Allen, 1979.
Southern Discomfort. New York, Harper, 1982; London, Severn House, 1983.
Sudden Death. New York, Bantam, 1983.
High Hearts. New York and London, Bantam, 1986.
Bingo. New York, Bantam, 1988.
Wish You Were Here, with Sneaky Pie Brown. New York, Bantam, 1990.
Rest in Pieces, with Sneaky Pie Brown. New York, Bantam, 1992.
Venus Envy. New York, Bantam, 1993.
Dolley: A Novel of Dolley Madison in Love and War. New York, Bantam, 1994.
Murder at Monticello; or, Old Sins, with Sneaky Pie Brown. New York, Bantam, 1994.

Plays

Television and film scripts: *I Love Liberty,* with others, 1982; *The Long Hot Summer,* 1985; *My Two Loves,* 1986; *The Alice Marble Story,* 1986; *Sweet Surrender,* 1986; *The Mists of Avalone,* 1987; *Table Dancing,* 1987; *The Girls of Summer,* 1989; *Selma, Lord, Selma,* 1989; *Rich Men, Single Women,* 1989; *The Thirty Nine Year Itch,* 1989.

Poetry

The Hand That Cradles the Rock. New York, New York University Press, 1971.
Songs to a Handsome Woman. Baltimore, Diana Press, 1973.
Poems. Freedom, California, Crossing Press, 1987.

Other

A Plain Brown Rapper (essays). Baltimore, Diana Press, 1976.
Starting from Scratch: A Different Kind of Writers Manual. New York, Bantam, 1988.

*

Critical Study: *Rita Mae Brown* by Carol M. Ward, New York, Twayne, 1993.

*   *   *

For a writer whose novels appear to be exclusively comic southern fiction, Rita Mae Brown has, in fact, produced a varied body of work. At the most basic level, her novels celebrate a particular image of the southern United States of America; they are funny, sassy, full of geographically specific language—expletives in particular seem to be strictly of the South rather than the North—and populated with hosts of astonishingly colorful characters.

Brown's writing is so particular to its location that her later novels *Bingo* and especially *High Hearts* have led to her being accused of falling into the trap of depicting the South as "wrong but romantic" and the North as "right but repulsive." This did not preclude her from being tipped seriously for the commission to write the sequel to *Gone with the Wind;* in fact, it was probably a main factor in the (ultimately unfounded) rumor that she *would* write it.

Considering the great success of her southern novels, it may be surprising to discover that her real claim to popular adulation is her parallel and entwined career as foremother of the modern lesbian novel. She is not an experimental writer in the style of Monique Wittig or Jeanette Winterson; she is not a stream of consciousness/coming out writer like Verena Stefan or early Michelle Roberts; but her lasting fame among lesbian readers rests primarily on her first novel *Rubyfruit Jungle* which charted hilariously the coming-out process of a young Southerner called Molly Bolt—a joke untranslatable outside of American carpentry circles—and her consequent discovery and assertion that a) it was cool to be queer, b) the only problem is other people's reactions, and c) the rest of the world had better just get used to it.

In these heady days of (fairly) free expression of sexuality, it is difficult to realize just what a bombshell Brown dropped onto a world in which the most famous lesbian novel was *The Well of Loneliness* and lesbians in other fiction almost always recanted, threw themselves into a purifying orgy of self-sacrifice or—more frequently—committed suicide in despair. It is not stretching the point to say that for the overwhelming majority of lesbians, *Rubyfruit Jungle* was the first book we ever read which said it was OK.

After such a success with a first novel, it was hardly surprising that her second *In Her Day* was to many a disappointment. It tries to deal with the still thorny issues of lesbian-feminism versus "political correctness," older and younger women, class, race and so on. All of this in a very slim volume. The book was published in one edition by a small US feminist press and disappeared without trace—except to obsessive collectors—until two years ago when it was republished. Interestingly, its long absence was the choice of the author who felt it was an inferior novel.

Brown's use of her own life for fiction is fascinating. While it is true that characters appear in *Rubyfruit Jungle, Six of One* and the latter's sequel *Bingo* who are clearly based on the same autobiographical raw material, the most obvious example is *Sudden Death.* With information clearly gathered during her highly public relationship with Martina Navratilova, Brown dissects the world of women's professional tennis with the satiric scalpel of an expert. A favorite game for some time after its publication was for the reader to try and identify the real-life models on which the characters were based.

Recently, attentive readers have found a shift in political values in her novels; it appears to be towards the right whilst retaining an undying feminism. A seeming contradiction, but then the Women's Movement had always intended to be a broad church. This reading is suggested by some of the apparently pro-Confederate sentiments in *High Hearts* and less than liberal stances taken by her main characters in *Bingo.*

Her writer's manual *Starting from Scratch* is probably best explained by her own assertion that she was broke after her messy divorce from Martina and needed to write something quickly. It is most memorable for being probably the first writer's manual since the 19th century which suggests that a putative writer must do nothing until they have spent some years mastering both Latin and Ancient Greek.

Wish You Were Here, her 1990 novel, marks something of a progression. Her novels have always been jointly dedicated to her animals but this, a competent if not particularly spectacular thriller, claims to have been co-written by her cat, Sneaky Pie Brown. Feline co-authorship is, I'm afraid to say, nothing new in women's writing of the late 20th century; I hope this is not a trend which will catch on. Meanwhile Brown is to be celebrated alongside a writer such as Armistead Maupin for proving that queer life also has its hilarious side, when the straight world lets it out.

—Linda Semple

BROWN, Rosellen

Nationality: American. **Born:** 1939. **Career:** Instructor in American and English literature, Tougaloo College, Mississippi, 1965-67; instructor in creative writing, Goddard College, Plainfield, Vermont, 1976, and University of Houston, Texas, 1982-85. Since 1989 instructor in creative writing, University of Houston. Visiting professor of creative writing, Boston University, 1977-78. **Awards:** National Endowmment for the Arts fellowship, 1973, 1982; Guggenheim fellowship, 1976; Great Lake College Association best first novel award, 1976, for *The Autobiography of My Mother;* Janet Kafka best novel award, 1984, for *Civil Wars; Ms. Magazine* Woman of the Year, 1984; American Academy and Institute of Arts and Letters award, 1987, for literature; Ingram-Merrill grant, 1989-90. **Address:** 1401 Branard, Houston, Texas 77006, U.S.A.

PUBLICATIONS

Novels

The Autobiography of My Mother. Garden City, New York, Doubleday, 1976.
Tender Mercies. New York, Knopf, 1978; London, Hutchison, 1979.
Civil Wars: A Novel. New York, Knopf, and London, Joseph, 1984.
Before and After. New York, Farrar Straus, 1992; London, Hodder and Stoughton, 1993.

Short Stories

Street Games. Garden City, New York, Doubleday, 1974.

Play

The Secret Garden, with Laurie MacGregor, adaptation of the novel by Frances Hodgson Burnett (produced, 1983).

Poetry

Some Deaths in the Delta, and Other Poems. Amherst, University of Massachusetts Press, 1970.
Cora Fry. New York, Norton, 1977.
Cora Fry's Pillow Book. New York, Farrar Straus, 1994.

Other

A Rosellen Brown Reader: Selected Poetry and Prose. Vermont, Middlebury College Press, 1992.

Editor, *The Whole World Catalog.* N.p., 1972.
Editor, *Men Portray Women, Women Portray Men.* N.p., 1978.

*   *   *

Rosellen Brown's characters—adults, teenagers, and children alike—are living on the edge, from the beginning to the end of her novels. These works start from the premise of lost innocence and move through the various permutations of damage that the condition wreaks upon the psyches of sensitive individuals. All of Brown's fictional marriages are in one stage or another of breakdown; most of her adolescents are experiencing extreme forms of alienation; all of her characters experience the cruel contingency of fate in the form of unhappy coincidence, accident, or death.

All of the novels use conditions of shock and horror to start off the narration. *Tender Mercies* begins with the boating accident of a young married couple. Through his macho bravado, the husband rams a motorboat, which he does not know how to steer, into his swimming wife, severing her spinal cord and rendering her a quadriplegic. *The Autobiography of My Mother* is narrated in part by a woman who, although she doesn't always take money for it, conducts her life somewhat like a prostitute. Meanwhile, her lawyer-mother encounters a series of clients whose conditions in poverty, jail, or the insane asylum are intended to horrify (though the mother herself is stoic as she submits to a forceful vaginal exam administered by black female convicts who want to demonstrate why they are angry). The civil-rights activist parents in *Civil Wars* are appointed legal guardians of children who have been raised by estranged relatives—estranged because they support the Ku Klux Klan. The orphaned daughter attempts suicide more than once. In *Before and After,* a middle-class, do-good family discovers that their son has murdered his girlfriend in a fit of rage at her name-calling.

As if these events were not enough, the narrations go on to describe how such crises, disasters, and shocks inevitably erode marriages. At the end of two of the three novels that are narrated by married partners, the spouses experience a qualified resolution of their relationship. In the third, the wife, after tolerating situations that would try the patience of Job, finally decides that she is through with her marriage. Working at the extremes of human experience, Brown analyzes the profound question of how much sadness the human mind is capable of absorbing without snapping. The human reader, however, may not be capable of absorbing all of Brown's plots, characters, and tone of sadness without losing interest. Although the plots are unique and different, the angst-ridden tone remains the same from one book to the next. Furthermore, the climaxes often arrive after too much delay. We may find ourselves reading on from morbid curiosity, simply to find out what happens: Did Jacob really kill his girlfriend, will Helen actually commit the suicide she obsesses about in her diary, will Renata's depression lead to insanity?

Brown's favored mode of narration contributes to this feeling of monotony: She switches back and forth between the interior monologues of her two main characters, usually spouses, whose private hatreds and sense of isolation become plots of their own, disconnected from the other half. These two subplots carry the narration without the necessary connection that makes for a coherent novel. Lacking are normal dramatic scenes that link characters: Caught between scenes of high-pitched crisis and interior monologues of despair, the scenes of quotidian family intercourse that do occur are laden with a sense of the ailing marriage and impending doom.

Brown illustrates how such sadness permeates spouses' relations with their children, parents, and friends—as well as with each other.

Though all the novels rely heavily on plot, suspense, and character, they go lightly on place description and a kind of omniscience that one becomes accustomed to in the postmodern novel: an omniscience that contains a forgiving irony and mutes the pain of contemporary married life. Brown creates beautiful moments in characters' heads, but rarely are they communicated to other characters, especially spouses. Perhaps this is her own version of postmodern consciousness: She perceives life as a series of private, disconnected moments rather than a crescendo toward a good or bad ending. Postmodern or no, however, there is only so much blood, guts, and gore—of body or mind—that one can take and still have a good read.

The poetry volume, *Cora Fry,* contains some of the same sentiments and events as the novels, such as a serious accident. This suggests that the writing is closely autobiographical, which is no problem in itself. In general, however, I think that human beings either like the angst of specific other beings or they do not. There are certain kinds of angst, or expressions of it, that we relate to better than others. And some readers may not like angst at all. Reading Rosellen Brown is a highly personal experience; hers isn't the angst for everybody.

—Jill Franks

———

BRYAN, Bryan. *See* **MOORE, Brian.**

———

BUECHNER, (Carl) Frederick

Nationality: American. **Born:** New York City, 11 July 1926. **Education:** Lawrenceville School, New Jersey, graduated 1943; Princeton University, New Jersey, A.B. in English 1947; Union Theological Seminary, New York, B.D. 1958: ordained a Minister of the United Presbyterian Church, 1958. **Military Service:** Served in the United States Army, 1944-46. **Family:** Married Judith Friedrike Merck in 1956; three children. **Career:** English Master, Lawrenceville School, 1948-53; Instructor in Creative Writing, New York University, summers 1953-54; head of the employment clinic, East Harlem Protestant Parish, New York, 1954-58; chairman of the Religion Department, 1958-67, and School Minister, 1960-67, Phillips Exeter Academy, New Hampshire. William Belden Noble Lecturer, Harvard University, Cambridge, Massachusetts, 1969; Russell Lecturer, Tufts University, Medford, Massachusetts, 1971; Lyman Beecher Lecturer, Yale Divinity School, New Haven, Connecticut, 1976; Harris Lecturer, Bangor Seminary, Maine, 1979; Smyth Lecturer, Columbia Seminary, New York, 1981; Zabriskie Lecturer, Virginia Seminary, Lynchburg, 1982; lecturer, Trinity Institute, 1990. **Awards:** O. Henry prize, 1955; Rosenthal award,

1959; American Academy award, 1982. D.D.: Virginia Seminary, 1983; Lafayette College, Easton, Pennsylvania, 1984; Cornell College, Mt. Vernon, Iowa, 1988; Yale University, New Haven, Connecticut, 1990; D.Litt.: Lehigh University, Bethlehem, Pennsylvania, 1985. **Agent:** Harriet Wasserman, 137 East 36th Street, New York, New York 10016. **Address:** Box 1145, Pawlet, Vermont 05761, U.S.A.

PUBLICATIONS

Novels

A Long Day's Dying. New York, Knopf, 1950; London, Chatto and Windus, 1951.
The Seasons' Difference. New York, Knopf, and London, Chatto and Windus, 1952.
The Return of Ansel Gibbs. New York, Knopf, and London, Chatto and Windus, 1958.
The Final Beast. New York, Atheneum, and London, Chatto and Windus, 1965.
The Entrance to Porlock. New York, Atheneum, and London, Chatto and Windus, 1970.
The Book of Bebb. New York, Atheneum, 1979.
   Lion Country. New York, Atheneum, and London, Chatto and Windus, 1971.
   Open Heart. New York, Atheneum, and London, Chatto and Windus, 1972.
   Love Feast. New York, Atheneum, 1974; London, Chatto and Windus, 1975.
   Treasure Hunt. New York, Atheneum, 1977; London, Chatto and Windus, 1978.
Godric. New York, Atheneum, 1980; London, Chatto and Windus, 1981.
Brendan. New York, Atheneum, 1987.
The Wizard's Tide. New York, Harper, 1990.
The Son of Laughter. San Francisco, HarperSanFrancisco, 1993.

Uncollected Short Story

"The Tiger," in *Prize Stories 1955: The O. Henry Awards,* edited by Paul Engle and Hansford Martin. New York, Doubleday, 1955.

Other

The Magnificent Defeats (meditations). New York, Seabury Press, 1966; London, Chatto and Windus, 1967.
The Hungering Dark (meditations). New York, Seabury Press, 1969.
The Alphabet of Grace (autobiography). New York, Seabury Press, 1970.
Wishful Thinking: A Theological ABC. New York, Harper, and London, Collins, 1973.
The Faces of Jesus, photographs by Lee Boltin. Croton-on-Hudson, New York, Riverwood, 1974.
Telling the Truth: The Gospel as Tragedy, Comedy, and Fairy Tale. New York, Harper, 1977.
Peculiar Treasures: A Biblical Who's Who. New York, Harper, 1979.
The Sacred Journey (autobiography). New York, Harper, and London, Chatto and Windus, 1982.

Now and Then (autobiography). New York, Harper, 1983.
A Room Called Remember: Uncollected Pieces. New York, Harper, 1984.
Whistling in the Dark: An ABC Theologized. New York, Harper, 1988.
Telling Secrets (autobiography). New York, Harper, 1991.
The Clown in the Belfry: Writings on Faith and Fiction. San Francisco, HarperSanFrancisco, 1992.
Listening to Your Life: Daily Meditations with Frederick Buechner, compiled by George Connor. San Francisco, HarperSanFrancisco, 1992.

*

Manuscript Collection: Wheaton College, Illinois.

Critical Studies: *Laughter in a Genevan Gown: The Works of Frederick Buechner 1970-1980* by Marie-Hélène Davies, Grand Rapids, Michigan, Eerdmans, 1983; *Frederick Buechner: Novelist and Theologian of the Lost and Found* by Marjorie McCoy, New York, Harper, 1988.

Frederick Buechner comments:

When I started out writing novels, my greatest difficulty was always in finding a plot. Since then I have come to believe that there is only one plot. It has to do with the way life or reality or God—the name is perhaps not so important—seeks to turn us into human beings, to make us whole, to make us Christs, to "save" us—again, call it what you will. In my fiction and non-fiction alike, this is what everything I have written is about.

*   *   *

The novels of Frederick Buechner represent a movement from a consideration of psychological textures to an assessment of the religious values that are expressed by those textures. The fact that Buechner is an ordained Presbyterian clergyman may not strike the reader of the earlier novels—*A Long Day's Dying, The Seasons' Difference,* and *The Return of Ansel Gibbs*—as particularly relevant to the interpretation of those novels. His early novels, indeed, may impress the casual reader as works that are in the tradition of Henry James, concerned as they are with the rather delicate and tenuously resolved relations among cultivated and privileged Americans. The characters in these novels are preoccupied with resolutions of their difficulties, but these resolutions go no farther than clarification of their identities in relation to each other. This clarification is conveyed in a style that was regarded, at the time of the novels' appearance, as oblique and over-worked. The actual course of events in the early novels issues, as indicated, in changes of orientation that can be spoken of as a clearing out of the psychological undergrowth that impedes the discovery of purpose and self-knowledge on the part of the chief characters. The course of the narratives is marked by a taste for ironic comedy—a comedy that records the experience of living in a world that, unlike the world of some older comedy, is bare of generally shared values. The values that are to be detached are values for a particular person and do not have much wider relevance.

It is in later novels—*The Final Beast, The Entrance to Porlock,* and *Lion Country*—that one can see Buechner moving, in an ironic and quite self-protective way, toward concerns that his ordination as a clergyman would suggest. He moves from concern with particular persons in special situations toward more inclusive concerns which announce that lives of individual characters are oblique annunciations of the general constraint and opportunity which all human beings can, if they are responsive, encounter. The psyche is also a soul—a focus of energy that achieves fulfillment by coming into relation with patterns that religion and mythology testify to. The style of the later work becomes simpler, and Buechner delights in reporting farcical aspects of American experience that found little place in his earlier work. And these farcical elements are organized by invocation of narrative patterns that are widely known. The narrative pattern that underpins *The Entrance to Porlock* is drawn from that item of popular culture, *The Wizard of Oz;* the motley company of his novel repeats and varies the quest that took Dorothy Gale and her companions along the Road of Yellow Bricks.

In *Lion Country* and the three novels that succeed it—*Open Heart, Love Feast,* and *Treasure Hunt*—the grotesque menagerie of characters has experiences that are organized by nothing less than the traditional patterns of the Christian religion itself. (The four novels are published together under the title of *The Book of Bebb.*) In this series, the Christian religion undergoes parody that on the surface is blasphemous, is offered variation that is ironical rather than confirming, and yet—in the long run—achieves the only kind of validation that is possible at the present time. At the very least the series is a successful counter-weight to novels that confirm conventional piety by exercises in conventional piety. Yet beneath the adultery, farce, and sheer violence of the Bebb series is a set of insights that are very close to the assertions of conventional Christianity. The conventionality—and the sincerity—of Buechner's views can be sampled in the theological ABC contained in *Wishful Thinking* and other meditations.

In summary Buechner can be seen as a novelist who at first was challenged by the sheer complexity of human behavior and who later finds that complexity comprehensible when linked with popular myth-work like the Oz books and, finally, with the self-mastery and self-discovery offered by the Christian religion.

—Harold H. Watts

BURKE, James Lee

Nationality: American. **Born:** Houston, 5 December 1936. **Education:** University of Southwest Louisiana, Lake Charles, 1955-1957; University of Missouri, B.A. 1959, M.A. 1960. **Family:** Married Pear Pail; four children. **Career:** Social worker, Los Angeles, 1962-64; reporter, Lafayette, Louisiana, 1964; U.S. Forest Service, Kentucky, 1965-66; English instructor, University of Southern Louisiana, Lafayette, Louisiana; English instructor, University of Montana, Missoula; English instructor, Miami-Dade Community College, Florida. Currently English professor, Wichita State University, Kansas. **Awards:** Bread Loaf fellowship, 1970; Southern Federation of State Arts Agencies grant, 1977; Guggenheim fellowship, 1989; Mystery Writers of America Edgar Allan Poe award, 1989. **Agent:** Philip Spitzer, 788 Ninth Ave., New York, New York 10019, U.S.A. **Address:** 338 North Quentin, Wichita, Kansas 62708, U.S.A.

PUBLICATIONS

Novels (series: Dave Robicheaux)

To the Bright and Shining Sun. New York, Scribner, 1970.
Lay Down My Sword and Shield. New York, Crewel, 1971.
The Lost Get-Back Boogie. Baton Rouge, Louisiana State University Press, 1986.
The Neon Rain (Robicheaux). New York, Holt, 1987; London, Mysterious Press, 1989.
Heaven's Prisoners (Robicheaux). New York, Holt, 1988; London, Mysterious Press, and London, Vintage, 1990.
Black Cherry Blues. Boston, Little Brown, 1989; London, Century, 1990.
A Morning for Flamingoes (Robicheaux). Boston, Little Brown, 1990; London, Arrow, 1993.
A Stained White Radiance (Robicheaux). New York, Hyperion, 1992; London, Arrow, 1993.
In the Electric Mist with Confederate Dead. New York, Hyperion, and London, Orion, 1993.
Dixie City Jam (Robicheaux). New York, Hyperion, and London, Orion, 1994 .
Burning Angel. New York, Hyperion, 1995.
Half of Paradise. New York, Hyperion, 1995.
Two for Texas. New York, Hyperion, 1995.

*   *   *

In his thirteen novels, James Lee Burke sets up a basic confrontation between the beauties of the natural world and the stark, cruel marginal existence of his characters. When he writes about the natural world of the Texas-Louisiana Gulf Coast with its swamps and bayou or the blue mountains of Montana, he produces a poetic and lyrical prose, filled with affirmation and awe, based solidly on his descriptions and evocations of the weather, light, aromas, and colors. Such a world appears Edenic and, for the most part, unspoiled. Burke writes with a Thoreauvian attention to detail and a Whitmanic delight in the sheer boundlessness of nature. Such a romantic sense of oneness and transcendence parallels his characters' often thwarted desire for escape, sex, occasional love, country music, and jazz.

Burke's characters pollute the world they inhabit. The ex-cons, prostitutes, mobsters, drug dealers and runners, alcoholics, bad cops, psychopathic killers, and mindless thugs occupy a Darwinian combat zone of existence, of life at the edge. Burke's men are crude and violent, driven by their own testosterone tactics in a raunchy moral wasteland that portrays violent predators in a sprawling, sleazy underworld of society and the soul. His women often partake of the same characteristics, except for the few who manage to love and survive. Burke depicts this world in a hard-edged, Hemingway-style prose that is cryptic and often crude, a style that balances precariously between sadism and sentiment, terror and tenderness.

The hero of many of Burke's novels is Dave Robicheaux, a former cop on the New Orleans police force, who stakes his claim to New Iberia, a small town in southern Louisiana. He's a barely reformed alcoholic still suffering from the dark depressions and nightmares from his service in the Vietnam War and the murder of his first wife, Annie Ballard, a social worker. As one of the walking wounded, he continually examines his own existential doubts and uncertainties. In recent books he has married Bootsie, the widow of a mob boss who has lupus, and they have adopted Alafair, an El Salvadorian orphan whom he had rescued from a plane crash. Robicheaux displays his own tough Cajun code of honor and right and wrong and emerges as a kind of knight errant in the seedy underworld that is his life.

Burke's plots are sprawling and elaborate with their interlocking network of rednecks, racists, and raunchy hitmen, served up in an intricate labyrinth of betrayals, double-dealings, frame-ups, and set-ups. In this grimly realistic and often nihilistic world, Robicheaux is usually able to find the connections beneath the murky mayhem, that touchstone of the mystery formula which assures us that some kind of rational order and moral victory can be achieved, however fitfully.

In *The Lost Get-Back Boogie* of 1986, an earlier novel that does not feature Robicheaux, Burke carefully lays out his landscape of prisons, dreary bars, holding cells, pickup trucks and gun racks, oil rigs and sleazy roadhouses, in which the ex-con, Iry Paret, tells the tale of his parole, released after having stabbed a man in a bar, and his journey to Montana from Louisiana to work on the ranch of his prison-buddy's father, Frank Riordan. In the course of the novel Paret, writing in the first-person, replaces Buddy Riordan, his friend from prison, by working well on the ranch and finally marrying Buddy's ex-wife Beth. In effect the story of this redneck's redemption is a complicated psychological process, for Iry's survival depends upon Buddy's death. Such Oedipal conflicts between "killer brothers" provide the novel with its terrible economy and vision that personal triumph necessarily involves personal betrayal. That dark psychological subtext pervades all of Burke's subsequent novels.

An example of his kind of plot can be seen in one of the later books, *In the Electric Mist with Confederate Dead* of 1993. Here Burke mixes the Robicheaux milieu and mystery with gothic overtones that involve the apparition of the Confederate general, John Bell Hood, who appears in an eerie hallucinatory manner to become Robicheaux's advisor and conscience. The circuitous and labyrithine plot involves the murder of a hooker, Robicheaux's memory of having witnessed the murder of a black man in the Atchafalaya Basin, and the return to New Iberia of the malignant mobster, Julie Balboni, to finance a Hollywood film there. Several murders and betrayals abound, Balboni's finally set afire in prison, and Robicheaux uncovers all the right solutions to the crimes.

James Lee Burke's novels build upon the "hard-boiled school" of American crime and detective fiction that was begun and carried on by Dashiell Hammett, Raymond Chandler, and Kenneth Millar writing as Ross Macdonald. Other contemporary writers continuing this tradition include Robert B. Parker, George V. Higgins, and Elmore Leonard. Such novels directly depict violent action in a world of total violence, corruption, and psychological mutants. Such writers create Dickensian characters who speak a tough, crude, naturalistic dialogue. Their vision of the world remains cruel, often heartless, relentlessly paranoid, and instinctually chaotic.

Burke brings to this hard-boiled school his own lyrical descriptions of the natural world, his own sense of loss for the Edenic world of his childhood in southern Louisiana, and his sounding of the psychological depths of guilt, obsession, and self-loathing that infect his characters. In using the mystery formula with its process of calculated revelation, he consistently exposes the darker, more frightening side of contemporary America, and even though the guilty may be captured and/or killed, that violent darker landscape remains brutally and masterfully intact.

—Samuel Coale

BURNS, Alan

Nationality: British. **Born:** London, 29 December 1929. **Education:** The Merchant Taylors' School, London; Middle Temple, London: called to the bar, 1956. **Military Service:** Served in the Royal Army Education Corps, 1949-51. **Family:** Married 1) Carol Lynn in 1954, one son and one daughter; 2) Jean Illien in 1980, one daughter. **Career:** Barrister in London, 1956-59; research assistant, London School of Economics, 1959; assistant legal manager, Beaverbrook Newspapers, London, 1959-62; Henfield fellow, University of East Anglia, Norwich, 1971; senior tutor in creative writing, Western Australian Institute of Technology, South Bentley, 1975; Arts Council writing fellow, City Literary Institute, London, 1976; associate professor and professor of English, University of Minnesota, Minneapolis, 1977-91. Since 1992, lecturer, Creative Writing Department, Lancaster University, England. **Awards:** Arts Council grant, 1967, 1969, and bursary, 1969, 1973; C. Day Lewis fellowship, 1973; Bush Foundation Arts fellowship, 1984. **Agent:** Diana Tyler, MBA Literary Agents Ltd., 45 Fitzroy St., London W1P 5HR, England. **Address:** Creative Writing Department, Lancaster University, Lancaster LA1 4YN, England.

PUBLICATIONS

Novels

Buster, in *New Writers One.* London, Calder, 1961; published separately, New York, Red Dust, 1972.
Europe after the Rain. London, Calder, 1965; New York, Day, 1970.
Celebrations. London, Calder and Boyars, 1967.
Babel. London, Calder and Boyars, 1969; New York, Day, 1970.
Dreamerika! A Surrealist Fantasy. London, Calder and Boyars, 1972.
The Angry Brigade: A Documentary Novel. London, Allison and Busby, 1973.
The Day Daddy Died. London, Allison and Busby, 1981.
Revolutions of the Night. London, Allison and Busby, 1986.

Uncollected Short Story

"Wonderland," in *Beyond the Words.* London, Hutchinson, 1975.

Play

Palach, with Charles Marowitz (produced London, 1970). Published in *Open Space Plays,* edited by Marowitz, London, Penguin, 1974.

Other

To Deprave and Corrupt: Technical Reports of the United States Commission on Obscenity and Pornography. London, Davis Poynter, 1972.
The Imagination on Trial: British and American Writers Discuss Their Working Methods, with Charles Sugnet. London, Allison and Busby, 1981.

*

Critical Study: Article by David W. Madden, in *British Novelists since 1960* edited by Jay L. Halio, Detroit, Gale, 1983.

* * *

Alan Burns's novels deserve the attention of serious readers. The first, *Europe after the Rain,* taking its title from a painting by Max Ernst, established him as a kind of infra-realist. Set in the unspecified future in a Europe devastated by internecine strife within "the party," it deals with ruined figures in a ruined landscape, purposelessly dedicated to "the work" which is the only thing the party will reward with the food necessary to keep alive. The unnamed narrator alone possesses any genuine purpose. His quest to find and take care of the daughter of the Trotskyite leader of the rebel forces is inspired by something like love, doubtfully implicit in his actions, later developed into a statement of hope which comes as the one redeeming human fact in a world blasted beyond the usual trappings of humanity, but arrived at only after much violence: a woman is flogged, a dog stabbed and its legs dislocated, people fight over corpses for the gold fillings in the teeth, a leg is wrenched off a corpse and eaten by a woman, other women pursue and stone and half-crucify and eventually beat to death the commander of the forces who are in power at the book's beginning. To this nightmarish action Burns applies a style which may be described as burnt-out. His sentences are mostly short, or built up of short phrases resting on commas where one might have expected full-stops, the total effect being slipped, stripped, and abrupt.

Celebrations is similarly uncompromising, with six characters and seven funerals. Williams, boss of a factory, has two sons, Michael and Phillip, whom he dominates. A hero to himself, Williams is a most uncertain personality, inconstant in his psychological attributes, extravagant in behavior which is nevertheless always reported in the same flat and colorless prose. Phillip's death, following an accident which necessitates the amputation of his leg, leaves an even sharper taste of doubt in the reader's mind—for while it throws his father and his brother into grim rivalry for the attention of his widow, Jacqueline, these affairs are chronicled with such irony that they hardly seem to occur. All the time, it appears, we are meant to be reminded of Kierkegaard's dictum, "The thought of death condenses and intensifies life," as Burns piles violence on violence, and funeral on funeral, abbreviating whole lives to a tapestry of gesture.

With *Babel* Burns seemed to have reached a dead end, though it confirms him in his role as infra-realist, anti-poet, steely perceiver of disconnections, writing as though he looks down on the rest of us from a private spaceship in unwilling orbit. Here he has assembled an ice-cold report on a world in chaos, stitching together clichés from the newspapers, fragments of misunderstood conversation, a babble of jokes and warnings. The cunningly fragmented styles owe too much to Burroughs and Ballard, and the comedy cannot quite conceal something merely self-disgusted in such furious insistence on unmeaning.

—Robert Nye

BURROUGHS, William S(eward)

Pseudonym: William Lee. **Nationality:** American. **Born:** St. Louis, Missouri, 5 February 1914. **Education:** John Burroughs School and Taylor School, St. Louis; Los Alamos Ranch School, New Mexico; Harvard University, Cambridge, Massachusetts, A.B. in anthropology 1936; studied medicine at the University of Vienna; Mexico City College, 1948-50. **Military Service:** Served in the United States Army, 1942. **Family:** Married 1) Ilse Herzfeld Klapper in 1937 (divorced 1946); 2) Jean Vollmer in 1945 (died 1951), one son (deceased). **Career:** Worked as a journalist, private detective, and bartender; now a full-time writer. Painter: exhibitions at Tony Shafrazi Gallery, New York; October Gallery, London, 1988; Kellas Gallery, Lawrence, Kansas, 1989. Lived for many years in Tangier and New York City; now lives in Lawrence. **Awards:** American Academy award, 1975. **Member:** American Academy, 1983. **Agent:** Andrew Wylie Agency, 250 West 57th Street, New York, New York 10107. **Address:** c/o Grove Press Inc., 841 Broadway, 4th Floor, New York, New York 10003, U.S.A.

PUBLICATIONS

Novels

Junkie: Confessions of an Unredeemed Drug Addict (as William Lee). New York, Ace, 1953; London, Digit, 1957; complete edition, as *Junky,* London, Penguin, 1977.
The Naked Lunch. Paris, Olympia Press, 1959; London, Calder, 1964; as *Naked Lunch,* New York, Grove Press, 1962.
The Soft Machine. Paris, Olympia Press, 1961; New York, Grove Press, 1966; London, Calder and Boyars, 1968.
The Ticket That Exploded. Paris, Olympia Press, 1962; revised edition, New York, Grove Press, 1967; London, Calder and Boyars, 1968.
Dead Fingers Talk. London, Calder, 1963.
Nova Express. New York, Grove Press, 1964; London, Cape, 1966.
The Wild Boys: A Book of the Dead. New York, Grove Press, 1971; London, Calder and Boyars, 1972; revised edition, London, Calder, 1979.
Short Novels. London, Calder, 1978.
Blade Runner: A Movie. Berkeley, California, Blue Wind Press, 1979.
Port of Saints. Berkeley, California, Blue Wind Press, 1980; London, Calder, 1983.
Cities of the Red Night: A Boy's Book. London, Calder, and New York, Holt Rinehart, 1981.
The Place of Dead Roads. New York, Holt Rinehart, 1983; London, Calder, 1984.
Queer. New York, Viking, 1985; London, Pan, 1986.
The Western Lands. New York, Viking, 1987; London, Pan, 1988.
Interzone. London, Picador, 1989.

Short Stories

Exterminator! New York, Viking Press, 1973; London, Calder and Boyars, 1974.
Early Routines. Santa Barbara, California, Cadmus, 1981.
The Streets of Chance. New York, Red Ozier Press, 1981.
Junky's Christmas and Other Stories. London, Serpents Tail, 1994.

Uncollected Short Stories

"The Ghost Lemurs of Madagascar," in *Omni* (New York), April 1987.

"The Valley," in *Esquire* (New York), September 1987.
"Twilight's Last Gleamings," in *Paris Review,* Winter 1988.

Play

The Last Words of Dutch Schultz (film script). London, Cape Goliard Press, 1970; New York, Viking Press, 1975.

Other

The Exterminator, with Brion Gysin. San Francisco, Auerhahn Press, 1960.
Minutes to Go, with others. Paris, Two Cities, 1960; San Francisco, Beach, 1968.
The Yage Letters, with Allen Ginsberg. San Francisco, City Lights, 1963.
Roosevelt after Inauguration. New York, Fuck You Press, 1964.
Valentine Day's Reading. New York, American Theatre for Poets, 1965.
Time. New York, "C" Press, 1965.
Health Bulletin: APO-33: A Metabolic Regulator. New York, Fuck You Press, 1965; revised edition, as *APO-33 Bulletin,* San Francisco, Beach, 1966.
So Who Owns Death TV?, with Claude Pelieu and Carl Weissner. San Francisco, Beach, 1967.
The Dead Star. San Francisco, Nova Broadcast Press, 1969.
Ali's Smile. Brighton, Unicorn, 1969.
Entretiens avec William Burroughs, by Daniel Odier. Paris, Belfond, 1969; translated as *The Job: Interviews with William S. Burroughs* (includes *Electronic Revolution*), New York, Grove Press, and London, Cape, 1970.
The Braille Film. San Francisco, Nova Broadcast Press, 1970.
Brion Gysin Let the Mice In, with Brion Gysin and Ian Somerville, edited by Jan Herman. West Glover, Vermont, Something Else Press, 1973.
Mayfair Academy Series More or Less. Brighton, Urgency Press Rip-Off, 1973.
White Subway, edited by James Pennington. London, Aloes, 1974.
The Book of Breeething. Ingatestone, Essex, OU Press, 1974; Berkeley, California, Blue Wind Press, 1975; revised edition, Blue Wind Press, 1980.
Snack: Two Tape Transcripts, with Eric Mottram. London, Aloes, 1975.
Sidetripping, with Charles Gatewood. New York, Strawberry Hill, 1975.
The Retreat Diaries, with *The Dream of Tibet,* by Allen Ginsberg. New York, City Moon, 1976.
Cobble Stone Gardens. Cherry Valley, New York, Cherry Valley Editions, 1976.
The Third Mind, with Brion Gysin. New York, Viking Press, 1978; London, Calder, 1979.
Roosevelt after Inauguration and Other Atrocities. San Francisco, City Lights, 1979.
Ah Pook Is Here and Other Texts (includes *The Book of Breeething, Electronic Revolution*). London, Calder, 1979; New York, Riverrun, 1982.
A William Burroughs Reader, edited by John Calder. London, Pan, 1982.
Letters to Allen Ginsberg 1953-1957. New York, Full Court Press, 1982.
New York Inside Out, photographs by Robert Walker. Port Washington, New York, Skyline Press, 1984.

The Burroughs File. San Francisco, City Lights, 1984.
The Adding Machine: Collected Essays. London, Calder, 1985; New York, Seaver, 1986.
Tornado Alley. Cherry Valley, New York, Cherry Valley Editions, 1988.
Interzone, edited by James Grauerholz. New York, Viking, and London, Pan, 1989.
Ghost of Chance, illustrated by George Condo. New York, Library Fellows of the Whitney Museum of American Art, 1991.
The Cat Inside. New York, Viking, 1992.
Everything Is Permitted: The Making of Naked Lunch, edited by Ira Silverberg. New York, Grove Weidenfeld, 1992.
The Letters of William S. Burroughs:1945-1959, edited by Oliver Harris. New York, Viking, and London, Picador, 1993.
My Education: A Book of Dreams. New York, Viking, 1994.

*

Film Adaptation: *Naked Lunch,* 1991.

Bibliography: *William S. Burroughs: A Bibliography 1953-1973* by Joe Maynard and Barry Miles, Charlottesville, University Press of Virginia, 1978; *William S. Burroughs: A Reference Guide* by Michael B. Goodman and Lemuel B. Coley, New York, Garland, 1990.

Critical Studies: *William Burroughs: The Algebra of Need* by Eric Mottram, Buffalo, Intrepid Press, 1971, revised edition, as *The Algebra of Need,* London, Boyars, 1991; *Contemporary Literary Censorship: The Case History of Burroughs' Naked Lunch* by Michael B. Goodman, Metuchen, New Jersey, Scarecrow Press, 1981; *With William Burroughs: A Report from the Bunker* edited by Victor Bokris, New York, Seaver, 1981, London, Vermilion, 1982; "William Burroughs Issue" of *Review of Contemporary Fiction* (Elmwood Park, Illinois), vol. 4, no. 1, 1984; *William Burroughs* by Jennie Skerl, Boston, Twayne, 1985; *Literary Outlaw: The Life and Times of William S. Burroughs* by Ted Morgan, New York, Holt, 1988, London, Bodley Head, 1991; *William S. Burroughs at the Front: Critical Reception 1959-1989* edited by Jennie Skerl and Robin Lydenberg, Carbondale, Southern Illinois University Press, 1991; *William Burroughs: El Hombre Invisible: A Portrait* by Barry Miles, London, Virgin, 1992, and New York, Hyperion, 1993.

*   *   *

William S. Burroughs is a novelist who is deeply involved with experimental writing and the investigation of his unconscious mind. In the years between his first book, *Junkie,* published in 1953 under the pseudonym of William Lee, and his most recent fiction, his narrative has been shaped by a series of intensely personal, sometimes eccentric ideas and unconventional prose techniques. Obsessively directed as a writer by what he calls the "dark side" of his mind, he feels invaded by what he describes as "the Ugly Spirit and maneuvered into a lifelong struggle" in which he says he has no choice except to write his way out.

The more than 29 books composing Burroughs's published fiction reflect his homosexuality and his 15 years of experience as a morphine and heroin addict. The motivation for *Junkie* was simple: he wanted to render in the most accurate and precise terms his experiences as a drug addict. This was the first time in American literature that drug addiction was presented nonjudgmentally as an individual choice, a type of solitary conditioning that was an alternative to the mass conditioning of conventional society. *Queer,* his next book, unpublished until 1985 but written 30 years earlier, was also autobiographical, created with a more complex intention during a brief period of withdrawal from junk after he accidentally shot and killed his wife in Mexico City. In his recent introduction to *Queer* Burroughs analyzes the creative process in which he initially became a writer, inventing what he calls the form of the "routine" to shock and amuse his audience during this period of his life when he felt himself "disintegrated, desperately in need of contact, completely unsure of himself and his purpose." Expressionistic routines became the basic structure of Burroughs's narrative style in much of his subsequent prose, a series of frantic, hallucinated, surreal episodes whose witheringly humorous tone masks a deadly serious commitment to writing. *The Yage Letters* is an epistolary "novel" based on his letter to Allen Ginsberg describing a journey to the Amazon jungle in search of the "final fix." It forms with *Junkie* and *Queer* what the poet Robert Creeley calls "a trilogy of despair" exploring sensory experience as an alternative to conventional social behavior and morality. It wasn't until after Burroughs moved from Mexico to Tangier and was cured of his heroin addiction in 1959 that he created the book generally regarded as his masterpiece, *Naked Lunch.*

The title of this volume was given to him by his friend Jack Kerouac, who helped type the manuscript from the thousand pages of notes Burroughs had kept during his addiction. The words "naked lunch" were meant to suggest what Burroughs sees as the book's theme: "That frozen moment when everyone sees what is on the end of every fork"—or as the critic Eric Mottram translates the image, "The moment a man realizes his cannibalism, his predatory condition, and his necessary parasitism and addictive nature." In *Naked Lunch* Burroughs engages himself totally with his nightmare experience, descending into the horrors of human physical disintegration and degradation with an unsettling calm and cold descriptive power reminiscent of Swift, entering the absolute nadir of existence where the physical tyranny of the junk habit has stripped bare what Burroughs envisions as the socio-political tyranny that controls our lives.

The Ticket That Exploded, The Soft Machine, and *Nova Express,* a trilogy assembled in Paris over the next few years from the remaining pages of notes accumulated in Tangier, strengthened Burroughs's literary reputation after *Naked Lunch.* The unnerving, sometimes viscerally disturbing routines involving sex and sadism in his work were admired by some readers—Anthony Burgess said, "Mr. Burroughs joins a small body of writers who are willing to look at hell and report what they see"—but his books also provoked violent critical response from many others. This controversy intensified during his next experimental phase of writing after he moved to London in 1966 and began to practice the cut-up method of composition with the American poet and painter Brion Gysin, introduced to him by Paul Bowles. Burroughs and Gysin collaborated on the books *Minutes to Go, The Exterminator,* and *The Third Mind.*

Burroughs regarded the cut-up method as an important evolutionary advance in the development of literature, a step beyond his narrative routines and Kerouac's technique of "spontaneous prose" composition. It was another way to help free the writer from the control of the standard sentence, which Burroughs (deadpan) told an interviewer from the *Paris Review* was "one of the great errors of Western thought" because it encouraged the conscious, rational mind and inhibited creativity. The technique of the cut-up was basically a juxtaposition of heterogeneous material; Burroughs felt that Eliot had used the method earlier in "The Waste Land." Experimenting with tapes and printed material, one of Burroughs's favorite procedures was to tape his own voice reading at random from magazines, newspapers, and books; then he would run the tape back and forth, inserting new material wherever it happened to stop, continuing until all the phrases were cut-up. Burroughs's English publisher John Calder realized that the cut-up was another way of producing mechanically what the writer's own creative processes had previously evoked by random association. Years later Burroughs was startled when Samuel Beckett told him that cut-ups weren't writing; they were plumbing. At the same time Burroughs was experimenting with cut-ups he also used his earlier narrative style in the other books he wrote in London: *The Wild Boys, Port of Saints,* the film script *The Last Words of Dutch Schultz,* and *Exterminator!,* a collection of short prose sketches that contains (along with *Junkie* and *Queer*), some of his most accessible writing.

Since Burroughs's return to live in the United States in 1974, he has continued experimenting with tapes and written cut-up collages, influencing a number of young writers and musicians. Under his influence, his son William Burroughs, Jr., wrote two fine autobiographical novels about addiction, *Speed* and *Kentucky Ham.* Burroughs's recent major fiction, *Cities of the Red Night* and *The Place of Dead Roads,* are long picaresque expressionistic novels in which several characters from his previous books appear—Doctor Benway, Clem Snide the Private Asshole, and the Wild Boys—along with new characters, as Burroughs experiments with satires of science fiction and the western. The form of the short, episodic, hallucinated routine still usually provides the basic structure of his narrative.

Burroughs is essentially a satirist who wants to reveal ways in which anyone in a position of authority exercises control over others. His routines dramatize his conviction that since our moral values are askew, police have a vested interest in crime, doctors in illness, governments in war, and the Drug Enforcement Administration in addition. Believing that human nature is evil throughout history, Burroughs feels the only possibility for good to evolve is through each individual's understanding his own nature and exorcising the cruelty and sadism that is innate in all of us; he says he exorcises the evil in his own mind by writing his routines.

Both Allen Ginsberg and Jack Kerouac credit him as a strong influence on their writing. The critic John Tytell recognizes that "Ginsberg's and Kerouac's pathway to beatitude stemmed from Burroughs's nightmare of devastation." Ginsberg feels that Burroughs's work, like his own, expresses "the change of consciousness that overcame the United States in the last two decades [since the 1960s] which resulted in disillusionment on the part of the general public with self-mystifying government. That was the first theme I picked up from him back in the 1940s—his contempt for the trappings of authoritarianism and his humor in seeing through military-police uniforms to the hairy cancerous body-corpse inside. And that leads later on to his cynicism about the outward forms and trappings of the ego itself."

If the farcical caricatures in Burroughs's brutal routines are a projection of his general cynicism about human nature, his attitude as a homosexual is sometimes specifically misogynistic. He said in *The Job,* "Women are a perfect curse. I think they were a basic mistake, and the whole dualistic universe evolved from this error. . . . Love is a con put down by the female sex." Yet while he feels he can make such sweeping statements, he is impatient with generalizations made by critics about his work. Burroughs insists that as a black humorist and writer he is transcribing "the still sad music of humanity." Of his writing he says, "I just make a little skit, that's all."

—Ann Charters

BURROWAY, Janet (Gay)

Nationality: American. **Born:** Tucson, Arizona, 21 September 1936. **Education:** The University of Arizona, Tucson, 1954-55; Barnard College, New York, B.A. (cum laude) in English, 1958; Cambridge University, B.A. (honours) in English 1960, M.A. 1965; Yale School of Drama, New Haven, Connecticut, 1960-61. **Family:** Married 1) Walter Eysselinck in 1961 (divorced 1973), two sons; 2) William Dean Humphries in 1978 (divorced 1981); 3)Peter Ruppert in 1993, one step-daughter. **Career:** Supply teacher and music director, Binghamton public schools, New York, 1961-63; costume designer, Belgian National Theatre, Ghent, 1965-70, and Gardner Centre for the Arts, University of Sussex, Brighton, 1965-71; lecturer in American Studies, University of Sussex, 1965-72; assistant to the Writing Program, University of Illinois, Urbana, 1972. Associate professor, 1972-77, since 1977 professor of English, and since 1986 McKenzie Professor of English Literature and Writing, Florida State University, Tallahassee. Visiting lecturer, Writers Workshop, University of Iowa, Iowa City, 1980. Fiction reviewer, *New Statesman,* London, 1970-71, 1975, and since 1991, *New York Times Book Review.* Since 1994, columnist, *New Letters* (Kansas City). **Awards:** Amoco award, for teaching, 1974; National Endowment for the Arts grant, 1976; Florida Fine Arts Council grant, 1983; FSU Distinguished Teacher award, 1992; Lila Wallace-Reader's Digest fellowship, 1993. **Agent:** Gail Hochman, Brandt and Brandt Inc., 1501 Broadway, New York, New York 10036. **Address:** 240 De Soto Street, Tallahassee, Florida 32303, U.S.A.

PUBLICATIONS

Novels

Descend Again. London, Faber, 1960.
The Dancer from the Dance. London, Faber, 1965; Boston, Little Brown, 1968.
Eyes. London, Faber, and Boston, Little Brown, 1966.
The Buzzards. Boston, Little Brown, 1969; London, Faber, 1970.
Raw Silk. Boston, Little Brown, and London, Gollancz, 1977.
Opening Nights. New York, Atheneum, and London, Gollancz, 1985.
Cutting Stone. Boston, Houghton Mifflin, and London Gollancz, 1992.

Uncollected Short Stories

"Embalming Mom," in *Apalachee Quarterly* (Tallahassee, Florida), Spring 1985.
"Winn Dixie," in *New Letters* (Kansas City), January 1986.

"Growth," in *New Virginia Review* (Richmond), Spring 1990.
"I'toi," in *Prairie Schooner,* Spring 1991.
"Dad Scattered," in *The Day My Father Died.* New York, Running Press, 1994.

Plays

Garden Party (produced New York, 1958).
The Fantasy Level (produced New Haven, Connecticut, 1961; Brighton, Sussex, 1968).
The Beauty Operators (produced Brighton, Sussex, 1968).
Poenulus; or, The Little Carthaginian, adaptation of a play by Plautus, in *Five Roman Comedies,* edited by Palmer Boive. New York, Dutton, 1970.

Television Plays: *Hoddinott Veiling,* 1970; *Due Care and Attention,* 1973.

Poetry

But to the Season. Weston super Mare, Somerset, Universities' Poetry, 1961.
Material Goods. Tallahassee, University Presses of Florida, 1981.

Other

The Truck on the Track (for children). London, Cape, 1970; Indianapolis, Bobbs Merrill, 1971.
The Giant Ham Sandwich (verse only; for children), with John Vernon Lord. London, Cape, 1972; Boston, Houghton Mifflin, 1973.
Writing Fiction: A Guide to Narrative Craft. Boston, Little Brown, 1982; 3rd edition, New York, HarperCollins, 1991; 4th edition, HarperCollins, 1995.

*

Manuscript Collection: Florida State University, Tallahassee.

Critical Studies: Article by Elisabeth Muhlenfeld, in *American Novelists since World War II,* 2nd series, edited by James E. Kibler, Jr., Detroit, Gale, 1980; "The Play in the Novel: *The Nuns* in *Opening Nights*" by Phyllis Zatlin, in *Modern Language Studies,* Summer 1993.

Janet Burroway comments:

I wrote my first novel, *Descend Again,* with the determination that it would be *fiction,* and not decorated autobiography. Therefore I set it in a town I knew only slightly, and in 1942, when I had been six years old. It was several years before I realized that it dealt with a heroine who, like myself, was driven by a desire to get out of Arizona and into a world of books.

I continued to choose subjects that seemed to me socially and politically "serious," eschewing concerns merely female, while certain themes chose me in spite of myself: the older-man-younger-woman relationship, near-suicide and the decision to live after all; the abandonment of children—even, recurrently, the image of proliferating garbage. I remember writing a scene in *The Buzzards,* when my children were toddlers, in which Eleanor walks out on her brood, myself thinking as I wrote: *I could never do this. Why do I keep writing about this?* Meanwhile my own boys pestered me to play and I kept sending them out of the room—"Can't you see mummy's working?"

After that novel I faced the fact that I had not considered women's lives sufficiently weighty for the content of fiction, and in the next book, *Raw Silk,* I faced my unchosen themes head on, beginning with the sentence, "This morning I abandoned my only child." The acknowledgement of gender as central to my identity has seemed to me a freeing and integrating change—freeing, even, to adopt a new breadth of attitude toward the global themes. I understand now why I kept fretting about all that garbage.

The greatest change in my work in the past five years has been in the process itself. I have paid deliberate attention to thwarting my linear, critical, perfectionist, left-brain proclivities, in favor of intuitive flow. It works; it makes for faster story, richer prose, more of the unexpected. The motto over my desk as altered, slightly but crucially, from "Don't Dread; Do" to "Writing is Easy. Not Writing is Hard." What's missing is mainly the imperative.

*   *   *

Janet Burroway depicts contemporary social issues through multiple points-of-view to convey strong, and sometimes nebulous, moral messages. Complicated relationships are neatly interconnected within sharply defined domestic and urban settings, as contrasting characters try to work out crises of conscience. The author's penchant for epigrams and symbols further unifies her narratives, but at the cost of excessive, self-conscious rhetoric. Likewise, while her abrupt and usually ambiguous endings avoid blatant didacticism, they also seriously mar the proportions of her careful structures. Stories do not seem to conclude so much as merely come to a halt. She also favors theatrical surprises which do not proceed necessarily from exigencies of plot but facilely exploit the sensational. These linguistic artifices and narrative ploys intrude more than they enlighten, weakening her otherwise admirable craftsmanship. Burroway's novels are well-paced, however, and she further enhances their popular appeal by providing plenty of practical information.

Eyes views the problems of race prejudice and of ethics in medicine and journalism through the individual perspectives of the four principal characters. Set in the South, the novel examines one day in the life of Dr. Rugg, an eye surgeon; his wife Maeve, who is pregnant at 40; their somewhat estranged son Hilary, a liberal reporter on a conservative paper; and Hilary's fiancée Jadeen, a junior high school teacher. Skillfully Burroway evokes the southern atmosphere and delineates the elaborate rituals of black-white relations as enacted by her sensitive protagonists. As a newly liberal and insecure daughter of an old Southern family, Jadeen's dilemma becomes acute: to refuse to teach an outrageously biased textbook and thus lose her job and alienate her genteel but bigotted mother, or to cave in and betray her recent convictions and lose her fiancée. Dr. Rugg, awkward in his charity and family relations and preoccupied in his profession, unwittingly destroys his career by casually mentioning his war-time experiments. Hilary, frustrated in his job and resentful of his famous father, carelessly misses the major scandal his father's seemingly innocuous lecture turns out to be—ironically, sent out on the national wires by Dodds, Rugg's soon-to-be-blind patient—which costs him and his mentor their positions. No totally satisfactory solution to these complications is possible. But Rugg heroically refuses to recant to save face for the State Department, and he serenely awaits his final heart-attack. Hilary,

given a last chance, refuses to compromise his principles, or betray his father. Jadeen, however, is not strong enough for the sacrifice and buckles under to the "system;" she resigns herself (somewhat illogically) to being a subservient, dull teacher, without Hilary. Only Maeve, always understanding if inarticulate, and calm, maintains stability amid the domestic chaos. At the end, Jadeen points a moral of sorts: "Thoughts are complex. Actions are not. That is the subject of tragedy." Burroway's vignettes are telling, especially when she describes racial tension in a black bar or the techniques of surgery, reporting, teaching. But that's the rub: she prefers to tell more than to show. Dialogue is often wooden, and despite the neat plotting, the separate thematic strands don't quite mesh. The melodrama ends slightly out of focus.

The Dancer from the Dance is an ambitious and often subtle attempt at a novel of manners, in which the young, strangely innocent yet wise Prytania naively brings about the destruction and near-collapse of the older and more sophisticated people irresistibly drawn to her. 60-year-old Powers, the sensitive but detached narrator, gives the hapless girl a job in his UNICEF office in Paris and entrée into his elegant world. Soon Prytania holds all in thrall. Stoddard, a young and unimaginative medical student, she leads on but finally cannot marry. Old Riebenstahl, a primitive sculptor and curious sage, finally commits suicide, because he has acted as go-between for her illicit affair with the talented mime Jean-Claude. Even the worldly wise Mme. de Verbois, with whom she stays, and finally Powers himself are cruelly touched by her strange power. The nuances of social behavior, the curious transformations of character, and the complex emotional entanglements are deftly portrayed in several delicately drawn scenes. Yet, for all that, Prytania remains a shadowy figure, and the narrative barely escapes incredibility. Further, although the pages are cluttered with more witticisms and aphorisms than a Restoration comedy, the general tone is more that of a middling French film about yet another blighted romance. The several ironies and crises come off as contrived and formulaic, and ultimately the novel sadly disappoints: such an anticlimax after so much art.

In *The Buzzards* Burroway turns to the political realm, employing, yet again, several narrators. But as we follow the campaign trail of Alex, the conservative but likeable Senator from Arizona, the multiple perspectives—interior monologues, set speeches, newspaper articles, letters—soon become redundant and tedious. Especially so are the fatuous epigrams which clog the journal of the sententious and most implausible manager, Galcher (he calls them Axioms of God; e.g., "We are not subtle enough to contrive a machine in which disintegration contributes to maintenance and manufacture"). Alex's cold, brittle, and marvelously inept wife, his disaffected son, and neurotic daughter Eleanor (whose near-suicide and Mexican abortion pose serious threats to his chances), like the "allegorical" Galcher, are definite liabilities—not only for Alex but for the reader, who has little reason to be interested in them, let alone to like them. Younger daughter Evie, a vivacious, all-American, plastic pom-pom girl, is equally off-putting, though depicted as an asset in Alex's uphill struggle for re-election. Nonetheless, Burroway still has incisive power to reveal the moral ambiguities, contradictions, and rationalizations of her characters, especially the women. But beyond showing the hectic pace and many stratagems of modern politicking, the novel's rationale is not quite clear. And when Evie is precipitously assassinated in the last few pages, the event seems not tragic but merely expedient in terminating a journey that has no real destination. That a writer of Janet Burroway's obvious talents in use of detail and perspective should ultimately be defeated by a lack of control or malfunction of these very elements is an unfortunate irony of her otherwise impressive work.

—Joseph Parisi

BUSCH, Frederick (Matthew)

Nationality: American. **Born:** Brooklyn, New York, 1 August 1941. **Education:** Muhlenberg College, Allentown, Pennsylvania, 1958-62, A.B. 1962; Columbia University, New York (Woodrow Wilson fellow, 1962), 1962-63, M.A. 1967. **Family:** Married Judith Burroughs in 1963; two sons. **Career:** Writer and editor, North American Précis Syndicate, New York, 1964-65, and *School Management* magazine, Greenwich, Connecticut, 1965-66. Instructor, 1966-67, assistant professor, 1968-72, associate professor, 1973-76, professor of English, 1976-87, and since 1987 Fairchild Professor of Literature, Colgate University, Hamilton, New York. Acting director, Program in Creative Writing, University of Iowa, Iowa City, 1978-79; visiting lecturer in creative writing, Columbia University, New York, 1979. **Awards:** National Endowment for the Arts grant, 1976; Guggenheim fellowship, 1980; Ingram Merrill Foundation fellowship, 1981; National Jewish Book award, 1985; American Academy award, 1986; PEN/Malamud award, for short story, 1991. Litt.D.: Muhlenberg College, 1980. **Address:** Department of English, Colgate University, Hamilton, New York 13346, U.S.A.

PUBLICATIONS

Novels

I Wanted a Year Without Fall. London, Calder and Boyars, 1971.
Manual Labor. New York, New Directions, 1974.
The Mutual Friend. New York, Harper, and Hassocks, Sussex, Harvester Press, 1978.
Rounds. New York, Farrar Straus, and London, Hamish Hamilton, 1980.
Take This Man. New York, Farrar Straus, 1981.
Invisible Mending. Boston, Godine, 1984.
Sometimes I Live in the Country. Boston, Godine, 1986.
War Babies. New York, New Directions, 1988.
Harry and Catherine. New York, Knopf, 1990.
Closing Arguments. New York, Ticknor and Fields, 1991.
Long Way from Home. New York, Ticknor and Fields, 1993.

Short Stories

Breathing Trouble and Other Stories. London, Calder and Boyars, 1974.
Domestic Particulars: A Family Chronicle. New York, New Directions, 1976.
Hardwater Country. New York, Knopf, 1979.
Too Late American Boyhood Blues. Boston, Godine, 1984.
Absent Friends. New York, Knopf, 1989.
The Children in the Woods: New and Selected Stories. New York, Ticknor and Fields, 1994.

Other

Hawkes: A Guide to His Fictions. Syracuse, New York, Syracuse University Press, 1973.
When People Publish (essays). Iowa City, University of Iowa Press, 1986.

*

Manuscript Collection: Ohio State University, Columbus.

Frederick Busch comments:

I write about characters I want to matter more than my own theories and more than my own delights. The great problem is to face the fullest implications of one's insights and fears—and to sustain the energy to make a usable shape from them. No: the great problem is to sit and write something worthy of the people on the page, and the good reader.

*   *   *

Frederick Busch is a humanist with an eagle eye fixed on the family. His are not like da Vinci's harmonious figure, however. They suggest Ted Hughes's more primal man: "Shot through the head with balled brains/ . . . Clubbed unconscious by his own heart/ . . . He managed to hear faint and far—'It's a boy!'" Pre-eminently, Busch celebrates that tenacity, somehow of the blood, by which we refuse to junk the perplexing intimacies in our lives.

Few writers attempt, let alone so effectively, to narrate from as many points of view. When his persona is a child or a woman, we do not disbelieve. Nor is there any bias in his work for male or female, or for adults as against children. Busch's descriptions are delineated with imagistic exaction and his conviction that work is grace allows him to particularize every type of labor with care. He is equally alert to the countryside or the city, to the barn or the hospital. Natural settings can be saving, as in "Trail of Possible Bones" (*Domestic Particulars*), or fearsome, as in "What You Might as Well Call Love" (*Hardwater Country*). Either way they are fixed in minutely apt detail. Likewise with work. Prioleau making a television hook-up (*Take This Man*), or Silver and Hebner at their pediatrics (*Rounds; Domestic Particulars*)—always, the enterprise is vividly present.

Frequently Busch's architecture renders plot in sundered pieces. One must be patient, wait for the late integration of narrative lines. It is time ill-spent with the too cryptic "You Have Been Warned" (*Breathing Trouble*); it is worthwhile with the adroit *Take This Man*. Busch's syntax is also significant. It can be terse, but is more often transcontinental. The goal is to let phrasing embody a character's thought process or immediate realization of place. A weakness is that Busch's dialogue has tended to repartee. Characters spontaneously produce the *mot juste*. Because their phrasing is closely woven into the works' *leitmotifs,* this seems a requirement. But in fiction so realistic, the pressure upon every utterance to be resonant has damaged plausible conversation, with its inevitable flatness. The problem lessens in *Rounds* and *Take This Man*. In *Invisible Mending,* Busch's best novel, such speech is germane.

I Wanted a Year Without Fall is legend passing from a father to his sleeping infant son. Its comic absurdity resides in parallels with *Pilgrim's Progress* and *Beowulf.* Ben recounts his adventures with Leo, who hits the road to escape urban destitution and a cuckold who wants his hide. Ben's complementary poverty is rural. *He* is fleeing a dead woman's voice. In a typical parody, Ben plays the Green Knight to an army of cockroaches. Here is the heroism of flight, not of the quest. Busch's anxious and ongoing preoccupation with the act of writing is central to the conclusion. Ben's last bardic utterance to his uncomprehending boy, "I will ask you to listen to an old time lay," is absurd indeed. Few will doubt this is a first novel.

Manual Labor concerns the struggle of Anne and Phil Sorenson to overcome the death of their unborn child. All three narrate the story, the immanent baby as the guiding voice. Anne writes an endless letter to her mother, but only in her mind. Phil keeps a journal, often contemplating the uses of narrative in the control of chaos. Death pervades their lives, including the suicide of a vagrant, Abe, whom they befriend in Maine. He had become an unhealthy focus of Anne's own suicidal attention. The novel esteems the victory of the couple over the nearly ubiquitous disintegration surrounding them. The key is labor, the manual labor of the two rebuilding an old house following the ruined labor of a childless mother. Phil's dictum, "You forget with your hands," is provided at the outset by the "child." Some, ponders Saul Maloff in *The New Republic,* will find the persona of the "bled away fetus" an "insuperable obstacle to . . . reading on."

Domestic Particulars is nearly a collection of stories, but its thirteen chapters are an integrated, episodic revelation of a family, as it endures between 1919 and the 1970s. Brooklyn, the Upper West Side, and Greenwich Village are extraordinarily detailed here. All conditions of the great national social ambiance hover pointedly over time and place. Again, domestic strife and the unexpected power of family affection are the essence. But the key figures, Claire and Mac and their son Harry, are much more tenuously bonded than the Sorensons. And the peace they make does not much alleviate the reader's sense of their limited natures and chary good will.

Pondering Busch's canon, one could not anticipate *The Mutual Friend.* It is, of course, about Dickens, but only the lonely figure of 1867 to 1870. No single Dickens emerges, however, because narrators vary. Dickens speaks through his own writing—including his entire will—but the "Chief's" companion, George Dolby, takes over and allows that it is difficult to guarantee precise accounts. And when he dies in a Fulham charity hospital, the Asian servant, Moon, tells us he'll be changing what we've had from Dolby. Busch, who believes we must accommodate the past narratively, nevertheless displays fiction's inevitable mutation of it.

Rounds joins the Sorensons, Elizabeth Bean (a school psychologist), and Eli Silver, M.D. The Sorensons still need children. Elizabeth is pregnant, unmarried, and unwilling to abort the fetus. At the outset, Silver is all but ruined. His inadvertence has cost his son's life and, in the disastrous aftermath of the tragedy, his marriage. Busch separates and eventually intersects his characters' stories, a common strategy in his work. Silver intends to save himself from alcohol and emotional collapse by unflagging and expert attention to his pediatric practice, which is presented with surpassing realism. But only the Sorensons' affectionate regard and Elizabeth's love for him finally achieve that. Silver's scrupulous decision to initiate the death of a little girl in her final agony is realized with superb ethical authenticity.

Gus has two fathers. At ten he goes to Anthony Prioleau, the biological one. His mother follows suit. The three are a family, strangely but abidingly. Tony and Ellen never marry. Hence, *Take This Man.* The novel gradually sketches in backgrounds—why Tony was a Conscientious Objector, why Ellen had a taste for leavetaking. The other father remains in emotional but not physical range, never betrayed by Gus, who nonetheless comes to love Ellen and Tony unreservedly. Gus's first meeting with Tony and Tony's passing are Busch at his emotional best. Two ministers, the Reverends Van Eyck and Billy Horsefall (a parody of Billy Joe Hargis), are Busch at his comic best.

Invisible Mending is equally hilarious and poignant. Though Zimmer, a "Jew manqué," fears loneliness, his Gentile wife shows him the door. Her love isn't equal to his self absorption. For the first four pages it is 1980; it requires 214 pages to get back there. Meanwhile, Zimmer recollects his wondrous days with Rhona Glinksy, librarian and Nazi hunter, and his marriage with Lillian. Lil avers that Zimmer "can make a secular mystery out of the holiest simplicity." Zimmer recollects himself as "the treacherous amphibian who waddled on the Christian sands and swam in the blood of Jews." When Rhona reappears in 1980, times past and present merge. But Zimmer's young son provides a new and imperative focus. *Invisible Mending* brings Philip Roth to mind, both *Portnoy's Complaint* and *The Ghost Writer.* The novel is entirely up to the comparison.

War Babies, a novella, follows Pete Santore's "mission of ignorant need" from Illinois to Salisbury, England. Son of a now-dead father who was imprisoned for treason after his return from the Korean war, Santore seeks Hilary Pennel, daughter of a dead British officer with whom Santore's father had been held captive. Just below full consciousness, Santore needs to expiate his father's sin, which he fears pertained not only to America but to this hero. Thus the adult children meet, have a brief affair and discover the paradoxical likeness of their fathers' emotional bequests. Hilary has experienced her father's fatal resistance to his captors as abandonment, as Santore has his father's collaboration. Pennel's inadvertent gift to his daughter proved to be his vicious jingoist subaltern, aptly named Fox. After surviving the camp, Fox has held Hilary thrall to both his horrifying memories of the war and his sexual needs. This has cost Hilary an authentic life and a serious measure of sanity. Santore's learning is deep and finely characterized, but the reader will most remember Fox, one of contemporary fiction's psychological horror shows. This is a disturbing, morally insightful book.

Absent Friends is a strong collection of stories. Those in which the "friends" are family, either dead or at a distance, are especially compelling. "From the New World," the first and longest, masterfully realizes a middle-aged son's relation to his dead father. But variety, both of absence and point of view about absence, gives the collection richness in subject and perspective. With Busch's last three novels, this work displays the author's ever intensifying effort to explicate the present by revealing its origins in a past equally personal and collective.

Harry and Catherine tells us more than we need to know about the enduring relationship of an unmarried couple, separated over a decade and brought together again through Harry Miller's employment by a senator from New York. The boss wants to work out his political posture toward an upstate country mall being constructed over the bones of slaves who had died of the plague after finding their way north on the underground railway. Far too serendipitously, Catherine Hollander's current lover, Carter Kreuss, is the contractor. Harry is honorably disposed to the dead and Carter's case for free enterprise is not without merit, especially given that the town fathers had long since secretively moved the bones from their original locale, a fact not worth much to a presidential aspirant. The novel is principally shaped, however, by the bond between Harry and the independent, morally centered Catherine.

Their endless, over-subtle exchanges strain patience. The novel's implausible integration of the characters' situations strains credulity.

—David M. Heaton

BYATT, A(ntonia) S(usan)

Nationality: British. **Born:** Antonia Susan Drabble, in Sheffield, Yorkshire, 24 August 1936; sister of Margaret Drabble, *q.v.* **Education:** Sheffield High School; The Mount School, York; Newnham College, Cambridge (open scholarship), B.A. (honours) in English 1957; Bryn Mawr College, Pennsylvania (English-Speaking Union fellow), 1957-58; Somerville College, Oxford, 1958-59, B.A. **Family:** Married 1) I.C.R. Byatt in 1959 (divorced 1969), one daughter and one son (deceased); 2)Peter J. Duffy in 1969, two daughters. **Career:** Teacher, Westminster Tutors, London, 1962-65; lecturer, Central School of Art and Design, London, 1965-69; extra-mural lecturer, 1962-71, lecturer, 1972-81, and senior lecturer in English, 1981-83, University College, London (assistant tutor, 1977-80, and tutor for admissions, 1980-82, Department of English). British Council Lecturer in Spain, 1978, India, 1981, and Korea, 1985. Deputy chair, 1986, and chair, 1986-88, Society of Authors Committee of Management; member, Kingman Committee, on the teaching of English, 1988-89. Associate, Newnham College, 1977-88. **Awards:** Arts Council grant, 1968; PEN Silver Pen, 1986; Booker prize, 1990, and *Irish Times*-Aer Lingus prize, 1990, both for *Possession.* D.Litt.: University of Bradford, 1987; University of York, 1991; University of Durham, 1991. Fellow, Royal Society of Literature, 1983. C.B.E. (Commander, Order of the British Empire), 1990. **Address:** 37 Rusholme Road, London SW15 3LF, England.

Publications

Novels

Shadow of a Sun. London, Chatto and Windus, and New York, Harcourt Brace, 1964.
The Game. London, Chatto and Windus, 1967; New York, Scribner, 1968.
The Virgin in the Garden. London, Chatto and Windus, 1978; New York, Knopf, 1979.
Still Life. London, Chatto and Windus, and New York, Scribner, 1985.
Possession: A Romance. London, Chatto and Windus, and New York, Random House, 1990.

Short Stories

Sugar and Other Stories. London, Chatto and Windus, and New York, Scribner, 1987.
Angels and Insects (novellas). London, Chatto and Windus, and New York, Random House, 1992.
The Matisse Stories. London, Chatto and Windus, 1993.

Uncollected Short Story

"Art Work," in *The New Yorker,* 20 May 1991.

Other

Degrees of Freedom: The Novels of Iris Murdoch. London, Chatto and Windus, and New York, Barnes and Noble, 1965.
Wordsworth and Coleridge in Their Time. London, Nelson, 1970; New York, Crane Russak, 1973; as *Unruly Times: Wordsworth and Coleridge in Their Time,* London, Hogarth Press, 1989.
Iris Murdoch. London, Longman, 1976.
Passions of the Mind (essays). London, Chatto and Windus, 1991; New York, Turtle Bay, 1992.

Editor, *The Mill on the Floss,* by George Eliot. London, Penguin, 1979.
Editor, with Nicholas Warren, *Selected Essays, Poems, and Other Writings,* by George Eliot. London, Penguin, 1990.

*

A.S. Byatt comments:

(1986) My novels are about habits of thought and imagination: the quartet I am writing combines a partly parodic "realist" first and last volumes, with a more experimental second and third. I am presently writing a novel, *Possession,* not in this quartet, and partly to do with history and the history of ideas, in the 19th century.

*   *   *

Although A.S. Byatt is among the best-known literary figures in England today, she has published only eight creative (as opposed to critical) books since her writing career began over 30 years ago. Until the publication of her third novel, *The Virgin in the Garden,* in 1978, her reputation owed more to her scholarly and critical writing, including the first book-length study of Iris Murdoch, *Degrees of Freedom,* and to the high quality of her literary journalism and reviewing than to her fiction; this was somewhat overshadowed by the very popular output of her younger and more prolific sister, Margaret Drabble. However, with *The Virgin in the Garden,* Byatt's first novel in over a decade and one of the most rewarding works of English fiction in the second half of the 1970s, she established herself as an important novelist in her own right, and confirmed this status in 1985 with *Still Life,* the first of three planned sequels to *The Virgin in the Garden.* By winning the Booker Prize in 1990 for her most recent novel, *Possession,* Byatt further enhanced her standing and has reached a wider audience than ever before.

Byatt's first two novels do not aim as high as her later ones, but both are substantial books, and they reveal a development towards the fusion of realism and symbolism in her more recent work. *Shadow of a Sun,* her first work of fiction, is essentially a straightforward piece of orthodox realism, whereas *The Game* makes extensive use of mythical and symbolic elements within a realistic framework.

The action of *Shadow of a Sun*—the title comes from a Ralegh poem—takes place in the shadow cast by Henry Severell, a major English novelist of visionary intensity who is prone to bouts of manic insanity. His teenage daughter, Anna, is the character most dominated by his overpowering personality, and the novel explores Anna's attempt to define herself as an independent being by liberating herself from parental, especially paternal, control and from her own conventionality. The book is a kind of *Bildungsroman,* tracing Anna's development from a very immature schoolgirl, who makes a protest by running away from school, to a Cambridge undergraduate made pregnant by one of her father's friends and most enthusiastic critics, Oliver Canning. In the inconclusive and open-ended final chapter, Anna, having rejected the possibility of a marriage of convenience with a well-to-do, kind-hearted, and mother-dominated fellow-student, asserts her new-found independence and maturity, and confronts the future.

Despite its ample scale, *Shadow of a Sun* concentrates on a very small, tightly knit group of characters, Henry Severell and his wife, Oliver Canning and his wife, and Anna herself. Byatt's second novel, *The Game,* is less claustrophobic in this respect, taking in a much wider spectrum of characters, from academics at Oxford and a Quaker community in Northumberland to fashionable television people in London and a homeless problem family. This range is one reason for the novel being more impressive than its predecessor, although there are obvious resemblances: a novelist is again a major participant, for example, and the erosion of a marriage features prominently. At the heart of *The Game* is the complex and basically antagonistic relationship between two sisters in their thirties, the unmarried Cassandra Corbett, an Oxford don specializing in medieval romance literature, and Julia Eskelund (her husband is Norwegian), a popular novelist who writes about the problems of contemporary women. Cassandra, a convert to Anglo-Catholicism from her family's Quakerism, is other-worldly; Julia, who becomes a participant in a regular arts programme on television and also has an affair with the producer, is decidedly modish. The game that gives the book its title is their elaborate Brontë-like childhood invention, which had literary analogues and opened up an entire imaginary world. Indeed, Cassandra, unlike her much more down-to-earth sister, still lives to a considerable extent in the realm of the imagination and has only a tenuous grasp of reality; the Arthurian imagery and symbolism—she is actually editing Malory—help to convey this. It is the re-entry into their lives of another part of their shared childhood experience, the now-famous zoologist and television personality Simon Moffitt, that revitalizes their teenage conflict over him and leads to Julia rapidly writing a cruel novel based on Cassandra and Simon. This in turn precipitates the tragic denouement of Byatt's novel with a mortally humiliated Cassandra finally retreating completely from reality by killing herself. Sibling rivalry finally culminates in death 20 years later. While the surface of *The Game* is realistic, Byatt introduces a mythic level by cleverly employing the symbolism of the Garden of Eden in relation to her characters; Simon's snakes, for example, clearly bring to mind the serpent.

Although much larger in scale than either of its predecessors, *The Virgin in the Garden* is but the first novel in an as yet untitled tetralogy in progress, which promises to be one of the most ambitious fictional undertakings of the postwar period, comparable to Lawrence Durrell's *Alexandria Quartet,* Doris Lessing's *The Children of Violence,* and Anthony Powell's *A Dance to the Music of Time.* The tetralogy aims to follow the lives of a group of characters during the second Elizabethan age, from the accession of the Queen in 1952 until the major Post-Impressionist exhibition held in London in 1980, but each novel, while advancing the chronology, is expected to have its own dominating motif or central symbol and was originally intended to be technically and stylistically distinctive. However, Byatt has found this latter plan very difficult, perhaps impossible, to implement for reasons explained in the second volume, *Still Life.*

After a short but complex and symbolically rich prologue set in 1968, *The Virgin in the Garden* narrates events in 1952-53, with occasional and brief forward-flashes that illuminate the characters from the advantageous perspective of hindsight. The novel, set in North Yorkshire, mainly in and around a public school, concentrates on the three children of the senior English master, Bill Potter, and the person each of them is most involved with: the eldest, Stephanie, a schoolteacher, and the curate she marries, much to the annoyance of her militantly agnostic father; Frederica, a brilliant and precocious schoolgirl, and the English teacher, poet, and playwright Alexander Wedderburn she falls in love with; the strange schoolboy, Marcus, and the biology teacher, a religious maniac, with whom he indulges in a lunatic, quasi-spiritual experiment.

One of the things the novel captures best is the festive atmosphere of Coronation year with its sense of promise and rebirth, of release from postwar privations, of a new Elizabethan age with just as much potentiality as that of the first Elizabeth. A main strand of the book is the production of Alexander's verse play about the Virgin queen, *Astraea,* in the garden of an Elizabethan country house—hence the title, although it also refers to Frederica, another virgin until the closing pages. The novel is, in fact, full of quotations and literary and mythological allusions, and is concerned with both English history and the English cultural tradition. While *The Virgin in the Garden* possesses an almost Victorian leisureliness in its depiction of detail and its analysis of characters, it is also a decidedly modernist work in the wake of *Ulysses,* since its meticulous realism is fused with symbolism. More conspicuously than in her previous fiction, Byatt draws her inspiration from Proust, one of her favourite novelists and a major influence on her work. Significantly, two of the three epigraphs to her next novel, *Still Life,* are from Proust.

If, as the title indicates, Elizabethan iconography plays an important part in structuring and unifying *The Virgin in the Garden,* the art of painting, as the title again suggests, performs an equivalent role in *Still Life.* The novel opens at the Post-Impressionist exhibition in 1980, and is pervaded by reference to the life and work of van Gogh, including a number of quotations from his famous letters. In *Still Life,* Alexander Wedderburn's new verse play, parallel to *Astraea* in its predecessor, is *The Yellow Chair,* which dramatizes the last phase of van Gogh's life and appropriates the title of one of his best-known paintings for its own title. The intrusive authorial "I," who must be equated with Byatt herself rather than interpreted as a deceptive metafictional device, comments reflexively on *Still Life* on several occasions, and describes her failure to achieve a style for the novel using the analogy of painting, as she had hoped. She had wanted to follow William Carlos Williams's injunction about "no ideas but in things" and to write "a novel of naming and accuracy" by using a language shorn of metaphor and figures of speech, an ambition shared by her character Alexander Wedderburn in writing *The Yellow Chair.* Like Wedderburn, she found that language, being inherently metaphorical and figurative, was against her, and she had to abandon her experimental aspirations for the book. As a result, *Still Life* is more of an orthodox sequel to *The Virgin in the Garden* than originally planned, and in some respects conforms to the traditional family saga, even though the use of flash-forward techniques and self-reflecting analysis, along with her intellectual arguments and philosophical speculations, ensure that its underlying realism is qualified by postmodernist perspectives on language, art, and reality itself.

As in *The Virgin in the Garden,* the narrative of *Still Life* has three main strands, one for each of the Potter children, and follows their lives during the mid and late 1950s, ending catastrophically with the accidental death of the eldest, Stephanie, electrocuted in her own kitchen. The closing chapters, dealing with this absurd yet horrific incident and its aftermath, are among the best in the book and are characterised by sombre intensity. In parallel with Stephanie's life as curate's wife and young mother are Marcus's development into a young scientist with a mystical apprehension of the world, and Frederica's career as an undergraduate at Newnham College, Cambridge, replete with intellectual and sexual adventures. Much of the vitality of the novel belongs to this part of the book, where Byatt's interest in ideas can be incorporated as an essential part of her academic characters' lives. Elsewhere the writing is at times laboured and lacks the freshness and dynamism of *The Virgin in the Garden,* perhaps because the major figures were so thoroughly described there. Byatt is, in fact, faced with the old, familiar problem confronting all writers of sequels and series: how to maintain the original momentum and avoid staleness. She anticipated the difficulty by resolving to write the novel in a totally different way from *The Virgin in the Garden,* but in the event found herself unable to do so.

After *Still Life* Byatt temporarily set aside her tetralogy to write a very long novel, *Possession,* but before publishing this she brought out her first collection of short fiction, *Sugar.* The 11 stories constituting this book are extremely varied in both length and content. "Rose-Coloured Teacups" is brief, while the title story, about the death of a father, is long, as is "Racine and the Tablecloth," about the conflict between a conformist schoolmistress and a rebellious schoolgirl. There is a story about a jinx in an East Asian setting ("The Dried Witch"), a kind of ghost story ("The July Ghost"), and an imaginary anecdote about Robert Browning in Italy ("Precipice-Encurled"). Several stories are about writing and writers, and they do contain an element of self-reflexivity even though the collection cannot be described as metafictional.

Two of these stories, "Precipice-Encurled" and "Sugar" itself, point almost subliminally in the direction of *Possession,* a novel of epic proportions written with great virtuosity. By providing the descriptive subtitle *A Romance,* Byatt emphasises her more radical departure from traditional realism than in her earlier fiction, in which she aimed to reconcile realism with modernist methods. Reminiscent of both John Fowles's *The French Lieutenant's Woman* and Peter Ackroyd's *Chatterton, Possession* is a thoroughgoing example of postmodernist fiction and even more self-consciously literary than her previous work. Like *The French Lieutenant's Woman,* although in a somewhat different way, *Possession* is simultaneously "Victorian" and "modern." The narrative, full of mystery and suspense as a "romance" should be, is a story of literary detection as two young academic researchers in the 1980s uncover more and more unsuspected biographical information about two apparently unconnected Victorian poets, Randolph Henry Ash and Christabel LaMotte. The novel contains a considerable amount of clever Victorian pastiche—supposedly the writings, in verse and prose, of the two poets. As the narrative moves to its bizarre and suitably "romantic" climax with a churchyard exhumation during a stormy night, the connections between Ash and LaMotte become increasingly clear, and at the same time the relationship between the 20th-century questors echoes that of their 19th-century subjects. The novel is, in fact, full of parallels and cross-references. There is no denying the brilliance of *Possession,* but now that the postmodernist heyday is past and even the leading American exponents of such fiction are talking about "the death of postmodernism," Byatt's novel seems, oddly enough, backward-looking rather than adventurous.

—Peter Lewis

C

CALISHER, Hortense

Nationality: American. **Born:** New York City, 20 December 1911.
Education: Hunter College High School, New York; Barnard College, New York, A.B. in philosophy 1932. **Family:** Married 1) H.B. Heffelfinger in 1935, one daughter and one son; 2) Curtis Harnack in 1959. **Career:** Adjunct professor of English, Barnard College, 1956-57; visiting professor, University of Iowa, Iowa City, 1957, 1959-60, Stanford University, California, 1958, Sarah Lawrence College, Bronxville, New York, 1962, and Brandeis University, Waltham, Massachusetts, 1963-64; writer-in-residence, 1965, and visiting lecturer, 1968, Univeristy of Pennsylvania, Philadelphia; adjunct professor of English, Columbia University, New York, 1968-70 and 1972-73; Clark Lecturer, Scripps College, Claremont, California, 1969; visiting professor, State University of New York, Purchase, 1971-72; Regents' Professor, University of California, Irvine, Spring 1976; visiting writer, Bennington College, Vermont, 1978; Hurst Professor, Washington University, St. Louis, 1979; National Endowment for the Arts Lecturer, Cooper Union, New York, 1983; visiting professor, Brown University, Providence, Rhode Island, 1986; guest lecturer, U.S.-China Arts Exchange, Republic of China, 1986. President, PEN, 1986-87; American Academy and Institute of Arts and Letters, 1987-90. Lives in New York City. **Awards:** Guggenheim fellowship, 1952, 1955; Department of State American Specialists grant, 1958; American Academy award, 1967; National Endowment for the Arts grant, 1967; Kafka prize, 1987; National Endowment for the Arts Lifetime Achievement award, 1989. Litt.D.: Skidmore College, Saratoga Springs, New York, 1980; Grinnell College, Iowa, 1986; Hofstra University, Hempstead, New York, 1988. **Member:** American Academy, 1977. **Agent:** Candida Donadio and Associates, 231 West 22nd Street, New York, New York 10011, U.S.A.

PUBLICATIONS

Novels

False Entry. Boston, Little Brown, 1961; London, Secker and Warburg, 1962.
Textures of Life. Boston, Little Brown, and London, Secker and Warburg, 1963.
Journal from Ellipsia. Boston, Little Brown, 1965; London, Secker and Warburg, 1966.
The Railway Police, and The Last Trolley Ride. Boston, Little Brown, 1966.
The New Yorkers. Boston, Little Brown, 1969; London, Cape, 1970.
Queenie. New York, Arbor House, 1971; London, W.H. Allen, 1973.
Standard Dreaming. New York, Arbor House, 1972.
Eagle Eye. New York, Arbor House, 1973.
On Keeping Women. New York, Arbor House, 1977.
Mysteries of Motion. New York, Doubleday, 1983.
The Bobby-Soxer. New York, Doubleday, 1986.
Age. New York, Weidenfeld and Nicolson, 1987.

The Small Bang (as Jack Fenno). New York, Random House, 1992.
In the Palace of the Movie King. New York, Random House, 1993.

Short Stories

In the Absence of Angels. Boston, Little Brown, 1951; London, Heinemann, 1953.
Tale for the Mirror: A Novella and Other Stories. Boston, Little Brown, 1962; London, Secker and Warburg, 1963.
Extreme Magic: A Novella and Other Stories. Boston, Little Brown, and London, Secker and Warburg, 1964.
The Collected Stories of Hortense Calisher. New York, Arbor House, 1975.
Saratoga, Hot. New York, Doubleday, 1985.

Uncollected Short Stories

"The Gig," *Confrontation,* 1986.
"The Evershams' Willie," in *Southwest Review* (Dallas), Summer 1987.
"The Man Who Spat Silver," (novella) in *Confrontation* (41), Summer/Fall 1989.
"The Nature of the Madhouse," in *Story* (Cincinnati), Spring 1990.
"The Iron Butterflies," in *Southwest Review,* Winter 1992.
"Blind Eye, Wrong Foot," in *American Short Fiction* (10), Summer 1993.

Other

What Novels Are (lecture). Claremont, California, Scripps College, 1969.
Herself (memoir). New York, Arbor House, 1972.
Kissing Cousins: A Memory. New York, Weidenfeld and Nicolson, 1988.

Editor, with Shannon Ravenel, *The Best American Short Stories 1981.* Boston, Houghton Mifflin, 1981.

*

Critical Studies: In *Don't Never Forget* by Brigid Brophy, London, Cape, 1966, New York, Holt Rinehart, 1967; article by Cynthia Ozick in *Midstream* (New York), 1969; "Ego Art: Notes on How I Came to It" by Calisher, in *Works in Progress* (New York), 1971; article by Kathy Brown in *Current Biography* (New York), November 1973; interview in *Paris Review,* Winter 1987; "Three Novels by Hortense Calisher" by Kathleen Snodgrass, in *Texas Studies in Literature and Language* (Austin), Winter 1989, and *The Fiction of Hortense Calisher* by Snodgrass, University of Delaware Press, 1994.

Hortense Calisher comments:

(1972) *False Entry* and *The New Yorkers* are connected novels; either may be read first; together they are a chronicle perhaps peculiarly American, according to some critics, but with European scope, according to others. *Journal from Ellipsia* was perhaps one of the first or the first serious American novel to deal with "verbal" man's displacement in a world of the spatial sciences; because it dealt with the possibility of life on other planets it was classed as "science fiction" both in the USA and in England. The *Dublin Times* understood it; its review does well by it. It also satirizes male-female relationships, by postulating a planet on which things are otherwise. In category, according to some, it is less an ordinary novel than a social satire akin to *Erewhon, Gulliver's Travels, Candide,* etc. *The Railway Police* and *The Last Trolley Ride*—the first is really a long short story of an individual, the second a novella built around an environs, a chorale of persons really, with four main parts, told in the interchanging voice of two men.

I usually find myself alternating a "larger" work with a smaller one, a natural change of pace. *Textures of Life,* for instance, is an intimate novel, of a young marriage, very personal, as *Journal* is not. After the latter, as I said in an interview, I wanted to get back to people. *The New Yorkers* was a conscious return to a "big" novel, done on fairly conventional terms, descriptive, narrative, leisurely, and inclusive, from which the long monologue chapters of the two women are a conscious departure. Its earlier mate, *False Entry,* has been called the only "metaphysical" novel in the America of its period—I'm not sure what that means, except perhaps that the whole, despite such tangible scenes as the Ku Klux Klan and courtroom episodes, is carried in the "mind" of one man. It has been called Dickensian, and in its plethora of event I suppose it is; yet the use of memory symbols and of psyche might just as well be French (Proust and Gide)—by intent it does both, or joins both ways of narration. *The New Yorkers* is more tied to its environs in a localized way; part of its subject *is* the environs.

Queenie is a satire, a farce on our sexual mores, as seen through the eyes of a "modern" young girl. As it is not yet out at this writing, I shall wait to be told what it is about.

(1986) *Standard Dreaming:* short novel narrated through the consciousness of a surgeon who believes the human race may be in process of dying off. *Herself:* the autobiography of a writer, rather than of the total life. Included are portions of critical studies, articles, etc., as well as several in toto (including one on the novel and on sex in American literature), and commentary on the writer's role in war, as a feminist, critic and teacher. *Eagle Eye:* the story of a young American non-combatant during and after the Vietnam War. Just as Queenie, in the novel of that name, confided in her tape-recorder, Bronstein addresses his computer. In 1974 some critics were bemused at this; time has changed that. *The Collected Stories:* preface by author begins with the much-quoted "A story is an apocalypse, served in a very small cup." *On Keeping Women: Herself* had broken ground in some of its aspects of what feminists were to term "womanspeak." I was never to be a conventional feminist; conventional thought is not for writers. But I had always wanted to do a novel from within the female feelings I did have from youth, through motherhood and the wish for other creation. This is that book. *Mysteries of Motion:* as in *Journal from Ellipsia* I continue concern for the way we live daily with the vast efforts and fruits of the scientists, and the terrors, without much understanding. Begun in 1977, before shuttles had flown or manmade objects had fallen to earth from orbit, this story of the first civilians in space is I believe the first novel of character (rather than so-called "science fiction") to be set in space. Because of that intent, the lives of all six people before they embark are an essential part of the story. What may happen to people, personality—and nations—in the space race, is what I was after. Though I researched minimally—just enough to know the language, or some of it—one critic commented that its technical details could not be faulted. I

imagined, rather than tried to be faithful to the momentary fact. And again, time has caught up with it, sadly so in the matter of "star wars." *Saratoga, Hot:* short works, called "little novels." Writing novels changes the short-story pen—the stories become novelistic, or mine do. The intent was "to give as much background as you can get in a foreground." *The Bobby-Soxer:* the story of the erotic and professional maturing of a young girl of the 1950s, as narrated by the woman she has become, it is also a legend of American provincial life, akin to the early novellas.

I have just completed a short novel called *Age,* and am resuming work on a novel set in Central Europe and the United States.

(1991) The working title of the book I refer to above as "a novel set in Central Europe and the United States" is *In the Palace of the Movie King.* I've been at work on this longer book in the background behind the shorter works that have emerged since the last longer work (*Mysteries of Motion*). It is certainly a more overtly political novel than any of the others, although that concern has been present in my work since the first stories.

This time the scene is Central Europe versus the U.S., as seen through the eyes of a filmmaker, Russian in origin, who grew up in Japan. Part of my interest has also been to see the U.S. as the visually obsessed nation it has fast become—through the eyes of a man who sees the world visually, rather than verbally. I hope thereby to free the book from what I think of as the de Tocqueville syndrome.

I am currently working on a shorter novel, set in England, where I have lived from time to time.

(1995) The "shorter work," set in England, is the novel, *The Small Bang,* published psuedonymously under the name Jack Fenno, to distinguish it from the other novel shortly to be published. As its title indicates, it poses the "small" bang that is human life against the "big bang" world views of the physicists. In the publisher's catalogue it is billed as a "mystery;" I wrote it as a novel purely, any novel being in a sense a "mystery" until its end.

On *In the Palace of the Movie King:* there comes a time for many of us when we feel seriously separated from the international intrigue that is happening all around us—and from the national picture also. Yet our domestic lives, urban or suburban or land-based, are always on that edge. I came to feel that I ought to be writing of what I thought of as "the long adventure"—that panorama, with documents, which would move through what we've been too trained to think of as the "thriller" novel. At the same time I must unite this with the domestic scene.

That's a nineteenth century ambition, from the books I cut my teeth on: Dickens, Victor Hugo, Mark Twain, and in my teens, the Russians. I miss their scope—if not necessarily their size. A sentence can embody the long view. But a novel so conceived will concentrate along that axis. What will the reader allow me to do for our twentieth century time? Meanwhile—my century feeding me what I ought to be seeing—in both the subtle and monumental. I was seeing the whole metaphor of "the third world." Censorship, yes, torture for the dissident, death because one differs. But the crux of it: they—the citizens of that third world I happen to know best, Middle Europe—they were locked in. My country was not. Is not.

The Gonchevs, the couple I wrote about, emerged through those mists, along with a vision of the whole wide-screen planet we are now. The time is just before that savage Balkan conflict we are now witnessing. When Gonchev, an apolitical man entirely, is shipped to the U.S.A. and cast in the role of "dissident," my own land emerges, as seen through his eyes. One strains like the devil not to be "author," authoring. There the emigrants and transcontinentals I've known all my life surely helped.

At times Gonchev's story is taken to be satirical, even hilarious. That's a relief.

*   *   *

Many readers first encounter Hortense Calisher through her widely anthologized short stories, then anticipate her novels. After reading them, however, they may come away vaguely unsatisfied though seldom quite dissatisfied. She is too gifted a writer for that.

It seems impossible for Calisher to write poorly: she is a master of language. Precise, powerful verbs give scenes life and immediacy. In "The Woman Who Was Everybody" an overqualified department store employee reluctantly faces the day: "She swung sideways out of bed, clamped her feet on the floor, rose and trundled to the bathroom, the kitchenette." Calisher's imagery is bountiful, original, and appropriate. In the same story, "the mornings crept in like applicants for jobs." Equal to language, Calisher has evidently observed and experienced how truth is revealed in the course of living and can reconstruct these epiphanies readily in characters.

Then why, since hers are among the best American short stories of this century, are Calisher's novels less successful? At least two reasons are likely. One is that it is impossible to sustain in the long form the power she packs into the short form. The small cast, limited setting, single problem of the short story let her build the work to a final revelation which suggests that, for better or worse, a life will never be quite the same again. This is the classic short story.

Calisher novels often merely elongate the story format. Substituting for traditional plot and subplot, there are series of revelations related to the central situation. (A young couple disclose aspects of themselves as they cope with an ill child in *Textures of Life*. Another couple, from the novella *Saratoga, Hot* actually reveal more about their horsey social set than themselves.) Whether the reader can sustain interest in longer works whose internal logic is random and whose continuity needs occasional propulsion by fortuitous revelation is a question. Certainly that *does* work in *The New Yorkers,* often called her most successful novel, an indulgent insight into family life. Ill-advised timing and treatment may have undercut Calisher's satirical novel, *Queenie.* The late 1960s were not laughing times and for many the new sexual freedom which Queenie fumbles toward was no laughing matter. What may be her least successful novel, *Mysteries of Motion,* distracts as much as discloses since six lives are revealed, and on a space journey at that. Better a bus ride in Brooklyn.

That more modest approach to setting is exactly what makes her short stories seem instantly relevant to our ordinary lives, that and the fact that each story—however brief—is also a life history of sorts. Calisher examines that life at a time of crisis and the reader comes away instructed in valuable experience. In the classic "One of the Chosen" a successful Jewish lawyer, Davy Spanner, always popular in his college days, has believed lifelong that he never needed the support of fraternity life and had comfortably rejected the early overtures of the campus societies. At a class reunion, a gentile classmate blurts out the unsettling truth that Spanner would *never* have been offered a serious membership bid.

Calisher's long interest in psychology and the supernatural is evident. Her life spans Freudianism and beyond, but psychology—eclectic and non-systematic—as it appears in her work at times is close to fantasy, at other times follows accepted dogma. "Heartburn" centers on the power of suggestion; "The Scream on 57th Street" treats fear. Both "work" just as her general grasp of family relationships seems valid, however it was acquired. On the other hand, *Standard Dreaming,* Calisher's unfortunate excursion into a dream world of searching characters, could be taken for a parody of surrealism.

Calisher's short stories and novellas may initially appear to be peopled by fully-rounded characters, but an overview of the stories reveals a high proportion of well-done types: the educated misfit, the eccentric family member, the young innocent, the at-odds mother-daughter (or husband-wife), the displaced southerner, the would-be radical. And type is all they need to be since hers are not primarily stories of character, but of complex situation, the result of long processes of cause and effect told in hints and subtleties. Where the Calisher protagonists have been, are now, and where they are probably going—or not going, depending on their revelations—*is* their story. Exactly *who* they are is incidental. Their external descriptions are often vivid, even witty, but their tastes and temperaments are revealed only to the degree that they serve the tale. If we flesh them out ourselves, it is a tribute to their creator's ability to write so that we *read* creatively.

The Collected Stories of Hortense Calisher, an enduring treasury of major works in her best genre, allows ready comparison of early and late works and reveals the consistency of Calisher's vision, even such traits as a vein of humor, a thread of the absurd, and a persistent interest in the power of the mind to direct fate. She is an eminently serious and concerned writer, despite the fatuous, the incompetents, the ditsy relatives, and the rattled authority figures who clamor for their share of attention in her works. Their truths are as true as anyone else's, Calisher suggests, and their numbers among us may be greater than we want to believe.

—Marian Pehowski

CALLOW, Philip (Kenneth)

Nationality: British. **Born:** Birmingham, 26 October 1924. **Education:** Coventry Technical College, 1937-39; St. Luke's College, Exeter, Devon, 1968-70, Teacher's Certificate 1970. **Family:** Married Anne Jennifer Golby in 1987 (third marriage); one daughter from previous marriage. **Career:** Engineering apprentice and toolmaker, Coventry Gauge and Tool Company, 1940-48; clerk, Ministry of Works and Minstry of Supply, 1949-51; clerical assistant, South West Electricity Board, Plymouth, 1951-66; Arts Council fellow, Falmouth School of Art, 1977-78; Creative Writing fellow, Open University, 1979; writer-in-residence, Sheffield City Polytechnic, 1980-82. **Awards:** Arts Council bursary, 1966, 1970, 1973, 1979; Society of Authors traveling scholarship, 1973; C. Day Lewis fellowship, 1973; Southern Arts Association fellowship, 1974. **Agent:** John Johnson Ltd., 45-47 Clerkenwell Green, London EC1R 0HT, England.

PUBLICATIONS

Novels

The Hosanna Man. London, Cape, 1956.
Common People. London, Heinemann, 1958.

A Pledge for the Earth. London, Heinemann, 1960.
Clipped Wings. Douglas, Isle of Man, Times Press, 1964.
Another Flesh. London, Allison and Busby, 1989.
  Going to the Moon. London, MacGibbon and Kee, 1968.
  The Bliss Body. London, MacGibbon and Kee, 1969.
  Flesh of Morning. London, Bodley Head, 1971.
Yours. London, Bodley Head, 1972.
The Story of My Desire. London, Bodley Head, 1976.
Janine. London, Bodley Head, 1977.
The Subway to New York. London, Martin Brian and O'Keeffe, 1979.
The Painter's Confessions. London, Allison and Busby, 1989.
Some Love. London, Allison and Busby, 1991.
The Magnolia. London, Allison and Busby, 1994.

Short Stories

Native Ground. London, Heinemann, 1959.
Woman with a Poet. Bradford, Yorkshire, Rivelin Press, 1983.

Uncollected Short Story

"Merry Christmas," in *New Statesman* (London), 22 December 1961.

Plays

The Honeymooners (televised 1960). Published in *New Granada Plays,* London, Faber, 1961.

Radio Plays: *The Lamb,* 1971; *On Some Road,* 1979.

Television Play: *The Honeymooners,* 1960.

Poetry

Turning Point. London, Heinemann, 1964.
The Real Life: New Poems. Douglas, Isle of Man, Times Press, 1964.
Bare Wires. London, Chatto and Windus-Hogarth Press, 1972.
Cave Light. Bradford, Yorkshire, Rivelin Press, 1981.
New York Insomnia and Other Poems. Bradford, Yorkshire, Rivelin Grapheme Press, 1984.
Icons. Bradford, Yorkshire, Blue Bridge Press, 1987.
Soliloquies of an Eye. Todmorden, Lancashire, Littlewood Press, 1990.
Notes over a Chasm. Bradford, Yorkshire, Redbeck Press, 1991.
Fires in October. Bradford, Yorkshire, Redbeck Press, 1994.

Other

In My Own Land, photographs by James Bridgen. Douglas, Isle of Man, Times Press, 1965.
Son and Lover: The Young D.H. Lawrence. London, Bodley Head, and New York, Stein and Day, 1975.
Van Gogh: A Life. London, Allison and Busby, and Chicago, Dee, 1990.
From Noon to Starry Night: A Life of Walt Whitman. London, Allison and Busby, and Chicago, Dee, 1992.

*

Manuscript Collection: University of Texas Library, Austin.

Critical Study: By Callow in *Vogue* (New York), 1 September 1969.

Philip Callow comments:

(1991) All my writing up to now has been autobiographical in style and content. My aim has simply been to tell the story of my life as truthfully as possible. In fact, this is impossible, and in the attempt to do so one discovers that another, spiritual, autobiography is taking shape. I now realize that by devising a narrative about total strangers based on events reported in a newspaper I reveal myself as nakedly as in a personal confession. Perhaps more so.

*   *   *

In all his earlier work Philip Callow is telling the same story—his life story. His "autobiography," *In My Own Land,* confirms a close approximation between himself and the "I" of the novels and the short stories in *Native Ground.* In his earliest novels he was seeking an idiom, which he found triumphantly in the freewheeling colloquialism of the trilogy *Going to the Moon, The Bliss Body,* and *Flesh of Morning.*

Callow's material is his working-class adolescence in the midlands, the experience of factory and clerical work there and in the west country, his artistic leanings and adult relationships. Louis Paul, Nicky Chapman, and Alan Lowry, the narrators respectively of *The Hosanna Man, Common People,* and *Clipped Wings,* and Martin Satchwell, the central character of *A Pledge for the Earth,* are prototypes for the Colin Patten of the trilogy, and its sequel *The Story of My Desire,* when Patten has qualified as a teacher. Parallels exist in the earliest books for the trilogy's other important characters, while in subsequent work the lecturer David Lowry, the central figure in *Janine,* and the poet and writer-in-residence Jacob Raby, the narrator of *The Subway to New York,* recall Patten.

Callow gives a full account of adolescence, describing the development of sexuality—more freely in the later books—as the boy grows up at the end of the war when "there was a ration even on questions." Then he has to adjust to life on the factory floor. Patten's painting and writing lead him into provincial artistic circles, amateur or bohemian and anarchic—the "city nomads." Callow's outstanding portrayal is Jack Kelvin, "the hosanna man" himself, a drop-out like Albert Dyer in *Clipped Wings,* who "sits up on a cliff like a dirty old monk;" in *Common People* there is the drunken Sunday painter, Cecil Luce, leader of the "Birmingham Twelve." With the public poetry readings by the "Callow-figure" Jacob Raby in *The Subway to New York* (and the painter Breakwell's fame in *The Painter's Confessions*), the wheel has come full circle.

A Pledge for the Earth was the earliest of Callow's third-person novels. The most overtly structured of his novels, it describes two generations of Satchwells in a framework of natural imagery, and culminates in 20-odd pages in the first person written by Martin Satchwell. In *Clipped Wings* Callow returned to first-person narration: "I decided that the only way is to plant yourself down in the very center of things, and then set out. In the same railway carriage, with all the others." With its new forceful, colloquial idiom, *Clipped Wings* is the key book in Callow's stylistic development, and made possible the trilogy. At the same time, he had begun to publish a good deal of poetry, which perhaps cross-fertilized his prose.

In the trilogy Callow ranged over his experiences freely with only a rough chronological surge onward: "Going back is pure instinct with me." The rationale of his method is in a sense anti-art: "Who believes in a book cut away from its writer with surgical scissors? I don't, I never did. I don't believe in fact and fiction, I don't believe in autobiography, poetry, philosophy, I don't believe in chapters, in a story." Callow's refusal to categorize is also embodied in his non-fiction *In My Own Land,* differentiated from his novels only by the use of real names.

Yours is an extended letter written by a young girl to her ex-lover, recalling that first unhappy love affair. In *The Story of My Desire* Callow continued the trilogy, with Colin's affair with the married Lucy, both cause and effect of the breakdown of his own marriage, in turn inextricably linked in a nexus of guilt with his mental breakdown. *Janine* describes the middle-aged David Lowry's relationship with the mixed-up young girl of the title. It is written in the third person, and from the opening sentence, "His name was Lowry," the man is referred to throughout by surname. Until a key moment late in the novel, Janine never calls David by name, so that the third-person narration has an active structural role.

The structural rationale in *The Subway to New York* is circular: "always with a woman you go in circles." Thus Marjorie of *The Story of My Desire,* already resurrected as Kate in *Janine,* reappears as Carmel in *The Subway to New York,* and Lucy of *The Story of My Desire* is Nell in *Subway.*

Callow's return to fiction after a break of 10 years (apart from the small-press short story collection *Woman with a Poet*) seems less directly autobiographical, though the subject matter of *The Painter's Confessions* enables him to explore how an artist—in the broad sense—uses his experience. The painter Francis Breakwell's "confessions" begin "Even before my sister's violent death I had felt this urge to use words, to tell a story that would be my own, yet irradiated in some way by hers." The narrative moves forward to her drowning, through her love for the unbalanced Celia. The central figure in Breakwell's life is his former mistress and model, Maggie, with whom he remains tenuously in touch. His marriage disintegrates through the novel but his American wife seems peripheral beside Maggie's presence from the past. As a contemporary painter aged 50, Breakwell seems unrealistically successful given his predominant old-fashioned abstract expressionism. Inevitably, Patrick White's classic *The Vivisector* casts a long shadow over any novel about a painter but especially here given Breakwell's expressionism.

There are lacunae in *The Painter's Confessions* but the rambling reminiscence form could be held to justify loose ends. The structure is more problematic in *Some Love,* a moving third-person novel about the under-privileged Johnnie, who, after time in a children's home, gets involved as a minor in an affair with Tina, a younger friend of his mentally unstable mother. Initially, the viewpoint is mainly Johnnie's, but, with the emergence of Tina midway as a major character, the viewpoint switches predominantly to her, with no apparent rationale. Callow's often unstructured way of writing becomes more difficult when it is not applied to the solid corpus of autobiographical fact. However, Callow is too good a writer for that decade's silence not to be our loss.

—Val Warner

CALVIN, Henry. *See* **HANLEY, Clifford (Leonard Clark).**

———

CAMPBELL, Marion (May)

Nationality: Australian. **Born:** Sydney, 25 December 1948. **Address:** 45 Arkwell Street, Willagee, Western Australia 6156, Australia.

PUBLICATIONS

Novels

Lines of Flight. Fremantle, Western Australia, Fremantle Arts Centre Press, 1985.
Not Being Miriam. Fremantle, Western Australia, Fremantle Arts Centre Press, 1989.

*   *   *

Marion Campbell is one of Australia's most powerful intellectual and postmodern writers and has an impressive reputation on the basis of two novels. Her first novel, *Lines of Flight,* is a work of luminous and startling intelligence, both elegant and playful. Through rival narrative modes, it is the story of Rita Finnerty, a young Australian artist in France, struggling to create a career, but struggling also to break free of the cloisters of other peoples' lives. Splinter scenes of her childhood and her early compositions emerge through the notion of cumulo-nimbus formations, but in France, amid emotional and artistic upheaval, the notion of *lignes de fuite* prevails, obedience to perspective and the lines of flight which taper to disappearance point.

Rita's involvement with Raymond, the entrepreneurial gay semiotician, and his two students, Gerard and Sebastien, becomes a locus of postmodern dissent and denial. Internal pressures in Rita's private world implode and the language too becomes implosive, yet the form of the novel remains precise, elegant, baroque. Campbell draws on spatial structures, such as framing and tripytch to cross the lines between art and self, between rival determinations of event, word, imagination, and vision. The development of Rita's painting in France and the sharp satire of the Australian art scene on her return to Australia, her disappearance even, are occasions of profound visual and spatial luminosity, her prose extraordinarily energetic and intellectually rich.

The novel is both witty and ludic, the scenes in France often droll, but beneath that surface there is a profound intellectual quest and a struggle to find in painting and in language areas of self-determination without confinement to the interstices of others' lives. Her writing is marked by the precision of elusive and complex notions and forms of trespass from the definitions and determinations of others. Campbell writes with

> . . . wild vertigo, intoxication of turning on my own
> axis in freed space. In a long greedy scrutiny of space from
> that pinnacle, I would see that crazy queue of arbitrarily
> fused selves, oh yes, from moments past recede, I would
> pluralize and scatter on horizons ebbing into horizons . . .

Narrative shifts and tilts with concentric planes, emanations, absences, default, space vacated, searching out the sacred, transgressing boundaries, as if the prose is on an inner spiral, measuring the space of self which defines and confines.

Campbell's forthcoming novel, tentatively entitled *Prowlers,* has a similar spatial construct playing over reversals of perspective and the sides of mirror and glass, again with tense and intense pressures of trespass and self-determination. Her second novel, *Not Being Miriam,* is about the "danger of certainty." In its composition of shifting frames about the tendencies of things, the world is "a tissue of complicated events only tending to occur." It is a fiercely celebratory vision, in which Campbell's remarkable energies and intelligence play across the intense inner dialogue of three women.

Through the interlocking stories of the three women, whose lives overlap, Campbell weaves a tapestry of lives compressed and defined by default. It is first the story of Bess, her childhood and her teaching life and her young son taken by the father to Italy, then her world as a middle-aged single woman. Through her sense of chaos and dissolution, of possibilities shrinking all around her, there is a quest for the center of gravity. When her own life palls and seems uninhabitable, she enters and enacts other lives, playing out putative selves, in her theater of masks.

Bess's story overlaps with that of Lydia from childhood in Nazi Germany to her adult life married to Harry; and the life of Elsie, Bess's working-class neighbor and the second wife of Roger, haunted by the presence of the first wife, the late Miriam, whose image is treasured openly by Roger. The women come together in the absence of Miriam, who stands as the figure of reference. Through Bess, Elsie and Lydia, Campbell conjures numerous images of woman. Each one is shadowed by antecedent figures: for Bess, Ariadne; for Elsie the second Mrs. de Winter from *Rebecca;* and for Lydia, Katerina Kepler, Johannes Kepler's mother, "the last musician of the spheres." One of the most remarkable sequences is about Katerina Kepler, suspected of witchcraft and doomed. Her voice plays out many of the notions of women caught in the ellipses of male lives.

The novel has a series of interesting structures, with filigree lines of narrative, a labyrinth of voices and threads which lock together in one startling moment. In the climactic courtroom sequence, Bess is charged with manslaughter. Amid voices of gossip and condemnation, where every gesture of the self, past and present, is suspect, there are echoes of the charges against Lindy Chamberlain in the notorious Australian case which ran through the 1980s. As Bess feels the collapse of the past, the collapse of all her rival selves, the condemnation of Bess becomes a dark enclosure, as if she is trapped in the ellipses of the *other,* reduced to a figure of others' purposes, a player in a collective script.

Through themes of mechanistic and quantum physics, Campbell explores the causal links which *tended* towards this effect, seeking the rip, the breach in the fabric of things. Amid narrative modes of theater and script, of acting out roles and guises of the self, literary and mythological references abound, from the prophecies of Cassandra, to impassioned writing about Ariadne and Theseus, or to the sisters in Genet's *The Maids,* with Bess forever playing out "this maid's revolt." *Not Being Miriam* is a bold and prismatic novel, in which voices spar in the deepest recesses of the self, while the narrative weaves in and out of the lives of women in a montage of voices. The prose is rich and crystalline, full of resonances and summonings of historical and mythological, literary and classical antecedents.

—Helen Daniel

CANNON, Curt. *See* **HUNTER, Evan.**

———

CAREY, Peter (Philip)

Nationality: Australian. **Born:** Bacchus Marsh, Victoria, 7 May 1943. **Education:** Geelong Grammar School; Monash University, Clayton, Victoria, 1961. **Family:** Married 1) Leigh Weetman; 2) Alison Summers in 1985, one son. **Career:** Worked in advertising in Australia, 1962-68 and after 1970, and in London, 1968-70; partner, McSpedden Carey Advertising Consultants, Chippendale, New South Wales, until 1988. Currently teacher, New York University and Princeton University. Lives in New York. **Awards:** New South Wales Premier's award, 1980, 1982; Miles Franklin award, 1981; National Book Council award, 1982, 1986; Australian Film Institute award, for screenplay, 1985; *The Age* Book of the Year award, 1985, 1994; Booker prize, 1988. Fellow, Royal Society of Literature. **Agent:** International Creative Management, 40 W. 57th St., New York, New York 10019, U.S.A.

PUBLICATIONS

Novels

Bliss. St. Lucia, University of Queensland Press, London, Faber, and New York, Harper, 1981.
Illywhacker. London, Faber, and New York, Harper, 1985.
Oscar and Lucinda. London, Faber, and New York, Harper, 1988.
The Tax Inspector. London, Faber, and New York, Knopf, 1992.
The Unusual Life of Tristan Smiln. London, Faber, and New York, Knopf, 1995.

Short Stories

The Fat Man in History. St. Lucia, University of Queensland Press, 1974; London, Faber, and New York, Random House, 1980; as *Exotic Pleasures,* London, Pan, 1981.
War Crimes. St. Lucia, University of Queensland Press, 1979.

Uncollected Short Story

"A Letter to Our Son," in *Best Short Stories 1989,* edited by Giles Gordon and David Hughes. London, Heinemann, 1989; as *The Best English Short Stories 1989,* New York, Norton, 1989.

Plays

Bliss: The Screenplay. St. Lucia, University of Queensland Press, 1986; as *Bliss: The Film,* London, Faber, 1986.

Screenplay: *Bliss,* with Ray Lawrence, 1987.

*   *   *

Peter Carey's short story collections, *The Fat Man in History* and *War Crimes,* established his reputation as one of Australia's most skilled and most innovative writers of short fiction. His stories break away from the Australian tradition of realism, experimenting with modes as diverse as absurdism, surrealism, science fiction, and the fable. "Report on the Shadow Industry" documents the terrors and addictions arising from a craze for buying packaged shadows; in "American Dreams" a man builds a mysterious replica of the town in which he lives, even sculpting the citizens' secrets and vices; and in "Peeling" a girl's clothing is unzipped and peeled away, followed by her flesh and her identity. . . . (Reviewers frequently compare Carey's work with that of Barthelme, Borges, García Márquez and Vonnegut.)

Stylistically, Carey's stories are distinguished by the way in which his fantasy worlds are rendered with the specific, particularised detail that is typical of traditional realism. Thematically, the stories are concerned with contemporary social reality: the insignificance and helplessness of the average citizen, and the rapacious cynicism of those with power or influence. "A Windmill in the West" deals with a lonely soldier guarding a line drawn across the uninhabited wasteland of Central Australia; he has long ago forgotten the rationale for his task, but he has neither the courage nor the authority to protest at the futility of his plight. 20th-century *angst* is outlined in "Conversations with Unicorns" as a man tries to warn a cave of unicorns that they will soon be discovered and destroyed by the march of human progress. Believing themselves to be immortal, the unicorns refuse to listen, and the man who seeks to save them must kill one of their number in order to make his point. Such are Carey's metaphors for the plight of western man.

Because Carey's stories are lean and laconic, and employ fantastic or non-specific settings, they have left room for the criticism that the author is a pessimist who is unable to deal with day-to-day realities in a "real" setting. However, Carey's novels refute this criticism by dealing with characters living "normal" lives in familiar Australian settings.

Bliss is the sad-but-funny story of middle-aged advertising executive Harry Joy, who experiences clinical death after a heart attack and revives with a radically different perception of reality. Death leads him to a recognition of "the worlds of pleasure and pain, bliss and punishment, Heaven and Hell." His second chance at life forces him into the task of trying to cope with a world that now seems like Hell; a world in which his son pushes drugs and commits incest while his wife is addicted to adultery, a world in which affluent citizens choose tawdry "progress" and cancer-inducing food additives above conservation and self-discipline.

Despite this description, *Bliss* is far from being a pessimistic novel. It is infused throughout with witty black humour, such as in Harry Joy's account of the caste system of "Hell," which ranges from Those in Charge (who inflict the torment) to the Actors (who robotically obey the orders they are given) to the Captives (who, like himself, can do nothing but suffer). Secondly, the characterization of Honey Barbara establishes that man *can* at least try to manipulate his own destiny. (An honest but streetwise country girl, Honey Barbara divides her life between a primitive backwoods rainforest community and the hellish city in which she earns money from prostitution and drug-dealing.) Most importantly, the final section of the novel offers a vision of bliss on Earth as Harry Joy escapes from the lunatic asylum to which his family has had him committed and joins Honey Barbara in her rainforest heaven.

Illywhacker (the word is slang for trickster, spieler, con-man) is the story of Herbert Badgery and three generations of his family, but the novel is also an examination of the lies and myths which underlie Australian history and culture. This is indicated by an epi-

graph from Mark Twain: "Australian history is almost picturesque. . . . It does not read like history, but like the most beautiful lies. . . . It is full of surprises and adventures, the incongruities, and contradictions, and incredibilities; but they are all true, they all happened."

The central lie of Australian history is revealed to be the assertion that Australia had no original owners; this ignores the claims of Australian Aborigines. But in two centuries of history this lie is shown to have spawned other lies, especially the belief that Australia is a free and independent land. The history of the Badgery family is a history of overseas domination continuing from one generation to another: Henry Badgery's 1920s dream of establishing an Australian aircraft industry is defeated by the importation of aircraft from overseas, his son's pet-shop only becomes successful because World War II brings American money into Australia, and the Badgery grandson can only continue the pet-shop business in the 1980s thanks to money invested by the Japanese. Yet Henry Badgery continues to believe (aggressively, pathetically) that with a few smooth lies, a bit of luck, and a confident swagger, he can be master of his own fate. *Illywhacker* celebrates the indomitable spirit of pioneers like Badgery, yet it also exposes the flaws in the nation and culture they helped to create.

Oscar and Lucinda, Carey's Booker prize-winning novel, also explores the legacy of Australian history. Narrated by the hero's great-grandson, a character of the 1950s, it concerns two guilt-ridden gamblers of the Victorian era, the most interesting being the heroine, Lucinda, who is ashamed to have been made wealthy by land stolen from the Aborigines. Both gamblers show traits of stubborn tenacity—the typical qualities of the Aussie "battler"—but neither is particularly admirable (or likeable). So once again Carey offers only a qualified celebration of the nation's achievements and character. Stylistically, *Oscar and Lucinda* pairs the racy intellectualism of modern Australia (from the 1950s narration) with the sombre, ponderous diction and moralizing of the Victorian era. But it's hard to see which era comes off best.

Carey is regarded as a major Australian novelist and his works are awaited with excitement by an eager readership . . . but some readers still long for his spare, chilling shorter fictions.

—Van Ikin

———

CARR, Jolyon. *See* **PARGETER, Edith (Mary).**

———

CASSILL, R(onald) V(erlin)

Nationality: American. **Born:** Cedar Falls, Iowa, 17 May 1919. **Education:** The University of Iowa, Iowa City, B.A. 1939 (Phi Beta Kappa), M.A. 1947; the Sorbonne, Paris (Fulbright fellow), 1952-53. **Military Service:** Served in the United States Army, 1942-46: Lieutenant. **Family:** Married Karilyn Kay Adams in 1956; three children. **Career:** Instructor, University of Iowa, 1948-52; editor, *Western Review,* Iowa City, 1951-52, *Colliers' Encyclopedia,* New York, 1953-54, and *Dude* and *Gent,* New York, 1958; lecturer, Columbia University and New School for Social Research, both New York, 1957-59, and University of Iowa, 1960-65; writer-in-residence, Purdue University, West Lafayette, Indiana, 1965-66. Associate professor, 1966-71, and professor of English, 1972-83, Brown University, Providence, Rhode Island; now emeritus. U.S. Information Service lecturer in Europe, 1975-76. Painter and lithographer: exhibitions—John Snowden Gallery, Chicago, 1946; Eleanor Smith Galleries, Chicago, 1948; Wickersham Gallery, New York, 1970. **Awards:** *Atlantic* "Firsts" prize, for short story, 1947; Rockefeller grant, 1954; Guggenheim grant, 1968. **Agent:** Candida Donadio and Associates, 231 West 22nd Street, New York, New York 10011. **Address:** 22 Boylston Avenue, Providence, Rhode Island 02906, U.S.A.

Publications

Novels

The Eagle on the Coin. New York, Random House, 1950.
Dormitory Women. New York, Lion, 1953.
The Left Bank of Desire, with Eric Protter. New York, Ace, 1955.
A Taste of Sin. New York, Ace, 1955; London, Digit, 1959.
The Hungering Shame. New York, Avon, 1956.
The Wound of Love. New York, Avon, 1956.
An Affair to Remember (novelization of screenplay; as Owen Aherne). New York, Avon, 1957.
Naked Morning. New York, Avon, 1957.
Man on Fire (novelization of screenplay; as Owen Aherne). New York, Avon, 1957.
The Buccaneer (novelization of screenplay). New York, Fawcett, 1958.
Lustful Summer. New York, Avon, 1958.
Nurses' Quarters. New York, Fawcett, 1958; London, Muller, 1962.
The Tempest (novelization of screenplay). New York, Fawcett, 1959.
The Wife Next Door. New York, Fawcett, 1959; London, Muller, 1960.
Clem Anderson. New York, Simon and Schuster, 1960.
My Sister's Keeper. New York, Avon, 1961.
Night School. New York, New American Library, 1961.
Pretty Leslie. New York, Simon and Schuster, 1963; London, Muller, 1964.
The President. New York, Simon and Schuster, 1964.
La Vie Passionée of Rodney Buckthorne: A Tale of the Great American's Last Rally and Curious Death. New York, Geis, 1968.
Doctor Cobb's Game. New York, Bantam, 1969.
The Goss Women. New York, Doubleday, 1974; London, Hodder and Stoughton, 1975.
Hoyt's Child. New York, Doubleday, 1976.
Labors of Love. New York, Arbor House, 1980.
Flame. New York, Arbor House, 1980.
After Goliath. New York, Ticknor and Fields, 1985.
The Unknown Soldier. Montrose, Alabama, Texas Center for Writers Press, 1991.

Short Stories

15 × 3, with Herbert Gold and James B. Hall. New York, New Directions, 1957.
The Father and Other Stories. New York, Simon and Schuster, 1965.

The Happy Marriage and Other Stories. West Lafayette, Indiana, Purdue University Press, 1967.
Three Stories. Oakland, California, Hermes House Press, 1982.
Patrimonies. Bristol, Rhode Island, Ampersand Press, 1988.
Collected Stories. Fayetteville, University of Arkansas Press, 1989.

Other

The General Said "Nuts." New York, Birk, 1955.
Writing Fiction. New York, Pocket Books, 1963; revised edition, Englewood Cliffs, New Jersey, Prentice Hall, 1975.
In an Iron Time: Statements and Reiterations: Essays. West Lafayette, Indiana, Purdue University Press, 1967.

Editor, *Intro 1-3.* New York, Bantam, 3 vols., 1968-70.
Editor, with Walton Beacham, *Intro 4.* Charlottesville, University Press of Virginia, 1972.
Editor, *Norton Anthology of Short Fiction.* New York, Norton, 1978; revised edition, 1981, 1985, 1989, 1994.
Editor, *Norton Anthology of Contemporary Fiction.* New York, Norton, 1988.

*

Manuscript Collection: Mugar Memorial Library, Boston University.

Critical Studies: "R.V. Cassill Issue" of *December* (Chicago), vol. 23, nos. 1-2, 1981 (includes bibliography).

R.V. Cassill comments:

(1972) My most personal statement is probably to be found in my short stories. If few of them are reliably autobiographical at least they grew from the observations, moods, exultations, and agonies of early years. If there is constant pattern in them, it is probably that of a hopeful being who expects evil and finds worse.

From my first novel onward I have explored the correspondences between the interior world—of desire and anxiety—and the public world of power—extra-social violences and politics. In *The Eagle on the Coin* I wrote of the ill-fated attempt of some alienated liberals, including a compassionate homosexual, to elect a Negro to the schoolboard in a small midwestern city. In *Doctor Cobb's Game* I used the silhouette of a major British political scandal as the area within which I composed an elaborate pattern of occult-sexual-political forces weaving and unweaving. Between these two novels, almost 20 years apart, I have played with a variety of forms and subject matter, but the focus of concern has probably been the same, under the surface of appearances. In *Clem Anderson* I took the silhouette of Dylan Thomas's life and within that composed the story of an American poet's self-destructive triumph. It probably is and always will be my most embattled work, simply because in its considerable extent it replaces most of the comfortable or profitable clichés about an artist's life with tougher and more painful diagrams.

But then perhaps my whole productive life has been a swimming against the tide. A midwesterner by origin, and no doubt by temperament and experience, I worked through decades when first the southern and then the urban-Jewish novel held an almost monopolistic grip on the tastes and prejudices of American readers. In my extensive reviewing and lecturing I have tried more to examine the clichés, slogans, and rallying cries of the time than to oppose or espouse them—thus leaving myself without any visible partisan support from any quarter. To radicals I have appeared a conservative, to conservatives a radical—and to both a mystification or, I suppose, I would not have been tolerated as long as I have been. As I grow older I love the commonplace of traditional thought and expression with a growing fervor, especially as their rarity increases amid the indoctrinating forces that spoil our good lives.

*   *   *

From the first novel, *The Eagle on the Coin,* and the early stories, R.V. Cassill's art shows a steady development from the autobiographical and the imitative to the fully dramatic capabilities of the mature novelist and short story writer. The range of his talent is wide: from near-pastoral impressions of midwestern America, to urban life in Chicago and New York, to his most technically accomplished work, *Doctor Cobb's Game,* based on the Profumo scandals in London.

Cassill's most complex work relies on four broad kinds of material: stories and novels about the midwest, most notably Iowa as in *Pretty Leslie;* stories and novels concerning academic life, as in "Larchmoor Is Not the World" and *The President;* materials about art and the artist's life (*Clem Anderson*); and finally materials of a less regional nature which may be called the vision of modernity found in the short story "Love? Squalor?" and *Doctor Cobb.* A second lesser-known order of Cassill's work consists of a dozen novels, "paperback originals" so-called because of the contractual circumstances of their first publication. For the most part *The Wound of Love, Dormitory Women,* and others await sophisticated literary evaluation. These shorter, often more spontaneous novels also exploit the same kinds of material. It should be well understood that these categories are intended to be only suggestive; the most ambitious work, for example, displays all these materials.

Beyond the technical accomplishments of any professional novelist, Cassill's most noteworthy literary quality is the "visual" nature of his prose fiction. There is a steady exploitation of color, of the precise, telling, visual detail, a sensitivity to proportion, and to the architectonics of scene. In fact Cassill began his artistic career as a painter, a teacher of art; from time to time he still exhibits his work. His fiction shows some of the same qualities as the Impressionists, the Post-Impressionists, and the German Expressionistic painters.

The literary influences are wide-ranging and interestingly absorbed. In general these influences are evoked when necessary rather than being held steadily as "models" in any neoclassic sense. Specifically, Cassill values Flaubert, James, Joyce, and especially D.H. Lawrence. Of a different order of specific influence would be *Madam Bovary,* Gissing's *New Grub Street,* and Benjamin Constant's *Adolphe* (1815). It is interesting that Cassill has written the best extant appreciation of *Adolphe.* Thus Cassill is a highly literary writer, with a broad, useful knowledge of American and European literatures; for many years he has been a teacher of contemporary literature and a writer-in-residence at universities, a professional reviewer, essayist, a discerning cultural commentator and critic.

The governing themes of Cassill's work are less easy to identify. A recurring situation is the nature and the resultant fate of a human pair, the destiny of a man or woman in the throes of new love, old love, marriage, or adultery. Closely bound to these concerns is the nature of love and responsibility; the implications of choice, loyalty, and liberty. Often there are conflicts generated between rationality and a merely emotional yearning—real or imag-

ined—genuine affection as against the implied necessity of sexual aggression or the ironies of "modern love." At times these relationships are between teacher and pupil, lovers, man and wife; between artist and patron, mistress, or the world "out there."

A fascination with these and other difficult themes places a heavy obligation on the novelist, especially in the matter of plot-structures and the handling of sex scenes. Throughout Cassill's work there is the insistence of the centrality of the sexual aspect of all human relationships. If in real life such concerns are seldom finally resolved, so is it in many novelistic structures which tend to rely on sexual involvements as a central motivation. Often, therefore, a story or a novel will begin with a vivid, strong situation which in the end is obscured or vague rather than suggestive or resolved. The reliance on the sexual drive as a compelling motive becomes more insistent in the later work.

Although he is primarily a novelist, Cassill's most sustained work is often in the short fiction, of which he is a master. The best stories focus on domestic scenes, memories of youth, the pathos of age, the casual lost relationship, conversations of art, ideas, literature, and the meaning of life itself.

Taken together, the stories, novels, and criticism show a strongly unified sensibility, a dedicated, energetic artist, a man in a modern world imaginatively and at times romantically comprehended, a man whose powerful gifts are his best protection against his own vision of America and of the midwest where modernity is rampant and the end is nowhere in sight.

—James B. Hall

CASTRO, Brian

Nationality: Australian. **Born:** Kowloon, Hong Kong, 16 January 1950. **Education:** University of Sidney, M.A. 1976. **Family:** Married Josephine Mary Gardiner in 1976. **Career:** Teacher, Mt. Druitt High School, New South Wales, 1972-76; assistant in languages, Lycee Technique, Paris, 1976-77; French master, St. Joseph's College, Hunter's Hill, NSW, 1978-79; journalist, Asiaweek magazine, Hong Kong, 1983-87. Since 1989 tutor of literary studies, University of Western Sydney. Writer-in-residence, Mitchell College, NSW, 1985; visiting fellow, Nepean College, Kingswood, NSW,1988. Since 1989 writer for *All-Asia Review of Books,* Hong Kong. **Awards:** Vogel-Australian prize, 1982, for *Birds of Paradise;* Australian Council of Literature Board grant, 1983, 1988; Victorian Premier's Literary Award, for *Double-Wolf* and *After China.* **Address:** c/o Allen and Unwin, 8 Napier Street, North Sydney 2059, Australia.

PUBLICATIONS

Novels

Birds of Passage. Sydney and London, Allen and Unwin, 1983.
Double-Wolf. Sydney, Allen and Unwin, 1991.
Pomeroy. Sydney, Allen and Unwin, 1991.
After China. Sydney, Allen and Unwin, 1992.
Drift. N.p., n.d.

*   *   *

Of Portuguese and Chinese-American parents, Brian Castro has much to do in his fiction with questions of identity and place, with the influence of the past upon the present, and with the relationship between language and experience. His first novel, *Birds of Passage,* concerns the history of that very much persecuted race in Australia, the Chinese. It documents—with brief, dispassionate understatement—the persecution of Castro's ancestors on the goldfields one hundred years ago and points to the rejection of their descendants today, but the purpose of the work is far from polemical. *Birds of Passage* is a parable about and an inquiry into the nature of identity and the relationship between past and present.

Its method is to juxtapose the narrative of Seamus O'Young, an ABC (Australian-born Chinese), and his ancestor, Lo Yun Shan, who came to Australia from Kwangtung in 1856 in search of gold. Sensitive, intelligent, but an outsider in Sydney, O'Young discovers a manuscript that Shan had left behind and from that starting point begins to retell his ancestor's story and, in effect, to reinvent it. Events 120 years apart are strikingly paralleled. An old man on the boat to Australia shares his food with Shan; we cut to Seamus being offered bread by two old men in a Sydney park. Different characters with the same name appear in the two halves. Even individual images are replicated. As he ponders and recreates the past, Seamus becomes possessed by it. He begins to age physically and to feel the return of his Chinese consciousness. Physical and psychoanalytic reasons are offered for this but are unconvincing speculations only. The truth is that Seamus seems, by the power of his imagination, to *become* his ancestor until finally they meet. At the end of the novel Shan returns to Kwangtung, deserted by his lover Mary Young, never to see the son he has fathered with her but in a truer sense having established a sense of continuity with the future: "He was on a different path now, in control of his destiny, and he brought with him something of the void he had experienced in Australia, the silence and the stillness that helped him to accept his microscopic role in the eternal recurrences of nature."

Birds of Passage has some of the faults one might expect in a first novel. The prose tends to become abstract or showily sententious at times, and Castro is prone to gesture at significances, to throw in names for their own sake, as with Seamus's casual meeting with Roland Barthes. But most of the time it is a tenderly written work, immensely sad without being in the least sense depressing.

Castro's second novel, *Double-Wolf,* is as much a tour de force as his first. Based on the celebrated case of Sergei Wespe, Freud's Wolf-Man, who experienced a childhood nightmare of wolves appearing in a tree outside his window (Freud built much of his theory of infantile sexuality based on it). It proceeds to spin a complex web of surmise and speculation involving primarily the relationship between Wespe and a fraudulent Australian-born psychoanalyst who calls himself Artie Catacomb. Castro has said in interviews that after picking up a copy of the Wolf-Man's memoirs in a second-hand bookshop he was drawn to the case, first because the Wolf-Man had always wanted to be a writer and second because Freud many years later asked Wespe to testify that what he had told him was true, a curious and uncharacteristic gesture of lack of self-confidence on the great man's part. Equally unusually Freud lent Wespe money during the Twenties when he was destitute.

Refusing to privilege any one narrator or narrative and meticulously listing date and place, Castro cuts between Catacomb, living out his last days in destitution at Katoomba in the Blue Mountains outside Sydney, and Wespe at various stages in his life—on his estate at Kherson, near Odessa, where he was born in 1887, in the Caucasus in 1906, Munich in 1910, and Vienna in 1972. Freud does not appear directly but is constantly a reported presence in the novel, and like much else in the novel he is often a comic one.

Strange things happened to Wespe when he was young. He watched his parents in the act of sex and saw his father crawl on all fours "and [hide] behind sofas with a wolf-mask over his face, springing up and terrifying the children, who ran screaming into the garden." He had an ecstatic sexual relationship with his sister, Anna. Two years older than himself, Anna, like his father and later like his wife, commits suicide. Wespe's response to Freud when he goes to be treated by him is an ambivalent and shifting one. Freud, it is hinted, in effect expropriates his client's writings while in turn the Wolf-Man's position as one of Freud's most celebrated cases gives him a certain status in the psychoanalytic world. It is one he adds to by becoming a successful author: "My book was a smash hit. Stayed on *The New York Times* best-seller list three months."

Through all this, Castro insists on the importance of play. Wespe tells us, "It was Freud who first taught me that parody comes before the paradigm, play before principle. The origin of man was a sort of partying without precedence." And again: "People have forgotten that life's a game. Play is the essence of thinking." The novel is full of jokes, puns, and wordplay ("The ego has landed"). Freud speaks like a character from the lower East side. In one of Castro's best gags, Wespe tells us, "When I got to Vienna I immediately visited Freud. He gave me an autographed copy of *From the History of an Infantile Neurosis.* I sold it for several hundred crowns to a fellow who came to see me. His name was Jung. . . ." In a neat reversal of Melville's famous opening the psychiatric entrepreneur Ishmael Liebmann says, "Call me Doctor Liebmann." There is an almost promiscuous variety of allusion, from references to wolves to Little Red Riding Hood to a guesthouse in Katoomba called the Aeneas. Part of the point that Castro is making is the not vastly original one of the problematic nature of truth. Wespe says of Freud's demand by what authority he writes what he writes, "I was dumbfounded. Did he believe that pornographers rendered something called the 'truth'? . . . Did he really mean to say that sexuality had firmer narrations than narrative, than a patient construction of scenes?" Similarly, he insists on the truth suggested in the title that reality is comprised of binary opposites. "A wolf is always a double," says Freud. Wespe says, "The Greeks understood how to be both true and false to themselves. Savagery and civilisation. Crudity and refinement." There are seven goats for seven wolves. *Double-Wolf* is an elegant and witty, if not always quite convincing, tour de force.

Given Castro's by now evident penchant for disconnectedness and fragmentation, the use of different narratorial personas and voices, the danger to his art lies in a heterogeneity of allusion so great that it makes finally for incoherence. This tends to happen in *Pomeroy,* his least typical and perhaps least successful novel. It is a novel of brilliant bits that finally don't make a whole. Pomeroy is a journalist cum detective cum aspiring writer who has been jilted by his cousin and former lover, Estrellita. He accepts a job in Hong Kong working for *I.D.* magazine, the initials standing variously for International Detective, Identity, Investigative Dialectics, and Indecent Disclosures. Pomeroy himself calls it Income for Destitutes. As the novel opens, however, he is living in Australia and has been summoned by Rory Halligan, the man whom Estrellita abandoned for him. In three sections, alternating first-person narration with third-person reportage, the novel crosses back and forth in time and space to tell the story of Pomeroy, one that leads finally to an anticipated end ("Give a man a chance to put off his own death").

As always with Castro the novel is full of jokes (Pomeroy's esky is covered with words from *Finnegans Wake,* which he reads as he almost drowns; there is a also letter in gloriously mangled English from Pomeroy's aunt complaining of his sexual activities) and allusions (to Shakespeare, Forster, Barthes, Housman). The esky is full of Hunter Valley wine. The novel both pays tribute to post-modernism and parodies it. The characters speak with incongruous sophistication: "That's why we're in the prison house of language. For us . . . there is really nothing outside the incriminating text. Just think . . . the mobster as reader." Castro is fond of repeating the injunction of E. M. Forster, the epitome of old-fashioned humanism, to "only connect," but the connections here are hard to follow.

Double-Wolf won Castro the Victorian Premier's Literary Award and he followed it the next year with *After China,* which achieved him the same honor. Once again, he exhibits his liking for rapidly shifting perspectives. A short novel, *After China* has almost as many scenes, neatly spliced together, as there are pages. Characteristically, it cuts between past and present, China and Australia, and first and third person to tell the story of the relationship between a Chinese architect, You Bok Man, and an unnamed but distinguished Australian writer of short stories. We learn little about the woman, apart from one brief episode devoted to her adolescence, except that it slowly becomes apparent that she is dying of cancer. The architect, however, eventually gives us his life story, from his training in Paris, imprisonment, impotence through an accident, and final escape in Shanghai, to a brief life in New York, to his current empty existence in the hotel he himself designed on the eastern coast of Australia, which is tumbling down around him. Castro's novels are nothing if not cosmopolitan and he himself points repeatedly to the extraordinarily complex cultural and racial background from which he comes.

Graver and more personal in tone than Castro's other novels, *After China* is also structurally a little simpler and more straightforward; it is a meditation on writing and its relation to sexuality and the relationship of both to immortality. The tales with which the architect "seduces" the writer and that become the substance of her final book are both from his own life and from ancient Chinese history and concentrate on this notion of immortality and its connection with the will to self-annihilation. The buildings that You designs are made deliberately difficult for their occupants. "When I built it," he says of his hotel, "I wanted people to be lost in it. The guest was not to come round again with any recognition or familiarity. Movement is discovery."

Similarly, we are told, "The Bauhaus and the Aufbau had attracted him because they opposed the unification of history, nationalism, and racial identity. He broke these things down into parts. Rearranged them." Doubleness is, of course, a central motif of Castro's work and fracturing goes hand in hand with unification. Perhaps the most appropriate of the many metaphors of binding and division that Castro offers us in the novel is that of the 16th-century pornographic painter in one of his stories, Tang Yin, who devises a fan that when opened from left to right depicts a traditional Chinese landscape and from right to left discloses an erotic painting. Tang Yin becomes famous when an imperial concubine catches sight of the fan open on the illicit side and takes a fancy to it.

Castro's most recent novel, *Drift,* takes now familiar themes and forms as far as they can go. It opens with a preface (reputedly written by one Thomas McGann in Tasmania in 1993) concerning the cult experimental author B. S. Johnson, who killed himself at the age of 40; it goes on to suggest that the novel itself is the last two thirds of Johnson's last projected work, a trilogy that he failed to complete. Based on a tiny passage in the only completed volume that McGann insists refers to Tasmania, McGann completes the trilogy, as Johnson had invited his readers to do, adopting the voice of the author. In addition, there are a number of other different narrative voices, including that of Johnson himself as well as Emma McGann, an aboriginal woman writing letters from Tasmania to Johnson that call him across the world.

In Castro's scenario, Bryan Stanley Johnson, or Byron Shelley Johnson, as he likes to dub himself ("he carried deep within a massive, debilitating romanticism"), journeys to Tasmania to meet the author of the letters. Slowly he becomes caught up in the predicament of the Aborigines, identifying with them, taking toxins that alter the color of his skin to the point where he becomes even blacker than the Aboriginals themselves: "Extinction. No longer white, unquestioning, biblical. No more dreams of primogeniture and ownership. No longer an author. What a relief."

Like Johnson, Castro is fond of wordplay, of allusions, and of arcane words; he loves puns, like his description of two sisters, "one grave, one acute," or the sign on McGann's Volkswagen, "-sabled driver." In everything he does he questions the simplistic notion that "writing is writing, life is life . . . and the former is always subordinate to the latter," which he quotes from an unsympathetic critic of Johnson. But like all of Castro's work the novel is fundamentally serious in its attempt to push his themes of estrangement and loss of identity as far as he can. From writing about being a person of Chinese origin in Australia he moves in this, his fifth novel, to the ultimate condition of exile, that of the aboriginal. The aim of the novel is best summed up in Johnson's final paradox: "What I am really doing is challenging the reader to prove his own existence as palpably as I am proving mine by the action of writing." By a combination of sheer linguistic brilliance and fundamental integrity Castro has succeeded in breaking through conventional labels such as "multicultural writer" to demonstrate the truth of his own expressed conviction: "Writing knows no boundaries. Its metaphors, its translations, are part of a migratory process, birds of passage, which wing from the subliminal to the page, leaving its signs for the reader."

—Laurie Clancy

CAULDWELL, Frank. *See* **KING, Francis (Henry).**

CAUTE, (John) David

Nationality: British. **Born:** Alexandria, Egypt, 16 December 1936. **Education:** Edinburgh Academy; Wellington College, Crowthorne, Berkshire; Wadham College, Oxford, M.A. in modern history, D.Phil. 1963; Harvard University, Cambridge, Massachusetts (Henry fellow), 1960-61. **Military Service:** Served in the British

Army, in Africa, 1955-56. **Family:** Married 1) Catherine Shuckburgh in 1961 (divorced 1970), two sons; 2) Martha Bates in 1973, two daughters. **Career:** Fellow, All Souls College, Oxford, 1959-65; visiting professor, New York University and Columbia University, New York, 1966-67; reader in social and political theory, Brunel University, Uxbridge, Middlesex, 1967-70; Regents' Lecturer, University of California, 1974; Benjamin Meaker Visiting Professor, University of Bristol, 1985. Literary and arts editor, *New Statesman,* London, 1979-80. Co-chair, Writers Guild of Great Britain, 1981-82. **Awards:** London Authors' Club award, 1960; Rhys Memorial prize, 1960. **Address:** 41 Westcroft Square, London W6 0TA, England.

Publications

Novels

At Fever Pitch. London, Deutsch, 1959; New York, Pantheon, 1961.
Comrade Jacob. London, Deutsch, 1961; New York, Pantheon, 1962.
The Decline of the West. London, Deutsch, and New York, Macmillan, 1966.
The Occupation. London, Deutsch, 1971; New York, McGraw Hill, 1972.
The Baby Sitters (as John Salisbury). London, Secker and Warburg, and New York, Atheneum, 1978.
Moscow Gold (as John Salisbury). London, Futura, 1980.
The K-Factor. London, Joseph, 1983.
News from Nowhere. London, Hamish Hamilton, 1986.
Veronica; or, The Two Nations. London, Hamish Hamilton, 1989; New York, Arcade, 1990.
The Women's Hour. London, Paladin, 1991.
Dr Orwell and Mr Blair. London, Weidenfeld and Nicolson, 1994.

Plays

Songs for an Autumn Rifle (produced Edinburgh, 1961).
The Demonstration (produced Nottingham, 1969; London, 1970). London, Deutsch, 1970.
The Fourth World (produced London, 1973).

Radio Plays: *Fallout,* 1972; *The Zimbabwe Tapes,* 1983; *Henry and the Dogs,* 1986; *Sanctions,* 1988.

Television Documentary: *Brecht & Co.,* 1979.

Other

Communism and the French Intellectuals 1914-1960. London, Deutsch, and New York, Macmillan, 1964.
The Left in Europe since 1789. London, Weidenfeld and Nicolson, and New York, McGraw Hill, 1966.
Fanon. London, Fontana, and New York, Viking Press, 1970.
The Illusion: An Essay on Politics, Theatre and the Novel. London, Deutsch, 1971; New York, Harper, 1972.
The Fellow-Travellers. London, Weidenfeld and Nicolson, and New York, Macmillan, 1973; revised edition, New Haven, Connecticut, Yale University Press, 1988.
Collisions: Essays and Reviews. London, Quartet, 1974.
Cuba, Yes? London, Secker and Warburg, and New York, McGraw Hill, 1974.

The Great Fear: The Anti-Communist Purge under Truman and Eisenhower. New York, Simon and Schuster, and London, Secker and Warburg, 1978.
Under the Skin: The Death of White Rhodesia. London, Allen Lane, and Evanston, Illinois, Northwestern University Press, 1983.
The Espionage of the Saints: Two Essays on Silence and the State. London, Hamish Hamilton, 1986.
Left Behind: Journeys into British Politics. London, Cape, 1987.
Sixty-Eight: The Year of the Barricades. London, Hamish Hamilton, 1988; as *The Year of the Barricades: A Journey Through 1968,* New York, Harper, 1988.
Joseph Losey: A Revenge on Life. London, Faber, 1994.

Editor, *Essential Writings,* by Karl Marx. London, MacGibbon and Kee, 1967; New York, Macmillan, 1968.

*

Critical Studies: Article by Caute, in *Contemporary Authors Autobiography Series 4* edited by Adele Sarkissian, Detroit, Gale, 1986; *Caute's Confrontations: A Study of the Novels of David Caute* by Nicolas Tredell, West Bridgford, Paupers' Press, 1994.

David Caute comments:

My novels are (perhaps) about: how people interpret the world to make themselves better and larger than they are; the helpless guilt of the self-aware; and the strategies of fictional narrative itself. Every private life is touched, or seized, by a wider public life.

*   *   *

In his novels, David Caute has always been concerned to dramatize and explore the complex relations between political commitment, the urge for power, and sexual desire. His fiction vividly portrays characters caught up in a range of struggles: African decolonization in *At Fever Pitch, The Decline of the West, News from Nowhere,* and *The K-Factor;* the attempt by the 17th-century Diggers to establish a free community in the England of Oliver Cromwell, in *Comrade Jacob;* the campus revolts of the 1960s in *The Occupation;* the social conflicts of 1980s Britain in *Veronica;* feminism in *The Women's Hour;* anti-communism in *Dr Orwell and Mr Blair.* Caute's sympathies are with the left, but never, in his novels, in an uncritical or dogmatic way; indeed, he is sharply aware of the bad faith and vanity that may be bound up with left-wing commitment, and he can present a sympathetic portrait of a right-wing figure, as he does in *Veronica.*

Caute's first four novels were primarily realistic, but showed signs of strain, as if another kind of writer were trying to get out. In the context of English fiction in the 1950s, *At Fever Pitch* was notable for the variety of narrative techniques it employed, from interior monologues to attempts to imitate the style of African folktales. At moments, *Comrade Jacob* moved into caricature and deliberate anachronism. *The Decline of the West* went further in the direction of caricature, and its exuberant style, endlessly generating similes and metaphors, was a distraction from the narrative and from the impact of specific scenes. *The Occupation,* however, triumphantly resolved these strains: here Caute found a form and style well suited to his talents, and to his concerns at the time.

The protagonist of *The Occupation* is a radical English academic, Steven Bright, working in the USA at the height of the 1960s student revolts. Roused by the tumults of the times, challenged by his students to live up to his radicalism, embroiled in fraught relationships with a range of women, Bright finds himself, and the novel he is in, falling apart. But this breakdown is a breakthrough for Caute: *The Occupation* mixes realism, fantasy, caricature, expressionism, and self-reflexive commentary in a way that vividly dramatizes its themes, but it also achieves aesthetic coherence through its skilful overall structure and the sustained pace, precision, and wit of its style. It is Caute's most frenetic but most assured achievement.

The Occupation was part of a trilogy that also included a play, *The Demonstration,* and a work of literary theory, *The Illusion.* This trilogy, which bore the overall title of *The Confrontation,* both advocated and sought to demonstrate a practice of politically committed writing that challenged and disrupted representation. Caute did not follow this up, however, and for the next thirteen years produced studies of modern history and politics. It was *Under the Skin,* his documentary account of the death of Ian Smith's Rhodesian regime, which heralded his return to fiction in *The K-Factor;* this short, fast-paced novel dramatized the identity crisis of Rhodesia in its last days, as definitions of reality were hotly disputed— were the black guerrillas, for example, to be seen as terrorists or freedom fighters? *The K-Factor* was followed by *News from Nowhere,* a long, serious, and absorbing chronicle of the fortunes of Richard Stern from his heady years as a Young Turk at the London School of Economics to his troubled existence as an ill-paid journalist in the twilight of white Rhodesia. *Veronica* explores the incestuous love of a Conservative Cabinet Minister for his half-sister, and *The Women's Hour* sharply and comically portrays the plight of an ageing, left-wing university lecturer who is accused of sexual harassment by a feminist colleague. *Dr Orwell and Mr Blair* offers a fictional memoir, supposedly written by a boy whom "Mr Blair" befriended, of George Orwell as he was developing the ideas for *Animal Farm.* All these novels are largely realistic, but they do sometimes highlight their own artifice, and call into question the veracity of representation in supposedly factual as well as fictional writing. They show neither the strain of Caute's early realist work nor the controlled frenzy of *The Occupation;* they are the work of a mature writer, skilled in his craft and balanced in his attitudes, who combines humour, scepticism, and clarity.

Caute's novels now comprise a significant body of work, but they have suffered some neglect. This is partly because they are difficult to classify. In their challenge to realism, they can be seen as postmodernist; in their political and ethical engagements, they subvert postmodernist playfulness. But it is precisely in this confrontation—between postmodernism and realism, politics and play, commitment and critical detachment—that their power and pleasure lies.

—Nicolas Tredell

CHAPPELL, Fred (Davis)

Nationality: American. **Born:** Canton, North Carolina, 28 May 1936. **Education:** Duke University, Durham, North Carolina, B.A. 1961, M.A. 1964. **Family:** Married Susan Nicholls; one son. **Career:** Since 1964 teacher of English, University of North Carolina, Greensboro. **Awards:** Sir Walter Raleigh prize, 1972; North Carolina award, 1980; Bollingen prize, 1985; World Fantasy awards, 1992, 1994; T.S. Eliot prize, 1993. **Agent:** Rhoda Weyr, 151 Bergen Street, New York, New York 14416, U.S.A.

PUBLICATIONS

Novels

It Is Time, Lord. New York, Atheneum, 1963.
The Inkling. New York, Harcourt Brace, 1965.
Dagon. New York, Harcourt Brace, 1968.
The Gaudy Place. New York, Harcourt Brace, 1972.
I Am One of You Forever. Baton Rouge, Louisiana State University Press, 1985.
Brighten the Corner Where You Are. New York, St. Martin's Press, 1989.
More Shapes Than One. New York, St. Martin's Press, 1991.

Short Stories

Moments of Light. Los Angeles, New South, 1980.

Poetry

The World Between the Eyes. Baton Rouge, Louisiana State University Press, 1971.
River. Baton Rouge, Louisiana State University Press, 1975.
The Man Twice Married to Fire. Greensboro, North Carolina, Unicorn Press, 1977.
Bloodfire. Baton Rouge, Louisiana State University Press, 1978.
Awakening to Music. Davidson, North Carolina, Briarpatch Press, 1979.
Earthsleep. Baton Rouge, Louisiana State University Press, 1980.
Driftlake: A Lieder Cycle. Emory, Virginia, Iron Mountain Press, 1981.
Midquest. Baton Rouge, Louisiana State University Press, 1981.
Castle Tzingal. Baton Rouge, Louisiana State University Press, 1985.
First and Last Words. Baton Rouge, Louisiana State University Press, 1988.
C. Baton Rouge, Louisiana State University Press, 1993.
Spring Garden: New and Selected Poems. Baton Rouge, Louisiana State University Press, 1995.

Other

The Fred Chappell Reader. New York, St. Martin's Press, 1987.
Plow Naked: Selected Writings on Poetry. Ann Arbor, University Michigan Press, 1993.

*

Manuscript Collection: Duke University, Durham, North Carolina.

Fred Chappell comments:

To be serious but not ponderous, or to be light but not frivolous: these are the qualities I strive for. They require clarity, and this is my strongest ambition.

*   *   *

Although Fred Chappell has perhaps been more widely renowned as a poet, he has written and published six novels since the 1960s. Since the publication in 1985 of *I Am One of You Forever,* set in the North Carolina mountains, Chappell has become recognized for his earlier achievements as an innovative and daring novelist. Indeed, the author's equally successful work in numerous genres, including short fiction and essays, is echoed by the variety exhibited within the novels. His books explore a range of themes and settings, captivating for their passages of beautiful prose, and also for their humor and pathos. Chappell's unusual handling of narrative structure, and his use of fantasy have contributed to his reputation as an experimental novelist.

Especially Chappell's early novels were considered experimental by many critics. *It Is Time, Lord,* written when Chappell was only 26 years old, presents in a fragmented narrative the spiritual journey of the narrator, James Christopher. The novel's action moves back and forth between the protagonist's present life and his childhood on a farm in Appalachia. The novel centers upon Christopher's suffering as he faces the memories of painful childhood experiences and the consequences of his own ineffectuality and lack of direction.

This impotence of will is further explored within Chappell's second novel, *The Inkling,* which concerns the dark side of human nature. The novel is highly allegorical, a treatment of the conflict between will and appetite. Like Chappell's first novel, *The Inkling* utilizes a unique narrative structure, beginning and ending at the same moment in time, framing the volatile circumstances in the life of the central character, Jan, and his emotionally disturbed sister, Timmie.

The themes of time, particularly the past, human suffering, and the struggle with temptation, are crucial within Chappell's early novels. However, within the third novel they are presented in extremity. The protagonist of *Dagon,* Peter Leland, is faced with a haunting past and incredible evil when he inherits his family farm in the southern mountains. He is pulled against his will by supernatural forces into a world of temptation and subsequent terror. A horror novel, *Dagon* is considered a vanguard of contemporary popular horror fiction, based in part on myths surrounding the pagan deity from which it takes its title. The novel also makes several allusions to works by H.P. Lovecraft, whose Cthulthu mythos are integral to the novel

The Gaudy Place, Chappell's fourth novel, is divergent from the early novels, and it is also quite different from the author's more recent fiction. Its setting, a fictionalized Asheville, North Carolina, its humorous tone, and its subject matter, set it apart and mark a new course in Chappell's longer fiction. This novel is also experimental in its use of shifting point of view. Each chapter is set within the consciousness and upon the circumstance of one of several characters whose lives are interwoven in the final pages. While there is in actuality no protagonist in *The Gaudy Place,* the distinct personalities coalesce to form a portrait of a unique urban community within Southern Appalachia.

Chappell's most recent novels, *I Am One of You Forever* and *Brighten the Corner Where You Are,* are markedly unique. However, they share with other of Chappell's novels thematic issues, an Appalachian setting, and fantastical moments. Unlike the horrific fantasy of *Dagon,* the fantasy in these two novels is utilized primarily for humorous effect. While some critics liken these surprisingly fantastical moments to the magical realism often employed by South American writers, according to Chappell they are in the tradition of the mountain tall tale. These two novels are quite simi-

lar to each other in some respects, primarily because they are the first two in a projected series of four novels which concern the Kirkman family. Each novel is narrated by the son, Jess. *I Am One of You Forever* concerns Jess's coming of age as he deals with divergent experiences and develops a sense of belonging. Chappell's 1989 novel, while also narrated by Jess, concerns a day in the life of his father, Joe Robert Kirkman, and the many amazingly coincidental, humorous, and touching occurrences which he faces. *Brighten the Corner Where You Are* traverses freely between stark realism and a world of fantasy, in which the protagonist converses freely with historic figures such as Socrates and Darwin.

The Fred Chappell Reader contains excerpts of Chappell's early novels, and Chappell's later novels are readily available. Unfortunately, for most readers it is difficult to find copies of *It Is Time, Lord* and *The Inkling.* These books have long been out of print. However, the early novels of Fred Chappell are being rediscovered by critics, and a new generation of readers is becoming aware of this unique American author.

—Susan O'Dell Underwood

CHARLES, Gerda

Nationality: British. **Born:** Liverpool. **Education:** Liverpool schools. **Career:** Journalist and reviewer for *New Statesman, Daily Telegraph, New York Times, Jewish Chronicle,* and other periodicals; television critic, *Jewish Observer,* London, 1978-79. **Awards:** James Tait Black Memorial prize, 1964; Whitbread award, 1971; Arts Council grant, 1972. **Address:** 22 Cunningham Court, London W9 1AE, England.

PUBLICATIONS

Novels

The True Voice. London, Eyre and Spottiswoode, 1959.
The Crossing Point. London, Eyre and Spottiswoode, 1960; New York, Knopf, 1961.
A Slanting Light. London, Eyre and Spottiswoode, and New York, Knopf, 1963.
A Logical Girl. London, Eyre and Spottiswoode, and New York, Knopf, 1967.
The Destiny Waltz. London, Eyre and Spottiswoode, 1971; New York, Scribner, 1972.

Uncollected Short Stories

"The Staircase," in *Vanity Fair* (London), April 1956.
"Rosh Hashanah in Five Weeks," in *Pick of Today's Short Stories 11.* London, Putnam, 1960.
"The Czech-Slovakian Chandelier," in *Modern Jewish Stories,* edited by Charles. London, Faber, 1963; Englewood Cliffs, New Jersey, Prentice Hall, 1965.
"A Mixed Marriage," in *Quest* (London), 1965.
"The Difference," in *Jewish Chronicle* (London), 24 November 1967.
"The Mitzvah," in *Jewish Chronicle* (London), March 1978.

Other

Editor, *Modern Jewish Stories.* London, Faber, 1963; Englewood Cliffs, New Jersey, Prentice Hall, 1965.

*

Critical Studies: "The World of Gerda Charles," in *Jewish Quarterly* (London), Summer 1967; "Facing the Music" by C.P. Snow, in *Financial Times,* 15 April 1971; "Gerda Charles: A Visionary Realist," in *Jewish Quarterly* (London), Summer 1971.

Gerda Charles comments:

(1991) Though I am known primarily as an Anglo-Jewish writer, my five novels all deal in general with what I have described (in my third book, *A Slanting Light*) as "the region of everyday hurt." My books are not concerned with extremes—which I believe to be largely unrelated to the real problems of living. They are not concerned with madness but rather with the job of maintaining sanity, dignity, and order. They advocate the unfashionable virtues of delicacy, tact, and generosity of heart within the context of day-to-day life.

*   *   *

The True Voice is an excellent first novel in which Gerda Charles develops a principal theme—the alienation felt by a person of talent when he is unable to articulate his aspirations and to communicate his inner intensities to others. After two disillusioning experiences with men, Lindy Frome finds that her only valid resource is the self, as she attains awareness of "the compassionate irony with which it was necessary to confront life; how flexibility, awareness and forgiveness were all."

With *The Crossing Point* Charles wrote her best book. She asserts through Rabbi Leo Norberg that Judaism is the most viable of religions for human beings since it is at "the crossing point" where opposites such as asceticism and sensuousness, mysticism and secularism, idealism and practicality converge. Boruch Gabriel is imposing as a presence but not as an influence since his conception of religion is literal and monolithic. His daughter, Sara, illustrates the true strength of Judaism as it gives her courage to face her father and her own life of impaired fulfillment. Rabbi Norberg is the novel's intellectual center. Humane and imaginative, he sometimes lacks the courage to act upon his insights. Knowing the best in Sara Gabriel, he chooses, out of a certain perversity and false pride, the second best, a calculating and fourth-rate woman, for wife. The characters, big with life, give the book its stature. They are human beings who also happen to be Jews, as they falter or triumph in achieving their destinies.

A Slanting Light is a notable if less arresting book. A psychically immolated American playwright, Bernard Zold, is protagonist. His chief antagonist is a power-hungry mother; his wife is superficial and his child unloving. He is a sufferer rather than a doer, a man of sympathetic imagination rather than of active confidence. For the narrator he is emblematic of "the whole role of the Jew in the historic life of the world's soul" and exemplifies "the human nature of society." Zold hardly achieves this archetypal dimension, and Charles's analysis of Zold as an artist lacks immediacy and exactitude. But as a novel exploring entangled relationships it has distinction and force.

In *A Logical Girl,* Charles's best book since *The Crossing Point,* Rose Morgan's views of what ought to be are in abrupt contrast with the way things are. In World War II in a seaside town, she develops from naive adolescence to maturity while the town is "invaded" by European and American troops. Her sensitivity allows her to see how selfish, impersonal, and degrading her associates and family often are, while they impress the world as models of virtue and propriety. The elements of deceit, inconsiderateness, and cruelty which all too often determine human relationships are the reflection in little of the injustices and sadism in the Nazi regime on the continent. Rose learns that human beings do not behave consistently and logically, that impulse is often triumphant over honesty. Charles finely controls her irony as she demonstrates in Rose how the individual who sees the truth is disregarded by most other people in their reverence for the flashy, the meretricious, and the materialistic.

The Destiny Waltz is Charles's longest and least satisfactory novel. It concerns the surviving influence of Paul Salomon, a great poet from the 1920s who had been passed over in his lifetime. At the instigation of a television company, Jimmy Marchant, a retired band leader and Paul's closest friend, meets Michele Sandburg, a college teacher in her forties who has written the best life of the poet. They are to help make a documentary film about Salomon's life. Much pathos and intense feeling develop when Jimmy realizes that in Michele he may yet find the happiness that eluded him in his marriage and sexual affairs. Yet Jimmy lacks interest and presence, and his moralizing, while genuine, is frequently labored. Again, Charles fails to make her artist believable; we have, in short, little idea of what Salomon's poetry was like. She does depict with assuredness the studio milieu, wherein prudential motives and the requirements of art are in locked conflict. In sum, Charles has overextended her materials for the value which accrues to them.

Charles has analyzed with sympathy and comprehension the spiritual misfit in modern life. Her insight into human nature is penetrating; and her eccentrics, as well as her fully developed figures, are authentic. She establishes the outlines of her characters economically by concentrated analysis and persuasive dialogue. As a stylist her prose is always perspicuous and perfectly modulated to convey a sense of Jamesian complexities in character and situation. Her main preoccupation is with the painful incursion of moral knowledge. The process whereby her protagonists determine "how to be" is fraught with anguish, on occasion with muted triumph, always with the ring of truth.

—Frederick P.W. McDowell

CHARYN, Jerome

Nationality: American. **Born:** New York City, 13 May 1937. **Education:** Columbia University, New York, B.A. (cum laude) 1959 (Phi Beta Kappa). **Family:** Married Marlene Phillips in 1965 (divorced). **Career:** Recreation leader, New York City Department of Parks, early 1960s; English teacher, High School of Music and Art, and School of Performing Arts, both New York, 1962-64; Lecturer in English, City College, New York, 1965; assistant professor of English, Stanford University, California, 1965-68; assistant professor, 1968-72, associate professor, 1972-78, and professor of English, 1978-80, Herbert Lehman College, City University of New York; Mellon Visiting Professor of English, Rice University, Houston, 1979; visiting professor, 1980, and lecturer in creative writing, 1981-86, Princeton University, New Jersey; Visiting Distinguished Professor of English, City College of New York, 1988-89. Founding editor, *Dutton Review,* New York, 1970-72; executive editor, *Fiction,* New York, 1970-75. Member of the Executive Board, PEN American Center, since 1984, International Association of Crime Writers, since 1988, and Mystery Writers of America, since 1989. Since 1986 member of Playwright/Director Unit, Actors Studio, New York. **Awards:** National Endowment for the Arts grant, 1979, 1984; Rosenthal Foundation award, 1981; Guggenheim grant, 1982. Chevalier, Order of Arts and Letters (France), 1989. **Agent:** Georges Borchardt Inc., 136 East 57th Street, New York, New York 10022, U.S.A.; or, Mic Cheetham, Anthony Sheil Associates, 43 Doughty Street, London WC1N 2LF, England. **Address:** 302 West 12th Street, Apartment 10-C, New York, New York 10014, U.S.A.; or, 1 rue Boulard, Paris 75014, France.

PUBLICATIONS

Novels

Once Upon a Droshky. New York, McGraw Hill, 1964.
On the Darkening Green. New York, McGraw Hill, 1965.
Going to Jerusalem. New York, Viking Press, 1967; London, Cape, 1968.
American Scrapbook. New York, Viking Press, 1969.
Eisenhower, My Eisenhower. New York, Holt Rinehart, 1971.
The Tar Baby. New York, Holt Rinehart, 1973.
The Isaac Quartet. London, Zomba, 1984.
   Blue Eyes. New York, Simon and Schuster, 1975.
    Marilyn the Wild. New York, Arbor House, 1976; London, Bloomsbury, 1990.
    The Education of Patrick Silver. New York, Arbor House, 1976.
   Secret Isaac. New York, Arbor House, 1978.
The Franklin Scare. New York, Arbor House, 1977.
The Seventh Babe. New York, Arbor House, 1979.
The Catfish Man: A Conjured Life. New York, Arbor House, 1980.
Darlin' Bill: A Love Story of the Wild West. New York, Arbor House, 1980.
Panna Maria. New York, Arbor House, 1982.
Pinocchio's Nose. New York, Arbor House, 1983.
War Cries over Avenue C. New York, Fine, 1985; London, Abacus, 1986.
The Magician's Wife. Tournai, Belgium, Casterman, 1986; New York, Catalan, 1987; London, Titan, 1988.
Paradise Man. New York, Fine, 1987; London, Joseph, 1988.
The Good Policeman. New York, Mysterious Press, 1990; London, Bloomsbury, 1991.
Elsinore. New York, Mysterious Press, and London, Bloomsbury, 1991.
Maria's Girls. New York, Mysterious Press, 1992; London, Serpent's Tail, 1994.
Montezuma's Man. New York, Mysterious Press, 1993.
Little Angel Street. New York, Mysterious Press, 1994.

Short Stories

The Man Who Grew Younger and Other Stories. New York, Harper, 1967.

Uncollected Short Stories

"The Blue Book of Crime," in *The New Black Mask.* San Diego, California, Harcourt Brace, 1986.
"Fantomas in New York," in *A Matter of Crime.* San Diego, California, Harcourt Brace, 1988.
"Young Isaac," in *The Armchair Detective* (New York), Summer 1990.

Other

Metropolis: New York as Myth, Marketplace, and Magical Land. New York, Putnam, 1986; London, Abacus, 1988.
Movieland: Hollywood and the Great American Dream Culture. New York, Putnam, 1989.

Editor, *The Single Voice: An Anthology of Contemporary Fiction.* New York, Collier, 1969.
Editor, *The Troubled Vision: An Anthology of Contemporary Short Novels and Passages.* New York, Collier, 1970.
Editor, *The New Mystery.* New York, Dutton, 1993.

*

Manuscript Collection: Fales Collection, Elmer Holmes Bobst Library, New York University.

Critical Studies: Introductions by Charyn to *The Single Voice,* 1969, and *The Troubled Vision,* 1970; "Notes on the Rhetoric of Anti-Realist Fiction" by Albert Guerard, in *Tri-Quarterly* (Evanston, Illinois), Spring 1974; "Jerome Charyn: Artist as Mytholept" by Robert L. Patten, in *Novel* (Providence, Rhode Island), Fall 1984; "Exploding the Genre: The Crime Fiction of Jerome Charyn" by Michael Woolf, in *American Crime Fiction,* London, Macmillan, 1988; Jerome Charyn issue of *The Review of Contemporary Fiction,* Summer 1992.

*   *   *

Jerome Charyn's work demonstrates a deep mistrust of the contemporary world, expressed frequently in alienation from mechanized or anti-humanistic institutions. At the same time, and in opposition to this perception, Charyn has celebrated humanity's heroic capacity for survival in the face of such alienation. A typical Charyn protagonist moves between worlds, between a landscape of urban decline and worlds of spiritual intensity and complexity where the capacity for magic and mayhem confronts the mundane and the menacing. Throughout his work he has imagined and reimagined America (most commonly New York City) into forms that repeatedly challenge and subvert the reader's perception of contemporary reality. A dark comedy meets fragments of spiritual persistence that finally affirm the fragile survival of flawed but beautiful humanity in the rubble of our civilization. The fiction is formed and informed both by an awareness of contemporary literary practice and by a moral consciousness deeply influenced by Jewish experience and perception. Of all the novelists characterized as Jewish-American, Charyn is the most radical and inventive. There is in the body of his work a restless creativity which constantly surprises and repeatedly undermines the reader's expectation.

His first novel, *Once Upon a Droshky,* explored a recurrent conflict in Jewish-American writing, that between father and son. The narrative voice, however, is that of the father and the language is in an English that is shaped by Yiddish speech structures. This creates a powerful comic narrative but it also reveals a sense of continuity with, and nostalgia for, the lost world of Yiddish-American culture. The father reflects a sense of moral justice while the son represents a legalistic, inhuman America. He embodies a future against which the voices of the past have little power except that accrued by spiritual strength and the sense that reality is ambiguous, containing both the known and the transcendent. It is characteristic of Charyn's originality that his first novel, published when he was 26, should be told through the perception of the father.

The world as this kind of ambiguous landscape places Charyn's work, in one context, in relation to Isaac Bashevis Singer's. In one of Charyn's most important novels, *War Cries over Avenue C,* for example, he goes into the innermost heart of the desolate inner city to invent a world of heroes and grotesques, angels and demons. Avenue C is a world without God. The novel is not, though, a grim record of urban decline. A Jewish girl with bad skin becomes magically transformed into a mythic and heroic figure, Saigon Sarah, while her lover returns from Vietnam as "The Magician" picking shrapnel, like dandruff, from his skull. Vietnam is carried like a drug into the twisted heart of New York. Charyn is not, though, solely representing the familiar issues of violence and degeneration in the city but a complex synthesis of moral collapse and spirituality, degradation and salvation.

Charyn's prose precisely reflects his themes. It makes startling conjunctions, dramatically synthesizes the magical and the mundane. He thrusts the reader out of the known world and then back into it with a radically altered perception. The experience is comic, violent, and profoundly serious.

Another aspect of Charyn's writing is his awareness of contemporary literary issues; he is an editor and critic of considerable sophistication. His knowledge of this field is shown in his use of the notions of fictionality and fable-making that characterizes, in part, post-realist and postmodern writing. This aspect of his work is most clearly illustrated in the novels of the early 1970s: *Eisenhower, My Eisenhower* and *The Tar Baby.* In the first novel he creates a fictional gypsy tribe of Azazians who are essentially comic figures with tails and a belief in an anarchic God. The novel is told in the first person by an Azazian gypsy, and Charyn's achievement is to use that comic voice to record a tragic history. The voice reveals a condition of persecution that transforms the fable of Azazian history into one that reflects all histories of ethnic alienation and persecution. Non-realism paradoxically offers an incisive analysis into the real predicament of the ethnic stranger. A similar strategy is found in *The Tar Baby.* The novel is a parody of a literary periodical which ostensibly honors the life of one Anatole Waxman-Weissman. The form gives Charyn the opportunity to create a succession of literary jokes reminiscent of Nabokov's *Pale Fire,* but the formal issues co-exist with a sense of Anatole as an archetypal ethnic outsider in a society and institution hostile to the creative imagination.

Charyn's view of his own creativity is of a process that comes close to mystical experience in its transfer between real and quasi-surreal worlds: "I start out each time to write a conventional story. All of a sudden, the story begins to shift. It's like a landslide—you're on one particular spot, and all of a sudden that spot disappears and you enter some other sort of crazy territory." These territories are rich indeed and they encompass many forms, from the Western landscape of *Darlin' Bill* to the immigrant history of America that informs *Panna Maria.* Of particular interest are two novels of quasi-mythical autobiography: *The Catfish Man* and *Pinocchio's Nose.* These frequently exuberant fables offer a kind of alternative history of Jewish America. This history counters the view of the Jews as an invariably upwardly mobile and successful immigrant group. Like the Azazians, Charyn's Jews remain on the edges of the world, occupying a territory that shifts and slides between alienation and magic. Charyn's Jews are in America but not always of it: a tribe apart.

Tribalism is, in fact, the mode in which he most frequently represents ethnicity. This is most clearly apparent in the crime novels that come close to offering an urban epic of major literary importance: *The Isaac Quartet* and *The Good Policeman.* In these five novels Charyn represents New York as a kind of tribal society populated by warring ethnic communities. The groups are intertwined in a system that blurs boundaries between good and evil, detective and criminal. In essence, the author uses the crime genre to complicate the nature of reality. He reverses a common objective of the form which frequently depends on a clear division between right and wrong, good and bad.

Charyn's view of the world is inclusive and complex. He grafts onto the form of the detective novel a set of strategies which permit those mystical transformations that are characteristic of a view of reality in which nothing stays simple or still. He is not essentially concerned with the mechanics of crime but he exploits the genre to approach the profoundest of paradoxes: the persistence of love and redemption in an ostensibly doomed and damned world. Within the violent disorder of contemporary experience, Charyn perceives the heroic nature of flawed humanity as it crawls towards some bizarre version of spiritual salvation.

Charyn is one of a handful of living American novelists who combine prolific output with stylistic originality and imaginative zest. Part of his claim to our attention is his unpredictability. He has taken hold of a vast range of American myths, locations, and dreams and reshaped these within his rich imagination. He melds that creativity with the fertile tradition of Jewish storytelling which traditionally envisages a spiritual potential within a mire of poverty and violence. The outcome is a deeply serious and profound vision of a world simultaneously half-catatonic at the edge of doom and heroically groping towards some version of God's grace.

—Michael Woolf

CHATTERJEE, Upamanyu

Nationality: Indian. **Born:** Bihar, India, 1959. **Career:** Currently, officer, Indian Administrative Service. **Address:** c/o Faber and Faber, Ltd., 3 Queen Square, London, WC1N 3AU, England.

PUBLICATIONS

Novels

English, August: An Indian Story. London, Faber, 1988.
The Last Burden. New Delhi, Viking, and London, Faber, 1993.

*   *   *

The corpus of Upamanyu Chatterjee is not vast but his is a powerful emergent voice in Indian postcolonial literature. Thus far he has published "The Assassination of Indira Gandhi" in 1986 and two novels, *English, August: An Indian Story* in 1988 and *The Last Burden* in 1993. Critics have found Chatterjee difficult to categorize in that the protagonists—August in *English, August* and Jamun in *The Last Burden*—just drift with no apparent purpose in life. Reviews of *English, August* liken August to Kingsley Amis's Lucky Jim as a portrayal of the angry young man. But such a comparison would thematically make August angrier, for this novel is focused on India's postcolonial condition and the necessity to decolonize.

English, August deals with August as a member of the Indian Administrative Service, a reincarnation of the Indian Civil Service, a behemoth left behind by the British to govern the country. A job in the IAS is highly sought after in postcolonial India; August, while appearing lackadaisical and self-centered and seeming to be its most inappropriate member, draws attention to a system which has become totally outmoded and out of touch with the needs of the Indian masses. Overtly, the novel attempts to do an expose of the IAS with its corruption and the tension which exists between the IAS officers representing the federal government and the state governments resulting in the victimization of the common people in the administrative nightmare in modern India.

Furthermore, there is a subtext of anger which is aimed not just at the IAS, but one which questions reality in India which is mediated by the English text or more particularly through Western eyes. For instance, watching Indian television, August makes references to *Peyton Place* and *Waiting for Godot,* which prompts his uncle to respond with "the *first* thing you are reminded of by something that happens around you, is something obscure and foreign, totally unrelated to the life and language around you." This particular theme pervades the novel and all the characters agree that postcolonial India is unreal, "a place of fantasy" and "confused metaphysics." To this extent, the IAS itself becomes a metaphor for India. Under the guise of decolonization, post-independence IAS once more reinscribes the colonial government as well as the profound sense of dislocation that a lot of Indians feel. Nationalism represented by the IAS can only be purchased by the homogenization of India and its people. The IAS and its policy of placing elite officers in locales and terrains they are unfamiliar with only goes further towards making it an inept administrative body, unable to cope with the intricacies of administering in a place and language alien to it. How can India/IAS decolonize then? August's only option is through taking a break from the IAS altogether.

If *English, August* is dark and bleak, *The Last Burden* comes to terms with and accepts such darkness. This novel of decolonization is truly "indigenous" in that its concern is not with India's relationship to the metropolitan centers but rather with middle-class life. It exposes the myth of the unity of the joint Hindu family (as opposed to the Western nuclear one) and its sense of duty, and dwells instead on the banality of urban life in India. The most striking aspect of this novel is the incredible language used by Chatterjee, which makes the reader oscillate between the beauty of the high serious prose and the ridiculous emotions that it covers. For instance, the novel is framed by the death of Jamun's mother. Upon being reprimanded at his demeanor and lack of sorrow at her impending death, Jamun retorts, "She isn't Indira Gandhi, you know, that we've to hurtle out into the streets and thwack our tits to voice our grief." Thus the chaos in the aftermath of Indira Gandhi's assassination is contextualized as hyperbole. Again, when Urmila dies, the doctor advises them to cremate the body, for the mourners "crack

up, if after a few hours, the cadaver they're half-worshipping exudes the wispiest pong." Thus Chatterjee's use of language is effective on two counts. First, his code-switching and inscription of the banal and the slang defuses the hyperbole and exaggerated emotions associated with death. Death becomes real and a part of life and not a farce. In addition, his treatment of language forcibly inflects the Indian and indigenous within the language reserved for the English canon and its system of cultural assumptions.

With *The Last Burden* and the deliberate indigenization of English, Chatterjee finds a solution to the postcolonial anxiety articulated in *English, August.*

—Radhika Mohanram

CHEUSE, Alan

Nationality: American. **Born:** Perth Amboy, New Jersey, 23 January 1940. **Education:** Rutgers University, New Brunswick, New Jersey, B.A. 1961, Ph.D. in comparative literature 1974. **Family:** Married 1) Mary Ethel Agan in 1964 (divorced 1972), one son; 2) Marjorie Pryse in 1975 (divorced 1984), two daughters; 3) Kristin O'Shee in 1991. **Career:** Toll taker, New Jersey Turnpike, 1961-62; speechwriter, 1965; reporter, Fairchild Publications, 1966; instructor in literature, Bennington College, Vermont, 1970-78; visiting writer, University of the South, 1984, University of Michigan, Ann Arbor, 1984-86, Universitity of Virginia, Charlottesville, and since 1987, George Mason University. Book critic, National Public Radio, *All Things Considered,* since 1984, producer and host, *Sound of Writing,* since 1989. **Awards:** National Endowment for the Arts fellowship, 1979-80. **Member:** National Book Critics' Circle. **Agent:** Nat Sobel, 146 East 19th Street, New York, New York 10003, U.S.A.

PUBLICATIONS

Novels

The Bohemians: John Reed and His Friends. Cambridge, Massachusetts, n.p., 1982.
The Grandmothers' Club. Salt Lake City, Utah, Peregrine Smith, 1986.
The Light Possessed. Salt Lake City, Utah, Peregrine Smith, 1990.

Short Stories

Candace and Other Stories. Cambridge, Massachusetts, n.p., 1980.
The Tennessee Waltz and Other Stories. Salt Lake City, Utah, Peregrine Smith, 1990.

Other

Fall Out of Heaven: An Autobiographical Journey. Salt Lake City, Utah, Peregrine Smith, 1987.

Editor, with Caroline Marshall, *The Sound of Writing.* New York, Doubleday, 1991.

Editor, with Caroline Marshall, *Listening to Ourselves*. New York, Doubleday, 1993.

*

Manuscript Collection: Alderman Library, University Of Virginia, Charlottesville.

Alan Cheuse comments:

Two notes about my stories. I tend to see them as pieces as much in the lyric mode as straight narrative, in which I work the language as closely as a poet might. So my stories are as close to writing lyric poetry as I will probably ever get.

As far as grouping them, I can see a rough geographical configuration. There are southern stories, western stories, and some eastern stories. I suppose in another ten or twenty years I'll have boxed the compass in short fiction. But I doubt if this has much to do with their meaning—it's a category that helps me keep track of them, is all, I think.

With regard to *Fall Out of Heaven,* I have to say that I would like to do more nonfiction, but I haven't yet found a new subject. In the case of this memoir-travel book, the subject was as personal as my own skin, and I had done all the research just by living and suffering. The travel part was the reward, I suppose, for having gone through the hellish rest of it, the battles with my father, the awful separation from my son that came when his mother and I divorced.

As far as finding an overall pattern in my work, who knows? No writer wants to think that he's finished searching for that, not before he himself is finished with life and work. Hemingway noticed certain patterns and began to parody himself. Faulkner kept on reaching and though the work fell off a bit it never became uninteresting. On goes the quest.

*   *   *

A. Cheuse is not only a prolific writer of fiction and nonfiction, but also a widely appearing commentator-critic-lecturer dealing with modern literature and—not least—a member of the writing faculty of George Mason University's MFA Program. Four of the topics he has addressed in his public-speaking engagements have a particular bearing on his concerns as an author. These are: "Writing for the Ear," "Imagining Ancestry," "Fathers and Fictions," and "The Elusive Matter of Form." In varying degrees these work together for Cheuse in his longer works, enabling him to be seen as an experimental, widely ranging littérateur of enormous power and troubling vision.

Cheuse's first novel, *The Bohemians: John Reed and His Friends,* is dedicated as follows: "For Fathers and Sons—Phil and Josh." Phil, Cheuse's father, died shortly after *The Bohemians* was written; Josh is Cheuse's teenage son by his first wife. Considering its emotional impact and the way its historic characters are made to come alive for the reader, *The Bohemians* is perhaps Cheuse's most noteworthy work of fiction. It is an imaginative re-creation of the life of America's premier communist, wherein Cheuse blurs the line between documentary journalism and action-packed adventure fiction while making use of the personal memoir. Reed was a polemical journalist fiercely opposed to America's entering World War I, yet he was committed to overthrowing the capitalist system and replacing it with a radical redistribution of power such as that envisioned by the Bolshevik faction of the American Communist Party.

Though Cheuse does not cite reference sources for his detailed "life" of this controversial figure, he seems to capture Reed's language, thereby enabling the reader to "hear" the fervent, irrepressible Reed in his comings and goings with associates on all levels of familiarity.

From childhood in Oregon to death from typhus in a Moscow hospital, Reed's life is played out in a largely first-person narrative pattern enriched through the inclusion of a postscript memoir by his wife, Louise Bryant, poetic inserts, a galaxy of important figures in Reed's life—each seeming to speak and act in propria persona—and a scattering of documentary details, real or imagined. Fascinating as are the occasional appearances of, among others, Lincoln Steffens, Max Eastman, Walter Lippmann, and Woodrow Wilson, Reed's stormy, sometimes tender, relationship with Louise Bryant makes an indelible impression on the reader. (Complicating their relationship was Reed's involvement with Edna St. Vincent Millay and Louise's with Eugene O' Neill.) Problematical as some of Cheuse's dramatic re-creations of Reed's personal history may appear, the live-voice dynamic of the supporting cast of *The Bohemians* lends plausibility to the book.

Hardly a novel in the literal sense, because it is not a fictional narrative, *Fall Out of Heaven: An Autobiographical Journey* integrates autobiographical episodes in Cheuse's life with an autobiographical manuscript left by his late father, a Russian immigrant and former captain and fighter pilot in the Soviet air force. The double-helix form of this experimental narrative, representing a heartfelt tribute to the parent with whom Cheuse had long had a tempestuous relationship, was foreshadowed in *The Bohemians,* written about six years before *Fall Out of Heaven.* Near the end of his life, John Reed tells his wife that he recently began "a novel in the form of a memoir" and then adds, "Or is it a memoir in the form of a novel? . . . Well, what the hell, to hell with form! Leave that to the bourgeois artistes!" The Alan Cheuse portion of *Fall Out of Heaven* is based on a sentimental journey Cheuse took with son Josh to the Far East in the mid-1980s. That journey in turn was based on a strange inner voice Alan Cheuse felt he had heard at his father's funeral almost four years earlier. It seemed to come from his father, directing Alan to go to Khiva. "Take your own son and go to Khiva, that little desert outpost in Uzbekistan where I spent my best youth, and I'll meet you there, and we'll see what happens next." Another unnatural visitation is recorded in *Fall Out of Heaven.* The day after Cheuse's friend, John Gardner (fiction writer, medievalist, academic), died in a motorcycle accident in 1982, he appeared to Cheuse in a vision and told him plainly to keep on working. This occurrence took place on the following day as well.

Cheuse's next novel, *The Grandmothers' Club,* is more of an "imagined" work—though still a reconstruction from a real-life story—than *The Bohemians.* It grew, he explains in an author's note, out of a *New York Times* news item he had read in the late 1970s, when he was beginning to write *The Bohemians.* "The president and CEO of United Brands," which had started out early in the 1800s "trading New England ice for Central American fruit, had jumped from a window high atop the Pan-Am building in midtown Manhattan," because of a "financial scandal, involving, among other things, bribery of high Latin government officials." He had begun "as a rabbinical student;" his most recent position, before entering "the world of corporate finance, had been assistant rabbi" in a Long Island synagogue. However, the central feature of this demanding novel is not the tarnished career of Manny Bloch the self-destructing rabbi but grandmother Minnie Bloch's narrative voice, shaping and projecting more than a mere saga of her anti-hero son. Minnie is a kind of tribal storyteller, creating a world of cultural experience behind Manny and his troubled family: for example, now a song title ("Mood Indigo," "Light My Fire"), now a commercial-history note on the development of the banana trade. Although some of the dialogue in *The Bohemians* (Lou Bryant and John Reed before his death, discussing their love and his writing achievement) suggests a parody of Hemingway at his weakest, the vocalized brooding sensibility of Minnie Bloch now and then evokes the powerful sweep and commanding presence of the overseeing narrator of Joyce's *Ulysses.*

As in *Fall Out of Heaven,* in *The Grandmothers' Club* there are also secret messages from beyond the realm of ordinary human experience. Manny Bloch's life has been permanently affected by the tragedy, when he was eight years old, of his father's death in a street accident. From time to time he senses that his dead father is delivering messages to him through the beak of a mysterious bird. At a crucial point in his life, when he finds himself wondering why he is going to the Temple on the High Holy Days, the experience of the oracle-bird's arrival is overwhelming and he falls to the ground. Then Manny hears his father's mandate: He must do what he must do, he must go where he must go. His father adds, "Midway in this life, a point I never reached, you must take a new road." Manny thereupon leaves the rabbinate so that he can enter his wife's family's shipping business, and he later becomes a powerful commercial entrepreneur. Manny's suicide, as described poetically by his super-sensitive, unusually articulate mother, provides what is perhaps the most beautifully written passage in the entire novel. In the end it is Manny's long-dead father who dominates Manny's life course and who thereby also exercises an indirectly damaging influence on two other members of Manny's star-crossed family, his wife and daughter.

Cheuse's latest novel, *The Light Possessed,* reveals a particular artistic and visual trait that he shared with the poet Emily Dickinson, a sensitivity to light. For example, in *The Grandmothers' Club,* Minnie Bloch tells about one of Manny's bird-visitations. The bird calls Manny's name, "and if sound can have a light, it's a bright light in the middle of the darkness that surrounds him, like a burning bush in a dark meadow, or a star against a black field of velvet, like that, all of the sunlight that was present a moment before condensed into the sound." Light is of much greater importance in the subsequent novel, which deals with 20th-century American art and one of our greatest artists. Cheuse offers us a fictionalized career study of Georgia O' Keeffe (here called Ava Boldin) against the background of her husband, Alfred Stieglitz (Albert Stigmar in the novel), numerous relatives, and fellow artists. One real-life character appears in propria persona: Stanley Edgar Hyman, Bennington College professor, literary critic, and free-living man-about-town.

Again in this novel there is the figure of the unnatural visitant. This time it is Eve, Ava's twin, who died at birth. When Ava was very young, she claimed that Eve appeared to her secretly, giving her information about future happenings. At the end of the book, it is this dead infant who has the last word, as she asks her sister (now so widely renowned for the use she has made of light in her scenes of the New Mexico desert) to clear up certain questions for her before she awakens from her dream. She wants to be shown, Eve pleads, "if color has a sound and how light creates music. And if the shape of things takes on a shade, visible near darkness . . . and . . . if light is the old metaphor for infinity, and . . . if color is light given in terms of the world." *The Light Possessed,* which contains a story line more difficult to follow than that of *The Grandmothers' Club,* exhibits to a fault three major features of the modernist mode in fiction: stream-of-consciousness narrative, jumbled

plot sequences, and multi-vocal rendition, as in for example, William Faulkner's *The Sound and the Fury.*

A number of Cheuse's short stories, originally appearing in various literary and mass-market magazines, were collected in *Candace and Other Stories;* all but the title story were published again in a collection titled *The Tennessee Waltz and Other Stories.* Although Cheuse clearly prefers to write novel-length, biographically based fiction (currently [1995] he is at work on another historical/biographical novel), he appears to favor "short takes," i.e., thin slices of life, as alternative fiction forms. Here his writing suggests somewhat the minimalist mode of certain stories by the late Raymond Carver. There is an underlying sadness in these tales of unhappy families and family members, each unhappy in a different way. Nashville and country music feature prominently in this assortment. Cheuse's real power as a writer of fiction is most pronounced when he has long pondered, perhaps brooded, over a complicated individual caught up in a formidable struggle with self and ominous circumstances. And though Cheuse in his fiction reflects touches of various contemporaneous authors, he is also capable of producing passages of rare poetic beauty as well as narratives with memorable personal voices, which in a sense sets him apart from some of the better known commercial writers with literary aspirations.

—Samuel I. Bellman

CHINODYA, Shimmer

Nationality: Zimbabwean. **Born:** Gweru, Zimbabwe, 30 May 1957. **Education:** University of Zimbabwe, B.A. (honors) in English 1979; University of Iowa, M.A. in creative writing 1985. **Family:** Married; two daughters and one son. **Career:** High school teacher, 1981-81; curriculum developer, 1983-87; editor, publisher and author, 1988-94; Dana Visiting Professor of creative writing, St. Lawrence University, 1995-96. **Awards:** Commonwealth Writers prize (African region), 1990, for *Harvest of Thorns;* Zimbabwe Writers award, 1990; Ragdale fellowship, Lake Forest, 1993. **Address:** 39 Lorraine Drive, Bluff Hill, P.O. Mabelreign, Harare, Zimbabwe.

PUBLICATIONS

Novels

Dew in the Morning. Gweru, Zimbabwe, Mambo Press, 1982.
Farai's Girls. Harare, Zimbabwe, College Press, 1984.
Child of War. Harare, Zimbabwe, College Press, n.d.
Harvest of Thorns. Harare, Zimbabwe, Baobab, 1989; Portsmouth, New Hampshire, Heinemann, 1991.

Other

Classroom Plays for Primary Schools. Harare, Longman Zimbabwe, 1986.
Traditional Tales of Zimbabwe, Books 1-6. Harare, Longman Zimbabwe, 1989.
Poems for Primary Schools. Harare, Longman Zimbabwe, 1990.

*

Shimmer Chinodya comments:
Read voraciously while still young!

*   *   *

This was your initiation on a rock, in the forests of hoary mountains, with a girl who smelt of blue soap and beans and gunpowder, who wore denims and boots and carried a bazooka on her back; a girl who cut her hair short like a boy and whose fingers were stone-stiff from hauling crates of ammo. You were surprised when she said "Thank you, I needed it," never having thought a woman could say that and you tried to say something nice back, wondering if she knew this was your first time. . . . You had left her there with your seed in her and would she have your child? . . . And what if she had your child? Would she deliver here in the camp? Would she carry the child in a strap together with her bazooka? Would the child look like you?

Thus muses Benjamin Tichafa, a.k.a. Pasi NemaSellout, the central character of Shimmer Chinodya's *Harvest of Thorns*, after he loses his virginity to a female comrade in a guerrilla camp. The passage encapsulates the central markers of Chinodya's writing: his concern for children, also demonstrated by his children's works; his profound humanism; and his sharp awareness that the personal and specific make up the broad political picture, giving it both its tragedy and its hope.

Critics have referred to *Harvest of Thorns* as a "coming-of-age" story; others emphasize its politics, reading it as a tale of Zimbabwe's fight for independence. It is these, and more. Chinodya demonstrates that unless people die—as some do, here—they must come of age, inescapably. What that means will be determined by idiosyncratic politics, in conjunction with the oral communication and awareness of community that alone can, in this novel, preserve humanity. Those communal values shape the novel's structure and content, imbuing it with a revolutionary vision belied by its straightforward and engaging style. Postmodern fireworks of language do not interrupt the story here; no narrator self-importantly trumpets about the difficulties of writing. Instead, we are caught up in the story of a young man—but one told in a way not imagined by the traditional bildungsroman.

Harvest of Thorns opens with Benjamin's return to his mother and the brother he accidentally crippled in childhood. After a few days of welcome, tensions grow, and his mother tells Benjamin's young foreign wife, whom he has brought home, that she must know who Benjamin truly is. Intriguingly, however, to show who Benjamin is requires circling into the past—this young man, as all of us, does not come from a vacuum. So, Chinodya recounts the youth of Shamiso, Benjamin's mother. We watch her attract the intentions of Clopas Tichafa, we see their courtship and wedding, and we follow their difficulty conceiving a child—which leads them to consult a doctor and a witch doctor and to attribute their final success to the Church of the Holy Spirit.

This early sequence shows the range of options to which people will turn in their quests. Beliefs, whether gained accidentally or not, determine the family structures in which children are brought up and in turn shape their reactions and their future paths. Through a wholly unpredictable path, his fanatical religious upbringing leads Benjamin to become the guerrilla Pasi NemaSellout.

Chinodya's treatment of the struggle again subverts expectations; battles and atrocities occur but are not central. Rather than glorifying young people fighting for a cause, Chinodya's narrative voice becomes distanced, describing day-to-day concerns. The tedium of finding food, staying dry, and getting enough sleep interweaves with struggles against the group's leader and telling stories around fires to explain the struggle to villagers. But the cause, even death, attract less thought than another interest: sex. Flirtation ends in a sudden, deadly raid by the opposing troops; or in tribal custom and virginity; or in orders to decamp.

Benjamin does grow up: by returning home, reversing the blind movement outward that led him to fight. The struggle, won at a heavy cost, has changed little in everyday life. When Benjamin embraces his place as a son, a brother, a husband, and a father, the novel questions the obstacles he had to overcome. Perhaps, Chinodya suggests, fewer causes and greater human compassion—between men and women, parents and children, neighbors and outsiders—offers the only hope for true political change.

—Victoria Carchidi

CLARK, Eleanor

Nationality: American. **Born:** Los Angeles, California, 6 July 1913; grew up in Roxbury, Connecticut. **Education:** Vassar College, Poughkeepsie, New York, B.A. 1934. **Family:** Married the writer Robert Penn Warren in 1952 (died 1989); one son and one daughter. **Career:** Editorial staff member, W.W. Norton, publishers, New York, 1936-39. Worked for the United States Office of Strategic Services, Washington, D.C., 1943-45. **Awards:** American Academy grant, 1947; Guggenheim fellowship, 1947, 1949; National Book award, for non-fiction, 1965. **Member:** American Academy. **Address:** 2495 Redding Road, Fairfield, Connecticut 06430, U.S.A.

PUBLICATIONS

Novels

The Bitter Box. New York, Doubleday, 1946; London, Joseph, 1947.
Baldur's Gate. New York, Pantheon, 1970.
Gloria Mundi. New York, Pantheon, 1979.
Camping Out. New York, Putnam, 1986.

Short Stories

Dr. Heart: A Novella and Other Stories. New York, Pantheon, 1974.

Uncollected Short Story

"Fortress and Raggedy Ann," in *Georgia Review* (Athens), Spring 1982.

Other

Rome and a Villa. New York, Doubleday, 1952; London, Joseph, 1953; revised edition, New York, Pantheon, 1975; Henley on Thames, Ellis, 1976.

The Song of Roland (for children). New York, Random House, 1960; London, Muller, 1962.

The Oysters of Locmariaquer. New York, Pantheon, 1964; London, Secker and Warburg, 1965.

Eyes, Etc.: A Memoir. New York, Pantheon, 1977; London, Collins, 1978.

Tamrart: 13 Days in the Sahara. Winston-Salem, North Carolina, Palaemon Press, 1984.

Editor, with Horace Gregory, *New Letters in America.* New York, Norton, 1937.

Translator, *The Dark Wedding,* by Ramón Sender. New York, Doubleday, 1943; London, Grey Walls Press, 1948.

*

Critical Studies: "Eleanor Clark Issue" of *New England Review* (Hanover, New Hampshire), Winter 1979.

Eleanor Clark comments:

(1972) I do not feel it is wise or in most cases helpful for writers to analyze their own work. In my case, I find it impossible, except to remark that, concerning impulse, motive and kind of personal involvement, I find no clear line of demarcation between my novels and nonfiction books (*Rome* and *Oysters*). This does not of course refer to essays—a different job altogether.

Can a woman be a good writer (artist) and a good mother? I have no idea. Are the two in conflict? Of course—so is art and everything else. Do I love and value my two children above my books? Certainly. Would I have stopped writing altogether if necessary for the children's happiness? Well, yes, but it would perhaps not have been physically possible—in the sense that one eats when hungry and scratches when itching—and with a little sleight-of-hand it was never quite necessary for too fatally long at a time. However, these facts do relate to *Baldur's Gate* having been written over a period of many years. It was in gestation, with false starts, long before that, but the home-town scene (the usual first novel) was too close. I disposed of it when young in a story, "Hurry, Hurry," found a built-in distance for my first published novel, *The Bitter Box,* and came to the perspective for the original one only years later, possibly through the fact of having children.

*   *   *

Twenty-four years separate Eleanor Clark's first novel and her second and in comparison one gives the impression of looking backward and the other of looking forward. *The Bitter Box,* though published in 1946, reflects the leftist social ferment of the 1930s. The novel's center is a timid, punctilious bank clerk named Mr. Temple who in his teller's cage serves efficiently, almost worshipfully, the symbol of capitalism until driven by a sense of oppression to search out and embrace another god vaguely defined as "the party," the official organ of which is the *Word.* His ultimate realization that both gods are false and corrupt is accompanied by an awakening to the redemptive influences of suffering and love. By painfully relinquishing the safety of a life of order and obedience he gradually learns to trust and to give of himself in concern for others. This theme of surrender into life, present also in *Baldur's Gate,* fails of effect in *The Bitter Box* largely because of a patronizing, detached point of view which creates a curiously remote and im-

probable hero whose political activism seems arbitrary rather than necessary and probable.

Baldur's Gate, an ambitious work rich in symbol and allusion, deals with a wealth of themes: the preservation of tradition, the search for values, the function of art, commercialism, ecology, among others. Eva Buckingham Hines relates the events in a complex style—disordered chronology, internal monologue, depth analysis—which complements her personal tortuous course out of the often painful and sometimes alluring memories of the past toward acceptance of the present and courage for the future. The memories derive from growing up in Jordan, an old Connecticut town rich in tradition and in the history of human weakness and error. And though she seems to be committed to the future, having married Lucas Hines and borne a son, in reality she is hostage to her past: to the pain and frustration of an indifferent and alcoholic mother, an ineffectual father, a corrupt brother, a once proud family socially disgraced, and to the memory of a love betrayed.

Her futile attempt to renew this early love affair with Jack Pryden and thus redeem the past is the motivating force behind many of the events, but it is the presence of the 70-year-old sculptor, Baldur Blake (the name suggesting his role as demigod and mystic), which lifts the novel above this rather trivial love affair. Having himself fought the battle of disillusionment with the heritage of the past, he returns to vision and creativity, like a fertility god in spring, revitalizing the whole community with promise that the future which destroys the past can also generate new beauty and harmony.

In the closing scene as Eva stands in the falling snow viewing the town dump, symbol of waste but also of change, the fundamental law of things, she reflects that his message had been "not to kid ourselves, about what art, home, love, Jordan, anything could ever mean to us again, and yet to keep capable of love, of work, of hope." The dream of a new community fails of realization, but the vision of the gate model Baldur never lived to complete remains, the "imitation of some large serenity always in the act of rising out of torment." The novel captures that torment and the courage to master it, but more frequently in the rhetoric than in the characters and situations. In the final analysis the plot and characters seem not quite the equal of the novel's deep philosophical vision.

—Dale K. Doepke

CLARKE, Arthur C(harles)

Nationality: British. **Born:** Minehead, Somerset, 16 December 1917. **Education:** Huish's Grammar School, Taunton, Somerset, 1927-36; King's College, London, 1946-48, B.Sc. (honours) in physics and mathematics 1948. **Military Service:** Flight Lieutenant in the Royal Air Force, 1941-46; served as Radar Instructor, and Technical Officer on the first Ground Controlled Approach radar; originated proposal for use of satellites for communications, 1945. **Family:** Married Marilyn Mayfield in 1954 (divorced 1964). **Career:** Assistant auditor, Exchequer and Audit Department, London, 1936-41; assistant editor, *Physics Abstracts,* London, 1949-50; since 1954, engaged in underwater exploration and photography of the Great Barrier Reef of Australia and the coast of Sri Lanka. Director, Rocket Publishing, London, Underwater Safaris, Colombo, and the Spaceward Corporation, New York. Has made numerous radio and television appearances (most recently as presenter of the television series *Arthur C. Clarke's Mysterious World,* 1980, and *World of Strange Powers,* 1985), and has lectured widely in Britain and the United States; commentator, for CBS-TV, on lunar flights of Apollo 11, 12 and 15; Vikram Sarabhai Professor, Physical Research Laboratory, Ahmedabad, India, 1980. **Awards:** International Fantasy award, 1952; Hugo award, 1956, 1969 (for screenplay), 1974, 1980; Unesco Kalinga prize, 1961; Boys' Clubs of America award, 1961; Franklin Institute Ballantine medal, 1963; Aviation-Space Writers Association Ball award, 1965; American Association for the Advancement of Science-Westinghouse Science Writing award, 1969; *Playboy* award, 1971; Nebula award, 1972, 1973, 1979; Jupiter award, 1973; John W. Campbell Memorial award, 1974; American Institute of Aeronautics and Astronautics award, 1974; Boston Museum of Science Washburn award, 1977; Marconi fellowship, 1982; Science Fiction Writers of America Grand Master award, 1986; Vidya Jyothi medal, 1986; International Science Policy Foundation medal, 1992; Lord Perry award, 1992. D.Sc.: Beaver College, Glenside, Pennsylvania, 1971. D.Litt.: University of Liverpool, 1995. Chair, British Interplanetary Society, 1946-47, 1950-53. Guest of Honor, World Science Fiction Convention, 1956. Fellow, Royal Astronomical Society; Fellow, King's College, London, 1977; Chancellor, University of Moratuwa, Sri Lanka, since 1979. C.B.E. (Commander, Order of the British Empire), 1989. **Agent:** David Higham Associates Ltd., 5-8 Lower John Street, London W1R 4HA, England; or, Scouil, Chichak, Galen Literary Agency, 381 Park Avenue, New York, New York 10016, U.S.A. **Address:** 25 Barnes Place, Colombo 7, Sri Lanka; or, Dene Court, Bishop's Lydeard, Taunton, Somerset TA4 3LT, England.

Publications

Novels

Prelude to Space. New York, Galaxy, 1951; London, Sidgwick and Jackson, 1953; as *Master of Space,* New York, Lancer 1961; as *The Space Dreamers,* Lancer, 1969.

The Sands of Mars. London, Sidgwick and Jackson, 1951; New York, Gnome Press, 1952.

Against the Fall of Night. New York, Gnome Press, 1953; revised edition, as *The City and the Stars,* London, Muller, and New York, Harcourt Brace, 1956.

Childhood's End. New York, Ballantine, 1953; London, Sidgwick and Jackson, 1954.

Earthlight. London, Muller, and New York, Ballantine, 1955.

The Deep Range. New York, Harcourt Brace, and London, Muller, 1957.

Across the Sea of Stars (omnibus). New York, Harcourt Brace, 1959.

A Fall of Moondust. London, Gollancz, and New York, Harcourt Brace, 1961.

From the Oceans, From the Stars (omnibus). New York, Harcourt Brace, 1962.

Glide Path. New York, Harcourt Brace, 1963; London, Sidgwick and Jackson, 1969.

An Arthur C. Clarke Omnibus [and *Second Omnibus*]. London, Sidgwick and Jackson, 2 vols., 1965-68.

Prelude to Mars (omnibus). New York, Harcourt Brace, 1965.

2001: A Space Odyssey (novelization of screenplay). New York, New American Library, and London, Hutchinson, 1968.

The Lion of Comarre, and Against the Fall of Night. New York, Harcourt Brace, 1968; London, Gollancz, 1970.

Rendezvous with Rama. London, Gollancz, and New York, Harcourt Brace, 1973.

Imperial Earth. London, Gollancz, 1975; revised edition, New York, Harcourt Brace, 1976.

The Fountains of Paradise. London, Gollancz, and New York, Harcourt Brace, 1979.

2010: Odyssey Two. New York, Ballantine, and London, Granada, 1982.

The Songs of Distant Earth. London, Grafton, and New York, Ballantine, 1986.

2061: Odyssey Three. New York, Ballantine, and London, Grafton, 1988.

Cradle, with Gentry Lee. London, Gollancz, and New York, Warner, 1988.

Rama II, with Gentry Lee. London, Gollancz, and New York, Bantam, 1989.

Beyond the Fall of Night, with Gregory Benford. New York, Putnam, 1990; with *Against the Fall of Night,* London, Gollancz, 1991.

The Ghost from the Grand Banks. New York, Bantam, and London, Gollancz, 1990.

The Garden of Rama, with Gentry Lee. London, Gollancz, and New York, Bantam, 1991.

Rama Revealed, with Gentry Lee. London, Gollancz, and New York, Bantam, 1993.

The Hammer of God. London, Gollancz, and New York, Bantam, 1993.

Short Stories

Expedition to Earth. New York, Ballantine, 1953; London, Sidgwick and Jackson, 1954.

Reach for Tomorrow. New York, Ballantine, 1956; London, Gollancz, 1962.

Tales from the White Hart. New York, Ballantine, 1957; London, Sidgwick and Jackson, 1972.

The Other Side of the Sky. New York, Harcourt Brace, 1958; London, Gollancz, 1961.

Tales of Ten Worlds. New York, Harcourt Brace, 1962; London, Gollancz, 1963.

The Nine Billion Names of God: The Best Short Stories of Arthur C. Clarke. New York, Harcourt Brace, 1967.

The Wind from the Sun: Stories of the Space Age. New York, Harcourt Brace, and London, Gollancz, 1972.

Of Time and Stars: The Worlds of Arthur C. Clarke. London, Gollancz, 1972.

The Best of Arthur C. Clarke 1937-1971, edited by Angus Wells. London Sidgwick and Jackson, 1973.

The Sentinel. New York, Berkley, 1983; London, Panther, 1985.

A Meeting with Medusa, with *Green Mars,* by Kim Stanley Robinson. New York, Tor, 1988.

Tales from Planet Earth. London, Century, 1989; New York, Bantam, 1990.

Play

Screenplay: *2001: A Space Odyssey,* with Stanley Kubrick, 1968.

Other

Interplanetary Flight: An Introduction to Astronautics. London, Temple Press, 1950; New York, Harper, 1951; revised edition, 1960.

The Exploration of Space. London, Temple Press, and New York, Harper, 1951; revised edition, 1959.

Islands in the Sky (for children). London, Sidgwick and Jackson, and Philadelphia, Winston, 1952.

The Young Traveller in Space (for children). London, Phoenix House, 1954; as *Going into Space,* New York, Harper, 1954; as *The Scottie Book of Space Travel,* London, Transworld, 1957; revised edition, with Robert Silverberg, as *Into Space,* New York, Harper, 1971.

The Exploration of the Moon. London, Muller, 1954; New York, Harper, 1955.

The Coast of Coral. London, Muller, and New York, Harper, 1956.

The Making of a Moon: The Story of the Earth Satellite Program. London, Muller, and New York, Harper, 1957; revised edition, Harper, 1958.

The Reefs of Taprobane: Underwater Adventures Around Ceylon. London, Muller, and New York, Harper, 1957.

Voice Across the Sea. London, Muller, 1958; New York, Harper, 1959; revised edition, London, Mitchell Beazley, and Harper, 1974.

Boy Beneath the Sea (for children). New York, Harper, 1958.

The Challenge of the Spaceship: Previews of Tomorrow's World. New York, Harper, 1959; London, Muller, 1960.

The First Five Fathoms: A Guide to Underwater Adventure. New York, Harper, 1960.

The Challenge of the Sea. New York, Holt Rinehart, 1960; London, Muller, 1961.

Indian Ocean Adventure. New York, Harper, 1961; London, Barker, 1962.

Profiles of the Future: An Enquiry into the Limits of the Possible. London, Gollancz, 1962; New York, Harper, 1963; revised edition, Harper, 1973; Gollancz, 1974, 1982; New York, Holt Rinehart, 1984.

Dolphin Island (for children). New York, Holt Rinehart, and London, Gollancz, 1963.

The Treasure of the Great Reef. London, Barker, and New York, Harper, 1964; revised edition, New York, Ballantine, 1974.

Indian Ocean Treasure, with Mike Wilson. New York, Harper, 1964; London, Sidgwick and Jackson, 1972.

Man and Space, with the editors of *Life.* New York, Time, 1964.

Voices from the Sky: Previews of the Coming Space Age. New York, Harper, 1965; London, Gollancz, 1966.

The Promise of Space. New York, Harper, and London, Hodder and Stoughton, 1968.

First on the Moon, with the astronauts. London, Joseph, and Boston, Little Brown, 1970.

Report on the Planet Three and Other Speculations. London, Gollancz, and New York, Harper, 1972.

The Lost Worlds of 2001. New York, New American Library, and London, Sidgwick and Jackson, 1972.

Beyond Jupiter: The Worlds of Tomorrow, with Chesley Bonestell. Boston, Little Brown, 1972.

Technology and the Frontiers of Knowledge (lectures), with others. New York, Doubleday, 1973.

The View from Serendip (on Sri Lanka). New York, Random House, 1977; London, Gollancz, 1978.

1984: Spring: A Choice of Futures. New York, Ballantine, and London, Granada, 1984.

Ascent to Orbit: A Scientific Autobiography: The Technical Writings of Arthur C. Clarke. New York and Chichester, Sussex, Wiley, 1984.

The Odyssey File, with Peter Hyams. New York, Ballantine, and London, Granada, 1985.

Astounding Days: A Science-Fictional Autobiography. London, Gollancz, 1989; New York, Bantam, 1990.

How the World Was One: Beyond the Global Village. London, Gollancz, and New York, Bantam, 1992.

By Space Possessed: Essays on the Exploration of Space. London, Gollancz, 1993.

The Snows of Olympus: A Garden on Mars. London, Gollancz, 1994.

Editor, *Time Probe: Sciences in Science Fiction.* New York, Delacorte Press, 1966; London, Gollancz, 1967.

Editor, *The Coming of the Space Age: Famous Accounts of Man's Probing of the Universe.* London, Gollancz, and New York, Meredith, 1967.

Editor, with George Proctor, *The Science Fiction Hall of Fame 3: The Nebula Winners 1965-1969.* New York, Avon, 1982.

Editor, *July 20, 2019: A Day in the Life of the 21st Century.* New York, Macmillan, 1986; London, Grafton, 1987.

*

Bibliography: *Arthur C. Clarke: A Primary and Secondary Bibliography* by David N. Samuelson, Boston, Hall, 1984.

Manuscript Collection: Mugar Memorial Library, Boston University.

Critical Studies: "Out of the Ego Chamber" by Jeremy Bernstein, in *New Yorker,* 9 August 1969; *Arthur C. Clarke* edited by Joseph D. Olander and Martin H. Greenberg, New York, Taplinger, and Edinburgh, Harris, 1977; *The Space Odysseys of Arthur C. Clarke* by George Edgar Slusser, San Bernardino, California, Borgo Press, 1978; *Arthur C. Clarke* (includes bibliography) by Eric S. Rabkin, West Linn, Oregon, Starmont House, 1979, revised edition, 1980; *Against the Night, The Stars: The Science Fiction of Arthur C. Clarke* by John Hollow, New York, Harcourt Brace, 1983, revised edition, Athens, Ohio University Press-Swallow Press, 1987; *Odyssey: The Authorized Biography of Arthur C. Clarke* by Neil McAleer, Chicago, Contemporary Books, and London, Gollancz, 1992.

Arthur C. Clarke comments:

I regard myself primarily as an entertainer and my ideals are Maugham, Kipling, Wells. My chief aim is the old SF cliché, "The search for wonder." However, I am almost equally interested in style and rhythm, having been much influenced by Tennyson, Swinburne, Housman, and the Georgian poets.

My main themes are exploration (space, sea, time), the position of Man in the hierarchy of the universe, and the effect of contact with other intelligences. The writer who probably had most influence on me was W. Olaf Stapledon (*Last and First Men*).

*   *   *

Arthur C. Clarke writes adventures of the near and far future, in which men seek knowledge and explore new environments. The most notable aspect of his fiction is the perfect welding of the expository passages, containing accurate but clear scientific explanations of how the adventures will sooner or later become possible, to the narrative passages.

Several of the adventures occur at or near the beginnings of exploration of a new environment. *Prelude to Space* fictionalizes what leads up to the first trip to the moon. *Earthlight* depicts the workings of the lunar colony, and *The Sands of Mars* does the same for that planet. *Islands in the Sky* explores the uses of space stations, and *The Deep Range* and *Dolphin Island* explore the uses of the sea, such as whale farming and cooperation with dolphins.

Three of Clarke's novels are primarily religious and philosophical. *Against the Fall of Night,* completed in 1946 and published in 1953, was rewritten as *The City and the Stars.* Diaspar, a city of the remote future, has (to paraphrase a favorite Clarke generalization) a technology so advanced that it cannot be distinguished from magic. But the city is a womb from which none of its citizens dare to escape until one courageous explorer goes on a quest for knowledge of the past, which opens up a new future for his society. In *Childhood's End* alien "Overlords" stop man's development of space travel until man, remade by his own unsuspected psychic powers, rises to a new level of childhood and moves toward the stars. The quest of David Bowman in *2001: A Space Odyssey* transforms him into Star-Child, who will "think of something" to move man up the ladder of evolution.

Clarke does in his stories (such as those collected in *Reach for Tomorrow, The Other Side of the Sky, Tales of Ten Worlds,* and *Tales from the White Hart*) what he does elsewhere—plus some things which he does not do elsewhere. "Breaking Strain," for example, is a study of contrasting personalities in crisis; "Hate" is a moral fable; "Transcience" is a nearly plotless poem written in prose which compares and contrasts three stages of man's existence.

Rendezvous with Rama, about an alien spaceship's mysterious visit to the solar system, is in some ways unique among Clarke's novels in that it allows the mystery to remain unexplained. Astronauts from Earth visit the vast ship, which is apparently now devoid of intelligent life and acting automatically; but they never do discover its origin and purpose. This is in contrast to *2001: A Space Odyssey,* in which the alien purpose is perhaps explained too thoroughly. Clarke's descriptive powers come marvellously to bear on the vast interior of the ship and the strange robotic forms which inhabit it.

What could Clarke do after *2001: A Space Odyssey* and *Rendezvous with Rama?* There is some, perhaps, inevitable, deflation in *Imperial Earth,* a novel about the American Quincentennial in 2276. Clarke assumes an Americanized world—indeed, solar system— after a rather vague "time of troubles." The prestige of the MacKenzie family, derived from centuries of prominence in diplomacy, is more significant than any remaining national power. Duncan MacKenzie's visit to earth from his native Titan fails to provide enough plot to sustain a novel. There are only technological bits and pieces of interest, such as an excursion on the raised ship *The Titanic.*

Clarke's full imaginative powers return with *The Fountains of Paradise,* one of his best novels. Clarke fuses a general technical idea of much interest—the space ladder as an alternative to rocketry—with the spirit of a particular place, a thinly disguised version of his homeland, Sri Lanka. A religious sect has inhabited the site of the space ladder for thousands of years, and Clarke lightly suggests a connection between their ancient presence and the scientific innovation which threatens them. The first sequel to *2001,* called *2010,* is disappointing. Although the book does contain some arresting ideas and images, the plot lacks unity and the style is prosaic.

Although Clarke's style can be wordy and pedestrian at times (as when he overexplains), at other times it is sparse and poetic.

His typical mode of narration—focusing all data through a first or second-person persona—generally facilitates his effective presentation of the concrete.

The universe challenges us, Clarke believes, by its inexhaustible beauty, strangeness, and richness. Unless we rise to the challenge by keeping our curiosity and extending our environment, both our art and our science will stagnate. The scientist is as likely to lack the necessary vision and spirit of adventure as the humanist; the romantic maverick is Clarke's protagonist. The eternal renewal of childhood is a never-ending expansion into the unknown is Clarke's theme.

—Curtis C. Smith

CLARKE, Austin C(hesterfield)

Nationality: Barbadian. **Born:** Barbados, 26 July 1934. **Education:** Combermere Boys' School, Barbados; Harrison's College, Barbados; Trinity College, University of Toronto. **Family:** Married Betty Joyce Reynolds in 1957; three children. **Career:** Reporter in Timmins and Kirkland Lake, Ontario, 1959-60; since 1963, freelance producer and broadcaster, Canadian Broadcasting Corporation, Toronto; scriptwriter, Educational Television, Toronto; Ziskind Professor of Literature, Brandeis University, Waltham, Massachusetts, 1968-69; Hoyt Fellow, 1968, and visiting lecturer, 1969, 1970, Yale University, New Haven, Connecticut; fellow, Indiana University School of Letters, Bloomington, 1969; Margaret Bundy Scott Visiting Professor of Literature, Williams College, Williamstown, Massachusetts, 1971; lecturer, Duke University, Durham, North Carolina, 1971-72; visiting professor, University of Texas, Austin, 1973-74; cultural and press attaché, Embassy of Barbados, Washington, D.C., 1974-76; writer-in-residence, Concordia University, Montreal, 1977. General manager, Caribbean Broadcasting Corporation, St. Michael, Barbados, 1975-76. Member, Board of Trustees, Rhode Island School of Design, Providence, 1970-75; vice-chair, Ontario Board of Censors, 1983-85. Since 1988 member, Immigration and Refugee Board of Canada. **Awards:** Belmont Short Story award, 1965; University of Western Ontario President's medal, 1966; Canada Council senior arts fellowship, 1967, 1970, and grant, 1977; Casa de las Americas prize, 1980; Toronto Arts award, for writing, 1993; Toronto Pride Achievement award, for writing, 1995. **Agent:** Phyllis Westberg, Harold Ober Associates, 425 Madison Avenue, New York, New York 10017, U.S.A. **Address:** 62 McGill Street, Toronto, Ontario M5B 1H2, Canada.

PUBLICATIONS

Novels

The Survivors of the Crossing. Toronto, McClelland and Stewart, and London, Heinemann, 1964.
Amongst Thistles and Thorns. Toronto, McClelland and Stewart, and London, Heinemann, 1965.
The Meeting Point. Toronto, Macmillan, and London, Heinemann, 1967; Boston, Little Brown, 1972.
Storm of Fortune. Boston, Little Brown, 1973.

The Bigger Light. Boston, Little Brown, 1975.
The Prime Minister. Toronto, General, 1977; London, Routledge, 1978.
Proud Empires. London, Gollancz, 1986.

Short Stories

When He Was Free and Young and He Used to Wear Silks. Toronto, Anansi, 1971; revised edition, Boston, Little Brown, 1973.
When Women Rule. Toronto, McClelland and Stewart, 1985.
Nine Men Who Laughed. Markham, Ontario, and New York, Penguin, 1986.
In This City. Toronto, Exile Editions, 1992.
There Are No Elders. Toronto, Exile Editions, 1994.

Other

The Confused Bewilderment of Martin Luther King and the Idea of Non-Violence as a Political Tactic. Burlington, Ontario, Watkins, 1968.
Growing Up Stupid under the Union Jack: A Memoir. Toronto, McClelland and Stewart, 1980.
A Passahe Back Home. Toronto, Exile Editions, 1994.

*

Manuscript Collection: McMaster University, Hamilton, Ontario.

Critical Studies: "The West Indian Novel in North America: A Study of Austin Clarke," in *Journal of Commonwealth Literature* (Leeds), July 1970, and *El Dorado and Paradise: Canada and the Caribbean in Austin Clarke's Fiction,* Centre for Social and Humanistic Studies, University of Western Ontario, 1989, both by Lloyd W. Brown; interview with Graeme Gibson, in *Eleven Canadian Novelists,* Toronto, Anansi, 1974; "An Assessment of Austin Clarke, West Indian-Canadian Novelist" by Keith Henry in *CLA Journal* (Atlanta), vol. 29, no. 1, 1985; *Austin C. Clarke: A Biography* by Stella Algoo-Baksh, University of West Indies Press, 1994.

Austin C. Clarke comments:

Whenever I am asked to give a statement about my work I find it difficult to do. All I can say in these situations is that I try to write about a group of people, West Indian immigrants (to Canada), whose life interests me because of the remarkable problems of readjustment, and the other problems of ordinary living. The psychological implications of this kind of life are what make my work interesting and I hope relevant to the larger condition of preservation. The themes are usually those of adjustment, as I have said, but this adjustment is artistically rendered in the inter-relationship of the two predominant groups of which I write: the host Jewish-Anglo Saxon group, and the black group (West Indian and expatriate black American).

*   *   *

Generally the discussion of West Indian fiction tends to focus exclusively on work written in England and the Caribbean. But the growing number of West Indian immigrants in Canada, especially over the last two decades, has given rise to a small but increasingly significant body of West Indian literature in that country. On the

whole, West Indian literature in Canada is dominated by the predictable and familiar themes of exile, but the theme is integrated here with the West Indian's response to Canada's much-touted ideal of a cultural mosaic—the notion that the country is, or ought to be, a harmonious aggregation of distinctive cultures which maintain their distinctiveness while blending with each other to create a diversified cultural whole.

But for West Indians the ideal of a cultural mosaic is not quite as simple as it sounds to the Anglo-Canadians who often espouse it. Given the usual disadvantages of being black in a predominantly white society, West Indians must choose between being integrated into a strange culture—at the cost of their cultural uniqueness and racial integrity—or being so dedicated to maintaining their black, West Indian identity that they risk being cultural and economic outsiders in their adopted homeland. This dilemma, one that is explored by the growing number of writers in Canada, dominates the writings of Austin C. Clarke, unquestionably the major West Indian writer in Canada at this time.

These Canadian issues are not the major concern in his earliest novels, or in his most recent. *The Survivors of the Crossing* and *Amongst Thistles and Thorns* are set in Barbados and they explore the twin evils of colonial self-hatred and Caribbean poverty. *The Prime Minister* is centered on the experiences of a West Indian writer, John Moore, who has returned to Barbados, to a government appointment, after 20 years in Canada. Significantly, Moore does not stay in Barbados: he returns to his Canadian home after discovering, to his mortification, that he no longer has a real place in Barbados.

Moore's experiences can be viewed as a paradigm of West Indians including Clarke himself, now living and writing in Canada. And it is logical enough that the Canadian presence dominates Clarke's fiction as a whole. His first collection of short stories includes works which take a close look at Canada as the West Indians' El Dorado. In "They Heard a Ringing of Bells" a group of West Indians discuss their experiences as immigrants—delighting in the sense of being released from Caribbean poverty while lambasting the hostility and indifference of white Canada to the West Indian presence. "Waiting for the Postman to Knock" is less ambivalent, more openly hostile to the adopted homeland. Enid, the heroine, is one of the most typical and enduring symbols of West Indian life in Canada—the lonely and isolated West Indian domestic servant who feels equally exploited by her white employer and by her West Indian lover (if she is lucky enough to find a lover). For other West Indians in Clarke's short fiction the problems of loneliness are compounded by racial self-hatred, especially in the lives of those who are achieving some degree of economic success at the cost of their racial pride or cultural integrity ("Four Stations in His Circle" and "The Motor Car").

These related themes of loneliness, self-hatred, and cultural exclusion are the main concerns of Clarke's Canadian trilogy, *The Meeting Point, Storm of Fortune,* and *The Bigger Light.* The three works center on the lives of a group of West Indians in Toronto—especially Bernice Leach, her sister Estelle, Boysie Cumberbatch, his wife Dots, and Henry White. *The Meeting Point* concentrates on Bernice's experiences as a maid in the home of the wealthy Burrmann family, and emphasizes the usual themes of sexual loneliness, cultural isolation, and the sense of economic exploitation.

Storm of Fortune shifts the focus to Estelle and her somewhat uneven struggle to gain a toehold in Canada. The novel also traces the failures of Henry White and his subsequent death, and, most important of all, it depicts the gradual emergence of Boysie

Cumberbatch, from shiftless *bon vivant* to ambitious small businessman with his own janitorial company. His success-story is continued in *The Bigger Light* which, despite some uneven writing, remains Clarke's most ambitious novel to date. Having devoted much of the preceding novels to the failures and half-successes in the West Indian community, Clarke concentrates here on a successful man, but one whose economic successes have not protected him from emotional failure (the gradual breakdown of his marriage and his increasing isolation from his less fortunate West Indian friends). And in fact his success as a *Canadian* businessman, in the Anglo-Saxon mould, has had the effect of encouraging a certain snobbery and a marked reserve towards matters of cultural and racial significance. In short he becomes increasingly hostile towards the issue of racial identity.

But in spite of his extreme and increasing isolation in the novel, Boysie is not an entire failure as a human being. His very isolation becomes a catalyst for a certain perceptiveness which allows him to recognize the real nature of his choices and the limitations of the world in which he has chosen to live. And as a consequence he remains the typical Clarke protagonist, one whose failures—economic and moral—are counterbalanced by a persistent ability to perceive their own lives, without self-deception or self-pity, as they really are. Given the persistent hostilities of the world in which they live, this kind of honest self-awareness is the most important quality of all—and Clarke invariably presents and invites judgements on his characters on the basis of their ability to achieve such an awareness.

These themes of isolation and self-conflict have increasingly been integrated with the issue of Canadian society and Canadian identity in Clarke's most recent writing. Canada is no longer a temporary (and deeply resented) resting-place for immigrants with a strong sense of *transience*. Clarke's fictional world, in his second collection of short stories, *When Women Rule,* is firmly located in the much touted Canadian ideal of social mosaic. These are stories about immigrants from Europe (Italians, "displaced" Central and Eastern Europeans), as well as from the Caribbean. They are almost all about middle-aged men whose familiar anxieties about aging, sexual relationships, and socio-economic success are interwoven with pervasive uncertainties about the directions of Canadian society—about the disruptive and challenging presence of "newer" immigrants, urban changes in metropolitan Canada, and the unsettling implications of female equality. And in one story, "Give It a Shot," these fears are shared even by a born-and-bred "Anglo-Canadian." Indeed, it is the central irony of this collection that the very idea of a Canadian mosaic, with its implicit promise of social harmony and individual success, binds Clarke's diverse Canadians together by virtue of its failure, rather than its fulfilment, in their lives. The ebullience and aggressive confidence of a Boysie Cumberbatch have given way to a middle-aged greyness, the newcomer's perpetual sense of youthfulness has been replaced by a depressing, numbing consciousness of death and aging. Canada, and the youthful idealism of its "mosaic" self-image, seem to have aged prematurely, like the anxious men who live and work in the anonymous apartment buildings of Clarke's Toronto.

Finally, it is noteworthy that Clarke's Canadian themes actually re-emphasize the most central, and universal, of all his themes—alienation. In their alienation from society, family, and even from their once-youthful selves, his middle-aged protagonists are the familiar isolates of much 20th-century fiction, ranging—in Clarke's work—from the canefields of Barbados to the chic boutiques and working-class bars of modern Toronto. And by way of emphasiz-

ing Clarke's insistence on the universality of alienation, it is only necessary to move from *When Women Rule* to his autobiography, *Growing Up Stupid under the Union Jack.* The title is no mere whimsy. The imperial reference sets the cultural theme—boyhood and adolescence in colonial Barbados. But the key word here is "stupid." It suggests the naiveté, the stunted self-consciousness of the (well educated) colonial, a culturally ingrained, institutionally enforced ignorance of one's history, society, and ethnicity. And, drawing on the Caribbean connotations of "stupid/tchupidness," it connotes absurdity as well as mental dullness. The colonial situation is the essence of the absurd because it both causes and symbolizes the condition of being isolated from one's self, one's cultural and personal roots. To be a colonial is therefore to be both the unique product of a concrete, specific process—colonial culture— and another archetype of 20th-century alienation. "Tchupidness" is simultaneously a Caribbean condition and a universal experience.

—Lloyd W. Brown

CLEARY, Jon (Stephen)

Nationality: Australian. **Born:** Sydney, New South Wales, 22 November 1917. **Education:** Marist Brothers School, Randwick, New South Wales, 1924-32. **Military Service:** Served in the Australian Imperial Forces in the Middle East and New Guinea, 1940-45. **Family:** Married Joy Lucas in 1946; two daughters (one deceased). **Career:** Prior to 1939 worked as a commerical traveler, bush worker, and commercial artist. Freelance writer, 1945-48; journalist, Government of Australia News and Information Bureau, London, 1948-49, New York, 1949-51; since 1945, full-time writer. Lives in New South Wales. **Awards:** Australian Broadcasting Commission prize, for radio drama, 1944; Australian Section prize, *New York Herald-Tribune* World Short Story Contest, 1950; Crouch gold medal, 1950; Mystery Writers of America Edgar Allan Poe award, 1974. **Agent:** John Farquharson Ltd., 162-168 Regent Street, London W1R 5TB. **Address:** c/o Harper Collins Publishers, 77-85 Fulham Palace Road, London W6 8JB, England.

PUBLICATIONS

Novels

You Can't See Round Corners. New York, Scribner, 1947; London, Eyre and Spottiswoode, 1949.
The Long Shadow. London, Laurie, 1949.
Just Let Me Be. London, Laurie, 1950.
The Sundowners. New York, Scribner, and London, Laurie, 1952.
The Climate of Courage. London, Collins, 1954; as *Naked in the Night,* New York, Popular Library, 1955.
Justin Bayard. London, Collins, 1955; New York, Morrow, 1956; as *Dust in the Sun,* New York, Popular Library, 1957.
The Green Helmet. London, Collins, 1957; New York, Morrow, 1958.
Back of Sunset. New York, Morrow, and London, Collins, 1959.
North from Thursday. London, Collins, 1960; New York, Morrow, 1961.

The Country of Marriage. New York, Morrow, and London, Collins, 1962.
Forests of the Night. New York, Morrow, and London, Collins, 1963.
A Flight of Chariots. New York, Morrow, 1963; London, Collins, 1964.
The Fall of an Eagle. New York, Morrow, 1964; London, Collins, 1965.
The Pulse of Danger. New York, Morrow, and London, Collins, 1966.
The High Commissioner. New York, Morrow, and London, Collins, 1966.
The Long Pursuit. New York, Morrow, and London, Collins, 1967.
Season of Doubt. New York, Morrow, and London, Collins, 1968.
Remember Jack Hoxie. New York, Morrow, and London, Collins, 1969.
Helga's Web. New York, Morrow, and London, Collins, 1970.
The Liberators. New York, Morrow, 1971; as *Mask of the Andes,* London, Collins, 1971.
The Ninth Marquess. New York, Morrow, 1972; as *Man's Estate,* London, Collins, 1972.
Ransom. New York, Morrow, and London, Collins, 1973.
Peter's Pence. New York, Morrow, and London, Collins, 1974.
The Safe House. New York, Morrow, and London, Collins, 1975.
A Sound of Lightning. New York, Morrow, and London, Collins, 1976.
High Road to China. New York, Morrow, and London, Collins, 1977.
Vortex. London Collins, 1977; New York, Morrow, 1978.
The Beaufort Sisters. New York, Morrow, and London, Collins, 1979.
A Very Private War. New York, Morrow, and London, Collins, 1980.
The Golden Sabre. New York, Morrow, and London, Collins, 1981.
The Faraway Drums. London, Collins, 1981; New York, Morrow, 1982.
Spearfield's Daughter. London, Collins, 1982; New York, Morrow, 1983.
The Phoenix Tree. London, Collins, 1984.
The City of Fading Light. London, Collins, 1985; New York, Morrow, 1986.
Dragons at the Party. London, Collins, 1987; New York, Morrow, 1988.
Now and Then, Amen. London, Collins, 1988; New York, Morrow, 1989.
Babylon South. London, Collins, 1989; New York, Morrow, 1990.
Murder Song. London, Collins, and New York, Morrow, 1990.
Pride's Harvest. London, HarperCollins, and New York, Morrow, 1991.
Dark Summer. New York, William Morrow, 1991; London, HarperCollins, 1992.
Bleak Spring. London, HarperCollins, 1993; New York, William Morrow, 1994.
Autumn Maze. London, HarperCollins, 1994.

Short Stories

These Small Glories. Sydney, Angus and Robertson, 1946.
Pillar of Salt. Sydney, Horwitz, 1963.

Plays

Screenplays: *The Siege of Pinchgut,* with Harry Watt and Alexander Baron, 1959; *The Green Helmet,* 1961; *The Sundowners,* 1961; *Sidecar Racers (Sidecar Boys),* 1975.

Radio Play: *Safe Horizon,* 1944.

Television Plays: *Just Let Me Be,* 1957 (England); *Bus Stop* series (2 episodes), 1961 (United States); *Spearfield's Daughter,* from his own novel, 1985 (United States).

*

Jon Cleary comments:

I write primarily to entertain, but, having stated that, I also write to inform about the world we live in. I have no overall theme, unless it is to affirm my belief that Man can, somehow, overcome the effects of his own disasters. I do my best not to be categorised, mainly because I want to keep fresh my enthusiasm for writing; but I'm afraid critics tend to overlook those books (such as *The Country of Marriage* and *The City of Fading Light*) in which I do not write about adventure in exotic places and I'm resigned now to being classified as an "adventure" writer. I have a principle that I will not write about a place I have not visited—this involves me in a lot of travel and is, I hope, opening me up for a book or two of wider scope in the future. I am, I suppose, an old-fashioned story-teller—but I feel that stories, combining action with character, will always be read. I hope so—the job opportunities for out-of-work novelists in their middle seventies are not too numerous.

*   *   *

Jon Cleary first appeared in print with a small collection of short stories titled *These Small Glories,* based on his experiences as an Australian soldier in the Middle East. Almost half a century later, he is the author of some forty books of fiction and possibly the most successful living Australian author. He writes to a meticulous routine and his novels appear in print runs of 25,000 and 300,000 paperback with the paperbacks being reprinted every third year or so.

His first and arguably best novel, *You Can't See Round Corners,* is the graphic documentation of the decline of a smart but hollow young man, Frankie McCoy, who deserts the army into which he has been conscripted and returns to Sydney. The novel captures the ambience of Cleary's beloved city very well and despite the wisecracking dialogue the prose carries overtones of a Graham Greene-ish kind of world-weariness; there is a good deal of Greene's Pinky from *Brighton Rock* in Cleary's hero.

Cleary's early novels are mostly set in Australia or figure Australian protagonists. His first big success came with *The Sundowners,* a novel set in the 1920s that concerns a drover who refuses to settle down and live the stable life his wife desires, and with the 14-year-old son and observer of the conflict. After that came *The Climate of Courage,* which follows a number of soldiers who have returned from fighting in the Middle East and are enjoying a break in Sydney before being sent to New Guinea. The first half of the novel deals with their romantic situations while on leave; the second sees them preparing for action and then involved in a disastrous retreat after being ambushed by the Japanese. The agonizing 35-day retreat over land is graphically portrayed. He followed this with *Justin Bayard;* set in the northwest of Australia it concerns a conscientious policeman who is forced into investigating the murder of his hostess on a distant station in the Kimberleys.

Both novels mingle realism with conventional romantic elements, but from *The Green Helmet* onwards, Cleary's work became both more commercial and more international and topical in tone. He notes rather disarmingly of himself that:

When I first started writing I had two models—Graham Greene and H.E. Bates. Then as time went by I realised I could never be that good. I wasn't aware of the amount of depth one would need to be a really significant writer. But enough people who knew what they were about said I had a natural talent for being a craftsman so I settled for that.

A very sound craftsman is, in fact, what he became. The novels are efficiently plotted, the dialogue is well done, though rather plentiful, and it is obvious that careful research, an element on which Cleary prides himself, goes into the settings. They range from predictable locations such as Sydney and London to the Middle East, India, China, the Andes, and parts of the United States. Most of the novels, though not all, are laced with frequent violent action, whether by men or nature, and the moral dilemmas of the characters are often resolved in a kind of imposed way.

As well as exploring what he calls in the title of one novel "the country of marriage," Cleary also examines in his novels the complex and ambivalent bonding of males, like the two astronauts in the ambitious *A Flight of Chariots,* or the two brothers in *The Green Helmet.* Occasionally, and with varying success, Cleary has moved away from the action novel, into the serious probing of *The Country of Marriage* and its marital and national tensions or in the feebly satirical treatment of the British pop and swingers' scene of the late 1960s, but his most popular novels deal with topical and public issues—the IRA, the Israel-Egypt Six Day War, the outbreak of hostilities between India and China—even if these are usually the background for the romantic entanglings of the protagonists.

Still writing well into his seventies, Cleary in his most recent novels has more or less abandoned international themes to concentrate instead on the figure of the Australian detective Scobie Malone, whom he introduced in *The High Commissioner* with the memorable opening sentence "'We want you to go to London,' said the Premier, 'and arrest the High Commissioner for murder.'" Scobie appears also in *Helga's Web* and *Ransom,* but in Cleary's recent work he has turned to him even more to attack what he sees as elements of corruption in contemporary Australian society. In *Dragons at the Party, Now and Then, Amen,* and *Babylon South,* he uses Scobie Malone, in the classic tradition of detective fiction, as an exemplar of an old-fashioned standard of morality which he sees as disappearing and which he himself embodies in much of his writing. A decent, if rather limited man, Malone lives in the modest Sydney suburb of Randwick, drives a six-year-old car, is a keen family man and has a vague kind of Catholic belief. In *Dark Summer,* the Gulf War is mentioned frequently but only as a background to the domestic theme of the importation of drugs and the romance between Malone's offsider Russ Clements and the general medical officer of the division of forensic medicine, a very attractive young German woman named Romy Keller. A Cleary regular, Jack Aldwych, makes an appearance as a retired gangster but more important is his son Jack Junior and the predatory woman he becomes involved with, Janis Eden, who is nominally a social worker.

Clearly's rather ambivalent attitude towards women emerges again in *Bleak Spring,* in which the displaced romantic energy of the novel resides, not in Clements, but in the growing sexual awareness of the new generation—the Malones' oldest daughter Claire and the young son of a neighbor Olive Rockne, as well as the lesbian relationship between Olive and the brilliant barrister Angela Bodalle. The later novels are written very much to a formula but it is a pleasant one and the writing and plotting are tight and efficient. Cleary has opinions about Australia but always feels that his first obligation is to entertain and hold the attention of the reader. In the words of one reviewer, he is a fine "page turner."

—Laurie Clancy

COBB, William (Sledge)

Nationality: American. **Born:** Eutaw, Alabama, 20 October 1937. **Education:** Livingston State College, 1957-61, B.A. in English 1961; Vanderbilt University, 1961-63, M.A. in English 1963; Breadloaf School of English, Middlebury College, 1967-68. **Family:** Married Loretta Douglas in 1965; one daughter. **Career:** Professor of English, 1963-89, and since 1989, writer-in-residence, both University of Montevallo, Alabama. **Awards:** *Story Magazine*'s Story of the Year Award, 1964; National Endowment for the Arts fellowship, 1978, for creative writing; Atlantic Center for the Arts grant, 1985, for playwriting; Alabama State Council on the Arts grant, 1985, for playwriting, and 1995, for fiction writing. **Agent:** Albert Zuckerman, Writers House, 21 West 26th St., New York, New York 10011, U.S.A. **Address:** 200 Shady Hill Drive, Montevallo, Alabama 35115, U.S.A.

PUBLICATIONS

Novels

Coming of Age at the Y. Columbia, Maryland, Portals Press, 1984.
The Hermit King. Columbia, Maryland, Portals Press, 1987.
A Walk Through Fire. New York, Morrow, 1992.
Harry Reunited. Montgomery, Alabama, Black Belt Press, 1995.

Uncollected Short Stories

"The Year of Judson's Carnival," in *The Sucarnochee Review,* 1961.
"A Single Precious Day," in *Livingston Life,* 1961.
"The Time of the Leaves," in *Granta,* 1963.
"The Stone Soldier," in *Story,* Spring 1964.
"'Suffer Little Children . . . ,'" in *Comment,* Spring 1967.
"The Iron Gates," in *Comment,* Winter 1968.
"The Hunted," in *The Arlington Quarterly,* Summer 1968.
"A Very Proper Resting Place," in *Comment,* Autumn 1969.
"An Encounter with a Friend," in *Inlet,* Spring 1973.
"Walk the Fertile Fields of My Mind," in *Region,* November 1976.
"Somewhere in All This Green," in *Anthology of Bennington Writers,* edited by John Gardner. Delbanco, 1978.
"The Night of the Yellow Butterflies," in *Arete,* Spring 1984.
"Old Wars and New Sorrow," in *The Sucarnochee Review,* Spring 1984.
"Faithful Steward of Thy Bounty." N.p., n.d.
"The Queen of the Silver Dollar," in *Amaryllis,* Spring 1995.

Plays

The Vine and the Olive (produced Livingston, 1961).
Brighthope (produced Montevallo, 1985).
Recovery Room (produced New Orleans, 1986).

Sunday's Child (produced Montevallo, 1986; New York, 1987).
A Place of Spring (produced New York, 1987).
Early Rains (produced New York, 1988).

*

Manuscript Collection: Vanderbilt University Library, Nashville, Tennessee.

William Cobb comments:

A strong influence, perhaps the strongest, on the structure of *Harry Reunited* is Robert Altman's wonderfully funny film *Nashville,* which I saw years ago when it was first released and have since watched countless times on video. I wanted to write a novel about a disparate group of people whose only real connection is something ephemeral—in this case a vague and distant past—whose lives touch others' lives in various ways as they pass through a sequence of events, and who are finally brought together and at the same time separated by one apocalyptic event. I did not, of course, want to retell *Nashville*. It had to be my own story.

Since I had not attended my own high school class's 25th reunion (I was somehow left off the invitation list; I'm still not sure what that says about me!), I was able to pose a hypothetical question to myself: What happens when a man goes back home, into an artificially created environment that attempts to mirror, even recreate, a period in his past, and he has to confront all the demons from that past? As I began to work on the novel all sorts of other nuances and themes began to appear, among them the inevitable facing of middle age, that middle passage in which we invariably begin to look both backward and forward with varying emotional consequences. And as a Southern writer, I've always been fascinated with the presence of the past, of our histories both individually and collectively, and with the notion of the abiding importance of "place," and as I wrote I found those themes emerging as well.

And I quickly fell in love with Bud Squires. Even though it's Harry's book, it is Bud's book, too, because it is he who provides the counterpoint to Harry's semi-comfortable life. It is Bud who is the avenging angel, and I was able, in a way, through my creation of Bud, to exorcise some of the guilt I suspect I still carried around with me for the cruel things I must have done in my own adolescence and which I have conveniently forgotten or blacked out. Bud became a wonderful comic character for me, a man who awakens, in varying degrees and in various startling ways, all the people in the book—and gives a kind of new life to them.

Finally, it was the comic mode that most drove me as I created this book. I very consciously wished to return to the comedy of my first novel, *Coming of Age at the Y,* and I wanted to paint this story with broad strokes. It is full of the kind of humor that I love, subtle and sly and almost slapstick at the same time. A humor of character. I *love* all these characters—Bernie Crease, as ineffectual as he is; Marie, as innocently slutty as she is; the foul-mouthed adolescents in the Sacristy before the Sunday morning service; the little black kid in the fish-net shirt; the three women at the yard sale; Cholly Polly, poor, poor Cholly Polly; Vera Babbs, the "message artist," and on and on; I love them all! That is the gift that comic writing like this gives back to the writer. I got the richest, warmest laughs of all. And I, too,—even though I was not invited—was finally reunited!

*　　*　　*

William Cobb studied with the last of the Fugitives at Vanderbilt, and his fiction is deeply rooted in the southern soil that the Agrarians revered; however, his political views have not always been in keeping with the conservative views of his mentors. Throughout his work there runs a deep respect for spirituality, the importance of family, and the necessity of maintaining a sense of place. Many readers feel that Cobb is at his best as a comic writer (his flair for the profane is certainly apparent); however, his more serious civil-rights novel, *A Walk Through Fire,* brought Cobb national acclaim. Cobb's body of work includes an impressive number of short stories, four novels, and three plays that were produced in New York.

Cobb's first national recognition came in 1964 when his story "The Stone Soldier" won the prestigious *Story Magazine*'s Story of the Year Award and was the title story in that year's collection. "The Stone Soldier" has since been anthologized a number of times. Cobb's flair for the vulgar was apparent in his vivid description of Lyman Sparks, a scalawag who preys on the families of Civil War soldiers. His "sausage legs" and "squiggly eyes" are indelibly printed in the reader's mind.

Another short piece of fiction was recognized as an outstanding contribution in the premier edition of *Arete. A Journal of Sport Literature,* published at San Diego State University. In "The Night of the Yellow Butterflies" the main characters are a minor league baseball coach and his star player, Luke Easter—who may or may not be an apparition. The theme of baseball, with its hopes and dreams—often lost ones—is recurrent in Cobb's work. This particular story weaves the real and the supernatural in a mysterious manner that is quite convincing.

There was some negative response to the bawdy nature of Cobb's satirical novel *Coming of Age at the Y.* Certainly, he took some chances writing a satirical coming-of-age story with a female protagonist (not always considered politically correct as early as the 1970s). However, it is hard to see how any reader could miss the tone of the book from its title. Though some readers felt that his heroine, Delores Lovelady, was a bit passive, most felt that it was a fine attack on sexism—loaded with irony. Lucille Weary, the "worldly" traveler on the Greyhound with Delores, is a wonderfully funny echo of *The Wife of Bath* cramped in a century full of the New South and Shoney's Big Boys.

Cobb's second novel, *The Hermit King,* is a more traditional coming-of-age novel. The main story line here is between two runaway adolescents and an old black man who has lived a hermit's life much like Thoreau's a century earlier in quiet protest to the setting tradition offers him. Cobb's descriptive power is clear.

Cobb also has an ear for dialogue that seemed to lead him inevitably to write for the stage. Horton Foote, who admired his work, suggested that he send a trilogy to H. B. Playwright's Studio in New York. All three plays were done there over a two-year period. Herbert Berghoff said that Cobb's plays are like Foote's plays in that they are domestic plays that deal with quiet human conflicts.

Cobb's third novel, *A Walk Through Fire,* was well received. Both *Library Journal* and *Publisher's Weekly* gave the book a strong endorsement in 1992, its year of publication, and the *West Coast Review of Books* declared it one of the most important books of the year. Caught up in an interracial triangle, the three main characters spin a story filled with passion and strength. The reader can see clearly Cobb's firm sense of place in the following scene, where O. B. Brewster, a white farm implement dealer (and former baseball player), offers to help an old black farmer plow his field:

The black earth turned smoothly on each side of the shiny blade. *I am not too far removed from this soil that I can't feel its message again, in my legs and in my heart.* The loamy earth was damp, and it smelled fecund and rich, fertile as life itself. Tears misted his eyes, one droplet spilling down his cheek, but he could not wipe his face because he held to the handles of the plow.

Reviewers have said that Cobb has undoubtedly had his turn at the plow in that soil. His description of the violence and pain of our collective history during those years is seared into the minds of his readers through the fire imagery that permeates the book. Most importantly, we are reminded that those with intense faith can walk through fire.

Many of Cobb's central characters have a quiet strength that comes from life lived close to the earth. The setting is almost always southern, but the struggles of the human heart transcend the regional boundaries and make valuable commentary on life in the last half of the 20th century in the United States.

—Chris Leigh

COE, Jonathan (Roger)

Nationality: British. **Born:** Birmingham, 19 August 1961. **Education:** Trinity College, Cambridge, 1980-83, B.A. (honours) in English literature; Warwick University, 1983-86, Ph.D in English literature. **Family:** Married Janine Maria McKeown in 1989. **Career:** Loan officer, Barclays Bank; poetry tutor, Warwick University; cabaret pianist; legal proofreader; arts journalist. **Agent:** Tony Peake, Peake Associates, 14 Grafton Crescent, London NW1 8SL, England.

PUBLICATIONS

Novels

The Accidental Woman. London, Buckworth, 1987.
A Touch of Love. London, Buckworth, 1989.
The Dwarves of Death. London, Fourth Estate, 1990.
What a Carve Up!. London, Viking, 1994; as *The Winshaw Legacy,* New York, Knopf, 1995.

Other

Humphrey Bogart: Take It and Like It. London, Bloomsbury, and New York, Grove, 1991.
James Stewart: Leading Man. London, Bloomsbury, and New York, Autumn, 1994.

*

Jonathan Coe comments:

My first impulse to write came from the films and television programmes I watched as a child: British film comedies such as *Kind Hearts and Coronets* and *I'm All Right, Jack,* and TV sitcoms like *Fawlty Towers.* At the same time I have a certain yearning to-wards the high European seriousness of great twentieth-century novelists such as Proust, Mann, and Musil, and my own novels have grown out of the tension between these two very different influences.

Another creative tension arises from my desire to reach a wide readership while remaining convinced that it is the novelist's job to innovate, to take formal risks and always attempt something new. I have never wanted to write historical or escapist fiction: contemporary Britain provides me with my source material.

An off-the-cuff list of all-time favourite writers would include Henry Fielding, Laurence Sterne, Charles Dickens, Dorothy Richardson, Rosamond Lehman, Bohumil Hrabal, Milorad Pavic, Flann O'Brien, and B.S. Johnson.

*   *   *

"Words are awkward sods, and very rarely say what you want them to say"—a thought expressed in Jonathan Coe's first novel, *The Accidental Woman.* The intractability of language seems to pre-occupy the young novelist. This slight tale of a young woman, Maria, to whom things happen, rather than who makes things happen, is haunted by an authorial voice that is never far from intervention. "Before the film they met for a drink, or at least they met at a place where drinks were served, and drank there." Such attention to detail is not uncommon in the first-time novelist; so keen to avoid cliché he is forever stopping the flow of the narrative to deconstruct the image: "Her hand was being held with a strength which it would not be inappropriate to compare to that of a vice."

The role of Maria reflects Coe's questing approach to narrative. Maria is the accidental woman; like one of Hardy's passive victims, things happen to her. Her actions never propel the narrative; the story is driven by her response to events. She marries Martin because she ate gammon.

In *A Touch of Love,* Coe eschews forthright authorial intrusion and tells a more direct story, although he does not completely forget his experimental roots. The story of Robin, a depressed postgraduate who is charged with indecency after a misunderstanding in a park, is seen from various viewpoints that allow the reader to build up a complete picture of his character. The clearest insight is allowed by the inclusion in the text of four of Robin's short stories. (The style of his work is reminiscent of *The Accidental Woman.*)

With *The Dwarves of Death,* Coe takes an enormous stride forward. The narrator, William, is a musician caught up in a murder case after being in the wrong place at the wrong time. Now, there is some heart (Maria and Robin had both been dealt their cards indifferently, even cruelly)—that is, William's frustrating relationship with the unreachable Madeline engenders the reader's sympathy. He gets us on his side early on, after all, by delivering blistering satirical salvos at Andrew Lloyd Webber's so-called music. Coe is experimenting. He constructs the novel like a popular song. It even has a middle eight—a hilarious account of waiting for a bus that never comes.

If Coe took a stride forward with *Dwarves,* he leaps to a higher plane with *What A Carve Up!.* Societal satire, savage political attack, rip-roaring farce, in-depth character study, deeply moving love story: It's all here, and every aspect of it works like a dream. Especially the oneness of it, the masterful way in which the author brings it all together. Ostensibly, at least to begin with, it's the story of a rich and powerful Yorkshire family, the Winshaws, and the story of writer Michael Owen, who is writing a book about the Winshaws for a vanity publisher. Tabitha Winshaw has been confined to an asylum, having overreacted to the death (she remains convinced it was no accident) of her brother, Godfrey. It's Tabitha who charges the Peacock Press with the task of finding someone to write the history of the Winshaws, and the more details that are revealed about the depths of greed and viciousness of her various relatives the more she emerges as the sanest of the bunch, despite being locked away.

Hilary Winshaw writes a vituperative, hawkish column for a right-wing tabloid; brother Roddy is a Cork Street gallerist sustaining the careers of talentless would-be artists. Henry becomes a Labour MP but veers sharply away from the party to become one of the powerful backroom thinkers and plotters behind the Conservatives' relentless drive to privatize everything they possibly can; Dorothy is a heartless factory farmer who becomes head of an insidious packaged-food business; Thomas is a merchant banker who involves himself in the film industry for the voyeuristic opportunities it will afford him; and Mark sells arms to Saddam.

Exploiting this extraordinary cast of characters to the full, Coe tears apart the body politic of British society and lays bare its corrupt heart. Because the author handles his material so assuredly, the reader never gets lost in the richness of detail. The appalling political machinations remain fascinating throughout the book, but what really draws the reader in is the character of Michael Owen, who you sense may be only partly fictional: Though he is nine years older than the author, there's a strong temptation to read Coe into part of the part of Michael, and not only because of playful references to Michael's published novels, whose titles are reworkings of *The Accidental Woman* and *A Touch of Love.*

The passages taken from Michael's works seem deeply personal, as does the relationship between Michael and Fiona. It's an indication, however, of how absorbing the action is throughout the book, that 90 pages elapse after Michael and Fiona's first embrace before the narrative returns to them. And although you do want to get back to them because you care for them now virtually as you would for real people, you remain captivated by all the many characters and narrative strands. This is partly due to ingenious plotting and a complicated structure that must have required the author constantly to go back and rework sections.

The scope of *What a Carve Up!* is dizzyingly ambitious, taking in the art world and factory farming; the depletion of the health service and the war against Saddam; the corruption of politicians and betrayal within the family; the philosophy that suggests that a course of events might be entirely accidental (harking back to Coe's first novel) set against elaborate and all-too-convincing conspiracy theories. It's a very brave novel and one that will have you laughing aloud and bursting into tears. The broad sweep and structure recall Michael Moorcock's *Mother London,* which was a masterpiece. In many respects, not least for the way in which the cinema metaphor is employed at the end of part one, that description would not be out of place here.

—Nicholas Royle

COETZEE, J(ohn) M(ichael)

Nationality: South African. **Born:** Cape Town, 9 February 1940. **Education:** The University of Cape Town, B.A. 1960, M.A. 1963; University of Texas, Austin, Ph.D. 1969. **Family:** Married in 1963 (divorced 1980); one son and one daughter. **Career:** Applications programmer, IBM, London, 1962-63; systems programmer, International Computers, Bracknell, Berkshire, 1964-65; Assistant Professor, 1968-71, and Butler Professor of English, 1984, State University of New York, Buffalo. Lecturer, 1972-83, and since 1984 Professor of General Literature, University of Cape Town. Hinkley Professor of English, Johns Hopkins University, Baltimore, 1986, 1989. **Awards:** CNA award 1978, 1980, 1983; James Tait Black Memorial prize, 1980; Faber Memorial award, 1980; Booker prize, 1983; Fémina prize (France), 1985; Jerusalem prize, 1987; *Sunday Express* Book of the Year award, 1990; Mondello prize (Italy), 1994. D.Litt.: University of Strathclyde, Glasgow, 1985; State University of New York, 1989. Life Fellow, University of Cape Town; Fellow, Royal Society of Literature, 1988; Honorary Fellow, Modern Language Association (U.S.A.), 1989. **Agent:** Murray Pollinger, 222 Old Brompton Road, London SW5 0BZ, England. **Address:** P.O. Box 92, Rondebosch, Cape Province 7700, South Africa.

PUBLICATIONS

Novels

Dusklands (two novellas). Johannesburg, Ravan Press, 1974; London, Secker and Warburg, 1982; New York, Viking, 1985.
In the Heart of the Country. Johannesburg, Ravan Press, and London, Secker and Warburg, 1977; as *From the Heart of the Country,* New York, Harper, 1977.
Waiting for the Barbarians. London, Secker and Warburg, 1980; New York, Penguin, 1982.
Life and Times of Michael K. London, Secker and Warburg, 1983; New York, Viking, 1984.
Foe. Johannesburg, Ravan Press, and London, Secker and Warburg, 1986; New York, Viking, 1987.
Age of Iron. London, Secker and Warburg, and New York, Random House, 1990.
The Master of Petersburg. London, Secker and Warburg, and New York, Viking, 1994.

Other

White Writing: On the Culture of Letters in South Africa. New Haven, Connecticut, Yale University Press, 1988.
Doubling the Point. Cambridge, Harvard University Press, 1992.

Editor, with André Brink, *A Land Apart: A South African Reader.* London, Faber, 1986; New York, Viking, 1987.

Translator, *A Posthumous Confession,* by Marcellus Emants. Boston, Twayne, 1976; London, Quartet, 1986.
Translator, *The Expedition to the Baobab Tree,* by Wilma Stockenström. Johannesburg, Ball, 1983; London, Faber, 1984.

*

Critical Studies: *The Novels of J.M. Coetzee* by Teresa Dovey, Johannesburg, Donker, 1988; *Countries of the Mind: The Fiction of J.M. Coetzee* by Dick Penner, Westport, Connecticut, Greenwood Press, 1989.

*   *   *

J.M. Coetzee's first book, *Dusklands,* foreshadowed the main direction and emphasis of his work. *Dusklands* consists of two novellas, one set in the U.S. State Department during the Vietnam era, while the other gives accounts of exploration and conquest by, in particular, one Jacobus Coetzee in southern Africa of the 1760s. Very different in setting, and 200 years apart in time, they are juxtaposed to offer a scarifying account of the fear and paranoia of imperialists and aggressors and the horrifying ways in which dominant regimes, "empires," commit violence against "the other" through repression, torture, and genocide. While Coetzee's work is firmly grounded in the violence and oppression of the South African situation out of which he writes, he regards it as "only one manifestation of a wider historical situation to do with colonialism, late colonialism, neo-colonialism." *Dusklands* also shows Coetzee's interest in the interplay between fiction and fact, author and subject, and in the importance of text and intertextuality. He is concerned with "dissecting" the "myths of our culture" and has engaged in a complex intertextual dialogue with Defoe's *Robinson Crusoe* as part of this demythologising process. Like Crusoe, Jacobus Coetzee must subdue the land and the people who inhabit it; but he does so by inflicting torture and death on the desert peoples who he feels have humiliated him and thwarted his imperial purpose.

In the Heart of the Country is narrated by the white South African spinster, Magda, who fantasises various bloody ways of disposing of the father with whom she lives on an isolated farm, and entering a new relationship, one not based on a gun and race superiority, with her erstwhile servants. But she cannot really dispose of the father or forge such a relationship however much she fictionally recreates her life. The "ghostly brown figures of the last people I knew" eventually abandon her. In this world where historical hatred and conflicts are irreconcilable, she cannot escape the polarities enshrined in the system to become "neither master nor slave, neither parent nor child but the bridge between."

Though the setting of *Waiting for the Barbarians* is unspecified, the novel can, like the earlier works, be read as a political fable of South Africa. A sympathetic but ineffectual liberal humanist, the narrator magistrate governs a frontier settlement at the edges of empire. A well-meaning man, he is nevertheless implicated in "the system" and is no match for the neo-fascist torturer, Colonel Joll, who persecutes the few pathetic "barbarians" (actually from a local fishing tribe) the Empire has succeeded in capturing. The barbarians are almost invisible, being largely a product of that nameless fear that haunts all conquering empires. The Empire is threatened from within, not from without, but it projects its paranoia onto the unknown "other." The barbarians remain unknown, and neither Joll's brutalities nor the magistrate's feeble attempts at love and restitution can bring them closer.

If the earlier narratives are recounted from the perspectives of those who are implicated in the imperial purpose, most of *Life and Times of Michael K* is told from the perspective of those it controls. Michael K attempts, in this highly political novel, to live outside politics and history. As is clear in Coetzee's earlier work, the "real heroes" are those who attempt to escape history, not those who connive in its making. Formerly a gardener in Cape Town, Michael K attempts to return his dying mother by makeshift cart to the farm of her childhood. She dies during the journey, but her son continues to the destination with her ashes. Here he is insulated from the civil and military terror that are both cause and effect of the breakdown of social order. In complete isolation he is able to discover the joys of cultivation. Though his desert produce barely allows him to subsist it offers a thoroughly magnificent apprehension of life and living. Predictably his painful desert idyll is terminated when he is captured and incarcerated as a guerrilla, but his sense of that one "tip of vivid green," the potential of life outside a corrupt society and even outside the casual and violent compassion of other fringe dwellers remains with him to the end.

Foe represents the climax of Coetzee's engagement with the imperial mythologies through rewriting of the colonialist topoi of *Robinson Crusoe.* Susan Barton is shipwrecked on an island inhabited by "Cruso" and Friday, who labor at constructing barren terraces. Friday is mute, having had his tongue cut out, possibly by slavers, possibly by Cruso himself. They are "rescued" from the island but Cruso dies on the voyage to England. On their arrival in London, Susan and Friday become "characters in search of an author," thus beginning their association with the elusive "Foe" and the novel's continuing complex exploration of authorship, writing, and betrayal, themes Coetzee takes up again in *The Master of Petersburg.* But *Foe* is also an inquiry into white liberal humanism and into the problem of white representations of the black majority; of the difficulty for South African blacks of finding "a voice," a way of speaking within the political and textual constraints that render them, like Friday, mute.

In *Age of Iron,* Coetzee's more cryptic address to the repressive South African politics in his earlier works is made overt in the South African setting. The white liberal protagonist, Mrs Curren, is dying of cancer, a disease as much of the apartheid South African State as of herself. The role of representation in the creation and perpetuation of such regimes is again a major issue, but this time it is the South African media (rather than the ur-text of imperialism) that is the violent instrument of "disinformation." The television's presentation of South Africa as "a land of smiling [white] neighbours" contrasts violently with the world of Mrs Curren's black "housegirl," Florence, and with the life (and death) Mrs Curren is forced to witness in Guguletu township. Mrs Curren admits to herself (and to her daughter in the United States to whom the letters that compose the novel are addressed) her complicity in the maintenance of this regime. But through her "witness" in the township and her increasingly close relationship with the vagrant Vercueil, she attempts to fight free of the constraints of her whiteness, eventually embracing her own death as the only apparent solution. Apartheid South Africa has, tragically, produced "children of iron" both white and black, and relationships between children and parents are of major concern.

In *The Master of Petersburg,* Coetzee examines the child products of another "age of iron" through Dostoevsky's relationship with his step-son, in a rather different context of violence and revolution, that of prerevolutionary St. Petersburg. In spite of the setting, there are echoes of South Africa in the poverty and violence sponsored by an oppressive regime and in the mysterious death of Dostoevsky's step-son, Pavel, who may have been murdered by one of his revolutionary comrades (Nechaev), or by the police, or who may have committed suicide. The novel is also about life and writing, and about the compelling authority of artistic genius, which is shown to be inescapably grounded in a betrayal as profound and obsessive as that of the revolutionary Nechaev himself.

—H.M. Tiffin

207

COHEN, Leonard (Norman)

Nationality: Canadian. **Born:** Montreal, Quebec, 21 September 1934. **Education:** McGill University, Montreal, B.A. 1955; Columbia University, New York. **Family:** Lived with Suzanne Elrod for several years; two children. **Career:** Composer and singer: has given concerts in Canada, the United States, and Europe. Lives in Montreal and Greece. **Awards:** McGill University literary award, 1956; Canada Council award, 1960; Quebec literary award, 1964; Governor-General's award, 1969 (refused), 1993; Canadian Authors Association award, 1985. D.L.: Dalhousie University, Halifax, Nova Scotia, 1971. **Address:** c/o Stranger Music Inc., 146 West 75th Street, Apartment 2-A, New York, New York 10023, U.S.A.

PUBLICATIONS

Novels

The Favorite Game. New York, Viking Press, and London, Secker and Warburg, 1963.
Beautiful Losers. Toronto, McClelland and Stewart, and New York, Viking Press, 1966; London, Cape, 1970.

Uncollected Short Stories

"Barbers and Lovers," in *Ingluvin 2* (Montreal), January-March 1961.
"Trade," in *Tamarack Review* (Toronto), Summer 1961.
"Luggage Fire Sale," in *Partisan Review* (New Brunswick, New Jersey), Winter 1961.
"Charles Axis," in *The Single Voice,* edited by Jerome Charyn. New York, Collier, 1969.

Plays

The New Step (produced Ottawa and London, 1972). Included in *Flowers for Hitler,* 1964; in *Selected Poems,* 1968.
Sisters of Mercy: A Journey into the Words and Music of Leonard Cohen (produced Niagara-on-the-Lake, Ontario, and New York, 1973).
A Man Was Killed, with Irving Layton, in *Canadian Theatre Review* (Downsview, Ontario), Spring 1977.

Poetry

Let Us Compare Mythologies. Montreal, Contact Press, 1956.
The Spice-Box of Earth. Toronto, McClelland and Stewart, 1961; New York, Viking Press, 1965; London, Cape, 1971.
Flowers for Hitler. Toronto, McClelland and Stewart, 1964; London, Cape, 1973.
Parasites of Heaven. Toronto, McClelland and Stewart, 1966.
Selected Poems 1956-1968. New York, Viking Press, 1968; London, Cape, 1969.
Leonard Cohen's Song Book. New York, Collier, 1969.
Five Modern Canadian Poets, with others, edited by Eli Mandel. Toronto, Holt Rinehart, 1970.
The Energy of Slaves. Toronto, McClelland and Stewart, and London, Cape, 1972; New York, Viking Press, 1973.
Two Views. Toronto, Madison Gallery, 1980.

Book of Mercy. Toronto, McClelland and Stewart, London, Cape, and New York, Villard, 1984.
Stranger Music: Selected Poems and Songs. London, Cape, and New York, Pantheon, 1993.

Recordings: *The Songs of Leonard Cohen,* Columbia, 1968; *Songs from a Room,* Columbia, 1969; *Songs of Love and Hate,* Columbia, 1971; *Live Songs,* Columbia, 1973; *New Skin for the Old Ceremony,* Columbia, 1974; *The Best of Leonard Cohen,* Columbia, 1975; *Death of a Lady's Man,* Warner Brothers, 1977; *Recent Songs,* CBS, 1979; *Various Positions,* CBS, 1985; *I'm Your Man,* CBS, 1987.

Other

Death of a Lady's Man (novel-journal). Toronto, McClelland and Stewart, 1978; London, Deutsch, and New York, Viking Press, 1979.

*

Bibliography: By Bruce Whiteman, in *The Annotated Bibliography of Canada's Major Authors 2* edited by Robert Lecker and Jack David, Downsview, Ontario, ECW Press, 1980.

Manuscript Collection: University of Toronto.

Critical Studies: *Leonard Cohen* by Michael Ondaatje, Toronto, McClelland and Stewart, 1970; *The Immoral Moralists: Hugh MacLennan and Leonard Cohen* by Patricia Morley, Toronto, Clarke Irwin, 1972; *Leonard Cohen: The Artist and His Critics* edited by Michael Gnarowski, Toronto, McGraw Hill Ryerson, 1976; *Leonard Cohen* by Stephen Scobie, Vancouver, Douglas and McIntyre, 1978; *Leonard Cohen: Prophet of the Heart* by Loranne S. Dorman and Clive L. Rawlings, London, Omnibus Press, 1990.

*   *   *

Few modern authors have presented critics so clearly as Leonard Cohen does with the problem of how to regard the writer who personifies the *Zeitgeist.* With astonishing rapidity, in the mid-1960s, Cohen passed from the obscurity of a romantic Canadian poet into the celebrity of an international pop singer who seemed to exemplify the decade's popular culture.

Time will decide how far, when fashion abandons him, Cohen's real qualities will sustain his standing as a writer. What the critic perceives even now is that the factors which made Cohen popular are those he shares with modish culture: conventionalism pretending to be independence; a slightly acrid romanticism merging into a solipsistic sentimentality; an echoing of past movements like the Decadence, Art Nouveau and Dada, which elevated style above substance. The fiction such movements have produced has usually been strained and eccentric. *The Picture of Dorian Gray,* the novels of Huysmans and, later Raymond Queneau, are examples.

Cohen stands in this company; his novels, *The Favorite Game* and *Beautiful Losers,* are interesting examples of black romance, and though *Beautiful Losers* projects a bizarre kind of splendor, as the novels of poets often do, it is a work of solitary fantasy that stands apart from the main stream of fiction in our time.

A shallowness of feeling, a solipsistic passionlessness masquerading as stylized passion, infects almost all of Cohen's writings. It is linked with the Pygmalion urge that is a dominant theme in his novels, exemplified in F.'s delusions of godly creativeness in *Beautiful Losers* and in the fantasies of occult power that haunt Breavman throughout *The Favorite Game*. "I want to touch people like a magician," he says to one of his mistresses, "to change them or hurt them, leave my brand, make them beautiful." To be beautiful, and to be a loser; both desires find their places in the romantic fancy; their juxtaposition in the title of Cohen's second novel is neither accidental nor inappropriate. The solipsist creates beauty within the mind and that is his only real world; he loses because the actual world does not correspond with his visionary world yet impinges on his life. F., the quasi-hero of *Beautiful Losers,* lives in flamboyant style; he is killed, in true decadent tradition, by syphilis.

Cohen's first novel, *The Favorite Game,* tells the development of a rich Montreal Jewish boy into a poet and folk singer; the resemblance's to Cohen's life are close enough to justify an assumption that this is the autobiographical novel with which many writers make their finest sacrifice to the muse of fiction. *The Favorite Game* is an episodic work, its shuffled time sequences strung along the thread of Breavman's affair with the all-American girl, Shell, most recent of his mistresses; the account of his experience becomes a kind of dialogue with Shell, from whom in the end he parts, as he has parted from her predecessors. His life has been measured off by relationships with girls, yet in none has Breavman been able to evade in passion that observing mind which is the alien participant.

Parallel to these uninvolved liaisons runs the continuing current of Breavman's friendship with Krantz, which survives all the broken love affairs. But the moment of real involvement comes when, working as a staff member in a Jewish summer camp, Breavman encounters the boy Martin, "a divine idiot" with a mathematical mania who spends his time counting grass blades and pine needles, and dies grotesquely when he is crushed by a bulldozer while killing and counting mosquitoes in a marsh.

Martin represents the other pole in Cohen's world to profane love. He is—albeit in disguise—of the company of saints, those exalted and obsessed ones to whom Cohen is always drawn. Destroyed saints appear often in his poems; Martin is one of them. Yet he dies at the peak of joy, rating his days at "98 per cent"—and the joyful saint is always in Cohen's world: Something about him so loves the world that he gives himself to the laws of gravity and chance. Far from flying with the angels, he traces with the fidelity of a seismograph needle the state of the solid bloody landscape. His house is dangerous and finite, but he is at home in the world. He can love the shapes of human beings, the fine and twisted shapes of the human heart.

To the Cohen alive to the call of sainthood as the complement of earthly love, the world takes on dual aspects. Breavman, inexperienced, sees decay everywhere. "The works themselves were corruption, the monuments were made of worms." But in *Beautiful Losers,* when "I" puts the classic decadent point about "the diamonds in the shit," F. replies, "It's all diamond." It is the unity in duality of the erotic and the spiritual that provides the bridge from *The Favorite Game* to *Beautiful Losers*. But, though there are many ways in which—in details of plot and imagery—the earlier novel anticipates its more ambitious successor, *Beautiful Losers* moves into a quite different category. Young artist novels can only be written once, and Cohen makes his escape in the same direction as Joyce, in the aestheticist reconstruction of life. *Beautiful Losers* is very much a work of artifice, and makes no concession to verisimilitude.

Of the three parts into which this novel is divided, the first contains the erratic musings of the onanist "I." Edith, his wife who has committed bizarre suicide, and F., the megalomaniac lover of them both, move in memory within a pattern which F. describes when de declares, "I was your journey and you were my journey and Edith was our holy star." Whether they have ever existed is not important, since they are absorbed in a timeless dream continuum where they are no more and no less real, no more and no less distant, than the Mohawk saint, Catherine Tekakwitha, three centuries dead, whose monumental holy masochism fascinates both F. and "I." F. becomes an industrialist who uses his unmanned factory for playing games, a member of Parliament quickly discredited, a leader of the Quebec underground, but these achievements are no more substantial than the grandiose fantasies which, one eventually realizes, are the products of a brain rotted by the pox.

This becomes evident in the wild inventions of the "Long Letter from F." In the central episode described in this document, F. and Edith, after packing "I" off on an absurd research assignment, set off for Argentina with a bag of erotic devices, and indulge in a long orgy in which they are ravished in turn by the "Danish vibrator" (a machine that develops and fulfills desires of its own) and finally bathe "three in a tub" with a waiter who provides human soap and turns out to be Hitler in exile.

Book III, an "Epilogue in the Third Person," closes with a description of the last dissolving days of "I," who has learnt to combine F.'s debauchery and Catherine Tekakwitha's self-mortifications in a regressive tree-house existence; he is saint and sinner, at once himself and F. and Edith, and he disappears in a puff of ambiguity.

Beautiful Losers is filled with interesting experiments, some of which belong to poetry rather than fiction; indeed there are passages which are actually concealed verse. But the burlesque element is overdone and the savage sexual comedy quickly palls. As a novel the book has no functioning unity; Cohen lacks the architectonic power with which Céline, for example, transformed similar material into self-consistent and convincing works of fiction.

—George Woodcock

COHEN, Matt(hew)

Nationality: Canadian. **Born:** Kingston, Ontario, 30 December 1942. **Education:** Fisher Park and Nepean high schools, Ottawa, graduated 1960; University of Toronto, 1960-64, B.A. 1964, M.A. in political science 1965. **Career:** Lecturer in Religion, McMaster University, Hamilton, Ontario, 1967-68; writer-in-residence, University of Alberta, Edmonton, 1975-76; visiting professor, University of Victoria, British Columbia, 1979-80; writer-in-residence, University of Western Ontario, London, 1981; taught at York University, Toronto, and University of Bologna, Italy, 1984. Chair, Canadian Writers' Union, 1985-86. **Awards:** Canada Arts Council senior award, 1977, 1985. **Address:** P.O. Box 401, Verona, Ontario K0H 2W0, Canada.

PUBLICATIONS

Novels

Korsoniloff. Toronto, Anansi, 1969.

Johnny Crackle Sings. Toronto, McClelland and Stewart, 1971.

The Disinherited. Toronto, McClelland and Stewart, 1974; London, Penguin, 1987.

Wooden Hunters. Toronto, McClelland and Stewart, 1975.

The Colours of War. Toronto, McClelland and Stewart, 1977; New York, Methuen, 1978; London, Penguin, 1987.

The Sweet Second Summer of Kitty Malone. Toronto, McClelland and Stewart, 1979; London, Penguin, 1987.

Flowers of Darkness. Toronto, McClelland and Stewart, 1981; London, Penguin, 1987.

The Spanish Doctor. Toronto, McClelland and Stewart, 1984; New York, Beaufort, and London, Penguin, 1985.

Nadine. Toronto and London, Viking, 1986; New York, Crown, 1987.

Emotional Arithmetic. Toronto, Lester and Orpen Dennys, 1990; New York, St. Martin's, 1995.

The Bookseller. Totonto, Knopf Canada, 1993.

Lives of the Mind Slaves. Toronto, Porcupine's Quill, 1994.

Short Stories

Columbus and the Fat Lady and Other Stories. Toronto, Anansi, 1972.

Too Bad Galahad. Toronto, Coach House Press, 1972.

Night Flights: Stories New and Selected. New York, Doubleday, 1978.

The Expatriate: Collected Short Stories. Toronto, General, 1981; New York, Beaufort, 1983.

Café le dog. Toronto, McClelland and Stewart, 1983; London, Penguin, 1985; as *Life on This Planet and Other Stories,* New York, Beaufort, 1985.

Living on Water. Toronto and New York, Viking, 1988; London, Viking, 1989.

Poetry

Peach Melba. Toronto, Coach House Press, 1974.

Other

The Leaves of Louise (for children). Toronto, McClelland and Stewart, 1978.

In Search of Leonardo. Toronto, Coach House Press, 1985.

Editor, *The Story So Far 2.* Toronto, Coach House Press, 1973.

Editor, with David Young, *The Dream Class Anthology: Writings from Toronto High Schools.* Toronto, Coach House Press, 1983.

Editor, with Wayne Grady, *Intimate Strangers: New Stories from Quebec.* Toronto and London, Penguin, 1986; New York, Penguin, 1987.

*

Manuscript Collection: Mills Memorial Library, McMaster University, Hamilton, Ontario.

*   *   *

In Matt Cohen's first book, *Korsoniloff,* a narrator possessed of dual consciousness confronts the reader with themes taken up and variously treated in Cohen's later work: that of the opacity of a character with little or no self-knowledge, and whose inner forces have been "misaligned." The novella is the journal of a schizophrenic professor of philosophy, Andre Korsoniloff, whose surname represents his alter ego. He does not yet "exist in the world," since his opposing selves together form a man who is essentially "unwhole and without judgement;" a man who is, however, wittily aware of this division within himself. We see Korsoniloff in the same way that he sees other characters, as being self-possessed and without need, but his one violent act—disturbing the peace at his mistress's wedding—renders credible his subsequent fantasies of suicide and murder.

Korsoniloff's potential for eruption also underscores the pop-hero of *Johnny Crackle Sings,* a star who cultivates "condition zero," his personal term for a state approaching Nirvana, as a retreat from pressure and decision. Rock idol of screaming schoolchildren, Johnny Crackle, born Johnny Harper, moves aimlessly, withdrawing into drug-induced illusions rather than reacting, another Cohen character "born without any destiny at all." He seems only subliminally aware that the rural landscape to which he continually returns has a calming effect upon him. When he moves to urban environments or travels abroad, he sinks back into his state of suspended animation. He and his girl-friend Jenny are finally married, and have a son, also Johnny. Crackle, in describing his reaction to the birth, sums himself up too: "Afterwards it was almost like I hadn't been there except like watching a movie."

Characters of Cohen's other books suffer from an uncultivated "condition zero," or (if one takes seriously *Too Bad Galahad,* distinguished more by Margaret Hathaway's illustrations than Cohen's literary merits), admit the quest for a Holy Grail of one sort or another, though they must perish finding it.

Cohen's short stories collected in *Columbus and the Fat Lady* can be whimsical, self-conscious, or embarrassingly weak. He is at his best with acutely observed psychological detail, as in "Janice;" stories with magical or fantastic elements are his least successful.

The Disinherited states what, in embryonic form, other books and characters have pointed to. The title applies to most of the characters in this novel, in which various forces of dispossession are at work. While it concentrates on the slow death of farmer Richard Thomas, and the alienation felt by his city-dwelling son, the novel flashes continually back and forth through four generations: young Erik Thomas and his adopted brother Brian, his father, his grandfather Simon Thomas, and his great-grandfather Richard, whose relative, a poet from England, had come to Canada as though to Canaan, like "Abraham being sent to father a new race of men." But those who came after him have been unable to accept the vision he wished them to inherit. The poet's son is mentally retarded and an outcast in the same way that other characters have been cast out, through human inadequacy or legal disheritance, from real and metaphoric promised lands. Richard is dying, Erik is not fully alive. With Erik begins the new breed; unlike his father, uncle or grandfather there is no heroic stance for him to assume: "A man has to know his own destiny," says Richard. Erik replies: "No-one has destinies any more. They live in apartments and breed goldfish."

The first and last chapters are the most successful of this book; here the basic dichotomy between the two generations and kinds of men stands out most clearly. As the book opens, Richard Thomas begins to succumb to the illness that kills him in the last pages, and is for the first time aware of the microscopic unknown workings of his body, an experience he explores in seemingly timeless detail throughout the rest of the book. Nature is revealed to him in an immediate and alarming fashion as he lies on the ground integrated into the landscape—a position symbolic of what Cohen makes him stand for in the book; and Richard Thomas has recurring dreams of being rooted in earth, hands and arms as branches growing up and out from soil. In the final chapter Erik returns to Toronto after his father's death, forcibly struck by the extent of his alienation from the city, sucking in peripheral lives like his. From his high-rise apartment he looks down aimlessly on the city, dispossessed of the farm, indispensable to no-one, not in pain, not even searching, but beginning to believe in the need for something other. *The Disinherited* is Cohen's most accomplished book, but he has not yet achieved balance, the kind of perspective that would allow him, instead of insisting on obscure eddies, to concentrate on the main currents he is obviously equipped to handle.

The Sweet Second Summer of Kitty Malone continues, in order to reverse, Cohen's earlier methods and preoccupations. The technique of rambling discourse and apparent digression is here a means towards a fine sense of organic time serenely apprehended. Middle age is not a prelude to the bitter winter of discontented and unfulfilled old age, but to the wisdom of uncynical experience as astonishing as an Indian Summer. Each character seems on the brink of "re-possession," an almost biblical dying to oneself in order to live. Thus Pat Frank loses the physical fight and is badly beaten, but wins understanding of himself and of Kitty. The major archetypes at the end of the novel are a simultaneous and almost indistinguishable funeral and wedding.

The Spanish Doctor is almost entirely a tumid pot-boiler. The horrors experienced by the Jews in 14th-century Spain are vitiated by the swash and buckle of the plot and the unlikely antics of the protagonist Avram Halevi. Son of a Jewish woman raped by Christians, a scientist in an age of superstition, fatally attractive to women, he would be redeemed, and the novel too, if he were played by Woody Allen.

—Barrie Davies

COLE, Barry

Nationality: British. **Born:** Woking, Surrey, 13 November 1936. **Education:** Balham Secondary School, London. **Military Service:** Served in the Royal Air Force, 1955-57. **Family:** Married Rita Linihan in 1958; three daughters. **Career:** Since 1958, staff member, Reuters news agency, London; reporter, 1965-70, and senior editor, 1974-94, Central Office of Information, London. Northern Arts Fellow, universities of Newcastle-upon-Tyne and Durham, 1970-72. **Address:** 68 Myddelton Square, London EC1R 1XP, England.

PUBLICATIONS

Novels

A Run Across the Island. London, Methuen, 1968.
Joseph Winter's Patronage. London, Methuen, 1969.
The Search for Rita. London, Methuen, 1970.
The Giver. London, Methuen, 1971.
Doctor Fielder's Common Sense. London, Methuen, 1972.

Poetry

Blood Ties. London, Turret, 1967.
Ulysses in the Town of Coloured Glass. London, Turret, 1968.
Moonsearch. London, Methuen, 1968.
The Visitors. London, Methuen, 1970.
Vanessa in the City. London, Trigram Press, 1971.
Pathetic Fallacies. London, Eyre Methuen, 1973.
The Rehousing of Scaffardi. Richmond, Surrey, Keepsake Press, 1976.
Dedications. Nottingham, Byron Press, 1977.

*

Barry Cole comments:

I have no general statement to make about my novels, but the epigraphs which precede *The Giver* may say more than any collected exegeses.

*   *   *

Barry Cole's novels have one striking thing in common. They are extremely well-written. It may, of course, be said that to write well is not so much a virtue in a novelist as a necessity. Yet the fact is that the majority of novelists lack Cole's gifts of verbal precision, wit, exact ear for conversation, and his feeling for the elastic possibilities of language, the way it can be stretched and twisted to provide unexpected meanings and insights. No doubt the fact that he is also a very fine poet accounts for much of his virtue as a writer of prose, but this should not be taken to mean that he writes poetic prose. On the contrary: his style is as free as possible from those encrustations of adjective and epithet that identify "fine" writing.

A Run Across the Island is a brilliant *tour de force* and for it Cole invented a form that he has found it possible to use for all his subsequent novels. Although by far the larger part of the novel is seen through the eyes of its hero, Robert Haydon, there is no straightforward narrative or division into chapters. Instead, we move about in time, each remembered detail or incident given a section, small or large, that is juxtaposed against others. By the end of the novel, however, the different incidents have been worked out and together compose one man's life, and it has been so resourcefully done that we have a much more *real* sense of a man's identity than we would have through a straightforward narrative.

The major theme of *A Run Across the Island* is, perhaps, of loneliness, of the difficulties of establishing relationships, of the slippery impermanence of friendship and love. And this theme is also present in the next novel. *Joseph Winter's Patronage* is, however, very different from *A Run Across the Island* in that its characters are almost exclusively old people. Indeed, the novel is mostly set in an Old People's Home, and the novelist manages with great sensitiveness to create the feeling of the Home itself and of its inhabitants. *Joseph Winter's Patronage* is the most touching and warmly sympathetic novel that Cole has so far written.

By contrast, *The Search for Rita* is the most glittering. It is an extremely elegant novel, but the elegance is not one that marks how far its author stands fastidiously aloof from life. It is rather that the mess of life is met by a keen-eyed wit that can be ironic, self-deprecatory, satiric, and bawdy by turns. Style means everything in a novel of this kind, and the novelist's style does not let him down.

—John Lucas

COLEGATE, Isabel (Diana)

Nationality: British. **Born:** Lincolnshire, 10 September 1931. **Education:** A boarding school in Shropshire and at Runton Hill School, Norfolk. **Family:** Married Michael Briggs in 1953; one daughter and two sons. **Career:** Literary agent, Anthony Blond Ltd., London, 1952-57. **Awards:** W.H. Smith Literary award, 1981. Hon. M.A.: University of Bath, 1988. Fellow, Royal Society of Literature, 1981. **Agent:** Peters Fraser and Dunlop, 503-504 The Chambers, Chelsea Harbour, Lots Road, London SW10 0XF, England. **Address:** Midford Castle, Bath BA1 7BU, England.

PUBLICATIONS

Novels

The Blackmailer. London, Blond, 1958.
A Man of Power. London, Blond, 1960.
The Great Occasion. London, Blond, 1962.
Statues in a Garden. London, Bodley Head, 1964; New York, Knopf, 1966.
The Orlando Trilogy. London, Penguin, 1984.
  Orlando King. London, Bodley Head, 1968; New York, Knopf, 1969.
  Orlando at the Brazen Threshold. London, Bodley Head, 1971.
  Agatha. London, Bodley Head, 1973.
News from the City of the Sun. London, Hamish Hamilton, 1979.
The Shooting Party. London, Hamish Hamilton, 1980; New York, Viking Press, 1981.
Deceits of Time. London, Hamish Hamilton, and New York, Viking, 1988.
The Summer of the Royal Visit. London, Hamish Hamilton, 1991; New York, Knopf, 1992.
Winter Journey. London, Hamish Hamilton, 1995.

Short Stories

A Glimpse of Sion's Glory. London, Hamish Hamilton, and New York, Viking, 1985.

*   *   *

The English will never turn Communist, they're such snobs. An English Communist could have a duke at gunpoint; if he asked him to stay for the weekend he'd drop the gun and dash off to Moss Brothers to hire a dinner-jacket.

(Agatha)

Isabel Colegate's fiction dramatizes the English obsession with aristocracy and sensitivity to the nuances of class, even in the 20th century when traditional aristocratic power was declining. Against a backdrop of post-World War II global unrest, Colegate's first three novels, *The Blackmailer, A Man of Power,* and *The Great Occasion,* depict both the aristocrats' alliances with new sources of wealth and their inability to comprehend the welfare state: ". . . a five-day week, holidays with pay, pensions, free this, free that . . . There's no sense of values" (*The Blackmailer*). Her later novels,

Statues in a Garden, The Orlando Trilogy, and *The Shooting Party,* root these changes in the disintegrating world immediately before and after World War I. *The Blackmailer,* a "self-making" man of lower-middle-class origins, extorts money from the widow of a Korean War hero primarily to gain entry to the hero's ancestral home and family and complete his identification with the dead man. The thriller elements are not a sound basis for Colegate's social satire, though her comedy supports the anti-romantic ending triggered by the heroine's class loyalties. (Similarly the recent story "Distant Cousins" in *A Glimpse of Sion's Glory* uneasily mixes a science-fiction thriller plot with cold war satire in the service of a plea for world peace and tolerance.)

The protagonist of *A Man of Power,* a capitalist of lower-middle-class origins who has risen through wartime opportunities, plans to wed an impoverished aristocratic beauty because of her "mystery" and ability to reshape his image; his first wife and former secretary is inadequate to the role: "It's always the wives that give them away." Upper-class characters respond as much to the protagonist's mystique as to his money: the aristocrat's daughter suffers a painful initiation into his chaotic world through her love for him. (Like the charismatic tycoon and the society beauty, the vulnerable young girl is a staple of Colegate's fiction.) Unfortunately, the novel's sentimentality undercuts the serious treatment of its themes.

The Great Occasion focuses on middle-class vulnerability by interweaving the lives of a magnate, whose success stemmed partly from his marriage to an upper-class wife, and his five daughters in a world that rejects his business integrity and their talents and idealism: ". . . I expect she'll soon level down to the others." The tone wavers because of Colegate's mixing of Waughesque satire with family saga, but her skill at maintaining several story lines anticipates *Statues in a Garden* and *The Shooting Party.* Like these later works, *The Great Occasion* presents the natural world as both ironical commentary on human futility and a source of reconciliation to existence.

Developed cinematically in short scenes, *Statues in a Garden* portrays a group of aristocrats just before World War I and flashes forward to the futures implicit in their actions. A quasi-incestuous affair, one of many in Colegate's fiction, between a society beauty and her nephew, whom she has adopted, suggests the destructive narcissism of aristocratic lives. The nephew and aunt proceed to dubious futures, his business speculations undermining the stability of her settled world. Colegate controls detail and tone, the heroine's uncomprehending ". . . not a very *close* sort of incest, surely?" perfectly defining her shallowness and ability to survive. Though the nephew's schematic significance as disturber of both sexual and economic order seems obtrusive, the novel uses this type of symbolism more gracefully than *The Orlando Trilogy.*

The protagonist of *Orlando King,* raised on a remote island by his adoptive father to protect him from civilization, carries a heavy symbolic burden besides his name: his hammer toes and damaged eyesight link him with Oedipus, as do, more obviously, his partial responsibility for his father's death and marriage to his aristocratic stepmother. The participants learn the truth only after many years: "'I suppose you really think . . . that I look old enough to be Orlando's mother.' 'Could be' he said.'" Though amusing, this dialogue puzzles; surely the stepmother's resultant breakdown and death and the consequences for the next generation make this stress on her superficiality misleading. Orlando's sense of guilt destroys his business and political careers in the England of the 1930s that is increasingly dominated by men like his father who capitalize on wartime connections and marriages to aristocrats. If such outsiders lust after class status, aristocrats display equal fascination with the challenge these newcomers represent. Orlando's initial success in emulating his father is presumably emblematic, but his other actions confuse the novel's political and social pattern. The incest motif seems especially intrusive: in *Orlando at the Brazen Threshold* he successfully pursues the mistress of his nephew, whom his daughter marries. Orlando's behavior seems motivated by a need to support the novel's symbolism and lacks the complexity that the interior monologues, letters, and searching dialogue initially promise. Similarly, the elliptical narration with flashwords and allusions to incidents as yet unknown to the reader creates an atmosphere of elusive reality puzzling to the characters through whose voices we perceive it; but then Colegate periodically destroys this rich ambiguity by over-explicit summary: "Stephen and Paul were Orlando's half-brothers. Their father Leonard had in the far-off and scarcely imaginable days of his youth also been the father of Orlando . . ." Colegate's epigrams about the inevitable failure of Communism in a class-obsessed society clash with her serious treatment of radicals, who seem as futile and foolishly motivated as her capitalists: Graham, who dies on the Loyalist side in Spain (*Orlando King*); Paul, who sells secrets to Russia during the Burgess era because of family problems (*Agatha*). Set during the Suez crisis, *Agatha* focuses on the girl's Forsteresque commitment to Paul rather than to England, partly because of Orlando's earlier ruthlessness. (Raymond, who defects to Russia in the title story of *A Glimpse of Sion's Glory,* has more ambiguous, even more attractive, motives than these earlier characters.)

Negative aristocratic images abound in the trilogy, sometimes mocking the physical effects of reclusiveness: "his little eyes directed their feeble gaze down the long organ through which his frail tones appeared to emerge (eugenically speaking, his breeding was a disaster)." Another aristocrat embodies more damning inadequacies, from 1930s appeasement, through Suez arrogance to personal betrayal of Agatha in the name of patriotism. Though Colegate effectively dramatizes the peculiar fusion of charm, decency, egotism, and plaintive misunderstanding that characterizes such aristocrats, her trilogy fails to provide an adequate political context that explains the contribution of this class to the general malaise of English civilization.

Like other Colegate characters, Sir Randolph Nettleby, protagonist of *The Shooting Party,* set in 1913, prophesies, "An age, perhaps a civilization, is coming to an end." The novel, Colegate's best, carefully places the Nettleby estate in its geographical and historical contexts and focuses on those details of dress and behavior that reveal the beauty and vulnerability of country life on the eve of destruction. Sir Randolph is at times over-generous in assessing his class: "If you take away the proper functions of an aristocracy, what can it do but play games too seriously?" But the novel's stress on the violence of these games redresses the balance: "It was hard to remember that the keen concentration of their hunting instinct was not directed at their fellow man." The callousness of a visiting Hungarian count, however, helps define, by contrast, the English commitment to their tenants and to their land. The highflown language and sentiments that impress servants have real substance. The narrowness of the aristocratic code, the complacency with which aristocrats experience their rituals is offset by their willingness to limit their freedom for the sake of standards: Hartlib's agonizing headaches are the price his inbred nerves exact for his performance as a hunter. However foolish, the codes of this class give form and meaning to their lives, including the duty to sacrifice these lives in

war. Restraining the epigrammatical tendencies that unbalanced earlier works, Colegate fuses an ironical view of society with a moving appreciation of its painful pleasures.

Colegate's story "The Girl Who Had Lived Among Artists" (*A Glimpse of Sion's Glory*) comes closest of all her work to the skill of *The Shooting Party.* Set in pre-World War II Bath, the story both illustrates and refutes the idea that "The snobbery of England in the 1930s was the real thing," as it examines the complex attitudes of the classes toward each other, the even more painful situation among civil servants and merchants in India, where the English condescend to each other and unite against the Indians, the desperate anxieties of European refugees who stress the superiority of their own culture, the ambiguous social position of clerics, and the special relation between artists and the upper classes (". . . there are three things that make people classless, talent, beauty, and something else I've forgotten"). What flaws this brilliantly conceived picture of the dangers of such a society is Colegate's attempt to pack so much rich material into a short story. Though the details are effective and the dialogue often chilling, the treatment is ultimately too truncated for such thematic wealth.

Colegate's 1988 novel, *Deceits of Time,* explores the mystery of a World War I hero's apparent pro-German activities before and during World War II and reveals the familiar milieu of social tensions and adjustments that *may* explain his actions. The middle-class biographer and Jewish holocaust survivor understandably learn much about themselves while investigating the hero's life, but the modest triumph of the novel is the gradual revelation of the character of the hero's aristocratic widow. Her values, however limited, are allowed their surprising victory. Despite the novel's occasionally fussy structure and tendency toward undramatic summary of other characters and their motives, this portrait is equal to the best in *The Shooting Party.* Colegate's fiction offers an impressive demonstration of genuine talent finding its strengths and continually refining its craft.

—Burton Kendle

COLLINS, Hunt. *See* **HUNTER, Evan.**

COLTER, Cyrus

Nationality: American. **Born:** Noblesville, Indiana, 8 January 1910. **Education:** Noblesville public schools; Youngstown University, Ohio; Ohio State University, Columbus; Kent College of Law, Illinois Institute of Technology, Chicago, J.D. 1940: admitted to the Illinois bar, 1940. **Military Service:** Served in the United States Army Field Artillery, Italy, 1942-46: Captain. **Family:** Married Imogene Mackay in 1943 (died 1984). **Career:** Worked for the YMCA, Youngstown, 1932-34, and Chicago, 1934-40; United States Government Deputy Collector of Internal Revenue, 1940-42; lawyer in Chicago, 1946-51; commissioner, Illinois Commerce Commission, Chicago, 1951-73; professor of creative writing,

1973-76, and Chester D. Tripp Professor of Humanities, 1976-78, Northwestern University, Evanston, Illinois; now emeritus. **Awards:** Iowa School of Letters award, 1970. D.Litt.: University of Illinois, Chicago, 1977. **Address:** 1115 South Plymouth Court, Chicago, Illinois 60605, U.S.A.

PUBLICATIONS

Novels

The Rivers of Eros. Chicago, Swallow Press, 1972.
The Hippodrome. Chicago, Swallow Press, 1973.
Night Studies. Chicago, Swallow Press, 1980.
A Chocolate Soldier. St. Paul, Minnesota, Thunder's Mouth Press, 1988.
City of Light. New York, Thunder's Mouth Press, 1993.

Short Stories

The Beach Umbrella. Iowa City, University of Iowa Press, 1970.
The Amoralists and Other Tales: Collected Stories. St. Paul, Minnesota, Thunder's Mouth Press, 1988; London, Penguin, 1991.

* * *

In his first volume of fiction, the stories collected as *The Beach Umbrella,* Cyrus Colter reveals a high purpose. The subject of each story, often an apparently small event, Colter recounts in the style of modern realism, keeping his authorial self unobtrusive while exploiting colloquial dialogue and entering briefly into the conscious minds of characters in order to develop the subject into a story intending no less than a dramatic *exemplum* of life in general. "The Lookout," for example, records the painful jealousy of a woman who discovers the frailty of what she had taken to be friendships; "Rescue," which tells of a woman finding herself unable to get out of a loveless relationship with a man and so agrees to marry him, has as a counterpart "Overnight Trip" in which a man becomes aware that he has lost his wife's love by sensing the joy she feels in going away from him ever so briefly. "An Untold Story" and "Moot" tell of death, one in violence and the other by natural causes, but though the subject is larger than in the other stories, these do not differ in suggesting the essential human condition is isolation and powerlessness before fate.

The Rivers of Eros introduces into Colter's writing a wider variety of characters, and the greater length of the novel form permits him to range more widely in time. His theme also undergoes some development. Set in a Chicago rooming house, *The Rivers of Eros* is presided over by the aging woman named Clotilda and, more importantly, by an act of adultery she committed many years before. The granddaughter living with her is the offspring of the child she conceived in adultery, and the environment of Clotilda's house can offer no alternative when the girl becomes involved in dangerous love affairs herself. The other people in Clotilda's world, with the exception of a promising grandson, are eccentric outsiders, inadequate to mitigate a situation that drives the granddaughter to attempt suicide and Clotilda to insanity as a result of guilt for her sexual transgression and for the fact that it seemed to set in motion a series of events that caused her daughter to be murdered. The last link in the chain Clotilda forges by murdering her grandchild. The development of Colter's theme in this book amounts to a broaden-

ing of fate into a conception of determinism (he says that Hobbes has especially influenced him). Evidently Colter is agnostic about the possibility of a purpose in the deterministic universe, but he is sure that the pattern of living once set in the personalities and characters of human beings is irreversible and normally painful. Though the situations he describes occur in the humanly constructed world of social and personal relationships, Colter's determinism allows no modification through social change or human will, because he finds neither social status and its consequent material environment nor any historical experience to be the source of life's direction. One is tempted to say that, though Colter's deterministic view of human life appears to be metaphysical, he bases it upon empirical observation. Realist that he is in style, he could deny any selectiveness in his choice of fictional material and say that he only shapes the truth into an exemplary tale.

In his second novel, *The Hippodrome,* an additional factor appears to be suggested by epigraphs taken from Dostoevsky's "The Man Who Lived Underground," Sartre's *La Nausée,* and Genet's *Miracle of the Rose.* That factor is an interest in the emotions of fear and anguish which he describes in the mind of a man who brutally murders his wife in jealousy and through curious circumstances becomes imprisoned in a house (the hippodrome) engaged in the business of providing sex shows for a voyeuristic clientele. The peculiar setting, the alienating effect it has on characters, and the protagonist's obsession with his macabre crime provide an effective representation of human extremity. Again, however, the accomplishment occurs within the style of realism. The suggestions of philosophical reflection result in a scene of elementary pondering on such ideas as motives as always selfish and the appropriateness of uncertainty as a way of life.

In his chosen style Colter is masterly. His imagination for situation is fertile, and his representation of characters instills them with interest. Thematically, however, his conceptions offer no challenge. Many sources outside literature are available to assert the popular "wisdom" of restricted determinism. Like the traditional tale-teller Colter renders consensual views in narrative, but the view of fate held by this tale-teller is insufficiently complex for a world as fluid as ours has become.

—John M. Reilly

COLVIN, James. *See* **MOORCOCK, Michael.**

CONDON, Richard (Thomas)

Nationality: American. **Born:** New York City, 18 March 1915. **Education:** Public schools in New York. **Military Service:** Served in the United States Merchant Navy. **Family:** Married Evelyn Hunt in 1938; two daughters. **Career:** Worked briefly in advertising; publicist in the American film industry for 21 years: worked for Walt Disney Productions, 1936-41, Hal Horne Organization, Twentieth

Century-Fox, 1941-45, Richard Condon Inc., 1945-48, Paramount, 1948-53, United Artists, 1953-57, and other firms; theatrical producer, New York, 1951-52. **Awards:** Writers Guild award, 1986; BAFTA award (U.K.), 1986. **Agent:** Harold Matson Company Inc., 276 Fifth Avenue, New York, New York 10001, U.S.A.; or, Abner Stein, 10 Roland Gardens, London SW7 3PH, England. **Address:** 3436 Asbury Avenue, Dallas, Texas 75205, U.S.A.

PUBLICATIONS

Novels

The Oldest Confession. New York, Appleton Century Crofts, 1958; London, Longman, 1959; as *The Happy Thieves,* New York, Bantam, 1962.
The Manchurian Candidate. New York, McGraw Hill, 1959; London, Joseph, 1960.
Some Angry Angel: A Mid-Century Faerie Tale. New York, McGraw Hill, 1960; London, Joseph, 1961.
A Talent for Loving; or, The Great Cowboy Race. New York, McGraw Hill, 1961; London, Joseph, 1963.
An Infinity of Mirrors. New York, Random House, 1964; London, Heinemann, 1967.
Any God Will Do. New York, Random House, 1964; London, Heinemann, 1967.
The Ecstasy Business. New York, Dial Press, and London, Heinemann, 1967.
Mile High. New York, Dial Press, and London, Heinemann, 1969.
The Vertical Smile. New York, Dial Press, 1971; London, Weidenfeld and Nicolson, 1972.
Arigato. New York, Dial Press, and London, Weidenfeld and Nicolson, 1972.
The Star-Spangled Crunch. New York, Bantam, 1974.
Winter Kills. New York, Dial Press, and London, Weidenfeld and Nicolson, 1974.
Money Is Love. New York, Dial Press, and London, Weidenfeld and Nicolson, 1975.
The Whisper of the Axe. New York, Dial Press, and London, Weidenfeld and Nicolson, 1976.
The Abandoned Woman. New York, Dial Press, 1977; London, Hutchinson, 1978.
Bandicoot. New York, Dial Press, and London, Hutchinson, 1978.
Death of a Politician. New York, Marek, 1978; London, Hutchinson, 1979.
The Entwining. New York, Marek, 1980; London, Hutchinson, 1981.
Prizzi's Honor. New York, Coward McCann, and London, Joseph, 1982.
A Trembling upon Rome. New York, Putnam, and London, Joseph, 1983.
Prizzi's Family. New York, Putnam, and London, Joseph, 1986.
Prizzi's Glory. New York, Dutton, and London, Joseph, 1988.
Emperor of America. New York, Simon and Schuster, and London, Joseph, 1990.
The Final Addiction. New York, St. Martin's Press, and London, Joseph, 1991.

Plays

Men of Distinction (produced New York, 1953).

Screenplays: *A Talent for Loving,* 1965; *The Summer Music,* 1969; *The Long Loud Silence,* 1969; *Prizzi's Honor,* with Janet Roach, 1985; *Arigato,* 1985.

Other

And Then We Moved to Rossenarra; or, The Art of Emigrating. New York, Dial Press, 1973.
The Mexican Stove: A History of Mexican Food, with Wendy Bennett. New York, Doubleday, 1973.
!Olé Mole! Great Recipes in the Classic Mexican Tradition, with Wendy Condon. Dallas, Taylor, 1988.

*

Manuscript Collection: Mugar Memorial Library, Boston University.

Richard Condon comments:

(1991) A writer may call himself an artist but he cannot sit down and consciously create art. What is art is not likely to be decided for decades or longer after the work has been produced—and then is often redecided—so we must not feel badly if we think of literature as entertainment rather than as transcendent enlightenment. The truest banner leading such a Children's Crusade should be blazoned: ENTERTAINMENT FOR THE SAKE OF LITERATURE. Any designation of any author's work as art, either by himself (shyly) or by his peers, is merely the kiss of a wish. Readers buy novels to be entertained, to be taken out of their own lives for a few hours, not to purchase the awe of the ages which will follow.

*   *   *

Richard Condon published his first novel, *The Oldest Confession,* at the age of 42; he had previously spent more than 20 years working as a publicist for the American film industry. Perhaps his fiction is best viewed in light of his prior Hollywood connection, for Condon is known primarily as the author of entertaining novels, novels that are what the public would term "good reads." Some of his more famous books (*The Manchurian Candidate, Winter Kills,* and *Prizzi's Honor,* for example) have been made into successful movies, furthering Condon's own claim of "What I *am* is a professional entertainer."

Condon's first novel defines many of the trademarks of his later works. Although the characters are involved in a highly unlikely plot of art theft and intrigue and the book lacks a certain depth, the author's fine writing and the book's sheer readability save it from the dismal fate of many first novels. Condon proves himself a very able, if not excellent, satirist, parodying everything from the art world to American politics. His subtlest, yet most significant, satire, however, is that of the thriller novel itself. It would seem as if the author sets out to parody the very genre in which he is working; such is the humor and ingenuity of the early Condon.

With the publication of his second novel, *The Manchurian Candidate,* Condon gained an even larger readership, one which was drawn to his eccentric brand of satire and espionage. This novel of political intrigue, brainwashing, murder, and incest is perhaps the best of the author's earlier works. The plot centers around the brainwashing by the Chinese of Richard Shaw, an American GI during the Korean War. Upon returning to the United States, Shaw is recommended for a Medal of Honor, not realizing that he has been the victim of an international plot. He is now the pawn in a dangerous game of political murder. As if he didn't have enough problems, he is also faced with an incestuous relationship with his mother, and a stepfather who bears a striking resemblance to Senator Joe McCarthy.

Condon's taking the absurd in any given situation to the extreme and examining the foibles and paranoia of modern American society soon won him wide public and critical acclaim. He became a type of cult novelist, being likened to Kerouac and Kafka. The novels published in the 1960s, although they still were read by avid fans, were greeted with less enthusiasm by critics. With each ensuing book, the mania and early satire gives way to an ever-increasing paranoia, a love of the too-grotesque, and an obsession with minute facts and statistics. This seeming divergence from his promising first novels lends credence to Condon's view of himself as the entertainer. Although the novels written in mid-career are neither satirical masterpieces nor realistic thrillers, they do combine moments of enjoyment with suspense.

Winter Kills re-established Condon's critical appeal. His best book since *The Manchurian Candidate, Winter Kills,* with is plot centering around the assassination of the wealthy, liberal Irish President Tim Kegan in 1960, could have back-fired in the hands of a less skillful novelist. The headline plot, as well as Condon's handling of it, raises paranoia to a high art, but Condon controls it to a much better extent in *Winter Kills* than in any of his more recent works.

—Sally H. Bennett

CONNELL, Evan S(helby), Jr.

Nationality: American. **Born:** Kansas City, Missouri, 17 August 1924. **Education:** Southwest High School, Kansas City; Dartmouth College, Hanover, New Hampshire, 1941-43; University of Kansas, Lawrence, 1946-47, A.B. 1947; Stanford University, California, 1947-48; Columbia University, New York, 1948-49. **Military Service:** Served as an aviator in the United States Navy, 1943-45. **Career:** Editor, *Contact* magazine, Sausalito, California, 1960-65. **Awards:** Saxton fellowship, 1952; Guggenheim fellowship, 1962; Rockefeller grant, 1967; Los Angeles *Times* award, for non-fiction, 1985. **Agent:** Don Congdon, 156 Fifth Avenue, Suite 625, New York, New York 10010. **Address:** Fort Marcy 13, 320 Artist Road, Santa Fe, New Mexico 87501, USA.

PUBLICATIONS

Novels

Mrs. Bridge. New York, Viking Press, 1958; London, Heinemann, 1960.
The Patriot. New York, Viking Press, 1960; London, Heinemann, 1961.
The Diary of a Rapist. New York, Simon and Schuster, 1966; London, Heinemann, 1967.
Mr. Bridge. New York, Knopf, and London, Heinemann, 1969.
The Connoisseur. New York, Knopf, 1974.
Double Honeymoon. New York, Putnam, 1976.

The Alchymist's Journal. Berkeley, California, North Point Press, 1991.

Short Stories

The Anatomy Lesson and Other Stories. New York, Viking Press, 1958.
At the Crossroads: Stories. New York, Simon and Schuster, 1965; London, Heinemann, 1966.
St. Augustine's Pigeon: The Selected Stories, edited by Gus Blaisdell. Berkeley, California, North Point Press, 1980.

Uncollected Short Stories

"A Cross to Bear," in *Foreign Service* (Kansas City), April 1947.
"The Flat-Footed Tiger," in *American Mercury* (New York), May 1949.
"The Most Beautiful," in *Tomorrow* (New York), September 1949.
"Filbert's Wife," in *Today's Woman* (New York), Summer 1950.
"Cocoa Party," in *Paris Review,* Autumn 1953.
"The Succubus," in *Gent* (New York), August 1957.
"Death and the Wife of John Henry," in *Transatlantic Review* (London), Spring 1960.
"The End of Summer," in *Premier 1* (Mobile, Alabama), n.d.
"Leon and Bebert Aloft," in *Carolina Quarterly* (Chapel Hill, North Carolina), Winter 1966.
"Puig's Wife," in *New Mexico Quarterly* (Albuquerque), Summer 1967.
"The Voyeur," in *Lillabulero* (Chapel Hill, North Carolina), Winter 1967.
"Undersigned, Leon and Bebert," in *Esquire* (New York), December 1969.
"Neil Dortu," in *Boston University Journal,* vol. 30, no. 1, 1977.

Poetry

Notes from a Bottle Found on the Beach at Carmel. New York, Viking Press, 1963; London, Heinemann, 1964.
Points for a Compass Rose. New York, Knopf, 1973.

Other

A Long Desire. New York, Holt Rinehart, 1979.
The White Lantern. New York, Holt Rinehart, 1980.
Son of the Morning Star: Custer and the Little Bighorn. Berkeley, California, North Point Press, 1984; London, Pavilion, 1985.

Editor, *I Am a Lover,* by Jerry Stoll. Sausalito, California, Angel Island, 1961.
Editor, *Woman by Three.* Menlo Park, California, Pacific Coast Publishers, 1969.

*

Manuscript Collection: Boston University Library.

Critical Studies: "After Ground Zero" by Gus Blaisdell, in *New Mexico Quarterly* (Albuquerque), Summer 1966.

*   *   *

In a short story, "The Trellis" (*The Anatomy Lesson*), a murder suspect, in the course of talking rings around a bewildered and suspicious police inspector, observes of the dead man, "He felt that time was passing and he seemed vaguely baffled and resentful of the fact, for he knew he had not done much." The observation might be made of almost any of Evan S. Connell's characters who lead generally privileged but ineffectual lives in the almost hermetic worlds of their private preoccupations.

Connell's reputation rests principally on *Mrs. Bridge* and *Mr. Bridge,* tales of an affluent couple who live in the Country Club district of Kansas City, Missouri, where Connell grew up. The Bridges appeared first in several short sketches collected in *The Anatomy Lesson;* and the two books about them are in no sense traditional novels, but rather montages of many short sketches out of which the reader gradually constructs his own portraits. While they are comfortably wealthy and enjoy an unruffled family life, the Bridges are indeed "vaguely baffled" by life, which the husband has dealt with by following formulas while his wife has floundered around. Their story is summed up by the final episode of *Mrs. Bridge,* in which one December morning the now widowed wife finds herself stuck in her Lincoln, half-out of the garage, so that she cannot open the car doors. She calls, "Hello out there;" but no one answers, "unless it was the falling snow." The Bridges are the kind of earnest, upper-middle-class suburbanites found especially in the American midwest (and probably any provincial culture without a strong local tradition) who have become wealthy without achieving the sophistication to enjoy their lives. One inquiring why so many talented young Americans flee to New York and San Francisco need only read the Bridges' story to find out. (Connell himself for many years lived near San Francisco, and writes mostly about New York.)

Between the Kansas City novels, Connell published *The Patriot,* a *Bildungsroman* about a young man from Kansas city who becomes a Naval air cadet during World War II and at last breaks free of the suffocating obligations he feels to family and country. Though published after the success of *Mrs. Bridge,* the novel is so much more traditional in form than his others and so much in the convention of first novels by sensitive young Americans, it seems surely an early work.

Connell's most remarkable achievement is *The Diary of a Rapist,* a *tour de force* in the form of a calendar year's diary entries in which 26-year-old Earl Summerfield, alienated by his ambitious wife and spiteful fellow Civil Service bureaucrats, is "tempted to keep a scrapbook of monstrous events," occurring daily in San Francisco. Ultimately, he is tempted also to commit monstrous acts and finally, as he has observed others do, to betray himself in his pathetic quest for attention. The disconcerting novel is diminished only by the usual problems of a work limiting the reader's perspective to the paranoid revelations of an unreliable narrator.

Since abandoning the Bridges, Connell has focused on Muhlbach, a New York insurance executive (though with a name borrowed—like others in the books—from those prominent in Kansas City). Like the Bridges, Muhlbach—a widower with a young son and daughter and a domineering housekeeper—first appears in short stories (collected in *At the Crossroads*). The first novel about him, *The Connoisseur,* is, in fact, hardly more than a long short story about Muhlbach's developing an obsession for pre-Columbian art, extended to book length by virtuoso passages displaying the author's vast erudition about folk arts. *Obsession* is indeed the theme of all the Muhlbach stories (perhaps of all Connell's work), as this anti-hero realizes when he thinks, "I can't distinguish real-

ity any longer, I'm gripped by an obsession. I suppose I should be alarmed, but as a matter of fact I'm not." Pre-Columbian art is entirely forgotten, however, in *Double Honeymoon,* in which Muhlbach becomes obsessed with an exotic young girl named Lambeth, whose erratic behavior culminates in suicide after she appears in the pornographic motion picture that gives the novel its title. The Muhlbach story—unlike the Bridges'—remains unresolved as he disappears into a crowd.

Connell's book-length poems defy summary because, like most of the novels, they are a montage of fragments drawn from the author's vast readings about ancient peoples and their cultures that show how he shares the skill of his dazzling speaker in "The Trellis."

—Warren French

COOK, David

Nationality: British. **Born:** Preston, Lancashire, 21 September 1940. **Education:** The Royal Academy of Dramatic Art, London, 1959-61. **Career:** Since 1961 professional actor. Writer-in-residence, St. Martin's College, Lancaster, 1982-83. **Awards:** Writers Guild award, 1977; American Academy E.M. Forster award, 1977; Hawthornden prize, 1978; Arts Council bursary, 1979; Southern Arts prize, 1985; Arthur Welton scholarship, 1991.; Odd Fellow Concern Book award, 1992. **Agent:** Greene and Heaton Ltd., 37 Goldhawk Road, London W12 8QQ. **Address:** 7 Sydney Place, London SW7 3NL, England.

PUBLICATIONS

Novels

Albert's Memorial. London, Secker and Warburg, 1972.
Happy Endings. London, Secker and Warburg, 1974.
Sunrising. London, Secker and Warburg, 1984; Woodstock, New York, Overlook Press, 1986.
Missing Persons. London, Secker and Warburg, 1986.
Crying Out Loud. London, Secker and Warburg, 1988.
Walter and June. London, Secker and Warburg, 1989.
    Walter. London, Secker and Warburg, 1978; Woodstock, New York, Overlook Press, 1985.
    Winter Doves. London, Secker and Warburg, 1979; Woodstock, New York, Overlook Press, 1985.
Second Best. London, Faber, 1991.

Uncollected Short Stories

"Finding Out," in *Mae West Is Dead,* edited by Adam Mars-Jones. London, Faber, 1983.
"Growing Away," in *Daily Telegraph* (London), 1994.

Plays

Square Dance (produced London, 1968).
If Only (televised 1984). Published in *Scene Scripts 3,* edited by Roy Blatchford, London, Longman, 1982.

Radio Play: *Pity,* 1989.

Television Plays: *Willy,* 1973; *Jenny Can't Work Any Faster,* 1975; *Why Here?,* 1976; *Couples* series, 1976; *A Place Like Home* series, 1976; *Repent at Leisure,* 1978; *Mary's Wife,* 1980; *Walter,* from his own novel, 1982; *Walter and June,* from his own novel, 1982; *If Only,* 1984; *Singles Week-end,* 1984; *Love Match,* 1986; *Missing Persons,* from his own novel, 1990; *Closing Numbers,* 1994; also scripts for Schools Television.

Screenplay: *Second Best,* from his own novel, 1994.

*

Film Adaptation: *Second Best,* 1994.

David Cook comments:

I began writing because I was an out-of-work actor, and needed an occupation which would be creatively satisfying. From the beginning, therefore, I brought an actor's concern with character to the task of writing fiction, and all my work is based on the same sort of act of empathy by which any actor brings life to an invented person. My discovery was that I now had to make this empathetic act for all my characters, not just one, seeing through their eyes, thinking their thoughts, feeling their feelings, and to do it without the help of a text; creating the text was up to me.

So the questions for me always are "Who are you?" "How do you live?" "How have you arrived at this condition?", and from the answers, logic will make a narrative. My first novel was about an old bag-lady whom I used to see sitting in doorways near South Kensington Station. I did not write a story; I wrote little pieces of what the details of her life might be, and after a while they began to form themselves into a story. All my work since, both the novels and the TV plays, has been based on empathy and research, and with a strong bias to those who have been called "the walking wounded." When I decided that my fifth novel, *Sunrising,* should be set in a time which was not my own, the research became different in kind. I could no longer walk to Fleetwood or work with autistic children, but had to find my material in books, and while it is not exactly easy for someone with no academic education whatever to gain access to Oxford's Bodleian Library, it was done. Now that I have the taste, for it, I shall write a sequel to *Sunrising* one day, but I do not anticipate that I shall abandon the walking wounded of the here and now; they press in too closely.

*   *   *

David Cook is a stage and television actor who began to write novels in the early 1970s. His first novel, *Albert's Memorial,* was acclaimed for its originality and its sharply detailed prose, and subsequent novels like *Happy Endings* and *Walter* won prestigious prizes. Finely and delicately crafted, Cook's novels build the interior perspectives of his characters with a meticulous sense of authenticity and convincing detail. Characteristically, Cook's characters are isolated, lonely, inward-dwelling creatures whose consciousness is limited by some form of impairment or crippling circumstance. Physical or emotional indigents, they wander through a world they perceive intensely, although never accurately, in only bits and pieces. The juxtaposition of their partial points of view, which Cook always sees sympathetically, with an assumed, seldom stated "normal" point of view provides the tension and the emotional energy of the novels. *Albert's Memorial,* for example, concentrates on two isolated creatures: Mary, who after her husband's death, tries to live in the cemetery where he is buried and later tramps to the seaside resort where they spent their honeymoon, interested only in the conversations she holds with him inside her head, and Paul, who establishes trivial routines in his more geographically circumscribed wanderings after his homosexual lover suddenly dies. In *Walter,* the world is seen through Walter's autistic point of view, tracing the origins and effects of the debility that has led to his being institutionalized. Cook's central characters are all dependent on others, or institutions, or fantasies, for a survival they cannot manage on their own.

Cook's characters welcome impingements on their isolation, respond to relationships that break through their defenses or their occluded and partial visions. In *Albert's Memorial,* Mary and Paul connect, finally living with each other and sharing the fantasy of Mary's phantom pregnancy (she has been raped while tramping, and mistakes symptoms because she and her husband had avoided having children by never fully consummating their love). The relationship exists in mutual dependency, as does that between Walter from the earlier novel and June, a more intellectually functioning although emotionally severely unstable resident of the mental institution, as they escape to wander England in *Winter Doves.*

Characters like Mary and Paul, Walter and June, are seen against the background of contemporary England. The reader is always aware of an ordinary England dimly seen through the distorted half-lens of the impaired, and Cook never explicitly and seldom even implicitly provides any significant social commentary. The understated conflict between the characters and the larger world is often effectively rendered as comedy, as in the scene in which Paul, consulting a doctor because he is worried that Mary's "pregnancy" may be endangered, is so haltingly unable to articulate his concern that the doctor tests him for gonorrhea and administers a preventive injection. Similarly, wandering characters, in *Winter Doves* and other novels, duplicate a muted version of the comic picaresque, as they clash with the society that they cannot understand. Cook frequently depicts representatives of the Welfare State who try to help or control the indigents. These representatives, nurses, social workers, custodians in mental hospitals, doctors, and bureaucrats, are generally benign and well-intentioned, although unable to touch or assuage the deeper disturbances of the central characters. England's postwar emphasis on the social services is seen as praiseworthy and humane, although never finally relevant, as if no social issue or characterization is ever as significant as is the tenuous establishment of the individual identity.

Much of that identity in Cook's fictional world is physical and direct. He concentrates on immediate experience, describing with acute sensitivity how his characters touch, feel, reason, and communicate. Long passages detail the tiring efforts necessary to establish oneself as a squatter in an uncompleted office building or the elaborate preparation for and physical progress of the homosexual love affair. In the emphasis on the physical and emotional, the detailed representation of how the impaired see and feel, Cook is attempting to shape his carefully developed prose to get at a primal quality within the human creature. Cook's versions of the primal are never aggressive or animalistic; rather, his novels are most frequently populated by birds, pigeons and doves, in both plot and metaphor. The birds suggest the delicacy, fragility, and tenuousness of identity, the only kind of precarious existence these impaired creatures can manage. Cook sees the bird-like fragility and tenacity of the creatures of limited consciousness with enormous sympathy that, because of his writing's directness, specificity, and lack of pretense, never descends to sentimentality.

—James Gindin

COOPER, Lettice (Ulpha)

Nationality: British. **Born:** Eccles, Lancashire, 3 September 1897. **Education:** St. Cuthbert's School, Southbourne; Lady Margaret Hall, Oxford, 1916-18, B.A. **Career:** Editorial assistant and drama critic, *Time and Tide,* London, 1939-40. Public relations officer, Ministry of Food, London, 1940-45. President, Robert Louis Stevenson Club, 1958-74; vice-chair, 1975-78, and president, 1979-81, English PEN Club. **Awards:** Arts Council bursary, 1968, 1979; Eric Gregory travelling scholarship, 1977. O.B.E. (Officer, Order of the British Empire), 1980. **Agent:** A.P. Watt Ltd., 20 John Street, London WC1N 2DL. **Address:** 95 Canfield Gardens, London NW6 3DY, England.

PUBLICATIONS

Novels

The Lighted Room. London, Hodder and Stoughton, 1925.
The Old Fox. London, Hodder and Stoughton, 1927.
Good Venture. London, Hodder and Stoughton, 1928.
Likewise the Lyon. London, Hodder and Stoughton, 1928.
The Ship of Truth. London, Hodder and Stoughton, and Boston, Little Brown, 1930.
Private Enterprise. London, Hodder and Stoughton, 1931.
Hark to Rover! London, Hodder and Stoughton, 1933.
We Have Come to a Country. London, Gollancz, 1935.
The New House. London, Gollancz, and New York, Macmillan, 1936.
National Provincial. London, Gollancz, and New York, Macmillan, 1938.
Black Bethlehem. London, Gollancz, and New York, Macmillan, 1947.
Fenny. London, Gollancz, 1953.
Three Lives. London, Gollancz, 1957.
A Certain Compass. London, Gollancz, 1960.
The Double Heart. London, Gollancz, 1962.
Late in the Afternoon. London, Gollancz, 1973.
Tea on Sunday. London, Gollancz, 1973.
Snow and Roses. London, Gollancz, 1976.
Desirable Residence. London, Gollancz, 1980.
Unusual Behaviour. London, Gollancz, 1986.

Uncollected Short Stories

"Frowning Caryatid," in *London Calling,* edited by Storm Jameson. New York, Harper, 1942.
"The Heavy Splash," in *Critical Quarterly* (Manchester), Autumn 1987.

Fiction (for children)

Blackberry's Kitten. Leicester, Brockhampton Press, 1961; New York, Vanguard Press, 1963.

The Bear Who Was Too Big. London, Parrish, 1963; Chicago, Follett, 1966.
Bob-a-Job. Leicester, Brockhampton Press, 1963.
Contadino. London, Cape, 1964.
The Twig of Cypress. London, Deutsch, 1965; New York, Washburn, 1966.
We Shall Have Snow. Leicester, Brockhampton Press, 1966.
Robert the Spy Hunter. London, Kaye and Ward, 1973.
Parkin. London, Harrap, 1977.

Other (for children)

Great Men of Yorkshire (West Riding). London, Lane, 1955.
The Young Florence Nightingale. London, Lane, 1960; New York, Roy, 1961.
The Young Victoria. London, Parrish, 1961; New York, Roy, 1962.
James Watt. London, A. and C. Black, 1963.
Garibaldi. London, Methuen, 1964; New York, Roy, 1966.
The Young Edgar Allan Poe. London, Parrish, 1964; New York, Roy, 1965.
The Fugitive King. London, Parrish, 1965.
A Hand upon the Time: A Life of Charles Dickens. New York, Pantheon, 1968; London, Gollancz, 1971.
Robert Louis Stevenson. London, Burns and Oates, 1969.
Gunpowder: Treason and Plot. London, Abelard Schuman, 1970.

Other

Robert Louis Stevenson. London, Home and Van Thal, 1947; Denver, Alan Swallow, 1948.
Yorkshire: West Riding. London, Hale, 1950.
George Eliot. London, Longman, 1951; revised edition, 1960, 1964.

*

Manuscript Collection: Eccles Public Library, Lancashire.

Lettice Cooper comments:

I want to write stories about people in depth, using the traditional form, but hoping to show how the unconscious pressures and situations are always there beneath the conscious pattern. I want to indicate both the inner and outer life of my characters, and to "explore the truth of the human situation."

*   *   *

Lettice Cooper has been writing novels for many years, and social historians of the future may well study them for their careful reflection of middle-class English life at various stages of this century. The worlds she described in her younger days may have gone, but this does not mean that the novels themselves have dated: technically and psychologically they still stand up well. Their settings are domestic, though their domesticity varies. In *Fenny,* one of the most ambitious and successful, we see some grandish Italian interiors; in *National Provincial,* lower middle-class North Country life; in *The Ship of Truth,* a young clergyman's home, penny-pinching through necessity; in *The New House,* an upper-middle-class family, suffocatingly cosy and financially quite secure; in *The Double Heart,* more townish and trendy people; in *Late in the Afternoon,* a smartish background in the main characters, very different ones in the others, who include a wandering hippie.

In some of the novels institutions stand behind the domesticity. In *Three Lives* it is an adult education college; in *We Have Come to a Country* an "occupational center for unemployed men" (the time is the mid-1930s). In these cases, the institutions are not just decorative backgrounds, realistically painted flats; we get inside them, learn how they work. Nothing in Cooper's novels is put in without a point or a place in the action, without being properly inserted and made familiar. Cooper is always professional, a writer whose care, and whose respect for her readers, deserve respect.

Two places are of primary importance in her novels—her native Yorkshire, standing rocklike and immovable, often a symbol of stability in a shifting world, sometimes of narrowness in a wider one (London beckons the young); and the country for which she feels the deep love of the enchanted (though knowledgeable) outsider: Italy, and more specifically Tuscany. Again and again the novels are set in, or have excursions to, one or other of these places. Both, in a sense, seem to represent homecoming.

If the settings of the novels are domestic, the action, as a rule, is unadventurous, in the sense of undramatic—except in terms of feelings and personalities. But this might be said, of course, of the majority of English fiction written by women, from *Middlemarch* downwards, and implies no narrowness of outlook. Cooper has kept fairly firmly within the worlds she knows and understands, but that they have opened out with the years is clear from *Late in the Afternoon,* in which, from the standpoint of an elderly woman, she deals sympathetically with the new young, and makes a splendidly unpatronising excursion into a working-class household touched but not radically altered by the new prosperity. From her domestic settings she deals, in fact, with the basic issues and problems: love and indifference, parental selfishness, the young's longing for escape, moral dilemmas, varying standards of behavior, of loyalty and truth. In what seems a straightforward way she concentrates much into seemingly simple scenes and passages; her strength lying in an intelligent understanding of human nature; in warmth tempered with briskness and humor, and in an intuitive interpretation of events, psychological and spiritual. At its simplest this concentration appears in her children's books, outstandingly good among which is *Bob-a-Job,* a small masterpiece of insight on that attractive menace, the predatory wolf-cub, out to help.

—Isabel Quigly

COOPER, William

Pseudonym: Harry Summerfield Hoff. **Nationality:** British. **Born:** Crewe, Cheshire, 4 August 1910. **Education:** Christ's College, Cambridge, M.A. in physics 1933. **Military Service:** Served in the Royal Air Force, 1940-45. **Family:** Married Joyce Barbara Harris in 1951 (died 1988); two daughters. **Career:** Schoolmaster, Leicester, 1933-40; assistant commissioner, Civil Service Commission, London, 1945-58. Part-time personnel consultant, United Kingdom Atomic Energy Authority, 1958-72, Central Electricity Generating Board, 1960-72, Commission of European Community, 1972-73; assistant director, Civil Service Selection Board, 1973-75; member of the Board, Crown Agents, 1975-77; adviser, Millbank Technical Services, 1975-77; personnel consultant, Ministry of Overseas Development, 1978. Adjunct professor of English, Syracuse University, London Center, 1977-90. Fellow, Royal Society of Literature. **Address:** 22 Kenilworth Court, Lower Richmond Road, London SW15 1EW, England.

PUBLICATIONS

Novels

Trina (as H.S. Hoff). London, Heinemann, 1934; as *It Happened in PRK,* New York, Coward McCann, 1934.
Rhéa (as H.S. Hoff). London, Heinemann, 1937.
Lisa (as H.S. Hoff). London, Heinemann, 1937.
Three Marriages (as H.S. Hoff). London, Heinemann, 1946.
Scenes from Provincial Life. London, Cape, 1950.
The Struggles of Albert Woods. London, Cape, 1952; New York, Doubleday, 1953.
The Ever-Interesting Topic. London, Cape, 1953.
Disquiet and Peace. London, Macmillan, 1956; Philadelphia, Lippincott, 1957.
Young People. London, Macmillan, 1958.
Scenes from Married Life. London, Macmillan, 1961.
Scenes from Life (includes *Scenes from Provincial Life* and *Scenes from Married Life*). New York, Scribner, 1961.
Memoirs of a New Man. London, Macmillan, 1966.
You Want the Right Frame of Reference. London, Macmillan, 1971.
Love on the Coast. London, Macmillan, 1973.
You're Not Alone: A Doctor's Diary. London, Macmillan, 1976.
Scenes from Metropolitan Life. London, Macmillan, 1982.
Scenes from Later Life. London, Macmillan, 1983.
Scenes from Provincial Life, and Scenes from Metropolitan Life. New York, Dutton, 1983.
Scenes from Married Life, and Scenes from Later Life. New York, Dutton, 1984.
Immortality at Any Price. London, Sinclair Stevenson, 1991.

Uncollected Short Stories

"Ball of Paper," in *Winter's Tales 1.* London, Macmillan, and New York, St. Martin's Press, 1955.
"A Moral Choice," in *Winter's Tales 4.* London, Macmillan, and New York, St. Martin's Press, 1958.

Plays

High Life (produced London, 1951).
Prince Genji (produced Oxford, 1968). London, Evans, 1959.

Other

C.P. Snow. London, Longman, 1959; revised edition, 1971.
Shall We Ever Know? The Trial of the Hosein Brothers for the Murder of Mrs. McKay. London, Hutchinson, 1971; as *Brothers,* New York, Harper, 1972.
From Early Life (memoirs). London, Macmillan, 1990.

*

Manuscript Collection: Humanities Research Center, University of Texas, Austin.

Critical Studies: *Tradition and Dream* by Walter Allen, London, Phoenix House, 1964, as *The Modern Novel in Britain and the United States,* New York, Dutton, 1964; introduction by Malcolm Bradbury to *Scenes from Provincial Life,* London, Macmillan, 1969; *William Cooper the Novelist* by Ashok Kumar Sinha, New Delhi, Jnanada, 1977.

William Cooper comments:

(1972) I don't know that I specially believe in artists making statements about their own work. An artist's *work* is *his* statement. And that's that. The rest is for other people to say. Perhaps a writer whose original statement has turned out obscure may feel it useful to present a second that's more comprehensible—in that case I wonder why he didn't make the second one first.

Speaking for myself, *Scenes from Provincial Life* seems to me so simple, lucid, attractive, and funny that anyone who finds he can't read it probably ought to ask himself: "Should I be trying to read books at all? Wouldn't it be better to sit and watch television or something?" I write about the real world and real people in it. And I stick pretty close to what I've had some experience of. That's why *Scenes from Metropolitan Life,* which is also simple, lucid, attractive and funny, was suppressed. *Scenes from Married Life,* makes the third of a trilogy. *Albert Woods* and *Memoirs of a New Man* are about goings-on in the world of science and technology; *You Want the Right Frame of Reference* in the world of arts—they have an added touch of wryness and malice. An unusual marriage is the core of *Young People* and of *Disquiet and Peace,* the former set in the provinces in the '30s, the latter in Edwardian upperclass London—its small group of admirers thinks it's a beautiful book. *The Ever-Interesting Topic* is about what happens when you give a course of lectures on sex to a boarding school full of boys: what you'd expect. *Shall We Ever Know?* is a day-by-day account of a most surprising and mystifying murder trial, a kidnapping for ransom in which no trace whatsoever of the body was ever found, and two men were found guilty of murder.

(1981) *Love on the Coast,* my only novel to be set outside England, is about some former "flower children" in San Francisco who are working their way back into society by running an "experimental" theater. And *You're Not Alone* is the diary of a London doctor, a retired GP of some distinction, to whom people come to confide their sexual quirks—as a start he tells them they are not alone.

(1986) In 1981 the 30-year suppression of *Scenes from Metropolitan Life* ended, allowing the trilogy to be published complete. The three novels fit together thus: *Provincial Life*—Boy won't marry Girl; *Metropolitan Life*—same Girl now won't marry Boy; *Married Life*—Boy meets another Girl and marries happily every after. In 1983 I published *Scenes from Later Life* as a companion volume to the trilogy, with the characters in their sixties and seventies, learning to cope with old age—in the final chapter I can make you laugh and make you cry within seven pages.

(1991) For my next novel I decided to make a change and embark on obvious satire. I completed a first draft which needed quite a lot of work, and two things happened which led me to put it aside. The first was a long drawn-out personal tragedy, on which I was persuaded to do a piece for *Granta* about the last stages—the most intimate thing I have ever written. The second was a friend's suggestion which caught my fancy, that I should try my hand at autobiography (from which I had previously had an aversion). I decided to write down things I could remember happening between the ages of 2 and 17 just as they came into my head—pure reminiscence unsullied by "research," *From Early Life,* short and delightful. And then I came back to my new departure, the satirical novel called *Immortality at Any Price.* The jacket by Willie Rushton discloses its nature—my response to a most wounding comment once made by an American reviewer: "Who wants to read a novel by a nice guy?" Well! . . .

* * *

William Cooper is the pen-name of a novelist who had already published four novels under his own name, H.S. Hoff, when in 1950 he emerged with a new literary identity, and won a new literary reputation, with *Scenes from Provincial Life*—a book which quickly became a classic of a new kind of postwar realism and undoubtedly had a very powerful influence on the development of the English novel in the 1950s and since. A delightful and tough-minded story set among young provincial intellectuals, in a British midland town that bears a close resemblance to Leicester, over the crucial months of change and crisis leading up to the outbreak of World War II, *Scenes from Provincial Life*—published at a time when new fictional directions were uncertain and no real postwar movement had shown itself—became the forerunner of a whole sequence of novels which, in the postwar years, were to treat local English life, and the familiar and ordinary experience of recognizable people, with a fresh, youthful, exploratory, and critical curiosity. There can be little doubt that the book did encourage, and often considerably influence, a number of younger writers like John Braine, David Storey, Stanley Middleton, and Stan Barstow, some of whom directly expressed their indebtedness; and it certainly helped writers thereafter to find a sense of direction in the period after the decline both of Modernism and the political fiction of the 1930s. Its force was strengthened by the fact that Cooper—along with C.P. Snow, Pamela Hansford Johnson, and some other younger writers like Kingsley Amis, Philip Larkin, and John Wain—was deliberately reacting against the Bloomsbury-dominated climate of "cultured" and cosmopolitan experimentalism, and was seeking out a form of fiction much more social, empirical, realistic, and humanly substantial in character, and concerned with a felt sense of texture and the issues of contemporary British life.

This spirit in writing has sometimes been characterized by critics as middlebrow, and it was self-defined as provincial. But it asserted a humanist vigor and a closeness to familiar life in the practice of serious British writing at a time when, in literary traditions in other countries, the break with the past was disquieting and the signs of literary strain were being felt. Joyce had seemed to bring the modern novel into a cul-de-sac, and Cooper and others pointed to the value of the native tradition, his argument clearly strengthened by the fact that his own novel was not just one of the first, but one of the best, of a kind. In time the tendency he represented was to come to seem a narrowed view of the direction of fiction, but Cooper represented this kind of novel in all its strength. *Scenes from Provincial Life* tells the story of Joe Lunn, the young science master at a provincial grammar school, and his friends, nonconforming emotional radicals who know they are distant witnesses to the world's great events, as a kind of conflict between the force of history and the force of the familiar. Fearful of a German occupation of Britain, they plan their exiles; but the day-to-day world of provincial life (especially their complex sexual relationships) seems all that matters, and they finally opt for it. The story was to go on through three more volumes, plotting the development of Joe's life as a scientific adviser to government, as a writer and a married man. *Scenes from Metropolitan Life,* written in the 1950s but not published for legal reasons until 1982, brings the story into the postwar world, the London scene, and the world of Whitehall, renewing Joe's relationship with his former mistress Myrtle in the context of urban sexual mores. *Scenes from Married Life,* which appeared in 1961, is, unusually in contemporary fiction, a celebration of marital life, reinforcing Cooper's gift for exploring the private underside of the public world in which Joe is now an important figure. *Scenes from Later Life* brings most of the characters forward into the world of the late 1970s, with Joe haunted by retirement and the ailments of his mother. But, despite a rising quota of pain, the characteristic Cooper good humor and the sense of celebration of the familiar prevails, and the sequence sustains the spirit with which it started. As in the novels of C.P. Snow, but without Snow's stoical and even tragic pessimism, we see the new bloods turn into the men of place and power in an age in which the scientist and technologist become important public figures. But Cooper's social history gives way to a history of the domestic and the familiar, a comedy of daily life done with great luminosity and delicacy.

Cooper's other novels are all marked by the same commitment to familiar life, and the same luminous good humor. One, *Disquiet and Peace,* is an historical novel, set in the high-society milieu of Edwardian political and drawing-room life as the strange death of Liberal England is taking place; another, *Love on the Coast,* takes radical Californian lifestyle as its subject. But most of his books are, in an approving sense of the term, "banal" novels—concerned, that is, with the world of everyday social and emotional experience, and capable of evoking a strong, strange sense of recognition. Set in the provinces, the suburbs, or the world of the urban middle-classes with its clubs and appropriate restaurants—the pieces of social experience Cooper knows and details very well—they describe with affection and understanding the way ordinary things happen to intelligent and skeptical people as they marry, breed families, have affairs, work at recognizable jobs, and worry about their sexual lives, their mortality, and their salaries. Many of them indeed belong to the world of the "new men" (one book is called *Memoirs of a New Man*) whose meritocratic ascent forms an important story in British social life. Like that of his friend C.P. Snow (on whom he has written warmly), Cooper's fiction relates the life of ordinary origins to the commonsense decencies of public life, and, as with Snow, his realistic pleasure in the world seems to have to do with the fact that it is open to his mobility and talent. Like Snow's fiction, Cooper's achievement bears some relation to that desire for a better world that fed the postwar years, and also explores many of its ambiguities and disappointments.

But if one of Cooper's best qualities is his powerful realism, another is his comedy and wit. If he deals with familiar life, he lights it up with a striking sense of human oddity, and of the quirks and unexpected outrages that exist in his very recognizable characters. The outrage is often added to by the cool, undercutting tone of his narrators themselves. Like Muriel, who in *Disquiet and Peace* is provoked to stirring up disorder by donning an eyeglass and then dropping it in her soup, Cooper has a way of stirring up the surface of his world by his oblique vision. The struggles of the characters for sexual, social, or material success become matters for very cool irony. His plots often turn on conflicts between traditional and more liberal values, and he writes with a moral edge, but is also capable of moving lightly away from it all, leaving the chaos to itself, as in *The Ever-Interesting Topic,* about a headmaster who tries to bring lectures on sex education into his public school. All

Cooper's books show a buoyant and vitalistic view of sexuality and an awareness of the way it undercuts so many of our social and moral pretensions. This comic vision is something he also handed on to his successors, and it makes his a realism of marvelous surprise, giving his books a sharp bite and clarity that distinguish them from Snow's sobered kind of realism. His Albert Woods and Joe Lunns may acquire influence, but they do not acquire sobriety. As a result they become attractive centers of vision, and that is especially true of Joe Lunn, who, in all the books where he is narrator, is both a performer in the chaotic and comic action and an artistic observer consciously knowing about fiction and busily interpreting, recalling, and shaping in a neat balance of sympathy and irony. Other narrative techniques are used in other novels, but they are usually distinguished by an adept mixture of sympathetic identification with lively characters and an ironic detachment from them.

With 17 novels over half a century to his credit, Cooper has contributed vitally to postwar British fiction. At times his committed support for realism and his distrust of writing in any way avant garde has been unfashionable and even inhibiting, though it has been an expression of his fierce literary individualism. Nonetheless his influence has been very considerable, and he did much to establish the "new realism" of British fiction from the 1950s onward. Though his own novels do vary somewhat in quality, they possess a very distinctive style, tone, and vision, and at their best a very cunning and powerful artistic control. Cooper's strengths are most apparent when—as in *Young People*—he is capturing the flavor of some distinctive period, milieu or generation, and then observing, with some cynicism, the characteristic, and comic, behavior of individuals within it. A strong admirer of the novelist H.G. Wells ("I loved it, enshrining Wells's message of optimism," Joe Lunn says of Wells's *The History of Mr. Polly* in *Scenes from Later Life*), and like him trained as a scientist, he can be compared with his master both for his concern with the way British society works and for his power to capture youthful, hopeful, buoyant pleasure from the stuff of ordinary life. At best, as in *Scenes from Provincial Life,* his balance of detail, reminiscence, sentiment, and irony comes together so exactly as to allow comparison with the great "artful realists," like Turgenev. Where many British novelists avoid the public world, of politics, government, law, and science, Cooper's books construct an important record of manners and moods, landscapes and cityscapes, social and historical changes, public operations and private and sexual emotions, in ways which are both morally and humanly illuminating and comically adept. Cooper has described his aim simply; it is "to tell the truth, laughing." These are the qualities that give the four novels of the *Scenes* series the classic status they now possess. Cooper has remained a vivid and influential writer, publishing in 1990 an autobiography of his midlands childhood, *From Early Life,* which captures his lower-middle-class social origins and ambitions with his familiar humane intelligence, and extends his chronicle of English life backwards to the years right after World War I. Meanwhile his late novel *Immortality at Any Price* deals in his sharp, cynical fashion with the raging competitiveness of the old, and turns on the principle that there is nothing like the animosity of old friends. Altogether, the long chronicle of his novels reminds us that the ability to see, illuminate, shape, and construct the experience of the ordinary and social world and to interpret the patterns of human behavior within it is something fundamental to the spirit of fiction.

—Malcolm Bradbury

COOVER, Robert (Lowell)

Nationality: American. **Born:** Charles City, Iowa, 4 February 1932. **Education:** Southern Illinois University, Carbondale, 1949-51; Indiana University, Bloomington, B.A. 1953; University of Chicago, 1958-61, M.A. 1965. **Military Service:** Served in the United States Naval Reserve, 1953-57: Lieutenant. **Family:** Married Maria del Sans-Mallafré in 1959; two daughters and one son. **Career:** Taught at Bard College, Annandale-on-Hudson, New York, 1966-67, University of Iowa, Iowa City, 1967-69, Columbia University, New York, 1972, Princeton University, New Jersey, 1972-73, Virginia Military Institute, Lexington, 1976, and Brandeis University, Waltham, Massachusetts, 1981. Since 1981 writer-in-residence, Brown University, Providence, Rhode Island. Fiction editor, *Iowa Review,* Iowa City, 1974-77. **Awards:** Faulkner award, 1966; Brandeis University Creative Arts award, 1969; Rockefeller fellowship, 1969; Guggenheim fellowship, 1971, 1974; American Academy award, 1976; National Endowment for the Arts grant, 1985; Rea award, for short story, 1987. **Agent:** Georges Borchardt Inc., 136 East 57th Street, New York, New York 10022, U.S.A.

PUBLICATIONS

Novels

The Origin of the Brunists. New York, Putnam, 1966; London, Barker, 1967.
The Universal Baseball Association, Inc., J. Henry Waugh, Prop. New York, Random House, 1968; London, Hart Davis, 1970.
The Public Burning. New York, Viking Press, 1977; London, Allen Lane, 1978.
Spanking the Maid. New York, Grove Press, 1982; London, Heinemann, 1987.
Gerald's Party. New York, Linden Press, and London, Heinemann, 1986.

Short Stories

Pricksongs and Descants. New York, Dutton, 1969; London, Cape, 1971.
The Water Pourer (unpublished chapter from *The Origin of the Brunists*). Bloomfield Hills, Michigan, Bruccoli Clark, 1972.
Hair o' the Chine. Bloomfield Hills, Michigan, Bruccoli Clark, 1979.
After Lazarus: A Filmscript. Bloomfield Hills, Michigan, Bruccoli Clark, 1980.
Charlie in the House of Rue. Lincoln, Massachusetts, Penmaen Press, 1980.
A Political Fable. New York, Viking Press, 1980.
The Convention. Northridge, California, Lord John Press, 1982.
In Bed One Night and Other Brief Encounters. Providence, Rhode Island, Burning Deck, 1983.
Aesop's Forest, with *The Plot of the Mice and Other Stories,* by Brian Swann. Santa Barbara, California, Capra Press, 1986.
A Night at the Movies; or, You Must Remember This. New York, Simon and Schuster, and London, Heinemann, 1987.
Whatever Happened to Gloomy Gus of the Chicago Bears? New York, Simon and Schuster, 1987; London, Heinemann, 1988.
Pinocchio in Venice. New York, Simon and Schuster, and London, Heinemann, 1991.

Plays

The Kid (produced New York, 1972; London, 1974). Included in *A Theological Position,* 1972.
A Theological Position (includes *A Theological Position, The Kid, Love Scene, Rip Awake*). New York, Dutton, 1972.
Love Scene (as *Scène d'amour,* produced Paris, 1973; as *Love Scene,* produced New York, 1974). Included in *A Theological Position,* 1972.
Rip Awake (produced Los Angeles, 1975). Included in *A Theological Position,* 1972.
A Theological Position (produced Los Angeles, 1977; New York, 1979). Included in *A Theological Position,* 1972.
Bridge Hand (produced Providence, Rhode Island, 1981).

Other

Editor, with Kent Dixon, *The Stone Wall Book of Short Fiction.* Iowa City, Stone Wall Press, 1973.
Editor, with Elliott Anderson, *Minute Stories.* New York, Braziller, 1976.

*

Critical Studies: *Fiction and the Figures of Life* by William H. Gass, New York, Knopf, 1970; *Black Humor Fiction of the Sixties* by Max Schulz, Athens, Ohio University Press, 1973; "Robert Coover and the Hazards of Metafiction" by Neil Schmitz, in *Novel 7* (Providence, Rhode Island), 1974; "Humor and Balance in Coover's *The Universal Baseball Association, Inc.*" by Frank W. Shelton, in *Critique 17* (Atlanta), 1975; "Robert Coover, Metafictions, and Freedom" by Margaret Heckard, in *Twentieth Century Literature 22* (Los Angeles), 1976; "The Dice of God: Einstein, Heisenberg, and Robert Coover" by Arlen J. Hansen, in *Novel 10* (Providence, Rhode Island), 1976; "Structure as Revelation: Coover's *Pricksongs and Descants*" by Jessie Gunn, in *Linguistics in Literature,* vol. 2, no. 1, 1977; *The Metafictional Muse: The Works of Robert Coover, Donald Barthelme, and William H. Gass* by Larry McCaffery, Pittsburgh, University of Pittsburgh Press, 1982; *Robert Coover: The Universal Fictionmaking Process* by Lois Gordon, Carbondale, Southern Illinois University Press, 1983; *Robert Coover's Fictions* by Jackson I. Cope, Baltimore, Johns Hopkins University Press, 1986; *Dissident Postmodernists: Barthelme, Coover, Pynchon* by Paul Maltby, Philadelphia, University of Pennsylvania Press, 1991; *Robert Coover: A Study of the Short Fiction* by Thomas E. Kennedy, New York, Twayne, 1992; *Comic Sense: Reading Robert Coover, Stanley Elkin, Philip Roth* by Thomas Pughe, Basel, Switzerland, Birkhäuser Verlag, 1994.

Robert Coover comments:

In reply to the question: "Why Do You Write?": Because art blows life into the lifeless, death into the deathless.

Because art's lie is preferable, in truth, to life's beautiful terror.

Because, as time does not pass (nothing, as Beckett tells us, passes), *it* passes the time.

Because death, our mirthless master, is somehow amused by epitaphs.

Because epitaphs, well-struck, give death, our voracious master, heartburn.

Because fiction imitates life's beauty, thereby inventing the beauty life lacks.

Because fiction is the best position, at once exotic and familiar, for fucking the world.

Because fiction, mediating paradox, celebrates it.

Because fiction, mothered by love, loves love as a mother might her unloving child.

Because fiction speaks, hopelessly, beautifully, as the world speaks.

Because God, created in the storyteller's image, can be destroyed only by His maker.

Because, in its perversity, art harmonizes the disharmonious.

Because, in its profanity, fiction sanctifies life.

Because, in its terrible isolation, writing is a path to brotherhood.

Because in the beginning was the gesture, and in the end to come as well: in between what we have are words.

Because, of all the arts, only fiction can unmake the myths that unman men.

Because of its endearing futility, its outrageous pretensions.

Because the pen, though short, casts a long shadow (upon, it must be said, no surface).

Because the world is re-invented every day and this is how it is done.

Because there is nothing new under the sun except its expression.

Because truth, that elusive joker, hides himself in fictions and must therefore be sought there.

Because writing, in all space's unimaginable vastness, is still the greatest adventure of all.

And because, alas, what else?

*   *   *

The change that has overtaken American fiction, Robert Coover has said, came about for two reasons. One is the familiar notion that the novel as a literary form is exhausted. We therefore need new ideas concerning what story writing is about, and we must search for new principles of fiction. The other is equally familiar: we have been pushed, in the modern world, to a state of extremity in which we face the obliteration of the race. This condition raises questions about the value of religion and of history. If these are meaningless, as now appears to be the case, then writers have recourse to the grotesque or to a nightmarish fiction or to a form of comedy, but not to tragedy, which is an "adolescent response to the universe." In his own fiction Coover has accordingly turned away from traditional realism. What he demonstrates in *Pricksongs and Descants,* which represents his earliest writing although published subsequent to his first novel, and in everything written since, is the conviction that reality, history, and truth are "made" or invented, that appearances are everything, that forms are really substance, that poetry is the art of subordinating facts to the imagination, and that objectivity is an impossible illusion. These are matters that he actually discusses, in the self-reflexive mode of modernist fiction, in his novels; all the points above come specifically from *The Public Burning.* Coover's aim is to dis-establish dogmatic confidence in the nature of reality, as his well-known story, "The Babysitter," so clearly demonstrates. It is a goal which rests on the premise, to which both Vladimir Nabokov and William H. Gass have given voice, that the author is a dictator or a god. In "The Magic Poker" the authorial voice announces that *I* have invented these characters, have dressed them and may well undress them, have endowed them with physical attributes but need not be bound by any anatomical reality; they will have or not have organs exactly as I decree. De-

spite these assertions, however, Coover cannot altogether free himself in his fiction from the sense-apprehensible reality which most of us acknowledge.

An alternative to the realistic novel which attempts to mirror life is a fiction which centers its attention upon language and technique. Language is a form of play, an expression of wit, and a source of joy. Language is an end in itself, rather than a means of expressing the ideas and feelings of characters and the culture. The magic of language becomes the supreme ordering principle of our existence. When Coover pushes these matters far enough, language transcends itself and becomes the culture. The play of language opens us to the literary strategies that are the means of defining and knowing the culture. The variety of techniques in *The Public Burning* offers the readiest example of Coover's conviction in this matter: he uses here, among others, the techniques of the drama, collage, montage, surrealism, opera, farce and slap-stick, the absurd, parody, and satire.

So much for Coover's version of the new ideas about fiction. Now as to history and religion, which are meaningless. Assuming the problematic nature of reality, Coover turns to myth in each of his first three novels. In *The Origin of the Brunists* a rational editor cynically invents a miracle which becomes the basis for a system of religious belief. This novel is an exercise in the creation of "truth;" the Brunist religion as an act of creation is a mirror-reflection of Coover's own creation of the novel itself. Coover is a mythmaker demonstrating how myth is made. In *The Universal Baseball Association, Inc., J. Henry Waugh Prop.,* Coover's most successful book, "real" events pass into myth and are expressed in recurring ritual. The primacy of the imagined world is established as a result of conflict with the "real" world, which is Coover's way of asserting the primacy of fiction. "The world itself being a construct of fictions," he has said, "I believe the fiction maker's function is to furnish better fictions with which we can re-form our notion of things." In this novel, both real and invented realms are merged and coalesce in time; a system of belief emerges which passes into myth or religion. The reality upon which Coover builds here is the history of baseball. The reality in *The Public Burning* is the espionage trial of Ethel and Julius Rosenberg, which Coover transmutes by way of folklore and history into the myth of America. He provides initiation into evil and the threat of evil in the conflict with the Phantom; sacrifices of the victims, who are to be executed; spectacle and saturnalia, since the execution, an orgasmic occasion, is staged by Cecil B. De Mille and others in Times Square; purification by fire; and rescue and preservation of the sacred flame—the atomic bomb—by Uncle Sam, the archetypal American hero. But Uncle Sam is also Sam Slick, the Yankee Peddler, who has his dark side. And much of the novel is narrated by Vice-President Richard Nixon, portrayed as treacherous, cunning, ruthless, paranoid, mean-spirited, vengeful, repressed, self-pitying, sentimental, lonely, and alienated. The mythic world is a self-encapsulated fiction. The judgment about the American myth and American heroes—real or symbolic—takes us out of the hermetic world of myth. In this novel, Coover validates equally the two realms and thus undercuts his expressed belief in the supremacy of fiction and the imagination.

In Bed One Night and Other Brief Encounters consists of nine short exercises in modernist writing. The most elaborated of these is "Beginnings," which demonstrates in its very existence and form the difficulties of writing, now that time and history, logic and causation, sequence and linearity have all been invalidated. In another piece, the protagonist realizes that everything that has happened to him has happened in language, which confirms William H. Gass's view that all we have in fiction is language, because there is nothing else. And in addition to this language play, the volume offers some effective surrealistic satire.

Spanking the Maid is a modernist novella constructed as an unending series of repetitions in a sado-masochistic sexual fantasy. Coover's technique, like the mode of "The Babysitter," repeats the same action over and over again, with minor alterations, in order to convey a sense of the instability of reality and of the impossibility of capturing it exactly. Mimesis is undermined and fantasy legitimated as a replacement for verisimilitude. Thus literary realism is thrashed as compulsively as the maid is whipped. Further, cause and effect relationships are destroyed, since the whipping is done 1) in accordance with the principles in a manual which is never shown to us or identified, or 2) for stated reasons that vary from page to page. In short, for no reason. Finally, the master and the maid, both nameless, are not characters in a fiction but automatons; or they are dream figures without being. The novella attacks the concept of ontology, as it does of rationality and reality. It lives, in no particularly vibrant way, in the rhythms of its repetition and in the sensuality of its male-oriented fantasy.

—Chester E. Eisinger

COPE, Jack

Nationality: South African. **Born:** Robert Knox Cope in Mooi River, Natal, 3 June 1913. **Education:** Durban High School. **Family:** Married Lesley de Villiers in 1942 (divorced 1956); two children. **Career:** Reporter, *Natal Mercury,* Durban, 1931-35; correspondent in London for South African Morning Newspapers, 1936-40; farmer, Natal, 1941-42; engaged in shark-fishing enterprise, Cape Town, 1943-45; director, South African Association of the Arts, Cape Town, 1946-48. Since 1949 freelance writer and reporter; founding editor, *Contrast,* Cape Town, 1960-79; editor, Mantis Editions, 1970s. **Awards:** South African Arts and Sciences Prose prize, 1959; British Council travel grant, 1960; Carnegie travel fellowship, 1966; South African Festival of the Soil award, 1970; CNA award, 1972; Argus Fiction prize and gold medal, 1972. D.Litt.: Rhodes University, Grahamstown, 1981. **Agent:** Shelley Power, INPRA, P.O. Box 149-A, Surbiton, Surrey KT6 5JH. **Address:** 21 Bearton Road, Hitchin, Hertfordshire SG5 1UB, England.

PUBLICATIONS

Novels

The Fair House. London, MacGibbon and Kee, 1955.
The Golden Oriole. London, Heinemann, 1958.
The Road to Ysterberg. London, Heinemann, 1959.
Albino. London, Heinemann, 1964.
The Dawn Comes Twice. London, Heinemann, 1969.
The Rain-Maker. London, Heinemann, 1971.
The Student of Zend. London, Heinemann, 1972.
My Son Max. London, Heinemann, 1977.

Short Stories

The Tame Ox. London, Heinemann, 1960.
The Man Who Doubted. London, Heinemann, 1967.
Alley Cat and Other Stories. London, Heinemann, 1973.
Selected Stories. Cape Town, Philip, 1986.
Tales of the Trickster Boy, with illustrations by Azaria Mbatha. Cape Town, Tafelberg, 1990.

Play

Nona: The Killing of the Cattle (produced Johannesburg, 1981).

Poetry

Lyrics and Diatribes. Cape Town, Stewart, 1948.
Marie: A South African Satire (as R.K. Cope). Cape Town, Stewart, 1949.
Jack Cope/C.J. Driver. Cape Town, Philip, 1979.

Other

Comrade Bill (biography). Cape Town, Stewart, 1943.
The Adversary Within: Dissident Writers in Afrikaans. Cape Town, Philip, London, Collings, and Atlantic Highlands, New Jersey, Humanities Press, 1982.

Editor, with Uys Krige, *The Penguin Book of South African Verse.* London, Penguin, 1968.
Editor, *Seismograph: Best South African Writing from Contrast.* Cape Town, Reijger, 1970.
Editor, *Under the Horizon: Collected Poems of Charles Eglington.* Cape Town, Purnell, 1977.

Translator, with William Plomer, *Selected Poems of Ingrid Jonker.* London, Cape, 1968.

*

Jack Cope comments:

Raised by a farming family on the South African veld a long way from anywhere, I had made up my mind at about 10 years of age that I was going to be a writer. How to do it was another thing. I am still on that search. It has been said that the art of writing lies in the struggle against the inability to write. I was a third generation from settlers in a practically empty region of Natal; white, English-speaking. Zulus came up from the warm bush country to work on the cold high-veld and they were often the only playmates I and my brothers had. We got to know them, liked them, learnt from them.

In the old stone farmhouse there were thousands of books—sermons, religious tracts and poetry, Victorian novels by "Ouida," Disraeli, Mrs. Gaskell, Wilkie Collins, Mrs. Henry Wood, etc. But there were also Fenimore Cooper, Kingsley, Defoe, Mark Twain, Dickens, Ruskin, Scott, William Morris, Thackeray; there were Shakespeare and all the English poets up to Browning. The Bible was part of one's life, though we were too far away to go to church more than a few times. I knew that I couldn't model myself on any of the writers I read—we had no Redskins, no sea or pirates, no rivers, lakes, forests, no cities, no factories, no art, no stage. Living in a mental desert what did one specially see and feel, let alone write about? We hunted and had guns and dogs and horses, but it was all so ordinary. At 12 I was sent 100 miles to boarding school into Durban, a seaport which seemed duller, more lonely even than the farm.

Then I left school, refused to enter university and went instead into a newspaper in Durban as an "apprentice." A mistake. I was ten years in journalism and never liked it. Learnt how not to write. One thing the newspaper business did for me—it got me out of South Africa and to London. I worked in Fleet Street. In four years I was almost flattened out into an Englishman. But there's the paradox, the nearer you are, the further you are away from a thing. Anyway I remained African. Language, blood, family, tradition were all on one side; but the break of nearly a century was too long. I belonged to Africa or to nowhere.

Of course I had long since made a mental holocaust of *white* race attitudes as no-one can like somebody born into them. Mad about Shaw and Morris, Russell, Marx, Ibsen, Pound(!), Eliot and O'Casey, I cultivated a polyglot creed, a sort of anarcho-social-communonihilist with a strong dash of pacifism. Wrote bad verse with an admiring eye on Yeats, Lawrence, or Pound, and my stories limped on crutches of Gorky, Bunin, Hemingway. No nationalism, no dogma, no traditionalism, I thought myself a citizen of that other country, The World. My time—the coming apocalypse.

The war drove me morosely from England home to Natal, to the farm, the loneliness. I tried to start writing consistently, seriously. To my astonishment and disgust I found I just couldn't. The novel I started with a family-historical background went through four re-writes over a period of 12 years—all torn up or burnt. Friends used to put down my typescript in embarrassment. The book was *The Fair House*. The fifth script I sent to London. Back came a cable from a young publisher, James MacGibbon: "Fair House is magnificent." I got very drunk. I'd like to believe it was true. But I know: it was shaky but a beginning. Meanwhile I was suddenly writing short stories that got accepted.

That was the break-out. I stumbled about after that but have made it a point not to get frozen into a "manner" (substitute for style) or be carried away by form. In each story and novel, as in my poems, I wanted all the elements, rhythm, structure, tone, to work separately and together within a different context and to be ruled by it. Each book, I hope, shifts a peg on. Eight novels so far, and a lot of stories—the objective is still to produce one good book by the time I pack in, and then I'll feel there was something in my dreams at the age of ten.

Writing in South Africa is not easy. There's a high voltage of tension. There's Censorship, intimidation; one's books get banned. But I don't believe in quitting; you can't see things straight from too great a distance, from exile. I am against writing dirt for sales or for its own sake. Life's full enough of dirt and if it gets into a book the context must give it an absolute necessity. I remain an African, and Africa somehow keeps a certain innocence, a certain newness and strength. It's not a political slogan. Or a garbage dump.

To fight against isolation I've always tried to work back from my own experience and to draw together the younger writers, raise critical standards, demand sound craftsmanship. I make translations from Afrikaans, Zulu, Sotho, Xhosa, and this I feel helps create links in a multi-national society. Writers cannot get a wide enough readership on the developing languages and therefore aim to master English or Afrikaans. To command a new language and learn to write in it is a mammoth task—one can be helped or encouraged, but there are no short cuts. In 1960 I took part in starting a two-language literary quarterly, *Contrast,* and edited it for 20 years.

The magazine has been a mouthpiece as well as workshop for many promising young poets, fiction writers, dramatists, artists; it now is called *New Contrast*.

South Africa still has a small enough population for writers living even thousands of miles apart to get to know each other. They come from every nationality, race, belief, outlook. Many are banned, exiled. But they form a kind of republic of talent rising above the jargon and propaganda, throwing shadows ahead.

In 1980 I came to England again, this time to write a novel from a new angle. My characters, although still African, have scattered outwards onto a wider stage.

*   *   *

Jack Cope is a South African writer whose work has attracted attention not only for its intrinsic merit as fiction—and Cope is undeniably a competent and at times a compelling story-teller with the power to create wholly believable fictional worlds—but more significantly, perhaps, because of the way in which he uses his South African material. His novels and short stories present a romanticized and initially attractive view of contemporary South Africa, derived partly, it would appear, from his own privileged position in the class-ridden and rigidly divided structures of South African society. The product of a liberal education, and to a large extent removed by birth and upbringing from the political struggles which have dominated South African history for the past 70 years, Cope can afford to regard his fellow South Africans, both black and white, with a large degree of tolerance, seeing them as actors in the great human drama rather than—as so often happens in South African fiction—as victims or oppressors. The landscape is always an important element in Cope's fiction, and he is particularly adept at evoking the great spaces of the South African deserts, the rugged sea coasts, and the lush sub-tropical settings of his native Natal. In his early stories, he also more than half seriously tends to invest the African landscape with a mystic quality, implying that powerful forces are at work helping to shape the destiny not only of the indigenous folk who still believe in witchcraft and sorcery but also of those more recent arrivals who have had the temerity to attempt to tame the wilderness.

Many of Cope's stories demonstrate a genuine concern for the sufferings of his black fellow citizens, whether such sufferings are caused by poverty or ignorance, or result from apartheid. Cope has however always avoided outright condemnation of this system, and has made it abundantly clear both in his critical writing and in his novels that he regards political involvement as an irrelevance at best, and at worst as exerting a corrupting influence on those who, like himself, should be concerned only with standards of excellence and with the republic of talent. Such views have ensured that Cope's work is free from the guilt-ridden breast-beating which characterizes so much writing by white South Africans, particularly those of Cope's generation who believed that committed literature could play a part in the struggle against the apartheid system, but they are also responsible for the fact that much of his work appears remote from the historical and political realities of South Africa today, and lacks interest for contemporary readers.

Cope's first three novels tackle themes which can be broadly categorized as historical, while the more recent work focuses more directly on the contemporary situation. *The Fair House* recreates a significant episode from colonial history centering on the last armed rising of the Zulu in 1902 and on the subsequent consolidation of white power. *Albino* explores white and black relationships through a story of family feuds and guilts. *The Golden Oriole* describes the abortive attempts of a black writer to gain acceptance in the white literary world of the 1930s, and is set against a background of black political intrigue. In all these novels as in *The Road to Ysterberg* Cope presents his black characters with a degree of sympathy and insight, but the novels themselves suggest that he regards attempts at social integration as misguided; and although he is by no means overtly or intentionally racist, he suggests very strongly that only those who accept and share western cultural values can be considered truly civilized.

The Dawn Comes Twice, loosely based on events in the early 1960s, dramatizes the efforts of a group of urban guerrillas to organize effective acts of sabotage. While this novel is relatively optimistic about the future of South Africa, *The Student of Zend* and *My Son Max* both demonstrate Cope's growing disillusion with the current political situation. Both novels are concerned with individuals who have tried to escape from a society which they perceive as narrow and personally frustrating. Both Jamie and Max are committed to a quest for personal fulfillment, which Cope presents in an almost romantic way as a "search for a goal beyond the self." Both men are, of course, doomed to failure; but while Jamie, the student of ancient religions, can at least choose exile in Switzerland if he so desires, there is only one outcome for the young black man, Max, who refuses to commit himself to the freedom struggle in which his comrades are involved: death at the hands of these comrades. In his earlier novels Cope had suggested that white society denied black people the right to live in a civilized way. In *My Son Max* he appears to imply that while whites may now be ready to accept black people (particularly if they are as "civilized" as Max is), it is black people themselves who now seek to deny each other this right in the name of an illusory struggle for "freedom."

—Ursula Edmands

COWAN, Peter (Walkinshaw)

Nationality: Australian. **Born:** Perth, Western Australia, 4 November 1914. **Education:** The University of Western Australia, Nedlands, B.A. in English 1940, Dip. Ed. 1946. **Military Service:** Served in the Royal Australian Air Force, 1943-45. **Family:** Married Edith Howard in 1941; one son. **Career:** Clerk, farm labourer, and casual worker, 1930-39; teacher, 1941-42; member of the faculty, University of Western Australia, 1946-50; Senior English Master, Scotch College, Swanbourne, Western Australia, 1950-62. Senior Tutor, 1964-79, and since 1979 Honorary Research Fellow in English, University of Western Australia. **Awards:** Commonwealth Literary Fund fellowship, 1963; Australian Council for the Arts fellowship, 1974, 1980; University of Western Australia fellowship, 1982; Patrick White prize, for literature, 1992. A.M. (Order of Australia), 1983. **Address:** Department of English, University of Western Australia, Nedlands, Western Australia 6009, Australia.

PUBLICATIONS

Novels

Summer. Sydney and London, Angus and Robertson, 1964.

Seed. Sydney and London, Angus and Robertson, and San Francisco, Tri-Ocean, 1966.
The Color of the Sky. Fremantle, Western Australia, Fremantle Arts Centre Press, 1986.
The Hills of Apollo Bay. Fremantle, Western Australia, Fremantle Arts Centre Press, 1989.
The Tenants. Fremantle, Western Australia, Fremantle Arts Centre Press, 1994.

Short Stories

Drift. Melbourne, Reed and Harris, 1944.
The Unploughed Land. Sydney, Angus and Robertson, 1958.
The Empty Street. Sydney and London, Angus and Robertson, and San Francisco, Tri-Ocean, 1965.
The Tins and Other Stories. St. Lucia, University of Queensland Press, 1973.
New Country, with others, edited by Bruce Bennett. Fremantle, Western Australia, Fremantle Arts Centre Press, 1976.
Mobiles. Fremantle, Western Australia, Fremantle Arts Centre Press, 1979.
A Window in Mrs. X's Place. Ringwood, Victoria, and New York, Penguin, 1986; London, Penguin, 1987.
Voices. Fremantle, Western Australia, Fremantle Arts Centre Press, 1988.

Other

A Unique Position: A Biography of Edith Dircksey Cowan 1861-1932. Nedlands, University of Western Australia Press, 1978.
A Colonial Experience: Swan River 1839-1888. Privately printed, 1979.
Maitland Brown: A View of Nineteenth-Century Western Australia. Fremantle, Western Australia, Fremantle Arts Centre Press, 1988.

Editor, *Short Story Landscape: The Modern Short Story.* Melbourne, Longman, 1964.
Editor, with Bruce Bennett and John Hay, *Spectrum 1-2.* Melbourne, Longman, 2 vols., 1970; London, Longman, 2 vols., 1971; *Spectrum 3,* Melbourne, Longman, 1979.
Editor, *Today: Short Stories of Our Time.* Melbourne, Longman, 1971.
Editor, *A Faithful Picture: The Letters of Eliza and Thomas Brown at York in the Swan River Country 1841-1852.* Fremantle, Western Australia, Fremantle Arts Centre Press, 1977.
Editor, with Bruce Bennett and John Hay, *Perspectives One* (short stories). Melbourne, Longman Cheshire, 1985.
Editor, *Impressions: West Coast Fiction 1829-1988.* Fremantle, Western Australia, Fremantle Arts Centre Press, 1989.

*

Critical Studies: "The Short Stories of Peter Cowan," 1960, and "New Tracks to Travel: The Stories of White, Porter and Cowan," 1966, both by John Barnes, in *Meanjin* (Melbourne); essay by Grahame Johnston in *Westerly* (Perth), 1967; "Cowan Country" by Margot Luke, in *Sandgropers* edited by Dorothy Hewett, Nedlands, University of Western Australia Press, 1973; "Behind the Actual" by Bruce Williams, in *Westerly* (Perth), no. 3, 1973; "Regionalism in Peter Cowan's Short Fiction" by Bruce Bennett, in *World Literature Written in English* (Guelph, Ontario), 1980;

"Practitioner of Silence" by Wendy Jenkins, in *Fremantle Arts Review* (Fremantle, Western Australia), vol. 1, no. 3, 1986; "Of Books and Covers: Peter Cowan" by Bruce Bennett, in *Overland 114* (Melbourne), 1989, and *Peter Cowan: New Critical Essays* by Susan Miller and edited by Bennett, Nedlands, University of Western Australia with The Centre for Studies in Australian Literature, 1992.

Peter Cowan comments:

Up to the present time writing has been for me as much something I wanted to do to please myself as something aimed solely at publication and any kind of wide audience. Now, I don't think this kind of attitude is any longer possible, and the chances for this kind of fiction have greatly diminished.

My writing may have been concerned as much with place as with people, though I have tried to see people against a landscape, against a physical environment. If isolation is one of the themes that occur frequently, particularly in the short stories, this is perhaps enforced by the Australian landscape itself. I am deeply involved in everything to do with the physical Australia, the land, its shapes and seasons and colors, its trees and flowers, its birds and animals. And its coast and sea.

I have been more interested in the short story than the novel. The technical demands of a short story are high, and seldom met, and through the short story a writer has perhaps a better chance of trapping something of the fragmentary nature of today's living.

I am, however, interested in some present forms of the novel and an attempting to work within these forms. Novel and short story now perhaps seem closer to one another.

*   *   *

Peter Cowan is a quietly introspective writer, and consequently his intensity of vision and his scrupulous craftsmanship can easily be underrated. He has shown a particular talent for the short story or novella, in which he can focus on a single relationship and explore a single line of feeling. His stories, written in a spare, taut style, have as a recurring theme the relationship of a man and a woman seeking relief from their loneliness in sexual love. Cowan is intent upon an inner reality: his characters are seldom individualized very far; they seem almost anonymous, and the sensuous reality of the external world is only faintly felt. His imagination is compelled by a painful awareness of the feelings of loneliness and alienation that lie beneath the surface of commonplace lives; and in exploring this territory he has become, more than is generally recognized, a significant interpreter of Australian realities.

In Cowan's first collection of stories, *Drift,* the preoccupations of his mature work are merely sketched in. Uneven in quality and stylistically in debt to Hemingway, the book nevertheless has a coherence and a unity of impression unexpected in the work of a young writer. Cowan has known his subject right from the start. Most of these early stories are set in the poor farming country of southwestern West Australia before World War II, and they centre on the lives of people who are emotionally unfulfilled or unable to express themselves in normal relationships.

Over the next 14 years Cowan wrote little. In his second collection, *The Unploughed Land,* he reprinted seven of his stories from *Drift,* along with six new stories, which represent a distinct advance in technique. These new stories include the much-anthologized "The Redbacked Spiders," a powerful story of a boy whose resentment at his brutal father leads to the man's death. The title story is an extended treatment of the pre-war country life about which he

writes in his first volume. In its evocation of that life it is one of his finest pieces, and it marks the end of the first phase of his development.

From this point onward Cowan has been more prolific and more varied—though compared with most writers he has a small and narrow output. In his third collection, *The Empty Street,* there is a noticeable shift in setting. Cowan now writes of people in suburbia, for whom the country is a refuge. The sense of being caught in an irresistible and disastrous historical process is expressed in a story like "The Tractor," which concerns the efforts of a hermit to stop the clearing of the land. Cowan's sympathies are with those who oppose "progress," but he sees their dilemma truly. "The Empty Street," a novella, is an impressive study of an unhappy middle-aged clerk, whose marriage is now a mere shell, and whose children are strangers to him: desperate to escape the pressures of a life that is meaningless to him, he collapses into schizophrenia and turns murderer. Cowan is especially responsive to the theme of the middle-aged, defeated, and desolate in marriage, groping for a way out. *The Tins and Other Stories* confirms the achievement of the earlier volumes, with stories like "The Rock" and "The Tins," in which Cowan is seen at his characteristic best.

In recent years Cowan has spent a great deal of time researching the history of his family, which has been prominent in the public life of West Australia since colonial times. This turning to the past has the appearance of being a retreat from the present, of which he takes such a bleak view in his fiction. But the collection, *Mobiles,* and, even more strikingly, *The Color of the Sky,* show, rather, that the sense of the past has sharpened and enlarged his sense of the present. Four of the seven stories in *Mobiles* are set in the stony northwest, beyond the limits of settlement or where settlement has failed. In these starkly rendered episodes human beings are no more than transitory figures in an enduring and inhospitable landscape. The longest story in the volume, "The Lake," reworks a favourite theme of 19th-century novelists—the "hidden valley" in the heart of the unexplored continent. In what is one of his most satisfying stories, the symbolic possibilities of the landscape—evoked here with more vividness than is usual in his writing—are subtly realized. This story points to a new strength in Cowan's writing which appears in his third and finest novel.

Peter Cowan's first two attempts at novels were not very successful. *Summer* is a short novel, more like two short stories that have been expanded and linked together. A businessman whose marriage has failed takes a job on the wheat bins, and in this lonely setting forms a relationship with the wife of the nearby storekeeper. The violent resolution is not well managed, and the central character tends to be a mouthpiece for Cowan's reflections on the spoiling of the natural environment. Yet there are some fine sequences establishing the relationship of the two lonely people in a solitary landscape.

In *Seed* Cowan set out to portray a group of middle-class families living in Perth. An Australian reader feels the force of his thesis about the boredom and frustration of suburban living, but it remains a thesis and seldom quickens into drama. It is a disappointing work, the result of Cowan's trying to write against the grain of his talent. He is not skilled at creating personalities or at suggesting the social facts of life, but in this rather old-fashioned, realistic novel the emphasis falls on just those aspects of his writing where he is weakest.

The Color of the Sky has the formal integrity and the imaginative vigour which the previous novels lacked. The narrator is a familiar enough Cowan creation—a man on his own, trying to make sense of his experience. In a visit to a place dimly remembered from a visit in childhood, the narrator is simultaneously exploring the past and the present, and much of the power of the narrative derives from the reader's realization of patterns only half-traced, elusive parallels, family likenesses, disturbing undercurrents and continuities. Both the past and the present contain events that could be sensationalized—drug-running, murder, illicit sexual liaisons—but Cowan's novel is a study of the consciousness of a man in search of himself. In the end, the narrator can no more complete the jigsaw puzzle of his family relationships than he can give shape to the incoherence of his own emotional and moral life, with its tangle of loose ends, evasions, and denials. This work is Cowan's most impressive treatment of (in his own words) "the fragmentary nature of today's living."

—John Barnes

COYNE, P.J. *See* MASTERS, Hilary.

CRACE, Jim

Nationality: British. **Born:** Brocket Hall, Lemsford, Hertfordshire, 1 March 1946. **Education:** Enfield Grammar School, Middlesex, 1957-64; Birmingham College of Commerce, 1965-68; University of London (external), B.A. (honours) in English 1968. **Family:** Married Pamela Ann Turton in 1975; one son and one daughter. **Career:** Volunteer in educational television, Voluntary Service Overseas, Khartoum, Sudan, 1968-69; freelance journalist and writer, 1972-86; since 1986 full-time novelist. **Awards:** Arts Council bursary, 1986; West Midlands Arts Literature grant, 1980; David Higham award, 1986; Whitbread award, 1986; *Guardian* Fiction prize, 1986; Antico Fattore prize (Italy), 1988; International prize for literature, 1989. **Address:** c/o Viking/Penguin, 27 Wrights Lane, London W8 5TZ, England.

PUBLICATIONS

Novel

The Gift of Stones. London, Secker and Warburg, 1988; New York, Scribner, 1989.
Arcadia. London, Cape, and New York, Atheneum, 1992.
Signals of Distress. London, Viking, 1994; New York, Farrar Straus, 1995.
The Slow Digestions of the Night (novella). London, Penguin, 1995.

Short Stories

Continent. London, Heinemann, 1986; New York, Harper, 1987.

Uncollected Short Stories

"Refugees," in *Socialist Challenge,* December 1977.
"Annie, California Plates" and "Helter Skelter, Hang Sorrow, Care'll Kill a Cat," in *Introduction 6: Stories by New Writers.* London, Faber, 1977.
"Seven Ages," in *Quarto,* 1980.

Plays

Radio Plays: *The Bird Has Flown,* 1977; *A Coat of Many Colours,* 1979.

*

Critical Study: *Jim Crace* by Judy Cooke, London, Book Trust and the British Council, 1992.

Jim Crace comments:

I count myself to be a traditional, old-fangled novelist rather than a conventional writer or a new-fangled modernist. I am more interested in the fate of communities than the catharsis of individuals. I owe more to the oral traditions of storytelling (rhythmic prose, moral satire, naked invention) than to the idiomatic, ironic, realist social comedies which typify post-war British fiction. My books are not an exploration of self. They are not autobiographically based. I do not write from experience. I focus on subjects—usually political or sociological, usually concerning the conflict between the old and new ways of humankind—which interest me, which seem worthy of exploration but of which I have no personal expertise. (I am surprised but not saddened to note that my novels are less progressive and more pessimistic than I am myself.) I shroud the offputting solemnity of my themes in metaphorical narratives which tease and subvert and flirt with the reader and which regard lies to be more eloquent than facts. Thus far, my novels seem to reach-and-preach the same conclusion: that everything new worth having, in both the private and public universes, is paid for by the loss of something old worth keeping. Those who do not like my novels consider them to be overwrought, passionless, schematic, and unEnglish.

*   *   *

Jim Crace has emerged as one of the more distinctive voices among English fiction writers of his generation. *Continent,* his first collection of seven related short stories, showed the influences of the Latin American "magical realists," especially Jorge Luis Borges and Gabriel Garcia Marquez, yet marshalled aspects of their aesthetic for purposes that were uniquely his own. The collection justly (if somewhat misleadingly) received the Whitbread award for the best first "novel" of 1986, as well as the David Higham award for the year's best first work of fiction. Crace's first work was widely hailed in America the following year and it is presently available in translation in 10 other languages at last count.

Crace may be considered a fabulist, insofar as his fictional worlds stress their distance from our own, and invite delight in the ability of both writer's and reader's imaginations to leap the gap. The stories of *Continent* take place, for example, in an exotic locale that seems to be Latin American, but often just as clearly is not—the fanciful names suggest some generic Third World. And Crace dips his pen in an unstable mixture of fiction and fact, a blend made popular by the fabulists of the Latin American "boom."

In "Cross Country," for instance, a visiting Canadian school-teacher, who amuses the villagers by his jogging, is suddenly pitted in a dramatic footrace against a native on horseback. Government soldiers in another story—"The World with One Eye Shut"—whisk an innocent man off the street into prison, where he succeeds in taking ingenious revenge. History and fantasy intertwine playfully here, and frighteningly. Like the mythical village of Macondo in Marquez's fiction, this "continent" is another "intricate stew of truths and mirages," and similarly captivating.

Crace writes gracefully in these stories, and with great assurance: "A fistful of grit he scattered in the grass so that it fell among the leaf joints like sleet." And he tells a good story. In "Sins and Virtues," perhaps the most likeable story in the collection, an aged calligrapher of the dying language Siddilic discovers that his work, pried loose from storefronts by visiting foreigners, is selling for high prices in America, especially in Chicago. A government minister orders the calligrapher to produce a vast amount of new work, to be sold abroad by the government. So the poor man, exhausted, is compelled to buy local forgeries of his work and pass them off as his own.

The ventriloquism that Crace practiced in *Continent*—the throwing of his voice, that is, to a new land not found on any of our maps—carries us back across the ages in *The Gift of Stones,* his second book and first novel. Here the novelist's imagination brings to vibrant and compelling life a few members of a clan of flint-carvers, just before the start of the Bronze Age. As in the stories, what is distinctive in Crace's work is the attention to language—not only in the finely crafted turns of detailed evocation, but in the awareness demanded by the plot itself of language's power to invent, impose, mislead, console. Crace's language is alive, a distinctive voice, an engaging character in itself. Life not only is the subject of, but is subject to, his artful words.

> We have heard my father talking—and we know the way he worked. We know that when he spoke he shaped the truth, he trimmed, he stretched, he decorated. He was to truth what every stoney was to untouched flint, a fashioner, a god. We know that when he said, "I'll keep it simple too, I won't tell lies," that this was just another arrow from his shaft by which we were transfixed. And so, again, we should beware when father claimed forgetfulness and said "Who knows what story I dished up for them that night? Who cares?" He knew, for sure. It was a turning-point for him—though, here again, his version was much tidier than truth.

Paradoxically, while the novel asserts the storyteller's power to transcend the ages, what causes anguish within the plot is the very passage of time itself. The narrator and her father (who tells part of the story himself) belong to a tribe that knows only how to chip and refine bits of flint into knives and other useful tools—yet this "gift" sets them apart from other communities who must barter with them for the fruits of such skill. By the novel's end, however, swiftly flying bronze-tipped arrows are not only killing individuals but threatening the group's very livelihood.

This theme, then—the great gift of consciousness, yet the greater losses to time's onward rush—beats centrally in both of Crace's early books. The tellers in his tales do transcend time, yet in doing so they memorialize loss. Still, the awareness of language as supplier of spurious compensations, of the stories we tell as futile consolations, is both counterbalanced and given weight by the sheer skill and austere beauty of Crace's writing.

> There was no ship upon the sea, just a rose-hip sun with fleshy canopies of cloud. Already shags and waterhuggers were flying off for the day's first fish. Fronds and frost and cobwebs gleamed with dew. Giant slugs were on the path. Rocks steamed.

Crace governs the race of chronology so as to yield a high degree of suspense. This may be the secret that makes his high-modernist prose so mainstream and readable. Crace celebrates the storyteller's skill, and its ironies, with a persuasiveness that is animated and reinforced by his own deft mastery of the art.

The Gift of Stones begins as an inquiry into how "my father" came to lose one of his arms below the elbow when he was seven years old. (Characteristically, the reader gets several "told" versions, and then "the truth;" and then the first in a string of surprises.) In the dynamics of reading, that missing arm *is* a hook. From such unpromising beginnings, in such a chill late-stoneage setting, Crace's memorable trio of characters engages the reader at levels of remarkable affective depth.

—Brian Stonehill

CREWS, Harry (Eugene)

Nationality: American. **Born:** Alma, Georgia, 6 June 1935. **Education:** The University of Florida, Gainesville, B.A. 1960, M.S.Ed. 1962. **Military Service:** Served in the United States Marine Corps, 1953-56: Sergeant. **Family:** Married Sally Ellis in 1960 (divorced); two sons. **Career:** English teacher, Broward Junior College, Fort Lauderdale, Florida, 1962-68. Associate professor, 1968-74, and since 1974 professor of English, University of Florida. **Awards:** Bread Loaf Writers Conference Atherton fellowship, 1968; American Academy award, 1972; National Endowment for the Arts grant, 1974. **Address:** Department of English, University of Florida, Gainesville, Florida 32601, U.S.A.

PUBLICATIONS

Novels

The Gospel Singer. New York, Morrow, 1968.
Naked in Garden Hills. New York, Morrow, 1969.
This Thing Don't Lead to Heaven. New York, Morrow, 1970.
Karate Is a Thing of the Spirit. New York, Morrow, 1971; London, Secker and Warburg, 1972.
Car. New York, Morrow, 1972; London, Secker and Warburg, 1973.
The Hawk Is Dying. New York, Knopf, 1973; London, Secker and Warburg, 1974.
The Gypsy's Curse. New York, Knopf, 1974; London, Secker and Warburg, 1975.
A Feast of Snakes. New York, Atheneum, 1976; London, Secker and Warburg, 1977.
All We Need of Hell. New York, Harper, 1987.
The Knockout Artist. New York, Harper, 1988.
Body. New York, Poseidon Press, 1990.
Scar Lover. New York, Poseidon Press, 1992.

Short Stories

The Enthusiast. Winston-Salem, North Carolina, Palaemon Press, 1981.
Two. Northridge, Lord John Press, 1984.

Uncollected Short Stories

"The Player Piano," in *Florida Quarterly* (Gainesville), Fall 1967.
"The Unattached Smile," in *Craft and Vision,* edited by Andrew Lytle. New York, Delacorte Press, 1971.
"A Long Wail," in *Necessary Fictions,* edited by Stanley W. Lindberg and Stephen Corey. Athens, University of Georgia Press, 1986.

Play

Blood Issue (produced Louisville, Kentucky, 1989).

Other

A Childhood: The Biography of a Place (on Bacon County, Georgia). New York, Harper, 1978; London, Secker and Warburg, 1979.
Blood and Grits. New York, Harper, 1979.
Florida Frenzy. Gainesville, University Presses of Florida, 1982.
Classic Crews (non-fiction pieces and previously published novels). New York, Poseidon Press, 1993; London, Gorse, 1994.

*

Critical Studies: *A Grit's Triumph: Essays on the Works of Harry Crews* edited by David K. Jeffrey, Port Washington, New York, Associated Faculty Press, 1983.

*   *   *

Harry Crews's novels establish him as the most astringent observer of contemporary good-old-boy culture, the grass roots of the South. An outrageous satirist of U.S. lie in general, Crews pits the empty materialism of our mainstream society against deep-South grotesques and misfits with results at once comic and horrific.

Beginning with *The Gospel Singer,* which probes the psychology of show-biz fundamentalism, Crews has invented a gallery of social, sexual, and spiritual outcasts who seek salvation in a civilization which offers them only *things.* The theme is expanded in *Naked in Garden Hills.* Fat Man, the 600-pound protagonist, lives in an abandoned phosphorus mine, where the earth has been eaten away, and he tries to eat the world itself. This is echoed in *Car,* in which Herman Mack vows to eat an entire 1971 Ford Maverick. A refugee from a junkyard, Mack revenges himself on the world by trying to consume and defecate it. *This Thing Don't Lead to Heaven* caricatures the old-folks industry, in which people are the used-up detritus of our society. In this novel, Jefferson Davis Munroe, a midget who works for a "graveyard chain," competes with Axel's Senior Club for the bodies (if not souls) of the dying.

In *Karate Is a Thing of the Spirit* Crews deals with the fads and obsessions of contemporary trendy culture. John Kaimon, its central character, wears a tee-shirt stenciled with William Faulkner's face and tries to find himself through an outlaw karate group. The story develops our sick fascination with sex and violence and the fear of love and belief which Crews sees as being at the focus of

our lives. *The Hawk Is Dying* portrays a more positive, even heroic, obsession, George Gattling's desire to "man" (train) a hawk in the prescribed medieval ritual. His attempt to fuse his soul with the raptor's is another way out of the stylized hell of a technologically focused world. George's need for belief is satisfied by the vitality of his hawk, its innate freedom and dignity.

The Gypsy's Curse returns to a world of physical violence and action with Marvin Molar, born with stunted legs, who walks on his hands and develops his upper body through exercise. In his upside-down world, he becomes sexually obsessed with Hester, a normal woman. The connection between possessiveness, "normality," sexuality, and strength is a basic Crews theme. It appears also in the savage burlesque of *A Feast of Snakes,* in which high school football, baton-twirling, weight-lifting, moonshine selling and rattlesnake hunting are intermixed as American rituals. The story ends, like *The Gospel Singer,* in an explosion of mortal violence, as Joe Lon Mackey, ex-state-champ quarterback, loses his slender grip on his own life.

Crews's satire is directed toward the triviality and rootlessness of our culture, its lack of belief. His characters search frantically for salvation through money, sex, social status, physical strength, mystical rites, through sheer acquisitiveness. Crews shows how these are false paths, failures. John Kaimon, in *Karate Is a Thing of the Spirit,* thinks:

> . . . he also knew he did not believe. The breath of little children would leave his flesh only flesh.
>
> Belief could see through glass eyes, could turn flesh to stone or stone to flesh. But not for him. He would walk through the world naked. He would bruise and bleed. He saw it clearly.

Crews sees clearly, through his scathing satire, that the absence of faith leads to violence, madness, death. His creatures search through a world of junkyards and abandoned mines and prisons for their authenticity through belief, and our world fails and maims them in savage ways.

All We Need of Hell is a gentler satire examining the folkways of modern marriage. It is a lighter "screwball comedy" of marriage and divorce. *The Knockout Artist* and *Body* re-imagine the body-soul dichotomy that haunts Crews. *The Knockout Artist* centers on Eugene Talmadge Biggs, a failed glass-jaw boxer whose "occupation" is to fight himself in the ring and ultimately knock himself out. This caricatures phony "sports" like professional wrestling and boxing and defines guilt and masochism as motive forces in our culture. *Body* lampoons the already-surreal world of body-building and physical-culture narcissism, echoing *Car* and *Karate Is a Thing of the Spirit.*

—William J. Schafer

CRICHTON, (John) Michael

Pseudonyms: John Lange; Jeffery Hudson; Michael Douglas. **Nationality:** American. **Born:** 23 October 1942. **Education:** Harvard University, Cambridge, Massachusetts, A.B.(summa cum laude) 1964 (Phi Beta Kappa): Harvard Medical School, M.D. 1969: Salk Institute, La Jolla, California (postdoctoral fellow), 1969-70. **Fam-**

ily: Married 1) Joan Radam in 1965 (divorced 1971); 2) Kathleen St. Johns in 1978 (divorced 1980); 3) Suzanne Childs (divorced); 4) Anne-Marie Martin in 1987, one daughter. **Career:** Visiting writer, Massachusetts Institute of Technology, Cambridge, 1988. **Awards:** Mystery Writers of America Edgar Allan Poe award, 1968, for *A Case of Need,* and 1980, for *The Great Train Robbery;* Association of American Medical Writers award, 1970, for *Five Patients: The Hospital Explained.* **Agent:** International Creative Management, 40 West 57th Street, New York, New York 10019, U.S.A.

PUBLICATIONS

Novels

A Case of Need (as Jeffery Hudson). Cleveland, World, and London, Heinemann, 1968.
The Andromeda Strain. New York, Knopf, and London, Cape, 1969.
Dealing; or, the Berkeley-to-Boston Forty-Brick Lost-Bag Blues (as Michael Douglas), with Douglas Crichton. New York, Knopf, 1971.
The Terminal Man. New York, Knopf, and London, Cape, 1972.
Westworld. New York, Bantam, 1974.
The Great Train Robbery. New York, Knopf, and London, Cape, 1975.
Eaters of the Dead: The Manuscript of Ibn Fadlan, Relating His Experiences with the Northmen in A.D. 922. New York, Knopf, and London, Cape, 1976.
Congo. New York, Knopf, 1980; London, Allen Lane, 1981.
Sphere. New York, Knopf, and London, Macmillan, 1987.
Jurassic Park. New York, Knopf, 1990; London, Century, 1991.
Rising Sun. New York, Knopf, and London, Century, 1992.
Disclosure. New York, Knopf, 1994.
The Lost World: A Novel. New York, Knopf, 1995.

Novels as John Lange

Odds On. New York, New American Library, 1966.
Scratch One. New York, New American Library, 1967.
Easy Go. New York, New American Library, 1968; London, Sphere, 1972; as *The Last Tomb* (as Michael Crichton), New York, Bantam, 1974.
The Venom Business. Cleveland, World, 1969.
Zero Cool. New York, New American Library, 1969; London, Sphere, 1972.
Drug of Choice. New York, New American Library, 1970; as *Overkill,* New York, Centesis, 1970.
Grave Descend. New York, New American Library, 1970.
Binary. New York, Knopf, and London, Heinemann, 1972.

Plays

Screenplays: *Westworld,* 1973; *Coma,* 1977; *The Great Train Robbery,* 1978; *Looker,* 1981; *Runaway,* 1984; *Jurassic Park,* with John Koepp, 1993; *Rising Sun,* with Philip Kaufman and Michael Backes, 1993.

Other

Five Patients: The Hospital Explained. New York, Knopf, 1970; London, Cape, 1971.

Jasper Johns. New York, Abrams, and London, Thames and Hudson, 1977.
Electronic Life: How to Think about Computers. New York, Knopf, and London, Heinemann, 1983.
Travels. New York, Knopf, and London, Macmillan, 1988.

*

Film Adaptations: *The Andromeda Strain,* 1971; *The Carey Treatment,* 1973, from the work *A Case of Need; Westworld,* 1973; *The Terminal Man,* 1974; *The Great Train Robbery,* 1978; *Jurassic Park,* 1993; *Rising Sun,* 1993; *Disclosure,* 1994.

Theatrical Activities:
Director: **Films**—*Westworld,* 1973; *Coma,* 1978; *The Great Train Robbery,* 1978; *Looker,* 1981; *Runaway,* 1984. **Television**—*Pursuit,* 1972; *E.R.* (executive producer), 1994.

*   *   *

Michael Crichton is a commercially successful writer widely known for over a half-dozen best-selling novels, most of which were subsequently adapted to films scripted by the author himself. In addition, he has produced an extraordinary array of lesser-known fiction, nonfiction, and film and television scripts, reflecting Catholic interests that range from archeology and medicine to crime and cybernetics. His steady stream of work, some of it under the pseudonyms John Lange and Jeffery Hudson, has led various critics to complain that his writing is too facile and superficial, but nobody can deny his great appeal to popular audiences.

Pure and simple, Crichton's familiar novels offer exciting if not provocative reading. They are always suspenseful and frequently thrilling. Although there are exceptions, as in *The Great Train Robbery,* his plots play off against modern technology and scientific theory as their lead characters try to deal with everything from averting a cataclysmic destruction of human life by an alien bacteria (*The Andromeda Strain*), to solving a murder in a high-tech cover-up within the cultural minefield of a powerful Japanese corporation operating in the United States (*Rising Sun*). In all of these "knowledge fiction" works, Crichton marshals convincing, fact-based details that disarm the reader and give his stories an aura of authenticity. He also treats his readers to short courses in relevant past and present scientific theory, ranging from Bernoulli's Law in *The Great Train Robbery* to the chaos theory advanced in his best-known novel, *Jurassic Park.* Intertwined with technology, some unresolved social and political problems are addressed in diverse works—sexual harassment and corporate ethics in *Disclosure* (1993), for example, and industrial espionage and animal rights in *Congo.*

Much of Crichton's fiction digs in at the borders of scientific knowledge then stealthily steps over the line. For example, in *Jurassic Park,* in which dinosaurs are cloned from the genetic residue of their great ancestors, Crichton moves a good distance over the frontier but never out of speculative range. In it, as in other works, like *The Andromeda Strain, The Terminal Man, Congo,* and *Sphere,* Crichton "documents" his story with seemingly authentic medical and laboratory records, media accounts, government and corporate communiqués, references to historical figures, and dozens of other convincing bits of evidence that blur the line between what is fact and what is fiction. Even when he slips out of the range of contemporary science and technology, as he does in

The Great Train Robbery, he relies on realistic detail. In *The Great Train Robbery,* the rich use of underworld argot and fact-based historical particulars about Victorian society, medicine, transportation, politics, and the industrial revolution leave the reader wondering whether the account is a factual reconstruction of an actual crime or a whole-cloth fabrication.

Crichton does not tread very deeply into character. His work is unabashedly plot driven, and his strengths are high-tech intrigue, suspense, and adventure, not in-depth character study. He narrates his novels from an omniscient, journalistic point of view, seldom approaching the core of his characters' beings. That approach is sometimes a virtue, particularly when it promotes an appropriate mystery, as in the case of the enigmatic Edward Pierce of *The Great Train Robbery,* but it tends to distance readers, leaving them with no empathetic hold on Crichton's chief players and certainly no indelible sense of them. Furthermore, many of his minor characters are wooden and one-dimensional "technospeakers," included largely to transmit scientific information or opinions, like disembodied heads. But even many of the main characters are simply too cerebral and mechanical. Most do not leave a vivid impression. The reader of *Congo,* for example, is much more likely to remember Amy, the gorilla, than any human character in the book.

Critics may carp, but to filmmakers Crichton must seem rather astute. Though few if any of his characters resonate in the reader's memory once his books are closed, they offer little challenge when it comes to cinematic adaptation. Films operate precisely where Crichton does in his fiction, at the sensory level, largely in a world of objective action, a world of external visual and aural images. An experienced director and scriptwriter, Crichton seems to fashion his novels with a filmmaker's sense of his craft. He can hardly be faulted for writing with an eye to the film adaptation of his work. In Hollywood, where he remains a hot literary property, the game changes: Characters becomes "roles" designed for box-office idols, and a good storyboard is what really matters.

—John W. Fiero

CRONE, Moira

Nationality: American. **Born:** Goldsboro, North Carolina, 10 August 1952. **Education:** Smith College, Northhampton, Massachusetts, 1970-74, B.A.(high honours); Johns Hopkins University, 1976-1977, M.A. **Family:** Married Rodger Kamenetz; two daughters. **Career:** Visiting professor, Johns Hopkins University, 1977-81; visiting professor, Goucher University, 1977-81. Since 1981 assistant, associate, and full professor of English, Louisiana State University, Baton Rouge, Louisiana. Co-editor, *City Lit,* 1980; editor and founder, *The New Delta Review,* 1983-86. **Awards:** Elliott Coleman award for fiction, 1977; Pirates Alley Faulkner Society Collin C. Diboll award for short story, 1993. Bunting Institute fellowship, Radcliffe College of Harvard University, 1987-88; National Endowment for the Arts Humanities Summer Institute fellowship, University of North Carolina at Chapel Hill, 1989; National Endowment for the Arts fellowship in fiction, 1990; fellowship to the Ragdale Foundation, 1995. **Address:** Louisiana State University, English Department, Allen Hall, Baton Rouge, Louisiana 70808, U.S.A.

PUBLICATIONS

Novels

The Life of Lucy Fern, Part One. New York, Cambridge, Adult Fiction, 1983.
The Life of Lucy Fern, Part Two. New York, Cambridge, Adult Fiction, 1983.
A Period of Confinement. New York, Putnam, 1986.

Short Stories

The Winnebago Mysteries and Other Stories. New York, Fiction Collective, 1982.

Uncollected Short Stories

"Easter," in *The Greycourt Review,* Spring 1973.
"Death and the Pastime Diner," in *The Greycourt Review,* Winter 1974.
"Defining Affairs," in *The Falcon,* Fall 1977.
"During a Night in the Winter," in *Gallimaufry 12: These Women,* 1978.
"Having Always Confused My Body with Hers," in *The Washington Review of the Arts,* Summer Fiction Issue, 1978.
"The Brooklyn Lie," in *The Falcon,* Winter 1979.
"Cleanliness," in *The City Paper* (Baltimore), 10 August 1979.
"Crocheting," in *Washington Review of the Arts,* Summer Fiction Issue, 1980.
"Kudzu," in *The Ohio Review,* Summer 1980.
"Aphasia," in *The Western Humanities Review,* Winter 1983.
"Oslo," in *The New Yorker* (New York), 28 May 1984.
"Paris Leaves Me Cold," in *Mademoiselle,* January 1985.
"German," in *American Voice,* Spring 1988.
"Just Outside the B.T.," in *The Southern Review,* Spring 1989.
"Plans," in *The Boston Sunday Globe Magazine,* 15 October 1989.
"Recovery," in *New Stories by Southern Women,* edited by Mary Ellis Gibson. Columbia, University of South Carolina Press, 1989.
"Just Outside the B.T.," in *New Stories from the South: The Year's Best, 1990,* edited by Shannon Ravenel. New York, Algonquin Books of Chapel Hill, 1990.
"Fever," in *Missouri Review,* Winter 1993.
"There Is a River in New Orleans," in *Negative Capability,* August 1994.
"Dream State," in *Gettysburg Review,* January 1995.
"Gaugin," in *North American Review,* Winter 1995.

*

Moira Crone comments:

I have always been interested, especially in my long fiction, in family relationships, particularly those of mother and daughters. I am also very drawn to the subject of women's emergence from the realm of the home and the family, into the wider world, and the price they must pay for this emergence, as well as its rewards. As an artist, I am very excited by the relationships between narrative and landscape, and between the story and the visual in general. Almost all my stories are written in first person, and therefore issues surrounding the fact, the act of telling, always excites me.

*   *   *

Moira Crone's first book consists of six short stories and a novella. The short narratives focus mainly on unhappy marriages resulting not only in disharmony between husbands and wives but also in negative effects on children. Crone especially emphasizes antagonisms between mothers and daughters. The stories are written in very crisp and vivid prose that is polished and possesses considerable narrative drive.

The Winnebago Mysteries is partly composed of letters written by the novella's characters. Ruth Stark is a 19-year-old who gives up her college studies and decides not to return home to her parents. While hitchhiking she is picked up by Clack Clark, who drives his Winnebago camper around the country anxious to avoid a permanent location and a routine job. Ruth writes letters to her mother and father from various locales. They in turn answer her letters even though no mailing is possible since Ruth gives them no return address.

Most of Ruth's letters are written to Gloria Stark, her mother, and they reflect many of the tensions in the marriage of Gloria and George. Gloria is a complaining, self-centered perfectionist who makes incessant demands on the family to live up to unrealistic expectations. She insists that a man's purpose is to produce babies so that a wife will have something to treasure after her brief love for the husband ends. Yet at the same time she maintains that the mother-daughter relationship is a curse in a world she finds disappointing and unhappy.

Despite this attitude there is ambivalence in the family relationship. Gloria abandons her husband and goes in search of Ruth. George Stark then leaves home to seek his wife and daughter. The family cannot get along with one another, yet they cannot leave one another alone. There is conflict, depression, and spite, but there is also attachment, dependency, and need. In setting out to search for her daughter, Gloria is in her own way mimicking Ruth's search. When they reunite, they are still separate as they engage in a hair-pulling melee; and the Winnebago, which Ruth has stolen after deserting Clack, crashes into a tree. The wrecked home, with its strange mysteries of family relationships and ambivalence of family life that is constantly shifting in moods and events, often crashing, is never fully beyond the hope of at least temporary repair. The impermanent permanence of home life is imaginatively and, at times, surrealistically symbolized and conveyed.

Crone's full-length novel, *A Period of Confinement,* develops in much more detail themes already treated in *The Winnebago Mysteries.* Alma Taylor, the novel's protagonist, is a teacher of painting as well as an artist. The novel is a tapestry of the difficulties involved in achieving and maintaining harmonious relationships both with family and friends. Alma's father had deserted her and her mother, yet he frequently reenters their lives. Although the mother has often been hostile to her husband both before and after the desertion, she can inexplicably rescue him when he is penniless and intoxicated and telephoning for help from a distant tavern. Alma feels a similar ambivalence, not only toward her parents but also toward other people in her life. One of her acquaintances has had a sex-change operation and is living with a woman friend. Another friend has left her husband for a lesbian lover. Alma herself has a confused and often ambivalent relationship with Richard Kaplan, both before and after they marry and while Alma bears his child.

Crone emphasizes that most people are scared of human relationships because so much can and does go wrong. When Alma attempts to become close with Richard's family, not only does his family set up difficulties, but even Richard does not want to let her into this desired unity. Parents are constantly doing things wrong,

and their adult offspring follow the same behavior in their own lives. Essentially, Crone stresses that people are always separated and often most alone even when seemingly together.

Crone presents her characters and themes with much sensitivity and perception. Even when we become exasperated with a character's behavior, we usually understand the reasons—often totally illogical and perverse—for the actions. A flaw in the novel is that on occasion Crone allows unconvincing and implausible coincidences to occur (for example, when Alma's father suddenly takes a romantic interest in a woman half his age who is involved in a lesbian relationship).

Crone's style is precise and vibrant. It takes on the aliveness of the characters. The prose is usually quick-paced but at the same time meditative and psychologically probing, demonstrating the keen intelligence of the author. It is surprising that Crone has not as yet written more than two novels. It appears that the repetitiveness of the novels' themes may limit her production unless she moves on to more varied topics.

—Paul A. Doyle

CROSS, Ian (Robert)

Nationality: New Zealander. **Born:** Wanganui, 1925. **Education:** Wanganui Technical College. **Family:** Married to Tui Tunnicliffe; four sons. **Career:** Associate Nieman Fellow in Journalism, Harvard University, Cambridge, Massachusetts, 1954-55; Robert Burns Fellow, University of Otago, Dunedin, 1959. Editor, *New Zealand Listener,* Wellington, 1973-77; since 1977, chair and chief executive, New Zealand on Air, Wellington. **Awards:** Hubert Church Prose award, 1962. **Address:** P.O. Box 98, Wellington, New Zealand.

PUBLICATIONS

Novels

The God Boy. New York, Harcourt Brace, 1957; London, Deutsch, 1958.
The Backward Sex. London, Deutsch, 1960.
After Anzac Day. London, Deutsch, 1961.
The Family Man. Auckland, Vintage, 1993.

Uncollected Short Story

"Love Affair," in *Atlantic* (Boston), January 1958.

Play

Television Play: *The City of No,* 1970.

Other

The Unlikely Bureaucrat: My Years in Broadcasting. Wellington, Allen and Unwin, 1988.

*   *   *

Ian Cross has written four novels of social concern, which explore the tensions in personal relationships, especially those given emphasis by the narrow experience of small communities. *The God Boy* presents this material through the eyes of a 13-year-old boy who has, two years previously, been a participant in a family tragedy which he observed but did not understand, and which has left its mark upon him. Torn between his father and his mother, young Jimmy reacts with violence and obsession, a classic case history. A clever child who has thought of himself as "chosen," he expects God to give him a helping hand, but no aid comes. He therefore sets up his own private "mutiny against God." The book is notable for its skilful handling of a difficult narrative mode, and for its successful evocation of the speech and ways of an average New Zealand boy. Irony thickens the texture. The reader is closely involved with Jimmy, and like the social worker whose concern this kind of situation so often becomes, begins to comprehend the disaster from within, with sympathetic insight.

The Backward Sex disappoints by being too similar in both manner and material. Raggleton, the coastal settlement of *The God Boy,* has become Albertville, but is otherwise the same place, with a wider range of wharves, sandhills, lupins, and suburban lives as befits the older teller, this time a boy of 17. The topic is the fumbling sexuality of adolescence, but the theme does not seem serious, and the novel is not far above the level of melodrama.

After Anzac Day is wider in both scope and narration. Four people share the telling: The Girl, whose life is going wrong (she is pregnant but unmarried); The Woman, wife of Rankin, ex-soldier and public servant, whose marriage has become a prison with "solitary cells" where the inmates do not even attempt to communicate; The Man, her husband, and The Old Man, her father. These four play out a domestic drama springing from the presence in the Woman's expensive well-oiled home of Jennie, The Girl, to whom her husband has unexpectedly extended a helping hand. Each narrator is given a short turn, which allows Cross to weave four different attitudes and backgrounds into the texture of his fictional world. Clearly, he means to raise wide social, personal, and even historical issues in the New Zealand of 1960. Had he succeeded fully, the elaborate narrative apparatus would have been justified, perhaps. But the problems of John and Margaret Rankin seldom lift above the level of private affairs; the story remains a family drama, without any transfer of significance to the wider issues. *The God Boy,* however, the best of these four novels, is a remarkable little work.

—Joan Stevens

————

CUNNINGHAM, E.V. *See* **FAST, Howard (Melvin).**

————

D

DABYDEEN, David

Nationality: Guyanian and British (immigrated to Britain, 1969). **Born:** Berbice, Guyana, 9 December 1956. **Education:** Cambridge University, 1974-78, B.A. (honours) in English 1978; London University, Ph.D. 1982. **Career:** Director, Centre for Caribbean Studies, University of Warwick. **Awards:** Cambridge University Quiller-Couch prize, 1978; Commonwealth Poetry prize, 1984; Guyana Literature prize, 1991. **Agent:** Curtis Brown, Ltd., Haymarket House, 28-29 Haymarket, London S.W.1 England. **Address:** c/o Centre for Caribbean Studies, University of Warwick, Coventry, England.

PUBLICATIONS

Novels

The Intended. London, Secker and Warburg, 1991.
Disappearance. London, Secker and Warburg, 1993.

Poetry

Slave Song. London, Dangaroo Press, 1984.
Coolie Odyssey. London, Hansib, 1988.
Turner. London, Cape, 1994.

Other

Hogarth, Walpole and Commercial Britain. London, Hansib, 1985.
Hogarth's Blacks: Images of Blacks in Eighteenth Century English Art. Manchester, Manchester University Press, 1987.
A Handbook for Teaching Caribbean Literature. London, Heinemann, 1988.

Editor, *The Black Presence in English Literature.* Manchester, Manchester University Press, 1985.
Editor, with Brinsley Samaroo, *India in the Caribbean.* N.p., Hansib Publishing Ltd., 1987.
Editor, with Paul Edwards, *Black Writers in Britain: An Anthology.* N.p., Columbia University Press, 1992.

* * *

As a writer, editor, professor, and critic, David Dabydeen is remarkably committed to critically exploring the literary contributions of the Caribbean diaspora and the often conflicting polyglot identities that emerge from diasporic movements to and fro homelands and *homeless lands* marked by racism, exploitation, and violence. Language—both the creolization of tongues and the overseer-institution of *standard* English—as an instrument of colonial bondage or the painful outcome of a brutal colonial past is also a central concern in Dabydeen's poetry and prose.

The Intended and *Disappearance* use Creole in ways that reveal a fascination with and resistance to *standard* English. First-person narrators in these bildungsroman-type novels start out by desiring assimilation and invisibility within white sociolinguistic norms. These norms are exemplified in an imagined purity and status associated with white bodies and *standard* English. Narrators in both novels are contrasted with characters and memories that recall them to the "angry, crude, energetic" (*Slave Song*) rawness associated with a Creole that has little patience for lyricism and cleanliness given the constantly intruding wounded history of its users. In *The Intended* and *Disappearance,* Dabydeen's focus shifts between England, Guyana, and Africa, playing with the intentions, memories, and desires of his fictional African and Asian diaspora in Britain. The writer juxtaposes his narrator's denial and shame with a series of narrative movements that double back on themselves, keeping the narrator both complicit and questioning as to the relationships between power and its consequences for race, gender, and empire.

The Intended presents a dilemma of diasporic writing. On the one hand, there is a pressure toward mimicry and the erasure of Black identity through the disciplinary projects of a seemingly apolitical aesthetics of reading practiced by some academic institutions. On the other hand, there is also a concentration on what Dabydeen called the "*folking* up" of Black literature that could lead to its being considered important only as an example of the ethnically exotic or aberrant ("On Not Being Milton: Nigger Talk in England Today"). *The Intended* problematizes these ambivalences by introducing the (ill) literate Joseph, who relentlessly questions the young student narrator and his friends in order to disrupt *the intended* narrative of mimicry. However, since Joseph sets fire to himself and dies, his influence on the narrator is mostly posthumous. It remains arguable, therefore, from the implications of Joseph's death, whether posing an alternate picture to colonial discourses can ever survive without tragic consequences. In *Disappearance,* the narrator is again compelled to move into the spaces between his present—as an engineer trained in Britain who resists cultivating a "sense of the past"—and the African masks on the walls of his landlady's home in Britain. Ironically, this time it is the *English* Mrs. Rutherford who discomfits the narrator's sense of history. The novel also takes Ireland into consideration in its questioning of imperialism. The narrator and Mrs. Rutherford share a curious blend of friendship that at times approaches a romantic closeness, and there is a sense of mystery associated with her past that complements the *disappearance* that the narrator has practiced with regard to his own racial history. However, as with *The Intended,* the narrative moves toward distancing the past but constantly undercuts itself by advancing right into those areas, destabilizing any security that the narrative might *intend* to offer the reader.

Dabydeen's poetry and fiction also contains overtones of riposte, overtones that are sporadically marked in the form of intertextual interrogations of well-known pieces of English literature, such as William Shakespeare's *The Tempest,* Joseph Conrad's *Heart of Darkness,* and John Milton's poetry. Some of his poems in *Slave Song, Coolie Odyssey,* and *Turner* write back to English paintings depicting blacks, such as those by Francis Wheatley and J. M. W. Turner, among others. These rejoinders come alongside his extensive research into the depictions of blacks and Indians in English art and society and into the history of indentured labor in the Caribbean. This research can be seen in his books *Hogarth's Blacks: Images of Blacks in Eighteenth Century Art and Society* and *A Handbook for Teaching Caribbean Literature;* as well as in books he has edited, such as *The Black Presence in English Literature;* or in books he has coedited, such as *Black Writers in Britain 1760-1890* and *India in the Caribbean*. Dabydeen's poems, unlike his fiction, offer translations in *standard* English that accompany their creolized texts. The poetry collections also offer introductions and contexts (which the novels do not) for ways in which he uses Creole. These introductions also serve to emphasize some of his major poetic concerns, concerns that are present also in his fiction.

The critical reception to Dabydeen's novels has been largely positive, except for a sharp critique on narrative complicity by Benita Parry. However, the complex and often tense ways in which gender, race, and identity configure in his writings deserve further and closer scrutiny that existing scholarship has offered.

—Marian Gracias

d'ALPUGET, Blanche

Nationality: Australian. **Born:** Sydney, 3 January 1944. **Education:** Sydney Church of England Girls' Grammar School. **Family:** Married Anthony Ian Camden Pratt in 1965; one son. **Career:** Journalist, president of the Australian Capital Territory branch of the Oral History Association of Australia. **Awards:** PEN Sydney Centre Golden Jubilee award for literature, 1981; *Age* Book of the Year award, 1981, for *Turtle Beach;* South Australian Government award for literature, 1982; New South Wales Premier's award for non-fiction, 1983, for *Robert J. Hawke.* **Member:** Women's Electoral Body; Women's International League for Peace and Freedom; Australian Labor Party; Oral History Association of Australia; Australian Society of Authors. **Agent:** Robert Gottlieb, William Morris Agency, 1350 Avenue of the Americas, New York, New York 10019, U.S.A. **Address:** 18 Urambi Village, Kambah, Australian Capital Territory 2902, Australia.

PUBLICATIONS

Novels

Monkeys in the Dark. Sydney, Aurora Press, 1980.
Turtle Beach. New York, Simon and Schuster, 1981.
Winter in Jerusalem. New York, Simon and Schuster, and London, Secker and Warburg, 1986.
White Eye. New York, Simon and Schuster, 1994.

Other

Mediator: A Biography of Sir Richard Kirby. Melbourne, Melbourne University Press, 1977.
Robert J. Hawke: A Biography. East Melbourne, Schwarts in conjunction with Landsdowne Press, 1982.

*   *   *

If it is true, as novelist Tom Keneally has often complained, that Australia lacks middle-brow writers who can write intelligent, absorbing fiction that deals with serious issues in a mature way, then Blanche d'Alpuget is the exception that proves the rule. She writes comparatively conventional novels that nevertheless are highly competent and engaging, show a keen interest in contemporary affairs, and engage with moral dilemmas in an accessible way without being shallow. She was one of the first Australian novelists to realize the relevance of Asia to Australian life and more recently has turned her attention to such contemporary issues as environmental destruction (and extremism in its defense), genetic engineering, and human cruelty to animals.

Monkeys in the Dark is set in Indonesia at the time of the attempted communist uprising but a year or so later than Christopher J. Koch's better known *The Year of Living Dangerously*. The revolution has been suppressed, Sukarno is still president though his power is clearly declining, and there is uneasy speculation in the air as to whether the communists will attempt another coup. It deals with Alexandra Wheatfield, a rather naive young woman working with the Australian consulate, and her relations with her first cousin and former lover, Anthony Sinclaire, as well as those with the militant Indonesian poet Maruli, with whom she falls in love. Although he does have some feeling for her, Maruli takes advantage of her diplomatic immunity to carry on his revolutionary activities. More wickedly, Anthony tricks her into coming back to him at the end of the novel by blackening Maruli's name. It is a gripping and well-plotted novel that captures the atmosphere of Indonesia in the wake of the uprising, but its pessimistic, even fatalistic, mood is summed up in the extract from a speech by Sukarno that gives the novel its title: "Oh, my people, if you abandon our history you will face a vaccuum. . . . Life for you will be no more than running amok. Running amok—like monkeys trapped in the dark!"

Turtle Beach is set in Malaysia, with the boat people arriving in the aftermath of the Vietnam War being greeted with hostility by local residents. When two hundred of them are drowned, the fish feed off their corpses and the livelihood of the fishermen is ruined, as people refuse to buy their produce. Ironies such as these abound in the novel. The heroine is again a reasonably attractive (not startlingly beautiful but with a seductively Monroe kind of voice) reporter in her late thirties, but unlike her predecessor, Judith Wilkes is a tough-minded careerist, determinedly carrying on with her work as she copes with a young family and a dying marriage to an ambitious political flunky back in Australia. Yet she has some of the same qualities as Alex: a tendency toward passivity, a weakness for sensual men, and a sense of idealism that renders her vulnerable to manipulation. Like Alex, she falls in love with one of the locals, Kanan, but is finally repelled by the fatalism of his Indian philosophy. Again the title of the novel embodies a metaphor to do with human helplessness in the face of larger historical movements. It comes from the turtles that battle against all odds to lay their eggs and bury them, only to have them dug up and sold or eaten by the local residents.

Winter in Jerusalem follows a relatively familiar format but with decreasing assurance. Its heroine is Danielle Green, a thirty-eight-year-old professional writer widowed after an unhappy marriage and with a teenage daughter in Sydney. She has arrived in Jerusalem to write the script for a film about an uprising of suicidal zealots in 73 A.D. and also to try and make contact with her father, whom she has not seen for many years. Although the novel has many of d'Alpuget's best qualities—her grasp of atmosphere, aphoristic wit, quick snapshots of characters—it is the least coherent and worse structured of her novels, heavily dependent on coincidence of an opportunistic kind. The theme of Danielle's relationship with her father is never explored in any depth and toward the end the action of the novel accelerates toward its upbeat resolution to a point that is almost laughable.

A gap of eight years followed before d'Alpuget published her fourth novel, *White Eye,* which again broke new ground for her. It is a kind of ecothriller, subsuming concerns the author has often spoken on in interviews in a popular format. Although written in a deliberately plain and simple style the novel has an extraordinarily intricate plot, involving illegal trafficking in chimpanzees between Thailand and Australia, genetic engineering, and an attempt to destroy the world. It opens dramatically with the discovery of the naked body of a woman who has been tortured, then shot. It will be the first of at least eight murders in the novel, some of them quite horrific. The protagonist, Diana Pembridge, is a quintessential d'Alpuget heroine, thirty-two years old, beautiful and patrician in appearance, but vulnerable and unfulfilled in reality. She is a passionate lover of nature without being a fanatic, and some of the finest writing in the novel is devoted to accounts of her falconing and her struggle to heal and release a wounded wedgetail eagle.

Against her is pitted John Parker, a deeply misogynistic man whose disgust with a proliferating human race drives him to invent a vaccine that will prevent it breeding: "He had succeeded in doing what every man, secretly, would like to do: he had created a vaccine that would sterilise all the other men on Earth." D'Alpuget has said that part of her aim was to preach against the excesses of environmentalists, but in Parker she has created not a zealot but a murderously pathological misanthrope with no redeeming qualities except a certain kind of mordant wit: Asked by a woman if he minds her smoking he replies amiably, "Not at all. Smoking helps reduce the population." It comes as no surprise to the reader to discover eventually that he is also a covert homosexual; gays in general get a bad press in this novel. Like all of d'Alpuget's work, *White Eye* is a carefully and thoroughly researched novel that at times indeed wears its learning a little ostentatiously. It alternates scenes of lyrical evocation of landscape and the beauty of the colony of birds that Diana looks after with descriptions of violence and cruelty. Like *Winter in Jerusalem* it suffers from a rushed ending in which Diana and a charismatic photographer cum environmentalist meet and fall in love in what seems seconds. D'Alpuget has admitted that she has difficulty in writing scenes of sexual love and this is evident here. The effect of love on Diana seems to be to turn her into a kind of travelling light show: "The colours around her body throbbed and flowed, rose-red, rose-pink, violet around her shoulders, orange around her and around her hands a bright, clear green." However, d'Alpuget does save a couple of ingenious twists in the plot till right near the end.

—Laurie Clancy

DATHORNE, O(scar) R(onald)

Nationality: British. **Born:** Georgetown, Guyana, 19 November 1934. **Education:** The University of Sheffield, Yorkshire, 1955-58, B.A. 1958, M.A. 1960, Ph.D. 1966; University of London, 1958-59, Cert.Ed. 1959, Dip.Ed. 1967; University of Miami, M.B.A., M.P.A. 1984. **Family:** Married Hildegard Ostermaier in 1959; one daughter and one son. **Career:** Lecturer, Ahmadu Bello University, Zaria, Nigeria, 1959-63, and University of Ibadan, Nigeria, 1963-66; Unesco consultant to the government of Sierra Leone, 1967-68; professor of English, Njala University College, University of Sierra Leone, Freetown, 1968-69; professor, Afro-

American Studies Department, University of Wisconsin, Madison, 1970, and Ohio State University, Columbus, 1971-77; professor of English and Director of American Studies, University of Miami, since 1977; currently, professor of English, University of Kentucky, Lexington. Editor, *Journal of Caribbean Studies,* Lexington. **Address:** Department of English, University of Kentucky, Lexington, Kentucky 40506, U.S.A.

PUBLICATIONS

Novels

Dumplings in the Soup. London, Cassell, 1963.
The Scholar-Man. London, Cassell, 1964.
Dele's Child. Washington, D.C., Three Continents Press, 1986.

Uncollected Short Stories

"The Wintering of Mr. Kolawole," in *Stories from the Caribbean,* edited by Andrew Salkey. London, Elek, 1965; as *Island Voices,* New York, Liveright, 1970.
"Hodge" and "The Nightwatchman and the Baby Nurse," in *Nigerian Radio Times* (Ibadan), 1967.
"Constable," in *Political Spider.* London, Heinemann, 1969.

Poetry

Kelly Poems. Privately printed, 1977.
Songs for a New World. Miami, Association of Caribbean Studies, 1988.

Other

The Black Mind: A History of African Literature. Minneapolis, University of Minnesota Press, 1974; abridged edition, as *African Literature in the Twentieth Century,* University of Minnesota Press, and London, Heinemann, 1976.
Dark Ancestor: The Literature of the Black Man in the Caribbean. Baton Rouge, Louisiana State University Press, 1981.
Imagining the World: Mythical Belief Versus Reality in Global Encounters. Westport, Connecticut, and London, Bergin and Garvey, 1994.
In Europe's Image: The Need for American Multiculturalism. Westport, Connecticut, Bergin and Garvey, 1994.

Editor, with others, *Young Commonwealth Poets '65.* London, Heinemann, 1965.
Editor, *Caribbean Narrative.* London, Heinemann, 1966.
Editor, *Caribbean Verse.* London, Heinemann, 1967.
Editor, with Willfried Feuser, *Africa in Prose.* London, Penguin, 1969.
Editor, *African Poetry for Schools and Colleges.* Yaba, Nigeria, Macmillan, 1969.
Editor, *Selected Poems,* by Derek Walcott. London, Heinemann, 1977.
Editor, *Afro World: Adventures in Ideas.* Milwaukee, University of Wisconsin Press, 1984.
Editor, *Caribbean Aspirations and Achievements.* Coral Gables, Florida, Association of Caribbean Studies, 1985.

*

Critical Studies: "Guyanese Writers" by Wilfred Cartey, in *New World* (Georgetown, Guyana), 1966; *The Islands in Between* by Louis James, London, Oxford University Press, 1968; *The Chosen Tongue* by Gerald Moore, London, Longman, 1969; *Homecoming* by James T. Ngugi, London, Heinemann, 1972, New York, Hill, 1973.

O.R. Dathorne comments:

(1972) My work has in general used situations which seemed near enough for me to handle. Black immigration in England, a Black man's quest for identity in Africa have been the starting points for what I hope have been larger involvements of the protagonist's new understanding of the world. Frequently, the "new" contact with reality cannot be resolved on a rational level and this is why in plays and poetry I have moved towards an intentionally "irrational" approach which expresses bewilderment.

I lived for 10 years in Africa; they taught me to be wary of novelty, as did the creative urges of young African writers like myself. Only incidentally, I became a "critic" of the new African literature; only incidentally, I was forced to learn about a man's world-view (which I had to understand) before I spoke. Only incidentally this led me back to myself and the large interrogatives concerning my history. Now I am aware of the manifestations of curious parallels in cultural experience and it is this I proclaim.

*   *   *

O.R. Dathorne's earlier fiction shows an eye for comic idiosyncrasy, in particular those of Africans and West Indians, and a lively interest in the predicament of the expatriate. Comedy is uppermost in *Dumplings in the Soup*. Here John Jiffey Jacket gets a room in a London tenement crowded with immigrant lodgers. They are dominated by Boffo, a genial non-rent-paying confidence man who enlivens the religious devotions of the local Shakers club with strong drinks, and lets his landlord's cellar to a newcomer from Africa for 50 pounds in advance. The book is lively and readable, but the comic exaggeration undermines the more serious undertones, and, ultimately, some of the comedy itself.

The Scholar-Man is a more complex and thoughtful work. Adam Questus, a West Indian, goes in search of Egor, an English-born mulatto who made such a strong impression on his childhood that Adam looks to him to show him a meaning in life. He teaches English at a university in an African state on the brink of independence. In his quest he visits a village where cult-drumming induces a trance in which he glimpses his slave-ancestry: however he is unable to endure the African ritual of the cult whip. He discovers that Egor has vanished. He runs away with an outcast girl and with her amid the mud and rain of the African bush glimpses the ambiguous "reality" he had been seeking.

Adam's search, with its echoes of Conrad's *Heart of Darkness,* is interwoven with comic satire on expatriate academic life and the political turmoil of a country exchanging one set of superstitions for another as it searches for its own identity. Some of the humour is somewhat forced, but in this second work the comedy also touches wider themes of identity and the wider reality.

His third novel, *Dele's Child,* which is a complex exploration of roots and ancestry, is more consistently serious. The novel moves across time and space. In America, Dele, with African ancestry, has a boy-child, Sunday, by one of three lovers. The story shifts from San Francisco to an African country in a state of revolution. Here the putative fathers, and Dele, search for both the meaning of

their past and a redemption of their present condition through working out their claims to the child. The novel shows Dathorne's deepening interest in aspects of African culture, including Yoruba religion and poetic form, as he experiments with ways to move beyond the conventions of European narrative into a form appropriate for an African-oriented consciousness.

—Louis James

DAVENPORT, Guy (Mattison, Jr.)

Nationality: American. **Born:** Anderson, South Carolina, 23 November 1927. **Education:** Duke University, Durham, North Carolina, B.A. 1948; Merton College, Oxford (Rhodes scholar), 1948-50, B.Litt. 1950; Harvard University, Cambridge, Massachusetts, Ph.D. 1961. **Military Service:** Served in the United States Army Airborne Corps, 1950-52. **Career:** Instructor, Washington University, St. Louis, 1952-55; assistant professor, Haverford College, Pennsylvania, 1961-63. Professor of English, 1963-92, and since 1992 professor emeritus, University of Kentucky, Lexington. Contributing editor, 1962-83, *National Review,* New York. Also book and magazine illustrator and designer. MacArthur fellow, 1991-96. **Awards:** Blumenthal-Leviton prize (*Poetry,* Chicago), 1967; American Academy Morton Dauwen Zabel award, 1981; Carter prize, for literary criticism, 1987. D.L.H.: University of Kentucky, 1992. **Address:** 621 Sayre Avenue, Lexington, Kentucky 40506, U.S.A.

PUBLICATIONS

Novel

The Bicycle Rider. New York, Red Ozier Press, 1985.

Short Stories

Tatlin! New York, Scribner, 1974.
Da Vinci's Bicycle: Ten Stories. Baltimore, Johns Hopkins University Press, 1979.
Eclogues: Eight Stories. Berkeley, California, North Point Press, 1981; London, Pan, 1984.
Trois Caprices. Louisville, Pace Trust, 1981.
The Bowmen of Shu. New York, Grenfell Press, 1983.
Apples and Pears and Other Stories. Berkeley, California, North Point Press, 1984.
The Bicycle Rider. New York, Red Ozier Press, 1985.
Jonah: A Story. New York, Nadja, 1986.
The Jules Verne Steam Balloon: Nine Stories. Berkeley, California, North Point Press, 1987.
The Drummer of the Eleventh North Devonshire Fusiliers. Berkeley, California, North Point Press, 1990.
A Table of Green Fields. New York, New Directions, 1994.
Seven Greeks. New York, New Directions, 1995.

Uncollected Short Stories

"August Blue," in *Antaeus* (New York), Spring-Autumn 1990.
"Juno of the Veii," in *Harper's* (New York), September 1990.

Poetry

Flowers and Leaves: Poems vel Sonata, Carmina Autumni Primaeque Veris Transformationum. Highlands, North Carolina, Jargon, 1966.
The Resurrection in Cookham Churchyard. New York, Davies, 1982.
Goldfinch Thistle Star. New York, Red Ozier Press, 1983.
Thasos and Ohio: Poems and Translations 1950-1980. Berkeley, Calfornia, North Point Press, and Manchester, Carcanet, 1986.

Other

Cydonia Florentia. Cambridge, Massachusetts, Lowell Adams House Printers, 1966.
Pennant Key-Indexed Guide to Homer's Iliad [and *Odyssey*]. Philadelphia, Educational Research Associates, 2 vols., 1967.
Do You Have a Poem Book on E.E. Cummings? Highlands, North Carolina, Jargon, 1969.
Jonathan Williams, Poet. Cleveland, Asphodel Book Shop, 1969.
The Geography of the Imagination: Forty Essays. Berkeley, California, North Point Press, 1981; London, Pan, 1984.
Cities on Hills: A Study of I-XXX of Ezra Pound's "Cantos." Ann Arbor, Michigan, UMI Research Press, and Epping, Essex, Bowker, 1983.
The Art of Lafcadio Hearn, with Clifton Waller Bennett, Charlottesville, University of Virginia Library, 1983.
Every Force Evolves a Form: Twenty Essays. Berkeley, California, North Point Press, 1987; London, Secker and Warburg, 1989.
A Balthus Notebook. New York, Ecco Press, 1989.
The Drawings of Paul Cadmus. New York, Rizzoli, 1990.
Charles Burchfield's Seasons. San Francisco, Pomegranate, 1994.

Editor, *The Intelligence of Louis Agassiz: A Specimen Book of Scientific Writings.* Boston, Beacon Press, 1963.

Translator, *Carmina Archilochi: The Fragments of Archilochos.* Berkeley, University of California Press, 1964.
Translator, *Sappho: Songs and Fragments.* Ann Arbor, University of Michigan Press, 1965.
Translator, *Archilochos, Sappho, Alkman: Three Lyric Poets of the Late Greek Bronze Age.* Berkeley, University of California Press, 1980.
Translator, *Herakleitos and Diogenes.* Berkeley, California, Grey Fox Press, 1980.
Translator, *The Mimes of Herondas.* Berkeley, California, Grey Fox Press, 1981.
Translator, *Maxims of the Ancient Egyptians,* by Boris de Rachewiltz. Louisville, Pace Trust, 1983.

*

Bibliography: "Guy Davenport: A Bibliographical Checklist," in *American Book Collector* (New York), March-April 1984.

Manuscript Collections: Rosenbach Library, Philadelphia; South Caroliniana Library, Columbia, South Carolina.

Critical Studies: "*Tatlin!;* or, The Limits of Fiction" by Richard Pevear, Spring 1975, and "Guy Davenport in Harmony," Autumn 1980, both in *Hudson Review* (New York).

Guy Davenport comments:

My talent is minor, my prose unskilled and contrived, my ideas derivative. In my stories I shape anecdotes about real people much as Parson Weems made a folktale hero of George Washington. This is not my intention: it is what happens when anybody writes about things in ignorance and from a distance. I have Panait Istrati wearing a flowery embroidered shirt; Marguerite Dorian tells me that he wouldn't be caught dead in one. In spite of doing research, this wrong-shirt effect usually turns up in every detail. I read some 40 books about prehistory to write the story "Robot," visited the site of Lascaux, talked with Jacques Marsal, have heard first-hand accounts of refugees fleeing the Germans across that part of France; and yet my story (which is about the discovery of the prehistoric cave at Lascaux in 1941) could not possibly have a single sentence of truth in it. From five to 10 years of such research go into every story; for one, 15. The stories are not what they seem to be about (what story is?), but I don't have any interpretation up my sleeve that I would insist on. My ambition is solely to get some effect, as of light on stone in a forest on a September day, that seems to me to be a duty to preserve, as a quality of our world, in a rhythm of words. I cannot write about myself or of emotions with which I am familiar. Fiction's essential activity is to imagine how others feel, what a Saturday afternoon in an Italian town in the second century looked like. I trust the world to speak for itself. If I write *rose,* there are roses to stand me good. When Louis Zukofsky wrote his *Eighty Flowers,* he went to the trouble to see each flower. Picture and description would not do. I have stood on my toes and touched Blériot's *Antoinette.* I've held Shelley's snuffbox in my hands, and have sat on the chair of Gertrude Stein's that Ezra Pound broke; I'll find a place for these encounters. I mention them because some such haptic event authenticates every detail in my writing. But for this invisible substantiality I would not write at all. In a sense my texts are translations of an obliterated original that can never be reconstituted. The story "Robot," for instance, is an afternoon looking for Indian arrowheads with my father in South Carolina (I feel certain). "The Dawn in Erewhon" is a translation and elaboration of a split second of a sunny morning in Amsterdam. "A Field of Snow on a Slope of the Rosenberg" is of course not about Robert Walser, but about Christopher Middleton's Robert Walser, and probably a translation of a moment in Paris 30 years ago, sitting in one of Joyce's *brasseries* (on the street where Rimbaud wrote *Les Illuminations*) when Chris and I saw a horse wearing a hat that made our day. "C. Musonius Rufus" is about Ezra Pound, or perhaps Virgil. "Au Tombeau de Charles Fourier" began in my head when I was reading Fourier on a bluff of the Ohio River and encountered the unknown word *quagga.* My feeling is that my stories just might, with luck, be included in the corporate attempt of writing in our time to understand how so hopeful a century as ours blundered so tragically as to be the most inhuman of them all.

* * *

Guy Davenport's a critic, poet, classicist, translator, teacher, and book illustrator who with the publication of *Tatlin!, Da Vinci's Bicycle, Eclogues* and *Apples and Pears* has become a master fictionist as well. These collections include novellae treating the Soviet constructivist V. Tatlin, the Dutch philosopher Adriaan van Hovendaal and friends, and the Modernist circle surrounding Stein and Picasso. Other stories feature Leonardo Da Vinci inventing a bicycle (to be ridden in battle, "a phalanx of these *due rote* bearing lancers at full tilt"), Kafka and Max Brod attending an air show where they brush shoulders with Wittgenstein, and most remarkably (and fictionally) "A photograph of Lenin reading *Iskra* at a Zurich cafe" which "accidentally includes over to the left James and Nora Joyce haggling with a taxi driver about the fare."

What strange yet telling juxtapositions of the Moderns, the very makers of our century. The fact that half of them are made up takes nothing from Davenport's achievement; indeed, he considers such combinations of fact and fantasy "necessary fictions" which in their very form of delight tell us much about our Postmodern selves. Ezra Pound spinning a fable about Yeats's body lost at sea by a drunken navy crew? Nietzsche signing the guestbook at a Rapallo inn with the caution, "Beware the beefsteak"? These are snapshots of the Modern, crafted by the same aesthetic in which, as part of an early photographic plate of fossils at the Museum of Natural History, "two gentlemen stand in the background, spectators at the museum. One wears a top hat and looks with neurotic intelligence at the camera. He is Edgar Allan Poe. The other gentleman is cross-eyed and ears a beret. God knows who he is."

History is a dream that strays into innocent sleep. This motto, from the heart of Davenport's fiction, helps tell why he feels the two modes must be mixed. "The mind is what it knows!" one of his characters insists. "It is nothing else at all, at all." Can our very nature be formed by the way we view history? Consider how that relatively new and most typically Modern of aesthetic media, the camera, composes things for us. Poe caught posing with a dinosaur Lenin and Joyce so casually compared in their own worlds of economics, all recorded by the chance photograph—"for the first time in the history of art," Davenport's story explains, "the accidental became the controlling iconography of a representation of the world."

Therefore *Tatlin!* and *Da Vinci's Bicycle* present imaginative exercises on characters who do not completely match up with our conventional readings of the past. The camera, by its very rigidity, rattles our perception and makes us see things we never knew were there; and so Davenport's fiction, using many of the same accidental and juxtapositional methods, attempts to do the same thing. Gertrude Stein is seen reading the Sunday comics to Picasso; ancient Greek philosophers invent a mechanical pigeon; President Richard Nixon, impressed by the Great Wall of China, bombs the DMZ to similarly impress his host. If any of these events did indeed happen, it was probably in other people's imaginations, for if history is a dream which strays into innocent sleep, so too may dreams contaminate (or perhaps enrich) history. In any event, Davenport concludes, we know reality only through our fictions, and his stories and novellae are attempts to structure those fictions according to the photographic, cinematic, and collagist natures of our time.

Eclogues and especially *Apples and Pears* are set in the world of Fourierist philosophy, and express Davenport's most complete vision. Adriaan van Hovendaal, the character whose sexual philosophy bloomed into the *ménage à trois* in *Tatlin!*'s "The Dawn in Erewhon," is now given a brood of children and network of friends within which to live his ideals of affection and sharing. The theme of apples and pears runs through this latter collection, providing a test of art against nature just as Adriaan's adventures allow philosophy to be measured against experience. As he and his friends establish an ideal communal household of love and culture, so Davenport creates a fictive world in which the activities of making art and love combine in a natural philosophy for which belief need rarely be suspended.

Nature and intelligence form an ideal balance in Davenport's ideal world. His characters respond to Fourier's notion of Harmony, which is based on the attractions of desire; "Apples and Pears" brashly gives these desires free rein. Through the novella's four sections characters undress, share beds and clothes, and make love in all combinations of sex and age. "Poetry in the Harmony will be a system of analogies and correspondences noted by children and gifted adults," Adriaan writes, and as author Davenport reifies this aesthetic with boldly physical affection. His people paint, write, and love each other's bodies in the same spirit of unfettered creativity and exchange. Davenport's frankness tests the limits of a philosophical ideal by writing out all the possibilities. If prose can contain them, then the vision is sound, just as in Fourier's grand plan.

Davenport's work of the 1980s concludes with an affirmation of both the aesthetic and ethical philosophies expounded in *Apples and Pears.* Portions of *The Jules Verne Steam Balloon* and *The Drummer of the Eleventh North Devonshire Fusiliers* combine to form a trilogy with this earlier work, centered as they are on the professed delights of the finest food and music, the adventures of learning, the enjoyment of nature, and the pleasures of adolescent male love (tempered with a healthy dose of heterosexual involvement for the adult protagonist, a teacher in a boys' school). Here Davenport develops his narrative technique to encompass a certain cubist fragmenting of the ongoing story by sectioning it into as many as 89 divisions, some of which are titled with consecutive numbers, others of which (in the manner of some of Roland Barthes's studies) are headed with key terms from the discourse at hand. That a philosophy stands behind these stories as a matter of advocacy is evident from a work that transcends the limits of genre, *A Balthus Notebook,* in which Davenport draws on not just art criticism and cultural commentary but also fictive meditation to convey the essence of the world as painted by Balthus, a style coming close to graphic equivalency with the world Davenport portrays in his stories.

—Jerome Klinkowitz

DAVIDSON, Lionel

Nationality: British. **Born:** Hull, Yorkshire, 31 March 1922. **Military Service:** Served in the Royal Naval Submarine Service, 1941-46. **Family:** Married 1) Fay Jacobs in 1949 (died 1988), two sons; 2) Frances Ullman in 1989. **Career:** Freelance magazine journalist and editor, 1946-59. **Awards:** Authors Club award, 1961; Crime Writers Association Gold Dagger, 1961, 1967, 1979. **Agent:** Curtis Brown, 28/29 Haymarket, London SW1Y 4SP, England.

PUBLICATIONS

Novels

The Night of Wenceslas. London, Gollancz, 1960; New York, Harper, 1961.
The Rose of Tibet. London, Gollancz, and New York, Harper, 1962.
A Long Way to Shiloh. London, Gollancz, 1966; as *The Menorah Men,* New York, Harper, 1966.

Making Good Again. London, Cape, and New York, Harper, 1968.
Smith's Gazelle. London, Cape, and New York, Knopf, 1971.
The Sun Chemist. London, Cape, and New York, Knopf, 1976.
The Chelsea Murders. London, Cape, 1978; as *Murder Games,* New York, Coward McCann, 1978.
Kolymsky Heights. London, Heinemann, and New York, St. Martin's, 1994.

Uncollected Short Stories

"Note to Survivors," in *Alfred Hitchcock's Mystery Magazine* (New York), May 1958.
"Where Am I Going? Nowhere!," in *Suspense* (London), February 1961.
"Indian Rope Trick," in *Winter's Crimes 13,* edited by George Hardinge. London, Macmillan, 1981.
"I Do Dwell," in *Winter's Crimes 16,* edited by Hilary Hale. London, Macmillan, 1984.

Fiction (for children) as David Line

Soldier and Me. New York, Harper, 1965.
Run for Your Life. London, Cape, 1966.
Mike and Me. London, Cape, 1974.
Under Plum Lake (as Lionel Davidson). London, Cape, and New York, Knopf, 1980.
Screaming High. London, Cape, and Boston, Little Brown, 1985.

*   *   *

A novelist in various genres, Lionel Davidson has become most widely known as a writer of mysteries, winning the Crime Writers Association Gold Dagger, an annual prize, three different times. His mystery stories are intricate and full of social and historical detail. *The Chelsea Murders* (published as *Murder Games* in the United States), for example, uses clues drawn from 19th-century literary and pre-Raphaelite figures. Each of the seven victims has the initials of one of the luminaries who lived in Chelsea, figures like Dante Gabriel Rossetti, Oscar Wilde, and Algernon Charles Swinburne; the mass killer, like one of the victims, has the initials of the satirist W.S. Gilbert. In addition, the clues, mailed to the police through different ingenious guises, are quotations from the writers, emphasizing the novel's resemblance to an intricate game. No clue is, in itself, more relevant than any of the others. *The Chelsea Murders* is also, like much of Davidson's fiction, socially referential, containing quick depictions of London porno clubs, film-making, language lessons for the acculturation of Arabs, a gay disco, and a jeans store on the King's Road. Within his quickly shifting and often comic scenes, Davidson pays deference to traditional elements in crime fiction, the establishment of time frame, the police procedure, and the use of disguise to confuse identity, although he allows himself little space for the treatment of motive, psychology, or any interior quality. His characterizations, like his characters themselves, are likely to operate in groups, and the most common theme in the mysteries is that of betrayal, the violation by one member of the ethos, the standards, or the lives of other members of the group.

Other of Davidson's novels shade the line dividing the mystery from the novel of espionage. One espionage novel is *Making Good Again* in which three lawyers in the 1960s, an Englishman, a German, and an Israeli, combine in an effort to find a long-missing German-Jewish banker or to decide what to do with the million Swiss francs still left in his name. Using various costumes and guises as they travel through the Bavarian forest and other parts of Europe, and shifting allegiances to various governments and national interests, they constantly confront echoes of Nazi feeling and raise questions about German guilt and possible reparations for crimes against the Jews and the rest of humanity. Again, the theme is betrayal; but the notion of a new international combination of responsibilities cannot sustain itself in a plot that involves a good deal of action and adventure. Another novel, published as *A Long Way to Shiloh* in England and *The Menorah Men* in the United States, combines adventure with a depiction of Israel in the 1960s. This novel places the search for a religious symbol originally lost or stolen from the Temple at Jerusalem against a background of contemporary Israel trying to develop a national identity through current forms of economic, social, sexual, and religious behavior.

Davidson manifests a considerable range among fictional genres, almost never writing the same kind of novel twice. *The Rose of Tibet* is pure adventure and travelogue, evoking that strange and isolated land held in by mountains. *Smith's Gazelle,* with considerable delicacy and sensitivity, deals with the excitements and problems of preserving a nearly extinct herd of deer, working its implicit argument for conservation into suggestions of a mythic statement about the origins of species. *Under Plum Lake* is a fantasy for children in which a young boy discovers a whole subterranean civilization underneath a familiar lake. Different as they are in genre and setting, all Davidson's novels depend on action and adventure, externalizing their themes and concerns into a constant involvement with a difficult, various, and morally confusing contemporary world.

Davidson's moral statements, however, never become obvious or heavy-handed. His humor and games are always visible, his social commentary more a matter of reference to or passing jabs at contemporary social phenomena than any sustained social criticism or analysis. His references, too, like those in *The Chelsea Murders,* are often literary, historical, or topical, references to other works or quick echoes of other styles that make the novels, especially those like *The Sun Chemist,* about the possible existence among Chaim Weitzmann's forgotten papers of a chemical formula that will free the world's industry from its dependence on Arab oil, sound derivative. Davidson has, as a novelist, not yet developed a strong or distinctive literary identity, but his protean skill, his deftness, his humor, and the excitement of the action and cleverness visible in all his novels, along with settings that always illustrate a responsiveness to the contemporary social and political world, have earned him a considerable and growing reputation.

—James Gindin

DAVIES, (William) Robertson

Nationality: Canadian. **Born:** Thamesville, Ontario, 28 August 1913. **Education:** Upper Canada College, Toronto; Queen's University, Kingston, Ontario; Balliol College, Oxford, 1936-38, B.Litt. 1938. **Family:** Married Brenda Mathews in 1940; three daughters. **Career:** Teacher and actor, Old Vic Theatre School and Repertory Company, London, 1938-40; literary editor, *Saturday Night,* Toronto, 1940-42; editor and publisher, Peterborough *Examiner,*

Ontario, 1942-63. Since 1960 professor of English, since 1962 Master of Massey College, and since 1981 Founding Master, University of Toronto. Governor, Stratford Shakespeare Festival, Ontario, 1953-71. **Awards:** Ottawa Drama League prize, 1946, 1947; Dominion Drama Festival prize, for play, 1948, 1949, for directing, 1949; Leacock medal, 1955; Lorne Pierce medal, 1961; Governor-General's award, for fiction, 1973; World Fantasy Convention award, for fiction, 1984; City of Toronto Book award, 1986; Canadian Authors' Association award, for fiction, 1986; Banff Centre award, 1986; Foundation for the Advancement of Canadian Letters award, 1986, 1990; Toronto Arts Lifetime Achievement award, 1986; U.S. National Arts Club Medal of Honor, 1987 (first Canadian recipient); Molson prize, 1988; Canadian Conference of the Arts diploma, 1988; Scottish Arts Council Neil Gunn International fellowship, 1988. LL.D.: University of Alberta, Edmonton, 1957; Queen's University, 1962; University of Manitoba, Winnipeg, 1972; University of Toronto, 1981; University of Prince Edward Island, Charlottetown, 1989; D.Litt.: McMaster University, Hamilton, Ontario, 1959; University of Windsor, Ontario, 1971; York University, Toronto, 1973; Mount Allison University, Sackville, New Brunswick, 1973; Memorial University of Newfoundland, St. John's, 1974; University of Western Ontario, London, 1974; McGill University, Montreal, 1974; Trent University, Peterborough, Ontario, 1974; University of Lethbridge, Alberta, 1981; University of Waterloo, Ontario, 1981; University of British Columbia, Vancouver, 1983; University of Santa Clara, California, 1985; Trinity College, Dublin, 1990; Oxford University, 1991; University of Wales, 1995; D.C.L.: Bishop's University, Lennoxville, Quebec, 1967; LL.D.: University of Calgary, Alberta, 1975; D.H.L.: Rochester University, Rochester, New York, 1983; Dowling College, New York, 1992; Loyola University, Chicago, 1994; D.S.L.: Thornloe University, Sudbury, Ontario, 1988; Diplome honoris causa: Royal Conservatory of Music, Toronto, 1994. Fellow, Balliol College, Oxford, 1986, and Trinity College, Toronto, 1987. Fellow, Royal Society of Canada, 1967, and Royal Society of Literature, 1984; Honorary Member, American Academy, 1981 (first Canadian elected). Companion, Order of Canada, 1972; Order of Ontario, 1988. **Agent:** Curtis Brown, 10 Astor Place, New York, New York 10003, U.S.A. **Address:** Massey College, 4 Devonshire Place, Toronto, Ontario M5S 2E1, Canada.

PUBLICATIONS

Novels

The Salterton Trilogy. Toronto and London, Penguin, 1986.
    Tempest-Tost. Toronto, Clarke Irwin, 1951; London, Chatto and Windus, and New York, Rinehart, 1952.
    Leaven of Malice. Toronto, Clarke Irwin, 1954; London, Chatto and Windus, and New York, Scribner, 1955.
    A Mixture of Frailties. Toronto, Macmillan, London, Weidenfeld and Nicolson, and New York, Scribner, 1958.
The Deptford Trilogy. Toronto and London, Penguin, 1983.
    Fifth Business. Toronto, Macmillan, and New York, Viking Press, 1970; London, Macmillan, 1971.
    The Manticore. Toronto, Macmillan, and New York, Viking Press, 1972; London, Macmillan, 1973.
    World of Wonders. Toronto, Macmillan, 1975; New York, Viking Press, 1976; London, W.H. Allen, 1977.

The Cornish Trilogy. Toronto and London, Penguin, 1991.
    The Rebel Angels. Toronto, Macmillan, 1981; New York, Viking Press, and London, Allen Lane, 1982.
    What's Bred in the Bone. Toronto, Macmillan, and New York, Viking, 1985; London, Viking, 1986.
    The Lyre of Orpheus. Toronto, Macmillan, and London, Viking, 1988; New York, Viking, 1989.
Murther & Walking Spirits. Toronto, McClelland and Stewart, New York, Viking, and London, Sinclair Stevenson, 1991.
The Cunning Man. Toronto, McClelland and Stewart, 1994; New York and London, Viking Penguin, 1995.

Short Stories

High Spirits: A Collection of Ghost Stories. Toronto and London, Penguin, 1982; New York, Viking Press, 1983.

Uncollected Short Story

"A Christmas Carol Reharmonized," in *Washington Post Book World,* 1982.

Plays

A Play of Our Lord's Nativity (produced Peterborough, Ontario, 1946).
Overlaid (produced Peterborough, Ontario, 1947). Included in *Eros at Breakfast and Other Plays,* 1949.
The Voice of the People (produced Montreal, 1948). Included in *Eros at Breakfast and Other Plays,* 1949.
At the Gates of the Righteous (produced Peterborough, Ontario, 1948). Included in *Eros at Breakfast and Other Plays,* 1949.
Hope Deferred (produced Montreal, 1948). Included in *Eros at Breakfast and Other Plays,* 1949.
Fortune, My Foe (produced Kingston, Ontario, 1948). Toronto, Clarke Irwin, 1949.
Eros at Breakfast (produced Ottawa, 1948). Included in *Eros at Breakfast and Other Plays,* 1949.
Eros at Breakfast and Other Plays. Toronto, Clarke Irwin, 1949.
At My Heart's Core (produced Peterborough, Ontario, 1950). Toronto, Clarke Irwin, 1950.
King Phoenix (produced Peterborough, Ontario, 1950). Included in *Hunting Stuart and Other Plays,* 1972.
A Masque of Aesop (for children; produced Toronto, 1952). Toronto, Clarke Irwin, 1952; in *Five New One-Act Plays,* edited by James A. Stone, London, Harrap, 1954.
A Jig for the Gypsy (produced Toronto and London, 1954). Toronto, Clarke Irwin, 1954.
Hunting Stuart (produced Toronto, 1955). Included in *Hunting Stuart and Other Plays,* 1972.
Leaven of Malice, adaptation of his own novel (as *Love and Libel,* produced Toronto and New York, 1960; revised version, as *Leaven of Malice,* produced Toronto, 1973). Published in *Canadian Drama* (Waterloo, Ontario), vol. 7, no. 2, 1981.
A Masque of Mr. Punch (for children; produced Toronto, 1962). Toronto, Oxford University Press, 1963.
Centennial Play, with others (produced Lindsay, Ontario, 1967). Ottawa, Centennial Commission, 1967.
Hunting Stuart and Other Plays (includes *King Phoenix* and *General Confession*), edited by Brian Parker. Toronto, New Press, 1972.

Brothers in the Black Art (televised 1974). Vancouver, Alcuin Society, 1981.

Question Time (produced Toronto, 1975). Toronto, Macmillan, 1975.

Pontiac and the Green Man (produced Toronto, 1977).

Television Play: *Brothers in the Black Art,* 1974.

Other

Shakespeare's Boy Actors. London, Dent, 1939; New York, Russell and Russell, 1964.

Shakespeare for Young Players: A Junior Course. Toronto, Clarke Irwin, 1942.

The Papers of Samuel Marchbanks (revised editions). Toronto, Irwin, 1985; New York, Viking, 1986; London, Viking, 1987.

The Diary of Samuel Marchbanks. Toronto, Clarke Irwin, 1947.

The Table Talk of Samuel Marchbanks. Toronto, Clarke Irwin, 1949; London, Chatto and Windus, 1951.

Renown at Stratford: A Record of the Shakespearean Festival in Canada 1953, with Tyrone Guthrie. Toronto, Clarke Irwin, 1953.

Twice Have the Trumpets Sounded: A Record of the Stratford Shakespearean Festival in Canada 1954, with Tyrone Guthrie. Toronto, Clarke Irwin, 1954.

Thrice the Brinded Cat Hath Mew'd: A Record of the Stratford Shakespearean Festival in Canada 1955, with Tyrone Guthrie. Toronto, Clarke Irwin, 1955.

A Voice from the Attic. New York, Knopf, 1960; revised edition, New York and Toronto, Penguin, 1990.

The Personal Art: Reading to Good Purpose. London, Secker and Warburg, 1961.

Marchbanks' Almanack. Toronto, McClelland and Stewart, 1967.

Stephen Leacock. Toronto, McClelland and Stewart, 1970.

What Do You See in the Mirror? Agincourt, Ontario, Book Society of Canada, 1970.

The Revels History of Drama in English 6: 1750-1880, with others. London, Methuen, 1975.

One Half of Robertson Davies: Provocative Pronouncements on a Wide Range of Topics. Toronto, Macmillan, 1977; New York, Viking Press, 1978.

The Enthusiasms of Robertson Davies, edited by Judith Skelton Grant. Toronto, McClelland and Stewart, 1979; London, Viking, 1990.

Robertson Davies, The Well-Tempered Critic: One Man's View of Theatre and Letters in Canada, edited by Judith Skelton Grant. Toronto, McClelland and Stewart, 1981.

The Mirror of Nature (lectures). Toronto, University of Toronto Press, 1983.

Conversations with Robertson Davies, edited by J. Madison Davis. Jackson, University Press of Mississippi, 1989.

Reading and Writing (lectures). University of Utah Press, 1994.

Editor, *Feast of Stephen: An Anthology of Some of the Less Familiar Writings of Stephen Leacock.* Toronto, McClelland and Stewart, 1970; as *The Penguin Stephen Leacock,* London, Penguin, 1981.

*

Bibliography: By John Ryrie, in *The Annotated Bibliography of Canada's Major Authors 3* edited by Robert Lecker and Jack David, Downsview, Ontario, ECW Press, 1981.

Manuscript Collection: National Archives.

Critical Studies: *Robertson Davies* by Elspeth Buitenhuis, Toronto, Forum House, 1972; *Conversations with Canadian Novelists 1* by Silver Donald Cameron, Toronto, Macmillan, 1975; *Robertson Davies* by Patricia A. Morley, Agincourt, Ontario, Gage, 1977; "Robertson Davies Issue" of *Journal of Canadian Studies* (Peterborough, Ontario), February 1977; *Robertson Davies* by Judith Skelton Grant, Toronto, McClelland and Stewart, 1978; *Here and Now 1* edited by John Moss, Toronto, NC Press, 1979; "The Master of the Unseen World" by Judith Finlayson, in *Quest* (Toronto), vol. 8, no. 4, 1979; *Studies in Robertson Davies' Deptford Trilogy* edited by Robert G. Lawrence and Samuel L. Macey, Victoria, British Columbia, English Literary Studies, 1980; *The Smaller Infinity: The Jungian Self in the Novels of Robertson Davies* by Patricia Monk, Toronto, University of Toronto Press, 1982; in *Canadian Writers and Their Work* edited by Robert Lecker, Jack David, and Ellen Quigley, Downsview, Ontario, ECW Press, 1985; *Robertson Davies* by Michael Peterman, Boston, Twayne, 1986; *Robertson Davies: Man of Myth* by Judith Skelton Grant, Toronto, Penguin, 1994.

Theatrical Activities:

Actor: **Plays**—Lord Norfolk in *Traitor's Gate* by Morna Stuart, London, 1938; Stingo in *She Stoops to Conquer* by Oliver Goldsmith, London, 1939; Archbishop of Rheims in *Saint Joan* by Shaw, London, 1939; roles in *The Taming of the Shrew* by Shakespeare, London, 1939.

Robertson Davies comments:

The theme which lies at the root of all my novels and several of my plays is the isolation of the human spirit. This sounds somewhat gloomy but I have not attempted to deal with it in a gloomy fashion but rather to demonstrate that what my characters do that might be called really significant is done entirely on their own volition and usually contrary to what is expected of them. This theme, which might be called in C.G. Jung's phrase "The Search for the Self," is worked out in terms of characters, usually young, who are trying to escape from early influences and find their own place in the world, but who are reluctant to do so in a way that will bring pain and disappointment to others, and particularly to people of the previous generation. As I say, this may not look like a theme for comedy but I find it so, and many readers of my books have assured me that they agree.

*　　*　　*

All Robertson Davies's novels embody responses to the revenge of the unlived life: "the only people who make any sense . . . are those who know that whatever happens to them has its roots in what they are," a character declares in *Tempest-Tost* and the novels proceed by exploring or exploding inner landscapes. The form resembles a psychoanalytical detective story with the plot revealing repressed selves by using the mode of social comedy. Even in *Tempest-Tost,* in the most socially restricted range of *The Salterton Trilogy,* aged Hector Mackilwraith attempts suicide over beautiful young Griselda. Where another author would cast for tragedy, Davies novel offers healing in the surfacing of the subconscious as a restorer of social harmony: "Hector slept."

A heavy injection of Jung makes *The Deptford Trilogy* somewhat akin to a prolonged Jungian analysis, especially *The*

Manticore, but Davies's wit sustains momentum. By *The Cornish Trilogy*, the Jungian matter has been absorbed into the novel's strategies allowing some experimentation with realism. *What's Bred in the Bone*, a revelation of the enigma of Francis Cornish, is narrated by Francis's psychic figures, his "daimons." *The Lyre of Orpheus* contains a commentary by the long dead E.T.A. Hoffman, while the narrator of *Murther & Walking Spirits* is killed in the opening sentence to describe the novel from a vivid afterlife. These playful gestures of experimentation are part of the witty pleasures of Davies's novels but are harnessed to conservative ends. Despite a declared interest in "the isolation of the human spirit," his humans find spiritual fulfillment in traditional lores and are antimodernist. An example is Dunstan Ramsay in *Fifth Business* who can only express himself in Saints' legends; also alchemy, Gypsy wisdom, and the Tarot in *The Cornish Trilogy*. For Davies, only discourses of European heritage like Anglo-Catholicism in the most recent *The Cunning Man* can express the archetypal energies of his contemporary Canadians. Those who fail to find integration through received western arts, like Boy Staunton, Davies most sustained portrait of a Canadian politician, die prematurely in overt or concealed suicide. The resulting conservative novels are wholly opposed to bourgeois values. Indeed, just as characters have to apprentice themselves to a diverse but Eurocentric heritage, so Davies paradoxically asserts Canadian identity through subservience to a highly selective cultural history.

Recent publication of *The Cunning Man* suggests that Davies may be engaged in a fourth trilogy since the novel's narrator, Dr. Jonathan Hullah, is the godfather of Connor Gilmartin, summarily executed before narrating *Murther & Walking Spirits*. The Arthurian theme of adultery recurs from *The Lyre of Orpheus* while both new "Toronto" novels have more than characters in common, sharing issues of spiritual healing and Canadian identity. Whereas Murther digs deep into colonial origins in England and Wales, *The Cunning Man* traces the transition of Toronto from a colonial to an international city with much nostalgic evocation of British heritage in the elaborate Anglo-Catholicism of St. Aidan's church and the mysterious death of saintly Father Hobbes during Good Friday Mass. A departure in Davies work is the presence of Native Canadians in the familiar quest for spiritual wholeness but despite Mrs. Smoke's efficacy in healing the child Jonathan Hullah, native culture is marginalized in favour of what appears to be Hullah's own adaptations of conventional western medicine. He becomes the "cunning man," the healer from English villages, we are told. As before, Davies employs wit, comedy, and Jungian themes to construct a Canadian identity that privileges white Anglo-Protestant origins, omitting other cultures and social inequalities. Davies typically opposes feminism, either by creating attractive female characters like Maria Magdalena Theotoky of *The Rebel Angels* who espouse traditional feminine positions or by portraying "modern" women like Esme Barron of *Murther & Walking Spirits* and *The Cunning Man* as unfaithful and ambitious. Although from *The Deptford Trilogy* on, sexuality occurs in great diversity, practitioners continue to identify non-traditional modes as "sin," however wholeheartedly embraced.

What is most attractive and compelling about Davies's novels is the celebration of art as a way of recovering psychic energies into the imagination. We have Francis Cornish's "soul picture," Monica Gall's singing in *The Salterton Trilogy*, Magnus Eisengrim, magician-artist from Deptford who alone can account for Boy Staunton in his final riddle, Arthurian opera in *The Lyre of Orpheus* and *The Cunning Man*'s exploration of Anglican ritual as art. As an artist of conservative values fused into social comedy and contributor to debates about Canadian identity, Davies should be read for his sharply argued nostalgia. Readers are encouraged to negotiate the didactic and religious tones of this author, obsessed with what's bred in the bone.

—S.A. Rowland

DAVISON, Liam

Nationality: Australian. **Born:** Melbourne, Victoria, 29 July 1957. **Education:** Melbourne State College, B.A. in education 1979. **Family:** Married Francesca White in 1983; one son and one daughter. **Career:** Taught creative writing, Peninsula College of Technical and Further Education. **Awards:** Australia Council/Literature Board fellowship, 1989, 1991; Marten Bequest Travelling Scholarship, 1992, for prose; National Book Council *Banjo* award, 1993, for fiction. **Address:** 1 Stephens Road, Mt. Eliza, Victoria 3930, Australia.

PUBLICATIONS

Novels

The Velodrome. Sydney, Allen and Unwin, 1988.
Soundings. St. Lucia, Australia, University of Queensland Press, 1993.
The White Woman. St. Lucia, University of Queensland Press, 1994.

Short Stories

The Shipwreck Party. St. Lucia, University of Queensland Press, 1989.

*

Manuscript Collection: University College, Australian Defence Force Academy, Campbell, Australia.

Liam Davison comments:

Much of my fiction is concerned with exploring the ways in which our knowledge of the past influences the way we perceive the world about us. Rather than writing historical fiction, I am interested in fiction that explores the notion of history itself and the relationship it bears with myth and story. Faulkner's notion of the past not being dead and not even being past yet, has had a strong influence on my work. I'm also interested in the idea of alternative and silenced histories which has a particular bearing on the post-colonial nature of Australian society and its attempts to redefine itself.

My third book *Soundings* integrates three narrative strands from different periods of Australian history, all set in the Westernport region of Victoria. While many have read it as a contemplation of the landscape of the region, it is also an exploration of the different cultural and historical perceptions and expectations imposed on a new land. *The White Woman* explores the notion of history in a quite different way. Operating largely as a re-working of a nineteenth century captivity myth about a virtuous white woman held captive by the Aborigines of Gippsland, it considers the power and consequences of story and the role it plays in shaping the way we live.

*   *   *

In four works of fiction, Liam Davison has made his mark among the younger generation of Australian novelists. He writes an elegant and cadenced yet earthly prose. Davison also has an individualistic preoccupation with humans' efforts to impose order on the world and to construct themselves by creating history, maps, roads, and canals. He is a landscape novelist, mapping the human psyche.

Davison's first novel, *The Velodrome,* is narrated by Leon, whose father, like his two friends Sam and Eric, is a passionate cyclist. Leon sees the three men constantly circle the cosmos on their biketrack, traveling eternally to the same spot and achieving "order."

In a cycling accident, Leon's father is killed and Eric is crippled. The two men and Leon's mother, now married to Eric, decide to find a new order by breaking the circle and making the long journey to the north of Australia. Traveling is a central theme in Davison's fiction, and most human interaction takes place on the road or on the water, shoulder-to-shoulder rather than face-to-face. There is a studied detachment in the prose, and dying is presented as an act of absentmindedness. Being murdered is more thought-provoking. Characters do not turn to other people but to the stories they use to make themselves; to God as benign cartographer, to "collecting the facts" into a shoe box of index cards, to measuring out life with the wheels of a well-made bike. *The Velodrome* may at times seem a little too self-conscious in its emotional distancing, but its narrative line is strong, its images reverberate, and its spare, nuanced prose lingers tantalizingly.

The Shipwreck Party, Davison's collection of stories, furthers his preoccupation with landscape as a taken rather than a given. A party is held on a grounded ship. Water flows through most of the subsequent fiction. Davison does not write about people in the landscape. Rather he focuses on the landscape or the seascape within the people. At the shipwreck, characters see the same but different things. Seeing is creating.

A story about a famous Australian convict, Buckley, who escaped to live with the Aborigines, signals two interests that become central. Unpursued, Buckley experiences "ironic disappointment." Characters are so busily creating a self in story that they are unable to read the stories of others. Each man is an island complete unto himself. And the causeway can offer drowning as well as welcome.

Also, in his two next novels, *Soundings* and *The White Woman,* Davison has moved from assiduous impersonality to a more emotionally energetic prose. His writing never risks death by flamboyance, but language has thawed and the grace of the prose takes on more force as both novels develop the interest in Australia's colonial past found earlier in Buckley.

If each person is an island, islands still have histories and changing shapes. *Soundings* is a deftly constructed novel covering three periods of Australian history. The first is the 1820s, predating the colony of Victoria. Wolfish sealers, French scientists, and the English explorer Hovell suspiciously track each other. Each sees a different country—and, in the indigenous people, a different species. Passionately calm, Davison stories a shame that even now is being only edgily owned by history.

Davison is not in any conventional sense "an historical novelist," but he deeply probes the ways in which we talk ourselves into being. History becomes the present trying to run away from itself. His second era is the 1900s, when swamplands were reclaimed for "progress." Canals are human bypass surgery on nature. Life might swamp them, but they leave scars of control. The natural world has signed no Geneva Convention for rules in war. There is a constant edge of absurdity in Davison's writing. The human animal is laughable but too busy making its story seriously important to notice. As one character remarks, "history's a lot safer than boats."

The third story is that of a contemporary landscape photographer who, with an old photo-finish camera, glimpses people long dead. Though sometimes a little contrived, this reinforces Davison's focus that seeing is inventing.

The White Woman, Davison's most powerful achievement yet, confirms that there are no absolutes in history, only ceremonial reunions or family squabbles of relatives. An old man looks back over half a century to 1847 when he took part in an expedition to rescue a white woman supposedly held captive by the Aborigines. As he relives his story, he makes clear "how much we needed her." His narrative takes on religious dimensions—"It was love" and "I still had faith in her." She is the white Madonna, enslaved by "savages, brutes, the very opposite of what we are ourselves." Such is history, official truth. The old man's truth is savagely different. Davison becomes a frontier novelist. The frontier is where civilization ends or behind which it has flourished for fifty thousand years.

Here Davison transcends fashionable political politeness. His most firmly modulated narrative brings into harmony his interest in history as the story we tell ourselves to make our dreams safe, his sense of landscape as invention, and his vision of the world as eternally elusive. All good stories are Revised Standard Versions and *The White Woman* has biblical rhythm and authority.

—John Hanrahan

DAWSON, Jennifer

Nationality: British. **Education:** Mary Datchelor School, London; St. Anne's College, Oxford, M.A. in history 1952. **Family:** Married Michael Hinton in 1964. **Career:** Has worked for Clarendon Press, Oxford, as a social worker in a mental hospital, and as a teacher. Lives in Charlbury, Oxfordshire. **Awards:** James Tait Black Memorial prize, 1962; Cheltenham Festival award, 1963; Fawcett prize, for *Judasland,* 1990. **Address:** c/o Virago Press, 20-23 Mandela Street, London NW1 0HQ, England.

PUBLICATIONS

Novels

The Ha-Ha. London, Blond, and Boston, Little Brown, 1961.
Fowler's Snare. London, Blond, 1962.
The Cold Country. London, Blond, 1965.
Strawberry Boy. London, Quartet, 1976.
A Field of Scarlet Poppies. London, Quartet, 1979.
The Upstairs People. London, Virago Press, 1988.
Judasland. London, Virago Press, 1989.

Short Stories

Penguin Modern Stories 10, with others. London, Penguin, 1972.
Hospital Wedding. London, Quartet, 1978.

*

Jennifer Dawson comments:

My greatest passion in life has always been music. I regard writing as a last resort, a *faute de mieux* for me. In a world where language has been eroded, gutted ("pre-emptive strike," "take-out" for the murder of eight million civilians, etc.) all art "aspires to the condition of music," which cannot be exploited, interpreted, which explores the lost places of the heart, which makes all things new. Two of my novels have had musicians as their main characters—studies of the composer/musician who for social and political reasons experience dryness, aridity, and cannot play any more. Politics creep, burst inevitably into my novels. They then become shrill, rhetorical, routine, etc.

One feeling that has haunted me all my life is that life, social life as we know it, is a kind of game with correct moves, correct remarks and replies, correct procedures. I don't know the rules. I have struggled in vain for the real life as opposed to the game of men-and-women.

But the thing that obsesses me most, and which I feel I shall never put into language, is the strangeness of life, its accidentalness. Here we all are on a tiny, blue-green balloon in the midst of naked gases, chambers of violence. The planet as an accident that has produced music, literature, art, and the extraordinary theme-and-variations of religions. Here we are, with our fitted carpets and Mixmasters and spin-dryers, stilted above the world, talking about mock O-levels, who is to be next Master of St. Judas's, how all the cars in St. John's Street seemed badly parked today. Here we are in the midst of nothingness, in the midst of a mystery, accidental and yet behaving politically and socially as though the bizarre nature of our life on this planet has not hit us yet. To me this freak of life (like a purple flower growing out of the dumped tippings of a Hoover-bag) is the invitation to a new kind of freedom. Only art can introduce us to this. But my art? *No!* It must be someone else's. I shall never succeed in saying what I want to say.

*   *   *

Novels which explore madness have certain qualities in common. They describe a world which is enclosed, static and ruled by obsessions; they are vivid, fragmented, highly personal documents in which only one character can be fully realized. This intensity is double-edged. It can exclude, and ultimately bore, the reader or it can provide him with a vision of life which has a relevance beyond the barriers of mental illness. Kafka's metaphors have been readily accepted and understood. Jennifer Dawson's *The Ha-Ha* is one of the few contemporary novels significant enough to deserve the appellation Kafkaesque.

The Ha-Ha is set in a mental hospital where the narrator, Jean, is slowly recovering from a breakdown. She has progressed from the ward and the company of the irretrievably mad; she is now allowed her own room and promised a suitable job, an eventual regrading. Even as the nurse explains these steps towards freedom, we see their sad irrelevance. Jean's private world is ready to obtrude at any moment; her existence is precarious, threatened by the anarchy in her own imagination. One of the most moving illustra-

tions of her plight is given in the description of her work as a librarian. She happily catalogues books for an elderly couple in the nearby town but is nonplussed by their casual, friendly conversation. When fine weather is mentioned she remarks "I wonder whether the monkeys would be better at the top or the bottoms of the trees." Her own company of animals, spotted, sleek, furred and quilled, wait relentlessly for the time when she will step back into their universe.

The inevitable relapse is brought about by her first real relationship, a love relationship, a love affair with another patient. Alastair is critical of doctors and routines; he alarms Jean by telling her the true nature of her illness and she panics when he leaves the hospital. She runs away, is picked up by the police and brought back to face "the black box crashing down around my head." It is at this point that the novel changes direction. Jean remembers Alastair for his anger; she begins to share his indignation, rejects the doctors and escapes for good, feeling that her own identity is worth more than any medical tag of health.

Schizophrenia is a disease that has received much attention from modern writers. It has been used to symbolize the artist's alienation from society and, by extension, presented as the condition of modern man, lost, lonely, unable to communicate. The schizophrenic is sometimes hailed as a prophet, whose view of life is not only as valid as that of his doctors but also morally superior to the standards they uphold. Dawson shares this fashionable, essentially romantic, attitude but her writing is without the stridency of propaganda. The parallels with Sylvia Plath's *The Bell Jar* are many and the prose is equally fine. Dawson has written further explorations of her subject but has not yet matched the sustained brilliance of this first novel.

—Judy Cooke

de BERNIÈRES, Louis

Nationality: British. **Born:** London, 8 December 1954. **Education:** Manchester University, B.A. (honors) in philosophy; Leicester Polytechnic, P.G.C.E.; University of London, M.A. (with distinction) in English. **Career:** Has held jobs as landscape gardener, mechanic, and carpenter; teacher for ten years. **Awards:** Commonwealth Writers prize, 1991, 1992. **Agent:** Lavinia Trevor, 6 The Glasshouse, 49A Goldhawk Rd., London W12 8QP, England.

PUBLICATIONS

Novels

The War of Don Emmanuel's Nether Parts. London, Secker and Warburg, 1990; New York, Morrow, 1991.
Señor Vivo and the Coca Lord. London, Secker and Warburg, and New York, Morrow, 1991.
The Troublesome Offspring of Cardinal Guzman. London, Secker and Warburg, 1992; New York, Morrow, 1994.
Captain Corelli's Mandolin. London, Secker and Warburg, and New York, Pantheon, 1994.

*

Louis de Bernières comments:

I like to read and write books on a grand scale. I am interested in situations where ordinary people are caught up in abuses of power or historical crises and events. I disapprove of "genre" literature. I have hundreds of influences, but was moved to to want to become a writer by Nicholas Monsarratt's "The Cruel Sea." I am much influence by the great Latin American writers, by Tolstoy and Cervantes, and by my studies in philosophy.

*　　*　　*

A novel by Louis de Bernières is like a series of brightly colored and boldly drawn murals that combine into an exotic epic of life, love, and struggle. His first three novels are set in an imaginary South American country and make full use of the stock resources of such a setting: political corruption and malpractice; murder, torture, and violence perpetrated by the military; revolutionary opposition, which sometimes also takes violent forms; drug trafficking and prostitution; *machismo* and exotic femininity; Roman Catholicism and native magic. These novels also spring large surprises; for example, a troop of *conquistadores,* frozen in a glacier for four centuries, who are brought back to life and have to adjust to the modern world. De Bernières's fourth and latest novel, *Captain Corelli's Mandolin,* is set on an imaginary Greek island invaded by the Italians during World War II, and, allowing for the difference of place and time, it has many of the same elements as his earlier works.

De Bernières is perhaps best seen as a mythic populist, who celebrates people in all their variety and idiosyncrasy and in their covert and overt resistance to oppression. In *The War of Don Emmanuel's Nether Parts,* the struggle of a band of guerrillas and a group of villagers against the depredations of the army culminates in the discovery of a half-buried Inca city, which they reinhabit and which becomes an intimation of Utopia; *Señor Vivo and the Coca Lord* sees the people of the city battling against the biggest drug baron of their country; and *The Troublesome Offspring of Cardinal Guzman* shows them resisting the drive of a new Inquisition to impose religious orthodoxy. In *Captain Corelli's Mandolin,* the oppressor is not only the invading Italians but also war itself, and de Bernières dramatizes both the cruelties of the conflict and the possibilities of transcending them through love.

Memorable characters people de Bernières's pages. Figures who recur in the South American novels include General Carlo Maria Fuerte, a true patriot and lover of the people, who, after his kidnap by guerrillas, learns the truth about the brutality of some of his army colleagues and exacts condign punishment before retiring to private life to pursue his interests as a lepidopterist and ornithologist; Dona Constanza Evans, the plump, idle wife of a wealthy landowner, who is also kidnapped by the guerrillas, who becomes leaner, fitter, and more desirable through sharing their strenuous life, and who eventually throws in her lot with them, not out of any political conviction but because of her passionate affair with one of the young fighters; and Remedios, the courageous and capable woman guerrilla chief, who falls in love with the leader of the revived *conquistadores* and presents a troubling and sometimes comic challenge to his patriarchal and feudal assumptions. Among the notable characters in *Captain Corelli's Mandolin* are the Captain himself, a handsome, cultured, and amusing Italian officer of whom, against her will, the daughter of the Greek house on which he is billeted becomes enamored; and Carlo Piero Guercio, a brave and strong Italian soldier tormented by his homosexuality and by

having to oppress the people whose ancestors exalted love between men.

In all his novels, de Bernières employs a form of magic realism, moving between vividly rendered incidents that stay within the confines of credibility, pastiches of anthropological and travel writing, and evocations of preternatural events and entities, such as the resurrection of the frozen *conquistadores* or the haunting figure of Parlanchina, a beautiful 19-year old girl killed by a land mine, who continues, after her death, to appear to, and speak with, her adoptive father. The novels are told from a variety of viewpoints and in a range of voices; the third person authorial narration is characterized by an impersonal quality that makes the novelist come across as the unflinching, but not uncompassionate, recorder of all that happens.

De Bernières's growing reputation has been significantly enhanced by *Captain Corelli's Mandolin.* He has found a way of writing fiction that enables him to engage with major issues of the 20th century—in particular, political and religious corruption and oppression—while retaining a keen perception of the pleasures of life, a sense of humor, a tempered anger, and a graceful utopianism. His novels do tend, however, to repeat the same formula—the move in his latest one from South America to Greece is more a shift of setting than of theme, structure, or style—and it remains to be seen whether his future work will continue to elaborate this formula or develop in a different and perhaps deeper way.

—Nicolas Tredell

de BOISSIÈRE, Ralph (Anthony Charles)

Nationality: Australian. **Born:** Port-of-Spain, Trinidad, 6 October 1907; moved to Australia, 1947; became citizen, 1970. **Education:** Queen's Royal College, Port-of-Spain, 1916-22. **Family:** Married Ivy Alcántara in 1935; two daughters. **Career:** Accounts clerk, 1927-28, and salesman, Standard Brands, 1929-39, both Trinidad; clerk, Trinidad Clay Products, 1940-47; auto assembler, General Motors-Holden, 1948, cost clerk in car repair shops, 1949-55, freelance writer, 1955-60, and statistical clerk, Gas and Fuel Corporation, 1960-80, all in Melbourne. **Agent:** Reinhard Sander, Department of Black Studies, Amherst College, Amherst, Massachusetts 01002, U.S.A. **Address:** 10 Vega Street, North Balwyn, Victoria 3104, Australia.

PUBLICATIONS

Novels

Crown Jewel. Melbourne, Australasian Book Society, 1952; London, Allison and Busby, 1981.
Rum and Coca-Cola. Melbourne, Australasian Book Society, 1956; London, Allison and Busby, 1984.
No Saddles for Kangaroos. Sydney, Australasian Book Society, 1964.

Uncollected Short Stories

"Booze and the Goberdaw" and "The Woman on the Pavement," in *From Trinidad,* edited by Reinhard Sander. New York, Africana, 1979.

Play

Calypso Isle, music by the author (produced Melbourne, 1955).

*

Manuscript Collection: The National Library of Australia.

Critical Study: *The Trinidad Awakening: West Indian Literature of the 1930s* by Reinhard Sander, Westport, Connecticut, Greenwood Press, 1988.

Ralph de Boissière comments:

I began writing *Crown Jewel* in 1935. As I am a slow writer who has rarely had much time to write I was still at it when the uprising took place in the oilfields of south Trinidad on 19 June 1937. I saw I was writing the wrong novel. The oil workers had lighted a torch to signal the breaking of the first bonds of colonialism, bonds which we novelists, short story writers, poets and artists who made up *The Beacon* group (after the name of the now-defunct magazine) had dared to dream would fall before our hatred of foreign masters and our urge to independence. A salesman at the time, I had come to know much of the oilfield area. From two of the important activists in the uprising I got important inside information on its origins, and I began again, discarding much of what I had already written.

I come from one of the best-known French-Creole families, families which, in days long gone, when cocoa was king, had been the real rulers of this British colonial outpost. But with 19 June 1937 my detestation of colonialism, simmering from childhood, and crudely expressed in a few short stories, now became clearly defined.

The second novel of the trilogy, *Rum and Coca-Cola,* deals with the war years when tens of thousands of American soldiers and civilians were building military bases on the island. The American military had in effect become our rulers. There is not the same tension as in *Crown Jewel* because everyone had a job and many had two. The conflicts were of a more subtle sort—the breaking down of British prestige, the mockery of former British might, under American occupation.

The third book of the trilogy, *Homeless in Paradise* (not yet published), covers the approach to Independence in 1962 and its immediate aftermath.

Readers sometimes want to know who was the real-life basis for such and such a character. It is both unwise and impossible to say because I am continually adding to and subtracting from people I have known and, what is more, putting myself into them as characters. The characters may have some resemblance to certain originals, that is all. It is in important crises that people truly reveal themselves: for the most part of our everyday lives we exhibit aspects of character that give only superficial insights into what we are made of. I chose a Black servant girl, Cassie, as one of the main figures in *Crown Jewel* because in Trinidad her class were the most oppressed, ill-paid, and despised among Blacks. In all of us there is potential of one kind or another, but I am thinking particularly of the potential of the human spirit to achieve greatness, something unsuspected by the individual until he or she is flung by events into a crucial situation which demands the utmost. Cassie has that potential. It made her a leader when the time came. There was no such woman as Cassie, but the point is, *there could have been.* In other more stable parts of the world there are fewer possi-bilities for the appearance of such characters because the social conflicts are not extreme or the time for their resolution is not ripe. This is evident in my third novel, *No Saddles for Kangaroos,* set largely in an automobile factory in Melbourne during the years of the Korean war; here I am dealing with different people at a different historical time.

In technology we have taken great leaps forward, but morally we lag far behind these attainments—which sometimes even threaten to destroy us. But under the surface of life there is always some urge, some movement to rise out of the mire, and it is this movement the writer should try to grasp, this spiritual strength that has to be encouraged. While a writer may profit greatly by displaying the potential for evil he fails if he does not also indicate the potential for creativity as well. The world does not need more hatred, gore, and contempt for life—especially now. It needs belief in the powers of ordinary people to achieve.

No Saddles for Kangaroos is based on experiences I and others had in the early 1950s. Those experiences, those times could produce a novel full of drama. But I find myself unable to write about other, quieter times in Australia because I wasn't born and schooled in that country. At the same time I am a West Indian who has become partly Australian without knowing it. Australia is in my blood, but home is still Trinidad, a home I intuitively, instinctively, emotionally understand as I do not understand Australia.

*   *   *

Ralph de Boissière's *Crown Jewel* and *Rum and Coca-Cola,* both published without much remark four decades ago in Australia, were rightly reissued in the 1980s and received with justified acclaim. They remain relevant because they give an unrivaled portrayal of two moments in Trinidad's recent past which are still very much alive in shaping its present. De Boissière's third novel, *No Saddles for Kangaroos,* deals with Cold-War politics in the Australian trade union movement, but it lacks the social inwardness and the shaping coherence that his own personal vantage point, as a white creole in a society moving towards black majority rule, gives his two Trinidadian novels.

Crown Jewel depicts Trinidadian society in the years between 1935 and 1937 when the black working class briefly threw aside the middle-class leaders who had diverted its power to their own ends and, through a series of bitter strikes and demonstrations began the process which led to universal suffrage, and political independence. *Rum and Coca-Cola* is set just before the end of World War II when the dollars from the American military presence changed Trinidad from a neglected and quasi-feudal British colony into a competitive market economy in which "we is all sharks, the stronger feedin' on the weaker." Both forces remain alive in Trinidadian society, the unfinished revolts of 1937 and 1970, and the individualistic consumer materialism which was fueled by the oil boom. Now that the boom has gone and social tensions rise, de Boissière's novels seem more relevant than ever.

Both novels are, in a Caribbean context, rare and largely successful attempts to create fictional models which give a panoramic view of their society. They give not merely a static or descriptive background against which characters perform, but a dynamic image of society created by the actions and social relationships of the characters. And, particularly in *Crown Jewel,* de Boissière shows individuals who are aware that it is they who make history.

There are limitations, both social and fictional in origin, to de Boissière's portrayal of his society. His portrayal of the Indian role in the social conflicts is inadequate and stereotyped, a consequence perhaps both of ignorance and his concern with coming to terms with his own denied black ancestry, which leads to the exclusion of the more significant relationship between people of African and Indian origin. De Boissière also has a naturalistic concern with narrative plausibility which condemns him to providing each of the major characters with some link of blood, service, or mutual acquaintance. This gives an image of Trinidad as a much more comfortable though quarreling social family than is, I think, intended by the overt picture of class warfare.

However, while most critics have agreed that *Crown Jewel* gives a detailed and vigorous social and historical portrayal of Trinidad, some have felt that its attempts at the development of a coherent literary design are undermined by its commitment to documentary realism. In fact, its relationship to historical reality is of a different kind. If one compares the fictional character of Le Maitre, the black trade union leader, with the historical person of "Buzz" Butler on whom it is based, one sees not the pursuit of topical detail but the simplification of the character in response to the needs of the novel's shaping pattern. Thus Le Maitre becomes a character of massive moral certainty and clear historical consciousness as a touchstone against which to measure the confused and tentative leanings of the three central intermediary characters towards the black working class.

It is de Boissière's concern with the moral choices facing this group, in particular the character of André de Coudray, like the author an idealistic and socially concerned French Creole, which shapes the novel. And because de Boissière is refreshingly honest in his recognition that de Coudray's commitment involved the destruction of his comfortably privileged world without any guarantee of a place in the new, he is convincing in making de Coudray's journey towards self-knowledge, social responsibility, and cultural pride an image for that of the whole society.

As befitting his perception of the individualism that the power of the American dollar stimulated in Trinidadian society, *Rum and Coca-Cola* places much greater emphasis on the inner lives of its major characters. In this period moral commitment is not so much a question of social action but of the attempt to stay true to one's perceptions of what one is and to principles which are being swept aside in a society engaged in a competitive struggle for survival, money and power.

In this novel the issue of choice is focused on the triangular relationship of three characters confused about who they are and how they should act in a Trinidad which denies their ideals. Fred Collingwood, a principled black working-class socialist is doomed because of his "moral strength in all its beauty" and he destroys the relationship with Marie, the woman he most loves, because he displaces his desire to change society onto her and in the process destroys her sense of worth. Indra, the part-Indian girl from a lower-middle-class family, struggles against a "terrible division of spirit" which affects her social and racial sensibilities. Even though she makes a commitment to the working-class movement she still feels cut off, "doomed at this time to a lonely pursuit of the dust they raised in their forward marching." But it is the character of Marie, trapped by the lightness of her color into believing that she can escape into whiteness, which provides the novel's tragic focus. Of the three main characters, she is the one to benefit most materially from the war-time boom, but her unremitting efforts to escape from her past of poverty and casual prostitution are made at the expense of her inner self. Her fate is tragic because she sees herself engaged in a battle for individual self-hood, but in the process becomes separated from what she most truly is and disintegrates as a personality.

Yet *Rum and Coca-Cola* does not succumb to pessimism. Indra's cry, "O my God! But what am I capable of" is agonized, but the possibilities of moral choice and the issues of human capacity remain central to de Boissière's vision. He sees Trinidad moving in a direction which he detests, but when he has Fred reflect on what has occurred, he shows him capable of taking something positive from it. He sees a society which is not yet free, but one in which old colonial illusions have been destroyed. "Now that walls had fallen, what lay exposed was a life of untrustworthy promises, treachery by those you trusted, servility . . ." And in this process of laying bare, Fred sees the generation of a new disabused awareness and "ideas which could be weapons."

—Jeremy Poynting

DEIGHTON, Len

Nationality: British. **Born:** Leonard Cyril Deighton in London, 18 February 1929. **Education:** Marylebone Grammar School, St. Martin's School of Art, and Royal College of Art, 1952-55, all London. **Military Service:** Served in the Royal Air Force. **Family:** Married Shirley Thompson in 1960. **Career:** Has worked as a railway lengthman, pastry cook, dress factory manager, waiter, illustrator, teacher, and photographer; art director of advertising agencies in London and New York; steward, British Overseas Airways Corporation, 1956-57; wrote weekly comic strip on cooking for the *Observer,* London, 1960s; founder, Continuum One literary agency, London. **Agent:** Jonathan Clowes Ltd., Iron Bridge House, Bridge Approach, London NW1 8BD, England.

PUBLICATIONS

Novels

The Ipcress File. London, Hodder and Stoughton, 1962; New York, Simon and Schuster, 1963.
Horse under Water. London, Cape, 1963; New York, Putnam, 1968.
Funeral in Berlin. London, Cape, 1964; New York, Putnam, 1965.
Billion-Dollar Brain. London, Cape, 1966; as *The Billion-Dollar Brain,* New York, Putnam, 1966.
An Expensive Place to Die. London, Cape, and New York, Putnam, 1967.
Only When I Larf. London, Joseph, 1968; as *Only When I Laugh,* New York, Mysterious Press, 1987.
Bomber. London, Cape, and New York, Harper, 1970.
Close-Up. London, Cape, and New York, Atheneum, 1972.
Spy Story. London, Cape, and New York, Harcourt Brace, 1974.
Yesterday's Spy. London, Cape, and New York, Harcourt Brace, 1975.
Twinkle, Twinkle, Little Spy. London, Cape, 1976; as *Catch a Falling Spy,* New York, Harcourt Brace, 1976.
SS-GB: Nazi-Occupied Britain 1941. London, Cape, 1978; New York, Knopf, 1979.
XPD. London, Hutchinson, and New York, Knopf, 1981.
Goodbye Mickey Mouse. London, Hutchinson, and New York, Knopf, 1982.

Game, Set and Match. London, Hutchinson, 1985; New York, Knopf, 1989.

Berlin Game. London, Hutchinson, 1983; New York, Knopf, 1984.

Mexico Set. London, Hutchinson, 1984; New York, Knopf, 1985.

London Match. London, Hutchinson, 1985; New York, Knopf, 1986.

Winter: A Berlin Family 1899-1945. London, Century Hutchinson, and New York, Knopf, 1987.

Spy Hook. London, Century Hutchinson, and New York, Knopf, 1988.

Spy Line. London, Century Hutchinson, and New York, Knopf, 1989.

Spy Sinker. London, Hutchinson, and New York, HarperCollins, 1990.

MAMista. New York, HarperCollins, 1991.

City of Gold. New York, HarperCollins, 1992.

Violent Ward. New York, HarperCollins, 1993.

Blood, Tears & Folly. London, Jonathan Cape, and New York, HarperCollins, 1993.

Faith. Bath, England, Chivers Press, and New York, HarperCollins, 1994.

Short Stories

Declarations of War. London, Cape, 1971; as *Eleven Declarations of War,* New York, Harcourt Brace, 1975.

Plays

Screenplay: *Oh! What a Lovely War,* 1969.

Television Plays: *Long Past Glory,* 1963; *It Must Have Been Two Other Fellows,* 1977.

Other

Action Cook Book: Len Deighton's Guide to Eating. London, Cape, 1965; as *Cookstrip Cook Book,* New York, Geis, 1966.

Ou Est le Garlic; or, Len Deighton's French Cook Book. London, Penguin, 1965; New York, Harper, 1977; revised edition, as *Basic French Cooking,* London, Cape, 1979; Berkeley, California, Creative Arts, 1987; revised edition, as *Basic French Cookery,* London, Century, 1990.

Len Deighton's Continental Dossier: A Collection of Cultural, Culinary, Historical, Spooky, Grim and Preposterous Fact, compiled by Victor and Margaret Pettitt. London, Joseph, 1968.

Fighter: The True Story of the Battle of Britain. London, Cape, 1977; New York, Knopf, 1978.

Airshipwreck, with Arnold Schwartzman. London, Cape, 1978; New York, Holt Rinehart, 1979.

Blitzkrieg: From the Rise of Hitler to the Fall of Dunkirk. London, Cape, 1979; New York, Knopf, 1980.

Battle of Britain. London, Cape, and New York, Coward McCann, 1980; revised edition, with Max Hastings, London, Joseph, 1990.

The Orient Flight L.Z. 127-Graf Zeppelin (as Cyril Deighton), with Fred F. Blau. N.p., Germany Philatelic Society, 1980.

The Egypt Flight L.Z. 127-Graf Zeppelin (as Cyril Deighton), with Fred F. Blau. N.p., Germany Philatelic Society, 1981.

ABC of French Food. London, Century Hutchinson, 1989; New York, Bantam, 1990.

Editor, *Drinks-man-ship: Town's Album of Fine Wines and High Spirits.* London, Haymarket Press, 1964.

Editor, *London Dossier.* London, Cape, 1967.

Editor, with Michael Rund and Howard Loxton, *The Assassination of President Kennedy.* London, Cape, 1967.

Editor, *Tactical Genius in Battle,* by Simon Goodenough. Oxford, Phaidon Press, and New York, Dutton, 1979.

*

Bibliography: *Len Deighton: An Annotated Bibliography 1954-85* by Edward Milward-Oliver, Maidstone, Kent, Sammler, 1985.

Critical Studies: *Secret Agents in Fiction: Ian Fleming, John le Carré, and Len Deighton* by L.O. Sauerberg, London, Macmillan, 1984; *The Len Deighton Companion* by Edward Milward-Oliver, London, Grafton, 1987.

*   *   *

Partly as a result of the work of Len Deighton, the spy story has replaced the formal detective novel as the relevant thriller for its time. While continuing the tradition of literary excellence that has distinguished British espionage fiction since the days of Somerset Maugham, Eric Ambler, and Graham Greene, both Deighton and his gifted contemporary John le Carré have contributed new energy, intelligence, and meaning to the novel of espionage. Ever since his first novel, *The Ipcress File,* Deighton has instructed a large reading public in some of the factual and emotional realities of espionage and counterespionage. Writing with a lively wit, a keen eye for the surfaces of modern life, a convincing sense of authenticity, and a genuine intellectual concern for what the dark side of governmental practice can mean, Deighton has revealed, in all of his novels, some of the sham and self-delusion of contemporary politics.

The spy novels employ a nameless first-person narrator who owes something to Raymond Chandler's Philip Marlowe in his breezy wisecracks and sometimes strained metaphors; beneath the wiseguy surface, however, he possesses some of Marlowe's decency and compassion. Resolutely working-class in background, education, and point of view, Deighton's hero is a professional spy who must do constant battle with the forces of the British Establishment in their full and whinnying glory as well as with whatever is on the other side. Frequently, in fact, his spy never knows precisely which side he is on, and is so often betrayed by his colleagues and superiors that it sometimes doesn't matter. Professional and personal betrayal mesh perfectly in the two separate trilogies about Bernard Samson, whose wife and colleague, Fiona, turns out to be a defecting Soviet agent in the middle of an immensely complicated operation. The double trilogy—*Berlin Game, Mexico Set, London Match,* and *Spy Hook, Spy Line,* and *Spy Sinker*—initially appeared to signal a certain finality in Deighton's exploration of contemporary international politics, but he has now resurrected the endless Samson saga in the first of a new series, *Faith,* which will, of course, be followed by *Hope* and *Charity.*

As the ambitiousness of the three trilogies indicates, a complicated sense of novelistic architecture supports Deighton's energetic style and disillusioned outlook. His books frequently delay revelation of method and meaning until their conclusions. As the protagonist solves whatever mystery has been confounding him, or wraps up a long and tangled investigation, the book reaches the end of an often puzzling and complex narrative structure. The complications of its subject and of its fictional development appear to blend perfectly: the construction artfully becomes an emblem of the meaning of espionage, as much as the usual anonymity of the narrator suggests something about the problem of identity in this troubled world.

Deighton's fictional and nonfictional researches into the history of World War II and his knowledge of Germany reflect some of the same concerns and interests of his espionage fiction. Like his spy novels, his war novels, *Bomber* and *Goodbye Mickey Mouse,* demonstrate his passion for authenticity along with a bittersweet attitude toward a past that is both glorious and ignoble. His generally unsuccessful *Winter* deals with the history of a particular family through the turmoil of two wars, economic collapse, and the rise of Nazism; characters in that novel recur in his Samson books, as if his oeuvre, in effect, constituted a single work in many volumes about some of the central events of the 20th century. Deighton has also dabbled in such odd areas of the modern landscape as fantasies of German victory in World War II (*SS-GB*) and a Graham Greeneish exploration of South American revolution (*MAMista*), which indicate an almost heroic attempt to comprehend the violence and horror of political conflict in our age.

Like le Carré again, Deighton has done much to advance our knowledge of the way spies and spying work and what they really mean in our time. For both writers the novel of espionage serves an emblematic function. It shows, all too convincingly, the sad history of treason that marks the real battle in the shadows—a spy seems always to betray one cause, one country, one person or another in order to accomplish his task. The contemporary reality of the Western world provides the necessary historical context for Deighton's writing; daily headlines indicate the truth of his fictional perceptions, and the Kafkaesque quality of international politics and modern life itself reflects the deeper truth of his books.

Because Deighton's novels invariably show the folly, imbecility, and corruption of the wealthy and privileged classes in England, they suggest something of the satiric flavor of the Angry Young Men, and his hero is somewhat of a Lucky Jim of espionage. Because they present a labyrinthine picture of undeclared war, conflicting loyalties, multiple betrayals, misuse of power, and complicated national alignments, they provide a useful image of the world we all inhabit. Their dominant emotions are those of our time—puzzlement, anxiety, cynicism, and guilt. They recognize, further, one of the major lessons of the modern English spy novel, that an entire class, long protected by its own sense of unity and privilege, has sold its birthright, as the sordid history of Burgess, Maclean, Philby, and Blunt, among others, has proved.

In his own flip, entertaining, and exciting style, Deighton treats essentially the same problem that haunts a great deal of English fiction, the timeless question of who will inherit the virtue of the nation, who will save England from itself. His works thus show some connections with books like *Adam Bede, Tess of the d'Urbervilles,* and *Lady Chatterley's Lover,* continuing in a highly unlikely form the theme of a nation and a class that, ultimately, have betrayed themselves. His work at its best indicates that the continuing vitality of the English novel itself may very well depend upon the popular and subliterary genres. As a spy novelist and simply as an author of British fiction, he deserves sympathetic reading and consideration with some of the better writers of his time.

—George Grella

DELANY, Samuel R(ay)

Nationality: American. **Born:** New York City, 1 April 1942. **Education:** The Dalton School and Bronx High School of Science, both New York; City College of New York (poetry editor, *Promethean*), 1960, 1962-63. **Family:** Married the poet Marilyn Hacker in 1961 (divorced 1980); one daughter. **Career:** Butler Professor of English, State University of New York, Buffalo, 1975; Fellow, Center for Twentieth Century Studies, University of Wisconsin, Milwaukee, 1977; since 1988 professor of comparative literature, University of Massachusetts. **Awards:** Nebula award, 1966, 1967 (twice), 1969; Hugo award, 1970. **Address:** Department of Comparative Literature, University of Massachusetts at Amherst, South College Bldg., Amherst, Massachusetts 01003, U.S.A.

PUBLICATIONS

Novels

The Jewels of Aptor. New York, Ace, 1962; revised edition, New York, Ace, and London, Gollancz, 1968; London, Sphere, 1971; Boston, Gregg Press, 1977.
The Fall of the Towers (revised texts). New York, Ace, 1970; London, Sphere, 1971.
  Captives of the Flame. New York, Ace, 1963; revised edition, as *Out of the Dead City,* London, Sphere, 1968; New York, Ace, 1977.
  The Towers of Toron. New York, Ace, 1964; revised edition, London, Sphere, 1968.
  City of a Thousand Suns. New York, Ace, 1965; revised edition, London, Sphere, 1969.
The Ballad of Beta-2. New York, Ace, 1965.
Babel-17. New York, Ace, 1966; London, Gollancz, 1967; revised edition, London, Sphere, 1969; Boston, Gregg Press, 1976.
Empire Star. New York, Ace, 1966.
The Einstein Intersection. New York, Ace, 1967; London, Gollancz, 1968.
Nova. New York, Doubleday, 1968; London, Gollancz, 1969.
The Tides of Lust. New York, Lancer, 1973; Manchester, Savoy, 1979.
Dhalgren. New York, Bantam, 1975; revised edition, Boston, Gregg Press, 1977.
Triton. New York, Bantam, 1976; London, Corgi, 1977.
The Ballad of Beta-2, and Empire Star. London, Sphere, 1977.
Empire: A Visual Novel, illustrated by Howard V. Chaykin. New York, Berkley, 1978.
Neveryóna; or, The Tale of Signs and Cities. New York, Bantam, 1983; London, Grafton, 1989.
Stars in My Pocket Like Grains of Sand. New York, Bantam, 1984.
Flight from Nevèrÿon. New York, Bantam, 1985; London, Grafton, 1989.
The Bridge of Lost Desire. New York, Arbor House, 1987.
The Straits of Messina. Seattle, Serconia Press, 1989.
Return to Nevèrÿon. London, Grafton, 1989; Hanover, New Hampshire, Wesleyan University Press, 1994.
They Fly at Ciron. Seattle, Incunabula, 1993.

Short Stories

Driftglass: 10 Tales of Speculative Fiction. New York, Doubleday, 1971; London, Gollancz, 1978.

Tales of Nevèrÿon. New York, Bantam, 1979; London, Grafton, 1988.

Distant Stars. New York, Bantam, 1981.

The Complete Nebula-Award Winning Fiction. New York, Bantam, 1986.

Other

The Jewel-Hinged Jaw: Notes on the Language of Science Fiction. Elizabethtown, New York, Dragon Press, 1977.

The American Shore: Meditations on a Tale of Science Fiction by Thomas M. Disch—"Angouleme." Elizabethtown, New York, Dragon Press, 1978.

Heavenly Breakfast: An Essay on the Winter of Love (memoir). New York, Bantam, 1979.

Starboard Wine: More Notes on the Language of Science Fiction. Pleasantville, New York, Dragon Press, 1984.

The Motion of Light in Water: Sex and Science Fiction Writing in the East Village 1957-1965. New York, Arbor House, 1988; with *The Column at the Market's Edge,* London, Paladin, 1990.

Wagner-Artaud: A Play of 19th and 20th Century Critical Fictions. New York, Ansatz Press, 1988.

Silent Interviews: On Language, Race, Sex, Science Fiction, and Some Comics. Hanover, New Hampshire, Wesleyan University Press, 1994.

Editor, with Marilyn Hacker, *Quark 1-4.* New York, Paperback Library, 4 vols., 1970-71.

Editor, *Nebula Winners 13.* New York, Harper, 1980.

*

Manuscript Collection: Mugar Memorial Library, Boston University.

Critical Studies: *The Delany Intersection: Samuel R. Delany Considered as a Writer of Semi-Precious Words* by George Edgar Slusser, San Bernardino, California, Borgo Press, 1977; *Worlds Out of Words: The SF Novels of Samuel R. Delany* by Douglas Barbour, Frome, Somerset, Bran's Head, 1979; *Samuel R. Delany* by Jane Weedman, Mercer Island, Washington, Starmont House, 1982; *Samuel R. Delany* by Seth McEvoy, New York, Ungar, 1983.

*   *   *

Samuel R. Delany's first novel, *The Jewels of Aptor,* is a novel of quests, both physical and philosophical, with mythological overtones, but is hardly distinguishable from other science-fiction novels of its time. In the three novels that followed (known collectively as *The Fall of the Towers*), Delany's strongly anti-war stance, his warning that a government can control, by manipulation of information, a citizenship that is metaphorically/literally asleep, were clear indications that Delany would become a writer who sets his narratives in the future in order to (as he has written of Ursula Le Guin) "force a dialogue with the here and now, a dialogue generally called science fiction." But Delany is not only a social thinker; he has immersed himself and his writings in the sciences, with archeology and linguistics uppermost among many.

A catchphrase from Delany's seventh published novel, *Empire Star,* best describes the layers of his work: "simplex, complex, mul-

tiplex." In the best of his work a complex question (the responsibilities of freedom, the shaping effect language has on thought) is worked through, and is interwoven with a fresh conception of a science (the study of myth, ethnomusicology) to produce a multiplex texture, a dense context that compels the reader to look at events in more than one light. Delany's greatest strength is as a conceptualist; his surfaces are kept deliberately simplex in most cases: adventure stories with daring heroes, strong beautiful women, and idiosyncratic aliens. *Empire Star,* probably the best point of entry into Delany's work, is very short, but has a complexity and a freshness that never flag, sustained by this multiplicity of levels, and particularly by many apparent paradoxes which Delany clears up on the last page by reminding the reader that human beings, their names, constructs, and actions, are very small parts of an infinite universe: "In this vast and multiplex universe there are almost as many worlds called Rhys as there are places called Brooklyn Bridge. It's a beginning. It's an end. I leave to you the problem of ordering your perceptions and making the journey from one to the other."

Between the Towers trilogy and *Empire Star* Delany wrote *The Ballad of Beta-2* and *Babel-17,* both of which revolve around linguistic puzzles. *Beta-2* is recognizably the work of a young author, while *Babel-17* is possessed of the mature Delany voice and complexity. The investigations reflect very different conceptions of the nature of language: in *Beta-2* language is a playful deceiver (even if the secrets it hides are tragic ones), while in *Babel-17* it is a threatening entity, an irresistible tyrant that shapes its users' thoughts.

The Einstein Intersection is a fascinating novel, and a very dense one. It is set in a highly mutated, possibly post-invasion, future. The plot is a variation on the Orpheus myth, but the subject of the novel's deepest probing is the author himself, his view of mythology, his ideas of how legendary figures from the Minotaur to Billy the Kid can be manipulated, and how their archetypal power can be used to charge a narrative. Notes from Delany's own journal serve as epigraphs for the chapters. And if the focus of *The Einstein Intersection* is on how Delany will use common experience and symbols, the space opera *Nova* is an investigation into how personal experience can become fiction. One character is trying to figure out how to write a novel from his experiences—the experiences we read about in this novel by Samuel R. Delany. Capt. Lorq von Ray filters ambivalent (multiplex) facts to sustain a subjective reality (fiction) that allows him to sustain his obsession to possess the powerful element Illyrion.

Introspective and self-referential elements are allowed to dominate the massive, though less successful, *Dhalgren.* Seven years in the making (the story collection *Driftglass* and the erotic novel *The Tides of Lust* appeared during the interval), *Dhalgren* appeared in 1975, but in its preoccupation with the idea of total freedom in the collapse of ordered civilization, and in the ways information is presented to the reader, this novel is a direct descendant of the experimental fictions of the 1960s. Parts of *Dhalgren* are presented in disruptive ways—text in double columns on a page, for example. Unfortunately, these techniques unbalance the work as a whole. The setting is vaguely mid-Armageddon, and the textual manipulations lack the emotional weight of the story elements. The reader is in effect asked to accept that a writer's notebook is as important as the end of civilization. Many readers remain unconvinced.

Triton concerns itself with sexual identity and role, but the depiction of the Triton colony, at once so alien and so close to our own experience, is undisrupted by authorial manipulations and the novel as a whole buoys up Delany's ideas more successfully than does *Dhalgren.* Here the male protagonist's identity crisis results in his undergoing a sex-change operation, which finally solves none of his problems. Sexual problems run deeper than the physical body, Delany shows us; they are rooted in our language and our ways of ordering our existence.

Since 1979 Delany has delved deeper into the questions of sexual and/vs. individual identity in two universes, universes which portray similar struggles in very different terms. In the Nevèrÿon books and in *Stars in My Pocket Like Grains of Sand* Delany's science of choice is semiology, a more complex science than most he's previously investigated. In the Nevèrÿon trilogy the surface is very simplex: a sword and cart civilization. Here the reader is free to ride on top of the stories, or dip down into the role exploration aspects, or even deeper, into the underlay of the theory of linguistic sign generation. To each reader according to his abilities and ambitions. But in *Stars in My Pocket* (and in "Omegahelm," the related short story in *Distant Stars*) plot elements are sparse, and theoretical discussions and long strings of fabulous detail (details which actually succeed in reordering a reader's response to some words: for example, we soon come to read "tall" as meaning "unattractive," and "he" as meaning "a sexually stimulating individual") are pushed to the fore. There is no easy ride in this universe.

Delany is presently at work on more Nevèrÿon stories and the other novel in the *Stars in My Pocket* universe diptych is presently "in the word processor." These, then, seem to be the universes which will carry Delany's work through the 1990s.

—William C. Bamberger

DeLILLO, Don

Nationality: American. **Born:** New York City, 20 November 1936. **Education:** Fordham University, Bronx, New York, 1954-58. **Awards:** Guggenheim fellowship, 1979; American Academy award, 1984; National Book award, 1985; *Irish Times*-Aer Lingus prize, 1989; PEN-Faulkner award for fiction, 1991. **Agent:** Wallace Literary Agency, 177 East 70th Street, New York, New York 10021, U.S.A.

PUBLICATIONS

Novels

Americana. Boston, Houghton Mifflin, 1971; London, Penguin, 1990.
End Zone. Boston, Houghton Mifflin, 1972; London, Deutsch, 1973.
Great Jones Street. Boston, Houghton Mifflin, 1973; London, Deutsch, 1974.
Ratner's Star. New York, Knopf, 1976; London, Vintage, 1991.
Players. New York, Knopf, 1977; London, Vintage, 1991.
Running Dog. New York, Knopf, 1978; London, Gollancz, 1979.
The Names. New York, Knopf, 1982; Brighton, Sussex, Harvester Press, 1983.
White Noise. New York, Viking, 1985; London, Pan, 1986.
Libra. New York and London, Viking, 1988.
Mao II. New York, Viking, and London, Jonathan Cape, 1991.

Uncollected Short Stories

"The River Jordan," in *Epoch* (Ithaca, New York), Winter 1960.
"Spaghetti and Meatballs," in *Epoch* (Ithaca, New York), Spring 1965.
"Take the 'A' Train," in *Stories from Epoch,* edited by Baxter Hathaway. Ithaca, New York, Cornell University Press, 1966.
"Coming Sun. Mon. Tues.," in *Kenyon Review* (Gambier, Ohio), June 1966.
"Baghdad Towers West," in *Epoch* (Ithaca, New York), Spring 1968.
"Game Plan," in *New Yorker,* 27 November 1971.
"In the Men's Room of the Sixteenth Century," in *The Secret Life of Our Times,* edited by Gordon Lish. New York, Doubleday, 1973.
"The Uniforms," in *Cutting Edges,* edited by Jack Hicks. New York, Holt Rinehart, 1973.
"Showdown at Great Hole," in *Esquire* (New York), June 1976.
"The Network," in *On the Job,* edited by William O'Rourke. New York, Random House, 1977.
"Creation," in *Antaeus* (New York), Spring 1979.
"Human Moments in World War III," in *Great Esquire Fiction,* edited by L. Rust Hills. New York, Viking Press, 1983.
"Walkmen," in *Vanity Fair* (New York), August 1984.
"Oswald in the Lone Star State," in *Esquire* (New York), July 1988.
"The Runner," in *Harper's* (New York), September 1988.
"Shooting Bill Gray," in *Esquire* (New York), January 1991.
"Pafko at the Wall," in *Harper's* (New York), October 1992.
"Videotape," in *Antaeus* (Hopewell, New Jersey), Autumn 1994.

Plays

The Engineer of Moonlight, in *Cornell Review* (Ithaca, New York), Winter 1979.
The Day Room (produced Cambridge, Massachusetts, 1986; New York, 1987). New York, Knopf, 1987.

*

Critical Studies: *In the Loop: Don DeLillo and the Systems Novel* by Thomas LeClair, Urbana, University of Illinois Press, 1988; *Introducing Don DeLillo* edited by Frank Lentricchia, Durham, North Carolina, and London, Duke University Press, 1991; *Don DeLillo* by Douglas Keesey, New York, Twayne, 1993.

*   *   *

"What writing means to me is trying to make interesting, clear, beautiful language. Working at sentences and rhythms is probably the most satisfying thing I do as a writer. I think after a while a writer can begin to know himself through his language. He sees someone or something reflected back at him from these constructions. Over the years it's possible for a writer to shape himself as a human being through the language he uses. I think written language, fiction, goes that deep. He not only sees himself but begins to make himself or remake himself. Of course this is mysterious and subjective territory. Writing also means trying to advance the art. Fiction hasn't quite been filled in or done in or worked out. We make our small leaps" (interview in *Anything Can Happen,* edited by Thomas LeClair and Larry McCaffery, 1983).

Of American novelists who began publishing in the 1970s, Don DeLillo is one of the most prolific and compelling. DeLillo believes, with his subway inspector in *Ratner's Star,* that existence is "nourished from below, from the fear level, the place of obsession, the starkest tract of awareness." His 10 novels are a spelunker's guide to American life, cool explorations of undergrounds and subcultures where the powers once housed in churches may now exist; football, rock music, film, terrorism, espionage, pure mathematics, technology. His characters experiment with crime and violence, burrow into bat caves and esoterica, travel to deserts and shut themselves in empty rooms to seek what can be called "subcedence," a private being far beneath the strictures, conditioning, and boredom of ego and ordinary life. Paralleling their quest is DeLillo's experiment with specialized languages, his search for a precision of style that will imply what he quotes Hermann Broch as calling "the word beyond speech." Consistent in motive and theme, DeLillo's work has a virtuoso variety of subject, form, and style. Like Pynchon, DeLillo knows the new modular man, component of large systems, consumer of banalities enlarged and projected by electronic media. His features are boredom, game-playing, narcissism, paranoia. Like Barth, DeLillo turns popular forms—the thriller, science fiction, the sports novel, the disaster book—against themselves and the reader's expectations. His books move toward vanishing points, not conclusions. Like Donald Barthelme, DeLillo records the babble of jargons—scientific, military, entertainment, and many others—that compete for power over silent reality. He can do aphorisms and slapstick, irony and meditation, linear plots and recursive structures. But for DeLillo, learning and craft are always the means to mystery, ways to manifest and pass through filters and occlusions, manufactured passions and trained gestures toward "the starkest tract of awareness," the primal and unnameable.

DeLillo thinks of his work as two parts: *Ratner's Star* and the nine realistic novels preceding and following this hybrid of *Alice in Wonderland* and science fiction. *Americana* is an extravagant, yet rather conventional, first novel, an on-the-road book full of observation and notebook philosophizing. Its protagonist, David Bell, leaves the politics of the New York City television industry to tour his small-town past and to cross the continent. As he travels, he both stores up and empties out experience, a signature of the DeLillo hero. In *End Zone* Gary Harkness, like Bell, moves West, away from civilization and towards an atavistic existence playing football for Logos College. The novel becomes a struggle between world (logos) and act, symbol systems and signal behavior, as the characters who surround Harkness try to claim him within their very different discourses. Probably DeLillo's best-known work, *End Zone* skilfully compresses into its football metaphor social, linguistic, and religious themes. *Great Jones Street* completes the protagonist's retreat. Bucky Wunderlick, a Mick Jagger-like rock star, drops out of his group to become "the least of what he was." Although *Great Jones Street* was largely unnoticed by reviewers, I think DeLillo's presentation of rock music, its motives, excesses, and voids, compares with West's treatment of the movies in *The Day of the Locust.*

Ratner's Star, like other encyclopedic novels of the 1970s—Barth's *Letters,* Gaddis's *JR,* Coover's *The Public Burning*—is more about processes than people, the paradoxical process of learning uncertainty. Trying to decipher a message from space, mathematical prodigy Billy Twillig finds that all abstract structures must be thought through and that a meta-language ("Have you emptied your system of meaning?" one character asks him) must be constructed. Dervish philosophers, inhabitants of holes, and other Alice-

like creatures rise up to give the reader a history of mathematics and a Godelian lesson: in "our press to measure and deliver . . . we implicate ourselves in endless uncertainty." A fiction about all fiction-making, *Ratner's Star* is a conceptual monster, a tail- and tale-eating beast worthy of Sterne, Carroll, or Escher.

The two short novels—*Players* and *Running Dog*—that follow *Ratner's Star* are more modest, scaled down to show the meager ways contemporaries try to fill up rather than map out voids. Conspirators in excitement, the protagonists hunt extremity in terrorism, sexual adventure, and pornography. The books, though, are subtracting machines, showing how little becomes less, a gradual divestment of humanness.

DeLillo's sensibilities were extended by his years of residence in Greece, which gave us *The Names,* and his sensitivity to life in the United States was reinvigorated by his return, out of which he wrote *White Noise,* a circling back to the themes of *Americana.* *The Names* is an international novel, set in the Mediterranean and the Middle East, that explores terror in all its manifestations—political, religious, family, and linguistic. *White Noise* is both a university book and a disaster book about a spillage—intellectual and toxic. DeLillo probes deep into "the fear level" of his mid-American family, to the Gladneys' thanatophobia and the ironically destructive defenses they set against it. In these two novels of the early 1980s, DeLillo shows both a new cultural range and greater emotional depth.

Libra gave DeLillo his first best-seller, a scrupulously researched and imaginatively constructed inquiry into paranoid killers, Lee Harvey Oswald and Jack Ruby. Although praised and damned for its conspiracy theory of CIA involvement in Kennedy's death, *Libra* succeeds through its psychological portraiture of two "undermen," one of whom (Oswald) lived within blocks of DeLillo in New York City. After finding in Oswald a distant double, DeLillo in *Mao II* explicitly examined the relation between the novelist and terrorist. Reclusive writer Bill Gray comes out of hiding and journeys to Beirut to lose himself or, possibly, regain himself by taking the place of a young hostage held by a Maoist group. If politics dominates these last two novels, DeLillo's most recent fiction—the novella "Pafko at the Wall," prologue to a much longer work—suggests that DeLillo is now returning to examine the religious experience of his youth, a paradoxically knotted source of and answer to the fear that marks his plays, stories, and novels.

—Thomas LeClair

DESAI, Anita

Nationality: Indian. **Born:** Anita Mazumbar, Mussoorie, 24 June 1937. **Education:** Queen Mary's Higher Secondary School, New Delhi; Miranda House, University of Delhi, B.A. (honours) in English literature 1957. **Family:** Married Ashvin Desai in 1958; two sons and two daughters. **Career:** Since 1963 writer; since 1988 Purington Professor of English, Mount Holyoke College. Helen Cam Visiting Fellow, Girton College, Cambridge, 1986-87; Elizabeth Drew Professor, Smith College, 1987-88; Ashby Fellow, Clare Hall, Cambridge, 1989. Since 1972 member of the Sahitya Academy English Board. **Awards:** Royal Society of Literature Winifred Holtby prize, 1978; Sahitya Academy award, 1979; *Guardian* award, for children's book, 1982; *Hadassah Magazine* award, 1989;

Tarak Nath Das award, 1989; Padma Sri award, 1989. Fellow, Royal Society of Literature, 1978; Girton College, Cambridge, 1988; Clare Hall, Cambridge, 1991. **Agent:** Deborah Rogers, Rogers Coleridge and White Ltd., 20 Powis Mews, London W11 1JN, England.

PUBLICATIONS

Novels

Cry, The Peacock. Calcutta, Rupa, n.d.; London, Owen, 1963.
Voices in the City. London, Owen, 1965.
Bye-Bye, Blackbird. New Delhi, Hind, and Thompson, Connecticut, InterCulture, 1971.
Where Shall We Go This Summer? New Delhi, Vikas, 1975.
Fire on the Mountain. New Delhi, Allied, London, Heinemann, and New York, Harper, 1977.
Clear Light of Day. New Delhi, Allied, London, Heinemann, and New York, Harper, 1980.
In Custody. London, Heinemann, 1984; New York, Harper, 1985.
Baumgartner's Bombay. London, Heinemann, 1988; New York, Knopf, 1989.

Short Stories

Games at Twilight and Other Stories. New Delhi, Allied, and London, Heinemann, 1978; New York, Harper, 1980.

Uncollected Short Stories

"Circus Cat, Alley Cat," in *Thought* (New Delhi), 1957.
"Tea with the Maharani," in *Envoy* (London), 1959.
"Grandmother," in *Writers Workshop* (Calcutta), 1960.
"Mr. Bose's Private Bliss," in *Envoy* (London), 1961.
"Ghost House," in *Quest* (Bombay), 1961.
"Descent from the Rooftop," in *Illustrated Weekly of India* (Bombay), 1970.
"Private Tuition by Mr. Bose," in *Literary Review* (Madison, New Jersey), Summer 1986.

Fiction (for children)

The Peacock Garden. Bombay, India Book House, 1974; London, Heinemann, 1979.
Cat on a Houseboat. Bombay, Orient Longman, 1976.
The Village by the Sea. London, Heinemann, 1982.

*

Critical Studies: *Anita Desai: A Study of Her Fiction* by Meena Belliappa, Calcutta, Writers Workshop, 1971; *The Twice-Born Fiction* by Meenakshi Mukherjee, New Delhi, Arnold-Heinemann, 1972; *The Novels of Mrs. Anita Desai* by B.R. Rao, New Delhi, Kalyani, 1977; *Anita Desai the Novelist* by Madhusudan Prasad, Allahabad, New Horizon, 1981; *Perspectives on Anita Desai* edited by Ramesh K. Srivastava, Ghaziabad, Vimal, 1984; *The Mind and Art of Anita Desai* by J.P. Tripathi, Bareilly, Prakash, 1986; *Stairs to the Attic: The Novels of Anita Desai* by Jasbir Jain, Jaipur, Printwell 1987; *The Novels of Anita Desai: A Study in Character and Conflict* by Usha Bande, New Delhi, Prestige, 1988; *Language*

and Theme in Anita Desai's Fiction by Kunj Bala Goel, Jaipur, Classic, 1989; *Voice and Vision of Anita Desai* by Seema Jena, New Delhi, Ashish, 1989; *Virginia Woolf and Anita Desai: A Comparative Study* by Asha Kanwar, New Delhi, Prestige, 1989; *The Fiction of Anita Desai* edited by R.K. Dhawan, New Delhi, Bahri, 1989; *Symbolism in Anita Desai's Novels* by Kajali Sharma, New Delhi, Abhinav, 1991; *Anita Desai's Fiction: Patterns of Survival Strategies* by Mrinalini Solanki, Delhi, Kanishka, 1992; *Human Bonds and Bondages: The Fiction of Anita Desai and Kamala Markandaya* by Usha Pathania, Delhi, Kanishka, 1992; *Cultural Imperialism and the Indo-English Novel: Genre and Ideology in R.K. Narayan, Anita Desai, Kamala Markandaya, and Salman Rushdie* by Fawzia Afzal-Khan, University Park, Pennsylvania State University Press, 1993.

Anita Desai comments:

I have been writing, since the age of 7, as instinctively as I breathe. It is a necessity to me: I find it is in the process of writing that I am able to think, to feel, and to realize at the highest pitch. Writing is to me a proccess of discovering the truth—the truth that is nine-tenths of the iceberg that lies submerged beneath the one-tenth visible portion we call Reality. Writing is my way of plunging to the depths and exploring this underlying truth. All my writing is an effort to discover, to underline and convey the true significance of things. That is why, in my novels, small objects, passing moods and attitudes acquire a large importance. My novels are no reflection of Indian society, politics, or character. They are part of my private effort to seize upon the raw material of life—its shapelessness, its meaninglessness, that lack of design that drives one to despair—and to mould it and impose on it a design, a certain composition and order that pleases me as an artist and also as a human being who longs for order.

While writing my novels, I find I use certain images again and again and that, although real, they acquire the significance of symbols. I imagine each writer ends by thus revealing his own mythology, a mythology that symbolizes his private morality and philosophy. One hopes, at the end of one's career, to have made some significant statement on life—not necessarily a water-tight, hard-and-fast set of rules, but preferably an ambiguous, elastic, shifting, and kinetic one that remains always capable of further change and growth.

Next to this exploration of the underlying truth and the discovery of a private mythology and philosophy, it is style that interests me most—and by this I mean the conscious labour of uniting language and symbol, word and rhythm. Without it, language would remain a dull and pedestrian vehicle. I search for a style that will bring it to vivid, surging life. Story, action, and drama mean little to me except insofar as they emanate directly from the personalities I have chosen to write about, born of their dreams and wills. One must find a way to unite the inner and the outer rhythms, to obtain a certain integrity and to impose order on chaos.

*   *   *

Whereas earlier Indian novelists were concerned with nationalist politics, protest and cultural assertion, Anita Desai is interested in the various changes which have affected lives since independence. Although her novels differ radically in subject matter, they attempt to find patterns in the chaos of modern India and modern life. At times this can result in the simplified optimism of *The Village by the Sea:* "You are going to give up your traditional way of living and learn a new way to suit the new environment that the factory will create at Thul so as to survive. Yes, you will survive." More complexly *In Custody* notes the decay of the great Muslim Urdu-language culture of north India since colonialism and partition; the last remaining great poet, carrier of the tradition, grows senile in a Delhi where Urdu poetry is used for the lyrics of sentimental cinema music.

An excellent stylist whose impressionistic sentences move the mind to imagine visual scenes, Desai is a less patient, less tolerant, more questioning social satirist than R.K. Narayan. She sees the same comedy of oversize characters, inefficiency, and deflated ambition as Narayan, but with less sympathy. Her up-beat, hopeful endings often seem imposed, a forced, formal drawing of the curtains on a farce or comedy which was leading towards a revelation of a dark world. Other novels reveal unsatisfied lives filled with illusions, lack of will, pettiness, misplaced duty, false ideals, and self-deception. The relationships between the characters and their lives are filled with subtexts; several of her novels are about the tensions between people related through family, childhood, friendship, admiration, or need. These people never live up to their ambitions, while the larger-than-life are small when seen closely. Desai's stories explore character through inaction; usually there is a wastage of the self, false choices, illusions, lack of will. Time takes its toll and those we have sympathized with are found to be foolish or wrong, while those who have been previously judged as superficial or weak are now seen in a better light.

The novels unexpectedly change direction. *Bye-Bye, Blackbird* appears a better written version of the Third World immigrant to England novel, but surprisingly veers off into the English countryside where epiphanies of the main characters lead to changed lives. *Voices in the City* starts as a Dostoevskian study in a young man's anguish and resentment, set in Calcutta, but becomes a record of a woman's search for purpose. *Clear Light of Day,* like Desai's previous books, first gives the impression of being about its male characters and then its focus shifts to the various roles, problems, and disillusionments of women.

In post-colonial India women have been radically affected by such matters as the increase of western-style education, choice in marriage partner, career expectations, and the loosening of the joint family. Desai, being an educated woman of half-European descent, is sensitively situated to record the crisis of the Indian colonial bourgeoisie after independence. This crisis leads to a sense of drifting lives, a general alienation and nostalgia. Each of Desai's novels focuses on a life at a particular stage. These lives, although set in a social context, are puzzling as more is implied than the stories offered about them. They are often marked by failure, withdrawals into the self, or self-assertions which at best are mediocre. The main characters have escaped confining limitations, but liberated they create an even more sterile existence. Desai's concern is with the lives of women, the limitations and handicaps placed on them by society and, as in *Where Shall We Go This Summer?* and *Clear Light of Day,* the difficulties they face in giving their lives purpose when they attempt to assert their identity.

Many of the lives she portrays are of wives, older women, sisters who are unable to break with their family, those who take responsibility for others, widows who want to be left alone. They are from the bourgeoisie, the upper-middle classes, or families which have gone down in the world economically since British rule without losing their English ways; they are from westernized families in which choice of life and independence for a woman is a moral and financial possibility. At first such women seem morally, although not financially, superior; they appear independent and have chosen their fate. As we read further, however, their choices seem traps and they are less free than others who were less favoured, less able to choose, more corrupted by realities. Are such lives grey because they are so misleadingly free and because they are so responsible? Virtue, sensitivity, fineness of perception, even freedom may not be as important as relationships, success, and adjustment. We are offered portraits of women trying to salvage dignity or hope from their lives only to be crushed by their own mediocrity. By contrast a few of the characters, usually artists, have a naturally irresponsible spirit, which allows them a true freedom in realizing themselves, far different from those of the failures.

Desai writes two basic novels, often mixing them together; there are novels about what men do and novels about what women feel. Although women also act, that is less relevant than the choices which lead to quiet desperation. In *Fire on the Mountain* we are inside the mind of an older woman who, after withdrawing from the family and social pressures of her former life, is unexpectedly made responsible for an independent, interesting great-granddaughter with whom ironically she is unable to make contact and who causes her death. When Desai writes of men it may be done very well and with great care, but it is external. *Bye-Bye, Blackbird* and *Voices in the City* begin with the lives of men and are focused on their actions, but the perspective shifts from the outside into the mind of a woman whose emotional life is a major concern of each novel. *In Custody* uses R.K. Naravan's comic territory of well-meaning, bumbling incompetence made more absurd when unexpectedly confronted by possibilities of achievement and fame. If males are judged by their successful actions in the public realm, the male poet and male teacher here are among the two most feminine characters Desai has created. While the comedy of *In Custody* shows the impossibility of returning to the womb of ambitionless resignation, the novel has its post-partition political-cultural dimension. Hindi-speaking Hindu India is now responsible for the preservation of the great Urdu culture of its former Muslim rulers.

On the evidence of Desai's recent books the long apprenticeship of her earlier novels was worthwhile. Her concerns have not changed, but whereas her early work seemed cluttered, arbitrary in form, and over-polished in style, the novels are now better structured, plotted and more implicit in psychology and characterization; instead of calling attention to her symbols, Desai now uses images functionally as part of a description of a scene.

—Bruce King

DESAI, Boman

Nationality: American. **Born:** Bombay, India, 4 March 1950. **Education:** Illinois Institute of Technology, 1969-71; Bloomsburg State College, 1971-72; University of Illinois at Chicago, B.A. 1977. **Family:** Married Marsha Lynne Dixon, 1972 (divorced 1976). **Career:** Has worked as telephone interviewer and demographics researcher. Currently, a secretary for Sears, Roebuck and Co., Chicago. **Award:** Illinois Arts Council award, 1990, for "Under the Moon;" *Stand Magazine* award, for "A Fine Madness." **Address:** 567 West Stratford, No. 305, Chicago, Illinois 60657, U.S.A.

PUBLICATIONS

Novels

The Memory of Elephants. London, Deutsch, 1988.
David and Charles. N.p., 1990.

Uncollected Short Stories

"The Blond Difference," in *Debonair* (Bombay), February 1986.
"Beauty and the Beast," in *Debonair* (Bombay), April 1988.
"Baby Talk," in *Debonair* (Bombay), April 1988.
"A Fine Madness," in *Stand,* Fall 1989.
"Underneath the Bombay Moon," in *Another Chicago Magazine,* 1989.

* * *

Boman Desai, who grew up in Bombay and was educated in the United States, began writing in 1976. It follows that his debut novel, *The Memory of Elephants,* would shuttle back and forth between Anglo and Indian worlds, neither critical nor laudatory, but clearly giving credence to the efficacy of both. Grounded in history, both panoramic and intimate, *The Memory of Elephants* is a visually evocative story chiefly concerned with memory—collective, personal, and perceived.

The novel's protagonist, Homi Seervai, is a brilliant Parsi from Bombay attending school in the United States. Homi has been conducting experiments on himself with a memory machine—a memoscan—that allows him to rewind to any memory he wishes to retrieve. He becomes so enamored of one particular memory that he overplays it, threatening to sever his synapses forever. As a result, he is now in a semiconscious state, without a short-term memory, and totally at the whim of an unrelenting past. Slipping in and out of time and space, Homi's memory takes him as far back as the 7th century, when the Parsis were driven from what is now Iran by the conquering Arabs. But most of his memories concern the last three generations, transporting readers into 19th-century India, England, even Scotland, and into the lives of his family's matriarchs.

The intriguing device of the memoscan is fairly inconsequential to the novel itself, although it certainly enhances the omniscience of the omniscient narrator. Homi not only remembers the past from his own perspective, he peeks into and actually participates in the perspectives of others. In this way he meets the long-dead Bapaiji, the strong-minded tomboy spurned by Navsari's most eligible bachelor and who visits Homi's memory dressed as a man, and Granny, whose happiest years were the four she spent in Cambridge and who never got beyond the single betrayal of her youth that established a lifetime of paranoia. Homi's own father returns to him in Highland regalia and attempts to teach him to dance the Scottish fling.

With these and many other familial trysts as his backdrops, the author is able to explore far deeper issues: the definition of self in a colonialized culture or, as the author puts it, "the pilgrimage to all things Anglo"; the strange contradiction of an India that is culturally chauvinistic yet submissive in its relation to England; and the freeing and fearsome aspects to being foreign, inside and outside of one's own culture.

Parsi words are interjected easily into the text without interrupting the narrative flow, and the author does a good job of explaining lingual distinctions, both quaint and exasperating. When presenting Indian perspectives on anything alien, the author is par-

ticularly adept, as when he describes a young American hippie having "a nimbus of cauliflower hair."

Especially persuasive are the passages describing Homi and his brother Rusi's struggles with cultural assimilation. Homi's observations of his host family—staid German farmers from Pennsylvania—are sympathetic and completely without condescension, even though he ultimately absorbs very little of their world.

Characters are drawn with warmth and penetrating satire. This is not a nostalgic memoir. We see these characters warts and all, and who they are is neither fixed nor immutable but changing and adaptive. Hence, the reader will often receive more than one perception of an event and, depending on the event itself, encounter different emphases and tones in much the same way that the memory functions, weeding out the things that are superfluous, selecting the things most strongly undergirded by emotion.

As the novel progresses, it becomes apparent that one memory has Homi held hostage. As he puts it, he could have "learned the password of whales" or "probed the memory of elephants." Instead, he is a cerebral slave to a single recollection—the night he lost his virginity. It is a nice touch on the author's part to suggest that it is a peculiar propensity of humans to shun the profoundly wise in favor of the emotionally and egoistically persuasive.

A somewhat anticlimatic ending does little to undermine this first excellent attempt by Desai; much can be expected from this promising novelist in the future.

—Lynda Schrecengost

DESANI, G(ovindas) V(ishnoodas)

Nationality: American. **Born:** Nairobi, Kenya, 8 July 1909; became United States citizen, 1979. **Career:** Came to Britain in 1926; journalist after 1928; correspondent for *Times of India,* Reuters, and Associated Press, 1935-45; lecturer on antiquities for Bombay Baroda and Central India Railway, late 1930s; lecturer, Imperial Institute, Council for Adult Education in the British Armed Forces, London and Wiltshire County Councils, and Royal Empire Society, and BBC broadcaster, during World War II; lived in Hindu and Buddhist monasteries in India, 1952-66, and Burma, 1960; special contributor and columnist ("Very High and Very Low"), *Illustrated Weekly of India,* Bombay, 1962-68. Fulbright-Hays Lecturer, 1968, professor of philosophy, 1969-79, and since 1979 professor emeritus, University of Texas, Austin. Visiting professor, Boston University, Summer 1979, and 1981. **Agent:** Stephen Greenberg, 1306 Guadalupe St., Austin, Texas 78701-1629. **Address:** c/o McPherson & Co., 81 Cornell Street, Kingston, New York 12401, U.S.A.

PUBLICATIONS

Novel

All about Mr. Hatterr: A Gesture. London, Aldor, 1948; as *All about H. Hatterr: A Gesture,* London, Saturn Press, 1950; revised edition, New York, Farrar Straus, 1951; revised edition, London, Bodley Head, and Farrar Straus, 1970; revised edition, New York, Lancer, 1972; London, Penguin, 1973; revised edition, Kingston, New York, McPherson, 1986.

Short Stories

Hali and Collected Stories. Kingston, New York, McPherson, 1990.

Play

Hali. London, Saturn Press, 1950; revised edition, Calcutta, Writers Workshop, 1967.

Other

Mainly Concerning Kama and Her Immortal Lord. New Delhi, Indian Council on Cultural Relations, 1973.

*

Critical Studies: *A Note . . . on G.V. Desani's "All about H. Hatterr" and "Hali"* edited by Khushwant Singh and Peter Russell, London and Amsterdam, Szeben, 1952; "The Dialogue in G.V. Desani's *All about H. Hatterr*" by D.M. Burjorjee, in *World Literature Written in English* (Arlington, Texas), November 1974; *G.V. Desani: Writer and Worldview* by Molly Ramanujan, New Delhi, Arnold Heinemann, 1984.

*   *   *

G.V. Desani's published fiction consists of a small number of short stories and one novel, *All about H. Hatterr.* In addition, he has published a prose poem, in dramatic form, titled *Hali,* which some critics consider his most significant work. *Hali* has also been called a "story of passion;" but whatever its classification, it serves as companion piece for Desani's novel. In both works the author is taking the measure of man—in *Hali,* ideal man, and in *All about H. Hatterr,* everyman or man as he really is in a far-from-perfect world. *Hali* is written in the prophetic and exalted style that its subject demands. In it the young hero, Hali, passes through fear, defeat, and sorrow to achieve a selfless, changeless, Christlike love for all humanity. Discarding deities that he had revered earlier, he now worships only his newly found God of Love, who is "eternally incarnated" in the human form.

H. Hatterr in *All about H. Hatterr* has accurately been described as "the mathematical opposite of Hali." The same may be said of the styles and the tones of the two works. A Eurasian born in Penang but a resident for long periods in India and England, H. Hatterr is indeed fitted for the role of everyman that Desani intends him to fill. The language employed by H. Hatterr as he narrates his "Autobiographical" is a mixture, wholly unique in literature, of cockney and babu English with liberal infusions of American slang, the argot of criminals, the jargon of the medical and legal professions, and literal translations from Hindi, the whole being sprinkled with quotations and misquotations from Shakespeare and other poets. Desani has aptly been called "a playboy of the English language, a juggler with words." His virtuosity in this respect is one of the chief pleasures and wonders of his novel: e.g., "Only a few days ago . . . I was sitting in my humble belle-vue-no view, cul-de-sack-the-tenant, a landlady's up-and-do-'em opportunity apartment-joint in India." H. Hatterr's incessant flow of vulgarisms, cynicisms, sarcasms, and malapropisms reflects the vulgarity-cum-naivety of his character as a 20th-century everyman. In contrast to Hali's religion of selfless love, H. Hatterr phrases his philosophy as follows: "To be easy and comfortable appears to be the aim of all man: even at

the expense of the other feller." H. Hatterr's application of this simple rule of conduct in seven "life-encounters" supplies the action of the novel. Each of the "encounters" is preceded by a humorous "Instruction," in which an eccentric guru voices some general truth about the human condition, and a "Presumption," which presents H. Hatterr's distortion of this truth. The "encounters" themselves are absurd and fantastic, and from each of them H. Hatterr emerges rather badly battered. But he always bounces back for more. "Life," he avers, "is no one-way pattern. It's *contrasts* all the way. And *contrasts* by Law! . . . I am not fed up with *Life* . . ." The fact that H. Hatterr enjoys the absurdity of life, at least as he leads it, serves to raise him somewhat above the stature of a mere buffoon and to give the reader the sense that the author's purpose is one of life-affirmation.

In his short fiction, G.V. Desani writes in one or the other of the two contrasting veins of *Hali* and *All about H. Hatterr.* Thus, "The Last Long Letter" records the ecstatic visions of a young man, a suicide, who casts his soul back into the opaque void of the universe, where it had been a light, as he has previously cast his jeweled ring into the depths of the sea to symbolize his belief that from time to time spirit illuminates matter but then withdraws, leaving all in chaos and darkness until its next coming. Other stories—"Mephisto's Daughter," "With Malice Aforethought," and "The Second Mrs. Was Wed in a Nightmare"—are fantasies, sometimes with a satiric sting, which further exemplify the talent that made *All about H. Hatterr* one of our century's major contributions to the literature of the absurd.

—Perry D. Westbrook

DESHPANDE, Shashi

Nationality: Indian. **Born:** Dharwad, 19 August 1938. **Education:** The University of Bombay, B.A. (honors) in economics 1956, diploma in journalism 1970, M.A. in English 1970; University of Mysore, Karnataka, B.L. 1959. **Family:** Married D.H. Deshpande in 1962; two sons. **Awards:** Raugammal prize, 1984; Nanjangud Tirumalamba award, for *The Dark Holds No Terrors,* 1989; Sahitya Academy award, 1990. **Address:** 409 41st Cross, Jayanagae V Block, Bangalore 560041, India.

PUBLICATIONS

Novels

The Dark Holds No Terrors. New Delhi, Vikas, 1980.
If I Die Today. New Delhi, Vikas, 1982.
Roots and Shadows. Bombay, Sangam, 1983.
Come Up and Be Dead. New Delhi, Vikas, 1985.
That Long Silence. London, Virago Press, 1988.
The Binding Vine. London, Virago Press, 1994.

Short Stories

The Legacy and Other Stories. Calcutta, Writers Workshop, 1978.
It Was Dark. Calcutta, Writers Workshop, 1986.
The Miracle and Other Stories. Calcutta, Writers Workshop, 1986.

It Was the Nightingale. Calcutta, Writers Workshop, 1986.
The Intrusion and Other Stories. New Delhi, Penguin India, 1994.

Play

Screenplay: *Drishte,* 1990.

Other (for children)

A Summer Adventure. Bombay, IBH, 1978.
The Hidden Treasure. Bombay, IBH, 1980.
The Only Witness. Bombay, IBH, 1980.
The Narayanpur Incident. Bombay, IBH, 1982.

*

Critical Studies: *Indian Women Novelists,* Vol. 5, Delhi, Prestige Books, 1991; *The Novels of Shashi Deshpande* by Sarabjit Sandhu, Delhi, Prestige Books, 1991.

Shashi Deshpande comments:

Though no writer in India can get away from the idea of social commitment or social responsibility, committed writing has always seemed to me to have dubious literary values. However, after 25 years of writing, I cannot close my eyes to the fact that my own writing comes out of a deep involvement with the society I live in, especially with women. My novels are about women trying to understand themselves, their history, their roles and their place in this society, and above all their relationships with others. To me, my novels are always explorations; each time in the process of writing, I find myself confronted by discoveries which make me rethink the ideas I started off with. In all my novels, from *Roots and Shadows* to *The Binding Vine,* I have rejected stereotypes and requestioned the myths which have so shaped the image of women, even the self-image of women, in this country. In a way, through my writing, I have tried to break the long silence of women in our country.

*   *   *

Shashi Deshpande's first book is *The Legacy,* a collection of short stories and since then she has published more than 60 stories. The authentic recreation of India, the outstanding feature of her stories, is a distinct feature of her novels also. There is nothing sensational or exotic about her India—no Maharajahs or snake charmers. She does not write about the grinding poverty of the Indian masses; she describes another kind of deprivation—emotional. The woman deprived of love, understanding, and companionship is the center of her work. She shows how traditional Indian society is biased against woman, but she recognizes that it is very often women who oppress their sisters, though their values are the result of centuries of indoctrination.

An early short story, "A Liberated Woman," is about a young woman who falls in love with a man of a different caste, and marries him in spite of parental opposition. She is intelligent and hardworking, and becomes a successful doctor, but her marriage breaks up because of her success. *The Dark Holds No Terrors,* Deshpande's first novel, seems to have grown out of this story. Sarita, the heroine, defies her mother to become a doctor, and defies caste restrictions by marrying the man she loves. Her husband Manu is a failure, and resents the fact that his wife is the primary

breadwinner. She uses Boozie to advance her career, and this further vitiates her relationship with Manu. Sarita goes to her parental home, but she cannot escape her past so easily. She realizes that her children and her patients need her, and finally reaches a certain clarity of thought: "All right, so I'm alone. But so's everyone else."

The next novel, *If I Die Today,* contains elements of detective fiction. The narrator, a young college lecturer, is married to a doctor, and they live on the campus of a big medical college and hospital. The arrival of Guru, a terminal cancer patient, disturbs the lives of the doctors and their families. Old secrets are revealed, two people murdered, but the tensions in the families is resolved after the culprit is unmasked. One of the memorable characters is Mriga, a 14-year-old girl. Her father, Dr. Kulkarni, appears modern and westernized, yet he is seized by the Hindu desire for a son and heir, and never forgives Mriga for not being a son; her mother, too, is a sad, suppressed creature, too weak to give Mriga the support and love a child needs to grow up into a well balanced adult.

Roots and Shadows describes the break-up of a joint family, held together by the money and authority of an old aunt, a childless widow. When she dies, she leaves her money to the heroine, Indu, a rebel. Indu left home as a teenager to study in the big city, and is now a journalist; she has married the man of her choice. But she realizes that her freedom is illusory; she has exchanged the orthodoxy of the village home for the conventions of the "smart young set" of the city, where material well-being has to be assured by sacrificing principles, if necessary. Indu returns to the house when her great-aunt dies after more than 12 years' absence. As she attempts to take charge of her legacy, she comes to realize the strength and the resilience of the village women she had previously dismissed as weak.

Deshpande's best work is her fifth novel, *That Long Silence.* The narrator Jaya, an upper-middle-class housewife with two teenage children, is forced to take stock of her life when her husband is suspected of fraud. They move into a small flat in a poorer locality of Bombay, giving up their luxurious house. The novel reveals the hollowness of modern Indian life, where success is seen as a convenient arranged marriage to an upwardly mobile husband with the children studying in "good" schools. The repetitiveness and sheer drabness of the life of a woman with material comforts is vividly represented, "the glassware that had to sparkle, the furniture and curios that had to be kept spotless and dust-free, and those clothes, God, all those never-ending piles of clothes that had to be washed and ironed, so that they could be worn and washed and ironed once again." Though she is a writer, Jaya has not achieved true self-expression. There is something almost suffocating about the narrowness of the narrator's life. The novel contains nothing outside the narrator's narrow ambit. India's tradition and philosophy (which occupy an important place in the work of novelists like Raja Rao) have no place here. We get a glimpse of Hinduism in the numerous fasts observed by women for the well being of husbands, sons or brothers. Jaya's irritation at such sexist rituals is palpable—it is clear that she feels strongly about the ill-treatment of the girl-child in India. The only reference to India's "glorious" past is in Jaya's comment that in Sanskrit drama, the women did not speak Sanskrit—they were confined to Prakrit, a less polished language, imposing a kind of silence on them. In spite of her English education, Jaya is like the other women in the novel, such as the half-crazed Kusum, a distant relative, or Jeeja, their poor maid-servant. They are all trapped in their own self-created silence, and are incapable of breaking away from the supportive yet stifling extended family. The narrow focus of the novel results in an intensity which is almost painful. All the characters, including Mohan, Jaya's husband, are fully realized, though none of them, including the narrator Jaya, are likable.

Deshpande usually has the heroine as the narrator, and employs a kind of stream-of-consciousness technique. The narrative goes back and forth in time, so the narrator can describe events with the benefit of hindsight. It would not be correct to term her a feminist, because there is nothing doctrinaire about her fiction; she simply portrays, in depth, the meaning of being a woman in modern India.

—Shyamala A. Narayan

DIDION, Joan

Nationality: American. **Born:** Sacramento, California, 5 December 1934. **Education:** California Junior High School and McClatchy Senior High School, both Sacramento; University of California, Berkeley, 1952-56, B.A. in English 1956. **Family:** Married John Gregory Dunne, *q.v.,* in 1964; one daughter. **Career:** Associate feature editor, *Vogue,* New York, 1956-63; moved to Los Angeles, 1964; columnist ("Points West"), with Dunne, *Saturday Evening Post,* Philadelphia, 1967-69, *Life,* New York, 1969-70, and "The Coast," *Esquire,* New York, 1976-77. Visiting Regents' Lecturer, University of California, Berkeley, 1975. Lives in New York. **Awards:** *Vogue* Paris prize, 1956; Bread Loaf Writers Conference fellowship, 1963; American Academy Morton Dauwen Zabel award, 1979. **Agent:** Lynn Nesbit, Janklow and Nesbit, 589 Madison Ave., New York, New York 10022, U.S.A.

PUBLICATIONS

Novels

Run River. New York, Obolensky, 1963; London, Cape, 1964.
Play It as It Lays. New York, Farrar Straus, 1970; London, Weidenfeld and Nicolson, 1971.
A Book of Common Prayer. New York, Simon and Schuster, and London, Weidenfeld and Nicolson, 1977.
Democracy. New York, Simon and Schuster, and London, Chatto and Windus, 1984.

Uncollected Short Stories

"The Welfare Island Ferry," in *Harper's Bazaar* (New York), June 1965.
"When Did the Music Come This Way? Children Dear, Was It Yesterday?," in *Denver Quarterly,* Winter 1967.
"California Blue," in *Harper's* (New York), October 1976.

Plays

Screenplays: *Panic in Needle Park,* with John Gregory Dunne, 1971; *Play It as It Lays,* with John Gregory Dunne, 1972; *A Star Is Born,* with John Gregory Dunne and Frank Pierson, 1976; *True Confessions,* with John Gregory Dunne, 1981; *Hills Like White Elephants,* with John Gregory Dunne and Frank Pierson, 1992;

Broken Trust, with John Gregory Dunne and Frank Pierson, 1995; *Up Close and Personal,* with John Gregory Dunne and Frank Pierson, 1995.

Other

Slouching Towards Bethlehem (essays). New York, Farrar Straus, 1968; London, Deutsch, 1969.
Telling Stories. Berkeley, California, Bancroft Library, 1978.
The White Album. New York, Simon and Schuster, and London, Weidenfeld and Nicolson, 1979.
Salvador. New York, Simon and Schuster, and London, Chatto and Windus, 1983.
Essays and Conversations, edited by Ellen G. Friedman. Princeton, New Jersey, Ontario Review Press, 1984.
Miami. New York, Simon and Schuster, 1987; London, Weidenfeld and Nicolson, 1988.
After Henry. New York, Simon and Schuster, 1992; as *Sentimental Journeys,* London, Harper Collins, 1993.

*

Critical Studies: *Joan Didion* by Mark Royden Winchell, Boston, Twayne, 1980, revised edition, 1989; *Joan Didion* by Katherine Usher Henderson, New York, Ungar, 1981.

*   *   *

Though very much a California writer, Joan Didion is not provincial. She uses her immediate milieu to envision, simultaneously, the last stand of America's frontier values pushed insupportably to their limits and the manifestations of craziness and malaise which have initiated their finale. And while her novels invite a feminist critique, her understanding of sexual politics is beyond ideology. Each of her major characters struggles with a demonic nihilism which is corroding the individual, the family, and the social organism. Affluent and glib, her people endure a relatively privileged despair which may initially suggest a narrow purview. But a considerable ability to render social and physical environment broadly is saving.

In addition to dialogue which rivals Albee's, Didion's finest gifts are her talents for keeping clean of self-indulgence and for realizing a moral dimension in lives veering *inevitably* out of control. Certain recurring features of her work constitute leitmotifs germane to their interpretation. These include newspaper headlines, phrases from popular ballads, cinematic jargon, snakes, and the genteel Christian educations of her females. All pertain to the disintegration of an orderly past into a chaotic present, perhaps Didion's most irreducible theme.

Run River follows the eroding marriage of Everett and Lily (Knight) McClellan through 20 years. Concomitantly it chronicles the collapse of a way of life and the betrayal of the land which had given an epoch its apparent order. Ryder Channing enters the McClellans' lives when he courts Everett's sister. Though Martha never misconceives his selfishness and venality, she kills herself when Channing quits her. Lily's many unfeeling liaisons express her isolation from her husband and fatally draw her into Channing's increasingly nihilistic orbit. In his futile attachment to their Northern California ranch, Everett lives at a tangent to Lily's very genuine crises. When Everett kills Channing, it is not simply because Channing and his sleazy economic machinations are the wave of

California's future, the perverse energy which turns redwoods to taco stands. Everett's suicide ends an era. But Lily's justifiable conclusion that Channing is guiltless, because he is a "papier-maché Mephistopholes," implies Didion's conviction that, however tawdry this interloper, he has only played upon a native tendency to ruin. Lily's survival implies her relatively greater, if tainted, adaptability and strength.

Play It as It Lays presents a culture beyond this metamorphosis. Consequently, it is set in Los Angeles where those tacky schemes of Ryder Channing are a *fait accompli* defining a whole state of being. Maria Wyeth's past is utterly disintegrated, her childhood home in Nevada having been detonated to oblivion by nuclear testing. Moribund, her marriage thins to extinction. With her brain-damaged daughter institutionalized and herself facing an abortion, Maria aimlessly drives the freeways to evade a ubiquitous dread.

Though Didion never politicizes abortion, she is morally obsessed with it. Lily and Maria endure the experience, but the treatment is fuller and more alarming here. A last straw, it pushes Maria closer to her counterpart and nemesis, BZ, another instance of modern demonic. Associated throughout with the serpent, this Hollywood Beelzebub tries with conscious nihilism to exploit Maria's drinking and sexual looseness. Maria's father, taking life as a crap game, had offered his case as a gambler and a cynic: "it goes as it lays, don't do it the hard way;" "overturning a rock [is] apt to reveal a rattlesnake." For Maria, this worldview is an affliction of passivity and anxiety, until she finally manages the small victory of rejecting BZ's invitation to join him in his successful suicide.

With *A Book of Common Prayer,* Didion suggests that the country is in the throes of metastasized California. So she invents an archetypal banana republic devoid of history. Boca Grande ("big mouth") yaps chamber of commerce propaganda and ingests North American residue. Charlotte Douglas, a San Francisco Pollyanna, weathers two difficult marriages: to a brilliant callous and cynical opportunist, and to a well-heeled radical lawyer. What she doesn't quite weather is the loss (à la Patty Hearst) of her daughter, Marin, "to history." Marin's situation is really very simple. She suffers from severe cases of banality and political jargon. But her new way of life tests to the limit Charlotte's too selective memory of the girl in Easter dresses. With the FBI agents who litter her house and the futility of her marriages at her back, she makes it to Boca Grande and a marginal life of good works for the suffering masses. She continues to put the best light on dark matters: stateside things like her brother's miserable existence on the old homestead in Hollister; Grande things like the Army's confiscation, for profit, of the people's cholera serum. She becomes oddly Sisyphean but holds out for the idea that we all remember what we need. Charlotte dies in the crossfire between Army and revolutionary forces, the guerilleros having decided that for once their insurrection is not going to be a State-sponsored melodrama. We come to like her and to wonder about the future of such folks as the Simbianese Liberation Army.

Democracy concerns the long and amorous liaison between Inez Victor, a politician's wife, and Jack Lovett. The latter embodies personal and social values lacking in and inconceivable to the husband, a congressman aspiring to the presidency. Southern California recollected and contemporary Southeast Asia, particularly Kuala Lumpur, provide settings in which the fabulous quality of Boca Grande yields to realism. The novel clearly depicts American and international political life in the very fast lane, and its ruinous effect on familiar relationships. But Inez Victor's moral tenacity and practical resolve to use the past ethically distinguish her from Didion's earlier protagonists. Technically the novel is fresh, if not unique, for cinematic effects which break linear narrative; and for including a narrator named Joan Didion, who remarks the discrete functions of journalism and fiction, both provinces of great success for the *real* author.

—David M. Heaton

DIXON, Stephen

Nationality: American. **Born:** New York City, 6 June 1936. **Education:** City College, New York, 1953-58, B.A. in international relations 1958. **Family:** Married Anne Frydman in 1982; two daughters. **Career:** Worked in various jobs, including bartender, waiter, junior high school teacher, technical writer, journalist, news editor, store clerk, and tour leader, 1953-79; lecturer, New York University School of Continuing Education, 1979-80. Assistant professor, 1980-83, associate professor, 1984-88, and since 1989 professor of English, Johns Hopkins University, Baltimore. **Awards:** Stanford University Stegner fellowship, 1964; National Endowment for the Arts grant, 1975, 1990; American Academy award, 1983; Train prize (*Paris Review*), 1985; Guggenheim fellowship, 1985; O. Henry prize, 1993. **Address:** Writing Seminars, Gilman 135, Johns Hopkins University, Baltimore, Maryland 21218, U.S.A.

PUBLICATIONS

Novels

Work. Ann Arbor, Michigan, Street Fiction Press, 1977.
Too Late. New York, Harper, 1978.
Fall and Rise. Berkeley, California, North Point Press, 1985.
Garbage. New York, Cane Hill Press, 1988.
Interstate. New York, Henry Holt, 1995.

Short Stories

No Relief. Ann Arbor, Michigan, Street Fiction Press, 1976.
Quite Contrary: The Mary and Newt Story. New York, Harper, 1979.
14 Stories. Baltimore, Johns Hopkins University Press, 1980.
Movies. Berkeley, California, North Point Press, 1983.
Time to Go. Baltimore, Johns Hopkins University Press, 1984.
The Play and Other Stories. Minneapolis, Coffee House Press, 1988.
Love and Will: Twenty Stories. Latham, New York, Paris Review Editions-British American, 1989.
All Gone: 18 Short Stories. Baltimore, Johns Hopkins University Press, 1990.
Friends: More Will and Magna Stories. Santa Maria, California, Asylum Arts, 1990.
Frog. Latham, New York, British American, 1991.
Long Made Short. Baltimore, Maryland, Johns Hopkins University Press, 1993.
The Stories of Stephen Dixon. New York, Henry Holt, 1994.

*

Manuscript Collection: Milton Eisenhower Library, Johns Hopkins University, Baltimore.

Critical Studies: "Stephen Dixon: Experimental Realism," in *North American Review* (Cedar Falls, Iowa), March 1981, and *The Self-Apparent Word,* Carbondale, Southern Illinois University Press, 1984, both by Jerome Klinkowitz; "Stephen Dixon Issue" of *Ohio Journal* (Columbus), Fall-Winter 1983-84 (includes bibliography); *The Dramaturgy of Style* by Michael Stephens, Carbondale, Southern Illinois University Press, 1985.

Stephen Dixon comments:

(1991) I've just about nothing to say about my work, I only write fiction. I don't write book reviews or any nonfiction. In fact the only book review I've written is a story called "The Book Review," about a character writing one. The only non-fiction work I've written since 1963, when I stopped writing news, and 1968, when I stopped being a technical writer, is a piece called "Why I Don't Write Nonfiction." which proves its point and appeared in the *Ohio Journal* issue devoted to my work. I write novels and short stories only and I like writing both but for different reasons. Novels because they continue, stories because they end. All my novels but *Fall and Rise,* started off as short stories and just grew. I would rather the reader interpret what I write than I interpret it for the reader. I don't want to give my life away in a statement. Not only is my life not very interesting but sometime in the future I might use, in my own way, part of my life for my fiction and then a reader might say "That comes from his uninteresting life." Better the reader know next to nothing about my life and how I write, where I get my ideas, and so on.

Best for the reader to read my work and say for himself what to make of it. I have no way, nor do I have the means, nor do I have the inclination to simplify my work by explaining it, elucidating about it, or simply saying what I think about it. I work at one work at a time, story or novel, and when I'm done with it I begin another work. That's how I keep busy and also keep myself from thinking about my work once I finish with it.

(1995) I'm still pretty much the same. Dying to find more time to write, since I also teach fulltime and run a household. My ambition is to teach just half a year so I can devote eight months a year to my writing. I find it difficult to do all at once, but I still manage to complete 250 finished fiction pages a year. I don't know why but I still think I have something to write and a continually changing writing style to write it in.

*   *   *

Stephen Dixon is a master of self-generating fiction. While eschewing the flamboyantly anti-realistic experiments of authors such as Ronald Sukenick and Robert Coover, Dixon nevertheless refuses to propel his narratives on the energy of represented action. Instead, he contrives circumstances so that everything that happens within his novels grows from the initial elements of his fiction. Developing from itself, his narrative ultimately has no pertinent reference beyond itself; yet that growth is so organic that it offers all the delight expectable from a more realistically referential piece of storytelling.

Dixon's method can be traced to his way of writing sentences. Often his action will take place grammatically, as subjects have to battle their way past intransigent verbs in order to meet their objects, and as modifying phrases pop up to thwart syntactic progress.

There are always modifications to everything, Dixon has learned, and his genius has been to apply this insight to the making of narratives.

His first novel, *Work,* finds this scheme in the workplace, as an image for both how hard it is to find employment and what a struggle it is to keep it. Hunting down a job takes his narrator fully one-third of the novel, and that turns out to be the easy part. Once he has signed on as a bartender in a New York City chain of restaurants, he has to cope with a prime ingredient of Dixon's fictionally generative world: in this case a self-contained universe of rules and relationships, which include how to mix drinks, charge for special orders, move customer traffic, scan the papers for conversation items, spot company spies, handle rush-hour jams, deal with the restaurant chain's union, thwart robberies, soothe tempers, counsel neurotics, and keep the whole mad dance of waiters, dishwashers, assistant managers, cashiers, and customers in step. And this is just three or four pages into the story. *Work* provides the ideal self-generating system for a Dixon novel.

Yet such a system also exists within the intimate relationship of a man and woman. *Too Late* borrows two favorite topics from Dixon's short stories—breaking off relationships and suffering through the endless complications of love—and rushes them through a breathless experience in the urban jungle, during which four days pass in an alternation of quick excitement and maniacal torture. The narrator's girlfriend has left him during a movie, the violence of which has sickened her. But she never arrives home, and tracing her disappearance becomes a full-time job. Not for the police, who want to brush it off as a jilting. Instead, the narrator's capabilities for worry (another self-generating machine for fiction) run through all the lurid possibilities, from abduction and rape to murder. The very worst fears are just what happen, as the ghouls who feed on sensational news rush into the narrator's life, and he himself experiences a Jekyll-and-Hyde transformation which costs him job, friends, and peace of mind. *Too Late* succeeds as a tangled web of disruptions and distractions, the very stuff of Dixon's fiction which is shown to be a built-in potential of city life.

Quite Contrary: The Mary and Newt Story assembles 11 related stories to form something less than a novel but much more than a story collection. Their unity, although established by subject and circumstance of action, comes from their address to the main concerns of Dixon's work: the fragility of human relationships and reality's dangerous tendency to run off into infinite digressions and qualifications. *Quite Contrary* treats the three-year off-and-on affair of a couple, familiar in Dixon's fiction, whose involvement breeds complications. Even their first meeting leads to a debate as to how they will leave to walk home. As their relationship develops, each finds fault: he is too demanding, she is noncommittal. Even breaking up becomes an endless complication, for if Newt tells a friend that he and Mary are "this time really through," a friend reverses his syntax to show that "Nah, you two are never really through. You're a pair: Tom and Jerry, Biff and Bang. You just tell yourselves you're through to make your sex better and your lives more mythic and poetic and to repeatedly renew those first two beatific weeks you went through." Here is Dixon's method established in the form of his sentences: the declaration that the pair (one *and* the other) are sundering their union leads directly to a restatement of that proposition in negative form, rebonding the relationship through a series of other conjunctions: mythic pairs, conjoined reasons, and most of all a grammatical structure which by virtue of more "ands" can string itself out indefinitely, just like their relationship which is commemorated in the final phrase.

Fall and Rise, a much longer and more ambitious novel, extends itself to its fullest fictional scope while requiring the least external circumstance. The affair which prompts it is the narrator's first sentence, "I meet her at a party." Its present tense is deliberate, for the narrator's voice moves through a constant set of possibilities to fill 245 closely-set pages with the action which devolves from just four or five hours of experience. Because so much of the narrator's action is made up of diffidence and fantasy, it has the character of fiction. In a Jamesian manner, Dixon examines every nuance, even of situations yet to transpire, and as a result the reader is caught up in the narrator's own imaginative experience. For one chapter, the narrative action is transferred to the object of these imaginative desires, and complications are amplified by having her point of view. The achievement of Dixon's work is that the smallest circumstance can expand to fill the space available, a reminder of fiction's infinite plenitude.

It is with *Frog* and *Interstate* that Dixon takes the novel form well past his standards for short stories, in both cases by contriving unique structural experiments. A massive work of 769 pages, *Frog* could be described as an initial collection of 14 stories followed by a novella, two additional stories, a second novella, a full-length novel, and a concluding story. All sections cover the life and times of a protagonist nicknamed "Frog," though only in the closing piece do readers learn the meritorious nature of this name. In the meantime, Frog himself is put through variations of circumstance, history, and identity, making the larger work contradictory in a close sense but universal in its ability to encompass all fictive possibilities. In character, the protagonist is much like the figures appearing in typical Dixon stories: so conscientious that he becomes worried to distraction, so earnest as to be compulsive, so anxious for everything to be right that he makes almost all things turn out hilariously wrong. Yet even more so than in a thematically organized collection, *Frog* gives a complete sense of this style of being, not just in itself but because of the historically improbable but imaginatively apt connections the reader is invited to draw. These same readerly connections motivate *Interstate,* a novel whose eight chapters retell a highway tragedy in competing forms. In the first, a father suffers when his little girl is shot and killed by a gunman in a passing car. Five subsequent versions focus on the different aspects of the tragedy, each with the hope that its effects can be mitigated, if not fully escaped. In the seventh, the killing is avoided, but at the cost of something worse. Only in the eighth and final chapter does all end well, allowing the reader to savor scenes of quiet domestic bliss that without the preceding versions would never merit fictive treatment. The protagonist is the usual Dixon type, but here pushed into literal life-or-death circumstances.

As prolific as his work has been, Dixon always has a great range of stories from which to assemble a new collection. In *The Play* his focus rests on narratives generated by the dynamics of interpersonal relationships. The volume's initial stories deal with a narrator leaving a relationship, while later pieces find a similarly dispositioned character dealing with other problems, more material and external, which nevertheless follow the same pattern of involved disinvolvement. *Love and Will* sees his characteristic protagonist more involved in the outside world, with the addition of stories told from a shared perspective, such as "Takes," in which a young woman's rape and attempted murder is considered (and worried about) by a range of bystanders who have varying amounts of information and differing degrees of involvement in her life. *All Gone* is Dixon's most thematically diverse yet technically unified collection in that almost every one of its 18 stories has its action

derive from partial, confused, or incorrect information. Yet Dixon's writing habits often bring him back to familiar characters in typical predicaments; Will and Magna, the couple who appear in the title story of *Love and Will,* have a book to themselves in *Friends,* where their life yields a post-Beckettian sense of going on in narrative language within the very snares that language sets for us. Even though dialogue or other narrative situations threaten to trap these characters, Dixon's genius is, like Beckett, to write their way out of it with an energy which produces a sense of life in itself. The multiplicity of such life is celebrated in *Long Made Short,* a story collection focused on the idea of subtraction—specifically, how many elements can be withdrawn from the narrative and still let the story survive. "Man, Woman, and Boy" displays the elemental nature of this technique, as a scene that begins with a marital breakup is put through structural mechanisms of reversal, subtraction, and retraction until a more desired result is achieved—the method of *Interstate* in miniature.

Dixon's reputation is built on his short stories, over 300 of which have been published and 60 of which are collected in *The Stories of Stephen Dixon.* This large assemblage, drawing on the work of nearly four decades, shows his method in highest profile and establishes his talent for self-generative form. In "Said" he runs through the rise and fall of a relationship simply by dropping all content and running through the "he said/she said" rhythm of a fight. "Time to Go" uses fantasy to recapture the memory of a long-dead father, as an image of the old man accompanies his son and the young man's fiancee as they select wedding rings, the father forever hectoring about price and size in a voice only his son can hear. In all cases they are self-generating, perfectly made examples of fiction's ability to delight simply by its own working.

—Jerome Klinkowitz

DOCTOROW, E(dgar) L(awrence)

Nationality: American. **Born:** New York City, 6 January 1931. **Education:** The Bronx High School of Science; Kenyon College, Gambier, Ohio, A.B. (honors) in philosophy 1952; Columbia University, New York, 1952-53. **Military Service:** Served in the United States Army, 1953-55. **Family:** Married Helen Setzer in 1954; two daughters and one son. **Career:** Editor, New American Library, New York, 1960-64; editor-in-chief, 1964-69, and publisher, 1969, Dial Press, New York; member of the faculty, Sarah Lawrence College, Bronxville, New York, 1971-78. Adjunct professor of English, 1982-86, and since 1987 Glucksman Professor of American and English Letters, New York University. Writer-in-residence, University of California, Irvine, 1969-70; Creative Writing Fellow, Yale School of Drama, New Haven, Connecticut, 1974-75; visiting professor, University of Utah, Salt Lake City, 1975; Visiting Senior Fellow, Princeton University, New Jersey, 1980-81. Director, Authors Guild of America, and American PEN. Lives in New Rochelle, New York. **Awards:** Guggenheim fellowship, 1972; Creative Artists Public Service grant, 1973; National Book Critics Circle award, 1976, 1990; American Academy award, 1976, and Howells medal, 1990; American Book award, 1986; PEN Faulkner award, 1990. L.H.D.: Kenyon College, 1976; Brandeis University, Waltham, Massachusetts, 1989; Litt.D.: Hobart and William Smith Colleges, Geneva, New York, 1979. **Member:** American Academy,

1984. **Agent:** International Creative Management, 40 West 57th Street, New York, New York 10019, U.S.A. **Address:** c/o Random House Inc., 201 East 50th Street, New York, New York 10022, U.S.A.

PUBLICATIONS

Novels

Welcome to Hard Times. New York, Simon and Schuster, 1960; as *Bad Man from Bodie,* London, Deutsch, 1961.
Big as Life. New York, Simon and Schuster, 1966.
The Book of Daniel. New York, Random House, 1971; London, Macmillan, 1972.
Ragtime. New York, Random House, and London, Macmillan, 1975.
Loon Lake. New York, Random House, and London, Macmillan, 1980.
World's Fair. New York, Random House, 1985; London, Joseph, 1986.
Billy Bathgate. New York, Random House, and London, Macmillan, 1989.
The Waterworks. London, Macmillan, 1994.

Short Stories

Lives of the Poets: Six Stories and a Novella. New York, Random House, 1984; London, Joseph, 1985.

Plays

Drinks Before Dinner (produced New York, 1978). New York, Random House, 1979; London, Macmillan, 1980.

Screenplay: *Daniel,* 1983.

Other

American Anthem, photographs by Jean-Claude Suarès. New York, Stewart Tabori and Chang, 1982.
Eric Fischl: Scenes and Sequences: Fifty-Eight Monotypes (text by Doctorow). New York, Abrams, 1990.

*

Bibliography: *E.L. Doctorow: An Annotated Bibliography* by Michelle M. Tokarczyk, New York, Garland, 1988.

Critical Studies: *E.L. Doctorow: Essays and Conversations* edited by Richard Trenner, Princeton, New Jersey, Ontario Review Press, 1983; *E.L. Doctorow* by Paul Levine, London, Methuen, 1985; *E.L. Doctorow* by Carol C. Harter and James R. Thompson, Boston, Twayne, 1990; *E.L. Doctorow* by John G. Parks, New York, Continuum Press, 1991; *Models of Misrepresentation: The Fiction of E.L. Doctorow* by Christopher D. Morris, Jackson, University Press of Mississippi, 1991.

*   *   *

Towards the end of E.L. Doctorow's novella *Lives of the Poets* his central character is discussing the art of writing with a fellow author. "Each book," he believes, "has taken me further and further out" so that the place or idea he started out from is now no more than "a weak distant signal from the home station." The same is only partly true of Doctorow himself. His novels for the most part revisit the same themes and places, in particular the America of the 1930s. What changes and excites is that the same themes and treatments when applied to different characters portray differing aspects of the America they are living through. Inevitably Doctorow's novels are considered very political.

Almost invariably (the exception being *Lives of the Poets*), Doctorow's central character is either a child or adolescent or else (*World's Fair*) an adult writing about his childhood. The central character is always a narrator. Again almost without exception, the child or adolescent becomes displaced from his roots, and the breakdown of family structure becomes a dominant ingredient in almost every novel. Doctorow himself may not have strayed "further and further out" as his novelist has, but his characters, seldom by choice, frequently do. In the more expressly political novel, especially *The Book of Daniel* and *Loon Lake,* this is a freedom granted to the character out of economic or political circumstances. Daniel's parents have been executed as Communists, while in *Loon Lake* the central character Joe is an economic migrant of the Depression, uprooted and adrift. In the less overtly political novels the circumstances behind the displacement become correspondingly less social. Billy Bathgate enjoys a freedom even Huckleberry Finn might envy due mainly to a mother who has little or no grasp either on him or on the world in general. Of the full-length novels, only *World's Fair* differs substantially, the displacement being one of time as the narrator looks back.

In each case Doctorow is drawing a parallel between the development of his central character and the development of America during the same period. *Ragtime* uses real historical figures as frequent landmarks in the narrator's childhood, intertwining his development and that of America. *The Book of Daniel* unfolds Daniel's discovery of the circumstances of his parents' execution alongside the portrayal of America's own discovery of Communism and the way the American government reacted to it. In *Loon Lake* the distorted, disjointed way Joe sees the world evokes the economic turmoil that has displaced him from his home. Similarly the World's Fair is both a forthcoming excitement for a small child and a symbol of hope for better times ahead. The displacement of the central figure in each case frees that figure to be a symbol of the wider environment, a product of the times. And, arguably, in each novel the child or adolescent learns whereas the world he has been thrown into does not: Billy Bathgate's era of childhood is ending as the era of gangsters is ending. He is a good luck charm who leaves the gangsters as the charm of childhood leaves him. By leaving, Billy is seen to have learned. He survives. The gang leader does neither.

As the central character in each novel develops and grows, the language with which that character expresses the narrative develops accordingly. *The Book of Daniel* begins in a confused manner, non-sequiturs exemplifying how Daniel takes in only exactly what he sees. He cannot yet put anything into context or draw conclusions. Similarly *Loon Lake* depicts the upheaval of the 1930s with sentences which lack formal structure, even verbs. It shows a time, historically, when established structure is shaken and falling. The effect of the language is like watching debris fall after an explosion. Slowly the language settles as in both novels the characters understand more of what has been happening. As with the history depicted, patterns emerge with time. In *World's Fair* time has elapsed, the language is therefore coherent, the patterns are clear.

Ragtime uses both techniques side by side. Some parts are written in a style which would not be out of place in a straight historical narrative. Elsewhere Doctorow uses the pauseless—breathless—sentences of Billy Bathgate. And in *Billy Bathgate* itself Doctorow appears to be using this device to make a further point. As a young child Billy is comical in the way he expresses himself and the adult world he comes to inhabit sees him as such. As Billy begins to come of age, and just begins to become articulate, it is the world that has laughed at him which is shown up as comical. Billy has the last laugh.

The characters in these novels, in their various ways, all offer what the wide-eyed Billy Bathgate at the end of his story calls "this bazaar of life."

—John Herbert

DONLEAVY, J(ames) P(atrick)

Nationality: Irish. **Born:** Brooklyn, New York, United States, 23 April 1926; became Irish citizen 1967. **Education:** A preparatory school, New York; Trinity College, Dublin. **Military Service:** Served in the United States Naval Reserve during World War II. **Family:** Married 1) Valerie Heron (divorced), one son and one daughter; 2) Mary Wilson Price in 1970 (divorced), one daughter and one son. **Awards:** London *Evening Standard* award, for drama, 1961; Brandeis University Creative Arts award, 1961; American Academy award, 1975. **Address:** Levington Park, Mullingar, County Westmeath, Ireland.

PUBLICATIONS

Novels

The Ginger Man. Paris, Olympia Press, and London, Spearman, 1955; New York, MacDowell Obolensky, 1958; complete edition, London, Corgi, 1963; New York, Delacorte Press, 1965.
A Singular Man. Boston, Little Brown, 1964; London, Bodley Head, 1964.
The Saddest Summer of Samuel S. New York, Delacorte Press, 1966; London, Eyre and Spottiswoode, 1967.
The Beastly Beatitudes of Balthazar B. New York, Delacorte Press, 1968; London, Eyre and Spottiswoode, 1969.
The Onion Eaters. New York, Delacorte Press, and London, Eyre and Spottiswoode, 1971.
A Fairy Tale of New York. New York, Delacorte Press, and London, Eyre Methuen, 1973.
The Destinies of Darcy Dancer, Gentleman. New York, Delacorte Press, 1977; London, Allen Lane, 1978.
Schultz. New York, Delacorte Press, 1979; London, Allen Lane, 1980.
Leila. New York, Delacorte Press, and London, Allen Lane, 1983.
DeAlfonce Tennis: The Superlative Game of Eccentric Champions: Its History, Accoutrements, Conduct, Rules and Regimen. London, Weidenfeld and Nicolson, 1984; New York, Dutton, 1985.
Are You Listening Rabbi Löw. London, Viking, 1987; New York, Atlantic Monthly Press, 1988.
That Darcy, That Dancer, That Gentleman. London, Viking, 1990; New York, Atlantic Monthly Press, 1991.

Short Stories

Meet My Maker the Mad Molecule. Boston, Little Brown, 1964; London, Bodley Head, 1965.

Uncollected Short Stories

"A Friend" and "In My Peach Shoes," in *Queen* (London), 7 April 1965.
"Rite of Love," in *Playboy* (Chicago), October 1968.
"A Fair Festivity," in *Playboy* (Chicago), November 1968.
"A Small Human Being," in *Saturday Evening Post* (Philadelphia), 16 November 1968.

Plays

The Ginger Man, adaptation of his own novel (produced London and Dublin, 1959; New York, 1963). New York, Random House, 1961; as *What They Did in Dublin, with The Ginger Man: A Play,* London, MacGibbon and Kee, 1962.
Fairy Tales of New York (produced Croydon, Surrey, 1960; London, 1961; New York, 1980). London, Penguin, and New York, Random House, 1961.
A Singular Man, adaptation of his own novel (produced Cambridge and London, 1964; Westport, Connecticut, 1967). London, Bodley Head, 1965.
The Plays of J.P. Donleavy (includes *The Ginger Man, Fairy Tales of New York, A Singular Man, The Saddest Summer of Samuel S*). New York, Delacorte Press, 1972; London, Penguin, 1974.
The Beastly Beatitudes of Balthazar B, adaptation of his own novel (produced London, 1981; Norfolk, Virginia, 1985).

Radio Play: *Helen,* 1956.

Other

The Unexpurgated Code: A Complete Manual of Survival and Manners, drawings by the author. New York, Delacorte Press, and London, Wildwood House, 1975.
Ireland: In All Her Sins and in Some of Her Graces. London, Joseph, and New York, Viking, 1986.
A Singular Country, illustrated by Patrick Prendergast. Peterborough, Ryan, 1989; New York, Norton, 1990.

*

Bibliography: By David W. Madden, in *Bulletin of Bibliography* (Westport, Connecticut), September 1982.

Critical Studies: *J.P. Donleavy: The Style of His Sadness and Humor* by Charles G. Masinton, Bowling Green, Ohio, Popular Press, 1975; *Isolation and Protest: A Case Study of J.P. Donleavy's Fiction* by R.K. Sharma, New Delhi, Ajanta, 1983.

* * *

Perhaps because of his transatlantic and multinational character, J.P. Donleavy defies easy classification and suffers from a certain critical neglect. His books blend some of the special literary qualities of all three—American, English, Irish—of his national traditions. He has a typically American zaniness, an anarchic and sometimes lunatic comic sense, mingled with an undertone of despair. He possesses an English accuracy of eye and ear for the look and sound of things, for the subtle determinants of class in appearances and accents, a Jamesian grasp of density of specification. Finally, his novels display an Irish wit, energy, and vulgarity as well as a distinctly Irish sense of brooding and melancholy. Like any Irish writer, he is inevitably compared to Joyce, but in this case the comparison is apt—his tone echoes the comic brevity and particularity of many parts of *Ulysses,* and his prose style often wanders into Joycean patterns.

Ever since his great success with *The Ginger Man,* which sometimes seems the template for almost all the later works, Donleavy has followed a sometimes distressing sameness of pattern and subject in his books. Roughly speaking, they are serio-comic picaresques that mix a close attention to verifiable reality with an increasingly outrageous sense of fantasy. Although the fantasy is always strongly sexual—and Donleavy writes about sex with refreshingly carnal gusto—it also dwells on the sensuousness, perhaps even the eroticism of all materiality. When he sinks his teeth into the dense texture of life, Donleavy imparts an almost sexual appetite to his prose, glorying in the things of this world to the virtual exclusion of all else. He writes with the same zest about such matters as gentlemen's clothing, wines, liquor, food, tobacco, women's bodies, the interior and exterior decorations of luxurious homes, all the lovingly itemized concretions that represent the good life. In his most recent novels, like *Schultz* and its successor, *Are You Listening Rabbi Löw,* Donleavy records, with no diminution in his sense of awe, the dithyrambic praise of the appetitive view of life as fully, comically, and joyously as in *The Ginger Man.*

Because of the basic similarity of characters, events, style, and structure in his books, they often seem initially a mere continual rewriting of the first and most famous novel. They pile, often rather randomly, episode upon outrageous episode, repeat the scenes of sex, of comic violence, of pratfalls and ridicule in the same fragmented sentences, and often appear to run out of steam rather than end. Few of his books possess a real sense of closure: the protagonist most often is left, like the Ginger Man, suspended midway between triumph and ignominy, humor and sadness, still completely himself but also touched by defeat and despair. Their constant, most powerful note is elegiac—the protagonist may continue on his crazy way but he inevitably recognizes the most final and undeniable fact of all, the fact of death. The last perception of Sebastian Dangerfield in *The Ginger Man* is a vision of horses: "And I said they are running out to death which is with some soul and their eyes are mad and teeth out." In *The Destinies of Darcy Dancer, Gentleman* and its sequels, *Leila* and *That Darcy, That Dancer, That Gentleman,* the fox hunt, which runs throughout the books, provides Dancer with the metaphors of mortality—"Till the Huntsman's blowing his long slow notes. Turn home. At end of day."

Schultz and *Are Your Listening Rabbi Löw* mix the perception of death with a jaunty, life-loving energy in a broader comic style than most of Donleavy's other works, as if the only solution to the perception of mortality is the relentless pursuit of physical gratification. The Jewish theatrical producer Schultz, who tries to succeed among the aristocratic sharks of London, is Donleavy's version of the Jamesian innocent American abroad. The books make their protagonist the butt of dozens of jokes but also the lovable scoundrel whose lunatic schemes somehow rescue him from his own preposterous ambitions and land him, rather shakily, on his feet. Like Darcy Dancer, he concludes his second, though perhaps

not final, appearance with the achievement of a sort of stasis—rich, successful, and loved, he cruises on a yacht with a beautiful, brilliant, and mad daughter of the British aristocracy.

His latest books suggest that Donleavy may be on the one hand simultaneously running out of energy and ideas, and on the other, attempting to bring his seemingly endless episodes to completion. In both *That Darcy, That Dancer, That Gentleman* and *Are You Listening Rabbi Löw* Darcy Dancer and Schultz ultimately achieve a state of apparent repose. With Donleavy, of course, one can never be fully sure; as his character Schultz realizes, "if you can balance on top, you can not only scratch your fanny but touch the moon. But don't count on anything."

Like all good comic writers, Donleavy grounds his vision in a dark view of the world; amid all his embracing vitality lurks a perception of the desperate need for comedy. His art derives from that perception—under the fully realized surfaces of life lie fear, guilt, and the dread of death. His books quite properly partake of the three national traditions with which he has associated himself; all three converge in his mixture of solemnity and humor and in the same mixture of resolution and disintegration that so often forms his conclusions. In his comic mode Donleavy is sometimes uproariously funny, sometimes brilliantly witty, sometimes just plain silly; often touched by a surprising melancholy, hedonistically devouring life but haunted by death, his novels end, at best, in a resounding "if." You may touch the moon, but don't count on anything.

—George Grella

DOUGLAS, Ellen

Nationality: American. **Born:** Josephine Ayeres in Natchez, Mississippi, 7 December 1921. **Education:** The University of Mississippi, Jackson, B.A. 1942. **Family:** Married Kenneth Haxton in 1945 (divorced); three sons. **Career:** Writer-in-residence, Northeast Louisiana University, Monroe, 1978-82, and since 1982 University of Mississippi; visiting professor, University of Virginia, Charlottesville, 1984; Welty Professor, Millsaps College, Jackson, 1988. **Awards:** Houghton Mifflin fellowship, 1961; Mississippi Institute of Arts and Letters award, 1979; Fellowship of Southern Writers award, 1989. **Agent:** R.L.R. Associates, 7 West 51st Street, New York, New York 10020, U.S.A. **Address:** 1600 Pine Street, Jackson, Mississippi 39202, U.S.A.

PUBLICATIONS

Novels

A Family's Affairs. Boston, Houghton Mifflin, 1961; London, Cape, 1963.

Where the Dreams Cross. Boston, Houghton Mifflin, 1968.

Apostles of Light. Boston, Hougton Mifflin, 1973.

The Rock Cried Out. New York, Harcourt Brace, 1979; London, Virago Press, 1990.

A Lifetime Burning. New York, Random House, 1982; London, Bodley Head, 1983.

Can't Quit You, Baby. New York, Atheneum, 1988; London, Virago Press, 1990.

Short Stories

Black Cloud, White Cloud. Boston, Houghton Mifflin, 1963

Uncollected Short Story

"On the Lake," in *Prize Stories 1963,* edited by Richard Poirier. New York, Doubleday, 1963.

Other

The Magic Carpet and Other Tales. Jackson, University Press of Mississippi, 1987.

*

Manuscript Collection: University of Mississippi Library, Jackson.

*   *   *

Ellen Douglas's novels, written over a period of 30 years, have consistently dealt with the South, with relationships between the individual and family, between men and women, and between blacks and whites. Never adopting a programmatic feminist stance, Douglas has nonetheless consistently made clear the difficulties faced by women in the world of Southern gentlemen and rednecks. Never adopting a stance of political activism, Douglas has also consistently stressed the close, complex, and ambiguous relationships between black and white Southern women. Throughout works notable for strong and sensitive characterizations, Douglas has created plots which test such humanistic values as love, responsibility, and respect for tradition against the impersonality, arrogant individualism, and materialism of the contemporary New South.

Her first novel, *A Family's Affairs,* won a Houghton Mifflin fellowship and was named one of the *New York Times* best novels of 1962. The novel focuses on the Anderson family during the years 1917-1948, when Kate, the family matriarch, dies at the age of 85. At the novel's center are five women: Kate, her three daughters, and a granddaughter. It is Anna through whose eyes we experience the family crises which make up the novel's plot—crises which usually result from the feckless behavior of the daughters' husbands and Kate's son. Their egocentric individualism contrasts with the women's sense of responsibility to the family and with what Anna calls at the end of the novel "the habit of moral consciousness."

Anna figures in one of the two novels and both of the short stories which form *Black Cloud, White Cloud,* Douglas's second book.

Here Douglas concentrates on the responsibilities of Southern whites to their black servants; the works attest to the complicated relationships between the races, acknowledging the guilt whites feel for their oppression of blacks and the difficulty of redeeming their relationships despite shared pasts.

Where the Dreams Cross is Douglas's weakest novel, attacking in obvious and easy ways the bigotry and greedy materialism of the New South's politicians and the empty-headed frivolity of Old and New Southern belles by contrasting those vices with the virtues of the beautiful but hard-drinking, scandalous but morally responsible heroine. *Apostles of Light,* however, deservedly won a nomination for the National Book award. Douglas here sensitively portrays the plight of the elderly, revealing the frustrations of her heroine, Martha, as, first, her mind and body begin to betray her, and as, eventually, her relatives begin to betray her as well. Torn between their sense of responsibility for Martha and their fear that she will become a financial burden to them, her relatives convert the old family mansion into a profitable nursing home, the ironically named Golden Age Acres. Douglas's powerful and contrasting characterizations of Martha with the home's villainous manager, who treated the elderly residents as prisoners, provide the novel's tension.

The Rock Cried Out won praise in the popular press for its portrayal of a young man's loss of innocence and for Douglas's original handling of elements of the Southern Gothic tradition. The novel chronicles the return of Alan McLaurin to Mississippi after years in Boston and his discovery that the car wreck which caused the death of his first love, Phoebe, was the result of a Ku Klux Klansman's bullet. The Klansman's confession of his crime during a 25-page monologue on the CB in his truck (which McLaurin overhears) marks a flaw in Douglas's narrative technique and strains the reader's credulity. However, McLaurin's maturation (his youthful idealism is gradually replaced by a worldly cynicism) is handled well, and Douglas portrays vividly the tensions in the South between both races and classes during the civil rights era. Here too Douglas reveals her angry sense that technology and materialism have replaced tradition values in the New South.

A Lifetime Burning takes the form of the diary of a 62-year-old English professor, Corinne, who discovers her husband George's infidelities and who writes in order to understand her own blindness, to make sense of what she had thought a "good" life with him, and to leave a record for their grown children. In the course of the six months during which Corinne keeps her diary, she first writes an absurdly comic (and perhaps false) account of George's affair with "The Toad," worries that his distaste for her aging body has motivated that affair, and eventually writes of George's affair with "The Musk-Rat," a male intern at the hospital where George practices. As critic Carol S. Minning has noted, Corinne's first diary entry makes it easier for her to accept the second, the comic anticipates the more shocking, the false anticipates the true. Throughout the novel invention anticipates confession; in dream begins reality. In Douglas's novel, as in the epistolary novels of the 18th century, Corinne writes so that she may find an order to the chaotic facts her life lacks; in her diary she seeks to illuminate the truth of human mystery, her own, her husband's, and her family's.

Douglas followed a collection of classic fairy tales, *The Magic Carpet and Other Tales,* with her best novel, *Can't Quit You, Baby.* It tells the stories of two middle-aged women, Cornelia—sheltered, privileged, white, and deaf—and her black servant, Julia or Tweet—experienced, vital, and enduring. As the women work at common household tasks in Cornelia's house, Julia's stories of her violent and poverty-ridden past awaken Cornelia's memories of crises in her own past. Julia's courage eventually helps Cornelia to survive the death of her husband, to endure her own grief, to live, and to help Julia sustain herself during a subsequent crisis. The novel also assesses the difficulties of story-telling; given the "deafness" of listeners such as Cornelia (or of the reader), how is a narrator such as Julia (or Douglas) to be heard? Intelligent, comic, and poignant, the novel validates the early claim of the New York Times Book Review that Douglas is "one of the best . . . American novelists."

—David K. Jeffrey

DOUGLAS, Michael. *See* **CRICHTON, (John) Michael.**

DOYLE, Roddy

Nationality: Irish. **Born:** Dublin, 1958. **Family:** Married; two sons. **Career:** Since 1980 teacher of English and geography, Greendale Community School, Kilbarrack, Dublin. **Award:** Booker prize, 1993, for *Paddy Clarke Ha Ha Ha.*

PUBLICATIONS

Novels

The Barrytown Trilogy. London, Secker and Warburg, 1992.
    The Commitments, Dublin, King Farouk, 1987; London, Heinemann, 1988; New York, Vintage, 1989.
    The Snapper. London, Secker and Warburg, 1990; New York, Penguin, 1992.
    The Van. London, Secker and Warburg, 1991; New York, Viking, 1992.
Paddy Clarke Ha Ha Ha. London, Secker and Warburg, 1993.

Plays

War. Dublin, Passion Machine, 1989.
Brownbread. London, Secker and Warburg, 1992.

Screenplays: *The Commitments,* an adaptation of his own novel, 1991; *The Snapper,* an adaptation of his own novel, 1993.

*

Film Adaptations: *The Commitments,* 1991; *The Snapper,* 1993.

*   *   *

Roddy Doyle's novels have fundamentally changed the possibilities open to any fictional representation of Ireland in the late twentieth century. Where Joyce had demolished the myth of rural Ireland as the only fit subject for "high" Irish literature by making Dublin the context for his fiction, Doyle has made Dublin the subject for a literature that questioningly straddles the boundaries between "high" and "popular," even deliberately "low," culture. Doyle's writing uses the urban in place of Joyce's sometimes urbane Dublin; his novels are set outside the literary confines of central Dublin, among the postwar housing estates and the disenfranchised population.

These two aspects of Doyle's work, his courting of the "popular" and the specific setting for his novels, have been apparent since his first work, *The Commitments.* Tracing the short life span of a soul group in "Barrytown," *The Commitments* self-consciously makes an iconic use of popular cultures and watches their mutation, examines their applicability, in the context of contemporary urban Ireland. The early comments in the novel—"the Irish are the niggers of Europe. . . . An' the northside Dubliners are the niggers

of Dublin"—need some skeptical scrutiny for their cultural resonance, but they undeniably enforce the continual assertion that Doyle's novels make: that Ireland cannot contemporarily be considered in a pre-1950s separatist mode. The terms of cultural reference in *The Commitments* are necessarily delimited by its subject matter (usually American soul music), but the hybrid "Dublin soul" that is briefly born in the narrative points the way forward in Doyle's fiction to a continual and politicized prioritization of all elements of lived culture over the strictures of readily available "literary" tropes. One influential model for the novel is the movie *The Blues Brothers,* which is referred to in the text and which in turn became the model for Alan Parker's film version of *The Commitments;* that the novel was so readily convertible into cinematic media testifies to its cultural influences and how they have structured Doyle's writing, which certainly owes more to film and television than it does to a tradition of "great" Irish writing.

The progression of Doyle's novels through *The Commitments, The Snapper, The Van,* and *Paddy Clarke Ha Ha Ha* might almost represent a strategy that captivates an audience before delivering a message. If *The Commitments* contained populism as well as the popular, the succeeding novels have become increasing hard-edged and interested in ever more troubling and difficult issues. *The Snapper* traces characters from the Rabbitte family (central to *The Commitments* and *The Van* also) through a teenage pregnancy—in Catholic Ireland, with contraception still having problematic connotations and abortion illegal, this is difficult enough in itself. But Doyle chooses to focus his text through Jimmy Rabbitte Sr., thus filtering social issues with feminist/gender issues attached through an almost archetypal (but challenged) male ego. Doyle's style, in his use of slang, dialect, and dialogue, remains relatively constant across *The Commitments* and *The Snapper,* and thus his readers feel themselves to be back in the groove of the first novel. However, where *The Commitments* narrates a temporary escape from pressing economic and social problems, *The Snapper* is able to confront those issues; the recognizable stylistics of humor and place retain their potentially comforting familiarity but the subject matter increasingly politicizes what Doyle writes.

The Van moves on, in both accomplishment and content, from *The Snapper.* Like the novels of Scottish contemporary James Kelman, Doyle's *The Van* is comfortable when almost narrativeless—indeed the same social context (unemployment) forces characters in the novels of both writers into periods of apparently unhealthy stasis. Doyle again makes Jimmy Sr. and his type of masculinity central to his fiction and traces the social and psychological effects of unemployment. The Van of the title is a chip van bought by Jimmy's similarly out of work friend, Bimbo, in which Jimmy begins to work. The strains on male relationships and friendships become clear when the ownership of the business venture becomes an issue. The old structures of working class male bonding are overthrown by economic circumstances which hint at the "enterprise culture's" intrusion into the Irish economy. And again Doyle uses popular culture, in this case Ireland's national soccer team, as a constant explanatory background for the sense of community and its breakdown that the novel hints at.

Paddy Clarke Ha Ha Ha is in many ways the most complex and rewarding of Doyle's novels. It steps back slightly from the overlapping but progressing narrative of what is now called the Barrytown Trilogy and looks to the formation of the communities on Dublin's housing estates in the 1950s and early 1960s. Paddy Clarke's childhood is concurrent with these social developments— their influence is mixed with his peculiar and carefully documented range of reading and the cruelties (inflicted and received) of childhood in a novel that builds with painstaking care toward an examination of the effects of marital breakdown on a child. *Paddy Clarke* promises even greater accomplishments from Doyle, who, despite his unsettled stature somewhere between the popular and the literary, is able to write novels that are political in the way that singing soul music in Dublin is, as Jimmy Jar says in *The Commitments,* "real politics."

—Colin Graham

DRABBLE, Margaret

Nationality: British. **Born:** Sheffield, Yorkshire, 5 June 1939; sister of A.S. Byatt, *q.v.* **Education:** Mount School, York; Newnham College, Cambridge, B.A. (honours) 1960. **Family:** Married 1) Clive Swift in 1960 (divorced 1975), two sons and one daughter; 2) the writer Michael Holroyd in 1982. **Career:** Deputy chair, 1978-80, and chair, 1980-82, National Book League. **Awards:** Rhys Memorial prize, 1966; James Tait Black Memorial prize, 1968; American Academy E.M. Forster award, 1973. D.Litt: University of Sheffield, 1976; University of Keele, Staffordshire, 1988; University of Bradford, Yorkshire, 1988. C.B.E. (Commander, Order of the British Empire), 1980. **Agent:** Peters Fraser and Dunlop, 503-504 The Chambers, Chelsea Harbour, Lots Road, London SW10 OXF, England.

PUBLICATIONS

Novels

A Summer Bird-Cage. London, Weidenfeld and Nicolson, 1962; New York, Morrow, 1964.
The Garrick Year. London, Weidenfeld and Nicolson, 1964; New York, Morrow, 1965.
The Millstone. London, Weidenfeld and Nicolson, 1965; New York, Morrow, 1966; as *Thank You All Very Much,* New York, New American Library, 1969.
Jerusalem the Golden. London, Weidenfeld and Nicolson, and New York, Morrow, 1967.
The Waterfall. London, Weidenfeld and Nicolson, and New York, Knopf, 1969.
The Needle's Eye. London, Weidenfeld and Nicolson, and New York, Knopf, 1972.
The Realms of Gold. London, Weidenfeld and Nicolson, and New York, Knopf, 1975.
The Ice Age. London, Weidenfeld and Nicolson, and New York, Knopf, 1977.
The Middle Ground. London, Weidenfeld and Nicolson, and New York, Knopf, 1980.
The Radiant Way. London, Weidenfeld and Nicolson, and New York, Knopf, 1987.
A Natural Curiosity. London and New York, Viking, 1989.
The Gates of Ivory. London and New York, Viking, 1991.

Short Stories

Hassan's Tower. Los Angeles, Sylvester and Orphanos, 1980.

Uncollected Short Stories

"A Voyage to Cytherea," in *Mademoiselle* (New York), December 1967.
"The Reunion," in *Winter's Tales 14,* edited by Kevin Crossley-Holland. London, Macmillan, and New York, St. Martin's Press, 1968.
"The Gifts of War," in *Winter's Tales 16,* edited by A.D. Maclean. London, Macmillan, 1970; New York, St. Martin's Press, 1971.
"Crossing the Alps," in *Mademoiselle* (New York), February 1971.
"A Day in the Life of a Smiling Woman," in *In the Looking Glass,* edited by Nancy Dean and Myra Stark. New York, Putnam, 1977.
"A Success Story," in *Fine Lines,* edited by Ruth Sullivan. New York, Scribner, 1981.
"The Dying Year," in *Harper's* (New York), July 1987.

Plays

Bird of Paradise (produced London, 1969).

Screenplays: *Isadora,* with Melvyn Bragg and Clive Exton, 1969; *A Touch of Love (Thank You All Very Much),* 1969.

Television Play: *Laura,* 1964.

Other

Wadsworth. London, Evans, 1966; New York, Arco, 1969.
Virginia Woolf: A Personal Debt. New York, Aloe, 1973.
Arnold Bennett: A Biography. London, Weidenfeld and Nicolson, and New York, Knopf, 1974.
For Queen and Country: Britain in the Victorian Age (for children). London, Deutsch, 1978; New York, Seabury Press, 1979.
A Writer's Britain: Landscape in Literature. London, Thames and Hudson, and New York, Knopf, 1979.
Wordsworth's Butter Knife: An Essay. Northampton, Massachusetts, Catawba Press, 1980.
The Tradition of Women's Fiction: Lectures in Japan, edited by Yukako Suga. Tokyo, Oxford University Press, 1985.
Case for Equality. London, Fabian Society, 1988.
Stratford Revisited: A Legacy of the Sixties. Shipston-on-Stour, Warwickshire, Celandine Press, 1989.
Safe as Houses: An Examination of Home Ownership and Mortgage Tax Relief. London, Chatto and Windus, 1990.
Angus Wilson: A Biography. London, Secker and Warburg, 1995.

Editor, with B.S. Johnson, *London Consequences* (a group novel). London, Greater London Arts Association, 1972.
Editor, *Lady Susan, The Watsons, Sanditon,* by Jane Austen. London, Penguin, 1974.
Editor, *The Genius of Thomas Hardy.* London, Weidenfeld and Nicolson, and New York, Knopf, 1976.
Editor, with Charles Osborne, *New Stories 1.* London, Arts Council, 1976.
Editor, *The Oxford Companion to English Literature.* Oxford and New York, Oxford University Press, 1985; concise edition, edited with Jenny Stringer, 1987.
Editor, *Twentieth Century Classics.* London, Book Trust, 1986.

*

Bibliography: *Margaret Drabble: An Annotated Bibliography* by Joan Garrett Packer, New York, Garland, 1988.

Manuscript Collections: Boston University; University of Tulsa, Oklahoma.

Critical Studies: *Margaret Drabble: Puritanism and Permissiveness* by Valerie Grosvenor Myer, London, Vision Press, 1974; *Boulder-Pushers: Women in the Fiction of Margaret Drabble, Doris Lessing, and Iris Murdoch* by Carol Seiler-Franklin, Bern, Switzerland, Lang, 1979; *The Novels of Margaret Drabble: Equivocal Figures* by Ellen Cronan Rose, London, Macmillan, 1980, and *Critical Essays on Margaret Drabble* (includes bibliography by J.S. Korenman) edited by Rose, Boston, Hall, 1985; *Margaret Drabble: Golden Realms* edited by Dorey Schmidt and Jan Seale, Edinburg, University of Texas-Pan American Press, 1982; *Margaret Drabble: Existing Within Structures* by Mary Hurley Moran, Carbondale, Southern Illinois University Press, 1983; *Guilt and Glory: Studies in Margaret Drabble's Novels 1963-1980* by Susanna Roxman, Stockholm, Almquist & Wiksell, 1984; *Margaret Drabble* by Joanne V. Creighton, London, Methuen, 1985; *The Intertextuality of Fate: A Study of Margaret Drabble* by John Hannay, 1986; *Margaret Drabble* by Lynn Veach Sadler, Boston, Twayne, 1986; *Margaret Drabble: Symbolic Moralist* by Nora Foster Stovel, San Bernardino, California, Borgo Press, 1989.

Margaret Drabble comments:

(1986) In this space I originally wrote that my books were mainly concerned with "privilege, justice and salvation," and that they were not directly concerned with feminism "because my belief in justice for women is so basic that I never think of using it as a subject. It is part of a whole." I stand by this, although the rising political consciousness of women has brought the subject more to the forefront in one or two of the later novels. I now see myself perhaps more as a social historian documenting social change and asking questions rather than providing answers about society: but my preoccupation with "equality and egalitarianism" remains equally obsessional and equally worrying to me, and if anything I am even less hopeful about the prospect of change.

*   *   *

With the appearance of her first novels in the early 1960s, Margaret Drabble gained a sizeable audience who felt their own discoveries and dilemmas in the contemporary world depicted with intelligence and immediacy. *A Summer Bird-Cage* presents a young woman, just after graduation from Oxford, alternately drawn to and repelled by her older sister, seen as brilliant and attractive, who marries a rich novelist. The marriage is ultimately hollow, and the young protagonist uses her recognition of this, as well as that of the marriage, affairs, and occupations of friends, to sort out her own approach to mature experience. The protagonist of *The Garrick Year* is more intimately involved. Married to an actor in a company playing in a provincial town, she falls in love with the producer and finally is able to draw away from the thickets of staged infidelities in her realization of her responsibility for her child. Moral issues, increasingly, become part of the protagonists' examinations of experience, as in *The Millstone,* in which a young academic, initially feeling "free" of the inhibitions of sexual morality and class, and, accidentally pregnant after a one-night stand, recognizes after the baby's birth that her concerns make her dependent on others,

on community, and *Jerusalem the Golden,* in which a young graduate from the North, attracted to the cosmopolitan life represented by a London family, must sort out her own allegiances and responses to issues of love and class. Although *The Waterfall* is more internal, more exclusively concerned with the isolating emotions the protagonist feels in her affair with her cousin's husband, this novel, like the other early ones, reflects directly many of the problems concerning freedom, responsibility, sexual behavior, families, occupation, class, and geography confronted by young women in contemporary Britain.

Drabble's protagonists are invariably intelligent and literary, trying seriously (although not solemnly) to relate what they experience to what they've read. Often they define themselves, either positively or negatively, as characters within the fictions of the 19th-century middle classes, the heroines in George Eliot's world confronting moral dilemmas, or those in Hardy's measuring themselves in the metaphorical terms of landscape. *The Waterfall* rings changes on Jane Austen plots and attitudes: the protagonist in *The Millstone* superimposes Bunyan's allegorical geography on the dark streets of contemporary London. The frequency and the importance of the references indicate that Drabble has always seen herself as part of an English literary tradition, a consciousness of defining the self through fiction.

In Drabble's later novels, the consciousness and function of fiction change. Points of view are deliberately interrupted, fictionality is overtly proclaimed and manipulated, sometimes comically and sometimes not. Drabble relies on questions in literary criticism over the past 20 years as well as on the tradition of English literature. Library reference is likely to be more general and pervasive, as in the epigraph of *The Ice Age* which quotes Milton's *Areopagetica* about "the puissant Nation rousing herself like a strong man after sleep" to illustrate the possibility of British "recovery" from a debilitating period, or the literary party, explicitly connected to the one in Virginia Woolf's *Mrs. Dalloway,* which concludes *The Middle Ground.* The frame of moral reference in the later novels is much wider, more international or more a statement concerning the condition of England, and the novels are more amenable to metaphorical readings. *The Needle's Eye* establishes various gardens in unlikely places, the London slums, the North, and in Africa, gardens that are conscious devices to preserve and nourish the human spirit. *The Realms of Gold* depicts an archeologist who collects both the shards of a public past in excavations in Africa and those of the private past of her family amidst the local and class deprivations of East Anglia, trying to combine the implications of all the relics into a fuller public and private life. *The Ice Age* focuses on the depression, sterility, and violence of Britain and the mid-1970s, problems demonstrated as private in the particular characters and rendered public through the metaphors of property development and misuse that dominate the novel. National "recovery" is seen, perhaps equivocally, as possible. *The Middle Ground,* again combining the public and private, tries to collect representatives of various cultures and classes in a contemporary London reclaimed from the septic wastes of its origins, a metaphor like that in Dickens's *Our Mutual Friend.* Drabble's self-conscious play with fictional perspectives keeps these metaphors away from the potential solemnity of the grandiose, yet the moral implications of the metaphors, the statements judging both personal and public conditions in England, are serious and controlling.

—James Gindin

DREWE, Robert

Nationality: Australian. **Born:** Melbourne, Victoria, 9 January 1943. **Education:** Hale School, Perth, Western Australia, 1952-60. **Family:** Married to Candida Baker (third marriage); four sons and two daughters. **Career:** Cadet journalist, Perth *West Australian,* 1961-64; journalist, 1964-65, and head of Sydney bureau, 1965-70, the *Age,* Melbourne; daily columnist, 1970-73, features editor, 1971-72, and literary editor, 1972-74, the *Australian,* Sydney; special writer, 1975-76, and contributing editor, 1980-83, the *Bulletin,* Sydney; writer-in-residence, University of Western Australia, Nedlands, 1979, and La Trobe University, Bundoora, Victoria, 1986; columnist, *Mode,* Sydney, and Sydney *City Monthly,* 1981-83; visiting writer-in-residence, South Bank Centre, London, and Brixton Prison, 1994. **Awards:** Australia Council fellowship, 1974, 1976, 1978, 1983, 1988; Walkley award for journalism, 1976, 1981; U.S. Government Leader grant, 1978; Victorian Arts fellowship, 1987; National Book award, 1987; Commonwealth Literary prize, 1990; Australian Artists Creative fellowship, 1993-96. **Agent:** Hickson Associates, 128 Queen Street, Woollahra, New South Wales 2025, Australia.

PUBLICATIONS

Novels

The Savage Crows. Sydney and London, Collins, 1976.
A Cry in the Jungle Bar. Sydney, Collins, 1979; London, Fontana, 1981.
Fortune. Sydney, Pan, 1986; London, Pan, 1987.
Our Sunshine. Sydney, Pan, 1991.
The Drowner. Sydney, Macmillan, 1995.

Short Stories

The Bodysurfers. Sydney, Fraser, 1983; London, Faber, 1984.
The Bay of Contented Man. Sydney, Pan, 1989; London, Pan, 1991.

Plays

The Bodysurfers, adaptation of his own story (produced Lismore, New South Wales, 1989).
South American Barbecue (produced Sydney, 1991).

Other

Editor, *The Picador Book of the Beach.* Sydney, Picador, 1993; London, Picador, 1994.

*

Manuscript Collection: University of Western Australia Library, Nedlands.

Critical Studies: "Making Connections" by Veronica Brady, in *Westerly* (Perth, Western Australia), June 1980; "The Littoral Truth" by Jim Crace, in *Times Literary Supplement* (London), 24 August 1984; "Beaches and Bruised Loves" by Jill Smolowe, in *Newsweek* (New York), 29 October 1984; "Cartoons for the Lucky Country"

by J.D. Reed, in *Time* (New York), 15 December 1986; "A New Angle on Our Uneasy Repose" by Helen Daniel, in Sydney *Morning Herald,* 18 November 1989; "Mining Dark Places" by Don Anderson, in *Age Monthly Review* (Melbourne), May 1990.

*   *   *

Robert Drewe is an important, highly original voice in Australian fiction. Like other writers before him, Drewe deals with the plight of the Australian Aborigines, scrutinizes Australia's uneasy relationship with Asia, and shows an overriding concern with questions of Australian national identity (especially in regard to the role of urban life). But Drewe's approach to these issues is original and provocative.

Whereas a novel about the Australian Aborigines will usually be set among Aborigines, or at least involve white people who live in areas inhabited by Aborigines, *The Savage Crows* deals with a white youth whose contact with Aborigines is at first only theoretical. Stephen Crisp is researching the early 19th-century events which led to the extinction of the Aborigines living in the island state of Tasmania. His source material is a document titled "The Savage Crows: My Adventures Among the Natives of Van Diemen's Land," which is the diary-journal of the clergyman G.A. Robinson, whose attempts to bring Christianity and civilization to the Tasmanian natives led to cultural misunderstanding, the spread of disease, and death.

Though Robinson was an actual historical figure, the Robinson journal is based upon a number of 19th-century documents and newspaper reports. *The Savage Crows* has been described as a "documentary novel," but its concerns extend beyond the fictional recreation of history. Drewe presents a number of moral contrasts: Robinson's "good intentions" and their deplorable outcome; Crisp's clinical, academic approach and the dire human suffering to which it is directed; the petty "problems" of affluent 20th-century suburbia beside the plight of early colonists and Aborigines.

A Cry in the Jungle Bar explores Australia's relationship with Asia, once again with focus upon the experiences of a single individual. The Jungle Bar is an attraction of the Asian Eden Hotel, and the "cry" of the title is an utterance of helpless western frustration in the face of Asian complexities. Australian Dick Cullen is a tall, beefy, former football player who now works for the United Nations in Manila. Like Stephen Crisp, Cullen is a researcher; an expert on animal husbandry, he is writing a book about water buffalo titled "The Poor Man's Tractor." More importantly, Cullen shares Crisp's desire to relate his own life to history (though Cullen is more interested in the future history of Australian-Asian relations), and he shares Crisp's struggle to come to terms with another race and culture.

Drewe presents a pessimistic, satirical view of the meeting of cultures. Cullen is marked indelibly a foreigner because of his massive physique, but also because of his inability to understand the subtle political divisions of Asia. (His Bangladeshi colleague, Z.M. Ali, is an enigma to him, and Cullen is bewildered when Ali's political activities lead to his expulsion.)

Fortune is written as a series of terse film-takes or cartoon-panels which tell the story of Don Spargo, a contemporary explorer who discovers a sunken treasure ship off the coast of Western Australia. This story has a "factual" basis (inasmuch as it is based upon a real-life character and posits the possible fate of a real-life 16th-century sailing ship, the *Fortuyn*) and in this sense it confirms the "journalistic" impulse in Drewe's writing. But the underlying themes are literary, for Spargo's story is a parable on contemporary issues, and the use of a young journalist as narrator raises postmodernist concerns about the nature of narrative: "Officially the reporter was simply the recorder of events, the objective conduit, but events had a habit of including the messenger in the disorder."

Drewe's novels feature an underlying concern with the malaise affecting suburban Australia. This is seen in the way in which Crisp, Cullen, and the journalist-narrator of *Fortune* are aloof and clinical about pressing human problems (each addressing social issues through reports and documentation, rather than experiencing the problems directly), and it is evident in the failed sexual relationships portrayed in each novel. The short stories in *The Bodysurfers* and *The Bay of Contented Man* develop these concerns in more detail, exploring the conflicts and contradictions in the national character. One of the epigraphs to *The Bodysurfers* is a statement from the polemical historian Manning Clark about the loss of national values: "Just as Samson after being shorn of his hair was left eyeless in Gaza, was this generation, stripped bare of all faith, to be left comfortless on Bondi Beach?" The stories contrast the carefree sensuality of Australian beach life (the nude sunbathers, the smell of suntan oil) with the characters' unconscious prurience and uneasiness about sexuality, and with the mundane anxieties and problems of urban life.

Drewe's portrayal of the beach culture is journalistically superb; to quote one reviewer: "It's all here—the oiled bodies, the smell of the salt, the heat of the sun, the sensuality." But Drewe also offers a provocative analysis of Australian life, hinting at an inability to untie the "masculine" and "feminine" aspects of the national culture. In many stories the beach embodies the Australian myth of physical action and carefree hedonism, but these simplistic masculine values are often dispelled by the comments or actions of the female characters. And in the story called "The Last Explorer" an aged adventurer, slowly dying in hospital, symbolically turns his back on the sea (symbol of the young, feminine, new Australia) and faces the desert (symbol of the dead "macho" world of exploration and masculine deeds).

—Van Ikin

DRIVER, C(harles) J(onathan)

Nationality: British. **Born:** Cape Town, South Africa, 19 August 1939. **Education:** St. Andrews College, Grahamstown; University of Cape Town, B.A. (honors) in English, B.Ed., and S.T.D. 1962; Trinity College, Oxford, M.Phil. 1967. **Family:** Married Ann Elizabeth Hoogewerf in 1967; two sons and one daughter. **Career:** President, National Union of South African Students, 1963-64; detained in 1964 under the "90 Day Law;" South African passport revoked, 1966. Assistant teacher, 1964-65 and 1967-68, and housemaster, International Sixth Form Center, 1968-73, Sevenoaks School, Kent; director of 6th Form Studies, Matthew Humberstone Comprehensive School, Humberside, 1973-78; principal, Island School, Hong Kong, 1978-83; headmaster, Berkhamsted School, Hertfordshire, 1983-89. Since 1989 master, Wellington College, Crowthorne, Berkshire. Research fellow, University of York, 1976. Fellow, Royal Society of Arts, 1984. **Agent:** John Johnson Ltd., 45-47 Clerkenwell Green, London EC1R 0HT. **Address:** Wellington College, Crowthorne, Berkshire RG11 7PU, England.

PUBLICATIONS

Novels

Elegy for a Revolutionary. London, Faber, 1969; New York, Morrow, 1970.
Send War in Our Time, O Lord. London, Faber, 1970.
Death of Fathers. London, Faber, 1972.
A Messiah of the Last Days. London, Faber, 1974.

Short Stories

Penguin Modern Stories 8, with others. London, Penguin, 1971.

Uncollected Short Story

"Impossible Cry," in *London Magazine,* February 1966.

Poetry

I Live Here Now. Lincoln, Lincolnshire and Humberside Arts, 1979.
Jack Copel/C.J. Driver. Cape Town, Philip, 1979.
Hong Kong Portraits. Oxford, Perpetua Press, 1986.
In the Water-Margins. Capetown, Snailpress, and London, Crane River Press, 1994.

Other

Patrick Duncan, South African and Pan-African. London, Heinemann, 1980.

Editor, with H.B. Joicey, *Landscape and Light:L Photographs and Poems of Lincolnshire and Humberside.* Lincoln, Lincolnshire and Humberside Arts, 1978.

*

C.J. Driver comments:

I am a writer and a teacher; the order depends on whether I am writing or teaching, but I am Master of a great national—and increasingly international—boarding school, so am kept busy in term. I write poems, though I do little about publishing them these days; I do much less reviewing than I used to, though I still read books; I spent two years writing the biography of Patrick Duncan, one of the tragic heroes of recent South African history; and I write novels. I believe profoundly that the novel is the "great book of life," and I hope that all my concerns as a human being enter my work as a novelist—love, marriage, children, homes, money, food, work, leisure—though my predominant concerns are with politics—in the widest sense—the relation of self and society, and the relation of conscious and unconscious minds. I would, at the moment, regard myself more as a poet than a novelist; but I hope the picture may change before the final curtain.

*   *   *

C.J. Driver is a South African writer whose four novels have earned him a considerable reputation. Not exclusively South African in stetting or in theme, the novels concentrate on a sometimes challenging and always recognizable view of contemporary society.

Elegy for a Revolutionary, the first and least satisfactory of the novels, uses Driver's own experience of underground political action in South Africa during the early 1960s. Like Nadine Gordimer's *The Late Bourgeois World,* it is an attempt to examine the motives and the fate of a group of young white "liberals" who turned to violence as a means of opposing the repressive Nationalist Government. Driver's analysis centers on the personality of the student leader, Jeremy, whom he sees as both traitor and, paradoxically, hero. The Weakness of the novel lies in its excessively uncritical view of Jeremy. Unlike Nadine Gordimer, who presents her revolutionary as an integral part of a wider social setting, Driver fails to create a context in which Jeremy's actions can be understood. And, although he is much concerned with psychological motivation, the discussion of Jeremy's peculiar family relationships and obscure guilts remain too abstract to be really credible.

In *Send War in Our Time, O Lord* Driver's main theme is the examination of the liberal conscience under stress. His portrayal of Mrs. Allen, a middle-aged white widow, discovering the inadequacy of her life-long moral code based on decency and tolerance, demonstrates his ability to create a convincing character. The setting (an isolated missionary settlement on South Africa's northern border) is also well-presented. The major weakness of this novel lies in its melodramatic and somewhat far-fetched plot, which involves terrorist activity, much police brutality, madness and two or three suicides, all graphically described. In the welter of violent action, the central issues (the failure of liberal values, the need for dynamic leadership, the nature of political commitment) are almost submerged.

Death of Fathers and *A Messiah of the Last Days* are both set in England, and show a much surer grasp of technique and theme than the earlier books. Driver's interest in details of violence and suffering are still in evidence, but now become part of a general vision of modern life. *Death of Fathers* has a close affinity with *Elegy for a Revolutionary,* although it is set in the confines of an English public school. Its central character is a schoolmaster, and, as in the earlier novel, he is both "heroic" (larger in every way than his colleagues) and "treacherous" (he betrays the confidence of his most brilliant and difficult pupil, in an attempt to "save" him). Again, Driver explores the nature of guilt, and the concept of betrayal, which appears, in his view, to be an inherent part of human experience. Friendship between two different but complementary male characters forms another strand in the novel, and is more competently handled here than in the earlier book.

In *A Messiah of the Last Days* Driver returns to a contemplation of political action. This time he makes his anti-establishment figures a group of idealistic young anarchists, the Free People, who set up a commune in a disused warehouse in London. Their leader, charismatic John Buckleson, projects such a powerful and attractive vision of a new society that he wins the allegiance of a number of eminently respectable people, as well as exciting the younger members of society. The most ambitious of the four novels, *A Messiah of the Last Days* contrasts a number of different life styles, and presents a complex image of contemporary Britain. Through the fast-moving story runs what is clearly, by now, Driver's most persistent theme: the need society has for a "leader" with a compelling vision, and its equal need to destroy him. Buckleson, who ends his life as a "vegetable" in a psychiatric ward, having been shot at close range by a former follower of his, is the latest version of Jeremy, sentenced to death for sabotage; of the terrorist leader, gunned down by the police; and of Nigel, the schoolboy who hanged himself. Skilled as Driver undoubtedly is in contriving variations

of his theme, one hopes that his interest in leadership and betrayal will not become obsessive.

—Ukrsula Edmands

DRURY, Allen (Stuart)

Nationality: American. **Born:** Houston, Texas, 2 September 1918. **Education:** Stanford University, California, B.A. 1939. **Military Service:** Served in the United States Army, 1942-43. **Career:** Editor, Tulare *Bee,* California, 1940-41; country editor, Bakersfield *California,* 1941-42; member, United Press Senate staff, Washington, D.C., 1943-45; national editor, *Pathfinder* magazine, Washington, D.C., 1947-53; member, Congressional staff, Washington *Evening Star,* 1954-59; political correspondent, *Reader's Digest,* 1959-63. Lives in Tiburon, California. **Awards:** Sigma Delta Chi award, for journalism, 1941; Pulitzer prize, for fiction, 1960. Lit.D.: Rollins College, Winter Park, Florida, 1961. **Member:** National Council on the Arts, Washington, D.C. **Agent:** The Lantz Office, 888 Seventh Avenue, Suite 2500, New York, New York 10106, U.S.A.

PUBLICATIONS

Novels

Advise and Consent. New York, Doubleday, 1959; London, Collins, 1960.

A Shade of Difference. New York, Doubleday, 1962; London, Joseph, 1963.

That Summer. London, Joseph, 1965; New York, Coward McCann, 1966.

Capable of Honor. New York, Doubleday, 1966; London, Joseph, 1967.

Preserve and Protect. New York, Doubleday, and London, Joseph, 1968.

The Throne of Saturn. New York, Doubleday, and London, Joseph, 1971.

Come Nineveh, Come Tyre: The Presidency of Edward M. Jason. New York, Doubleday, 1973; London, Joseph, 1974.

The Promise of Joy: The Presidency of Orrin Knox. New York, Doubleday, and London, Joseph, 1975.

A God Against the Gods. New York, Doubleday, and London, Joseph, 1976.

Anna Hastings: The Story of a Washington Newspaperperson. New York, Morrow, 1977; London, Joseph, 1978.

Return to Thebes. New York, Doubleday, and London, Joseph, 1977.

Mark Coffin, U.S.S.: A Novel of Capital Hill. New York, Doubleday, 1979; as *Mark Coffin, Senator,* London, Joseph, 1982.

Decision. New York, Doubleday, and London, Joseph, 1983.

The Roads of Earth. New York, Doubleday, 1984; London, Joseph, 1985.

Pentagon. New York, Doubleday, 1986; as *The Destiny Markers,* London, Severn House, 1988.

Hill of Summer. N.p., Windsor Publishing Corporation, 1989.

Toward What Bright Glory? New York, Morrow, and London, Severn House, 1990.
Into What Far Harbor?: A Novel. New York, Morrow, and London, Severn House, 1993.

Uncollected Short Stories

"Something," in *The Best from Fantasy and Science Fiction 10,* edited by Robert P. Mills. New York, Doubleday, 1961; London, Gollancz, 1963.
"No More Tears," in *Good Housekeeping* (New York), February 1971.

Other

A Senate Journal 1943-1945. New York, McGraw Hill, 1963.
Three Kids in a Cart: A Visit to Ike and Other Diversions. New York, Doubleday, 1965.
"A Very Strange Society:" A Journey to the Heart of South Africa. New York, Simon and Schuster, 1967; London, Joseph, 1968.
Courage and Hesitation: Notes and Photographs of the Nixon Administration. New York, Doubleday, 1971; as *Courage and Hesitation: Inside the Nixon Administration,* London, Joseph, 1972.
Egypt: The Eternal Smile, photographs by Alex Gotfrydx. New York, Doubleday, 1980.

*

Manuscript Collection: Hoover Institution, Stanford, California.

Critical Studies: *Political Fiction, The Spirit of the Age, and Allen Drury* by Tom Kemme, Bowling Green, Ohio, Popular Press, 1987.

*   *   *

Allen Drury's experiences as a journalist, especially as a political correspondent in Washington, D.C., have left their mark, for better or worse, on his novels and non-fiction. Almost all his fiction is concerned with political warfare in the United States, with attacks by the media upon politicians when in power and opposition, and with the external enemies of the United States. These enemies are shown as unprincipled, ungrateful, and malicious both when making their verbal assaults in the United Nations, an institution that is not usually shown in a flattering light, and when physically attacking American installations. Communist Russia, the archfoe, is made completely villainous, particularly in *The Throne of Saturn* and *Come Nineveh, Come Tyre.* In the former, Russian astronauts try to destroy American space craft far above the earth; in the latter, Russia invades Alaska and humiliates a foolishly idealistic left-wing president. Even in *Pentagon* (1986), the Soviets are still scheming against the United States. Whether *glasnost* and the collapse of the monolithic U.S.S.R. will cause Drury to find another external enemy remains to be seen, but the internal forces undermining his country will probably remain the same: pacifists, woolly-minded liberals and, in his most recent fiction, the spread of violence and the alarming reactionary growth of vigilantism (e.g. the justice now! movement in *Decision*) are Drury's targets.

Of his novels, *Advise and Consent* is the first published and the best. It would undoubtedly benefit from severe pruning, but there is a momentum built upon a melodramatic presentation of events that carries the reader along, even if he is wary of the hysterical undertone of the book. In the detailing of Congressional infighting

and the tension of significant debates in the Senate, Drury is at his strongest. Here his years as a member of the United Press Senate Staff are effectively used. He is not so strong, however, when presenting the actions of the president or the left-wingers. As in later books, many characters are stereotypes. Even in this book, a Pulitzer prize winner, he uses incidents that appear contrived (even though they have real life counterparts) and characters that are mere puppets.

Subsequent novels carry on the story of political struggles and national alarms through outbreaks of "liberal"-inspired violence and presidential assassination. Instead of refining, distilling, and subtilizing the promising material and fictional technique of *Advise and Consent,* he seems to have been pushed by an increasing fear for the preservation of traditional American values and institutions into composing novels that are more overtly propagandistic statements of his conservative political beliefs than aesthetically pleasing books. Readers who share his deep distrust of liberals and his hatred of Communism may accept his fiction more readily, but they too may find his conservative preachings too heavy and his plots, especially in their violent conclusions, too contrived and sensational. Even characters such as Orrin Knox, who are interestingly depicted in the early novels, begin to pall in the later works. The use of melodramatic incident (often to compensate for feeble characterization) is strikingly exemplified in *Preserve and Protect,* which opens with the death of President Harley M. Hudson in a fiery plane crash and (on the last page) concludes with the assassination before a huge crowd of either the presidential or the vice-presidential nominee—in movie-serial fashion we are not told which one. The failure to identify the victims is deliberate since Drury is thereby able to give us two novels as sequels. In *Come Nineveh, Come Tyre,* Orrin Knox, the stalwart conservative, is identified as the victim. Thus Edward Montoya Jason, the liberal but too-malleable vice-presidential nominee assumes the highest office; but, exploited by NAWAC (National Anti-War Activities Congress) and Communist imperialists, he brings the country to abject international defeat. The alternative with Jason dead and Knox alive, is given in *The Promise of Joy.*

Drury returns to Washington with *Anna Hastings,* but the focus has shifted. The ruthless rise of the liberal newspaper-woman has interest and excitement, but the novel is often a sermon on the dangers of liberalism. In *Mark Coffin, U.S.S. Drury* comes back to the U.S. Senate, a scene he knows so well. The hero, the intelligent young senator from California, too naive to be completely credible, has to survive great political pressure and a scandal. The author's favorite, indeed obsessive, theme is dominant once again in *Hill of Summer.* The usual elements of the realistic novel—plot, characterization, dramatic scene—are subordinated to the message that the United States is not sufficiently prepared to meet the Soviet menace. At the end of the novel, world war is temporarily averted. The theme is even more clearly and repetitiously sounded in *The Roads of Earth,* for both an authorial prefatory note and the novel itself monotonously declare that the Soviet Union is set on destroying the United States; pre-emptive strikes against Russian manifestations of power are advocated. The staunch incumbent American president forces the Russians to retreat. Many of the characters are once again stereotyped as good or bad in *Decision,* but Drury centers this novel on the Supreme Court and the prevalence of violent crime in America: the highest court has to decide the case of a vicious Harvard graduate, a hippie, who has blown up an atomic power station and made the daughter of one of the judges hearing the case into a human vegetable. The issues are important—indeed one of the valuable aspects of his fiction is that he forces the American reader to face disquieting facts about the nature of American society and the corruption of its politics—and the author does distinguish the different kinds of left-wing or liberal thought. The presentation of an immense amount of information about the judicial process adds realism to much of the book, but some of the action relies too much on coincidence, and the violent, breathless, and sensational ending is too contrived.

Non-American readers are probably irritated by the obtrusive patriotism and the condescension shown for foreigners. Drury seems unable or unwilling to present stereotypes or caricatures in his fiction. Lord Claude Maudulayne, the British Ambassador, is an example. In addition, by failing to develop credible characters for the ambassadors at the UN or in Washington, he loses the chance to utilize them as a kind of Greek chorus commenting on American tragedies. On the other hand, a moderate and balanced view of foreigners is given in *"A Very Strange Society:" A Journey to the Heart of South Africa.* Perhaps he is too ready to depreciate the achievements of black African nations, but he acknowledges the complex problems of a multi-racial society.

In 1986, he produced another enormous novel, *Pentagon,* which is weighed down with a multitude of characters and details. Much of the book deals with the Pentagon's failure to formulate a plan to respond effectively to the Soviet military adventuring in the Pacific. Despite some suspenseful episodes, much of the book plods along. Once again, however, Drury shows his detailed and informed knowledge of the way the American government and its agencies work or fail to work. Clearly, he is passionately interested in his subject and in converting his readers to his point of view. He is a Cassandra for the 20th-Century American reader.

Two of Drury's novels of he late 1970s, *A God Against the Gods and Return to Thebes,* are set in ancient Egypt. In the former, Akhenaten and his beautiful wife Nefertitti are locked in a power struggle with the priesthood; in the sequel, Akhenaten is murdered, Tutankhaten succeeds him; then he too is murdered. Like most of Drury's novels, these two are concerned with the struggle for power. Both novels are well researched and have exciting scenes, but the characterization is simplistic and the dialogue insufficiently differentiated.

His main claim to fame, however, is his series of political novels, structured around the beliefs and actions of Americans during the 1960s, 1970s, and 1980s—some of the novels might indeed be read as *romans a clef.* In the 1970s American history betrayed Allen Drury: his right-wing heroes—at least their equivalents in real life— were found guilty through such investigations as Watergate of the very crimes he attributes to his left-wing villains. He was equally unfortunate in his non-fiction. *Courage and Hesitation: Notes and Photographs of the Nixon Administration* (1971) is a tribute, with only a few cautionary statements, to "a decent and worthy man, leading an administration composed, for the most part, of decent and worthy men." To overcome the unkind cuts of history, Drury must either develop a greater political sensitivity or take more seriously his role as a creator of fiction. It must be said in Drury's defense, however, that the recent opening up of Soviet archives shows that some of his fears of Soviet ambitions and American traitors have more basis than left-wing critics were prepared to accept. Unfortunately, his recent fiction has become so melodramatic and hortatory in its insistence on the United States staunchly resisting the Russian threat that, even in the current conservative era many readers will be so alienated by the intrusive ideology that they will overlook the good qualities of his fiction.

—James A. Hart

DUBUS, Andre

Nationality: American. **Born:** Lake Charles, Louisiana, 11 August 1936. **Education:** McNeese State College (now University), Lake Charles, B.A. 1958; University of Iowa, Iowa City, M.F.A. 1966. **Military Service:** Served in the United States Marine Corps 1958-64: Captain. **Family:** Married 1) Patricia Lowe in 1958 (divorced 1970), four children; 2) Tommie Gail Cotter in 1975 (divorced 1977); 3) Peggy Rambach in 1979 (divorced 1989), two daughters. **Career:** Creative writing teacher, Bradford College, Massachusetts, 1966-84. Since 1984 visiting teacher, University of Alabama, Birmingham, and Boston University. Crippled by automobile, 1986. **Awards:** National Endowment for the Arts fellowship, 1985; MacArthur Foundation award, 1988-93. **Agent:** Philip G. Spitzer, 50 Tulmage Farm Lane, East Hampton, New York 11937, U.S.A. **Address:** 753 East Broadway, Haverhill, Massachusetts 01830, U.S.A.

PUBLICATIONS

Novel

The Lieutenant. New York, Dial Press, 1967.

Short Stories

Separate Flights. Boston, Godine, 1975.
Adultery and Other Choices. Boston, Godine, 1977.
Finding a Girl in America: Ten Stories and a Novella. Boston, Godine, 1980.
The Times Are Never So Bad: A Novella and Eight Short Stories. Boston, Godine, 1983.
We Don't Live Here Anymore. New York, Crown, and London, Pan, 1984.
Land Where My Fathers Died (single story). Winston-Salem, North Carolina, Wright, 1984.
Voices from the Moon and Other Stories, with David Godine. Boston, Godine, 1984; London, Pan, 1987.
The Last Worthless Evening: Four Novellas and Two Short Stories. Boston, Godine, 1986.
Blessings (single story). Elmwood, Connecticut, Raven Editions, 1987.
Selected Stories. Boston, Godine, 1988.
Into the Silence. Cambridge, Masssachusetts, Green Street Press, 1988.

Other

Broken Vessels (essays). Boston, Godine, 1991.

*   *   *

Late one night in July 1986 Andre Dubus was the first to arrive at the scene of a serious accident. He pulled to the far side of the road and while dashing across to help the victims of the accident was struck by another vehicle. One of his legs was amputated and he lost most of the mobility of the other. The cruel consequence of a heroic nature moved to action might have been from one of his own stories. Dubus writes of the triumph of altruism over selfishness, and the endurance of a human capacity for goodness in the face of all the forces that assail it—poverty, jealousy, cowardice, lust, and especially that dull anomie that comes from working too long for too little in return. Surely, one thinks, these are conditions that would decimate the spirit. Instead, Dubus stands resolutely with that small group of contemporary writers who believe that transcendent heroism is the common property of every one of us.

Dubus's fictions are short, though far longer than the average minimalist and dirty realists' stories that have been in vogue in the 1970s and 1980s. Still, he is a short story writer only on the technicality of length. Otherwise his works feel like novels, so profoundly and so fully drawn are his characters, so important their stories. His people work, love, wonder, hope, pray, and sometimes murder in the rundown industrial towns of the Merrimack river valley of Massachusetts. Dubus knows the location intimately, and in reading his stories the reader feels that he has drunk with his characters in their bars, eaten in the roadhouses with them, played softball and driven off to hunt with them, slept with them in their beds, and even inhabited their minds while they have struggled with questions of justice, faith, and mortality. Dubus has repaid them with absolute frankness, yet not once has he demeaned them.

Dubus is a Catholic writer, and, whether devout or lapsed, his characters tend to return to their religious instruction for ways to understand or alter their predicaments. He is also a political writer, and for each story that turns on a question of faith there is another that reveals the injustices of our institutions and laws, and of our racist and class attitudes. But Dubus is not didactic, unless the lesson is that we are bigger than we suspect and that learning who we are and where we are is never easy. At the heart of Dubus's realism, then, is the double assumption that his characters, wholly and humanly complicated, are defined within and against a complicated set of ethical and social structures. It is this settling of one complexity on another that imbues Dubus's work with its force.

"Land Where My Fathers Died" is among the strongest of his stories, it also illustrates much of Dubus's approach. Multiple voices, multiple perspectives, collect themselves to render a story of justifiable homicide, sexual coercion, mistaken accusation, and, finally, the heroic assertion of faith, not in the infallibility of the legal system, but in the necessity of risking one's freedom in order to uphold the rule of law. "Land Where My Fathers Died" shares with the story "Rose" a confidence in the essential nobility of characters whose violence erupts when those dearest to them are abused. The story of a woman who has murdered her husband to protect her babies—only to have the state exonerate the crime but take the children away—"Rose" uses a framing narrator to give the woman voice. He is also a post facto collaborator, whose own past and beery present provide energy and ambiguity. A similar method is used in "After the Game," a story of lapidary concision, in which a professional baseball player who speaks only Spanish loses his mind. His story is told by an American whose unpredictable sympathy turns out to be complete.

Most often provision of a sympathetic center is left to the reader. In a story like "The Pretty Girl" the process can be disconcerting; we are asked to move from sympathy for a victim and enter into the wild rationalizations of a rapist. In "Adultery," we pull together the three points of view of a love triangle, composed of a philandering husband who suddenly has the tables turned on him as his wife takes a lover, a former priest who, having renounced his vocation, finds that he is dying of cancer. Like the novella, *Voices from the Moon*, "Adultery" brings readers through the ambiguities of multiple perspectives to a still point of understanding and hope.

This is basically the same movement of another religious work, "A Father's Story," though here the dialogue does not rise from several points of view, but is only imagined, or wished for, as a Catholic father, covering for his daughter's irresponsibility, argues the necessity of his failure with a silent God.

Dubus has few real peers. Certainly he is as important as Raymond Carver, for the pathos of his vision and for his role in the renaissance of the American short story. As a Catholic writer, he is a successor to Flannery O'Connor in his concern for anchoring the spirit against the disruptions and perjuries of life in the modern world. No American writer since the young John Dos Passos has so thoroughly understood and described the American working class. He has much in common with Frederick Busch, whose honesty, inextinguishable humanity, and compassion are similarly refreshing, and who, with Dubus, is one of only two contemporary American fiction writers who can bring this cold reader to tears. Finally, Dubus is bigger than the sum of all comparisons, no matter how flattering. The man has a genius for the invasion of his readers; sooner or later your address is on his list.

—Mark A.R. Facknitz

DUCKWORTH, Marilyn

Nationality: New Zealander. **Born:** Marilyn Adcock, Auckland, New Zealand, 10 November 1935. **Education:** Victoria University of Wellington, 1953, 1956. **Family:** Married 1) Harry Duckworth 1955 (dissolved 1964); 2) Ian Macfarlane, 1964 (dissolved 1972); 3) Daniel Donovan, 1974 (died 1978); 4) John Batstone, 1985; four daughters. **Career:** Full-time writer. Has held positions in public relations, nurse aiding, factory work and library work. **Awards:** Scholarship in Letters, 1961, 1972, 1993; New Zealand award for achievement, 1963; Katherine Mansfield fellowship, 1980; New Zealand Book award, 1985, for fiction; Fulbright Visiting Writers fellowship, 1986; Australia New Zealand Exchange fellowship, 1989; Victoria University of Wellington Writers fellowship, 1990; Hawthornden Writers fellowship, Scotland, 1994; Sargeson Writers fellowship, Auckland, 1995. O.B.E. (Officer, Order of the British Empire), 1987. **Member:** New Zealand Society of Authors. **Agent:** Tim Curnow, Curtis Brown (Australia) Pty. Ltd., P.O. Box 19, Paddington, New South Wales 2021, Australia.

PUBLICATIONS

Novels

A Gap in the Spectrum. Auckland, Hutchinson, 1959.
The Matchbox House. London, Hutchinson, 1960; New York, Morrow, 1961.
A Barbarous Tongue. London, Hutchinson, 1963.
Over the Fence Is Out. London, Hutchinson, 1969.
Disorderly Conduct. Auckland, Hodder and Stoughton, 1984.
Married Alive. Auckland, Hodder and Stoughton, 1985.
Rest for the Wicked. Auckland, Hodder and Stoughton, 1986.
Pulling Faces. Auckland, Hodder and Stoughton, 1987.
A Message from Harpo. Auckland, Hodder and Stoughton, 1989.
Unlawful Entry. Auckland, Random Century, 1992.

Seeing Red. Auckland, Random House, 1993.
Leather Wings. Auckland, Random House, 1995.

Short Stories

Explosions on the Sun. Auckland, Hodder and Stoughton, 1989.
Fooling (novella). Auckland, Hazzard Press, 1994.

Poetry

Other Lovers' Children. Christchurch, New Zealand, Pegasus Press, 1975.

*

Marilyn Duckworth comments:

In my fiction I focus on the tension between individuals' need for each other and their need for independence. I'm fascinated by the words and the devices they use to conceal and reveal these needs.

Critic Heather Murray has said of my work that I espouse no ideology and that I refuse to dress my novels in the current colours of political correctness. My characters "continue to search, perchance to make sense of the existential void in which they haplessly float."

*   *   *

Throughout a prolific career Marilyn Duckworth has been fascinated by the human condition. Archetypal character Sophie in *Disorderly Conduct* realizes on the final page that her "disorder" is life itself:

What she suffers from is the human condition, no less. . . . She can expect a succession of bizarre and distressing symptoms. Small disasters, small rejections, dripping like acid onto her nerves and burrowing into her sense of well being. Life is a sexually transmitted terminal disease.

From her first novel, Duckworth broke with the certainties of the great tradition of the English novel, with its underpinning faith in a benevolent God and an ordered universe. Rather, in the uncertainties of existentialism, she found a way of bringing some sanity to the human condition. To Duckworth, the traditional English novel was male in themes, values, and modes of expression. She prefers to take a line from Virginia Woolf in seeking a female form of narrative, a system of values, which Duckworth hoped readers would accept as necessarily different but valid, and also from Muriel Spark, whose characters, Duckworth said in a series of radio talks on women's writing in 1960, exude a sense of female normality and completeness: They are "rarely martyrs, rarely self-pitying, and in spite of their eccentricities appear totally sane."

As has been Duckworth's own life—wife to four husbands, mother of four, stepmother to several more—the lives of her predominantly female characters are domestic and suburban. Distinctly unheroic, they stand revealed amid a daily round of chores, pregnancy, children, falling in and out of love, knitting, gardening, and caring for aging parents. They are flawed individuals for whom the reader feels varying amounts of sympathy and, often, considerable irritation. The only constant is change, for as Kevin Ireland has written, theirs is "a wonky world, where thunder resounds in-side the cupboards and a whirlwind lurks behind the curtains." Duckworth uses a bare minimum of description and explanation; she is particularly skilled at crisp, pithy dialogue, and her plots unwind at speed.

Duckworth's characters echo the journey toward independence women have made from the 1950s. In *A Barbarous Tongue,* Frieda, as a teenage unmarried mother, still hopes for happiness, which she finds (again on the last page) in a daring break for independence from family ties, away from her young inadequate lover, in the arms of an older lover, who warns her, "Only children expect to be happy." Frieda is the new generation of women who shocked a puritan society by seeking independence from it and from family, to exist as sexual beings, sentient, passionate, and instinctive. It seemed Frieda—and Duckworth—were returning to a pre-Christian, barbarous age.

As women have been engaged in redefining their status in society, so changing gender roles occupy a prominent and recurring place in Duckworth novels. Power games among siblings, female violence, incest, and homosexuality (especially lesbianism) upset any notion of the stable family unit. In *Seeing Red,* Duckworth examines the complex web of destructive family ties. *Pulling Faces* transposes the traditional roles of man as leader and woman as dependent follower: In a tragicomic love story that combines elements of science fiction, social satire, and thriller, Stuart seeks to bind the elusive Gwyn in a conventional union. Towing her caravan wherever she likes, she eludes her mother and child and Stuart; she alters her mind with drugs and is ultrasecretive about her movements, playing childhood games of pulling faces to disguise self. Yet with a machine she tries to bind others to her by capturing their thoughts on videotape. It is a chilling and ironic foretaste to a computer age where personal independence has been achieved and people communicate (still inadequately) by machine.

Disorderly Conduct, Unlawful Entry, and *A Message from Harpo* are sophisticated studies of women as daughters, wives, and mothers. Duckworth is skilled at creating believable families. Aging mothers entrap the young, but they are redeemed by some small nobility of character. Children devour the strength of their mother with their selfish demands but are saved from complete monsterhood by honesty and quite disarming acts of kindness and unexpected selflessness. Duckworth is particularly good at the intimate conversation of families.

In Duckworth's latest novella, *Fooling,* Ros feels the strain of her independence (won for her by several generations of Duckworth's earlier women): "A woman of the nineties is expected to want control of her life—but not necessarily self-control—to be centred and self-sufficient, but not, of course, self-centred. It isn't easy." Ros is honest in an age when everyone else is fooling. She still wants love, but her hopes (and perhaps Duckworth's also) of finding lasting happiness are fading: "Ros, you're going to have to grow up one day. You're 28 years old—aren't you?—and this is the real world. The freaky old real world."

—Heather Murray

DUFF, Alan

Nationality: New Zealander. **Born:** Rotorua, 26 October 1950. **Education:** Two years of high school. **Family:** Married Joanna

Harper; two sons and three daughters. **Awards:** PEN Best First Book award, 1991. **Agent:** William Morris Agency, 1350 Avenue of the Americas, New York, New York 10019, U.S.A.

PUBLICATIONS

Novels

Once Were Warriors. Auckland, Tandem Press, 1990; Honolulu, University of Hawaii Press, 1994; London, Random House, 1995.
One Night Out Stealing. Auckland, Tandem Press, 1991; Honolulu, University of Hawaii Press, 1992.
State Ward. Auckland, Vintage, 1994.

Other

Maori: The Crisis and the Challenge. Auckland, HarperCollins, 1993.

*

Alan Duff comments:
Main influence: Contemporary American, Faulkner, Selby Jr., Doctorow, Gurganis, Styron.

*   *   *

Alan Duff is the enfant terrible of contemporary Maori novelists. Like Witi Ihimaera and Patricia Grace he focuses on the debilitating effect urban life has had on Maori. But the violent, drunken underworld of *Once Were Warriors* and *One Night Out Stealing* makes the cityscapes of Grace and Ihimaera look positively genteel. Even the violence of Keri Hulme's *The Bone People* is quite different in kind and ultimately less threatening, in that it is a personal idiosyncrasy rather than a generic phenomenon.

Duff's formula for resolving the problems of the urban Maori is likewise very distinctive. In his journalism and in his book-length survey of Maoridom, *Maori: The Crisis and the Challenge,* he has stressed the need for orthodox Western education, and—putting into practice Beth's dreams in the opening pages of *Once Were Warriors*—he has personally instigated a campaign to get books into every underprivileged Maori household. Conversely he is wont to express contempt for many aspects of traditional Maori culture—though there have been signs recently of some softening in his attitudes.

Duff's politically incorrect views are most clearly reflected in his novels in Grace Heke's excursions from the Pine Block ghetto to gaze on the plush Trambert house in *Once Were Warriors* and in Sonny's much more intimate inspection of the Harland mansion in *One Night Out Stealing.* Typically Duff exaggerates the gap between these two worlds. The Harlands and the Tramberts, with their love of fine music, art, and furniture, are extreme examples of Pakeha patrician taste, and the deep impression that their music in particular makes on the deprived Maori onlookers gets dangerously close to sentimentality.

However, Pakeha are not depicted entirely uncritically in Duff's work. The men in particular have their shortcomings, ranging from Mr Harland's penchant for pornographic pictures to the outright pedophilia of Mr Dekka in *State Ward.* And in *One Night Out Steal-*

ing the hardened recidivist, Jube McCall, is a Pakeha, while his softer side-kick, Sonny Mahia, is Maori.

In fact Duff's novels, more clearly than his journalism, do explore specifically Maori solutions for the Maori problems which he illustrates so graphically—solutions that are ultimately much closer to those proposed by Ihimaera, Grace, and Hulme than Duff the journalist would have us believe.

Towards the end of *Once Were Warriors* Beth reestablishes contact with her *marae* in the countryside, just outside the city where the rest of the action takes place: Twin Lakes (presumably a fictional verson of Rotorua—not Auckland, where the film of the novel is set). The funeral of her daughter Grace takes place on this *marae,* presided over by "the paramount chief of the tribe," Te Tupaea. And a little later, after Beth has succeeded in throwing her aggressive husband Jake out of the house, she brings to town "a village committee," including Te Tupaea, to help her reestablish a sense of mission among the Pine Block Maori.

Beth's "project" is ostensibly a very practical one; she attempts to wean her people away from their reliance on state funding (notably the unemployment benefit) and to foster instead a spirit of "self-help." So, for example, she organises the building of "a changing room and shower block" for a "newly ploughed and sown rugby field" conveniently donated by the benevolent Trambert family.

However, all this practical "self-help" is underpinned by a strong dedication to traditional Maori culture, though it is the more aggressive aspects of that culture (the "warrior" heritage, particularly as exemplified in the *haka*) that are emphasised most. So, although this novel eventually embraces a kind of primitivism, like the novels and stories of Ihimaera, Grace, and Hulme, Duff's is a harder form of primitivism than theirs.

In fact it is not always easy to distinguish between the admirable aggression of the traditional "warriors" and the degenerate aggression of Jake Heke and his drunken mates. This confusion becomes particularly troubling in the final pages of the book, where scenes from Beth's "project" alternate with scenes from the last days in the life of Beth's son Nig, who has joined a Maori gang (the Brown Fists). The gang violence is presumably meant to act as a foil for the noble primitivism of the *haka,* but it is hard not to sense a deep kinship between the two. In fact the film of *Once Were Warriors* presented the gang in a very positive light.

Meanwhile, in the background, the exiled Jake Heke, growing wiser as he lives rough and consorts with other down-and-outs, looks like a more realistic hope for the future. As a detached observer of Maori culture he actually occupies a position somewhat similar to Duff's own.

One Night Out Stealing has less to say about traditional Maori culture, but *State Ward* is built around the kind of liberating journey from city to country that features in the work of many Maori authors. George, a native Maori speaker, helps Charlie to escape from Riverton Boys' Home, where they have both been confined, and takes him back, not to Charlie's home in Twin Lakes, but to the Maori heartland of Ruapotiki (evidently a place not far away from the Waituhi of Ihimaera's novels). Here George burns down the house haunted by the evil spirit (*kehua*) that has dogged his career hitherto, and celebrates the pair's "freedom."

To convey the tough concerns of his novels Duff has developed a strikingly idiomatic and hard-hitting form of interior monologue that is flexible enough (particularly in *One Night Out Stealing*) to accommodate varying states of inebriation and drug use in the characters. *State Ward* is generally regarded as his weakest novel because of its departure from this confrontational style. There are, however, two good reasons for this: the book deals with younger characters than its predecessors, and it was originally written for radio, which requires a more accessible presentation.

—Richard Corballis

DUFFY, Maureen (Patricia)

Nationality: British. **Born:** Worthing, Sussex, 21 October 1933. **Education:** Trowbridge High School for Girls, Wiltshire; Sarah Bonnell High School for Girls; King's College, London, 1953-56, B.A. (honours) in English 1956. **Career:** Schoolteacher for five years. Co-founder, Writers Action Group, 1972; joint chair, 1977-78, and president, 1985-89, Writers Guild of Great Britain; chair, Greater London Arts Literature Panel, 1979-81; vice-chair, 1981-86, and since 1989 chair, British Copyright Council; since 1982 chair, Authors Lending and Copyright Society; vice-president, Beauty Without Cruelty; fiction editor *Critical Quarterly,* Manchester, 1987; since 1992 vice-president, European Writers Congress. **Awards:** City of London Festival Playwright's prize, 1962; Arts Council bursary, 1963, 1966, 1975; Society of Authors travelling scholarship, 1976. Fellow, Royal Society of Literature, 1985. **Agent:** Jonathan Clowes Ltd., Ironbridge House, Bridge Approach, London NW1 8BD. **Address:** 18 Fabian Road, London SW6 7TZ, England.

PUBLICATIONS

Novels

That's How It Was. London, Hutchinson, 1962; New York, Dial Press, 1984.
The Single Eye. London, Hutchinson, 1964.
The Microcosm. London, Hutchinson, and New York, Simon and Schuster, 1966.
The Paradox Players. London, Hutchinson, 1967; New York, Simon and Schuster, 1968.
Wounds. London, Hutchinson, and New York, Knopf, 1969.
Love Child. London, Weidenfeld and Nicolson, and New York, Knopf, 1971.
I Want to Go to Moscow: A Lay. London, Hodder and Stoughton, 1973; as *All Heaven in a Rage,* New York, Knopf, 1973.
Capital. London, Cape, 1975; New York, Braziller, 1976.
Housespy. London, Hamish Hamilton, 1978.
Gor Saga. London, Eyre Methuen, 1981; New York, Viking Press, 1982.
Scarborough Fear (as D.M. Cayer). London, Macdonald, 1982.
Londoners: An Elegy. London, Methuen, 1983.
Change. London, Methuen, 1987.
Illuminations. London, Sinclair Stevenson, 1991.
Occam's Razor. London, Sinclair Stevenson, 1993.

Plays

The Lay-Off (produced London, 1962).
The Silk Room (produced Watford, Hertfordshire, 1966).

Rites (produced London, 1969). Published in *New Short Plays 2,* London, Methuen, 1969.
Solo, Old Thyme (produced Cambridge, 1970).
A Nightingale in Bloomsbury Square (produced London, 1973). Published in *Factions,* edited by Giles Gordon and Alex Hamilton, London, Joseph, 1974.

Radio Play: *Only Goodnight,* 1981.

Television Play: *Josie,* 1961.

Poetry

Lyrics for the Dog Hour. London, Hutchinson, 1968.
The Venus Touch. London, Weidenfeld and Nicolson, 1971.
Actaeon. Rushden, Northamptonshire, Sceptre Press, 1973.
Evesong. London, Sappho, 1975.
Memorials of the Quick and the Dead. London, Hamish Hamilton, 1979.
Collected Poems. London, Hamish Hamilton, 1985.

Other

The Erotic World of Faery. London, Hodder and Stoughton, 1972.
The Passionate Shepherdess: Aphra Behn 1640-1689. London, Cape, 1977; New York, Avon, 1979.
Inherit the Earth: A Social History. London, Hamish Hamilton, 1980.
Men and Beasts: An Animal Rights Handbook. London, Paladin, 1984.
A Thousand Capricious Chances: A History of the Methuen List 1889-1989. London, Methuen, 1989.

Editor, with Alan Brownjohn, *New Poetry 3.* London, Arts Council, 1977.
Editor, *Oroonoko and Other Stories,* by Aphra Behn. London, Methuen, 1986.
Editor, *Love Letters Between a Nobleman and His Sister,* by Aphra Behn. London, Virago Press, 1987.
Editor, *Five Plays,* by Aphra Behn. London, Methuen, 1990.

Translator, *A Blush of Shame,* by Domenico Rea. London, Barrie and Rockliff, 1968.

*

Manuscript Collection: King's College, University of London.

Critical Study: *A Female Vision of the City* by Christine Sizemore, Knoxville, University of Tennessee Press, 1989.

*   *   *

Maureen Duffy is a prolific novelist, poet, and playwright whose work has consistently developed in range and importance. *That's How It Was* won her immediate acclaim for its simplicity and forcefulness. It is a moving account of the relationship between a mother and daughter; their existence is poor, insecure, even brutal, but transcended by mutual love. "I grew six inches under the light touch of her hand," explains the narrator. The little girl has an acute sense of social isolation and a fierce loyalty to the one constant figure in her universe; her mother's death is thus cause for more than grief, it brings total despair. The loneliness, restlessness, and sexual hunger which spring from the situation are the dominating themes of each subsequent novel.

Realism is the touchstone of Duffy's style; like many other observers of working-class life, she is at her best when she relies on accurate, detailed reportage and at her weakest when tempted by sentiment. *The Paradox Players* is an example of her writing at its most compelling. It describes a man's retreat from society to live for some months in a boat moored on the Thames. The physical realities of cold, snow, rats, and flooding occupy him continually and the hardship brings him peace. He is a novelist, suffering from the hazards peculiar to that profession and has some pertinent comments to make about the vulnerability of the writer. "When I saw the reviews I could have cut my throat. You see they're very kind to first novels for some mistaken reason but when the poor bastard follows it up with a second and they see he really means it they tear its guts out." The experience of winter on the river restores his faith in his own ability to survive.

Duffy's observations are acute, her use of dialogue witty and direct; this authenticity is complemented by an interest in the bizarre, the fantastic. Her best-known book uses these qualities to great effect in a study of lesbian society which is both informative and original. *The Microcosm* begins and ends in a club where the central characters meet to dance, dress up, and escape from the necessity of "all the week wearing a false face." Their fantasies are played out in front of the juke box; then the narrative follows each woman back into her disguise, her social role. Steve is Miss Stephens, a schoolmistress; Cathy is a bus conductress; Matt works in a garage. Their predicament as individuals, the author suggests, extends beyond the interest of their own minority group. A plea is made for tolerance, understanding, and that respect without which the human spirit must perish. "Society isn't a simple organism with one nucleus and a fringe of little feet, it's an infinitely complex structure and if you try to suppress any part . . . you diminish, you mutilate the whole." *Wounds* and *Love Child* reaffirm this belief.

—Judy Cooke

DUNDY, Elaine

Nationality: American. **Born:** New York City, 1927. **Education:** Sweet Briar College, Virginia. **Family:** Married the writer Kenneth Tynan in 1951 (marriage dissolved 1964); one daughter. **Career:** Actress; worked for the BBC, London; directed the Winter Workshop of the Berkshire Festival; also journalist. **Agent:** Andrew Hewson, John Johnson Ltd., 45-47 Clerkenwell Green, London EC1R 0HT, England.

PUBLICATIONS

Novels

The Dud Avocado. London, Gollancz, and New York, Dutton, 1958.
The Old Man and Me. London, Gollancz, and New York, Dutton, 1964.
The Injured Party. London, Joseph, 1974.

Uncollected Short Stories

"The Sound of a Marriage," in *Queen* (London), 1965.
"Death in the Country," in *Vogue* (New York), 1974.

Plays

My Place (produced London, 1962). London, Gollancz, 1962; New York, French, 1963.
Death in the Country, and The Drowning (produced New York, 1976).

Screenplay: *Life Sign,* 1975.

Other

Finch, Bloody Finch. London, Joseph, and New York, Holt Rinehart, 1980.
Elvis and Gladys: The Genesis of the King. New York, Macmillan, and London, Weidenfeld and Nicolson, 1985.
Ferriday, Louisiana. New York, Fine, 1990.

*   *   *

In *The Dud Avocado* and *The Old Man and Me,* Elaine Dundy employs first-person, reflective narrators who self-consciously and self-indulgently record and evaluate their experiences in Paris and Soho. The narrators relate their stories in a candid, energetic, witty style, spiced with parenthetical revelations, word association games, and sensory impressions. Their language is often the jargon of the Beat-hipster; audacious, flippant, nervous, saucy. Their tone is the good-humored self-mockery of the cocktail party confession, the stage whisper, the open diary. The narrators are deliberate storytellers, replaying moments from their pasts, exposing their naivety and limitations, and benefiting from hindsight.

Sally Jay in *The Dud Avocado* is the contemporary American innocent abroad, superficially hip to the decadent Left Bank and "running for her life." Caught in the ambiguity between naivety and sophistication, she is in pursuit of "freedom" and the ability "to be so sharp that I'll always be able to guess right . . . on the wing." She expends her time and innocence in a disorganized, impulsive debauch with the avant-garde of Paris.

Through a series of wrong guesses, she eventually is schooled in the ways of the world. The glamorous, daring, free world of Paris is revealed as pretentious, opportunistic, grotesque. Her romantic vision of the rebellious life is destroyed when she understands that her would-be lover is a pimp and that her life in Paris has exposed her to "too much prostitution." She declares herself a dud avocado—a seed without life potential.

In flight to Hollywood, the narrator confronts her runaway life strategy and determines that some "unrunning" is called for to "[lay] the ghost once and for all." She seeks out the role of librarian and schools herself in cynicism until she recognizes the life which she wishes to embrace. Giddy with optimism, she accepts the love and marriage proposal of a famous photographer and embarks on a new life with "an entirely new passport," the new self emerging from the old like the growth of an avocado seedling from the stone of the old fruit: "It's zymotic!" The narrator survives her initiation experience ready to "Make voyages. Attempt them. That's all there is."

Betsy Lou in *The Old Man and Me* is older and more experienced than Sally Jay, but like Sally Jay, she is on a quest which leads to greater self-knowledge. Motivated by puerile revenge, she journeys to London to recover her "stolen" inheritance from C.D. McKee. As his unknown heir, she plans to hasten the recovery of her money by any means necessary—lying, cheating, masquerading, or attempting murder. She partially achieves her declared end, and in the process realizes her injustice to those in her past, the reasons for the loss of her father's love, and her love for C.D. despite his age and possession of her money. Thus she corrects her mistaken view of her past and sees the futility of trying to salve emotional loss with money.

Betsy Lou's relationship to C.D. is never linear and controllable. The very complexity of the relationship betrays her ambiguity over her past, her present motives, and her unconscious needs. She loves/hates him, recognizes that he is/is not a father figure, accepts/rejects him as teacher, is repulsed/excited by his lust, and wishes him dead/fears for his life. This confusion drives her to abandonment in jazz, drink, dope, and sex, which results in C.D.'s collapse and her self-confrontation and confession.

Betsy Lou's declaration of her identity, her deceit, and her desire for C.D. comes too late. He rejects the contrite Betsy Lou, gives her fifty percent of her money, and leaves her with the advice that she "use it. See its power to corrupt or save. . . . Learn from our stupidities." She is left with what she initially wanted "only . . . because it was mine."

In both novels the narrators are left at the point of departure. For Sally Jay the future appears glorious with possibility. She sees her new life as "the end. The end. The last word." However, the author implies that Sally Jay has ended one cycle of learning experiences and is beginning another with her marriage. One is reminded of Stefan's description of the Typical American Girl as the avocado, "So green—so eternally green." She has experienced growth and is more worldly wise, but her final pronouncement indicates that her maturation is not complete. The process has just begun. Similarly, Betsy Lou is left facing her future. She hasn't Sally Jay's confidence of joy, but rather experiences a sense of unreality. She has no delusions about the future, and the past "seems (to) never really (have) happened." She is no longer directed by spurious monetary goals; instead she suffers the bewilderment of a hollow victory. Thus, while both narrators experience an epiphany, that moment of awareness is tinged with irony.

Dundy is an entertaining novelist who rehearses the familiar theme of initiation with adeptness and flair. However, her craftsmanship and energy do not always compensate for her characters' lack of psychological depth nor for her rather formulaic situations. Her novels do not provoke new or refined insights, but they do provide moments of engaging and refreshing humor.

—Deborah Duckworth

DUNN, Nell (Mary)

Nationality: British. **Born:** London in 1936. **Education:** A convent school. **Family:** Married the writer Jeremy Sandford in 1956 (marriage dissolved); three sons. **Awards:** Rhys Memorial prize, 1964; Susan Smith Blackburn prize, for play, 1981; *Evening Standard* award, for play, 1982; Society of West End Theatre award, 1982. **Agent:** Curtis Brown, 162-168 Regent Street, London W1R 5TB.

PUBLICATIONS

Novels

Poor Cow. London, MacGibbon and Kee, and New York, Doubleday, 1967.
The Incurable. London, Cape, and New York, Doubleday, 1971.
I Want, with Adrian Henri. London, Cape, 1972.
Tear His Head Off His Shoulders. London, Cape, 1974; New York, Doubleday, 1975.
The Only Child: A Simple Story of Heaven and Hell. London, Cape, 1978.

Short Stories

Up the Junction. London, MacGibbon and Kee, 1963; Philadelphia, Lippincott, 1966.

Plays

Steaming (produced London, 1981; Stamford, Connecticut, and New York, 1982). Ambergate, Derbyshire, Amber Lane Press, 1981; New York, Limelight, 1984.
Sketches in *Variety Night* (produced London, 1982).
I Want, with Adrian Henri, adaptation of their own novel (produced Liverpool, 1983; London, 1986).
The Little Heroine (produced Southampton, 1988).

Screenplay: *Poor Cow,* with Ken Loach, 1967.

Television Plays: *Up the Junction,* from her own stories, 1965; *Every Breath You Take,* 1988.

Other

Talking to Women. London, MacGibbon and Kee, 1965.
Freddy Gets Married (for children). London, MacGibbon and Kee, 1969.
Grandmothers Talking to Nell Dunn. London, Chatto and Windus, 1991.

Editor, *Living Like I Do.* London, Futura, 1977; as *Different Drummers,* New York, Harcourt Brace, 1977.

* * *

Nell Dunn begins with vignettes or fragmental episodes to build a picture of British urban life. Much like Charles Dickens, with his newspaper sketches and small portraits of London street life, she began her career with a set of brilliant realistic snapshots of the mod world. In *Up the Junction* she collected these sketches, which in effect are much like the 17th-century Theophrastan "character." They deal primarily with young working-class Britons in their milieu, incised in photographic reportage, built on their dialect, street signs, bits of popular music, the clichés and repetitious folk-wisdom of ghetto life. The feeling for the nagging, obstinate details of daily life is very strong—the sketches demonstrate how complex yet unrewarding most of these lives can be.

In *Poor Cow* Dunn develops the same method of terse, richly detailed sketches into a more unified form, a novel centering on the life of one young woman. Ironically named Joy, she becomes a "poor cow" through the constant erosion of her life. At 22 she has gone through one luckless marriage, and her life moves centrifugally around Jonny, her son. Joy drifts into casual prostitution, random affairs with anchorless men. She worries constantly about her looks, her body, her sexual responsiveness, the prospects of aging. Life is intractable, and wishes evaporate in the face of simple necessities. Joy's role as a mother is a transference of her egocentrism to Jonny, as an extension of her former hopes for herself. Her own life has run down a blind alley, but her son's life may be different. As she clings to Jonny, Joy invents a bitter epitaph for her youth: "To think when I was a kid I planned to conquer the world and if anyone saw me now they'd say, 'She's had a rough night, poor cow.'"

A vision of the confusion and oppressiveness of modern life is extended in *The Incurable*, which deals with a middle-class woman, Maro, whose life collapses in crisis. Maro's husband develops multiple sclerosis, and her formerly orderly and manageable existence is destroyed. She falls into a state of anomie which, like her husband's progressive disease, eats up her life. She too is "incurable," although her malaise is mental and spiritual. Her children's cannibalistic demands and the relentless pressure of everyday routine erode her will and energy: "She felt like some country that had been oppressed for a long time and was slowly rising up and throwing over its oppressors. She was making a revolution but the bloodshed was horrifying and how many lives would be lost and when was it going to end and would she ever make the country of the free spirits?"

Tear His Head Off His Shoulders is another set of related vignettes and episodes in the lives of women. The narrative revolves around the sexual obsessions and conflicts of women, viewed in retrospect. The vernacular style and complex combination of nostalgia and revulsion give a bittersweet flavor to the work. A strong "fascination of the abomination" feeling makes the stories of sexual compulsion convincing.

In *The Only Child* Dunn constructs a novel again focused on sexual obsession and possessiveness—of a mother for her son. We follow Esther Lafonte through Dunn's careful sensual details as she drifts from her over-comfortable marriage to a search for her identity—sexual and spiritual—in her 19-year-old son, Piers. At one point she speaks for all of Dunn's lost women: "I want to get in, I want to be somebody, I have a feeling that I could have done very much more with my life, that I could be doing more now, I want to be a part of things."

Dunn's special province is the mind and spirit of the beleaguered woman—a view from the "oppressed country" of the woman trapped by circumstances. The vignettes she presents deal with developing sexuality, the allure of the pop world, the deadly immobility of domestic responsibilities. Her recent fiction extends this vision to the perimeters of middle-class life.

—William J. Schafer

DUNNE, John Gregory

Nationality: American. **Born:** Hartford, Connecticut, 25 May 1932. **Education:** Princeton University, New Jersey, A.B. in English 1954. Married Joan Didion, *q.v.,* in 1964; one daughter. **Career:** Staff writer, *Time*, New York, 5 years; columnist ("Points West"), with

Didion, *Saturday Evening Post,* Philadelphia, 1967-69; regular contributor, *Esquire* and the *New York Review of Books.* **Agent:** Janklow and Nesbit, 598 Madison Ave., New York, New York 10022, U.S.A.

PUBLICATIONS

Novels

Vegas: A Memoir of a Dark Season. New York, Random House, and London, Quartet, 1974.
True Confessions. New York, Dutton, 1977; London, Weidenfeld and Nicolson, 1978.
Dutch Shea, Jr. New York, Simon and Schuster, and London, Weidenfeld and Nicolson, 1982.
The Red, White and Blue. New York, Simon and Schuster, and London, Weidenfeld and Nicolson, 1987.
Playland. New York, Random House, 1994; London, Granta, 1995.

Plays

Screenplays (with Joan Didion): *Panic in Needle Park,* 1971; *Play It as It Lays,* 1972; *A Star Is Born,* also with Frank Pierson, 1976; *True Confessions,* 1981; *Hills Like White Elephants,* 1992; *Broken Trust,* 1995; *Up Close and Personal,* 1995.

Other

Delano: The Story of the California Grape Strike, photographs by Ted Streshinsky. New York, Farrar Straus, 1967; revised edition, 1971.
The Studio. New York, Farrar Straus, 1967; London, W.H. Allen, 1970.
Quintana and Friends (essays). New York, Dutton, 1978.
Harp. New York, Simon and Schuster, 1989.
Crooning. New York, Simon and Schuster, 1991.

*   *   *

His wife and sometime collaborator, Joan Didion, is undoubtedly better known than he, but John Gregory Dunne certainly deserves a measure of critical attention. Like his wife he has carved out a successful career as a versatile writer.

In addition to novels he has written essays, articles, columns, and books of contemporary journalism that combine objective observation with a generous quantity of personal display, confession, and self analysis. Whatever his subject, method, or venue of publication, he generally returns over and over again to his family history, financial standing, and ethnic and religious background: Hartford, Connecticut, apparently prosperous, middle-class, Irish Catholic.

The numerous essays, articles, and columns, (the early ones written with his wife), cover a large range of subjects that challenge the writer not only eager to speak his mind, but also desperate to meet deadlines and make an honest buck; many of them, nevertheless, are penetrating, intelligent, and informative. Luckily, Dunne has strong opinions on a great many subjects and can communicate those opinions clearly, forcefully, and often humorously; he has a keen eye for sham and hypocrisy and a constructive sense of rage and outrage. His early columns tend to reflect something of the sweet haze of the 1960s, but the later ones show a more characteristic tone of weary, cynical anger creeping into his voice.

In one of the most useful books about the business of making movies, *The Studio,* Dunne provides not only important information but also a valuable corrective to the highflown nonsense of film theorists and critics about the art of film.

Dunne's very personal confessional style surfaces most obviously in *Vegas,* the record of his recovery from a nervous breakdown, a subject roughly akin to Melville's Great White Whale for contemporary writers, and in *Harp,* an impressionistic memoir that begins with a brother's suicide, chronicles a number of deaths in his family, and culminates in his own cardio-vascular troubles. Because it also discusses other matters, including some of the fascinating processes of the author's own methods, it is actually somewhat more interesting than it sounds. For the son of a Hartford surgeon who attended private schools and graduated from Princeton, Dunne rather overdoes the Studs Lonigan role; for readers from the working class, he hardly seems the rough diamond of the tough, impoverished Irish ghetto. In *Harp* the generative narcissism of any writer finally gives way to the self pity of a poseur.

His novels clearly benefit from his journalism, since they also turn on the same subjects that engage his nonfiction, exploring with a good deal more energy and bite contemporary American politics and public behavior and the variousness of Irish American life. *True Confessions, Dutch Shea, Jr.,* and *The Red, White and Blue* reflect that variousness with some of the sensitivity and accuracy of a novelist of manners in the mold of John O'Hara. They constitute a contemporary trilogy that in this case perhaps really does deserve comparison with James T. Farrell's monumental *Studs Lonigan;* certainly Dunne seems to be the only American writer, except for Norman Mailer, still concerned with the Irish experience.

Dunne himself has stated that the three books attempt to show some of the history of the levels, from working class to upper class, that the Irish inhabit in America and how they have fared in this century. As a result, they concern themselves with historical events, from a famous murder case to national politics, in the public arena, while examining the lives and fortunes of some particular families. They also examine the traditional figures of Irish American life, literature, and cinema—policemen, priests, and politicians. In the process, his books touch on some of the major public events of the last 50 years.

True Confessions is based on the notorious unsolved Black Dahlia murder case of the 1940s, and uses one of those brother combinations of 1930s movies—Tom Spellacy, a detective, and Desmond, a priest. The fascinating murder investigation opens up a complicated tangle of religion, politics, and corruption in Los Angeles, a story told in the tough, cynical, funny, and wised-up manner of traditional American gangster and detective fiction. It is a brilliant, moving, and heartfelt performance, far superior to anything else Dunne has written. Less successful, *Dutch Shea, Jr.* revolves around the personal and public tragedy of a criminal lawyer's loss of his daughter, coyly hinting at but holding off the completion of its haunting and horrific background subject. Like *True Confessions,* however, the book handles its characters and especially its dialogue with considerable skill and confidence; it addresses, sometimes with defensive humor, the daily curse of criminality and the horrors of terrorism. The third volume of the trilogy, *The Red, White and Blue* reads at times like a *roman à clef* based on the history of some of the most successful Irish families in America, which of course means the Kellys and the Kennedys. With considerable ambition, the book takes aim at the all too familiar hypoc-

risy, horror, and tragedy of the waning decades of the 20th century—the culpability of politicians, the waste of war, the conspiracies of the media. This novel repeats the cynicism of the first two, but goes far beyond, to achieve a tone and a conclusion of utter despair, which though appropriate to its subject may signal the depths of the author's own reaction to contemporary American life.

Dunne's ethnicity, worn like a flag, seems somewhat anachronistic in a time when his fellow Irish Americans have practically become WASPs. At the same time, it has generated three good novels, some autobiographical writing, and numerous articles and essays, which means the concept remains useful to the writer, a notion that automatically endows it with meaning and value. The subject may no longer possess its former richness, however, and the author may have to look elsewhere. He may have now reached something of a crossroads in his career.

His bestselling novels and several screenplays have enabled him to enjoy some of the material rewards of the literary life that elude so many other writers, but like so many successful people in any field of endeavor, he has begun to question the importance and validity of his success. His new awareness of his own mortality, the serial losses of a number of loved ones, his own inherent cynicism, and perhaps even a certain Irish bitterness and melancholy have induced a gloom that his wisecracking cannot lighten. Any further success with fiction will depend on whether he can conquer the depression that imbues his recent nonfiction; at present, he appears to be overwhelmed by the sadness of both his own and his nation's recent history.

—George Grella

DUNNETT, (Lady) Dorothy

Nationality: British. **Born:** Dorothy Halliday in Dunfermline, Fife, 25 August 1923. **Education:** James Gillespie's High School, Edinburgh; Edinburgh College of Art; Glasgow School of Art. **Family:** Married Alastair (later Sir Alastair) M. Dunnett in 1946; two sons. **Career:** Assistant press officer, Scottish government departments, Edinburgh, 1940-46; member of the Board of Trade Scottish Economics Department, Glasgow, 1946-55; non-executive director, Scottish Television plc, Glasgow, 1979-92. Since 1950 professional portrait painter; since 1986 trustee, National Library of Scotland; since 1990 a direcctor of the Edinburgh Book Festival. **Awards:** Scottish Arts Council award, 1976; St. Andrews Presbyterian College award, Laurinburg, North Carolina, 1993. Fellow, Royal Society of Arts, 1986. **Agent:** Curtis Brown, 162-168 Regent Street, London W1R 5TB, England. **Address:** 87 Colinton Road, Edinburgh EH10 5DF, Scotland.

PUBLICATIONS

Novels (Dolly books prior to *Bird of Paradise* published as Dorothy Halliday in UK)

The Game of Kings. New York, Putnam, 1961; London, Cassell, 1962.
Queens' Play. London, Cassell, and New York, Putnam, 1964.
The Disorderly Knights. London, Cassell, and New York, Putnam, 1966.

Dolly and the Singing Bird. London, Cassell, 1968; as *The Photogenic Soprano,* Boston, Houghton Mifflin, 1968.

Pawn in Frankincense. London, Cassell, and New York, Putnam, 1969.

Dolly and the Cookie Bird. London, Cassell, 1970; as *Murder in the Round,* Boston, Houghton Mifflin, 1970.

The Ringed Castle. London, Cassell, 1971; New York, Putnam, 1972.

Dolly and the Doctor Bird. London, Cassell, 1971; as *Match for a Murderer,* Boston, Houghton Mifflin, 1971.

Dolly and the Starry Bird. London, Cassell, 1973; as *Murder in Focus,* Boston, Houghton Mifflin, 1973.

Checkmate. London, Cassell, and New York, Putnam, 1975.

Dolly and the Nanny Bird. London, Joseph, 1976; New York, Knopf, 1982.

King Hereafter. London, Joseph, and New York, Knopf, 1982.

Dolly and the Bird of Paradise. London, Joseph, 1983; New York, Knopf, 1984.

Niccolò Rising. London, Joseph, and New York, Knopf, 1986.

The Spring of the Ram. London, Joseph, 1987; New York, Knopf, 1988.

Race of Scorpions. London, Joseph, 1989; New York, Knopf, 1990.

Scales of Gold. London, Joseph, 1991; New York, Knopf, 1992.

Moroccan Traffic. London, Chatto and Windus, 1991; as *Take a Fax to the Kasbah,* New York, Harcourt Brace Jovanovich, 1992.

The Unicorn Hunt. London, Joseph, 1993; New York, Knopf, 1994.

To Lie with Lions. London, Joseph, 1995.

Other

The Scottish Highlands, with Alastair M. Dunnett, photographs by David Paterson. Edinburgh, Mainstream, 1988.

*

Bibliography: In *Book and Magazine Collector 53* (London), August 1988.

Critical Study: *The Dorothy Dunnett Companion* by Elspeth Morrison, London, Joseph, 1994.

*   *   *

Dorothy Dunnett's fame as a best-selling novelist has been built on two major series of historical romances, a long novel on Macbeth which startled and impressed academic historians, and a series of modern thrillers apparently thrown off with ease as a diversion from her other work.

She came comparatively late to writing, having previously established a reputation as a portrait painter and sculptress. This artistic versatility in itself offers clues to her literary achievement. As a painter she has a remarkable ability to create instantly recognizable likenesses. Her sitters are portrayed with nicely calculated chiaroscuro, their faces and figures standing out against closely observed and romantically ordered backgrounds. As a sculptress she controls the modeling of her subjects with skill, shaping her material into volumes that satisfy from whatever angle they are viewed.

Dunnett's first major series, six novels known as the Lymond saga, opens in turbulent 16th-century Scotland, torn by war and intrigue both in its relations with England and in the domestic struggles of its noble families for power at court. This is the period of Henry VIII's rough dynastic wooing of the infant Mary, Queen of Scots, for his son Edward; it is the period also of the Reformation and the clash between the old Catholic order and Protestantism.

The hero of the saga, Francis Crawford of Lymond and later Comte de Sevigny, is condemned as a rebel and forced into exile. The six volumes of the saga recount his clandestine return to Scotland, his quest for the truth about his lineage and rightful inheritance, the adventures which take the wide-ranging story and its characters to France, Russia, Turkey and the Netherlands, and the final denouement of the intricate web of mystery surrounding Lymond's birth. As befits popular romances there is a happy ending; but a great deal goes on before it is delivered.

With each volume of this sprawling tale there is an extraordinary proliferation of sub-plots. The array of major and minor figures, both historical and fictitious, is so numerous that the reader might well get lost in the crowd had the author not prefaced each volume with lists of the leading characters, asterisked if they are her own inventions. Her research into historical events, places, people, their homes, dress and comportment, are so accurate and detailed that the reader can, like the author before starting to write, visit the scenes of the action and, book in hand, calculate the angle of a bow-shot or see where a duel or a lovers' meeting was arranged. Dunnett's stamina in historical and topographical research is indefatigable; and she seemingly cannot bear to throw anything away unused.

In many hands this accumulation of detail would make the story founder. But the author has such energy, such narrative pace, such inventiveness, wit and vitality, that the story is driven forward at breath-taking speed and the reader is kept easily afloat on the running tide of her prose. She has also a deft way with intelligent and witty women and their handling of intelligent, and not so intelligent, men. There is freshness and charm in the love scenes, muscle in the fights and swordplay.

The qualities of the Lymond saga were perceived and promoted by the publisher's editor who discovered *Gone with the Wind.* A suggestion that Dunnett's next novel should be about Mary, Queen of Scots, or Prince Charles Edward Stuart, ground tilled enough by others, was countered with a proposal to write a book about Macbeth. Hardly known to the public apart from the matter of Shakespeare's play, Macbeth and his world were pursued by the author through countless 11th-century sources, including those for Thorfinn, Earl of Orkney, who shared common ancestry with Macbeth and according to some accounts was his foster-brother. Eventually she became convinced that Macbeth and Thorfinn were possibly the same person, presented to the world for reasons of secret intrigue as two individuals. The coincidence of dates and common activities in extending and consolidating the kingdoms of the Northern Isles, Caithness, and Alba into the beginnings of a recognizable Scotland made the identification plausible if not proven beyond doubt. Armed with this historical thesis Dunnett wrote *King Hereafter,* a blockbuster of a novel whose claim to the popular title of saga is greater than that of the Lymond cycle.

Meantime she was also publishing a series of thrillers, revolving around the portrait painter, yachtsman and Secret Service agent Johnson Johnson and his yacht *Dolly.* An enterprising feature of these suspense stories is that each is narrated by the girl in the case—all of whom, it seems, are intimidated and repelled by Johnson's bifocal spectacles. The thrillers with their different narrators' voices are great fun, substituting for the classic car chase some hard sailing in foul weather in seas as far apart as the Caribbean and the Scottish Minches.

Dunnett's second long historical series, published under the generic title *The House of Niccolò,* takes us to the 15th century and the rise of the merchant class in Flanders, France, and Venice, financed by Florentine and Genoese bankers and trading throughout Europe and the Mediterranean. Again there has been a massive accumulation of source material for the detailed *mises-en-scène;* again the characters are highlighted in the foreground of the composition; again the author's sparkling style and swift pace make the work immensely readable. Dunnett fans—and there is now an association of them, known as the Dorothy Dunnett Convention—await each new volume in the series with whetted appetite.

—Stewart Sanderson

DUTTON, Geoffrey (Piers Henry)

Nationality: Australian. **Born:** Anlaby, South Australia, 2 August 1922. **Education:** Geelong Grammar School, Victoria, 1932-39; University of Adelaide, 1940-41; Magdalen College, Oxford, 1946-49, B.A. 1949. **Military Service:** Served in the Royal Australian Air Force, 1941-45: Flight lieutenant. **Family:** Married 1) Ninette Trott in 1944 (divorced 1985), two sons and one daughter; 2) Robin Lucas in 1985. **Career:** Senior lecturer in English, University of Adelaide, 1954-62; Commonwealth Fellow in Australian Literature, University of Leeds, 1960; visiting professor, Kansas State University, Manhattan, 1962. Editor, Penguin Australia, Melbourne, 1961-65, Australian Writers and Their Work series, 1962-66, *Bulletin Literary Supplement,* Sydney, 1980-84, and *Australian Literary Quarterly,* Sydney, 1984-88; editorial director, Sun Books Pty. Ltd., 1965-80. Co-founder, *Australian Letters,* Adelaide, 1957, and *Australian Book Review,* Kensington Park, 1962. **Awards:** Grace Leven prize, 1959. Officer, Order of Australia, 1976. **Member:** Australian Council for the Arts, 1968-70, Commonwealth Literary Fund Advisory Board, 1972-73, and Australian Literature Board, 1973-78. **Agent:** Curtis Brown (Australia) Pty. Ltd., P.O. Box 19, Paddington, New South Wales 2021, Australia.

PUBLICATIONS

Novels

The Mortal and the Marble. London, Chapman and Hall, 1950.
Andy. Sydney and London, Collins, 1968.
Tamara. Sydney and London, Collins, 1970.
Queen Emma of the South Seas. Melbourne and London, Macmillan, and New York, St. Martin's Press, 1976.
The Eye-Opener. St. Lucia, University of Queensland Press, 1982.
Flying Low. St. Lucia, University of Queensland Press, 1992.

Short Stories

The Wedge-Tailed Eagle. Melbourne, Macmillan, 1980.

Poetry

Night Flight and Sunrise. Melbourne, Reed and Harris, 1944.
Antipodes in Shoes. Sydney, Edwards and Shaw, 1958.
Flowers and Fury. Melbourne, Cheshire, 1962.
On My Island: Poems for Children. Melbourne, Cheshire, 1967.
Poems Soft and Loud. Melbourne, Cheshire, 1967.
Findings and Keepings: Selected Poems 1940-1970. Adelaide, Australian Letters, 1970.
New Poems to 1972. Adelaide, Australian Letters, 1972.
A Body of Words. Sydney, Edwards and Shaw, 1977.
Selective Affinities. Sydney, Angus and Robertson, 1985.
New and Selected Poems. Sydney, Angus and Robertson, 1993.

Other

A Long Way South (travel). London, Chapman and Hall, 1953.
Africa and Black and White. London, Chapman and Hall, 1956.
States of the Union (travel). London, Chapman and Hall, 1958.
Founder of a City: The Life of William Light. Melbourne, Cheshire, and London, Chapman and Hall, 1960.
Patrick White. Melbourne, Lansdowne Press, 1961; revised edition, London and New York, Oxford University Press, 1971.
Walt Whitman. Edinburgh, Oliver and Boyd, and New York, Grove Press, 1961.
Paintings of S.T. Gill. Adelaide, Rigby, 1962.
Russell Drysdale (art criticism). London, Thames and Hudson, 1964; revised edition, as *Russell Drysdale: A Biographical and Critical Study,* Sydney and London, Angus and Robertson, 1981.
Tisi and the Yabby (for children). Sydney and London, Collins, 1965.
Seal Bay (for children). Sydney and London, Collins, 1966.
The Hero as Murderer: The Life of Edward John Eyre, Australian Explorer and Governor of Jamaica, 1815-1901. Melbourne, Cheshire, and London, Collins, 1967.
Tisi and the Pageant (for children). Adelaide, Rigby, 1968.
Australia's Last Explorer: Ernest Giles. London, Faber, 1970.
Australia since the Camera: From Federation to War 1901-1904. Melbourne, Cheshire, 1972.
White on Black: The Australian Aborigine Portrayed in Art. Melbourne, Macmillan, 1974.
A Taste of History: Geoffrey Dutton's South Australia. Adelaide, Rigby, 1978.
Patterns of Australia, photographs by Harri Peccinotti. Melbourne and London, Macmillan, 1981.
Impressions of Singapore, photographs by Harri Peccinotti. Melbourne and London, Macmillan, 1981.
S.T. Gill's Australia. Melbourne, Macmillan, 1981.
The Australian Heroes. Sydney, Angus and Robertson, 1981; London, Angus and Robertson, 1982.
The Prowler (for children). Sydney, Collins, 1982.
Country Life in Old Australia. South Yarra, Victoria, O'Neill, 1982.
In Search of Edward John Eyre. Melbourne, Macmillan, 1982.
Out in the Open: An Autobiography. St. Lucia, University of Queensland Press, 1984.
Snow on the Saltbush: The Australian Literary Experience. Ringwood, Victoria, Viking, 1984.
The Australian Collection: Australia's Greatest Books. Sydney, Angus and Robertson, 1985.
The Squatters: An Illustrated History of Australia's Pastoral Pioneers. South Yarra, Victoria, O'Neill, 1985.

Sun, Sea, Surf, and Sand: The Myth of the Beach. Melbourne, Oxford University Press, 1985.

The Innovators: The Sydney Alternatives in the Rise of Modern Art, Literature, and Ideas. Melbourne, Macmillan, 1986.

The Book of Australian Islands. Melbourne, Macmillan, 1986.

Kenneth Slessor. Gosford, New South Wales, Ashton Scholastic, 1987.

Arthur Streeton 1867-1943: A Biographical Sketch. Brisbane, Oz, 1987.

Tom Roberts 1856-1931: A Biographical Sketch. Brisbane, Oz, 1987.

Famous Australian Art: Frederick McCubbin. Brisbane, Oz, 1987.

Henry Lawson. Gosford, New South Wales, Ashton Scholastic, 1988.

Waterways of Sydney: A Sketchbook. Melbourne, Dent, 1988.

Kanga Creek: Havelock Ellis in Australia. Sydney, Pan, 1989.

Russell Drysdale 1912-1981: A Biographical Sketch. Moorebank, New South Wales, Mallard Press, 1989.

Images of Melbourne: A Sketchbook, illustrated by Kay Stewart. Ferntree Gully, Victoria, Houghton Mifflin, 1989.

Kenneth Slessor: A Biography. Ringwood, Victoria, Viking, 1991.

Country Childhoods. St. Lucia, University of Queensland Press, 1992.

Editor, *The Literature of Australia.* Melbourne, Penguin, 1964; revised edition, 1976, 1985.

Editor, *Modern Australian Writing.* London, Fontana, 1966.

Editor, *Australia and the Monarchy: A Symposium.* Melbourne, Sun, 1966.

Editor, with Max Harris, *The Vital Decade: 10 Years of Australian Art and Letters.* Melbourne, Sun, 1968.

Editor, with Max Harris, *Australia's Censorship Crisis.* Melbourne, Sun, 1970.

Editor, *The Australian Uppercrust Book.* Melbourne, Sun, 1971.

Editor, with Max Harris, *Sir Henry Bjelke, Don Baby, and Friends.* Melbourne, Sun, 1971.

Editor, *Australian Verse from 1805: A Continuum.* Adelaide, Rigby, 1975.

Editor, *Republican Australia?* Melbourne, Sun, 1977.

Editor, *The Illustrated Treasury of Australian Stories.* Melbourne, Nelson, 1986.

Editor, *The Australian Bedside Book: A Selection of Writings from the Australian Literary Supplement.* Melbourne, Macmillan, 1987.

Editor, *The Poetic Language: An Anthology of Great Poems of the English Speaking World.* Melbourne, Macmillan, 1987.

Translator, with Igor Mezhakoff-Koriakin, *Bratsk Station,* by Yevgeny Yevtushenko. Melbourne, Sun, 1966; New York, Doubleday, 1967; London, Hart Davis, 1968.

Translator, with Igor Mezhakoff-Koriakin, *Fever and Other New Poems,* by Bella Akhmadulina. Melbourne, Sun, 1968; New York, Morrow, 1969; London, Owen, 1970.

Translator, with Igor Mezhakoff-Koriakin, *Little Woods: Recent Poems,* by Andrei Voznesensky. Melbourne, Sun, 1972.

Translator, *Kazan University and Other New Poems,* by Yevgeny Yevtushenko. Melbourne, Sun, 1973.

*

Manuscript Collection: Australian National Library, Canberra.

Geoffrey Dutton comments:

(1972) My three novels, although completely different in characters and in settings, have all basically dealt with the same theme, that of Australian innocence as against the experience of "older" countries. In more detail, *The Mortal and the Marble* deals with the impact of European migrants on Australia after the second world war; *Andy* with the idiocy of war, especially in a country on whose soil it is never fought: *Tamara* with the impact on an intelligent but relatively unsophisticated Australian scientist of the complex world of Soviet Russian poetry.

(1986) *Queen Emma of the South Seas,* a fictionalized account of an historical figure, deals with Emma Coe, a Samoan-American, who in the late 19th century from a trading-post in what became German New Guinea established a commercial empire in the South-West Pacific. *The Eye-Opener* is a satirical novel about two confidence-men and the Adelaide Festival of Arts.

* * *

Geoffrey Dutton is one of Australia's most versatile writers: poet, biographer, novelist, short story writer, editor, travel writer, literary and art critic and essayist. His biographies include those of two of Australia's most famous explorers, Edward John Eyre and Ernest Giles.

Dutton's six novels to date reflect this versatility and a cosmopolitanism that stems from his upbringing as the son of one of South Australia's pioneer colonizers and pastoralists; his education at Oxford University; his wide travels, about which he has written extensively; and, especially, his several sojourns in Russia where he established friendships with, and eventually published translations of the work of the poets Yevgeny Yevtushenko and Anna Akhmatova.

Dutton's first and the least considerable of his novels, *The Mortal and the Marble,* with an Anglo-Australian setting, is partly the story of a young marriage and partly a study of national differences. But he was on sure ground with his next novel, *Andy,* a lively, picaresque tale of a devil-may-care flying instructor, set against Northern Australia and the Pacific during World War II and based on Dutton's own experiences as a pilot in the Royal Australian Air Force.

As a novel that explores the sheer beauty and exhilaration of flying it invites comparison with the similar writing of Saint-Exupéry. Andy's is an enduring portrait of a born leader, whether of the pious, intellectual fellow-flyer who worships him; the black-marketeer who will do anything for him, even below cost; or his roistering, women-chasing comrades. If the novel occasionally borders on farce it is nevertheless a shrewdly observed and often disturbing account of the excesses and follies of warfare. The climax is worthy of the hero—an adventure involving an enchanting refugee girl, a captured Japanese officer, an airplane, a volcano in eruption, and a sort of Circe's island where the more violent human emotions find their expression and outlet.

For his third novel, *Tamara,* Dutton turned to his Russian travels and experiences, and his appreciation of Russian poetry. Angus James, friend of poets, lover of wine, poetry, and the other pleasures of living, and, incidentally, a distinguished Australian agronomist, is in Moscow for a conference of soil scientists. By a happy accident he finds himself co-opted as an Australian delegate at a festival to celebrate the 800th anniversary of the birth of the Georgian epic poet, Shota Rustaveli. His total ignorance of the latter's work in no way inhibits Angus's enjoyment of the festival. And then, through mists of rhetoric and strawberry-tasting wine, he catches his first glimpse of Tamara: black-haired, beautiful, and Russia's most esteemed woman poet. They meet and they love until the pressure of politics and ideologies comes heavily to bear upon their idyll. This is a novel about poets by a poet: in its simplicity, its lyricism, its rich yet economical evocations of Georgia and the Georgians, it is, in the truest sense, a deeply romantic story. Dutton's sensitive evocations of Russian mores and idiosyncrasies emerge in many fine passages, as, for instance: "Their praises like their curses come straight from the soul. Although they have many secrets they have no hypocrisies in their personal relationships."

For *Queen Emma of the South Seas* Dutton spent many months of research in the South Pacific area. It is based on the life of the Samoan-American woman who built a 19th century trading empire covering half an ocean and became known throughout the Pacific as Queen Emma. Her fantastic exploits, her commercial genius, her beauty and magnetic personality, her many lovers and fierce passions, her extraordinary rise to fame and finally her mysterious death in Monte Carlo in 1913, have become a full-blooded legend. Her story is filled with adventure, love and pomp and ceremony, with lust and political and commercial intrigue. The settings include the idyllic paradise of pre-colonial Samoa; the primitive brutality and cannibalism of the early New Guinea tribes; the boisterous society of Sydney and San Francisco at the turn of the century; the court of Kind Kalakaua; Berlin's Royal Palace. Dutton ranges through them all, fashioning a colorful slice of history into an exotic and remarkable novel, deftly handling the technique of recording Emma's story through narratives by herself, her father, her brother and sisters, traders, missionaries, planters, diplomats and lovers.

Finally, Dutton has extended his versatility to that of satirist in *The Eye-Opener,* a witty and irreverent account, as fiction, of the preparations in Adelaide, one of the most conservative of Australian cities, for its Festival of Arts in the early 1960s. Consciously literary with its allusions and with sardonic swipes at Adelaide's high society and its obstacle course of dinners and cocktail parties, it is at once a clever comic creation and a shrewd examination of life in Australia—the Australia that denigrates "the bloody Poms" and yet is so servilely and profoundly Anglophile.

Perhaps Dutton's main achievement as a novelist is that with his erudite, polished, and uninhibited writing (exemplified also in his many short stories) he has brought new dimensions of sophistication to modern Australian fiction.

—Clement Semmler

E

EASTLAKE, William (Derry)

Nationality: American. **Born:** New York City, 14 July 1917. **Education:** Bonnie Brae School; Caldwell High School, New Jersey; Alliance Française, Paris, 1948-50. **Military Service:** Served in the United States Army during World War II: Bronze Star. **Family:** Married Martha Simpson in 1943 (divorced 1971). **Career:** Writer-in-residence, Knox College, Galesburg, Illinois, 1967, University of New Mexico, Albuquerque, 1967-68, University of Southern California, Los Angeles, 1968-69, University of Arizona, Tucson, 1969-71, and United States Military Academy, West Point, New York, 1975. Vietnam correspondent, *Nation*, New York, 1968. **Awards:** Ford grant, 1964; Rockefeller grant, 1966; Les Lettres Nouvelles award (France), 1972; Western Literature Association award, 1985. D.Litt.: University of Albuquerque, 1970. **Address:** 966 Coy Road, Bisbee, Arizona 85603, U.S.A.

PUBLICATIONS

Novels

Go in Beauty. New York, Harper, 1956; London, Secker and Warburg, 1957.
The Bronc People. New York, Harcourt Brace, 1958; London, Deutsch, 1963.
Portrait of an Artist with Twenty-Six Horses. New York, Simon and Schuster, 1963; London, Joseph, 1965.
Castle Keep. New York, Simon and Schuster, 1965; London, Joseph, 1966.
The Bamboo Bed. New York, Simon and Schuster, 1969; London, Joseph, 1970.
Dancers in the Scalp House. New York, Viking Press, 1975.
The Long Naked Descent into Boston: A Tricentennial Novel. New York, Viking Press, 1977.

Short Stories

Jack Armstrong in Tangier and Other Escapes. Flint, Michigan, Bamberger, 1984.
Prettyfields: A Work in Progress (novella), with *The Man Who Cultivated Fire and Other Stories* by Gerald Haslam. Santa Barbara, California, Capra Press, 1987.

Uncollected Short Stories

"Ishimoto's Land," in *Essai* (Geneva, Switzerland), Summer 1952.
"Two Gentlemen from America," in *Hudson Review* (New York), Fall 1954.
"Homecoming," in *Quarto* (New York), Fall 1954.
"The Barfly and the Navajo," in *Nation* (New York), 12 September 1959.
"A Long Day's Dying," in *The Best American Short Stories 1964,* edited by Martha Foley and David Burnett. Boston, Houghton Mifflin, 1964.

"Little Joe," in *The Best American Short Stories 1965,* edited by Martha Foley and David Burnett. Boston, Houghton Mifflin, 1965.
"Something Big Is Happening to Me," in *New American Story,* edited by Robert Creeley and Donald Allen. New York, Grove Press, 1965.
"What Nice Hands Held," in *Gallery of Modern Fiction,* edited by Robie Macauley. New York, Salem Press, 1966.
"Three Heroes and a Clown," in *Evergreen Review Reader 1957-1967,* edited by Barney Rosset. New York, Grove Press, 1968.
"Now Lucifer Is Not Dead," in *Evergreen Review* (New York), November 1968.
"The Message," in *New Mexico Quarterly* (Albuquerque), Winter 1968.
"The Hanging at Prettyfields," in *Evergreen Review* (New York), February 1969.
"The Biggest Thing since Custer," in *Prize Stories 1970: The O. Henry Awards,* edited by William Abrahams. New York, Doubleday, 1970.
"The Death of Sun," in *The Best American Short Stories 1973,* edited by Martha Foley. Boston, Houghton Mifflin, 1973.
"Mrs. Gage in Her Bed of Pain with a Nice Cup of Gin," in *Ms.* (New York), March 1977.
"Don't Be Afraid, The Clown's Afraid Too," in *South Shore* (Au Train, Michigan), vol. 1, no. 2, 1978.
"Inside the Belly of the Whale," in *Bisbee Times* (Bisbee, Arizona), March 1982.
"The Writer as a Young Man," in *Taos Review* (Taos, New Mexico), no. 2, 1990.
Untitled chapter from novel in progress, *The Journal* (Columbus, Ohio), vol. 16, no. 1, 1992.

Poetry

A Child's Garden of Verses for the Revolution (includes essays). New York, Grove Press, 1971.

*

Critical Studies: "The Novels of William Eastlake" by Delbert W. Wylder, in *New Mexico Quarterly* (Albuquerque), 1965; *Covering Ground: Essays for Now* by Donald Phelps, New York, Croton Press, 1969; "Of Cowboys, Indians and the Modern West" by Peter M. Kenyon, in *Sage* (Las Vegas, Nevada), Winter 1969; *William Eastlake* by Gerald Haslam, Austin, Texas, Steck Vaughn, 1970; "William Eastlake Issue" of *Review of Contemporary Fiction* (Elmwood Park, Illinois), Spring 1983; article by Eastlake, in *Contemporary Authors Autobiography Series* edited by Dedria Bryfonski, Detroit, Gale, 1984; *William Eastlake; High Desert Interlocutor* by W.C. Bamberger, San Bernardino, California, Borgo Press, 1993; *The Work of William Eastlake* by W.C. Bamberger, San Bernardino, California, Borgo Press, 1994.

William Eastlake comments:

(1972) As long as we are serving a life sentence on this earth there has got to be something to make the time go easy. The thing to work at is to be the best writer on earth, or the best magician, for writing is magic, and like all the things that are important you do it all alone. As I expressed it in *The Bronc People:*

> "You can't give anyone anything."
> "You mean I've got to do it alone?"
> "Yes."
> "But the missionary says no man is an island."
> "Well, he is."
> "You think the missionary got that saying from another preacher?"
> "Yes."
> "We've got to go it all alone?"
> "Yes, we do."

A Child's Garden of Verses for the Revolution is a comment on the end of America and the west, the only part of the earth I really know. But the artist is sentenced and elected as medicine man because he holds out hope. That is his job. That is what he was hired for. My hope is in the youth of the world. The people of the earth turn more and more to the writer, the medicine man, as their tribal leaders fail them. And as our present tribal leaders are unworthy even of the dignity of death, the medicine man, through his novels, fulfills man through artistic re-enactment.

> Once upon a time there was a time. The land here in the Southwest had evolved slowly and there was time and there were great spaces. Now a man on horseback from atop a bold mesa looked out over the violent spectrum of the Indian Country—into a gaudy infinity where all the colors exploded soundlessly. "There is not much time," he said.

The death of all of us worthy of death is enacted by the Indian medicine man. Death he calls "Something big is happening to me." Any place the writer, the medicine man, the shaman, lives is the center of the earth.

> Below at the post, the exact center and the capital of the world for The People, two Indians crouched at the massive stone root of the petrified-wood house where it made its ways into the ground.
> "This crack," the indian said, tracing it with his brown finger.
> "They can fix it," Rabbit Stockings said.
> "No. And perhaps even The People cannot stop something come apart and beginning here at the center of the world."

The artist's job is to hold the world together. What the politicians cannot do with reality the artist does with magic, even if the artist is an epileptic Dostoievsky, a failed Melville working in a customs house, a wandering Walt Whitman peddling his *Leaves of Grass* from door to door. The artist finds life everlasting in his magic. William Shakespeare is still very much alive. God is pronounced dead.

*   *   *

At first glance William Eastlake appears to be America's most paradoxical literary artist. Although he was born in New York and grew up in New Jersey and although he traveled widely in Europe after World War II and for some years lived and worked in Los Angeles, he purchased land in an isolated, remote area of New Mexico and there for some years lived the life of the small-spread rancher and literary man. Eastlake thereby became a strongly committed regionalist and one of the most astute observers of present-day American Indian life. Although isolated, Eastlake's concerns were always with national policy, our establishment in Washington and in Vietnam, or the significance of American poverty at home as against American explorations of outer space. On the one hand he appears to seek a kind of peace in a remote area, yet he remains angry at fellow provincials of limited vision, the rednecks and un-enlightened army colonels. If Eastlake protests the fate of Mexican, Indian, and Black persons in America, he cannot defend, in the name of a beloved democracy, the violence and the turmoil in our urban centers and on the country roads of out-yonder America. His lifestyle suggests the pursuit of calm by association with Nature; yet the work presents a sharp focus on the evils of modernity in an idiom which combines the sardonic and the realistic along with an acceptance of the implied values of both ritual and myth. If these paradoxes are real, then their resolution in Eastlake's work suggests an artist of uncommon personal stability and unusual dedication to his own view of the world. If there is tension implicit in these paradoxical roles, the result is artistic production of a high order.

From the centers of these contradictive conflicts emerge his most significant works. Ostensibly the materials are Indians and tourists; cattlemen and brute geography; the neon market towns and the sagebrush. Beneath this closely observed, naturalistic surface, however, the concern is the modes of right conduct, the normal propositions implicit in actions, the attitudes toward life of the protagonists. Irony, humor, and fantasy are everywhere, and thus the true position of the authorial voice behind the prose fictions is not always easy to discern. In moral considerations a continued reliance on irony is no position at all.

Nevertheless, the pervading irony—and compassion—suggest Eastlake's American literary tradition and major influence. His overt search for materials (the move to New Mexico), his stints as war correspondent in Vietnam, his running commentary on cultural and political policy suggest the tradition of the 19th-century correspondent/writer: Stephen Crane, Jack London, and more recently Hemingway. Likewise, the concern for a "moral center," for Justice, for the destiny of America and its people suggests Walt Whitman, poet, editor, "correspondent" of an earlier age. Of the direct literary influences, however, Hemingway is the most significant: the terse understatement, the stripped-down dialogue, the concept of the character, the close focus on the details of war, the sometimes anti-intellectual, anti-bookish, anti-cultural stances strongly suggest the Hemingway of the early novels and the war-correspondent years. Many commonplaces from the criticism of Hemingway, for example, the kind of commentary which identifies the strong romantic element in his work, could be applied as well to Eastlake. If the two men in a great many ways are comparable literary talents, Eastlake's exemplary management of his own talent may prove ultimately the more productive. Eastlake is a model of affirmative experience in the matter of attaining a balance between artistic necessity and humanitarian concern.

Of the novels *The Bronc People* and the short fictions in the same vein attract the most critical attention. Although *Castle Keep* became a successful film and was widely translated, the novel increasingly becomes an example of a book less effective as a whole than the sum of its sometimes brilliant episodes. The Vietnam materials, the journalistic snap shots and quasi-interviews, are repetitive and are less effective together than when they appeared singly in the *Nation*. The poetry of *A Child's Garden of Verses for the Revolution* purports to be "revolutionary" but on balance fails either to move the reader or to offer an effective program beyond the necessity of mutual respect, a change of heart; the commitment is always firm, and a strong sensibility is apparent everywhere.

At full artistic maturity, Eastlake now lives in the country which was significant and stimulating to his early work: on the border of Arizona and Old Mexico. A recent collection of short fiction, *Jack Armstrong in Tangier,* is largely retrospective, a summary. The literary quality is high, the artistic intention lofty; at least four of the stories have claimed space in major anthologies. The cumulative effect of these stories is strong in large part because of the authorial voice behind them, this voice characterized by irony, humor, and wit; in addition, there is the sharp observation of the significant detail, and an unwavering—if often bleak—estimate of the human condition broadly considered.

—James B. Hall

EKWENSI, Cyprian (Odiatu Duaka)

Nationality: Nigerian. **Born:** Minna, Niger State, 26 September 1921. **Education:** Government School, Jos, 1931-36; Government College, Ibadan, 1936-41; Higher College, Yaba, 1941-43; School of Forestry, Ibaban, 1942-45; Achimota College, Gold Coast, 1943; School of Pharmacy, Yaba, 1947-49; Chelsea School of Pharmacy, University of London, 1951-56; University of Iowa, Iowa City, 1974. **Family:** Married to Eunice Anyiwo; five children. **Career:** Teacher, Igbobi College, Yaba, 1947-49; lecturer, School of Pharmacy, Lagos, 1949-51; pharmacist superintendent, Nigerian Medical Services, 1956-57; head of features, Nigerian Broadcasting Corporation, 1957-61; director, Federal Information Services, 1961-67; director-general, Broadcasting Corporation of Biafra, during Nigerian civil war, 1967-70; proprietor, East Niger Chemists and East Niger Trading Company since 1970; chairman, East Central State Library Board, 1972-75; managing director, Star Printing and Publishing Company, 1975-79; consultant, *Weekly Trumpet* and *Daily News,* both Anambra State, and *Weekly Eagle,* Imo State, 1980-81; commissioner for information, Anambra State, 1983. Member of the Board of Governors, Federal Radio Corporation, Lagos, 1985; chairman, Anambra State Hospitals Board, 1986-88. **Awards:** Dag Hammarskjöld International award, 1968. **Agent:** David Bolt Associates, 12 Heath Drive, Send, Surrey GU23 7EP, England. **Address:** 12 Hillview, P.O. Box 317, Enugu, Anambra State, Nigeria.

PUBLICATIONS

Novels

When Love Whispers. Onitsha, Nigeria, Tabansi Bookshop, 1947.
People of the City. London, Dakers, 1954; revised edition, London, Heinemann, 1963; New York, Fawcett, 1969.
Jagua Nana. London, Hutchinson, 1961; New York, Fawcett, 1969.
Burning Grass: A Story of the Fulani of Northern Nigeria. London, Heinemann, 1962.

Beautiful Feathers. London, Hutchinson, 1963.
Iska. London, Hutchinson, 1966.
Survive the Peace. London, Heinemann, 1976.
Divided We Stand. Enugu, Fourth Dimension, 1980.
Jagua Nana's Daughter. Ibadan, Spectrum, 1986.
For a Roll of Parchment. Ibadan, Heinemann, 1987.

Short Stories

Lokotown and Other Stories. London, Heinemann, 1966.
Restless City and Christmas Gold with Other Stories. London, Heinemann, 1975.

Fiction (for children)

The Leopard's Claw. London, Longman, 1950.
The Drummer Boy. London, Cambridge University Press, 1960.
The Passport of Malam Ilia. London, Cambridge University Press, 1960.
Yaba Roundabout Murder. Lagos, Tortoise, 1962.
The Rainmaker and Other Stories. Lagos, African Universities Press, 1965.
Trouble in Form Six. London, Cambridge University Press, 1966.
Juju Rock. Lagos, African Universities Press, 1966.
Coal Camp Boy. Lagos, Longman, 1973.
Samankwe in the Strange Forest. Ikeja, Longman Nigeria, 1973.
The Rainbow-Tinted Scarf and Other Stories. London, Evans, 1975.
Samankwe and the Highway Robbers. London, Evans, 1975.
Motherless Baby. Enugu, Fourth Dimension, 1980.
Gone to Mecca: A Story. Ibadan, Heinemann, 1991.
Masquerade Time. N.p., Heinemann, 1991.
King for ever! Oxford, Heinemann, 1992.

Other (for children)

Ikolo the Wrestler and Other Ibo Tales. London, Nelson, 1947.
An African Night's Entertainment: A Tale of Vengeance. Lagos, African Universities Press, and London, Deutsch, 1962.
The Great Elephant-Bird (folktale). London, Nelson, 1965.
The Boa Suitor. London, Nelson, 1966.

Other

Editor, *Festac Anthology of Nigerian New Writing.* Lagos, Federal Ministry of Information, 1977.

*

Critical Study: *Cyprian Ekwensi* by Ernest Emenyona, London, Evans, 1974.

*   *   *

Cyprian Ekwensi's first publications preceded by several years the flourishing of Nigerian writing signalled by the accomplished worker of Chinua Achebe and Wole Soyinka. He has little in common with them. He abjured their high seriousness and literary experiment. Ekwensi was university-trained, but in pharmacy, so that he was not involved in the intellectual debates of the humanities. He sees himself as a storyteller and in that guise he has also produced some delightful children's books.

The question of audience has always been a controversial issue in African literature. Many writers seem to give prime consideration to gaining international recognition. Ekwensi seems indifferent to such aspirations and serves local readers. His first work, *When Love Whispers,* was one of the famous "Onitsha market novels." These are slender, crudely printed tales of young passion, aimed at the increasing number of buyers educated to minimal literacy in English who seek untaxing romantic gratification. With this background Ekwensi has never received the kind of attention that has followed Achebe's career, from critics intent on analyzing complexity. Their attitude unfairly ignores Ekwensi's particular gifts. No one has better explored the nature of modern Nigeria, especially Lagos, in a time of violent post-independence transition. He is a writer who draws upon the experience of the great city rather than the revered cultural tradition which preoccupies many others. No other Nigerian has so exactly caught the rhythm of the streets, bars, and night clubs which entertain an entirely new class. He exposes the lives of ambitious and frustrated young people as they try to carve for themselves an existence unthinkable two decades before. They are separated from the impoverished and hopeless squatters at one extreme and on the other from the wealthy Lebanese and Nigerian financial manipulators who make gross profits from the chaotic circumstances of modern Lagos. Through their eyes we see the city almost as a personality, exuding temptation and challenge along with its fraudulent contriving and brutal misery. The city has a glitter which irresistibly entices and allures men and women alike. Ekwensi's themes are crude but he presents this society with a vivid eye for the locale and an ear reponsive to the slang and varied accents of its inhabitants.

The title of Ekwensi's first full-length novel, *People of the City,* defines his source. There are several plots, linked by the experiences of Amusa Sango, a jazz musician by night and by day a journalist for the aptly named *West African Sensation.* Sango's jobs indicate the new prospects opening up, and they allow Ekwensi to use Sango as a means of penetrating society at various levels. All the familiar types are present: the wealthy Syrians; the pathetic whores, some crudely confident, others trapped by their innocence; muggers and thieves; good time girls and their boyfriends—all find satisfaction, or escape, in drinking and dancing. Ekwensi despises his evident villains and sympathises with their victims but he is not moralistic in the absolute sense of Achebe. He devises a spicy mixture of romance and melodrama but he offers no overall condemnation of the politics which sustain his realistic world. His short stories, collected in *Lokotown,* follow the same pattern.

With *Jagua Nana,* Ekwensi moves towards a more calculated structure and a convincing diction that ranges from elevated rhetoric to idiomatic pidgin. The book is given substance by two remarkably effective characters: Jagua Nana herself, an aging prostitute, and Uncle Taiwo, the archetypal corrupt politician. The title is emblematic of this divided society, bringing together two measures of success as it is viewed in Lagos. From Western literature comes Zola's depiction of Nana, the arrogant and successful whore. Surprisingly the accolade Jagua does not attribute to Nana the sleek grace of the wild cat; it refers instead to the British Jaguar car—a comparison which neatly reveals the materialist admiration for expensive and foreign possessions.

The problem with Ekwensi is that a reader has to sift through so much triviality to find the nuggets of convincing description. Jagua falls in love, falls out, becomes the mistress of a Lagos politician and a village chief while seeking her destiny. Throughout these excessive and improbable adventures Jagua maintains a certain dig-

nity. She is a survivor in a vicious world. Ekwensi tries to set town against country as moral extremes. When Jagua returns to her home village she finds a calm order and courteous generosity lacking in her Lagos life. In the village she finds she can assume the status of wife rather than whore. Yet the presentation of this conversion is a little bland and one feels that Jagua, like Ekwensi, is unlikely to wish to exchange the sinful city for the peace of the countryside.

Not even Achebe's Nanga (in *A Man of the People*) is quite such a hideously plausible character as Uncle Taiwo, his friendly title indicating well that surface geniality which conceals the rapacity of the politician. There is a cheerful bravado about Taiwo. He is totally without hypocrisy. His desires are so open, so utterly amoral, he achieves the dangerous capacity to be likeable. His death provides Jagua with an illegal cache of money which allows her to consider exchanging prostitution for the more honorable career of a market woman.

The novels *Beautiful Feathers* and *Iska* have impressive moments but they lack the underlying energy of some of the author's previous work. It is as if Ekwensi is being a little too careful, seeking a more legitimate reputation. The themes remain the same, the difficulties for honest men and decent women to survive in this corrupt and venal society. Wilson Iyari, the main character of *Beautiful Feathers,* is a visionary who believes in the brotherhood of man. Perhaps for this reason he is a far less assured character than wicked Uncle Taiwo. Like many writers, Ekwensi finds villainy easier to represent that idealism. Regrettably, Wilson's generous principles seem so surprising that the happy ending strikes one as artificial.

In a similar way the heroine of *Iska,* Filia, seems bloodless against the pepper of Jagua. Certainly she is infinitely more modest, but virtue makes her bland. National politics is the new dimension in this book. It describes the Hausa-Ibo tribal conflict which anticipated the terrible calamity of the Biafran war. Regrettably, Ekwensi does not let this intense background animate the events of his novel, but merely uses it as a platform to deliver homilies on the problems of tribal loyalties and national goals. This intrusive preaching tone suits few writers, certainly not Ekwensi. For his achievement one needs to look back at his exuberant earlier works. Despite their technical limitations and banal plots, these works live for their vivid, if ultimately depressing, vision of modern Nigeria. The experiences portrayed are not communicated through the Western-educated intellectuals of Achebe's novels but from "the people of the city" who struggle to survive and so need hectic frivolity as an antidote to despair. Numerically, at least, Ekwensi is celebrating a far larger population and perhaps one more nearly attuned to the situation in contemporary Lagos.

—John Povey

ELDRED-GRIGG, Stevan (Treleaven)

Nationality: New Zealander. **Born:** Grey Valley, New Zealand, 5 October 1952. **Education:** University of Canterbury, Christchurch, 1970-74, M.A. (honours) 1975; Australian National University, 1975-78, Ph.D. 1978. **Family:** Married in 1976 (marriage dissolved, 1994); three sons. **Career:** Postdoctoral fellow, University of Canterbury, 1981; writing fellow, l986, scholar-in-letters, 1991, Victoria University; New Zealand writing fellow, University of

Iowa, Iowa City. **Awards:** A.W. Reed memorial book award, 1984; Commonwealth Writers prize, 1988. **Agent:** Curtis Brown, P.O. Box 19, Paddington, New South Wales 2021, Australia.

PUBLICATIONS

Novels

Oracles and Miracles. Auckland and New York, Penguin, 1987.
The Siren Celia. Auckland, Penguin, 1989.
The Shining City. Auckland, Penguin, 1991.
Gardens of Fire. Auckland, Penguin, 1993.
Mum. Auckland, Penguin, 1995.

Short Stories

Of Ivory Accents (novella). N.p., n.d.

Play

Radio Play: *Oracles and Miracles,* from his own novel, 1989.

Other

A Southern Gentry: New Zealanders Who Inherited the Earth. Wellington, Reed, 1980.
A New History of Canterbury. Dunedin, McIndoe, 1982.
New Zealand Working People, 1890-1990. Palmerston North, Dunmore Press, 1990.
My History, I Think. Auckland, Penguin, 1994.
Pleasures of the Flesh. N.p., n.d.

*

Manuscript Collection: Macmillan Brown Library, University of Canterbury, Christchurch, New Zealand.

Stevan Eldred-Grigg comments:

I'm a provincial writer, a writer of social comedy. My province is Canterbury, centred on the city of Christchurch. It's the comedy of a little white world, a small society, a very precise place. My novels resemble my province, a province whose history is as long or short as the history of the novel. A province civil, sociable, not unconcerned with style.

We write, though. We lie. We make meanings where there can be no meaning.

* * *

In the mid-1980s Stevan Eldred-Grigg switched his attention from history to fiction in order to challenge the customary "literary portrait of working class life" in New Zealand, which he saw as being "very remote from working class reality."

I knew . . . that most of the people who had written serious history and fiction in New Zealand during the middle years of the twentieth century had been male and Pakeha. I also knew . . . that most had been middle class. . . . The worker who turned up in the pages of mid twentieth century literature was almost always a man. . . . And these working men were not only male, they were usually also itinerant, solitary and homeless. The working man was Man Alone. He lived in a world of "casual workers and rouseabouts," "station hands and street loungers."

In a series of short stories and in his celebrated first novel, *Oracles and Miracles*—though not in a much earlier novella, *Of Ivory Accents,* which predates his socialist convictions—Eldred-Grigg set out to focus on the city rather than the country and on women rather than men. Rehabilitation of the Maori he has evidently left to New Zealand's rapidly expanding body of Maori writers.

Oracles and Miracles does not have a strong story line. Based on interviews with actual working-class women (and originally conceived as an oral history), it simply documents the lives of Ginnie and Fag from their births in 1929 through the Depression and World War II to their twenty-first birthdays. The method is akin to the realism of Arnold Bennett, but it must be said that Eldred-Grigg is not yet as adept as Bennett at suggesting human depth beneath the welter of surface detail.

Ginnie, who does not deviate from the working-class context of her birth, enables Eldred-Grigg to evoke what he calls the "grit and texture" of the times. Her working-class dialect is particularly well realized. Fag's voice is different since—like Eldred-Grigg's own mother, incidentally—she has realized the Cinderella myth by marrying out of her class and has cleaned up her idiom. Whereas Ginnie makes political statements unconsciously (as when she observes that "the two words 'good' and 'work' didn't have anything to do with one another"), Fag can stand apart from her upbringing and comment on it quite explicitly. Thus when she shows her husband-to-be (who, incidentally, closely resembles Eldred-Grigg's own father) round the working-class suburb where she grew up, she tells us that she "started to see it in a new way, thinking how strange it was that to him all this seemed interesting, important, this dreary old stamping ground of South Christchurch." Here she has become the mouthpiece for Eldred-Grigg's own concern about the destruction of working-class culture by the capitalist ideology of consumerism promulgated by the media of the day—including a popular magazine called *Miracles and Oracles.*

Ironically, at the very moment when she recognizes the authenticity of working-class culture, Fag is already in the process of deserting it for what turns out to be a sterile bourgeois existence. Ginnie, on the other hand, finds a partner from within the working class and seems happier at the end. The novel has been criticized for its naive implication that "it's better to be working class and know it as long as you marry for love." The author himself insists that he did not intend this moral and that what he calls "the tragedy" of both sisters "is not that they don't find love but that they do."

These problems with the conclusion to *Oracles and Miracles* are not resolved by the disappointing sequel, *The Shining City.* Fag is still married—happily enough, it would seem, though she continues to live in a sterile middle-class suburb, where her behavior and idiom (now considerably closer to her working-class origins than they were in the earlier book) mark her out as an eccentric. But she is a minor character in the book, whereas Ginnie scarcely features. Instead the focus is on the formative years of two young men of the next generation: Fag's son, Ashley, and his cousin, Christopher, a scion of pure patrician stock.

The Shining City is in effect the obverse of *Oracles and Miracles* in that it focuses on the exploiting class rather than the exploited class. Eldred-Grigg the historian had already critiqued the Canterbury squattocracy mercilessly in his early works, *A Southern Gentry, A New History of Canterbury,* and *Pleasures of the Flesh.* In *The Shining City* and—more memorably—in *The Siren Celia* and *Gardens of Fire* he levels the same critique in fictional form. In all three novels an exploited working class is glimpsed from time to time, but the primary focus is on the foibles and corrupt practices of the landed gentry.

Gardens of Fire is closely based on fact. It is a compelling reconstruction of the disastrous fire of 1947 that destroyed Ballantynes—Christchurch's premier department store. Forty-one employees died in the blaze, and Eldred-Grigg's account rests the blame for their deaths squarely on the shoulders of their bosses.

The Siren Celia is based not on fact but on an earlier work of New Zealand fiction—George Chamier's *A South Sea Siren,* first published in 1895 and reprinted in 1970. Eldred-Grigg explains that he took from Chamier's novel "all the bits that I thought worked really well and reinforced the themes I wanted to take up. I fed these chunks into my computer. Then I deconstructed them all and built them up again the way I wanted them." Other material is introduced from Chamier's earlier novel, *Philosopher Dick,* and from the writings of Sarah Amelia Courage.

His principal purpose in modifying Chamier was, he explains, to emphasize "questions of gender and class." So the landed gentry of Canterbury are effectively satirized, and the siren (who in Chamier's account was—according to one critic—"altogether too snaky and sinuous for modern belief") is shown to be the victim of a series of boorish and incompetent men. It is in his depiction of one of these men, the protagonist, Richard Raleigh, that Eldred-Grigg departs most radically from his source. Chamier's "philosopher Dick" finally abjures the siren, takes up an honest profession, and seems set to marry the respectable Alice Seymour; Eldred-Grigg shows him degenerating into a corrupt entrepreneur with whom the siren is finally unfortunate enough to contract a marriage. Eldred-Grigg has done to Chamier precisely what Shaw's *Plays Unpleasant* did to the Victorian well-made play.

Eldred-Grigg also felt that Chamier "didn't have the ability to dramatize" and tried to remedy this deficiency. He wisely cut the chapters in Chamier that amount to miniature Socratic dialogues led by "philosopher Dick" (Raleigh), but his version of the actual events of the story is really no more dramatic than Chamier's; as in *Oracles and Miracles* and *The Shining City,* the text conveys little sense of felt experience, even when Raleigh purports to be succumbing to the charms of the siren.

—Dick Corballis

ELKIN, Stanley (Lawrence)

Nationality: American. **Born:** Brooklyn, New York, 11 May 1930. **Education:** The University of Illinois, Urbana, 1948-60, B.A. 1952, M.A. 1953, Ph.D. in English 1961. **Military Service:** Served in the United States Army, 1955-57. **Family:** Married Joan Jacobson in 1953; two sons and one daughter. **Career:** Instructor, 1960-62, assistant professor, 1962-66, associate professor, 1966-69, since 1969 professor of English, and since 1983 King Professor of Modern Letters, Washington University, St. Louis. Visiting lecturer, Smith College, Northampton, Massachusetts, 1964-65; visiting pro-

fessor, University of California, Santa Barbara, Summer 1967, University of Wisconsin, Milwaukee, Summer 1969, Yale University, New Haven, Connecticut, 1975, and Boston University, 1976. **Awards:** Longview Foundation award, 1962; *Paris Review* prize, 1965; Guggenheim fellowship, 1966; Rockefeller fellowship, 1968; National Endowment for the Arts grant, 1971; American Academy grant, 1974; Rosenthal Foundation award, 1980; *Southern Review* award, 1981; National Book Critics Circle award, 1983; Brandeis University Creative Arts award, 1986. L.H.D.: University of Illinois, Urbana, 1986. **Member:** American Academy, 1982. **Address:** Duncker Hall, Washington University, St. Louis, Missouri 63130, U.S.A.

PUBLICATIONS

Novels

Boswell. New York, Random House, and London, Hamish Hamilton, 1964.
A Bad Man. New York, Random House, 1967; London, Blond, 1968.
The Dick Gibson Show. New York, Random House, and London, Weidenfeld and Nicolson, 1971.
The Franchiser. New York, Farrar Straus, 1976.
George Mills. New York, Dutton, 1982.
The Magic Kingdom. New York, Dutton, 1985.
The Rabbi of Lud. New York, Scribner, 1987.
The Macguffin. New York, Simon and Schuster, 1991.

Short Stories

Criers and Kibitzers, Kibitzers and Criers. New York, Random House, 1966; London, Blond, 1968.
The Making of Ashenden. London, Covent Garden Press, 1972.
Searches and Seizures. New York, Random House, 1973; as *Alex and the Gypsy,* London, Penguin, 1977.
The Living End. New York, Dutton, 1979; London, Cape, 1980.
Early Elkin. Flint, Michigan, Bamberger, 1985.
Van Gogh's Room at Arles: Three Novellas. New York, Hyperion, 1993.

Plays

The Six-Year-Old Man (screenplay). Flint, Michigan, Bamberger, 1987.
The Coffee Room (radio play). Louisville, Kentucky, Contre Coup Press, 1987.

Other

Stanley Elkin's Greatest Hits (omnibus). New York, Dutton, 1980.
Why I Live Where I Live (essay). University City, Missouri, Contre Coup Press, 1983.
Pieces of Soap: Essays. New York, Simon and Schuster, 1990.

Editor, *Stories from the Sixties.* New York, Doubleday, 1971.
Editor, with Shannon Ravenel, *The Best American Short Stories 1980.* Boston, Houghton Mifflin, 1980.

*

Manuscript Collection: Washington University Library, St. Louis.

Critical Studies: *Humanism and the Absurd* by Naomi Lebowitz, Evanston, Illinois, Northwestern University Press, 1971; *City of Words* by Tony Tanner, London, Cape, and New York, Harper, 1971; *The Jewish Writer in America* by Allen Guttman, New York, Oxford University Press, 1971; *Beyond the Wasteland* by Raymond Olderman, New Haven, Connecticut, Yale University Press, 1972; *The Fiction of Stanley Elkin* by Doris G. Bargen, Bern, Switzerland, Lang, 1980; *Reading Stanley Elkin* by Peter J. Bailey, Boston, Houghton Mifflin, 1985; *Stanley Elkin* by David C. Dougherty, Boston, Twayne, 1990; *Comic Sense: Reading Robert Coover, Stanley Elkin, Philip Roth* by Thomas Pughe, Basel, Switzerland, Birkhäuser Verlag, 1994.

Stanley Elkin comments:

I don't know what to say about my work. What I like best about it, I suppose, are the sentences. What I like least about it is my guess that probably no one is ever moved by it.

*   *   *

"[Writing] is a matter of feeling one's way. It is not instinctive. It's a question of using a pencil, erasing, creating a palimpsest of metaphor right there on the page. One gets a notion of the conceit and one is inspired to work with it as a draftsman might work with some angle that he is interested in getting down correctly. That's where all the fun of writing is for me. I don't read much non-fiction because the non-fiction I do read always seem to be so badly written. What I enjoy about fiction—the great gift of fiction—is that it gives language an opportunity to happen. What I am really interested in after personality are not philosophic ideas or abstractions or patterns, but this superb opportunity for language to take place." (Interview in *Anything Can Happen,* edited by Thomas LeClair and Larry McCaffery, 1983.)

"Surely the point of life was the possibility it always held out for the exceptional. The range of the strange," says Dick Gibson, Stanley Elkin's disc jockey and fellow word man. The point, too, of Elkin's fiction which is exceptional because sentence for sentence, metaphor for metaphor, no novelist in America writes as energetically and musically as Elkin. His books display the "range of the strange": not the exotic or esoteric, but ordinary life made extraordinary by his imaginative participation in it, the usual seen and said with unusual clarity. "The world is a miracle," adds franchiser Ben Flesh, but, he goes on for himself and for Elkin, you have to "Drive up and down in it. . . . Look close at it. See its moving parts, its cranes and car parks and theater districts." Elkin has pressed his nose to the American showcase, heard all the sellers of self and thing, has eaten Colonel Sanders chicken and slept in Holiday Inns. Everything—and this is the secret of Elkin's prose—is available for the sentences that turn us back to our franchised and media-furrowed land with new apprehension and appreciation.

"Drive drives the world," to quote Dick Gibson again. Elkin's heroes are obsessives, common men with uncommon appetites, bad men because they refuse to compromise, good men for the same reason. The professional wrestler in *Boswell,* Elkin's first novel, is obsessed with death and with what he calls "The Great." Like his predecessor James, Boswell seeks out the exceptional. Feldman, entrepreneur hero of *A Bad Man,* is driven to make the ultimate sale, either in his bargain basement or in the prison to which he is sent. Dick Gibson of *The Dick Gibson Show* and Ben Flesh of

The Franchiser must have destinies, must feel chosen for the services they render. Gibson as a late-night Miss Lonelyhearts of the air, Flesh as provider of the goofy comfort of familiar franchises. For these characters, fixation turns an occupation into a life, and Elkin turns their lives into success stories for a shrinking America: modest means transformed by the gaiety of will.

Like his characters, Elkin's prose is willful, obsessive, omnivorous. Here is Dick Gibson describing quiet: "I was in a trance, a catalepsy, a swoon, a brown study, a neutral funk. I was languid, gravid, the thousand-pound kid in Miriam's room, sensitized as human soup. And if I heard her at all it was in my ilium I listened—as deep as that—harkened in my coccyx, my pajama strings all ears, and my buttons and the Kleenex under my pillow." The series of synonyms tries to exhaust meaning as the extravagant metaphors, hyperbole, and refurbished clichés try to extend it. Elkin's models are oral and colloquial—the pitch of his salesman father, the oratory he wrote about in Faulkner's work, the shop talk he collects. His purposes are performance—Elkin loves the comic high-wire—and defamiliarization, the artistic recovery of "all the derelict and marooned, the ditched and scavenged. Debris, dregs, lees. Dregs addicts. All the multitudinous slag of the ordinary."

While Elkin's stories in *Criers and Kibitzers, Kibitzers and Criers* are widely anthologized, and the three novellas in *Searches and Seizures* are much admired, Elkin's gifts are those of the novelist. He describes himself as a "putter-inner." Because shorter forms do not allow Elkin room for the accretion of character that marks the novels, situations and people in the stories can seem simply eccentric. In the novels, repetition of image and action, rhetorical intensity, even digressions and included tales, have a cumulative effect. *The Living End,* a triad of long stories about heaven and hell, is an exception, for here a whole cosmos is created, laced and grained with detail. The most widely read of Elkin's books, *The Living End* ranges from the life of a Minneapolis-St. Paul liquor salesman to the secrets God held back from man ("why dentistry was a purer science than astronomy, biography a higher form than dance" and more), encompassing the banalities of conventional wisdom and the profundities of last things. Not since Melville shook Ahab's fist at heaven has an American novelist written so affectingly about the problem of Evil, the bugs in the divine "state of the art."

In the award-winning *George Mills* and in *The Magic Kingdom,* Elkin extends his imagination—to medieval Europe, Sultanic Turkey, and impoverished contemporary St. Louis in *George Mills*—and deepens his sensibility, treating with high comedy and passionate precision the holiday of terminally ill children in Disney's and Elkin's "Magic Kingdom." For a very long time a "writer's writer," Elkin has in these books brought his dense prose to bear on people's subjects, the strangeness of loss, the wearing down of life and lives, and, finally, in the face of the "sapped, the unsound, the impaired, the unfit," the ecstasy of creation, the very long-odds possibility of love.

—Thomas LeClair

ELLIOTT, Janice

Nationality: British. **Born:** Derby, 14 October 1931. **Education:** Nottingham High School for Girls; Oxford University, 1950-53, B.A. (honours) 1953. **Family:** Married Robert Cooper in 1959;

one son. **Career:** Journalist, *House and Garden, House Beautiful, Harper's Bazaar,* and *Sunday Times,* all London, 1954-62; since 1964 freelance reviewer, *Sunday Telegraph, Sunday Times, Times,* and *New Statesman,* all London. **Awards:** Southern Arts award, 1981. Fellow, Royal Society of Literature, 1989. **Agent:** Vivien Green, Richard Scott Simon Ltd., 43 Doughty Street, London WC1N 2LF, England. **Address:** Dolphin House, Trafalgar Square, Fowey, Cornwall PL23 1AX, England.

PUBLICATIONS

Novels

Cave with Echoes. London, Secker and Warburg, 1962.
The Somnambulists. London, Secker and Warburg, 1964.
The Godmother. London, Secker and Warburg, 1966; New York, Holt Rinehart, 1967.
The Buttercup Chain. London, Secker and Warburg, 1967.
The Singing Head. London, Secker and Warburg, 1968.
Angels Falling. London, Secker and Warburg, and New York, Knopf, 1969.
The Kindling. London, Secker and Warburg, and New York, Knopf, 1970.
England Trilogy:
   A State of Peace. London, Hodder and Stoughton, and New York, Knopf, 1971.
   Private Life. London, Hodder and Stoughton, 1972.
   Heaven on Earth. London, Hodder and Stoughton, 1975.
A Loving Eye. London, Hodder and Stoughton, 1977.
The Honey Tree. London, Hodder and Stoughton, 1978.
Summer People. London, Hodder and Stoughton, 1980.
Secret Places. London, Hodder and Stoughton, 1981.
The Country of Her Dreams. London, Hodder and Stoughton, 1982.
Magic. London, Hodder and Stoughton, 1983.
The Italian Lesson. London, Hodder and Stoughton, 1985; New York, Beaufort, 1986.
Dr. Gruber's Daughter. London, Hodder and Stoughton, 1986.
The Sadness of Witches. London, Hodder and Stoughton, 1987.
Life on the Nile. London, Hodder and Stoughton, 1989.
Necessary Rites. London, Hodder and Stoughton, 1990.
City of Gates. London, Hodder and Stoughton, 1992.
Figures in the Sand. London, Sceptre, 1994.

Short Stories

The Noise from the Zoo. London, Hodder and Stoughton, 1991.

Other (for children)

The Birthday Unicorn. London, Gollancz, 1970.
Alexander in the Land of Mog. Leicester, Brockhampton Press, 1973.
The Incompetent Dragon. London, Blackie, 1982.
The King Awakes. London, Walker Books, 1987.
The Empty Throne. London, Walker Books, 1988.

*

Janice Elliott comments:

I have always tried to avoid writing in a way that might invite categorisation in either subject matter or treatment. The result is a body of work ranging from the bizarre and darkly magical (*Dr. Gruber's Daughter, Magic, The Sadness of Witches*) to the social realism of the England Trilogy and the poignancy of *Secret Places*— set in the war-time Midlands where I grew up.

I make frequent use of myth, which fascinates me (most overtly in *The Singing Head*). So does modern history (*Angels Falling* set in Britain 1901–68; *Life on the Nile,* Egypt today and in the 1920s). The domestic scene has interested me only when it is set in and interacts with, the larger, outer world (e.g. the menace of the authoritarian state in *Necessary Rites*). A sense of place is vital to me, even when I have invented a country (*The Country of Her Dreams*).

I have been consistent only in my aspiration, my attempt each time to try something that will set me a fresh challenge as a writer. I am consistent too, in my conviction that style is not the icing on the cake but an organic and essential element in a good novel. If there is one recurring theme it may be the fall from grace, the image of exile from the garden.

In the last decade I have felt an urge to get out of England (mentally, imaginatively, and physically), and so made use of a number of foreign settings (*The Italian Lesson, Life on the Nile*).

I have also been more drawn by humour, sometimes to the forefront, more often as a bright, sharp thread in the weave. I believe that as a result, my novels may become more accessible to a wider audience.

Given my inclination to dash off in different directions, I have been lucky in my critical reception. Not that I could have done otherwise. I am an entirely intuitive writer, often astonished to find myself where I am and in what company (e.g. with Hitler in an attic in North Oxford in *Dr. Gruber's Daughter*).

*   *   *

Most of Janice Elliott's carefully crafted novels share the same background (the affluent English middle-class), the same period of time, the same preoccupation with the menopausal crises of well-established marriages, and, to a surprising extent, the same characters under different names. The Farmers of *The Italian Lesson,* the Tylers of *Summer People,* the Contis of *Magic,* the Watermans of *The Sadness of Witches,* the Franklands of *Necessary Rites,* appear to be all in admired and envied perfect marriages, while in private they are becoming estranged, even hostile to one another. Infidelity in thought and deed is commonplace, but the real issue seems to be a questioning of the need to continue living together.

The stress is on women's strength and ability to survive while men crack up and break. When disaster strikes, women will instinctively carry on with the daily round, knowing its therapeutic value ("cooking being an orderly process, a gesture, in a small way, against chaos.") Repeatedly Elliott emphasises the value of feminine friendships ("Friends . . . are family nowadays, which is why there is so much kissing. For whatever reason, we seem to feel the need to touch"), in which there is unspoken understanding, the "dolphin language, mind to mind communication."

It is perhaps inevitable in these times when modish, half-understood cults and myths are elbowing out Christianity, that the bond between women should take the surprising form of a witches' coven, as in *Magic*.

Set against the praise of friendships between women is the recurrent theme of the absence of any such understanding between a mother and her daughter. Hinted at in *The Italian Lesson,* it is openly declared in *Summer People* ("she never cared for her mother because they were alike. And who can bear for long speaking to a mirror?"), and in *The Sadness of Witches* and *Necessary Rites.*

Conversely Elliott emphasizes the strength of the bond between a mother and her adolescent son (*Summer People, The Sadness of Witches, Necessary Rites*). There is a marked similarity both of physical appearance and of turn of mind between all these boys, as there is also between the young girls who float in and out of these people's houses and lives: long-haired, bare-foot flower children with little in the way of conversation and a terrifying egocentricity.

Some of the minor characters too bear an uncanny resemblance to one another (Felix Wanderman in *The Italian Lessons* and Max Stiller in *Life on the Nile* are both wise, elderly, Jewish, widowed, close to death—and sporting the same tufts of cottonwool after shaving).

Such similarities may perhaps be expected in a novelist who restricts herself largely to chronicle one small section of society. They are not due to a poverty of imagination; when she chooses Elliott can exercise her imagination with astonishing results: in *Dr. Gruber's Daughter* Adolf Hitler is hiding in a North Oxford attic, while his daughter, the offspring of an incestuous affair with his half-sister, roams leafy Oxford, a wraith from hell, in search of human and feline victims to devour. In *Magic* Sir Oliver and his housekeeper practise the skill of out-of-body experiences, and in *The Sadness of Witches* Martha, like the witches in *Macbeth,* can cause storms at sea and wreck or save boats.

The style is plain, straightforward; indeed in *The Italian Lesson* the short sentences seem to mimic those of the heroine's Italian phrase book. The form is usually that of a straight narrative; the horrors of bomb scares, car crashes, oil spills, murder, and suicide are all the more telling for this plainness. Only in *Life on the Nile* do we find a more complex form: the present-day story of Charlotte Hamp's experiences in Egypt is interwoven with extracts from the diary of her great-aunt who had lived in Egypt in the 1920s and was murdered there.

Characteristic perhaps of most novels which present life through a women's eyes are the descriptions of the small pleasures with which women shore up their lives. But always there is an undercurrent of unease beneath the calm surface ("a small daily terror"). In this respect particularly Elliott is a true chronicler of her chosen society.

—Hana Sambrook

ELLIS, Alice Thomas

Pseudonym for Anna Margaret Haycraft. **Nationality:** British. **Born:** Anna Margaret Lindholm in Liverpool, 9 September 1932; grew up in Penmaenmawr, Wales. **Education:** Bangor County Grammar School, Gwynedd; Liverpool School of Art; postulant, Convent of Notre Dame de Namur, Liverpool. **Family:** Married the publisher Colin Haycraft in 1956; four sons and one daughter (and one daughter and one son deceased). **Career:** Director, Duckworth, publishers, London. Columnist ("Home Life"), the *Spectator,* London, the *Universe,* London, 1989-91; and for *The Catholic Herald.* **Awards:** Welsh Arts Council award, 1977; *Yorkshire Post* award, 1986. **Address:** 22 Gloucester Crescent, London NW1 7DY, England.

PUBLICATIONS

Novels

The Sin Eater. London, Duckworth, 1977.
The Birds of the Air. London, Duckworth, 1980; New York, Viking Press, 1981.
The 27th Kingdom. London, Duckworth, 1982.
The Other Side of the Fire. London, Duckworth, 1983.
Unexplained Laughter. London, Duckworth, 1985; New York, Harper, 1987.
The Inn at the Edge of the World. London, Viking, 1990.
The Summerhouse Trilogy. London, Penguin, 1991; New York, Penguin, 1994.
   The Clothes in the Wardrobe. London, Duckworth, 1987.
   The Skeleton in the Cupboard. London, Duckworth, 1988.
   The Fly in the Ointment. London, Duckworth, 1989.
Pillars of Gold. London, Viking, 1992.

Uncollected Short Story

"Away in a Niche," in *Spectator* (London), 21-28 December 1985.

Other

Natural Baby Food: A Cookery Book (as Brenda O'Casey). London, Duckworth, 1977; as Anna Haycraft, London, Fontana, 1980.
Darling, You Shouldn't Have Gone to So Much Trouble (cookbook; as Anna Haycraft), with Caroline Blackwood. London, Cape, 1980.
Home Life. London, Duckworth, 1986.
Secrets of Strangers, with Tom Pitt-Aikens. London, Duckworth, 1986.
More Home Life. London, Duckworth, 1987.
Home Life 3. London, Duckworth, 1988.
Loss of the Good Authority: The Cause of Delinquency, with Tom Pitt-Aikens. London, Viking, 1989.
Home Life 4. London, Duckworth, 1989.
A Welsh Childhood, photographs by Patrick Sutherland. London, Joseph, 1990.

Editor, *Mrs. Donald,* by Mary Keene. London, Chatto and Windus, 1983.
Editor, *Wales: An Anthology.* London, Collins, 1989.

*　　*　　*

In all her books Alice Thomas Ellis takes the form of the upper-class social comedy and turns it inside out, with mordant, often uncomfortable wit, satire (some of it quite savage), and a gift for dialogue which means much more than is apparent, in a background which alternates between the country (usually Wales) and London, patches of which must be regarded as the author's own territory.

Her first novel, *The Sin Eater,* is set in Wales, where the Welsh have given up farming and taken to preying on the holidaymaker. In a country house, near a small resort which has declined since its pre-war heyday, the Captain, patriarch of the family, lies dying, unable to speak or move. Only a matter of time, says the doctor, cheerfully. Not much grief is shown by the family assembling to say goodbye to him. Henry, the eldest son and heir, lives with his wife

Rose and the twins in the family home. Visiting are younger brother Michael, his wife Angela, and Edward, a Fleet Street literary journalist, object of Angela's love (or lust). Ministering incompetently to the household is Phyllis, her son Jack ("Jack the Liar") and Gomer, Phyllis's adored but highly unpleasant grandson. The outsider is Ermyn, youngest daughter of the house, back from a secretarial course in London, regarded by the rest as half-witted (in fact she is slightly deaf, following measles in childhood, but no one has noticed). Rose (like Ellis) is a Roman Catholic, a brilliant organizer, one who arranges food, houses, and circumstances to disconcert others. Angela (who hates her) is disoriented by being put in a room newly arranged in 1930s style. A killing meal is eaten shortly before the cricket match of village versus Squire. When the village wins, for the first time, there follows a vengeful and dismaying Welsh saturnalia. Rose loves only the twins (absent from all but the first and last page of the novel) and the terrifying denouement is a fitting end to the outpouring of spite and malice so deftly observed.

Christmas is a family time, and in *The Birds of the Air,* Mrs. Marsh decides to invite all the family, to try to cheer Mary, whose grief will neither disappear, nor be assuaged. Mary's sister Barbara has just discovered her husband's infidelity by overhearing a sniggered comment that suddenly makes sense. She is on the way to a breakdown. Mary's grief is an indescribable agony, unhelped by her Catholicism, over the death of her illegitimate son, Robin. Everyone is embarrassed by Mary's grief. Barbara makes an exhibition of herself, getting drunk and pursuing Hunter, who rejects her. Social embarrassment to the last degree forms the basis for some hard, sharp things said about the nature of grief, love, and family life.

The 27th Kingdom (shortlisted for the Booker prize in 1982) is set in Chelsea in the 1950s, where Aunt Irene (of distant Russian descent) lives with her nephew Kyril in a pretty little house. Chelsea is still very socially mixed, and the cast includes the O'Connors, a large family of criminal Cockneys, and a passing parade of casual lodgers. The outsider and new lodger is Valentine, who wishes to be a nun, but has been sent out to see more of the world by Reverend Mother, who is Aunt Irene's sister. Valentine is, most inconveniently, a saint, as well as being very beautiful, and black. As in all the novels, the four last things of the Catholic Church—death and judgment, heaven and hell—loom in the background. Aunt Irene loves Kyril, but recognizes that he is evil and wicked. Both she and Mrs O'Connor, the Cockney matriarch, recognize the goodness of Valentine. Once again, it's very funny, and slightly more gentle in tone. Food plays its part, and so does Focus, a charming, beautiful, and amusing cat.

The Other Side of the Fire brings together a number of themes which can be claimed as standard ingredients in the Ellis novel. Claudia Bohannon is the second wife of Charles—they have two children of their own (absent at boarding school). Claudia finds herself inexplicably and shamingly in love with her stepson, Philip. Her confidante is Sylvie (living in the country, there are few congenial people around). Sylvie has given up love, and company, and has become a witch—or not, depending on how you view her. Certainly she has a familiar in the dog Gloria, evil-tempered and a perfect nuisance, rather like Sylvie's ex-husband, as one of the characters points out. Evvie, Sylvie's daughter, is writing a romantic novel along very predictable lines, containing stock characters like a Scottish vet with a dull fiancée, a housekeeper, a beautiful promiscuous girl, a mad Laird. Unfortunately and hilariously the characters from the novel invade life, and vice versa. Claudia is sweet

but dim—it takes a brick dropped by Evvie before she realizes what everyone else knows—that Philip is a charming and unscrupulous homosexual. The book meditates on various forms of love—and its transitory nature—touching all but the maternal, which, as in *The Sin Eater,* is so important that it is never mentioned.

Unexplained Laughter is set in Wales, where Lydia, a tough London journalist, has retreated to get over a broken heart. With her is Betty, who is nice, but a bore. The only company (typically, a small group of characters at each other's throats) is a family. Hywel, a farmer, is married unhappily to Elizabeth; Angharad, his youngest sister, is speechless and considered mad but is not as mad as all that; Beuno, the younger brother, is studying for the ministry. There is also the doctor, formerly Elizabeth's lover. Lydia is witty and cruel. It is only when she starts hearing unexplained laughter in the air round the cottage, and she talks to Beuno about the existence of God and the devil that she begins to develop into a more human being and allows herself to become fond of others. The devil is at work; they are a nasty bunch, with exceptions. Beuno is some kind of saint, Betty is pleasant and dull, Angharad is a visionary, and Lydia is improving her soul. Beuno exorcises the laughter, and it disappears. Whatever it was, he considered it evil.

These short novels are written with an uncanny ear for contemporary dialogue, the flash of steel beneath the apparently harmless words. There is a great deal said about the Catholic church, life, death, food, love, children, and the existence of evil, the devil in our midst ("Stan" Lydia calls him, a nickname for "Satan"). Only in the short story, "Away in a Niche," in which a tired housewife swaps places with the local saint for the three worst days of Christmas, do we get anything like a cheerful, happy conclusion.

—Philippa Toomey

ELLIS, Bret Easton

Nationality: American. **Born:** Los Angeles, 7 March 1964. **Education:** Bennington College, Vermont, B.A. 1986. **Agent:** International Creative Management, 40 West 57th Street, New York, New York 10019, U.S.A.

PUBLICATIONS

Novels

Less Than Zero. New York, Simon and Schuster, 1985; London, Pan, 1985.
The Rules of Attraction. New York, Simon and Schuster, 1987; London, Picador, 1988.
American Psycho. New York, Vintage, and London, Picador, 1991.
The Informers. New York, Knopf, and London, Picador, 1994.

*   *   *

Bret Easton Ellis's four novels to date explore the accidie (apathy, boredom) and alienation of the "brat pack" or "blank generation" of affluent white youth in the United States in the 1980s. Whether set in Los Angeles (*Less Than Zero* and *The Informers*) or in a New England college (*The Rules of Attraction*) or New

York (*American Psycho*), each of these novels represents the homogenizing and dehumanizing effect of late capitalist consumer culture. Through his cipher-like characters, who are mostly distinguished from each other only by the brand names of their designer clothes, Ellis traces the metonymies of desire in a culture where sex and the body are commodified and, like drugs, alcohol, and MTV, are addictively consumed.

The desire for excess that is underlain by ennui is recorded in an affectless and "stunned" prose style that is arguably mimetic of a "depthless" postmodern culture. Each of the novels has occasioned controversy as to whether this flat style merely reproduces the nihilistic lassitude of its characters or whether, through verisimilitude, Ellis is indeed offering a critique of the ethics of the society that he represents. This controversy culminated in the critical reception of *American Psycho,* Ellis's tale of serial killing and mass murder in yuppie Manhattan. This novel was variously perceived as a devastating indictment of the erosion of ethics by capitalism in the Reaganite 1980s, as a virulent brand of pornography thinly veiled as mainstream art for the middle classes, and as simply an aesthetic failure because it did not manage to create a metaphor for the violence that it repetitively detailed.

Arguably, each of Ellis's novels expresses a yearning for a meaningful reality that seems inaccessible through the inauthentic simulations of consumer culture. *Less Than Zero,* which begins with the observation that "people are afraid to merge on the freeways in Los Angeles," a statement of disconnection that becomes a refrain in the novel, describes the spiraling loss of ethical bearings experienced by the narrator, Clay, as he spends a Christmas vacation in Los Angeles, away from his college in the East. The various forms of consumption—sex, shopping, drugs, alcohol—that dominate the lives of Clay and his peers fail to signify for Clay. He is haunted by the menacing extremity of the desert, by reports of random violence and disaster, and by childhood memories that disclose psychic violence within a family where, in the end, "nobody's home." Passivity becomes voyeurism and consumption becomes pornographic spectacle as Clay is an unresisting witness to scenes of forced prostitution and gang rape. Nathaniel West's Hollywood of the 1930s is echoed by the broodingly apocalyptic vision of Los Angeles in the 1980s with which Ellis leaves us: "The images I had were of people being driven mad by living in the city. Images of parents who were so hungry and unfulfilled that they ate their own children."

The East Coast, an absent referent that would potentially signify in Ellis's first novel, fails to offer an authentic alternative to the artifice of Los Angeles in his second novel, *The Rules of Attraction.* The interior monologues of the three main characters and their somewhat indeterminate peers register the fluidity of desire that is sometimes shaped by romantic narratives but that ultimately is "haphazard and random . . . episodic, broken . . . [showing] no sense of events unfolding from prior events," to quote from the epigraph by Tim O'Brien, which serves to interpret the ensuing trajectory of the novel.

Ellis's apparent withholding of explicit moral comment on the spiritual impoverishment of the culture that his novels represent was critically perceived as being more problematic in his detailed account of the activities of Patrick Bateman, the eponymous "American Psycho." In contrast to the classic realist novel, here no "deep" psychological exploration of or explanation for the protagonist's actions is offered. Instead, the reader is immediately introduced into the hermetic world of New York consumer culture with the opening words of the novel: "Abandon all hope ye who enter here. . . ."

The randomness of desire that was the subject of *The Rules of Attraction* is now replaced by a deterministic consumerism whereby the serial killer is the parodic extremity of a cultural logic that reifies people and stimulates an addiction to excess that only violence can temporarily assuage.

If the relation between author, text, and reader is ambiguous in *American Psycho,* authorial comment seems foregrounded through the narrative strategies of Ellis's most recent novel, *The Informers.* An impressionistic composite of narrative voices, this novel presents the estrangement between the generations and between the sexes in affluent Los Angeles. Images of anomie and personal and familial dissociation are interwoven with scenes of sexual violence that accelerate as the novel shifts into gothic fantasy, with vampires preying on their victims, and then moves toward a conclusion with the depiction of the sexual assault, torture, and murder of a child. The willfully blind romantic fantasy that concludes the novel would seem to draw attention to the cultural disavowal of what Ellis, speaking of the 1980s, has described as "the absolute banality of a perverse decade."

—Joanna Price

ELLROY, James

Nationality: American. **Born:** 1948. **Family:** 1) married (divorced 1991); 2) Helen Knode. **Career:** Has held a variety of jobs, including country club caddy, 1965-84. Since 1984, full-time writer. **Agent:** Nat Sobel, Sobel Weber Assc., 146 East 19th St., New York, New York 10003, U.S.A. **Address:** 84 Siwanoy Blvd., Eastchester, New York 10707, U.S.A.

PUBLICATIONS

Novels

Brown's Requiem. New York, Avon, 1981; London, Allison and Busby, 1984.

Clandestine. New York, Avon, 1982; London, Allison and Busby, 1984.

Blood on the Moon. New York, Mysterious Press, 1984; London, Allison and Busby, 1985.

Because the Night. New York, Mysterious Press, 1984; London, Century, 1987.

Suicide Hill. New York, Mysterious Press, 1986; London, Century, 1988.

Killer on the Road. New York, Mysterious Press, 1986.

Silent Terror. New York, Mysterious Press, 1986; London, Arrow, 1990.

L.A. Quartet:

    The Black Dahlia. New York, Mysterious Press, 1987; London, Mysterious Press UK, 1988.

    The Big Nowhere. New York, Mysterious Press, 1988; London, Mysterious Press UK, 1989.

    L.A. Confidential. New York and London, Mysterious Press, 1990.

White Jazz. New York, Knopf, and London, Random House, 1992.

American Tabloid. New York, Knopf, and London, Century, 1995.

Short Stories

Hollywood Nocturnes. New York, Knopf, 1994; as *Dick Contino's Blues and Other Stories.* London, Arrow, 1994.

Other

Murder and Mayhem: An A-Z of the World's Most Notorious Killers. London, Arrow, 1992.

*   *   *

Labeling James Ellroy a writer of hardboiled crime or *noir* fiction oversimplifies his contribution to American imaginative writing. Although his earliest novels belong to the generic crime mode perfected by masters like Chandler, Cain, and MacDonald, the originality of recent works like *Dick Contino's Blues* and *American Tabloid* compel a different critical attention. After ten successful works of a pulp fiction both unsentimental and romantic, this unorthodox author began to depict life in America at the end of the 20th century as a remembered story of comically exaggerated criminality.

Similar traits stamp Ellroy's first two novels, *Brown's Requiem* and *Clandestine,* as the work of a gifted but unpracticed author: disturbed cops corrupted by the crime world they are supposed to combat; redeeming women who are (or were) hookers; sprawling, ill-managed plots loaded with depravity and violence. The second book replicates the framework of the murder of Ellroy's mother (which occurred in 1958 and remains unsolved), and it includes a portrait of himself as the young boy he was at the time of her death. His next projects were a long saga of the caper-filled life of gangster Bugsy Siegel and an extended epic of the Los Angeles underworld that concluded with the city's burning down. Persuaded to abandon *The Confessions of Bugsy Siegel,* Ellroy reworked and published the L.A. epic as *Blood on the Moon* in 1984. With his next two novels, *Because the Night* and *Suicide Hill,* it formed a trilogy about the brilliant but tainted L.A. cop, Lloyd Hopkins, described by *New York* magazine contributor Martin Kihn as "an evil-genius . . . [who] becomes by the end of the series the archetypal Ellroy cop, indistinguishable from his prey and tortured by guilt." These were followed in 1986 by *Killer on the Road,* narrated by a serial killer named Martin Plunkett. Then Ellroy returned to the city and time of his own genesis—Los Angeles, from the late 1940s until 1958—to produce the four novels that constitute the "L.A. Quartet": *The Black Dahlia, The Big Nowhere, L.A. Confidential,* and *White Jazz.* Published between 1987 and 1992, they catapulted James Ellroy into the top rank of new, original crime fiction authors.

These progressively baroque stories of corruption, depravity, and violence turn Los Angeles into an emblematic urban inferno for our time. *The Black Dahlia*'s hero is the sensitive ex-boxer, Bucky Bleichert, who joins the LAPD after World War II and is soon plunged into the famous 1947 "Black Dahlia" murder case, a social storm whipped up by the discovery of a young woman's mutilated body in a Los Angeles vacant lot. Obsessively pursuing a solution to the case (in reality it went unsolved), the naive Bleichert is personally transformed through a violent plot that parallels both the course of the murder investigation and the path of his relationships with fellow cops, a kindred detective partner, their shared lover, and a sexually irresistible female in her twenties who perversely relives the sordid career of the mysterious "Black Dahlia." Called by Harlan Ellison "the shocker other writers would kill to

have written," *The Black Dahlia* is dedicated to "Geneva Hilliker Ellroy 1915-1958," and inscribed "Mother: Twenty-nine Years Later, This Valediction in Blood."

The heroes of the next three novels of the "L.A. Quartet" live, like Bucky Bleichert, in the region between morally unredeemable personal lives and the enveloping swamp of American urban corruption. Harboring terrible personal secrets, they are driven to accomplish something honest in their compromised lives, while also furiously compelled to identify the wellsprings of their spiritual torture. They move through plots that compound sensational incident and crazy complication at exponentially gathering paces, leading to tensilely wrought climaxes. Their adventures are narrated with a progressively condensed, high-energy expressiveness that mimics the several dictions of mainstream newspaper, sensational tabloid, gossip magazine, municipal bureaucracy, advertising agency, and police communication. Ellroy gives them speech and thought that convincingly captures the talk and intelligence of working cops, established gangsters, ethnic Los Angelenos, and most of the numerous types who populate the city's sprawling lowlife.

In *The Big Nowhere,* Ellroy employs a multiple point-of-view, his trio of compromised heroes carrying a three-strand plot that focuses on the early-1950s hunt for Communists in the movie business, the conspiracy between organized crime and the LAPD, and the growing phobia about homosexuality in American society. Young sheriff's deputy Danny Upshaw transforms his buried secret of unadmitted homosexuality into an obsessive zeal to prosecute the perpetrators of a string of revoltingly perverse sex murders. His counterparts, an ambitious police sergeant and an expulsed city cop turned private security guard, are similarly driven to compensate for self-perceived failures of character. The corrupt social system ultimately does them all in, leaving the Irish-born, diabolically conniving LAPD detective, Dudley Smith, to rule over the criminal infestation that defines American life more and more into the 1950s.

Dave Klein, the hero of *White Jazz,* is the most morally tortured cop-hero of the "Quartet." A sublimated incestuous relationship with his sister not only prevents his finding pleasure in women, but also shackles him psychologically to every prurient vice assignment. Everything in his barely tolerable environment stimulates his murderous inclinations, and his history of quasi-official executions and betrayals allows his departmental superiors to expose him to deadly hazards. Klein nevertheless succeeds in enlisting our sympathy, both by wrestling with his inner torment and by regarding his repulsive world honestly. In the most extreme act of unlawfulness yet committed by an Ellroy cop-hero, he exacts a ferocious revenge on the plot's lead villains, as penalty for which he suffers a beating so thorough that his physiognomy requires rebuilding. Thus disguised, he escapes his avengers and finds the freedom to set down this supposed "memoir" of horrible events in Los Angeles of the mid-1950s which we are reading.

The theme of an archetypal villainy rooted in the police mentality itself may dominate the four novels of the "L.A. Quartet," but Ellroy also injects them with an increasingly comic serum by portraying many of the secondary characters—especially the historically documentable gangsters and celebrities—as familiar caricatures. Although it seems clear that he means to suggest thereby the ludicrous influence wrought on the American imagination by these publicity-fashioned personalities, with their outlandish behavior and bizarrely demotic lingo, some critics have found it callously offensive of Ellroy to bestow such unacceptable views and articulateness upon both his demi-heroes and their low-life confreres. But this presumed political incorrectness is also quite authentic, both behaviorally and linguistically. Indeed, the characters' aggregate argot constitutes a colorfully "hip" language all its own, a kind of fictively vulgar tongue for late century. These figures may therefore be heard as speaking in the submerged "voice of our time," uttering the unspoken views of a sickened national conscience. On this matter, Ellroy is quoted by Kihn as saying: "I think that social revisionism and political correctness make for very, very bad crime novels."

The 1994 collection of short pieces, *Hollywood Nocturnes,* offers an excellent sampling of Ellroy's developing dark-comic rendition of the world as a kaleidoscopic cartoon of corruption. The centerpiece of the compendium is the novella, *Dick Contino's Blues,* whose first-person narrator is the documentable Contino himself, a reasonably successful pop singer and accordionist of the 1950s. Ellroy has him tell a manic adventure story set in southern California, a tale of grade-Z Hollywood movies, sexual hustling, extortion, murder, and drug-dealing, enacted with a breathless brio by gangsters, politicians, moguls, detectives, and a gallery of L.A. citizenry—car salesmen, beat cops, real estate brokers, singers, hookers, waitresses, Disney artists, bureaucrats, small-time hoodlums, and every kind of proto-lounge lizard. In short, it is the usual Ellroy circus, but performing in a more than usually bizarre Ellroy plot.

Together with its introductory essay, "Out of the Past," *Dick Contino's Blues* encapsulates all the energies and impetuses of Ellroy's literary quest for his own life's significance, a creative destiny he has been pursuing unwittingly (it turns out) since the age of 30, when, after almost dying from drug and alcohol abuse three years earlier, he finally decided to start writing. His impetus for the novelistic experiment came from a recalled image of the entertaining Contino in a 1958 television appearance, an image that coalesced with a photograph, sent to him years later by a friend, taken of the ten-year-old Ellroy on June 22, 1958, minutes after he was told that his mother had been found murdered. As he relates in "Out of the Past:"

> The photo held me transfixed; its force transcended my many attempts to exploit my past for book sales. An underlying truth zapped me: my bereavement, even in that moment, as ambiguous. I'm already calculating potential advantages, regrouping as the officious men surrounding me defer to the perceived grief of a little boy.

After he had framed the photo and stared at it for "a good deal of time," he writes, "Spark point: late '50s memories re-ignited." In his sparked memory, the "grade-Z movie" *Daddy-O* that Contino made after his career had been torpedoed by a charge of draft-dodging merges with Ellroy's awakening perception that the "L.A. Quartet" novels contain the significant secrets still locked in his own memory; these secrets now promise an emergent clarity because they have been re-contextualized by the chance juxtaposition of shocked boy's photo and lounge entertainer's television image, both deriving from the late 1950s. "Because I knew—instinctively—that he held important answers. I sensed that he could powerfully spritz narrative detail and fill up holes in my memory, bringing Los Angeles in the late '50s into some sort of hyper-focus." Memory, for Ellroy, is "that place where personal recollections collide with history."

Finding the 63-year-old Dick Contino in Las Vegas, the author of ten money-making crime novels confirmed the feeling that he was about to change direction in his writing. In two days of conversations—about how to adjust to shifting popular taste, what con-

stitutes quality in popular entertainment, why the audience cannot be deprived of their easy entertainment—Ellroy solidified his sense that his "world had tilted toward a new understanding of my past." After the accordionist had serenaded him for his forty-fifth birthday, Ellroy says: "I asked Dick if he would consent to appear as the hero of a novella and my next novel." These would be books about "fear, courage and heavily compromised redemptions." Contino agreed, saying: "Good, I think I've been there."

These insights and the narrative action of *Dick Contino's Blues* make it possible to appreciate Ellroy's earlier fiction for more than the raw, sensational, titillating effects of its plots and narrative energies. At a deeper level, the maniacal violence and cold-bloodedness in them manifest the author's passionate need to understand the fullness of his half-buried personal memory, which had both haunted and eluded him. As he says, quoting Jung: "What is not brought to consciousness comes to us as fate." He refers both to his finding of Dick Contino and to his fictive sallies into the period shared by Contino's mid-life and his own childhood, the American post-Korea 1950s.

In *American Tabloid,* the novel he was writing as he also plotted the Contino novella, Ellroy breaks away from Los Angeles as his main fictive venue. The crime chronicler's American version of the City of Dis now spreads out to encompass all the sites of the momentous events leading to the assassination of John F. Kennedy. And the plot, tapping the several modes of contemporary American fiction that have already engaged this modern mythic material, gleefully tangles up the high-fictional doings of the Mafia, the CIA, the Kennedys, J. Edgar Hoover, Jimmy Hoffa, and the sundry organizations involved in early 1960s civil rights, racket-busting, Kennedy electioneering, the Bay of Pigs, and anti-Communism, not to omit a menagerie of Hollywood and showbiz characters ranging from Marilyn Monroe to Howard Hughes.

Miami, Chicago, New York, Los Angeles, New Orleans, and several other purviews of the Mob, the CIA, and the FBI intertwine to form a plot terrain that could compete, in its sweep and detail, with the combined features of Dali, Brueghel, Villon, and Rabelais. This ground is traversed with extreme modern facility by the novel's three maculate heroes: Kemper Boyd, a stone-souled free agent of conspiracy and a genius at multiple role-playing; Ward Littell, a guilt-infected repository of self-destructiveness and Jesuit-schooled moral absolutism, deteriorating sympathetically into a helpless American amorality; and Pete Bondurant, the hired hitman and dope-runner carried over from his minor role in *White Jazz* to discharge the duties of an old-fashioned fictional heavy who turns out to be a romantic. An introductory note, presuming the would-be narrative authority to "tell it like it is," declares that America, having long since lost its innocence, now needs to look at its recent traumatic history from the point of view of the "bad little men" who have actually shaped it. These duly become the characters of Ellroy's most picaresque novel to date. *American Tabloid* presents the historic adventures of all the American rogues one can imagine participating in the early 1960s' *commedia* of Camelot, Cuba, and the CIA.

James Ellroy has declared that he wants to recreate the entire history of 20th-century America—"the story of bad white men"—through crime fiction, thereby becoming "the Tolstoy of the crime novel." With the Contino novella and *American Tabloid,* he revealed a bold new direction to this design. He would not merely insert historical personages into his stories and rewrite their lives' facts, as docu-novelists like Norman Mailer and Don DeLillo were still doing; he would appropriate a still-living, modest entertainment figure from those "bad old days" like Dick Contino and make him the "improved" narrative hero of his memorial crime fictions. In this process, he would also refine the comic sensibility that has been growing through his years of holding off the demons of personal bitterness and egomania. As his friend Joseph Wambaugh told Martin Kihn: "I always suspect that beneath [his anger and intensity] there's a performer there. . . . You sort of know you're being put on when you're with James Ellroy—maybe even when you read him, in a sense." Ellroy's fictional performances, inspired by their fiercely unsentimental vision of our times, do indeed disclose a Beckett-like comedian who, spawned in Los Angeles, California, in the middle of the century, seems destined to chronicle its absurd, criminal course ironically—as if it were his own life's perfect metaphor.

—Peter W. Ferran

ELY, David

Nationality: American. **Born:** Chicago, Illinois, 19 November 1927. **Education:** The University of North Carolina, Chapel Hill, 1944-45; Harvard University, Cambridge, Massachusetts, 1947-49, B.A. 1949; St. Antony's College, Oxford (Fulbright scholar), 1954-55. **Military Service:** Served in the United States Navy, 1945-46, and the United States Army, 1950-52. **Family:** Married Margaret Jenkins in 1954; four children. **Career:** Reporter, St. Louis *Post-Dispatch,* 1949-50, 1952-54, 1955-56; administrative assistant, Development and Resources Corporation, New York, 1956-59. **Awards:** Mystery Writers of America Edgar Allan Poe award, for short story, 1962. **Address:** P.O. Box 1387, East Dennis, Massachusetts 02641, U.S.A.

PUBLICATIONS

Novels

Trot: A Novel of Suspense. New York, Pantheon, 1963; London, Secker and Warburg, 1964.
Seconds. New York, Pantheon, 1963; London, Deutsch, 1964.
The Tour. New York, Delacorte Press, and London, Secker and Warburg, 1967.
Poor Devils. Boston, Houghton Mifflin, 1970.
Walking Davis. New York, Charterhouse, 1972.
Mr. Nicholas. New York, Putnam, 1974; London, Macmillan, 1975.
A Journal of the Flood Year. New York, Fine, and London, Phoenix, 1992.

Short Stories

Time Out. New York, Delacorte Press, 1968; London, Secker and Warburg, 1969.
Always Home and Other Stories. New York, Fine, 1991.

Uncollected Short Stories

"The Wizard of Light," in *Amazing* (New York), March 1962.
"The Alumni March," in *Cosmopolitan* (New York), 1962.

"McDaniels' Flood," in *Elks Magazine* (Chicago), 1963.
"The Captain's Boarhunt," in *Saturday Evening Post* (Philadelphia), 21 March 1964.
"The Assault on Mount Rushmore," in *Cavalier* (New York), July 1969.
"The Carnival," in *Antaeus* (New York), 1971.
"The Light in the Cottage," in *Playboy* (Chicago), 1974.
"Starling's Circle," in *Ellery Queen's Mystery Magazine* (New York), July 1976.
"The Running Man," in *Ellery Queen's Mystery Magazine* (New York), December 1976.
"The Weed Killer," in *Ellery Queen's Mystery Magazine* (New York), May 1977.
"The Temporary Daughter," in *Seventeen* (New York), April 1978.
"The Rich Girl," in *Seventeen* (New York), July 1978.
"The Looting of the Tomb," in *Ellery Queen's Scenes of the Crime,* edited by Ellery Queen. New York, Davis, 1979; London, Hale, 1981.
"The Marked Man," in *Best Detective Stories of the Year 1980,* edited by Edward D. Hoch. New York, Dutton, 1980.
"Methuselah," in *Atlantic* (Boston), March 1980.

*   *   *

David Ely's fiction describes the cost and conditions of freedom—what an ordinary man must do to understand himself and his world. His novels are shaped like thrillers; in each a man is driven onto a quest (initially for the wrong motives) which ultimately leads him to himself, to his unconscious mind, his heart. The novels describe with remarkable sensitivity individuals coping with worlds that are alien, inimical and all-powerful. The triumph of the individual spirit in hostile modern milieu is accompanied by pain and sorrow, loss of innocence and simple comfort, but it brings both self-knowledge and peace.

Trot, Ely's first novel, is subtitled "A Novel of Suspense" and predicates the world of all of Ely's fiction: an alien, minatory and hostile environment, in this case the Paris underworld after World War II. An Army CID man, Sergeant Trot, abruptly becomes the victim in a case on which he is assigned. Suspected of corruption and murder, he hides with the criminals he has stalked. The inversion of his world causes him to reassess his concepts of justice and freedom. Finally he is able to reinstate himself by breaking an extortion-murder plot by escaped Nazis. But the significant victory is Trot's own self-revelation.

In *Seconds,* probably Ely's best-known novel, a Babbitt-like man, a cipher known only by the code name "Wilson," abandons his comfortable but aimless upper-middle-class existence when a mysterious corporation offers him a new life, a second chance. He is surgically rehabilitated and supplied a total identity as a successful artist, but the new freedom proves too painful and challenging. Wilson disintegrates under the stress of his open and unfamiliar world of freedom and nonconformity. "I never had a dream," he says when he returns to the corporation to be erased.

The Tour deals with the same theme in a more terrifying form. A parable of American imperialism and military-scientific manipulation of other cultures, it describes a "tour" designed to provide jaded bourgeois travelers with ultimate thrills in a mythical Central American banana republic. The tour includes episodes of sex, jungle survival and guerrilla fighting, carefully staged for the fuddled gringos. Behind the scenes a test is made on an automated counter-insurgency weapon, a robot tank which wipes out a starveling guerrilla band (and its builders) and nearly decimates the tour. The novel develops as an analogue for U.S. involvement in Southeast Asia and for other paramilitary "tours" of policy. It is similar in shape to Peter Matthiessen's important *At Play in the Fields of the Lord.*

Poor Devils attacks the sociological concepts of poverty and its alleviation. Another parable, it describes the slow education of a history professor, Aaron Bell, who stumbles onto a Project Nomad, a genocidal agency for a "final solution" to poverty, a technological bureau that fights poverty with coldly mechanical games theory and supertechnology. Bell's education leads him to discover the futility of his life and his career, the absurdity of history and ideals faced with amoral technology. The old man he has pursued, Lundquist, a "picaresque saint," teaches him finally that he must discover (or invent) his values himself. Bell opts out of the system of research and manipulation to become a Whitmanesque wanderer, following the "Lundquist heresy, the preamble written short for men in too big a hurry to read much: *Life, liberty, and the pursuit.*"

An allegorical study of personality in existentialist terms, *Walking Davis* describes Pierce Davis, who decides to walk around the world. Setting out from Spark, Iowa, Davis makes a Robinson Crusoe voyage of survival and self-discovery, finally plumbing all his human resources and learning that "You can't build a monument to a hero. If a man's a hero, he builds his own." His walk leads him into a strange union with nature and himself, stripped of all pretense like Camus's Sisyphus, reduced to one essential human function—questing.

Mr. Nicholas describes the complete symptomology of paranoia, centering on an executive in the surveillance industry who becomes convinced that "He was being watched everywhere and all the time." The protagonist, Henry Haddock, eventually adjusts to a life without privacy, wherein his public function subsumes his whole personality, and he becomes reconciled to a world without privacy, without self. The story develops allegorically in that it describes a whole world pressed and overcrowded, when personal rights are lost to the pressure of the many.

Ely's novels are all parables of the New Babbitt redeemed, the affluent and self-satisfied "Executive Man" freed to make real, life-or-death decisions, to direct his life and test the morality of his society. The transformations are costly, painful and sometimes tragic, but they are real and significant actions, leaps of faith which give meaning to the small existences Ely depicts.

—William J. Schafer

EMECHETA, (Florence Onye) Buchi

Nationality: British. **Born:** Lagos, Nigeria, 21 July 1944. **Education:** Methodist Girls' High School, Lagos; University of London, B.Sc. (honors) in sociology 1972. **Family:** Married Sylvester Onwordi in 1960 (separated 1969); two sons and three daughters. **Career:** Librarian, 1960-64; library officer, British Museum, London, 1965-69; youth worker and resident student, Race, 1974-76; community worker, Camden Council, London, 1976-78; visiting lecturer at 11 universities in the United States, 1979; senior research fellow and visiting professor of English, University of Calabar, Nigeria, 1980-81; lecturer, Yale University, New Haven, Connecticut, 1982. Since 1982, lecturer, University of London. Proprietor, Ogwugwu Afo Publishing Company, London; since 1979, mem-

ber of the Home Secretary's Advisory Council on Race. **Address:** 7 Briston Grove, London N8 9EX, England.

PUBLICATIONS

Novels

Adah's Story. London, Allison and Busby, 1983.
In the Ditch. London, Barrie and Jenkins, 1972.
Second-Class Citizen. London, Allison and Busby, 1974; New York, Braziller, 1975.
The Bride Price. London, Allison and Busby, and New York, Braziller, 1976.
The Slave Girl. London, Allison and Busby, and New York, Braziller, 1977.
The Joys of Motherhood. London, Allison and Busby, and New York, Braziller, 1979.
Destination Biafra. London, Allison and Busby, 1982.
Double Yoke. London, Ogwugwu Afo, 1982; New York, Braziller, 1983.
The Rape of Shavi. London, Ogwugwu Afo, 1983; New York, Braziller, 1985.
A Kind of Marriage. London, Macmillan, 1986.
Gwendolen. London, Collins, 1989; as *The Family,* New York, Braziller, 1990.
Kehinde. Oxford, Heinemann, 1994.

Fiction (for children)

Titch the Cat. London, Allison and Busby, 1979.
Nowhere to Play. London, Allison and Busby, 1980.
The Moonlight Bride. Oxford, Oxford University Press, 1980.
The Wrestling Match. Oxford, Oxford University Press, 1981; New York, Braziller, 1983.
Naira Power. London, Macmillan, 1982.

Plays

Television Plays: *A Kind of Marriage,* 1976; *The Ju Ju Landlord,* 1976.

Other

Our Own Freedom, photographs by Maggie Murray. London, Sheba, 1981.
Head above Water (autobiography). London, Ogwugwu Afo, 1986.

*   *   *

The title *Second-Class Citizen* which Buchi Emecheta chose for one of her most successful novels constitutes a very fair summary of the major theme which she explores. She always feels for the oppressed and presents their plight in a way that engages the reader's sympathy. From childhood on she observed life in Nigeria, and since her early twenties she has looked at the ways of the west through the skeptical, appraising eyes of a trained sociologist. And what she has seen, whether in Africa or England, has been a bleak picture of antagonisms and tyranny. There are flashes of humor and moments of happiness, but generally she depicts the scouring of human relationships by the desire of the powerful to dominate and exploit those who are weaker.

Married life she depicts as a battle of the sexes, and if some white males are shown in a bad light, that is nothing compared with the portrayal of the Nigerian men. Francis, in *Second-Class Citizen,* is a Nigerian immigrant in London whose thoughtlessness is the ruin of his more gifted wife; lazy, egotistical, and feckless, he compounds every problem that confronts the pair in their struggle to make ends meet, and his sexual demands and irresponsibility about parenthood leave Adah a physical wreck, distraught and without a penny in her pocket. In *The Joys of Motherhood* we become aware of the mordant irony of the title as the novel chronicles the misfortunes of Nnu Ego, a simple Nigerian girl who comes to Lagos to marry and suffers every kind of humiliation as her husband proves himself incapable of overcoming the admittedly difficult circumstances of his wretched existence. Her agony reaches its peak when, in accord with custom, he takes as his second wife the widow of his brother and thoroughly enjoys the tensions this naturally creates.

Tyranny and heartlessness outside the domestic sphere also rouse Emecheta's ire. For many young people in Nigeria education seems to offer a route towards self-fulfillment, but *Double Yoke* shows what the price can be when a young girl tries to cope with the rival claims of tradition and modernity within a system which fundamentally has little to offer that is really valid. The cynicism of the whole enterprise is revealed when the heroine realizes she must trade sexual favors with her professor if she is to gain the examination results she covets. Once she has qualifications she will perhaps be able, like Adah in *Second-Class Citizen,* to go to the United Kingdom and enjoy what it has to offer. In fact, as *Second-Class Citizen* and its grim predecessor, *In the Ditch,* show, London is a hostile world where racialism is rife and housing is squalid. There is the welfare state, of course, yet it operates in such a way that a talented and qualified young woman is gradually but inexorably pauperized and deskilled. *Destination Biafra* is a chilling account of a different sort of horror, the disastrous civil war that ripped Nigeria apart in the difficult times immediately after the withdrawal of the inadequate colonial powers. No atrocity is too cruel for men in brief authority, and though Emecheta has sympathy for everyone, it is natural that the women are shown as those who suffer the most.

Gwendolen changes the focus to some degree, presenting the plight of Caribbean immigrants in London primarily through the perspective of the difficulties that a young girl has in finding any sort of fulfillment as a child and teenager in a culture which means very little to her at any time. A perfect symbol of this failure of integration lies in the fact that even her own family finds pronouncing her rather highfalutin name impossibly difficult. Emecheta is far from ascribing all her heroine's ills to the failure of the citizens of her adopted country to take her to their heart, though there are some criticisms, especially of the education service, that strike home. Gwendolen's misfortunes had, however, already begun before she ever left Jamaica, and in London tensions within the immigrant community are shown to be particularly damaging. Beneath the psychological problems of immigrants there runs, moreover, the deep current of protest at the exploitation of women by men whose sexual demands are never diminished by any sense of their only too apparent personal inadequacies and general fecklessness.

Few will seek to deny that Emecheta has grounds for the complaints she makes about marital relationships in particular and about the interplay of social and political forces in general. Yet she loads

the dice a little too much. The girls and women she takes as her heroines always possess something which places them above the ordinary run of those with whom they mix. Birth or superior intelligence makes them outstanding. But it also has the unfortunate consequence of making them atypical of the group they represent. There is too some idealization of rural society in Nigeria in former times. It certainly had merits, which colonial powers were stupid not to recognize, yet by concentrating on the more advantaged members of such communities Emecheta distorts the picture. The problem becomes most acute in *The Rape of Shavi,* a somewhat mannered allegorical tale of Europeans who are fleeing from an impending cataclysm, and who have the privilege of insight into an almost Utopian Africa.

For the most part, however, Emecheta's mode is realistic, and though *Destination Biafra* contains some devastating pictures of the pretentiousness and luxurious lifestyle of upper-class Nigerians, she generally concerns herself with the straightforward portrayal of the underprivileged. There is some description of locales, with Nigerian names for plants, foodstuffs, and fabrics adding a dash of local color which sometimes contrasts, especially in the earlier novels, a little too obviously with literary allusions in a dated English tradition. Dialogue is invariably crisp, highlighting important turns in the narrative or enhancing characterization. Above all, Emecheta is a storyteller. The title of her novels, like the chapter headings, are direct and explicit, helping the reader to see the way forward through narratives that have the power to convince as well as the capacity to arouse sympathy with the misfortunes depicted.

—Christopher Smith

ENGLISH, Isobel

Nationality: British. **Born:** London, 9 June 1925. **Education:** A convent school in Somerset. **Awards:** Katherine Mansfield-Menton prize, 1974. **Address:** 10 Gardnor Rd, London NW3, England.

PUBLICATIONS

Novels

The Key That Rusts. London, Deutsch, 1954.
Every Eye. London, Deutsch, 1956; New York, Crowell, 1959.
Four Voices. London, Longman, 1961.

Short Stories

Life after All and Other Stories. London, Martin Brian and O'Keeffe, 1973.

Uncollected Short Story

"Promises," in *New Stories 1,* edited by Margaret Drabble and Charles Osborne. London, Arts Council, 1976.

Play

Meeting Point, in *New Review* (London), 1976.

Other

The Gift Book, illustrated by Barbara Jones. London, Parrish, 1964.

*

Critical Study: Interview in *Friends and Friendship* by Kay Dick, London, Sidgwick and Jackson, 1974.

*   *   *

Isobel English's particular angle of vision, focusing on the various implications of an action and intricate suppositions of hidden motivation, inclines her naturally towards first-person narration. For her, experience must necessarily be filtered through the eye of one particular observer, with an implicit question as to the nature of the filter in each case.

The Key That Rusts deals with the love-affair of the narrator's married step-brother and a friend, culminating in the latter's madness. The narrator both reveals much of herself in her account of this, and is insidiously affected by the action. The flashbacks to her childhood, as she revisits her old convent school, introduce another scale of values, though without necessarily any acceptance of "the security of faith," and complicated by the implications of the metamorphosis of her schoolgirl love, Felicity, into Mother Peter.

Confusion of time sequences to bring out thematic continuity is taken further in the more stylized *Every Eye,* with its exploitation of photographic imagery. Here, the narrator's holiday journey across Europe is accompanied by a journey through her memory, reconstructing her youthful love-affair with the middle-aged Jasper. Although in these memories the narrator is ostensibly one of the two chief protagonists, it yet seems appropriate for the journey through place to reveal that her role in Jasper's life was subsidiary to Cynthia's, whose presence has permeated the book. The closing factual substantiation of the relationship between Jasper and Cynthia is a highly skilful sleight-of-hand. English's quirky phrasing is well suited both to the piquant past and the contented present which her narrator juxtaposes; the style has shed the occasional overselfconsciousness of her previous book.

Middle-class characters similar to those of the earlier books reappear in *Four Voices,* but here English introduces the middle-class failures, Mona and Pentry. Pentry has sunk to the level of a men's hostel, though the exigencies of the plot keep the setting mostly middle-class. In fact, the accidents of marriage unite the characters in the same family—an institution which fascinates English in all three novels. However, it is doubtful whether the slightly clumsy narrative technique—inspired by the radio?—justifies the wider range of characterization. In any case the technique of blending monologues "spoken" by the main characters, once used, is probably a dead end for this author.

English's stories, collected in *Life after All and Other Stories,* show an individual and accomplished use of the form. In general she dispenses with the first-person narrator on the smaller scale of the short story. An exception, "Running Away," describes a convent school childhood, while Sebastian's mother in "The Crucifix after Cellini" is cast in the same mould as the Catholic dévoté in *Four Voices.* English's preoccupation with the extended family runs through several stories, including the longest, "One of the Family," which like *The Key That Rusts* confronts mental illness. Her material ranges from the Jewish background of this story to an evoca-

tion of an American academic's homosexual haunts and cronies in "Saying Goodbye." Only one story, "Nobody Came," is unsuccessful, failing to avoid cliché in its treatment of lonely old age; but "Cousin Dot," partly in verse is an interesting if light-weight attempt to handle a similar subject.

The middle-class ambience of English's work recalls Elizabeth Bowen and Elizabeth Taylor. Her power lies in her ironic control of nuance: "She frayed away the edges of her last days in the flat in a sadly distracted manner, that had behind it a great strength of purpose." There is a rare but all the more effective grotesqueness in her humor: "Then he said 'Granny,' and two heads reared up off their pillows like old tortoises, but fell back again when they saw him." This highly individual voice is only occasionally blurred by imprecision.

—Val Warner

ERDRICH, (Karen) Louise

Nationality: American. **Born:** Little Falls, Minnesota, 7 June 1954. **Education:** Dartmouth College, Hanover, New Hampshire, B.A. 1976; Johns Hopkins University, Baltimore, M.A. 1977. **Family:** Married Michael Anthony Dorris in 1981; three sons and three daughters. **Career:** Visiting poetry teacher, North Dakota State Arts Council, 1977-78; creative writing teacher, Johns Hopkins University, 1978-79; visiting fellow, Dartmouth College, 1981. Member, Turtle Mountain Band of Ojibwa. **Awards:** MacDowell fellowship, 1980; Yaddo fellowship, 1981; Nelson Algren award, for story, 1982; National Book Critics Circle award, 1984; Virginia Sully prize, 1984; Sue Kaufman award, 1984; *Los Angeles Times* Book award, 1985; Guggenheim fellowship, 1985. **Address:** c/o Harper Collins, 10 East 53rd Street, New York, New York 10022, U.S.A.

PUBLICATIONS

Novels

Love Medicine. New York, Holt, 1984; London, Deutsch, 1985.
The Beet Queen. New York, Holt, 1986; London, Hamish Hamilton, 1987.
Tracks. New York, Holt, and London, Hamish Hamilton, 1988.
Crown of Columbus, with Michael Dorris. New York and London, Harper Collins, 1991.
The Bingo Palace. New York and London, Harper Collins, 1994.
The Bluejay's Dance. New York and London, Harper Collins, 1995.

Uncollected Short Stories

"Scales," in *The Best American Short Stories 1983,* edited by Shannon Ravenel and Anne Tyler. Boston, Houghton Mifflin, 1983; as *The Year's Best American Short Stories,* London, Severn House, 1984.
"American Horse," in *Earth Power Coming,* edited by Simon J. Ortiz. Tsaile, Arizona, Navajo Community College Press, 1983.
"Destiny," in *Atlantic* (Boston), January 1985.
"Mister Argus," in *Georgia Review* (Athens), Summer 1985.

"Flesh and Blood," in *Buying Time,* edited by Scott Walker. St. Paul, Minnesota, Graywolf Press, 1985.

"Saint Marie," in *Prize Stories 1985,* edited by William Abrahams. New York, Doubleday, 1985.

"Fleur," in *Prize Stories 1987,* edited by William Abrahams. New York, Doubleday, 1987.

"Snares," in *The Best American Short Stories 1988,* edited by Shannon Ravenel and Mark Helprin. Boston, Houghton Mifflin, 1988.

"A Wedge of Shade," in *Louder than Words,* edited by William Shore. New York, Vintage, 1989.

"Crown of Thorns," in *The Invisible Enemy,* edited by Miriam Dow and Jennifer Regan. St. Paul, Minnesota, Graywolf Press, 1989.

"Matchimanito," in *The Best of the West 2,* edited by James Thomas and Denise Thomas. Layton, Utah, Peregrine Smith, 1989.

"The Bingo Van," in *New Yorker,* 19 February 1990.

"Happy Valentine's Day, Monsieur Ducharme," in *Ladies' Home Journal* (New York), February 1990.

"The Leap," in *Harper's* (New York), March 1990.

"Best Western," in *Vogue* (New York), May 1990.

"The Dress," in *Mother Jones* (San Francisco), July-August 1990.

"The Island," in *Ms.* (New York), January-February 1991.

Poetry

Jacklight. New York, Holt, and London, Sphere, 1990.
Baptism of Desire. New York, Harper Collins, 1991.

*   *   *

In Louise Erdrich's third novel, certain members of the Pillager Kashpaw families are behind in paying the government their annual fees on the reserve land that has always been theirs but that is now under government control. To raise the money at the last moment, they work for several days and nights gathering cranberry sticks and stripping the bark to sell to the tonic dealer. Nanapush comments that: "The thin pungent odor stuck to us, lodged in our clothes, and would be with us forever as the odor of both salvation and betrayal."

This episode encapsulates the tragic paradox with which the Chippewa in Erdrich's novels struggle, and illuminates the central concerns of the relatively few families and individuals on and around the North Dakota Chippewa reservation who survive and persist despite the threats to their community and culture by modern white "progress." Taken together, the novels act as a record of change on a general historical level, and of loss of a vital culture and system of knowledge. Erdrich shows that the sources of potential salvation are memory, and family and community cohesion, and she sensitively traces the causes of betrayal—alcohol, government money, the cutting up and conversion of native land into "property," the pervasion of Catholicism—and the effects of betrayal by individuals of traditional Chippewa culture and of each other.

Together Erdrich's first three novels cover the years 1912 to 1984; *Tracks* covers the earliest years and the other two chronologically dovetail to cover the later decades between them. The novels share certain characters, but each focuses on different families, interdependencies, complex loyalties, and threads of identity among the reservation Chippewa and the local whites with whom some become involved or bear children. The notion of intertwining threads of identity is reinforced by multiple point-of-view narration. Through Nanapush, Erdrich shows most effectively how the key to forming

and sustaining identity is collective and individual memory, which takes the form of his storytelling and upholding of the oral tradition.

One of the two narrators and a central character of *Tracks,* Nanapush is a wordsmith who shapes Chippewa experience from the raw material of history and experience, noting that "Only looking back is there a pattern." His "patterns" are the "tracks" for others to follow. Nanapush's storytelling becomes both figuratively and literally a means of survival and preservation. *Tracks* is the most powerful of the three novels because, in its evocation of Chippewa perspective and beliefs, it relies as much on the power of the unsaid as on the said. The plots of Erdrich's novels become increasingly spare and her characteristic use of multiple narrative voices is increasingly refined.

Love Medicine and *The Beet Queen* shift among several narrative voices, as each novel is made up of a loose collection of intertwining narratives and perspectives; in *The Beet Queen,* the narratives converge in a beautifully controlled movement toward the single day of the blackly humourous parade that finds the central characters in Argus, where Dot is to be crowned Beet Queen. In *Tracks,* the number of narrative voices has been pared down to two—Nanapush's and Pauline Puyat's—which alternate and are adeptly controlled to offer conflicting visions of the same events and people, as well to include statements on the reliability of each other. Erdrich uses the interplay and juxtaposition of Nanapush's and Pauline's narratives to expose the increasing unreliability of Pauline's, together with which, her mixed blood symbolizes the twistedness and confusion that arises when two cultures collide.

Pauline's increasing madness is shown as at least partly the result of white teachings—specifically orthodox Catholicism—gone awry in her head: she is a warper of stories, of memory, and experience, as is Sita in *The Beet Queen.* One of the strengths of Erdrich's fiction (and poetry) is the richness of specific recurrent images and symbols that connote spiritual states and qualities of life; Pauline, because of her affiliation with death and with division of family and community, is a bird of prey.

By the end of *Tracks,* Pauline becomes Sister Leopolda, and she appears as this sadistic Catholic sister with a "black intelligence" in the first two novels. *Love Medicine* focuses on the Kashpaw family branches, delineating in particular Nector's, and that of his brother Eli, who maintains traditional ways. Nector's wife Marie, who was persecuted, as a child, by Leopolda, as an adult takes in several children who have fallen "in the dark spaces" between couplings of various members of the extended family. Erdrich makes the gradual disclosure of the identity of the biological parents of some of these children as potent with meaning for the reader as for the children.

The Beet Queen is set in Argus, the local town inhabited largely by many German-Americans, and focuses on female legacy. When Adelaide Adare spontaneously takes off into the sky with a stunt pilot, abandoning her three children by a married man, her daughter Mary goes to Argus to live with the Kozkas, her German Aunt, uncle, and cousin (Sita) at their butcher shop—which she eventually takes over—and a network of interrelations ensues among Mary, her brother Karl, and a few of the Indian families of the other two novels. *The Beet Queen* culminates in a symbolic overturning of Adelaide's initial betrayal: Dot, the child of Karl and the Indian Celestine James, sees the "thread of flight" running through her paternal grandmother and her father, and attempt to escape her family through flight, but returns to the ground to find her mother waiting steadfastly for her return, and "want[s] to lean into her the way wheat leans into wind. . . ."

It should be noted that Erdrich's Chippewa are far from mere two-dimensional victims: her fiction serves to subvert stereotypes of the North American native and the rural poor. Their highly individualized flaws, weaknesses, and idiosyncrasies are given as careful attention as their strengths, accord with Nature, and insights, and create much of the black humour in the novels.

—Diane Watson

————

ERICSON, Walter. *See* **FAST, Howard (Melvin).**

————

ESSOP, Ahmed

Has also written as Ahmed Yousuf. **Nationality:** Indian. **Born:** Dabhel, Surat, 1 September 1931. **Education:** The University of South Africa, Pretoria, B.A. 1956, B.A. (honours) in English 1964. **Family:** Married Farida Karim in 1960; four children. **Career:** Teacher at a secondary school, Eldorado Park, Johannesburg, 1980-85. **Awards:** English Academy of Southern Africa Schreiner award, 1979. **Address:** P.O. Box 1747, Lenasia, Johannesburg 1820, South Africa.

PUBLICATIONS

Novels

The Visitation. Johannesburg, Ravan Press, 1980.
The Emperor. Johannesburg, Ravan Press, 1984.

Short Stories

The Hajji and Other Stories. Johannesburg, Ravan Press, 1978; as *Hajji Musa and the Hindu Fire-Walker,* Columbia, Louisiana, Readers International, 1988.
Noorjehan and Other Stories. Johannesburg, Ravan Press, 1990.

Poetry

The Dark Goddess (as Ahmed Yousuf). London, Mitre Press, 1959.

*

Manuscript Collection: National English Literary Museum, Grahamstown, South Africa.

Critical Studies: "Mr. Sufi Climbs the Stairs: The Quest and the Ideal in Ahmed Essop's *The Visitation*" by Eugenie Freed, in *Theoria* (Pietermaritzburg, Natal), May 1988; "Straightforward Politics and Ironic Playfulness: The Aesthetic Possibilities of Ahmed Essop's *The Emperor*" by Antje Hagena, in *English in Africa* (Grahamstown, Cape Province), October 1990.

*   *   *

Ahmed Essop's fiction displays a marvelously realized sense of place and the ability to regard human nature, even at its most absurdly self-centered or viciously craven, as still worthy of some pity. Fordsburg, within metropolitan Johannesburg, is in Essop's writing what Malgudi is in R.K. Narayan's. Both are Indian places; their inhabitants have Indian names, often speak with similar accents, and would not feel entirely lost culturally if translated to each others' towns. In Fordsburg the women wear saris and there are "the raucous voices of vendors . . . the spicy odors of Oriental foods, the bonhomie of communal life." Older Fordsburgians usually speak Gujarati or Urdu and try to preserve traditional customs like arranged marriages. Hindu and Muslim religious observances exist side by side, with both rivalry and some merging at the edges (as in the Caribbean) rather than as potential sources of communal violence. As in Trinidad and Guyana, the Indian proletariat and the educated alike speak a regional variety of English, illustrated by this passage of invective from "Hajji Musa and the Hindu Fire-Walker":

> "You liar! You come and tell me dat good-for-nutting Dendar boy, dat he good, dat he ejucated, dat he good prospect. My foot and boot he ejucated! He sleep most time wit bitches, he drink and beat my daughter. When you go Haj? You nutting but liar. You baster! You baster!"

The Afrikaans word "baster" (bastard) here signals the South African provenance of Essop's fiction about the largest population of Indian origin outside the sub-continent. Indeed Hindu and Muslim can taunt each other safely, in the knowledge that historically they have more in common than with members of other South African communities.

With its extension Newtown, Fordsburg seems to be based upon realities of Essop's childhood and youth before and during the 1950s campaign of passive resistance to apartheid, when there was a stronger sense of "Indianness," despite socializing and sexual encounters across racial boundaries. More secular and less traditional is Lenasia, beyond the Johannesburg perimeter, where *The Emperor* is set, a government-built township for the decanting of Fordsburg Indians, thus allowing white suburbs around Fordsburg to expand conveniently and cheaply.

It is in *The Hajji and Other Stories* that the life of Fordsburg/Newtown is most engagingly and unpretentiously set forth. Nearly half the stories are satirizations of human beings falling short of the high standards of personal and social behavior that they profess: Dr. Kamal's political cowardice in "The Betrayal," Yogi Khrishnasiva's covert fornication in his pursuit of spiritual liberation in "The Yogi," the holy men forced to seek refuge in the cinema and watch a film on "The Prophet" so as to escape the public violence they have stirred up as a protest against the screening of that film, the irrepressible Hajii Musa, in hospital with badly burned feet, dismissing Hindu fire-walking as "showmanship" after his own unsuccessful attempt. At his best, Essop strips pretense, hypocrisy, untruth, and deviousness from his characters and shows the naked humanity beneath, but with an imaginative and delicate understanding of the humiliation that people suffer when thus exposed, as in "The Hajii," where obdurate refusal to condone a brother's past apostasy results only in self-inflicted hurt and spiritual aridity, or the 70-year-old father's pathetic defeat when his new young second wife divorces him, Muslim-fashion, in preference for his own son. Some of the stories are competent psychological studies, as of the victim-figure in "The Target," or of the self-important (unto insanity) high school headmaster in "Gladiators," of the ambivalently dedicated political characters eventually left utterly isolated in "Ten Years" and "In Two Worlds." A frequent theme is the loss of human dignity, whether of the genuine or the merely outward kind. Occasionally Essop unnecessarily resorts to melodrama and sensationalism, as in "Labyrinth" and "Mr. Moonreddy."

The novel, *The Visitation,* sparkles with lively ideas and flashes of invention that on the whole don't quite coalesce. Mr. Sufi, a wealthy, complacent property owner, married but with a satisfying concubine discreetly housed in each of his apartment buildings, conducts his life quietly and respectably, even turning his monthly payment of protection money to the racketeer Gool into a polite little social ceremony. By the simple expedient of delivering large quantities of obviously stolen electric lamps to Sufi's home, Gool gains the blackmailer's firm hold upon a timid victim. Ironically, the lamps usher Sufi into an existence of darkness, fear, panic, and hallucination. As Gool and his thugs take over Sufi's very life, including his rent-collecting, like a supernatural visitation, he gradually realizes that they are doing crudely and violently what he has always done urbanely but equally ruthlessly. Even his love-life is reduced, when he witnesses Gool's sexual contortions with one of his former concubines. Clearly Gool is a doppelgänger, revealing to Sufi his own true nature—selfish, sensual, and sadistic—which he'd tried

to cloak respectably. The weakness is that Gool becomes a mere caricature of criminality. The narrative might have been even more persuasive had Gool's wilder actions been incorporated in Sufi's hallucinations.

Caricature as a substitute for characterization is a legitimate satirist's tool, though probably more successful within the narrower compass of a short story than in the fuller extent and more subtle shadings of a novel. The Lenasia headmaster, Mr. Dharama Ashoka, the central character in *The Emperor,* is a "stooge" Indian, a creature of the apartheid state with an unassuageable appetite for power. The ludicrous story of his rise and downfall is also the tragedy of his wrong-headedness. The author's ingenious schema isn't really credible—an analysis, in one persona, of both arrogance and its necessary pettinesses in exercising power, with Ashoka as a possible figuring of the apartheid state and his opponents as the resistance. But Essop's ultimate interest in human individuality undercuts such a reading, making Ashoka at the end (like Sufi in *The Visitation*), a man to be pitied in the hour of his humiliating self-knowledge.

—Arthur Ravenscroft

F

FAIRBAIRNS, Zoë (Ann)

Nationality: British. **Born:** Tunbridge Wells, Kent, 20 December 1948. **Education:** St. Catherine's School, Twickenham, Middlesex, 1954-67; University of St. Andrews, Fife, Scotland, 1967-72, M.A. in modern history 1972; College of William and Mary, Williamsburg, Virginia, 1969-70. **Career:** Editor, Campaign for Nuclear Disarmament newspaper *Sanity*, London, 1973-74; freelance journalist, 1975-82; poetry editor, *Spare Rib*, London, 1978-82; fiction reviewer, *Everywoman*, London, 1990-93. Since 1993 subtitler, Independent Television Facilities Centre, West London. C. Day Lewis Fellow, Rutherford School, London, 1977-78; creative writing tutor, City Literary Institute, 1978-82, Holloway Prison, 1978-82, Wandsworth Prison, 1987, Silver Moon Women's Bookshop, 1987 and 1989, and Morley College, 1988 and 1989, all London; writer-in-residence, Bromley schools, Kent, from 1981, and Deakin University, Geelong, Victoria, 1983, Sunderland Polytechnic, Tyne and Wear, 1983-85, and Surrey County Council, 1989. **Awards:** Fawcett prize, 1985; British Council travel grant 1990. Lives in London. **Agent:** A.M. Heath, 79 St. Martin's Lane, London WC2N 4AA, England.

PUBLICATIONS

Novels

Live as Family. London, Macmillan, 1968.
Down: An Explanation. London, Macmillan, 1969.
Benefits. London, Virago Press, 1979; New York, Avon, 1982.
Stand We at Last. London, Virago Press, and Boston, Houghton Mifflin, 1983.
Here Today. London, Methuen, and New York, Avon, 1984.
Closing. London, Methuen, 1987; New York, Dutton, 1988.
Daddy's Girls. London, Methuen, 1991.

Short Stories

Tales I Tell My Mother, with others. London, Journeyman Press, 1978; Boston, South End Press, 1980.
More Tales I Tell My Mother, with others. London, Journeyman Press, 1987.

Uncollected Short Stories

"Relics," in *Despatches from the Frontiers of the Female Mind,* edited by Jen Green and Sarah Lefanu. London, Women's Press, 1985.
"Spies for Peace: A Story of 1963," in *Voices from Arts for Labour,* edited by Nicki Jackowska. London, Pluto Press, 1985.
"Covetousness," in *The 7 Deadly Sins,* edited by Alison Fell. London, Serpent's Tail, 1989.
"By the Light of the Silvery Moon," in *By the Light of the Silvery Moon,* edited by Ruth Petrie. London, Virago, 1994.

Play

Details of Wife (produced Richmond, Surrey, 1973).

Other

Study War No More. London, CND, 1974.
No Place to Grow Up, with Jim Wintour. London, Shelter, 1977.
Peace Moves: Nuclear Protest in the 1980s, with James Cameron, photographs by Ed Barber. London, Chatto and Windus, and Bridgeport, Connecticut, Merrimack, 1984.

Editor, *Women's Studies in the UK,* compiled by Oonagh Hartnett and Margherita Rendel. London, London Seminars, 1975.

*

Zoë Fairbairns comments:

I don't want to comment on my own work, but I'm always pleased and interested to receive comments from readers. (How will I know who you are or what you think, if you don't tell me?) Write to me c/o my agent—I will do my best to reply.

*   *   *

Zoë Fairbairns is, deservedly, one of the most popular feminist fiction writers working in Britain. Her pacey novels are very much a part of mainstream fiction, making their appeal much broader than that of many more overtly polemical books. At first glance her work seems straight genre fiction; science fiction in *Benefits;* the multigenerational family saga in *Stand We at Last;* the crime thriller in *Here Today.* However, what Fairbairns does is to take each genre and transform it for her own use.

The main theme underlying each of these works is the gradual, irresistible raising of feminist consciousness. Other themes are the complexity of relationships between the sexes; loneliness; the powerlessness of need; and the ever-changing yet somehow constant problems faced by women, whether they be women of the future, the past, or today. Fairbairns approaches all her characters with realism, sympathy, and a great deal of wit. Though her male characters tend to be lightly sketched, her women make up for this lack of depth; they are humorous, deep-thinking, and self-critical; and whenever a character seems to be slipping close to social stereotype, the author quickly steps in with a touch of irony.

Take, for example, the two main characters in *Here Today.* On the one hand there is Catherine, a 30-year-old virgin, feminist, and teacher who, having been made redundant, finds herself thrown into the world of temporary office employment. Shocked by the exploitation of her fellow temps by the employers and job agencies, she sets about undermining the temping system. On the other hand there is fashion-conscious Antonia, one-time self-satisfied "Temp of the Year," who is shaken out of her complacency both by the advent of word-processing which threatens her livelihood and by a bad case of genital herpes which brings about the end of her marriage. Drawn together in an uneasy alliance through their loneliness and their common need to earn a living, the two women embark on an adventurous road to self-fulfillment, fraught with contrasts between the traditional middle- and working-class attitudes to love and work.

The concept of romantic love, though not a central theme, plays a part in Fairbairns's novels. Men tend to be either saints or sinners—and, surprisingly, the saints predominate. In *Here Today,* Catherine forms a close relationship with Frank, a union leader who's extremely sympathetic to the women's movement. In *Benefits,* in many ways the most pessimistic of her books, we are presented with the enlightened, too-good-to-be-true Derek, who bends over backwards not to oppress his journalist wife, Lynn. However, the cold dictates of a superbureaucracy intent on controlling the reproductive rights of its women drives Lynn away from "the women's pages of the *Guardian*" towards a more radical feminism epitomized by Collindeane Tower, an abandoned block of council flats which has become home to a leaderless feminist community. As Lynn struggles with mixed feelings about her marriage and her own fertility, the women of Collindeane form ranks against Family, a political party dedicated to restoring so-called "family values" by methods of giving or holding back government benefits to those women who do or do not reproduce. The novel takes us from the late 1970s through to a 21st century where family planning has become government planning and the fabric of a once-prosperous society is, like Collindeane, crumbling away. Though *Benefits* is a science-fiction novel, the futuristic views of post-industrial Britain depicted in it are, at times, too close to aspects of present reality to be comfortable; poverty and decay are rife in all aspects of society; the Family Party eventually brings about its own destruction; and leaderless feminism seems to lead nowhere. The result is a powerful, chilling, somewhat depressing book.

Despite her preoccupation with the present lot of women, Fairbairns seems more at home when writing about the future or the past. Nowhere is this more evident than in *Stand We at Last,* perhaps the most ambitious of her novels. In her own words "a family saga with a feminist background," it traces the lives of a succession of women, starting in 1855 with the adventurous Sarah who emigrates to Australia hoping to make her fortune as a farmer, and ending with Jackie, a single parent living on a hippie commune in 1970s England. As in her other books, the writer remains true to the genre she has chosen: all of Life is present in this 600-page saga—births, suicides, miscarriages, abortions, raised hopes, dashed ambitions—not to mention love, passion, and sexual guilt. But this is no ordinary rags-to-riches saga; as in all Fairbairns's novels, ambitions are spiritual rather than material; children and men seem to be the rocks on which women's ambitions founder; and in order to break out of the cycle set up by her predecessors, the modern heroine must give up her man rather than get him in the end.

Though the themes in Fairbairns's writing are constant, each novel remains quite distinct in style. Her female characters, who are primarily ordinary people with ordinary problems, manage somehow to be extraordinarily interesting. Her plots are imaginative and gripping. One wonders with interest what genre she will choose to subvert next.

—Judith Summers

FARAH, Nuruddin

Nationality: Somali. **Born:** Baidoa, 24 November 1945. **Education:** Istituto di Magistrale, Mogadiscio, Somalia, 1964; Panjab University, Chindigarh, India, 1966-70; University of London, 1974-75; University of Essex, Colchester, 1975-76. **Family:** Divorced, one son; remarried in 1992, one daughter. **Career:** Clerk-typist, Ministry of Education, and secondary school teacher, 1969-71, Mogadiscio; teacher, Wardhiigley Secondary School, 1970-71; lecturer, Somali National University, Mogadiscio, 1971-74; guest professor, Bayreuth University, Germany, 1981; associate professor, University of Jos, Nigeria, 1981-83; visiting professor, University of Minnesota, Minneapolis, Autumn 1988, State University of New York, Stony Brook, Spring 1989, and Brown University, Providence, Rhode Island, Autumn 1991. Since 1990 professor, Makerere University, Kampala, Uganda. **Awards:** Unesco fellowship, 1974; English-Speaking Union award, 1980; Corman Artists fellowship, 1990; Tucholsky award for literary exiles (Sweden), 1993; Cavour prize (Italy), 1993. **Agent:** Curtis Brown, 162-168 Regent Street, London W1R 5TB, England.

PUBLICATIONS

Novels

From a Crooked Rib. London, Heinemann, 1970.
A Naked Needle. London, Heinemann, 1976.
Sweet and Sour Milk. London, Allison and Busby, 1979; St. Paul, Minnesota, Graywolf Press, 1992.
Sardines. London, Allison and Busby, 1981; St. Paul, Minnesota, Graywolf Press, 1992.
Close Sesame. London, Allison and Busby, 1983; St. Paul, Minnesota, Graywolf Press, 1992.
Maps. London, Pan, 1986; New York, Pantheon, 1987.
Gifts. London, Serif, 1992.

Uncollected Short Story

"Why Dead So Soon?" in *Somali News* (Mogadiscio), 1965.

Plays

A Dagger in Vacuum (produced Mogadiscio, 1970).
The Offering (produced Colchester, Essex, 1975).
Yussuf and His Brothers (produced Jos, Nigeria, 1982).

Radio Play: *Tartar Delight,* 1980 (Germany).

*   *   *

It is characteristic of Nuruddin Farah's writing that the reader reaches the end of his fourth novel, *Sardines,* and wonders what link there is between the title and the text. There is one, but it has to be teased out by a participating reader. The novels are, in the widest sense, political but are never simplistic or predictable. Farah is concerned to show the pressure of the Somalian regime on individual psyches; in five of his novels, all of which are set in Somalia, he concentrates on characters who are obsessed, or become obsessed, with the failure of the revolution or with the General, the head of the "revolutionary" state who has acquired 99 names, like God, and is worshipped with such phrases as "there is no General but our General." In all his novels, Farah limits the narrative by using the partial and restricted point of view of his central characters, thus making the reader enact the characters' own frustration and confusion in trying to make sense of a society whose leaders deliberately mislead, deceive, and betray their people.

Farah resembles no other African novelist in subject-matter or style. He is interested in experimental writers who portray extreme emotional and psychological states: Koschin's favourite novel in *A Naked Needle* is *Wuthering Heights* and he and Medina, in *Sardines,* refer to Soyinka's *The Interpreters.* Farah uses epigraphs in a stimulating manner, and they range from Somali proverbs to Beckett, Melville, Kafka, Ted Hughes, and Blake. Perhaps the most unusual aspect of Farah's fiction, especially in a writer who comes from a mainly Islamic society, is its sensitive depiction of women. The central characters in two of his novels, *From a Crooked Rib* and *Sardines,* are women; the dilemmas and pitfalls of a liberated woman in a profoundly reactionary society are explored brilliantly in *Sardines* though Farah has so far not extended his imaginative sympathy to white women: Nancy, in *A Naked Needle,* is lumpish and predatory. Women like Medina, in *Sardines,* are shown to bear the brunt of all the contradictory interwoven cultural strands that contribute to modern Somalia: tribalism, Islamic and Italian influences, a Marxist regime dominated by Soviet involvement, European culture imposed on an oral tradition. Medina thinks:

> In this century, the African is a guest whether in Africa or elsewhere. A guest. The technology; the ideology; the living cells of power which throb with confidence; the intellectual make-up from which we derive our source of power; the contradictions which breathe life into us. If not a guest, then slave to a system of thoughts, a system of a given economic rerouting.

Farah is not politically naive or specifically anti-Soviet; his implicit theme is the imprisoning effect of outside intervention in Somalian life. Loyaan, in *Sweet and Sour Milk,* sees "a nation regimented, militarised. A nation disciplined and forced to obey the iron-hand directing the orchestra of groans and moans."

One of the incidental pleasures of reading Farah's fiction is that characters recur in his imaginary world; Farah uses the centrality of family life within Somali society as a metaphor for the state. The novels are dedicated to members of Farah's own family, and he involves the reader in the sense of community by creating links between the novels. The young Ebla of the first novel reappears as a middle-aged woman in *Sardines;* the fates of Koschin in *A Naked Needle* and Loyaan in *Sweet and Sour Milk* are revealed in later novels, and the end of *Sardines* anticipates the action of *Close Sesame.* The interconnectedness of the texts reflects on the society depicted, in which the intellectual elite is small, with a family-like intensity about its bonding and its betrayals.

From a Crooked Rib is the least political of the novels. The point of view is almost exclusively that of Ebla, a girl from a nomadic tribe who escapes from an arranged marriage only to become a victim of male sexual attitudes in Mogadiscio. Her naivety gradually disappears as she tries and fails to make her way in a man's world: "Why is it only the sons in the family who are counted? For sure this world is a man's—it is his dominion. It is his and is going to be his as long as women are oppressed, as long as women are sold and bought like camels, as long as this remains the system of life. Nature is against women. . . . Aren't men the law?"

A Naked Needle takes place in one day in Mogadiscio during which Koschin passively accepts the arrival of an Englishwoman who is determined to marry him. Koschin himself is on the verge of a nervous breakdown, and is therefore rather too confusing a medium through which to communicate the situation to the reader. There are powerful passages, such as the chapter in which Koschin shows Nancy the city, but Koschin's are the only judgments given and he is so egotistical, bitter, and cruel to Nancy that the political

issues are clouded by his diseased consciousness. In *Sweet and Sour Milk,* however, the reader is made acutely aware of the cunning of the post-revolutionary regime through Loyaan, a non-political innocent whose twin brother dies mysteriously at the beginning of the novel. The use of the plot is subtle: the reader expects to find out who killed Soyaan and shares Loyaan's experience as he gains wisdom and cynicism, and begins to unravel the mystery. But the answer is never found, and the reader's frustration mirrors that of the protagonist whose integrity cannot crack the manipulative power of the General and his minions. It is never clear who the minions or who the political activists are.

Sardines is similarly about people caught in a trap, or a tin. Our admiration of Medina, a journalist who has the courage to fight the General with all the weapons at her disposal, is tempered at the end when we see the precociousness of her daughter, Ubax, and the dangerous situation in which she has helped to place her husband, family, and friends. It is impossible to win in such a situation: Ubax embodies the difficulties for she, at eight, is charming and independent but also insolent and forlorn, longing for an ordinary mother. The language of the novel shows the weakness as well as the strengths of Farah's style. Even in a novel that explores the horrors of female circumcision this simile is strained: "the night which opened up like the teased lips of a vagina." There are persistent mixed metaphors which clutter a prose that, as its best, uses metaphor powerfully: "No, she wasn't a guest any more. She was a full and active participant in the history of her country."

Close Sesame is in a sense a reply to the monstrous Idil in *Sardines,* an orthodox Muslim who is determined that her granddaughter shall be circumcised. The title *Close Sesame* suggests the loss of legendary riches, which take the form of a character, old Deeriye, also a devout Muslim, who is a source of comfort to his grandson and of traditional and political wisdom to his family and friends. His romantic devotion to his dead wife, Nadiifa, is uncharacteristic of Farah's fiction; he integrates ancient lore with political commitment, and dies attempting to avenge his son's death by assassinating the General. This gesture perhaps suggests that political idealism is ultimately incompatible with religious devotion as Deeriye pulls out his prayer-beads instead of his revolver when the crucial opportunity to shoot the General arrives.

Farah's 1986 novel, *Maps,* is more experimental than his earlier fiction, with some chapters written in the first person, some in the third, and some in the second. This reflects the central character's problems with his identity. Askar's mother dies when he is born and he is adopted by an Ethiopian, Misra. His experiences parallel those of his place; the battle for Ogaden rages while Misra suffers terrible pain in aborting a baby she conceived by her Somali lover. Maps, definitions, and boundaries are questions throughout the novel, partly through surreal episodes, as when Askar mysteriously menstruates at the beginning of the war. Farah never repeats his effects, and this novel emphatically takes a new direction.

—Angela Smith

FARMER, Beverley

Nationality: Australian. **Born:** 1941. **Family:** Divorced, one son. **Address:** c/o University of Queensland Press, P.O. Box 42, St. Lucia, Queensland 4067, Australia.

PUBLICATIONS

Novel

Alone. Carlton South, Victoria, Sisters, 1980.
The Seal Woman. St. Lucia, University of Queensland Press, 1992.
The House in the Light. St. Lucia, University of Queensland Press,
    1995.

Short Stories

Milk. Fitzroy, Victoria, McPhee Gribble, and New York, Penguin, 1983.
Home Time. Fitzroy, Victoria, McPhee Gribble, and New York, Pen-
    guin, 1985.
A Body of Water: A Year's Notebook. St. Lucia, University of
    Queensland Press, 1990.
Place of Birth. London, Faber, 1990.

*   *   *

Beverley Farmer made her reputation initially as a writer of short and shortish fiction but more recently has turned to full-length novels. Her first book was a novella *Alone,* published in 1980 but written ten years before and set even earlier in 1959. Like most of her work it has closely autobiographical overtones. A student at Melbourne University has been having an affair with another young woman which ends when she becomes too importunate. In total despair, but quite rationally, she decides to end her life unless her former lover comes to see her before Sunday, the day of her eighteenth birthday. *Alone* describes in clinical tones exactly what the girl, Shirley Nunne, does during the last hours of her life, before she comes to the moment of her final decision. Although, as often with Farmer, the writing can sometimes be exaggeratedly sensuous to the point of over-ripeness, more often it ranges from the poetic conjuring up of atmospheric detail through the meticulously objective description of physical processes to a painstaking rendition of harshly Australian idiomatic speech. It is a haunting and gifted novel.

Farmer confirmed the promise of this work with two fine collections of short stories, *Milk* and *Home Time.* Nearly all the stories in the first collection concern the interaction between the cultures of Greece and Australia and the misunderstandings that occur, but their authenticity and almost elemental strength and intensity of feeling make them far more than merely sociological. Although frequently the protagonist is a young woman involved with a Greek man, the stories have a variety of voices and protagonists. The most impressive quality is the author's ability to confront and immerse herself in the experience of her characters, no matter how distressing it is, without becoming self-pitying or maudlin. Violence—whether psychic or physical—is never far away; if it does not actually occur it hovers on the outskirts of the stories, constantly threatening as it does in "Sally's Birthday." Frequently, especially when the victim is a woman, it takes the form of humiliation or violation of some kind. Estrangement, too—husband from wife, parent from child, Greek from Australian—is another pervasive element. Almost the sole source of comfort and consolation lies in the children who often appear in the collection, and whose joys and griefs ("The little tragedies of children") are lovingly and tenderly evoked.

Many of the same themes recur in *Home Time.* Here again, few relationships are seen to be in any way harmonious; most are riddled with tension and often verge on violence. The sense of estrangement can be both emotional and geographical. In "Place of Birth," Bell (who appears in two stories) is pregnant and agonizing over whether to leave Greece and return to Australia. She receives little consolation from her husband: "You're a stubborn, selfish, cold-blooded woman, Bell." Several of the stories are set in Greece but the sense of isolation is not confined to place. Whether she is called Bell or Anne or Barbara, the protagonist is usually alone or caught up in an unhappy relationship. There are signs, however, that certain veins of ore have been fairly solidly mined. In particular, there is a self-consciousness about the stories, many of which feature a protagonist who is a writer. They are bleak and desolate stories, enlivened by a sensuous awareness of landscape, especially in the ones set in Greece, and an extraordinarily acute ear for dialogue.

Farmer waited five years, a period of apparent sterility, to publish her first full-length novel, *A Body of Water.* Sub-titled "A Year's Notebook," it is in fact exactly that, her jottings from February 1987 to February of the following year. It records her friendships, love affairs, conversations, thoughts, and, above all, her reading. Interspersed with the diary entries, which begin with the gloomy statement "My forty-sixth birthday, and no end in sight to the long struggle to come to terms with this isolation, this sterility," are the five stories she managed to complete during the year. The reader is thus in the privileged and fascinating position of reading not only the fiction but the process of how it came to be written, how it emerged from the writer's unconscious and finally took shape. In the post-modernist tradition the novel is not about anything so much as itself. It is about the process of writing, not the result; however, in the end the theme of artistic and personal sterility threatens to invade the book like a virus. In addition, there is a good deal of overblown writing: "Tide coming in, a stiff wind. A black ship out, a white ship in. A flash out on the gray water—a pilot boat catching the sun. The dunes have grown fine long green hairs all over—their skin shows through." Much of the novel is taken up with the author's study of Zen Buddhism.

Bleakness and solitude are themes of Farmer's most recent fiction also. *The Seal Woman* is a Danish woman named Dagmar Mikkelsen, who has come to live in a seaside resort in Victoria for a few months at the invitation of two absent Australian friends whose house she is minding. She falls in love with Martin, muses over her past, the husband she lost at sea, and the child she could not have. Like *A Body of Water* this is a highly self-conscious, literary novel that makes constant allusion to other forms of narrative, including fiction, poetry, film, and above all myth. Dense with imagery and symbolism, the novel finally abandons itself completely to myth in the final chapter in the story of the tragic seal woman whose fate runs in counterpoint to Dagmar's own: at the end, having left her faithless lover to return home, she finds herself joyfully with his child.

In *The House in the Light* Farmer has returned to the familiar country of the short stories and her alter ego Bell. Now fifty years old, divorced, with her son a student and living his own life, and with her ex-husband's new wife about to give birth, Bell has returned to the Greek village she married in to celebrate Easter. It is eight years since she has been back and twenty years since she first celebrated the Greek Easter with her then husband. Her former father-in-law has recently died but the family still welcomes her ambivalently into their midst. The novel takes us through the week of Easter day by day. It is almost a dramatic meditation, an account of a private mental struggle: Bell has to reconcile past affections and allegiances with the changed circumstances she finds herself in, to tread the line between respect for the hospitality and culture of her hosts, especially her aging mother-in-law, and a fierce insistence on her own very different values, which she will neither abandon nor deny. Again, it becomes apparent that the most central fact in the universe of Beverley's fiction is solitude. Her characters are mostly physical and mental isolates and Bell is no exception. At the end, though, in a beautifully written scene, Bell and the family come to some kind of tentative accommodation. *The House in the Light* is a profoundly desolate but moving novel.

—Laurie Clancy

———

FARREFF, M.J. *See* **KEANE, Molly.**

———

FAST, Howard (Melvin)

Pseudonyms: E.V. Cunningham; Walter Ericson. **Nationality:** American. **Born:** New York City, 11 November 1914. **Education:** George Washington High School, New York, grauated 1931; National Academy of Design, New York. **Military Service:** Served with the Office of War Information, 1942-43, and the Army Film Project, 1944. **Family:** Married Bette Cohen in 1937 (died 1994); one daughter and one son, the writer Jonathan Fast. **Career:** War correspondent in the Far East for *Esquire* and *Coronet* magazines, 1945. Taught at Indiana University, Bloomington, Summer 1947; imprisoned for contempt of Congress, 1947; owner, Blue Heron Press, New York, 1952-57. Since 1989 weekly columnist, New York *Observer.* Founder, World Peace Movement, and member, World Peace Council, 1950-55; currently, member of the Fellowship for Reconciliation. American-Labour Party candidate for Congress for the 23rd District of New York, 1952. Lives in Greenwich, Connecticut. **Awards:** Bread Loaf Writers Conference award, 1933; Schomburg Race Relations award, 1944; Newspaper Guild award, 1947; Jewish Book Council of America award, 1948; Stalin (now Soviet) International Peace prize, 1954; Screenwriters award, 1960; National Association of Independent Schools, award, 1962; Emmy award, for television play, 1976. **Agent:** Sterling Lord Literistic Inc., 1 Madison Avenue, New York, New York 10010, U.S.A.

PUBLICATIONS

Novels

Two Valleys. New York, Dial Press, 1933; London, Dickson, 1934.
Strange Yesterday. New York, Dodd Mead, 1934.
Place in the City. New York, Harcourt Brace, 1937.
The Call of Fife and Drum: Three Novels of the Revolution. Secausus, New Jersey, Citadel Press, 1987.
Conceived in Liberty: A Novel of Valley Forge. New York, Simon and Schuster, and London, Joseph, 1939.

The Unvanquished. New York, Duell, 1942; London, Lane, 1947.
The Proud and the Free. Boston, Little Brown, 1950; London, Lane, 1952.
The Last Frontier. New York, Duell, 1941; London, Lane, 1948.
The Tall Hunter. New York, Harper, 1942.
Citizen Tom Paine. New York, Duell, 1943; London, Lane, 1946.
Freedom Road. New York, Duell, 1944; London, Lane, 1946.
The American: A Middle Western Legend. New York, Duell, 1946; London, Lane, 1949.
The Children. New York, Duell, 1947.
Clarkton. New York, Duell, 1947.
My Glorious Brothers. Boston, Little Brown, 1948; London, Lane, 1950.
Spartacus. Privately printed, 1951; London, Lane, 1952.
Fallen Angel (as Walter Ericson). Boston, Little Brown, 1952; as *The Darkness Within,* New York, Ace, 1953; as *Mirage* (as Howard Fast), New York, Fawcett, 1965.
Silas Timberman. New York, Blue Heron Press, 1954; London, Lane, 1955.
The Story of Lola Gregg. New York, Blue Heron Press, 1956; London, Lane, 1957.
Moses, Prince of Egypt. New York, Crown, 1958; London, Methuen, 1959.
The Winston Affair. New York, Crown, 1959; London, Methuen, 1960.
The Golden River, in *The Howard Fast Reader.* New York, Crown, 1960.
April Morning. New York, Crown, and London, Methuen, 1961.
Power. New York, Doubleday, 1962; London, Methuen, 1963.
Agrippa's Daughter. New York, Doubleday, 1964; London, Methuen, 1965.
Torquemada. New York, Doubleday, 1966; London, Methuen, 1967.
The Hunter and the Trap. New York, Dial Press, 1967.
The Crossing. New York, Morrow, 1971; London, Eyre Methuen, 1972.
The Hessian. New York, Morrow, 1972; London, Hodder and Stoughton, 1973.
The Immigrants:
The Immigrants. Boston, Houghton Mifflin, 1977; London, Hodder and Stoughton, 1978.
Second Generation. Boston, Houghton Mifflin, and London, Hodder and Stoughton, 1978.
The Establishment. Boston, Houghton Mifflin, 1979; London, Hodder and Stoughton, 1980.
The Legacy. Boston, Houghton Mifflin, and London, Hodder and Stoughton, 1981.
Max. Boston, Houghton Mifflin, 1982; London, Hodder and Stoughton, 1983.
The Outsider. Boston, Houghton Mifflin, 1984; London, Hodder and Stoughton 1985.
The Immigrant's Daughter. Boston, Houghton Mifflin, 1985; London, Hodder and Stoughton, 1986.
The Dinner Party. Boston, Houghton Mifflin, and London, Hodder and Stoughton, 1987.
The Pledge. Boston, Houghton Mifflin, 1988; London, Hodder and Stoughton, 1989.
The Confession of Joe Cullen. Boston, Houghton Mifflin 1989; London, Hodder and Stoughton, 1990.
The Trial of Abigail Goodman. New York, Crown, 1993.
Seven Days in June. New York, Crown, 1994.

Novels as E.V. Cunningham

Sylvia. New York, Doubleday, 1960; London, Deutsch, 1962.
Phyllis. New York, Doubleday, and London, Deutsch, 1962.
Alice. New York, Doubleday, 1963; London, Deutsch, 1965.
Lydia. New York, Doubleday, 1964; London, Deutsch, 1965.
Shirley. New York, Doubleday, and London, Deutsch, 1964.
Penelope. New York, Doubleday, 1965; London, Deutsch, 1966.
Helen. New York, Doubleday, 1966; London, Deutsch, 1967.
Margie. New York, Morrow, 1966; London, Deutsch, 1968.
Sally. New York, Morrow, and London, Deutsch, 1967.
Samantha. New York, Morrow, 1967; London, Deutsch, 1968; as
    The Case of the Angry Actress, New York, Dell, 1984.
Cynthia. New York, Morrow, 1968; London, Deutsch, 1969.
The Assassin Who Gave Up His Gun. New York, Morrow, 1969;
    London, Deutsch, 1970.
Millie. New York, Morrow, 1973; London, Deutsch, 1975.
The Case of the One-Penny Orange. New York, Holt Rinehart,
    1977; London, Deutsch, 1978.
The Case of the Russian Diplomat. New York, Holt Rinehart, 1978;
    London, Deutsch, 1979.
The Case of the Poisoned Eclairs. New York, Holt Rinehart, 1979;
    London, Deutsch, 1980.
The Case of the Sliding Pool. New York, Delacorte Press, 1981;
    London, Gollancz, 1982.
The Case of the Kidnapped Angel. New York, Delacorte Press,
    1982; London, Gollancz, 1983.
The Case of the Murdered Mackenzie. New York, Delacorte Press,
    1984; London, Gollancz, 1985.
The Wabash Factor. New York, Delacorte Press, 1986; London,
    Gollancz, 1987.

Plays

The Hammer (produced New York, 1950).
Thirty Pieces of Silver (produced Melbourne, 1951). New York,
    Blue Heron Press, and London, Lane, 1954.
General Washington and the Water Witch. London, Lane, 1956.
The Crossing (produced Dallas, 1962).
The Hill (screenplay). New York, Doubleday, 1964.
David and Paula (produced New York, 1982).
Citizen Tom Paine, adaptation of his own novel (produced
    Williamstown, Massachusetts, 1985). Boston, Houghton Mifflin,
    1986.
The Novelist (produced Williamstown, Massachusetts, 1987).
The Second Coming (produced Greenwich, Connecticut, 1991).

Screenplay: *The Hessian,* 1971.

Television Plays: *What's a Nice Girl Like You . . . ?,* 1971; *The
    Ambassador* (*Benjamin Franklin* series), 1974; *21 Hours at
    Munich,* with Edward Hume, 1976.

Poetry

Never to Forget the Battle of the Warsaw Ghetto, with William
    Gropper. New York, Jewish Peoples Fraternal Order, 1946.
Korean Lullaby. New York, American Peace Crusade, n.d.

Other

The Romance of a People (for children). New York, Hebrew Pub-
    lishing Company, 1941.

Lord Baden-Powell of the Boy Scouts. New York, Messner, 1941.
Haym Salomon, Son of Liberty. New York, Messner, 1941.
The Picture-Book History of the Jews, with Bette Fast. New York,
    Hebrew Publishing Company, 1942.
Goethals and the Panama Canal. New York, Messner, 1942.
The Incredible Tito. New York, Magazine House, 1944.
Intellectuals in the Fight for Peace. New York, Masses and Main-
    stream, 1949.
Tito and His People. Winnipeg, Contemporary Publishers, 1950.
Literature and Reality. New York, International Publishers, 1950.
Peekskill, U.S.A.: A Personal Experience. New York, Civil Rights
    Congress, and London, International Publishing Company, 1951.
Tony and the Wonderful Door (for children). New York, Blue Heron
    Press, 1952; as *The Magic Door,* Culver City, California, Peace
    Press, 1979.
Spain and Peace. New York, Joint Anti-Fascist Refugee Commit-
    tee, 1952.
The Passion of Sacco and Vanzetti: A New England Legend. New
    York, Blue Heron Press, 1953; London, Lane, 1954.
The Naked God: The Writer and the Communist Party. New York,
    Praeger, 1957; London, Bodley Head, 1958.
The Howard Fast Reader. New York, Crown, 1960.
The Jews: Story of a People. New York, Dial Press, 1968; Lon-
    don, Cassell, 1970.
The Art of Zen Meditation. Culver City, California, Peace Press,
    1977.
Time and the Riddle: Thirty Zen Stories. Boston, Houghton Mifflin,
    1981.
Being Red: A Memoir. Boston, Houghton Mifflin, 1990.
War and Peace. Armonk, New York, Sharpe, 1992.
The Sculpture of Bette Fast. Armonk, New York, Sharpe, 1995.

Editor, *The Selected Work of Tom Paine.* New York, Modern Li-
    brary, 1946; London, Lane, 1948.
Editor, *The Best Short Stories of Theodore Dreiser.* Cleveland,
    World, 1947.

*

Manuscript Collections: University of Pennsylvania, Philadelphia;
University of Wisconsin, Madison.

Critical Studies: *History and Conscience: The Case of Howard Fast*
by Hershel D. Meyer, Princeton, New Jersey, Anvil Atlas, 1958; *Counterpoint* by Roy Newquist, New York, Rand McNally, 1964.

Howard Fast comments:

(1972) From the very beginning of my career as a writer, my
outlook has been teleological. Since my first work was published
at a very early age—my first novel at the age of 18—my philosophical position was naturally uncertain and in formation. Yet the
seeds were there, and by the end of my first decade as a writer, I
had clearly shaped my point of view. In the light of this, both my
historical and modern novels (excepting the entertainments I have
written under the name of Cunningham) were conceived as parables
and executed as narratives of pace and, hopefully, excitement. I discovered that I had a gift for narrative in the story sense; but I tried
never to serve the story, but rather to have it serve my own purpose—a purpose which I attempted in a transcendental sense.

In other words, I was—and am—intrigued by the apparent lunacy of man's experience on earth; but at the same time never ac-

cepted a pessimistic conclusion or a mechanical explanation. Thereby, my books were either examinations of moments or parables of my own view of history. As a deeply religious person who has always believed that human life is a meaningful part of a meaningful and incredibly wonderful universe, I found myself at every stage in my career a bit out of step with the current literary movement or fashion. I suppose that this could not have been otherwise, and I think I have been the most astounded of any at the vast audiences my work has reached.

Since I also believe that a person's philosophical point of view has little meaning if it is not matched by being and action, I found myself willingly wed to an endless series of unpopular causes, experiences which I feel enriched my writing as much as they depleted other aspects of my life. I might add that the more I have developed the parable as a form of literature, the more convinced I become that truth is better indicated than specified.

All of the above is of course not a critical evaluation of my work; and I feel that a writer is the last person on earth capable of judging his own work as literature with any objectivity. The moment I cease to feel that I am a good writer, I will have to stop writing. And while this may be no loss to literature, it would be a tragic blow to my income.

As for the books I have written under the name of E.V. Cunningham, they are entertainments, for myself primarily and for all others who care to read them. They are also my own small contribution to that wonderful cause of women's liberation. They are all about wise and brave and gallant women, and while they are suspense and mystery stories, they are also parables in their own way.

*   *   *

Howard Fast has written in virtually every genre—novels, plays, poems, filmscripts, critical essays and short stories—and in a number of subgenres of fiction, including science fiction, social satire, historical and contemporary novels, spy thrillers, and moral allegories. He began publishing novels at the age of 18 and has kept up a brisk pace of production.

His strongest fictional gifts are a talent for swift, interesting narrative, the vivid portrayal of scenes of action, especially of violence, and an uncluttered style only occasionally marred by sentimental lapses. Although he became identified in the 1940s as a publicist for the Communist Party line, his novels reveal an intensely emotional and religious nature which eventually clashed with his left-wing allegiances. His ideals reflect a curious compound of slum-culture courage, Jewish concern for social justice, self-taught history, Cold-war Stalinism and, in his later years, Zen Buddhism. His entire literary career embodies his deepest beliefs: that life has moral significance, that the writer must be socially committed, that literature should take sides.

After two youthful blood-and-thunder romances, Fast found his métier in a series of class-conscious historical novels of the American Revolution. *Conceived in Liberty* heralded the loyalty of the common soldier; *The Unvanquished* celebrated the dogged persistence of George Washington (despite his aristocracy and wealth, Fast's favorite hero); and *Citizen Tom Paine* glorified our first professional revolutionary. Fast then championed anonymous heroes of other races: *The Last Frontier* is a spare but moving account of the heroic flight in 1878 of the Cheyenne Indians to their Powder River home in Wyoming; *Freedom Road* recounts the amazing social experiments of black Southern legislatures in the Reconstruc-

tion era. The best selling of the popular novels of the early 1940s, *Freedom Road* shows great power in its scenes of violent conflict but it is melodramatic and tendentious. By contrast, the poetically evocative *Last Frontier,* perhaps his best novel, enlists profound sympathy through great control and objectivity, and evades the pitfalls of "noble redskin" sentimentality.

In 1946 *The American* detailed the rise and fall of Illinois Governor John Peter Altgeld, who was politically defeated after he pardoned three anarchists convicted of bomb-throwing in Haymarket Square in 1886. Although Fast's novels had reflected Marxist thought since his youthful conversion to socialism, his propagandizing became too obtrusive with *Clarkton* in 1947. This proletarian strike novel of life in the Massachusetts textile mills revealed his inability to maintain the necessary distance to interpret contemporary events soundly. He returned in 1948 to the historical novel with *My Glorious Brothers,* a stirring account of the Maccabees and the 30-year Jewish resistance to Greek-Syrian tyranny. This success was duplicated with *Spartacus,* the largely imagined story of the gladiatorial revolt against Rome in 71 BC. *Spartacus* was self-published in 1951 after the author was blacklisted for Communist activities and had spent three months in federal prison for contempt of Congress. But, predictably, Fast's other works of the early 1950s were failures in proportion to their nearness to the present day: *The Passion of Sacco and Vanzetti* recounted sentimentally the last hours of the doomed Italian anarchists; *Silas Timberman* depicted an academic victim of a McCarthyite witchhunt; and *The Story of Lola Gregg* described the FBI pursuit and capture of an heroic Communist labor leader. These self-published works of imprisoned martyrs, abounding in Christ-figures and symbolic Judases, reflect their author's bitter sense of entrapment and isolation, for he could neither publish with established houses nor leave the country.

In 1957 Fast publicly quit the Communist Party after the Hungarian revolution and then described his tortured apostasy in *The Naked God.* He soon revisited Jewish history as a favored novelistic subject with *Moses, Prince of Egypt; Agrippa's Daughter,* and *Torquemada.* He returned, with a more mature vision, thrice more to the American revolution in *April Morning, The Crossing,* and *The Hessian.* In other historical novels he continued to re-examine earlier themes: *The Winston Affair* deals with the court-martial of an American murderer, homosexual and anti-Semite who nevertheless deserves and wins justice in a military court, while *Power* shows the corruption by power by a John L. Lewis-type of labor leader: *Agrippa's Daugther* rejects the "just-war" theory of *My Glorious Brothers* in favor of Rabbi Hillel's pacifism.

Most readers saw Fast in two new guises (or disguises), as author of science-fiction stories and as a writer of "entertainments" in the manner of Graham Greene. These late science fiction or "Zen stories" include stories in *The Edge of Tomorrow, The Hunter and the Trap* and *The General Zapped an Angel* (late gathered into one volume, *Time and the Riddle*). The dozen or so "entertainments" are written under the pseudonym E.V. Cunningham, most built around the female title characters. Both the science fiction and the Cunningham novels criticize American institutions and values with wit and humor, and all show the deft hand of the professional storyteller at work. A newer series of Cunningham thrillers stars Masao Masuto, a Japanese-American detective of the Beverly Hills Police Department and a Zen Buddhist. In these, character holds the main appeal, especially that of family-man Masuto.

More recently, Fast has achieved repeated bestsellerdom with an immigrant-saga that has grown to several large novels, starting with

The Immigrants and including, *The Immigrant's Daughter.* These volumes trace the Italian, Dan Lavette, and his family while newly arrived Italians, Jews, Orientals, and others struggle against the entrenched wealth and prejudice of old-line Americans. Beginning with the San Francisco earthquake of 1906, the series energetically sweeps across 20th-century American history and recent world events. No longer ax-grinding, Fast uses well his own rich experiences for the first time, and he is at the top of his admirable narrative form.

—Frank Campenni

FAULKS, Sebastian

Nationality: British. **Born:** Newbury, 20 April 1953. **Education:** Wellington College; Emmanuel College, Cambridge, 1974, B.A. (honours). **Family:** Married Veronica Youlten in 1989; one son and one daughter. **Career:** Teacher of English and French, International School of London, 1975-79; journalist, *Daily Telegraph,* London, 1979-82; feature writer, *Sunday Telegraph,* 1983-86; literary editor, *Independent,* London, 1986-89. Since 1989 deputy editor, *Independent on Sunday.* Radio broadcaster, British Broadcasting Corp. Editor, *New Fiction Society,* 1978-81. **Address:** c/o *Independent,* 40 City Road, London E.C.1, England.

PUBLICATIONS

Novels

A Trick of the Light. London, Bodley Head, 1984.
The Girl at the Lion d'Or. London, Hutchinson, 1989.
A Fool's Alphabet. London, Hutchinson, and Boston, Little Brown, 1992.
Bird Song. London, Hutchinson, 1993.

*   *   *

Although Sebastian Faulks had already published *A Trick of Light,* it actually was his second novel, *The Girl at the Lion d'Or,* that received critical acclaim. He was praised for his sensitive characterization of a love story, related in a traditional manner and placed in France in the 1930s, where there is disquiet about fascist and communist threats. The title refers to a hotel, *Lion d'Or,* in Janvilliers, a small town where the "girl" is Anne from Paris, taken on as waitress there. She is orphaned under circumstances she keeps secret.

The opening of the novel, when Anne is driven from the railway station to the Lion d'Or, is detailed and sets the pace and style of the prose. Everything en route is observed in camera like detail, as are the appearances and nature of the characters. The plot is romantic and highly improbable, under the *mores* of class society of the period. Anne is spotted by a middle-aged Jewish lawyer, Hartmann, when she serves drinks at the hotel bar. He lives in a rambling country house with his wife, Christine, and accepts Anne's offer of domestic help on her hotel day off. Hartmann pays for her to have superior lodgings, as they have fallen in love and their relationship becomes sexual.

For Anne, the affair, which is her first, is her only experience of any love. Faulks conveys, with understanding, Anne's naivete in the affair and her innocent enthusiasm for her lover. Her love breaks through any social awkwardness, and her previous deep hurts from life help to confer on her a sympathy that is entirely deserved. She tells Hartmann how her father, a brave soldier in World War I, refused, with other men, to obey the command of a bullying officer, which would have meant death for them all, and shot him to save the men's lives. He in turn was ordered by an officer to be shot, and his name became publicly disgraced as a murderer. The lies and gossip about her father in the village where Anne lived unhinged her mother, who took her own life.

Hartmann, who barely loves his wife, feels strengthened by Anne's revelations. He is disturbed by his own experiences of the Great War and the general malaise of France. Despite the locale, the atmosphere is not particularly French, but the dominant image is of Hartmann's brooding house, with the clutter of bric-a-brac and old books. Shoddy repairs result in the collapse of part of it, a portent of what happens to the Hartmann-Anne affair. When a troublemaker allows Christine to know about her husband's mistress, Hartmann ends the relationship very abruptly, although broken hearted. Anne has no choice but to begin life again in Paris. She now knows that love is possible and life-enriching, which makes her new wound endurable.

A Fool's Alphabet is accomplished but perhaps too contrived to succeed as memorable fiction. Pietro Russell, of partial Italian descent, searches for influences on his own character from Italy. These occur as flashbacks from childhood, when he determines to pass a night in a place that starts with each letter of the alphabet. Thus, 26 chapters in random chronology slowly reveal Pietro's life, in which his mother died when he was young, and his quest for love as an adult. Pietro is quite uninteresting, but he achieves his ambition with the exception of X—which is Xianging in China, the symbolic dream city—representing the places he can never visit.

Bird Song is almost an unqualified success, but one wonders if the extreme length of the novel was necessary for the statement of the theme—suffering in World War I and its aftermath, reverberating to the late 1970s. In the war scenes the contrasting characters and their diverse backgrounds provide different ways of survival from which the other men can learn. No detail of deprivation is spared, whether it is of lice in clothing or filthy food, because for Faulks there is no glory in war, only the fact that the full horror of war had to be experienced to be understood. *Bird Song* is a forceful attempt to convey that reality, largely through the character of Stephen Wraysford, who is an officer on the western front in 1916.

The long opening of over one hundred pages of *Bird Song* takes places six years previously, when Wraysford, a rather neurotic man, lodges with a family in Amiens to study textiles and falls in love with a Isabella, a daughter with whom he elopes. After she becomes pregnant and unexpectedly leaves him, Wraysford's emotional life is shocked into a stupor. As a soldier, he is considered coldhearted. The officers' language is embarrassingly "old school tie," with the back-slapping, false bonhomie of the English tradition. One is unsure if Faulks means to be satirical or not. In any case, it is a little too precious. The same stricture applies to Wraysford's love scenes, which touch on sentimentality but vividly recall when he is emotionally frigid. But the men who dig the trenches communicate directly, and Faulks gives these characters more than a light sketch. They are important for their self-reliance, drawing strength from their individual experiences of the past. In the case of Jack Firebrace, who digs the mine tunnels under enemy lines, the conditions of war are better than his poverty-riddled life in London. His survival of everything with courage, including the death of his son, makes a deep impression on Wrayford, who unlocks his suppressed feelings when he is wounded and left for dead in a tunnel. Wraysford concludes the meaning of life is the continuity of human love. The exuberant birdsong of the title, the twittering of birds that starts when the gun fire stops, echoes through to 1979 in an epilogue. Wraysford's pregnant grandchild, Elizabeth, learns the truth of her origin, and Faulks accentuates his belief in redeeming the past when the baby is born by a description of rapturous exultation as the living proof of goodness from past tragedy.

—Geoffrey Elborn

FAUST, Irvin

Nationality: American. **Born:** New York City, 11 June 1924. **Education:** City College of New York, B.S. 1949; Columbia University, New York, M.A. 1952, D.Ed. 1960. **Military Service:** Served in the United States Army, 1943-46. **Family:** Married Jean Satterthwaite in 1959. **Career:** Teacher, Manhattanville Junior High School, New York, 1949-53; guidance counselor, Lynbrook High School, Long Island, 1956-60. Since 1960 director of Guidance and Counselling, Garden City High School, Long Island. Taught at Columbia University, Summer 1963, New School for Social Research, New York, 1975, Swarthmore College, Pennsylvania, 1976, City College, 1977, and University of Rochester, New York, Summer 1978. **Awards:** O. Henry prize, 1983 and 1986; Charles Angoff award, for fiction, 1994. **Agent:** Gloria Loomis, Watkins Loomis Agency Inc., 150 East 35th Street, New York, New York 10016. **Address:** 417 Riverside Drive, New York, New York 10025, U.S.A.

PUBLICATIONS

Novels

The Steagle. New York, Random House, 1966.
The File on Stanley Patton Buchta. New York, Random House, 1970.
Willy Remembers. New York, Arbor House, 1971.
Foreign Devils. New York, Arbor House, 1973.
A Star in the Family. New York, Doubleday, 1975.
Newsreel. New York, Harcourt Brace, 1980.
Jim Dandy. New York, Carroll and Graf, 1994.

Short Stories

Roar Lion Roar and Other Stories. New York, Random House, and London, Gollancz, 1965.
The Year of the Hot Jock and Other Stories. New York, Dutton, 1985.

Uncollected Short Stories

"Action at Vicksburg," in *New Black Mask* (Orlando, Florida), Fall 1985.

"Artie and Benny," in *Michigan Quarterly Review* (Ann Arbor), Spring 1989.
"Let Me Off Uptown," in *Fiction* (New York), 1991.
"Black Auxiliaries," in *The Literary Review* (Madison, New Jersey), Summer 1994.

Other

Entering Angel's World: A Student-Centered Casebook. New York, Columbia Teachers College Press, 1963.

*

Critical Studies: By Richard Kostelanetz, in *The New American Arts,* New York, Horizon Press, 1965, in *Tri-Quarterly* (Evanston, Illinois), Winter 1967, and in *On Contemporary Literature,* New York, Avon, 1967; by R.V. Cassill, in *New York Times Book Review,* 29 August 1971; interview with Matthew Bruccoli, in *Conversations with Writers 2,* Detroit, Gale, 1978; by Martin Tucker in *Confrontation* (Brookville, New York), Fall 1994.

Irvin Faust comments:

(1972) It seems to me that thus far my work has dealt with the displacement and disorganization of Americans in urban life; with their attempt to find adjustments in the glossy attractions of the mass media—movies, radio, TV, advertising, etc.—and in the image-radiating seductions of our institutions—colleges, sports teams, etc. Very often this "adjustment" is to the "normal" perception a derangement, but perfectly satisfying to my subjects.

Recently my work has moved out to include suburban America and also back in historical directions. My characters to this date have been outside of the white anglo-saxon milieu, but have included Jews, Blacks, Puerto Ricans and the so-called Ethnic Americans.

Both *Roar Lion Roar* and *The Steagle* were published in France (Gallimard) and I feel the reviews were most perceptive, leading me to muse that perhaps, unbeknownst to me, I am quite close to the French literary sensibility.

(1995) *Jim Dandy* continues my exploration of the psychology and actuality of wars since 1898. This time I've dug into the Italo-Ethiopian conflict of 1936, which pre-figured World War II. We are still living with its ramifications, and fiction helps us to understand these relationships.

*   *   *

In his novels and short stories, Irvin Faust has attempted (as he said of one novel), "to show the rise and fall of this nation over the last forty years." Were this all, he would be essentially a social historian disguised as fictional chronicler of our times. Faust, however, has managed to weave together a substantial number of additional themes, drawing upon his background as Jew, New Yorker, veteran, husband, and professional guidance counselor. The integration of these materials, when successful, produces a rich tapestry of life in contemporary urban America, especially when played off against the past, both mythicized and actual.

His first fictional book, *Roar Lion Roar,* treated with sensitive compassion the interior lives of disturbed adolescents of minority backgrounds. In the title story, Ishmael Ramos, a janitor at Columbia University, so identifies with the "ivory leak" school that he kills himself when the football team loses. Most of the protagonists of these stories are insane but even the sane have been mind-molded by the mass media or warped by the pressures of recent history. Indeed, Faust's major theme of the forming and deforming of personality by an empty culture in a violent, chaotic world may here have found its most solid embodiment.

The broader canvas of the novel form permitted Faust the breadth and depth needed to convey the specificity of a conflicted culture in its dizzying impact upon the individual. In Faust's first novel, *The Steagle,* English Professor Harold Weissburg develops a multiple personality while his sense of self disintegrates during the Cuban missile crisis. The title is a composite-name formed from two football teams, the Steelers and the Eagles. Thus, as the United States shifts from "good neighbor" to threatening nuclear power, Weissburg, in desperate flight across the country, becomes Bob Hardy (brother of Andy, of the wholesome movie family), gangster Rocco Salvato, a football hero, a flying ace, and, finally Humphrey Bogart. In *The File on Stanley Patton Buchta* his protagonist is an undercover policeman, Vietnam veteran, and college graduate who infiltrates both a para-military rightist group within the police department and a New Left organization. He is further divided in romantic loyalty to an all-American blonde beauty and a black militant on whom he is spying. Perhaps because the hero is not fully realized, or because the material lacks the historical density which the author prefers, this fairly conventional novel lacks impact.

Faust's next two novels, however, are probably his best to date. *Willy Remembers* features the redoubtable Willy Kleinhans, who at 93 is an embodiment and archive of America in the 19th century. The history he recalls is badly scrambled but curiously apt: Grover Cleveland is confused with baseball-pitcher Grover Cleveland Alexander; John F. Kennedy melds with McKinley, another assassinated President; Admiral and Governor Dewey, Franklin and Teddy Roosevelt likewise interchange. The Haymarket Riot, the frame-up of Tom Mooney, prohibition, and T.R. at San Juan hill all whiz by as kaleidoscopic snapshots. Despite Willy's anti-semitism, curmudgeonly judgments and angry confusion, he is a likable and likely representative of his time and place. Although R.V. Cassill rightly praised *Willy Remembers* for its "overlapping stereotypes of urban and national memory" and the novel's "Joycean complexity," Faust does not always guide the reader adequately along these high-speed, involuted memory-trips. The novel does display, nevertheless, a marked advance in control of point-of-view and the blend of fantasy and realism. With *Foreign Devils* Faust achieves mastery in weaving together the items of popular culture, the myths by which many Americans live, and the disintegrating personality of a Jewish writer. His hero, Sidney Benson (born Birnbaum), is separated from his wife and living partly off his mother's earnings from a candy store. Inspired by President Nixon's trip to China, Benson, who has suffered from writer's block, begins a novel about the Boxer rebellion. This melodrama, or novel-within-the novel, is an exquisite parody of the swashbuckling accounts of Richard Harding Davis, and is perhaps the chief attraction of *Foreign Devils.* The action in the present, except for Benson's reunion at the end with his father (who had deserted his family years ago), is cluttered with topical references, both a shortcoming and an attraction in Faust's fiction.

Faust's *A Star in the Family* and *Newsreel* show flashes of power as each book scans recent American history, but he is in danger of repeating himself. The tale of vaudevillian Bart Goldwine, protagonist of *A Star in the Family,* consists of interviews conducted by Goldwine's biographer, plus longer memoiristic accounts by

Goldwine. The reproduction of showbusiness patter, street talk, fan magazine prose, courtship, and family discussions is flawless in evoking the cynicism and innocence of the last generation. Showman Goldwine's impression of John F. Kennedy is abruptly ended by the assassination; his long decline thereafter is symbolically entwined with the decline of American vitality and national will. In *Newsreel* former Army Captain Manny "Speed" Finestone is again the victim of his times. Linked spiritually with his wartime "chief," Dwight Eisenhower', Speed cannot escape contrasting the purity of the great crusade against Hitler with the materialism of the affluent 1950s, the cold war mentality, and the slaying of President Kennedy (Chapter 29 is simply "11/22/63"). Finestone's inability to write, his failed romances with two Jewish women and an Irish girl, his unraveling into psychosis are all played against national deterioration in a cultural wasteland. Other previous themes and motifs are also present: sex and sports, the abandoning father, the Jew fighting his ethnic identity, the writer supported by his mother, the use of dialogues with other selves or fantasy-heroes. Although their repeated use suggests personal concerns that are insufficiently integrated into fiction, Faust continues to portray both interior individual lives and cultural tension with skill and sincerity.

—Frank Campenni

FEDERMAN, Raymond

Nationality: American. **Born:** Paris, France, 15 May 1928; emigrated to the United States in 1947; became citizen, 1953. **Education:** Columbia University, New York, 1954-57, B.A. (cum laude) 1957 (Phi Beta Kappa); University of California, Los Angeles, 1957-63, M.A. 1958; Ph.D. in French 1963. **Military Service:** Served in the United States Army 82nd Airborne Division in Korea, 1951-54: Sergeant. **Family:** Married Erica Hubscher in 1960; one daughter. **Career:** Jazz saxophonist, 1947-50; lecturer and assistant professor, University of California, Santa Barbara, 1959-64. Associate professor of French, 1964-68, professor of French and comparative literature, 1968-73, professor of English and comparative literature, 1973-89, and since 1990 Distinguished Professor, State University of New York, Buffalo. Since 1994 the Melodia E. Jones Chair of Literature, SUNY-Buffalo. Visiting professor, University of Montreal, 1970, Hebrew University, Jerusalem, 1982-83; and University of California, San Diego, 1986. Co-editor, *Mica* magazine, Santa Barbara, 1959-64; co-director, Fiction Collective, New York, 1977-80. **Awards:** Guggenheim fellowship, 1966; *Panache* Experimental Fiction prize, 1971; Steloff prize, 1972; Camargo Foundation fellowship, 1977; Fulbright fellowship, 1982; National Endowment for the Arts fellowship, 1985; New York State Foundation for the Arts fellowship, 1985; American Book award, 1986; DAAD fellowship (Berlin), 1990. **Address:** 46 Four Seasons West, Eggertsville, New York 14226, U.S.A.

PUBLICATIONS

Novels

Double or Nothing: A Real Fictitious Discourse. Chicago, Swallow Press, 1971; revised edition, Fiction Collective Two, 1991.

Amer Eldorado (in French). Paris, Stock, 1974.

Take It or Leave It. New York, Fiction Collective, 1976.

The Voice in the Closet (bilingual edition), with *Echos à Federman,* by Maurice Roche. Madison, Wisconsin, Coda Press, 1979.

The Twofold Vibration. Bloomington, Indiana University Press, and Brighton, Harvester Press, 1982.

Smiles on Washington Square. New York, Thunder's Mouth Press, 1985.

Playtexts/Spieltexte (prose and poetry, in English and German). Berlin, LCB-DAAD, 1990.

To Whom It May Concern. Boulder, Colorado, Ficton Collective 2, 1990.

Uncollected Short Stories

"The Man on the Bridge" (as Robin St. Gill), in *Mica* (Santa Barbara, California), vol. 1, no. 1, 1960.

"False Evidence," in *Kolokon,* Summer 1966.

"Histoire du Ballon," in *West Coast Review* (Burnaby, British Columbia), Fall 1969.

"The Captain and the Kids," in *Assembling,* edited by Richard Kostelanetz. New York, Assembling Press, 1970.

"Suspension," in *UCLAN Review Magazine* (Los Angeles), Winter 1970.

"Au pied du livre," in *Sub-Stance 5-6* (Madison, Wisconsin), Summer 1973.

"An Impromptu Swim," in *Out of Sight* (Wichita, Kansas), April 1974.

"Inside the Thing," in *Oyez Review* (Berkeley, California), Fall 1974.

"Setting and Tripping," in *Statements,* edited by Jonathan Baumbach. New York, Braziller, 1975.

"Self-Plagiaristic Autobiographical Poem in Form of a Letter from Here and Elsewhere," in *Oyez Review* (Berkeley, California), new series 5, 1977.

"Hat Missive," "Questionnaire," and "Hats Hats Hats," in *Milk 11-12,* 1978.

"Premembrance," in *Mississippi Review* (Hattiesburg), Fall 1978.

"Parcifal in Hamburg," in *Chicago Review,* Spring 1980.

"Moinous, Nam, and Dostoevsky," in *Paris Review,* Fall 1981.

"The Rigmarole of Contrariety," in *Story Quarterly 15-16* (Northbrook, Illinois), 1982.

"Moinous and Scuette: A Love Story of Sorts," in *Sub-Stance* (Madison, Wisconsin), Spring 1983.

"Displaced Person," in *Denver Quarterly,* Spring 1984.

"Report from the World Federation of Displaced Writers," in *American Made,* edited by Mark Leyner, Curtis White, and Thomas Glyn. New York, Fiction Collective, 1986.

"Last Night's Dream," in *Caliban* (Laguna Beach), 1988.

"A Letter from the Galaxy," in *Mississippi Review* (Hattiesburg), 1988.

"A Love Story of Sorts," in *The Before Columbus Fiction Anthology,* New York and London, Norton, 1991.

"Driving on Highway 290," in *Black Ice* (Boulder, Colorado), 1991.

"D'une parenthèse à l'autre," in *TXT* (Paris), 1991.

"The Story-Teller," in *Black Ice* (Boulder, Colorado), 1992.

"The Line," in *Alaska Quarterly Review* (Fairbanks), 1993.

"The Interrogators," in *Caliban* (Laguna Beach), 1994.

"Crisis in the Oversexed Society," in *Iowa Review* (Iowa City), 1994.

"The Gravediggers," in *Private* (Chicago), 1994.

"The Excavation of the Gravediggers," in *Private* (Chicago), 1994.

"The Voice," in *Cups* (San Francisco), 1994.

Plays

Radio Plays: *The Twofold Vibration,* adapted from his own novel, 1990; *Double or Nothing,* adapted from his own novel, 1992; *Playtexts/Spieltexte,* adapted from his own novel, 1992; *Smiles on Washington Square,* adapted from his own novel, 1992; *The Voice in the Closet,* adapted from his own novel, 1992; *To Whom It May Concern,* adapted from his own novel, 1992.

Poetry

Among the Beasts (bilingual edition). Paris, Millas Martin, 1967.

Me Too. Reno, Nevada, West Coast Poetry Review Press, 1976.

Duel/Duel (in English, French, and German). Berlin, Stopover Press, 1991.

Now Then/Nun Denn. Freiburg, Germany, Edition Isele, 1992.

Other

Journey to Chaos: Samuel Beckett's Early Fiction. Berkeley, University of California Press, 1965; London, Cambridge University Press, 1966.

Samuel Beckett: His Works and His Critics: An Essay in Bibliography, with John Fletcher. Berkeley, University of California Press, 1970.

Surfiction: Der Weg der Literatur. Frankfurt, Suhrkamp, 1992.

Critifiction: Postmodern Essays. Buffalo, State University of New York Press, 1993.

Eine Version Meines Lebens. Augsberg, Germany, Verlag, 1993.

Editor, *Cinq Nouvelles Nouvelles.* New York, Appleton Century Crofts, 1970.

Editor, *Surfiction: Fiction Now—and Tomorrow.* Chicago, Swallow Press, 1975; revised edition, Athens, Ohio University Press-Swallow Press, 1981.

Editor, with Tom Bishop, *Samuel Beckett.* Paris, L'Herne, 1976.

Editor, with Lawrence Graver, *Samuel Beckett: The Critical Heritage.* London, Routledge, 1979.

Translator, *Poems,* by Jacques Temple. Santa Barbara, California, 1964.

Translator, *Temporary Landscapes* (bilingual edition), by Yvonne Caroutch. Venice, Mica, 1965.

Translator, with Genevieve James, *Detachment,* by Michel Serres. Athens, Ohio University Press, 1990.

*

Critical Studies: *The End of Intelligent Writing* by Richard Kostelanetz, New York, Sheed and Ward, 1974; "The Choice of Invention" by Harris Dienstfrey, in *Fiction International 2* (Canton, New York), 1974; *Literary Disruptions* by Jerome Klinkowitz, Urbana, University of Illinois Press, 1975, revised edition, 1980; interviews, with Charlotte Meyers in *Story Quarterly* (Northbrook, Illinois), Fall 1982, with Larry McCaffery in *Contemporary Literature* (Madison, Wisconsin), Fall 1983, and in *Anything Can Happen: Interviews with Contemporary American Novelists* edited by McCaffery and Thomas LeClair, Urbana, University of Illinois Press, 1983; *The Novel as Performance: The Fiction of Ronald Sukenick and Raymond Federman* by Jerzy Kutnik, Carbondale, Southern Illinois University Press, 1986; "Narrative Disarticulation and the Voice in the Closet Complex in Raymond Federman's

Fiction" by Marcel Cornis-Pop, in *Critique* (Santa Rosa, California), Winter 1988; "Raymond Federman's America: Take It or Leave It" by David Dowling, in *Contemporary Literature* (Madison, Wisconsin), Fall 1989; *Criteria of Identity: A Comparative Analysis of Raymond Federman and Jasper Johns* by Eva-Maria Erdpohl, Frankfurt, New York, and Paris, Verlag, 1992.

Raymond Federman comments:

Although my work has been labeled "experimental" and "avant-garde," and it is true my fiction departs radically from conventional narrative forms, I do believe that it speaks to the reality of our modern times. That does not mean it is realistic; on the contrary, I am not interested in writing fiction which represents the world, but which improves reality. My main concern is with language, but not a language which reproduces meaning but which produces new meaning. I have expressed my position on fiction in several theoretical essays, in particular the essay/manifesto "Surfiction" (*Partisan Review,* 1973), and more recently in "Imagination as Playgiarism" (*New Literary History,* 1977). I believe that my novels form a coherent project which is an effort on my part to come to terms with both my personal experiences (especially during World War II, and as an immigrant in America) and the recent historical events in which I have participated as a writer and a human being. The distinction I make, however, is that I do not think that my life and history are the sources of my fiction, but that in fact my fiction is what invents my life and history. In other words, the stories I write are my life.

(1995) I often wonder if being a writer, becoming a writer is a gift one receives at birth, or if it happens accidentally in the course of one's life. I am always envious—and suspicious too—of those who say to me: "I wrote my first poem when I was eight years old, and published my first story when I was fifteen." It makes me feel that perhaps I wasted the first twenty-five years of my life.

Even today, after the millions of words I have scribbled (in English and in French) for more than thirty years, with seven novels in print, another about to be published, one more in progress, and two abandoned, four volumes of poems, several books of essays and criticism, hundreds of loose pieces of prose and poetry in magazines, and much more unpublished, I often doubt that I am a writer. More than thirty years trying to convince myself of this fact. Thirty-eight years, to be exact, since my first published poem in a college magazine in 1957—a five line poem entitled "More or Less." It went like this:

> From Cambrian brain-
> Less algae sprung the ten-ton
> Flesh and bone reptile
> Then man from Ape till bodi-
> Less brain shall inherit the Earth

A ponderous little poem which certainly does not indicate that I was then or would ever become a writer. Even now I believe I am still working at becoming one, and perhaps I shall die never knowing whether or not I was a real writer. It seems to me that everything I write (and few days pass that I do not sit at my desk to work) is a preparation for the great book that someday will make of me the real writer. Meanwhile my books are published, reviewed, discussed, analyzed, criticized, translated, praised and attacked, a couple even received literary prizes, and still I am not sure.

The other day my best fan, my lovely daughter Simone, on the phone from New York City (collect of course) says to me, without malice, lovingly in fact: "Hey, Pop, I think I know what your epitaph will be, I mean, you know, what should be written on your tombstone: OUT OF PRINT!" What gentle brutality. She's got it right though, there is brutality in what writers do. Writing is such an inhuman thing to be doing, so brutally asocial, unnatural. So much against nature. No wonder writers suffer fits of doubt and despair.

No, I do not think I was born a writer (even though I too can doubt and despair like a true writer), but the accidents of my life may have helped make of me a writer. If I was given a gift at all which forced me to write, it was what happened to me, often in spite of myself, during the first 25 years of my life. Much of the fiction I have written found its source in those early years.

In a recent article about my fiction, the critic Marcel Cornis-Pope states, rightly so I suppose, that "unlike some of his metafictional contemporaries, [Federman] has been blessed (or cursed) with enough biography for several epic cycles, condemned to string out the story of his life endlessly in various fictions." The first 25 years of my life certainly contained enough drama, enough adventures, misadventures and misfortunes to inspire several novels. I lived those years oblivious to myself and to the sordid affairs of the world around me, unaware that the experiences I was living, or I should say enduring, would someday make a writer of me. My life began in incoherence and discontinuity, but also with doubt and uncertainty, and my work has undoubtedly been marked by this. Perhaps that is why it has been called experimental.

*   *   *

Raymond Federman established himself as a critic before he turned to novel-writing. His books and essays about Samuel Beckett seem to have shaped his career as a novelist just as surely as Beckett's early criticism on Joyce and Proust pointed the way to his fiction from *More Pricks Than Kicks* to the *Molloy* trilogy. Federman once called Beckett's fiction "le roman du langage." He was trying on this occasion to distinguish between André Gide's *Counterfeiters,* which he saw as "primarily a reflection on fiction by fiction," and Beckett's work, which is more "a reflection on fiction by its own language."

Federman's novels are, among other things, showcases for "linguistic play" and "narrative joy" (as Jerome Klinkowitz points out in his *Literary Disruptions*). Like Beckett, Federman is enviably bilingual and moves with ease between English and French. His novels seem to profit from experiments—verbal, visual, and narrative—he has observed on both the American and French fictional scenes.

Double or Nothing, his first novel, is described on the dustjacket as "a *concrete* novel—*concrete,* as in *concrete poetry*." Each page seems to go its own visual and verbal way. All classical distinctions between image and word appear to be rendered obsolete. *Double or Nothing* is what the French might call a "roman-en-train-de-se-faire." We witness the growing pains of writing a novel while we see the grudging, halting fleshing-out of a story which involves the arrival in America of a 19-year-old immigrant. Everything is tentative, every detail of the story is subject to the caprices of the narrator. Hence names change as they do in Beckett ("In fact I'll change all the names eventually. Has to be"), situations alter on retelling, digressions wear down the narrative at every turn. It seems to take the immigrant as long to disembark from his boat as it does Tristram Shandy to get born. Catalogues, inventories, all sorts of spatial devices slow down time and arrest any kind of forward movement.

The same complex, digressive, unlinear telling characterizes *Take It or Leave It.* This novel is more completely "a reflection on fiction by its own language" than *Double or Nothing.* This "exaggerated second-hand tale," as it is called on the title page, seems less eccentric typographically than its predecessor but much denser verbally and narratively. In a certain sense it is part of the tradition of the French voyage-of-discovery-of-America, a tradition which includes Céline's *Journey to the End of the Night* and Butor's *Mobile.* (There are even references to Céline in the text, such as "here go back and reread the arrival of Bardamu in New York in le Voyage.")

The telling of *Take It or Leave it* has more than its share of exhilaration (a word used appropriately as the title of the sixth chapter of the novel). Words seem to explode on the page as Frenchy's adventures are recounted from his days with the 82nd Airborne Division in North Carolina through his trip north to Camp Drum in early 1951. These adventures, which offer something of a narrative line, are eclipsed at every turn by an elaborate series of subtexts which comment on such unrelated matters as the differences between French and English, the theories of Derrida, and the terrible legacy of the holocaust. There is room in this unpaginated novel for almost anything its creator chooses to place within its covers. Titles of Federman's earlier works are paraded before us as well as a brief biographical sketch of the author when he retreats behind the mask of Hombre De La Pluma. This *opera aperta* (Umberto Eco's words) keeps opening-out and breaking down the walls of conventional fiction. The novelist freely enters the frame of his novel and creator and creatures come to confront one another on equal terms.

Even on this crowded canvas, with its "story that cancels itself as it goes," the presence of Beckett is unmistakable. Federman at one point embellishes a line from *Murphy:* "MUST I BITE THE HAND THAT STARVES ME SO THAT IT CAN STRANGLE ME BETTER?" At another he nods fondly to his mentor: "In complete LESSNESSness my friend Sam would say where nothing is even less than nothing."

The Voice in the Closet seems to honor Beckett at every turn. Just as the Irish writer achieved such remarkable economy of means in his recent prose, so has Federman realized a startling process of reduction here. *The Voice in the Closet,* which looks more like an art book than fiction, contains three texts: parallel English and French versions of a work by Federman (*The Voice in the Closet/La Vois dans le Cabinet de Débarras*), with a piece by Maurice Roche, *Echos* (dedicated to Federman), sandwiched in between. The Federman work, with its disturbing hermetic words and cadences, is unpunctuated and unparagraphed in both languages. Here is the way the author described *The Voice in the Closet* in a recent letter: "A complex double book—system of mirrors, echoes, boxes within boxes to accommodate my plural voice."

Federman's career as writer and critic seems reduced to a few words and images in this text. A reading of the two earlier novels as well as a knowledge of his criticism and poetry would seem a prerequisite for any understanding of *The Voice in the Closet.* A forbidding Mallarméan density should keep away all but the most serious students of recent Franco-American literature. While the author hid behind a series of masks or disguises in *Double or Nothing* and *Take It or Leave It,* he emerges here as "federman" (or as "namredef" or "featherman") and Beckett quite simply as "sam." The matters of Jewishness ("the yellow star on my chest") and the experience of the holocaust ("the empty skins already remade into lampshades") are perhaps more sharply focused here than anywhere else in Federman's' work.

The focus continues into *The Twofold Vibration,* the title of which is taken from Beckett's *The Lost Ones.* The Irish writer's presence is once again everywhere in evidence, both in storytelling technique and in frequent reference, such as ". . . he sounded like old Winnie sinking into her mound of earth, you know in *Happy Days,* casually observing her own burial." The text is thickened by Federman's accustomed digressions to a variety of writers and works. Thus Dostoevsky's narrow escape from the firing squad in 1849 is given five pages and Henry James's ritualistic shaving of his beard as the 19th century ended is offered a lengthy paragraph. The present time of *The Twofold Vibration* is New Year's Eve 1999. An unnamed old man is about to be "deported to the space colonies." (This sounds like science fiction but we are assured it is something different: "call it exploratory or better yet extemporaneous fiction.") Three narrators tell this old man's story from his birth in 1918, through his holocaust experiences, his amorous and gambling indulgences, his marriage and divorce, to the unlikely final happenings at the "spaceport." As with Federman's previous fiction, *The Twofold Vibration* is a constant witness to the frustrations and difficulties of writing a novel. Despite the eccentricities of telling, of composition, and even of typography and punctuation (commas everywhere, no periods), there is something agreeably old-fashioned about this work. It seems to be part of the leisurely picaresque tradition. It also, in an intriguing way, confronts contemporary issues and involves itself in the history of literature and thought.

Smiles on Washington Square offers a narrative which circles about an "initial encounter across a smile" between a man and a woman. This "almost" meeting between Moinous (a literary alter ego Federman has cultivated in his earlier fiction) and Sucette is precisely dated as occurring on March 15, 1954, during the McCarthy hearings. The rest of the text abounds in problematical turns, which feature words like should, would, could, perhaps, and if. Federman flirts with the device of the novel-within-the-novel, somewhat in the manner of Gide's *Counterfeiters,* when he has Sucette work on a short story which mirrors events in *Smiles on Washington Square.* The narrative is cleverly made to exist on a variety of levels, with fiction triumphing over fact, imagination over reality. Moinous, the French immigrant, and Sucette, the Bostonian with the social conscience, have a life together only when their creator posits hypothetical situations: "It would probably be a good place in the love story of Moinous & Sucette for her to suggest that perhaps they should go to her apartment where Sucette could then read her story to Moinous."

The typography, punctuation, and paragraphing here are all quite regular, suggesting perhaps that Federman has tired somewhat of his experiments with disrupting the appearance of his text. Yet the tentative nature of reality with a "story that cancels itself as it goes" (words from *Take It or Leave It*) seem to survive intact from the early fiction. Federman makes interesting use of the present tense through much of his narrative, capturing the illusion of what Gertrude Stein once called "a continuous present." There is less of Beckett in *Smiles on Washington Square* than in the rest of Federman's work. The writer who comes to mind is Marguerite Duras.

Federman turns to the epistolary form ("the epistolary fragments you have before you") in *To Whom It May Concern.* The preoccupations of the earlier novels resurface—the problematic nature of the compositional act, the centrality of the holocaust, the difficulties of attaching names to people and places, the blurring of the line separating myth from reality—but everything seems more finely tuned here. The literary echoes are less frequent but just as haunting, with references to Rimbaud's *Une Saison en enfer,* Diderot's *Jacques le fataliste,* and even an oblique glance at Styron's *Sophie's Choice.*

An unnamed letter writer gradually fleshes out a narrative about Sarah and her cousin who are on the verge of a reunion after a separation of 35 years. The telling moves back and forth in time to accommodate the life stories of these two survivors and several generations of family members. The author of the letters worries insistently about "how to stage the story of Sarah and her cousin," as process seems to matter as much as progress. We get a privileged view of this author's workshop as he circles around his subject only to admit on the final page: "I realized that their story would always remain unfinished . . ." Intermittently we get something of Federman's poetics, especially in a statement like ". . . I would gladly sacrifice all the tricks and gimmicks that have sustained me so far if I could rid myself of the imposture of realism, that ugly beast that stands at bay ready to leap in the moment you begin scribbling your fiction."

—Melvin J. Friedman

FEINSTEIN, Elaine

Nationality: British. **Born:** Bootle, Lancashire, 24 October 1930. **Education:** Wyggeston Grammar School, Leicester; Newnham College, Cambridge, B.A. in English 1952, M.A. 1955. **Family:** Married Arnold Feinstein in 1956; three sons. **Career:** Editorial staff member, Cambridge University Press, 1960-62; lecturer in English, Bishop's Stortford Training College, Hertfordshire, 1963-66; assistant lecturer in literature, University of Essex, Colchester, 1967-70. **Awards:** Arts Council grant, 1970, 1979, 1981; Daisy Miller award, for fiction, 1971; Kelus prize, 1978. Fellow, Royal Society of Literature, 1980. **Agent:** Rogers Coleridge and White, 20 Powis Mews, London W11 1JN; (plays and film) Lemon Unna and Durbridge, 24-32 Pottery Lane, London, W11 4LZ, England.

PUBLICATIONS

Novels

The Circle. London, Hutchinson, 1970.
The Amberstone Exit. London, Hutchinson, 1972.
The Glass Alembic. London, Hutchinson, 1973; as *The Crystal Garden,* New York, Dutton, 1974.
Children of the Rose. London, Hutchinson, 1975.
The Ecstasy of Dr. Miriam Garner. London, Hutchinson, 1976.
The Shadow Master. London, Hutchinson, 1978; New York, Simon and Schuster, 1979.
The Survivors. London, Hutchinson, 1982; New York, Penguin, 1991.
The Border. London, Hutchinson, 1984; New York, Boyars, 1989.
Mother's Girl. London, Century Hutchinson, and New York, Dutton, 1988.
All You Need. London, Century Hutchinson, 1989; New York, Viking, 1991.
Loving Brecht. London, Hutchinson, 1992.
Dreamers. London, Macmillan, 1994.

Short Stories

Matters of Chance. London, Covent Garden Press, 1972.
The Silent Areas. London, Hutchinson, 1980.

Plays

Lear's Daughters (produced London, 1987).

Radio Plays: *Echoes,* 1980; *A Late Spring,* 1982; *A Captive Lion,* 1984; *Marina Tsvetayeva: A Life,* 1985; *A Day Off,* from the novel by Storm Jameson, 1986; *If I Ever Get on My Feet Again,* 1987; *The Man in Her Life,* 1989; *The Temptations of Dr. William Fosters,* 1991.

Television Plays: *Breath,* 1975; *Lunch,* 1982; *Country Diary of an Edwardian Lady* series, from work by Edith Holden, 1984; *A Brave Face,* 1985; *The Chase,* 1988; *A Passionate Woman* series, 1989.

Poetry

In a Green Eye. London, Goliard Press, 1966.
The Magic Apple Tree. London, Hutchinson, 1971.
At the Edge. Rushden, Northamptonshire, Sceptre Press, 1972.
The Celebrants and Other Poems. London, Hutchinson, 1973.
Some Unease and Angels: Selected Poems. London, Hutchinson, and University Center, Michigan, Green River Press, 1977.
The Feast of Euridice. London, Faber, 1980.
Badlands. London, Century Hutchinson, 1986.
City Music. London, Hutchinson, 1990.
Selected Poems. London, Carcanet, 1994.

Other

Bessie Smith. London, Penguin, 1985.
A Captive Lion: The Life of Marina Tsvetayeva. London, Century Hutchinson, and New York, Dutton, 1987.
Marina Tsvetayeva. London and New York, Penguin, 1989.
Lawrence's Women. London and New York, HarperCollins, 1993.

Editor, *Selected Poems of John Clare.* London, University Tutorial Press, 1968.
Editor, with Fay Weldon, *New Stories 4.* London, Hutchinson, 1979.
Editor, *PEN New Poetry.* London, Quartet, 1988.

Translator, *The Selected Poems of Marina Tsvetayeva.* London, Oxford University Press, 1971; revised edition, Oxford and New York, Oxford University Press, 1981.
Translator, *Three Russian Poets: Margarita Aliger, Yunna Moritz, Bella Akhmadulina.* Manchester, Carcanet, 1979.
Translator, with Antonia W. Bouis, *First Draft: Poems,* by Nika Turbina. London, Boyars, 1988.

*

Manuscript Collection: Cambridge University.

Critical Study: Article by Peter Conradi, in *British Novelists since 1960* edited by Jay L. Halio, Detroit, Gale, 1983.

Elaine Feinstein comments:

My earliest fiction was very much an extension of my poetry, but as the novels have moved away from a single narrative voice to explore a wider territory, I have largely abandoned those rhythms and have come to prefer the traditional clarity of prose.

*   *   *

Lena, in Elaine Feinstein's first novel, *The Circle,* realizes *à propos* her husband "that she would have to take it up again. Her separate life. Her lonely life, the music of words to be played with, the books . . . they would be her refuge; her private world. As his was this of the laboratory. And she must now move as securely into that . . . and find magic." However, in the general context of Feinstein's work, which shows a progressive widening of focus, this is broader than a feminist prescription. Subsequent novels are dominated by men and women in search of "magic," partly via illegitimate means in *The Ecstasy of Dr. Miriam Garner,* and both actively and contemplatively through religion in *The Shadow Master.* "Magic" may be partially embodied in people, as in *The Amberstone Exit,* with Emily's fascination with the glamorous Tyrenes, the local rich family, and in *The Ecstasy of Dr. Miriam Garner,* with Miriam's fascination with the brilliant but brutal Stavros; in both novels there is a strong erotic element in the fascination, and Emily's youthful hunger for sexual experience, which comes to focus on Max Tyrene, anticipates Miriam's more sophisticated desire for Stavros. Similarly, in *Mother's Girl* Halina as a student is infatuated with the brilliant don Janos, while in *All You Need* middle-aged Nell falls for glamorous, powerful Theo.

The fundamental source of "magic" is inevitably "the music of words." For Lena and Emily it is joy in intoxicating language, and for Nell who aspires to writing poetry, and so it could be for the poet Hans in *The Border* were he not, as a part-Jew, persecuted by Hitler, while in the title story of *The Silent Areas* poetry must be "the words that ran in the blood of freezing men without food. Or the minds of the half-mad in lonely cells." In *The Shadow Master,* before the closing religious acceptance, the search for magic meant apocalyptic action. Thus, unfashionably, Feinstein is concerned with validation for people's lives outside as well as inside human relationships.

Perhaps drawing on her experience as a poet, in her first novel, *The Circle,* Feinstein used technical devices, notably spaces within paragraphs, intended for immediacy but in practice often distracting, and later abandoned. A staple technique throughout her work is the juxtaposition of different time-sequences. In *The Circle* this is unstructured, while *The Amberstone Exit* opens in a maternity ward where Emily is having her baby and swings back over the events bringing her there, with the two time-sequences running together toward the end.

The Glass Alembic is about a more mature woman, Brigid, and for the first time focuses on a group. Two passages from this novel are reworked with different names and alternative endings in the stories "Complicity" and "Strangers" (*The Silent Areas*). Brigid's arrival in Basel where her husband is a biochemist is a catalyst for various human reactions in the scientific community. The setting of Paracelsus-haunted Basel is merely coincidentally metaphoric of the action. By contrast, the settings are integral in *Children of the Rose,* which evokes Collaborationist tensions in present-day Provence and the reactions of Jews, once refugees, on revisiting Poland.

In *The Ecstasy of Dr. Miriam Garner* Feinstein plaits a strand of narrative from medieval Toledo with a glamorous female

academic's life into a mystery story with spiritual side-lights. *The Shadow Master* is set mainly in Turkey, where an international religious and political apocalyptic movements begins, leading indirectly to the explosion of "a small nuclear device." In *The Survivors* Feinstein follows two Jewish émigré families in Liverpool, one rich and one poor, from 1914 to 1956, when Diana, the offspring of a surprising marriage linking the families, agonizes "So many had died in mud and fire for being Jewish. To give it up seemed a gross betrayal." This two-family saga not only describes the difficulties Jews found in Britain but also delineates both through the successor generations and within generations the characters' very different attitudes to their Jewishness. As the book ends, West Indians are moving into some of the old Jewish quarters.

The Border also draws on Feinstein's Jewish background. Through various narrative devices, notably the use of diaries kept by the scientist Inge and her husband the poet Hans, Feinstein highlights the personal and increasingly the political strains put upon the marriage. The book follows the part-Jewish couple's flight from Vienna to Paris and beyond, in 1983. In this powerful novella, where Walter Benjamin appears, "the border" is metaphoric as well as actual. The book is a technical *tour de force,* and a deeply moving human text.

Mother's Girl deals with the effect of the Holocaust on the next generation. As a child, Halina was sent to Britain in 1939 from Budapest. The novel is a story within a story, as Halina recounts her life to her much younger American half-sister before their father's funeral: this form brings out the continuing effects of a terrible and incompletely known past. The fate of Halina's mother, an unsung underground heroine, never emerges. Her debonair, womanizing father reappeared after the war though without revealing his wartime experience until dying, nursed by Halina. Meanwhile Halina was temporarily and unhappily married to Janos, who had known her father in wartime Budapest.

If through circumstances of history Halina cannot fully understand herself, neither can Nell in *All You Need,* through her own fault. Her husband's sudden arrest for fraud precipitates her into moving to London with her 12-year-old daughter and earning her own living. Some readers may feel less sympathy for her climb into the media world of the late 1980s than Feinstein does: middle-class Nell with a Cambridge degree was a privileged person who had chosen to become a housewife.

So far, *The Border* is Feinstein's major achievement, bringing together all her greatest strengths—the examination of a long-term relationship between a man and a woman, where both are treated equally sympathetically, with a poet's use of language, and a witnessing to history, however dark.

—Val Warner

FIEDLER, Leslie A(aron)

Nationality: American. **Born:** Newark, New Jersey, 8 March 1917. **Education:** New York University, B.A. 1938 (Phi Beta Kappa); University of Wisconsin, Madison, M.A. 1939, Ph.D. 1941; Harvard University, Cambridge, Massachusetts (Rockefeller fellow), 1946-47. **Military Service:** Served in the United States Naval Reserve, 1942-46: Lieutenant. **Family:** Married 1) Margaret Ann Shipley in 1939 (divorced 1973), three sons and three daughters;

2) Sally Smith Andersen, 1973, two step-children. **Career:** Assistant professor, 1947-48, associate professor, 1948-52, professor of English, 1953-64, and chair of the department, 1954-56, University of Montana, Missoula. Since 1965 professor of English, currently Samuel Clemens Professor, State University of New York, Buffalo. Fulbright Lecturer, University of Rome, 1951-52, University of Bologna and Ca Foscari University, 1952-53, and University of Athens, 1961-62; Gauss Lecturer in Criticism, Princeton University, New Jersey, 1956-57; lecturer, University of Sussex, Brighton, and University of Amstrdam, 1967-68; visiting professor, University of Vincennes, Paris, 1970-71. Fellow, Indiana University School of Letters, Bloomington, 1953; associate fellow, Calhoun College, Yale University, New Haven, Connecticut, 1969. Advisory editor, *Ramparts* magazine, New York, 1958-61; literary adviser, St. Martin's Press, New York, 1958-61. **Awards:** *Furioso* poetry prize, 1951; *Kenyon Review* fellowship, for non-fiction, 1956; American Academy grant, 1957; American Council of Learned Societies grant, 1960, 1961; Guggenheim fellowship, 1970. **Address:** Dept. of English, SUNY at Buffalo, Buffalo, New York 14260, U.S.A.

PUBLICATIONS

Novels

The Second Stone: A Love Story. New York, Stein and Day, 1963; London, Heinemann, 1966.
Back to China. New York, Stein and Day, 1965.
The Messengers Will Come No More. New York, Stein and Day, 1974.

Short Stories

Pull Down Vanity and Other Stories. Philadelphia, Lippincott, 1962; London, Secker and Warburg, 1963.
The Last Jew in America. New York, Stein and Day, 1966.
Nude Croquet and Other Stories. New York, Stein and Day, 1969; London, Secker and Warburg, 1970.

Uncollected Short Stories

"And We'll All Feel Gay," in *New Directions 10.* New York, New Directions, 1948.
"Amphibious Operation," in *Harper's Bazaar* (New York), March 1948.
"Dear Friends and Gentle Hearts," in *Epoch* (Ithaca, New York), Fall 1949.
"For the Record," in *Quarterly Review of Literature* (Chapel Hill, North Carolina), Winter 1952.
"What Used to Be Called Dead," in *Kenyon Review* (Gambier, Ohio), Winter 1990.

Other

An End to Innocence: Essays on Culture and Politics. Boston, Beacon Press, 1955.
The Jew in the American Novel. New York, Herzl Press, 1959.
Love and Death in the American Novel. New York, Criterion, 1960; London, Secker and Warburg, 1961; revised edition, New York, Stein and Day, 1966; London, Cape.

No! In Thunder: Essays on Myth and Literature. Boston, Beacon Press, 1960; London, Eyre and Spottiswoode, 1963.
The Riddle of Shakespeare's Sonnets. New York, Basic Books, 1962.
Waiting for the End. New York, Stein and Day, 1964; as *Waiting for the End: The American Literary Scene from Hemingway to Baldwin,* London, Cape, 1965.
The Return of the Vanishing American. New York, Stein and Day, and London, Cape, 1968.
Being Busted. New York, Stein and Day, and London, Secker and Warburg, 1970.
The Collected Essays of Leslie Fiedler. New York, Stein and Day, 2 vols., 1971.
The Stranger in Shakespeare. New York, Stein and Day, 1972; London, Croom Helm, 1973.
To the Gentiles. New York, Stein and Day, 1972.
Cross the Border, Close the Gap. New York, Stein and Day, 1972.
A Fiedler Reader. New York, Stein and Day, 1977.
Freaks: Myths and Images of the Secret Self. New York, Simon and Schuster, 1978; London, Penguin, 1981.
The Inadvertent Epic: From Uncle Tom's Cabin to Roots. Toronto, Canadian Broadcasting Corporation, 1979; New York, Simon and Schuster, 1980.
What Was Literature? Class Culture and Mass Society. New York, Simon and Schuster, 1982.
Pity and Fear: Myths and Images of the Disabled in Literature Old and New, with others. New York, International Center for the Disabled, 1982(?).
Olaf Stapledon: A Man Divided. New York and Oxford, Oxford University Press, 1983.
Fiedler on the Roof: Epistle to the Gentiles (essays). Boston, Godine, 1991.

Editor, *The Art of the Essay.* New York, Crowell, 1958; revised edition, 1969.
Editor, *Selections from The Leaves of Grass,* by Walt Whitman. New York, Dell, 1959.
Editor, with Jacob Vinocur, *The Continuing Debate: Essays on Education.* New York, St. Martin's Press, 1965.
Editor, with Arthur Zeiger, *O Brave New World.* New York, Dell, 1968.
Editor, with Houston A. Baker, Jr., *English Literature: Opening Up the Canon.* Baltimore, Johns Hopkins University Press, 1981.

*

Manuscript Collection: State University of New York, Buffalo.

Critical Study: *Leslie A. Fiedler* by Mark Royden Winchell, Boston, Twayne, 1985.

Leslie A. Fiedler comments:

My chief interest in the field of fiction has always been the exploration of the comic possibilities inherent in the elusive distinctions between races and generations, as well as between East and West, and Europe and America. I have also been deeply concerned with the difficulties of knowing who is one's father, or is not, for that matter. None of this, however, has seemed to me a proper occasion for tears.

*   *   *

There is no doubt that Leslie A. Fiedler aimed from his professional beginnings to be not just a critic but a genuine all-round man-of-letters, publishing not only controversial essays but also poetry and fiction soon after his literary debut; and he has followed all these muses, as well as a powerful one for public speaking, throughout his career. His fiction is, by common consent, less interesting and less original than his criticism (and his poetry even less substantial); and few critics of conscience have ever honored his imaginative work in print. In his opening critical essays, eventually collected as *An End to Innocence,* Fiedler established a knack for controversial argument, full of far-fetched connections and exaggerated remarks, all expressed in equally provocative prose; few since Mencken have provoked so much outrage. Rejecting the simple sentence along with the simplistic idea, Fiedler concocted a robust style composed of long and convoluted clause-compounded sentences riddled by paradoxes, parentheses, and charming self-ironies. However, only the tough-minded intelligence behind this forceful style, rather than the characteristic language, informs his fictions, which nonetheless reflect certain ideas in his criticism (which, in turn, sometimes mentions, if not quotes, his fiction!). The key theoretical text is the brilliant title essay opening his second collection, *No! In Thunder,* where Fiedler argues that the great modern writers have responded to ideals, institutions, and even people with uncompromised negation—the Melvillian cry of "No! in Thunder" indicating a complete stripping down that reveals inadequacy, deceit, failure, and the impossibility of perfection. "The No! in Thunder is never partisan," Fiedler writes, "it infuriates Our Side as well as Theirs, reveals that all Sides are one, insofar as they are all yea-sayers and hence all liars."

The title of his first collection of stories, *Pull Down Vanity,* announces the characteristic strategy of his fiction, for most of the pieces here are shaped around the uncovering of illusory images presented by a person or group; and in this stripping away of human artifice is unveiled another favorite Fiedler theme of universal culpability. Thus, these stories are structured around actions of exposure and embarrassment—a technique admittedly indebted to Nathanel West's *The Day of the Locust* (1939). Thus, should readers come to believe that one of Fiedler's characters might be honest and good, the rug is pulled out before the story is done, leaving that character too sprawled in the fundamental mud. In "Nude Croquet" a busty young thing darkens a party's room and then leads a group of middle-aging "intellectuals" in playing croquet in the buff. Not at all uncomfortable, she flaunts her fresh figure, forcing the others to uncover both their masked bodily defects and, then, their spiritual vanities. One has body hair different in color from that on her head, another a withered leg, a third is flat-chested, while on another level one is insanely jealous, another has never completed his projected and much-announced masterpiece, a third has "sold out" to the commercial theater. When the group's slightly older idol collapses from over-exertion and dies of a heart attack, the girl screams a long blast as the lights go on. "Molly-o," Fiedler writes, "confronted them in the classic pose of nakedness surprised, as if she knew for the first time what it meant to be really nude." Discovering one's nudity is, symbolically, recognizing comparable inadequacies and culpability.

Fiedler's first and best novel takes for its unusual subject the demonic attachment of unrelated twins who, once childhood friends, re-encounter each other over a dozen years. One character speaks of "a comedy of confused identities," and these confusions are not only witty, but also difficult to summarize. The novel's protago-
nist, Clem Stone, is an unsuccessful writer, while his friend is Mark Stone, an eminent TV intellectual and existentialist rabbi. In the past, Clem was named Mark Stone, and the present Mark's last name was Stein. But as the present Mark changed his surname, Clem, overshadowed by the most successful Mark, became known as Mark the second, or Mark Twain. As the historical author Twain's real identity was Samuel Clemens, Stone takes the first name of Clem. The two Stones have always competed for the same goals, and before the novel is over, Clem seduces Mark's pregnant wife. The novel is similarly erudite in its joking, as in one scene Mark pummels his wife with a rolled-up copy of a magazine entitled *Thou;* and he is described, of course, as unable to stop stuttering "I-I-I-I." Long on such literary gags and arch symbols, *The Second Stone* is also short on credible surface and literary importance.

The protagonist of Fiedler's second novel, *Back to China,* is a college teacher in Montana, whose career in some respects parallels Fiedler's own—a Jew from the East teaching in the West, with a reputation for being the most famous radical on campus, the author of several books, a former wartime Japanese interpreter in the Far East; but whereas Fiedler himself has been a father several times over, Baro Finklestone's main problem is that he and his wife are childless. The reason, as we learn through a series of flashbacks, is that Finklestone's life, as well as the book's plot, turned upon a vasectomy, an irreparable voluntary sterilization, that he underwent in China. His reasons for doing this are never made entirely clear—indeed, the act itself is barely credible—and the novel never quite emerges from a mire of absurdities. Indeed, this slide toward preposterousness, which comes from mixing too much realistic, highly detailed, almost pedantic satire with more wholly symbolic fantasy—a mismating of Sinclair Lewis with Franz Kafka—becomes even more pronounced in the three novellas collected as *The Last Jew in America;* and Fiedler's next book of fiction, *Nude Croquet,* adds four slighter stories to those previously collected. A more suggestive step comes in *Being Busted,* an autobiographical memoir devoid of proper names, that successfully elevates to imaginative myth not only Fiedler's 1967 arrest on a marijuana related charge but also his responses to the life styles of his children, for Fiedler ranks among the few writers of his post-fifty generation to suffer genuine confrontation and rebirth.

If Fiedler the critic is ambitious and original, as well as appreciative of eccentricity, the novelist is rather conventional in style, structure, and subject-matter—his own fiction scarcely acknowledging the innovative literature praised in his criticism; and the impact of his recent rebirth has so far been more intellectual than artistic. A truth of literature's past apparently unremembered in all this effort is that critics as major as Fiedler have rarely produced consequential fiction, try as much as they otherwise might. With his encompassing theme of deflation, Fiedler's fiction suggests that marriage is insufferable, that adultery is inevitable and just as inevitably disappointing; and his fictions deal as well with ambivalent attitudes toward paternity, slavish obsessions with seduction's ulterior motives, and the terrors of American professors and intellectuals. This rather limited range is, needless to say perhaps, closer to more prosaic writing that to what Fiedler the critic has defined as the great tradition of American imaginative prose.

—Richard Kostelanetz

FIGES, Eva

Nationality: British. **Born:** Eva Unger in Berlin, Germany, 15 April 1932; came to England in 1939. **Education:** Kingsbury Grammar School, 1943-50; Queen Mary College, University of London, 1950-53, B.A. (honours) in English 1953. **Family:** Married John George Figes in 1954 (divorced 1963); one daughter and one son. **Career:** Editor, Longman, 1955-57, Weidenfeld and Nicolson, 1962-63, and Blackie, 1964-67, publishers, London. Since 1987 co-editor, Macmillan Women Writers series. **Awards:** *Guardian* Fiction prize, 1967; C. Day Lewis fellowship, 1973; Arts Council fellowship, 1977-79; Society of Authors traveling scholarship, 1988. Fellow, Queen Mary and Westfield College, 1990. **Agent:** Rogers Coleridge and White Ltd., 20 Powis Mews, London W11 1JN. **Address:** 24 Fitzjohn's Avenue, London N.W.3, England.

PUBLICATIONS

Novels

Equinox. London, Secker and Warburg, 1966.
Winter Journey. London, Faber, 1967; New York, Hill and Wang, 1968.
Konek Landing. London, Faber, 1969.
B. London, Faber, 1972.
Days. London, Faber, 1974.
Nelly's Version. London, Secker and Warburg, 1977; New York, Pantheon, 1988.
Waking. London, Hamish Hamilton, 1981; New York, Pantheon, 1982.
Light. London, Hamish Hamilton, and New York, Pantheon, 1983.
The Seven Ages. London, Hamish Hamilton, 1986; New York, Pantheon, 1987.
Ghosts. London, Hamish Hamilton, and New York, Pantheon, 1988.
The Tree of Knowledge. London, Sinclair Stevenson, 1990; New York, Pantheon, 1991.
The Tenancy. London, Sinclair Stevenson, 1993.

Uncollected Short Stories

"Obbligato, Bedsitter," in *Signature Anthology.* London, Calder and Boyars, 1975.
"On the Edge," in *London Tales,* edited by Julian Evans. London, Hamish Hamilton, 1983.

Plays

Radio Plays: *Time Regained,* 1980; *Dialogue Between Friends,* 1982; *Punch-Flame and Pigeon-Breast,* 1983; *The True Tale of Margery Kempe,* 1985.

Television Plays: *Days,* from her own novel, 1981.

Other

The Banger (for children). London, Deutsch, and New York, Lion Press, 1968.
Patriarchal Attitudes: Women in Society. London, Faber, and New York, Stein and Day, 1970.
Scribble Sam (for children). London, Deutsch, and New York, McKay, 1971.
Tragedy and Social Evolution. London, Calder, 1976; New York, Persea, 1990.
Little Eden: A Child at War (autobiography). London, Faber, 1978; New York, Persea, 1987.
Sex and Subterfuge: Women Novelists to 1850. London, Macmillan, 1982; New York, Persea, 1988.

Editor, *Classic Choice 1.* London, Blackie, 1965.
Editor, *Modern Choice 1* and *2.* London, Blackie, 2 vols., 1965-66.
Editor, with Abigail Mozley and Dinah Livingstone, *Women Their World.* Gisburn, Lancashire, Platform Poets, 1980.

Translator, *The Gadarene Club,* by Martin Walser. London, Longman, 1960.
Translator, *The Musicians of Bremen: Retold* (for children). London, Blackie, 1967.
Translator, *The Old Car,* by Elisabeth Borchers. London, Blackie, 1967.
Translator, *He and I and the Elephants,* by Bernhard Grzimek. London, Deutsch-Thames and Hudson, and New York, Hill and Wang, 1967.
Translator, *Little Fadette,* by George Sand. London, Blackie, 1967.
Translator, *A Family Failure,* by Renate Rasp. London, Calder and Boyars, 1970.
Translator, *The Deathbringer,* by Manfred von Conta. London, Calder and Boyars, 1971.

*   *   *

"I am using a different grid which I have first to construct by a painful process of trial and error," writes Eva Figes. In outright reaction against what she sees as the continuing conservative realist tradition of British fiction Figes resumes the modernist task of reshaping the novel and questioning the assumptions on which it is built. In her novels, as in those of Virginia Woolf (surely the greatest influence on her work), Figes seeks to bring together the properties of formal art and the intensities of the inner self. Here, life takes place between the acts, and we catch it unawares in the lives of ordinary people: Janus, the old man dying alone in his council house in *Winter Journey,* or Lily, the spinster sister and aunt who measures the subtly shifting relationships in *Light.* As Figes explores the self concealed behind the artifice of manners, the most elusive moments of existence are redefined in her novels as the prerequisite for creative vitality, and continuity is found in the lyric hoard of memories through which her characters resist the flux of time. In *Winter Journey* the presentation of a series of psychological states in place of a continuous narrative or plot results in an intense poetic lyricism. The same kind of unbroken texture, or openness and continuity, is found in *Light* (Figes's finest work to date), where Claude, artist and philosopher, explains: "Everything is always in flux . . . it was both his overriding difficulty and essential to him."

But there are darker realities here too. A sense of menace underlies the lyrical affirmation of the novels, and there is a corresponding sense that only a continuous style can soothe a narrative which is subject to unexpected disruptions and dislocations. "My starting-point is inevitably Kafka," Figes claims, and there are echoes of Beckett too in her novels' unresolved ambivalence about their own representational activity. The negative energies of solipsism and angst are inseparable from the moments of heightened consciousness in the fragmented autobiography of Janus' winter journey. And in *Light,* Claude's fragile images of perfection are troubled by the motifs of transience and death. In the final analysis, perhaps the most fascinating and complex aspect of Figes's novels is that they do follow the Modernist tradition of showing art and memory as creative of a new order of reality. But they also remain firmly located in the destructive elements of historical time that many classic modernists would seek to bypass. The power and potency of the recurrent images of holocaust in her novels seem to reveal the author's deepest motivations for writing: "I am a European wrestling with a different reality," she says. "A piece of shrapnel lodges in my flesh, and when it moves, I write."

—Sandra Kemp

FINDLEY, Timothy

Nationality: Canadian. **Born:** Toronto, Ontario, 30 October 1930. **Education:** Rosedale Public School, Toronto; St. Andrews College, Aurora, Ontario; Jarvis Collegiate, Toronto; Royal Conservatory of Music, Toronto, 1950-53; Central School of Speech and Drama, London. **Career:** Stage, television, and radio actor, 1951-62; charter member, Stratford Shakespearean Festival, Ontario, 1953; contract player with H.M. Tennent, London, 1953-56; toured U.S. in *The Matchmaker,* 1956-57; studio writer, CBS, Hollywood, 1957-58; copywriter, CFGM Radio, Richmond Hill, Ontario. Playwright-in-residence, National Arts Centre, Ottawa, 1974-75; writer-in-residence, University of Toronto, 1979-80, Trent University, Peterborough, Ontario, 1984, and University of Winnipeg, 1985. Chair, Writers Union of Canada, 1977-78; president, English-Canadian Centre, International P.E.N., 1986-87. **Awards:** Canada Council award, 1968, 1978; Armstrong award, for radio writing, 1971; ACTRA award, for television documentary, 1975; Governor General's award, 1977; City of Toronto Book award, 1977, 1994; Anik award, for television writing, 1980; Canadian Authors Association prize, 1985, 1991, 1994; Western Magazine award, 1988; Government of Ontario Trillium award, 1989; Mystery Writers of America Edgar Allan Poe award, 1989; National Radio award, 1989, 1990; Gabriel award, 1990; Crime Writers of Canada award, 1994, for drama; Toronto Arts award, 1994; Gemini award, 1995. D.Litt.: Trent University, 1982; University of Guelph, Ontario, 1984; York University, Ontario, 1989; Lakehead University, Ontario, 1995. Officer, Order of Canada, 1986. **Agent:** Virginia Barber Literary Agency, 353 West 21st Street, New York, New York 10011, U.S.A. **Address:** Stone Orchard, Box 419, Cannington, Ontario L0E 1E0, Canada.

PUBLICATIONS

Novels

The Last of the Crazy People. New York, Meredith Press, and London, Macdonald, 1967.
The Butterfly Plague. New York, Viking Press, 1969; London, Deutsch, 1970.

The Wars. Toronto, Clarke Irwin, 1977; New York, Delacorte Press, and London, Macmillan, 1978.
Famous Last Words. Toronto, Clarke Irwin, and New York, Delacorte Press, 1981; London, Macmillan, 1987.
Not Wanted on the Voyage. Toronto, Viking, 1984; New York, Delacorte Press, and London, Macmillan, 1985.
The Telling of Lies. Toronto, Penguin, 1986; London, Macmillan, and New York, Dell, 1988.
Headhunter. Toronto, HarperCollins, 1993; New York, Crown, 1994.
The Piano Man's Daughter. Toronto, HarperCollins, and New York, Crown, 1995.

Short Stories

Dinner Along the Amazon. Toronto and London, Penguin, 1984; New York, Penguin, 1985.
Stones. Toronto, Penguin, 1988; New York, Delta, 1990.

Uncollected Short Stories

"Island" and "The Long Walk" in *The Newcomers,* edited by Charles E. Israel. Toronto, McClelland and Stewart, 1979.

Plays

The Paper People (televised 1968). Published in *Canadian Drama* (Toronto), vol. 9, no. 1, 1983.
The Journey (broadcast 1971). Published in *Canadian Drama* (Toronto), vol. 10, no. 1, 1984.
Can You See Me Yet? (produced Ottawa, 1976). Vancouver, Talonbooks, 1977.
John A. Himself music by Berthold Carriere (produced London, Ontario, 1979).
Strangers at the Door (radio script), in *Quarry* (Kingston, Ontario), 1982.
Daybreak at Pisa: 1945, in *Tamarack Review* (Toronto), Winter 1982.
The Stillborn Lover (produced London, 1993). Winnipeg, Blizzard, 1993.
The Trials of Ezra Pound, adapted from her own radio play.

Screenplays: *Don't Let the Angels Fall,* 1970; *The Wars,* 1983.

Radio Plays and Documentaries: *The Learning Stage and Ideas* series, 1963-73; *Adrift,* 1968; *Matinee* series, 1970-71; *The Journey,* 1971; *Missionaries,* 1973; *The Trials of Ezra Pound,* 1990.

Television Plays and Documentaries: *Umbrella* series, 1964-66; *Who Crucified Christ?,* 1966; *The Paper People,* 1968; *The Whiteoaks of Jalna* (7 episodes), from books by Mazo de la Roche, 1971-72; *The National Dream* series (8 episodes), with William Whitehead, 1974; *The Garden and the Cage,* with William Whitehead, 1977; *1832 and 1911 (The Newcomers* series), 1978-79; *Dieppe 1942,* with William Whitehead, 1979; *Other People's Children,* 1981; *Islands in the Sun* and *Turn the World Around (Belafonte Sings* series), with William Whitehead, 1983.

Other

Imaginings, with Janis Rapaport, illustrated by Heather Cooper. Toronto, Ethos, 1982.

Inside Memory: Pages from a Writer's Workbook. Toronto, Harper Collins, 1990.

*

Bibliography: *Timothy Findley: An Annotated Bibliography* by Carol Roberts and Lynne Macdonald, Downsview, Ontario, ECW Press, 1990.

Manuscript Collection: Historical Resources Branch, National Archives of Canada.

Critical Studies: *Eleven Canadian Novelists* by Graeme Gibson, Toronto, Anansi, 1973; *Conversations with Canadian Novelists* by Silver Donald Cameron, Toronto, Macmillan, 1973; "An Interview with Timothy Findley," in *University of Toronto Review,* 1980; "Timothy Findley Issue" of *Canadian Literature* (Vancouver), Winter 1981; *Timothy Findley* by Wilfred Cude, Toronto, Dundurn Press, 1982; "The Marvel of Reality" (interview) with Bruce Meyer and Brian O'Riordan, in *Waves* (Toronto), vol. 10, no. 4, 1982; "Prayers Against Despair" by Gilbert Drolet, in *Journal of Canadian Fiction 33* (Montreal), 1982; "Whispers of Chaos" by Eugene Benson, in *World Literature Written in English* (Guelph, Ontario), Autumn 1982; *Second Words: Selected Critical Prose* by Margaret Atwood, Toronto, Anansi, 1982, Boston, Beacon Press, 1984; "The Dubious Battle of Storytelling: Narrative Strategies in Timothy Findley's *The Wars*" by Simone Vauthier, in *Gaining Ground: European Critics on Canadian Literature* edited by Robert Kroetsch and Reingard M. Nischik, Edmonton, Alberta, NeWest Press, 1985; *Timothy Findley's "The Wars": A Study Guide,* Toronto, ECW Press, 1990, and *"Front Lines": The Fiction of Timothy Findley,* Toronto, ECW Press, 1991, both by Lorraine York; *Moral Metafiction: The Novels of Timothy Findley,* Toronto, ECW Press, 1991; *Praying for Rain: Timothy Findley's Not Wanted on the Voyage,* Toronto, ECW Press, 1992, both by Donna Pennee; *Timothy Findley: Stories from a Life* by Carol Roberts, Toronto, ECW Press, 1994; *Writing on Trial: Timothy Findley's Famous Last Words* by Diana Brydon, Toronto, ECW Press, 1995.

Timothy Findley comments:

There are some who say you should only and always write about what you know. If I had taken this advise, then all my books would be about the theatre, rabbits and cats, a fairly standard version of family life and the road between the farm where I live and the City of Toronto. The fact is, only the rabbits and the cats have made it into my fiction—in one book as the companions of a man in World War I and in another as stowaways on Noah's Ark. Without apology, I must admit that I cannot imagine why I have written what I have. It does occur to me, however, that a thread runs through all my work that has to do with unlikely people being confronted with uncommon events.

*   *   *

Timothy Findley began writing fiction in his early twenties and contributed a story to the first issue of *Tamarack Review* in 1956, but during this earlier period he was largely involved in acting, playing at the first Stratford Festival (1953) and later touring in Britain and the United States. In several ways the theatrical career he would eventually abandon had its effect upon his later writing. His novels show him to be highly conscious of the dramatic po-

tentialities in human relationships, and very often he seems in fiction to be moving in that area between actuality and illusion where we accept the backdrop for what it pretends to be and willingly allow the devices of *trompe-l'oeil* to go unchallenged. When he was acting in Thronton Wilder's play *The Matchmaker* Wilder encouraged him to continue with fiction, advice that finally led him to devote himself fulltime to writing in the 1960s and his own early thirties.

Since that time, Findley has published six novels and two books of short stories, *Dinner Along the Amazon* and *Stones,* whose very title suggests the lapidary art and laconic manner of his shorter fictions. His novels expand into broader, looser forms, which is in keeping with his emergence as a kind of historical novelist, for history, and in particular the relationship between individual and community, is his favourite but not necessarily his most tractable material. In all his novels, whatever our vantage point, we look back into a past that for most of us is completed, finished business, but for Findley is a stage on which to enact dramas in which his characters respond to the situation the world presents, accepting or reacting.

In his first novel, *The Last of the Crazy People,* he presents the 1960s in southern California, where a child, obsessed by the futility of his family's existence in a world that war has robbed of meaning, eventually kills the people he most loves as the logic of childhood and the logic of insanity blend together. In *The Butterfly Plague* he takes us to the late 1930s in Hollywood, where the fate of a family threatened with an inherited disease parallels the breakdown of civilization in Europe during the same decade.

The two great conflicts that mark off that period are the settings for what may to date be Findley's major novels, *The Wars* and *Famous Last Words,* the first dominated by the senseless slaughters of what we used to call the Great War, and the second set in World War II with the bizarre and dread-ridden years that led up to it. In such novels rewriting is the key concept, for unlike past historical novelists, Findley is not seeking to present the past "as it must have been." He is taking history into the world of the imagination and in the process creating his own myths by which the lessons of history are made more clear.

At the same time, Findley's research is always impeccable. He knows the periods of which he writes in depth, and in *The Wars* he actually creates a deeper illusion of authenticity by presenting the story as the product of an intensive reconstruction of events, even to the extent of inventing taped interviews with the survivors who remember Robert, the hero, and his quixotic attempt to rescue a great troop of horses doomed to a pointless death on the western front. But *The Wars* is not merely the product of research, of vestigial records piled one on top of the other. It is a work of the imagination, of literature, and though history, as Auden once said "cannot help or pardon," literature can offer understanding and compassion. When Clive, the soldier poet in *The Wars,* is asked "Do you think we'll ever be forgiven for what we've done?" ("we" meaning his generation) he answers: "I doubt we'll ever be forgiven. All I hope is—they'll remember we were human beings."

Famous Last Words is a work of elaborate artifice, in which fictional figures mingle with people who actually lived and were famous and yet played such artificial roles that they have become as manipulable as the puppets of the imagination. The narrator is actually an offspring of the mind of one of the characters, for Ezra Pound—who appears in the novel in one of his fascistic rages—invented Hugh Selwyn Mauberley, the narrator of *Famous Last Words,* as a minor figure in one of his poems. A fugitive collaborationist at the end of the war in a deserted Alpine hotel, Mauberley writes on the walls and ceilings the story of the strange plots in which he and his associates, including the Duke of Windsor and Mrs. Simpson, sought to make use of fascism for their own ends and merely became more deeply mired. Aestheticism and fascism, the lesson seems to read, led to the same dead end. Yet, finally, as a manifestation of the urge to live that lies at the heart of even most extreme aestheticism, there is Mauberley's own remark, as he remembers the caves of Altamira and reproduces their smoke-ringed handprint above his own engraved message: "Some there are who never disappear. And I knew I was sitting at the heart of the human race—which is its will to say *I am.*" In such a neo-Cartesian statement—which echoes that of Clive in *The Wars,* style becomes its own morality, and understanding assumes more importance than help or pardon.

Not Wanted on the Voyage is an elusive novel that takes us far from the world of modern war and political intrigue, back to Genesis and the world before history. Yet still the devices of transforming the past are there, and still we are faced with the presentation in new guides of figures that for long, until the first books of the Old Testament retreated into myth, were regarded as being just as historical as Alfred the Great or Napoleon. It is the retold story of the flood and the building and voyage of the Ark, but seen largely through the eyes of humbler creatures, such as Motyll the Cat. It reads, in fact, rather like a thinly disguised fictional tract on behalf of gnosticism, for Yahweh is presented—like the Old Testament God by the Gnostics—as a crude and cruel tyrant, personification of all the evil forces and not in any sense creative. Present throughout is God's rebel child, the androgynous Lucy-Lucifer who accompanies the voyage, but perhaps in the end the most obdurate rebel is Mrs. Noyes, the gin-toping wife of Dr. Noyes (Noah), who realizes that the only true world is that which she and Motyll hold in memory, and who, when the dove comes back with the olive twig, makes her own prayer.

> She prayed. But not to the absent God. Never, never again to the absent God, but to the absent clouds, she prayed. And to the empty sky. She prayed for rain.

Like a good Gnostic, Mrs. Noyes has rejected the prospect of a sanitized work remade by evil Yahweh and his equally evil vivisecting minister, Dr. Noyes. She prefers to remember the old magical world with its dragons and demons and fairies and its community between humankind and thinking, talking animals.

Findley describes his sixth novel, *The Telling of Lies,* as "a mystery," and indeed it is so in the double sense that a crime is committed and we have to know the criminal, but at the same time we have to judge the victim and the crime, which in itself is a judgment.

The scene is an old hotel on the Maine coast where a group of American and Canadian patrician families have been wintering for a couple of generations. As Nessa Van Horne, a photographer and landscape architect, is walking on the beach early one morning, she sees a great iceberg that has floated overnight into the bay; it will remain through the novel as a portentous symbol of the indifference of nature. Later in the day, on the beach before the hotel, an ancient billionaire dies mysteriously; his empire in pharmaceutical products has become so vast that he boasts of owning one half of the world and renting the rest.

The situation is immediately complicated when a doctor closely connected with the President of the United States unexpectedly appears and commandeers the body. Nessa is further mystified when

no reports of the death appear in the newspapers, and she and another doctor—her cousin's husband—begin to act as amateur detectives. In the process they find that the murder of Conrad Maddox has embarrassed a whole series of American government departments with which he has contracts, so that a gathering of politicians and high bureaucrats takes place in a hotel down the beach. Maddox's mistress is kidnapped by the presidential doctor and his associates, and Nessa and her friends rescue her with difficulty.

It turns out that the authorities are less than anxious to find the murderer or bring the case to court, particularly as the killing was actually done—with a tube of poisoned sun lotion—by the wife of a man who had been turned into a human vegetable by the experimental use of Maddox's medicaments. So nobody is brought to justice but, in a sense, justice is done. However, the virtues of *The Telling of Lies* do not reside entirely in the detective element, which is a slow revealing of the obvious, or the sombre moral, but as much in the acuity with which personal relations within a limited social class are examined and in the atmospheric luminosity with which the beach and its life are portrayed, almost like Boudin in prose.

—George Woodcock

FISCHER, Tibor

Nationality: British. **Born:** Stockport, 15 November 1959. **Education:** Cambridge University. **Career:** Works as a freelance journalist. **Agent:** Nicholas Ellison Inc., 55 Fifth Ave., New York, New York 10003, U.S.A.

PUBLICATIONS

Novels

Under The Frog. Edinburgh, Polygon 1992; New York, New Press, 1994.
The Thought Gang. Edinburgh, Polygon, 1994; New York, New Press, 1995.

*   *   *

That Tibor Fischer's first novel was shortlisted for Britain's most prestigious literary award, the Booker Prize, may have had something to do with its subject: Hungary from the end of World War II to the Uprising of 1956. But it is Fischer's treatment of his subject, his specific style as well as his overall approach, that sets the novel apart. Eschewing the elegiac quality of another Hungarian novel that covers much the same period, George Konrad's *Feast in the Garden,* the absurdist, blackly humorous *Under the Frog* is closer in tone to Czech novelist Milan Kundera's *The Joke* and Polish writers Tadeusz Borowski's *This Way to the Gas* and *Ladies and Gentlemen* and Tadeusz Konwicki's *A Minor Apocalypse.*

Fischer's odd title derives from a Hungarian saying meaning "nothing could be worse." For the novel's main character, Gyorgi Fischer, things in fact can be worse and usually become so. What this member of the Locomotive basketball team fears is that he may never be "given a future to lose." What he wants is to get out of the country; any place will do: if not Sweden, then Poland, and if not Poland, then Rumania or China or even Korea during the war, which, he believes, would be better than postwar Hungary. Pragmatic and apolitical, perhaps to a fault, he occupies the middle ground between idealists like his Polish girlfriend Jadwiga and opportunists like Farago, once a petty thief, then head of his district's "Nazi franchise," and now local secretary of the Communist Party. Gyorgi is an opportunist of a different stripe: too cynical to be an idealist, too moral to blow with the prevailing winds. The real horror in this novel is not that good people like Jadwiga who are committed to justice and freedom should die; nor is it that in the world Fischer describes even a little power seems to corrupt absolutely. Rather it is that so many people should find themselves in much the same position as the father of Gyorgi's friend, Tibor Pataki. Arrested in 1951, the elder Pataki must endure interrogation and torture before being released to face a different kind of humiliation, "having been judged too dull" to be a conspirator. In a world of opportunists and optimists, of a Catholic Church that "wasn't too topheavy with brilliance," and of a national infatuation with defeat born of centuries of invasions (from Mongol hordes to Soviet tanks), there is something understandable if not altogether noble in Gyorgi's choosing cynical detachment, self-interest, noncooperation, and, finally, escape. Getting what he wants does not bring relief, however. Once across the border, Gyorgi, like Lot's wife, looks back and turns not to a pillar of salt but to tears.

Fischer has described his second novel, *The Thought Gang,* as "a short book about all human knowledge and experience." The apparent flippancy of his remark matches the apparent flippancy of this playfully structured but nonetheless serious novel. Pushing his fondness for unfamiliar words and usages even further than he did in *Under the Frog* and employing a variety of mutually exclusive structural devices, Fischer creates a form that matches perfectly the character of its protagonist-narrator. Born on 9 May 1945 (the day after VE Day), Eddie Coffin has spent the last 30 years "in the thought trade," the philosophy "biz." On the run from the London police, he joins forces with the one-armed, one-eyed Hubert to form the Thought Gang, specializing in bank robberies with a philosophical twist. In a novel this fragmented having a plot this wayward dealing with the misadventures of a hero this antiheroic, the reader may well ask (as the novel does), "What's going on here?" and whether what is going on amounts to anything more than a "good deal of blagging" (nonsense-making). As in the art of Donald Barthelme, another writer fond of collage, blague, and cultural debris, the range of literary and subliterary reference is impressively diverse. The entire novel may be read as a weirdly angled takeoff on Boethius's *Consolation of Philosophy,* with opening gambit adapted from Kafka's *The Trial,* plot from *Bonnie and Clyde,* title from Orwell's *1984,* parts of the structure from Nietzsche's *The Will to Power,* and additional material from the Keystone Kops, Charlie Chaplin, and François Rabelais, among others. All this adds up to a great deal more than just another (and by now belated) example of postmodern plagiarism and randomness. *The Thought Gang* irreverently takes to task the entire Western philosophical tradition, from the earliest Ionians (Eddie's specialty) to the currently fashionable deconstructionists. In a world in which "brute force works," philosophy is either irrelevant or merely one kind of "biz" among others. Although it lacks *Under the Frog*'s sense of historical immediacy and prefers flights of cartoonish fantasy and intellectual slapstick to direct satire, *The Thought Gang* is nonetheless a deeply committed work, as the references to other failures of the postwar moral and political imagination—Vietnam, Afghanistan, and Sarajevo—clearly indicate. Near novel's end, Eddie makes his and

Fischer's point clearer still. "It's embarrassing that the answer is so simple, so right in front of us. The sages have said so, but like most of the truths, we're bored with it. Change it round, say it backwards, make it foreign: evol, evol, evol. Unstealable money."

—Robert A. Morace

FITZGERALD, Penelope (Mary)

Nationality: British. **Born:** Penelope Mary Knox in Lincoln, 17 December 1916. **Education:** Wycombe Abbey; Somerville College, Oxford, B.A. (honors) in English 1939. **Family:** Married Desmond Fitzgerald in 1941 (died 1976); one son and two daughters. **Career:** Teacher with Westminster Tutors, London. **Awards:** Booker prize, 1979; British Academy Crawshay prize, for non-fiction, 1985. **Address:** c/o Harper Collins, 77-85 Fulham Palace Road, London W6 8JB, England.

<small>**PUBLICATIONS**</small>

Novels

The Golden Child. London, Duckworth, 1977; New York, Scribner, 1978.
The Bookshop. London, Duckworth, 1978.
Offshore. London, Collins, 1979; New York, Holt, 1987.
Human Voices. London, Collins, 1980.
At Freddie's. London, Collins, 1982; Boston, Godine, 1985.
Innocence. London, Collins, 1986; New York, Holt, 1987.
The Beginning of Spring. London, Collins, 1988; New York, Holt, 1989.
The Gate of Angels. London, Collins, 1990.

Uncollected Short Stories

"The Axe," in *The Times Anthology of Ghost Stories.* London, Cape, 1975.
"The Prescription," in *New Stories.* London, Hutchinson, 1983.
"At Hiruharama," in *New Writing,* edited by Malcolm Bradbury and Judith Cooke. London, Minerva, 1992.
"The Means of Escape," in *Infidelity,* edited by Marsh Rowe. London, Chatto and Windus, 1993.

Other

Edward Burne-Jones: A Biography. London, Joseph, 1975.
The Knox Brothers: Edmund ("Evoe") 1881-1971, Dillwyn 1883-1943, Wilfred 1886-1950, Ronald 1888-1957. London, Macmillan, and New York, Coward McCann, 1977.
Charlotte Mew and Her Friends: With a Selection of Her Poems. London, Collins, 1984; Reading, Massachusetts, Addison Wesley, 1988.

Editor, *The Novel on Blue Paper,* by William Morris. New York, AMS Press, and London, Journeyman Press, 1982.

*

Manuscript Collection: Humanities Research Center, University of Texas, Austin.

Penelope Fitzgerald comments:

(1981) I've done short novels so far because I like economy and compression; I don't think long novels are necessarily better than short ones, any more than tall men are necessarily better than short men—it's a different form, that's all. Tolstoy's *Master and Man* is the great example.

I try to get the movement and counter-movement of the novel and its background to go together. *Offshore* was set in the Thames houseboat community and I wanted the movement of the novel to rise and ebb like the tidal river. *Human Voices* was set in Broadcasting House in the old days of wartime radio, and the narration as far as possible is through voices and music.

I write from my own experience and places where I've worked and from what I can judge of the feelings of other people, particularly when they are quiet by nature and prefer not to give away too much. Sometimes readers write and ask why I can't manage to produce a happy ending, but I don't see where to find one except in the considerate endurance of the human beings I have known.

*   *   *

Penelope Fitzgerald's first novel, *The Golden Child,* was a delightful, intelligent, and witty detective story. Even in a genre which does not call for such qualities, her characters are wholly believable—kind, vain, ambitious, or suffering. Her second, *The Bookshop,* was a "straight" novel, very short but beautifully composed and filled with flashing insights into the concealed, shaping currents of human behavior. Her third novel, *Offshore,* equally short and memorable though not quite as outstanding as *The Bookshop* won the Booker prize, But for this award and its attendant and focusing publicity, many people would never have discovered her, the best possible argument for the awarding of literary prizes, despite the absurdity of so many choices.

Before the novels, however, there were biographies of Edward Burne-Jones, the Victorian painter, and of the four famous Knox brothers, one of whom, Evoe (who became editor of *Punch*), was Fitzgerald's father. Both volumes were competently written, well researched, smoothly put together, and, above all, accurate. The author has that rare quality of engaging the reader's absolute trust. And though the biographies lack the acute and astonishing insights of the novels, Fitzgerald makes up for this by a brilliant ability to select other people's words: marvelously apt quotations which strikingly illuminate the narrative. Just one example from *Burne-Jones,* perfectly placed in context, is from a letter from his wife to George Eliot: "My heart smites me that I have somewhat resembled those friends who talk only of themselves to you." How revealing of the Victorian concept of good behavior. That one phrase, in its delicacy, its self-accusation, is like a gleam of light shed on the entire English, upper-middle-class sensibility of the time.

It is, nevertheless, said by someone else. Fitzgerald's real talents only begin to reveal themselves in the novels. She evidently needs the imaginative freedom of fiction before she can take wing—though perhaps "plunge" would be a better word since she goes so deep. Give someone an enviably cultivated and civilized background, a First at Somerville, what seems to have been a wonderfully lively and interesting life, marriage and three bright children, and what kind of novels would one expect? Clever-academic? Grand-historical? The novel of manners? Even polished Women's Rights? Not a

bit of it. Even in *The Golden Child,* for all its wit in portraying the jockeying for position of scholarly men in museums, she has an eye for the uncertainties which govern all our lives. She sees the tiny sources of terrible distress. In *The Bookshop,* about a pleasant intelligent widow trying to run a bookshop in a small town, the theme is betrayal—sometimes from spite, sometimes from the baffling resentment always aroused by intelligence allied to modesty, sometimes from the equally inexplicable fury felt by the well-placed towards the less lucky, and sometimes from pure laziness. She sees the vast importance of small truths. Human beings, she says, are "divided into exterminators and exterminatees with the former, at any given moment, dominating." The book is a sad little masterpiece yet it sparkles with wit. and who could not admire a writer who can speak of an M.P. as "a brilliant, successful and stupid young man"?

Offshore deals with the fortunes, or rather misfortunes, of a variety of people living on houseboats on a stretch of the Thames. There are children who speak in a curiously formalized, almost Ivy Compton-Burnett style; their mother, beautiful and incapable; a stiff, competent, unhappily married man; and many others, all struggling to find a degree of fullness in their lives. Faced with the possibility of finally losing her estranged husband, the beautiful Nenna says: "I feel unemployed. I don't know what I'm going to think about if I'm not going to worry about him all the time." Fitzgerald sees with extraordinary perception what all our other women novelists, however famous, do not—that the root of love is not sex but occupation, the having something to do.

It is, again, startling to find that such a privileged life and nurturing should produce such understanding of what it is like to live on infinitely lower levels, socially, intellectually, and even emotionally. How did she manage to create a character like ten-year-old Christine, the working-class child in *The Bookshop;* perky, helpful, shrewd, impatient, and, in the end, like everyone else, a betrayer? Perhaps partly because, like her heroine in the same book: "In the end she valued kindness above everything."

These three novels are so good in their different ways that it is difficult to know how to avoid even further superlatives about the next two without sounding unbearably fulsome. *Human Voices* is set inside the BBC during World War II. The text abounds in that endemic BBC disease, intialitis: RPD, ADDG, RPA. They strew the pages but with such laughing satire that they do not irritate. The evocation of wartime London, the food, the black-outs, the people—from the irreproachable to the silly—is superb. Fitzgerald's style remains unique; at once broad and subtle, hilarious and heartbreaking, the whole laced with an astounding, psychological truth.

At Freddie's again exhibits her talents. It is set in a decrepit drama school, specializing in training children for the stage. The owner, Freddie (a sort of cross between Lilian Bayliss and Joan Littlewood), is a monstrous, towering creation—and a survivor ("She knew that she was one of those people . . . whom society has mysteriously decided to support at all costs"). The children are impishly observed, as are the actors and the whole backstage world. But there are also desolation and failure. (Who else has noticed that shoulders, far more than faces, can speak of grief?)

The Booker prize notwithstanding, Fitzgerald has never achieved the "flavor of the month" publicity of other winners. But compare her to some of our contemporary heavyweight women novelists, the politicos, the feminists, the sex-obsessed, the fairy-tale tellers, the working-class snapshotters, and she emerges with distinction. If one must find a fault it may be that people in real life do not so readily confess their faults and deficiencies as do her characters.

Indeed, if they did, most of our lives would be spent in moments of horrified silence followed by rushed getaways. In this sense only does she swerve slightly from life as it is. But it is a small price to pay for such perception.

Fitzgerald's next novels abandon England, if not entirely the English, altogether. *Innocence* is set in the Florence of the early 1950s, the characters drawn mainly from the slightly tattered fringes of the Italian upper classes. The Ridolfis have a long history of somewhat eccentric, not to say wacky ancestors. Their present day representative is Chiara, 18 years old, English-convent educated, rather beautiful. She falls in love with Salvatore, a thirtyish, bad-tempered neurologist and, with the help of her convent friend, Barney (whose other name must surely be Joan Hunter Dunne), pursues him, albeit in her own highly individual way. He, comically (the acrimonious in love are always comic) fighting it to the last, loves her too and they marry, but with Fitzgerald's usual, marvelous understanding of what tiny significances of behavior turn people on or off—seldom to do with sex—there are many misunderstandings, ("Come back," shouts the doctor at one point, "I'm saying what I don't mean") before, literally in the last paragraph, there is a happy ending. Around these two a sometimes absurd gallery of Italians cavort and talk, Chiara's father, her mad aunt, her austere uncle; their crumbling lives and fortunes and fates play out their roles, including financial shenanigans. It is Fitzgerald territory all right though the earlier, deeper note of pain is missing.

One has to say that this is still somewhat muted in *The Beginning of Spring,* though the situation is potentially far more anguished. Frank Reid is an Englishman whose father founded a smallish printing works in Moscow where Frank, Russian-born though still very English, runs it. His wife Nellie, also English, has deserted him and their three children without explanation. He struggles to run his home, his business, his life without her. The year is 1913.

What was it like to live a kind of bourgeois, English life in Czarist Russia at that time? To the Fitzgerald wit, dialogue, and exquisitely economic natural description has here been added another ingredient: *fact.* The novel teems with facts; facts about how people actually lived in that even now totally unknown time and place, though the Moscow she describes as that "powerful, slow-moving muddle" conveys a faintly contemporary Slav image. But the facts abound: from cutlery to cooking, from petty officialdom to servants' wages, from the curiously villagey ambiance of "dear, slovenly, mother Moscow" to the sledges and galoshes, and even to the workings of the printing press which Fitzgerald manages to make miraculously unboring.

All the Fitzgerald virtues are in evidence; but, as with *Innocence,* there are some reservations. Frank seems to suffer more from a transitory passion for his slightly mysterious housekeeper (*is* she a spy?) than from his strangely unquestioned abandonment by his wife. His children seem equally incurious. Nobody apparently suffers very much. A somehow unbelievable, reasonable placidity surrounds the situation. One misses *explanation*—especially for Nellie's return in the very last sentence. Perhaps it is *un*-reasonable for the reader to expect it. There are in any case a great many pleasures, among them the sheer skill with which Fitzgerald re-creates an unknown country and time.

—Gerda Charles

FLANAGAN, Thomas

Nationality: American. **Born:** Thomas James Bonner Flanagan in Greenwich, Connecticut, 5 November 1923. **Education:** Amherst College, Massachusetts, B.A. 1945; Columbia University, New York, M.A. 1948, Ph.D. in English 1958. **Military Service:** Served in the United States Naval Reserve, 1942-44. **Family:** Married Jean Parker in 1949; two daughters. **Career:** Instructor, 1949-52, and assistant professor, 1952-59, Columbia University; assistant professor, 1960-67, associate professor, 1967-73, professor, 1973-78, and chair of the Department of English, 1973-76, University of California, Los Angeles. Since 1978 professor of English, State University of New York, Stony Brook. **Awards:** American Council of Learned Societies grant, 1962; Guggenheim fellowship, 1962; National Book Critics Circle award, 1979. **Agent:** Robin Straus Agency, Inc., 229 E. 79th St., New York, New York 10021, U.S.A. **Address:** Department of English, State University of New York, Stony Brook, New York 11794, U.S.A.

PUBLICATIONS

Novels

The Year of the French. New York, Holt Rinehart, and London, Macmillan, 1979.
The Tenants of Time. New York, Dutton, and London, Bantam, 1988.
The End of the Hunt. New York, Dutton, 1994.

Uncollected Short Stories

"The Cold Winds of Adesta" April 1952, "The Point of Honor" December 1952, "The Lion's Mane" March 1953, "This Will Do Nicely" August 1955, "The Customs of the Country" July 1956, and "Suppose You Were on the Jury" March 1958, all in *Ellery Queen's Mystery Magazine* (New York).
"The Fine Italian Hand," in *Ellery Queen's Book of First Appearances,* edited by Ellery Queen and Eleanor Sullivan. New York, Dial Press, 1982.

Other

The Irish Novelists 1800-1850. New York, Columbia University Press, 1959.

*   *   *

Thomas Flanagan has written three novels of historical fiction that describe some of the most turbulent episodes in the history of Ireland. His first novel, *The Year of the French,* was based on an actual historical event in which a French military force landed at Killala, County Mayo, Ireland on 22 August 1798. The French, who came ostensibly to free Ireland from British rule, were apparently more interested in embarrassing and harassing the English than in actually aiding the Irish. The French troops were joined by many peasants and various Irish rebel organizations. After marching through much of western and central Eire and winning several battles, they were eventually badly defeated at Ballinamuk, near Longford, by a vastly superior army led by Lord Cornwallis, whose success redeemed his tarnished experience in America. One of the most fascinating aspects of Flanagan's novel, which gives it an epic quality, is his attempt to portray in depth all sides and viewpoints in the conflict: the high-born and the peasants, the Catholics and the Protestants, the French, Irish, and British military units, the clergy, the schoolmasters, the merchants—these and other groups are delineated with flesh and blood realization. At one point Flanagan even switches the scene to England and conveys a memorable portrait of an absentee landlord. Among the personages who beguile the reader are Arthur Broome, the local Anglican clergyman in Killala; Owen MacCarthy, the heavy-drinking itinerant poet and hedgerow schoolmaster; Jean-Joseph Humbert, the wily, pragmatic French general; Malcolm Elliott, an upper-class Protestant estate holder committed to a more equitable economic order; and Captain Ferdy O'Donnell, a courageous, sensitive rebel leader.

Fictional characters are interrelated with real-life figures such as Wolfe Tone, George and John Moore, Dennis Browne, and Maria Edgeworth. The social, political, economic, and historical background and climate are presented and examined in thorough detail. Flanagan effectively intersperses dialogue and description with numerous imaginary diaries and memoirs of the era, and this technique adds immeasurably to the verisimilitude.

The novel is also distinguished by capturing the scene with marvellously rendered poetic lyricism exemplified in both the written and spoken language of the period. The book is a mellifluous delight—many of the pages are sheer poetry glowing with beauty and picturesque phrasing. Further, *The Year of the French* possesses considerable narrative drive.

The book is not without flaws. Flanagan's portrayal of the Catholic clergy is virulently hostile, whereas the Protestant ministers are always presented as decent individuals. Flanagan also understates the suffering and oppression the common people had to endure. He takes a distastefully snobbish attitude toward them on several occasions. He also unduly fantasizes about a magical humanitarian union between Catholics and Protestants, which is certainly desirable but, as he presents it, totally unconvincing.

Flanagan's second novel, *The Tenants of Time,* deals with the Fenian Rising in Kilpeder in 1867, the Land Wars, the Phoenix Park killings, and the career of Charles Stewart Parnell. Although Flanagan still conveys vividly the beauty of the Irish countryside and the lilt of the language, this novel does not have the consistency of lyricism that distinguished his previous book. Flanagan's poetic sensibility is effective in portraying the old Fenian schoolmaster Hugh MacMahon; at other times the prose is frequently flat and uninspired. Flanagan tries also to present too many characters in too many different locations. As a consequence, the book frequently becomes sketchy and superficial.

The End of the Hunt, Flanagan's third novel, however, recaptures much of the force, lyricism, and convincing historical re-creation of his first book. He now focuses on the violent years after the 1916 Easter Rebellion when Irish rebel forces fought the English with guerrilla-style warfare and, then, after the British had granted the country Free State status, a civil war broke out between those Irish groups who wanted a Republic, completely independent of England, and their fellow countrymen who were willing to accept the Free State arrangement. Flanagan depicts with considerable force the conflicts, betrayals, terrorism, and treachery that marked this era. Numerous scenes are unforgettable, with Frank Lacy's ambush at Dawson Crossings typical of the intensity of Flanagan's descriptions. Once again, historical personages, such as Eamon DeValera, Winston Churchill, and rebel leader Michael Collins, enter the narrative. Flanagan succeeds once more in conveying the musicality of the Irish language, whether spoken by uneducated farmers or by the intellectual leaders of the rebellion during battles, or in secret hideouts, or in the back rooms of public houses. The realism of speech and characterization is compelling, and the historical events in themselves provide a fast-paced, natural narrative movement.

The novel's only serious weakness is the love story between well-bred rebel Christopher Blake and the widowed Janice Nugent. It is obvious that this material has been superimposed on the narrative to add romantic interest. In general, throughout his writings, Flanagan is not as sure-handed in portraying female characters as he is in describing males.

After the relative failure of his second novel, several critics felt that Flanagan would not continue to write gripping fiction. His latest novel, however, disproves that notion and gives hope for more successful novels in the future.

—Paul A. Doyle

FOOTE, Shelby

Nationality: American. **Born:** Greenville, Mississippi, 17 November 1916. **Education:** The University of North Carolina, Chapel Hill, 1935-37. **Military Service:** Served in the United States Army, 1940-44: Captain, and Marine Corps, 1944-45. **Family:** Married Gwyn Rainer in 1956 (second marriage); two children. **Career:** Novelist-in-residence, University of Virginia, Charlottesville, November 1963; playwright-in-residence, Arena Stage, Washington, D.C., 1963-64; writer-in-residence, Hollins College, Virginia, 1968. **Awards:** Guggenheim fellowship, 1955, 1956, 1957; Ford fellowship, for drama, 1963; Fletcher Pratt award, for non-fiction, 1964, 1974; University of North Carolina award, 1975. D.Litt.: University of the South, Sewanee, Tennessee, 1981; Southwestern University, Memphis, Tennessee, 1982; University of North Carolina, Chapel Hill, 1992; University of South Carolina, 1991; University of Notre Dame, South Bend, Indiana, 1994. **Member:** Society of American Historians, 1980; American Academy of Arts and Letters, 1994. **Address:** 542 East Parkway South, Memphis, Tennessee 38104, U.S.A.

PUBLICATIONS

Novels

Tournament. New York, Dial Press, 1949.
Follow Me Down. New York, Dial Press, 1950; London, Hamish Hamilton, 1951.
Love in a Dry Season. New York, Dial Press, 1951.
Shiloh. New York, Dial Press, 1952.
Jordan County: A Landscape in Narrative (includes stories). New York, Dial Press, 1954.
September September. New York, Random House, 1978.
Stars in Their Courses. New York, Random House, 1994.
The Beleaguered City. New York, Random House, 1995.

Play

Jordan County: A Landscape in the Round (produced Washington, D.C., 1964).

Other

The Civil War: A Narrative:
1. *Fort Sumter to Perryville.* New York, Random House, 1958; London, Bodley Head, 1991.
2. *Fredericksburg to Meridian.* New York, Random House, 1963; London, Bodley Head, 1991.
3. *Red River to Appomattox.* New York, Random House, 1974; London, Bodley Head, 1991.

The Novelist's View of History. Winston-Salem, North Carolina, Palaemon Press, 1981.
Conversations with Shelby Foote, edited by William C. Carter. Jackson, University Press of Mississippi, 1989.

*

Manuscript Collection: Southern Historical Collection, University of North Carolina, Chapel Hill, North Carolina.

Critical Studies: "Shelby Foote Issue" (includes bibliography) of *Mississippi Quarterly* (State College), October 1971, and *Delta* (Montpellier, France), 1977; *Shelby Foote* by Helen White and Redding Sugg, Boston, Twayne, 1982; *Shelby Foote: Novelist and Historian* by Robert L. Phillips, University of Mississippi Press, 1992.

*   *   *

Shelby Foote appears to succeed as a historian, not as a novelist; his multi-volume history *The Civil War: A Narrative* shows his ability to best advantage. However, one should remember that his entree into the literary world came as a promising novelist. His novels show a serious craftsman at work.

Foote experimented with technique. *Tournament* is a character study—approaching biography—with an objective omniscient point of view. *Follow Me Down* takes a single plot but incorporates a multiple point of view. This method is interesting because it allows eight characters—including protagonist and minor characters—to comment in a limited first person viewpoint on their reactions to a violent murder. *Love in a Dry Season* is a *tour de force* in which the author links two separate stories centered on the subject of money by a character who tries and fails to obtain a place in the financial elite of a small delta town. *Shiloh* enters the domain of historical fiction as the author recreates that Civil War battle through the eyes of six soldiers from both camps. Unlike the viewers in *Follow Me Down,* these narrators describe different aspects of the three-day confrontation, and only by adroit maneuvering does the author bring the respective narratives into contact. The battle, therefore becomes the hero of the novel. *Jordan County* is a collection of seven tales or episodes ranging from 1950 backwards to 1797. In each case the locale is Bristol, Jordan County, Mississippi. As his previous novel focused on a single battle, so this chronicles human drama of a fictional area, which becomes the only constant in a world of flux.

With the exception of his historical novel, all of Foote's novels are located in his microcosm, the delta country around Lake Jor-

dan. This fictive locale includes two counties, Issawamba and Jordan, Solitaire Planatation, and the town of Bristol on the Mississippi River. Through a habit of cross reference, Foote links episodes from one novel to another. For instance, the novella "Pillar of Fire" (*Jordan County*) relates the story of Isaac Jameson, founder of Solitaire Plantation and a patriarch of the delta, while *Tournament* supplies information about the man, Hugh Bart, who brought Solitare back from devastation by war and reconstruction.

Foote's use of setting, as well as style, subject matter, themes, and characterization, invites comparison with his geographical neighbor, Faulkner, but Foote's accomplishments suffer thereby. Foote is competent, not great. Normally his style is simple, lean, and direct; it seldom takes on richly suggestive qualities. Most of his themes move in the negative, anti-social direction: violence instead of peace; lust rather than love; avarice, power, and pride instead of self-sacrifice; and loneliness rather than participation in community. At his best Foote deals effectively with dramatic situations and characterizations, for example, the concatenation of episodes in the life of Hugh Bart or Luther Eustis's murder (*Follow Me Down*); however, Harley Drew's career (*Love in a Dry Season*) of lust and avarice seems an exploitation of violence rather than art. Foote chronicles events in the realistic tradition without conveying a larger insight than the particular—an insight necessary for him to achieve a significant place in southern literature.

—Anderson Clark

FORD, Jesse Hill (Jr.)

Nationality: American. **Born:** Troy, Alabama, 28 December 1928. **Education:** Vanderbilt University, Nashville, B.A. 1951; University of Florida, Gainesville, M.A. 1955; University of Oslo (Fulbright fellow), 1961. **Military Service:** Served in the United States Navy, in the Far East, 1951-53. **Family:** Married 1) Sally Davis in 1951 (divorced 1975), two sons and two daughters; 2) Lillian Pellettieri in 1975. **Career:** Reporter, Nashville *Tennesseean,* 1950-51; editorial news writer, University of Florida, 1953-55; medical news writer, Tennessee Medical Association, Nashville, 1955-56; public relations executive, American Medical Association, Chicago, 1956-57. Since 1986 guest editorialist, *USA Today* newspaper. Fellow, Center for Advanced Study, Wesleyan University, Middletown, Connecticut, 1965. **Awards:** *Atlantic* "Firsts" award, 1959; Guggenheim fellowship, 1966; Mystery Writers of America Edgar Allan Poe award, for short story, 1976. D.Litt.: Lambuth College, Jackson, Tennessee, 1966. **Agent:** Harold Ober Associates, 425 Madison Avenue, New York, New York 10017. **Address:** X-4-500 Plantation Court, Nashville, Tennessee 37221, U.S.A.

PUBLICATIONS

Novels

Mountains of Gilead. Boston, Little Brown, 1961.
The Liberation of Lord Byron Jones. Boston, Little Brown, 1965; London, Bodley Head, 1966.
The Feast of Saint Barnabas. Boston, Little Brown, and London, Bodley Head, 1969.

The Raider. Boston, Little Brown, 1975.

Short Stories

Fishes, Birds, and Sons of Men: Stories. Boston, Little Brown, 1967; London, Bodley Head, 1968.

Uncollected Short Stories

"Collector," in *Atlantic* (Boston), February 1968.
"Doctor," in *Atlantic* (Boston), June 1969.
"Destruction," in *Esquire* (New York), July 1969.
"Debt," in *Atlantic* (Boston), June 1972.
"The Jail," in *The Edgar Winners,* edited by Bill Pronzini. New York, Random House, 1980.
"Big Boy," in *Stories from Tennessee,* edited by Linda Burton. Knoxville, University of Tennessee Press, 1983.

Plays

The Conversion of Buster Drumwright: The Television and Stage Scripts (televised 1959). Nashville, Vanderbilt University Press, 1964; musical version, as *Drumwright!* (produced Knoxville, Tennessee, 1982).

Screenplay: *The Liberation of L.B. Jones,* with Stirling Silliphant, 1970.

Television Plays: *The Conversion of Buster Drumwright,* 1961; *The Lynching of Michael Donald,* 1988; *Murder in the Chapel,* 1989.

Other

Mister Potter and His Bank (biography of Edward Potter, Jr.). Nashville, Commerce Union Bank, 1977.

*

Bibliography: *Jesse Hill Ford: An Annotated Check List* by Helen White, Memphis, Tennessee, Memphis State University, 1974.

Manuscript Collection: Memphis State University, Tennessee.

Jesse Hill Ford comments:

(1981) In 1963 I found to my surprise that I had been working on the same story for ten years and that bits and pieces of it had by then appeared in several short stories, one play, and one novel. The second novel continued the story. In the third novel, *The Feast of Saint Barnabas,* I tried, but failed to escape the one long story I began in 1953, the story I have, fitfully to be sure, been writing ever since. If one reads all my books and stories the pattern will emerge in tenuous connections and sometimes indicated only by the appearance of a name carried forward, or backward, from one generation into another. The story begins in the western district of Tennessee in the American South and it probably will end there someday, far off in the future I hope, even though I am now 51 years old and still attempting to write it all down, not just the tragic events, but also the happy ones, and not just the earth-shaking things, but also the small moments that have been of such singular importance to the people I work to portray.

(1986) I owe special thanks to Edward Weeks and his wife, Phoebe-Lou Adams Weeks. Towards the end of his 35-year stint as editor of *The Atlantic Monthly* he and Phoebe-Lou, his associate editor, discovered and encouraged me, as did Peter Davison, who was then with the Atlantic Monthly Press. The unselfish efforts of these gifted people brought out the best in me. It is thanks to them that I've been privileged to devote the fresh hours of each day since 1957 to writing, and to live by and for it.

*   *   *

One generation removed from the modern Southern Renaissance, Jesse Hill Ford has begun to establish his legitimate place in that literary heritage. He has shown ability to treat universal themes embodied in the subjects—people, attitudes, events—of a particular geographic region, the American South. The greater portion of Ford's work—including two novels, *The Liberation of Lord Byron Jones* and *Mountains of Gilead,* and several short stories collected in *Fishes, Birds, and Sons of Men*—is set in the author's fictional 20th-century microcosm, Somerton, Sligo County, Tennessee. Through the continuity of locale and the cross reference to particularly prominent families and community events, the reader of Ford's fiction absorbs one writer's observation of the diversified southern consciousness.

Ford's observation covers an impressive range of themes. For example, the theme of innocence to experience has several dimensions. Simple childhood reminiscences in "The Cave" and "The Cow" respectively lead a child to intuit the fact of evil and of death, although the child can not articulate these experiences. In another short story, "A Strange Sky," Ford deals directly with the effects of this progression to experience in the life of his adult protagonist, Patsy Jo. She examines her past life, especially the seduction and manipulation by her irresponsible childhood lover, who has continually postponed marriage. Now past her marriageable prime, Patsy Jo reaches a point of maturity by severing her relationship as mistress. In the hunting story, "Savage Sound," the same theme is used differently. The protagonist does not move from innocence to experience; rather, he is responsible for teaching his young whippets to kill rabbits and, thereby, for changing the dogs' loving natures to that of vicious predators.

Violence as a theme pervades all of Ford's fiction. A catalogue of physical violence includes assault and battery, automobile wrecks, arson, rape, adultery, rusty coat hanger abortion, castration, cattle-prodding humans, drowning, man-slaughter in self-defense, premeditated murder, and even a bizarre homicide effected by the chomping jaws of a hay-bailing machine. Psychological violence, often a concomitant of the physical, makes Ford's characters also an emotionally mangled humanity. Both facets of violence show that in Ford's chaotic world egocentric modern man chooses to satisfy his own desires at the expense of his fellow man.

The violence in Ford's fiction is often an adjunct of the revenge theme. His drama, *The Conversion of Buster Drumwright,* produced first as a television play and later expanded for the stage, links murder, a desire for blood revenge, and religion. Ford's plot functions in such a way as to discredit the impulse toward revenge and sanction the worth, if not the authenticity, of the Christian message of repentance, forgiveness, and salvation. *Mountains of Gilead,* Ford's first novel, artistically uneven, offers a perceptive characterization of a southern father caught in the dilemma of avenging his daughter's violated honor while remembering the unhappy consequences of his own early marital infidelity. That the father follows the code of revenge, despite his own moral inconsistency, allows the plot to resolve—after a blood bath, suicide, and time interval—in a melodramatic reunion and marriage of the estranged youthful lovers.

Another significant theme is racial injustice, prejudice, and discrimination in Ford's south. The short story "Bitter Bread" recounts the agony and humiliation of a black man whose wife dies in a hospital corridor because they have no money for admission. Ford continues this theme of racial injustice in his second novel, *The Liberation of Lord Byron Jones.* Somerton's respectable black mortician, L.B. Jones, in seeking a divorce from his young, promiscuous wife, precipitates his own violent "liberation," his murder by the white policeman involved in the miscegenous affair. Jones is a believably tragic character as well as a representative of the oppressed southern Negro. Other characters—with varying degrees of success—demonstrate typical attitudes including that of White Citizen's agitator, socially conservative and moderate whites, and simple and militant blacks. Ford takes another viewpoint in the third novel, *The Feast of Saint Barnabas,* by focusing on the forces operating in a southern racial riot. He shows a rich black man manipulating the violent elements in the community for selfish gains. While this novel contains plenty of action, it lacks dimensions of characterization and even psychological suffering which underscore themes of the two earlier impressive works.

As an imaginative craftsman, Ford writes especially well in the short story genre. In this particular genre, in contrast to a drift in his longer works toward the melodramatic or the maudlin, Ford welds dramatic action, effective characterization, and vivid imagery into a thematic unity. His talents in the short story are in the best of Southern Renaissance literary tradition. His narration is simple; his style is clear and direct. In the shorter pieces he handles point of view with strict control, and while *The Liberation* offers a multiple point of view, Ford uses his short story technique of control from section to section. Of primary importance are his vivid eye for details, which often function both literally and symbolically, and his fine ear for dialogue. His sense of humor moves from the rockingly jovial to the grimly ironic, and his best characters possess the complexity and vitality of a gifted artist's imagination.

—Anderson Clark

FORD, Richard

Nationality: American. **Born:** Jackson, Mississippi, 16 February 1944. **Education:** Public schools in Jackson, 1950-62; Michigan State University, East Lansing, 1962-66, B.A. 1966; Washington University Law School, St. Louis, 1967-68; University of California, Berkeley, 1968-70, M.A. 1970. **Family:** Married Kristina Hensley in 1968. **Career:** Assistant professor of English, Williams College, Williamstown, Massachusetts, 1978-79; lecturer, Princeton University, New Jersey, 1980-81; teacher, Harvard University, 1994. **Awards:** Guggenheim fellowship, 1977; National Endowment for the Arts fellowship, 1978, 1983; New York Public Library Literary Lion award, 1989; American Academy award, 1989; Echoing Green Foundation award, 1991. **Agent:** Amanda Urban, International Creative Management, 40 West 57th Street, New York, New York 10016, U.S.A.

PUBLICATIONS

Novels

A Piece of My Heart. New York, Harper, 1976; London, Collins, 1987.
The Ultimate Good Luck. Boston, Houghton Mifflin, 1981; London, Collins, 1989.
The Sportswriter. New York, Vintage, and London, Collins, 1986.
Wildlife. New York, Atlantic Monthly Press, and London, Collins, 1990.
Independence Day. New York, Knopf, 1995.

Short Stories

Rock Springs. New York, Atlantic Monthly Press, 1987; London, Collins, 1988.

Play

Screenplay: *Bright Angel,* 1991.

Other

Editor, with Shannon Ravenel, *The Best American Short Stories 1990.* Boston, Houghton Mifflin, 1990.
Editor, *The Granta Book of the American Short Story.* London, Granta, 1991.

*

Richard Ford comments:

I'm stymied in an attempt to introduce my work. I wish I could write something about it that would make it seem wonderful and irresistible. My belief is, though, that anybody's work ought to introduce itself from its first moment, and I would prefer to take my chances that way rather than to put on the critic's cap regarding my own efforts or risk confusing my later opinions about my book or my story or my essay with any of their actual effects. Writers, in my experience, often gain very lofty opinions of their *oeuvres* once their *oeuvres* are out of writerly control. Any number of wondrous intentions, structures, and philosophical underpinnings can be made to dress up a simple story after the fact. I've probably been guilty of it myself, though it's only human.

*   *   *

Near the end of *The Sportswriter,* Frank Bascombe tells a young woman in whom he's interested that he never lets himself feel sorry for anyone he writes about, "since the next person you're liable to feel sorry for is you, and then you're in real trouble." While the settings of Richard Ford's fiction range from Montana to Arkansas to Mexico to New Jersey, his theme seems to remain constant. Emotional entanglements are to be avoided—emotional entanglements with the past, the future, philosophy and religion, other sides of one's self, other people.

In *A Piece of My Heart,* after eight years of marriage to Jackie, Robard Hewes leaves their home in Bishop, California, and drives his truck to the Arkansas bank of the Mississippi River. There, in the sleepy town of Helena, he takes up again with Beuna, with whom he had a brief affair 12 years earlier. He has been led to do this because for a year Beuna, married to an obsessed minor-league pitcher, has been writing him letters persuading him to come see her and renew their affair. Robard, whose own marriage has lost some of its flavor, knows that fooling with another man's wife is risky business. But having made his decision to do it, he is bent on carrying out his mission.

In Arkansas, Robard encounters Sam Newel, just down from Chicago, where he was about to complete his education in the law. The two men end up sharing quarters on an island that is the destination of hunting parties from out of state. Sam has been urged to spend some time on the island by his girlfriend Beebe, who thinks Sam needs to raise his "tolerance for ambiguity" and to learn to keep going "when nothing is very clearly defined," a notion that sounds very much like the poet John Keats's "negative capability."

Although it is obvious that Sam has a precarious hold on life, Robard does not like him or offer him anything resembling pity. Nor does Sam see anything in Robard worthy of his respect. Sam, burdened with intellect and guilt, thinks Robard is an impulsive fool. That Robard is not a reflective person clearly, in the view of the author, is very much to his credit; when called by his instincts, Robard acts. Sam's troubles are due to his willingness to dwell on the same old issues.

A Piece of My Heart is divided into seven parts. The first and last and two parts in the middle are Robard's; three alternate parts in the middle are Sam's. The effect of this path-crossing is that Sam is moved away from his Hamlet-like tendencies and Robard begins to reflect, in particular to realize his mistake in leaving Jackie. His realization, though, comes too late, for he is shot as a trespasser before he can start back to California.

Ford's second novel, *The Ultimate Good Luck,* is about 31-year-old Harry Quinn's adventures in Oaxaca, Mexico, where he is trying to gain the release from prison of a young American drug smuggler. Quinn is a more thoughtful Robard. Just as Robard left Jackie, Quinn too let a good woman get away from him. But he is given a chance to get Rae back when she writes and asks whether he would be interested in helping to get her brother out of a Mexican prison. As a former Marine helicopter pilot in Vietnam, Quinn has the skills and cast of mind needed for dealing with corrupt prison officials and the Mexican underworld.

Unlike Sam Newel, Quinn, despite the horrors of Vietnam, will not let the past take hold of him. He is determined to live in the present. Putting the past firmly behind him allows him to act. Not worrying about the future either, he is free of anxiety. Quinn is convinced that the ultimate good luck comes only to those who live in the present. What Quinn learns, though, is that even living in the present is not sufficient for outrunning loneliness. Thus he is glad for the opportunity to win Rae back.

Quinn, whose language is spare and hardboiled, is a typical Ford protagonist. In language and temperament, Quinn is very much a descendent of Ernest Hemingway's heroes. Near the beginning of this novel is one of the best pieces of descriptive prose to be found in all of Ford's writing, and it too is reminiscent of Hemingway. It is a description of two teenage Mexican boys boxing. At first they haven't the heart to hit each other, but the bout ends with one boy poking the other's eyeball out of its socket.

The Sportswriter is Ford's best-known novel. The influence of John Keats is heavily felt in this novel, in both a negative and a positive way. Keats anguished over impermanence and the transience of living things, but Ford's sportswriter, Frank Bascombe, denounces that attitude and does so in language that calls up recollections of Keat's great odes. Bascome, who has given up his career as a writer of fiction, likes sportswriting because athletic con-

tests teach that there are "no transcendent themes in life." When a contest is over, it's over, finished. That's the way life is, and any other view is a lie. Athletes are completely happy living in the present. Their selves are not divided; they have no encounters with existential dread. The athlete "isn't looking around the sides of his emotions to wonder about alternatives for what he's saying or thinking about."

Thus Bascombe, like Quinn, is very tough on himself and has little tolerance for sentimentalities; he is a very harsh realist. When an acquaintance who clearly is suicidal reaches out to him after they have been on a fishing trip off the Jersey coast, Bascombe responds with anything but compassion. Just as Keats in one of his letters coldly points out that a friend's misfortune will give him "the pleasure of trying the resources of his spirit," Bascombe too is content to merely observe and is reluctant to commiserate. When the man shoots himself, Bascombe has no regrets whatsoever regarding his behavior.

A pervasive problem in all of Ford's fiction, is his philosophizing. His protagonists' statements of hard-earned wisdom come off as muddled epigrams, neither clear nor particularly wise. Ford is extremely adept at making his scenes of conflict vivid and powerful. Whatever meaning there might be in what happens to his characters should be left to readers to infer. The overlay of philosophy only throws a fog over his great scenes.

—Paul Marx

FORREST, Leon

Nationality: American. **Born:** Chicago, Illinois, 8 January 1937. **Education:** Hyde Park High School, 1951-55, Wilson Junior College, 1955-56, and Roosevelt University, 1957-58, all Chicago; University of Chicago, 1959-60, 1962-64. **Military Service:** United States Army, 1961-62: public information specialist. **Career:** Editor of community newspapers, Chicago, 1965-69; associate editor, 1969-72, and managing editor, 1972-73, *Muhammad Speaks* (Black Muslim newspaper), Chicago. Associate professor, 1973-84, since 1984 professor, and since 1985 chair of the Department of African-American Studies, Northwestern University, Evanston, Illinois. President, Society of Midland Authors, 1981-82. "Leon Forrest Day" observed in Chicago, 1985. **Address:** Department of African-American Studies, Northwestern University, Arthur Andersen Hall, 2003 Sheridan Road, Evanston, Illinois 60208, U.S.A.

PUBLICATIONS

Novels

There Is a Tree More Ancient Than Eden. New York, Random House, 1973.
The Bloodworth Orphans. New York, Random House, 1977.
Two Wings to Veil My Face. New York, Random House, 1984.
Divine Days. Chicago, Another Chicago Press, 1992.

Uncollected Short Stories

"Packwood's Sermon by Firelight," in *Massachusetts Review* (Amherst), Winter 1977.

"Oh Jeremiah of the Dreams," in *Callaloo* (Lexington, Kentucky), May 1979.
"Oh Say Can You See," in *Story Quarterly* (Northbrook, Illinois), 1982.
"Inside the Body of a Green Apple Tree," in *Iowa Review* (Iowa City), vol. 14, no. 1. 1984.
"Sub-Rosa," in *Tri-Quarterly* (Evanston, Illinois), Summer 1984.

Plays (libretti)

Re-Creation, music by T.J. Anderson (produced Chicago, 1978).
Soldier Boy, Soldier, music by T.J. Anderson (produced Bloomington, Indiana, 1982).

Other

The Furious Voice for Freedom. Mount Kisco, New York, Bell, 1992.
Relocations of the Spirit: Essays. Wakefield, Rhode Island, Asphodel Press/Bell, 1994.

*   *   *

Ralph Ellison's enthusiastic foreword to *There Is a Tree More Ancient Than Eden* helped to launch Leon Forrest as a novelist. The novel is a *tour de force,* not easy to get into and requiring constant participation from the reader, but offering great rewards. The narrator is Nathan Witherspoon, a mulatto boy attending his mother's funeral, although the five parts of the novel encompass a much wider scope. "The Lives" provides biographical information about the major characters and serves to start Nathan on his way to the confrontations in "The Nightmare" and "The Dream" which focus on his own experience. He then launches into "The Vision" and arrives at "Wakefulness." The influences of Faulkner's *The Sound and the Fury* and Joyce's *Ulysses* are discernible but the structure is more deeply informed by the patterns of oral narration in folk sagas. Recurring themes and symbols weave a vivid, complex texture of images and motifs in terms of violence, rapes, lynchings, and also ecstasies, flights, illuminations.

The past is all-important; it is seen as a burden, for the white branch of Nathan's family included slave traders and their Dupont relatives are still openly racist. Nathan wavers between the despairing voices of his own father and of Jamestown Fishbond and the hope embodied by his aunt and guide, Hattie Breedlove. Fishbond is Nathan's relative on the slave side and extreme poverty and racial oppression have made him a modern instance of the Africans transported during the Middle Passage. His sister Madge likewise tries to hold on to her Christian faith in spite of many setbacks but she is ultimately defeated.

Most of the narrative happens wholly within Nathan's consciousness (indeed the final monologue seems inspired by Molly Bloom's soliloquy in *Ulysses*), but a number of historical characters appear, such as Abraham Lincoln who is depicted as divided between his desire to keep the nation whole and his mission as the Emancipator. However, images and words are more important than themes: Forrest derives from black oral tradition his constant use of hymns, spirituals, church scenes, and biblical phrases typical of the black preacher. Folk sermon, lament, and chant mingle with angel-like apparitions and the sensation of being given a pair of wings. In the finale of the "Vision" section, a Christ figure is torn to pieces, crucified or lynched. The novel does not end in salvation but simply on the metaphorical road to it: the mulatto protagonist has taken stock of his divided heritage and one can hope his confidence will be restored by his acceptance of his, and his people's, history.

The mosaic-like composition makes the novel difficult reading, but, in a way similar to Ellison's *Invisible Man,* the juxtaposition of echoing episodes and characters makes them reverberate and enrich the whole. In his latest novel Forrest uses again a large number of characters and the same way of developing his story, which is centered around the symbolic image of the "bleeding tree," the Christian Cross and/or the instrument of lynching about which Billie Holiday sang in "Strange Fruit." *The Bloodworth Orphans* pursues the exploration of American genealogy begun *There Is a Tree More Ancient Than Eden* but extends it, by way of the Genesis myth of the lost children of Israel, into a complex metaphor of bastardy located at the heart of American national identity. The Bloodworths are, all of them, at least symbolically, orphans in search of ancestors: twelve chapters and many characters and episodes are united through the theme of abandonment. The descendants of P.F. Pourty Bloodworth are all more or less cast away and doomed to perish, but as in the Oedipus story, they are saved and raised by foster parents so that their prototypical experience becomes mirror for all the forsaken children in the novel, youngsters like Jonathan Bass or Rachel Flowers, all exposed to drift in quest of roots and anchorage in a chaotic world. Likewise, Regal Pettibone and LaDonna Scales are heirs to a past of incest. Admittedly Noah Grandberry and Nathan find a baby right in the middle of a gang war, as though turmoil also produces the hope of regeneration. Violence, however, seems to prevail, and Carl Rae, the son of Rachel Flowers, is shot down, and nearly cut in two. Rachel herself is a dominant character, central in a scene of conversion and a dying soliloquy. Her strong Baptist faith leads her to self-denial and sacrifice. Contrasting with such well-meaning but disoriented characters is the scheming, all powerful con-man W.W.W. Ford. He is a sort of trickster straight from Afro-American folklore and creation myths alike, the leader who manipulates the crowd and deceives it as he pretends to act as its mentor. A hustler, he enacts his own entombment and resurrection in order to attract more followers. One finds echoes *Invisible Man* in this elaborate novel, but also reference to myths of Osiris, Oedipus, and Orpheus which transform episodes from Afro-American history and experience into metaphors for humanity at large. The strength of the novel derives from its superlative use of folk forms, notably the art of the black preacher represented by Reverend Packwood. Yet Forrest also employs, at times, a grotesque, surrealistic treatment.

Two Wings to Veil My Face use similar types of characters and situations: is there a hint of Ishmael Reed's "neo hoodoo" aesthetics in Aunty Foisty, the conjure woman who has hexed I.V. Reed? Again, Forrest subtly draws upon the oral tradition of folk beliefs and projects black situations onto a wider framework through the half-veiled use of Greek myths. All Forrest's fictions seem to blend into one attempt at spinning a web of verbal connections. His novels are palimpsests, radical attempts to renew black fiction, not along metafictional and self-reflexive perspectives but by the contrapuntal arrangement of the timeless processes of popular tale-telling and the innovative techniques of modernism used by Joyce and Faulkner.

—Michel Fabre

FORSTER, Margaret

Nationality: British. **Born:** Carlisle, Cumberland, 25 May 1938. **Education:** Carlisle and County High School for Girls, 1949-56;

Somerville College, Oxford (scholar), 1957-60, B.A. in modern history 1960. **Family:** Married the writer Hunter Davies in 1960; two daughters and one son. **Career:** Teacher, Barnsbury Girls' School, London, 1961-63; chief non-fiction reviewer, London *Evening Standard,* 1977-80. Fellow, Royal Society of Literature, 1975. **Agent:** Tessa Sayle Agency, 11 Jubilee Place, London SW3 3TE. **Address:** 11 Boscastle Road, London NW5 1EE, England.

PUBLICATIONS

Novels

Dames' Delight. London, Cape, 1964.
Georgy Girl. London, Secker and Warburg, 1965; New York, Berkley, 1966.
The Bogeyman. London, Secker and Warburg, 1965; New York, Putnam, 1966.
The Travels of Maudie Tipstaff. London, Secker and Warburg, and New York, Stein and Day, 1967.
The Park. London, Secker and Warburg, 1968.
Miss Owen-Owen Is at Home. London, Secker and Warburg, 1969; as *Miss Owen-Owen,* New York, Simon and Schuster, 1969.
Fenella Phizackerley. London, Secker and Warburg, 1970; New York, Simon and Schuster, 1971.
Mr. Bone's Retreat. London, Secker and Warburg, and New York, Simon and Schuster, 1971.
The Seduction of Mrs. Pendlebury. London, Secker and Warburg, 1974.
Mother Can You Hear Me? London, Secker and Warburg, 1979.
The Bride of Lowther Fell: A Romance. London, Secker and Warburg, 1980; New York, Atheneum, 1981.
Marital Rites. London, Secker and Warburg, 1981; New York, Atheneum, 1982.
Private Papers. London, Chatto and Windus, 1986.
Have the Men Had Enough? London, Chatto and Windus, 1989.
Lady's Maid. London, Chatto and Windus, 1990; New York, Doubleday, 1991.
The Battle for Christabel. London, Chatto and Windus, 1991.
Mothers' Boys. London, Chatto and Windus, 1994.

Play

Screenplay: *Georgy Girl,* with Peter Nichols, 1966.

Other

The Rash Adventurer: The Rise and Fall of Charles Edward Stuart. London, Secker and Warburg, 1973; New York, Stein and Day, 1974.
William Makespeace Thackeray: Memoirs of a Victorian Gentleman. London, Secker and Warburg, 1978; as *Memoirs of a Victorian Gentleman,* New York, Morrow, 1979.
Significant Sisters: The Grassroots of Active Feminism 1839-1939. London, Secker and Warburg, 1984; New York, Knopf, 1985.
Elizabeth Barrett Browning: A Biography. London, Chatto and Windus, 1988; New York, Doubleday, 1989.
Daphne du Maurier: A Biography. London, Chatto and Windus, and New York, Doubleday, 1993.

Editor, *Drawn from Life: The Journalism of William Makepeace Thackeray.* London, Folio, 1984.

Editor, *Selected Poems of Elizabeth Barrett Browning.* London, Chatto and Windus, and Baltimore, Johns Hopkins University Press, 1988.

* * *

Since the publication of her first novel, *Dames' Delight,* more than 25 years ago, Margaret Forster has written well over a dozen novels. In all of them she is preoccupied with human relationships or, to put it more precisely, with the impact of one person on another, with the possibility—or impossibility—of any real change in someone's character and outlook on life through emotional involvement with someone else. (She seems to declare her interest in character in the very choice of her titles; it is hardly an accident that so many of her novels carry someone's name, that badge of personal identity, in the title.)

Hers is a characteristically feminine preoccupation; even today love, whether within or outside marriage, or between those tied by the unbreakable blood knot, remains all-important to women, and Forster acknowledges this. Her perception of the impact of love seems to have changed somewhat, grown softer perhaps, over the years. In *Georgy Girl* behind all the clowning and laughter there hides a bleak, loveless little world, and George herself, so full of fierce, all-embracing love for children, has very little real lasting love to spare for her relationships with adults. In *The Travels of Maudie Tipstaff* Maudie, disappointed with her visits to her children, readily accepts the explanation of her disappointment offered in her son Robert's chilling words: "Two people are always two people . . . I'm on my own, and you, Mother, are on your own." In *Mr. Bone's Retreat,* however, we sense a change; Mr. Bone retreats indeed from his position of determined non-involvement, and slowly and with hesitation comes to accept the possibility of receiving graciously the love that is offered: "Love had to be accepted. The quality of the gift was what mattered."

The process of change does not, however, culminate in the happy ending of a romantic novel. In *The Seduction of Mrs. Pendlebury* Alice Oram nearly destroys Mrs. Pendelbury by demanding love and reassurance for her own doubts and insecurities which Rose Pendlebury cannot give. Her demands cannot be met because a personality cannot change totally without breaking in the violence of the change; the relationship between the two women sours into obsession and near madness. As in *Mr. Bone's Retreat* the young intruder acts as a catalyst, while remaining largely unchanged herself; her resilience and her strength in the possession of a future full of rich possibilities save her from disaster. For Mrs. Pendlebury salvation lies in flight to the isolation of a small seaside bungalow, set well back from its neighbors and screened so well by trees. However powerful human relationships are, they cannot radically alter a person's character, and tampering with people is a dangerous hobby.

In two more recent novels, *The Bride of Lowther Fell* and *Marital Rites,* the note of cautious acceptance of love is sounded more clearly. Alexandra, the liberated young woman in *The Bridge of Lowther Fell,* admits at the very end of her tale: "The lessons are learned. No man is an island, and no woman either." In *Marital Rites,* though Robert and Anna Osgood come through their marriage crisis shattered and diminished, marriage itself, the conventional and convenient symbol of lasting love, survives triumphant; the value of giving and accepting love, and being altered by it, is tacitly acknowledged. The love between mother and daughter, crippling and even destructive, is the theme of *Private Papers* and *Have* the Men Had Enough? Though the emphasis in both novels is on the negative aspects of the relationship, yet affection and love are both there, implicit or openly declared.

There is always a touch of irony in a human relationship, in its misconceptions, its wishful attempts to make others see us as we see ourselves. Forster recognizes this irony and uses it, sometimes as part of the very structure of her novels. Not always as overtly as in *Mother Can You Hear Me?* where Angela's struggle against the emotional demands of her elderly mother is counterpointed by italicized passages recording her vain attempts to bring up her own daughter free of the crushing burden of filial guilt. A similar device is employed in *Private Papers* where Mrs. Butler's written record of her family's history is mocked and contradicted by her eldest daughter's interpolations, giving a radically different version of the same events. In *The Travels of Maudie Tipstaff,* too, Maudie's picture of herself and her children's perception of her behavior are offered with silent irony, the mutual miscomprehensions stressing the theme of human isolation. In *The Seduction of Mrs. Pendlebury* and in *Mr. Bone's Retreat* the same technique is used more subtly, and instead of the juxtaposition of two contrasting pictures there are oblique backward glances, slowly altering a remembered incident or conversation.

In all her novels Forster's style is plain, deliberately downbeat, letting the pathos and the irony speak for themselves. The impersonal third-person narrator tells the story in short sentences, except when—as in *The Seduction of Mrs. Pendelbury*—she is voicing the thoughts of her characters. Then the sentences stretch and curl, following the course of thought. In her more recent novels Forster dispenses with the impersonal narrator, using instead the diary form (in *Private Papers*) or two first-person narrators speaking in turn (in *Have the Men Had Enough?*). Though in *Lady's Maid* the impersonal authorial voice is heard again, it is interrupted by Elizabeth Wilson's letters, the plain, bleak style matching the drab existence of Elizabeth Barrett Browning's maid.

Like so many women novelists writing today, Forster has a sharp eye for domestic detail, for the social comedy of our times. She is very much a town dweller (except in *The Bride of Lowther Fell* where she clearly draws on her Cumbrian memories, as well as— nostalgically—on those of North London). She can sum up in a few telling phrases the gentrification process in Islington ("large removal van, stacked with pine tables and brass bedsteads"), a council house in Cornwall ("The cheap cotton, flowered curtains had never fitted and let in too much light"), middle-class life in Highgate (instant coffee always offered with apologies, a sluttish daily help tolerated as a sop to social conscience). All this has been done often, but is done here extremely well. (It should be added that in *Have the Men Had Enough?,* written from personal experience of the effect of senile dementia on a family, comedy turns to tragedy in the well-observed scenes in the geriatric ward of a mental hospital.)

She reproduces variants of speech with equal accuracy. Her characters come to us with full credentials of class and educational background. It is when she moves beyond the everyday that her skill fails her. Larger-than-life characters like the eponymous Miss Owen-Owen and Fenella Phizackerley may astonish us by their behavior, but they do not convince. Over Miss Owen-Owen the shadow of Miss Jean Brodie lies very heavily indeed; Fenella, the reader of popular women's magazines imprisoned inside a creature of breathtaking beauty, remains the impossible heroine of some extravagant fairy tale. The heroine of *The Bride of Lowther Fell* (a book subtitled "a Romance," and boldly inviting by its very title a comparison with the Victorian novel) is no more convincing than the con-

trived plot. It is interesting to note here that in her recent novel *Lady's Maid* Forster turns from pastiche Victorian romance to a realistic, disturbing picture of that endlessly fascinating period.

—Hana Sambrook

FORSYTH, Frederick

Nationality: British. **Born:** Ashford, Kent, in 1938. **Education:** Tonbridge School, Kent. **Military Service:** Served in the Royal Air Force 1956-58. **Family:** Married Carrie Forsyth in 1973; two sons. **Career:** Journalist, *Eastern Daily Press,* Norwich, and in King's Lynn, Norfolk, 1958-61; reporter for Reuters, London, Paris, and East Berlin, 1961-65; reporter, BBC Radio and Television, London, 1965-67; assistant diplomatic correspondent, BBC, 1967-68; freelance journalist in Nigeria, 1968-70; television presenter, *Soldiers* series, 1985, and *Frederick Forsyth Presents* series, 1989-90. Lives in London. **Awards:** Mystery Writers of America Edgar Allan Poe award, 1971, 1983. **Address:** c/o Hutchinson Pub Group Ltd., 62-65 Chandos Pl, London WC2N 4NW, England.

PUBLICATIONS

Novels

The Day of the Jackal. London, Hutchinson, and New York, Viking Press, 1971.
The Odessa File. London, Hutchinson, and New York, Viking Press, 1972.
The Dogs of War. London, Hutchinson, and New York, Viking Press, 1974.
The Shepherd. London, Hutchinson, 1975; New York, Viking Press, 1976.
The Devil's Alternative. London, Hutchinson, 1979; New York, Viking Press, 1980.
The Fourth Protocol. London, Hutchinson, and New York, Viking Press, 1984.
The Negotiator. London and New York, Bantam, 1989.
The Deceiver. London, Corgi, and New York, Bantam, 1991.
The Fist of God. London and New York, Bantam, 1994.

Short Stories

No Comebacks: Collected Short Stories. London, Hutchinson, and New York, Viking Press, 1982.

Play

Screenplay: *The Fourth Protocol,* 1987.

Other

The Biafra Story. London, Penguin, 1969; as *The Making of an African Legend: The Biafra Story,* 1977.
Emeka (biography of Chukwuemeka Odumegwu-Ojukwu). Ibadan, Spectrum, 1982.

*   *   *

Frederick Forsyth achieved considerable commercial success with his first book, *The Day of the Jackal,* and in his subsequent novels he has followed the same basic formula: start with a plausible international crisis, keep a number of narrative threads moving at all times, scatter violent or erotic incidents liberally through the story, explain the secrets of criminal and police activity in minute detail, build toward an explosive climax, end with an unexpected twist of plot. The formula has produced a series of bestsellers, all a notch above standard popular fare, all already made or likely to be made into commercial films.

The Day of the Jackal represents the best elements of the Forsyth formula. A group of disgruntled veterans of the Algerian war hire a professional assassin from England, code-named the Jackal, to kill President De Gaulle for betraying the French cause in North Africa. Forsyth adds an abundance of peripheral plots and characters, many based on actual events of the time. We are jolted back and forth between two centers of intrigue: the solitary assassin meticulously planning each step of the murder and the special police unit trying to track him down. Forsyth's fascination with detail draws us into the story. We learn how to acquire false passports, how to obtain a custom-made rifle, how to travel around Europe under a variety of identities, and how, conversely, police forces of different nations cooperate to prevent the assassination. Facing a complex plot and an overabundance of characters, we follow events without understanding the human motives behind them. But though we never get inside the main figure, the Jackal, we are willing to ascribe it to the nature of the character: a professional assassin keeps his own counsel, revealing nothing of himself to anyone. Thus a fundamental shortcoming in Forsyth's work, an unwillingness or inability to create convincing characters, works to his advantage in *The Day of the Jackal.*

The same flaw is more apparent, and less defensible, in the novels that followed. *The Odessa File* concerns a young German journalist's attempt to infiltrate an organization of influential former SS officers and to locate one war criminal in particular. The theme of hunter and hunted is repeated from the earlier book, but the absence of full characters seems glaring here. So too with *The Dogs of War,* a novel about mercenaries overthrowing an African dictator, and *The Devil's Alternative,* about a series of international events that brings the world to the brink of nuclear war. In *The Fourth Protocol* however, as in *The Day of the Jackal,* the more shadowy the people, the more real they seem. The novel describes an ingeniously complex Soviet plot to undermine the British government, with intelligence experts from each side anticipating and thwarting each other's moves.

The Negotiator follows the Forsyth pattern to a point, with the kidnapping and murder of a liberal American president's son serving as the entree into a more complicated story of right-wing conspiracies in both the Soviet Union and the United States to undermine stability in the Middle East. Untypically, Forsyth tries, without much success, to humanize his title character by creating a love interest for the otherwise solitary hero. Another solitary hero is Sam McCready, the unifying figure in *The Deceiver,* four stories of counterespionage. McCready, a veteran agent of British Intelligence, personally outwits such enemies of freedom as the Soviets, Libyans, IRA, Castro, and Colombian drug lords. A recurring theme is the careerism or ineptitude of MIA and CIA bureaucrats whose rules McCready must violate to defeat an enemy who knows no rules.

Forsyth's plots have the short-term advantages and the long-term problems of dealing with topical world affairs. His latest venture,

The Fist of God, is set during the 1991 Gulf War and includes, in addition to its fictional characters, inside glimpses of the major players in that conflict: George Bush, Margaret Thatcher, Norman Schwarzkopf, and Saddam Hussein. Here Forsyth finds material to fit his strengths: international intrigue, behind-the-scenes manipulation of events, and weapons derived from high technology. The novel works well because the Gulf War event lends itself to the Forsyth formula.

All Forsyth's novels include a wealth of detail on matters well beyond the experience of their readers, yet they convey a compelling atmosphere of verisimilitude. We learn how experts make and plant bombs, smuggle weapons, infiltrate secret agencies; we learn how terrorists operate, how world leaders confer and conspire, how spies attend to their daily chores. But all of this detail does not produce convincing human beings. The events seem real, at least plausible, but not the people.

Forsyth himself is candid about his work. He recognizes the need for thorough research into his material, knowing that the credibility of his plots lies in his attention to realistic detail. He sees himself, moreover, as a strictly commercial writer, and his language is crisp and direct, without grace or pretension. Proficient within his genre, Forsyth has the intelligence and good taste not to stray beyond it.

—Robert E. Lynch

FOSTER, David (Manning)

Nationality: Australian. **Born:** Sydney, New South Wales, 15 May 1944. **Education:** The University of Sydney, B.Sc. in chemistry 1967; Australian National University, Canberra, Ph.D. 1970. **Family:** Married 1) Robin Ruth Bowers in 1965 (marriage ended); 2) Gerda Hageraats in 1975; has four daughters and two sons. **Career:** Research fellow, U.S. Public Health Service, Philadephia, 1970-71; senior research officer, University of Sydney Medical School, 1971-72. **Awards:** Australian Literature Board fellowships, 1973-91; *The Age* award, 1974; Marten Bequest award, 1978; Australian National Book Council award, 1981; New South Wales Premier's fellowship, 1986; Australian creative fellowship, 1992-95. **Address:** Ardara, Bundanoon, New South Wales 2578, Australia.

PUBLICATIONS

Novels

The Pure Land. Melbourne, Macmillan, 1974; New York, Penguin, 1985.

The Empathy Experiment, with D.K. Lyall. Sydney, Wild and Woolley, 1977.

Moonlite. Melbourne, Macmillan, 1981; London, Pan, 1982; New York, Penguin, 1987.

Plumbum. Ringwood, Victoria, Penguin, 1983.

Dog Rock: A Postal Pastoral. Ringwood, Victoria, and New York, Penguin, 1985.

The Adventures of Christian Rosy Cross. Ringwood, Victoria, London, and New York, Penguin, 1986.

Testostero. Ringwood, Victoria, and New York, Penguin, 1987.
The Pale Blue Crochet Coathanger Cover. Ringwood, Victoria, Penguin, 1988.
Mates of Mars. Ringwood, Victoria, Penguin, 1991.

Short Stories

North South West: Three Novellas. Melbourne, Macmillan, 1973.
Escape to Reality. Melbourne, Macmillan, 1977.
Hitting the Wall: Two Novellas. Ringwood, Victoria, and London, Penguin, 1989.

Poetry

The Fleeing Atalanta. Adelaide, Maximus, 1975.

Other

Editor, *Self Portraits.* Canberra, Australian National Library, 1991.

*

Manuscript Collection: Australian Defence Force Academy Library, Canberra.

*　　*　　*

David Foster's background as a scientist is very much in evidence in his fiction, in his interest in concepts such as entropy and in his vast and eclectic vocabulary, which is full of technical words. For instance, his first book, *North South West,* contains sentences such as "We will fall before their arrows as before the nematocysts of a coelenterate." The stories foreshadow Foster's directions in other ways too, in their ambivalent dichotomy of country and city and in the writer's political conservatism: "I functioned as the opponent of all liberalism," one of his characters says. In "Mobil Medley," a kind of latterday *Canterbury Tales,* there is again a significant remark from the narrator which is applicable to Foster's fiction in general. "His words never settled fully about the object, but created a diversion to themselves, leaving the naked."

Foster's second book and first novel, *The Pure Land,* is an unusual and at times parodic example of that familiar Australian fictive stand-by, the generational novel. Divided into three parts, it tells the stories of three generations of a family, with only minor connecting links between the largely discrete sections. Beginning in Sydney it crosses to the United States before returning to its original base and finally petering out in a series of unanswered letters. *The Empathy Experiment* is set some time in the future and in a city something like Canberra, to judge from its obsessive bureaucracy. It concerns a scientist named FX and his experiments in harnessing the forces of empathic identification with his subjects. Although there are mad puns and various bizarrely comic incidents, the book is less playful than most of Foster's work. What emerges eventually from the novel's frantic improvisation is an angry satire of scientific experimentation which ignores the rights of its victims. *Escape to Reality* is Foster's only collection of short fiction to date. Like much of his work, it is concerned with outsiders or outlaws of some kind, and is written in a coolly objective, unjudging way, often in the first person. The collection is full of voices, the narrator's and other characters', in the many dialogues. In the longest and best story, "The Job," the narrator Billie is a petty criminal

who is picked up on his release by another petty criminal, Brian. The story follows a familiarly circular pattern, with Billie waiting outside the jail at the end to pick up another released man, just as Brian had waited for him.

By now Foster had made a mark as a writer but still gave the impression of a talent of considerable, if somewhat cerebral, intelligence, deeply uncertain as to the direction in which it wanted to go. It is with the novels of the 1980s and especially *Moonlite,* still probably the best work, that he seems to find that direction and that personal voice. It is a less coldly written but still ingenious narrative of the picaresque adventures of one Finbar ("Moonbar") MacBuffie which amount to something like an allegorical account of the history of immigration to Australia. It is a wittily parodic novel, reminiscent in many ways of John Barth and especially of *The Sot-Weed Factor.* Foster displays his characteristic fascination with language, using arcane or self-invented words, punning vigorously, giving characters names like the Marquis of Moneymore and Grogstrife and employing a variety of dialects as well as a multitude of satiric targets, from academic scholarship and Christianity through advocates of temperance to Australian myths of heroism and identity.

Plumbum is written in a mode which Foster makes his own from *Moonlite* onwards, a self-conscious but also surreal, highly inventive but sometimes irritatingly cerebral comedy. It concerns a group of young musicians who form a heavy metal band, but the satiric targets are lost in the medley of competing voices and increasingly frantic pace. *Dog Rock* is a country town, population 776 of which the narrator D'Arcy D'Oliveres has been postman for ten years. A murderer known only as the Queen's Park Ripper is terrorising the town's citizens by progressively eliminating them. The novel is a parody of the detective genre, with an abundance of improbable clues and an impossibly complicated plot. Foster returned to Dog Rock and D'Arcy D'Oliveres later with the slight but genially witty *The Pale Blue Crochet Coathanger Cover.*

The Adventures of Christian Rosy Cross, which Foster has said he considers his magnum opus, is another picaresque novel, or parody of one. Its hero is born in 1378, the son of Comte de Rosencreutz who manages to finish off his own wife by immediately after the birth engaging in violent sexual intercourse with her. The novel recounts his adventures up until the age of 23, after which, we are told at the end, "By judicious speculation he acquires a modest income, and spends the remaining years of his life, till his death in 1483, keeping fit, playing the harpsichord, cultivating bulbs, arguing with his neighbour over who should build the new boundary fence, and striving to improve the local breed of dog." Foster speaks in his introduction of his conviction that our present age resembles that of Christian Rosy Cross but the connections he claims with modern parallels are tenuous and much of the humour is built on simple-minded juxtapositions between modern and medieval ("Would you care to see some filthy woodcuts?"). *Testostero* is sub-titled "a comic novel" but is in fact a laboured, tedious farce involving Noel Horniman, talented but ockerish Australian poet, and Leon Hunnybun, limp-wristed English aristocrat, who discover in the course of the novel that they are twins. *Hitting the Wall* is actually two novellas of which one, "The Job," is reprinted from *Escape to Reality.*

On the face of it, Foster would seem to have an imagination as original and inventive as almost any contemporary Australian novelist and he commands an astounding range of material. But that imagination seems difficult for him to harness and like Barth and perhaps Thomas Pynchon, he reads better in bits and pieces than in toto. There are brilliantly original gags but no normative centre against which to place them. Perhaps he might do well to take note of one of his own witty scientific analogues from *Plumbum:* "You will sometimes see a middle-aged man holding the jaws of his mind open with every intellectual prop and pole at his disposal. In such a state he resembles a bivalve mollusc, constrained to sup whatever shit floats by."

—Laurie Clancy

FOWLES, John (Robert)

Nationality: British. **Born:** Leigh-on-Sea, Essex, 31 March 1926. **Education:** Bedford School, 1940-44; Edinburgh University, 1944; New College, Oxford, B.A. (honors) in French 1950. **Military Service:** Served in the Royal Marines, 1945-46. **Family:** Married Elizabeth Whitton in 1956. **Career:** Lecturer in English, University of Poitiers, France, 1950-51; teacher at Anargyrios College, Spetsai, Greece, 1951-52, and in London, 1953-63. **Awards:** Silver Pen award, 1969; W.H. Smith Literary award, 1970; Christopher award, 1981. **Address:** c/o Jonathan Cape Ltd, 20 Vauxhall Bridge Road, London SW1V 2SA, England.

PUBLICATIONS

Novels

The Collector. London, Cape, and Boston, Little Brown, 1963.
The Magus. Boston, Little Brown, 1965; London, Cape, 1966; revised edition, Cape, 1977; Little Brown, 1978.
The French Lieutenant's Woman. London, Cape, and Boston, Little Brown, 1969.
Daniel Martin. Boston, Little Brown, and London, Cape, 1977.
Mantissa. London, Cape, and Boston, Little Brown, 1982.
A Maggot. London, Cape, and Boston, Little Brown 1985.

Short Stories

The Ebony Tower: Collected Novellas. London, Cape, and Boston, Little Brown, 1974.

Plays

Don Juan, adaptation of the play by Molière (produced London, 1981).
Lorenzaccio, adaptation of the play by Alfred de Musset (produced London, 1983).
Martine, adaptation of a play by Jean Jacques Bernard (produced London, 1985).

Screenplay: *The Magus,* 1968.

Poetry

Poems. New York, Ecco Press, 1973.
Conditional. Northridge, California, Lord John Press, 1979.

Other

The Aristos: A Self-Portrait in Ideas. Boston, Little Brown, 1964; London, Cape, 1965; revised edition, London, Pan, 1968; Little Brown, 1970.
Shipwreck, photographs by the Gibsons of Scilly. London, Cape, 1974; Boston, Little Brown, 1975.
Islands, photographs by Fay Godwin. London, Cape, 1978; Boston, Little Brown, 1979.
The Tree, photographs by Frank Horvat. London, Aurum Press, 1979; Boston, Little Brown, 1980.
The Enigma of Stonehenge, photographs by Barry Brukoff. London, Cape, and New York, Summit, 1980.
A Brief History of Lyme. Lyme Regis, Dorset, Friends of the Lyme Regis Museum, 1981.
A Short History of Lyme Regis. Wimborne, Dorset, Dovecote Press, 1982; Boston, Little Brown, 1983.
Land, photographs by Fay Godwin. London, Heinemann, and Boston, Little Brown, 1985.
Lyme Regis Camera. Stanbridge, Dorset, Dovecote Press, 1990; Boston, Little Brown, 1991.

Editor, *Steep Holm: A Case History in the Study of Evolution.* Sherborne, Dorset, Allsop Memorial Trust, 1978.
Editor, with Rodney Legg, *Monumenta Britannica,* by John Aubrey. Sherborne, Dorset Publishing Company, 2 vols., 1981-82; vol. 1, Boston, Little Brown, 1981.
Editor, *Thomas Hardy's England,* by Jo Draper. London, Cape, and Boston, Little Brown, 1984.

Translator, *Cinderella,* by Perrault. London, Cape, 1974; Boston, Little Brown, 1975.
Translator, *Ourika,* by Claire de Durfort. Austin, Texas, Taylor, 1977.

*

Bibliography: "John Fowles: An Annotated Bibliography 1963-76" by Karen Magee Myers, in *Bulletin of Bibliography* (Boston), vol. 33, no. 4, 1976; *John Fowles: A Reference Guide* by Barry N. Olshen and Toni A. Olshen, Boston, Hall, 1980; "John Fowles: A Bibliographical Checklist" by Ray A. Roberts, in *American Book Collector* (New York), September-October, 1980; "Criticism of John Fowles: A Selected Checklist" by Ronald C. Dixon, in *Modern Fiction Studies* (Lafayette, Indiana), Spring 1985.

Manuscript Collection: University of Tulsa, Oklahoma.

Critical Studies: *Possibilities* by Malcolm Bradbury, London, Oxford University Press, 1973; *The Fiction of John Fowles: Tradition, Art, and the Loneliness of Selfhood* by William J. Palmer, Columbia, University of Missouri Press, 1974; *John Fowles: Magus and Moralist* by Peter Wolfe, Lewisburg, Pennsylvania, Bucknell University Press, 1976, revised edition, 1979; *Etudes sur The French Lieutenant's Woman de John Fowles* edited by Jean Chevalier, Caen, University of Caen, 1977; *John Fowles* by Barry N. Olshen, New York, Ungar, 1978; *John Fowles, John Hawkes, Claude Simon: Problems of Self and Form in the Post-Modernist Novel* by Robert Burden, Würzburg, Königshausen & Neumann, and Atlantic Highlands, New Jersey, Humanities Press, 1980; *John Fowles* by Robert Huffaker, New York, Twayne, 1980; "John Fowles Issue" of *Journal of Modern Literature* (Philadelphia), vol. 8, no.

2, 1981; *Four Contemporary Novelists* by Kerry McSweeney, Montreal, McGill-Queen's University Press, 1982, London, Scolar Press, 1983; *John Fowles* by Peter J. Conradi, London, Methuen, 1982; *Fowles, Irving, Barthes: Canonical Variations on an Apocryphal Theme* by Randolph Runyon, Columbus, Ohio State University Press, 1982; *The Timescapes of John Fowles* by H.W. Fawkner, Rutherford, New Jersey, Fairleigh Dickinson University Press, 1983; *Male Mythologies: John Fowles and Masculinity* by Bruce Woodcock, Brighton, Harvester Press, 1984; *The Romances of John Fowles* by Simon Loveday, London, Macmillan, 1985; "John Fowles Issue" of *Modern Fiction Studies* (Lafayette, Indiana), Spring 1985; *The Fiction of John Fowles: A Myth for Our Time* by Carol M. Barnum, Greenwood, Florida, Penkevill, 1988; *The Art of John Fowles* by Katherine Tarbox, Athens, University of Georgia Press, 1988; *Form and Meaning in the Novels of John Fowles* by Susana Onega, Ann Arbor, Michigan, UMI Research Press, 1989; *John Fowles: A Reference Companion* by James R. Aubrey, New York, Greenwood Press, 1991; *Point of View in Fiction and Film: Focus on John Fowles* by Charles Garard, New York, P. Lang, 1991; *John Fowles's Fiction and the Poetics of Postmodernism* by Mahmoud Salami, Rutherford, Fairleigh Dickinson University Press, 1992; *Something and Nothingness: The Fiction of John Updike and John Fowles* by John Neary, Carbondale, Southern Illinois University Press, 1992; *Understanding John Fowles* by Thomas C. Foster, Columbia, University of South Carolina Press, 1994.

*　　*　　*

John Fowles is a highly allusive and descriptive novelist. In all his fictions, situations and settings are carefully and lavishly done: the French country landscape of "The Cloud" (*The Ebony Tower*); the blues and purples of the stark New Mexican mountains, the soft rainy contours of Devon in various greens and greys, the bleak and menacing deserts of Syria, all in *Daniel Martin*. Most frequently, Fowles's richly painted settings conceal a mystery, as in the title story of *The Ebony Tower*, in which an old English painter has created his "forest" in France, like that of Chrétien de Troyes, a "mystery island" to break away from the closed formal island into "love and adventure and the magical." The lush Greek island of *The Magus* conceals mystery and magic, a stage for the complicated and elaborate series of theatricals that enchant, enslave, and instruct a young Englishman who has taken a teaching job there. The five 18th-century travellers in *A Maggot* go through the deep vales and caverns near Exmoor, which lead to death for one, to a vision of paradise that may have helped establish a new religion for another, and to unknowable disappearance for a third. Often, Fowles's characters, like Nicholas Urfe in *The Magus* or the interrogating magistrate in *A Maggot*, try to solve the mysteries, to make sense of what happens as they confront new worlds, but they are not entirely successful. Frequently, as in the short story "The Enigma," in which a solid, stable, middle-aged Tory M.P. simply disappears, Fowles does not resolve the mystery and concentrates on the implications for others in living in terms of what is finally unknown.

In staging his mysteries, in choosing what to reveal and what to conceal, Fowles has often been seen by readers as manipulative. Such manipulation, however, is not merely a matter of tricks, ingenious switches, or "the God-game." Rather, the sense of "reality" as something that has to be manipulated, rearranged, in order to be understood is central to Fowles's conception of both the nature and the function of fiction. When victimized by a mock trial in the culminating theatrical invented for him, Nicholas Urfe realizes that he is only getting what he has deserved, for "all my life I had tried to turn life into fiction, to hold reality away." *Mantissa,* the title itself suggesting a trivial addition to literature, consists of a debate between the novelist and his erotic muse about the nature of fiction which satirizes simplistic solipsistic positions like "Serious modern fiction has only one subject: the difficulty of writing serious modern fiction." The novelist's manipulation is more complex and immediately recognizable in *The French Lieutenant's Woman,* which is full of parodies of old novelistic devices, switches in time and history, and frequent interruptions of the Victorian narrative that acknowledge the author's deliberate arrangements. The reader is constantly led to question what "Victorian" means, to recognize the texture of anachronism, parody, research, quotations from Marx, Darwin, Victorian sociological reports, Tennyson, Arnold, and Hardy as various means of demonstrating the conditional nature of time and history, the necessity of locating oneself in the present before one can understand anything of the past. The novel also has three endings, not simply as a form of prestidigitation, but as a demonstration that three different possible resolutions, each characterizing a different possible perspective itself historically definable, are consistent with the issues and characters Fowles has set in motion. *A Maggot* deploys strategies of similar contemporary interruptions, like the child opening a gate for the travellers on horse-back who is thrown a farthing that falls "over her bent crown of no doubt lice-ridden hair," or the actor playing a London merchant who changes from "anachronistic skinhead" to "Buddhist monk," to present a conflict between legalistic dialogue and the origins of religion or art, later explained as a version of the universal conflict between the left-lobed brain and the right, in terms of its modern genesis in the socially static period of the 1730s. Only in *Mantissa* and in parts of *Daniel Martin* do Fowles's speculations about the nature of fiction become arid and modish.

The allusive references of Fowles's ingenious fictions have generally widened and deepened over the course of his development. In his first novel, *The Collector,* more sensational than those that followed, Fowles attempted to probe psychologically and sociologically on a single plane of experience, to demonstrate what in a young man of one class caused him to collect, imprison, and dissect the girl from another class he thought he loved. The fabrications of *The Magus* extend further into history, legend, and myth, exploring various kinds of Gods, of perspectives "real" and imaginary (one can never finally draw a line between the two) that negate human freedom. A number of the long stories of *The Ebony Tower,* like "Eliduc," retell ancient myths or recreate them in contemporary terms. *The French Lieutenant's Woman,* with all its literary, historical, and artistic allusions, shows what of the story is of the past, what of the present, and what indeterminate, for history, for Fowles, invariably includes much of the time and perspective of the historian. Thematically, *Daniel Martin* is, in some ways, an expansion of *The French Lieutenant's Woman,* an analysis of Fowles's own generation, the last in England that might still be characterized as Victorian, "brought up in some degree of the nineteenth century since the twentieth did not begin until 1945." *Daniel Martin* also makes explicit a theme implicit in Fowles's earlier fiction, the paralyzing and complicated effects of all the guilts originating in the Victorian past, what he calls a "pandemic of self-depreciation" that leads to emotional insularity and to the capacity to live gracefully with loss rather than expending effort to change. In this novel, which ranges geographically (America, Italy, and the

Middle East, as well as England) and historically (past wars and cultural legends), the guilt and self-depreciation are also attached to attractions to lost civilizations, the American Indians, the Minoans, the Etruscans, and the contemporary English. *A Maggot,* following the metaphor of the "larval stage of a winged create," but also, according to Fowles, meaning in the 18th century a "whim or quirk . . . an obsession," expands its terms historically into a vision of possible humanity, an "almost divine maggot" attempting social and religious change against "reason, convention, established belief."

Until the fictional focus on the mother and the creation of Ann Lee, the historical founder of the Shaker religion, in *A Maggot,* Fowles's central characters have been isolated, rational, self-punishing males who attempted to join with independent, passionate, and enigmatic women. As the voice of the author in *The French Lieutenant's Woman* claims, he may be simply transferring his own inabilities to understand the enigmatic female into the safety of his historically locatable Victorian story. The sexual focus, however, with its attendant guilts and metaphorical expansions, is characteristic, and the novels develop the rational and sometimes manipulative means the male uses to try to understand and control the amorphous and enigmatic female. The male is always limited, his formulations and understandings only partial. And, in his frustration, the necessity that he operate in a world where understanding is never complete, he acts so as to capture (*The Collector*), desert (*The Magus*), betray (*The French Lieutenant's Woman*), relate to through art (*Mantissa*), or both betray and finally recover (*Daniel Martin*) the female he can only partially comprehend. In *A Maggot,* the prestidigitating male finally disappears from the fiction entirely, leaving the woman, who incorporates both whore and saint, to bring forth significant life herself. Fowles has treated his constant metaphorical focus on relationships between the sexes with growing insight, sympathy, and intelligence, as well as with a fascinating complexity of sociological, historical, and psychological implications of the incessant human effort involved.

—James Gindin

FRAME, Janet (Paterson)

Nationality: New Zealander. **Born:** Dunedin, 28 August 1924. **Education:** Oamaru North School; Waitaki Girls' High School; University of Otago Teachers Training College, Dunedin. **Awards:** Hubert Church Prose award, 1952, 1964, 1974; New Zealand Literary Fund award, 1960; New Zealand Scholarship in Letters, 1964, and Award for Achievement, 1969; University of Otago Robert Burns fellowship, 1965; Buckland Literary award 1967; James Wattie award, 1983, 1985; Commonwealth Writers prize, 1989. D.Litt.: University of Otago, 1978. C.B.E. (Commander, Order of the British Empire), 1983. **Address:** P.O. Box 1118, Palmerston North, New Zealand.

PUBLICATIONS

Novels

Owls Do Cry. Christchurch, Pegasus Press, 1957; New York, Braziller, 1960; London, W.H. Allen, 1961.

Faces in the Water. Christchurch, Pegasus Press, and New York, Braziller, 1961; London, W.H. Allen, 1962.
The Edge of the Alphabet. Christchurch, Pegasus Press, New York, Braziller, and London, W.H. Allen, 1962.
Scented Gardens for the Blind. Christchurch, Pegasus Press, and London, W.H. Allen, 1963; New York, Braziller, 1964.
The Adaptable Man. Christchurch, Pegasus Press, New York, Braziller, and London, W.H.Allen, 1965.
A State of Siege. New York, Braziller, 1966; London, W.H. Allen, 1967.
The Rainbirds. London, W.H. Allen, 1968; as *Yellow Flowers in the Antipodean Room,* New York, Braziller, 1969.
Intensive Care. New York, Braziller, 1970; London, W.H. Allen, 1971.
Daughter Buffalo. New York, Braziller, 1972; London, W.H. Allen, 1973.
Living in the Maniototo. New York, Braziller, 1979; London, Women's Press, 1981.
The Carpathians. London, Bloomsbury, and New York, Braziller, 1988.

Short Stories

The Lagoon: Stories. Christchurch, Caxton Press, 1952; revised edition, as *The Lagoon and Other Stories,* 1961; London, Bloomsbury, 1991.
The Reservoir: Stories and Sketches. New York, Braziller, 1963.
Snowman, Snowman: Fables and Fantasies. New York, Braziller, 1963.
The Reservoir and Other Stories. Christchurch, Pegasus Press, and London, W.H. Allen, 1966.
You Are Now Entering the Human Heart. Wellington, Victoria University Press, 1983; London, Women's Press, 1984.

Poetry

The Pocket Mirror. New York, Braziller, and London, W.H. Allen, 1967.

Other

Mona Minim and the Smell of the Sun (for children). New York, Braziller, 1969.
An Autobiography. Auckland, Century Hutchinson, 1989; London, Women's Press, 1990; New York, Braziller, 1991.
   1. *To the Is-Land.* New York, Braziller, 1982; London, Women's Press, 1983.
   2. *An Angel at My Table.* Auckland, Hutchinson, New York, Braziller, and London, Women's Press, 1984.
   3. *The Envoy from Mirror City.* Auckland, Hutchinson, New York, Braziller, and London, Women's Press, 1985.

*

Film Adaptations: *An Angel at My Table,* 1991.

Bibliography: By John Beston, in *World Literature Written in English* (Arlington, Texas), November 1978.

Critical Studies: *An Inward Sun: The Novels of Janet Frame,* Wellington, New Zealand University Press, 1971, and *Janet Frame,*

Boston, Twayne, 1977, both by Patrick Evans; *Bird, Hawk, Bogie: Essays on Janet Frame* edited by Jeanne Delbaere, Aarhus, Denmark, Dangaroo Press, 1978; *Janet Frame* by Margaret Dalziel, Wellington, Oxford University Press, 1981; *The Ring of Fire: Essays on Janet Frame* edited by Jeanne Delbaere, Sydney, Dangaroo Press, 1992; *I Have What I Gave: The Fiction of Janet Frame* by Judith Dell Panny, New York, Braziller, 1993.

* * *

"All dreams," Janet Frame writes in her 1970 novel *Intensive Care,* "lead back to the nightmare garden." And all nightmares lead circuitously into truth. In all her novels, the looming threat of disorder, violent and disrupting, persistently attracts those that it frightens, for it proves more fertile, more imaginatively stimulating, more genuine, and more real than the too-familiar world of daily normality. The tension between safety and danger recurs as her characters—voyaging into strange geographies (like the epileptic Toby Withers in *The Edge of the Alphabet*), or madness (like Daphne in *Owls Do Cry,* or Istina Navet in *Faces in the Water*), or other people's identities (like Ed Glace in *Scented Gardens for the Blind*), or mirrors (like Vic in *The Adaptable Man*), or death (like Godfrey Rainbird in *The Rainbirds*)—discover both the mental deliberation that the safe state, in oxymoronic creativity, engenders, and the disembodying that danger contrives. The opening of *Faces in the Water* demonstrates the author's thematic density and sardonic touch:

> They have said that we owe allegiance to Safety, that he is our Red-Cross God who will provide us with ointment and . . . remove the foreign ideas, the glass beads of fantasy, the bent hair-pins of unreason embedded in our minds. On all the doors which lead to and from the world they have posted warning notices and lists of safety measures to be taken in extreme emergency. . . . Never sleep in the snow. Hide the scissors. Beware of strangers. . . . But for the final day . . . they have no slogan. The streets throng with people who panic, looking to the left and the right, covering the scissors, sucking poison from a wound they cannot find, judging their time from the sun's position in the sky when the sun itself has melted and trickles down the ridges of darkness into the hollows of evaporated seas. Nightmares and madness, the education in the nature of Apocalypse and survival, become not mere metaphors of sanity, but direct training in the reactivation of the mind's perceiving eyes.

By "shipwrecking" oneself in mad geographies, however (Frame speaks in one novel of "an affliction of dream called Overseas"—as in another she observes that OUT is in man, is what he fears, "like the sea"), one places oneself on "the edge of the alphabet," in possession perhaps of insight, but no longer capable of communicating with the people who stay within regulated boundaries. Malfred Signal, in Frame's weakest novel, *A State of Siege,* for example, leaves her old self to live on an island and to find the perspectives of "the room two inches behind the eyes." What she discovers, when the elements besiege her, is fear, but all she can do then is silently utter the strange new language that she clutches, alone, into seacalm and death. Like Ed Glace in *Scented Gardens,* who researches the history of the surname *Strang* and (discovering *strong, Strange,* and *Danger* along the way) wonders if people are merely anagrams, Malfred lives in a mad mirror world of in-

tensely focused perception that anagrammatic Joycean punning-distorting day-to-day language—tries to render. As *Owls Do Cry* had earlier specified, in the shallow suburban character of Chicks, the "safe" world deals in language, too, as a defence against upset, hiding in the familiarity of conventional clichés and tired similes. What the brilliant punning passages of *The Rainbirds* show is what the title poem of *The Pocket Mirror* implies: that convention will not show ordinary men the "bar of darkness" that are optically contained within the "facts of light"; "To undeceive the sight a detached instrument like a mirror is necessary." Or her narratives. But even that vantage point is fraught with deceit. Superstition, like convention, and Platonic forms, like safe order, can all interfere with true interpenetration with "actuality." And to find the live language—the "death-free zone" of Thora Pattern, in *Edge of the Alphabet*—as a novelist inevitably dealing with day-to-day words becomes an increasingly difficult task the stronger the visionary sense of the individual mind on its own. Turnlung, the aging New Zealand writer in New York, in *Daughter Buffalo,* finds the challenge particularly acute; his exile to "a country of death" brings him into bizarrely creative contact with a young doctor, but in the epilogue to the story, he wonders if he has dreamed everything. What matters, as Turnlung puts it, is that "I have what I gave." To conceive is to create some kind of reality, however unconventional the act, the result, and the language of rendering the experience may seem.

There are passages in France that are reminiscent of Doris Lessing—like the apocalyptic scenes of *Scented Gardens* and *Intensive Care,* the one anticipating the atomic destruction of Britain and the birth of a new language, the other observing the destruction of animals in Waipori City (the computerized enactment of the Human Delineation Act which will identify the strong normal lawabiding "humans" and methodically, prophylactically, eliminate the rest), and the ironic intensification of a vegetable human consciousness. In the earlier novel, particularly, the author emphasizes the relationship between the "safety dance of speech" and a kind of Coleridgean death-in-life, and that between winter (the gardenless season) and madness, life-in-death, "Open Day in the factory of the mind." *The Rainbirds,* the writer's gentlest, most comic (however hauntingly, macabrely, relentlessly discommoding) book, takes up the metaphor in its story of a man *pronounced* dead after a car accident. Though Godfrey Rainbird lives, the official pronouncement, the conventional language, the public utterance, takes precedence over the individual spiritual actuality, depriving him of his job, his children, public acceptance, and so on. Indeed, he only becomes acceptable when he has "died" a second time, when his story is sufficiently distanced into legend and into the past to become a tourist attraction. But if you visit the grave in the winter, Frame adds, you must create the summer flowers within yourself. Summer gardens are openly available even to the spiritually blind; winter gardens are not. Her quiet acceptance, however, of that (mad, winter) power to change seasons within the mind expresses her most optimistic regard of humanity. And as *Living in the Maniototo* reaffirms, there is an ordering potentiality in the recognition of any person's several selves.

Intensive Care more broodingly evokes the same theme and provokingly points out the difference between the hospitalization of the body and the intensive care required to keep the mind truly alive. When the second world war is long over and the computer mentality takes over after the next impersonal War, all fructifying abnormality seems doomed; Deciding Day will destroy that which is not *named* human. Through the sharp memory of the supposedly dull Milly Galbraith, who is one of the few to appreciate an ancient surviving pear-tree, and the damningly conciliatory (and then expiatory) attitudes of Colin Monk, who goes along with the system, valuing Milly too late to save her, the apocalyptic days of Waipori City are told. Behind them both looms the mythical presence of Colin's twin Sandy, the Reconstructured Man, made of metal and transplanted part, who is also the Rekinstruckdead Man, a promise of technological finesse and an accompanying sacrifice of man's animal warmth and spiritual being. Milly is exterminated; Sandy is myth; Colin, declared human, breathes:

> I was safe, I had won.
> I had lost. I began losing the first day, when the news of the Act came to me and I signed the oath of agreement. Why of course, I said, I'll do anything you ask, naturally, it's the only way, the only solution, as I see it, to an impossible situation, as if situations needed solving, I mean, looked at objectively, as it must be seen to be. . . .
> The skimming words and phrases that need leave no footprints; one might never have been there, but one had spoken; and the black water lay undisturbed beneath the ice; and not a blade of grass quivered or a dead leaf whispered; a race of words had lived and died and left no relic of their civilization.
> As it must be seen to be, looked at objectively. . . .

The ironies multiply around each other. Language reasserts its fluid focus; the Society for the Prevention of Cruelty to Vegetation plants new pear trees on the Livingstone estate; the computer (not having been programmed for nostalgia) fails to account for the new enthusiasm for old abnormalities; and the Sleep Days cannot erase the time of the fires from the mind of Colin Monk. The mind survives. That her commitment to the spiritual independence of such perception is made so provocative is a tribute to Frame's arresting skill with images. She has an uncanny ability to arouse the diverse sensibilities of shifting moods and to entangle in language the wordless truths of her inner eye.

Language (always a motif in these works) is the central subject of the later novels *Living in the Maniototo,* with its artificial California setting, and the futuristic *The Carpathians.* The characters here contend not so much with a world outside themselves as with the kinds of world their imaginations create. Trained in words, they construct fantasies with the power of reality, often mistakenly accepting these ostensible "realities" as fixed truths. While most characters see only what they expect, some are given the gift of transcending their own verbal limitations. Understanding the *processes* of language is essential. Readers of the later novels are guided into limited insights: once the authoritarianism of their conventional expectations is exposed, they are offered a chance to glimpse alternative possibilities—within themselves, and consequently also in the "ordinary" world.

—W.H. New

FRAME, Ronald (William Sutherland)

Nationality: British. **Born:** Glasgow, 23 May 1953. **Education:** High School of Glasgow, 1962-71; University of Glasgow, 1971-75, M.A. 1975; Jesus College, Oxford, 1975-79, B.Litt. 1979.

Awards: Betty Trask award, for first novel, 1984; Samuel Beckett award, 1986; Television Industries award, 1986; Scottish Arts Council award, 1987. **Address:** c/o Hodder and Stoughton Ltd, 47 Bedford Square, London WC1B 3DP, England.

PUBLICATIONS

Novels

Winter Journey. London, Bodley Head, 1984; New York, Beaufort, 1986.
A Long Weekend with Marcel Proust: Seven Stories and a Novel. London, Bodley Head, 1986.
Sandmouth People. London, Bodley Head, 1987; as *Sandmouth,* New York, Knopf, 1988.
A Woman of Judah: A Novel and Fifteen Stories. London, Bodley Head, 1987; New York, Norton, 1989.
Penelope's Hat. London, Hodder and Stoughton, 1989; New York, Simon and Schuster, 1991.
Bluette. London, Hodder and Stoughton, 1990.
Underwood and After. London, Hodder and Stoughton, 1991.
Winter Journey. London, Sceptre, 1993.

Short Stories

Watching Mrs. Gordon and Other Stories. London, Bodley Head, 1985.
Walking My Mistress in Deauville: A Novella and Nine Stories. London, Hodder and Stoughton, 1992.
The Sun on the Wall: Three Novels. London, Hodder and Stoughton, 1994.

Uncollected Short Stories

"Rowena Fletcher," in *Winter's Tales 3* (new series), edited by Robin Baird-Smith. London, Constable, and New York, St. Martin's Press, 1987.
"Trio-3 Stories," in *20 Under 35,* edited by Peter Straus. London, Sceptre, 1988.

Plays

Paris: A Television Play; with Privateers (includes story). London, Faber, 1987.

Radio Plays: *Winter Journey,* 1985; *Twister,* 1986; *Rendezvous,* 1987; *Cara,* 1988; *Marina Bray,* 1989.

Television Plays: *Paris,* 1985; *Out of Time,* 1987.

*

Ronald Frame comments:

My characters are caught between an imagined freedom to determine their lives and the machinations of fate. I write about the circular nature of time as we experience it, about repetitions and coincidences working through generations. About social ritual as a mental stabilizer.

"History" to me is a kind of grand opera bouffe, scarcely believable sometimes. Social contact too is a complex game, perhaps a more serious one, of bluffs and evasions and all graduations of "truth."

I'm interested in the compelling power of imagination. My characters are inward, inhabiting a landscape of memory and desire, but are also ironically aware of how other people see them: I prefer my descriptions to come through, say, self-reflections in mirrors or window glass, or to be read in the facial reactions of others. I try to bring my third-person narratives as close to the first-person perspective as I can.

I hope I don't deal in heroes and villains. I write quite formally, but within that structure I mean to follow illogic where necessary; violence is implied, and it may appear the more desperate by contrast with this ambience of control.

While dissecting, I aim to preserve some essential mystery about my characters, so that not everything should be knowable, to themselves or to us. They partly live through received images—cinematic, for instance—and I appreciate that in writing about a period like the 1950s, as I frequently do, I'm approaching it through its own legend. I don't hold with research and verifiable realism; much more important to me is atmosphere, the evocation of a world—an approximately detailed but spiritually authentic world—which I can use to pit my individuals against the process of historical change. I hope the atmosphere will lure the reader, and induce for a short time a spell that might prove consistent and credible—and enjoyable.

*   *   *

Ronald Frame belongs to that select group of male novelists who write almost exclusively from the female point of view; indeed he has been described as the poet of *thé dansant,* obsessed with the minutiae of women's lives. Although in a novel like *Sandmouth People* he is capable of creating a whole range of characters reflecting different social strata and both sexes—in this case representative of a small English resort town during the 1950s—his preference is clearly for the female personality and it is noticeable that the most memorable characters are women. In this record of a day in the life of a non-descript English town, Frame creates the milieu of a social comedy in which his characters reveal themselves through their past and present lives, most notably Nanny Filbert whose hidden secrets are resurrected once more to haunt her. Other characters also remain in the memory: Lady Sybil de Castellet, representing the old monied aristocracy who dreams only of death, or Penelope Prentice, middle-class and wealthy who carries on a covert affair with Norman Pargiter, "Sandmouth's own success story," or Meredith Vane, the sub-Bloomsbury local author. All these, and a supporting cast of lesser lights, give the novel its knowing tone of a darker existence lying below the surface of a middle-class life so carefully depicted by Frame. It is indicative of the author's wit that he introduces a repertory company visiting Sandmouth to play Terence Rattigan's *Harlequinade,* a quintessential description of English middle-class life.

Although *Sandmouth People* is only his second novel—it was preceded by *Winter Journey* and by two collections of short stories—it is a good starting point for exploring Frame's fictional world. Similar to it in range of experience and in choice of background is *A Woman of Judah* which was published in a single volume with 15 short stories—Frame is an excellent creator of shorter fiction. Once again the time is the past, in this case England during one of the long hot summers of the 1930s, and the background is again peopled with a selection of suitably enigmatic characters. The story is told by Pendlebury, an elderly judge, reminiscing some 50 years after events which had a profound effect on him during his days as

an articled clerk in rural Essex. While that is the starting point, Frame's main interest is the friendship which Pendlebury strikes up with a couple called Davies: he is the local doctor and she appears to Pendlebury in all her "glowing well-scrubbed voluptuousness." Slowly but surely the novel starts to revolve around her and young Pendlebury is drawn ever more deeply into her life. Although he desires her she remains curiously aloof and yet, following her husband's suspicious death, she continues to haunt Pendlebury, allowing him no peace in the years to come. It is a strange and diverting novel which manages to seduce the reader into joining a claustrophobic and closed society inhabited by basically dishonest people.

In his next two novels, *Penelope's Hat* and *Bluette,* the themes which Frame had been exploring in his earlier fiction come to fruition in a new and precocious way. *Penelope's Hat* is basically the story of an English novelist who disappeared in 1979 leaving only her straw hat as a clue to her fate. Seven years later she resurfaces in Australia, but this is not a literary whodunit; rather it is a novel of layers which have to be drawn back to reveal the different stages of Penelope's life—her childhood in Borneo and the return to postwar Britain, Cornish summer holidays, her life as a young girl during World War II and the awakening of sexual desire. Different hats at various stages of her life punctuate the passing of the years and provide clues about Penelope but the novel's real fascination is the central character herself. Here Frame displays an uncanny ability to unravel the strands of her past, to make sense of her obsessions with expensive clothes, silk stockings, even hats. Luxury is a key word in Penelope's life and Frame revels in the goods which provide it—precious perfumes, fast cars, and designer-labelled clothes. Penelope might have hidden herself under several hats but Frame has the measure of her personality and the overall effect is of hearing whispered conversations behind half-closed doors.

It could be said that in *Bluette* Frame wrote a sequel; even the opening sentence is a promise of the exotic story that is about to unfold—"Follow the finger of Destiny." Like Penelope in the previous novel Catherine Hammond, the main character, occupies a world that is part reality and part make-believe and which flits disconcertingly between the two. At different stages she works in a nightclub, as an actress and, later still, in an upper-class brothel, but throughout she manages to retain her integrity, largely it has to be said through her ability to surround herself with the finer things of life. Vast, sprawling and eclectic, *Bluette* is both a saga and deeply touching story of a woman's search to find something which approaches fulfillment and happiness. It marks Frame as one of the most innovative writers of his generation.

—Trevor Royle

FRANCIS, Dick

Nationality: British. **Born:** Richard Stanley Francis in Tenby, Pembrokeshire, 31 October 1920. **Education:** Maidenhead County Boys' School, Berkshire. **Military Service:** Served as a Flying Officer in the Royal Air Force, 1940-45. **Family:** Married Mary Margaret Brenchley in 1947; two sons. **Career:** Amateur National Hunt (steeplechase) jockey, 1946-48; professional, 1948-57: National Hunt champion, 1953-54. Racing correspondent *Sunday Express,* London, 1957-73. Chairman, Crime Writers Association, 1973-74.

Awards: Crime Writers Association Silver Dagger award, 1965, Gold Dagger award, 1980, Diamond Dagger award, 1989; Mystery Writers of America Edgar Allan Poe award, 1969, 1981. L.H.D.: Tufts University, Medford, Massachusetts, 1991. O.B.E. (Officer, Order of the British Empire), 1984. **Agent:** John Johnson, 45-47 Clerkenwell Green, London EC1R 0HT, England. **Address:** P.O. Box 30866 S.M.B., Grand Cayman, British West Indies.

PUBLICATIONS

Novels

Dead Cert. London, Joseph, and New York, Holt Rinehart, 1962.
Nerve. London, Joseph, and New York, Harper, 1964.
For Kicks. London, Joseph, and New York, Harper, 1965.
Odds Against. London, Joseph, 1965; New York, Harper, 1966.
Flying Finish. London, Joseph, 1966; New York, Harper, 1967.
Blood Sport. London, Joseph, 1967; New York, Harper, 1968.
Forfeit. London, Joseph, and New York, Harper, 1969.
Enquiry. London, Joseph, 1970; New York, Harper, 1971.
Rat Race. London, Joseph, 1970; New York, Harper, 1971.
Bonecrack. London, Joseph, 1971; New York, Harper, 1972.
Smokescreen. London, Joseph, and New York, Harper, 1972.
Slay-Ride. London, Joseph, and New York, Harper, 1973.
Knock-Down. London, Joseph, 1974; New York, Harper, 1975.
High Stakes. London, Joseph, 1975; New York, Harper, 1976.
In the Frame. London, Joseph, 1976; New York, Harper, 1978.
Trial Run. London, Joseph, 1978; New York, Harper, 1979.
Whip Hand. London, Joseph, 1979; New York, Harper, 1980.
Reflex. London, Joseph, 1980; New York, Putnam, 1981.
Twice Shy. London, Joseph, 1981; New York, Putnam, 1982.
Banker. London, Joseph, 1982; New York, Putnam, 1983.
The Danger. London, Joseph, 1983; New York, Putnam, 1984.
Proof. London, Joseph, 1984; New York, Putnam, 1985.
Break In. London, Joseph, and New York, Putnam, 1986.
Bolt. London, Joseph, 1986; New York, Putnam, 1987.
Hot Money. London, Joseph, 1987; New York, Putnam, 1988.
The Edge. London, Joseph, 1988; New York, Putnam, 1989.
Straight. London, Joseph, and New York, Putnam, 1989.
Longshot. London, Joseph and New York, Putnam, 1990.
Comeback. London, Joseph, and New York, Putnam, 1991.
Driving Force. London, Joseph, and New York, Putnam, 1992.
Decider. London, Joseph, and New York, Putnam, 1993.
Wild Horses. London, Joseph, and New York, Putnam, 1994.
Come to Grief. London, Joseph, and New York, Putnam, 1995.

Uncollected Short Stories

"The Gift," in *Winter's Crimes 5,* edited by Virginia Whitaker. London, Macmillan, 1973.
"A Day of Wine and Roses," in *Sports Illustrated* (New York), May 1973.
"A Carrot for a Chestnut," in *Stories of Crime and Detection,* edited by Joan D. Berbirch. New York, McGraw Hill, 1974.
"The Big Story," in *Ellery Queen's Crime Wave.* New York, Putnam, and London, Gollancz, 1976.
"Nightmare," in *Ellery Queen's Searches and Seizures.* New York, Davis, 1977.
"Twenty-One Good Men and True," in *Verdict of Thirteen,* edited by Julian Symons. London, Faber, and New York, Harper, 1979.

"The Day of the Losers," in *Ellery Queen's Mystery Magazine* (New York), 9 September 1981.

Play

Screenplay: *Dead Cert,* 1974.

Other

The Sport of Queens: The Autobiography of Dick Francis. London, Joseph, 1957; revised edition, 1968, 1974, 1982, 1988; New York, Harper, 1969.
Lester: The Official Biography. London, Joseph, 1986; as *A Jockey's Life: The Biography of Lester Piggott,* New York, Putnam, 1986.

Editor, with John Welcome, *Best Racing and Chasing Stories 1-2.* London, Faber, 2 vols., 1966-69.
Editor, with John Welcome, *The Racing Man's Bedside Book.* London, Faber, 1969.

*

Critical Studies: *Dick Francis* by Melvyn Barnes, New York, Ungar, 1986; *Dick Francis* by J. Madison Davis, Boston, Twayne, 1989; *Dick Francis: Steeplechase Jockey* by Bryony Fuller, London, Joseph, 1994.

*   *   *

"Dying slowly of bone cancer the old man, shrivelled now, sat as ever in his great armchair, tears of lonely pain sliding down crepuscular cheeks." Hardly the opening words one expects in a top-selling thriller. Yet they are what Dick Francis chose to write at the start of his thirty-third novel, *Wild Horses,* and they tell us at once that the book will be more than a simple thriller. As, though in a less immediately obvious way, were each of its thirty-two predecessors.

There is perhaps a reason for this. Dick Francis did not come to fiction until he was approaching 40 and had already had a highly successful career in horse racing, ending as Champion jockey. Then, too, his life had not been without profound trouble. So it should be no surprise that his books, though designed first to entertain, each ask, with more pointedness or less, about one aspect of existence or another, the question, "How should we live?"

His method is to write a first version and then to read it aloud on to tape. I suspect that it is this process that accounts for the first of his virtues, the extreme easiness of his style. But easy reading generally comes from hard work first, and Francis has said that producing a novel is "just as tiring" as race riding. Besides the style, there are solid plots underneath the whole; concluding events have reasonable and likely causes. There is the continuing pull of the story, so that you are all the time wanting to know what will happen next. You get told what you want to know, too, and not something just a little bit different, a mistake less skilled authors often make. And at the same time you are made to want to know some new thing.

Then there is the language. Francis chooses straightforward words and never wastes them. (Though in his later books he uses, where needed, something more resonant, such as the "crepuscular" in the passage quoted earlier.) This virtue comes perhaps from his sense of timing, a gift he brought with him from racing to writing. The art of judging at just what moment to put a new fact into the reader's head, whether the fact is as important as the discovery of a body (most adroitly done in *Slay-Ride*) or just some necessary detail, is one that Francis shares with the masters of his craft.

But more important than the pacing, or plot, or even skillful story-telling, are the people writers invent for their stories. It is through people that the storyteller affects an audience. The people in Francis's books are as real as real-life people. Perhaps the best example of the kind of human being in his pages is the girl the hero either loves or comes to love. There is not one in every book (Francis has succeeded in bringing considerable variety to thrillers that might, with their customary Turf settings or references, have become formula affairs), but she has featured often enough to be easily identifiable as a certain sort of person. She will have some grave handicap, such as needing to live in an iron lung, or simply being widowed, or, as in *The Danger,* having been the victim of a cruel kidnapping. Many thriller writers would not dare to use such people because the reality of their situation would show up the tinsel world around them. But Francis is tough enough, and compassionate enough, to be able to write about such things.

His knowledge of the effects of tragedy comes from his own experience. While his wife was expecting their first child she was struck down by poliomyelitis and confined to an iron lung. It is from personal experience, too, that the typically stoic Francis hero comes. One of the few complaints that have been made about the books is that the hero (usually a different one each time, a jockey, a horse-owner, a trainer, a painter, a film star, an accountant, a photographer, a merchant banker) is too tough to be credible. But the fact is that most critics are not used to taking actual physical hard knocks; Francis, the jumps jockey, was. So if you look carefully at what he says happens when one of his heroes gets beaten up (as almost invariably they do) you find that, unlike many a pseudo-Bond or carbon-copy private eye, he gets really hurt and recovers only as fast as a physically fit and resilient man would in real life.

A Francis hero will have another important characteristic: he will be a man not scared of judging. He weighs up the police he meets and sees them for what they are: tough men, good men, nasty men, weak men, tough women, greedy women, sensitive women. And, more than this, the Francis books make judgments on a wider scale. By its particular choice of hero each one addresses some particular human dilemma. *Slay-Ride,* for instance, though it might seem to be no more than a good story about dirty work on the Norwegian race-courses, is in fact a book about what it is like to be the parent of children, to give these hostages to fortune, to be taking part in the continuing pattern of human existence. Similarly *Reflex* is about the need to accept inevitable change, and *Twice Shy* is about the acquiring of maturity.

The Edge, though an exciting puzzle set on a Canadian train with a cargo of bloodstock and a posse of actors playing a "murder mystery," is fundamentally about the need (to quote) "to retain order," and all its events reflect this. In *Straight* Francis takes the last yards of a jumps race course, "the straight," as illustrating a man facing the end of a particular career (a jockey, once again), but he also goes deeper by saying something about that human ideal of being "straight." It is such subtle themes that give the Francis books the weight that lifts them right out of the run of good but ordinary thrillers.

—H.R.F. Keating

FRAYN, Michael

Nationality: British. **Born:** Mill Hill, London, 8 September 1933. **Education:** Sutton High School for Boys; Kingston Grammar School, Surrey; Emmanuel College, Cambridge, B.A. 1957. **Military Service:** Served in the Royal Artillery and Intelligence Corps, 1952-54. **Family:** Married Gillian Palmer in 1960 (marriage dissolved 1990); three daughters. **Career:** Reporter, 1957-59, and columnist, 1959-62, the *Guardian,* Manchester and London; columnist, the *Observer,* London, 1962-68. Lives in London. **Awards:** Maugham award, 1966; Hawthornden prize, 1967; National Press award, 1970; *Evening Standard* award, for play, 1976, 1981, 1983, 1985; Society of West End Theatre award, 1977, 1982; British Theatre Association award, 1981, 1983; Olivier award, 1985; New York Drama Critics Circle award, 1986; Emmy award, 1990. Honorary Fellow, Emmanuel College, 1985. **Agent:** Elaine Greene Ltd., 37 Goldhawk Road, London W12 8QQ, England.

PUBLICATIONS

Novels

The Tin Men. London, Collins, 1965; Boston, Little Brown, 1966.
The Russian Interpreter. London, Collins, and New York, Viking Press, 1966.
Towards the End of the Morning. London, Collins, 1967; as *Against Entropy,* New York, Viking Press, 1967.
A Very Private Life. London, Collins, and New York, Viking Press, 1968.
Sweet Dreams. London, Collins, 1973; New York, Viking Press, 1974.
The Trick of It. London, Viking, 1989; New York, Viking, 1990.
A Landing on the Sun. London, Viking, 1991.
Now You Know. London, Viking, 1993.

Plays

Zounds!, with John Edwards, music by Keith Statham (produced Cambridge, 1957).
Jamie, On a Flying Visit (televised 1968). With *Birthday,* London, Methuen, 1990.
Birthday (televised 1969). With *Jamie, On a Flying Visit,* London, Methuen, 1990.
The Two of Us (includes *Black and Silver, The New Quixote, Mr. Foot, Chinamen*) (produced London, 1970; Ogunquit, Maine, 1975; *Chinamen* produced New York, 1979). London, Fontana, 1970; *Chinamen* published in *The Best Short Plays 1973,* edited by Stanley Richards, Radnor, Pennsylvania, Chilton, 1973; revised version of *The New Quixote* (produced Chichester, Sussex, and London, 1980).
The Sandboy (produced London, 1971).
Alphabetical Order (produced London, 1975; New Haven, Connecticut, 1976). With *Donkeys' Years,* London, Eyre Methuen, 1977.
Donkeys' Years (produced London, 1976). With *Alphabetical Order,* London, Eyre Methuen, 1977.
Clouds (produced London, 1976). London, Eyre Methuen, 1977.
The Cherry Orchard, adaptation of a play by Chekhov (produced London, 1978). London, Eyre Methuen, 1978.

Balmoral (produced Guildford, Surrey, 1978; revised version, as *Liberty Hall,* produced London, 1980; revised version, as *Balmoral,* produced Bristol, 1987). London, Methuen, 1987.

The Fruits of Enlightenment, adaptation of a play by Tolstoy (produced London, 1979). London, Eyre Methuen, 1979.

Make and Break (produced London, 1980; Washington, D.C., 1983). London, Eyre Methuen, 1980.

Noises Off (produced London, 1981; New York, 1983). London, Methuen, 1982; New York, French, 1985.

Three Sisters, adaptation of a play by Chekhov (produced Manchester and Los Angeles, 1985; London, 1987). London, Methuen, 1983.

Benefactors (produced London, 1984; New York, 1985). London, Methuen, 1984.

Wild Honey, adaptation of a play by Chekhov (produced London, 1984; New York, 1986). London, Methuen, 1984.

Number One, adaptation of a play by Jean Anouilh (produced London, 1984). London, French, 1985.

Plays I (includes *Alphabetical Order, Donkeys' Years, Clouds, Make and Break, Noises Off*). London, Methuen, 1986.

The Seagull, adaptation of a play by Chekhov (produced Watford, Hertfordshire, 1986). London, Methuen, 1986.

Clockwise (screenplay). London, Methuen, 1986.

Exchange, adaptation of a play by Trifonov (broadcast 1986; produced Southampton, Hampshire, 1989; London, 1990). London, Methuen, 1990.

Uncle Vanya, adaptation of a play by Chekhov (produced London, 1988). London, Methuen, 1987.

Chekhov: Plays (includes *The Seagull, Uncle Vanya, Three Sisters, The Cherry Orchard,* four vaudevilles). London, Methuen, 1988.

The Sneeze, adaptation of works by Chekhov (produced Newcastle-upon-Tyne and London, 1988). London, Methuen, and New York, French, 1989.

First and Last (televised 1989). London, Methuen, 1989.

Look Look (as *Spettattori,* produced Rome, 1989; as *Look Look,* produced London, 1990). London, Methuen, 1990.

Listen to This: 21 Short Plays and Sketches. London, Methuen, 1991.

Audience: A Play in One Act. London, French, 1991.

Here: A Play in Two Acts. London, French, 1994.

Screenplay: *Clockwise,* 1986.

Radio Play: *Exchange,* from a play by Trifonov, 1986.

Television Plays and Documentaries: *Second City Reports,* with John Bird, 1964; *Jamie, On a Flying Visit,* 1968; *One Pair of Eyes,* 1968; *Birthday,* 1969; *Beyond a Joke* series, with John Bird and Eleanor Bron, 1972; *Laurence Sterne Lived Here* (*Writers' Houses* series), 1973; *Imagine a City Called Berlin,* 1975; *Making Faces,* 1975; *Vienna: The Mask of Gold,* 1977; *Three Streets in the Country,* 1979; *The Long Straight* (*Great Railway Journeys of the World* series), 1980; *Jerusalem,* 1984; *First and Last,* 1989.

Other

The Day of the Dog (*Guardian* columns). London, Collins, 1962; New York, Doubleday, 1963.

The Book of Fub (*Guardian* columns). London, Collins, 1963; as *Never Put Off to Gomorrah,* New York, Pantheon, 1964.

On the Outskirts (*Observer* columns). London, Fontana, 1967.

At Bay in Gear Street (*Observer* columns). New York, Fontana, 1967.

Constructions (philosophy). London, Wildwood House, 1974.

Great Railway Journeys of the World, with others. London, BBC Publications, 1981; New York, Dutton, 1982.

The Original Michael Frayn: Satirical Essays, edited by James Fenton. Edinburgh, Salamander Press, 1983.

Editor, *The Best of Beachcomber,* by J.B. Morton. London, Heinemann, 1963.

*   *   *

Three of Michael Frayn's novels, the first, fourth, and fifth, are highly original, a satire and fantasies; the second and third, on the other hand, are conventional. The second, *The Russian Interpreter,* concerns an English research student in Moscow who serves as interpreter for a mysterious businessman (he seeks ordinary Russians for exchange visits), and the pair become involved with a Russian girl. Though Moscow's streets and weather are described, soon the action is moving swiftly. Books are stolen and sought, somebody is tricking somebody, espionage or smuggling is occurring, and we read on eagerly, awaiting explanations. Even when the student is imprisoned, Frayn focuses on his comic efforts to obtain a towel, and the novel remains a good, cheerful read.

The American title of the third novel points to opposing inertia and conformity; the English one, only a little more relevantly, to the subject of being in the mid-thirties (the hero "had spent his youth as one might spend an inheritance, and he had no idea of what he had bought with it"). Frayn's 37-year-old is a feature editor, worrying about repairs to his Victorian house with West Indian neighbors in S.W.23 and dreaming of escape, hopefully through appearances on a television panel. The plot is vehicle for comedy about a newspaper office, with a few shrewd observations, as when a girl reflects: "She wasn't a girl at all, in any sense that the fashion magazines would recognize. She was just a young female human being, fit only to be someone's cousin or aunt." Some passages suggest Frayn intends more, a fuller study of his hero's marriage and serious focus on the future of newspapers (a cynical, pushy graduate challenges the office's ways), but these are not pursued.

The Tin Men, the first book, is about the William Morris Institute of Automation Research and its eccentric scientists. A thin plotline turns on a new wing, the arrangements for the Queen to open it, and the TV company that plans to finance it. Most of the fun is about computers: the automating of football results because the Director believes "the main object of organized sports and games is to produce a profusion of statistics," the programmed newspaper, which prints the core of familiar stories such as "I Test New Car" and "Child Told Dress Unsuitable by Teacher," and Delphic I, the Ethical Decision Machine, which expresses its moral processes in units called pauls, calvins, and moses. Amid clever jokes, Frayn shows anxiety about the dangerous possibilities of computers and the limitations of the men responsible for them.

A Very Private Life begins "Once upon a time there will be a little girl called Uncumber." In her world, "inside people" remain all their lives in windowless houses, supplied by tube and tap and using drugs—Pax, Hilarin and Orgasmin—for every experience. In very brief chapters, Frayn explains how life has grown more private, first physically, then through drugs to cope with anger and uncertainty. Dissatisfied Uncumber meets a man through a wrong number on "holovision" and goes to the other side of the world to visit him. The compelling story is part fairy tale, part fantasy, part morality, so that we ask "Is it plausible?" and "What is the moral?" Frayn's inspiration was contemporary America, where he noticed dark glasses used to hide feelings, and city people buying disused farmhouses to be alone in. He touches on penology, longevity, the treatment of personality, but concentrates on technology making possible a new kind of isolation which excludes uncomfortable realities. And Frayn the moralist never dominates Frayn the story-teller.

Even better is *Sweet Dreams*—clever, entertaining, dazzling. A typical middle-aged, middle-class Londoner is killed and finds himself in a Heaven where he can fly, speak any language, change his age, and retrieve long-lost possessions. He is set to invent the Matterhorn, returns to England and writes an official report on its condition, drops out to the simple country life and bounces back as right-hand man to God (who proves to be a blend of Freddie Ayer and A.J.P. Taylor, and says "To get anything done at all one has to move in tremendously mysterious ways"). Slowly we realize the hero's Heavenly evolution is markedly similar to his earthly one. Frayn tells with wit and flourish his shrewd, sardonic and deceptively charming fable.

After 16 years during which Frayn established a big reputation as a playwright, and also translated Chekhov's plays, he returned to the novel in 1989 with a highly original work which, however, was linked more closely with a real world than the fantasies. *The Trick of It* is told through the letters of a young lecturer in English to a friend in Australia. These describe how he first meets the successful woman novelist he studies (he refers to her as a "MajWOOT," a major writer of our time) and marries her. He thinks that he can improve her next novel; is disturbed that the work which follows is about his mother and does not mention him; tries to write fiction himself, then discovers he has not "the trick of it"; finally values his letters (which we are reading) only to learn that the recipient has lost them. The tone is playful, yet Frayn has insights into creativity and the relation of critic to creator.

A Landing on the Sun is less ingenious, although it cleverly unfolds as narrative and explores significant ideas. A civil servant investigates a mysterious death from 17 years earlier, of a man involved with a "policy unit" on "the quality of life," headed by an Oxford philosopher. Frayn writes of the bureaucratic world while pursuing the concept of "happiness" and the intriguing way in which the searcher becomes caught up with the object of his search.

Now You Know is about an elderly man with a varied past who runs an organization devoted to freedom of information. Gradually all the characters emerge as having something to hide and as misinterpreting the behaviour of others. Frayn's subject this time seems to be truth and when lying may be justified. Audaciously, the novel resembles a play, being told in a series of dramatic monologues.

These three most recent novels have in common wit, elegance, page-turning storytelling, and a playful treatment of serious themes.

—Malcolm Page

FREELING, Nicolas

Nationality: British. **Born:** London, 3 March 1927. **Education:** Schools in England, Ireland, and France; attended University of Dublin. **Military Service:** Served in the Royal Air Force, 1945-47. **Family:** Married Cornelia Termes in 1954; four sons and one daughter. **Career:** Hotel and restaurant cook throughout Europe, 1945-60. **Awards:** Crime Writers Association Gold Dagger, 1964; Grand Prix de Roman Policier, 1964; Mystery Writers of America Edgar Allan Poe award, 1966. **Agent:** Curtis Brown, 162-168 Regent Street, London W1R 5TB, England; or, 10 Astor Place, New York, New York 10003, U.S.A. **Address:** Grandfontaine, 67130 Schirmeck, France.

PUBLICATIONS

Novels

Love in Amsterdam. London, Gollancz, and New York, Harper, 1962; as *Death in Amsterdam,* New York, Ballantine, 1964.
Because of the Cats. London, Gollancz, 1963; New York, Harper, 1964.
Gun Before Butter. London, Gollancz, 1963; as *Question of Loyalty,* New York, Harper, 1963.
Valparaiso (as F.R.E. Nicolas). London, Gollancz, 1964; as Nicolas Freeling, New York, Harper, 1965.
Double-Barrel. London, Gollancz, 1964; New York, Harper, 1965.
Criminal Conversation. London, Gollancz, 1965; New York, Harper, 1966.
The King of the Rainy Country. London, Gollancz, and New York, Harper, 1966.
The Dresden Green. London, Gollancz, 1966; New York, Harper, 1967.
Strike Out Where Not Applicable. London, Gollancz, and New York, Harper, 1967.
This Is the Castle. London, Gollancz, and New York, Harper, 1968.
Tsing-Boum. London, Hamish Hamilton, 1969; as *Tsing-Boom!,* New York, Harper, 1969.
Over the High Side. London, Hamish Hamilton, 1971; as *The Lovely Ladies,* New York, Harper, 1971.
A Long Silence. London, Hamish Hamilton, 1972; as *Aupres de ma Blonde,* New York, Harper, 1972.
A Dressing of Diamond. London, Hamish Hamilton, and New York, Harper, 1974.
What Are the Bugles Blowing For? London, Heinemann, 1975; as *The Bugles Blowing,* New York, Harper, 1976.
Lake Isle. London, Heinemann, 1976; as *Sabine,* New York, Harper, 1978.
Gadget. London, Heinemann, and New York, Coward McCann, 1977.
The Night Lords. London, Heinemann, and New York, Pantheon, 1978.
The Widow. London, Heinemann, and New York, Pantheon, 1979.
Castang's City. London, Heinemann, and New York, Pantheon, 1980.
One Damn Thing after Another. London, Heinemann, 1981; as *Arlette,* New York, Pantheon, 1981.
Wolfnight. London, Heinemann, and New York, Pantheon, 1982.
The Back of the North Wind. London, Heinemann, and New York, Viking Press, 1983.
No Part in Your Death. London, Heinemann, and New York, Viking, 1984.
A City Solitary. London, Heinemann, and New York, Viking, 1985.
Cold Iron. London, Deutsch, and New York, Viking, 1986.
Lady Macbeth. London, Deutsch, 1988.

Not as Far as Velma. London, Deutsch, and New York, Mysterious Press, 1989.

Sand Castles. London, Deutsch, 1989; New York, Mysterious Press, 1990.

Those in Peril. London, Deutsch, 1990; New York, Mysterious Press, 1991.

The Pretty How Town. London, and, as *The Flanders Sky,* New York, Scribner, 1991.

You Who Know. London, Little Brown, and New York, Mysterious Press, 1993.

The Seacoast of Bohemia. London, Little Brown, and New York, Mysterious Press, 1994.

Uncollected Short Stories

"The Beach Murder" May 1969, "Van der Valk and the Old Seaman" August 1969, "Van der Valk and the Four Mice" November 1969, "Van der Valk and the Young Man" December 1969, "Van der Valk and the High School Riot" March 1970, "Van der Valk and the Great Pot Problem" April 1970, "Van der Valk and the Wolfpack" August 1970, "Van der Valk and the False Caesar" February 1972, "Van der Valk and the Man from Nowhere" May 1972, "Van der Valk: The Train Watcher" April 1973, "Van der Valk and the Cavalier" January 1974, and "Van der Valk and the Spanish Galleon" August 1975, all in *Ellery Queen's Mystery Magazine* (New York).

"Van der Valk and the Two Pigeons," in *Ellery Queen's Magicians of Mystery.* New York, Davis, 1976.

Other

Kitchen Book. London, Hamish Hamilton, 1970; as *The Kitchen,* New York, Harper, 1970.

Cook Book. London, Hamish Hamilton, 1971.

The Kitchen Book and The Cook Book. Boston, Godine, 1990.

Criminal Convictions. Boston, Godine, and London, Owen, 1994.

*

Nicolas Freeling comments:

I am known as a crime novelist, an expression meaningless unless preceded by the word "commercial," meaning one who writes a series on a similar theme purely for entertainment value and to make a living. This describes my activities accurately enough, but not my ideas, nor my ambitions.

The advantage of this method is that the public for crime novels is large, appreciative, faithful, and generous. For this I am extremely grateful. There is a corresponding large disadvantage: that one is held to and bound by a rigid formula. Any originality or variation in theme is severely discouraged by a sharp drop in sales; this rigidity is the enemy of progress and growth. The writer is expected to concentrate exclusively upon telling an entertaining story, which is indeed the first basic element of the novelist's craft, and to introduce elements of mystery and suspense, melodramatic and largely artificial. The crime novelist who attempts art, his natural function and legitimate ambition, is asking for trouble.

Few commercial crime novelists make the attempt. Most are content to work in purely mechanical fashion, with no artistic or literary pretension whatever. The result is that they receive no critical attention—indeed they need none, for their public rarely bother with book reviews and has small interest in literary effort—and have small ambition, being content with a commercial operation and financial success.

It does not seem to me that the "crime" novelist should have such limited and materialistic ambitions.

Raymond Chandler agreed. He thought that it should be possible to write a crime "entertainment" which would rejoin the main stream of fiction. It would be about basic human themes and predicaments, of which crime, obviously a phenomenon of much social importance, with increasing impact upon the lives of any and all of us, would be the predominant subject, not necessarily the only subject.

I wish to attempt this ambitious design.

So far I have failed, and am not much ashamed because the ambition is high and the technical problems posed very considerable. Only the best European novelists—Stendhal, Dostoievsky, Conrad are the examples which come first to mind—have succeeded, and then often partially or imperfectly. A real human being, when involved in a traumatic situation such as a crime creates, behaves destructively—towards himself, towards society, and towards I may add the structure and coherence of a novel. This creates pitfalls for the novelist, the most obvious being to fall into mere sociological observation, documentary journalism in the interests of veracity. Also the behavior of a criminal (a man by definition set at odds with his society) raises wide moral, metaphysical, and philosophic problems. To disregard these is to write a play with no third act. Many technically accomplished writers dodge ethical problems of right and wrong on the ground of "tolerance" and because their own ethical, not to say religious beliefs are vague, and often because they are frightened to appear unfashionable.

It has become too fashionable to disregard the craftsmanship of form, shape, and rhythm, on the grounds that this is mere artificial mechanical contrivance. Such a notion is both immature and superficial: without form there is no art. The public insists, rightly, that a crime novel shall rebound continually in interest and excitement, and shall culminate, that is to say end in a climax.

I intend to keep trying.

(1995) When I wrote the [above] "selfcritical" comment, I was largely alone in the field, and in believing that crime fiction could take a more ambitious or "literary" path. Since then, several writers (e.g., Charyn, Constantine) have written very good crime fiction, outside the sex-and-violence gang. There were and are many in Europe, but who do not fit into the still widely accepted but narrow and impoverished "mystery" category.

*   *   *

Love in Amsterdam began Nicolas Freeling's career as a writer of novels which have an almost startling verisimilitude: their dialogue, setting, and action convey a feeling of exact observation at work. Freeling's Van der Valk is a Dutch detective who is human, individual, unorthodox. He has both compassion and a stern compulsion to solve the puzzles that are presented to him. His thoughts as he proceeds in his investigations are shown clearly to us; we share in his intellectual unraveling of problems of human behavior; and we believe in the reflections and the actions because the characters are real and the locale so effectively re-created. The flavor of Dutch life, the tempo of Amsterdam, the attitudes of the Dutch emerge convincingly in *Love in Amsterdam;* they are consolidated in *Because of the Cats,* an unfolding of the terrifying ruthlessness displayed by a gang of Dutch teenagers, morally corrupted and warped. This story is set partially in a seaside town of about sixty thousand people, half an hour by train from Amsterdam, "a new town, the pride of Dutch building and planning." Here is where Van der Valk displays his intuition: his process of investigation is hardly orthodox; he becomes friendly with the local whore, and understands the parents' relations with their children as he probes into their activities. The tempo of the novel is skillfully varied, and the final speeding up comes with an inevitability which holds the reader's horrified attention. The effect of Freeling's narration is heightened by the skeptical comments, the iconoclastic attitude with which he invests his policeman. Van der Valk's humanity gains by his lack of illusion.

This Is the Castle showed a deepening in Freeling's powers of characterization. The story revolves around the Swiss menage of a successful novelist, a neurotic yet likable man, whose tensions and foibles are seen through his own eyes and his wife's. The relationship between the novelist and his wife (to whom he is God), his secretary-mistress, his Spanish servants, his sons, and above all, his teenage daughter are unfolded with skill and sympathy; the visiting publisher and the American journalist arrive in time for a shooting of a macabre kind. This novel explores the blurred edges between the writer's imagination and the real events of his life: it does much to convey the effort of writing, the nervous strain between books, the dangerous seductiveness of the daydream. It moves away from the genre of *roman policier.*

Freeling's next *roman policier, Tsing-Boum,* carries on this deeper interest in human nature. The parallel with Simenon's writing becomes clearer, and indeed Van der Valk mentions Maigret twice in his story of the murder of the wife of a dull Dutch sergeant. She is machine-gunned in her dull municipal flat during a television gangster serial. She leaves behind a daughter whose father is unknown, and as Van der Valk investigates he finds himself puzzling out the connections between this Mevrouw Zomerlust and Dien Bien Phu. This allows Freeling to explore the French surrender there and the complex aftermath: a case of cowardice, revenge, blackmail, jealousy, violence. The Dutch police Commissaire, older now (and suffering from wounds incurred in an earlier novel), regards his quarry with sympathy as well as severity, and the pathos of the story is effectively built up, with constant reminders of humanity's frailties as well as moments of bravery.

In *Valparaiso* Freeling develops further his uniting of person and place. Into Porquerolles he brings a second rank Parisian film star. Her coming has an explosive effect upon Raymond, who has drifted around the Mediterranean for years, nourishing a dream of crossing the Atlantic in his boat the *Olivia.* The need to refit the *Olivia* tempts Raymond into crime. The story has a seeming inexorability. The slow lazy tempo of life in Porquerolles gives way to an equally Mediterranean urgency, and the narrative tautens as Raymond becomes more deeply emitted in the consequences of what seemed a perfect plan for the quick acquisition of the money which would enable him to act out his dream. In *Valparaiso* Freeling again shows his Simenon-like capacity to absorb atmosphere, to assess how far it is created by and how much it affects the human beings whose lives he presents in such concentrated description, such revealing action and inaction.

After ten novels centering on Van der Valk, Freeling developed a French equivalent, Henri Castang. The new setting is an imaginary French city, and in *The Night Lords* Freeling explored differences between French and British legal institutions, for a British High Court Judge and his family on holiday in France are caught up in the machinery of the law when their Rolls-Royce is found to have a naked female corpse in its boot.

Strasbourg is the scene for *The Widow* in which Van der Valk's widow Arlette, now married to an Englishman, become a private detective, and tumbles into a narcotics racket. The suspense is, as usual, well maintained and Arlette's mental processes deftly sketched in, amid the continuous and sinister action. Freeling manages to mix the detail well; his city is alive, Arlette and her husband lucky to do so. *Castang's City,* however, is deliberately not Strasbourg: but it is a convincing French provincial city, in which Freeling's Commissaire Richard is an elegant foil to Castang, and his Colette Delavigne, the judge of instruction, a charming, intelligent French woman. There is a good deal of information in this novel about French provincial life, and French ways of dealing with crime; but this does not intrude unduly on the action. The action requires the detailed information supplied copiously in dialogue for the story to come alive, which, thanks to the careful creation not only of inanimate detail but of human idiosyncracies, it does, most convincingly too. Freeling's own attitudes burst out of his narration from time to time, and this gives his story an extra credibility since we are asked to share in his detached examination of characters who move through the novel with an apparent reality of their own.

A City Solitary is sensitive in its explorations of a writer's feelings, thoughts, ideals lost and regained. It moves swiftly in its tale of a ruthless robbery, the casual cruelty which later turns into a kidnapping in which the hostages aid their captor, convincingly, in a dash across France to the Belgian border. It tells its story well, as Freeling's novels always have; it blends realistic details evocatively with the emotional intensity engendered by the strange though entirely credible situation, in which Walter, his wife, and his son are involved, as well as Miriam Lebreton, an attractive young French woman who is a skilled advocate. This is, as is usual with Freeling's fiction, more than a crime novel; it is a penetrating psychological study of the main character whose memories blend with his reflections upon his own past and present, as well as on the nature of human life. This provides surprises, just as the narration provides the suspense to be expected as Freeling unrolls the actions of the story in his usual masterly way.

In *Sand Castles,* another Van der Valk story, Freeling captures the ambiance of the coastal area of North Holland skillfully. Arlette is more to the fore in this account of her husband's holiday, which turns into an investigation of a nasty racket: indecent photographs of children. This, however, leads him into something even nastier, one of those sinister conspiracies: an apparent murder, an actual one, an attempted one, of Van der Valk and Arlette. Freeling's technique has changed. The narrative can be more staccato than before, the thoughts that run in Van der Valk's mind now race, and the dialogue is crisper, for we become involved in the thoughts, the actions, and the speech of a highly intelligent couple. As usual the places are pictured deftly, casually but convincingly: this, particularly to anyone who knows the locale, is the mark of Freeling's particular genius.

—A. Norman Jeffares

FREEMAN, Gillian

Nationality: British. **Born:** London, 5 December 1929. **Education:** The University of Reading, Berkshire, 1949-51, B.A. (honors) in English literature and philosophy, 1951. **Family:** Married

Edward Thorpe in 1955; two daughters. **Career:** Copywriter, C.J. Lytle Ltd., London, 1951-52; schoolteacher in London, 1952-53; reporter, *North London Observer,* 1953; literary secretary to Louis Golding, 1953-55. Lives in London. **Agent:** Richard Scott Simon, Anthony Sheil Associates, 43 Doughty Street, London WC1N 2LF, England.

PUBLICATIONS

Novels

The Liberty Man. London, Longman, 1955.
Fall of Innocence. London, Longman, 1956.
Jack Would Be a Gentleman. London, Longman, 1959.
The Leather Boys (as Eliot George). London, Blond, 1961; New York, Guild Press, 1962.
The Campaign. London, Longman, 1963.
The Leader. London, Blond, 1965; Philadelphia, Lippincott, 1966.
The Alabaster Egg. London, Blond, 1970; New York, Viking Press, 1971.
The Marriage Machine. London, Hamish Hamilton, and New York, Stein and Day, 1975.
Nazi Lady: The Diaries of Elisabeth von Stahlenberg 1933-1948. London, Blond and Briggs, 1978; as *The Confessions of Elisabeth von S,* New York, Dutton, 1978; as *Diary of a Nazi Lady,* New York, Ace, 1979.
An Easter Egg Hunt. London, Hamish Hamilton, and New York, Congdon and Lattès, 1981.
Love Child (as Elaine Jackson). London, W.H. Allen, 1984.
Termination Rock. London, Unwin Hyman, 1989.

Uncollected Short Stories

"The Soufflé" in *Courier* (London and New York), May 1955.
"Pen Friend," in *Woman's Own* (London), December 1957.
"The Changeling," in *London Magazine,* April 1959.
"The Polka (Come Dance with Me)," in *Woman's Own* (London), December 1962.
"Kicks," in *Axle Quarterly* (London), Summer 1963.
"Dear Fred," in *King* (London), June 1965.
"Venus Unobserved," in *Town* (London), July 1967.
"A Brave Young Woman," in *Storia 3,* edited by Kate Figes. London, Pandora Press, 1989.

Plays

Pursuit (produced London, 1969).

Screenplays: *The Leather Boys,* 1963; *That Cold Day in the Park,* 1969; *I Want What I Want,* with Gavin Lambert, 1972; *Day after the Fair,* 1986.

Radio Plays: *Santa Evita,* 1973; *Field Day,* 1974; *Commercial Break,* 1974.

Television Plays: *The Campaign,* 1965; *Man in a Fog,* 1984; *Hair Soup,* 1991.

Ballet Scenarios: *Mayerling,* 1978; *Intimate Letters,* 1978; *Isadora,* 1981.

Other

The Story of Albert Einstein (for children). London, Vallentine Mitchell, 1960.
The Undergrowth of Literature. London, Nelson, 1967; New York, Delacorte Press, 1969.
The Schoolgirl Ethic: The Life and Work of Angela Brazil. London, Allen Lane, 1976.
Ballet Genius: Twenty Great Dancers of the Twentieth Century, with Edward Thorpe. Wellingborough, Northamptonshire, Thorsons, 1988.

*

Manuscript Collection: University of Reading, Berkshire.

Critical Study: *Don't Never Forget* by Brigid Brophy, London, Cape, 1966, New York, Holt Rinehart, 1967; *Friends and Friendship* by Kay Dick, London, Sidgwick and Jackson, 1974.

Gillian Freeman comments:

I have always been concerned with the problems of the individual seen in relation to society and the personal pressures brought to bear because of moral, political or social conditions and the inability to conform. This is reflected in all my work to date, although I have never set out to propound themes, only to tell stories. After 12 novels I am able to make my own retrospective assessment, and I find recurring ideas and links of which I was unconscious at the time of writing.

My first six novels are in some way concerned with the class system in England, either as a main theme (*The Liberty Man, Jack Would Be a Gentleman*) or as part of the background (*The Leather Boys*). Although the rigid class patterns began to break up soon after the last war and have changed and shifted, they still remain subtle delineations that I find absorbing. In *The Liberty Man* there is the direct class confrontation in the love-affair between the middle-class school teacher and the cockney sailor. In *Fall of Innocence* I was writing about the sexual taboos of the middle class attacked by an outsider, a young American girl. This element, the planting of an alien into a tight social structure, reappears constantly in my novels—atheist Harry into the Church of England parish in *The Campaign;* the Prossers in *Jack Would Be a Gentleman* from one class area into an elevated one in the same town; the cross-visiting of Freda and Derek in *The Liberty Man;* strongest of all, Hannah in *The Alabaster Egg,* transplanted from Munich of the 1930s to postwar London. This is the theme pursued in *The Marriage Machine,* with Marion, from rural England, unable to adapt completely to life in the United States and battling against her-in-laws (also uprooted from Europe) for the mind of her young son. In *Jack Would Be a Gentleman* the theme is the sudden acquisition of money without the middle- or upper-class conditioning which makes it possible to deal with it. *The Campaign* has the background of a seedy seaside parish, against which the personal problems of a cross-section of individuals (all involved in a fund-raising campaign) are exacerbated; God and Mammon, the permissive society, the Christian ethics. *The Leather Boys* is the story of two working-class boys who have a homosexual affair; *The Leader* explores fascism in a modern democracy, which, on both sides of the Atlantic, throws up a sufficient number of people who are greedy, ruthless, intolerant, bigoted and perverted enough to gravitate towards the extreme right. In *Nazi Lady* the socially climbing heroine, Elisabeth, records in her diary her joy in meeting Hitler. in *The Alabaster Egg,* which I consider my best work to date, Hannah also meets Hitler and there is another fictitious diary, an historical memoir of a lover of Ludwig II. This earlier novel contains several of my recurring themes—fascism, homosexuality, the main characters all victims of the prevailing political scenes. There are parallels between Hitler's Germany and Bismarck's reflecting in two love affairs which end in betrayal. I used real as well as imaginary characters, linking fiction and reality closely, and did so, too, in *Nazi Lady. An Easter Egg Hunt* is concerned with the disappearance of a schoolgirl during Word War I—another character wrenched from her normal environment, a refugee from France now living in England's Lake District where the war harshly changes the lives of the four main protagonists. *Love Child,* in the psychological thriller genre, is about the problem of surrogate motherhood in both England and the United States. Once more, the heroine, feckless and easygoing Gwen, is thrust into a new society. In *Termination Rock* the narrator, Joanna, finds herself with an alter ego, Victorian Ann, the two stories paralleled as both of them travel to and in America. Whether Joanna's journey is into the paranormal or whether there is a psychological and logical explanation, is for the reader to decide. This novel, with its double time scale, has links with both *The Alabaster Egg* and *The Marriage Machine,* and also continues my fascination with the United States. *The Marriage Machine, Love Child,* and *Termination Rock,* in different ways and in different periods, deal with the adaptation to life in North America.

My choice of Einstein for a children's biography—a highly individual man whose life was spent in trying to eliminate the frontiers of prejudice—and the thesis of *The Undergrowth of Literature* (the need for fantasy in the sexually disturbed) illustrate my interest in and compassion for those unable to conform to the accepted social mores. To some extent my film writing has also dealt with social and sexual distress, as did my short play for The National Theatre, *Pursuit.* The ballet scenarios for Kenneth MacMillan, although the subjects were not selected by me, again present individuals who are "outsiders"—Prince Rudolf in *Mayerling* and the strong, passionate and wayward Isadora Duncan.

*   *   *

Since her first novel, *The Liberty Man,* Gillian Freeman has shown an outstanding ability to get inside the skin of characters from very different social backgrounds. It should be remembered that *The Liberty Man* was considerably in advance of its time in its truly empathic conveyance of a working-class character (Derek, a naval rating) who becomes involved in an affair with an intellectual and middle-class woman. This book appeared when the prevailing literary method of portraying working-class people still tended to be by projecting the image of the well-intentioned but clumsy, scruffy, and inarticulate "little man." The unusual power of *The Liberty Man,* however, does not rest only in its portrait of Derek, but in his relationship with Freda, the middle-class school teacher, through which Freeman analyses resonances between people from extremely diverse social groups, and between the inner experiences of the individual and the externals that he sees in operation around him.

Freeman is, in a sense, the writer of the archetypal anti-Cinderella story. She has acute honesty and a flair for precise, almost wickedly unerring observation of detail and motive. In her novels, despite changes of fortune (*Jack Would Be a Gentleman* is a good example) people's lives are *not* transformed, and their basic inad-

equacies remain. Her novels are preoccupied with frustration and fallibility; she frequently manages, however, by well-timed injections of compassion, to lift a book's mood of inadequacy and doubt into warmth and well-being that are almost physical in the strength of their expression.

Freeman observes and analyses the vagaries of human nature but rarely makes moral judgments. She highlights complexities in apparently "ordinary" or superficial characters, and makes her jaded sophisticates capable of sudden deep and challenging emotions. She explores conflicts between ambition and conscience, and the primitive feelings that underlie the veneer of our civilization. Permeating some of her narratives is a sense that the protective social structure we strive to perpetuate is deeply flawed. She is, in this context, extremely concerned with nonconformity—the healthily truculent attitudes of the working classes; the bewildered responses of the unconscious homosexual; the rootlessness of the young that can sometimes find expression only in violence (*The Leather Boys*).

Freeman's novels are synonymous with power and panache, though these qualities are often expressed in low-key and even throwaway language. She is in this respect quintessentially English, and until *The Alabaster Egg* her preoccupations were with issues particularly pertinent to English society. *The Alabaster Egg* is her most trenchant and telling work. It is about the pursuit of political power, and this is counterpointed by a probing of the exploitation of human beings at the personal level. Her setting is wider than in the earlier novels; it is no longer England but Europe—or the world—and the focus, significantly, is Germany—the vortex of 20th-century "civilization," corruption, and decay.

Her earlier stories were concerned with displacement, in particular with the catalytic effect of an alien presence in a close-knit and apparently secure social structure (*Fall of Innocence, The Campaign*). *The Alabaster Egg* highlights an ironic reversal of this theme of dissociation; Hannah, the book's heroine, has the misfortune to be a Jew in Nazi Germany. She does not, however, see herself as an alien. In her own estimation she is as much a German as a Jew. Her situation, of course, stresses one of the most pernicious effects of Nazi racist policies—the enforced separation of certain people from their own communities, from the only group to which they had felt a sense of belonging. Hannah's tragic but resilient story has parallels with happenings in the time of Bismarck. Her love affair with a "real" German is illuminated by her readings from the diary of the homosexual lover of King Ludwig II. This affair—like Hannah's—ends in bewilderment and betrayal.

Having written compellingly from the viewpoint of a sensitive and intelligent Jewish woman caught up in the hideousness of fascism, Freeman goes on to write as if from the inside about a passionate supporter of Hitler's ideologies in *Nazi Lady.* This originally appeared as a factual diary; it was so convincing that one critic pronounced it "unquestionably genuine." Genuineness, of course, does not have to be a matter of fact but of mood, and in this sense *Nazi Lady* is genuine, although it is a work of fiction. Freeman says that it was inspired by her publisher's observations on the extraordinary dichotomy between the anguishes of the battles of Stalingrad and the "good life" enjoyed at the same time by influential civilians in Germany.

In *Nazi Lady* the heroine's initial enthusiasm for Nazism is presented with subtlety and conviction. Elisabeth is German; to English readers she is possibly a slightly glamorized amalgam of Marlene Dietrich, Irma Greeser, and whatever the Nazi slogan "Strength through Joy" suggested. As well as being brittle she is beautiful, and her experiences are macabrely fascinating.

Freeman combines fact and fiction with aplomb. (For example, Elisabeth has to accept expert but distasteful seduction by Goebbels in order to save her husband from the rigors of the Russian Front.) In the end, all her convictions are reduced to ashes, as both her son and her husband become victims of Nazi ruthlessness and fanaticism. But she survives—and marries an American from the liberating forces.

An Easter Egg Hunt, is set in a girls' school during Word War I, and it is not only an intriguing mystery story on its own account but memorable for its evocation of Angela Brazil's schoolgirl adventures. School was, of course, regarded by Angela Brazil as the (essentially neatly ordered) world in microcosm; but Freeman recognizes bizarre and eccentric elements even in the innately conservative and sheltered confines of school life. She adeptly creates and manipulates her adolescent characters without excesses or sentimentality, and they are in fact far removed from Brazil's colorful but artless embodiments of schoolgirlishness.

The narrative style of all Freeman's novels is perfectly suited to her sensitive but down-to-earth approach. Her prose is robust and direct; her plots are constructed with economy and excellence, and the stories seem to vibrate with energy and insight.

—Mary Cadogan

FRENCH, Marilyn

Nationality: American. **Born:** Marilyn Edwards in New York City, 21 November 1929. **Education:** Hofstra College (now University), Hempstead, Long Island, B.A. 1951, M.A. 1964; Harvard University, Cambridge, Massachusetts, Ph.D. 1972. **Family:** Married Robert M. French in 1950 (divorced 1967). **Career:** Instructor, Hofstra University, 1964-68; assistant professor of English, College of the Holy Cross, Worcester, Massachusetts, 1972-76; artist-in-residence, Aspen Institute for Humanistic Study, 1972; Mellon fellow, Harvard University, 1976. **Agent:** Sheedy Literary Agency, 41 King Street, New York, New York 10014, U.S.A.

PUBLICATIONS

Novels

The Women's Room. New York, Summit, 1977; London, Deutsch, 1978.
The Bleeding Heart. New York, Summit, and London, Deutsch, 1980.
Her Mother's Daughter. New York, Summit, and London, Heinemann, 1987.
Our Father. Boston, Little Brown, 1994; New York, Penguin, 1995.

Other

The Book as World: James Joyce's Ulysses. Cambridge, Massachusetts, Harvard University Press, 1976; London, Abacus, 1982.
Shakespeare's Division of Experience. New York, Summit, and, London, Cape, 1981.
Beyond Power: On Women, Men, and Morals. New York, Summit, and London, Cape, 1985.

The War against Women. New York, Summit, and London, Hamilton, 1992.

* * *

The narrator of Marilyn French's phenomenally best-selling first novel, *The Women's Room,* leaves the subject of men's pain "to those who know and understand it, to Philip Roth and Saul Bellow and John Updike and poor wombless Norman Mailer." French's own most extensive treatment of male suffering appears not in her three long feminist fictions but in *The Book as World: James Joyce's Ulysses,* where she describes Stephen Dedalus's emotional paralysis and Leopold Bloom's moral heroism. By accepting his "participation in the human condition," Stephen can accept his own feelings and act in ways that will end his crippling numbness. "Such an end," says French,"is not equivalent to reaching some new Jerusalem where everything will become clear; it offers merely survival, the ability to live and grow." Stephen thus anticipates the shell-shocked female survivors of French's novels, who pass through their own nightmarish versions of Joyce's Nighttown.

French suggests that the endurance of Bloom and Stephen is "an affirmation of the human race;" the endurance of her protagonists—Mira, Dolores, and Anastasia—is a tribute to the "feminine principle" that offers the race's best hope for the future. In *Beyond Power,* French calls for a new synthesis of traditionally conflicting female and male values: "For women, as for society at large, it is necessary to reach out both to the dishonored body, discredited emotion, to blood and milk; and to self-control, power-to, assertive being in the world. Only by incorporating both can we attain integrity." French attributes much of the world's suffering to an obsession with patriarchal structures of power, a major concern too of her second novel, *The Bleeding Heart.* Pleasure, in the deep sense of felicity, must replace power as society's highest good. French's fictional women have several experiences of delight. Among the most memorable is the New Year's Eve dance in *The Women's Room,* where men and women, young and fortyish, join in a circle of "color and motion and love." Mira returns to the image as "a moment of grace vouchsafed them by something divine." Unfortunately, episodes of mutual nurturance are much less common than years of lonely anguish. French's central characters undergo agonies so severe that, as she says of Bloom and Stephen, "survival alone is a triumph."

Even as a girl, Mira Ward realizes that "Women are victims by nature." Almost raped by her boyfriend Lanny, she tearfully marries the gentle and intelligent Norm. Disinterested in sex and horrified at Mira's dreams of someday earning a doctoral degree, Norm makes her feel like "a child who had stumbled, bumbled into the wrong house." Almost two decades later, the divorced Mira still feels out of place even though she is finally working toward her long-deferred goal. French's novel opens in 1968 with Mira uneasily enrolled at Harvard. Supported by a women's group, which includes the outspoken Val, Mira gains a strong sense of woman's value that enables her to survive the rape of Val's daughter, Val's death in a confrontation between radical feminists and police, and even the break-up of her passionate affair with Ben, who asks her to delay her career by accompanying him to Africa and bearing his child. Only in the closing pages does it become clear that the somewhat cynical narrator—who considers her protagonist to be "a little ridiculous"—is actually Mira, now "unbearably alone" as she walks a Maine beach and waits for the fall semester to begin at the community college where she teaches English. Haunted by nightmares of a vacant-eyed man who pursues her with a phallic pipe and pen-knife, Mira nevertheless feels that it is "time to begin something new, if I can find the energy, if I can find the heart."

French's second novel lacks the narrative complexity, the large groups of characters, and the scope of *The Women's Room,* which traced Mira's growth from a naïve 1950s housewife to an independent woman of the 1970s against the cultural backdrop of the Eisenhower years, the assassinations of the Kennedys and Martin Luther King, Kent State, and My Lai. A tenured professor and author of two books, Dolores Durer—the bleeding heart of the title—seems to have achieved even greater success than Mira in recovering from an even worse marriage and divorce. Yet she feels like a "walking robot," and, celibate for years, her body is "dying of thirst." An affair with Victor Morrissey, an American businessman whom Dolores meets in England, relieves the sexual dryness but reconfirms her belief that "Women always end up paying" because the world follows "Men's rules, still, always." Victor does, however, encourage Dolores to share with him her most terrible memory, the suicide of her daughter Elspeth, thus enabling her to feel again. Freed from her repeated identification with Lot's pillar-of-salt wife, Dolores refuses a potentially numbing marriage to Victor (as Mira refused Ben) and prepares to return to her students and good woman friends.

Her Mother's Daughter, French's most experimental novel, incorporates struggles of three generations: Anastasia Stevens, a world-famous photographer; Belle, her often silent mother, who has a symbolically "defective heart;" and her immigrant grandmother, Frances. Striving to avoid the misery of her mother and grandmother, the twice-divorced Anastasia comes closer than French's earlier women to achieving the freedoms more usually associated with a man's life, but in learning a masculine self-control she so thoroughly masters her feelings that she "cannot find them myself." Anastasia's progress toward emotional recovery begins with the women's movement, a lesbian relationship with Clara Traumer, her reconciliation with the son and daughter who have grieved her, and—perhaps most significant—her mother's unprecedented words of praise: "I will never forget how sweet you were to me." French's three novels illuminate a distinction she makes between the "feminine" plots of comedy and the "masculine" plots of tragedy in "Shakespeare's Division of Experience": "We lose, but we replace, we substitute: we go on. This is as profound a truth as that we lose and cannot replace, we die."

—Joan Wylie Hall

FRIEDMAN, Bruce Jay

Nationality: American. **Born:** New York City, 26 April 1930. **Education:** De Witt Clinton High School, Bronx, New York; University of Missouri, Columbia, 1947-51, B.A. in journalism 1951. **Military Service:** United States Air Force, 1951-53: Lieutenant. **Family:** Married 1) Ginger Howard in 1954 (divorced 1977), three children; 2) Patricia J. O'Donohue in 1983, one daughter. **Career:** Editorial director, Magazine Management Company, publishers, New York, 1953-64. Visiting professor of literature, York College, City University, New York, 1974-76. **Address:** P.O. Box 746, Water Mill, New York 11976, U.S.A.

PUBLICATIONS

Novels

Stern. New York, Simon and Schuster, 1962; London, Deutsch, 1963.
A Mother's Kisses. New York, Simon and Schuster, 1964; London, Cape, 1965.
The Dick. New York, Knopf, 1970; London, Cape, 1971.
About Harry Towns. New York, Knopf, 1974; London, Cape, 1975.
Tokyo Woes. New York, Fine, 1985; London, Abacus, 1986.
The Current Climate. New York, Atlantic Monthly Press, 1989.

Short Stories

Far from the City of Class and Other Stories. New York, Frommer-Pasmantier, 1963.
Black Angels. New York, Simon and Schuster, 1966; London, Cape, 1967.
Let's Hear It for a Beautiful Guy and Other Works of Short Fiction. New York, Fine, 1984.
Collected Short Fiction. New York, Fine, 1995.

Uncollected Short Story

"Pitched Out," in *Esquire* (New York), July 1988.

Plays

23 Pat O'Brien Movies, adaptation of his own short story (produced New York, 1966).
Scuba Duba: A Tense Comedy (produced New York, 1967). New York, Simon and Schuster, 1968.
A Mother's Kisses, music by Richard Adler, adaptation of the novel by Friedman (produced New Haven, Connecticut, 1968).
Steambath (produced New York, 1970). New York, Knopf, 1971.
First Offenders, with Jacques Levy (also co-director: produced New York, 1973).
A Foot in the Door (produced New York, 1979).
Sardines (produced New York, 1994).
Have You Spoken to Any Jews Lately? (produced New York, 1995).

Screenplays: *Stir Crazy,* 1980; *Splash,* with others, 1984; *Dr. Detroit,* with others, 1988.

Other

The Lonely Guy's Book of Life. New York, McGraw Hill, 1978.
The Slightly Older Guy. New York, Simon and Schuster, 1995.

Editor, *Black Humor.* New York, Bantam, and London, Corgi, 1965.

*

Critical Study: *Bruce Jay Friedman* by Max F. Schulz, New York, Twayne, 1974.

Theatrical Activities:
Director: **Play**—*First Offenders* (co-director, with Jacques Levy), New York, 1973.

*   *   *

For good or ill, Bruce Jay Friedman seems destined to be forever linked with the literary phenomenon of the 1960s known as "black humor." In his foreword to *Black Humor,* an anthology he edited in 1965, Friedman ducks the business of rigid definition, insisting that each of the 13 writers represented is separate and unique, but he does suggest that "if there is a despair in this work, it is a tough, resilient brand and might very well end up in a Faulknerian horselaugh." For Friedman, style is a function, an extension, of the disorderly world that surrounds him. As he puts it, there is a "fading line between fantasy and reality, a very fading line, a god-damned, almost invisible line." Friedman's slender fiction—as well as his drama and his screenplays—are pitched on this precarious edge. In such a world, the *New York Times* is "the source and fountain and bible of black humor," while television news convinces Friedman, perhaps too easily, that "there is a new mutative style of behavior afoot, one that can only be dealt with by a new, one-foot-in-the-asylum style of fiction." We are hardly surprised when a contemporary novelist declines rather than develops, when he or she adds increasingly smaller additions to the original house of fiction. For Friedman, *Stern* doubled as his debut and his most accomplished novel. It's all there in *Stern:* the uneasy Jewishness, the ulcers, the suburban situation. But the sense of terror it generates is actualized, altogether convincing, located in a compactness that never quite appears again in Friedman's fiction.

Stern is, in short, the angst-ridden apartment dweller, nose pressed against suburbia while visions of extra rooms dance in his head: "As a child he had graded the wealth of people by the number of rooms in which they lived. He himself had been brought up in three in the city and he fancied people who lived in four were so much more splendid than himself." Alas, as Stern quickly discovers, he is not one of the Chosen People who can make the exodus from the bondage of crowded apartments to the Promised Land of suburban living. He is, at best, a reluctant pioneer, a man who misses the cop on the beat, the delicatessen at the corner.

Stern is a contemporary variation on the classical schlemiel, one victimized by darkly comic fantasies of his own making, rather than by accidents. Besieged by problems on all sides—caterpillars devour his garden, neighborhood dogs attack him on a nightly basis—Stern pictures the police as "large, neutral-faced men with rimless glasses who would accuse him of being a newcomer making vague troublemaking charges." Especially if he complains about the threatening dogs: "They would take him into a room and hit him in his large, white, soft stomach." And so he swallows his impulse to protest, only to imagine himself "fighting silently in the night with the two gray dogs, lasting eight minutes and then being found a week later with open throat by small Negro children." Friedman's subsequent works confirmed two facts: that he is equally at home in the novel (*A Mother's Kisses*), the short story (*Far from the City of Class*), or the play (*Steambath*); and that he is a flashy writer of limited scope. For example, in *A Mother's Kisses,* the psychodynamics of black humor shrink to Momism and the difficulties of getting into college. As always, excess is the heart of Friedman's matter:

He [Joseph] saw himself letting a year go by, then reapplying only to find himself regarded as a suspicious leftover fellow, his application tossed onto a pile labeled "repeaters," not to be read until all the fresh new ones had been gone through. Year after year would slip away, until finally, at thirty-seven, he would enter night school along

with a squad of newly naturalized Czechs, sponsored by labor unions and needing a great many remedial reading sessions.

Joseph's American-Jewish mother begins as a vulgar cliché, and Friedman's touch merely raises it to a second power. When Joseph went away to summer camp, mother struck a camp of her own just across the lake; when Joseph finally sets off for Kansas Land Grant Agricultural (where courses like "the History and Principles of Agriculture" and "Feed Chemistry" comprise the curriculum) Mom insists on coming too.

And yet, there are moments in *A Mother's Kisses* when the terrors of contemporary life are rendered with sharp, metaphysical precision:

A long line had formed in the men's room, leading to a single urinal, which was perched atop a dais. When a fellow took too long, there were hoots and catcalls such as "What's the matter, fella, can't you find it?" As his turn came nearer, Joseph began to get nervous. He stepped before the urinal finally, feeling as though he had marched out onto a stage. He stood there a few seconds, then zipped himself up and walked off. The man in back of him caught his arm and said, "You didn't go. I watched."

Little of Kakfa's flavor is lost in the translation. And the hand that descends to unmask our smallest deception strikes us as real, all too real.

The problem, of course, is that Friedman throws off brilliantly comic moments without the inclination to turn them into sustained, comic fictions. He remains the perennial sophomore, chortling at what can only be called sophomoric jokes. In *The Dick,* for example, Friedman means to draw a parallel between sexuality and crime-fighting, as the title of the novel and the name of its beleaguered protagonist, LePeters, suggest. One bad joke begets another. When LePeters has his psychological interview, the conversation owes more to Hollywood than to Henry James:

"What do you think all these guns around her represent?" he asked LePeters in a lightning change of subject.

"Oh, I don't know," said LePeters. "Phalluses, I guess." Actually, he had dipped into a textbook or two and was taking a not-so-wild shot.

"Not bad," said Worthway, lifting one crafty finger in the Heidelberg style and making ready to leave. "But some of them are pussies, too."

About Harry Towns focuses on a moderately successful screenwriter, one given to verbal razzle-dazzle, urbane irony, and just enough innocence to be amazed about the money producers stuff into his pockets and the girls who fall into his bed. One shorthand way of putting it might be this: the Sexual Revolution caught Harry Towns with his pants up. The result is a man in his forties (formerly married, now anguishing through a permanent "temporary separation") trying too hard to be trendy and protesting too much about enjoying it. No doubt Friedman's biographer will, one day, point out just how "biographical" the stories in fact were.

In *Tokyo Woes,* Friedman introduces Mike Halsey, a more circumspect protagonist—at least in the sense that he is more routinized, more circumspect, than the likes of Harry Towns: "Normally, Mike was a fellow who liked to stay close to his beat. Once he bought newspapers in one place, that's where he bought them." In short, Halsey "was a fellow who kept to the center of the road, although he had to admit that every time he swerved off a bit it had worked out nicely." A short chapter later (indeed, all the chapters in *Tokyo Woes* run to fewer than ten pages), Halsey is on his way to Tokyo, where comic misadventures and sexual peccadilloes will follow him like the night the day. For Friedman followers, the highjinks are all to predictable, all too self-consciously offered up.

With *The Current Climate,* Friedman returns to Harry Towns, the Hollywood wordsmith he had invented as a comic projection of the writing business and himself. Harry is still crazy after all these years—still frisky, still foolish, and still likely to be found in a writers' bar where sex and drugs are the major attractions.

Friedman relates Harry's escapades in short, choppy sentences and with appropriately coarse language, but if the result has its comic moments, they tell us precious little about the scriptwriting racket and even less about who the Harry Towns under the highjinks really is.

For nearly two decades, Friedman has been a steady worker in the vineyards of Hollywood. One learned to look quickly as his name, and the other credits, rolled over the silver screen. The heyday of the black humorist was over. Some, like Ken Kesey, dropped out. And some, like Bruce Jay Friedman, apparently found the medium their "message" had been looking for all along.

—Sanford Pinsker

G

GADDIS, William

Nationality: American. **Born:** New York City in 1922. **Education:** Harvard University, Cambridge, Massachusetts, 1941-45. **Family:** Has one son and one daughter. **Career:** Worked for the *New Yorker*, 1946-47; lived in Latin America, Europe, and North Africa, 1947-55; freelance writer of speeches, corporate communications, and filmscripts, 1956-1970s; distinguished visiting professor at Bard College, 1977; contributor to periodicals including *Atlantic, New Yorker, New York Times,* and *Harper's*. **Awards:** American Academy grant, National Institute of Arts and Letters grant, 1963; National Endowment for the Arts grant, 1966, 1974; National Book award, Rockefeller grant, 1976; Guggenheim Fellowship, 1981; MacArthur prize, 1982; nomination for PEN/Faulkner award, 1985. **Member:** American Academy and Institute of Arts and Letters, 1984. **Agent:** Candida Donadio and Associates, 231 West 22nd Street, New York, New York 10011, U.S.A.

PUBLICATIONS

Novels

The Recognitions. New York, Harcourt Brace, 1955; London, MacGibbon and Kee, 1962.
JR. New York, Knopf, 1975; London, Cape, 1976.
Carpenter's Gothic. New York, Viking, 1985; London, Deutsch, 1986.
A Frolic of His Own. New York, Poseidon Press, 1994.

*

Critical Studies: *City of Words* by Tony Tanner, London, Cape, and New York, Harper, 1971; *A Reader's Guide to William Gaddis's The Recognitions* by Steven Moore, Lincoln, University of Nebraska Press, 1982, and *In Recognition of William Gaddis* edited by Moore and John Kuehl, Syracuse, New York, Syracuse University Press, 1984; "William Gaddis Issue" of *Review of Contemporary Fiction* (Elmwood Park, Illinois), vol. 2, no. 2, 1982; *American Fictions 1940-1980* by Frederick Karl, New York, Harper, 1983; *Carnival of Repetition: Gaddis's The Recognitions and Postmodern Theory* by John Johnston, Philadelphia, University of Pennsylvania Press, 1990; *Fire the Bastards!* by Jack Green, Normal, Illinois, Dalkey Archive Press, 1992; *The Ethics of Indeterminacy in the Novels of William Gaddis* by Gregory Comnes, Gainesville, University Press of Florida, 1994.

*   *   *

John W. Aldridge well describes *The Recognitions* as an attempt to create "a satirical portrait of no less than the entire modern world . . . through a most intricate 956-page exploration of such arcane matters as art forgery, counterfeiting, false religious rhetoric, ambidextrous sexuality, the fraudulence of political life, and the masquerades of intellectual and artistic society." As one might suspect—given the fact that the novel is dense in style, has little plot, and is encyclopedic in scope (treating in Joycean fashion everything from the origins and varieties of religious belief to every major period in human history)—it was greeted with a mixed reception. Even today, while it is regarded by many as one of the most brilliant works of our century, it has a small reading public. *JR,* Gaddis's second novel, similarly difficult to read and gargantuan in size, has led many highly respected critics to question if the effort involved in reading his books is equal to its rewards. *Carpenter's Gothic,* Gaddis's third, shorter, and less dense work, has been universally applauded as rich and artful and is clearly the least intimidating of his novels.

Throughout, Gaddis imposes his vast erudition and epistemological questions on the corrupt contemporary world. It is a world overwhelmed by technology and big business—the money and efficiency ethic—and characterized by the demise of human relationships. This he captures in the corruption of language and all apparent communicative patterns—from painting to public media. Gaddis focuses upon the human suffering and alienation that exist in a society of hypocrisy, greed, and fraudulence. He searches for redemption with the recurrent question of whether or not the individual can assert any control within such a world, as well as within the larger universe that may lack design or purpose. Beneath all of society's counterfeit structures, after all, may lie chaos rather than order and the simplicity of basic form. Although his vision is often grim and his satire black, Gaddis implies the power of human love and the transcending possibilities of artistic creation. The acceptance of self and the effort to create or extend toward some fundamental unity may at least restore balance to the chaotic and entropic universe.

The Recognitions has over 50 characters whose paths cross and who contrast and parallel one another within a vast number of subplots. Gaddis echoes Joyce, Rilke, Dante, Eliot, Augustine, Melville, and dozens more. The novel also covers a 30-year period and takes place in New York, New England, Paris, Italy, and Spain. Wyatt Gwyon, its central figure, is the son of an eccentric clergyman, who rejects the ministry to become an artist, and who then rejects his own original work (his aunt accused him years before of trying to assume God's creative function) to copy the Old Flemish Masters who "found God everywhere." Although he leaves his father and wife to become a counterfeit artist and is exploited by a series of people, like Rectall Brown, his is a pilgrimage to discover the counterfeits of contemporary life. He arrives ultimately at a Spanish monastery and (in blinding insight or madness?) goes beyond copying the "falsifications" of the Masters to arrive at final truth—by erasing their canvases. He departs, presumably having had the ultimate epiphany, having "seen" the simple truth behind all artifice and structure.

The novel is filled with recognitions and failed recognitions, of forgeries on every conceivable level, social, aesthetic, scientific, sexual, religious, and political. There is a sense that the individual has surrendered all sense of mystery, wonder, feeling, and belief to science, technology, psychology, and commerce. Wyatt tries to get beyond the contemporary disease of egotism to original truths, as Gaddis pursues the distinctions between the real and fictional. What lies behind all human enterprise (a forgery), he asks: Is it form, chaos, or God? In the end, it may be that art and reality are, after all, the same. Both may be constructs over and against chaos.

What Wyatt finally accomplishes is a spatial, spiritual, and truly creative experience, a "recognition" of the unity of all living and nonliving things. He goes beyond art, which like life, and all human relationships and systems, separates ("afraid of spaces"), to gain a sense of the intermingling of life and death. This occurs in a bizarre scene where he eats bread mistakenly made from his father's ashes.

Although *JR* is vast in scope, its most immediate focus is the corruptive power of money in a society marked by wasted human relationships and aborted creative potentiality. Beneath Gaddis's concentration upon the immediate and topical is once again his sense of cosmic meaninglessness. The novel, moreover, lacks any formal organization: it has no chapter divisions; sentences are often unfinished; it utilizes minimal punctuation. The book consists of uninterrupted speeches in dialogues and monologues. Its spare plot centers on an 11-year-old boy, rejected by both his family and society, who is a student at an ultramodern school on Long Island. An emblem of his society, which teaches wheeling and dealing rather than thinking and feeling, the illiterate JR—with torn sweater, open sneakers, and running nose—having mastered Wall Street jargon, puts into practice the lessons of his time and place. Horatio Alger magnified (and satirized) a hundredfold, he builds a paper empire that touches the political, cultural, and social power bases of our society. Gaddis focuses on the decadence of the people involved in all his maneuvering. In their midst, however, is the "hero" Edward Bast, the one-time composer at the school (fired for sneaking some truths about Mozart into his television lesson). Bast is taken over by JR, who becomes his business agent. At the end, Bast gives up financial security to return to art, and JR, who has never actually realized (i.e., cashed in on) his paper empire, pleads for the respect of personal values. One's worth, it appears, depends upon one's acts—in an existential sense.

Although *JR*'s canvas appears smaller than that of *The Recognitions* and the story takes place in New York and Long Island during a few months, it is even more difficult to read. With little description, narrative, or characterization (which is handled through dialect variations), one has a hard time assigning speeches, even though Gaddis utilizes a remarkable variety of spoken styles. One has no difficulty, however, focusing upon his predominant image of American life as one of corruption, lovelessness, and easy surrender. This is an insane world where friendship and love, on any level, are betrayed. Language mirrors the separation of the individual from his world and the entropy of that very world. People no longer listen to one another, or if they do, they don't hear what is said. Language, so studded with bureaucratic and political jargon, has lost any "meaning."

Though less dense, *Carpenter's Gothic* retains Gaddis's vision of human corruption and lovelessness. Its bizarre and complex plot revolves around an immoral and scheming veteran, Paul Booth, who works as a media consultant for a fundamentalist preacher, the Reverend Elton Ude. Paul's ambitions are vast. He would transform a local drowning incident into a religious miracle and spread the word as far as Africa. His wife, Elizabeth, is no less ambitious, as she pursues an insurance fraud and, along with her vulgar brother Billy (with whom she has inherited a mining combine), schemes to embrace power and gold in Africa. The backdrop for the ill-doings of this family trinity is the rented, gothic house of the geologist-novelist, Mister McCandless. It is a house built in that architectural style noticeably appealing on the outside but inwardly ill-functioning and frequently unseemly. Indeed, it is McCandless, the prince of darkness, the perverse and eternal host, who not only

designs several significant plot events—he seduces Elizabeth by falsely claiming discovery of the gold—but he also speaks out the novel's grotesque prophecies of doom. A mad evangelist, it is through his words and house—all tied to the Gothic—that Gaddis achieves a final statement. It is a "vision of a disorder which . . . [is] beyond any . . . man to put right," about the failure of modern faith (irrevocably distorted from that of history's first great Carpenter, Jesus). It is a comment on contemporary America, whose "grand solutions" have inevitably turned to "nightmare." The modern world, the author sadly concludes, has turned Gothic in its decay and grotesque violence, indeed in its every dimension, "a patchwork of conceits . . . [and] deceptions," orderly and beautiful on the outside but irreversibly distorted within.

The first sentence of *A Frolic of His Own* reveals its subject, one all too familiar to many in the modern world: "Justice?—You [may] get justice in the next world, in this world, you have the law." Although the novel is lighter in tone and easier to read than Gaddis's earlier fiction, it is still marked by extraordinary plays in language—moving across a variety of dialects, archaic and modern usages, and a storehouse of referents that include virtually every category one can imagine. Specifically, *A Frolic of His Own* focuses on the law, as Gaddis treats, plot-wise, the various suits in which a middle-aged college instructor, Oscar Crease, is involved directly and indirectly. First, Crease has been run over by his own car while he was working on it; he is hence both victim and the victimizer. (Is he, the car manufacturer, or the insurance company responsible?) In addition, he has written a play, *Once at Antietam,* based on the experiences of his grandfather in the Civil War, which has been turned into a full-blown blockbuster (*The Blood in the Red, White and Blue*) by a Hollywood mogul. Crease's problems, juxtaposed against several other suits to which he is tangentially related (like a dog trapped in a sculpture and a death during a river baptism), encourage the reader, as the title would wish, "to frolic" in his own confabulated world of legal, often illogical, and infuriating litigious life arrangements. Gaddis's remarks about legalese admit not only of the absurdity of litigation as a favorite contemporary pastime but of the meaningless of language in every human endeavor: "Law is . . . language," he writes at one point, soon adding: "Every profession is a conspiracy against the public, every profession protects itself with a language of its own. . . . Language confronted by language turning language itself into theory till it's not about what it's about it's only about itself turned into a mere plaything." As Oscar, that is to say, Gaddis, the last "civilized man," rages against the misuses of language, so-called culture, corrupt human relations, and most prominently, the law, and he excoriates the very nature of the modern American quest: money. This is one of Gaddis's funniest inventions, and despite its occasionally thorny prose, *A Frolic of His Own* is one of his most readable books.

—Lois Gordon

GAINES, Ernest J(ames)

Nationality: American. **Born:** Oscar, Louisiana, 15 January 1933. **Education:** Vallejo Junior College; San Francisco State College, 1955-57, B.A. 1957; Stanford University, California (Stegner fellow, 1958), 1958-59. **Military Service:** Served in the United States Army, 1953-55. **Career:** Writer-in-residence, Denison University,

Granville, Ohio, 1971, Stanford University, Spring 1981, and Whittier College, California, 1982. Since 1983 professor of English and writer-in-residence, University of Southwestern Louisiana, Lafayette. **Awards:** San Francisco Foundation Joseph Henry Jackson award, 1959; National Endowment for the Arts grant, 1966; Rockefeller grant, 1970; Guggenheim grant, 1970; Black Academy of Arts and Letters award, 1972; San Francisco Art Commission award, 1983; American Academy award, 1987; National Book Critics Circle award, 1994, and Pulitzer prize, 1994, both for *A Lesson Before Dying*. D.Litt.: Denison University, 1980; Brown University, Providence, Rhode Island, 1985; Bard College, Annandale-on-Hudson, New York, 1985; Louisiana State University, Baton Rouge 1987; D.H.L.: Whittier College, 1986. **Agent:** JCA Literary Agency, 242 West 27th Street, New York, New York 10001. **Address:** 932 Divisadero St., San Francisco, California 94115, U.S.A.

PUBLICATIONS

Novels

Catherine Carmier. New York, Atheneum, 1964; London, Secker and Warburg, 1966.
Of Love and Dust. New York, Dial Press, 1967; London, Secker and Warburg, 1968.
The Autobiography of Miss Jane Pittman. New York, Dial Press, 1971; London, Joseph, 1973.
In My Father's House. New York, Knopf, 1978.
A Gathering of Old Men. New York, Knopf, 1983; London, Heinemann, 1984.
A Lesson Before Dying. New York, Knopf, 1993.

Short Stories

Bloodline. New York, Dial Press, 1968.

Uncollected Short Stories

"The Turtles," in *Transfer* (San Francisco), 1956.
"Boy in the Doublebreasted Suit," in *Transfer* (San Francisco), 1957.
"My Grandpa and the Haint," in *New Mexico Quarterly* (Albuquerque), Summer 1966.

Other

A Long Day in November (for children). New York, Dial Press, 1971.
Porch Talk with Ernest Gaines, with Marcia Gaudet and Carl Wooton. Baton Rouge, Louisiana State University Press, 1990.

*

Manuscript Collection: Dupree Library, University of Southwestern Louisiana, Lafayette.

Critical Studies: "Human Dignity and Pride in the Novels of Ernest Gaines" by Winifred L. Stoelting, in *CLA Journal* (Baltimore), March 1971; "Ernest J. Gaines: Change, Growth, and History" by Jerry H. Bryant, in *Southern Review* (Baton Rouge, Louisiana),

October 1974; "Bayonne ou le Yoknapatawpha d'Ernest Gaines" by Michel Fabre in *Recherches Anglaises et Américaines 9* (Strasbourg), 1976; "To Make These Bones Live: History and Community in Ernest Gaines's Fiction" by Jack Hicks, in *Black American Literature Forum* (Terre Haute, Indiana), Spring 1977; "Ernest Gaines: 'A Long Day in November'" by Nalenz Puschmann, in *The Black American Short Story in the 20th Century* edited by Peter Bruck, Amsterdam, Grüner, 1978; "The Quarters: Ernest J. Gaines and the Sense of Place" by Charles H. Rowell, in *Southern Review* (Baton Rouge, Louisiana), Summer 1985.

Ernest J. Gaines comments:

I have tried to show you a world of my people—the kind of world that I came from.

*   *   *

The fictive world of Ernest J. Gaines, as well as certain technical aspects of his works, might be compared to that of William Faulkner. But useful as such a comparison may be, it should not be pursued to the point of obscuring Gaines's considerable originality, which inheres mainly in the fact that he is Afro-American and very much a spiritual product, if no longer a resident, of the somewhat unique region about which he writes: south Louisiana, culturally distinguishable from the state's Anglo-Saxon north, thus from the nation as a whole, by its French legacy, no small part of which derives from the comparative ease with which its French settlers and their descendants formed sexual alliances with blacks.

Gaines's Afro-American perspective enables him to create, among other notable characters both black and white, a Jane Pittman (*The Autobiography of Miss Jane Pittman*) whose heroic perseverance we experience, rather than a housekeeping Dilsey (*The Sound and the Fury*) for whom we have little more than the narrator's somewhat ambiguous and irrelevant assurance that "She endured." In general, Gaines's peculiar point of view generates a more complex social vision than Faulkner's, an advantage Gaines has sustained with dramatic force and artistic integrity. Gaines's fictive society consists of whites, blacks, and creoles, presumably a traditionally more favored socio-economic class of African American given to fantasies of racial superiority to those of darker skin, fantasies of the kind the Martinican psychiatrist Frantz Fanon explores in *Black Skin, White Masks*.

The Gainesian counterparts of the Sartorises and Snopeses (the moribund aristocracy and parvenu "poor white trash" respectively of Faulkner's mythical Mississippi county) are the south Louisiana plantation owners, mostly of French extraction, and the cajuns, of French extraction but of lesser "quality." The cajuns are inheriting and spoiling the land and displacing the creoles and blacks, the former tragically though not irrevocably doomed by a persistent folly, the latter a people of promise who have never really betrayed their African heritage.

All Gaines's works reflect the inherent socio-economic intricacy of this quadruplex humanity, though we are never allowed to lose sight of its basic element of black and white. In his apprentice first novel *Catherine Carmier,* for instance, we see the sickly proscribed love of Jackson, who is black, and Catherine, daughter of an infernally proud creole farmer, as a perverted issue of the miscegenation that resulted from the white male's sexual exploitation of black people. This mode of victimization assumes metaphoric force in Gaines's works, figuring forth in historical perspective the oppression of black people generally. The fictive plantation world, then, is uniquely micro-cosmic. It is south Louisiana, the south, the nation as a whole. This aspect is explored, for example, in the title story of *Bloodline*. Copper, a character of mythopoeic proportion, the militant young son of a now deceased white plantation owner and a black woman field hand, stages a heroic return, presumably from his education in school and in the world at large, to claim his heritage: recognition of kinship by an aristocratic white uncle and his rightful share of the land. In *In My Father's House,* and for the first time, Gaines deals with the black father-son relationship, and explores a neglected aspect of African American life: the perplexities of the public vs. private person relative to individual responsibility. The Reverend Phillip Martin, a grass roots Civil Rights leader in the fictional south Louisiana town of St. Adrienne, is forced to confront his wayward past when his estranged son Etienne, reminiscent of Copper, comes to claim paternal recognition and redress of grievances.

In *A Gathering of Old Men* Gaines extends the thematic concerns of his earlier novels into a new South setting, employing a multiple first-person point of view in the manner of Faulkner's *As I Lay Dying.* The conflict between blacks and cajuns comes to a cinematically stylized, somewhat surrealistic climax and resolution as several old black men gather in mutual militant defense of one of their number who has been accused of killing Cajun farmer Beau Boutan, confronting the local sheriff as well as the slain man's avenging father, "retired" nightrider Fix Boutan. The result is a gripping allegorical tale of race relations in the new South resonant with the Gainesian theme of individual responsibility, this time for holding ground in the wake of the civil rights gains of the 1960s and 1970s.

In Gaines's 1993 novel *A Lesson Before Dying,* set in 1940, individual responsibility is highlighted again. Wiggins, the novel's narrator, is a young school teacher and one among a number of Gainesian tutelary figures. Wiggins is pressured by his elders into assuming the responsibility of mentor to Jefferson, a young black manchild who awaits execution for having taken part in the murder of a white storekeeper, a crime for which he is apparently unjustly convicted in a racist environment. A National Book Critics Circle award winner and recipient of the Pulitzer Prize for fiction in 1994, *A Lesson* chronicles the young Jefferson's gradual assumption of responsibility, under Wiggins's increasingly committed mentorship, for assimilating the attributes of manhood before he dies in the electric chair. In one of Gaines's characteristic ironies, Wiggins's mentorship of Jefferson contributes to his own edification as well.

—Alvin Aubert

GALLANT, Mavis

Nationality: Canadian. **Born:** Mavis de Trafford Young in Montreal, Quebec, 11 August 1922. **Education:** Schools in Montreal and New York. **Career:** Worked in Montreal, early 1940s; reporter, Montreal *Standard*, 1944-50; has lived in Europe since 1950, and in Paris from early 1960s. Writer-in-residence, University of Toronto, 1983-84. **Awards:** *Canadian Fiction* prize, 1978; Governor-General's award, 1982; Canada-Australia literary prize, 1984. Honorary degree: Université Sainte-Anne, Pointe-de-l'église, Nova Scotia, 1984. Officer, Order of Canada, 1981. **Agent:** Georges Borchardt Inc., 136 East 57th Street, New York, New York 10022, U.S.A. **Address:** 14 rue Jean Ferrandi, 75006 Paris, France.

PUBLICATIONS

Novels

Green Water, Green Sky. Boston, Houghton Mifflin, 1959; London, Deutsch, 1960.
A Fairly Good Time. New York, Random House, and London, Heinemann, 1970.

Short Stories

The Other Paris. Boston, Houghton Mifflin, 1956; London, Deutsch, 1957.
My Heart Is Broken: Eight Stories and a Short Novel. New York, Random House, 1964; as *An Unmarried Man's Summer,* London, Heinemann, 1965.
The Pegnitz Junction: A Novella and Five Short Stories. New York, Random House, 1973; London, Cape, 1974.
The End of the World and Other Stories. Toronto, McClelland and Stewart, 1974.
From the Fifteenth District: A Novella and Eight Short Stories. New York, Random House, and London, Cape, 1979.
Home Truths: Selected Canadian Stories. Toronto, Macmillan, 1981; New York, Random House, and London, Cape, 1985.
Overhead in a Balloon: Stories of Paris. Toronto, Macmillan, 1985; London, Cape, and New York, Random House, 1987.
In Transit: Twenty Stories. Markham, Ontario, Viking, 1988; New York, Random House, 1989; London, Faber, 1990.
Across the Bridge: Stories. New York, Random House, 1993.

Uncollected Short Stories

"Good Morning and Goodbye" and "Three Brick Walls," in *Preview* (Montreal), December 1944.
"A Wonderful Country," in *Standard Magazine* (Montreal), 14 December 1946.
"The Flowers of Spring," in *Northern Review* (Montreal), June-July 1950.
"Madeline's Birthday," in *The New Yorker,* 1 September 1951.
"Thieves and Rascals," in *Esquire* (New York), July 1956.
"A Short Love Story," in *Montrealer,* June 1957.
"The Old Place," in *Texas Quarterly* (Austin), Spring 1958.
"Crossing France," in *The Critic* (Toronto), December 1960-January 1961.
"Willi," in *The New Yorker,* 5 January 1963.
"Paolo and Renata," in *Southern Review* (Baton Rouge, Louisiana), Winter 1965.
"A Report," in *The New Yorker,* 3 December 1966.
"The Rejection," in *The New Yorker,* 12 April 1969.
"The Burgundy Weekend," in *Tamarack Review* (Toronto), Winter 1979.
"A Revised Guide to Paris," in *The New Yorker,* 11 February 1980.
"From Sunrise to Daybreak," in *The New Yorker,* 17 March 1980.
"Dido Flute, Spouse to Europe," in *The New Yorker,* 12 May 1980.
"From Gamut to Yalta," in *The New Yorker,* 15 September 1980.
"Europe by Satellite," in *The New Yorker,* 3 November 1980.
"Mousse," in *The New Yorker,* 22 December 1980.
"Mau to Lew: The Maurice Ravel-Lewis Carroll Friendship," in *Exile* (Toronto), vol. 7, nos. 3-4, 1981.
"French Crenellation," in *The New Yorker,* 9 February 1981.
"This Space" and "On with the New in France," in *The New Yorker,* 16 July 1981.

"La Vie Parisienne," in *The New Yorker,* 19 October 1981.
"Siegfried's Memoirs," in *The New Yorker,* 5 April 1982.
"Treading Water," in *The New Yorker,* 24 May 1982.
"The Concert Party," in *The Best American Short Stories 1989,* edited by Margaret Atwood and Shannon Ravenel. Boston, Houghton Mifflin, 1989.
"In a War," in *The New Yorker,* 30 October 1989.
"Across the Bridge," in *The New Yorker,* 18 March 1991.

Play

What Is to Be Done? (produced Toronto, 1982). Montreal, Quadrant, 1984.

Other

The Affair of Gabrielle Russier, with others. New York, Knopf, 1971; London, Gollancz, 1973.
Paris Notebooks: Essays and Reviews. London, Bloomsbury, and New York, Random House, 1988.

*

Bibliography: By Judith Skelton Grant and Douglas Malcolm, in *The Annotated Bibliography of Canada's Major Authors 5* edited by Robert Lecker and Jack David, Downsview, Ontario, ECW Press, 1984.

Manuscript Collection: Fisher Library, University of Toronto.

Critical Studies: "Mavis Gallant Issue" of *Canadian Fiction 28* (Prince George, British Columbia), 1978; *Mavis Gallant: Narrative Patterns and Devices* by Grazia Merler, Ottawa, Tecumseh Press, 1978; *The Light of Imagination: Mavis Gallant's Fiction* by Neil K. Besner, Vancouver, University of British Columbia Press, 1988; *Reading Mavis Gallant* by Janice Kulyk Keefer, Oxford, Oxford University Press, 1989; *Figuring Grief: Gallant, Munro, and the Poetics of Elegy* by Karen E. Smythe, Montreal, McGill Queens' University Press, 1992.

*   *   *

The characters who move through the fiction of Mavis Gallant are unwilling exiles and victims, born or made. Her first collection of short stories, *The Other Paris,* clearly sets the tone of her work: in a series of impersonal, almost clinical sketches the lonely and displaced struggle against an indifferent or hostile world. A naive American girl, engaged to a dull American in Paris, wonders why her colorless days have no connection with the legendary "other Paris" of light and civility; a pathetic American army wife in Germany faces her stale marriage and a rootless future; a bitter, unforgiving set of brothers and sisters gathers after the funeral of their mother, a dingy Romanian shopkeeper in Montreal; a cow-like Canadian girl with Shirley Temple curls is repeatedly deceived by seedy fiancés; a traveler staying in a Madrid tenement watches a petty bureaucrat trying to justify the new order "to which he has devoted his life and in which he must continue to believe." These anti-romantic glimpses of dislocation and despair are rendered in deliberately hard, dry prose, reminiscent, like their subject matter, of Joyce's *Dubliners.* The narrative manner is flat, unadorned, without any relieving touches of wit—or, it seems, compassion (save

for the best of the stories, "Going Ashore," in which a sensitive child is dragged from port to port by a desperate, amoral mother). Although there is an admirable consistency of theme and feeling in these stories, and a high degree of professional skill, there is little here to suggest the brilliance of Gallant's later work and her gradual mastery of longer, more demanding fictional forms.

The title of the next collection, *My Heart Is Broken,* reveals a continuation of the same concerns. Yet there is a good deal more vigor here, and an indication as well that the author, if not her characters, may be taking some pleasure in the sharpness of her perceptions. There is also the first clear suggestion of a problem which is to become of major importance in Gallant's later work: the eccentricity and near-madness to which her losers may be driven by want or isolation. Gallant has an appallingly accurate eye for the desperation of the shabby genteel, the Englishwomen who live at the edge of poverty in unfashionable pensions out of season, and a shrewd eye as well for the vulgarities of those who try to keep up the pretense of well being. And there is at least one completely successful story, "An Unmarried Man's Summer" which manages to combine many of the earlier preoccupations with a degree of wit and energy not present before.

Gallant's first experiment with longer fiction, *Green Water, Green Sky,* despite a vivid central section, suffers from an uncertainty of focus. Three of the four parts of the novella offer peripheral views of the breakdown of a young American wife, raised abroad and now living in Paris. The reasons for her drift into madness are never fully explained, although the blame must in part rest with a vain and foolish mother. Florence remains an intriguing and pathetic puzzle; our questions are unanswered, our sympathies largely unresolved. A second short novel, "Its Image on the Mirror" (*My Heart Is Broken*), is an unqualified success, partly because the point of view is strictly limited to one character—a device which is the source of some ambiguity here as well as consistency. The faintly repressed family hostilities which have appeared in various guises in the earlier work are now given sustained treatment. The narrator, Jean, who has always suffered from a sense of drabness and compromise in contrast to her beautiful younger sister, tries to come to terms with her ambivalent feelings. After years of apparent freedom and romance the spoiled Isobel makes what seems to be an unhappy and confining marriage; looking back, Jean is able to move towards compassion and acceptance. But to what degree is she using the narrative as a kind of revenge for the years she was forced to take second place? Is her sympathy finally untainted by satisfaction? The reader has no means of deciding, precisely because the author makes no comments on Jean's reminiscences. The uncertainty we feel at the end of the work, however, is entirely appropriate: Jean herself is still divided between love, pity and jealousy.

A Fairly Good Time is a splendidly complex full-length novel. Again the plot is familiar and simple in outline: a well-off, still young Canadian woman passes over the borders of sanity as her second marriage, to a Parisian journalist, dissolves. The reasons for her collapse, again, are hinted at rather than developed: an eccentric, domineering mother, a happy first marriage cruelly ended by a freak accident, the frustrating sense of isolation in a foreign world of would-be intellectuals and amoral opportunists—all of these play a partial role. This time, however, Gallant operates directly inside the mind of her heroine, and the result is a spectacular *tour de force:* the writing is disconcertingly vivid, full of the unmediated poetry of near-hallucination, yet nothing is irrelevant or misplaced. Shirley's madness has a kind of honesty about it which attracts the users and manipulators around her. The sane world of her husband's family and the Maurel family, into whose civil wars she is thrust, seems finally to offer much less integrity than her own world of memories and fantasies. At the conclusion there is just a hint that Shirley may be returning to reality, as she learns to moderate her hopes: "if you make up your mind not to be happy," runs the epigraph from Edith Wharton, "there's no reason why you shouldn't have a fairly good time."

There are no ideas in Gallant's work, no set of theses. The strong and willful may or may not succeed; the sensitive will almost certainly pay for their gifts. And if they endure, as Shirley may, or as Jean does in "Its Image on the Mirror," the only wisdom is a kind of expensive stoicism:

> We woke from dreams of love remembered, a house recovered and lost, a climate imagined, a journey never made. . . . We would waken thinking the earth must stop now, so that we could be shed from it like snow. I knew, that night, we would not be shed, but would remain, because that is the way it was. We would survive, and waking— because there was no help for it—forget our dreams and return to life.

This is not exactly hopeful, but neither is it completely despairing: perhaps if we learned to moderate our hopes we might have a fairly good time. But Gallant's more recent collections *The Pegnitz Junction* and *From the Fifteenth District* seem to deny even this modest possibility. The mood here is that of *The Other Paris;* the effect is considerably more oppressive, however, since Gallant has extended the range of her style. The relatively dry, understated manner of the first books has now been replaced by a highly poetic technique in which feelings are conveyed by sudden, uncanny, and yet astonishingly precise images. Yet as before, her characters do not act, they are acted upon; they suffer, but in the end it hardly seems to matter. Life dwindles away and with it everything which gave pleasure, so perhaps nothing had much substance to begin with. The conclusion of "An Autobiography" (*The Pegnitz Junction*) is typical. A middle-aged woman thinks about her failure to hold onto the love of a shiftless young man called Peter (the cause of the failure is left undefined, these things just "happen"):

> These are the indecisions that rot the fabric, if you let them. The shutter slams to in the wind and sways back; the rain begins to slant as the wind increases. This is the season for mountain storms. The wind rises, the season turns; no autumn is quite like another. The autumn children pour out of the train, and the clouds descend upon the mountain slopes, and there we are with walls and a ceiling to the village. Here is the pattern on the carpet where he walked, and the cup he drank from. I have learned to be provident. I do not waste a sheet of writing paper, or a postage stamp, or a tear. The stream outside the window, deep with rain, receives rolled in a pellet the letter to Peter. Actually, it is a blank sheet on which I intended to write a long letter about everything—about Véronique. I have wasted a sheet of paper. There has been such a waste of everything; such a waste.

"The only way to be free," reflects one of the battered characters in *From the Fifteenth District,* "is not to love." This is the freedom of isolation, madness, and death, but perhaps any escape from being is preferable to the pain of living. Thus Piotr, for example, the

central figure in the novella "Potter," welcomes the imagined prospect of his death: "Oh, to be told that there were only six weeks to live! To settle scores; leave nothing straggling, to go quietly." Yet even death may offer no release. In "From the Fifteenth District," a truly harrowing prose-poem—it can hardly be called a story—the pathetic ghosts of the dead complain to the "authorities" that the memories of life and the intrusions of the still-living make any final rest impossible.

—Elmer Borklund

GALLOWAY, Janice

Nationality: Scottish. **Born:** Kilwinning, Scotland, 2 December 1956. **Education:** Glasgow University, M.A. 1978. **Family:** Has one son. **Career:** Welfare rights worker, 1976-77; teacher of English, Strathclyde Regional Council, Ayrshire, Scotland, 1980-89. **Awards:** Scottish Arts Council book award, 1990, and MIND book of the year/Allan Lane award, 1991, both for *The Trick Is to Keep Breathing; Cosmopolitan*/Perrier award, 1991, for short story writing; Scottish Arts Council book award, 1991, for *Blood.* **Agent:** Cathie Thomson, 23 Hillhead Street, Hillhead, Glasgow G12 8PX, Scotland. **Address:** 25 Herriet Street, P.O. Hokshields, Glasgow G41 2NN, Scotland.

PUBLICATIONS

Novel

The Trick Is to Keep Breathing. Edinburgh, Polygon, 1989; Normal, Illinois, Dalkey Archive Press, 1994.
Foreign Parts. London, Vintage, 1995.

Short Stories

Blood. London, Secker and Warburg, and New York, Random House, 1991.

Other

Editor, with Hamish Whyte, *New Writing Scotland 8.* Aberdeen, Aberdeen University Press, 1990.
Editor, with Hamish Whyte, *Scream, If You Want to Go Faster.* Aberdeen, Association for Scottich Literary Studies, 1991.
Editor, with Marion Sinclair, *Meantime.* N.p., 1991.
Editor, with Hamish Whyte, *Pig Squealing.* Aberdeen, Association for Scottich Literary Studies, 1992.
Editor, with Hamish Whyte, *New Writing Scotland 9.* Aberdeen, Aberdeen University Press, 1991.
Editor, with Hamish Whyte, *New Writing Scotland 10.* Aberdeen. Aberdeen University Press, 1992.

*   *   *

Hailed by novelist John Hawkes as "a Scottish Poe of the lower middle class," Janice Galloway writes a grimly detached yet eerily familiar fiction that combines minimalist style, formal innovation, contemporary subject matter, and Gothic sensibility. In a bleak and sometimes blackly humorous manner, she chronicles various forms of social and psychological oppression, particularly as experienced by women.

Her novel, *The Trick Is to Keep Breathing,* creates an unnerving atmosphere of fragility and menace as it traces one woman's efforts over the course of several weeks to deal with the death of her married lover. "This Is the Way Things Are" in the post-Trollope world of the novel's ironically, indeed oxymoronically named narrator-protagonist, Joy Stone: straitened, empty, in-between in every sense, caught for the most part (as is the reader) in a perpetual, numbing present. On the one hand, Joy is too independent and intelligent to accept the bromides dispensed by the modern therapeutic community; on the other, she cannot entirely escape feeling that she is the problem: inadequate and therefore guilty, insufficiently persistent in her behavior or "realistic" in her attitude. Compounding her situation is the fact that she is a woman (depression and suicide run in the family on the female side) and a Scot. "Love/Emotion = embarrassment: Scots equation. Exceptions are when roaring drunk or watching football. Men do rather better out of this loophole." Joy does rather worse in any and all of her roles: teacher, friend, patient, lover, Other Woman, "harridan," and would-be princess awaiting the arrival of her prince.

Withdrawing further into herself, perhaps dangerously so, and out of necessity making do with the little that is financially and psychologically available to her, she fills in the blank that her life has become with writing that proves just as compelling as it is disturbing. At once highly fragmented and omnivorously, obsessively multifarious, her narrative includes the postcards she receives from her one (geographically distant) friend, the replies she writes, the lists she compiles, the pop-song lyrics she hears on the radio, the advice columns she reads in the tabloids, dramatized scenes depicting her brief encounters with others, painful memories, even marginalia. Surveying the contemporary wasteland from her bleak council housing estate on the outskirts of Glasgow, shoring the fragments against the ruin but without benefit of T. S. Eliot's "mythic method" and all it metaphysically implies, Joy seems less the latest version of the hysterical woman, the madwoman in the attic, than the female writer in a room not quite her own (it belongs to her dead lover) but able nonetheless to write in a voice at once entirely original yet filled with the echoes of Galloway's literary precursors, chief among them Plath, Kafka, Scheherazade, Stevie Smith, James Kelman, the Dickinson of "After Great Pain," the Beckett of *The Unnamable,* and *Krapp's Last Tape.*

Where Galloway's novel takes something comparatively small and expands it, minutely and almost unbearably, the twenty-two stories that make up *Blood* move in the opposite direction toward an equally intense and unnerving compression. Long or short, Galloway's goal remains the same: giving voice to repressed narratives. In the novel Joy claims that she cannot actually scream; she can only write "it" down. In the collection, "Things stick . . . in her throat that she would never say," her "voice full of splinters." The five "Scenes from the Life" take the form of little plays having little or no dialogue. In "Two Fragments," a woman remembers her mother's macabre versions of how her father lost two fingers and her grandmother an eye—not during the war but while hungrily eating fish and chips, not while breaking a piece of coal but while trying to kill a cat by boiling it alive. "Faire Ellen and the Wanderer Returned" retells the Odysseus myth from a contemporary Penelope's point of view. Stories such as "Love in a Changing Environment" take literary minimalism to a chilly and chilling extreme, whereas the phantasmagoric "Plastering the Cracks" re-

calls the repressed protagonist of Roman Polanski's *Repulsion.* Throughout the collection there is the sense of trust and especially of innocence betrayed: The father who tricks his young son into falling from the fireplace mantle in order to teach him the lesson, "Trust nae cunt," the woman who comes to the aid of an elderly man who has stumbled only to have him strike out at her. In the title story that opens the collection a young girl's having a tooth extracted becomes a horrific study in female shame, and in the haunting novella-length "A Week with Uncle Felix" at collection's end, speechlessness and sexuality come together in a particularly suspenseful and disturbing manner wholly characteristic of Galloway's larger aesthetic and unprogrammatically feminist concerns.

—Robert A. Morace

GANGEMI, Kenneth

Nationality: American. **Born:** Bronxville, New York, 23 November 1937. **Education:** Rensselaer Polytechnic Institute, Troy, New York, B.Mgt.E. 1959; San Francisco State College (now University), California. **Military Service:** Served in the United States Navy, 1960-61. **Family:** Married Jana Fisher in 1961. **Awards:** Stegner fellowship, 1968; PEN grant, 1975; Creative Artists Public Service fellowship, 1976. **Address:** 211 E. Fifth St., New York, New York 10003, U.S.A.

PUBLICATIONS

Novels

Olt. New York, Orion Press, and London, Calder and Boyars, 1969.
Corroboree: A Book of Nonsense. New York, Assembling Press, 1977.
The Volcanoes from Puebla. London, Boyars, 1979.
The Interceptor Pilot. London, Boyars, 1980.

Poetry

Lydia. Los Angeles, Black Sparrow Press, 1970.

*   *   *

A literary innovator whose works have often had their first appearance in French translation or in British editions, Kenneth Gangemi has distinguished himself as an uncompromising perfectionist whose fiction makes none of those gestures toward popularity that made similar developments part of mainstream American fiction in the later 1960s and 1970s. Without foregrounding techniques or dramatizing his pose as an anti-illusionistic writer, Gangemi has fashioned a style of narrative that at times questions itself comically and always highlights the pleasure of having referential materials from the world being transformed into the makings of literary art.

His short novel *Olt* remains the best introduction to Gangemi's fiction. Although it qualifies as anti-fiction (in the terms of refusing to capitalize on the effects of suspended disbelief), not a single convention of traditional fiction is violated. The characterization of

Gangemi's protagonist, Olt, is coherent, and the narrative action of his adventures is linear. Gangemi's style is clear and concise. Yet none of these familiar aspects is used to accomplish the customary aim of narrative. There are no flashes of insight or moments ponderous with great meaning, and certainly no accumulation of wisdom that might add up to a conclusive point. Instead Gangemi fashions a narrative life in which his on-going language constitutes an experiential flow of life, as Olt's existence is generated by the fact that he lives within a sentence structure capable of accommodating an infinite series of actions. "Olt knew he would never see a meteor striking an iceberg, a bat falling into snow, or a clown on a nun," for instance. "He knew he would never go to a party and talk to thunderstorm experts, roller-coaster experts, vampire experts, sailplane experts, dinosaur experts, or volcano experts. He knew that he would never design bear grottos, furnish a time capsule, live in an orange grove, wade in a vat of mercury," and so forth. Even though all of these objects exist in the world, and even though syntax makes it possible to combine them, what readers know about the world confirms that seeing a bat fall into snow is among the unlikeliest of possibilities. Yet these sentences of Gangemi's have linked them linguistically, the word "not" preserving the narrative from utter nonsense. Readers can therefore delight in the combinatory action of language without having to suspend disbelief. Free of any obligation to add up to something, these fictive objects can be appreciated in and of themselves.

In *Corroboree*—like *Olt*, a short novel of about 60 pages—Gangemi uses similar found objects to constitute a style. These objects predominate over narrative, and where narrative exists it is often for the sake of a self-referential joke, such as the quickly summarized story of a man who makes a fortune in the shipping industry by realizing cargoes of ping-pong balls need not be insured against sinking. Gangemi's talent for construing off-base situations leads to such real-life observations as noting a woman at the Hong Kong Hilton suggesting a trip to Chinatown and considering the effect of filling a cello with jello. As a result, language is allowed to become its own subject without such artificial devices as concrete forms on the page or devices such as featuring a writer writing a story about a writer writing a story about a writer. . . .

Gangemi's most successful work is *The Volcanoes from Puebla*. As a transfictional narrative, it combines the most useful aspects of both the novel and the travel memoir by discarding those factors which prove overly determining for each form: in the case of fiction, the need for a developing story, and in the memoir a dedication to the chronology of time and integrity of space. In *The Volcanoes from Puebla,* the only true narrative results from the reader coming to an appreciation of Mexico as a sensual experience, while the autobiographical element of this experience is countered by the adventure being broken down by alphabetical points of reference. The references themselves are various, as idiosyncratic as a system devised by Jorge Luis Borges to show off its own infinite cleverness. While "Calle Bolivar" rates a description as a street in Mexico City, so do "Helmets" (as part of a motorcyclist's gear) and "Mexican Day" (as a reflection on typical daily rhythms). Read in this jigsaw-puzzle manner, the book stresses the materials of experience themselves, apart from any of the typical travelog conventions which by prioritizing such materials tend to falsify the experience. The test of Gangemi's effectiveness as a writer is how well he is able to hold this experience together, fragmented as it is by the alphabetical structure and antisystematics of its categories. Soon the reader sees how the author himself is experiencing Mexico free from traditional constraints—letting buses pass by while he appreciates the pleasure of waiting at the bus stop, seeing a beautiful girl walk by with a baby coati-mundi on her shoulder and not knowing whether to look at her or at the coati-mundi. *The Volcanoes from Puebla* is itself experienced by the reader just this way, free of both fictive narrative and biographical consequence.

The ultimate effect of Gangemi's art is seen in what is his most conventional narrative, a full-length novel titled *The Interceptor Pilot*. Its plot is traditional and has the interest of a politically pertinent action thriller: during the Vietnam War an American pilot volunteers his service in defense of the North against bombing by his own countrymen. The key to this novel is that it is told as simply and as sparely as possible; indeed, the form implied is that of the film treatment, a bare-bones, present-tense indication of how the camera is supposed to capture the action ("The scene is . . . ," "The time is . . ."). Here Gangemi has taken just the element that his earlier fiction discarded, and now employs it to do the work that in other cases would be accomplished by detailed characterization, careful imagery, and complexly contrived action (all of which the movie treatment assumes will be displayed for the camera). Again like a film *The Interceptor Pilot* ignores every element except what can be seen; being so limited, it must rely on such cinematic devices as montage and quick cutting. What happens in the narrative becomes a dynamic collage in which each object remains itself just as much as it functions as an agent of action: kills stenciled beneath an airplane cockpit railing, a copy of *Le Monde* tossed on the seat of a French journalist's car, TOP SECRET stamped on an Air Force document. Just as the objects of *Olt, Corroboree,* and *The Volcanoes from Puebla* function as narrative and not just referential materials, the lightness and clarity of Gangemi's prose allows similar objects to take on similar artistic importance in *The Interceptor Pilot*.

—Jerome Klinkowitz

GARNER, Helen

Nationality: Australian. **Born:** Helen Ford in Geelong, Victoria, 7 November 1942. **Education:** Manifold Heights State School; Ocean Grove State School; The Hermitage, Geelong; Melbourne University, 1961-65, B.A. (honors) 1965. **Family:** Married 1) William Garner in 1968, one daughter; 2) Jean-Jacques Portail in 1980. Teacher, Werribee High School, 1966-67, Upfield High School, 1968-69, and Fitzroy High School, 1971-72, all Victoria; journalist, *Digger,* 1973; lived in Paris, 1978-79. **Career:** Writer-in-residence, Griffith University, Nathan, Queensland, 1983, and University of Western Australia, Nedlands, 1984. Melbourne theater critic, *National Times,* Sydney, 1982-83. Since 1981 feature writer, *Age,* Melbourne. Since 1985 member of the Australia Council Literature Board. **Awards:** Australia Council fellowship, 1978, 1979, 1980, 1983; National Book Council award, 1978; New South Wales Premier's award, 1986. **Address:** 849 Drummond St., North Carlton, Victoria 3054, Australia.

PUBLICATIONS

Novels

Monkey Grip. Melbourne, McPhee Gribble, 1977; London, Penguin, 1978; New York, Seaview, 1981.

Moving Out (novelization of screenplay), with Jennifer Giles. Melbourne, Nelson, 1983.
The Children's Bach. Melbourne, McPhee Gribble, 1984.
Cosmo Cosmolino. Ringwood, Victoria, McPhee Gribble, 1992; London, Bloomsbury, 1993.

Short Stories

Honour, and Other People's Children: Two Stories. Melbourne, McPhee Gribble, 1980; New York, Seaview, 1982.
Postcards from Surfers. Melbourne, McPhee Gribble, 1985; New York, Penguin, 1986; London, Bloomsbury, 1989.

Play

The Stranger in the House, adaptation of a play by Raymond Demarcy (produced Melbourne, 1982; London, 1986).

Other

La Mama: The Story of a Theatre. Melbourne, McPhee Gribble, 1988.

*

Critical Study: "On War and Needlework: The Fiction of Helen Garner" by Peter Craven, in *Meanjin* (Melbourne), no. 2, 1985.

*   *   *

Helen Garner's novels deal with the fractured relationships of "alternative" living in Melbourne. Against a background of communes and shared houses, the drug scene, rock bands, cooperative movies, suburb, and beach, her characters try to form relationships and cope with their inevitable failure. Her fiction explores the point at which freedom stops and irresponsibility begins. It is a world in which women with love to spare try to deal with men who have "the attention span of a stick insect" who monopolize them one minute and ignore them the next. There is a sympathetic, fatalistic cast to her writing. Most of her characters could be summed up by the line: "Their mother was dead and they were making a mess of things." *Monkey Grip* is Nora's account of her obsessive love for Javo, a junkie. They belong to a subculture where drugs define the real and the tolerable, where there is no tomorrow only today, and therefore where commitments to another person are infinitely redefinable. "I'm not all that worried about futures. I don't want to love anyone forever." Nora's love, her habit of "giving it all away," is as addictive as Javo's heroin habit, and makes her as vulnerable. She supports and is supported by other women, sometimes finding herself consoling or being consoled by a sexual rival. The pain and the jealousy are intense but in the curiously reticent unreticence of this culture, protest about exploitation is limited to declarations as inadequate as, "That makes me feel bad." By the end of the novel Nora has achieved some degree of detachment from Javo, but there is no guarantee that the cycle will not be repeated with another exploitingly helpless male.

Honour, and Other People's Children is a pair of novellas which show characters similar to those in *Monkey Grip* at a later stage in their lives. Each involves separation. In "Honour" a woman who has been separated for five years from her husband is shocked by his asking for a divorce in order to remarry. Instead of the commune life he now wants "a *real* place to live, with a back yard where I can plant vegies, and a couple of walls to paint, and a dog—not a bloody room in a sort of railway station." Despite their five-year separation Elizabeth still feels a residual bonding which is now threatened. Relationships in this book are much more richly delineated than in the first novel. Here they are products of shared experience, shared jokes and personal rituals, family connections and mutual awareness. When Frank's father is about to die, it is Elizabeth who accompanies him on the visit. Their child stands in the middle of an awkward triangle wanting all to live together and not comprehending the nuances and difficulties of the situation. However her instinct is right, and ex-wife and future wife tentatively feel towards some sort of acquaintance, even friendship, symbolized by the balanced seesaw of the story's conclusion.

"Other People's Children" moves the focus away from heterosexual relationships to the declining friendship between two women who have been the nucleus of a shared house, and have gradually become abrasive towards each other. Over years in the same household Scotty has come to love Ruth's daughter, Laurel, and hers is the greatest loss when the house breaks up. Loving other people's children gives no rights, not even the limited access granted to the non-custodian parent by the divorce court. Ruth's relationship with the self-protective Dennis shows the same sort of male manipulation used by Javo in *Monkey Grip*, while Madigan, to whom Scotty turns for companionship, is so torn between misogyny and the need for acceptance that he ranks as the most destructive of Garner's male characters.

The Children's Bach extends Garner's range of characters, and puts them in a new arrangement. Whereas previous novels concentrated on the isolation of characters and on the failures of bonding, this novel offers at least one couple in a successful relationship: "She loved him. They loved each other. They were friends." Dexter and Athena embody an innocence which characters in the earlier novels seem never to have had. Their marriage is stable and caring despite the strains put on it by their retarded second son who has a musical sense but not speech. Set against them are Dexter's old friend from university days, Elizabeth, her lover Philip, and her younger sister, Vicky. There is a clash of values in this novel, and a sense that characters are redefining their perspectives instead of being depicted at a stage when they are already locked into a fixed way of seeing, and surviving in, the world.

Music has always been an important motif in Garner's books, and here it becomes dominant. In earlier works it offered, like sex or drugs, a way of immersion or escape. It is associated with most of the characters in this novel, and it generally suggests sanity and harmony. While Philip uses music to exploit people, it is a mark of Athena's unglamorous dedication to making life work, and of Dexter's uncomplicated gusto.

Postcards from Surfers is a collection of stories which offers vignettes on the ways people relate and report themselves to others. In the title story a woman holidaying with her parents who have retired to the seaside writes a series of postcards to a former lover which she does not post because it's "too late to change it now." Other stories tell of chance meetings, visits, trips in Europe and Australia. Males in this collection continue to be selfish, manipulative, and arrogant but Garner ends some of the stories more hopefully in the manner of *The Children's Bach.* Women trying to make something of their lives ("The Life of Art") are always going to find males unsatisfactory, but they can support each other. Women are always going to be racked by passion for men who want them less continuously and exclusively, but it is possible to "hang on until the spasm passes."

—Chris Tiffin

GARRETT, George (Palmer, Jr.)

Nationality: American. **Born:** Orlando, Florida, 11 June 1929. **Education:** Sewanee Military Academy; The Hill School, graduated 1947; Princeton University, New Jersey, 1947-48, 1949-52, B.A. 1952, M.A. 1956, Ph.D. 1985; Columbia University, New York, 1948-49. **Military Service:** Served in the United States Army Field Artillery, 1952-55. **Family:** Married Susan Parrish Jackson in 1952; two sons and one daughter. **Career:** Assistant professor, Wesleyan University, Middletown, Connecticut, 1957-60; visiting lecturer, Rice University, Houston, 1961-62; associate professor, University of Virginia, Charlottesville, 1962-67; writer-in-residence, Princeton University, 1964-65; professor of English, Hollins College, Virginia, 1967-71; professor of English and writer-in-residence, University of South Carolina, Columbia, 1971-73; senior fellow, Council of the Humanities, Princeton University, 1974-77; adjunct professor, Columbia University, 1977-78; writer-in-residence, Bennington College, Vermont, 1979, and University of Michigan, Ann Arbor, 1979-84. Since 1984 Hoyns Professor of English, University of Virginia, Charlottesville. President of Associated Writing Programs, 1971-73. United States poetry editor, *Transatlantic Review,* Rome (later London), 1958-71; Contemporary Poetry Series editor, University of North Carolina Press, Chapel Hill, 1962-68; co-editor, *Hollins Critic,* Virginia, 1965-71; Short Story Series editor, Louisiana State University Press, Baton Rouge, 1966-69. Since 1970 contributing editor, *Contempora,* Atlanta; since 1971 assistant editor, *Film Journal,* Hollins College, Virginia; since 1972 co-editor, *Worksheet,* Columbia, South Carolina; since 1981 editor, with Brendan Galvin, *Poultry: A Magazine of Voice,* Truro, Massachusetts; since 1988 fiction editor, *The Texas Review;* contributing editor, *Chronicles,* Rockford, Illinois. Vice-Chancellor, 1987-92, and since 1992 Chancellor, Fellowship of Southern Writers. **Awards:** *Sewanee Review* fellowship, 1958; American Academy in Rome fellowship, 1958; Ford grant, for drama, 1960; National Endowment for the Arts grant, 1967; *Contempora* award, 1971; Guggenheim fellowship, 1974; American Academy award, 1985; New York Public Library Literary Lion award, 1988; T. S. Eliot award, 1989; PEN/Malamud award for short fiction, 1990. Cultural Laureate of Virginia, 1986; Hollins College medal, 1992. D. Litt.: University of the South (Sewanee), 1994. **Agent:** Jane Gelfman, John Farquharson Ltd., 250 West 57th Street, New York, New York 10107, U.S.A. **Address:** 1845 Wayside Place, Charlottesville, Virginia 22903, U.S.A.

PUBLICATIONS

Novels

The Finished Man. New York, Scribner, 1959; London, Eyre and Spottiswoode, 1960.
Which Ones Are the Enemy? Boston, Little Brown, 1961; London, W. H. Allen, 1962.
Do, Lord, Remember Me. New York, Doubleday, and London, Chapman and Hall, 1965.
Death of the Fox. New York, Doubleday, 1971; London, Barrie and Jenkins, 1972.
The Succession: A Novel of Elizabeth and James. New York, Doubleday, 1983.

Poison Pen. Winston-Salem, North Carolina, Wright, 1986.
Entered from the Sun. New York, Doubleday, 1990.

Short Stories

King of the Mountain. New York, Scribner, 1958; London, Eyre and Spottiswoode, 1959.
In the Briar Patch. Austin, University of Texas Press, 1961.
Cold Ground Was My Bed Last Night. Columbia, University of Missouri Press, 1964.
A Wreath for Garibaldi and Other Stories. London, Hart Davis, 1969.
The Magic Striptease. New York, Doubleday, 1973.
To Recollect a Cloud of Ghosts: Christmas in England. Winston-Salem, North Carolina, Palaemon Press, 1979.
An Evening Performance: New and Selected Short Stories. New York, Doubleday, 1985.

Uncollected Short Stories

"The Other Side of the Coin," in *Four Quarters* (Philadelphia), (6), 1957.
"The Rare Unicorn," in *Approach* (Wallingford, Pennsylvania), (25), 1957.
"The Only Dragon on the Road," in *Approach* (Wallingford, Pennsylvania), (31), 1959.
"3 Fabliaux," in *Transatlantic Review* (London), (1), 1959.
"The Snowman," in *New Mexico Quarterly* (Albuquerque), (29), 1959.
"Two Exemplary Letters," in *Latitudes* (Houston), (1), 1967.
"Jane Amor, Space Nurse," in *Fly by Night,* 1970.
"There Are Lions Everywhere," "How Can You Tell What Somebody's Thinking on the Telephone," and "Moon Girl," all in *Mill Mountain Review* (Roanoke, Virginia), Summer 1971.
"Here Comes the Bride," in *Gone Soft* (Salem, Massachusetts), (1), 1973.
"Live Now and Pay Later," in *Nassau Literary Magazine* (Princeton, New Jersey), 1974.
"Little Tune for a Steel String Guitar," in *Sandlapper* (Columbia, South Carolina), (9), 1976.
"Soldiers," in *Texas Review* (Huntsville), (3), 1982.
"Wine Talking," in *Quarterly West* (Salt Lake City), (20), 1985.
"Ruthe-Ann," in *Texas Review* (Huntsville), (6), 1985.
"Genius Baby," in *Chattahoochie Review* (Dunwoody, Georgia), 1986.
"Dixie Dreamland," in *South Carolina Review* (Clemson), (19), 1986.
"The Confidence Man," in *Necessary Fictions,* edited by Stanley W. Lindberg and Stephen Corey. Athens, University of Georgia Press, 1986.
"Captain Barefoot Tells His Tale," in *Virginia Quarterly Review* (Charlottesville), Spring 1990.
"Velleities and Vicissitudes," in *Sewanee Review* (Tennessee), Fall 1990.

Plays

Sir Slob and the Princess: A Play for Children. New York, French, 1962.
Garden Spot, U.S.A. (produced Houston, 1962).
Enchanted Ground. York, Maine, Old Gaol Museum Press, 1981.

Screenplays: *The Young Lovers,* 1964; *The Playground,* 1965; *Frankenstein Meets the Space Monster,* with R.H.W. Dillard and John Rodenbeck, 1966.

Television Plays: *Suspense* series, 1958.

Poetry

The Reverend Ghost. New York, Scribner, 1957.
The Sleeping Gypsy and Other Poems. Austin, University of Texas Press, 1958.
Abraham's Knife and Other Poems. Chapel Hill, University of North Carolina Press, 1961.
For a Bitter Season: New and Selected Poems. Columbia, University of Missouri Press, 1967.
Welcome to the Medicine Show: Postcards, Flashcards, Snapshots. Winston-Salem, North Carolina, Palaemon Press, 1978.
Luck's Shining Child: A Miscellany of Poems and Verses. Winston-Salem, North Carolina, Palaemon Press, 1981.
The Collected Poems of George Garrett. Fayetteville, University of Arkansas Press, 1984.

Other

James Jones (biography). New York, Harcourt Brace, 1984.
Understanding Mary Lee Settle. Columbia, University of South Carolina Press, 1988.
My Silk Purse and Yours: The Publishing Scene and American Literary Art. Columbia, University of Missouri Press, 1992.
The Sorrows of Fat City: A Selection of Literary Essays and Reviews. Columbia, University of South Carolina Press, 1992.
Whistling in the Dark: True Stories and Other Fables. New York, Harcourt Brace, 1992.

Editor, *New Writing from Virginia.* Charlottesville, Virginia, New Writing Associates, 1963.
Editor, *The Girl in the Black Raincoat.* New York, Duell, 1966.
Editor, with W.R. Robinson, *Man and the Movies.* Baton Rouge, Louisiana State University Press, 1967.
Editor, with R.H.W. Dillard and John Moore, *The Sounder Few: Essays from "The Hollins Critic."* Athens, University of Georgia Press, 1971.
Editor, with O.B. Hardison, Jr., and Jane Gelfman, *Film Scripts 1-4.* New York, Appleton Century Crofts, 4 vols., 1971-72.
Editor, with William Peden, *New Writing in South Carolina.* Columbia, University of South Carolina Press, 1971.
Editor, with John Graham, *Craft So Hard to Learn.* New York, Morrow, 1972.
Editor, with John Graham, *The Writer's Voice.* New York, Morrow, 1973.
Editor, with Walton Beacham, *Intro 5.* Charlottesville, University Press of Virginia, 1974.
Editor, with Katherine Garrison Biddle, *The Botteghe Oscure Reader.* Middletown, Connecticut, Wesleyan University Press, 1974.
Editor, *Intro 6: Life As We Know It.* New York, Doubleday, 1974.
Editor, *Intro 7: All of Us and None of You.* New York, Doubleday, 1975.
Editor, *Intro 8: The Liar's Craft.* New York, Doubleday, 1977.
Editor, with Michael Mewshaw, *Intro 9.* Austin, Texas, Hendel and Reinke, 1979.

Editor, with Sheila McMillen, *Eric Clapton's Lovers and Other Stories from the Virginia Quarterly Review.* Charlottesville, University Press of Virginia, 1990.
Editor, with Mary Flinn, *Elvis in Oz: New Stories and Poems from the Hollins Creative Writing Program.* Charlottesville, University Press of Virginia, n.d.
Editor, with Susan Stamberg, *The Wedding Cake in the Middle of the Road.* New York, Norton, 1992.
Editor, with Paul Ruffin, *That's What I Like (About the South).* Columbia, University of South Carolina Press, 1993.

*

Bibliography: In *Seven Princeton Poets,* Princeton University Library, 1963; "George Garrett: A Checklist of His Writings" by R.H.W. Dillard, in *Mill Mountain Review* (Roanoke, Virginia), Summer 1971; *George Garrett: A Bibliography 1947-1988* by Stuart Wright, Huntsville, Texas Review Press, 1989.

Manuscript Collection: Duke University, Durham, North Carolina.

Critical Studies: By James B. Meriwether, in *Princeton University Library Chronicle* (New Jersey), vol. 25, no. 1, 1963; "George Garrett Issue" of *Mill Mountain Review* (Roanoke, Virginia), Summer 1971; "Imagining the Individual: George Garrett's *Death of the Fox*" by W. R. Robinson, in *Hollins Critic* (Hollins College, Virginia), August 1971; "The Reader Becomes Text: Methods of Experimentation in George Garrett's *The Succession*" by Tom Whalen, in *Texas Review* (Huntsville), Summer 1983; "George Garrett and the Historical Novel" by Monroe K. Spears, in *Virginia Quarterly Review* (Charlottesville), Spring 1985; *To Come Up Grinning: A Tribute to George Garrett* edited by Paul Ruffin and Stuart Wright, Huntsville, Texas Review Press, 1989; *Understanding George Garrett* by R.H.W. Dillard, Columbia, University of South Carolina Press, 1989.

George Garrett comments:

(1972) I feel I am only just beginning, still learning my craft, trying my hand at as many things, as many ways and means of telling as many stories as I'm able to. I hope that this will always be the case, that somehow I'll avoid the slow horror of repeating myself or the blind rigor of an obsession. I can't look back, I'm not ashamed of the work I've done, but it is done. And I am (I hope) moving ahead, growing and changing. Once I've seen something into print I do not re-read it. I have tried always to write out of experience, but that includes imaginative experience which is quite as "real" to me and for me as any other and, indeed, in no way divorces from the outward and visible which we often (and inaccurately) call reality. I only hope to continue to learn and to grow. And to share experience with my imaginary reader. I use the singular because a book is a direct encounter, a conversation between one writer and one reader. Though I couldn't care less how many, in raw numbers, read my work, I have the greatest respect for that one imaginary reader. I hope to manage to please that reader before I'm done, to give as much delight, or some sense of it, as I have received from reading good books by good writers.

(1986) Years and scars, and various and sundry books, later, I would not change much in my earlier statement, innocent as it was. Now that I am in my mid-fifties I would not use the word *hope* so much. Naturally I have less hope for myself; though I insist on maintaining high hopes for the best of the young writers I teach. And I have every intention, with and without hope, to continue working, trying to learn my craft always (never to *master* it), still seeking, sometimes finding my imaginary reader. I know more than a decade's worth of darker, sadder things than I did in 1972. So does the world. So goes the world. Well, I have learned a full deck of new jokes, also, and never ceased to taste good laughter. If some hopes have faded and been abandoned, faith, which is altogether something else, has replaced them. And the old dog learns new tricks. One: to turn to the light and live on it until it's gone. Another: to be as open as I can until my book is closed.

(1991) In 1989 I was suddenly 60 years old, older than I had planned to be or ever imagined. Not that a whole lot has changed (I was and am still a viable candidate for the American Tomb of the Unknown Writer); but I did finish my Elizabethan trilogy; and now I have a new publisher and have embarked on three related American novels, coming out of our recent history. I am not planning to live forever, but I would like to finish telling these stories and some others on my mind. Meantime I'm a grandfather and have the pleasure of seeing a generation and a half of former students writing and publishing books on their own. And I am sometimes surprised by the kindness of strangers. The world is not (all claims to the contrary) a kinder or gentler place; but, somewhat to my cynical chagrin, I keep discovering worthy and amazing creatures in it.

(1995) Is there anything to add? Years-now I'm 65 and counting. And still working as hard as I can, hoping to get the work done, hoping, from here on, the work will simply speak for itself.

*   *   *

Directness, seriousness, a Chaucerian comic sense which in no way conflicts with that seriousness, imaginative vigor, sheer intelligence, and a rich variety of matter and manner—these qualities mark the fiction of George Garrett. An American, a southerner, Garrett has published seven novels, a collection of short novels, five collections of stories (including the major collection of new and selected stories, *An Evening Performance*), seven books of poems (including *The Collected Poems*), plays and screenplays, and a respectable body of critical work (including a biography of James Jones and a monograph on the fiction of Mary Lee Settle). This output reveals his energy and the scope of his interests, and they offer some indication of the seriousness with which he pursues his vocation as writer. Garrett approaches his world and his work with an Elizabethan forcefulness and range, directly and with all his strength.

Garrett is a Christian artist—not a pietist, but a writer whose very sense of the living world is infused with an Augustinian Christian understanding. He is a realist and not a fabulist, but, because of his Christian belief, his work is never far from parable, his direct reality always shaped by the enigmas of the spirit. His seven novels are very different each from each in subject and texture, but together they form a quest for a narrative structure sufficient to the expression of his increasingly more complex view of the ways of the world. *The Finished Man* is a novel of modern Florida politics; *Which Ones Are the Enemy?* takes place in Trieste during the American occupation following World War II; *Do, Lord, Remember Me* concerns the shattering visit of an evangelist to a small Southern town; *Death of the Fox* is an account of the events, exterior and interior, of the last two days of Sir Walter Raleigh's life; *The Succession* is a synoptic recreation of the events surrounding the suc-

cession of James I to the throne of Queen Elizabeth; *Poison Pen* (a new novel built upon the ruins of a larger, unfinished novel to have been called *Life with Kim Novak Is Hell*) is an acidly satirical examination of American public lives, illusion and reality, and the real and illusory nature of fiction itself; *Entered from the Sun* is an Elizabethan mystery novel which explores the illusion and impenetrable reality surrounding Christopher Marlowe's death. But they are all products of the same central concerns—a blessing of the dark and fallen world, a knowledge of the power of the imagination to enter that dark world and create and sustain values in it, a faith in the possibility of redemption and salvation even in the very process of the fall into sin and death, and a commitment to the individual moment as the sole window on eternity.

Garrett's major works thus far are the novels in his Elizabethan historical trilogy. In *Death of the Fox* all of his major thematic concerns come together in the person of Ralegh, the soldier, the politician, the sailor, the poet, and the morally creative man. In his imaginative union with Ralegh, Garrett fuses present and past into an artistic whole which is both truth and lie—the disappointing truth which nevertheless burns ideally in the imagination and dreams of the beholder (as in Garrett's earlier short story, "An Evening Performance") and the saving lie of love (as in his poem "Fig Leaves") which enables us "to live together." *The Succession* both extends and fulfills the stylistic and formal advances of *Death of the Fox* by presenting a thoroughly researched and vividly written account of English and Scottish life in the years succeeding, following, and pivoting upon the succession in 1603, and at the same time developing an aesthetic meditation on the creation and revelation of meaning in the succession of moments that makes up the nexus of time. Set in 1597, *Entered from the Sun* brings the trilogy round full circle, allowing Ralegh to be viewed this time from the outside rather than from within, and commenting both upon the way time conceals truth and the way the fictive imagination attempts to penetrate those concealing veils—commenting, therefore, upon itself and upon the trilogy as a whole.

How he will develop as he moves beyond these major milestones of his career (the Elizabethan trilogy, the collected stories, and the collected poems) is fascinating to contemplate. Garrett has always continued to grow and change in his work while so many of his contemporaries have faltered or simply repeated themselves book after book. His importance becomes clearer year by year as the magnitude of his exploration of reality (outward and inward) reveals itself with each new and startlingly original book.

—R.H.W. Dillard

GASS, William H(oward)

Nationality: American. **Born:** Fargo, North Dakota, 30 July 1924. **Education:** Schools in Warren, Ohio; Kenyon College, Gambier, Ohio, 1942-43, 1946-47, A.B. 1947; Ohio Wesleyan University, Delaware, 1943; Cornell University, Ithaca, New York, 1947-50, Ph.D. 1954. **Military Service:** Served in the United States Navy, 1943-46: Ensign. **Family:** Married 1) Mary Pat O'Kelly in 1952, two sons and one daughter; 2) Mary Alice Henderson in 1969, two daughters. **Career:** Instructor in Philosophy, College of Wooster, Ohio, 1950-54; assistant professor, 1954-60, associate professor, 1960-65, and professor of philosophy, 1966-69, Purdue

University, Lafayette, Indiana. Since 1969 professor of philosophy, now David May Distinguished University Professor in the Humanities and director, International Writers Center, both Washington University, St. Louis. Visiting lecturer in English and philosophy, University of Illinois, Urbana, 1958-59. **Awards:** Longview Foundation award, 1969; Rockefeller fellowship, 1965; Guggenheim fellowship, 1969; American Academy award, 1975; Award of Merit medal, 1979; National Book Critics Circle award, for criticism, 1986. L.H.D.: Kenyon College, 1973; George Washington University, Washington, D.C., 1982; Purdue University, 1985. **Member:** American Academy, 1983. **Agent:** International Creative Management, 40 West 57th Street, New York, New York 10019. **Address:** International Writers Center, Campus Box 1071, One Brookings Drive, Washington University, St. Louis, Missouri 63130-4899, U.S.A.

PUBLICATIONS

Novels

Omensetter's Luck. New York, New American Library, 1966; London, Collins, 1967.
Willie Masters' Lonesome Wife (essay-novella). New York, Knopf, 1971.
The Tunnel. New York, Knopf, 1995.

Short Stories

In the Heart of the Heart of the Country and Other Stories. New York, Harper, 1968; London, Cape, 1969.
The First Winter of My Married Life. Northridge, California, Lord John Press, 1979.
Culp. New York, Grenfell Press, 1985.

Uncollected Short Stories

"The Clairvoyant," in *Location 2* (New York), 1964.
"The Sugar Crock," in *Art and Literature 9* (Paris), 1966.
"We Have Not Lived the Right Life," in *New American Review 6,* edited by Theodore Solotaroff. New York, New American Library, 1969.
"The Cost of Everything," in *Fiction* (New York), vol. 1, no. 3, 1972.
"Mad Meg," in *Iowa Review* (Iowa City), Winter 1976.
"Koh Whistles Up a Wind," in *Tri-Quarterly 38* (Evanston, Illinois), 1977.
"Susu, I Approach You in My Dreams," in *Tri-Quarterly 42* (Evanston, Illinois), 1978.
"August Bees," in *Delta 8* (Montpellier, France), May 1979.
"The Old Folks," in *The Best American Short Stories 1980,* edited by Stanley Elkin and Shannon Ravenel. Boston, Houghton Mifflin, 1980.
"Why Windows Are Important to Me," in *The Best of Tri-Quarterly,* edited by Jonathan Brent. New York, Washington Square Press, 1982.
"Uncle Balt and the Nature of Being," in *The Pushcart Prize 7,* edited by Bill Henderson. Wainscott, New York, Pushcart Press, 1982.
"Family Album," in *River Styx.* St. Louis, Big River Association, 1986.

Other

Fiction and the Figures of Life. New York, Knopf, 1970.
On Being Blue. Boston, Godine, 1976; Manchester, Carcanet, 1979.
The World Within the Word: Essays. New York, Knopf, 1978.
The House VI Book, with Peter Eisenman. Boston, Godine, 1980.
Habitations of the Word: Essays. New York, Simon and Schuster, 1985.
Words about the Nature of Things. St. Louis, Washington University, 1985.
A Temple of Texts. St. Louis, Washington University, 1990.

*

Bibliography: "A William H. Gass Bibliography" by Larry McCaffery, in *Critique* (Atlanta), August 1976.

Manuscript Collection: Washington University Library, St. Louis.

Critical Studies: "Omensetter's Luck" by Richard Gilman, in *New Republic* (Washington, D.C.), 7 May 1966; "The Stone and the Sermon" by Saun O'Connell, in *Nation* (New York), 9 May 1966; "Nothing But the Truth" by Richard Howard, in *New Republic* (Washington, D.C.), 18 May 1968; interview with Thomas Haas in the *Chicago Daily News,* 1 February 1969; *City of Words* by Tony Tanner, London, Cape, and New York, Harper, 1971; "The Well Spoken Passions of William H. Gass" by Earl Shorris, in *Harper's* (New York), May 1972; "But This Is What It Is Like to Live in Hell," in *Modern Fiction Studies* (Lafayette, Indiana), Autumn 1974; "Against the Grain: Theory and Practice in the Work of William H. Gass" by Ned French, in *Iowa Review* (Iowa City), Winter 1976; *The Metafictional Muse: The Works of Robert Coover, Donald Barthelme, and William H. Gass* by Larry McCaffery, Pittsburgh, University of Pittsburgh Press, 1982.

William H. Gass comments:

I think of myself as a writer of prose rather than a novelist, critic, or storyteller, and I am principally interested in the problems of style. My fictions are, by and large, experimental constructions; that is, I try to make things out of words the way a sculptor might make a statue out of stone. Readers will therefore find very little in the way of character or story in my stories. Working in the tradition of the Symbolist poets, I regard the techniques of fiction (for the contemporary artist) as in no way distinct from the strategies of the long poem.

*   *   *

William H. Gass, a philosopher and literary critic as well as a fiction writer, derives from and is closely allied to the *symbolistes,* Gertrude Stein, Ortega y Gasset, John Crowe Ransom and the New Critics generally, Borges, Robbe-Grillet, Sarraute, and the structuralists. He believes that language is all in all; that words are not agents to instruct or direct us in fiction but that they exist there for their own sake; that the novelist must keep us imprisoned in his language, because there is nothing beyond it; and that the only events in novels are linguistic events. Metaphor is the means by which concepts are expressed in fiction. The writer, furthermore, does not simply render a world; he makes one out of language, creating imaginary objects and imaginary lives. He works toward the purity of prose fiction and the autonomy of art. He works against the concept of mimesis, that is the imitation of "reality," partly because it is futile for the artist to strive for the illusion of life, and partly because he has no obligation to life. His commitment is to aesthetic satisfaction achieved through metaphorical language; it is to writing as process.

Omensetter's Luck, is accordingly, an exercise in the use of language, which in this instance is a prose that strives constantly to be like poetry or music. The words are better than experience, are, indeed, the experience, and the book is intended to be about language and writing. To give himself ample opportunity to exercise his writing capabilities, Gass designed the novel in three sections, each written in a different mode: the first in the narrative, the second in the lyric, and the third in the rhetorical and dramatic modes. The rhythms and images of the Bible, the baroque qualities of Sir Thomas Browne, the technical virtuosity of Flaubert, the stream of consciousness of Joyce all contribute to the writing of the novel in full freedom from the conventional principles of realism and the traditional values of humanism. Nevertheless, lurking behind this dedication to process are narrative and theme, those Gass-identified enemies to the purity of art. The novel dramatizes a conflict between Omensetter, a natural force who represents being-in-nature, and Jethro Furber, a man of religion and thought, obsessed with death and sex. Attractive as he is, Omensetter demonstrates the inadequacies of mindless and spiritless being, while Furber shows us the failure to fuse successfully word, belief, and action in such a way as to elevate the spirit. In short, Gass has drawn, perhaps despite himself, upon the mythological dimensions of Christianity.

While the title story in Gass's *In the Heart of the Heart of the Country* is confessedly modeled on reality, the collection as a whole is experimental. "The Pedersen Kid" is deliberately designed to call into question the nature of reality and the possibility of truth, matters that must live side by side with Gass's concern for the shape of his sentences and the relation of sentence to sentence in the paragraph. In the stories generally, the narrative voice struggles to get inside the characters and with words, magic words, steal their souls away and play with them.

But even more thoroughly committed to experimentalism is *Willie Masters' Lonesome Wife,* in which conventional narrative is largely discarded. The book offers instead a pastiche of various materials: reminiscences of the narrator, little essays on words and the imagination by the author, a variety of typographical play, authorial abuse of the reader, a parody of pornography, and footnotes. All this is designed to destroy the character and form of traditional fiction and to offer opportunities, once the old patterns of linear and logical thought, linear time, and linear print are broken up, for free-wheeling use of the imagination. The book is an experience in art, as Gass tells us at the end, where he inserts a motto: You have fallen into art—return to life. In *Willie Masters' Lonesome Wife* Gass gives himself to self-indulgent play, maximizing the freedom that the author, a god-like figure in Gass's view, justifiably claims in his dedication to the autonomy of art.

—Chester E. Eisinger

GEE, Maggie (Mary)

Nationality: British. **Born:** Poole, Dorset, 2 November 1948. **Education:** Horsham High School for Girls; Somerville College, Oxford (open scholarship), B.A. 1969, M.Litt. 1972, Ph.D. in English 1980. **Family:** Married Nicholas Rankin in 1983; one daughter. **Career:** Editor, Elsevier International Press, Oxford, 1972-74; research assistant, Wolverhampton Polytechnic, 1975-79; Eastern Arts writing fellow, University of East Anglia, Norwich, 1982; since 1987 honorary visiting fellow, Sussex University, 1987. Lives in London. **Agent:** Jonathan Lloyd, Curtis Brown, 4th Floor Haymarket House, 28/29 Haymarket, London SW1Y 4SP, England.

PUBLICATIONS

Novels

Dying, In Other Words. Brighton, Harvester Press, 1981; Boston, Faber, 1984.
The Burning Book. London, Faber, 1983; New York, St. Martin's Press, 1984.
Light Years. London, Faber, 1985; New York, St. Martin's Press, 1986.
Grace. London, Heinemann, 1988; New York, Grove Weidenfeld, 1989.
Where Are the Snows. London, Heinemann, 1991; New York, Ticknor and Fields, 1992.
Lost Children. London, HarperCollins, 1994.

Uncollected Short Stories

"Rose on the Broken," in *Granta 7* (Cambridge), 1982.
"Mornington Place," in *London Tales,* edited by Julian Evans. London, Hamish Hamilton, 1983.

Plays

Over and Out (broadcast, 1984). Published in *Literary Review* (London), February 1984.

Radio Play: *Over and Out,* 1984.

Other

Editor, *For Life on Earth.* Norwich, University of East Anglia, 1982.

*

Maggie Gee comments:

My chief 20th-century models are probably Woolf, Nabokov, and Beckett. But I was also raised on the great 19th-century writers like Dickens and Thackeray. And I loved *stories:* I read and reread my mother's copy of Hans Christian Andersen. I wanted to write stories myself; and I always felt that the difficulty of much 20th-century "serious" writing must be a problem, not a virtue. If I was difficult, it was despite myself. On the one hand I wanted to write new things, and tell the absolute truth according to my perception of it, which often seems to demand new ways of writing: on the other hand, I've become increasingly aware of the importance of an audience.

My first published novel, *Dying, In Other Words,* is probably the most difficult technically. It is a bizarre kind of thriller. Moira's body is found on the pavement one morning. The police assume it is suicide; yet the milkman who found the body turns out to be a mass-murderer, far too many of Moira's surviving acquaintances start to die in their turn, and increasingly often the sound of typing can be heard in Moira's "empty" room . . . is she still alive, and writing the story? The novel is a circle; and when it returns inevitably to the point of Moira's death, we find it was neither suicide nor murder, after all. . . .

The Burning Book is a variation on the family saga. Two English working families, the Ships and the Lambs, shop-keepers and railway-workers, try to live their own lives, interrupted by two world wars and the threat of a third. One theme of the book is the stupidity of nuclear weapons, which endanger all stories and the continuity embodied in families. There are flashbacks to Hiroshima and Nagasaki. The family itself isn't perfect; violence and frustration inside it counterpoint violence and frustration outside. On a small scale, though, humans can learn to do better. The central couple, Henry and Lorna, finally learn to love each other by the last chapter of the book, when they go for a winter picnic in an earthly Eden, Kew Gardens. By a stupid irony, the public world of war-like headlines breaks in on their "happy ending." *Light Years* is an inverted romance, set in 1984. The lovers, Lottie and Harold, split up on the first page of the novel, and are apart through the year (and 52 chapters) that the book lasts, though perhaps things change in the very last chapter. . . . The longer they are separated, the more they love each other. Meanwhile, the earth turns full circle, and the seasons, the stars, and the planets play their part in the very formal structure of this book. It is my "easiest" book I think— short chapters, short sections within the chapters, with much "lighter" looking pages: all of which was intended to help express a rather rare commodity in 20th-century literature—happiness.

Retrospectively, I realized that each of these three books was an attempt to write a new version of a popular genre—thriller, family saga, romance—to appeal to basic emotions, and use basic narrative drives, but to re-work the genre in my own way, and to surprise my readers. All I am conscious of at the time of writing, though, is a desire to show the truth, in ways I never can in speech, and a desire to make structures as beautiful as I can.

(1995) *Grace* is an anti-nuclear thriller, whose form and themes both depend on ideas of splitting and one-ness—splitting of the atom, of the male and female sides of ourselves, of families, of society.

Where Are the Snows is a panoramic global love-story, the story of Christopher and Alexandria, a bourgeois couple who give up family and roots for love. They are both archetypal tourists—thinking they can buy the planet and use it as a backdrop for their personal drama—and embodiments of the "transcendental homelessness" that Georg Lukacs saw as central to the novel form. I was writing about a fantasy of eternal youth and romance that runs aground on the rocks of bodily aging, and about our human need for something wider than a couple bond; about the loneliness and greed of contemporary western society; about our selfish desire to have everything for ourselves, within our own individual life-spans, and a consequent contempt for the future and the past, most obviously shown in my central couple's abandonment of Christopher's teenage children, and Alexandra "forgetting" to have children of her own—until it is too late.

Lost Children is a British book, like *Grace*. It is about the process of dealing with loss—of a teenage daughter, Zoe, who runs away from home, in the first instance. But the bereaved mother, Alma, is driven back to her own lost childhood as she tries to understand what has happened; is it the working-through of an older pattern of unhappiness that has driven her daughter away in 1993?

The 90s London of the novel is full of poverty and literal lost, homeless children, a darker city than the already troubled London of *Light Years,* a decade earlier. The personal question the book asks is one that particularly concerns the middle-aged, like Alma— how can we understand our parents? How can we understand and forgive ourselves as parents?

The Keeper of the Gate (work in progress) is about the difficult transition between centuries, and that between life and death. One of London's last Park Keepers has a stroke and faces death. In his absence in the hospital, a racial murder takes place in a park which for a hundred years has never known a major crime. Meanwhile, the middle-class children of this working-class man jostle for position around his bed and try to understand their parents, themselves, and the frightening future. The sub-text of this book is the loss of public space, the breakdown of public order, the lost notion of truly shared society—and how black and white can live together.

*   *   *

In her as yet short career as a novelist Maggie Gee has gained the reputation of an experimentalist. Technically innovative would be the way I would prefer to describe her work, and this is certainly true of her first novel *Dying, In Other Words.* Beginning with the dramatic suicide of a young writer, Moira Penny, *Dying, In Other Words* could have been a brightly written but run-of-the-mill suspense thriller, and in some ways it is. But it is considerably more than that, for Penny's suicide is dropped, as it were, into the pool of lives around her and the ripples spread and impinge on the lives of others and, what makes the novel remarkable, on the continuum of the past and present of those lives. *Dying, In Other Words* has been described as a "Chinese box of a novel" and that is well put. As the novel progresses the implications of Penny's suicide reach further and further into the lives of others. But while the past impinges, the future overshadows, and in *Dying, In Other Words* there are already dark hints of the Armageddon to come. What her characters are unaware of is as important as that of which they are aware: "What Bill didn't know was that the girl he evoked, with her long brown limbs and her full yellow rose bud skirt and her underwear smelling of lemon perfume and seaweed died six months later in a car crash." Gee encourages an awareness that her characters exist in a fiction. She pushes beyond this and writes in her second novel *The Burning Book:* "All of us live in a novel, and none of us do the writing. Just off the stage there are grim old men planning to cut the lighting." Thus Gee can be seen, in spite of (or perhaps because of) her experimentation, to be in the tradition of Fielding and Dickens where the author is ever-present, ready to comment or intervene.

If the ghost of the future is fleetingly glimpsed in *Dying, In Other Words,* it positively haunts *The Burning Book.* Indeed that is its theme and purpose as it explores the loves, joys, frustrations, quarrels, hates, degradations and pettinesses of Lorna and her family. "In an ordinary novel," Gee interpolates, "that would be the whole story," but the shadow cast on the future by Hiroshima and Nagasaki darkens the final episode in this everyday story of ordinary folk. It is to Gee's purpose that they are so ordinary, even petty, in their thoughts and relationships, and it is a tribute to her narrative skills that she carries us with them through their dull and messy lives. Because it is their very dullness and messiness that allow us to identify with them and make their final pointless agonizing destruction so telling and poignantly horrifying. As a nuclear warning the book certainly succeeds; and it succeeds as a work of literature as well.

Nevertheless, *The Burning Book* leaves two largish questions. One is that if Gee wishes her fears and anxieties for our future to be more universally understood, and the passion I sense behind her novels suggests she does, then she may well have to find less sophisticated means to her end. The other question is that having written the terminal novel where does she go? Where she went immediately was to her novel *Light Years*. "An oddly simple and old fashioned love story" one reviewer has described it. But all Gee's stories as such are simple and old fashioned: the story of a mysterious suicide in *Dying, In Other Words,* an everyday family saga in *The Burning Book.* It is what she makes of this material that leaves it far from simple and old fashioned. The narrative of Harold and Ottie in *Light Years* can be enjoyed on the story level alone, but Gee's intentions are more involved. She can entertain and does, but she has no wish to entertain alone: her narratives reflect a wider, less immediate, context. Sometimes, in order to do this, she has to rely on her author's interpolations and interventions and there is a danger that these can become digressive or intrusive and defeat their purpose. But there is no danger that Gee will cease to look with a compassionate but unblinking eye at a world in which there are no happy endings.

In her novel *Grace* there are signs that Gee is solving the problem posed by *The Burning Book. Grace* has the pace and structure of a superior thriller in the style of Ruth Rendell. The threads of the story and the lives they describe gradually and skillfully converge and intermesh. In addition *Grace* is finely written. Take this description of the seaside town where much of the action takes place:

> They do not have their grandeur, these white hotels, set square to the waves, with their flags streaming backwards, flying in splendor from the prevailing winds. Salt eats the paint every winter, and the wood and plaster underneath; each spring they repaint it, and if the walls have shrunk you would hardly detect it from one year to the next . . . in a few decades, the loss might show.
>
> Coming each year to the white hotels—The Empire, The Sandhurst, The Majestic, The Windsor—the regular guests never notice. Though may be the porter looks older, and that waitress is no longer here, retired, they suppose, to the country cottage she chatted about as she served the soup.

The description is graphic, but it is more than a visual description for there is something of the continuity of decay in it and in it something of the spirit of place. Though in this case we might call it the dispirit of place! Whatever we call it catches the place and its atmosphere beautifully. I quote this as an example of the quality of Gee's writing in *Grace.* But as her earlier novels have led us to expect the context of *Grace* and the lives of its characters is a much wider one. The context is of a world of fall-out from Chernobyl, of the trains running through our suburbs carrying nuclear waste, and of the murder of Hilda Murrell. The drama of *Grace* with its overlapping and interlocking lives and situations is played out against this background which impinges and is as fundamental to the story as Hardy's countryside is to his novels. *Grace* can be seen as an exciting and considerable advance in the art of Gee's novels.

—John Cotton

GEE, Maurice (Gough)

Nationality: New Zealander. **Born:** Whakatane, 22 August 1931. **Education:** Avondale College, Auckland, 1945-49; University of Auckland, 1950-53, M.A. in English 1953; Auckland Teachers College, 1954. **Family:** Married Margaretha Garden in 1970, two daughters; one son from previous relationship. **Career:** Schoolteacher, 1955-57; held various jobs, 1958-66; assistant librarian, Alexander Turnbull Library, Wellington, 1967-69; city librarian, Napier Public Library, 1970-72; deputy librarian, Teachers Colleges Library, Auckland, 1974-76. Since 1976 full-time writer; writing fellow, Victoria University of Wellington, 1989. **Awards:** New Zealand Literary Fund scholarship, 1962, 1976, 1986, 1987, and Award of Achievement, 1967, 1973; University of Otago Robert Burns fellowship, 1964; Hubert Church Prose award, 1973; New Zealand Book award, 1976, 1979, 1982, 1991; James Tait Black Memorial prize, 1979; Wattie award, 1979, 1993; New Zealand Children's Book of the Year award, 1984; New Zealand Library Association Esther Glen Medal, 1986. D.Litt.: Victoria University of Wellington, 1987. **Agent:** Richards Literary Agency, P.O. Box 31240, Milford, Auckland 9. **Address:** 41 Chelmsford Street, Ngaio, Wellington, New Zealand.

PUBLICATIONS

Novels

The Big Season. London, Hutchinson, 1962.
A Special Flower. London, Hutchinson, 1965.
In My Father's Den. London, Faber, 1972.
Games of Choice. London, Faber, 1976.
Plumb. London, Faber, 1978.
Meg. London, Faber, 1981; New York, St. Martin's Press, 1982.
Sole Survivor. London, Faber, and New York, St. Martin's Press, 1983.
Prowlers. London, Faber, 1987.
The Burning Boy. London, Faber, 1990.
Going West. London, Faber, 1992.
Crime Story. Auckland, Viking, 1994; London, Faber, 1995.

Short Stories

A Glorious Morning, Comrade. Auckland, Auckland University Press-Oxford University Press, 1975.
Collected Short Stories. Auckland and London, Penguin, 1986; New York, Penguin, 1987.

Fiction (for children)

Under the Mountain. Wellington, London, and New York, Oxford University Press, 1979.
The World Around the Corner. Wellington, Oxford University Press, 1980; Oxford and New York, Oxford University Press, 1981.
The Halfmen of O. Auckland and Oxford, Oxford University Press, 1982; New York, Oxford University Press, 1983.
The Priests of Ferris. Auckland and Oxford, Oxford University Press, 1984; New York, Oxford University Press, 1985.
Motherstone. Auckland and Oxford, Oxford University Press, 1985.

The Fire-Raiser. Auckland, Oxford University Press, 1986.
The Champion. Auckland, Oxford University Press, 1989.
The Fat Man. Auckland, Viking, 1994.

Plays

Television Series: *Mortimer's Patch,* 1980; *The Fire-Raiser,* from
his own story, 1986; *The Champion,* from his own story, 1989.

Other

Nelson Central School: A History. Nelson, Nelson Central School
Centennial Committee, 1978.

*

Bibliography: "Maurice Gee: A Bibliography" by Cathe Giffuni,
in *Australian and New Zealand Studies in Canada* (London,
Ontario), no. 3, Spring 1990.

Critical Studies: "Beginnings" by Gee, in *Islands* (Auckland),
March 1977; *Introducing Maurice Gee* by David Hill, Auckland,
Longman Paul, 1981; Trevor James, in *World Literature Written
in English* (Guelph, Ontario), vol. 23, no. 1, 1984; Lawrence Jones,
in *Landfall* (Christchurch), September 1984; *Maurice Gee* by Bill
Manhire, Auckland, Oxford University Press, 1986; *Leaving the
Highway: Six Contemporary New Zealand Novelists* by Mark Wil-
liams, Auckland, Auckland University Press, 1990.

*   *   *

With the trilogy of novels comprising *Plumb, Meg* and *Sole Survivor* (published between 1978 and 1983), Maurice Gee established
himself as one of the most distinguished of living New Zealand
writers and indeed as a decidedly prominent figure in his country's
short literary history. Whether this status makes him a major novelist in the totality of contemporary literature written in English is
less clear and more controversial.

Gee first attracted attention in the mid and late 1950s with a few
stories published in New Zealand's best-known literary periodical,
Landfall, and was highly praised by British reviewers in 1961 for
his two stories published in the New Authors series. For complex
reasons characteristic of new countries founded by colonization,
the short story has flourished in New Zealand, and Gee's initial
success in the genre might have encouraged him to adhere to it in
the manner of his great predecessor Katherine Mansfield, rather
than turn to the longer form of the novel, which has taken longer
to acclimatize successfully there than in such countries as Australia
and Canada. However, Gee committed himself to the novel early
in his career and his output of stories is small—regrettably so, because some of his most powerful writing is to be found in the genre.
His best stories, such as the well-known "The Losers" (1959) and
the even more memorable "Eleventh Holiday" (1961),
unostentatiously transcend their surface realism and immediate situations to reverberate with archetypal significance; he possesses the
really good story writer's gift of being able to imply much more
than he states, so that the events described take on a universal, symbolic dimension. Gee concentrates on various aspects of provincial
and small-town petit-bourgeois life in New Zealand, and favourite
themes include isolation, loneliness, the effects of ageing (especially old age), the conflict between conformity and nonconformity,

and the emotional and spiritual claustrophobia of a middle-class
society in which philistinism and aggression are never far beneath
the respectable veneer. In his stories Gee casts a cold eye on New
Zealand without employing the alienating devices of the dedicated
satirist; he therefore achieves a balance between sympathy and criticism.

Gee's first novel, *The Big Season,* is a compressed
Bildungsroman about the central character's quest for selfhood and
identity in a humanly stifling environment, and in this respect recalls such novels as Joyce's *Portrait of the Artist as a Young Man*
and Lawrence's *Sons and Lovers.* Rob Andrews seems to be destined to conform to all the expectations of his very conservative
milieu. He is an excellent rugby player (which probably carries more
prestige in New Zealand than anywhere else), joins his father's small
business, becomes engaged to a nice, wholesome girl, and has the
makings of a future pillar of the blinkered community. Yet Rob
also contains within himself the rebellious streak of the outsider.
The short Prologue, set in 1946 and 1947, describes Rob's
voyeuristic interest as a child in a local boarding house considered
by his parents and their circle to be a den of iniquity and vice and
therefore completely out of bounds. The main narrative in 1958
deals with Rob's crisis of loyalty and responsibility for his own
life when he becomes involved with a small group of social outcasts, principally the burglar and ex-convict Bill Walters, whom he
had encountered at the boarding house as a child. Torn between the
security of bland conformity and the risks of freedom, Rob eventually rejects the world he knows, repudiating its values with a public
act of defiance, but he also precipitates a disaster among his new
associates. Rob's victory over the forces of conservatism is heavily
qualified, and the conclusion, as Rob leaves his home town to begin a new life in Auckland, is open-ended. The strengths of *The
Big Season* lie in Gee's control of the narrative as it builds up
to its dramatic showdown and in the skill with which he invests
the particulars of an individual case-history with symbolic meaning. Gee is less impressive at dealing with Rob's inner life and
psychological development, but the main reservation—and this
is to be a recurrent one—is that his prose is too flat and unex-
citing, too drably realistic, to do justice to the overall imaginative conception.

Structurally and technically Gee's second novel, *A Special
Flower,* is more complex and adventurous than its straightforward
predecessor. While adhering to third-person narration, Gee alters
the main point of view in every section or chapter, marking the
change by a character's name rather than orthodox numbering. By
means of these shifting perspectives, Gee achieves narrative rela-
tivism as opposed to the omniscience of *The Big Season,* and his
unconventional handling of time enhances the effect. The first of
the two main sections deals chronologically with the unexpected
marriage of a seemingly confirmed bachelor in middle age, the eminently respectable Donald Pinnock, to a woman 20 years his junior and of a decidedly lower social position, Coralie Marsh. The
marriage soon flounders, Coralie leaving her husband for a well-
known footballer, who in turn discards her after making her pregnant and also after Donald's suicide, triggered off by her demand
for a divorce. In the second section, Gee puts the clock back to
before Donald's death, this time concentrating more on Coralie than
on members of the Pinnock family. Only after her husband's death
does Coralie come to a full appreciation of his love for her, and
this eventually leads to a reconciliation between Coralie and Donald's
mother and sister as their hatred gives way to understanding—understanding that, for Donald, Coralie provided a gust of fresh air,

offering him his one chance of freedom from the inhibiting confines of New Zealand middle-class propriety and decorum. The short third section, describing Coralie's life with the Pinnocks as she awaits the birth of her baby, gives the novel a more positive and optimistic conclusion than *The Big Season,* despite the tragedy of Donald's death.

The mother-son relationship also plays a prominent part in his third novel, *In My Father's Den,* which opens with a murder, ends with the identification of the killer, but is only incidentally a story of mystery and detection. After a Prologue in the form of a newspaper cutting about the killing of Celia Inverarity, a schoolgirl at Wadesville College near Auckland in May 1969, the novel consists of two intercut strands, both narrated by Paul Prior, an unmarried teacher at Celia's school and a prime suspect. One of these is restricted to a few days at the time of the murder, while the other is his life story, told in historical slices such as "1928-1937." The crime prompts Paul to review his entire life, especially in relation to the emotionally and humanly paralysing forces of small-town and suburban New Zealand, embodied in Wadesville. As a literary intellectual who has spent part of his life abroad, Paul is an outsider in his own country. He is strongly contrasted with Celia's father, Charlie, a rough, crude patriarch who marries Paul's former girlfriend and opposes his daughter's educational interests. Charlie represents an ugly, unacceptable face of middle-class New Zealand that manifests itself in the threats, abuse, and violence directed against Paul after Celia's death because, being a Camus-like *étranger,* he is wrongly assumed by the community to be the murderer. In fact, the killer is Paul's conventional and conformist brother, Andrew, a man stunted by his Oedipal relationship with his mother and by the pressures of New Zealand society. *In My Father's Den,* is among other things, a searing indictment of that smug, one-dimensional society.

In *Games of Choice* Gee's examination of a New Zealand family as it virtually disintegrates during a few days over Christmas acquires something of the intensity of Greek tragedy, although the events are much less bloody and extreme, despite the brutal killing of a pet cat with a garden fork. The pressures precipitating catastrophe have built up over many years because the marriage of Kingsley Pratt, a provincial bookseller, and his wife Alison has long been a sham based on empty convention. The departure of their two children from home in pursuit of their own identities is a key factor in dissolving the bonds that have held the family together, often in a mutually enervating, even destructive, configuration. Parents and children are involved in games of choice, quests for freedom. With his wife leaving him for another man, his student daughter having an affair with a much older lecturer, and his son deciding to join the army in defiance of the family's commitment to pacifism, Kingsley is left with his old father Harry, whose memories include his political activities as an idealistic socialist. In one sense the novel is very narrow in its focus, but Gee succeeds in adding an historical and political dimension by giving the Pratt family emblematic as well as realistic status.

Since the late 1970s Gee has written a substantial body of fiction for children and television scripts, but his principal imaginative undertaking has been the extremely ambitious trilogy of novels about the Plumb family, *Plumb, Meg,* and *Sole Survivor.* Many of the ingredients of the trilogy are present in his earlier novels: the emotional complexity of family life with its blend of loyalty and antagonism, mutual care and incomprehension, love and hate; the relationship between individual and community and between private and public life; conformist acceptance and nonconformist rebellion; relativity of viewpoint. But the scale of trilogy allows Gee to be more expansive and wide-ranging than ever before so that he is able to produce a saga of New Zealand life covering about a hundred years, from the late 19th century to the 1980s, and including six generations while concentrating on three. Because the trilogy incorporates so much of New Zealand's short history since British colonization and includes a number of real-life politicians and major events, it takes on the air of a national epic in the way that a three-generation family saga set in England could not possibly do. Structurally the three novels are similar in that each is a first-person narrative in which the narrator surveys his or her life from the vantage point of a fictional present, where the immediate action provides a framework for recollecting and reconsidering the past. Roughly twenty years separate the fictional presents of the three novels, *Plumb* being set in the 1940s while *Sole Survivor* brings the cycle to a conclusion in the early 1980s. Gee acknowledges that his family history was an important source of inspiration, especially for the first novel; the eponymous narrator George Plumb is partly based on Gee's maternal grandfather, whose wife was in turn the model for Plumb's wife Edith. In a trilogy containing a number of memorable characters, Plumb is certainly the most extraordinary and interesting. He is a flawed hero, a failed saint, a dedicated idealist of religious and political vision whose moral integrity and over-active conscience blind him to part of the truth about both himself and the world he inhabits. His quest for absolutes and his desire to build a New Jerusalem in New Zealand are undermined by the uncompromising fanaticism that motivates him. Although not a tragic novel, *Plumb* is full of tragic irony.

After the spiritual and ideological crises of *Plumb, Meg* seems restrained, but in its own way it is equally panoramic. The narrator, Meg Sole, née Plumb, is the youngest of George and Edith's twelve children and very much her father's favourite. A considerable part of her narrative overlaps chronologically with her father's in *Plumb,* but Meg offers her own view of events previously mentioned and introduces a wide range of new material, not only in the later chapters after George's death in 1950. The enormous size of the Plumb family does, of course, mean that there are many parallel strands, only a few of which can be given prominence in any one novel. Towards the end of her memoir, Meg accurately calls it "a tale of deaths," and the novel conveys a characteristically mid- and late 20th-century sense of entropy in contrast to the passionate 19th-century romanticism and utopianism embodied in Plumb in the earlier novel, although that too runs down as the century advances.

Just as George Plumb's death is reported in *Meg,* Meg's horrific death by fire in a domestic accident is related in the punningly titled *Sole Survivor,* narrated by one of her three children, the journalist Raymond Sole, equally punningly known as R. Sole. This is another "tale of deaths," specifically triggered off by the murder of Douglas Plumb, a grandson of George and therefore one of Raymond's numerous cousins, as well as being a cabinet minister. If *Plumb* is the most religious of the three novels and *Meg* the most domestic, *Sole Survivor* is the most political, with fictional and nonfictional elements combined (Douglas is a member of Muldoon's National Government). In *Sole Survivor* Raymond interweaves a selective account of his own life from childhood to middle age with a parallel account of Douglas's career. Even when young, Douglas always put self-interest first, and Raymond recalls his cousin's ruthless pursuit of his own advantage and of power, from the sexual to the political. Douglas's expediency and aggressive opportunism are a total perversion of his grandfather's high-minded dedication to his socialist conception of Man, and the story of Douglas's carefully engineered ascent to prominence, almost to the premiership, is, paradoxically, also a story of decline and fall and entropy—the collapse and disintegration of George Plumb's unrealistic yet noble ideals at both the personal and political levels. The nemesis of Douglas's death does not cancel out what his life represents about the nature of success in the 20th century. The ending of *Sole Survivor* and the trilogy as a whole is open-ended rather than pessimistic, but the emphasis is on the failure to realize the New Zealand dream, the slide from heroic vision to debased materialism. Gee's achievement in encompassing the general through the particular and in sustaining a high level of imaginative input makes the trilogy one of the two or three outstanding works of fiction by a New Zealander in the postwar period.

The two adult novels Gee has published since the trilogy, *Prowlers* and *The Burning Boy,* continue his exploration of the particularities of New Zealand life, drawing in particular on his home town of Nelson. *Prowlers* is a highly compressed and selective family saga, spanning much of the 20th century and narrated by a distinguished scientist and public servant, the octogenarian Sir Noel Papps. He is prompted to review his own long life when his grandniece Kate picks his brains for information about his equally famous sister Kitty, a leading figure in the Labor Party for many years. While Kate researches the past in order to write a biography of her grandmother, Noel reminisces about his experiences and friendships in the town of Jessop from his childhood at the time of World War I up to the 1980s. In their different ways Noel and Kate prowl through history and memory. The narrative oscillates between past and present, but instead of presenting a methodical account of Noel's and Kitty's careers in the public arena, it focuses more on their personal relationships and other aspects of their private lives. What emerges is a series of interrelated vignettes and episodes cohering into a panoramic tapestry of Jessop during most of its history, but with the emphasis on the richness and quirkiness of emotional experience—on what it is to be human.

In both the trilogy and *Prowlers* Gee offers a broad historical overview of his characters' lives. In *The Burning Boy,* on the other hand, the time span in the mid-1980s is quite short, generating a greater dramatic intensity. At the symbolic level Gee orchestrates his narrative around the four elements of fire, water, air, and earth in a subtle and unostentatious manner. The novel, which falls into three main sections ("Spring Rain," "Dry Times," and "Fire"), opens with the burned boy of the title, a badly scarred victim of an accident in which another boy died, and ends with a devastating bush fire, which threatens the town of Saxton and kills one of the main characters. At the literal level Gee handles the relatively large cast of equally important characters and the complex network of their relationships with sophistication. By presenting a cross-section of Saxton, from its most puritanical and outwardly respectable inhabitants to its violent criminal elements, Gee creates a vivid portrait of an entire community while projecting the principal characters with considerable depth and complexity. The specific context is provincial New Zealand, but the inner conflicts and interpersonal tensions that Gee analyses are typical of all modern Western societies. Gee succeeds in universalising the microcosm of Saxton.

—Peter Lewis

GELLHORN, Martha (Ellis)

Nationality: American. **Born:** St. Louis, Missouri, in 1908. **Education:** The John Burroughs School, St. Louis; Bryn Mawr College, Pennsylvania. **Family:** Married 1) the writer Ernest Hemingway in 1940 (divorced 1945); 2) T. S. Matthews in 1954 (divorced 1964); one son. **Career:** Correspondent for *Collier's Weekly* in Spain, 1937-38, Finland, 1939, China, 1940-41, England, Italy, France, and Germany, 1943-45, and Java, 1946; for the *Guardian* in Vietnam, 1966, and Israel, 1967; and for *New Statesman* in El Salvador, 1983, and Nicaragua, 1985. Lives in London and Wales. **Awards:** O. Henry award, 1958. **Agent:** Gillon Aitken, Aitken and Stone Ltd., 29 Fernshaw Road, London SW10 0TG, England. **Address:** 72 Cadogan Sq., London S.W.1, England.

PUBLICATIONS

Novels

What Mad Pursuit. New York, Stokes, 1934.
A Stricken Field. New York, Duell, 1940; London, Cape, 1942.
Liana. New York, Scribner, and London, Home and Van Thal, 1944.
The Wine of Astonishment. New York, Scribner, 1948; as *Point of No Return,* New York, New American Library, 1989.
His Own Man. New York, Simon and Schuster, 1961.
The Lowest Trees Have Tops. London, Joseph, 1967; New York, Dodd Mead, 1969.

Short Stories

The Trouble I've Seen. New York, Morrow, and London, Putnam, 1936.
The Heart of Another. New York, Scribner, 1941; London, Home and Van Thal, 1946.
The Honeyed Peace. New York, Doubleday, 1953; London, Deutsch, 1954.
Two by Two. New York, Simon and Schuster, and London, Longman, 1958.
Pretty Tales for Tired People. New York, Simon and Schuster, and London, Joseph, 1965.
The Weather in Africa. London, Allen Lane, 1978; New York, Dodd Mead, 1980.
The Short Novels of Martha Gellhorn. London, Sinclair Stevenson, 1991; as *The Novellas of Martha Gellhorn,* New York, Knopf, 1993, and London, Picador, 1994.

Plays

Love Goes to Press, with Virginia Cowles (produced London, 1946; New York, 1947). Lincoln, University of Nebraska Press, 1995.

Television Play: *Venus Ascendant,* 1963.

Other

The Face of War. New York, Simon and Schuster, and London, Hart Davis, 1959; revised edition, London, Sphere, 1967, London, Virago Press, 1986.

Travels with Myself and Another. London, Allen Lane, 1978; New York, Dodd Mead, 1979.
The View from the Ground. New York, Atlantic Monthly Press, 1988; London, Granta, 1989.

*

Manuscript Collection: Boston University.

Critical Studies: *Nothing Ever Happens to the Brave: The Story of Martha Gellhorn* by Carl E. Rollyson, (Carl Edmund), New York, St. Martin's, 1990.

*   *   *

Some novelists are born to their craft. Others are made. Among the latter kind are those who, while possessing no striking originality of gift or of vision, have nonetheless an ability to handle prose, to depict scenes, and to control narrative flow which make them very similar in kind to the good journalist (and the gifts of novelist and journalist do, after all, cross at a great many points). Martha Gellhorn is one of the better "made" writers. None of her novels can be considered a masterpiece, none has pioneered a new kind of fiction and in none do we experience that all-important shock of recognition that comes when we encounter a genuinely original voice. Yet that said it has to be added that if her novels never surprise they rarely disappoint. At the very least there is about them a cool, controlled craftsmanship that rewards our interest in them.

Gellhorn is without doubt remarkable for the utterly candid manner in which she understands and makes the most of her gifts. She does not try to overreach herself; she knows, none better, what she can and what she cannot do, and she keeps her fiction within the scope of her abilities. As a result she is incapable of falling disastrously flat, as is so often the way with would-be "great" writers who lack her sure self-knowledge. On the other hand, it is no good expecting her to take the kind of dangerous risk which is perhaps necessary for the production of major art. Gellhorn is modest, efficient, clever, and above all she is content to move within limits which she knows she can encompass.

Much of her ability as a novelist is bound up with her ability as a journalist, and in this respect it is worth noting that as a journalist she is first-rate. She produced a searingly accurate and moving account of her journey to Vietnam to investigate the effect America's war was having on the unhappy people of that country. And what more than anything else comes across from her reports is her candor, her real feeling for people no matter what the color of their skins or their political ideologies, and the openness, even perhaps acute vulnerability of her conscience. She did not produce bleeding-heart journalism—and indeed all her writing, fiction especially, is remarkable for the wry toughness of her stance towards life (a kind of controlled stoicism which it would probably be unfair to say she derived from her one-time husband, Ernest Hemingway, but which has striking affinities with his steely self-containment). But for all that, there is in her accounts of life in Vietnam a real tenderness of regard for individuals which shows how easily the novelist and journalist blend into each other. For her fiction is good in its controlled but never dispassionate observation of different people caught up in fates which they can neither control nor ignore.

In this respect *A Stricken Field* and *The Trouble I've Seen* are works in which Gellhorn's powers of judicious, sympathetic, wry,

and compassionate observation of human beings are at their best. And although both suffer from what is really a muddied narrative (in neither does she manage to tell the story as well as she might), they succeed admirably in bringing home to us their touching sense of how other people live and suffer privately.

However, *The Weather in Africa,* although it makes use of her expected skills is, if compared to the stories of Nadine Gordimer, sadly lacking in political sophistication. Even the best of these tales do not really rise above humdrum reporting supplied by a heart-on-the-sleeve narrator.

Of all her novels it is *Liana* which seems most fully to embody her virtues and which is least marred by her faults. True, there is a suspiciously Hemingway-like handling of the dialogue—Gellhorn is always at her weakest in this area—but for the rest there is a sharpness, a truth of observation in the studies of Liana herself and of Marc that would make the novel worth reading if there were nothing else to commend it. Add to that, however, the keen feeling for atmosphere, emotional as well as environmental, and you have a fine piece of fiction, *Liana* alone assures Gellhorn a respectable place among the order of good if not great novelists.

—John Lucas

GHOSE, Zulfikar

Nationality: British. **Born:** Sialkot, Pakistan, 13 March 1935. **Education:** Keele University, England, B.A. in English and philosophy 1959. **Family:** Married in 1964. **Career:** Cricket correspondent, the *Observer,* London, 1960-65; teacher in London, 1963-69. Since 1969 professor of English, University of Texas, Austin. **Awards:** Arts Council of Great Britain bursary, 1967. **Agent:** Aitken, Stone and Wylie, 29 Fernshaw Road, London SW10 0TG, England. **Address:** Department of English, University of Texas, Austin, Texas 78712, U.S.A.

PUBLICATIONS

Novels

The Contradictions. London, Macmillan, 1966.
The Murder of Aziz Khan. London, Macmillan, 1967; New York, Day, 1969.
The Incredible Brazilian:
    The Native. London, Macmillan, and New York, Holt Rinehart, 1972.
    The Beautiful Empire. London, Macmillan, 1975; Woodstock, New York, Overlook Press, 1984.
    A Different World. London, Macmillan, 1978; Woodstock, New York, Overlook Press, 1985.
Crump's Terms. London, Macmillan, 1975.
The Texas Inheritance (as William Strang). London, Macmillan, 1980.
Hulme's Investigations into the Bogart Script. Austin, Texas, Curbstone Press, 1981.
A New History of Torments. New York, Holt Rinehart, and London, Hutchinson, 1982.
Don Bueno. London, Hutchinson, 1983; New York, Holt Rinehart, 1984.

Figures of Enchantment. London, Hutchinson, and New York, Harper, 1986.
The Triple Mirror of the Self. London, Bloomsbury, 1991.

Short Stories

Statement Against Corpses, with B.S. Johnson. London, Constable, 1964.

Uncollected Short Stories

"The Absences," in *Winter's Tales 14,* edited by Kevin Crossley-Holland. London, Macmillan, and New York, St. Martin's Press, 1968.
"A Translator's Fiction," in *Winter's Tales 1* (new series), edited by David Hughes. London, Constable, and New York, St. Martin's Press, 1985.

Poetry

The Loss of India. London, Routledge, 1964.
Jets from Orange. London, Macmillan, 1967.
The Violent West. London, Macmillan, 1972.
Penguin Modern Poets 25, with Gavin Ewart and B.S. Johnson. London, Penguin, 1974.
A Memory of Asia. Austin, Texas, Curbstone Press, 1984.
Selected Poems. Karachi, Oxford University Press, 1991.

Other

Confessions of a Native-Alien (autobiography). London, Routledge, 1965.
Hamlet, Prufrock, and Language. London, Macmillan, and New York, St. Martin's Press, 1978.
The Fiction of Reality. London, Macmillan, 1983.
The Art of Creating Fiction. London, Macmillan, 1991.
Shakespeare's Mortal Knowledge. London, Macmillan, 1993.

*

Critical Studies: Zulfikar Ghose issue of *The Review of Contemporary Fiction,* 9 (2), Summer 1989; *Structures of Negation: The Writings of Zulfikar Ghose* by Chelva Kanaganayakam, Toronto, University of Toronto Press, 1993.

*   *   *

Zulfikar Ghose's five stories in *Statement Against Corpses* repeatedly concern the metaphysics that unites thought with action, life with death, success with failure, aspirations with accomplishment. "The Zoo People" is the best of these. Thematically complex, linguistically assured, subtle in its evocation of character, delicate in its responses to landscape, provocative in its approach to time, it probes the mind of the English émigré Emily Minns, as she comes to terms with physical and metaphysical perception in an India alien to her upbringing. Is an animal more beautiful in the wild than in a zoo, she asks—and what happens if, taking a cage away, one discovers "primitive wildness" *instead* of beauty? Her ultimate answer arises from her increased sensitivity to Indian paradoxes and her adaptation of them to her "European Enlightenment" patterns of thought:

Absolute barrenness was a reality with which she now felt a sympathy. There were rocks and rocks: each, whether a pebble or a boulder, was a complete, homogeneous, self-sufficient mass of matter in itself; each stood or lay in the dust at perfect peace with the universe which did no more to it than round its edges; each was there in its established place, a defiant mass of creation, magnificently aloof, without ancestry and without progeny.

Order, in other words, is within her mind's eye.

The Contradictions not only continues the metaphor of barrenness, but also structures itself on East-West logical oppositions. The "assertions" that open the book explore an Englishman's inhibited barriers against India, and India's human fecundity nonetheless. The "contradictions" that close it are set in England and pick up each theme and symbol from the first half of the book—not in order to refute them, but to complete them. The English rationalist philosophers must be blended with India's atemporality; material welfare must be glimpsed concurrently with the nominal importance of the colour of silk squares; Sylvia's English miscarriage must encourage her to appreciate what her experience of India did not directly allow: that an "area of nothingness" might possess "an odd attraction, and in this darkness, a disturbing power."

Attached ambivalently to a landscape of heart as well as a landscape of mind, Sylvia spirals towards a point of balance between antitheses. For Ghose himself, as his autobiography clearly announces, the point of balance is represented by the tenuous hyphen in "native-alien." Pakistan, India, British India, Britain, and the USA are all part of his experience, and all necessary to him, in conjunction. In another short story, "Godbert," the antithesis is conveyed by a different metaphor: "Donald . . . looked at horizons whereas John examined the texture of cobblestones." Later in the story, in a similar tense vein, Ghose writes: "One chooses a way of life. Or life imposes its own pattern upon one despite oneself." Such a dilemma lies at the core of Ghose's ambitious and moving novel *The Murder of Aziz Khan,* about a peasant farmer's futile effort to preserve his traditional land from industrial expansion, political roguery, blatant thuggery, and the power of money in other people's hands.

The metaphysics of perception and cultural tension continues to preoccupy Ghose in his later novels. Though *Crump's Terms,* the reflections of a London schoolteacher, is a weak foray into wry social comedy, the three volumes of *The Incredible Brazilian* show the author to be highly imaginative. Influenced by Márquez and others, these three books—*The Native, The Beautiful Empire,* and *A Different World*—tell the marvelous, almost picaresque narratives of a single character named Gregório, who in a series of reincarnations is variously native, explorer, soldier, planter, merchant, marketeer, writer, and revolutionary. In writing out the three "lives" of the three books, Gregório confronts various ethical, historical, and mythological claims to both the territory and the idea of Brazil: native land, European colony, and new nation. Beyond the claim to the land lies the claim to the future, he writes, and he asks if cultural contact must necessitate corruption, if power is really man's only motivation, and in a closing and magnificently eloquent irony, if efforts to prevent violence inevitably prove destructive. This knot of abstract ideas gives the work its breadth of vision; its success derives also from Ghose's skill in telling a vivid, concrete narrative.

Even more successful are Ghose's further forays into patterns of imaginative adventure. *A New History of Torments* and *Don Bueno* take prototypical quest cycles and turn them into contemporary adventures of the psyche. *A New History of Torments* follows the life of a young man from his rural South American home to a pleasure-palace island, only to watch him destroy himself after he becomes unwittingly entangled in an incestuous love. With a related setting, *Don Bueno* watches generations of young men grow up to inherit their fate: inevitably they pursue, kill off, and then replace their fathers—secure only in their blindness to the effects of time on their own ambition.

Figures of Enchantment, using metatextual and magic realist techniques, turns more consciously to analyze artifice, and probes the experience of exile in yet another way. Focusing on the *figures* of representation and imaginative understanding (each of the characters, or "figures," for example, exists as a "figure" or "type" in other character's eyes), the novel draws the attention to its own syntax. It makes clear that "figurative" language both constructs versions of reality and removes people from any "natural" or "unmediated" relation with the external world.

By turns poetic, comic, and dramatic, these novels are engaging narratives: they also constitute a continuing analysis of power: of its workings, and of its basis in the economics of ownership and desire.

—W.H. New

GHOSH, Amitav

Nationality: Indian. **Born:** 11 July 1956. **Education:** Delhi University, India, B.A. in history, M.A. in sociology; Oxford University, diploma in social anthropology, Ph.D.; Institut Bourguiba des Langues Vivants Tunis, diploma in Arabic. **Family:** Married Deborah Ann Baker in 1990. **Career:** Since 1986 lecturer in sociology, Delhi School of Economics, Delhi University. Contibutor to *Indian Express* (New Dehli), *Granta* (Cambridge), and *The New Republic* (Washington, D.C.). **Award:** Academy of Letters, India, annual prize, 1990. **Agent:** Wylie, Aitken and Stone, 250 West 57th Street, New York, New York 10107, U.S.A.

PUBLICATIONS

Novels

The Circle of Reason. London, Hamilton, and New York, Viking, 1986.
The Shadow Lines. New Delhi, Ravi Dayal, and London, Bloomsbury, 1988; New York, Viking, 1989.

Other

The Relations of Envy in an Egyptian Village. Trivandrum, Centre for Development Studies, 1982.
In an Antique Land. New Delhi, Ravi Dayal, 1992; New York, Knopf, 1993; London, Penguin, 1994.

Translator, *The Slave of Ms. H.* Calcutta, Centre for Studies in Social Sciences, 1990.

*   *   *

Amitav Ghosh's fictional world is one of restless narrative motion. His central figures are travelers and diasporic exiles—exemplars of "the migrant sensibility" that Salman Rushdie calls "one of the central themes of this century of displaced persons." If in Rushdie's metaphor "the past is a country from which we have all emigrated," then Ghosh's conflation of time and space—and of distinct times and distant spaces—is even more radical. He treats national borders and conceptual boundaries as permeable fictions to be constantly transgressed. Through the multiple crisscrossings enabled by a free-ranging narrative, discrete binaries of order and category give way to a realm of mirror images and hybrid realities. Reason becomes passion, going away is also coming home, and the differences between us and them, now and then, here and there are disrupted by the itinerant maps of a roaming imagination.

The Circle of Reason follows Indian characters from a Bengali village to an Egyptian town to an outpost in the Algerian Sahara. This first novel begins by making comic hay of unlikely conjunctions. The scientific Reason of Balaram's obsession melds Hindu notions of purity and Western notions of cleanliness with Pasteur's microbiology; his vision of social progress through weaving suggests both Gandhi's nationalist self-sufficiency and a global multi national economy whose technology "recognizes no continents and no countries." This eccentric version of Reason is almost wiped out by forces of unreason: ambition and paranoia, territoriality and violence.

Balaram's last disciple, the mysterious Alu, is chased across oceans and continents as a narrative of shifting, spooling time within fixed village space gives way to a linear-time, picaresque story spread across the international space of diaspora. In al-Ghazira, Alu's charismatic socialism quixotically links the eradication of germs with the elimination of money. The final scenes in El Oued are more earnest and down-to-earth, favoring the migrant's adaptive "making do" and "being huma" over the purist strictures of science and religious tradition. Nevertheless, Reason and the past both circle back in the form of Balaram's favorite book, *Life of Pasteur,* which has also traveled from Bengal to Algeria and which Alu can now "reverently" cremate.

Ghosh's second novel is more somber, less fanciful in its politics, and quite stunning in the power with which its formal experiments in sequence and location resonate thematically. *The Shadow Lines* traces nearly a half-century of interlocking relations among three generations of two families, one Indian and one British, giving perhaps the definitive fictional demonstration of Benedict Anderson's dictum that nations are "imagined communities." When the same Hindu-Muslim conflict can take place simultaneously in Dhaka and Calcutta, the unnamed narrator must abandon his common-sense assumption "that distance separates, that it is a corporeal substance" and his belief "in the reality of nations and borders." The self, like the cosmopolitan cities it lives in, becomes a palimpsest, sedimented with history, memory, and others that the self has absorbed. The narrative mode echoes this intricate layering with its looping, Russian-doll-like nestling of stories within stories, place within place, memory within actuality.

The narrator, with his internationalized consciousness, wallows in an empowering sense of simultaneity and correspondence. Growing up with Tridib in Calcutta, he can "know" wartime London neighborhoods and see the English boy Nick Price as a spectral mirror image. His grandmother's confusion between her childhood Dhaka and the present-day foreign city becomes symptomatic of a violence done to people by artificial borders and partitions (poignantly allegorized in her family's divided house). If the novel valorizes the search for undivided space and coexisting time, however, it refuses to endorse self-serving appropriations of "other" realities. When Ila compares her pleasure at bohemian living with that of wartime radicals, the narrator rails at the "easy arrogance" by which she assumes "that times and places are the same because they happen to look alike, like airport lounges." But after a futile argument about whether her London or his Calcutta is the site of real history and important politics, he realizes the shaky ground on which he too claims possession of people and places he has largely invented.

Ghosh thus recognizes the political stakes involved in drawing connecting lines, like airline routes, across the shadow lines of national space and historical period. His globe-shrinking project enables not only integration but also juxtaposition. The controlling metaphor of the airport lounge makes this point brilliantly: as replicated space (they all look alike) and individual place (each one is distinctive); as both attached to and detached from its national home; as a place where departures rub shoulders with arrivals, where everyone is always on the move. Full of complex cross-cultural encounters, *The Shadow Lines* makes a unique contribution to the debates over "difference" and "otherness" that have galvanized our contemporary postcolonial world.

—John Clement Ball

GIBSON, Graeme

Nationality: Canadian. **Born:** London, Ontario. **Education:** University of Western Ontario. **Family:** Married 1) Shirley Mann (divorced); 2) Margaret Atwood, *q.v.;* three sons. **Career:** Teacher of English, Ryerson Polytechnical Institute, Toronto, 1961-68; writer-in-residence, University of Waterloo, 1982-83. Founding member, Book and Periodical Development Council, 1975, chair, 1976, executive director, 1977. **Awards:** Scottish Canadian Exchange fellowship, 1978. **Member:** Amnesty International; Federation of Ontario Naturalists; Writers' Development Trust. **Address:** c/o Writers' Union of Canada, 24 Ryerson Ave., Toronto, Ontario M5T 2P3, Canada.

PUBLICATIONS

Novels

Five Legs. Toronto, Anansi, 1969.
Communion. Toronto, Anansi, 1971.
Perpetual Motion. New York, St. Martin's Press, 1982.
Gentleman Death. Toronto, McClelland and Stewart, 1993.

Other

Eleven Canadian Novelists Interviewed by Graeme Gibson. Toronto, Anansi, 1972.
St. Vincent and the Grenadines: Bequia, Mustique, Canouan, Mayreau, Tobago Cays, Palm, Union, PSV: A Plural Country, with Jill Bobrow, Margaret Atwood, and Raquel Welch; photographs by Dana Jinkins, Stockbridge, Massachusetts, Concepts, 1985.

How to Build a Clone Computer: The Clone Building Seminar. Independence, Missouri, Computer Training Corp., 1993.

*   *   *

Graeme Gibson has a solid reputation among Canadian novelists, based on both his fictional writings and his activities in cultural politics. His first two novels, *Five Legs* of 1969 and *Communion* two years later, are relatively short works, with decidedly modernist styles; *Perpetual Motion* of 1982 has a more clearly delineated narrative and narrator; and *Gentleman Death,* published in 1993, cuts between a writer's life and lives in his writings. In 1973 Gibson also contributed a collection of interviews titled *Eleven Canadian Novelists;* although not itself fiction, this work reveals something of Gibson's concerns about the professional pursuit of writing in questions repeated to different writers.

Five Legs, Gibson's first novel, tells the story of the gathering of several people for the funeral of a student acquaintance. Its first half consists of the perspective of Lucan Crackell, a university lecturer and mentor of the deceased, who has been commandeered into attending the funeral, as well as driving some others to it. The novel's modernist style blends objective dialogue between characters with verbalized thought in a manner that strongly recalls James Joyce. The opening of the novel might almost be a re-presentation of Bloom's breakfast in *Ulysses,* as Crackell prepares breakfast for his wife and assembles his clothes for the funeral. In the course of his thoughts, we find a realistic psychological portrayal of a petty and critical mind. Gibson uses Crackell's profession as an English lecturer to interweave motifs of literary death and rebirth with the conscious, social, "real-world" action of funeral preparations themselves. Allusions to Milton's "Lycidas," among other elegies, lend texture to the novel. These notes are blended with an ironic tone introduced by Crackell himself, whose thoughts transform the traditional elegiac "Who would not sing for Lycidas?" to the blacker "Who would not weep?" when he thinks of Martin Baillie, nipped in his prime by a hit-and-run driver. Gibson skillfully interweaves hints of *Hamlet, Romeo and Juliet,* T. S. Eliot's characters in "Prufrock" and "Gerontion," Browning's monologues, and other literary reflections on death. Some risk is taken that the text may become too self-consciously literary, however; readers may not feel like discerning between the literary mind of Crackell and the book itself.

The second half of the novel adopts the viewpoint of one of Crackell's passengers, the dead Baillie's friend Felix Oswald. He, like Crackell, muses about his life and dislikes. The novel leaves an impression of an anarchic despair, tempered with a glimmer of hope.

The brief sequel *Communion* traces Felix Oswald after his graduation from school, as he works for a veterinarian. In a slightly more coherent diction, Gibson moves toward a static closure that shows Felix breaking a dying epileptic husky from its cage and releasing it into the wild. Themes of abnormality and frustration are symbolically presented, often in analogy between Oswald and the dog.

Perpetual Motion diverges from *Five Legs* and *Communion* stylistically and fictionally, telling the story of Robert Fraser, a farmer in 19-century Canada, whose plowing uncovers the skeleton of a mammoth in his field. His discovery brings him into contact with the world of Victorian pseudoscience, and he becomes seduced by the dream of building a perpetual motion machine in the form of an orrery, a working model of the solar system. His pursuit becomes obsessive and appears elusive as well, until he in a moment of inspiration makes the mammoth bone he discovered years earlier a part of his machine. It then starts to move, and gradually gains speed until it flies to pieces.

In *Perpetual Motion* Gibson investigates the implications of technology from a sophisticated perspective, mixing the dream of total human control over the machine with images of extinction, both of the mammoth and of the passenger pigeon. Gibson also introduces aspects of the tall tale and magic realism into *Perpetual Motion:* throughout the book, characters tell tales of the fabulous, and the creation of perpetual motion itself falls into this category, making the book itself a version of the fantastic epic. But Gibson's tale is one with a moral: the human costs of technological fixation are seen in Fraser's family, as they suffer under his monomania.

Gentleman Death is Gibson's return to the literary scene after eleven years. Ultimately, this novel reconciles its narrator with mortality, but his growth into this resolution is painful. Gibson essentially triangulates his book between the life of the Torontonian novelist Robert Fraser (coincidentally the great-grandson of the protagonist of *Perpetual Motion*) and the plot lives of two of his characters, travellers from Toronto to Britain and Germany. The interweaving of elements of Fraser's life with those of the characters he is laboring to bring to life is slightly disorienting, but gradually encircles the great unspoken in Fraser's soul: the source of his writing block and his greatest sadness, the death of his brother. In a conclusion that feels like the resolution of Woolf's *To the Lighthouse,* Gibson shows how love of people and place can bridge the life of the present and ghosts of the past.

—Ron Jenkins

GIBSON, William (Ford)

Nationality: American. **Born:** Conway, South Carolina, 17 March 1948. **Education:** University of British Columbia, B.A. 1977. **Family:** Married Deborah Jean Thompson in 1972; one daughter and one son. **Awards:** Hugo award, Philadelphia Science Fiction Society Philip K. Dick memorial award, Nebula award, Porgie award, all 1985, and Australian Science Fiction Convention Ditmar award, all for *Neuromancer.* **Agent:** Martha Millard Literary Agency, 204 Park Avenue, Madison, New Jersey 07940, U.S.A.

PUBLICATIONS

NOVELS

Neuromancer. New York, Ace, 1984, London, HarperCollins, 1994.
Count Zero. New York, Arbor House, 1986.
Mona Lisa Overdrive. New York, Bantam, 1988.
The Difference Engine, with Bruce Sterling. London, Gollancz, 1990; New York, Bantam, 1991.
Virtual Light. New York, Bantam, and London, Viking, 1993.

Play

Dream Jumbo (text to accompany performance art; produced, Los Angeles, 1989).

*

Film Adaptation: *Johnny Mnemonic,* 1995.

Critical Study: *William Gibson* by Lance Olsen, San Bernardino, California, Borgo Press, 1992 (includes bibliography).

*   *   *

In 1922, T. S. Eliot published a review of Joyce's *Ulysses,* coining the now famous phrase "mythical method" to describe how Joyce created an effect of order in the chaos of modern fragmentation by invoking old stories and myths as compositional forms. In his "cyberpunk" trilogy that dominated science fiction of the 1980s (*Neuromancer, Count Zero, Mona Lisa Overdrive*), and in his bestseller of the early nineties (*Virtual Light*), William Gibson has demonstrated the continuing vitality of this "method" and come up with some new developments of his own. There are strong plots in his novels, but they have little to do with the characters who inhabit them, who for the most part don't know much at all about the plot they are acting in. In *Neuromancer,* the "cowboy" computer-jockey Case—like the reader—only discovers at the end that he has been acting out a scheme composed by a seemingly omniscient and nearly omnipotent embodiment of artificial intelligence (AI) that merged with another AI to become the "matrix." In the later two novels the AI/matrix chooses to manifest itself in the form of Voodoo beings called Loa. As the initiated Beauvoir explains to the novice Bobby, in *Count Zero,* we don't have to worry about "whether it's a religion or not. It's just a *structure.* Lets you an' me discuss some things that are happening. . . . What it's about is getting things *done.*" Gibson reports in an interview that all he knows about Voodoo he found by accident in an issue of *National Geographic* just when he needed to find a way to "get things done" in his second novel: "That probably has a lot to do with the way I write—stitching together all the junk that's floating around in my head." This self-reflexivity in the writing, together with self-effacing creative modesty and tactics of conspicuously parodic pastiche, place Gibson's work within the discourse of postmodernism. Recycled clichés are the staple of his work, shared with the knowing reader who is hip to the ironic game being played with cultural artifacts.

Gibson's publishing career began the same year MTV hit the video market (1981), and his style reflects some of the same tactics and pace, where mundane music is transformed into a montage-collage of rapid-fire imagery in a placeless and timeless stream-of-consciousness continuum. Like the typical MTV presentation, his work seems designed to force a sensory overload onto a reader who can't keep up with the frantic pace. Oft-quoted lines from *Neuromancer* describe the effect nicely: "Night City was like a deranged experiment in social Darwinism, designed by a bored researcher who kept one thumb permanently on the fast-forward button." The sensory overload is reflected in a stylistic saturation that has been aptly characterized as a "neon epic style," a breathless linguistic texture that sweeps lyrically through mental states of stressed-out tension and drug highs, with an exhilaratingly desperate hallucinatory intensity, in a futuristic reenactment of the film noir cityscape of movies like *Blade Runner* (1982) or *The Terminator* (1984). Things slow down a bit in the second and third novels of the trilogy, to allow for more complex character development and for a shift from major male characters to female ones. Things slow still more in *Virtual Light,* where we find a female main character who is a bicycle courier in San Francisco, physically transporting bits of information like a rider for the Pony Express.

Gibson's work has an uneasy relationship to the genre of science fiction, comparable to what's called a "crossover" performance in the music world. In the early period of sci-fi, the conventional goal was to expand human consciousness into outer space, under the secure control of scientist adventurers who combined the classical liberal virtues of morality with the forces of technological production. Gibson represents a strong turn away from this outward-bound surge, toward a more problematic contemporary frontier of science that is focused inwards, on an infinity of microcosms rather than the old-fashioned infinity of open space. Gibson's fiction follows the investments of current scientific research in the practical/theoretical fields of communication, data storage, miniaturization, artificial intelligence, bionic prosthetics, neurochemistry, genetics, and surgical interventions while continuing the exploration of paranoid subject positions inaugurated by the "serious" writers who inspired and influence him, like William Burroughs, J. G. Ballard, and Thomas Pynchon.

Paradoxically, the fact that Gibson himself knows no science ("I have no grasp of how computers *really* work," he admits in an interview), enables him to be all the more convincing to the millions of his readers who also know nothing about science. Like Edgar Rice Burroughs, who knew nothing of Africa, Gibson creates characters who glide mentally through cyberspace as effortlessly as Tarzan glided through the jungles of the dark continent. "My ignorance had allowed me to romanticize them [computers]" he admits, and our ignorance allows us to accept the romanticized exaggerations. Gibson's famous invention, "cyberspace," is technically sheer nonsense, but since it exists as a form of belief, it also has a certain kind of reality, as "a consensual hallucination experienced daily by billions of legitimate operators, in every nation."

The cyberpunk movement leapt to prominence in the early 1980s, with Gibson at its helm, as an apparent manifestation of countercultural art. Ten years later, with the appearance of his fourth novel on the *New York Times* best-seller list, the inevitable question must be raised: Can there be an authentic countercultural literature that achieves popularity and also resists becoming an imitation of itself suitable for mass consumption? Gibson himself refers to the cyberpunk movement as "mainly a marketing strategy—and one that I've come to feel trivializes what I do." The 1990s will be the critical period for this young author, who has without question an impressive talent.

—Thomas A. Vogler

GILCHRIST, Ellen (Louise)

Nationality: American. **Born:** Vicksburg, Mississippi, 20 February 1935. **Education:** Vanderbilt University, Nashville; Millsaps College, Jackson, Mississippi, B.A. in philosophy 1967; University of Arkansas, Fayetteville, 1976. Has three sons. **Career:** Broadcaster on National Public Radio 1984-85; also journalist. **Awards:** Mississippi Arts Festival poetry award, 1968; *New York Quarterly* award, for poetry, 1978; National Endowment for the Arts grant, 1979; *Prairie Schooner* award, 1981; Mississippi Academy award, 1982, 1985; Saxifrage award, 1983; American Book award, 1985; University of Arkansas Fulbright award, 1985; Mississippi Institute Arts and Letters award, for literature, 1985, 1990, 1991. **Address:** c/o Little Brown, 34 Beacon St., Boston, Massachusetts 02108, U.S.A.

PUBLICATIONS

Novels

The Annunciation. Boston, Little Brown, 1983; London, Faber, 1984.
The Anna Papers. Boston, Little Brown, 1988; London, Faber, 1989.
Net of Jewels. Boston, Little Brown, and London, Faber, 1992.
Anabasis: A Journey to the Interior. Jackson, University of Mississippi, 1994.
Starcarbon: A Meditation on Love. Boston, Little Brown, and London, Faber, 1994.

Short Stories

In the Land of Dreamy Dreams: Short Fiction. Fayetteville, University of Arkansas Press, 1981; London, Faber, 1982.
Victory over Japan. Boston, Little Brown, 1984; London, Faber, 1985.
Drunk with Love. Boston, Little Brown, 1986; London, Faber, 1987.
Light Can Be Both Wave and Particle. Boston, Little Brown, 1989; London, Faber, 1990.
I Cannot Get You Close Enough: Three Novellas. Boston, Little Brown, 1990; London, Faber, 1991.
The Blue-Eyed Buddhist and Other Stories. London, Faber, 1990.

Play

Television Play: *A Season of Dreams,* from stories by Eudora Welty, 1968.

Poetry

The Land Surveyor's Daughter. Fayetteville, Arkansas, Lost Road, 1979.
Riding Out the Tropical Depression: Selected Poems 1975-1985. New Orleans, Faust, 1986.

Other

Falling Through Space: The Journals of Ellen Gilchrist. Boston, Little Brown, 1987; London, Faber, 1988.

*   *   *

Ellen Gilchrist is one of America's best contemporary fiction writers. Her reputation presently rests on two novels, three novellas, and five volumes of superb stories. Throughout her work, some characteristics remain constant. Usually presented from a woman's point of view, the fiction includes convincing male figures. Gilchrist satirizes the foibles and arrogance of both sexes. Her women are not better than men, but their notably bad behavior is more often presented positively—as a sign of strength, a refusal to be victimized, or a daring determination to get pleasure through an outrageous act or verbal exchange. Most of her characters are self-centered, and their egoism can have both positive and negative effects. Gilchrist frequently employs an ironic juxtaposition of agony and comedy. Her stories usually present a series of scenes, with heavy use of dialogue and relatively little narrative comment. The stories generally close abruptly after a climactic episode. Narrators are either the main character, speaking in the first person, or an emotionally detached and critical observer. The settings, frequently in the South, include New Orleans, the rural Louisiana Delta, Oklahoma, North Carolina, Alabama, Mississippi, and Arkansas—although some stories in recent books take place in San Francisco, in Maine, and even in Istanbul.

In her first two volumes of stories, *In the Land of Dreamy Dreams* and *Victory over Japan,* Gilchrist includes a number of stories exploring the drug culture, alcoholism, diet faddism, and prescription drug abuse. The early stories include some of great violence. Among the early stories related to drugs are "The President of the Louisiana Live Oak Society," which presents child-pushers; "The Gauzy Edge of Paradise," which focuses on drug faddists (a topic pursued later in "The Last Diet" in *Drunk with Love*); and "Defender of the Little Falaya." In some of these, Gilchrist skillfully contrasts the disorientation and hilarity induced by drugs with the dullness of the individuals' lives in their lucid states. *Victory over Japan* includes two sequences of compelling stories: one focusing on the engaging 19-year-old Nora Jane Whittington, introduced in *In the Land of Dreamy Dreams,* and the other on Crystal Weiss, who "manages to have a good time" while detesting her rich lawyer husband, Manny. "Miss" Crystal gains a sympathetic dimension, because in four of the stories she is seen through the eyes of her tolerant black maid, Traceleen, the only fully-developed black person in Gilchrist's work. Gilchrist's strengths throughout all of her collections of short stories lie in comic satire and the creation of highly memorable characters. Her satire sometimes misfires in its harshness or repetitiveness, as in her predictable sniping at religion, and she tends to overuse stereotypes—Jewish lawyers, sex-starved wives, black servants, Chinese-Americans, nuns, and tennis players at country clubs. Such stereotypical minor characters function effectively in many of the satiric stories but lessen the impact of the two novels. In *The Annunciation* Amanda sustains the novel well in her childhood and early adolescence as she innocently enjoys incest and as she suffers a nightmarish and life-changing cesarean at the age of 14. In the final chapters, Amanda also responds with a moving and dramatic range of emotion to the challenge of bearing a child in her forties after more than twenty-five years of infertility. But Amanda is unconvincing both in her conversion to scholarly research at the University of Arkansas and her affair with the working-class student who makes love as beautifully as he plays the guitar. This novel possesses many of the strengths of the stories: forceful scenes, aggressive, stubborn, reckless characters, interesting eccentrics, and abundance of dialogue. In two stories in *Light Can Be Both Wave and Particle* ("The Song of Songs" and "Life on Earth") Gilchrist has recently provided alternative endings for *The Annunciation,* which should revive interest in the novel. Gilchrist's second novel, *The Anna Papers,* lacks the orderly structure of the first. It breaks into several episodic narratives, punctuated by letters, journal notes, and other fragments that comprise the papers of the author Anna Hand. Anna discovers she has cancer, returns home to Charlotte, North Carolina for a final year, and then drowns herself. Her dutiful sister, Helen Abadie, with reluctance and resentment, is sorting through Anna's papers as Anna's literary co-executor. The informing presence of Anna, the pointed statements and questions she left behind in her papers, the re-creation of her life by the friends who gather for a memorable six-day wake, the appearance of the New England poet, Mike Carmichael (literary co-executor with Helen) and—most of all—

the surprising and refreshing renewal of the deadened life and spirit of Helen Abadie blend sorrow, anger, and comedy in *The Anna Papers.*

Anna Hand is central in Gilchrist's other recent fiction: in "Anna, Part I" in *Drunk with Love* and in all three novellas (*Winter, De Haviland Hand, Summer in Maine*) collected in *I Cannot Get You Close Enough.* She appears also in many references in the other recent publications, especially in *Light Can Be Both Wave and Particle.* The titles of these last two books by Gilchrist are provided by Anna in her papers, and both refer to the conflict between individualism and connection with others. The words, quoted near the end of *A Summer in Maine,* are Anna's last words and were addressed to her lover, the "married physician": "I cannot get you close enough. . . . We never can get from anyone else the things we need to fill the endless terrible need, not to be dissolved, not to sink back into sand, heat, broom, air, thinnest air. And so we revolve around each other." The words imply not only her recognition of the failure of this love affair and of her year's efforts to forge strong bonds within her family before her death, but also her recognition of universal human inability to fully relate to others. Similarly, she chooses *Light Can Be Both Wave and Particle* to be the title of her "one last book." The title implies again that one is a separate and inconsequential particle in the universe, but it also suggests that one can tenuously or temporarily identify the self with the great waves of nature and of human history. The first two novellas in *I Cannot Get You Close Enough* chronicle Anna's two major efforts to establish solidity in her unstable family. *Winter* recounts her journey to the slums of Istanbul to expose the irresponsibility of Daniel Hand's wife, Sheila, in order to assure Anna that custody of her niece, Jessica, now 15, will remain with the Hand family. Jessica, a beautiful and talented pianist and dancer, is a slow learner and despises school. The second novella, *De Haviland Hand,* describes Anna's efforts, including a trip to a Cherokee community in rural Tahlequah, Oklahoma, to prepare the way for Daniel's other 15-year-old daughter, Olivia de Haviland Hand, to join the Hand enclave. (Spring Deer, Olivia's mother, died during childbirth, after her brief marriage to Daniel. Daniel was never notified of Olivia's existence.) Olivia has grown up fearing sex and childbirth as precursors of death, and consequently shuns the attention of boys. Achievement in horseback riding and getting high grades in school have become obsessions. She decides eventually to follow Anna by choosing a career as a writer and also to become a famed research scientist. At the close of *A Summer in Maine,* Jessica is pregnant and enters an ill-advised marriage. Olivia cries out that, if she is not accepted by Harvard, she will, like Anna, drown herself. This novella allows Gilchrist to gather at the rented house in Maine several figures from New Orleans who appeared memorably in her earlier books. They include the Weiss family (Miss Crystal, her husband, Manny, their children, King and Crystal Anne, their maid Traceleen and her niece, Andria); Lydia, a painter; Noel, an aging actress, who fears possible publication of her intimate correspondence with Anna Hand; and Alan Dalton, a handsome tennis player who causes estrangement between Lydia and Miss Crystal. The formerly inhibited and unimaginative Helen Abadie and the poet/literary co-executor arrive (as lovers), adding to the gossip and excitement in this novella. In other recent books, Gilchrist rewards faithful readers by returning to still more familiar figures. For example, in *Drunk with Love* Rhoda Manning appears at different ages—childhood, puberty, adolescence, and early marriage—in "Nineteen Forty-one," "The Expansion of the Universe," and "Adoration." Traceleen returns in a monologue,

"Traceleen at Dawn," comically recalling Miss Crystal's attempt to quit drinking. In *The Anna Papers* Miss Crystal and Phelan Manning and other longtime companions enliven a six-day wake. In *Light Can Be Both Wave and Particle* Rhoda Manning again dominates three stories: as a child in "The Time Capsule," an adult in "Blue Hills at Sundown," and as a 53-year-old woman, "having run out of men" in the very long story, "Mexico." Rhoda, her brother, Dudley, and cousin Saint John attempt to prove in several days in Mexico that they can still have as wild a time as in their youth. The story, however, includes three sobering events: their attendance at a bull-fight, Rhoda's reckless arranging of a liaison with the champion matador, and a disastrous visit to Dudley's insecurely fenced compound, where wild animals are procured by thrill-seeking hunters. In the end, Rhoda finds herself, as in childhood, angry and dependent on her brother, but always willing to take risks for pleasure and excitement. Nora Jane Whittington, the anarchist, bandit, and lover of Sandy in *In the Land of Dreamy Dreams* and *Victory over Japan,* also returns in the title story of *Drunk with Love*—pregnant and with two lovers. She gives birth to twins in "The Starlight Express" in *Light Can Be Both Wave and Particle,* a story in which Gilchrist also introduces her most intriguing new character, a Chinese geneticist, Lin Tan Sing, who will surely reappear in another volume.

—Margaret B. McDowell

GILL, Brendan

Nationality: American. **Born:** Hartford, Connecticut, 4 October 1914. **Education:** Yale University, New Haven, Connecticut, A.B. 1936. **Family:** Married Anne Barnard in 1936; five daughters and two sons. **Career:** Since 1936 regular contributor to the *New Yorker* magazine: film critic, 1961-67; since 1968 drama critic. President, Municipal Art Society, New York; vice-president, Victorian Society in America, Philadelphia; member, Board of Directors, Film Society of Lincoln Center, New York. **Awards:** American Academy grant, 1951; National Book award, 1951. **Address:** c/o The New Yorker, 25 West 43rd Street, New York, New York 10036, U.S.A.

PUBLICATIONS

Novels

The Trouble of One House. New York, Doubleday, 1950; London, Gollancz, 1951.
The Day the Money Stopped. New York, Doubleday, and London, Gollancz, 1957.

Short Stories

The Malcontents. New York, Harcourt Brace, 1973.
Ways of Loving: Two Novellas and Eighteen Stories. New York, Harcourt Brace, 1974; London, Joseph, 1975.

Uncollected Short Stories

"Adriance Prize," in *Saturday Evening Post* (Philadelphia), 22 February 1941.

"Together," in *Saturday Evening Post* (Philadelphia), 8 August 1941.
"Choice," in *New Yorker,* 16 August 1941.
"King Barney the First," and "All the Right People," in *Stories of School and College Life,* edited by Robert J. Cadigan. New York, Appleton, 1941.
"Scientific Mind," in *With a Merry Heart,* edited by Paul J. Phelan. New York, Longman, 1943.
"Interest in Boys," in *New Yorker,* 21 August 1943.
"Grand Old Man," in *Virginia Quarterly Review* (Charlottesville), October 1943.
"Helpmeet," in *New Yorker,* 20 November 1943.
"More Like Home," in *Cross-Section 1944,* edited by Edwin Seaver. New York, Fischer, 1944.
"Privilege," in *World's Great Tales of the Sea,* edited by William McFee. Cleveland, World, 1944.
"Will's Girl," in *Collier's* (Springfield, Ohio), 28 October 1944.
"The Test," in *The Best American Short Stories 1945,* edited by Martha Foley. Boston, Houghton Mifflin, 1945.
"Mother Coakley's Reform," in *Our Father's House,* edited by Mariella Gable. New York, Sheed and Ward, 1945.
"The Guide," in *New Yorker,* 21 April 1945.
"Fall from Grace," in *Collier's* (Springfield, Ohio), 20 December 1945.
"Fine Start," in *Collier's* (Springfield, Ohio), 9 February 1946.
"A Little Rain," in *Fireside Book of Yuletide Tales,* edited by Edward Wagenknecht. Indianapolis, Bobbs Merrill, 1948.
"Night Bus to Atlanta," in *Girls from Esquire,* edited by Frederic A. Birmingham. New York, Random House, 1952.

Play

La Belle (produced Philadelphia, 1962).

Poetry

Death in April and Other Poems. Windham, Connecticut, Hawthorn House, 1935.
Wooings: Five Poems. Verona, Italy, Plain Wrapper Press, 1980.

Other

Cole: A Book of Cole Porter Lyrics and Memorabilia, with Robert Kimball. New York, Holt Rinehart, 1971; as *Cole: A Biographical Essay,* London, Joseph, 1972.
Tallulah. New York, Holt Rinehart, 1972; London, Joseph, 1973.
Happy Times, photographs by Jerome Zerbe. New York, Harcourt Brace, 1973; London, Joseph, 1974.
Here at "The New Yorker." New York, Random House, and London, Joseph, 1975.
The U.S. Custom House on Bowling Green. New York, New York Landmarks Conservancy, 1976.
Lindbergh Alone. New York, Harcourt Brace, 1977.
Summer Places, photographs by Dudley Witney. Toronto, McClelland and Stewart, and New York, Methuen, 1978.
The Dream Come True: Great Houses of Los Angeles, photographs by Derry Moore. New York, Harper, and London, Thames and Hudson, 1980.
John F. Kennedy Center for the Performing Arts. New York, Abrams, 1982.
Many Masks: A Life of Frank Lloyd Wright. New York, Putnam, 1987; London, Heinemann, 1988.

A New York Life: Of Friends and Others. New York, Posiedon Press, 1990.

Editor, *States of Grace: Eight Plays,* by Philip Barry. New York, Harcourt Brace, 1975.

Editor, *The Portable Dorothy Parker,* New York, Viking, 1991.

*   *   *

> A Fly mounted a curtain in the sun, and
> the fly's shadow mounted the shadow of
> lace, like a dream threading a dream.
>
> *(The Trouble of One House)*

Reversing conventional causation, Brendan Gill's novels and short stories dramatize a present that seems to create, rather than derive from, a densely textured past. Both novels ostensibly focus on immediate problems in upper-middle-class Irish Catholic families—the death of a young mother in *The Trouble of One House,* and the dispute over a father's will in *The Day the Money Stopped.* But the books reveal the past to be as alive and insistent as the present, perhaps more insistent, since in *Money* questions from the past demand solution with an urgency which transcends mere significance for the present, and the dead lawyer father compels greater interest than his son, Charlie Morrow, the protagonist. And in *House,* the nuances of the characters' previous relationships with each other not only explain their responses to Elizabeth's death, but actually seem forced into life for the first time by that death.

This creation by the present of a vital new past does not, however, totally overshadow the more conventional themes of the shaping power of the past, and its continual struggle with the present. Dependent on fragile and illusory human memory, the force of the past can nevertheless guide the present, as does the unlabelled photograph that begins and ends *House.* The last thing the dying Elizabeth sees is this picture of her children, an aid to memory at the moment her memory fades. But the photograph will dominate the father as long as his memory functions: "There was no indication of where the picture had been taken, or when, or by whom. A stranger would have been able to make nothing of it. It was just a picture of three children on a beach. But they were his children; he was theirs. From now on, he was theirs forever." Objects and places redolent with meaning from the past also stimulate conflict in the present: the dead Elizabeth's sister and mother-in-law vie for her chair at the dining table in *House,* and Charlie is intimidated by his father's office chair in *Money.* The cemetery opposite the office window has been a trysting place for as long as Charlie can remember, an image that reinforces the struggle between past and present in his own consciousness. In the story "The Cemetery" a doctor's son confronts the mingled accomplishment and futility of his father's life in a similar office opposite a symbolic cemetery. The American heroine of Gill's recent novella *The Malcontents* redefines herself through the order precariously preserved by an antique mirror, a sign of the 18th-century obsession with the elegance of a remoter past: "In the depths of the intricately carved frame of the mirror, elderly mandarins holding parasols sauntered through latticed pavilions, dreaming that they were butterflies. The mantel and the mirror—all that survived of a red-brick Georgian house in the ferny depths of Sussex—had come up at auction in London, and Claire had outbid the richest magnate in the world in order to make them

hers. . . . Claire bowed to her image among the mandarins, and said, 'Well! So I am a nice person, after all!'"

Money is a *tour de force* creating past and present largely through dialogue during Charlie's brief visit to his father's office. (This abundant dialogue, concentrated time, and a single setting presumably facilitated Maxwell Anderson's dramatic adaptation.) But despite the technical skill of the book, *Money* suffers from Gill's failure to endow Charlie with the charm to which the other characters unvaryingly respond. Though *House* is the better novel, the supporting characters act with a vitality denied Elizabeth, who, like Browning's Pippa, merely stimulates others without herself undergoing much change or awareness. Her sister and undertaker brother-in-law perform with an arresting combination of vulgarity and pathos; Father Degnan and Monsignor Brady are dramatized with a blend of satire and compassion that rivals the best of J. F. Powers; and Elizabeth's daughter awakens to sex on the day of her mother's death in an episode sustaining a complex tone of serious irony. But these brilliant vignettes and characterizations threaten to unbalance the novel, since Elizabeth's character fails to act as a unifying force.

Though *House* is a competent, often moving, work, Gill's major accomplishments are his short stories, which escape the structural problems of the novels. Harry Carter in "Something You Just Don't Do in a Club" is a convincing version of the successful scoundrel, a figure familiar in Gill's fiction, but, like Charlie Morrow in *House,* incapable of sustaining an entire novel. Admittedly, there are some early *Saturday Evening Post* stories, "King Barney the First," "Adriance Prize," and "All the Right People," in which prep school or Yale Protagonists manage, through a series of plot contrivances and unmotivated epiphanies, to avoid becoming adult versions of Charlie Morrow. But, contemporary with these works and continuing through the present are a wealth of first-rate *New Yorker* pieces, including Gill's finest, "Triumph," which undercuts, without destroying, an impoverished dowager's distorted reminiscences of an elegant past. The couple in "Helpmeet" provide a grimmer version of the relationship between the undertaker and his wife in *House;* the episode in the novel loses some of its strength to the overall diffuseness of the work, while the story preserves its power intact. "Grand Old Man," the most effective of Gill's clerical stories, dramatizes the same ambivalent struggle between religious innocence and practicality as does *House.* "Interest in Boys" portrays a girl like Elizabeth's daughter, awakening to sexuality and learning that the object of her excitement is a young priest. As in all his best fiction, Gill uses this sudden revelation to illuminate both character and the nature of religious commitment.

Like his biographies *Cole* and *Tallulah,* Gill's story "Fat Girl" and novellas "Last Things" and *The Malcontents* compassionately pursue the new theme of unconventional sexuality, its attendant violence, and its occasional delicate balances: "Jack and Fletcher would go on being lovers, Laura and Harry would go on being man and wife, and Laura and Jack would be lovers in every respect except that of sex" ("Last Things"). A continuity underlies these apparent innovations, however. Although the international theme of *The Malcontents* allows Gill to chart the wanderings of the very rich, and although the protagonists of both novellas finally transcend the family or sexual relationships that dominated their early lives (and much of Gill's early fiction), ultimately these novellas seem secularized versions of "And Holy Ghost" and other religious stories. Harry, having buried his wife, escaped the ministrations of his conventional offspring, and shot his beloved, ailing dog, is apparently ready for "Last Things," while Claire, surviving the death of her antagonist mother, the independence of her son, and the waning of her sexuality "looked forward to enjoying the emptiness for a while. . . . Long ago, she had predicted that she would be coming to the simplest things last."

—Burton Kendle

GLANVILLE, Brian (Lester)

Nationality: British. **Born:** London, 24 September 1931. **Education:** Newlands School; Charterhouse School, Surrey, 1945-49. **Family:** Married Elizabeth Pamela De Boer in 1959; two sons and two daughters. **Career:** Literary adviser, Bodley Head, publishers, London, 1958-62. Since 1958 sportswriter for the *Sunday Times,* London. **Awards:** Berlin Film Festival award, for documentary, 1963; British Film Academy award, for documentary, 1967; Thomas Coward Memorial award, 1969; Sports Council Reporter of the Year award, 1982. **Agent:** John Farquharson, 162-168 Regent Street, London W1R 5TB. **Address:** 160 Holland Park Avenue, London W.11, England.

PUBLICATIONS

Novels

The Reluctant Dictator. London, Laurie, 1952.
Henry Sows the Wind. London, Secker and Warburg, 1954.
Along the Arno. London, Secker and Warburg, 1956; New York, Crowell, 1957.
The Bankrupts. London, Secker and Warburg, and New York, Doubleday, 1958.
After Rome, Africa. London, Secker and Warburg, 1959.
Diamond. London, Secker and Warburg, and New York, Farrar Straus, 1962.
The Rise of Gerry Logan. London, Secker and Warburg, 1963; New York, Delacorte Press, 1965.
A Second Home. London, Secker and Warburg, 1965; New York, Delacorte Press, 1966.
A Roman Marriage. London, Joseph, 1966; New York, Coward McCann, 1967.
The Artist Type. London, Cape, 1967; New York, Coward McCann, 1968.
The Olympian. New York, Coward McCann, and London, Secker and Warburg, 1969.
A Cry of Crickets. London, Secker and Warburg, and New York, Coward McCann, 1970.
The Financiers. London, Secker and Warburg, 1972; as *Money Is Love,* New York, Doubleday, 1972.
The Comic. London, Secker and Warburg, 1974; New York, Stein and Day, 1975.
The Dying of the Light. London, Secker and Warburg, 1976.
Never Look Back. London, Joseph, 1980.
Kissing America. London, Blond, 1985.
The Catacomb. London, Hodder and Stoughton, 1988.

Short Stories

A Bad Streak and Other Stories. London, Secker and Warburg, 1961.

The Director's Wife and Other Stories. London, Secker and Warburg, 1963.
Goalkeepers Are Crazy: A Collection of Football Stories. London, Secker and Warburg, 1964.
The King of Hackney Marshes and Other Stories. London, Secker and Warburg, 1965.
A Betting Man. New York, Coward McCann, 1969.
Penguin Modern Stories 10, with others. London, Penguin, 1972.
The Thing He Loves and Other Stories. London, Secker and Warburg, 1973.
A Bad Lot and Other Stories. London, Penguin, 1977.
Love Is Not Love and Other Stories. London, Blond, 1985.

Plays

A Visit to the Villa (produced Chichester, Sussex, 1981).
Underneath the Arches, with Patrick Garland and Roy Hudd (produced Chichester, Sussex, 1981; London, 1982).

Screenplay (documentary): *Goal!,* 1967.

Radio Plays: *The Diary,* 1987; *I Could Have Been King,* 1988.

Television Documentary: *European Centre Forward,* 1963.

Other

Cliff Bastin Remembers, with Cliff Bastin. London, Ettrick Press, 1950.
Arsenal Football Club. London, Convoy, 1952.
Soccer Nemesis. London, Secker and Warburg, 1955.
World Cup, with Jerry Weinstein. London, Hale, 1958.
Over the Bar, with Jack Kelsey. London, Paul, 1958.
Soccer round the Globe. London, Abelard Schuman, 1959.
Know about Football (for children). London, Blackie, 1963.
World Football Handbook (annual). London, Hodder and Stoughton, 1964; London, Mayflower, 1966-72; London, Queen Anne Press, 1974.
People in Sport. London, Secker and Warburg, 1967.
Soccer: A History of the Game, Its Players, and Its Strategy. New York, Crown, 1968; as *Soccer: A Panorama,* London, Eyre and Spottiswoode, 1969.
The Puffin Book of Football (for children). London, Penguin, 1970; revised edition, 1984.
Goalkeepers Are Different (for children). London, Hamish Hamilton, 1971; New York, Crown, 1972.
Brian Glanville's Book of World Football. London, Dragon, 1972.
The Sunday Times History of the World Cup. London, Times Newspapers, 1973; as *History of the Soccer World Cup,* New York, Macmillan, 1974; revised edition, as *The History of the World Cup,* London, Faber, 1980, 1984.
Soccer 76. London, Queen Anne Press, 1975.
Target Man (for children). London, Macdonald and Jane's, 1978.
The Puffin Book of Footballers. London, Penguin, 1978; revised edition, as *Brian Glanville's Book of Footballers,* 1982.
A Book of Soccer. New York, Oxford University Press, 1979.
Kevin Keegan (for children). London, Hamish Hamilton, 1981.
The Puffin Book of Tennis (for children). London, Penguin, 1981.
The Puffin Book of the World Cup (for children). London, Penguin, 1984.

The British Challenge (on the Los Angeles Olympics team), with Kevin Whitney. London, Muller, 1984.

Editor, *Footballer's Who's Who.* London, Ettrick Press, 1951.
Editor, *The Footballer's Companion.* London, Eyre and Spottiswoode, 1962.
Editor, *The Joy of Football.* London, Hodder and Stoughton, 1986.

*

Critical Study: "Khaki and God the Father" in *A Human Idiom* by William Walsh, London, Chatto and Windus, 1965.

Brian Glanville comments:
(1972) There has, I suppose, been some tendency to categorize my work under three headings; that which deals with Italy (*Along the Arno, A Cry of Crickets, A Roman Marriage*), that which deals with Jewish life (*The Bankrupts, Diamond*), and that which deals with professional football (*The Rise of Gerry Logan* and many of the short stories). I think I might accept the categorization of the two Jewish novels, but it scarcely places *The Olympian,* which uses an athlete as its figure, athletics as its theme, or rather as its metaphor; or *A Second Home,* which is narrated in the first person by a Jewish actress—and has been bracketed with *A Roman Marriage,* itself narrated by a young girl. Again, one can, and does, use similar material for widely different purposes.

A large disenchantment with the conventional novel and its possibilities has, I think, led one gradually away from it, to more experimental methods. Like many novelists of serious intentions, one lives uneasily from one novel to the elusive next, always questioning and trying to establish the validity of the form.

*   *   *

Brian Glanville has written of his novels that "large disenchantment with the conventional novel . . . has, I think, led one gradually away from it, to more experimental methods." Each novel from this prolific writer has demonstrated that impatience; his need to break away from the manners of the traditional novel and from its central narrative line to a more fluid exposition of his thought has meant that the action frequently unfolds through his characterization instead of through the plot. In *A Roman Marriage* the story is told by the young English girl who has allowed herself to be trapped into a futile, claustrophobic marriage to a handsome young Italian; and through her outraged consciousness we experience, too, the suffocation of her husband's clinging, over-protective mother as the tentacles of family life cut the girl off from reality and draw her in to a nightmare. Similarly the tensions and cabalistic integrity of the family are strikingly unfolded in his Jewish novels such as *The Bankrupts, Diamond,* and *A Second Home.*

A further strength of the novels in this latter group is Glanville's sure ear for the cadences of everyday speech. The Jewish patois is never forced to gain its effect through comic music-hall over-indulgence but is allowed to expose itself through Glanville's feeling for the poetic possibilities of the spoken language. Although the unforced ease of his dialogue gives it a down-to-earth integrity, Glanville never allows it to become mundane or demeaning, and the simplicity of effect is a structural strength of all his writing.

As a commentator on professional sport Glanville has also written several novels about the stamina and passion that make up the modern athlete. In *The Olympian* a young miler, Ike Low, is torn between his passion for his wife Jill and the almost sexual release that he finds in winning races. Against their uneasy relationship stands the ambiguous figure of Sam Dee, Ike's trainer, who acts as both *agent provocateur* and chorus over their slowly disintegrating marriage. The narrative is broken up with journalese and taut, film-like dialogue as the drama of Ike's racing career draws to an unexpected climax. *The Dying of the Light* is perhaps Glanville's most profound and satisfying sporting novel to date. Although it is described as "a football novel," it is in effect a parable of contemporary life. Len Rawlings, a footballing hero in the post-war years, slumps gradually to the bottom of the ladder in a world where the aged and the losers are quickly forgotten. In desperation he turns to petty crime but finds salvation in the love of his daughter, so unlike him in character, but the only one to understand the terrifying loneliness of his personal predicament. As in all Glanville's novels, the moralizing is made manifest by its absence—Rawlings may have broken the law but it is the law of the jungle that is at fault, the "sporting" code that allows a talented man to be driven to despair through no fault of his own.

Contemporary obsessions of another kind are examined in *Never Look Back,* a novel that explores the world of rock and roll bands and the attitudes of its denizens: the stars, their managers and hangers-on, the agents and the crooks. The documentary detail is impressive but Glanville's mastery of language and skillful handling of dialogue convey subtle shifts of feeling, and they also constantly change his and the reader's focus on this kaleidoscopic world. Above all, Glanville shows that he is one of the few contemporary novelists capable of tackling and expressing the values, or lack of them, in our rapidly changing society.

—Trevor Royle

GLOAG, Julian

Nationality: British. **Born:** London, 2 July 1930; son of the writer John Gloag. **Education:** Rugby School, Warwickshire; Magdalene College, Cambridge. **Military Service:** Served in the British Army, 1949-50. **Family:** Married 1) Elise Piquet in 1963 (divorced 1966); 2) Danielle Haase-Dubosc in 1968 (divorced 1981); one son and one daughter. **Career:** Researcher, *Chambers's Encyclopaedia,* London, 1954-56; assistant editor, Ronald Press, New York, 1956-59; editor, Hawthorn Books, New York, 1961-63. Fellow, Royal Society of Literature, 1970. Lives in Paris. **Agent:** Georges Borchardt Inc., 136 East 57th Street, New York, New York 10022, U.S.A.; Richard Scott Simon Ltd., 43 Doughty Street, London WC1N 2LF, England; Michelle Lapautre, 6 rue Jean Carriès, 75007 Paris, France.

PUBLICATIONS

Novels

Our Mother's House. New York, Simon and Schuster, and London, Secker and Warburg, 1963.
A Sentence of Life. New York, Simon and Schuster, and London, Secker and Warburg, 1966.

Maundy. New York, Simon and Schuster, and London, Secker and Warburg, 1969.

A Woman of Character. New York, Random House, and London, Weidenfeld and Nicolson, 1973.

Sleeping Dogs Lie. London, Secker and Warburg, and New York, Dutton, 1980.

Lost and Found. New York, Linden Press, and London, Secker and Warburg, 1981.

Blood for Blood. London, Hamish Hamilton, and New York, Holt Rinehart, 1985.

Only Yesterday. London, Hamish Hamilton, 1986; New York, Holt, 1987.

Love as a Foreign Language. London, Sinclair Stevenson, 1991.

Plays

Television Plays: *Only Yesterday,* from his own novel, 1986; *The Dark Room,* 1988.

Other

The American Nation: A Short History of the United States (revised edition), with John Gloag. London, Cassell, 1955.

*

Manuscript Collection: Mugar Memorial Library, Boston University.

* * *

Julian Gloag is a novelist with quite remarkable gifts of observation. His portrayals of human life, whether in Britain or in France, which he has made his home in recent years, are thoroughly persuasive and his characters come across as human beings who are compellingly convincing both in their psychology and in the marvelously accurate dialogue in which they express themselves and, no less significantly, betray their inner selves. At times, though, especially in his earlier work, Gloag felt obliged to find for his stories situations that go just too far beyond plausibility and to construct plots that are over-ingenious and tax the reader's powers of concentration. Increasing simplicity, conveyed with undiminished veracity and insight, is the mark of Gloag's later, more mature work.

Our Mother's House is striking in its cool narration of a horrifyingly macabre tale. After the death of their mother, her seven children, the offspring of various fathers and ranging in age from toddlers to teenagers, seek to hide her death from the authorities and the prying neighbors. They do so for fear of being consigned to an orphanage. Soon, somewhat in the fashion of William Golding's *Lord of the Flies* but in a London suburban setting, there develops a society with a clearly defined and strictly ordered hierarchy. When problems arise, the children gather at the tabernacle they have erected over the grave which they laboriously dug for their mother's corpse, and consult her spirit. The uneasy situation is disturbed by the return of the dead woman's husband, which, far from resolving problems, leads at first to further disaster before finally law and order is restored.

The situations are extreme in *A Sentence of Life,* which is a gripping variant on the traditional murder mystery. Jordan Maddox, a quiet, well-meaning man who works for a publishing house, did not kill his secretary, but when questioned by Chief Superinten-

dent George neglects to tell the whole truth. Whichever way he turns, however hard he tries to escape from suspicion, evidence keeps on turning up which seems to point unambiguously the finger at him. An extra dimension is added by a number of flashbacks which, far from clearing Jordan, appear to lend credibility to the detective's suspicions about his motives and actions. Finally things are sorted out as Jordan's solicitor uncovers unexpected information about the past of the victim.

Blood for Blood is also a murder mystery with some intriguing differences. At first it seems that the issue is simply one of discovering who murdered the barrister Vivian Winter with such excessive violence. Gradually, though, we learn more and more about the character from his friend Ivor Speke, a minor writer with a past complicated by personal tragedies, and we eventually realize that Vivian was not at all what he seemed to be at the outset, but instead something disturbingly different. The novel moves in the world of the comfortably-off middle classes, but there is a sense of fragility in all that is depicted, and, like Vivian in his legal practice, Ivor has to make forays into less privileged parts of society. Initial sympathies are gently transformed as the focus subtly changes from the classic question of who committed the crime to the more intriguing problem of deciding who the characters really are.

With a middle-aged hero, crippled by polio, who, like Ivor Speke, has rather failed to make his way in life and now works listlessly as a village schoolmaster, dreaming of the novel which might have made his name, *Lost and Found* is based on a complex and initially confusing structure of quite brief and remarkably vivid interlocking flashbacks. Against the backcloth of what might be seen as a saga of successive generations' hopes and calamities in rural France in the period since World War II, Gloag again presents a story which ultimately focuses on the hero's self-discovery.

Short, with its plot reduced to a bare minimum, but with every character evoked with a host of idiosyncrasies that ring true, and set against the precisely detailed background of a comfortable London suburb, *Only Yesterday* recounts an apparently simple event: a middle-aged son, another schoolmaster who wishes he were a better writer, comes for the weekend to tell his aged parents that he has given up his job and left his wife; after a while his daughter also arrives. There is a good deal of gentle humor, but that only adds to what has rightly been hailed by the critics as a brilliant portrayal of old age and what the realization of old age and death must mean both to the elderly and to younger generations.

—Christopher Smith

GLOVER, Douglas (Herschel)

Nationality: Canadian. **Born:** Simloe, Ontario, 14 November 1948. **Education:** York University, Toronto, 1966-69, B.A. in philosophy; University of Edinburgh, 1969-71, M.Litt. in philosophy; University of Iowa, Iowa City, 1980-82, M.F.A. in creative writing. **Family:** Married Helen Edelman in 1990; two sons. **Career:** Lecturer in philosophy, University of New Brunswick, Saint John, 1971; reporter, *The Evening Times-Globe,* Saint John, New Brunswick, 1972; reporter, *The Examiner,* Peterborough, Ontario, 1973-75; copy editor, *The Montreal Star,* 1975; copy editor, *The Star-Phoenix,* Saskatoon, Saskatchewan, 1979. Since 1991 lecturer in English, Skidmore College, Saratoga Springs, New York, and since 1994 faculty, Norwich University, Montpelier, Vermont. Writer-in residence, University of New Brunswick, Fredericton, 1987, State University of New York, Albany, 1992-94. Fiction editor, *The Iowa Review,* 1980-81. Since 1991 editor, with Maggie Helwig, *Coming Attractions,* Oberon Press, Ottawa. Since 1994 host, *The Book Show,* National Public Radio, Albany. **Awards:** Canadian Fiction Magazine annual prize, 1984, and Literary Press Group award, 1986, both for "Dog Attempts to Drown Man in Saskatoon"; Canadian National Magazine awards gold medal, 1990, for "Story Carved in Stone"; New York Foundation for the Arts Artists' fellowship, 1994. **Address:** R.R. 1, Waterford, Ontario, Canada N0E 1Y0.

PUBLICATIONS

Novels

Precious. Toronto, Seal, 1984.
The South Will Rise at Noon. Toronto. Viking, 1988; New York, Viking, 1989.
The Life and Times of Captain N. Toronto, McClelland and Stewart, and New York, Knopf, 1993.

Short Stories

The Mad River and Other Stories. Windsor, Black Moss Press, 1981.
Dog Attempts to Drown Man in Saskatoon. Vancouver, Talonbooks, 1985.
A Guide to Animal Behaviour. Fredericton, Goose Lane, 1991.

Other

Editor, with Maggie Helwig, *Coming Attractions 91-94,* 4 vols. Ottawa, Oberon Press, 1991-94.
Editor, with Diane Schoemperlen, *Coming Attractions 95.* Ottawa, Oberon Press, 1995.

*

Critical Studies: In *Canadian Fiction Magazine,* 65, 1989; in *Paragraph,* 13 (1), 1991; in *The New Story Writers* edited by John Metcalf, Quarry Press, 1992; in *Matrix,* 40, Summer 1993.

Douglas Gover comments:

Most of what I write comes from a place so personal, so intimate, and so painful that I cannot write about it except as fiction. Elements of my style—the obsessive repetitions, the phantasmagoria of images, allusions and comparisons, the mix of comedy and violence, the grotesquerie which is the joke of horror—were always present, but have been reinforced by reading the novels of the late great French Canadian writer Hubert Aquin, especially *Blackout* and *The Antiphonary.* Nabokov lurks somewhere. And back of Nabokov the ghost of Viktor Shklovsky telling us to make things "strange."

I like to write stories that touch the mind and the heart at once, stories that don't necessarily mean but which nonetheless refer to the world's miraculous complexity, its unexpectedness, its divine playfulness. I write about love and memory, the weight of memory and history and the multifarious messages of culture and the past

which run through us and, briefly, use us before passing on. What is the self that's being used and what is using it? I ask. And how do lovers love? Why are people cruel? And whither the words, when the wind blows . . . ?

As an individual I find it difficult to separate the rhetorical from the personal. I am a nomad, an expatriate, a wandering Canadian (which is worse than just being a Canadian, I am doubly displaced, a Canadian squared), and I can no longer tell whether that's because I am a writer or why I am a writer. Some mornings I wake up and it's a problem. Some mornings I wake up and it's a dance.

*   *   *

Since 1981, Douglas Glover has yoked highly cerebral concerns with a witty and passionate style, a steadily growing array of techniques serving an increasingly complex vision. "Life has a way of complicating itself," the narrator says in "The Obituary Writer" (from *A Guide to Animal Behavior*). In many Glover stories, as in "Pender's Visions" (*The Mad River and Other Stories*) and in the title story of *Dog Attempts to Drown Man in Saskatoon,* the writer embraces that complexity in a flexible style that has steadily grown in power and resource. A further example is "A Man in a Box" (*A Guide to Animal Behavior*) in which a pandemonic, logorrheic universe swirls within the confines of an obsessed derelict's cardboard shelter.

The same growth can be traced in his novels. *Precious* is a rococo play on mystery-novel conventions, whose antihero is a much-married newspaper reporter in a small Lake Ontario shoreline community ("It seemed to me that I had spent a lifetime, more or less, in towns just like Ockenden, changing buses to get to other towns"). *The South Will Rise at Noon,* after a start somewhat straining suspension of disbelief, builds to brilliant comedy in telling of one Tully Stamper's misadventures in Gomez Gap, Florida, scene of a preposterous cinematic re-creation of a Civil War battle.

To some extent *Precious* and *The South Will Rise at Noon* amount to a novelist's accomplished apprenticeship. But *The Life and Times of Captain N.,* a story of violent border transactions set in the Niagara frontier, 1779-81, marks a breakthrough, the first thirty pages or so of it among the most engaged and involving Canadian prose in recent years. The novel bodies forth a startlingly vivid historical imagination (in a favorable notice *The New Yorker* said the book belongs to the "Apocalypse The" school of historical fiction), previously only hinted at in a few stories like "Swain Corliss, Hero of Malcolm's Mills (Now Oakland, Ontario), November 6, 1814" in *A Guide to Animal Behavior.* ("The Indians skinned and butchered Edwin Barton's body, Ned having no further use for it.") Amid a treacherous landscape of shattered alliances, psychological as much as political, Glover tells of Captain Hendrick Nellis, Tory guerrilla and "redeemer" of Indian-abducted whites; his son, Oskar, whom Hendrick kidnaps to fight the Yankee rebels; and Mary Hunsacker, a German immigrant girl captured and culturally assimilated by the Mississauga tribe. Then there are the Mohawk, Oneida, Cayuga, Onondaga, and Seneca—Iroquoian shape-shifters viciously caught in a no-holds-barred conflict between Loyalists and "Bostonians." The narrative language, especially that of the psychically riven Oskar, is a virtuoso mix of period-sensitive verisimilitude and the shifting premises of the postmodern.

Glover has thought and written extensively about the art of fiction; more importantly, his stories and novels are not just five-finger exercises on the theme of extreme situations but work out a deeply felt, still-evolving vision. Complexity is never achieved at the expense of clarity.

—Fraser Sutherland

GODDEN, (Margaret) Rumer

Nationality: British. **Born:** Sussex, 10 December 1907. Educated privately and at Moira House, Eastbourne, Sussex. **Family:** Married 1) Laurence Sinclair Foster in 1934 (died), two daughters; 2) James Lesley Haynes Dixon in 1949 (died 1973). **Career:** Director of a children's ballet school, Calcutta, in the 1930s. **Awards:** Whitbread award, for children's book, 1973. **Agent:** Curtis Brown, 162-168 Regent Street, London W1R 5TB; or, 10 Astor Place, New York, New York 10003, U.S.A. **Address:** c/o Macmillan Publishers Ltd., 4 Little Essex Street, London WC2R 3LF, England.

PUBLICATIONS

Novels

Chinese Puzzle. London, Davies, 1936.
The Lady and the Unicorn. London, Davies, 1937.
Black Narcissus. London, Davies, and Boston, Little Brown, 1939.
Gypsy, Gypsy. London, Davies, and Boston, Little Brown, 1940.
Breakfast with the Nikolides. London, Davies, and Boston, Little Brown, 1942.
A Fugue in Time. London, Joseph, 1945; as *Take Three Tenses: A Fugue in Time,* Boston, Little Brown, 1945.
The River. London, Joseph, and Boston, Little Brown, 1946.
A Candle for St. Jude. London, Joseph, and New York, Viking Press, 1948.
A Breath of Air. London, Joseph, 1950; New York, Viking Press, 1951.
Kingfishers Catch Fire. London, Macmillan, and New York, Viking Press, 1953.
An Episode of Sparrows. New York, Viking Press, 1955; London, Macmillan, 1956.
The Greengage Summer. London, Macmillan, and New York, Viking Press, 1958.
China Court: The Hours of a Country House. London, Macmillan, and New York, Viking Press, 1961.
The Battle of the Villa Fiorita. London, Macmillan, and New York, Viking Press, 1963.
In This House of Brede. London, Macmillan, and New York, Viking Press, 1969.
The Peacock Spring. London, Macmillan, 1975; New York, Viking Press, 1976.
Five for Sorrow, Ten for Joy. London, Macmillan, and New York, Viking Press, 1979.
The Dark Horse. London, Macmillan, 1981; New York, Viking Press, 1982.
Thursday's Children. London, Macmillan, and New York, Viking, 1984.
Coromandel Sea Change. London, Macmillan, and New York, Morrow, 1991.
Pippa Passes. London, Macmillan, and New York, Morrow, 1994.

Short Stories

Mooltiki and Other Stories and Poems of India. London, Macmillan, and New York, Viking Press, 1957.
Swans and Turtles: Stories. London, Macmillan, 1968; as *Gone: A Thread of Stories,* New York, Viking Press, 1968.
Indian Dust, with Jon Godden. London, Macmillan, 1989; as *Mercy, Pity, Peace and Love,* New York, Morrow, 1990.

Fiction (for children)

The Dolls' House, London, Joseph, 1947; New York, Viking Press, 1948; as *Tottie,* London, Penguin, 1983.
The Mousewife. London, Macmillan, and New York, Viking Press, 1951.
Four Dolls. London, Macmillan, 1983; New York, Greenwillow, 1984.
Impunity Jane: The Story of a Pocket Doll. New York, Viking Press, 1954; London, Macmillan, 1955.
The Fairy Doll. London, Macmillan, and New York, Viking Press, 1956.
The Story of Holly and Ivy. London, Macmillan, and New York, Viking Press, 1958.
Candy Floss. London, Macmillan, and New York, Viking Press, 1960.
Mouse House. New York, Viking Press, 1957; London, Macmillan, 1958.
Miss Happiness and Miss Flower. London, Macmillan, and New York, Viking Press, 1961.
Little Plum. London, Macmillan, and New York, Viking Press, 1963.
Home Is the Sailor. London, Macmillan, and New York, Viking Press, 1964.
The Kitchen Madonna. London, Macmillan, and New York, Viking Press, 1967.
Operation Sippacik. London, Macmillan, and New York, Viking Press, 1969.
The Old Woman Who Lived in a Vinegar Bottle. London, Macmillan, and New York, Viking Press, 1972.
The Diddakoi. London, Macmillan, and New York, Viking Press, 1972.
Mr. McFadden's Hallowe'en. London, Macmillan, and New York, Viking Press, 1975.
The Rocking Horse Secret. London, Macmillan, 1977; New York, Viking Press, 1978.
A Kindle of Kittens. London, Macmillan, 1978; New York, Viking Press, 1979.
The Dragon of Og. London, Macmillan, and New York, Viking Press, 1981.
The Valiant Chatti-Maker. London, Macmillan, and New York, Viking Press, 1983.
Fu-Dog. London, MacRae, 1989.

Plays

Screenplays: *The River,* with Jean Renoir, 1951; *Innocent Sinners,* with Neil Patterson, 1958.

Poetry (for children)

In Noah's Ark. London, Joseph, and New York, Viking Press, 1949.
St. Jerome and the Lion. London, Macmillan, and New York, Viking Press, 1961.

Other

Rungli-Rungliot (Thus Far and No Further). London, Davies, 1943; as *Rungli-Rungliot Means in Paharia, Thus Far and No Further,* Boston, Little Brown, 1946; as *Thus Far and No Further,* London, Macmillan, 1961.

Bengal Journey: A Story of the Part Played by Women in the Province 1939-45. London, Longman, 1945.

Hans Christian Andersen: A Great Life in Brief. London, Hutchinson, and New York, Knopf, 1955.

Two under the Indian Sun (autobiography), with Jon Godden. London, Macmillan, and New York, Knopf, 1966.

The Tale of the Tales: The Beatrix Potter Ballet. London, Warne, 1971.

Shiva's Pigeons: An Experience of India, with Jon Godden. London, Chatto and Windus, and New York, Viking Press, 1972.

The Butterfly Lions: The Story of the Pekingese in History, Legend, and Art. London, Macmillan, 1977; New York, Viking Press, 1978.

Gulbadan: Portrait of a Rose Princess at the Mughal Court. London, Macmillan, 1980; New York, Viking Press, 1981.

A Time to Dance, No Time to Weep (autobiography). London, Macmillan, and New York, Morrow, 1987.

A House with Four Rooms (autobiography). London, Macmillan, and New York, Morrow, 1989.

Editor, *Round the Day, Round the Year, The World Around: Poetry Programmes for Classroom or Library.* London, Macmillan, 6 vols., 1966-67.

Editor, *A Letter to the World: Poems for Young Readers,* by Emily Dickinson. London, Bodley Head, 1968; New York, Macmillan, 1969.

Editor, *Mrs. Manders' Cookbook,* by Olga Manders. London, Macmillan, and New York, Viking Press, 1968.

Editor, *The Raphael Bible.* London, Macmillan, and New York, Viking Press, 1970.

Translator, *Prayers from the Ark* (verse), by Carmen de Gasztold. New York, Viking Press, 1962; London, Macmillan, 1963.

Translator, *The Creatures' Choir* (verse), by Carmen de Gasztold. New York, Viking Press, 1965; as *The Beasts' Choir,* London, Macmillan, 1967.

*

Manuscript Collection: Mugar Memorial Library, Boston University.

Critical Study: *Rumer Godden* by Hassell A. Simpson, New York, Twayne, 1973.

*   *   *

Rumer Godden inherited a love of language from her philologist father. In whatever vein of fiction she writes—and there have been several—her work is informed with a loving sense of the color and shape and rhythm of the words she chooses. It is not surprising that she is also a poet and has published two narratives in verse: *In Noah's Ark* and *St. Jerome and the Lion.*

The traditional novel of individual lives, however, is her natural medium. She thinks as a novelist. When she came to collect some of her short stories (*Swans and Turtles*), she chose to string them together as a "thread," with notes to tell how they had arisen from remembered incidents in her own life. In this sense her novels, too, can be seen to reflect her autobiography.

Three themes, which sometimes interweave, have predominated in the novels and stories: the lives of foreigners in an exotic land (she grew up in India and has often returned there); the religious life (paralleling her own conversion to Roman Catholicism); and the secret lives and thoughts of children viewing their elders through their own fresh eyes. From the latter grows a fourth theme, of imaginative and playful fantasy, which is particularly evident in her many books for children but also occurs in such a novel as *A Breath of Air,* her modern version of *The Tempest.* In evaluating her novels, one is inclined to give most critical weight, in the Indian group, to *Breakfast with the Nikolides,* a poignantly perceptive study of inter-racial relations, and the beautiful short novel, *The River,* about a childhood tragedy in the mysterious aura of Indian tradition (which she helped Jean Renoir to make into an exceptional motion picture). Experimentally, *China Court,* evoking an English household through several generations with its sense of past and present running concurrently, is perhaps the most interesting. She had earlier tried a similar experiment, less successfully, in *A Fugue in Time,* set in wartime London. Among the books with a religious theme, *In This House of Brede* has the peculiar fascination of a special way of life (a contemporary English Catholic nunnery) shown in intimate detail. She completed it in Lamb House at Rye, the long-time home of Henry James where she lived for some years by invitation of its owners, the British National Trust.

The public at large has most loved *Black Narcissus,* about an Anglican sisterhood in India, written before her conversion; *An Episode of Sparrows,* a tender story of street-urchins in London; and *The Greengage Summer,* a mystery involving a family of English children on their own in a French hotel. All three became successful motion pictures.

She writes her adult novels at long intervals, with time for reflection, while children's books and lesser writings continue. *The Peacock Spring* is a shorter work of young love between an English girl and a native boy in India. *Five for Sorrow, Ten for Joy,* came 10 years after *Brede.* It renewed the theme of devoted convent life, but in another country, France, and with something quite unexpected added: before the convent came life in a Paris brothel, a murder that might appear as a crime of passion, and years of penitence in a women's prison. In terms of rather ordinary humans, though often in unusual situations, Godden wins sympathy by dealing thoughtfully and hopefully with some persistent verities.

Although Godden can be regarded as a "senior" writer on grounds of age and reputation, nothing she writes is dated or shows her to be out of touch with contemporary society, to judge by the observations she presents in her fiction. Perhaps because her work is of a dependably high standard and extremely accessible to the reader, Godden's output since *Ten for Sorrow, Five for Joy* has not always been noticed by critics. Because much of her work has required factual knowledge of a specialised nature, such as the workings of juvenile courts for *An Episode of Sparrows,* Godden researches scrupulously, without ever letting the factual matter seem contrived. It is a technique she uses in *Pippa Passes,* a novel set in Venice. The germ of *An Episode of Sparrows* grew from a chance remark by a London busybody neighbour, but an Edwardian novel about Venice inspired Godden to devise a contemporary story where the city in its moods is as important as the characters. The shifting light matches the rather confused thoughts of Pippa, a young English dancer of star qualities with a corps de ballet. Her first experience of love is for Nico, a handsome gondolier. At first deliberately understated is the rival affection for her of her ballet mistress Angharad, a lesbian, who scarcely conceals her sexual feelings for her loved one under the guise of protective discipline. The progress of the ballet performance, the feelings of fame, and Pippa's reaction are a sympathetic study of young womanhood facing a crisis of identity in what she wants and expects to gain from life. But the turning point of the novel is more than just Agharad's attempted seduction of Pippa. It is a brutal attempted rape, and its effect not only forces Pippa to be aware of her true heterosexual identity, but also to be confronted by her emotions about everything for the first time. The shock of Nico's desertion is experienced as a powerful and hurtful reality, rather than just an adolescent transient mood of little impact. In short, she has grown up.

—Marshall A. Best, updated by Geoffrey Elborn

GODFREY, Dave

Nationality: Canadian. **Born:** Winnipeg, Manitoba, 9 August 1938. **Education:** Harvard University, Cambridge, Massachusetts, 1957; University of Toronto, 1957-58; University of Iowa, Iowa City, 1958-60, 1963, 1965-66, B.A. 1960, M.F.A. 1963, Ph.D. 1966; Stanford University, California, 1960-61, M.A. 1963; University of Chicago, 1965. **Family:** Married Ellen Swartz in 1963; two sons and one daughter. **Career:** Acting head of the English Department, Adisadel College, Cape Coast, Ghana, 1963-65; assistant professor of English, 1966-68 and 1969-74, and visiting professor, 1975-76, Trinity College, Toronto; writer-in-residence, Erindale College, Toronto, 1973-74; visiting professor, 1974-75, and associate professor of English, 1976-77, York University, Toronto. Associate professor and head of the Creative Writing Department, 1977-82, and since 1982 professor of English, University of Victoria, British Columbia. Co-founder, House of Anansi, publishers, Toronto, 1966-70; general editor, Canadian Writers series, McClelland and Stewart, publishers, Toronto, 1968-72; co-founding editor, New Press, Toronto, 1969-73; fiction editor, *Canadian Forum,* Toronto, 1971-72. Since 1972 editor, Press Porcépic, Erin, Ontario, later Victoria, British Columbia; since 1982 vice-president, Inter-Provincial Association for Telematics and Telidon. President, Association of Canadian Publishers, 1972-73. **Awards:** University of Western Ontario President's medal, 1965; Canada Council award, 1969; Governor-General's award, 1971. **Address:** Department of English, University of Victoria, Victoria, British Columbia V8W 2Y2, Canada.

PUBLICATIONS

Novel

The New Ancestors. Toronto, New Press, 1970.

Short Stories

Death Goes Better with Coca-Cola. Toronto, Anansi, 1967.
New Canadian Writing 1968, with Clark Blaise and Lewis Stein. Toronto, Clarke Irwin, 1969.
Dark Must Yield. Erin, Ontario, Press Porcépic, 1978.

Other

I Ching Kanada. Erin, Ontario, Press Porcépic, 1976.
The Telidon Book. Victoria, British Columbia, Press Porcépic, 1981; Reston, Virginia, Reston Publishing, 1982.
The Elements of CAL: The How-To Book on Computer-Aided Learning, with Sharon Sterling. Victoria, British Columbia, Press Porcépic, 1982.
Computer-Aided Learning Using the NATAL Language, with Jack Brahan. Victoria, British Columbia, Press Porcépic, 1984.

Editor, with Bill McWhinney, *Man Deserves Man.* Toronto, Ryerson Press, 1967.
Editor, *Gordon to Watkins to You: A Documentary of the Battle for Control of the Canadian Economy.* Toronto, New Press, 1970.
Editor, with Robert Fulford and Abraham Rotstein, *Read Canadian: A Book about Canadian Books.* Toronto, Lorimer, 1972.
Editor, with Douglas Parkhill, *Gutenberg Two.* Erin, Ontario, Press Porcépic, 1979; 4th edition, Victoria, British Columbia, 1984.
Editor, *Empire and Communications,* by Harold A. Innes. Victoria, British Columbia, Press Porcépic, 1986.

*

Critical Studies: Article by Dorah Hood, in *Oxford Companion to Canadian History and Literature* edited by Norah Story, Toronto, New York, and London, Oxford University Press, 1967; by Margaret Laurence, in *Ellipse* (Quebec), Fall 1970, and in *Mysterious East* (Fredericton, New Brunswick), December 1970; Phyllis Grosskurth, in *Canadian Forum* (Toronto), April 1971; *Sex and Violence in the Canadian Novel* by John Moss, Toronto, McClelland and Stewart, 1977.

Dave Godfrey comments:

I am most interested in that portion of literature where myth meets social realities; literary dogma concerning the purity of fantasy or of realism does not interest me. The Canadian environment has influenced me greatly although I write mainly about people from cultures other than my own. A good part of my twenties was spent traveling about the U.S. and Africa. I strive for great complexity in my writing because that is how I find life; I do not believe the writer has a duty to simplify or interpret life for his readers; his major tasks are to be as intelligent as possible and to take flights of imagination into bodies, minds, and situations other than his own.

*   *   *

In both its form and content Dave Godfrey's fiction reflects the nationalistic political stance that colors his career. As an emerging writer in the 1960s, Godfrey initiated several attempts to define Canadian literary consciousness through policies affecting the publishing industry and through fiction that addressed the issue of foreign influence in Canada. His activities in publishing, including the founding of House of Anansi Press, New Press, and Press Porcépic, as well as the controversial *Gordon to Watkins to You: A Documentary of the Battle for Control of the Canadian Economy,* testified to his early commitment to fostering a national literature by increasing awareness of Canadian writing and culture. More recently, he has become involved in writing about new communication modes, an interest that has prompted him to theorize about the impact of computer and electronic technology on contemporary society.

As this brief description of Godfrey's changing concerns may suggest, he is a writer committed to questioning and to change. In his fiction this commitment makes him an innovator in the best sense of the word. His stories are marked by the characteristics associated with the French *nouveau roman* and with metafictional theories of narrative. Godfrey consistently undermines conventional notions of plot, characterization, and narrative perspective. He juxtaposes time frames, intercuts settings, reveals character through flashback and fantasy, and allows his stories to be told from several points of view which inevitably contradict each other and force the reader to question the narrative act itself. Godfrey's experimentation, however, is not purely formal, since each of his works can be interpreted, implicitly and explicitly, as bearing on his understanding of Canada and what he perceives to be the various predicaments involving the nation.

His experimental, nationalistic stance is suggested by the title of his first collection of stories, *Death Goes Better with Coca-Cola,* a book that explores the connection between American Coca-Cola culture and death—a death that Godfrey writes against in a series of densely-textured tales about various forms of life-giving liberation. The first of these stories—and certainly the one most widely anthologized—is "The Hard-Headed Collector," an intricate examination of the conflict between a symbolic group of (extinct) Canadian artists attempting to locate themselves in the midst of a pervading American influence on the arts, embodied in the person of an art collector who has sold out to American power and patronage. All of the stories in the collection are subtle and complex, and all rely for their interpretation on an understanding of the murder metaphor that pervades the book: the numerous killers we encounter are Americans or foreigners and therefore threats to an independent and "alive" Canada.

Godfrey's only novel, *The New Ancestors,* is a brilliant Canadian *nouveau roman* set in Ghana. Although the book is set abroad, it is clear that Godfrey saw in an African struggle for independence important parallels with Canada's desire for a similar independence from foreign control. Thus the novel can be read in allegorical terms. But it can also be appreciated for Godfrey's experiments with perspective, in that the story is told from four vastly different viewpoints which must be interpreted individually and collectively before the tragic story can emerge. *The New Ancestors* is not easy reading, but it rewards careful study and demonstrates Godfrey's ability to evoke atmosphere and human emotion with subtlety and power.

I Ching Kanada, which must be doubly read as "I Sing Canada," is a series of prose-poem meditations based on the hexagrams of the *I Ching,* a source that also informs *Death Goes Better with Coca-Cola.* The book presents no final message or overall coherence because Godfrey is interested in exploring the relationship between chance and the movement toward nationhood. If the meditations are also seen as reflections on selfhood, as some commentators have suggested, then *I Ching Kanada* becomes a metafictional text through which Godfrey reveals himself, his fiction, and the relationship he sees between the two.

Dark Must Yield is also highly experimental, but here he returns to the short story mode familiar to readers of his first collection. The stories, however, are more compressed, less overtly political, and more subtly structured than those in the earlier volume, perhaps because Godfrey chose to emphasize psychological, rather than social processes. In one of the first assessments of Godfrey's work, published in 1974, Frank Davey reached a conclusion that still applies today. He found that Godfrey's involvement with contemporary theories of art and communications has created for him "a deserved reputation as a resourceful and uncompromising prose experimenter."

—Robert Lecker

GODWIN, Gail (Kathleen)

Nationality: American. **Born:** Birmingham, Alabama, 18 June 1937. **Education:** Peace Junior College, Raleigh, North Carolina, 1955-57; University of North Carolina, Chapel Hill, 1957-59, B.A. in journalism 1959; University of Iowa, Iowa City, 1967-71, M.A. 1968, Ph.D. in English 1971. **Family:** Married 1) Douglas Kennedy in 1960 (divorced); 2) Ian Marshall in 1965 (divorced 1966). **Career:** Reporter, Miami *Herald,* 1959-60; consultant, U.S. Travel Service, United States Embassy, London, 1962-65; researcher, *Saturday Evening Post,* New York, 1966; Instructor in English, 1967-70, and lecturer at the Writers Workshop, 1972-73, University of Iowa, instructor and fellow, Center for Advanced Studies, University of Illinois, Urbana, 1971-72; American specialist, United States Information Service, Brazil, 1976; lecturer, Vassar College, Poughkeepsie, New York, 1977, and Columbia University, New York, 1978, 1981. **Awards:** National Endowment for the Arts grant, 1974, and fellowship, for libretto, 1978; Guggenheim fellowship, 1975; St. Lawrence award, 1976; American Academy award, 1981; Thomas Wolfe Memorial award, 1988; Janet Kafka award, 1988. **Agent:** John Hawkins and Associates, 71 West 23rd Street, Suite 1600, New York, New York 10010. **Address:** P.O. Box 946, Woodstock, New York 12498, U.S.A.

PUBLICATIONS

Novels

The Perfectionists. New York, Harper, 1970; London, Cape, 1971.
Glass People. New York, Knopf, 1972.
The Odd Woman. New York, Knopf, 1974; London, Cape, 1975.
Violet Clay. New York, Knopf, and London, Gollancz, 1978.
A Mother and Two Daughters. New York, Viking Press, and London, Heinemann, 1982.
The Finishing School. New York, Viking, and London, Heinemann, 1985.
A Southern Family. New York, Morrow, and London, Heinemann, 1987.
Father Melancholy's Daughter. New York, Morrow, and London, Deutsch, 1991.
The Good Husband. New York, Ballantine, and London, Deutsch, 1994.

Short Stories

Dream Children. New York, Knopf, 1976; London, Gollancz, 1977.
Mr. Bedford and the Muses. New York, Viking Press, 1983; London, Heinemann, 1984.

Uncollected Short Stories

"Fate of Fleeing Maidens," in *Mademoiselle* (New York), May 1978.

"The Unlikely Family," in *Redbook* (New York), August 1979.
"Over the Mountain," in *Antaeus* (New York), 1983.

Plays

The Last Lover, music by Robert Starer (produced Katonah, New
York, 1975).
Journals of a Songmaker, music by Robert Starer (produced Phila-
delphia, 1976).
Apollonia, music by Robert Starer (produced Minneapolis, 1979).

Recordings: *Anna Margarita's Will* (song cycle), music by Robert
Starer, C.R.I., 1980; *Remembering Felix,* music by Robert Starer,
Spectrum, 1987.

Other

Editor, with Shannon Ravenel, *The Best American Short Stories
1985.* Boston, Houghton Mifflin, 1985.

*

Manuscript Collection: Southern Collection, University of Northern Carolina Library, Chapel Hill.

Critical Studies: "*The Odd Woman:* Literature and the Retreat from
Life" by Susan E. Lorsch, in *Critique* (Atlanta), vol. 20, no. 2,
1978; "Reaching Out: Sensitivity and Order," in *Recent American
Fiction by Women* by Anne Z. Mickelson, Metuchen, New Jersey,
Scarecrow Press, 1979; interview and "Gail Godwin and Southern
Womanhood" by Carolyn Rhodes, both in *Women Writers of the
Contemporary South* edited by Peggy Whitman Prenshaw, Jack-
son, University Press of Mississippi, 1984; *Gail Godwin* by Jane
Hill, New York, Twayne, 1992.

Gail Godwin comments:

Since I began writing fiction I have been most interested in creating
characters who operate at a high level of intelligence and feeling as
they go about trying to make sense of the world in which they find
themselves, and as they make decisions about how to live their lives.

*   *   *

In her fiction Gail Godwin depicts the choices that modern
women make. Whether within marriage or the single life, motherhood or career, these choices necessitate compromise, and none
brings complete happiness. Godwin's characters often explore their
options through art as they create or analyze images that may reveal or even change reality. A common crisis that precipitates this
artistic endeavor or self-exploration is a death in the family, and
within renewed family relationships, either nuclear or extended,
Godwin's characters defend, dismiss, or display their choices.

Godwin demonstrates the effects of lack of choice in her first
two novels, both violent and oppressive tales. In *The Perfectionists* Dane Empson's rage against her stifling marriage erupts when
she beats her husband's illegitimate son. Obsessed with sexual acts
in which she is either completely powerless or powerful, Dane
views any relationship as invasive. Francesca Bolt, a passive princess in *Glass People,* makes not even basic decisions about food
and clothes. She may "open out" like a beautiful flower but only if
husband Cameron provides the container. Like Dane Empson,

Francesca longs for a dark angel to transport her to her "true but
unknown destiny." Neither Dane nor Francesca finds the strength
to leave her marriage.

In her most insightful novel to date, *The Odd Woman,* Godwin
creates Jane Clifford, an academic who researches life in order to
control it. Unlike Dane Empson and Francesca Bolt, Jane believes
in relationships, in perfect unions, like that of Marian Evans
(George Eliot) and George Henry Lewes, in which men and women
can communicate but retain separate identities. If she can analyze
her married lover's words, Jane believes she can discover his feelings. And to some extent she succeeds, for in a rare moment Jane
experiences Gabriel completely. However, she cannot sustain her
moment, and her analyses usually lead her away from reality toward melodramas with faceless villains.

The fictive present in *The Odd Woman* begins with Jane's
grandmother's death, an event that forces Jane's rediscovery of family relationships. Within her family and in George Gissing's *The
Odd Women,* a novel for her next teaching assignment, Jane explores women's choices. Although she hates her aggressive stepfather, the man with whom her mother makes an apparent compromise, Jane still cheers for women who strive for marriage. She
destroys the family myth about great-aunt Cleva who ran away with
a villain actor in the melodrama *The Fatal Wedding.* Caught between the world of literature in which every plot seems probable
and reality in which married lovers seldom leave their wives, Jane
struggles with her own possibilities. She rejects total withdrawal
into literature after living in isolation the winter she writes her dissertation. Gerda, her radical feminist *doppelgänger,* cannot convince
her to give up on men, but neither will Jane continue to play the
role of Understanding Mistress. Jane's insomnia functions as her
muse, and keeping herself open to relationships may free the ending of the Jane Clifford Story, with all its Aristotelian requirements.
At the end of the novel, back in her apartment, Jane may not have
found an Eliot-Lewes union, but she clings to her belief that one
can "organize the loneliness and the weather and the long night
into something of abiding shape and beauty."

Moving the reader closer to the main character through first-person point of view and less reliance on interior monologue than in
The Old Woman, Godwin nevertheless continues her reflections
on the thin line between reality and imagination, between art and
life in *Violet Clay.* The title character in *Violet Clay* searches idly
for her options in "the book of Old Plots" while she projects herself into the romance novels she illustrates for a living. The death
of Violet's Uncle Ambrose serves as catalyst for change when he
commits suicide in his Adirondack cabin. Ambrose's note to Violet
reads: "I'm sorry, there's nothing left." Violet sketches his face and
interprets the punctuation in the note until she realizes that the "nothing" is artistic inspiration. When Violet realizes the meaning of
Ambrose's note, she takes up serious art again, and the goal in the
fictive present becomes the proper artistic subject. Violet finally remembers Ambrose's advice: write about (or create) something you
want to happen. Art is a way of seeing life rather than postponing
it, Violet learns. In her portrait of her neighbor Samantha De Vere,
a woman who survives incest and rape, Violet captures the human
spirit and earns artistic recognition. Exploring relationships and testing possibilities through artistic expression contribute to Violet's
growth; as she states, "Sam put me into proportion, as Ambrose
put me into perspective." Godwin continues to explore this connection between art and life in her two short story collections,
Dream Children and *Mr. Bedford and the Muses.*

Each female character in *A Mother and Two Daughters* represents one choice for women. Cate, the academic who chooses abortion, Lydia, the divorcée who returns to school and career, and Nell, the widow who finds contentment in a second husband, all receive narrative attention in Godwin's longest novel to date. Although Godwin reduces her focus on art to a few comments on *The Scarlet Letter,* the theme of that novel is clearly relevant: "Can the individual spirit survive the society in which it has to live?" The society in *A Mother and Two Daughters* is that of the family, which Cate and Lydia's sibling rivalry threatens to pull apart after their father's death. Although blinded by misunderstanding, Lydia and Cate experience much the same anxiety and desire, as Lydia writes a research paper on Eros, a "striving for what one lacks," and Cate defines hope as "keeping a space ready for what you did want, even though you didn't know what it would be until it came." Neither daughter wants to close off her possibilities, whatever her destiny might bring.

In the most intense scene in the novel, Cate and Lydia explode at each other in anger. They express their resentment of their childhood roles: Cate as rebel, Lydia as dutiful daughter. After the fight, their neglect causes their father's cabin to burn, the fire taking with it not only childhood possessions but much of the sisters' anger. In the peace that follows, Lydia and Cate incorporate each other into their lives, and the connections between Lydia's real family and Cate's extended one allow each to survive as individual spirits: "Do you remember? . . . Does it still hurt here? . . . Oh, it all passes, but that's the beauty of it, too." Music written by Lydia's son Dickie unites the family in the final scene.

"Your soul craves that constant heightening of reality only art can give you," Ursula DeVane tells Justine Stokes in *The Finishing School* and thus continues Godwin's theme of art affecting life. Fourteen-year-old Justine, grieving for her dead father and grandparents, turns to 44-year-old Ursula for friendship. 26 years later Justine still struggles to understand that tragic summer. Curiosity about that tragedy, Godwin's portrayal of eccentric Ursula, and her sensitive depiction of adolescent Justine propel the reader through *The Finishing School.* Much like Muriel Spark's Jean Brodie, Ursula DeVane serves as muse to the innocent. Always "keep moving forward and making new trysts with life," Ursula advises Justine, and you'll never grow old. However, the time comes when the student becomes independent and sees her teacher as flawed rather than ideal. This inevitability forms the essential part of Ursula's definition of tragedy: the "something terrible" that happens when a person lives out her own "destiny." The intensity of their relationship causes Justine to betray Ursula much as Ursula betrayed her own mother. The adult Justine realizes that now she must use "all the fate" that has happened to her and "make possible what still may happen." Her yearnings and torments strengthen her acting talent: "As long as you can go on creating new roles for yourself, you are not vanquished," Justine concludes, much as Ursula would. In Godwin's fictional world, roles for women are artistically created and recreated until they become real.

—Mary M. Lay

GOLD, Herbert

Nationality: American. **Born:** Cleveland, Ohio, 9 March 1924. **Education:** Columbia University, New York, B.A. 1946, M.A. 1948; the Sorbonne, Paris (Fulbright scholar), 1949-51. **Military**

Service: Served in the United States Army, 1943-46. **Family:** Married 1) Edith Zubrin in 1948 (divorced 1956), two daughters; 2) Melissa Dilworth in 1968 (divorced 1975), one daughter and two sons. **Career:** lecturer in philosophy and literature, Western Reserve University, Cleveland, 1951-53; lecturer in English, Wayne State University, Detroit, 1954-56. Visiting professor, Cornell University, Ithaca, New York, 1958, University of California, Berkeley, 1963, Harvard University, Cambridge, Massachusetts, 1964, Stanford University, California, 1967, and University of California, Davis, 1973-79. **Awards:** Inter-American Cultural grant, to Haiti, 1950; *Hudson Review* fellowship, 1956; Guggenheim fellowship, 1957; American Academy grant, 1958; Longview Foundation award, 1959; Ford fellowship, for drama, 1960; Sherwood Anderson prize, 1989. L.H.D.: Baruch College, City University, New York, 1988. **Address:** 1051-A Broadway, San Francisco, California 94133, U.S.A.

PUBLICATIONS

Novels

Birth of a Hero. New York, Viking Press, 1951.
The Prospect Before Us. Cleveland, World, 1954; as *Room Clerk,* New York, New American Library, 1955.
The Man Who Was Not With It. Boston, Little Brown, 1956; London, Secker and Warburg, 1965; as *The Wild Life,* New York, Permabooks, 1957.
The Optimist. Boston, Little Brown, 1959.
Therefore Be Bold. New York, Dial Press, 1960; London, Deutsch, 1962.
Salt. New York, Dial Press, 1963; London, Secker and Warburg, 1964.
Fathers: A Novel in the Form of a Memoir. New York, Random House, and London, Secker and Warburg, 1967.
The Great American Jackpot. New York, Random House, 1970; London, Weidenfeld and Nicolson, 1971.
Swiftie the Magician. New York, McGraw Hill, 1974; London, Hutchinson, 1975.
Waiting for Cordelia. New York, Arbor House, 1977; London, Hutchinson, 1978.
Slave Trade. New York, Arbor House, 1979.
He/She. New York, Arbor House, 1980; London, Severn House, 1982.
Family: A Novel in the Form of a Memoir. New York, Arbor House, 1981; London, Severn House, 1983.
True Love. New York, Arbor House, 1982; London, Severn House, 1984.
Mister White Eyes. New York, Arbor House, 1984; London, Severn House, 1985.
A Girl of Forty. New York, Fine, 1986.
Dreaming. New York, Fine, 1988.

Short Stories

15 x 3, with R.V. Cassill and James B. Hall. New York, New Directions, 1957.
Love and Like. New York, Dial Press, 1960; London, Deutsch, 1961.
The Magic Will: Stories and Essays of a Decade. New York, Random House, 1971.

Stories of Misbegotten Love. Santa Barbara, California, Capra Press, 1985.
Lovers and Cohorts: Twenty-Seven Stories. New York, Fine, 1986.

Other

The Age of Happy Problems (essays). New York, Dial Press, 1962.
Biafra Goodbye. San Francisco, Twowindows Press, 1970.
My Last Two Thousand Years (autobiography). New York, Random House, 1972; London, Hutchinson, 1973.
The Young Prince and the Magic Cone (for children). New York, Doubleday, 1973.
A Walk on the West Side: California on the Brink (stories and essays). New York, Arbor House, 1981.
Travels in San Francisco. New York, Arcade, 1990.
The Best Nightmare on Earth: A Life in Haiti. New York, Prentice Hall Press, and London, Grafton, 1991.
Bohemia. New York, Simon and Schuster, 1993.

Editor, *Fiction of the Fifties: A Decade of American Writing.* New York, Doubleday, 1959.
Editor, with David L. Stevenson, *Stories of Modern America.* New York, St. Martin's Press, 1961; revised edition, 1963.
Editor, *First Person Singular: Essays for the Sixties.* New York, Dial Press, 1963.

*

Herbert Gold comments:

Subjects: Power, money, sex and love, intention in America.
Themes: The same.
Moral: Coming next time.

*   *   *

In Herbert Gold's introduction to *Fiction of the Fifties,* he makes a distinction between fiction which *avows* and fiction which *controls.* The fiction which avows is a rather faithful transcription of the immediate and personal experience of the writer; such fiction makes use of the writer's own experience of his past and the section of social life where that experience took place. The other sort of fiction makes an attempt to present the experiences of persons who indeed are not the writer; these experiences are given clarity by an effort of the imagination which takes the writer outside himself and immerses him in circumstances that are not his own. All this is done by the exercise of *control.*

These interesting categories can be used to classify Gold's own fiction. A great deal of that fiction falls into the first category, that of avowal, as one can see from an inspection of his autobiographical *My Last Two Thousand Years.* This book is a narrative of Gold's own life, a life that finds its way into several of his novels. It was a life in which, as the son of a Jewish immigrant who settled in Cleveland, Gold experienced a difficult youth in the shadow of a strong father who had found a place for himself in an alien society. Gold's narrative relates his own struggles to detach himself from his father's ambitions for him, and to achieve his own goals, in New York and elsewhere, as student, critic, and novelist. All this was a process of self-discovery that demanded acts of will and personal heroism. This self-discovery, as Gold relates it, also involved a succession of painful relationships: marriage, parenthood, divorce, and a second marriage, with various temporary relationships along the way.

These are all matters that various other novelists would regard as private. So are they for Gold. But they are also the stuff of much of his fiction. These are the novels which *avow* (or assert) the essentials of the writer's own life. Such fiction contrasts with other novels in which Gold borrows and reshapes elements of other lives; it is in these latter novels that Gold *controls* the experiences of other persons and also depicts social patterns which the writer does not know directly and immediately.

Gold's frequent adherence to the dictum of Sir Philip Sidney's muse—"Fool . . . look in thy heart and write"—is illustrated by an excellent novel, *Fathers,* which is subtitled "A Novel in the Form of a Memoir." The novel tells of the relation between an immigrant father and his son; it is a vivid recollection of matters that Gold also puts down in *My Last Two Thousand Years. Fathers* offers homage to a courageous father and to the equally courageous son who chooses to turn aside from his father. The novel offers a convincing texture of loyalty and enmity. The same section of Gold's life appears in *Therefore Be Bold* which, however, centers attention on "Daniel Berman's" adolescent years in Cleveland: his encounters with poetry and sex and his bitter first experience of anti-Semitism.

Other novels, one can judge, are transcriptions of Gold's own experience of self-assertion and self-discovery in the New York literary world. Thus, *Swiftie the Magician* displays Gold's creative imagination moving onwards from his youth and assessing a man's attempts to find his own way through the jungles of professional and emotional life that surround a person in the second half of the 20th century. The novel relates the involvement of a writer with three women: an East Coast innocent, a West Coast "experienced" young woman, and the hard-bitten Swiftie, a "magician" who knows what the score is in a rough world. *Salt* gives the reader a more complex version of such pursuits of identity. Two men—one a complacent Wasp and the other once more an alter ego for Gold—move from woman to woman, the Wasp learning little and the young Jew from Cleveland a great deal.

Such are the novels in which Gold reworks the stuff of his own life. But there are other novels in which Gold is exercising *control*—is, in more conventional literary language, inventing persons not himself and following the courses of their experiences. *Birth of a Hero* follows the attempts of a middle-aged business man, Reuben Flair, a faceless cipher, to become a man fully aware of what he has done, in marriage and beyond marriage. As in other novels by Gold, the outlines of Reuben's achievement are cloudy, but a sense of travel and change is conveyed. In *The Prospect Before Us* Gold moves still farther afield. In this novel the chief person is Harry Bowers, manager of a run-down motel in Cleveland. A level of life—low, raunchy, and cruel, and quite different from the world of the novels of avowal—is presented in colors that convince. And there is no touch of the frequent father-son situation; Harry Bowers allows a black woman to rent a room in his motel and is hounded for what he has done. *The Man Who Was Not With It* allows us to inhabit the awareness of a carnival worker. Here, however, there is an approach to the themes of the novels of avowal. Bud, the carnie, is saddled with two fathers: one, his real one in Pittsburgh, and the other a carnival barker. The barker delivers Bud from his drug habit (and falls foul of it himself) and hovers like a threatening cloud over the early weeks of Bud's marriage: a relation that links this novel with other work of Gold. In *The Great American Jackpot* the persona is also not Gold's own (the hero is a Berkeley student of the 1960s), but the student's preoccupations are not unfamiliar. Al Dooley loves and hates his teacher, a black sociologist; Dooley tries to find out who he is in the arms of two girls; and, finally, he asserts his identity by breaking out: in this instance, by robbing a bank and experiencing the farce of American justice. Dooley reappears in *Waiting for Cordelia* where he is doing a thesis on prostitution in the San Francisco area. A madam (Cordelia) and Marietta, a woman eager to become a reforming mayor of San Francisco, enrich Dooley's research. In the course of writing his study, Dooley faces Gold's usual questions about the nature of love and the sadness and the loneliness which hamper its realization. Similar preoccupations mark the early novel, *The Optimist*, in which Burr Fuller makes his way through a failed marriage and achieves some mastery of the mysteries of love and career. And similar struggles mark *True Love* where the subject is the uneasiness of middle age; a "respectable" man is harassed by the dreams of his youth and by his fears about his later life. Will the late discovery of "true love" allay these discontents? In all, a considerable variety. It is a variety bound together by a style that is generally pervasive save for variations that reflect the different social levels reproduced. A certain vigor results from the determined contemporary quality of Gold's references, including commercial products and public diversions, and even turns of speech. What usually holds this variety together is Gold's own sense of the worth of what he is doing. The language of the novels is a considerable support to the portions of wisdom that appear in the novels.

—Harold H. Watts

GOLDMAN, William

Nationality: American. **Born:** Chicago, Illinois, 12 August 1931; brother of the writer James Goldman. **Education:** Highland Park High School; Oberlin College, Ohio, 1948-52, B.A. in English 1952; Columbia University, New York, 1954-56, M.A. in English 1956. **Military Service:** Served in the United States Army, 1952-54: Corporal. **Family:** Married Ilene Jones in 1961 (divorced); two daughters. **Awards:** Oscar, for screenplay, 1970, 1977. **Address:** 50 East 77th Street, New York, New York 10021, U.S.A.

PUBLICATIONS

Novels

The Temple of Gold. New York, Knopf, 1957.
Your Turn to Curtsy, My Turn to Bow. New York, Doubleday, 1958.
Soldier in the Rain. New York, Atheneum, and London, Eyre and Spottiswoode, 1960.
Boys and Girls Together. New York, Atheneum, 1964; London, Joseph, 1965.
No Way To Treat a Lady (as Harry Longbaugh). New York, Fawcett, and London, Muller, 1964; as William Goldman, New York, Harcourt Brace, and London, Coronet, 1968.
The Thing of It Is. . . . New York, Harcourt Brace, and London, Joseph, 1967.
Father's Day. New York, Harcourt Brace, and London, Joseph, 1971.
The Princess Bride: S. Morgenstern's Classic Tale of True Love and High Adventure: The "Good Parts" Version, Abridged. New York, Harcourt Brace, 1973; London, Macmillan, 1975.

Marathon Man. New York, Delacorte Press, 1974; London, Macmillan, 1975.
Magic. New York, Delacorte Press, and London, Macmillan, 1976.
Tinsel. New York, Delacorte Press, and London, Macmillan, 1979.
Control. New York, Delacorte Press, and London, Hodder and Stoughton, 1982.
The Color of Light. New York, Warner, and London, Granada, 1984.
The Silent Gondoliers (as S. Morgenstern). New York, Ballantine, 1984.
Heat. New York, Warner, 1985; as *Edged Weapons,* London, Granada, 1985.
Brothers. New York, Warner, and London, Grafton, 1986.

Uncollected Short Stories

"Something Blue," in *Rogue* (New York), 1958.
"Da Vinci," in *New World Writing 17.* Philadelphia, Lippincott, 1960.
"Till the Right Girls Come Along," in *Transatlantic Review 8* (London), Winter 1961.
"The Ice Cream Eat," in *Stories from the Transatlantic Review,* edited by Joseph F. McCrindle. New York, Holt Rinehart, 1970.

Plays

Blood, Sweat and Stanley Poole, with James Goldman (produced New York, 1961). New York, Dramatists Play Service, 1962.
A Family Affair, with James Goldman, music by John Kander (produced New York, 1962).
Butch Cassidy and the Sundance Kid (screenplay). New York, Bantam, and London, Corgi, 1969.
The Great Waldo Pepper (screenplay). New York, Dell, 1975.

Screenplays: *Masquerade,* with Michael Relph, 1964; *Harare (The Moving Target),* 1966; *Butch Cassidy and the Sundance Kid,* 1969; *The Hot Rock (How to Steal a Diamond in Four Uneasy Lessons),* 1972; *The Stepford Wives,* 1974; *The Great Waldo Pepper,* 1975; *All the President's Men,* 1976; *Marathon Man,* 1976; *A Bridge Too Far,* 1977; *Magic,* 1978; *The Princess Bride,* 1987; *Heat,* 1987; *Misery,* 1990; *Memoirs of an Invisible Man,* with Robert Collector and Dana Bodner, 1992.

Television Film: *Mr. Horn,* 1979.

Other

The Season: A Candid Look at Broadway. New York, Harcourt Brace, 1969; revised edition, New York, Limelight, 1984.
Wigger (for children). New York, Harcourt Brace, 1974.
The Story of "A Bridge Too Far." New York, Dell, 1977.
Adventures in the Screen Trade: A Personal View of Hollywood and Screenwriting. New York, Warner, 1983; London, Macdonald, 1984.
Wait Till Next Year: The Story of a Season When What Should've Happened Didn't and What Could've Gone Wrong Did, with Mike Lupica. New York, Bantam, 1988.
Hype and Glory. New York, Villard, and London, Macdonald, 1990.

*

Critical Study: *William Goldman* by Richard Andersen, Boston, Twayne, 1979.

*   *   *

William Goldman is a successful novelist, film scenarist, playwright, critic, and children's book author who focuses much of his attention on the illusions by which men and women live. These illusions often make existence more miserable than it need be and provide a core from which all of Goldman's protagonists seek to escape. Ironically, what they escape to is more often than not other illusions, which, because of the artificial distinctions society attaches to them, rarely satisfy their human needs.

When Raymond Trevitt's desperate attempts to protect the ideals of his childhood from adult realities in *The Temple of Gold* inadvertently cause the deaths of his closest friends, he leaves his home, but discovers only frustration and intolerance elsewhere. In *Your Turn to Curtsy, My Turn to Bow,* Chad Kimberly is driven by his ambitious illusions into believing he is a new Messiah, whose schizophrenic demands frighten the novel's protagonist, Peter Bell, into a life of escapist day-dreaming. Ambition is not the only illusion that drives the characters of *Boys and Girls Together* to New York; most of them are escaping from the unbearable circumstances of their home lives. Nevertheless, their hopes for self-improvement are dashed by unsuccessful love affairs, domineering parents, professional failures, embarrassing social exposures, and suicide. In *Soldier in the Rain,* Eustis Clay and Maxwell Slaughter cannot free themselves from the military-economic complex of which they are so much a part.

The great American illusions about success are the central concerns of *The Thing of It Is . . .* and *Father's Day,* in which the talented, rich, but quirky Amos McCracken spends a tremendous amount of money trying to save his marriage and then his relationship with his daughter. In the end, his guilt-ridden personal failures lead him to create fantasies that enable him to fulfill the images he has of himself but that also pose a serious threat to the safety and well-being of others.

Unlike Amos McCracken or Kit Gil of *No Way to Treat a Lady,* Westley and Buttercup of *The Princess Bride,* Babe Levy of *Marathon Man,* and Corky Withers of *Magic* cannot retreat to a fabulous land to try to make themselves whole; they already live in fabulous land, where they are constantly assaulted by its empirical and psychological facts. Forced to encounter a vast confusion of fact and fiction, to deal with pain and death, and to seek power against forces that are difficult to pinpoint and consequently understand, the protagonists of these three novels must stay rooted in social systems that attempt to deny their vitality while creating illusions that life is what it should be.

Combining the everyday reality of Goldman's early novels with the fabulous reality of his later works, *Tinsel* tells the story of three women who desperately try to escape from the boredom of their daily lives to the fame and fortune of movie stardom, which, like all illusions, eludes them. As he did in *Marathon Man* and *Magic,* Goldman divides this into many chapters, so short and so different from any other in terms of setting and action that they flash by the reader like scenes in a movie. Because of their length, Goldman can keep simultaneously occurring stories running vividly in the reader's imagination without making any significant connections between them. When the individual stories eventually come together, Goldman continues flashing different scenes containing markedly different actions at such a pace that reading Goldman's story about

the film industry becomes as close to a cinematic experience as literature can provide.

With *The Color of Light* Goldman returned to the themes of innocence and loss that concerned him in his early novels, only this time around he discusses them as subjects for writing. Unfortunately, this serious book, like some of his early serious novels, wasn't as well received as it should have been, and Goldman returned to the fabulist landscape of *Marathon Man* and *Magic* in *Control* and *Heat.* But he passed through fantasyland on the way just as he did in 1973 with *The Princess Bride. The Silent Gondoliers* tells us why the gondoliers in Venice no longer sing. Even they have lost their innocence in a world from which there is no escape.

Perhaps because of his popularity or the reputation he has established in Hollywood (many of his novels have been adapted to the screen), many critics have misunderstood or underrated Goldman's works. Perhaps these critics have been confused by Goldman's use of multiple modes—novel of manners, confessional journal, psychological novel, social satire, romantic parody, black humor novel, detective story, spy novel, radical protest novel, soap opera, absurdist novel, and more—within a wide frame of genres. Whatever the reason, Goldman is an extraordinarily talented and prolific writer whose incorporation of cinematic techniques with conventional narrative forms mark a significant contribution to the novel tradition.

—Richard Andersen

GORDIMER, Nadine

Nationality: South African. **Born:** Springs, Transvaal, 20 November 1923. **Education:** A convent school, and the University of the Witwatersrand, Johannesburg. **Family:** Married 1) G. Gavron in 1949; 2) Reinhold Cassirer in 1954; one son and one daughter. **Career:** Visiting lecturer, Institute of Contemporary Arts, Washington, D.C., 1961, Harvard University, Cambridge, Massachusetts, 1969, Princeton University, New Jersey, 1969, Northwestern University, Evanston, Illinois 1969, and University of Michigan, Ann Arbor, 1970; Adjunct Professor of Writing, Columbia University, New York, 1971; presenter, *Frontiers* television series, 1990. **Awards:** W.H. Smith Literary award, 1961; Thomas Pringle award, 1969; James Tait Black Memorial prize, 1972; Booker prize, 1974; Grand Aigle d'Or prize (France), 1975; CNA award, 1975; Scottish Arts Council Neil Gunn fellowship, 1981; Common Wealth award, 1981; Modern Language Association award (U.S.A.), 1981; Malaparte prize (Italy), 1985; Nelly Sachs prize (Germany), 1985; Bennett award (U.S.A.), 1986; Royal Society of Literature Benson medal, 1990; Nobel prize, 1991, for literature. D.Lit.: University of Leuven, Belgium, 1980; D.Litt.: Smith College, Northampton, Massachusetts, 1985; City College, New York, 1985; Mount Holyoke College, South Hadley, Massachusetts, 1985; Harvard University, 1986; Yale University, New Haven, Connecticut, 1986; Columbia University, 1987; New School for Social Research, New York, 1987; University of York, 1987. Honorary Member, American Academy of Arts and Sciences, 1980; Honorary Fellow, Modern Language Association (U.S.A.), 1985. **Agent:** A.P. Watt Ltd., 20 John Street, London WC1N 2DR, England; or, Russell and Volkening Inc., 50 West 29th Street, New York, New York 10001, U.S.A.

PUBLICATIONS

Novels

The Lying Days. London, Gollancz, and New York, Simon and Schuster, 1953.

A World of Strangers. London, Gollancz, and New York, Simon and Schuster, 1958.

Occasion for Loving. London, Gollancz, and New York, Viking Press, 1963.

The Late Bourgeois World. London, Gollancz, and New York, Viking Press, 1966.

A Guest of Honour. New York, Viking Press, 1970; London, Cape, 1971.

The Conservationist. London, Cape, 1974; New York, Viking Press, 1975.

Burger's Daughter. London, Cape, and New York, Viking Press, 1979.

July's People. London, Cape, and New York, Viking Press, 1981.

A Sport of Nature. London, Cape, and New York, Knopf, 1987.

My Son's Story. London, Bloomsbury, and New York, Farrar Straus, 1990.

None to Accompany Me. London, Bloomsbury, and New York, Farrar Straus, 1994.

Short Stories

Face to Face. Johannesburg, Silver Leaf, 1949.

The Soft Voice of the Serpent and Other Stories. New York, Simon and Schuster, 1952; London, Gollancz, 1953.

Six Feet of the Country. London, Gollancz, and New York, Simon and Schuster, 1956.

Friday's Footprint and Other Stories. London, Gollancz, and New York, Viking Press, 1960.

Not for Publication and Other Stories. London, Gollancz, and New York, Viking Press, 1965.

Penguin Modern Stories 4, with others. London, Penguin, 1970.

Livingstone's Companions. New York, Viking Press, 1971; London, Cape, 1972.

Selected Stories. London, Cape, 1975; New York, Viking Press, 1976; as *No Place Like,* London, Penguin, 1978.

Some Monday for Sure. London, Heinemann, 1976.

A Soldier's Embrace. London, Cape, and New York, Viking Press, 1980.

Town and Country Lovers. Los Angeles, Sylvester and Orphanos, 1980.

Something Out There. London, Cape, and New York, Viking, 1984.

Crimes of Conscience. London, Heinemann, 1991.

Plays

Television Plays and Documentaries: *A Terrible Chemistry* (*Writers and Places* series), 1981 (UK); *Choosing for Justice: Allan Boesak,* with Hugo Cassirer, 1985 (USA and UK); *Country Lovers, A Chip of Glass Ruby, Praise,* and *Oral History* (all in *The Gordimer Stories* series), 1985 (USA); *Frontiers* series, 1990 (UK).

Other

African Lit. (lectures). Cape Town, University of Cape Town, 1972.

On the Mines, photographs by David Goldblatt. Cape Town, Struik, 1973.

The Black Interpreters: Notes on African Writing. Johannesburg, Spro-Cas Ravan, 1973.

What Happened to Burger's Daughter; or, How South African Censorship Works, with others. Johannesburg, Taurus, 1980.

Lifetimes: Under Apartheid, photographs by David Goldblatt. London, Cape, and New York, Knopf, 1986.

Reflections of South Africa, edited by Kirsten Egebjerg and Gillian Stead Eilersen. Herning, Denmark, Systime, 1986.

The Essential Gesture: Writing, Politics, and Places, edited by Stephen Clingman. London, Cape, and New York, Knopf, 1988.

Conversations with Nadine Gordimer, edited by Nancy Topping Bazin and Marilyn Dallman Seymour. Jackson, University Press of Mississippi, 1990.

Writing and Being. Cambridge, Harvard University Press, 1995.

Editor, with Lionel Abrahams, *South African Writing Today.* London, Penguin, 1967.

*

Bibliography: *Nadine Gordimer, Novelist and Short Story Writer: A Bibliography of Her Works* by Racilia Jilian Neil, Johannesburg, University of the Witwatersrand, 1964.

Critical Studies: *Nadine Gordimer* by Robert F. Haugh, New York, Twayne, 1974; *Nadine Gordimer* by Michael Wade, London, Evans, 1978; *Nadine Gordimer* by Christopher Heywood, Windsor, Berkshire, Profile, 1983; *The Novels of Nadine Gordimer: Private Lives/ Public Landscapes* by John Cooke, Baton Rouge, Louisiana State University Press, 1985; *The Novels of Nadine Gordimer: History from the Inside* by Stephen Clingman, London, Allen and Unwin, 1986; *Nadine Gordimer* by Judie Newman, London, Macmillan, 1988; *Critical Essays on Nadine Gordimer* edited by Rowland Smith, Boston, Hall, 1990.

Theatrical Activities:
Director: **Television—***Choosing for Justice: Allan Boesak,* with Hugo Cassirer, 1985.

*   *   *

Despite Nadine Gordimer's international status as one of the finest living writers in English, her work is rooted in her native country, South Africa, where she has remained throughout her career. Her social confinement within a white, liberal, English, and middle-class position, in a diverse and divided country, has been a source of strength and weakness in her writing. On the one hand, she has ruthlessly exposed the limitations of Western, liberal humanism as a way of life in apartheid society, yet many of her characters have remained located within these very limitations, even while struggling against them.

Most of Gordimer's main characters are involved in the very serious business of finding suitable moral apparatus to cope with the excruciating *mental* difficulties of living white, with a conscience, in a minority within a greater South African minority. Viewed as a group, Gordimer's male and female protagonists show a parallel development of consciousness towards a point at which most moral options appear to be exhausted (two of her later heroes end up running away, blindly, to nowhere).

In Helen Shaw, Jessie Stilwell, and Liz van den Sandt, the heroines of *The Lying Days, Occasion for Loving,* and *The Late Bour-*

geois World, respectively, Gordimer charts the development from the racially exclusive confines of a white childhood in South Africa, to the discovery of (and disillusion with) the "freedom" of adult liberal thinking, and from there to the point where personal sacrifice becomes necessary for the sake of political integrity. In *The Lying Days,* Helen Shaw triumphs against the provincial narrowness and racial bigotry of her parents' mining village existence, yet she discovers that she, too, is sealed within her social limitations when she watches, from behind the windscreen of a car, a riot in a black township in which a man is shot dead by the police. As is the case with a number of Gordimer's characters, Helen Shaw's sense of moral failure is realised within and suggested by the failure of a love relationship in which certain moral suppositions function as a way of life. She goes away, to Europe, aware of a need for new sustenance, but essentially disillusioned. She is succeeded by Jessíe Stilwell, an older version of Helen, back from Europe, now married and running a family, and committed to a makeshift liberal ideology, because the general (white) South African way of life is unacceptable. Yet this ideology is shown to be vulnerable and in danger of hypocrisy by the action of the novel, in which Jessie's world is "invaded" by an illicit love affair between a black artist and a young woman from England who, with her white musicologist husband, is a guest in the Stilwell home. The liberal idea of openness is belied by Jessie's wish to be left to her own kind of semi-romantic isolation, and all legitimate human reactions to the situation are bedevilled by a factor the Stilwels profess not to take undue account of—skin colour. In *The Late Bourgeois World* the developments in *The Lying Days* and *Occasion for Loving* find a conclusion. For Liz van den Sandt, the old liberal "way of life" is already dead when the book opens—her liberal-activist former husband has just committed suicide—while her present existence is nothing more than a kind of helpless withdrawal, reflected by a particularly pallid love affair she is conducting. She faces her moment of truth when a black friend, an activist, challenges her to step outside the sealed area of sensibility and conscience, and *do* something to help, at considerable personal risk. Thirteen years later, in *Burger's Daughter,* Rosa Burger appears: she is the daughter of the generation which did in fact take the struggle further from where Liz van den Sandt was poised at the end of *The Late Bourgeois World.* But now the process goes into reverse: Rosa's father dies while in prison for Marxist "subversion," and Rosa finds herself unable simply to go on from where her father and his kind were stopped by politically repressive authority. She is heir to the failure of left-wing activism among whites in South Africa, and she settles for an occupation as a physiotherapist at a black hospital (treating Soweto riot victims), before she too is detained and committed to trial, merely on the basis of her connections with the nether-world of political dissent.

Gordimer's other major female protagonist, Hillela in *A Sport of Nature,* encapsulates and transcends all her predecessors. Hillela's story, told in a dingy factual and documentary manner, encompasses an upbringing in a liberal South African household, political activity in exile and marriages to an ANC activist as well as to the leader of an African State. But the novel awkwardly mixes a documentary style with a picaresque form (Hillela's travels and adventures). Although Hillela completely breaks free of the barriers constraining her predecessors, the novel comes across as stodgy and contrived.

Gordimer's male heroes differ in that they either come in from the outside, or they represent a significantly non-liberal approach to life in South Africa. *A World of Strangers,* in which the new post-1948 apartheid society is anatomised with great clarity, shows the rapid disillusionment of a young Englishman, Toby Hood, who comes to South Africa determined to live a "private life." An altogether different kind of disillusionment faces the more mature and intellectually well-equipped figure of Colonel Evelyn James Bray, hero of *A Guest of Honour.* He returns to the newly independent African state to witness the realisation of ideals of freedom for which, as a colonial civil servant, he was deported. The political situation gradually slips out of control, and Bray is killed as a result of a misunderstanding that underscores the ambiguity of any European's role in Africa.

It is as though all illusions of a meaningful political existence for whites have been stripped bare when Mehring the technologist appears in Gordimer's Booker prize-winning masterpiece, *The Conservationist.* This is a novel of immense symbolic power and great descriptive beauty. For once, Gordimer's main protagonist is representative of far more than just the white English liberal: he is simply white, South African, of ambiguous European heritage, rich, and politically conservative. His symbolic struggle in the book is a struggle for possession of the land against its black inheritors. Mehring (and by implication the whole of white South Africa) loses the struggle. It is thus not surprising that the protagonists of Gordimer's most recent novel, *July's People,* find themselves being run off the land. They escape revolution by running away with, and becoming captives of, their lifelong black servant, July.

Gordimer's most recent male creation, Sonny in *My Son's Story* is a "coloured" activist whose extramarital love affair with a white woman is reconstructed by his writer-son, Will. This is a highly readable and unusual novel for Gordimer, although the parameters of love and politics, of public commitment and personal betrayal, are shown to invade each other tellingly, as often happens in Gordimer's fiction.

—Leon de Kock

GORDON, Giles (Alexander Esme)

Nationality: British. **Born:** Edinburgh, 23 May 1940. **Education:** Edinburgh Academy, 1948-57. **Family:** Married 1) Margaret Anna Eastoe in 1964 (died 1989); two sons (one deceased, 1994) and one daughter; 2) Margaret Anne McKernan in 1990, two daughters. **Career:** Advertising executive, Secker and Warburg, publishers, London, 1962-63; editor, Hutchinson Publishing Group, London, 1963-64, and Penguin Books, London, 1964-66; editorial director, Victor Gollancz, publishers, London, 1967-72. Since 1972 partner, Anthony Sheil Associates, literary agents, London. Lecturer in Creative Writing, in London, for Tufts University, Medford, Massachusetts, 1971-76; C. Day Lewis Fellow in Writing, King's College, London, 1974-75; lecturer in drama, in London, for Hollins College, Virginia, 1984-85. Editor, *Drama* magazine, London, 1982-84; theater critic, *Spectator,* London, 1983-84, *Punch* and *House Magazine,* both London 1985-87, and *London Daily News,* 1988. Since 1993 books' columnist, London *Times.* **Member:** Arts Council of Great Britain Literature Panel, 1966-69, and Society of Authors Committee of Management, 1973-75. **Awards:** *Transatlantic Review* prize, 1966; Scottish Arts Council grant, 1976, Fellow. Royal Society of Literature, 1990. **Agent:** Sheil Land Associates Ltd., 43 Doughty Street, London WC1N 2LF, England. **Address:** 6 Ann St., Edinburgh EH4 1PG, Scotland.

PUBLICATIONS

Novels

The Umbrella Man. London, Allison and Busby, 1971.
About a Marriage. London, Allison and Busby, and New York, Stein and Day, 1972.
Girl with Red Hair. London, Hutchinson, 1974.
100 Scenes from Married Life: A Selection. London, Hutchinson, 1976.
Enemies: A Novel about Friendship. Hassocks, Sussex, Harvester Press, 1977.
Ambrose's Vision: Sketches Towards the Creation of a Cathedral. Brighton, Harvester Press, 1980.

Short Stories

Pictures from an Exhibition. London, Allison and Busby, and New York, Dial Press, 1970.
Penguin Modern Stories 3, with others. London, Penguin, 1970.
Farewell, Fond Dreams. London, Hutchinson, 1975.
The Illusionist and Other Fictions. Hassocks, Sussex, Harvester Press, 1978.
Couple. Knotting, Bedfordshire, Sceptre Press, 1978.

Uncollected Short Stories

"The Line-up on the Shore," in *Mind in Chains,* edited by Christopher Evans. London, Panther, 1970.
"The Partition," in *Triangles,* edited by Alex Hamilton. London, Hutchinson, 1973.
"Crampton Manor," in *The Ninth Ghost Book,* edited by Rosemary Timperley. London, Barrie and Jenkins, 1973.
"Peake," in *The Eleventh Ghost Book,* edited by Aidan Chambers. London, Barrie and Jenkins, 1975.
"Morning Echo," in *The Sixteenth Pan Book of Horror Stories,* edited by Herbert Van Thal. London, Pan, 1975.
"In Spite of Himself," in *The Twelfth Ghost Book.* London, Barrie and Jenkins, 1976.
"Horses of Venice," in *The Thirteenth Ghost Book,* edited by James Hale. London, Barrie and Jenkins, 1977.
"The Necessary Authority," in *The Midnight Ghost Book,* edited by James Hale. London, Barrie and Jenkins, 1978.
"Room, With Woman and Man," in *New Stories 3,* edited by Francis King and Ronald Harwood. London, Hutchinson, 1978.
"Liberated People," in *Modern Scottish Short Stories,* edited by Fred Urquhart and Gordon. London, Hamish Hamilton, 1978.
"The Red-Headed Milkman," in *The Punch Book of Short Stories,* edited by Alan Coren. London, Robson, 1979.
"Screens," in *Labrys 4* (Hayes, Middlesex), 1979.
"Mask," in *The After Midnight Ghost Book,* edited by James Hale. London, Hutchinson, 1980; New York, Watts, 1981.
"Drama in Five Acts," in *New Terrors 2,* edited by Ramsey Campbell. London, Pan, 1980.
"Madame Durand," in *Punch* (London), 19 November 1980.
"The Indian Girl," in *Winter's Tales 27,* edited by Edward Leeson. London, Macmillan, 1981; New York, St. Martin's Press, 1982.
"Three Resolutions to One Kashmiri Encounter," in *Scottish Short Stories 1981.* London, Collins, 1981.
"Your Bedouin," in *Logos* (London), 1982.
"The South African Couple," in *Scottish Short Stories 1983.* London, Collins, 1983.

"A Bloomsbury Kidnapping," in *London Tales,* edited by Julian Evans. London, Hamish Hamilton, 1983.
"Father Christmas, Father Christmases," in *A Christmas Feast,* edited by James Hale. London, Macmillan, 1983.
"The Wheelchair," in *New Edinburgh Review 61,* 1983.
"The Battle of the Blind," in *New Edinburgh Review 65,* 1984.
"Hans Pfeifer," in *Winter's Tales 1* (new series), edited by David Hughes. London, Constable, and New York, St. Martin's Press, 1985.
"Mutual of Omaha," in *Critical Quarterly* (Manchester), Winter 1988.

Plays

Radio Plays: *Nineteen Policemen Searching the Sedway Shore,* 1976; *The Jealous One,* 1979; *Birdy,* from the novel by William Wharton, 1980.

Poetry

Landscape Any Date. Edinburgh, M. Macdonald, 1963.
Two and Two Make One. Preston, Lancashire, Akros, 1966.
Two Elegies. London, Turret, 1968.
Eight Poems for Gareth. Frensham, Surrey, Sceptre Press, 1970.
Between Appointments. Frensham, Surrey, Sceptre Press, 1971.
Twelve Poems for Callum. Preston, Lancashire, Akros, 1972.
One Man Two Women. London, Sheep Press, 1974.
Egyptian Room, Metropolitan Museum of Art. Rushden, Northamptonshire, Sceptre Press, 1974.
The Oban Poems. Knotting, Bedfordshire, Sceptre Press, 1977.

Other

Book 2000: Some Likely Trends in Publishing. London, Association of Assistant Librarians, 1969.
Walter and the Balloon (for children). London, Heinemann, 1973.
The Twentieth-Century Short Story in English: A Bibliography. London, British Council, 1990.
Aren't We Due a Royalty Statement?: A Stern Account of Literary, Publishing and Theatrical Folk. London, Chatto and Windus, 1993.

Editor, with Alex Hamilton, *Factions: Eleven Original Stories.* London, Joseph, 1974.
Editor, with Michael Bakewell and B.S. Johnson, *You Always Remember the First Time.* London, Quartet, 1975.
Editor, *Beyond the Words: Eleven Writers in Search of a New Fiction.* London, Hutchinson, 1975.
Editor, with Dulan Barber, *"Members of the Jury—": The Jury Experience.* London, Wildwood House, 1976.
Editor, *Prevailing Spirits: A Book of Scottish Ghost Stories.* London, Hamish Hamilton, 1976.
Editor, *A Book of Contemporary Nightmares.* London, Joseph, 1977.
Editor, with Fred Urquhart, *Modern Scottish Short Stories.* London, Hamish Hamilton, 1978; revised edition, London, Faber, 1982.
Editor, *Shakespeare Stories.* London, Hamish Hamilton, 1982.
Editor, *Modern Short Stories 2: 1940-1980.* London, Dent, 1982.
Editor, with David Hughes, *Best Short Stories 1986 [-1995].* London, Heinemann, 10 vols., 1986-95; vols. 4-6 as *The Best English Short Stories 1989-1991.* New York, Norton, 3 vols., 1989-91.

Editor, *English Short Stories: 1900 to the Present.* London, Dent, 1988.

Editor, with David Hughes, *The Minerva Book of Short Stories 1-6.* London, Minerva, 6 vols., 1990-95.

* * *

Relationships lie at the root of Giles Gordon's novels and short stories, relationships between man and woman, woman and woman, man and man, husband and wife, lover and lover—and also the relationship between the writer and the reader. In his first novel, *The Umbrella Man,* Gordon was content to view the burgeoning affair between Felix and Delia from the outside, using the technique that a film director might bring to bear in building up a scene from different camera angles. This is a device of which Gordon is particularly fond, and its exposition is seen to good effect in his story "Nineteen Policemen Searching the Solent Shore."

About a Marriage is a more straightforward narrative in which the seeming detritus of modern married life assumes a form that the protagonists, the husband and wife, can understand. A reasonably well-off couple Edward and Ann, move from a bland acceptance of their marriage to a blazing revelation of the strengths of their relationship and of the bond that exists between them. Their love is based not so much on a romantic attachment, although that is also present, as on the many-sided passions and frustrations that ultimately give each partner a vivid insight into their own strengths and weaknesses. Of growing importance in this novel is Gordon's mastery of dialogue and his relaxed ability to enter the minds of his characters who cease to exist as mere ciphers and have grown into stark, living creatures.

Enemies ("A Novel about Friendship") is in the now-familiar Gordon mold of a terse examination of how people relate to each other in familiar and not so familiar circumstances, but its stylistic achievement lies in his ability to strip the central narrative line to a series of scenes which embody sharp dialogue with an internalization of the characters' thoughts and emotions. The Hiltons live in an unspecified European country, and the action centers on the events of a few days while they are being visited by their parents and friends from England. Events outside their house, which at the beginning of the novel seems to be so secure against outside interference, threaten the fabric of their cozy world as it becomes a microcosm of a beleaguered society with all its concomitant stresses. Faced with the center falling away, the adults find their relationships shifting uneasily before they reach the triumphant conclusion of the salving power of their own friendships.

100 Scenes from Married Life picks up again the story of Edward and Ann. The intensity of their love for each other is still apparent, but growing self-doubt and encroaching middle age, with its sense of the loss of youth and vitality, gnaw at Edward's vitals. Interestingly, as if to prove the security of their marriage, Gordon disconcertingly opens the first scene with Edward returning from a week in Venice with his mistress. The novel's title reflects Gordon's debt to Ingmar Bergman's *Scenes from a Marriage,* and in a series of 18 scenes he has captured the warm, womblike, yet claustrophobic story of a close relationship. The inscription is from Philip Roth's *My Life as a Man:* "You want subtlety, then read *The Golden Bowl.* This is life, bozo, not high art." And there are many echoes from Roth's and John Updike's style in Gordon's low-key examination of the matter of middle-class life.

With those two American writers he also shares an interest in language and the economy of its use. At his best he is able to strip his sentences to an almost surreal invisibility which is allied disconcertingly to a lively, sparkling wit. His first collection of what Gordon calls "short fictions," *Pictures from an Exhibition,* was stylistically naive but there was a sense of innovatory excitement as he adopted the attitude of the detached observer in his frequently startling revelations. *Farewell, Fond Dreams* continued many of the same conventions but it showed a surer touch as Gordon risked some breathtaking conceits in his mixture of fact and fantasy, as in the sequence "An attempt to make entertainment out of the war in Vietnam." *The Illusionist and Other Fictions* showed a return to calmer waters, with Gordon seeming to take a fresh interest in the traditional structure of the short story, although he can never lose sight completely of their liquid, three-dimensional possibilities. Critics have been frequently exasperated by the audacious verve of much of Gordon's writing, but he remains one of the few British writers interested in pushing the possibilities of the novel to their outer limits.

—Trevor Royle

GORDON, Mary (Catherine)

Nationality: American. **Born:** Long Island, New York, 8 December 1949. **Education:** Holy Name of Mary School, Valley Stream, New York; Mary Louis Academy; Barnard College, New York, B.A. 1971; Syracuse University, New York, M.A. 1973. **Family:** Married 1) James Brain in 1974 (marriage dissolved); 2) Arthur Cash in 1979, one daughter and one son. **Career:** English teacher, Dutchess Community College, Poughkeepsie, New York, 1974-78; lecturer, Amherst College, Massachusetts, 1979. **Awards:** Janet Kafka prize, 1979, 1982. **Address:** c/o Viking Penguin, 375 Hudson Street, New York, New York 10014, U.S.A.

PUBLICATIONS

Novels

Final Payments. New York, Random House, and London, Hamish Hamilton, 1978.
The Company of Women. New York, Random House, and London, Cape, 1981.
Men and Angels. New York, Random House, and London, Cape, 1985.
The Other Side. New York, Viking, 1989; London, Bloomsbury, 1990.

Short Stories

Temporary Shelter. London, Bloomsbury, and New York, Random House, 1987.
The Rest of Life: Three Novellas. New York, Viking, 1993.

Uncollected Short Stories

"Vision," in *Antaeus* (New York), Spring 1989.
"Separation," in *Antaeus* (New York), Spring-Autumn, 1990.
"At the Kirks'," in *Grand Street* (New York), Winter 1990.

Other

Good Boys and Dead Girls and Other Essays. New York, Viking, and London, Bloomsbury, 1991.

*   *   *

For Mary Gordon, *tout comprendre* is emphatically not *tout pardonner.* Guilt rages through her fiction like a prairie fire, sweeping her heroines to and fro between the poles of autonomy and dependence, religious faith and neurosis, greed for life and masochistic self sacrifice. Although reviewers have celebrated her 19th-century virtues—irony, intellect, powerful moral themes, and such classically realist skills as an eye for detail, an ear for dialogue, and a gift for the creation of memorable characters—Gordon's overarching concerns are recognizably modern: the exploration of the female psyche, the relations between parents and children, and between feminism and patriarchal religion.

In her first novel, *Final Payments,* the seductive securities of dependence are explored through the relationship of Isabel Moore to her bedridden father, a Catholic intellectual whom she nurses for 11 years. Trapped by sexual guilt, Isabel is effectively cut off in a time warp, until his death. Set free, she makes a venture into the world of the 1970s, only to recoil again into renunciation, sacrificing her life anew to the odious Margaret Casey as a penance for a second sexual transgression. Although Isabel is ultimately rescued (an embryonic feminist moral) by two close female friends, she has only just begun to learn how to put paid to the obligations imposed by both father and faith. Gordon's heroines tend to rebel against a dominant father figure, adopt a surrogate father, and reconcile themselves in some fashion, learning the deficiencies of patriarchal institutions in the process. Felicitas, the heroine of *The Company of Women,* is no exception. As the daughter of one of five women (the company of the title) each devoted to Father Cyprian, a conservative Catholic intellectual, Felicitas gets away only temporarily, is impregnated, and returns, to bequeath to her daughter her mixed heritage of Catholicism and liberation. Unfathered (by careful plotting) Linda shares the same group of good and bad fairy-godmothers as Felicitas, but without the patriarch's overriding authority. Catholic values have been feminized and "macho clericalism" crippled and humanized. (The novel's intertextual allusions to *Jane Eyre* are no accident).

With *Men and Angels,* however, Gordon leaves behind the subculture of Catholicism, in favor of a broader exploration of women's relation to artistic and social structures. When Anne Foster, dismissed as merely a college wife, has the chance to investigate the life of a (fictional) neglected American painter, Caroline Watson, she faces a dilemma: how to tell a woman's story as fully and as realistically as possible. As biographer Anne sets out to rescue Caroline from obscurity, so her childminder, Laura, in the grip of religious obsession, sets out to save Anne from the lusts of the flesh. The feminist rescue mission is therefore attended with tragic ironies. Just as Anne seeks a nurturing foremother and role model in Caroline, so Laura pursues Anne. The dead female artist is lovingly investigated and re-created at the price of a living girl. Laura's scorn for the "Religion of Art" indicates her potentially strong affiliations with Gordon's father, and makes her a splendid vehicle for an exploration of the tragic consequences of the phallocentric appropriation of religious experience. Dividing its narration between third-person, realist Anne and Laura's fantastic stream of consciousness, the novel sets up a series of mirrorings and doublings, both

in terms of character and narrative mode, in order to investigate the utility to women of models and precedents, the means by which a woman's story may best be told, and the benefits of realist modes of representation in dealing with women's issues. Anne's representation of Caroline is re-presented by Laura, with major events twice told, in realism and in fantasy, to ironic effect. Though Laura's chapters are shorter (as befits the Pyrrhic psychomachia, the body of the text is Anne's) they are technically and psychologically compelling. Laura's experiences are organized according to the fantasies of male culture, and a quality of fascinated horror accrues to them. Gordon often uses fairy tale and melodrama to sharpen the menace of her plots. Domestic horror stalks her characters, whether in the shape of witch-housekeepers (Laura, Margaret), bad fairies, terrible mothers or passive, masochistic victims.

Gordon's own essay on the difference between writing a story as a fairy tale or as realist fiction is memorably embodied in "A Writing Lesson," one of the 20 stories collected in *Temporary Shelter.* Two others, a five-voiced story "Now I Am Married," and "Delia" anticipate in theme and structure Gordon's latest novel, *The Other Side,* which marries an Irish family saga with a popularization and updating of two founder figures of Modernism. Ulysses-like, 88-year-old Vincent MacNamara returns after an absence to his wife Ellen, a demented Penelope, now dying. Through the events of one day, 14th August 1985, the Woolfian narrative recounts their lives, together with those of their children, grandchildren and great-grandchildren, moving through the individual consciousnesses of some dozen family members. Gordon's psychological themes now expand to the national stage. Mother Ireland, rather than mothers, is rejected—America is no longer "the other side" but home—yet the dying matriarch remains a brooding presence. Although religion has largely evaporated on the moving staircase of American immigrant striving, Ellen's granddaughter Cam displays a recognizable mixture of idealism, self-sacrifice, dutifulness and self-love and her awareness that unhappiness is "the sickle-cell anemia of the Irish" pervades the book. Slowly the "other side" to each story comes into focus, as the jigsaw of memories from different individuals finally coheres into a three-dimensional pattern, revealing the inner significance of each apparently contingent event.

Although critical attention has centered upon her feminist response to Catholicism, Gordon would be a first-rate novelist if she were an atheist. Fiercely intellectual, unafraid to unite modernist irony with popular plot and pace, clearly non-androcentric, Gordon has produced five books in little more than a decade, and will clearly remain a figure to watch.

—Judie Newman

GOVER, (John) Robert

Nationality: American. **Born:** Philadelphia, Pennsylvania, 2 November 1929. **Education:** Girard College, Philadelphia; University of Pittsburgh, B.A. in economics 1953. **Family:** Married 1) Mildred Vitkovich in 1955 (divorced 1966); 2) Jeanne-Nell Gement in 1968; two sons. **Career:** Held a variety of jobs, including reporter on various newspapers, in Pennsylvania and Maryland, until 1961. **Address:** K8 River's Bend, Carney's Point, New Jersey 08069, U.S.A.

PUBLICATIONS

Novels

J.C. Kitten Trilogy. Berkeley, California, Reed, 1982.
    One Hundred Dollar Misunderstanding. London, Spearman, 1961; New York, Grove Press, 1962.
    Here Goes Kitten. New York, Grove Press, 1964; London, Mayflower, 1965.
    J.C. Saves. New York, Simon and Schuster, 1968; London, Arrow, 1979.
The Maniac Responsible. New York, Grove Press, 1963; London, MacGibbon and Kee, 1964.
Poorboy at the Party. New York, Simon and Schuster, 1966.
Going for Mr. Big. New York, Bantam, 1973; London, Arrow, 1979.
To Morrow Now Occurs Again (as O. Govi). Santa Barbara, California, Ross Erikson, 1975.
Getting Pretty on the Table (as O. Govi). Santa Barbara, California, Capra Press, 1975.

Short Story

Bring Me the Head of Rona Barrett. San Francisco, Hargreaves, 1981.

Other

Voodoo Contra. York Beach, Maine, Weiser, 1985.

Editor, *The Portable Walter: From the Prose and Poetry of Walter Lowenfels.* New York, International Publishers, 1968.

*

Bibliography: *Robert Gover: A Descriptive Bibliography* by Michael Hargreaves, Westport, Connecticut, Meckler, 1988.

Manuscript Collection: Boston University.

Robert Gover comments:

His trilogy, *One Hundred Dollar Misunderstanding, Here Goes Kitten,* and *J.C. Saves,* captures in two characters relations between Black and White in America, especially as it evolved during the 1960s.

J.C. Holland first meets Kitten while he is a university sophomore and she a 13-year-old prostitute. In the second book, J.C. is public relations director of the local political party in power and encounters Kitten as a nightclub singer, or "B-girl." In the third, he finds her ducking police gunfire during a "race riot." *The Maniac Responsible* examines the *why* of a rape-murder case. The protagonist, Dean, becomes so involved in the invisible mental process that led to the brutal slaying that he becomes "possessed." Gover uses Joycean techniques to vivify his character's mental world.

Poorboy at the Party mythologizes the split between rich and poor in America. Randy, the main character, goes with his wealthy friend to a party in a large mansion containing art treasures. Conflicting emotions and values plant seeds of frustration and the party erupts into a violent orgy of destruction.

Going for Mr. Big is the tale of a pimp and his two ladies and a millionaire and his wife. Luke Small is a self-styled revolutionary with a lust to pull down the rich and powerful, but his "campaign"

to conquer Malcolm McMasters first backfires, then resolves itself in a meaningful togetherness that is outside the prevailing economic system.

To Morrow Now Occurs Again, published under Gover's penname O. Govi, is a surrealist romp through a mythical land called all Damnation, which is one big Plantation where Big Money is the Holy Spirit. The protagonist, Big I and little me, soul and ego of one entity, is baffled by the situation he finds himself in. The Rat Doctor, whose experimental maze of millions of rats is periodically studied to show the workings of society and shed light on the religion of Big Money, does not deter Big I from asserting that his currency is eternal.

Victor Versus Mort, a novella published only in Portuguese, pits two archetypal forces against each other in an American social setting. In the end, the main character's worldly successes are eclipsed by death.

Getting Pretty on the Table, also a novella, carries into a suburban orgy a game played by pimps and prostitutes. The game combines psychic therapy and spiritual cleansing.

*   *   *

In the "After Words" to *J.C. Saves* (the last volume of the trilogy begun with *One Hundred Dollar Misunderstanding* and *Here Goes Kitten*), Robert Gover tell us that at the beginning "I had no preconceived idea where these two characters would lead me, their author." Unfortunately, the reader's sharing of that aimlessness is such that he arrives at the last page of the last volume with the sense that the trilogy is completed only because the author has told him so. There is no reason why the characters might not go on in book after book, *ad infinitum,* like the Rover Boys. When J.C. Holland, the white middle-class protagonist, and Kitten, his black prostitute love, achieve their partial understanding at the end of *J.C. Saves,* it is clear that the slightest alteration provided by another time and other circumstances will be enough to set another story in motion. For the fact is that this is formula fiction: shake up the characters, move them to a new starting point, put them in motion, follow the formula, and you have another book. The other works, from *Poorboy at the Party* through *Getting Pretty on the Table,* play variations on the same basic themes.

Yet there is an honesty in Gover, a vision of the life about him and a quality of writing that raises him above the level of either the pulp pornographer or the slick composer of bestsellers. However much he taxes the reader's impatience with shallow characterizations, absurd plot manipulations, gratuitous sex, and moral implications that are occasionally downright silly, he is at times an accomplished satirist. One must only imagine his books in the form of Classic Comics, illustrated by cartoonists for *Mad Magazine,* to be made aware how sure is his touch of the particular grotesque exaggeration that comically, or cruelly, reveals a specific truth. His are not realistic novels, but verbal comic strips, sharing a good many of the virtues and faults of such a paradigm of the genre as Norman Mailer's *An American Dream.*

In large measure he is a moralist—disgusted at times, bitter and angry at others, but always subordinating the matter to the message. And the message is always the same: the Anglo-Saxon American power structure has created a society in which sex and violence are so perversely twisted together that there is no place for honest respect and affection between individuals, classes, or races. Never showing what society might be, he concentrates his attention on the extremes of actuality that he sees as emblematic of the whole. In some respects his most memorable statement is *The Maniac Responsible,* where he parallels the movements of a reporter covering a brutal sex murder with the man's movements while attempting to seduce his teasingly voluptuous neighbor. Finally driven by circumstances (the natural circumstances, the author suggests, of the American way of life) and his own sensitivity, he becomes a suspect in the murder and breaks down into an admission that he, himself, is the maniac responsible (as we all are) for the rape and murder of the girl.

Sex is in the forefront of all Gover's novels. However, the human failures he depicts are not to be blamed on sex, but rather on the failure of its right use, the tendency to treat the other human beings as a means rather than an end. Significantly, in the twisted world of Gover's vision the individual who seems best to know how to use her sex is Kitten, the African-American prostitute. Significantly, too, the Kitten trilogy, *Poorboy at the Party,* and *The Maniac Responsible* all end in rejections of the middle-class societies they have portrayed.

—George Perkins

GRACE, Patricia (Frances)

Nationality: New Zealander. **Born:** Wellington in 1937. **Education:** Green Street Convent, Newtown, Wellington; St. Mary's College; Wellington Teachers' College. **Family:** Married; seven children. **Career:** Has taught in primary and secondary schools in King Country, Northland, and Porirua. **Awards:** Maori Purposes Fund Board grant, 1974; New Zealand Literature Fund grant, 1975, 1983; Hubert Church Prose award, 1976; Children's Picture Book of the Year award, 1982; Victoria University Writing fellowship, 1985; Wattie award, 1986; New Zealand Fiction award, 1987; New Zealand Maori Scholarship in Letters, 1988, 1992-93; Literary Fund grant, 1990; Victoria University Archive Project grant, 1993; LiBeraturepreis (Germany), 1994. D.H.L.: Victoria University, 1989. **Address:** Box 54111, Plimmerton, New Zealand.

PUBLICATIONS

Novels

Mutuwhenua: The Moon Sleeps. Auckland, Longman Paul, 1978; London, Women's Press, 1988.
Potiki. Auckland, Penguin, 1986; London, Women's Press, 1987.
Cousins. Auckland, Penguin, 1992.

Short Stories

Waiariki. Auckland, Longman Paul, 1975.
The Dream Sleepers and Other Stories. Auckland, Longman Paul, 1980.
Electric City and Other Stories. Auckland, Penguin, 1987.
Selected Stories. Auckland, Penguin, 1991.
The Sky People. Auckland, Penguin, 1994.
Collected Stories. Auckland, Penguin, 1995.

Other (for children)

The Kuia and the Spider. Auckland, Longman Paul, 1981; London, Penguin, 1982.

Watercress Tuna and the Children of Champion Street. Auckland, Longman Paul, 1984; London, Penguin, 1986.
He aha te mea nui?, Ma wai?, Ko au tenei, Ahakoa he iti (Maori readers). Auckland, Longman Paul, 4 vols., 1985.
The Trolley. Auckland, Penguin, 1993.
Areta and the Kahawai. Auckland, Penguin, 1994.

Other

Wahine Toa: Women of Maori Myth, paintings by Robyn Kahukiwa. Auckland, Collins, 1984.

*   *   *

Perhaps it is inevitable that, as a New Zealand writer of short stories whose subject matter is the intimate, self-sufficient world of the family, Patricia Grace should suggest certain similarities with Katherine Mansfield. Both deal with themes such as the passing of innocence, the constraints of daily routine and close relationships, and the elusiveness of answers to life's meaning and purpose. Both seek to retrieve the past through a receptive and finely tuned consciousness, and cultivate a narrative style whose modulations extend from haunting lyricism to crisp exposition.

Yet when a reference to Katherine Mansfield actually occurs in one of Grace's short stories, "Letters from Whetu," it signals not their affinity only, but their separateness as well. For Mansfield (as for the little girl in her "How Pearl Button was Kidnapped"), Maori life could only be, at best, a momentary escape from the *pakeha* values of time, money, and respectability. For Grace, writing 70-odd years later and from an insider's point of view, the life is binding, vital, and unified, qualities which are figured in the recurring images of the extended family gathered within the home or at some other spot of cherished ground often located by the sea. Their shared activities—feast-making, or gardening, or collecting mussels, or diving for *kina*—combine the dual aspects of work and play, and participate in the rhythm of the tides, the seasons, growth, and decay.

Even so, the life Grace celebrates bears the ineradicable marks of *pakeha* encroachments and *pakeha* progress. Old ways and old names are often put aside for the sake of seeming modern; land is abandoned for work in the cities; roads and buildings appear in places which were once held to be *tapu.* In a number of the short stories ("Transition," "And So I Go," "Letters from Whetu"), an awareness that the world is large and that new ways must be learned is explicitly stated. But running against this, and through all of Grace's writing, is the stronger and more insistent feeling of displacement and loss, and of an obligation to keep alive what remains of the old inheritance. The objective correlative of this burden of consciousness is the land, and in her best work—notably the short story "Journey" and her second novel *Potiki*—the complexity of this symbol, and therefore of the Maori experience, is fully and imaginatively developed.

At the basis of "Journey" is the very real issue of land ownership, dramatized here as a confrontation between the old Maori who claims the right to leave his land sub-divided among his heirs according to Maori custom, and the government department which has appropriated his land and the entire locality for development. Between the two parties there is no communication possible, a situation underlined by the differences in their language. One argues for people and their need for houses, the other enumerates the engineering problems; one speaks from first-hand experience of the nature of the soil and the vegetables it will produce, the other resorts to maps and plans and the abstractions of "aesthetic aspects."

"Journey" is characteristic of Grace's stories in that the action is sited in the consciousness of the main character. Virtually all her early work accesses this consciousness by way of first person narration. In the first of her novels, *Mutuwhenua,* the "I" is a young Maori woman who—like the sisters in another celebrated story, "A Way of Talking"—moves between the the worlds of Maori and *pakeha,* using a different idiom and even a different name in each. In the *pakeha* world she is Linda, and she says things like "I happen to like Graeme"—a remark which prompts her grandmother to scold, "Happen to like, happen to like, what's that talk? You talk like them already."

But it is Linda's alter ego Ngaio who dominates the story, bringing to it not just a Maori idiom but—for the first half anyway—a distinctively oral structure. The story begins on the eve of Ngaio's marriage to Graeme but continually flashes back as Ngaio recalls episodes from her childhood, so that the marriage does not take place until the book is more than half-way through. Then, disappointingly, the format changes; the traumatic events which follow the marriage are set down in chronological order, with only a few stagey questions and premonitions to suggest an oral structure.

In her subsequent work Grace's narrative technique has become increasingly adventurous and assured. The early reliance on the first person gives place to third and even (in one section of *Cousins*) second person narratives, the former (e.g. in "Journey") using a species of free indirect discourse which enables her still to suggest oral Maori usage. And the subtle use of Maori myth as an undercurrent in several of the stories (e.g. the Rangi and Papa creation myth in "Between Earth and Sky" and "Sun's Marbles") reinforces this effect.

All these threads come together in her second and most celebrated novel, *Potiki.* Both it and the later *Cousins* are organized rather like Faulkner's *As I Lay Dying,* with the viewpoints of several members of one family arranged in distinct but overlapping chapters—or (as they are constantly called in *Potiki*) "stories." Some of *Potiki's* stories are told in third-person free indirect discourse, but the two principal characters, Roimata and Toko, tell theirs in the first person.

Toko is a crippled child with a "special knowing" who epitomizes the state of Maori culture—physically broken but spiritually profound. Given that his death saves his endangered people, that his mother's name is Mary and that his father is either an itinerant called Joseph or a carved figure of great spiritual significance in the *wharenui,* Toko has obvious affinities with Christ. In other ways—not least his success in catching a huge eel while out fishing with his brothers—he is akin to the mythical Maori trickster Maui.

This blend of Maori and Christian myths may suggest that Grace wants to preach accommodation between Maori and *pakeha* ways. She certainly does so in *Mutuwhenua,* where Ngaio's mission is evidently to marry the *pakeha* Graeme and make him accept some traditional Maori ways. She succeeds, and the book can be seen as an allegory which recommends that New Zealand society become a bicultural melting-pot, though the force of the allegory is compromised by the insipid depiction of Graeme, who never challenges Maori ways but, like a male version of patient Griselda, accepts what he cannot understand. The plot of *Potiki,* on the other hand, comes to a less comfortable conclusion. The Maori community must adopt aggressive tactics to preserve their integrity and their land from the threat of *pakeha* capitalism, and the book ends with the two races in uneasy juxtaposition. The blend of Maori and *pakeha*

in Toko may be seen as a muted counterpoint to this stand-off, or it may be simply an indication that—like most contemporary Maori authors—Grace takes Christianity to be a traditional feature of Maori culture; Toko may be Christ-like, but this does not give him any significant affinity with the *pakeha.*

Though Grace claimed in a recent interview that she has "never thought about the political element" in her work, she would seem to have become an angrier, more committed writer between *Mutuwhenua* and *Potiki.* Stories like "Journey," "Going for the Bread," and "House of the Fish" tend to the same conclusion. But other recent stories (e.g. "Ngati Kangaru") bring a note of levity to the treatment of Maori grievances, while still others (e.g. "Flower Girls" and "My Leanne") show that Grace is not impervious to the darker side of contemporary Maori society to which authors like Alan Duff have recently drawn attention.

She is—as a recent critic has observed—"far too good and various a writer to allow herself only one side of any story," and her novel *Cousins* bears out this point. Makareta, the most articulate of the three protagonists, becomes a Maori activist, but only after she has escaped the stifling atmosphere of the *whanau* where she was born and the arranged marriage which its formidable old matriarch sought to impose on her. (She marries instead a *pakeha* who is even less substantial than *Mutuwhenua's* Graeme.) The *whanau* is not entirely discredited, however; Missy steps happily into Makareta's role (including the arranged marriage), and the return there of the book's third protagonist, Mata, after a desolate life in the city, seems to constitute a happy ending for the book.

—Shirley Chew, updated by Richard Corballis

GRAHAM, Winston (Mawdsley)

Nationality: British. **Born:** Victoria Park, Manchester, 30 June 1910. **Family:** Married Jean Mary Williamson in 1939 (died 1992); one son and one daughter. **Career:** Chair, Society of Authors, London, 1967-69. **Awards:** Crime Writers Association prize, 1956. Fellow, Royal Society of Literature, 1968. O.B.E. (Officer, Order of the British Empire), 1983. **Agent:** A.M. Heath, 79 St. Martin's Lane, London WC2N 4AA. **Address:** Abbotswood House, Buxted, East Sussex TN22 4PB, England.

<small>PUBLICATIONS</small>

Novels

The House with the Stained-Glass Windows. London, Ward Lock, 1934.
Into the Fog. London, Ward Lock, 1935.
The Riddle of John Rowe. London, Ward Lock, 1935.
Without Motive. London, Ward Lock, 1936.
The Dangerous Pawn. London, Ward Lock, 1937.
The Giant's Chair. London, Ward Lock, 1938.
Strangers Meeting. London, Ward Lock, 1939.
Keys of Chance. London, Ward Lock, 1939.
No Exit: An Adventure. London, Ward Lock, 1940.
Night Journey. London, Ward Lock, 1941; New York, Doubleday, 1968.

My Turn Next. London, Ward Lock, 1942.
The Merciless Ladies. London, Ward Lock, 1944; revised edition, London, Bodley Head, 1979; New York, Doubleday, 1980.
The Forgotten Story. London, Ward Lock, 1945; as *The Wreck of the Grey Cat,* New York, Doubleday, 1958.
Ross Poldark: A Novel of Cornwall 1783-1787. London, Ward Lock, 1945; as *The Renegade,* New York, Doubleday, 1951.
Demelza: A Novel of Cornwall 1788-1790. London, Ward Lock, 1946; New York, Doubleday, 1953.
Take My Life. London, Ward Lock, 1947; New York, Doubleday, 1967.
Cordelia. London, Ward Lock, 1949; New York, Doubleday, 1950.
Night Without Stars. London, Hodder and Stoughton, and New York, Doubleday, 1950.
Jeremy Poldark: A Novel of Cornwall 1790-1791. London, Ward Lock, 1950; as *Venture Once More,* New York, Doubleday, 1954.
Warleggan: A Novel of Cornwall 1792-1793. London, Ward Lock, 1953; as *The Last Gamble,* New York, Doubleday, 1955.
Fortune Is a Woman. London, Hodder and Stoughton, and New York, Doubleday, 1953.
The Little Walls. London, Hodder and Stoughton, and New York, Doubleday, 1955; abridged edition, as *Bridge to Vengeance,* New York, Spivak, 1957.
The Sleeping Partner. London, Hodder and Stoughton, and New York, Doubleday, 1956.
Greek Fire. London, Hodder and Stoughton, and New York, Doubleday, 1958.
The Tumbled House. London, Hodder and Stoughton, 1959; New York, Doubleday, 1960.
Marnie. London, Hodder and Stoughton, and New York, Doubleday, 1961.
The Grove of Eagles. London, Hodder and Stoughton, 1963; New York, Doubleday, 1964.
After the Act. London, Hodder and Stoughton, 1965; New York, Doubleday, 1966.
The Walking Stick. London, Collins, and New York, Doubleday, 1967.
Angell, Pearl and Little God. London, Collins, and New York, Doubleday, 1970.
The Black Moon: A Novel of Cornwall 1794-1795. London, Collins, 1973; New York, Doubleday, 1974.
Woman in the Mirror. London, Bodley Head, and New York, Doubleday, 1975.
The Four Swans: A Novel of Cornwall 1795-1797. London, Collins, 1976; New York, Doubleday, 1977.
The Angry Tide: A Novel of Cornwall 1798-1799. London, Collins, 1977; New York, Doubleday, 1978.
The Stranger from the Sea: A Novel of Cornwall 1810-1811. London, Collins, 1981; New York, Doubleday, 1982.
The Miller's Dance: A Novel of Cornwall 1812-1813. London, Collins, 1982; New York, Doubleday, 1983.
The Loving Cup: A Novel of Cornwall 1813-1815. London, Collins, 1984; New York, Doubleday, 1985.
The Green Flash. London, Collins, 1986; New York, Random House, 1987.
Cameo. London, Collins, 1988.
The Twisted Sword: A Novel of Cornwall 1815-1816. London, Chapmans, 1990; New York, Carroll and Graf, 1991.
Stephanie. London, Chapmans, 1992; New York, Carroll and Graf, 1993.
Tremor. London, Macmillan, 1995.

Short Stories

The Japanese Girl and Other Stories. London, Collins, 1971; New York, Doubleday, 1972; selection, as *The Cornish Farm,* Bath, Chivers, 1982.

Uncollected Short Stories

"The Circus," in *Winter's Crimes 6,* edited by George Hardinge. London, Macmillan, and New York, St. Martin's Press, 1974.
"Nothing in the Library," in *Winter's Crimes 19,* edited by Hilary Hale. London, Macmillan, 1987.

Plays

Shadow Play (produced Salisbury, 1978).
Circumstantial Evidence (produced Guildford, Surrey, 1979).

Screenplays: *Take My Life,* with Valerie Taylor and Margaret Kennedy, 1948; *Night Without Stars,* 1951.

Television Play: *Sleeping Partner,* 1967.

Other

The Spanish Armadas. London, Collins, and New York, Doubleday, 1972.
Poldark's Cornwall, photographs by Simon McBride. London, Bodley Head, 1983.

*

Winston Graham comments:

I look on myself simply as a novelist. I have written—always—what I wanted to write and not what I thought people might want me to write. Reading for me has always been in the first place a matter of enjoyment—otherwise I don't read—and therefore I would expect other people to read my books for the enjoyment they found in them—or not at all. Profit from reading a novel should always be a by-product. The essence to me of style is simplicity, and while I admit there are depths of thought too complex for easy expression, I would despise myself for using complexity of expression where simplicity will do.

If there has been a certain dichotomy in my work, it is simply due to a dichotomy in my own interests. I am deeply interested in history and deeply interested in the present; and I find a stimulus and a refreshment in turning from one subject and one form to another.

I like books of suspense at whatever level they may be written, whether on that of Jane Austen or of Raymond Chandler; so I think all my books of whatever kind contain some of that element which makes a reader want to turn the page—the "and then and then" of which E.M. Forster speaks. This can be a liability if over-indulged in; but so of course can any other preference or attribute.

Although I have always had more to say in a novel than the telling of a story, the story itself has always been the framework on which the rest has depended for its form and shape. I have never been clever enough—or sufficiently self-concerned—to spend 300 pages dipping experimental buckets into the sludge of my own subconscious. I have always been more interested in other people than in myself—though there has to be something of myself in every character created, or he or she will not come to life. I have always been more interested in people than in events, but it is only through events that I have ever been able to illuminate people.

*   *   *

Of the 40 novels Winston Graham has published over some 57 years, many of the modern ones are in some way concerned with crime. But they are not, in the usual sense of the term, "crime stories." In them, crime is a kind of catalyst speeding and provoking action, rather than an end in itself or a sufficient reason for the story, as it is in thrillers. It is seen as an aberration in otherwise normal lives, something non-criminal people, generally respectable and middle-class, may slip into or become involved with, gradually, almost imperceptibly, for all kinds of reasons—greed, love, loyalty, even a sudden impulse, but not through a "professional" criminal background. It is not surprising that his novel *Marnie* became one of Hitchcock's most successful films—since Hitchcock too is interested in the way ordinary people may become entangled in the bizarre.

Graham has written straightforward thrillers, and what Michael Gilbert wrote in choosing *The Little Walls* for his "classics of detection and adventure" series applies to the other novels equally well. It was, he says, "the very best of those adventure stories which introduce what has come to be known in critical jargon as the anti-hero . . . a useful portmanteau expression to describe someone who undertakes the hero's role, without the hero's normal equipment." The characters in all Graham's novels are, in fact, floundering and all-too-human amateurs, realistically placed in a present-day life that includes jobs and domesticity well observed, and with a normal proneness to fear, indiscretion, and lack of nerve; caught in the end by their moral attitudes, by those who love them, by grief, conscience, and the realistic eye of their creator, who knows that their amateur status fails to give them the professional's coolness, his moral indifference.

Graham's sinners are nearly all racked by their sins, and he is fascinated both by the "congenital" liars and outsiders (Marnie, or the crook-lover in *The Walking Stick*), who are conditioned by their past yet devotedly loved in the present, and by their victims, or the victims of circumstances, mistakes, impulses, devotions: the narrator of *After the Act,* for instance, who pushes his ailing wife off a balcony, then finds he cannot face the mistress he ostensibly did it for. Graham values suspense; and, for his own fiction, at least, believes in action rather than analysis as the means to bring his characters to life.

His novels can roughly be divided into two, the modern and the historical. To the historical novels he brings the same *kind* of realism that he does to the present day. Through *Cordelia,* the Poldark novels set in 18th-century Cornwall, or *The Forgotten Story,* another tale about ordinary people involved in murder, this time at the turn of the last century, one walks familiarly. Graham has the good historical novelist's ability to suggest, rather than describe, the physical surroundings; above all to avoid gadzookery and picturesqueness. As he can get the feel of an insurance office, a printing works, or an auctioneer's, so he can walk into the past, giving the sense and atmosphere of it rather than the physical detail, making one breathe its air.

—Isabel Quigly

GRAU, Shirley Ann

Nationality: American. **Born:** New Orleans, Louisiana, 8 July 1930. **Education:** Booth School, Montgomery, Alabama, 1938-45; Ursuline Academy, New Orleans, 1945-46; Sophie Newcomb College, Tulane University, New Orleans (associate editor, *Carnival;* Lazarus Memorial medal, 1949), 1946-50, B.A. 1950 (Phi Beta Kappa); graduate study, Tulane University, 1950-51. **Family:** Married James Kern Feibleman in 1955; two sons and two daughters. **Career:** Creative writing teacher, University of New Orleans, 1966-67. **Awards:** Pulitzer prize, 1965. LL.D.: Rider College, New Jersey; D.Litt.: Spring Hill College, Alabama. **Agent:** Brandt and Brandt, 1501 Broadway, New York, New York 10036. **Address:** 210 Baranne Street, Suite 1120, New Orleans, Louisiana 70112, U.S.A.

PUBLICATIONS

Novels

The Hard Blue Sky. New York, Knopf, 1958; London, Heinemann, 1959.
The House on Coliseum Street. New York, Knopf, and London, Heinemann, 1961.
The Keepers of the House. New York, Knopf, and London, Longman, 1964.
The Condor Passes. New York, Knopf, 1971; London, Longman, 1972.
Evidence of Love. New York, Knopf, and London, Hamish Hamilton, 1977.
Roadwalkers. New York, Knopf, 1994.

Short Stories

The Black Prince and Other Stories. New York, Knopf, 1955; London, Heinemann, 1956.
The Wind Shifting West. New York, Knopf, 1973; London, Chatto and Windus, 1974.
Nine Women. New York, Knopf, 1986.

Uncollected Short Stories

"The Things You Keep," in *Carnival* (New Orleans), December 1950.
"The Fragile Age," in *Carnival* (New Orleans), October 1951.
"The First Day of School," in *Saturday Evening Post* (Philadelphia), 30 September 1961.
"The Beginning of Summer," in *Story* (New York), November 1961.
"The Empty Night," in *Atlantic* (Boston), May 1962.
"The Loveliest Day," in *Saturday Evening Post* (Philadelphia), 5 May 1962.
"One Night," in *Gentlemen's Quarterly* (New York), February 1966.
"The Young Men," in *Redbook* (New York), April 1968.

*

Critical Study: *Shirley Ann Grau* by Paul Schlueter, Boston, Twayne, 1981.

*   *   *

Shirley Ann Grau may be described as a Southern writer, whose range is sometimes narrowly regional. She may also, therefore, be described as a local colorist whose observations of custom and character suggest an anthropologist at work in a fictional mode. She is a white author who deals with blacks and the black sub-culture, which makes her an anomaly in a period of black militancy. And she is finally a novelist of manners who is sharply aware of the collapse of conventional behavior patterns in modern life. The pervasive style and mood of her work may be summed up best in the terms tough, cold, and realistic. The toughness and the apparent realism seem to reveal a debt to Hemingway. She is never sentimental, and almost always she maintains sufficient distance from her characters to depict them with an objectivity that is sometimes little short of chilling. At her best she displays a kind of cold power. But she is, in general, a limited writer. She lacks originality, especially in her treatment of African-Americans and of the South. More seriously, she lacks the complex vision that enables her both to see around and to penetrate deeply into her subject. She is a competent writer who stands at some distance from the center of the Southern Renaissance.

Her best work to date is *The Keepers of the House,* a novel about a southern family. The story concerns Will Howland who inherits a great deal of land and acquires more. After the death of his wife, he brings a black girl into his house and has by her three children who survive. Late in the book, it is revealed that Will had secretly married the girl. He is portrayed as a good, compassionate man whose miscegenation arose out of love. His white granddaughter marries a man who enters politics, joins the Klan, runs for governor, and makes racist speeches. One of Will's children by the black woman reveals that his father is related to a racist politician. As a result of the revelation, the latter is ruined and the Howland family estate attacked. The estate endures, and the daughter revenges herself upon the town.

Grau is fully aware that the glamorous past may be a trap, as one of her short stories reveals. But she also knows that family traditions which are rooted in the past may endow life in the present with an illuminating sense of time and a stabilizing sense of place; in these ways the past provides a sense of continuity which enriches life in the present. This novel centers on these conceptions of life, which are characteristically Southern and which mark the work of other contemporary Southern writers as different as Robert Penn Warren and Eudora Welty. The treatment of inter-racial love here, made acceptable by marriage, appears to be an apologia for Southern miscegenation, which is, of course, usually conceived in much harsher terms. The same is true of the manipulation of racial animosities in politics, which in itself is authentic enough in the novel. But in depicting the defeat of the racist, Grau seems to depart from her characteristically objective stance.

That stance she had maintained in *The Hard Blue Sky,* which reveals her talent for local color. The scene is an island in the Gulf of Mexico inhabited by characters of French and Spanish descent. The principal conflict is between them and the inhabitants of another island who are Slavic in descent. A boy from one island marries a girl from another; the marriage precipitates a feud. Added to the violence of men is the violence of nature, displayed when a hurricane sweeps through the Gulf. Grau does not dwell on the quaintness of character or place in her novel, and she does not patronize her characters, although the temptation to do so must have been quite real, since she conceives them as primitives. She looks at them coldly and clearly, dramatizing their attitudes toward life but passing no judgment on their behavior. These are people who recognize no canons of respectability, who admit of no restraints

on their passions, and who recognize no guilt. Their sexual attitudes are thus quite free, sex being simply in the natural order of things, and their tendency towards violence is always close to the surface, since they believe that a good fight is healthy. Their life is hard and the hazards of nature, whether snakes or wind, make it harder.

Her treatment of the characters in this novel is the same, generally speaking, as her treatment of African-Americans throughout her fiction. Her composite African-American lives an unstructured life in which he obeys appetite and impulse in a naturally selfish movement toward gratification. His morality is virtually non-existent, but casual if apparent at all. His capacity for violence is like that of the islanders. This black does not rise to the level of self-consciousness. Ralph Ellison might say that he is a stereotype, perceived because the white writer suffers from a psychic-social blindness caused by the construction of the inner eye; that is, either Grau is blind or the real African-American is invisible.

Grau's chief contribution to the novel of manners is *The House on Coliseum Street.* Although it is an inferior work, it demonstrates, as some of her short stories have, that she understands the various kinds of moral corruption that mark modern life. She knows that the contemporary world is without values, and she makes divorce and sexual promiscuity the obvious signs, in this novel, of the disintegration of well-to-do society.

The Condor Passes is another family novel, melodramatic in plot but of interest for its method: much of the story is told from the five points of view of the five major characters. *Evidence of Love,* like James Gould Cozzen's *By Love Possessed,* concerns the varieties of love, some a burdensome chore, as Grau shows in the sensitive and effective section on the old mother who, content in her loneliness, awaits the coming of death. The title story of her collection *The Wind Shifting West* displays Grau's feel of water and sky, but only occasionally do the other stories reveal the detachment and power which distinguish her fictional voice at its best.

—Chester E. Eisinger

GRAY, Alasdair (James)

Nationality: Scottish. **Born:** Glasgow, 28 December 1934. **Education:** Whitehill Senior Secondary School, 1946-52; Glasgow Art School (Bellahouston traveling scholarship, 1957), 1952-57, diploma in mural painting and design 1957. **Family:** Married 1) Inge Sorensen in 1962 (divorced 1970); one son; 2) Morag McAlpine in 1991. **Career:** Art teacher, Lanarkshire and Glasgow, 1958-61; scene painter, Pavilion and Citizens' theaters, Glasgow, 1961-63; freelance painter and writer, Glasgow, 1963-76; artist recorder, People's Palace Local History Museum, Glasgow, 1976-77; writer-in-residence, Glasgow University, 1977-79. Since 1979 freelance writer and painter. **Address:** Dog and Bone Books, 175 Queen Victoria Drive, Glasgow G14 9BP, Scotland.

PUBLICATIONS

Novels

Lanark: A Life in Four Books. Edinburgh, Canongate, and New York, Harper, 1981.

1982, Janine. London, Cape, and New York, Viking, 1984.

The Fall of Kelvin Walker: A Fable of the Sixties. Edinburgh, Canongate, 1985; New York, Braziller, 1986.

Something Leather. London, Cape, 1990; New York, Random House, 1991.

McGrotty and Ludmilla; or, The Harbinger Report. Glasgow, Dog and Bone, 1990.

Poor Things. London, Bloomsbury, 1992; New York, Harcourt Brace, 1993.

A History Maker. Edinburgh, Canongate, 1994; New York, Harcourt Brace, 1995.

Short Stories

The Comedy of the White Dog. Glasgow, Print Studio Press, 1979.

Unlikely Stories, Mostly. Edinburgh, Canongate, 1983; New York, Penguin, 1984.

Lean Tales, with Agnes Owens and James Kelman. London, Cape, 1985.

Ten Tales Tall and True. London, Bloomsbury, 1993; New York, Harcourt Brace, 1994.

Plays

Jonah (puppet play; produced Glasgow, 1956).

The Fall of Kelvin Walker (televised 1968; produced on tour, 1972).

Dialogue (produced on tour, 1971).

The Loss of the Golden Silence (produced Edinburgh, 1973).

Homeward Bound (produced Edinburgh, 1973).

Tickly Mince (revue), with Tom Leonard and Liz Lochhead (produced Glasgow, 1982).

The Pie of Damocles (revue), with others (produced Glasgow, 1983).

Radio Plays: *Quiet People,* 1968; *The Night Off,* 1969; *Thomas Muir of Huntershill* (documentary), 1970; *The Loss of the Golden Silence,* 1974; *The Harbinger Report,* 1975; *McGrotty and Ludmilla,* 1976; *The Vital Witness* (on Joan Ure), 1979.

Television Plays and Documentaries: *Under the Helmet,* 1965; *The Fall of Kelvin Walker,* 1968; *Triangles,* 1972; *The Man Who Knew about Electricity,* 1973; *Honesty* (for children), 1974; *Today and Yesterday* (3 plays; for children), 1975; *Beloved,* 1976; *The Gadfly,* 1977; *The Story of a Recluse,* 1986.

Poetry

Old Negatives: Four Verse Sequences. London, Cape, 1989.

Other

Self-Portrait (autobiography). Edinburgh, Saltire Society, 1988.
Why Scots Should Rule Scotland. Edinburgh, Canongate, 1992.

*

Manuscript Collections: Scottish National Library, Edinburgh; Hunterian Museum, Glasgow University.

Theatrical Activities:
Actor: **Television**—*The Story of a Recluse,* 1986.

Critical Study: *The Arts of Alasdair Gray* edited by Crawford and Naion, Edinburgh, Edinburgh University Press, 1991.

Alasdair Gray comments:
Lanark was planned as a whale, *1982, Janine* as an electric eel, *The Fall of Kelvin Walker* as a tasty sprat. Of the short stories I think "A Report to the Trustees" has the most honestly sober prose, "Five Letters from an Eastern Empire" the most inventive fancy, "Prometheus" the greatest scope.

(1995) My stories try to seduce the reader by disguising themselves as sensational entertainment, but are propaganda for democratic welfare—state Socialism and an independent Scottish parliament. My jacket designs and illustrations—especially the erotic ones—are designed with the same high purpose.

* * *

Alasdair Gray came late to the novel and was in middle life when *Lanark* his first and most successful novel was published. Prior to that he had been a painter and a scriptwriter and visual influences bear heavily on all his work: even his book jackets are designed by him. His eye for detail and his taste for color combine especially well in his short stories which were published together under the title *Unlikely Stories, Mostly.* Some stories in this collection are long, such as "Logopandocy" a pastiche in the writings of Sir Thomas Urquhart of Cromartie whom Gray much admires; others short, and two, "A Likely Story in a Non-Marital Setting" and "A Like Story in a Domestic Setting," only five lines long. Some are set in modern everyday life, others in a fantastic other world; above all, they are rich in imaginative background detail. His story "Five Letters from the Eastern Empire" is set in the time of Marco Polo and the letters are supposedly written by Bohum the Chinese emperor's tragic poet, to his parents and they describe the court—"the evergreen garden"—in all its magnificence and all its cruelty. On the other hand it is an evocative description of the lives led by the divinely justified and the sharp, cinematic cuts and finely observed detail make it seem an exercise in scriptwriting. On another level it is a parable of power that oppresses, of a backsliding emperor whom Bohu discovers to be an "evil little puppet, and all the cunning, straightfaced, pompous men who use him."

Although Gray makes considerable use of myth and parable in his fiction and delights in creating imaginative worlds and societies, the matter of Scotland is never far away from the heart of his fiction. In *1982, Janine,* the hero, an aging, divorced alcoholic, insomniac supervisor of security installations tells his story while sitting in the dingy bedroom of a small Scottish hotel: to him, his native country and his fellow countrymen are subjects of disgust. "The truth is that we are a nation of arselickers, though we disguise it with surfaces: a surface of generous, openhanded manliness, a surface of dour practical integrity, a surface of futile, maudlin defiance like when we break goalposts and windows after football matches on foreign soil and commit suicide on Hogmanay by leaping from fountains in Trafalgar." Although this novel is only loosely connected to the reality of present-day Scotland, and more concerned with the general human condition as experienced in the narrator's drunken reverie, *1982, Janine* is rich in Scottish literary allusions. In one section the narrator meets a pantheon of Scottish poets in an Edinburgh pub; in another Gray's richly lyrical exploration of time, space, and inebriation is reminiscent of Hugh MacDiarmid's long poem, "A Drunk Man Looks at the Thistle." That Gray should be so concerned with Scotland and yet repelled by it—a classic theme in Scottish cultural life—should come as little surprise to readers of *Lanark*. In this phantasmagoric exploration of modern city life Gray has an index of plagiarisms, a recurring literary device in his fiction, and this includes an entry on the Scottish novelist George Douglas Brown (1869-1902): "Books 1 and 2 owe much to the novel *The House with the Green Shutters* in which heavy paternalism forces a weak-minded youth into dread of existence, hallucination and crime." In Brown's novel, Gourlay, a wealthy self-made man is ruined by his monstrous self-willed nature and his son is castrated both by his malignancy and by the squalid ethics of Barbie, the mean town in which the Gourlays live. Although Duncan Thaw, the narrator of *Lanark* is not subjected to similar pressures he has to cope with a loveless family and the dreary drudgery of growing to maturity in a far-from-idealized version of the city of Glasgow. To escape from the numbing mindlessness of his life Thaw finds himself in a world which might yet be; this is the afterlife to which he is condemned after a death which is half accidental and half suicidal. Called Unthank it contains echoes of his life on earth in Scotland but is peopled by creatures which have the power of transmogrification.

For all the brilliance of his imaginative inventiveness, Gray showed himself to be on less secure ground in these fantasy sections and was at his best in dealing with the realities of modern life; indeed his descriptions of life in post-war Scotland have a sure and naturalistic touch. This virtue resurfaces in *Something Leather,* a quirky meandering novel which examines the nature of female sexuality as experienced by three different women, Senga, Donalda and June. As has become *de rigueur* in Gray's novels there is also a full cast of supporting characters, including the self-deluding and destructive Tom who bears a close resemblance to Duncan Thaw. Gray has spiced the narrative with a number of erotic cameos—the effect is of reading a number of short stories—but the end result is curiously asexual.

Most of Gray's writing leaves an impression of linguistic inventiveness and artistic energy but his later fiction, including the bizarre *McGrotty and Ludmilla,* has revealed a growing impatience with the confines of the novel's form. In "Critic-Fuel," an epilogue to *Something Leather* he made the surprising admission that he had run out of interest in his writing, hence the change to female central characters. "Having discovered how my talent worked it was almost certainly defunct. Imagination will not employ whom it cannot surprise." Time will tell if Gray can be lured back to the narrative strengths of *Lanark,* to date his most accomplished piece of work.

—Trevor Royle

GRAY, Stephen Richard

Nationality: South African. **Born:** Cape Town, South Africa, 1941. **Education:** St. Andrew's College, Grahamstown; University of Cape Town; Cambridge University, B.A. in English, M.A. in English; Iowa State University, M.A. in creative writing; Rand Afrikaans University, Johannesburg, D.Litt and Ph.D 1978. **Career:** Lecturer in English, Aix-en-Provence, two years; professor of English, Rand Afrikaans University, Johannesburg, until 1991. Since 1991 full-time writer. Editor, *Granta,* and director, Cambridge Shakespeare Group, both while a student at Cambridge; writer-in-

residence, 1982, University of Queensland, Australia. **Address:** P.O. Box 86, Crown Mines, South Africa, 2025.

PUBLICATIONS

Novels

Local Colour. Johannesburg, Ravan Press, 1975.
Visible People. Cape Town, Philip, and London, Collins, 1977.
Caltrop's Desire. Cape Town, Philip, and London, Collins, 1980.
Time of Our Darkness. Johannesburg and London, Muller, 1988.
Born of Man. Yeoville, South Africa, Justified Press, and London, Gay Men's Press, 1989.
War Child. Johannesburg, Justified Press, 1991; London, Serif, 1993.
Season of Violence. Sydney, Dangaroo Press, 1992.
Drakenstein. Johannesburg, Justified Press, 1994.

Plays

Schreiner: A One-Woman Play. Cape Town and London, Philip, 1983.

Poetry

It's About Time, edited by Douglas Livingstone. Cape Town, Philip, 1974.
Hottentot Venus, and Other Poems. Cape Town, Philip, and London, Collins, 1979.

Other

The Assassination of Shaka by Mhlangane Dingane and Mbopa on 22 September 1828 at Dukuza by Which Act the Zulu Nation First Lost Its Empire, with woodcuts by Cecil Skotnes. Johannesburg, McGraw Hill, 1974.
Southern African Literature: An Introduction. Cape Town, Philip, London, Collins, and New York, Barnes and Noble, 1979.
Douglas Blackburn. Boston, Twayne, 1984.
John Ross: The True Story. N.p., 1987.
Human Interest and Other Pieces. Johannesburg, Justified Press, 1993.
Accident of Birth. Fordsburg, Johannesburg, COSAW, 1993.

Editor, *Writer's Territory.* Cape Town, Longman Southern Africa, 1973.
Editor, *On the Edge of the World: Southern African Stories of the Seventies.* Johannesburg, Donker, 1974.
Editor, *A World of Their Own: Southern African Poets of the Seventies.* Johannesburg, Donker, 1976.
Editor, *Mhudi,* by Solomon T. Plaatje. London, Heinemann, 1978.
Editor, *Theatre One: New South African Drama.* Johannesburg and London, Donker, 1978.
Editor, *Modern South African Stories.* Craighall, South Africa, Donker, 1980.
Editor, *Stormwrack,* by C. Louis Leipoldt. Cape Town, Philip, 1980.
Editor, *Turbott Wolfe,* by William Plomer. Johannesburg, Donker, 1980.
Editor, *Theatre Two: New South African Drama.* Johannesburg, Donker, 1981.

Editor, *Fugard.* Johannesburg, McGraw Hill, 1982.

Editor, *Modern South African Poetry.* Craighall, South Africa, Donker, 1984.

Editor, with David Schalkwyk, *Modern Stage Directions: A Collection of Short Dramatic Scripts.* Pinelands, Cape Town, Maskew Miller Longman, 1984.

Editor, *Three Plays,* by Stephen Black. Craighall, Donker, 1984.

Editor, *The Penguin Book of Southern African Stories.* Harmondsworth, Middlesex, Penguin, 1985.

Editor, *Selected Poems,* by William Plomer. Craighall, South Africa, Donker, 1985.

Editor, *Bosman's Johannesburg.* Cape Town, Human and Rousseau, 1986.

Editor, *Herman Charles Bosman.* Johannesburg, McGraw Hill, 1986.

Editor, *Market Plays.* Craighall, South Africa, Donker, 1986.

Editor, *The Penguin Book of South African Verse.* London, Penguin, 1989.

Editor, *My Children! My Africa! and Selected Shorter Plays,* by Athol Fugard. Johannesburg, Witwatersrand University Press, 1990.

Editor, *The Natal Papers of "John Ross": Loss of the Brig Mary at Natal with Early Recollection of That Settlement and Among the Caffres,* by Charles Campbell Maclean. Durban, Killie Campbell Africana Library, 1992.

Editor, *South Africa Plays.* London, Hern, 1993.

*   *   *

In addition to his significant work as a poet, playwright, editor, and novelist, Stephen Gray is a prominent literary critic in his native South Africa. Always one to blur the boundaries between categories (be they generic or sociopolitical), Gray frequently combines these writerly personae, revisiting and reassessing his own fiction in his essays. As he has noted on more than one occasion, the legacy of apartheid has forced the South African writer into a position of negotiating between cultural extremes, into crossing multiple and manifold borders. This "hybrid" aesthetic, this "translational" ethic, is well represented in Gray's eight published novels, which regularly transgress the margins of race, class, and sexuality.

Gray's first novel, *Local Colour,* displays many of the central preoccupations that recur throughout his entire oeuvre: experimentation with form; a facility with the finer details of setting; a penchant for exploring the limits of racial and sexual taboos, in this case so-called miscegenation. A five-part satirical allegory set in Saldanha Bay, a remote outpost near the Cape, the narrative is a fragmentary and complex amalgam of Western literary conventions (interior monologue, epistolary romance) and African modes of oral storytelling (fable, myth). In the main section of the novel, while an American oil tanker burns and lists offshore, Beattie, Chris, and Alex hatch a plot to swindle Beattie's dying Aunt Miriam out of her property. What begins as a mere act of greed soon turns into an epic quest for the truth about Miriam's relationships with the legendary Captain McBlade and Elsabie, her colored maid. This quest motif, which is given even more satirical treatment in Gray's next novel, *Visible People,* juxtaposes the prejudices inherent in a dominant white mode of perception against the historical contingencies of the indigenous landscape, with decidedly ambivalent results.

The dialectic between past, present, and future operates at some level in all of Gray's novels, but two in particular are concerned with specific watershed moments in South African history. In

Caltrop's Desire, on the eve of the 1948 national elections, a dying war correspondent records the waning moments of white liberalism in South Africa and anticipates an even bloodier future for the country under apartheid. In *John Ross,* Gray writes against the grain of both early-19th-century historical documentation and late-20th-century popular mythmaking (Gray's "novel" was meant as a companion volume to the 1987 South African television serial, *John Ross: An African Adventure*), offering readers "the true story" of the young, redheaded Scottish lad who was shipwrecked at Port Natal in 1825 and subsequently became a member of King Shaka's Zulu court. Drawing attention to both the factual authenticity and the fictionality of his texts, Gray illuminates the often contradictory ways in which history gets written and stories get told.

The bond between dispossessed child and powerful adult is examined further in *Time of Our Darkness.* Here, however, Gray reverses the races of his central characters; he also complicates their relationship by introducing homosexual desire into the admixture of competing social differences. Nine years after the 1976 Soweto uprising, Disley Mashinini, a young black boy from the townships, transfers into Saint Paul's, an all-white private school. He is soon receiving more than just extracurricular instruction from his teacher, Pete Walker. Gray maps this potentially explosive territory forthrightly and candidly, underscoring South Africa's erotic investments in the more visible markers of identity, such as race. In this regard, Disley proves to be the wiser of the two protagonists. "'You know, but you don't want to know,'" Pete quotes him as saying at the outset of the novel. "That was the theme of our relationship."

Gay subcultural affiliation receives an altogether more vernacular treatment in *Born of Man.* Adopting a narrator with a distinctively camp idiom and filling his text with all manner of playful posturing by members of the extended community of Bairnsford Nursery, Gray reinscribes homosexual difference in ways that signify strength, attitude, and ironic pride.

Although most of Gray's novels are highly metafictional (in *Born of Man,* for example, Gray revisits the epistolary genre via the word processor), *Drakenstein* is by far Gray's most self-reflexive work to date. Clearly having fun with some of the basic tenets of postmodern theory, he uses the generic codes of the horror story—fictional *and* cinematic—precisely in order to undermine and subvert them. In confronting the horrific crimes of the past and the present in order to imagine a future for postapartheid South Africa at its time of transition, the narrator, John Raeburn, like the monster in *Frankenstein,* must also confront the horrors of his own fragmented subjectivity. "Who is this I," he asks at the end of the novel, "impatient but regretful, spitting out his flesh? Which I—I—I—half these sentences begin with I." This referentially unstable first-person pronoun, which surfaces throughout Gray's fiction, has gradually grown more introspective over the course of his career. The autobiographical experiments of *Accident of Birth* and some of the short pieces in *Human Interest* are, in many ways, a natural progression from the childhood reminiscences that make up *War Child.* In the opening sketch of *Human Interest,* Gray notes that even before he had "grown to any consciousness of how morally *wrong* apartheid was," he nevertheless understood "that I must become someone who would write about those aspects of life that were not recorded, were never mentioned, not even imagined to exist." Four decades later, decades that comprise a "time of darkness" from which South Africa is only now emerging, Gray has clearly made good on his teenaged vow.

—Peter Dickinson

GREENBERG, Joanne

Pseudonym: Hannah Green. **Nationality:** American. **Born:** Brooklyn, New York, 24 September 1932. **Education:** American University, Washington, D.C., B.A. **Family:** Married Albert Greenberg in 1955; two sons. **Career:** Medical officer, Lookout Mountain Fire Department; certified emergency medical technican. Since 1983, adjunct professor of anthropology, Colorado School of Mines, Golden. **Awards:** Frieda Fromm-Reichman memorial award, 1967; National Jewish Welfare Board Harry and Ethel Daroff award, 1963, and William and Janice Epstein award, 1964, both for *The King's Persons;* New York Association of the Deaf Marcus L. Kenner award, 1971; Christopher book award, 1971, for *In This Sign;* Rocky Mountain Women's Institute award, 1983; Denver Public Library Bookplate award, 1990; Colorado Author of the Year award, 1991. D.L.: Western Maryland College, 1977. D.H.L.: Gallaudet College, 1979. J.H.L.: University of Colorado, 1987. **Agent:** Wallace Literary Agency, 1977 East 70th Street, New York, New York 10021, U.S.A. **Address:** 29221 Rainbow Hill Road, Golden, Colorado 80401, U.S.A.

PUBLICATIONS

Novels

The King's Persons. New York, Holt, and London, Gollancz, 1963.
The Monday Voices. New York, Holt, and London, Gollancz, 1965.
In This Sign. New York, Holt, 1968; London, Gollancz, 1970.
The Dead of the House. Garden City, New York, Doubleday, 1972.
Founder's Praise. New York, Holt, 1976.
A Season of Delight. New York, Holt, 1981.
The Far Side of Victory. New York, Holt, and London, Gollancz, 1983.
Simple Gifts. New York, Holt, and London, Gollancz, 1986.
Age of Consent. New York, Holt, and London, Gollancz, 1987.
Of Such Small Differences. New York, Holt, and London, Gollancz, 1988.
No Reck'ning Made. New York, Holt, 1993.

Short Stories

Summering: A Book of Short Stories. New York, Holt, and London, Gollancz, 1966.
Rite of Passage. New York, Holt, 1971; London, Gollancz, 1972.
High Crimes and Misdemeanors. New York, Holt, 1979; London, Gollancz, 1980.
With the Snow Queen and Other Stories. New York, Arcade, 1991.

Other

I Never Promised You a Rose Garden (as Hannah Green). New York, Holt, and London, Pan, 1964.
In the City of Paris (as Hannah Green; for children). Garden City, New York, Doubleday, 1985.

*

Film Adaptation: *I Never Promised You a Rose Garden,* 1977.

*   *   *

Joanne Greenberg, also known as Hannah Green, is a writer whose style lends itself to the mature reader yet simultaneously presents themes suitable for all ages. Greenberg addresses the persistent doubts that plague all of us by relating stories of others in need. Though the scenarios in which her characters find themselves may be unfamiliar to the average reader, the emotions they feel while enmeshed in the plotlines are universal in appeal and scope. Her works include magazine publications, short stories, novels, and a movie adaptation of her book, *I Never Promised You a Rose Garden.*

Greenberg wrote *I Never Promised You a Rose Garden* under the pseudonym Hannah Green. In this book, she details the struggle of a 16-year-old girl fighting for her sanity. The descriptive and, at times, poetic uses of language bring the reader inside the character's world of fantasy. The depiction of the brilliant psychiatrist grappling with the reality of her own life while immersed in the treatment of her patient is explicitly detailed and well written. As Greenberg's personal encounter with mental problems was a basis for the character's ordeal with psychosis and schizophrenia, her empathy for her character is clearly evident.

Another popular book, *In This Sign,* was heralded by those both within and outside of the deaf community. The themes of loneliness, isolation, and of being different are dramatically brought to life by the experiences of Greenberg's characters. She transforms the occurrences within the realm of her deaf character into common circumstances with which we can all identify. Readers can gain an affinity for the handicapped through edification and education that is expertly interwoven into the story line.

In another book, *Of Such Small Differences,* Greenberg expands the reader's mind to encompass the daily trials and tribulations of a character who is not only deaf but also blind. The leading character's experiences and ensuing love affair are portrayed as one might relate a story told by one friend to another. The primary difficulties handled by the protagonist are those of anyone involved in a growing relationship. It is a love story. The physical disabilities are secondary in the development of the characters' union.

In *Simple Gifts,* we also see people somewhat "out of sync" with the world around them. Their lives are complicated by secrets long thought buried. Love, for them, usually comes after much turmoil, when it is least expected.

One of Greenberg's sadder stories is *The Far Side of Victory.* This book examines such themes as crime and punishment of the human soul. One's guilt or innocence is primarily determined by the ability to cope with life's adversities. In the search for truth and meaning, there lies the experience of love and loss.

In *Age of Consent,* Greenberg strongly portrays the mysterious loner no one ever really knew. By examining a character's life following untimely death at the hands of murderers, Greenberg cleverly utilizes the technique of flashback. The investigators are forced to look at their own lives as the impact of both the life and death of the main character is revealed. Once again we see a study in solitude; of being alone in the company of many.

A book that includes references to actual historical events is *Founder's Praise.* This book details the climb of a family through hard times during the history of the United States. Their belief in the goodness of people through religion and morality guides them into their future.

Greenberg has also written several collections of short stories. In one book, *Summering,* her tales again reflect the themes of love and misunderstanding, loneliness and friendship. We are subsequently captivated by her imaginative characterizations and narratives that uniquely embody her freshness and innovation. In another book of short stories, *With the Snow Queen and Other Stories,* she writes of people we know. We can relate to people with basic human needs, even in peculiar situations. In one story, she employs the unconventional tact of having a character break through the "third wall" to "speak" directly to the reader. Her range of unusual topics runs the gamut from time travel to the solemnity of the life of a monk. Another collection, *High Crimes and Misdemeanors,* utilizes much humor and fantasy. Yet Greenberg is still able to embroil the readers in the particulars of her characters that most closely link us all to the hopes, fears, and dreams of life. Additionally, this book contains several stories that derive from Greenberg's religious background.

Greenberg's popularity lies in both her creativity and her originality. Her ability to incorporate common themes into uncommon situations makes her a most readable author.

—Laurie Schwartz Guttenberg

GRISHAM, John

Nationality: American. **Born:** Jonesboro, Arkansas, 8 February 1955. **Education:** Mississippi State University, B.S. in accounting 1977; University of Mississippi, LL.D in 1981. **Family:** Married Renee Jones; three children. **Career:** Practiced law, Southaven, Mississippi, 1981-91; member Mississippi House of Representatives, 1984-90. **Address:** c/o Doubleday, 666 Fifth Avenue, New York, New York 10103, U.S.A.

PUBLICATIONS

Novels

A Time to Kill. New York, Wynwood Press, 1989; London, Century, 1993.
The Firm. New York, Doubleday, and London, Century, 1991.
The Pelican Brief. New York, Doubleday, and London, Century, 1992.
The Client. New York, Doubleday, and London, Century, 1993.
The Chamber. New York, Doubleday, and London, Century, 1994.
The Rainmaker. New York, Doubleday, and London, Century, 1995.

*

Film Adaptations: *The Firm,* 1993; *The Pelican Brief,* 1993; *The Client,* 1994.

*   *   *

John Grisham hit the best-seller lists as a kind of publishing phenomenon, a blockbuster novelist whose books are instant hits and are snapped up by Hollywood even before they hit the bookstores. Grisham writes a type of novel that might best be described as a "legal procedural." His books deal with the law and those who practice it. If, as surveys indicate, Americans are antilawyer, they are certainly not antilaw novel. Grisham and others have made the legal novel vastly popular with the American reading public.

There are probably two main reasons for Grisham's popularity

among contemporary readers. First, Grisham invites his reader into the often confusing and arcane world of legal practice. He cuts through the "heretofores" and "whereases" to simplify law for the reader. He shows how the law works, how lawyers work, why the law sometimes doesn't work, and what's going on when we can't see legal workings. Furthermore, he does this with a page-turning style that is hard to resist for those curious about the legal system in this country.

Second, Grisham suggests to his readers that the law can be made to work for all of us, even neophytes, even in the face of huge companies with high-priced representation, even against overwhelming odds, even against government oppression. Grisham's protagonists are always underdogs. They may be law students (*The Pelican Brief*), brand new lawyers (*The Firm, The Chamber, The Rainmaker*), or practicing lawyers fighting against great odds (*A Time to Kill, The Client*). Whatever the situation, the message is powerful and seductive. Americans hold strongly and dearly the belief that we are all equal under the law and that all of us have a chance to win if our cause is right, never mind the reality of expensive attorneys.

One of Grisham's gifts is that he is able to make sympathetic to the reader even those characters who might ordinarily have no claim to those sympathies. In *The Chamber,* for instance, Grisham presents his readers with a character who deserves the death penalty, if indeed anyone ever has. He is a multiple murderer, an unrepentant racist—a virtual compendium of all that could possibly be wrong with a character facing capital punishment. Still, it would be the hard-hearted reader who could reach the end of this book and not feel sorry for the death of an old man who glories in a last gift of Eskimo Pies.

Grisham's first book, *A Time to Kill,* is probably his weakest, although that could be said of most first novels. He introduces plot lines and characters that he fails to develop sufficiently or to tie up neatly at the end. By his second book, *The Firm,* he has overcome those problems quite thoroughly. Grisham likes introducing involved plot lines and twists and weaving them into a fast-paced whole. One almost suspects that he considers complexity a personal challenge, taking it on in the way one might consider constructing a puzzle.

Although his novels are generally well edited and fairly seamless, *The Chamber* showed signs of a syndrome unfortunately common to blockbuster writers, one that sometimes appears after their first few novels. When writers become so valuable to their publishers that publishers are afraid to edit them, sloppiness in the minor aspects of editing may begin to pop out, and that is the case with *The Chamber.* In one instance, Grisham goes to some lengths to portray an African-American prison guard as an engaging character then refers to him as having "shuffled" along the corridor. It's a lapse that must jump out at readers sensitive to racial issues and is inexplicable in a book in which race relations are central to the plot. Other editing problems surface in this book, as well, suggesting that Grisham may need to pay more attention to his editors and vice versa.

No such problems surface in *The Rainmaker,* the novel following *The Chamber;* perhaps the writer has been made aware of the editing lapses.

Overall, Grisham's work is well constructed, tightly plotted, fast paced, and, if undemanding, certainly exciting for the reader looking for a hard-to-put-down novel.

—June Harris

GRUMBACH, Doris (Isaac)

Nationality: American. **Born:** New York City, 12 July 1918. **Education:** Washington Square College, A.B. 1939; Cornell University, M.A. 1940. **Military Service:** U.S. Navy WAVES. **Family:** 1) married Leonard Grumbach, 1941 (divorced 1972), four children; 2) companion of Sybil Pike. **Career:** Title writer for Metro-Goldwyn-Mayer, New York City, 1940-41; proofreader and copyeditor, Time, Inc., 1941-42; associate editor of *Architectural Forum*, 1942-43; English teacher at Albany Academy for Girls, Rochester, New York, 1952-55; held a variety of positions from instructor to professor of English at College of St. Rose, Albany, New York, 1952-73; literary editor for *The New Republic*, 1973-75; professor of American literature, American University, Washington, D.C., 1975-85. Columnist for *Critic*, 1960-64; *National Catholic Reporter*, 1968-76; *New York Times Books Review*, 1976-83; *Saturday Review*, 1977-78; and *Chronicle of Higher Education*, 1979-84. Contributor of reviews and criticism to *New York Times Books Review*, *Chicago Tribune*, *Commonweal*, *Los Angeles Times*, *Nation*, *Washington Post*, *New Republic*, National Public Radio, and the *MacNeil-Lehrer Newshour*. Board of directors, 1984-89, and executive board, 1985-91, PEN/Faulkner. **Member:** American Association of University Professors, Phi Beta Kappa. **Agent:** Maxine Groffsky, 2 Fifth Avenue, New York, New York 10011, U.S.A.

PUBLICATIONS

Novels

The Spoils of Flowers. Garden City, New York, Doubleday, 1962.
The Short Throat, the Tender Mouth. Garden City, New York, Doubleday, 1964.
Chamber Music. New York, Dutton, and London, Hamish Hamilton, 1979.
The Missing Person. New York, Putnam, and London, Hamish Hamilton, 1981.
The Ladies. New York, Dutton, and London, Hamish Hamilton, 1984.
The Magician's Girl. New York, MacMillan, 1987.
The Book of Knowledge. New York, Norton, 1995.

Other

The Company She Kept (biography). New York, Coward, 1967.
Coming into the End Zone (autobiography). New York and London, Norton, 1991.
Extra Innings: A Memoir. New York, Norton, 1993.
Fifty Days of Solitude. Boston, Beacon Press, 1994.

Recordings: *The Craft of My Fiction*, Archive of Recorded Poetry and Literature, 1985.

* * *

Immediately apparent in Doris Grumbach's fiction is its decency. She prefaces some of her novels without resorting to the usual disclaimer, "no relationship to anyone living or dead," but declares her characters as typifying numerous individuals: "This novel is a portrait, not of a single life but of many lives melded into one." However, her stereotypes attracted the most pejorative criticism of her work and are likely to be the reason that her most widely acclaimed books are recent nonfictional memoirs.

Her novels' inflammatory scenes and subjects are treated delicately, with an unfashionable sense of niceness. *The Ladies* is a polite narrative of an 18th-century lesbian relationship between Eleanor, who at seven decides to "be a boy, and then a man," and Sarah, whose "steps were prim and careful." Leaving behind authoritarian fathers and hand-wringing mothers, the women spend their first night together in a cold barn where "they put their arms about each other, ignoring the wet discomforts of their clothes, seeking to dry themselves in the heat of their creature love." Later, free and established in Wales, "they lay close together," which does not explain the trouble to which they have gone. More warmth has already occurred in a scene from Eleanor's childhood, masturbating on a stone lion and "never allowing herself to believe that in her ecstasy it was she who dampened his granite back."

Nor are we given more than an implication of a physical relationship between *Chamber Music*'s Caroline and Anna: "the way we moved together at the start of sleep to lie close, often in each other's arms, the sense of creature warmth and security we kindled between our two bodies as we touched." Grumbach relies upon the imagination of her audience to equate "creature love" or "creature warmth and security" with passion.

Lovemaking is more vividly portrayed in *The Magician's Girl* through Minna's reverie after Lowell has left her bed: "Enlivened by the pressure of his young presence, she greeted his entry with moisture long absent from the unused region of her sex." Readers spoiled by the power of a D.H. Lawrence novel or desensitized by pulp fiction may have jaded tastes, but also Grumbach seems to be writing to an easily offended, past generation. She sacrifices credibility by making scant distinction between friendship, love, and sex.

She is much less ambiguous about other themes, such as the lonely survivor, the wasted lives of those who wait for excitement to come to them. *Chamber Music*'s heroine Caroline is "raised by a lovely, heartbroken mother," and the book concludes with Caroline's observation that, "Conceived in the age of the Centennial's bentwood sofa, I lived an almost empty life into an overcrowded and hectic century." *The Ladies*' Sarah barely sustains herself with memories, indeed the ghost, of Eleanor. *The Magician's Girl* leaves the ineffectual Liz musing that she is "the one left. Odd woman out. Or in. Still afloat, still kicking," but without direction.

Sarah alone finds peace with herself: "After a time of crying at her fears and her life's small tragedies, she never shed a tear again." Likewise, in *Magician's Girl,* Minna loses the fear taught by her mother, and although "Minna Grant's first memory, at five, was of terror," she leaves "fearless." By contrast, Caroline's worst fear is realized as she is "deserted by the single point of light, the one glowing coal, in a long, cold, dark life." Franny has no personality, only her stage persona: "Eddie Puritan, the agent of her real self, the slate man for all her inner takes, was the only one . . . who thought Fanny Marker was a person. And then, of course, he died." As a homosexual ("nance"), he was the only man who had not been a sexual threat.

Despite all of the unusual, improbable, or unexpected situations that actually happen to people and which Grumbach employs in her novels, she nonetheless maintains a detachment from her characters, unlike Charles Dickens's or John Irving's emotive qualities. Grumbach readers feel little sympathy for those who will cry no more, little arousal from those who snuggle faithfully rather than intimately, little compassion for those who never really lived. What then engages us so deeply about these characters who reveal their worst flaws and banalities, their deepest fears, and self-knowledge, but realism? What Grumbach's critics fault her for is intermixing realism and romanticism. Her books are not intended for readers who need to identify with hyperbolic characters, rather for those with enough sense of self to know that they too are at times ordinary, prudish, or in need of a cuddle.

—Maril Nowak

GUERARD, Albert (Joseph)

Nationality: American. **Born:** Houston, Texas, 2 November 1914. **Education:** Stanford University, California, B.A. 1934, Ph.D. 1938; Harvard University, Cambridge, Massachusetts, M.A. 1936. **Military Service:** Served in the Psychological Warfare Branch of the United States Army, 1943-45: Technical Sergeant. **Family:** Married Mary Maclin Bocock in 1941; three daughters. **Career:** Instructor in English, Amherst College, Massachusetts, 1935-36; instructor, assistant professor, and associate professor of English, 1938-54, and professor of English, 1954-61, Harvard University; professor of literature, Stanford University, 1961-85, now emeritus. **Awards:** Rockefeller fellowship, 1946; Fulbright fellowship, 1950; Guggenheim fellowship, 1956; Ford fellowship, 1959; *Paris Review* prize, 1963; National Endowment for the Arts grant, 1967, 1974. **Member:** American Academy of Arts and Sciences. **Agent:** Clyde Taylor, Curtis Brown, 10 Astor Place, New York, New York 10003. **Address:** 635 Gerona Road, Stanford, California 94305, U.S.A.

PUBLICATIONS

Novels

The Past Must Alter. London, Longman, 1937; New York, Holt, 1938.
The Hunted. New York, Knopf, 1944; London, Longman, 1947.
Maquisard: A Christmas Tale. New York, Knopf, 1945; London, Longman, 1946.
Night Journey. New York, Knopf, 1950; London, Longman, 1951.
The Bystander. Boston, Little Brown, 1958; London, Faber, 1959.
The Exiles. London, Faber, 1962; New York, Macmillan, 1963.
Christine/Annette. New York, Dutton, 1985.
Gabrielle: An Entertainment. New York, Fine, 1992.
The Hotel in the Jungle. Stanford, California, CSLI, 1995.

Uncollected Short Stories

"Davos in Winter," in *Hound and Horn* (Cambridge, Massachusetts), October-December 1933.
"Tragic Autumn," in *The Magazine* (Beverly Hills, California), December 1933.
"Miss Prindle's Lover," in *The Magazine* (Beverly Hills, California), February 1934; revised edition, in *Wake* (Cambridge, Massachusetts), Spring 1948.
"Turista," in *The Best American Short Stories of 1947,* edited by Martha Foley. Boston, Houghton Mifflin, 1947.

"The Incubus," in *The Dial* (New York), vol. 1, no. 2, 1960.
"The Lusts and Gratifications of Andrada," in *Paris Review,* Summer-Fall 1962.
"On the Operating Table," in *Denver Quarterly,* Autumn 1966.
"The Journey," in *Partisan Review* (New Brunswick, New Jersey), Winter 1967.
"The Rabbit and the Tapes," in *Sewanee Review* (Tennessee), Spring 1972.
"The Pillars of Hercules," in *Fiction* (New York), December 1973.
"Bon Papa Reviendra," in *Tri-Quarterly* (Evanston, Illinois), Spring 1975.
"Post Mortem: The Garcia Incident," in *Southern Review* (Baton Rouge, Louisiana), Spring 1978.
"Diplomatic Immunity," in *Sequoia* (Stanford, California), Autumn-Winter, 1978.
"The Poetry of Flight," in *Northwest Magazine* (Portland, Oregon), 22 January 1984.
"Suspended Sentence," in *Sequoia* (Stanford, California), Winter 1988.
"The Mongol Orbit," in *Sequoia* (Stanford, California), Centennial Issue, 1989.

Other

Robert Bridges: A Study of Traditionalism in Poetry. Cambridge, Massachusetts, Harvard University Press, and London, Oxford University Press, 1942.
Joseph Conrad. New York, New Directions, 1947.
Thomas Hardy: The Novels and Stories. Cambridge, Massachusetts, Harvard University Press, 1949; London, Oxford University Press, 1950; revised edition, 1964.
André Gide. Cambridge, Massachusetts, Harvard University Press, and London, Oxford University Press, 1951; revised edition, 1969.
Conrad the Novelist. Cambridge, Massachusetts, Harvard University Press, 1958; London, Oxford University Press, 1959.
The Triumph of the Novel: Dickens, Dostoevsky, Faulkner. New York, Oxford University Press, 1976; London, Oxford University Press, 1977.
The Touch of Time: Myth, Memory, and the Self. Stanford, California, Stanford Alumni Association, 1980.

Editor, *Prosateurs Américains de XXe Siécle.* Paris, Laffont, 1947.
Editor, *The Return of the Native,* by Thomas Hardy. New York, Holt Rinehart, 1961.
Editor, *Hardy: A Collection of Critical Essays.* Englewood Cliffs, New Jersey, Prentice Hall, 1963.
Editor, *Perspective on the Novel,* special issue of *Daedalus* (Boston), Spring 1963.
Co-Editor, *The Personal Voice: A Contemporary Prose Reader.* Philadelphia, Lippincott, 1964.
Editor, *Stories of the Double.* Philadelphia, Lippincott, 1967.
Editor, *Mirror and Mirage.* Stanford, California, Stanford Alumni Association, 1980.

*

Manuscript Collection: Stanford University Library, California.

Critical Studies: *The Modern Novel in America* by Frederick Hoffman, Chicago, Regnery, 1951; *The Hero with the Private Parts* by Andrew Lytle, Baton Rouge, Louisiana State University Press, 1966; "The Eskimo Motor in the Detection Cell" by Paul West, in *Southern Review* (Baton Rouge, Louisiana), Winter 1979; *The Touch of Time,* 1980, "The Past Unrecaptured: The Two Lives of Lya de Putti," in *Southern Review* (Baton Rouge, Louisiana), Winter 1983, and "Divided Selves," in *Contemporary Authors Autobiography Series 2* edited by Adele Sarkissian, Detroit, Gale, 1985, all by Guerard; "The New Historical Romance" by David Levin, in *Virginia Quarterly Review* (Charlottesville), Spring 1986.

Albert Guerard comments:

My work has been notably affected by wartime experience (political intelligence work in France) and by the pressures and ambiguities of the subsequent cold war. I have tried without success to put the political subject aside; thousands of unpublished pages, many of them angry, testify to inescapable contemporary pressures.

Maquisard, written immediately after the 1944 events it describes, is an affectionate record of wartime comradeships among men who had been in the underground. Apologetically subtitled *A Christmas Tale,* it is the slightest of my novels and was the most warmly received. *Night Journey,* my most complex and most substantial novel, is more truthful in its picture of the political and moral devastation caused by American-Soviet rivalries in a world as deceptive, and as self-deceptive, as that of *1984.* It was, on publication, repeatedly compared to Orwell's book. The confession of Paul Haldan (wandering and evasive, with his final crime left undescribed, and indeed undetected by most readers) is that of a liberal "innocent" who can accept neither his mother's sexual betrayals nor his country's systematic abuse of power and liberal ideology, nor its threatened use of germ warfare. Haldan's night journey into temporary regression takes him into the middle European city of his childhood, disrupted by the two great powers and betrayed by both. The ambiguities of an undeclared war are internalized by Paul Haldan, and his psycho-sexual anxieties projected onto the screen of public conflict. *The Exiles* (based on a journey to Cuba, Haiti, and Santo Domingo during the turmoil of 1959) explores deception and self-deception in the tragi-comic context of Caribbean propaganda and political intrigue. It dramatizes the conflict of a quixotic Trujillo assassin incorrigibly drawn to the exiled statesmen he is supposed to destroy. Manuel Andrada appears to be the most winning of my fictional creations.

In *The Hunted,* an earlier novel and conventionally realistic in technique, psycho-sexual anxieties and monumental vanities reflect public disorders in a small New England college just before World War II. Oedipal conflicts and fantasies, dramatized fairly unconsciously in *The Past Must Alter,* are central to *Night Journey* and to *The Bystander,* another story of romantic love vitiated by immaturity and regression. The technique of *The Bystander* is that of the French *récit,* with the motives either concealed or distorted by the narrator-protagonist. But the story is also of a collision between American "innocence" and European compromise. One of my central aims has been to avoid, while writing fairly complex psychological novels, the deadening burden of explicit and accurate analysis. *The Bystander*—very easy to read, perhaps too easy to read—requires, to be truly understood, the closest attention to hint, to image, to nuance of voice and style.

In *Christine/Annette* I wanted to bring a number of perspectives and narrative methods to bear on the ambiguous case of an actress who changes her name and even her personality several times. We see her through fragments of her own journal, her son's reconstructive memoir, a former lover's screen play, brief oral histories by old friends, a few letters. No two versions entirely agree. A good young writer urged me to simplify my novel in accord with contemporary taste by making it more "linear," with a clear story line and third-person narration. But I kept to my ambiguities and contradictory witnesses, knowing they were true to a past that was irrecoverable and had become mythical. I was much pleased by a reviewer who found in this novel a combination of Proust's impressionism and the post-modern qualities of Italo Calvino.

I was bemused by the turbulent self-destructive life of Louise Brooks, but even more by that of Lya de Putti, a Hungarian star of silent films whom I met when I was ten years old. She left husband and infant daughters to become an actress, and the children were led to believe she was dead. More than 50 years later I met the daughters, and was struck by their loyalty to the lost mother and to the father who had kept them in ignorance. I knew none of this family history when I brought a remembered "Lia" briefly into my first novel of 1937. But the loyalty of the daughters, as well as Lya de Putti's turbulent life, is reflected in *Christine/Annette.*

Gabrielle was subtitled "An Entertainment" after the model of Graham Greene, who thus labeled his less complex novels. The subtitle may have been a mistake. Although structured as a psychological thriller, *Gabrielle* is a serious political satire. More than ever before I was conscious, as I wrote, of an earlier work as an ideal model: Voltaire's *Candide.* The immediate provocation for the novel was the misguided and complacent attitude of the State Department toward Latin America.

The Hotel in the Jungle is laid in 1870, 1922, and 1982, with two characters appearing in both 1870 and 1922 and two appearing in both 1922 and 1982. The setting is a resort hotel located in Santa Rosalia, an isolated Indian village in southern Mexico. The novel is based on the premise that the filibuster William Walker might not have been executed after his loss of Nicaragua and on the hypothesis that the poet Mina Loy, looking for her disappeared husband the poet-boxer Arthur Cravan, might have come to Santa Rosalia at the same time as the former heavyweight champion Jack Johnson. Cravan had fought Johnson in Barcelona and hoped to enlist Johnson in a boxing academy in Mexico. In 1982 a woman scholar, bemused by the disappearance of one major character in 1922 and another in 1982, comes to Santa Rosalia to investigate the ambiguous past. The final owner of the hotel was Cyrus Cranfield, an entrepreneur who resembles in some ways Howard Hughes.

*　　*　　*

Albert Guerard's seven novels, published over a period of nearly 50 years, have shown a steady progression in technique and a constant reconsideration of theme. Nearly all his novels represent a controlled madness, a largely successful attempt to valorize political/psychological issues in a modern world where the center cannot hold. Guerard concentrates on intense moments of introspective terror and possibility for brooding protagonists trapped in futile or apocalyptic situations. The subjects of his major works of literary criticism—Hardy, Conrad, Gide, Dickens, Dostoevsky, Faulkner—and his admiration for the macabre humor and sexual fantasies of anti-realists liked Joyce, Kafka, Nabokov, Hawkes, Pynchon, Barthelme lead Guerard to a kind of fiction that refuses linear narration and embraces time distortion, untrustworthy observers, and ambiguous relationships. Dangerously close to the critical praise gained by the academic novelist, with its ensuing commercial failure, Guerard has never wavered from his commitment to the novel as complex experiment. As he states in *The Triumph of the Novel,* the effects he seeks are inventive fantasy, intuitive psychology, solitary obsessions, and political trauma.

Guerard's first novel, *The Past Must Alter,* deals with his major theme, a young man fascinated by his abortive desire for a beautiful older woman and bothered by an implausible relationship with a shadowy father. Drives to gamble and to test himself obsess and threaten the youth. *The Hunted* takes a more traditional fictional approach—the story of a waitress who marries an arrogant college instructor, of her increasing disillusion with his weakness and growing awareness of her own strength. *The Hunted* has a special quality that comes not from this anti-love story, nor from the New England rural college setting, but from a near-Faulknerian treatment of a violent flood and of a hunt for a doomed mythomaniac, the Bomber, who awakens the aggressions of the truly lost "normal" inhabitants and releases the female protagonist. Equally familiar in form is *Maquisard.* Subtitled, deliberately, "A Christmas Tale"—and Guerard's most commercial novel—the short book deals with a group of maquis and an American officer during the last months of World War II. Brilliantly compressed, coming close to but ultimately avoiding sentimentality, the novel is Guerard's most positive statement: the personal comradeship, solidarity, and dedication to a cause formed in combat allow the characters to act out their loyalties and sacrifices as well as to discover emotional and political possibilities that can sustain them in the postwar world. The book is warm, dramatic, lyrical.

In *Night Journey* Guerard creates this postwar world as a surreal one that joins varieties of betrayals. Paul Haldan (even the name echoes Conrad) betrays—deserts, literally—his superior officer in a move that re-enacts Haldan's guilt towards his father's death. Even darker themes of sexual betrayals by a form of projected rape and political betrayal by a military maneuver that alternately liberates and abandons a city qualify *Night Journey* as a work of inward and outer deception and destruction. Certainly Guerard's most imaginative and ambitious book, this novel is intelligent, probing, and yet, like many works of the psycho-political genre, ultimately lacking in human vitality. The madness is too controlled; the passion is too spent.

The Bystander concentrates on personal relations. Anthony, a young man in France, pursues the actress subject of his adolescent dreams. Poor and self-destructive, Anthony does attain his erotic desires, only to discover in Christiane a fundamental pragmatist who can reject passion for financial support from an older man. The book circles back on itself and is as much about loss as about gain. Tormented, sensual, self-lacerating, this anti-hero remains one of Guerard's most fascinating psychological portraits. *The Exiles* returns to the Conrad-Greene political arena that Guerard is drawn to as powerfully as to the psychological realm. (Indeed, sections of two unpublished political novels have appeared during the past decade in magazines; *Suspended Sentence,* which concerns an aging middle-European political exile, and *Still Talking,* a post-holocaust vision of wandering armies across a destroyed landscape.) Guerard's most comic effort, *The Exiles* satirizes Central American political refugees and their hangers-on and sympathetically presents a comic/tragic secret agent who combines absolute loyalty to a dictator and emotional commitment to a dissident, quasi-revolutionary poet. The comedy of Manuel Andrada's maneuverings in Boston is effective; the tragedy of his self-immolation in his beloved homeland is moving. Guerard's use of an objective, rather colorless narrator, however, mutes both the laughter and terror.

Constantly dedicated to the writing of fiction despite his careers as professor and critic. Guerard finally achieves his aim of defini-

tively catching his fascination with his earliest subject—the love of an innocent young man for a more experienced lovely actress . . . only for Charles Strickland the actress is in reality his lost mother, and the novel *Christine/Annette* is at once a rewriting of the past and an acceptance of the present. The book is indeed a triumph, easily Guerard's finest. He is lyrical and humorous, wistful and historical, tough-minded and sensitive. Part detective story, part family romance, part *bildungsroman,* part American and European social history, *Christine/Annette* is largely about the mystery of identity. The search for the mother, in all its Freudian and Jungian potentials, takes place in the real, richly evoked worlds of Paris and Berlin, Houston and Los Angeles. The narration is equally sure and varied—autobiography, movie script, objective frame, letters—and the film trope superbly sustained. The novel displays a confidence that comes from years of successful writing, certainly, but the special quality of this 1985 work is its freshness, its variety, its flexibility, its combination of an open, experimental structure, an authentic voice, and a traditional theme of loss, search, and discovery. Like Shakespeare's *The Tempest* or Faulkner's *The Reivers,* Guerard's novel of his mature years recapitulates his earlier concepts and techniques. The book provides as well a sparkle and energy, an argument with himself rather than with others that in Yeats's formulation leads not to political rhetoric but to lyrical achievement.

—Eric Solomon

GUNESEKERA, Romesh

Nationality: British (originally Sri Lankan, immigrated to England).

PUBLICATIONS

Novel

Reef. London, Granta, 1994; New York, New Press, 1995.

Short Stories

Monkfish Moon. New Delhi, Penguin, London, Granta, and New York, New Press, 1992.

*   *   *

Romesh Gunesekera belongs to an increasingly important strand of British and American fiction—that written by immigrants haunted by their mother country, often inspired by it while harboring ambivalent feelings—a strand that has produced major novelists such as V.S. Naipaul, Salman Rushdie, and Isaac Bashevis Singer. Gunesekera's first book, *Monkfish Moon* is a collection of nine stories, drawing on both Sri Lanka where he grew up, and England where he has settled down, and he forms a kind of uneasy bridge between them. The volume is slim, but each story is distinct in spite of a common motif of refurbishing dilapidated interiors and of building crisscrosses with an ironic theme of severance, parting, fracture, and failure. The context is Sri Lanka's contemporary history and "history is not a simple matter," one of the characters reminds us. Its most striking feature is violence created by the Tamil terrorist group, the Liberation Tigers of Tamil Eelam in the North and East, and by the now-suppressed Sinhala group, the Janata Vimukti Peramuna or People's Liberation Front in the South. Gunesekera does not confront the violence but allows it to enter his stories obliquely. He shows it as harming personal life and personal relations and as having altered the paradisal image of Sri Lanka of the past. In "A House in the Country," it is the Southern insurgency that sunders the developing relationship between the master, newly returned from England, and the servant. It is the Northern insurrection that separates the Tamil husband and Sinhala wife (as the former surrenders to racist feelings) in "Batik." It ruins the Sinhala clerk's dreams and ambitions in regard to returning to the mother country in "Storm Petrel". All of these stories are set in London: the turbulence at home crosses the seas and injures the expatriates.

Gunesekera's stories are finely tuned. His language is apparently simple, yet tactile and precise. Except for "Batik," which has a happy conclusion (the husband and wife are reconciled), the stories are open-ended, closing on a note of irresolution or fracture, and they generate melancholy, a condition characteristic of the exile, but one shared by those at home at the present time. Probably, the title—a note informs the reader that monkfish are not found in the ocean around Sri Lanka—is meant to express Gunesekera's view that: "Sri Lanka is a place where the mythic is very strong." Salman Rushdie considers Gunesekera's book as giving "notice of a fine writer in the making."

Reef confirms Rushdie's opinion regarding Gunesekera's promise, though the writer is still in the making. The novel too is set in Sri Lanka during its recent restive history, and the violence does enter the story, yet it is marginal. Here it is confined to brief references in the main and not woven into the story except at the end. It is always presented as reportage or reported, and the novel does not convey a sense of history (certainly not for Sri Lankans who have lived through it, though reviewers in the West and Gunesekera himself gave it prominence in the press). The strength of the novel lies in its treatment of individual lives and personal relations and in his characteristic use of language. The growth of its hero-narrator, Triton, is the center of interest. Named appropriately after a minor Greek sea-god, it is the household of a marine biologist, Mister Salgado, that he enters as a servant. After his immediate superior, Joseph (whom he hated justifiably), is sacked and the cook, Lucy, retires to her village, he remains as the sole factotum. Triton is given to cooking as the expression of his creativity, and his culinary delights described by Gunesekera with tastebud-titillating exactitude. Triton is aware at the beginning that his "head was like a balloon that had only a few puffs of air in it," but he is content to make Salgado his whole world. One of Gunesekera's original titles for the novel was *His Master's Voice,* and yet Triton does develop an individuality and identity. After Salgado moves to England, he finally is able to break with Salgado, though Triton is still limited by his only skill to a position as the owner of a small snack bar.

Salgado too changes and his story too is important. At the beginning an idle-rich, theorizing proto-environmentalist, he later involves himself in a government project to save the coral reef in the South. But he is drawn away from it when he falls hopelessly in love with Miss Nili, and they adopt the lifestyle of urban socialites. Nili's entrance into the household generates an element of sociosexual tension in Triton, but it is submerged under his role as servant. Eventually, after a late-night slanging match wherein Salgado accuses Nili of infidelity, they part. Salgado leaves for England, but decides to return to Sri Lanka to seek his old lover when

he learns that she had suffered during the early 1980s troubles. Gunesekera is arguably one of the top twenty young British novelists.

—D.C.R.A. Goonetilleke

GURGANIS, Allan

Nationality: American. **Born:** Rocky Mount, North Carolina, 11 June 1947. **Education:** Rocky Mount Senior High, 1965; Philadelphia Academy of Fine Arts, 1965-66; Sarah Lawrence College, Bronxville, New York, 1970-72. **Military Service:** United States Navy, 1966-70. **Career:** Desk clerk and salesperson of art reproductions, 1969-70; night watchman in a vitamin factory, 1970-72; professor of fiction writing, University of Iowa, Iowa City, 1972-74, Stanford University, Stanford, California, 1974-76, Duke University, Durham, North Carolina, 1976-78, Sarah Lawrence College, Bronxville, New York, 1978-86, and University of Iowa Writers' Workshop, 1989-90. Artist, with paintings in many private and public collections. Member of board, Corporation of Yaddo; cofounder, "Writers for Harvey Gantt." **Awards:** Jones lecturer, Stanford University; PEN prizes for fiction; National Endowment for the Arts grants; Ingram Merrill award; Wallace Stegner fellowship. **Agent:** c/o International Creative Management, 40 West 57th Street, New York, New York 10019, U.S.A.

PUBLICATIONS

Novel

Oldest Living Confederate Widow Tells All. New York, Knopf, and London, Faber, 1989.

Short Stories

Good Help, with illustrations by the author. Rocky Mount, North Carolina Wesleyan College Press, 1988.
Blessed Assurance: A Moral Tale (novella). Rocky Mount, North Carolina Wesleyan College Press, 1990.
White People: Stories and Novellas. New York, Knopf, and London, Faber, 1991.
The Practical Heart. Rocky Mount, North Carolina Wesleyan College Press, 1993.

*

Critical Study: "Black and Blue and Gray: An Interview with Allan Gurganis" by Jeffrey Scheuer, in *Poets and Wrtiers,* November-December 1990.

*　　*　　*

Allan Gurganus is an old-fashioned storyteller. The stories he tells are multi-layered and contain strong, varied voices. While both his novel, *Oldest Living Confederate Widow Tells All,* and his short story collection, *White People,* are set primarily in the South, he should not be considered a "Southern Writer" solely. In American literature, the oral tradition that feeds his ability with voice and character is strongly associated with that region, but Gurganus covers territory that is all-American by bringing uniquely American questions to light, all somehow having to do with how Americans perceive themselves.

In *Oldest Living Confederate Widow Tells All,* a 99-year-old woman named Lucy Marsden relates stories that take place during more than a century of time, from the beginnings of the Civil War to the 1980s. At the time of its publication, some critics were happy to see, in light of recent literary trends toward the abstract, the minimal, and the eccentric, the emergence of such a "big" story; others considered the premise unequal to the task of carrying such a sizeable narrative. Lucy tells stories of her life and the life of her Civil War veteran husband, whom she had married when she was 15. She regales us with tales of his experiences before she was even born, becoming her husband's voice. Indeed, she even takes on the voice of his one-time slave, Castalia, as well as many others. This multiple-narrator role makes her at once story and storyteller, participant and omniscient observer. While this raises interesting questions about narrative authority, it also presents a fascinating experience for the perceptive reader, for there is also the author to consider. Through Lucy, he has entered and presented male and female lives, historical lives, young and old lives, warrior lives—American lives that embrace and reflect more than one American epoch, more than one American region.

In addition to all of this, there is more than the Civil War being fought here, although many issues from the other battles contained in the book are related to that war between the states. Sex, race, class, age—all those words which so efficiently assume the -ism suffix—are concepts in conflict within the novel. Gurganus has much to say about it all. However, at the core of the novel's resolution is forgiveness and the hope it can bring. Because of this, the comparison to at least one other Southern writer may come quickly to mind, for Flannery O'Connor's famous "Moment of Grace" resembles the theme closely. There is also Gurganus's sense of humor to tempt us into such a comparison. But it is his use of voice which makes the humor effective, the theme accessible. The author has quite an ear and quite an imagination, and it is his accuracy with the female voice that is most impressive.

Gurganus has said that he chose Lucy as narrator for this novel because he wanted a new version/vision of history that had not before been solicited: that of a female who was neither rich nor beautiful. He is successful in this; but in Castalia, the former Marsden slave, he is successful in giving us the vision of a female who was neither rich nor beautiful (in a white man's world) nor white. The Captain himself is not a particularly likeable character; still, he too has his sympathetic side and his own particularly strong

voice. But again—we hear this voice only through Lucy and, thus, must be cautious about what we conclude from it.

It is a long book; and the plot, although guided by chronology, is not strictly linear in its construction. There are many side roads taken, even to Africa during the slave trade. Although necessary to the theme of his/her-story that the author is illuminating, this technique is often cited as the weakness of the book. But for those who enjoy an old-fashioned story treated with respect in the telling, *Oldest Living Confederate Widow Tells All* lives up to the promise of its title. It is rather like sitting around the kitchen table listening to previous generations tell what they know about family members and small town denizens in anecdotal but wise and witty tones. What could be more American?

In *White People,* Gurganus's collection of short stories and novellas, we are given just such an image in the opening passages of "A Hog Loves Its Life." The boy Willie and his grandfather, "hiding" from the other relatives, are forced into a "story-hour" by Willie's ignorance of local lore. The story of this novella, and the story within the story, are fine examples of what a writer can do with a talent for voice. The ritual engaged in by these two characters is related in tones of solemnity balanced by humor. It is important to the participants, and to the reader, that each understands the significance of what is being told at both levels—that of the grandfather telling the tale and the boy/man retelling it. As with *Oldest Living Confederate Widow Tells All,* the narrator is both story and storyteller. Gurganus's narrative constructions resemble the double helix of DNA: simultaneously, and deceptively, simple and complex.

Embedded in the themes weaving through the various tales of the collection is a penetrating look at what the passage of time and the losses it naturally brings, can mean to our individual sense of hope and forgiveness. One of the most often mentioned and poignant of the stories is "Blessed Assurance," the final novella of the collection. In telling the story of an aging, Southern, white man looking back on his days as a college student who sold funeral insurance to poor blacks in the late 1940s, Gurganus requires that the reader look carefully at the loss of youthful innocence and naiveté, the use of exploitation in race relations, the burden of guilt—and the absurdity of all these things. For that sense of humor is here, too, at the base of this and the other tales.

The author seems to possess a core belief in the terrible beauty of daily survival; and this belief transcends geography, gender, age, race, and sexual orientation. In this way, Gurganus contributes to contemporary American literature while retaining an old-fashioned faith in, and a sizeable talent for, the telling of the tale.

—Maggi R. Sullivan

H

HAILEY, Arthur

Nationality: British and Canadian. **Born:** Luton, Bedfordshire, 5 April 1920; emigrated to Canada in 1947: became citizen, 1952. **Education:** Elementary schools in England. **Military Service:** Served as a pilot in the Royal Air Force, 1939-47: Flight Lieutenant. **Family:** Married 1) Joan Fishwick in 1944 (divorced 1950), three sons; 2) Sheila Dunlop in 1951, one son and two daughters. **Career:** Office boy and clerk, London, 1934-39; assistant editor, 1947-49, and editor, 1949-53, *Bus and Truck Transport,* Toronto; sales promotion manager, Trailmobile Canada, Toronto, 1953-56. Since 1956 freelance writer. **Awards:** Canadian Council of Authors and Artists award, 1956; Best Canadian TV Playwright award, 1957, 1958; Doubleday Prize Novel award, 1962. **Address:** Lyford Cay, P.O. Box N. 7776, Nassau, Bahamas.

PUBLICATIONS

Novels

Flight into Danger, with John Castle. London, Souvenir Press, 1958; as *Runway Zero-Eight,* New York, Doubleday, 1959.
The Final Diagnosis. New York, Doubleday, 1959; London, Joseph-Souvenir Press, 1960; as *The Young Doctors,* London, Corgi, 1962.
In High Places. New York, Doubleday, and London, Joseph-Souvenir Press, 1962.
Hotel. New York, Doubleday, and London, Joseph-Souvenir Press, 1965.
Airport. New York, Doubleday, and London, Joseph-Souvenir Press, 1968.
Wheels. New York, Doubleday, and London, Joseph-Souvenir Press, 1971.
The Moneychangers. New York, Doubleday, and London, Joseph-Souvenir Press, 1975.
Overload. New York, Doubleday, and London, Joseph-Souvenir Press, 1979.
Strong Medicine. New York, Doubleday, and London Joseph-Souvenir Press, 1984.
The Evening News. New York, Doubleday, and London, Doubleday-Souvenir Press, 1990.

Plays

Flight into Danger (televised 1956). Published in *Four Plays of Our Time,* London, Macmillan, 1960.
Close-up on Writing for Television. New York, Doubleday, 1960.

Screenplays: *Zero Hour,* with Hall Bartlett and John Champion, 1958; *The Moneychangers,* 1976; *Wheels,* 1978.

Television Plays: *Flight into Danger,* 1956 (USA); *Time Lock* 1962 (UK); *Course for Collision,* 1962 (UK); and plays for *Westinghouse Studio One, Playhouse 90, U.S. Steel Hour, Goodyear-Philco Playhouse,* and *Kraft Theatre* (USA).

*

Critical Studies: *I Married a Best Seller* by Sheila Hailey, New York, Doubleday, and London, Joseph-Souvenir Press, 1978.

Arthur Hailey comments:

My novels are the end product of my work and are widely available. Therefore I see no reason to be analytical about them.

Each novel takes me, usually, three years: a year of continuous research, six months of detailed planning, then a year and a half of steady writing, with many revisions.

My only other comment is that my novels are the work of one who seeks principally to be a storyteller but reflect also, I hope, the excitement of living here and now.

* * *

Arthur Hailey has developed and virtually perfected a highly efficient and extremely successful (and profitable) process of novel writing. Whether he is writing about doctors (*The Final Diagnosis, Strong Medicine*) or airline pilots (*Flight into Danger*), hotels (*Hotel*) or airports (*Airport*), government (*In High Places*) or industry (*Wheels*), he follows the same formula. Each of his novels is filled with enough information about the subject of his exhaustive research to satisfy the most curious reader; there are enough character types to appeal to the widest possible audience; everything is interwoven into a complex web of plots and sub-plots to satisfy every reader's desire for a good, suspenseful story.

Hailey writes documentary fiction, or what has been called "faction," that is, a mixture of the real and the fictitious. After spending a year of research for each novel, Hailey is prepared to give his reader as much factual information as he can work into the novel. Consequently, only his characters and situations are imaginary, and they are sometimes only slightly fictitious.

To speak of any Hailey novel is to speak of every Hailey novel for there is little to distinguish one from the rest except subject matter. Each novel shares the same characteristic strengths and weaknesses. *Airport* is a typical example. The action of the novel is centered at a fictitious Chicago airport during one of the worst blizzards in the city's history. To give his reader an inside look at the operations of a major airport and into the lives of the people responsible for its existence, Hailey devises several plots; an airliner is stuck in the snow, blocking a runway and causing emergency situations in the air; an air-traffic controller is planning suicide; a trans-Atlantic airliner is about to take off with a bomb aboard; a stewardess has discovered she is pregnant; a group of local citizens is demonstrating against the excessive noise of the airport. The novel follows each plot to its conclusion, but not before the reader's intellectual curiosity about airports and his emotional curiosity about the characters are satisfied.

The narrative is slick and fast-moving, the information is interesting, the prose is readable, but the seams in Hailey's fabric too often show through. In order to introduce all his researched information into the novel, he is frequently forced to construct irrelevant sub-plots or to break the flow of the narrative for a lecture on such things as the safety records of commercial airlines or the pressures suffered by air-traffic controllers. To manage all his characters, he is forced into a "holding pattern" of his own. The focus of the novel shifts from one character to another as Hailey abandons characters temporarily only to return to them later when their number in the rotation comes up again. Consequently what unity there is in the book is provided only by the subject matter. The characters themselves are paper thin, reduced to simple dimensions; they are so typical that they could be interchanged from one novel to the next with little difficulty.

Wheels is much like *Airport* in its intention and its execution. The main difference is its lack of dramatic suspense; there is less drama to be derived from the introduction of a new car, the primary plot device in the novel, than from the naturally more exciting subjects of the earlier novels.

Hailey is a good popular novelist. He has learned what his audience expects and his audience knows what to expect from him; the reciprocal arrangement ought to ensure a continuing place for Hailey's novels on the bestseller lists for years to come.

—David Geherin

HALEY, Russell

Nationality: New Zealander (originally English: immigrated to Australia, 1961, then to New Zealand, 1966). **Born:** Dewsbury, England, 1934. **Education:** University of Auckland, M.A. in English, 1970. **Address:** c/o Viking Penguin, 375 Hudson St., New York, New York 10014, U.S.A.

PUBLICATIONS

Novels

The Settlement. Auckland and London, Hodder and Stoughton, 1986.
Beside Myself. Auckland and New York, Penguin, 1990.

Short Stories

The Sauna Bath Mysteries and Other Stories. Auckland, Mandrake Root, 1978.
Real Illusions: A Selection of Family Lies and Biographical Fictions in Which the Ancestral Dead Also Play Their Part. Wellington, Victoria University Press, 1984; New York, New Directions, 1985.
The Transfer Station. N.p., 1989.

Poetry

The Walled Garden. Auckland, Mandrake Root, 1972.
On the Fault Line and Other Poems. Paraparaumu, New Zealand, Hawk Press, 1977.

Other

Hanly: A New Zealand Artist. Auckland, Hodder and Stoughton, 1989.

Editor, with Susan Davis, *The Penguin Book of Contemporary New Zealand Short Stories.* Auckland and New York, Penguin, 1989.

*   *   *

The Sauna Bath Mysteries and Other Stories established Russell Haley's reputation as a pioneering writer of postmodernist experimental fiction with affinities with writers such as Nabakov, Beckett, John Barth, Robert Coover, and Thomas Pynchon. This has been confirmed in the achievement of his two novels, *The Settlement* and *Beside Myself,* and the series of interlinked stories that are collected in *The Transfer Station.* These extend the narrative strategies of his short stories, such as the classic "Barbados—A Love Story," into ambitious performances in which he collapses the boundaries between fiction and reality, overlapping dream, memory, and experience and undermining epistemological certainties. Such metafictional constructions do more than challenge the reader's ingenuity. Haley, who came to New Zealand from England in the 1960s, has masterminded the characteristic dilemmas of the hero who is displaced due to "migratio" and whose extreme self-consciousness as subject and paranoid distrust of the world transforms a condition of existential disease into an absurdist vision of life.

The Settlement, partly inspired by public conflict over the Springbok tour of New Zealand in 1981, leaves the reader with minimalized certainties. In The Settlement at Moorfields, identified first as a convalescent home and later as a mental asylum, in which the middle-aged hero, Walter Lemanby, finds himself after falling from his roof, images of menacing control abound—mysterious installations, searchlights, helicopters, curfews, nameless uniformed assailants. They point either to civil unrest or to the existence of a centralized, totalitarian state that represses the individual; they are reinforced in the plot in the sinister, masked figure of Dr. Grimshaw. Yet Haley draws attention to the fictionality of his omniscient hero by creating a narrative break after 50 pages in an italicized passage, implying that he is the "secret collaborator within this text" who "threw the stone" by creating its circumstances, and then he starts over again. This authorial self-consciousness is reminiscent of the challenge issued to the reader in "Barbados—A Love Story" as to who should throw the first stone, call the narrator's bluff, and so undermine the fictionality of his creation.

Haley's foregrounding of the process of writing through metafictional games that stress the artifice of illusion and the fictional nature of subjectivity, however, rarely lapses into linguistic solipsism. His narratorial self-consciousness is both artful and endearing. Walter's struggles to familiarize himself with an alien world, to reorder experience by labeling his landscape, are intensely personal if not moving. In *Beside Myself,* a sequence of unsettling experiences destabilize the hero's attempts to impose order on his life: A heady sexual encounter with a woman he meets at a party, followed by the revelation of his best friend's death, lead to comical yet painful struggles to understand himself. In these works lyrical moments appear sporadically, creating sudden shifts of tone.

In his more recent writing Haley gestures nostalgically toward values of longing, loss, and love. The nine linked stories in *The Transfer Station,* an extended meditation on the meaning of death, represent the aging protagonist's bereavement at the death of his wife. The nearby Transfer Station, a rubbish dump on the outskirts of Auckland that chews up detritus and waste, has a unifying function as a symbol of death in its most dehumanized form as a sought-after memorable extinction of life. This is articulated by the two teenage girls whom the narrator befriends briefly and whose memory becomes a preoccupation until he is able to reaffirm the value of his own life. Cumulatively these stories convey the impression of a mind in a state of psychological dislocation recovering its mental balance. The customary zaniness and humor of Haley's heroes, although functioning near the surface of the text, are partly displaced into the girls' vision of life as brief, juvenile, yet imaginatively enduring.

Just as patterns of displacement characterize Haley's fiction, so too does the antilinear, multidirectional narrative and an insistence on the fragmented and uncertainly known nature of reality as conveyed through language. In his novels and in stories such as "Looping the Loop," 'Barbados—A Love Story," or "The Balkan Transformer," he uses fantasy, dream transformations, and the uncertainties of memory to present events as occurring in the context of the multiple possibilities of the narrator's mind. Yet he insists equally on the physical presence of the body—its inevitable habits of defecation, erection, eating, and sleeping—as a point of entry into the often comical collusion between his narrators' self-conscious subjectivity and the constraints imposed by physical existence.

Haley's innovative humor is most immediately accessible in his short stories, whereas his two novels explore more fully the tragicomic conditions of existential angst leading to an absurdist worldview; at his best he has produced some of the liveliest, most engaging postmodern fiction yet to have been written in New Zealand.

—Janet Wilson

HALL, James B(yron)

Nationality: American. **Born:** Midland, Ohio, 21 July 1918. **Education:** Miami University, Oxford, Ohio, 1938-39; University of Hawaii, Honolulu, 1938-40; University of Iowa, Iowa City, B.A. 1947, M.A. 1948, Ph.D. 1953; Kenyon College, Gambier, Ohio, 1949. **Military Service:** United States Army, 1941-46. **Family:** Married Elizabeth Cushman in 1946; five children. **Career:** Writer-in-residence, Miami University, 1948-49; instructor, Cornell University, Ithaca, New York, 1952-53; writer-in-residence, University of North Carolina, Greensville, 1954; assistant professor, 1954-57, associate professor, 1958-60, and professor of English, 1960-65, University of Oregon, Eugene; director of the Writing Center, and professor of English, University of California, Irvine, 1965-68. Since 1968, professor of literature, and Provost of College V. University of California, Santa Cruz. Writer-in-residence, University of British Columbia, Vancouver, Summer 1956; guest artist, Pacific Coast Festival of Art, Reed College, Portland, 1958; writer-in-residence, University of Colorado, Boulder, 1963. Co-founding editor, *Northwest Review*, Eugene, Oregon, 1957-60; founder and director, University of Oregon Summer Academy of Contemporary Arts, Eugene, 1959-64. Editorial consultant, Doubleday and Company, publishers (West Coast staff), 1960; cultural specialist, United States Department of State, Washington, 1964. **Awards:** Octave Thanet prize, 1950; Yaddo grant, 1952; Oregon Poetry prize, 1958; Chapelbrook fellowship, 1967; Institute of Creative Arts fellowship, 1967; Balch Fiction prize, 1967. **Address:** 1080 Patterson #901; Eugene, Oregon 97401, U.S.A.

PUBLICATIONS

Novels

Not by the Door. New York, Random House, 1954.
TNT for Two. New York, Ace, 1956.

Racers to the Sun. New York, Obolensky, 1960; London, Corgi, 1962.
Mayo Sergeant. New York, New American Library, 1967.

Short Stories

15 x 3, with Herbert Gold and R.V. Cassill. New York, New Directions, 1957.
Us He Devours. New York, New Directions, 1964.
The Short Hall: New and Collected Stories. Athens, Ohio University Press, 1980.
I Like It Better Now. Fayetteville, University of Arkansas Press, 1992.

Poetry

The Hunt Within. Baton Rouge, Louisiana State University Press, 1973.
Bereavements. Brownsville, Oregon, Story Line Press, 1991.

Other

The Art and Craft of the Short Story. N.p., 1995.

Editor, with Joseph Langland, *The Short Story.* New York, Macmillan, 1956.
Editor, *The Realm of Fiction: 61 Short Stories.* New York, McGraw Hill, 1965; revised edition, 1970, 1977.
Editor, with Barry Ulanov, *Modern Culture and the Arts.* New York, McGraw Hill, 1967; revised edition, 1972.
Editor, *John Barleycorn: Alcoholic Memoirs,* by Jack London. Santa Cruz, California, Western Tanager Press, 1981.
Editor, with Hotchkiss and Shears, *Perspectives on William Everson.* Blackfoot, Idaho, Castle Peak Editions, 1992.

*

James B. Hall comments:

Although the novels are interesting, the central significance of the work resides largely in the short stories; the poetry is various, and by intention ancillary to the prose.

The novels, short stories, and poetry are thematically interrelated. The reccurring motifs are the effects of competition on individuals in a system of modified capitalism such as obtains in the United States. Thus acquisitive, frustrated, evasive protagonists reccur, some of them mad or nearly so. Extreme conduct in a hostile world is not infrequent; the adjustments which protagonists make vary from callous acceptance or the exploitation of others to withdrawal, revenge, and self-destruction. In general, the work shows the difficulty of remaining human in a competitive, non-Darwinian world fashioned in large part by a democratic society. Specifically, *Racers to the Sun* traces the "rise" and fall of a motorcycle racer who builds his own machine; the hero is injured (used up), and then is dropped by those who exploited his talent for machinery and speed. Likewise, in the typical short stories, "Us He Devours" and "The Claims Artist," the protagonists are in some ways laudable, but in the end are victims of their own and of society's demands. A typical poem, "Pay Day Night," treats the counterproductive nature of experience in another bureaucracy, the Army.

The short stories are experimental, highly compressed, and exploit language poetically for artistic effect. They are condensed statements that very often extend the possibilities of the genre. Many of the stories are anthologized; because they are complex they apparently "teach well" in classrooms.

(1995) Increasingly the short forms of imaginative writing claim most of my attention: the short story, poetry, nonfiction articles. This comes as no surprise for increasingly the literary artist under (finance) capitalism has the obligation to justify corporate investment, and the long forms, such as the novel, presently require greater sponsorship by the publisher and more author-time dedicated to promotion(s) of the work. This drift has evident impact on modernist (and post-modernist) work and is suggested merely as ways the writer's "work place" has changed in the past twenty years. No practicing writer may claim exemption therefrom; nevertheless, work of high literary quality does get written, published, and read. The new writer, I think, faces the greatest challenges for, among other things, the institutions which once offered some order of literary apprenticeship now offer too early specialization from which there seems no rise and no return.

*   *   *

James B. Hall is of that generation of writers who hit the beaches of American literature following World War II. Like Mailer and Vonnegut, Hall is a veteran. Unlike them, however, he did not write a war novel and get a literary Purple Heart. His medals are yet in the drawer. Along with having grown up on a farm, his military experiences are significant to an understanding of his social vision, and to the imagery and tropes in many of the short stories, especially "The Snow Hunter," "The Rumor of Metal," and "The War in the Forest," (in *I Like It Better Now*).

The three stories mentioned above are also typical of the way Hall works. They are compressed and complex, very close to poetry. The imagery is both precise and evocative; scenic and narrative paragraphs are modulated; the swift and brief dialogue often in counterpoint to the description elements. Character in Hall's stories and novels develops within a particular phenomenological environment. In other words, character is what character does in the world.

Here is a passage from Hall's second novel, *Racers to the Sun*. Though of course he doesn't know it, Harold "Speedy" Hill is about to enter his last race. The way that Speedy sees the arriving motorcycles is at the same time beautiful and threatening:

> Delicate, the red, black, and sun-burst orange racing machines reared imperceptibly as their trailers stopped. They were vicious and lovely, imperious and chaste in orange or bone-white paint, the waspish handle bars curved downward over the front wheels, the magnetoes humped, fetal-like, in the coarse belly of the engine.

In *Not by the Door*, Hall has already discovered how to use scene to flesh out character. The Reverend Howard Marcham, an Episcopal minister in his first pastorate, has gotten himself into somewhat of a moral pickle. He decides to take a drive in the country, parks his car and goes for a walk. He comes upon a water moccasin sleeping on a willow branch. The snake has recently shed its skin. Hall makes the most of the biblical and mythological reference to sin, evil and rebirth. But he does it subtly, by scenic description. As a reader one "gets it" as an after-image. By this method of writing, Hall is very much a poet. The prose fiction is as burnished as a Spenserian stanza. In Hall's case, the genre boundaries

among lyric, short story, and novel dissolve, and this in particular makes him a singular voice in contemporary fiction.

The Reverend Marcham is also typical of many of Hall's male characters. Very often the personae suggest some aspect of the author as self-critical. Unlike Hall, brought up Methodist, Howard Marcham is already a notch up, because he is an Episcopalian. Hall's protagonists fight to get ahead in the social world: fight for control of a motorcycle, a race, a yacht, a woman, real estate, or money; attempt to put a rein on personal anarchy but often end up in self-destruction. Howard Marcham is a pastor without spiritual depth, and he lacks a feeling for community. The reverend also prefigures *Mayo Sergeant*, an even emptier and more venal person.

We get to the last novel, with its much darker and sardonic social canvas, by way of *Racers to the Sun*. It is in the second novel that Hall begins to strike the note of class conflict and of the brutal nature of capitalism. Harold "Speedy" Hill and his boss, Jeffcoat, at the novel's beginning, are two of Hall's most sympathetic male characters. The author's rural upbringing, and his stint as a labor officer on the German docks during the occupation, are obviously influences on his social point of view. Hall favors the rural and urban working classes, those who try to make an honest living with their hands. No other prose writer writes so lovingly of tools and machinery as Hall in *Racers to the Sun*.

Generally, the female characters in his fiction come off better than the males. Lucern "Gunner" Greener in the racing novel is an exception. The daughter of a motorcycle agency owner, she gives herself to the winners. As soon as Hill is injured, she leaves him flat out. Gunner is a sexual metaphor for a system that uses people for its own needs and then dumps them. The motorcycle agency and the racing track owners drop the hero, too, when they can no longer profit from his status as a winner.

Whereas the system uses Speedy Hill, Mayo Sergeant uses women and the sleight-of-hand world of real estate as he glad-hands and charms and screws his way up the social ladder in Cutlass Bay, until he moves into the Moorish house on the hill and takes part possession of the racing yacht, *Indus*. The novel is narrated by Roberte "Bombie" Glouster, who lost his foot in the World War II. Glouster represents "old money" in Cutlass Bay, and is in love with the very wealthy Hildy Moorish himself. At first Roberte befriends Mayo, who arrives from nowhere; but then he is taken in by Mayo and cuckolded as well. There is something of both Gatsby and Willy Loman in Mayo Sergeant, but Hall's novel perhaps surpasses the other two works in its savage judgment of the way we live. Hall's vision is indeed Dantean here, Hall's own version of Hell. There is not one likeable character in *Mayo Sergeant*, either male or female. But the novel should be reissued, for it contains some of the finest prose in American fiction today. And if the portrait of America is an unlikeable one, that is Hall's very point.

— Bill Witherup

HALL, Rodney

Nationality: Australian. **Born:** Solihull, Warwickshire, England, 18 November 1935; immigrated to Australia during his childhood. **Education:** City of Bath Boys' School; Brisbane Boys' College; University of Queensland, Brisbane, B.A. 1971. **Family:** Married Maureen Elizabeth MacPhail in 1962; three daughters. **Career:**

Freelance scriptwriter and actor, 1957-67, and film critic, 1966-67, Australian Broadcasting Corporation, Brisbane. Tutor, New England University School of Music, Armidale, New South Wales, summers 1967-71 and 1977-80; youth officer, Australian Council for the Arts, 1971-73; lecturer in recorder, Canberra School of Music, 1979-83. Since 1962 advisory editor, *Overland* magazine, Melbourne; since 1967 poetry editor, *The Australian* daily newspaper, Sydney. Traveled in Europe, 1958-60, 1963-64, 1965, and the United States, 1974. Australian Department of Foreign Affairs Lecturer in India, 1970, 1981, Malaysia, 1972, 1980, and Europe, 1981, 1983, 1984. **Awards:** Australian National University Creative Arts fellowship, Canberra, 1968; Commonwealth Literary Fund fellowship, 1970; Literature Board fellowship, 1973, 1976, 1982, 1986, 1990; Grace Leven prize, 1974; Miles Franklin award, Australian Natives Association award, and Barbara Ramsden award, all 1982, all for *Just Relations;* Victorian Premier's literary award, 1989, for *Captivity Captive.* **Address:** c/o Penguin Books, P.O. Box 257, Ringwood, Victoria 3134, Australia.

PUBLICATIONS

Novels

The Ship on the Coin: A Fable of the Bourgeoisie. St. Lucia, University of Queensland Press, 1972.

A Place Among People. St. Lucia, University of Queensland Press, 1975.

Just Relations. Ringwood, Victoria, Penguin, 1982; London, Allen Lane, and New York, Viking Press, 1983.

Kisses of the Enemy. Ringwood, Victoria, Penguin, 1987; New York, Farrar Straus, 1988; London, Faber, 1989.

Just Relations. London and Boston, Faber, 1990.

A Dream More Luminous than Love: The Yandilli Trilogy. Sydney, Picador Australia, 1994; New York, Noonday Press, 1995.

Captivity Captive. Melbourne, McPhee Gribble, New York, Farrar Straus, and London, Faber, 1988.

The Second Bridegroom. Ringwood, Victoria, McPhee Gribble, and London, Faber, 1991.

The Grisly Wife. Sydney, Macmillan, and London, Faber, 1993.

Poetry

Penniless till Doomsday. London, Outposts, 1962.

Four Poets, with others. Melbourne, Cheshire, 1962.

Forty Beads on a Hangman's Rope: Fragments of Memory. Newnham, Tasmania, Wattle Grove Press, 1963.

Eyewitness. Sydney, South Head Press, 1967.

The Autobiography of a Gorgon. Melbourne, Cheshire, 1968.

The Law of Karma: A Progression of Poems. Canberra, Australian National University Press, 1968.

Heaven, In a Way. St. Lucia, University of Queensland Press, 1970.

A Soapbox Omnibus. St. Lucia, University of Queensland Press, 1973.

Selected Poems. St. Lucia, University of Queensland Press, 1975.

Black Bagatelles. St. Lucia, University of Queensland Press, 1978.

The Most Beautiful World: Fictions and Sermons. St. Lucia, University of Queensland Press, 1981.

Recording: *Romulus and Remus,* University of Queensland Press, 1971.

Other

Social Services and the Aborigines, with Shirley Andrews. Canberra, Federal Council for Aboriginal Advancement, 1963.

Focus on Andrew Sibley. Brisbane, University of Queensland Press, 1968.

J.S. Manifold: An Introduction to the Man and His Work. Brisbane, University of Queensland Press, 1978.

Australia, Image of a Nation, 1850-1950, with David Moore. Sydney, Collins, 1983.

Journey Through Australia. Richmond, Victoria, Heinemann, and London, Murray, 1989; as *Home, A Journey through Australia.* Port Melbourne, Minerva, 1990.

Editor, with Thomas W. Shapcott, *New Impulses in Australian Poetry.* Brisbane, University of Queensland Press, 1968.

Editor, *Australian Poetry 1970.* Sydney, Angus and Robertson, 1970.

Editor, *Poems from Prison.* Brisbane, University of Queensland Press, 1973.

Editor, *Australians Aware: Poems and Paintings.* Sydney, Ure Smith, 1975.

Editor, *Voyage into Solitude,* by Michael Dransfield. Brisbane, University of Queensland Press, 1978.

Editor, *The Second Month of Spring,* by Michael Dransfield. Brisbane, University of Queensland Press, 1980.

Editor, *The Collins Book of Australian Poetry.* Sydney, Collins, 1981; London, Collins, 1983.

Editor, *Collected Poems* by Michael Dransfield. St. Lucia, University of Queensland Press, 1987.

*   *   *

One of Australia's most prolific writers, Rodney Hall established his reputation first as a poet before turning to fiction. His early novelistic ventures were less than successful. *The Ship on the Coin* is a rather heavy-handed satire based on the "Creosus" travel agency, which rebuilds a quinquereme and invites customers to row their own ship for a holiday. The scheme is wildly successful but the allegory concerning voluntary subservience to the United States ("Buy your way into slavery now") seems somewhat dated today and the comedy is very broad. *A Place Among People* is a more sensitively written novel about a small town just out of Brisbane called Battery Spit. Set in the 1950s, a period where bigotries and conformist attitudes are skillfully conveyed, it concerns the nonconformist (intellectual, aboriginal) Collocott who is persecuted by the townspeople. The central incident involves the town's attempt to drive a black woman, Daisy Daisy, out of their midst and onto a reservation the blacks call Prison Island and Collocott's stubborn defiance of them in defense of her. However, it is relatively benign and even optimistic in many of its views. When it finally comes to the crunch only 11 of the townspeople actually turn up outside Collocott's house to force him to release Daisy, and others among them come unexpectedly to his aid. Many of the characters achieve minor victories over their own lesser instincts, and of the unorthodox hero Collocott the novel concludes, "He wavered on the brink of life." Occasional obscurities aside, *A Place Among People* is an intelligent and graceful novel.

Hall established his reputation, however, with his third novel, *Just Relations.* A long, complex, and sometimes overwritten book, it is set in the ironically named Whitey's Fall, a declining former

gold town peopled by a set of aging eccentrics, whose only religion is "Remembering." There is Felicia Brinsmead, a 73-year-old
spinster who has never had her hair cut so that it hangs over her
like a huge, dirty web and who believes that she is the mother of a
12-year-old boy, Fido. There is the narcissistic Mr. Ping, who willfully destroys his fading beauty. There is the spirit of Kel McAlon,
who has killed himself. In the local pub a group of people are sitting around drinking; they are aged between 80 and 114. Into this
community comes beautiful 34-year-old Vivien Lang, with whom
the teenager Billy Swan falls in love, to the scandal of some of the
town. To it also comes Senator Frank Halloran to inform the community that a highway is being built through to bring the town to
life. All but one of the 49 residents are outraged. Their creed is
summed up by Uncle, Billy's grandfather, who proudly lists the
examples of "progress" that he has opposed—hospital, old people's
home, police station, jail, school, highways, and the draft. Hall
seems to intend the community to be a paradigm of a dying Australia that he sees as infinitely superior to the current one. The book
is unnecessarily long and the writing often clumsy, particularly in
any of the scenes to do with sex: "Her fingers fluttered round him,
giant butterflies afraid to alight but fatally attracted by the honey
hidden in him." The presence of Patrick White is felt at times in the
deliberately dissonant rhythms of the prose, and there is a positive
smorgasbord of techniques brought to bear as the novel moves between past and present, employing all kinds of texts—diaries, newspaper reports, letters—to illuminate the theme. Nevertheless, the
conception is original and eventually the novel gains conviction,
particularly through the beautifully realized figures of the women
and its fine treatment of landscape.

In *Kisses of the Enemy,* Hall returns to political satire with a
novel set in the near future. Australia has become a republic under
the leadership of Bernard Buchanan, who represents the multinational Interim Freeholdings Incorporated of Delaware; Buchanan,
in fact, is really the front man for the company's Luigi Squarcia
and Australia is rapidly becoming the puppet state of the United
States. Hall manages to draw this parable out to over 600 pages,
but though the object of the satire is legitimate enough, the novel
rarely comes to life and the jokes are even more labored than in
The Ship on the Coin. For instance, Buchanan is very fat at the
start of the novel, with two men carrying him around; at the height
of his power the retinue has grown to eight and still later, when
his power begins to decline, he simultaneously begins to lose
weight. The very topicality of the satire ensures that the jokes become dated.

Just Relations apart, Hall's major novelistic achievement to date
is found in his three most recent novels, *Captivity Captive* (published 1988 but set in 1888), *The Second Bridegroom* (1991, 1836),
and *The Grisly Wife* (1993, 1898). Hall has finally drawn these
together as a trilogy under the title *A Dream More Luminous than
Love,* or the Yandilli trilogy. According to the author, the first volume grew out of the Gatton murders, the macabre killing of three
siblings in New South Wales in 1898. Then, according to an interview he gave, "Hall began working on an earlier setting and then
realized that, ideally, there should be an even earlier novel, introducing the theme of the white presence and—almost immutably—
that of the Aborigines." *The Grisly Wife* is the middle novel in terms
of chronology and the only one to have a woman as its narrator,
though all three are monologues. Hall explained, "In the two outside books I had two male voices, a pagan outcast from the Isle of
Man and a working-class Catholic. Symmetry required me to have
the voice of a Protestant middle-class woman." All three books have

the same setting, the backwoods of south coastal New South Wales,
where Hall himself now lives and which critics frequently compare to William Faulkner's Yoknapatawpha County as an example
of a novelist creating his own fictive territory. All three are monologues spoke in an almost unnaturally eloquent, even poetic voice,
though Hall has gone out of his way to anticipate this objection by
giving each of his narrators a background of literacy. The convict
forger in *The Second Bridegroom* learned about words from his
mother and how to use them from his trade as a printer. Catherine
Byrne, the eponymous wife, is the daughter of an Anglican clergyman. And Patrick Malone was the one child (of ten) chosen by his
brutal father to be educated outside the closed family by a learned
old Catholic priest.

The Second Bridegroom is the story of an unnamed youth told
(we eventually learn) to the widow of his master with whom he
has fallen blindly in love and who he wrongly believes to have at
least some sympathy for him. Transported to Australia in the "Fraternity" for the forgery of a 15th-century document, he is manacled
to Gabriel Dean, whose mistreatment of him drives him to strangle
the man. He then escapes into the bush and joins a tribe of Aborigines who make him their king. When the tribe attack a settlement, killing a young woman and then most of the rest of the settlers and setting fire to their property, the narrator takes the guilt
upon himself as having somehow willed it: "The truth was this,
that while the Men knew no word of my language they must have
known my thoughts. So, they had felt my fury and sensed my need.
They had obeyed. I had given orders as sure as if I spoke them."

Although the Aborigines are not individualized and the narrator
never learns even a single word of their language, their mode of
life is shown to be inherently superior to that of the whites. The
narrator quickly adjusts to their ways of thinking. When he comes
upon a white settlement after a few months in the wilderness he
speaks of their efforts to "tame" and fence the land in horrified
terms of "the sheer scale of violence." He notes the Aborigines'
generosity and selflessness toward himself, their patience with his
clumsiness, and their refusal to steal more food than they need.
The theme of the novel is perhaps best summed up in one of the
narrator's many bouts of sententiousness: "I want you to understand that there is something to be understood out there, something
free of the law, free of any comforting faith in a God whose motives may be explained through our own, something that has to
become the map of my heart."

The Grisly Wife is a monologue delivered by Catherine Byrne
before a silent audience, which we discover only at the end to be a
sergeant who has come to inquire about the murder of the three
Malone siblings, her neighbors and the subject of *Captivity Captive.* We learn also that Catherine believes he is inquiring about a
different murder, that of the unnamed narrator of *The Second Bridegroom.* The year is 1898 and not the least of Hall's concerns is the
intrusion of the secular and scientific world upon the kind of messianic faith inspired in Catherine and her female friends by the charismatic preacher Muley Moloch. There is mention of Charles Darwin, for instance, of Richard Wagner as some kind of herald of a
new age, and of new scientific phenomena such as cameras,
lawnmowers, and steam trains. Muley marries Catherine after she
has been impressed by his apparent feat of levitation and then persuades a group of eight women to sail with him to Australia and
found a new community on the south coast of New South Wales,
christening them the Household of Hidden Stars. One by one the
women die of consumption at the mission they establish, as the
prophet's hold on them diminishes. Eventually the survivors kick

him out after he shoots and kills a wild white man (the escaped convict).

This is an almost ostentatiously feminist novel, as *The Second Bridegroom* concerns itself conspicuously with environmental issues. A sense of close camaraderie grows among the women, especially after they dismiss Muley, and extends eventually to a close friendship between Catherine and Louisa Theuerkauf, the woman she had once hated. Protests against male authority keep emerging in the text, particularly in Catherine's constant reproaches of Sergeant Arrell, her silent audience. "Tenderness grows among us," we are told of the women, and they embrace frequently.

In *Captivity Captive,* Barney Barnett, the unsuccessful suitor of one of the girls shot and clubbed to death on a remote New South Wales farm, has confessed to the crime on his deathbed, but it soon becomes clear that his claim is merely a piece of retrospective self-aggrandizement. One of the surviving siblings sets out to tell the story of what actually happened. It does not take the reader too long to find out who the actual killer is, but the question of why remains almost as much of an enigma at the end as at the beginning. In a prose that is in turn poetic, highly self-conscious, rhetorical, and obsessive, Hall explores the relationship between guilt and innocence, captive and tyrant.

For all its occasional stylistic excesses, the trilogy is an impressive attempt to reexplore and rewrite white Australian history. One of the key themes in all three novels is the sense that the land was not empty but was seized by white people; hence the constant presence of the Aborigines, seen as ghosts or demons by the whites, hovering constantly around the outskirts of the narratives, their presence both a threat and an admonishment to the whites: "They were briefly there and soon gone but it was evident to me that they knew more than we had ever believed possible," Catherine says in *The Grisly Wife.* One critic has gone so far as to suggest that "Each of these characters attempts to live and reenact a myth, to take on some self-imposed mantle of immortality: the Second Bridegroom, the Second Coming or the Second Fall from Grace. Each fails."

—Laurie Clancy

HALLIGAN, Marion

Nationality: Australian. **Born:** Marion Mildred Crothall, Newcastle, New South Wales, 16 April 1940. **Education:** University College, 1957-62, B.A.(honours) in education 1962. **Family:** Married Graham James Halligan in 1963; one daughter and one son. **Career:** Teacher, Canberra High School, Australian Capital Territory, 1963-65, Canberra Church of England Girls' Grammar School, 1974-86. Since 1993, chair of literature, Board of Australia Council. Writer-in-residence, Charles Stuart University, Riverina, 1990. **Awards:** Patricia Hackett prize for best creative contribution to *Westerly,* 1985; Butterly/Earla Hooper award, for short story; Steele Rudd award, 1989, and Braille book of the year, 1989, for *The Living Hothouse;* Geraldine Pascall award, 1990, for critical writing; Australia/New Zealand Exchange, 1991; Keesing Studio Cite Internationale des Arts, Paris, 1991; Award for Gastronomic writing, 1991, for *Eat My Words; Age* book of the year, 1992, ACT book of the year, 1993, 3M talking book of the year, 1993, and Nita B. Kibble award, 1994, for *Lovers' Knots;* The Newton-John award, 1994. **Agent:** Margaret Connolly, 37 Ormond Street,

Paddington, New South Wales 2021, Australia. **Address:** 6 Caldwell Street, Hackett, Australian Capital Territory 2602, Australia.

PUBLICATIONS

Novels

Self Possession. Brisbane, University of Queensland Press, 1987.
The Hanged Man in the Garden. Melbourne, Penguin, 1989.
Spider Cup. Melbourne, Penguin, 1990.
Lovers' Knots. Melbourne, Heinemann, 1992; London, Minerva, 1995.
Wishbone. Melbourne, Heinemann, 1994.

Short Stories

The Living Hothouse. Brisbane, University of Queensland Press, 1988.
The Worry Box. Melbourne, Heinemann, 1993.

Play

Gastronomica (produced Melbourne Festival, 1994).

Other

Out of the Picture. Canberra, National Library of Australia, 1990.
Eat My Words. Sydney, Angus and Robertson, 1990.

*

Manuscript Collection: National Library of Australia, Canberra.

Marion Halligan comments:

I am interested in words and stories. I think that when you find the words you find out what it is you want to say. Stories are what people are good at, both telling them and listening to them. In both fiction and non-fiction story-telling is important, though it may not always be simple; sometimes narratives are hidden.

Looking back over my writing I realise it is often about choice and chance, though I don't start with these notions. And I write about ordinary lives, and how amazing they are.

*   *   *

Marion Halligan's fiction moves through daily life to its structuring fantasies, personal and cultural. Her narratives of "what if" interrupt routine: Beyond the ordinary, other worlds beckon. At the beginning of "The Orangery," found in her third collection of short stories, *The Worry Box,* a woman sits on a train reading. From the seat opposite a stranger breaks into her containment. Lift your eyes, he admonishes her. The world is there to see. Get off at the next stop and visit the stationmaster's orangery. When the train halts, she looks out the window at orange trees covered with flower and fruit and, yielding to a sudden desire to breathe the sharp scented air of orange blossom, she puts down her book and follows the man. Suddenly the narrative, moving along a trajectory of erotic seduction, veers off into death. Anticipating elegance and artifice, the woman encounters explosion, a bomb blast, bodies in bits. What was she doing there? Did she choose, or was she lured? Where were the meanings for this violent intrusion?

Questions like these have disturbed Halligan's writing since she began publishing seriously in 1981. She is a writer of unease and yet a celebrator of story and the senses. In less than ten years she has become one of Australia's best-known writers, highly regarded for her work across an unusual range of forms. Her short stories, which have won many prizes, appear in literary and mainstream magazines, are read on national radio, and are frequently anthologized. The first collection, *The Living Hothouse,* with its stories set in Australia, New Zealand, and France, won the Steele Rudd Award and the Braille Book of the Year Award. Since that initial book, she has published over six years two more collections of short fiction, four novels, and a work of nonfiction. Her most ambitious novel to date, *Lovers' Knots,* won the *Age* Book of the Year Award. Set in the coastal town of Newcastle, where Halligan grew up and went to university, the novel begins as if it were a family saga covering the century 1911-2011, but its narrative denies the conventional chronology evoked and shatters into the fragments caught by photographs.

Halligan is fascinated by story and, refusing as she does the borders of telling, her narratives surface in unexpected places. She has written the libretto for a children's opera, a trilogy of plays for the Melbourne Theater Company, and the narratives to accompany photographs in *Out of the Picture,* commissioned by the National Library of Australia. Above all, however, she is admired for writing food. Food and story, she has said, are the most important things in life. Together they are irresistibly seductive. We cannot live without them. Probably her work of widest appeal is *Eat My Words* (winner of the Prize for Gastronomic Writing), a book of food and story set largely in France and loosely structured as autobiography. Its sequel, *A Second Helping* (to be published in 1996), will within a framework of travel through France offer readers another helping of words. Metaphor and reality took a new twist in Halligan's œuvre during 1994 when the patrons dining in five opulent 19th-century restaurants in Melbourne ate their way through menus specially devised as accompaniments for theater pieces performed between courses. Each of Halligan's five "Gastronomicas," commissioned by the Melbourne International Festival, was created for the particular eating space and drew for its stories on writers like Dickens and Wilde selected as fitting that restaurant. Diners ate the highest of cuisine amid the best of story.

Such pampering of desire takes strange twists in Halligan's most recent novel, *Wishbone.* Like the fairy tales where wishes come true to the considerable consternation of those careless with words, the wealthy characters in this fable of contemporary Australia find themselves swept up in narratives of murder, sex, and intrigue they never anticipated in their wishing. In the materialistic culture imagined, the opportunities for pleasures and indulgence abound, but no narrative of desire is genuinely to be wished. This novel has received little of the critical praise accorded *Lovers' Knots.* Perhaps those who delighted in the humor, warmth, and poignancy of the preceding novel are uncomfortable with the wicked wit and uncompromising satire of *Wishbone.* Gender may play its part. Although women writers in Australia have incorporated the satiric moment into their fiction, the sustained narratives of satire have belonged predominantly to men (such as Patrick White, Frank Moorhouse, and Morris Lurie). Marion Halligan is praised for writing the meals set on Australian tables; making a meal of Australia may be another matter, may be unbecoming in a woman writer. If the cultural cringe is gone from Australian readers, the gender cringe still seems to linger.

—Lucy Frost

HAMMOND INNES, (Ralph)

Nationality: British. **Born:** Horsham, Sussex, 15 July 1913. **Education:** Cranbrook School, Kent, 1927-31. **Military Service:** Served in the British Army Artillery, 1940-46: Major. **Family:** Married Dorothy Mary Lang in 1937 (died 1989). **Career:** Staff member, *Financial News,* London, 1934-40. **Awards:** C.B.E. (Commander, Order of the British Empire), 1978. D.Litt.: Bristol University, 1985. **Agent:** Curtis Brown, 14th Floor, Haymarket House, 28/29 Haymarket, London SW1Y 4SP. **Address:** Ayres End, Kersey, Ipswich, Suffolk IP7 6EB, England.

PUBLICATIONS

Novels

The Doppleganger. London, Jenkins, 1937.
Air Disaster. London, Jenkins, 1937.
Sabotage Broadcast. London, Jenkins, 1938.
All Roads Lead to Friday. London, Jenkins, 1939.
Wreckers Must Breathe. London, Collins, 1940; as *Trapped,* New York, Putnam, 1940.
The Trojan Horse. London, Collins, 1940.
Attack Alarm. London, Collins, 1941; New York, Macmillan, 1942.
Dead and Alive. London, Collins, 1946.
The Killer Mine. London, Collins, and New York, Harper, 1947; as *Run by Night,* New York, Bantam, 1951.
The Lonely Skier. London, Collins, 1947; as *Fire in the Snow,* New York, Harper, 1947.
Maddon's Rock. London, Collins, 1948; as *Gale Warning,* New York, Harper, 1948.
The Blue Ice. London, Collins, and New York, Harper, 1948.
The White South. London, Collins, 1949; as *The Survivors,* New York, Harper, 1950.
The Angry Mountain. London, Collins, 1950; New York, Harper, 1951.
Air Bridge. London, Collins, 1951; New York, Knopf, 1952.
Campbell's Kingdom. London, Collins, and New York, Knopf, 1952.
The Strange Land. London, Collins, 1954; as *The Naked Land,* New York, Knopf, 1954.
The Mary Deare. London, Collins, 1956; as *The Wreck of the Mary Deare,* New York, Knopf, 1956.
The Land God Gave to Cain. London, Collins, and New York, Knopf, 1958.
The Doomed Oasis. London, Collins, and New York, Knopf, 1960.
Atlantic Fury. London, Collins, and New York, Knopf, 1962.
The Strode Venturer. London, Collins, and New York, Knopf, 1965.
Levkas Man. London, Collins, and New York, Knopf, 1971.
Golden Soak. London, Collins, and New York, Knopf, 1973.
North Star. London, Collins, 1974; New York, Knopf, 1975.
The Big Footprints. London, Collins, and New York, Knopf, 1977.
Solomon's Seal. London, Collins, and New York, Knopf, 1980.
The Black Tide. London, Collins, 1982; New York, Doubleday, 1983.
High Stand. London, Collins, 1985; New York, Atheneum, 1986.
Medusa. London, Collins, and New York, Atheneum, 1988.
Isvik. London, Chapmans, 1991.
Target Antarctica. London, Chapmans, 1993.

Plays

Screenplay: *Campbell's Kingdom,* with Robin Estridge, 1957.

Television Play: *The Story of Captain James Cook,* 1975.

Other (for children) as Ralph Hammond

Coco's Gold. London, Collins, and New York, Harper, 1950.
Isle of Strangers. London, Collins, 1951; as *Island of Peril,* Philadelphia, Westminster Press, 1953.
Saracen's Tower. London, Collins, 1952; as *Cruise of Danger,* Philadelphia, Westminster Press, 1954.
Black Gold on the Double Diamond. London, Collins, 1953.

Other

Harvest of Journeys. London, Collins, and New York, Knopf, 1960.
Scandinavia, with editors of Life. New York, Time, 1963.
Sea and Islands. London, Collins, and New York, Knopf, 1967.
The Conquistadors. London, Collins, and New York, Knopf, 1969.
Hammond Innes Introduces Australia, edited by Clive Turnbull. London, Deutsch, and New York, McGraw Hill, 1971.
The Last Voyage: Captain Cook's Lost Diary. London, Collins, 1978; New York, Knopf, 1979.
Hammond Innes' East Anglia. London, Hodder and Stoughton, 1986.

Editor, *Tales of Old Inns,* by Richard Keverne, revised edition. London, Collins, 1947.

*

Manuscript Collection: Mugar Memorial Library, Boston University.

Hammond Innes comments:

Writing and traveling can be kept in separate compartments of time. But the organization and preparation for journeys and voyages cannot. And this is a major problem, for I need the familiarity of my own home and the peace of the country in order to write. I need my books and my maps and charts around me. I also need to live with it seven days a week, for I am a painfully slow writer, usually discarding far more than appears in the final work.

I find it very difficult to be certain at what point I became conscious of the role travel was to play in my writing. I think probably after the war. I had cut my writing teeth in the Great Depression of the early 1930s, a particularly insular period that I believe to have been the result of the mud and blood of Flanders. To earn my living, however, I worked as a journalist on a London daily. My starting wage was a now unbelievable 17s. 6d. a week, and at the time I counted myself fortunate to get the job, for most newspapers were firing, not hiring, staff. All through the 1930s I had to be content to discover my own country, so that when I finally did go abroad it was at H.M.'s expense—a voyage round the Cape, my destination the Western desert.

I was 27 when I joined the services. I felt the best years of my life were being wasted. It was only when I was demobilized, and had taken the plunge and abandoned journalism for full-time writing, that I realized what a wealth of experience I had been soaking up.

As a youngster, my imagination had been fired by geography almost as much as by literature. On my return to England after the war, I was made strongly aware that, whilst I had been absorbing the atmosphere of the old world of the Mediterranean, the vast majority of the British people had been locked up in their island fortress for six long years. I had characters and backgrounds that seemed to interest them. There is always an element of luck in everything, and in writing the luck is to find that what you want to write, and therefore what you write best, is what people happen to want to read.

I wanted to write about far-off places and people. Because of that I determined to plough back as much of my royalties as possible into travel. And looking back now, how glad I am that I did. A writer has no business, no land, no factory that he can call his own. His capital assets are all in his head, and one of the very few things that can't be taxed, expropriated, or in any way filched by others, is personal experience.

This was a conscious decision, the only one I have ever made about my writing. The rest has developed in the normal haphazard way of things. I cannot even say what it is that draws me at a certain period of time to a certain part of the world. The choice would appear to be intuitive. But I can say that, as with the voyages under sail, a lot of preparation is necessary. The research, the books, the maps, the visits to London to seek out the right contacts. This is all necessary, so that when one arrives in the country itself there is a sense of familiarity; by which I mean that the people and their way of life are at least within one's comprehension. And the journey itself needs to be planned—meetings with ministers, industrialists, writers to get the overall picture, and then, with the country's problems clear in mind, a prolonged stay in one area so that one gets to grips with the people themselves.

Returning, one begins a long, slow process of rendering down. The mind is too often overflowing with all that one has absorbed, and the only way I know to rid oneself of this embarrassment of riches is to write a travel piece—hence my two books in search of background. Even then, it may be two or three years before I am ready to start on the novel, for if it is to be real, the story has to grow out of the background. And in the case of remote areas like the Labrador, or Addu Atoll in the Indian Ocean, there is probably only one real story line that will achieve my purpose and show what the country and the people are really like.

It may appear from this that I am a highly organized writer. I wish this were so. It would make my life a lot easier if it were. But at least by building on a background of very personal travel I know what I am trying to achieve. And whether I succeed or not, it is at least a start to have the goal clear in mind.

*   *   *

Hammond Innes is one of the foremost thriller writers of his day. Like John Buchan—a writer whom he much resembles—he believes that there is only a thin dividing line between the claims of civilization and the slide into anarchy, between the warm room and the savage out-of-doors. For that reason Hammond Innes's characters often find themselves in conflict as much with their environment—the sea, the polar regions, the desert—as with other men. *Maddon's Rock,* one of his earliest sea tales is ostensibly about a ghost ship which never sank during World War II, but that is only an undercurrent to his main theme of the crew's defiance of the gale-swept ocean. The theme of man against the sea is also central to *The Mary Deare* and *Atlantic Fury,* both of which contain excellent and moving descriptions of man's age-old battle with the elements. Innes is equally at home in the services—he served as a Royal Artillery officer during World War II—and his novels *Attack Alarm* and *The Trojan Horse* both deal with infiltration of enemy agents into Britain's defense establishment. His strong clear prose makes for compulsive reading, and his attention to detail—essential to the writer of thrillers—enables readers to feel that they are actually involved in the action at the height of any crisis.

These abilities are not confined to his books about the sea. *The White South* is set in the Antarctic and *Campbell's Kingdom* and *The Land God Gave to Cain* in Canada, yet the sense of place and his concern with background detail remain constant factors. Like all his novels these are excellent entertainments, and his hard-hitting action always flows along at a great pace. At the back of each adventure, too, lies the theme of redemption, with each hero having to pass through a necessary ordeal before good is allowed to triumph. Thus, in *Dead and Alive* the central character, David Cunningham, has to endure many trials before he feels again the "strange contentment" of being once more in command of his own ship. This early Hammond Innes adventure story acts as a pointer to much of his later fiction. Cunningham, scarred by his wartime experiences, becomes a partner in a dubious trading enterprise, using a landing craft in the Mediterranean: part of his mission is to discover the whereabouts of a young Anglo-French girl who has gone missing in Italy. While in Naples, Cunningham and his partners become drawn into the post-war black market and are forced to fight their way through the garish haunts of petty criminals and racketeers before the girl, Monique, is found and all obstacles have been overcome.

Critics of Hammond Innes's style have claimed that because his adventures tend to follow a pattern he only writes to a proven formula. This is to miss both the point of many of his plots and also his concern with morality. His belief that his heroes must face a necessary ordeal before virtue can triumph is no idle bow to the basic convention of the thriller plot. Hammond Innes is frequently at pains to point out that by enduring danger and risking his life the hero not only becomes a better person but also enriches the lives of those around him. In *The Strode Venturer*, for example, the Englishman in the central role might be a typical post-colonial adventurer interested only in exploiting a market for manganese in the Maldive Islands, but through his actions the primitive islanders are also enabled to establish their own claims. In this case, the hero is neither a paragon nor a superman but an ordinary man caught up in a dangerous position from which he can escape only by virtue of his own quick-thinking.

Characterization is another strong point of Hammond Innes's fiction, even though he does tend to rely on the stock figure of the clean-limbed young Englishman as his central character. His villains excite neither fear nor pity: they are usually ruthless men motivated by greed, envy, or politics. In most novels the most telling opponent is the environment, and in addition to his concern with natural detail, Hammond Innes also has the ability to draw natural adversaries almost as if they were human beings. An avalanche, volcanic explosion, or gale at sea in an Hammond Innes novel can often be possessed of stealth, cunning, or strength, attributes which one normally associates with the human race. His prose is conventional, but his sense of place and his ability to evoke it manages to transport his readers to the far-flung regions of the world.

—Trevor Royle

HANLEY, Clifford (Leonard Clark)

Pseudonym: Henry Calvin. **Nationality:** British. **Born:** Glasgow, Scotland, 28 October 1922. **Education:** Eastbank School, Glasgow. Conscientious objector in World War II. **Family:** Married Anna E. Clark in 1948 (died 1990); one son and two daughters. **Career:** Reporter, Scottish Newspaper Services, Glasgow, 1940-45; subeditor, *Scottish Daily Record,* Glasgow, 1945-57; feature writer, *TV Guide,* Glasgow, 1957-58; director, Glasgow Films Ltd., 1957-63; columnist, Glasgow *Evening Citizen,* 1958-60; television critic, *Spectator,* London, 1963. Visiting professor, Glendon College, York University, Toronto, 1979-80. **Awards:** Oscar award, 1960, for *Seawards the Great Ships.* **Member:** Close Theatre Management Committee, Glasgow, 1965-71, Inland Waterways Council, 1967-71, and Scottish Arts Council, 1967-74; vice-president, 1966-73, and president, 1974-77, Scottish PEN; Scottish chairman, Writers Guild of Great Britain, 1968-73. **Agent:** Curtis Brown, 162-168 Regent Street, London W1R 5TB, England. **Address:** 35 Hamilton Drive, Glasgow G12 8DW, Scotland.

PUBLICATIONS

Novels

Love from Everybody. London, Hutchinson, 1959; as *Don't Bother to Knock,* London, Digit, 1961.
The Taste of Too Much. London, Hutchinson, 1960.
Nothing But the Best. London, Hutchinson, 1964; as *Second Time Round,* Boston, Houghton Mifflin, 1964.
The Hot Month. London, Hutchinson, and Boston, Houghton Mifflin, 1967.
The Red-Haired Bitch. London, Hutchinson, and Boston, Houghton Mifflin, 1969.
Prissy. London, Collins, 1978.
Another Street, Another Dance. Edinburgh, Mainstream, 1983; New York, St. Martin's Press, 1984.

Novels as Henry Calvin

The System. London, Hutchinson, 1962.
It's Different Abroad. London, Hutchinson, and New York, Harper, 1963.
The Italian Gadget. London, Hutchinson, 1966.
The DNA Business. London, Hutchinson, 1967.
A Nice Friendly Town. London, Hutchinson, 1967.
Miranda Must Die. London, Hutchinson, 1968; as *Boka Lives,* New York, Harper 1969.
The Chosen Instrument. London, Hutchinson, 1969.
The Poison Chasers. London, Hutchinson, 1971.
Take Two Popes. London, Hutchinson, 1972.

Plays

The Durable Element (produced Dundee, Scotland, 1961).
Saturmacnalia, music by Ian Gourlay (produced Glasgow, 1965).
Oh for an Island, music by Ian Gourlay (produced Glasgow, 1966).
Dick McWhittie, music by Ian Gourlay (produced Glasgow, 1967).
Jack o' the Cudgel (produced Perth, 1969).
Oh Glorious Jubilee, music by Ian Gourlay (produced Leeds, 1970).

The Clyde Moralities (produced Glasgow, 1972).

Screenplay: *Seawards the Great Ships,* 1960; *The Duna Bull,* 1972.

Television Plays: *Dear Boss,* 1962; *Down Memory Lane,* 1971; *Alas, Poor Derek,* 1976.

Poetry

Rab Ha': The Glasgow Glutton. Glasgow, General District Libraries, 1989.

Other

Dancing in the Streets (autobiography). London, Hutchinson, 1958.
A Skinful of Scotch (travel). London, Hutchinson, and Boston, Houghton Mifflin, 1965.
Burns Country: The Travels of Robert Burns. Newport, Isle of Wight, Dixon, 1975.
The Unspeakable Scot. Edinburgh, Blackwood, 1977.
Poems of Ebenezer McIlwham. Edinburgh, Gordon Wright, 1978.
The Biggest Fish in the World (for children). Edinburgh, Chambers, 1979.
A Hypnotic Trance. Edinburgh, BBC Scotland, 1980.
The Scots. Newton Abbot, Devon, David and Charles, and New York, Times, 1980.
Another Street, Another Dance. Edinburgh, Mainstream, 1983.
Glasgow: A Celebration. Edinburgh, Mainstream, 1984.
The History of Scotland. London, Hamlyn, and New York, Gallery, 1986.
The Sheer Gall, with Willie Gall. Edinburgh, Mainstream, 1989.
Gall in a Day's Work, with Willie Gall. Edinburgh, Mainstream, 1989.

*

Clifford Hanley comments:

(1972) *Dancing in the Streets,* my first published book, was written at the suggestion of my publisher, who wanted a book about the city of Glasgow. At the time I thought it a rather pedestrian recital of childhood memories and was taken aback by its critical and commercial success (it is still used as background reading in schools of social studies and urbanology). My first novel, *Love from Everybody,* written previously but published later, was frankly intended as a light entertainment, to make money, and was later filmed as *Don't Bother to Knock.* Having then retired from journalism, I wrote what I considered my first serious work, *The Taste of Too Much,* as a study of "ordinary" adolescence, without crime and adventitious excitement, and it may well be my most successful book in the sense of fully achieving the author's original conception. In the subsequent novels under my own name, I think my intention was to look at some areas of life—a businessman's troubles, the family situation, the agonies of work in the theater—simply in my own way, without reference to fashionable literary conceptions. I have often been surprised when people found the novels "funny" because their intention was serious; but an author can't help being what he is. I do see the human condition as tragic (since decay and death are the inevitable end), but I don't distinguish between comedy and tragedy. Funerals can be funny too, and life is noble and absurd at the same time. I also insist on distinguishing between seriousness and solemnity, which are opposite rather than similar. On looking back, I realize that the tone of

the novels tends to be affirmation rather than despair. This may be a virtue or a fault, or an irrelevance—a novelist should probably leave such judgments to critics and simply get on with what he must do. Maybe they also betray some kind of moral standpoint of which I was unconscious. This was explicit, in fact, in my first professionally produced play, *The Durable Element,* which was a study of the recurrent urge to crucify prophets. It was also deliberate in *The Chosen Instrument,* a pseudonymous Henry Calvin ten years later, in which a contemporary thriller mode was used to do a sort of feasibility study on the New Testament mythology. (The intention was so well disguised that no critic noticed it).

But I suppose cheerfulness keeps breaking through. I am an entertainer as well as novelist, and the two may be compatible. My first commandment as a writer is not at all highfalutin. It is Thou Shalt Not Bore. *A Skinful of Scotch* is an irreverent guide to one man's Scotland and was written for fun. So, originally, were the Henry Calvin thrillers. I enjoy reading thrillers and I adopted the pen-name simply to feel uninhibited. The thriller too is a morality, but the morality is acceptable only if it has character and pace. These are not intellectual mysteries but tales of conflict between good and evil. My later work for the theater was exclusively devoted to calculated entertainment and I am glad that people were actually entertained. I find now that I see life in more somber terms, but whether this will show in future novels is hard to tell. It may even be a temporary condition.

(1991) Self-assessment has always struck me as a futile exercise, in the sense that we can study a bug through a microscope, but we can't study the microscope through itself. I wrote my novels for fun or from internal compulsion (the two are the same, maybe) but have always seen myself as an entertainer, so they were intended for the reader's fun, which could include laughter, fear, enlightenment, puzzlement, and any other response.

They are not bad, probably. I did feel I hit the target with *The Taste of Too Much* (a committee title I don't like too much) in picturing the pangs of teenage love. School pupils agreed, especially girls, and it seems nothing has changed in 30 years. *Nothing But the Best* was partly stolen from life, and when I myself was widowed in 1990 I was interested in how my own responses followed those of the hero. *Another Street, Another Dance* was compulsive. The heroine, Meg, came into my mind fully formed, I was back in the time and place of my autobiographical first book *Dancing in the Streets.* It went onto the typewriter at the rate of 4,000 to 7,000 words a day with no hesitation because Meg was in the room with me. A very strange experience.

The Henry Calvin thrillers were entirely for fun, and I can only hope readers have shared it. (Odd, how many Scottish writers have hidden under pseudonyms). Henry was my father's name, and I picked Calvin because in these light tales virtue would triumph over vice, and to hell with some of the grim realities.

Not sure if I'll produce any more. I am now lazy, and comfortably fixed—a serious disincentive to work. But I am being nagged by an idealistic young New Yorker on a voyage of discovery through working-class and academic Glasgow, and I fear I shall have to let him right into the brain to dictate his misadventures and revelations. He is taking over, and I mildly resent that, but life is real and life is earnest, and the gravy is our goal, still.

*   *   *

Humor is never far away from the prose writings of Clifford Hanley. Although it is not officially a work of fiction and is based largely on his childhood experiences, his autobiographical study *Dancing in the Streets* gives the best clue to his literary technique. Partly, its success was due to Hanley's ability to realize the sharp and witty cadences of Glasgow patois; partly, too, it was his by no means dispassionate discovery of objective gaiety in a city in which it is not a common commodity. But the main reason for the book's place as Hanley's seminal work was his ability to work himself and his own comic experiences into a punchy and furiously paced narrative. Thus, when he came to write his first novel, *Love from Everybody,* he not only confirmed his competence to write with wit and humor about people and places, but he also gave notice that in his future fiction his persona was never going to be far absent from his writing.

This gift is seen to good advantage in *The Taste of Too Much,* a sensitive study of adolescence clearly based not only on his own experiences in Glasgow but also on his observations of the lives of young people in the city during the late 1950s. (Hanley was then working as a journalist for a Glasgow newspaper). Once again, as in *Dancing in the Streets,* the central theme is of a clever boy who is about to make good in the world, but in this instance, Peter Haddow, the intelligent and sensitive teenager, has to come face-to-face with a reality that is not always comic. The pinpricks of parental co-existence, an exasperating older sister, a ghoulish younger one, and an outrageous Aunt Sarah make young Peter's life miserable at times, yet shining like a candle in a wicked world is the gleam of his first love for the fabulous Jean Pynne. Although lightly written, *The Taste of Too Much* perceptively records Peter Haddow's adolescent feelings, and its modern council-estate setting marks it as a precursor of the later Scottish school of proletarian romanticism.

In his subsequent novels it became obvious that although Hanley had not lost his comic touch he was striving too hard to achieve his humorous effects. *The Red-Haired Bitch,* with its promising plot combining historical romance and modern reality, is superficially treated, Hanley being unable to sustain the historical motif of Mary Queen of Scots and the *realpolitik* of Glasgow's gangland. An earlier novel, *The Hot Month,* suffered from similar flaws with Hanley treating the Scots Calvinist ethos in comic fashion before plunging on to an attempt at analysis.

Hanley found his touch again in *Another Street, Another Dance* which takes a panoramic view of Glasgow from the troubled years of the Depression and Red Clydeside to the events of World War II and the beginning of the end of the city's great industrial supremacy. Much of the action is seen through the eyes of the family of Meg Macrae, a young girl from the western islands of Scotland who has come to terms with the big city and all its associated problems. Through her we come face to face with the reality of spiritual and physical poverty, drunkenness, wretched housing conditions, bad schooling, and furtive sex. Her triumphant ability to rise above those problems and to overcome a series of harrowing domestic disasters without ever losing grasp of her essential femininity gives the book its main theme and provides the backbone to Hanley's narrative, yet it is his sure ear for Glasgow dialogue and his compassion for all of the characters—good and bad—which finally beguile the reader.

Hanley has also written several modest detective novels under the mischievous pseudonym of Henry Calvin; but he is at his most successful when he remains in Glasgow, a city which nourishes his fiction and provides him with a realistic backdrop, and whose people offer unfailingly witty patterns of speech.

—Trevor Royle

HANNAH, Barry

Nationality: American. **Born:** Meridian, Mississippi, 23 April 1942. **Education:** Mississippi College, Clinton, B.A. 1964; University of Arkansas, Fayetteville, M.A. 1966, M.F.A. 1967. **Family:** Divorced; three children. **Career:** Member of the Department of English, Clemson University, South Carolina, 1967-73; writer-in-residence, Middlebury College, Vermont, 1974-75; member of the Department of English, University of Alabama, University, 1975-80; writer for the director Robert Altman, Hollywood, 1980; writer-in-residence, University of Iowa, Iowa City, 1981, University of Mississippi, Oxford, 1982, 1984, 1985, and University of Montana, Missoula, 1982-83. **Awards:** Bellaman Foundation award, 1970; Bread Loaf Writers Conference Atherton fellowship, 1971; Gingrich award (*Esquire*), 1978; American Academy award, 1979. **Address:** c/o Houghton Mifflin Company, 2 Park St., Boston, Massachusetts 02108, U.S.A.

PUBLICATIONS

Novels

Geronimo Rex. New York, Viking Press, 1972.
Nightwatchmen. New York, Viking Press, 1973.
Ray. New York, Knopf, 1980; London, Penguin, 1981.
The Tennis Handsome. New York, Knopf, 1983.
Power and Light. Winston-Salem, North Carolina, Palaemon Press, 1983.
Hey Jack! New York, Dutton, 1987.
Boomerang. Boston, Houghton Mifflin, 1989.
Never Die. Boston, Houghton Mifflin, 1991.

Short Stories

Airships. New York, Knopf, 1978; London, Vintage, 1991.
Two Stories. Jackson, Mississippi, Nouveau Press, 1982.
Black Butterfly. Winston-Salem, North Carolina, Palaemon Press, 1982.
Captain Maximus. New York, Knopf, 1985.
Bats Out of Hell. Boston, Houghton Mifflin/Seymour Lawrence, 1993.

Uncollected Short Story

"Sources Agree Rock Swoon Has No Past," in *Harper's* (New York), June 1986.

Other

In Honor of Oxford at One Hundred and Fifty. Grenada, Mississippi, Salt-works, 1987.

*

Critical Study: *Barry Hannah* by Mark J. Charney, New York, Twayne, 1992.

*   *   *

Barry Hannah's favored form is the monologue, his subject matter the grotesqueries of American life. Hannah's work includes incidents of beheading, a car wreck in the upper branches of an oak tree, a man who saves himself from drowning by balancing on the tip of a car aerial, a walrus's sexual attack on a woman who is having an affair with her nephew, and a drowned man who jump starts himself using a bus battery. "But that's farfetched, and worse than that, poetic, requiring a willing suspension of disbelief along with a willing desire to eat piles of air sausage," complains a character in *Nightwatchmen* while trying to make sense of a senseless death. A reader must bring along this willingness when reading Hannah.

Geronimo Rex, Hannah's first novel, is a long song of remembrance, an ode to southern adolescence, his discoveries of music and women and firearms and, perhaps most importantly, the extra spark style can give to life. Style is very important to Hannah's characters; this and endurance are the virtues they admire and aspire to. Style is also a large element in Hannah's writing: in *Geronimo Rex* impressionistic sentences that at first seem a beginning writer's excesses grate against the coming-of-age context, stylize the barstool braggart tone of voice: "I felt very precise in the oily seat; I was a pistol leaking music out of its holster." Far from being excesses the mature Hannah would weed out, sentences such as these (what Thomas McGuane admiringly referred to as Hannah's "moon-landing English") come to dominate the later works, from *Airships* on.

In the stories collected in *Airships* much of the traditional connective tissue of setting and exterior atmosphere is absent, leaving us with thick, nervous monologues by emotionally damaged men and women with a lot of style. Even the Civil War stories (which are enough alike to suggest Hannah may once have planned a Civil War novel) are narrated by characters with a jaded, violent sensibility identical with that of Hannah's characters from a hundred years later—particularly those with some involvement in the Vietnam War in their past. (Vietnam and the Civil War thread through much of Hannah's work.) Sentences such as "Levaster did not dream about himself and French Edward, although the dreams lay on him like the bricks of an hysterical mansion," mix southern gothic with an updated "hardboiled dick" tone, sometimes moving past intelligibility into a private impressionistic flow. At other times this same mix produces beautiful straight-to-the-heart images: "There is a poison in Tuscaloosa that draws souls toward the low middle." Plots are sketchy here, short portraits or sketches of fragmented lives. Characters, as in much of the work that follows, tend to stand or sit around listlessly, or to strike poses that accentuate their stylized speeches.

The title character in the short novel *Ray* is hardly a character at all, serving for the most part as a kind of tuning fork adjusted to the pitches of certain kinds of misery, those that reflect his own. Dr. Ray is a drinker, an adulterer, and perhaps a little too free with his drug prescriptions. Dr. Ray was a pilot during the Vietnam War, and has begun confusing this experience with what he knows of the Civil War. Others living the low middle life around Dr. Ray get ahead or fall, but his yearnings are too huge or too vague, too subject to change, and he remains stalled in a stasis of half-hearted healing, sex, and war memories.

The Tennis Handsome was expanded from a story in *Airships.* The title character, French Edward, sustains brain damage when he is nearly drowned trying either to save or to kill his mother's lover, who is also his old tennis coach. French Edward is still able to continue his career as a tennis pro through the Svengali-like attentions of Levaster, an unsavory old friend who likes to shoot people with a gun loaded with popcorn. The story version ends with everyone admiring, even taking solace in, French Edward's mindless grace and endurance, his perfect second of "blazing" serve. In the novel French Edward phases in and out, sometimes shocking himself into lucidity, writing poetry, finding religion, and generally frustrating everyone around him. Despite its brevity *The Tennis Handsome* seems to sprawl.

Captain Maximus, Hannah's second story collection, is even more spare, more knife-edged than *Airships.* Again these vignettes are filled with people consumed by yearning, but devoid of hope. Only in "Idaho," an ode to the late poet Richard Hugo which captures some of the poet's own style, and in "Power and Light," a reflection on the travails of working women, does Hannah's tone lighten at all, and only marginally.

Standing apart from his other works is Hannah's second novel, *Nightwatchmen.* While the novel's grotesqueries outnumber those of the other novels, it is a much more emotional, caring work. The writing here is much less stylized, and conflicts are not kept at a callous distance. Hannah's other works are plotted concentrically or in parallel lines, with groups of characters having some experience in common rather than sharing some common experience; only in *Nightwatchmen* do lives truly intersect in any significant way. The primary narrator, Thorpe Trove, is open and vulnerable, concerned for the people around him. He spends two years solving the mysteries of who knocked a half dozen people unconscious, and who then beheaded two nightwatchmen. When Thorpe records the stories of the "innocent" parties involved it becomes clear that they care only for their own fears and defenses. In the end the whodunit aspect is overshadowed by the realization of how much the other characters have in common with The Knocker and The Killer.

Mississippi State Press published *Boomerang* and *Never Die* in 1991, which was quickly followed by *Bats out of Hell,* a collection of stories that brings with it the same flair for the grotesque as *Airships.* Reviews of the collection were mixed, but given that the reader agrees to bring along a generous willingness to suspend disbelief, there is much to enjoy. Again, the Civil War provides the setting when the Confederate soldiers win the Union troops by playing Tchaikovsky in the title story, "Bats out of Hell Division."

The War in Vietnam also recurs as a shaping force in Hannah's short pieces. For example, in "I Taste Like a Sword," which appeared in *The Oxford American,* a character named Fagmost pukes at football games "but smiling." When he is dragged off by policeman, we see a glimpse of him that calls to mind the 1960s in the United States: ". . . him all wet in his lumpy flowered shirt and dirty beard." The narrator tells us that the veteran ". . . had a good four year war behind [him] and was carried down the street by a flock of children on Memorial Day."

The usual monologue is delivered by a waiter whose sense of humor saves him from the start. He speaks of his father: ". . . now I realize he might have been interesting although something about my devoted apathy in my teens wouldn't let me like him." By the end of the story, we have seen through his eyes and find him endearing, worthy of the same compassion as Flannery O'Connor's flawed characters. His father, a helicopter technology expert who was exposed to poisonous gas during the war, cries out on his deathbed, "God bless war otherwise the pestilent hordes rising up to level us. There you'd really have your flat plains." Hannah's work continues to be "farfetched and worse than that, poetic," yet the vision seems more tender.

—William C. Bamberger, updated by Loretta Cobb

HANNON, Ezra. *See* **HUNTER, Evan.**

———

HANSEN, Ron(ald Thomas)

Nationality: American. **Born:** Omaha, Nebraska, 8 December 1947. **Education:** Holy Angels Grade School, 1953-62; Creighton Preparatory School, 1962-66; Creighton University, Omaha, 1966-70, B.A. in English 1970; University of Iowa, Iowa City, 1972-74, M.F.A. in creative writing 1974; Stanford University, California, (Stegner fellow), 1977-78. **Military Service:** Served in the United States Army, Adjutant Generals Corps, 1970-72: Lieutenant. **Family:** Married Julie Vinsonhaler in 1985 (divorced 1993). **Career:** Jones Lecturer, Stanford University, 1978-81; fellow, University of Michigan, Ann Arbor, 1981-84; lecturer, University of Iowa, 1985; assistant professor, Cornell University, Ithaca, New York, 1985-86; associate professor, State University of New York, Binghamton, 1988-89. Since 1989 associate professor, University of California, Santa Cruz. **Awards:** National Endowment for the Arts fellowship, 1979, 1987; American Academy of Arts and Letters award, 1989; Guggenheim fellowship, 1990; Lyndhurst Foundation fellowship, 1992. **Agent:** Peter Matson, Sterling Lord Literistic, 1 Madison Avenue, New York, New York 10010. **Address:** c/o Benjamin F. Porter College, University of California, Santa Cruz, California 95064, U.S.A.

PUBLICATIONS

Novels

Desperadoes. New York, Knopf, 1979; London, Souvenir Press, 1980.
The Assassination of Jesse James by the Coward Robert Ford. New York, Knopf, 1983; London, Souvenir Press, 1984.
Mariette in Ecstasy. New York, HarperCollins, 1991; London, Picador, 1995.

Short Stories

Nebraska. New York, Atlantic Monthly Press, 1989.

Plays

Screenplay: *Mariette in Ecstasy,* 1995.

Television Play: *Blue Movie* (*Private Eye* series), 1987.

Other

The Shadowmaker (for children). New York, Harper, 1987.

Editor, *You Don't Know What Love Is: Contemporary American Stories.* Princeton, New Jersey, Ontario Review Press, 1987.
Editor, with Jim Shepard, *You've Got to Read This: Contemporary American Writers Introduce Stories That Held Them in Awe,* HarperCollins, 1994.

*

Film Adaptations: *Mariette in Ecstasy,* 1995.

Manuscript Collection: Creighton University, Omaha, Nebraska.

Ron Hansen comments:
While I don't think of myself as a historical novelist, I do use history in my novels on the principle that Isak Dinesen first expressed: that a writer can own the past, but not the present. I have also been interested in the uses of genres: the western, the ghost story, the mystery, religious hagiography, and the *Bildungsroman.* Examples of those experiments can be seen in my published novels and stories, and also in works that are forthcoming or still in progress. If asked what school of writing I find myself most comfortable in, I would probably say that of the fabulators, but I have been influenced by writers as different as John Irving and John Updike, William H. Gass and E.L. Doctorow, John Gardner and Thomas McGuane; indeed my greatest influence may be the filmmaker Ingmar Bergman. I see all my scenes cinematically before I try to transcribe them. In childhood I hoped to be a painter; perhaps that shows in my work.

*   *   *

Ron Hansen occupies an unusual position in modern American fiction. While most of his contemporaries have turned their attention to the modern urban scene, Hansen has chosen instead to write about quite a different place and period—a place and a period, moreover, that have not generally been regarded as fit subjects for "serious" fiction. His tales of the Wild West (he has published a volume of short stories as well as three novels) occupy, indeed, a curious half-way house between popular and high culture; between the worlds of art and entertainment.

Desperadoes, his first book, tells the story of the notorious Dalton gang, who terrorized Kansas and what is now Oklahoma in the 1880s and 1890s. Narrated in the first person by Emmett, adoring younger brother of the band's leader, Bob Dalton, it is a fast-paced, almost breathless account of the robbers' progress from horse stealing, through train hold-ups, to their final bloody liquidation on the streets of their hometown, Coffeyville. It is a story full of violence and drama—a story, also, full of humor and irony, for at the beginning of the novel the brothers are peace officers on the right side of the law, and by the end they are popular heroes and Hollywood stars. *Desperadoes,* in fact, might be called a meditation on our need for heroes—a description which in no way lessens its value as entertainment, or its quite unusual skill in recreating the language, habits, and mentality of the time. It is this last quality, perhaps, that most clearly separates it from the general run of Westerns: seldom, indeed, has the past been brought so uncannily to life.

The Assassination of Jesse James by the Coward Robert Ford, Hansen's second work, is far more ambitious. Like *Desperadoes* the story is set in the Wild West, and like *Desperadoes* it focuses on the relationship between an admiring youngster and the leader of a robber band. Bob Ford's relations with Jesse James, however, are far removed from the simple adoration of Emmett for Bob Dalton. Ford, that is, not merely wishes to be *like* James; in a sense he wants to *become* James, a fact the older man is uncomfortably aware of. Initially tolerated, Ford eventually becomes an object of fear and distrust—a fear and distrust he fully reciprocates, while still maintaining an almost mystical awe of the great villain. In the end he feels obliged to murder James, so becoming, in his own way, as famous, or infamous, as the man he has killed. Haunted by his act, and persecuted by hatred and contempt, he flees westward, but cannot escape retribution: he too, ultimately, is gunned down. *The Assassination of Jesse James by the Coward Robert Ford* in fact, has something like the inevitability of Greek tragedy about it—though, like *Desperadoes,* it is fully and completely authentic in its use of 19th-century American language and custom. All in all it marks a definite advance on the earlier book.

An ironical comment on our need for heroes; an articulation of ancestral voices; a recreation of jaded American myth—Hansen's fiction can be studied for any and all of these. Perhaps, though, it is their most obvious virtue that recommends them: the fact that they are, simply, a superb read.

—John O'Leary

HARDWICK, Elizabeth (Bruce)

Nationality: American. **Born:** Lexington, Kentucky, 27 July 1916. **Education:** The University of Kentucky, Lexington, A.B. 1938, M.A. 1939; Columbia University, New York, 1939-41. **Family:** Married the poet Robert Lowell in 1949 (divorced 1972); one daughter. **Career:** Adjunct Associate Professor, Barnard College, New York. Founder and advisory editor, *New York Review of Books.* **Awards:** Guggenheim fellowship, 1948; George Jean Nathan award, for criticism, 1966; American Academy award, 1974; for belles lettres and criticism, 1992. **Member:** American Academy, 1977. **Address:** 15 West 67th Street, New York, New York 10023, U.S.A.

PUBLICATIONS

Novels

The Ghostly Lover. New York, Harcourt Brace, 1945; London, Virago Press, 1986.
The Simple Truth. New York, Harcourt Brace, and London, Weidenfeld and Nicolson, 1955.
Sleepless Nights. New York, Random House, and London, Weidenfeld and Nicolson, 1979.

Uncollected Short Stories

"People on the Roller Coaster," in *O. Henry Memorial Award Prize Stories of 1945.* New York, Doubleday, 1945.
"Saint Ursula and Her Eleven Thousand Virgins," in *Yale Review* (New Haven, Connecticut), March 1945.
"The Mysteries of Eleusis," in *The Best American Short Stories 1946,* edited by Martha Foley. Boston, Houghton Mifflin, 1946.
"What We Have Missed," in *O. Henry Memorial Award Prize Stories of 1946.* New York, Doubleday, 1946.
"The Temptations of Dr. Hoffman," in *Partisan Review* (New Brunswick, New Jersey), Fall 1946.
"The Golden Stallion," in *The Best American Short Stories 1947,* edited by Martha Foley. Boston, Houghton Mifflin, 1947.
"Evenings at Home," in *The Best American Short Stories 1949,* edited by Martha Foley. Boston, Houghton Mifflin, 1949.

"The Friendly Witness," in *Partisan Review* (New Brunswick, New Jersey), April 1950.
"A Florentine Conference," in *Partisan Review* (New Brunswick, New Jersey), May-June 1951.
"A Season's Romance," in *New Yorker,* 10 March 1956.
"The Oak and the Axe," in *New Yorker,* 12 May 1956.
"The Classless Society," in *Stories from The New Yorker 1950-1960.* New York, Simon and Schuster, 1960.
"The Purchase," in *The Best American Short Stories 1960,* edited by Martha Foley and David Burnett. Boston, Houghton Mifflin, 1960.
"Two Recent Triumphs," in *Gallery of Modern Fiction,* edited by Robie Macauley. New York, Salem Press, 1966.
"The Faithful," in *The Best American Short Stories 1980,* edited by Stanley Elkin and Shannon Ravenel. Boston, Houghton Mifflin, 1980.
"The Bookseller," in *The Best American Short Stories 1981,* edited by Hortense Calisher and Shannon Ravenel. Boston, Houghton Mifflin, 1981.
"Back Issues," in *New York Review of Books,* 17 December 1981.
"On the Eve," in *New York Review of Books,* 20 December 1983.
"Shot!: A New York Story," in *The New Yorker,* September 1993.

Other

A View of My Own: Essays in Literature and Society. New York, Farrar Straus, 1962; London, Heinemann, 1964.
Seduction and Betrayal: Women and Literature. New York, Random House, and London, Weidenfeld and Nicolson, 1974.
Bartleby in Manhattan and Other Essays. New York, Random House, and London, Weidenfeld and Nicolson, 1983.

Editor, *Selected Letters,* by William James. New York, Farrar Straus, 1961.
Editor, with Robert Atwan, *Best American Essays 1986.* New York, Ticknor and Fields, 1986.

*

Elizabeth Hardwick comments:

(1995) I am presently collecting my short stories written over the years, and also a collection of essays published since 1983. It is dismaying to me that writing does not become easier after all these years at the task. It is consoling to think that one makes greater demands on oneself, and yet I am not sure that is the case. The only part I truly enjoy about writing is revision: often, or so it appears to me, making something out of nothing. Perhaps in the long run a rather stupid problem confronts the writer more often than not: having something to say.

*   *   *

For over two decades, Elizabeth Hardwick's reputation as a tough-minded, occasionally wry, critic has been secure. Her career as a novelist has been less certain. Her first novel, *The Ghostly Lover,* published in 1945, was promising, but its early feminist slant was not rightly appreciated. A novel about Marian Coleman who learns that she cannot settle for the comforts of a man, it offers telling glimpses into her life, the life of her restless parents, the hot, lazy days in the South, the grubby days studying in New York, and the dreams of the ghostly men who pursue her. Marian knows the value of concealment; the book confirms her suspicion that love is not "the hard, demanding surrender she had imagined." Marian suffers from a peculiar emptiness, one that comes from knowing that what men want from her is not in her, but is "tuned to a certain imaginary pitch in women" that men have invented. The novel closes with Marian's act of independence: she walks unseen away from her lover who has come to the station to meet her. She knows that to accept him would be to accept marriage and not to care about motives. Hardwick's next novel, *The Simple Truth,* appeared a decade later. Tightly plotted, probing the motives behind a frightful act, the novel examines the death of a beautiful college girl, Betty Jane Henderson, who died in her boyfriend's rooming-house, after hours. The trial of the boyfriend, Rudy, dominates the book. It is examined from numerous perspectives, most important those of two curious onlookers, the affable, married Mr. Parks and the middle-aged, married Anita Mitchell who is drawn to the case to investigate the working of the unconscious. The truth about the act, late at night, in a rooming-house where two lovers frolicked and struggled, ultimately emerges, but equally as interesting is the picture of the psyches of the characters who become caught up in the trial. These two early novels were competent—the writing was careful; the characters, ordinary, but true, surprisingly often; the plots were slightly thin.

Sleepless Nights appeared in 1979 and broke a silence of more than 20 years. It should make Hardwick's name. Its form is novel, daringly breaking the strictures of her earlier narrative style. The autobiographical component of the novel is openly confronted, and handled effectively. Roaming like an insomniac from one recollection to another, the book continually surprises us with its fleeting memories of rooms we have all known, feelings we have felt, losses we have never remedied. In retrospect, Hardwick's earlier novels show a niggling regret on the author's part that the story is not a little more important, that life for women is not a little more adventuresome. *Sleepless Nights* reflects a more mature sensibility—one that has learned that ordinary experience needs no apology.

Sleepless Nights offers a record of life's obscenities. The insomniac narrator is identified as "Elizabeth" in the novel. The book is a queer blend of autobiography and fiction. Hardwick's decision to create a persona with her own name heightens our sense of how life informs fiction. The Elizabeth of this book is very nearly the Elizabeth Hardwick who lives, the woman who is a career journalist, writer, reviewer for *Partisan Review* and the *New York Review of Books,* and the ex-wife of the poet Robert Lowell. The memories and imaginings of the persona curl about the lives of deprived souls, of which Elizabeth is one. There is Josette, the Boston cleaning-lady, a victim of "unfair diseases," with her "breasts hacked off by cancer." There is Billie Holiday, self-destructive, haunting, pure style, who died in agony, with the police at her bedside, denied in her last hours the drugs her body craved. Elizabeth wonders at the "sheer enormity" of Holiday's vices. There is Alex A., Elizabeth's bachelor friend, an intellectual and failed academic who does not marry the woman who might have made his life different. There is her other half, the partner of the "we" she alludes to. She complains of his tyranny by the weak, women. He reads and writes all day, drinks quarts of mild, smokes cigarettes, and complains when she plays jazz records. There is her mother, bearer of nine children; childbearing is "what she was always doing, and in the end what she had done." There is the neighborhood prostitute, Juanita, who died of "prodigious pains and sores." This is a bitter, troubling book of memories to keep us all awake. But if the dose is bitter, it is also life. The laundress, the cleaning-lady, the Boston

spinster, the middle-aged persona whose divorce has brought her back to her old territory, the talk of a mother, troubled that her son cannot cope and the complaints of a couple too long married are all authentic. The style is often sparse; the details are selected with startling directness and simplicity; yet the whole is very full.

—Carol Simpson Stern

HARDY, Frank

Has also written as Ross Franklyn. **Nationality:** Australian. **Born:** Francis Joseph Hardy in Southern Cross, Victoria, 21 March 1917; brought up in Bacchus Marsh. **Education:** State schools. **Military Service:** Served in the Australian Army, 1942-46 (staff member, *Salt* army magazine). **Family:** Married Rosslyn Couper in 1939; one son and two daughters. **Career:** Joined Communist Party of Australia, 1939; freelance writer: President, Realist Writers Group, Melbourne and Sydney, 1945-74; co-founder, Australian Society of Authors, Sydney, 1968-74; President, Carringbush Writers, Melbourne, 1980-83. **Awards:** Logie award, for television script, 1972; Television Society award, 1973; 3 Literature Board grants. **Agent:** Jill Hickson Associates, 137 Regent Street, Chippendale, New South Wales 2008. **Address:** 9/76 Elizabeth Bay Road, Elizabeth Bay, New South Wales 2011, Australia.

PUBLICATIONS

Novels

Power Without Glory. Melbourne, Realist, 1950; London, Laurie, 1962.
The Four-Legged Lottery. London, Laurie, 1958.
The Outcasts of Foolgarah. Melbourne, Allara, 1971; London, Panther, 1975.
But the Dead Are Many: A Novel in Fugue Form. London, Bodley Head, 1975.
Who Shot George Kirkland? A Novel about the Nature of Truth. Melbourne, Arnold, 1981.
Warrant of Distress. Carlton, Victoria, Pascoe, 1983.
The Obsession of Oscar Oswald. Carlton, Victoria, Pascoe, 1983.

Short Stories

The Man from Clinkapella and Other Prize-Winning Stories. Melbourne, Realist, 1951.
Legends from Benson's Valley. London, Laurie, 1963.
The Yarns of Billy Borker. Sydney, Reed, 1965.
Billy Borker Yarns Again. Melbourne, Nelson, 1967.
The Great Australian Lover and Other Stories. Melbourne, Nelson, 1972.
It's Moments Like These. Melbourne, Gold Star, 1972.
The Loser Now Will Be Later to Win. Carlton, Victoria, Pascoe, 1985.
Hardy's People: Stories of Truthful Jones. Fairfield, Victoria, Pascoe, 1986.

Plays

Black Diamonds (produced Sydney, 1956).

The Ringbolter (produced Sydney, 1964).
Who Was Harry Larsen? (produced 1985).
Faces in the Street: An Epic Drama. Westgate, New South Wales, Stained Wattle Press, 1990(?).
Mary Lives! Sydney, Currency Press, 1992.

Other

Journey into the Future (on the Soviet Union). Melbourne, Australasian Book Society, 1952.
The Hard Way: The Story Behind Power Without Glory. London, Laurie, 1961.
The Unlucky Australians (on the Gurindji). Melbourne, Nelson, 1968; revised edition, Melbourne, Gold Star, 1972.
The Needy and the Greedy: Humorous Stories of the Racetrack, with Athol George Mulley. Canberra, Libra, 1975.
You Nearly Had Him That Time and Other Cricket Stories, with Fred Trueman. London, Paul, 1978.
A Frank Hardy Swag, edited by Clement Semmler. Sydney, Harper, 1982.
Great Australian Legends. Surry Hills, New South Wales, Hutchinson, 1988.
Retreat Australia Fair and Other Great Australian Legends. Milsons Point, New South Wales, Hutchinson, 1990.

*

Bibliography: In *A Frank Hardy Swag,* 1982.

Manuscript Collection: Australian National Library, Canberra.

Theatrical Activities:
Actor: **Play**—role in *Black Diamonds,* Sydney, 1956.

*   *   *

Though Frank Hardy has written a number of Australia's best short stories (including the "classic" yarn "The Load of Wood"), he is best known as a novelist. His first novel, *Power Without Glory,* was a long social-realist exposé of corruption in Australian society and political life. The central character, John West, rises above his humble working-class beginnings and amasses wealth, power, and influence; he abandons all concern for the working man, loses all human compassion and decency, and drives his wife to adultery and his children to despair.

Though its prose style is merely workaday and its structure crude (but serviceable), the novel has three enduring strengths. It tells a long story with clarity; it is imbued with a powerful, angry sincerity; and it combines the suspense of fiction with the fascinating factual insights of a journalistic "exposé." The "factuality," however, became the source of controversy when it was alleged that *Power Without Glory* was a disguised portrait of the Melbourne personality John Wren. Hardy was taken to court over the claim that he had defamed Wren's wife by portraying her as having committed adultery. (The story of his trial and acquittal, together with an account of the researching and writing of the novel, is told in Hardy's non-fiction book *The Hard Way.*) *Power Without Glory* established Hardy's concern with socio-political subjects, but his distinctive handling of structure and narrative point of view does not emerge until his second novel, *The Four-Legged Lottery.* Taking as its epigraph the comment that horse-racing has "ceased to be

a valiant sport" and has become "a lottery, with four-legged tickets," Hardy uses the corruption of the Australian horse-racing industry as a metaphor for the injustice and corruption of Australian capitalism. By an ingenious plot construction, the novel combines a third-person account of race-track life with a first-person analysis of the ills of betting (written from the prison cell of a man who has seen his mate driven to death by punting debts).

In his best novel, *But the Dead Are Many,* Hardy uses a similar but more ambitious structure. Sub-titled "A Novel in Fugue Form," the work concerns the disappearance and apparent suicide of John Morel, a leading figure in the Australian Communist Party, and the efforts of Morel's friend, Jack, to retrace Morel's final journey and discover the reasons for his death. Morel's story points to a crisis of confidence in the moral standards of the Communist Party, for Morel has come to see his comrades' ideals as a reflection of Stalinism. But Morel's story becomes the story of another man, the communist intellectual Nicolai Buratakov, whose writings converted Morel to communism. Attempting to understand the reasons why Buratakov was put on trial and executed in Moscow in 1938, Morel's faith in his ideology becomes as weak as the morality of Stalinist practice.

Describing the intentions behind this novel, Hardy claims a desire to speak for the generation of Australian communists born at the time of the Russian revolution and compelled to live through the failure of capitalism (such as the Great Depression) only to witness the collapse of the Utopian dream in the brutality of Stalinism and the Soviet response to events in Hungary. The novel succeeds in this aim, but achieves even more: it is also a study of suicide, an examination of the relationship between the individual and the group, and (less successfully, perhaps) an attempt to explore the concepts of death and transcendence. The novel also breaks new ground in Australian fiction, using character and plot to expound themes that are simultaneously social, psychological and ideological. *But the Dead Are Many* is one of the major works of Australian literature in the 1970s.

Who Shot George Kirkland? (sub-titled "A Novel About the Nature of Truth") is equally ambitious but less successful. The novel clearly draws upon Hardy's own experience in the writing of *Power Without Glory,* for it uses a character named Ross Franklyn, and Hardy has admitted (in the 1971 "Prologue" to *The Hard Way*) that Ross Franklyn is his own pseudonym. Decades after facing criminal charges over a story of adultery in his novel *Power Corrupts,* Franklyn despairingly wonders whether or not the story was true. His source was a Melbourne underworld figure named Alan Hall, and Franklyn recalls that Hall also claimed to have shot the gangster named George Kirkland. If the claim about Kirkland can be shown to be true, presumably the story of the adultery would also be true.

Instead of questioning this spurious logic, the novel proceeds to add complications to its structure and concerns. Ross Franklyn commits suicide without discovering who shot Kirkland, and it is left to a young researcher to retrace Franklyn's final uncertainties and seek to discover the truth. The events which subsequently unfold are used to assert the view that "the truth resides in memory and memory is clouded . . . the recollections of any individual are conditioned by the general truths by which he or she has tried to live." However, the accuracy of such a view is scarcely demonstrated by researchers who fail to take notes, conduct research interviews when drunk, or freely admit they may have "embroidered" their material! Far from being a novel about the nature of truth, *Who Shot George Kirkland?* is merely an indictment of slip-shod research.

Like his comic novel *The Outcasts of Foolgarah,* Hardy's latest novel, *The Obsession of Oscar Oswald,* is disappointingly slight and suffers from the thinness of its characterization. Though published in 1983, the novel purports to be a 1985 manuscript proving that "In *1984,* George Orwell got it all wrong!" Obsessed with the Hire Purchase system (and the capitalist society which supports it), Oscar Oswald sets out to prove that Orwell "ignored the capitalist 'free' market with its built-in cycle of boom, bust and war": "It was not Big Brother but Big Business exploiting the poor . . . not Double Think picking the minds of the intellectuals but Capitalists picking the pockets of the poor." Hardy has written an accurate literary epitaph for himself, using the words of the young researcher in *Who Shot George Kirkland?:* he "wrote truly of and for the common man. His overall theme is in his concern for the way the ordinary man is cheated by those who manipulate him, and he invests this theme with greater urgency and power than any other writer."

—Van Ikin

HARRIS, Mark

Nationality: American. **Born:** Mark Harris Finkelstein in Mount Vernon, New York, 19 November 1922. **Education:** The University of Denver, B.A. in English 1950, M.A. in English 1951; University of Minnesota, Minneapolis, Ph.D. in American Studies 1956. **Military Service:** Served in the United States Army, 1943-44. **Family:** Married Josephine Horen in 1946; one daughter and two sons. **Career:** Reporter, *Daily Item,* Port Chester, New York, 1944-45, *PM,* New York, 1945, and International News Service, St. Louis, 1945-46; writer for *Negro Digest* and *Ebony,* Chicago, 1946-51. Member of the English Department, San Francisco State College, 1954-68, Purdue University, Lafayette, Indiana, 1967-70, California Institute of the Arts, Valencia, 1970-73, Immaculate Heart College, Los Angeles, 1973-74, and University of Southern California, Los Angeles, 1973-75; professor of English, University of Pittsburgh, 1975-80. Since 1983 professor of English, Arizona State University, Tempe. Fulbright Professor, University of Hiroshima, 1957-58; visiting professor, Brandeis University, Waltham, Massachusetts, 1963. **Awards:** Ford grant, for theater, 1960; American Academy grant, 1961; Guggenheim fellowship, 1965, 1974; National Endowment for the Arts grant, 1966. D.H.L.: Illinois Wesleyan University, Bloomington, 1974. **Member:** San Francisco Art Commission, 1961-64; U.S. Delegate, Dartmouth Conference, Kurashiki, Japan, 1974. **Address:** Department of English, Arizona State University, Tempe, Arizona 85287, U.S.A.

PUBLICATIONS

Novels

Trumpet to the World. New York, Reynal, 1946.
City of Discontent: An Interpretive Biography of Vachel Lindsay, Being Also the Story of Springfield, Illinois, USA, and of the Love of the Poet for That City, That State, and That Nation, by Henry W. Wiggen. Indianapolis, Bobbs Merrill, 1952.
The Southpaw: by Henry W. Wiggen: Punctuation Inserted and Spelling Greatly Improved. Indianapolis, Bobbs Merrill, 1953.

Bang the Drum Slowly, by Henry W. Wiggen: Certain of His Enthusiasms Restrained. New York, Knopf, 1956.
A Ticket for a Seamstitch, by Henry W. Wiggen: But Polished for the Printer. New York, Knopf, 1957.
Something about a Soldier. New York, Macmillan, 1957; London, Deutsch, 1958.
Wake Up, Stupid. New York, Knopf, 1959; London, Deutsch, 1960.
The Goy. New York, Dial Press, 1970.
Killing Everybody. New York, Dial Press, 1973.
It Looked Like For Ever. New York, McGraw Hill, 1979.
Lying in Bed. New York, McGraw Hill, 1984.
Speed. New York, Fine, 1990.
The Tale Maker. New York, Fine, 1994.

Uncollected Short Stories

"Carmelita's Education for Living," in *Esquire* (New York), October 1957.
"Conversation on Southern Honshu," in *North Dakota Quarterly* (Grand Forks), Summer 1959.
"The Self-Made Brain Surgeon," in *The Best American Short Stories 1961,* edited by Martha Foley and David Burnett. Boston, Houghton Mifflin, 1961.
"La Lumière," in *Denver Quarterly,* Fall 1983.
"Hi, Bob!," in *Arizona Quarterly* (Tuscon), Summer 1986.
"Titwillow," in *Michigan Quarterly Review* (Ann Arbor), Summer 1986.
"Flattery," in *Sequoia* (Stanford, California), Winter 1988.
"From the Desk of the Troublesome Editor," in *Virginia Quarterly Review* (Charlottesville), Summer 1989.

Plays

Friedman & Son (produced San Francisco, 1962). New York, Macmillan, 1963.
The Man That Corrupted Hadleyburg, adaptation of the story by Mark Twain (televised, 1980). Published in *The American Short Story 2,* edited by Calvin Skaggs, New York, Dell, 1980.

Screenplay: *Bang the Drum Slowly,* 1973.

Television Plays: *The Man That Corrupted Hadleyburg,* 1980; *Boswell for the Defence,* 1983 (UK); *Boswell's London Journal,* 1984 (UK).

Other

Mark the Glove Boy; or, The Last Days of Richard Nixon (autobiography). New York, Macmillan, 1964.
Twentyone Twice: A Journal (autobiography). Boston, Little Brown, 1966.
Public Television: A Program for Action, with others. New York, Harper, 1967.
Best Father Ever Invented: The Autobiography of Mark Harris. New York, Dial Press, 1976.
Short Work of It: Selected Writing. Pittsburgh, University of Pittsburgh Press, 1979.
Saul Bellow, Drumlin Woodchuck. Athens, University of Georgia Press, 1980.
Diamond: Baseball Writings of Mark Harris. New York, Fine, 1994.

Editor, *Selected Poems,* by Vachel Lindsay. New York, Macmillan, 1963; London, Collier Macmillan, 1965.

Editor, with Josephine and Hester Harris, *The Design of Fiction.* New York, Crowell, 1976.

Editor, *The Heart of Boswell.* New York, McGraw Hill, 1981.

*

Manuscript Collection: University of Delaware Library, Newark.

Critical Study: *Mark Harris* by Norman Lavers, Boston, Twayne, 1978.

Mark Harris comments:

(1972) I have written eight novels. I think that a constant line travels through them. I didn't know this was happening while it was happening, but I can see it now, looking back after a quarter of a century since my first novel was published.

They are about the writer. That is, if you will, they are about the artist. Which is to say, if you will, they are about the one man against his society and trying to come to terms with his society, and trying to succeed within it without losing his own identity or integrity.

My novels are always very carefully written. Since hard work makes the writing look easy, there exist stupid reviewers and critics who think I (and others) just slam these writings out. My books are all constructed with great care. Nothing is missing from any of them in the way of plot. I forget nothing.

Of course, although I am spiritually at the center of my novels (every novel is mainly about one man), I am disguised as poet or baseball player or professor or historian. I am always a minority person in some sense, either because I am fictionally left-handed or, most recently, gentile in a Jewish milieu. (My first book was about a black man in a white milieu). I don't know why this is so. I believe that it is most deeply the result of being a Jew, but it may be attributable to other things I am not fully aware of. Maybe I was just born that way. It is a mystery.

Subject and theme: sometimes these aren't really stated in the works, and people feel disappointed. They want to know what they shouldn't: where does the author stand? In my heart, if not always dogmatically in my books, I stand for human equality and peace and justice.

I also stand for writing well: I don't believe that good ends can come of false or shoddy or hasty means. Books must be beautiful so that the world is put into a mood of beauty. Books mustn't merely *say* but must, on the other hand, *exist* as beauty.

I am opposed to the reduction or paraphrase of works of art. Thus I feel that I may on this page already have written more than I should.

*   *   *

Mark Harris's fiction and autobiography share several themes: the problems of racism and racial justice, the dilemma of violence and pacifism, the price of individualism and the forms of democracy and social justice. His work is dominated by genial comedy, a gentle optimistic view of man's possibilities and capacities, and Harris has pursued his own life through his fiction. His journal-auto-biographies *Mark the Glove Boy* and *Twentyone Twice* complement fictionalized self-portraits like pitcher-author Henry Wiggen (*The Southpaw, Bang the Drum Slowly, A Ticket for a Seamstitch*), boxer-novelist-teacher Lee Youngdahl (*Wake Up, Stupid*), soldier-pacifist

Jacob Epstein (*Something about a Soldier*) and historian-diarist Westrum (*The Goy*).

Harris's novels depict individuals in pursuit of themselves, discovering through self-analysis, experience, and observation who they are and what their lives mean. His first novel, *Trumpet to the World,* follows a black man through self-discovery and self-education to his rejection of war and violence and his attempts to reach the world through writing. He suffers poverty, hatred, and violence but also discovers friendship and love. Through determination and courage, he overcomes dehumanizing conditions to become fully alive, a fully functioning man. The baseball tetralogy (*The Southpaw, Bang the Drum Slowly, A Ticket for a Seamstitch, It Looked Like For Ever*) describes the career of Henry W. Wiggen, a young man who succeeds in big-league baseball. In a Lardneresque style, Wiggen writes the journal of his maturity as an athlete and a man. Wiggen grapples with the mysteries of love, the problem of hatred and violence, becomes reconciled with the finality of death. Each story shows Wiggen's growth, mentally and spiritually, and his progress down a road to self-understanding and reconciliation. Overtly a comedy of athletics and folk-hero rambunctiousness, the four books also form a study of pacifism, love and justice.

Something about a Soldier turns explicitly to the problems of violence and nonviolence which appear in the earlier novels. In it Jacob Epp (Epstein) discovers the importance of his identity, the meaning of love and loyalty, and the relationship between violence and justice. A young, very bright, but naive recruit, Jacob rejects the Army and the war (World War II), militantly works for justice and equality for black people and begins to understand love and friendship. He rejects death for life, war for peace, goes AWOL, and through meditation in prison comes to self-reconciliation.

In *Wake Up, Stupid* Harris uses the epistolary form to follow a crisis of insecurity in the life of a man who is successful as an athlete, teacher, and writer. Lee Youngdahl, during a lull in artistic creativity, takes up letter-writing to occupy his imagination. Comic crises of his fantasy life involve all his friends and enemies and lead him to a final understanding of his needs and desires, the sources of his imagination. *Lying in Bed* continues Harris's exploration of marital comedy through the viewpoint of Lee Youngdahl. Older and wiser in the ways of love and literature, Youngdahl extends his imaginative self-analysis and reviews his love affairs, real and fictive, as he tries to defend his virtuous monogamy and his need for varied romance.

The Goy continues the theme of self-discovery. In it, Westrum, a midwestern gentile who has married an eastern Jew, pursues his identity through a massive, life-long journal. He comes to understand, through the journal, his relationship with the Jews in his life, his father's virulent anti-semitism, his own obsession with history, his relationship with his son, his wife, and his mistress. The past, through his journal and his study of history, ultimately explains his present.

In *Killing Everybody* Harris explores opposing passions of love and rage, life-giving and death. The novel deals with the madness of the world and of individuals caught up in its madness. It studies revenge and charity, physical love and sexual fantasy, a dialectic skillfully developed as a complex dance between four central minds. The story moves more deeply into the roots of modern psychic life than Harris's earlier fiction, and he confronts a massive theme— civilization and its discontents.

All of Mark Harris's fiction is comic in conception, and sports and games are at the center of the work, especially the social games which are the substance of comedy of manners. Lee Youngdahl, in

Wake Up, Stupid, analyzes American literature in a statement epitomizing Harris's own work:

> What is it that thrusts Mark Twain and Sherwood Anderson into one stream, and Henry James into another? ... It has so much to do with a man's early relationship to the society of boys and games—that miniature of our larger society of men and business, with its codes and rules, its provision for imagination within these rules, with winning, losing, timing, bluffing, feinting, jockeying, with directness of aim and speech and with coming back off the floor again.

Harris's fiction is solidly within this tradition which translates social games into comedy, a comedy which explains our secret lives more clearly than any social or psychological theory.

—William J. Schafer

HARRIS, (Theodore) Wilson

Nationality: British. **Born:** New Amsterdam, British Guiana, now Guyana, 24 March 1921. **Education:** Queen's College, Georgetown. **Family:** Married 1) Cecily Carew in 1945; 2) Margaret Whitaker in 1959. **Career:** Government surveyor in the 1940s, and senior surveyor, 1955-58, Government of British Guiana; moved to London in 1959. Visiting lecturer, State University of New York, Buffalo, 1970; writer-in-residence, University of the West Indies, Kingston, Jamaica, and Scarborough College, University of Toronto, 1970; Commonwealth Fellow in Caribbean Literature, Leeds University, Yorkshire, 1971; visiting professor, University of Texas, Austin, 1972, and 1981-82, University of Mysore, 1978, Yale University, New Haven, Connecticut, 1979, University of Newcastle, New South Wales, 1979, and University of Queensland, St. Lucia, 1986; Regents' Lecturer, University of California, Santa Cruz, 1983. Delegate, National Identity Conference, Brisbane, and Unesco Symposium on Caribbean Literature, Cuba, both 1968. **Awards:** Arts Council grant, 1968, 1970; Guggenheim fellowship, 1973; Henfield fellowship, 1974; Southern Arts fellowship, 1976; Guyana fiction prize, 1987; Premio Mondello International award, 1992. D.Litt.: University of the West Indies, 1984; University of Kent, Canterbury, 1988. **Address:** c/o Faber and Faber Ltd., 3 Queen Square, London WC1N 3AU, England.

PUBLICATIONS

Novels

The Guyana Quartet. London, Faber, 1985.
    Palace of the Peacock. London, Faber, 1960.
    The Far Journey of Oudin. London, Faber, 1961.
    The Whole Armour. London, Faber, 1962.
    The Secret Ladder. London, Faber, 1963.
Heartland. London, Faber, 1964.
The Eye of the Scarecrow. London, Faber, 1965.
The Waiting Room. London, Faber, 1967.
Tumatumari. London, Faber, 1968.
Ascent to Omai. London, Faber, 1970.

Black Marsden: A Tabula Rasa Comedy. London, Faber, 1972.
Companions of the Day and Night. London, Faber, 1975.
Da Silva da Silva's Cultivated Wilderness, and Genesis of the Clowns. London, Faber, 1977.
The Tree of the Sun. London, Faber, 1978.
The Angel at the Gate. London, Faber, 1982.
Carnival. London, Faber, 1985.
The Infinite Rehearsal. London, Faber, 1987.
The Four Banks of the River of Space. London, Faber, 1990.
Resurrection at Sorrow Hill. London and Boston, Faber, 1993.
The Carnival Trilogy. London, Faber, 1993.

Short Stories

The Sleepers of Roraima. London, Faber, 1970.
The Age of the Rainmakers. London, Faber, 1971.

Poetry

Fetish. Privately printed, 1951.
The Well and the Land. Georgetown, Magnet, 1952.
Eternity to Season. Privately printed, 1954; revised edition, London, New Beacon, 1979.

Other

Tradition, The Writer, and Society: Critical Essays. London, New Beacon, 1967.
History, Fable, and Myth in the Caribbean and Guianas. Georgetown, National History and Arts Council, 1970.
Fossil and Psyche (lecture on Patrick White). Austin, University of Texas, 1974.
Explorations: A Selection of Talks and Articles, edited by Hena Maes-Jelinek. Aarhus, Denmark, Dangaroo Press, 1981.
The Womb of Space: The Cross-Cultural Imagination. Westport, Connecticut, Greenwood Press, 1983.
The Radical Imagination: Lectures and Talks, edited by A. Riach and M. Williams. Liège, Belgium, Université de Liège, 1992.

*

Manuscript Collections: University of the West Indies, Mona, Kingston, Jamaica; University of Texas, Austin; University of Indiana, Bloomington; University of Guyana, Georgetown.

Critical Studies: *Wilson Harris: A Philosophical Approach* by C.L.R. James, Port of Spain, University of the West Indies, 1965; *The Novel Now* by Anthony Burgess, London, Faber, and New York, Norton, 1967, revised edition, Faber, 1971; essay by John Hearne, in *The Islands in Between* edited by Louis James, London, Oxford University Press, 1968; *Wilson Harris and the Caribbean Novel* by Michael Gilkes, Trinidad and London, Longman, 1975; *Enigma of Values* edited by Kirsten Holst Petersen and Anna Rutherford, Aarhus, Denmark, Dangaroo Press, 1975; *The Naked Design: A Reading of Palace of the Peacock,* Aarhus, Denmark, Dangaroo Press, 1976, and *Wilson Harris,* Boston, Twayne, 1982, both by Hena Maes-Jelinek; *West Indian Literature* edited by Bruce King, London, Macmillan, 1979; "The Eternal Present in Wilson Harris's *The Sleepers of Roraima* and *The Age of the Rainmakers*" by Gary Crew, in *World Literature Written in English* (Arlington, Texas), Autumn 1980; "Limbo, Dislocation, Phantom Limb" by

Nathaniel Mackey, in *Criticism* (Detroit), Winter 1980; *Wilson Harris and the Modern Imagination: A New Architecture of the World* by Sandra E. Drake, Westport, Connecticut, and London, Greenwood Press, 1986; *The Literate Imagination: Essays on the Novels of Wilson Harris* edited by Michael Gilkes, London, Macmillan, 1989; *Wilson Harris: The Uncompromising Imagination* edited by Hena Maes-Jelinek, Aarhus, Kangaroo Press, 1991.

Theatrical Activities:

Actor: **Television**—*Da Silva da Silva*, 1987.

Wilson Harris comments:

(1972) *Palace of the Peacock* through *The Guyana Quartet* and successive novels up to *The Sleepers of Roraima* and *The Age of the Rainmakers* are related to a symbolic landscape-in-depth—the shock of great rapids, vast forests and savannahs—playing through memory to involve perspectives of imperiled community and creativity reaching back into the Pre-Columbian mists of time.

I believe that the revolution of sensibility of defining community towards which we may now be moving is an extension of the frontiers of the alchemical imagination beyond an *opus contra naturam* into an *opus contra ritual*. This does not mean the jettisoning of ritual (since ritual belongs in the great ambivalent chain of memory; and the past, in a peculiar sense, as an omen of proportions, shrinking or expanding, never dies); but it means the utilization of ritual as an ironic bias—the utilization of ritual, not as something in which we situate ourselves absolutely, but as an unraveling of self-deception with self-revelation as we see through the various dogmatic proprietors of the globe within a play of contrasting structures and anti-structures: a profound drama of consciousness invoking contrasting tones is the variable phenomenon of creativity within which we are prone, nevertheless, to idolize logical continuity or structure and commit ourselves to a conservative bias, or to idolize logical continuity or anti-structure and commit ourselves to a revolutionary bias. Thus we are prone to monumentalize our own biases and to indict as well as misconceive creativity. A capacity to digest as well as liberate contrasting figures is essential to the paradox of community and to the life of the imagination.

*   *   *

With the publication in 1990 of *The Four Banks of the River of Space*, Wilson Harris completed a trilogy of novels which began with *Carnival* and continued through *The Infinite Rehearsal*. Although each book involves different characters and locations, when taken together, they form a complex revision of three crucial texts of Western Culture: *The Odyssey, The Divine Comedy,* and *Faust*. This is the culmination of a process which began with Harris's first novel, *Palace of the Peacock*, published 30 years earlier, and has continued through 26 volumes of fictional prose, criticism and verse.

Like Blake, Harris is a visionary, and his work is the complex literary expression of a vision which offers redemptive hope. For Harris, creativity is an intrinsic value in all the forms taken by the expressions of the intuitive imagination. Harris's prose is not seductively mimetic, like that of a realist novel. Rather, it demands concentrated attention as it works through continual disclosures of its own ambivalence. For example, the opening of *Palace of the Peacock* seems to describe a character on horseback "approaching at breakneck speed." A shot rings out, the man falls dead and a second man approaches (an unnamed "I"). The narrative seems

straightforward, but close scrutiny of Harris's language reveals ambivalent meanings. The word "breakneck" suddenly suggests that the man has been hanged, not shot, and the noise of the gunshot may be the sound of the trapdoor dropping. Harris puns repeatedly on "I"/"eye" and brings together "one dead seeing eye" and "one living closed eye" to suggest that the contemplative man of vision and the unimaginative man of action are not absolute types but only aspects of a complex wholeness, wherein no individual has absolute authority. Harris extends this notion radically in the *Carnival* trilogy, where cultural archetypes like Ulysses are seen to be no longer viable as the property of any single culture, but demand to be shared among cultures globally.

Thus the journey upriver into the rainforests of Guyana which forms the narrative "line" of *Palace* is better understood as a prismatic perspective which reveals the "characters" as parts of a vast, interrelated family. They are the representatives of numerous cultures, scattered from pole to pole by the processes of imperialism and colonialism. Though they are symbolic, the symbolism is unreliable and inconstant.

The strategy of Harris's novels is therefore to draw hope from a narrative which would seem to be linear and closed by opening it up to historical and geographical dimensional senses and formal experimentation. Although ostensibly "set" in South America, *Palace* is as much an inquiry into the nature of language and literary form as it is a story of conquistadors striking out for El Dorado. Indeed, the forbidding opacities and dazzling visions of the Guyanese rainforests seem sometimes to act metaphorically for Harris's written English, its adamantine immediacy and allusive depths. The name of the principal character, Donne, echoes that of the late Renaissance poet who stands at the end of the medieval world and at the beginning of the modern, at the point where colonial expansion began. Harris is hopefully signaling an equally transitional period. He addresses the questions of the dissolution of personal identity and "the open wound of human history" in ways which are significant not only in terms of "Caribbean literature" or "post-colonial literature", but rather in terms of modern literature in English.

The three novels which follow *Palace* are thematically distinct as they deal with slavery and indenture on the rice plantations, the imposition of law on frontier society and finally the rise of the modern state. But throughout *The Guyana Quartet*, themes and characters from past and present meet and mingle with each other. The space between the hinterland of forest and the cultivated coastal areas is shifting, just as language is a vast repository of unarticulated expression, an "enabling" or "womb-like space." As Harris has said, "The human person has very deep resources. We tend to live our lives on the surface and eclipse those deep and incredible resources. It happens on the individual as well as on the cultural level."

After the *Quartet*, Harris embarked upon a further cycle of novels beginning with *Heartland*, whose main character vanishes into the jungle (as Harris's own stepfather did), leaving only fragments of letters and notes. *The Eye of the Scarecrow, The Waiting Room, Tumatumari,* and *Ascent to Omai,* delve further into questions about the condition of irretrievable absence and loss. Yet for Harris, even the most dreadful conditions are intricately and indissolubly linked to processes of change which might reveal a further regeneration of possibility. Such regeneration is never glib or easy. But it is this motivating and empowering sense which Harris works through, as catastrophe and deprivation is understood to be in a difficult but actual relationship with emergent reality. Two volumes of short stories were followed by *Black Marsden*, subtitled "A Tabula Rasa

Comedy," and set mainly in Scotland. Harris recognized in Scotland and in Scottish literature an implicit quality of diverse cultural and linguistic layers which corresponded with his understanding of the Caribbean, a country whose people were both exploiters and exploited, both a tributary and a backwater of empire. In *Black Marsden,* he takes a recognizable motif from Scottish fiction (the Devil as familiar tempter) and loads it with the unfamiliar depths of his vision. The following novels continued this process in Mexico, London, and most recently through the *Carnival* trilogy, in which the philosophical understanding of the relations between absence and presence, possession and loss, paradise, purgatory, and hell, is presented in fictional terms with diamond clarity and refractive depth.

Harris's peculiar distinction among modern novelists is threefold. He imagines in a complex dynamic and changing condition aspects of that condition which are normally held to be separate and static. He understands that imaginative act to be a radical departure from normal imaginative procedures, which are frequently run along familiar lines. And he embodies this in a major and invigorating sequence of novels which break down the rigidities of the form as drastically as they reconfirm potential in the protean forms of humanity.

—Alan Riach

HARRISON, Jim

Nationality: American. **Born:** James Thomas Harrison in Grayling, Michigan, 11 December 1937. **Education:** Michigan State University, East Lansing, B.A. in comparative literature 1960, M.A. in comparative literature 1964. **Family:** Married Linda King in 1960; two daughters. **Career:** Assistant professor of English, State University of New York, Stony Brook, 1965-66. Lives in Michigan. **Awards:** National Endowment for the Arts grant, 1967, 1968, 1969; Guggenheim fellowship, 1969. **Agent:** Robert Datilla, 233 East 8th Street, New York, New York 10028. **Address:** Box 135, Lake Leelanau, Michigan 49653, U.S.A.

PUBLICATIONS

Novels

Wolf. New York, Simon and Schuster, 1971; London, Flamingo, 1993.
A Good Day to Die. New York, Simon and Schuster, 1973; London, Flamingo, 1993.
Farmer. New York, Viking Press, 1976; London, Flamingo, 1993.
Legends of the Fall (novellas). New York, Delacorte Press, 1979; London, Collins, 1980.
Warlock. New York, Delacorte Press, and London, Collins, 1981.
Sundog: The story of an American foreman, Robert Corvus Strang, as told to Jim Harrison. New York, Dutton, 1984; London, Heinemann, 1985.
Dalva. New York, Dutton, 1988; London, Cape, 1989.
The Woman Lit by Fireflies (three novellas). Boston, Houghton Mifflin, 1990; London, Weidenfeld and Nicolson, 1991.
Julip. Boston, Houghton Mifflin/Seymour Lawrence, and London, Flamingo, 1994.

Uncollected Short Story

"Dalva: How It Happened to Me," in *Esquire* (New York), April 1988.

Poetry

Plain Song. New York, Norton, 1965.
Locations. New York, Norton, 1968.
Walking. Cambridge, Massachusetts, Pym Randall Press, 1969.
Outlyer and Ghazals. New York, Simon and Schuster, 1971.
Letters to Yesenin. Fremont, Michigan, Sumac Press, 1973.
Returning to Earth. Ithaca, New York, Ithaca House, 1977.
Selected and New Poems 1961-1981. New York, Delacorte Press, 1982.
The Theory and Practice of Rivers. Seattle, Winn, 1986.
The Theory and Practice of Rivers and New Poems. Livingston, Montana, Clark City Press, 1989.

Other

Natural World, with Diana Guest. Barrytown, New York, Open Book, 1983.
Just Before Dark: Collected Nonfiction. Livingston, Montana, Clark City Press, 1991.

*   *   *

A reviewer for the *Times* observed that Jim Harrison is "a writer with immortality in him." Archivist Bernard Fontana, of the University of Arizona, has expressed his belief in the quality of Harrison's work in another way: "To read Jim Harrison is to be tattooed." Harrison's early reputation was founded on four volumes of poetry. In 1971, his first novel, *Wolf,* was published. *Wolf* is the story of one man's quest for identity and freedom through the primal levels of nature and sex. The novel's themes and northern Michigan location drew critical comparisons to Ernest Hemingway's Nick Adams stories.

Two years after *Wolf, A Good Day to Die* appeared as a statement about the decline of America's ecological systems. In a blending of Edward Abbey's *The Monkey Wrench Gang* and Hemingway's *The Sun Also Rises,* readers are presented with three characters who are launched on a cross-country trek to blow up a dam and rescue the Grand Canyon. A modern day Tom Sawyer and Huck Finn and an earthy Becky Thatcher are faced with the bankruptcy of the American dream. The novel also illustrates the author's fascination with Native Americans and begins a thematic interest that is found in other novels.

Farmer is a *Lolita*-like account of a country school teacher coming to grips with middle age while caught between two love affairs—one with a nymphet student and the other with a widowed co-worker who was his childhood sweetheart.

Harrison's first three novels resulted in many attacks by critics who saw him as a stereotype of the Hemingway myth: a writer obsessed with the macho male activities of hunting, drinking, and manly sex. In later novels Harrison would confront these criticisms head-on.

After *Farmer,* Harrison entered into an unusual contract with the actor Jack Nicolson. For $15,000 in advance of writing and publication, Nicholson purchased half the film rights to Harrison's yet-to-be-written project. Harrison produced three novellas which were published in book form under the title of *Legends of the Fall.* The first novella, "Revenge," is the story of a love affair between Cochran; an ex-fighter pilot; and Miryea, the wife of a Mexican gangster. "The Man Who Gave Up His Name" chronicles Nordstrom's divorce, his run-ins with the New York underworld and his attempt to form a new life built around a new identity. *Legends of the Fall* is an epic story that spans 50 years and tells the tale of William Ludlow and his three sons. The story is filled with beautiful characterizations and with great action from its beginning, when the brothers ride out to Calgary to join the Canadian army and fight in World War I; to its end, when Ludlow confronts Irish bootleggers who have come to kill one of his sons.

Published in 1981, *Warlock* parodies nearly everything for which critics had taken Harrison to task. Johnny Lundgren, a.k.a. Warlock, becomes a private detective after he loses his job as a foundation executive. Unable to handle women, earn the devotion of his dog or remember to load his pistol, he bumbles through a series of adventures on the behalf of a deranged physician. *Sundog,* subtitled "The story of an American foreman, Robert Corvus Strang, as told to Jim Harrison," is a piece of fiction presented as a true tale. Strang recounts the story of his life, his several marriages and children, dozens of lovers, and his work on giant construction projects around the world.

Dalva, which was published in 1988, contains two stories: a tale of a middle-aged women's search for her out-of-wedlock child as well as her tribulations with her almost-boyfriend professor; and a story of her pioneer ancestor, an Andersonville survivor and naturalist whose diaries vividly tell of the destruction of the Plains Indian way of life by Anglo invasion.

The Woman Lit by Fireflies is a collection of three novellas. The first, "Brown Dog" is the comic memoir of an ex-Bible college student who loves to eat, drink, and chase women and his discovery of an Indian chief submerged in Lake Superior. "Sunset Limited" concerns a group of Sixties radicals who reunite to rescue an old friend held in a Mexican jail. "The Woman Lit by Fireflies" is the story of a woman who walks away from her husband at an Interstate Welcome Center near Davenport, Iowa and is a tale of transfiguration and discovery.

—Tom Colonnese

HARROWER, Elizabeth

Nationality: Australian. **Born:** Sydney, New South Wales, 8 February 1928. **Career:** Lived in London 1951-58; worked for the Australian Broadcasting Commission, Sydney, 1959-60; reviewer, Sydney *Morning Herald,* 1960; worked for Macmillan and Company Ltd., publishers, Sydney, 1961-67. **Awards:** Commonwealth Literary Fund fellowship, 1968; Australian Council for the Arts fellowship, 1974. **Address:** 5 Stanley Avenue, Mosman, New South Wales 2088, Australia.

Publications

Novels

Down in the City. London, Cassell, 1957.

The Long Prospect. London, Cassell, 1958.
The Catherine Wheel. London, Cassell, 1960.
The Watch Tower. London, Macmillan, 1966.

Uncollected Short Stories

"The Cost of Things," in *Summer's Tales 1,* edited by Kylie Tennant. Melbourne and London, Macmillan, and New York, St. Martin's Press, 1964.
"English Lesson," in *Summer's Tales 2,* edited by Kylie Tennant. Melbourne and London, Macmillan, and New York, St. Martin's Press, 1965.
"The Beautiful Climate," in *Modern Australian Writing,* edited by Geoffrey Dutton. London, Fontana, 1966.
"Lance Harper, His Story," in *The Vital Decade,* edited by Geoffrey Dutton and Max Harris. Melbourne, Sun, 1968.
"The Retrospective Grandmother," in *The Herald* (Melbourne), 1976.
"A Few Days in the Country," in *Overland* (Melbourne), 1977.

*

Critical Studies: "The Novels of Elizabeth Harrower" by Max Harris, in *Australian Letters* (Adelaide), December 1961; *Forty-Two Faces* by John Hetherington, Melbourne, Cheshire, 1962; "Elizabeth Harrower's Novels: A Survey," in *Southerly* (Sydney), no. 2, 1970, and *Recent Fiction,* Melbourne, Oxford University Press, 1974, both by R.G. Geering; *The Directions of Australian Fiction 1920-1974* by D.R. Burns, Melbourne, Cassell, 1975; "The Novels of Elizabeth Harrower" by Robyn Claremont, in *Quadrant* (Sydney), November 1979; Nola Adams, in *Westerly* (Nedlands, Western Australia), September 1980; "Deep into the Destructive Core" by Frances McInherny, in *Hecate* (St. Lucia, Queensland), vol. 9, nos. 1-2, 1983; "Down in the City: Elizabeth Harrower's Lost Novel" by Rosie Yeo, in *Southerly* (Sydney), no. 4, 1990; "The Watch Tower: Bluebeard's Castle" by Deirdre Coleman, in *(Un)common Ground* edited by A. Taylor and R. McDougall, Bedford Park, South Australia, CRNLE, 1990.

*   *   *

An ideal introduction to Elizabeth Harrower's work is the short story "The Beautiful Climate," since it provides a paradigm of her fictional universe. It is a world in which selfish men manipulate their women and material possessions in a vain attempt to achieve happiness; frustrated by their blind male egotism, they become subject to fits of smoldering violence and frequent relapses into bouts of alcoholism and morbid self-pity. The woman's role is to suffer, to pity, and to provide the innocent seeing eye for the narrative. In "The Beautiful Climate" the paranoiac male is Mr. Shaw, who secretly buys a holiday island, reduces his wife and daughter to domestic slavery there, then sells the place behind their backs. The consciousness that develops from innocent passivity to partial sad wisdom is the daughter's, who reflects her creator in turning from psychology to literature as a guide to truth. The same basic situations and characters recur throughout the novels; and the tormented relationship between father and daughter in this short story might seem to offer a psychological clue to the novelist's preoccupation with male domination.

In *Down in the City,* a very remarkable first novel, Harrower traces the disenchantment that follows when the heroine exchanges the empty security of her wealthy bay-side suburb in Sydney for the puzzling ups and downs of her husband's shady business world. In describing the characteristic claustrophobia of the flat-dwelling city wife, she succeeds wonderfully well in evoking the typical sights and sounds of Sydney and in establishing a connection between climate and states of mind. And the hero, who oscillates between his classy wife and his obliging mistress, reflects the conflicting drives and split personality of many an Australian business man.

What distinguishes Harrower's second novel, *The Long Prospect,* from all her others is that the malevolent main character is a woman not a man. But once again the viewpoint is through an innocent seeing eye; in this case, it is a child's. By the end of the novel, she has plumbed the seedy adult world to its depths. The scene in which four irredeemably corrupt adults spy on the 12-year-old and her middle-aged friend, transferring their own "atmosphere of stealth" onto the innocent pair, is only one of many pieces of superb psychological drama in this accomplished novel.

While the third novel, *The Catherine Wheel,* laudably attempts to extend the range of the fictional world by having its setting in London bed-sitter-land, it is a somewhat disappointing work that hardly prepares the reader for the splendid fourth novel, *The Watch Tower.* The conspicuous success in *The Watch Tower* lies in the creation of Felix Shaw, the Australian business man, who climaxes a series of similar portraits and shares the surname of the father in "The Beautiful Climate." But equally subtle is the analysis of pity, through the contrasted characters of Shaw's two victims, who show that pity may enslave as well as ennoble (this a continuous preoccupation in the novels). Shaw's capriciousness, his bursts of petty pique and rage, his resentment at others' success, his dark nihilism, brutal aggression, unrecognized homosexuality and alcoholism, all point to a profound psychic disorder. But it is the novelist's triumph to suggest that this disorder is at least partly the product of a society that worships materialism and masculinity.

In most of her work, Harrower combines sharp observation of individual life with a searching critique of Australian society. Although she lacks the resilient vitality of such English novelists as Margaret Drabble, her vision of a male-dominated society is depressingly authentic. She has been highly praised and compared favorably with Patrick White, but her unflattering, somewhat drab and disenchanted view of Australian life is now winning her the wide local readership her work certainly deserves.

—John Colmer

———

HART, Veronica. *See* **KELLEHER, Victor.**

———

HASLUCK, Nicholas (Paul)

Nationality: Australian. **Born:** Canberra, 17 October 1942; son of the politician and diplomat Sir Paul Hasluck. **Education:** The University of Western Australia, Nedlands, 1960-63, LL.B. 1963; Oxford University, 1964-66, B.C.L. 1966. **Family:** Married Sally Anne

Bolton in 1966; two sons. **Career:** Lawyer, admitted to Supreme Court of Western Australia as barrister and solicitor, 1968. Deputy Chairman, Australia Council, 1978-82. **Awards:** *The Age* Book of the Year award, 1984. **Member:** A.M. (Order of Australia), 1986. **Agent:** Murray Pollinger, 222 Old Brompton Road, London SW5 0B2, England. **Address:** 14 Reserve Street, Claremont, Western Australia 6010, Australia.

PUBLICATIONS

Novels

Quarantine. Melbourne and London, Macmillan, 1978; New York, Holt Rinehart, 1979.
The Blue Guitar. Melbourne and London, Macmillan, and New York, Holt Rinehart, 1980.
The Hand That Feeds You: A Satiric Nightmare, photographs by the author. Fremantle, Western Australia, Fremantle Arts Centre Press, 1982.
The Bellarmine Jug. Ringwood, Victoria, Penguin, 1984.
Truant State. Ringwood, Victoria, Penguin, 1987; New York, Penguin, 1988.
The Country Without Music. Ringwood, Victoria, Viking, 1990.
The Blosseville File. Ringwood, Victoria, Penguin, 1992.
A Grain of Truth. Ringwood, Victoria, Penguin, 1994.

Short Stories

The Hat on the Letter O and Other Stories. Fremantle, Western Australia, Fremantle Arts Centre Press, 1978.

Poetry

Anchor and Other Poems. Fremantle, Western Australia, Fremantle Arts Centre Press, 1976.
On the Edge, with William Grono. Claremont, Western Australia, Freshwater Bay Press, 1980.
Chinese Journey, with C.J. Koch. Fremantle, Western Australia, Fremantle Arts Centre Press, 1985.

Other

Collage: Recollections and Images of the University of Western Australia, photographs by Tania Young. Fremantle, Western Australia, Fremantle Arts Centre Press, 1987.
Offcuts from a Legal Literary Life. Nedlands, University of Western Australia Press, 1993.

*

Critical Studies: Review by Martin Seymour-Smith, in *Financial Times* (London), 15 June 1978; article by Helen Daniel, in *The Age Monthly Review* (Melbourne), December 1984; *Liars* by Helen Daniel, Ringwood, Victoria, Penguin, 1988.

*		*		*

Nicholas Hasluck's first novel, *Quarantine,* introduced the combination of intrigue, dark humour, and fable that have become characteristic of Hasluck's style. In an ominous, rundown hotel on the bank of the Suez canal, the passengers of a cruise ship are unaccountably held in isolation under the sinister charge of the proprietor Shewfik Arud and the dipsomaniac Dr. Magro. The exiles themselves are caught between the menacing Burgess and the moral hero of the story, David Shears, who loses his life through the moral cowardice of the narrator. Parallels with Camus's *La Peste* do not deny the individuality of Hasluck's brand of mordant absurdism.

The more restrained *The Blue Guitar,* unusually for an Australian novel, is concerned with commerce, and is set in a vividly-evoked urban jungle (recognisably Sydney). As a speculator, Dyson Garrick attempts to promote the inventor Herman's "blue guitar" that automatically creates music. His quest is idealistic (the title directs us to Wallace Steven's poem "Things as they are are changed by the blue guitar") but also tangled in the temptations of commercial exploitation, and this conflict leads to Garrick's own moral disintegration as he finally betrays his friend.

The Hand That Feeds You subtitled "A Satiric Nightmare," turns to a science-fiction framework for its satirical fantasy of an Australia controlled by the trade unions and the mass media, where paid work has become taboo, tax evasion and social handouts the ideal. A product of New Right thinking of the early 1980s, the novel lacks the universality of *The Bellarmine Jug,* his most complex and assured novel to date.

The Bellarmine Jug explores the roots of Australian identity on both personal and social levels, using techniques from the spy thriller and a legal examination that probes each layer of truth to reveal alternative realities. In 1948, student unrest in the Grotius Institute, Den Haag, is linked to an attempt by the authorities to suppress evidence that the 1629 mutiny of the *Batavia* off Western Australia was led by the son of Grotius, codifier of international law and founder of the institute. The evidence has implications for the status of Grotius, the institute, and the relationship between authority and rebellion. As the mutiny is envisaged as leading to atrocities surrounding a Rosicrucian settlement of the Abrolhos islands, it is also conjecturally linked to the first white settlement of Australia. The plot moves between Holland, London, and Australia, implicating issues such as the British atomic tests in the Monte Bellow islands, and Australian involvement in Sukarno's independence movement, to question the nature of international law, human rights, and individual morality. Exploring these through a taut and compelling narrative, the novel rates amongst the finest Australian novels of the 1980s.

Truant State is set in Western Australia in the heady days of the 1920s and the depression of the 1930s. It is narrated by the young Jack Taverne, an immigrant from England, whose father becomes caught in the illusory hopes of the era. There is a vivid recreation of the conflict between the trades unions, and the reactionary West Guard secret society which sought seccession for Western Australia (the "truant state" of the title). A subtext involves D.H. Lawrence's *Kangaroo* which also draws on the Fremantle riots and the right-wing secret organisations. The novel, which shows Hasluck's characteristic interweaving of personal, social, and metaphysical issues, with detective intrigue, is remarkable for its regional evocation of the fictional Butler's Swamp and Western Australia between the wars. The short stories of *The Hat on the Letter O* show Hasluck's technical versatility, and they are interesting as background to the novels.

In his most recent fiction, *The Country Without Music, The Blosseville File,* and *A Grain of Truth,* Hasluck, like John O'Hara and William Faulkner, has created an imaginary territory through which to explore contemporary actuality. Blosseville and the Baie de Baudin, and the off-shore islands of Depuis and Gournay, provide a subtle and complex milieu through which to explore historical and political issues of Western Australia. *The Country Without Music* is set on the island of Gournay, the site of a penal colony founded by French Revolutionaries. The ruins of the "panopticon" prison—Jeremy Bentham's model of penal reform—and the preserved guillotine stand as the ambivalent ideals of rational justice on which the island's administrator tries to build a modern capitalist society. But it is "without music" (or soul), and at the climax the island folk interact violently with authority in the rituals of Carnival.

If that novel explores political justice within the role of history, Hasluck's most recent work, *A Grain of Truth* turns directly to issues of contemporary law, and the novel is set on the mainland in Blosseville. The central character, the lawyer Michael Cheyne, finds himself standing for human rights against the weight of apparent justice within the legal system. The novel, which has an optimistic ending, underlines Hasluck's conviction that life is a conflict between the structures of social order—exemplified by the law—and the anarchy that lies at the core of human experience. Hasluck has declared that it is the "kind of quirky unpredictable exotic side of things" beneath the rational surface that is the task of literature to explore. Hasluck continues to develop his highly individual vein of intelligent and inventive fiction.

—Louis James

HASSLER, Jon

Nationality: American. **Born:** Minneapolis, Minnesota, 30 March 1933. **Education:** St. John's University, B.A. 1955; University of North Dakota, M.A. 1961. **Family:** Married (divorced), two sons and one daughter; remarried. **Career:** High school teacher of English for ten years; faculty member, Bemidji State University and Brainerd Community College. Since 1980 writer-in-residence, St. John's University. **Awards:** Friends of American Writers Novel of the Year, 1978, for *Staggerford;* Guggenheim grant, 1980; Society of Midland Authors Best Fiction award, 1987, for *Grand Opening.* D.Litt.: Assumption College, Massachusetts, 1993; University of North Dakota, 1994. **Address:** St. John's University, Collegeville, Minnesota 56321, U.S.A.

PUBLICATIONS

Novels

Staggerford. New York, Atheneum, and London, Deutsch, 1977.
Simon's Night. New York, Atheneum, and London, Deutsch, 1979.
The Love Hunter. New York, Morrow, and London, Weidenfeld and Nicolson, 1981.
A Green Journey. New York, Morrow, 1985; London, Allen, 1986.
Grand Opening. New York, Morrow, 1987.
North of Hope. New York, Ballantine, 1990.
Dear James. New York, Ballantine, 1993.
Rookery Blues. New York, Ballantine, 1995.

Poetry

The Red Oak and Other Poems. Privately printed, 1968.

Other

Four Miles to Pinecone (for children). New York, Warne, 1977.
Jemmy (for children). New York, Atheneum, 1980.

*

Manuscript Collection: St. Cloud State University, St. Cloud, Minnesota.

Critical Study: *An Interview with Jon Hassler* (includes bibliography), Minneapolis, Dinkytown Antiquarian Bookstore, 1990.

*   *   *

Until very recently, only one comprehensive essay had ever been published about Jon Hassler—by Andrew Greeley in a Catholic journal. Why this should be so is not greatly surprising. Hassler is a very traditional writer with exciting, real, complex, and intriguing subject matter. But his strengths are quiet and (on the surface) unremarkable. And he is not bold and audacious like so many of our writing personalities—like, say, Norman Mailer or Camille Paglia—and takes no overt political position. He is always present in his novels but he never identifies wholly with any of his major characters like Agatha McGee in *Staggerford* (his first novel) or Peggy Benoit in *Rookery Blues* (his most recent one). In fact, I would go so far as to say that although he is strongly attracted to characters like Agatha, Peggy, and Simon Shea, they don't much resemble him and often do things or take positions that he would probably not take himself. The only character he has created that is even remotely autobiographical is the young protagonist/observer of *Grand Opening*, Brendan Foster, whose father, like Hassler's, owns a grocery store in a small, rural Minnesota town called Plum.

Hassler's presence is subtle, quiet, and apparently unobtrusive. He is absorbed in what he is writing about and as indifferent to public recognition (as a persona) as Andrew Wyeth the painter. He does not take bold political positions, even though he sometimes seems obsessed with Church politics and the behaviors of the priests, sisters, and laypersons who people many of his novels. In some cases, he defuses potentially explosive conflicts by turning them into high comedy, as he does in *Staggerford*, with the confrontation between whites (or Anglos) and Native Americans, or in the strike action that takes place in *Rookery Blues*.

His four predominantly "Catholic" novels (*Simon's Night, A Green Journey, North of Hope,* and *Dear James*) more closely resemble the Barchester and distinctly Anglican novels of Anthony Trollope than they do the Catholic novels of Graham Greene (to whom he is sometimes compared). Like Trollope he is more fascinated with the political infighting and machinations of a huge and powerful Church that is in a state of transition than he is in the spiritual or mystical character of its clergy and laypeople. He is intrigued by the fact that laypeople like Agatha McGee and Simon Shea, both highly traditional Catholics, take vows and commitments more seriously than many of the clergy and are, in fact, "better Catholics." Shea, for instance, in one of Hassler's very best novels, *Simon's Night*, remains faithful for 20 years, not so much to

the woman whom he marries early and who runs off with one of his colleagues as to their marriage vows. He gives up a warm and passionate relationship with one of his students who has seduced him not because he doesn't love this young woman but because he regards his vows to his unfaithful wife, Barbara, as binding. And Agatha McGee, who, at 67 and on the verge of retirement from her teaching position in a religious elementary school, is startled nearly out of her mind when she discovers that an older Irishman named James O'Hannon—with whom she has engaged in a long and deeply personal correspondence—is in fact a priest. This violates her whole conception of herself as a Catholic and her conception also of what it is proper—and sacred—for a priest to do and not do. Yet the power of that friendship and its personal if not sexual intimacy fuels the action of two novels, *A Green Journey* and *Dear James.*

In a radio interview, Hassler once said that he likes to challenge his protagonists. This means, first of all, that his characters are fully alive to him, as if they were actors in a repertory company or simply real, breathing human beings. Sometimes, as with Agatha McGee and her friend, James O'Hannon, they are central to more than one novel, larger than that one canvas. They are fully alive to him but also creatures of his own imagination and in the end they challenge him—his creative ability to make them work convincingly in new contexts and sometimes highly complex plots.

As a mark of his traditional practice, Hassler never uses stream of consciousness and other techniques perfected by such early modernists as James Joyce, Virginia Woolf, and Dorothy Richardson, even though he regularly enters the minds and sensibilities of his protagonists. Nor does he use first person singular narrative as perfected by Mark Twain in *The Adventures of Huckleberry Finn* or the soliloquy familiar to readers of Melville's *Moby-Dick.*

What Hassler does use with increasing mastery and fluidity are three other mnemonic techniques: flashbacks, journal entries, and letters. He does this because he knows all too well that what a particular character does in the present is strongly conditioned by what he or she has done or believed in the past. In his most recent novel, *Rookery Blues,* he inserts five two- or three-page flashbacks (set in italics) at various and appropriate points in the novel to tell us crucial things—in a very funny way—about each of the five members of the Icejam Quintet, the jazz group that forms the heart and soul of the book from beginning to end. In *Staggerford,* he uses the sometimes extensive journal entries written by protagonist Miles Pruitt about his early love life, especially his attraction to Carla Carpenter, the high school girl whom his brother seduces. In *Dear James* (as the title suggests), he makes extensive and highly dramatic use of some of the letters that Agatha McGee writes to James O'Hannon (but only mails to him much later) and the letters that she has saved from him.

Traditionally, plot is character in action or, in Hassler's case, many characters in action. For a novel to succeed, the protagonist and other major characters must first of all be rich and interesting in themselves; second, the actions they are involved in should be at least worthy of that depth and flow from it. Thus Simon Shea, in *Simon's Night,* is both an excellent college professor and a strong, believing Catholic. As the novel opens, he has retired from his college position and commits himself to a weirdly comic nursing home because he feels he is losing his ability to remember anything significant and is thus ready to cash in his chips. The young female doctor who regularly visits that home immediately decides that Simon is too interesting and has too much to live for to give up and in essence put himself to sleep or to death. She engineers his reunion with his wife, Barbara, and the novel ends with their beginning life together anew.

That Hassler is fascinated by richly compelling individuals who have sacrificed themselves to principle of one sort or another is equally manifest in his two later Agatha McGee-James O'Hannon novels, *A Green Journey* and *Dear James,* both of which test Agatha's rigidly held Catholic principles; she, like Simon Shea, is forced by the external circumstances of her life and her age to compromise that rigidity. This compromise grows out of the depth and richness of Agatha's character, her resilience, and the fact that she acts finally out of a character that those rigidly held principles don't explain.

In *Rookery Blues,* his most complex, funniest, and most satisfying novel to date, he manages to control in every respect the five protagonists—each radically different from one another—who make up the Icejam Quintet: Victor Dash is a hotheaded labor organizer, who happens also to be an aptly hotheaded drummer in the quintet; Neil Novotny is a poor teacher and an obsessed but dreadful novelist, who thinks he is in love with Peggy Benoit; Leland Edwards is a conservative, mother-bound professor and opponent of the teachers' strike Dash foments, who is a superb jazz pianist; Connor is a good portrait painter obsessed with doing paintings of mothers and daughters, who is a bass player and in a dreadfully unhappy marriage; and Peggy Benoit herself is a beautiful music professor and blues singer, who falls in love with Connor and eventually succeeds in wresting Connor away from his marriage. Any one or two of these characters might well have been the subject of a novel because each is fully, comically, ironically developed, but their interreactions and their roles in the external tensions of Rookery State University together form a complex, comic, and believable series of actions.

What makes Hassler such an interesting and engaging novelist—and what will probably make him outlast all or almost all of his flashier contemporaries—is not just that he is unashamedly a traditional novelist but that he does so well what he does, that he involves the reader so deeply in his characters that no matter who we might be we really care about them, talk about them as if they were very real and interesting people. Limited, sometimes myopic, often obsessive, they work their slow and ironic ways through recognizable and familiar situations or even rather unlikely ones (like the relationship between Agatha McGee and James O'Hannon) as if they were familiar. We come to know many of his characters better than we know most people and even ourselves (sometimes). I suspect that Jon Hassler will come to be recognized as a major 20th-century novelist.

—C.W. Truesdale

HAU'OFA, Epeli

Nationality: Tongan. **Born:** Papua New Guinea, 7 December 1939, to missionary parents. **Education:** Tupou College, Tonga, 1951-55; Lelean Memorial School, Fiji, 1956-59; Armidale High School, New South Wales, 1960; University of New South Wales, Kensington, 1961-64; McGill University, Montreal, 1965-68, M.A.; Australian National University, Canberra, 1970-75, Ph.D. in social anthropology 1975. **Family:** Married Barbara Hau'ofa in 1966; two children. **Career:** Senior Tutor, University of Papua New Guinea,

Port Moresby, 1968-70; research fellow, University of the South Pacific, Suva, Fiji, 1975-77; visiting fellow, University of New South Wales, 1977; deputy private secretary to the King of Tonga, in Nuku'alofa, 1978-81; director, University of the South Pacific Rural Development Centre, Nuku'alofa, Tonga, 1981-83. Reader, from 1983, and currently professor of sociology, University of the South Pacific. Visiting fellow, Centre for Pacific Studies, University of Auckland, 1985. Consultant to the Asian Development Bank, 1979, and the World Bank, 1980. Co-founder and co-editor, *Faikava,* a Tongan literary journal. **Address:** School of Social and Economic Development, University of the South Pacific, P.O. Box 1168, Suva, Fiji.

PUBLICATIONS

Novel

Kisses in the Nederends. Auckland, Penguin, 1987.

Short Stories

Tales of the Tikongs. Auckland, Longman Paul, 1983; New York, Penguin, 1988.

Other

Our Crowded Islands, photographs by Randy Thaman. Suva, Fiji, Institute of Pacific Studies, 1977.
Corned Beef and Tapioca: A Report on the Food Distribution Systems in Tonga. Canberra, Australian National University Development Studies Centre, 1979.
Mekeo: Inequality and Ambivalence in a Village Society. Canberra, Australian National University Press, 1981.

*   *   *

Comic writers are always welcome. Epeli Hau'ofa's humorous *Tales of the Tikongs* consists of linked short stories about a South Pacific island so small that it is left off maps owing to the difficulty of finding "a dot sufficiently small to represent it faithfully and at the same time big enough to be seen without the aid of a microscope." The Tikongs have become Christians and work so hard praying on Sunday that it takes a six-day rest to recover. They practise the Christian virtue of forgiveness: "when five very, very important men discovered that they had together helped themselves to half a million dollars of public money to which they had no right to help themselves, they prayed for God's forgiveness, they forgave each other, and they neither had to resign from their very important jobs nor return any money to anyone." They are also "expert tellers of half-truths, quarter-truths, and one-percent truths." When Inoke forges and cashes a cheque for $100 and is caught, he swears on the Bible that it was the fault of the cashier who supposedly misread a $1.00 cheque.

While Hau'ofa's stories often have a satiric relationship to actual events and persons in the South Pacific, they show an amused appreciation of the trickster and swindler. At times satire is blended with a tolerance of extravagance, outrageousness, and absurdity which approaches moral anarchy and fun for its own sake. His Holiness Bopeep Dr. Toki Tumu, "a descendent of one of the thieves of Captain Cook's chamber pot," comes from Chamber Island. Seeing that the Tikongs are "thoroughly conditioned" by the many church bells on the island, he conditions them to his bell-ringing and sets up his own church, "based on the Doctrine of the Infallibility of the Bopeep"; "The Bopeep can do anything he wants, for his decisions and actions are spotless in the eyes of the Lord." Besides gaining absolute control of church finances ("all financial transactions of the Church shall, unless otherwise decreed by His Holiness, remains forevermore Unwritten"), and "taking his cue from benighted Melanesian cargo cult leaders," he assembles a harem as "it is a necessity that he experience the suffering and agony of sin in order to transcend earthly pleasures." While Hau'ofa, for the sake of his art, appears amused at the comedy of human relations, including the ways people use and exploit each other, the *Tales* are explicitly satiric of institutionalized injustice: "organized religion was the most effective instrument, in Tiko at least, for the attainment of wealth, power and renown"; "White lambs abound in Australia . . . because no sheep of tinted fleece is ever allowed into that spotless land." These are more than tales of charming, roguish, eccentric natives and the foibles of foreign-aid experts. Although satire at its best can appear self-contradictory and anarchistic, the *Tales* have many of the same concerns as writing after national independence in other parts of the Third World. The stories show the various ways European culture and politics have affected the South Pacific, leaving a conformist middle class and a corrupt elite, a legacy of church dominance, inappropriate forms of education and educational qualifications, and subservience to and dependence on foreigners. Although the islanders' way of life was not destroyed despite Christianity and colonialism, national independence led to increased dependence. At Independence the local rulers and their relatives change their English clothes for a melange of "Afro-shirts and other Third World clothes" and take over from the colonial administration positions for which they are not trained or qualified. Mistrusting and feeling threatened by their own new university graduates, so that the skilled and talented flee the country, they fill the resulting vacancies with foreign experts, technical advisers, youthful volunteers, and the well-paid employees of United Nations organizations.

Manu, the character closest to the author's sympathies, wears a shirt lettered with "Over Influenced" on the front and "Religion and Education Destroy Original Wisdom" on the back. There is the obvious symbolism of Ole Pasifikiwei who during his spare time collects oral traditions which he records in school exercise books until he attracts the attention of an Australian cultural aid official. Now supported by an annual grant, trips abroad, duty-free goods, and a committee, he progresses to forming the National Council for Social, Economic, and Cultural Research, which is placed by "the Great International Organization on the list of the Two Hundred Least Developed Committees—those in need of urgent, generous aid." Within six years Ole applies for 14 million dollars for his organization, is given honorary doctorates, and loses his old exercise books with the oral records. "He has since shelved his original sense of self-respect and has assumed another, more attuned to his new, permanent role as a first-rate, expert beggar." If at times *Tales of the Tikongs* seems artless, that can be an art. Four of the stories were revised from previous publication and show improvements along with expansion. One of the additions is an example of an Australian expert attempting to communicate in pidgin:

> "Me big brother, you little brother. You me help Tiko come up all same big fela rich country. Plenty plenty ice cream, sweet sweet all same lollies from Heaven. All right?"

"Me doan know."

"You no can savvy? Gawd! Me talk talk all same simple something na you no can savvy! Whassamatter? Me think think head belong you too much dumdum na full up shit something no good true! All right, me all same try one more time yet, na you try savvy good or I'll bloody well bash your coon head in, O.K.?"

That is from "The Tower of Babel." The book starts with allusions to Genesis in "The Seventh and Other Days" and works its way through "The Second Coming" to its final revelation, the corruption of Ole by an organization with the acronym MERCY in "The Glorious Pacific Way," the title of which is itself a reference to the way nationalist values are manipulated by the rulers and elite. Manu says, "the Pacific Way belongs to regional Elites, Experts, Wheeler-dealers, and Crooks!" Even when not being so explicit, Hau'ofa provides social comment through the ludicrous, mocking parody, topical allusions, and witty malice.

—Bruce King

HAUSER, Marianne

Nationality: American (originally French; granted U.S. citizenship, 1944). **Born:** Sreasbourg, Alsace, France, 11 December 1910. **Education:** University of Berlin; Sorbonne. **Family:** Married Frederic Kirshberger (divorced); one son. **Career:** Journalist, French and Swiss newspapers and periodicals; lecturer, Department of English, Queens College, New York, 1962-79; held various teaching positions, including positions at New York University and New School until 1988. **Awards:** Rockefeller grant; National Endowment for the Arts grant. **Agent:** Perry Knowlton, Curtis Brown, 1 Astor Pl., New York, New York, U.S.A. **Address:** 2 Washington Square Village, apt. 13-M, New York, New York 10012, U.S.A.

PUBLICATIONS

Novels

Monique. Zurich, n.p., 1934.
Shadow Play in India. Vienna, n.p., 1937.
Dark Dominion. New York, Random House, 1947.
The Choir Invisible. London, Gollancz, 1958; New York, McDowell Obolensky, 1959.
Prince Ishmael. New York, Stein and Day, 1963; London, Michael Joseph, 1964.
The Talking Room. New York, Fiction Collective, 1976.
The Memoirs of the Late Mr. Ashley: An American Comedy. N.p., Sun and Moon Press, 1986.
Me and My Mom. N.p., Sun and Moon Classics, 1993.

Short Stories

A Lesson in Music. N.p., 1964.

Uncollected Short Stories

"The Colonel's Daughter," in *Tiger's Eye,* March 1948.

"The Rubber Doll," in *Mademoiselle,* 1951.
"Mimoun of the Mellah," in *Harper's Bazaar,* 1966.
"The Seersucker Suit," in *Carleton Miscellany,* 1968.
"O-To-Le-Do," in *Parnassus,* 14(1).
"Weeds," in *Denver Quarterly,* 1983.
"It Isn't So Bad That It Couldn't Be Worse," in *City,* 9, 1984.
"Blatant Artifice," in *Hallwalls,* 1986.
"Heartlands Beat," in *Fiction International,* 1988.
"The Missing Page," in *Witness,* 1989.
"No Name on the Bullet," in *Fiction International,* 1991.
"Scandal at the Bide-a-Wee Nursing Home for Mature Seniors," in
    Fiction International, 1992.

*

Manuscript Collection: Florida University, Gainsville.

Marianne Hauser comments:
    To write without compromise or an eye on the market.

*   *   *

Early on in Marianne Hauser's first major work, *Prince Ishmael*—an historical novel based on the legend of Caspar Hauser—the narrator observes, "I wasn't ready for reality black or white." This same inability to relate to a world of dizzying complexity and ambiguity through linguistic systems that reduce experience to simple binary categories is evident in all of Hauser's fiction; it also expresses Hauser's personal conviction that "reality" is a dynamic, multilayered process for which the conventions of traditional realism—with its empirical biases and emphasis on causal relationships and logic—are ill-equipped to represent. This conviction has resulted in a series of novels and stories that weave together dream and waking reality, the known and unknown, the perverse and banal, and the poetic and idiomatic into darkly humorous fables of great emotional power, uniqueness, and universal relevancy. Yet ironically enough it has been precisely the uniqueness and poetic intensity of Hauser's fiction that has thus far relegated her work to relative popular and critical obscurity—a situation that is almost certain to change as feminist and postmodern critics discover her works.

In a career that now spans some six decades, Marianne Hauser has published a total of eight books of fiction; these include an early novel written in German, *Shadow Play in India,* and seven subsequent English-language works: a story collection, *A Lesson in Music,* and five novels—*Dark Dominion, The Choir Invisible, Prince Ishmael, The Talking Room, Memoirs of the Late Mr. Ashley: An American Comedy,* and *Me and My Mom.* In the most extended and perceptive analysis of Hauser's work to date, Ewa Ziarek, writing in the Fall 1992 issue of *Contemporary Literature,* noted: "Marianne Hauser's fiction represents an interesting intersection between experimentation challenging literary conventions and feminist concerns. Significantly, both interests converge on the issue of articulating specifically feminine desires—sexual, reproductive, and linguistic." Yet, despite such recurrent themes—which have found their expression in remarkably rich, subtle, and evocative prose mannerisms—it would be a mistake to view her works solely or even primarily as feminist documents. Although several of her major novels—for example, *Me and My Mom* and *The Talking Room*— have been narrated by women and have focused on psychological issues peculiar to women's experiences, others have male narrators and can't be said to be specifically feminist in orientation. This isn't to deny the importance of Hauser's work from feminist perspectives—indeed, *The Talking Room* ranks with Marilynne Robinson's *Housekeeping* and Toni Morrison's *Beloved* as among the most significant and original feminist novels of the past 20 years; rather what needs to be stressed is that although Hauser's work has naturally always expressed viewpoints and concerns central to her own experiences as a woman, it has also consistently been concerned with expressing larger, more universal issues. Central to all her works, for example, has been an emphasis on human loneliness and the need for people to escape from isolation, understand their origins, and find erotic fulfillment. There is also a persistent fascination with epistemological and metaphysical issues—the role of dreams, fantasy, and language in constructing memory and our sense of the waking world; a suspicion of empiricism and linguistic categories and a corresponding appreciation of storytelling and personal reverie in making sense of our lives.

Despite such thematic commonalties, the language, style, and tone of her work has undergone significant transformations over the last five decades. The precise, almost classical prose of *Dark Dominion*—which depicts a strange, haunting relationship between a nondreaming New York psychiatrist, his wife (whom he wins when he analyzes her dreams), her obsessively devoted brother, and her lover—has loosened; and Hauser has increasing incorporated American idioms, slapstick, and absurdist humor. She has also been increasingly adventurous in devising experimental formal strategies suited for portraying her sense of the permeability of dream and waking reality. The obsessions explored in *Dark Dominion*—the role of the imagination in shaping one's response to life, the search for and discovery in the "dark dominio" of the unconscious as a multilayered space in which phantom and reality coexist to create the drama of the self, and the difficulty in inhabiting a coherent "self"— continue through her next two books, *The Choir Invisible,* which is set in a small town in the Midwest, and *Prince Ishmael,* a fictional account of the Caspar Hauser legend.

Her most recent novels, *The Talking Room, The Memoirs of the Late Mr. Ashley: An American Comedy,* and *Me and My Mom* all display a command of American lingoes and cultural references that range effortlessly from urban to rural, straight to gay, highbrow to lowbrow—all the voices a chorus of pathos, absurdity, lyricism, and beauty that sing the bittersweet song of the America Hauser found herself living when she took up permanent residency there beginning in 1937. From her earliest work, Hauser has explored how dreams, the unconscious, and the irrational affect our perception of the "real"; but with her last three novels (as well as her more recent short stories), this notion is no longer so much an element of "theme" but finds its expression as a fully integrated aspect of her style. Thus, to enter her recent fiction is to find oneself in a unsettling landscape where the strange becomes familiar and the familiar strange—a realm where people, events, and associations ebb and flow with the logic of dreams. Partly this effect comes from connections that make no rational sense but which are brought together by Hauser's ability to ground her fiction in details that are vivid and sensual; it arises too from the playfulness of her language and her willingness to let go of the linear in favor of something wilder and less predictable.

It was Hauser's 1976 novel, *The Talking Room,* where she first found a voice and a method uniquely her own. The plot of *The Talking Room* is as simple as it is outrageous. The book is narrated by B, a pregnant 13-year-old girl who is the daughter of a lesbian couple (her mother, V, and her lover J) who are living in a deserted neighborhood of New York City. Fearful of being forced by her "Aunt" J to have an abortion, B hides her pregnancy under the pretense of being fat and stays in her room. There she attempts to uncover the mystery of her origins (was she perhaps a test-tube baby?) by sifting through the many voices that drift up into her "talking room." These voices—which include those of her own imagination, the turbulent sounds of V and J arguing and reminiscing from downstairs, the funny and surrealistic chitchat of their eccentric friends, and the radio (which provides political and pop culture references)—combine to form what Ewa Ziarek described as a "polyphonic compositio" that "makes it impossible to uncover the simplicity of origin in the maternal body." Ziarek goes on to note the ways that B's search for a matrilineal genealogy reinforces a metafictional critique of the "traditional idea of authorship as a conscious begetting, grounded in the intentionality of the author." This critique, in turn, links up to Hauser's ongoing presentation of the limitations of rationality and the ways that the search for one's self and one's origins are ultimately limited by the fact that the self is never a discrete entity but a plurality of different selves whose "essences" are themselves shifting perpetually in a state of transformation.

—Sinda Gregory

HAWKES, John (Clendennin Burne, Jr.)

Nationality: American. **Born:** Stamford, Connecticut, 17 August 1925. **Education:** Trinity School, 1940-41; Pawling High School, 1941-43; Harvard University, Cambridge, Massachusetts, 1943-49, A.B. 1949. **Military Service:** Served as an ambulance driver with the American Field Service in Italy and Germany, 1944-45. **Family:** Married Sophie Goode Tazewell in 1947; three sons and one daughter. **Career:** Assistant to the production manager, Harvard University Press, 1949-55; visiting lecturer, 1955-56, and instructor in English, 1956-58, Harvard University. Assistant professor, 1958-62, associate professor, 1962-67, professor of English, 1967-73, T. B. Stowell University Professor, 1973-88, and since 1988 Professor of English Emeritus, Brown University, Providence, Rhode Island. Visiting assistant professor, Massachusetts Institute of Technology, 1959; special guest, Aspen Institute for Humanistic Studies, Colorado, 1962; staff member, Utah Writers Conference, summer 1962, and Bread Loaf Writers Conference, Vermont, summer 1963; Visiting Professor of Creative Writing, Stanford University, California, 1966-67; Visiting Distinguished Professor of Creative Writing, City College of the City University of New York, 1971-72. Member, Panel on Educational Innovation, Washington, D.C., 1966-67. **Awards:** American Academy of Arts and Letters grant, 1962; Guggenheim fellowship, 1962; Ford fellowship, 1964; Rockefeller fellowship, 1968; Foreign Book prize (France), 1974, 1986. A.M.: Brown University, 1962. **Member:** American Academy of Arts and Sciences, 1973; American Academy of Arts and Letters, 1980. **Agent:** Lynn Nesbit, Janklow and Nesbit, 598 Madison Avenue, New York, New York 10022. **Address:** 18 Everett Avenue, Providence, Rhode Island 02906, U.S.A.

PUBLICATIONS

Novels

The Cannibal. New York, New Directions, 1949; London, Spearman, 1962.
The Beetle Leg. New York, New Directions, 1951; London, Chatto and Windus, 1967.
The Lime Twig. New York, New Directions, 1961; London, Spearman, 1962.
Second Skin. New York, New Directions, 1964; London, Chatto and Windus, 1966.
The Blood Oranges. New York, New Directions, and London, Chatto and Windus, 1971.
Death, Sleep, and the Traveler. New York, New Directions, 1974; London, Chatto and Windus, 1975.
Travesty. New York, New Directions, and London, Chatto and Windus, 1976.
The Passion Artist. New York, Harper, 1979.
Virginie: Her Two Lives. New York, Harper, 1982; London, Chatto and Windus, 1983.
Adventures in the Alaskan Skin Trade. New York, Simon and Schuster, 1985; London, Chatto and Windus, 1986.
Whistlejacket. New York, Weidenfeld and Nicolson, 1988; London, Secker and Warburg, 1989.
Sweet William: A Memoir of Old Horse. New York, Simon and Schuster, 1993.

Short Stories

The Goose on the Grave, and The Owl: Two Short Novels. New York, New Directions, 1954; *The Owl* published separately, 1977.
Lunar Landscapes: Stories and Short Novels 1949-1963. New York, New Directions, 1969; London, Chatto and Windus, 1970.
The Universal Fears. Northridge, California, Lord John Press, 1978.
Innocence in Extremis. Providence, Rhode Island, Burning Deck, 1985.

Uncollected Short Stories

"The Heart Demands Satisfaction," in *Vogue* (New York), 15 January 1964.
"Island Fire," in *Hellcoal Annual* (Providence, Rhode Island), Spring 1979.
"Two Shoes for One Foot," in *The Best of Tri-Quarterly,* edited by Jonathan Brent. New York, Washington Square Press, 1982.
"A Little Bit of the Old Slap and Tickle," in *New Directions 50.* New York, New Directions, 1986.

Plays

The Wax Museum (produced Boston, 1966; New York, 1977). Included in *The Innocent Party,* 1966.
The Questions (produced Stanford, California, 1966). Included in *The Innocent Party,* 1966.
The Innocent Party: Four Short Plays. New York, New Directions, 1966; London, Chatto and Windus, 1967.
The Undertaker (produced Boston, 1967). Included in *The Innocent Party,* 1966.

The Innocent Party (produced Boston, 1968). Included in *The Innocent Party,* 1966.

Poetry

Fiasco Hall. Privately printed, 1943.

Other

Humors of Blood and Skin: A John Hawkes Reader. New York, New Directions, 1984.

Editor, with others, *The Personal Voice: A Contemporary Prose Reader.* Philadelphia, Lippincott, 1964.
Editor, with others, *The American Literary Anthology 1: The 1st Annual Collection of the Best from the Literary Magazines.* New York, Farrar Straus, 1968.

*

Bibliography: *Three Contemporary Novelists: An Annotated Bibliography* by Robert M. Scotto, New York, Garland, 1977; *John Hawkes: An Annotated Bibliography* by Carol A. Hryciw, Metuchen, New Jersey, Scarecrow Press, 1977, revised edition, as *John Hawkes: A Research Guide,* New York, Garland, 1986.

Manuscript Collection: Houghton Library, Harvard University, Cambridge, Massachusetts.

Critical Studies: *The Fabulators* by Robert Scholes, New York, Oxford University Press, 1967; *Hawkes: A Guide to His Fictions* by Frederick Busch, Syracuse, New York, Syracuse University Press, 1973; *Comic Terror: The Novels of John Hawkes* by Donald J. Greiner, Memphis, Memphis State University Press, 1973, revised edition, 1978; *John Hawkes and the Craft of Conflict* by John Kuehl, New Brunswick, New Jersey, Rutgers University Press, 1975; *A John Hawkes Symposium* edited by Anthony C. Santore and Michael N. Pocalyko, New York, New Directions, 1977; *A Poetry of Force and Darkness: The Fiction of John Hawkes* by Eliot Berry, San Bernardino, California, Borgo Press, 1979; *John Fowles, John Hawkes, Claude Simon: Problems of Self and Form in the Post-Modernist Novel* by Robert Burden, Würzberg, Königshausen & Neumann, and Atlantic Highlands, New Jersey, Humanities Press, 1980; *John Hawkes* by Patrick O'Donnell, Boston, Twayne, 1982; "John Hawkes Issue" of *Review of Contemporary Fiction* (Elmwood Park, Illinois), vol. 3, no. 3, 1983; *Unbodied Hope: Narcissism and the Modern Novel* by Lawrence Thornton, Lewisburg, Pennsylvania, Bucknell University Press, 1984; *Understanding John Hawkes* by Donald J. Greiner, Columbia, University of South Carolina Press, 1985.

John Hawkes comments:

(1991) In the Spring of 1964, at the University of Wisconsin, I was interviewed by a gracious and extraordinary member of that English faculty, John Enk. About midway through our conversation I made the following statement:

My novels are not highly plotted, but certainly they're elaborately structured. I began to write fiction on the assumption that the true enemies of the novel were plot, character, setting and theme, and having once abandoned these familiar ways of thinking about fiction, totality of vision or structure was really all that remained. And structure—including verbal and psychological coherence—is still my largest concern as a writer. Related or corresponding event, recurring image or recurring action, these constitute the essential substance or meaningful density of my writing. . . . This kind of structure can't be planned in advance but can only be discovered in the writing process itself. The success of the effort depends on the degree and quality of consciousness that can be brought to bear on fully liberated materials of the unconscious. I'm trying to hold in balance poetic and novelistic methods in order to make the novel a more valid and pleasurable experience.

This is a fair statement, I think, and despite the obvious changes that have occurred in my fiction over this past quarter century, I stand by it now. However, a single sentence in this passage has come to haunt me over the years, especially recently, when Tom Wolfe quoted it to indicate what's wrong with so-called post-modernist fiction, and *Time* magazine included my name in an essay on Wolfe only to take me to task for so outrageously denying the traditional elements of fiction. For me the main part of that sentence is "familiar ways of thinking about fiction," and then and now I really meant to rebel against banality in reading and writing as much as anything else. My lighting on those "true enemies," without which the novel probably would disappear, was a youthful flourish—but as I say, one that I cannot denounce or retract at this late date. Having made my refusal, I am happy to say that long ago, in Buffalo, even my friend John Barth objected to my rejection of, especially, plot, and Barth is a man to listen to. In my work, setting has always meant creating a world; some of my later characters are more deeply created than earlier figures, theme for me has generally remained exposing the truth about our cruel natures in apposition to our capacities for questing after the ideal; but plot is a matter I've struggled with, generally without too much success. My plots tend to be sleights-of-hand, though I've attempted to coerce results from causes, and have increasingly come to admire not only Barth's great plots but those as exemplified, say in Faulkner's *The Reivers,* a novel I denied myself all these years but have just now enjoyed to the full. Finally, I distrust all theories about the novel. Writing for me is often painful, sometimes satisfying. We write what we must and as best as we're able, and a gifted writer can make anything out of anything. Of course there are those who have written encouragingly and with splendid original insight about the novel. To them, and to writers who persist in envisioning, I am grateful.

*   *   *

John Hawkes, perhaps the most original American novelist since Faulkner, bears only superficial resemblances to other contemporary innovators. His work is distinctly less philosophical and less parodic than that of Barth, Nabokov, Pynchon, Durrell, Borges. And if he chooses to create fictional worlds, rather than represent ours—fictional worlds in which one man on a motorcycle may occupy a third of Germany, or a Caribbean island wander in space and time—these visionary landscapes yet seem genuine dynamic projections of our real underground lives. Childhood terror, oral fantasies and castration fears, fears of regressions and violence, profound sexual disturbances—these (rather than the spatial inventions of science fiction or of Nabokov's *Ada*) are the components of Hawke's myths and of the "places" he calls Germany or America or England.

Hawkes claims to have recognized at the outset of his career four enemies: plot, character, setting, theme. Haunting chordal insistences and recurring images replace plot; the symbols of nightmare and neurosis and of the preconscious serve for character; a general vision of deterioration and collapse offers a semblance of theme. All these, and the dark hallucinatory landscapes, are redeemed by humor and by what Tony Tanner calls the "complicated and wrought fabric of his style." To a degree rare even in contemporary literature ugly materials—violence, suffering, deliberately reversed sympathies, magnified obscenities of landscape or human form—become things of beauty. Are the visions of violence and collapse prompted, as the author has occasionally insisted, by a belief in order and love? These stylized, distanced enormities maintain a very powerful hold on us, even as we enjoy them aesthetically, in part because they are rarely explained. This is the one thing Hawkes has in common with Robbe-Grillet; his world is unexplained. Hawkes's fictional world simply and dynamically, even magically, *is*.

Such originality and uncompromising difficulty long restricted Hawkes to an underground audience. *The Cannibal*, written while the author was a Harvard undergraduate, drew some attention because it appeared to be a powerful symbolic commentary on the American occupation of a diseased, deteriorated Germany. The ruined landscape of 1945 is juxtaposed against a Germany of 1914, already doomed; there is a vision of history as fated yet inconsecutive and absurd. But at least a few readers were drawn rather by powerful scenes of grotesque transformation and psychic substitution (as cannibalism for homosexual assault) and by the nervous, exceptionally brilliant phrasing. *The Cannibal* is, for some readers, the masterpiece of American avant-garde fiction.

The Beetle Leg is a cooler vision, at times parodic, often comic, of a mythical American west and sexless wasteland in which helpless persons somnambulistically wander. This excellent novel had few readers at first; *The Goose on the Grave* (a volume containing also *The Owl*) was also almost completely ignored. It has been reissued, with several stories added, as *Lunar Landscapes*. These darkly playful short novels are laid in 20th-century Italy and in a fictionalized San Marino locked in medieval legend and ritual: "two sides of a single dream," Tony Tanner has remarked, "centering on human violence in a hostile terrain—sudden deaths in still squares." (Tanner's essay in *City of Words* is one of the best brief introductions to Hawkes's work.)

By 1961, with *The Lime Twig*, a number of major writers and critics had discovered Hawkes, and this novel has become a favorite in American college classrooms. Moreover, Hawkes had by now moved to a more conscious understanding of his own materials and methods, and even some distance toward realism and narrative suspense. Parody of the detective novel form is merely the thin surface or pretext, in *The Lime Twig*, for another powerful vision of violence and tormented sexuality, this time laid in a bleakly plausible wartime and post-war England. Freudian substitutions and displacements are clearly evident as such, and are therefore oddly comic (an injection in the place of sexual penetration, or beating by a truncheon as rape). Yet the writing is so powerful that we continue to experience fascination and terror, even as we coolly watch the author's game. Few novels have dramatized so powerfully ultimate threats to identity.

With *Second Skin*, which lost the National Book award to Saul Bellow's *Herzog* by one vote, Hawkes reached a much larger au-

dience. And now for the first time the concealed affirmations and sympathies of the earlier books come to the surface in a vision of death and disaster (in America and on a north Atlantic island) succeeded by pastoral bliss on a wandering southern island. The narrator has survived the suicide of father, wife, daughter, and, escaped from a world of impotence, has become an artificial inseminator of cows. He is also, possibly, the father of the child of the black Catalina Kate, whom he shares with his messboy Sonny. Some of the dark materials of Hawkes's earlier fiction are present, even on that lush tropical island—a monstrous iguana, for instance, clinging to Catalina Kate's back. But the final vision of equanimity is genuine, reinforced by a conversational style of Nabokovian loveliness.

Hawkes has clearly moved from the brilliant groping of a wholly original, half-conscious, at times primitive visionary to the wholly conscious artistry and calculated rhetoric of a novelist who is also a gifted literary critic and professor of English (at Brown University). The writing of several tightly constructed plays, collected as *The Innocent Party*, may have contributed to Hawkes's development toward a more open and public art. *The Blood Oranges* has only a few scenes of wildly antirealist invention, though it has many moments of original and exquisite writing. Its comic treatment of two couples who have exchanged partners, yet still live together, often seems both to parody Ford's *The Good Soldier* and to satirize the gravity with which middle-class Americans, in the 1960s, contemplated their sexual anxieties. In one respect *The Blood Oranges* is like its predecessors. The Mediterranean world of "Illyria"—recalling *Twelfth Night* as *Second Skin* evoked *The Tempest*—is absolutely plausible, and absolutely Hawkes's own.

Hawkes's later fictions, reveal a more and more conscious and suave art. *Death, Sleep, and the Traveler* is perhaps the slightest of the later novels, and in its ambiguities and comic sexuality is even closer than *The Blood Oranges* to Nabokovian fictional games. In place of a quaternion of lovers there are now three sexual triangles, with the pleasures of "sharing" and complicity, and those of fellatio, even more overt than before. *Travesty*, on the other hand, is a masterpiece of first-person narration, though the very existence of the narrator's interlocutors remains problematic. The *données* of the fiction, while superficially melodramatic, invite a teasing, speculative, even philosophical voice reminiscent of Clamence's voice in Albert Camus's *The Fall:* the narrator and only speaker driving fast toward a deliberate murder and suicide that will crash the car against an already designated wall far ahead; beside him "Henri," who has been the lover of both the narrator's wife and his daughter, who is riding in the back seat. In a statement of cosmic skepticism as absolute as Camus's the car's journey becomes, metaphorically, that of the earth's "progress through the fortress of space." Between the Creation (the mechanic's last adjustments) and "the life of the mind that holds the moving car to the road there is nothing, nothing at all"; or there is only "design and debris."

With *The Passion Artist* Hawkes returned deliberately to the fictional world of *The Cannibal*, its bleak city and devastated landscape reflecting the psychic impotence of its protagonist, its gratuitous violence stemming from a revolt in a penal institution for women. The misogynous imagination evident in powerful pages throughout Hawkes's fiction is now allowed altogether free play; the familiar sexual materials (castration fear and fear of engulfment, Oedipal configurations, etc.) are wholly unrepressed and virtually undisplaced. The first 50 or 60 pages of *The Passion Artist* may seem disappointingly methodical and realistic to the lover of the audacities of *The Cannibal*. But the later portions of the novel, energized by a remarkable dream sequence, recover the tension and terror, the dynamic fantasies and stylistic beauties of the best earlier work. The circumstance is virtually unique in modern literature: that of a suave, immensely skilled conscious artist remanipulating the powerful dreams and atavistic energies of 30 years before.

An increasing sophistication and poetic delicacy, but also an increasing serenity, is evident in three of the four books Hawkes published between 1982 and 1985. *Virginie* could well mark the culmination of a love affair with France, where Hawkes spends some of his years freed from teaching, and with French literature. In 1980 in Provence "we knew we had come to the end of the line in a long search for vineyards, rude beams, red tiles, Picasso's dancing goats, literary voluptuousness" (*Humors of Blood and Skin*). Hawkes hoped to write a novel based on the life of the Marquis de Sade, but could not. In *Virginie* he did capture the calm, suave, graceful, highly formal manner in which Sade recites his litany of horrors.

The *tour de force,* entirely credible within its enclosed world, has a nine-year-old girl tell her two complementary lives—one as the innocent student of an artist in the erotic education of women, a man known only as Seigneur; the other as the still innocent inhabitant of a Paris brothel. The first life is lived in 1740, the second in 1945. Even more striking than this Nabokovian game with time is the successful combination of the child's fresh wondering vision of things, even the most depraved things, and her rich suave voice capable of expressing the author's gnomic wit and philosophical insight. *Virginie*, like the pornography it occasionally parodies, establishes fiction's autonomy from the "real" real world. Sexual manipulation, misogynous fantasies of omnipotence, real erotic bliss—all exist in a realm of poetic artifice.

Humors of Blood and Skin, subtitled "*A John Hawkes Reader,*" offers a not entirely fortunate selection of four short stories and extracts from 10 novels. The selections were not made by Hawkes, but presumably had his approval. The stories, placed at the beginning of the volume, would put a new reader on the wrong track, and the pages from *The Cannibal, Second Skin,* and *Travesty* are far from the best. On the cover is a reclining Bacchic Hawkes, nude to the waist and about to address a listener, with a demure young woman (his daughter) in the background. The genial but not complacent serenity of the later Hawkes is evident in the 11 autobiographical notes, prefatory musings rather, that introduce the selections. The author looks back on past turmoil as quietly as Conrad did in his prefaces, but much less evasively than Conrad. He examines good-humoredly the fears and obsessions behind his fiction, the psychic sources as well as the sources in lands visited, books read, anecdotes heard, traumatic experiences remembered. An Alaskan childhood, from ages 10 to 15 and nine months as a driver with the American Field Service ("not so much horrific as bizarre") have left obvious marks on the fiction. But earlier still were "nightly asthma attacks and listening to the thumping and snorting of the horses in the riding stable that adjoined our back yard then in Old Greenwich, Connecticut," also a "trim young girl" contemplated at the age of six. "I think that my writing has always depended in one way or another on those first configurations of suffocation, faint stirrings of desire, and horses."

Horses are ancient and terrifying in *The Cannibal* and *The Lime Twig* and explicitly sexual in *The Passion Artist,* where they are associated with initiation by powerful women and with fears of castration. But it is the horse who suffers and is overcome in *Virginie,* where Seigneur organizes the ceremonial extraction of a horse's tooth. (The tooth becomes the fragment of a glacier in *Ad-*

ventures in the Alaskan Skin Trade!) In *Innocence in Extremis* art has totally prevailed. Both dressage and the carefully staged mounting of a mare are emblematic of the artist who exerts power by subduing violence. *Innocence in Extremis,* though nominally an offshoot of the Alaskan novel, is more closely allied to *Virginie:* a stately saraband danced by an American family visiting their French aristocratic connection, and witnessing both the mounting of the mare and the ritualized treading of grapes by village virgins. This long story or very short novel is a flawless exercise in style.

Adventures in the Alaskan Skin Trade, much the longest of the novels, and the most realistic in method, represents a surprising departure from the dark intensities of *The Passion Artist* and the cameo perfection of *Virginie.* Hawkes's wife, he says, urged him to "try relaxing into the pleasures of autobiographical fiction"—autobiographical though the narrator Sunny is a disillusioned 39-year-old proprietress of a Juneau brothel, thinking back on her childhood discovery of Alaska and on the legendary exploits of her father "Uncle Jake," a reckless, improvident, sentimentally meddling heroic adventurer and chronic failure. The novel is very nearly as warm and un-neurotic as Faulkner's *The Reivers,* and the inhabitants of the two brothels are similarly good-natured. Hawkes's Gallicized imagination has here allowed itself to expand into the most traditional of American modes: the tomboy childhood on the last frontier, with a wily and garrulous father to cope with bears, Indians, glaciers and steep cliffs, a leaking boat, a small smashed plane. The father's disappearances and hairbreadth escapes and abrupt returns seem to parody the tall tales of 19th-century southwestern humor and even the serialized movies of the 1920s. Each escape introduces a new yarn.

Adventures in the Alaskan Skin Trade is perhaps the one "big novel," sprawling and vigorous, that a number of American writers attempt at some late moment in their careers. There is far more realistic detail of landscape, weather, flora, clothing, furniture than in any earlier book. And Alaska is a real place, though mythical exploits occur there. Sunny recreates her childhood vision of things—innocent yet probing, vivid, at times immoral—with the authenticity of *Great Expectations* and *David Copperfield.* By contrast the gloomy present and recent past of the brothel, with some attention to Sunny's own sexual history, seem contrived and unimportant. A few archetypal dreams echo powerful dreams in the earlier books, and in these the author's true voice is dominant. But Sunny's waking voice, and the yarn-spinning voice of her father, are wandering and diffuse, colloquially slack of syntax. The conversational ease is "in character," a further realism. But something is lost for the reader committed to the beautiful rhythms, great compression, and metaphorical intensity of the earlier books.

In *Whistlejacket* Hawkes returns to the visual intensity and cold unsentimental detachment of earlier work, and to the imaginative association of horses and women, horses and sexuality, that is central to *The Lime Twig* and *The Passion Artist.* But the powerful inward, at times psychoanalytic, exploration of childhood trauma and adult regression of *The Passion Artist* is now replaced by an art at times as ruthlessly uninterpretive and visual as Robbe-Grillet's in *The Voyeur.* The change is implicit in the fact that the narrator Mike, adopted son of the rich, horse-loving Van Fleet family, is a professional photographer who long fails to discern the lust and cruelty in the hidden lives of his adoptive family. He is as passive a spectator as Dowell of *The Good Soldier.* His amoral preoccupation with lights and shadows, with the lines and curves and masses of clothing, furniture, and flesh, are stronger than his own flickerings of erotic desire. He is entirely taken by surprise when his foster sister Virgie invites him to her bed, then orders him to proceed to his foster mother's. The novel's tone and quiet perversities suggest a close affinity with Peter Greenaway's film, *The Draughtsman's Contract*.

Whistlejacket is, given its narrator's measured voice and photographer's eye, a further step in the author's progression from compressed, visionary, anti-realist narrative to a slower moving and more realistic art. The overall structure, however, is once again unusual, with two disparate narratives linked thematically by their pictures of obsessively serious and unsentimental artists. The first section is rambling and genial autobiography, with an hilarious account of the boy Michael's first hunt on a remarkable Faulknerian horse. The family owns a painting of a horse named Whistlejacket by the 18th-century English painter George Stubbs. The novel's second section, "The Horse Painter," takes us back to Stubbs's quiet life and describes his methodical dissection both of the horse model and of the cadaver of a pregnant woman. Out of intense commitment and repulsive process may come both medical knowledge and beautiful works of art.

The surface materials of *Whistlejacket* are closer to those of realistic mainstream fiction than any of the earlier novels: a photographer and his models, a rich family with its hidden drama of sexual sharing, a social gathering culminating in a fox hunt. So too the even pace of narration, and the precise but seldom metaphorical language, with generally realistic dialogue and a reasonable and unhurried narrator who watches the events with a calm eye. The presence of an implied author behind the narrator, and of Hawkes behind both, is less pronounced than in the early work, although familiar pleasures and eccentricities remain: a man kicked to death after going into a horse's stall and a balled up stocking as an instrument of sex, both echoing *The Lime Twig*.

After more than 40 years of always original yet carefully wrought uncommercial fiction Hawkes would appear to be established as one of the great contemporary writers, although he is still resisted by those who expect a novel to represent ordinary reality and to be easy to read. (His most noticeable weakness, one shared by Garcia Marquez, is in producing dialogue that purports to be realistic.) A voluminous criticism has applauded his work, sometimes for the wrong reasons. Only a few books in the vast library of Faulkner criticism do justice to his comic side and to his mastery of language. And this is also true for Hawkes. In his novels comedy may intrude at any moment on the most appalling violence. And everything he has written has many moments of stylistic power and grace.

As a poetic novelist, caring most about language and the imagination, Hawkes has wanted "to try everything" (to use Joyce's comment on himself), and he has gone very far. There will probably be further movements in the career of this great artist.

—Albert Guerard

HAZZARD, Shirley

Nationality: American. **Born:** Sydney, New South Wales, Australia, 30 January 1931; became U.S. citizen. **Education:** Queenwood School, Sydney. **Family:** Married the writer Francis Steegmuller in 1963. **Career:** Staff member, Combined Services Intelligence, Hong Kong, 1947-48, United Kingdom High Commissioner's Of-

fice, Wellington, New Zealand, 1949-50, and United Nations Headquarters, New York (General Service Category), 1951-61. **Awards:** American Academy award, 1966; Guggenheim fellowship, 1974; O. Henry award, 1977; National Book Critics Circle award, 1981. **Address:** 200 East 66th Street, New York, New York 10021, U.S.A.

PUBLICATIONS

Novels

The Evening of the Holiday. New York, Knopf, and London, Macmillan, 1966.
People in Glass Houses: Portraits from Organization Life. New York, Knopf, and London, Macmillan, 1967.
The Bay of Noon. Boston, Little Brown, and London, Macmillan, 1970.
The Transit of Venus. New York, Viking Press, and London, Macmillan, 1980.

Short Stories

Cliffs of Fall and Other Stories. New York, Knopf, and London, Macmillan, 1963.

Uncollected Short Stories

"The Flowers of Sorrow," in *Winter's Tales 10,* edited by A.D. Maclean. London, Macmillan, and New York, St. Martin's Press, 1964.
"Forgiving," in *Ladies' Home Journal* (New York), August 1964.
"Comfort," in *New Yorker,* 24 October 1964.
"The Evening of the Holiday," in *New Yorker,* 17 April 1965.
"Out of Itea," in *New Yorker,* 1 May 1965.
"Nothing in Excess," in *New Yorker,* 26 March 1966.
"A Sense of Mission," in *New Yorker,* 4 March 1967.
"Swoboda's Tragedy," in *New Yorker,* 20 May 1967.
"Story of Miss Sadie Graine," in *New Yorker,* 10 June 1967.
"Official Life," in *New Yorker,* 24 June 1967.
"The Separation of Dinah Delbanco," in *New Yorker,* 22 July 1967.
"The Everlasting Delight," in *New Yorker,* 19 August 1967.
"Statue and the Bust," in *McCall's* (New York), August 1971.
"Sir Cecil's Ride," in *Winter's Tales 21,* edited by A.D. Maclean. London, Macmillan, 1975; New York, St. Martin's Press, 1976.
"A Long Story Short," in *Prize Stories 1977: The O. Henry Awards,* edited by William Abrahams. New York, Doubleday, 1977.
"A Crush on Doctor Dance," in *Winter's Tales 24,* edited by A.D. Maclean. London, Macmillan, 1978; New York, St. Martin's Press, 1979.
"Something You'll Remember Always," in *New Yorker,* 17 September 1979.
"She Will Make You Very Happy," in *New Yorker,* 26 November 1979.
"Forgiving," in *Ladies' Home Journal* (New York), January 1984.
"The Meeting," in *The Faber Book of Contemporary Australian Short Stories,* edited by Murray Bail. London, Faber, 1988.
"The Place to Be," in *Prize Stories 1988,* edited by William Abrahams. New York, Doubleday, 1988.
"In These Islands," in *New Yorker,* 18 June 1990.

Other

Defeat of an Ideal: A Study of the Self-Destruction of the United Nations. Boston, Little Brown, 1972; London, Macmillan, 1973.
Coming of Age in Australia (lectures). Sydney, Australian Broadcasting Corporation, 1985.
Countenance the Truth: The United Nations and the Waldheim Case. New York, Viking, 1990; London, Chatto and Windus, 1991.

*

Critical Studies: "Patterns and Preoccupations of Love: The Novels of Shirley Hazzard" by John Colmer, in *Meanjin* (Melbourne), December 1970; *Recent Fiction* by R.G. Geering, Melbourne, Oxford University Press, 1974; "Shirley Hazzard: Dislocation and Continuity" by Robert Sellick, in *Australian Literary Studies* (Hobart), October 1979; "Shirley Hazzard Issue" of *Texas Studies in Literature and Language* (Austin), vol. 25, no. 2, 1983.

*   *   *

Shirley Hazzard is a slow, painstaking writer who seems to have known where she was going in her art right from the beginning. Her first published work, the 10 stories in *Cliffs of Fall and Other Stories,* is like the rest of her fiction with the exception of *People in Glass Houses* in that it is concerned with the tensions, complications, and disappointments of adult sexual love. The stories involve doubles, triangles, and sometimes quadrilaterals of people caught up with one another in complex webs of relationships, the trails of which are traced out in the subtle, witty, biting prose that is Hazzard's trademark. Usually the stories are told from the perspective of the female protagonist and often, as is the case with much of Hazzard's fiction, they are set in a fairly recent past. The scenes range from England to the United States and in one case Switzerland. Sometimes they consist simply of observation of manners at some occasion or gathering—"The Party," "The Weekend," "The Picnic"—but almost invariably they are chronicles of pain and betrayal.

The Evening of the Holiday is a short novel, a simple and rather inconclusive account of a love affair between a woman named Sophie and an Italian, Tancredi, who is separated from his wife but cannot gain a divorce under Italian law, a situation that occurs in several of these stories. It is a tender, elegantly written book with a strong but rather cryptic sense of fatalism hanging over it. *People in Glass Houses* is a brilliantly funny and scathing collection of eight interrelated stories concerning an unnamed "Organization" which is transparently the United Nations, where Hazzard worked for a time. The stories are linked, not merely by the reappearance of several characters such as Mr. Bekkus, Clelia Kinglake, Swoboda, Rodriguez-O'Hearn, and others but by the repetition of the savage criticisms that the author offers in each story. In her view, the U.N. is characterized by petty and insensitive bureaucracy, a determination to squeeze out the individual and the gifted, an absence of personal feeling and a refusal to promote loyal and efficient, if limited, employees such as Swoboda and Dinah Delbanco. It is especially unfair in the last respect to women. Hazzard's interest in language itself, always strong in her fiction, has never been livelier or more intense than in this book and she constantly points to bureaucratic inertia, insensitivity, and finally

lack of human feeling by concentrating on the way people use language. The interest surfaces early in the figure of Algie Wyatta, rebel, iconoclast, and therefore doomed, who collects contradictions in terms such as "military intelligence," "competent authorities" and "easy virtue." The egregious Mr. Bekkus is characterized in terms of his employment of jargon. The story "The Flowers of Sorrow" hinges around an important personage intruding a personal note into his speech— "In my country . . . we have a song that asks, Will the flowers of joy ever equal the flowers of sorrow"—and the diverse but almost always disparaging reaction to this on the part of his staff.

The Bay of Noon is again a short novel, set in Naples and dealing with the complex relationships worked out among four people from a perspective of some 12 or 15 years later. The story is told in the first person by Jenny, an English girl sent to Italy as a translator, who becomes involved with Gioconda, her lover Gianni and a Scot named J.P. (Justin) Tulloch. Hazzard brings to her treatment of the familiar theme of love and its entanglements all the sophisticated techniques she has been steadily developing in her fiction and which culminate in her finest and most ambitious novel, *The Transit of Venus.* The language is packed with literary allusion. There are aggressively bracketed interpolations, such as a violent attack on the military. There is a flash forward to Tulloch's eventual death in a plane crash, a recurring event in Hazzard's fiction. It is an enjoyable but finally rather lightweight novel that has an uncharacteristic look of improvisation about its plot.

But Hazzard's masterpiece and the basis of her reputation is undoubtedly *The Transit of Venus.* A young Australian woman travels to England with her sister, has a relationship with a worthless man, is reduced to material poverty and emotional impoverishment, out of which she is rescued by a rich, liberal-minded, middle-aged American. However, the novel moves on to the deeply melancholy ending of the death of its heroine Caroline (Caro) Bell in an air crash and the post-fictive suicide of Ted Tice, the man she has finally realized she loved and was on the way to meet. The novel is about love and about truth, about the difference between those who love truly and those who exploit emotions for selfish ends. It is also about chance and the contingent, specifically the accident referred to in the title by which Australia came to be discovered by Captain Cook.

The motif of Venus itself becomes an important one in the novel, along with a number of others of which perhaps the most important is that of the shipwreck. Caro is indeed a child of Venus in that for her, love is a total commitment; it is part of her complete emotional honesty, her belief in the possibility of an excellence and distinction that are not necessarily related to any demonstrable achievement or worldly success but may consist solely in a life of constant personal integrity: "the truth has a life of its own," she says. *The Transit of Venus* is an unfashionably romantic novel. Coupled with this, however, is the fact that in terms of structure and technique it is also ruthlessly calculating, even cold-blooded. This paradoxical combination has upset many of its critics. The novel is structured around an inferential method that makes heavy demands on the reader's ability to connect different events and personages, and demonstrates the author's almost lordly superiority over and distance from her material. Of these demands, the most important is the suicide of Ted Tice which, though mentioned explicitly early in the novel, takes place after its close and can be worked out by the reader only by carefully following a number of clues scattered carefully throughout its pages. However, the meticulous—sometimes almost too meticulous—craftsmanship of the novel and the elegance and subtle wit of the style are a delight and almost unique among contemporary Australian fiction writers.

—Laurie Clancy

HEATH, Roy A(ubrey) K(elvin)

Nationality: Guyanese. **Born:** British Guiana, now Guyana, 13 August 1926. **Education:** Central High School, Georgetown; University of London, 1952-56, B.A. (honours) in French 1956; called to the bar, Lincoln's Inn, 1964. **Family:** Married Aemilia Oberli; three children. **Career:** Treasury clerk, Georgetown, 1944-51; clerical worker, London, 1951-58; primary school teacher, Inner London Education Authority, 1959-68. Since 1968 French and German teacher, Barnet Borough Council, London. **Awards:** Guyana Theatre Guild award, 1972; *Guardian* Fiction prize, 1978; Guyana Literature prize, 1989. **Agent:** Bill Hamilton, A.M. Heath, 79 St. Martin's Lane, London WC2N 4AA. **Address:** c/o Allison and Busby Ltd, 44 Hill St, London W1X8LB, England.

PUBLICATIONS

Novels

A Man Come Home. London, Longman, 1974.
The Murderer. London, Allison and Busby, 1978; New York, Persea, 1992.
Kwaku; or, The Man Who Could Not Keep His Mouth Shut. London, Allison and Busby, 1982.
Orealla. London, Allison and Busby, 1984.
The Shadow Bride. London, Collins, 1988.
The Armstrong Trilogy. New York, Persea, 1994.
From the Heat of the Day. London, Allison and Busby, 1979.
One Generation. London, Allison and Busby, 1981.
Genetha. London, Allison and Busby, 1981.

Uncollected Short Stories

"Miss Mabel's Burial," in *Kaie* (Georgetown, Guyana), 1972.
"The Wind and the Sun," in *Savacou* (Kingston, Jamaica), 1974.
"The Writer of Anonymous Letters," in *Firebird 2,* edited by T.J. Binding. London, Penguin, 1983.
"Sisters," in *London Magazine,* September 1988.
"The Master Tailor and the Lady's Skirt," in *Colours of a New Day: New Writing for South Africa,* edited by Sarah Lefanu and Stephen Hayward. London, Lawrence and Wishart, and New York, Pantheon, 1990.
"According to Marx," in *So Very English,* edited by Marsha Rowe. London, Serpent's Tail, 1991.

Play

Inez Combray (produced Georgetown, Guyana, 1972).

Other

Art and History (lectures). Georgetown, Guyana, Ministry of Education, 1984.
Shadows Round the Moon: Caribbean Memoirs. London, Collins, 1990.

*

Roy A.K. Heath comments:

A Man Come Home relates the story of a large working-class Guyanese family whose mores provide a striking contrast to those of their middle-class brethren. *From the Heat of the Day* and *One Generation* are the first two parts of a trilogy treating the condition of the middle classes in Guyana in the 20th century. *Genetha* completes the trilogy and shows the heroine faced with the choice of joining the Catholic church, returning to a life of prostitution, or living with her aunts in a stifling middle-class atmosphere. *Kwaku* is the tale of a trickster figure. Orealla, the unseen haven for the main character in the novel of that title, is real, yet imagined.

I see myself as a chronicler of Guyanese life in this century.

*   *   *

Roy A.K. Heath's eight novels, beginning with *A Man Come Home* and concluding with the most recent, *The Shadow Bride,* represent a distinctive body of fictive insights into contemporary Guyanese society. It blends traditional social realism with local folklore and myths to dramatize the everyday lives of the poor and the lower middle class in the capital, Georgetown, and, occasionally, in the rural hinterlands. Indeed, it is this kind of blending, or interweaving, that makes for one of Heath's distinctive strengths as a novelist. The folk myths of "obeah" or voudun ("voodoo"), the strict orthodoxies of biblical morality, local legends drawn from Amerindian or East Indian sources—these all co-exist with the empirical "realities" of everyday village life, the familiar routine of middle-class home life, or the rough-and-tumble of the streets and slumyards of Georgetown's impoverished districts. Heath's is a world of popular beliefs and customs which determine the perceptions and choices of his characters; and the very diversity of values and viewpoints, not only within the community but also within any single individual, dramatizes the discrete complexities of the social milieu, complicates the very notion of moral judgment or social choices in the recurrent tensions between classes, religious traditions, and cultural backgrounds, and, finally, challenges conventional assumptions about "social realism" in prose fiction.

This discreteness also goes hand in hand with Heath's other strength—his ability to evoke a given environment and its social milieu (urban slum, middle-class neighborhood, rural village, and so forth), bringing to life the sights and sounds of a family dining room or a Georgetown whorehouse in vivid, richly suggestive vignettes. In his more recent fiction, especially in the impressively crafted *Kwaku,* he has shown signs of developing a flair for a lively, effective prose style as well as for credible characterization; but even in the previous novels where thinness of characterization and of style is often a problem, Heath's reader is always aware of a provocative intelligence perpetually raising questions about the nature of social reality and of moral judgments in a vividly realized world. These questions are integrated with recurrent themes which typify all of Heath's fiction: the inevitable obsession with material success in a society dominated by poverty, and the price of success as well as of failure; the conflict between the needs and desires of the private self and the restrictive conventions of a world in which ideals of family responsibility, social respectability, and moral conventions are paramount; and that unending war between the sexes in which mutual exploitiveness and shared dependency, hostility and desire all seem to mirror tensions and contradictions in human society as a whole. In turn all of these conflicts center on a fundamental dilemma which links all the novels, the dilemma of freedom: for whether the quest be freedom from poverty or from some intolerable marriage, Heath's rebel-protagonists must always wrestle, usually inconclusively, with certain unresolved contradictions—it seems all but impossible to flee from poverty without losing a part of one's basic humanity in the process of amassing wealth; the despised spouse (Heath's marriages are invariably wretched) is also an integral, indispensable part of one's self; and the young rebels against family and conventional morality soon discover that the target of their rebellion is also an ineradicable part of themselves.

In *A Man Come Home* the chief rebel is Archie "Bird" Foster who tries to escape from the poverty of Georgetown's slum-yards by entering into a liaison with one of the legendary "Water People" of Guyanese folklore, a "Fair Maid," or witch. She gives him unlimited wealth on condition that he returns regularly to her bed at her bidding. Now wealthy, he quickly collects the usual trappings of middle-class affluence—an ostentatious house in the suburbs, expensive habits, and a wife (in the person of his long-suffering girlfriend from the slum-yard). The legendary materials provide Heath with a rather obvious and ready-made allegory on the middle-class aspirations of the poor, and the moral cost of acquiring wealth in exchange for one's humanity—for the contract with the Fair Maid is, in effect, a Faustian pact. His marriage, his ties with the rest of his family and with his old friends all conflict with that pact, and when he reneges on his agreement with the Fair Maid in order to re-establish the "normal" relationships and "respectable" conventions of his society, she exacts the inevitable price: he dies in a car accident which also claims the life of his sister's children.

Bird's tragedy is not isolated, for even the most isolated of Heath's characters are bound up with their families and the rest of society. The deaths of the children therefore emphasize that Bird's tragedy has become a family disaster. His sister never recovers from her loss, and her marriage eventually collapses. At the same time his father's household continues the steady decline which actually started before Bird's misadventures. Egbert Foster, the father, tries, unsuccessfully, to establish peace in a home in which his mistress envies the social life and sexual activity of her young daughter Melda. She administers a savage beating from which Melda never recovers fully, spending the rest of her life as an idiot. In the meanwhile the older woman enters upon an affair with one of Bird's slum-yard friends (who is also Melda's lover), then betrays him to her husband's inevitable violence. Viewed in the context of the Foster family as a whole, then, it becomes clear that Bird's liaison with the Fair Maid is not only an allegory on the moral dilemmas of poverty and materialism; it is also a mythological re-enactment of sexual conflicts and contradictions. The weakness and domination, the mutual exploitation, the futile obsession with escape and freedom—these are not only the patterns of Bird's ill-fated liaison with the Fair Maid, but also the familiar, repetitive patterns in his family and among his friends.

This grim vision of sexual relationships dominates *The Murderer,* where the waste and mutual destructiveness of many conventional relationships are explored through the experiences of ab-

normal psychology—a narrative strategy which allows Heath to juxtapose images of the "normal" or "conventional" with patterns of "abnormality" in order to challenge settled assumptions about these terms. The murderer is an archetypal psychotic: Galton Flood has been scarred by a wretched childhood in which his sexuality and social instincts were repressed or warped by the ridicule and harshness of a domineering mother who also made life miserable for her husband. His parents' marriage is a model of the shared resentment and contempt which characterize sexual unions in Galton's world, and when he becomes an adult he is deeply suspicious of women, a suspiciousness that is aggravated by his general inability to socialize. When he does marry, he chooses a wife whose prior experience (with an older lover and a dependent but unloving father) has convinced her that men are unreliable and weak beneath the usual male bravado. The marriage quickly fails because of Galton's jealousy and because of the unsociability which prevents him from developing a stable career. His jealousy is the first symptom of criminal insanity. He kills his wife, and although he confesses the murder to both her family and to his own, he is never brought to justice. He ends up, instead, as a street derelict, a relatively harmless idiot who is supported by his kind-hearted brother. Galton's inability to function as part of the family unit or in society at large is partly counteracted by the generosity and family loyalties of his older brother; but Heath's main achievement is to evoke ironic parallels between Galton's "abnormal" obsessions and those familiar habits of possessiveness and abusiveness which characterize the sexual relationships of "normal" people. "Abnormal" psychology is as much an allegory of the "real" world here, as "supernatural" events are in *A Man Come Home.*

Heath's other family tragedy, the tragedy of the Armstrong family, is the subject of his Georgetown trilogy, *From the Heat of the Day, One Generation,* and *Genetha.* The first work traces the history of the parents' marriage (Sonny Armstrong, from a poor, relatively uneducated background, resents his wife's middle-class family even before he marries her). It is a history of failing affections and growing isolation on both sides, a growing misery which inevitably affects the two children, Genetha and Rohan, and which concludes with the death of Mrs. Armstrong. *Her* misery, at least, ends with her death. He drowns his in drink, until he dies as a derelict pensioner, early in *One Generation.* The second novel describes Rohan's flight from the Georgetown family home, away from the possessive caring of his sister, to a Civil Service job in rural Guyana where he falls in love with a married woman while living with her sister. He is killed by his impoverished East Indian assistant who envies him his social standing and relative prosperity. His murderer is never discovered, and his impunity reinforces the grim realities which lend an air of inevitability and repetition to the trilogy as a whole: Rohan's personal life has been as wasted as his parents'; his sexual relationships have been equally fraught with betrayals and exploitation; and he, too, leaves behind him a legacy of hurt. The inheritors of that legacy are Dada, the mother of his unborn child, who has been victimized by his duplicity with her sister, and his own sister, Genetha, whom he has abandoned to face life alone as a single, inexperienced girl in Georgetown. Finally, in the third part of the trilogy, Genetha recalls her late mother by virtue of her loneliness and isolation, her inability to develop satisfactory relationships with men, and the perpetual tension between her need for the middle-class respectability of her mother's family and her dislike of the family's suffocating propriety. She ends as a total dependent on the family's former maid, now a very successful "madam" of a Georgetown whorehouse (another "success" acquired at the cost of one's humanity). Esther, like Mr. Armstrong before her, despises the middle-class attitudes of Genetha and the late Mrs. Armstrong, but the eventual bond between Genetha and Esther transcends the barriers, for it has been strengthened by their common experiences as women in a world of weak, bullying men.

Kwaku, the hero of the novel of the same name, is no bully, but he is another weak, insecure male whose dependency on his wife (Gwendoline) and his close, lifelong friend (Blossom) has been intensified by the fact that as a social misfit he has never made friends among the villagers with whom he has grown up. Like the other figures of poverty in Heath's fiction, he tries to make money, succeeding for a while as a "healer" in the small town of New Amsterdam. But his insecurity, his need to brag and command respect, leads to his downfall: he runs afoul of the village fisherman when he fails to "cure" the latter's family problems. The fisherman retaliates by resorting to obeah: Gwendoline becomes blind and the family sinks into utter destitution. Kwaku's children rebel or are forced to leave home for sheer survival, and both Kwaku and Gwendoline end up as a drunken pair of derelicts in New Amsterdam. It is worth noting that, to his credit, Kwaku never deserts his family in order to resuscitate his business as "healer"— despite the fact that the expenses of supporting a blind wife and eight children make it impossible for him to start up his business again. But the familiar irony with which Heath handles family and love remains the final judgment here. Kwaku is loyal to his family because he needs them. As he himself recognizes, his love for his wife is a kind of possessiveness—a possessiveness which we can easily recognize, in some of its most repulsive forms, in Gwendoline. Unlike Gwendoline, Blossom is fiercely independent—but her own marriage survives, after a fashion, because she has bullied her own husband into his (accepting) place, even manipulating him into "accepting" a child which, he himself knows, he never fathered. In the uncompromising realism of Heath's 20th-century vision, Wilfred's marital happiness with Blossom is the happiness of the Swiftian fool in *A Tale of a Tub*—a state of being well deceived. It is the kind of "happiness" which exemplifies the solid achievements and rich possibilities of Heath's narrative irony.

—Lloyd W. Brown

HELLENGA, Robert (Riner)

Nationality: American. **Born:** Milwaukee, Wisconsin, 5 August 1941. **Education:** University of Michigan, Ann Arbor, 1959-63, B.A. (with high honors) 1963 (Phi Beta Kappa); The Queen's University at Belfast, Northern Ireland (exchange fellowship), 1963-64; University of North Carolina, Chapel Hill (Woodrow Wilson fellow), 1964-65; Princeton University, New Jersey (NDEA Title IV fellowship), 1965-68, Ph.D. in English 1968. **Family:** Married Virginia Hellenga in 1963; three daughters. **Career:** Co-director, Newberry Library Seminar in the Humanities, Chicago, 1973-76; National Endowment for the Humanities fellowship, University of Chicago, 1975-76; director, Associated Colleges of the Midwest program in Florence, Italy, 1982-83. Since 1968, professor of English, Knox College, Galesburg, Illinois. **Awards:** Illinois Arts Council, fellowship in creative writing, 1981, artist's grant, 1983, 1984, 1987, 1990, artist's literary award, 1985; PEN Syndicated award, 1988 for fiction; National Endowment for the Arts artist's

fellowship, 1989. **Agent:** Harold Ober Associates, 425 Madison Avenue, New York, New York 10017, U.S.A. **Address:** 343 North Prairie Street, Galesburg, Illinois 61401, U.S.A.

PUBLICATIONS

Novel

Sixteen Pleasures. New York, Soho, and London, Hodder/Headline, 1994.

Uncollected Short Stories

"Russian Dreams," in *Iowa Review,* Fall 1973.
"A Lover's Pinch," in *Chicago Review,* January 1975.
"The Mountain of Lights," in *California Quarterly,* 21, 1982.
"Strange Bedfellows," in *Columbia,* (7), 1982.
"Green of Real Green," in *Ascent,* (10), December 1984.
"Class of '59," in *Farmer's Market,* (3), January 1984.
"The Minstrels," in *Farmer's Market,* (2), Fall 1985.
"Pockets of Silence," in *Chicago Tribune Magazine,* 29 January 1989.
"Where I Want to Be," in *Triquarterly,* (81), Spring-Summer 1991.
"I Speak a Little French," in *Crazyhorse,* (43), Winter 1992.
"The Second Coming," in *Mississippi Valley Review,* (23), Fall 1992.
"O Happy Men, If Love Which Rules the Stars Rule Your Hearts," in *Crazyhorse,* (47), Winter 1994.

*

Robert Hellenga comments:

I like to write about things I don't understand—Italy, for example, or works of art, or the desire for transcendence—because I believe that at the heart of every story there's something mysterious, something that can't be explained. If it could be explained, there wouldn't be any need for a story. Three contemporary novels that have pointed me in this direction are: *The Finishing School* and *Father Melancholy's Daughter* (Gail Godwin); and *Family Portraits* (Sue Miller).

*   *   *

Adding to a theme previously explored by Dante and Frost, Robert Hellenga sets out to illustrate the spiritual bankruptcy that often follows when people despair over choices made during life's crossroads. *The Sixteen Pleasures,* his first novel, lectures that only one road can be traveled and that looking back upon the one not taken only leads to more bad choices and a wrongly held sense of failure. "What I wanted most was denied to me," the protagonist is told by a convent superiora who chose to become a nun after years of unsuccessfully trying for a child with her husband. "You come up against something, a roadblock, you're so sure of the direction you're going in, the road you want to take, that it's inconceivable. But a bridge has been washed out. You have to find some other way. . . . We can't make any sense out of life until we give up our deepest hopes, until we stop trying to arrange everything to suit us."

Set in Italy in 1966, *The Sixteen Pleasures* follows protagonist Margot Harrington, a 29-year-old American book conservator who travels to Florence to help save priceless books and arts from the overflowing banks of the Arno but ends up rescuing her own self-identity. Trips to Italy during her teen years had proved to be an overwhelming influence; during a stay there after her senior year in high school, she had enthusiastically planned her life's course: Radcliffe, a career as a research chemist, marriage, a family. Instead, she spent her early twenties nursing her dying mother and the rest of her life regretting the roads she had not taken. The person Margot might have been but for different choices is venerated through her conversations with a "ghostly double," Margeaux, a woman she imagines to be wiser, more beautiful, and more successful than she and who influences her every decision. Even while journeying to Italy, Margot worries again about whether she has made the correct choice.

Once there, she sets about helping a convent save its tiny water-logged library. Margot and the nuns eventually discover a book containing 16 erotic drawings by Marcantonio Raimondi and 16 accompanying sonnets by Pietro Aretino, the last copy of the most famous and most scandalous example of Renaissance erotica. With the convent under financial pressure, the Madre Badessa—the Mother Abbess—asks Margot to discreetly determine the book's value and sell it. As she goes about restoring the book, she begins an affair with a much older married man, the head restorer of works of fine arts in Tuscany, hoping that love, marriage, and children will give her life distinction. Instead, he betrays her, and she begins to see that successfully restoring and selling the Aretino and keeping her promise to the Madre Badessa are the keys to establishing her self-harmony. In the end, she admits, "God's will is our peace."

The Sixteen Pleasures is a remarkably entertaining read, with lively dialogue and strong narration. Conflict within the Church contributes to the greater conflict of self, and Hellenger's knowledgeable mix of Catholicism and Italian art history and mystique provides for an exotic setting, yet he successfully deals with very inclusive themes of regret, grief, acceptance, self-discovery, and fatalism.

—Heather B. Hayes

HELLER, Joseph

Nationality: American. **Born:** Brooklyn, New York, 1 May 1923. **Education:** Abraham Lincoln High School, New York, graduated 1941; University of Southern California, Los Angeles, 1945-46; New York University, B.A. 1948 (Phi Beta Kappa); Columbia University, New York, M.A. 1949; Oxford University (Fulbright scholar), 1949-50. **Military Service:** Served in the United States Army Air Force in World War II: Lieutenant. **Family:** Married 1) Shirley Held in 1945, one son and one daughter; 2) Valerie Humphries. **Career:** Instructor in English, Pennsylvania State University, University Park, 1950-52; advertising writer, *Time* magazine, New York, 1952-56, and *Look* magazine, New York, 1956-58; promotion manager, *McCall's* magazine, New York, 1958-61. **Awards:** American Academy grant, 1963; Médicis prize (France), 1985. **Member:** American Academy, 1977. Hon. fellow, St. Catherine's College, Oxford University, 1991. **Address:** c/o International Creative Management, 40 W. 57th St., New York, New York 10019, U.S.A.

PUBLICATIONS

Novels

Catch-22. New York, Simon and Schuster, 1961; London, Cape, 1962.
Something Happened. New York, Knopf, and London, Cape, 1974.
Good as Gold. New York, Simon and Schuster, and London, Cape, 1979.
God Knows. New York, Knopf, and London, Cape, 1984.
Picture This. New York, Putnam, and London, Macmillan, 1988.
Closing Time: A Sequel to Catch-22. New York and London, Simon and Schuster, 1994.

Uncollected Short Stories

"I Don't Love You Anymore," in *Story* (New York), September-October 1945.
"Castle of Snow," in *Atlantic* (Boston), May 1947.
"Bookies, Beware!," in *Esquire* (New York), March 1948.
"Girl from Greenwich," in *Esquire* (New York), June 1948.
"A Man Named Flute," in *Atlantic* (Boston), August 1948.
"Nothing to Be Done," in *Esquire* (New York), August 1948.
"MacAdam's Log," in *Gentlemen's Quarterly* (New York), December 1959.
"World Full of Great Cities," in *Nelson Algren's Own Book of Lonesome Monsters,* edited by Algren. New York, Lancer, 1962; London, Panther, 1964.
"Love, Dad," in *Playboy* (Chicago), December 1969.
"The Day Bush Left," in *Nation* (New York), 4 June 1990.

Plays

We Bombed in New Haven (produced New Haven, Connecticut, 1967; New York, 1969; London, 1971). New York, Knopf, 1968; London, Cape, 1969.
Catch-22, adaptation of his own novel. New York, Delacorte Press, and London, French, 1973.
Clevinger's Trial, adaptation of chapter 8 of his novel *Catch-22* (produced London, 1974). New York, French, 1973; London, French, 1974.

Screenplays: *Sex and the Single Girl,* adapted from the work by David R. Schwartz, 1964; *Casino Royale* (uncredited), 1967; *Dirty Dingus Magee,* adapted from the work by Tom and Frank Waldman, 1970.

Other

No Laughing Matter (autobiographical), with Speed Vogel. New York, Putnam, and London, Cape, 1986.

*

Bibliography: *Three Contemporary Novelists: An Annotated Bibliography* by Robert M. Scotto, New York, Garland, 1977; *Joseph Heller: A Reference Guide* by Brenda M. Keegan, Boston, Hall, 1978.

Critical Studies: "Joseph Heller's *Catch-22*" by Burr Dodd, in *Approaches to the Novel* edited by John Colmer, Edinburgh, Oliver and Boyd, 1967; "The Sanity of *Catch-22*" by Robert Protherough, in *Human World* (Swansea), May 1971; *A Catch-22 Casebook* edited by Frederick T. Kiley and Walter McDonald, New York, Crowell, 1973; *Critical Essays on Catch-22,* Encino, California, Dickinson Seminar Series, 1974, and *Critical Essays on Joseph Heller,* Boston, Hall, 1984, both edited by James Nagel; "Something Happened: A New Direction" by George J. Searles, in *Critique* (Atlanta), vol. 18, no. 3, 1977; *From Here to Absurdity: The Moral Battlefields of Joseph Heller* by Stephen W. Potts, San Bernardino, California, Borgo Press, 1982; *Joseph Heller* by Robert Merrill, Boston, Twayne, 1987; *The Fiction of Joseph Heller: Against the Grain* by David Seed, London, Macmillan, 1989; *Understanding Joseph Heller* by Sanford Pinsker, Columbia, University of South Carolina Press, 1991; *Joseph Heller* by Judith Ruderman, New York, Continuum, 1991.

*   *   *

Joseph Heller has a better claim than any other American to having written the definitive novel of modern war—if universal response to his definition of that war is any measure. People now know as "catch-22" the circular bureaucratic formula they had learned from experience. In Heller's book the "catch" works simply. Anyone who is crazy can be grounded from flying bombing missions; all he has to do is ask, but if he should ask he can't possibly be crazy. The unyielding absurdity of Heller's routine could be observed as easily in Flanders and Vietnam as in the air war over Europe that was the setting of his novel.

Catch-22 is a burlesque epic built upon the "catch-22" routine. Vaudeville, comic strips, and animated cartoons all inspire its basic structure and pace, which is not to say that Heller is flippant or callous. Far from it. It is his special talent to render his war epic in the formats of popular culture, then juxtapose it with the feelings it provokes in such men as his hero, Yossarian—feelings also bordered in film frames and comic strip panels. Yossarian is determined to "live forever or die in the attempt." Almost as often as assorted characters perform the catch-22 routine, he relives the moment in the air over Avignon when the wounded gunner, Snowden, lay "spilling his secret all over the back of the plane." "Ou sont les neigedens . . ." Yossarian murmurs over his crewman's body, touching the secret with heartbreaking word play.

Yossarian struggles to survive in a system in which a Lieutenant Scheisskopf necessarily moves through the ranks to become a general. Another name from the folklore of humor is Captain Aardvark, "Good Old Arfie," who can ignore the suffering he sees because he can't quite hear it. The chaplain is an Anabaptist, and the soldier in white is a plaster-cast embodiment of the system with a circuitry of tubes running into and out of what is alleged to be his body. There is the Unknown Soldier killed on his first mission before he has a chance to unpack his bags and get to know his comrades. His name, it turns out, is Mudd. In the world of *Catch-22,* a conversation begins with someone inventing the rumor that Germans are now using the Le Page anti-aircraft gun to spray webs of mucilage over formations of Allied bombers and ends with official confirmation that Le Page guns at Bologna have inflicted losses on the squadron by shooting webs of mucilage over formations of its planes. *Catch-22* is a brilliant, if exhausting, mosaic of comic invention fired by abiding rage.

Something Happened seems to be the effort to write as complicated a book as *Catch-22* about the mean, narrow life of a New York corporation executive. Bob Slocum is an insensitive man who knows himself quite well. "A friend in need is no friend of mine,"

he says. His "Snowden" is the older girl who teased him when he was an office boy and left the rest of his agitated sex life short of fulfillment. Slocum is a mimic and an echolaliac who cannot resist imitating the defects of those who suffer at his hands. One recognizes the comic techniques of *Catch-22* applied to something deadlier and more polished than Heller's undoubted masterpiece.

After these two extraordinarily ambitious books, critics were harsh with *Good as Gold,* a novel often funnier than *Catch-22* and always funnier than *Something Happened,* but it is also an uneasy mixture of two comic inspirations. One was to have Bruce Gold try to write about "The Jewish experience in America" despite his headlong striving after every token of assimilation. The other was to burlesque the career of Henry Kissinger. Accordingly, Gold is a plodding intellectual who even-handedly covets Washington power and tall gentile girls. His father bullies him, and his prospective father-in-law addresses him with anti-semitic epithets: his closest gentile friend admits that if worst came to worst he wouldn't hide him. The Washington fantasies are less effective than the bitter comedy involving Gold and his father, which is a little surprising given the similarities between Heller's top government brass and the military of *Catch-22.*

The narrator of *God Knows* is David, psalmist, King of Israel, and the archetypal Jewish ironist, wit, and standup comic. His storytelling is a torrent of anachronism that flows brilliantly as when, for example, David's modernisms give readers a precise notion of the scruffy little town that he hands on to Solomon as Jerusalem, site for the temple God has forbidden him to build. The middling or rapid-fire anachronisms can be seen in David's view of another town: "The city of Hebron is not Versailles, you know." The richest language Heller has ever used rests on his anachronisms, as when the psalmist proclaims his own place among all the poets ("How the mighty have fallen. Proud of that line. That goneff, William Shakespeare . . .") and when the king laments one son ("Absalom, my son") only to disparage his plodding successor ("You're a hard man, Shlomo.") Of course, Heller is unable to resist describing Michal as the first Jewish-American Princess and exploiting David's reputation as eulogist by having him proclaim Abner as "the noblest Israelite of them all."

In *Picture This,* the narrator observes the Averrhoes reading Aristotle's *Nicomachean Ethics* 41 times without understanding a single word. Something like that experience awaits the reader of *Picture This* if he should attempt to picture the fiction that encompasses Rembrandt, Aristotle, Heller, assorted ancient Athenians, 17th-century Dutchmen, and addled capitalist art collectors everywhere. Heller imagines Rembrandt painting "Aristotle Contemplating the Bust of Homer." Rembrandt slaves under a commission yet is beguiled by knowing that he can color cloth and medals as no one else can. Nothing else interests him. Aristotle is aware of the burgherish limits enclosing Rembrandt's genius, which his ever sharp eyes and classifying mind recognize at its worth. Rembrandt is virtually ignorant of both his subjects, man and bust. Proceeding from this studio sitting—or ignoring it—Heller discourses on major fallacies of the ancient sages, particularly Plato, and on the Peloponnesian War, where the world's foremost democracy sends a doomed force overseas on "the rise of the Dutch Republic, which could be subtitled "money talks." It all gets noticeably Hellerian with such comments as: "There are people willing to pay a great deal to own the most expensive painting in the world. They will not pay as much for one that costs less."

No Laughing Matter is a collaboration with Heller's close friend, Speed Vogel, on the writer's struggle with the Guillain-Barré syndrome. Writing alternate passages, they describe Heller's recovery from the debilitating and often disabling virus.

Some critics see *Closing Time: A Sequel to Catch 22* as a brilliant conclusion to Heller's career, though others feel that the book suffers by comparison to the earlier work. It is satisfying for long-time readers of Heller to revisit Yossarian and to see his response to aging and to eventual death. There is still a great deal to enjoy: a president who is goofy enough to start a nuclear war by accident, a descent into hell, an aging protagonist who still longs for the nurses. Readers would get an interesting view of Heller's lifespan by reading his entire works, from the youthful exuberance, through the doubt of middle years, to the final passage of death and dying. There is wisdom here worth savoring.

—David Sanders, updated by Loretta Cobb

HELWIG, David (Gordon)

Nationality: Canadian. **Born:** Toronto, Ontario, 5 April 1938. Educated at Stamford Collegiate Institute; University of Toronto, B.A. in English 1960; University of Liverpool, 1960-62, M.A. 1962. **Family:** Married Nancy Keeling in 1959; two daughters. **Career:** Member of the Department of English, Queen's University, Kingston, Ontario, 1962-80; literary manager, CBC television drama, 1974-76. **Address:** 106 Montreal Street, Kingston, Ontario K7K 3E8, Canada.

PUBLICATIONS

Novels

The Day Before Tomorrow. Ottawa, Oberon Press, 1971; as *Message from a Spy,* Don Mills, Ontario, PaperJacks, 1975.
The Glass Knight. Ottawa, Oberon Press, 1976.
Jennifer. Ottawa, Oberon Press, 1979; New York, Beaufort, 1983.
The King's Evil. Ottawa, Oberon Press, 1981; New York, Beaufort, 1984.
It Is Always Summer. Toronto, Stoddart, and New York, Beaufort, 1982.
A Sound Like Laughter. Toronto, Stoddart, and New York, Beaufort, 1983.
The Only Son. Toronto, Stoddart, and New York, Beaufort, 1984.
The Bishop. New York, Viking, and London, Penguin, 1986.
A Postcard from Rome. New York, Viking, 1988.
Old Wars. New York, Viking, 1989.
Of Desire. New York, Viking, 1990.
The Beloved. Ottawa, Oberon Press, 1992.

Uncollected Short Stories

"Presences" and "Things That Happened Before You Were Born," in *The Narrative Voice,* edited by John Metcalf. Toronto, McGraw Hill Ryerson, 1972.
"Avia da Capo," in *80: Best Canadian Stories,* edited by Clark Blaise and John Metcalf. Ottawa, Oberon Press, 1980.

Plays

A Time in Winter (produced Kingston, Ontario, 1967). Included in *Figures in a Landscape,* 1967.
The Hanging of William O'Donnell (produced Toronto, 1970).
Barnardo Boy (opera libretto), music by Clifford Crawley (produced Kingston, Ontario, 1981).

Poetry

Figures in a Landscape. Ottawa, Oberon Press, 1967.
The Sign of the Gunman. Ottawa, Oberon Press, 1969.
The Best Name of Silence. Ottawa, Oberon Press, 1972.
Atlantic Crossings. Ottawa, Oberon Press, 1974.
A Book of the Hours. Ottawa, Oberon Press, 1979.
The Rain Falls Like Rain. Ottawa, Oberon Press, 1982.
Catchpenny Poems. Ottawa, Oberon Press, 1983.
The Hundred Old Names. Ottawa, Oberon Press, 1988.

Other

A Book about Billie (documentary on Billie Miller). Ottawa, Oberon Press, 1972; as *Inside and Out: The Story of Billie, Junkie, Pimp, Booster, Robber, and Conman,* Don Mills, Ontario, PaperJacks, 1975.

Editor, with Tom Marshall, *Fourteen Stories High: Best Canadian Stories of 71.* Ottawa, Oberon Press, 1971.
Editor, with Joan Harcourt, *72, 73, 74* and *75: New Canadian Stories.* Ottawa, Oberon Press, 4 vols., 1972-75.
Editor, *Words from Inside.* Kingston, Ontario, Prison Arts, 1972(?).
Editor, *The Human Elements: Critical Essays* (and *Second Series*). Ottawa, Oberon Press, 2 vols., 1978-81.
Editor, *Love and Money: The Politics of Culture.* Ottawa, Oberon Press, 1980.
Editor, with Sandra Martin, *83, 84, 85, 87* and *88: Best Canadian Stories.* Ottawa, Oberon Press, 5 vols., 1983-89.
Editor, with Sandra Martin, *Coming Attractions 1-4.* Ottawa, Oberon Press, 4 vols., 1983-86.
Editor, with Maggie Helwig, *Coming Attractions 5.* Ottawa, Oberon Press, 1987.
Editor, with Maggie Helwig, *1989: Best Canadian Short Stories.* Ottawa, Oberon Press, 1989.
Editor, *The Best Canadian Stories,* with Maggie Helwig. Ottawa, Oberon Press, 1991.

*

Manuscript Collection: McMaster University, Hamilton, Ontario.

Critical Studies: "Bourgeois and Arsonist," in *Harsh and Lovely Land* by Tom Marshall, Vancouver, University of British Columbia Press, 1979; "David Helwig's Kingston Novels: This Random Dance of Atoms" by Diana Brydon, in *Present Tense* edited by John Moss, Toronto, NC Press, 1985.

* * *

David Helwig's novels, in particular the Kingston tetralogy (*The Glass Knight, Jennifer, It Is Always Summer, A Sound Like Laughter*), give universal, humane enigmas a local habitation. The setting, Kingston, is chosen for definite reasons. Founded by United

Empire Loyalists and former capital of Canada, the city epitomized values and traditions which somehow by the 1970s were in shards. From Kingston, with its proximity to Montreal, Ottawa, and Toronto, there is the added awareness of the English and French centers of politics, economics, and culture.

At another level the books may be read as a commentary on Book IV especially of Plato's *Republic*. Helwig wrestles with the disparity between the modern city and modern civilization and the ideal symbol of the city as the expression of the virtues of justice, wisdom, courage, and temperance. Plato's words, "We must not pursue complexity nor great variety in the basic movements, but must observe what are the rhythms of a life that is orderly and brave . . ." form the epigraph of *The Glass Knight* and *Jennifer*. Here, though the ideal is tarnished and debased, the characters are at least haunted by intimations of a lost order. The final two novels, *A Sound Like Laughter* and *It Is Always Summer* are without epigraphs, implying that the opposites of the ideal, injustice, madness, cowardice, violent license, and sensual excess, are paramount.

A brief reading of character and event in each book supports such assertions. Helwig takes major images of control from Western cultural history and associates his characters with them. Plato is always important, but in *The King's Evil* it is the saintly figure of Edward the Confessor and his ability (handed down to future monarchs) to cure the ills of humankind, who is pervasive. In *The Glass Knight,* chivalric ideals and Freudian explanation are associated with the central character Robert Mallon poring over *Civilization and Its Discontents*. Likewise, Robert's ex-wife Jennifer is absorbed in questions of responsibility and moral choice raised by George Eliot's *Middlemarch* and Elizabeth his mistress is drawn to the unworldly romanticism of Saint-Denys-Garneau.

Helwig forces his readers to see beyond the pragmatic and material glue of a society which in actuality is in ruins. Moral, and therefore legal and political, consensus is gone. Thus the sensitive and intelligent, like Robert and Jennifer, are driven to suicide, and the shallow, unscrupulous, and morally reprehensible, like Charlie or Remnant or Anne, survive. Helwig's vision of contemporary Ontario is a more despairing *Wasteland,* for if there is an approximation to the Fisher King here it is the suicidal Mallon whose name suggests (he planned a book on the F.L.Q. crisis) the French for corruption and dishonesty.

—Barrie Davis

HIGGINS, Aidan

Nationality: Irish. **Born:** Celbridge, County Kildare, 3 March 1927. **Education:** Celbridge Convent; Killashee Preparatory School; Clongowes Wood College, County Kildare. **Family:** Married Jill Damaris Anders in 1955; three sons. **Career:** Copywriter, Domas Advertising, Dublin, early 1950s; factory hand, extrusion moulder, and storeman, London, mid-1950s; puppet-operator, John Wright's marionettes, in Europe, South Africa, and Rhodesia, 1958-60; scriptwriter, Filmlets (advertising films), Johannesburg, 1960-61. British Arts Council grants; James Tait Black Memorial prize, 1967; DAAD grant (Berlin), 1969; Irish Academy of Letters award, 1970; American-Irish Foundation grant, 1977. Lives in Kinsale, County Cork. **Address:** c/o Secker and Warburg, Michelin House, 81 Fulham Road, London SW3 6RB, England.

PUBLICATIONS

Novels

Langrishe, Go Down. London, Calder and Boyars, and New York, Grove Press, 1966.
Balcony of Europe. London, Calder and Boyars, and New York, Delacorte Press, 1972.
Scenes from a Receding Past. London, Calder, and New York, Riverrun Press, 1977.
Bornholm Night-Ferry. Dingle, County Kerry, Brandon, and London, Allison and Busby, 1983.
Lions of the Grunewald. London, Secker and Warburg, 1993.

Short Stories

Felo de Se. London, Calder, 1960; as *Killachter Meadow,* New York, Grove Press, 1961; revised edition, as *Asylum and Other Stories,* Calder, 1978; New York, Riverrun Press, 1979.
Helsingør Station and Other Departures: Fictions and Autobiographies 1956-1989. London, Secker and Warburg, 1989.

Plays

Radio Plays (UK): *Assassination,* 1973; *Imperfect Sympathies,* 1977; *Discords of Good Humour,* 1982; *Vanishing Heroes,* 1983; *Texts for the Air,* 1983; *Winter Is Coming,* 1983; *Tomb of Dreams,* 1984 (Ireland); *Zoo Station,* 1985; *Boomtown,* 1990.

Other

Images of Africa: Diary 1956-60. London, Calder and Boyars, 1971.
Ronda Gorge and Other Precipices: Travel Writings 1959-1989. London, Secker and Warburg, 1989.
Donkey's Years: Memories of a Life as Story Told. London, Secker and Warburg, 1995.
Samuel Beckett. London, Secker and Warburg, 1995.

Editor, *A Century of Short Stories.* London, Cape, 1977.
Editor, *Colossal Gongorr and the Turkes of Mars,* by Carl, Julien, and Elwin Higgins. London, Cape, 1979.

*

Manuscript Collection: University of Victoria, British Columbia.

Critical Studies: By David Holloway, in *The Bookman* (London), December 1965; "Maker's Language" by Vernon Scannell, in *Spectator* (London), 11 February 1966; in *New Leader* (London), 25 September 1967; Morris Beja, in *Irish University Review* (Dublin), Autumn 1973; "Aidan Higgins Issue" of *Review of Contemporary Fiction* (Elmwood Park, Illinois), Spring 1983.

*   *   *

In his attempt to escape the traditional constraints of Irish fiction, Aidan Higgins has emerged as an Irish internationalist, firmly grounded in his Irish experience and yet devoted to an extensive view. In *Asylum and Other Stories* he drifts from the dilapidated Irish big house of "Killaghter Meadow" through the seedy England of "Asylum" and the decadent German cosmopolitanism of "Winter Offensive" to the stultifying South Africa of "Southfall on Cape Piscator." The collection displays an amalgam of literary sources—Higgins's answer to Frank O'Connor's "lonely voice." Among his characters are Beckettian down-and-outs such as Eddy Brazill in "Asylum," whose rise from hopelessness to mindlessness is synchronized with the fall to lunacy of his Anglo-Irish alcoholic benefactor. There is Borges's fascination with doubles and mirrors, and Proust's with time and space. And Higgins's scenery is as barren as Eliot's waste land. Yet the collection is dominated by the influence of Joyce's *Dubliners*. Higgins's "leaded windows" also have "blind views," and his inert characters are also unable to share in any form of intercourse. Like Joyce, Higgins enlivens morbidity with flashes of—mostly verbal—irony, as when he has "as angelic line of chorus girls" in "Asylum" sing "*Coming over Jordan* out of key." In "Winter Offensive," irony gives way to a sarcastic depiction of Herr Bausch's "sole preoccupation, . . . venery not so pure not so simple."

Langrishe, Go Down details the sinking of the languid inhabitants of the big house that in "Killaghter Meadow" was "flooded unsolicited on a mixed bag of male and female gentry come to pay . . . their last respects." The novel is Higgins's dismissal of Irish regional fiction in the light of major international events. As the Langrishe sisters, vestiges of the big house, prepare for their dying fall, Germany is rising to war. The novel is framed by political events; when, at the start, Helen Langrishe suffers the nausea of her marvelously detailed bus-ride home, the paper on her lap reports the Spanish Civil War, and when she dies in the end a chapter factually reports Germany's invasion of Austria. The main part of the book is set in 1932 and skillfully combines Irishism and internationalism in the love affair of Imogen Langrishe, the only big house maiden with a trace of sexuality, and the German Otto Beck, a toned-down version of Herr Bausch, and Higgins's least constrained character. The German hunter's invasion of Springfield and Imogen, his poaching on the estate and his indifferent departure parallel the factual framework of the novel.

Although *Balcony of Europe* begins and ends in gray Ireland, it is not concerned with the tensions between Irish fiction and world events. The only reminders of the external reality are the bombers that continually contour the sky over Andalusia, where the main part of the book, the adulterous affair between Dan Ruttle, passionate Irish artist, and the American Jewess, Charlotte Bayless, is set. Instead, Ruttle's experiences are probed in an almost continuous first-person narrative which attempts to do for fiction what Husserl did for philosophy. In *Langrishe*, Higgins's interest in phenomenology remained subservient to the narrative, but it determines the shape of *Balcony*. Higgins tries to coalesce the moment of experience and expression. Plot is largely sacrificed for a number of cognitive tableaux, held together by cross-references and a distinctively idiosyncratic voice. As a result, the novel is dominated by a technique of Beckettian repetitions, ellipses, and grammatical distortions to which are added spices of Sterne and numerous quotations from Yeats. Rather than drawing us to Dan Ruttle's point of view, Higgins's technique emphasizes his labored and insistent symbolism. Higgins, for example, transforms the eagles from *A Portrait of the Artist* into the bombers that in turn are associated with the ghost of Ruttle's mother flying to heaven and with a football that is kicked in the air on a Spanish beach.

Scenes from a Receding Past adds further scraps to the memory of Dan Ruttle from his early childhood and adolescence to his early maturity. The book is set in Sligo, but we are told in a note that

Sligo stands for Celbridge, the author's birthplace and the parish near the big house in *Langrishe*, which bears out Higgins's contention that most of his books follow his life "like slug-trails." Again, Joyce is very much in evidence in verbal reminiscences. Young Ruttle's *bildung* is quite similar to young Stephen's. The pangs of growing up are projected unto Ruttle's brother, the inflexible and intransigent Wally, who ends up in a lunatic asylum. Interleaved are records, and records of records, including a—faulty—Dutch Mass Card, a clothes list for La Sainte Union Convent, and two pages from the score book for the Fifth Oval, August 20-23, 1938. In the final part, Ruttle meets and woos Olivia Orr, a girl from New Zealand who hovers in the background of *Balcony of Europe* as his unhappy wife; the present and glimpses of their past intermingle in a mixture of mawkish poetry and matter-of-fact prose that is disrupted by a page-long list of names for the baby which Olivia loses in her fifth month.

The epistolary form of *Bornholm Night-Ferry* is a logical follow-up to the snap-shot technique of *Scenes from a Receding Past*. It enables Higgins to combine successfully post-modernism and his timeless gift for detail. The novel is as full of linguistic distortions, chronological jumps, and occasional lyricism as any of his works, but they are sustained by the form and add to the tension of the extra-marital affair of a Danish girl with poor English and an Irish writer with poor commonsense. And between Elin Marstrander's tell-tale errors in English and Finn Fitzgerald's passionate errors in decorum, Higgins introduces an implied narrator-as-archivist who identifies letters and diaries as they come to him, far more in charge than his camouflaged counterpart who emerged on the last page of *Balcony of Europe* to ask us if we "are still awake."

—Peter G.W. van de Kamp

HIGGINS, George V(incent)

Nationality: American. **Born:** Brockton, Massachusetts, 13 November 1939. **Education:** Rockland High School, Massachusetts; Boston College, A.B. in English 1961; Stanford University, California, 1961-62, M.A. 1965; Boston College Law School, Brighton, Massachusetts, J.D. 1967; admitted to the Massachusetts bar, 1967. **Family:** Married 1) Elizabeth Mulkerin in 1965 (divorced 1979), one daughter and one son; 2) Loretta Lucas Cubberley in 1979. **Career:** Reporter, *Journal* and *Evening Bulletin*, Providence, Rhode Island, 1962-63; bureau correspondent, Springfield, Massachusetts, 1963-64, and journalist, Boston, 1964-66, Associated Press; researcher, Guterman Horvitz and Rubin, attorneys, Boston, 1966-67; legal assistant, Administrative Division and Organized Crime Section, 1967, Deputy Assistant Attorney General, 1967-69, and Assistant Attorney General, 1969-70, Commonwealth of Massachusetts; Assistant U.S. Attorney for the District of Massachusetts, 1970-73, and Special Assistant U.S. Attorney, 1973-74; president, George V. Higgins, Inc., Boston, 1973-78; partner, Griffin and Higgins, Boston, 1978-82. Since 1988 professor, Boston University. Consultant, National Institute of Law Enforcement and Criminal Law, Washington, D.C., 1970-71; instructor in trial practice, Boston College Law School, 1973-74 and 1978-79; columnist, Boston *Herald American*, 1977-79, Boston *Globe*, 1979-85, and *Wall Street Journal*, New York, 1984-87. Visiting professor, State University of New York, Buffalo, 1988. Lives in Milton, Massachusetts. **Awards:** D.H.L.: Westfield State College, Massachusetts, 1986. **Address:** Creative Writing Program, Department of English, Boston University, 236 Bay State Rd., Boston, Massachusetts 02215, U.S.A.

PUBLICATIONS

Novels

The Friends of Eddie Coyle. New York, Knopf, and London, Secker and Warburg, 1972.

The Digger's Game. New York, Knopf, and London, Secker and Warburg, 1973.

Cogan's Trade. New York, Knopf, and London, Secker and Warburg, 1974.

A City on a Hill. New York, Knopf, and London, Secker and Warburg, 1975.

The Judgment of Deke Hunter. Boston, Little Brown, and London, Secker and Warburg, 1976.

Dreamland. Boston, Little Brown, and London, Secker and Warburg, 1977.

A Year or So with Edgar. New York, Harper, and London, Secker and Warburg, 1979.

Kennedy for the Defense. New York, Knopf, and London, Secker and Warburg, 1980.

The Rat on Fire. New York, Knopf, and London, Secker and Warburg, 1981.

The Patriot Game. New York, Knopf, and London, Secker and Warburg, 1982.

A Choice of Enemies. New York, Knopf, and London, Secker and Warburg, 1984.

Penance for Jerry Kennedy. New York, Knopf, and London, Deutsch, 1985.

Impostors. New York, Holt Rinehart, and London, Deutsch, 1986.

Outlaws. New York, Holt, and London, Deutsch, 1987.

Wonderful Years, Wonderful Years. New York, Holt, and London, Deutsch, 1988.

Trust. New York, Holt, and London, Deutsch, 1989.

Victories. New York, Holt, 1990; London, Deutsch, 1991.

The Mandeville Talent. New York, Holt, and London, Little Brown, 1991.

Defending Billy Ryan. New York, Holt, 1992; London, Little Brown, 1993.

Bomber's Law. New York, Holt, 1993; London, Little Brown, 1994.

Short Stories

Old Earl Died Pulling Traps. Columbia, South Carolina, Bruccoli Clark, 1984.

The Sins of the Fathers. London, Deutsch, 1988.

Other

The Friends of Richard Nixon. Boston, Little Brown, 1975.

Style Versus Substance: Boston, Kevin White, and the Politics of Illusion. New York, Macmillan, 1984.

The Progress of the Seasons: Forty Years of Baseball in Our Town. New York, Holt, 1989.

On Writing: Advice to Those Who Write to Publish (or Would Like To). New York, Holt, 1990.

*

Critical Studies: "Very Nearly GBH: Savouring the Texts of George V. Higgins" by Michael J. Hayes, in *American Crime Fiction: Studies in the Genre* edited by Brian Docherty, London, Macmillan, and New York, St. Martin's Press, 1988; "The Voices of George V. Higgins" by Graham Daldry, in *Watching the Detectives: Essays on Crime Fiction* edited by Daldry and Ian A. Bell, London, Macmillan, 1990; "Getting It Right: The Novels of George V. Higgins" by Edward L. Galligan, in *The Sewanee Review,* no.2, 1992.

George V. Higgins comments:

In retrospect I think *A Choice of Enemies* represented some sort of watershed in my development as a writer. At the time I was not aware that I was doing things that I had not done before, but it seems to me now that that book was the fruition of an evolutionary development I began with *The Friends of Eddie Coyle* twelve years before. *Coyle* although the first published was the fifteenth book I had written. I did not plan to write it almost entirely in dialogue; that just seemed the most efficient way of telling the story. Similarly, with *Enemies,* I did not intentionally strive to combine storytelling with trial practice, but as it turned out that was what I did.

Trial lawyers, though lacking the liberties of novelists to usher witnesses back and forth to lend chronological order to the presentation, nevertheless employ those summoned as surrogate narrators, each adding his or her piece to make the puzzle whole. Trial lawyers—barristers, if you like—depend upon the triers of fact (whether jurors or judges) to inspect the testimony laid before them and arrive at their own conclusions. And trial lawyers are uncomfortably aware, as they go about their tasks, that those judgments of what happened may disagree with their own.

It distresses me when slothful or stupid readers declare that my books have no plots. Such reactions indicate that the readers have not been paying attention. The characters do not appear to provide cheap yucks; they appear when they do because they are telling their own stories. When it works right, I am replacing the omniscient author with the omniscient reader. That reader for the money gets what amounts to a valid warrant to observe and to eavesdrop upon all the actions and conversations material to the unfolding story. At the end, the reader should be able to judge whether their conduct was morally and ethically good. I won't do it for him.

I realize this demands a good deal of the reader. I recognize that not all readers desire quite so much exercise. Nevertheless, the books that I have most enjoyed have been those by writers who made me partner in their schemes, and since I am the first reader as well as the scribbler, those are the kind I try to write. After all, if we're not going to have any fun doing this, why bother?

*   *   *

The opening sentence of George V. Higgins's first published novel, *The Friends of Eddie Coyle,* immediately immerses its readers in his fictional world: "Jackie Brown at twenty-six, with no expression on his face, said that he could get some guns." Not only does the content lead us into the characteristic Higgins milieu of Boston low-life and crime, and not only does the dead-pan announcement set the emotional tone for the whole book, the wonderful rhythm and cadence of the sentence introduces the author's outstanding technical dexterity and originality in capturing speech and mood. In many ways, that first novel is representative of Higgins's later work. The plot concerns the betrayal and death of a small-time crook, but it is no ordinary crime story. Its narrative is intricately assembled from apparently isolated fragments, and conducted for the most part through vivid and compelling dialogue, at once realistic and highly stylised. The tone is uncompromisingly sombre and wholly unsentimental, conveying a great sense of knowingness, and a worldliness verging on cynicism. By a combination of extraordinarily disciplined use of speech and consistently downbeat themes, Higgins achieves an originality and distinctiveness denied most crime writers.

In his subsequent fiction these technical devices are further refined, and the conflict between idealism and cynicism is variously addressed. *The Digger's Game* returns to Boston and to another loser, an Irish bar-owner heavily in debt to the mob, owing these dangerous men a great deal of money he does not have. Through his complex social connections—he has a brother who is a priest, a beautiful mercenary wife and some well-connected customers—the Digger's struggle obliquely reveals the grasping and competitive ethos of urban America. Criminal activities become in all Higgins's novels dramatisations and intensifications of the everyday course of contemporary life, rather than occasional deviations from any more stable moral patterns. Crime is endemic in society and criminals are only slightly worse (and less successful) than allegedly more respectable citizens. Their frank and self-revelatory dialogue does not, however, turn Higgins's criminals into romantic outlaws, or oppressed victims. They remain as barren, joyless figures, subject to random and casual violence, deprived of the opportunity to participate fully in their world.

After another superbly bleak low-life novel, *Cogan's Trade,* the author turned his attention to the even dirtier world of politics. In *A City on a Hill* his venue moves from Boston to the Washington of Nixon's post-Watergate administration, where shabby careerists jostle for position in a moral ghost town, kept alert only by envy and intrigue. Sex, drink, and petty ambitions keep the political insiders alive in a world of spiritual bankruptcy. Through the persistent use of dialogue, Higgins remains aloof from the squalor which he unsparingly lays before us. It seems always as though he assembles his fictions, rather than that he commandeers or directs them, and that no point of idealism or judgment can be found. However, in *The Judgment of Deke Hunter, A Year or So with Edgar, Kennedy for the Defense, A Choice of Enemies,* and *Penance for Jerry Kennedy* Higgins explores individual lives in the police force, the press, the law, and the judiciary to explore the possibilities of integrity and honesty in the complex institutional machinery of politicised life. These are impressive books, but the emergence of positive features from Higgins's quasi-neutral style is perhaps less successfully handled than would be the case if he had adopted a more normative or judgmental approach. By taking on the role of Diogenes and searching for an honest man in a dishonest world, Higgins seems to impose limits on his imaginative faculties, which are more successfully animated by plausible storytellers and confidence tricksters than by embattled purveyors of the truth.

Since the mid-1980s, Higgins has turned again to low-life, albeit the low-life of respectable citizens, writing a series of quite exceptional novels, in which a whole complex of issues surrounding personal and political integrity are uncovered with the greatest precision and scepticism. *Impostors* moves through a world of slick deceivers, characters who lie to each other so unremittingly that the novelist has no need to take on the responsibility of truth-telling.

He allows us to overhear multiple conversations, all in conflict with each other, all serving the interests of the speakers. By piecing these stories together, sifting their contradictions and assessing their motives, readers can reassemble a version of a scandal of 20 years previously, and begin to see who covered up what for whom and why. *Outlaws* is even better, dealing with the bruised and distorted (and self-deceiving) idealism of 1970s radicals turned to crime. Once again, Higgins uses cumulative dialogue to enhance the presentation of a cast of crooks and frauds, and in a brilliant trial scene he reveals the hypocrisies of a legal system in cahoots with a corrupt government. *Wonderful Years, Wonderful Years* brings together a crooked contractor who tries to hide his schizophrenic wife from a divorce hearing, a chauffeur with a past who seems to keep accidentally killing people (though only pretty worthless people), and a wider world of political intrigue. It may be that in this novel the interpersonal drama, involving a rather lurid connection with AIDS, is less successfully connected to broader issues, and Higgins surprisingly creates relatively likeable characters. Such is not the case in *Trust,* which explores the multiple mendacities and deceptions of an ex-jailbird turned used car salesman. This novel, which is a suitable sample of his recent work, has brought its author into even greater prominence, and he is seen now more often alongside serious "dirty realist" writers like Richard Ford than in the broad context of crime fiction. After these diverse and intense books, there can be no doubt that Higgins is one of the most serious and technically adept novelists writing today. His unsurprised account of everyday confusion and corruption has continued in fine novels like *Victories, The Mandeville, Talent, Defending Billy Ryan,* and *Bomber's Law.* Many enthusiastic readers will await the unfolding of more of Higgins's saga of Boston life, although even his most ardent fan would be unlikely to buy a used car from him.

—Ian A. Bell

HILL, Carol

Nationality: American. **Born:** Carol DeChellis, New Jersey, 20 January 1942. **Education:** At Chatham College, Pittsburgh, 1957-61, B.A. in history 1961. **Career:** Publicist, Crown Publishers, 1965-67, and Bernard Geis Associates, 1967-69, both New York; publicist, 1969-71, and editor, 1971-73, Pantheon Books, New York; publicity manager, Random House, New York, 1973-74; senior editor, William Morrow, publishers, New York, 1974-76; senior editor, editor-in-chief, vice-president, and publisher, Harcourt Brace Jovanovich, New York, 1976-79. Since 1980 full-time writer. Formerly, actress at Judson Poets Theatre, New York, and in summer stock, Gateway Playhouse, New Jersey. **Agent:** Lynn Nesbit, Janklow and Nesbit Associates, 598 Madison Avenue, New York, New York 10022. **Address:** 2 Fifth Avenue, Apartment 19-U, New York, New York 10011, U.S.A.

PUBLICATIONS

Novels

Jeremiah 8:20. New York, Random House, 1970.
Let's Fall in Love. New York, Random House, 1974; London, Quartet, 1975.

An Unmarried Woman (novelization of screenplay). New York, Avon, and London, Coronet, 1978.
The Eleven Million Mile High Dancer. New York, Holt Rinehart, 1985; as *Amanda and the Eleven Million Mile High Dancer,* London, Bloomsbury, 1988.
Henry James' Midnight Song. New York, Poseidon Press, 1993.

Uncollected Short Stories

"The Shameless Shiksa," in *Playboy* (Chicago), September 1969.
"Gone," in *Viva* (New York), November 1974.
"Lovers," in *Viva* (New York), April 1975.

Play

Mother Loves (produced New York, 1967).

Other

Subsistence U.S.A., photographs by Bruce Davidson, edited by Jamie Shalleck. New York, Holt Rinehart, 1973.

*

Manuscript Collection: Mugar Memorial Library, Boston University.

*   *   *

Carol Hill writes with a wit and sense of the absurd that some critics have likened to the bizarre humor found in the novels of Tom Robbins. Her characters are varied, genuine, and somewhat offbeat. The protagonists usually find themselves in absurd situations sometimes of their own making, but often coming as a surprise. Contemporary issues are interwoven in the plots, although they are not necessarily central to the stories.

In her first novel, *Jeremiah 8:20,* peace marchers protesting the war in Vietnam and problems of racial integration affect the rather unusual hero of this novel. Jeremiah Francis Scanlon, fat, balding, and 39, is a bookkeeper of mediocre abilities who has worked for the same company for almost 20 years. After years of living in the protective environment of his parents' suburban home he has taken the plunge and moved to New York City, not far from his place of employment. He rents a room in a boarding house that comes complete with a cast of strange and unusual characters. Hill's talent for delineating a varied array of individuals is evident in her description of Jeremiah, the social misfit; Miles, a part-time actor who specializes in female roles and is often seen prancing around the house in full costume and makeup; his friend Jocko, a pseudo-revolutionary and a cynic who excels in debate and delights in flustering his opponent. There are also two ladies: a prim old maid, and a wasp-tongued librarian who secretly yearns for Jocko. Although Jeremiah seems the most unlikely sort of protagonist to carry a novel, Hill makes us care for this pathetic, befuddled man who suffers great loneliness and despair. He does not, however, give up on life, but in a strangely courageous way keeps seeking an answer to his misery. Admittedly the answer he comes up with—that there is a secret held by Negroes that will end all his problems—seems absurd, but we have come to know Jeremiah so well that we can believe he would believe such nonsense.

The humor in *Jeremiah* is dark, though not oppressive. In Hill's next two novels the tone is lighter. *Let's Fall in Love* has a $10,000-a-shot hooker caught up in a web of murder and intrigue. This book has plenty of sex, including some very strange forms of coupling, a considerable departure from her first novel (about which, she says, people complained because there was not enough sex). *Let's Fall in Love* offers Hill's usual humor, and satire that some readers may find shocking, others erotic. Although this novel sold well, in the author's own estimation it lacked the power of her first. With *The Eleven Million Mile High Dancer* Hill is back on form although writing in a very different vein from *Jeremiah.* She combines her flare for the comic with a layman's knowledge of physics, a concern for the environment, and a natural penchant for fantasy. And here again is a multitude of characters.

The heroine is Amanda Jaworski, pilot, particle physicist, ardent feminist (most of the time), America's leading lady astronaut, and free spirit who roller skates through the NASA complex in red and white striped non-regulation shorts. She lives with a cat named Schrodinger who spends 23 out of 24 hours in a catatonic state that Amanda believes must be a form of narcolepsy. Meanwhile Amanda, a champion of female rights, finds herself wildly in love with the ultimate macho man, Bronco McCloud. He was "devastating in the most literal sense of the word. It was quite exciting to be devastated by McCloud, and he knew it. His business was devastation not love. And this was why women adored him." Fortunately for Amanda there is another man in her life, Donald Hotchkiss, who is as masculine as Bronco, but capable of loving Amanda in a way she deserves to be loved. Love is an important theme in Hill's works: Jeremiah spent an entire novel in a desperate, futile search for it, while Amanda not only receives love in its many guises but returns it in abundance.

Bringing everything together is an intricate plot in which Amanda is selected to make an 18-month journey to Mars, but is diverted from this mission by the Great Cosmic Brain who kidnaps Schrodinger. The GCB is a disgustingly huge, bloated snake-like creature that discharges a foul odor with every exhalation. He is earth's creator and he is angry that humankind seems so ready to destroy itself either with nuclear weapons or pollution of the air and water. Amanda is helped in her search for Schrodinger by a tough-talking subatomic particle named Oozie. Their adventure in another dimension brings all Hill's imaginative skills to the fore. She amazes the reader with ever more exotic creatures and situations, culminating in a starry spin through space with the Dancer of the title. Throughout the story she intersperses quotes from scientists writing on the new physics which show how strange our world of reality can be (Paul Davies: "One of the more bizarre consequences of quantum uncertainty is that matter can appear more or less out of nowhere"). So perhaps the wild imaginings of Hill are not so farfetched after all.

Her literary style is often blunt, filled with contemporary jargon, and always to the point. She demonstrates the feelings of her characters by letting the reader eavesdrop on internal conversations. In this way she shows the desperate unhappiness and bewilderment suffered by Jeremiah as well as the gutsy determination and deep-felt love that drive Amanda to the ends of the universe to save Schrodinger. Although the themes of her books have varied greatly, there is one element that permeates them all—her ability to portray the human condition in all of its terrible and wonderful ways, and to portray even the darkest moments with plenty of wit.

—Patricia Altner

HILL, Susan (Elizabeth)

Nationality: British. **Born:** Scarborough, Yorkshire, 5 February 1942. **Education:** Grammar schools in Scarborough and Coventry; King's College, University of London, B.A. (honours) in English 1963. **Family:** Married the writer and editor Stanley Wells in 1975; three daughters (one deceased). **Career:** Since 1963 full-time writer: since 1977 monthly columnist, *Daily Telegraph,* London. Presenter, *Bookshelf* radio program, 1986-87. **Awards:** Maugham award, 1971; Whitbread award, 1972; Rhys Memorial prize, 1972. Fellow, Royal Society of Literature, 1972, and King's College, 1978. **Address:** Longmoor Farmhouse, Ebrington, Chipping Campden, Glos GL55 6NW England.

PUBLICATIONS

Novels

The Enclosure. London, Hutchinson, 1961.
Do Me a Favour. London, Hutchinson, 1963.
Gentleman and Ladies. London, Hamish Hamilton, 1968; New York, Walker, 1969.
A Change for the Better. London, Hamish Hamilton, 1969.
I'm the King of the Castle. London, Hamish Hamilton, and New York, Viking Press, 1970.
Strange Meeting. London, Hamish Hamilton, 1971; New York, Saturday Review Press, 1972.
The Bird of Night. London, Hamish Hamilton, 1972; New York, Saturday Review Press, 1973.
In the Springtime of the Year. London, Hamish Hamilton, and New York, Saturday Review Press, 1974.
The Woman in Black: A Ghost Story. London, Hamish Hamilton, 1983; Boston, Godine, 1986.
Air and Angels. London, Sinclair Stevenson, 1991.
The Mist in the Mirror. London, Mandarin, 1993.
Mrs. de Winter. London, Sinclair Stevenson, and Thorndike, Maine, Thorndike Press, 1993.

Short Stories

The Albatross and Other Stories. London, Hamish Hamilton, 1971; New York, Saturday Review Press, 1975.
The Custodian. London, Covent Garden Press, 1972.
A Bit of Singing and Dancing. London, Hamish Hamilton, 1973.
Lanterns Across the Snow (novella). London, Joseph, 1987; New York, Potter, 1988.

Uncollected Short Story

"Kielty's," in *Winter's Tales 20,* edited by A.D. Maclean. London, Macmillan, 1974; New York, St. Martin's Press, 1975.

Plays

Lizard in the Grass (broadcast 1971; produced Edinburgh, 1988). Included in *The Cold Country and Other Plays for Radio,* 1975.
The Cold Country and Other Plays for Radio (includes *The End of Summer, Lizard in the Grass, Consider the Lilies, Strip Jack Naked*). London, BBC Publications, 1975.

On the Face of It (broadcast 1975). Published in *Act 1,* edited by David Self and Ray Speakman, London, Hutchinson, 1979.
The Ramshackle Company (for children; produced London, 1981).
Chances (broadcast 1981; produced London, 1983).

Radio Plays: *Taking Leave,* 1971; *The End of Summer,* 1971; *Lizard in the Grass,* 1971; *The Cold Country,* 1972; *Winter Elegy,* 1973; *Consider the Lilies,* 1973; *A Window on the World,* 1974; *Strip Jack Naked,* 1974; *Mr. Proudham and Mr. Sleight,* 1974; *On the Face of It,* 1975; *The Summer of the Giant Sunflower,* 1977; *The Sound That Time Makes,* 1980; *Here Comes the Bride,* 1980; *Chances,* 1981; *Out in the Cold,* 1982; *Autumn,* 1985; *Winter,* 1985; *I am the King of the Castle, Susan Hill,* London, Longman, 1990.

Television Play: *Last Summer's Child,* from her story "The Badness Within Him," 1981.

Other (for children)

One Night at a Time. London, Hamish Hamilton, 1984; as *Go Away, Bad Dreams!,* New York, Random House, 1985.
Mother's Magic. London, Hamish Hamilton, 1986.
Suzy's Shoes. London, Hamish Hamilton, 1989.
I Won't Go There Again. London, Walker Books, 1990.
Septimus Honeydew. London, Walker Books, 1990.
Stories from Codling Village. London, Walker Books, 1990.
The Collaborative Classroom. with Tim Hill. Portsmouth, New Hampshire, Heinemann, 1990.
A Very Special Birthday. London, Walker, 1992.
Beware, Beware, with illustrations by Angela Barrett. Cambridge, Massachusetts, Candlewick Press, and London, Walker, 1993.
The Christmas Collection, with illustrations by John Lawrence. Cambridge, Massachusetts, Candlewick Press, and London, Walker, 1994.
  Can It Be True? A Christmas Story. London, Hamish Hamilton, and New York, Viking Kestrel, 1988.
  The Glass Angels. London, Walker, 1991. Cambridge, Massachusetts, Candlewick, 1992.
  King of Kings. Cambridge, Massachusetts, Candlewick, 1993; London, Walker Books, 1994.
  White Christmas. London, Walker, and Cambridge, Massachusetts, Candlewick, 1994.

Other

The Magic Apple Tree: A Country Year. London, Hamish Hamilton, 1982; New York, Holt Rinehart, 1983.
Through the Kitchen Window. London, Hamish Hamilton, 1984.
Through the Garden Gate. London, Hamish Hamilton, 1986.
Shakespeare Country, photographs by Rob Talbot. London, Joseph, 1987.
The Lighting of the Lamps. London, Hamish Hamilton, 1987.
The Spirit of the Cotswolds, photographs by Nick Meers. London, Joseph, 1988.
Family. London, Joseph, 1989; New York, Viking, 1990.
Crown Devon: The History of S. Fielding and Co. Stratford Upon Avon, Jazz, 1993.

Editor, *The Distracted Preacher and Other Tales,* by Thomas Hardy. London, Penguin, 1979.

Editor, with Isabel Quigly, *New Stories 5.* London, Hutchinson, 1980.

Editor, *People: Essays and Poems.* London, Chatto and Windus, 1983.

Editor, *Ghost Stories.* London, Hamish Hamilton, 1983.

Editor, *The Parchment Moon: An Anthology of Modern Women's Short Stories.* London, Joseph, 1990; as *The Penguin Book of Modern Women's Short Stories,* 1991.

Editor, *The Walker Book of Ghost Stories.* London, Walker Books, 1990; as *The Random House Book of Ghost Stores,* New York, Random House, 1991.

Editor, *Contemporary Women's Short Stories.* London, Joseph, 1995.

*

Manuscript Collection: Eton College Library, Windsor, Berkshire.

Critical Study: *Susan Hill: I'm the King of the Castle* by Hana Sambrook, London, Longman, 1992.

*   *   *

One striking feature of Susan Hill's novels is the wide-ranging diversity of the experience they depict; and another, a maturity of understanding remarkable in a writer who began publishing her work at the age of only 19.

From the first she has shown a painful awareness of the dark abysses of the spirit—fear, grief, loneliness, and loss. A recurring early theme is that of lives warped and ruined by the selfishness of maternal domination. In *A Change for the Better* Deirdre Fount struggles in vain to break the shackles of dependence forged by her overbearing mother. The boy Duncan in the short story "The Albatross" is the impotent victim of a similar situation, dogged by the mother-created image of his own inadequacy. Driven finally over the brink of desperation, he does achieve his desired freedom, however brief, through a climactic act of violence.

Hill has always been especially perceptive in her portrayal of children. One of her most memorable novels, *I'm the King of the Castle,* is a penetrating study of mounting tensions in a bitter conflict between two 11-year-old boys. This arises when a widower engages a new housekeeper, who brings with her a son the same age as his own. The peevish weakling already in possession is outraged at this invasion of his cherished territory, and in a subtle campaign of persecution, relentlessly hounds the hapless intruder towards an inevitably tragic denouement.

Hill's sensitive insight into the behavior and motivations of the young is matched by equal acuteness in delineating the problems and attitudes of those at the opposite end of the human life-span. *Gentleman and Ladies,* a novel simultaneously funny and sad, observes with a shrewdly amused yet compassionate eye the daily life and personalities of the inmates of an old people's home. The same intuitive sympathy informs the short story called "Missy." Through a dying woman's fragmentary memories—frustratingly interrupted by the ministrations of brisk nurse and single visitor—the author intimately identifies with the thought-processes of extreme age.

Hill's gift of imaginative projection into worlds of experience far removed from her own is nowhere more apparent than in *Strange Meeting.* Probably her most notable *tour de force,* this is set in the trenches of Flanders during the 1914-18 war, and depicts with power, and at times almost intolerable poignancy, the doomed friendship of two young officers drawn together by their mutual daily contact with destruction and imminent death. There is also an irresistible attraction between opposite temperaments and family backgrounds: the reserved, introspective Hilliard finding inhibition magically thawed in the warmth of his companion Barton's easy, outgoing generosity.

The impact of actuality in this novel, both in its factual detail and the immediacy of involvement in the responses of combatants, is an astonishing achievement for a young woman. *Strange Meeting* also exemplifies Hill's capacity—comparatively rare among women novelists either past or present—for the convincing depiction of life from a male viewpoint. *The Bird of Night* is another highly original novel of great intensity which surveys a close relationship between two men. The central character is a poet, Francis Croft, whose tormented struggle against intermittent but increasing insanity is chronicled by the withdrawn scholar Lawson, whose life becomes devoted to care of his friend. The first-person masculine narrative of *The Woman in Black,* published after a silence of some years in her career as a novelist, provides a further instance of this aspect of Hill's talent. An atmospherically charged ghost story, it is related in a formal, rather stately past idiom, although carefully unlocated in any particular time. Full of Jamesian echoes and undercurrents, it traces with chilling compulsiveness the progress of a mysterious and sinister haunting.

Her adventurous charting of such varied areas of experience—childhood and old age, loyalties between men, the horrors of war and of insanity—demonstrates this versatile writer's ability to participate truthfully in many states of mind and conditions of life. But this does not preclude her treatment of the more conventionally "feminine" subject. Perhaps more than any of her books, *In the Springtime of the Year* has a direct appeal for a readership of women. Its heroine is a young widow cruelly bereaved after a short and happy marriage; and it movingly explores the successive stages of her grief, from initial angry refusal to accept the fact of loss through a gradual coming to terms and adjustment to her changed situation. The surrounding countryside, evoked with poetic precision, plays a key role in Ruth's final renewal of hope. This echoes the author's own belief in the restoring influence of rural rhythms and simplicities, reflected in her volumes of essays, such as *The Magic Apple Tree, Through the Kitchen Window,* and *Through the Garden Gate.*

—Margaret Willy

HILLIARD, Noel (Harvey)

Nationality: New Zealander. **Born:** Napier, Hawke's Bay, 6 February 1929. **Education:** Gisborne High School, 1942-45; Victoria University, Wellington, 1946-50; Wellington Teachers College, 1954-55. **Family:** Married Kiriwai Mete in 1954 (died 1990); four children. **Career:** Journalist, *Southern Cross,* Wellington, 1946-50; teacher, Khandallah School, Wellington, 1955-56, and District High School, Mangakino, 1956-64; chief sub-editor, *New Zealand Listener,* Wellington, 1965-70; sub-editor, *New Zealand's Heritage* and *New Zealand Today,* 1972-73; deputy editor, *New Zealand's Nature Heritage,* 1973-74; full-time writer, 1974-77; sub-editor, Wellington *Evening Post,* 1977-91. Chair, Mangakino-Pouakani

Maori Executive Committee, and delegate to the Waiariki District Council of Maori Executive Committees, 1962-64. **Awards:** Hubert Church Prose award, 1961; New Zealand Literary Fund scholarship, 1963, 1975; University of Otago Robert Burns fellowship, 1981. **Address:** 28 Richard Street, Titahi Bay, Wellington, New Zealand.

PUBLICATIONS

Novels

Maori Girl. London, Heinemann, 1960.
Power of Joy. Christchurch, Whitcombe and Tombs, and London, Joseph, 1965; Chicago, Regnery, 1966.
A Night at Green River. Christchurch, Whitcombe and Tombs, and London, Hale, 1969.
Maori Woman. Christchurch, Whitcombe and Tombs, and London, Hale, 1974.
The Glory and the Dream. London, Heinemann, 1978.

Short Stories

A Piece of Land: Stories and Sketches. Christchurch, Whitcombe and Tombs, and London, Hale, 1963.
Send Somebody Nice: Stories and Sketches. Christchurch, Whitcombe and Tombs, and London, Hale, 1976.
Selected Stories. Dunedin, McIndoe, 1977.

Other

We Live by a Lake (for children), photographs by Ans Westra. Auckland, Heinemann, 1972.
Wellington: City Alive, photographs by Ans Westra. Christchurch, Whitcoulls, 1976.
Mahitahi/Work Together: Some Peoples of the Soviet Union. Moscow, Progress, 1989.
Nude Chooks Stun Farmer! Auckland, Reed Books, 1992.

*

Bibliography: *Noel Hilliard: A Preliminary Bibliography* by Jeffrey Downs, Wellington, National Library of New Zealand, 1976.

Critical Studies: *The New Zealand Novel 1860-1965,* Wellington, Reed, 1966, and *New Zealand Short Stories,* Wellington, Price Milburn, 1968, both by Joan Stevens; *New Zealand Fiction since 1945,* Dunedin, McIndoe, 1968, and *New Zealand Novels,* Wellington, New Zealand University Press, 1969, both by H. Winston Rhodes; "The Maori and Literature 1938-65" by Bill Pearson, in *The Maori People in the Nineteen-Sixties,* Auckland, Paul, 1968; *A Descriptive Account of Social Attitudes in the Fiction of Noel Hillard* by T.J. Mullinder, Christchurch, University of Canterbury, 1974; "The Persistence of Realism: Dan Davin, Noel Hilliard, and Recent New Zealand Short Stories" by Lawrence Jones, in *Islands 20* (Auckland), December 1977; *The New Zealand Novel* by Kevin Cunningham, Wellington, Department of Education, 1980; *Noel Hilliard: La tetralogia di Netta Samuel* by Tiziana Nisini, Rome, University of Rome, 1985; *Barbed Wire and Mirrors: Essays on New Zealand Prose* by Lawrence Jones, Dunedin, University of Otago Press, 1987.

Noel Hilliard comments:

My principal area of interest has been life in New Zealand today, and particularly how Maori and Pakeha view and behave towards each other. All my writing has been about working people. Since 1978 my work has been mainly in journalism except for a study of Soviet ethnic minorities based on visits there in 1982 and 1986.

*   *   *

Maori Girl, Noel Hilliard's first novel, made an immediate impact on its readers. It appeared at a time when many New Zealanders were becoming uncomfortably aware that all was not well with race relations in their country; and the story of Netta Samuel's early life in a Maori farming community, together with her painful experiences when she arrived alone in the city, were as disturbing as they were impressive. The competence and sincerity of the author could hardly be questioned. Yet the realistic portrayal and unrelenting exposure of discriminatory practices caused some to disparage the novel as mere documentary and to complain that Hilliard was too obviously writing to a thesis.

Although complete in itself, *Maori Girl* proved to be the prelude to a theme. It was the first of a series of novels that can be said to be without parallel in New Zealand fiction. When *Power of Joy* appeared and was followed at intervals by *Maori Woman* and *The Glory and the Dream,* it became apparent that the whole tetralogy had been devised and orchestrated to give life and form to a much more complex theme than had been surmised. If the first novel had evoked the childhood and youth of a Maori girl, forced to endure the pressures of a bi-racial society, *Power of Joy* followed the development of a Pakeha or European boy who almost unconsciously discovers his sense of identity in the spirit of earth, in tree and river and hill, in all his natural New Zealand surroundings, and is forced to resist the traditional pressure of his conventional but poverty-stricken family background. Both are significant variations of the theme of growing up in New Zealand. With *Maori Woman* the lives of these two become interwoven and entangled in a harsh city-world of dominant Pakehas and under-privileged Maoris. In the final book of the tetralogy Maori girl and Pakeha boy have come together, to find unity through a process of adjustment, to discover harmony in difference.

Hilliard has certainly been intent on exploring relations between Maoris and Pakehas, and unmasking discriminatory practices, but his aim has been far more comprehensive. He has been even more intent on revealing the human implications of cultural diversity, on identifying his leading characters with the spirit of place and with their inherited but distinctive traditions. He has attempted to reveal and dramatize the tensions that are produced in the community at large and in the unitary family of mixed race from the different ways of life of Maori and Pakeha. However, the major difficulty in such an ambitious undertaking is that of achieving both individuality and typicality, of avoiding the special case and of refraining from the temptation to stereotype characters and their responses to particular situations. This must always be a daunting task for any writer whose aim is not confined to entertainment of a trivial kind. The measure of Hilliard's achievement is that he succeeds not only in establishing his leading characters in an authentic setting and involves the reader in their problems of adjustment, but also in introducing subsidiary themes and characters to illuminate and give further meaning to his many-sided treatment of human relations in a bi-racial community.

In the midst of writing this quartet of novels Hilliard produced a number of short stories. A group of these shorter pieces contains episodes in the lives of two Maori children, and the involvement of the whole family in the simple rhythms of work, play, and ceremonial occasions; but other stories touch on Maori-Pakeha relations and on aspects of the ordinary life of ordinary New Zealanders, generally with implications that have some social significance. Hilliard has always shown his preference for dealing with subjects and people that are of the earth.

Besides these stories Hilliard has written *A Night at Green River*, a novel with the very simple theme of a Pakeha farmer's need for assistance in stacking his hay. Its patterned development emphasizes the different values of Pakeha and Maori, especially in relation to material wealth and possessions, to the gospel of work and to human dignity. *A Night at Green River* becomes a comic parable that has relevance to the human predicaments caused when two races with different life-styles and aspirations attempt to mingle. As a lively parable it achieves a rare distinction and enhances Hilliard's reputation for providing valuable insights to the mental and emotional processes that collide when European and Polynesian come together.

—H. Winston Rhodes

HINDE, Thomas

Pseudonym for Sir Thomas Willes Chitty, Baronet. **Nationality:** British. **Born:** Thomas Willes Chitty in Felixstowe, Suffolk, 2 March 1926; succeeded to the baronetcy, 1955. **Education:** Winchester School, Hampshire; University College, Oxford. **Military Service:** Served in the Royal Navy, 1944-47. **Family:** Married Susan Elspeth Glossop (i.e., the writer Susan Chitty) in 1951; one son and three daughters. **Career:** Worked for Inland Revenue, London, 1951-53; staff member, Shell Petroleum Company, in England, 1953-58, and in Nairobi, Kenya, 1958-60. Granada Arts Fellow, University of York, 1964-65; visiting lecturer, University of Illinois, Urbana, 1965-67; visiting professor, Boston University, 1969-70. Fellow, Royal Society of Literature. **Address:** Bow Cottage, West Hoathly, near East Grinstead, Sussex RH19 4QF, England.

Publications

Novels

Mr. Nicholas. London, MacGibbon and Kee, 1952; New York, Farrar Straus, 1953.
Happy as Larry. London, MacGibbon and Kee, 1957; New York, Criterion, 1958.
For the Good of the Company. London, Hutchinson, 1961.
A Place Like Home. London, Hodder and Stoughton, 1962.
The Cage. London, Hodder and Stoughton, 1962.
Ninety Double Martinis. London, Hodder and Stoughton, 1963.
The Day the Call Came. London, Hodder and Stoughton, 1964; New York, Vanguard Press, 1965.
Games of Chance: The Interviewer, The Investigator. London, Hodder and Stoughton, 1965; New York, Vanguard Press, 1967.
The Village. London, Hodder and Stoughton, 1966.

High. London, Hodder and Stoughton, 1968; New York, Walker, 1969.
Bird. London, Hodder and Stoughton, 1970.
Generally a Virgin. London, Hodder and Stoughton, 1972.
Agent. London, Hodder and Stoughton, 1974.
Our Father. London, Hodder and Stoughton, 1975; New York, Braziller, 1976.
Daymare. London, Macmillan, 1980.

Other

Do Next to Nothing: A Guide to Survival Today, with Susan Chitty. London, Weidenfeld and Nicolson, 1976.
The Great Donkey Walk, with Susan Chitty. London, Hodder and Stoughton, 1977.
The Cottage Book: A Manual of Maintenance, Repair, and Construction. London, Davis, 1979.
Sir Henry and Sons: A Memoir. London, Macmillan, 1980.
A Field Guide to the English Country Parson. London, Heinemann, 1983.
Stately Gardens of Britain, photographs by Dmitri Kasterine. London, Ebury Press, and New York, Norton, 1983.
Forests of Britain. London, Gollancz, 1985.
Just Chicken, with Cordelia Chitty. Woodbury, New York, Barron's, 1985; London, Bantam Press, 1986.
Capability Brown: The Story of a Master Gardener. London, Hutchinson, 1986; New York, Norton, 1987.
Courtiers: 900 Years of English Court Life. London, Gollancz, 1986.
Tales from the Pump Room: Nine Hundred Years of Bath: The Place, Its People, and Its Gossip. London, Gollancz, 1988.
Imps of Promise: A History of the King's School, Canterbury. London, James and James, 1990.
Paths of Progress: A History of Marlborough College. London, James and James, 1992.
Highgate School: A History. London, James and James, 1993.

Editor, *Spain: A Personal Anthology.* London, Newnes, 1963.
Editor, *The Domesday Book: England's Heritage, Then and Now.* London, Hutchinson, and New York, Crown, 1985.

*

Manuscript Collection: University of Texas, Austin.

Critical Studies: In *New York Herald Tribune,* 24 May 1953; *The Angry Decade* by Kenneth Allsop, London, Owen, 1958; *Times Literary Supplement* (London), 26 May 1961, 27 October 1966, 7 November 1968, 11 September 1970; *Observer* (London), 7 June 1964; *New York Times,* 9 August 1967; *Books and Bookmen* (London), September 1974.

Thomas Hinde comments:

I write novels because I like novels and I like trying to make my own. These aim to be—but unfortunately hardly ever succeed in being—the novels I will like best of all. Just as my taste in novels changes, so the sort of novel I try to write changes. I also believe in the importance of the novel—one of the few places where individual art as opposed to script-conference art can still flourish. I believe that it can and will change and develop, however fully explored it seems at present. I believe that people will go on wanting to read novels. But however much I am convinced by these logical arguments of the vitality, value, and survival of the form, the real reason why I go on writing novels remains personal: despite its anxiety and difficulties, I like the process, and, despite disappointments, I am still excited by the results which I aim for.

*   *   *

When in 1957, American popular journalism first discovered the "Angry Young Men," Thomas Hinde was listed, in articles in *Time* and *Life,* along with Kingsley Amis, John Wain, and John Braine, as one of the principal progenitors of the "Movement." *Happy as Larry,* Hinde's second novel, had just been published and the novel's protagonist was a rather feckless young man who lost menial jobs, was vaguely trying to write, and irresponsibly drifted away from his wife. Yet the designation of "Angry Young Men," over-generalized and inappropriate as it was for all the writers to whom it was applied, was particularly inappropriate for Hinde. Far from "angry" or defiantly rebellious, Hinde's protagonist wanders about apologetically, full of guilt, trying to help a friend recover a lost photograph that might be used for blackmail. His indecision, inhibitions, and constant self-punishment characterize him far more consistently than do any articulate attitudes toward society. In addition, Hinde's point of view in the novel is far from an unqualified endorsement of his protagonist's actions and attitudes. The ending, like the endings of most of Hinde's novels, is left open, without any definitive or summarizable statement. And the kind of judgment frequently assumed in popular accounts of novelists, the clarion call for a new way of life or the castigation of depraved contemporary morality, is entirely absent.

At the same time, however, in other terms, *Happy as Larry* is a novel of the 1950s. The protagonist's wandering, his lack of certainty, his allegiance only to close personal friends, his inhibitions and apologies, his insistence on self as a starting point for value, are all characteristic of much of the serious fiction of the decade. London, too, shrouded in rain, and gloom, spotted with crowded pubs that provide the only refuge, is also made the grim postwar city. In addition, Hinde uses a frequent symbol in fiction, the photograph, as central to the plot of his novel. In a world in which identity was regarded as shifting, unreliable, unknowable, only the photograph, the fixed and permanent image, could give identity any meaning, although that meaning, far more often than not, was itself a distortion, an over-simplification, occasion for blackmail. In fact, Hinde's novels most characteristically begin with categories definable in terms of other novels and novelists, with genres to which the reader is accustomed.

His first novel, *Mr. Nicholas,* chronicles the struggles of a young Oxonian, home on holidays, to define himself against his domineering and insensitive father. Another novel, *For the Good of the Company,* deals with the struggles for definition and power within the business combine, the complex organization that seemed a microcosm to depict human efforts to maintain a sense of rational control. *The Cage* and *A Place Like Home* are Hinde's African novels, *The Cage* a particularly sensitive and effective treatment of a young British colonial girl in Kenya attempting to retain her ties to the world of her parents while simultaneously understanding sympathetically the emerging black society. *The Village* establishes, without sentimentality or nostalgia, the world of the small English village about to be leveled by bulldozers and flooded for a new reservoir. *High* is Hinde's American visit novel, an account of the 40-year-old British writer teaching at an American university, including the familiar device of a novelist character writing a novel which is itself partly reproduced within the novel. In other words, the

themes, techniques, concerns, and atmosphere of Hinde's novels are all familiar, all representative of their time and place—the heroine of *The Cage* often sounds like a more restrained Doris Lessing heroine, the protagonist of *High* is well established in a lineage that stretches back to Eric Linklater—yet Hinde is also an individual novelist of great skill with an individual sense of texture and intelligence.

Hinde is frequently at his best in describing the sensitivities of his young characters—their introspections, their naivety, their commitments to attitudes and to people they cannot entirely understand. The heroine of *The Cage,* unable to untangle the racial antagonisms she does not entirely understand, thinks her young colonial boyfriend will kill the black man he thinks she's been sleeping with, over-dramatizing a conflict she cannot solve. The young budding capitalist in *For the Good of the Company* makes love to the boss's daughter but cannot really fathom all the perplexities of her emotions. He is loyal to the enigma he has partially observed and partially constructed, always wondering how much he has made up himself. A similarly intelligent sensitivity characterizes the love affair in *The Village* between the harassed local doctor and the opportunistic young stockbroker's wife, an affair in which love is created out of mutual desperation. Hinde's sensitivity is applied not only to personal relationships, but to exterior atmospheres as well. Each novel contains many descriptions of weather, rich and subtle evocations of different climates and seasons—equally acute whether England, America or Africa—that are shaped carefully to suit the emotions or the problems of the characters. Weather is both the material for physical description and a principal means of controlling the atmosphere of the novel.

Hinde's novels are also full of action, concerned with plot. Yet the plots never reach definitive conclusions, never entirely resolve the issues they present. The protagonist of *Happy as Larry* finally finds the photograph, but may or may not become a solid citizen and create a home for his faithful wife. The young capitalist in *For the Good of the Company* is enmeshed in the system and, at the end, like his boss, is about to live his past over again. But whether or not he will be any wiser is an open question. *The Village* ends with the feeling that the old English village is probably doomed, as much from its own hypocrisies and inadequacies as from an insensitive "urban bureaucracy," but the fight to save the village is not completely finished. Hinde's novels are, in a way, slices of recognizable contemporary life, a life in which people live and react, in which things happen although those things are not irremediably conclusive, and in which judgment is superficial or irrelevant. And these slices, communicated with a rich sense of personal and historical atmosphere, are never distorted by conversion into an object lesson or part of a message. In fact, Hinde, as author, keeps his distance. He can use familiar themes effectively because he treats them from a distance, stands far enough away to demonstrate a compassionate irony or an intelligent sympathy with his fictional world, a world effectively communicated because, like our larger world, it is one not easily reduced to understandable principles or judgments.

—James Gindin

HINES, (Melvin) Barry

Nationality: British. **Born:** Barnsley, South Yorkshire, 30 June 1939. **Education:** Ecclesfield Grammar School, 1950-57;

Loughborough College of Education, Leicestershire, 1958-60, 1962-63, teaching certificate. **Family:** Divorced; one daughter and one son. **Career:** Teacher of physical education in secondary schools in London, 1960-62, Barnsley, 1963-68, and South Yorkshire, 1968-72; Yorkshire Arts Fellow in Creative Writing, University of Sheffield, 1972-74; East Midlands Arts Fellow in Creative Writing, Matlock College of Further Education, Derbyshire, 1975-77; Fellow in Creative Writing, University of Wollongong, New South Wales, 1979; Arts Council Fellow, Sheffield City Polytechnic, 1982-84. **Awards:** Writers Guild award, for screenplay, 1970; Society of Authors traveling scholarship, 1989. Fellow, Royal Society of Literature, 1977; Honorary Fellow, Sheffield City Polytechnic, 1985. **Agent:** Lemon Unna and Durbridge Ltd., 24 Pottery Lane, London W11 4LZ. **Address:** 323 Fulwood Road, Sheffield, Yorkshire S10 3BJ, England.

PUBLICATIONS

Novels

The Blinder. London, Joseph, 1966.
A Kestrel for a Knave. London, Joseph, 1968; as *Kes,* 1974.
First Signs. London, Joseph, 1972.
The Gamekeeper. London, Joseph, 1975.
The Price of Coal. London, Joseph, 1979.
Looks and Smiles. London, Joseph, 1981.
Unfinished Business. London, Joseph, 1983.
The Heart of It. London, Joseph, 1994.

Uncollected Short Stories

"First Reserve," in *Argosy,* 1967.
"Another Jimmy Dance," in *Dandelion Clocks,* edited by Alfred Bradley and Kay Jamieson. London, Joseph, 1978.
"Christmas Afternoon," in *The Northern Drift,* edited by Alfred Bradley. London, Blackie, 1980.

Plays

Billy's Last Stand (televised 1970; produced Doncaster, Yorkshire, 1984; London, 1985).
Two Men from Derby (televised 1976; produced London, 1989). Published in *Act Two,* edited by David Self and Ray Speakman, London, Hutchinson, 1979.
Kes, with Allan Stronach, adaptation of the novel by Hines (produced Oldham, Lancashire, 1979). London, Heinemann, 1976.
The Price of Coal (includes *Meet the People* and *Back to Reality*) (televised 1977; produced Nottingham 1984). London, Hutchinson, 1979.

Screenplays: *Kes,* with Ken Loach, 1969; *Looks and Smiles,* 1981.

Television Plays: *Billy's Last Stand,* 1970; *Speech Day,* 1973; *Two Men from Derby,* 1976; *The Price of Coal (Meet the People* and *Back to Reality),* 1977; *The Gamekeeper,* 1979; *A Question of Leadership* (documentary), with Ken Loach, 1981; *Threads,* 1984; *Shooting Stars,* 1990; *Born Kicking,* 1992.

*

Critical Studies: *The Silent Majority: A Study of the Working Class in Post-War British Fiction* by Nigel Gray, London, Vision Press, and New York, Barnes and Noble, 1973; *Fire in Our Hearts* by Ronald Paul, Gothenburg, Sweden, Gothenburg Studies in English, 1982; "Miners and the Novel" by Graham Holderness, in *The British Working-Class Novel in the Twentieth Century* edited by Jeremy Hawthorn, London, Arnold, 1984.

Barry Hines comments:

My novels are mainly about working-class life. They are about people who live on council estates or in small terraced houses. The men work in mines and steelworks, the women in underpaid menial jobs—or, increasingly, are on the dole. I feel a strong sense of social injustice on behalf of these people which stems from my own mining background. The hardness and danger of that life (my grandfather was killed down the pit, my father was injured several times) formed my attitudes and made me a socialist.

My political viewpoint is the mainspring of my work. It fuels my energy; which is fine, as long as the characters remain believable and do not degenerate into dummies merely mouthing my own beliefs. However, I would rather risk being didactic than lapsing into blandness—or end up writing novels about writers writing novels. If that happens it will be time to hang up the biro.

My books are all conventional in form. They have a beginning, a middle, and a sort of ending (mainly in that order), with the occasional flashback thrown in. I think, after seven novels, I've now probably exhausted this form and need to explore different ways of telling a story, using some of the more fractured techniques I employ in writing film scripts.

*   *   *

The setting of all Barry Hines's novels is the working-class community of his native West Riding of Yorkshire. But every new work has dealt with another section or facet of this community, a new experience or dilemma as encountered by a representative, if highly individualized, figure from this class.

The author began his writing career in the wake of the late 1950s and 1960s movement in which a whole generation of northern working-class novelists had come to the fore, imprinting themselves on the map of English literary history through an unblinking representation of their native milieu and its language. Like Alan Sillitoe, Keith Waterhouse, Brendan Behan, or Sid Chaplin, Hines is initially concerned with the problems of young people. Like David Storey's *This Sporting Life,* Hines's first novel *The Blinder* considers professional football as an escape route from the working class, and Lenny Hawk is clearly akin to Arthur Seaton or Arthur Machin in his unbounded confidence, ready wit, and aggressiveness, though his gifts—intellectual as well as physical—reach far beyond the football pitch.

However, almost from the outset, certainly from *A Kestrel for a Knave* onward, Hines has found his own voice. It is not only an angry voice denouncing class prejudice and class privilege, and attacking the shortcomings of the once celebrated affluent society. It has also a cautiously hopeful ring emanating from the creative, defiant, and ultimately invincible qualities which his working-class characters display, often against overwhelming opposition. Thus *The Blinder* ends with Lenny publicly throwing torn-up sterling notes in the face of the powerful mill owner and football club director Leary who has sought to take revenge on the young soccer star by aiming to destroy his brilliant career through ugly intrigue.

And even Billy Casper, despite being more isolated than ever after the violent death of the hawk which he has reared and looked after with the care and devotion that he has never himself received from any human being, will, we feel, somehow carry on unsubdued, a victim but also an Artful Dodger of the ways of the adults.

A Kestrel for a Knave, better known by the title of the acclaimed film adaptation *Kes,* remains Hines's best-know and bestselling novel to date. It is technically an accomplished work, breaking up the story of a day in the life of an undersized lad from a one-parent family through a series of skillfully interwoven flashbacks. It has a number of memorable scenes (e.g., Billy before the careers officer), some of which have entered textbooks. What they convey is not only a sense of the complete breakdown of communication between adults and the adolescent but also his consequent negative perception of social relations and institutions—the family, school, law, work. Significantly, his one point of succor and fulfillment in an otherwise hostile and crippling environment lies outside society—the hawk, trained but not tamed, embodying strength, pride, and independence.

The author pursues this theme in *The Gamekeeper* just as the previous novel had developed the school subject from *The Blinder.* If *A Kestrel for a Knave* could be read as an affirmation of the Lawrentian opposition between an alienating and degrading urban-industrial world and a fuller, more aware natural life, *The Game-keeper* demonstrates that the author has either emancipated himself from this view or has never fully endorsed it. For the life of George Purse, who works on a ducal estate rearing and protecting pheasants from predators and poachers alike, is unspectacular and bare of romanticism. It is true that he has chosen this ill-paid job precisely in order to get away from the heat and dust of shiftwork in a steel mill. But the contentment and pride that he finds in his occupation are questioned and subverted by its inherent contradictions: the game is preserved for no other reason than to provide the Duke and his shooting party with the maximum bag; the gamekeeper's family suffers from the isolation imposed by living in a far-off cottage; chasing the poachers implies turning against members of his own class. Gamekeeping may thus be a personal alternative to industrial labor, but this form of living in direct contact with natural processes cannot shed capitalist relations of property and domination.

With *The Price of Coal* Hines returns to the industrial working class, this time confronting squarely such central issues as the nature of the work underground, the relationship between management and workforce, and the exigencies of an industrial policy to which, despite nationalization, the interests of the men remain firmly subordinated. The miners of this novel—the author has here visibly widened his cast even though he retains a central working-class family—are a singularly class-conscious and humorous breed; the way they poke fun at the absurdly exaggerated preparations for the impending Royal Visit to the colliery shows them drawing upon unfailing sources of resilience.

The militant spirit and satirical perspective of *The Price of Coal* clearly owe something to the 1972 and 1974 strikes in the industry, which goes to show how close to the thoughts and feelings of ordinary working people Hines has remained over the years, how loyal to his roots and faithful to his socialist humanist creed. The episodic structure of this terse narrative, its revealing juxtaposition of contrasting scenes and parts, and the dominance of dialogue derive in part from cinematographic techniques. The film version of *The Price of Coal* did, in fact, precede the novel by two years, and it is important to remember that Hines is a television playwright

and filmscript writer as well as a novelist. He has been lucky to find a congenial interpreter of his material in the film director Ken Loach, whose documentary realist approach successfully transposed *Kes, The Gamekeeper, The Price of Coal,* and *Looks and Smiles* onto the screen, and has thus enabled the author to reach new audiences at home and abroad.

—H. Gustav Klaus

HOAGLAND, Edward (Morley)

Nationality: American. **Born:** New York City, 21 December 1932. **Education:** Deerfield Academy; Harvard University, Cambridge, Massachusetts, 1950-54, A.B. 1954. **Military Service:** Served in the United States Army, 1955-57. **Family:** Married 1) Amy Ferrara in 1960 (divorced 1964); 2) Marion Magid in 1968; one daughter. **Career:** Taught at the New School for Social Research, New York, 1963-64, Rutgers University, New Brunswick, New Jersey, 1966, Sarah Lawrence College, Bronxville, New York, 1967 and 1971, City College, New York, 1967-68, University of Iowa, Iowa City, 1978 and 1982, Columbia University, New York, 1980-81, Bennington College, Vermont, 1987-95, and University of California, Davis, 1990 and 1992. Editorial writer, *New York Times,* 1979-89. Since 1985 general editor, Penguin Nature Library, New York. **Awards:** Houghton Mifflin fellowship, 1956; Longview Foundation award, 1961; Guggenheim fellowship, 1964, 1975; American Academy traveling fellowship, 1964, and Vursell Memorial award, 1981; O. Henry award, 1971; New York State Council on the Arts fellowship, 1972; Brandeis University citation, 1972; National Endowment for the Arts grant, 1982; New York Public Library Literary Lion award, 1988; National Magazine award, 1989; Lannan fellowship, 1993. **Member:** American Academy, 1982. **Address:** P.O. Box 51, Barton, Vermont 05822, U.S.A.

PUBLICATIONS

Novels

Cat Man. Boston, Houghton Mifflin, 1956.
The Circle Home. New York, Crowell, 1960.
The Peacock's Tail. New York, McGraw Hill, 1965.
Seven Rivers West. New York, Summit, 1986.

Short Stories

City Tales, with *Wyoming Stories,* by Gretel Ehrlich. Santa Barbara, California, Capra Press, 1986.
The Final Fate of the Alligators. Santa Barbara, California, Capra Press, 1992.

Other

Notes from the Century Before: A Journal from British Columbia. New York, Random House, 1969.
The Courage of Turtles: Fifteen Essays about Compassion, Pain, and Love. New York, Random House, 1971.

Walking the Dead Diamond River (essays). New York, Random House, 1973.

The Moose on the Wall: Field Notes from the Vermont Wilderness. London, Barrie and Jenkins, 1974.

Red Wolves and Black Bears (essays). New York, Random House, 1976.

African Calliope: A Journey to the Sudan. New York, Random House, 1979; London, Penguin, 1981.

The Edward Hoagland Reader, edited by Geoffrey Wolff. New York, Random House, 1979.

The Tugman's Passage (essays). New York, Random House, 1982.

Heart's Desire: The Best of Edward Hoagland. New York, Summit, 1988; London, Collins, 1990.

Balncing Acts (essays). New York, Simon and Schuster, 1992.

Editor, *The Circus of Dr. Lao,* by Charles Finney. New York, Vintage, 1983.

Editor, *The Mountains of California,* by John Muir. New York and London, Penguin, 1985.

Editor, *The Maine Woods,* by Henry David Thoreau. New York, Penguin, 1988.

Editor, *Walden,* by Henry David Thoreau. New York, Vintage, 1991.

Editor, *Steep Trails,* by John Muir. Sierra Club, 1994.

*   *   *

In the years since he published his first novel, *Cat Man* (1956), Edward Hoagland has gradually developed a reputation as one of America's leading essayists and a distinctive creator of fiction about both city life and the wilderness. His circus and boxing novels have been labeled required reading for those interested in these activities. In all his novels and many of his short stories, he shows a detailed, often first-hand knowledge of occupations where brawn or physical skills are more important than intellect. His essay, "Big Cats," is a deft description of the cat family; *Cat Man* is a novel of circus life that contains sordid but not unrealistic detail about the human struggles unseen by the spectators; and *The Circle Home* is a novel full of information about the training of boxers and life among the destitute. In his third but not best novel, *The Peacock's Tail,* he still shows an interest in the lower classes, for the protagonist is a young white man who gradually loses cultural and racial prejudice as he works among the urban poor. In his most recent novel, *Seven Rivers West,* a small group of white men and two women make an arduous journey through the Canadian west.

His prose style, though varied, is often unembellished, staccato, and unpretentious; yet since his narrators and central characters are usually lower class people, relatively uneducated and inarticulate, the straightforward colloquial prose is appropriate. In its direct, deflationary tone, the beginning of his short story, "The Final Fate of the Alligators," is a succinct introduction to most of his main characters: "In such a crowded, busy world the service each man performs is necessarily a small one. Arnie Bush's was no exception." Yet the lack of subtle, intellectual prose does not mean that the author offers no insights. A description of leopards in motion ends, for example, with a deft comment: "Really, leopards are like machines. They move in a sort of perpetual motion. Their faces don't change; they eat the same way, sleep the same way, pace much the same as each other. Their bodies are constructed as ideally as a fish's for moving and doing, for action, and not much room is left for personality." Regrettably, the final clause may aptly be applied to his characters, for many of them are so busy learning survival techniques in an uncaring world that their personalities are never fully developed. We may believe in them, but we are not always interested in them. The lack of interest sometimes results from the brevity of a character's role or the analysis devoted to it. Thus when characters fall back into self-destructive habits such as self-pity or alcoholism, we feel little sympathy. We impatiently dismiss them as born losers. On reflection, however, we may realize that we lack the compassion that Hoagland has for the urban poor or the uneducated easterner following his dream.

An accurate and just sense of Hoagland's strengths and weaknesses in prose style, narrative technique, characterization, and thought may be obtained from *The Circle Home,* the story of Denny Kelly, an irresponsible 29-year-old who has failed and continues to fail as a prize fighter and husband. In prose direct and at times colorful, the author demonstrates a close knowledge of the world of third-rate boxers.

> A lively fight: One-hand found occasion to maneuver into every foot the ring provided. He'd be close, mining in the belly, and spring back with a lithe light antelope-type movement. Often when his left returned from thrusts his arms dropped by his sides to balance him. Those leaps, narrow body straight upright and turning in the air to face the way he wanted, were the essence of his style. . . .

The author seems intent, not upon muckraking, but upon having readers understand the world of boxers and boxing. The reader comes to know Denny through the straight chronological flow of his attempted comeback, and through a series of flashbacks that chronicle his irresponsible and immature behavior as a husband and father. In re-creating the flow of events Hoagland shows a keen ear for dialogue. The end of the novel, however, is weak: Denny, contrite yet once more, phones to inform his wife that he is determined (because of *his* miseries) to return and to be henceforth a good family man. The title, *The Circle Home,* suggests that at last he will be truly home, but because he has failed so often before and has shown no true deep reformation, the reader may prophesy further backsliding. If we are meant to view Denny's future optimistically, the author's compassion for the dwellers in the "lower depths" has led him to a sentimental conclusion.

Seven Rivers West contains some of Hoagland's best fictional writing. Set in the Canadian west of the 1880s, not yet settled by Europeans, though it has been touched by them, it gives a vivid and detailed look at the white men pressing on with their railroad and seeking their future in the territory of the Indians, some of whom are still defiant, others already tainted by an alien civilization. Hoagland makes us appreciate both the energy and activities of the native people, and the magnificent challenge of the landscape. John Updike rightly praised it for being "wonder-ful." The conclusion of the novel, however, is somewhat disappointing in its treatment of Cecil Roop's capture of a bear he has long sought and the depiction of the mythic Bigfoot.

From his works as a whole, Hoagland appears as a careful writer who, steeped in firsthand knowledge of his material, attempts with some humor and considerable compassion to show us men and women struggling first to survive and then to improve themselves or the world. There is, indeed, a definite sense of the author's feelings and involvement in the fiction and essays. (One reviewer objected to Hoagland exposing his neuroses in his travel essays.) But Hoagland does not hesitate to acknowledge the autobiographical aspects of his fiction. In the foreword to *City Tales,* he says:

I found at the end of the 1960s that what I wanted to do most was to tell my own story; and by the agency of my first book of nonfiction, *Notes From the Century Before*—which began as a diary intended only to fuel my next novel—I discovered that the easiest way to do so was by writing directly to the reader without filtering myself through the artifices of fiction. By the time another decade had passed, however, I was sick of telling my own story and went back to inventing other people's, in a novel I hope will be finished before this book you are holding comes out.

Because Hoagland has the skill to make vivid the plight of the unprivileged, whether in the city or in the wilderness, he deserves the esteem that has gradually gained during his writing career.

—James A. Hart

HOBAN, Russell (Conwell)

Nationality: American. **Born:** Lansdale, Pennsylvania, 4 February 1925. **Education:** Lansdale High School; Philadelphia Museum School of Industrial Art, 1941-43. **Military Service:** Served in the United States Army Infantry, 1943-45: Bronze Star. **Family:** Married 1) Lillian Aberman (i.e., the illustrator Lillian Hoban) in 1944 (divorced 1975), one son and three daughters; 2) Gundula Ahl in 1975, three sons. **Career:** Magazine and advertising agency artist and illustrator; story board artist, Fletcher Smith Film Studio, New York, 1951; television art director, Batten Barton Durstine and Osborn, 1951-56, and J. Walter Thompson, 1956, both in New York; freelance illustrator, 1956-65; advertising copywriter, Doyle Dane Bernbach, New York, 1965-67. Since 1967 full-time writer; since 1969 has lived in London. **Awards:** Christopher award, 1972; Whitbread award, 1974; Ditmar award (Australia), 1982; John W. Campbell Memorial award, 1982. Fellow, Royal Society of Literature, 1988. **Agent:** David Higham Associates Ltd., 5-8 Lower John Street, London W1R 4HA, England.

PUBLICATIONS

Novels

The Lion of Boaz-Jachin and Jachin-Boaz. London, Cape, and New York, Stein and Day, 1973.
Kleinzeit. London, Cape, and New York, Viking Press, 1974.
Turtle Diary. London, Cape, 1975; New York, Random House, 1976.
Riddley Walker. London, Cape, and New York, Summit, 1980.
Pilgermann. London, Cape, and New York, Summit, 1983.
The Medusa Frequency. London, Cape, and New York, Atlantic Monthly Press, 1987.
The Moment under the Moment. London, Cape, 1992.

Uncollected Short Story

"Schwartz," in *Encounter* (London), March 1990.

Fiction (for children)

Bedtime for Frances. New York, Harper, 1960; London, Faber, 1963.
Herman the Loser. New York, Harper, 1961; Kingswood, Surrey, World's Work, 1972.
The Song in My Drum. New York, Harper, 1962.
London Men and English Men. New York, Harper, 1962.
Some Snow Said Hello. New York, Harper, 1963.
The Sorely Trying Day. New York, Harper, 1964; Kingswood, Surrey, World's Work, 1965.
A Baby Sister for Frances. New York, Harper, 1964; London, Faber, 1965.
Bread and Jam for Frances. New York, Harper, 1964; London, Faber, 1966.
Nothing to Do. New York, Harper, 1964.
Tom and the Two Handles. New York, Harper, 1965; Kingswood, Surrey, World's Work, 1969.
The Story of Hester Mouse Who Became a Writer. New York, Norton, 1965; Kingswood, Surrey, World's Work, 1969.
What Happened When Jack and Daisy Tried to Fool the Tooth Fairies. New York, Four Winds Press, 1965.
Henry and the Monstrous Din. New York, Harper, 1966; Kingswood, Surrey, World's Work, 1967.
The Little Brute Family. New York, Macmillan, 1966.
Save My Place, with Lillian Hoban. New York, Norton, 1967.
Charlie the Tramp. New York, Four Winds Press, 1967.
The Mouse and His Child. New York, Harper, 1967; London, Faber, 1969.
A Birthday for Frances. New York, Harper, 1968; London, Faber, 1970.
The Stone Doll of Sister Brute. New York, Macmillan, and London, Collier Macmillan, 1968.
Harvey's Hideout. New York, Parents' Magazine Press, 1969; London, Cape, 1973.
Best Friends for Frances. New York, Harper, 1969; London, Faber, 1971.
The Mole Family's Christmas. New York, Parents' Magazine Press, 1969; London, Cape, 1973.
Ugly Bird. New York, Macmillan, 1969.
A Bargain for Frances. New York, Harper, 1970; Kingswood, Surrey, World's Work, 1971.
Emmet Otter's Jug-Band Christmas. New York, Parents' Magazine Press, and Kingswood, Surrey, World's Work, 1971.
The Sea-Thing Child. New York, Harper, and London, Gollancz, 1972.
Letitia Rabbit's String Song. New York, Coward McCann, 1973.
How Tom Beat Captain Najork and His Hired Sportsmen. New York, Atheneum, and London, Cape, 1974.
Ten What? A Mystery Counting Book. London, Cape, 1974; New York, Scribner, 1975.
Dinner at Alberta's. New York, Crowell, 1975; London, Cape, 1977.
Crocodile and Pierrot, with Sylvie Selig. London, Cape, 1975; New York, Scribner, 1977.
A Near Thing for Captain Najork. London, Cape, 1975; New York, Atheneum, 1976.
Arthur's New Power. New York, Crowell, 1978; London, Gollancz, 1980.
The Twenty-Elephant Restaurant. New York, Atheneum, 1978; London, Cape, 1980.

The Dancing Tigers. London, Cape, 1979.
La Corona and the Tin Frog. London, Cape, 1979.
Flat Cat. London, Methuen, and New York, Philomel, 1980.
Ace Dragon Ltd. London, Cape, 1980.
The Serpent Tower. London, Methuen, 1981.
The Great Fruit Gum Robbery. London, Methuen, 1981; as *The Great Gumdrop Robbery,* New York, Philomel, 1982.
They Came from Aargh! London, Methuen, and New York, Philomel, 1981.
The Battle of Zormla. London, Methuen, and New York, Philomel, 1982.
The Flight of Bembel Rudzuk. London, Methuen, and New York, Philomel, 1982.
Ponders (Jim Frog, Big John Turkle, Charlie Meadows, Lavinia Bat). London, Walker, and New York, Holt Rinehart, 4 vols., 1983-84; 1 vol. edition, London, Walker Books, 1988.
The Rain Door. London, Gollancz, 1986; New York, Crowell, 1987.
The Marzipan Pig. London, Cape, 1986; New York, Farrar Straus, 1987.
Monsters. London, Gollancz, and New York, Scholastic, 1989.
Jim Hedgehog's Supernatural Christmas. London, Hamish Hamilton, 1989; New York, Clarion, 1992.
Jim Hedgehog and the Lonesome Tower. London, Hamish Hamilton, 1990; New York, Clarion, 1992.
M.O.L.E. Much Overworked Little Earthmover, with Jan Pienkowski. London, Cape, 1993.
The Court of the Winged Serpent. London, Cape, 1994.

Plays

The Carrier Frequency, with Impact Theatre Co-operative (produced London, 1984).
Riddley Walker, adaptation of his own novel (produced Manchester, 1986).
Some Episodes in the History of Miranda and Caliban (opera libretto), music by Helen Roe (produced London, 1990).

Television Play: *Come and Find Me,* 1980.

Poetry (for children)

Goodnight. New York, Norton, 1966; Kingswood, Surrey, World's Work, 1969.
The Pedalling Man and Other Poems. New York, Norton, 1968; Kingswood, Surrey, World's Work, 1969.
Egg Thoughts and Other Frances Songs. New York, Harper, 1972; London, Faber, 1973.

Other (for children)

What Does It Do and How Does It Work? Power Shovel, Dump Truck, and Other Heavy Machines. New York, Harper, 1959.
The Atomic Submarine: A Practice Combat Patrol under the Sea. New York, Harper, 1960.

Critical Studies: *Through the Narrow Gate: The Mythological Consciousness of Russell Hoban* by Christine Wilkie, Rutherford, New Jersey, Fairleigh Dickinson University Press, and London, Associated University Presses, 1989.

*   *   *

Russell Hoban's six novels for adults have a compelling strangeness made up of the most elusive aspects of myth, riddle, history, fantasy, philosophy, and humor. For many readers this is a deeply intriguing mixture which has made him something of a cult author. Drop the title of his most-discussed book, *Riddley Walker,* into any literary conversation and it will divide the group into three parties, the excited supporters who believe it to be one of the great underestimated novels of the 20th century, the bored opposition who didn't get past page six because it was "odd," and the remainder who've never heard of Russell Hoban. This last group is smaller since the success of the film *Turtle Diary* which follows the bare plot of Hoban's third novel, but with scarcely a shadow of the book's power.

Turtle Diary is the most approachable of Hoban's works for readers familiar with the "realist" novel, although its structure is unusual. The first chapter is a kind of journal note by William G. who works in a London bookshop and whose deliberately limited life is metaphorically connected to the lives of the giant turtles he visits in the London Zoo. Chapter 2 is an apparently unrelated narration by Neaera H., an author of children's books, but now in a state of block about a water-beetle she had hoped would become a new character. As William and Neaera meet and join forces to free the turtles the parallel narration continues, creating two characters of powerful immediacy, and allowing the reader to know far more about them than either is willing to reveal to the other. Like all Hoban's major characters these two are seekers, looking for answers, or even the right questions, about the meaning of life. The starting point is often a sudden perception of the extraordinariness of the ordinary, whether it's the daily human routine or the world of landscape and natural objects.

Animals are often used by Hoban as metaphors, or totems, or familiars. Through them he questions reality and identity, Thing-in-Itself. What a turtle is to itself remains a riddle for Neaera and William. The lion in *The Lion of Boaz-Jachin and Jachin-Boaz,* Hoban's first novel for adults, begins as a figure in a lion-hunt Boaz-Jachin sees carved in relief upon a tomb. It develops as a richly ambiguous image during his search for his father and the map of life his father has promised him. Like many other objects in the internal worlds of Hoban's narrators, the lion becomes increasingly "real," and moves into the external world with farcical, sad, moving, results. Although some of the black comedy, like the outrageously funny scene in the asylum, is similar to the surrealism of Samuel Beckett, the bleakness is always moderated in Hoban's work by a far more benign, optimistic view of the world than Beckett's. Love is possible, even probable, in Hoban's world, though it is always love with toughness, risk, and no certainties. Like life, it requires courage, hope, and a sense of humour.

Kleinzeit and *The Medusa Frequency* have hints of Beckett too, but also of Charlie Chaplin, Woody Allen, and "magic realism." *Kleinzeit* tells Ward Sister that his name means "hero" in German, but his rival explains that it really means "smalltime," and the unheroic hero, struggling with inner states which have become inseparable from outer, is often at the center of Hoban's novels. Gifts are given to Kleinzeit as he leaves the hospital with Ward Sister, "cured" of his "dismemberment," if not of the pains in his hypotenuse, diapason, and stretto. God gives the lovers a week free of electricity-strikes to start them off on their joint life, Hospital gives a week's postponement of Kleinzeit catching the flu, and Death gives Kleinzeit the power to draw with a calligraphy brush in "one fat sweep" of black ink, a perfect circle, symbol of harmony and completion. But although the symbols in Hoban's novels are often universal ones, and frequently have a classical source, like the recurrent Orpheus and Eurydice myth, their particular appearances are always full of wit and unexpected application. The Orpheus and Eurydice myth allows scope to some of Hoban's strongest interests, the need to love which has as its dark side the possibility of loss and death, the power of memory and history, and the urge to make sense of experience by remaking it in song, story, and art.

Hoban has fun with names and words in all his books, but *Riddley Walker* is, among other things, an extended examination of the connections between language and the world. The action is narrated by Riddley Walker himself in an extraordinary dialect, a cross between phonetic Cockney, mixed regional, and corrupted remnants of computer-speak, which succeeds brilliantly in suggesting the language of England over two thousand years after the "1 Big 1," a nuclear explosion around 1997 A.D. With no words for half the abstractions we take for granted, Riddley expresses ideas of religion, science, and art in terms of the practical things he knows, and the resulting metaphors are exhilarating. The two parts of Riddley's name hint at the two aspects of his adventures, mental and physical, during the ten days after he earns manhood in his tribe. "Walker is my name and I am the same. Riddley Walker. Walking my riddles where ever they've took me and walking them now on this paper the same." One of the great pleasures of Hoban's novels lies in the participation demanded from the reader. In this novel the distant past of Riddley's society, known to him only from scraps of myth, song, and game, is the reader's 20th-century present. There are continual shocks in the collision between our own and Riddley's view of events. A very funny scene satirizes "expert" interpretation of the past when Goodparley explains the meaning of a manuscript dating from the 20th century.

Pilgermann, Hoban's most violent and disturbing novel, is an equally startling use of history to ask philosophical questions, but this time with a complexity of biblical and Islamic allusions. The pilgrim-hero is a Jew in the 11th century, another of Hoban's seekers on whom the riddles of life suddenly force an imperative physical journey and metaphysical quest. Any answers come through connections demonstrated, not merely told.

—Jennifer Livett

HODGINS, Jack

Nationality: Canadian. **Born:** John Stanley Hodgins in Comox Valley, Vancouver Island, British Columbia, 3 October 1938. **Education:** Tsolum School, Courtenay, British Columbia; University of British Columbia, Vancouver, 1956-61, B.Ed. 1961. **Family:** Married Dianne Child in 1960; one daughter and two sons. **Career:** Teacher, Nanaimo District Senior Secondary School, British Columbia, 1961-80; visiting professor, University of Ottawa, 1981-83; visiting professor, 1983-85, and currently professor of creative writing, University of Victoria, British Columbia. Writer-in-residence, Simon Fraser University, Burnaby, British Columbia, 1977, and University of Ottawa, 1979; Canadian Department of External Affairs lecturer, Japan, 1979. **Awards:** University of Western Ontario President's medal, for short story, 1973; Canada Council award, 1980; Governor-General's award, 1980; Canada-Australia award, 1986. **Agent:** Bella Pomer Agency, 22 Shallmar Boulevard, Toronto, Ontario M5N 2Z8. **Address:** Creative Writing Dept., University of Victoria, Box 1700, Victoria, British Columbia, Canada V8W 2Y2.

PUBLICATIONS

Novels

The Invention of the World. Toronto, Macmillan, 1977; New York, Harcourt Brace, 1978.
The Resurrection of Joseph Bourne; or, A Word or Two on Those Port Annie Miracles. Toronto, Macmillan, 1979.
The Honorary Patron. Toronto, McClelland and Stewart, 1987.
Innocent Cities. Toronto, McClelland and Stewart, 1990.

Short Stories

Spit Delaney's Island: Selected Stories. Toronto, Macmillan, 1976.
The Barclay Family Theatre. Toronto, Macmillan, 1981.
Beginnings: Samplings from a Long Apprenticeship: Novels Which Were Imagined, Written, Re-Written, Submitted, Rejected, Abandoned, and Supplanted. Toronto, Grand Union, 1983.

Uncollected Short Stories

"The God of Happiness," in *Westerly,* (Nedlands, Australia) 4, 1968.
"Promise of Peace," in *The North American Review,* New Ser. 6(4), 1969.
"A Matter of Necessity," in *The Canadian Forum,* January 1970.
"The Graveyard Man," in *Descant* (Fort Worth, Texas) 15(4), 1971.
"Witness," in *Alphabet* 18-19, 1971.
"Edna Pike, on the Day of the Prime Minister's Wedding," in *Event: Journal of the Contemporary Arts,* 2(1), (1972).
"Open Line," in *The Antigonish Review* 9, 1972.
"Passing by the Dragon," in *Island: Vancouver Island's Quarterly Review of Poetry and Fiction,* (Nanaimo, British Columbia), 2, 1972.
"The Importance of Patsy McLean," in *Journal of Canadian Fiction,* 2(1), 1973.
"In the Museum of Evil," in *Journal of Canadian Fiction,* 3(1), 1974.
"Silverthorn," in *Forum* (Houston) 12(1), 1974.
"Great Blue Heron," in *Prism International,* 14(2), 1975.
"A Conversation in the Kick-and-Kill: July," in *Sound Heritage,* (Victoria, British Columbia), 6(3), 1977.
"The Invention of the World," in *Viva,* February 1978.
"Spit Delaney's Nightmare," in *Toronto Life,* January 1978.
"Miss Schussnigg's First Spring," in *Peter Gzowski's Spring Tonic,* edited by Peter Gzowski. Edmonton, Alberta, Hurtig, 1979.
"Victims of the Masquerade," in *Interface,* 4(8), 1981.
"Change of Scenery," in *Small Wonders: New Stories by Twelve Distinguished Canadian Writers,* edited by Robert Weaver. Toronto, CBC, 1982.
"The Day of the Stranger," in *Chatelaine,* December 1982.
"Faller Topolski's Arrival," in *True North/Down Under* (Lantzville, British Columbia), 1, 1983.
"The Crossing," in *Vancouver Magazine,* February 1985.
"Earthquake," in *The Canadian Forum,* March 1986.
"Loved Forever," in *Books in Canada,* August-September 1988.
"Balance," in *Paris Transcontinental: A Magazine of Short Stories* 7, 1993.

"Galleries," in *O Canada 2,* edited by Cassandra Pybus, *Meanjin* (Parkville, Victoria), 54, 1995.

"In the Forest of Discarded Pasts," in *Paris Transcontinental: A Magazine of Short Stories,* 11, c. 1995.

"Over Here," in *Prism International,* 33(3), 1995.

Other

Teachers' Resource Book to Transition II: Short Fiction, with Bruce Nesbitt. Vancouver, CommCept, 1978.

Teaching Short Fiction, with Bruce Nesbitt. Vancouver, CommCept, 1981.

Left Behind in Squabble Bay (for children), illustrated by Victor Gad. Toronto, McClelland and Stewart, 1988.

A Passion for Narrative: A Guide for Writing Fiction. Toronto, McClelland & Stewart, 1993; New York, St. Martin's Press, 1994.

Over Forty in Broken Hill: Unusual Encounters Outback and Beyond. St. Lucia, University of Queensland Press, 1992.

A Passion for Narrative: A Guide for Writing Fiction. Toronto, McClelland and Stewart, 1993.

Editor, with W.H. New, *Voice and Vision.* Toronto, McClelland and Stewart, 1972.

Editor, *The Frontier Experience.* Toronto, Macmillan, 1975.

Editor, *The West Coast Experience.* Toronto, Macmillan, 1976.

Editor, with Bruce Nesbitt, *Teaching Short Fiction; A Resource Book to "Transitions II: Short Fiction."* Vancouver, CommCept, 1978.

*

Bibliography: "Jack Hodgins," in *The Writers' Union of Canada: A Directory of Members,* edited by Ted Whittaker, Toronto, The Writers' Union of Canada, 1981; "Hodgins, Jack (1938-)" by Helen Hoy, in her *Modern English-Canadian Prose: A Guide to Information Sources,* Detroit, Gale Research, 1983; "Hodgins, Jack (1938-)" by Allan Weiss, in his *A Comprehensive Bibliography of English-Canadian Short Stories, 1950-1983,* Toronto, ECW Press, 1988; "Selected Bibliography" by David [L.] Jeffrey, in his *Jack Hodgins and His Works,* Toronto, ECW Press, 1989.

Manuscript Collection: The National Library of Canada, Ottawa, Ontario.

Critical Studies: "The Mind of the Artist: The Soul of the Place," in *Essays on Canadian Writing,* 5, 1976, "Fantasy in a Mythless Age" in *Essays on Canadian Writing,* 9, 1977-78, "Thinking about Eternity," in *Essays on Canadian Writing,* 20, 1980-81, all by J.R. (Tim) Struthers; "An Interview with Jack Hodgins" by Jack David, in *Essays on Canadian Writing,* 11, 1978; "Jack Hodgins and the Island Mind," in *Canada Emergent: Literature/Art,* edited by James Carley, *Book Forum,* 4, 1978, "A Crust for the Critics," in *Canadian Literature,* 84, 1980, "It Out-Hodgins Hodgins: Burlesque and the Freedoms of Fiction," in *Essays on Canadian Writing,* 26, 1983, and *Jack Hodgins and His Works,* Toronto, ECW Press, 1989, all by David L. Jeffrey; "Jack Hodgins" by Geoff Hancock, in his *Canadian Writers at Work: Interviews with Geoff Hancock,* Toronto, Oxford University Press, 1987; "Haunted by a Glut of Ghosts: Jack Hodgins' *The Invention of the World*" by Robert Lecker, in *Essays on Canadian Writing,* 20, 1980-81; "Canadian Burlesque: Jack Hodgins' *The Invention of the World*" by Susan

Beckmann, in *Essays on Canadian Writing,* 20, 1980-81; "Western Horizon: Jack Hodgins" by Alan Twigg, in his *For Openers: Conversations with 24 Canadian Writers,* Madeira Park, British Columbia, Harbour, 1981; "*The Barclay Family Theatre*" by Ann Mandel, in *The Fiddlehead,* 134, 1982; "An Interview with Jack Hodgins" by Peter O'Brien, in *Rubicon* (Montreal), 1, 1983; "Irish and Biblical Myth in Jack Hodgins' *The Invention of the World*" by Jan C. Horner, in *Canadian Literature,* 99, 1983; "Isolation and Community in Jack Hodgins's Short Stories," in *Recherches Anglaises et Américaines,* 16, 1983, "Jack Hodgins: Interview," in *Kunapipi* 9(2), 1987, and "Magic Realism in Jack Hodgins's Short Stories," in *Recherches Anglaises et Nord-Américaines* 20, 1987, all by Jeanne Delbaere-Garant; "Jack Hodgins' *The Invention of the World* and Robert Browning's 'Abt Vogler'" by Laurence Steven, in *Canadian Literature,* 99, 1983; "Brother XII and *The Invention of the World,*" in *Essays on Canadian Writing,* 28, 1984, and "Lines and Circles: Structure in *The Honorary Patron*" in *Canadian Literature,* 128, 1991, both by JoAnn McCaig; "Disbelieving Story: A Reading of *The Invention of the World*" by Frank Davey, in *Present Tense, The Canadian Novel,* edited by John Moss, vol. 4, Toronto, NC Press, 1985; "'If Words Won't Do, and Symbols Fail': Hodgins' Magic Reality" by Cecilia Coulas Fink, in *Journal of Canadian Studies,* 20(2), 1985; "The Invention of a Region: The Art of Fiction in Jack Hodgins' Stories" by Waldemar Zacharasiewicz, in *Gaining Ground: European Critics on Canadian Literature,* edited by Robert Kroetsch and Reingard M. Nischik, Edmonton, NeWest, 1985; "Jack Hodgins's Island: A Big Enough Country" by Allan Pritchard, in *University of Toronto Quarterly,* 55, 1985; "Jack Hodgins and the Sources of Invention," in *Essays on Canadian Writing* 34, 1987, "Jack Hodgins," in *A Sense of Style: Studies in the Art of Fiction in English-Speaking Canada,* Toronto, ECW Press, 1989, "Hodgins's 'Pack of Crazies': *The Resurrection of Joseph Bourne*" and "On the Edge of Something Else: Jack Hodgins's Island World," both in *An Independent Stance: Essays on English-Canadian Criticism and Fiction,* Erin, Ontario, Porcupine's Quill, 1991, all by W.J. Keith; "Out on the Verandah: A Conversation with Jack Hodgins" by Alan Lawson and Stephen Slemon, in *Australian-Canadian Studies* 5(1), 1987; "Jack Hodgins: Interview" by Russell McDougall, in *Kunapipi,* 12(1), 1990; "Reader's Squint: An Approach to Jack Hodgins' *The Barclay Family Theatre*" by Simone Vauthier, in *Modes of Narrative: Approaches to American, Canadian, and British Fiction,* edited by Reingard M. Nischik and Barbara Korte, Würzburg, Germany, Königshausen and Neumann, 1990; *The Counterfeit and the Real in Jack Hodgins' "The Invention of the World"* by Carol Langhelle, Lund, Sweden, Nordic Association for Canadian Studies—L'Association Nordique d'études Canadiennes, 1992; *How Stories Mean* edited by John Metcalf and J.R. (Tim) Struthers, Erin, Ontario, Porcupine's Quill, 1993.

Jack Hodgins comments:

(1981) I write fiction in order to free myself of those shadowy creatures that walk briefly across the back of my mind and then return to grow into living breathing people who aren't satisfied to live in my skull: Spit Delaney, the engineer who falls apart when his steam locomotive is sold to a museum; Maggie Kyle, the gorgeous "loggers' whore" who sets herself up a new life in the ruins of a failed utopian colony; Joseph Bourne, the famous poet who dies and returns to life in a tiny town on the edge of the world; Jacob Weins, the small-town mayor never seen without a different costume on, who after his town has slid off the mountain and into the sea has to search for a new role for himself, and a new costume. Writing them down is a way of getting rid of them. It is also, I hope, a way of sharing them—of allowing other people to love them too, as I must do myself before I'm through with them. I write fiction in order to explain their mysteries to myself—what makes them tick?—but always in the process of writing uncover more mystery than I solve. I write fiction in order to nail down a place before it disappears. If much has been made of the fact that most of my stories are set on Vancouver Island, it is not just that there is some excitement in introducing a part of the world seldom represented before in fiction. The place is changing while I look at it and I want to get the trees, the rocks, the beaches down right before they disappear. I also feel that if I nail the place down right, the people who walk around in it will be just that much more convincing to the reader, wherever he is in the world. I write fiction, finally, for the same reason the magician creates *his* illusions—in order to start something magical happening in the audience's (reader's) mind. If the critics insist on calling me a "magic realist" it isn't because I distort reality or indulge in fantasy but because I see the magic that's already there.

*   *   *

Jack Hodgins is a strongly regional writer in the sense that up to now, though he has lived elsewhere, he has never departed in his fiction from Vancouver Island, the fairly circumscribed region where he was born and spent his childhood and young manhood. Yet, in common with the best of regional writers, he finds the local a staging point for the universal, and his novels and stories owe their appeal largely to his recurrent theme that—as Frank Davey put it in the *Oxford Companion to Canadian Literature*—"imagination can redeem or transcend the physical," a theme exemplified in the title as well as in the action of his most considerable work—and earliest novel—*The Invention of the World.* Given such a vision, his work is necessarily comic in character, and its humour seems to spring from a temperamental inability on the author's part to see life as other than good, prospects as other than expansive, human nature as other than extravagant in its potentialities.

Hodgins was reared in an area of Canada that runs to excess, the rural north of Vancouver Island, which represents the country's westernmost edge of settlement. Until recently it still counted as a frontier area, attracting with its fine scenery and its good winters a rich variety of eccentrics who populated its fishing villages, stump farms, and logging camps. The present writer inhabited the same area for a period, and can give a certificate of authenticity to the rustic society with its peculiar behavior patterns that Hodgins makes the setting of his fictions. Imagine the oddities of Erskine Caldwell's deep southern villages transferred to the green wilderness of far western Canada, and one might get an image of the kind of world Hodgins portrays, except that his optimistic vision lacks Caldwell's darker shadows and his work is in any case interesting enough to be read for itself without referring it back to models.

Hodgins's first book was a group of loosely linked stories, *Spit Delaney's Island;* Spit Delaney himself, wild and often shocking in the unconventionality of his behavior, is the first of Hodgins's roguish and exuberant heroes who live by their dreams and in the process expose the futility limited lives of the literal-minded.

Hodgins in fact practices a latter-day picaresque fiction. His central characters are often variants on the classical picaro, the ultimately redeemable rogue. His novels take on the loose structure of the picaresque romance, and in the process, as his evident master

Cervantes did in *Don Quixote,* he constantly intertwines parables with the deceptions of verisimilitude.

The Invention of the World is still to date the most satisfying of Hodgins's longer fictions and the most representative of his writing. It is a mingling, which does not always blend well, of the eccentrically regional and the extravagantly parabolical. A larger-than-life evangelist (based on an actual confidence trickster who once operated in the same area under the name of Brother Twelve) persuades a whole Irish village to follow him to Vancouver Island and form a community subservient to his wishes. In a way the evangelist thus invents a world, but it is a false one; the real heroine and creative spirit of the book is the exuberant and promiscuous Maggie Kyle, eventual bride in an epic and Brueghelesque wedding in which the island loggers break out into ferocious battle. Maggie is not only a splendidly complex personality; she also spans the literary genres and approaches, from Joycean interior monologue to vitalist action.

His broad grasp of a variety of literary approaches, and his intent to use them in comic affirmation have given Hodgins short-term advantages. But they also offer long-term perils, for his second novel, *The Resurrection of Joseph Bourne,* though it is even more emphatically vitalist than *The Invention of the World* in its insistence on the power of the human imagination to make its own terms with existence, is not merely less plausible mimetically, but also less satisfying on the parabolic level, since Hodgins fails to reinvigorate his "resurrected" poet Joseph Bourne into a convincing personification of the life principle.

The problems of sustaining exaggerative fantasy are shown in a volume of stories Hodgins published in 1981, *The Barclay Family Theatre.* It is the most shallow and facile of his books, a series of stories concerning the daughters of a single backwoods family and their disconcerting impact on the world. The stories all seem to suffer from the strain of surprising the reader with ever greater extravagance, and the authenticity of characterization is correspondingly diminished. Hodgins had clearly come to the point where the possibilities of his existing material and his current methods were almost exhausted.

Considering his situation in his own terms, Hodgins would have to invent a new world for himself—or perhaps reinvent an old one—if he were to continue the process of creative change needed for any writer to outlive his early promise. For the time being, at least, Hodgins has answered the challenge by producing a striking number and variety of new works that range widely in both a geographical and a generic sense. These include a children's book, *Left Behind in Squabble Bay,* a travel book, *Over 40 in Broken Hill,* based on an expedition with Australian writer Roger McDonald, a creative writing text, *A Passion for Narrative,* a growing group of as yet uncollected stories, and two more novels: one, *The Honorary Patron,* divided between Europe and Vancouver Island, and another, *Innocent Cities,* divided between Australia and Vancouver Island. It remains to be seen whether this variety of literary activity represents an end in itself, however satisfying or unsatisfying, or rather a means leading forward, or perhaps back, to something more important.

Clearly conscious of the need to change, Hodgins has done so most strikingly in his novel *Innocent Cities.* It is, in its own way, a historical novel, set in Victoria during the 1880s, the period of lull between the Cariboo and the Klondike gold rushes. The famed historical figures of early British Columbia are mainly ghosts in the background; at the same time Hodgins has said that his novel was inspired by an actual family history. It begins, like *The Resurrec-*

tion of Joseph Bourne, with the arrival in the "innocent city" of a mysterious woman who thrusts herself with determination into the life of the small community and captures—or rather recaptures in the midst of a fine subplot of various bigamies—the flamboyant hotelier James Horncastle. It is all Dead Sea Fruit, for Horncastle frustrates her by dying, while her younger sister, who has followed her to Victoria, happily marries the visionary builder, Logan Sumner. *Innocent Cities* may be seen, then, as a work of parody and palimpsest; what Hodgins has written is an imitation Victorian novel presented through an ironic modern sensibility.

—George Woodcock, updated by J.R. (Tim) Struthers

HOFF, Harry Summerfield. *See* **COOPER, William.**

HOFFMAN, Alice

Nationality: American. **Born:** New York City, 16 March 1952. **Education:** Adelphi University, Garden City, New York, B.A. 1973; Stanford University, California (Mirelles fellow), M.A. 1975. **Family:** Married to Tom Martin; two sons. Lives in Boston, Massachusetts. **Awards:** Bread Loaf Writers Conference Atherton scholarship, 1976. **Address:** c/o Putnam, 200 Madison Avenue, New York, New York 10016, U.S.A.

PUBLICATIONS

Novels

Property Of. New York, Farrar Straus, 1977; London, Hutchinson, 1978.
The Drowning Season. New York, Dutton, and London, Hutchinson, 1979.
Angel Landing. New York, Putnam, 1980; London, Severn House, 1982.
White Horses. New York, Putnam, 1982; London, Collins, 1983.
Fortune's Daughter. New York, Putnam, and London, Collins, 1985.
Illumination Night. New York, Putnam, and London, Macmillan, 1987.
At Risk. New York, Putnam, and London, Macmillan, 1988.
Seventh Heaven. New York, Putnam, and London, Virago Press, 1991.
Turtle Moon. New York, Putnam, and London, Macmillan, 1992.
Second Nature. New York, Putnam, and London, Macmillan, 1994.
Practical Magic. New York, Putnam, and London, Macmillan, 1995.

Uncollected Short Stories

"Blue Tea," in *Redbook* (New York), June 1982.
"Sweet Young Things," in *Mademoiselle* (New York), June 1983.

"Sleep Tight," in *Ploughshares* (Cambridge, Massachusetts), vol. 15, no. 2-3, 1989.

*   *   *

Alice Hoffman's female protagonists have much in common. They are all drawn to dangerous men: a saboteur, a gang leader, a drug-dealing older brother, a nihilistic singer. They are all estranged from their parents, though most have strong relationships with their grandparents or someone of their grandparents' age. These older people are often fortunetellers of some kind. There is a strong undercurrent of magic in Hoffman's work.

In Hoffman's first novel, *Property Of,* the unnamed narrator attaches herself to McKay, a gang leader whose life is dedicated to the notion of honor as the gang had adapted it to the violent world of The Avenue, gang territory on the edge of New York City. When she leaves McKay it is because his glittering image and his honor have both crumbled. Hoffman brings almost nothing new to this old-hat situation, and only in the scattered passages where the narrator meditates on deeper things does her language come alive. The neo-hardboiled style dialogue is undermined by an unrealistic candor between characters who hardly know one another. Hoffman tries to pass this off as cool detachment, but it is clearly narrative strategy; a way to delineate character without much development. Hoffman's interest in ceremonial or ritual behavior, and in personal myth-making that will continue to be a part of all her work is present here, though muffled by the screen of toughness. There is also the first of many magic charms and talismans: a locket with a human tooth inside given the narrator by Monty, an older man who tries to look out for her.

Property Of's narrator, like many of Hoffman's women, seeks a life of magic. She contrasts the "little magic" of herbs and that nature that fights its way up through the concrete with the "big magic" of alcohol and drugs. "Difficult to categorize, until, of course, the consequences are seen. The little magic only causes a smile, but the big magic always seems to end up in the slammer or at a wake." In the last sentence of the novel she smiles.

The Drowning Season is the story of Esther the White and her granddaughter Esther the Black. The generation between these two women, Esther the Black's parents, are both lost: her father to his compulsion to drown himself every summer, and her mother to drink and dream of escape to the desert. Esther the White and the caretaker who loves her try to help the younger Esther come to grips with the emptiness of her life.

Like *The Drowning Season, Angel Landing* is set on the shore of a large cove. Two women live in a nearly empty boarding house across the bay from a nuclear plant under construction. When the plant is sabotaged the younger of the women, Natalie, discovers who "the bomber" is and finds herself falling in love with him. This "dangerous" man works his way through his feelings of alienation through his commitment to Natalie. Aunt Minnie, the older woman and owner of the boarding house, encourages Natalie in the relationship, even when she knows the man is "the bomber." As in *Property Of* the parts of this novel that are timely—the protesting over the nuclear plant, the struggle for better conditions in an old age home—clutter the story and add little. And again there is the unbelievable openness: Finn, the "bomber," who had been completely closed up, speaks his first emotionally committed words to Natalie in front of five strangers at a Thanksgiving dinner. After a *deus ex machina* helps Finn escape prosecution, he and Natalie run off to Florida, ending the novel on a hopeful but vague note.

White Horses is a difficult novel. The writing is as emotional and poetic as Hoffman's best work, but there is no character with which a reader might comfortably identify, or even sympathize. Aversion or pity are the likely responses. Young Teresa spends her life waiting for an "Aria," a mythical kind of outlaw lover, whose image has been passed down to her from her mother. The mother passes up real love while she waits, surrendering the myth only as she is dying. Both Teresa and her mother believe Teresa's brother Silver is an Aria, and Teresa enters into an incestuous relationship with him. Mother and daughter are both caught between the romance of the wild outlaw lover and the harsh life of attachment to the self-centered cruel Silver. Teresa breaks away from this destructive love only in the last pages.

Fortune's Daughter is a story of nurturing, and of "female mythology" as the jacket copy reads. Rae Perry is pregnant by a cruel and dangerous man, Jessup. Here the older woman Rae (who has cut herself off from her parents) turns to is Lila, a fortune-telling woman whose illegitimate daughter was given up at birth. She helps Rae, though her tea-leaf reading turns up the image of a dead baby. The dead child, however, turns out to be Lila's daughter, and Lila has to choose between isolating herself with the ("actual") ghost of her dead child, or giving it up and accepting her childless life with her supportive husband—who had a dangerous reputation when she met him. (In all Hoffman's novels women are the real movers, the instigators. The men run in circles raising dust, but accomplish little.) Lila chooses the living. Rae does not cut herself off completely from Jessup, and their relationship is left an open question at the novel's end.

Turtle Moon again invokes the theme of magic and mysticism, this time in a community of divorcees, Verity, Florida, a place where sea turtles migrate during the month of May. When the sea turtles mistake "the glow of streetlights for the moon, people go a little bit crazy;" marriages crumble and affairs begin. The story of Verity is the story of Lucy Rosen and her twelve-year-old son Keith, who find out just how bad life can be when the turtles migrate. A woman in Lucy's apartment building, also a runaway wife from New York, is murdered and Lucy's son rescues the victim's baby daughter and runs off, making him suspect in the murder. When Verity native Julian Cash investigates the murder and the missing children, he becomes romantically involved with Lucy, and another of Hoffman's female protagonists is drawn to a reckless man.

In *Second Nature,* there's a primal blend of the mysterious and the commonplace as compelling as the moon-besotted turtles found in *Turtle Moon.* Stephen and Robin are a modern-day Beauty and the Beast; Stephen, now an attractive man, was a feral child raised by wolves and Robin the woman who falls under his spell. It is when Robin tries to hide Stephen away in the small island community where she lives that the love story unfolds. By the end of the story the astute reader has taken Hoffman's foreshadowing as the inevitable ending of a good fairy tale, and the magic has worked again.

In Hoffman's eleventh novel, *Practical Magic,* another tale of love, the magic is not so much practical as predictable. As in earlier novels, Hoffman's older generation of characters are seers. Sally and Gillian are two orphaned sisters who live with their two aunts, women who grow strange herbs to make their magical brews and who are visited by lovesick women seeking their love potions and charms. Shunned by superstitious classmates, Sally and Gillian finally flee the small New England town in an attempt to flee the mysteries of love, which is always one step behind them. They cannot escape the magic of love and of life, even when it takes a malevolent form. Unlike earlier Hoffman stories, by the end of the story the overwhelming dose of magic becomes as hard to swallow as the aunts' mysterious love potions.

Hoffman seems content to rework her favored themes and ideas again and again, but usually manages to keep them fresh. Of the several tellings of the Hoffman story, *Fortune's Daughter* is surely the finest, with *The Drowning Season* not far behind. In attempting to keep her ideas always fresh, Hoffman's strengths at times seem to verge on self parody, seen occasionally in *At Risk* and *Seventh Heaven.*

—William C. Bamberger, updated by Sandra Ray

HOGAN, Desmond

Nationality: Irish. **Born:** Ballinasloe, County Galway, 10 December 1950. **Education:** Garbally College, Ballinasloe, 1964-69; University College, Dublin, 1969-73, B.A. in English and philosophy 1972, M.A. 1973. **Career:** Writer and actor with Children's T. Company theatre group, Dublin, 1975-77; moved to London, 1977: teacher, 1978-79; writer-in-residence, University of Glasgow, 1989. **Awards:** Hennessy award, 1971; Irish Arts Council grant, 1977; Rooney prize (USA), 1977; Rhys Memorial prize, 1980; *Irish Post* award, 1985. **Agent:** Rogers Coleridge and White Ltd., 20 Powis Mews, London W11 1JN, England.

PUBLICATIONS

Novels

The Ikon Maker. Dublin, Co-op, 1976; London, Writers and Readers, and New York, Braziller, 1979.
The Leaves on Grey. London, Hamish Hamilton, and New York, Braziller, 1980.
A Curious Street. London, Hamish Hamilton, and New York, Braziller, 1984.
A New Shirt. London, Hamish Hamilton, 1986.
The Edge of the City. London, Faber, 1993; Boston, Faber, 1994.
A Farewell to Prague. London, Faber, 1995.

Short Stories

The Diamonds at the Bottom of the Sea and Other Stories. London, Hamish Hamilton, 1979.
Children of Lir: Stories from Ireland. London, Hamish Hamilton, and New York, Braziller, 1981.
Stories. London, Pan, 1982.
The Mourning Thief and Other Stories. London, Faber, 1987; as *A Link with the River,* New York, Farrar Straus, 1989.

Plays

A Short Walk to the Sea (produced Dublin, 1975). Dublin, Co-op, 1979.
Sanctified Distances (produced Dublin, 1976).
The Ikon Maker, adaptation of his own novel (produced Bracknell, Berkshire, 1980).

Radio Play: *Jimmy,* 1978 (UK).

Television Play: *The Mourning Thief,* 1984 (UK).

* * *

The writings of Desmond Hogan testify to the strength of the creative impulse, and the fragility of those who carry it within them. In his novels and stories he depicts the struggles of isolated individuals to assert and define themselves in the face of social pressures. The tragedies he explores—whether set in rural Ireland or urban Britain—present a vision of human frailty, with characters unable to withstand the force of their own destructive passions and the smothering proprieties of the world. They are rendered vulnerable to attack by their fellows, succumbing to a collective psychological violence whose inevitable outcome is madness and suicide. The mental hospital and the dark depths of the river are images that recur constantly in Hogan's fiction. Equally common to his work are other images, the ikon objects used by his characters to give meaning to their lives.

The Ikon Maker, Hogan's first novel, describes the close, obsessional relationship between a mother and son in a remote part of Galway. Charting its growth from the boy's childhood, through the trauma of a friend's early death, and later through his travels among hippies, homosexuals, and IRA activists in England, Hogan portrays compellingly the son's desire for freedom and the fierce, all-consuming need of the mother who pursues him in a doomed effort to re-establish the original bond between them. Building up his narrative from a pattern of terse, fragmented sentences, the author draws the threads of plot neatly together, his style at once jagged and poetic. Diarmaid, the quiet, self-contained youth creating his own inner world through "ikons" of collage, and the mother struggling to suppress her rampant life-force, are both memorable. Here too, as elsewhere in his works, Hogan reveals the bleak, stultifying nature of life in rural Ireland, and its gradual change under the impact of the modern world with its television and terrorism.

The Leaves on Grey has as its central point the friendship ripening into love, of three privileged youngsters in 1950s Dublin. Growing up in a world where the ideals of the Easter Rising have already been betrayed, forming an elite distinct from their fellows, the three friends see themselves as being chosen for a noble destiny, prospective arbiters of their country's regeneration. Liam the mystic intellectual, Sarah with her religiously charged sexuality, and the narrator Sean together experience the varieties of love and loss, pursuing in their different ways the search for fulfillment. The suicide of Liam's mother, a beautiful Russian émigré, binds them closer, and shadows the course of their future lives. Hogan evokes with subtlety the characters and their shifting perceptions, and once more employs his "splintered" technique of short, sharp sentences to good effect. He also uses a device not unlike Joyce's epiphany, fixing on moments of revelation and insight which bridge chronological time and emphasize the continuity of human experience. (This device, as well as the fragmented style, is used later in the more ambitious *A Curious Street*). *The Leaves on Grey* contains the symbol which most appropriately sums up the nature of Hogan's art: the stained glass window, here the last act of creation by a dying artist, in which broken shards are fitted together and transformed by light into a vision of beauty, perfectly encapsulates the method—and the achievement—of this writer.

A Curious Street is arguably the most impressive of Hogan's novels. Taking as its beginning the suicide of Alan Mulvanney, a teacher and unpublished writer, in Athlone in 1977, the story is presented in the form of a memoir by its half-English narrator, son of the woman with whom Mulvanney enjoyed a brief, frustrating affair. Scanning these two lives and the lives of those closest to them, the narrative glides freely in and out of time, going back to explore previous generations, returning to touch on an intense three-fold friendship involving the narrator himself. The novel appears to expand outward, branching through families and friends, delving by way of Mulvanney's unpublished writings into the traumas of the past—the Cromwellian invasion, the devastating famine of the 1840s, the 1916 revolution. Hogan's treatment of his subject is nothing less than inspired. As ever, he constructs from broken splinters of sentences, adroitly marshalling his devices—potted "biographies" of his numerous characters, spreading outward from the novel's core, dream-vision passages from history and legend that still strike echoes in the modern Irish consciousness, the transcendent moment linking the experience of successive generations. *A Curious Street* probes at the purity and the loss of innocence, the brutal violence that lurks in family relationships, the destructive power of creativity. Images of the quest, of constant journeyings in search of peace through a wartorn land, and of the ever-present threat of death and madness haunt the pages. Recent writings yield fresh explorations of those themes central to the author's fiction, touching once more on vulnerability, alienation and exile, the struggle for self-assertion in the face of tribal disapproval. *The Mourning Thief and Other Stories* is perhaps the most accessible, childhood memories resurfacing in the flawed hero-figures of "Teddyboys" and "The Man from Korea". "Afternoon" gives a moving account of an ancient tinker queen's adventures, while the title story examines the conflict between a young pacifist and his dying father, a former I.R.A. activist now troubled by the bombings in the North. The stories of Lebanon Lodge provide further variations on the theme—the Irish-Jewish actor of the title-story recalling the birth and death of love from exile in England, the murderous response of a rural village to illicit love in "The Players", the fraught marriage of a Catholic beauty queen and her violent clergyman husband in "The Vicar's Wife". By turns gentle and savage, Hogan's vision challenges with undeniable conviction.

A Farewell to Prague shows the author at his least accessible and most complex. The novel follows its narrator, Des, in his wanderings through Europe and the United States, his dream-visions and reminiscences. Des recounts his bisexual love affairs, his bond with the unattainable Eleanor and the doomed Marek, who later dies of AIDS. Nightmare memories pervade the text, of World War II concentration camps and racial hatred, a scenario viewed as beginning again in wartorn Croatia. As always, Hogan builds his work from disparate visual images, bringing alive the wastelands and high-rise blocks of Prague, the desolation of rural Ireland, the dirt roads of Georgia. At the heart of his narrative is the quest for love, the fight to maintain the self against the tribal will. His distrust of the herd and its values is given perhaps its most ferocious expression to date: "Community leads to fascism, the swastikas in the churches, the lilies of the valley under Hitler." His positive images are of artistic creation, the familiar talismans of the stained glass window, the ancient Russian religious ikons. In these later works, as in all his writings, Hogan assembles the shards of experience to produce a literary ikon of his own, light shining through a sequence of moments seized from the passage of time.

—Geoff Sadler

HOLLINGHURST, Alan

Nationality: British. **Born:** Stroud, Gloucestershire, 26 May 1954.
Education: Magdalen College, Oxford, B.A. in English 1975,
M.Litt. 1979. **Career:** Lecturer of English, Magdalen College, 1977-
78; Somerville College, 1979-80, and Corpus Christi College,
1981, all Oxford University, and University of London, 1982; assistant editor, 1982-90, and since 1990 poetry editor, *Times Literary Supplement,* London, 1982-90. **Address:** c/o Times Literary
Supplement, Priory House, St. John's Lane, London EC1M 4BX,
England.

PUBLICATIONS

Novel

The Swimming-Pool Library. London, Chatto and Windus, 1988;
New York, Vintage, 1989.
The Folding Star. London, Chatto and Windus, and New York,
Pantheon, 1994.

Poetry

Confidential Chats with Boys. Oxford, Sycamore Press, 1982.

Other

Translator, *Bajazet,* by Jean Racine. London, Chatto and Windus,
1991.

*   *   *

With the publication of *The Swimming-Pool Library* in 1988,
British writer Alan Hollinghurst emerged as one of the most articulate voices in the expanding field of contemporary gay fiction.
The success of Hollinghurst's novel arose from its erotically
charged depiction of contemporary gay life in London, as well as
from its attempt to articulate that ever-elusive "gay sensibility" that
so many gay writers claim to understand but can never, it seems,
adequately describe.

Stylistically and thematically, Hollinghurst places his novel within
a richly intertextual framework of other gay texts, characters, events,
and literary traditions. The novel is peopled with various gay historical characters, such as E.M. Forster and Ronald Firbank, and it
draws eclectically upon various alternative forms of expression that
have historically served the clandestine needs of the gay community, such as camp, pink prose, and classical mythology. Throughout *The Swimming-Pool Library* echoes of other homosexual writers can be heard. These include, for example, the Genet-like encounter with a gang of skinheads, or the Firbank-like thematics
found in the novel's racist commodification of the black male body.
The novel's proliferation of witty aphorisms and anecdotes reminds
one of Wilde, while its meditative moments and search for sexual
identity are reminiscent of Proust.

The novel's narrative revolves around two historically separate,
yet thematically comparable, events that expose the continuity and
insidiousness of oppression used by British authorities against homosexuals throughout the last two centuries. When, for example,
the novel's modern-day protagonist is naively told that sexual op-

pression is no longer an issue and that it belongs to another time,
to "another world," he responds with what is surely the most important utterance of the novel: "it isn't another world . . . it's going
on in London almost every day." Oppression and bigotry, as
Hollinghurst's novel reveals, continued as frequently in Thatcher's
Britain as they did during any other place or time.

The central narrative takes place in London during the summer
of 1983, "the last summer of its kind," and describes, with tragicomic flourish, the amorous adventures of 25-year-old Will
Beckwith, whose primary concern, he writes, is "making passes at
anything in trousers." Hollinghurst's Will Beckwith, like White's
unnamed narrator and Andrew Holleran's Malone, is one of the
most memorable characters of recent gay fiction. That summer, Will
writes, "I was riding high on sex and self-esteem—it was my time,
my *belle époque.*" Egotistical and unreflective, Will lives a privileged life of luxury, supported by his wealthy grandfather. During
the course of the summer, Will meets an elderly and eccentric homosexual, Lord Charles Nantwich, and their unlikely alliance forms
the cornerstone of the novel's detective-like narrative. Will is commissioned by the older man to write his biography because, as a
character tells Will, "he thinks you will understand." In the process
of reading through Charles's journal entries Will discovers that in
1954 his own grandfather, as the former Director of Public Pros-
ecutions, was responsible for entrapping and imprisoning Charles,
along with many other homosexual men, for the sin of "male vice."
When a similar event happens to James, Will's best friend, he is
outraged and takes action to prevent history from cruelly repeating
itself: "I decided that if necessary, and if it might save James, I
would testify in court . . . and so perhaps do something, though
distant and symbolic, for Charles, and for Lord B's other victims."
In this act of defiance against his own grandfather, and, in turn,
against the whole legal system which suppresses homosexual expression, Will puts aside his over-developed ego for the first time
and becomes aware of his communal identity with other homosexuals. These "experiences," declares Will, "gave me an urge to
solidarity with my kind." The suffering of Charles and James ultimately serves as a catalyst for Will's own developing sense of responsibility and underscores the central theme of Hollinghurst's
novel: the journey toward liberation can only begin when one acknowledges a political responsibility to a community under siege.

Although *A Swimming-Pool Library* brilliantly achieved what the
author intended, it can never be granted the status of a "classic" in
general fiction. To achieve that universality, such a novel would
have to embody a world where gay and heterosexual characters,
including women, are integrated equally. Sexual description would
have to be balanced against the rather obvious, deliberate purpose
of much of *A Swimming-Pool Library,* and also his next novel, *A
Folding Star,* where one feels that Hollinghurst is aware of the market demands of readers whose main concern is the enjoyment of
gay erotic description. *A Swimming-Pool Library* partly delineated
a gay world where frequency of sex on demand was easily achieved
and nearly all the sexual partners were unrealistically physically
perfect—it was amongst the last fiction of its kind that could do
so. Since the advent of AIDS, the moral responsibility in writing
of safe sex became obligatory, something Hollinghurst is conscious
of in *A Folding Star.*

A Folding Star, with its exceptionally clear prose, is more impressive than Hollinghurst's first novel, for the charmed world of
the 1980s is replaced by a broader range of personalities as well as
more introspection. Hollinghurst also gives a welcome unblinkered
handling of his main character, Edward Manners: gay, physically

unattractive in his early thirties, and fond of a drink. The unrelenting ugliness of the Belgium town where Manners has arrived to teach English to two boys corresponds to Manners' hopeless and obsessional love for one of his pupils, the attractive and seventeen-year-old Luc Altidore. Hollinghurst's vivid account of the semi-underworld of gay life, represented here by a bar called "The Casette" and its inhabitants, is far less self-conscious than that of *A Swimming-Pool Library,* with more engaging and likeable characters. He also makes Manners a rounded portrait by relating flashbacks of his childhood experiences, often with comic humour and a strong awareness of the ridiculous. The circumstances of Edward Manners' love force him into repeated self-examination, as he knows he cannot yet escape the grip of this temporary insanity. He does have sex with Luc, an experience that has physical satisfaction but ridicules any hopes of love. The theme of loyalty and betrayal, traitors and victims, connects the main topic with the subplots. Although *A Folding* Star makes a significant contribution towards lifting gay fiction out of a narrow gay ghetto, it is not quite broad enough to escape limitations of the label of "genre writing."

—Thomas Hastings, updated by Geoffrey Elborn

HOOD, Hugh

Nationality: Canadian. **Born:** Hugh John Blagdon Hood in Toronto, Ontario, 30 April 1928. **Education:** De La Salle College, Toronto; St. Michael's College, University of Toronto, 1947-55, B.A. 1950, M.A. 1952, Ph.D. 1955. **Family:** Married Ruth Noreen Mallory in 1957; two sons and two daughters. **Career:** Teaching fellow, University of Toronto, 1951-55; associate professor, St. Joseph College, West Hartford, Connecticut, 1955-61; professor titulaire, Department of English Studies, University of Montreal, 1961-95. **Awards:** University of Western Ontario President's medal, for story, 1963, for article, 1968; Women's Canadian Club of Toronto Literary award, 1963; Beta Sigma Phi prize, 1965; Canada Council grant, 1968, award, 1971, 1974, and Senior Arts grant, 1977; Province of Ontario award, 1974; City of Toronto award, 1976; Queen's Jubliee medal, 1977; QSPELL award, 1988; 125th anniversary of Canadian Confederation medal, 1992; University of Montreal medal for distinguished service, 1995. Officer, Order of Canada, 1988. **Address:** 4242 Hampton Avenue, Montreal, Quebec H4A 2K9, Canada.

Publications

Novels

White Figure, White Ground. Toronto, Ryerson Press, and New York, Dutton, 1964.
The Camera Always Lies. New York, Harcourt Brace, 1967.
A Game of Touch. Don Mills, Ontario, Longman, 1970.
You Can't Get There from Here. Ottawa, Oberon Press, 1972; New York, Beaufort, 1984.
The New Age/Le nouveau siècle:
 The Swing in the Garden. Ottawa, Oberon Press, 1975.
 A New Athens. Ottawa, Oberon Press, 1977.
 Reservoir Ravine. Ottawa, Oberon Press, 1979.

 Black and White Keys. Downsview, Ontario, ECW Press, 1982.
 The Scenic Art. Toronto, Stoddart, 1984.
 The Motor Boys in Ottawa. Toronto, Stoddart, 1986.
 Tony's Book. Toronto, Stoddart, 1988.
 Property and Value. Toronto, Anansi, 1990.
Be Sure to Close Your Eyes. Toronto, Anansi, 1993.
Dead Men's Watches. Toronto, Anansi, 1995.
Five New Facts about Giorgione (novella). Windsor, Ontario, Black Moss Press, 1987.

Short Stories

Flying a Red Kite. Toronto, Ryerson Press, 1962.
Around the Mountain: Scenes from Montreal Life (sketches). Toronto, Peter Martin, 1967.
The Fruit Man, The Meat Man, and The Manager. Ottawa, Oberon Press, 1971.
Dark Glasses. Ottawa, Oberon Press, 1976.
Selected Stories. Ottawa, Oberon Press, 1978.
None Genuine Without This Signature. Downsview, Ontario, ECW Press, 1980.
August Nights. Toronto, Stoddart, 1985.
A Short Walk in the Rain. Erin, Ontario, Porcupine's Quill, 1989.
The Isolation Booth. Erin, Ontario, Porcupine's Quill, 1991.
You'll Catch Your Death. Erin, Ontario, Porcupine's Quill, 1992.

Play

Friends and Relations, in *The Play's the Thing: Four Original Television Dramas,* edited by Tony Gifford. Toronto, Macmillan, 1976.

Other

Strength Down Centre: The Jean Béliveau Story. Toronto, Prentice Hall, 1970.
The Governor's Bridge Is Closed: Twelve Essays on the Canadian Scene. Ottawa, Oberon Press, 1973.
Scoring: The Art of Hockey, illustrated by Seymour Segal. Ottawa, Oberon Press, 1979.
Trusting the Tale (essays). Downsview, Ontario, ECW Press, 1983.
Unsupported Assertions (essays). Concord, Ontario, Anansi, 1991.

Editor, with Peter O'Brien, *Fatal Recurrences: New Fiction in English from Montréal.* Montreal, Véhicule Press, 1984.

*

Bibliography: "A Bibliography of Works by and on Hugh Hood," in *Before the Flood: Our Examination round His Factification for Incamination of Hugh Hood's Work in Progress,* edited by J.R. (Tim) Struthers, Downsview, Ontario, ECW Press, 1979, and "Hugh Hood: An Annotated Bibliography" also by Struthers, in *The Annotated Bibliography of Canada's Major Authors: Volume Five,* edited by Robert Lecker and Jack David, Downsview, Ontario, ECW Press, 1984; "Hood, Hugh (1928-)" by Allan Weiss, in his *A Comprehensive Bibliography of English-Canadian Short Stories, 1950-1983,* Toronto, ECW Press, 1988.

Manuscript Collection: The University of Calgary Libraries, Alberta.

Critical Studies: "Grace: The Novels of Hugh Hood" by Dennis Duffy, in *Canadian Literature* 47, 1971; "An Interview with Hugh Hood," in *World Literature Written in English,* (11)1, 1972, and "An Interview with Hugh Hood," in *Le Chien d'or/The Golden Dog,* 3, 1974, both by Victoria G. Hale; "An Interview with Hugh Hood," in *Journal of Canadian Fiction* (2)1, 1973, and "Space, Time and the Creative Imagination" in *Journal of Canadian Fiction,* 3(1), 1974, both by Pierre Cloutier; "Hugh Hood and His Expanding Universe," in *Journal of Canadian Fiction,* 3(1), 1974, and "Formal Coherence in the Art of Hugh Hood" in *Studies in Canadian Literature,* 2, 1977, both by Kent Thompson; "An Interview with Hugh Hood" by Robert Fulford, in *The Tamarack Review,* 66, 1975; "Near Proust and Yonge: That's Where Hugh Hood Grew Up and Why He's Making a 12-Novel Bid for Immortality" by Linda Sandler, in *Books in Canada,* December 1975; *The Comedians: Hugh Hood and Rudy Wiebe* by Patricia A. Morley, Toronto, Clarke Irwin, 1977; "Hugh Hood and John Mills in Epistolary Conversation" by Hugh Hood and John Mills, in *The Fiddlehead,* 116, 1978; *Before the Flood: Our Exagmination round His Factification for Incamination of Hugh Hood's Work in Progress,* Downsview, Ontario, ECW Press, 1979, and *The Montreal Story Tellers: Memoirs, Photographs, Critical Essays,* Montreal, Véhicule Press, 1985, both edited by J.R. (Tim) Struthers; "Hugh Hood" in *Profiles in Canadian Literature,* edited by Jeffrey M. Heath, vol. 2, Toronto, Dundurn Press, 1980, and "A Secular Liturgy: Hugh Hood's Aesthetics and *Around the Mountain,*" in *Studies in Canadian Literature,* 10, 1985, both by Struthers; "The Case for Hugh Hood," in *An Independent Stance: Essays on English-Canadian Criticism and Fiction,* Erin, Ontario, Porcupine's Quill, 1991, and "The Atmosphere of Deception: Hugh Hood's 'Going Out as a Ghost'," in *Writers in Aspic,* edited by John Metcalf, Montreal, Véhicule Press, 1988, and "Hugh Hood," in *A Sense of Style: Studies in the Art of Fiction in English-Speaking Canada,* Toronto, ECW Press, 1989, all by W.J. Keith; "Hugh Hood's Celebration of the Millenium's End" by Geoff Hancock, in *Quill and Quire,* November 1980; "Field of Vision: Hugh Hood and the Tradition of Wordsworth" by Anthony John Harding, in *Canadian Literature,* 94, 1982; "'Incarnational Art': Typology and Analogy in Hugh Hood's Fiction" by Barry Cameron, in *The Fiddlehead,* 133, 1982; *On the Line: Readings in the Short Fiction of Clark Blaise John Metcalf and Hugh Hood* by Robert Lecker, Downsview, Ontario, ECW Press, 1982; "Tradition and Post-Colonialism: Hugh Hood and Martin Boyd" by Diana Brydon, in *Mosaic: A Journal for the Interdisciplinary Study of Literature,* 15(3), 1982; "Faith and Fiction: The Novels of Callaghan and Hood" by Barbara Helen Pell, in *Journal of Canadian Studies,* 18(2), 1983; *Hugh Hood* by Keith Garebian, Boston, Twayne, 1983; "Hugh Hood's Edenic Garden: Psychoanalysis Among the Flowerbeds" by Patrick J. Mahony with a reply by Hugh Hood, in *Canadian Literature,* 96, 1983; *Hugh Hood and His Works,* Toronto, ECW Press, 1985, and "Onward to the New Age," in *Books in Canada* October 1990, both by Keith Garebian; *Pilgrim's Progress: A Study of the Short Stories of Hugh Hood* by Susan Copoloff-Mechanic, Toronto, ECW Press, 1988; "On the Trail of Hugh Hood: History and the Holocaust in *Black and White Keys*" by Dave Little, in *Essays on Canadian Writing* 44, 1991; "Changing Metropolis and *Urbs Eterna:* Hugh Hood's 'The Village Inside'" by Simone Vauthier, in her *Reverberations: Explorations in the Canadian Short Story,* Concord, Ontario, House of Anansi Press, 1993; *Canadian Classics: An Anthology of Short Stories,* Toronto, McGraw-Hill Ryerson, 1993, and *How Stories Mean,* Erin, Ontario, Porcupine's Quill, 1993, both edited by John Metcalf and J.R. (Tim) Struthers; "A *Scriptible* Text" by John Mills, in *Essays on Canadian Writing* 50, 1993; "The History of Art and the Art of History: Hugh Hood's *Five New Facts About Giorgione*" by Alex Knoenagel, in *Mosaic: 27(1),* 1994.

Hugh Hood comments:

(1971) My interest in the sound of sentences, in the use of colour words and the names of places, in practical stylistics, showed me that prose fiction might have an abstract element, a purely formal element, even though it continued to be strictly, morally realistic. It might be possible to think of prose fiction the way one thinks of abstract elements in representational painting, or of highly formal music. . . . It's the seeing-into-things, the capacity for meditative abstraction, that interests me about philosophy, the arts and religious practice. I love most in painting an art that exhibits the transcendental element dwelling in living things. I think of this as true super-realism. And I think of Vermeer, or among American artists of Edward Hopper, whose paintings of ordinary places, seaside cottages, a roadside snack bar and gasoline station, have touched some level of my own imagination which I can only express in fictional images. . . . Like Vermeer or Hopper or that great creator of musical form, Joseph Haydn, I'm trying to concentrate on knowable form as it lives in the physical world. These forms are abstract, not in the sense of being inhumanly non-physical but in the sense of communicating the perfection of the essences of things—the formal realities that create things as they are in themselves. A transcendentalist must first study the things of this world, and get as far inside them as possible. . . . That is where I come out: the spirit is totally *in* the flesh. If you pay close enough attention to things, stare at them, concentrate on them as hard as you can, not just with your intelligence, but with your feelings and instincts, you will begin to apprehend the forms in them. . . . The illuminations in things are there, really and truly *there,* in those things. They are not run over then by the projective intelligence, and yet there is a sense in which the mind, in uniting itself to things, creates illumination in them. . . . The poetry of Wordsworth supplies us again and again with examples of this imaginative colouring spread over incidents and situations from everyday life. . . . Like Wordsworth, I have at all times endeavoured to look steadily at my subjects. I hope my gaze has helped to light them up.

(1978) I am trying to assimilate the mode of the novel to the mode of fully-developed Christian allegory, in ways that I don't fully understand. I want to be more "real" than the realists, yet more transcendent than the most vaporous allegorist. In short, I am following what I conceive the method of Dante. . . . Now let me put it to you that since I am *both* a realist and a *transcendentalist allegorist* that I cannot be bound by the forms of ordinary realism.

(1979) I think it would be marvellous for Canada if we had one artist who could move easily and in a familiar converse with Joyce, and Tolstoy, and Proust; and I intend to be that artist if I possibly can; and I am willing to give the rest of my life to it. I don't say that to put down Margaret Atwood or to make Margaret Laurence seem insignificant. That isn't my point at all. I want simply—and I think every artist does—to do what I think I can do as fully, and as powerfully, and as many-modally, and as exhaustively, as I can. . . . I really want to endow the country with a great imperishable work of art. If I do, it will be the first one that we have. I think it would make an enormous difference to the confidence of this country if we did have one thing like the plays of Shakespeare or *War and Peace* or *A la recherche du temps perdu,* and we knew it, and were sure of it. *Jalna,* ha, ha, won't do. It isn't good enough. I think that *The New Age* and the works of mine which go with it and around it *will* be good enough, and I think it will do a lot for the country.

(1995) I am now, February 1995, at work on the eleventh volume (of twelve) in the novel sequence *The New Age/Le nouveau siècle,* which I've been working on since I began to make notes for the project in late 1966. The first volume actually appeared, as *The Swing in the Garden,* in 1975, and the final book in the series is scheduled for publication at the end of 1999 when the "new age" will really be directly in front of us as new century and new millenium. At this moment I can feel myself beginning to wonder how it will feel to write the closing page. Now I can suspect what Gibbon, Proust, and Joyce of *Finnegans Wake* (17 years in the making) must have gone through towards the end, an end that Proust unfortunately never saw. Temptations and distractions of a long work!

*   *   *

Hugh Hood is a writer in whom pedantry wars with creative gifts of a high order. His best work so far occurs in his short stories which demonstrate his mastery at revealing what is immense through what is small. He is an indefatigable explorer of human aspiration, conveying much of its mystery, heroism, and comedy. An impassioned drive towards some symbolic victory is celebrated seriously or gaily in such stories as "Silver Bugles, Cymbals, Golden Silks" (*Flying a Red Kite*), "The Pitcher" (*Dark Glasses*), and "Le Grand Déménagement" (*Around the Mountain*). His art is at its finest in "Looking Down from Above" (*Around the Mountain*), where separate characters connect in a visionary moment of great beauty, crowded like a medieval tapestry with life: "inscrutable but undeniable."

Hood's earlier novels have something of this imaginative intensity, as in the burning warehouse scene (*A Game of Touch*), an incident pivotal to the hero's fate and a keystone in the novel's structure. However, Hood is unable to control the tone of his prose over the long course of a novel. When the painter in *White Figure, White Ground* retreats to the safety of his old manner and family life, Hood's point of view is unclear. Although the hard urbanity and narrow sympathies of the wife offend, it is uncertain whether the artist's glorification of her is to be received with irony or approval. In *The Camera Always Lies,* a romance, Hood's continuing problem with creating likable characters re-emerges. A romance requires archetypal figures on whom fantasies can be projected: yet "virtuous" Rose Leclair, suffering through near-death and rebirth, is a bore, the hero who saves her an overbearing prig. Precise detail of film financing, production, and costume design merely throws into relief Hood's difficulty with his characters. *You Can't Get There from Here,* set in an imaginary African nation, is both a study of struggle in a new society and "Christological [except] . . . that the Christ figure does not rise again. . . ." Because he is writing satire and allegory, Hood must be excused for missing opportunities of further defining the two tribes, and of describing the personal history of his sketchy hero; but his Cabinet villains need sharper outlines to succeed either as allegory or satire.

When Hood attempts in *The New Age,* a serial novel in twelve volumes of which eight have been completed, to work on the scale of "Coleridge, Joyce, Tolstoy, and Proust," his inadequacies become obvious. He is striving for "a very wide range of reference without apparent connection on the surface which nonetheless will yield connections and networks and links and unities if you wait and allow them to appear." Moving back and forth through time, the huge project includes passages of philosophy, social history, topography, and lectures on a broad variety of topics, as well as the fictionalized incidents of his own life.

As a simultaneous "realist and transcendental allegorist" (his admitted aim), Hood falls short in these novels, for although characters and events have a formal importance, they rarely achieve emotive significance. The marriage in *A New Athens,* for instance, is never felt as the redemptive force intended, because Edie is no more than a shadow, and Matt Goderich remains, as one character observes, "a pompous ass." Too often Hood offers neither psychological nor pictorial realism, but the factuality of an encyclopedia or a catalogue. Obsessive lists of, for example, baseball players (*The Swing in the Garden*) suggest an inability to select. Local history and neighborhood cartography too often supply the substance rather than the raw material of these fictions. Pedantic tenacity in description cannot of itself invest places or objects with meaning, nor is Hood's style sufficiently adept, usually, to produce this result by its own power. He even slips into bathos with the showpiece engagement scenes in *A New Athens* and *Reservoir Ravine.* His uninspired prose has created a bland, provincial world where values do not develop organically, but are imposed from without. Only when he writes of marvels does the reader's interest freshen, as with the appearance of the visionary painter (*A New Athens*). Striving to write a masterpiece, Hood is so concerned with large patterns and themes that he fails to breathe life into the material of which these patterns are composed. Heterogeneity can succeed only for the writer gifted enough to consume disparate materials in the unifying fire of his art; but, with one third of the sequence still to come, Hood may yet produce work on a level comparable to that of the short stories.

Of course critical assessments may vary strikingly from one person to another; indeed, judgments frequently say as much about readers' assumptions as they do about writers' achievements. Perhaps genius needs to create—that is, to educate—its own audience, an audience that appreciates and quite possibly revels in the idiosyncrasies that some readers find disconcerting. A number of volumes so far in Hood's sequence, including *The Swing in the Garden, A New Athens, Black and White Keys, Property and Value,* and *Dead Men's Watches,* have been received with considerable enthusiasm by individual reviewers and critics. With time—and with the altered understanding that further attention, different assumptions, and a broader perspective can bring—*The New Age* may win the distinguished audience that its advocates believe it deserves. With the completion of the last two of twelve volumes as we reach a new millenium, the overall design and the inner workings of the sequence will certainly become clearer. Perhaps then *The New Age* will stand as Hood envisioned it twenty-five years earlier: "I hope it will be an enormous image, an enormous social mythology, an enormous prism to rotate, to see yourself and your neighbors and friends and your grandparents."

—Margaret Keith, updated by J.R. (Tim) Struthers

HOPE, Christopher

Nationality: South African. **Born:** Christopher David Tully Hope in Johannesburg, 26 February 1944; moved to Europe in 1975.

Education: Christian Brothers College, Pretoria, 1952-60; University of the Witwatersrand, Johannesburg, 1963-65, B.A. 1965, M.A. in English 1970; University of Natal, Durban, 1968-69, B.A. (honours) 1969. **Military Service:** Served in the South African Navy, 1962. **Family:** Married Eleanor Marilyn Klein in 1967; two sons. **Career:** English teacher, Halesowen Secondary Modern School, 1972; editor, *Bolt,* Durban, 1972-73; writer-in-residence, Gordonstoun School, Elgin, Morayshire, 1978. Lives in London. **Awards:** English Academy of Southern Africa Pringle award, 1974; Cholmondeley award, for poetry, 1978; David Higham prize, 1981; Natal University Petrie Arts award, 1981; Silver Pen award, 1982; Arts Council bursary, 1982; Whitbread award, 1985; CNA award, 1989. Fellow, Royal Society of Literature. **Agent:** Deborah Rogers, Rogers Coleridge and White Ltd., 20 Powis Mews, London W11 1JN, England.

PUBLICATIONS

Novels

A Separate Development. Johannesburg, Ravan Press, 1980; London, Routledge, and New York, Scribner, 1981.
Kruger's Alp. London, Heinemann, 1984; New York, Viking, 1985.
The Hottentot Room. London, Heinemann, 1986; New York, Farrar Straus, 1987.
My Chocolate Redeemer. London, Heinemann, 1989.
Serenity House. London, Macmillan, 1992.

Short Stories

Private Parts and Other Tales. Johannesburg, Bateleur Press, 1981; London, Routledge, 1982; as *Learning to Fly,* London, Minerva, 1990.
Black Swan (novella). London, Hutchinson, and New York, Harper, 1987.
The Love Songs of Nathan J. Swirsky. London, Macmillan, 1993.

Uncollected Short Stories

"Carnation Butterfly," in *London Magazine,* April-May 1985.
"Strydom's Leper," in *Colours of a New Day: Writing for South Africa,* edited by Sarah Lefanu and Stephen Hayward. London, Lawrence and Wishart, and New York, Pantheon, 1990.

Plays

Radio Plays: *Box on the Ear,* 1987; *Better Halves,* 1988.

Television Plays: *Ducktails,* 1976; *Bye-Bye Booysens,* 1979; *An Entirely New Concept in Packaging,* 1983.

Poetry

Whitewashes, with Mike Kirkwood. Privately printed, 1971.
Cape Drives. London, London Magazine Editions, 1974.
In the Country of the Black Pig and Other Poems. Johannesburg, Ravan Press, and London, London Magazine Editions, 1981.
Englishmen. London, Heinemann, 1985.

Other

The King, The Cat, and the Fiddle (for children), with Yehudi Menuhin. Tonbridge, Kent, Benn, and New York, Holt Rinehart, 1983.
The Dragon Wore Pink (for children). London, A. and C. Black, and New York, Atheneum, 1985.
White Boy Running: A Book about South Africa. London, Secker and Warburg, and New York, Farrar Straus, 1988.
Moscow! Moscow! London, Heinemann, 1990.

Editor, *Life Class: Thoughts, Exercises, Reflections of an Itinerant Violinist,* by Yehudi Menuhin. London, Heinemann, 1986.

*

Christopher Hope comments:

Writing has always seemed to me to be a rather mischievous occupation. I write not to change the world but to undermine it, since the models on offer seem pretty dull most of the time. Much of life is odd and disorganized. Many people who pretend to be sure about things are either ingenuous or wicked. They are also often charlatans. One wants to record their utterances as a warning to others.

I was lucky enough to grow up in South Africa, a place where the lethal folly of what everyone assured me was "normal" life outstripped even the most audacious imaginations. For a writer, this was wonderful training. It taught me about the sheer inventiveness of life. And it gave me a subject—the triumph of power and the terminal comedy provided by those who wield it.

*   *   *

Christopher Hope is a leading example of an important new group of white South African writers who have broken free of the traditional mold of liberal realism in South African fiction. These writers have cast off the predictable and often sterile tones of superior intellectual humanism or impassioned but helpless outrage against apartheid. Seen against the seriousness and moral sanctimony of the liberal idiom, Hope's writing is positively liberating. His vision is black, wicked, and surreal, and his satire and humor have a measure of viciousness which seems peculiarly appropriate to South Africa. In the case of two of his novels, *A Separate Development* and *Kruger's Alp,* one feels that here, at last, is a writer who has the measure of the system; who, indeed, has found a language of fiction which matches the system point by point for ruthlessness, power, subtlety, and the ability to knock down targets.

Hope, who has been living in voluntary exile in London since 1976, has also published several volumes of poetry and a collection of short stories, *Private Parts.* In the stories, as in the novels, Hope's unusual blend of familiar reality and bizarre, surreal inventiveness is apparent. Increasingly in his fiction, Hope has created a special space for himself halfway between the real and the bizarre, showing how interchangeable these categories are and establishing newly capacious and flexible fictional conventions for himself.

Like Herman Charles Bosman and Tom Sharpe before him, Hope demonstrates how endlessly funny South African life is when seen from a great and merciless distance. In *A Separate Development* the notions of mixed blood and miscegenation, so tragically dealt with by such South African heavyweights as Sarah Gertrude Millin and Alan Paton, not to mention André Brink, become a mainspring for blackish and farce-filled comedy. The novel's young first-person narrator, Harry Moto, thrives on irony and absurdity. He has little choice, having grown up as a white South African and then being forced to take refuge as a "black" denizen of Johannesburg. Moto scrambles the categories: his darkish skin and somewhat frizzy hair suggest certain irregularities in his ancestry, and through no fault of his own he becomes a comic victim. In Harry Moto, Hope achieves what has always remained impossible for South African writers in their more serious efforts: to combine or unify black and white experience in a country which reduces such unification to a fictional pipe-dream. By discarding the heavy mantle of serious liberalism, Hope happily indulges in that pipe-dream. Moto, who has grown up spending idle hours around swimming pools and ruminating about sex, finally goes "black" under the weight of neurotic moral condemnation because he was caught in an advanced state of intimacy with a wealthy white girl at a school-leaving dance. Given Harry's hue of skin, this situation is humiliatingly close to sexual immorality, and Harry faces absolute disapproval from his parents, who see in him tangible evidence of their deep psychological fears about mixed blood. Harry disappears to become a black, working first as a runner for an Indian clothing merchant, and later as a "living proof" assistant to a man who sells skin-lightening creams to infinitely deluded blacks. He ends up as the invisible "boy" collecting trays from cars at a roadhouse, and finally as a detainee writing his story to stay alive.

If *A Separate Development* is an unusually deft first novel, then *Kruger's Alp* is a truly remarkable effort for a second novel. More "serious" in effect, the novel demonstrates literary artifice and fictional inventiveness of masterful proportions. Hope combines modern political mystery with historical myth, revelatory allegorical structure with acid-strength satire. This amalgam is based on a wide vision of present and past South African experience, in which social and historical myth is reformulated and given new meaning. Hope's principal point of reference in this novel is John Bunyan's *The Pilgrim's Progress*. As in Bunyan's allegory, there is a dream of revelation as a narrative vehicle, a physical journey of discovery and a mythic destination. Like Bunyan's Christian, Hope's main protagonist, Blanchaille (white-bait), is obsessed with the idea of escape. Whereas Christian is filled with a sense of doom because he realizes that "our city will be burned with fire from heaven," Blanchaille is envisioned as experiencing the acute anxiety of a "despised sub-group within a detested minority [waiting] for the long-expected wrath to fall on them and destroy them." Blanchaille's anxiety is fueled by the news that a former friend of his, a top fiscal official, has been murdered, apparently by his own government for political reasons.

As boys, Blanchaille and the murdered official, Tony Ferreira, both served under a prophesying and idiosyncratic Irish priest, Father Lynch. Lynch was obsessed with and preached the truth of the missing Kruger millions, a great hoard of gold which the Boer War president of the Transvaal republic, Paul Kruger, is reputed to have taken away with him into exile in Switzerland. As interpreted in this novel, Kruger is supposed to have established a "shining city" ("celestial city" in *The Pilgrim's Progress*) for white South Africans seeking an ultimate haven after lifetimes of trekking. Ferreira was killed because he uncovered massive irregular spending on huge projects to buy world opinion (the situation is closely modeled on the Information Scandal which rocked South Africa in the late 1970s), and these efforts to find a haven in world opinion constitute only one of several equivalents of the Kruger myth. Blanchaille is set off by Father Lynch on an allegorical journey of

revelation to Kruger's "white location in the sky" in Switzerland. It is a journey which goes backwards and forwards at the same time, into the heart of the mythic secrets of white South African existence. The Kruger refuge is recognizable as the mythic basis of an escape syndrome cutting across all periods and categories in white South African history. The notion of pilgrims seekings a promised land remains a key interpretation of this history, today as much as in earlier times.

In *The Hottentot Room* a group of South African exiles find a fellow sufferer in Frau Katie, a German Jew and refugee from Nazi Germany. Frau Katie presides over the Hottentot Room, a London club for South African expatriates. The novel's protagonist, Caleb Looper, is an expatriate who joins the club, but he is a spy for the South African regime, while the habitués of the club are enslaved to illusions about themselves and their former homeland. These illusions, as well as the secret of betrayal in their midst, all find a correlative, or mythical resonance, in Frau Katie's story. But there is self-deception at the heart of *her* sustaining myth, and a complementary self-deception in all the "Hottentots" who use her story for their own ends. The novel is an intricately patterned fable which says much about the condition of exile, but the artifice often protrudes uncomfortably—a constant damper for a novelist as inventive as Hope.

Hope's next work, a novella *Black Swan,* exhibits his satirical and ironic skill at its pared-down best. The story of an idiosyncratic black township boy who wants to be a ballet dancer but is eventually executed as an enemy of the state is a superb example of Hope's ability to create fictions which reveal the victory of the cruel over the poignant in South African life.

Hope's most recent novel, *My Chocolate Redeemer,* tells the story of a friendship between a French-English girl and the deposed head of a black African state. It is set in France and a fictional African country called Zanj, and relies heavily on principles borrowed from the New Physics about truth being a function of observation. It would appear as though Hope may be trying to move away from South Africa as subject matter, but *My Chocolate Redeemer* has little in it to maintain interest or arouse excitement. It lacks Hope's usual ironic punch, and survives merely as an odd but forgettable novel by an excellent writer. One hopes that the dislocations of voluntary exile are not beginning to take a toll on this writer.

—Leon de Kock

HOSPITAL, Janette Turner

Nationality: Australian. **Born:** Melbourne, Victoria, 12 November 1942. **Education:** The University of Queensland, St. Lucia, Brisbane, B.A. in English 1965; Queen's University, Kingston, Ontario, M.A. 1973. **Family:** Married Clifford G. Hospital in 1965; one son and one daughter. **Career:** Teacher, Queensland, 1963-66; librarian, Harvard University, Cambridge, Massachusetts, 1967-71; lecturer in English, Queen's University, and St. Lawrence College, Kingston, Ontario, 1971-82. Since 1982 full-time writer. Writer-in-residence, Massachusetts Institute of Technology, Cambridge, 1985-86, 1987, 1989; University of Ottawa, Ontario, 1987; University of Sydney, New South Wales, 1989; La Trobe University, Melbourne, Australia, 1990-93; Boston University, fall 1991; adjunct professor of English, La Trobe University, 1990-93. Lived in the United States, 1967-71, and India, 1977, and 1990. Currently divides year between Australia, Boston, and Paris. **Awards:** Seal award (Canada), 1982; Atlantic First citation from Atlantic Monthly, 1978; CDC Literary Prize, for short story, 1986; Fellowship of Australian Writers Fiction award, 1988; Torgi award, Canadian Association for the Blind, 1988; Australian National Book Council award, 1989. **Agent:** Jill Hickson Associates, P.O. Box 271, Woollahra, New South Wales 2025, Australia; or, Molly Friedrich,, Literary Agent, 708 Third Ave., 23rd Floor, New York, New York 10017, U.S.A.

PUBLICATIONS

Novels

The Ivory Swing. Toronto, McClelland and Stewart, 1982; New York, Dutton, and London, Hodder and Stoughton, 1983.
The Tiger in the Tiger Pit. Toronto, McClelland and Stewart, 1983; New York, Dutton, and London, Hodder and Stoughton, 1984.
Borderline. Toronto, McClelland and Stewart, New York, Dutton, and London, Hodder and Stoughton, 1985.
Charades. St. Lucia, University of Queensland Press, 1988; New York and London, Bantam, 1988.
A Very Proper Death (as Alex Juniper). Melbourne, Penguin, 1990; New York, Scribner, 1991.
The Last Magician. London, Virago, and New York, Holt, 1992.

Short Stories

Dislocations. Toronto, McClelland and Stewart, 1986; Baton Rouge, Louisiana State University Press, 1988.
Isobars. St. Lucia, University of Queensland Press, 1990; Baton Rouge, Louisiana State University Press, 1991; London, Virago, 1992.

*

Critical Studies: Introduction by Helen Daniel to *Virago Modern Classics* edition of *Borderline,* 1990; Janette Turner Hospital issue of LINQ Magazine, (Queensland, Australia), 17(1) 1990; "Recent Australian Writing: Janette Turner Hospital's Borderline" by Michael Wilding, in *Working Papers in Australian Studies,* Australian Studies Center, University of London, 1988; "The Commonplace of Foreignness: the Fictions of Janette Turner Hospital" by Sabrina Achilles, in *Editions,* (Sydney), 1989; "Charades: Searching for Father Time: Memory and the Uncertainty Principle" by Sue Gilett, in *New Literature's Review* (Australia), 21, Summer 1991; "Janette Turner Hospital" by Elspeth Cameron in *Profiles in Canadian Literature, No. 8,* edited by Jeffrey M. Heath, Toronto, Dundum Press, 1991.

Janette Turner Hospital comments:

In childhood, I felt like a space voyager, traveling daily between two alien worlds, daily mediating between them, decoding mutually unintelligible sign systems, an instinctive semiotician from the age of six. This was the result of growing up within a subculture of evangelical fundamentalist Pentecostalism (in which almost everything was forbidden to me) within the wider culture (encountered at school each day) of boisterous working-class anti-religious subtropical Australia. The incantatory rhythms of the King James version of the bible (especially the Psalms), read aloud at the fam-

ily dinner-table every night for the first 20 years of my life until I left home, are a dominant influence on my prose, as are the jagged, irreverent, piquant, slangy bush-ballad rhythms of working-class Australia. My weirdly cross-cultural childhood turned out to be a good rehearsal for the rest of my life, which, by happenstance (economic, academic, and marital) rather than by deliberate choice, has been culturally nomadic. I have lived for extended periods of time in the U.S.A., Canada, India, and England, although for some time I have been spending an increasing portion of each year back in Australia, and the drift of things is toward a permanent return.

All my writing, in a sense, revolves around the mediation of one culture (or subculture) to another. Wherever I am, I live about equally (in terms of company kept and haunts frequented) in the rarefied academic/literary/cultural worlds and the netherworlds of working-class pubs/cops/street people/gutter people (with, I must confess, an instinctive preference for the latter). I mix easily in both worlds, I switch accent and idiom easily. I have, in general, (there are always individual exceptions on both sides), a higher moral opinion of the denizens of the netherworld than of pillars of the community.

My first novel *The Ivory Swing,* was written after a period of living in a village in South India and explored the fact that, regardless of the degree to which educated and enlightened individuals of western and Asian cultures bend over backwards to understand and appreciate one another, there are certain basic and intractable differences that, given a particular course of events, will result in insoluble dilemmas and cataclysms. Since then, all my novels and short stories have explored the same basic situation of clashing perspectives (particularly the clash between the socially favored and the disempowered) but have stayed within a western framework.

The themes of dislocation and connection are constant in my work. So are the themes of moral choice and moral courage. I am always putting my characters into situations of acute moral dilemma (this encompasses the political), to find out what they will do. This is, it seems to me, the question of maximum interest about the human species: what will she, or he, do under extreme pressure? The attempt to find a fictional form which will bridge the disparate worlds I explore has meant that I have often seen myself categorized as "postmodernist." I don't object to this, except that I am disturbed when I read Terry Eagleton, a critic whom I esteem, extolling modernism but finding postmodernism morally nihilistic. I object. (His definition of the term is too narrow). I have passionate moral and political commitments (though I like to feel that these can be surmised but cannot be precisely located in my work. I would like to think that my writing forces the reader to make inner moral and political choices and alignments, but does not tell the reader what such alignments should be).

Stylistically, I probably have more in common with poets and formalists than with other politically *engagé* writers and postmodernists. Words, images, rhythms are of major sensual importance to me. I have an erotic relationship with language. (Ironically, this goes back to those family bible readings. The stern prophets of the Old Testament were voluptuous with words.) I am a feminist who has frequently been trashed by literary "career feminists." I am, it seems, "ideologically unsound." Apparently I'm much too exuberant about female sexuality, seeking, for example, to redeem and reclaim words like "slut;" and much too fond of male characters.

All labels, in fact, are a bad fit. I'm a maverick and a guerrilla.

*   *   *

Janette Turner Hospital's work is intellectually sophisticated writing which spirals through mysteries and indeterminacies but never loosens its tug on the senses. Much of her work is about the borderlines of things, of art and self, of time and space, borders which curve and mutate, shimmering and chimerical. Intellectually compelling yet fiery and dynamic, her work is baroque, elegant yet with a sensuous energy and immediacy.

Hospital is a writer of many places—Canada, Boston, India, Australia and the Queensland rainforests. The workings of dislocation and rivalries of place shape much of her work. Time doubles back and places overlap, as memories cluster and jostle. In her two powerful short story collections, *Dislocations* and *Isobars,* the Australian landscape underlies the icy surface of Canada, memories of Queensland surface in multiple exposure. In *Isobars,* many of the stories are littoral, on beaches and shores, in the surf of memory and underwater memories wait to surface unbidden. Isobar lines of memory run through time and space, linking continents and eras in unexpected conjunctions.

While her major novels are *Borderline* and *Charades,* Hospital's earlier novels are assured, polished and crisp. In her first, *The Ivory Swing,* borderlines of time and place are already blurred and reality is serpentine. Living in a South Indian village with her husband, Juliet is besieged by memories of Canada and her lover. Caught up in conflicts of Indian proprieties and rigidities, Juliet swings between two worlds, shackled by her own conflicting impulses. In *The Tiger in the Tiger Pit,* her second novel, through the interwoven voices of a family, memories and dissonant images of the past break through into the present. Through the family's gathering for a golden wedding anniversary, Hospital explores the nature of familial wounds and damage persisting through time. The voices of the children and the parents run discordant through change and loss, dream and fear, but through a musical metaphor, the novel becomes the composition of a family symphony, reaching through themes of harmony towards celebration and hope.

Themes of coevality, damage persisting through time, and time as a cycle or a somersault, run throughout Hospital's work. Her third novel, *Borderline,* is an outstanding work, a tense and intense mystery thriller about boundaries and borders of art, reality, fiction, perception, dream, vision, and memory. Through contestant versions of events runs a sense of sinister forces at work in mysterious ways, clandestine agencies within a Dantesque vision of urban worlds. Here dreams intersect, as if the characters have stumbled into one another's dreams and are locked now in the frames of one another's worlds.

From the beginning when a refrigerated truck carrying illegal immigrants is stopped at the Canada-US border, mysteries entangle Gus, the insurance salesman, and Felicity, art historian and curator of a private gallery. Chance accomplices, they are caught up in the consequences of smuggling one woman across the border—Dolores Marquez, La Magdalena, (also known as La Desconocida, the unknown or unknowable one) whose image becomes an icon with shifting patterns of meaning. The mysteries run serpentine: La Magadalena's fate after her disappearance, the identity of a murdered woman, the identity of Hunter, the sinister figure who pursues Felicity, and the secret Salvadoran organization in hiding from the immigration authorities.

While the narrative moves forward with tightening intrigue, Hospital undermines its movement with contestant notions of art and truth. The narrator, Jean-Marc, is reconstructing events prior to the disappearance of Gus and Felicity. A piano tuner, he links the art of "tempering" to his construction of narrative, attuning dynamics and harmonics of meaning. Within the multiple frames of the narrative, Borgesian possibilities shimmer in front of the reader: the possibility that the whole grows out of Felicity's memory of a Perrugino painting, and her nightmarish images of herself being entrapped within the frames of paintings. Between narrator and Felicity run Borgesian notions of the dreamer being dreamed. The novel becomes an extraordinary blend of the political and the postmodern, moving in and out of memory, dream, the guises and masks of self, the borders of truth, art and imagination, while sustaining subtle and tense mysteries.

In *Charades,* Hospital draws on the logic of quantum physics, tempering paradoxes of meaning, the whole a graceful and sinuous work, always compelling. Here nothing is fixed, not time, not history, not even matter, which is "one of our most persistent illusions." The novel is a world of correspondences, of synchronicity and Borgesian dreaming, a world which keeps recreating itself—a fine-spun web of tales, in which the tale-telling opens up mysteries of time and meaning.

Throughout the novel, Hospital traffics in quantum notions of space and time, and Heisenberg's principle of uncertainty, proposing the *necessity* of uncertainty. There are rippling notions of the self as a hologram, supernova occurrences, the event horizon, wave and particle theories, complementarity, all of which are combined with the age-old tradition of tale-telling, of Scheherazade and the Thousand and One Nights. Charade's tales are told to her lover, the Boston physicist, Koenig, over the nights of a year plus one. Through the tales, the novel becomes both a series of tangled mysteries and a dynamic portrayal of Charade's own past in Queensland, growing up in the Queensland rainforests. Charade herself intrigues: chameleon, wry, commanding, her mind leaping, with a baroque intelligence. She seems to Koenig a hologram figure, a presence of lucent spirals and hairlines of light. Perhaps he has invented Charade, or they are figures in dreams, or perhaps she is a configuration of his guilt which comes in "a thousand and one guises and plays many games." The novel has a pervasive sense of the past pushing its consequences through into the present in a meditation on time and reprieve.

Charades becomes a mystery of origins—of Charade herself, of the universe, of story, and in a muted way the origins of Australia. The novel has a lucid inventiveness, dancing through curves and loops of uncertainty and contingency, curving through paradoxes and circles of meaning, holding contradictory notions in easy conjunction, with coincidences clustering around obsessions in weird and wonderful ways. Tales, memories, imaginings, illusions, even legends, all cluster together in a tangled hierarchy of "planes and spheres and tales which can never intersect." Charged with energy, Hospital's work has sheen and elegance, as she explores contradictions of time and space, through rivalries and revenants, transgressing boundaries of self, art, and figure.

—Helen Daniel

HOWARD, Elizabeth Jane

Nationality: British. **Born:** London, 26 March 1923. Educated privately; trained as an actress at the London Mask Theatre School and with the Scott Thorndike Student Repertory; acted in Stratford-on-Avon, and in repertory theatre in Devon. **Military Service:**

Served as an air raid warden in London during World War II. **Family:** Married 1) Peter M. Scott in 1942 (divorced 1951), one daughter; 2) James Douglas-Henry in 1959 (divorced); 3) Kingsley Amis, *q.v.,* in 1965 (divorced 1983). **Career:** Worked as a model, and in radio and television broadcasting, 1939-46; secretary, Inland Waterways Association, London, 1947-50; editor, Chatto and Windus Ltd., London, 1953-56, and Weidenfeld and Nicolson Ltd., London, 1957; book critic, *Queen* magazine, London, 1957-60. Honorary artistic director, Cheltenham Literary Festival, 1962; co-artistic director, Salisbury Festival, 1973. Fellow, Royal Society of Literature. Lives in Suffolk. **Awards:** Rhys Memorial prize, 1951; *Yorkshire Post* award, 1983. **Agent:** Jonathan Clowes Ltd., Iron Bridge House, Bridge Approach, London NW1 8BD, England.

PUBLICATIONS

Novels

The Beautiful Visit. London, Cape, and New York, Random House, 1950.
The Long View. London, Cape, and New York, Reynal, 1956.
The Sea Change. London, Cape, 1959; New York, Harper, 1960.
After Julius. London, Cape, 1965; New York, Viking Press, 1966.
Something in Disguise. London, Cape, 1969; New York, Viking Press, 1970.
Odd Girl Out. London, Cape, and New York, Viking Press, 1972.
Getting It Right. London, Hamish Hamilton, and New York, Viking Press, 1982.
The Light Years. London, Macmillan, and New York, Pocket Books, 1990.
Making Time. London, Macmillan, and New York, Pocket Books, 1991.
Confusion. London, Macmillan, and New York, Pocket Books, 1993.

Short Stories

We Are for the Dark: Six Ghost Stories with Robert Aickman. London, Cape, 1951.
Mr. Wrong. London, Cape, 1975; New York, Viking Press, 1976.

Plays

Screenplays: *The Very Edge,* 1963; *Getting It Right,* 1989.

Television Plays: *The Glorious Dead (Upstairs, Downstairs* series), 1974; *Skittles (Victorian Scandals* series), 1976; *Sight Unseen (She* series), 1977; *After Julius,* from her own novel, 1979; *Something in Disguise,* from her own novel, 1980.

Other

Bettina: A Portrait, with Arthur Helps. London, Chatto and Windus, and New York, Reynal, 1957.
Howard and Maschler on Food, with Fay Maschler. London, Joseph, 1987.
Cooking for Occasion, with Fay Macshler. London, Macmillan, 1994.

Editor, *The Lover's Companion: The Pleasure, Joys, and Anguish of Love.* Newton Abbot, Devon, David and Charles, 1978.

Editor, *Green Shades: An Anthology of Plants, Gardens, and Gardeners.* London, Aurum Press, 1990.

*

Elizabeth Jane Howard comments:

I consider myself to be in the straight tradition of English novelists. I do not write about "social issues or values"—I write simply about people, by themselves and in relation to one another. The first aim of a novel should be readability. I do not write (consciously, at least) about people whom I know or have met.

My methods are to be able to write in one sentence what my novel is to be about, to test this idea for several months, and then to invent situations that will fit the theme. I make the people last—to suit the situations. I write only one draught and rarely make any alterations to it. Occasional cutting has sometimes seemed necessary. I write about 300 words a day with luck and when I am free to do so. I do it chiefly because it is the most difficult thing that I have ever tried to do.

I began by writing plays when I was 14. Before that I wrote 400 immensely dull pages (since destroyed) about a horse. I have also written a film script of *The Sea Change* with Peter Yates, but this has not yet been produced. I would very much like to write a good play, and, indeed, come to that, a first rate novel.

*   *   *

All Elizabeth Jane Howard's novels are distinguished by sharp and sensitive perceptions about people—their loves, their guilts, the damage they wittingly or unwittingly do to others. Sometimes, the perceptions are worked into satirical set pieces, like the treatment of a group of feckless post-Oxford young people sponging in London in *Something in Disguise.* Often the satire is more gentle and generous, like that of the patriotic major in *After Julius* who combines long, boring speeches about the past with silent sensitivity to the human dramas around him. Howard's protagonists, often simple, gentle young girls from a variety of backgrounds, are treated with a great deal of sympathy, with respect for their quiet intelligence and their capacity to feel for others. Any tendency toward the mawkish or sentimental is carefully controlled by a prose that works on sharp and often comic juxtapositions of images: the heavy-handed Colonel, trying to appear sympathetic to others in *Something in Disguise,* is "about as jocular and useless as the Metro-Goldwyn-Mayer Lion," in *The Sea Change* a young actress tries desperately to impress a playwright by showing a knowledge of his plays, "broadcasting her innocuous opinions like weed killer on a well kept lawn," the repressed and deferential hairdresser who is the central character in *Getting It Right* begins by noticing a wealthy and demanding client whose face has the "apoplectic bloom of unpeeled beetroot" and eyes "the shade of well-used washing-up water," and then proceeds, in a moment of personal conflict, to discover his mind like a "partially disused branch railway line."

The careful control visible in Howard's prose is also apparent in the structure of her novels. Sometimes, as in all of *The Sea Change* and most of *After Julius,* the novel consists of alternate narrations from the point of view of a small number of closely connected characters. Each episode is seen from at least two points of view, started by one character, taken up by the next who then moves the narrative on a little further until a third character takes it up. In *After Julius* the action of the novel is confined to a three-day weekend, although most of the characters are engaged in sorting out casual connections of current problems to the heroic death of Julius at Dunkerque 20 years earlier. *Something in Disguise* compresses action into three segments: April, August, and December of a single year. *The Long View* begins with a marriage breaking up in 1950 and its consequences for the couple's children, then traces the marriage back, through several precisely dated stages of problem and uneasy reconciliation, to its desperate origin in 1926. The past invariably leads to the present in Howard's fictional world, and the structural control often indicates both a working out of causation in human affairs and a kind of moral control, an insistence on a combination of awareness, responsibility, and refusal to hurt others in order to end the painful isolation of contemporary dilemmas.

More tightly controlled, and showing characters able to resolve their dilemmas more positively than do some other novels, *After Julius* depends, to some extent, on a rather striking coincidence. A young woman, visiting her mother for the week-end, finds her London lover, whom she had thought in Rome, arriving, with his wife, for dinner, and the affair explodes in a scene where fireworks are literal as well as symbolic. The structured plot shapes a novel in which moral or immoral actions eventually reveal themselves, in which moral judgment insists that characters take publicly visible responsibility for their actions. Similarly, in *Odd Girl Out* the young girl, amoral from a conventional point of view, who visits a young couple who have established a self-sufficient "island" in ten years of marriage and, in turn, sleeps with each of the partners, refuses to lie and insists on confronting both together to try to establish the "truth" of a three-way love that could nourish a child. Although the *ménage à trois,* full of ironic parallels and other forms of structural compression, cannot work for these three characters, the young girl who proposes it is seen as more moral, more willing to face the consequences of her actions and her emotions, than is the superficially more respectable couple. Virtue, in Howard's world, is not fragmented or buried, never the private gesture of an alienated sensibility; rather, actions have consequences, visible and direct, on the people closest to one.

Knowing and facing the past allows all three of the central women in *After Julius* some kind of resolution of their current dilemmas, but Howard's endings are not always so positive. In *The Sea Change* an aging playwright, who has longed for a renewal of youth in loving a young girl brought up in a village parsonage, and his wife, who has lost her only child, can understand and forgive each other in an acknowledgment of mutual pain and loss. The acknowledgment, the assumption of responsibility, allows them to survive, although it is far from a triumphant resolution. In *Something in Disguise* the resolution is melodramatic. The mother, a war widow who has raised her children alone, finally marries a retired army colonel to whom both her children object. Underneath the colonel's blunt, dull, insensitive exterior, the author slowly reveals, is the criminal heart of a man who tries gradually to poison his wife for her money, as he has poisoned two previous wives. And the daughter, who unpredictably marries a man who is both exciting and considerate, both a successful man of the world and a paragon of simple understanding and virtue, is desolate when the man is killed in an auto accident, having been sent on a fool's errand by one of the inconsiderate. Although moral judgment on each of the characters is clear enough, the plot punishes with an intensity that seems, somewhat sensationally, to detract from the emphasis on moral choice in some of the other novels. In *Getting it Right* melodrama and sensationalism recede into the background, useful for the hairdresser's discovery of sex, but not finally relevant to his moral choices that require the careful adjustment of both his con-

cern for others' pain and his need to establish a satisfying life for himself.

Howard's carefully shaped moral tales are also dense with descriptions and references that convey the social texture of the times. *The Long View* is skillful in recreating both the sense of the wealthy English in southern France between the wars and the austerely genteel dinner party of 1950. *The Sea Change* contrasts the conventional life in the village parsonage with that of the 1950s playwright conveying a young girl to London, New York, and a Greek island. *After Julius* is brilliant with settings: the tiny attic office of the editorial staff of an old, respectable publishing firm; the spacious, chintzy Tudor of the mother's house in Sussex; the cheerful chaos of a young doctor's and his family's crowded flat. *Something in Disguise* contains a terrifying portrait of daily life in the pseudo-Spanish surroundings of the "distinguished" house on a new suburban housing estate. Within these tartly observed and wholly recognizable environments, certain types appear in novel after novel. The apparently dull retired Army officer, either basically sensitive and kindly or basically cruel and criminal, represents an older England, an irrelevant survival. The confident man of the world, playwright in *The Sea Change,* doctor in *After Julius,* international businessman in *Something in Disguise* (though quickly parodied in *Getting It Right*), generally has not allowed charm, success, or the modern world to distort his basically simple sense of responsibility. But all these men are seen from the point of view of women, and the novels reiterate a constant sense that women are more responsible, more affectionate, more genuinely concerned with others than men are. After the dinner party that opens *The Long View,* the men rejoin the women "having discussed the fundamentals as superficially as the women in the drawing room discussed the superficialities fundamentally." *Getting It Right* switches the emphasis to the young lower-middle class male hairdresser discovering his need for risking conflict and responsibility, his recognition that one "can't take out a kind of emotional insurance policy with people." The three principal women in the novel have known this all along.

Howard's intelligent and sensitive heroines are, however, far from independent. They often regret or seek to rediscover the wise father lost. The benign and revered village parson father in *The Sea Change* is killed in a bicycle accident; fathers in other novels are killed in World War II; still other fathers, like the one in *The Long View,* are remote and indifferent or, like the actor who deserts his family in a melodramatic sub-plot in *Odd Girl Out,* completely irresponsible. The heroines seek protection, look for the man who might replace the absent father and make smoothly decisive all the hard and complex edges of a difficult world. They want to be safe and cosseted, a desire that can lead to the aridity of *The Long View,* the self-discovery of *After Julius,* or the impossible fantasies of *Something in Disguise* and *Odd Girl Out.* The complexities of the search for protection are stated explicitly near the end of *Odd Girl Out,* when the couple turns the amoral young girl who proposed it into a scapegoat who can be exorcised. Yet they cannot return to their "island": "Each thought of what he had to do to sustain life for the other; each considered his efforts and translated them into nobility and unselfish determination." The roles are not equivalent, for, a few pages later, at the very end of the novel, the wife realizes that she, who had thought herself protected originally, must now become the principal protector. And they will not have a child. In Howard's fictional world sympathetic and competent mothers, who abound, are not enough. Heroines need the wisdom, the control, and the safety of the responsible and caring father, a safety dimly seen, always lost, and invariably over-compensated for. Looking for safety, always precarious in a world of airplanes and betrayals, requires a great deal of risk, sensitivity, and control. Howard's great distinction is that the search for safety is presented with such rare and intelligent discrimination.

—James Gindin

HOWARD, Maureen

Nationality: American. **Born:** Maureen Keans in Bridgeport, Connecticut, 28 June 1930. **Education:** Smith College, Northampton, Massachusetts, B.A. 1952. **Family:** Married 1) Daniel F. Howard in 1954 (divorced 1967), one daughter; 2) David J. Gordon in 1968; 3) Mark Probst, 1981. **Career:** Worked in publishing and advertising, 1952-54; lecturer in English, New School for Social Research, New York, 1967-68, 1970-71, and since 1974, and at University of California, Santa Barbara, 1968-69, Amherst College, Massachusetts, Brooklyn College, and Royale University. Currently, Member of the School of the Arts, Columbia University, New York. **Awards:** Guggenheim fellowship, 1967; Radcliffe Institute fellowship, 1967; National Book Critics Circle award, 1979; Merrill fellowship, 1982. **Address:** c/o Penguin, 375 Hudson Street, New York, New York 10014, U.S.A.

PUBLICATIONS

Novels

Not a Word about Nightingales. London, Secker and Warburg, 1960; New York, Atheneum, 1962.
Bridgeport Bus. New York, Harcourt Brace, 1965.
Before My Time. Boston, Little Brown, 1975.
Grace Abounding. Boston, Little Brown, 1982; London, Abacus, 1984.
Expensive Habits. New York, Summit, and London, Viking, 1986.
Natural History. New York, Norton, 1992.

Uncollected Short Stories

"Bed and Breakfast," in *Yale Review* (New Haven, Connecticut), March 1961.
"Sherry," in *The Best American Short Stories 1965,* edited by Martha Foley and David Burnett. Boston, Houghton Mifflin, 1965.
"Three Pigs of Krishna Nura," in *Partisan Review* (New Brunswick, New Jersey), Winter 1971-72.
"Sweet Memories," in *Statements,* edited by Jonathan Baumbach. New York, Braziller, 1975.

Other

Facts of Life (autobiography). Boston, Little Brown, 1978.

Editor, *Seven American Women Writers of the Twentieth Century.* Minneapolis, University of Minnesota Press, 1977.
Editor, *The Penguin Book of Contemporary American Essays.* New York, Viking, 1984.

*   *   *

In her award-winning autobiography, *Facts of Life,* Maureen Howard explains the conflict between her goals and her father's hopes for her: "I think because I loved him, coarse and unlettered as he pretended to be, that he would have known from experience that our lives do not admit the fictional luxury of alternate endings." Howard's fiction reflects this view that alternate endings are illusive. As her characters attempt to recreate their stories, they discover that the past has predetermined their lives. One cannot alter personality; one can only understand, accept, and grow within the frame of individual talent. At the end of *Facts of Life,* Howard describes herself at 23: "I am beginning. My life is beginning which cannot be true." Her life began long ago, her character determined years before that moment. That the majority of Howard's fictional characters are female seems coincidental; in her introduction to *Seven American Women Writers of the Twentieth Century,* Howard asserts her preference for universal concerns: "To my mind this is the most egalitarian manner in which to study women's literature—to presume that these women are artists first and do not have to be unduly praised or their reputations justified on grounds of sex." In Howard's novels, discovery and acceptance of one's own character challenge both genders.

When Professor Albert Sedgely, in *Not a Word about Nightingales,* prolongs his sabbatical in Italy, he wants "to take his life as it was and alter its limits as though he lived in a theatrical set, movable flats—and having created a new scene, then he could shift his tastes, his emotions, even his appearance." To create this illusive possibility, Howard emphasizes Albert's daughter Rosemary's reaction. As with Henry James's Strether in *The Ambassadors,* Rosemary, sent to bring Albert back, is so charmed by his new personality and environment that she ignores her pledge until she discovers Albert's affair with Carlotta Manzini. Sexual awakening so threatens Rosemary, her mother Anne, and even Albert that all three retreat to narrow and confined lives. Is this the novel that Howard alludes to in *Facts of Life* as her "mannered academic novel," that displays a "sense of order as I knew it in the late fifties and early sixties with all the forms that I accepted and even enjoyed: that was the enormous joke about life—that our passion must be contained if we were not to be fools"? If so, at least Albert's final decision rests on acknowledgment of his own character; that his love for Carlotta is "incomplete" and his business with Anne "unfinished" brings Albert home.

With humor Howard tackles the same questions in *Bridgeport Bus.* Although Howard shifts point of view frequently between her protagonist Mary Agnes Keely and other characters, the central question belongs to Mary Agnes: is "the mutually destructive love of mother and daughter more substantial than tidy freedom"? Howard's readers view Mary Agnes's attempts as recorded in her journals. When Mary Agnes begins her affair with Stanley Sarnicki, she records the event twice: first as "a thirty-five-year-old virgin would write it—the easy dodge and genteel fade-out," and then "done by a thirty-five-year-old lady *writer* who fancies herself a woman of experience when really there will always be something too delicate about her sensibility." Mary Agnes cannot escape her own nature, despite the different journal entries. As in her play, "The Cheese Stands Alone," one of several creative interludes in her journal, Mary Agnes recognizes that her fate is "inextricably woven" to her mother's. She returns, pregnant and unmarried, to help her mother die. Truth and fiction are not always discernible in Mary Agnes's journal, but as her friend Lydia comments, "she has in fact got at us in every meaningful respect." Mary Agnes's "triumph" is that she knows that "it was not a great sin to be, at last, alone." She has grown within her limits.

By sharing personal histories, Laura Quinn in *Before My Time* exchanges spirits with her cousin's son, Jim Cogan. At the end of the novel, a more responsible Jim returns to face drug charges while Laura writes of personal rather than public feelings. However, Howard states clearly, "Whoever compares the present and the past will soon perceive that there prevail and always have prevailed the same desires and passions." Although beneficial, this ending reflects an awakening, not a creation, of character. To develop the pedagogy to instruct young Jim, Laura resees her brother Robert's failed relationship with their father; silently to Jim, Laura urges, "Think that this story is your answer: Robert and all my honesty and self-knowledge are here for you at last. Think before you run." Howard also offers histories of other family members. The most successful story, that of Jim's twin siblings Cormac and Siobhan, parallels Jim and Laura's as the twins have similar desires but are out of step with each other. Mary Agnes Keely may have had "triumph" in *Bridgeport Bus,* but at the end of *Before My Time,* Laura Quinn's new doubt is as "sweet"; the confines of her personality contain newly tapped emotion.

Because Howard's characters in *Grace Abounding* remain isolated from each other, the reader senses little more than ongoing struggle at the end of this novel. Within shifts of point of view and time frame, each character attempts to discern what in the past enlightens the present. The reader first meets Maude and Elizabeth Dowd in shock after Frank Dowd's death; widow Maude and daughter Elizabeth, "unable to speak of their abandonment," "have drawn off into private desolation." Maude's mother, lost in the world of senility, and her nurse die soon after. Years later, neither Maude's nor Elizabeth's husbands know their wives' true natures. In a disturbing scene, three-year-old Warren, a victim of child abuse who is locked within himself, dies before Maude, now a psychologist, can reach him. Only the mad poet Mattie appears to have a whole life, but, after her death, her heir inadvertently burns all her poems. After the first two sections of the novel, "Sin" and "Sorrow," the reader expects in the final "Grace Note" some resolution but encounters instead Theodore Lasser, Maude's husband's son, a priest more concerned with public relations than spiritual needs. Where then is that "grace abounding"? The last line holds some answer: "The young priest stumbles back and forth from bush to lemon tree, brushing and brushing at cold cobwebs that will fade with the morning dew." The reader knows that Theodore's ghostly cobwebs stem from unresolved conflicts with his father. *Grace Abounding* may well serve as Howard's warning rather than model: to accept limits, one must discover, know, and then share one's nature.

—Mary M. Lay

HUDSON, Jeffery. *See* **CRICHTON, (John) Michael.**

HUGHES, David (John)

Nationality: British. **Born:** Alton, Hampshire, 27 July 1930. **Education:** Eggar's Grammar School, Alton; King's College School,

Wimbledon; Christ Church, Oxford (editor, *Isis*), B.A. in English 1953, M.A. 1965. **Military Service:** Served in the Royal Air Force, 1949-50. **Family:** Married 1) the actress and director Mai Zetterling in 1958 (divorced 1976); 2) Elizabeth Westoll in 1980; one daughter and one son. **Career:** Assistant editor, *London Magazine,* 1953-54; editor, *Town* magazine, London, 1960-61; documentary and feature film writer in Sweden, 1961-68; lived in France, 1970-74; editor, New Fiction Society, 1975-77, 1981-82; film critic, *Sunday Times,* London, 1982-83. Since 1982 film critic, *Mail on Sunday,* London. Assistant visiting professor, University of Iowa, Iowa City, 1978-79 and 1987, and University of Alabama, University, 1979; visiting associate professor, University of Houston, 1986. **Awards:** W.H. Smith Literary award, 1985; Welsh Arts Council prize, 1985. Fellow, Royal Society of Literature, 1986. **Agent:** Anthony Sheil Associates, 43 Doughty Street, London WC1N 2LF, England.

PUBLICATIONS

Novels

A Feeling in the Air. London, Deutsch, 1957; as *Man Off Beat,* New York, Reynal, 1957.
Sealed with a Loving Kiss. London, Hart Davis, 1959.
The Horsehair Sofa. London, Hart Davis, 1961.
The Major. London, Blond, 1964; New York, Coward McCann, 1965.
The Man Who Invented Tomorrow. London, Constable, 1968.
Memories of Dying. London, Constable, 1976.
A Genoese Fancy. London, Constable, 1979.
The Imperial German Dinner Service. London, Constable, 1983.
The Pork Butcher. London, Constable, 1984; New York, Schocken, 1985.
But for Bunter. London, Heinemann, 1985; as *The Joke of the Century,* New York, Taplinger, 1986.

Uncollected Short Stories

"The Coloured Cliffs," in *Transatlantic Review* (London), Spring 1961.
"Rough Magic," in *Shakespeare Stories,* edited by Giles Gordon. London, Hamish Hamilton, 1982.

Plays

Flickorna (screenplay). Stockholm, PAN/Norstedt, 1968.

Screenplays (with Mai Zetterling): *Loving Couples,* 1964; *Night Games,* 1966; *Dr. Glas,* 1967; *The Girls,* 1968.

Television Play: *The Stuff of Madness,* with Mai Zetterling, from story by Patricia Highsmith, 1990.

Other

J.B. Priestley: An Informal Study of His Work. London, Hart Davis, 1958; Freeport, New York, Books for Libraries, 1970.
The Road to Stockholm and Lapland. London, Eyre and Spottiswoode, 1964.
The Cat's Tale (for children), with Mai Zetterling. London, Cape, 1965.

The Seven Ages of England. Stockholm, Swedish Radio, 1966.
The Rosewater Revolution: Notes on a Change of Attitude. London, Constable, 1971.

Editor, *Memoirs of the Comte de Gramont,* translated by Horace Walpole. London, Folio Society, 1965.
Editor, *Sound of Protest, Sound of Love: Protest-Songs from America and England.* Stockholm, Swedish Radio, 1968.
Editor, *Evergreens.* Stockholm, Swedish Radio, 1977.
Editor, *Winter's Tales 1* (new series). London, Constable, and New York, St. Martin's Press, 1985.
Editor, *The Stories of Ernest Hemingway.* London, Folio Society, 1986.
Editor, with Giles Gordon, *Best Short Stories 1986* [*1988*]. London, Heinemann, 3 vols., 1986-88.
Editor, with Giles Gordon, *Best Short Stories 1989* [*1991*]. London, Heinemann, 3 vols., 1989-91; as *The Best English Short Stories 1989* [*1991*]. New York, Norton, 3 vols., 1989-91.
Editor, with Giles Gordon, *The Minerva Book of Short Stories 1-6.* London, Minerva, 6 vols., 1990-94.

*   *   *

David Hughes takes war for his subject, but he is certainly not concerned to make stirring adventures out of the sordid tragedies, mass killings, and crowd emotions of armed conflict, nor to contrive intellectual puzzles out of the intrigues of international enmity. His business is with individuals and the way that their lives have been shaped (and frequently grossly distorted) by the wars of this century.

His skillful control of his subject matter, his ingenuity as a story teller, and his subtle and powerful delineation of character enable him to create unforgettable novels out of his chosen material. He seldom makes overt judgments. His characters may condemn themselves out of their obsessions and stored guilt, but their creator insists that, whatever they may have done to other people, they are themselves frail and vulnerable, and therefore, in some respects at least, lovable. However much the readers are kept at a distance by the way Hughes structures his novels, they are never allowed to forget that he is dealing with people not ciphers.

The history of the war-torn first half of this century is epitomized in *Memories of Dying* in which Flaxman, a prosperous business man on the brink of a nervous breakdown is suddenly caught up into the consciousness of his old history teacher, Hunter. As Flaxman flies to the south of France, in a vain attempt to escape from the pressures of work and family, he finds his mind invaded by thoughts of his home town and the aged lonely man who once taught him, now engaged in the impossible task of writing a history of the world that will present the facts honestly to future generations of schoolchildren. It is an act of penitence, for in the first world war Hunter through accident and panic shot one of his fellow officers. For years thereafter he carried the man's wallet around with him, vowing that he would marry the widow whose photograph it contained. He achieved his aim. He located the woman, who had turned into a lonely alcoholic, married her, and had one son. At the outbreak of World War II he insisted that she should leave their home for a more remote cottage. In that place, of his choosing, she was killed by a random air raid. History had not finished with Hunter. Sometime in the years of unsteady peace, his son was found dead of drugs and alcohol in an Oxford college.

Like Hunter, the narrator of *The Imperial German Dinner Service* tries to make some reparative and creative response to the war-torn century into which he has been born. In his case, his task takes the symbolic form of collecting the scattered pieces of a dinner service made in Edwardian England as a gift for the Kaiser. Many threads are drawn into his search, for Hughes is determined to show, yet again, how individual needs are woven into public events. As his obsessed narrator journeys to meet his unlikely contacts in the countries of western Europe and Scandinavia, and ultimately reaches the precarious geology of Iceland in his search for the fragile pieces of china, he is reconstructing his own life as well as searching for the innocence of an impossible golden age. Each bit of the dinner service is adorned with an English scene, which he has visited at some time with his estranged wife. So, as Europe is torn, so is he, both by the torments of his marriage to an ambitious Sunday columnist (who discovered the first plate of the dinner service and so set him off on his quest) and the futility of his own work as a freelance journalist.

Ernst Kestner, the protagonist of *The Pork Butcher,* Hughes's most important and serious novel so far, is also on a quest. A widower from Thomas Mann's town of Lubeck, he is dying of lung cancer and determined that his final act shall be a confrontation with the guilt of his wartime past. So he goes to Paris to take his coldly neurotic, self-obsessed daughter (who has married a Frenchman) on a weekend trip to the village where he had been stationed in the 1940s. In that village, Kestner had met Jannie and become so infatuated with her that he wrote home to his German fiancée breaking off the engagement. The letter never arrived, for the day he posted it, the order came that the village was to be "punished," the inhabitants were to be lured to the central square and shot, and the whole place was to be abandoned. In the numbed brutality of that act, Kestner killed the girl he loved. Now, like Hunter, he is determined to make some amends, even if all he can do is to give himself up to the mayor of the restored village. Beating the usual intransigence of local bureaucracy, he manages to talk to the mayor and gradually realizes that the man is Jannie's brother. When the mayor also recognizes to whom he is talking, he drives the car in which he is conveying Kestner with such wild fury that it is involved in a fatal accident. The mayor is killed; and Kestner, now badly injured, has to end his life with a double guilt on his shoulders. This irony underlines the impossibility of making amends either internationally or personally for the obscenities of war.

But for Bunter takes up the same theme in a strangely light-hearted vein. Hughes imagines that Billy Bunter (the fat boy of Greyfriars, who entertained generations of schoolboys) has survived into the 1980s, and is now ready to confess his own responsibility for the horrors of the century he has lived through. Once again Hughes makes his point: none of us, not even the most unlikely, can shelve responsibility for the times we live in.

—Shirley Toulson

HULME, Keri

Nationality: New Zealander. **Born:** Christchurch, 9 March 1947. **Education:** North Beach primary school; Aranui High School; Canterbury University, Christchurch. **Career:** Formerly, senior postwoman, Greymouth, and director for New Zealand television; writer-in-residence, Canterbury University, 1985. **Awards:** New Zealand Literary Fund grant, 1975, 1977, 1979, and scholarship in letters, 1990; Katherine Mansfield Memorial award, for short story, 1975; Maori Trust Fund prize, 1978; East-West Centre award, 1979; ICI bursary, 1982; New Zealand writing bursary, 1984; Book of the Year award, 1984; Mobil Pegasus prize, 1985; Booker prize, 1985; Chianti Ruffino Antico Fattor award, 1987. **Address:** Okarito, Private Bag, Hokitika Post Office, Westland, New Zealand.

PUBLICATIONS

Novels

The Bone People. Wellington, Spiral, 1983; London, Hodder and Stoughton, and Baton Rouge, Louisiana State University Press, 1985.
Lost Possessions (novella). Wellington, Victoria University Press, 1985.

Short Stories

The Windeater/Te Kaihau. Wellington, Victoria University Press, 1986; London, Hodder and Stoughton, and New York, Braziller, 1987.

Uncollected Short Stories

"See Me, I Am Kei," in *Spiral 5* (Wellington), 1982.
"Floating Words," in *Prize Writing,* edited by Martyn Goff. London, Hodder and Stoughton, 1989.
"The Plu-perfect Pawa," in *Sport 1* (Wellington), 1989.
"Hinekaro Goes on a Picnic and Blows Up Another Obelisk," in *Subversive Acts,* edited by Cathie Dunsford. Auckland, New Women's Press, 1991.

Poetry

The Silences Between (Moeraki Conversations). Auckland, Auckland University Press-Oxford University Press, 1982.
Strands. Auckland, Auckland University Press, 1991.

Other

Homeplaces: Three Coasts of the South Island of New Zealand, with photographs by Robin Morrison. Auckland, Hodder and Stoughton, 1989; London, Hodder and Stoughton, 1990.

*

Critical Studies: "In My Spiral Fashion" by Peter Simpson, in *Australian Book Review* (Kensington Park), August 1984; "Spiraling to Success" by Elizabeth Webby, in *Meanjin* (Melbourne), January 1985; "Keri Hulme: Breaking Ground" by Shona Smith, in *Untold 2* (Christchurch); *Leaving the Highway: Six Contemporary New Zealand Novelists* by Mark Williams, Auckland, Auckland University Press, 1990.

Keri Hulme comments:

I have a grave suspicion that Life is a vast joke: we are unwitting elements of the joke.
It is not a nice or kind joke, either.
I write about people who are in pain because they can't see the joke, see the point of the joke.

What I write is fantasy-solidly-based-in-Reality, everyday myths.
I rarely write out of a New Zealand context and, because I am lucky enough to be a mongrel, draw extensively from my ancestral cultural heritages—Maori (Kai Tahu, the South Island tribe), Scots (the Orkneys), and English (Lancashire). (Remember that the Pakeha elements of my ancestry predominate, but they have been well-sieved by Aotearoa.) I want to touch the raw nerves in NZ—the violence we largely cover up; the racism we don't acknowledge; the spoliation of land & sea that has been smiled at for the past 150 years—and explore *why* we (Maori & Pakeha) have developed a very curious type of humor which not many other people in the world understand, like, or appreciate and which is a steel-sheathed nerve I want to hide inside.
I'm not particularly serious about anything except whitebaiting. (Whitebait are the fry of NZ galaxids: they are a greatly relished and *very* expensive-about $75NZ a kilo—delicacy. I whitebait every season.)

*   *   *

Keri Hulme comes from the heartland of New Zealand—the South Island's west coast—and, perhaps as a consequence, she has developed an idiom which remains distinctively New Zealand even when it is feeding on the great traditions of English, Irish, American, and other (notably sufic) literature. This New Zealandness is the most immediately striking feature of the work for which she is best know, *The Bone People.*
The Maori phrases which permeate the text immediately proclaim its provenance. But the texture of the English which she writes is also unmistakably New Zealand. Many writers before her have managed a passable imitation of Kiwi pub argot, but Hulme is one of the first to have succeeded in giving a characteristic account of the speech and thoughts of New Zealanders as educated and intelligent as her protagonist, Kerewin Holmes. In passages like the following one can sense the typical rhythms and accents ("thunk"), the half-suppressed obscenities ("whateffers"), the gentle ironies and not-so-gentle prejudices ("Poms" are Englishmen) of New Zealand's more articulate denizens. (Kerewin has just discovered that her young protégé, Simon Gillayley, may have aristocratic Irish blood):

> Ah hell, urchin, it doesn't matter, you can't help who your forbears were, and I realized as I thunk it, that I was reveling in the knowledge of my whakapapa and solid Lancashire and Hebridean ancestry. Stout commoners on the left side, and real rangatira on the right distaff side. A New Zealander through and through. Moanawhenua bones and heart and blood and brain. None of your (retch) import Poms or whateffers.

The uncovering of Simon's background constitutes one strand of the plot of *The Bone People,* but ultimately—like the plots of many of Hulme's short stories—it turns out to be an inconclusive strand. All we can be sure of is that he comes from a background of violence and drug-dealing. The more detailed clues lead nowhere, and it seems that Hulme intended merely to tease her readers with these elements of a "well-made" plot, and that her real interest lay elsewhere. As Kerewin begins to check out Simon's Irish background she apologizes for "dragging" the reader "out of the cobweb pile, self-odyssey." The phrase highlights not only the book's principal concern (Kerewin's mental and spiritual progress) but also one of its dominant images (the spider's web, which at different times represents entanglement and intricate harmony).

Even more prominent than the spider and its web is the traditional Maori (and sufic) motif of the spiral. Kerewin lives in a tower full of spirals, notably a spiral staircase and a double spiral engraved on the floor: "one of the kind that wound your eyes round and round into the center where surprise you found the beginning of another spiral that led your eyes out again to the nothingness of the outside . . . it was an old symbol of rebirth, and the outward-inward nature of things. . . ." At the beginning of the book Kerewin has clearly begun a downward spiral into "nothingness." Her Tower, conceived as a "hermitage," "a glimmering retreat," has become an "abyss," a "prison," She is entangled in a web of self-absorption and materialism.

Into her life walks Simon, who is her opposite in almost every respect. She is dark (though only one-eighth Maori); he is fair. She is "heavy shouldered, heavy-hammed, heavy-haired"; he is lithe, almost skeletal. She is wonderfully articulate; he is a mute. (Again Hulme teases our expectations of a "well-made" plot by holding out the promise that he will eventually learn to speak. He does not.) She is obsessed by her possessions, and fears as a consequence that she has "lost the main part" of life; he is "rough on possessions," but has a sense of the deeper aura of things. She shrinks from touching others; he and his adoptive father (Joe) are, as Hulme has subsequently put it, "huggers and kissers deluxe." She is clever; he is trusting—two terms which are juxtaposed in the book. She is associated with the moon; he is a "sunchild." She is an introvert; he and Joe are extroverts.

Symbol-hunters have been quick to latch on to Simon's character, but they have so far been baffled by the diffuseness of the portrait. Hulme herself claims that she writes "from a visual base and a gut base rather than sieving it through the mind," and so it is probably futile to search for any conscious allegorical design in the book. A psycho-analytical approach offers greater rewards. Many aspects of *The Bone People*—notably the dreams (which often foretell the future), the paintings, the search for "wholeness" (and the dance imagery which accompanies it), the emphasis on myth, the eclectic attitude to religion, the disdainful attitude towards sex, and the mandala-like tricephalos which anticipates the asexual harmony ("commensalism") achieved by the principal characters at the end—suggest the influence of Jung. Jung also provides as good an explanation as any of Simon's relationship with Kerewin.

The book is full of projections and personifications of deviant aspects of the characters' personalities. Kerewin's more cynical thoughts are attributed to an inner voice labeled "the snark"; her violent tendencies turn at length into a palpable cancer; and the mysterious character who helps her to grapple with this cancer ("a thin wiry person of indeterminate age. Of indeterminate sex. Of indeterminate race") appears to be a projection of her own enfeebled self. Similarly Simon (who was originally conceived as a figment of Kerewin's dreams and not as an independent character) may be seen as her "shadow"—the embodiment of everything she has lost by withdrawing from society. This includes not only positive factors like trust and responsiveness to touch but also negative ones, especially violence.

Simon brings with him a long history of violence, culminating in the savage beatings inflicted on him by Joe. Kerewin's spiraling descent is accompanied and to a large extent occasioned by her recognition of this violence, and the nadir of her "self-odyssey" comes when she gives way to violence herself. At the same time an orgy of violence (effectively amplified by the recurrent images of knives and splintered glass) erupts among the other characters, so that at the end of the third part of the novel Simon is hospital-ized, Joe (wounded) is in jail, one minor character is dead, another seriously ill, and Kerewin's Tower has been reduced to a single story.

Many readers feel that Hulme should have left the book there—that, as in much of her other fiction (of which the fine story "Hooks and Feelers" and the novella *Lost Possessions* are the most accessible examples) it is the violence, and especially the violence that wells out of love, which is the most compelling element. But Hulme added a fourth section and an epilogue in which the principals, aided by a set of unorthodox assistants and (except in Simon's case) by a deep draught of Maori culture, spiral back towards "rebirth," "wholeness," and harmony.

In a recent interview Hulme has acknowledged that the ending owes something to Jung, which encourages the notion advanced here that the whole novel is susceptible to a Jungian interpretation. Just who is really the focus of this interpretation—Kerewin Holmes or her virtual namesake, Keri Hulme—is a question difficult to resolve. Hulme concedes that the three protagonists emerged from her dreams. (She keeps a dream diary, and at least one of the dreams in *The Bone People*—Kerewin's at Moerangi—is lifted straight from it.) Much of the material also seems quasi-autobiographical. Time will tell if she can write effectively on less personal subjects.

—Richard Corballis

HUMPHREY, William

Nationality: American. **Born:** Clarkesville, Texas, 18 June 1924. **Education:** Southern Methodist University, Dallas; University of Texas, Austin. **Family:** Married to Dorothy Humphrey. **Career:** Teacher at Bard College, Annandale-on-Hudson, New York, 7 years, and briefly at Smith College, Northampton, Massachusetts, and Yale University, New Haven, Connecticut; lived in Italy for 7 years, then in Lexington, Virginia; now lives in Hudson, New York. **Awards:** American Academy award, 1962. **Address:** c/o Delacorte Press, 666 Fifth Avenue, New York, New York 10103, U.S.A.

PUBLICATIONS

Novels

Home from the Hill. New York, Knopf, and London, Chatto and Windus, 1958.
The Ordways. New York, Knopf, and London, Chatto and Windus, 1965.
Proud Flesh. New York, Knopf, and London, Chatto and Windus, 1973.
Hostages to Fortune. New York, Delacorte Press, 1984; London, Secker and Warburg, 1985.
No Resting Place. New York, Delacorte Press, and London, Secker and Warburg, 1989.
September Song. Boston, Houghton Mifflin/Seymour Lawrence, 1992.

Short Stories

The Last Husband and Other Stories. New York, Morrow, and London, Chatto and Windus, 1953.

A Time and a Place: Stories. New York, Knopf, 1968; as *A Time and a Place: Stories of the Red River Country,* London, Chatto and Windus, 1969.
The Collected Stories. New York, Delacorte Press, 1985; London, Secker and Warburg, 1986.

Other

The Spawning Run: A Fable. New York, Knopf, and London, Chatto and Windus, 1970.
Ah, Wilderness! The Frontier in American Literature. El Paso, Texas Western Press, 1977.
Farther Off from Heaven. New York, Knopf, and London, Chatto and Windus, 1977.
My Moby Dick. New York, Doubleday, 1978; London, Chatto and Windus, 1979.
Open Season: Sporting Adventures. New York, Delacorte Press, 1986.

*

Critical Study: *William Humphrey* by James W. Lee, Austin, Texas, Steck Vaughn, 1967; *William Humphrey* by Mark Royden Winchell, Boise, Idaho, Boise State University, 1992.

*   *   *

Locale is a potent force in most of William Humphrey's best work. Three of his novels and nearly all of his successful short stories are set in the Red River country of northeast Texas. Humphrey should not, however, be dismissed as nothing more than a regionalist. Like Faulkner, with whom he is often compared, Humphrey uses locale as a framework for the discussion of universal issues.

Home from the Hill, Humphrey's first and certainly his best novel, is both a first-class *Bildungsroman* and a family tragedy of mythic dimensions. Much of the novel concerns young Theron Hunnicutt's passage to manhood, a journey largely related to his hunting experiences. The most powerful force in the novel, however, is Theron's father, Captain Wade—wealthy cotton planter, legendary hunter, notorious philanderer—more an embodiment of Texas myth than an actual flesh-and-blood man. The House of Hunnicutt is destined to have the father's sins visited upon it. The captain is murdered by the crazed father of a pregnant teenage girl in a highly ironic case of mistaken identity. Following the primitive code of manhood learned from his father and other hunting men, Theron pursues the murderer and eventually kills him. Theron then retreats to the recesses of Sulphur Bottom, an almost impenetrable swamp, presumably to die alone. Hannah Hunnicutt, the long-suffering wife, is taken away to a Dallas asylum where she spends the last 15 years of her life. Though often compelling, *Home from the Hill* contains more than a touch of melodrama, and the last third of the novel is too much a series of coincidences.

While Humphrey's first novel is a melodramatic tragedy, his second is a mock epic. *The Ordways* is a panoramic novel spanning four generations. Its first section largely concerns the journey of the blinded Civil War veteran, Thomas Ordway, and his wife, Ella, along with both the remains and the tombstones of their kindred from eastern Tennessee to northeast Texas. Most of the rest of the novel concerns the 1898 journey of Sam Ordway, who traverses much of Texas in an attempt to find his kidnapped son. Despite his solemn oath to search to the ends of the earth if necessary, Sam Ordway is no avenging western hero, no believer in the primitive

code of manhood that governs the life of Theron Hunnicutt and, for that matter, the lives of Sam's own Texas neighbors. His quest becomes picaresque and includes such events as a political rally in the small town of Paris, Texas, a jailing in Dallas on charges of intent to commit murder, and a stint with a traveling circus. In the best picaresque tradition, *The Ordways* ends happily, though in this case the hero fails in his quest. The reunion of father and son takes place some 30 years after Sam's journey. The strength of the novel is in its evocation of late 19th-century Texas. The author also includes an enlightening discourse on the relationship of the Southerner to his past. The book's major weakness is in the extent of the episodic account of Sam's travels. Though highly entertaining at points, this segment often seems like nothing more than a collection of incidents. One wishes for an end to the sequence long before it comes.

Humphrey has written of the southerner: "Clannishness was and is the key to his temperament." *Proud Flesh,* his third novel, is about clannishness gone berserk. Centering on the death of matriarch Edwina "Ma" Renshaw, the novel is highly grotesque and often hilarious. Grotesquerie piles upon grotesquerie. When the family physician pronounces Edwina dead, he is forced to spend an additional three-day vigil at her bedside, just to make sure that his judgment has not been premature. An irrationally guilt-ridden oldest daughter entombs herself in the storm cellar, vowing never to emerge, an event which leads to the formation of a new religious cult. Finally, the dead matriarch's body is stored in a local cold storage plant while two Renshaws are dispatched to New York City to search for the family "black sheep," Edwina's favorite, who must return home before the funeral takes place. The novel's weakness is the same as that of *The Ordways* and even more apparent. More a collection of incidents than a coherent novel, *Proud Flesh* is allowed to continue far too long.

Humphrey's fourth novel, *Hostages to Fortune,* differs markedly from his first three in setting, theme, and tome. Set in the northeast, the novel concerns the agonized struggle of Ben Curtis, a 50-year-old writer and onetime avid fly fisherman, to rebuild his life after a series of personal tragedies— the suicides of both his beloved god-daughter and his teenage son, the supposedly accidental death of his best friends, and the break-up of his marriage of 20 years. Having barely failed in a suicide attempt, the convalescing writer, hoping to regain the desire to go on living, journeys to a fishing lodge where he has spent some of his happiest moments. The novel consists largely of flashbacks which cover most of the significant events of Curtis's adult life. Curtis's tormented attempts to understand both his son's suicide and the demise of his once-happy marriage constitute some of the most poignant passages in Humphrey's fiction. Though *Hostages to Fortune* lacks the mythic dimension of *Home form the Hill,* Humphrey's tortured writer is among his most sympathetic creations.

Most of Humphrey's short stories are competent, and some are first-rate. Among the best are "The Shell," an account of a young man's growth to self-awareness as he struggles to free himself from the shadow of his deceased father, a legendary hunter; "A Fresh Snow," a sensitive of a lonely southern girl in a northern industrial city; "The Ballad of Jesse Neighbors," a tale of an ill-fated "poreboy" in Depression-era Red River Country who, as a victim of society and circumstance, recalls Hardy's Tess; and "Mouth of Brass," perhaps Humphrey's best story, a sensitive young narrator's recounting of his first experience with racial prejudice and small-town cowardice.

In addition to his fiction, Humphrey has written two slender volumes on fishing. *The Spawning Run* and *My Moby Dick,* a critical study, *Ah, Wilderness! The Frontier in American Literature,* and a poignant autobiographical work, *Farther Off from Heaven*. Though uneven, his work is quite readable. In his ability to evoke his native region, Humphrey has few if any equals.

—Craig Hudziak

HUMPHREYS, Emyr (Owen)

Nationality: British. **Born:** Prestatyn, Clwyd, Wales, 15 April 1919. **Education:** University College of Wales, Aberystwyth, 1937-39; University College of North Wales, Bangor, 1946-47. **Military Service:** Served as a relief worker in the Middle East and the Mediterranean during World War II. **Family:** Married Elinor Myfanwy Jones in 1946; three sons and one daughter. **Career:** Teacher, Wimbledon Technical College, London, 1948-50, and Pwllheli Grammar School, North Wales, 1951-54; producer, BBC Radio, Cardiff, 1955-58; drama producer, BBC Television, 1958-62; freelance writer and director, 1962-65; lecturer in drama, 1965-72, and Honorary Professor, 1988, University College of North Wales. Since 1972 freelance writer. **Awards:** Maugham award, 1953; Hawthornden prize, 1959; Welsh Arts Council award, 1972, 1975, 1979, for non-fiction, 1984; Gregynog fellowship, 1974; Society of Authors traveling scholarship, 1979; Welsh Arts Council Book of the Year, 1992, for *Bonds of Attachment*. D.Litt.: University of Wales, Cardiff, 1990. Honorary Fellow, University of Wales, 1987. **Agent**: Anthony Sheil Associates, 43 Doughty Street, London WC1N 2LF, England. **Address:** Llinon, Pen-y-berth, Llanfairpwll, Pnys Môn, Gwynedd LL61 5YT, Wales.

PUBLICATIONS

Novels

The Little Kingdom. London, Eyre and Spottiswoode, 1946.
The Voice of a Stranger. London, Eyre and Spottiswoode, 1949.
A Change of Heart. London, Eyre and Spottiswoode, 1951.
Hear and Forgive. London, Gollancz, 1952; New York, Putnam, 1953.
A Man's Estate. London, Eyre and Spottiswoode, 1955; New York, McGraw Hill, 1956.
The Italian Wife. London, Eyre and Spottiswoode, 1957; New York, McGraw Hill, 1958.
Y Tri Llais (in Welsh). Llandybie, Dyfed, Llyfrau'r Dryw, 1958
A Toy Epic. London, Eyre and Spottiswoode, 1958.
The Gift. London, Eyre and Spottiswoode, 1963.
Outside the House of Baal. London, Eyre and Spottiswoode, 1965.
National Winner. London, Macdonald, 1971.
Flesh and Blood. London, Hodder and Stoughton, 1974.
The Best of Friends. London, Hodder and Stoughton, 1978.
The Anchor Tree. London, Hodder and Stoughton, 1980.
Jones. London, Dent, 1984.
Salt of the Earth. London, Dent, 1985.
An Absolute Hero. London, Dent, 1986.
Open Secrets. London, Dent, 1988.
Bonds of Attachment. London, Macdonald, 1991.

Short Stories

Natives. London, Secker and Warburg, 1968.
Miscellany Two. Bridgend, Glamorgan, Poetry Wales Press, 1981.

Uncollected Short Stories

"Down in the Heel on Duty," in *New English Review* (London), 1947.
"Michael," in *Wales* (London), vol. 7, nos. 26-27, 1947.
"A Girl in the Ice" and "The Obstinate Bottle," in *New Statesman* (London), 1953.
"Mrs. Armitage," in *Welsh Short Stories.* London, Faber, 1959.
"The Arrest," in *Madog 3* (Barry), 1977.

Plays

King's Daughter, adaptation of a play by Saunders Lewis (produced London, 1959; as *Siwan,* televised, 1960). Published, as *Siwan,* in *Plays of the Year 1959-60,* London, Elek, 1960.
Dinas, with W.S. Jones. Llandybie, Dyfed, Llyfrau'r Dryw, 1970.

Radio Plays: *A Girl in a Garden,* 1963; *Reg,* 1964; *The Manipulator,* 1970; *Etifedd y Glyn,* 1984; *The Arrest,* 1985.

Television Plays and Documentaries: *Siwan,* 1960; *The Shining Pyramid,* from a story by Arthur Machen, 1979; *Y Gosb* (The Penalty), 1983; *Wyn ir Lladdfa* (Lambs to the Slaughter), 1984; *Hualau* (Fetters), 1984; *Bwy yn Rhydd* (Living Free), 1984; *Angel o'r Nef* (An Angel from Heaven), 1985; *Teulu Helga* (Helga's Family), 1985; *Cwlwm Cariad* (A Love Knot), 1986; *Twll Ole* (A Hole), 1987; *Yr Alwad* (The Call), 1988; *The Triple Net,* 1988; *Yr Alltud* (The Exile), 1989; *Dyn Perig* (A Dangerous Fellow), 1990; *Outside Time,* 1991; *Dwr Athân* (Fire and Water), 1991.

Poetry

Roman Dream, music by Alun Hoddinott. London, Oxford University Press, 1968.
An Apple Tree and a Pig, music by Alun Hoddinott. London, Oxford University Press, 1969.
Ancestor Worship: A Cycle of 18 Poems. Denbigh, Gee, 1970.
Landscapes, music by Alun Hoddinott. London, Oxford University Press, 1975.
Penguin Modern Poets 27, with John Ormond and John Tripp. London, Penguin, 1979.
The Kingdom of Bran. London, Holmes, 1979.
Pwyll a Riannon. London, Holmes, 1979.

Other

The Taliesin Tradition: A Quest for the Welsh Identity. London, Black Raven Press, 1983; revised edition, Chester Springs, Pennsylvania, Dufour, 1990.
The Triple Net: A Portrait of the Writer Kate Roberts 1891-1985. London, Channel 4 Television, 1988.
The Crucible of Myth. Swansea, University of Swansea, 1990.

*

Bibliography: *A Bibliography of Anglo-Welsh Literature 1900-1965* by Brynmor Jones, Swansea, Library Association, 1970.

Manuscript Collection: National Library of Wales, Aberystwyth.

Critical Studies: *The Novel* 1945-1950 by P.H. Newby, London, Longman, 1951; *Y Ilenor a'i Gymdeithas* by A. Llewelyn Williams, London, BBC, 1966; *The Dragon Has Two Tongues* by Glyn Jones, London, Dent, 1968; *Ysgrifau Beirniadol VII* by Derec Llwyd Morgan, Denbigh, Gee, 1972; Jeremy Hooker and Andre Morgan, in *Planet 39* (Llangeitho Tregaron, Dyfed), 1977; *Emyr Humphreys,* Cardiff, University of Wales Press, 1980, and "Land of the Living," in *Planet 52* (Llangeitho Tregaron, Dyfed), 1985, both by Ioan Williams; "Channels of Grace: A View of the Earlier Novels of Emyr Humphreys," in *Anglo-Welsh Review 70* (Tenby, Dyfed), 1982, and article in *British Novelists 1930-1959* edited by Bernard Oldsey, Detroit, Gale, 1983, both by Roland Mathias; *Emyr Humphreys* by M. Wynn Thomas, Caernarvon, Pantycelyn, 1989.

* * *

The preoccupations of Emyr Humphreys are peculiarly Welsh, and since there are very few Welsh novelists writing in English who spring from or have assimilated the Welsh Nonconformist heritage, his work has few parallels in that of his contemporaries. Humphreys manifests in his novels a Puritan seriousness about the purpose of living, about the need for tradition and the understanding of it, and about the future of the community (usually seen as Wales) as well as the good of the individual. Welsh Nationalist as well as Christian, he re-emphasised in 1953 that "personal responsibility is a Protestant principle" and saw himself as engaged in writing the

Protestant novel. His interest in the non-realist novel is minimal and his technical experimentation is limited to the use, in *A Man's Estate,* of a number of narrators and, in *Outside the House of Baal,* to an interleaving of narratives in which the past rapidly catches up with the present.

His first two novels, *The Little Kingdom* and *The Voice of a Stranger,* are concerned respectively with idealism betrayed by false leadership and idealism bludgeoned by Knavery. Their conclusions are pessimistic. The earlier of those themes appears again in *A Toy Epic.* But with *A Change of Heart* begins Humphreys's concern with the Christian belief in the gradual progress of society towards *the good* and the means by which *good* is transmitted from generation to generation. Heredity is soon discarded in favour of answers more complex. Perhaps the finest of the earlier novels which pursue this theme is *Hear and Forgive,* and of the later, *Outside the House of Baal.* In this book Humphreys faces the apparently total defeat of his Calvinistic Methodist minister, leaving the reader only with the silence which might make room for faith. Since the problems involved plainly need the longest time scale possible, Humphreys's more recent novels (with the exception of *The Anchor Tree,* which is a digression, with the same preoccupations, into his Welsh-American experience) were intended as a quartet, the fourth of which, *National Winner,* he wrote first. The appearance of the first and second, *Flesh and Blood* and *The Best of Friends,* has, however, been accompanied by the intimation that the quartet is now to be a sextet, so that *Salt of the Earth* still leaves two gaps in the sequence. *Jones* is a single-volume study of the refusal of responsibility.

—Roland Mathias

HUNTER, Evan

Pseudonyms: Curt Cannon; Hunt Collins; Ezra Hannon; Richard Marsten; and Ed McBain. **Nationality:** American. **Born:** Salvatore A. Lombino, New York City, 15 October 1926. **Education:** Evander Childs High School, New York; Cooper Union, New York, 1943-44; Hunter College, New York, B.A. 1950 (Phi Beta Kappa). **Military Service:** United States Navy, 1944-46. **Family:** Married 1) Anita Melnick in 1949 (divorced), three sons; 2) Mary Vann Finley in 1973, one step-daughter. **Career:** In the early 1950s taught in vocational high schools and worked for Scott Meredith Literary Agency, New York. Lives in Norwalk, Connecticut. **Awards:** Mystery Writers of America Edgar Allan Poe award, 1957, and Grand Master award, 1985. **Agent:** John Farquharson Ltd., 250 West 57th Street, New York, New York 10107, U.S.A.; or, 162-168 Regent Street, London, W1R 5TB, England.

PUBLICATIONS

Novels

The Big Fix. N.p., Falcon, 1952; as *So Nude, So Dead* (as Richard Marsten), New York, Fawcett, 1956.
The Evil Sleep! N.p., Falcon, 1952
Don't Crowd Me. New York, Popular Library, 1953; London, Consul, 1960; as *The Paradise Party,* London, New English Library, 1968.
Cut Me In (as Hunt Collins). New York, Abelard Schuman, 1954; London, Boardman, 1960; as *The Proposition,* New York, Pyramid, 1955.
The Blackboard Jungle. New York, Simon and Schuster, 1954; London, Constable, 1955.
Second Ending. New York, Simon and Schuster, and London, Constable, 1956; as *Quartet in H,* New York, Pocket Books, 1957.
Tomorrow's World (as Hunt Collins). New York, Avalon, 1956; as *Tomorrow and Tomorrow,* New York, Pyramid, 1956; as Ed McBain, London, Sphere, 1979.
Strangers When We Meet. New York, Simon and Schuster, and London, Constable, 1958.
I'm Cannon—For Hire (as Curt Cannon). New York, Fawcett, 1958; London, Fawcett, 1959.
A Matter of Conviction. New York, Simon and Schuster, and London, Constable, 1959; as *The Young Savages,* New York, Pocket Books, 1966.
Mothers and Daughters. New York, Simon and Schuster, and London, Constable, 1961.
Buddwing. New York, Simon and Schuster, and London, Constable, 1964.
The Paper Dragon. New York, Delacorte Press, 1966; London, Constable, 1967.
A Horse's Head. New York, Delacorte Press, 1967; London, Constable, 1968.
Last Summer, New York, Doubleday, 1968; London, Constable, 1969.
Sons. New York, Doubleday, 1969; London, Constable, 1970.
Nobody Knew They Were There. New York, Doubleday, and London, Constable, 1972.
Every Little Crook and Nanny. New York, Doubleday, and London, Constable, 1972.

Come Winter. New York, Doubleday, and London, Constable, 1973.
Streets of Gold. New York, Harper, 1974; London, Macmillan, 1975.
Doors (as Ezra Hannon). New York, Stein and Day, 1975; London, Macmillan, 1976
The Chisholms: A Novel of the Journey West. New York, Harper, and London, Hamish Hamilton, 1976.
Walk Proud. New York, Bantam, 1979.
Love, Dad. New York, Crown, and London, Joseph, 1981.
Far from the Sea. New York, Atheneum, and London, Hamish Hamilton, 1983.
Lizzie. New York, Arbor House, and London, Hamish Hamilton, 1984.
Criminal Conversations. New York, Warner, 1994.

Novels as Richard Marsten

Runaway Black. New York, Fawcett, 1954; London, Red Seal, 1957.
Murder in the Navy. New York, Fawcett, 1955; as *Death of a Nurse* (as Ed McBain), New York, Pocket Books, 1968; London, Hodder and Stoughton, 1972.
The Spiked Heel. New York, Holt, 1956; London, Constable, 1957.
Vanishing Ladies. New York, Permabooks, 1957; London, Boardman, 1961.
Even the Wicked. New York, Permabooks, 1958; as Ed McBain, London, Severn House, 1979.
Big Man. New York, Pocket Books, 1959; as Ed McBain. London, Penguin, 1978.

Novels as Ed McBain

Cop Hater. New York, Permabooks, 1956; London, Boardman, 1958.
The Mugger. New York, Simon and Schuster, 1956: London, Boardman, 1959.
The Pusher. New York, Simon and Schuster, 1956; London, Boardman, 1959.
The Con Man. New York, Permabooks, 1957; London, Boardman, 1960.
Killer's Choice. New York, Simon and Schuster, 1958; London, Boardman, 1960.
Killer's Payoff. New York, Simon and Schuster, 1958; London, Boardman, 1960.
April Robin Murders, with Craig Rice (completed by McBain). New York, Random House, 1958; London, Hammond, 1959.
Lady Killer. New York, Simon and Schuster, 1958; London, Boardman, 1961.
Killer's Wedge. New York, Simon and Schuster, 1959; London Boardman, 1961.
'Til Death. New York, Simon and Schuster, 1959; London, Boardman, 1961.
King's Ransom. New York, Simon and Schuster, 1959; London, Boardman, 1961.
Give the Boys a Great Big Hand. New York, Simon and Schuster, 1960; London, Boardman, 1962.
The Heckler. New York, Simon and Schuster, 1960; London, Boardman, 1962.
See Them Die. New York, Simon and Schuster, 1960; London, Boardman, 1963.
Lady, Lady, I Did It! New York, Simon and Schuster, 1961; London, Boardman, 1963.

Like Love. New York, Simon and Schuster, 1962; London, Hamish Hamilton, 1964.
Ten Plus One. New York, Simon and Schuster, 1963; London, Hamish Hamilton, 1964.
Ax. New York, Simon and Schuster, and London, Hamish Hamilton, 1964.
The Sentries. New York, Simon and Schuster, and London, Hamish Hamilton, 1965.
He Who Hesitates. New York, Delacorte Press, and London, Hamish Hamilton, 1965.
Doll. New York, Delacorte Press, 1965; London, Hamish Hamilton, 1966.
Eighty Million Eyes. New York, Delacorte Press, and London, Hamish Hamilton, 1966.
Fuzz. New York, Doubleday, and London, Hamish Hamilton, 1968.
Shotgun. New York, Doubleday, and London, Hamish Hamilton, 1969.
Jigsaw. New York, Doubleday, and London, Hamish Hamilton, 1970.
Hail, Hail, The Gang's All Here! New York, Doubleday, and London, Hamish Hamilton, 1971.
Sadie When She Died. New York, Doubleday, and London, Hamish Hamilton, 1972.
Let's Hear It for the Deaf Man. New York, Doubleday, and London, Hamish Hamilton, 1973.
Hail to the Chief. New York, Random House, and London, Hamish Hamilton, 1973.
Bread. New York, Random House, and London, Hamish Hamilton, 1974.
Where There's Smoke. New York, Random House, and London, Hamish Hamilton, 1975.
Blood Relatives. New York, Random House, 1975; London, Hamish Hamilton, 1976.
Guns. New York, Random House, 1976; London, Hamish Hamilton, 1977.
So Long as You Both Shall Live. New York, Random House, and London, Hamish Hamilton, 1976.
Long Time No See. New York, Random House, and London, Hamish Hamilton, 1977.
Goldilocks. New York, Arbor House, 1977; London, Hamish Hamilton, 1978.
Calypso. New York, Viking Press, and London, Hamish Hamilton, 1979.
Ghosts. New York, Viking Press, and London, Hamish Hamilton, 1980.
Rumpelstiltskin. New York, Viking Press, and London, Hamish Hamilton, 1981.
Beauty and the Beast. London, Hamish Hamilton, 1982; New York, Holt Rinehart, 1983.
Ice. New York, Arbor House, and London, Hamish Hamilton, 1983
Jack and the Beanstalk. New York, Holt Rinehart, and London, Hamish Hamilton, 1984.
Lightning. New York, Arbor House, and London, Hamish Hamilton, 1984.
Snow White and Rose Red. New York, Holt Rinehart, and London, Hamish Hamilton, 1985.
Eight Black Horses. New York, Arbor House, and London, Hamish Hamilton, 1985.
Another Part of the City. New York, Mysterious Press, 1985; London, Hamish Hamilton, 1986.
Cinderella. New York, Holt, and London, Hamish Hamilton, 1986.

Poison. New York, Arbor House, and London, Hamish Hamilton, 1987.

Puss in Boots. New York, Holt, and London, Hamish Hamilton, 1987.

Lullaby. New York, Morrow, and London, Hamish Hamilton, 1987.

The House That Jack Built. New York, Holt, and London, Hamish Hamilton, 1988.

Downtown. New York, Morrow, and London, Heinemann, 1989.

Three Blind Mice. New York, Arcade, 1990.

Vespers. New York, Morrow, and London, Heinemann, 1990.

Widows. London, Heinemann, 1991.

Kiss. London, Heinemann, 1992.

Mary, Mary. London, Heinemann, 1992.

Mischief. London, Hodder and Stoughton, 1993.

Short Stories

The Jungle Kids. New York, Pocket Books, 1956.

I Like 'em Tough (as Curt Cannon). New York, Fawcett, 1958

The Last Spin and Other Stories. London, Constable, 1960.

The Empty Hours (as Ed McBain). New York, Simon and Schuster, 1962; London, Boardman, 1963.

Happy New Year, Herbie, and Other Stories. New York, Simon and Schuster, 1963; London, Constable, 1965.

The Beheading and Other Stories. London, Constable, 1971.

The Easter Man (a Play) and Six Stories. New York, Doubleday, 1972; as *Seven,* London, Constable, 1972.

The McBain Brief. London, Hamish Hamilton, 1982; New York, Arbor House, 1983.

McBain's Ladies: The Women of the 87th Precinct. New York, Mysterious Press, and London, Hamish Hamilton, 1988.

McBain's Ladies Too. New York, Mysterious Press, 1989; London, Hamish Hamilton, 1990.

Uncollected Short Stories

"Ticket to Death," in *Best Detective Stories of the Year 1955,* edited by David Coxe Cooke. New York, Dutton, 1955.

"Classification: Dead" (as Richard Marsten), in *Dames, Danger, and Death,* edited by Leo Margulies. New York, Pyramid, 1960.

"Easy Money," in *Ellery Queen's Mystery Magazine* (New York), September 1960.

"Nightshade" (as Ed McBain) in *Ellery Queen's Mystery Magazine* (New York), August 1970.

"Someone at the Door," in *Ellery Queen's Mystery Magazine* (New York), October 1971.

"Sympathy for the Devil," in *Seventeen* (New York), July 1972.

"Weeping for Dustin," in *Seventeen* (New York), July 1973.

"The Analyst," in *Playboy* (Chicago), December 1974.

"Dangerous Affair," in *Good Housekeeping* (New York), March 1975.

"Eighty Million Eyes" (as Ed McBain), in *Ellery Queen's Giants of Mystery.* New York, Davis, 1976.

"Stepfather," in *Ladies' Home Journal* (New York), June 1976.

"What Happened to Annie Barnes?," in *Ellery Queen's Mystery Magazine* (New York), June 1976.

Plays

The Easter Man (produced Birmingham and London, 1964; as *A Race of Hairy Men,* produced New York, 1965). Included in *The Easter Man (a Play) and Six Stories,* 1972.

The Conjuror (produced Ann Arbor, Michigan, 1969).

Screenplays: *Strangers When We Meet,* 1960; *The Birds,* 1963; *Fuzz,* 1972; *Walk Proud,* 1979.

Television Plays: *Appointment at Eleven* (Alfred Hitchcock Presents series), 1955-61; *The Chisholms* series, from his own novel, 1978-79; *The Legend of Walks Far Woman,* 1982.

Other (for children)

Find the Feathered Serpent. Philadelphia, Winston, 1952.

Rocket to Luna (as Richard Marsten). Philadelphia, Winston, 1952; London, Hutchinson, 1954.

Danger: Dinosaurs! (as Richard Marsten). Philadelphia, Winston, 1953.

The Remarkable Harry. New York and London, Abelard Schuman, 1961.

The Wonderful Button. New York, Abelard Schuman, 1961; London, Abelard Schuman, 1962.

Me and Mr. Stenner. Philadelphia, Lippincott, 1976; London, Hamish Hamilton, 1977.

Other (as Ed McBain)

Editor, *Crime Squad.* London, New English Library, 1968.

Editor, *Homicide Department.* London, New English Library, 1968.

Editor, *Downpour.* London, New English Library, 1969.

Editor, *Ticket to Death.* London, New English Library, 1969.

*

Manuscript Collection: Mugar Memorial Library, Boston University.

Evan Hunter comments:

(1972) The novels I write under my own name are concerned mostly with identity, or at least they have been until the most recent book. (I cannot now predict what will interest or concern me most in the future.) I change my style with each novel, to fit the tone, the mood, and the narrative voice. I have always considered a strong story to be the foundation of any good novel, and I also apply this rule to the mysteries I write under the Ed McBain pseudonym. Unlike my "serious" novels, however, the style here is unvaried. The series characters are essentially the same throughout (although new detectives appear or old ones disappear from time to time, and each new case involves a new criminal or criminals). The setting is the same (the precinct and the city), and the theme is the same—crime and punishment. (I look upon these mysteries, in fact, as one *long* novel about crime and punishment, with each separate book in the series serving as a chapter.) I enjoy writing both types of novels, and consider each equally representative of my work.

*   *   *

The vividness and immediacy of the author's prose, coupled with the timeliness of his subject, drew considerable attention to Evan Hunter's novel *The Blackboard Jungle.* This story of a young teacher confronting the brutal realities of a big city vocational high school was praised for its realism and for opening to fiction an area of public concern that had begun to attract national attention in the United States. *Second Ending* was an even more aggressively topical novel, tracing the effects of drugs on four young New Yorkers. The central character, a young trumpet player who has been addicted for two years, draws the other characters together, and they are all altered in some way by his descent toward death. Some of the novel's episodes, which were termed "sensational" at the time of publication, now no longer seem so unique, and despite the awkwardness with which portions of the novel are narrated, Hunter's power as a storyteller moved his characters unerringly toward the slough of mutual desperation.

In *Strangers When We Meet* Hunter elected to describe a more muted kind of action in which a young architect, happily married and the father of two children, drifts into an affair with a suburban neighbor. Hunter showed a keen eye for the minute details that slowly gather round the illicit relationship, creating a highly realistic impression of a young man unable to cope with conflicting loyalties. Nonetheless, his characters finally seem insignificant—certainly not sufficiently strong to carry the philosophical baggage that the author gives them in an improbable conclusion.

A Matter of Conviction was a return to the mode of social protest that Hunter had developed so successfully in his two earlier novels. A polemic against the forces in society that make young men into killers, it was too contrived to offer more than passing interest. *Mothers and Daughters,* which chronicles the youth and maturity of four middle-class women—their dreams and their loves—is a more substantial work, despite its occasional melodrama.

Much of Hunter's fiction is over-written: striving for a realistic thickness, it bogs down in minutiae, and while the author writes with a high and consistent degree of professionalism, his vision rarely penetrates beneath the elaborate surfaces that his prose projects. *Last Summer* is a major exception to this adroit verbosity. It is told with an unforgettable simplicity and directness, which nonetheless conveys the author's own highly sophisticated point of view. During a summer holiday two teenage boys and a girl explore an Atlantic island, tell each other the "truth," and dominate a shy young girl. Their experiences end in violence, which vividly symbolizes the moral degeneracy of their society.

Few contemporary writers can match the versatility and consummate professionalism of Evan Hunter. His work includes a highly successful series of detective novels published under the pseudonym of Ed McBain; a science-fiction novel for children; a comic cops-and-robbers novel, *A Horse's Head,* written with great inventiveness and wit; and a spirited children's book in verse, illustrated by his own sons. *Sons* tells the story of three generations of a Wisconsin family, powerfully challenging some of the basic presumptions of the American Dream; *The Paper Dragon* is a densely plotted intriguing story of a five-day plagiarism trial; and *Buddwing* plunges its amnesiac hero into the heart of a Washington Square riot, a hold-up, and a crap game. *Nobody Knew They Were There* takes a futuristic look at the innate forces of violence that assail man's attempt to achieve world peace. Throughout a varied and highly prolific career, Hunter has produced a body of work distinguished for its sound craftsmanship, although only one of his novels, *Last Summer,* clearly demonstrates the art which such craft should sustain.

—David Galloway

HUNTER, Kristin (Elaine)

Nationality: American. **Born:** Kristin Elaine Eggleston, Philadelphia, Pennsylvania, 12 September 1931. **Education:** Charles Sumner School and Magnolia Public School, both Philadelphia; Haddon Heights High School, New Jersey, graduated 1947; University of Pennsylvania, Philadelphia, 1947-51, B.S. in education 1951. **Family:** Married 1) Joseph Hunter in 1952 (divorced 1962); 2) John I. Lattany in 1968. **Career:** Philadelphia columnist and feature writer, Pittsburgh Courier, 1946-52; teacher, Camden, New Jersey, 1951; copywriter, Lavenson Bureau of Advertising, Philadelphia, 1952-59; research assistant, School of Social Work, University of Pennsylvania, 1961-62; copywriter, Wermen and Schorr, Philadelphia, 1962-63; information officer, City of Philadelphia, 1963-64, 1965-66; director of health services, Temple University, Philadelphia, 1971-72; director, Walt Whitman Poetry Center, Camden, 1978-79. Lecturer in creative writing. 1972-79, adjunct professor of English, 1980-83, and since 1983 senior lecturer in English, University of Pennsylvania. Writer-in-residence, Emory University, Atlanta, 1979. **Awards:** Fund for the Republic prize, for television documentary, 1955; Whitney fellowship, 1959; Bread Loaf Writers Conference De Voto fellowship 1965; Sigma Delta Chi award, for reporting, 1968; National Council on Interracial Books for Children award, 1968; National Conference of Christians and Jews Brotherhood award, 1969; Christopher award, 1974; Drexel citation, 1981; New Jersey Council on the Arts fellowship, 1982, 1985; Pennsylvania Council on the Arts fellowship, 1983. **Agent**: Don Congdon Associates, 156 Fifth Avenue, Suite 625, New York, New York 10010. **Address:** 721 Warwick Road, Magnolia, New Jersey 08049, U.S.A.

PUBLICATIONS

Novels

God Bless the Child. New York, Scribner, 1964; London. Muller, 1965.
The Landlord. New York, Scribner, 1966; London, Pan, 1970.
The Survivors. New York, Scribner, 1975.
The Lakestown Rebellion. New York, Scribner, 1978

Uncollected Short Stories

"To Walk in Beauty," in *Sub-Deb Scoop* (Philadelphia), 1953.
"Supersonic," in *Mandala* (Philadelphia), vol. 1, no. 1, 1956.
"There Was a Little Girl," in *Rogue* (New York), 1959.
"An Interesting Social Study," in *The Best Short Stories by Negro Writers,* edited by Langston Hughes. Boston, Little Brown, 1967.
"Debut," in *Negro Digest* (Chicago), June 1968.
"Honor among Thieves," in *Essence* (New York), April 1971.
"The Tenant," in *Pennsylvania Gazette* (Philadelphia).
"Bleeding Berries," in *Callaloo* (Lexington, Kentucky), vol. 2, no. 2, 1979.
"The Jewel in the Lotus," in *Quilt 1* (Berkeley, California), 1981.
"Bleeding Heart," in *Hambone* (Santa Cruz, California), 1983.
"Perennial Daisy," in *Nightsun* (Frostburg, Maryland), 1984.
"Brown Gardenias," in *Shooting Star Review* (Pittsburgh), Fall, 1989.

Fiction (for children)

The Soul-Brothers and Sister Lou. New York, Scribner, 1968; London, Macdonald, 1971.
Boss Cat. New York, Scribner, 1971.
The Pool Table War. Boston, Houghton Mifflin, 1972
Uncle Daniel and the Raccoon. Boston, Houghton Mifflin, 1972.
Guests in the Promised Land: Stories. New York, Scribner, 1973.
Lou in the Limelight. New York, Scribner, 1981.

Plays

The Double Edge (Produced Philadelphia, 1965).

Television Play: *Minority of One,* 1956

*

Critical Studies: *From Mammies to Militants: Domestics in Black American Literature* by Trudier Harris, Philadelphia, Temple University Press, 1982, and article by Sondra O'Neale, in *Afro-American Fiction Writers after 1955* edited by Harris and Thadious M. Davis, Detroit, Gale, 1984.

Kristin Hunter comments:

The bulk of my work has dealt—imaginatively, I hope—with relations between the white and black races in America. My early work was "objective," that is, sympathetic to both whites and blacks, and seeing members of both groups from a perspective of irony and humor against the wider backdrop of human experience as a whole. Since about 1968 my subjective anger has been emerging, along with my grasp of the real situation in this society, though my sense of humor and my basic optimism keep cropping up like uncontrollable weeds.

*   *   *

In her first two novels Kristin Hunter played upon the contradictions between reality as it is experienced by the black urban poor and the false optimism of popular story. *God Bless the Child* parodies the tale of the enterprising but low-born youngster who, since the origins of middle-class fiction, has set out to achieve a place in society by the application of nerve and energy. In the case of Rosie Fleming, however, her vitality leads to failure, for by setting up as a small entrepreneur in the numbers game she earns the enmity of the white men who manage the poor people's version of finance capitalism. Despite her portrayal of the relentless power that destroys Rosie, Hunter is not resigned to a sense of human powerlessness. A sympathetic and complex portrayal of three generations of black women conveys an intensely humanistic conception of character, which in her second novel, *The Landlord,* becomes the basis for an optimistic theme. The formal foundation of this book is the novel of maturation. Its main character, determined to "become a man" by exercising mastery over his tenants, is frustrated and tricked at every turn as they disabuse him of the mythology of white male dominance. Against his will, and contrary to the assumptions of middle-class convention the landlord forms an admiration and appreciation for the diverse styles by which blacks cope with life's troubles, large and small.

Following publication of *The Landlord* Hunter occupied herself with stories of ghetto life directed toward younger readers. Like the adult novels that preceded them, these children's books reject the idealizations of popular genres while preserving a belief in the capacity of the black underclass to transform their lives by the power of their spirit. In both the adult and children's books the message has been that society's "victims" refuse the dehumanization that either social relations or a literature of pity would assign them.

This insider's view, informed by Hunter's commitment to the verve and quality of black life, led her to write two additional adult novels that must be termed celebrations. The first signifies by its title, *The Survivors,* its author's devotion to the rendition of character traits that enable a middle-aged dressmaker and a street kid to form an emotional and practical alliance that enables them both to overcome the predacious circumstances of the neighborhood. There are more than enough coincidence and pathos in the plot, but that is a small price to pay for the vibrancy of humor and characterization.

It is with *The Lakestown Rebellion,* however, that Hunter achieves the fulfillment of her craft. This story of a small black township, originally settled by fugitive slaves, battling against plans to build a highway that will destroy their homes, renews the tradition of the folk tricksters. A range of ingenious, zany, and simply unusual characters play the entire repertory of stereotypical roles popularly assumed to be black in order to stop the encroachment of "progress" upon their lives. The wit of the novel's conception perfectly suits Hunter's optimistic humanism. The book is so enjoyable one is almost unaware that it is also a symbolic reenactment of cultural history, but there can be no missing the fact that it places Hunter squarely in the tradition of Afro-American fiction at one of its best moments.

—John M. Reilly

I

IGNATIEFF, Michael

Nationality: Canadian. **Born:** Toronto, Ontario, 12 May 1947. **Education:** Upper Canada College, Toronto; University of Toronto, B.A., 1969; Harvard University, Boston, (teaching fellow in social studies), 1971-74, Ph.D., 1975; Cambridge University (research fellow, King's College), 1978-84, M.A., 1978. **Family:** Married Susan Barrowclough in 1977; one son and one daughter. **Career:** Reporter, *The Globe and Mail,* 1966-67; assistant professor of history, University of British Columbia, 1976-78; broadcaster, Channel 4, London, 1986. Since 1987, broadcaster, British Broadcasting Corp, London. Visiting fellow, École des Hautes Études, Paris, 1985; Alistair Horne Fellow, St. Anthony's College, Oxford, 1993-95. Editorial columnist, *The Observer,* 1990-93. **Awards:** Canadian Governor General's award, 1988, Heinemann prize, 1988, both for *The Russian Album.* **Agent:** Sheil Land Associates, 43 Doughty Street, London WC1N 2LF, England. **Address:** 37 Baalbec Road, London N5 1QN, England.

PUBLICATIONS

Novels

Asya. London, Chatto and Windus, and New York, Knopf, 1991.
Scar Tissue. London, Chatto and Windus, 1993; New York, Farrar Straus, 1994.

Plays

1919 (screenplay), with Hugh Brody. London, Faber, 1985.

Other

A Just Measure of Pain: The Penitentiary in the Industrial Revolution, 1750-1850. London, Macmillan, 1978.
The Needs of Strangers. London, Chatto and Windus, and New York, Viking, 1984.
The Russian Album. London, Chatto and Windus, and New York, Viking, 1987.
Blood and Belonging. London, BBC, 1993; New York, Farrar Straus, 1994.

Editor, with Jeffrey Rose, *Religion and International Affairs.* Toronto, Anansi, 1968.
Editor, with Istvan Hont, *Wealth and Virtue: The Shaping of Political Economy in the Scottish Enlightenment.* Cambridge, Cambridge University Press, 1983.

*   *   *

Michael Ignatieff arrived at fiction by the route of introspection, through sensitive and intelligent effort to understand both his personal and historical moment. He has produced two novels, *Aysa* and *Scar Tissue,* but his arrival as a fiction writer emerges organically from earlier prose works.

Trained as an historian, Ignatieff gravitated to social philosophy in *The Needs of Strangers,* a study of the issue of social responsibility in the modern state that focuses on the relationship between material and emotional needs, the question of rights to the fulfillment of needs, and a history of the concept of needs. He then produced *Blood and Belonging,* an intense, personal, and philosophical study of the pain-filled nationalisms in the Balkans, Northern Ireland, Germany, Ukraine, Quebec, and Kurdistan. In these volumes he demonstrates a rare balance between analysis and personal involvement, commitment conditioned by historical perspective.

Ignatieff won the 1988 Governor General's Award for Non-Fiction (the Canadian Pulitzer Prize) for *The Russian Album,* his account of his family's White Russian history and emigration to England and, later, Canada. In it he dramatizes life under the tsars in terms of the personal lives of his ancestors, including his grandfather, who was minister of education under Nicholas II, the last tsar.

From his knowledge of the Russian past comes *Aysa,* the life of a Russian princess who escapes to France and, much later, to England. The novel is enriched both by historical accuracy of detail and by the development of Aysa herself from a self-willed rich child to a suffering and perceptive woman. It is patently not stereotyped, for many of its emigres are prosperous and able, aware that the Russia they have left is gone yet constantly orbiting around things Russian, such as the struggle between the motherland and Hitler. It has a fatalism to its shape, coming to a conclusion when the 90-year-old Aysa finds the grave of her first husband in Moscow's Novodevichy cemetery. Although it owes structural debts to the sweeping historical epic novel, *Aysa* is anchored to the intimate life of a woman whose stature grows gently in the reader's eyes until she stands as a marker of strength of will mixed with keen self-knowledge drawn from the century of pain.

Scar Tissue is a book dominated by such a searing immediacy of anguish that it is, simply, hard to read. Yet it is so powerful and its subject matter so central to human experience that it exerts a grip on the imagination matched only by other unrelentingly direct fictions, like those of Samuel Beckett. It is the retrospective story of a man experiencing the degeneration and death of his mother from neurological disease and its effects on family, on love, on loyalty. Beyond that it subtly places the situation of one death and one family in medical and philosophical frameworks that go to the heart of human experience.

When, Ignatieff asks, does selfhood disappear when the mind is breaking apart—when memory goes, when recognition goes, when the plague overtakes the pathways in the brain? Is there always a self inside? And, if so, how horribly chaotic must be the terrible collage of the unlinked present and past, the life always lived among strangers because even loved ones are not remembered?

What makes these questions truly excruciating is the intense emotional and intellectual perspective of the middle-aged professor whose mother is dying. In an immense leap from the conventional omniscient chronological narration of Aysa, Ignatieff has mastered a style that mixes time and allows for the flows of feeling and language. The narrator looks backward for the first signs of his mother's change and charts the slow decline as it drags her loving husband to self-sacrifice and death and then immerses the narrator himself in a struggle of responsibility that ruins his marriage, damages his relationship with his brother, and nearly ruins his life.

Towering above all this affliction is his growing knowledge that he is seeing his own destiny, for his brother, who has become a neuroscience researcher, makes clear the condition is genetic. The narrator sees the scans of his mother's brain, strangely beautiful abstract colored designs, and he sees the patterns of the damaged chromosomes that mark the start of the cascade of tiny events of disease. As he struggles to continue to see his once vital, gifted mother as a person, she loses her personhood before his eyes, and he comes face to face with protracted living death.

The narrator's voice is so intense that criticism has been leveled at the autobiographical elements of the text. But that is to mistake its real achievement. *Scar Tissue* marks the emergence of a fully disciplined and original writer who communicates the deepest and most painful of human questions through the lives it portrays.

—Peter Brigg

IHIMAERA, Witi (Tame)

Nationality: New Zealander. **Born:** Gisborne, 7 February 1944. **Education:** Te Karaka District High School, 1957-59; Church College of New Zealand, 1960-61; Gisborne Boys High School, 1962; University of Auckland, 1963-66; Victoria University, Wellington, 1968-72, B.A. 1972. **Family:** Married Jane Cleghorn in 1970. **Career:** Cadet reporter, Gisborne *Herald,* 1967; journalist, Post Office Headquarters, Wellington, 1968-72; information officer, 1973-74, Third Secretary, Wellington, 1975-78, Second Secretary, Canberra, 1978, and First Secretary, Wellington, 1979-85, Ministry of Foreign Affairs; New Zealand Consul, New York, 1986-88; Counsellor on Public Affairs, New Zealand Embassy, Washington, D.C., 1989; lecturer, University of Auckland, 1990-95. **Awards:** Freda Buckland Literary award, 1973; James Wattie award, 1974, 1986; University of Otago Robert Burns fellowship, 1974; Scholarship in Letters, 1990; Katherine Mansfield fellowship, 1993. **Address:** 2 Bella Vista Road, Herne Bay, Auckland, New Zealand.

PUBLICATIONS

Novels

Tangi. Auckland and London, Heinemann, 1973.
Whanau. Auckland, Heinemann, 1974; London, Heinemann, 1975.
The Matriarch. Auckland and London, Heinemann, 1986.
The Whale Rider. Auckland, Heinemann, 1987; London, Heinemann, 1988.
Bulibasha. Auckland, Penguin, 1994.
Nights in the Gardens of Spain. Auckland, Secker and Warburg, 1995.

Short Stories

Pounamu, Pounamu. Auckland, Heinemann, 1972; London, Heinemann, 1973.
The New Net Goes Fishing. Auckland, Heinemann, 1977; London, Heinemann, 1978.
Dear Miss Mansfield: A Tribute to Kathleen Mansfield Beauchamp. Auckland, Viking, 1989; New York, Viking, 1990.

Other

Maori. Wellington, Government Printers, 1975.
New Zealand Through the Arts: Past and Present, with Sir Tosswill Woollaston and Allen Curnow. Wellington, Friends of the Turnbull Library, 1982.

Editor, with D.S. Long, *Into the World of Light: An Anthology of Maori Writing.* Auckland, Heinemann, 1982.
Editor, *Te Ao Marama: Maori Writing Since the 1980s, Vols. 1-4.* Auckland, Reeds, 1992-94.

*

Critical Studies: "Participating" by Ray Grover, in *Islands* (Auckland), Winter 1973; "Tangi" by H. Winston Rhodes, in *Landfall* (Christchurch), December 1973; "Maori Writers," in *Fretful Sleepers and Other Essays* by Bill Pearson, Auckland, Heinemann, 1974; *The Maoris of New Zealand* by Joan Metge, London, Routledge, 1977; *Introducing Witi Ihimaera* by Richard Corballis and Simon Garrett, Auckland, Longman Paul, 1984.

Witi Ihimaera comments:

There are two cultural landscapes in my country, the Maori and the Pakeha (European), and although all people, including Maori, inhabit the Pakeha landscape, very few know the Maori one. It is important to both Maori and Pakeha that they realize their dual cultural heritage, and that is why I began to write. Not to become the first Maori novelist but to render my people into words as honestly and as candidly as I could; to present a picture of Maoritanga which is our word for the way we feel and are, in the hope that our values will be maintained. I like to think that I write with both love—aroha—and anger in the hope that the values of Maori life will never be lost. So far I have written about exclusively Maori people within an exclusively Maori framework, using our own oral tradition of Maori literature, our own mythology, as my inspiration. Cultural difference is not a bad thing, it can be very exciting, and it can offer a different view of the world, value system, and interpretation of events. This is what I would like to offer: a personal vision of Maori life as I see it, the Maori side of New Zealand's dual heritage of culture.

*   *   *

Witi Ihimaera writes with a keen awareness of his cultural heritage and a profound commitment to the values and traditions of his people. A central feature of his imaginative landscape is the *whanau,* or extended family community, an emotional and cultural bastion eroded by urbanization and social fragmentation. Writing with "both love and anger," Ihimaera documents the traditional Maori way of life and the changes it has undergone since the coming of the Pakeha. Although his early works can be seen as pastoral and elegiac, Ihimaera does not idealize his subjects, rather he renders their trials and conflicts, joys and sorrows, shortcomings and strengths, with remarkable honesty and clarity. Drawing upon the rich resources of Maori myth and legend, he blends the past with the present, evoking the ancestral framework of historical continuity that is an essential part of Maoritanga. His work proclaims the vitality and significance of New Zealand's "other culture," one that Ihimaera suggests enriches the lives of Maori and Pakeha alike.

Many of the stories in Ihimaera's first collection, *Pounamu, Pounamu,* are set in the village of Waituhi, the geographical and cultural hearth—and heart—of the Whanau A Kai, to which much of his subsequent fiction returns. Both celebration and lamentation, they are lyrical evocations of a rural, communal way of life that is rapidly becoming a thing of the past. *Pounamu,* or greenstone— semi-precious jade traditionally used to make weaponry and jewelry—is Ihimaera's symbol of Maoritanga, and he contrasts it with the cold, glittering attractions of Pakeha culture in "the emerald city." One story in particular, "The Whale," dramatizes the conflicting claims of tradition and change, as an old man sits in the meeting house mourning the decay of the world that he knew and the loss of the young to the city's siren call. It is his granddaughter who articulates the dilemma that the young people face: "The world isn't Maori any more. But it's the world I have to live in. You dream too much. Your world is gone. I can't live it for you. Can't you see?"

Ihimaera's first novel, *Tangi,* is an extended meditation on the subject of *Pounamu, Pounamu*'s concluding story: Tama Mahana's return from Wellington (the emerald city) to attend the burial of his father. Structured by the ceremonial patterns of the funeral itself, *Tangi* is a work that mines the emotional intensity of loss and the communal rituals surrounding death. It is at once a mourning of the dead and an affirmation of the living, for Tama's personal grief and memories are tempered by the spirit of love and kinship that draws the community together on such occasions. Past, present, and future interconnect as Tama's individual response to his father's death is framed by the history of his *whanau,* and the mythic history of Maori legend: the separation of Rangitane, the sky father, from Papatuanuku, the earth mother, so that their children could dwell in the light. Coming to terms with his loss is, for Tama, a voyage of self-discovery and a recognition of his responsibility to uphold the tradition that is his father's legacy. Thus, Tama's journey into the future is focused through the myth of creation that underpins the novel, the separation of earth and sky that allowed "the dawning of the first day."

If, through the single consciousness of an individual, Ihimaera introduced his readers to the communal basis of Maoridom, then *Whanau* gives that extended grouping full fictional rein. Since the whanau is the combination of the land and its people, Ihimaera's approach is utterly in keeping with his title and theme. In an interrelated series of vignettes spanning a single day, he captures the lives of the individuals who compose the Whanau A Kai. Although deftly drawn, no one character in this novel could be said to be central; rather, it is the whanau itself that is the subject and focus. Through the reflections of sorrowing elders, disillusioned adults, and rebellious adolescents, *Whanau* records the slow disintegration of the traditional way of life as Pakeha culture encroaches and many of the young people willingly embrace its values at the expense of their Maoritanga. But it also symbolically affirms the strength of the cultural ties that bind this community as the *whanau* come together to search for their missing *kaumatua,* the revered patriarch who is their living link with the past.

The New Net Goes Fishing heralded a new streak of anger in Ihimaera's writing that would find its most clear expression in *The Matriarch.* Framed by two stories that allude to *The Wonderful Wizard of Oz, The New Net Goes Fishing* examines Maori in the urban setting of the emerald city. Although a few of the stories register success or acceptance in the Pakeha world, many focus on the conflicts arising from an impersonal, alien environment and the clash of two different value systems. Although this collection often proffers a bleak view of race relations, it does conclude on a note

of hope. Returning to Waituhi after twenty years in Oz, an old man stresses the need for his people to experience the best of both worlds. The complexities of Maori-Pakeha concourse, however, and his need to find a new means with which to express it, prompted a self-imposed hiatus. Nearly ten years later, Ihimaera broke his silence with a novel of epic historical proportions, *The Matriarch.*

Unabashedly aggressive, *The Matriarch* constitutes Ihimaera's battle cry. Mixing fact and fiction, biography and autobiography, myth and "reality," Ihimaera imaginatively reconstructs New Zealand colonial history from a Maori perspective. The novel challenges the claims of official history even as it declares its own contingency, and the inadequacy of any history to enclose and explain its subject. The woman warrior of the novel's title is Artemis Riripeti Mahana, the enigmatic figure who dominated the narrator's youth and who now dominates his memories as he struggles to understand her. His recollective investigation leads him further back to two significant ancestors, the warrior prophet, Te Kooti, and the politician, Wi Pere Halbert. All three are linked by a common cause: the fight to retain Maori land under Maori control, and this theme is the driving force behind the various histories and narrative styles that compose the novel. Although Maori myth-history and spirituality feature prominently in *The Matriarch,* Ihimaera draws freely upon European history and culture: the trials of his people are likened to those of the Israelites in Egypt, and the matriarch's instruction of her grandson is liberally interspersed with snatches of Verdi (in a symbolic paralleling of nationalist struggles). Although the matriarch herself remains shadowed by historical controversy, her political legacy is clear: "to fight the Pakeha you must learn to be like him. You must become a Pakeha, think like him, act like him and, when you know that you are in his image then turn your knowledge to his destruction." Critics are divided over the success of Ihimaera's unwieldy epic; what cannot be denied, however, is the scope and power of this ambitious work.

Ihimaera's next two works can be termed "occasional": *The Whale Rider* was written in anticipation of a visit by his teenage daughters, and the collection *Dear Miss Mansfield* marks the centenary celebrations of New Zealand's most famous writer. While *The Whale Rider* returns to the mythic territory of Ihimaera's ancestry in a lyric and positive revisioning of *Pounamu, Pounamu*'s "The Whale," *Dear Miss Mansfield* is a response to the work of an equally important literary ancestor, Katherine Mansfield. The titular letter that opens the collection is a song of homage to the divine Miss M., but the stories themselves evoke the subversive notion of "writing back" that characterizes *The Matriarch.* Playing Maori variations on Mansfield's themes, or retelling some of her most famous short stories from a Maori perspective, Ihimaera presents the other side of Mansfield's New Zealand in a self-conscious, intertextual refashioning. Ihimaera interprets his world through the lens of Maori culture, but he is also aware that that culture is not a static entity. Although *The Matriarch* and *Dear Miss Mansfield* proclaim that the Maori cannot be subsumed under the banner of Pakeha history, they also demonstrate that the latter has become a part of an ongoing Maori genealogy. Like the old man of "Return from Oz," Ihimaera incorporates the best of both worlds.

Bulibasha: King of the Gypsies continues the exploration of New Zealand's dual cultural heritage in Ihimaera's typical blend of fiction and autobiography. In some ways, *Bulibasha* is the paternal complement to *The Matriarch,* since the central relationship of the narrator with his grandparent is intermingled with the history of the tribe. With this novel, however, Ihimaera eschews metafictional bricolage in favor of a straightforward Bildungsroman concerning the anxiety of influence. The king of the novel's title is the Mahana family patriarch, a powerful economic and religious leader who rules the familial shearing gangs with an iron fist. Set against Bulibasha is the rival Poata clan, and his grandson, Simeon, whose verbal audacity and intellectual pursuits label him as *whakahihi:* too big for his boots. It is from Simeon's precocious perspective that the twin rivalries are related, and, like the matriarch, it is he who both challenges and upholds the traditions of his people. Set in the era of Ihimaera's youth, *Bulibasha* examines generational conflict and social change, offering an often humorous insight to the oral histories of which family legends are made. Simeon's perceptions testify to the intermingling of cultural landscapes: family dramas are often recounted and comically illuminated by the conventional plots of the American movies that Simeon watches so avidly; the ritualized conflicts between the two clans are the rivalries of Montagues and Capulets, and his heretical challenges to Bulibasha's authority are those of a mortal intent on toppling Olympus. The novel concludes with a resounding deconstruction of Bulibasha's mythic status, but Simeon's assumption of responsibility prompts a recognition of his grandfather's guiding principle: the family always comes first.

For Ihimaera, *Bulibasha* concerns the challenge of surviving familial influence and establishing one's separate identity. His most recent novel, *Nights in the Gardens of Spain,* explores the conflict between family and sexual identity. Equally as autobiographical as his earlier work, *Nights in the Gardens of Spain* nevertheless represents a radical new departure in Ihimaera's writing. The central character is Pakeha, a university lecturer torn between the love of his wife and two daughters, and his sexuality as a gay man. A coming out novel, *Nights* traces David's exploration of his sexual identity and the social and emotional complexities of being married and being gay. Many of the minor characters in the novel are satiric caricatures, and the narrator's characterization is an odd blend of cardboard gay Everyman and particularized individuality. Although *Nights* presents a provocative foray into the steamroom gardens of gay culture, the emotional center of the book—and of its web of Peter Pan allusions—lies in the narrator's powerful and often anguished relationship with his young daughters. *Nights in the Gardens of Spain* is Ihimaera's novelistic declaration that his writing need not necessarily be restricted to exclusively Maori issues. It also indicates, as one commentator has noted, that the category "Maori writer" is not one in which Ihimaera can be expected to stay.

—Jackie Buxton

IRELAND, David

Nationality: Australian. **Born:** Lakemba, New South Wales, 24 August 1927. **Family:** Married 1) Elizabeth Ruth Morris in 1955 (divorced 1976), two sons and two daughters; 2) Christine Hayhoe in 1984. **Career:** Worked as a greenskeeper, in factories, and at an oil refinery. **Awards:** *Adelaide Advertiser* award, 1966; Miles Franklin award, 1972, 1977, 1980; *The Age* Book of the Year award, 1980. **Member:** Order of Australia, 1981.

PUBLICATIONS

Novels

The Chantic Bird. London, Heinemann, and New York, Scribner, 1968.
The Unknown Industrial Prisoner. Sydney and London, Angus and Robertson, 1971.
The Flesheaters. Sydney and London, Angus and Robertson, 1972.
Burn. Sydney and London, Angus and Robertson, 1975.
The Glass Canoe. Melbourne and London, Macmillan, 1976.
A Woman of the Future. Ringwood, Victoria, Allen Lane, and New York, Braziller, 1979; London, Penguin, 1980.
City of Women. Ringwood, Victoria, Allen Lane, 1981.
Archimedes and the Seagle. Ringwood, Victoria, Viking, 1984; London, Viking, 1985; New York, Penguin, 1987.
Bloodfather. Ringwood, Victoria, Penguin, 1987; London, Hamish Hamilton, 1988.

Uncollected Short Story

"The Wild Colonial Boy," in *Winter's Tales 25,* edited by Caroline Hobhouse. London, Macmillan, 1979; New York, St. Martin's Press, 1980.

Play

Image in the Clay (produced Sydney, 1962). Brisbane, University of Queensland Press, 1964.

*

Critical Study: *Double Agent: David Ireland and His Work* by Helen Daniel, Ringwood, Victoria, Penguin, 1982; *Atomic Fiction: The Novels of David Ireland* by Ken Gelder, Brisbane, University of Queensland Press, 1993.

*   *   *

David Ireland is one of Australia's most innovative prose stylists. His first three novels depict a world that is in its "industrial adolescence," obsessed with profit and production to the point where those who do not contribute to industry (the poor, the aged, the unemployed) are treated as failures and misfits—as social lepers. *The Chantic Bird* offers this view in semi-comic fashion, its alienated teenage narrator providing a jaded running commentary on existence: "If there is no other life, why is this one so lousy?" Written in the absurdist-surrealist mode, but viewing its subject matter more somberly, *The Flesheaters* is set in a boarding-house for the poor and unemployed.

To counter the pervasive "functional" mentality (which insists that all human activity must have a public and profit-making purpose, Ireland's fictions insist upon the psychic value to the individual of such "useless" (but natural) activities as day-dreaming, fantasizing, and self-expression. Realistic treatments merge with fantasy sequences, and oblique viewpoints reveal familiar behavior from unusual angles. (Some of these effects verge on magical-realism, and Ireland has acknowledged his interest in South American writers of this school.) Ireland structures his works as scattered fragments, like elaborate mosaics constructed from tiny pieces, and this presentation clearly reflects not only his sense of the fragmentation of experience but also a celebration of its gloriously frustrating diversity.

Arguably the best of Ireland's early novels, *The Unknown Industrial Prisoner* portrays the life of workers in a foreign-owned Sydney oil refinery, examining their plight piece by piece and layer by layer until the fragmented mosaic builds into a microcosm of Australian industrial society. Ireland himself worked for a time in such a refinery, and the novel provides an absurdist (but acutely authentic) record of the dehumanization of the workforce, the emasculation of management, and the laziness and inefficiency of both employer and employee.

The Unknown Industrial Prisoner is an angry and rigorous account of the absurdities of industrialism. But Ireland is Australia's most intensely *analytical* writer, and it should therefore come as no surprise that he is prepared to question the assumptions behind his own angry sense of injustice. This analytic quality is seen in frequent bitter references to the workers as "the soil" in which the "money tree" of industry is growing. This is primarily an image of protest at exploitation and degradation, but it can also be seen as a wholly natural organic image (for if there is to be a "money tree" there must be "soil" to sustain it). Instead of accepting social realities at face value, Ireland digs for underlying assumptions and implications.

Monotonous conformity is the keynote of Ireland's vision of Australian society. He sees Australians as tame and insipid, bowed in philistine worship to the god of materialism. *The Chantic Bird* portrays the people of Sydney sitting at home at night, "filling in insurance policies on their fowls, their wrought-iron railings, concrete paths, light globes, their health, funeral expenses, borers, carpets," and so on; *The Glass Canoe* deals with characters who escape this monotony by drowning their woes in "amber fluid" (beer). A bawdy and violent celebration of life in a Sydney pub, *The Glass Canoe* portrays the urban drinkers as the last of a colorful "tribe" which preserves values (such as mateship and "macho" brawniness from Australia's mythic past.

Though the writer of this essay would defend Ireland's earlier novels, most critical opinion favors the works of his "second phase." These recent novels have moved more clearly in the direction of fable, the prose style has become remarkably agile and witty, and the author's earlier concern with specific political issues has broadened into a preoccupation with the inner world of the imagination. The later novels are more mellowed and sensuous without having lost any of their radical analytical edge.

A Woman of the Future is Ireland's first attempt to create a full-scale female character, but—more importantly—it is an attempt to confront Australia's dauntingly masculine national self-image. It deals with the outlook and adventures of an intellectually gifted young female about to take crucial end-of-school exams before venturing upon life in the larger world. By setting the novel some years in the future, Ireland allows himself to extrapolate the effects of current social problems (especially unemployment), but the novel's chief concern is to draw a parallel between the young heroine stepping out into life, and her country—Australia—stepping out into nationhood. Ireland has argued in an interview that "women seem more open [than men] to experience and to new things," and *A Woman of the Future* attempts to redefine the national consciousness in these terms. But the book is also concerned with female sexuality, and many of its sexual episodes proved controversial (some because they were explicit, some because they addressed female sexuality in allegedly male language).

City of Women pursues these preoccupations, but often by questioning them. Ostensibly, the novel is set in the city of Sydney after all males have been expelled, and tells the story of an aging mother's loneliness after her daughter has joined an engineering project in the heart of the continent. Challenging the premise that women have an outlook different to that of men, Ireland portrays the city of women as being no different from the former city of men. The functions of bully or criminal or whinger are still fulfilled—but by women, not men (which suggests that the basic humanity of the sexes is more important than their differences). However, this judgment in turn is questioned when the novel's ending reveals that the City of Women exists only in the mind of the eccentric central character. Though frequently criticized as a "cop out," this unexpected denouement is an effective means of insisting upon the value of individual viewpoint and perception.

As if having had enough of women, Ireland's most optimistic novel takes a dog as its central character. *Archimedes and the Seagle* is the memoir of a dog in the city of Sydney . . . but it is also a deliberately (and successfully) "upbeat" novel, celebrating the joys of life and the beauties of nature even in the midst of a huge city's urban sprawl. The novel asserts Ireland's optimism about the world, re-affirming his preoccupation with fantasy and individual perception. It is a slight work, but successfully exuberant.

Bloodfather is generally considered to be Ireland's best work to date. A *Bildungsroman,* presented in the by now familiar fragmentary "mosaic" pattern, it clearly draws deeply upon aspects of Ireland's own experience. The life of young David Blood is traced from infancy to his teenage years, recording the child's evolving perception of his environment, his growing awareness that he needs a God (and that this God will provide him with his life's work). But the book's richness lies not in *what* it is about but the *way* it deals with that material; in the words of reviewer Mary Rose Liverani, "The sources of pleasure in *Bloodfather* are too many to explore in a very brief review: enjoyment of characters who are portrayed with uninhibited affection, exploration of religious, moral and social issues in language that is genuinely fresh and unexpected, and the affirmation of the god-like in mankind and the universe."

—Van Ikin

IRVING, John (Winslow)

Nationality: American. **Born:** Exeter, New Hampshire, 2 March 1942. **Education:** Phillips Exeter Academy, Exeter, graduated 1962; University of Pittsburgh 1961-62; University of Vienna, 1963-64; University of New Hampshire, Durham, B.A. (cum laude), 1965; University of Iowa, Iowa City, M.F.A. 1967. **Family:** Married 1) Shyla Leary in 1964 (divorced 1981), two sons; 2) Janet Turnbull in 1987. **Career:** Taught at Windham College, Putney, Vermont, 1967-69; lived in Vienna, 1969-71; writer-in-residence, University of Iowa, 1972-75; assistant professor of English, Mount Holyoke College, South Hadley, Massachusetts, 1975-78. **Awards:** Rockefeller grant, 1972; National Endowment for the Arts grant, 1974; Guggenheim grant, 1976; American Book Award, for paperback, 1980. **Agent:** Sterling Lord Literistic, 1 Madison Avenue, New York, New York 10010. **Address:** c/o William Morrow Inc., 105 Madison Avenue, New York, New York 10016, U.S.A.

PUBLICATIONS

Novels

Setting Free the Bears. New York, Random House, 1969; London, Corgi, 1979.
The Water-Method Man. New York, Random House, 1972; London, Corgi, 1980.
The 158-Pound Marriage. New York, Random House, 1974; London, Corgi, 1980.
The World According to Garp. New York, Dutton, and London, Gollancz, 1978.
The Hotel New Hampshire. New York, Dutton, and London, Cape, 1981.
The Cider House Rules. New York, Morrow, and London, Cape, 1985.
A Prayer for Owen Meany. New York, Morrow, and London, Bloomsbury, 1989.
A Son of the Circus. New York, Random House, and London, Bloomsbury, 1994.

Short Stories

Trying to Save Piggy Snead. London, Bloomsbury, 1993.

Uncollected Short Stories

"A Winter Branch," in *Redbook* (New York), November 1965.
"Weary Kingdom," in *Boston Review,* Spring-Summer 1968.
"Almost in Iowa," in *The Secret Life of Our Times,* edited by Gordon Lish. New York, Doubleday, 1973.
"Lost in New York," in *Esquire* (New York), March 1973.
"Brennbar's Rant," in *Playboy* (Chicago), December 1974.
"Students: These Are Your Teachers!," in *Esquire* (New York), September 1975.
"Vigilance," in *Ploughshares* (Cambridge, Massachusetts), no. 4, 1977.
"Dog in the Alley, Child in the Sky," in *Esquire* (New York), June 1977.
"Interior Space," in *Fiction* (New York), no. 6, 1980.
"Trying to Save Piggy Sneed," in *The Bread Loaf Anthology of Contemporary American Short Stories,* edited by Robert Pack and Jay Parini. Hanover, New Hampshire, University Press of New England, 1987.

*

Manuscript Collection: Phillips Exeter Academy, Exeter, New Hampshire.

Critical Studies: Introduction by Terrence DuPres to *3 by Irving* (omnibus), New York, Random House, 1980; *Fowles, Irving, Barthes: Canonical Variations on an Apocryphal Theme* by Randolph Runyon, Columbus, Ohio State University Press, 1982; *John Irving* by Gabriel Miller, New York, Ungar, 1982; *Understanding John Irving* by Edward C. Reilly, Columbia, South Carolina, University of South Carolina Press, 1991.

Theatrical Activities:
Actor: **Film**—*The World According to Garp,* 1982.

*   *   *

The publication of *The World According to Garp* was an important event in contemporary American literature. For John Irving himself, of course, the novel's reception must have been extremely gratifying: the book neatly divided his career forever into the pre- and post-*Garp* periods. Initially a little-known academic novelist whose first three books—*Setting Free the Bears, The Water-Method Man,* and *The 158-Pound Marriage*—rapidly sought the remainder lists, he suddenly found himself inundated by critical superlatives and, no doubt, positively drenched in money. He achieved that rare combination of literary acclaim and wide readership that every writer dreams of. The success of *Garp,* following the previous achievement of E.L. Doctorow's *Ragtime,* indicated that after many years of stifling academicism, fiction may have finally graduated from college and ventured out into the arena of ordinary life. Because many professors seem to believe that literature was written exclusively to be studied in their courses and because far too many writers receive their training in those courses, a great deal of American writing has been marked by a sterile obsession with technique for its own sake, a conscious avoidance of traditional subjects, a fatal attraction to critical theory, and a perverse desire to appeal only to a coterie of initiates.

Irving's works in general, and *Garp* most spectacularly, signal the return of fiction to its proper and honorable concerns—a close engagement with the stuff of real life, a profound compassion for humanity, and—inextricably and possibly even causally connected to these qualities—great dedication to the narrative process, to storytelling itself. Irving cares deeply for his characters and their stories and makes his readers care for them as well; in doing so he places his work in the great lineage of the novel. Only a bold and innovative writer could venture so daringly backward into the literary past. His three most significant books at this point in his career—*The World According to Garp, The Cider House Rules,* and *A Prayer for Owen Meany*—indicate that this late 20th-century American novelist also participates in the traditions of the 19th-century English novel. Long, leisurely narratives, densely populated with eccentrics, attentive to the whole lives of virtually all the characters, replete with coincidence and foreshadowing, full of allusions to specific writers and works, his novels combine a Dickensian richness of character and emotion with a Hardyesque sense of gloom and doom.

In addition to his refreshingly old-fashioned qualities, Irving also demonstrates his appropriateness to his own time and place. His novels are in many ways as contemporary as those of any of his peers. In addition to a growing sense of topicality, most fully realized in *A Prayer for Owen Meany,* they display all the familiar landmarks of the American literary countryside: violence, grotesquerie, a certain craziness, a racy, energetic style, and a powerful interest in the fiction-making process. They differ from one another in manner, matter, and merit—*The 158-Pound Marriage* seems his weakest performance—but they also share certain peculiarly Irvingesque subjects that create their special zany charm. Until *The Cider House Rules,* his books all dealt with such matters as academia, art, children, marital triangles and quadrangles, wrestlers, writers, sexual mutilation, Vienna, and bears. Bears creep through his first book and also show up in the long story "The Pension Grillparzer," that appears in *The World According to Garp* as well as *The Hotel New Hampshire.*

The pre-*Garp* Irving is lively, comic, whimsical, a writer whose works display immense confidence, a kind of assured easiness rare in a young beginner, far beyond the usual condescending cliches about promise. *Setting Free the Bears* is a revitalized American picaresque improbably set in Austria; the goal of its protagonist's lunatic quest is suggested in its title and works out to be as improbable as its location. *The Water-Method Man* deals with the sexual escapades, personal failures, and professional problems of a more or less lovable rogue wonderfully named Bogus Trumper; it explores, with rich glee, some fascinating notions about the creation of art from the chaos of Trumper's life, through the medium of avant-garde filmmaking and Trumper's absurd doctoral dissertation.

Whatever the value of his earlier work, however, in retrospect it seems a preliminary for *The World According to Garp,* which entirely altered Irving's career. The novel is written with enormous energy and strength, clearly the work of writer in full command of his material and his method. Although its style presents no particular problems and its plot moves in a leisurely, straightforward manner, the novel seems radically experimental for its complicated narrative progress. Its ostensibly simple story of the life of T.S. Garp from conception to death is interrupted by a number of other fictions from "The Pension Grillparzer" to a horribly violent account of rape, murder, and despair, Garp's own novel, *The World According to Bensenhaver;* the book also includes bits from Garp's mother's autobiography, *A Sexual Suspect,* other short stories, and parts of the biography of Garp that will only be written after his life and the book are over. In an action that must have called for some courage, Irving even includes an epilogue, detailing the lives of his characters after the main events of his major fiction have concluded: once again, in reverting to the methods of the past the author seems daringly innovative.

The actual subjects and events of *Garp,* just as unusual as its narrative archaism, come to dominate all of Irving's works. Although the novel itself was almost universally regarded as comic and, in Irving's words, "life affirming," it is an immensely sad and troubling book, haunted by violence, savagery, fear, horror, and despair. From beginning to end a bleeding wound gapes across the book: Garp's mother slashes a soldier in a theater; his father dies of a terrible war wound; his wife bites her lover's penis off in the same automobile accident that kills one of Garp's sons and half-blinds the other; and Garp's own novel, *The World According to Bensenhaver,* employs one of the most vivid rape scenes in all of literature. The relationship between sexuality and mutilation is emphasized through virtually every character—from Roberta Muldoon, the transsexual former football player to the man-hating feminists who cut out their own tongues to commemorate the maiming of a rape victim; Garp himself is assassinated by a cult member, the sister of the girl who was responsible for his sexual initiation.

Irving's fascination with sex-related violence and sexual mutilation winds disturbingly through most of his works, from the gang rapes of *The Cider House Rules* through the *hijras*—transvestite eunuchs—of India and the transsexual serial murderer Rahul in *A Son of the Circus.* Along with the bizarre and horrific narratives and the close attention to the character and life of the artist, the theme of sexual mutilation suggests something about the creative act itself. Throughout his works, art is generated out of sex, fear, pain, blood, and guilt; experiencing all these, Irving's artists create their fictions, which also make up a large part of the books about them, sometimes even as in *A Son of the Circus,* attempting to "write" life as if it were their own narrative. Sex, art, life, and the interpretation of both provide his rich and often puzzling structures, sometimes leading away from their initially simple, comic narrative lines into a region of horror, grotesquerie, insanity, and myth.

The post-*Garp* Irving, no longer the obscure academic writer, was rapidly transformed into the celebrity author, attentive to sales, publicity, and movie rights. He soon began to appear on the television talk shows, demonstrating his recipe for breaded veal cutlet; dressed in wrestler's togs and flexing his wrestler's muscles, he brooded handsomely in full color for readers of slick magazines. His good looks, his popularity, and his willingness to publicize his books and films earned him a more than literary fame and no doubt a more than literary fortune—his post-*Garp* works are copyrighted by something called Garp Enterprises Ltd. *The Hotel New Hampshire* and *The Cider House Rules* demonstrate the pernicious influence of success. The former continues some of the subjects of its predecessor, boiling over with violence and whimsy—a gang rape, a plane crash, suicide, terrorism, a lesbian in a bear suit, and a flatulent dog named Sorrow. Although the obsessions remain intact, they seem mechanical and perfunctory in style and substance; the laborious drollery and the easy cynicism, along with the specious profundities of the repeated catch phrases and verbal tags, read like warmed-over Vonnegut.

The Cider House Rules, on the other hand, shows that the author can move away from a possibly fatal self-imitation in new directions. Irving discovers for the first time the depths and possibilities of his natural penchant for Dickensian storytelling by inventing a truly Irvingesque place, an orphanage where abortions are performed. Though heavily dependent on the kind of research that hinders so many academic authors, *The Cider House Rules* recaptures some of the original Garpian compassion. The quirkiness of style and the fascination with genital wounds and sexual pain remain, but they are mixed with less labored touches of lightness and a good deal of love.

The Dickens and the Hardy influences flourish in *A Prayer for Owen Meany,* his finest work after *Garp,* which shows the author once again in full command of his considerable gifts and more fully aware of the tradition in which he works. Returning to the autobiographical mode that fuels the energy of *Garp,* Irving once again reports terrible events in a straightforward, even comic style, invents some remarkable people—especially the title character—and explores some of his favorite subjects. In addition, he more explicitly confronts his repeated theme of problematic paternity and this time attempts to provide reason and causality for what he had previously presented as the horrible mischancing of coincidence and fate; in *A Prayer for Owen Meany* Irving has found religion, specifically Christianity. He employs a nicely orchestrated set of typically unusual symbols and a variety of people and events to express the religious dimension, which encompasses the primitive and mythic as well as the various Protestant orthodoxies. As a result the book suggests a more energetic but less lapidary and learned John Updike.

The novel, along with the long, rather disordered exploration of India in *A Son of the Circus,* demonstrates that Irving has challenged himself in new ways; instead of settling for the sort of repetition that pleases far too many readers, he has chosen to break new ground. In a relatively brief time and at a relatively young age, John Irving has become a major contemporary novelist. His considerable body of work displays originality, development, and richness of subject and theme. His startling mixture of humor and sorrow, accessibility and complexity, clarity and confusion, of strong narrative with humane vision, of horrified despair with life-affirming comedy seems perfectly suited to end-of-century culture and literature. The chord he struck in a large and varied public with *Garp* continues to resonate; his works still appeal to a readership that encompasses many levels of literacy, an indication of their timeliness and power.

—George Grella

ISHIGURO, Kazuo

Nationality: British. **Born:** Nagasaki, Japan, 8 November 1954. **Education:** Woking County Grammar School for Boys, Surrey, 1966-73; University of Kent, Canterbury, B.A. (honors) in English and Philosophy 1978; University of East Anglia, Norwich, M.A. in creative writing 1980. **Career:** Community worker, Renfrew Social Works Department, 1976; social worker, 1979-80, and re-settlement worker, West London Cyrenians Ltd., 1979-80. **Awards:** Winifred Holtby prize, 1983; Whitbread award, 1986; Booker prize 1989. D.Litt.: University of Kent, 1990. Fellow, Royal Society of Literature. **Agent:** Deborah Rogers, Rogers Coleridge and White Ltd., 20 Powis Mews, London W11 1JN, England. **Address:** c/o Faber and Faber, 3 Queen Square, London WC1N 3AU, England.

PUBLICATIONS

Novels

A Pale View of Hills. London, Faber, and New York, Putnam, 1982.
An Artist of the Floating World. London, Faber, and New York, Putnam, 1986.
The Remains of the Day. London, Faber, and New York, Knopf, 1989.

Uncollected Short Story

"A Family Supper," in *The Penguin Book of Modern British Short Stories,* edited by Malcolm Bradbury. London, Viking, 1987; New York, Viking, 1988.

Plays

Television Plays: *A Profile of Arthur J. Mason,* 1984; *The Gourmet,* 1986.

*   *   *

Kazuo Ishiguro has established a considerable reputation on the strength of only three novels, resulting in his being awarded the Booker prize in 1989 for *The Remains of the Day.* However, as each of these novels is crafted in an inimitable, meticulously observed manner, it is not surprising that Ishiguro was given this literary accolade so early on in his writing career.

The three novels are characterized by the way the calm expository style, and seemingly unimportant concerns of the narrators, disguise a world fraught by regrets, unresolved emotional conflicts, and a deep yearning to recapture (and make sense of) the past. In the case of *A Pale View of Hills* and *An Artist of the Floating World,* the central figures are, like Ishiguro, Japanese by birth, and their personal desires to excavate the past indicate not only a troubled personal history, but much broader issues concerned with Japanese society in the immediate post-war period.

Ishiguro's first full-length work, *A Pale View of Hills,* is set in present-day rural England, where Etsuko, a Japanese widow comes to terms with her elder daughter's recent suicide. The sad event of the present precipitates memories of the past, and leads the mother to recall certain aspects of her life in Nagasaki just after the war. In particular, she remembers her friendship with the displaced, inde-

pendent, and rather cruel Sachiko, a woman once of high rank, now living in poverty with her neglected, willful daughter, Mariko. An elegant, elliptical composition, this novel (or perhaps more precisely novella) hints at connections between Etsuko's Nagasaki days and her present-day English existence. Her half-understood relationship with the enigmatic Sachiko and Mariko prefigures her problematic one with her own daughters, while Sachiko's displacement from her class, and, with the vagrant woman's enthusiastic espousal of all things American, her turning away from her race anticipate Etsuko's future anomie.

A striking feature of this confident first novel is the underlying sense of the macabre that pervades Etsuko's memories, particularly in her recollection of the strange, perhaps not entirely imaginary, woman whom young Mariko claims to know, and who appears like a character from a Japanese folk tale. This hinting at sinister possibilities, coupled with the way that Ishiguro with the skill of a miniaturist delicately shapes the story around shifting perspectives and selective memories, marks out *A Pale View of Hills* as a compelling and intriguing debut work.

While Etsuko's narrative betrays hesitation and uncertainty from the beginning, the narrator of *An Artist of the Floating World* is a much more robust creation. It is 1948 and Masuji Ono, a painter who has received great renown for his work, some of which was decidedly nationalistic in its objectives, reconsiders his past achievements in the light of the present. As with the previous novel, little of consequence seems to happen. Over a number of months, Ono is visited by his two daughters, is involved in marriage negotiations on the part of one of them, re-visits old artist colleagues, drinks in the "Migi-Hidari," and, in a beautifully evoked scene, attends a monster movie with his grandson. However, these seemingly mundane domestic occurrences gradually force the elderly painter to review his past to reveal a complex personal history of public and private duties, professional debts and ambitions, and possible culpability in Japan's recent military past. More obviously than in *A Pale View of Hills,* the central character is both an individual and a representative figure. Through Ono's re-visiting of his past life, Ishiguro describes very skillfully an artist's training and work conditions before the war, raising much more general questions about artistic and personal responsibility during this contested period in Japan's history.

Ono's "floating world" is "the night-time world of pleasure, entertainment and drink," frequented by fellow artists. The narrators of all Ishiguro's novels inhabit "floating worlds" distinct from the much visited, and joyfully described, pleasure-quarter. For them the old assumptions they held about their lives are under scrutiny, leaving them to try to make sense of the brave new "floating worlds" they inhabit. In *The Remains of the Day,* Ishiguro examines the changed cultural climate of post-war England through the attempts by Stevens, a "genuine old-fashioned English butler" (in the words of his American employer), to make sense not only of the present but, more acutely, of the past. As with the other novels, this tale of self and national discovery is precisely dated. In July 1956 the butler of the late Lord Darlington sets forth on a motoring holiday, accompanied by Volume III of Mrs Jane Symons's *The Wonders of England,* to meet Miss Kenton, housekeeper at Darlington Hall during the inter-war years.

In the previous novels, Ishiguro raises questions about the relationship between personal and public morality. In the figure of Stevens, he presents public and domestic behavior as indivisible. Stevens has renounced family ties in order to serve his masters, having given up many years of his life to Darlington. As he sojourns in the West Country, Stevens reconsiders his time in service to the English aristocracy. *The Remains of the Day,* like the novels with Japanese settings, is distinguished by the skilled use of first-person narration. Here the stiff formality and prim snobbery of the butler's voice are maintained throughout, demonstrating the way that Stevens has renounced his individuality in order to serve well, and creating also some splendid moments of comedy when the events narrated are inappropriately described in such dignified and constrained tones.

In Ishiguro fashion, the "truth" is gradually hinted at through summoning up memories of things passed, and Stevens has to admit that his former master to whom he has devoted a good part of his life was possibly an incompetent amateur diplomat who was manipulated by National Socialists in the 1930s. However, as with the previous novels, the confrontation with an earlier, at times misguided, self offers hope for the future, and the endings of these precisely composed books are gently optimistic, rather than painfully elegiac, celebrating people's capacity for adaptation, understanding, and change.

—Anna-Marie Taylor

IYAYI, Festus

Nationality: Nigerian. **Born:** 1947. Educated in Nigeria; University of Bradford, Yorkshire, Ph.D. 1980. **Career:** Economic correspondent for several newspapers in Bendel; industrial training officer, Bendel State University, Ekpoma. Currently lecturer in business administration, University of Benin, Benin City. **Awards:** Association of Nigerian Authors prize, 1987; Commonwealth Writers prize, 1988. **Address:** Department of Business Administration, University of Benin, PMB 1154, Ugbowo Campus, Benin City, Nigeria.

PUBLICATIONS

Novels

Violence. London, Longman, 1979.
The Contract. London, Longman, 1982.
Heroes. London, Longman, 1986.

*   *   *

". . . those who carry the cross for society always get crucified in the end . . ."

(Heroes)

Festus Iyayi's three novels, *Violence, The Contract,* and *Heroes,* expose the abject penury and disenfranchisement that constitute the social reality of the majority of Nigerians. In language that is often vitriolic and stinging, Iyayi's protagonists potently display his contempt for the rampant corruption that strangles contemporary Nigeria. Businesspersons, politicians, generals, and other officials hoard the country's wealth and power at the expense of the working class. This base depravity of the ruling class manifests itself in various forms and ultimately trickles down to the ruled class. In each of Iyayi's novels the real tragedy is this: those of the ruled class are either forced or coerced to absorb their oppressor's abuse. They in turn release their anger and frustration not upon the deserving ruling class, but rather upon and amongst themselves. Iyayi, however, does weave threads of hope within each of the three narratives via truculent calls by the main characters to defy their oppressors en masse and fight for their civil rights as well as for the future of their country.

Violence usually connotes physical abuse, but in his first novel, *Violence,* Iyayi redefines it as a continual, demoralizing structure that eliminates hope, pride, self-esteem, health, and the ability to live independently. Having to always rely on borrowed naira from those that are more fortunate leaves deep scars of shame and guilt. Iyayi's violence creeps into the corners of the pneuma of the lower classes, the have-nots, and renders them feeling helpless against the machine powered solely by money, corruption, and opportunity.

Obofun and Queen exemplify Nigeria's corrupt, monied class. Obofun makes his millions by winning coveted building contracts through his connections in the government and through the relinquishing of percentages of the contracts' total worth to those who award them. His wife, Queen, sleeps with other men to get what she wants—namely supplies, which are otherwise expensive and scarce, for her hotels.

When Idemudia, a typical, destitute laborer, is fortunate enough to find work, the conditions at the site are deplorable. If he wants to keep his job and be able to feed himself and his wife, Adisa, then he has to swallow the maltreatment. If he chooses to fight the system, to organize the workers against his boss, Queen, and to ask for higher wages and better conditions, then he risks being fired and subsequent starvation.

One of the most effective passages in *Violence* is a series of lines from a play performed at a local hospital. Iyayi utilizes this poignant and very effective device to convey his definition of violence. Idemudia witnesses this play, is educated and inspired by the actor who denounces violence and advocates resistance, and then leads his co-workers in threatening to strike for better wages and conditions.

Iyayi's writing continues to be mordacious and gripping in his second novel, *The Contract.* The main character, Ogie, returns to Benin after an absence of four years and is amazed and disgusted at how quickly and completely the city has decayed. There is filth and chaos everywhere. He learns that the government awards contracts for building hospitals, roads, and low-cost housing, then demands percentages for awarding the contract. This practice leaves little or no money for building the structures the contract was for—resulting often in inferior and often abandoned projects. The people of Benin live in squalor while a few wealthy, corrupt officials get fatter. Anything can be bought or sold. Men will even offer their wives for a favored chance at winning a contract, or lie, cheat, and even kill for fortunes.

Like Idemudia in *Violence,* Ogie's abomination of the stark contrasts of wealth and poverty in his hometown is potently conveyed. He swears he will fight the system of which even his father is a part. He takes a job at the council and soon finds himself tortuously torn and confused over right and wrong. He continues to reaffirm decent convictions, but eventually compromises his values to become "corruption with a human face." He decides he cannot beat the system entirely, but can take the money he receives from the contract percentages and invest it in Benin and local businesses, rather than hoard it in a Swiss bank account.

Heroes, Iyayi's third and latest novel, is set against the background of Nigeria's civil war in the late 1960s. As in his previous work, Iyayi's style is forceful and bold. Once again, he cries out against the injustices in Nigeria through well-crafted characters and electrifying writing.

Osime is a journalist and supports the vociferous calls for a united Nigeria and those denouncing the Biafran soldiers and exalting the Federal troops. He sees the Federal troops as the saving force for Nigeria. But when the Federal troops shoot and kill his girlfriend's father without cause in cold blood, he begins to realize that there is more to the war than he had originally thought.

Osime quickly sees that even though the Biafran and Federal troops commit wretched crimes, the generals and the officers are the real enemies of the people of Nigeria. The soldiers have learned to become murderers from the military's officers—they are merely instruments of destruction under the orders of officers who seek power, territory, and fortune.

Osime's solution is the formation of a third army—one that fights the greedy politicians, businesspersons, and generals. A total revolution, powered by the third army, could eliminate the corrupt officials reigning at the top of all sectors of Nigerian society and replace it with rule by those who love the land, work the land, and therefore respect it and its inhabitants.

Iyayi's criticism of Nigerian society is relentless in all three novels, but even amongst the dire revelations and depressing reality of the polarities of privation and opulence in Nigeria, he offers an encouraging creed for social change: "A people are never conquered. Defeated, yes, but never conquered. . . ." (*Heroes*) Iyayi's masterful prose indeed has a message for us all.

—Susie deVille

JACOBSON, Dan

Nationality: British. **Born:** Johannesburg, South Africa, 7 March 1929. **Education:** The University of the Witwatersrand, Johannesburg, 1946-49, B.A. 1949. **Family:** Married Margaret Pye in 1954; three sons and one daughter. **Career:** Public relations assistant, South African Jewish Board of Deputies, Johannesburg, 1951-52; correspondence secretary, Mills and Feeds Ltd., Kimberley, South Africa, 1952-54. Fellow in Creative Writing, Stanford University, California, 1956-57; visiting professor, Syracuse University, New York, 1965-66; visiting fellow, State University of New York, Buffalo, 1971, and Australian National University, Canberra, 1980; lecturer, 1976-80, reader, 1980-88, professor of English, 1988-94, University College, London. Since 1994, professor emeritus, University College, London. Vice-chair of the Literature Panel, Arts Council of Great Britain, 1974-76. **Awards:** Rhys Memorial prize, 1959; Maugham award, 1964; H.H. Wingate award (*Jewish Chronicle*, London), 1978; Society of Authors traveling scholarship, 1986; J.R. Ackerley award, for autobiography, 1986. Fellow, Royal Society of Literature, 1974. **Agent:** A.M. Heath, 79 St. Martin's Lane, London WC2N 4AA, England; or, Russell and Volkening Inc., 50 West 29th Street, New York, New York 10001, USA.

PUBLICATIONS

Novels

The Trap. London, Weidenfeld and Nicolson, and New York, Harcourt Brace, 1955.
A Dance in the Sun. London, Weidenfeld and Nicolson, and New York, Harcourt Brace, 1956.
The Price of Diamonds. London, Weidenfeld and Nicolson, 1957; New York, Knopf, 1958.
The Evidence of Love. London, Weidenfeld and Nicolson, and Boston, Little Brown, 1960.
The Beginners. London, Weidenfeld and Nicolson, and New York, Macmillan, 1966.
The Rape of Tamar. London, Weidenfeld and Nicolson, and New York, Macmillan, 1970.
The Wonder-Worker. London, Weidenfeld and Nicolson, 1973; Boston, Little Brown, 1974.
The Confessions of Josef Baisz. London, Secker and Warburg, 1977; New York, Harper, 1979.
Her Story. London, Deutsch, 1987.
Hidden in the Heart. London, Bloomsbury, 1991.
The God-Fearer. London, Bloomsbury, 1992; New York, Scribner, 1993.

Short Stories

A Long Way from London. London, Weidenfeld and Nicolson, 1958.
The Zulu and the Zeide. Boston, Little Brown, 1959.
Beggar My Neighbour. London, Weidenfeld and Nicolson, 1964.
Through the Wilderness. New York, Macmillan, 1968.

Penguin Modern Stories 6, with others. London, Penguin, 1970.
A Way of Life and Other Stories, edited by Alix Pirani. London, Longman, 1971.
Inklings: Selected Stories. London, Weidenfeld and Nicolson, 1973; as *Through the Wilderness,* London, Penguin, 1977.

Play

Radio Play: *The Caves of Adullan,* 1972.

Other

No Further West: California Visited. London, Weidenfeld and Nicolson, 1959; New York, Macmillan, 1961.
Time of Arrival and Other Essays. London, Weidenfeld and Nicolson, and New York, Macmillan, 1963.
The Story of the Stories: The Chosen People and Its God. London, Secker and Warburg, and New York, Harper, 1982.
Time and Time Again: Autobiographies. London, Deutsch, and Boston, Atlantic Monthly Press, 1985.
Adult Pleasures: Essays on Writers and Readers. London, Deutsch, 1988.
The Electronic Elephant: A Southern Africa Journey. London, Hamilton, 1994.

*

Bibliography: *Dan Jacobson: A Bibliography* by Myra Yudelman, Johannesburg, University of the Witwatersrand, 1967.

Manuscript Collections: National English Literary Museum, Grahamstown, South Africa; University of Texas, Austin.

Critical Studies: "The Novels of Dan Jacobson" by Renee Winegarten, in *Midstream* (New York), May 1966; "Novelist of South Africa," in *The Liberated Woman and Other Americans* by Midge Decter, New York, Coward McCann, 1971; "The Gift of Metamorphosis" by Pearl K. Bell, in *New Leader* (New York), April 1974; "Apollo, Dionysus, and Other Performers in Dan Jacobson's Circus," in *World Literature Written in English* (Arlington, Texas), April 1974, and "Jacobson's Realism Revisited," in *Southern African Review of Books,* October 1988, both by Michael Wade; "A Somewhere Place" by C.J. Driver, in *New Review* (London), October 1977; *Dan Jacobson* by Sheila Roberts, Boston, Twayne, 1984; "Stories" by John Bayley, in *London Review of Books,* October 1987; "Intolerance" by Julian Symons, in *London Review of Books,* October 1992; "The Mother's Space" by Sheila Roberts, in *Current Writing* (South Africa) 5(1), 1993; "Weapons of Vicissitude" by Richard Lansdown, in *The Critical Review* (Australia) 34, 1994.

Dan Jacobson comments:
My novels and stories up to and including *The Beginners* were naturalistic in manner and were written almost entirely about life in South Africa. This is not true of the novels I have written subsequently.

*　　*　　*

Dan Jacobson's first two novels, *The Trap* and *A Dance in the Sun,* marked him as a writer of considerable ability, with an interest in typically South African "problems." Since then, he has developed rapidly to become one of South Africa's best known and most interesting novelists.

The two early novels are both concerned with the tensions inherent in the extremely close, almost familial, relationships between white employer and black employee, which tend to develop in the particular kind of farm community Jacobson describes. Both embody what might be described as allegorical statements about the South African situation. Jacobson implies that the inhabitants of the country are trapped in their own environment and condemned to perform a ritualistic "dance in the sun." To an outsider this can only appear to be a form of insanity. This vision of South Africa leaves out of account, or, at best, finds irrelevant, the group (English speaking, liberal, white) to which Jacobson himself belongs, and it is, therefore, not surprising that he should have chosen to live and work abroad.

For some years, however, his novels continued to deal with South African subjects. *The Evidence of Love* tells the story of a black man and a white woman who fall in love and attempt to defy South African law and custom by living together. The novel treats the theme of interracial love in a more relaxed and naturalistic way than is usual in South African fiction, and also highlights aspects of the individual struggle for freedom and the achievement of self-identity. *The Price of Diamonds* focuses on shady dealings and financial corruption in a small town in South Africa, and reveals Jacobson's quite considerable gift for comedy.

The Beginners, which, together with the collection of stories *A Long Way from London,* established Jacobson's position as a writer of stature, is an ambitious and substantial novel. The story of three generations of an immigrant Jewish family, it offers a penetrating, subtle, and complex analysis of what it means to be a "demi-European at the foot of Africa" and a "demi-Jew" in the modern world. The novels which follow *The Beginners* are not concerned with South Africa directly, nor are they naturalistic in manner. But two of the three later novels deal with political tensions and power struggles, and in so doing appear to have deliberate parallels with the contemporary situation in South Africa. Jacobson's continuing interest in South Africa is also reflected in his collection of autobiographical pieces, *Time and Time Again,* in which he reflects, among other things, on the way in which his perceptions of the country have changed since the days when he could see it only as a place from which he had to escape.

The Rape of Tamar is a witty and sophisticated reconstruction of an episode at the court of the biblical King David, focusing on a power struggle between the aging king and his politically ambitious sons. *The Wonder-Worker,* set in contemporary London, explores the world of a sensitive and lonely character whose inability to establish meaningful relationships leads inevitably to his complete alienation from the world around him, but, paradoxically, also to his ability to understand people completely. Jacobson's novel, *The Confessions of Joseph Baisz,* is a brilliantly inventive and deeply disturbing fantasy: the "extraordinary autobiography" of an emotionally stunted individual who discovers very early in his bleak life that he is capable of loving only those people whom he has first betrayed. Set in an imaginary country with a nightmarish but distinctly recognizable resemblance to South Africa, the novel is wholly convincing in its portrayal of a society whose members illustrate what Baisz calls "the iron law: the wider their horizons, the narrower their minds."

Like other contemporary South African novelists, Jacobson has written some excellent short stories. Many of them probe the guilts and fears of white South Africans living in the midst of what they regard as an alien and hostile black culture. Two stories which are among the best things he has done are "The Zulu and the Zeide" and "Beggar My Neighbour." The former contrasts the small-minded meanness of a wealthy Jewish businessman with the unaffected humanity of the black servant he employs to care for his ailing father; while "Beggar My Neighbour" movingly evokes the world of a young white boy forced to come to terms with the cruel realities of a racist society through his chance meeting with two black children. In these stories, as in all his work, Jacobson's special skills are displayed: detailed observation, economic presentation, and a compassionate but objective analysis of the varieties of human behavior.

—Ursula Edmands

JACOBSON, Howard

Nationality: British. **Born:** Manchester, 25 August 1942. **Education:** Stand Grammar School, 1953-60; Downing College, Cambridge, 1961-64, B.A. in English 1964. **Family:** Married Rosalin Sadler in 1978; one son from a previous marriage. **Career:** Lecturer, University of Sydney, New South Wales, 1965-68; supervisor, Selwyn College, Cambridge, 1969-72; senior lecturer, Wolverhampton Polytechnic, West Midlands, 1974-80. Presenter, *Traveller's Tales* television series, 1991; currently freelance book reviewer, the *Independent,* London. **Agent:** Peters Fraser and Dunlop, 503-504 The Chambers, Chelsea Harbour, Lots Road, London SW10 0XF, England.

PUBLICATIONS

Novels

Coming from Behind. London, Chatto and Windus, 1983; New York, St. Martin's Press, 1984.
Peeping Tom. London, Chatto and Windus, 1984; New York, Ticknor and Fields, 1985.
Redback. London, Bantam Press, 1986; New York, Viking, 1987.
The Very Model of a Man. London, Viking, 1992; New York, Overlook Press, 1994.

Uncollected Short Story

"Travelling Elsewhere," in *Best Short Stories 1989,* edited by Giles Gordon and David Hughes. London, Heinemann, 1989; as *The Best English Short Stories 1989,* New York, Norton, 1989.

Other

Shakespeare's Magnanimity: Four Tragic Heroes, Their Friends and Families, with Wilbur Sanders. London, Chatto and Windus, and New York, Oxford University Press, 1978.
In the Land of Oz (travel). London, Hamish Hamilton, 1987.

Roots Schmoots: Journey Among Jews. London, Viking, 1993; New York, Overlook, 1994.

*

Howard Jacobson comments:

It is an irony not lost on novelists that though they inveigh against all characterizations of their work in reviews, in profiles, and even on the covers of their own books, the moment they are invited to describe themselves, they say they would rather not.

I too, would rather not. Except to say that an argument about the nature of comedy—an argument I go on having largely with myself—is at the back of everything I write. The familiar formula, that comedy stops where tragedy begins, is unsatisfactory to me. The best comedy, I maintain, deals in truths which tragedy, with its consoling glimpses of human greatness, cannot bear to face. Comedy begins where tragedy loses its nerve. That's the sort of comedy I try to write, anyway.

*   *   *

"You know what novelists are like—they spill their guts on every page and claim it's plot." So Barney Fugelman is told by his second wife Camilla in Howard Jacobson's second novel, *Peeping Tom.* That fiction writers must draw on their own experience in order to give their work a ring of truth is something of a truism, but Jacobson's easy familiarity with Lancashire, Wolverhampton, Cambridge, Cornwall, and Australia and his sharply observed portrayals of academic life and the urban Jewish psyche give his bawdy, scatological books a piquant verisimilitude. The themes which pervade his novels—ideological duplicity, cultural self-consciousness, sexual ambivalence, and gnawing self-doubt—could make some readers uncomfortable as they recognize themselves within his glass, were it not for the verve and aplomb of the humor with which they are relayed. And although Jacobson's protagonists often share the same individual afflictions and obsessions—identity crises, failed relationships, self-conscious Judaism, robustly masculine sexual preoccupations—and inhabit similar *milieux* (characters occasionally put in appearances in one another's novels), the underlying issues have universal appeal and are dealt with in a way which is simultaneously reassuring and thought-provoking.

Sefton Goldberg, the subject of Jacobson's first novel and only third-person narrative *Coming from Behind,* is a man with a great future behind him. Manchester born, Cambridge educated and now doomed to ignominy in his post at a Midlands polytechnic which is in the throes of merging with the local football club, he spends his days applying unsuccessfully for every available academic post and skirmishing with colleagues. He is jealously obsessed with the success of these colleagues' publications while he himself, as yet unpublished, plans to write a tome on failure, which trait in himself is another obsession. Doggedly leading the lifestyle of a transient visitor, his condition is aggravated by his refusal to make the best of his situation and environment. He is finally granted an interview for a post in Cambridge, only to discover that he is to be in competition with, and interviewed by, his former students. The result is a success which is so thoroughly compromised on all sides that it is practically a Pyrrhic victory: a success achieved through a failure to fail consummately.

In Jacobson's most ribald book, *Peeping Tom,* Barney Fugelman discovers under hypnosis that he is somehow reincarnated from (or possibly related to) Thomas Hardy and, it transpires, the Mar-

quis de Sade. Incest, voyeurism, troilism and auto-erotic hanging all feature in the plot as the sexual predilections of the narrator's alter-egos manifest themselves through him, helping to precipitate his downfall and the ruin of his two marriages. What is being examined is the confusion of sexual and personal identities: Barney has two unwanted guests in his psyche and cannot tell if he is loved for himself, for Hardy, or for de Sade. Nor is it made easy for him to get a purchase on his real self in terms of his psychological make-up or his personal history. His parents swap spouses with their neighbors and so, compounded by his mother's intimations and revelations, Barney is never sure of his true relationship to Rabika Flatman, his father's paramour and the object of his own erstwhile voyeuristic fantasies. The discovery that Mr. Flatman is in fact his real father merely completes the symmetry, it is the resolution of the comic mechanism.

His most recent novel, *Redback,* is remarkable not least of all because the logistics of the plot neatly mirror Clive James's semi-autobiographical trilogy, *Unreliable Memoirs.* But James—himself namechecked within—tells a vastly different story to that of Leon Forelock, who leaves Cambridge with a degree in Moral Decencies and is assigned by the CIA to purge Australia of its non-conformist elements. Castigating homosexuals, drug-takers, and anyone voicing an opinion remotely left of the far-right, he censors and bans his way through University campuses and bookstalls. But Leon practices much of what he preaches against and relishes the privileges of the Englishman abroad while setting obscure questions on Langland's *Piers Plowman* as a test for prospective immigrants. The narrative is informed, however, by Forelock's epiphanic conversion, the occasion of which is a bite inflicted by the venomous redback spider of the title. Given a new outlook on humanity, doomed to suffer a myriad of recurring symptoms which include priapism and kept under surveillance by his former employers, Leon overtly embraces all that is radical and bohemian in the world. His priapism is a metaphor for the contradictions of his moral condition: the rampant impotence of his own self.

Jacobson's work has been compared to that of Kingsley Amis, Malcolm Bradbury and David Lodge and rightly so, for he exhibits many themes, nuances and preoccupations in common with them. Certain elements of his work do lack finesse: tendencies toward stereotypical characters and meandering narrative are apparent on occasions, as is what some might claim to be an unhealthy dwelling on all things phallic. Nonetheless, his characters evoke pathos even in their more grotesque or puerile moments, his plots are thoughtful and rounded and his wit is dry and infectious. After less than a decade spent writing in his chosen genre, Jacobson seems set to become a major force in English comic fiction.

—Liam O'Brien

JAMES, Kelvin Christopher

Nationality: Trinidadian (immigrated to United States, U.S. citizenship pending). **Born:** Port of Spain, Trinidad. **Education:** University of West Indies (St. Augustine), B.S. (honors) in zoology and chemistry 1967; Columbia University, New York, M.A. in 1975, M.Sc. in education 1976, and doctorate in science education, 1978. **Career:** Science researcher, Department of Agriculture, Trinidad, 1961-64; high school science teacher, Trinidad, 1968-70; technologist in chemistry lab, Harlem Hospital, 1970-76. Since 1980, full-time writer. **Awards:** New York Foundation for the Arts award, 1989. **Agent:** Joy Harris, 156 Fifth Ave., Suite 617, New York, New York 10010, U.S.A. **Address:** 1295 Fifth Ave., New York, New York 10029, U.S.A.

PUBLICATIONS

Novel

Secrets. New York, Random House, 1993.

Short Stories

Jumping Ship and Other Stories. New York, Random House, 1992.

* * *

Trinidadian writer Kelvin Christopher James began writing full-time in 1980. Prior to that he taught high school science in Sangre Grande before emigrating to New York, where he worked as a lab technician at Harlem Hospital Center and eventually earned a Ph.D. in science education from Teachers College, Columbia University. His background in zoology contributes richly to the lush, sensual landscapes in both of his works.

In his debut collection of short stories—*Jumping Ship and Other Stories*—James paints a bold canvas of savage sexuality, physical and mental incarceration, and bloody revenge. The first five stories are set in the Caribbean, followed by two transitional tales of immigrants making the difficult adjustment to a new country. The remaining stories take place in a hard-edged, gritty Harlem. At a first glance, the collection appears desultory in theme. But a closer look reveals an intriguing evocation of ritual that is a unifying thread through most of the stories—in the intense games of sibling rivalry in "Littleness"; in the rote cruelties of the street in "Guppies"; in the inscrutable circumstances of an Obeah voodoo ceremony in "Tripping." These rituals, both terrifying and essential, bring into sharp relief the visceral quality of life for many of the characters.

The descriptive language of the stories is potent and visual, if occasionally self-conscious. At times, the violence of the Harlem tales seems to be gratuitous, and one wishes for a little more narrative cohesion to lend them some purposefulness. Still, the author is quite effective with a story like "Home is the Heart," in which a father severs the bonds of his youth in order to form a stronger alliance with his son.

In James's second work, the novel *Secrets,* he seems more at ease and in his natural element. Here the author uses idiomatic language and natural description to good effect: The fecund earth—the ripening fruit and buzzing flies of island life—mirror a young girl's sexual coming-of-age. And as with most mythopoeic tales, the prosaic becomes profound. An expedition in search of *balata,* an elusive, pulpy fruit that nests high in the trees, transcends the commonplace to become a virtual odyssey.

The story is told from the viewpoint of Uxann, a plump, bookish Catholic schoolgirl, who steals mangoes from her neighbor, cooks mouthwatering meals for her Paps, and gossips mercilessly with best friend Keah. The author captures convincingly the easy rhythms and musings of a typically self-absorbed adolescent, and from the opening sentences he thrusts the reader into her almost excessively sensual, dangerously naive world. But soon the novel and Uxann's life take on the character of a folktale, with the discovery of a snake in her island's Garden of Eden. Uxann's journey becomes at once universal and disturbingly out of the ordinary. The author is commended for retelling an age-old story in such an imaginative way and for capturing a young girl's sexual odyssey with candor and insight.

In both these works, James unearths the darker forces that lie in wait beneath the surface, whether they be in a tropical jungle or an asphalt one.

—Lynda Schrecengost

JAMES, P(hyllis) D(orothy)

Nationality: British. **Born:** Oxford, 3 August 1920. **Education:** Cambridge Girls' High School, 1931-37. During World War II worked as a Red Cross nurse and at the Ministry of Food. **Family:** Married Ernest Connor Bantry White in 1941 (died 1964); two daughters. **Career:** Prior to World War II, assistant stage manager, Festival Theatre, Cambridge; principal administrative assistant, North West Regional Hospital Board, London, 1949-68; principal, Home Office, in police department, 1968-72, and criminal policy department, 1972-79. Justice of the Peace, Willesden, London, 1979-82, and Inner London, 1984. Chair, Society of Authors, 1984-86; governor, BBC, and board of the British Council, 1988-93; chair, Arts Council Literature Advisory Panel, 1989-92. Lives in London. **Awards:** Crime Writers Association award, 1967, Silver Dagger award, 1971, 1975, 1986, Diamond Dagger award, 1987. D.Litt.: Buckingham, 1992; London, 1993; Hertfordshire, 1994; Glasgow, 1995. Associate Fellow, Downing College, Cambridge, 1986; Fellow, Institute of Hospital Administrators, Royal Society of Literature, 1987, and Royal Society of Arts. O.B.E. (Officer, Order of the British Empire), 1983. Baroness, 1991. **Agent:** Greene & Heaton, Ltd., 37 Goldhawk Road, London W12 8QQ, England.

PUBLICATIONS

Novels

Cover Her Face. London, Faber, 1962; New York, Scribner, 1966.
A Mind to Murder. London, Faber, 1963; New York, Scribner, 1967.
Unnatural Causes. London, Faber, and New York, Scribner, 1967.
Shroud for a Nightingale. London, Faber, and New York, Scribner, 1971.
An Unsuitable Job for a Woman. London, Faber, 1972; New York, Scribner, 1973.
The Black Tower. London, Faber, and New York, Scribner, 1975.
Death of an Expert Witness. London, Faber, and New York, Scribner, 1977.
Innocent Blood. London, Faber, and New York, Scribner, 1980.
The Skull Beneath the Skin. London, Faber, and New York, Scribner, 1982.
A Taste for Death. London, Faber, and New York, Knopf, 1986.
Devices and Desires. London, Faber, 1989; New York, Knopf, 1990.
The Children of Men. London, Faber, 1992; New York, Knopf, 1993.

Original Sin. London, Faber, 1994; New York, Knopf, 1995.

Uncollected Short Stories

"Moment of Power," in *Ellery Queen's Murder Menu.* Cleveland, World, 1969.

"The Victim," in *Winter's Crimes 5,* edited by Virginia Whitaker. London, Macmillan, 1973.

"Murder, 1986," in *Ellery Queen's Masters of Mystery.* New York, Davis, 1975.

"A Very Desirable Residence," in *Winter's Crimes 8,* edited by Hilary Watson. London, Macmillan, 1976.

"Great-Aunt Ellie's Flypapers," in *Verdict of Thirteen,* edited by Julian Symons. London, Faber, and New York, Harper, 1979.

"The Girl Who Loved Graveyards," in *Winter's Crimes 15,* edited by George Hardinge. London, Macmillan, and New York, St. Martin's Press, 1983.

"Memories Don't Die," in *Redbook* (New York), July 1984.

"The Murder of Santa Claus," in *Great Detectives,* edited by D.W. McCullough. New York, Pantheon, 1984.

"The Mistletoe Murder," in *The Spectator* (London), 1991.

"The Man Who Was 80," in *The Man Who.* London, Macmillan, 1992.

Play

A Private Treason (produced Watford, Hertfordshire, 1985).

Other

The Maul and the Pear Tree: The Ratcliffe Highway Murders, 1811, with Thomas A. Critchley. London, Constable, 1971; New York, Mysterious Press, 1986.

*

Critical Study: *P.D. James* by Norma Siebenheller, New York, Ungar, 1981; *P.D. James* by Richard B. Gidez, Boston, Hall, 1986.

*   *   *

Starting from a conventional first detective story, *Cover Her Face,* P.D. James has moved toward fiction in which criminal investigation provides merely a loose structure for characterization, atmosphere, and theme, which now seem most important to her. In this assault on generic boundaries, she resembles, but is more determined than, Dorothy L. Sayers, Josephine Tey, and Ngaio Marsh. Consequently, James's detectives—Cordelia Gray (private and young) and Adam Dalgliesh (professional and middle-aging)—have been absent from or muted in recent works.

Commander Dalgliesh resembles other detectives created by women writers: tall, dark, attractive, and frangible (he is ill, bashed, or burned in half his novels). "When the Met . . . want to show that the police know . . . what bottle to order with the *canard à l'orange* . . . , they wheel out Dalgliesh," a hostile chief inspector says. Sensitive under seeming coldness, he has published several volumes of poetry. Before his first appearance, Dalgliesh's wife has died in childbirth, but in successive novels her presence dies away. At one time readers hoped that Cordelia Gray would take her place, but romantic notes have ceased to be struck; Cordelia has disappeared, and Inspector Kate Miskin, introduced in *A Taste*

of Death has not replaced her. In fact, few James characters are happily married, and there are no juvenile leads to assert the normality of love. There are, however, close, psychologically incestuous brother-sister relationships.

James once told an interviewer that she believes detective fiction can lessen our fear of death. Yet her details of what happens after death—the doctor's fingers penetrating the orifices of the female body, the first long opening cut of an autopsy—are scarcely reassuring. Other shocks of mortality include the skulls of plague victims packed cheekbone to cheekbone in the crypt of Courcy Castle in *The Skull Beneath the Skin,* James's most gothic novel, and boatloads of the elderly sailing out to die in *The Children of Men.*

Although few of James's settings are as conventional as the house party in *Skull,* her action generally takes place in closed, often bureaucratic communities: e.g., a teaching hospital, a psychiatric clinic, a forensic laboratory, or a nuclear power station, organizations which draw, no doubt, upon the author's own administrative experiences.

In terms of plot, James is most successful when dealing with the processes of investigation and is weakest in motivation. She has said she thinks in terms of film sequences; her latest novels contain variants of the "chase," and the long "panning" shots and close-ups in which she relentlessly describes interiors have become at times an intrusive mannerism. Perhaps her best, most controlled use of domestic detail occurs in *Innocent Blood,* where Phillipa furnishes a flat to greet her just-released murderess mother. Indeed, this violent *Lehrjahr* with its slower discoveries, its ambiguities, and its psychological images in "the wasteland between imagination and reality" is James's best claim to consideration as a "serious" novelist.

James's characters have always thought and talked about truth, faith, responsibility, and justice, even if not profoundly. But in the books that follow *Innocent Blood,* plot is almost lost amid talkiness and theme. The nature of Sir Paul Berowne's religious experience in *A Taste for Death,* for instance, is more important and less explicable than the identity of his blood-happy killer. In *Devices and Desires* (title drawn from the Book of Common Prayer) a nuclear power station and a ruined abbey confront each other, perhaps adversarially, in one of James's bleak coastal landscapes. They are surrounded by serial murder, terrorism, anti-nuclear and pro-animal protesters, cancer, drowning, anti-racism, a libel suit—all pretexts and conveniences for a plot which the novel is not about. Dalgliesh is present, but almost a bystander, although he finds a corpse and almost dies in the fire that consumes the killer. Since then he has appeared in *Original Sin,* heading the investigation into the deaths of a young publisher and his sister, but is even more detached, except for brief bravura scenes, which demonstrate his sureness of touch and of technique. Instead, Kate Miskin is to the fore, with a Jewish detective who tries to be an atheist. The "original sin" is presumably the Nazi murder long ago of a woman and her two children, whom her husband finally avenges by murdering the two children of the man responsible. Ironically, however, they had merely been adopted to satisfy a childless wife, whose infertile husband is not particularly fond of his "offspring."

In *The Children of Men,* a futurist thriller, published between *Devises and Desires* and *Original Sin,* James opts for brutality. The year is 2021; mankind has lost the power to reproduce, and Xan is Warden of England. The narrator, Xan's cousin and once his advisor, is attracted to a tiny protest group, "The Five Fishes," and particularly to Julian, who is almost miraculously pregnant. To escape Xan's protective care, they embark on a wild drive, during which the religious Luke is bludgeoned to death by a band of "Painted Faces." Julian bears a son, but her midwife is murdered. When Xan appears, the narrator shoots him and becomes Warden in his stead. He signs a cross on the newborn's head. But, the reader wonders, will the state of the world really improve? In a 1985 interview, James described herself as born with a sense "that every moment is lived, really, not under the shadow of death but in the knowledge that this is how it's going to end." This sense now dominates her fiction.

—Jane W. Stedman

JANOWITZ, Tama

Nationality: American. **Born:** San Francisco, California, 12 April 1957. **Education:** Barnard College, New York, B.A. 1977; Hollins College, Virginia, M.A. 1979; Yale University, New Haven, Connecticut, 1980-81. **Career:** Model, Vidal Sassoon, London and New York, 1975-77; assistant art director, Kenyon and Eckhardt, Boston, Massachusetts, 1977-78; writer-in-residence, Fine Arts Works Center, Provincetown, Massachusetts, 1981-82; since 1985 freelance writer. **Awards:** Bread Loaf Writers fellowship, 1975; Janoway Fiction prize, 1976, 1977; National Endowment award, 1982. **Agent:** Jonathan Dolger, 49 East 96th Street, New York, New York 10028. **Address:** c/o Crown Publishers, 201 E. 50th St., New York, New York 10022, U.S.A.

PUBLICATIONS

Novels

American Dad. New York, Putnam, 1981; London, Picador, 1988.
A Cannibal in Manhattan. New York, Crown, 1987; London, Pan, 1988.
The Male Cross-Dresser Support Group. New York, Crown, and London, Picador, 1992.

Short Stories

Slaves of New York. New York, Crown, 1986; London, Picador, 1987.

Uncollected Short Stories

"Conviction," in *The New Generation,* edited by Alan Kaufman. New York, Doubleday, 1987.
"Case History No.179: Tina," in *Between C and D,* edited by Joel Rose and Catherine Texier. New York, Penguin, 1988.

*   *   *

Among reports emanating from the front line of the war of attrition presently being waged in the name of normality, few can match Tama Janowitz's commentaries on the race of fakes, freaks, and flakes who inhabit the sprawling no-man's land of social non-achievement. Janowitz's characters are the walking wounded, the holed-in-the-water hapless fools who, by accident or design (never

their own), just happened to get in the way of the action. Patrolling the space bordered on one side by total obscurity, on another by bizarre notoriety and on a third by a spectacular failure, the objective of these curiosities, stated or otherwise, is to seek another boundary, the crossing of which will mean acceptance into the ranks of the adequate.

In *American Dad,* a tale of familial disaffection, the part of principal loser is assigned to Earl Przepasniak, aided, in an admirable supporting role by his mother Mavis, a neglected poet. The awe-inspiring shadow of father and husband Robert falls over them both. Przepasniak senior's reputation rests not so much upon an ability to practice his profession (psychiatry) as on his talents in another field: "Can you imagine what it is for me, five-foot-six-inches," asks Earl "to live up to a six-foot-tall Dad whose sexual prowess is mythical in the northwestern corner of a certain New England state?" Following the inevitable divorce of his parents, Earl takes refuge in his mother's house, at one stage resorting almost to complete misanthropy, with the aim of escaping his father's admonishing glare. Having developed the feminine side of Earl's nature and made a virtue of his mawkishness Janowitz finishes the novel with the death of Mrs. Przepasniak, the end of Earl's reclusivity, and sends him, completely unanchored, slipping back into society, struggling with his independence and the demands of shaping an identity.

American Dad is many things—an imaginative view of current family life, a semi-parodic interpretation of the "coming of age" saga, an extravagant joke at the hero's expense (with a predictable but nevertheless agreeable punch-line) and a subtle dissection of the place of analysis, not only psychological, in contemporary culture—but above all a statement about what it is to lack overtly masculine merit in a seemingly male oriented meritocracy.

Janowitz's second major publication, *Slaves of New York,* a cluster of connected short stories, exhibits an array of aspiring Greenwich Village artists, gallery owners and their associates. Akin here to the season-ticket-holding spectator of a perpetually losing side, Janowitz casts her gaze around the sparse crowd of her fellow disaster addicts and is rewarded with a splendid display of self-delusion, clashing colors, and reckless hope. Eleanor, an extension of the female aspects of Earl Przepasniak, appears in several pieces, forming a loose link within the book but, more importantly, providing the remark which stamps a larger thematic imprint on the whole of Janowitz's output—"It's hard for me to figure out how to be a social being." Slaves not really of New York, but more shackled by their own modish attitudes and the self-promoting opinions of others, Janowitz's cast of egos and spaced-out oddities people a highly artificial environment of which they can only barely make sense. Taken in isolation, the stories in *Slaves of New York* lack the epigrammatic sparkle that enlivened *American Dad* and, as a whole, have not the dynamism of the earlier work. Neither of these problems is apparent in Janowitz's second novel *A Cannibal in Manhattan.*

Transplanted from his native island of New Burnt Norton to even more fierce surroundings, Mgungu Yabba Mgungu, the eponymous "cannibal" relates the history of his intended journey toward greater civilization. Mgungu, nominal leader of the withered and disenfranchised Lesser Pimbas and possessor of the recipe for a narcotic which has made his tribal life even more bearable during 65 years of indolence has, we soon discern, been brought to America solely to be exploited. That this only becomes explicit through the knowing use of extra-narrative devices deployed by Janowitz is testimony to the sophistication of her wit and the profundity of Mgungu's gullibility.

Duped at every turn, unwittingly implicated in a horrendous crime, abandoned by his erstwhile sponsors, this distinctly unmythical savage slides towards vagrancy and is eventually apprehended in typically ridiculous circumstances. Yet, his mind-numbing naiveté, his fondness for drink, his unenviable record as a chief and his occasionally incongruous use of language serve to alert us to the possibility that he may not be wholly reliable. Manipulating her characters with a barely concealed Nabokovian glee, Janowitz draws a world of drug-dealing, treachery, and self-aggrandizement, underpinning it with an alternative landscape of itinerancy, drunken camaraderie, and self-destruction.

Mgungu's passage through the first sphere is a journey of missed connections and plans gone awry, allowing the reader plenty of space to fill in the details—his trawl through the second, leaves less to the imagination. Guilty or innocent, Mgungu is a thoroughly engrossing guide to his own misfortune and the richly inventive tale of a decline into contemporary civilization is both stunningly funny, and damningly true.

Although seeming to avoid overtly political statements in her fiction, Janowitz addresses the issues of feminism, racism, capitalism and cultural imperialism in a genuinely original and surprising manner, containing equal elements of humor, seriousness, and warmth. Calling her the poet of the inept fails to fully convey the breadth of her ability, and is at any rate, somewhat ironic, for she is undoubtedly a writer of superior quality.

—Ian McMechan

JENKINS, (John) Robin

Nationality: British. **Born:** Cambuslang, Lanarkshire, Scotland, 11 September 1912. **Education:** Hamilton Academy; Glasgow University, 1931-35, B.A. (honors) in English 1935, M.A. 1936. **Family:** Married Mary McIntyre Wyllie in 1937; one son and two daughters. **Career:** Teacher at Dunoon Grammar School; Ghazi College, Kabul, Afghanistan, 1957-59; British Institute, Barcelona, 1959-61; and Gaya School, Sabah, Malaysia, 1963-68. **Awards:** Frederick Niven award, 1956. **Address:** Fairhaven, Toward, by Dunoon, Argyll PA23 7UE, Scotland.

PUBLICATIONS

Novels

So Gaily Sings the Lark. Glasgow, Maclellan, 1951.
Happy for the Child. London, Lehmann, 1953.
The Thistle and the Grail. London, Macdonald, 1954.
The Cone-Gatherers. London, Macdonald, 1955; New York, Taplinger, 1981.
Guests of War. London, Macdonald, 1956.
The Missionaries. London, Macdonald, 1957.
The Changeling. London, Macdonald, 1958.
Love Is a Fervent Fire. London, Macdonald, 1959.
Some Kind of Grace. London, Macdonald, 1960.
Dust on the Paw. London, Macdonald, and New York, Putnam, 1961.
The Tiger of Gold. London, Macdonald, 1962.

A Love of Innocence. London, Cape, 1963.
The Sardana Dancers. London, Cape, 1964.
A Very Scotch Affair. London, Gollancz, 1968.
The Holy Tree. London, Gollancz, 1969.
The Expatriates. London, Gollancz, 1971.
A Toast to the Lord. London, Gollancz, 1972.
A Figure of Fun. London, Gollancz, 1974.
A Would-Be Saint. London, Gollancz, 1978; New York, Taplinger, 1980.
Fergus Lamont. Edinburgh, Canongate, and New York, Taplinger, 1979.
The Awakening of George Darroch. Edinburgh, Harris, 1985.
Just Duffy. Edinburgh, Canongate, 1988.
Poverty Castle. Nairn, Balnain, 1991.

Short Stories

A Far Cry from Bowmore and Other Stories. London, Gollancz, 1973.

Uncollected Short Story

"Exile," in *Modern Scottish Short Stories,* edited by Fred Urquhart and Giles Gordon. London, Hamish Hamilton, 1978.

*   *   *

Scotland, Spain, Afghanistan— the countries in which he has lived—have provided the backdrops for much of Robin Jenkins's writing, and it is his uncanny ability to realize those settings and the people who inhabit them which has given so much immediate strength to his fictional output. "You must write about people you know best," Jenkins has written, "and they are the ones you were born and brought up with." His Scottish novels— *So Gaily Sings the Lark, Happy for the Child, The Thistle and the Grail, The Cone-Gatherers, Guests of War, The Missionaries, The Changeling, Love Is a Fervent Fire, A Love of Innocence, The Sardana Dancers, A Toast to the Lord, A Would-Be Saint, Fergus Lamont, The Awakening of George Darroch,* and *Just Duffy*— tend to focus on the sterner aspects of Calvinism. The best of the early novels, *The Cone-Gatherers,* set on the patrician country estate of Lady Runcie-Campbell, follows to its bitter conclusion the enmity between Duror the gamekeeper and Calum, a simple-minded hunchback who gathers pine cones for their seeds. Loss of innocence is also a central theme of *The Changeling* and *Guests of War,* and is transformed in Jenkins's later novels to a yearning for the level of grace that transcends human frailty.

In all his work Jenkins's writing is characterized by his probing insights into the paradox that makes human relationships both loving and self-destructive, and by his skillful delineation of character and psychological make-up. Poverty, too, is a central issue, whether it be the spiritual poverty which disfigures men like Mungo Niven, the self-deluding hero of *A Very Scotch Affair,* or the physical poverty of the slums of Drumsagart in *The Thistle and the Grail.* Yet, despite his moral stance and his round condemnation of a society which breeds those twin evils, Jenkins is not without mercy. The reader is invited to examine the reasons which make Niven such an unattractive character and to understand how other factors, such as religion, upbringing, and heredity have helped to warp his life. Even when Niven commits adultery, sympathy for his stupidity is never far away from Jenkins's narrative. Similarly, the citizens of the mean town of Drumsagart experience a moment of grace when their football team wins a cup competition. Irony is never far away from Jenkins's literary style.

Nowhere is this virtue seen to better advantage than in a recent novel, *The Awakening of George Darroch*. Set in 1843, the year of the Disruption (the schism in the Church of Scotland over livings and privileges which led to the foundation of the Free Church of Scotland), it follows the crisis of conscience which affects George Darroch, a minister of the church whose parish is in a typically grim and Jenkinsian small Scottish town. On one level Darroch's dilemma is political in origin. Should he follow the dictates of his conscience and side with the Free Church reformers, or should he allow himself to be tempted into staying with the established church? At that level the arguments for following the first option are his engrained beliefs in the necessity for change, beliefs which he wishes to make manifest; balanced against these is his brother-in-law's promise of a rich living in a decent country area. On another level, Darroch is besieged by a moral problem. To throw in his lot with the reformers means that he will have to sacrifice his family and their well-being.

As time passes and the day of the "Disruption" meeting comes closer, Darroch sways from one direction to the other, much to the dismay of his family who expect him not only to remain constant to the established church but also to have the good sense to accept the offer of a new and more agreeable parish. When he eventually makes the fateful decision to join the reformers it seems, superficially, that Darroch is doing so to expiate past sins, in the full knowledge that he is of the Elect. But Jenkins is too clever a writer and too committed a critic of the effects of extreme Calvinism to allow Darroch such a simple exit. It is not religious faith which carries Darroch forward but simple hypocrisy: the important motive for him is not the action itself but the view which others will have of his part in it.

Despite the maturity of the writing and the sense of culmination which suggested that he had little more to say on the subject, Jenkins returned once more to the matter of sin and betrayal in *Just Duffy*. This is set in contemporary small-town Scotland, a world which the author obviously detests; Duffy lives in a bleak, urban, and uncaring environment in which achievement and greed are preferred to the more ordinary values of respect and friendship. Never addressed by his Christian name of Thomas—hence the title—Duffy is the only child of an unmarried mother and, considered stupid, he occupies a never-never land between leaving school as a simpleton and entering a world dominated by despair and poverty. Instead of accepting meekly what is offered to him, Duffy declares war on society, indulging in a growing number of meaningless actions until he commits the ultimate crime of murder. Although Jenkins reserves much sympathy for his central character, he also makes clear that Duffy's crimes are born of a frightful innocence which allows him to imagine that he can act with impunity. Eventually, Duffy retreats into the silence of madness, the only justification he can discover for what he has done.

Although Jenkins is capable of ranging easily and fluently over a wide range of social backgrounds, his vision of the demonic state of the world and the salving balm of love remain the central motifs. Anger, sexual disappointments, the betrayal of innocence are emotions never far from the surface, and like Edwin Muir (1887-1959) Jenkins is aware of the fall from grace and the widening gulf between man and Eden.

—Trevor Royle

JHABVALA, Ruth Prawer

Nationality: American. **Born:** Ruth Prawer in Cologne, Germany, of Polish parents, 7 May 1927; sister of the writer S.S. Prawer; moved to England as a refugee, 1939; became British citizen, 1948; now U.S. citizen. **Education:** Hendon County School, London; Queen Mary College, University of London, 1945-51, M.A. in English literature 1951. **Family:** Married C.S.H. Jhabvala in 1951; three daughters. Lived in India, 1951-75, and in New York City from 1975. **Awards:** Booker prize, 1975; Guggenheim Fellowship, 1976; Neil Gunn International fellowship, 1978; MacArthur fellowship, 1984; Academy of Motion Picture Arts and Sciences award for screenplay (Oscar), 1987, 1992. **Agent:** Harriet Wasserman, 137 East 36th Street, New York, New York 10016. **Address:** 400 East 52nd Street, New York, New York 10022, U.S.A.

PUBLICATIONS

Novels

To Whom She Will. London, Allen and Unwin, 1955; as *Amrita,* New York, Norton, 1956.
The Nature of Passion. London, Allen and Unwin, 1956; New York, Norton, 1957.
Esmond in India. London, Allen and Unwin, and New York, Norton, 1958.
The Householder. London, Murray, and New York, Norton, 1960.
Get Ready for Battle. London, Murray, 1962; New York, Norton, 1963.
A Backward Place. London, Murray, and New York, Norton, 1965.
A New Dominion. London, Murray, 1972; as *Travelers,* New York, Harper, 1973.
Heat and Dust. London, Murray, 1975; New York, Harper, 1976.
In Search of Love and Beauty. London, Murray, and New York, Morrow, 1983.
Three Continents. London, Murray, and New York, Morrow, 1987.
Poet and Dancer. London, Murray, and New York, Doubleday, 1993.

Short Stories

Like Birds, Like Fishes and Other Stories. London, Murray, 1963; New York, Norton, 1964.
A Stronger Climate: Nine Stories. London, Murray, 1968; New York, Norton, 1969.
An Experience of India. London, Murray, 1971; New York, Norton, 1972.
Penguin Modern Stories 11, with others. London, Penguin, 1972.
How I Became a Holy Mother and Other Stories. London, Murray, and New York, Harper, 1976.
Out of India: Selected Stories. New York, Morrow, 1986; London, Murray, 1987.

Uncollected Short Stories

"Parasites," in *New Yorker,* 13 March 1978.
"A Summer by the Sea," in *New Yorker,* 7 August 1978.
"Commensurate Happiness," in *Encounter* (London), January 1980.
"Grandmother," in *New Yorker,* 17 November 1980.

"Expiation," in *New Yorker,* 11 October 1982.
"Farid and Farida," in *New Yorker,* 15 October 1984.
"The Aliens," in *Literary Review* (Madison, New Jersey), Summer 1986.

Plays

A Call from the East (produced New York, 1981).

Screenplays: *The Householder,* 1963; *Shakespeare Wallah,* with James Ivory, 1965; *The Guru,* 1968; *Bombay Talkie,* 1970; *Autobiography of a Princess,* 1975; *Roseland,* 1976; *Hullabaloo over Georgie and Bonnie's Pictures,* 1978; *The Europeans,* 1979; *Jane Austen in Manhattan,* 1980; *Quartet,* 1981; *Heat and Dust,* 1983; *The Bostonians,* 1984; *A Room with a View,* 1986; *Madame Sousatzka,* with John Schlesinger, 1988; *Mr. and Mrs. Bridge,* 1990; *Howard's End,* 1992; *The Remains of the Day,* 1993; *Jefferson in Paris,* 1995.

Television Play: *The Place of Peace,* 1975.

Other

Meet Yourself at the Doctor (published anonymously). London, Naldrett Press, 1949.
Shakespeare Wallah: A Film, with James Ivory, with *Savages,* by James Ivory. London, Plexus, and New York, Grove Press, 1973.
Autobiography of a Princess, Also Being the Adventures of an American Film Director in the Land of the Maharajas, with James Ivory and John Swope. London, Murray, and New York, Harper, 1975.

*

Film Adaptations: *The Householder,* 1963; *Heat and Dust,* 1983.

Critical Studies: *The Fiction of Ruth Prawer Jhabvala* by H.M. Williams, Calcutta, Writer's Workshop, 1973; "A Jewish Passage to India" by Renee Winegarten, in *Midstream* (New York), March 1974; *Ruth Prawer Jhabvala* by Vasant A. Shahane, New Delhi, Arnold-Heinemann, 1976; *Silence, Exile and Cunning: The Fiction of Ruth Prawer Jhabvala* by Yasmine Gooneratne, New Delhi, Orient Longman, and London, Sangam, 1983; *Cross-Cultural Interaction in Indian English Fiction: An Analysis of the Novels of Ruth Prawer Jhabvala and Kamala Markandaya* by Ramesh Chadha, New Delhi, National Book Organisation, 1988; *The Fiction of Ruth Prawer Jhabvala* by Laurie Sucher, London, Macmillan, 1989; *The Novels of Kamala Markandaya and Ruth Prawer Jhabvala* by Rekha Jha, New Delhi, Prestige, 1990; *Passages to Ruth Prawer Jhabvala* edited by Ralph J. Crane, New Delhi, Sterling, 1991, and *Ruth Prawer Jhabvala* by Crane, New York, Twayne, 1992.

Ruth Prawer Jhabvala comments:

(1972) The central fact of all my work, as I see it, is that I am a European living permanently in India. I have lived here for most of my adult life and have an Indian family. This makes me not quite an insider but it does not leave me entirely an outsider either. I feel my position to be at a point in space where I have quite a good view of both sides but am myself left stranded in the middle. My work is an attempt to charter this unchartered territory for myself. Sometimes I write about Europeans in India, sometimes about Indians in India, sometimes about both, but always attempting to present India to myself in the hope of giving myself some kind of foothold. My books may appear objective but really I think they are the opposite: for I describe the Indian scene not for its own sake but for mine. This excludes me from all interest in all those Indian problems one is supposed to be interested in (the extent of Westernisation, modernity vs. tradition, etc! etc!). My work can never claim to be a balanced or authoritative view of India but is only one individual European's attempt to compound the puzzling process of living in it.

(1981) In 1975 I left India, and am now living in and writing about America—but not for long enough to be able to make any kind of comment about either of these activities.

(1986) I have now lived in the U.S. for ten years and have written one novel, several stories, and several film scripts about the experience. I cannot claim that India has disappeared out of—synonymously—myself and my work; even when not overtly figuring there, its influence is always present. But influence is too weak a word—it is more like a restructuring process: of one's ways of thinking and being. So I would say that, while I never became Indian, I didn't stay totally European either.

*   *   *

In a writing career which now spans 40 years, Ruth Prawer Jhabvala has successfully combined the writing of novels, short stories, and screenplays. She is perhaps best known as a novelist of India, even as a novelist who interprets India for the Western reader, but her most recent novels introduce a shift in setting—to America and England—and reveal a desire to combine her own triple European, Indian, and American experiences in her fiction.

Jhabvala's life of exile and expatriation has placed her in an unusual position among novelists who write about India, and has enabled her to write about that country from the ambiguous position of an outsider who is also an intimate insider. All Jhabvala's fiction up to *Heat and Dust* (with the exception of two short stories) is set in India. For the most part Jhabvala has avoided the harsher problems of post-Independence India (the communal violence, the political unrest, etc) in these novels, and, except in *Heat and Dust,* she has also avoided the subject of the British Raj. In her early work Jhabvala focuses on the domestic and social problems of predominantly middle-class urban Indians living in Delhi in the years following Independence. Her first two novels, *To Whom She Will* and *The Nature of Passion,* both deft comedies of manners in an Austenish vein, treat the subjects of arranged marriage and romantic love and explore the conflicts which arise as the modern, Western views of characters like Amrita, or Viddi and Nimmi clash with the traditional values of their families. Both novels express the author's obvious delight in all she found in her newly adopted country. But she was not blind to the overwhelming social problems facing India. In *Get Ready for Battle,* those problems are confronted as far as the limits of her domestic drama will allow; this is Jhabvala's darkest portrait of modern India, and the last of her novels to deal primarily with Indian characters.

In her next three novels, *A Backward Place, A New Dominion,* and *Heat and Dust,* Jhabvala moves away from the presentation of India, to a portrayal of the Westerner in India, a subject she had already introduced in *Esmond in India,* and an interest in the effect of India on her Western characters. She explores the problems faced by expatriate Westerners (mostly women) and the world of often fraudulent gurus encountered by the young Western seekers who flocked to India in the 1960s and 1970s. This shift in emphasis is also reflected in her short stories—all nine stories in *A Stronger Climate* are concerned with Westerners in India—and in her screenplays—in such films as *Shakespeare Wallah, The Guru,* and *Autobiography of a Princess.*

In *A Backward Place* Jhabvala considers whether or not it is possible for some Europeans to live in India and survive, and through the character of Judy, she shows that it is possible if one is willing to adopt Indian values. In *A New Dominion* and *Heat and Dust,* Jhabvala again shows that Westerners can remain in India and survive, as Miss Charlotte does, and as both Olivia and the unnamed narrator of *Heat and Dust* do, but the question of whether this is desirable remains largely unanswered in her fiction. For the first time, these two novels move out of Delhi and beyond the confines of the largely domestic, interior settings of her earlier novels. The landscape, the heat and the dust, become increasingly important metaphors which show how unsuitable India is for most of the Westerners who populate Jhabvala's fiction. Quite different narrative techniques are employed, too—the straightforward realist narrative method of the earlier novels gives way to a more experimental form in which the reader is addressed directly, through monologues, letters, and journal entries, both by characters and the author herself. Jhabvala attributes these innovations to the influence of her writing for the cinema.

Heat and Dust contains two parallel stories, skillfully interwoven to contrast two time periods 50 years apart. The earlier of the two stories, Olivia's story, set in 1923, invites comparison with E.M Forster's *A Passage to India.* The later story, that of the unnamed narrator, which began in response to her reading of Olivia's letters, updates the 1923 story, and reveals Jhabvala's postmodernist interest in the effect of text on life.

Since moving to America, Jhabvala's interest has moved away from Indian subjects and settings. *In Search of Love and Beauty,* focuses on a group of German and Austrian refugees in New York, and Jhabvala writes for the first time on a sustained level about the German-Jewish background she knew as a child. At the center of this novel and of her next novel, *Three Continents,* is a concern with the search for identity and heritage—and an attempt to explain and understand the sense of alienation and expatriation which has been her own experience as well as that of many of her Western characters. While these novels represent a new phase in Jhabvala's writing career, it is clear to the reader familiar with her oeuvre that the concerns of her Indian fiction have not been entirely left behind; both novels share much in common with her later Indian fiction. The guru figures, Leo of *In Search of Love and Beauty,* and the Rawul of *Three Continents,* recall, among others, the unprincipled Swami of *A New Dominion,* while the seekers of these novels are variations on the young questing figures like Lee of *A New Dominion* and Katie of "How I Became a Holy Mother," for example. An interesting development is that for the first time in her fiction Jhabvala explores the backgrounds of the Western characters who populate her Indian fiction.

In her 1993 novel, *Poet and Dancer,* India as a locale is altogether absent, and the presence of an Indian mother and son is too peripheral to the main narrative to bring the spirit of the place into the novel. And so in some ways *Poet and Dancer* marks the greatest shift to date in Jhabvala's career as a novelist. In other ways, though, there is still common ground between this work and her earlier fiction. At the heart of this novel is an exploration of the dichotomy between good and evil—played out through the destructive relationship between Angel and her cousin Lara whose love

Angel obsessively pursues—which is reminiscent of the destructive relationships between the many seekers and bogus gurus found in her earlier work.

Ruth Prawer Jhabvala's reputation as a writer of fiction has been built around her Indian novels, particularly the Booker prize-winning *Heat and Dust.* Her more recent novels show that she can write equally well about America and Europe, and suggest that she is an international writer who deserves to be numbered amongst the best novelists writing in English today.

—Ralph J. Crane

JOHNSON, Charles (Richard)

Nationality: American. **Born:** Evanston, Illinois, 23 April 1948. **Education:** Southern Illinois University, Carbondale, B.A. in journalism 1971, M.A. in philosophy 1973; State University of New York, Stony Brook, 1973-76. **Family:** Married Joan New in 1970; two children. **Career:** Reporter and cartoonist, Chicago *Tribune,* 1969-70; member of art staff, St. Louis *Proud,* Missouri, 1971-72; assistant professor, 1976-79, associate professor, 1979-82, and since 1982 professor, University of Washington, Seattle. Since 1978 fiction editor, *Seattle Review.* **Awards:** Governor's award for literature, 1983; *Callaloo* creative writing award, 1985; National Book award, 1991. **Address:** c/o Antheneum Publishers, Macmillian Publishing Company, 866 3rd Avenue, New York, New York 10022; c/o University of Washington, Department of English, Seattle, WA 98105 U.S.A.

PUBLICATIONS

Novels

Faith and the Good Thing. New York, Viking, 1974.
Oxherding Tale. Bloomington, Indiana University Press, 1982; London, Blond and Briggs, 1983.
Middle Passage. New York, Atheneum, 1990; London, Picador, 1991.

Short Stories

The Sorcerer's Apprentice: Tales and Conjuration. New York, Atheneum, 1986; London, Serpent's Tail, 1988.

Plays

Olly Olly Oxen Free. New York, French, 1988.

Television Writing: *Charlie's Pad* series, 1971; *Charlie Smith and the Fritter Tree,* 1978; *For Me Myself,* 1982; *A Place for Myself,* 1982; *Booker,* with John Allmann, 1984.

Other

Black Humor (cartoons). Chicago, Johnson, 1970.
Half-Past Nation Time (cartoons). Westlake Village, California, Aware Press, 1972.

Being and Race: Black Writing since 1970. Bloomington, Indiana Press, and London, Serpent's Tail, 1988.

*   *   *

Charles Johnson's most recent novel *Middle Passage* is a pastiche of 19th-century American sea-faring literature. It won the 1990 National Book award, received much critical acclaim, and has been favorably compared to Melville's *Moby Dick*. In *Middle Passage* Rutherford Calhoun, a newly-freed slave, seeks to avoid his personal responsibilities by working his passage on board a slave clipper bound for Africa. During his time on ship Rutherford has to confront his own identity; this search for the self is a recurring concern of Johnson's and lies at the heart of his work.

Johnson's novels contain a diverse range of characters who constantly examine and re-examine the nature of self, and are continually confronted by central philosophical dilemmas. Nothing is certain in Johnson's world and his characters struggle incessantly, at times trying to find a black role in white society, or trying to define their own identity, or trying to define America herself. Johnson uses particular situations to explore fundamental themes of black American history such as the connections, and resultant tensions between race and sexuality, and race and class. His novels are fascinating, mysterious, and unusual, if at times difficult to comprehend. He is a deeply philosophical writer whose works are littered with scholarly erudition firmly rooted in the science of phenomenology. Everything he writes is deliberate, and Johnson is a conscious stylist who pays detailed attention to structure and method. His writing tends to fuse a combination of traditional narrative forms producing a highly individual tone and style.

The use of parable is an important element in Johnson's work. Reb's great grandfather Rakhal (*Oxherding Tale*), was a powerful member of the Allmuseri tribe who was cheated out of half his land by Akbar the village king. Akbar then became a Moslem and hated Rakhal for holding fast to the old religion. As an act of revenge Rakhal promised a storm that would rain madness down upon the village. Akbar naturally stored away all the fresh water he could and remained sane while all the villagers drank from the waters of insanity. Uncertain as to Rakhal's motives, Akbar wandered among his tribe shouting "I'm sane, you're not," but none of his subjects would listen as they all believed it was the king who was mad. Eventually Akbar drinks from the waters of insanity thus completing Rakhal's revenge. Here, and throughout Johnson's writing, myth and parable are used as a means of revealing truths. "Menagerie, A Child's Fable" in *The Sorcerer's Apprentice* is an incisive allegory about Mankind's ignorance and intolerance. A pet-shop owner leaves his animals alone for days and Berkeley, the guard dog, is forced to take control being the most trustworthy. For a while all is well, but soon the monkey convinces Berkeley to open a few of the cages—some animals being more equal than others—and chaos ensues. Berkeley struggles to get everyone to live together in harmony—"For Christ's sake, we're all animals"—but fails. As a result of this inability to cohabit peacefully the shop is burnt down and their world destroyed.

A natural companion of allegory and parable is the supernatural, and this features strongly in much of Johnson's fiction. He has been criticized for overuse of the supernatural purely for reasons of effect but this is to misunderstand both the author and his intentions. The fantastic and uncanny play an important role which is similar to that of Johnson's use of allegory. Contact with the supernatural creates an understanding of things real. Through experience of the fantastic the characters arrive at an earthly entelechy which would not otherwise be attainable. In "Popper's Disease"—a brilliantly comic short story that is structurally if not semantically reminiscent of Edgar Allan Poe—a spaceship crashes close to Dr. Henry Popper's car. Hearing painful screams from within, he enters the spaceship which is strongly symbolic of the womb and finds an alien the size of a fence post and similar to a boiled crayfish with a terminal but as yet undiagnosed illness. The alien has been sent to earth for quarantine purposes—this "other" world uses earth as a place for outpatients—until he either recovers or dies. After heaving many sighs the creature eventually explodes. The doctor, locked in the ship, has little else to do except discover the root cause of the illness. This he succeeds in doing and it transpires that the alien suffered from an incurable existential illness—the self. Through his contact with the alien and the ensuing examination, Popper discovers previously unknown facts about his own life.

As this story suggests there is an innate sense of comedy in Johnson's writing. Moses Green acquires Mingo, a native Allmuseri, as a slave and decides to train him in his own image ("Education of Mingo"). Mingo proves adept at imitating the ways of his master but unfortunately confuses two types of behavior. Instead of killing chickens and being polite to other people, Mingo spends hours talking to the chickens and murders several of Moses's friends. Johnson's comedy is not merely restricted to narrative situations, but it permeates his entire work from character depiction's to a style of dialogue which is often Wodehousian in its wit: "Peggy Undercliff gave me what I have often read described in popular fiction as the 'eye', though I'll not swear on it, never having seen the 'eye' at such close range before." Johnson concentrates on the aspirations and experiences of black Americans, but there is a rich diversity in his fictional characterization. Ebenezer Falcon, the captain of *The Republic* (*Middle Passage*) is an embittered dwarf who in many ways is a microcosm of the new American republic eager to push back frontiers and prepared to bully others to take what is not offered. In *Oxherding Tale* Horace Bannon is the apocalyptic soul catcher who has tattoos of his victims on his chest. All of Johnson's characters are fully drawn portraits yet it is in the main characters that Johnson's ability to depict the individual is most successfully realized. His heroes and heroines never start off as rounded or completed personalities, rather they go through a progression during the narrative that is the equivalent of a journey from innocence to experience. Faith Cross, Andrew Hawkins, and Rutherford Calhoun are all innocents to begin with but through their experiences of events and contact with the multifarious characters of Johnson's fiction they confront their own identity and come to know themselves. Experience is one of the essentials of life and this is a central theme for Johnson.

The narrator of "Alethia" is a bookish professor who knows all there is to know about the human sciences. He is, however, ignorant in life and receives a practical education from one of his students. For Johnson, academia and scholarship have an important role and philosophy is an integral part of Johnson's vision. Especially influential are the philosophical doctrines of the Far East which provide a direction in life for the prematurely-old hypochondriac postman in China, as well as being important for other of Johnson's protagonists. But the role of learning becomes redundant without actual life experience.

Although multifaceted, specific semantic concerns dominate Johnson's prose. The idea of the "middle passage" is crucial—an entire book and a chapter in *Oxherding Tale* receiving this name. The passage marks a period of time in the lives of Johnson's heroes when the past and the future have little or no significance. Only the immediate present matters and it is in moments of crisis and stress that the characters come to understand most about their lives. Rutherford Calhoun fights daily for his own survival and that of his mates on board *The Republic* and only in the middle of a huge storm after a life-endangering mutiny on a ship riddled with disease and plague can Rutherford confront his own nature and reach a genuine understanding of his true self.

It is during this "middle passage" that Johnson's principal intent as an author is realized. Faith Cross, Andrew Hawkins, and Rutherford Calhoun (as well as the protagonists in *The Sorcerer's Apprentice*) have to face the question "Who am I?". As black Afro-Americans there are many obstacles on the way to finding a solution to this philosophical dilemma. White people in a white society do not have such obstacles in their path. Neither do the Allmuseri, a people vital to Johnson's prose. As a tribe of racial purity they too are free to consider the nature of their own identity, at least until they undergo integration into American Society. As soon as this happens the obstacles appear because before being able to afford the comparative luxury of determining the self, black Americans must first come to terms with their environment and social surroundings. This is the heart of Johnson's prose and all his works confront the question of black identity in America. There is in black America, and America in general, a multiplicity of origin and culture. By definition, purity cannot exist and Johnson views America as a polymorphous culture full of cultural mongrels. His literature seeks primarily to reach an understanding of this reality.

—Harry Bucknall

JOHNSON, Colin. *See* MUDROOROO.

JOHNSON, Denis

Nationality: American. **Born:** Munich, Germany, in 1949. **Awards:** American Academy Kaufman prize, 1984; Whiting Foundation award, 1986. **Address:** c/o Robert Cornfield, 145 W. 79th Street, New York, New York 10024, U.S.A.

PUBLICATIONS

Novels

Angels. New York, Knopf, 1983; London, Chatto and Windus, 1984.
Fiskadoro. New York, Knopf, and London, Chatto and Windus, 1985.
The Stars at Noon. New York, Knopf, 1986; London, Faber, 1987.
Resuscitation of a Hanged Man. New York, Farrar Straus, 1991.

Short Stories

Jesus' Son. New York, Farrar, Straus, 1992.

Uncollected Short Stories

"The Taking of Our Own Lives," in *Three Stances of Modern Fiction,* edited by Stephen Minot and Robley Wilson, Jr. Cambridge, Massachusetts, Winthrop, 1972.
"There Comes after Here," in *Atlantic* (Boston), April 1972.
"Tattoos and Music," in *North American Review* (Cedar Falls, Iowa), Spring 1977.
"Two Men," in *New Yorker,* 19 September 1988.
"Work," in *New Yorker,* 14 November 1988.
"The Bullet's Flight," in *Esquire* (New York), March 1989.
"Car-Crash While Hitchhiking," in *Paris Review,* Spring 1989.
"Dirty Wedding," in *New Yorker,* 5 November 1990.

Poetry

The Man among the Seals. Iowa City, Stone Wall Press, 1969.
Inner Weather. Port Townsend, Washington, Graywolf Press, 1976.
The Incognito Lounge and Other Poems. New York, Random House, 1982.
The Veil. New York, Knopf, 1987.

*   *   *

Denis Johnson's first two novels, *Angels* and *Fiskadoro,* delineate the lives of outcasts on the fringes of their societies. The first is a contemporary urban novel whose characters drift into tragedy and moral and physical decline; still, it is a novel of hope. In the second, though the landscape is bleaker, an even deeper, more elemental hope for human survival is posited. Johnson brings his considerable gifts as a poet to help explore the possibilities of persistence and redemption in two separate worlds, one in decline, the other struggling to be born.

The surface of *Angels* is sensational, melodramatic, and even savage at times. Occasionally the characters are presented as cartoon-like as Johnson depicts the contemporary world in ways that bring this work close to the absurdist novel; however, *Angels* is finally a novel more in the realistic mode, and the self-conscious gothicism is meant as a comment on the irrationalism and hysteria that have become commonplace in descriptions of contemporary urban life in the United States.

The two lower-class characters, Jamie Mays and Bill Houston, an ex-sailor and ex-convict, are losers who travel across America in a state of radical drift. What we see is a society spiritually blighted by vacuous radio, movies, and TV, and superstitious cults that function as ersatz religions; all these derive from the human need for moral purpose and personal transcendence that have everywhere been lost and which only serve to disguise the destructive forces that lay just beneath the surface, often represented in images of self-immolation: "Scarlet light and white heat awoke her. She was in flames. . . . It was not her clothing, but her flesh itself that was burning." The setting of this hallucination is a mental ward where Jamie is taken after a psychotic break precipitated by a rape that is motivated by an almost indifferent sadism, itself the amoral outcome of a society spiritually lost, one in which self-identity is always at risk: "For a second standing in line behind a half dozen people, she felt as if no one part of herself was connected to any other." Bill Houston becomes involved in a bank robbery during which he kills a bank guard, but given the circumstances of his life, it is difficult to determine moral culpability. Mainly for political reasons, he is sentenced to die in the gas chamber, but the angel of light finally prevails and Bill's life is at the end given moral dimension in his epiphany at the moment of death: "He got it right in the dark between heartbeats, and rested there. And then he saw that another one wasn't going to come. That's it. That's the last. He looked at the dark. I would like to take this opportunity, he said, to pray for another human being." This is the angel of light, corresponding to Jamie's return to sanity and wholeness, and is the hope that infuses the end of the novel. However, no such hope is held out for a social healing.

Fiskadoro, Johnson's second novel, set in the Florida Keys two generations after the nuclear holocaust, is also a novel about survival, this time removed from an urban environment and put in the larger social context of the entirety of human society.

The question posed at the center of the novel is "What must be done to ensure the rebirth of civilization?" Several alternate societies coexist, and it is their clash and intermingling that provide the answer. Mr. Cheung represents the old pre-nuclear society built on art and rationalism; members of his group meet to try and reconstruct the Western (and to some extent, the Eastern) tradition from the bits and pieces of it that have survived: various artifacts, a book on nuclear war, a clarinet, spent radiation-sensitive buttons that declare the wearers believers in reason and science. The anti-culture, represented by Fiskadoro, a young teen, clashes with the defunct culture when Fiskadoro comes to Mr. Cheung (who is manager of the bedraggled Miami Symphony Orchestra) for clarinet lessons, as if asking Cheung to integrate him into the old cultural tradition. However, Fiskadoro has no talent for music and fails to master the instrument until at the end of the novel when he is transformed.

Fiskadoro becomes the leader of the new order, but only after he spends days among the jungle savages who destroy his memory through drugs and primitive ritual, which includes self-inflicted circumcision. This memory loss fits Fiskadoro as the harbinger, and perhaps founder, of the new world struggling to be born because, Johnson says, memory is the faculty through which history lives and culture is transmitted; memory severed makes rebirth possible. After the cleansing, the historical cycle will again be put in motion: "Everything we have, all we are, will meet its end, will be overcome, taken up, washed away. But everything came to an end before. Now it will happen again. Many times. Again and again." Alternating action at the end of the novel juxtaposes Fiskadoro's rebirth with that of Cheung's grandmother, a ship-wrecked Vietnamese refugee who is the offspring of a Western Father and Asian mother. She spends 20 hours in the sea awaiting rescue: "The shock of finding herself here where she'd always been was like a birth." She has obvious parallels with Fiskadoro: ". . . saved not because she hadn't given up, because she had, and in fact she possessed no memory of the second night. . . ." Thus Johnson integrates within this complex poetic novel the themes of social and individual regeneration. The work at times strains to keep these and other elements in balance and manages often enough to make this ambitious work succeed.

—Peter Desy

JOHNSON, Diane

Nationality: American. **Born:** Diane Lain in Moline, Illinois, 28 April 1934. **Education:** Stephens College, Columbia, Missouri,

1951-53, A.A. 1953; University of Utah, Salt Lake City, B.A. 1957; University of California, Los Angeles (Woodrow Wilson fellow), M.A. 1966, Ph.D. 1968. **Family:** Married 1) B. Lamar Johnson, Jr., in 1953, two sons and two daughters; 2) John Frederic Murray in 1968. **Career:** Member of the Department of English, University of California, Davis, 1968-87. **Awards:** American Association of University Women fellowship, 1968; Guggenheim fellowship, 1977; American Academy Rosenthal award, 1979; Strauss Living award, 1987. **Agent:** Lynn Nesbit, New York, New York. **Address:** 24 Edith Street, San Francisco, California 94133, U.S.A.

PUBLICATIONS

Novels

Fair Game. New York, Harcourt Brace, 1965.
Loving Hands at Home. New York, Harcourt Brace, 1968; London, Heinemann, 1969.
Burning. New York, Harcourt Brace, and London, Heinemann, 1971.
The Shadow Knows. New York, Knopf, 1974; London, Bodley Head, 1975.
Lying Low. New York, Knopf, 1978; London, Bodley Head, 1979.
Persian Nights. New York, Knopf, and London, Chatto and Windus, 1987.
Health and Happiness. New York, Knopf, 1990; London, Chatto and Windus, 1991.

Uncollected Short Story

"An Apple, An Orange," in *Prize Stories 1973,* edited by William Abrahams. New York, Doubleday, 1973.

Play

Screenplay: *The Shining,* with Stanley Kubrick, 1980.

Other

The True History of the First Mrs. Meredith and Other Lesser Lives. New York, Knopf, 1972; London, Heinemann, 1973.
Terrorists and Novelists. New York, Knopf, 1982.
Dashiell Hammett: A Life. New York, Random House, 1983; as *The Life of Dashiell Hammett,* London, Chatto and Windus, 1984.
Natural Opium. New York, Knopf, and London, Chatto and Windus, 1993.

*

Critical Studies: Article by Judith S. Baughman, in *Dictionary of Literary Biography Yearbook 1980* edited by Karen L. Rood, Jean W. Ross, and Richard Ziegfeld, Detroit, Gale, 1981; *Women Writers of the West Coast: Speaking of Their Lives and Careers* edited by Marilyn Yalom, Santa Barbara, California, Capra Press, 1983.

Diane Johnson comments:

(1986) I try not to think about my novels in sum too directly; but I guess I think of them as serious comic novels on subjects of contemporary concern. At the moment I'm writing a novel (set in

Iran) about being American, and about political meddling, being a woman, relationships and ideas. I think these are pretty much the subjects of my other novels too. This is the first one not set in California.

*   *   *

In *Fair Game,* Diane Johnson's first novel, the characters' movement is toward pairing off and finding stability, despite some outward denials that this is what they want. The characters here are "types": the frustrated virgin, the ambitious executive, the frustrated executive, the ambitious writer, and the libidinous eccentric writer (clearly modeled on Henry Miller). Only in some of the matchmaking and in making the woman writer the author of a children's book taken up by intellectuals, does Johnson show much originality in dealing with the clichéd material.

Beginning with *Loving Hands at Home* the momentum of the characters' lives tends toward the splitting of bonds between people; man-woman love relationships in particular require heroic efforts to sustain them. In Johnson's later novels the women characters stand almost completely alone.

On the first page of *Fair Game* a man is said to have a knack for finding "moments of truth" in the course of any experience. Most of Johnson's protagonists are sensitized—at times to an obsessive degree—to this search for epiphanies. In *The Shadow Knows* N. Hexam is haunted by her premonition of evil and probes every occurrence for significance; Ouida in *Lying Low* believes in "old" magic, and watches for signs. And, as Karen Fry says in *Loving Hands at Home,* "It is odd how events follow suspicions, as if, by wondering about things, you cause them to happen." This is often the case in Johnson's work, though the characters are never prepared for the form these conjured-up events ultimately take. Despite this hunger for signs (and, in the early novels, a glut of psychiatrists) Johnson's characters are not particularly inward-looking; the outside world has to nudge or shake them. Karen Fry, for example, discovers she is unhappy with her life only after she impulsively accepts a motorcycle ride from a stranger and falls off: "A pratfall in the middle of Santa Monica Boulevard is too large a symbol to be overlooked." Karen, married into a tradition-bound Mormon family, longs to be like a shiftless girl she knew when she was younger; a girl who, in Karen's mind, directed her own fate in defiance of convention. Karen finally does free herself, becomes "shiftless," and takes up residence on the sand at the Pacific beach. There she creates her own symbol: a huge baroque sandcastle she contentedly lets the waves destroy because she knows she has done her work on it well.

In *Burning* the jolt that forces Barney and Bingo Edwards to look at themselves is the removal of a high hedge that kept out the sight of the disturbing, passionate lives of their psychiatrist neighbor and his patients. Bingo is a perfect wife, "infinitely erudite . . . witty when she wasn't depressed," and the mother of two. But when she stands-in for a junkie mother whose children are about to be taken by the state her truthful answers to a bank of psychological tests classify her as an unfit mother. Here, as in all Johnson's novels except *Fair Game,* the main female character encounters women who personify hidden aspects of her own makeup: in Bingo's case, the unfit mother and promiscuous women. With their protective hedge gone, Bingo and Barney are infected with the neighbor's passions and the neighborhood burns—literally.

If the problem in these first three novels is how to attain and manage a passion-filled, self-determinate life, the problem in *Lying*

Low and *The Shadow Knows* is not one of escaping the clichéd life, but how to be protected from slipping out of such a life into something truly horrible. In *Lying Low* Marybeth lives "underground," in fear of imprisonment for her part in a political bombing that took a life. Her life of passionate commitment has led her to a decade of the most mundane, restricted kind of life. Marybeth's landlady, Theo, is a dancer who chose the unsung life rather than risk failure trying to become a prima ballerina. Marybeth and Ouida, a Brazilian girl who is hiding from officials who want to have her deported, hide and live in fear of discovery, but when tragedy comes it comes not to them but to Theo while she is trying to move out of her mundane life and do something worthwhile for others.

The Shadow Knows is Johnson's most complex novel, partly because its subject is the indeterminate, lurking nature of evil. N. Hexam begins the new year with a prophetic dread she interprets as a premonition that she will be murdered. As in *Loving Hands at Home,* the root of her fear is "the realization that life can change on you, can darken like a rainy day; wretchedness and dread can overtake the lightest heart." It is this dread that is N. Hexam's worst enemy. For her evil is a closing circle with its center nowhere and its circumference all around her. (Johnson has said that *The Shadow Knows* was in part intended to show how race relations stood at the time of its writing, 1974, but the blackness of the two women that figure most prominently in N. Hexam's life is not their most important attribute: what is important about these women is that they live out two of N. Hexam's own possible fates: life drives one mad, while the other is killed by a violent man.)

All through *The Shadow Knows* N. Hexam tries to solve the puzzle of how and from where the anticipated evil will strike. The method she uses is to conceive an ideal Famous Inspector, someone part lover and part Sherlock Holmes, to whom she compares her own efforts at finding the answers she seeks. (Still, she knows such a Famous Inspector would be unable to understand her fears, because he would be male. Here, more clearly than in her other novels, Johnson insists there is a basic irreconcilable difference between women and men based in their different fears.) When a real life counterpart of this Famous Inspector appears, his name is Dyce, "suggesting the tincture of chance." He tells her many mysteries are insoluble, and so is the voice not of reason but of reality. As in *Lying Low* the anticipated evil does manifest itself, though in a form N. Hexam never anticipates. Her reaction is one of relief: now that she truly knows evil ("I . . . have taken on the thinness and the lightness of a shadow . . .") she can live with it.

—William C. Bamberger

JOHNSTON, Jennifer (Prudence)

Nationality: Irish. **Born:** Ireland, 12 January 1930; daughter of the dramatist Denis Johnston. **Education:** Park House School, Dublin; Trinity College, Dublin. **Family:** Married 1) Ian Smyth in 1951, two sons and two daughters; 2) David Gilliland in 1976. **Awards:** Pitman award, 1972; *Yorkshire Post* award, 1973, 1980; Whitbread award, 1979. Fellow, Royal Society of Literature, 1979; member, Aosdana. D.Litt.: University of Ulster, Coleraine, 1984. **Address:** Brook Hall, Culmore Road, Derry BT48 8JE, Northern Ireland.

PUBLICATIONS

Novels

The Captains and the Kings. London, Hamish Hamilton, 1972.
The Gates. London, Hamish Hamilton, 1973.
How Many Miles to Babylon? London, Hamish Hamilton, and New York, Doubleday, 1974.
Shadows on Our Skin. London, Hamish Hamilton, 1977; New York, Doubleday, 1978.
The Old Jest. London, Hamish Hamilton, 1979; New York, Doubleday, 1980.
The Christmas Tree. London, Hamish Hamilton, 1981; New York, Morrow, 1982.
The Railway Station Man. London, Hamish Hamilton, 1984; New York, Viking, 1985.
Fool's Sanctuary. London, Hamish Hamilton, 1987; New York, Viking, 1988.
The Invisible Worm. London, Sinclair Stevenson, 1991; New York, Carroll and Graf, 1993.

Uncollected Short Stories

"Trio," in *Best Irish Short Stories 2,* edited by David Marcus. London, Elek, 1977.
"The Theft," in *Irish Ghost Stories,* edited by Joseph Hone. London, Hamish Hamilton, 1977.

Plays

The Nightingale and Not the Lark (produced Dublin, 1979). London, French, 1981.
Indian Summer (produced Belfast, 1983).
Andante un Poco Mosso, in *The Best Short Plays 1983,* edited by Ramon Delgado. Radnor, Pennsylvania, Chilton, 1983.
The Porch (produced Dublin, 1986).

*

Critical Study: "Three Writers of the Big House: Elizabeth Bowen, Molly Keane and Jennifer Johnston" by Bridget O'Toole, in *Across a Roaring Hill: The Protestant Imagination in Modern Ireland* edited by Gerald Dawe and Edna Longley, Belfast, Blackstaff Press, 1985.

*   *   *

Jennifer Johnston is often described as a Big House novelist, writing in the tradition (beginning with Maria Edgeworth and continuing to William Trevor) of those who delineate the plight of the Anglo-Irish, strangers alike in Ireland and England, living an attenuated half-life of divided loyalties and allegiances in crumbling houses filled with the ghostly remains of better days and a broader culture, more and more alienated from the world of the native Irish around them, treated by their former inferiors with, at best, indifference, at worst, open hostility.

There are, of course, reasons for grounding Johnston in this tradition. All her novels focus on a situation in which a member of the Anglo-Irish is led to try to overcome their political and personal isolation by creating a relationship, across the barriers of national identity, class, religion, and political allegiance, with a mem-

ber of the native Irish. This attempt is doomed to failure from the start; the barriers to be surmounted being too well entrenched in time and history.

Yet, in spite of the apparent familiarity of the setting and subject matter, and even the depiction of family relationships in her novels, it is far too limiting to regard Johnston merely as a Big House novelist. In a 1987 article she said:

What the characters in my books are trying to do . . . is to keep for a few moments their heads above the waters of inexorable history. "I know that in the end I will drown," they shout. "But at this moment I am waving."

This statement encapsulates a central aspect of Johnston's parable-like novels. The personal and the historical are so intertwined, with metaphors and allusions resonating from one sphere to the other, that it is impossible to say whether what is paramount is a portrait of class at a crucial historical juncture, modulated through the experiences of particular characters or the examination of personal situations of alienation, loneliness, choice, and the necessity for and function of art against the determining and limiting background of time, history, and tradition.

Most of Johnston's characters are would-be artists, musicians, or writers. They are concerned with the relationship between art and life; the formality and perfection of art and the shapelessness and failure of life. Many of them look for subjects for their art and, because she has a fondness for first-person, retrospective narratives, that subject is often their own lives and the crucial moments when the choices that determined the shape of those lives were made. To this extent, many of her novels are *Bildungsroman*—portraits of the artist as a young man or woman, even if recollected from age or at the point of death. The themes that are crucial in this, essentially personal, focus are the forces of family, society, and tradition that entrap the writer. As Alex Moore shapes his life before his execution (*How Many Miles to Babylon?*) he makes it clear that it is his rejection by his cold, manipulative mother and the social pressures that compel him, against his own inclination, to be "an Officer and a Gentleman" that have led directly to his impending death. The focus seems to be less on the background of World War I or the 1916 rising than on Alex's sense of silence and isolation in the murderous battle between his parents. However, it is also clear that Alex's parents represent different allegiances, different senses of history. He is caught in more than a personal impasse. He is torn between conflicting roles, identities, allegiances. His attempt to escape in his companionship with Jerry Crowe, cannot succeed. The "inexorable" force of "history" is against it. That history conditions Jerry Crowe, too. One of the achievements of Johnston's novels is her capacity to suggest levels of complexity beneath the apparent simplicity and lyricism of her prose. Jerry is not presented as the stereotyped "peasant" living in harmony with the land and his own senses, the opposite to Alex's repressed intellectualism. Jerry too is sent to his death by his mother and is, in his way, as alienated from his home and class as is Alex. In the presentation of these destructive mothers (and in the naming of the horse which the two young men train for the Morrigan, the Celtic Goddess of war), Johnston is extending the scope of her themes from conflicted nationalisms to a consideration of the human capacity for violence.

It is noticeable that all of her novels deal with war in one form or another. Two are set against the background of World War I. *The Old Jest* and *Fool's Sanctuary* deal with the period of the Black and Tans. *Shadows on Our Skin* and *The Railway Station Man* are concerned with the modern IRA. *The Christmas Tree* is centrally concerned with the holocaust. In one sense, Johnston's novels represent an answer to the question of whether it is possible to deal with the reality of contemporary violence in the north without being programmatic or strident. She is able to do this because the violence is seen as both almost unimportant and as a permanent part of human experience. The essential question about war and death is how the experience is used, and in this aspect, there has been a notable development in the novels. The early ones concentrate on defeat. The wave before the drowning is very subdued; the characters are in retreat from life, insulating themselves behind writing, drinking, or accepting that there is no possibility of a relationship with the world or with another individual. In the later novels, however, the outlook is more hopeful. Even though Constance Keating dies (*The Christmas Tree*) she has left behind her a child who will provide hope for Jacob's future, and she has got young Bridie May to arrange her papers into a, finally, publishable book. The latest novel, *The Invisible Worm,* is the most ambitious to date, providing in its story of incest and abuse of a daughter by her successful politician father, a chilling metaphor of the state of modern Ireland, and a new variation of Johnston's old reworking of the stereotype of "Mother Ireland." It also continues to suggest that moments of personal happiness can be snatched in spite of violence and madness and that the ghosts of the past which haunt all Johnson's characters, can be appeased.

—Anne Clune

JOLLEY, (Monica) Elizabeth

Nationality: Australian. **Born:** Monica Elizabeth Knight in Birmingham, England, 4 June 1923; moved to Australia, 1959; became citizen, 1978. **Education:** Friends' School, Sibford, Oxfordshire, 1934-40; St. Thomas' Hospital, London (orthopaedic nursing training), 1940-43; Queen Elizabeth Hospital, Birmingham (general training), 1943-46. **Family:** Married Leonard Jolley; two daughters and one son. **Career:** Salesperson, nurse, and domestic, 1960s. Part-time tutor in creative writing, Fremantle Arts Centre, Western Australia, from 1974; part-time tutor in English from 1978, writer-in-residence, 1982, and since 1984 half-time tutor in English, Western Australian Institute of Technology, Bentley; half-time lecturer and writer-in-residence from 1986, and since 1989 honorary writer-in-residence, Curtin University of Technology, Perth, Western Australia. Writer-in-residence, Scarborough Senior High School, Winter 1980, and Western Australian College of Advanced Education, Nedlands, 1983. President, Australian Society of Authors, 1985-86. **Awards:** State of Victoria prize, for short story, 1966, 1981, 1982; Sound Stage prize, for radio play, 1975; Wieckhard prize, 1975; Australian Writers Guild prize, for radio play, 1982; *Western Australia Week* prize, 1983; *The Age* Book of the Year award, 1983, 1989; Australia Council Literature Board senior fellowship, 1984; New South Wales Premier's award, 1985; Australian Bicentennial National Literary award, 1986; Miles Franklin award, 1987; Fellowship of Australian Writers Ramsden plaque, 1988; Australian Literary Society Gold Medal award, 1991, for *Cabin Fever;* The France-Australia award, 1993, for translation of *The Sugar Mother;* The Premier of West Australia's prize, 1993,

for *Central Mischief;* National Book Connail Banjo award, 1994, for *The Georges' Wife.* D.Tech.: Western Australian Institute of Technology, 1986. Officer, Order of Australia, 1988. **Agent:** Caroline Lurie, Australian Literary Management, 2-A Armstrong Street, Middle Park, Victoria 3206. **Address:** 28 Agett Road, Claremont, Western Australia 6010, Australia.

PUBLICATIONS

Novels

Palomino. Collingwood, Victoria, Outback Press, and London, Melbourne House, 1980; New York, Persea, 1987.
The Newspaper of Claremont Street. Fremantle, Western Australia, Fremantle Arts Centre Press, 1981; New York, Viking, 1987; London, Penguin, 1988.
Mr. Scobie's Riddle. Ringwood, Victoria, Penguin, 1983; New York, Penguin, 1984; London, Penguin, 1985.
Miss Peabody's Inheritance. St. Lucia, University of Queensland Press, 1983; New York, Viking, 1984; London, Viking, 1985.
Milk and Honey. Fremantle, Western Australia, Fremantle Arts Centre Press, 1984; New York, Persea, 1986; London, Viking, 1987.
Foxybaby. St. Lucia, University of Queensland Press, and New York, Viking, 1985; London, Viking, 1986.
The Well. Ringwood, Victoria, London, and New York, Viking, 1986.
The Sugar Mother. Fremantle, Western Australia, Fremantle Arts Centre Press, and New York, Harper, 1988; London, Viking, 1989.
My Father's Moon. Ringwood, Victoria, and London, Viking, and New York, Harper, 1989.
Cabin Fever. Ringwood, Victoria, Viking, 1990; London, Sinclair Stevenson, and New York, Harper Collins, 1991.
The Georges' Wife. Ringwood, Victoria, Viking, 1993.
The Orchard Thieves. Ringwood, Victoria, Viking, 1995.

Short Stories

Five Acre Virgin and Other Stories. Fremantle, Western Australia, Fremantle Arts Centre Press, 1976.
The Travelling Entertainer and Other Stories. Fremantle, Western Australia, Fremantle Arts Centre Press, 1979.
Woman in a Lampshade. Ringwood, Victoria, Penguin, 1983; New York and London, Penguin, 1986.
Stories. Fremantle, Western Australia, Fremantle Arts Centre Press, 1984; New York, Viking, 1988; London, Penguin, 1989.

Uncollected Short Stories

"The Talking Bricks," in *Summer's Tales 2,* edited by Kylie Tennant. Melbourne and London, Macmillan, and New York, St. Martin's Press, 1965.
"The Rhyme," in *Westerly* (Nedlands, Western Australia), no. 4, 1967.
"The Sick Vote," in *Quadrant* (Sydney), vol. 12, no. 5, 1968.
"The Well-Bred Thief," in *South Pacific Stories,* edited by Chris and Helen Tiffin. St. Lucia, Queensland, SPACLALS, 1980.
"Mark F," in *The True Life Story of . . . ,* edited by Jan Craney and Esther Caldwell. St. Lucia, University of Queensland Press, 1981.

"Night Report," "It's about Your Daughter Mrs. Page" and "Poppy Seed and Sesame Rings," in *Frictions,* edited by Anna Gibbs and Alison Tilson. Fitzroy, Victoria, Sybylla, 1982.

"Night Runner," in *Room to Move,* edited by Suzanne Falkiner. Sydney, Allen and Unwin, 1985.

"Bathroom Dance," in *Transgressions,* edited by Don Anderson. Ringwood, Victoria, Penguin, 1986.

"Frederick the Great Returns to Fairfields," in *Portrait: A West Coast Collection,* edited by B.R. Coffey and Wendy Jenkins. Fremantle, Western Australia, Fremantle Arts Centre Press, 1986.

"This Flickering, Foxy Man, My Father," in *Vogue Australia* (Sydney), October 1986.

"Mr. Berrington," in *Australian Literary Quarterly,* April 1987.

"Melon Jam," in *The Crankworth Bequest and Other Stories,* edited by Jennifer Haynes and Barry Carozzi. Adelaide, Australian Association for the Teaching of English, 1987.

"A Miracle of Confluence," in *Landfall* (Christchurch), no. 2, 1988.

"727 Chester Road," in *Southern Review* (Adelaide), vol. 21, no. 3, 1988.

"The Fellmonger," in *Eight Voices of the Eighties,* edited by Gillian Whitlock. St. Lucia, University of Queensland Press, 1989.

"My Mother's Visit," in *Westerly* (Nedlands, Western Australia), vol. 34, no. 4, 1989.

"The Widow's House," in *Expressway,* edited by Helen Daniel. Ringwood, Victoria, Penguin, 1989.

"The Goose Path," in *Best Short Stories 1990,* edited by Giles Gordon and David Hughes. London, Heinemann, 1990; as *The Best English Short Stories 1990,* New York, Norton, 1990.

"The Widder Tree Shadder Murder," in *Crimes for a Summer Christmas,* edited by Stephen Knight. Sydney, Allen and Unwin, 1990.

Plays

Woman in a Lampshade (broadcast 1979). Published in *Radio Quartet,* Fremantle, Western Australia, Fremantle Arts Centre Press, 1980.

Radio Plays: *Night Report,* 1975; *The Performance,* 1976; *The Shepherd on the Roof,* 1977; *The Well-Bred Thief,* 1977; *Woman in a Lampshade,* 1979; *Two Men Running,* 1981; *Paper Children,* 1988; *Little Lewis Has Had a Lovely Sleep,* 1990.

Poetry

Diary of a Weekend Farmer. Fremantle, Western Australia, Fremantle Arts Centre Press, 1993.

Other

Travelling Notebook: Literature Notes. Fremantle, Western Australia, Arts Access, 1978.
Central Mischief. Ringwood, Victoria, Viking, 1992.

*

Manuscript Collection: Mitchell Library, Sydney.

Critical Studies: Articles by Jolley and by Laurie Clancy, in *Australian Book Review* (Melbourne), November 1983; Helen Garner, in *Meanjin* (Melbourne), no. 2, 1983; "Between Two Worlds" by A.P. Riemer, in *Southerly* (Sydney), 1983; "The Goddess, the Art-

ist, and the Spinster" by Dorothy Jones, in *Westerly* (Nedlands, Western Australia), no. 4, 1984; Joan Kirkby, in *Meanjin* (Melbourne), no. 4, 1984; Martin Harrison, in *The Age Monthly Review* (Melbourne), May 1985; *Elizabeth Jolley: New Critical Essays* edited by Delys Bird and Brenda Walker, Sydney, Angus and Robertson, 1991.

Elizabeth Jolley comments:

(1991) In my writing I try to explore and celebrate the small things in human life. I am interested in people and their needs and feelings. I work with imagination from moments of truth and awareness. Characters stay with me for years.

*   *   *

Elizabeth Jolley has had perhaps the most meteoric rise to fame of any Australian writer over the last two decades. Apart from stories in anthologies and journals Jolley had had no work published until 1976 when, at the age of 53, her collection *Five Acre Virgin and Other Stories* appeared under the aegis of the newly formed Fremantle Arts Centre Press. Since then her rate of publication has been as phenomenal as the rise in critical acclaim of her work. The stories were written over a period of 16 years prior to publication in book form and show already her peculiar combination of unsentimental realism and original, often bizarre humor. The title itself suggests one of the most pervasive themes in her early work. "There's nothing like having a piece of land," a protagonist in several of the stories says. "Having a piece of land" is crucial to the characters in these works, many of whom are dispossessed or migrants or both. They have come from Vienna, where the author's father grew up, or the Black Country of England where she herself lived, or Holland from where the recurring figure of Uncle Bernard migrated. They struggle all their lives to buy the talismanic five acres only to find out that they cannot live off them. They lie and blackmail in order to stay on other people's land. Adam, in "Adam's Wife," one of the most powerful and somber stories that Jolley has written, even marries a retarded woman in order to gain possession of her miserable shack and few acres.

Jolley's second collection, *The Travelling Entertainer,* contains her longer stories from much the same period and shows her going back and revising and reworking the same material—themes, characters, landscapes, situations and motifs, even names. As well as the preoccupation with land again, the stories contain many elements that appear throughout her work: allusions to music (especially Beethoven), to literature (especially Tolstoy), the interest in nursing homes and hospitals, the figure of the defeated salesman, the migrants from Holland and the Black Country including Uncle Bernard again, and the first of Jolley's many treatments of lesbian relationships and of women offering themselves to other women as a form of comfort or consolation or even occasionally as a means of achieving power. A lesbian relationship is at the center of her first and least typical novel, *Palomina,* which was written partly in the late 1950s, partly in 1962, and then rewritten over 1970, 1973, and 1974 before finally appearing in 1980. It is a lyrical, even reverential account of a love affair between a 60-year-old deregistered doctor and another woman barely half her age. It is totally devoid of her usual humor and sense of the incongruous and despite the then controversial subject the two women behave with such relentless nobility towards each other that they threaten to become merely boring. *The Newspaper of Claremont Street* is vintage Jolley, not her most profound book but a delightfully amusing and at times quite poignant one. The heroine of this novella is a cleaning woman known as Newspaper, or Weekly, because she gathers gossip from her rich clients and passes it on to the rest of the community.

Mr. Scobie's Riddle placed her instantly in the forefront of Australian novelists. Set in the appalling nursing home of St. Christopher and St. Jude, the novel gives full vent to her penchant for mordant and grotesque humor; it is both hilarious and horrifying and yet its triumph is that it avoids the extremes of seeing the aged people of the home as either the victims of society's cruelty and indifference on the one hand, or merely comic eccentrics on the other. *Woman in a Lampshade* is an assured collection of stories, though there is little in it to surprise readers of the author's earlier work, while *Miss Peabody's Inheritance* is an earlier novella, rewritten, which cuts back and forth between two separate and interrelated stories. At the end of the book, the two stories, England and Australia, converge in an unexpected way to make a comment on a theme that increasingly concerns Jolley in her later work, the relationship between life and art, and between reality and fantasy.

Throughout the 1980s Jolley continued her prolific output, confirming her reputation and winning all major Australian literary awards at some stage or other. The short novel *Milk and Honey* is a strange parable and a darkly disturbing, somber book. *Foxybaby,* on the other hand, returns more to the bizarrely comic and almost surreal mode of *Mr. Scobie's Riddle. The Well* is a fusion of Grimm fairytale (there are many images and motifs to do with fairytales) and psychological thriller, about two women who lower a man down into a well after they believe they have killed him in a car accident. The significance of the well itself, as both fact and symbol, steadily expands as disturbing ripples swell out from the initial action. The title of *The Sugar Mother* refers to the surrogate mother used by one of the characters in this strange but delicate novel in which most of the meanings are both subterranean and suggestive, the comedy present but muted and somber.

But perhaps Jolley's finest achievements have come most recently with the publication of *My Father's Moon* and *Cabin Fever.* Here Jolley has returned to her roots, to what Yeats called "the foul rag and bone shop of the heart," in order to reassess her life and work. What the critic Helen Daniel said of *My Father's Moon*—that it is "the novel at the heart of all her work"—is equally true of its successor and the two books read in fact like the first two parts of a closely autobiographical and linked trilogy. Their protagonist is Vera or Veronica Wright and the setting is England in all the misery of its immediate post war austerity. *My Father's Moon* depicts her as a young girl, growing up to become a student nurse during the war and becoming pregnant by a worthless doctor. By the time of *Cabin Fever* her lover is dead, she has given birth to a daughter and become a qualified nurse. Vera speculates at one point on "Whether things are written down or they dwell somewhere within and surface unbidden at anytime." The two novels are a record of that unbidden surfacing, a confrontation with the events of the past and all their shaping of the novelist's subsequent art.

—Laurie Clancy

JONES, Gayl

Nationality: American. **Born:** Lexington, Kentucky, 23 November 1949. **Education:** Connecticut College, New London, B.A. in English 1971; Brown University, Providence, Rhode Island, M.A.

1973, D.A. 1975. **Career:** Member of the Department of English, University of Michigan, Ann Arbor, 1975-83. **Awards:** Howard Foundation award, 1975; National Endowment for the Arts grant, 1976. **Address:** c/o Lotus Press, P.O. Box 21607, Detroit, Michigan 48221, U.S.A.

PUBLICATIONS

Novels

Corregidora. New York, Random House, 1975; London, Camden, 1988.
Eva's Man. New York, Random House, 1976.

Short Stories

White Rat. New York, Random House, 1977.

Uncollected Short Stories

"Almeyda," in *Massachusetts Review* (Amherst), Winter 1977.
"Ensinança," in *Confirmation,* edited by Amiri and Amina Baraka. New York, Morrow, 1983.

Play

Chile Woman. New York, Shubert Foundation, 1975.

Poetry

Song for Anninho. Detroit, Lotus Press, 1981.
The Hermit-Woman. Detroit, Lotus Press, 1983.
Xarque. Detroit, Lotus Press, 1985.

Other

Liberating Voices: Oral Tradition in African American Literature. Cambridge and London, Harvard University Press, 1991.

*

Critical Studies: *Engendering the Subject: Gender and Self-Representation in Contemporary Women's Fiction* by Sally Robinson, Albany, State University of New York Press, 1991; *Bridging the Americas: The Literature of Paula Marshall, Toni Morrison and Gayl Jones* by Stelamaris Coser, Philadelphia, Temple University Press, 1994.

*   *   *

Gayl Jones's first novel, *Corregidora,* focuses on the lingering effects of slavery in black America—specifically on its sexual and psychological manifestations in the life of Ursa Corregidora, a Kentucky blues singer. The great granddaughter of a Portuguese plantation owner who fathered not only her grandmother but also her mother, and who used his progeny both in the fields and in his own whorehouse, Ursa is unable to free herself of painful and obsessive family memories. In each personal relationship she finds yet again the sickness of the master-slave dynamic. Her short-lived first marriage is convulsive with desire, possessiveness, humiliation, and violence; her second, safer, marriage fails as she cannot forget the first. In relating Ursa's story, Jones shows the difficulty of loving when abusive relationships have been naturalized by cultural continuity, when so much has been taken that one's only dignity is in withholding. Her taut and explicit idiom, sometimes plainly narrative, sometimes wildly stream-of-consciousness, captures the nuances of a tormented sexuality that is both specific to black experience and symptomatic of our troubled gender system. "I knew what I still felt. I knew that I still hated him. Not as bad as then, not with the first feeling, but an after feeling, an aftertaste, or like an odor still in a room when you come back to it, and it's your own." The book's ending, almost unbearably intense but strangely hopeful, suggests that we may begin to heal ourselves only as we confront the deep sexual hatred that pervades our lives.

Whereas *Corregidora* allows us to perceive the construction of personality as historical process, *Eva's Man* offers a very different kind of experience, one that many readers have found profoundly disturbing. Eva Canada, the main character of the novel, tells her tale from an institution for the criminally insane, where she has been imprisoned for a hideous sexual crime of murder and dental castration. Like Ursa, Eva has been damaged by abuse and by a legacy of violence; unlike the protagonist of *Corregidora,* she has no sense of how her past motivates her present. As she speaks her disjointed narrative, an ugly story disrupted by flashes of recalled nastiness, she remains alien to us, a personality beyond promise or repair.

> I put my hand on his hand. I kissed his hand, his neck. I put my fingers in the space above his eyes, but didn't close them. They'd come and put copper coins over them. That's why they told you not to suck pennies. I put my forehead under his chin. He was warm. The glass had spilled from his hand. I put my tongue between his parted lips. I kissed his teeth.

In *Eva's Man,* Jones takes us into the pathological mind, and we do not find ourselves there. As the tidy reader-protagonist identification is denied us, we are left with the horror of what we can't sympathetically imagine. Jones's unflinching violation of our strongest taboos—made all the more chilling by her starkly controlled prose—raises a number of questions about the roles of writers, readers, and cultural conventions. Beyond shock value, what does a writer achieve in presenting the truly sordid? Is our understanding necessarily dependent upon the protagonist's understanding? What do disturbing books demand of us that comforting ones do not? How must we see the world in order to change it? The stories that make up *White Rat* suggest that Jones is intent on keeping those questions before us. The majority of these pieces ("Legend," "Asylum," "The Coke Factory," "The Return," "Version 2," "Your Poems Have Very Little Color in Them") are about madness or extreme psychic alienation. Some ("The Women," "Jevata") address the painful complications of desperate sexual arrangements. The most attractive, of course, are those few ("White Rat," "Persona," "The Roundhouse") that hint at successful human connection despite overwhelming odds. Like *Eva's Man,* most of the stories in *White Rat* challenge our notions of what fiction should do. What we make of Gayl Jones's work depends largely on what we are willing to perceive as the function of art—on how, as readers, we enter into the dialogue.

—Janis Butler Holm

JONES, (Morgan) Glyn

Nationality: British. **Born:** Merthyr Tydfil, Glamorgan, 28 February 1905. **Education:** Castle Grammar School, Merthyr Tydfil; St. Paul's College, Cheltenham, Gloucestershire. Married Phyllis Doreen Jones in 1935. **Career:** Formerly a schoolmaster in Glamorgan; now retired. First chair, Yr Academi Gymreig (English Section). **Awards:** Welsh Arts Council prize, for non-fiction, 1969, and Premier award, 1972. D.Litt.: University of Wales, Cardiff, 1974. **Agent:** Laurence Pollinger Ltd., 18 Maddox Street, London W1R 0EU, England. **Address:** 158 Manor Way, Whitchurch, Cardiff CF4 1RN, Wales.

PUBLICATIONS

Novels

The Valley, The City, The Village. London, Dent, 1956.
The Learning Lark. London, Dent, 1960.
The Island of Apples. London, Dent, and New York, Day, 1965; revised edition, Cardiff, University of Wales Press, 1992.

Short Stories

The Blue Bed. London, Cape, 1937; New York, Dutton, 1938.
The Water Music. London, Routledge, 1944.
Selected Short Stories. London, Dent, 1971.
Welsh Heirs. Llandysul, Dyfed, Gomer, 1977.

Play

The Beach of Falesá (verse libretto), music by Alun Hoddinott (produced Cardiff, 1974). London, Oxford University Press, 1974.

Poetry

Poems. London, Fortune Press, 1939.
The Dream of Jake Hopkins. London, Fortune Press, 1954.
Selected Poems. Llandysul, Dyfed, Gomer, 1975.
The Meaning of Fuchsias. Newtown, Gregynog Press, 1987.
Selected Poems, Fragments, and Fictions. Bridgend, Glamorgan, Poetry Wales Press, 1988.
The Story of Heledd, with T.J. Morgan; edited by Jenny Rowland and engravings by Harry Brockway. Newtown, Powys, Gwasg Grefynog, 1994.

Other

The Dragon Has Two Tongues: Essays on Anglo-Welsh Writers and Writing. London, Dent, 1968.
Profiles: A Visitor's Guide to Writing in Twentieth Century Wales, with John Rowlands. Llandysul, Dyfed, Gomer, 1980.
Setting Out: A Memoir of Literary Life in Wales. Cardiff, University College Department of Extra Mural Studies, 1982.
Random Entrances to Gwyn Thomas. Cardiff, University College Press, 1982.

Editor, *Poems '76.* Llandysul, Dyfed, Gomer, 1976.

Translator, with T.J. Morgan, *The Saga of Llywarch the Old.* London, Golden Cockerel Press, 1955.

Translator, *What Is Worship?,* by E. Stanley John. Swansea, Wales for Christ Movement, 1978.

Translator, *When the Rose-bush Brings Forth Apples* (Welsh folk poetry). Gregynog, Powys, Gregynog Press, 1980.

Translator, *Honeydew on the Wormwood* (Welsh folk poetry). Gregynog, Powys, Gregynog Press, 1984.

*

Bibliography: By John and Sylvia Harris, in *Poetry Wales 19* (Bridgend, Glamorgan), 3-4, 1984.

Manuscript Collection: National Library of Wales, Aberystwyth.

Critical Studies: Article by Iolo Llwyd, in *South Wales Magazine* (Cardiff), Autumn 1970; *Glyn Jones* by Leslie Norris, Cardiff, University of Wales Press, 1973, and article by Norris in *British Novelists 1930-1959* edited by Bernard Oldsey, Detroit, Gale, 1983; Harri Pritchard-Jones, in *Welsh Books and Writers* (Cardiff), Autumn 1981; David Smith, in *Arcade* (Cardiff), February 1982.

Glyn Jones comments:

I began my literary life as a poet. In 1934 I first became friendly with Dylan Thomas, who suggested I should write short stories, as he himself was doing then. My first published book was a volume of short stories, *The Blue Bed.* This was written when the great industrial depression was at its most intense in South Wales and the longest story in the book takes this for its subject. South Wales, industrial and agricultural—this is the theme in all the stories in *The Blue Bed.* Indeed, all my prose, and much of my poetry, is concerned with this region. The novel *The Valley, The City, The Village,* which is partly autobiographical, tries to convey what it was like to grow up in South Wales; *The Learning Lark* deals with learning and teaching in the area; *The Island of Apples* describes childhood and its fantasies in a closely knit community in the Welsh valleys.

The Water Music has stories about both the industrial east of South Wales (Glamorgan) and the agricultural west (Carmarthen, Pembroke, Cardigan). To quote my publisher—I have "carried the medium [i.e., the imaginative short story] to an unexcelled synthesis of realism and fantasy, magic and humor. From the regional contrasts of industrialism and pastoralism, modernity and tradition, he builds up a world of convincing beauty, and expresses himself in a prose style of unusual poetic vitality." I would accept this as a statement of what I have *tried* to do in my short stories. Whether I've done it is of course quite another question.

*   *   *

"While using cheerfully enough the English language, I have never written in it a word about any country other than Wales, or any people other than Welsh people," wrote Glyn Jones in *The Dragon Has Two Tongues.* This deliberate limitation of his material is the only reason I can suggest for any kind of restriction to the general recognition his gifts deserve.

Certainly his stories and novels, although they share a Welsh background, are set in widely separate countries of the mind, pose different problems, and offer to us recognizable human situations. His prose, too, is very much more than the "cheerful use" of the English language. Always exuberant and seemingly spendthrift ("I fancy words," he says in his poem, "Merthyr"), it is also exact, muscular, very energetic. He can range from elegant and mannered writing—and the use of a vocabulary so exotic that it upset some reviewers of his first novel, *The Valley, The City, The Village*—to the direct, racy, almost physical style, the true, idiosyncratic speaking voice we find in some of the stories and in the two later novels.

His Wales commonly has two contrasting faces, that of the idyllic land of country happiness opposing the suppurating mining towns where the ugly, comical people are unfailingly kindly. But it also exists as a metaphysical universe, and the young people who are to be found in almost everything Jones writes are given early experience of both Heaven and Hell. To some extent this duality reflects Jones's own early life; during his impressionable boyhood he lived in the grimy steel and coal town of Merthyr Tydfil, but spent significant periods in Llanstephan, a beautiful Carmarthenshire village.

His identification with the scenes and characters of his imagination is absolutely complete, and it is noticeable that many of these stories and all three of his novels are told in the first person. Many critics, indeed, thought *The Valley, The City, The Village* largely autobiographical, although this story of a young painter, aware of his vocation but forced by the obstinate love of his grandmother to go to university to train as a preacher, has only tenuous links with Jones's own life. It is the quality of Jones's visual imagination and the unjudging tolerance that lies behind his observation that make his young artist credible.

For in the end Jones's love of his people is the illuminating quality of his work. He has created a whole gallery of memorable characters, some of them fully realized, some of whom enter his pages but once. He sees their blemishes, particularly their physical shortcomings, as clearly as their virtues, but to him they are lovable because their faults are the faults of human beings. Even in *The Learning Lark,* that picaresque send-up of the state of education in a corrupt mining valley where teachers have to bribe their way to headships, there is no scalding satire. Both bribed and bribers are seen as only too human and the book is full of gargantuan laughter.

The world of childhood and adolescence, that magical period when the real and the imagined are hardly to be distinguished, has been a particularly fertile area of Jones's concern. *The Water Music,* for example, is a collection of stories about young people: of his three novels only one is set entirely in the world of adults, and even that one has some very realistic schoolboys in it.

The Island of Apples is a full-scale exploration of the world of adolescence, seen through the eyes of the boy Dewi. It is a remarkable novel, using a prose which is obviously the boy's voice, yet flexible and powerful enough to describe an enormous range of events and emotions. Its sensitivity, its combination of dreamlike confusion and the clear, unsentimental observation which is the adolescent state of mind, the excitement with which the boy invests the commonplace with the exotic, are perfectly balanced attributes of a work which is as individual and complete as *Le Grand Meaulnes,* that other evocation of vanishing youth.

Perhaps the greatest of Jones's qualities is that of delight in the created world and the people who inhabit it. If he writes of a small and often shabby corner of that world—the first story in *The Blue Bed* is called "I Was Born in the Ystrad Valley" and it is to Ystrad that he returns for *The Island of Apples*—yet his writing is a celebration, an act of praise. To this end he has shaped his craftsmanship and inspiration, and his achievement is permanent and real.

—Leslie Norris

JONES, Gwyn

Nationality: British. **Born:** Blackwood, Monmouthshire, 24 May 1907. **Education:** Tredegar Grammar School; University College, Cardiff, 1924-29, B.A. 1927, M.A. 1929. **Family:** Married 1) Alice Rees in 1928 (died 1979); 2) Mair Sivell in 1979. **Career:** Schoolmaster, 1929-35; lecturer, University College, Cardiff, 1935-40; professor of English language and literature, University College of Wales, Aberystwyth, 1940-65, and University College, Cardiff, 1965-75. Ida Beam Visiting Professor, University of Iowa, Iowa City, 1982. Editor, *Welsh Review,* Cardiff and Aberystwyth, 1939, 1944-48; director, Penmark Press, Cardiff, 1939-60. President, 1951-52, and Honorary Life Member, 1979, Viking Society for Northern Research; Chairman, Welsh Arts Council, 1957-67. **Awards:** Welsh Arts Council award, 1973; Christian Gauss award, for non-fiction, 1973. D.Litt.: University of Wales, Cardiff, 1977; University of Nottingham, 1978; University of Southampton, Hampshire, 1983. Freeman of Islwyn, Gwent, 1988. Fellow, University College, Cardiff, 1980, and University College of Wales, Aberystwyth, 1987, of Welsh Academy, 1990. Knight, 1963, and Commander's Cross, 1987, Order of the Falcon (Iceland). C.B.E. (Commander, Order of the British Empire), 1965. **Address:** Castle Cottage, Sea View Place, Aberystwyth, Dyfed, Wales.

PUBLICATIONS

Novels

Richard Savage. London, Gollancz, and New York, Viking Press, 1935.
Times Like These. London, Gollancz, 1936.
The Nine-Days' Wonder. London, Gollancz, 1937.
Garland of Bays. London, Gollancz, and New York, Macmillan, 1938.
The Green Island. London, Golden Cockerel Press, 1946.
The Flowers Beneath the Scythe. London, Dent, 1952.
The Walk Home. London, Dent, 1962; New York, Norton, 1963.

Short Stories

The Buttercup Field and Other Stories. Cardiff, Penmark Press, 1945.
The Still Waters and Other Stories. London, Davies, 1948.
Shepherd's Hey and Other Stories. London, Staples Press, 1953.
Selected Short Stories. London, Oxford University Press, 1974.

Other

A Prospect of Wales. London, Penguin, 1948.
Welsh [and Scandinavian] Legends and Folk-Tales Retold (for children). London, Oxford University Press, 2 vols., 1955-56; New York, Walck, 2 vols., 1965.
The First Forty Years: Some Notes on Anglo-Welsh Literature (lecture). Cardiff, University of Wales Press, 1957.

The Norse Atlantic Saga, Being the Norse Voyages of Discovery and Settlement to Iceland, Greenland, America. London and New York, Oxford University Press, 1964; revised edition, Oxford, Oxford University Press, 1986.
The Legendary History of Olaf Tryggvason (lecture). Glasgow, Jackson, 1968.
A History of the Vikings. London and New York, Oxford University Press, 1968; revised edition, Oxford, Oxford University Press, 1984.
Kings, Beasts, and Heroes. London and New York, Oxford University Press, 1972.
Babel and the Dragon's Tongue (lecture). Southampton, Hampshire, University of Southampton, 1981.
The Novel and Society (lecture; in Welsh and English). Bangor, North Wales Arts Association, 1981.
Background to Dylan Thomas and Other Explorations. Oxford, Oxford University Press, 1992.

Editor, with E.M. Silvanus, *Narrative Poems for Schools.* London, Rivingtons, 3 vols., 1935.
Editor, *Prose* [and *Poems*] *of Six Centuries.* London, Rivingtons, 2 vols., 1935-36.
Editor, *Welsh Short Stories.* London, Penguin, 1940.
Editor, with Gweno Lewis, *Letters from India,* by Alun Lewis. Cardiff, Penmark Press, 1946.
Editor, *Salmacus and Hermaphroditus.* London, Golden Cockerel Press, 1951.
Editor, *Circe and Ulysses: The Inner Temple Masque,* by William Browne. London, Golden Cockerel Press, 1954.
Editor, *Welsh Short Stories.* London, Oxford University Press, 1956.
Editor, *Songs and Poems of John Dryden.* London, Golden Cockerel Press, 1957.
Editor, *The Metamorphosis of Publius Ovidius Naso.* London, Golden Cockerel Press, 1958.
Editor, *The Poems and Sonnets of Shakespeare.* London, Golden Cockerel Press, 1960.
Editor, with Islwyn Ffowc Elis, *Twenty-Five Welsh Short Stories.* London, Oxford University Press, 1971.
Editor, *The Oxford Book of Welsh Verse in English.* London and New York, Oxford University Press, 1977.
Editor, with Michael Quinn, *Fountains of Praise: University College, Cardiff, 1883-1983.* Cardiff, University College Cardiff Press, 1983.

Translator, *Four Icelandic Sagas.* London, Allen and Unwin, and Princeton, New Jersey, Princeton University Press, 1935.
Translator, *The Vatnsdalers' Saga.* London, Oxford University Press, and Princeton, New Jersey, Princeton University Press, 1944.
Translator, with Thomas Jones, *The Mabinogion.* London, Golden Cockerel Press, 1948; New York, Dutton, 1950; revised edition, London, Dent, 1975; revised edition, London, Dent, 1993.
Translator, *Sir Gawain and the Green Knight.* London, Golden Cockerel Press, 1952.
Translator, *Egil's Saga.* Syracuse, New York, Syracuse University Press, 1960.
Translator, *Eirik the Red and Other Icelandic Sagas.* London and New York, Oxford University Press, 1961.

*

Bibliography: "The Writings of Gwyn Jones: A Checklist" by Paul Bennet Morgan, in *New Welsh Review* (Lampeter, Dyfed), Winter 1988.

Critical Study: *Gwyn Jones* by Cecil Price, Cardiff, University of Wales Press, 1976.

*   *   *

Gwyn Jones did not begin as an "Anglo-Welsh" writer—that is, as a Welshman writing in English about Wales; his first book was a weighty historical novel, *Richard Savage,* in which he traced the decline of the 18th-century poet against a richly described background peopled with a large number of real and imaginary characters. The same ability to conjure up the very smell of a bygone age is apparent in his *Garland of Bays,* an even longer, picaresque novel in which the story of Robert Greene is used to link striking pictures of Elizabethan life—in country and city, in university and prison, at home and abroad. In between these considerable undertakings he produced a Manchester novel—*The Nine-Days' Wonder*—in which there is an attempt to depict part-time criminals living otherwise ordinary lives, and his first book with a Welsh background—*Times Like These,* a novel of the General Strike of 1926 as it affected life in a South Wales mining valley.

All Jones's fiction after 1938 is set in Wales, but he seems to have largely avoided the themes most immediately associated with Anglo-Welsh writers from South Wales. It is true that a part of *The Flowers Beneath the Scythe* recalls pit disasters, unemployment, and poverty in the Welsh valleys between the wars, but the filter is the middle-class guilt-feelings of the hero, and the novel is equally concerned with the horrors of trench warfare, the rise of the dictators, the debate about pacifism, the challenge of World War II—in short, it looks retrospectively at some of the major preoccupations of the period covered. *The Walk Home,* too, reaches out to more general themes; here Jones returns to the historical novel, though this time the place is 19th-century Wales and the hero the victim not of his own folly and weakness but of Evil incarnate in experienced, ruthless men.

Of the volumes of short stories, *The Buttercup Field* is the most conventionally "Anglo-Welsh" and it sounds notes of comedy and whimsy heard more rarely in the two later collections. The dominant features of the more impressive stories in this and the later volumes are strong story lines, dramatic—even melodramatic—situations, and that acceptance of the importance and dignity of ordinary people which so often informs serious regional fiction. The characters and settings are Welsh, certainly, but the Welshness is taken for granted as the elemental situations take hold of the author's imagination.

Orthodox in structure, Jones's fiction has been notable for the energy of its narrative style, the vividness of its descriptive passages, and the boldness of its characterization; it has been most successful when the material has been sufficiently distanced in the exercise of an outstanding talent for research, whether historical or cultural. Many readers will find it interesting to note the tensions between the writer's fascination with crime and violence and his tacit acceptance of the most humane standards of his time, between the shrewdness of his even-toned reflections on human nature and a strain of romanticism not always held in check, between occasional self-indulgence and a strong, versatile prose style rooted in detailed observation and firm self-discipline.

—Roy Thomas

JONES, Madison (Percy, Jr.)

Nationality: American. **Born:** Nashville, Tennessee, 21 March 1925. **Education:** Vanderbilt University, Nashville, A.B. 1949; University of Florida, Gainesville, 1950-53, A.M. 1951. **Military Service:** Served in the United States Army in the Corps of Military Police, Korea, 1945-46. **Family:** Married Shailah McEvilley in 1951; two daughters and three sons. **Career:** Farmer in Cheatham County, Tennessee, 1940s; instructor in English, Miami University, Oxford, Ohio, 1953-54, and University of Tennessee, Knoxville, 1955-56. Member of the Department of English from 1956, writer-in-residence, 1967-87, and professor of English, 1968-87, Auburn University, Alabama; now emeritus. **Member:** Alabama Academy of Distinguished Authors; Fellowship of Southern Writers. **Awards:** *Sewanee Review* fellowship, 1954; Alabama Library Association Book award, 1968; Rockefeller fellowship, 1968; Guggenheim fellowship, 1973; Lytle prize, for short fiction, 1992. **Agent:** Harold Matson Company, Inc., 276 Fifth Avenue, New York, New York 10001. **Address:** 800 Kuderna Acres, Auburn, Alabama 36830, U.S.A.

PUBLICATIONS

Novels

The Innocent. New York, Harcourt Brace, and London, Secker and Warburg, 1957.
Forest of the Night. New York, Harcourt Brace, 1960; London, Eyre and Spottiswoode, 1961.
A Buried Land. New York, Viking Press, and London, Bodley Head, 1963.
An Exile. New York, Viking Press, 1967; London, Deutsch, 1970; as *I Walk the Line,* New York, Popular Library, 1970.
A Cry of Absence. New York, Crown, 1971; London, Deutsch, 1972.
Passage Through Gehenna. Baton Rouge, Louisiana State University Press, 1978.
Season of the Strangler. New York, Doubleday, 1982.
Last Things. Baton Rouge, Louisiana State University Press, 1989.

Uncollected Short Stories

"The Homecoming," in *Perspective* (St. Louis), Spring 1952.
"Dog Days," in *Perspective* (St. Louis), Fall 1952.
"The Cave," in *Perspective* (St. Louis), Winter 1955.
"Home Is Where the Heart Is," in *Arlington Quarterly* (Texas), Spring 1968.
"A Modern Case," in *Delta Review* (Memphis, Tennessee), August 1969.
"The Fugitives," in *Craft and Vision,* edited by Andrew Lytle. New York, Delacorte Press, 1971.
"The Family That Prays Together Stays Together," in *Chattahoochee Review* (Dunwoody, Georgia), Winter 1983.
"A Beginning," in *Homewords,* edited by Douglas Paschall. Knoxville, University of Tennessee Press, 1986.
"Zoo," in *Sewanee Review,* Summer 1992.
"Before the Winds Came," in *Oxford American* (Oxford, Mississippi), Winter 1994.

Other

History of the Tennessee State Dental Association. Nashville, Tennessee Dental Association, 1958.

*

Film Adaptation: *I Walk the Line,* 1970, from the novel *An Exile.*

Manuscript Collection: Emory University, Atlanta; Auburn University, Alabama.

Critical Studies: By Ovid Pierce, in *New York Times Book Review,* 4 July 1971; Joseph Cantinella, in *Saturday Review* (New York), 9 July 1971; Reed Whittemore, in *New Republic* (Washington, D.C.), July 1971; *Separate Country* by Paul Binding, London and New York, Paddington Press, 1979; interview, in *Southern Quarterly* (Hattiesburg, Mississippi), Spring 1983; in *The History of Southern Literature* edited by Louis Rubin, Louisiana State University Press, 1986.

Madison Jones comments:

Generally, on a more obvious level, my fiction is concerned with the drama of collision between past and present, with emphasis upon the destructive elements involved. More deeply, it deals with the failure, or refusal, of individuals to recognize and submit themselves to inevitable limits of the human condition.

*   *   *

There is a homogeneity of theme which links together into a coherent body the published fiction of Madison Jones. The setting of these books is invariably Jones's native south. But whether their time be late 18th-century settlement days or the region's more recent past, his unvarying song is abstraction, ideology, and its consequences. *The Innocent,* his first novel, set in rural Tennessee immediately after the coming of modernity, treats of the attempts by a young southerner, Duncan Welsh, to repent of earlier impiety and reestablish himself upon inherited lands in inherited ways. The enterprise is a failure because of Duncan's deracinated preconception of it. Welsh "sets up a grave in his house." Soon he and his hopes are buried in another.

A Cry of Absence again focuses on a fatal archaist, a middle-aged gentlewoman of the 1960s who is anything but innocent. Hester Glenn finds an excuse for her failures as wife, mother and person in a self-protective devotion to the tradition of her family. But when her example proves, in part, responsible for her son's sadistic murder of a black agitator, Hester is driven to know herself and, after confession, to pay for her sins with suicide.

A kind of Puritanism distorts Mrs. Glenn. In *The Innocent* the error is a perversion of the Agrarianism of Jones's mentors (Lytle, Davidson). But in his other novels the informing abstractions are not so identifiably southern. Jones's best, *A Buried Land,* is set in the valley of the Tennessee River during the season of its transformation. Percy Youngblood, the heir of a stern hill farmer (and a central character who could be any young person of our century), embraces all of the nostrums we associate with the futurist dispensation. He attempts to bury the old world (represented by a girl who dies aborting his child) under the waters of the TVA; but its truths (and their symbol) rise to haunt him back into abandoned modes of thought and feeling. In *An Exile* Hank Tawes, a rural

sheriff, is unmanned by a belated explosion of passion for a bootlegger's daughter. His error has no date or nationality, but almost acquires the force of ideology once Tawes recognizes that, because he followed an impulse to recover his youth, his "occupation's gone." *Forest of the Night* tests out an assumption almost as generic, the notion that man is inherently good. An interval in the Tennessee "outback" is sufficient to the disabusement of Jonathan Cannon. There is no more telling exposé of the New Eden mythology.

In all of Jones's fiction there operates an allusive envelope embodied in a concrete action and supported by an evocative texture. That action is as spare as it is archetypal; and in every case its objective is to render consciousness. Jones is among the most gifted of contemporary American novelists, a craftsman of tragedy in the great tradition of his art.

—M.E. Bradford

JONES, Marion Patrick

Nationality: Citizen of Trinidad and Tobago. **Born:** Trinidad. **Family:** Married. **Career:** Librarian and social anthropologist. A founder of Campaign Against Racial Discrimination, London. **Address:** c/o Columbus Publishers, 64 Independence Square, Port of Spain, Trinidad.

PUBLICATIONS

Novels

Pan Beat. Port of Spain, Columbus, 1973.
J'Ouvert Morning. Port of Spain, Columbus, 1976.

*   *   *

The relatively limited contributions of women writers to Caribbean literature has been one of the long-standing curiosities about the region. In the area of prose fiction there has been a small handful of women novelists, and from the English-language Caribbean in particular there have only been Sylvia Wynter of Jamaica, the Barbados-born Paule Marshall of the United States, and Merle Hodges and Marion Patrick Jones of Trinidad. Jones therefore belongs to a rather small circle in Caribbean literature, one that has unfortunately been slow—with the exception of Paule Marshall—to attract significant attention from students and teachers of the literature. And on the basis of her published works it is clear that Jones has carved out a distinctive niche for herself within that small circle.

Thus far, at any rate, she has chosen to concentrate on domestic drama as the main staple of her novels. For example, both *Pan Beat* and *J'Ouvert Morning* center on middle-class marriages in Port of Spain, Trinidad, each work concentrating on not one but several couples, on the quality of the marriages (invariably bad and getting worse), on the circle within which the couples move (usually since their childhood), and on a social background that is experiencing the growing pains of new nationhood. And in the case of *J'Ouvert Morning* this all spans three generations. As this synopsis is intended to imply, Jones's fiction usually borders on soap opera. Her plots are endless strands of unrelieved misery that are interwoven in a pattern of endless conflicts and unmitigated wretchedness.

In *Pan Beat,* for example, the narrative events are sparked by Earline MacCardie's return home to Trinidad for a holiday visit. As a high-schooler she was associated with the Flamingoes steel band. After high school she and David Chow, a member of the band, emigrated to England. He committed suicide after their estrangement, and she promptly turned to prostitution to assuage her grief—and to express her resentment at his suicide. Then she had subsequently married a British homosexual in New York (where she has been "passing" as a white Brazilian). Now that she is in Trinidad her husband breaks off the marriage, and she discovers that her former friends have been just as unhappy as she has been abroad: another old boyfriend, Louis Jenkins, is a futile, left-wing radical who is eventually killed in a gang war during Earline's visit; Louis's wife, Denise, enjoys some success, but merely as an insipid, commercially popular artist; Alan Hastings is a highly paid oil refinery worker who divides his time between a disastrous marriage and an affair with Earline herself. Of the two persons who have managed to avoid the endemic miseries of marriage, Tony Joseph is a desperately lonely prude of a civil servant, while Leslie Oliver, a Roman Catholic priest, is tormented by his sexual passion for Denise Jenkins.

The middle-class miseries of *J'Ouvert Morning* are less convoluted, largely because Jones mercifully concentrates on a smaller, more tightly knit group of sufferers in this novel—the Grant family. But their collective wretchedness is no less acute. Helen and Mervyn Grant have worked hard to secure a good education and middle-class affluence for their children. But one daughter, Elizabeth, is a well-known city drunk whom everyone knows as "Stinking Fur Liz." Their son, John, is a wealthy Port of Spain doctor with an unhappy marriage and a rebellious son, John Jr. Eventually John Jr.'s rebelliousness leads to an anti-government, left-wing plot that ends in his death at the hands of the police. The novel itself ends with the abortive suicide attempt by John Jr.'s distraught mother.

In spite of the soap operatic quality of her narrative materials, Jones's novels succeed as riveting documents of a troubled society in a state of transition. Jones's Trinidad has left official colonialism behind, but it has not yet discovered a vital sense of its own direction and purpose. It is soulless, without a driving motive, except the predictable trappings of neo-colonial values and the second-hand middle-class aspirations that have been handed down from Europe and the United States. The present tragedies and failures of her characters therefore reflect the unfulfilled promise of a generation that grew up in the years before independence. The empty successes of her achievers demonstrate the limitations of the neocolonial imitativeness that too often thwarts the growth of a healthy national consciousness. The radical dissidents like Louis Jenkins or John Jr. are equally failures in their own way: their radicalism is too often a self-destructive aimlessness that merely underscores their irrelevance in a society which is completely indifferent to them and their revolutionary messages.

Moreover, all of this remains convincing in the long run, because, despite Jones's melodramatic tendencies, the characters are vividly drawn and the language—especially in *J'Ouvert Morning*—is original and invigorating. Thus far she has demonstrated considerable promise, one that should be fulfilled to a significant degree if she continues to integrate an engaging narrative language with both disturbing social insights and a formidable grasp of the human personality.

—Lloyd W. Brown

JONES, Mervyn

Nationality: British. **Born:** London, 27 February 1922. **Education:** Abbotsholme School, Derbyshire; New York University, 1939-41. **Military Service:** Served in the British Army, 1942-47: Captain. **Family:** Married Jeanne Urquhart in 1948; one son and two daughters. **Career:** Assistant editor, 1955-60, and dramatic critic, 1958-66, *Tribune,* London; assistant editor, *New Statesman,* London, 1966-68. **Awards:** Society of Authors traveling scholarship, 1982. **Agent:** Scott Ferris Associates, 15 Gledhow Gardens, London S.W.5. **Address:** 1 Evelyn Mansions, Carlisle Place, London SW1P 1NH, England.

PUBLICATIONS

Novels

No Time to Be Young. London, Cape, 1952.
The New Town. London, Cape, 1953.
The Last Barricade. London, Cape, 1953.
Helen Blake. London, Cape, 1955.
On the Last Day. London, Cape, 1958.
A Set of Wives. London, Cape, 1965.
John and Mary. London, Cape, 1966; New York, Atheneum, 1967.
A Survivor. London, Cape, and New York, Atheneum, 1968.
Joseph. London, Cape, and New York, Atheneum, 1970.
Mr. Armitage Isn't Back Yet. London, Cape, 1971.
Holding On. London, Quartet, 1973; as *Twilight of the Day,* New York, Simon and Schuster, 1974.
The Revolving Door. London, Quartet, 1973.
Strangers. London, Quartet, 1974.
Lord Richard's Passion. London, Quartet, and New York, Knopf, 1974.
The Pursuit of Happiness. London, Quartet, 1975; New York, Mason Charter, 1976.
Nobody's Fault. London, Quartet, and New York, Mason Charter, 1977.
Today the Struggle. London, Quartet, 1978.
The Beautiful Words. London, Deutsch, 1979.
A Short Time to Live. London, Deutsch, 1980; New York, St. Martin's Press, 1981.
Two Women and Their Man. London, Deutsch, and New York, St. Martin's Press, 1982.
Joanna's Luck. London, Piatkus, 1984.
Coming Home. London, Piatkus, 1986.
That Year in Paris. London, Piatkus, 1988.

Short Stories

Scenes from Bourgeois Life. London, Quartet, 1976.

Uncollected Short Stories

"The Foot," in *English Story 8,* edited by Woodrow Wyatt. London, Collins, 1948.

"The Bee-Keeper," in *English Story 10,* edited by Woodrow Wyatt. London, Collins, 1950.
"Discrete Lives," in *Bananas* (London), 1978.
"Five Days by Moonlight," in *Encounter* (London), November 1978.
"Living Together," in *Woman* (London), 1979.

Plays

The Shelter (produced London, 1982).

Radio Plays: *Anna,* 1982; *Taking Over,* 1984; *Lisa,* 1984; *Generations,* 1986.

Other

Guilty Men, 1957: Suez and Cyprus, with Michael Foot. London, Gollancz, and New York, Rinehart, 1957.
Potbank (documentary). London, Secker and Warburg, 1961.
Big Two: Life in America and Russia. London, Cape, 1962; as *The Antagonists,* New York, Potter, 1962.
Two Ears of Corn: Oxfam in Action. London, Hodder and Stoughton, 1965; as *In Famine's Shadow: A Private War on Hunger,* Boston, Beacon Press, 1967.
Life on the Dole. London, Davis Poynter, 1972.
Rhodesia: The White Judge's Burden. London, Christian Action, 1972.
The Oil Rush, photographs by Fay Godwin. London, Quartet, 1976.
The Sami of Lapland. London, Minority Rights Group, 1982.
Chances: An Autobiography. London, Verso, 1987.
A Radical Life: The Biography of Megan Lloyd George. London, Hutchinson, 1991.
Michael Foot. London, Gollancz, 1994.

Editor, *Kingsley Martin: Portrait and Self-Portrait.* London, Barrie and Rockliff, and New York, Humanities Press, 1969.
Editor, *Privacy.* Newton Abbot, Devon, David and Charles, 1974.

Translator, *The Second Chinese Revolution,* by K.S. Karol. New York, Hill and Wang, 1974.

*

Critical Study: Chapter by Kiernan Ryan, in *The Socialist Novel in Britain* edited by H. Gustav Klaus, Brighton, Harvester Press, 1982.

Mervyn Jones comments:

(1981) I have become known as a political novelist, although only two of my books—*Joseph* and *Today the Struggle*—could be defined strictly as political novels, and some others are deliberately limited to the study of personal relationships. Probably, this reveals how rarely most British novelists concern themselves with the political framework of life. Taking account of that framework does, I think, extend the novel's range. But I also think, decidedly, that a novel ceases to be a novel when it does not have human character and human experience at its center. Those interested in my views on the matter are referred to a *Guardian* interview, 9 July 1979.

I have never planned a recurrent theme in my writing, but when I consider it I believe that there is one: the nobility and irony of idealism. I take both the nobility and the irony to be realities. This is the subject of *Strangers,* the novel with which I am least dissatisfied and by which I should wish to be judged.

*   *   *

Mervyn Jones is a fine storyteller whose skill continues to improve after some 40 years of writing. While some of his novels are about a broad variety of characters, and tend to be built on his journalistic experience, his specialty seems to be the problems of those people who have enough time and money to enable them to reflect on life. The conflicts between their ideals and their experiences, or between values related to ideals, are the themes of *The New Town, Mr. Armitage Isn't Back Yet, Strangers, Joanna's Luck,* and the short stories "The Syndrome" and "Happiness Is . . ." How these people reconcile themselves to reality while retaining their ideals or, more often, how they retain ideals that have less and less to do with their actions and decisions is of primary interest to Jones. He has said that the theme of the nobility and irony of idealism is a recurrent one in his writing, and crucial to his depiction of this theme is his calculated distance from his characters. They are intellectual rather than emotional; their thoughts are clear, their emotions suppressed; and if they seem to lack depth, it may be because this lack is an aspect of the modern middle-class idealist.

Strangers, the novel by which Jones has said he would like to be judged, is the best example of his study of the problems of idealism. Andrew Stanton is a pacifist who refuses to live in his native South Africa, and whose refusal to fight in the Second World War has alienated him from his conservative family. He has devoted himself to the ideal of fighting the pure evil in the world with the pure good of compensatory charitable actions. His first wife was a frail survivor of a concentration camp, who was killed by a sniper in Israel. His young second wife, Val, marries him out of her own idealism and faith in him. When Andrew leaves to work with refugees in Uganda, Val is left with a house full of charity cases: a pregnant teenager on the run from her parents, an American on the run from the draft, and a foreign student who runs off with a local schoolgirl. As Andrew and Val struggle in their separate situations, both are confronted with the futility of charity, but while Val sheds specific failures to become more hopeful, Andrew, after a major success, is cruelly struck by the failure of his ideals.

A Short Time to Live is a more cynical view of the idealist. A charismatic journalist with a conscience, Michael Kellet, dies mysteriously on a Pacific island. Each of the old school-friends, teacher, ex-wife, and widow who attend his funeral is carefully examined, as the solution to the mystery gradually becomes apparent. None of them cherishes much of any ideal, except the old teacher, secure in his faith in education, and each is laid bare with a cold, journalistic precision that could have been that of the dead Kellet.

Joanna's Luck is a study of one of the children of the idealists of the 1960s. Joanna's mother and father are ex-hippies, described with the snide acceptance of a disillusioned young woman of the 1980s: the one is still smoking dope and wearing beads at 48, the other has shed it all to become a prosperous businessman. Locked in the thoughts of their era, they cannot comprehend why Joanna cares so much about finding a rewarding job or about wanting to feel close to a man before she goes to bed with him. Joanna is bright, but muddled in her emotions, lonely and drifting. It is not until she drifts into situations that force decisions that she begins to analyze her own emotions and beliefs with the same clarity that she had applied to her work in social research. Jones has always written sympathetically about women, but here he extends that to a deeper, fuller portrayal of a character.

The Beautiful Words is probably Jones's finest book to date, combining his excellent storytelling with interesting characterization. Here he contrasts a sensitive, full description of his main character, Tommy, with flatter, colder perceptions of the many people

Tommy encounters but cannot understand. Tommy is a handsome boy of 17 with the mind of a very small child. After a life of being shunted among relatives, he becomes a homeless drifter. All that his confused mind can offer for consolation in times of loneliness, fear, and despair are the "beautiful words" his one kind aunt taught him to memorize. He wanders into the home of a prostitute, who cares for him and has him do her cleaning, but her pimp uses him for a robbery and he gets beat up by the police. Lost, he lives with the dossers and drunks on London's Embankment until he finds an empty house and becomes a squatter. Others move in and care for him in a haphazard way, finally dumping him on Belle, a rich and greedy old woman who uses him as a watchdog. The story is about how all of these people deal with the responsibility of innocence as much as what it is like for poor Tommy to be an innocent, and Jones tells the sad story with compassion.

Because of their topical nature, some of Jones's novels date quickly, but not those which delve deeply into the effort of modern people trying to find something to believe and to live by it. For the craft of his storytelling alone, Jones continues to be well worth reading.

—Anne Morddel

JONG, Erica

Nationality: American. **Born:** Erica Mann in New York City, 26 March 1942. **Education:** The High School of Music and Art, New York; Barnard College, New York (George Weldwood Murray fellow, 1963), 1959-63, B.A. 1963 (Phi Beta Kappa); Columbia University, New York (Woodrow Wilson fellow, 1964), M.A. 1965; Columbia School of Fine Arts, 1969-70. **Family:** Married 1) Michael Werthman in 1963 (divorced 1965); 2) Allan Jong in 1966 (divorced 1975); 3) the writer Jonathan Fast in 1977 (divorced 1983), one daughter; 4) Kenneth David Burrows in 1989. **Career:** Lecturer in English, City College, New York, 1964-66, 1969-70, and University of Maryland European Division, Heidelberg, Germany, 1967-68; instructor in English, Manhattan Community College, New York, 1969-70. Since 1971 instructor in poetry, YM-YWHA Poetry Center, New York. Member of the literary panel, New York State Council on the Arts, 1972-74. Since 1991 president of Author's Guild. **Awards:** Academy of American Poets award, 1963; Bess Hokin prize (*Poetry*, Chicago), 1971; New York State Council on the Arts grant, 1971; Madeline Sadin award (*New York Quarterly*), 1972; Alice Fay di Castagnola award, 1972; National Endowment for the Arts grant, 1973; Creative Artists Public Service grant, 1973; International Sigmund Freud prize, 1979. **Agent:** Ed Victor Ltd., 162 Wardour Street, London W1V 3AT, England.

PUBLICATIONS

Novels

Fear of Flying. New York, Holt Rinehart, 1973; London, Secker and Warburg, 1974.
How to Save Your Own Life. New York, Holt Rinehart, and London, Secker and Warburg, 1977.

Fanny, Being the True History of the Adventures of Fanny Hackabout-Jones. New York, New American Library, and London, Granada, 1980.
Parachutes and Kisses. New York, New American Library, and London, Granada, 1984.
Serenissima: A Novel of Venice. Boston, Houghton Mifflin, and London, Bantam, 1987.
Any Woman's Blues. New York, Harper, and London, Chatto and Windus, 1990.

Uncollected Short Stories

"From the Country of Regrets," in *Paris Review,* Spring 1973.
"Take a Lover," in *Vogue,* April 1977.

Poetry

Fruits and Vegetables. New York, Holt Rinehart, 1971; London, Secker and Warburg, 1973.
Half-Lives. New York, Holt Rinehart, 1973; London, Secker and Warburg, 1974.
Here Comes and Other Poems. New York, New American Library, 1975.
Loveroot. New York, Holt Rinehart, 1975; London, Secker and Warburg, 1977.
The Poetry of Erica Jong. New York, Holt Rinehart, 1976.
Selected Poems 1-2. London, Panther, 2 vols., 1977-80.
At the Edge of the Body. New York, Holt Rinehart, 1979; London, Granada, 1981.
Ordinary Miracles: New Poems. New York, New American Library, 1983; London, Granada, 1984.
Becoming Light: Poems: New and Selected. New York, HarperCollins, 1991.

Other

Four Visions of America, with others. Santa Barbara, California, Capra Press, 1977.
Witches (miscellany). New York, Abrams, 1981; London, Granada, 1982.
Megan's Book of Divorce: A Kid's Book for Adults. New York, New American Library, 1984; London, Granada, 1985.
The Devil at Large: Erica Jong on Henry Miller. New York, Turtle Bay, and London, Chatto and Windus, 1993.
Fear of Fifty: A Midlife Memoir. New York, HarperCollins, 1994.

*

Critical Studies: Interviews in *New York Quarterly 16,* 1974, *Playboy* (Chicago), September 1975, and *Viva* (New York), September 1977; article by Emily Toth, in *Twentieth-Century American-Jewish Fiction Writers* edited by Daniel Walden, Detroit, Gale, 1984; "Isadora and Fanny, Jessica and Erica: The Feminist Discourse of Erica Jong" by Julie Anne Ruth, in *Australian Women's Book Review* (Melbourne), September 1990.

*   *   *

Erica Jong is an impressive poet who writes in the confessional vein of Anne Sexton, Robert Lowell, Sylvia Plath, and John Berryman. She also creates an energetic, garrulous, witty, and tender verse, both erudite and earthy, about the conflict between sexuality and inhibiting intelligence, about death (and one's impulse both toward and away from suicide), the problems of sexual and creative energy (both consuming and propelling), and the hunger for love, knowledge, and connecting. Although she has aligned herself with the feminist movement, her poetry goes beyond the dilemma of being a woman in a male-dominated world, or for that matter, a Jew in an urban culture, to the ubiquitous need for human completeness in a fiercely hostile social and cosmic world.

Jong distinguishes her poetic and fictional forms: "In poetry I could be pared down, honed, minimal. In the novel what I wanted was excess, digression, rollicking language, energy, and poetry." Her stated preference was always for the novel that made one believe "it was all spilled truth." To be sure, "excess," "energy," and "rollicking language" are terms that well describe her fiction, along with its absolute quest for truth.

Fear of Flying is a funny, moving, and deeply serious book. "Nothing human was worth denying," her heroine, Isadora Wing, says, "and even if it was unspeakably ugly, we could learn from it, couldn't we?" Isadora, a picaresque heroine, is a bright, pretty, Jewish, guilt-ridden writer, who accompanies her Chinese-American, child psychiatrist husband, Bennett Wing, to a psychoanalytic congress in Vienna. Torn between the stability of marriage and her sexual fantasies for the "zipless fuck," she abandons Bennett for Adrian Goodlove, an illiterate, sadistic, but very sexy London psychiatrist. Adrian is a selfish and pompous bully, whose words arouse her as much as his sexual promise. (Bennett, though "often wordless," is a far better lover.) Her excursions into the past, where we meet her family and childhood world, her brilliant but sad and mad first husband, and her various sexual partners, are drawn in an earthy and ebullient fashion. But beneath all the bravura is Isadora's basic lack of fulfillment. Sex is only the apparent means toward connecting and feeling alive, an outlet that confounds desperation and freedom. It is only a temporary departure from guilt, an illusory means of flying. Isadora's life remains tortured. The end of the book only half-heartedly suggests some sort of insight and the half-believed: "People don't complete us. We complete ourselves." Isadora has struggled to write as a means of self-discovery and as a sublimated but illusory fulfillment for the frustrations of the real world. She retains an unremitting sense of guilt, vulnerability, childish impulsiveness, and romanticism.

The less successful sequel, *How to Save Your Own Life,* focuses on Isadora's literary success, her divorce from Bennett, and her subsequent move to Hollywood with its virtually limitless number of disappointments, sexual and otherwise. As Jong again portrays it, the plight of the woman is to be torn between her own restlessness and the bourgeois virtues of marriage. She illustrates poignantly and powerfully how a woman's greatest fear is of being alone, and yet her deepest wish is to break free as "hostage" to her own "fantasies," her "fears," and "false definitions."

Fanny, Being the True History of the Adventures of Fanny Hackabout-Jones is an extraordinary tour de force. In the style (with careful modifications) and spirit of the 18th century, it tells of the tragic and comic fortunes of the beautiful and brilliant young Fanny, whose picaresque adventures en route to becoming a writer and member of the gentry include everything from membership in a witches' coven (really a modern sisterhood), a brothel, and a pirate ship to a series of sexual adventures with the likes of Alexander Pope, Jonathan Swift, and Theophilus Cibber. It is a rich, racy, and enormously funny and serious book—moving, at times to the extreme, in its focus on love, friendship, motherhood, and courage. It

is filled with serious, playful, and frequently ironic references to an enormous body of literature. (Fanny is conversant with Homer, Virgil, Horace, Boileau, La Rochefoucauld, Voltaire, Locke, and Pascal.) Although as a character, Fanny speaks with a 1980s consciousness, the kind of woman she represents might have lived during any age for, to quote Jong's stated intention in creating her, Fanny transcends her own time. *Fanny,* as a character and novel, embodies, above all, an unflagging and uncompromising search for truth.

"A Woman is made of Sweets and Bitters. . . . She is both Reason and Rump, both Wit and Wantonness," Fanny remarks, in an observation that is applicable to all of Jong's females, including her Isadora Wing character in *Parachutes and Kisses.* Here Jong portrays the famous, rich, brilliant, and beautiful writer, now nearly 40 and separated from her husband. Isadora once again possesses a prodigious sexuality, but it is now accompanied by a purposive loneliness. Although she would seem to have reconciled her sexuality with her personal and professional responsibilities—mainly as mother and writer—it is the quest for love that remains her driving force. Isadora relates her experiences with a series of lovers—including a real estate developer, rabbi, antiques dealer, plastic surgeon, and medical student—but the need for love and security remains insatiable. Isadora may long ago have given up the fear of flying, but she remains, in many ways, the woman she described herself as in the earlier works: "My life had been a constant struggle to get attention, not to be ignored, to be the favored child, the brightest, the best, the most precocious, the most outrageous, the most adored." Such is her relationship with parents, lovers, and not least of all, the world.

Serenissima, another historical novel and tour de force of the order of the Rabelaisian *Fanny,* is set in the Venice of Shakespeare's *The Merchant of Venice.* It is filled not only with details and characters from Shakespeare's life and plays but also with echoes from any number of other Elizabethan writers, as well as often hilarious reminders of numerous more modern authors—from Byron and Ruskin to Dylan Thomas, Henry James to James Joyce. Jessica Pruitt, a middle-aged, jet-setting movie star, has come to Venice as a judge for the Film Festival. Although she plans to play Jessica in a "filmic fantasy" of *The Merchant of Venice,* she is forced to remain in Italy, since she has become ill. She takes this as the occasion to embark upon a trip back in time to 16th-century Venice. The city, with its grand history, labyrinthine canals, and reflexive surfaces, permits not just her thorough investigation of the Bard himself—in all his natural (i.e., sexual), as well as social and literary capabilities—but it provides the means for a personal journey into her own female identity, in fact and fantasy. It is a pagan rite de passage in preparation for her future. She is, after all, 43—an ageing woman who must survive within a professional and everyday world that adulates youth; even Shakespeare's heroine, Jessica, is a celebration of youth.

Once back in time, in Shakespeare's Venice, she is a reborn Jessica. She cavorts with an enormous retinue of suitors and even fancies herself as Shakespeare's Dark Lady, among any number of other real and fantasized roles. Amid all the disguises, ruses, and exposes, however, Jong casts a number of tasteless scenes, such as the incredible romping of the Bard with his own creations (like Juliet), or with specifically important people who lived during his lifetime, like his patron, the Earl of Southampton. Jong portrays, for example, Shakespeare and Southampton with a courtesan posing as a boy. They were, she writes, "a three-backed beast that pants and screams and begs for mercy." The reader may be similarly offended by Jessica's numerous attempts to describe "Will's stiff staff." Jong remains at her best linguistically, in her use of quotes and puns. When Jessica first meets Shakespeare, for example, in the Ghetto Vecchio, he says to her: "Who ever loved, who loved not at first sight?" and "What's in a name? A rose by any other name would smell as sweet."

Any Woman's Blues portrays yet another "sexaholic," as Jong's newest sexual Wonderwoman, Leila Sand, describes herself. Presumably authored by Isadora Wing (which we learn in a foreword and afterword), the novel deals with an artist in her mid-forties. Leila's (midlife) crisis, as the epigraph announces, is that "the blues ain't nothing/but the facts of life." Despite all her celebrity, Leila fears that her talent is waning; she must also come to terms with drugs and alcohol; most importantly, she must confront her masochistic relationship with a young, blond WASP named Darton Veneble Donegal IV. (When she first sees him he is "helmeted like Darth Vader.") On the one hand, Leila says, in the typical poor prose of the novel: "He rarely said anything that wasn't loving, sweet, and dear. He spoke, in fact, like a Hallmark greeting card." But she adds: "It was just that his actions belied his words." Dart, her "great primitive god," is also, a "con man, a hustler, a cowboy, a cocksman, an addict." He is also well celebrated for being "born with an erection." As Leila tries, still like Isadora in *Fear of Flying,* to "get free" and be her own person, she utters the cloying: "Life . . . is a feast. It is there for the taking. You have only to . . . love one another, thank God, and rejoice. At its most simple, it is a prayer." Leila's words ring hollow: "Give, give, give! is the cry of the gods. It rhymes with: "Live, live, live! Why else are we passing through this sublunary sphere?" Such a conclusion—and the language in which it is couched—is unworthy of the lusty, witty, and utterly unrepentant Jong persona, whose wild and wicked adventures we have otherwise enjoyed in seven books thus far.

Having coined the term "zipless fuck" in *Fear of Flying,* virtually a classic in its portrayal of female libido, Jong now uses the word "whiplash" to describe what she calls the "women of her generation." Once more, in her autobiographical novel form, Jong focuses on many women who grew up during the respectable 1950s and feminist 1960s—women who burned their bras but subsequently had children and discovered the joys of simple motherhood. The book rings painfully true for many women torn between career and motherhood, sexuality and traditional reserve, and even feminism as opposed to femininity. Subtitled "A Midlife Memoir," *Fear of Fifty* more importantly deals with the "terror" women experience when they realize they are no longer young and beautiful. Although Jong appears less concerned with her body (while still capable of great sexual prowess), her words ring true in such statements as: "I wander around," wondering if "I have the right to my immortal soul." Perhaps she laments her earlier romans à clef and the devastating impact they must have had on her barely disguised characters; now she says: "Writing matters only if it . . . ripens your humanity."

—Lois Gordon

JORDAN, Neil

Nationality: Irish. **Born:** Sligo in 1950. **Education:** University College, Dublin. **Career:** Co-founder, Irish Writers Co-operative, 1974. Lives in Bray, County Wicklow. **Awards:** Arts Council bur-

sary, 1976; *Guardian* Fiction prize, 1979; Cannes Film Festival Palme d'Or, 1986; Sorrento Film Festival De Sica award, 1986; Academy Award, 1992. **Address:** c/o Faber and Faber, 3 Queen Square, London WC1N 3AU, England.

PUBLICATIONS

Novels

The Past. London, Cape, and New York, Braziller, 1980.
The Dream of a Beast. London, Chatto and Windus, 1983; New York, Random House, 1989.
Sunrise with Sea Monster. London, Chatto and Windus, 1994; New York, Random House, 1995.

Short Stories

Night in Tunisia and Other Stories. Dublin, Co-op, 1976; London, Writers and Readers, 1979.

Uncollected Short Stories

"A Bus, a Bridge, a Beach" and "The Old-Fashioned Lift," in *Paddy No More.* Nantucket, Massachusetts, Longship Press, 1978.
"The Artist" and "The Photographer," in *New Writing and Writers 16.* Atlantic Highlands, New Jersey, Humanities Press, 1979.

Plays (screenplays)

Mona Lisa, with David Leland. London, Faber, 1986.
Angel. London, Faber, 1989.
High Spirits. London, Faber, 1989.

Screenplays: *Angel* (*Danny Boy*), 1982; *The Company of Wolves,* with Angela Carter, 1984; *Mona Lisa,* with David Leland, 1986; *High Spirits,* 1988; *The Miracle,* 1991; *The Crying Game,* 1992.

*

Theatrical Activities:
Assistant director: **Film**—*Excalibur* (John Boorman), 1981; Director: **Films**—*Angel* (*Danny Boy*), 1982; *The Company of Wolves,* 1984; *Mona Lisa,* 1986; *High Spirits,* 1988; *We're No Angels,* 1990; *The Miracle,* 1991; *The Crying Game,* 1992; *Interview with the Vampire,* 1994.

*　　*　　*

Neil Jordan is one of the most talented of the new generation of Irish writers. His book of short stories, *Night in Tunisia,* put his name on the map and this was quickly followed by his novel *The Past.* He has scripted and directed several notable feature films, and says that for him the disciplines of film-making and written fiction have never been mutually exclusive. "I don't know any novelists, particularly the younger ones, who aren't working in film. In the fifties, people used to talk about the death of the novel and saw television as a threat to writing. Now the writers have pushed their way in."

Born in Sligo in 1950, Jordan has lived for some time in Dublin, a city which he made the setting for his second novel, *The Dream of a Beast.* In this book Dublin is a place of heightened intensity, where opposing forces of beauty and ugliness hold an uneasy balance and the mood can shift quickly from vision into nightmare. Jordan says of his home town: "It's in a strange state these days. It's become a very small city. The economic recession hit much faster there than in larger places; the poverty there is more extreme, the wreckage is so visible." In *Beast*—as in the film *Angel*— Jordan's comment on, and portrayal of, the situation is conveyed in a narrative that juxtaposes lyricism and squalor, love and death. The effect is often baffling and disturbing but never essentially pessimistic. He writes so well, sentence by sentence, that it is the clarity and energy of his work which remain in the mind. In *Dream of a Beast* a man loses every previously held point of reference; he becomes "beastly," non-rational, lost to his wife and child and to his work, lost to his own perception of himself transformed physically. This is a journey into grief and confusion, even madness, but at the same time an initiation into mystery: "I walked forward. There were doors off the corridor, with rooms leading to more doors. What I had assumed to be devoid of life I soon found to be a bestiary. A deep-piled room seethed with mice. A moth watched me from a filing-cabinet. His eyes, full of the wisdom of the ages and the fierceness of his few hours here, seemed to require my attention."

There are two strong complementary elements in Jordan's work: an ability to pull the reader into the narrative, the subjective dream, and an equally forceful sense of good old-fashioned storytelling. The situations he describes are dramatic, the characters easily recognisable. He says of his "beast" that "it wasn't really Kafka, more the B Movie feature, the Creature from the Black Lagoon, the sort of fabulous monster you find in children's fiction." He has made good use of his own work in children's theatre and his close involvement with the world of music. Jazz and rhythm and blues played a great part in *Angel.*

Not surprisingly, Angela Carter's fables have a great appeal for Jordan and his adaptation of her story "The Company of Wolves" made another successful film. His description of Carter's "highly visual and dramatic imagination, her ability to combine this with a sense of ironic perspective on what she describes" could as well be related to his own work. While continuing to direct and script films, Jordan remains committed to the novel form.

—Judy Cooke

JORGENSON, Ivar. *See* **SILVERBERG, Robert.**

JOSHI, Arun

Nationality: Indian. **Born:** 1939. **Education:** Attended schools in India and the United States. **Career:** Director, Shri Ram Centre for Industrial Relations.

PUBLICATIONS

Novels

The Foreigner. Bombay and London, Asia Publishing House, 1968.
The Strange Case of Billy Biswas. Bombay, London, and New York, Asia Publishing House, 1971.
The Apprentice. Bombay and New York, Asia Publishing House, 1974; London, Asia Publishing House, 1975.
The Last Labyrinth. New Delhi, Vision, 1981.
City and the River. New Delhi, Vision, 1990.

Short Stories

The Survivor: A Selection of Stories. New Delhi, Sterling, 1975.

Other

Shri Ram: A Biography, with Khushwant Singh. London and New York, Asia Publishing House, 1968.
Laia Shri Ram: A Study in Entrepreneurship and Industrial Management. New Delhi, Orient Longman, 1975.

*

Critical Studies: *Arun Joshi: A Study of His Fiction* edited by N. Radhakrishnan, Gandhigram, Tamilnadu, Gandhigram Rural Institute, 1984; *The Fictional World of Arun Joshi,* New Delhi, Classical, 1986, and *The Novels of Arun Joshi,* New Delhi, Prestige, 1992, both edited by R.K. Dhawan.

*   *   *

Arun Joshi is a novelist who, more strongly than most, has brought to his work that detachment from the everyday, while still acknowledging its existence, which is perhaps India's particular gift to the literature of the world. The rising up into the transcendental is a trait that has increasingly marked out his novels from his first, *The Foreigner*—where the young hero, after experiencing life and love in America, is, back in Delhi, at last persuaded by a humble office worker that sometimes detachment lies in actually getting involved—on up to *The City and the River,* which takes place wholly in an imaginary land.

To venture as a writer into such territory it is necessary to be equipped with the means to make the everyday credible and sharply present. This Joshi was from the start well able to do, as his early short stories, subsequently collected in *The Survivor,* clearly show. "The Gherao" tells simply and effectively of how a young college teacher arrives at maturity when his aged Principal is subjected to that peculiar Indian form of protest action, the *gherao,* the preventing of a target figure from moving anywhere or receiving any succor.

The Strange Case of Billy Biswas is the story of a young, rich, American-educated Indian who ends up in the wilderness of central India living as a semi-naked "tribal" seeking a meaning to things above and beyond all that everyday civilization can provide. A key to Joshi's whole intent can be found in the words he puts into the mouth of his narrator; as he grows old he realizes that the most futile cry of man is his impossible wish to be understood.

The Apprentice, Joshi's third novel, takes his search for understanding man's predicament one step further toward the transcendental. Its central figure is a man essentially docile and uncourageous whose life more or less parallels the coming into being of postcolonial India. Eventually gaining a post in the civil service, he ends, as many real-life civil servants did, by taking a huge bribe. But in the final pages he comes to see that at least corrupt man can strive to do just a little good—he cleans shoes at a temple—and that while there are in the world young people still untainted, there is a spark of hope.

In *The Last Labyrinth,* the hero, if that always is not too strong a term for the men Joshi puts at the center, is a man crying always "I want! I want!" and not knowing what it is he desires, in some ways a parallel figure to Saul Bellow's Henderson, the rain king. His search takes him, however, to infinitely old Benares, a city seen as altogether intangible, at once holy and repellent, and to an end lost in a miasma of nonunderstanding. But the way there is gripping. Joshi writes with a persuasive ease and illuminates the outward scene with telling phrase after telling phrase.

Finally we come to *The City and the River,* where the city is not the Delhi or the Bombay Joshi has elsewhere described so concretely but a wholly intangible place, removed from time, where yet a man can be seen wearing jeans. Joshi, in his search for a way to describe the meaning of things, has now come to a world akin to those of science fiction or perhaps to the mystical poetry of Blake writing of "Golgonooza the spiritual Fourfold London eternal." But all the while there are digs or sly hints at the current ills of Indian society and, by implication, of all societies everywhere. And in the final pages, where the wild river sweeps over the whole complex city, there is, again, sounded that faint note of hope. The question is not of success or failure, an old yogi tells his disciple, the question is of trying.

—H.R.F. Keating

JOSIPOVICI, Gabriel (David)

Nationality: British. **Born:** Nice, France, 8 October 1940. **Education:** Victoria College, Cairo, 1950-56; Cheltenham College, Gloucesteshire, 1956-57; St. Edmund Hall, Oxford, 1958-61, B.A. in English 1961. **Family:** Married in 1963. **Career:** Lecturer, 1963-74, reader, 1974-80, part-time reader, 1981-84, and since 1984 professor of English, University of Sussex, Brighton. Northcliffe Lecturer, University College, London, 1981. **Awards:** *Sunday Times* award, for play, 1970; South East Arts prize, 1978. **Agent:** John Johnson, 45-47 Clerkenwell Green, London EC1R 0HT. **Address:** Department of English, University of Sussex, Falmer, Brighton, Sussex BN1 9RH, England.

PUBLICATIONS

Novels

The Inventory. London, Joseph, 1968.
Words. London, Gollancz, 1971.
The Present. London, Gollancz, 1975.
Migrations. Hassocks, Sussex, Harvester Press, 1977.
The Echo Chamber. Brighton, Harvester Press, 1980.

The Air We Breathe. Brighton, Harvester Press, 1981.
Conversations in Another Room. London, Methuen, 1984.
Contre-Jour: A Triptych after Pierre Bonnard. Manchester, Carcanet, 1986.
The Big Glass. Manchester, Carcanet, 1991.
In a Hotel Garden. Manchester, Carcanet, 1994.
Moo Pak. Manchester, Carcanet, 1995.

Short Stories

Mobius the Stripper: Stories and Short Plays (includes the plays *One, Dreams of Mrs. Fraser, Flow*). London, Gollancz, 1974.
Four Stories. London, Menard Press, 1977.
In the Fertile Land. Manchester, Carcanet, 1987.

Plays

Dreams of Mrs. Fraser (produced London, 1972). Included in *Mobius the Stripper,* 1974.
Evidence of Intimacy (produced London, 1972).
Flow (produced Edinburgh and London, 1973). Included in *Mobius the Stripper,* 1974.
Echo (produced London, 1975). Published in *Proteus 3,* 1978.
Marathon (produced London, 1977). Published in *Adam* (London), 1980.
A Moment (produced London, 1979).
Vergil Dying (broadcast 1979). Windsor, SPAN, 1981.

Radio Plays: *Playback,* 1973; *A Life,* 1974; *Ag,* 1976; *Vergil Dying,* 1979; *Majorana: Disappearance of a Physicist,* with Sacha Rabinovitch, 1981; *The Seven,* with Jonathan Harvey, 1983; *Metamorphosis,* from the story by Kafka, 1985; *Ode for St. Cecilia,* 1986; *Mr. Vee,* 1988; *A Little Personal Pocket Requiem,* 1990.

Other

The World and the Book: A Study of Modern Fiction. London, Macmillan, and Stanford, California, Stanford University Press, 1971; revised edition, Macmillan, 1979.
The Lessons of Modernism and Other Essays. London, Macmillan, and Totowa, New Jersey, Rowman and Littlefield, 1977.
Writing and the Body: The Northcliffe Lectures 1981. Brighton, Harvester Press, 1982; Princeton, New Jersey, Princeton University Press, 1983.
The Mirror of Criticism: Selected Reviews 1977-1982. Brighton, Harvester Press, and New York, Barnes and Noble, 1983.
The Book of God: A Response to the Bible. New Haven, Connecticut, Yale University Press, 1988.
Steps: Selected Fiction and Drama. Manchester, Carcanet Press, 1990.
Text and Voice. Manchester, Carcanet, 1992.

Editor, *The Modern English Novel: The Reader, The Writer, and the Work.* London, Open Books, and New York, Barnes and Noble, 1976.
Editor, *The Sirens' Song: Selected Essays,* by Maurice Blanchot. Brighton, Harvester Press, and Bloomington, Indiana University Press, 1982.

*

Critical Studies: Interview with Bernard Sharratt, in *Orbit* (Tunbridge Wells, Kent), December 1975; "True Confessions of an Experimentalist" by Josipovici, and interview with Maurice Kapitanchik, in *Books and Bookmen* (London), 1982; article by Linda Canon and Jay L. Halio, in *British Novelists since 1960* edited by Halio, Detroit, Gale, 1983; interview with Timothy Hyman, in *Jewish Quarterly* (London), 1985; James Hansford, in *Prospice* (Portree, Isle of Skye), 1985; essay by Josipovici, in *Contemporary Authors Autobiography Series 8* edited by Mark Zadrozny, Detroit, Gale, 1988; "Bonnard and Josipovici" by Jean Duffy, in *Word and Image,* 9(4), October-December 1993.

*   *   *

"Modern art," says Gabriel Josipovici in *The Lessons of Modernism,* "moves between two poles, silence and game." In his own novels the game is that of verbal art; the silence is that of unanswered questions. Conversations abound, explanations are sought, inquiries are pursued, but answers are always lacking. Characters experience an overwhelming pressure to speak, like a weight on the chest. But there is no narrator with authority to pronounce on the truth. The reader is drawn into puzzled involvement, impotent attentiveness, and pleasure in the play of the text.

In *The Inventory* a young man is constructing a list of the contents of a flat in which an old man and his son Sam used to live. They are both now dead. The precision of the inventory contrasts with the uncertainty of what he hears about their lives from Susan who tells him stories about her experiences of the two men. Why did Sam suddenly leave? Was he in love with Susan? Did she love him? Are her stories based on memory or invention? The novel is almost entirely in dialogue form and its effect depends on the author's precise control of rhythm, pace, and tone. It demonstrates his fascination with the musical, kinesthetic, and dramatic aspects of speech which he has explored equally in his work for radio and theater.

In *Words* Louis and his wife Helen are visited by Jo, who was once Louis's girlfriend and who may or may not also have had an affair with his brother Peter. The reader learns about the characters only through what they say to each other. Conversations return again and again to certain nagging questions. What happened years ago when Louis and Jo separated? Are either of them in earnest now when they talk about going away together? Are they serious or are they playing games? We only have their words to go on and words always leave open a variety of possible interpretations: cheerful banter or wounding aggression, flirtation or contempt, honesty or evasion? *The Present* represents a change in fictional technique, for in this novel even the basic narrative situation is left undecided. The narrative, in the present tense, simultaneously develops stories in a number of different possible directions. The present leaves the future open. Reg and Minna share a flat with Alex; Minna is in hospital after a breakdown and dreams or imagines her life with Reg; Minna is married to Alex and they live with their two daughters in the country; Alex is dead having thrown himself from the window of Reg and Minna's flat. The stories interweave, each compelling but inconclusive.

Since 1977 Josipovici has written his most ambitious and accomplished work, including the major radio play *Vergil Dying* and the novels *Migrations* and *The Air We Breathe.* In these novels he moves further away from the conventions of realist narrative. Whereas the early novels (and *The Echo Chamber*) are constructed around inconclusive stories and are primarily in dialogue form the later novels are constructed around multiple repetitions of fragmentary scenes and haunting images.

In *Migrations* a man lies on a bed in an empty room; a man collapses in an urban street; an autistic child fails to communicate with uncomprehending adults; a man talks in an over-furnished room with an unsympathetic woman, and so on. The text migrates restlessly from scene to scene: "You try to find a place to stop, roots . . . attempt to find a resting place for the imagination." "A series of places. Each must be visited. In turn. Then it will be finished. Then they will disappear." Temporary stillness and a disturbing sense of the physicality of speech, of words in the mouth, are achieved as the narrative voice repeats certain rhythms, images, and sound patterns and occasionally settles on certain sensuous sentences: "The black sky presses on his face like a blanket." "The sun streams in through the closed panes." "Silence drains away from him in dark streams." There is a poetic preoccupation with certain elemental forces, water and light, motion and rest, air and breath, which are to become an explicit theme of inquiry in *The Air We Breathe.*

In *Conversations in Another Room* an old woman, Phoebe, lies in bed. She shares her flat with a companion and is visited regularly by her niece. The narration is in the present tense and is mostly dialogue, at times very funny. The conversations circle around unanswered questions about Phoebe's husband who vanished without trace, and her son David whose marriage has broken up. In the hall the niece's boyfriend sits under a convex mirror, occasionally jotting in a notebook. To the reader's surprise, towards the end of the book there is suddenly a section in an unfamiliar and unidentified voice, in the first person. We do not know what the relationship is between this voice and the characters in Phoebe's flat. The voice says: "Perhaps we cannot write about our real selves, our real lives, the lives we have really lived. They are not there to be written about. The conversation always goes on in another room." *Contre-Jour* derives from a fascination with the French painter Pierre Bonnard. The first half of the novel is in the voice of his daughter, who has left home. The second half is in the voice of his wife. She compulsively bathes as her husband sits and sketches her. She voices her complaints and her unhappiness about her daughter's behavior. She writes odd notes and pins them around the house. We begin to realize that she is seriously disturbed. Perhaps the daughter does not exist at all but is made up as a consolation or a demented irritant by the painter's wife. We hear only short fragments of the painter's own speech as they are quoted by the women. Through all of his wife's miseries he continues, apparently serenely, to paint. Is his absorption in his work immensely cruel or is it that he has extraordinary patience? At the end we read a short, formal letter from the painter to a friend announcing the death of his wife. It has come to seem that the main subject of the work is the painter himself even though we scarcely hear his own voice directly. We view him only in the negative shapes he makes against the background of those who surround him, against the light.

One central image from *Migrations* can serve as an index of Josipovici's concerns as a novelist. The friends and relations of Lazarus wait outside the tomb, excited, anticipating a miracle. Lazarus emerges and slowly unwinds the linen cloth. He unwinds and unwinds and when he is finished there is nothing there, nothing but a little mound of dust. There is nothing in the center. There is no central meaning. As Josipovici says in *The Lessons of Modernism* the modern writer, like Eliot's Prufrock, rejects the role of Lazarus, "come back from the dead, come back to tell you all."

—John Mepham

JUST, Ward

Nationality: American. **Born:** Michigan City, Indiana, 5 September 1935. **Education:** Trinity College, Hartford, Connecticut, 1953-57. **Family:** Has two daughters, one son; married Sarah Catchpole, 1983. **Career:** Reporter, *Newsweek,* Chicago and Washington, 1959-62; *The Reporter Magazine,* Washington, 1962-63; *Newsweek,* London and Washington, 1963-65; *The Washington Post,* Washington and Saigon. **Awards:** Overseas Press Club award, 1968; National Magazine award, 1970, for non-fiction, and 1980, for fiction; Chicago *Tribune* Heartland award for fiction, 1989, for "Jack Gance." **Address:** RFD 342, Vineyard Haven, Massachusetts 02568, U.S.A.

PUBLICATIONS

Novels

A Soldier of the Revolution. New York, Knopf, and London, Weidenfeld and Nicolson, 1970.
The Congressman Who Loved Flaubert. Boston, Atlantic, and London, Little Brown, 1973.
Stringer. Boston, Atlantic, 1974.
Nicholson at Large. Boston, Atlantic, 1975.
A Family Trust. Boston, Atlantic, and London, Secker, 1978.
Honor, Power, Riches, Fame and the Love of Women. New York, Dutton, 1979.
In the City of Fear. New York, Viking, 1982.
The American Blues. New York, Viking, 1984.
American Ambassador. Boston, Houghton Mifflin, and London, Serpent's Tail, 1987.
Jack Gance. Boston, Houghton Mifflin, and London, Hale, 1989.
The Translator. Boston, Houghton Mifflin, 1991.
Ambition and Love. Boston, Houghton Mifflin, 1994.

Short Stories

Twenty-One: Selected Stories. Boston, Houghton Mifflin, 1990.

Other

To What End. New York, Knopf, 1968.
Military Men. New York, Knopf, 1970.

*

Manuscript Collection: Cranbrook School Archives, Bloomfield Hills, Michigan.

Critical Studies: "Just Deserts" by Tad Friend, *GQ,* June 1990; "Just So: The Odyssey of a Quintessentially American Novelist" by Dinitia Smith, *New York Magazine,* 19 August 1991.

*   *   *

Though Ward Just has distinguished himself as a journalist, he has also produced an impressive body of fiction. As a novelist, he has been compared favorably with Ernest Hemingway and Henry James. Much of his work centers around war—portrayed by the keen eye of a journalist—as is often true of Hemingway; however, his characters and their settings seem more Jamesian in their affluence and jaded sophistication. It is as if Just has felt the pulse of America for the past 50 years and produced "our story," one that is frighteningly familiar. The primary criticism of Just's work is that his action is slow and plodding. Although his characters are articulate and witty, they often do just sit and talk, especially in his fine piece on Washington during Vietnam, *In the City of Fear.*

Stringer, published in 1974 during the era of disillusion that followed Watergate, received mixed reviews. The general response was that this was a small book with flaws but a powerful look at the Vietnam War and the society that lived through it. In the opening scene, when Stringer savors the taste of chocolate and limeaid through a high that captures his readers with the physical surroundings, he might well be a Hemingway character discovering watercress except that this war is different for the individual soldier who feels more alienated than heroic. The main character does not feel connected to the war anymore than he does to his education, his career as a journalist, or to his family.

In his next novel, *Nicholson at Large,* Just captures the spirit of Washington as it reflects whatever else is going on in the nation. Many readers, however, felt that the work revealed flaws of an early novelist who, nonetheless, showed promise. Other reviewers insisted that this novel was more than promising—that it had, in fact, established Just as a serious writer to be watched. In 1978, *A Family Trust* was widely praised for its insightful treatment of family conflict. The word "promising" was less audible but still heard in response to Ward Just.

With *In the City of Fear,* the promise came to fruition almost without dispute. Just was praised for the convincing character of Colonel Sam Joyce and for his satirical look at some of Washington's key figures, including the presidents (even if he does not name them). One of the most stirring scenes in the book helps to illustrate the realization of Just's ability to portray strong female characters. Sheila has disrupted the chatter of a Washington dinner party (attended by military men, politicians, newspaper men, and their wives) by producing a poignant photo of her young son, who is in Vietnam. The photo quiets even the most enthusiastic war conversationalists, and Marina muses:

> Watching Sheila now, Marina was surprised at her—forbearance. At the general forbearance of women—Sheila's, Jo's, her own. It would not last, they concealed so much. She knew the tempo of the dance was increasing.... They would all go to pieces, men would leave their wives and women their families. Children would disappear. There would be heart attacks and suicides and breakdowns and no one would be as he or she had been. The thin would grow fat, and the fat would grow fatter. They were all fighting the same war, in this murderous twilight of the American century. Now she was drawn to Sheila, tired and distraught, her grief worn like a black badge of courage.

She goes on to say they were all beguiled in the way that Henry James once described "women traveling in exotic Italy." The echo of James is significant in the middle of this musing, but even more so is the echo of Stephen Crane's badge of courage. No wonder this book brought Just praise as a sensitive, distinguished writer of our time.

The American Blues, a first-person narrative, is disarming, given the close relationship of journalism and fiction that readers of Just already grapple with. His work often reads more like a factual account than a novel, particularly here.

The theme of father and son pitted against one another recurs in *The American Ambassador,* when William and Bill Jr., a diplomat and a terrorist respectively, struggle in the exciting backdrop of international intrigue. Not surprisingly, *The Translator,* which appeared in 1991, covers the historic lifting of the Iron Curtain. An American woman in Paris marries a refugee who has become a linguist—a skill that leads to international intrigue again. Critics found this a gloomy portrayal of humanity as it nears the 21st century, but none of them were arguing that a more hopeful picture is deserved.

With *Ambition and Love* Just moves away from the political scene and gives the reader a delightful "tour" of Paris through the eyes of an artist, who may well be Just's strongest female character, and her lover, who is a writer. The critical response to this novel has been quite positive. Just is certainly a writer to watch.

—Loretta Cobb

K

KAPLAN, Johanna

Nationality: American. **Born:** New York City, 29 December 1942.
Education: The High School of Music and Art, New York; University of Wisconsin, Madison; New York University, B.A. 1964; Columbia University Teachers College, M.A. in special education 1965. **Career:** Since 1966 teacher of emotionally disturbed children in New York public schools at Mount Sinai Hospital, New York. **Awards:** Creative Artists Public Service grant, 1973; National Endowment for the Arts grant, 1973; Jewish Book Council Epstein award, 1976; Wallant award, 1981; Jewish Book award, 1981; Smilen-*Present Tense* award, 1981. **Agent:** Georges Borchardt Inc., 136 East 57th Street, New York, New York 10022. **Address:** 411 West End Avenue, New York, New York 10024, U.S.A.

PUBLICATIONS

Novel

O My America! New York, Harper, 1980.

Short Stories

Other People's Lives. New York, Knopf, 1975.

Uncollected Short Stories

"Not All Jewish Families Are Alike," in *Commentary* (New York), January 1976.
"Family Obligations," in *Forthcoming* (New York), March 1983.
"Close Calls," in *Commentary* (New York), May 1986.
"Christmas Party," in *City Journal* (New York), Winter 1995.

*   *   *

By all the laws of literary logic, Johanna Kaplan should not have a career at all, much less an increasingly successful one. She began publishing short fiction about American-Jewish life in the early 1970s, at a time when the tapestry of American-Jewish life seemed threadbare, when sheer exhaustion had taken its toll on imaginative transformations of American-Jewish material, when critics and reviewers alike outraced themselves to say "Enough already!" *Other People's Lives* proved how wrong the nay-sayers had been. In this collection of five short stories and a novella, Kaplan made us aware, once again, of how vital, how dynamically alive, renderings of the American-Jewish milieu could be—especially if one had Kaplan's ear for speech rhythms and an instinctive grasp of our time, our place. Here, for example, is a snippet from the title story:

When your mother wrote that book [a character hectors a disaffected daughter], it was the Age of Conformity. And I'm not just talking about gray flannel suits! What I'm talking about is all those people who got caught up—they couldn't help themselves—in the whole trend and sway and

spirit of the times. Not that I got trapped into it even then. Because it always seemed escapist and reactionary to me. And that's all that was going on—the flight to the suburbs! Your own *lawn.* Your own *house.* Your own *psyche.* Your own little *garden*—and for some people, not so little! And *that,* Julia darling, was what your mother was up against! Forget the city and live in the trees! And these were genuinely progressive people, not just ordinary *shtunks!*

Kaplan's congenial turf is the ordinariness of ordinary New York Jewish life. You walk into her stories as if through a crowded living room—never as an invited, "formal" guest, but, rather, as some distant cousin catching up on family gossip. It is a world where one's childhood is fixed forever in the mind of an aunt, even when that "child" is now an adult, and a psychiatrist to boot:

"Naomi!" the aunt said, jumping up from a green plastic chair that could easily have come from the office of a dentist with no eye for the future.
"I know," Naomi said. "My panti-hose are crooked. I'll go to the ladies' room and fix them."
"*When* did I—"
"All right, then, I'll go to the *men's* room and fix them . . ."

But that much said about the comic ironies, the delicately shaded satire of Kaplan's stories, what *lasts* in these fictions are the complex privacies that simmer just beneath the surface. In "Sour or Suntanned, It Makes No Difference," for example, a ten-year-old protagonist who hates, absolutely *hates,* the regimen and artificiality of a summer camp ("at flag lowering you joined hands and swayed . . . in swimming you had to jump for someone else's dripping hand. . . . There was no reason to spend a whole summer hugging them"), is confused, and frightened, by the part she must play in a camp production directed by a visiting Hebrew playwright. The story's concluding sentence, brilliantly written and hauntingly evocative, might stand for many of the stories in *Other People's Lives:* "standing there on the stage, a little girl in braids and a too-long dress who would end up not dead, Miriam promised herself that never again in her life would anyone look at her face and see in it what Amnon did, but just like the girl who could fake being dead, she would keep all her aliveness a secret."

O My America! extended the range and depth of Kaplan's fiction. It is, on one level, the story of Ezra Slavin, a crusty, unremitting social critic who dies at an anti-war rally in 1972. As an obituary puts it:

From very early in his career, Mr. Slavin was harshly critical of the anomic trends of urban, mechanized American life, yet his vision of the city as a place of "limitless, tumultuous possibility" was a lyrical, even celebratory one. "I have had a lifelong affair with the idea of America," Mr. Slavin once said. "And when people find that difficult to believe, I remind them of that flintier vision which is bound to result when love is unrequited."

That, one might say, is the "official," the pundit's, version of Ezra Slavin and what he stood for. *O My America!,* on the other hand, is that life told in flashback by his daughter Merry, one of his six children and part of what can only be called a complicated, free-form and exasperatingly extended "family."

The result is a canvas large enough for Kaplan to pour in a satiric history of immigrant Jewish life, to sketch minor characters by the dozen and to deepen the connections between American Jews and contemporary versions of the American Dream. Even more impressive, *O My America!* opened new possibilities for American-Jewish fiction, at a time when its dimensions seemed limited to pale re-tellings of Borsht Belt jokes or to pale imitations of major writers like Bernard Malamud, Saul Bellow, and Philip Roth. Even the most skeptical reviewers admitted that if Kaplan's fiction were the norm, there would be plenty of American-Jewish novels to kick around, for some time to come.

—Sanford Pinsker

KATZ, Steve

Nationality: American. **Born:** New York City, 14 May 1935. **Education:** Cornell University, Ithaca, New York, 1952-56, A.B. (honors) 1956; University of Oregon, Eugene, M.A. in English 1959. **Family:** Married Patricia Bell in 1956 (divorced 1979); three sons. **Career:** Staff member, English Language Institute, 1960, and faculty member, University of Maryland Overseas, 1961-62, both Lecce, Italy; Assistant Professor of English, Cornell University, 1962-67; Lecturer in Fiction, University of Iowa, Iowa City, 1969-70; writer-in-residence, Brooklyn College, New York, 1970-71; Assistant Professor of English, Queens College, New York, 1971-75; Associate Professor of English, Notre Dame University, Indiana, 1976-78. Since 1978 Associate Professor of English, and Director of Creative Writing, 1978-81, University of Colorado, Boulder. Has also worked for the Forest Service in Idaho, in a quicksilver mine in Nevada, and on dairy farms in New York State; since 1971 teacher of Tai Chi Chuan. **Awards:** National Endowment for the Arts grant, 1976, 1981; Creative Artists Public Service grant, 1976. **Agent:** Georges Borchardt Inc., 136 East 57th Street, New York, New York 10022. **Address:** 3060 8th Street, Boulder, Colorado 80302, U.S.A.

PUBLICATIONS

Novels

The Lestriad. Lecce, Italy, Milella, 1962; Flint, Michigan, Bamberger, 1987.
The Exagggerations of Peter Prince. New York, Holt Rinehart, 1968.
Posh (as Stephanie Gatos). New York, Grove Press, 1971.
Saw. New York, Knopf, 1972.
Moving Parts. New York, Fiction Collective, 1977.
Wier and Pouce. College Park, Maryland, Sun and Moon, 1984.
Florry of Washington Heights. Los Angeles, Sun and Moon, 1988; London, Serpent's Tail, 1989.

Short Stories

Creamy and Delicious: Eat My Words (in Other Words). New York, Random House, 1970.

Stolen Stories. New York, Fiction Collective, 1984.
43 Fictions. Los Angeles, Sun and Moon, 1991.

Play

Screenplay: *Grassland* (*Hex*), with Leo Garen, 1972.

Poetry

The Weight of Antony. Ithaca, New York, Eibe Press, 1964.
Cheyenne River Wild Track. Ithaca, New York, Ithaca House, 1973.
Journalism. Flint, Michigan, Bamberger, 1990.

*

Critical Studies: *The Life of Fiction* by Jerome Klinkowitz, Urbana, University of Illinois Press, 1977; "Fiction and the Facts of Life" by J.K. Grant, in *Critique* (Atlanta), Summer 1983; article by Sinda J. Gregory and Larry McCaffery, in *Dictionary of Literary Biography Yearbook 1983* edited by Mary Bruccoli and Jean W. Ross, Detroit, Gale, 1984.

Steve Katz comments:

(1991) The nature of our work is determined by our peculiar collaborative procedures. There are nine Steve Katz and each of us makes a contribution to each piece. Three of the Steve Katz are women, putting them in a minority, but allowing, at least, for some female input into all of the work, which sometimes invokes misogyny, but because of the female component in its composition transcends that inference. We break down into three groups of three, each one with a woman at its pivot most of the time, though sometimes the women collaborate as a separate cadre. Three of us live in New York City, three travel all over North America, and sometimes to South America, and are stationed in Boulder, Colorado, and the third three never rest as travelers of the remaining world. Sometimes for variety one Steve Katz from the New York triumvirate will replace one Steve Katz from the world travelers and etc., generally without disruption or conflict. Some of the works can be written by only five of us (this blurb, for instance), and some by seven. In these instances we arbitrarily eliminate the four Steve Katz, or the two, by a process we call "blistering." For more information about this process please contact our agent. We have never before revealed our method of composition because we had expected great financial gain from this unique procedure. Since this has not been forthcoming, voilà!

*   *   *

Steve Katz's fictions are woven from two distinct strands: from playful fable-like tales, often of serious intent, and from disruptive watch-the-writer-writing materials. The proportions in which these two narrative impulses are mixed vary from book to book, and give each its individual character.

Experiments in textual disruption dominate and shape *The Exagggerations of Peter Prince.* Devices used include crossed-out pages, notices of deleted passages, partially whited-out ads, and authorial injunctions to the characters and to the author himself. Despite the emphasis on technical manipulations, the emotional contour of a caring young man's struggles to do the right thing comes through—both from Peter Prince and from Katz. Katz's hope here, as in most of his quasi-autobiographical fiction, is that by writing

Peter Prince he will invent for himself a better life. It is an admission of uncertainty about the future that the novel has no ending, that the planned ending is lost in the "archives of the unwritten." (The ending was to have been "America, with a rock and roll band at the castle, and all the new dances, formal and primitive . . ." This scene does appear, 16 years later, as "The Death of Bobby Kennedy" in *Wier and Pouce*.) Between disruptive passages Katz also shows himself to be a visually oriented writer, with a gift for evoking realistic detail: ". . . trees like candelabra, holding vultures, their gray and carmine heads flickering, and the small dark kites circling the umbrella crowned acacias." With the stories in *Creamy and Delicious* Katz's neo-fable style hits its stride. This book collects the "Mythologies," satirical reworkings and defacings of the stories and images of Wonder Woman, Nancy and Sluggo, Dickens, and Greek mythology. The writing here shares with *Peter Prince* a tense feel, and a need to discomfit or shock the reader: "Wonder Woman was a dike, but she was nice." The plain speech style is in places extended and stylized, with results not unlike some of Gertrude Stein's work: "A man there was called Thomas who in the aged long ago time before I was a boy was the man of many creatures, a many-creatured man in the hills before my youth. . . ." Katz's disruptive side is here confined to two short, comparatively unsuccessful pieces, and some short poems. Katz followed this collection with the erotic novel *Posh,* which he wrote in six weeks.

With *Saw* Katz finds his mature voice. The disruptive and the fabulous are blended in a much more confident and relaxed, even whimsical, way. Characters in the novel include Eileen, who feeds a puppy to a hawk; a sphere from the center of the earth; a cylinder; a talking fly; and an astronaut from a distant galaxy—who, as Katz confesses midway through the book, is really the author. The Astronaut has come to Earth seeking a substance which can revitalize his world, a substance which is an amalgam of "ambition, greed, bullshit, pride, envy, bourbon, and smut." If we can credit the authorial interruptions in *Saw,* this is identical with Katz's idea of the substance of fiction. So in some ways *Saw* is about, not the process, but the experience of creating fiction. The final chapter (titled "The First Chapter") is a detailed account of a long hot day filled with poets and worries, and concludes with Katz getting away from it all in the more genial company of The Astronaut; leaving his everyday life behind and going off to explore his fictional world.

Beginning with "Female Skin" in *Moving Parts* Katz's fables move into new territory, become more deeply reflective of modern life and concerns than was possible through the more conventionally satirical characters of the earlier "Mythologies." "Female Skin" takes literally the metaphorical idea of getting inside another's skin. Called a novel, *Moving Parts* contains stories, diary entries, photographs, and a log of encounters with the number 43. Katz's playful side is evident everywhere: a photograph of Katz with a beard is followed by one of a barber shop, then one of a clean-shaven Katz. The author's face is one more "moving part" employed in the process of creating his fiction.

In *Stolen Stories* the literary experimentalist and the fable-wright once again speak separately. Half the pieces here are disembodied monologues, which are disruptive not in the sense of any authorial intrusion, but through their staccato, Burroughs-like use of language ("come in: this is my tent: you carry the sickness:"). These monologues succeed only in evoking the sounds of the experiences and states Katz deals with, with little of the emotional depth of his best work. The fabulous stories here are Katz's best. "Friendship" makes a convincing case for cannibalism being the logical and loving end toward which all friendships should move. "Death of the Band"

crosses John Cage-style compositional ideas with psychotic urban violence to prophesy a new musical form.

Wier and Pouce is Katz's masterpiece, an encapsulation of the spiritual/ideological crisis in America since the 1950s. (*Wier and Pouce* is a very American novel: it begins and ends with ball games.) The writing style varies to mirror the temper of the times, from the Horatio Algerish first chapter, through anagramic and alphabetical sections (covering roughly the years of Katz's early literary experiments), before settling into the mature Katz voice.

Dusty Wier is clearly Katz's stand-in here, but he is also representative of everyone who grew up in those times hoping for a better American Way to manifest itself. E. Pouce embodies the arrogance and ambition of the dark side of that Way: among his other deeds he drops napalm on his own party—this in the wake of "The Death of Bobby Kennedy," that is, of the death of 1960s idealism. Episodes and images subtly mirror one another from scene to scene and country to country, reinforcing the universal feel Katz is striving to establish. Fiction's role here is spelled out for the reader: "When the day gets short people must make up stories just to get through the nights." As at the end of *Peter Prince,* Katz here is uncertain about what is to come: an impossibly high fly ball is falling toward a long-dormant giant's glove as the novel closes.

—William C. Bamberger

KAVANAGH, Dan. *See* BARNES, Julian (Patrick).

KEANE, Molly

Pseudonym: M.J. Farrell. **Nationality:** Irish. **Born:** Mary Nesta Skrine, County Kildare, 4 July 1904. **Family:** Married Robert Lumley Keane in 1938 (died 1947). **Agent:** Murray Pollinger, 222 Old Brompton Road, London SW5 0BZ, England. **Address:** Dysert, Ardmore, County Waterford, Ireland.

PUBLICATIONS

Novels

Good Behaviour. London, Deutsch, and New York, Knopf, 1981.
Time after Time. London, Deutsch, 1983; New York, Knopf, 1984.
Loving and Giving. London, Deutsch, 1988; as *Queen Lear,* New York, Dutton, 1989.

Novels as M.J. Farrell

The Knight of the Cheerful Countenance. London, Mills and Boon, 1928.
Young Entry. London, Mathews and Marrot, 1928; New York, Holt, 1929.

Taking Chances. London, Mathews and Marrot, 1929; Philadelphia, Lippincott, 1930.

Mad Puppetstown. London, Collins, 1931; New York, Farrar and Rinehart, 1932.

Conversation Piece. London, Collins, 1932; as *Point-to-Point,* New York, Farrar and Rinehart, 1933.

Devoted Ladies. London, Collins, and Boston, Little Brown, 1934.

Full House. London, Collins, and Boston, Little Brown, 1935.

The Rising Tide. London, Collins, 1937; New York, Macmillan, 1938.

Two Days in Aragon. London, Collins, 1941.

Loving Without Tears. London, Collins, 1951; as *The Enchanting Witch,* New York, Crowell, 1951.

Treasure Hunt. London, Collins, 1952.

Plays as M.J. Farrell

Spring Meeting, with John Perry (produced London, 1938; New York, 1939). London, Collins, 1938.

Ducks and Drakes, with John Perry (produced London, 1941).

Guardian Angel (produced Dublin, 1944).

Treasure Hunt, with John Perry (produced London, 1949). London, Collins, 1950.

Dazzling Prospect, with John Perry. London, French, 1961.

Other

Red Letter Days, with Snaffles (as M.J. Farrell; on hunting). London, Collins, 1933.

Molly Keane's Nursery Cooking. London, Macdonald, 1985.

Molly Keane's Ireland: An Anthology, with Sally Phipps. London, HarperCollins, 1993.

*

Critical Studies: "Three Writers of the Big House: Elizabeth Bowen, Molly Keane and Jennifer Johnston" by Bridget O'Toole, in *Across a Roaring Hill: The Protestant Imagination in Modern Ireland* edited by Gerald Dawe and Edna Longley, Belfast, Blackstaff Press, 1985; "The Persistent Pattern: Molly Keane's Recent Big House Fiction" by Vera Kreilkamp, in *Massachusetts Review* (Amherst), Autumn 1987.

*   *   *

The career of Irish novelist Molly Keane falls into two chronological periods. In the first, between 1928 and 1961, she published 11 Big House novels under the pseudonym M.J. Farrell. Keane was herself born and raised in an Edwardian country house of the Protestant Ascendancy, and she explores this insular and philistine world of field-sports, eccentric relatives, bad debts, and secrets both above and below stairs with varying degrees of satire in all her work. Even if we accept her own story that she only began writing to increase a meager dress allowance, it would be wrong to see the Farrell novels as nothing more than mere apprentice-work for the second phase of her career represented by three mature novels of the 1980s, when her return to writing gained more serious critical attention, and the reprinting of all the earlier titles. Although patchy, the best of the early works show Keane's ability to expose the private fears and obsessions of a bankrupt class whose hands were rapidly slipping from the reins of power.

Apart from the elusive adolescent romance *The Knight of the Cheerful Countenance* published by Mills and Boon, and according to Keane "best forgotten," her career begins with *Young Entry,* a work dominated by the youthful, indiscreet, heiress Prudence Lingfield Turrett. Prudence is typical of Keane's exclusively female narrator-heroines, whose youthful mobility within the social and spatial hierarchy of the house, is exploited to cast an ironic eye over the world of hunting, shooting, fishing, and flirting. In Prudence's overbearing guardian Gus, we have a pale ancestor of the strong matriarch figures who quietly tyrannize the domestic world of the later novels. The romantic enthusiasm of this overparodic first work is already held in check in *Taking Chances,* a social comedy with more pointed ironies, which takes off with the arrival from London of scatter-brained, femme fatal, Mary Fuller, (armed with numerous suitcases and ratty terrier,) who is immediately perceived as "a factor for disturbance." Many Keane plots follow this pattern, exploiting the disruptive effects of the arrival of a potentially anarchic outsider to expose the emotional fragility behind the crumbling edifice of the doomed Ascendancy. Predatory Aunt Edythe in the same novel is the forerunner to later "mad aunts," whose dottiness all too often thinly disguises a vindictive need to enviously thwart youthful enthusiasms.

Mad Puppetstown gives more historical focus to the theme of extinction or adaptation, as it traces the fate of the Chevington family from its hey-day in a pre-World War I "Golden Age," through the Troubles and the uprising. Within the comic *Full House,* Keane tackles the taboo surrounding mental illness anticipating her late more subtle explorations of domestic psychological complexities. She had already expanded the emotional range of the Big House genre in *Devoted Ladies,* which some claim to be the first Irish novel with a lesbian theme. Such early explorations anticipate the marginal role of homosexuality in the plots of *Good Behaviour* and *Time after Time.* The success of *The Rising Tide* was followed by *Two Days in Aragon,* in which the wider Irish political context, only implicit elsewhere, is confronted head-on, if portentously and sentimentally, when the wild-blooded heroine Grania falls in love with a member of Sinn Fein. *Loving Without Tears* and *Treasure Hunt* mark the end of this first period of creativity. Throughout these novels, female relatives or devoted governesses inadequately fill the emotional vacuum created in the heroines by deceased, departed, or emotionally cold mothers. Maternal instincts are invariably misdirected towards dogs, furniture or gardening and fathers are well-meaning but ineffectual, hen-pecked patriarchs. Any genuine affection for daughters finds inadequate expression through the competitive, masculine language of hunt, stable, and dog kennel.

For personal reasons Keane abandoned her literary career for more than 20 years, before emerging from silence and pseudonymity in 1981 with *Good Behaviour,* another account of an Ascendancy girlhood. Early chapters are dominated by the comically pathetic presence of the governess Mrs. Brock, dismissed from her last post for encouraging a young boy to read poetry. The war-wounded father and his decline into bed-ridden dependency upon the soothing attentions of a loving housemaid is portrayed with some sympathy, but again Keane's real strength lies in the use of grotesque, black comedy to expose self-delusion and cruelty, and the deep chasm separating the ruling Ascendancy from their Catholic servants. When the maid hears the news of her husband's death in the trenches, "she was kneeling at the brass harpstrings of some piece of Regency rubbish, and collapsed like a dead frog, Mummie said. Such a good thing she wasn't standing up or she'd certainly have fallen on something and broken it, and we'd only just finished washing those Waterford glass rummers." There is a shocking inevitability in the way we finally witness the daughter/narrator growing up into another version of her selfish, cynical, and cruel mother. *Good Behaviour* shows Keane's earlier strength as a comedienne of manners supported by more subtle characterisation and pointed description. Like Surtees, she is detailed about dress, like Thackeray she is skilful with food. Whilst her detailed, almost precious evocations of furnishings are reminiscent of those of her contemporary Denton Welch, there is something ruthlessly Swiftian in Keane's pursuit of her characters into dressing-room and lavatory!

In *Time after Time,* Keane views similar material from a more contemporary perspective. The elderly, impoverished Swifts of Durraghglass—three eccentric sisters, April, May, and Baby June and their one-eyed brother Jasper—defiantly cling to youthful memories of the golden days when their "darling Mummie" presided over ball and garden-party, but they are left trapped in a crumbling house and an incestuous emotional web of petty cruelties and resentments. The outsider here is long-lost Jewish Cousin Leda whose arrival stirs up the emotional dust. She discovers that while April trades the family heirlooms for "Pot," and May's flower-arranging demonstrations form a cover for her kleptomania, June flirts with the stable-lad, and Jasper flirts with a neighbouring monk. This somewhat camp depiction of old-age, shifts uneasily between racy, domestic satire and wordy psychological explanation.

But Keane's powers are far from diminished in *Loving and Giving,* in which Nicandra tells the story of her childhood, haunted by her mother's desertion and her father's financial struggles. Keane's comic skills shine in the opening accounts of generous, but eccentrically self-indulgent Aunt Tossie in bed with her parrot and bottle of Scotch. Elsewhere a blacker comedy exposes the social blindness of the Ascendency: "One morning, on his way to breakfast, Dada saw her kneeling on the left-hand flight of the double staircase; thinking she was saying her prayers, she bent so low, Dada stepped past her politely. After breakfast someone found her sprawled in difficult death." Farce gives way to pathos when we witness Tossie's perversely symbiotic relationship with her loyal servant "Silly-Willy," who tends to her every whim in the reduced circumstances of a caravan parked beside the French-windows of the leaky dining-room. In the distance a deserted Dada, unable to afford any more race-horses, ends his days "breaking in" a motor mower on the overgrown lawns of his decaying estate. As it closes the novel takes on symbolic resonances with an acutely observed power struggle for Tossie's affections enacted between Willy and the newly divorced Nicandra, who is haunted by childhood memories of sado-sexual cruelties she once inflicted on the mentally retarded peasant boy. Here, as in all Keane's work, acute social satire is surrounded by an ambiguous aura of nostalgia.

While Keane's novels are open to criticism for their limited thematic range, she has lent genuine literary skill and fresh psychological depth to the Big House novel. Her subtle explorations of the obsessive and cruel psychology of Ascendency women would benefit from recent developments in feminist and psycho-analytic cortical theory.

—David Shuttleton

KELLEHER, Victor

Pseudonym: Veronica Hart. **Nationality:** British (also a citizen of Australia). **Born:** Victor Michael Kitchener Kelleher in London,

19 July 1939. **Education:** The University of Natal, Pietermaritzburg, South Africa, B.A. in English 1962; University of St. Andrews, Fife, Dip. Ed. 1963; University of the Witwatersrand, Johannesburg, B.A. (honors) 1969; University of South Africa, Pretoria, M.A. 1970, D.Litt. et Phil. 1973. **Family:** Married Alison Lyle in 1962; one son and one daughter. **Career:** Junior lecturer in English, University of the Witwatersrand, 1969; lecturer, then senior lecturer, in English, University of South Africa, 1970-73; lecturer in English, Massey University, Palmerston North, New Zealand, 1973-76; senior lecturer, 1976-84, and associate professor of English, 1984-87, University of New England, Armidale, New South Wales. **Awards:** Patricia Hackett prize, for short story, 1978; West Australian Young Readers' Book award, 1982, 1983, 1993; Australia Council fellowship, 1982, 1989-91, 1995-98; Australian Children's Book of the Year award, 1983, 1987; Australian Science Fiction Achievement award, 1984; Australian Children's Book Council Honour award, 1987, 1991; Australian Peace prize, 1989; Koala award, 1991; Hoffman award, 1992, 1993; Cool award, 1993. **Address:** 1 Avenue Rd., Clebe, New South Wales 2037, Australia.

PUBLICATIONS

Novels

Voices from the River. London, Heinemann, 1979; St. Lucia, University of Queensland Press, 1991.
The Beast of Heaven. St. Lucia, University of Queensland Press, 1984.
Em's Story. St. Lucia, University of Queensland Press, 1988.
Wintering. St. Lucia, University of Queensland Press, 1990.
Micky Darlin'. St. Lucia, University of Queensland Press, 1992.
Double God (as Veronica Hart). Melbourne and London, Mandarin, 1994.
The House That Jack Built (as Veronica Hart). Melbourne and London, Mandarin, 1994.

Short Stories

Africa and After. St. Lucia, University of Queensland Press, 1983; as *The Traveller,* 1987.

Other (for young adults)

Forbidden Paths of Thual. London, Kestrel, 1979.
The Hunting of Shadroth. London, Kestrel, 1981.
Master of the Grove. London, Kestrel, 1982.
Papio. London, Kestrel, 1984; as *Rescue,* New York, Dial Books, 1992.
The Green Piper. Melbourne, Viking Kestrel, 1984; London, Viking Kestrel, 1985.
Taronga. Melbourne, Viking Kestrel, 1986; London, Hamish Hamilton, 1987.
The Makers. Melbourne, Viking Kestrel, 1987.
Baily's Bones. Melbourne, Viking Kestrel, 1988; New York, Dial Press, 1989.
The Red King. Melbourne, Viking Kestrel, 1989; New York, Dial Press, 1990.
Brother Night. London, MacRae, 1990; New York, Walker, 1991.
Del-Del. London, MacRae/Random House, 1991; New York, Walker, 1992.
To the Dark Tower. London, MacRae/Random House, 1992.

Where the Whales Sing. Melbourne and London, Viking, 1994.
Parkland. Melbourne, Viking, 1994.

*   *   *

Although he has spent considerable periods of time in several countries it is his experiences in Africa that dominate Kelleher's fiction. He says of himself, "Central Africa, where I was to spend a good portion of the next twenty years [after leaving England], did more to alter my attitudes and prospects than anything before or since," and he speaks also of his immense grief at being compelled to leave it. His first novel *Voices from the River* is, like most of his work, a study of the many forms that racism and also racial interaction generally can take and of the necessity of finding what is universal in human nature that can overcome the superficialities of differences in the color of skin. The voices belong to five different people, two brothers, Davy and Jonno, their father Cole, whom one or both of them murder, and two policemen, Samuels and Priestly, who are temperamentally and philosophically poles apart. In its complex structure and deliberate, even willful creation of uncertainty about motive and even fact, the novel seems influenced by Faulkner. Kelleher's view of Africa and Africans is far from misty-eyed. In many ways the novel could be read as a critique of the philanthropic liberalism of Samuels who returns after retirement to England but the fact that he is killed because, as Priestly had predicted, he is too trusting and sentimental, is offset by the large numbers of Africans at his funeral.

Africa and After contains fifteen stories, seven set in Africa, one bridging story which looks back upon Africa from self-imposed exile, and seven set in Australia, where Kelleher finally settled. The first half of the book is far better than the second. The material itself is richer and Kelleher's imagery seems engaged by it in a way that is not true of the later stories where the view of human behavior is often reductive and even cynical, the observations of an uninvolved outsider.

Kelleher has spoken of his wish to write in a diverse variety of modes. He is a very successful writer of young adult fiction and, more recently, has published two bloodthirsty novels of terror under the pseudonym of Veronica Hart. Even his third book of adult fiction under his own name, *The Beast of Heaven,* represents another radical departure from anything he had written previously. The novel is set 100,000 years after a nuclear holocaust that has taken place in the year 2027 and is a moral fable about the merit of continuing the human race. Two computers, the survivors of a war which destroyed the "Ancients" who created them, debate the issue while the only survivors, the peaceful Gatherers, struggle amid the desolate landscape to eke out a living and to evade the predatory Houdin, the Beast of Heaven. It is an ingeniously constructed and often lyrically written novel which leads ineluctably to an apocalyptic ending of dreadful irony. Reviewers have mentioned Dylan Thomas in connection with it but a more appropriate analogy would be with Yeats' "The Second Coming."

Em's Story returns us to Africa and the question of race. A young woman named Eva is asked by her grandmother Emma Wilhelm to write the story of an heroic trek she undertook sixty years before. Rebelling against her German ancestors and their virtual extinction of the Hereros she offers shelter to a Herero tribesman and then makes love to him. After he is murdered by her father she sets out on her journey north to rejoin the remnants of the tribe she has come to accept as her own people. Sixty years later her granddaughter undertakes the same journey in circumstances which, as she

observes, are markedly different, bent on a similar mission of reconciliation and recovery of her personal identity. Kelleher cuts frequently between past and present and the similarity of Eva's circumstances to those of Em are pointedly stressed but the novel's emphasis is on the healing and hopeful qualities of Eva's journey across the bridge between white and black Africa.

Wintering is set in Australia in 1988, the year of the bicentennial, but returns to many of the same themes as his earlier fiction. The narrator, a young man named Jack Rudd, writes out his story in between visiting his friend Benny who lies comatose in hospital. The novel cuts rapidly between the present—Benny's condition and Jack's struggle to revive his relationship with his Aboriginal former girlfriend Bridget—and the past of a year before, and the events that led to Benny's destruction and the end of the relationship. Once again, Kelleher finds the soil of Australia a little too arid to write the kind of novel he had in mind; his 1960s white radicals are hardly more complex or interesting than his Redfern Aboriginals and the upbeat ending of the novel is both startling and unconvincing. Nevertheless, the pleasures to be found in this work are those in all of his fiction—a fine ear for dialogue, a command of narrative, an ability to evoke landscape, and more importantly and less definably, a fundamental integrity in the way he approaches the issues that concern him.

The same qualities are evident in his most recent work for adults, *Micky Darlin',* in which the author has returned to the first of his three countries for his material. *Micky Darlin'* consists of a number of interrelated stories which together comprise a history of the sprawling Donoghue family of Irish expatriates, spread over many years and narrated by the eponymous Micky. Beginning in the early 1940s in wartime London when Micky is of preschool age, they take us through the following decade when Micky has grown to be a young adult, the witness and recorder of the family's progressive disintegration over the different generations. More or less abandoned by his weak mother and alcoholic father, Micky has been brought up by his grandparents, Nan and Gramps, but when Gramps dies in a foolish accident, the family falls apart and the embittered Micky feels forsaken yet again. In the hands of a lesser writer the Donoghues would be almost Irish stereotypes—constantly drinking, brawling, angrily divided from another over questions of religion—but Kelleher's unsentimental, sharply observant prose brings them alive.

—Laurie Clancy

KELLEY, William Melvin

Nationality: American. **Born:** Bronx, New York, 1 November 1937. **Education:** Fieldston School, New York; Harvard University, Cambridge, Massachusetts (Read prize, 1960), 1957-61. **Family:** Married Karen Gibson in 1962; two children. **Career:** Writer-in-residence, State University College, Geneseo, New York, Spring 1965; teacher, New School for Social Research, New York, 1965-67, and University of the West Indies, Mona, Jamaica, 1969-70. **Awards:** Dana Reed Literary prize, Harvard University, 1960; Bread Loaf Writers Conference grant, 1962; Whitney Foundation award, 1963; Rosenthal Foundation award, 1963; *Transatlantic Review* award, 1964; Black Academy of Arts and Letters award, 1970. **Address:** The Wisdom Shop, P.O. Box 2658, New York, New York 10027, U.S.A.

PUBLICATIONS

Novels

A Different Drummer. New York, Doubleday, 1962; London, Hutchinson, 1963.
A Drop of Patience. New York, Doubleday, 1965; London, Hutchinson, 1966.
Dem. New York, Doubleday, 1967.
Dunfords Travels Everywheres. New York, Doubleday, 1970.

Short Stories

Dancers on the Shore. New York, Doubleday, 1964; London, Hutchinson, 1965.

Uncollected Short Stories

"Jest, Like Sam," in *Negro Digest* (Chicago), October 1969.
"The Dentist's Wife," in *Women and Men, Men and Women,* edited by William Smart. New York, St. Martin's Press, 1975.

* * *

William Melvin Kelley's novels to date have dealt with interracial conflict, but the emphasis has been on the examination of characters, black and white, and the myths with which they delude themselves. His novels pose no "solutions" to the conflict but the solution of self-understanding, and his depiction of the relationships—loving and competitive—between men and women and blacks and whites combines compassion, objectivity, and humor.

His first novel, *A Different Drummer,* set realistically rendered characters in a fantasy plot. From multiple points of view he displayed the reactions of the whites of a fictional Southern state to the spontaneous grass-roots emigration of the state's blacks. A minor incident in *A Different Drummer* concerns Wallace Bedlow, who is waiting for a bus to take him to New York City, where he plans to live with his brother, Carlyle. Bedlow appears only that one time, but he surfaces again in "Cry for Me," probably the best short story in *Dancers on the Shore,* in which he becomes a famous folk singer. In that story the themes of one's public image versus the true self and commercialism versus art are explored.

These themes are developed further in Kelley's second novel, *A Drop of Patience.* The protagonist is a blind, black jazz musician, whose intuitive experimentation is contrasted to the intellectualization of critics, and whose love of music comes into conflict with the commercialization of music. More important than these themes, however, is the development of the character himself, who passes through various rites of passage as he learns to deal with sex, love, racism, and fame.

Carlyle Bedlow, who appeared in several of the stories in *Dancers on the Shore,* reappears in *Dem,* Kelley's third novel. "Lemme tellya how dem folks live," the novel begins. It goes on to show dem white folks living out their myths of white superiority, masculine prerogative, and soap-opera escapism. They are such victims of the pernicious myths of their culture that they are no longer even a threat to black people.

Racial conflict nearly disappears amidst the experimentation and fantasy of *Dunfords Travels Everywheres,* Kelley's own clever and original permutation of *Finnegans Wake.* A triptych in plot, style, and character, *Dunfords Travels Everywheres* is an ambitious short

novel; it succeeds in being clever, but as an exploration into character it's less satisfying than his earlier novels.

Kelley has shown himself a skillful craftsman in a variety of styles and approaches. In his stories and in his first three novels his exploration of character develops as the character seeks—or refuses to seek—a unity between the person he feels he is and the personality he or society thinks he should be. This is true also in one of the three interwoven stories of *Dunfords Travels Everywheres.* In the other two stories a playful fantasy dominates. If Kelley's fiction has a direction, it's one that moves from seriousness and psychological probing to fantasy, playfulness, and comedy.

—William Borden

KELLY, M(ilton) T(errence)

Nationality: Canadian. **Born:** Toronto, 30 November 1946. **Education:** Glendon College, York University, B.A. 1970; University of Toronto, B.Ed. 1976. **Family:** Married Lynn King, two sons. **Career:** Since 1970 journalist; since 1989, contributor and interviewer, TVO's Imprint. **Awards:** Books in Canada's Best First Novel award, 1978; Governor General's award for literature, 1987. **Member:** Champlain Society.

PUBLICATIONS

Novels

I Do Remember the Fall. Toronto, Simon and Pierre, 1978.
The Ruined Season. Windsor, Ontario, Black Moss Press, 1982.
A Dream Like Mine. Don Mills, Ontario, Stoddart, 1987; New York, Warner, 1992.
Out of the Whirlwind. Don Mills, Ontario, Stoddart, 1995.

Short Stories

The More Loving One. Windsor, Ontario, Black Moss Press, 1980.
Breath Dances Between Them: Stories by M.T. Kelly. Don Mills, Ontario, Stoddart, 1991.

Plays

The Green Dolphin, Toronto, Playwrights Canada, n.d.

Screenplay: *Clearcut,* 1991.

Television Play: *Wildfire, The Legend of Tom Longboat,* 1983.

Poetry

Country You Can't Walk In. Waterloo, Ontario, Penumbra Press, 1979; as *Country You Can't Walk In and Other Poems,* Waterloo, Ontario, Penumbra Press, 1984.

*

Manuscript Collection: National Library of Canada, Ottawa.

*   *   *

From *I Do Remember the Fall* to *Out of the Whirlwind,* the course of M.T. Kelly's work has seen consistent preoccupations and decisive changes of direction. Constant to his work has been a Celtic lyricism, an extraordinary porousness to landscape and the weather, and characters who rub each other raw emotionally and, in related fashion, are viscerally obsessed with odors, textures, and the physiological states of their own and others' bodies. Yet there have been changes, too. Stylistically, Kelly's syntax, at first almost Faulknerian, has been greatly simplified. The psychological concerns of his early work have broadened into more public, even political, expressions. For example, the distinctive treatment of female characters—ambiguous goddesses deeply troubling to men yet rendered with great empathy—remains constant, but social and ecological issues also become involved. As well, there has been a kindred shift in locales: Since 1977 more and more of his work has been placed outside Toronto, scene of his play *The Green Dolphin* and the stories of *The More Loving One* and *Breath Dances Between Us,* and outside urban areas generally. Thus *I Do Remember the Fall* is chiefly set in small-city Saskatchewan, but *The Ruined Season* (and the poetry collection *Country You Can't Walk In*) takes place in northern Ontario, *A Dream Like Mine* on an Indian reserve in northwestern Ontario, and *Out of the Whirlwind* in the Northwest Territories.

Such settings both aid and hinder Kelly's characters in working out their destinies. In the title novella of *The More Loving One,* John Cooper dabbles in the shallow waters of psychodrama, shucks off his marriage for the sake of a new woman, but finds that she can only truly live in his mind's eye: In this and the collection's other stories, sensations tell painful truths. In the often hilarious *I Do Remember the Fall,* the self-mocking Randy Gogarty moves toward a better understanding of himself amid low comedy, vocational intrigues, and poignant domestic politics. For Michael Leary, the protagonist of *The Ruined Season,* northern Ontario is "the empty country of his imagination," and its rocks, rivers, and black spruce compel him to take new bearings. Kelly's most popularly and critically successful novel has been *A Dream Like Mine,* which won the 1987 Governor General's Award. With cinematic vividness (it was in fact filmed as *Clearcut* in 1989, directed by Richard Bugiski and starring Iroquois actor Grahame Greene), the novel takes on a polluting paper mill and a retaliatory kidnapping as well as, more broadly, the world of Indian spirituality, sometimes in scenes of great power, more rarely lapsing into authorial special pleading.

However, Kelly's best work may be his most recent: *Out of The Whirlwind* (the title is taken from the *Book of Job*), tells of the ill-fated canoe expedition of three Torontonians and a northern Alberta teenager and unites such Kelly themes as claustrophobic human conflict and the absolute otherness of nature. With great compression—the book is barely longer than a novella—it achieves the understated wisdom and poetic force of a New Testament parable.

In his response to the north—a mingled awe, reverence, and terror—as well as his attitudes toward wildlife and indigenous peoples, Kelly somewhat resembles many other Canadian writers in that his work elaborates the archetypes (or stereotypes) some critics have specified as distinctive to Canada. But his style and psychosexual preoccupations mark him as one of a kind.

—Fraser Sutherland

KELMAN, James

Nationality: Scottish. **Born:** Glasgow, 9 June 1946. **Education:** Greenfield School, Stonedyke School, and Hyndland School, all Glasgow, 1951-61. University of Strathclyde, Glasgow, 1975-78, 1981-82. **Family:** Married Marie Connors in 1969; two daughters. **Career:** Has worked at a variety of semi-skilled and labouring jobs. Scottish Arts Council Writing fellowship, 1978-80, 1982-85. **Awards:** Scottish Arts Council bursary, 1973, 1980, and book award, 1983, 1987, 1989; Cheltenham prize, 1987; James Tait Black Memorial prize, 1990; Booker McConnell Prize, 1994. **Agent:** Cathie Thomson, 23 Hillhead Street, Glasgow G12. **Address:** 244 West Princess Street, Glasgow G4 9DP, Scotland.

PUBLICATIONS

Novels

The Busconductor Hines. Edinburgh, Polygon Press, 1984.
A Chancer. Edinburgh, Polygon Press, 1985.
A Disaffection. London, Secker and Warburg, and New York, Farrar Straus, 1989.
How Late It Was, How Late. London, Secker and Warburg, 1994.

Short Stories

An Old Pub Near the Angel. Orono, Maine, Puckerbrush Press, 1973.
Three Glasgow Writers, with Tom Leonard and Alex Hamilton. Glasgow, Molendinar Press, 1976.
Short Tales from the Nightshift. Glasgow, Print Studio Press, 1978.
Not Not While the Giro and Other Stories. Edinburgh, Polygon Press, 1983.
Lean Tales, with Alasdair Gray and Agnes Owens. London, Cape, 1985.
Greyhound for Breakfast. London, Secker and Warburg, and New York, Farrar Straus, 1987.
The Burn. London, Secker and Warburg, 1991.

Plays

The Busker (produced Edinburgh, 1985).
Le Rodeur, adaptation of the play by Enzo Cormann (produced Edinburgh, 1987).
In the Night (produced Stirling, 1988).
Hardie and Baird: The Last Days (produced Edinburgh, 1990). London, Secker and Warburg, 1991.

Radio Play: *Hardie and Baird: The Last Days,* 1978.

Screenplay: *The Return,* 1990.

Other

Some Recent Attacks: Essays Cultural and Political. Stirling, Scotland, AK Press, 1992.

Editor, *An East End Anthology.* Glasgow, Clydeside Press, 1988.

*

Manuscript Collection: Mitchell Library, Glasgow.

Critical Studies: "Patter Merchants and Chancers: Recent Glasgow Writing" in *Planet* (Aberystwyth), no. 60, 1986-87, and article in *New Welsh Review,* (Aberystwyth), no. 10, 1990, both by Ian A. Bell.

James Kelman comments:

Glasgow is a post-industrial city; its culture comprises many different cultural traditions: I work within this.

*   *   *

James Kelman has established himself as one of the most compelling new voices in British fiction. Combining intense local affiliation with the west of Scotland and great stylistic inventiveness, he represents commitment and integrity, frankness and exuberance, and has been compared with Kafka and Beckett. His first novel, *The Busconductor Hines* takes a sombre subject, but articulates its central character through a mixture of impersonal reports and stream-of-consciousness imaginings. Kelman ignores the conventions of orthodox "realist" fiction in favour of a kaleidoscopic juxtaposition of fact and fantasy, in tribute to the imaginative capacities of "ordinary people." Here is a sample:

> Life is too serious.
> Hunch the shoulders and march. The furtively fast figure. One fine morning Hines R. was arrested. Crackle crackle crackle. We have this fantasy coming through on the line sir should we tape it and hold it against him or what. Naw but honest sir he's just a lowly member of the transport experience; he slept in a little and perforce is obliged to walk it to work, having missed the bastarn omnibus. A certain irony granted but nothing more, no significance of any insurrectionary nature.

It may be tempting to read this as a purely formal experiment, and relax into appreciating the multivocal texture of the writing. However, the stylistic extravaganza is always at the service of a purposive exploration of Hines's world, and the book retains its human centre in moving descriptions of Hines at work and at home.

Kelman's second novel, *A Chancer,* adopts a different approach. It portrays a young man without qualities, with no attempt to investigate what goes on inside his head. Instead, it narrates his day-to-day existence as he drifts and gambles—a perennial interest of Kelman's—without overt or coercive authorial intrusion. The novel is interspersed with brief scenes where Kelman scrupulously describes events, and just as scrupulously keeps his distance. Such reluctance to invade his character's privacy is yet another way of resisting the pseudo-omniscience of more conventional third person narrative. It challenges us to make sense of events, without allowing us any special privileges. The formal features are not decorative, but are ways of identifying the limits of knowledge. What we eventually see through the sombre narrative is a life of purposelessness and indecision, lived within day-to-day privations, invigorated by the austerity of its unadorned, skeletal telling.

In his collections of short fictions, *Greyhound for Breakfast* and *The Burn,* Kelman shows more of his range. Some stories are brief vignettes, less than a page long, an anecdotal form he has experimented with from his earliest full collection—*Not Not While the Giro*—onwards. Others are more elaborately developed, in alter-

nating moods of wit, exhilaration, exasperation, and despair. They are certainly the most diverse and exuberant collections of recent years, with the power and intensity and wit of the prose encapsulating very large social and political concerns within miniaturist sketches.

"Greyhound for Breakfast" is an exceptional piece, showing the author at his best. Without ornament, it recounts a couple of hours in the life of a character and his newly-acquired greyhound. It sounds comic, a not-very-shaggy dog story, but it is not. Ronnie has bought the dog for more money than he really has, and as the day goes on he can find no good reason for having done so. He had a half-formed idea of entering it in races, but this soon seems ridiculous. As he wanders, more and more of his life begins to look absurd. He has no job, no proper communication with his wife, his son has just left home, and the whole business of living seems meaningless. As the story ends, the narrative drifts into a wonderfully controlled and frightening stream-of-consciousness reverie. The nihilism is deeply unsettling, representing the inarticulate yearnings and unsatisfied desires of an ordinary man undergoing the alienations of contemporary urban life. Kelman's language is of necessity frank, but never gratuitously so, dramatising the painful struggle towards articulacy of the most complex emotions. The dog is used as a symbol, but to call it that suggests a cruder, more schematic technique than Kelman offers. The story is typically suggestive, enigmatic, and nuanced. Without overly directive authorial intervention, the connections between individual lives and the circumstances which prescribe them are made. Although Kelman's work is insistently angry, it is angry on behalf of his subjects, rather than exasperated with them.

The same intensity and the same humanity can be found in Kelman's 1989 novel, *A Disaffection,* which returns to the fabric of interior and exterior description. This book puts on display a Glasgow school teacher at the moment when he sees the paucity of his own life. It offers an engagement with the traditional concerns of the social realist novel, but also a more tense mixture of moods than in comparable work by David Storey or Alan Sillitoe. Kelman uses his very flexible style to move inside and outside Doyle's head, to maintain scrupulous attention to him and his fantasies. The novel becomes an unsentimental education, taking us through Doyle's crisis of confidence. Although it is an attack on the constraints and hypocrisies of the State educational system, it is a much more broadly-based revelation of a culture clinging onto the vestiges of its self-esteem.

Doyle's yearnings for something better, represented by the strange pair of pipes he finds and his unsatisfied fancy for a fellow-teacher, become a way of intensifying and demonstrating not only Doyle's own malaise, but also broader national circumstances. At times, the political leanings are explicit. Kelman uses the book to insinuate a disturbing critique of those who believe in the possibilities of change from within. Doyle struggles all the way through under the pressures to effect change, pressures which are much greater than he fully realises. In very powerful scenes with his parents and his unemployed brother, he enacts his alienation from the conditions of their lives, yet he has found nothing to replace their dignity. In the classroom and the staffroom, the futility of trying to educate people genuinely in circumstances so adverse is made very clear.

Yet the book is neither a simple diatribe, nor a purely personal vision. Kelman introduces complex framing devices through Doyle's interests in Hölderlin and Pythagorean philosophy. As in *The Busconductor Hines* the author seems very close to his character, but these references, like the frequent allusions to Hamlet, are ways of introducing new perspectives, and encouraging distance. At times, Kelman shows a Swiftian taste for irony, using that form as the only possible way of coping with the revealed awfulness of the world. We are not allowed to hold Doyle in contempt, and the sharp oscillations in the narrative between wit and horror are both compulsive and disturbing.

In 1994 Kelman's novel *How Late It Was, How Late* won the Booker McConnell Prize, a highly prestigious award. Yet this harrowing tale of blindness and affliction provoked an extraordinary controversy in Britain. Unable to see the book's deep humanity, many critics castigated its harsh language and its intense concentration on the lives of the dispossessed. *How Late It Was, How Late* is Kelman's toughest book yet, his most clearly focussed and uncompromising. His fascinating style, combining the darkest humour with glimpses of the horror of everyday life, allows him to produce narratives capable of the caustic and the tender, the intimate and the aloof. Moving in and out of the central figure's consciousness makes possible a fully human realisation of an individual's plight, and a recognition of the material circumstances that impose such pressure. More recently, Kelman has written plays (notably *Hardie and Baird*) and numerous political pamphlets, and his development is clearly continuing.

—Ian A. Bell

KENEALLY, Thomas (Michael)

Nationality: Australian. **Born:** Sydney, New South Wales, 7 October 1935. **Education:** St. Patrick's College, Strathfield, New South Wales; studied for the priesthood 1953-60, and studied law. **Military Service:** Australian Citizens Military Forces. **Family:** Married Judith Mary Martin in 1965; two daughters. **Career:** High school teacher in Sydney, 1960-64; lecturer in drama, University of New England, Armidale, New South Wales, 1968-69; lived in the U.S., 1975-77; visiting professor of English, University of California, Irvine, 1985; Berg Professor of English, New York University, 1988. **Member:** Australia-China Council, 1978-83; member of the advisory panel, Australian Constitutional Commission, 1985-88; member, Australian Literary Arts Board, 1985-88; president, National Book Council of Australia, 1985-89; chairman, Australian Society of Authors, 1987. **Awards:** Commonwealth Literary Fund fellowship, 1966, 1968, 1972; Miles Franklin award, 1968, 1969; Captain Cook Bicentenary prize, 1970; Royal Society of Literature Heinemann award, 1973; Booker prize, 1982; Los Angeles *Times* award, 1983;. Fellow, Royal Society of Literature, 1973, American Academy of Arts and Sciences, 1993; Officer, Order of Australia, 1983. **Agent:** Deborah Rogers, Rogers, Colleridge and White, 20 Powis Mews, London W11 1JN, England.

PUBLICATIONS

Novels

The Place at Whitton. Melbourne and London, Cassell, 1964; New York, Walker, 1965.
The Fear. Melbourne and London, Cassell, 1965; as *By the Line,* St. Lucia, University of Queensland Press, 1989.

Bring Larks and Heroes. Melbourne, Cassell, 1967; London, Cassell, and New York, Viking Press, 1968.
Three Cheers for the Paraclete. Sydney, Angus and Robertson, 1968; London, Angus and Robertson, and New York, Viking Press, 1969.
The Survivor. Sydney, Angus and Robertson, 1969; London, Angus and Robertson, and New York, Viking Press, 1970.
A Dutiful Daughter. Sydney and London, Angus and Robertson, and New York, Viking Press, 1971.
The Chant of Jimmie Blacksmith. Sydney and London, Angus and Robertson, and New York, Viking Press, 1972.
Blood Red, Sister Rose. London, Collins, and New York, Viking Press, 1974.
Moses the Lawgiver (novelization of television play). London, Collins-ATV, and New York, Harper, 1975.
Gossip from the Forest. London, Collins, 1975; New York, Harcourt Brace, 1976.
Season in Purgatory. London, Collins, 1976; New York, Harcourt Brace, 1977.
A Victim of the Aurora. London, Collins, 1977; New York, Harcourt Brace, 1978.
Passenger. London, Collins, and New York, Harcourt Brace, 1979.
Confederates. London, Collins, 1979; New York, Harper, 1980.
The Cut-Rate Kingdom. Sydney, Wildcat Press, 1980; London, Allen Lane, 1984.
Schindler's Ark. London, Hodder and Stoughton, 1982; as *Schindler's List,* New York, Simon and Schuster, 1982.
A Family Madness. London, Hodder and Stoughton, 1985; New York, Simon and Schuster, 1986.
The Playmaker. London, Hodder and Stoughton, and New York, Simon and Schuster, 1987.
Towards Asmara. London, Hodder and Stoughton, 1989; as *To Asmara,* New York, Warner, 1989.
Flying Hero Class. London, Hodder and Stoughton, and New York, Warner, 1991.
Woman of the Inner Sea. N.p., Doubleday and Hodder, 1992.
Jacko. N.p., Heinemann, 1993.
A River Town. London, Reed Books, 1995.

Uncollected Short Story

"The Performing Blind Boy," in *Festival and Other Stories,* edited by Brian Buckley and Jim Hamilton. Melbourne, Wren, 1974; Newton Abbot, Devon, David and Charles, 1975.

Plays

Halloran's Little Boat, adaptation of his novel *Bring Larks and Heroes* (produced Sydney, 1966). Published in *Penguin Australian Drama 2,* Melbourne, Penguin, 1975.
Childermass (produced Sydney, 1968).
An Awful Rose (produced Sydney, 1972).
Bullie's House (produced Sydney, 1980; New Haven, Connecticut, 1985). Sydney, Currency Press, 1981.
Gossip from the Forest, adaptation of his own novel (produced 1983).

Screenplays: *The Priest* (episode in *Libido*), 1973; *Silver City,* with Sophia Turkiewicz, 1985.

Television Writing (UK): *Essington,* 1974; *The World's Wrong End* (documentary; *Writers and Places* series), 1981; *Australia* series, 1987.

Other

Ned Kelly and the City of Bees (for children). London, Cape, 1978; Boston, Godine, 1981.

Outback, photographs by Gary Hansen and Mark Lang. Sydney and London, Hodder and Stoughton, 1983.

Australia: Beyond the Dreamtime, with Patsy Adam-Smith and Robyn Davidson. London, BBC Publications, 1987; New York, Facts on File, 1989.

Child of Australia (song), music by Peter Sculthorpe. London, Faber Music, 1987.

Now and in Time to Be: Ireland and the Irish, photographs by Patrick Prendergast. N.p., Panmacmillan, n.p., Ryan, and n.p., Norton, 1992.

*

Manuscript Collections: Mitchell Library, Sydney; Australian National Library, Canberra.

Critical Study: *Thomas Keneally* by Peter Quartermaine, London, Arnold, 1991.

Theatrical Activities:

Actor: **Films**—*The Devil's Playground,* 1976; *The Chant of Jimmie Blacksmith,* 1978.

Thomas Keneally comments:

(1972) I would like to be able to disown my first two novels, the second of which was the obligatory account of one's childhood—the book then that all novelists think seriously of writing.

I see my third novel as an attempt to follow out an epic theme in terms of a young soldier's exile to Australia.

The fourth and fifth were attempts at urbane writing in the traditional mode of the English novel: confrontations between characters whose behaviour shows layers of irony and humour, in which all that is epic is rather played down.

For *A Dutiful Daughter,* the best novel I have written (not that I claim that matters much), I have turned to myth and fable, as many a novelist is doing, for the simple reason that other media have moved into the traditional areas of the novel.

(1986) I can see now that a great deal of my work has been concerned with the contrast between the new world—in particular Australia—and the old; the counterpoint between the fairly innocent politics of the new world and the fatal politics of Europe. One of the most remarkable phenomena of my lifetime has been the decline of both the British Empire and the European dominance in the world. As a colonial, I was just getting used to these two phenomena and adjusting my soul to them when they vanished, throwing into doubt the idea that artists from the remote antipodes must go into the northern hemisphere to find their spiritual source and forcing me to reassess my place in the world as an Australian.

Blood Red, Sister Rose, for example, concerned a European aboriginal, a potent maker of magic, Joan of Arc. *Gossip from the Forest* concerned the war, World War I, by which Europe began its own self destruction. These books are characteristic of my middle period, the historical phase, when in a way, coming from a fairly innocent and unbloodied society, I was trying to work Europe out. There was some of this too in *Schindler's Ark.* In my last book, *A Family Madness,* you have Australian ingenuousness and the ancient, complicated and malicious politics of Eastern Europe standing cheek by jowl.

I feel it is significant that *A Family Madness* is set in 1985. I believe the historic phase is nearly over for me and was merely a preparation for the understanding of the present. Time—and future work—will tell.

*   *   *

With twenty-one novels published over the past four decades, Thomas Keneally has grown to be one of Australia's most interesting, as well as its most prolific, novelists. His work is noted for its range of material, from his most familiar setting, Australia's past, to such various subjects as Joan of Arc, the American Civil War, the Holocaust, and contemporary Africa. Despite his diverse subjects, however, Keneally brings a consistently humanistic point of view, an eye for accuracy of detail, and a knack for engaging storytelling, all of which account both for his wide readership and critical acclaim.

Australia's colonial relation to Britain provides the setting for *The Playmaker* (adapted by Timberlake Wertenbaker for the stage as *Our Country's Good*). Keneally uses a seemingly insignificant detail from the history of the Sydney Cove prison and converts it into a compelling metaphor for his country's birth. When an idealistic British officer is asked to stage Farquhar's restoration comedy *The Recruiting Officer* with a cast of convicts, he, they, and we come to a new understanding of the meaning of human dignity and freedom. A less uplifting account of Australia's past is *The Chant of Jimmy Blacksmith,* also inspired by a real event in Australian history. The imposition of European ways on one aborigine leads to his ritualistic killing of a number of white women, and while we never feel that we really enter the mind of the title character, this distance between character and reader is precisely the effect Keneally sought. The Australian setting is also dominant in *Woman of the Inner Sea,* whose sophisticated heroine, having lost her two children in a fire, finds in the basic values of the Outback the strength to confront her grief and throw off her unwarranted guilt. Again in his most recent novel, *A River Town,* Keneally uses the origin of a rural settlement to convey the essential identity of Australia: outcasts coming together to form a community and, through their diversity, to define a national character.

When it is not the primary setting, Australia is often involved indirectly in Keneally's novels, such as *Passenger,* in which the story of an Irish girl's pregnancy is narrated by her unborn child. While living in London, she is writing a historical novel about a group of Irish prisoners being transported to Australia for their part in the Rebellion of 1798. The determination of the fetal narrator to survive parallels that of the Irish rebels, and, in fact, the birth eventually does take place in Australia. The influence of history is also apparent in *A Family Madness* in which an Australian worker falls in love with his boss's daughter and becomes involved with their haunted past in Byelorussia during World War II. Keneally uses the double plot structure again in *To Asmara* where the Eritrean guerrilla war against Ethiopia mirrors the prior struggles of the main character, the journalist Darcy, to reconcile his European heritage with his determination to help the Australian tribes. In all these novels Keneally's native Australia is a vital presence regardless of where the story takes his characters.

When Keneally chooses historical material from foreign sources, the effect is usually less engaging. *Blood Red, Sister Rose,* his version of the Joan of Arc legend, and *Confederates,* set in Northern Virginia during the summer of 1862, both feature typical Keneally heroes—realistically earthy characters caught up in the historical moment—but despite a wealth of historical detail, neither the Maid of Orleans nor the Virginian farmer-turned-soldier really seem to live in their respective worlds. Even Stonewall Jackson, who figures prominently in *Confederates,* has more Australian pluck than Southern grit in him.

Two novels dealing with the world wars, on the other hand, display considerable insight and power. The diplomats in *Gossip from the Forest,* gathered at Compiegne in the fall of 1918 to negotiate an armistice, are compelling characters. The cultured German delegate, Matthias Erzbergen, finds himself in an impossible political bind, as he tries to deal with the imperious Marshall Foch, who takes full advantage of his superior position. The tenuous political alliances of the period are reflected in the negotiations at Compiegne, with the tragic realization that an opportunity for peace is lost and another war becomes inevitable. Even more compelling is *Schindler's List,* the story of a Catholic industrialist who ran an arms factory using workers from concentration camps. The Oskar Schindler of Keneally's novel is as enigmatic as the man seems to have been in life, conveying no sense of high moral principle even while he was saving hundreds of Polish Jews by convincing the gullible Nazis that his factory's productivity depended on their labor. The narrative voice in *Schindler's List* is detached and distant, as if Keneally is determined to allow Schindler to maintain his privacy, a hero we need not like or even understand. This fascinating ambiguity of character was lost in Stephen Spielberg's popular film based on Keneally's book.

The clash of cultures, a recurring theme in Keneally's work, dominates *Flying Hero Class,* in which an airplane carrying Barramatjara tribal dancers from New York to Frankfurt is hijacked by a group of Palestinians. The hijackers try to convince the aborigines that theirs is a common cause, but without much success. The danger is averted by the courage of Frank McCloud, the troupe's manager and supposed exploiter. Although contrived, the novel summarizes Keneally's ambivalence toward cultural assimilation. Rejecting the comforting liberal assumption that cultural diversity is to be cherished and celebrated, he more often shows the inevitability of misunderstanding and conflict when cultures collide, whether it be as direct as the murderous outburst of a Jimmie Blacksmith or as subtle as the Australian journalist's inability to express his emotions to an Eritrean woman in *To Asmara.*

Given his steady output and his often risky choices of material, Keneally has maintained a remarkable level of quality in his work, which, at its very best—as in *The Playmaker* and *Schindler's List*— is a testament to the power of the historical imagination and to the novelist's craft.

—Robert E. Lynch

KENNEDY, A.L.

Nationality: Scottish.

PUBLICATIONS

Novels

Looking for the Possible Dance. London, Secker and Warburg, 1993.

So I Am Glad. London, Cape, 1995.

Short Stories

Night Geometry and the Garscadden Trains. London, Secker and Warburg, 1990.
Now That You're Back. London, Cape, 1994.

Other

Editor, with James McGonigal. *A Sort of Hot Scotland.* Aberdeen: Association for Scottish Literary Studies, 1994.
Editor, with Hamish Whyte. *The Ghost of Liberace.* Aberdeen: Association for Scottish Literary Studies, 1993.

*   *   *

Throughout her work to date, Scottish writer A.L. Kennedy has explored the potentially infinite spaces within "ordinary" people's minds. Kennedy's novels and short stories focus on the mental and emotional confinement that is caused by isolation, psychic and physical violence within personal relationships, and enclosure within the ritualized routines of "the average shape of the day." These conditions are frequently met with an obsessive striving for control and the repetition of violence. Yet Kennedy's works also express a yearning for connection and an almost religious sense of the expansiveness of human life as glimpses are gained of a potentiality that exceeds the trammels of the quotidian. Her characters frequently represent a desire to perceive a larger, more harmonious pattern beyond both their own psychic turmoil and the apparent political and social chaos of the late twentieth century.

These concerns are introduced in Kennedy's first collection of short stories, *Night Geometry and the Garscadden Trains.* Here, in her already notably economic style, Kennedy writes of "small people" who, "withered by lack of belief," "live their lives in the best way they can with generally good intentions and still leave absolutely nothing behind." In her second collection of short stories, *Now That You're Back,* Kennedy, returning to the minds of "small people," explores the fine distinctions between normality and perversity as she probes the points at which isolation and estrangement produce what is perceived as obsession and deviance. As Kennedy ventriloquizes her characters' voices, several of the stories being written in the form of dramatic monologues, she confers upon them an impression of bodilessness, a fitting signifier of their disconnection from the world. Yet her characters seek that correspondence through which "a spasm of what I might call completeness" may be attained.

Kennedy retains her focus on subtle gradations of psychic spaces in her first novel, *Looking for the Possible Dance,* where she explores the way in which her protagonist's relationship with her father inscribes that with her lover. Here, as in her other works, Kennedy's exploration of parental legacy is allusive rather than diagnostic as she displays the proximity between pleasure and pain, particularly the pleasure that is sought through self-denial. Through one of the novel's central structural metaphors, that of the dance, Kennedy weaves together several of the novel's main concerns. Margaret's father's words at a Methodist ceilidh are echoed in her reflection that the search for meaningful political opposition in Britain in the 1980s was "looking for the possible dance, the step, the move to beat them all." The possibility that the discrete spaces that individuals occupy may be choreographed into an overarching pattern is adumbrated by the novel's concluding image: "Margaret walks to one door and sinks into brilliant air, becoming first a moving shadow, then a curve, a dancing line."

The concerns of Kennedy's earlier works are strikingly elaborated in her most recent novel, *So I Am Glad*. Like the characters of her short stories, Kennedy's narrator, Jennifer Wilson, has learned "to enjoy a small, still life," achieving a "calmness" that is "empty space . . . a pause." Having been made a voyeur, as a child, of her parents' violent sexual practices, she now pathologizes other people's emotions as "moles . . . violent, tunnelling mammals." Jennifer's desire to free herself from her body and its emotional history is facilitated by her work as a radio commentator, a "professional enunciator." The novel recounts her attempt to discover the identity of her lover who, it transpires, is Cyrano de Bergerac, reincarnated in late-20th-century Scotland. This fantastic device enables Kennedy to explore further a number of the concerns of her earlier works. De Bergerac becomes a vehicle for metaphysical speculation that is the more poignant as it is incorporated into Jennifer's mourning for his inevitable loss and her search for the words to articulate this. Through de Bergerac's estranged perspective, he is able to comment on the "madness" of the late 20th century, defamiliarizing horrors to which, it is implied, the reader may have become acculturated. De Bergerac's history of dueling is extended through his verbal parrying with Jennifer as he explains, "The point is that single moment when you truly touch another person. You reach to them with a word, a thought, a gesture." The duel codifies the desire for violence that is elsewhere in the narrative less successfully contained, whether in scenes of sadomasochistic sex or the political atrocities that are the subject of Jennifer's news broadcasts.

In *So I Am Glad*, as in Kennedy's earlier works, the movement between the personal and the political, between the poetic and the polemic, is uneven, the power of Kennedy's work lying in her painterly detailing of psychic spaces rather than in the large brush strokes with which she comments on the political turbulence of recent decades. Her work is, however, already notable for its combination of wit, precision, and restraint with bold imaginative gestures.

—Joanna Price

KENNEDY, William (Joseph)

Nationality: American. **Born:** Albany, New York, 16 January 1928. **Education:** Siena College, Loudonville, New York, B.A. 1949. **Military Service:** Served in the United States Army, 1950-52: sports editor and columnist for Army newspapers. **Family:** Married Ana Daisy Dana Segarra in 1957; two daughters and one son. **Career:** Assistant sports editor and columnist, Glens Falls *Post Star,* New York, 1949-50; reporter, Albany *Times-Union,* 1952-56; assistant managing editor and columnist, *Puerto Rico World Journal,* San Juan, 1956; reporter, Miami *Herald,* 1957; Puerto Rico correspondent for Time-Life publications, and reporter for Dorvillier business newsletter and Knight newspapers, 1957-59; founding managing editor, San Juan *Star,* 1959-61; full-time writer, 1961-63; special writer, 1963-70, and film critic, 1968-70, Albany *Times-Union;* book editor, *Look,* New York, 1971. Lecturer, 1974-82, and since 1983 professor of English, State University of New York, Albany; visiting professor of English, Cornell University, Ithaca, New York,

1982-83. Since 1957 freelance magazine writer and critic; brochure and special project writer for New York State Department of Education and State University system, New York Governor's Conference on Libraries, and other organizations; director, New York State Writers Institute. **Awards:** Puerto Rican Civic Association of Miami award, 1957, NAACP award, 1965, Newspaper Guild Page One award, 1965, and New York State Publishers award, 1965, all for reporting; National Endowment for the Arts fellowship, 1981; Siena College Career Achievement award, 1983; MacArthur Foundation fellowship, 1983; National Book Critics Circle award, 1984; Celtic Foundation Frank O'Connor award, 1984; Before Columbus Foundation award, 1984; New York Public Library award, 1984; Pulitzer prize, 1984; Governor's Arts award, 1984; Brandeis University Creative Arts award, 1986. L.H.D.: Russell Sage College, Troy, New York, 1980; Siena College, 1984; Rensselaer Polytechnic Institute, Troy, New York, 1987; Long Island University, Greenvale, New York, 1989; D.Litt.: College of St. Rose, Albany, 1985. D.H.L.: Skidmore College, 1991; Fordham University, 1992; Trinity College, 1992. Commander, Order of Arts and Letters, France, 1993. **Agent:** Liz Darhansoff Literary Agency, 1220 Park Avenue, New York, New York 10128. **Address:** R.D. 3, Box 508, Averill Park, New York 12018, U.S.A.

PUBLICATIONS

Novels

The Ink Truck. New York, Dial Press, 1969; London, Macdonald, 1970.
Legs. New York, Coward McCann, 1975; London, Cape, 1976.
Billy Phelan's Greatest Game. New York, Viking Press, 1978; London, Penguin, 1983.
Ironweed. New York, Viking Press, 1983; London, Penguin, 1984.
Quinn's Book. New York, Viking, and London, Cape, 1988.
Very Old Bones. New York, Viking, 1992.

Uncollected Short Stories

"The Secrets of Creative Love," in *Harper's* (New York), July 1983.
"An Exchange of Gifts," in *Glens Falls Review* (Glens Falls, New York), no. 3, 1985-86.
"The Hills and the Creeks (Albany 1850)," in *Harper's* (New York), March 1988.

Plays

The Cotton Club (screenplay), with Francis Ford Coppola. New York, St. Martin's Press, 1986.

Screenplay: *The Cotton Club,* with Francis Ford Coppola, 1984; *Ironweed,* 1987.

Other

Getting It All, Saving It All: Some Notes by an Extremist. Albany, New York State Governor's Conference on Libraries, 1978.
O Albany! Improbable City of Political Wizards, Fearless Ethnics, Spectacular Aristocrats, Splendid Nobodies, and Underrated Scoundrels. Albany and New York, Washington Park Press-Viking Press, 1983.

The Capitol in Albany (photographs). New York, Aperture, 1986; as *Albany and the Capitol,* London, Phaidon, 1986.
Charlie Malarkey and the Belly Button Machine (for children), with Brendan Kennedy. Boston, Atlantic Monthly Press, 1986; London, Cape, 1987.
Charlie Malarkey and the Singing Moose (for children), with Brendan Kennedy. Viking Children's Books, 1994.
Riding the Yellow Trolley Car. New York, Viking, 1993.

*

Bibliography: "A William Kennedy Bibliography" by Edward C. Reilly, in *Bulletin of Bibliography* 48(2), June 1991.

Critical Studies: "The Sudden Fame of William Kennedy" by Margaret Croyden, in *New York Times Magazine,* 26 August 1984; *Understanding William Kennedy* by J.K. Van Dover, Columbia, University of South Carolina Press, 1991; *William Kennedy* by Edward C. Reilly, Boston, Twayne, 1991.

*   *   *

In *O Albany!,* William Kennedy's "urban biography" of Albany, New York, he describes himself as "a person whose imagination has become fused with a single place." This fusion has proved an impressive resource and theme in his novels which present an expansive yet intimate fictional and historical tableau of Albany life. While there is a humanist breadth of vision in Kennedy's writings—he views Albany as a city "centered squarely in the American and human continuum"—his treatment of the city is closely focused on the lives and histories of Irish-Americans. His novels pay detailed attention to the culture and politics of this ethnic group, exploring both the local historical conditions and the internal mechanisms of ethnic identity, and illuminating the rich interplay of history, myth, and memory as these give meaning to the lives of Irish-Americans.

Kennedy offers his readers a richly detailed world where language is always inventive. The interactions of realism and romance, and of historical and mythical vision in his novels have led many critics to describe them as "magic realist." The lyrical treatment of larger-than-life characters and use of vernacular humor also suggest the influences of American strains of imaginative journalism and oral storytelling. If there is a "magic" in the narratives it is the sense of intimacy they convey. The sounding of a common past and shared memories is an important element in Kennedy's writings and in having places, characters, and everyday objects animated by reminiscence and anecdote he shows how the past may be kept alive in "memory and hearsay." Kennedy's first novel, *The Ink Truck,* is a black comedy which details the pathetic attempts of a small group of strikers to keep alive a failed strike against their newspaper employers. The true center of the novel is Bailey, a garrulous loner who invents crazy plots to challenge the newspaper company. Like the other strikers, Bailey is caught in the paradoxes of ideal and action which emerge from supporting a lost cause, but Kennedy draws his protagonist with an irrepressible energy and wit which mark his repeated failures with curious heroism. Although there is clearly a satirical intention to illuminate the way American society can both foster and thwart idealism, the narrative relies a little too heavily on the egotistical rhetoric and surreal imaginings of Bailey. If he is a failed hero there is little to draw the reader into his predicament.

Legs deals with a form of hero in the character of Jack "Legs" Diamond, the prohibition gangster-cum-celebrity whose life story is narrated by Marcus Gorman, a lawyer who is simultaneously attracted to and perturbed by this "venal man of integrity." Diamond is an entertainer who is able to act out his fantasies and appetites in public, only to find that he is "created anew" by the media who draw on, add to, and manipulate his glamour. Kennedy interweaves history and myth in his characterization of Diamond as a powerful public figure who finds that fame is not a force he can control: "Jack had imagined his fame all his life and now it was imagining him." Kennedy uses Gorman to mediate the multiple and conflicting documents, stories and cultural references surrounding Diamond's life. *Legs* is less a close study of what motivated this particular criminal than an examination of how he became a product of America's "collective imagination." In *Billy Phelan's Greatest Game* Kennedy shows a more localized interest in how memory and myth circulate in the everyday actions and discourses of Albany's Irish-Americans in the 1930s. Billy Phelan, a young Irish-American hustler, has his world turned upside down when he is caught up in the kidnapping of Charlie McCall, son of the city's political boss. While Kennedy keeps the kidnap plot moving steadily along it is clear that his real interest is in exploring how an ethnic past is absorbed into the present day lives of his characters. Billy's encounters with the McCalls reveal a political network which maintains its power by endorsing and exploiting a rhetoric of family, morality, and loyalty that draws heavily on mythicized immigrant experiences. Kennedy also identifies rich seams of a common or collective memory which establishes a knowledge of the past in stories and anecdotes engendered by commonplace stimuli. In detailing and juxtaposing multiple rememorisations of the Irish-American past he shows how all members of the ethnic group, not only the politically powerful, are engaged in reconstructing the past to meet the demands of the present.

Ironweed, a Pulitzer prize-winner, is widely viewed as Kennedy's finest novel to date. The novel is closely connected to *Billy Phelan's Greatest Game* in terms of character, event, theme, and temporal setting. Francis Phelan, father of Billy and the "Ironweed" of the title, is a vagrant who returns to Albany after 22 years "on the bum," a partly self-induced exile sustained by the guilt he feels about the deaths of a scab he felled during a strike and of his 13-day-old son Gerald whom he accidentally dropped and killed. On his return to Albany he confronts voices and images of ghosts which press him to re-examine his past. Returning to a community which has projected him into myth Francis reaches no clear resolution of his need to locate himself "in time and place," but he does discover that in releasing memories and sharing them with others he is able tentatively to embrace much that he has repressed. Kennedy brilliantly meshes fantasy and realism in this narrative, examining both the inner confusions of his protagonist's ethnic identity and the powerful cultural and social forces which willfully idealize or obscure aspects of the ethnic past.

Set in mid-19th-century Albany, *Quinn's Book* is the narrative of Daniel Quinn, an orphaned boy who witnesses such major historical events as the Underground Railroad, the Civil War and the New York draft riots. While there is a wealth of historical detail in this novel it is the apocalyptic opening—as Albany experiences freak disasters of fire and flood—and the surreal tinge to the events which imaginatively fire the narrative. Kennedy evokes a spirit world which shadows the lives of his characters providing sometimes comic, sometimes frightening perspectives on the past, present, and future. A sense of prescience grips the narration as Daniel grows to become the journalist-writer who views his life as a "great canvas of the imagination." As in his earlier novels Kennedy intermingles fact and fantasy, but is perhaps more ambitious with his historical sweep, constructing a phantasmagoria of human actions and desires that denies any simple patternings or resolutions.

In Kennedy's novels the Irish-American past is always under construction, its reinvention important to the patterning of social relations in the present. Kennedy is a speculative historian of this ethnic past, self-consciously aware that he is himself playing a part in its reinvention. He skillfully dissolves distinctions between the real and the fictional as his writings explore how memory and fantasy can influence historical understanding. In *Billy Phelan's Greatest Game* he offers an ironical authorial note: "Any reality attaching to any character is the result of the author's creation, or of his own interpretation of history. This applies not only to Martin Daugherty and Billy Phelan, to Albany politicians, newsmen, and gamblers, but also to Franklin D. Roosevelt, Thomas E. Dewey, Henry James, Damon Runyon, William Randolph Hearst, and any number of other creatures of the American imagination."

—Liam Kennedy

———

KENTON, Maxwell. *See* **SOUTHERN, Terry.**

———

KESEY, Ken (Elton)

Nationality: American. **Born:** La Junta, Colorado, 17 September 1935. **Education:** A high school in Springfield, Oregon; University of Oregon, Eugene, B.A. 1957; Stanford University, California (Woodrow Wilson fellow), 1958-59. **Family:** Married Faye Haxby in 1956; four children (one deceased). **Career:** Ward attendant in mental hospital, Menlo Park, California; president, Intrepid Trips film company, 1964. Since 1974 publisher, *Spit in the Ocean* magazine, Pleasant Hill, Oregon. Served prison term for marijuana possession, 1967. **Awards:** Saxton Memorial Trust award, 1959. **Address:** 85829 Ridgeway Road, Pleasant Hill, Oregon 97455, U.S.A.

PUBLICATIONS

Novels

One Flew over the Cuckoo's Nest. New York, Viking Press, 1962; London, Methuen, 1963.
Sometimes a Great Notion. New York, Viking Press, 1964; London, Methuen, 1966.
Demon Box. New York, Viking, and London, Methuen, 1986.
Caverns, with others. New York, Viking, 1990.
The Further Inquiry. New York, Viking, 1990.
Sailor Song. New York, Viking, 1992; London, Black Swan, 1993.
Last Go Round, with Ken Babbs. New York, Viking, 1994.

Short Story

The Day Superman Died. Northridge, California, Lord John Press, 1980.

Uncollected Short Stories

"The First Sunday in October," in *Northwest Review* (Seattle), Fall 1957.
"McMurphy and the Machine," in *Stanford Short Stories 1962,* edited by Wallace Stegner and Richard Scowcroft. Stanford, California, Stanford University Press, 1962.
"Letters from Mexico," in *Ararat* (New York), Autumn 1967.
"Excerpts from Kesey's Jail Diary," in *Ramparts* (Berkeley, California), November 1967.
"Correspondence," in *Tri-Quarterly* (Evanston, Illinois), Spring 1970.
"Once a Great Nation," in *Argus* (College Park, Maryland), April 1970.
"Dear Good Dr. Timothy," in *Augur* (Eugene, Oregon), 19 November 1970.
"Cut the Motherfuckers Loose," in *The Last Whole Earth Catalog.* San Francisco, Straight Arrow, 1971.
"The Bible," "Dawgs," "The I Ching," "Mantras," "Tools from My Chest," in *The Last Supplement to the Whole Earth Catalog-The Realist* (New York), March-April 1971.
"Over the Border," in *Oui* (Chicago), April 1973.
"'Seven Prayers' by Grandma Whittier," in *Spit in the Ocean 1-5* (Pleasant Hill, Oregon), 1974-79.

Other

Kesey's Garage Sale (miscellany; includes screenplay *Over the Border*). New York, Viking Press, 1973.
Little Tricker the Squirrel Meets Big Double the Bear (for children). New York, Viking, 1990.
The Sea Lion: A Story of the Sea Cliff People (for children). New York, Viking, 1991.

*

Manuscript Collection: University of Oregon, Eugene.

Critical Studies: *The Electric Kool-Aid Acid Test* by Tom Wolfe, New York, Farrar Straus, 1968, London, Weidenfeld and Nicolson, 1969; *Ken Kesey* by Bruce Carnes, Boise, Idaho, Boise State College, 1974; "Ken Kesey Issue" of *Northwest Review* (Eugene, Oregon), vol. 16, nos. 1-2, 1977; *Ken Kesey* by Barry H. Leeds, New York, Ungar, 1981; *The Art of Grit: Ken Kesey's Fiction,* Columbia, University of Missouri Press, 1982, and *One Flew over the Cuckoo's Nest: Rising to Heroism,* Boston, Twayne, 1989, both by M. Gilbert Porter; *Ken Kesey* by Stephen L. Tanner, Boston, Twayne, 1983; *On the Bus: The Legendary Trip of Ken Kesey and the Merry Pranksters* by Ken Babbs, photographs by Rob Bivert, New York, Thunder's Mouth Press, 1989, London, Plexus, 1991.

* * *

Ken Kesey's celebrity and critical reputation were instantly established with the publication of his first two novels. *One Flew Over the Cuckoo's Nest* was a widely popular commercial success as a novel and was also successful in its adaptations for stage and screen. *Sometimes a Great Notion* was initially received with some critical reservations. Seen as an ambitious but not altogether satisfying attempt to enter the rank of great American novels, it has since received more favorable attention from the academic critics, though it has not found a secure place in the established canon of contemporary American literature. After finishing it, Kesey announced a shift from "literature" to "life," and achieved a great deal of public notoriety in the process of making the change. He was frequently public news during the late 1960s, forming a band of "Merry Pranksters" (reported on at length in Tom Wolfe's *The Electric Kool-Aid Acid Test*) who attempted to live life as a work of comic fiction. His arrest and conviction for marijuana possession made still more news and provided experiences that he would frequently exploit in his writing. Stray and often occasional pieces of a miscellaneous nature were published in countercultural venues during the late 1960s and early 1970s, suggesting that perhaps a new project was in the works, and some of these were assembled in *Kesey's Garage Sale,* an apt title for a collection of miscellaneous items. In 1986 a more ambitious collection was assembled for *Demon Box,* a series of largely autobiographical pieces that continued to look back in time to the historical period of Kesey's public notoriety. The volume is loosely united by a first-person narrator whose name, Devlin Deboree (pronounced *debris*), hints at a devil-may-care attitude towards social and artistic conventions, and at the disorganized, self-consciously problematic value of his observations.

Both of Kesey's early novels are richly northwestern and regional in setting and atmosphere, with a strong sense of the incursion of the white man on the Indian's land and way of life. The emphasis is a bit one-sided in *Cuckoo's Nest,* which is set in a mental institution and has for its stream-of-consciousness narrator a "dumb" (thought to be deaf, but in fact choosing not to speak) Indian nicknamed Chief, whose father was the last chief of his tribe. The novel can be read as an allegory of how the invaders have been driven to subjugate the Native Americans because they are a reminder of what must be sacrificed in the process of western civilization and its discontents, and an exploration of the power struggle between a desire to be free and the fearful consequences of that freedom. Most of the characters confined in the institution could leave if they wished; but their fear of the outside is more intense than their hatred of the inside, until the raucous protagonist McMurphy comes along to inspire their lapsed self-confidence and zest for life. Recognizable as a tragicomic parodic microcosm of the world we all live in, the book captures and reflects the reality of a Walt Disney world, as perceived through the eyes of the "Big Chief" who used to be on the bright red covers of the writing tablets of children all over the United States, but who is now pretending to be a vegetable in a nut house. What he sees is "Like a cartoon world, where the figures are flat and outlined in black, jerking through some kind of goofy story that might be real funny if it weren't for the cartoon figures being real guys . . ." The comic-book quality has lent itself nicely to dramatic production, as have the compactness and wild humor of the novel. These qualities also tempt one to allegorize, but at the same time mock the attempt as absurd, for the work is not itself allegorical. It is a report on the way people choose to see themselves and their world in allegorical or comic-book fashion. The reality of the villain, "Big Nurse," is as exaggerated by the characters who fear and hate her as it is by the novelist. It is their insecurity and weakness that feed her power and make her "big," while the institution, with its equipment and routines, becomes the pretext for sociological and cultural myths pushed to an exaggerated but all-too-plausible extreme. The prefrontal lobotomy performed on McMurphy at the end is any operation on or treatment of or way of seeing a man designed to limit him for his own sake, to protect him from his own human nature. The Big Nurse is that spirit which loves the "idea" of man so much it can't allow individual men to exist.

Sometimes a Great Notion was Kesey's stab at writing the great American novel in a Faulknerian mode, and it deserves more attention than can be given it here. Like an *Absalom, Absalom!* set in Oregon, intensely regional, with elaborate and intricately complex narrative structure (flashbacks, shifts of point of view), the work demands several readings. With such attention, what at first seem like gratuitous confusions and exploitations of narrative technique begin to emerge as the necessary supports for a novelistic structure which commands respect even though it fails in the end to achieve its full potential. In this novel Kesey aimed high, and he came impressively close to his target. The publication two decades later of *Demon Box* produces the effect of a long-deferred anti-climax. Lingering colloquially and nostalgically over his acquaintances and escapades in the 1960s and 1970s, in a deliberately naive reportage style, this work often succeeds in capturing the colloquial idiom of prison life or Hell's Angels banter, but it does little to enhance Kesey's reputation as an innovative writer of the first rank. As if aware of this critical judgment, Kesey deliberately prefaced the book with a poem called "TARNISHED GALAHAD—*what the judge called him at his trial,*" two lines of which ask and answer the significant question:

> Tarnished Galahad—did your sword get rusted?
> Tarnished Galahad—there's no better name!

—Thomas A. Vogler

KIDMAN, Fiona

Nationality: New Zealander. **Born:** Fiona Judith Eakin, Hawera, 2 March 1940. **Family:** Married Ian Kidman in 1960; one daughter, one son. **Career:** Librarian, Rotorua Boys High 1961-62; wrote and produced radio plays in the 1970s, has taught creative writing, and has been a weekly columnist for *The Listener;* President of the New Zealand Book Council, since 1992. **Awards:** New Zealand Scholarship in Letters, 1981, 1985, 1995; Mobil Short Story award, 1987; Arts Council award for achievement, 1988; New Zealand Book award, 1988, for fiction; Writers Fellow, Victoria University, 1988; OBE (Officer, Order of the British Empire). **Member:** New Zealand Writers' Guild; New Zealand Book Council. **Agent:** Ray Richards, Richards Literary Agency, P.O. Box 31-240, Milford, Auckland 9, New Zealand. **Address:** 28 Rakan Rd., Hataitai, Wellington 3, New Zealand.

PUBLICATIONS

Novels

A Breed of Women. Ringwood, Victoria, Harper and Row, 1979; New York, Penguin, 1988.

Mandarin Summer. Auckland, Heinemann, 1981.
Paddy's Puzzle. Auckland, Heinemann, 1983; London, Penguin, 1985; as *In the Clear Light,* New York, Norton.
The Book of Secrets. Auckland, Heinemann, 1987.
True Stars. Auckland, Random Century, 1990.

Short Stories

Mrs Dixon and Friend. Auckland, Heinemann, 1982.
Unsuitable Friends. Auckland, Century Hutchinson, 1988.
The Foreign Woman. Auckland, Vintage, 1993.

Play

Search for Sister Blue. Wellington, New Zealand, Reed, 1975.

Poetry

Honey and Bitters. Christchurch, New Zealand, Pegasus Press, 1975.
On the Tightrope. Christchurch, New Zealand, Pegasus Press, 1978.
Going to the Chathams, Poems 1977-84. Auckland, Heinemann, 1985.
Wakeful Nights, Poems Selected and New. Auckland, Vintage, 1991.

Other

Palm Prints. Auckland, Vintage, 1994.
Gone North, with Jane Ussher. Auckland, Heinemann, 1984.
Wellington, with Grant Sheehan. Auckland, Random House, 1989.

*

Manuscript Collection: Alexander Turnbull Library, Wellington, New Zealand.

Fiona Kidman comments:

I was brought up in the northern part of New Zealand in isolated country areas, an only child whose family moved a lot, and was hard-up. Perhaps because of this, I have often examined the situation of people who live at "the edge" and find it difficult to communicate. My work has been identified to some extent with the feminist movement in New Zealand, particularly my historical novel, *The Book of Secrets,* (winner of the New Zealand Book award, 1988) which examined the life of migrant Scottish women on their journeys from Scotland to Nova Scotia, and ultimately New Zealand. My most recent short story collection *The Foreign Woman,* (runner-up to New Zealand Book award, 1994) has been likened to the work of Alice Munro—a great, but probably undeserved, compliment.

*   *   *

In her novels and short stories Fiona Kidman depicts New Zealand women, both contemporary and historical, writing in a style of social realism that sympathetically delineates the fates of these usually rebellious heroines against the social values that threaten to engulf them. Her forte is in capturing the atmosphere of small towns like Waipu. She does this brilliantly in her first novel, *A Breed of Women,* which created something of a sensation in New Zealand as it broke social taboos. Kidman exposes the narrow-minded, conformist mentality of bourgeois New Zealand and the limited choices open to her heroine. Harriet, a bright but unsophisticated farm girl,

falls into the hands of milkbar cowboys, and ends up in a shotgun marriage to a Maori. She traces her fortunes from this familiar scenario into a second marriage, family and middle age, deftly splitting the focus of attention between Harriet and her friend Leonie to give contrasting pictures of unfulfilled women, women who are driven to take risks and seek alternative sources of happiness outside marriage. This provided a near-perfect paradigm for middle-class New Zealand women of the late 1970s.

Her second novel, *Mandarin Summer,* owes more to the genre of Gothic horror, for it tells a disturbing story successfully by evoking a macabre atmosphere. Set in 1946 in a small Northland community, it narrates the encounter between a wealthy, decadent European family and their hangers-on and a New Zealand family, the Freemans, who have been duped into buying unsuitable land from the Europeans. In a neat reversal of colonial history, the Machiavellian Brigadier Barnsley coerces the Freemans into a servitude which embroils them in his disputes and passions. Although the scenes concerning his opium-addicted, incarcerated wife, his Jewish mistress, and the final conflagration that destroys the homestead are inspired by *Jane Eyre,* the novel exerts a weird fascination, and explores a new twist on the theme of incest. Its local setting is authentically captured through the observations of Emily, the 11-year-old narrator, who sees more than is good for her, even though at times her retrospective child's point of view slips into adult reportage. Kidman distorts the lens of romantic fiction here and tells a tale that is implausible, yet compelling.

Although the second half of *Paddy's Puzzle* is also set at the end of World War II, the novel opens on the small town of Hamilton during the 1930s depression. The traumas caused by Winnie's pregnancy, poverty, and her husband's abandonment of the family to seek work anticipate the abortive, juvenile love affair of her heroine Clara, whom Winnie has also raised. But her early life does not entirely explain Clara's subsequent fate—a life of abandonment in prostitution, and then tuberculosis—outlined in a grim account of her dying days in Paddy's Puzzle, a tenement slum for prostitutes on Karangahape Road. Through this cityscape Kidman explores the seedy side of life during the war with pathos and dramatic flair. Although Clara's death might convey a message about the afflictions women suffered at a time of limited social support systems, the writing reveals less a political agenda than a fascination with forms of self-entrapment and marginal states of existence.

In *The Book of Secrets* Kidman returns to historical fiction, telling the lives of three women through letters, journals, and dreams, and exploring the world view of the isolated, strangely unemancipated figure of Maria who lives in solitude as a witch. Her story has its roots in fact: the account of the charismatic figure of Reverend McLeod who led his followers from poverty-stricken Scotland to Nova Scotia and New Zealand is true, but its real interest is in the three generations of women who enact some pattern of retribution through their association with him. Isabella defies him, is raped and goes mad; her daughter, Annie, submits to his order; and Maria eventually achieves some kind of spiritual victory. The theme of hidden lives once more demands negotiation with the religious and social values which reflect an irrational patriarchal power structure capable of determining women's fates. But Kidman lets her story take its path rather than imposing a determinedly feminist pattern on her historical sources.

Kidman's *True Stars* tells a contemporary story of love, betrayal, politics, and death in the last days of Lange's Labour government. Her subjects are the citizens of Weyville: the left wing yuppies who rose to prominence at the time of the 1981 Springbok tour and gained a political voice through their freshly elected Labour MP, Kit Kendall, the Maori activists, and the drop-out generation. Together they represent a range of topical issues in New Zealand of the 1980s, including the need to confront a collapsing dream with the reality of a nearly defunct government; but it is the victimization of Kit's wife, Rose, and her conflicting family and social loyalties that signals the full extent of those confused times. Kidman here shows her strengths as a journalist, capturing with immediacy the class and social divisions of the times, the tensions of small-town politics as played out against a national context, and the personal dilemmas faced by the middle-aged Rose. In a tightly organized plot, she ties together these different strands in such a way that each interacts with the other to create a thrilling denouement.

Kidman has won many prizes for her writing, but she may well be remembered best for her short stories. Her three volumes show a flair comparable to John Updike's for the traumas of marital infidelity, marital break-up, and failed relationships. These themes are often foregrounded but never so consistently as when she traces the mixed fortunes of Peter and Bethany Dixon. Her confidence is apparent in her animated style, her control of structure and a sense of ease with a more restricted form. As with the novels, her prose is economical, yet often sensual. In the genre of social realism, Kidman must rank of one of New Zealand's most accomplished writers of the late 20th century. Although she reaffirms social truths, she also questions social conformity, and never better so than when dealing with the immediate past.

—Janet Wilson

KIELY, Benedict

Nationality: Irish. **Born:** Dromore, County Tyrone, 15 August 1919. **Education:** Christian Brothers' schools, Omagh; National University of Ireland, Dublin, B.A. (honours) 1943. **Family:** Married Maureen O'Connell in 1944; three daughters and one son. **Career:** Journalist in Dublin, 1939-64. Writer-in-residence, Hollins College, Virginia, 1964-65; visiting professor, University of Oregon, Eugene, 1965-66; writer-in-residence, Emory University, Atlanta, 1966-68. Since 1970 visiting lecturer, University College, Dublin. **Awards:** American-Irish Foundation award, 1980; Irish Academy of Letters award, 1980. **Member:** Council, and President, Irish Academy of Letters. **Address:** c/o The Irish Times, Westmoreland Street, Dublin, Ireland.

PUBLICATIONS

Novels

Land Without Stars. London, Johnson, 1946.
In a Harbour Green. London, Cape, 1949; New York, Dutton, 1950.
Call for a Miracle. London, Cape, 1950; New York, Dutton, 1951.
Honey Seems Bitter. New York, Dutton, 1952; London, Methuen, 1954.
The Cards of the Gambler: A Folktale. London, Methuen, 1953.
There Was an Ancient House. London, Methuen, 1955.
The Captain with the Whiskers. London, Methuen, 1960; New York, Criterion, 1961.

Dogs Enjoy the Morning. London, Gollancz, 1968.
Proxopera. London, Gollancz, 1977; Boston, Godine, 1987.
Nothing Happens in Carmincross. London, Gollancz, and Boston, Godine, 1985.

Short Stories

A Journey to the Seven Streams: Seventeen Stories. London, Methuen, 1963.
Penguin Modern Stories 5, with others. London, Penguin, 1970.
A Ball of Malt and Madame Butterfly: A Dozen Stories. London, Gollancz, 1973.
A Cow in the House and Nine Other Stories. London, Gollancz, 1978.
The State of Ireland: A Novella and Seventeen Stories. Boston, Godine, 1980; London, Penguin, 1982.
A Letter to Peachtree and Nine Other Stories. London, Gollancz, 1987; Boston, Godine, 1988.
God's Own Country. London, Minerva, 1993.

Other

Counties of Contention: A Study of the Origins and Implication of the Partition of Ireland. Cork, Mercier Press, 1945.
Poor Scholar: A Study of the Works and Days of William Carleton 1794-1869. London, Sheed and Ward, 1947; New York, Sheed and Ward, 1948.
Modern Irish Fiction: A Critique. Dublin, Golden Eagle, 1950.
All the Way to Bantry Bay and Other Irish Journeys. London, Gollancz, 1978.
Ireland from the Air. London, Weidenfeld and Nicolson, and New York, Crown, 1985.
Yeats' Ireland: An Illustrated Anthology. London, Aurum Press, and New York, Crown, 1989.
Drink to the Bird: A Memoir. London, Methuen, 1991.

Editor, *The Various Lives of Keats and Chapman and The Brother,* by Flann O'Brien. London, Hart Davis MacGibbon, 1976.
Editor, *The Penguin Book of Irish Short Stories.* London, Penguin, 1981.
Editor, *Dublin.* Oxford and New York, Oxford University Press, 1983.

*

Critical Studies: *Benedict Kiely* by Daniel J. Casey, Lewisburg, Pennsylvania, Bucknell University Press, 1974; *Benedict Kiely* by Grace Eckley, New York, Twayne, 1974.

*   *   *

Myth and legend, the heroic and the mock-heroic, form the central strands to the short stories of Benedict Kiely. He relies heavily on the Irish genius for creating epic myths about man, his heroic deeds and his human frailties. Although his fiction is largely set in the County Tyrone of his boyhood, a landscape that he knows intimately and with a sense of delight, it is transformed in a story like "A Journey to the Seven Streams" to a land of eternal and universal childhood. The trip to the stone-fiddle beside Lough Erne in Hookey Baxter's whimsical motor car takes on the aspect of a pilgrimage to a shrine or the tale of travellers in a magic, dreamlike land who have to face numerous adventures and dangers.

In a second collection, *A Ball of Malt and Madame Butterfly,* Kiely confirmed that although his work continues to be rooted in the Ireland that he knows so well, it has a breadth of vision and humanity in its subject matter and literary style that raises it above the merely provincial. The Tyrone of his childhood and the Dublin of his formative years are favorite backdrops for his novels where the mood changes from the mock-epic to the mock-gothic romance in a work like *The Captain with the Whiskers* with its memorable scene of the mad captain drilling his three sons in Boer War uniforms in the doomed big house; and in *Dogs Enjoy the Morning* with its satirical mixture of pub gossip and idle anecdote in the grotesque, but finely drawn, village of Cosmona where a newspaper reporter remarks, aptly enough, that "all human life is here." Kiely is at his best when he is writing short stories in which fantasy, satire, anecdote, and comic inventiveness play vital parts. The stories in *A Letter to Peachtree* are all told from a narrator's point of view, often as rambling comic monologues, and the end result is similar to listening to saloon bar badinage or half-heard eclectic conversations. Much of it is very funny and in each story the voice of the narrator is of paramount importance. A countryman reminisces about the past in a Dublin pub, attempting to put faces to half-remembered acquaintances in long-forgotten incidents; a writer attends a curious re-enactment of the events of 1690; a "secret poltroon" desires the girls at the dancing class and in the title story an American is caught up in other people's lives as he attempts to write about an Irish writer. It is not stretching a point to compare Kiely's later short stories to the great classical short fiction written by his fellow countrymen Frank O'Connor and Sean O'Faolain.

A new note in Kiely's work was struck with the publication of *Proxopera* in 1977, a savagely indignant novel with its anger directed against all men of violence in Ireland. The title comes from an "operation proxy" when an elderly grandfather, Binchey, is forced by three terrorists holding his family ransom to take a bomb into the neighboring town. The background is again Tyrone, but the mood is at once savage in Binchey's outrage at the terrorism that Ireland has helped to spawn, and at once an elegy for the nonsectarian, chivalrous past of his own childhood. Everything is seen through the enraged consciousness of Binchey and his sense of loss that nothing, his past, his family, the countryside and his relationship to them, will ever be the same again.

The same theme is continued—although this time on a larger canvas—in *Nothing Happens in Carmincross,* a novel which is constructed with enormous skill, layer upon layer, until its final and devastating act of violence. Mervyn Kavanagh, the central character, has a career as an academic in America, but has retained a great love for his native Ireland. Unlike many Irish-Americans, though, he has no love for terrorism; this cannot save him from the reality he has to confront when, on a visit to Ireland, he is brought face to face with the violence of his country's past and present history.

At the novel's end the reader is left with the certainty that another meaningless act of horror is about to become just another memory, part of the historical process: in that sense Kiely has faced up courageously to the peculiar tragedy of the Irish situation. In contrast to his morbid theme Kiely writes with zest and grace, humor and irony, in a style which is totally individual, the cadences of his language pointing and counterpointing feelings and ideas.

—Trevor Royle

KINCAID, Jamaica

Nationality: American. **Born:** Elaine Potter Richardson in St. John's, Antigua, 25 May 1949. **Education:** Princess Margaret girls' school, Antigua; New School for Social Research, New York; Franconia College, New Hampshire, **Family:** Married Allen Evan Shawn; one daughter and one son. **Career:** Since 1974 contributor, and currently staff writer, *The New Yorker.* **Awards:** American Academy Morton Dauwen Zabel award, 1984. Honorary doctorate: Williams College; Colgate University. **Address:** The New Yorker, 25 West 43rd Street, New York, New York 10036, U.S.A.

PUBLICATIONS

Novels

Annie John. New York, Farrar Straus, and London, Pan, 1985.
Lucy. New York, Farrar Straus, 1990; London, Cape, 1991.

Short Stories

At the Bottom of the River. New York, Farrar Straus, 1983; London, Pan, 1984.
Annie, Gwen, Lily, Pam, and Tulip, illustrated by Eric Fischl. New York, Library Fellows of the Whitney Museum of American Art, 1986.

Uncollected Short Stories

"Autobiograph of a Dress," in *Grand Street Magazine.*

Other

A Small Place. New York, Farrar Straus, and London, Virago Press, 1988.

*   *   *

Jamaica Kincaid is a talented writer, who has so far published four arresting books of fiction: *At the Bottom of the River; Annie John; Lucy;* and *Annie, Gwen, Lily, Pam, and Tulip.* Her work has been described variously as elegant, beguiling, gentle, graceful, dazzling, poetic, and lyrical. Her fiction is sensuous, evocative, and sometimes erotic. The meanings are elusive in her first, second, and fourth books, and they emerge gradually from an almost hypnotic litany which is marked by repetition, echoes, and refrains as well as by brilliant descriptions of people, objects, and geography. The third book, the novel *Lucy,* departs from this characteristic style in its plain prose. In the first two books Kincaid uses the narrative voice of a girl preoccupied with love and hate for a mother who caresses her only child one moment and then berates her as "the slut you are about to become." The child's father, 35 years older than her mother, is seldom with his wife and daughter and has had more than 30 children by various women, who jealously seek his wife's death through *obeah* rites. In the 10 meditative sections of *At the Bottom of the River,* neither the child nor her homeland (Antigua in the West Indies) have names; in *Annie John* both do. In *Annie John,* Annie ages from 10 to 17 giving the second book greater continuity and a more specific chronology. In both books the narrator describes her experiences and reflects upon them in monologues which complement one another but could stand separately. In both of these episodic works Kincaid achieves a degree of aesthetic unity through her careful and sparse selection of characters, an emphasis on the relative isolation of the child, a preoccupation with the mother/daughter relationship, and the use of a distinctive narrative voice. Kincaid reflects the childlike simplicity and apparent naivety of the speaker, even while she conveys Annie John's sophisticated vision of her cultural milieu, her sexual awakening, her responses to nature, and her sensitivity to events, persons, and influences possessing symbolic overtones. Hypnotically talking to herself, Annie John uses parallel phrases reminiscent of biblical poetry. She is keenly receptive to sense impressions—sounds, scents, and colors. These two books offer insight into the nature of a typical girl's growth to maturity, but they also offer analysis of an atypical and highly sensitive child as she moves inevitably toward psychological breakdown, which occurs when she is 15.

Annie John lives in constant conflict with her unpredictable mother. She must choose always to submit or to resort to lies, trickery, and even open rebellion. In both books, transitions from everyday school and home life into the psychic are lacking as Kincaid shifts abruptly from realistic depiction of the Caribbean milieu to disclosure of the child's dreams and fantasies. At the most intense crisis of her protagonist's experiences Kincaid approaches the mythic and archetypal. She projects the unusual and timeless aspects of the mother/daughter relationship as an alternate merging and separating of two spirits. Annie John also views the strength of a mature woman symbolically—as the shedding of the skin, so that a woman stands up naked, vulnerable, and courageous before the world and leaves her protective covering rolled into a ball in the corner. The child in both books recites rules dictated by her mother, defining the female role in household routines and in social behavior. Some of these chants are ominous: "This is how to make a good medicine for a cold; this is how to make a good medicine to throw away a child before it even becomes a child . . . this is how to bully a man; this is how a man bullies you." The narrator in *At the Bottom of the River* parodies the commandments as she mischievously recites, "this is how to spit up in the air if you feel like it, and this is how to move quick so that it doesn't fall on you."

The protagonist in both books moves into the disordered and the surreal as in dreams she walks with her mother through caves, empty houses, and along the shores of the sea. She dreams of happy marriage to a "red woman," who seems to be her mother (or an idealized mother-substitute), who wears skirts "big enough to bury your head in," and who will make her happy by telling stories that begin with "Before you were born."

In *at the Bottom of the River* the most notable explorations of the visionary and contemplative mind of the child occur in the sections entitled "Wingless" and "My Mother" and most disturbingly in "Blackness." In *Annie John* the girl's narrative of her mental and physical breakdown, marked by hallucinations, appears in "The Long Rain," and her illness is concurrent with rain that continues for 10 weeks. Annie John's mother and maternal grandmother treat her with medications supplied by a British physician, but they also use—in spite of her father's objections—various *obeah* potions and rituals. In her fantasy the child never loses all contact with reality. At the bottom of the river of her mind, trust exists as cold, hard, and uncompromising as rocks embedded below moving water. Moving into the surreal or unconscious, she does not quite abandon her world of household routine, the rigors of her life at school, or her sensitivity to the details of external nature. In the midst of a visionary passage, she startles the reader with a meditative statement based upon her observations of concrete realities: "I covet the rocks and the mountains their silence." On the closing page of *At the Bottom of the River,* the girl finds direction and substance, not so much in her visionary flights as in familiar objects: books, a chair, a table, a bowl of fruit, a bottle of milk, a flute made of wood. As she names these objects, she finds them to be reminders of human endeavor, past and present, though in themselves they are transient. She identifies herself as part of this endeavor as it betokens a never-ending flow of aspiration and creativity. She declares: "I claim these things then—mine—and now feel myself grow solid and complete, my name filling up my mouth." Annie John admires the courage and wildness of an imaginary "red girl," whom her mother denounces. Near the close of *Annie John,* the girl moves away, implying that Annie John no longer needs this double. Such kinship—even with an imagined role-model—determines her positive self-identity in the last analysis as a human being and as a part of nature. As she leaves at 17 to study nursing in England, she stands quietly and stoically on the ship, watching her mother become a mere dot in the distance.

The protagonist of *Lucy* similarly leaves Antigua at 19 to become an au pair, caring for the children of a rich white couple in New York, and studying in night school, with nursing as a possible goal. Lucy Josephine Potter's mother is considered to be saintly, although Lucy suspects she angrily named her Lucifer at birth. Her father, like Annie John's, is a philanderer, with mistresses who have borne his many children and who jealously threaten his wife through *obeah* schemes. But Lucy, except for occasional moments in this novel, presents herself as a relatively unemotional, detached, and self-centered woman, far different from Annie John. Her tough cynicism may arise primarily from resentment of her parents and from her anger at what she perceives as an oppressive island background. She despises the negative impact on her education of historic British imperialism, the exploitation of the island's beauty by Antiguan promoters of tourism, and the corruption of Antiguan politicians. At home she was punished for her healthy refusal to regard Columbus as a hero for his part in the "discovery" of West Indies, and she suffered silently the failure of books and teachers to recognize black African heritage in Antiguan students.

In general, however, Lucy's emotional repression is so great that she is a far less vibrant character than Annie John, whose imagination, passion, amusing impudence, and open laughter and grief make her unforgettable. Annie John's sensitive response to surroundings transformed the most mundane and familiar objects into art, but Lucy in her new surroundings allows herself to notice and remember only a few selected scenes. Protectively, she closes her mind and heart to new people and events, as if to cut herself off from the future and the present. She has already cut herself off from the past in her refusal even to open any letters from home. Only for a moment does she feel guilt upon learning a month late of her father's death. She sends her penniless mother a little money, but no message, and then burns all the unread letters from home. Yet when Peggy, her Irish apartment-mate, speaks of having "outgrown" her parents, Lucy is startled. She thinks she has never known anyone who could think of parents as pests, rather than as people "whose presence you are reminded of with each breath you take." At such rare moments, Lucy reveals the difficulty with which she maintains her cold isolation from emotion and intimacy. In all of her relationships, she seeks to appear detached. When her employer, Mariah, who is 40 confides that her marriage is breaking up, Lucy simply wants to declare, "Your situation is an everyday thing. Men behave in this way all the time. . . . Men have no morals." Lucy contends that she and Peggy have nothing in common except that they feel at ease when together. She manages to learn to love only one of the four children she cares for. Her companionship with Peggy and Peggy's sister lessens; her evenings with young men she meets at night school provide welcome and exciting sexual experience but no warmth and love. She remains always critical in evaluating their skill in arousing her but never viewing them as people worthy of love. On the last page we glimpse Lucy without her protective mask. She lies alone in her bed and on the first white page of a book Mariah has given her, she writes: "I wish I could love someone so much that I would die from it." Her tears fall on the page and blur the words. Kincaid's writing style—a plain prose lacking the imagery, cadence, and brilliant descriptions of the earlier books—reinforces the rigidity of the mask that Lucy hides behind throughout most of the novel.

Kincaid's fourth book of fiction, *Annie, Gwen, Lily, Pam, and Tulip,* blends literature with visual art in the evocative meditations of five young women in this collaboration with the artist Eric Fischl. Kincaid's text and Fischl's full-page lithographs of the women—nude, loosely draped, or shadowed—appear on alternate pages in this beautifully designed fine-press book. Kincaid's interest in photography flourished in university night classes in New York before she began publishing stories, and in her effort to blend her writing with visual art, she feels kinship with Virginia Woolf, James Joyce, and other modernists. The speeches of the five women resemble the style of *At the Bottom of the River,* and bear close resemblance also to the Song of Solomon in their relating of the beauty of women's bodies to nature imagery—animals, birds, mountains, and valleys. The influence of Woolf, particularly in *The Waves,* may also be evident. Though usually idyllic, the tone becomes ominous at times. As their thoughts dip into the unconscious, one senses their loving concern for one another, but the meanings are elusive and the abstraction of the poetic monologues seems to demand the abstraction of the visual artistry of Fischl's lithographs.

—Margaret B. McDowell

KING, Francis (Henry)

Pseudonym: Frank Cauldwell. **Nationality:** British. **Born:** Adelboden, Switzerland, 4 March 1923. **Education:** Shrewsbury School; Balliol College, Oxford, B.A. in English, 1949, M.A. 1951. **Career:** Poetry reviewer, the *Listener,* London, 1945-50; worked for the British Council, 1949-63: lecturer in Florence, 1949-50, Salonika, 1950-52, and Athens 1953-57; assistant representative, Helsinki, 1957-58; regional director, Kyoto, 1959-63. Literary reviewer, 1964-78, and theatre reviewer, 1978-89, *Sunday Telegraph,* London. Since 1978 fiction reviewer, *Spectator,* London. Member of the Executive Committee, 1969-73, vice-president, 1977, and president, 1978-85, English PEN; International President, PEN, 1986-89; chair, Society of Authors, 1975-77; member of the Royal Literary Fund Committee, 1977-89; member of the Executive Committee, National Book League, 1980-81. **Awards:** Maugham award, 1952; Katherine Mansfield-Menton prize, 1965; Arts Council bur-

sary, 1966; *Yorkshire Post* award, 1983. Fellow, Royal Society of Literature, 1952; resigned, then re-elected, 1967. O.B.E. (Officer, Order of the British Empire), 1979; C.B.E. (Commander, Order of the British Empire), 1985. **Agent:** A.M. Heath, 79 St. Martin's Lane, London WC2N 4AA. **Address:** 19 Gordon Place, London W8 4JE, England.

PUBLICATIONS

Novels

To the Dark Tower. London, Home and Van Thal, 1946.
Never Again. London, Home and Van Thal, 1948.
An Air That Kills. London, Home and Van Thal, 1948.
The Dividing Stream. London, Longman, and New York, Morrow, 1951.
The Dark Glasses. London, Longman, 1954; New York, Pantheon, 1956.
The Firewalkers: A Memoir (as Frank Cauldwell). London, Murray, 1956.
The Widow. London, Longman, 1957.
The Man on the Rock. London, Longman, and New York, Pantheon, 1958.
The Custom House. London, Longman, 1961; New York, Doubleday, 1962.
The Last of the Pleasure Gardens. London, Longman, 1965.
The Waves Behind the Boat. London, Longman, 1967.
A Domestic Animal. London, Longman, 1970.
A Game of Patience. London, Hutchinson, 1974.
The Needle. London, Hutchinson, 1975; New York, Mason Charter, 1976.
Danny Hill: Memoirs of a Prominent Gentleman. London, Hutchinson, 1977.
The Action. London, Hutchinson, 1978.
Act of Darkness. London, Hutchinson, and Boston, Little Brown, 1983.
Voices in an Empty Room. London, Hutchinson, and Boston, Little Brown, 1984.
The Woman Who Was God. London, Hutchinson, and New York, Weidenfeld and Nicolson, 1988.
Punishments. London, Hamish Hamilton, 1989; New York, Viking, 1990.
Visiting Cards. London, Constable, 1990.
The Ant Colony. London, Constable, 1991.
The One and Only. London, Constable, 1994.

Short Stories

So Hurt and Humiliated and Other Stories. London, Longman, 1959.
The Japanese Umbrella and Other Stories. London, Longman, 1964.
The Brighton Belle and Other Stories. London, Longman, 1968.
Penguin Modern Stories 12, with others. London, Penguin, 1972.
Flights (2 novellas). London, Hutchinson, 1973.
Hard Feelings and Other Stories. London, Hutchinson, 1976.
Indirect Method and Other Stories. London, Hutchinson, 1980.
One Is a Wanderer: Selected Stories. London, Hutchinson, 1985; Boston, Little Brown, 1986.
Frozen Music (novella). London, Hutchinson, 1987; New York, Harper, 1988.
Secret Lives (novella). London, Constable, 1991.

Plays

Far East (produced Coventry, 1980).

Radio Plays: *The Prisoner,* 1967; *Corner of a Foreign Field,* 1969; *A Short Walk in Williams Park,* from a story by C.H.B. Kitchin, 1972; *Death of My Aunt,* from the novel by C.H.B. Kitchin, 1973; *Desperate Cases,* 1975.

Poetry

Rod of Incantation. London, Longman, 1952.

Other

Japan, photographs by Martin Hürlimann. London, Thames and Hudson, and New York, Viking Press, 1970.
Christopher Isherwood. London, Longman, 1976.
E.M. Forster and His World. London, Thames and Hudson, and New York, Scribner, 1978.
Florence, photographs by Nicolas Sapieha. New York, Newsweek, 1982.
Florence: A Literary Companion. London, Murray, 1991.
Yesterday Came Suddenly. London, Constable, 1993.

Editor, *Introducing Greece.* London, Methuen, 1956; revised edition, 1968.
Editor, *Collected Short Stories,* by Osbert Sitwell. London, Duckworth, 1974.
Editor, with Ronald Harwood, *New Stories 3.* London, Hutchinson, 1978.
Editor, *Prokofiev by Prokofiev: A Composer's Memoir,* translated by Guy Daniels. London, Macdonald and Jane's, 1979.
Editor, *My Sister and Myself: The Diaries of J.R. Ackerley.* London, Hutchinson, 1982.
Editor, *Writings from Japan,* by Lafcadio Hearn. London, Penguin, 1984.
Editor, *Twenty Stories: A South East Arts Collection.* London, Secker and Warburg, 1985.

*

Manuscript Collection: Humanities Research Center, University of Texas, Austin.

Critical Studies: Essay by King, in *Leaving School,* London, Phoenix House, 1957; "Waves and Echoes: The Novels of Francis King" by John Mellors, in *London Magazine,* December 1975-January 1976; "Francis King's Obscured Passions" by Barbara Hardy, in *European Gay Review,* vols. 6-7, 1991; "Francis King" by Val Warner, in *Dictionary of Literary Biography,* Detroit, Gale Research.

Francis King comments:

(1972) Except for the period of my schooling and the war, mine has, until the last decade, always been an itinerant life. As a child, I was brought up alternately in India and Switzerland (the country of my birth); subsequently I worked for the British Council in Italy, Greece, Egypt, Finland and Japan. This desire always to set off for another destination is reflected in my novels. Of course, certain themes in them are constant; but I have never wished to be identified with only one type of fiction. Perhaps this has harmed me in

popular esteem; the public tends to like its novelists to write the same novel over and over again.

Foreign places have always provided me with imaginative stimulation and the majority of my books have foreign settings. Most English novelists, like the society from which they derive, seem to me to be too much preoccupied with differences of class, which obscure for them differences more profound between human beings. In choosing so often to write about "abroad," I have, perhaps subconsciously, attempted to avoid this class-obsession.

I believe strongly in national character, and a recurrent theme of my books is the way in which people struggle to break out of the patterns of national behavior in which they have been imprisoned since birth.

Critics sometimes say that they find my work "depressing" and my readers sometimes ask why I never write about "nice" people or "normal" people—not surprisingly perhaps, since mine is an attitude of profound, if resigned, pessimism about the world. I do not expect people to behave consistently well, and my observation is that few of them do. But I should like to think that the tolerance and compassion that I genuinely feel are also reflected in my writing.

I have always been preoccupied with style and form. I feel that I am most successful in achieving both if the reader is unconscious of any straining for them.

In my early books, written at a period of loneliness in my own life, isolation is a recurrent theme; in my later books I see now that envy and jealousy—to my mind the least attractive of human traits—have taken over.

My biggest and most successful novels were *The Custom House* and *Act of Darkness.* The novel that comes nearest to saying what I wanted to say—and that cost me most—was *A Domestic Animal.*

* * *

Francis King's first novel, *To the Dark Tower,* is his most experimental. In some of the stories in *The Japanese Umbrella* he adopts Isherwood's trick of using a narrator to whom he gives his own name, and *The Firewalkers,* subtitled "a memoir," was first published under the pseudonym of Frank Cauldwell, who is also the narrator, and who first appeared as a novelist in *To the Dark Tower.* King's stress on the plurality of truth, as formulated in the early story "A True Story" (*So Hurt and Humiliated*), led him to write from both first- and third-person angles in *The Custom House* and *The Last of the Pleasure Gardens. The Action,* actually about a novel, seems redolent with echoes from King's previous work. The bawdy *Danny Hill,* with much linguistic humor, purports to be an 18th-century text by John Cleland and is written by King in that idiom, modernized. The very structure of *Voices in an Empty Room,* linking three separate stories of attempts at communication with the dead, mirrors death's arbitrary cut-off and residual loose ends.

The themes of separation and loss recurring throughout King's work may be traced to his second novel, *Never Again,* a moving evocation of childhood and adolescence in India and at an English prep school. In his third novel, *An Air That Kills,* there is a lyricism, often negated, in the spirit of Housman's poem whence the title comes. *The Dividing Stream,* a complex novel set in Florence, is imbued with a sense of decay and the melancholy that pervades much of King's world. These moods are articulated in the stark ending of *The Dark Glasses,* as Patrick recognizes "the terrible, morbid beauty of this world." Yet the Greek setting seems to make for an easier sensuous acceptance: in *The Dark Glasses* King evokes the natural beauty of Corfu, while *The Firewalkers* is a mainly happy reminiscence of a group of friends in Athens centered on the dilettante and metaphorical firewalker, Colonel Grecos. In *The Man on the Rock* King succeeds in impersonating as narrator the parasitic Spiro, a character utterly removed from the self-effacing King/Cauldwell persona. King is as skillful with the short story form as the novel, with some of the stories in his first collection, *So Hurt and Humiliated,* set in Greece. So is the second novella in *Flights,* "The Cure," which like the other, "The Infection," set in Hungary, has political overtones.

King's most ambitious book to date, *The Custom House,* also has political implications. In this long, complex novel he focuses on a cross-section of Japanese society, both from within and through western eyes. King's writing is always rich in ambivalence; he found congenial material in Japanese formalism, recording "the echoes which surround events, not merely after they have taken place but also before them." Yet the novel has his characteristic intense sensuousness hedged with negatives. Like the collection of short stories, *The Japanese Umbrella, The Waves Behind the Boat* is set in Japan, though its theme of incest and dishonesty concerns expatriates, including the woman narrator.

Christine Cornwell in *The Widow* is outstanding among King's female portraits. The novel's opening illustrates his skill in manipulating the reader's sympathy in a few pages as he highlights alternately her unlikeable and likeable traits. His evocation of wartime London in part 2 of *The Widow* is complemented by his account of civilian rural experience, chiefly through the eyes of a 17-year-old land-girl, in *A Game of Patience.* In *The Last of the Pleasure Gardens* King shows how a severely retarded child exacerbates beyond endurance the weaknesses in a marriage. Most of the short stories in *The Brighton Belle* are studies in decay, symbolized in the town itself. *A Domestic Animal,* about unreciprocated homosexual love, is a poignant and powerful study of sexual jealousy; the narrator's attitude to Pam recalls the narrator's attitude to Anne in *An Air That Kills,* although the novels are different in tone.

The darkness of *The Needle,* about a doctor's love for her weak brother, is expressed too in some of the stories in *Hard Feelings.* The stories in *Indirect Method* are either set abroad or involve foreigners in Britain. *The Action,* about the libel action threatened against Hazel's novel on the eve of publication, incidentally reveals much about King's understanding of the novel form; the ending, as Hazel begins a new story, is something of a writer's credo. *Act of Darkness,* set mainly in 1930's India, focuses on a child's murder apparently by someone in his family circle; it is a major novel of suspense with powerful psychological depths. *Voices in an Empty Room* shows para-normal communication as mainly fraudulent, though the only certainty is doubt.

The affirmative novella *Frozen Music,* set in contemporary India, shows an elderly Englishman "giving" his young Finnish wife to his son, her lover, in an extraordinary act of love. In *The Woman Who Was God* Ruth, unable to accept that her son's death in an African commune was accidental, travels there and confronts its charismatic leader, "Mother." Through King's skillful sleight-of-hand narrative, Ruth not "Mother" emerges as playing God—with a destructiveness stemming from inability to understand her son. The moving *Punishments* opens in 1981 with Michael dreaming about his trip to Germany in 1948 in a party of students including the woman he married. The novel then describes that visit among Germans forced to see themselves as punished and guilty, the setting for Michael's seduction by a male German student: "And no

future experience of my whole life was ever to be so thrilling." *Visiting Cards* is a brilliant comic novel set at a World Association of Authors conference, presided over by the undistinguished Amos Kingsley, mistakenly elected as Kingsley Amis. The serious underlying issue is whether public agitation is necessarily in the interests of imprisoned writers if it further alienates their governments.

Though always a skillful storyteller, King's outstanding quality through all his work is his understanding of a wide range of characters' emotions. He is a master of implication, and writes with unnerving precision, strength, and sensitivity.

—Val Warner

KING, Thomas

Nationality: Canadian citizen. **Born:** Sacramento, California, 24 April 1943. **Career:** Currently Chair of American Indian Studies, University of Minnesota.

PUBLICATIONS

Novels

Medicine River. Toronto, Penguin, 1989.
A Coyote Columbus Story. Toronto, Douglas and McIntyre, 1992.
Green Grass, Running Water. Toronto, HarperPerennial, and Boston, Houghton Mifflin, 1993.

Short Stories

One Good Story, That One. Toronto, HarperPerennial, 1993.

*   *   *

As chair of American Indian Studies at the University of Minnesota and a native person himself, Thomas King has more than a passing interest in native issues. His fiction explores what it means to be native in a predominantly white culture. However, his writing does not simply separate native elements from a corrupt white influence or mythologize native life, strategies that tend to create dehumanizing stereotypes of indigenous peoples as members of a "vanishing race" or as "noble savages." Rather, King sees the native experience as hybrid. King himself is of mixed European and native background, and he appears to understand ethnicity as an inherently unstable set of self-created fictions, to be treated ironically rather than merely accepted. His writing is playfully satiric; with broad humor he debunks both white and native misconceptions of native life. Storytelling transgresses the racial or social limits that all human beings place upon themselves and injects a welcome complexity into narrow-minded understandings of human experience.

The native person in King's work often acts as a detached observer, pointing with amazement and disbelief to the self-interested behavior within North American culture. Lionel James, one of many storytellers who inhabit King's Medicine River, is mystified by what he calls this "crazy world." He can't understand why people want to fly him to Japan to recite, and he worries about his audiences "living in the past like that," listening to other people's "old" stories instead of making up their own. In a tall tale from *One Good Story, That One,* native people are depicted literally as aliens who end up being carted off in flying saucers by blue coyotes. King's native people, particularly the elders, are outsiders in a technocratic world gone amuck; they offer fragments of bewildered commentary on the absurdity of the standards and ideals to which most "modern" North Americans conform.

However, native people are not exempted from the pressures of that crazy world. Often, King's characters embrace what many might see as nontraditional roles. Will, the narrator of *Medicine River,* is a photographer who plays in the all-native basketball league. Lionel, in *Green Grass, Running Water,* is a TV salesman. King wants to subvert narrow preconceptions of who an "Indian" ought to be. In "A Seat in the Garden," two white farmers—having visions of an "Indian" spirit who stands in their garden chanting a parody of the refrain from W. P. Kinsella's *Shoeless Joe,* "If you build it, he will come"—seek the advice of three native men they assume are mystical, only to be tricked into building them a bench. The taciturn, all-knowing "Indian," King suggests, is a false stereotype and reflects little of actual native life, which is as "normal" as that of whites. King's native person plays a dual role, at once participant and critic, a member of mainstream society and social misfit. King's satire hinges on this duality, with its troubling, comic contradictions.

Coyote, the shape-shifting trickster, becomes particularly important in King's later fiction. In *Green Grass, Running Water,* Coyote plays the double roles of creator and subversive, ardent listener and avid story-wrecker, slipping between the novel's surreal narrative framework (where the "mythical" aspects of the text unfold) and the mundane. In *A Coyote Columbus Story,* Coyote's recklessness makes her both a friend to native people and agent of their demise as King rewrites the history of the "discovery" of the New World. In "One Good Story, That One," an old speaker is asked to tell a "good Indian story" to some anthropologists, thereby feeding them back a version of the biblical creation myth with added coyotes and TV sets. Nothing is pure or simple when Coyote is around. King's Coyote stories are metanarratives, tales about telling tales, and their circularity is tied directly to the duplicitous nature of Coyote, who is constantly undoing and rewriting whatever human beings might take for granted.

All of King's texts are about the act of narration. Often, King constructs stories within stories or interweaves one tale with another. The narrative of *Medicine River* is constructed through juxtapositions of Will's memories of childhood and Toronto with his current situation; King builds parallels between past events and present life to suggest how we give shape to our lives by telling stories about our experiences. In *Green Grass, Running Water,* several narrative threads are interlaced as King explores the complex interdependence of fiction and fact, story and truth. Key figures in every one of his fictions are always storytellers, young and old, mythical and real, who fabricate a world of words. Storytelling is the means by which we, as readers and participants in King's work, learn to appreciate our place in all the worlds of our own making.

—Kevin McNeilly

KINGSLEY, Johanna. *See* **PERUTZ, Kathrin.**

KINGSTON, Maxine Hong

Nationality: American. **Born:** Maxine Ting Ting Hong, Stockton, California, 27 October 1940. **Education:** University of California, Berkeley, A.B. 1962, teaching certificate, 1965. **Family:** Married Earll Kingston in 1962; one son. **Career:** Teacher of English and mathmatics, Sunset High School, Hayward, California, 1965-67; teacher of English, Kahuku High School, Hawaii, 1967; teacher, Kahaluu Drop-In School, 1968; teacher of English as a second language, Honolulu Business College, Hawaii, 1969; teacher of language arts, Kailua High School, Hawaii, 1969, and Mid-Pacific Institute, Honolulu, 1970-77. Since 1977 visiting associate professor of English, Univeristy of Hawaii, Honolulu. **Awards:** National Book Critics Circle award, 1976, for nonfiction; *Mademoiselle* award, 1977; Anisfiel-Wolf Race Relations award, 1978; National Education Association writing fellowship, 1980; American Book award, 1981, for nonfiction; Arts Commission award, 1981. **Address:** c/o. Alfred A. Knopf Inc., 201 East 50th Street, New York, New York 10022, U.S.A.

PUBLICATIONS

Novel

Tripmaster Monkey, His Fake Book. New York, Knopf, and London, Pan, 1989.

Other

The Woman Warrior: Memoirs of a Girlhood Among Ghosts. New York, Knopf, 1976; London, Allen Lane, 1977.
China Men. New York, Knopf, 1980; London, Pan, 1981.
The Making of More Americans. Honolulu, Hawaii, InterArts, 1980.
Through the Black Curtain. Berkeley, University of California Press, 1987.

*

Critical Studies: *Approaches to Teaching Kingston's 'The Woman Warrior',* edited by Shirley Geok-Lim, New York, Modern Language Association of America, 1991; *Articulate Silences: Hisaye Yamamoto, Maxine Hong Kingston, Joy Kogawa,* by King-Kok Cheung, Ithaca, Cornell University Press, 1993.

*   *   *

Myth, legend, history, and biography are so seamlessly blended in Maxine Hong Kingston's books that it is often difficult to know how to categorize them. Are *The Woman Warrior: Memoirs of a Girlhood Among Ghosts* and *China Men* works of non-fiction? Officially, they are cataloged as such, but in the deepest sense of reader's experience they seem more akin to fairy tales, folkloric stories, even epic poems. Based on the history and myth passed on to Kingston by members of her immediate family, as well by "story-talkers" in the Stockton, California, community where she grew up, the result is a species of magical realism, one that continually hovers between fact and the imagination, between what was and what might have been.

Kingston regards *The Woman Warrior* and *China Men* as a single large book, despite the fact that each was published separately. Moreover, she often confuses, willfully or no, family members who actually lived with those she invents. This penchant for blurring the distinctions between the actual and the invented has occasioned some criticism, especially among those who feel that Kingston plays fast and loose with history, but most reviewer-critics showered her with praise.

No doubt categories matter when one is handing out literary prizes (both *The Woman Warrior* and *China Men* received awards for general excellence in non-fiction), and the confusion of actuality and invention may be worth quarreling about, but what matters finally are the stories themselves—and they are quite good. Indeed, one would be hard-pressed to think of books that detail the joys and pains of growing up within a strictly defined ethnic community that could match Kingston's sentence for sentence, paragraph for paragraph, page for page. She is, quite simply, a marvelous writer.

Moreover, Kingston so experiments with form that the result is a species of algebra: stories that interlock or comment on each other; life lessons that creep inextricably out of mythic depths; and perhaps most of all, an eerie sense of that the burdens of the past rest securely on the shoulders of those in the present. Kingston herself straddles two vibrant worlds, each as menacing as it is mysterious.

The Woman Warrior is dominated by Kingston's mother (Brave Orchid, in the book) and the other women of China—ghosts of the heart, all—who formed her sensibility and willed her strength. By contrast, *China Men* focuses on the man who labored for 15 years in a laundry to pay for Brave Orchid's passage. The books beg to be read as an inseparable pair, as yin and yang are seen as opposite sides of a unified principle.

In Kingston's culture, it is the women who use story as a means to understanding and survival. By contrast, Chinese men tend toward silence, which forces Kingston to invent multiple versions of what may have happened in her father's past. No doubt some must have wondered if Kingston could write as penetratingly about men as she clearly did about women, especially given the restricted circumstances under which Chinese women traditionally functioned. The worries, however, were unfounded, for the effect of *China Men* is as riveting as it is daring. In Kingston's skillful hands, myth is not only a source of refuge and inspiration, but also of power. Kingston works not as a professional Sinologist, but, rather, as a creative writer; and the result is the construction of a deeper truth than facts normally allow for.

Kingston's two extraordinary books remind us that what James Joyce, an Irishman on the other side of the world, set out to accomplish when his protagonist set off to forge on the smithy of his soul "the uncreated conscience of my race" can also happen when a young Chinese-American writer sets out to discover who she is amid the rich tapestry of memory and the imagination.

—Sanford Pinsker

KINSELLA, W(illiam) P(atrick)

Nationality: Canadian. **Born:** Edmonton, Alberta, 25 May 1935. **Education:** Eastwood High School, Edmonton, graduated 1953; University of Victoria, British Columbia, B.A. in creative writing 1974; University of Iowa, Iowa City, 1976-78, M.F.A. 1978. **Family:** Married 1) Myrna Salls in 1957, two children; 2) Mildred Clay in 1965 (divorced 1978); 3) Ann Knight in 1978. **Career:** Clerk, Government of Alberta, 1954-56, and manager, Retail Credit Co., 1956-61, both Edmonton; account executive, City of Edmonton, 1961-67; owner, Caesar's Italian Village restaurant, 1967-72, editor, *Martlet,* 1973-74, and cab driver, 1974-76, all Victoria, British Columbia; assistant professor of English, University of Calgary, Alberta, 1978-83. Since 1983 full-time writer. **Awards:** *Edmonton Journal* prize, 1966; *Canadian Fiction* award, 1976; Alberta Achievement award, 1982; Houghton Mifflin Literary fellowship, 1982; *Books in Canada* prize, 1982; Canadian Authors Association prize, 1983; Leacock medal, for humor, 1987. **Address:** 14881 Marine Drive, no. 201, White Rock, British Columbia V4B 1C2, Canada.

PUBLICATIONS

Novels

Shoeless Joe. Boston, Houghton Mifflin, 1982; London, Allison and Busby, 1988.
The Iowa Baseball Confederacy. Boston, Houghton Mifflin, 1986.
Box Socials. Toronto, HarperCollins, 1991; New York, Ballantine, 1992.

Short Stories

Dance Me Outside. Ottawa, Oberon Press, 1977; Boston, Godine, 1986.
Scars. Ottawa, Oberon Press, 1978.
Shoeless Joe Jackson Comes to Iowa. Ottawa, Oberon Press, 1980; Dallas, Southern Methodist University Press, 1993.
Born Indian. Ottawa, Oberon Press, 1981.
The Ballad of the Public Trustee. Vancouver, Standard, 1982.
The Moccasin Telegraph and Other Indian Tales. Toronto, Penguin, 1983; Boston, Godine, 1984; London, Arrow, 1985.
The Thrill of the Grass. Toronto and London, Penguin, 1984; New York, Viking, 1985.
The Alligator Report. Minneapolis, Coffee House Press, 1985.
The Fencepost Chronicles. Toronto, Collins, 1986; Boston, Houghton Mifflin, 1987.
Red Wolf, Red Wolf. Toronto, Collins, 1987; Dallas, Southern Methodist University Press, 1990.
Five Stories. Vancouver, Hoffer, 1987.
The Further Adventures of Slugger McBatt. Toronto, Collins, and Boston, Houghton Mifflin, 1988.
The Miss Hobbema Pageant. Toronto, Harper Collins, 1989.
The Dixon Cornbelt League and Other Baseball Stories. Toronto, HarperCollins, 1993.

Uncollected Short Stories

"These Changing Times" (as Felicien Belzile), in *Civil Service Bulletin* (Edmonton), vol. 35, no. 9, October 1955.

"I Walk Through the Valley" (as Felicien Belzile), in *Civil Service Bulletin* (Edmonton), vol. 36, no. 1, January 1956.

"I Was a Teen-age Slumlord," in *Edmonton Journal,* 27 May 1966.

"Hofstadt's Cabin," in *Edmonton Journal,* 14 June 1966.

"The Jackhammer," in *Edmonton Journal,* 24 June 1966.

"Something Evil This Way Comes," in *Edmonton Journal,* September 1966.

"Night People Never Come Back," in *Martlet* (Victoria, British Columbia), 10 February 1972.

"White Running Shoes," in *View from the Silver Bridge,* vol. 2, no. 1, May 1972.

"Children of the Cartomancy," in *Martlet* (Victoria, British Columbia), November 1972.

"Does Anyone Know How They Make Campaign Buttons?," in *Karaki* (Victoria, British Columbia), January 1973.

"Broken Dolls" (as Leslie Smith), in *Martlet* (Victoria, British Columbia), Fall 1973.

"The Snow Leprechaun," in *This Week* (Coquitlam, British Columbia), 9 March 1974.

"Famines" (as Angie Jean Jerome), in *Martlet* (Victoria, British Columbia), Spring 1974.

"A Literary Passage at Arms; or, TX vs. BK," in *Iowa City Creative Reading Series Magazine,* Spring-Summer 1977.

"The Elevator," in *Canadian Fiction* (Vancouver), nos. 40-41, 1981.

"Intermediaries," in *Scrivener* (Montreal), Spring 1982.

Poetry

Rainbow Warehouse, with Ann Knight. Lawrencetown Beach, Nova Scotia, Potterfield Press, 1989.

Other

Two Spirits Soaring: The Art of Allen Sapp, The Inspiration of Allan Ganor. Toronto, Stoddart, 1990.

The First and Last Annual Six Towns Area Old Timers' Baseball Game, with wood engravings by Gaylord Schanilec. Minneapolis, Coffee House Press, 1991.

*

Bibliography: *W.P. Kinsella: A Partially-Annotated Bibliographic Checklist (1953-1983)* by Ann Knight, Iowa City, Across, 1983.

Manuscript Collection: National Library of Canada, Ottawa.

Critical Studies: "Down and Out in Montreal, Windsor, and Wetaskiwin" by Anthony Brennan, in *Fiddlehead* (Fredericton, New Brunswick), Fall 1977; "Don't Freeze Off Your Leg" Spring 1979, and "Say It Ain't So, Joe" Spring-Summer 1981, both by Frances W. Kaye, in *Prairie Schooner* (Lincoln, Nebraska); article by Brian E. Burtch, in *Canadian Journal of Sociology* (Edmonton), Winter 1980; essay by Anne Blott, in *Fiddlehead* (Fredericton, New Brunswick), July 1982; Marjorie Retzleff, in *NeWest Review* (Edmonton), October 1984; "Search for the Unflawed Diamond" by Don Murray, in *NeWest Review* (Edmonton), January 1985; *The Fiction of W.P. Kinsella: Tall Tales in Various Voices* by Don Murray, Fredericton, New Brunswick, York Press, 1987.

*   *   *

Before the publication of his best-known novel, W.P. Kinsella had already written extensively about baseball in four short story collections. *Shoeless Joe* (filmed as *Field of Dreams*) is preeminently a paean to baseball as it was once played when it was the national pastime, before inflated salaries, players' disputes, and artificial turf. The novel is almost studiously old-fashioned in its unabashed lyricism and unmitigated affirmation of life and love. *Shoeless Joe* has nothing in common with either the modernist or postmodernist traditions, and very little with the realist tradition. It posits the possibility of achieving the Whitmanesque dream, but denies that *Democratic Vistas* had ever been written. Its antecedent is J.D. Salinger's *The Catcher in the Rye,* but only Holden Caulfield's vision of a world redeemed through his sister Phoebe's innocence. *Shoeless Joe* is, in many ways, a plea for a return to the Edenic dream in which the serpent appears only to be crushed. Although Kinsella's novel often seems to be all surface, it can be read on the levels of love story, tall tale, and myth.

Shoeless Joe affirms the absolute redemptive power of human love. Ray Kinsella, the narrator and main character, makes love to his wife Annie who "sings to me, love songs in tongues, bird songs thrilling and brilliant as morning," and he marvels that he "can love her so much . . . that [their] love puts other things in perspective." (The reader may suspect that Kinsella owes more to E.E. Cummings's views of love and his detestation of technology than he does to any novelist.) Above all, baseball has the power to unite in love those estranged by time and emotional distance. Eddie Scissons, an old player, advised Ray that to be reconciled with his dead father he must realize that they "both love the game. Make that your common ground, and nothing else will matter."

But it is baseball mythologized and raised to the levels of magic and religion that has the transcendent power. As a Moses of the midwest, Ray hears a voice tell him "If you build it, he will come"; the "he" is Shoeless Joe Jackson, a member of the infamous 1919 Black Sox team that fixed the World Series. So bidden, Ray erects a baseball stadium, replete with bleachers and lights, on his Iowa farm, which is soon peopled with the entire Chicago team that nightly play their opponents on a field of planted grass, undefiled by the artificial turf of modern playing fields. But only those who firmly believe in magic and love the game can see the players or the action, when "all the cosmic tumblers have clicked into place and the universe appears for a few seconds, or hours, and shows you what is possible." Ray's twin brother, Richard, is not privy to the shades because his "eyes are blind to the magic," and he must ask Ray to "teach me how to see."

At times Kinsella puts too great a burden on baseball's redemptive power by giving it too many of the trappings of religion and myth. J.D. Salinger (whom Ray, obeying the voice, has kidnapped from his home in New Hampshire, and who soon becomes Ray's mythic accomplice) eulogizes that people will "watch the game, and it will be as if they have knelt in front of a faith healer, or dipped themselves in magic waters where a saint once rose like a serpent and cast benedictions to the wind like peach petals." Playing baseball is like being "engaged in a pagan ceremony," and as Eddie "Kid" Scissons says, "I know there are many who are troubled, anxious, worried, insecure. What is the cure? . . . The answer is in the word, and baseball is the word," and those who heed the message "will be changed by the power of the living word." The game becomes too freighted with symbolism to survive the attributions. Then there is the question of evil, which in this Garden takes two forms. One is Ray's wife's brother who contrives to buy Ray's land and plans to turn it into part of a vast computerized farm, destroying the stadium and playing field. Needless to say, his brother-in-law is foiled; technology cannot prevail against the pastoral ideal. The second is Eddie Scissons who has lied about his baseball triumphs and is punished by striking out in a game he is allowed to play as a returned youth; the serpent head cane he fondles is too intrusive and obvious a symbol.

But *Shoeless Joe* has a great many strengths, in particular its sustained lyricism and Kinsella's love for the literal game and its authentic rituals. It is worth noting that in his recent short story collection *The Thrill of the Grass* Kinsella continues to write about baseball; his lyricism is unabated, but he usually avoids the excesses that mar *Shoeless Joe.*

In *The Iowa Baseball Confederacy,* much of the same imagery of magic and religion recurs. Gideon Clarke finds himself inspired by the presence of his absent father to carry the family tradition forward and prove to the historians and to the Chicago Cubs that the Confederacy did exist. Matthew, the father, dreams a wife named Maudie who steps out of a carnival side show and into his life at least long enough to produce Gideon, whose shoulder-length white hair and strange blue eyes set him apart in the same way that his father was set apart even before the lightning bolt struck him during his first contact with Maudie. These characters continue the tradition of "being dipped in magic waters" that offer healing to a modern world through the ritual of baseball. The stakes of the game are high here: the losers will be consigned to everlasting oblivion. Of course, there is the suggestion that baseball is eternal, and the winners will bask in it forever.

Box Socials, a strong affirmation of love, is set in rural Canada, outside Edmonton. The central hero is one who does not quite make it in the big leagues, but he is admired in his community. All the families take box lunches to church socials, and their social lives are centered around the activity. Kinsella offers a generous portrait of rural Alberta, some touching pictures of life out on the plains.

Throughout Kinsella's work, there is a refreshing belief that love is possible and that life is good. He lifts us to the level of myth where we, too, can walk taller.

—Peter Desy, updated by Loretta Cobb

KNOWLES, John

Nationality: American. **Born:** Fairmont, West Virginia, 16 September 1926. **Education:** Phillips Exeter Academy, Exeter, New Hampshire, graduated 1945; Yale University, New Haven, Connecticut, B.A. 1949. **Career:** Reporter, Hartford *Courant,* Connecticut, 1950-52; freelance writer, 1952-56; associate editor, *Holiday* magazine, Philadelphia, 1956-60. Writer-in-residence, University of North Carolina, Chapel Hill, 1963-64, and Princeton University, New Jersey, 1968-69. **Awards:** Rosenthal Foundation award, 1961; Faulkner Foundation award, 1961; National Association of Independent Schools award, 1961. **Address:** c/o Dutton, 2 Park Ave., New York, New York 10016, USA.

PUBLICATIONS

Novels

A Separate Peace. London, Secker and Warburg, 1959; New York, Macmillan, 1960.

Morning in Antibes. New York, Macmillan, and London, Secker and Warburg, 1962.
Indian Summer. New York, Random House, and London, Secker and Warburg, 1966.
The Paragon. New York, Random House, 1971.
Spreading Fires. New York, Random House, 1974.
Vein of Riches. Boston, Little Brown, 1978.
Peace Breaks Out. New York, Holt Rinehart, 1981.
A Stolen Past. New York, Holt Rinehart, 1983; London, Constable, 1984.
The Private Life of Axie Reed. New York, Dutton, 1986.

Short Stories

Phineas: Six Stories. New York, Random House, 1968.

Other

Double Vision: American Thoughts Abroad. New York, Macmillan, and London, Secker and Warburg, 1964.
Backcasts: Memories and Recollections of Seventy Years as a Sportsman. Fowlerville, Michigan, Wilderness Adventure, 1993.

*

Manuscript Collection: Beinecke Library, Yale University, New Haven, Connecticut.

*   *   *

John Knowles writes, in general, not about his home turf but about New England or Europe. Only one novel, *Vein of Riches,* and that not his best, is about West Virginia, his childhood home. His fictional world is a cultivated, cosmopolitan, somewhat jaded world. He is a fine craftsman, a fine stylist, alert to the infinite resources and nuances of language. Yet, as he says, he is one of the live-around-the-world people, rootless, nomadic, and making a virtue of that rootlessness. He is a connoisseur of different cultures but master of none—or perhaps of one only, the sub-culture of the New England prep school. One defect of this very cosmopolitanism is the feeling of alienation that Knowles feels from his fictional world. As a veteran of many cultures he finds this trait an advantage when he writes graceful travel essays for *Holiday* magazine. He finds it a disadvantage when he wishes to create for *Vein of Riches* a thoroughly credible fictional character.

A Separate Peace, his first novel, is also by far his most important. It is a prep school novel about Gene Forrester and his close friend, Finney, and the studied set of ambiguities and ambivalences arising from the intense and complex relationship between the two. Gene, beset by a love-hate attitude toward Finney, causes Finney to suffer a serious injury and still later is the putative cause of his death from a second injury. But Finney's death is preceded by Gene's reconciliation with him, a redemptive act which to some degree assuages his feeling of guilt. Thus, the novel recounts Gene's initiation into manhood and into both worldly and moral maturity. Fifteen years after Finney's death, Gene returns to Devon to conclude the novel by thinking—"Nothing endures, not a tree, not love, not even a death by violence." What does endure is the extraordinary popularity of this novel with prep school and college students.

Knowles's later books display his writing grace but not the inner strength of *A Separate Peace.* His second novel, *Morning in*

Antibes, has a pot-pourri of comatose characters revolving about the deracinated Nicolas Petrovich Bodine in a kind of latter day *The Sun Also Rises;* it lacks, however, the Hemingway tone, atmosphere, and taut dialogue. The people are phony and maybe the novel is too. The long passivity of Nick makes him seem to move under water. The novel fails in characterization.

Indian Summer follows Cleet Kinsolving, World War II vet, in his jousting with his friend, Neil Reardon, Irish Catholic and heir to multi-millions (seemingly modeled on John Kennedy). Cleet's conviction, which he shares with T.S. Eliot's Sweeney, is that each man needs to do someone in. A good deal of cultural primitivism is spread about, but again the characters are unconvincing. *The Paragon* describes Lou Colfax, a brilliant, handsome sophomore in love with a beautiful actress four years older than he. In spite of the Yale ambiance and a plethora of cocktail parties and beautiful people the intended "Gatsby glamour" never comes to this novel. Perhaps because we miss the "yellow cocktail music" of *Gatsby,* perhaps because the characters remain partially developed. *Spreading Fires,* a brief novel of decadence and homosexual vagaries set in the south of France, deals with madness, potential madness, and the low life of the upper class.

Vein of Riches is a study of the great coal boom of 1910-1924 in a West Virginia town. Knowles shows a house, a family, and an industry, and the interactions of the three; he employs one of the central themes of American fiction, money versus land. It is a pleasant novel but the characters again are given perfunctory treatment. We do not have the empathy and zest that bubbled up from *A Separate Peace.* Coal does not interest Knowles the way New England prep school life did.

Peace Breaks Out is set in Devon School, New Hampshire, and is an attempt by Knowles to revisit the scene of his greatest fictional success, *A Separate Peace.* The parallels between the two novels are very strong: the place is the same school, the time is five years later and the crux of the plot is the wrongful death of a disliked schoolmate, Hochschwender, who dies of heart failure after being tortured by four of his classmates. Again, as in *A Separate Peace,* there is a legacy of guilt suffered by the four survivors. Knowles is much at home in the world of the private school and depicts it with grace and clarity. But it has all been done before in his earlier and better novel and thus lacks freshness and spontaneity. Many readers will find the excessive hypocrisy of Wexford, the ringleader of the torturers, a little unrealistic. This novel will not achieve the status of *A Separate Peace,* although it is well crafted and knowledgeably written.

In summary, Knowles is intelligent, highly literate, a skilled and sensitive craftsman and stylist. He is knowledgeable of the world, tolerant, a connoisseur of many cultures. He possesses in his own person that bifocal vision which he praises in *Double Vision.* He has created one extraordinary novel, *A Separate Peace,* which for many young people has truly caught the *zeitgeist.* There is also a negative side. Every novel but his first suffers from one fundamental defect—the characters are not plausible. There is not a single memorable woman character in his fiction and only two male characters—Gene Forrester and Phineas—that stay in our memory. The result is an imperfect empathy and a resultant lack of reader interest. In general his male protagonists are inert, deracinated, ambivalent, depersonalized, dehumanized. Why does Knowles create such types? Only he can answer this definitively, but perhaps he gives us the answer in his book *Double Vision* where he argues against roots and for rootlessness, the new form of nomadism. "We need to be nomadic and uprooted today," he maintains. As he says, he is not regional, does not come from a town or a city. He is one of the live-around-the-world people. So he is and so are the characters in his books. This is his fundamental failure and it is a major one. He may yet overcome this and give us again a convincing, brilliant novel as was *A Separate Peace.*

—Ruel E. Foster

———

KNOX, Calvin M. *See* **SILVERBERG, Robert.**

———

KNOX, Elizabeth (Fiona)

Nationality: New Zealander. **Born:** Wellington, 15 February 1959. **Education:** Tawa College, 1972-76; Victoria University, Wellington, 1983-86, B.A. in English 1986. **Family:** Married Fergus Barrowman in 1989, one son. **Career:** Clerk, Department of Inland Revenue, 1977-78; printer, Butterworths, and PPTA, 1980-81; insurance underwriter, 1981; publicity officer, National Museum, 1983-84; assistant editor of *Sport,* 1988-93; tutor in film studies, Victoria University, 1989-95. **Awards:** PEN award, 1988, and fellowship, 1991; New Zealand Book award, 1993. **Address:** 74 Glen Rd., Kelburn, Wellington, New Zealand.

PUBLICATIONS

Novels

After Z-Hour. Wellington, Victoria University Press, 1987.
Paremata. Wellington, Victoria University Press, 1989.
Treasure. Wellington, Victoria University Press, 1992.
Pomare. Wellington, Victoria University Press, 1994.

Uncollected Short Stories

"From the Treasury," in *Sport* (Wellington), April 1989.
"After Images," in *New Zealand Listener* (Wellington), March 1990.
"Post Mortem," in *Landfall* (Christchurch), March 1990.
"The Sword," in *Sport* (Wellington), October 1990.
"Sex of Metals," in *Now See Hear!* edited by Ian Wedde and Gregory Burke. Wellington, Victorian University Press, 1990.
"Afraid," in *Sport* (Wellington), April 1991.
"Take as Prescribed," in *Soho Square 4.,* edited by Bill Manhire. London, Bloomsbury, 1991.
"Fiona Pardington," in *Pleasures and Dangers,* edited by Wystan Curnow and Trish Clark. Auckland, Moet and Chandon/Longman Paul, 1992.
"Going to the Gym," in *Into the Field of Play,* edited by Lloyd Jones. N.p., Tandem, 1992.
"A Doubtful Guest," in *Stout Centre Review,* February 1992.
"The Black Disc (*Treasure 2.2*)," in *Metro,* May 1992.

Plays

Screenplay: *The Dig (Un Certain Regard)*, 1994.

*   *   *

In an essay entitled "Origins, Authority and Imaginary Games" published in 1988 in the first issue of *Sport,* Elizabeth Knox told the story of an imaginary game which she, her sisters, and friends had been playing for more than 15 years. The game began as a pastime for imaginative children, but over the years it became more elaborate, creating its own history. The separate worlds of the game have merged and intertwined, and the game itself has expanded and contracted at different times to take in new players or release old ones. Characteristically Knox asserts that she remembers parts of the game's history more vividly than she does her own. The game gave rise to an early unpublished novel, but traces of it are also to be found in her first two novels. Years of playing the game have confirmed Knox's sense of herself as a storyteller, and may also explain the unexpected maturity of the writing that reviewers have noted.

After Z-Hour is told in first-person narrative form by three people trapped in an old house during a storm: Jill, Basil, and Kelfie. The structure of alternating voices suggests that it may have begun as a game episode; one of its characters, Kelfie, seems more complete than most of the others, as though he has strayed into this tale from somewhere else. The house is located in a recognizable South Island landscape, the brooding, massive Takaka Hill, unstable, unsafe, riddled with potholes and tunnels. The novel itself shifts unpredictably: at first it seems that the house may be haunted, and the voice of its ghost joins that of the other three. Later it modulates briefly from ghost story to crime thriller, when Kelfie discovers one of the other characters disposing of a body from the boot of his car, and the genre changes again to psychological drama. The novel's attention is focused on memory: from Jill's straightforward, though harrowing, recollections of the death of her stepdaughter, to the persistent voice of Mark, the dead soldier, recalling his time in the trenches of France during World War I. Memory is given substance by extracts from letters and entries from a diary.

Paremata is set in the summer of 1969. The central character, Lex, is one of a group of children who play in the hills of Paremata, a seaside suburb near Wellington. The world of the children, with its shifting enmities and allegiances, is vividly recreated. Knox seems to be less at ease with the adults; there are hints of plot (difficulties in the marriage of Lex's parents, for instance) but the children are central. Knox is interested in the way in which they make sense of the world, the acuteness of their observations. Cathy, for instance, comments, "Sometimes I think people believe being happy and being respectable are the same thing," while Lex is amazed to discover that people will destroy what is theirs for the sake of a vengeful gesture. She recognizes, too, that atheism may be "valiant, gallant," but that disaster might "smash the shell of the sky," so she believes in the power of the shaman in the game while noting the inconsistency of such belief. *Paremata* is a sensuous and spicy evocation of the world of children.

Treasure is Knox's third novel, and is more ambitious than the first two. The "surrounding story" is set in contemporary Wellington, New Zealand; the "interior story" in White Steppes, North Carolina, in the 1970s. The Wellington story concerns Kath, a graduate student, and Martin, her supervisor, with whom she is having an unsatisfactory affair. Kath works at the local museum, where one of her colleagues, Frances Kirby, has been sent a mysterious black disc with peculiar physical properties. Kath's friend is concerned about her sister, who has become involved with a fundamentalist Christian group. Once these stories have been established, the inner story takes over. It concerns Mayhew Quitman, a young boy who goes to White Steppes, North Carolina, when his mother decides to return to her close-knit family. The family business is religion, and Mayhew's cousin is being brought up to follow in his preacher father's footsteps. Mayhew is not a believer, but he discovers he has the ability to heal the sick (which his uncle takes credit for). The two stories come together in one final episode, when all the characters attend, in various ways, the Miracle Healing Rally in Wellington—and Frances Kirby passes the black disc to Mayhew. Although *Treasure* is more complex and richer than *After Z-Hour,* it too shifts genre subtly and unpredictably. While structurally the novel is flawed, the character of Mayhew Quitman is well drawn and in Knox's evocation of the world of White Steppes we have her some of her strongest writing to date.

—Anne French

KOCH, C(hristopher) J(ohn)

Nationality: Australian. **Born:** Hobart, Tasmania, 16 July 1932. **Education:** Clemes College; St. Virgil's Christian Brothers College; Hobart State High School, 1946-50; University of Tasmania, Hobart, 1951-54, B.A. 1954. Has one son. **Career:** Until 1972, radio producer, Australian Broadcasting Commission, Sydney. **Awards:** *The Age* Book of the Year award, 1978; Australian National Book award, 1979; Miles Franklin award, 1986. **Agent:** Curtis Brown, 27 Union Street, Paddington, New South Wales 2021, Australia.

PUBLICATIONS

Novels

The Boys in the Island. London, Hamish Hamilton, 1958; revised edition, Sydney, Angus and Robertson, 1974.
Across the Sea Wall. London, Heinemann, 1965; revised edition, Sydney and London, Angus and Robertson, 1982.
The Year of Living Dangerously. Melbourne, Nelson, and London, Joseph, 1978; New York, St. Martin's Press, 1979.
The Doubleman. London, Chatto and Windus, 1985; New York, McGraw Hill, 1986.
Highways to a War. N.p., 1995.

Plays

Screenplay: *The Year of Living Dangerously,* with Peter Weir and David Williamson, 1983.

Other

Chinese Journey, with Nicholas Hasluck. Fremantle, Western Australia, Fremantle Arts Centre Press, 1985.

Crossing the Gap: A Novelist's Essays. London, Chatto and Windus, 1987.

*

Manuscript Collection: Australian National Library, Canberra.

Critical Studies: "In the Shadow of Patrick White" by Vincent Buckley, in *Meanjin* (Melbourne), no. 2, 1961; "The Novels of C.J. Koch" by Robyn Claremont, in *Quadrant* (Sydney), 1980; "Asia, Europe and Australian Identity: The Novels of Christopher Koch," May 1982, and "Asia and the Contemporary Australian Novel," October 1984, both by Helen Tiffin, in *Australian Literary Studies* (St. Lucia, Queensland); "*Pour mieux sauter:* Christopher Koch's Novels in Relation to White, Stow and the Quest for a Post-colonial Fiction," in *World Literature Written in English* (Guelph, Ontario), 1983, and "Living Dangerously: Christopher Koch and Cultural Tradition," in *Quadrant* (Sydney), September 1985, both by Paul Sharrad; "Oedipus in the Tropics: A Psychoanalytical Interpretation of C.J. Koch's *The Year of Living Dangerously*" by Xavier Pons, in *Colonisations* (Toulouse), 1985; "Expanding Other-world: The Achievement of C.J. Koch" by Andrew Sant, in *The Age Monthly Review* (Melbourne), June 1985; "The Envenomed Dreams of C.J. Koch" by Laurie Clancy, in *Island* (Hobart, Tasmania), Winter 1985.

C.J. Koch comments:

(1991) I began by writing verse, but gave my main attention to the novel from the age of 19. I believe that the novel can be a poetic vehicle, and that it has taken over the function of narrative poetry in this century. By this I do not mean that it uses the techniques of verse; nor do I mean that it can replace the lyric.

My first two novels were youthful and over-written. I have cut and revised both, and am now more satisfied with them. I don't expect to do this again, since I feel that I reached the stage of mastering my craft with *The Year of Living Dangerously.*

Two things preoccupy me as a novelist: the way in which many people search for a world just outside normal reality; and dualities: the dualities that run through both the human spirit and the world itself. It is the effort to reconcile these contradictions that makes for the pathos and drama I am interested in. Perhaps an Australian is attuned to duality more than some other writers, since he comes from a country born of Europe, but lying below Asia.

*   *   *

C.J. Koch (who originally signed himself Christopher Koch) had his first poem accepted when he was 17 and still at school; he began his first novel when he was only 19. He wrote two novels, which were well received both critically and commercially, but was then silent until, at the age of 40, he left his senior position at the Australian Broadcasting Commission to devote himself full-time to writing. Since then he has established himself as one of Australia's finest contemporary practitioners of fiction. Koch substantially revised his first two novels; he sees his earlier work as being marred by over-writing, and the changes are mostly in the direction of cutting and paring the prose, as well as making the scenes to do with sexuality slightly more explicit.

As well as a fine book of essays, *Crossing the Gap,* which do much to illuminate his own art, Koch has published three new novels since 1978, with another due for release at the end of 1995. His

concerns in all of his books remain remarkably consistent, as do the imagery and symbolism through which he explores. He is especially preoccupied with the nature of reality and illusion and the relationship between them. Subordinate to this, but also important, is the Conradian question of whether it is not, after all, necessary to live by illusion if one is to live at all. Waking up and growing up are, for Koch's earlier and younger characters especially, conditions to be feared: "They were growing up. It was what Shane had seen, before any of them. It was a thing that happened when you did not want it, and sooner than you expected," the protagonist of *The Boys in the Island* thinks, as he ponders on a fellow adolescent who is driven to suicide by exactly that realisation. In his most recent fiction Koch has returned almost obsessively to this question of the tyranny of time and the desire to return to the past.

The Boys in the Island tells the story of a sensitive young boy from the age of six (in 1936) through his school days and adolescence to his final, reluctant initiation into early manhood. Francis falls in love with a young girl who suddenly, heartbreakingly, abandons him. He fails his exams and travels from Tasmania to Melbourne, where he becomes involved in a meaningless life of petty crime. Then the suicide of a friend and his own near-death in a car crash send him back to his home to reassess his life and accept unprotestingly what the author calls "the iron bonds of his imminent adulthood." Despite the familiarity of the material, Koch's keen ear for colloquial speech, his sensuous command of natural detail, and the delicate restraint with which his understated prose conveys the boy's confusion and distress give the novel a fresh and poignant flavour.

Across the Sea Wall opens with Robert O'Brien, a 29-year-old journalist, looking back over an affair he had six years ago. Fleeing from an imminent marriage and the terrors of the life of a staid suburbanite working for his future father-in-law, O'Brien and a schoolhood friend take a boat to Naples. En route he falls in love with Ilsa Kalnins and they skip the boat at Ceylon. But eventually O'Brien discovers that he is a suburbanite after all. He cannot accept the challenge of Ilsa's love or believe in its sincerity when confronted with the facts that his friends bring against her character, and he returns to Australia. Two years later she appears in Sydney and they make plans to marry but once again O'Brien abandons her. In its original form especially, *Across the Sea Wall* is over-written—the descriptions of India in particular, finely done though they are, go on much too long—but the novel has many shrewd touches of characterisation and the same sensitivity in dealing with the impact of love on the uninitiated and the failure of the males to respond adequately to its demands that is a recurring theme in Koch's work.

The Year of Living Dangerously is set in Indonesia in 1965, the last year of Sukarno's regime. The Sukarno of this novel is a man who seemed originally to embody the hopes and dreams of his people (as well as those of an Australian-Chinese dwarf named Billy Kwan who is in the country as a press photographer) but who now has lost himself in grandiose schemes and the pursuit of private gratification. A coup is being prepared against him and it is this that provides the spectacular climax to the novel. Slowly, as Billy begins to see through Sukarno, his idealistic allegiance to and hope in a saviour begin to switch towards Guy Hamilton, the journalist who has been sent out to replace Billy's previous boss. Once again, the novel is told in the first person, this time by a narrator identified only as "Cookie" or by the initials he supplies to his occasional footnotes, R.J.C. Through the use of diaries, speaking through the voices of various characters, using purloined documents from Billy Kwan's private files, speculating and inventing when he cannot know for certain, the narrator builds up layer after layer of texture upon the basic structure of the narrative. At the end Koch tries, unfashionably and audaciously, to suggest Hamilton's final redemption and capacity to love as he ascends into insight via partial blindness.

The central character in *The Doubleman* is Richard Miller, a thoughtful, complex man but an observer rather than a participant in life. His tendency to retreat into himself is exacerbated by the fact that he contracts poliomyelitis as a child, is dependent on crutches for a long time, and develops a heavy psychological dependence on worlds of fantasy and illusion. Although barred from an active physical life, he is drawn towards his athletic cousin Brian Brady, who is both simpler and more adventurous than himself; such binary oppositions are common in Koch's fiction. Miller leaves his native Tasmania and follows Brady and his friend Darcy Burr to the mainland where he pursues a career as a radio actor (illusion again) and the other two form a musical group. When the three men come together again, it is in Sydney several years later. Miller is now a successful radio producer, moving into television; Burr, Brady, and eventually Miller's emigre wife Katrin form a folk group called Thomas and the Rymers, and it is inevitable that he will become entangled in the complex moral and ethical choices that confront Koch's protagonists sooner or later.

Like *The Year of Living Dangerously* , the novel is compelling reading; its narrative power is intense and firmly sustained. Koch's finely sensuous imagination can conjure up the burning, windless atmosphere of a Sydney summer as skilfully as the cold, haunted isolation of the Tasmania of his boyhood and adolescence. As with his previous novel, comparisons with Graham Greene come to mind—the superb sense of place and atmosphere, the conviction of the ambiguous and double-edged nature of innocence—and in fact Greene expressed his admiration for the novel.

Koch is a slow and painstaking writer and nine years separated his previous novel from *Highways to a War.* However, in an author's note to the novel Koch tells us that it will be followed later in the year by *Out of Ireland,* the two forming a diptych entitled *Beware of the Past,* a quotation from a poem "Warning" by the Australian James McAuley. A major connecting link is that Mike Langford, the protagonist of *Highways to a War,* is the illegitimate great-great-grandson of Robert Devereux, whose story is told in *Out of Ireland* but whose presence is felt faintly in this novel.

Highways to a War takes us back in some ways to the territory of *The Year of Living Dangerously.* This time the locale is Vietnam and then Cambodia (after a beautifully written section on Tasmania) rather than Indonesia, but the period is the 1960s as well as 1970s, and again the confrontation is between an Australian innocent and a world of Asian complexity and suffering that leaves him vulnerable and bewildered. Langford is an idealised, if also deeply romanticised character; he is even, if we are to believe the ending, a Christ figure who attracts his own Judas in the person of the secret operative Aubrey Hardwick. His friends speak of his serenity, his almost womanly gentleness, his heroic courage, and his chivalry towards the weaker and the dispossessed. But he is also a man fatally in love with the past. His ex-lover Diana says of him, "He told me once that the past used to get into his dreams at night," and although it is not primarily his own fault, his relations with women—Maureen Maguire, Diana, Claudine Phan, Kim Ahn, and finally Ly Keang—are all doomed ones that he spends his life, unsuccessfully and in the end fatally, trying to keep alive.

The novel opens arrestingly. "In April 1976, my friend Michael Langford disappeared inside Cambodia." An old school friend of

the narrator, Ray Barton, Langford is nearly 40 and has been covering the war in Vietnam and Cambodia for eleven years as a photographer, winning himself a worldwide reputation. At the urging of Diana, Barton travels to Bangkok to see if he can find out what happened to his old friend. As he did in *The Year of Living Dangerously,* Koch tells the story by adding layer upon layer, voice upon voice, so that the effect is of a kind of palimpsest that has been painted over repeatedly, with each portrait of the main character adding to or contradicting the ones previously offered. As well as Ray's tactful, self-effacing commentary we have the audio tapes that Langford kept meticulously for over a decade and that are the only thing he managed to send out of Phnom Penh before it fell. These in turn are succeeded and supplemented by long passages of narrative by Harvey Drummond and Jim Feng in their different voices, which offer new insights into Langford's character and history. The effect is of a rich and multi-faceted tapestry of meanings that involve not just Langford himself but the history of the Vietnam war and of Asia during the turbulent and bloody decade that the novel covers. The history of Langford's being slowly sucked into the vortex of the war becomes a history of that decade and what Koch sees, even though he is careful not to take sides, as its betrayals.

Like *The Doubleman,* though, this novel is very much concerned with the past, its inescapability and its irrecoverability; presumably the second part of the "diptych" will reinforce this theme. In the fine mixture of irony and tenderness with which he treats the heroism and fatal flaws of his protagonist one is reminded of an author whom Koch very much admires, Scott Fitzgerald. Langford's passion for his lover Ly Kean is inextricably tied up with his passion for her country, Cambodia, which is described with wonderfully vivid affection. "My impression was that for Langford," his colleague Drummond says, "she became Cambodia." When she disappears there, leaving Langford stranded in Bangkok, he has only one final, fateful choice: "You want to know why he did it—why he went over the border," Drummond tells Barton. "He went to get back into the past."

—Laurie Clancy

KOGAWA, Joy

Nationality: Canadian. **Born:** Toronto, 6 June 1935. **Family:** Has one son and one daughter. **Awards:** Books in Canada First Novel award, 1981, Canadian Authors Association Book of the Year award, 1981, Before Columbus Foundation's American Book award, 1982, and American Library Association Notable Book award, 1982, all for *Obasan;* Ryerson Polytechnical Institute fellowship, 1991; Urban Alliance Race Relations award, 1994; Grace MacInnis Visiting Scholar award, 1995. D.L.: University of Lethbridge, 1991; Simon Fraser University, 1993. D.Litt: University of Guelph, 1992. **Member:** Officer, Order of Canada, 1986. **Address:** 447 Montrose Ave., Toronto, Ontario M6G 3H2, Canada; and 845 Semlin Dr., Vancouver, British Columbia V5l 4J6, Canada.

PUBLICATIONS

Novels

Obasan. Toronto, Dennys, 1981; New York, Anchor, 1994.

Itsuka. New York, Viking, 1992; revised edition, New York, Penguin, 1993.

Poetry

The Splintered Moon. St. John, University of New Brunswick, 1967.
A Choice of Dreams. Toronto, McClelland and Stewart, 1974.
Jericho Road. Toronto, McClelland and Stewart, 1977.
Woman in the Woods. Oakville, Ontario, Mosiac Press, 1985.

Other

Naomi's Road (for children). Toronto, Oxford University Press, 1986.

*

Critical Studies: *Articulate Silences: Hisaye Yamamoto, Maxine Hong Kingston, Joy Kogawa* by King-Kok Chueng, Ithaca, Cornell University Press, 1993.

*   *   *

Joy Kogawa, after several collections of poetry, published her first novel, *Obasan,* in 1981. It and its sequel, *Itsuka,* written eleven years later, show Kogawa's poetic origins, as they are extremely lyrically written books. *Obasan* is the story of the internment of Japanese Canadians and Canadians of Japanese descent during the World War II. In so doing, it is one of few fictional accounts of the North American treatment of ethnic Japanese during this period, others being Carlos Bulosan's *America is in the Heart* of 1943, John Okada's *No-No Boy,* written in 1957, Jean Wakatsuki Houston and Jones Houston's *Farewell to Manzanar* of 1974, and Maxine Hong Kingston's 1980 novel, *China Men.*

Obasan ("aunt") is a unique and successful blending of the literary, the historical, and the autobiographical. Kogawa's novel is the account of two families' experiences told primarily from the point of view of Naomi Nakane, a schoolteacher in Alberta in 1972. The occasion of her uncle's death brings her brother (Stephen), her widowed aunt (Aya Obasan), and another aunt (Emily) together for the first time in years and precipitates a series of recollections and revelations about the war that begin when Naomi was about six (and Kogawa herself about seven). The war leads to the dissolution of Naomi's parents' families, the Nakanes and the Katos, and the seizure of their property. Naomi, her brother, father, aunt, and uncle are shunted progressively further east as the internment proceeds through and after the war, ending in Canada in 1949.

Obasan's narrative is essentially retrospective, a backward movement into Naomi's childhood seeded by a packet of materials given to her by her Aunt Emily. They lead to a series of memories of childhood as seen through the consciousness of the young Naomi, and shaped by the literary consciousness of Kogawa, who delineates a texture of symbols that become the personal metaphoric language of this book. Thus, a loaf of "stone bread" baked by her uncle just before his death becomes a symbol of a Eucharistic sort as it is eaten by his grieving relatives. It also serves as a symbol of the Japanese exile to the prairies as it is connected to the manna of Moses' people in Egypt in *Obasan*'s epigraph. Kogawa develops a rich texture of personal and biblical symbolism throughout to reinforce her themes.

The novel moves into the present gradually, and the past and present are linked in the import of some documentary materials which have been kept from Naomi and Stephen until their adulthood. Naomi, who has grown up with a mixture of puzzlement and misplaced guilt about the failure of her mother to return from Japan, is eventually initiated into the horrors of her death in the atomic bombing at Nagasaki through a letter from the distant past.

This news breaks the silence of the past in *Obasan,* and begins the process of final healing. Aunt Emily, a fully Canadianized "word warrior" who crusades for publicity or compensation in the Japanese cause, and Aya Obasan, Naomi's ancient aunt who still has only rudimentary English after spending most of her life in Canada, seem diametrically opposed in their cultural adaptations. Secretiveness about the fate of Naomi and Stephen's mother is perhaps the only thing they have in common. Yet this novel does not attempt to dichotomize attitudes to silence into "good" or "bad," and itself negotiates the fine line between telling the past and giving the present room to grow. *Obasan* explores language, euphemism, and silence; traces the ties of the self to family and place; and initiates the process of healing.

Itsuka ("someday") resumes Naomi's story in Toronto in 1983, and traces her involvement in the Japanese-Canadian fight for redress for the internment, as Joy Kogawa was herself involved. The novel, like *Obasan,* is simultaneously mixed-up in both the personal and the political, but in *Itsuka* the sharp line that Naomi has tried to maintain between the two in her life becomes blurred. *Itsuka* also shows Naomi's personal development in her tentative romance with Cedric, a priest involved in her political world.

In *Itsuka,* Kogawa tells a story well worth telling, but perhaps not so successfully fictionalized. At many points the narrative verges on the didactic, and the psychology of Naomi remains static and somewhat tangential to the politics of the tale she narrates.

—Ron Jenkins

KOPS, Bernard

Nationality: British. **Born:** London, 28 November 1926. **Education:** Attended London elementary schools to age 13. **Family:** Married Erica Gordon in 1956; four children. **Career:** Has worked as a docker, chef, salesman, waiter, lift man, and barrow boy; writer-in-residence, London Borough of Hounslow, 1980-82; lecturer in Drama, Spiro Institute, 1985-86, Surrey, Ealing, and Inner London education authorities, 1989-90, and City Literary Institute, London, 1991. **Awards:** Arts Council bursary, 1957, 1979, 1985, 1990, 1991; C. Day Lewis fellowship, 1981-83. **Agent:** John Rush, Sheil Land Associates, 43 Doughty St., London WC1N 2LF, England. **Address:** 35 Canfield Gardens, Flat 1, London N.W.6, England.

PUBLICATIONS

Novels

Awake for Mourning. London, MacGibbon and Kee, 1958.
Motorbike. London, New English Library, 1962.
Yes from No-Man's Land. London, MacGibbon and Kee, 1965; New York, Coward McCann, 1966.

The Dissent of Dominick Shapiro. London, MacGibbon and Kee, 1966; New York, Coward McCann, 1967.

By the Waters of Whitechapel. London, Bodley Head, 1969; New York, Norton, 1970.

The Passionate Past of Gloria Gaye. London, Secker and Warburg, 1971; New York, Norton, 1972.

Settle Down Simon Katz. London, Secker and Warburg, 1973.

Partners. London, Secker and Warburg, 1975.

On Margate Sands. London, Secker and Warburg, 1978.

Plays

The Hamlet of Stepney Green (produced Oxford, London, and New York, 1958). London, Evans, 1959.

Goodbye World (produced Guildford, Surrey, 1959).

Change for the Angel (produced London, 1960).

The Dream of Peter Mann (produced Edinburgh, 1960). London, Penguin, 1960.

Stray Cats and Empty Bottles (produced Cambridge, 1961; London, 1967).

Enter Solly Gold, music by Stanley Myers (produced Wellingborough, Northamptonshire, and Los Angeles, 1962; London, 1970). Published in *Satan, Socialites, and Solly Gold: Three New Plays from England,* New York, Coward McCann, 1961; in *Four Plays,* 1964.

Home Sweet Honeycomb (broadcast 1962). Included in *Four Plays,* 1964.

The Lemmings (broadcast 1963). Included in *Four Plays,* 1964.

Four Plays (includes *The Hamlet of Stepney Green, Enter Solly Gold, Home Sweet Honeycomb, The Lemmings*). London, MacGibbon and Kee, 1964.

The Boy Who Wouldn't Play Jesus (for children; produced London, 1965). Published in *Eight Plays: Book 1,* edited by Malcolm Stuart Fellows, London, Cassell, 1965.

David, It Is Getting Dark (produced Rennes, France, 1970). Paris, Gallimard, 1970.

It's a Lovely Day Tomorrow, with John Goldschmidt (televised 1975; produced London, 1976).

More Out Than In (produced on tour and London, 1980).

Ezra (produced London, 1981).

Simon at Midnight (broadcast 1982; produced London, 1985).

Some of These Days (produced London, 1990).

Sophie! Last of the Red Hot Mamas (produced London, 1990).

Dreams of Anne Frank (produced London, 1993).

Who Shall I Be Tomorrow (produced London, 1993).

Playing Sinatra (produced London, 1993).

Call in the Night (produced West Yorkshire, 1995).

Golem (produced London, 1995).

Radio Plays: *Home Sweet Honeycomb,* 1962; *The Lemmings,* 1963; *Born in Israel,* 1963; *The Dark Ages,* 1964; *Israel: The Immigrant,* 1964; *Bournemouth Nights,* 1979; *I Grow Old, I Grow Old,* 1979; *Over the Rainbow,* 1980; *Simon at Midnight,* 1982; *Trotsky Was My Father,* 1984; *Kafe Kropotkin,* 1988; *Colour Blind,* 1989; *Congress in Manchester,* 1990; *The Ghost Child,* 1991; *Soho Nights,* 1991; *Sailing with Homer,* 1994; *Protocols of Fire,* 1995.

Television Plays: *I Want to Go Home,* 1963; *The Lost Years of Brian Hooper,* 1967; *Alexander the Greatest,* 1971; *Just One Kid,* 1974; *Why the Geese Shrieked* and *The Boy Philosopher,* from stories by Isaac Bashevis Singer, 1974; *It's a Lovely Day Tomorrow,* with John Goldschmidt, 1975; *Moss,* 1975; *Rocky Marciano Is Dead,* 1976; *Night Kids,* 1983; *The Survivor,* serial, 1991-92.

Poetry

Poems. London, Bell and Baker Press, 1955.

Poems and Songs. Northwood, Middlesex, Scorpion Press, 1958.

An Anemone for Antigone. Lowestoft, Suffolk, Scorpion Press, 1959.

Erica, I Want to Read You Something. Lowestoft, Suffolk, Scorpion Press, and New York, Walker, 1967.

For the Record. London, Secker and Warburg, 1971.

Barricades in West Hampstead. London, Hearing Eye, 1988.

Other

The World Is a Wedding (autobiography). London, MacGibbon and Kee, 1963; New York, Coward McCann, 1964.

Neither Your Honey nor Your Sting: An Offbeat History of the Jews. London, Robson, 1985.

Editor, *Poetry Hounslow.* London, Hounslow Civic Centre, 1981.

*

Manuscript Collections: University of Texas, Austin; Indiana University, Bloomington.

Critical Studies: By Colin MacInnes, in *Encounter* (London), May 1960; "The Kitchen Sink" by G. Wilson Knight, in *Encounter* (London), December 1963; "Deep Waters of Whitechapel" by Nina Sutton, in *The Guardian* (London), 6 September 1969.

*   *   *

The novels of Bernard Kops are an extension of his work as poet and playwright. His prose is rhythmic, almost ritualistic, and his plots unfold through dialogue. He is concerned with Jewishness, with the Jew as outsider to the world at large, and as a trapped insider in the claustrophobic atmosphere of the tightly knit Jewish family in which a child can find it almost impossible to grow up. So 16-year-old Dominick in *The Dissent of Dominick Shapiro* is driven to run away from home and join a collection of drop-outs protesting against established society; and in *By the Waters of Whitechapel* Aubrey, at 35, can only free himself from his financial and emotional dependency on his mother by indulging in far-fetched fantasies of a prospective career which will bring him wealth and fame.

These goals have indeed been realized by the successful Jewish businessman, Daniel Klayman, in *Partners,* but his achievement leads him to madness. At the very height of his powers, while the house-warming celebrations for his new St. John's Wood home are in progress, he goes crazy. Lionel is his partner in lunacy, a projected *doppelgänger,* who pushes him into killing his new neighbor's dog, and which eventually engineers the situation which makes him responsible for the death of his beloved son, Zachary. Until that moment, despite the disastrous party, Daniel manages to disguise his madness by running away from his wife and family, and by pretending that Lionel is a real person, who is going to become a partner in his business and so relieve him of the stress and strain which has caused his strange behavior.

The lengths that the mad will go to in attempts to hide their condition is the theme of Kops's most mature novel, *On Margate Sands*. Here he abandons his Jewish concern for one which affects the whole of society, and which is even more urgent in Britain now than it was when this novel was published. He wrote his study of five former patients of a psychiatric hospital in the light of the 1975 Parliamentary White Paper on the revised services to the mentally ill as a result of new drug treatments. Because their sickness can be more or less controlled by "Happy tabs" as their warden landlady calls them, Brian, Larry, Dolores, Buzz, and Michelle can exist in sheltered accommodation outside the hospital.

On Margate Sands should be compulsory reading for any planners concerned with the present widespread closure of psychiatric hospitals, who still believe that "Community care" is anything more than a socially acceptable phrase. Kops's confused characters experience the reality of being "post-mad" in a society that is both fearful and uncaring. The owners of the run-down seaside hotel in which they are housed are clearly on to a money-making enterprise, squeezing their sick lodgers into cramped rooms, and kicking them out of the house during the daylight hours. The five of them walk the streets and lounge on the beach, and the "pre-mad" citizens of Margate and the frenzied holidaymakers do their best to ignore them.

Yet this is not simply a novel of social concern. It is one which could only have been written by a poet, for it demands that the reader experience the simultaneous levels of rational thought and irrational emotional response that lead to the bizarre and anti-social behavior of the insane. Like most of Kops's characters, Brian, the most integrated of the quintet, is a middle-aged man still in thrall to his parents, even though they are long dead. His emotional life stopped at the age of seven; and although he is both intellectually aware and well read (the novel's title comes from a quotation from T.S. Eliot with which he is familiar—"On Margate Sands/I can connect/Nothing with nothing") he is incapable of controlling the violent impulses that push him back into his past. Yet he is capable of a real, non-sexual affection for the adolescent boy, Buzz, and is seriously concerned when the lad runs off with a group of dropouts, who can be compared with the hippies that Dominick linked up with in the previous novel. In Brian's estimation, and in that of his creator, the Alternative Society offers its "ragged and self-indulgent" adherents a life that is no better than the killing waste of time experienced by former psychiatric patients at the mercy of the community.

Despite his wretched and crazy behavior, Brian has courage, determination and an ability to appreciate reality and the cruelty of the machine age. In a lyrical, rural passage, the old man Larry recalls family holidays in the Kent hop fields; so all five go off in search of the farm where he spent those childhood, summer days. Of course it has been mechanized, and this abrupt encounter with present reality is the fulcrum of the novel. His companions return to Margate, but Brian goes off on his own, tablet-less, on a quest for his lost sister and a sane and normal life. It cannot be achieved. In a state far worse than the one in which he set out he returns to Margate beach. His story of tragic waste is repeated in thousands of case studies, but it takes a poet to enable the "pre-mad" to enter the turbulent, sad world of the "post-mad."

—Shirley Toulson

KOSTELANETZ, Richard (Cory)

Nationality: American. **Born:** New York City, 14 May 1940. **Education:** Brown University, Providence, Rhode Island, A.B. 1962 (Phi Beta Kappa); Columbia University, New York (Woodrow Wilson fellow, 1962-63, and International fellow, 1963-64), M.A. 1966; King's College, London (Fulbright fellow, 1964-65). **Career:** Program associate, John Jay College, New York, 1972-73; guest artist, WXXI-FM radio, Rochester, New York, 1975, 1976, Syracuse University, New York, 1975, Cabin Creek Center for Work and Environmental Studies, 1978, Electronic Music Studio, Stockholm, 1981, 1983, 1984, 1986, 1988, Brooklyn College Center for Computer Music, New York, 1984, Dennis Gabor Laboratory Museum of Holography, 1985, 1989, and Experimental Television Laboratory, Oswego, New York, 1985, 1986, 1987, 1989, 1990; visiting professor, University of Texas, Austin, 1977; artist-in-residence, Mishkenot Sha'ananim, Jerusalem, 1979, and DAAD Kunstlerprogramm, Berlin, 1981-83. Co-founder, Assembling Press, 1970-82; contributing editor, *Lotta Poetica,* Villa Nuova, Italy, 1970-71, *Arts in Society,* Madison, Wisconsin, 1970-75, the *Humanist,* Buffalo, 1970-78, *New York Arts Journal,* 1980-82, *Rampike Magazine,* Toronto, since 1987, and *Liberty,* since 1989. Proprietor, Future Press, since 1976, and Words and Music, since 1982; since 1977 co-editor and publisher, *Precisely.* Visual poetry and related language art exhibited at galleries and universities since 1975. **Awards:** New York State Regents fellowship, 1963-64; Pulitzer fellowship, 1965; Guggenheim fellowship, 1967; National Endowment for the Arts grant, 1976, 1978, 1979, 1980, 1981, 1982, 1985, 1986, 1990; Vogelstein Foundation fellowship, 1980. **Address:** P.O. Box 444, Prince Street Station, New York, New York 10012-0008, U.S.A.

PUBLICATIONS

Novels

In the Beginning. Somerville, Massachusetts, Abyss, 1971.
One Night Stood. New York, Future Press, 1977.
Tabula Rasa. New York, RK Editions, 1978.
Exhaustive Parallel Intervals. New York, Future Press, 1979.
Flipping. New York, Archae, 1991.
Intermix. New York, Archae, 1991.

Short Stories and Novellas

Accounting. Brescia, Italy, Amodulo, 1972; Sacramento, California, Poetry Newsletter, 1973.
Ad Infinitum. Friedrichsfehn, Germany, International Artists' Cooperation, 1973.
Modulations. Brooklyn, New York, Assembling Press, 1975.
Openings and Closings. New York, D'Arc, 1975.
Constructs. Reno, Nevada, West Coast Poetry Review, 1975.
Come Here. New York, Assembling Press, 1975.
Extrapolate. New York, Assembling Press, 1975.
Three Places in New Inkland, with others. New York, Zartscorp, 1977.
Constructs Two. Milwaukee, Membrane, 1978.
Foreshortenings and Other Stories. Willits, California, Tuumba Press, 1978.

Inexistences. New York, RK Editions, 1978.
And So Forth. New York, Future Press, 1979.
More Short Fictions. New York, Assembling Press, 1980.
Epiphanies. West Berlin, Literarisches Colloquium Berlin, and New York, RK Editions, 1983.
Constructs Three. New York, Archae, 1991.
Constructs Four. New York, Archae, 1991.
Constructs Five. New York, Archae, 1991.
Constructs Six. New York, Archae, 1991.
March. Mentor, Ohio, Generator, 1991.
Fifty Constructivist Stories. New York, Archae, 1991.
Openings. Evanston, Illinois, Depth Charge, 1995.

Plays

Epiphanies (produced Grand Forks, North Dakota, 1980).
Lovings (produced New York, 1991).

Screenplays and Video Scripts: *Openings and Closings,* with Bart Weiss, 1975; *Three Prose Pieces,* 1975; *Declaration of Independence,* 1979; *Constructivist Fictions,* with Peter Longauer, 1979; *Epiphanies,* 1980; *A Berlin Lost,* with Martin Koerber, 1985; *Partitions,* 1986; *Home Movies Reconsidered: My First Twenty-Seven Years,* 1987; *Seductions,* 1987; *Relationships,* 1987; *Video Writing,* 1987; *Video Fictions,* 1988; *Video Poems,* 1988; *Video Strings,* 1989; *Kinetic Writings,* 1989; *Turfs/Grounds/ Lawns,* 1989.

Radio Scripts: *Audio Art,* 1978; *Text-Sound in North America,* 1981; *Glenn Gould as a Radio Artist,* 1983; *Hörspiel USA,* 1983; *Audio Writing,* 1984; *Nach Weissensee,* with Martin Koerber and Michael Maassen, 1984; *Radio Comedy Made in America Today,* 1986; *Hörspielmacher Tony Schwartz,* 1987; *New York City Radio,* 1988; *Orson Welles as an Audio Artist,* 1988; *Norman Corwin as an Audio Artist,* 1991.

Poetry

Visual Language. New York, Assembling Press, 1970.
I Articulations, with *Short Fictions.* New York, Kulchur, 1974.
Portraits from Memory. Ann Arbor, Ardis, 1975.
Word Prints. Privately printed, 1975.
Rain Rains Rain. New York, Assembling Press, 1976.
Numbers: Poems and Stories. New York, Assembling Press, 1976.
Illuminations. Woodinville, Washington, and New York, Laughing Bear-Future Press, 1977.
Numbers Two. Columbus, Ohio, Luna Bisonte, 1977.
Richard Kostelanetz. New York, RK Editions, 1980.
Turfs Arenas Fields Pitches. Battleground, Indiana, High/Coo Press, 1980.
Arenas Fields Pitches Turfs. Kansas City, BK Mk-University of Missouri, 1982.
Behold Visual Poetry. Phoenix, Arizona, eXpEriMenTal Press, 1991.
Solos, Duets, Trios, and Choruses. Milwaukee, Membrane, 1991.
Partitions. Patagonia, Arizona, Bright Moments, 1992.
Repartitions-IV. Port Charlotte, Florida, Runaway Spoon, 1992.
Wordworks: Poems New and Selected. Rochester, New York, BOA, 1993.
MoRepartitions. Port Charlotte, Florida, Runaway Spoon, 1994.

Recordings: *Experimental Prose,* Assembling Press, 1976; *Audio Art,* RK Editions, 1977; *Asdescent* and *Anacatabasis,* RK Editions, 1978; *Audio Writing,* RK Editions, 1984; *Complete Audio Writing,* RK Editions, 1985; *The Drunken Boat,* RK Editions, 1986; *Turfs Arenas Fields Pitches,* RK Editions, 1988; *America's Game,* RK Editions, 1988; *Onomatopoeic,* RK Editions, 1988; *Yiddish,* RK Editions 1990.

Holograms: *Antitheses,* RK Editions, 1985; *Abracadabra,* RK Editions, 1987; *Ambiguity,* RK Editions, 1987; *Hell/Elle,* with Eduardo Kac, RK Editions, 1987; *Ho/Log/Rap/Her,* RK Editions, 1987; *Ho/Log/Rap/Hy,* RK Editions, 1987; *Madam/Adam,* RK Editions, 1987.

Other

The Theatre of Mixed-Means: An Introduction to Happenings, Kinetic Environments, and Other Mixed-Means Performances. New York, Dial Press, 1968; London, Pitman, 1970.
Master Minds: Portraits of Contemporary American Artists and Intellectuals. New York, Macmillan, 1969.
The End of Intelligent Writing: Literary Politics in America. New York, Sheed and Ward, 1974.
Recyclings: A Literary Autobiography. New York, Assembling Press, 1974; augmented edition, New York, Future Press, 1984.
Grants and the Future of Literature. New York, RK Editions, 1978.
Wordsand. Burnaby, British Columbia, Simon Fraser Gallery, 1978.
Twenties in the Sixties: Previously Uncollected Critical Essays. Westport, Connecticut, Greenwood Press, 1979.
"The End" Essentials, "The End" Appendix. Metuchen, New Jersey, Scarecrow Press, 1979.
Metamorphosis in the Arts. New York, Assembling Press, 1980.
Autobiographies. Santa Barbara, California, Mudborn, 1981.
The Old Poetries and the New. Ann Arbor, University of Michigan Press, 1981.
Reincarnations. New York, Future Press, 1981.
American Imaginations. West Berlin, Merve, and New York, RK Editions, 1983.
Autobiographien New York Berlin. West Berlin, Merve, 1986.
The Grants-Fix: Publicly Literary Granting in America. New York, RK Editions, 1987.
The Old Fictions and the New. Jefferson, North Carolina, and London, McFarland, 1987.
Prose Pieces/Aftertexts. Calexico, California, Atticus Press, 1987.
Conversing with Cage (interviews with John Cage). New York, Limelight, 1988; London, Omnibus Press, 1990.
On Innovative Music(ian)s. New York, Limelight, 1989.
Unfinished Business: An Intellectual Non-history 1963-1989. New York, RK Editions, 1990.
The New Poetries and Some Old. Carbondale, Southern Illinois University Press, 1990.
Politics in the African-American Novel. Westport, Connecticut, Greenwood Press, 1991.
References. East Lansing, Michigan, Ghost Dance, 1991.
On Innovative Art(ist)s. Jefferson, North Carolina, McFarland, 1992.
A Dictionary of the Avant-Gardes. Chicago, A Cappella, 1993.
On Innovative Performance(s). Jefferson, North Carolina., McFarland, 1994.
An ABC of Contemporary Reading. San Diego, California, San Diego State University Press, 1995.
Crimes of Culture. Brooklyn, New York, Autonomedia, 1995.

Fillmore East: Recollections of Rock Theater, Twenty-Five Years After. New York, Schirmer, 1995.
Radio Writings. Union City, New Jersey, Leggiere, 1995.

Editor, *On Contemporary Literature: An Anthology of Critical Essays on Major Movements and Writers of Contemporary Literature.* New York, Avon, 1964; revised edition, 1969.
Editor, *The New American Arts.* New York, Horizon Press, 1965; London, Collier Macmillan, 1968.
Editor, *Twelve from the Sixties.* New York, Dell, 1967.
Editor, *The Young American Writers: Fiction, Poetry, Drama, and Criticism.* New York, Funk and Wagnalls, 1967.
Editor, *Beyond Left and Right: Radical Thought for Our Time.* New York, Morrow, 1968.
Editor, *Imaged Words and Worded Images.* New York, Outerbridge and Dienstfrey, 1970.
Editor, *Possibilities of Poetry: An Anthology of American Contemporaries.* New York, Dell, 1970.
Editor, *John Cage.* New York, Praeger, 1970; London, Allen Lane, 1971.
Editor, *Moholy-Nagy.* New York, Praeger, 1970; London, Allen Lane, 1972.
Editor, *Assembling,* and *Second* through *Eleventh Assembling.* New York, Assembling Press, 12 vols., 1970-81.
Editor, *Future's Fictions.* New York, Panache, 1971.
Editor, *Human Alternatives: Visions for Our Time.* New York, Morrow, 1971.
Editor, *Social Speculations: Visions for Us Now.* New York, Morrow, 1971.
Editor, *In Youth.* New York, Ballantine, 1972.
Editor, *Seeing Through Shuck.* New York, Ballantine, 1972.
Editor, *Breakthrough Fictioneers: An Anthology.* New York, Something Else Press, 1973.
Editor, *The Edge of Adaptation: Man and the Emerging Society.* Englewood Cliffs, New Jersey, Prentice Hall, 1973.
Editor, *Essaying Essays.* New York, OOLP, 1975.
Editor, *Language and Structure.* New York, Kensington Arts, 1975.
Editor, *Younger Critics of North America: Essays on Literature and the Arts.* Fair Water, Wisconsin, Margins, 1977.
Editor, *Esthetics Contemporary.* New York, Prometheus, 1977.
Editor, *Assembling Assembling.* New York, Assembling Press, 1978.
Editor, *Visual Literature Criticism: A New Collection.* Carbondale, Southern Illinois University Press, and London, Feffer and Simons, 1979.
Editor, *Text-Sound Texts.* New York, Morrow, 1980.
Editor, *The Yale Gertrude Stein* (selection). New Haven, Connecticut, Yale University Press, 1980.
Editor, *Scenarios.* New York, Assembling Press, 1980.
Editor, *Aural Literature Criticism.* New York, Precisely-RK Editions, 1981.
Editor, *American Writing Today.* Washington, D.C., Voice of America Forum Series, 2 vols., 1981.
Editor, *The Avant-Garde Tradition in Literature.* Buffalo, New York, Prometheus, 1982.
Editor, *The Literature of SoHo.* New York, Shantih, 1983.
Editor, with Bejamin Hrushovski, *The Poetics of the New Poetries.* New York, RK Editions, 1983.
Editor, with Stephen Scobie, *Precisely Complete.* New York, RK Editions, 6 vols., 1985.
Editor, *Gertrude Stein Advanced: An Anthology of Criticism.* Jefferson, North Carolina, McFarland, 1990.

Editor, *Merce Cunningham: Dancing in Time and Space.* Chicago, A Cappella, 1992.
Editor, *John Cage, Writer.* New York, Limelight, 1993.
Editor, *Writings About John Cage.* Ann Arbor, Michigan, University of Michigan Press, 1993.
Editor, *Nicolas Slonimsky: the First 100 Years.* New York, Schrimer, 1994.
Editor, *A Shorter Baker's Biographical Diction of Musicians.* New York, Schrimer, 1995.
Editor, *Another E.E. Cummings.* New York, Norton, 1995.

*

Critical Studies: Article by Dick Higgins, in *Postmodern Fiction* edited by Larry McCaffery, Westport, Connecticut, Greenwood Press, 1986; "Richard Kostelanetz as a Breakthrough Fictioneer" by Jerome Klinkowitz, in *Asylum* (Santa Maria, California), vol. 2, no. 4, 1987; "Toward a Critical Understanding of Richard Kostelanetz's Single Sentence Stories" by Raymond Gomez, in *Critique: Studies in Contemporary Fiction,* 35(4), Summer 1994.

Richard Kostelanetz comments:

In nearly 30 years' exploration of fiction writing, I have produced 1) a novella with no more than two words to a paragraph (and then, in one published form, no more than two words to a book page); 2) a story with only single-word paragraphs; 3) stories that are narrated through a series of shapes that are composed exclusively of words or letters; 4) stories consisting exclusively of words whose meaning changes with the introduction not of other words but of different shapes or nonverbal imagery; 5) stories composed entirely of nonrepresentational line-drawings that metamorphose so systematically that each image in the sequence belongs only to its particular place; 6) stories composed of just cut-up photographs whose chips move symmetrically through narrative cycles; 7) individual sentences that are either the openings or the closings of otherwise unwritten stories; 8) separate modular fictions of photographs that can be read in any order, of line-drawings whose positions in a sequence are interchangeable (and thus can be shuffled), of sentences that are recorded in systemic ways to produce different emphases of the same words and gestures, if not radically different stories; 9) circular stories that flow from point to point but lack beginnings or ends; 10) narratives, one as long as a book, composed exclusively of numerals; 11) a story composed of 16 different (but complementary) stories interwoven in print in 16 different typefaces and on audiotape told in 16 purposefully different amplifications of a single voice; 12) a modular fiction whose sentences are reordered in systemic ways to produce different emphases of the same words and gestures, if not radically different stories; 13) over two thousand single-sentence fictions representing the epiphanies of over two thousand otherwise unwritten stories; 14) manuscripts of stories (*Epiphanies*) that have been offered to periodical editors not to publish *in toto* but for them to make their own selections that can then be ordered and designed to their particular tastes; 15) fiction books published in formats ranging from conventional spine-bound volumes to such alternatives as tabloid-sized newsprint books, loose-leaf books (whose pages are gathered in an envelope), and accordion books that are 4 inches high and several feet long; 16) a film and a videotape whose imagery is nothing other than words telling stories; 17) a film with symmetrical abstract fictions (described in #5 above) that metamorphose in systemic sequence; 18) fictions that exist primarily on audiotape—that cannot be performed live, whose printed version is no more than a score for its realization; 19) a film composed of verbal and visual epiphanies that have no connection to each other, either vertically or horizontally, other than common fictional structure; 20) Truly "minimal" fictions no more than three words in length; 21) a cycle of 127 erotic fictions, each one word longer than its predecessor, beginning with a one-word story, up to 64 words, and then each one word less, down to another one-word story; 22) perhaps a few other departures whose character cannot yet, for better or worse, be neatly encapsulated; 23) the purest *oeuvre* of fiction, as fiction, uncompromised by vulgar considerations, that anyone has ever done; 24) no conventional fiction—absolutely none—which is to say nothing that could pass a university course/workshop in "fiction writing" (and get me a job teaching such), and no familiar milestone from which simpleminded critics could then measure my "departure." Even though these fictions of mine have appeared in over three dozen literary magazines, and over a dozen volumes of these fictions have appeared in print, there have been few reviews of individual books, no commercial contracts, no offers from small presses to do a second book, no grants for fiction writing, no inclusion in surveys of contemporary fiction, no public acknowledgment of my alternative purposes in creating and publishing fiction; only one story was ever anthologized by someone else (Eugene Wildman, in his *Experiments in Prose* [1969]). Does anyone care? Should anyone care (other than me)? (Should I care? If so, how? Should I have written this?) What should be made of the fact that no one else—absolutely no one else visible to us—is making fiction in these ways?

*   *   *

Richard Kostelanetz's experimental fiction reflects a formalist program that he has elaborated in his writings as a critic, anthologist, and memoirist. He takes as his "principal assumption . . . that the foundation of experimental literature is a history of formal innovation." On the basis of this assumption, he asserts that "the canon of modernist fiction—Kafka, Stein, Faulkner, Joyce, Beckett, Borges—establishes a tradition of the new" and comprises the only "relevant succession of precedents for the present"; but he adds that several subsequent "post-realist, post-symbolist 'avant-gardes'" now have extended that succession. On the basis of this extended succession, he founds his own experimentalist practice. He has intended "to extend poetry and fiction into other media and, conversely, to discover how other media could best be used for publishing poetry and fiction;" and he has devised a "constructivism" that, in his words, "represents an extreme, perhaps ultimate, development of formalism in fiction." Kostelanetz's program commits him to a particular polemics. He assails publishing conventions that virtually proscribe "pronounced stylistic originality" and, especially, "predominantly visual fiction;" and he argues that "only a philistine would dare dismiss an unfamiliar creation as 'not-fiction'" and characterizes as such critics who accept the abstract and the non-representational in painting but not in fiction. Koselanetz's defense of such fictional practice, however, does not entirely satisfy. He argues that even the most non-representational fictions are mimetics of the "constructive process" itself; that formally experimental fictions can sensitize the reader to "unfamiliar forms in everyday experience;" that such fictions tend to emphasize "kinds of information and perceptions that were previously foreign to literature"; and that such fictions are "culturally progressive" *because* they are "formally progressive." But he also tends to strip these classical avant-garde arguments from their specific ideological bases and ends up appealing generally to what Meyer Schapiro has characterized as a modernist ideology of individual accomplishment in which "artistic integrity required a permanent concern with self-development and the evolution of art." This appeal is implicit in Kostelanetz's assertion that "the sum of my artworks is ultimately about the discovery of possibilities—not only in the exploitation of media but in art and, by extension, in oneself as a creative initiator." Because he is a polemicist, Kostelanetz has sought to isolate the definition of fiction on which his program rests. He begins with negative propositions. He asserts that "words need not be the building blocks of fiction, or sentences the frame, or human beings the 'characters;'" and he asserts that statement in fiction is neither the referential statement he identifies with such expository prose forms as history and journalism nor the "concise, static, generally formalized statement" he identifies with poetry. He then proceeds to his positive definition. Fiction is "a frame filled with a circumscribed world of cohesively self-relating activity," the frame necessarily containing "some kind of movement from one point to another," some internal "diversity and change," some form of "sequential[ity]" or "internal event." Fiction, then, might be made of any material and might therefore exist in any medium; it might be referential but need not be; it need be only dynamic and, for reasons unexplained but locatable in his formalist assumptions, framed. One inclined to challenge Kostelanetz's premises and his reasoning might conclude that they have led him to mistake necessary conditions for sufficient conditions.

It should be obvious that the radically minimalist fiction predicated on Kostelanetz's definition does not resemble fiction in any usual acceptation, and no more so when he is exploring the possibilities of the print medium than when he is exploring those of audiotape, videotape, or film. His annotated "Inventory of My Fictions" lists 41 works. They include visual fictions, such as the "alphabet novellas" *In the Beginning* and *Ad Infinitum: A Fiction,* in each of which Kostelanetz explored how "images in sequence could tell a story by themselves, apart from any additional language." They include numerical fictions, ranging from early concretist pieces such as *Accounting* to more sophisticated mathematical variations such as *Exhaustive Parallel Intervals,* "a book-length narrative, perhaps a novel," in which Kostelanetz attempted "to see whether I could create a Literature composed of numbers alone." They include his "constructivist" works *Constructs* and *Constructs Two,* each comprising "sequential four-sided symmetrical line-drawings that metamorphose in systemic sequence;" the accordian books *Modulations* and *Extrapolate,* "constructivist novella(s) that can be read from one end to the other and back again;" *Tabula Rasa: A Constructivist Novel,* comprising approximately 1,000 pages, "blank with exception of the title page from which subsequent content can be inferred," and *Inexistences: Constructivist Fictions;* "a collection of stories, likewise blank with the exception of the title page from which subsequent contents can be inferred." And they include sophisticated verbal pieces: "One Night Stood," an early "story" comprising two-word paragraphs on the theme of "boy meets girl," becomes *One Night Stood,* printed "in two radically different book formats," in one of which each two-word phrase "take(s) up the entire page of a book, thereby expanding the 'story' into a minimal *novel;" Openings and Closings,* comprising "single sentence fictions" that "were meant to be either the *opening* sentences of hypothetical stories that might have followed or the *closing* sentences of stories that might have come before," finds its companion piece in *Epiphanies,* comprising single-sentence fictions "that are meant to be . . . the key lines in the middle—the epiphany that, in James Joyce's theory, tells the narrative and reveals everything around it." Whether new works or new realizations of printed works, his explorations in other media are equally provocative, at once exuberantly audacious and fastidiously formalitic.

—Charles Caramello

KROETSCH, Robert (Paul)

Nationality: Canadian. **Born:** Heisler, Alberta, 26 June 1927. **Education:** Schools in Heisler and Red Deer, Alberta; University of Alberta, Edmonton, B.A. 1948; McGill University, Montreal, 1954-55; Middlebury College, Vermont, M.A. 1956; University of Iowa, Iowa City, Ph.D. 1961. **Family:** Married 1) Mary Jane Lewis in 1956 (divorced 1979), two daughters; 2) Smaro Kamboureli in 1982. **Career:** Laborer and purser, Yellowknife Transportation Company, Northwest Territories, 1948-50; information specialist (civilian), United States Air Force Base, Goose Bay, Labrador, 1951-54; assistant professor, 1961-65, associate professor, 1965-68, and professor of English, 1968-78, State University of New York, Binghamton. Professor of English, 1978-85, and since 1985 Distinguished Professor, University of Manitoba, Winnipeg. Artist-in-residence, Calgary University, Alberta, Fall 1975, University of Lethbridge, Alberta, Spring 1976, and University of Manitoba, 1976-78. Co-founder, *Boundary 2* magazine, Binghamton, 1972. **Awards:** Bread Loaf Writers Conference grant, 1966; Governor-General's award, 1970; Killam award, 1986. Fellow, Royal Society of Canada, 1986. **Agent:** Sterling Lord, 10 St. Mary Street, Suite 510, Toronto M4Y 1P9. **Address:** Department of English, University of Manitoba, Winnipeg, Manitoba R3T 2N2, Canada.

PUBLICATIONS

Novels

But We Are Exiles. Toronto, Macmillan, 1965; London, Macmillan, and New York, St. Martin's Press, 1966.
The Words of My Roaring. Toronto and London, Macmillan, and New York, St. Martin's Press, 1966.
The Studhorse Man. Toronto, Macmillan, and London, Macdonald, 1969; New York, Simon and Schuster, 1970.
Gone Indian. Toronto, New Press, 1973.
Badlands. Toronto, New Press, 1975; New York, Beaufort, 1983.
What the Crow Said. Toronto, General, 1978.
Alibi. Toronto, Stoddart, and New York, Beaufort, 1983.
The Puppeteer. Toronto, Random House, 1993.

Play

The Studhorse Man, adaptation of his own novel (produced Toronto, 1981).

Poetry

The Stone Hammer: Poems 1960-1975. Nanaimo, British Columbia, Oolichan, 1975.

The Ledger. London, Ontario, Applegarth Follies, 1975.
Seed Catalogue. Winnipeg, Turnstone Press, 1977.
The Sad Phoenician. Toronto, Coach House Press, 1979.
The Criminal Intensities of Love as Paradise. Lantzville, British Columbia, Oolichan, 1981.
Field Notes: Collected Poems. Toronto, General, and New York, Beaufort, 1981.
Advice to My Friends. Toronto, Stoddart, 1985.
Excerpts from the Real World: A Prose Poem in Ten Parts. Lantzville, British Columbia, Oolichan, 1986.
Completed Field Notes: The Long Poems of Robert Kroetsch. Toronto, McClelland and Stewart, 1989.

Other

Alberta. Toronto, Macmillan, and New York, St. Martin's Press, 1968.
The Crow Journals. Edmonton, Alberta, NeWest Press, 1980.
Labyrinths of Voice: Conversations with Robert Kroetsch, with Shirley Neuman and Robert Wilson. Edmonton, Alberta, NeWest Press, 1982.
Letter to Salonika. Toronto, Grand Union, 1983.
The Lovely Treachery of Words: Essays Selected and New. Toronto, Oxford University Press, 1989.

Editor, with James Bacque and Pierre Gravel, *Creation* (interviews). Toronto, New Press, 1970.
Editor, *Sundogs: Stories from Saskatchewan.* Moose Jaw, Saskatchewan, Thunder Creek, 1980.
Editor, with Smaro Kamboureli, *Visible Visions: The Selected Poems of Douglas Barbour.* Edmonton, Alberta, NeWest Press, 1984.
Editor, with Reingard M. Nischik, *Gaining Ground: European Critics on Canadian Literature.* Edmonton, Alberta, NeWest Press, 1985.

*

Bibliography: "An Annotated Bibliography of Works by and about Robert Kroetsch" by Robert Lecker, in *Essays on Canadian Writing* (Toronto), Fall 1977.

Manuscript Collection: University of Calgary Library, Alberta.

Critical Studies: *Robert Kroetsch* by Peter Thomas, Vancouver, Douglas and McIntyre, 1980; "Robert Kroetsch Issue" of *Open Letter* (Toronto), Spring 1983 and Summer-Fall 1984; *Robert Kroetsch* by Robert Lecker, Boston, Twayne, 1986.

Robert Kroetsch comments:

(1991) My novels, often set on the open plains and in the new cities of the Canadian West, border on the comic and hint of the bawdy. The critic Linda Hutcheon has called me the champion of postmodern in Canada because of the experimental nature of my work. I think of myself as a storyteller trying to tell stories amidst the radical discontinuities of contemporary life.

*   *   *

From his first novel, *But We Are Exiles,* to his latest one, *Alibi,* Robert Kroetsch has consistently attempted to reconcile two of his abiding passions: his personal attraction to the literal realities of Canada's rural west, and his artistic desire to transform those realities into various myths, to redefine them by the mere process of telling about them. If our fictions make *us* real, as he has said on many occasions, then everything in our world is transformed by those fictions, too, as long as the fictions last, as it were. And this is the central problem about realistic fiction as he sees it: since it has a beginning, a middle, and an end, it does not last, and the process of transformation is both limited and finite. But if we don't have to worry about beginnings and endings, or if they remain confused for us, then we are continually involved in the process of recreation ourselves, and the realities we once were so sure of take on new and forever changing shapes.

Inevitably, there will be a gap between the intellectualizing of such ideas and their workings out in fiction, and to many readers Kroetsch is more convincing in a critical work like *Labyrinths of Voice* than in his novels that try to dramatize these theories, like his surrealistic *What the Crow Said*. Reality keeps intruding itself in his fiction, and so passionate is Kroetsch about these realities that they, and not the theories, carry the weight of his fiction. The day-to-day activities aboard the *Nahanni Jane* in his first novel, the politics, the beer parlors, and the funeral parlors of *The Words of My Roaring*, the conjoining evidences of man's past and present along the Red Deer River in *Badlands*, the erotic fantasies and realities in spas around the world in *Alibi*: these are the components that give substance and credibility to his novels. *The Studhorse Man* and *Gone Indian* succeed, too, where *What the Crow Said* does not, because they do have tangible landscapes across which we can precisely trace the wanderings of Hazard Lepage and Jeremy Sadness, and their mythical increments assume conviction because of that. *What the Crow Said* is unique amongst Kroetsch's novels in that all its components violate the criteria of empirical reality, and in a sense we have to allow ourselves to be carried along by words that have no tangible referents. It is Kroetsch at his best as a postmodernist, but not at his best as a novelist, for it lacks that fusion of imagination and reality that give his other six novels their power.

As a novelist, Kroetsch is shaped by his belief in a prevailing duality that finds its mythical manifestations in such patterns as the death/rebirth cycle, the quest for identity, the *doppelgänger* motif, the narcissus theme. All of these informed even his first novel which is essentially his most realistic one; Peter Guy's literal role there as a pilot on a riverboat on the MacKenzie allowed Kroetsch to use these mythical accretions as natural extensions of Guy's situation. The novel derives much of its power from Kroetsch's exploitation of the element of water, deriving in turn from his familiarity with his landscape: the absence of water on the dry prairies, where Peter and Mike first meet; the hot springs in the Rockies, where their immersion constitutes a rebirth; the wide expanse of the MacKenzie, in effect all water and no land, where Peter and Mike achieve their final death/rebirth resolution.

In this respect, this first novel anticipates many water-related events of his later works: the drowning of Jonah Bledd in *The Words of My Roaring* and the coming of the apocalyptic rain; Hazard Lepage's and Eugene Utter's trial by flood in *The Studhorse Man;* Dawe and his crew floating towards the past on the Red Deer River in *Badlands;* and, most obviously, Dorf's uncontrollable obsessions with spas in *Alibi*. In one sense, this latest novel can be seen to constitute an obligatory conclusion to the quest for water first launched in *But We Are Exiles,* though in tone or vision, Kroetsch has moved from the tragic to the comic in the process.

River valleys, spring floods, rains, spas, ingredients of the realities and dreams of rural westerners, have become for Kroetsch brilliantly workable symbols in his creation of his fictional worlds.

The male quest, whether for identity, sexuality, power, or death and resurrection, constitutes another recurring motif in Kroetsch's fiction, particularly in what is called his *Out West* trilogy. Built on a fusion of the myth of Genesis and the reality of Alberta's 1935 election, *The Words of My Roaring* chronicles the ascension of the undertaker, Johnnie Judas Backstrom, as he not only defeats the old party incumbent, Doc Murdoch (who had brought Johnnie into the world), but also sexually captures his daughter. The comic tone of this novel camouflages some of its grim realities, like poverty, drought, suicide, auction sales, but the novel's conclusion, like the election itself, can be seen as either the end or the beginning, and within this perspective, its picaresque hero represents the triumph of a new form of chaos over an old, outdated order.

The action of *The Studhorse Man* takes place some 10 years later, just as World War II comes to an end, which helps to transform Hazard Lepage's literal quest into a comic odyssey. The realistic narrative, with its precise times, places, and events moves quite readily into surrealistic and mythological dimensions, and Kroetsch's startling achievement here is how easily he makes us believe that Hazard and Poseidon belong in all three worlds, done in part through his manipulation of the sexual quest. Hazard's earthy sexuality, his lust for Martha kept active by numerous women he encounters on his odyssey, is balanced against his need to reserve Poseidon's rampant sexuality for the right mare to ensure the survival of his breed. It is the studhorse man who triumphs here, for his last sexual act bestows life upon Martha, while the studhorse is pressed into service to provide ingredients for the artificial controlling of life.

Formally, *The Studhorse Man* reflects a number of post-modernist tendencies, from its sense of discontinuity, its fusion of the biographical and autobiographical forms, to the story shaping itself without the traditional rules of narration. It points in these respects to the third work of the trilogy, *Gone Indian,* with its stichomythic structure, its simultaneous narration and narrative revision as Jeremy Sadness exchanges his messages with his graduate professor back in Binghamton. Kroetsch here reflects a novel treatment of the duality pattern, as he structures Sadness's quest in the form of a total identity change, to transform himself into another Grey Owl. The novel lacks the sustaining humor of *The Studhorse Man,* depending unduly on extravagant incidents that do not rise organically out of the fictional ingredients that always made the earlier work plausible, despite its outrageous scenes. Some of the familiar academic games in *Gone Indian,* the infidelities and in-jokes add at best only minor complications to Jeremy's situation, but that he has only one sentence of his dissertation written after nine years, and that he is sexually impotent in a prone position, obviously give him good reason to come to this "far, last edge of our civilization" to start over again. Like Hazard, he is resurrected into death by his final sexual success, and thus can follow his idol, Grey Owl, who also "died into a new life."

The resurrective powers that Bea Sunderman and Martha Proudfoot demonstrated in these last two novels suggest amongst other things their ability, like Faulkner's Dilsey, to survive time, and Kroetsch's next two novels put even more weight on the female adaptability. *Badlands* in effect is a chronicle of distortions and obsessive ambition transformed into truth by the two women who survived this folly, Anna Dawe and Anna Yellowbird, both of whom have been twisted by the actions of William Dawe and his crew. Dawe's daughter at 45 has been denied love and life; Anna Yellowbird has given of her body and life to those men, and then was discarded, much like the bones and the relics they dug up and left behind. Now in league with one another, they make the reverse trip up the river to its source in the Rockies, undoing, as it were, and unrecording all of Dawe's achievements.

In *What the Crow Said* the opposition between the male and female worlds is firmly entrenched—only men are allowed in the beer parlor and in the card game—but the female world gets even with a vengeance. In the more than a dozen marriages in this novel, all the husbands die, except for Liebhaber, some in most gruesome ways, while all the wives survive. This expendability of husbands fulfills, too, the sexual message of Vera's orgasmic cry at the outset, that no mortal man can ever satisfy her after her seduction by the swarm of bees. But it is an extravagant way to make a point, and reflects the fact that the novel's many interplays of cosmic jokes, silences, overlappings of time, and circumstantial exaggerations do not sufficiently come together to create a consistent success.

With *Alibi* Kroetsch has in a sense come full circle from his earlier serious concerns with the quest myths that characteristically had as their goals such respectable revelations as identity, sexuality, or a death/rebirth possibility. But the quest order here—"Find me a spa, Dorf"—is not so much a comment on Deemer's greed or stupidity as it is on the hero's eagerness to continue playing the ritual of the games even when its realization is impossible. It gives Kroetsch the excuse (the alibi) to poke fun at himself, and as a result he has written one of his richest and bawdiest works to date. He is back in a credible, realistic world again, much as he was in *Exiles,* but in that he takes a rest here from the word games of his previous novel, *Alibi* is informed by a refreshing spontaneity. It may well mark the end (or the beginning) of a significant stage in Kroetsch's fictional development.

—Hallvard Dahlie

KUREISHI, Hanif

Nationality: British. **Born:** Bromley, England, 5 December 1954. **Education:** King's College, London, B.A. **Career:** Film director, playwright, screenwriter, novelist; writer-in-residence, 1981 and 1985-86, Royal Court Theatre, London. **Awards:** Themes Television Playwright award, 1980, for *The Mother Country;* George Devine award, 1981; *Evening Standard* award, 1985, for screenplay; Rotterdam Festival's Most Popular Film award, New York Film Critics' Circle Best Screenplay award, and National Society of Film Critics' Best Screenplay award, all 1986, all for *My Beautiful Launderette;* Whitbread book of the Year award, and Booksellers Association of Great Britain and Ireland first novel category, both 1990, both for *The Buddha of Suburbia.* **Agent:** Sheila Lemon, Lemon and Durbridge Ltd., 24 Pottery Lane, London W11 4 LZ, England.

PUBLICATIONS

Novels

The Buddha of Suburbia. London, Faber, and New York, Viking, 1990.

The Black Album. London, Faber, 1995.

Plays

Soaking Up the Heat (produced London, 1976).
The Mother Country (produced London, 1980).
The King and Me (produced London, 1980).
Borderline (produced London, 1981). London, Metheun, 1981.
Cinders, adaptation of a play by Janusz Glowacki (produced London, 1981).
Tomorrow—Today! (produced London, 1981).
Birds of Passage (produced London, 1983). London, Amber Lane, 1983.
Outskirts, The King and Me, Tomorrow—Today! London, River Run Press, 1983.
Mother Courage, adaptation of a play by Bertold Brecht (produced London, 1984).
My Beautiful Launderette and The Rainbow Sign (screenplay). London, Faber, 1986.

Screenplays: *My Beautiful Launderette,* 1985; *Sammy and Rosie Get Laid,* 1987.

Radioplays: *You Can't Go Home,* 1980; *The Trial,* adaptation the novel by Franz Kafka, 1982.

*   *   *

Hanif Kureishi's fiction is a conglomeration of influences; youth culture, the British-Asian experience, sexuality and experimentation, politics and resistance. *The Buddha of Suburbia* and *The Black Album,* in including these influences, make a political aesthetic of their interaction. The ironies of adolescence explored in *The Buddha of Suburbia* depend on the ability of the reader to see wry and sly humor in the meeting of unstable cultural entities; but more significantly Kureishi's version of British-Asian identity insists on critiquing the reification of that identity and implies a necessary and layered complexity in the politics of identity in general. For this reason, Kureishi's novels make him an extraordinarily perceptive commentator on the complexities of postcoloniality and immigrant experiences, a perception that he has applied to the status of Asian identity in the widest contexts of post-1960s Britain.

The Buddha of Suburbia, Kureishi's first novel, opens with an uncovering of the "Indianess" and Englishness of the adolescent Karim. Karim asserts his right to describe himself as an "Englishman" but this soon becomes qualified ("a funny sort of Englishman") and then shifts to a discussion of "the odd mixture of continents and blood, of here and there, of belonging and not belonging, that makes me so restless and easily bored." Already established then is the assumption that the novel will examine this movement from cultural fixity to flux and that the ability to recognize the constituent parts of the result of these changes is a vital outcome in itself. *The Buddha of Suburbia* begins from a similar position to that described autobiographically by Kureishi in "The Rainbow Sign" (published with the script of *My Beautiful Laundrette* in 1986): "From the start I tried to deny my Pakistani self. I was ashamed. It was a curse and I wanted to be rid of it. I wanted to be like everyone else." *The Buddha* has a narrative starting point in which Karim and his father, Haroon, are archetypally "like everyone else"—Haroon is the perfect civil servant, Karim behaves like the typical adolescent. Yet the novel is spurred by events that begin to transform both characters, as Haroon adopts a comically (but never entirely ridiculed) Buddhist personality, whereas Karim develops along the unpredictable cultural and sexual trajectories of teenage life.

The Buddha of Suburbia opens up these moments of stasis. Its narrative progresses almost without the participation of its main characters; their lives are affected by perceptions of their identity constructed by those around them, and Kureishi continually emphasizes the importance of particular versions of being Indian/Muslim that resurface. *The Buddha,* for example, is scathing in its satire of the apparently well intentioned liberal left in Britain and its overindulgence in the "East" as a site of mysticism and spirituality. Indeed most of the humor associated with Haroon in the novel depends on the discrepancy between his Islamic roots and his newfound Buddhism. Edward Said's notion that the West constructs a monolithic East for its own purposes is neatly played out through Haroon, yet with an irony at the expense of the "West" that is in some ways lacking in Said. Thus a fixed "India" cultural identity, desired and projected by those liberal spiritualists who come to Haroon's meditations, is never allowed to settle; it is undermined by their own inability to see Haroon's "inauthenticity" because of their preconceptions.

Whereas Kureishi scrutinizes liberal Western mysticism in *The Buddha of Suburbia,* he uses his second novel to examine a more serious "usage" of marginalized racial groups in the metropolis. *The Black Album* is set during the Rushdie affair (when a *fatwa* was imposed by Iran's spiritual leader upon Salman Rushdie, au-

thor of *The Satanic Verses*) and takes the brave step (considering Kureishi's credentials during the Rushdie affair as someone outspoken in his defense of Rushdie) of attempting to enter the thought processes involved in the anger caused by *The Satanic Verses.* Shahid, the novel's central character, is placed between the familiar poles of an essentialist Asian identity (in this case anti-Rushdie fundamentalism) and Western liberalism. But *The Black Album* (and this is part of its comparative seriousness) produces other options within these polarities. The apparently insupportable monolithic ideology of cultural essentialism represented by Chad and Riaz is given an attraction through its ability to produce a sense of cultural cohesion, community, and comfort. From the liberal Western pole splinters Brownlow, who is used as an example of the Western leftist tendency to overprioritize the marginality of marginal groups—this becomes a drama playing out a guilt that is apparently purged if reversed. *The Black Album* is thus more complex than *The Buddha of Suburbia* in the delineation of race in British society that it offers; it is also a more serious and intense piece of writing, dealing with the same issues in a more threatening, highly charged context. Kureishi's fiction has thus moved along the trajectories of the experience of postcolonial immigration in Britain with intelligence and irony, developing a more complex attitude to political issues and continually exploring narrative and writing stylistics to place that experience in its political and (popular) cultural context.

—Colin Graham

L

LAMMING, George (Eric)

Nationality: Barbadian. **Born:** Carrington Village, 8 June 1927. **Education:** Roebuck Boys' School; Combermere School. **Career:** Teacher in Trinidad, 1946-50; moved to England, 1950; host of book review programme, BBC West Indian Service, London, 1951. Writer-in-residence, University of the West Indies, Kingston, 1967-68. Co-editor of Barbados and Guyana independence issues of *New World Quarterly,* Kingston, 1965 and 1967. **Awards:** Guggenheim fellowship, 1954; *Kenyon Review* fellowship, 1954; Maugham award, 1957; Canada Council fellowship, 1962. D.Litt.: University of the West Indies, Cave Hill, Barbados, 1980. **Address:** 14-A Highbury Place, London N.5., England.

PUBLICATIONS

Novels

In the Castle of My Skin. London, Joseph, and New York, McGraw Hill, 1953.
The Emigrants. London, Joseph, 1954: New York, McGraw Hill, 1955.
Of Age and Innocence. London, Joseph, 1958; New York, Schocken, 1981.
Season of Adventure. London, Joseph, 1960.
Water with Berries. London, Longman, 1971; New York, Holt Rinehart, 1972.
Natives of My Person. London, Longman, and New York, Holt Rinehart, 1972.

Uncollected Short Stories

"David's Walk," in *Life and Letters* (London), November 1948.
"Of Thorns and Thistles" and "A Wedding in Spring," in *West Indian Stories,* edited by Andrew Salkey. London, Faber, 1960.
"Birds of a Feather," in *Stories from the Caribbean,* edited by Andrew Salkey. London, Elek, 1965; as *Island Voices,* New York, Liveright, 1970.
"Birthday Weather," in *Caribbean Literature,* edited by G.R. Coulthard. London, University of London Press, 1966.

Other

The Pleasures of Exile. London, Joseph, 1960; Ann Arbor, University of Michigan Press, 1992.
Influencia del Africa en las literaturas antillanas, with Henry Bangou and René Depestre. Montevideo, Uruguay, I.L.A.C., 1972.
The Most Important People, with Kathleen Drayton. Bridgetown, Barbados, Drayton, 1981.

Editor, *Cannon Shot and Glass Beads: Modern Black Writing.* London, Pan, 1974.

*

Bibliography: *George Lamming: A Select Bibliography,* Cave Hill, Barbados, University of the West Indies Main Library, 1980.

Critical Studies: *The Novels of George Lamming* by Sandra Pouchet Paquet, London, Heinemann, 1982; *Anancy in the Great House: Ways of Reading West Indian Fiction* by Joyce Jonas, New York and London, Greenwood Press, 1990; *Caliban in Exile: The Outsider in Caribbean Fiction* by Margaret Paul Joseph, New York and London, Greenwood Press, 1992.

Theatrical Activities:
Director: **Play**—*Meet Me at Golden Hill,* Barbados, 1974.

* * *

The critical reception of George Lamming's first four novels fell short of their real merits and originality. It is often said that Lamming demands too much of the reader; it might be truer to say that the reader demands too little of Lamming. West Indian fiction has often been distinguished by a certain energy and rhetorical glow but not, except in the work of Lamming and Wilson Harris, by much complexity of form or texture. Right from his first book, *In the Castle of My Skin,* Lamming made it clear that the real complexity of West Indian experience demanded some adequate response of its writers. He has since elaborated this view in an important essay called "The Negro Writer and His World," where he wrote: "To speak of his [the Negro Writer's] situation is to speak of a general need to find a center as well as a circumference which embraces some reality whose meaning satisfies his intellect and may prove pleasing to his senses. But a man's life assumes meaning first in relation to other men . . ." *In the Castle of My Skin* may at first appear to be an autobiography of childhood, but it soon becomes apparent that the book is also the collective autobiography of a Barbadian village moving through the break-up of the old plantation system dominated by the Great House and into the new age of nationalism, industrial unrest and colonial repression. The four boys who stand at the center of the book are given a more or less equal importance though it is "George" who ultimately registers the meaning of their disparate experiences as they are driven asunder by education, travel, and emerging social distinctions.

The collective quality already evident in this, the most personal of all Lamming's books, is more strongly present in *The Emigrants.* Here the portrait is of one boatload of the black emigrants (the title is significant, for it stresses what they leave as well as what they find) who flocked from the Caribbean to Britain between 1950 and 1962. On the boat the emigrants discover a new identity as "West Indians," only to lose it again as they fly centrifugally apart under the stresses of life in an alien culture.

The Emigrants is the saddest of all Lamming's books, because there is almost no focus of hope amid so much disillusionment and despair. By contrast both *Of Age and Innocence* and *Season of Adventure* are powerfully positive books in which what is shed is a set of values adhering to the older generation, those who are unable to match the pace and tendency of the times. *Of Age and Innocence* is set in San Cristobal, a fictional Caribbean island colony rapidly approaching independence. The dominant generation of islanders is unable to break away from its class and racial identities to work together for a new society which will redeem the past of slavery and colonialism, but it is throughout juxtaposed to the generation of its children, who struggle towards that meaning which the nationalist leader Shepherd has glimpsed and then lost again.

> I had always lived in the shadow of a meaning which others had placed on my presence in the world, and I had played no part at all in making that meaning, like a chair which is wholly at the mercy of the idea guiding the hand of the man who builds it. . . . But like the chair, I have played no part at all in making that meaning which others use to define me completely.

Shepherd is destroyed by the forces of the past, but the children look out through the flames of destruction which end the novel towards a future they have already presaged in their games. At the center of *Season of Adventure* stands another unawakened character, the "big-shot coloured" girl Fola, whose father is a West Indian police officer imbued with all the old ideas of order, dominance, and segregation. A visit to a Voduñ ceremony awakens her to the real capacity of her nature for self-discovery and self-renewal. This awakening by ancestral drums is in itself a cliché of Caribbean literature, but here it escapes banality by the intensity of Lamming's lyrical style and the bizarre violence of much of the action. *Season of Adventure* is in some ways the finest of his novels, just as *The Emigrants* is certainly the weakest. Yet the hesitancy which overtakes the drums at the end of the novel, in the very moment of their triumph as the expression of popular values, is analogous to the problem of language Lamming faces in projecting a West Indian culture which will be truly united, consistent and free: "But remember the order of the drums . . . for it is the language which every nation needs if its promises and its myths are to become a fact."

After a silence of more than 10 years, Lamming published two new novels within a year. These were powerfully contrasted in style and theme. *Water with Berries* is superficially a naturalistic novel about three West Indian artists living difficult and ever more lonely lives in modern London. Gradually, however (and the quotation of Caliban in the title gives a clue), the reader becomes aware that this is a study of what happens when Caliban comes to Prospero's original home. The revenges of history work themselves out through characters who are helpless to prevent completing the bizarre and violent patterns of the past. Each of the friends is an aspect of Caliban and each passes through an extreme personal crisis at the novel's end. But Derek, erect upon the stage before a howling audience, having completed the rape of Miranda at last, or Teeton, erect upon a northern island after destroying his last links with the racial past, have at least sketched the possibilities of freedom from these tyrannies of history.

Natives of My Person is more of an extended reverie upon certain dominant themes in Atlantic mythology—the demonic captain, the slave-ship, the imprisoned Amerindian prince, the crew variously haunted by tragedy and terror—which are treated like themes in music. The style is deliberately wrought from the timbers of 17th-century maritime prose, in which this mythology finds its roots. Hence the novel voyages freely in the dimension of space-time, deriving its structure simply from the musical resolution of its dominant themes. This is a work of great beauty, originality, and difficulty, which may finally prove to be Lamming's most important achievement.

—Gerald Moore

LANGE, John. *See* **CRICHTON, (John) Michael.**

LAVIN, Mary

Nationality: Irish. **Born:** East Walpole, Massachusetts, United States, 11 June 1912; moved with her family to Athenry, Ireland, 1923. **Education:** East Walpole schools; Loreto Convent, Dublin; University College, Dublin, B.A. (honors) in English 1934; National University of Ireland, Dublin, M.A. (honors) 1938. **Family:** Married 1) William Walsh in 1942 (died 1954), three daughters; 2) Michael MacDonald Scott in 1969 (died 1990). **Career:** French teacher, Loreto Convent, early 1940s. President, Irish PEN, 1964-65. **Awards:** James Tait Black Memorial prize, 1944; Guggenheim fellowship, 1959, 1962, 1972; Katherine Mansfield-Menton prize, 1962; Ella Lynam Cabot fellowship, 1971; Eire Society gold medal (U.S.A.), 1974; Gregory medal, 1974; American Irish Foundation award, 1979; Allied Irish Bank award, 1981. D.Litt.: National University of Ireland, 1968. President, Irish Academy of Letters, 1971-73. **Address:** Apartment 5, Gilford Pines, Gilford Road, Sandymount, Dublin 4, Ireland.

PUBLICATIONS

Novels

The House in Clewe Street. Boston, Little Brown, and London, Joseph, 1945.
Mary O'Grady. Boston, Little Brown, and London, Joseph, 1950.

Short Stories

Tales from Bective Bridge. Boston, Little Brown, 1942; London, Joseph, 1943.
The Long Ago and Other Stories. London, Joseph, 1944.
The Becker Wives and Other Stories. London, Joseph, 1946; as *At Sallygap and Other Stories,* Boston, Little Brown, 1947.
A Single Lady and Other Stories. London, Joseph, 1951.
The Patriot Son and Other Stories. London, Joseph, 1956.
Selected Stories. New York, Macmillan, 1959.
The Great Wave and Other Stories. London, Macmillan, and New York, Macmillan, 1961.
The Stories of Mary Lavin. London, Constable, 3 vols., 1964-85.
In the Middle of the Fields and Other Stories. London, Constable, 1967; New York, Macmillan, 1969.
Happiness and Other Stories. London, Constable, 1969; Boston, Houghton Mifflin, 1970.
Collected Stories. Boston, Houghton Mifflin, 1971.
A Memory and Other Stories. London, Constable, 1972; Boston, Houghton Mifflin, 1973.
The Shrine and Other Stories. London, Constable, and Boston, Houghton Mifflin, 1977.
Selected Stories. London, Penguin, 1981; New York, Penguin, 1984.
A Family Likeness and Other Stories. London, Constable, 1985.
In a Café and Other Stories. Dublin, Town House, 1995.

Other (for children)

A Likely Story. New York, Macmillan, 1957.
The Second-Best Children in the World. London, Longman, and Boston, Houghton Mifflin, 1972.
The Story of the Widow's Son. Mankato, Minnesota, Creative Education, 1993.

*

Bibliography: By Paul A. Doyle, in *Papers of the Bibliography Society of America 63* (New York), 1969; *Mary Lavin: A Check List* by Ruth Krawschak, Berlin, Krawschak, 1979.

Manuscript Collections: Southern Illinois University, Carbondale; Mugar Memorial Library, Boston University.

Critical Studies: Preface by Lavin to *Selected Stories,* 1959, and by V.S. Pritchett to *Collected Stories,* 1971; *Mary Lavin* by Zack Brown, Lewisburg, Pennsylvania, Bucknell University Press, 1975; *Mary Lavin* by Richard F. Peterson, Boston, Twayne, 1978; "Mary Lavin Issue" of *Irish University Review* (Dublin), Autumn 1979; *Mary Lavin, Quiet Rebel: A Study of Her Short Stories* by A.A. Kelly, Dublin, Wolfhound Press, and New York, Barnes and Noble, 1980; forward by Thomas Kilroy to *In a Café,* 1995; preamble by Elizabeth Walsh Pearoy to *In a Café,* 1995.

*   *   *

Mary Lavin has obvious gifts for fiction: she can tell a story, invent characters and give them vivid speech, a life of their own, settings described economically yet evocatively. But she has more also, a capacity for selecting those moments of crisis when the world passes by but time stops still as the meaning of life is suddenly crystallized for some person. She first showed this gift in her short stories, which are Chekhovian in scope. *Tales from Bective Bridge* contained "Love Is for Lovers" where Mathew, an elderly bachelor, is attracted and then repelled by Mrs. Cooligan, a widow. His sudden nausea at the thought of her, of her love of warmth, of her dog, of cushions, of her orange dress, occurs one summer day in her garden. She tips a half dead fly out of her tea: the fly shakes the liquid out of his wings, as though celebrating his release. But the lazy fat dog swallows him. The whole Saturday afternoon's lesson is there, and we are prepared for Mathew's thoughts that evening: he had been trying to go back, to his dreams of a slender girl, a sweet cool fragrant marriage: "But you couldn't go back, ever."

These sudden moments of perception enrich her stories which also explore the differences between dream and reality. The story "Magenta," for instance, in *The Becker Wives* builds slowly and remorselessly up to a climax where the girl's quickly invented stories about the supposed actress who employs her, lending her her clothes, are punctured by the small mistake of her being 20 minutes too late for the train back, so that she cannot replace the clothes she has stolen.

There is a remorseless quality about Lavin's fiction which marks her two novels, *The House in Clewe Street* and *Mary O'Grady.* In both she displays an impressive skill in handling different ages in family groupings. *The House in Clewe Street* explores a boy's growing up under the care of two aunts, and his sudden rebellion and running away with the servant girl. In this story Lavin explores the tyranny given by the possession of both money and ruthless self-confidence and shows its crippling effect upon Gabriel, the pro-

tagonist. The story is, in essence, about the gradual undermining of his innocence. He does not question or rebel, without the outside stimulus given by his friend Sylvester. The exploration of his school, his growing interest in Onny the servant, his jealousy of her friendships in Dublin are all unfolded with the precision of a surgeon's skill. Yet this is no clinical novel, for we are aware of a compassionate attitude on the part of the author towards her characters. They have choice, they even enjoy the after effects of making a wrong choice. They are indeed children to whom Yeats's lines might well apply: "young/We loved each other and were ignorant."

In *Mary O'Grady* we are given the history of a family living in a Dublin suburb: a devoted husband and wife, their children growing up, and becoming adults, one going to America and eventually returning, one studying to become a priest, the girls finding husbands. The emotional content is rich and varied, the mother's strength impressive, the children's development into adults charted with convincing knowledge.

If the reader were to concentrate upon one specific aspect of Lavin's storytelling capacity and the subtle human understanding which informs all her fiction it might well be upon that delicate stage where adolescence asserts independence, is critical of parents while half ashamed of being so, yet determined to escape from the round of accustomed family life. In *Mary O'Grady,* for instance, there is the brilliantly evoked evening when the daughters are visited for the first time by the two engineering students who fall in love with them. The shyness, the gaucherie, the gradually developing friendliness of the family are handled with an assurance which not only encourages the reader to accept the narrator's unobtrusive, tactful guidance, but reinforces the sympathetic interest created from the beginning of the novel.

The secret of Lavin's success is, perhaps, to be found in that ability she possesses of taking her readers into her confidence, sharing with them her panoptic survey of those characters whom she regards in a kindly yet detached fashion. She has an awareness of the comedy as well as the tragedy of human life. She relishes its absurdities, weaves them into the tapestry, and keeps her proportions right. Her stories are set in Ireland, but her characters are universal. They may speak with the accents of the Irish countryside or of the city of Dublin, their particular modes of tact or forthrightness may be Irish in emphasis or accent, but these are people who exist anywhere in the world, given the author's ability to see them with insight, and, like Lavin, to portray them with realistic compassion, in their actions and in their self-revealing speech. She believes a writer distills the essence of his thought in a short story, that this kind of writing is only looking closer into the human heart. Her themes are loneliness, despair, escape, paralysis, and frustration: her strength comes from the impersonal objectivity with which she depicts unhappy characters. Ultimately she is an enduring writer, because the irony which is the mainstay of her technique is matched by penetrating insight into human thought and its effect on behavior.

—A. Norman Jeffares

le CARRÉ, John

Pseudonym for David John Moore Cornwell. **Nationality:** British. **Born:** Poole, Dorset, 19 October 1931. **Education:** Sherborne

School, Dorset; St. Andrew's Preparatory School; Bern University, Switzerland, 1948-49; Lincoln College, Oxford, B.A. (honours) in modern languages 1956. **Family:** Married 1) Alison Ann Veronica Sharp in 1954 (divorced 1971), three sons; 2) Valerie Jane Eustace in 1972, one son. **Career:** Tutor, Eton College, Berkshire, 1956-58; member of the British Foreign Service, 1959-64: second secretary, Bonn Embassy, 1961-64; consul, Hamburg, 1963-64. **Awards:** British Crime Novel award, 1963; Maugham award, 1964; Mystery Writers of America Edgar Allan Poe award, 1965, and Grand Master award, 1984; Crime Writers Association Gold Dagger, 1978, 1980, and Diamond Dagger, 1988; James Tait Black Memorial prize, 1978; Nikos Kasanzakis prize, 1991. Honorary doctorate: University of Exeter 1990. Honorary fellow, Lincoln College, 1984. **Agent:** David Higham Associates, 5-8 Lower John Street, London W1R 4HA, England.

PUBLICATIONS

Novels

Call for the Dead. London, Gollancz, 1961; New York, Walker, 1962; as *The Deadly Affair,* London, Penguin, 1966.
A Murder of Quality. London, Gollancz, 1962; New York, Walker, 1963.
The Spy Who Came In from the Cold. London, Gollancz, 1963; New York, Coward McCann, 1964.
The Looking-Glass War. London, Heinemann, and New York, Coward McCann, 1965.
A Small Town in Germany. London, Heinemann, and New York, Coward McCann, 1968.
The Naive and Sentimental Lover. London, Hodder and Stoughton, 1971; New York, Knopf, 1972.
The Quest for Karla. London, Hodder and Stoughton, and New York, Knopf, 1982.
Tinker, Tailor, Soldier, Spy. London, Hodder and Stoughton, and New York, Knopf, 1974.
The Honourable Schoolboy. London, Hodder and Stoughton, and New York, Knopf, 1977.
Smiley's People. London, Hodder and Stoughton, and New York, Knopf, 1980.
The Little Drummer Girl. London, Hodder and Stoughton, and New York, Knopf, 1983.
A Perfect Spy. London, Hodder and Stoughton, and New York, Knopf, 1986.
The Russia House. London, Hodder and Stoughton, and New York, Knopf, 1989.
The Secret Pilgrim. London, Hodder and Stoughton, and New York, Knopf, 1991.
The Night Manager. London, Hodder and Stoughton, and New York, Knopf, 1993.
Our Game. London, Hodder and Stoughton, and New York, Knopf, 1995.

Uncollected Short Stories

"Dare I Weep, Dare I Mourn," in *Saturday Evening Post* (Philadelphia), 28 January 1967.
"What Ritual Is Being Observed Tonight?," in *Saturday Evening Post* (Philadelphia), 2 November 1968.

Play

Television Play: *Smiley's People,* with John Hopkins, from the novel by le Carré, 1982.

Other

The Clandestine Muse. Portland, Oregon, Seluzicki, 1986.
Vanishing England, with Gareth H. Davies. Topsfield, Massachusetts, Salem House, 1987.

*

Critical Studies: *John le Carré* by Peter Lewis, New York, Ungar, 1985, London, Lorrimer, 1986; *The Novels of John le Carré: The Art of Survival,* Oxford, Blackwell, 1985, and *Smiley's Circus: A Guide to the Secret World of John le Carré,* London, Orbis, 1986, both by David Monaghan; *John le Carré* by Eric Homberger, London, Methuen, 1986; *Taking Sides: The Fiction of John le Carré* by Tony Barley, Milton Keynes, Buckinghamshire, Open University Press, 1986; *Corridors of Deceit: The World of John le Carré* by Peter Wolfe, Bowling Green, Ohio, Popular Press, 1987; *The Quest for John le Carré* edited by Alan Bold, London, Vision Press, and New York, St. Martin's Press, 1988.

*   *   *

Though John le Carré has written two thrillers, *Call for the Dead* and *A Murder of Quality,* it was when *The Spy Who Came In from the Cold* was published that it became obvious that a new talent for writing a different kind of spy story had emerged. Le Carré caught a new mood of chilling horror in this picture of the beastliness underlying the espionage of the cold war, for this is a novel which shows how man's capacity for inhumanity to man and woman is heightened through the process of espionage. The style matches the material. The moods evoked are of gray despair. The tone is cold, almost clinical. The conversations convince; they have the authentic texture of contemporary speech. And the details of the British, Dutch and German background are painted in with a casual assurance. The story is unfolded, given fresh twists, until the reality of life itself becomes warped. Leamas, the British agent, is created convincingly; he carries out his role of defector only to find that his own people have framed him, in order to frame Fiedler, an East German who has discovered the truth about Mundt, his chief.

This is a world of intellectual skills applied arbitrarily, of brilliance without scruple, of brutality without restraint. The inexorable march of the story continues: its destiny is disaster, the same kind of disaster which opens its account of the effects of treason and betrayal. And yet in the final moment Leamas returns for Liz, the English communist party member who befriended him in London, who has been brought to East Germany to testify against him. Before their final moments, before they attempt to cross the Berlin wall, he makes his apology to her. To him it seems the world has gone mad. His life and hers, their dignity, are a tiny price to pay. They are, ultimately, the victims of a temporary alliance of expediency. His people save Mundt because they need him, "so that," he says to her, "the great moronic mass that you admire can sleep soundly in their beds at night. They need him for the safety of ordinary crummy people like you and me." He sees the loss of Fiedler's life as part of the small-scale war which is being waged, with a wastage of innocent life sometimes, though it is still smaller than other wars. Leamas doesn't believe in anything, but he sees people cheated, misled, lives thrown away, "people shot and in prison, whole groups and classes of men written off for nothing." Her party, he remarks, was built on the bodies of ordinary people, and she remembers the German prison wardress describing the prison as one for those who slow down the march, "for those who think they have the right to err."

Le Carré's next book, *The Looking-Glass War,* carries his exploration of the work of intelligence services further. This story opens impressively, with the death of a courier who has gone to Finland to pick up films made by the pilot of a commercial flight apparently off course over Eastern Germany. An unconfirmed report indicates the likelihood of a rocket site there. Then a small intelligence unit is authorized to put an agent into the area. The preparations are described in detail: the recruiting and training of the agent, the ineptitude involved, and the rivalry among the different agencies—and ultimately the schooled indifference with which the older professionals see their scheme fail abysmally. They are already planning the future, disowning the agent whose slow broadcasting on single frequencies on an obsolete radio has doomed him to capture. The story is well told; it explores the stresses and the vanities, the dangerous risks, even delusions, which beset the world of intelligence; it has a curious pathos, accentuated by the naivety and decency of the young man Avery which is opposed in fury by Haldane, who has become a technician: "We sent him because we needed to; we abandon him because we must."

In *A Small Town in Germany* there is an enlarging of scope. Here is a story of the British Embassy in Bonn, from which secret files—and Leo Harting—have vanished. Turner comes from London to investigate. His interrogations of some of the Embassy staff are brilliant. The pattern of thieving, of treachery, of insinuation, of making himself indispensable, of using others, emerges slowly as Turner tries to build up his picture of Leo Harting. The contrasts of personalities as Turner painstakingly pursues his inquiries give this picture depth, and yet the nature of the vanished man remains elusive. The complications of the British negotiations in Brussels where German support is necessary, the student riots, and the ugly neo-nazism give the man-hunt an extreme urgency. The attitude of the German authorities, and that of the Head of Chancery, surprise Turner. And the events he unravels surprise the reader.

The novel has a continuous tension; the discoveries of the investigator are cumulative; and finally his aggressive desire to hunt out the missing man turns to a sympathetic understanding of just what Harting has been doing. At this point his attitude differs markedly from that of the Head of Chancery. To a certain extent his reactions are parallel to those of Avery in *The Looking-Glass War.* Both are younger men, outside the orthodoxies of their elders, possessed ultimately of more humanity, though they have no capacity to influence the final stages of the story. The difference lies between the character who professes to control the processes of his own mind and the character who believes we are born free, we are not automatons and cannot control the processes of our minds. The novel is, in fact, about the problems of forgetting, and about the problems of idealism, innocence, and practical politics; and the incidental picture it gives of the complex working life of an Embassy provides a very suitable background against which political issues can be spotlit.

The Naive and Sentimental Lover lacks the punch and energy of his earlier works. In them the tendency of the characters to be warped, maimed, frustrated men and women mattered little because the action backed by skillful description carried the plot forward at such headlong speed that analysis of character *per se* was less important than the actions taken by the participants. In this novel there is a need for a deeper analysis of character, and this does not seem to have been fully achieved, while the story does not move with the same sureness. However, it is likely that le Carré was experimenting with a new genre, and just as *The Spy Who Came In from the Cold* needed preliminary studies this may herald a development in character depiction similar to his earlier advances in technique and architectonic power in *The Spy Who Came In from the Cold,* which will remain as a chilling exposé of the continuous underground battle of intelligence services.

Tinker, Tailor, Soldier, Spy and *The Honourable Schoolboy* are both surpassed by *Smiley's People,* the narrative art of which is combined with a sympathetic compassion for its characters. Here le Carré shows Smiley torn by loyalties, uncovering instead of covering up the murder of an ex-agent, and in the process peeling layer after layer from the mystery of betrayal, getting steadily closer to his old enemy the Russian Karla. The story moves deliberately, the details are amassed, but the tension is maintained right to the climax. This is a *tour de force* because its present action demands an understanding of the past, and that past is revealed so skillfully that its actions live as a pressing part of the present. The reader is involved in the characters' memories, their evasions and searchings.

In *The Little Drummer Girl* le Carré portrays the violent conflicts of Arab and Israeli, moving his characters freely about Europe as he tightens the tense atmosphere created by terrorism. His characters are meticulous in their attention to detail; he conveys the concentration, the ruthlessness, the tyranny of abstract concepts made utterly inhuman. This is a story in which several ways of looking at life—and the deaths of victims—are juxtaposed convincingly; the effect is achieved through le Carré's capacity to create confidence in his readers through an inside knowledge of how terrorists and counter-terrorists operate.

A Perfect Spy and *The Russia House* both show le Carré's maturity, his established mastery of his medium. In *The Russia House* he moves to the new situation in the Soviet Union and brings alive the nature of its strange society. Deftly he indicates the effect of *glasnost,* the shift from suppression of public debate to new speculation, new credulity, new idealism, all balanced by old shortages, old skepticism, old inertias. The analysis is effective, the shifting pattern of change suggested with subtlety, the tension maintained. Bailey, the blundering British publisher, and Katya, the unselfish Russian woman with whom he falls in love, hold our attention, watched over by the British and American intelligence agents. It is convincing, at times moving, always exciting; it blends irony with a sense of the absurdity of suspicion, while at the same time suggesting the need for political caution in reacting to the unpredictable turmoil of the contemporary Soviet scene.

—A. Norman Jeffares

LEE, SKY

Nationality: Canadian. **Born:** Port Alberni, British Columbia, 1952. **Education:** University of British Columbia, B.A.; Douglas College, diploma in nursing. **Family:** Has one son. **Career:** Nurse and writer.

PUBLICATIONS

Novels

Disappearing Moon Cafe. Vancouver, Douglas and McIntyre, 1990;
    Seattle, Washington, Seal Press, 1991.
Bellydancer. Vancouver, Press Gang, 1994.

Short Stories

Teach Me to Fly, Skyfighter! and Other Stories, with Paul Yee.
    Toronto, Lorimer, 1983.

*   *   *

In "All Spikes but the Last" (1957), F. R. Scott rebukes E. J.
Pratt for failing in his epic, *Towards the Last Spike* (1952), to acknowledge the contribution Chinese laborers made in finishing the
transnational Canadian Pacific Railway. "Where are the coolies in
your poem, Ned? / Where are the thousands from China who swung
their picks with bare hands at forty below?" Who, Scott asks, "has
sung their story?"

A revisionist narrative returning presence to historical absence,
defying silence with song and story, *Disappearing Moon Cafe* tells
the story of Vancouver's Chinese community, whose role in British Columbia's development has, until recently, been disregarded.
SKY Lee's novel is a formidable addition to the growing, though
relatively small, body of Chinese-Canadian literature. Epic in scope
and intent, spanning four generations and nearly a century (1892
to 1986), *Disappearing Moon Cafe* weighs the cultural cost of survival, particularly for generations of Chinese-Canadian women, and
charts the tangled connections between Wong Gwei Chang, who is
entrusted by the Chinese community with the responsibility of collecting the bones of laborers who died building the railway and
returning them to China for burial, and his descendants. Great-
granddaughter Kae Ying Woo, inspired by her pregnancy, narrates
the story and exposes murky familial secrets. Like her ancestor,
Kae searches for her family's bones. Powerful vignettes, flashbacks, multiple perspectives, and temporal juxtapositions are features of her narrative as she wrestles with the problems of knowing and representing the past. At times, though, the sameness of
Lee's narration and its occasional inchoateness restrain the promising elasticity of her invention.

Lee's family saga deals with repatriation and assimilation, the
tug between cultures. The young migrants maintain connections
with China to protect themselves from the Canadian wilderness and
nativism. But as they settle down and have families, as the Canadian government restricts passage between China and Canada, and
as China is politically transformed and then isolated, their Canadian-born children forge new identities, negotiating the conflicting
demands of the old world, where customs and laws are clear, and
the new, where values are less certain. For some, such as relocated
village teenager Wong Choy Fuk, this is easy. He proves "amazingly quick to shed his bumpkin ways in favour of a more cocky
western style." Indeed, the cafe of the title is symbolically divided
in two. One section, "a nostalgic replica of an old-fashioned Chinese teahouse," is very popular with "homesick Chinese clientele;"
the other, a "more modern counter-and-booth section," enchants
Choy Fuk: "He loved the highly polished chrome and brightly lit
glass, the checkerboard tiles on the floor, the marble countertop.
And except for the customers, his mother, and perhaps the cacti,
there was nothing Chinese about it."

The family plays an important role offsetting the dislocations of
immigration. Mui Lan, Gwei Chang's Chinese wife, expends considerable malicious energy ensuring that the Wong name does not
evaporate. Although her obsession with her daughter-in-law's fertility may appear to be a traditional Chinese concern, conditions in
Canada—the Canadian government imposed an expensive head tax
and then prohibited Chinese immigration for many years, thus obstructing the possibility of family reunion—helped shape and exacerbate this concern also.

The genealogy of the Wong family, a potential dynasty, structures *Disappearing Moon Cafe.* Maintaining a pure lineage is impossible, as Kae discovers when she probes the secrets, allegiances,
demands, and contradictions of family. Anything is permissible, so
long as a son is born and the Wong name perpetuated. Security,
honor, and prestige, for example, will be Fong Mei's reward on
the condition that she let her husband, Choy Fuk, who we later
learn is impotent, sleep with Song An, a waitress at Disappearing
Moon Cafe. The Wong family tree prefaces the story; primarily
Chinese, it includes aboriginal Shi'atko and an anonymous French-
Canadian woman, although both are nominal figures. Positioning
the family tree at the start of the narrative and thus disclosing the
infidelities and incest that motivate various characters does, however, drain the narrative of much of its tension.

Lee's 1994 short story collection, *Bellydancer,* augments her
range of characters, if not her colloquial prose, which favors explanation and exclamation over ellipsis. Some stories focus on Chinese-Canadian experience and expand upon themes addressed in
Disappearing Moon Cafe—"Broken Teeth" is about conflict between a mother born in China and her Canadian-born daughter,
and the marvelous "The Soong Sisters" revolves around a genealogy only slightly less complicated than the Wong family's. Others
consider relationships: heterosexual, lesbian, and, in "Safe Sex,"
something mysterious that transcends gender altogether.

—Stephen Milnes

———

LEE, William. *See* **BURROUGHS, William S(eward).**

———

LE GUIN, Ursula K(roeber)

Nationality: American. **Born:** Berkeley, California, 21 October
1929; daughter of the anthropologist Alfred L. Kroeber. **Education:** Radcliffe College, Cambridge, Massachusetts, A.B. in French
1951 (Phi Beta Kappa); Columbia University, New York (Faculty
fellow; Fulbright fellow, 1953), M.A. in romance languages 1952.
Family: Married Charles A. Le Guin in 1953; two daughters and
one son. **Career:** Instructor in French, Mercer University, Macon,
Georgia, 1954, and University of Idaho, Moscow, 1956; department secretary, Emory University, Atlanta, 1955; taught writing
workshops at Pacific University, Forest Grove, Oregon, 1971, University of Washington, Seattle, 1971-73, Portland State University,
Oregon, 1974, 1977, 1979, 1995, in Melbourne, Australia, 1975,

at the University of Reading, England, 1976, Indiana Writers Conference, Bloomington, 1978 and 1983, and University of California, San Diego, 1979. **Awards:** Boston *Globe-Horn Book* award, 1968; Nebula award, 1969, 1975 (twice), 1990; Hugo award, 1970, 1973, 1974, 1975; National Book award, 1972; Newbery Silver Medal award, 1972; *Locus* award (twice), 1973, 1984; Jupiter award, 1975 (twice), 1976; Gandalf award, 1979; Lewis Carroll Shelf award, 1979; University of Oregon Distinguished Service award, 1981; Janet Kafka award, 1986; Prix Lectures-Jeunesse (France), 1987; Pushcart prize, 1991; Harold Vursell award, 1991; Oregon Institute of Literary Arts H.L. Davis award, 1992; *Hubbub* Annual Poetry award, 1995; *Asimov's* Reader's award, 1995. Guest of Honor, World Science Fiction Convention, 1975. D.Litt.: Bucknell University, Lewisburg, Pennsylvania, 1978; Lawrence University, Appleton, Wisconsin, 1979; D.H.L.: Lewis and Clark College, Portland, 1983; Occidental College, Los Angeles, 1985. Lives in Portland, Oregon. **Agent:** Virginia Kidd, 538 East Harford Street, Milford, Pennsylvania 18337, U.S.A.

PUBLICATIONS

Novels

Rocannon's World. New York, Ace, 1966; London, Tandem, 1972.
Planet of Exile. New York, Ace, 1966; London, Tandem, 1972.
City of Illusions. New York, Ace, 1967; London, Gollancz, 1971.
The Left Hand of Darkness. New York, Ace, and London, Macdonald, 1969.
The Lathe of Heaven. New York, Scribner, 1971; London, Gollancz, 1972.
The Dispossessed: An Ambiguous Utopia. New York, Harper, and London, Gollancz, 1974.
The Word for World Is Forest. New York, Putnam, 1976; London, Gollancz, 1977.
Earthsea. London, Gollancz, 1977; as *The Earthsea Trilogy,* London, Penguin, 1979.
A Wizard of Earthsea. Berkeley, California, Parnassus Press, 1968; London, Gollancz, 1971.
The Tombs of Atuan. New York, Atheneum, 1971; London, Gollancz, 1972.
The Farthest Shore. New York, Atheneum, 1972; London, Gollancz, 1973.
Malafrena. New York, Putnam, 1979; London, Gollancz, 1980.
The Eye of the Heron. New York, Harper, and London, Gollancz, 1983.
Always Coming Home. New York, Harper, 1985; London, Gollancz, 1986.
Tehanu: The Last Book of Earthsea. New York, Atheneum, and London, Gollancz, 1990.
Buffalo Gals, Won't You Come Out Tonight, illustrated by Susan Seddon Boulet, San Francisco, Pomegranate Artbooks, 1994.

Short Stories

The Wind's Twelve Quarters. New York, Harper, 1975; London, Gollancz, 1976.
The Water Is Wide. Portland, Oregon, Pendragon Press, 1976.
Orsinian Tales. New York, Harper, 1976; London, Gollancz, 1977.
The Compass Rose. New York, Harper, 1982; London, Gollancz, 1983.

The Visionary: The Life Story of Flicker of the Serpentine, with *Wonders Hidden,* by Scott Russell Sanders. Santa Barbara, California, Capra Press, 1984.
Buffalo Gals and Other Animal Presences (includes verse). Santa Barbara, California, Capra Press, 1987; as *Buffalo Gals,* London, Gollancz, 1990.
Searoad. New York, HarperCollins, 1991; London, Gollancz, 1992.
A Fisherman of the Inland Sea: Science Fiction Stories, New York, HarperPerennial, 1994.

Fiction (for children)

Very Far Away from Anywhere Else. New York, Atheneun, 1976; as *A Very Long Way from Anywhere Else,* London, Gollancz, 1976.
Leese Webster, New York, Atheneum, 1979; London, Gollancz, 1981.
The Beginning Place. New York, Harper, 1980; as *Threshold,* London, Gollancz, 1980.
The Adventure of Cobbler's Rune, New York, Virginia, Cheap Street, 1982.
Solomon Leviathan's Nine Hundred and Thirty-First Trip Around the World. New Castle, Virginia, Cheap Street, 1983.
A Visit from Dr. Katz. New York, Atheneum, 1988; as *Dr. Katz,* London, Collins, 1988.
Catwings. New York, Orchard, 1988.
Catwings Return. New York, Orchard, 1989.
Fire and Stone. New York, Atheneum, 1989.
A Ride on the Red Mare's Back. New York, Orchard, 1992.
Fish Soup. New York, Atheneum, 1992.
Wonderful Alexander and the Catwings. New York, Orchard, 1994.

Plays

No Use to Talk to Me, in *The Altered Eye,* edited by Lee Harding. Melbourne, Norstrilia Press, 1976; New York, Berkley, 1980.
King Dog (screenplay), with *Dorstoevsky,* by Raymond Carver and Tess Gallagher. Santa Barbara, California, Capra Press, 1985.

Poetry

Wild Angels. Santa Barbara, California, Capra Press, 1975.
Tillai and Tylissos, with Theodora K. Quinn. N.p., Red Bull Press, 1979.
Torrey Pines Reserve. Northridge, California, Lord John Press, 1980.
Gwilan's Harp. Northridge, California, Lord John Press, 1981.
Hard Words and Other Poems. New York, Harper, 1981.
In the Red Zone. Northridge, California, Lord John Press, 1983.
Wild Oats and Fireweed. New York, Harper, 1988.
Blue Moon over Thurman Street. Portland, Oregon, NewSage Press, 1993.
Going Out with Peacocks and Other Poems. New York, HarperPerennial, 1994.

Other

From Elfland to Poughkeepsie (lecture). Portland, Oregon, Pendragon Press, 1973.
Dreams Must Explain Themselves. New York, Algol Press, 1975.

The Language of the Night: Essays on Fantasy and Science Fiction, edited by Susan Wood. New York, Putnam, 1979; revised edition, London, Women's Press, 1989.

Dancing at the Edge of the World: Thoughts on Words, Women, Places. New York, Grove Press, and London, Gollancz, 1989.

The Way the Water's Going: Images of the Northern California Coastal Range, photographs by Ernest Waugh and Alan Nicolson. New York, Harper, 1989.

Editor, *Nebula Award Stories 11.* London, Gollancz, 1976; New York, Harper, 1977.

Editor, with Virginia Kidd, *Interfaces.* New York, Ace, 1980.

Editor, with Virginia Kidd, *Edges.* New York, Pocket Books, 1980.

Editor, with Brian Attebery, *The Norton Book of Science Fiction: North American Science Fiction, 1960-1990.* New York, Norton, 1993.

Recordings: *The Ones Who Walk Away from Omelas,* Alternate World, 1976; *Gwilan's Harp and Intracom.* Caedmon, 1977; *The Earthsea Triology,* Colophone, 1981; *Music and Poetry of the Kesh,* Valley Productions, 1985; *Rigel Nine: An Audio Opera,* Charisma, 1985; *The Left Hand of Darkness,* Warner, 1985; *The Word for World Is Forest,* Book of the Road, 1986.

*

Bibliography: *Ursula K. Le Guin: A Primary and Secondary Bibliography* by Elizabeth Cummins Cogell, Boston, Hall, 1983.

Manuscript Collection: University of Oregon Library, Eugene.

Critical Studies: *The Farthest Shores of Ursula K. Le Guin* by George Edgar Slusser, San Bernardino, California, Borgo Press, 1976; "Ursula Le Guin Issue" of *Science-Fiction Studies* (Terre Haute, Indiana), March 1976; *Ursula Le Guin* by Joseph D. Olander and Martin H. Greenberg, New York, Taplinger, and Edinburgh, Harris, 1979; *Ursula K. Le Guin: Voyage to Inner Lands and to Outer Space* edited by Joseph W. De Bolt, Port Washington, New York, Kennikat Press, 1979; *Ursula K. Le Guin* by Barbara J. Bucknall, New York, Ungar, 1981; *Ursula K. Le Guin* by Charlotte Spivack, Boston, Twayne, 1984; *Approaches to the Fiction of Ursula K. Le Guin* by James Bittner, Ann Arbor, Michigan, UMI Research Press, and Epping, Essex, Bowker, 1984; *Understanding Ursula K. Le Guin* by Elizabeth Cummins Cogell, Columbia, University of South Carolina Press, 1990.

*   *   *

Ursula K. Le Guin's earliest works attracted, almost exclusively, the devoted audience of science-fiction readers. *Rocannon's World, Planet of Exile,* and *City of Illusions* are interconnected novels which depict a situation entirely familiar to such readers. Earth and other planets of a far-future "League of All Worlds" are peopled by "Human" races which must struggle to recognize one another as such. The League prepares to meet a rather vaguely defined invasion from afar. Heroes out of touch with lost civilization undertake quests of self-discovery, or get the enemy's location through to headquarters just in time to repel the invasion. In short, Le Guin offers us space opera, although the delicate tone, the theme of communication, and the imagery of light and darkness suggest her future development.

With *The Left Hand of Darkness, The Word for World Is Forest,* her *Earthsea* fantasy trilogy, and *The Disposessed,* Le Guin moved to another level, and began, deservedly, to attract an audience outside the science-fiction ghetto. The treatment of androgyny in *The Left Hand of Darkness* has made the book into a minor classic. The League of All Worlds has been succeeded by a non-imperialistic "Ekumen," which sends a lone envoy, Genly Ai, to make an alliance with the isolated planet Winter (Gethen). The Ekumen has no wish to subdue Winter but to extend "the evolutionary tendency inherent in Being; one manifestation of which is exploration." Subverting the stock situation of civilization brought to the savages, Le Guin has Ai learn at least as much from the relatively primitive Gethenians as they from him. Gethenians mate only once a month, and they may adopt alternatively male and females roles. We heard at one point that "the King is pregnant." Ai, a male chauvinist, learns how difficult it is to think of our fellow humans as people rather than as men and women. When he forms an alliance with a Gethenian called Estraven, Ai learns how close together the words "patriot" and "traitor" can be. Ai's loyalty begins to shift from the Ekumen to Gethen, but this shift is a precondition of his mission's success. Conversely, Estraven's loyalty shifts to Ai, but only because he loves his country well enough to want Ai to succeed.

Although Ai and Estraven grow closer to one another, a vast distance also remains between them. Humans are alienated from one another in a wintry universe. But hope springs from the melancholy. The universe is dark but young, and spring will follow winter. The book reverberates with a non-theistic prayer: "Praise then darkness and Creation unfinished."

Although they meet as equal individuals, Ai and Estraven are members of differing societies. Le Guin would insist on Aristotle's definition of people as social animals. In her ambivalent utopia *The Dispossessed,* Le Guin preserves this insistence—while making it equally clear that anarchism is one of her centers of value. The book is an important break in science fiction's anti-utopian trend. A scientist, Shevek, moves to and fro between an anarchist utopia which is becoming middle-aged, and a world—obviously analogous to our own—that is divided between propertarian (capitalist) and statist (communist) countries. Nowhere does he find full self-expression; conversely, full self-expression requires one's participation in a society. In alternating chapters which disrupt sequential chronology, Shevek moves both away from the anarchist utopia and back toward it. Le Guin identifies herself both as a stylistic artist and as a thinker. Her stark, wintry worlds are philosophically rich with dialectic Taoism and the co-reality of such opposites as light and darkness, religion and politics, and language and power. In *A Wizard of Earthsea* the magician has power over things when he knows their true names, so that his power is the artist's power. Le Guin plays with the notion, in "The Author of the Acacia Seeds and Other Extracts from *The Journal of the Association of Therolinguistics,*" that ants, penguins, and even plants might be producing what could be called language and art.

Since writing *The Dispossessed,* Le Guin has been turning in the direction of fantasy. *Malafrena* is a compelling mixture of fantasy and historical fiction. Le Guin sets the imaginary country of Orsinia into central Europe in the 19th century. It is Itale Sorde's story: he rejects the ease of an inherited landed estate (Malafrena) to work for revolution against Orsinia's domination by the Austrian Empire. After being jailed for several years and after a failed insurrection in 1830, he returns to Malafrena, but there are hints that he will leave again. True voyage is return, and structure and theme coalesce, as in *The Dispossessed.*

In her recent works Le Guin often presents us with the ambiguity of revolution, once again the theme of a long short story, "The Eye of the Heron." A colony of young counter-culturalists attempts to break away from their elders, with typically ambiguous results. A central paradox in Le Guin's fiction is her simultaneous recognition of the need for harmony and the need for revolt.

Praise for Le Guin has been high—too uniformly high. Her style is unexceptional and her desire for peace and harmony borders on sentimentality at times. But she has taken important steps toward blending politics and art in her novels, and she is still experimenting with both form and content. Thus *Always Coming Home* both returns to the anthropological format of *The Left Hand of Darkness* and greatly expands that format. Le Guin has gathered together stories, folklore, histories, and other materials into what she calls "an archaeology" of primitive people living in a far-future northern California. The central story (occupying only a small part of the book) is of the coming of age of the woman "Stone Telling," whose mother lives in the peaceful Valley, which is integrated with nature, and whose father is of the war-like Condor people. Stone Telling leaves her valley to join her father for a while, but she becomes "woman always coming home" when she returns, her to-and-fro motion reminding us of *The Dispossessed.* When we discover that the Condor can build bridges and that they have electric lights, we may wonder how their traditional culture is supposed to have survived. But Le Guin's ability to capture the language, culture, and thought of primitive people is, despite some lapses, generally remarkable.

Harmony with nature is more than just a greeting card sentiment in Le Guin's short story collection *Buffalo Gals and Other Animal Presences* and the novel *Buffalo Gals, Won't You Come out Tonight.* In *Animal Presences,* the gap between the natural world and the human has become a virtual chasm. Shifting points of view allow even a lab rat his voice of protest. But voice alone is not sufficient to narrow the gap: one must set fire to complacency, open oneself up to hearing voices other than one's own, as in the story "May's Lion," about a woman who transcends her fears to help a mountain lion to die. The intriguing novella *Buffalo Gals, Won't You Come out Tonight,* which first appeared in the *Magazine of Fantasy and Science Fiction,* is a parable of the disintegrating relationship between humankind and the natural world. A remarkably resilient girl-child survives a plane crash only to find herself in different plane of reality, a desert world not unlike pre-settlement America, where the line between animals and man is less clearly drawn. As the girl becomes increasingly aware of the sour smell of humanity and its encroachments, she becomes more and more uprooted and unsure of her place. She eventually returns to her own people, but with an eye, both figuratively and literally, to seeing the world differently. Although occasionally heavy-handed, the story is compelling and visually rich. The girl protagonist speaks with the recognizable and sympathetic voice of a child.

The short story collection, *Searoad,* reveals how definitions of mainstream fiction and science fiction are not mutually exclusive. Though clearly a work of realistic fiction, the novel contains aspects of myth and ritual that fall into the realm of fantasy. Each story can be read as a separate entity, yet each contributes to one unified vision. This vision is unabashedly feminist, and as such is chiefly and somewhat exclusively concerned with the lives of women. Set in the small resort town of Klatsand, located on the Oregon coast, the stories contrast the different ways in which males and females communicate, the first being authoritative and unyielding, the other conversational and communal. This rigid polarity marks one of the problems with the novel, especially in terms of its persuasiveness. Male characters are impotent, if not downright evil; female characters are still waters running effortlessly deep. This seems to diminish rather than enhance believability. In addition, one questions the validity of rejecting outright the male world as a means of acquiring personal freedom. Nonetheless, characterization is compelling enough to sustain interest. One admires the resiliency of women who have also recognized the incontrovertibility of choice, or as the character Jilly in the story "In and Out" realizes, "doing something wasn't just a kind of practice for something that would keep happening. . . . You didn't get to practice."

In *A Fisherman of the Inland Sea,* Le Guin returns to science fiction, with a disparate collection of tales, both humorous and serious, that asserts many of the recurrent themes in her work: the responsibility we have to nature; cultural diversity and ethnic tolerance; the importance of communication in spite of the inadequacies of language; and the interdependency of peoples. Among the most compelling stories in the collection is "Newton's Sleep," which casts a circumspect eye on the elitism of technology and suggests the need for the irrational, for the unknown and unseen in our lives. As with all of the author's work, this collection seeks to expand and challenge the reader's ideas as to what it means to be human.

—Curtis C. Smith, updated by Lynda Schrecengost

LELCHUK, Alan

Nationality: American. **Born:** Brooklyn, New York, 15 September 1938. **Education:** Brooklyn College, B.A. 1960; University College, London, 1962-63; Stanford University, California, M.A. 1963, Ph.D. in English 1965. **Family:** Married Barbara Kreiger in 1979; two sons. **Career:** Assistant professor of English, 1966-75, and writer-in-residence, 1975-81, Brandeis University, Waltham, Massachusetts. Since 1985 professor of English, Dartmouth College, Hanover, New Hampshire. Visiting writer, Amherst College, Massachusetts, 1982-84; writer-in-residence, Haifa University, Israel, 1986-87. Associate editor, *Modern Occasions* quarterly, Cambridge, Massachusetts, 1970-72. Guest, Mishkenot Sha'Ananim, Jerusalem, 1976-77. **Awards:** Yaddo Foundation grant, 1968, 1971, 1973; MacDowell Colony fellowship, 1969; Guggenheim fellowship, 1976; Fulbright grant, 1986. **Agent:** Georges Borchardt, 136 East 57th Street, New York, New York 10022. **Address:** RFD 2, Canaan, New Hampshire 03741, U.S.A.

PUBLICATIONS

Novels

American Mischief. New York, Farrar Straus, and London, Cape, 1973.
Miriam at Thirty-four. New York, Farrar Straus, 1974; London, Cape, 1975.
Shrinking: The Beginning of My Own Ending. Boston, Little Brown, 1978.
Miriam in Her Forties. Boston, Houghton Mifflin, 1985.
Brooklyn Boy. New York, McGraw Hill, 1989.
Playing the Game. Dallas, Baskerville, 1995.

Uncollected Short Stories

"Sundays," in *Transatlantic Review 21* (London), Summer 1966.
"Of Our Time," in *New American Review 4,* edited by Theodore Solotaroff. New York, New American Library, 1968.
"Winter Image," in *Transatlantic Review 32* (London), Summer 1969.
"Cambridge Talk," in *Modern Occasions 1* (Cambridge, Massachusetts), Fall 1970.
"Hallie of the Sixties," in *Works in Progress 6* (New York), 1972.
"Doctor's Holiday," in *Atlantic* (Boston), March 1981.
"New Man in the House," in *Boston Globe Magazine,* 29 March 1987.
"Adventures of a Fiction Boy," in *Partisan Review* (Boston), Fall 1989.

Plays

Screenplays: *Tippy,* with Jiri Weiss, 1978; *What Ashley Wants,* with Isaac Yeshurun, 1987.

Other

On Home Ground (for children). New York, Harcourt Brace, 1987.

Editor, with Gerson Shaked, *Eight Great Hebrew Short Stories.* New York, New American Library, 1983.

*

Manuscript Collection: Mugar Memorial Library, Boston University.

Critical Studies: By Philip Roth in *Esquire* (New York), September 1972; "Lelchuk's Inferno" by Wilfrid Sheed, in *Book-of-the-Month Club News* (New York), March 1973; "The Significant Self" by Benjamin DeMott, in *Atlantic* (Boston), October 1974; "Faculty in Fiction: Images of the Professor in Recent Novels" by Frances Barasch, in *Clarion* (New York), June 1982; "Aaron's Rod" by Sven Birkerts, in *New Republic* (Washington, D.C.), 5 February 1990.

Alan Lelchuk comments:

Some points about my fiction: A realism of extreme sensibilities and modernism of content . . . the intensity and ambiguity of the sensual life . . . a blurring of the line between the comic and the serious . . . vibrating the odd strings of obsession . . . character through sexuality, and sexuality as (native) social gesture . . . a mingling of lofty thought and contemporary vulgarity . . . playing out the deep comic disorders of our culture . . . some unnerving fables and comic myths of our time camouflaged by realistic garb and inhabited by real souls . . .

*   *   *

Alan Lelchuk's first four novels recreate that rich Jewish-American intellectual life which synthesizes John Garfield with Bakunin. These cautionary tales dramatize the self-destructiveness inherent in political, artistic, and sexual revolt, the three frequently fused, as an academician (*American Mischief*), a woman photographer (*Miriam at Thirty-four, Miriam in Her Forties*), and a novelist (*Shrinking*) painfully test the boundaries of contemporary experi-

ence. *American Mischief,* Lelchuk's variation on *The Possessed,* explores 1960s campus upheaval through the contrapuntal voices of a radical student, Lenny Pincus ("Not the son of Harry and Rose Pincus of Brooklyn, but a boy with fathers like Reston and Cronkite, mothers such as Mary McCarthy and Diana Trilling"), and a liberal dean, Bernard Kovell ("a kind of Americanized version of Romanov-Quixote, a European Liberal-Idealist turned Massachusetts sensualist, tilting simultaneously at foolish theories and female bodies"). A wealth of political and literary allusions threatens to overwhelm the novel, as the protagonists share both their private agonies and extensive bibliographies with the reader. But the novel impresses with its vivid style, ultimately sane perspective, and brilliant bursts of imagination: the notorious episode detailing Norman Mailer's symbolically appropriate bloody end manages to outdo an already bizarre reality. Like Lelchuk's other novels, *American Mischief* attempts narrative complexity by telling its story through a variety of "documents": Lenny's preface; Kovell's journal focusing on his six mistresses; his lengthy speech during a campus uprising, interlarded with Lenny's comments; Lenny's "Gorilla Talk," an account of radical activities that occupies more than half the book. This stylistic attempt to heighten the dialectical tension between the two men fails because their voices sound so alike from the beginning that the fusion of their ideologies into a statement of concern for man's ultimate victimization seems predictable.

Victimization goes even further in *Miriam at Thirty-four.* The heroine's sexual experimentation (three lovers with a variety of backgrounds and tastes) parallels her exploration of the Cambridge setting, which is "a male with secrets . . . one whom she could arouse by uncovering different parts of his anatomy and photographing them." This obsession with exposing truth leads Miriam to take sexually revealing pictures of herself and exhibit them at a prestigious gallery to the sounds of "early Dylan, trio sonatas (Tartini? Bach?), the Beatles." Her final breakdown results from the uncomprehending responses of her audience: "they were cannibals who had just feasted on human flesh with no time yet for digestion. And the flesh was herself, Miriam." To provide multiple views of Miriam, Lelchuk supplements the narrative with her letters and notebook ("her self-therapy kit, her doctor between covers, her book of reason, reflection, questions . . .") Shorter and less ambitious than *American Mischief,* the novel primarily conveys Miriam's pathos and leaves the sources of her disaster uncertain: a society that simultaneously seeks and savages the new, or the self-destructive urges that are implicit in Miriam's authentic artistry? A similar uncertainty pervades *Shrinking,* which chronicles the breakdown of novelist/academician Lionel Solomon, victimized by both inner doubts and a hostile world epitomized by Tippy, a predatory young woman who humiliates him sexually, reveals his inadequacies in an *Esquire* exposé, and leads him on a strange journey into Hopi country. Elaborately narrated, *Shrinking* includes a foreword and afterword by Solomon's psychiatrist, letters from other characters, and the text of Tippy's article with Solomon's comments. The article forces a comparison of Tippy's version with the "real" experience, a contrast that underscores the novel's obsession with truth: "what happens in life, when put into fiction, can sound 'in poor taste' and be near impossible to write about." This apologia and Lelchuk's witty parodies of reviewers almost disarm criticism, but cannot obscure the catch-all quality of the book: essays on Hopi culture and Melville, however they reflect the workings of Solomon's mind, are too long for the effects they achieve, and Lelchuk's wit seems more forced, less outrageous than in *American Mischief.*

Miriam in Her Forties lacks much of the excitement and the sense of discovery of *Miriam at Thirty-four,* despite the weaknesses of the original. The sequel provides Miriam with an overly facile ability to analyze and resolve the types of problems that threatened to destroy her 10 years earlier. The rape by a black man that triggered her breakdown in the original seems to have strengthened her to the extent that she now responds to a renewed threat from the rapist by using gangster-government ties to imprison him on trumped-up charges. She then helps arrange his release and rehabilitation, though the outcome of these efforts is left ambiguous. Like the teenage Aaron of Lelchuk's latest novel, *Brooklyn Boy,* who is seduced by a Jamaican librarian, Miriam must investigate the meaning of black-white sexuality. She may reject such a relationship for herself, as she does the lesbian overtures of a feminist artist, but she certainly considers the possibilities. Besides, she already has commitments to an emblematic Israeli, and WASP surgeon, with whom she experiences Maileresque sex in an almost deserted medical school lecture hall, and she has recently come to accept the validity of masturbation (in an implicit tribute to Roth). These teasing echoes of slightly older contemporaries seem appropriate in a writer very conscious of his place in the pantheon of American-Jewish authors and give the book some leavening wit. Significantly, despite her anxieties and occasional bouts of dangerous sex, Miriam sometimes echoes Bellow's Sammler in her sense of being the one sane person in a lunatic world: "In short, one is ready at last for the higher stage—wisdom, contemporary-style. So, wisdom, where do you reside?" The novel's chief weakness, in addition to the sentimentalized treatment of Miriam's son and some easy anti-Cambridge satire, is the third-person narrative voice which often unconvincingly infuses Miriam's experiences with an instant analysis that sounds more like the author's notes than a transcript of Miriam's mind. This technique threatens to stifle her distinctiveness and to parody her responses to serious issues.

Brooklyn Boy and *Playing the Game* are Lelchuk's most conventional work thus far, though both novels introduce material that almost unbalances their narrative flow. *Brooklyn Boy* is an expansion of the slightly earlier *On Home Ground* (designed "for young readers"). The novel develops Aaron's obsession with the Dodgers and the resultant conflict with his European-born father, who has a different set of priorities for his son, but then the novel seems to abandon this theme to trace Aaron's interest in writing and his job as a deckhand on a freighter that in the final scene heads up the Congo so that Aaron can complete his education with blacks begun in his affair with the Jamaican librarian. Unfortunately, the most lively sections of *Brooklyn Boy* are the excerpts from Aaron's school reports on local history. Though the novel shifts, early on, to a first-person narrative, it fails to provide Aaron with a plausible voice, and the reader has met variants of the character in other coming-of-age works (*On Home Ground,* which focuses on the father-son relation, is on its own terms the stronger of the two narratives).

Sidney Berger, the protagonist of *Playing the Game,* a 51-year-old assistant coach with a Ph.D. in history, is given the opportunity to coach basketball at an ivy-league college and manages to produce a Cinderella team that attracts international media coverage. The team members suggest a World War II bomber crew film—black, Hispanic, native American, white ethnic, and even a Soviet Jew. Some of the boys have problems that hint at serious tensions later on, but these problems, like Berger's with the college and the NCAA, get easily resolved, primarily through Berger's commitment to coaching and basic decency. What inspires the team to victorious exploits is Berger's practice of half-time reading from key American writers like Parkman and Thoreau, whose prose apparently awes the players into an almost mystical awareness of the meaning of America, a prose that stimulates them to a better game than elaborate discussions of strategy or the personal humiliations inflicted by some coaches would have accomplished. One problem with these long excerpts, aside from their breaking the tension of the novel, is that the prose and its ideas are more exciting than anything in the framework narrative and leave the reader reluctant to return to the main story, a reluctance stemming partly from the stereotyped portraits of the players and various college and sports officials. Berger's voice, which narrates the story, seems at times a surrogate for the author's views on sports, education, and current American values, and only rarely conveys the idiosyncratic flavor of Lelchuk's earlier protagonists.

Lelchuk's shift to the relatively conventional material of these last two novels perhaps provides a breathing space from the bravura performances of earlier works. Admirers of Lelchuk's talent anticipate a return to his distinctive voice, often brilliant, often charmingly irrelevant to the apparent themes of the books, and often suggesting an underlying despair that the writing can only imperfectly capture.

—Burton Kendle

LEONARD, Elmore

Nationality: American. **Born:** New Orleans, Louisiana, 11 October 1925. **Education:** The University of Detroit, 1946-50, Ph.B. in English 1950. **Military Service:** Served in the United States Naval Reserve, 1943-46. **Family:** Married 1) Beverly Cline in 1949 (divorced 1977); 2) Joan Shepard in 1979 (died 1993), two daughters and three sons; 3) Christine Kent in 1993. **Career:** Copywriter, Campbell Ewald advertising agency, Detroit, 1950-61; writer of industrial and educational films, 1961-63; director, Elmore Leonard Advertising Company, 1963-66. Since 1967 full-time writer. **Awards:** Western Writers of America award, 1977; Mystery Writers of America Edgar Allan Poe award, 1984; Michigan Foundation for the Arts award, 1985. **Agent:** Michael Siegel and Associates, 502 Tenth St., Santa Monica, California 90402, U.S.A.

PUBLICATIONS

Novels

The Bounty Hunters. Boston, Houghton Mifflin, 1953; London, Hale, 1956.
The Law at Randado. Boston, Houghton Mifflin, 1955; London, Hale, 1957.
Escape from Five Shadows. Boston, Houghton Mifflin, 1956; London, Hale, 1957.
Last Stand at Saber River. New York, Dell, 1959; as *Lawless River,* London, Hale, 1959; as *Stand on the Saber,* London, Corgi, 1960.
Hombre. New York, Ballantine, and London, Hale, 1961.
Valdez Is Coming. London, Hale, 1969; New York, Fawcett, 1970.
The Big Bounce. New York, Fawcett, and London, Hale, 1969.
The Moonshine War. New York, Doubleday, 1969; London, Hale, 1970.

Forty Lashes Less One. New York, Bantam, 1972.

Mr. Majestyk (novelization of screenplay). New York, Dell, 1974; London, Penguin, 1986.

Fifty-Two Pickup. New York, Delacorte Press, and London, Secker and Warburg, 1974.

Swag. New York, Delacorte Press, 1976; London, Penguin, 1986; as *Ryan's Rules,* New York, Dell, 1976.

The Hunted. New York, Delacorte Press, 1977; London, Secker and Warburg, 1978.

Unknown Man No. 89. New York, Delacorte Press, and London, Secker and Warburg, 1977.

The Switch. New York, Bantam, 1978; London, Secker and Warburg, 1979.

Gunsights. New York, Bantam, 1979.

City Primeval: High Noon in Detroit. New York, Arbor House, 1980; London, W.H. Allen, 1981.

Gold Coast. New York, Bantam, 1980; London, W.H. Allen, 1982.

Split Images. New York, Arbor House, 1982; London, W.H. Allen, 1983.

Cat Chaser. New York, Arbor House, 1982; London, Viking, 1986.

Stick. New York, Arbor House, 1983; London, Allen Lane, 1984.

LaBrava. New York, Arbor House, 1983; London, Viking Press, 1984.

Glitz. New York, Arbor House, and London, Viking, 1985.

Bandits. New York, Arbor House, and London, Viking, 1987.

Touch. New York, Arbor House, 1987; London, Viking, 1988.

Freaky Deaky. New York, Arbor House, and London, Viking, 1988.

Killshot. New York, Arbor House, and London, Viking, 1989.

Get Shorty. New York, Delacorte Press, and London, Viking, 1990.

Maximum Bob. New York, Delacorte Press, and London, Viking, 1991.

Rum Punch. New York, Delacorte Press, and London, Viking, 1992.

Pronto. New York, Delacorte Press, and London, Viking, 1993.

Riding the Rap. New York, Delacorte Press, and London, Viking, 1995.

Uncollected Short Stories

"Trail of the Apache," in *Argosy* (New York), December 1951.

"Red Hell Hits Canyon Diablo," in *Ten Story Western,* 1952.

"Apache Medicine," in *Dime Western,* May 1952.

"You Never See Apaches," in *Dime Western,* September 1952.

"Cavalry Boots," in *Zane Grey's Western* (New York), December 1952.

"Long Night," in *Zane Grey's Western 18* (London).

"The Rustlers," in *Zane Grey's Western 29* (London), 1953.

"Under the Friar's Ledge," in *Dime Western,* January 1953.

"The Last Shot," in *Fifteen Western Tales,* September 1953.

"Trouble at Rindo's Station," in *Argosy* (New York), October 1953.

"Blood Money" in *Western Story* (London), February 1954.

"Saint with a Six-Gun," in *Frontier,* edited by Luke Short. New York, Bantam, 1955.

"3:10 to Yuma," in *The Killers,* edited by Peter Dawson. New York, Bantam, 1955.

"The Hard Way," in *Branded West,* edited by Don Ward. Boston, Houghton Mifflin, 1956.

"No Man's Gun," in *Western Story* (London), May 1956.

"Moment of Vengeance," in *Colt's Law,* edited by Luke Short. New York, Bantam, 1957.

"The Tall T," in *The Tall T and Other Western Adventures.* New York, Avon, 1957.

"The Rancher's Lady," in *Wild Streets,* edited by Don Ward. New York, Doubleday, 1958.

"Only Good Ones," in *Western Roundup,* edited by Nelson Nye. New York, Macmillan, 1961.

"The Boy Who Smiled," in *The Arbor House Treasury of Great Western Stories,* edited by Bill Pronzini and Martin H. Greenberg. New York, Arbor House, 1982.

"The Nagual," in *The Cowboys,* edited by Bill Pronzini and Martin H. Greenberg. New York, Fawcett, 1985.

"The Captive," in *The Second Reel West,* edited by Bill Pronzini and Martin H. Greenberg. New York, Doubleday, 1985.

"Law of the Hunted Ones," in *Wild Westerns,* edited by Bill Pronzini and Martin H. Greenberg. New York, Walker, 1986.

"The Colonel's Lady," in *The Horse Soldiers,* edited by Bill Pronzini and Martin H. Greenberg. New York, Fawcett, 1987.

"Jugged" in *The Gunfighters,* edited by Bill Pronzini and Martin H. Greenberg. New York, Fawcett, 1987.

"The Tonto Woman," in *The Arizonans,* edited by Bill Pronzini and Martin H. Greenberg. New York, Fawcett, 1989.

"The Big Hunt," in *More Wild Westerns,* edited by Bill Pronzini. New York, Walker, 1989.

Plays

Screenplays: *The Moonshine War,* 1970; *Joe Kidd,* 1972; *Mr. Majestyk,* 1974; *Stick,* with Joseph C. Stinson, 1985.

Television Play: *High Noon, Part II: The Return of Will Kane,* 1980.

*

Manuscript Collection: University of Detroit Library.

Critical Study: *Elmore Leonard* by David Geherin, New York, Ungar-Continuum, 1989.

*   *   *

Elmore Leonard is one of those rare authors who began as a pulp writer and ended top of the bestseller lists. More impressive, however, is his feat of moving from being considered a mere genre novelist to being credited with elevating the crime novel to new levels of artistic achievement.

Leonard began as a writer of Westerns, turning out stories for the pulps that still flourished in the 1950s. One of his early novels, *Hombre,* the story of a white man raised by Indians whose bravery saves the lives of his fellow stagecoach passengers, was selected by the Western Writers of America as one of the 25 best Westerns of all time.

With *The Big Bounce* in 1969, Leonard switched to writing about the contemporary scene. Set in the author's home state of Michigan, the novel describes the dangerous encounter between Jack Ryan, an ex-convict, and Nancy Hayes, a restless 19-year-old with a thirst for thrills. *The Big Bounce* highlights the two kinds of characters that would become trademarks of Leonard's fiction: those who run afoul of the law, and those who become involved with those who do.

In 1972, after reading George V. Higgins's *The Friends of Eddie Coyle,* a comic novel about the activities of a small-time Boston hoodlum narrated through colorful dialogue and extended monologues, Leonard began to experiment with new ways of telling his stories. He found that by relying more on dialogue he could effectively shift the burden of storytelling to his characters. The result was *Fifty-Two Pickup,* his first major success as a crime novelist.

Fifty-Two Pickup is the story of a Michigan businessman named Harry Mitchell who is being framed by a trio of low-life characters for the murder of his mistress. Like many of Leonard's protagonists, Mitchell is an easygoing guy until pushed. Then he takes control of the situation and single-handedly extricates himself from his predicament.

In 1978, Leonard was commissioned by a local newspaper to write a non-fiction profile of the Detroit police. Though he planned to spend only a few days hanging around police headquarters, he ended up staying for two and a half months, soaking up atmosphere, listening to the cops and criminals, lawyers and witnesses who passed through the squad room. This rich assortment of colorful characters provided a new source for the distinctive sounds and speech rhythms that would heighten the realism of his fiction.

The first novel that resulted from this experience was *City Primeval,* also his first book to feature a policeman as protagonist. Raymond Cruz, a Detroit Police Homicide Lieutenant, crosses paths with Clement Mansell, a killer known (with ample reason) as the "Oklahoma Wildman." Their final showdown reads like the climax to one of Leonard's early Westerns. (Appropriately, the novel is subtitled *High Noon in Detroit.*) Besides exciting action, the novel also owes its success to its authentic characters and unflinching realism.

Convinced of the benefits of research on his fiction, Leonard now began employing a part-time researcher to assist him in his efforts. No amount of background research can guarantee a novel's success. However, combined with Leonard's gift for creating fresh and believable characters and dialogue that unerringly rings true, research provides a factual grounding that enhances an already solid core of believability. Such a combination resulted in some of the most notable crime novels in recent American fiction.

Glitz is a good example. Vincent Mora is an off-duty Miami policeman who is recuperating from a bullet wound in sunny Puerto Rico. There he meets and takes a liking to a young woman named Iris Ruiz. When she plunges to her death from a hotel room in Atlantic City, where she has gone to work as a hostess, Mora heads north to investigate. Soon he is engaged in a deadly cat-and-mouse game with Teddy Magyk, a sociopathic ex-convict who seeks revenge on Mora for having sent him to prison.

Thanks to Leonard's extensive research, the reader enjoys an insider's peek behind the scenes at the Atlantic City casinos and gets to meet the distinctive inhabitants of that world. Vincent Mora and Teddy Magyk give life to *Glitz,* while the setting and colorful supporting cast flesh it out in vivid detail.

Leonard employs a similar recipe with equal success in novels like *Stick, LaBrava, Bandits, Freaky Deaky, Killshot* and *Get Shorty.* However, he is careful never to repeat a stale formula. The settings vary from Miami Beach to New Orleans to Hollywood and back to Detroit, and each novel introduces a fresh cast of memorable characters and plots filled with unpredictable twists.

Though his novels are about serious—often deadly—matters, they also reveal Leonard's gift for comedy, especially comic dialogue. Leonard has a talent for mimicking voices that capture the distinctive personality of the speaker. Once these characters open their mouths, they open their minds, and the result is fiction filled with amusingly offbeat points of view.

Leonard is sometimes mistakenly categorized as a mystery writer. Though suspenseful, his novels contain little mystery. Instead, they are novels about character and, because many of those characters are either criminals or policemen, novels about crime. The best of them are rich in texture, authentic in detail, and colorful in the richness and variety of character and voice. Over the past two decades, Leonard has produced an impressive body of fiction that exemplifies what the crime novel in the hands of a talented artist is capable of achieving.

—David Geherin

LESSING, Doris (May)

Pseudonym: Jane Somers. **Nationality:** British. **Born:** Doris May Tayler in Kermanshah, Persia, 22 October 1919; moved with her family to England, then to Banket, Southern Rhodesia, 1924. **Education:** Dominican Convent School, Salisbury, Southern Rhodesia, 1926-34. **Family:** Married 1) Frank Charles Wisdom in 1939 (divorced 1943), one son and one daughter; 2) Gottfried Lessing in 1945 (divorced 1949), one son. **Career:** Au pair, Salisbury, 1934-35; telephone operator and clerk, Salisbury, 1937-39; typist, 1946-48; journalist, Cape Town *Guardian,* 1949; moved to London, 1950; secretary, 1950; member of the Editorial Board, *New Reasoner* (later *New Left Review*), 1956. **Awards:** Maugham award, for fiction, 1954; Médicis prize (France), 1976; Austrian State prize, 1981; Shakespeare prize (Hamburg), 1982; W.H. Smith Literary award, 1986; Palermo prize (Italy), 1987; Mondello prize (Italy), 1987; Cavour award (Italy), 1989. Honorary doctorate: Princeton University, New Jersey, 1989; Durham, 1990; Warwick, 1994; Bard College, New York, 1994; Harvard, 1995. Associate member, American Academy, 1974; Honorary Fellow, Modern Language Association (U.S.A.), 1974. **Agent:** Jonathan Clowes Ltd., Iron Bridge House, Bridge Approach, London, NW1 8BD, England.

PUBLICATIONS

Novels

The Grass Is Singing. London, Joseph, and New York, Crowell, 1950.
Children of Violence:
    Martha Quest. London, Joseph, 1952; with *A Proper Marriage,* New York, Simon and Schuster, 1964.
    A Proper Marriage. London, Joseph, 1954; with *Martha Quest,* New York, Simon and Schuster, 1964.
    A Ripple From the Storm. London, Joseph, 1958; with *Landlocked,* New York, Simon and Schuster, 1966.
    Landlocked. London, MacGibbon and Kee, 1965; with *A Ripple From the Storm.* New York, Simon and Schuster, 1966.
    The Four-Grated City. London, MacGibbon and Kee, and New York, Knopf, 1969.
Retreat to Innocence. London, Joesph, 1956; New York, Prometheus, 1959.
The Golden Notebook. London, Joseph, and New York, Simon and Schuster, 1962.
Briefing for a Decent into Hell. London, Cape, and New York, Knopf, 1971.
The Summer Before the Dark. London, Cape, and New York, Knopf, 1973.

The Memoirs of a Survivor. London, Octagon Press, 1974; New York, Knopf, 1975.

Canopus in Argos: Archives:

Shikasta. London, Cape, and New York, Knopf, 1979.

The Marriages Between Zones Three, Four, and Five. London, Cape, and New York, Knopf, 1980.

The Sirian Experiments. London, Cape, and New York, Knopf, 1980.

The Making of the Representative for Planet 8. London, Cape, and New York, Knopf, 1982.

The Sentimental Agents. London, Cape, and New York, Knopf, 1983.

The Diaries of Jane Somers. New York, Vintage, and London, Joseph, 1984.

The Diary of a Good Neighbour (as Jane Somers). London, Joseph, and New York, Knopf, 1983.

If the Old Could— (as Jane Somers). London, Joseph, and New York, Knopf, 1984.

The Good Terrorist. London, Cape, and New York, Knopf, 1985.

The Fifth Child. London, Cape, and New York, Knopf, 1988.

Short Stories

This Was the Old Chief's Country. London, Joseph, 1951; New York, Crowell, 1952.

Five: Short Novels. London, Joseph, 1953.

No Witchcraft for Sale: Stories and Short Novels. Moscow, Foreign Language Publishing House, 1956.

The Habit of Loving. London, MacGibbon and Kee, and New York, Crowell, 1957.

A Man and Two Women. London, MacGibbon and Kee, and New York, Simon and Schuster, 1963.

African Stories. London, Joseph, 1964; New York, Simon and Schuster, 1965.

Winter in July. London, Panther, 1966.

The Black Madonna. London, Panther, 1966.

Nine African Stories, edited by Michael Marland. London, Longman, 1968.

The Story of a Non-Marrying Man and Other Stories. London, Cape, 1972; as *The Temptation of Jack Orfkney and Other Stories,* New York, Knopf, 1972.

Collected African Stories. New York, Simon and Schuster, 1981.

1. *This Was the Old Chief's Country.* London, Joseph, 1973.

2. *The Sun Between Their Feet.* London, Joseph, 1973.

(Stories), edited by Alan Cattell. London, Harrap, 1976.

Jack Orkney. London, Cape, 2 vols., 1978; as *Stories,* New York, Knopf, 1 vol., 1978.

London Observed: Stories and Sketches. London, and New York, HarperCollins, 1992.

Uncollected Short Stories

"The Case of the Foolish Minister" (as Doris M. Wisdom), in *Rafters* (Salisbury, Rhodesia), November 1943.

"A Sense of Humour" (as D.M. Wisdom), in *Rafters* (Salisbury, Rhodesia), December 1943.

"Esperanto and Others" (as D.M. Wisdom), in *Rafters* (Salisbury, Rhodesia), April 1944.

"Politics and Alister Warren," in *Labour Front* (Salisbury, Rhodesia), September 1948.

"The Twitching Dog," in *N.B.* (Salisbury, Rhodesia), January 1949.

"Fruit from the Ashes," in *Trek* (Johannesburg), October 1949.

"Pretty Puss," in *Trek* (Johannesburg), March 1950.

"Womb Ward," in *New Yorker,* 7 December 1987.

"The Real Thing," in *Partisan Review* (Boston), Fall 1988.

"Debbie and Julie," in *Antaeus* (New York), Spring 1989.

"Among the Roses," in *Ladies' Home Journal* (New York), April 1989.

Plays

Before the Deluge (produced London, 1953).

Mr. Dollinger (produced Oxford, 1958).

Each His Own Wilderness (produced London, 1958). Published in *New English Dramatists,* London, Penguin, 1959.

The Truth about Billy Newton (produced Salisbury, Wiltshire, 1960).

Play with a Tiger (produced Brighton and London, 1962; New York, 1964). London, Joseph, 1962; in *Plays by and about Women,* edited by Victoria Sullivan and James V. Hatch, New York, Random House, 1973.

The Storm, adaptation of a play by Alexander Ostrovsky (produced London, 1966).

The Singing Door (for children), in *Second Playbill 2,* edited by Alan Durband. London, Hutchinson, 1973.

The Making of the Representative for Plant 8 (opera libretto), music by Philipo Glass, adaptation of the novel by Lessing (produced London, 1988).

Television Plays: *The Grass Is Singing,* from her own novel, 1962; *Care and Protection* and *Do Not Disturb* (both in *Blackmail* series), 1966; *Between Men,* 1967.

Poetry

Fourteen Poems. Northwood, Middlesex, Scorpion Press, 1959.

Other

Going Home. London, Joseph, 1957; revised edition, London, Panther, and New York, Ballantine, 1968.

In Pursuit of the English: A Documentary. London, MacGibbon and Kee, 1960; New York, Somon and Schuster, 1961.

Particularly Cats. London, Joseph, and New York, Simon and Schuster, 1967.

A Small Personal Voice: Essays, Reviews, Interview, edited by Paul Schlueter. New York, Knopf, 1974.

Prisons We Choose to Live Inside. Montreal, CBC, 1986; London, Cape, and New York, Harper, 1987.

The Wind Blows Away Our Words, and Other Documents Relating to Afghanistan. London, Pan, and New York, Vintage, 1987.

Particularly Cats and More Cats. London, 1989; as *Particularly Cats . . . and Rufus,* illustrated by James McMullen, New York, Knopf, 1991.

The Doris Lessing Reader. London, Cape, and New York, Knopf, 1990.

African Laughter: Four Visits to Zimbabwe. London, and New York, HarperCollins, 1992.

Under My Skin. London, and New York, HarperCollins, 1994.

*

Bibliography: *Doris Lessing: A Bibliography* by Catharina Ipp, Johannesburg, University of the Witwatersrand Department of Bibliography, 1967; *Doris Lessing: A Checklist of Primary and Secondary Sources* by Selma R. Burkom and Margaret Williams, Troy, New York, Whiston, 1973; *Doris Lessing: An Annotated Bibliography of Criticisim* by Dee Seligman, Westport, Connecticut, Greenwood Press, 1981; *Doris Lessing: A Descriptive Bibliography of Her First Editions* by Eric T. Brueck, London, Metropolis, 1984.

Critical Studies (selection): *Doris Lessing* by Dorothy Brewster, New York, Twayne, 1965; *The Novels of Doris Lessing* by Paul Schlueter, Carbondale, Southern Illinois University Press, 1973; *Doris Lessing,* London, Longman, 1973, and *Doris Lessing: Critical Studies* edited by Annis Pratt and L.S. Dembo, Madison, University of Wisconsin Press, 1974; *The Tree Outside the Window: Doris Lessing's Children of Violence* by Ellen Cronan Rose, Hanover, New Hampshire, University Press of New England, 1976; *The City and the Veld: The Fiction of Doris Lessing* by Mary Ann Singleton, Lewisburg, Pennsylvania, Bucknell University Press, 1977; *The Novelistic Vision of Doris Lessing: Breaking the Forms of Consciousness* by Roberta Rubenstein, Urbana, University of Illinois Press, 1979; *Doris Lessing: The Problem of Alienation and the Form of the Novel* by Rotraut Spiegel, Frankfurt, Germany, Lang, 1980; *From Society to Nature: A Study of Doris Lessing's Children of Violence* By Ingrid Holmquist, Gothenburg, Studies in English, and Atlantic Highlands, New Jersey, Humanities Press, 1980; *Notebooks/Memoirs/Archives: Reading and Rereading Doris Lessing* edited by Jenny Taylor, London and Boston, Routledge, 1982; *Substance under Pressure: Artistic Coherence and Evolving Form in the Novels of Doris Lessing* by Betsy Draine, Madison, University of Wisconsin Press, 1983; *Doris Lessing* By Lorna Sage, London, Methuen, 1983; *Transforming the World: The Art of Doris Lessing's Science Fiction,* Westport, Connecticut, Greenwood Press, 1983; and *The Unexpected Universe of Doris Lessing: A Study of Narrative Technique,* Greenwood Press, 1985, both by Katherine Fishburn; *The Implicit Feminism of Doris Lessing's The Four-Gated City* by Lisa Maria Hogeland, Stanford, California, Stanford University Press, 1983; *Doris Lessing* by Mona Knapp, New York, Ungar, 1984; *Doris Lessing and Women's Appropriation of Science Fiction* by Mariette Clare, Birmingham, University of Birmingham Centre for Contemporary Cultural Studies, 1984; *Doris Lessing* edited by Eve Bertelsen, Johannesburg, McGraw Hill, 1985; *Critical Essays on Doris Lessing* edited by Claire Sprague and Virginia Tiger, Boston, Hall, 1986; *Rereading Doris Lessing: Narrative Patterns of Doubling and Repetition* by Claire Sprague, Chapel Hill, University of North Carolina Press, 1987, and *In Pursuit of Doris Lessing: Nine Nations Reading* edited by Sprague, London, Macmillan, 1990; *The Theme of Enclosure in Selected Works of Doris Lessing* by Shirley Budhos, Troy, New York, Whitston, 1987; *Doris Lessing: The Alchemy of Survival* edited by Carey Kaplan and Ellen Cronan Rose, Athens, Ohio University Press, 1988; *Doris Lessing* by Ruth Whittaker, London, Macmillan, 1988; *Doris Lessing* by Jeannette King, London, Arnold, 1989; *Understanding Doris Lessing* by Jean Pickering, Columbia, University of South Carolina Press, 1990.

*   *   *

Doris Lessing's writings extend the boundaries of fiction, experiment with different genres, explore the worlds of Africa, Britain, and Space, and offer a socio-political and cultural commentary upon the postmodern world. She is a descendant of those 19th-century women writers who made poverty, class conflict, women's suffrage, and slavery the subjects of their novels. She is a writer of epic scope and startling surprises. Her novels range from social realism to science fiction with brief forays into speculative mysticism and fables of horror. After completing five books in her science-fiction sequence, *Canopus in Argos,* in 1983, Lessing startled her public by turning away from the Antarctic cold of two of her planetary realms and returning to novels of postwar London with its welfare state, terrorists, and aging population. Two of these recent books, *The Diary of a Good Neighbour* and *If the Old Could—*, were originally published under the pseudonym of Jane Somers; the third, *The Good Terrorist,* offers a detailed psychological and political portrait of a group of radicals-turned-terrorists living in London in a dilapidated council flat. Her most recent novella, *The Fifth Child,* tells the chilling tale of a changeling, a goblin-child, and questions whether this child is actually the incarnation of evil, a bad seed, a genetic freak, or is it the mother who is deeply disturbed, projecting her own fears and ambivalence regarding the child onto a child who might, in fact, be nearly normal, or minimally retarded, had he not been so cruelly treated by his family and relatives who thought they had an evil "alien" in their midst?

The Antartic expeditions of Britain's once revered, now tarnished hero, Robert Falcon Scott, profoundly influenced Lessing's *The Sirian Experiments* and *The Making of the Representative for Plant 8,* not only by providing her with an understanding of the landscape of paralyzing ice and snow, but by offering her insights into the social processes of Scott's time—the Edwardian era of fierce nationalistic pride and Imperial longings—and of ours. Her four most recent books, a complete departure from her science-fiction vein, nonetheless continue her preoccupation with human behavior and social processes. Two depict, with graphic psychological realism and rich naturalistic detail, the ordinary day-to-day life of an unmarried, middle-aged career woman living in London and tending society's outcast aged, and belatedly trying to love and give—something she was always too busy to do. The third recounts the life of a group of squatters whose radical spirits transform them into revolutionaries. Many greeted *The Golden Notebook,* written in 1962, as Lessing's feminist manifesto, underestimating its critique of the twin gods, Communism and Freud. Almost two decades later, Lessing is pioneering in writing novels of aging and dying, confronting the pressing social problems they entail and depicting the grim reality we so often ignore or repress. Her fierce reformist spirit pervades her writing; her anger very much with her, she nonetheless tempers her disillusionment with a wisdom learned through living. Her uncanny gift for knowing characters deeply is very much in evidence.

Lessing's books have always articulated her ideas, whether they be about women's orgasms, Armageddon, or utopia. More often than one would expect from so prolific a writer, she is sufficiently imaginative to integrate smoothly her ideas into her narrative. Even more to her credit is that her writing is continually evolving and is unusual in its breadth. Her plunge into science fiction seemed entirely unexpected. In its incipient stages, in *Briefing for a Descent into Hell,* it was startling and seemed to mark a change as radical as Picasso's when he moved from the Blue Period to Abstract Cubism. With more reflection, one can discover the thread that connects *The Golden Notebook* to her science-fiction sequence, *Canopus in Argos;* but it is hard to think of a writer of her stature in the past half-century who has demonstrated such range.

Her career began with *The Grass Is Singing,* a gem of a book. Set in Rhodesia, it charts with an economy rare in Lessing's works the dissolution of a couple's relationship. After Lessing left Africa in 1949, she devoted 10 years to the *Children of Violence* series which explored exhaustively the theme of the "free Woman" long before it was fashionable. It also displayed Lessing's preoccupation with politics, which many have criticized as tedious. *The Golden Notebook* is the best of her works from this period despite its obvious flaws. It is as much a book about writing as it is an exploration of women's relationships with each other and men. In many ways it ought to be compared to Gide's *The Counterfeiters*—the writer's quest to capture the self intended in fiction, not a different, diminished, or enhanced self; the journey through madness that this task requires—the visions of violence it calls up are integral to both books. Both descend from Joyce; both require a sophisticated audience who enjoys unraveling puzzles; both mirror an age when the Heisenberg Uncertainty Principle threatens the reliability of all narrators and estranges the artist from world and self.

In the 1970s came the unexpected turn to science fiction. Lessing's interest in extra-sensory perception first emerged in *Landlocked.* Madness had been seen as a state offering Anna Wulf a respite from the obsessional insistence upon the self that Saul Green spattered out like machine-gun bullets in *The Golden Notebook.* In *Briefing for a Descent into Hell* Lessing took her interest in madness a step further. Calling the book a work of "inner space fiction," she built a story around Charles Watkins, a 50-year-old classics professor who is found wandering on Waterloo Bridge and is confined for a stay in a psychiatric hospital. Two doctors, of conflicting views, struggle to bring back his memory while he follows a visionary journey in which he enjoys a different, higher identity— one conferred upon him by the Crystal—and one that ordained that he enter earth, hell, as part of a Descent Team whose mission is to show the mad, ego-obsessed humans that they are part of a larger harmony. Lessing, following R.D. Laing, explores the possibility that only the mad are sane. But much more intriguing than this idea is Lessing's decision to fashion the language and metaphors of madness from the idiom of science fiction and the visions experienced through ESP. The inner journey of this modern Odysseus is traveled on the space-time warp of science fiction. The regions he visits are vividly depicted. The language which attempts to capture the visions Watkins is experiencing is one where words are understood by their sounds, not their connotative meanings. "I" glides into "aye" and "eye" as Watkins's mind seems to float in limbo, carrying his body through an unfamiliar medium, revealing images from the visionary realm. Lessing sustains this style, interrupted by only the curt notations of the two psychiatrists, for over a hundred pages. The effect is startling. At times one almost drowns in verbiage, but the flow of the vision is interrupted with the banal observations of the doctors or the staccato questioning of the patient. Undoubtedly, Lessing's style will cost her some readers, but those who bear with her will find themselves caught up in this bizarre account and caring very much whether this amnesiac will tenaciously hang on to his visionary self or succumb to the pressures of the doctors and society and return to the ordinary realm where he is merely a slightly eccentric don. Watkins's hold on the link between the two ways of seeing is most precarious. The reader must try to decide whether Felicity, Constancia, and Nancy, creatures in his visions, correspond with his wife, Felicity, his mistress, Constance, and the wife of a friend. We are also left puzzling whether Miles and Watkins are at some level identical, and whether it matters at all since others in the Descent Team seem still to be around. Also, of course, there is

the possibility that Watkins is nothing more than temporarily schizophrenic, though the weight of the story seems to negate this alternative. This book introduces all the ideas and the paraphernalia of science fiction that dominate the *Canopus in Argos* sequence. In its ambiguous treatment of Watkins's identity, it anticipates questions raised in *The Fifth Child.*

Shikasta and *The Marriages Between Zones Three, Four, and Five* are the first works in the sequence. In the first a compilation of reports, historical documents, letters, and psychiatric diagnoses is used to unfold the story of Johor's three visits to Shikasta (Earth), the last taking place in the final phase just following the Third World War. Johor is an emissary from the galactic Empire of Canopus, sent to Shikasta to report on the colony. It is Johor's task to educate those who survive the Third World War to their true place in a larger planetary System, where cosmological accidents have heavily contributed to the blighted human condition, and where Shammat, the criminal planet of another galactic empire, has temporarily obstructed the lock that will connect Shikasta to Canopus. A Chronicler from zone Three is the narrator of the second book. He tells one of the myths that accounts for man's fallen state and reveals the will of the Powers that the potentates of three hitherto separate zones are to marry and so hasten the evolutionary design that governs the six zones encircling Earth. The myth he tells is of the marriage of Al-Ith, Queen of Zone Three, to Ben Ata, ruler of Zone Four, and, later, the marriage of Ben Ata to Vahshi, ruler of Zone Five. Two births follow. The marriages alter the Zones, estrange their monarchs from the old dispensation, and bring about alterations which enable all the peoples to move between the Zones to explore again, in new metaphors, the human qualities responsible for the catastrophic happenings in this century, and the nature of the kinds of relationships men and women must make and the kinds of societies that must be constructed to move humans to a higher consciousness. *The Marriage Between Zones Three, Four, and Five* is far more lyrical than *Shikasta.* The Chronicler uses songs and pictures to capture the mythic dimension of the story he tells. *The Sirian Experiments* recounts the colonial experiments practiced upon Shikasta, leading its people into their 20th century of Destruction. *The Making of the Representative for Planet 8* tells of Johor's journeys to the planet and the ordeal that he and Doeg, the narrator of the novel, along with other representatives, encounter when the planet begins to freeze to death. Doeg comes to understand his part in the Canopean grand design and recognizes finally the mystical transformation which makes him both many and one and enables him to transcend time and space, entering the realm of all possibility under the tutelage of the Canopean Agents. The last book in the series, *The Sentimental Agents,* is the most disappointing. The history of invasions and conquests of the Volyen Empire enables Lessing to reflect on Klorathy's educational process and his attempts to free the Volyens from the power of words and rhetoric, and teach them the power of thought. The book aspires to place itself in the tradition of Plato, Rousseau, Mill, and Orwell as a novel about an educational project, but it is over-written and the ideas seem tedious. Her old concerns abound—how a revolutionary is made; why man has created a world he cannot manage; that history is a repetition of invasion and conquest with the oppressors of one age the oppressed of the next—but the narrative frame is predictable and the ideas simplistic.

Lessing's last four books return her to the kind of fiction she was writing before she tackled science fiction. *The Summer Before the Dark, The Memoirs of a Survivor,* and the ambitious *The Golden Notebook* are of a piece with her recent writing. *The Sum-*

mer Before the Dark is one of Lessing's most perfectly crafted novels. Compact, tightly constructed, it tells the moving story of a woman's coming to terms with aging. Kate Brown, the 45-year-old mother of four children, all grown, and the wife of a neurologist of some standing, is a woman who has lived her married years making accommodations, to her husband's choices and to the needs of her children. In the summer of the story, events unexpectedly leave Kate Brown without family responsibilities and alone in London for the first time since her marriage. She holds a job briefly, depending again on the talents that the sympathetic understanding of mothering taught her. Then she has a brief affair with a young man on the continent. Both fall sick; Kate returns to London where she lies ill, preoccupied with the recurring dream of a seal which she must complete. She loses weight; her brightly tinted red hair becomes brassy, then banded in gray. In the last phase of the story, she shares quarters with a young woman who is struggling with her own coming of age. The two women work upon each other; Kate's dream is completed; both separate to enter another stage of their lives—the young woman choosing marriage, children, even responsibility; Kate, returning to her husband, with her hair gray, as a woman who acts for her own reasons, not merely to please others.

The Memoirs of a Survivor is an even more remarkable book, and equally as mature. It is the memoirs of a nameless woman who has survived "it," a nameless war that has left the cities of England empty shells, with conclaves of people living barricaded in their apartments while the gangs of youths roam the streets and the air is so polluted that hand-driven machines are necessary to purify it. The narrator retells how she lived through this period; how she came by a child, Emily, who was entrusted to her care; how she entered a space behind the white walls of her living-room, and inhabited others rooms, from earlier times, and witnessed the traumatic moments of Emily's youth spent with her real parents. She struggles to tell in words how the two worlds, at first so different, began to impinge upon one another. She contrasts what she calls "personal" moments of experience with others that she labels "impersonal." Both reside in the world behind the wall. The story blends the dreamy, prophetic, timeless moments behind the wall where some heightened consciousness, some visionary powers, exist, with a dispassionate, often chilling, realistic account of "ordinary" life in a ravaged London apartment. Always, when the narrator goes behind the wall, she seeks, with a sense of urgency, the inhabitant of the other house, those other gardens. The protagonist's memoirs end with her account of how they somehow came through the darkest times, and realized that the worst was over, that something new would be built. The final paragraphs describe the moment when the walls opened again, and she saw the face she had sought so long, the inhabitant of that hidden world. And that presence takes the hands of Emily, her boyfriend, and the evil child who had terrorized the London streets and leads them into the garden. It is a mystical moment, transfiguring, mysterious, and a consummate end for this exquisitely crafted book.

In *The Diary of a Good Neighbour* Jane Somers, like Kate Brown, is a middle-aged, seemingly successful woman, but, unlike Kate, she is childless and recently widowed with only a career to give her definition. To compensate for her lack of relationships and to try to come to terms with cancer and dying—she had faced neither when her husband was terminally ill—she befriends an elderly woman, Maudie, whom she has met in a corner store. The book offers an extraordinarily moving, also frightening, story of this stubborn old woman's final years, living in a council flat, tended to by Meals on Wheels, day nursing, a cadre of Home Helpers, and the volunteer Good Neighbours. Lessing diligently details the life of the 90-year-old woman, alone in London, too ill to care for herself, too proud to let others help her, and too angry to let friendship or death come easily to her. Soiled in her own clothing, almost too weak and brittle to walk to the unheated lavatory in the hall outside her flat, or to light her meager fire, far beyond any ability to clean her rooms or even dress or bathe. Maudie fiercely clings to her independence, refusing to be put in a home or a hospital which she knows will only mark her end. This is a novel about our time, aging, and society's refusal to differentiate between growing old and dying. It calls forth Lessing's gifts—a precise eye for detail, an absorption in the quotidian, a psychological understanding of people, and the ability to tell a story. The book is full of stories—Maudie's, the elderly Anne's, another of the women Jane comes to help, and, of course Jane's. The second book in the series is less successful. *If the Old Could—* tells a triter story of Jane's affair with a married man whose unhappy daughter shadows them and whose son baffles her with his unexpected declaration of love. The portions that deal with the elderly, however, are again excellent. Lessing, in both these books, forces the reader to see the elderly. After reading the books, I found myself looking searchingly at the solitary old people sitting on benches, or queuing in the grocery store, or shuffling to a bus, and more important, I looked forward and within.

The Good Terrorist is absorbing, so apt is its portrait of Alice Mellings, a 36-year-old over-aged adolescent, and her "family" of squatters. Alice's instincts are motherly; her zeal to save council flats from being condemned makes her a valuable friend for other, younger, motley members of the Communist Centre Union who join her as a squatter. Her rages are instantaneous and inexplicable to her. Immersed in her day-to-day life, we witness her transformation into a terrorist.

The Fifth Child again demonstrates Lessing's ability to defy labels and forge in new directions. Although its world relates back to a world she revealed in both *Briefing for a Descent into Hell* and *Memoirs of a Survivor,* the tale is told in a new and disquieting form. It begins with a too idyllic account of a pair of young Londoners and their old-fashioned dream of a large family, housed in a mammoth Victorian mansion, comfortably away from the strife of the city. After recounting a cycle of yearly house parties and the arrival of four healthy children, it moves to the birth of the fifth child and the disastrous consequences. Folk ingredients, elements of *Frankenstein,* and images of gnomes and trolls and distant ancestors of the Nebelung haunt the imagination of the mother as her child grows. Mysterious stranglings of animals, and, later, a beating of a classmate, and then thefts and worse crimes occur. All seem the work of the demon child and the idyll of a happy family disintegrates. Throughout the book, we are conscious not only of the desperate plight of the mother of this hapless child, but also of deeper societal unrest. As in many of her other novels, Lessing questions whether there is a higher dimension, or whether mankind has reverted to some darker, primitive age where troll-like creatures dominate the land.

It is too early to assess Lessing's place in literary history. Her imagination is too rich. What can be said is that she is deeply concerned with the human condition, and hungry to explore new dimensions, to redefine relationships. Her writings reflect a nearly obsessive effort to find a way through the historical ravages of this century to a condition beyond the one of personal unhappiness that plagues so many human relationships. Her novels try to teach us how better to manage our world; they expose a world out of control.

—Carol Simpson Stern

LEVIN, Ira

Nationality: American. **Born:** New York City, 27 August 1929.
Education: Drake University, Des Moines, Iowa, 1946-48; New
York University; 1948-50, A.B. 1950. **Military Service:** Served
in the United States Army Signal Corps, 1953-55. **Family:** Married 1) Gabrielle Aronsohn in 1960 (divorced 1968), three sons; 2)
Phyllis Finkel in 1979 (divorced 1982). **Awards:** Mystery Writers
of America Edgar Allan Poe award, 1954, and Special Award, 1980.
Agent: Harold Ober Associates, 425 Madison Avenue, New York,
New York 10017, U.S.A.

PUBLICATIONS

Novels

A Kiss Before Dying. New York, Simon and Schuster, 1953; London, Joseph, 1954.
Rosemary's Baby. New York, Random House, and London, Joseph, 1967.
This Perfect Day. New York, Random House, and London, Joseph, 1970.
The Stepford Wives. New York, Random House, and London, Joseph, 1972.
The Boys from Brazil. New York, Random House, and London, Joseph, 1976.
Sliver. New York, Bantam, and London, Joseph, 1991.

Plays

No Time for Sergeants, Adaptation of the novel by Mac Hyman
(produced New York, 1955; London, 1956). New York, Random House, 1956.
Interlock (produced New York, 1958). New York, Dramatists Play
Service, 1958.
Critic's Choice (produced New York, 1960; London, 1961). New
York, Random House, 1961; London, Evans, 1963.
General Seeger (produced New York, 1962). New York, Dramatists Play Service, 1962.
Drat! That Cat!, music by Milton Schafer (produced New York, 1965).
Dr. Cook's Garden (also director: produced New York, 1967). New
York, Dramatists Play Service, 1968.
Veronica's Room (produced New York, 1973; Watford,
Hertfordshire, 1982). New York, Random House, 1974; London, Joseph, 1975.
Deathtrap (produced New York and London, 1978). New York,
Random House, 1979; London, French, 1980.
Break a Leg (produced New York, 1979). New York, French, 1981.
Cantorial (produced Stamford, Connecticut, 1984; New York,
1989). New York and London, French, 1990.

*

Critical Study: *Ira Levin* by Douglas Fowler, Mercer Island,
Washington, Starmont, 1988.

Theatrical Activities:
Director: **Play**—*Dr. Cook's Garden,* New York, 1967.

The heroine of *Rosemary's Baby* is overwhelmed by the "elaborate . . . evil" of the witches' coven through whose agency she has
unknowingly borne Satan's child, which now lies in a black bassinet with an inverted crucifix for a crib toy. Elaborateness is, indeed, the chief characteristic of both evil and good in Ira Levin's
novels. Bud Corless of *A Kiss Before Dying* makes neat lists of
ways to arrange his pregnant girlfriend's "suicide" and to win her
eldest sister's love. In *This Perfect Day* all human actions are ostensibly directed by a world computer and everyone must touch
his identification bracelet to scanners before he can do anything,
go anywhere, or receive any supplies. The novel's hero, Chip (or
Li RM35M4419, to give him his "nameber") fights system with
system in a complicated expedition to disable UniComp's memory
banks. The first dozen pages of *The Boys for Brazil* describe, course
by course, Dr. Mengele's dinner party-*cum*-briefing for the assassination of 94 retired civil servants, each of whom has unwittingly
adopted a clone of Hitler, produced by the Doctor, who now intends to recreate Hitler's family environment.

Such procedures provide the sustaining interest and suspense of
Levin's novels, combining neatness and system with Satanism, secrets, universal surveillance, violence, and death. Rosemary uses a
scrabble set to work out the anagram which identifies her friendly
neighbor Roman Castevet as devil-worshipping Steven Marcato.
In *A Kiss Before Dying* Dorothy's provision of "Something old,
Something new, Something borrowed, And something blue" enables her sister to deduce that Dorothy intended marriage, not suicide. The husbands of *The Stepford Wives* make speaking, moving
replicas of their spouses. They begin with seemingly innocuous
sketches of each real wife and tape recordings of her voice; they
end by killing her off-stage. Levin increases the "reality" of such
sinister processes by mingling them with ordinary routines of eating, pregnancy, moving to a new house, etc.

Both good and bad characters must, at times, revise their elaborate plans on the spur of the crisis. Their expedients are ingenious,
often complex, and the pleasure of following Levin's details is
enough to make some of his novels re-readable when their surprise is over.

The forward movement and acceleration of the plots are further
complicated by sudden reversals, single or double, overt or psychological, in which characters (and often readers) are temporarily
disoriented. For example, Rosemary, arriving at the logical conclusion that her husband had joined the coven, "didn't know if she
was going mad or going sane." Joanna cannot tell if her best friend
is still a person or has become an automaton. (She *is* an automaton, and stabs Joanna). Although the reader is sometimes prepared
for these discoveries, there are also unexpected shocks, such as
when Rosemary, thinking herself safe, sees her witch-obstetrician
enter, or when Chip, suddenly taken prisoner by a trusted teammember, discovers that betrayal is really recruitment by the elite
subterranean programmers. The effect on the reader of such continual reversals and realignments is a constant uneasiness as to his
personal safety and moral identity, which produces horror very successfully in *Rosemary's Baby,* but rather mechanically in *This Perfect Day* and *The Stepford Wives.* No doubt Levin's constant readers now anticipate his surprises, which may account for his increasing detail of violence as excitement in *The Boys from Brazil.*

Occasionally and chiefly in *This Perfect Day,* Levin's literary antecedents are apparent. His shock techniques are essentially those of Ambrose Bierce and Villiers de l'Isle Adam. Bud's slow plunge into a vat of molten copper recalls H.G. Wells's "The Cone" with its archetypal death by blast furnace. The world of UniComp is essentially a Brave New World with a Big Brother mentality, but controlled by a mad scientist out of Edgar Rice Burroughs, who rejuvenates through body transference. In short, Levin has drawn upon the almost inescapable traditional materials of his genre, but he uses them intelligently and individually.

Increasingly, Levin's novels imply larger significances. Looking at the copper smelter, the murderer says seriously, "It makes you realize what a great country this is." Rosemary's subtly evil apartment house is owned by the church next door, and there are seemingly casual references to the Death of God. An ideal universe of "the gentle, the helpful, the loving, the unselfish" is the vision of a power-joyful egoist. Even the intelligent Stepford husbands in a strange feminist fable want only big-breasted, floor-waxing, mindless wives. A wise old Nazi-hunter, clashing with a radical rabbi, refuses to let 94 teenage Hitlers be exterminated for the sake of future Jewish safety, saying, "This was *Mengele's* business, killing children. Should it be ours?" These moral paradoxes, undeveloped though they are, both extend and intensify the disquieting uncertainty which had been Levin's chief characteristic.

His latest novel, *Sliver,* 15 years after *The Boys from Brazil,* seems, however, almost a parody of earlier motifs. There is the sinister apartment house of *Rosemary's Baby,* now dominated by the corrupting power of television. Its owner, Peter Henderson, a hi-tech Peeping Tom, has bugged every room for closed circuit TV and watches the most intimate lives of his tenants—the soap operas God sees. Like God, Peter rewards and punishes, while manipulating a plot to avenge his actress-mother's death. There is also the violent fall of *A Kiss Before Dying* as Peter pushes Kay (less innocent and sympathetic than Rosemary) backward through a window—although she manages to hold on while her cat claws out his eyes. Levin's processes in this novel have become pedestrian, and there is no real shock of reversal since Kay has known of and participated in Peter's surveillance. Nor is a reader likely to be much disquieted by learning that three other New York buildings have been similarly wired. Instead, *Sliver* is basically a melodramatic parable about television, for which Levin himself wrote in its golden age. Then, a character says, it was more real because shows were live. Now it corrupts, and Sam Yale, Peter's intended victim, points out that "tv madness" was bound to come. He and Kate give in quickly to the lure of Peter's multiple screens, even while disapproving. Levin's style is now abrupt, especially at first, appropriate to "short takes," but becoming a mannerism.

—Jane W. Stedman

LEVINE, (Albert) Norman

Nationality: Canadian. **Born:** Ottawa, Ontario, 22 October 1923. **Education:** York Street School and High School of Commerce, Ottawa; Carleton College, Ottawa, 1945; McGill University, Montreal, 1946-49, B.A. 1948, M.A. 1949; King's College, London, 1949-50. **Military Service:** Served in the Royal Canadian Air Force, 1942-45: Flying Officer. **Family:** Married 1) Margaret Payne in 1952 (died 1978), three daughters; 2) Anne Sarginson in 1983. **Career:** Employed by the Department of National Defence, Ottawa, 1940-42; lived mainly in England, 1949-80; head of the English Department, Barnstaple Boys Grammar School, Devon, 1953-54; resident writer, University of New Brunswick, Fredericton, 1965-66. **Awards:** Canada Council fellowship, 1959, and Arts award, 1969, 1971, 1974. **Address:** Penguin Books, 10 Alcorn Avenue, Toronto, Ontario M4V 3B2, Canada.

PUBLICATIONS

Novels

The Angled Road. London, Laurie, 1952.
From a Seaside Town. London, Macmillan, 1970.

Short Stories

One Way Ticket. London, Secker and Warburg, 1961.
I Don't Want to Know Anyone Too Well: 15 Stories. London, Macmillan, 1971.
Selected Stories. Ottawa, Oberon Press, 1975.
In Lower Town, photographs by Johanne McDuff. Ottawa, Commoners', 1977.
Thin Ice. Ottawa, Deneau, and London, Wildwood House, 1980.
Why Do You Live So Far Away? A Novella and Six Stories. Ottawa, Deneau, 1984.
Champagne Barn. Toronto and London, Penguin, 1984; New York, Penguin, 1985.
Something Happened Here. Toronto and London, Viking, 1991.

Poetry

Myssium. Toronto, Ryerson Press, 1948.
The Tight-Rope Walker. London, Totem Press, 1950.
I Walk by the Harbour. Fredericton, New Brunswick, Fiddlehead, 1976.

Other

Canada Made Me. London, Putnam, 1958.
The Beat & the Still. Toronto, North Edition, 1990.

Editor, *Canadian Winter's Tales.* Toronto and London, Macmillan, 1968.

*

Manuscript Collections: University of Texas, Austin; York University, Toronto.

Critical Studies: "The Girl in the Drugstore" by Levin, in *Canadian Literature 41* (Vancouver), 1969; interview in *Canadian Literature 45* (Vancouver), 1970; Philip Oakes, in *Sunday Times* (London), 19 July 1970; Alan Heuser, in *Montreal Star,* 26 September 1970; *Times Literary Supplement* (London), 3 December 1971; Maurice Capitanchik, in *Books and Bookmen* (London), September 1972; Frederick Sweet, in *Profiles in Canadian Literature 4* edited by Jeffrey M. Heath, Toronto, Dundurn, 1982; George Galt, in *Saturday Night* (Toronto), June 1984; "A Small Piece of Norman

Levine" (interview) by Michael Winter, in *TickleAce 26* (St. John's, Newfoundland), Winter 1993.

Norman Levine comments:

For anyone who wants to know where to begin, I suggest that the start would be *Canada Made Me, From a Seaside Town,* then *Champagne Barn.*

I wrote in the *Atlantic Advocate:* "When you go to a writer's work—it is into his personal world that you enter. What he is doing is paying, in his own way, an elaborate tribute to people and places he has known."

*   *   *

Norman Levine has always been remarkable for the reserve of his writing; but it took him some years to learn what best to withhold and what to reveal. In his early autobiographical stories and novel, *The Angled Road,* he was "trying to cut out [his] past, to cover . . . up" his origins as the Canadian-bred son of a Jewish street-peddler. As if to compensate for this leaching of color from his material, he was also experimenting with patches of vulgar prose-poetry. While teaching himself to write simply and directly, he came to terms with his personal history. Now, in *Thin Ice,* although his range is narrow, he shapes his stories with the unmistakable authority of a writer who has found his subject and style.

Speaking for the most part in the first person, Levine relates in neutral prose incidents from his Canadian upbringing and his years in England. Certain worlds are revealed which he leaves and is drawn back to: Jewish society, life at McGill University summer cottages by the Richelieu, the tourist villages of Cornwall, poverty in a small town. He has achieved the outsider's vantage point from which he turns a telephoto lens on ordinary people and events. The danger of his method is that when it miscarries, as sometimes it does, the reader is left with a commonplace, colorless anecdote that adds up to nothing. His later stories and novel do not differ greatly from his travel narrative, *Canada Made Me,* except in being increasingly crafted, concise, and superficially detached. Although he has escaped the heavy cold of Montreal and the intimate squalor of lower Ottawa, he takes with him wherever he goes his Canadian melancholy and taste for failure.

In drawing on his personal past, Levine often returns to the same scenes, characters, and even fragments of conversation, as if he were unable to invent afresh or to leave behind any of his life. An Englishman awaiting the flowering of a large cactus, a woman without a nose, a prowling man whom a couple nicknames "the house detective," are only a few of many recurrent elements in the work of this man who mines his own writings, word for word, as well as his past. The friction of repeated use has polished his memories until all that is inessential has worn away, leaving a smooth pebble of experience.

Levine consistently avoids evocative vocabulary, choosing instead to make a plain statement of fact in language so empty of implication that it becomes mysterious. It is as if he is trying to create prose as objective as the reality he perceives. Yet, in his best work, when everything possible has been jettisoned, a core of emotion remains. He writes in short, often broken, sentences that correspond to the fragmentary moments of human contact in his tales. Sometimes an ugly expression such as "less worse" (*Canada Made Me*) has been selected as the only way of expressing what he means, but at other times a sentence muddles into ambiguity that adds nothing, or an angularity almost illiterate. Except for brief periods, Levine

lived in England from 1949 until 1980, so it is not surprising that he somewhat lost his grasp of Canadian idiom and fact. His use of such expressions as "the School of Seven," "motorways," "left luggage," and "do some walks" is evidence of the distance he traveled from his native speech. Even his distinguished German translator, Heinrich Böll, the Nobel prize-winner, must have felt it a hopeless task to convey in all its aspects Levine's continual shuttling between England and Canada.

Although Levine says little about his feelings, one cannot miss the passion that concentrates his prose and sends him back to places and people he cannot forget. His journeys are the counterpart of the sexual hunger that runs through *From a Seaside Town.* His appetite for experience and his enjoyment of the grotesque have so far saved him from the sterility that threatens autobiographical writers in middle age. In his low-keyed world even tiny incidents stand out like figures against a landscape of snow. They may mean nothing or anything, but to him they have an importance which the reader feels, but never entirely understands.

—Margaret Keith

LEWIS, Janet

Nationality: American. **Born:** Chicago, Illinois, 17 August 1899. **Education:** The Lewis Institute, Chicago, A.A. 1918; University of Chicago, Ph.B. 1920. **Family:** Married the writer Yvor Winters in 1926 (died 1968); one daughter and one son. **Career:** Passport Bureau clerk, American Consulate, Paris, 1920; proofreader, *Redbook* magazine, Chicago, 1921; English teacher, Lewis Institute, 1921-22; editor, with Howard Baker and Yvor Winters, *Gyroscope,* Palo Alto, California, 1929-30. Lecturer, Writers Workshop, University of Missouri, Columbia, 1952, and University of Denver, 1956; visiting lecturer, then lecturer in English, Stanford University, California, 1960, 1966, 1969, 1970. **Awards:** Friends of American Literature award, 1932; Shelley Memorial award, for poetry, 1948; Guggenheim fellowship, 1950; Los Angeles *Times* Kirsch award, 1985. **Address:** 143 West Portola Avenue, Los Altos, California 94022, U.S.A.

PUBLICATIONS

Novels

The Invasion: A Narrative of Events Concerning the Johnston Family of St. Mary's. New York, Harcourt Brace, 1932.
The Wife of Martin Guerre. San Francisco, Colt Press, 1941; London, Rapp and Carroll, 1967.
Against a Darkening Sky. New York, Doubleday, 1943.
The Trial of Sören Qvist. New York, Doubleday, 1947; London, Gollancz, 1967.
The Ghost of Monsieur Scarron. New York, Doubleday, and London, Gollancz, 1959.

Short Stories

Goodbye, Son, and Other Stories. New York, Doubleday, 1946.

Uncollected Short Stories

"At the Swamp," in *The Best Short Stories of 1930,* edited by Edward J. O'Brien. Boston, Houghton Mifflin, 1930.

"La Pointe Chegiomegon," in *Hound and Horn* (Portland, Maine), October-December 1931.

"A Still Small Voice," in *McCall's* (New York), 1946.

"The Breakfast Cup," in *Saturday Evening Post* (Philadelphia), 27 February 1965.

Plays (opera libretti)

The Wife of Martin Guerre, music by William Bergsma, adaptation of the novel by Lewis (produced New York, 1956). Denver, Swallow, 1958; as *The Wife,* Santa Barbara, California, Daniel, 1988.

The Last of the Mohicans, adaptation of the novel by Cooper, music by Alva Henderson (produced Wilmington, Delaware, 1976).

A Birthday of the Infanta, adaptation of the story by Wilde, music by Malcolm Seagrave (produced Carmel, California, 1977). Los Angeles, Symposium Press, 1979.

Mulberry Street, music by Alva Henderson. Onset, Massachusetts, Dermont, 1981; as *West of Washington Square* (produced San Jose, California, 1988), Santa Barbara, California, Daniel, 1988.

The Swans. Santa Barbara, California, Daniel, 1986.

The Legend, music by Bain Murray, adaptation of the novel *The Invasion* by Lewis (produced Cleveland, 1987). Santa Barbara, California, Daniel, 1987.

Poetry

The Indians in the Woods. Bonn, Germany, Monroe Wheeler, 1922; Palo Alto, California, Matrix Press, 1980.

The Wheel in Midsummer. Lynn, Massachusetts, Lone Gull Press, 1927.

The Earth-Bound 1924-1944. Aurora, New York, Wells College, 1946.

The Hangar at Sunnyvale 1937. San Francisco, Book Club of California, 1947.

Poems 1924-1944. Denver, Swallow, 1950.

The Ancient Ones. Portola Valley, California, No Dead Lines, 1979.

Poems Old and New 1918-1978. Athens, Ohio University Press-Swallow Press, 1981.

Late Offerings. Florence, Kentucky, Barth, 1988.

The Dear Past. Edgewood, Kentucky, Barth, 1994.

Other

The Friendly Adventure of Ollie Ostrich (for children). New York, Doubleday, 1923.

Keiko's Bubble (for children). New York, Doubleday, 1961; Kingswood, Surrey, World's Work, 1963.

The U.S. and Canada, with others. Green Bay, University of Wisconsin Press, 1970.

*

Manuscript Collection: Stanford University Library, California.

Critical Studies: By Richard F. Goldman, in *Musical Quarterly* (New York), July 1956; "The Legacy of Fenimore Cooper," in *Essays in Criticism* (Brill, Buckinghamshire), July 1959, and "The Historical Novels of Janet Lewis," in *Southern Review* (Baton Rouge, Louisiana), January 1966, both by Donald Davie; "Genius Unobserved" by Evan S. Connell, Jr., in *Atlantic* (Boston), December 1969; "Patriarchal Women: A Study of Three Novels by Janet Lewis" by Ellen Killoh, in *Southern Review* (Baton Rouge, Louisiana), Spring 1974; "Janet Lewis Issue" of *Numbers* (Cambridge, Massachusetts), Winter 1989-90; interview with Mickey Pearlman and Katherine Usher Henderson, in *Inter/View: Talks with America's Writing Women,* Lexington, University Press of Kentucky, 1990; *Landscape, Memory, and the Poetry of Janet Lewis* by Brigitte Carnochan, California, The Stanford University Libraries and the Department of English, Stanford University, 1995.

Janet Lewis comments:

(1972) It is difficult to know what to say about my own work. Most of it needs little if any explanation. In regard to *The Invasion* I can state that I meant to write history as if I were writing fiction. It is in every way, in so far as I could manage, faithful to the facts and the events. When it comes to the three novels based on the famous cases of circumstantial evidence, I can only state again that I intended to write history as if it were fiction. I remained in each case as faithful to the facts as I could, but I was so far from them in time and space that I needed to invent rather freely, in order to clothe the facts with life. In the case of *Martin Guerre* I began with a very brief account of the events, and have learned bit by bit since the day the book was first published more and more about the truth of the matter, so that now, 30 years later, I have at hand the ultimate source for the story, the account by one of the judges, Jean de Coras. My story of Martin Guerre is fiction, but it is very close indeed to the known facts.

*   *   *

Janet Lewis is admired as one of the purest stylists in contemporary fiction, and as a novelist who continued to write quietly probing dramas of psycho-moral ambiguity with almost total disregard for the changing fashions of American fiction. She is to be compared, in the quiet integrity of her art, with Willa Cather, Caroline Gordon, and her friend Elizabeth Madox Roberts. Only her modest volume of short stories (*Goodbye, Son*) and the slowpaced, intelligent, at times dreary *Against a Darkening Sky* are contemporary in scene. Her reputation rests instead on her four historical novels, one related to her own part-Indian background, the others laid in remote European times.

The Invasion occupies a surprisingly satisfying border region between fiction and history, and contains some of the loveliest prose in modern American literature. Its singular achievement is to present without pretentiousness or strain an Indian culture from within (the Ojibway of the Lake Superior area), and its gradual change and slow obliteration over a century and a half. The family chronicle extends from 1791, when we meet the 14-year-old Woman of the Glade, who married the trader John Johnston, to the death in 1944 of Anna Maria Johnston, the Red Leaf. The novel is the work of a poet recording delicate nuances of landscape and mood, and of a scrupulous historian contemplating with equanimity the inevitable outrages of human passion and eroding time. It combines with remarkable success an intimate immersion in scene (a succession of lived moments) and a flow of time that is calm as well as swift. The chronicle's exceptional authenticity is strengthened by the fact that the famous ethnologist, linguist, and Indian agent Henry Rowe Schoolcraft is a central figure in the family history.

Three very different historical novels are based on incidents recorded in Phillips's *Famous Cases of Circumstantial Evidence,* an early 19th-century work. *The Trial of Sören Qvist,* laid in 17th-century Denmark, is the story of a saintly pastor executed for a crime he did not commit. This is a spare and dramatic novel, but meditative too, like everything Lewis has written. *The Ghost of Monsieur Scarron* is the product of years of research, some of it in a part of Paris that has not greatly changed since 1694. It is the minutely realistic story of a book-binder falsely accused of authoring a libelous pamphlet directed against Louis XIV and Madame de Maintenon. The evocation of the Paris of that time is remarkable.

The best of these novels, one of the greatest short novels in American literature, is *The Wife of Martin Guerre,* a quietly authentic, immaculately written story of a man whose physical "double" (but far more considerate and more loving than the original) returns to claim the wife of a soldier supposed dead in the wars of 16th-century France. Here as in her other two novels of ambiguous crime and punishment Lewis dramatizes, always calmly, situations exerting extreme pressure on her characters. The marriage of Martin Guerre and Bertrande de Rols, at 11, is of its time, and so too the execution 21 years later. A sentence from Lewis's "Foreword" suggests the human understanding underlying all her work. "The rules of evidence vary from century to century, and the morality which compels many of the actions of men and women varies also, but the capacities of the human soul for suffering and for joy remain very much the same."

—Albert Guerard

LIM, Catherine

Nationality: Singaporean (naturalized). **Born:** Kedah, Malaysia, 23 March 1942. **Education:** University of Malaysia, B.A. (honours) in English 1963; National University of Singapore, M.A. in applied linguistics 1979, Ph.D. 1987. **Family:** Married in 1964 (divorced 1980); one daughter and one son. **Career:** Education officer, 1965-78; deputy director of curriculum development, Institute of Singapore, 1979-85; lecturer in sociolinguistics, Seameo Regional Centre, Singapore, 1989-90. **Address:** 18 Leedon Heights, #07-05, Farrer Road, Singapore 1026.

PUBLICATIONS

Novel

The Serpent's Tooth. Singapore, Times Books International, 1982.

Short Stories

Little Ironies: Stories of Singapore. Singapore and Portsmouth, New Hampshire, Heinemann, 1978.
Or Else, the Lightning God and Other Stories. Singapore and Portsmouth, New Hampshire, Heinemann, 1980.
They Do Return. Singapore, Times Books International, 1983.
The Shadow of a Shadow of a Dream: Love Stories of Singapore. Singapore, Times Books International, 1987.

O Singapore!: Stories in Celebration. Singapore, Times Books International, 1989.
Deadline for Love and Other Stories. Singapore, Heinemann, 1992.
The Woman's Book of Superlatives. Singapore, Times Books International, 1993.
The Best of Catherine Lim. Singapore, Heinemann, 1993.

Poetry

Love's Lonely Impulses. Singapore, Heinemann, 1992.

*

Critical Studies: "Catherine Lim and the Singapore Short Story in English" by Robert Yeo, in *Commentary,* 2, 1981; "An Interview with Catherine Lim" by Siti Rohaini Kassim, in *Southeast Asian Review of English,* December 1989; in *Literary Perspectives on Southeast Asia: Collected Essays* by Peter Wicks, 1991.

Catherine Lim comments:

Absorbing, enduring interest in the Chinese culture of my childhood; aware of my unusual position as an English-educated Chinese writing in English, with a perspective inevitably coloured by the fact of straddling two worlds.

*   *   *

Catherine Lim is the author of one novel, *The Serpent's Tooth,* and eight collections of short stories, vignettes of Singaporean life. Her writing is fuelled by the energies generated by incongruities of many kinds, which power both its themes and also its manner. Lim's main themes are the clashes between generations and cultures, the disparity of attitudes and lifestyles found amongst the various income-groups, and the discrepancy between the society's ever-improving economic profile and its state of moral poverty. While the themes are large ones, they are expressed within a context of the mundane, in terms of the bric-a-brac of everyday life which lend these themes concreteness and believability. The authorial voice is generally ironic though not uncompassionate, the irony exploiting the territory between differing levels of awareness (e.g., between author, reader, and characters) and pointing sharply to the complacence and the unthinking selfishness displayed by individuals that must be remedied. Lim, however, seldom intrudes judgement; action is allowed to serve as its own comment, and the discrepancies, blandly presented, (e.g., Angela in *The Serpent's Tooth* spends 5,000 dollars on a birthday dinner whereas 17 dollars and 25 cents is undreamed-of wealth to Ah Bah in "Ah Bah's Money") insist on the reader's attention, engendering social/moral awareness even if none should have existed before.

The Serpent's Tooth brings together many of the concerns treated of separately in the short stories. As its reference to *King Lear* makes clear, it is on one level about ingratitude and thankless children. But more importantly, it is about the tensions born of the different assumptions and perspectives brought to bear upon things and events, by the main character, Angela and her mother-in-law, (and to a lesser extent, by other members of the extended family). The one stands for the modern, English-speaking Singaporean, for whom money stands in place of culture, the other is an adherent of traditional Chinese beliefs and practices, impervious to change in the world around. They are each other's serpents, each seeing the other as the cause of separation from her child, each making life intolerable for the other, yet ironically unaware of her own short-comings and insensitivity. What emerges here, and in the short stories, is a sketch of a culture/society comprising morally indifferent and solipsistic individuals. Neither set of values (modern or traditional) is seen as being above reproach. The antique bed belonging to the mother-in-law serves as a vehicle by which both the callousness of the older generation: a bondmaid (who subsequently bled to death) has been raped on it, and also the mercenary tendencies of the younger generation, concerned only with the value of the antique, are exposed.

Certain of the short stories (e.g. "Gold Dust," "Miss Pereira," and "Deadline for Love") examine the disparity between economic plenty and emotional/spiritual starvation, and the groping of the individual for meaning un-indexed by the ownership of material things. However, genuine piety or spirituality is seldom encountered in Lim's stories; instead, what is made to substitute for this is a shallow and formal worship of supernatural forces. These forces must be propitiated, not out of devotion, but from a desire to avert ill-fortune ("Or Else the Lightening God") or to increase wealth. Kindness goes ill-repaid ("A.P. Velloo") and hopes are, more often than not, thwarted. Thus, while as a body of work, Catherine Lim's stories stand as testimony to culture in transit, the older traditions particular to race becoming slowly eradicated or homogenized, they also stand as an indictment of materialism on the increase which threatens to destroy things of intangible value.

—Susan Ang

LITVINOFF, Emanuel

Nationality: British. **Born:** London, 30 June 1915. **Military Service:** Served in the Royal West African Frontier Force, 1940-46: Major. **Family:** Married Cherry Marshall in 1942 (divorced); four children. **Career:** Before World War II, worked in tailoring, cabinet-making, and the fur trade; after the war worked as a journalist and broadcaster, and founded the journal, *Jews in Eastern Europe,* London. Since 1958 director, Contemporary Jewish Library, London. **Awards:** Wingate Award (*Jewish Chronicle,* London), 1979. **Agent:** David Higham Associates, 5-8 Lower John Street, London W1R 4HA, England.

PUBLICATIONS

Novels

The Lost Europeans. New York, Vanguard Press, 1959; London, Heinemann, 1960.
The Man Next Door. London, Hodder and Stoughton, 1968; New York, Norton, 1969.
A Death Out of Season. London, Joseph, 1973; New York, Scribner, 1974.
Blood on the Snow. London, Joseph, 1975.
The Face of Terror. London, Joseph, and New York, Morrow, 1978.
Falls the Shadow. London, Joseph, and New York, Stein and Day, 1983.

Short Stories

Penguin Modern Stories 2, with others. London, Penguin, 1969.
Journey Through a Small Planet. London, Joseph, 1972.

Uncollected Short Stories

"The God I Failed," in *The Guardian* (London), 1966.
"Call Me Uncle Solly," in *The Listener* (London), 1967.

Plays

Magnolia Street Story, adaptation of a novel by Louis Golding (produced London, 1951).

Television Plays: *Another Branch of the Family,* 1967; *Marriage and Henry Sunday,* 1967; *A Dream in the Afternoon,* 1967; *Foxhole in Bayswater,* 1968; *A Foot in the Door,* 1969; *The World Is a Room,* 1970; *Warm Feet, Warm Heart,* 1970; *The Kazmirov Affair,* 1971.

Poetry

Conscripts: A Symphonic Declaration. London, Favil Press, 1941.
The Untried Soldier. London, Routledge, 1942.
A Crown for Cain. London, Falcon Press, 1948.
Notes for a Survivor. Newcastle upon Tyne, Northern House, 1973.

Other

Editor, *Soviet Anti-Semitism: The Paris Trial.* London, Wildwood House, 1974.
Editor, *The Penguin Book of Jewish Short Stories.* London, Penguin, 1979.

*

Emanuel Litvinoff comments:

(1991) My novel *The Lost Europeans* is haunted by the Holocaust. It describes the morbid psychological obsessions of victim and persecutor in a situation where former German Jews return to Germany after the war and confront their erstwhile neighbors.

The Man Next Door is, in a sense, related to this theme. Its central character is a conventional suburban Englishman of the middle-class whose personality begins to disintegrate under the encroachments of middle-age, accompanied by a sense of social and sexual failure. In the process, a mild and commonplace xenophobia turns to rabid hatred of Jews and Negroes of the kind so hideously expressed by the Nazis.

A Death Out of Season, Blood on the Snow and *The Face of Terror* comprise a trilogy following the fortunes of a group of young revolutionaries in the early years of the century, through the Russian Revolution, civil war and famine, to their final disillusion and bitterness in the Stalinist purges of the mid-1930s.

Falls the Shadow, written in thriller form, shows how the Nazi holocaust intertwines with modern life in Israel, raising moral issues that Israel must still come to terms with.

My short stories, set in the milieu of the London Jewish East End, celebrate the idealism, pain, and promise of adolescence.

(1995) Gusts of that Revolution blew with Siberian bleakness through my East End tenement. . . . My parents' flight from Russia saved me, my seven brothers and one sister from the holocausts of starvation and Nazism. I am connected to these tragedies with the guilt and obsession of a survivor, and they inform almost everything I have written.

*   *   *

Emanuel Litvinoff's short stories describe the atmosphere of a close Jewish community in London's East End where he grew up between the wars. The stories contain some poignant and sometimes verbose semi-autobiographical sketches of adolescence, as in "A View from the Seventh Floor":

> "What do you do on week-ends?" I stammered.
> "On Saturday," she whispered, without lifting her head, "I go to the synagogue with my aunt." Soft black hair curled on the nape of her slender neck and I was tormented by her narrow, sleepy Russian eyes. I wanted to say something miraculous and unforgettable, or so sharp, cruel and eloquent it would remain a fresh wound all of her life. But instead I said: "Does your aunt shave on Shabbos?"

In the same story, Litvinoff mentions his early feelings of rootlessness which inform much of his later work: "In those days I had the shadowy premonition that unless my life was shattered to pieces and I could put it together differently, I'd never, never be myself."

As Litvinoff approaches maturity, he becomes increasingly aware of his "ancestry of misfortune." He regards it as mere chance that he was born in Whitechapel. His home could as easily have been in Hitler's Germany or Stalin's Russia. Litvinoff's first novel, *The Lost Europeans,* develops this ideas and examines the restless lives of a few World War II survivors. The novel is set in post-war Berlin, where ex-nazis and communists, hedonistic young Aryans, whores, and a few Jews live in awkward peace. Martin Stone, a London accountant, takes time off to visit the city of his childhood and claim the legal restitution of his family's fortune. The war-blighted Berliners whom Martin meets involuntarily inflame his smoldering bitterness. There is Hugo Krantz, a fellow Jew, once the witty doyen of Berlin's theater circles, now a fat businessman in relentless pursuit of sensual pleasures, and the friend who betrayed him to the SS. Hugo arranges accommodation for Martin in the guesthouse of his oldest friend, Frau Goetz. Her gothic hair-do and bird-like charm cannot conceal the marks of Auschwitz. Every Berliner is a victim. In the parks and pastryshops and honky tonk bars, Martin feels once more "the poisons moving in the bloodstream, the familiar throbbing of the diseased night." But it is in this city that Martin meets Karin, a docile factory worker from the eastern sector. She too is a victim—raped in childhood by conquering Russian soldiers. In order to offer her his love, Martin must expiate Karin's years of numbness and resolve his own haunting resentments.

Litvinoff's descriptions of the strange personal lives of Hugo and Frau Goetz are especially good, and Hugo's foray into the ambiguous and dangerous world of intelligence agents has all the atmosphere of a first-rate spy thriller. But just as the pace is getting really hot, we are back with the dour, curiously faceless Martin. The impact of each story—Martin's and Hugo's—is reduced rather than enhanced by its entanglement with the other. Nevertheless, *The Lost Europeans* is a very readable and frequently compelling account of the obsessions of German Jews and their former persecutors.

The Man Next Door focuses on Harold Bollam, a man who blossomed early in life. Boarding school, the army, and a spell as a store manager in West Africa supported and strengthened his hawkish sentiments on class and race. Back in England he finds life somewhat bewildering:

> The country had gone mad for gimmicks. Young smart alecks were getting in everywhere. Long-haired pop-singers bought up the stately homes, public opinion media were in the hands of queers and sensation-mongers who made England look cheap in the eyes of the world. Cheap, indeed, when black college boys became prime ministers of ridiculous "independent" states, dined with the Queen and lectured the British on the what's-what of democracy.

Middle-age does not mellow a man like Bollam; failures and frustrations pile upon him. Relations with his fretful wife Edna are bleak; prospects for promotion at International Utilities dwindle daily; sex is a combat between flesh and despair; his children, away at boarding school, are strangers. When the Winstons (born Weinsteins) move in next door, Bollam's resentments and fears become obsessions. His wife, his colleagues, the Blacks, the Jews, and especially the Jews next door, are all conspiring to degrade and defeat him. Obsession turns to paranoia and Bollam seeks insane revenge. ". . . as soon as the Winstons arrived he'd guessed it would end badly. They didn't fit. Apart from being Jews, there was something alien and disruptive about them. They were the kind who carried the germ of misfortune wherever they went, like spores of an invisible cancer . . ."

The Man Next Door has a certain morbid fascination, but it lacks the authenticity of Litvinoff's first novel. The characters are somewhat stereotyped, his portrayal of Bollam's grim and neurotic life occasionally verges on the glib, and the analogy between Bollam's retrogression and the rise of nazism is not always effective.

Litvinoff's obsession with Jewish persecution has further opened out in recent work. *A Death Out of Season, Blood on the Snow,* and *The Face of Terror* constitute a trilogy of historical novels which seek to portray the experience of revolutionary and Stalinist Russia, and have been highly praised by reviewers. Though these novels have complicated and dazzling plots, the double agents, summaries of Russian history, and rather conventional iconography lack real conviction. Much more original is *Falls the Shadow.* The plot is genuinely unusual (a SS torturer masquerading as a Jewish victim, complete with concentration camp tattoo, and an obsessed police investigator). The moral problems (does living the life of an orthodox Jew for 40 years balance having been an SS torturer?) and the convincing description of suburban life in Tel Aviv give strength to the work, though the messages are rather thumped home, the reader continually nudged into historical awareness.

Litvinoff writes about people whose painful history has left them bitter, tormented, and potentially destructive. At his best he is a compelling storyteller, but his characters' obsessions bludgeon rather than inform the reader.

—Roland Turner

LIVELY, Penelope (Margaret)

Nationality: British. **Born:** Penelope Margaret Low in Cairo, Egypt, 17 March 1933; came to England, 1945. **Education:** Boarding school in Sussex, 1945-51; St. Anne's College, Oxford, B.A. (honors) in modern history 1956. **Family:** Married Jack Lively in 1957; one daughter and one son. **Career:** Has been presenter for BBC Radio program on children's literature; regular reviewer for newspapers and magazines in England. **Awards:** Library Association Carnegie Medal, 1974; Whitbread award, 1976; Southern Arts Association prize, 1979; Arts Council National Book award, 1980; Booker prize, 1987. Fellow, Royal Society of Literature, 1985. **Agent:** Murray Pollinger, 222 Old Brompton Road, London SW5 OB2, England.

PUBLICATIONS

Novels

The Road to Lichfield. London, Heinemann, 1977; New York, Grove Weidenfeld, 1991.
Treasures of Time. London, Heinemann, and New York, Doubleday, 1979.
Judgement Day. London, Heinemann, 1980; New York, Doubleday, 1981.
Next to Nature, Art. London, Heinemann, 1982.
Perfect Happiness. London, Heinemann, 1983; New York, Dial Press, 1984.
According to Mark. London, Heinemann, 1984; New York, Beaufort, 1985.
Moon Tiger. London, Deutsch, 1987; New York, Grove Press, 1988.
Passing On. London, Deutsch, 1989; New York, Grove Weidenfeld, 1990.
City of the Mind. London, Deutsch, 1991.
Cleopatra's Sister. London, Viking, and New York, HarperCollins, 1993.

Short Stories

Nothing Missing But the Samovar and Other Stories. London, Heinemann, 1978.
Corruption and Other Stories. London, Heinemann, 1984.
Pack of Cards: Stories 1978-86. London, Heinemann, 1986; New York, Grove Press, 1989.

Plays

Television Plays: *Boy Dominic* series (3 episodes), 1974; *Time Out of Mind,* 1976.

Other (for children)

Astercote. London, Heinemann, 1970; New York, Dutton, 1971.
The Whispering Knights. London, Heinemann, 1971; New York, Dutton, 1976.
The Wild Hunt of Hagworthy. London, Heinemann, 1971; as *The Wild Hunt of the Ghost Hounds,* New York, Dutton, 1972.
The Driftway. London, Heinemann, 1972; New York, Dutton, 1973.
The Ghost of Thomas Kempe. London, Heinemann, and New York, Dutton, 1973.
The House in Norham Gardens. London, Heinemann, and New York, Dutton, 1974.
Going Back. London, Heinemann, and New York, Dutton, 1975.

Boy Without a Name. London, Heinemann, and Berkeley, California, Parnassus Press, 1975.
A Stitch in Time. London, Heinemann, and New York, Dutton, 1976.
The Stained Glass Window. London, Abelard Schuman, 1976.
Fanny's Sister. London, Heinemann, 1976; New York, Dutton, 1980.
The Voyage of QV66. London, Heinemann, 1978; New York, Dutton, 1979.
Fanny and the Monsters. London, Heinemann, 1979.
Fanny and the Battle of Potter's Piece. London, Heinemann, 1980.
The Revenge of Samuel Stokes. London, Heinemann, and New York, Dutton, 1981.
Uninvited Ghosts and Other Stories. London, Heinemann, 1984; New York, Dutton, 1985.
Dragon Trouble. London, Heinemann, 1984; New York, Baron, 1989.
Debbie and the Little Devil. London, Heinemann, 1987.
A House Inside Out. London, Deutsch, 1987; New York, Dutton, 1988.

Other

The Presence of the Past: An Introduction to Landscape History. London, Collins, 1976.
Oleander, Jalaranda: A Childhood Perceived. London, Viking, 1994.

*

Critical Study: *Penelope Lively* by Mary H. Moran, New York, Twayne, 1993.

* * *

From the late 1970s and through the 1980s Penelope Lively has been one of the favorite writers of the literary panelists. Already a much-lauded writer of children's fiction, Lively entered mainstream adult fiction with *The Road to Lichfield* which was shortlisted for the 1977 Booker prize. Since then her work has regularly appeared on the shortlists for the major British fiction prizes, and in 1987 *Moon Tiger* was the Booker winner. The aspects of her work which have endeared her to the literary judges are those which have also found favor with a middle-brow, middle-class fiction audience: she writes in precise and elegant prose without ever descending into preciosity; she tells a good story about believable middle-class characters and situations; she engages with matters of serious moral and intellectual concern without pretension, pedantry or ponderousness; she is witty, ironic, and intelligent. In short, she offers a good read which provides food for thought; she exercises her readers' intelligence and occasionally pricks their conscience, and she subtly undermines their certainties even as she (ultimately) comforts and consoles them.

Lively is a writer who is fascinated, even obsessed, with history, and the connections between the past and present. Her major characters are both professionally and privately concerned with the past: Hugh Paxton (*Treasures of Time*) is an archaeologist who discovers that digging up the past also disturbs the present; Mark Lamming (*According to Mark*) is a literary biographer whose researches begin to reveal a new view of the past, and whose own life becomes enmeshed with the subject of his research; Claudia Hampson (*Moon Tiger*) is a maverick popular historian who constructs her own history of the world (and, more particularly, the history of her own world) as she lies dying of cancer.

Virtually all of Lively's novels are concerned with the remembrance of things past. The female narrator of *Going Back* (first published as a children's book in 1975, but reissued in 1990 on the adult list) sets the tone for virtually all of Lively's subsequent fiction: "There's what you know happened, and what you think happened. And then there's the business that what you know happened isn't always what you remember. Things are fudged by time. . . . The things that should matter—the stepping-stones that marked the way, the decisions that made one thing happen rather than another—they get forgotten. You are left with islands in a confused and layered landscape . . ." Time and again Lively uses a death as the means of mapping these islands and investigating their archaeological and geological layers. Almost all of her novels focus on characters in the process of coming to terms with their own approaching death, or the (usually) recent death of someone who has played a crucial part in their lives.

Perfect Happiness, for example, charts the process by which Frances Brooklyn takes up the threads of a life which has been totally disorientated by the death of her husband with whom she has lived in the state referred to in the title. Coming to terms with the present and learning to believe in a future involves a complex revisiting of the past. As well as being a very powerful novel about love and grief this book also offers a picture of two sharply contrasted female lives: Frances, who has dedicated her adult life to her marriage and her adopted children, who now faces life without her husband and must adjust to the departure of her children into their own adult lives, and Chloe, her sister-in-law, the powerful independent journalist who has resolutely avoided marriage and motherhood, whose choices are thrown into sharp relief by her own illness, the decision of her long-time lover to marry a younger woman, and the gradually revealed truth about a crucial incident in her past. The novel persistently juxtaposes and compares the nature and the consequences of the specific choices they have made, and the particular conditions and constraints under which women choose.

Claudia Hampson (*Moon Tiger*) is a character who has been denied the possibility of "perfect happiness" by the death of her lover in the western desert campaign of 1941. The life-shaping influence of this and other experiences is gradually unfolded in Lively's most complex and formally ambitious work to date. The structure of this narrative embodies the perception of Claudia, the historian that, "The voice of history . . . is composite. Many voices; all the voices that have managed to get themselves heard. Some louder than others, naturally." *Moon Tiger* tangles and untangles the voices that surround and have surrounded the central character, so that in the end we hear a different story from the one she is telling herself as she faces the end of her life.

Passing On gives quite a different perspective on the process of coming to terms with a life whose meaning has been defined by someone who is now dead. The death of their domineering mother is the catalyst for a crisis in the lives of Helen and Edward Glover, the middle-aged, unmarried, shabby genteel brother and sister at the center of this novel. As this subtle and gripping narrative unfolds both the reader and the two main characters discover and re-examine the forces that have shaped these two lives. Both characters become temporarily "deranged" as they adjust to life without the repressive presence of their mother, as they reassess the implications of roads not taken, and learn more about the exact nature of their mother's intervention in their lives.

Like most of Lively's characters Edward and Helen are decent, serious-minded, sensitive people. They hang on and come through,

their basic human decency intact. In particular, and in sharp contrast to their sister Louise, who fled the family home at the earliest opportunity, they resist the seductive and corrupting pressures of the materialism of modern life. Their resistance is figured in their bemused and unimpressed response to London in the 1980s and in their resolute refusal to sell the Britches (an oasis of undeveloped land behind their family home) to a local developer, even when he tries to blackmail them (using Edward's homosexuality). As is often the case in Lively's work rural England is used as a focus for an examination of change and an affirmation of continuity.

Thatcher's London, and the evils of property developers (in the shape of the menacing Mr. Rutter who first attempts to bribe, and then threatens the novel's central character) play a more prominent part in Lively's most recent novel *City of the Mind,* another story of death and renewal. This time the death in question is the death of the marriage of the central character, Matthew, a moderately successful architect, whose tentative re-entry into life and love provides the main narrative thread. This narrative of a single life is set in the context of a narrative (or series of narratives) about past and present London, whose rapidly changing face and increasingly chaotic mixture of architectural styles are used to figure the palimpsest of a living history. In her latest novel Lively also engages in the kind of time travel she uses in her children's fiction, with narrative vignettes from London's past: a child searching for food, a Victorian paleontologist, an Arctic explorer, an air-raid warden. As always it is when writing about the past that Lively writes with most passion and imagination.

—Lyn Pykett

LODGE, David (John)

Nationality: British. **Born:** London, 28 January 1935. **Education:** St. Joseph's Academy, London; University College, London, 1952-55, 1957-59, B.A. (honors) in English 1955; M.A. 1959; University of Birmingham, Ph.D. 1967. Military Service: served in the Royal Armoured Corps, 1955-57. **Family:** Married Mary Frances Jacob in 1959; two sons and one daughter. **Career:** Assistant, British Council, London, 1959-60. Assistant lecturer, 1960-62, lecturer, 1963-71, senior lecturer, 1971-73, reader, 1973-76, and professor of modern English literature, 1976-87, University of Birmingham; now honorary professor. Since 1987 full-time writer. Visiting associate professor, University of California, Berkeley, 1969; Henfield Writing Fellow, University of East Anglia, Norwich, 1977. Chairman of the Booker prize judges, 1989. **Awards:** Harkness Commonwealth fellowship, 1964; *Yorkshire Post* award, 1975; Hawthornden prize, 1976; Whitbread award, for fiction and for book of the year, 1980; *Sunday Express* Book-of-the-Year award, 1988. Fellow, Royal Society of Literature, 1976, University College, London, 1982, and Goldsmiths' College, London, (honorary), 1992. **Address:** English Department, University of Birmingham, Birmingham B15 2TT, England.

PUBLICATIONS

Novels

The Picturegoers. London, MacGibbon and Kee, 1960.

Ginger, You're Barmy. London, MacGibbon and Kee, 1962; New York, Doubleday, 1965.

The British Museum Is Falling Down. London, MacGibbon and Kee, 1965; New York, Holt Rinehart, 1967.

Out of the Shelter. London, Macmillan, 1970; revised edition, London, Secker and Warburg, 1985; New York, Penguin, 1989.

Changing Places: A Tale of Two Campuses. London, Secker and Warburg, 1975; New York, Penguin, 1979.

How Far Can You Go? London, Secker and Warburg, 1980; as *Souls and Bodies,* New York, Morrow, 1982.

Small World: An Academic Romance. London, Secker and Warburg, 1984; New York, Macmillan, 1985.

Nice Work. London, Secker and Warburg, 1988; New York, Viking, 1989.

Paradise News. London, Secker and Warburg, 1991.

Therapy. New York, Viking, and London, Secker, 1995.

Uncollected Short Stories

"The Man Who Couldn't Get Up," in *Weekend Telegraph* (London), 6 May 1966.

"My First Job," *London Review of Books,* 4 September 1980.

"Hotel des Boobs," in *The Penguin Book of Modern British Short Stories,* edited by Malcolm Bradbury. London, Viking, 1987; New York, Viking, 1988.

"Pastoral," in *Telling Stories,* edited by D. Minshull. London, Hodder and Stoughton, 1992.

Plays

Between These Four Walls (revue), with Malcolm Bradbury and James Duckett (produced Birmingham, 1963).

Slap in the Middle (revue), with others (produced Birmingham, 1965).

The Writing Game (produced Birmingham, 1990). London, Secker and Warburg, 1991.

Television Writing: *Big Words . . . Small Worlds* (also presenter), 1987; *Nice Work,* from his own novel, 1989; *The Way of St. James* (also presenter), 1993; and *Martin Chuzzlewit* (adapted from Charles Dickens), 1994.

Other

About Catholic Authors (for teenagers). London, St. Paul Publications, 1958.

Language of Fiction. London, Routledge, and New York, Columbia University Press, 1966; revised edition, Routledge, 1984.

Graham Greene. New York, Columbia University Press, 1966.

The Novelist at the Crossroads and Other Essays on Fiction and Criticism. London, Routledge, and Ithaca, New York, Cornell University Press, 1971.

Evelyn Waugh. New York, Columbia University Press, 1971.

The Modes of Modern Writing: Metaphor, Metonymy, and the Typology of Modern Literature. London, Arnold, and Ithaca, New York, Cornell University Press, 1977.

Working with Structuralism: Essays and Reviews on Nineteenth- and Twentieth-Century Literature. London, Routledge, 1981.

Write On: Occasional Essays 1965-1985. London, Secker and Warburg, 1986.

After Bakhtin: Essays on Fiction and Criticism. London and New York, Routledge, 1990.

The Art of Fiction. New York, Viking, and London, Secker and Penguin, 1992.

Editor, *Jane Austen: "Emma": A Casebook.* London, Macmillan, 1968; Nashville, Aurora, 1970(?).

Editor, with James Kinsley, *Emma,* by Jane Austen. London, Oxford University Press, 1971.

Editor, *Twentieth-Century Literary Criticism: A Reader.* London, Longman, 1972.

Editor, *Scenes of Clerical Life,* by George Eliot. London, Penguin, 1973.

Editor, *The Woodlanders,* by Thomas Hardy. London, Macmillan, 1974.

Editor, *The Best of Ring Lardner.* London, Dent, 1984.

Editor, *The Spoils of Poynton,* by Henry James. London, Penguin, 1987.

Editor, *Modern Criticism and Theory: A Reader.* London, Longman, 1988.

Editor, *Lucky Jim,* by Kingsley Amis. London, Penguin, 1992.

*

Manuscript Collection: University of Birmingham Library.

Critical Studies: Interview with Bernard Bergonzi, in *Month* (London), February 1970, "The Decline and Fall of the Catholic Novel," in *The Myth of Modernism and Twentieth-Century Literature* by Bergonzi, Brighton, England, Harvester Press, 1986, *Exploding English: Criticism, Theory, Culture* by Bergonzi, Oxford, England, n.p., 1990; *David Lodge* by Bergonzi, Plymouth, England, n.p., 1995. "The Novels of David Lodge" by Michael Parnell, in *Madog* (Barry, Wales), Summer 1979; article by Dennis Jackson, in *British Novelists since 1960* edited by Jay L. Halio, Detroit, Gale, 1983; *Novelists in Interview* by John Haffenden, London and New York, Methuen, 1985; *The Dialogic Novels of Malcolm Bradbury and David Lodge* by Robert A. Morace, Carbondale, Southern Illinois University Press, 1989; *Modern Critics in Practice: Critical Portraits of British Literary Critics* by P. Smallwood, London, n.p., 1990; *David Lodge: How Far Can You Go?* by M. Moseley, San Bernardino, California, n.p., 1991; *Faithful Functions: The Catholic Novel in British Literature* by T. Woodman, n.p., Milton Keynes, 1991.

David Lodge comments:

(1972) My novels belong to a tradition of realistic fiction (especially associated with England) that tries to find an appropriate form for, and a public significance in, what the writer has himself experienced and observed. In my case this experience and observation include such things as: lower-middle-class life in the inner suburbs of South East London; a wartime childhood and a postwar "austerity" adolescence; Catholicism; education and the social and physical mobility it brings; military service, marriage, travel, etc. My first, second, and fourth novels are "serious" realistic novels about such themes, the last of them, *Out of the Shelter,* which is a kind of Bildungsroman, being, as far as I am concerned, the most inclusive and most fully achieved.

My third novel, *The British Museum Is Falling Down,* was something of a departure in being a comic novel, incorporating elements of farce and a good deal of parody. I plan to write more fiction in the comic mode, as I enjoy the freedom for invention and stylistic effect it affords. On the other hand, I have not (like many contemporary writers) lost faith in traditional realism as a vehicle for serious fiction. The writer I admire above all others, I suppose, is James Joyce, and the combination one finds in his early work of realistic truthtelling and poetic intensity seems to me an aim still worth pursuing.

As an academic critic and teacher of literature with a special interest in prose fiction, I am inevitably self-conscious about matters of narrative technique, and I believe this is a help rather than a hindrance. I certainly think that my criticism of fiction gains from my experience of writing it.

(1981) Since writing the above I have come to have less faith in the viability of the traditional realistic novel of the kind that seeks, by suppressing the signs that it is written and narrated, to give the illusion of being a transparent window upon the real. This shift of attitude does not entail abandoning the novel's traditional function of engaging with, organizing and interpreting social-historical experience—merely being open about the necessarily conventional and artificial ways in which it does so. My last two works of fiction, therefore, have a prominent "metafictional" thread running through them through which the self-consciousness about fictional technique referred to above is allowed some play in the texts themselves— licenced by comedy in *Changing Places*, but with more serious thematic intent in *How Far Can You Go?*

*   *   *

David Lodge's novels use and stay close to material that he knows well. Without being overtly autobiographical, they often draw on personal experience: a lower-middle-class South London childhood and adolescence in *The Picturegoers* and *Out of the Shelter*, military service in *Ginger, You're Barmy*, and academic life in his "campus" novels. Lodge was brought up as a Catholic and some of his novels examine the culture and customs of English Catholic life. His emphasis is sociological rather than theological, providing sharp but affectionate observations of the lives of a minority group. In *The British Museum Is Falling Down* he gives brisk comic treatment to the human problems arising from the Catholic ban on contraception. In *How Far Can You Go?*, a longer and more serious-minded novel (though none of his fiction is without comic elements), Lodge traces the lives of a group of middle-class English Catholics from the early 1950s when they are students at London University, to the late 1970s when they are approaching middle age and have lived through the transformations of Catholicism which followed the Vatican Council.

Though he is an entertaining and sharp-eyed recorder of personal and social embarrassment, Lodge is a good-humored writer, and rather too genial to be a thoroughgoing satirist. These qualities are apparent in the three novels set wholly or partly in the city of Rummidge and its university, which form a sequence with recurring characters, covering the years from 1969 to 1986. Lodge describes their settings as imaginary places which for the purposes of fiction occupy "the space where Birmingham is to be found on maps of the so-called real world." They draw on Lodge's long career as a university teacher of English between 1960 and 1987, during which time he published several academic critical books in addition to his fiction. *Changing Places* is subtitled "A Tale of Two Campuses": Rummidge is contrasted with Plotinus, a celebrated Californian university which bears much the same relation to Ber-

keley as Rummidge does to Birmingham. Philip Swallow, a mild, amiable, unsophisticated lecturer in English at Rummidge, goes to Plotinus as an exchange professor; in return Rummidge gets one of the biggest guns at Plotinus, the high-powered Professor Morris Zapp, who comes to England to escape his marital problems. The story moves, with a wealth of inventiveness, back and forth between Swallow in Plotinus and Zapp in Rummidge, each coping with different kinds of culture shock. They end up having exchanged not only jobs but wives; the reader is left uncertain whether the exchange will be permanent. *Changing Places* exploits polarities to splendid comic effect: Britain and America, the Midlands and San Francisco Bay, English academic life and American. Zapp and Swallow are representative types, well observed and culturally placed: the ruthless professional Zapp wants to be the greatest expert on Jane Austen in the world, even though he dislikes her novels; the dithering Swallow likes the whole of English literature so much that he can never find a "field" to specialize in, to the amused incredulity of the Americans.

In *Small World*, set ten years on, Zapp is divorced and even more famous; Swallow and his wife are together again, though he is now more worldly and has achieved some modest academic success. It is a formally elaborate novel, making use of the conventions of the epic romances of the Italian Renaissance, where narratives are interwoven, the characters have frequent and surprising adventures, and a beautiful maiden flits elusively in and out of the narrative. It opens in Rummidge but moves over the globe, as the academic participants fly from one conference or lecturing engagement to another. There is a rich mixture of comedy, sex, and scholarship, sometimes all on the same plate. *Small World* is learned and allusive— among other things, it offers an ordinary reader's guide to structuralism—but at the same time farcical, fast-moving, and highly entertaining.

Nice Work is set wholly in Rummidge, when the university is suffering from the financial cuts of the 1980s. Zapp and Swallow put in appearances, but the principal characters are new, a man and woman who are completely different types but whose lives become fascinatingly entwined. Vic Wilcox runs a local engineering works; he is tough, energetic, and good at his job but socially and emotionally insecure. Robyn Penrose teaches English and Women's Studies at the university. She is a recognizable figure of the age: attractive, intellectual, and self-assured, an articulate feminist and supporter of left-wing causes, at home in the abstruse reaches of critical theory. But she is also narcissistic and naive, and entirely ignorant of the industrial world (represented by Wilcox, the factory, and its workers) into which she finds herself thrown. She is an expert on the Victorian "Condition of England" novel, and *Nice Work* is Lodge's own essay in the genre, surveying Margaret Thatcher's England. The unfashionably happy ending has what looks like a deliberately Victorian air. In this novel, Lodge, like Robyn, takes a good look at the world outside the academy—*Nice Work* appeared soon after he had taken early retirement from teaching— with rewarding results.

His next novel, *Paradise News*, returns to the Catholic topics of *How Far Can You Go?* and takes them further still. The central character, Bernard Walsh, is an ex-priest in his forties, from the South London Irish milieu of Lodge's first novel. He is a sad, lonely figure who has lost not only faith but hope; he makes a meagre living as a part-time, unbelieving lecturer in theology at a non-denominational college. His life picks up when he and his cantankerous widower father travel to Hawaii, where Bernard's expatriate aunt has lived for many years and where she is now dying of cancer. Hawaii, the self-styled island paradise, is contrasted in Bernard's thoughts with the Christian heaven which he used to preach about and can no longer believe in. But in Hawaii he unexpectedly finds love, and, if not faith, a renewed sense of hope. In this gentle, quietly moving novel Lodge takes another look at the themes and some of the settings of his earlier work; but it is a little lacking in the ingenuity and wit that readers have come to expect in his fiction.

Those qualities, though, are triumphantly present in *Therapy,* which Lodge published soon after his 60th birthday. It is the story, told in the first person, of Tubby Passmore, a successful and prosperous television scriptwriter. He has most things he could want in life, including, he believes, a stable and happy marriage. He wonders, therefore, why he is consumed by anxiety and dread, neuroses which have sent him to a variety of therapists, and which make him an avid reader of Kierkegaard, the Danish philosopher who wrote books with titles that Tubby finds irresistible: *Fear and Trembling, The Concept of Dread,* and *Sickness Unto Death.* Tubby's world falls apart when his wife suddenly leaves him after 30 years, not for anyone else but because she finds him too moody and boring to live with any longer. Tubby is shattered but he survives and fights back in ways which involve him in farcical humiliations, especially when he tries, in late middle age, to get some sexual variety into his life. He resembles the heroes of many American novels, who undergo all kinds of personal, professional, and sexual disasters, but who remain fiercely articulate and opinionated in the midst of everything—an English cousin of Saul Bellow's Herzog, perhaps. *Therapy* shows Lodge at the top of his form, comic, thoughtful, and continually surprising.

—Bernard Bergonzi

LOVELACE, Earl

Nationality: Trinidadian. **Born:** Taco, Trinidad, 13 July 1935. **Family:** Married; two sons, one daughter. **Career:** Proofreader, *Trinidad Guardian,* 1953-54; civil servant: agricultural assistant in Jamaica, 1956-66; journalist, *Trinidad and Tobago Express,* 1967; lecturer in English, University of the District of Columbia, 1971-73; writer-in-residence, Hartwick College, Oneonta, New York, 1986. Since 1977 teacher, University of the West Indies, Saint Augustine, Trinidad. **Awards:** B.P. Independence award, 1965; Pegasus Literary award, 1966; Guggenheim fellowship, 1980; National Endowment for the Humanities grant, 1986. **Address:** c/o Andre Deutsch, 105 Great Russell St., London WC1B 3LJ, England.

Publications

Novels

While Gods Are Falling. London, Collins, 1965; Chicago, Regnery, 1966.
The Schoolmaster. London, Collins, and Chicago, Regnery, 1968.
The Dragon Can't Dance. London, Deutsch, 1979; Washington, D.C., Three Continents Press, 1981.
The Wine of Astonishment. London, Deutsch, 1982; New York, Vintage, 1984.

Short Stories

A Brief Conversation and Other Stories. London, Heinemann, 1988.

Plays

The New Hardware Store (produced London, 1985). Included in *Jestina's Calypso and Other Plays,* 1984.
Jestina's Calypso and Other Plays (includes *The New Hardware Store* and *My Name Is Village*). London, Heinemann, 1984.
The Dragon Can't Dance, adaptation of his own novel (produced London, 1990).

*

Bibliography: "Earl Lovelace: A Bibliography" by Chezia Thompson-Cager, in *Contributions in Black Studies,* 8, 1986-87.

Manuscript Collection: The Lovelace Archives, Port of Spain, Trinidad.

Critical Studies: "In Search of the West Indian Hero: A Study of Earl Lovelace's Fiction" by Marjorie Thorpe, in *Critical Issues in West Indian Literature,* edited by Erika Sollish Smilowitz and Roberta Quarles Knowles, Parkersburg, Iowa, Caribbean, 1984; "Salvation, Self, and Solidarity in the Work of Earl Lovelace" by Norman Reed Cary, *World Literature Written in English,* Spring 1988; "Earl Lovelace's Bad Johns, Street Princes and the Masters of Schools" by Chezia Thompson-Cager, in *Imagination, Emblems, and Expressions,* edited by Helen Ryan, Bowling Green, Ohio, Bowling Green University Popular Press, 1992.

* * *

Earl Lovelace is primarily a wonderful storyteller. He holds one's interest whether through exciting dialogue which rings true, or by his descriptive ability and his portrayal of the inner conflicts which puzzle his characters.

To say that he is an excellent storyteller is in no way to belittle his work; nor is it to deny that his work embodies values and has its serious moral concerns. But his great ability as a writer of fiction, i.e., as a writer who through images works at a deeper level than that of the preacher or "social scientist," is much downgraded by the kind of statement made by one reviewer about two of Lovelace's novels: "This tension between the ideal and the reality (of Trinidad and Tobago's 'national motto' "all o' wi is one") creates the chief interest of both *The Wine of Astonishment* and *The Dragon Can't Dance.*" Thank heavens there is much more to both novels than that! There is, for one thing, Lovelace's control of the Trinidadian language, and his constant concern with the ambiguous relationship between change and progress. The arrival of the Schoolmaster, the behavior of Ivan Morton (the new "Independence" politician), the coming of "good behavior" and sponsorship to the Steel Bands, the passing of the stick fighters and stick fighting—all these are developed, in different novels, subtly, and at a subconscious level, as signs and images of the profit and loss of change, and also of the inevitability of some of the changes and of the disturbance that they necessarily bring in their wake.

One of the changes occurs in the relationship between the rural and urban styles of living. At the beginning of *While Gods Are Falling* Walter, much to the distress of his wife, wishes to leave the confusion, "scuffling," and sycophancy of Port of Spain. He wishes to return to the country, where he grew up—none too happily—but where he feels he can be "a man," full of spirit and independence. The concern with being one's own person—with "being a man"—to use the old formulation—constantly appears in Lovelace's work.

But then again one must not forget that Lovelace is mainly a storyteller. A story uses and recounts disparate elements which create a pattern and make sense and give satisfaction only when they come together in a certain way under the master's hand. Lovelace holds our attention without being trivial or facile. He not only pleases by verisimilitude, he also enables aspects of the significance of the life of a people, and of individual persons, to dawn upon us. When, for instance, in *The Schoolmaster,* Christiana confesses to the priest that she is with child by the Schoolmaster, who has seduced her, the priest is dismayed, and we read, as she stares at his face turned sideways in the confessional: "And now the priest's ear gazed at her, and she saw now that it was a pool, a deep pool and her mother was sitting on the bank there, waiting for her in her long white dress . . . waiting for her." In this way Lovelace begins to prepare us for the only solution which Christiana, betrothed to Pedro, can find to her predicament, a predicament—be it noted—which has risen out of the fact that it was part of progress to set up a school and to bring a schoolmaster to the "backward," "illiterate" village. Those who helped with this necessary and progressive step are the ones who suffer most from the unfortunate consequences of the move!

This paradoxical, non-linear relationship between change and progress is often made palpable in Lovelace's fiction. In *The Dragon Can't Dance* those who would have been, in the old days, ornaments of the village as stick fighters become nuisances in the city as "Bad Johns," and the old struggles of would-be warriors become competitions between sponsored bands; it is no longer the warrior as musician, but the musician as would-be competitor.

In *The Wine of Astonishment* a son goes off from the restrictions of the village to the wider opportunities of the city—never to be heard from again. And Ivan Morton, the people's man, moves from his more than adequate home to the vacated "great house" without even taking a "favorite" chair along. For a long time he seems to do nothing for the bell-ringing Baptists who have worked to vote him in, and when he does help to remove the ban from their mode of worship, it seems too late. The old Spirit deserts them. And yet at the end, as Ma, the wonderful narrator of the tale, turns the corner "where Miss Hilda living," she says, as she passes the carnival tent, "I listening to the music; for the music that those boys playing on the steelband have in it that same Spirit that we miss in our church: the same Spirit; and listening to them, my heart swell and it is like resurrection morning. I watch Bee, Bee watch me, the both of us bow, nod, as if, yes, God is great, and like if we passing in front of something holy." So ends the book which 145 pages before had started: "God don't give you more than you can bear, I say . . ." One has a slight feeling of uneasiness about Ma's firm feeling that "the steelband have in it the same Spirit that we miss in our church." But then *she* should know!

Lovelace often has a dramatic way of presenting his characters and images. Think of the opening dialogue in *While Gods Are Falling.* He has a very good feeling for, and ability to bring to life, the complicated reality of Trinidad society—"everybody wanted to see Mr. Ramroop dance because he danced in the awkward East Indian fashion, a waltz, a castilliane or a calypso." There we have Vienna, Spain, Afro-Trinidad, and the Asian as perceived by others! Lovelace's ability to handle the English and Trinidadian lan-

guages recommends him strongly to our attention. But particularly in England he should be read because his excellent fiction is a good antidote to the limited view often touted by many, including Caribbean Heritage people, of the rich variety and mixture that is Caribbean culture.

He takes his ability to enshrine the full Trinidadian—and Caribbean—experience in suitable images to further levels of perfection in his short story collection *A Brief Conversion.* In doing so he fulfills one of the oldest desires of writers of fiction: to mix the useful with the pleasurable, as the Preface to *Gil Blas* puts it. The story after which this collection takes its name stirs one's sensibilities, and touches one's heart as the growing up of the young boy, Travey, and the family relationships enveloping him, are put to us, often through great Trinidad conversations. The husband-wife relationship—for the parents decide to have a proper church wedding after living together and producing children for years—is lovingly and humorously portrayed: the strong woman is not quite as strong as she seems, and the man not quite as feckless as the critical observer might imagine.

This short story along with the portrayal of Miss Ross—*Call Me "Miss Ross" For Now*—confirms what we knew of this writer before, that he has the master's touch, and in being hilarious at times he is in no way frivolous but deeply serious. One must wonder, though, in reading this recent collection of short stories whether Lovelace missed a novel or two by not letting some of these mustard seeds grow to lovely leafy trees?

—John J. Figueroa

LUDWIG, Jack (Barry)

Nationality: Canadian. **Born:** Winnipeg, Manitoba, 30 August 1922. **Education:** St. John's High School, Winnipeg; University of Manitoba, Winnipeg, B.A. 1944; University of California, Los Angeles, Ph.D. 1953. **Family:** Married Leya Lauer in 1946; two daughters. **Career:** Instructor, Williams College, Williamstown, Massachusetts, 1949-53; Assistant and Associate Professor, Bard College, Annandale-on-Hudson, New York, 1953-58, and University of Minnesota, Minneapolis, 1958-61. Since 1961 Professor of English, State University of New York, Stony Brook. Co-editor, *Noble Savage,* New York, then Cleveland, 1960-62. Chairman, Humanities Group, International Seminar, Harvard University, Cambridge, Massachusetts, summers 1963-66. Writer-in-residence, University of Toronto, 1968-69; playwright-in-residence, Stratford Shakespearean Festival Workshop, Ontario, 1970; writer-in-residence, Banff Center, Alberta, Summer 1974; Visiting Professor, University of California, Los Angeles, Summer 1976. **Awards:** Longview Foundation award, 1960; *Atlantic* Firsts award, 1960; O. Henry award, 1961, 1965; Canada Council award, 1962, and Senior Arts fellowship, 1967, 1975. **Address:** Box A, Setauket, New York 11733, U.S.A.

PUBLICATIONS

Novels

Confusions. Greenwich, Connecticut, New York Graphic Society, and London, Secker and Warburg, 1963.

Above Ground. Toronto and Boston, Little Brown, 1968.
A Woman of Her Age. Toronto, McClelland and Stewart, 1973.

Short Story

Requiem for Bibul. Agincourt, Ontario, Book Society of Canada, 1967.

Uncollected Short Stories

"Orlick Miller and Company," in *Commentary* (New York), January 1960.
"Thoreau in California," in *Noble Savage 1* (New York), April 1960.
"Meesh," in *Tamarack Review* (Toronto), Autumn 1961.
"Death Was the Glass," in *Midstream* (New York), Winter 1961.
"Celebration on East Houston Street," in *Tamarack Review* (Toronto), Spring 1963.
"Einstein and This Admirer," in *London Magazine,* September 1965.
"A Death of One's Own," in *Tamarack Review* (Toronto), Winter 1968.
"Shirley," in *Tamarack Review,* (Toronto), Spring 1969.

Plays

The Alchemist, adaptation of the play by Ben Jonson (produced Stratford, Ontario, 1969).
Bustout, with Peter Scupham (produced Stratford, Ontario, 1969).
Ubu Rex, adaptation of a play by Alfred Jarry (produced Stratford, Ontario, 1970).

Television Play: *Hedda Gabler,* from the play by Ibsen, 1979.

Poetry

Homage to Zolotova. Banff, Alberta, Banff Centre Press, 1974.

Other

Recent American Novelists. Minneapolis, University of Minnesota Press, 1962.
Hockey Night in Moscow. Toronto, McClelland and Stewart, 1972; revised edition, as *The Great Hockey Thaw; or, The Russians Are Here!,* New York, Doubleday, 1974.
Games of Fear and Winning: Sports with an Inside View. New York, Doubleday, 1976.
The Great American Spectaculars: The Kentucky Derby, Mardi Gras, and Other Days of Celebration. New York, Doubleday, 1976.
Five-Ring Circus: The Montreal Olympics. New York, Doubleday, 1977.

Editor, with Richard Poirier, *Stories: British and American.* Boston, Houghton Mifflin, 1953.
Editor, with Andy Wainwright, *Soundings: New Canadian Poets.* Toronto, Anansi, 1970.

*

Jack Ludwig comments:

(1991) Winnipeg, Los Angeles, New York, London were for me never centers of abstraction. Doubtless each city had its moral paralytics; doubtless I didn't run into them often. A liar and a truth-teller have always been equally fascinating to me. The imagination's scale of values is not easily coerced. When I look at Brueghel's paintings I see life without categories, without underlined morals, without tilting: the paltry and exalted, the sleazy and the grand are great challenges to the image that alone makes for realization. Comedy and tragedy are different, but, to the imagination, equal. I reject the Eliot and Pound notions about the past giving shape to the formless present. Whether literature rises out of Dublin or Rome, New York or London, it begins, as Yeats finally recognized, in "A mound of refuse or the sweepings of a street."

*   *   *

Taken together, all of Jack Ludwig's several voices are the voice of a civilized North American; also the voice of a cultured man. His culture, a culture he wears with ease, comes more from the roots of things genuine than from the academy alone. It comes from underground. Ludwig was born into the Jewish community of Winnipeg. He knows it in North America and in its European roots; his own, in Odessa; he knows much of its rich Yiddish and Hasidic backgrounds. In reading him one may think of Mordecai Richler or Philip Roth or I.B. Singer.

To a degree all his writing voices one central, pervasive concern. With his emphasis included, it reads: ". . . *re-educate yourself, kid, but do it with ebullience*" (*Recent American Novelists,* 1962). Was he advising then, in the early 1960s, what the 1970s took as the quest; namely, alternative modes of doing almost everything in everyday life, alternative modes to those which have come to threaten everyday life on almost every hand? The difference would lie with the rarity of ebullience in much of that quest. But in Ludwig it carries the reader joyously, if he be willing and aware. As it does, even in such a short story as "Meesh" in which the hero, in that poignant Yiddish mode, is forced daily to sacrifice himself for *un*worthy kin with hardly a murmur of dissent. And as it carries the reader, even when he is telling of his summer spent on the vacant floor of the old Ryan Building in downtown Winnipeg where he wrote *Confusions.*

So in *Confusions,* Ludwig celebrates life and vitality. Even the mock epic hero Joe Galsky (a Roxbury Jew)/Joseph Gillis (a Harvard graduate) does so in his confusions ("confissions"), troubled as he is by trying to follow what his creator refers to as a kind of North American credo, the putting of "Second Things First," second things such as "status-establishing, career-making and image-projecting." Galsky/Gillis will need to admit, "I am confused, therefore I am." One wonders if Ludwig may intend this to mean in part somewhat what Alan Watts means about the wisdom of insecurity in his book of that title. At any rate, Galsky/Gillis refuses to accept mephistophelean aid. He will not seek success as a novelist, if it means creating the kind of book he could not believe in. His closing words echo: "Look on me, ye unmighty, and live a little." Rabbinical spirit prevails.

In *Above Ground,* Ludwig celebrates life and vitality, more in a lyric than satiric way, not the least sexual vitality, even though, or perhaps because, the hero, Joshua, has had to spend almost all his formative years in hospital rooms due to a crippling ailment of the hip-bone. And that sexual vitality appeals. It has been suggested (by D.O. Spettigue, in *Queen's Quarterly,* 1968) that the women in Joshua's life may be "death-figures," especially since two of them, his dying mother and an amazing, neurotic mistress, pose "threats to his living integrity." But one wonders. The novel carries such a constant lyricism.

In his extended essay *Recent American Novelists,* Ludwig writes as though he were already thinking of the form this second of his novels would take. "Serious fiction shows definite signs of turning from Kafkaesque 'Underground Man' to Tolstoian or Conradian 'Aboveground Man,' the hero who breaks out of his real or symbolic, sealed-off rooms to re-enter the world of action and history . . ." (*The New Romans,* 1968). At any rate, when his hero Joshua does find himself free of those "symbolic" (at least) "sealed-off rooms," he "re-enters" a world of vital sexual activity which Ludwig celebrates without self-consciousness. Again, in praising Saul Bellow's *The Adventures of Augie March* in *The New Romans,* Ludwig says, "history becomes a dimension of a hero's awareness—if not yet his acts." And he seems to describe the kind of novel *Above Ground* was going to become, one in which the sexual could find honest expression in the hero's awareness. Lastly, *Above Ground* seems to be a novel written in the open form as he had earlier conceived it: ". . . an open form, a way of writing *about* almost anything with almost unlimited scope—i.e.; the limits are imposed not by the chosen form of the novel, but rather, as they should be, by the author's own limitations of talent, imagination, and knowledge." Two simple sentences from this same essay seem to define Joshua's growing consciousness. "He lives as an aware Aboveground Man. The man aware knows there is limitless fiction in the fall of a sparrow." And now the woman becoming aware in *A Woman of Her Age* shows that life at 85 years can crowd limitless fiction into the span of a single Friday—*shabbes*—of a single spring day between Montreal's Westmount and Saint Lawrence Main.

In the dozen dazzling and discontinuous chapters of *A Woman of Her Age,* Ludwig brings together within the same pages, although not within the same dramatic scenes, two of his most unforgettable short story characters. They are Doba Goffmann, a now-85-year-old ex-radical, displaced from the Montreal Jewish community of the Main to Westmount and pampering wealth; and "the chicken-slaughterer's daughter Shirley," similarly displaced, but also disoriented by a second marriage and motherhood, and estranged from Doba Goffmann since the death of Jimmy, her first husband, and Doba's favorite among her devoted sons. Ludwig's almost breathless shifts of focus among memory, fantasy, and present event give effects in his narrative resembling as much as anything perhaps the fluid, fantastic, and comic imagery in many a Chagall canvas of Jewish subject. As he draws his interlocking dramatic portraits of Doba and Shirley, and of the various men in their present lives, Ludwig undercuts the confusions and hypocrisies of "success" while again finding stature in the comic vitality of the seemingly anti-heroic. As Dave Godfrey has suggested, "It's life on every page."

What better way to bring this to a stop than to hear Ludwig speak again: ". . . the novel has broken through, and broken out. Liberated from the tyranny of symbolic smallness it has attempted to become *the* literary form to catch the visible world in all its complexity, clangor, and untriumphant celebration. Our times have a tonality the novel cannot ignore."

—Herbert C. Burke

LURIE, Alison

Nationality: American. **Born:** Chicago, Illinois, 3 September 1926. **Education:** Radcliffe College, Cambridge, Massachusetts, A.B. in history and English 1947. **Family:** Married Jonathan Peale Bishop, Jr., in 1948 (divorced 1985); three sons. **Career:** Lecturer, 1968-73, adjunct associate professor, 1973-76, associate professor, 1976-79, and since 1979 professor of English, Cornell University, Ithaca, New York. **Awards:** Yaddo Foundation fellowship, 1963, 1964, 1966; Guggenheim fellowship, 1965; Rockefeller grant, 1968; New York State Council on the Arts grant, 1972; American Academy award, 1979; Pulitzer prize, 1985; Prix Femina Etranger (France), 1989. **Address:** Department of English, Cornell University, Ithaca, New York 14853, U.S.A.

PUBLICATIONS

Novels

Love and Friendship. London, Heinemann, and New York, Macmillan, 1962.
The Nowhere City. London, Heinemann, 1965; New York, Coward McCann, 1966.
Imaginary Friends. London, Heinemann, and New York, Coward McCann, 1967.
Real People. New York, Random House, 1969; London, Heinemann, 1970.
The War Between the Tates. New York, Random House, and London, Heinemann, 1974.
Only Children. New York, Random House, and London, Heinemann, 1979.
Foreign Affairs. New York, Random House, 1984; London, Joseph, 1985.
The Truth about Lorin Jones. Boston, Little Brown, and London, Joseph, 1988.

Short Stories

Women and Ghosts. New York, Doubleday, and London, Heinemann, 1994.

Uncollected Short Stories

"Hansel and Gretel," in *New Story 2* (New York), 1951.
"Fat People," in *Vogue* (New York), October 1989.

Other (for children)

The Heavenly Zoo: Legends and Tales of the Stars. London, Eel Pie, 1979; New York, Farrar Straus, 1980.
Clever Gretchen and Other Forgotten Folktales. New York, Crowell, and London, Heinemann, 1980.
Fabulous Beasts. New York, Farrar Straus, and London, Cape, 1981.
Don't Tell the Grown-ups: Subversive Children's Literature. Boston, Little Brown, and London, Bloomsbury, 1990; as *Not in Front of the Grown-ups: Subversive Children's Literature,* London, Cardinal, 1991.
Cap o'Rushes. London, BBC, 1991.

Other

V.R. Lang: A Memoir. Privately printed, 1959; in *Poems and Plays,* by V.R. Lang, New York, Random House, 1975.

The Language of Clothes. New York, Random House, 1981; London, Heinemann, 1982.

Steve Poleskie, Artflyer, with Stephen Foster. Southampton, Hampshire, John Hansard Gallery, 1989.

Editor, *The Oxford Book of Modern Fairy Tales.* Oxford, Oxford University Press, 1993.

*

Manuscript Collection: Cornell University Library, Ithaca, New York.

Critical Study: *Alison Lurie* by Richard Hauer Costa, New York, Twayne, 1992.

*   *   *

It is difficult to think of any other North American writer who has held up the mirror to the nature of the professional middle classes as exactly and as wittily as Alison Lurie. From *Love and Friendship* (1962) all the way through to *The Truth about Lorin Jones* (1988), the customs and usages, fancies and foibles, of comfortable (usually East Coast) America are carefully scrutinized with Lurie's wryly amused, detached, yet not unsympathetic gaze.

Events that could have become the stuff of American tragedy in another writer's hands—marital breakdown, illicit sexual passion, madness, problems of artistic creation, loss of innocence, crisis in personal identity, emotional neglect—are transformed deftly and sharp-wittedly by Lurie into a compelling comedy of affluent U.S. life. The reader's pleasure is further enhanced by the meticulously composed and poised nature of Lurie's prose, and her ability to create vigorous characters and to spin an engaging tale.

In particular, Lurie is skilled at describing North American campus life and the idiosyncratic behavior of U.S. academics. Her novels are self-referential, employing recurrent characters usually connected with the successful, confident and combative Zimmern family. The Lurie reader looks forward to further acquaintanceship with the aggressive and influential critic Leonard D. Zimmern, for example, and the Zimmern brood are used to represent the fortunes of artistic and intellectual life in postwar East Coast America.

All her novels depict characters who are subject to rapid, and often unexpected, changes which precipitate crises in previous and usually smoothly organized existences. Rational academics join crazy religious sects, careful WASP wives have affairs with unsuitable musicians and artists, besuited historians turn beatnik, while refined East Coast ladies on vacation in London have passionate flings with waste-disposal engineers from Tulsa. Like fellow campus chroniclers David Lodge and Malcolm Bradbury, Lurie obviously enjoys the narrative strategy of placing her characters in unfamiliar surroundings, testing their previous relationships and assumptions to the limit.

Thus in *Love and Friendship* upper-class metropolitan Emily Turner finds her relationship with her rather insensitive academic husband tried by her new life as college wife in an inward-looking rural community. *The Nowhere City,* set in Los Angeles, shows how Californian attitudes gradually reshape the social presumptions of historian Paul Cattleman and his New England wife, Katherine. *Imaginary Friends* explores how two sociologists, much given to behavior models, are forced into serious reconsideration of their own identities and actions by their fieldwork among the religious group, the Truth Seekers, in a small town in rural New York State. This questioning of self and motive results in Lurie's possibly most hilarious episode when the two rationalists cast off their professional clothing in preparation for a supreme being's arrival in Sophis.

In *Real People,* an intimate novel about the act of writing, successful novelist Janet Belle Smith finds her principles tested and her status as happily married woman threatened during her transposition from well-run home to the less rule-bound atmosphere of the writer's retreat, Illyria. *The War Between the Tates* sees Erica's orderly home and long-established marriage completely transformed by the presence of her "nasty, brutish and tall" teenage offspring and husband Brian's absence due to fluffy-headed and hippyish Wendee, while the adults in *Only Children* (the only novel without a contemporary setting) shed their adult social apparel and behave in an often childish manner, when weekending on a rural retreat in the Catskill Mountains during the Depression.

The search for self-knowledge when an accepted life is disrupted becomes even more pronounced in Lurie's later novels. *Foreign Affairs,* played out in London, is the only novel set abroad, and, here in a Jamesian fashion, a group of North American exiles are challenged by the people and customs of the Old World. But it is *The Truth about Lorin Jones* that tries most ambitiously and strenuously to combine the novel of social displacement with the quest for self-knowledge. Here art historian Polly Alter, in her attempt to write a biography of a prematurely deceased artist, discovers an "alter ego" in her subject, and, on her visit to Key West to search for Lorin's past, finds her own life under question, as it becomes increasingly entwined with that of the dead painter.

Lorin Jones (born Lolly Zimmern) is seen as a young girl in *Only Children,* in which novel, as might be expected from Lurie's own academic research into children's literature and authorship of books for children, the child's view of adult behavior is portrayed very sensitively and winningly. Also present in this novel, and indeed discernible throughout her work, is the sense that Lurie's adults themselves crave the release from responsibility, decision-making, and conventional behavior that is present in a happy childhood. Many of her central figures are products of less than contented childhoods (a point not labored in any way by Lurie), and the topsy-turvy, fantastic ways they choose to change their lives reflect such a desire for liberation as an adult.

Lurie's work is intelligent, entertaining and consistently well crafted, and, like that of an earlier novelist with a superior talent for social portraiture, Jane Austen, the American writer's books provide us with a very keen and real understanding of the everyday life and aspirations of a particular group of people.

—Anna-Marie Taylor

LURIE, Morris

Nationality: Australian. **Born:** Melbourne, Victoria, 30 October 1938. **Education:** Melbourne High School; Royal Melbourne Institute of Technology. Divorced; one son and one daughter. **Career:** Worked in advertising, early 1960s; lived in Europe and Morocco, 1965-72, then in Melbourne. **Address:** c/o Penguin Books, P.O. Box 257, Ringwood, Victoria 3134, Australia.

PUBLICATIONS

Novels

Rappaport. London, Hodder and Stoughton, 1966; New York, Morrow, 1967.

The London Jungle Adventures of Charlie Hope. London, Hodder and Stoughton, 1968.

Rappaport's Revenge. London, Angus and Robertson, 1973.

Flying Home. Collingwood, Victoria, Outback Press, 1978; London, Penguin, 1982.

Seven Books for Grossman. Ringwood, Victoria, Penguin, 1983.

Madness. Sydney, Angus and Robertson, 1991.

Short Stories

Happy Times. London, Hodder and Stoughton, 1969.

Inside the Wardrobe: 20 Stories. Fitzroy, Victoria, Outback Press, 1975; New York, Horizon Press, 1978.

Running Nicely. Melbourne, Nelson, and London, Hamish Hamilton, 1979.

Dirty Friends. Ringwood, Victoria, Penguin, 1981; New York, Penguin, 1983.

Outrageous Behaviour: Best Stories. Ringwood, Victoria, Penguin, 1984; London and New York, Penguin, 1985.

The Night We Ate the Sparrow: A Memoir and Fourteen Stories. Ringwood, Victoria, and New York, Penguin, 1985.

Three Stories. Melbourne, Grossman Press, 1987.

Two Brothers, Running: Seventeen Stories and a Movie. Ringwood, Victoria, Penguin, 1990.

Plays

Waterman: Three Plays (includes *Jangle, Jangle; A Visit to the Uncle; Waterman*). Collingwood, Victoria, Outback Press, 1979.

Other (for children)

The Twenty-Seventh Annual African Hippopotamus Race. London, Collins, and New York, Simon and Schuster, 1969.

Arlo the Dandy Lion. London, Collins, and New York, McGraw Hill, 1971.

Toby's Millions. Ringwood, Victoria, Kestrel, 1982; London, Penguin, 1983.

The Story of Imelda, Who Was Small. Melbourne, Oxford University Press, 1984; Oxford, Oxford University Press, 1985; Boston, Houghton Mifflin, 1988.

Night-Night! Seven Going-to-Bed Stories. Melbourne, Oxford University Press, 1986.

Heroes. North Ryde, New South Wales, Methuen, 1987.

Alison Gets Told. Crows Nest, New South Wales, ABC Enterprises, 1990.

What's That Noise? What's That Sound? Milsons Point, New South Wales, Random Century, 1991.

Other

The English in Heat. Sydney and London, Angus and Robertson, 1972.

Hack Work. Collingwood, Victoria, Outback Press, 1977.

Public Secrets. Melbourne, Sun, 1981.

Snow Jobs. Carlton, Victoria, Pascoe, 1985.

Whole Life: An Autobiography. Fitzroy, Victoria, McPhee Gribble, 1987.

My Life as a Movie and Other Gross Conceits: 24 Essays Sportifs. Fitzroy, Victoria, McPhee Gribble-Penguin, 1988.

Editor, *John Hepworth, His Book.* Sydney, Angus and Robertson, 1978.

* * *

Morris Lurie is one of Australia's most prolific writers, centering himself firmly in the fabulist tradition, or, more colloquially, as a spinner of yarns. The son of Jewish immigrant parents, Lurie shares the call of ancient European traditions, practiced and firmly clung to by the older migrant group among whom he grew up, and about whom he writes so well, with the irresistible sense of freedom from such tradition which Australian life produced for the boy and young man in the 1950s and early 1960s.

Lurie, like Judah Waten before him, explores this conflict between the New World and the Old in compassionate, yet humorous, terms, finding a voice for hundreds of thousands of people caught up in the postwar migration and refugee flood which brought so much to Australian life and culture. Here was a different tradition, neither English nor Celtic, but firmly Euro-centered, and just as firmly Jewish, transported to a country which neither understood nor appreciated what that tradition would eventually offer.

Little wonder, then, that four of Lurie's novels, *Rappaport, The London Jungle Adventures of Charlie Hope, Rappaport's Revenge,* and *Flying Home,* as well as many of his short stories, focus on the theme of the young Australian attempting to cope with cultural traditions learned first from books and the memories of his parents and their friends, yet having to be confronted firsthand and experienced personally before any of their richness or folly can be assessed. It is not for nothing that Charlie Hope finds London a jungle and capers about with shrewd simian nimbleness, or that Rappaport, having received something of a drubbing when he first arrived in London, nevertheless manages to exact his revenge, financially and culturally, when he is safe and sound back in Australia.

Lurie's major work is the novel *Flying Home.* It is both a love story, as Leo Axelrod seeks to understand the mystery of his lover Marianne, and a novel which seeks to explore the confused and confusing tangle of roots and origins which migrant families carry within their displaced baggage. Leo comes to realize that he will never exorcise, much less comprehend, his demons until he visits Israel, for somewhere in that promised land lies the secret to his own self and the ambiguities which enclose his relationship with his parents and grandparents. As he reflects:

> It was the way I was brought up, it was what *they* felt. They didn't like Australia. Well, it wasn't even a matter of like. They ignored it. They pretended it wasn't there. Australia was an unfortunate thing that had happened to them; that Hitler had done, that's all it was to them. An accident. A terrible accident. It wasn't the real world. The real world was Bialystock, Poland, Europe. . . . So that's where I was born, that's where I grew up, that's where I lived. Nowhere. In a black cage.

The conflict between the "nowhere" of Australia and the "real world" of Europe is exigent and drives Leo to explore that "real world" in search of his self and his true home. This exploration of the mystery of family relationships—their tortuous and often painful ambiguities—and the search for a locus, a spiritual natal place, are the predominant themes of Lurie's work until the early 1980s.

During the 1970s his trips to the U.S.A. provided him with a rich source of material for exploring the Jewish community in that country of immigrants, and allowed him to see how a more established and larger community handled the translocation from Europe to a new country of considerable freedom and material progress. Several of his books of reportage, *Hack Work* and *Public Secrets,* for example, contained witty and ebullient pieces on the Jewish community in America, particularly in New York. His novella *Seven Books for Grossman* explores the mad and funny world of the Jewish fantasist, coping with sexual anarchy, a maddening intelligence, and a material culture at war with ancient demons which demand guilt and obeisance to vestigial traditions. As book tumbles after book (*Dirty Friends, Outrageous Behaviour, The Night We Ate the Sparrow* and *Two Brothers, Running* are recent story collections), Lurie shows himself not only as an acute and funny social observer, but as something of a transcultural anthropologist. His interest in the quirky, the outrageous, the madcap, in no way diminishes his exploration of the roots of human behavior and ideals.

Despite, or perhaps because of, the steady and voluminous flow of his work, Lurie remains a professional craftsman. His style is colloquial and confessional, brimming with witty aphorisms and incisive dialogue. His humor teeters on the brink of the absurd, often the anarchistic, and his later works show a considerable freedom of imagination, particularly when he, or his fictive creations, explore sexual situations, as though, by having confronted a range of taboos in his earlier work, he has earned for himself the freedom to move unselfconsciously wherever his keen nose for the funny, the eccentric, or the absurd, might lead him.

One aspect of his work often overlooked by critics as though it were secondary to his short stories, essays, and novels is his attention to and success in children's fiction. His first foray into this field was as far back as 1969 with *The Twenty-Seventh Annual African Hippopotamus Race,* followed by *Arlo the Dandy Lion, The Story of Imelda, Who Was Small,* and several other stories. These simple, homespun yarns have proved immensely popular with young children, partly because Lurie manages the difficult feat of containing his narrative within the perspective of a child's eye and allowing his fictive heroes moderate, but not overwhelming, success in a world seen as competitive, but not threatening.

When one looks at the range and volume of Lurie's work, one can only admire his dedication to the creative tasks and his skill as a craftsman. Where some have found a certain sameness about his earlier works and their concentration on the young Jewish male, squirming his way to maturity through the mess of memory, tradition, and lore imposed upon him, others have seen in his humor and aphoristic style, his sharp eye for the idiosyncratic, and his keen sense of human folly a writer deeply concerned for the constant rediscovery of human values and human freedom. Behind the sophisticated wit, the mock-heroic style of so much of his works, lies a writer making sense of the modern world, noting its curiosities and failures of sensibility, but realizing, through his imaginative creations, the human capacity to survive with sadness, but also with humor.

—D.J. O'Hearn

LYTLE, Andrew (Nelson)

Nationality: American. **Born:** Murfreesboro, Tennessee, 26 December 1902. **Education:** Sewanee Military Academy, Tennessee; Exeter College, Oxford, 1920; Vanderbilt University, Nashville, B.A. 1925 (Phi Beta Kappa); Yale University School of Drama, New Haven, Connecticut, 1927-29. **Family:** Married Edna Langdon Barker in 1938 (died 1963); three daughters. **Career:** Professor of history, Southwestern College, Memphis, Tennessee, 1936; professor of history, University of the South, Sewanee, Tennessee, and managing editor, *Sewanee Review,* 1942-43; lecturer, 1946-48, and Acting Head, 1947-48, University of Iowa School of Writing, Iowa City; lecturer in creative writing, University of Florida, Gainesville, 1948-61; lecturer in English, 1961-67, and professor of English, 1968-73, University of the South, and editor, *Sewanee Review,* 1961-73. **Awards:** Guggenheim fellowship, 1940, 1941, 1960; National Endowment for the Arts grant, 1966; University of the South Brown fellowship, 1978, 1981; Lyndhurst Foundation prize, 1985; Ingersoll Foundation prize, 1986. Litt.D.: Kenyon College, Gambier, Ohio, 1965; University of Florida, 1970; University of the South, 1973; D.H.L.: Hillsdale College, Michigan, 1985. **Address:** Monteagle SS Assembly, Monteagle, Tennessee 37356, U.S.A.

PUBLICATIONS

Novels

The Long Night. Indianapolis, Bobbs Merrill, 1936; London, Eyre and Spottiswoode, 1937.
At the Moon's Inn. Indianapolis, Bobbs Merrill, 1941; London, Eyre and Spottiswoode, 1943.
A Name for Evil. Indianapolis, Bobbs Merrill, 1947.
The Velvet Horn. New York, McDowell Obolensky, 1957.

Short Stories

A Novel, A Novella and Four Stories. New York, McDowell Obolensky, 1958.
Alchemy. Winston-Salem, North Carolina, Palaemon Press, 1979.
Stories: Alchemy and Others. Sewanee, Tennessee, University of the South, 1984.

Uncollected Short Story

"Old Scratch in the Valley," in *Virginia Quarterly Review* (Charlottesville), 1935.

Other

Bedford Forrest and His Critter Company (biography). New York, Minton Balch, 1931; London, Eyre and Spottiswoode, 1939; revised edition, New York, McDowell Obolensky, 1960.
The Hero with the Private Parts: Essays (literary criticism). Baton Rouge, Louisiana State University Press, 1966.
A Wake for the Living: A Family Chronicle. New York, Crown, 1975.
The Lytle/Tate Letters, with Allen Tate, edited by Thomas Daniel Young and Elizabeth Sarcone. Jackson, University Press of Mississippi, 1987.

Southerners and Europeans: Essays in a Time of Disorder. Baton Rouge, Louisiana State University Press, 1988.
From Eden to Babylon: The Social and Political Essays of Andrew Nelson Lytle, edited by M.E. Bradford. Washington, D.C., Regnery, 1990.
Kristin: A Reading. Columbia and London, University of Missouri Press, 1992.

Editor, *Craft and Vision: The Best Fiction from The Sewanee Review.* New York, Delacorte Press, 1971.

*

Bibliography: *Andrew Nelson Lytle: A Bibliography 1920-1982* by Stuart Wright, Sewanee, Tennessee, University of the South, 1982; *Andrew Lytle, Walker Percy, Peter Taylor: A Reference Guide* by Victor A. Kramer, Boston, Hall, 1983.

Manuscript Collections: Joint University Libraries (Vanderbilt University), Nashville, Tennessee; University of Florida Library, Gainesville.

Critical Studies: "Andrew Lytle Issue" of *Mississippi Quarterly* (State College), Fall 1970; *The Form Discovered: Essays on the Achievement of Andrew Lytle* edited by M.E. Bradford, Jackson, University and College Press of Mississippi, 1973; "Novels as History: The Art of Andrew Lytle" by Gregory Wolfe, in *Continuity* (Bryn Mawr, Pennsylvania), Fall 1984; *The Southern Vision of Andrew Lytle* by Mark Lucas, Baton Rouge, Louisiana State University Press, 1986.

Andrew Lytle comments:

My work is best described in the rendition of the fiction I have done and in the critical reading of other books. An artist is not a scientist. He discovers his theme and subject as he writes. When he has dealt totally with either, and brought it all out, he is done for.

*   *   *

The art of Andrew Lytle is clearly within the tradition of Flaubert, James, and Joyce. It is the work of a man who has thought carefully about what a novel is supposed to be, a gifted critic, editor, and advisor to many younger novelists who have honored his example in their own best production. Lytle's novels are dramatic in the modern sense. They render from within a felt life gathered to some central image or cluster of images, and project that life from the post of observation where resides "the author's seeing eye." The result of this procedure in Lytle's reader is something like a shock, a full and simultaneous engagement of all the faculties in a moment of illumination.

His first novel, *The Long Night,* is a powerful evocation of the character of ante-bellum southern society. Yet it is not *about* history—except as his times can be said to converge upon Pleasant McIvor, the central character. The plot here is Celtic in overtone and the issue revenge. But the Civil War interrupts the enactment of McIvor honor, reminding Pleasant that it is possible to offend his own dignity by pursuing it privately in a time when the future survival of such values is very much at stake. Pleasant's extravagance is perceived and judged by a younger kinsman who refuses to extend it into later days.

Lytle's *At the Moon's Inn* (and the related novella *Alchemy*) discovers form and meaning in the Spanish conquest of Eldorado. Both novel and novella "occur" from the viewpoint of an engaged spectator who, after being overcome by the vital presence of a conquistador, sees in his captain the Promethean pride which dissolved Christendom. In *At the Moon's Inn* Tovar draws back from the delusion of a worldly beatitude at the behest of De Soto's ghost. The nameless speaker in *Alchemy* retreats from Pizarro after years of reflection on the adventure in Peru. The two conquerors are counters for modernity in being representative of Columbus, their prototype of feudal Spain gone awry.

A Name for Evil is Lytle's Tennessee revelation of abstract and self-delusive traditionalism. It is, for an Agrarian, a contributor to the southern manifesto *I'll Take My Stand,* and devoted champion of the "landed interest," an amazing book. Henry Brent attempts to restore the patriarchy on land cursed by the self-centered severity of his ancestor, Major Brent. As in James's *The Turn of the Screw,* a wicked history prevails over him. Henry hates the Major too much. The "why" of his ruin is revealed ironically in his account of its unfolding. His Eden is too private for an Eve. Wife, unborn child, and therefore the entire enterprise, are the victims.

The Velvet Horn is Lytle's masterpiece. Again the scene is the Tennessee of his fathers. The Fall of Man is there re-enacted in the context of another excessive isolation. Years later, Lucius Cree is compelled by ostensible father and by mother and uncle to learn of it. First Captain Cree and then the Cropleighs "pay" for the boy's education. Yet (thanks to them) he comes forth complete from his own loss of innocence to seek a "Paradise within, greater by far." The book is, as Caroline Gordon has written, a "landmark in American fiction."

—M.E. Bradford

M

MACAULEY, Robie (Mayhew)

Nationality: American. **Born:** Grand Rapids, Michigan, 31 May 1919. **Education:** Kenyon College, Gambier, Ohio, A.B. 1941; University of Iowa, Iowa City, M.F.A. 1950. **Military Service:** Served in the United States Army, in the Counter Intelligence Corps, 1942-46. **Family:** Married 1) Anne Draper in 1948 (died 1973), one son; 2) Pamela Painter in 1979. **Career:** Instructor in English, Bard College, Annandale-on-Hudson, New York, 1946-47, and University of Iowa, 1947-50; assistant professor, Woman's College of the University of North Carolina, Greensboro, 1950-53; assistant professor, 1953-58, associate professor, 1959-61, and professor of English, 1961-66, Kenyon College, and editor, *Kenyon Review,* 1959-66; fiction editor, *Playboy,* Chicago, 1966-77; adjunct professor, University of Illinois, Chicago Circle, 1975-78. Since 1988 adjunct professor, Harvard University Extension, Cambridge, Massachusetts. Senior editor, 1978-83, and since 1984 executive editor, Houghton Mifflin, publishers, Boston; United States Delegate, PEN Conference, Tokyo, 1957, and Brazil, 1960; State Department lecturer, Australia, 1962; since 1990, co-director, Ploughshares International Writing Seminar, Emerson College European Center, Kasteel Well Netherlands. **Awards:** *Furioso* prize, 1949; Rockefeller fellowship, 1958; Guggenheim fellowship, 1964; Fulbright fellowship, 1964; O. Henry award, 1967; John Train award, 1990. D.Litt.: Kenyon College, 1986. **Agent:** Witherspoon Associates, 200 West 57th Street, New York, New York 10019, U.S.A. **Address:** P.O. Box 792, South Wellfleet, Massachusetts 02663-0792, U.S.A.

PUBLICATIONS

Novels

The Disguises of Love. New York, Random House, 1952; London, Harrap, 1954.
A Secret History of Time to Come. New York, Knopf, 1979; London, Corgi, 1983.

Short Stories

The End of Pity and Other Stories. New York, McDowell Obolensky, 1957; London, Harrap, 1958.

Uncollected Short Stories

"Dressed in Shade," in *Prize Stories 1967: The O. Henry Awards,* edited by William Abrahams. New York, Doubleday, 1967.
"For Want of a Nail," in *Cosmopolitan* (New York), October 1967.
"That Day," in *Playboy* (Chicago), November 1967.
"Ellen's Dream" (as A. Dumbarton), in *Playboy* (Chicago), July 1971.
"The Barrington Quality," in *Ellery Queen's Aces of Mystery.* New York, Davis, 1975.
"Silence, Exile, and Cunning," in *Paris Review* (New York), Spring 1990.

"Lost," in *New England Living* (Manchester, New Hampshire), September 1991.

Other

Technique in Fiction, with George Lanning. New York, Harper, 1964; revised edition, 1987.
The Seven Basic Quarrels of Marriage, with William Betcher. New York, Villard, 1991.

Editor, *Gallery of Modern Fiction: Stories from the Kenyon Review.* New York, Salem Press, 1966.
Editor, with Larzer Ziff, *America and Its Discontents.* Waltham, Massachusetts, Xerox, 1971.

*

Manuscript Collection: University of North Carolina, Greensboro.

*   *   *

Robie Macauley's prose, like the best poetry, has a startling economy of means and precision of language. Macauley seems to have applied certain poetic theories of his teacher at Kenyon College, John Crowe Ransom, to the demands of fiction. It is not surprising that a writer so attentive to technique should have produced his own poetics of the novel. The book which Robie Macauley wrote with George Lanning, *Technique in Fiction* (appropriately dedicated to Ransom), serves as an addendum to his own practices as a novelist and story writer and asserts his feelings about the importance of craft. The introduction points to the inseparability of the functions of critic and creator, distantly echoing a famous remark of Charles Baudelaire: "The best modern critics of fiction, from the standpoint of technique, and probably the only critics that the beginning writer will find of any specific help, are those who write fiction themselves."

Macauley's *The Disguises of Love* is the enviable product of years spent in close and sympathetic relationship with the best novels from Jane Austen through Joyce. Several reviewers were disturbed at certain things they saw and expressed mild discomfort. Thus Anthony West, writing in the *New Yorker,* saw in the novel the "reversal of masculine and feminine roles" which gives it, in the end, "a nonsensical quality." Stanley Edgar Hyman (*Hudson Review*) started with West's argument and proceeded to find "accounts of homosexual relations . . . disguised as accounts of heterosexual relations" in good Proustian fashion. Macauley roundly expressed his disapproval of this reading by turning Hyman's evidence from the text against him to assure us that he had in no sense tampered with gender.

Indeed, Macauley's temptress Frances (a name which Hyman suggests should more accurately be spelled "Francis") has very little in common with Albertine, Gilberte, Andrée, or Proust's other menwomen. In accustomed heterosexual fashion she manages to take to bed with her the straight-laced college professor and paterfamilias Howard Graeme. The novel is shaped by the twists and turns of their love affair. Macauley sets up three "successive centres" (Henry James's expression in the preface to *The Wings of the*

Dove) who alternate in the telling of the story; they are: Howard, his wife Helen, and their son Gordon. Howard's voice is stuffy and pedantic; Helen's has the unmistakable ring of the soap opera; Gordon's is precocious, mischievous, and ironical. The tellings have in common an unreliability. Howard mistakenly believes Gordon is "in fact pretty much an average boy with all the insensitivity of the average boy . . . " Helen accepts Howard's pretense that he is writing a book and resists the notion that he is carrying on a love affair. Gordon believes that it is his mother rather than his father who has a lover. The unraveling of the various threads of misunderstanding is performed by outsiders.

The Disguises of Love, in a sense, is an academic novel. It has in common with the best examples of the genre, like Kingsley Amis's *Lucky Jim* and Mary McCarthy's *The Groves of Academe,* the uncomfortable feeling that "teaching is the one job where you can hang on for years after you go completely bad" (Howard's words). Macauley knows the precise cadence of academic exchange and reproduces it convincingly at a musical gathering at Professor Llewellen's house and again at a party of the U.F.W.G. (University Faculty Wives' Group), with Helen Graeme acting as one of the hostesses. Three of the eleven stories in Macauley's *The End of Pity* are also concerned with academics. "The Academic Style" and "The Chevigny Man" are set on college campuses while "A Guide to the Muniment Room" involves a professor in England on "a literary pilgrimage." Stuffiness, phoniness, the narrow devotion to one's "special subject" are exposed in all three.

The first four stories in *The End of Pity* have to do with military experiences, removed from the front lines, involving Counter-Intelligence Corps personnel. Macauley mentions in his superb introduction to Ford's *Parade's End* that "some of us went to war ourselves"; these stories seem to represent a glance over his left shoulder at the absurdities and ironies of his own World War II encounters. The remaining four stories have fairly little in common. Two, "The Invaders" and "The Wishbone," end in moments of violence. "Legend of the Two Swimmers" is faintly reminiscent to Katherine Anne Porter's "Old Mortality" with its family secrets and legends, "Windfall" involves the unexpected gesture of another of Macauley's heroes overwhelmed by events; the difference is, however, that Vanderbilt acts with a decisiveness and affirmation which elude most of the other characters in *The Disguises of Love* and *The End of Pity.*

After a long stint as fiction editor of *Playboy,* Macauley returned to novel-writing with *A Secret History of Time to Come.* The humanistic soundings of *The Disguises of Love* have been replaced by the technological rumblings of this second novel. Just as Macauley suffered at the hands of certain reviewers with his first novel, so in periodicals as dissimilar as the *New York Times Book Review* and the *Magazine of Fantasy and Science Fiction* his credentials as a science-fiction writer were placed seriously in doubt. In this post-holocaust novel we are confronted with a landscape of the future which resembles the frontier of much 19th-century American literature. Like a good many philosophers of history—Vico immediately comes to mind—Macauley appears to accept a cyclical view of human endeavor, with its inevitable *ricorso.* He expresses this position structurally by beginning and ending his novel with the same words. The book begins with the diary notations ("my recollective therapy") of a black newspaperman-turned-revolutionary in Chicago. His writing is charged with elegance and a sense of mission: "All revolutions must have the same standard footage and stock shots, I think. The vehicles and the clothes are different, but Paris in 1789, Moscow in 1917, Johannesburg in 1968 must

have told the same stories to the eye." These journal entries at first alternate with the third-person account of a traveler named Kinkaid; then the diary stops and Kinkaid's story becomes the only narrative. It is all an account of "time to come," but Kinkaid's adventures occur far in the future while the diarist's jottings are close to our own period.

Macauley links up the journal with the account of Kinkaid's adventures by having the traveler see the black diarist "on the horizon of his dreams" and finally, at the end of his journey, uncover "a dusty book" which turns out to be that journal itself. *A Secret History of Time to Come,* like so many novels with an apocalyptic bent, walks a thin line between dream and reality.

—Melvin J. Friedman

———

MacCREIGH, James. *See* **POHL, Frederik.**

———

MacLAVERTY, Bernard

Nationality: Irish. **Born:** Belfast, Northern Ireland, 14 September 1942. **Education:** Queen's University, Belfast, B.A. (honors) in English 1974, diploma in education 1975. **Family:** Married Madeline McGuckin in 1967; three daughters and one son. **Career:** Medical laboratory technician, Belfast, 1960-70; teacher of English, St. Augustine's High School, Edinburgh, 1975-78, and Islay High School, 1978-81; writer-in-residence, University of Aberdeen, 1983-85. Since 1981 full-time writer. **Awards:** Northern Ireland Arts Council award, 1975; Scottish Arts Council award, 1978, 1981, 1982; Pharic McLaren award, for radio play, 1981; Jacobs award, for television play, 1982; Irish *Sunday Independent* award, 1983; London *Evening Standard* award, for screenplay, 1984. **Address:** 26 Roxburgh Street, Hillhead, Glasgow G12 9AP, Scotland.

PUBLICATIONS

Novels

Lamb. London, Cape, and New York, Braziller, 1980.
Cal. London, Cape, and New York, Braziller, 1983.

Short Stories

Secrets and Other Stories. Belfast, Blackstaff Press, 1977; New York, Viking, 1984.
A Time to Dance and Other Stories. London, Cape, and New York, Braziller, 1982.
The Great Profundo and Other Stories. London, Cape, 1987; New York, Grove Press, 1988.
Walking the Dog and Other Stories. London, Cape, 1994; New York, Norton, 1995.

Uncollected Short Stories

"For My Wife's Eyes Only," in *Redbook* (New York), February 1985.

"A Foreign Dignitary," in *Best Short Stories 1989,* edited by Giles Gordon and David Hughes. London, Heinemann, 1989; as *The Best English Short Stories 1989,* New York, Norton, 1989.

"Life Drawing," in *The Oxford Book of Irish Short Stories,* edited by William Trevor. Oxford and New York, Oxford University Press, 1989.

Plays

Screenplays: *Cal,* 1984; *Lamb,* 1986.

Radio Play: *My Dear Palestrina,* from his own story, 1980.

Television Plays: *My Dear Palestrina,* from his own story, 1980; *The Real Charlotte,* from the novel by Somerville and Ross, 1991.

Other (for children)

A Man in Search of a Pet. Belfast, Blackstaff Press, 1978.
Andrew McAndrew. London, Walker, 1989.

*

Critical Study: "An Introduction to the Stories of Bernard MacLaverty" by Arnold Saxon, in *Journal of the Short Story in English,* Spring 1987.

*   *   *

Bernard MacLaverty's writing is distinguished by its unusually adept combination of craft and compassion. So far, he has produced three collections of short stories and two novels, and every one of his volumes has appeared in the lists of the more prestigious literary awards. His first book, *Secrets and Other Stories,* won the first of his numerous Scottish Arts Council book awards, and introduces his recurrent themes of loneliness, alienation, and the awkwardnesses of human contact. Although less assured and varied than his later writing, it is an invigorating start. These themes and moods are also apparent in his first novel, *Lamb,* in which a priest, losing faith in the institutionalized religion he serves, seeks to pursue a path of genuine charity and tries to liberate the spirit of one of the boys in his care by running off with him. In a very poignant narrative, the gesture of release is construed as a kidnapping, and the priest's attempt to express real selfless love becomes confused and complicated, leading to a tragic conclusion. MacLaverty handles the complex relationship between the priest and the boy with great dignity and circumspection. The restrained passion of the writing is remarkable, and the tenderness with which the two figures are presented is moving and uplifting. Through this relationship, MacLaverty shows how modern British society makes it almost impossible for individuals to make full contact with one another.

After this promising debut as a novelist, MacLaverty issued his most successful book to date, the collection of stories called *A Time to Dance.* Like only a few of his contemporaries (James Kelman, Alan Spence, William Trevor), MacLaverty has a genuine affinity with the form of the short story. The 10 pieces in this collection show great versatility in tone, where the events are made sometimes gentle and touching, sometimes amusing, and sometimes they hint at great depths of passion. Remarkably, MacLaverty can write stories of poignancy and melancholy without ever falling into vapidity or sentimentality. Although the level of writing is consistently high, and the uniform literary craftsmanship is unquestionable, the best story is clearly "My Dear Palestrina," in which a rather callow young Irish boy is introduced to a whole new world of mystery and intensity by his sad and exotic music teacher. The story, like *Lamb* and much of MacLaverty's other writing, uses the relationship between two unlikely people as a way of exploring the limits of permissible contact in society. In this tale, the narrow-minded atmosphere of rural Ireland is obliquely evoked, and the context provides a way of exploring the frustrated lives of the participants.

MacLaverty's next book was another novel, *Cal,* in which his by now established themes work themselves out in a more urgent and stressful political environment. Thematically, it is a study of guilt, carried on through the central character, and with an intensity unusual in recent British writing, it treats the situation in Northern Ireland with the seriousness it deserves. Cal lives as a Catholic in Protestant Ulster. He has an unpleasant job in an abattoir, and his home life with his father is made miserable by Loyalist pressure. He becomes rather helplessly involved in para-military activities, including the murder of a prominent Protestant. Thereafter, he drifts into a doomed liaison with the murdered man's family, and falls in love with his widow. Inevitably, he is betrayed, and the book ends on a somber note of retributive justice. *Cal* is one of those rare novels which deals with the human stories behind day-to-day news headlines. It takes the situation in Ulster, and personalizes the tragedy of sectarian conflict, without intrusive partisanship. Cal himself remains as much of a victim as a perpetrator, and we see that the woman he loves, Marcella, is, despite her affluence, just as wounded by her environment and disabled as he is. By being successfully filmed, *Cal* has done much to bring MacLaverty into public prominence. However, good though the film is, it fails to record or reproduce the emotional texture of the book, and simplifies the intensity of its smallest scenes.

MacLaverty's most recent book is another collection, *The Great Profundo,* which again offers a series of encounters and incidents which resonate in the memory. Amid some good stories of the embarrassments of childhood and growing up—particularly the darkly comic "More Than Just the Disease"—the book touches on issues of loss and dignity. In the title story, a student encounters a remarkable sword-swallower, and hears of the magic of his life in circumstances which are now humiliating. In the small touches, MacLaverty economically conveys a great deal about scene and situation. His humane concerns with the lives of marginalized figures, and his efforts to understand the lengths people go to in order to maintain their sense of themselves, make him an involving and powerful writer, from whom much may be expected in the future.

—Ian A. Bell

MADDEN, (Jerry) David

Nationality: American. **Born:** Knoxville, Tennessee, 25 July 1933. **Education:** Knox High School, Knoxville; Iowa State Teachers

College (now University of Northern Iowa), Cedar Falls, 1956; University of Tennessee, Knoxville, B.S. 1957; San Francisco State College, M.A. 1958; Yale Drama School (John Golden fellow), New Haven, Connecticut, 1959-60. **Military Service:** Served in the United States Army, 1955-56. **Family:** Married Roberta Margaret Young in 1956; one son. **Career:** Instructor in English, Appalachian State Teachers College, Boone, North Carolina, 1958-59, and Centre College, Danville, Kentucky, 1960-62; lecturer in creative writing, University of Louisville, Kentucky, 1962-64; member of the Department of English, Kenyon College, Gambier, Ohio, and assistant editor, *Kenyon Review,* 1964-66; lecturer in creative writing, Ohio University, Athens, 1966-68. Writer-in-residence, 1968-92, director, Creative Writing Program, 1992-94, and since 1994, director, United States Civil War Center, all Louisiana State University, Baton Rouge. **Awards:** Rockefeller grant, 1969; National Endowment for the Arts prize, 1970; Bread Loaf Writers Conference William Raney fellowship, 1972. **Address:** 614 Park Boulevard, Baton Rouge, Louisiana 70806, U.S.A.

PUBLICATIONS

Novels

The Beautiful Greed. New York, Random House, 1961.
Cassandra Singing. New York, Crown, 1969.
Brothers in Confidence. New York, Avon, 1972.
Bijou. New York, Crown, 1974.
The Suicide's Wife. Indianapolis, Bobbs Merrill, 1978.
Pleasure-Dome. Indianapolis, Bobbs Merrill, 1979.
On the Big Wind. New York, Holt Rinehart, 1980.

Short Stories

The Shadow Knows. Baton Rouge, Louisiana State University Press, 1970.
The New Orleans of Possibilities. Baton Rouge, Louisiana State University Press, 1982.

Uncollected Short Stories

"My Name Is Not Antonio," in *Yale Literary Magazine* (New Haven, Connecticut), March 1960.
"Hair of the Dog," in *Adam* (Los Angeles), April-November 1967.
"The Master's Thesis," in *Fantasy and Science Fiction* (New York), July 1967.
"Nothing Dies But Something Mourns," in *Carleton Miscellany* (Northfield, Minnesota), Fall 1968.
"The Day the Flowers Came," in *The Best American Short Stories 1969,* edited by Martha Foley and David Burnett. Boston, Houghton Mifflin, 1969.
"A Voice in the Garden," in *English Record* (Oneonta, New York), October 1969.
"Traven," in *Short Stories from the Little Magazines,* edited by Jarvis Thurston and Curt Johnson. Chicago, Scott Foresman, 1970.
"Home Comfort," in *Jeopardy* (Bellingham, Washington), March 1970.
"No Trace," in *The Best American Short Stories 1971,* edited by Martha Foley and David Burnett. Boston, Houghton Mifflin, 1971.

"Night Shift," in *Playboy's Ribald Classics 3.* Chicago, Playboy Press, 1971.
"A Secondary Character," in *Cimarron Review* (Stillwater, Oklahoma), July 1972.
"The Spread-Legged Girl" (as Jack Travis), in *Knight* (Los Angeles), October 1972.
"The Singer," in *Scenes from American Life: Contemporary Short Fiction,* edited by Joyce Carol Oates. New York, Vanguard Press, 1973.
"Here He Comes! There He Goes!," in *Contempora* (Atlanta, Georgia), Summer 1973.
"Wanted: Ghost Writer," in *Epoch* (Ithaca, New York), Fall 1973.
"The World's One Breathing," in *Appalachian Heritage* (Pippa Passes, Kentucky), Winter 1973.
"Hurry Up Please, It's Time," in *The Botteghe Oscure Reader,* edited by George Garrett and Katherine Garrison Biddle. Middletown, Connecticut, Wesleyan University Press, 1974.
"The Hero and the Witness," in *New Orleans Review,* vol. 4, no. 3, 1974.
"On the Big Wind," in *The Pushcart Prize 5,* edited by Bill Henderson. Yonkers, New York, Pushcart Press, 1980.
"Putting an Act Together," in *Southern Review* (Baton Rouge, Louisiana), Winter 1980.
"Code-a-Phone," in *Crescent Review* (Winston-Salem, North Carolina), vol. 1, no. 1, 1983.
"Lights," in *New Letters* (Kansas City), Winter 1984-85.
"Rosanna," in *South Dakota Review* (Vermillion), Summer 1985.
"Was Jesse James at Rising Fawn?," in *South Dakota Review* (Vermillion), Autumn 1985.
"Willis Carr at Bleak House," in *The Bread Loaf Anthology of Contemporary American Short Stories,* edited by Robert Pack and Jay Parini. Hanover, New Hampshire, University Press of New England, 1987.
"Gristle," in *Appalachian Heritage* (Berea, Kentucky), Spring-Summer 1988.
"Children of the Sun," in *New Letters* (Kansas City), Summer 1988.
"The Invisible Girl," in *The Southern California Anthology 7.* Los Angeles, University of Southern California Master of Professional Writing Program, 1989.
"The Demon in My View," in *Southern Review* (Baton Rouge, Louisiana), Spring 1989.
"Crossing the Lost and Found River," in *Chattahoochie Review* (Dunwoody, Georgia), Winter 1989.
"James Agee Never Lived in This House," in *Southern Review* (Baton Rouge, Louisiana), Spring 1990.
"A Forgotten Nightmare," in *The Southern Californian Anthology* (Los Angeles), 1991.
"The Last Bizarre Tale," in *Southern Short Stories.* Huntsville, Texas, Huntsville Texas Review Press, 1991.
A Survivor of the Sinking of the Sultana," in *Appalachian Heritage* (Berea, Kentucky), 1992.
"If the Ash Heap Begins to Glow Again . . . " in *Louisiana English Journal* (Eunice, Louisiana), October 1993.
"Fragments Found on the Field," in *Gulf Coast Collection* (Montrose, Alabama), 1994.
"Hairtrigger Pencil Lines," in *Louisiana Cultural Vistas Magazine* (New Orleans), Spring 1994.

Plays

Call Herman in to Supper (produced Knoxville, Tennessee, 1949).

They Shall Endure (produced Knoxville, Tennessee, 1953).

Cassandra Singing (produced Knoxville, Tennessee, 1955). Published in *New Campus Writing 2,* edited by Nolan Miller, New York, Putnam, 1957; (expanded version, produced Albuquerque, New Mexico, 1964).

From Rome to Damascus (produced Chapel Hill, North Carolina, 1959).

Casina, music by Robert Rogers, lyrics by Joseph Matthewson (produced New Haven, Connecticut, 1960).

In My Father's House, in *First Stage* (Lafayette, Indiana), Summer 1966.

Fugitive Masks (produced Abingdon, Virginia, 1966).

The Day the Flowers Came (produced Baton Rouge, Louisiana, 1974). Chicago, Dramatic Publishing Company, 1975.

Other

Wright Morris. New York, Twayne, 1965.

The Poetic Image in Six Genres. Carbondale, Southern Illinois University Press, 1969.

James M. Cain. New York, Twayne, 1970.

Harlequin's Stick, Charlie's Cane: A Comparative Study of Commedia dell'Arte and Silent Slapstick Comedy. Bowling Green, Ohio, Popular Press, 1975.

A Primer of the Novel, For Readers and Writers. Metuchen, New Jersey, Scarecrow Press, 1980.

Writers' Revisions: An Annotated Bibliography of Articles and Books about Writers' Revisions and Their Comments on the Creative Process, with Richard Powers. Metuchen, New Jersey, Scarecrow Press, 1981.

Cain's Craft. Metuchen, New Jersey, Scarecrow Press, 1985.

Revising Fiction: A Handbook for Writers. New York, New American Library, 1988.

The Fiction Tutor. Fort Worth, Texas, Harcourt Brace, 1990.

Editor, *Tough Guy Writers of the Thirties.* Carbondale, Southern Illinois University Press, 1968.

Editor, *Proletarian Writers of the Thirties.* Carbondale, Southern Illinois University Press, 1968.

Editor, *American Dreams, American Nightmares.* Carbondale, Southern Illinois University Press, 1970.

Editor, *Rediscoveries: Informal Essays in Which Well-Known Novelists Rediscover Neglected Works of Fiction by One of Their Favorite Authors.* New York, Crown, 1971.

Editor, with Ray B. Browne, *The Popular Cultural Explosion: Experiencing Mass Media.* Dubuque, Iowa, William Brown, 2 vols., 1972.

Editor, *Nathanael West: The Cheaters and the Cheated.* Deland, Florida, Everett Edwards, 1973.

Editor, *Remembering James Agee.* Baton Rouge, Louisiana State University Press, 1974.

Editor, *Creative Choices: A Spectrum of Quality and Technique in Fiction.* Chicago, Scott Foresman, 1975.

Editor, with Virgil Scott, *Studies in the Short Story.* New York, Holt Rinehart, 1975; 6th edition, 1984.

Editor, with Peggy Bach, *Rediscoveries II.* New York, Carroll and Graf, 1988.

Editor, *8 Classic American Novels.* San Diego, Harcourt Brace, 1990.

Editor, *The World of Fiction* (short stories). Fort Worth, Texas, Holt Rinehart, 1990.

Editor, with Peggy Bach, *Classics of Civil War Fiction.* Jackson, University of Mississippi, 1991.

Editor, *A Pocketful of Prose: Contemporary Short Fiction.* Fort Worth, Texas, Harcourt Brace, 1992.

*

Bibliography: "A David Madden Bibliography 1952-1981" by Anna H. Perrault, in *Bulletin of Bibliography* (Westport, Connecticut), September 1982.

Manuscript Collection: University of Tennessee Library, Knoxville.

Critical Studies: "A Conversation with David Madden," and "The Mixed Chords of David Madden's *Cassandra Singing*" by Sanford Pinsker, in *Critique* (Atlanta), vol. 15, no. 2, 1973; "An Interview with David Madden," in *The Penny Dreadful* (Bowling Green, Ohio), vol. 3, no. 3, 1974; "The Story Teller as Benevolent Con Man" by Madden, in *Appalachian Heritage* (Pippa Passes, Kentucky), Summer 1974; interviews in *Southern Review* (Baton Rouge, Louisiana), vol. 11, no. 1, 1975, *New Orleans Review,* Spring 1982, and *Louisiana Literature* (Hammond), Fall 1984; by Jeffrey Richards in *Contemporary Poets, Dramatists, Essayists, and Novelists of the South,* edited by Robert Bain and Joseph M. Flora, Westport, Connecticut, Greenwood Press, 1994.

David Madden comments:

I've been trying all my life to pass the test F. Scott Fitzgerald set for himself. "The test of a first-rate intelligence is the ability to hold two opposed ideas in the mind at the same time and still retain the ability to function." Camus's concept of the absurd helped clarify Fitzgerald's: one's life should be a self-created contradiction of the fact that life is basically absurd. A similar polarity has given some form to my art as well as my life. It was not books but my grandmother's storytelling and the movies' charged images that inspired me to write. My first literary hero was the Dionysian Thomas Wolfe; then came the Apollonian James Joyce. In the tensions between those two extremes I have tried to shape my own work. I have practiced for a long time now the concept that it is between the limitations externally imposed by the form I'm working in and limitations I imposed on myself in the writing of a specific work that I experience genuine and productive freedom. Two metaphors of the artist (and the teacher) are useful for me: the magician and the con man. As with the magician's techniques of illusion, art works by a phantom circuit; and the relationship between writer and reader is like that between the con man and his mark, except that the climax (the sting) is beneficial for both. For me, the function of fiction is to create imaginary words; discipline and technique enable me to cause that to happen. And in that process I consider my reader as an active collaborator.

(1995) Because it is on the crest of a single great wave of creative energy that I enter up all the activities in my life and in my writing, I reject the perception that the fact that I have not published a novel in 15 years is evidence of diminished capacity. In all that time, I have researched and revised *Sharpshooter,* a Civil War novel, and published 14 chapters from it. I have also created the United States Civil War Center. I have the first draft of a book that provides a unique perspective on ancient London Bridge (1110 to 1828). I have always worked simultaneously on five major projects, while taking up dozens of other life and literary projects. Surfing on the one great, never-ending wave of creative force is the life-work for me.

*   *   *

Much of David Madden's fiction is autobiographical. Like Lucius Hutchfield in *Bijou,* Madden goes over his personal history again and again, remolding details. Incidents appear in more than one work; short stories are absorbed into novels; the short novel *Brothers in Confidence* becomes the first half of the longer novel *Pleasure-Dome,* as Madden works at perfecting the tale of his life. Arranged in chronological order Madden's fictional autobiography would begin with two stories from *The Shadow Knows,* "The Pale Horse of Fear" and the title story, then continue on through *Bijou, The Beautiful Greed, Pleasure-Dome,* to the elegiac story "The World's One Breathing."

Madden's goal is to transport his readers into "the Pleasure-Dome." As Lucius says in the novel of that name, "Everyday life is an effort to disentangle facts and illusions. There are rare moments in our lives when we transcend captivity in fact-and-illusion through pure imagination and dwell in the Pleasure-Dome, a luminous limbo between everyday experience and a work of art." Lucius knows well the value of a good story. He is an aspiring writer, and his older brother is a con man—which for Madden is nearly the same thing: "The relationship between the storyteller and the listener is like that between the con man and his mark," Madden has said. Madden himself is at his best when emulating the oral storytelling style he learned from his grandmother when he was growing up in the Tennessee hills, the setting of much of his fiction.

In the stories collected in *The Shadow Knows* the characters are caught between the knowledge that their old lives—in many cases rural or small town lives—are disappearing, and that the new lives available to them are spiritually unsatisfying. Madden's world here is primarily one of moonshiners and county fairs, motorcycles and coalmines, but a few of these stories are set outside the mountains. "Love Makes Nothing Happen," set in Alaska, is the best of these, while "The Day the Flowers Came," set in some faceless suburb, is maudlin and unbelievable. Two of the mountain stories here turn up as Lucius's memories in *Bijou.*

Bijou picks up Lucius's story in early adolescence, when he becomes an usher in a movie theater. Lucius tries to reinvent his life in the image of the films he sees. The Bijou itself is a symbol of the exotic mysteries of adulthood: ". . . the Bijou . . . seemed foreign, beyond his life, as if he were entering a special Bijou experience prematurely. The Bijou was somehow for other people, people who were superior to him because they'd had Bijou experiences he hadn't had." The promising framework of the theater as Lucius's doorway into adulthood is unfortunately overloaded with page after page of movie synopses, and undercut by the repetitive nature of his experiences with the other characters. We last see Lucius lurking about Thomas Wolfe's house, ready to give up films for the idea of the writer's life.

The Beautiful Greed relates the adventures of a young man named Alvin (who is just a little older than Lucius at the end of *Bijou*) on a merchant marine voyage to South America. This novel was Madden's first, and it seems thin in almost all regards when compared to his later works, though the plot here is unusually straight for Madden.

Pleasure-Dome is perhaps Madden's finest novel to date, despite a structure of two clumsily hinged together story lines. Lucius Hutchfield is once again the main character. He has been in the merchant marine and has become a writer since the events of *Bijou.* Lucius spends the first half of the novel trying to free his younger brother from jail by using his storytelling gifts. But it is the eldest brother, the con man, who succeeds in this—by telling taller tales than those Lucius tells. The second half is a cautionary tale about the responsibilities of being a storyteller. A boy's outlaw side lies dormant until Lucius awakens it with a story about Jesse James. The boy tries to emulate the outlaw's success with a young woman, with disastrous results. Though the boy goes to prison he is happy: he has on some small scale entered the world of legendary figures.

Cassandra Singing, the story of a wild boy and his invalid sister, is generally considered one of Madden's least autobiographical works, but it would be more accurate to say that Madden's character is here split between Lone and his sister Cassie. Lone is the motorcycle rider, the one with the need to escape the small world of the hills, while bedridden Cassie's life is in touch with the country's oral tradition, through the songs and stories she knows. That these two lie down together as the novel's end may be more of a self-portrait than a suggestion of incest. *On the Big Wind* is a loose string of satiric sketches with obvious targets, tied together by the voice of Big Bob Travis, nomadic radio announcer. The most telling thing here is "The World's One Breathing," spliced in from *The Shadow Knows.*

The Suicide's Wife stands apart from the rest of Madden's work. It is the story of a woman, and a story of the city. The language and plot are very spare and straightforward. Ann Harrington's husband kills himself, leaving "a vacuum into which *things* rushed." The novel is the story of Ann's struggle to gain a command over these "things," which is also the struggle to open herself to possibilities: "Before, I had never really imagined possibilities. Since she never caused events, they just happened, and she took them as they came." Ann's triumph over the foreboding world of "things" is symbolized by her successful quest to earn a driver's license, an official recognition of her right to take herself where she wants to go.

—William C. Bamberger

MAILER, Norman (Kingsley)

Nationality: American. **Born:** Long Branch, New Jersey, 31 January 1923. **Education:** Boys' High School, Brooklyn, New York, graduated 1939; Harvard University, Cambridge, Massachusetts (associate editor, *Harvard Advocate*), 1939-43, S.B. (cum laude) in aeronautical engineering 1943; the Sorbonne, Paris, 1947. **Military Service:** Served in the United States Army, 1944-46: Sergeant. **Family:** Married 1) Beatrice Silverman in 1944 (divorced 1951), one daughter; 2) Adele Morales in 1954 (divorced 1961), two daughters; 3) Lady Jeanne Campbell in 1962 (divorced 1963), one daughter; 4) Beverly Bentley in 1963 (divorced 1979), two sons; 5) Carol Stevens in 1980 (divorced 1980); 6) Norris Church in 1980, one son. **Career:** Co-founder, 1955, and columnist, 1956, *Village Voice,* New York; columnist ("Big Bite"), *Esquire,* New York, 1962-63, and *Commentary,* New York, 1962-63. Member of the Executive Board, 1968-73, and president, 1984-86, PEN American Center; Independent Candidate for Mayor of New York City, 1969. Lives in Brooklyn, New York. **Awards:** *Story* prize, 1941; American Academy grant, 1960; National Book award, for non-fiction, 1969; Pulitzer prize, for non-fiction, 1969, 1980;

MacDowell medal, 1973; National Arts Club gold medal, 1976.
D.Litt.: Rutgers University, New Brunswick, New Jersey, 1969.
Member: American Academy, 1985. **Agent:** Scott Meredith Literary Agency, 845 Third Avenue, New York, New York 10022. **Address:** c/o Rembar, 19 West 44th Street, New York, New York 10036, U.S.A.

PUBLICATIONS

Novels

The Naked and the Dead. New York, Rinehart, 1948; London, Wingate, 1949.
Barbary Shore. New York, Rinehart, 1951; London, Cape, 1952.
The Deer Park. New York, Putnam, 1955; London, Wingate, 1957.
An American Dream. New York, Dial Press, and London, Deutsch, 1965.
Why Are We in Vietnam? New York, Putnam, 1967; London, Weidenfeld and Nicolson, 1969.
A Transit to Narcissus: A Facsimile of the Original Typescript, edited by Howard Fertig. New York, Fertig, 1978.
Ancient Evenings. Boston, Little Brown, and London, Macmillan, 1983.
Tough Guys Don't Dance. New York, Random House, and London, Joseph, 1984.
Harlot's Ghost. New York, Random House, and London, Joseph, 1991.

Short Stories

New Short Novels 2, with others. New York, Ballantine, 1956.
Advertisements for Myself (includes essays and verse). New York, Putnam, 1959; London, Deutsch, 1961.
The Short Fiction of Norman Mailer. New York, Dell, 1967.
The Short Fiction of Norman Mailer (not same as 1967 book). New York, Pinnacle, 1981; London, New English Library, 1982.

Plays

The Deer Park, adaptation of his own novel (produced New York, 1960; revised version, produced New York, 1967). New York, Dial Press, 1967; London, Weidenfeld and Nicolson, 1970.
A Fragment from Vietnam (as *D.J.,* produced Provincetown, Massachusetts, 1967). Included in *Existential Errands,* 1972.
Maidstone: A Mystery (screenplay and essay). New York, New American Library, 1971.

Screenplays: *Wild 90,* 1968; *Beyond the Law,* 1968; *Maidstone,* 1971; *The Executioner's Song,* 1982; *Tough Guys Don't Dance,* 1987.

Poetry

Deaths for the Ladies and Other Disasters. New York, Putnam, and London, Deutsch, 1962.

Other

The White Negro. San Francisco, City Lights, 1957.

The Presidential Papers. New York, Putnam, 1963; London, Deutsch, 1964.
Cannibals and Christians. New York, Dial Press, 1966; London, Deutsch, 1967.
The Bullfight. New York, Macmillan, 1967.
The Armies of the Night: The Novel as History, History as a Novel. New York, New American Library, and London, Weidenfeld and Nicolson, 1968.
Miami and the Siege of Chicago: An Informal History of the Republican and Democratic Conventions of 1968. New York, New American Library, and London, Weidenfeld and Nicolson, 1968.
The Idol and the Octopus: Political Writings on the Kennedy and Johnson Administrations. New York, Dell, 1968.
Of a Fire on the Moon. Boston, Little Brown, 1971; as *A Fire on the Moon,* London, Weidenfeld and Nicolson, 1971.
The Prisoner of Sex. Boston, Little Brown, and London, Weidenfeld and Nicolson, 1971.
The Long Patrol: 25 Years of Writing from the Works of Norman Mailer, edited by Robert F. Lucid. Cleveland, World, 1971.
King of the Hill: On the Fight of the Century. New York, New American Library, 1971.
Existential Errands. Boston, Little Brown, 1972; included in *The Essential Mailer,* 1982.
St. George and the Godfather. New York, New American Library, 1972.
Marilyn: A Novel Biography. New York, Grosset and Dunlap, and London, Hodder and Stoughton, 1973.
The Faith of Graffiti, with Mervyn Kurlansky and John Naar. New York, Praeger 1974; as *Watching My Name Go By,* London, Mathews Miller Dunbar, 1975.
The Fight. Boston, Little Brown, 1975; London, Hart Davis MacGibbon, 1976.
Some Honorable Men: Political Conventions 1960-1972. Boston, Little Brown, 1976.
Genius and Lust: A Journey Through the Major Writings of Henry Miller, with Henry Miller. New York, Grove Press, 1976.
The Executioner's Song: A True Life Novel (on Gary Gilmore). Boston, Little Brown, and London, Hutchinson, 1979.
Of Women and Their Elegance, photographs by Milton H. Greene. New York, Simon and Schuster, and London, Hodder and Stoughton, 1980.
The Essential Mailer. London, New English Library, 1982.
Pieces and Pontifications (essays and interviews). Boston, Little Brown, 1982; London, New English Library, 1983.
Huckleberry Finn: Alive at 100. Montclair, New Jersey, Caliban Press, 1985.
Conversations with Norman Mailer, edited by J. Michael Lennon. Jackson, University Press of Mississippi, 1988.
Pablo and Fernande: Portrait of Picasso as a Young Man. New York, Talese, 1994.

*

Bibliography: *Norman Mailer: A Comprehensive Bibliography* by Laura Adams, Metuchen, New Jersey, Scarecrow Press, 1974.

Critical Studies (selection): *Norman Mailer* by Richard Foster, Minneapolis, University of Minnesota Press, 1968; *The Structured Vision of Norman Mailer* by Barry H. Leeds, New York, New York University Press, 1969; *Sexual Politics* by Kate Millett, New

York, Doubleday, 1970, London, Hart Davis, 1971; *Norman Mailer: The Man and His Work* edited by Robert F. Lucid, Boston, Little Brown, 1971; *Norman Mailer* by Richard Poirier, London, Collins, and New York, Viking Press, 1972; *Norman Mailer: A Collection of Critical Essays* edited by Leo Braudy, Englewood Cliffs, New Jersey, Prentice Hall, 1972; *Down Mailer's Way* by Robert Solotaroff, Urbana, University of Illinois Press, 1974; *Norman Mailer: A Critical Study* by Jean Radford, London, Macmillan, and New York, Barnes and Noble, 1975; *Existential Battles: The Growth of Norman Mailer* by Laura Adams, Athens, Ohio University Press, 1976; *Mankind in Barbary: The Individual and Society in the Novels of Norman Mailer* by Stanley T. Gutman, Hanover, New Hampshire, University Press of New England, 1976; *Norman Mailer* by Philip Bufithis, New York, Ungar, 1978; *Norman Mailer,* Boston, Twayne, 1978, and *Norman Mailer Revisited,* New York, Twayne, 1992, both by Robert Merrill; *Norman Mailer: The Radical as Hipster* by Robert Ehrlich, Metuchen, New Jersey, Scarecrow Press, 1978; *Norman Mailer's Novels* by Sandy Cohen, Amsterdam, Rodopi, 1979; *Norman Mailer, Quick-Change Artist* by Jennifer Bailey, London, Macmillan, 1979, New York, Barnes and Noble, 1980; *Acts of Regeneration: Allegory and Archetype in the Work of Norman Mailer* by Robert J. Begiebing, Columbia, University of Missouri Press, 1980; *An American Dreamer: A Psychoanalytic Study of the Fiction of Norman Mailer* by Andrew M. Gordon, Rutherford, New Jersey, Fairleigh Dickinson University Press, 1980; *Mailer: A Biography* by Hilary Mills, New York, Empire, 1982, London, New English Library, 1983; *Mailer: His Life and Times* by Peter Manso, New York, Simon and Schuster, and London, Viking, 1985; *Mailer's America* by Joseph Wenke, Hanover, New Hampshire, University Press of New England, 1987; *Radical Fictions and the Novels of Norman Mailer* by Nigel Leigh, London, Macmillan, 1990; *The Lives of Norman Mailer* by Carl Rollyson, New York, Paragon House, 1991; *Norman Mailer* by Brian Morton, London, Arnold, 1991.

Theatrical Activities:

Director: **Films**—*Wild 90,* 1968; *Beyond the Law,* 1968; *Maidstone,* 1971; *Tough Guys Don't Dance,* 1987.
Actor: **Films**—his own films, and *Ragtime,* 1981.

*   *   *

A formal distinction between fiction and non-fiction, or between fiction and journalism, is not the most helpful way to approach either the direction or the value of Norman Mailer's work. Involving himself directly with public events as well as private concerns, reporting on activities as diverse as protest marches, prizefights, the moon landing, political conventions, and the life of the first man executed for murder in America in more than ten years, Mailer characteristically blurs, argues about, and plays with the conventional categories of fiction and non-fiction. The public events he reports become metaphors that clarify and demonstrate the issues he sees as significant, apocalyptic, or destructive about contemporary America. This combination of reporting with a personal fictive vision underlies some of Mailer's best and most searching prose, like *The Armies of the Night* or much of *The Executioner's Song.* Mailer began his career with a much more conventional idea of the difference between fiction and non-fiction, for, in the early novel *The Deer Park,* he had Sergius O'Shaugnessy, the young Air Force veteran trying to become a writer in the "new" Hollywood offshoot of Desert D'Or, smugly certain that "a newspaperman is ob-

sessed with finding the facts in order to tell a lie, and a novelist is a galley-slave to his imagination so he can look for the truth." More central to Mailer's later, more complicated, fiction and reporting is another statement from the same novel, the remark by Charles Eitel, the failed and (in the 1950s) politically suspect Hollywood writer and director, musing that "the artist was always divided between his desire for power in the world and his desire for power over his work." This emphasis on power, on the capacity to change both public and private circumstances, is never far from the center of Mailer's consciousness.

Rather than using any formal means of distinguishing one example of Mailer from another, the reader recognizes that a problem of selectivity, of what to include and what to exclude, is always visible. At times, Mailer seems to concentrate too repetitiously for too long on the relatively trivial or excessively personal, as in the rather stereotyped and remote satire of Hollywood in *The Deer Park,* all the legalisms of the last third or so of *The Executioner's Song,* or the defense of his own part in literary squabbles at the beginning of *The Prisoner of Sex.* Frequently, as he recognized himself in *The Presidential Papers,* he lacks a sense of proportion, is not sure about "how to handicap the odds."

Mailer's considerable literary ambition and the popular success of his first novel, *The Naked and the Dead,* published when he was just 25, placed his own development as a writer in a highly public focus. In spite of all the claims (many of them not from Mailer himself) about the "new" voice of his generation, his first three novels were somewhat literary and derivative. *The Naked and the Dead,* the novel about the platoon fighting both the Japanese and its own army on a Pacific island during World War II, shows considerable allegiance to the fiction of Hemingway and Dos Passos, as well as deference to the ethnic mix visible in Hollywood films made during the war. *Barbary Shore,* probably the best of the three novels, taking place in a Brooklyn rooming house after the war, using characters to debate all the various perspectives of radical politics in the 1930s, and ending with no resolution for the young alienated writer, is reminiscent of James T. Farrell. And *The Deer Park,* depicting the Hollywood world of drugs, pimps, mate-swapping, and politics, contains echoes of Fitzgerald and Nathanael West without the force of originality of either, all seen at a great distance, as if the chronicle of events could shock with nothing of the feelings rendered. Although interesting, often competent, and (particularly *Barbary Shore*) full of excellent description, this fiction was more distinctive in aim than in achievement. Mailer's perspective, however, changed considerably in the middle and late 1950s, a change first visible in the 1957 essay *The White Negro,* a recognition of the clash of cultures and the violence endemic in American life. In that essay, as well as in the work that followed, Mailer began to associate imagination and creativity with the position of a sociological minority, a potentially healthy underside of American life. As he later, in *The Presidential Papers,* explained, he had not earlier acknowledged his own secret admiration for his violent characters in *The Naked and the Dead,* his own obsession with violence. From *The White Negro* on, although still disapproving strongly of the "inhuman" or abstract violence of technology, Mailer recognized the possibilities of creative change through violence, both in himself and in others. He also began to probe himself more consciously as a metaphor for the larger world he described.

Mailer regards his central characters, whether in the persona of himself in works like *The Armies of the Night* or *Miami and the Siege of Chicago* or through fictional personae in the novels *An American Dream, Why Are We in Vietnam?,* or *Ancient Evenings,* as "existential" heroes who constantly test the possible edges of human experience. Always in conflict, within themselves and with others, they dare, like Rojack walking around the parapet of the terrace high above New York, possible destruction in order to live all the possibilities of the self. Through action, they create the self, as Rojack does through murder, varieties of sexual experience, escape, criminality, and understanding. The self-creation involves a good deal of fear, as well as overcoming fear, for the hero must break away from the safe and familiar, acknowledging violence and destruction within himself. In *Why Are We in Vietnam?,* the novel of Texans on a bear hunt in Alaska, a metaphor that coalesces all those attitudes, tests, totems, and taboos that explain the American presence in Vietnam, the young voice, D.J., must create himself by recognizing and overcoming his own fear of the bear. The most frequent action in Mailer's work, which overcomes stasis and safety, is sex, the direct relationship with another being. In *Ancient Evenings* sexuality extends to procreation and lineage, speculations about new means of explaining human continuity and change. Each sexual encounter is a victory over isolation and abstraction, and, as Mailer explains in *The Prisoner of Sex,* he objects to masturbation and contraception because, in different ways, they prevent the fullest exploration of direct physical relationship. Mailer has always implicitly thought of sex in these terms, ending *The Deer Park* with a God-like voice intoning "think of Sex as Time, and time as the connection of new circuits." Yet the full development of self-creation through sexual experience, the sense of the orgasm as "the inescapable existential moment," detailed variously and explicitly, is in the work that follows *The White Negro.*

Mailer's "existentialism" is not simply private self-definition. In the first place, he frequently argues that existentialism is rootless unless one hypothesizes death as an "existential continuation of life," so that how one dies, how one faces destruction, matters. In addition, and emphasized much more frequently, Mailer's "existential" values are also social, the public consequences of definitions at the edges of experience. Social conflict is always visible, men defining themselves through the active public and social metaphors of parties, prize-fights, and wars. War (and Mailer frequently distinguishes "good" wars from "bad") has the possibility, seldom actually achieved, of changing the consciousness of a sufficient number of people to alter the whole society. Mailer began his definition of "existential politics" in 1960, with his essay called "Superman Comes to the Supermarket," on the nomination of John Kennedy for president at the convention in Los Angeles. He called Kennedy an "existential" leader because he displayed the capacity to commit himself to the "new" when "the end is unknown," a contrast to the safety and the public predictability of the Eisenhower years, although Mailer doubted that Kennedy had the "imagination" to create a wholly beneficial revolution. Yet, for Mailer, the potentiality for change and revolution, for self-creation on a public scale, is always there, a human impulse that if repressed or thwarted causes "cancer" on either the individual or social level. In these terms, Mailer, through subsequent "reports" on protests, political conventions, and public events, propounds both a vision and an analysis of contemporary American society.

In rather undiscerning popular terms, Mailer is often accused of a monstrous ego. Yet, the persona of "Norman Mailer," as it develops through many of the "journalistic" works, is highly complicated and self-critical, a metaphor for all the possibilities in contemporary man that the author can visualize and understand. As he explains in *The Armies of the Night,* he can accept the ambivalences of all the personae he adopts, "warrior, presumptive general, ex-political candidate, embattled aging enfant terrible of the literary world, wise father of six children, radical intellectual, existential philosopher, hard-working author, champion of obscenity, husband of four battling sweet wives, amiable bar drinker, and much exaggerated street fighter, party giver, hostess insulter." But the one persona he finds "insupportable" is that of "the nice Jewish boy from Brooklyn," the one with which he began, which would deny his possibility to change and create himself. The personae of his later fiction are also complicated and carefully structured voices: the violent explosions, sensitivities, challenges, and social concerns of Rojack in *An American Dream* (still, to some extent, literary, as one critic, Richard Poirier, has explained, "both a throwback to Christopher Marlowe and . . . a figure out of Dashiell Hammett"); the scatology, sensitivity, fear, bravery, and self-recognition of D.J. in *Why Are We in Vietnam?* These voices, rhetorical and linguistic creations of a point of view, effectively express much of Mailer's complexity, although they lack something of the arch self-criticism (though not the humor) and the multiplicity of the persona of Norman Mailer who enriches *The Armies of the Night* and *Of a Fire on the Moon,* and whose implicit and more self-abnegating presence created *The Executioner's Song.* As personae, creative and capacious as they are, Rojack and D.J. can sound slightly more insistent, missing something of the "Norman Mailer" acknowledged incapacity to represent immediately all of America.

More recent examples of Mailer's fiction extend the personae into different forms. *Ancient Evenings,* an ambitious novel on which he worked for more than a decade, magnifies Mailer's scope as cultural historian. Set in Egypt over two centuries more than a thousand years before Christ, the novel locates the historical genesis and implications of many of Mailer's ideas concerning sexuality, lineage, violence, public power, society, and religion. Critically regarded as either the most probing or most pretentious of Mailer's fictions, *Ancient Evenings* manifests the enormous intellectual risks which the persona confronts. A much more limited and comic side to Mailer is visible in *Tough Guys Don't Dance,* his contemporary extension of Dashiell Hammett's world. The form, the multiple killings and suicides, as well as their discovery by the "macho" narrator who could have but, in fact, did not commit them, leaves room for many characteristic digressions. In addition to the central charting of the "tough guy" lineage, Mailer includes pages on topics such as the geological and historical topography of Provincetown, the implications of different uses of adjectives in the prose of Hemingway and Updike, the horrors for an addict of giving up smoking, and the inverse relationship between cancer and schizophrenia—all done with a sharp infusion of the comic that fits both the style and substance of Mailer's personae.

As a writer, Mailer is variously talented. He is a superb journalist, always aware of the differences between what an observer sees directly and what he creates. He is an excellent literary critic, as in his attack on Kate Millett and his defenses of Henry Miller and D.H. Lawrence in *The Prisoner of Sex.* He can describe pictorially and movingly, as in *Of a Fire on the Moon,* or select brilliantly to chronicle American life, as in most of *The Executioner's Song.* More than any of these, he is consciously, seriously, humorously, and often convincingly the heir to a tradition of American visionaries, the writer who can create, in terms of the imagination, a new consciousness for his time and his country. In spite of his prolixity, his repetition, his occasional tendency to simplify polarities (his arguments against "technology" can become rant that denies his own understanding of science), and his occasional insistence on the literal applications of his own metaphors (as in parts of *The*

Prisoner of Sex), Mailer has achieved something of his own revolutionary form in transforming the consciousness of others.

—James Gindin

MAJOR, Clarence

Nationality: American. **Born:** Atlanta, Georgia, 31 December 1936. **Education:** The Art Institute, Chicago (James Nelson Raymond scholar), 1952-54; Armed Forces Institute, 1955-56; New School for Social Research, New York, 1972; Norwalk College, Connecticut; State University of New York, Albany, B.S. 1976; Union Graduate School, Yellow Springs and Cincinnati, Ohio, Ph.D. 1978. **Military Service:** Served in the United States Air Force, 1955-57. **Family:** Married 1) Joyce Sparrow in 1958 (divorced 1964); 2) Pamela Ritter in 1980. **Career:** Research analyst, Simulmatics, New York, 1966-67; director of creative writing program, Harlem Education Program, New Lincoln School, New York, 1967-68; writer-in-residence, Center for Urban Education, 1967-68, and Teachers and Writers Collaborative, Columbia University Teachers College, 1967-71, both New York; lecturer, Brooklyn College, City University of New York, 1968-69, Spring 1973, 1974-75, Cazenovia College, New York, Summer 1969, Wisconsin State University, Eau Claire, Fall 1969, Queens College, City University of New York, springs 1972, 1973, and 1975, and Fall 1973, Sarah Lawrence College, Bronxville, New York, 1972-75, and School for Continuing Education, New York University, Spring 1975; writer-in-residence, Aurora College, Illinois, Spring 1974; assistant professor, Howard University, Washington, D.C., 1974-76, and University of Washington, Seattle, 1976-77; visiting assistant professor, University of Maryland, College Park, Spring 1976, and State University of New York, Buffalo, Summer 1976; associate professor, 1977-81, and professor, 1981-89, University of Colorado, Boulder. Director of Creative Writing, 1991-93, and since 1989 professor, University of California, Davis. Visiting professor, University of Nice, France, 1981-82, Fall 1983, University of California, San Diego, Spring 1984, and State University of New York, Binghamton, Spring 1988; writer-in-residence, Albany State College, Georgia, 1984, and Clayton College, Denver, Colorado, 1986, 1987; distinguished visiting writer, Temple University, Philadelphia, Fall 1988; guest writer, Warren Wilson College, 1988. Editor, *Coercion Review,* Chicago, 1958-66; staff writer, *Proof* and *Anagogic and Paideumic Review,* Chicago, 1960-61; associate editor, *Caw,* New York, 1967-70, and *Journal of Black Poetry,* San Francisco, 1967-70; reviewer, *Essence* magazine, 1970-73; columnist 1973-76, and contributing editor, 1976-86, *American Poetry Review,* Philadelphia; editor, 1977-78, and since 1978 associate editor, *American Book Review,* New York; associate editor, *Bopp,* Providence, Rhode Island, 1977-78, *Gumbo,* 1978, *Departures,* 1979, and *par rapport,* 1979-82; member of the editorial board, *Umojo,* Boulder, Colorado, 1979-80; editorial consultant, Wesleyan University Press, Middletown, Connecticut, 1984, and University of Georgia Press, Athens, 1987; since 1986 fiction editor, *High Plains Literary Review,* Denver. Also artist: individual shows—Sarah Lawrence College, 1974; First National Bank Gallery, Boulder, Colorado, 1986. **Awards:** National Council on the Arts award, 1970; National Endowment for the Arts grant, 1970, 1975, 1979; Creative Artists Public Service grant, 1971;

Fulbright-Hays Exchange award, 1981; Western States Book award, for fiction, 1986; Pushcart prize, for short story, 1989. **Agent:** Susan Bergholtz, 340 West 72nd Street, New York, New York 10023. **Address:** Department of English, Sproul Hall, University of California, Davis, California 95616, U.S.A.

PUBLICATIONS

Novels

All-Night Visitors. New York, Olympia Press, 1969.
NO. New York, Emerson Hall, 1973.
Reflex and Bone Structure. New York, Fiction Collective, 1975.
Emergency Exit. New York, Fiction Collective, 1979.
My Amputations. New York, Fiction Collective, 1986.
Such Was the Season. San Francisco, Mercury House, 1987.
Painted Turtle: Woman with Guitar. Los Angeles, Sun and Moon Press, 1988.

Short Stories

Fun and Games. Duluth, Minnesota, Holy Cow! Press, 1990.

Uncollected Short Stories

"Church Girl," in *Human Voices 3* (Homestead, Florida), Summer-Fall 1967.
"An Area in the Cerebral Hemisphere," in *Statements,* edited by Jonathan Baumbach. New York, Braziller, 1975.
"Dossy O," in *Writing under Fire,* edited by Jerome Klinkowitz and John Somer. New York, Dell, 1978.
"Tattoo," in *American Made,* edited by Mark Leyner, Curtis White, and Thomas Glynn. New York, Fiction Collective, 1987.

Poetry

The Fires That Burn in Heaven. Privately printed, 1954.
Love Poems of a Black Man. Omaha, Nebraska, Coercion Press, 1965.
Human Juices. Omaha, Nebraska, Coercion Press, 1965.
Swallow and Lake. Middletown, Connecticut, Wesleyan University Press, 1970.
Symptoms and Madness. New York, Corinth, 1971.
Private Line. London, Paul Breman, 1971.
The Cotton Club: New Poems. Detroit, Broadside Press, 1972.
The Syncopated Cakewalk. New York, Barlenmir House, 1974.
Inside Diameter: The France Poems. Sag Harbor, New York, and London, Permanent Press, 1985.
Surfaces and Masks. Minneapolis, Coffee House Press, 1988.
Some Observations of a Stranger at Zuni in the Latter Part of the Century. Los Angeles, Sun and Moon Press, 1989.
Parking Lots. Mount Horeb, Wisconsin, Perishable Press, 1992.

Other

Dictionary of Afro-American Slang. New York, International, 1970; as *Black Slang: A Dictionary of Afro-American Talk,* London, Routledge, 1971.
The Dark and Feeling: Black American Writers and Their Work. New York, Third Press, 1974.
Juba to Jive: A Dictionary of African-American Slang. New York, Viking, 1994.

Editor, *Writers Workshop Anthology*. New York, Harlem Education Project, 1967.

Editor, *Man Is Like a Child: An Anthology of Creative Writing by Students*. New York, Macomb's Junior High School, 1968.

Editor, *The New Black Poetry*. New York, International, 1969.

Editor, *Calling the Wind: Twentieth Century African-American Short Stories*. New York, Harper Collins, 1993.

Editor, *The Garden Thrives: Twentieth Century African-American Poetry*. New York, Harper Collins, 1995.

*

Bibliography: "Clarence Major: A Checklist of Criticism" by Joe Weixlmann, in *Obsidian* (Fredonia, New York), vol. 4, no. 2, 1978; "Toward a Primary Bibliography of Clarence Major" by Joe Weixlmann and Clarence Major, in *Black American Lierature Forum* (Terre Haute, Indiana), Summer 1979.

Critical Studies: In *Interviews with Black Writers* edited by John O'Brien, New York, Liveright, 1973; "La Problematique de la communication" by Muriel Lacotte, unpublished dissertation, University of Nice, 1984.

*   *   *

"In a novel, the only thing you have is words," Clarence Major told the interviewer John O'Brien. "You begin with words and you end with words. The content exists in our minds. I don't think it has to be a reflection of anything. It is a reality that has been created inside of a book." Major's fiction exists as a rebellion against the stereotype of mimetic fiction—that telling a story, one of the things fiction can do, is the only thing fiction can do.

His first novel, *All-Night Visitors,* is an exercise in the imaginative powers of male sexuality. Major takes the most physical theme—the pleasure of the orgasm—and lyricizes it, working his imagination upon the bedrock and world of sense not customarily indulged by poetry. The pre-eminence of the imagination is shown by blending Chicago street scenes with fighting in Vietnam—in terms of the writing itself, Major claims that there is no difference. His second novel, *NO,* alternates narrative scenes of rural Georgia life with a more disembodied voice of fiction, and the action advances as it is passed back and forth, almost conversationally, between these two fictive voices. In both books, language itself is the true locus of action, as even the most random and routine development is seized as the occasion for raptures of prose (a fellatio scene, for example, soon outstrips itself as pornography and turns into an excuse for twelve pages of exuberant prose).

Major's best work is represented in his third and fourth novels, *Reflex and Bone Structure* and *Emergency Exit.* In the former, he describes an action which takes place legitimately within the characters' minds, as formed by images from television and film. "We're in bed watching the late movie. It's 1938. *A Slight Case of Murder.* Edward G. Robinson and Jane Bryan. I go into the bathroom to pee. Finished, I look at my aging face. Little Caesar. I wink at him in the mirror. He winks back./I'm back in bed. The late show comes on. It's 1923. *The Bright Shawl.* Dorothy Gish. Mary Astor. I'm taking Mary Astor home in a yellow taxi. Dorothy Gish is jealous." Throughout this novel, which treats stimuli from social life and the output of a television set as equally informative, Major insists that the realm of all these happenings is in language itself. "I am standing behind Cora," he writes. "She is wearing a thin black nightgown. The backs of her legs are lovely. I love her. The word standing allows me to watch like this. The word nightgown is what she is wearing. The nightgown itself is in her drawer with her panties. The word Cora is wearing the word nightgown. I watch the sentence: the backs of her legs are lovely."

As a result, the action of this novel takes place not simply in the characters' behavior but in the arrangements of words on the page. Here Major makes a significant advance over the techniques of his innovative fiction contemporaries. Many of them, including Ronald Sukenick (in *Up*) and John Barth (in the stories of *Lost in the Funhouse*), took a metafictive approach, establishing fiction's self-apparency and anti-illusionism by self-consciously portraying the writer writing his story. In *Reflex and Bone Structure,* however, Major accomplishes the task of making the words function not as references to things in the outside world but as entities themselves; the action is syntactic rather than dramatic, although once that syntactic function is served the action, as in the paragraph cited, can return for full human relevance. Indeed, because the activity is first located within the act of composition itself, the reader can empathize even more with the intensity of feeling behind it.

Emergency Exit is Major's most emphatic gesture toward pure writing, accomplished by making the words of his story refer inward to his own creative act, rather than outward toward the panoramic landscape of the socially real. The novel's structure makes this strategy possible. *Emergency Exit* consists of elementary units of discourse; words, sentences, paragraphs, vignettes, and serial narratives. The novel is composed of equal blocks of each, spread out and mixed with the others. At first, simple sentences are presented to the reader. Then elements from these same sentences (which have stood in reference-free isolation) recur in paragraphs, but still free of narrative meaning. The plan is to fix a word, as word, in the reader's mind, apart from any personal conceptual reference—just as an abstract expressionist painter will present a line, or a swirl of color, without any reference to figure. Then come a number of narratives, coalescing into a story of lovers and family. When enough sections of the serial narrative have accumulated to form a recognizable story, we find that the independent and fragmentary scenes of the sentences and paragraphs have been animated by characters with whom we can now empathize. Forestalling any attempt to rush off the page into incidental gossip is the memory and further repetition of these words—whether they be of black mythology, snatches of popular song, or simply brilliant writing—all within Major's arresting sentences and paragraphs. A word, an image, or scene which occurs within the narrative leads the reader directly back to the substance of Major's writing. All attention is confined within the pages of the book.

Silent as a writer for the better part of a decade, though actively engaged in teaching, speaking, and world travel, Major takes the occasion of his fifth novel, *My Amputations,* to comment on his own identity as a writer and person. His protagonist, named Mason Ellis, has a biography which matches Major's own, and his responsiveness to black music and folklore recalls the techniques of *Emergency Exit.* Mason's writing is like a closet he steps into in a recurring dream: a "door to darkness, closed-off mystery" through which his muse leads him in search of his personal and literary identities, both of which have been assumed by an "Impostor" nearly a decade ago (when Major's last novel was written). Mason's personal struggle has been with "the unmistakable separation of Church and State," which for him produces an unbearable polarity between spirit and body, mentality and sexuality, and eventually a contradiction between "clean" and "dirty" which he refuses to accept. His muse must guide him away from this middle ground of separation where he languishes; imprisoned in various forms of life (which correspond to Major's background growing up in Chicago and serving in the Air Force), he must literally "write his way out" by constructing a different paradigm for God's interests and Caesar's. Falsely jailed while "the Impostor" continues his career, Mason joins a group of urban terrorists who rob a bank to finance their dreams—in his case, the recovery of his role as novelist. To do this, Mason adopts the pose of the black American writer abroad, living in Nice and speaking at various universities across Europe. But at every stage the concerns of State intervene, as each country's particular style of political insurgency disrupts his visit. Even his idealistic goal of Africa is torn by conflicts of body and spirit, and he finds himself either caught in the crossfire of terrorists or imprisoned as a political suspect. These circumstances, while being complications in the narrative, prompt some of the novel's finest writing, as Major couches Mason's behavior in a linguistic responsiveness to the terroristic nature of our times. The achievement of *My Amputations* is its conception of Mason Ellis as a creature of the world's signs and symbols. He moves in a world of poetic constructions, where even crossing the street is an artistic adventure: "Mason Ellis sang 'Diddie Wa Diddie' like Blind Blake, crossed the street at Fifth Avenue and Forty-Second like the Beatles on the cover of *Abbey Road* and reaching the curb leaped into the air and coming down did a couple of steps of the Flat Foot Floogie." Not surprisingly, Major points his character toward a tribal sense of unity in Africa, pre-colonial and hence pre-political, where the separations of "Church" and "State" do not exist.

With his novels *Such Was the Season* and *Painted Turtle: Woman with Guitar* Major makes his closest approach to narrative realism, yet in each case the mimesis is simply a technical device that serves an equally abstract purpose. *Such Was the Season* is ostensibly a gesture toward that most commercially conventional of formats, the family saga, as a nephew from Chicago returns to the Atlanta home of an old aunt who helped raise him. His visit, however, entails not just the usual thematics of family history and a touch of matriarchy but rather a spectrum study of African-American culture in its many forms, from bourgeois society to political power-playing. Because the narrator is Aunt Eliza herself, the novel becomes much more a study in language than social action, however, for the emphasis remains not on the events themselves but upon her blending them into an interpretive narrative. That Major is ultimately interested in these aesthetic dimensions rather than in the simply social is evident from *Painted Turtle,* in which the story of a native American folksinger's career is told only superficially by the episodic adventures surrounding her work; at the heart of her story is the nature of her poetic expression, passages of which are reproduced as transcriptions of her songs—which are unlike any folksongs the reader may have heard, but much like the linguistic constructions Aunt Eliza fashions in the previous novel as a way of making the emerging reality of her family meaningful to her.

—Jerome Klinkowitz

MALGONKAR, Manohar (Dattatray)

Nationality: Indian. **Born:** Bombay, 12 July 1913. **Education:** Karnatak College, Dharwar; Bombay University, B.A. (honours) in English and Sanskrit 1936. **Military Service:** Served in the Maratha Light Infantry, 1942-52: Lieutenant Colonel. **Family:** Married Manorama Somdutt in 1947; one daughter. **Career:** Professional big-game hunter, 1935-37; cantonment executive officer, Government of India, 1937-42. Owner, Jagalbet Mining Syndicate, 1953-59. Since 1959 self-employed farmer in Jagalbet. Independent candidate for Parliament, 1957, and Swatantra Party candidate, 1962. **Address:** P.O. Jagalbet, Londa, Belgaum District, India.

PUBLICATIONS

Novels

Distant Drum. Bombay, Asia Publishing House, 1960; London and New York, Asia Publishing House, 1961.
Combat of Shadows. London, Hamish Hamilton, 1962; Thompson, Connecticut, InterCulture, 1968.
The Princes. London, Hamish Hamilton, and New York, Viking Press, 1963.
A Bend in the Ganges. London, Hamish Hamilton, 1964; New York, Viking Press, 1965.
The Devil's Wind: Nana Saheb's Story. New York, Viking Press, and London, Hamish Hamilton, 1972.
Shalimar. New Delhi, Vikas, 1978.
The Garland Keepers. New Delhi, Vision, 1980.
Bandicoot Run. New Delhi, Vision, 1982.
Cactus Country. New Delhi, Viking Penguin, 1991.

Short Stories

A Toast in Warm Wine. New Delhi, Hind, 1974.
In Uniform. New Delhi, Hind, 1975.
Bombay Beware. New Delhi, Orient, 1975.
Rumble-Tumble. New Delhi, Orient, 1977.
Four Geaves and Other Stories. New Delhi, Viking Penguin, 1989.

Play

Spy in Amber (screenplay). New Delhi, Hind, 1971.

Other

Kanhoji Angrey, Maratha Admiral: An Account of His Life and His Battles with the English. Bombay, London, and New York, Asia Publishing House, 1959; as *The Sea Hawk,* New Delhi, Vision, 1978.
The Puars of Dewas Senior. Bombay, Orient Longman, 1963.
Chhatrapatis of Kolhapur. Bombay, Popular Prakashan, 1971.
Dead and Living Cities. New Delhi, Hind, 1978.
The Men Who Killed Gandhi. Madras, Macmillan, 1978; London, Macmillan, 1979.
Cue from the Inner Voice: The Choice Before Big Business. New Delhi, Vikas, 1980.
Inside Goa (travel). Panaji, Government of Goa, 1983.
Princess: The Autobiography of the Dowager Maharani of Gwalior, with Vijayaraje Scindia. London, Century Hutchinson, 1985; as *The Last Maharani of Gwalior,* Albany, State University of New York Press, 1987.
Dropping Names. New Delhi, Lotus, 1991.

*

Critical Studies: *An Area of Darkness* by V.S. Naipaul, London, Deutsch, 1964, New York, Macmillan, 1965; "Purdah and Caste Marks" by Malgonkar, in *Times Literary Supplement* (London), 4 June 1964; *Eating the Indian Air* by John Morris, London, Hamish Hamilton, 1968; *Manohar Malgonkar* by G.S. Amur, New Delhi, Arnold-Heinemann, and New York, Humanities Press, 1973; *Manohar Malgonkar* by James Y. Dayananda, New York, Twayne, 1974.

Manohar Malgonkar comments:

(1991) Praise can embarrass but it does not call for a rejoinder. Censure often does, so here goes. Those who disparage my work think that (1) I write with one eye on Hollywood, (2) my writing is "withdrawn" from the reality of my country's poverty as well as the reality of the four-letter word, and (3) I inject my values and politics and prejudices into my writings.

Well, I do strive to write the sort of novel I also like to read, full of meat, exciting, well-constructed, plausible and with a lot of action—in short, to tell a good story. If this is what Hollywood also likes, good for Hollywood and, I hope, some day for me too. I know one admits this rather shamefacedly, as one might say "I'm afraid I do chew paan," or "Yes, I do use a night shirt." At the same time, I often think of myself as belonging to the advance guard in the swing back of the romantic novel. The peddlers of erotica and drug dreams may churn out best sellers, but these are not novels; and the interminable ramblings about a day in the life of somebody or the other are like dissecting the veins in every single leaf of a cabbage. All this was a phase and it has had too long a run, but you cannot go on playing with a cabbage forever. The novel will be back, plot, action and all; the signs are already there.

Withdrawn? I maintain that my novels are close enough to the ground to pass off for straight history. The withdrawal is seen in my refusal to be trapped in the dirt and misery of India. The social life of millions of Indians centres around the dustbins of cities. Granted. But mine doesn't, and for me to write about it would be as insincere as a white man writing about Harlem life. And this is perhaps related to my other "withdrawal"—the disrelish for the language of graffiti. For two years during my army service, I was in daily contact with British and other ranks and can thus claim to have acquired a fairly full vocabulary of raw words which I can use far more naturally than those who discovered a handful of them since *Fanny Hill* came out as a paperback. I don't use them for the same reason that I don't have my characters talking in local accents: they would show up as being utterly false to my style.

But the third point of criticism I accept as a kind of compliment. I believe that it is the thinking man's business to influence. In a country such as ours, where democracy itself is threatening to throttle individual freedom, it is the duty of every writer to do so.

* * *

Essentially a romantic novelist of action, Manohar Malgonkar adds the freshness of an exotic scene and the novelty of a bi-focal viewpoint to an expert use of tried and true Western techniques. English is his own first language and his life style is westernized (unlike his compatriot R.K. Narayan, for example). He had a university education and is a man of cosmopolitan culture, widely read; but he has lived for the past many years on a remote estate in the heart of India. He commands a lively and colloquial English, full of vivid metaphors. He uses dialogue fluently. One thinks of affinities to Conrad on the one hand and John Masters on the other.

In the earliest of his novels first published in the West, *Combat of Shadows,* he writes of British tea planters in the last years of the British Raj, somewhat in the vein of a disillusioned Kipling; he is able to mock the pukka-sahib Establishment by letting the reader see it through the eyes of its own cynics and outcasts. But it is primarily a story of love and derring-do rather than social comment. *The Princes,* on the other hand, deals with the old Indian aristocracy before the Princely States were absorbed in the new India, and with the painful transition. This has been his most widely read, most thoughtful, and perhaps most distinguished work. Here E.M. Forster comes to mind.

A Bend in the Ganges, though politically objective, echoes recent history in its personal love story set against the cruelty of a great civil disaster—the Indian-Pakistani split of 1947. Two other novels of post-Independence days, still unpublished in the West, reflect his involvement with current Indian politics, in which he has participated from a minority position to the right of the dominant Congress Party. One is an adventure story of the Indian take-over of Goa; the other a character study of a land-owning politician in a country district.

The Devil's Wind goes back a century to the so-called "Indian Mutiny," never before presented from the Indian point of view. He narrates it in the person of Nana Saheb, an actual princely leader of the rebellion and a notorious villain in British eyes. Neither a hero nor an anti-hero, he is the kind of ambiguous character that Malgonkar delights in. In being an historical novel, and in its marked change of sympathy toward the British, this is a new departure; but in style and in storytelling qualities, particularly its violence, it has the characteristics of his other best novels.

While Malgonkar's books all have thoughtful overtones, he is first of all the storyteller. He enjoys heroic characters fighting the odds and struggling with inner conflicts. He understands how to stretch the reader's willing suspension of disbelief for the sake of a dramatic confrontation. He makes graphic the hunt for a rogue elephant or a tiger; the crude violence of a human massacre; the tragic dislocations of civil war, from the burning of a single house to bombers over a great city. He bridges the nostalgia of India's past with the turbulence of her present.

—Marshall A. Best

MALOUF, David

Nationality: Australian. **Born:** David George Joseph Malouf in Brisbane, Queensland, 20 March 1934. **Education:** Brisbane Grammar School, 1947-50; University of Queensland, Brisbane, 1951-54, B.A. (honours) in English 1954. **Career:** Lecturer, University of Queensland, 1955-57; teacher, St. Anselm's College, England, 1962-68; lecturer, University of Sydney, 1968-77. **Awards:** Australian Literature Society gold medal, 1974, 1983; Grace Leven prize, 1975; James Cook award, 1975; Australia Council fellowship, 1978; New South Wales Premier's prize, for fiction, 1979; *The Age* Book of the Year award, 1982; Commonwealth prize for fiction, 1991; Prix Femina Étranger, 1991; Miles Franklin award, 1991; New South Wales award for fiction, 1991. **Address:** 53 Myrtle St., Chippendale, New South Wales 2008, Australia.

PUBLICATIONS

Novels

Johnno. St. Lucia, University of Queensland Press, 1975; New York, Braziller, 1978.
An Imaginary Life. New York, Braziller, and London, Chatto and Windus, 1978.
Child's Play, with Eustace and the Prowler. London, Chatto and Windus, 1982; as *Child's Play, The Bread of Time to Come: Two Novellas,* New York, Braziller, 1982.
Fly Away Peter. London, Chatto and Windus, 1982.
Harland's Half Acre. London, Chatto and Windus, and New York, Knopf, 1984.
The Great World. London, Chatto and Windus, 1990; New York, Pantheon, 1991.
Remembering Babylon. London, Chatto and Windus, and New York, Knopf, 1993.

Short Stories

Antipodes. London, Chatto and Windus, 1985.

Plays

Voss (opera libretto), music by Richard Meale, adaptation of the novel by Patrick White (produced Sydney, 1986).
Blood Relations. Sydney, Currency Press, 1988.
Baa Baa Black Sheep (opera libretto). London, Chatto and Windus, 1993.

Poetry

Four Poets, and others. Melbourne, Cheshire, 1962.
Bicycle and Other Poems. St. Lucia, University of Queensland Press, 1970; as *The Year of the Foxes and Other Poems,* New York, Braziller, 1979.
Neighbours in a Thicket. St. Lucia, University of Queensland Press, 1974.
Poems 1975-76. Sydney, Prism, 1976.
Selected Poems. Sydney, Angus and Robertson, 1980.
Wild Lemons. Sydney, Angus and Robertson, 1980.
First Things Last. St. Lucia, University of Queensland Press, 1980; London, Chatto and Windus, 1981.
Poems, 1959-89. St. Lucia, University of Queensland Press, 1992.

Other

New Currents in Australian Writing, with Katharine Brisbane and R.F. Brissenden. Sydney and London, Angus and Robertson, 1978.
12 Edmondstone Street (essays). London, Chatto and Windus, 1985.
Johnno, Short Stories, Poems, Essays, and Interview, edited by James Tulip. St. Lucia, University of Queensland Press, 1990.

Editor, with others, *We Took Their Orders and Are Dead: An Anti-War Anthology.* Sydney, Ure Smith, 1971.
Editor, *Gesture of a Hand* (anthology of Australian poetry). Artarmon, New South Wales, Holt Rinehart, 1975.

*

Manuscript Collections: University of Queensland, St. Lucia; Australian National University Library, Canberra.

Critical Studies: Interviews in *Commonwealth 4* (Rodez, France), 1979-80, *Meanjin 39* (Melbourne), and *Australian Literary Studies* (Hobart, Tasmania), October 1982; "David Malouf as Humane Allegorist" by James Tulip, in *Southerly* (Sydney), 1981; "David Malouf and the Language of Exile" by Peter Bishop, in *Australian Literary Studies* (Hobart, Tasmania), October 1982; "David Malouf's Fiction" by P. Pierce, in *Meanjin* (Melbourne), vol. 41, no. 4, 1982; "Discoveries and Transformations: Aspects of David Malouf's Work" by L.T. Hergenhan, in *Australian Literary Studies* (Hobart, Tasmania), May 1984; "Secret Companions: The Continuity of David Malouf's Fiction" by M. Dever, in *World Literature Written in English* (Guelph, Ontario), vol. 26, no. 1, 1986; "David Malouf's *Child's Play* and 'The Death of the Author'" by S. Woods, in *Australian Literary Studies* (Hobart, Tasmania), May 1988; "Body Talk: The Prose of David Malouf" by N. Mansfield, in *Southerly* (Sydney), vol. 49, no. 2, 1989; *Australia in Mind: Thirteen Influential Australian Thinkers* by M. Thomas, Sydney, Hale and Iremonger, 1989; "Mapping the Local in the Unreal City" by E. Ferrier, in *Island* (Sandy Bay, Tasmania), no. 41, 1989; *Imagined Lives: A Study of David Malouf* by P. Neilsen, St. Lucia, University of Queensland Press, 1990; *Sheer Edge: Aspects of Identity in David Malouf's Writing* by Karin Hansson, Lund, Lund University Press, 1991; *David Malouf* by Ivor Indyk, Melbourne and Oxford, Oxford University Press, 1993.

*   *   *

David Malouf was already an established and well-regarded poet when he published his first novel in 1975. His career seems to have taken a decisive turn for it is primarily prose works that he has published since 1980, including two major novels, some novellas, a book of short stories, and one of autobiographical essays. Malouf writes the prose one might expect from a poet, rich in precise and elaborated metaphor, intensely lyrical, symbolic, almost visionary at times, and at others built on passages of powerfully realised concrete detail.

His novels show a continuous interest in certain themes and images. He is fascinated by opposites, for example by Australia and Europe which are not only at opposite ends of the earth but also make possible contrary forms of experience. He often returns to images of life on the periphery; in *An Imaginary Life* Ovid is exiled to the limits of the known world, and in *Harland's Half Acre* Frank Harland lives in a tent by the Pacific Ocean. At the margins there can still just about be a certain innocence, an intensity of relationship with nature, a way of being relatively at ease with time and death. In each of Malouf's novels there is a main pair of male characters who embody these opposites (in the centre/on the periphery of society and culture) whose tense, ambivalent relationship is the central theme of the novel. Through them Malouf creates a view which is simultaneously "from both sides," as though he needed to come back again and again to these fundamentally different forms of life and to create a space in which a choice between them can be avoided.

In other respects his novels show very little continuity, for in overt subject matter they are extraordinarily diverse. Malouf's first novel, *Johnno,* is about growing up in suburban Brisbane during and after World War II. It contains much autobiographical material, to some of which Malouf has recently returned in the essays in *12*

Edmondstone Street. The hero, Johnno, is like a character from the Paris of Sartre or Cortazar, a 1950s existentialist but stranded in a subtropical suburb at the wrong end of the earth, full of angst and the wildness of an untamed spirit. The narrator is nicknamed Dante, and he tells the tale of Johnno's life without ever resolving his ambivalence towards him. On the one hand Johnno seems to be an authentic fresh wind blowing away the suffocating, humid atmosphere of Brisbane life; on the other he is irresponsible, reckless, and ultimately self-destructive (he dies in a swimming incident that was quite probably suicide). The narrator maintains an affectionate though ironic distance from this wild hero, and uses him as a way of exploring his own youthful indecisions about family, about Europe, and about work. A strength of the novel is its convincing and moving depiction of life in Brisbane, but its interest by far transcends this particularity.

On the face of it Malouf's next novel, *An Imaginary Life,* could hardly be more different. It tells the imaginary story of the Roman poet Ovid, living in exile in a village on the edge of the known world in the most appallingly harsh conditions and entirely cut off from his own family and culture. The novel vividly realises the hardness of the very long winters, the bleakness of the landscape, but also the power of the symbolic life of the village community (its shamanistic rituals, its burial ground, its hunting expeditions). Ovid becomes obsessed with a child who is discovered living wild among wolves in the forest. He is captured and brought into the village where the poet begins to teach him to speak. Ovid gradually realises, however, that it is the boy who is the teacher. Ovid increasingly identifies him with a mysterious child of whom he had visions when he was himself very young. Forced to flee the village together, Ovid is led by the boy through vast grasslands and is taught to observe insects, plants and the earth. At last he finds the place where he will die. His exile and journey have been an education. He has put behind him the frivolity of his life as an urban poet and has been forced into regions of experience beyond the limits of his imagination. There, on the margins, he has found peace and truth. It is a novel of rather grand themes and enigmatic visions.

Fly Away Peter contains some of Malouf's most powerful writing. It is again a story of exile, only in this case it turns out to be catastrophic. Jim, a young Queenslander, has a strong sense of having found his place when he becomes the warden of a bird sanctuary on the Queensland coast. He is a silent young man, at ease when observing with endless, meticulous patience the markings and migrations of the birds. His life is marginal, since world history does not pass through this remote region, but it is harmless, innocent, and rich in detailed experience of nature. The migrating birds, however, remind him that it is possible to span the immense distances that separate him from Europe. His friend and employer, Ashley Crowther, is a sophisticated and educated man who has recently returned from the heartlands of European culture in Cambridge and Germany. They could not be more different. But these differences and distances are to count for nothing, for it is 1914 and in that other hemisphere a war begins. Jim and Ashley migrate to Europe and to that horrific negation of all landscape, the trenches and mud of World War I. Jim's life, and eventual death, in the trenches are written with great intensity. It is perhaps Malouf's most symbolic novel, built around a series of collapsing opposites (Europe and Australia, innocence and cruelty, history and nature). Little episodes and images come to carry a great weight of meaning. As in all of his novels, and here particularly successfully, Malouf constructs a perspective that allows life to be seen "from both sides."

He brings together the opposite poles of human capacity, the patient and loving receptiveness to nature, and the obliterating cruelty of war, each described with visionary intensity.

The novella *Child's Play* may be the oddest and least successful of Malouf's attempts to write "from both sides." On the one hand, he creates a man of great learning, an immensely important author with a central role in modern Italian culture. On the other, there is a terrorist who is to assassinate him. We are shown a strange office where a group of terrorists work with the discipline and industry of a community of scholars in a library, studying their victims and plotting murder. The story is told in the first person by the killer, who becomes obsessed with his victim and with his reflection on the role of meaningless coincidence and brute accident in human affairs. But this personification of metaphysical themes does not convince.

A similar problem affects at least some of the short stories in *Antipodes.* It is as if they strain to be about matters of too great significance. Many of the stories are about particularly crucial or traumatic episodes in the lives of the characters (first sex, death of loved ones, and so on). The events are so weighty that the attempt to encompass them within the short story format does not allow that expansion of metaphor and slow preparation of the more visionary moments which Malouf achieves in his novels. As a consequence the writing is uneven and sometimes hovers dangerously close to cliché.

In *Harland's Half Acre* Malouf successfully returns to a more ambitious format. It is his longest novel since *Johnno,* and tells the long life stories of an eccentric Queensland painter, Frank Harland, and of the narrator, a Brisbane lawyer, Phil Vernon. As in all of his novels, the characters form a pair of opposites. Harland is the son of an impoverished farmer and always lives on the margins of society, sometimes as a swagman roaming the state jobless during the Great Depression, at another period painting in an abandoned cinema on a pier in the coastal town of Southport. In the last period of his life, even though he is by then celebrated and wealthy, he lives in a tent in the bush near the ocean. Phil Vernon, who helps to sort out his affairs and to protect him and his brother, has an utterly different life trajectory. He comes from a small-business family always struggling against possible disasters. He chooses the safe and orderly life of a lawyer. Both of their lives are shaped by significant family deaths. Europe and its wars have an indirect impact on this peripheral society. Scenes of concentration camps are shown at the newsreel cinemas in Brisbane. A slave camp of derelict tramps and winos is discovered on the outskirts of the city. The tidal wave of cruelty and inhumanity which has swept across Europe has reached these remote shores. As in all Malouf's work, we get in this novel a strong sense of the power of family attachments and loyalties and of the memories of childhood experience. The novel celebrates endless small acts of kindness and of anger that shape our lives. It is the quality of Malouf's writing that is, here as in all of his novels, the most notable feature of his work.

—John Mepham

MANGIONE, Jerre

Nationality: American. **Born:** Gerlando Mangione in Rochester, New York, 20 March 1909. **Education:** Syracuse University, New

York, B.A. 1931. **Family:** Married Patricia Anthony in 1957. **Career:** Staff writer, *Time* magazine, New York, 1931; book reviewer, New York *Herald Tribune,* 1931-35, and the *New Republic,* New York, 1931-37; book editor, Robert M. McBride Company, New York, 1934-37; national coordinating editor, Federal Writers' Project, 1937-39; information specialist, 1940-42, special assistant to the United States Commissioner, 1942-48, and editor-in-chief of the *Monthly Review,* 1944-48, Immigration and Naturalization Services of the United States Department of Justice; advertising and public relations writer for various firms in New York and Philadelphia, 1948-61. Lecturer, 1961-63, associate professor, 1963-68, professor of English and director of the Writing Program, 1968-78, acting director, Italian Studies Center, 1978-80, and since 1978, Emeritus Professor of American Literature, University of Pennsylvania, Philadelphia. Visiting lecturer, Bryn Mawr College, Pennsylvania, 1967-68; visiting professor, Trinity College, Rome, Summer 1973, and Queens College, City University of New York, 1980. Editor-in-chief, *WFLN Philadelphia Guide,* 1959-61; advisory editor, *Humanist,* 1979. National president, Friends of Danilo Dolci Inc., New York, 1969-71; member of the Executive Council, American-Italian Historical Association, 1980. **Awards.** Guggenheim fellowship, 1946; Fulbright fellowship, 1965; Rockefeller grant, 1968; American Philosophical Society grant, 1971; Philadelphia Athenaeum award, 1973; American Institute for Italian Culture award, 1979; National Endowment for the Arts grant, 1980, 1984; American-Italian Historical Association special award, 1983; Empedocles prize (Italy), 1984; Pennsylvania Governor's award, 1989; Leonardo Da Vinci award, 1989; Columbus Countdown Society International Arts award, 1990, 1992; Mariano DiVito Human Achievement award, 1993. M.A. 1971, and D.Litt. 1980, University of Pennsylvania; L.H.D.: State University of New York, Brockport, 1987. Commander, Order of the Star of Italian Solidarity, 1971; Fellow, Society of American Historians, 1974. **Address:** 3300 Darby Road, no. 7315, Haverford, Pennsylvania 19041, U.S.A.

PUBLICATIONS

Novels

Mount Allegro. Boston, Houghton Mifflin, 1943; revised (nonfiction) edition, New York, Columbia University Press, 1981.
The Ship and the Flame. New York, Wyn-Current, 1948.
Night Search. New York, Crown, 1965; as *To Walk the Night,* London, Muller, 1967.

Short Stories

Life Sentences for Everybody (fables). New York and London, Abelard Schuman, 1966.

Other

Reunion in Sicily. Boston, Houghton Mifflin, 1950.
A Passion for Sicilians: The World Around Danilo Dolci. New York, Morrow, 1968; as *The World Around Danilo Dolci,* New York and London, Harper, 1972.
America Is Also Italian. New York, Putnam, 1969.
The Dream and the Deal: The Federal Writers' Project 1935-1943. Boston, Little Brown, 1972.

Mussolini's March on Rome (for children). New York, Watts, 1975.
An Ethnic at Large: A Memoir of America in the Thirties and Forties. New York, Putnam, 1978.
La Storia: Five Centuries of the Italian American Experience, with Ben Morreale. New York, HarperCollins, 1992.

*

Bibliography: "Jerre Mangione: A Bibliography," in *VIA (Voices in Italian Americana),* Fall 1993.

Manuscript Collection: University of Rochester, Rochester, New York.

Critical Studies: In *Current Biography 1943* edited by Maxine Block, New York, Wilson, 1943; *The Italian in America* by Lawrence Frank Pisani, New York, Exposition Press, 1957; "Jerre Mangione: The Sicilian Sources" by Ben Morreale, in *Italian Americana* (Buffalo), Fall-Winter 1981; "Jerre Mangione: American Writer with Sicilian Roots" by Lloyd Bruno, in *Il Caffe* (Rome), July-August 1982; *Immigrant Autobiography in the United States* by William Boelhower, Verona, Essedue, 1982; "My House Is Not Your House: Jerre Mangione and Italian/American Autobiography," in *Multi-Cultural Autobiography: American Lives,* edited by James Robert Payne, Knoxville, University of Tennessee Press, 1992; "A Tribute to Jerre Mangione" by Fed Gardaphe, "Jerre Mangione: The Man and His Work" by Bernard Weisberger, "An Interview with Jerre Mangione" by Frank Salamone, and "Humor, Ethnicity, and Identity in Jerre Mangion's *Storia*" by John Lowe, all in *VIA (Voices in Italian Americana),* Fall 1993.

Jerre Mangione comments:

(1981) As a writer I am motivated by the need to understand myself and the world around me. This need was first nourished by the circumstances of being born and raised among Sicilian relatives in an urban American environment. That experience, which is the substance of my first book, *Mount Allegro,* accentuated for me the sharp contrast between the philosophical values of the old world and those of the new. It also succeeded in casting me in the role of the outsider who, belonging to neither world, tries to create his own world by the writing of fiction. Two of my novels, *The Ship and the Flame* and *Night Search,* are efforts in that direction, and for that reason may be more truly autobiographical than the four books I have written in the first person, namely *Mount Allegro, Reunion in Sicily, A Passion for Sicilians,* and *An Ethnic at Large.* Although *Mount Allegro* is somewhat fictional in content, it is a basic part of this series which extends over a span of 50 years and deals largely with my public identity as a Sicilian-American observing the people and places he knows best.

My other books are more simply explained.

Life Sentences for Everybody consists of fables dealing with contemporary characters. "Life Sentences" were inspired by the challenge of telling a story within the confines of a single sentence. These are, frankly, exercises in procrastination (I was trying to work on a novel when I wrote the first batch), which gave me more pleasure than I usually derive from the act of writing. At least two critics have written that "Life Sentences" represent a new genre. And that too is pleasurable, for who doesn't enjoy being an innovator?

I have also written two social histories: *America Is Also Italian,* a brief telling of the Italian-American immigrant saga; and *The Dream and the Deal,* an account of the Federal Writers' Project of the thirties. These two histories were written because I was personally involved in both of them and felt that they needed to be told.

(1986) Despite all my books of memoirs, my first love remains fiction. Yet I must confess to a certain fickleness—for when I'm writing fiction I long to be writing nonfiction, and vice versa. I'm reminded of Italo Svevo's Zeno who when he was with his wife longed to be with his mistress, and vice versa. Presently I long to write a new draft of an unpublished novel gathering dust in a desk drawer while I work on my *magnum opus,* a social history of the Italian American experience during the past century.

*   *   *

Jerre Mangione's prose style is straightforward and lively. Because he often employs a first person narration his work conveys the impression of conversation liberally sprinkled with anecdote and description. Much of it is factual or semifictional accounting of the author's experiences. The ordering of this material is subtle and it is only at the end of the book such as *Mount Allegro* or *A Passion for Sicilians* that one sees the cumulative effect of the massing of seemingly unrelated detail.

At the heart of Mangione's prose are the mountains, temples, and people of Sicily. He draws from his Sicilian relatives, his acquaintances in all levels of Sicilian society, and his extensive travels on the island a wealth of fascinating detail. On one level the last chapters of *Mount Allegro, Reunion in Sicily,* and *A Passion for Sicilians* function as travel books to introduce the reader to a land, comparatively untouched by tourism, which has fascinated and lured observers like D.H. Lawrence by its forbidding beauty. The ruined Greek temples of Agrigento, the hilltop castle of Mussolmeli built atop a Saracen fortification, the beautiful fishing village of Scopello are tantalizingly described. But the slums of Palermo are not forgotten. Villages with beautiful mountain views but no water, and hovels where ten people live in one room are painted with the same force and clarity.

His presentation of people is no less effective. The transplanted families of the Mount Allegro section of Rochester, New York, who try to keep Sicily alive there with their gregariousness, their intimate brand of Catholicism, their devotion to food, and their resignation to *destinu* are presented with warmth and vitality. Their Sicilian counterparts are also sympathetically and clearly drawn, but the author's partisanship is not blind. Danilo Dolci, for instance, who is studied at length in *A Passion for Sicilians,* is presented as a complex man who desires approval but sometimes courts dissension, who attracts and alienates followers. The reader is allowed to sort out for himself the powers and foibles of this pacifist and his programs for economic and social reform.

Mangione displays similar talents in his fiction. In the novel, *The Ship and the Flame,* which deals with the development of the will to act in Stiano Argento, a Sicilian refugee from fascism, we are presented with the action as Stiano experiences it and we see his need to act taking shape. He is a passenger, with his wife and daughter, on a Portuguese ship filled with people fleeing several European countries. Although they have been issued entrance visas to Mexico, they find when they arrive there that these visas are not authentic and that Mexican officials will not allow them to land. Goaded to action by the suicide of his friend Josef Renner, the love of Tereza Lenska, and the bravery of Peter Sadona, Stiano helps secure permission for most of them to land in the United States. If there are problems with Mangione's method in this book

they are shown in Stiano's frustrated love affair with Tereza. Although reviewers at the time seem to have found it torrid, the effect today is quite the opposite. The limits permissible for sexual description have changed so much in the intervening years that a reader now finds it hard to believe in the force of this passion.

Books like *Mount Allegro* and *A Passion for Sicilians* fare better. In these the material remains interesting even though not current. The process of assimilation in America is a fascinating one and the stories of *Mount Allegro* enliven our understanding of what has happened and is occurring. Social action is a continuing interest to us: Dolci's work goes on and it is important to be shown that imperfect people can accomplish much and a single life can affect the lives of others.

—Barbara M. Perkins

MANKOWITZ, (Cyril) Wolf

Nationality: British. **Born:** London, 7 November 1924. **Education:** East Ham Grammar School, London; Downing College, Cambridge, M.A. in English 1946. **Military Service:** Served as a volunteer coal miner and in the British Army during World War II. **Family:** Married Ann Margaret Seligmann in 1944; four sons. **Career:** Play and film producer: with Oscar Lewenstein, 1955-60; independently, 1960-70; with Laurence Harvey, 1970-72. Owner, Pickwick Club restaurant, London, 1963-70; also antique and art dealer. Moved to Ireland in 1971. Since 1982 adjunct professor of English, and adjunct professor of theatre arts, 1987-88, University of New Mexico, Albuquerque. Honorary Consul to the Republic of Panama in Dublin, 1971. Exhibition of Collages, Davis Gallery, Dublin, 1990. **Awards:** Society of Authors award, for poetry, 1946; Venice Film Festival prize, 1955; BAFTA award, 1955, 1961; Oscar, for screenplay, 1957; Film Council of America Golden Reel, 1957; *Evening Standard* award, for play, 1959; Cork Film Festival International Critics prize, 1972; Cannes Film Festival grand prize, 1973. **Address:** The Bridge House, Ahakista, Durrus, near Bantry, County Cork, Ireland; or, 2322 Calle Halcon, Sante Fe, New Mexico 87505, U.S.A.

PUBLICATIONS

Novels

Make Me an Offer. London, Deutsch, 1952; New York, Dutton, 1953.
A Kid for Two Farthings. London, Deutsch, 1953; New York, Dutton, 1954.
Laugh Till You Cry: An Advertisement. New York, Dutton, 1955; included in *The Penguin Wolf Mankowitz,* 1967.
My Old Man's a Dustman. London, Deutsch, 1956; as *Old Soldiers Never Die,* Boston, Little Brown, 1956.
Cockatrice. London, Longman, and New York, Putnam, 1963.
The Biggest Pig in Barbados: A Fable. London, Longman, 1965.
Raspberry Reich. London, Macmillan, 1979.
Abracadabra! London, Macmillan, 1980.
The Devil in Texas. London, Royce, 1984.
Gioconda. London, W.H. Allen, and New York, Freundlich, 1987.

The Magic Cabinet of Professor Smucker. London, W.H. Allen, 1988.
Exquisite Cadaver. London, Deutsch, 1990.
A Night with Casanova. London, Sinclair Stevenson, 1991.

Short Stories

The Mendelman Fire and Other Stories. London, Deutsch, and Boston, Little Brown, 1957.
Expresso Bongo: A Wolf Mankowitz Reader. New York, Yoseloff, 1961.
The Blue Arabian Nights: Tales of a London Decade. London, Vallentine Mitchell, 1973.
The Days of the Women and the Nights of the Men: Fables. London, Robson, 1977.

Plays

Make Me an Offer, adaptation of his own novel (televised 1952; revised version, music and lyrics by Monty Norman and David Heneker, produced London, 1959).
The Bespoke Overcoat (produced London, 1953). London, Evans, 1954; New York, French, n.d.
The Baby, adaptation of a work by Chekhov (televised 1954; produced London, 1981). Included in *Five One-Act Plays,* 1955.
The Boychik (produced London, 1954).
It Should Happen to a Dog (televised 1955; produced Princeton, New Jersey, 1967; London, 1977). Included in *Five One-Act Plays,* 1955.
Five One-Act Plays. London, Evans, 1955; New York, French, n.d.
The Mighty Hunter (produced London, 1956). Included in *Five One-Act Plays,* 1955.
The Last of the Cheesecake (produced London, 1956). Included in *Five One-Act Plays,* 1955.
Expresso Bongo, with Julian More, music and lyrics by David Heneker and Monty Norman (produced London, 1958). London, Evans, 1960.
Bells; or, The Ballad of Dr. Crippen, with Beverley Cross, music by Monty Norman (produced London, 1961).
Pickwick, music and lyrics by Cyril Ornadel and Leslie Bricusse, adaptation of the novel by Dickens (produced London, 1963). New York and London, French, 1991.
Passion Flower Hotel, music and lyrics by Trevor Peacock and John Barry, adaptation of the novel by Rosalind Erskine (produced London, 1965).
The Samson Riddle (produced Dublin, 1972; as *Samson and Delilah,* produced London, 1978). London, Vallentine Mitchell, 1972.
Jack Shepherd, music by Monty Norman (produced Edinburgh, 1972; as *Stand and Deliver,* produced London, 1972).
Dickens of London (televised 1976). London, Weidenfeld and Nicolson, 1976; New York, Macmillan, 1977.
The Hebrew Lesson (screenplay). London, Evans, 1976.
The Irish Hebrew Lesson (produced London, 1978; New York, 1980).
Iron Butterflies (produced Albuquerque, 1985). Two acts published in *Adam International Review* (London), 1984.

Screenplays: *Make Me an Offer,* with W.P. Lipscomb, 1954; *A Kid for Two Farthings,* 1955; *The Bespoke Overcoat,* 1955; *Trapeze,* 1955; *Expresso Bongo,* 1959; *The Two Faces of Dr. Jekyll* (*House of Fright*), 1960; *The Millionairess,* with Ricardo Aragno, 1960; *The Long and the Short and the Tall* (*Jungle Fighters*), with Willis Hall, 1961; *The Day the Earth Caught Fire,* with

Val Guest, 1961; *Waltz of the Toreadors,* 1962; *Where the Spies Are,* with James Leasor and Val Guest, 1965; *Casino Royale,* with others, 1967; *La Vingt-cinquième Heure* (*The Twenty-fifth Hour*), 1967; *The Assassination Bureau,* with Michael Relph, 1969; *Bloomfield* (*The Hero*), with Richard Harris, 1970; *Black Beauty,* with James Hill, 1971; *The Hebrew Lesson,* 1972; *Treasure Island,* with Orson Welles, 1973; *The Hireling,* 1973; *Almonds and Raisins* (documentary), 1983.

Television Plays: *Make Me an Offer,* 1952; *The Baby,* 1954; *The Girl,* 1955; *It Should Happen to a Dog,* 1955; *The Killing Stones,* 1958; *Love Is Hell,* 1966; *Dickens of London* series, 1976; *Have a Nice Death,* from the story by Antonia Fraser (*Tales of the Unexpected* series), 1984.

Poetry

XII Poems. London, Workshop Press, 1971.

Other

The Portland Vase and the Wedgwood Copies. London, Deutsch, 1952.
Wedgwood. London, Batsford, and New York, Dutton, 1953; revised edition, London, Barrie and Jenkins, 1980.
Majollika and Company (for children). London, Deutsch, 1955.
ABC of Show Business. London, Oldbourne Press, 1956.
A Concise Encyclopedia of English Pottery and Porcelain, with R.G. Haggar. London, Deutsch, and New York, Hawthorn, 1957.
The Penguin Wolf Mankowitz. London, Penguin, 1967.
The Extraordinary Mr. Poe: A Biography of Edgar Allan Poe. London, Weidenfeld and Nicolson, and New York, Summit, 1978.
Mazeppa: The Lives, Loves, and Legends of Adah Isaacs Menken: A Biographical Quest. London, Blond and Briggs, and New York, Stein and Day, 1982.

*

Manuscript Collection: Mugar Memorial Library, Boston University.

Theatrical Activities:
Director: **Film**—*The Hebrew Lesson,* 1972.

Wolf Mankowitz comments:

I have written a novel whenever a story idea has held my attention long enough. There has been no intended overall pattern to them: they vary totally, making it difficult for publishers who prefer me to write the same successful story again and again.

*   *   *

Wolf Mankowitz writes in the tradition of the Yiddish storyteller, holding his audience by a powerful blend of cynicism and sentiment. His narration is simple and direct; his subject matter ranges from life in London's East End to the manipulations of the antique trade and show business. This material gives him a scope for satire that he exploits to the full. He pokes gentle fun at the characters of whom he is fond and tears the others apart. Above all, he cares that people should care, whether for 18th-century English pottery or for their religion or for the happiness of their children. His villains are those with no emotions to hide.

Make Me an Offer is about a man who cares obsessively for Wedgwood and is both lucky and unscrupulous enough to track down the object of his passion, an early copy of a Portland vase. It is a fantasy rooted in the reality of double dealing, bluff, and auction rigging. The central character knows all the tricks he needs and has no illusions about his profession; Mankowitz makes him attractive for his humour, his knowledge, and his genuine love of beauty. "Who knew better than he that nothing is given, that everything passes, the woods decay. He was the ultimate human being. He resigned himself to making a profit." The immediate success of this novella, which was made into a prize-winning musical, is paralleled by the acclaim given to *A Kid for Two Farthings*. This is a celebration of the author's Cockney childhood, told with a warmth and pathos that are wholly irresistible. "Life is all dreams—dreams and work," says the tailor Kandinsky to his six-year-old friend Joe. Joe's dream comes true: he goes to the market to buy a unicorn and finds one, the kid of the title and of the Passover song.

Mankowitz conveys the flavour of Jewish life in anecdote and dialogue; he lets moral values and social attitudes emerge out of business confrontations and family relationships. "The Mendelman Fire" is a particularly fine treatment of paternal love, told by Mr. Mendelman's admiring accountant, a man who "could make a company for twelve pounds and liquidate it for five." Many of the stories in this collection are set in Russia and have the charm of folktale, a form which, transposed to the West Indies, is used in *The Biggest Pig in Barbados*.

Perhaps the most original of the novels is *My Old Man's a Dustman,* a study of survival and friendship at the lowest levels of human experience. It takes place in a Beckett-like landscape of shacks and rubbish-tips but is lightened by Cockney songs and Cockney cheek. *Cockatrice* is a far more bitter book in a far plushier setting. We meet the hero, Daniel Pisarov, in "a Regency bed with swans' heads": like everything else, this belongs to his boss, the film producer whom he is vainly trying to double-cross. Mankowitz takes a grim pleasure in putting Danny through the hoops of ambition and corruption; in the film industry, the story suggests, no dreams are realised, only the nightmares come true.

One can imagine that *The Devil in Texas,* a satire written with unhesitating fluency about the excesses of American academia, gave Mankowitz enormous pleasure to create. The anti-hero, for he has to be so in a fable based on the damnation of Faust, is Dr. Oliver Stanley, who studies one of the obscurer areas of theology in a university that bears more than a little resemblance to the University of Texas at Austin. Originally from Cambridge, England, Stanley is now researching at the University City of Longhorn and is dependent on a grant that may or may not be renewed. Mankowitz projects the harmless, slightly stuffy English academic prototype in Stanley, but his full name, with its wry reference to Laurel and Hardy, at once makes him a comical figure. In order to keep his research programme, Stanley sells his soul to the beautiful, elusive Dr. Armorian, who devises fantastic and entirely worthless projects for him to study. The plot is the vehicle for Mankowitz's observations on American society, an exposé of nepotism and excessive material greed, where a colossal excess of money seems to buy anything available but sincerity. Stanley's new office, gained when his further research programme is guaranteed, is fantastic, with the latest electronic gadgetry. However, none of it is conducive to genuine scholarly research.

Texas, famed for the biggest of everything, represents more than the confines of the university that has lost sight of the human soul and individual needs. The pressure of a society where everyone must have everything is emphasized by the loss of individual personality and basic human values of feeling, in a cast of characters who nearly all have the same surname. Their crass vulgarity and pride in having the best stresses their lack of concern for those who have nothing, and they are blessed by having no such misfits in their perfect money-dominated world. When remarking that verbal magic has gone, Stanley is roundly rebuked and told the magicians of the world are Vidal Sassoon, Falchi, Cartier, and Rolex, and that the "invocations today are Master Charge, Visa and American Express, and Diners and Texas First National Bank." Mankowitz is anything but gentle in shredding the various layers he examines, but the verve with which he writes makes *The Devil in Texas* completely convincing.

The theme of fantastic magic, invocations of dead Jewish alchemists, and a panoply of the fake sciences dominates *Abracadabra,* a futurist novel set in 2013. The reflections of Benjámin Abarbanel, an old Jewish man, occur when he is unwillingly cast into "The Barbara Castle Rest Home for Senior Citizens," where he is attended to by robotic nurses who cannot answer his questions. Even his memories are manipulated by a machine, which projects on a screen the past and the present like a film. As Abarbanel recalls his adolescence as an evacuee during World War II, Mankowitz relentlessly savages present-day uncaring society, where individuals have ceased to matter and politicians are celebrated as new gods. *Abracadabra* is an attack on a British Thatcher-created world, the promised utopia that never came to be. As in all his writing, Mankowitz has a dry humour and constantly plays with words. But his purpose is serious, and he informs as he entertains. With Mankowitz, the unlikely plot is unimportant, and the more preposterous the character, the more one is curious to understand his purpose in the novel. The past of the boy Abarbanel, with its "forties" period flavour and its cast of richly drawn characters, contrasts pointedly with the empty, featureless, but allegedly comfortable life that aged Abarbanel has to endure.

—Judy Cooke, updated by Geoffrey Elborn

MANTEL, Hilary (Mary)

Nationality: British. **Born:** Glossop, Derbyshire, 6 July 1952. **Education:** The London School of Economics, 1970; Sheffield University, Yorkshire, B. Jurisprudence 1973. **Family:** Married Gerald McEwen in 1972. **Career:** Social worker in a geriatric hospital, 1974-75; teacher of English, Botswana, 1977-80, lived in Saudi Arabia, 1981-86. **Awards:** Naipaul Memorial prize, for travel writing, 1987; Winifred Holtby prize, 1990; Cheltenham fiction prize, 1991; Soultrem Arts Literary prize, 1991; Sunday Express Book of the Year prize, 1992. Fellow, Royal Society of Literature, 1990. **Agent:** Bill Hamilton, A.M. Heath, 79 St. Martin's Lane, London WC2N 4AA, England.

PUBLICATIONS

Novels

Every Day Is Mother's Day. London, Chatto and Windus, 1985.
Vacant Possession. London, Chatto and Windus, 1986.

Eight Months on Ghazzah Street. London, Viking, 1988.
Fludd. London, Viking, 1989.
A Place of Greater Safety. London, Viking, 1992; New York, Athenaeum, 1993.
A Change of Climate. London, Viking, 1994.
An Experiment in Love. London, Viking, 1995.

Uncollected Short Stories

"Poor Children" (as Hilary McEwen), in *Punch* (London), 21 February 1979.
"Something for Sweet," in *Literary Review* (London), December 1986.
"Alas for the Egg," in *Best Short Stories 1987,* edited by Giles Gordon and David Hughes. London, Heinemann, 1987.
"A Dying Breed," in *London Magazine,* April-May 1987.
"Dog Days," in *Encounter* (London), May 1987.

*

Hilary Mantel comments:

My first two novels are set in the north of England, in 1974 and 1984 respectively. *Every Day Is Mother's Day* tells the story of Muriel Axon and her mother Evelyn, two reclusive women who live together in mutual disgust, united only by their fear of the outside world. Their peculiar lives touch the lives of their neighbors at many points, but true contact is never made. Muriel Axon becomes mysteriously pregnant, and at the end of the story there are two violent deaths.

The mood of this book is comic and satirical, with excursions into the fantastic; at times it has the flavor of a ghost story. Some of the ideas come from a short period I spent as a hospital social worker. At a deeper level, I was interested by different theories of mental health and illness, and especially by Bruno Bettelheim's writings on autism. Muriel's internal world consists of a series of terrifying misapprehensions about the nature of cause and effect; but her major problem is that there is a gap where her imagination should be. Because of this gap, she cannot put herself in anyone else's place, or guess what their feelings might be. So she is equipped to evolve from a pathetic person into a wicked one.

Vacant Possession takes up Muriel's story 10 years later. Released from a long-stay mental hospital, which is closing as a result of government policy, Muriel returns to her old haunts and begins to wreak havoc in the lives of the new owners of her mother's house.

Here I wanted to make some topical points about the hospital closures and the kinds of problems they might create; sadly, the points remain topical several years on. I also wanted to expand the character of Muriel to its logical limits. Since she had no center—no soul, really—it is possible for her to assume other identities at will. In one incarnation she is a cleaning woman called Lizzie Blank; in another, she is a depressive hospital orderly called Poor Mrs. Wilmot. She has the knack of finding out the fears and vulnerabilities of the people around her, and dealing with them accordingly.

Vacant Possession is superficially less serious than *Every Day Is Mother's Day.* It has a faster pace, more jokes per page, and a more farcical plot-line. As epigraph to the first book I used a quotation from Pascal: "Two errors: one, to take everything literally; two, to take everything spiritually." When reading anything I have written, my *ideal* reader would hear that warning in mind.

My third novel *Eight Months on Ghazzah Street* is a psychological thriller set in Saudi Arabia, where I lived for some years.

My fourth novel, *Fludd* is a comedy set in the north of England in the 1950s in a fictitious moorland village. The main characters are nuns and priests. Here I used motifs, mishaps and miseries from my own Catholic childhood; but the book is not a satire on the Church. Its central device is the notion of alchemy. I wanted to explore what alchemy meant, as a liberating and creative process, and to see what form my own earliest memories would take if I worked to transform them into fiction.

*   *   *

Hilary Mantel's four novels offer a curious graph of a novelist's preoccupations and of her development. Her first two novels, *Every Day Is Mother's Day* and *Vacant Possession,* are unusual in that they deal with the same people and, up to a point, with the same events. This has been done before, of course (by Lawrence Durrell, for example, in the first three volumes of his *Alexandrian Quartet*), but while other novelists use this method to present different views of the same events, this has not been Mantel's approach.

In *Every Day Is Mother's Day* the madness, infanticide, and matricide in the Axon household are described mostly through Mrs. Axon's eyes (giving us some idea of her marriage to the horrible Mr. Axon, now mercifully dead), and in *Vacant Possession* the same events are recalled by her daughter Muriel in a flashback that asserts her hate for her mother, yet tells us nothing of the cunning ways in which Muriel reinforced her mother's belief in the evil spirits possessing the house (it is left to the reader to guess at these from Mrs. Axon's terrors in the first book). The action in *Vacant Possession* then moves forward however to two more murders committed by Muriel and two by her mad landlord. There is a terrible neatness about the second book: multiple links never thought of in the first book are now established between the Axons and their neighbors, the Sidneys, and Isobel, the social worker, her husband and her father.

Coincidences abound, all part of a carefully worked out pattern, and what happens has the inevitability of a fairy tale. Mantel's preoccupation is with evil, with human wickedness which pursues its ends singlemindedly and appears to triumph, at least in the first novel. At the end of *Vacant Possession,* however, Muriel Axon is back in her old house: like a dreadful sorcerer's apprentice she has called up spirits that will destroy her—retribution at last.

It is unusual for a novelist to return to the same characters and the same preoccupations in a second novel, apparently to dispense belated justice. Yet there is no moral tone, the appalling deeds are described with a chilling unemotional impartiality. Only the images hint perhaps at the author's distaste: a blind shoots up "with a soft flurry like the exit of a family of rats," Mrs. Axon eats cold baked beans with her fingers out of a cut-glass ashtray.

Mantel's third book, *Eight Months on Ghazzah Street,* is a very different kind of novel. Presumably based on personal experiences, and written out of the shock and outrage of living in a society that has little time for Western liberal ideals and none for Western women, it is a mixture of a thriller (with no clear-cut solution of the mystery) and a record (some of it in diary form) of the heroine's progress, or disintegration. Frances Shore came to Saudi Arabia to join her husband, a civil engineer. A cartographer, she is not permitted to work in the Kingdom, finds the expatriate society uncongenial, and tries to make friends with two young women neighbors, one a Pakistani, one a Saudi. An Englishman is murdered, there are hints of Fundamentalist plots, of gun-running. The end of the novel finds Frances and her husband silent, defeated, waiting to leave for good. There are no real villains, just a clash of two worlds, two cultures, two moralities, and, in the end, a deep dislike of the hot, dusty city and its ways.

In her latest book, *Fludd,* Mantel returns to good and evil manifested in the everyday world. Fludd, who seems to be a reincarnation of the 16th-century mystical theosophist and alchemist Robert Fludd, comes to the Northern village of Fetherhoughton as curate to the Roman Catholic priest, Father Angwin. Like a catalyst in a chemical process he brings change to the village: the traditional old faith is reinforced; the cruel Mother Perpetua of the local convent apparently meets the devil and is burnt; a young nun, Sister Philomena, escapes with Fludd, spends the night with him and is left to face the unknown world with confidence born out of love. There is perhaps a devil in the shape of the local tobacconist, and there is a miracle: the priest's housekeeper is cured of a disfiguring wart. There is some unexpected kindness, another miracle perhaps (the old nuns help Philomena to run away), and in the end the message is reassuring: "the ways of the wicked shall perish."

It should be stressed that there is much to amuse the reader in Mantel's novels, surprisingly so given the grim events that take place. She has a wicked sense of the absurd (Colin Sidney's kitchen units were put up "with the help of a screwdriver provided and simple instructions in Japanese"), and a sharp eye for detail. This latter quality she shares of course with most present-day novelists (surely there has never been a period of literary endeavor so dedicated to documenting the minutiae of daily living down to the last brand name), but in her descriptions of the present-day world, evil, banal but powerful, is caught and held for the reader to inspect and recognize.

—Hana Sambrook

MARKANDAYA, Kamala

Pseudonym for Kamala Purnaiya Taylor. **Nationality:** Indian. **Born:** 1924. **Education:** Madras University. **Family:** Married; one daughter. **Career:** Journalist; now full-time writer. Lives in London. **Awards:** National Association of Independent Schools award (U.S.A.), 1967; English-Speaking Union award, 1974. **Address:** c/o Chatto and Windus, 20 Vauxhall Bridge Road, London SW1V 2SA, England.

PUBLICATIONS

Novels

Nectar in a Sieve. London, Putnam, 1954; New York, Day, 1955.
Some Inner Fury. London, Putnam, 1955; New York, Day, 1956.
A Silence of Desire. London, Putnam, and New York, Day, 1960.
Possession. Bombay, Jaico, London, Putnam, and New York, Day, 1963.
A Handful of Rice. London, Hamish Hamilton, and New York, Day, 1966.
The Coffer Dams. London, Hamish Hamilton, and New York, Day, 1969.
The Nowhere Man. New York, Day, 1972; London, Allen Lane, 1973.

Two Virgins. New York, Day, 1973; London, Chatto and Windus, 1974.
The Golden Honeycomb. London, Chatto and Windus, and New York, Crowell, 1977.
Pleasure City. London, Chatto and Windus, 1982; as *Shalimar,* New York, Harper, 1983.

*

Critical Studies: *Kamala Markandaya* by Margaret P. Joseph, New Delhi, Arnold-Heinemann, 1980; *Cross-Cultural Interaction in Indian English Fiction: An Analysis of the Novels of Ruth Prawer Jhabvala and Kamala Markandaya* by Ramesh Chadha, New Delhi, National Book Organisation, 1988; *The Novels of Kamala Markandaya and Ruth Prawer Jhabvala* by Rekha Jha, New Delhi, Prestige, 1990; *Cultural Imperialism and the Indo-English Novel: Genre and Ideology in R.K. Narayan, Anita Desai, Kamala Markandaya, and Salman Rushdie* by Fawzia Afzal-Khan; *Human Bonds and Bondages: The Fiction of Anita Desai and Kamala Markandaya* by Usha Pathania, Delhi, Kanishka, 1992.

*   *   *

Kamala Markandaya is one of the best of contemporary Indian novelists. Her novels are remarkable for their range of experience. *Nectar in a Sieve* is set in a village and examines the hard agricultural life of the Indian peasant; *Some Inner Fury,* which includes a highly educated woman and her English lover who are torn apart by the Quit India campaign of the time, has to do with the quarrel between Western and Indian influences, as they are focussed in a marriage; *A Silence of Desire* deals with the middle class, and *A Handful of Rice* with the city poor; *Possession* moves from the West End of London to a South Indian village, and is centred on the conflict of Eastern spirituality with Western materialism; *The Coffer Dams* is a highly contemporary examination of the activities of a British engineering firm which is invited to build a dam in India. Markandaya has not the same intimacy and familiarity with all these areas of life, and she has indeed been criticised by Indian critics for a certain lack of inwardness with the life of the Indian poor. Her particular strength lies in the delicate analysis of the relationships of persons, particularly when these have a more developed consciousness of their problems, and particularly when they are attempting to grope towards some more independent existence. She has, too, the genuine novelist's gift for fixing the exact individuality of the character, even if she is less successful at establishing it in a reasonably convincing social context. She has been most successful and at her best, an impressive best, in dealing with the problems of the educated middle class, and she has a gift in particular for delineating the self-imposed laceration of the dissatisfied.

Perhaps Markandaya's most achieved and characteristic work is *A Silence of Desire.* It is a delicate, precise study of husband and wife, although the wife has less actuality than the husband, Dandekar, a nervy, conscientious, petty government clerk. He is rocked off his age-old balance by his wife's strange absences, excuses, and lies. It turns out that she has a growth and is attending a Faith Healer. The husband is by no means a Westernised person, but he is to some degree secular and modern, and the situation enables the author to reflect on the tensions, the strength and the inadequacies and aspirations of middle-class Indian life. The book is gentle in tone but sharp in perception, and the mixture of moods, the friction of faith and reason, the quarrel of old and young, are beautifully pointed. There are conventional, perfunctory patches in the novel, but Markandaya shows a very high skill in unravelling sympathetically but unflinchingly the structure of the protagonist's motives and the bumbling and stumbling progress of his anxieties.

Towards the end of *A Silence of Desire* there occurs a suggestion in an encounter between Sarojini and Dandekar, the husband and wife, of a theme which clearly much engages Markandaya. The wife reverences the tulasi tree as embodying the divine spirit, whereas the husband understands its purely symbolic function. "You with your Western notions, your superior talk of ignorance and superstition . . . you don't know what lies beyond reason and you prefer not to find out. To you the tulasi is a plant that grows in earth like the rest—an ordinary common plant. . . ." She is preoccupied with the opposition between a cerebral, Western—and, she seems to be suggesting, a narrowly Benthamite—habit of mind and the more inclusive, the more ancient and ritualistic Indian sensibility. This is a theme which works its way in and out of *Possession,* in which the artist Valmiki is discovered and taken over by Lady Caroline Bell, a relationship which appears to offer itself as a tiny image of India's being taken over by Britain. Neither Valmiki nor Lady Caroline is irresistibly convincing. There is a certain put-up, slightly expected, air about them. The novel's merit lies in the clarity and point of the prose, in an unusual metaphorical capacity and in a gift for the nice discrimination of human motives.

Markandaya's failure as yet is to establish a context as impressively real and as sympathetically grasped as her central characters. She is very much more conscious in *A Handful of Rice* of the context, in this case an urban one, which nevertheless still suffers from a lack of solidity. Ravi, on the other hand, the central character, an educated peasant, is seen with the coolest and most accurate eye and realised with a very considerable creative skill. Nor does this novel offer any easy solution or any obvious superiority of one side of a spiritual dilemma over the other. The novel ends flatly and hopelessly but rightly in a way which suggests the achievement by the author of a bleaker and more necessary kind of wisdom.

—William Walsh

MARKFIELD, Wallace (Arthur)

Nationality: American. **Born:** Brooklyn, New York, 12 August 1926. **Education:** Abraham Lincoln High School, New York; Brooklyn College, B.A. 1947; New York University, 1948-50. **Family:** Married Anna May Goodman in 1949; one daughter. **Career:** Film critic, *New Leader,* New York, 1954-55; worked as a publicist and in public relations for several years. **Awards:** Guggenheim fellowship, 1965; National Endowment for the Arts grant, 1966. **Address:** c/o Bruccoli Clark, 2006 Sumter Street, Columbia, South Carolina 29201, U.S.A.

PUBLICATIONS

Novels

To an Early Grave. New York, Simon and Schuster, 1964; London, Cape, 1965.

Teitlebaum's Window. New York, Knopf, 1970; London, Cape, 1971.
You Could Live If They Let You. New York, Knopf, 1974.
Radical Surgery. New York, Bantam, 1991.

Short Story

Multiple Orgasms. Bloomfield Hills, Michigan, Bruccoli Clark, 1977.

Uncollected Short Stories

"Notes on the Working Day," in *Partisan Review* (New Brunswick, New Jersey), September-October 1946.
"Ph.D.," in *These Your Children,* edited by Harold U. Ribalow. New York, Beechhurst Press, 1952.
"The Patron," in *Partisan Review* (New Brunswick, New Jersey), January 1954.
"The Country of the Crazy Horse," in *Commentary* (New York), March 1958.
"The Big Giver," in *Midstream* (New York), Summer 1958.
"A Season of Change," in *Midstream* (New York), Autumn 1958.
"Eulogy for an American Boy," in *Commentary* (New York), June 1962.
"The Decline of Sholem Waldman," in *My Name Aloud,* edited by Harold U. Ribalow. New York, Yoseloff, 1969.
"Under the Marquee," in *Jewish-American Stories,* edited by Irving Howe. New York, New American Library, 1977.

*

Critical Studies: "Wallace Markfield Issue" of *Review of Contemporary Fiction* (Elmwood, Illinois), vol. 2, no. 1, 1982.

*   *   *

Philip Roth helped enormously, if inadvertently, to make people conscious of Wallace Markfield by referring to him in *Portnoy's Complaint.* "The novelist, what's his name, Markfield, has written in a story somewhere that until he was fourteen he believed 'aggravation' to be a Jewish word." Roth is referring to "The Country of the Crazy Horse," which sets the tone and milieu of New York Jewish life that carries through all of Markfield's work: the story begins in this way, "As the train began the long crawl under the tunnel to Brooklyn. . . ." Markfield's characters travel by subway or Volkswagen as they negotiate the impossible distances separating the boroughs of New York City and encounter the unique kind of aggravation which is part of their Jewish vantage point.

Stanley Edgar Hyman spoke of Markfield's first novel, *To an Early Grave,* as a more modest *Ulysses* and as "Mr. Bloom's Day in Brooklyn." The part of *Ulysses* it most nearly resembles is the sixth episode, "Hades." Joyce's "creaking carriage" has been replaced by a Volkswagen; Paddy Dignam has turned into a young writer named Leslie Braverman; and the four mourners who attend the Dignam funeral, Martin Cunningham, Leopold Bloom, John Power, and Simon Dedalus, give way to the more literary foursome of Morroe Rieff, Holly Levine, Felix Ottensteen, and Barnet Weiner. The Jew, Leopold Bloom, feels uncomfortable and unwanted among his Christian companions during the ride to the cemetery. Braverman and his mourners are Jews, as are the other characters who figure prominently in *To an Early Grave.* Their conversation on the way to the cemetery reflects the urban chic of New York

City, with its literary quarterlies, its literary critical conscience ("And he hissed softly, 'Trilling . . . Leavis . . . Ransom . . . Tate . . . Kazin . . . Chase . . .' and saw them, The Fathers, as though from a vast amphitheater, smiling at him, and he smiled at them"), its intellectual's obsession with popular culture, its carefully placed Yiddishisms.

Markfield has been fascinated by Joyce since his early story "Notes on the Working Day"; there are nods here toward the Joyce of *Finnegan's Wake* ("There Goes Everyman, Here Comes Everybody, the H.C.E. of our culture-lag") and toward the Joyce of *Ulysses* ("Leopold Bloom of the garment center" and "Leopold fat-belly Bloom"). When the Volkswagen of *To an Early Grave* arrives at a chapel, Braverman's four friends are treated to an elaborate funeral oration by a rabbi, which seems indeed to be the Jewish equivalent of the terrifying sermons which dominate chapter three of Joyce's *A Portrait of the Artist as a Young Man*. Here is a sample of the rabbi's language: "*That* on the Day of Judgment *in* the Valley of Jehoshaphat you'll be called up. *Either* to everlasting life *or* to such a shaming there's no imagining *how* terrible." Markfield manages to turn this into a wonderfully comic scene when the four mourners discover on examining the corpse that they have attended the wrong funeral. The novel ends with the most sympathetic of the four mourners, Morroe Rieff, finally breaking into tears—the only genuine tears shed in all of *To an Early Grave*—but the humorous and satirical effects in character and situation linger on; the comic survives the fleeting attempts at tragedy.

Teitlebaum's Window is the Brighton Beach-Coney Island version of the *Bildungsroman,* the Jewish boy, Simon Sloan, coming of age between the Depression years and the beginnings of World War II. *To an Early Grave* takes place during a single day, a Sunday, while *Teitlebaum's Window* covers a ten-year period. Joyce continues to be very much on Markfield's mind in this novel, especially in the use of certain impressionistic techniques and symbolic patterns. The narrative proceeds in a vastly complicated way, with traditional storytelling methods giving way frequently to diary notations, letters, classroom notes, and snatches of monologue. Many of the chapters begin with a single convoluted sentence which may go on for several pages: dating the events, reintroducing characters, referring to celebrities in the political, film and comic book worlds, and quoting the signs in Teitlebaum's store window (for example, "There will always be an England but there will not always be such a low low price on belly lox"). These long sentences act rather like the interchapters in Virginia Woolf's *The Waves*. The references to Teitlebaum's window offer the novel a symbolic design and supply the reader with a useful *point de repère*.

Teitlebaum's Window is a vintage American-Jewish novel. Here the mother-son confrontation is quite as convincingly realized as it was in *Portnoy's Complaint*. Markfield's Jewish mother, with her "dropped stomach," gargantuan stutter, constant aggravation, and dislocated syntax, is quite as believable in her own way as Sophie Portnoy.

You Could Live If They Let You continues Markfield's concern with Jewish subjects, but is less closely plotted than either of the previous novels. It offers what is probably, according to reviewers, another version of the Lenny Bruce saga, following closely on the heels of Albert Goldman's book *Ladies and Gentlemen, Lenny Bruce!!* and Bob Fosse's film *Lenny*. The Lenny Bruce character appears under the name Jules Farber and he has a Boswell in the person of Chandler Van Horton (whom one is tempted to think of as a non-Jewish Albert Goldman). The novel is dedicated to "the wisest men of our time—the stand-up comics" and indeed its nar-

rative procedures often remind us of the staccato verbal habits of a Lenny Bruce or a Woody Allen.

Farber's stand-up comic delivery favors the incongruous, the unexpected: 'Plehnt hah treee in Eretz Yisroel for Norman Vincent Peale"; "Readings from Kierkegaard, Kafka and Julia Child"; "it's Bobby Fischer's end game and Thomas Aquinas quoting from William Buckley and Bella Abzug buying two-and-a-half pounds of the best flanken. . . ." It is consistently irreverent as it takes on such formidable adversaries as the Anti-Defamation League, American rabbis, the Modern Language Association of America, and the world of popular culture. There is seemingly no end to the literary echoes and allusions: "cold, iron-hard epiphany which Farber favored"; "because every carhop and every checkout girl and every chippy and every cellar-club thumper is Molly Boom and Madeline *[sic]* Herzog." (Joyce is unmistakably a presence here as he was in Markfield's earlier fiction!)

We not only hear the voice of Farber, the "vertical monologist," but also that of Chandler Van Horton and that of Farber's sister, Lillian Federman. Farber's life story is eventually fleshed out in bits and pieces as we find out about his autistic son, Mitchell, and his Christ Therapist estranged wife, Marlene. We find Markfield's latest hero to have the same Jewish awareness and identity as the characters in *To an Early Grave* and *Teitlebaum's Window*. He shares with them the assurance that "there are certain things only a Jewish person can understand" and that "when you're in love the whole world is Jewish; and perhaps, in fact, even when you're not in love." We recognize the Markfield touch most emphatically when Farber proclaims: "I got a terminal case of aggravation."

—Melvin J. Friedman

MARKSON, David (Merrill)

Nationality: American. **Born:** Albany, New York, 20 December 1927. **Education:** Union College, Schenectady, New York, B.A. 1950; Columbia University, New York, M.A. 1952. **Military Service:** Served in the United States Army, 1946-48: staff sergeant. **Family:** Married Elaine Kretchmar in 1956; one daughter and one son. **Career:** Staff writer, Albany *Times-Union,* New York, 1944-46, 1948-50; rigger, Weyerhauser Timber Company, Molalla, Oregon, 1952; editor, Dell, publishers, 1953-54, and Lion Books, 1955-56, both New York; freelance writer, 1956-64; assistant professor of English, Long Island University, Brooklyn, New York, 1964-66. Since 1966 freelance writer; part-time lecturer, Columbia University, 1979-87. **Address:** 215 West 10th Street, New York, New York 10014, U.S.A.

PUBLICATIONS

Novels

Epitaph for a Tramp. New York, Dell, 1959; as *Fannin,* New York, Belmont, 1971.
Epitaph for a Dead Beat. New York, Dell, 1961.
Miss Doll, Go Home. New York, Dell, 1965.
The Ballad of Dingus Magee. Indianapolis, Bobbs Merrill, 1966; London, Blond, 1967.

Going Down. New York, Holt Rinehart, 1970.
Springer's Progress. New York, Holt Rinehart, 1977.
Wittgenstein's Mistress. Elmwood Park, Illinois, Dalkey Archive
Press, 1988; London, Cape, 1989.

Uncollected Short Stories

"Be All My Sins Remembered," and "Healthy Kate," both in *Review of Contemporary Fiction* (Elmwood Park, Illinois), Summer 1990.

Play

Screenplay: *Face to the Wind,* 1974.

Poetry

Collected Poems. Normal, Illinois, Dalkey Archive Press, 1993.

Other

Malcolm Lowry's Volcano: Myth, Symbol, Meaning. New York,
Times Books, 1978.

Editor, *Great Tales of Old Russia.* New York, Pyramid, 1963.

*

Critical Study: John Barth/David Markson issue of *Review of Contemporary Fiction* (Elmwood Park, Illinois), Summer 1990.

*   *   *

In a letter to David Markson, Malcolm Lowry wrote that "a book is a much harder proposition than a human being." This could be Markson's motto, as he found it easy to form friendships with well-known writers such as Lowry, Dylan Thomas, and Jack Kerouac in his youth, but only found widespread success for his own work with *Wittgenstein's Mistress,* a book rejected 54 times before its publication in 1988. His fiction falls into several distinct phases. First, there are three self-conscious paperback "entertainments," two of which feature detective Harry Fannin investigating murders in a bohemian setting. One example of the bookishness of these thrillers is an episode in *Epitaph for a Tramp,* when Fannin reads part of a literature paper in a student's apartment praising *The Recognitions* by William Gaddis as a significant work of American fiction: this at a time when few were aware of its existence, let alone its worth. There are also references for those in the know to Kerouac and Nabokov in *Epitaph for a Dead Beat,* and *Miss Doll, Go Home* experiments with multiple points of view in a way deliberately reminiscent of Faulkner. But despite the intertextual games, none of these early novels aspire to be anything other than good crime stories.

Markson's transition away from commercial genre fiction begins with *The Ballad of Dingus Magee,* a satire on the Western which received mixed notices. One reviewer thought that it was "stacked with enough sagebrush clichés to make it high Campfire," while Leslie Fiedler admired its inversion of stereotypes and well-crafted prose. Nineteen-year-old Magee's gunslinging encounters with cowards instead of tough guys and ugly saloon whores should have been ideal for the cinema, but even a Joseph Heller screenplay couldn't make up for the miscasting of Frank Sinatra in the

lead role of M.G.M.'s *Dirty Dingus Magee.* This came out in 1970, the year in which *Going Down* was published, a novel begun a decade earlier. Set in an imaginary Mexican village which echoes Lowry's Quauhnahuac, this close psychological study of three characters—Steve Chance, Fern Winters, and Lee Suffridge—is difficult fare. This is partly because of its extravagant diction, and its density of allusions to Shakespeare, Eliot and others. But the book also flirts with sensationalism, such as the opening image of a girl with a withered hand carrying a machete. What was widely overlooked, as the critics brandished their own sharp instruments, was the vim of this dark study of despair.

Markson's unique timbre became clearly audible in *Springer's Progress,* thanks to a major stylistic innovation. Paragraphs with only one or two sentences form short chapters with an average length of only a few pages, and this fractured structure acts as a corrective to Markson's leanings toward excess. Lucien Springer—a 47-year-old heavy drinker with writer's block—cheats on his wife Dana and chases the "sensuously cartilaginous" neck (and other zones) of Jessica Cornford. Springer's lust for language matches his libido, and he stuffs his head with "all sorts of quirky, disjunct quotations" as he tries to write at least "a phrase or three worth some lonely pretty girl's midnight underlinings." The title recalls Bunyan, and Springer is a comic Everyman who finds certain consolations as he saunters through the wilderness of this world.

Wittgenstein's Mistress adopted a similar style (clusters of short sentences) but a more tragic tone a decade or so later. This monologue represents the attempts of Kate, who believes that she is the last person alive, to rebuild a world with the baggage of misquotes and half-remembered cultural anecdotes which clutter her memory. Markson's original plan of presenting a science-fiction scenario—with a female Crusoe as the only survivor of a global catastrophe—was shelved in favor of a more open-ended situation, which foregrounds the central question of Kate's sanity as she typewrites messages to the void in her Long Island beach house. The best evidence comes from her distinctive fragmentation of thought, which is typical of the schizophrenic who tries to link together disparate facts on the basis of accidental similarity of sound or coincidence of sense. Her elementary propositions, to use a Wittgensteinian term, connect Cimabue to Giotto to Taddeo Gaddi and Perugino to Raphael to Giulio Romano as if she were playing intellectual dominoes. But the family resemblances between many of her ideas are faint: the numbers on the dominoes simply do not match. Furthermore, these language games seem to be a means of avoiding both the general horror of her situation, and the more personal sorrow associated with the death of her mother from cancer and her son from meningitis. Markson's achievement in this book is to marry his prodigious literary knowledge with a more minimalist approach suggested to him by Lowry in one of his last letters: "Do you know which stars are which and what bird is flying over your head and what flower blossoming? If you don't the anguish of *not* knowing is a very valid field for the artist."

—Barry Lewis

MARLATT, Daphne

Nationality: Canadian (originally Maylasian, immigrated to Canada in 1951). **Born:** Daphne Shirley Buckle, Melbourne, Australia, 11

July 1942. **Education:** University of British Columbia, Vancouver, 1960-64, B.A.; University of Indiana, Bloomington, 1964-67, M.A. 1968. **Family:** Married G. Alan Marlatt in 1963 (divorced 1971), one son; companion of 1) Roy Kinooka, 1975-82; 2) Betsy Warland, 1982-94; 3) Bridget MacKenzie, since 1994. **Career:** Has taught at University of British Columbia, University of Victoria, University of Saskatchewan, University of Western Ontario, Simon Fraser University, University of Calgary, Mount Royal College, University of Alberta, McMaster University, University of Manitoba; second vice chair of the Writers' Union of Canada, 1987-88. **Awards:** MacMillan and Brissenden award for creative writing, Canada Council award. **Member:** Founding member of West Coast Women and Words Society. **Address:** c/o The Writers' Union of Canada, 24 Ryerson Avenue, Toronto, Ontario M5T 2P3, Canada.

PUBLICATIONS

Novels

Ana Historic. Toronto, Coach House, 1988; London, Women's Press, 1990.

Poetry

Frames of a Story. Toronto, Ryerson, 1968.
leaf leaf/s. Los Angeles, Black Sparrow, 1969.
Rings. Vancouver, Vancouver Community Press, 1971.
Vancouver Poems. Toronto, Coach House, 1972.
Steveston, photographs by Robert Minden. Vancouver, Talonbooks, 1974.
Our Lives. Carrboro, North Carolina, Truck Press, 1975.
The Story, She Said. Vancouver, Monthly Press, 1977.
What Matters: Writing 1968-70. Toronto, Coach House, 1980.
Net Work: Selected Writing, edited by Fred Wah. Vancouver, Talonbooks, 1980.
here & there. Lantzville, Island Press, 1981.
How to Hug a Stone. Winnipeg, Turnstone, 1983.
Touch to My Tongue. Edmonton, Longspoon, 1984.
Double Negative, with Betsy Warland. Charlottetown, Gynergy Books, 1988.
Salvage. Red Deer, Red Deer College Press, 1991.
Ghost Works. Edmonton, NeWest Press, 1993.
Two Women in a Birth, with Betsy Warland. Toronto, Guernica, 1994.

Play

Radio Play: *Steveston,* 1976.

Other

Zócalo. Toronto, Coach House, 1977.

Editor, *Lost Language: Selected Poems of Maxine Gadd.* Toronto, Coach House Press, 1982.
Editor, *Telling It: Women and Language Across Cultures.* Vancouver, Press Gang, 1990.

Translator, *Mauve,* by Nicole Brossard. Montreal, Nouvelle Barre du Jour/Writing, 1985.

*

Manuscript Collection: The National Library of Canada, Ottawa, Ontario.

Critical Studies: *"I Quote Myself"; or, A Map of Mrs. Reading: Re-siting "Women's Place" in "Anna Historic"* by Manina Jones, Toronto, University of Toronto Press, 1993; *The Country of Her Own Body: Ana Historic,* by Frank Davey, Toronto, University of Toronto Press, 1993; *Translation A to Z: Notes on Daphne Marlatt's "Ana Historic"* by Pamela Banting, Edmonton, NeWest Press, 1991.

Daphne Marlatt comments:

Although I think of myself as a poet first, I began writing both fiction and lyric poems in the early 1960s. My collections of poetry have usually had a loose narrative shape as I tend to write in sequences, or "books." As an immigrant, I'd long held the ambition to write an historical novel about Vancouver, but *Ana Historic* actually critiqued and broke open the genre, as it also increased my fascination with the potential for openness in the novel form. Influenced by the development of "fiction/theory" in Quebec by feminist writers there, I see open structures combined with a folding or echoing of women's experiences in different time periods as a way to convey more of the unwritten or culturally overwritten aspects of what it means to be alive as a woman today.

*   *   *

With the arguable exception of *Zócalo,* a Mexican travel memoir she wrote in 1977, *Ana Historic* of 1988 is Daphne Marlatt's first novel. Heavily influenced by the French feminism filtering through Quebec women's writing at the time she wrote it, *Ana Historic* continues to excite attention from feminist critics interested in the politics of language, history, colonialism, gender, race, and sexuality.

Ana Historic is really two novels in one. In the course of doing historical research in the Vancouver City Archives for her professor husband, Richard, protagonist Annie Anderson discovers two short references to a Mrs. Richards, who comes to Vancouver in 1873 to teach school. Obsessed by the way official history erases Mrs. Richards's life, Annie begins writing a novel that imagines the life Ana Richards (Annie supplies a first name for her) might have had. This novel becomes *Ana Historic*'s embedded narrative. Annie's writing of this novel continually interrupts itself with reminiscences of her mother, Ina, now dead, and metacritical reflections on the process of writing itself. Underneath all of this reflective activity, in the narrative present, Annie moves slowly but steadily away from her relationship with her husband toward a sexual relationship with a woman named Zoe.

Only recently have critics focused on the lesbian aspects of Marlatt's work. Initial criticism of *Ana Historic* emphasized formal continuities with Marlatt's earlier writing. Certainly the etymological play in the text shows the same careful attention to language that one finds in her poetry. This poetic wordplay reaches its height in *Touch To My Tongue,* a book of prose poems, and the critical essay published along with it, "musing with mothertongue." In "musing," Marlatt follows Julia Kristeva in theorizing language as a living, maternal body of expressive potential that has been bastardized by patriarchy's insistence on singularity, hierarchy, and mastery. In *Ana Historic,* Marlatt demonstrates how patriarchal language excludes women from the dominant narrative of official history, but through both Annie's embedded narrative and the novel's etymological wordplay, she also shows a way in which women might be written back into history.

Feminist critics were swift to pick up on *Ana Historic* as an empowering story for women. But just as the term "woman" grew increasingly complicated by vectors of race, class, and sexuality at the end of the 1980s, so did readings of Marlatt's fiction gain in complexity. Rather than focusing on Annie as a literary Everywoman, critics have begun to examine the relationships among all the characters in the novel. Particularly important to this inquiry is the status of the Native Canadian characters in the embedded narrative, because it is against their silence that Ana Richards—and, by extension, white Canadian women generally—understand their particular subject positions. In turn, the examination of native figures in the novel has opened up the possibility for considering Ina's colonial background and Annie's uneasy Canadian identity.

This recognition of specific subject positions contextualizes the lesbian ending of the story. Although *Ana Historic* is perhaps most easily read as a lesbian-feminist utopia that ultimately abandons history in favor of imagination, a critical reader can see in the novel an argument for rethinking gender, historically and imaginatively, in conjunction with race, sexuality, colonialism, and post-colonialism. It is such scope that makes Marlatt's fiction significant.

—Heather Zwicker

MARS-JONES, Adam

Nationality: British. **Born:** London, 26 October 1954. **Education:** Cambridge University, B.A. 1976, M.A. 1978. **Career:** Film critic and reviewer, the *Independent,* London. **Awards:** Maugham award, 1982. **Agent:** Peters Fraser and Dunlop, 503-504 The Chambers, Chelsea Harbour, Lots Road, London SW10 0XF. **Address:** 42B Calabria Road, Highburn, London N5 1HU, England.

PUBLICATIONS

Novels

The Waters of Thirst. London, Faber, 1993; New York, Knopf, 1994.

Short Stories

Lantern Lecture and Other Stories. London, Faber, 1981; as *Fabrications,* New York, Knopf, 1981.
The Darker Proof: Stories from a Crisis, with Edmund White. London, Faber, 1987.
Monopolies of Loss. London, Faber, 1992; New York, Knopf, 1993.

Other

Venus Envy. London, Chatto and Windus, 1990.

Editor, *Mae West Is Dead: Recent Lesbian and Gay Fiction.* London, Faber, 1983.

*   *   *

Few writers have established a reputation on as slight an output as Adam Mars-Jones. In the decade since *Lantern Lecture* (comprising three prose pieces totaling under 200 pages), Mars-Jones, though active as an arts journalist, has published only half a book of short stories, *The Darker Proof* with Edmund White, where he abandoned the experimentalism that had distinguished his first collection.

The opening and title piece of *Lantern Lecture* outlines the life of eccentric landowner Philip Yorke. The story is told in the present tense in a series of two-paragraph sections. In the opening section, Philip's christening is described in the first paragraph and his Memorial Service in the second: "The fame of his house and of his own appearances on television attracts a large crowd. The overflow is awkwardly accommodated in the adjoining Church Hall, by chance the site of Philip's last magic-lantern lecture only weeks before his death." In fact, Mars-Jones's prose sections are the linguistic equivalent of lantern-slides. About halfway through, the reader becomes aware that the order of the pair of paragraphs in each section has been reversed with the first paragraph about his later life and the second about his earlier life, so that the second paragraph of the final section reproduces the first paragraph of the opening section with the odd significant change.

The second prose piece is entitled "Hoosh-Mi," which we later learn "is a nonsense word coined by Princess Margaret as a child, and means (as a noun) mixed food of any sort, or by extension . . . 'disorderly jumble . . .' small" The piece opens with an off-course rabies-infected American hoary bat infecting a dog, who turns out to be no less than a royal corgi and who infects Queen Elizabeth II. Her condition becomes apparent on "walkabout" in Australia when she attacks a sightseer's hat; decline through hydrophobia follows until Prince Philip authorizes euthanasia. A key element in this *tour de force* is the interpolation in the narrative of a speech by Dr. John Bull on "Royalty and the Unreal" at the Annual Dinner of the Republican Society. Thus the absurdity of royalty is shown both in theory and practice in this subversive tale.

The third prose piece, "Bathpool Park," focuses on the trial of Donald Neilson, the so-called "Black Panther," who after a series of post office robberies involving three murders kidnapped 17-year-old Lesley Whittle of whose murder he was also convicted. (Mars-Jones acknowledges indebtedness to Harry Hawkes's *The Capture of the Black Panther.*) Mars-Jones intercuts his description of the behavior in court of all those concerned, including the insignificant marshal-cum-judge's-social-secretary, with reconstructions of Neilson's crimes. In invented dialogue between the two barristers, after Neilson's sentencing, Mars-Jones suggests possibilities that could not emerge in court through the inevitably flawed working of both legal procedure and the preceding police investigation, in turn handicapped by the press. This is the most ambitious of the three pieces in *Lantern Lecture:* while maintaining the witty, dissecting style of the two previous pieces, Mars-Jones must encompass the suffering caused by Neilson, which indeed he achieves.

It's all the more disappointing, therefore, that when Mars-Jones wrote four stories about AIDS sufferers and those involved with them—lovers, friends, "buddies," families etc.—in *The Darker Proof,* he jettisoned his experimentalism. Possibly, he opted here for conventional techniques to write as vividly as possible about a few individuals, whereas in "Bathpool Park" the focus was not on individuals but the judicial machine.

The opening story "Slim" is a 10-page interior monologue by a man with AIDS about his "buddy," that is his helper from "the

Trust," presumably the Terrence Higgins Trust. In his state of permanent exhaustion, he imagines a World War II ration-book "only instead of an allowance for the week of butter or cheese or sugar, my coupons say One Hour of Social Life, One Shopping Expedition, One Short Walk. I hoard them, and I spend them wisely."

The other three stories are all in the third person, longer and plotted. "An Executor" follows the "buddy" Gareth's attempts to fulfill the charge laid on him by the dying Charles—whose moment of death in hospital we witness—to find a suitable recipient for his leather clothes. "A Small Spade" describes a weekend spent in Brighton by schoolteacher Bernard and his lover Neil, the young HIV-positive hairdresser from New Zealand. Because a bad splinter in Neil's fingernail "like a small spade" takes them to out-patients, Bernard fully comprehends "A tiled corridor filled with doctors and nurses opened off every room he would ever share with Neil."

All the main characters in these three stories are deeply sympathetic, unlike architect Roger in "The Brake," who ranges across America as well as London fully exploiting his sex-appeal in search of his perfect lover, while smoking heavily, taking drugs and overeating. The unfortunate Larry "became very attached." Though warned by a doctor to "put the brake on," Roger carries on until a faulty heart-valve forces a change of life-style, roughly coinciding with the beginning of the AIDS crisis: "he made his accommodation. In the end, he found it easier to give up men than to give up the taste, even the smell, of fried bacon."

It's ironic, given Mars-Jones's fully justified attack on the tabloid press in "An Executor," that in his stories AIDS appears to be exclusively confined to Western gay men. And Western gay men with a certain level of income. This is not the world of the terminally ill struggling along on inadequate Social Security benefits. Given that the book is subtitled "Stories from a Crisis," it seems fair to harbor these worries—though the subtitle may have been the publisher's rather than the author's choice.

Albeit devoid of the exciting experimental structures of *Lantern Lecture,* the same basic strengths of Mars-Jones's writing come through in *The Darker Proof.* The humor, fully retained in the later stories, springs from an awareness of the maximum possible motivations and interpretations of any action, and his subject matter of whatever kind, is imbued with absolute precision.

—Val Warner

MARSHALL, Owen

Nationality: New Zealander. **Born:** Owen Marshall Jones in Te Kuiti, 17 August 1941. **Education:** Timaru Boy's High School; University of Canterbury, Christchurch, 1960-63, M.A. (honours) in history 1963; Christchurch Teachers College, teaching diploma, 1964. **Family:** Married Jacqueline Hill in 1965; two daughters. **Career:** Deputy rector, Waitaki Boys High School, Oamaru, 1983-85; deputy principal, Craighead Diocesan School, Timaru, 1986-91. Since 1993, tutor, Aoraki Polytechnic, Timaru. Literary fellow, University of Canterbury, 1981. **Awards:** Lillian Ida Smith award, 1986, 1988; Queen Elizabeth II Arts Council scholarship, 1987; *Evening Standard* award, for short story, 1987; American Express award, for short story, 1987; New Zealand Literary Fund scholarship in letters, 1988, and Distinction award, 1989; University of

Otago's Robert Burns fellowship, 1992. **Agent:** Glenys Bean, 15 Elizabeth Street, Freeman's Bay, Auckland. **Address:** 10 Morgan's Road, Glenwood, Timaru, New Zealand.

PUBLICATIONS

Novel

A Many Coated Man. Dunedin, Longacre, 1995.

Short Stories

Supper Waltz Wilson and Other New Zealand Stories. Christchurch, Pegasus Press, 1979.
The Master of Big Jingles and Other Stories. Dunedin, McIndoe, 1982.
The Day Hemingway Died. Dunedin, McIndoe, 1984.
The Lynx Hunter and Other Stories. Dunedin, McIndoe, 1987.
The Divided World: Selected Stories. Dunedin, McIndoe, 1989.
Tomorrow We Save the Orphans. Dunedin, McIndoe, 1992.
The Ace of Diamonds Gang. Dunedin, McIndoe, 1993.

Play

Radio Play: *An Indirect Geography,* 1989.

*

Critical Studies: "The Naming of Parts: Owen Marshall" by Vincent O'Sullivan, in *Sport 3* (Wellington), 1989; *Barbed Wire and Mirrors: Essays on New Zealand Prose* by Lawrence Jones, Dunedin, University of Otago Press, 1987; *In the Same Room* edited by Alley and Williams, Auckland, Auckland University Press, 1992.

*   *   *

In an essay in *Sport* Owen Marshall has written of his growing interest in books during his childhood and of his early attempts at writing, including two unpublished novels. He turned to the short story form in the mid-1970s and published his first piece in the New Zealand *Listener* in 1977. It was the beginning of a success which has been sustained since then, and which has gained him recognition as one of the most substantial short story writers in present-day New Zealand.

By 1979 he was able to present a collection of 14 stories to the Christchurch publisher Pegasus Press. *Supper Waltz Wilson and Other New Zealand Stories* was financed by the author in a venture well-justified by the publication's success and by its favourable reviews. Frank Sargeson's praise helped confirm Marshall's reputation as an important new writer, and from then on his stories began to appear regularly in New Zealand periodicals and anthologies of contemporary fiction as well as being broadcast by Radio New Zealand. Three further books made Marshall's work widely available over these years: *The Master of the Big Jingles, The Day Hemingway Died,* and *The Lynx Hunter.* These were followed by *The Divided World,* a retrospective selection of his work in 1989, and more recently a new collection, *Tomorrow We Save the Orphans,* and a further selection, *The Ace of Diamonds Gang and Other Stories.*

Marshall's stories fit easily into a tradition of realism that has long been one of the strengths of the New Zealand short story; they serve, moreover, to extend and enhance that tradition. The narratives frequently describe a middle or lower-middle class New Zealand world, with its Anglo Saxon parameters of conventionality. It is a world that is frequently small town or rural in its perspectives, and masculine in its point of view, though Marshall treats his female characters with more subtlety and sensitivity than has traditionally been associated with male New Zealand writers. In some of his most successful stories—the title stories of his first two volumes, for example, or in "Kenneth's Friend," "Valley Day," and "The Paper Parcel"—his characters recall childhood and adolescence, the rites of passage, and the awareness of an impinging world that the young have to take into account. There are similar cool recognitions in his stories that tell of young adults who perceive the realities of an older generation's experiences of life, as in "The Day Hemingway Died," "A Poet's Dream of Amazons," and the superb study of a son's vision of his dying father—"The Seed Merchant." In Marshall's fictional world the sense of loss or of poignancy that habitually accompanies such awareness is not allowed to deteriorate into sentimentality. Indeed, Marshall is distinctive among the New Zealand writers who have treated such themes for his quiet ironic detachment, and for the clear-eyed recognitions (akin to those of his literary predecessor Maurice Duggan) of inevitability and common culpability in his little scenes from the human comedy.

Characterisation, perhaps even more than plot, is of principal importance to Marshall, and his proclivity for first person narration allows him both the opportunities for narrative insights, and the possibilities of unconscious ironic self-revelation on the part of his protagonists. He handles dialogue fluently and has a sharp ear for the cadences and nuances of the local idiom, but it is perhaps in his settings, of places and people alike, that New Zealand readers most clearly recognise an indigenous writer of considerable ability. Sargeson very early saw that Marshall could move us to "experience an environment which has mysteriously become a character in its own right"; the idea is as valid in Marshall's latest work as in his earliest.

Marshall's reputation still rests on his work as a short story writer at the present time, though his first novel, A Many Coated Man, written when he held the Robert Burns fellowship at the University of Otago in 1992, was published in 1995. A novel that is both wry and tragicomic, it looks at the politics and society of a New Zealand some years into the future from our own time when immense social and economic changes are reconstructing the nation and its sense of identity. It reveals many of the skills that have made Marshall's stories so popular, though tonal unevennness and a sense that the writer is possibly less assured in writing fiction on this scale, have meant a muted critical response to the book thus far.

A literary tradition of strength and vitality in the field of the short story has distinguished New Zealand writing since the late 1930s, and Marshall is clearly one of the most important contemporary exponents of the form. The last 10 years have seen an increasing interest in the postmodern ludic invention in prose; some of New Zealand's best new writers have pursued this interest, but Marshall has to a considerable extent chosen to remain within an older tradition of realism that gives priority to characterisation and plot narration. Though some of the stories in The Lynx Hunter and the title story of The Divided World show an increasing preparedness to work experimentally with new forms and with nonrealist modes of presentation, Marshall is still primarily a teller of tales. His writings seek to remind us of the known and the forgotten alike; their narrative vision suggest the wish to reveal sympathies that are never sentimental, seldom other than compassionate, and always couched in the language of one who is thoroughly sensitive to the power of words.

—W.S. Broughton

MARSHALL, Paule

Nationality: American. **Born:** Paule Burke, Brooklyn, New York, 9 April 1929. **Education:** Brooklyn College, B.A. (cum laude) 1953 (Phi Beta Kappa); Hunter College, New York, 1955. **Family:** Married 1) Kenneth E. Marshall in 1950 (divorced 1963), one son; 2) Nourry Menard in 1970. **Career:** Librarian, New York Public Library; staff writer, Our World, New York, 1953-56; taught creative writing at Yale University, New Haven, Connecticut, Columbia University, New York, University of Iowa, Iowa City, and University of California, Berkeley, 1984. **Awards:** Guggenheim fellowship, 1961; Rosenthal award, 1962; Ford grant, for drama, 1964; National Endowment for the Arts grant, 1966, 1977; Creative Artists Public Service fellowship, 1974; Before Columbus Foundation award, 1984. **Address:** 407 Central Park West, New York, New York 10025, U.S.A.

PUBLICATIONS

Novels

Brown Girl, Brownstones. New York, Random House, 1959; London, W.H. Allen, 1960.
The Chosen Place, The Timeless People. New York, Harcourt Brace, 1969; London, Longman, 1970.
Praisesong for the Widow. New York, Putnam, and London, Virago Press, 1983.
Daughters. New York, Atheneum, 1991; London, Serpent's Tail, 1992.

Short Stories

Soul Clap Hands and Sing. New York, Atheneum, 1961; London, W.H. Allen, 1962.
Reena and Other Stories. Old Westbury, New York, Feminist Press, 1983; as Merle and Other Stories, London, Virago Press, 1985.

Uncollected Short Story

"To Da-duh, in Memoriam," in Afro-American Writing 2, edited by Richard Long and Eugenia Collier. New York, New York University Press, 1972.

*

Critical Study: Bridging the Americas: The Literature of Paule Marshall, Toni Morrison, and Gayl Jones by Stelamaris Coser, Philadelphia, Temple University Press, 1994.

* * *

In "From the Poets in the Kitchen," her contribution to "The Making of a Writer" series in the *New York Times Book Review* (9 January 1983), Paule Marshall declares the sources of her art to be the expressive talk she heard as a young girl among her mother's friends as they sat around a table in the basement kitchen of her Brooklyn brownstone home. For these immigrants from Barbados, language was therapy for the tribulations they endured as invisible citizens of a new land—invisible because black, female, and foreign. But talk was more than that, too, for the West Indian dialect, syntactically unique and metaphorically inventive, sustained these women whom Marshall characterizes, in the words of James Weldon Johnson's famous poem, as "unknown bards" in the nurturing culture of home while in exile. In their native everyday speech Marshall's forebears, mothers, and kin in Marshall's mind and imagination, affirmed themselves in the world through spontaneously creative use of the idiom, which bears in its forms and sound the conception of life, the philosophy, that embodies an Afro-Caribbean heritage. Finding the means for later generations to emulate the kitchen poets she knew in her childhood is the burden of Marshall's fiction.

Marshall's "unknown bards" of reminiscence experienced their place in an affirmative culture naturally, because after all one hardly needs to reflect upon the significance involved in the intimate possession of language, but the protagonists of her fiction must struggle with necessities that either sever their connection to an affirmative culture or encourage them to find identity in the values of individualism. Her first published story, "The Valley Between" (1954), relates the contest between a wife's wish to return to school to prepare for a career and her husband's resentment of the apparent departure from a conventional woman's role. The conflict encodes Marshall's own experience in an early marriage while also restricting its significance through the fact that the fictional characters are white. *Brown Girl, Brownstones,* her first novel, can also be read as partly autobiographical, but in this case the author's story is inserted into a typified set of circumstances. The book traces the maturation of young Selina Boyce beyond a loving father, whose incapacity for the get-ahead life of New York City issues in romantic dreams of a big-paying job or self-sufficiency on two acres of inherited land home in Barbados, and beyond, as well, the equally deadening illusions of her mother who sacrifices her being to the successful Bajan's goal of property ownership. Selina's autonomy is welcome, except that Marshall's pleasing rendition of Barbados English and folk-say, definitely a version of the kitchen talk of the instinctive poets she knew in her childhood, makes it clear that Selina's necessary sacrifice of community tragically likens her to the mass of other rootless Americans.

Each of the four stories in *Soul Clap Hands and Sing,* Marshall's second published volume of fiction, shows the ways individual animation is replaced in modern life by a protective but deadening routine. Whether in "Barbados," "Brooklyn," "British Guiana," or "Brazil" an aged man discovers that in seeking ease he has in fact lost the surety of selfhood. Yet, despite these protagonists it is not entirely correct to present the accomplishment of *Soul Clap Hands and Sing* as solely the tales of wasted men, since in the construction of the plot for each narrative Marshall sets up a relationship with a woman more vital than the man to develop the point of the Yeatsian epigraph, that the older man has become "a paltry thing." Thus the geographic breadth given to the condition of modern rootlessness by the range of settings is accompanied in each story by evidence of Marshall's continuing interest in the distinctive roles women can assume in society. A later story, "Reena" (1962), re-

turns the theme of the unique concerns of female identity to the center of the narrative, where it remains for all of Marshall's later work. "Reena" investigates the matrimonial and political choices made by an educated black woman, using the occasion of a wake for Reena's aunt as opportunity to frame the matter of self-definition within consideration of the continuities and differences between two generations of women. "Reena" together with "To Da-duh, in Memoriam," the story of a nine-year-old girl exchanging boasts about the size and energy of New York City for an introduction to the flora and fauna of Barbados from her grandmother, establish the focus for Marshall's mature fiction: the importance of lineage in the lives of women on the cusp of historical change.

Her first major novel, *The Chosen Place, The Timeless People,* reveals that focus to be profoundly political as well as intensely personal. The book records the encounter of an American research team with the "backward" people inhabiting Bournehills, the wasted corner of an island resembling perhaps Barbados but signifying the entire Caribbean. Marshall sympathetically portrays both aliens and natives in terms of the motives of guilt and frustration by which they characterize their own lives. As Merle Kinbona, a woman of Bournehills whose residence in England included schooling in painfully exploitive relationships along with professional training, assumes predominance in the narrative personal drama is translated into general social meaning. A native of the island despite her "modernization," Merle shares the timelessness of the people to whom the experience of slavery and particularly the momentary success of the rebellion of Cuffee Ned remain palpably present. On a level as deep as culture and as unavailable to measurement as the subconscious, they know that technological change is nothing compared to the redemption presaged in Cuffee's rebellion, and in their integrity they will settle for nothing less. The politics of the novel are conservative in a way that is unknown in parliaments or organized parties. This conservative politics grows from knowledge that the configurations of character and the complex relationships of love or resentment gain their shape from historical cultures.

With *Praisesong for the Widow* Marshall tentatively completes the exploration of black women's relationship to their history. Having begun with Selina Boyce, a young adult intent on gaining personal independence before all else, and then continuing with the narrative of Merle Kinbona, who seeks a viable cause beyond herself in middle age, Marshall carries her study forward with Avey Johnson, the 64-year-old widow who leaves her friends on a cruise ship for reasons she cannot articulate though they are as compelling as a subconscious drive. Juxtaposing memory of the past with present setting, the narrative recalls Avey's relationship to her great aunt who brought alive the tale of slaves who had left Ibo Landing, South Carolina, to walk home across the sea to Africa, and traces the course of Avey's marriage to Jay, who with respectability assumed the proper name of Jerome and the distant manner of a man mistaking status for integrity. Avey understood the value of middle-class security, but the loss of joy and spontaneity subsequent to its attainment has left her bereft in age. The sense of loss originates as an individual's trouble, its remedy lies in regaining a sense of collectivity; therefore, the later sections of the novel are structured around the symbolic rituals of a journey to Carriacou and the ceremonies of the blacks who annually return to the island to "beg pardon" of their ancestors and to dance the "nation dances" that survive from their African origins. By these means *Praisesong for the Widow* leads Avey through her crisis of integrity so that she can re-experience the connection to collective history she once felt as a child, reclaim her original name of Avatara (for which Avey is the diminutive), and join the movements of traditional dance that link her in body and spirit to her heritage.

Unquestionably more deliberate in its aesthetic form than the talk of the West Indian women in her childhood kitchen, Paule Marshall's stories share qualities with that speech while also distinguishing itself as markedly literary. Full of rich detail, the best of her writing brings character and incident alive in the vivid manner of popular tale telling. Informed, however, by a reflexivity that is absent from the creations of "unknown bards," the tales Marshall makes into novels reach beyond simulation of folk art, beyond the surface realism, nostalgia, or elementary denunciations of modernization that would constitute the easy and simple responses to historical transformation of traditional culture. Instead Marshall makes complex literature of the proposition that every woman needs to gain the power to speak the language of her elder kinswomen.

—John M. Reilly

MARSTEN, Richard. *See* **HUNTER, Evan.**

MASON, Bobbie Ann

Nationality: American. **Born:** Mayfield, Kentucky, 1 May 1940. **Education:** The University of Kentucky, Lexington, 1958-62, B.A. 1962; State University of New York, Binghamton, M.A. 1966; University of Connecticut, Storrs, 1972. **Family:** Married Roger B. Rawlings in 1969. **Career:** Writer, Mayfield *Messenger,* 1960, and Ideal Publishers, New York; contributor to numerous magazines including *Movie Star, Movie Life,* and *T.V. Star Parade,* 1962-63; assistant professor of English, Mansfield State College, Pennsylvania, 1972-79. Since 1980, contributor to *The New Yorker.* **Awards:** Hemingway award, 1983; National Endowment award, 1983; Pennsylvania Arts Council grant, 1983, 1989; Guggenheim fellowship, 1984. **Agent:** Amanda Urban, International Creative Management, 40 West 57th Street, New York, New York 10019, U.S.A.

PUBLICATIONS

Novels

In Country. New York, Harper, 1985; London, Chatto and Windus, 1986.
Spence + Lila. New York, Harper, 1988; London, Chatto and Windus, 1989.
Feather Crowns. New York, Harper, and London, Chatto and Windus, 1993.

Short Stories

Shiloh and Other Stories. New York, Harper, 1982; London, Chatto and Windus, 1985.

Love Life. New York, Harper, and London, Chatto and Windus, 1989.

Uncollected Short Story

"With Jazz," in *New Yorker,* 26 February 1990.

Other

The Girl Sleuth: A Feminist Guide to the Bobbsey Twins, Nancy Drew, and Their Sisters. New York, Feminist Press, 1975.
Nabokov's Garden: A Nature Guide to Ada. Ann Arbor, Michigan, Ardis, 1976.

*

Manuscript Collection: University of Kentucky, Lexington.

Critical Studies: "Making Over or Making Off: The Problem of Identity in Bobbie Ann Mason's Short Fiction" in *Southern Literary Journal* (Chapel Hill, North Carolina), Spring 1986, and "Private Rituals: Coping with Changes in the Fiction of Bobbie Ann Mason" in *Midwest Quarterly* (Pittsburg, Kansas), Winter 1987, both by Albert E. Wilhelm; "Finding One's History: Bobbie Ann Mason and Contemporary Southern Literature" in *Southern Literary Journal* (Chapel Hill, North Carolina), Spring 1987, and "Never Stop Rocking: Bobbie Ann Mason and Rock-and-Roll" in *Mississippi Quarterly* (Jackson), Winter 1988-89, both by Robert H. Brinkmeyer, Jr.; "The Function of Popular Culture in Bobbie Anne Mason's *Shiloh and Other Stories* and *In Country*" by Leslie White, in *Southern Quarterly* (Hattiesburg, Mississippi), Summer 1988; "Bobbie Ann Mason: Artist and Rebel" by Michael Smith, in *Kentucky Review* (Lexington), Autumn 1988; "Downhome Feminists in *Shiloh and Other Stories*" by G.O. Morphew, in *Southern Literary Journal* (Chapel Hill, North Carolina), Spring 1989.

*   *   *

Despite some notable exceptions—Toni Morrison, Louise Erdich, the late Raymond Carver—recent American fiction is still primarily concerned with white, middle-class people of a certain education. To some extent this is inevitable, for it is the background of most writers, and writers tend to write what they know.

The distinction of Bobbie Ann Mason's writing is her characters, who do not fit this usual mold. Gone are East and West Coast urban professionals; Mason's fiction—three novels and two collections of short stories—is full of people who have never left western Kentucky, never been to a big city, for whom a trip to the shopping mall in Paducah is a highlight. They are usually poor and uneducated. This does not mean they are unaware, however; although they may not be able to articulate their thoughts, characters in Mason's work are always sensing problems and coming to understandings about their lives. Mason's great strength is her ability to give a voice to people who do not have a strong grasp of words, and to do so without condescension.

Her style is unadorned and unobtrusive, much the way her characters speak and think. Nothing really outlandish or earth-shattering happens. Mason's recent short novel *Spence + Lila* is "simply" about an older woman having operations to remove a cancerous breast and unclog hardened neck arteries. She goes to the hospital, she has the operations, she has visitors, she goes home again. But the novel is not "simple"—it explores family relationships and feelings that have been taken for granted until this crisis. The question of articulating feelings arises—whether it is necessary, whether words can ever adequately describe feelings. With his wife hospitalized, her prospects for survival uncertain, Spence wrestles with how to express his feelings for her.

> At times there is no way on earth he can say what he feels. . . . He knows what he *wants* to say, and he imagines saying it to Lila, but it takes guts to . . . lavish loving feelings on someone. If only he could, he would say, "Lila, you and me have been together a long time, and we've been through a lot together." He laughs to himself. How phony that would be. It sounds like something on television. He has never said those things because he would feel as though he were speaking lines. Real love requires something else, something deeper. And sometimes a feeling just goes without saying.

Mason's stories and novels are littered with culture-specific references—to name-brand products, fast-food restaurants, stores, pop music, and above all, television shows. *The Phil Donahue Show, Mork and Mindy, M*A*S*H, WKRP in Cincinnati*—all are part of a common culture central to people's lives. Characters constantly turn to television as a point of reference and comparison. In "Old Things" a photograph of a scene from *Charlie's Angels* takes its place among family pictures in a photo album. In "Midnight Magic" couples compare themselves to couples appearing on *The Newlywed Game*.

Television is particularly prevalent in *In Country*, probably Mason's best-known work, particularly since it was made into a film (such as her characters might go to see). The book concerns Sam, a teenager whose father died in the Vietnam War before she was born, and Sam's Uncle Emmett, a Vietnam vet. Sam's mother has remarried and moved to Lexington, but Sam has remained in her old home with Emmett, who ostensibly looks after her—though Sam often feels it is the other way around. Both are obsessed in different ways with the Vietnam War—Emmett trying to come to terms with his memories, Sam wanting to understand more about the war that killed her father and thus altered her own life.

Every night Sam and Emmett religiously watch reruns of *M*A*S*H*, the half-hour comedy-drama set during the Korean War. For both *M*A*S*H* is a reflection of the conflicts they face, and they depend on it as a standard by which they measure their own concerns, behavior, and ability to cope. In a key scene Sam confronts Emmett with the brutality of the war she has learned about first-hand from reading her father's journal. As Emmett tries to explain the attitudes men had to take on in order to survive in such a bewildering and hostile territory, he seems about to break down, and Sam compares his behavior with that of a character in a particular *M*A*S*H* episode: "She waited. She thought he was going to come out with some suppressed memories of events as dramatic as that one that caused Hawkeye to crack up in the final episode of *M*A*S*H*. But nothing came." Sam continues encouraging Emmett to describe some of his memories of the war, and when he finally does she immediately relates them to TV movies and documentaries about Vietnam that she has seen, to process his information into something more familiar to her experience. Through television she attempts to bridge the gap between her own limited experience and the wider world.

Television and other pop culture references can also bridge the gap between characters and readers. The assumption that we too have seen that last episode of *M*A*S*H* brings us that much closer to the lives of Sam and Emmett. Unfortunately such aesthetic assumptions do not always translate well over space and time. Mason's references to popular culture are so specific that they may become obsolete very quickly. Will Bruce Springsteen still be considered a hero in 20 years' time? Will people even know who he is? After all, many people born after 1970 do not know who the Beatles were. Moreover, many references are already alien to those who have not shared the culture; who outside of the United States would understand a reference in the story "The Retreat" to "quicker picker-upper" paper towels? A minor detail it may be, but the accumulation of such details may finally alienate readers not familiar with American culture.

This is not to belittle Mason's characters. Certainly their crises and resolutions are universal—but the cultural markers that signal these issues are not, and it is hard not to think that ultimately Mason's writing is as trapped by her culture as her characters are. But maybe expecting her fiction to extend beyond the borders of the United States and the present time is asking too much. For now her work speaks for a group of people who have not had much say before, and perhaps that is enough; as her character Spence says, "Using the right simple words at the right time requires courage enough."

—Tracy Chevalier

MASSIE, Allan

Nationality: British. **Born:** Singapore in 1938. **Education:** Glenalmond College, Perthshire; Trinity College, Cambridge. **Family:** Married; three children. **Awards:** Niven award, 1981; Scottish Arts Council award, 1982, 1987; Society of Authors travelling scholarship, 1988. Fellow, Royal Society of Literature. **Address:** Thirladean House, Selkirk TD7 5LU, England.

PUBLICATIONS

Novels

Change and Decay in All Around I See. London, Bodley Head, 1978.
The Last Peacock. London, Bodley Head, 1980.
The Death of Men. London, Bodley Head, 1981; Boston, Houghton Mifflin, 1982.
One Night in Winter. London, Bodley Head, 1984.
Augustus: The Memoirs of the Emperor. London, Bodley Head, 1986; as *Let the Emperor Speak,* New York, Doubleday, 1987.
A Question of Loyalties. London, Hutchinson, 1989.
Tiberius. London, Hodder and Stoughton, 1990.
The Hanging Tree. London, Heinemann, 1990.
The Sins of the Father. London, Hutchinson, 1991.
Caesar. London, Hodder and Stoughton, 1993.
These Enchanted Woods. London, Hutchinson, 1993.
The Ragged Lion. London, Hutchinson, 1994.

Uncollected Short Story

"In the Bare Lands," in *Modern Scottish Short Stories,* edited by Fred Urquhart and Giles Gordon. London, Hamish Hamilton, 1978.

Other

Muriel Spark. Edinburgh, Ramsay Head Press, 1979.
Ill Met by Gaslight: Five Edinburgh Murders. Edinburgh, Harris, 1980.
The Caesars. London, Secker and Warburg, 1983; New York, Watts, 1984.
A Portrait of Scottish Rugby. Edinburgh, Polygon, 1984.
Colette. London, Viking, and New York, Penguin, 1986.
101 Great Scots. Edinburgh, Chambers, 1987.
Byron's Travels. London, Sidgwick and Jackson, 1988.
The Novelist's View of the Market Economy. Edinburgh, David Hume Institute, 1988.
Glasgow: Portrait of a City. London, Barrie and Jenkins, 1989.
The Novel Today: A Critical Guide to the British Novel 1970-1989. London, Longman, 1990.

Editor, *Edinburgh and the Borders: In Verse.* London, Secker and Warburg, 1983.
Editor, *PEN New Fiction 2.* London, Quartet, 1987.

*   *   *

Allan Massie occupies a curious place in Scottish letters. As a journalist and political commentator he embraces the politics of the conservative new right; in newspaper columns and elsewhere he has espoused the economic dogma of Margaret Thatcher (the British prime minister between 1979 and 1990), yet he is also a novelist of rare talent whose sympathies belong to the corrupted and the downtrodden, whatever their rank in society. All too often his critics are confused by the apparent contradictions between his public and his private face. In fact, a key to his thinking can be found in his novels about the emperors Augustus and Tiberius. Like Robert Graves before him, Massie uses the Roman world as suitable material with which to reconstruct the lives of these two very different men but then he goes a step further. In both he finds something of the loneliness of power and the constant battle between a temptation to use it for good or as a diabolic agency which can only corrupt and destroy. A recurring theme in both novels—parts of a planned trilogy—is the realisation that for rulers to do nothing is an evasion of responsibility yet action itself creates the possibility of doing wrong.

The idea is taken a stage further in *A Question of Loyalties* which takes a sympathetic view of the confusion of political ideologies in the establishment of Vichy France in 1940. Although this novel is rich in historical detail and contains real-life characters like Petain and de Gaulle, Massie's real concern is with the moral corruption of Lucien, the main character and a force behind the creation of a Vichy government. His life is recalled by Etienne his son and the action swings across Europe and between the modern world and the events of World War II as the moral ambiguities in both men's lives become ever apparent. It is an inventive and intellectually satisfying novel.

When Massie's first novel, *Change and Decay in All Around I See,* was first published, comparisons were made with the young Evelyn Waugh. The analogy was not fanciful. Atwater, the central character would feel equally at home in the flawed world of *Decline and Fall,* and the wasteland of 1950s London created by Massie is a timeless city in which social and spiritual life has slumped to a new ebb. The theme of things falling apart is explored further in *The Last Peacock,* a sensitive comedy of manners set among the Scottish landed gentry. Massie returned to Scotland

in his fourth novel, *One Night in Winter,* but it is a very different country from the place he previously portrayed. Whereas his earlier preoccupations had been social, Massie plunged into the world of Scottish nationalist politics. Dallas Graham looks back from his middle-class London middle age to the years of his young manhood in Scotland when he found himself drawn into a bizarre coterie of nationalists and their fanatical camp followers. A murder lies at the heart of the novel, but Massie's theme is the tragedy of overweening ambition and flawed motives. Fraser Donnelly, a self-made man who espouses political nationalism, has his career ruined when fantasy overcomes his sense of reality, but Massie's concern seems to be less with the murder which Donnelly commits than with the effect it has on young Graham. In that sense, Donnelly's rise and fall seem to mirror the imperfect political ambitions of those who take up the cause of nationalism.

Political nationalism of a different kind also informs Massie's best novel to date, *The Death of Men.* In this modern parable of terrorism and politics, the scene is set in Rome in the summer of 1978, a period of political instability in Italy. Corrado Dusa, senior minister in the ruling Christian Democratic Party and a leading proponent of resolving the crisis of dissent and violence permeating his country, is mysteriously kidnapped, and a tangled series of political trails leads to the involvement of his son in the kidnap. At this point in the novel there are echoes of the uneasy relationship between Lucien and Etienne in *A Question of Loyalties.*

The action is based loosely in the events surrounding the real-life kidnap and murder of the Italian politician Aldo Moro in 1978, but it would be misleading to draw too many parallels between *The Death of Men* and those real events; neither would it be accurate to describe Massie's novel as a *roman à clef.* Writing with great assurance, Massie transforms the style into a fast-moving thriller, building up to a conclusion which, however expected it might be, is still cleverly handled. His gallery of characters all play expected roles and the Italian background is expertly and lovingly described: there are few better pictures of life in the inner city of modern Rome. And in the near distance Massie keeps open his moral options. Terrorism is roundly condemned, but he never loses sight of the question which is central to its occurrence: what are the political conditions which bring it into existence?

—Trevor Royle

MASTERS, Hilary

Pseudonym: P.J. Coyne. **Nationality:** American. **Born:** Kansas City, Missouri, 3 February 1928. **Education:** Davidson College, 1944-46; Brown University, 1948-52, B.A. **Military Service:** United States Navy (naval correspondent), 1946-47. **Family:** Married 1) Robin Owett Watt in 1954 (divorced); 2) Polly Jo McCulloch in 1955 (divorced); 3) Kathleen E. George in 1954; one son, two daughters. **Career:** Theatrical press agent, New York, 1952-56; journalist and founder, *The Hyde Park Record,* Hyde Park, New York. Since 1983 professor of English, Carnegie Mellon University, Pittsburgh, Pennsylvania. **Awards:** Yaddo fellowship, 1980, 1982; Fulbright Lecturer, Finland, 1983. **Member:** Authors Guild. **Agent:** Christina Ward, Box 515, North Scituate, Massachusetts 02060, U.S.A. **Address:** Department of English, Carnegie Mellon University, Pittsburgh, Pennsylvania 15213, U.S.A.

PUBLICATIONS

Novels

The Common Pasture. New York, Macmillan, 1967.
An American Marriage. New York, Macmillan, 1969.
Palace of Strangers. New York, World, 1971.
Clemmons. New York, Godine, 1985.
Cooper. New York, St. Martin's Press, 1987.
Manuscript for Murder (as P.J. Coyne). New York, Dodd, Mead, 1987.
Strickland: A Romance. New York, St. Martin's Press, 1990.

Short Stories

Hammertown Tales. N.p., Stuart Wright, 1987.
Success. New York, St. Martin's Press, 1992.

Other

Last Stands: Notes from Memory. New York, Godine, 1982.

*

Hilary Masters comments:

My approach to my work is to sit down and try to do a little bit of it every morning. Earliest influence at age eight was Robinson Crusoe. Since then everyone I read has been an "influence." Most particularly H. James, Faulkner, Wright Morris, J. Conrad, etc.

*   *   *

Critics often see similarities between the writings of Hilary Masters and his father, poet Edgar Lee Masters. Thus, Hilary Masters's fictional characters, created with bold strokes, are ordinary people caught up in ordinary events that reshape their lives. Increasingly, Masters sharpens his use of locale often, placing a character in a detailed building or neighborhood. His most characteristic technique is filtering the past through memory to inform a character's present. Often a shift in time occurs without warning as a present event replays an earlier one in a character's consciousness. Deftly done, these shifts demonstrate Master's control of plot and character.

His early novels, *The Common Pasture* and *An American Marriage,* reveal the roots of these characteristics. The former elaborates on the tensions between folks in a small town over 24 hours as they prepare for a community-day celebration. Masters economically draws stock characters as he develops his theme of corrupting power. The latter novel places an American college professor and one of his students, now his wife, in Ireland. Masters wittily sends up the Irish, visiting professorships, newlyweds, and the CIA as he moves the story line back and forth between Ireland and America. *Palace of Strangers,* set in upstate New York, follows a congressional primary as it progresses through smoke-filled rooms and done-deal politics. Cynically told through the newcomer's campaign manager, the novel was faulted for this narrator's keener interest in his own sexual prowess. Masters himself ran for political office in New York; thus the novel's noted credibility.

The memoir, *Last Stands: Notes from Memory,* transcends pure autobiography as it lovingly portrays the author's maternal grand-parents, Molly and Thomas Coyne, who raised him, and his poet father and mother, Ellen, who he joined during the summers. Placing in the foreground his own memories of these four people most important in his childhood, Masters uses their memories to create an historical portrait of America that includes the 1983 Columbia Exposition; immigrants moving across America; American myths of the American West, as feisty Grandpa Gee Gee relives on-site Custer's battle at the Little Big Horn; and Edgar Lee Masters's success and waning as a poet while living in the Chelsea Hotel and being visited by other 1930s poets. All these are set against the organization and determination of his mother as she earns a master's degree in teaching and supports her family, even in widowhood. Masters's skillful mixture of three generations highlights the importance of family in one's life. Stylistically, his stream-of-consciousness technique allows him to use his father's and grandfather's letters to him, poems, allusions to music, remembered conversations, and events, particularly his grandfather's suicide, his father's near-penniless demise, and their somber funerals.

His later novels, *Clemmons, Cooper,* and *Strickland,* form a "Harlem Valley Trilogy." Masters's wit and humor come through best in these novels, where family and understanding the past play crucial roles in self-understanding. The first two portray men who have fled Manhattan, seeking organized lives in the solitude of lazy country towns; their memories or imaginations contrast the quotidian. In *Clemmons,* the eponymous protagonist's reveries move between his past and current relationships with his mother, his Southern wife, and mistresses as he frets over the complications created by the upcoming marriage of an estranged daughter. Rich comedy results when his New York mistress, his daughters, and his almost divorced wife converge on the family farm as he attempts simultaneously to paint the house and flee the festivities. As in other works, small incidents have enormous consequences; for instance, a reconciling family squabble erupts when Clemmons corrects the spelling of the son-in-law's rock album, *Find Stanley Livingston.*

Cooper continues Masters's use of upstate New York as a peaceful background for family turmoil; in this instance, Jack Cooper sells old magazines in Hammertown while he churns out World War I adventure tales and, in an echo of Grandpa Gee Gee, corresponds with a veteran flying ace whose wartime memories result in Cooper/Masters writing an exciting, lively, detailed story of World War I dogfights, which is in sharp contrast to the boring life from which Ruth, his promiscuous wife, seeks escape. Additional, somber, and melancholy echoes of *Last Stands* appear in both novels in the form of failed poets, infidelities, and suicides. And neither protagonist escapes life's confounding complications.

This darker vein continues in *Strickland: A Romance* as Masters alternates Vietnam War experiences with events in the life of former war correspondent Carrol Strickland, now a 60-year-old widower living in upstate New York with his 15-year-old daughter. Fantasizing his war experiences, Strickland tries to recapture lost emotions through their pathetic simulation.

Masters's short stories continue his vivid sketches of place and the use of a present incident to spark a memory that infuses understanding into the now. The melancholy stories of *Hammertown Tales* portray a small, dying town in upstate New York; the 16 stories of *Success* show Masters's sensitivity to ordinary people who long for the unretrievable past.

—Judith C. Kohl

MATHERS, Peter

Nationality: Australian. **Born:** Fulham, London, England, in 1931; brought to Australia as an infant. **Education:** Sydney Technical College. **Family:** Married in 1961 (divorced); two daughters. **Career:** Worked as a farmer, laborer, in wool-classing, in a brewery, and for the public service in Victoria, 1950s-early 1960s; lived in Europe, mainly in London, 1964-67, and worked as a researcher; theater adviser, University of Pittsburgh, 1968. **Awards:** Miles Franklin award, 1967. **Address:** c/o The Almost Managing Company, 83 Faraday St., Carlton, Victoria 3053, Australia.

PUBLICATIONS

Novels

Trap. Melbourne, Cassell, 1966; London, Sphere, 1970.
The Wort Papers. Melbourne, Cassell, 1972; London, Penguin, 1973.

Short Stories

A Change for the Better. Adelaide, Wav, 1984.

*   *   *

Peter Mathers is the author of only three books of fiction, yet he is undoubtedly one of the best of the generation of Australian fiction writers that followed in the wake of White, Stead, and Xavier Herbert. Though he was born in England, his work is marked by a deep strain of Australian nationalism, a conscious attempt at mythologizing Australian experience.

His first novel, for instance, begins as the story of the eponymous Jack Trap, part-Aboriginal, but as it continues its concerns steadily widen until finally it takes in, with the discussion of Trap's forebears, the whole savage history of the Aboriginal race over the last 200 years: its shooting down and poisoning by white settlers, exploitation by businessmen and missionaries, abuse and mistreatment by foremen and fellow workers, and, finally, assaults by police and jailing by magistrates. If the novel is dominated by the angry, ebullient presence of its central character, the author makes it clear nevertheless that Jack is in part the product of a whole history of exploitation, cruelty, and contemptuous indifference on the part of white people. Trap is a misfit—neither craven nor surly, neither in society nor wholly out of it. Although he schools himself to patience, he is prone to violent eruptions at periodic intervals, and the result is always, "six months from an understanding magistrate." He is resentful of his Aboriginal features and hopes they will not be recognized but at the same time he "marries" an Aboriginal woman and his final scheme is to lead a party of followers across the continent to the Narakis Mission.

Despite its subject matter, *Trap* is essentially a comic novel with its author much given to word play, puns, and episodes of slapstick. In *The Wort Papers* Mathers takes both his concerns and his experiments with language a good deal further, virtually out of the realm of social realism altogether. Style in *The Wort Papers* is not merely the means of recording the rebellious and independent freedom to which the protagonist aspires, but it is also the means of achieving it. The last word in the novel is MATTERS, the name of

the protagonist's alter ego and the mysterious writer who has hovered on its outskirts throughout the narrative.

Although it is concerned with a smaller period of time than *Trap*—roughly from the 1930s onward—*The Wort Papers* is similarly involved with questions of identity and mythic journeys inland; there are two series of journeys which are described in comic and even parodic terms. The first third of the novel is taken up with the various expeditions of William Wort, and his attempt to define himself in terms of a sense of Englishness. Like his son later, William is constantly "In Flight," Mathers's awareness that William's peregrinations carry him over territory already covered by other Australian writers such as Patrick White is shown by the heading of one section: "Journey and Employers (& obligatory bushfire)."

William's son Percy is an explorer, but whereas earlier explorers and even his father had traveled on foot or on horseback, Percy mounts a 500c.c. Norton motorbike. Whereas they had traveled into the heart of the inland, he sticks mostly to the cities, and his predicaments are urban ones, often taking a farcical form. Where their enemies were droughts or hostile natives, Percy's are figures of bureaucratic authority—policemen, mysterious representatives of the A.S.I.O. (the Australian equivalent of the C.I.A.), and recalcitrant bosses and bar-keepers.

Percy's acts of insurrection are embodied in the language of the novel itself. Wort's words are exuberant, very funny, and finally surreal weapons fired by his "sturdy, 350 shot Remington." At the end of the novel Percy dies but his doppelgänger Matters is still around. It is the artist, the word-maker, who in Mathers's view survives.

A gap of 12 years separates *The Wort Papers* from Mathers's third book of fiction, a collection of short stories titled *A Change for the Better,* and when it did appear it was greeted by sympathetic reviewers with no more than respectful disappointment. The distinguishing elements of Mathers's writing—the compression, density, and self-conscious linguistic play—have been taken as far as they can possibly go, to the point where the style is cryptic, rather than merely compressed, not so much self-conscious as hermetic. The title story is both witty and accessible. It tells of a young boy with homosexual inclinations who is therefore the scandal of his country district. Eventually he is discovered peering through the bathroom at a girl bathing. The outraged parents send for his father but are deeply chagrined at his reaction of delight: at least his sexual proclivities indicate "a change for the better." Another story that works well is "Like a Maori Prince," which returns the reader to the territory of the novels: a black man poses as a Maori Prince in order to escape the tag of "Lairy Boong" and is treated with fawning respect by the whites of the town. For the most part, though, the stories are marked by long exchanges of almost indecipherable puns and one-liners. One of the characters in "Like a Maori Prince" comments on the pun that "People have been run out of town for better jokes." There are enough bad ones in this collection to cause a mass exodus.

Mathers continues to write constantly but like Malcolm Lowry is never able to consider a work finished and is deeply reluctant to relinquish it to a publisher. Like Lowry, also, it is probable that much of his writing will be published posthumously, a suggestion that delights the author when it is put to him.

—Laurie Clancy

MATHEWS, Harry (Burchell)

Nationality: American. **Born:** New York City, 14 February 1930. **Education:** Harvard University, Cambridge, Massachusetts, B.A. 1952. **Military Service:** Served in the United States Navy, 1949-50. **Family:** Married 1) Niki de Saint Phalle in 1949 (divorced 1961), one son and one daughter; 2) Marie Chaix. **Career:** Publisher and editor with John Ashbery, Kenneth Koch, and James Schuyler, *Locus Solus,* New York, 1960-62; part-time teacher, Bennington College, Vermont, 1978, 1979-80; Hamilton College, New York, 1979; Columbia University, New York, 1982-83; Brown University, Providence, Rhode Island, 1988; Temple University, Philadelphia, 1990. Since 1989 Paris editor, *Paris Review,* Paris and New York. **Awards:** National Endowment grant, 1982; American Academy award, 1991. **Agent:** Maxine Groffsky, 2 Fifth Avenue, New York, New York 10011, U.S.A. **Address:** 67 Rue de Grenelle, 75007 Paris, France.

PUBLICATIONS

Novels

The Conversions. New York, Random House, and London, Weidenfeld and Nicolson, 1962.
Tlooth. New York, Doubleday, 1966; Manchester, Carcanet, 1987.
The Sinking of the Odradek Stadium and Other Novels (includes *The Conversions* and *Tlooth*). New York, Harper, 1975; Manchester, Carcanet, 1985.
Cigarettes. New York, Weidenfeld and Nicolson, 1987; Manchester, Carcanet, 1988.
The Journalist. Boston, Godine, 1994.

Short Stories

Selected Declarations of Dependence (includes verse). Calais, Vermont, Z Press, 1977.
Country Cooking and Other Stories. Providence, Rhode Island, Burning Deck Press, 1980.
Singular Pleasures. New York, Grenfell Press, 1988.
The American Experience. London, Atlas Press, 1991.

Poetry

The Ring: Poems 1956-1969. Leeds, Juilliard, 1970.
The Planisphere. Providence, Rhode Island, Burning Deck Press, 1974.
Trial Impressions. Providence, Rhode Island, Burning Deck Press, 1977.
Armenian Papers: Poems 1954-1984. Princeton, New Jersey, Princeton University Press, 1987.
Out of Bounds. Providence, Rhode Island, Burning Deck Press, 1989.
A Mid-Season Sky: Poems 1954-1989. Manchester, Carcanet, 1991.

Other

20 Lines a Day (journal). Elmwood Park, Illinois, Dalkey Archive Press, 1988.
The Orchard (on Georges Perec). Flint, Michigan, Bamberger, 1988.

The Way Home: Collected Longer Prose. London, Atlas Press, 1989.

Translator, *The Laurels of Lake Constance,* by Marie Chaix. New York, Viking Press, 1977.
Translator, *The Life: Memoirs of a French Hooker,* by Jeanne Cordelier. New York, Viking Press, 1978.
Translator, *Blue of Noon,* by Georges Bataille. New York, Urizen, 1978; London, Boyars, 1979.

*

Critical Study: Harry Mathews issue of *Review of Contemporary Fiction* (Elmwood Park, Illinois), Fall 1987 (includes checklist by William McPheron); "Locus Solu et Socii: Harry Mathews and John Ashbery" by Christopher Sawyer-Lauçanno, in *The Continual Pilgrimage: American Writers in Paris, 1944-1960,* New York, Grove Weidenfeld, 1992; *Harry Mathews* by Warren Leamon, New York, Twayne, 1993.

*   *   *

Harry Mathews takes semiotics out of the seminar and makes it live as fiction. Language is anything but transparent for him. He is not a self-centered performer, or a member of the Look Ma, I'm Writing! school. Nor does he make us uncomfortably aware of ourselves as readers. But (although he ridicules McLuhan) Mathews does treat his medium as his message; language, in its multimeaning, ambiguous, tragicomic potential, is itself his subject matter. His first three novels are in fact intricate allegories of the reader or listener caught in the act of interpretation.

The distinctive appeal of Mathews's novels lies in their extraordinarily rich and playful linguistic texture, rather than in the plot structures that are relatively straightforward and easy to recount. *The Conversions* begins when its anonymous narrator is given a golden ceremonial adze by a wealthy eccentric named Grent Wayl. The adze is engraved with a series of seven mysterious scenes which the narrator attempts, tentatively, to explain. When Wayl dies, a provision in his will turns the narrator's mild curiosity into exegetical zeal, by conferring immense wealth on the person who can answer three riddles: 1) When was a stone not a king?; 2) What was *La Messe de Sire Fadevant?*; and 3) Who shaved the Old Man's beard?

The riddles all have to do with the engravings on the adze, and all seem to depend upon puns. Along with the narrator, the reader gradually learns of a secret society that has persisted through the centuries despite repeated persecution, a society that, in a ceremony involving the golden adze, crowns its leader King and calls him Sylvius. An impostor named Johnstone once claimed falsely to be Sylvius—hence the "stone" that was "not a king." *La Messe de Sire Fadevant* devolves upon musical and translingual puns: *Sire* denotes not a noble title but two musical notes, while *Fadevant* places a third note in front: *fa-si-re.* Tracking down a Mass that begins with these notes, the narrator finds that its words shed further light upon the followers of Sylvius. The third riddle stumps him, however, and he abandons the quest, seemingly inconclusively, at the end of the novel.

Mathews' second novel, *Tlooth* achieved some renown when Martin Gardner described it glowingly in *Scientific American.* Its narrator and protagonist (whose name and even gender are concealed until close to the end) spends the novel pursuing a fellow ex-convict, for reasons that are tucked away as an aside to a footnote on the first page. (It appears that the object of pursuit, a criminally perverse surgeon, unnecessarily amputated two fingers from the left hand of the narrator, who until then had been a violinist.)

"Texts True and False" (one of *Tlooth's* chapter titles) litter the trail of vengeance, as do documents in a dozen lingos, clashing symbols, and uncracked codes. "Tlooth" itself, the sound uttered by a bizarre oracle, is, when properly construed, a prophecy that comes true: the narrator, now turned dentist, succeeds in strapping the object of her pursuit into her own dentist's chair. Mercifully for both reader and quarry, no painful drilling takes place, for reasons not to be divulged here.

An epistolary novel, *The Sinking of the Odradek Stadium* presents the letters of two correspondents, Zachary McCaltex, an American treasure-hunter from Miami, and Twang, his obscurely Asian wife, answering in comically bad but meliorative English from various spots in Italy. The two of them are pursuing, by diverse machinations, a fortune in gold hidden in a chest and then lost by the Medici family. Again much of the action consists of the perusal, translation, interpretation, and verification of a host of documents, maps, clues, and false leads. In the very last letter of the book we learn that Twang has actually gotten her hands on the gold, and is about to ship it to Zachary via the freighter *Odradek Stadium*. Only the novel's title hints at what happens next.

In *Cigarettes,* his fourth novel, Mathews makes a fresh departure, overlaying his earlier artificial principles of construction with a richly textured family chronicle set among a certain privileged set of New Yorkers in the late 1930s and the early 1960s. The narrative proceeds nonlinearly, by focusing in turn on pairs of characters, at moments of considerable drama in their lives. We have fraud among friends in the insurance business; painters, critics, gallery owners; homosexual couples in scenes of bondage and domination. Schemes and betrayals, illnesses and disappointments make of the novel a quick-paced tumult of emotional highs and lows. Filial guilt and obligation play prominent roles.

One passage in *Cigarettes* offers a capsule summary of Mathews's esthetic program; ostensibly it describes an art-history essay:

> Morris was showing him what writing could do. He advanced the notion that creation begins by annihilating typical forms and procedures, especially the illusory "naturalness" of sequence and coherence. Morris did more than state this, he demonstrated it. He made of his essay a minefield that blew itself up as you crossed it. You found yourself again and again on ground not of your choosing, propelled from semantics into psycho-analysis into epistemology into politics. These displacements seemed, rather than willful, grounded in some hidden and persuasive law that had as its purpose to keep bringing the reader back fresh to the subject.

The intentional fallacy notwithstanding, this passage offers the clearest exposition of Mathews's practice now in print. It is deepened by Lewis's paraphrase: "one can't really *describe* anything. So you pretend to describe—you use words to make a false replica. Then we're absorbed by the words, not by the illusion of a description. You also defuse reactions that might get in our way."

The characters of *Cigarettes,* like their namesake, are consumed by a certain self-destructive yet elegant passion. More than their predecessors in Mathews's fiction, they are defined not by their

arbitrary utility to a quest pattern, but by their relations of loyalty, betrayal, and abuse. By the novel's end, several mysteries—including the forging of new links between love and language—are illuminated as if by the striking of a match in a darkened room.

—Brian Stonehill

MATTHEWS, Jack

Nationality: American. **Born:** John Harold Matthews in Columbus, Ohio, 22 July 1925. **Education:** Ohio State University, Columbus, 1945-49, 1952-54, B.A. in classics and English 1949, M.A. in English 1954. **Military Service:** Served in the United States Coast Guard, 1943-45. **Family:** Married Barbara Jane Reese in 1947; two daughters and one son. **Career:** Post office clerk, Columbus, 1950-59; associate professor, 1959-62, and professor of English, 1962-64, Urbana College, Ohio; associate professor, 1964-70, professor of English, 1971-77, and since 1978 Distinguished Professor, Ohio University, Athens. Distinguished Writer-in-Residence, Wichita State University, Kansas, 1970-71. **Awards:** Florence Roberts Head award, 1967; Quill award (*Massachusetts Review,* Amherst), 1967; Guggenheim grant, 1974; Ohio Arts Council award, 1989. **Agent:** Ann Elmo Agency, 60 East 42nd Street, New York, New York 10165. **Address:** 24 Briarwood Drive, Athens, Ohio 45701, U.S.A.

PUBLICATIONS

Novels

Hanger Stout, Awake! New York, Harcourt Brace, 1967.
Beyond the Bridge. New York, Harcourt Brace, 1970.
The Tale of Asa Bean. New York, Harcourt Brace, 1971.
The Charisma Campaigns. New York, Harcourt Brace, 1972.
Pictures of the Journey Back. New York, Harcourt Brace, 1973.
Sassafras. Boston, Houghton Mifflin, 1983.

Short Stories

Bitter Knowledge. New York, Scribner, 1964.
Tales of the Ohio Land. Columbus, Ohio Historical Society, 1978.
Dubious Persuasions. Baltimore, Johns Hopkins University Press, 1981.
Crazy Women. Baltimore, Johns Hopkins University Press, 1985.
Ghostly Populations. Baltimore, Johns Hopkins University Press, 1987.
Dirty Tricks. Baltimore, Johns Hopkins University Press, 1990.
Storyhood as We Know It and Other Tales. Baltimore and London, Johns Hopkins University Press, 1993.

Poetry

An Almanac for Twilight. Chapel Hill, University of North Carolina Press, 1966.
In a Theater of Buildings. Marshall, Minnesota, Ox Head Press, 1970.

Other

Collecting Rare Books for Pleasure and Profit. New York, Putnam, 1977.
Booking in the Heartland. Baltimore, Johns Hopkins University Press, 1986.
Memoirs of a Bookman. Athens, Ohio University Press, 1990.

Editor, with Elaine Gottlieb Hemley, *The Writer's Signature: Idea in Story and Essay.* Chicago, Scott Foresman, 1972.
Editor, *Archetypal Themes in the Modern Story* (anthology). New York, St. Martin's Press, 1973.
Editor, *Rare Book Lore: Selections from the Letters of Ernest J. Wessen.* Athens, Ohio University Press, 1992.

*

Manuscript Collections: Ohioana Library, Ohio Departments Building, Columbus; Alden Library, Ohio University, Athens.

Critical Studies: "That Appetite for Life So Ravenous" by Dave Smith, in *Shenandoah* (Lexington, Virginia), Summer 1974; "One Alternative to Black Humor: The Satire of Jack Matthews" by Stanley W. Lindberg, in *Studies in Contemporary Satire* (Cambridge Springs, Pennsylvania), vol. 1, no. 1, 1977; "Jack Matthews and the Shape of Human Feelings" by Elmer F. Suderman, in *Critique* (Atlanta), vol. 21, no. 1, 1979.

Jack Matthews comments:

I think of every literary work as a place where three classes of people come together: the author, the reader, and the characters. The work is importantly, if not solely, definable in terms of these three classes and their relationships to one another and to the story (or poem) which is the arena of their convention. Thus, every story can be viewed as, in varying degrees, an occasion and ceremony of passionate learning.

All stories are philosophical probes, hypotheses, heuristic journeys, maps of powerful and conceivable realities, speculations, ceremonies of discovery. All these, every one. Some attempts to write a good story work beautifully; others prove sadly unworthy, false, flat, silly. Nevertheless, an author should have the courage and energy to experiment constantly and knowledgeably (i.e., remembering and adding to his craft), even in his awareness that he will often miss whatever mark is there, and knowing also that whatever can conceivably happen to him and come out of him will ultimately be found to have taken place within his signature.

Man's character is his fate, but he should never let this fact inhibit his real freedom of the real moment. I celebrate this truth in my stories, as well as in the act of writing them.

*   *   *

Many contemporary fiction writers—especially in America—are displaced persons: they don't really live *in* any particular location, they merely reside there. But Jack Matthews's mature imagination lives in the American heartland where it was shaped. In fact, Matthews is at his best when he is taking the pulse of Middle America (not merely a geographical area, of course, but a state of consciousness extending far beyond Matthews's native Ohio). In his six novels (and in many of his remarkable short stories) the reader can sense the wide-open spaces of the Midwest, the often-

closed minds of its inhabitants, the limitless possibilities of success and failure, the comic and the tragic in ironic balance. Like Sinclair Lewis, Matthews captures the essence of Middle America. He does so, however, without the didacticism of Lewis and with more of the comic and a surer control of the dramatic.

Matthews's early novels are all rather short, though they are richly developed and populated with memorable characters—originals with much more than just literary validity, ranging from gas-station attendants and warehouse laborers to used-car salesmen and battered cowboys. Most of them are essentially innocents, viewed with unsentimental compassion as they try to cope with what they see of the confusion around them; but they carry their innocence in interestingly differing ways.

The most openly naive of his characters is "Hanger" Stout, the narrator of Matthews's first novel, who relates a poignant but truly funny account of how he was tricked into competing for the championship of a nonexistent sport ("free-hanging" by one's hands). Genuinely unaware of how much others are using him, and often unaware of the refreshing comedy in his tale, "Hanger" emerges from his experiences relatively untouched, still kind and trusting, a most convincing original.

Less convincing is the self-conscious narrator of *Beyond the Bridge,* a middle-aged man who narrowly escapes death when the Silver Bridge collapses, plunging a number of people into the Ohio River. Knowing that his family expects him to be crossing the bridge at that hour, he seizes this unique chance to shed all his responsibilities, to disappear and begin a new life elsewhere. Such a break with one's past is not that easy, Matthews demonstrates, and the novel offers some nicely detailed moments in the mind of the neurotic narrator. When compared to Matthews's other fiction, however, the action here seems excessively internalized, and the symbolism often too overt.

Matthews's ironic sense of humor surfaces as witty sexual satire in *The Tale of Asa Bean,* where the innocent is a former Ph.D. candidate in philosophy now working in an A & P grocery warehouse. Asa, burdened with an IQ of more than 170 and an overactive libido, is a compulsive verbalist with a tendency to drop recondite phrases (often in Latin) at inappropriate moments—a habit that regularly scares off the women he so desperately wants. "What ironic man can make love?" Asa agonizes, "And yet, how can man achieve truth, understanding, humor, manhood, without irony?" But Asa's hilarious misadventures end triumphantly—despite himself—in a brilliant demonstration of wit and verbal precision, a winning performance.

In *The Charisma Campaigns* Matthews takes a calculated risk in creating a character who is announced as possessing magnetic charisma—and, indeed, convincingly projects it on the page. A used-car dealer in a small Ohio town, Rex McCoy plays with a full deck of corny sales slogans and gimmicks, but like nearly all of Matthews's characters, he moves far beyond any stereotyped model. His cunning machinations and energetic naivety, his success in selling cars and his failures in other aspects of life, all blend into a fascinating portrait. It is easy to agree with Anthony Burgess, who proclaimed it "an American classic." This is a superb novel—Matthews's finest accomplishment to date.

In *Pictures of the Journey Back,* set in the early 1970s, Matthews portrays a trip from Kansas to Colorado by three disparate characters: a weathered ex-rodeo hand, a confused college girl estranged from her mother, and the girl's hippie lover, an aspiring filmmaker. The cowboy insists upon returning the girl to her dying mother because, he argues, it is "only right," and the boyfriend accompanies them to make a film of the total experience. Here is the vehicle for the unending dialectics of youth *vs.* age, freedom *vs.* tradition, appearance *vs.* reality, etc. More ambitious technically than his earlier work, *Pictures* employs a shifting point of view to examine a concern that occupies much of Matthews's fiction—a sense that something is slowly being lost: "the sacred ideals of one's family and culture," as Matthews sees it, "what the Romans termed *Pietas.*"

In his most recent (and longest) novel, Matthews sets the action in 1840 on the American frontier. The protagonist/narrator of *Sassafras* is Thad Burke, a young phrenologist who takes his show from village to village, lecturing and "reading" the heads of a wild assortment of soldiers, Indians, settlers, and whores. Thad's Candide-like journey is not without its moving and painful lessons, but Matthews infuses a marvelous comic energy into this picaresque novel, and the dominant tone is that of a boisterous tall tale. Like Huck Finn, Thad is a splendid innocent—despite his natural "sass" and the sophistication he thinks he has acquired.

All of Matthews's novels have distinct merit, inviting and convincingly sustaining subsequent readings, but it would be a serious mistake to measure his achievement solely by these longer works. During the past four decades, well over 200 of his stories have appeared in major American quarterlies and magazines (with a number of them reprinted in prize anthologies), and significantly, this is the genre that has been receiving most of his energies in recent years.

Of the six splendid collections of Matthews's stories that have been published, perhaps the best is the thematically integrated *Tales of the Ohio Land,* which is particularly rich in its blend of history and myth. Unfortunately, neither this nor his first collection, *Bitter Knowledge,* is easily available, but his last four volumes are all in print, thanks to Johns Hopkins University Press. These include *Dubious Persuasions, Crazy Women* ("dedicated to all those who will understand how negotiable and variously ironic the title is"), *Ghostly Populations,* and *Dirty Tricks.* Together they provide solid evidence of Matthews's range and versatility, his sure powers of observation, and his compassionate understanding of the human comedy.

Engaging wit and irony have been characteristic of Matthews's writing from the start, and both are strongly present in his latest gatherings of stories. His irony is increasingly darker, however, and his characters' obsession with memory and its distortions plays a more dominant role in this later work, much of which deals with death. For the most part, these are stories with deceptively simple and ordinary surfaces, but they are driven by powerful and ominous undercurrents, which often fuse the local and regional with the archetypal. Few can do it better. Without question, Matthews has established himself as one of America's finest storytellers.

—Stanley W. Lindberg

MATTHIESSEN, Peter

Nationality: American. **Born:** New York City, 22 May 1927. **Education:** Hotchkiss School, Connecticut; Yale University, New Haven, Connecticut, B.A. in English 1950; the Sorbonne, Paris, 1948-49. **Family:** Married 1) Patricia Southgate in 1951 (divorced); 2) Deborah Love in 1963 (died 1972), two children; 3) Maria Eckhart in 1980. **Career:** Commercial fisherman, 1954-56. Has made an-

thropological and natural history expeditions to Alaska, the Canadian Northwest Territories, Peru, New Guinea (Harvard-Peabody expedition, 1961), Africa, Nicaragua, and Nepal. Co-founder, 1952, and editor, *Paris Review.* Trustee, New York Zoological Society, 1965-79. **Awards:** *Atlantic* Firsts award, 1951; American Academy award, 1963; National Book award, for nonfiction, 1979; Brandeis University Creative Arts award, 1979; American Book award, for nonfiction, 1980; John Burroughs medal, 1982; Philadelphia Academy of Sciences gold medal, 1984. **Member:** American Academy of Arts and Letters, 1974. **Address:** Bridge Lane, Sagaponack, Long Island, New York 11962, U.S.A.

PUBLICATIONS

Novels

Race Rock. New York, Harper, 1954; London, Secker and Warburg, 1955; as *The Year of the Tempest,* New York, Bantam, 1957.
Partisans. New York, Viking Press, 1955; London, Secker and Warburg, 1956; as *The Passionate Seekers,* New York, Avon, 1957.
Raditzer. New York, Viking Press, 1961; London, Heinemann, 1962.
At Play in the Fields of the Lord. New York, Random House, 1965; London, Heinemann, 1966.
Far Tortuga. New York, Random House, 1975; London, Collins, 1989.
Killing Mister Watson. New York, Random House, and London, Collins, 1990.

Short Stories

Midnight Turning Gray. Bristol, Rhode Island, Ampersand Press, 1984.
On the River Styx and Other Stories. New York, Random House, and London, Collins, 1989.

Uncollected Short Stories

"Fifth Day," in *Atlantic* (Boston), September 1951.
"A Replacement," in *Paris Review 1,* Spring 1953.
"Lina," in *Cornhill* (London), Fall 1956.

Other

Wildlife in America. New York, Viking Press, 1959; London, Deutsch, 1960; revised edition, Viking, 1987.
The Cloud Forest: A Chronicle of the South American Wilderness. New York, Viking Press, 1961; London, Deutsch, 1962.
Under the Mountain Wall: A Chronicle of Two Seasons in the Stone Age. New York, Viking Press, 1962; London, Heinemann, 1963.
The Shorebirds of North America. New York, Viking Press, 1967; as *The Wind Birds,* 1973.
Oomingmak: The Expedition to the Musk Ox Island in the Bering Sea. New York, Hastings House, 1967.
Sal Si Puedes: Cesar Chavez and the New American Revolution. New York, Random House, 1970.
Blue Meridian: The Search for the Great White Shark. New York, Random House, 1971.
Everglades: Selections from the Writings of Peter Matthiessen, edited by Patricia Caulfield. New York, Ballantine, 1971.

Seal Pool (for children). New York, Doubleday, 1972; as *The Great Auk Escape,* London, Angus and Robertson, 1974.

The Tree Where Man Was Born, with *The African Experience,* photographs by Eliot Porter. New York, Dutton, and London, Collins, 1972.

The Snow Leopard. New York, Viking Press, 1978; London, Chatto and Windus, 1979.

Sand Rivers (on the Selous Game Reserve), photographs by Hugo van Lawick. New York, Viking Press, and London, Aurum Press, 1981.

In the Spirit of Crazy Horse. New York, Viking Press, 1983; revised edition, Viking, and London, Harper Collins, 1991.

Indian Country. New York, Viking, 1984; London, Collins, 1985.

Nine-Headed Dragon River: Zen Journals 1969-1982. Boston, Shambhala, and London, Collins, 1986.

Men's Lives: The Surfmen and Baymen of the South Fork. New York, Random House, 1986; London, Collins, 1988.

African Silences. New York, Random House, 1991.

African Shadows. New York, Harry Abrams, 1993.

*

Bibliography: *Peter Matthiessen: A Bibliography 1952-1979* by D. Nicholas, Canoga Park, California, Orirama Press, 1980.

*   *   *

Peter Matthiessen has a dream of mankind living gracefully in the world, one species of many in an organic relationship. Unlike earlier American authors given to a version of this dream, Matthiessen can have no illusions. He writes with our contemporary knowledge that the "natural man," whose free application of energy to the environment was for earlier Americans to be the means of achieving a paradise, has wrought ecological disaster. Materially that disaster derives from the rapacious application of technology to the subjugation of nature, and Matthiessen's works of nonfiction are its historical record reporting the extinction and threatened destruction of animal species, the fateful meetings of representatives of industrial society with people yet to experience even the agricultural revolution, and the desperate resistance of American farm workers to the culminating stage of exploitation. Philosophically, the disastrous consequences of the traditional American dream result from the theoretical separation of society, usually conceived of as oppressive, and the individual, always assumed to be noble; thus, people celebrating individualism but nonetheless required to construct a social system find that their rejection of the claims of fraternity does not foster sturdy independence but merely produces anomie. The counterpart of his historical record of the destruction of the natural environment, Matthiessen's first novels are a representation of this disabled American character.

Writing evocatively of his own generation and social class in *Race Rock,* he links four young Americans in exploring the directions their lives have taken since their adolescence in the same seacoast setting. The shifting viewpoint and intermingling of recollection and present event provide the sense of movement we associate with growth, but it is ironic since there has been no growth. Two of the male characters—George and Sam—are the ineffectual products of middle-class culture: uncertain of vocation, implausible in deeds, in short unable to complete the arc between thought and action because they doubt the efficacy of their thought. Providing the apex of a triangle is a woman who, though female and, there-

fore, less intensively drawn by the romance of achievement, is herself ungratified. Her fulfillment must come through the ineffectual males to one of whom she has been married and with the second of whom she is involved in a love affair. The point of reference for all three is Cady, a man whose natural capacity to act let him bully them in childhood. As adults these four are bound as they were in adolescence into personally destructive relationships. Cady's irresponsible brutishness has merely become more lethal. He still seeks to get what he wants according to a base code of individual force, while George, Sam, and Eve ambivalently resent and admire his dominance. For Matthiessen the behavior of the characters has explanation, but no excuse. Carefully avoiding extenuating circumstances that would lift their personal responsibility, he shows that they have neither the direction nor the will to exist in other than an unjustifiably predatory arrangement.

In *Partisans* Matthiessen again focuses upon an ineffectual son of the American bourgeoisie. Barney Sand, alienated from family and culture, proceeds on a search for a revolutionary who had befriended him as a child. By means of a descent into Parisian working class life on which Barney is led by a Stalinist Party functionary named Marat, Matthiessen parallels the physical search with an inquiry into the motives for revolutionary action. The Brechtian portrayal of proletarian conditions denies Barney the clarity available to those who think in the abstract. The bestial lives of the poor make sympathy, or even the belief in their natural rectitude, impossible for Barney, and a politics without idealism is beneath his consideration. All that Matthiessen permits Barney to grasp is that revolutionaries have strong convictions for which they will sacrifice— the man for whom he searches gives life and reputation. But since there can be no doubt that revolutionary forces are in motion, the failure to comprehend must lie in Barney. Matthiessen seems to be suggesting that so long as thought and action are held to be categorically separate, as they are in Barney's mind, no motive will be sufficient for action and no action entirely justifiable. It is integration of both in practice that makes a revolutionary, and comprehension of that fact is necessary for modern men to make their lives adequately human.

Technically Matthiessen's neatest explication of character occurs in *Raditzer.* The figure who gives his name to the book is a passive-aggressive, physically weak and socially a parasite, yet able to strike through the mask of civilized respectability and mastery to reveal in those he victimizes a deep-seated guilt and bewildering remorse. The kinship Raditzer insists he shares with the respectable Navy men whose tenuous security he undermines conveys, as in *Race Rock,* Matthiessen's perception of the split between thought and action that manifests itself in the indecisiveness of American men. The tight narrative construction enforcing psychological parallels goes beyond the earlier novel, however, making it evident in *Raditzer* through the substance of style that the leading characters of the book amalgamate into a general type.

Successful though he has been in the manner of psychological realism, Matthiessen's developing vision has required that he exceed the form of his first three novels, and in *At Play in the Fields of the Lord* he introduces to fiction the comprehensiveness of philosophical anthropology. Carrying the ineffectual civilized types he has previously described into the jungle of South America, Matthiessen strips away the protective coloration they gain from their native culture; thus, they are as exposed as the jungle Indians to the test of survival. As the narrative increasingly centers upon the grand attempt of a reservation-trained North American Indian to reclaim his past by immersing himself in the natural and cultural world of the primitive South American Indians, three levels of meaning emerge. The first concerns the historical conflict between modern technological civilization and the less developed societies whose destruction is only a matter of time. Through imaginative sympathy with both Indians and whites Matthiessen, then, establishes a second theme of the unity of desire to humanize the world. For the Indians this involves a balanced relationship to nature that yet allows a sense of transcendence. For the North Americans sharing the same impulse the desire is domination. Certainly their technology will eventually dominate but for the time being they are alone with only personal resources inadequate to sustain their sanity. Finally, on a third level of meaning he reveals both Indians and whites to be lonely beings who must find salvation through development of community that embraces the total material and social world.

Thematically more spare than the previous novels, *Far Tortuga* embodies in literary technique itself the forces of the natural and human world that might make a community. The crew of a Grand Cayman fishing boat going about the business of sailing to the turtle banks off Nicaragua communicates in dialogue detached from expository context. Their speech, afloat as they are, concerns the specifics of job and personality but is imbued with the sense that fishing has come upon hard times. Tales of past voyages, former captains, and historical events imply the decline their way of life has suffered because excessive fishing has depleted marine life. Impressionistic description of sea and weather and time dominates the narrative just as natural forces dominate the watery world. There is no significant plot to the narrative, for at sea the men cannot be a cause of their destiny, and, for the same reason, narrative movement is simply temporal. Human purpose appears in the novel's title, which refers to a legendary bay where fishing is eternally good, but that very purpose has sustained material nature as the ultimate force in human life.

Matthiessen's fiction and nonfiction are one. As he writes in *Sal Si Puedes:* "In a damaged human habitat, all problems merge." The good life will be achieved, if at all, only when man and society and nature are equally nurtured and cherished.

—John M. Reilly

MAVOR, Elizabeth (Osborne)

Nationality: British. **Born:** Glasgow, 17 December 1927. **Education:** St. Leonard's School, St. Andrews, Scotland; St. Anne's College, Oxford (editor, *Cherwell*), 1947-50, B.A. in history, M.A. **Family:** Married Haro Hodson in 1953; two sons. **Address:** c/o Hutchinson, 20 Vauxhall Bridge Road, London SW1V 2SA, England.

PUBLICATIONS

Novels

Summer in the Greenhouse. London, Hutchinson, 1959; New York, Morrow, 1960.
The Temple of Flora. London, Hutchinson, 1961.
The Redoubt. London, Hutchinson, 1967.
A Green Equinox. London, Joseph, 1973.

The White Solitaire. London, Hutchinson, 1988.

Other

The Virgin Mistress, A Study in Survival: The Life of the Duchess of Kingston. London, Chatto and Windus, and New York, Doubleday, 1964.
The Ladies of Llangollen: A Study in Romantic Friendship. London, Joseph, 1971; New York, Penguin, 1984.

Editor, *Life with the Ladies of Llangollen.* London, Viking, 1984.
Editor, *The Grand Tour of William Beckford: Selections from Dreams, Waking Thoughts, and Incidents.* London, Penguin, 1986.
Editor, *Fanny Kemble: The American Journals.* London, Weidenfeld and Nicolson, 1990.
Editor, *The Grand Tours of Katherine Wilmot: France 1801-3 and Russia 1805-7.* London, Weidenfeld and Nicolson, 1992.
Editor, *The Captain's Wife: The South American Journals of Maria Graham 1821-23.* London, Weidenfeld and Nicolson, 1993.

*   *   *

The strength of Elizabeth Mavor's writing is her sensuous evocation of nature, gardens, art, and sex. The quirky interest in the past apparent in her earlier novels flowered in *The White Solitaire* into a full-scale historical novel. Each of her four earlier novels centres on a woman in love, around whom revolve questions of the justification of adultery, and who pits herself against time, past or future.

In Mavor's first novel, *Summer in the Greenhouse,* the predominant mood of lyrical reminiscence contrasts with the stylized and fantastic plotting on which it is hinged. The middle-aged Claire Peachey recounts the sad love affair of her youth to a child and a young man who see "not so much Mrs. Peachey's house and the walks and flower-beds about it as the buildings and monuments of Florence beneath an identical burning sky in that June of 1895." Mrs. Peachey is observed through the granddaughter of her old admirer; the child's quest for the Fra Angelico painting of "the face," which she has seen reproduced, brings the adults together after 45 years. Though anticipated throughout the book, this encounter remains a *tour de force,* upstaged by the radio announcement of Britain's entry into World War II.

Mavor extends the range of broad comedy in *The Temple of Flora,* which switches from rural fun reminiscent of *Cold Comfort Farm* to sometimes serious theology. Dinah Gage's aspirations to reform the semipagan village of Thrussel are complicated by her tangling with a local youth. In a heavily symbolic but hilarious climax, a bull disrupts the harvest festival, which has already transformed the church into the temple of the title. The novel shifts to a consideration of the eternal triangle in which Dinah now involves herself. In the closing farewell scenes, as she decides to renounce her married lover, Mavor successfully treads a dizzy tightrope between poignance and ridicule, with Dinah's wish for "a sacramental relationship between him and me so that I could live apart from him with courage and a belief that I was doing something true and creative."

In *The Redoubt* Mavor broke away from the third-person narration of her two previous novels for a mixture of first- and third-person narration which she retained in *A Green Equinox* and *The White Solitaire,* though in all three books the potentialities of this freedom are left unexplored. In *The Redoubt,* too, she extended her range of characterization with the publican Lil, who is her only full-scale lower-class portrait before the 18th-century figures of *The White Solitaire.* The novel is set over the weekend of the 1953 East Coast floods, as Eve gives birth to a child. Through flashbacks grafted on to the chaos of the floods and the proverbial reliving of the past before drowning, the flickering validity of a childhood friendship comes across, "a kind of marriage in that childhood moment." Mavor's most experimental writing in any of her novels shows Eve's mind, in labour, ranging across history in hysterical metaphors for her life and predicament now. But the novel's ending is facile as Eve, who wishes that the father of her child were not her abandoned husband, but Faber, her rediscovered—married—and now drowned childhood friend and recent lover, resolves that "it is out of his death that my own life must be remade somehow."

A Green Equinox ends on a similar note after a death: "'Now,' she had said, 'do without me!'" Earlier, it had ranged even wider than *The Temple of Flora,* and fuses its diverse material better in an ironical circular structure. It follows Hero Kinoull's search for "Heaven now" in her successive loves for Hugh Shafto, the rococo expert, his wife and his mother, in Beaudesert—to be found on the same allegorical map as Thrussel. The novel partially resolves itself into a meditation on age, as Hero's third love is seen as the most lyrical; old Mrs. Shafto's gardens and model boats—"a love for the miniature" —recall Faber's in *The Redoubt. A Green Equinox* combines the bathetic comedy of saving the Bunyan Elm with a plethora of dramatic disasters—car accident, typhoid epidemic, near-drowning, drowning, and fire. Complete with metaphysical overtones, all this is crammed into six months which culminate in Hero's defiance of time; the reader has been initially forewarned of her "love affair, sexual almost, with the lost past." The rococo, "the worst and most provocative of all styles," subsumes all the ramifications of this tale under its imagery.

In *The Virgin Mistress,* the earlier of her historical biographies, Mavor affirmed that "a human personality is not mewed up in its own life-span." She has an antiquarian fascination with objects, just as Imogen in *Summer in the Greenhouse* listening to Mrs. Peachey's story was spellbound by "all the props of the play that had been." In *A Green Equinox,* the extended metaphor of rococo frivolity permitted her even greater licence for lyricism and satire.

The White Solitaire relates the life of the pirate Mary Read (1693-1715). This book tellingly musters a huge amount of historical and geographical detail as context for Read, whose roles included trooper in Marlborough's army as well as innkeeper in Holland with her husband. At the beginning, Mavor prints "the only known biography" of Read from Johnson's *A General History of the Robberies and Murders of the Most Notorious Pirates* (probably written by Defoe), though as there seems no structural rationale for outlining Read's drift into piracy in advance, it might have been better printed as an appendix at the end. If the rationale for Mavor's use of extended extracts supposedly from Read's journal is to point to the contrast between Read as seen by others and by herself—most of his/her life disguised as a man with consequent sexual complications—this technique isn't fully developed. Mary Read seems a less vivid presence in the novel than Eve or Hero in their contexts. In fact, Eve's and Hero's motivations don't bear very close scrutiny, and *The White Solitaire* albeit using "given" historical material parallels this interesting author's weakness elsewhere—overreliance on exciting plot.

—Val Warner

MAXWELL, William (Keepers)

Nationality: American. **Born:** Lincoln, Illinois, 16 August 1908. **Education:** The University of Illinois, Urbana, B.A. 1930; Harvard University, Cambridge, Massachusetts, M.A. 1931. **Family:** Married Emily Gilman Noyes in 1945; two daughters. **Career:** Member of the Department of English, University of Illinois, 1931-33. From 1936, in the art department, then fiction editor, *New Yorker;* retired 1976. **Awards:** Friends of American Writers award, 1938; American Academy award, 1958, and Howells medal, 1980; American Book award, for paperback, 1982. D.Litt.: University of Illinois, 1973. **Member:** President, National Institute of Arts and Letters, 1969-72. **Address:** 544 East 86th Street, New York, New York 10028, U.S.A.

PUBLICATIONS

Novels

Bright Center of Heaven. New York, Harper, 1934.
They Came like Swallows. New York, Harper, and London, Joseph, 1937.
The Folded Leaf. New York, Harper, 1945; London, Faber, 1946.
Time Will Darken It. New York, Harper, 1948; London, Faber, 1949.
The Chateau. New York, Knopf, 1961.
So Long, See You Tomorrow. New York, Knopf, 1980; London, Secker and Warburg, 1989.

Short Stories

Stories, with others. New York, Farrar Straus, 1956; as *A Book of Stories,* London, Gollancz, 1957.
The Old Man at the Railroad Crossing and Other Tales. New York, Knopf, 1966.
Over by the River and Other Stories. New York, Knopf, 1977.
Five Tales. Omaha, Nebraska, Cummington Press, 1988.
Billie Dyer and Other Stories. N.p., 1992.

Uncollected Short Stories

"Billie Dyer," in *New Yorker,* 15 May 1989.
"Fable Begotten of an Echo of a Line of Verse by W.B. Yeats," in *Antaeus* (New York), Spring-Autumn 1990.

Other

The Heavenly Tenants (for children). New York, Harper, 1946.
The Writer as Illusionist (lecture). New York, Unitelum Press, 1955.
Ancestors. New York, Knopf, 1971.
The Outermost Dream: Essays and Reviews. New York, Knopf, 1989.

Editor, *The Garden and the Wilderness,* by Charles Pratt. New York, Horizon Press, 1980.
Editor, *The Letters of Sylvia Townsend Warner.* London, Chatto and Windus, 1982; New York, Viking Press, 1983.
Editor, with Susanna Pinney, *Selected Stories,* by Sylvia Townsend Warner. London, Chatto and Windus, 1988.

*   *   *

The subjects of William Maxwell's major novels vary, but the sensibility that informs them is a Midwestern one. In both *They Came like Swallows* and *The Folded Leaf,* for example, the novelist is reworking and focusing his recollections of an Illinois boyhood and college experience. The materials he draws on in these novels he thus shares with somewhat older writers like Sinclair Lewis and Sherwood Anderson. But these novelists were involved in labors of repudiation; their work was marked by what has been called the "revolt from the village," by a keen sense that the Midwestern setting was a stultifying one from which the writer, by a satirical and unflattering report, had to separate himself. This accent of mockery and dismissal is absent from Maxwell's novels, which render the texture of Midwestern life in the early decades of this century. It is an accent which is absent from Maxwell's *Ancestors,* a work of nonfiction which gives an attentive account of the writer's forebears.

In general, then, there is a cherishing of the provincial limitations that other writers have found galling. There is, in most of the novels, a precise if not loving recollection of the diversions and the limited esthetic taste that created upper-class, prosperous sensibility in "downstate" Illinois towns. *They Came like Swallows,* for example, tells of the impact of a mother's death on a decent and conventional Illinois household. *Time Will Darken It* is an account of a protracted visit which Southern relatives pay and the disruption that the visitors bring to what was a moderately happy family. *The Folded Leaf,* which the French critic Maurice Coindreau has referred to as the best novel about college experience, tells of the adolescent and college experiences of two young Midwestern men; it leaves them on the threshold of an uneasy maturity, a maturity far short of ideal, but the only maturity that is open to them under Midwestern conditions.

The clearest indications of Maxwell's attitude toward his American materials appears in two novels: *The Folded Leaf* and *So Long, See You Tomorrow. The Folded Leaf* is about the "coming of age" of two boys; the author draws explicit parallels between the boys' rather casual passage from youth to maturity and the "rites of passage" that anthropologists and students of comparative religion describe in the tradition-oriented societies they study. *So Long, See You Tomorrow* also deals with the friendship of two boys. It is friendship terminated by the sensational crime and death of the father of one of the boys. Here also Maxwell deals with studious attention to matters that other writers handle sensationally or ironically. Maxwell even allows us to see how he has collected his materials—old newspapers—as a first step to his imaginative reconstruction. Both novels contain controlled attention, free of animus.

The same sort of attention is offered adult experience in *The Chateau.* The American travelers at the center of this novel undergo contacts with an enigmatic culture—that of the French—which are a series of challenges that are neither mockingly presented, as in Sinclair Lewis's *Dodsworth,* nor offered as proof of American superiority, as in Booth Tarkington's *The Plutocrat.* Rather is Maxwell's prevailing note that of detached comprehension, the same sort of comprehension that the anthropologist offers the alien culture that he wishes to grasp. The anthropologist does not question the values of his "informants"; he reports those values. Such is also the attitude of Maxwell toward the aspirations of the characters he creates.

—Harold H. Watts

McBAIN, Ed. *See* **HUNTER, Evan.**

McCABE, Patrick

Nationality: Irish. **Born:** Clones, County Monaghan, Ireland, 27 March 1955. **Education:** St. Patrick's Training College, Dublin. **Family:** Married Margot Quinn in 1981, two daughters. **Career:** Since 1980 teacher, Kingsbury Day Special School, London. **Awards:** *Irish Press* Hennessy award, 1979, for *The Call;* Aer Lingus award, 1992 **Address:** Kingsbury Day Special School, Kingsbury, London N.W.9, England.

PUBLICATIONS

Novels

Music on Clinton Street. Dublin, Raven Arts Press, 1986.
Carn. N.p., Aidan Ellis, 1989.
The Butcher Boy. London, Picador, 1992; New York, Fromm International, 1993.
The Dead School. London, Picador, and New York, Dial Press, 1995.

Plays

Radio Plays: *Ulster Final,* 1984; *Frontiers,* 1984; *The Adventures of Shay Mouse,* 1983; *Belfast Days,* n.d.; *The Outing,* n.d.; *The Butcher Boy,* n.d.

Other

The Adventures of Shay Mouse: The Mouse from Longford (for children). Dublin, New Island, 1994.

*   *   *

Patrick McCabe's third novel, *The Butcher Boy,* earned him a considerable amount of critical acclaim, including an Aer Lingus Award and a space on the short list for the 1992 Booker Prize. It identified him as a representative voice for a new generation of Irish writers. Like colleagues Roddy Doyle and Dermot Bolger, Patrick McCabe expresses a sense of dislocation from what is normally perceived as the Irish literary tradition. His novels resist both the romantic nationalism of Yeats and the modernist mythologizing of Joyce; they remain firmly rooted in the everyday lives of ordinary people in mid-20th-century Ireland. His characters, primarily lower-middle class or working class, belong to a generation born well after the struggle for independence. They have little time for nationalism, which they view as overly nostalgic and peripheral, surviving only in old men's stories and songs sung after a few too many pints.

Indeed, McCabe's characters seem more steeped in British and American popular culture. Francie Brady's narration of *The Butcher Boy* is littered with references to British comic books and American TV shows. He frequently assumes different accents and phraseology in his narration, reflecting both his desire to remain in the world of childhood innocence, of comic books and cowboy games, and his sense of alienation from his town and his culture. Malachy Dudgeon of *The Dead School* woos his love interest by impersonating Jack Nicholson and later chooses the Tubes hit "White Punks on Dope" as his anthem. *Carn*'s Sadie Rooney, in her desire to escape the stultifying atmosphere of her town, fantasizes about moving to London and living out *True Romance* story lines. Benny Dolan, Sadie's future husband, mixes the American image of the itinerant biker with enthusiasm for the local football team and a superficial form of nationalism by decorating his Yamaha with appropriate stickers. The town of *Carn*'s boom era is accompanied by a gradual assimilation of American culture, culminating in the opening of the "tavern-cum-roadhouse," the Turnpike Inn, which is decorated with American flags and pictures of Davy Crockett and John F. Kennedy. Whether foreign popular culture signifies escape or affluence, the ideal it represents is never achievable, and the desire that marks so many of McCabe's characters leads ultimately to inertia or destruction.

Patrick McCabe's novels revel in the absurd futility of his characters' lives. They each try their best to rebel against an overwhelming sense of predetermination, yet their rebellion only brings them closer to their inescapable fate. Each of his novels is saturated with a stifling atmosphere of impeding doom, and the combination of this atmosphere with the primarily comic tone in the voices of his narrators produces a strange sense of dislocation in the reader.

Francie Brady's stubborn innocence and humor make him an incredibly appealing narrator. The early parts of *The Butcher Boy*, which portray his relationship with childhood friend Joe Purcell, his mother's suicide, and his father's sense of angry hopelessness, evoke a certain amount of empathy for Francie, who seems only to be trying to make the best of an impossible situation. As the novel progresses, this empathy finds itself conflicting with the increasing awareness of Francie's madness and his tendency toward violence. Despite his clearly psychotic actions, however, his desperate quest for affection, intimacy, and recognition keep the reader fluctuating between empathy and revulsion.

This kind of vicious circle is a predominant motif in McCabe's fiction. The contradictory position provoked by the narration of *The Butcher Boy* is reflected thematically in each of his novels but is perhaps best exemplified by his newest release, *The Dead School*. The two teachers portrayed in *The Dead School* belong to different generations and have correspondingly different worldviews and lifestyles. Yet their meeting results in much more than a conflict between Raphael Bell's high standards and old-fashioned authoritarian teaching style and Malachy Dudgeon's if-it-feels-good-do-it approach to life. Other forces are at work, it seems, and neither character is fated to succeed in his attempt to model himself according to the image idealized by his generation. For Raphael, the younger Malachy represents all the evils of a generation that is rapidly declaring his way of life extinct. Malachy is only one small pocket of the grand conspiracy against him; more insidious are the developments in the media, represented by Terry Krash (a radio personality who declares that Raphael's favorite traditional music radio show has "gone out with the ark") and the figure of Ms. Evans, the feminist parents' advocate who is single-handedly secularizing Raphael's school. It is not Malachy that defeats Raphael but the process of evolution and Raphael's own stubborn rigidity. And though Malachy identifies Raphael as the major contributor to his downfall, it is instead his own incompetence, shiftlessness, and inability to accept responsibility for his own actions and his own

fate that lead him to acid-induced madness. The sense of inevitability and despair produced by the parallel decline of both protagonists is not a result of the irreconcilability of two generations but the realization that neither seems to have a place in the world. Each teacher is a mirror for the other in his attempt to live out an ideal, and neither ideal can survive in the constant flux of 20th-century culture.

—Victoria A. Smallman

McCANN, Edson. *See* **POHL, Frederik.**

McCARTHY, Cormac

Nationality: American. **Born:** Charles McCarthy, Providence, Rhode Island, 20 July 1933. **Education:** University of Tennessee. **Military Service:** United States Air Force, 1953-56. **Family:** Married 1) Lee Holman in 1961 (divorced), one child; 2) Anne de Lisle, 1967 (divorced). **Awards:** Ingram-Merrill Foundation grant for creative writing, 1960; William Faulkner Foundation award, 1965, for *The Orchard Keeper;* Rockefeller Foundation grant, 1966; MacArthur Foundation grant, 1981; National Book award, 1992, for *All the Pretty Horses;* Lyndhurst Foundation grant; Institute of Arts and Letters award. American Academy of Arts and Letters traveling fellowship to Europe, 1965-66; Guggenheim fellowship, 1976. **Agent:** Amanda Urban, International Creative Management, 40 West 57th Street, New York, New York 10019, U.S.A.

PUBLICATIONS

Novels

The Orchard Keeper. New York, Random House, 1965; London, Picador, 1994.
Outer Dark. New York, Random House, 1968; London, Picador, 1994.
Child of God. New York, Random House, 1974; London, Chatto and Windus, 1975.
Suttree. New York, Random House, 1979; London, Chatto and Windus, 1980.
Blood Meridian; or, The Evening Redness in the West. New York, Random House, 1985; London, Picador, 1989.
All the Pretty Horses. New York, Knopf, 1992; London, Picador, 1993.
The Crossing. New York, Knopf, and London, Picador, 1994.

Plays

The Stonemason: A Play in Five Acts. Hopewell, New Jersey, Ecco Press, 1994.

Television Play: *The Gardener's Son,* 1977.

*

Critical Studies: *The Achievement of Cormac McCarthy* by Vereen M. Bell, Baton Rouge, Louisiana State University Press, 1988; *Perspectives on Cormac McCarthy* edited by Edwin T. Arnold and Dianne C. Luce, Jackson, University Press of Mississippi, 1993; *Notes on 'Blood Meridian'* by John Sepich, Louisville, Kentucky, Bellarmine College Press, 1993.

*   *   *

Many contemporary writers who enjoy an academic following are themselves academics, or are at least willing to address academic audiences through readings or interviews. Cormac McCarthy is unusual in this sense, though he evades the spotlight along with other notorious hermits like J.D. Salinger and Thomas Pynchon. Unlike Salinger and Pynchon, McCarthy's reputation in the academic world and with a widespread general audience has come about only in the late 1980s, even though the first of his seven novels was published in 1965. The delay in recognition for McCarthy is perhaps due to the fact that he doesn't fit comfortably among his contemporaries; his writing seems to connect best with an older tradition, one which explores the often tragic implications of the rugged individual trying to survive the hostile North American frontier. While narrating the lives of his rough-hewn outsiders, McCarthy subtly reveals a profound awareness of literary tradition; he is frequently compared to Faulkner and Melville. Yet McCarthy's ability to tell stories, notably his command of descriptive language and his unfailing ear for dialogue, ultimately supersedes the allusive aspects of his work.

The critical connection to Faulkner is most apparent in McCarthy's first four novels which take place in and around his native Tennessee, and which are characterized by Faulknerian prose style and themes. From the opening page of his first novel *The Orchard Keeper,* which describes how a piece of barbed-wire fence has grown and tangled itself throughout an elm tree, we are conscious of being in a world where something human and malignant has tainted the landscape. *The Orchard Keeper* is less concerned with detailing the life of its protagonist, John Wesley Rattner, than with showing the deterioration of the social order of Rattner's community. The characters in this community struggle in vain for some sense of cultural value; the implication is that revenge and survival instincts will prevail over any sense of community, or even common respect for others. The novel's ending involves one character's feverish search for a platinum plate rumored to be in the head of the corpse of Kenneth Rattner, John Wesley's father. This profiteering disrespect for the traditional sanctity of human life and the rights of others is evident to a greater degree in *Outer Dark,* McCarthy's second novel, which examines the result of incest between a brother and sister. The child borne of their incest, initially abandoned, becomes the object of the individual searches of Culla and Rinthy Holme. On their journeys, they meet with characters who exploit, mistreat, or abuse them to various degrees. The social order that was deteriorating in McCarthy's first novel seems entirely dissolved in his second. His third novel, *Child of God,* puts no more faith in the future of humanity. Lester Ballard, the protagonist, metamorphoses from a potentially dangerous outsider to a necrophilic sociopath, hunted by his fellow townspeople in a labyrinth of caves under Sevier County, Tennessee. Taken together, these first three novels provide a bleak vision of the rural South and its tragic history; they are also the source of some of McCarthy's most experimental prose, revealing his masterful command of idiom and gift for description, the beauty of which provides a stark contrast to the subject matter.

Suttree, McCarthy's fourth novel, stands apart from his first three novels in more than one way. Though it is also about an outsider drifting through eastern Tennessee, the tone is somewhat more affirmative. *Suttree* is considerably longer than its predecessors, and McCarthy uses the space to make the protagonist, Cornelius Suttree, human in a way that his other characters are not. Suttree, a fisherman, seems to have some regard for the future; his objective is not merely to survive the circumstances of his social condition, but also to embody some version of grace, in contrast to the band of misfits who surround him. His life continues even after incarceration, a period of mental illness, repeated nights of drunken brawling, and two failed attempts at love. *Suttree* is more humorous than McCarthy's other work, and notably less violent, especially when placed next to *Blood Meridian,* his fifth novel. *Blood Meridian* may in fact be the most violent novel in recent literary history. It focuses on a group of mid-19th-century bounty hunters who roam the Texas-Mexico border murdering Indians for their scalps. Moving away from the type of a unified single character he created in *Suttree,* McCarthy depicts his band of marauders as archetypes— three are known as the judge, the ex-priest, and the kid. Amidst all the bloodshed—the same disregard for the sanctity of human life evident in McCarthy's first three novels—one can sense something intensely philosophical in *Blood Meridian;* these killers, so alien to the reader's world, represent a more fundamental element of human nature than we would care to admit.

McCarthy updates the landscape from *Blood Meridian* to the 20th century in order to confront some element of human experience again in his most recent novels, *All the Pretty Horses* and *The Crossing,* which constitute the first two volumes of "The Border Trilogy." *All the Pretty Horses* contains McCarthy's familiar convention of characters bent on surviving unfavorable circumstances. John Grady Cole, without hope for a future in his hometown, sets forth on horseback with his friend Lacey Rawlins into Mexico, where they attempt to make a living breaking horses on a farm. The romance of this journey vanishes abruptly when they find themselves in a Mexican prison, where their survival is threatened by hostile prisoners. Billy and Boyd Parnham face similar hostility in *The Crossing;* their journey into Mexico is necessitated by revenge and a sense of duty to family and to nature. The necessity that the youthful protagonists grow up quickly in the face of harsh external circumstances gives their journeys into Mexico mythical import. McCarthy relies much more on his ear for dialogue in these novels than on his gift for description; consequently, his more recent prose reads more like Hemingway than Faulkner. The first two books of the Border Trilogy seem more concerned with getting the story out than with reveling in the sound and texture of language, and consequently may be less obscure to a general readership than his earlier novels. But whether one chooses to read the denser, earlier novels, or the more accessible Border Trilogy, it is indisputable that McCarthy is worth reading as the heir apparent to various American literary traditions and as a storyteller with a gift for both description and dialogue.

—D. Quentin Miller

McCAULEY, Sue (Montgomery)

Nationality: New Zealander. **Born:** Dannevirre, 1 December 1941. **Family:** Married 1) Denis McCauley in 1962, one son and one daughter; 2) Pat Hammond in 1979. **Career:** copywriter, New Zealand Broadcasting Corporation, Napier, 1959-61; journalist, *New Zealand Listener,* Wellington, 1961-62, Taranaki *Herald,* New Plymouth, 1963-64, and Christchurch *Press,* 1964-65; writer-in-residence, University of Auckland, 1986. **Awards:** New Zealand Book award, 1983; Mobil award, for radio play, 1982; New Zealand Literary Fund grants. **Agent:** Glenys Bean, 15 Elizabeth Street, Freeman's Bay, Auckland. **Address:** 59 Laurence Street, Christchurch 1, New Zealand.

PUBLICATIONS

Novels

Other Halves. Auckland, Hodder and Stoughton, 1982; London, Hodder and Stoughton, 1983; New York, Penguin, 1985.
Then Again. Auckland, Hodder and Stoughton, 1986; London, Hodder and Stoughton, 1987.
Bad Music. Auckland, Hodder and Stoughton, 1990.

Uncollected Short Stories

"The Alternative Life," in *New Zealand Listener* (Wellington), 1976.
"Mothers Day," "John Harrison Is a Drip," "The Puzzle," and "Pansy," all in *Thursday Magazine* (Auckland), 1970s.
Waiting for Heathcliff (produced Christchurch, 1988).

Screenplay: *Other Halves,* adaptation of her own novel, 1984.

Radio Plays: *The Obituary,* 1967; *The Evening Out,* 1968; *ABC,* 1970; *Robbie,* 1972; *Crutch,* 1975; *Minor Adjustment,* 1975; *Some Without a Sigh,* 1975; *Letters to May,* 1977; *The Ordinary Girl,* 1978; *When Did He Last Buy You Flowers?,* 1980; *The Voice Despised,* 1980; *The Missionaries,* 1981; *Isobel, God and the Cowboy,* 1981; *The Ezra File,* 1982; *Thank You Buzz Aldrin,* 1982; *The Man Who Sleeps with His Mother,* 1983; *Family Ties,* 1986; *Waiting for Heathcliff,* adaptation of her own play.

Television Plays: *As Old as the World,* 1968; *Friends and Neighbours,* 1973; *The Shadow Trader* series, 1989; *Shark in the Park* (episodic), 1991; *Married,* 1993; *Matrons of Honour,* 1993; *Marlin Bay,* with Greg McGee, 1993.

Other

Editor, *Erotic Writing.* New York, Penguin, 1992.

*

Sue McCauley comments:

Writers for screen and radio are never asked to provide an introduction to their work. That may be why I feel more comfortable in the role of script writer—being taken seriously is a terrifying thing. Another plus about writing for screen is that, providing you have an IQ over 50, you can sample the genre and feel needed. But (and I say this after many years in journalism) prose fiction is still the only medium I know where a writer is allowed to tell the truth (at least as s/he perceives it). And every so often that freedom feels hard to resist.

All three of my novels have been about modern social attitudes and personal relationships. They have focused on people of low-to-average education and limited financial means—not by way of a political statement but because, as a person of low-to-average education and limited financial means, these have been the kind of people I know best.

However, in style all the novels are, I believe, unalike. I was attempting different things and driven by different motivations. *Other Halves* grew out of personal anger and *Then Again* out of generalized fear. *Bad Music,* my third novel was, I suspect, something of a reaction to the cultural circles that had been prepared (somewhat diffidently) to embrace me on account of my having written two novels. *Bad Music* I wrote just to please myself and other people with bad attitudes.

I've been writing for a living for 30 years and I don't think I've yet got the hang of it. But I do have one simple philosophy—the reader is a friend and should not be subjected to boredom, posturings or . . . I would say lies, but lies are a kind of fiction. I'm afraid the only word that suits it is . . . bullshit.

*   *   *

"Making music is like any skill," remarks Hal, a musician in Sue McCauley's third novel, *Bad Music.* "The more you do it, the better you get. If you listen to some of the great bands in their earlier years they sound like a pack of uncoordinated roosters. At eighteen you think you've discovered the ultimate sound but in fact you're barely acquainted with the instrument you play. I'm glad I'm finally getting to be an old codger."

McCauley, in her first novel *Other Halves,* could hardly be accused of being unacquainted with her instrument. Rather she is finely attuned to her craft, demonstrating an acute ear for the vernacular and a clear understanding of the social issues which inform her three novels. Although each has a specificity of time and place, this is not in itself a limitation, for the issues McCauley addresses have resonances throughout Western culture even though some of the details may differ.

Such is the case with *Other Halves.* The protagonist, Liz Harvey, admits herself as a voluntary patient to a psychiatric hospital, leaving behind acquaintances who "looked like the cover photo of a knitting pattern or a soap packet" and a marriage in which, according to "clear headed and convincing" husband Ken: "our main problem was your loss of individuality. That may sound hard, but it is true. There came a point where I couldn't respect you anymore. While I was growing, you were regressing."

This is, however, no novel of suburban neurosis or of women and madness, for here she encounters the streetwise, arrogant, 16-year-old Maori boy, Tug. Illiterate, semi-articulate in English and even more so in Maori, dislocated from his extended family, owing loyalty initially only to his street kid gang. Admitted for treatment by the judicial system, he is arguably as powerless and as dispossessed as is she.

The parallels between the oppression of women and that of a colonized, indigenous people are readily drawn by the reader, and in *Other Halves* Liz and Tug's problematic relationship encapsulates the rising challenge to the dominant discourse by both women and Maori. This discomfiture at the growing awareness of social injustices such as lack of education, lack of job opportunities, poverty, and homelessness invites a typical official response:

> "But my point is," he stabbed his finger towards her, "it's only *you* who sees these things as problems. You with your middle-class values. I'll guarantee Thomas [Tug] never thought of himself as having problems until some well-intentioned social worker told him he had them. . . . But that's what happens when people start shoveling their middle-class values onto other races."

The analysis offered by one of the women is couched not in the elegant, academic language of Betty Friedan, but as "I dunno how the fuck I'm gonna manage here. It's not really my chosen environment." The chosen environment of *Then Again,* Motuwairua, is an indication of McCauley's corrosive wit. One literal translation is Island of the Spirit/Soul, and it is there that a motley cross-section of society chooses to live in order to escape from or retreat from the pressures and demands of a materialistic, self-absorbed, corrupt and corrupting "civilization." Despite its name this is no utopia but a microcosm of the larger society where each character's needs and goals are crystallized, experience sharpened and intensified. The single mother, Maureen, escapes with her three small children from a sadistic marriage to a tumbledown shanty only to find herself under the scrutiny of an impersonal Welfare system and an anonymous, vindictive neighbor. Worn down by economic and emotional insecurity plus the demands made upon her by her children, her response to her younger son's bringing her a thing of beauty, "a large, perfect, transparent shell of which once may have been a cicada or a cricket. She told him, cruel and deadpan, that the thing he held was called a mother. See, she said, her children have eaten her all away."

In contrast with the self effacing, almost faceless Maureen, the seismic, ebullient Josie "fair, fat and forty-six" refuses to marry her lover of seven years standing because she "can't be certain that the act of marriage doesn't in itself precipitate divorce." Nonetheless, her relationship is kept alive by occasional partner swapping and frequent fantasy. Despite her amorous nature she is well aware of the negative effects of patriarchal power:

> "Need a rooster," said old Bill. "Keeps the hens happy." "Too right," said Geoff. But Josie had seen how the hens run and cringe when he saunters past. She's seen them trapped in corners, rammed against the netting like an old mat being shaken. Eyes closed, beaks open, thinking of Mother England. Happy?

By placing this perception within the consciousness of a thoroughly heterosexual woman, the political statement assumes an unexpected potency and illustrates the wry humor which characterizes McCauley's work.

McCauley is careful to give her characters, on the whole, a credible inner life, a suitable motivating force, allowing each to explore and express appropriate concerns ranging from the anger and pain of a young, alienated boy in search of a friend, the emotional inadequacy of an embittered, sensitive, alcoholic ex-journalist to those of the outwardly secure and stroppy group of lesbian feminist separatists. She avoids the stereotypical by rarely allowing her charac-

ters to become pompous or didactic, avoids overkill by diffusing statements with varying doses of self-knowledge, wit, and humor.

The elements of wit, humor, appropriate concerns, an ear for the vernacular, and appreciation of social concerns and social change, an understanding of human nature and experience, the ability to explore the inner life and the irreverence towards sacred cows coalesce in *Bad Music*. The text appears deceptively simple, for it seems to imply and express a yearning for the Golden Age of innocence, when Elvis Presley ruled the air waves and would-be pop stars acted out rebellion in fantasy shoot-outs at the local cinema and played at the Town Hall.

Bad music (i.e. popular music), creates and reflects the aspirations of the age, but nostalgia by its very nature is selective. "We were hearing in our hearts . . . everything was bigger and younger and faster and freer. . . ." The remembered innocence and yearning is juxtaposed with the cruel reality of music and groupies, the drug subculture where a "muso" will inform on his mate in order to avoid a bust, where recycled dreams are as tatty and unfashionable as the recycled clothing the protagonist, Kath, attempts to sell.

Bad Music is an investigation of the power of myth, of how popular culture persuades our perception, of how nostalgia clouds rational memory. It speaks, as do her previous two novels, for the inarticulate and dissects with skill and elegance, a society renowned for its taciturnity. Perhaps the irrepressible Audrey in *Other Halves* voices the author's function:

> "They told me you're not into talking. Well, that's okay. I can take it or leave it. I tend to talk quite a bit myself so I hope you don't mind if I sometimes do the talking for both of us."

—Caroline Steemson

McELROY, Joseph (Prince)

Nationality: American. **Born:** Brooklyn, New York, 21 August 1930. **Education:** Williams College, Williamstown, Massachusetts, 1947-51, B.A. 1951; Columbia University, New York, 1951-52, 1954-56, M.A. 1952, Ph.D. in English 1961. **Military Service:** Served in the United States Coast Guard 1952-54. **Family:** Married 1) Joan Leftwich in 1961, one daughter; 2) Barbara Ellmann in 1988, one son. **Career:** Instructor and assistant professor of English, University of New Hampshire, Durham, 1956-62. Since 1964 professor of English, Queens College, City University of New York. Visiting professor, Johns Hopkins University, Baltimore, 1976, Columbia University, 1978, University of Paris, 1981, and New York University, 1984; Visiting Scholar, Temple University, Philadelphia, 1991. Writer-in-residence, Northwestern University, Evanston, Illinois, 1977; Hurst Professor, Washington University, St. Louis, 1979. Lives in New York City. **Awards:** Rockefeller grant, 1968; Ingram-Merrill Foundation grant, 1970, 1985; Creative Artists Public Service grant, 1973; National Endowment for the Arts fellowship, 1973, 1986; Guggenheim fellowship, 1976; American Academy award, 1977; D.H. Lawrence fellowship, 1979. **Agent:** Melanie Jackson Agency, 250 West 57th Street, New York, New York 10107, U.S.A.

PUBLICATIONS

Novels

A Smuggler's Bible. New York, Harcourt Brace, 1966; London, Deutsch, 1968.
Hind's Kidnap: A Pastoral on Familiar Airs. New York, Harper, 1969; London, Blond, 1970.
Ancient History. New York, Knopf, 1971.
Lookout Cartridge. New York, Knopf, 1974.
Plus. New York, Knopf, 1977.
Ship Rock, A Place: From Women and Men, A Novel in Progress. Concord, New Hampshire, Ewert, 1980.
Women and Men. New York, Knopf, 1987.
The Letter Left to Me. New York, Knopf, 1988.

Uncollected Short Stories

"The Accident," in *New American Review 2,* edited by Theodore Solotaroff. New York, New American Library, 1968.
"The Future," in *The Best American Short Stories 1981,* edited by Hortense Calisher and Shannon Ravenel. Boston, Houghton Mifflin, 1981.
"The King's Reforms," in *New York Journal of the Arts,* Spring 1981.
"The Departed Tenant," in *New Yorker,* 23 November 1981.
"The Man with the Bag Full of Boomerangs in the Bois de Boulogne," in *Partisan Review* (Boston), vol. 51, no. 1, 1984.
"Preparations for Search," in *Formations* (Wilmette, Illinois), Spring 1984.
"Daughter of the Revolution," in *Prize Stories 1985,* edited by William Abrahams. New York, Doubleday, 1985.
"Canoe Repair," in *Review of Contemporary Fiction* (Elmwood Park, Illinois), Spring 1990.

*

Manuscript Collection: Middlebury College, Vermont.

Critical Studies: "Joseph McElroy Issue" of *Review of Contemporary Fiction* (Elmwood Park, Illinois), Spring 1990 (includes bibliography by Steven Moore).

*   *   *

Joseph McElroy explores the many implications of symmetries between the behavior of electrons and the behavior of humans. The flow of traffic in our cities, the pulse of blood through one's aorta, the dash of information through a computer from keyboard to printout: McElroy adumbrates these analogies, and assesses their intent. This is, of course, in addition to the imaginative depth and human scope that we have a right to expect from one of the major writers of the period.

A Smuggler's Bible introduced McElroy's first readers to a new world of narrative discontinuities, multiple viewpoints, and a heightened modernist sense that the telling is inseparable from the tale. Eight numbered chapters are divided from each other by discursive intrusions from a witty if disembodied narrator. David Brooke, on board ship from New York to London, is determined to bring coherence to seven autobiographical manuscripts he has written himself. Formally, then, we are in a universe parallel to that of Doris Lessing's *The Golden Notebook,* but the narrative mentality is con-

siderably wider-ranging and more freely associative in McElroy. The novel's title refers to a hollowed-out copy of a Bible used for purposes of contraband; McElroy fills it with a trove of metaphoric readings for the ways in which we smuggle meanings beneath a host of impostures in daily life.

In *Hind's Kidnap: A Pastoral on Familiar Airs* Jack Hind, a six-foot-seven New Yorker, is obsessed with the kidnapping, seven years earlier, of a four-year-old boy named Hershey Laurel. Hind spends the novel accumulating clues—some of them imagined, some apparently real—in an effort to solve the crime. It emerges that sleuthing means to dislodge information from its context—that the very act of perception qualifies as a kind of kidnapping. McElroy uses such master metaphors as smuggling, in the first novel, and kidnapping here, to cast a polarized light over the action which revolves prismatically for the reader's surprise, recognition, and delight.

Ancient History, as McElroy has described in a remarkable self-study ("Neural Neighborhoods and Other Concrete Abstracts," *Tri-Quarterly,* Fall 1975), extrapolates certain concepts of time and narrative form that he learned from Michel Butor's novel *Degrees.* "Concrete abstracts" may define the characters as well as the plot, since the principals are named, alphabetically, Al, Bob, Cy, and Dom. Upon Dom's death, Cy begins to examine the lives of Bob, a city dweller, and Al, a country boy. The novel explores spatial relationships analogous to field theory in physics; its subtitle, accordingly, denotes "a new time, or state like time, or state of being outside or beside time."

Lookout Cartridge may well be McElroy's masterpiece; of his seven novels to date, it is the one most often compared to William Gaddis's *The Recognitions* and Thomas Pynchon's *Gravity's Rainbow.* It concerns the efforts by one Cartwright to track down the thief of several rolls of film from a clandestinely shot movie which may or may not have captured scenes of political crime. The locations shift speedily and often between New York, London, and Stonehenge, where part of the film was shot, as the narrative, following Cartwright's thoughts closely, veers from the comically pedantic to the cosmically profound. Analog and digital models of computing are presented as analogies of human fate and freedom, and the concept of human divinity itself glimmers behind much of the action. In the opinion of many, *Lookout Cartridge* is one of the most unjustly overlooked novels in the American canon. Amid much else it offers a knowledgeable survey of the mindsets of London and New York. The novel suspends itself, figuratively speaking, on an airplane's flightpath between the English and the American, much as *A Smuggler's Bible* had done by ship. McElroy's Anglo-American binocularity recalls that of Henry James.

Plus, offering in its title to negate the negators, is the most abstract of McElroy's already challenging fiction. The main character is called IMP PLUS where IMP stands for "Interplanetary Monitoring Platform." "He" has been distilled from a disembodied human brain, a conceit reminiscent of Isaac Asimov's "positronic brain."

The novel's strangely unnerving conclusion mentions "a power raised to wholeness by camouflage," adding camouflage to smuggling and kidnapping as master metaphors for the dishonesty of consciousness. *Plus* suggests an artificial angel—a high-tech, human artifact that manages a plausible mimesis of something divine. Lessing, in other ways entirely different, neighbors McElroy in "intellectual science fiction" too.

Women and Men (another way, *inter alia,* of saying "plus") comprises 1192 pages, and not for that reason alone McElroy's sixth novel, upon its publication in 1987, invited comparisons both to Joyce's major work and to that of Tolstoy. The electron model suggests polarity, so McElroy slips over his lens the polarizing filter of sex. How women behave, how men behave, a "division of labor" susceptible to extensive and minute study. Grace Kimball and Jim Mayn share overlapping orbits—they inhabit the same New York apartment house—but they never meet. Around and about and through them pass a large cast of relations both distinctive and familiar. Binary rhythms—such as the links and contrasts of knowledge, or the inhaling and exhaling at every level of life—animate a novel that itself claims to breathe. A chorus-like collective voice speaks in occasional interstitial chapters, called "breathers." As before, McElroy eschews continuity, and seems to follow André Gide's dictum, "*Ne jamais profiter de l'élan acquis*" (roughly, never to take advantage of the narrative's momentum). The demands upon the reader, and the corresponding rewards, are strong.

A much briefer novel, and perhaps the most accessible introduction to McElroy's work, *The Letter Left to Me* tells of a late father's letter of advice delivered to the 15-year-old narrator by his mother. The narrator observes, with some particularity, his own reactions to the letter, the response of his family, and, when he gets to college, that of everyone around him—for his mother sends a copy of the letter to the Dean, who has it distributed to the college community. The novel offers a placid and nearly affectless surface, quite *à la nouveau roman,* beneath which ripples a potent pathos, the loss of father and the loss of missed opportunities.

McElroy's career attests to his refusal to confuse language with life, conjoined to a refusal to let life pass unwitnessed by words. His intelligence and achievement are unique in American letters.

—Brian Stonehill

McEWAN, Ian (Russell)

Nationality: British. **Born:** Aldershot, Hampshire, 21 June 1948. **Education:** Woolverstone Hall School; University of Sussex, Brighton, B.A. (honours) in English 1970; University of East Anglia, Norwich, M.A. in English 1971. **Family:** Married Penny Allen in 1982 (divorced 1995); two stepdaughters and two sons. Lives in Oxford. **Awards:** Maugham award, 1976; *Evening Standard* award, for screenplay, 1983. D.Litt.: University of Sussex, 1989; University of East Anglia, 1993. Fellow, Royal Society of Literature, 1984. **Address:** c/o Jonathan Cape Ltd., 20 Vauxhall Bridge Road, London SW1V 2SA, England.

PUBLICATIONS

Novels

The Cement Garden. London, Cape, and New York, Simon and Schuster, 1978.
The Comfort of Strangers. London, Cape, and New York, Simon and Schuster, 1981.
The Child in Time. London, Cape, and Boston, Houghton Mifflin, 1987.
The Innocent. London, Cape, and New York, Doubleday, 1990.
Black Dogs. London, Cape, and New York, Doubleday, 1992.

Short Stories

First Love, Last Rites. New York, Random House, and London, Cape, 1975.
In Between the Sheets. London, Cape, 1978; New York, Simon and Schuster, 1979.

Uncollected Short Stories

"Intersection," in *Tri-Quarterly* (Evanston, Illinois), Fall 1975.
"Untitled," in *Tri-Quarterly* (Evanston, Illinois), Winter 1976.
"Deep Sleep, Light Sleeper," in *Harpers and Queen* (London), 1978.

Plays

The Imitation Game: Three Plays for Television (includes *Solid Geometry* and *Jack Flea's Birthday Celebration*). London, Cape, 1981; Boston, Houghton Mifflin, 1982.
Or Shall We Die? (oratorio), music by Michael Berkeley (produced London, 1983; New York, 1985). London, Cape, 1983.
The Ploughman's Lunch (screenplay). London, Methuen, 1985.
Soursweet (screenplay). London, Faber, 1988.
A Move Abroad: Or Shall We Die? and *The Ploughman's Lunch.* London, Pan, 1989.

Screenplays: *The Ploughman's Lunch,* 1983; *Soursweet,* 1989; *The Good Son,* 1994.

Radio Play: *Conversation with a Cupboardman,* 1975.

Television Plays and Films: *Jack Flea's Birthday Celebration,* 1976; *The Imitation Game,* 1980; *The Last Day of Summer,* from his own short story, 1983.

Other (for children)

Rose Blanche. London, Cape, 1985.
The Daydreamer. London, Cape, and New York, HarperCollins, 1994.

*

Critical Studies: "*The Cement Garden* d'Ian McEwan" by Max Duperray, in *Études Anglaises* (Paris), vol. 35, no. 4, 1982; "McEwan/Barthes" by David Sampson, in *Southern Review* (Adelaide), March 1984.

*   *   *

With the publication of three books between 1975 and 1978, Ian McEwan was promoted during the late 1970s as one of the most exciting new talents in English fiction for many years. Like Martin Amis, the other literary *enfant terrible* of the 1970s, McEwan won the Somerset Maugham award for his first book, a collection of stories called *First Love, Last Rites,* which also achieved a *succès de scandale.* McEwan, like Amis, immediately acquired notoriety as a "shocking sensationalist" on the basis of work neither shocking nor sensational—except, it appears, in England. Admittedly, McEwan's subject matter is often potentially lurid and pornographic, with sex, perversion, and bodily functions featuring frequently, but his actual treatment of these is highly controlled and even reticent.

It is easy to damn McEwan as obscene or praise him as liberated by isolating the "dirty" bits, but both responses reveal more about the commentators than about McEwan since they are based on misrepresentation.

Nevertheless, there is something obsessional in his early work, a quality not evident when his stories are read separately, but conspicuous enough when encountered in a collection. Several stories in *First Love, Last Rites* include scenes of male masturbation, and the title story involves copulation during menstruation. "Homemade" is about a teenage boy, determined to lose his virginity, who seduces his 10-year-old sister during a game of Mummies and Daddies; "Disguises" treats a teenage boy forced to dress as a girl; "Solid Geometry" features a pickled penis; "Butterflies" concerns a lonely man who almost inadvertently becomes the sex killer of a nine-year-old girl. McEwan's second collection, *In Between the Sheets,* is similar in this respect, featuring bondage, bestiality, a sex doll, and teenage lesbianism, while the first story, actually called "Pornography," culminates in a penis amputation performed as an act of revenge. Although *The Cement Garden,* his third book but first novel, is less replete with the more bizarre and deviant aspects of sexuality, it still contains incest, adolescent sex games, and childhood transvestism. Again there is a considerable emphasis on the sexually confused world of adolescents and teenagers.

Yet obsessional as he is, McEwan is no more a pornographer than T.S. Eliot is in that poem full of gloomy sexuality, *The Waste Land.* In a number of his stories, McEwan, too, is depicting an existential void, an emotional and spiritual waste land of frustration, lovelessness, noncommunication, isolation, and *la nausée,* and he finds some of his objective correlatives in sexual behaviour. His reputation as a "shocking" writer has probably arisen not because he writes about sex and perversion but because he deals with them in such an antiromantic and unerotic way. When he focuses on masturbation, or lovemaking with nonhuman substitutes, or the link between disease and sex, McEwan severs the connection between sex and meaningful fulfilment and is therefore radically undermining the importance sex has assumed in Western society as a substitute for religion, with orgasm replacing God. One thing McEwan most decidedly is not is titillating.

Sex is an important source of objective correlatives for McEwan, as it was for Eliot, but it is far from being the only one. It is significant that in the first paragraph of *First Love, Last Rites* the narrator of "Homemade" says, "this story is about Raymond and not about virginity, coitus, incest and self-abuse," suggesting that the sex, prominent though it is, is not there just for its own sake. In the ironically entitled "Butterflies" the images of widespread industrial decay, the "brown stinking water" of the canal, and the boys torturing a cat in a scrap yard, all correspond to the emotional sterility, stifled passion, and inner wasteland of the narrator himself. The futuristic and dystopian "Two Fragments: March 199-" (*In Between the Sheets*), which is strongly reminiscent of Doris Lessing's *The Memoirs of a Survivor* in its prophetic portrayal of a disintegrating civilization, employs similar imagery to convey McEwan's bleak, joyless vision of the human condition. The house occupied by the orphaned children in *The Cement Garden,* a fable about the fallen and apparently irredeemable world of adolescence and therefore bearing some resemblance to Golding's *Lord of the Flies,* is an island in a sea of demolition and desolation, and the symbolism of this urban wilderness, like that of the nature-destroying cement garden itself, is as clear as those of the polluted Thames and the dust heaps in Dickens's *Our Mutual Friend,* to take an example other than *The Waste Land.*

McEwan's mastery of the short story is unquestionable. The outstanding example in his first collection is the title story, "First Love, Last Rites," a complex study of adolescence on the verge of adulthood, awakening to the potency of sexual love, the possibility of parenthood, and the reality of death. This compact and electrifying story builds up to a horrific climax with the brutal killing of a pregnant rat, an event that has a profound effect on the narrator. The title story of *In Between the Sheets* is also very memorable, but not perhaps as stunning as the longest and only American one in the collection, "Psychopolis," a word summing up the city where it is set, Los Angeles, the symbolic "unreal city" of many writers' wasteland. While containing an abundance of the "outrageous" ingredients for which he is famous, this story is really about dislocation, incoherence, futility, and the impossibility of achieving wholeness in the pluralist, multi-faceted psychopolis we have created for ourselves where truth is so ambiguous and uncertain. The admirable technical control of his stories is not so evident in *The Cement Garden,* where the first-person narration by a teenager is less consistently sustained than it might be, the adolescent consciousness sometimes appearing to have an adult awareness of the situation. McEwan appears to have approached the writing of the longer form with some trepidation, and *The Cement Garden* might have been more satisfactory had it been concentrated into a long story rather than extended into a novel, short though it is.

With *The Cement Garden* McEwan exhausted one particular creative vein. This first phase has been much admired for the stylish power with which he conveys his own variant of the grotesque, but is not altogether immune to the charge that there is something intellectually modish in his underlying nihilism, morbidity, and gothicism. The first sign of an important and unexpected change of direction in his work was one of the best British television plays in recent years, *The Imitation Game,* which differs from his fiction of the 1970s in being conventionally realistic and committedly polemical. Dealing with British intelligence during World War II, the play cogently yet subtly articulates an antiwar, pro-feminist argument about male hegemony and patriarchal values, especially the threat they pose to the future of civilization. McEwan's libretto for a television oratorio, *Or Shall We Die?,* specifically about the danger of a nuclear holocaust, presents similar ideas in a more overtly propagandist way. His second short novel, *The Comfort of Strangers,* introduces related themes but much more obliquely and without the element of doctrinaire provocation appropriate to the mass medium of television but undesirable in the one-to-one author-reader relationship of fiction. Set in Venice, although neither the city nor its sights are ever mentioned by name, *The Comfort of Strangers* is an impressionistic, dreamlike narrative that finally bursts into violent nightmare. By describing the encounter between an almost androgynous English couple on holiday in the city and a totally different couple they meet there, McEwan explores the nature of human relationships, especially between the sexes, and how patriarchal societies implicitly endorse domination and brutality.

After the publication of *The Comfort of Strangers* John Fletcher said of McEwan that he might "turn out to be a mere nine-days'-wonder in the British literary scene" and six years elapsed before the publication of his next novel, *The Child in Time.* This confirmed that McEwan, now a father, had undergone something of a sea-change as a writer, shedding many of the preoccupations of his early fiction. *The Child in Time* is about marriage, parenthood, and the adult-child relationship, but McEwan approaches his themes more in terms of absence than presence, simultaneously placing the personal issues in a public context of politics and science. The abduction and unknown fate of their five-year-old daughter traumatises the lives of the central character Stephen Lewis and his wife Julie. Stephen is a writer of children's books and as a result has been appointed to a committee dealing with the Prime Minister's pet project, the Official Commission on Childcare. After the "unthinkable" and "impossible" has happened to them, Stephen and Julie struggle to come to terms with their loss, and their suffering leads them to a new awareness of what love, loyalty, and caring can mean. Although they move apart for a time, the novel ends positively with the birth of another child to Julie, suggesting that although the past cannot be undone it may be redeemed.

With *The Innocent,* a strange love story set in Berlin during the Cold War, McEwan again attempts something different, exploiting the potential of the spy novel without actually writing one. He bases parts of his narrative on an actual CIA-MI6 surveillance operation in 1955-56 using a tunnel under the Wall and even introduces real-life characters, notably the notorious British double agent George Blake. The political, emotional, and sexual "innocent" who enters this world of intrigue and deception, a veritable wilderness of mirrors, is a young British Post Office technician, Leonard Marnham. For Leonard, who works on communications systems needed in the tunnel, Berlin proves to be a rite of passage and an initiation by fire, especially when he begins an affair with a young German woman, Maria. The killing of her brutal husband and the horrific disposal of his dismembered body in the tunnel brings a grisly, grotesque dimension into the novel, recalling McEwan's early fiction, but the moving, upbeat conclusion is even more positive than that of *The Child in Time,* in which the couple's reunion is at the expense of their social and political involvement. In *The Innocent,* Leonard and Maria necessarily separate after Otto's death, but in the final chapter, set 30 years later, it is clear that what was lost can be found and regained. At the personal as well as the political level, there is a promise of hope and renewal.

The Child in Time attempted to deal with the political by being set in an ultra-Thatcherite Britain of the near-future with privatized beggars on the streets, public transportation abolished, and government committees regulating education and childcare. The reunion of Stephen and Julie represents a retreat from an unpleasant public world into the private world of the nuclear family. The novel also sets up an opposition between "masculine" rationality and "feminine" intuition, or even mysticism: the plot hinges on an "out of time" experience in which Stephen "sees" his own parents some 40 years earlier, sitting in a pub discussing whether or not his mother should have an abortion. She later tells Stephen that she thought she "saw" the face of a child floating outside the pub window on that day, which convinced her that it—Stephen himself—had a right to live.

In his latest novel, *Black Dogs,* McEwan continues his attempt to engage with the contemporary political situation whilst undermining this attempt with a similar and dangerously oversimplified polarization of the mystical-feminine and the rational-masculine. Here, the narrator's parents-in-law, June and Bernard, represent these oppositions: idealistic communists just after the war, both believed in the possibility of a better future until June's encounter, on their honeymoon in France, with the black dogs of the title convinced her of both the existence of absolute evil and of a numinous power that saved her life. The narrator's conversations with June and Bernard not only reinforce this polarization, but, much more subtly, suggest the different versions of the past that we construct for ourselves according to our views of the world. The story of June's encounter with the dogs is tantalizingly suggested in the early stages of the novel, when the narrator visits her in the nursing home where she is dying with a view to writing a memoir of her life: it is finally told with McEwan's precise and chilling clarity, which evokes the heat and beauty of the limestone hills of the Languedoc in the South of France as well as June's terror. Here we also learn that the black dogs were owned and used by the Gestapo when they arrived in the area to suppress the resistance: McEwan cannot resist including a report of the "rumour" that the dogs had been trained to rape women. The narrator also visits Berlin with Bernard in November 1989 to celebrate the fall of the Wall: Bernard is injured in an attempt to defend a young Turk against a gang of skinhead racists. To reinforce a fairly obvious point about the persistence of evil, McEwan has the narrator and his wife-to-be visit Majdanek concentration camp in Poland, an otherwise gratuitous episode except that it is where they fall in love.

Although the narrator says that he remains undecided between the world views of Bernard and June, the narrative is weighted towards the latter, and the sketchy and rather programmatic attempts at political contextualization leave social and human agency mystified. The black dogs are still there, some 50 years later, "fading as they move into the foothills of the mountains from where they will return to haunt us, somewhere in Europe, in another time." McEwan's skill remains that of brilliantly evoking reactions of fear, pain, loss, or love in precisely defined situations and locations: his plots are cleverly, but too simplistically, constructed on an over-schematic opposition that he attempts to link with political ideas or events in novels much too brief (*Black Dogs* is only 174 pages long) to bear their weight.

—Peter Lewis, updated by Nicola King

McGAHERN, John

Nationality: Irish. **Born:** Leitrim, 12 November 1934. **Education:** Presentation College, Carrick-on-Shannon, County Leitrim; St. Patrick's Training College, Dublin; University College, Dublin. **Family:** Married 1) Annikki McGahern; 2) Madeline Green in 1973. **Career:** Primary school teacher, St. John the Baptist Boys School, Clontarf, 1956-64; research fellow, University of Reading, Berkshire, 1968-71; Visiting O'Connor Professor of Literature, Colgate University, Hamilton, New York, 1969, 1972, 1978, 1980; Northern Arts Fellow, University of Newcastle, 1974-76. Lives near Mohill, County Leitrim. **Awards:** [AE] Memorial award, 1962; Macauley fellowship, 1964; Arts Council award, 1966, 1968, 1971, 1978; Society of Authors travelling scholarship, 1975; American Irish Foundation award, 1985. Fellow, Royal Society of Literature; member, Aosdana. **Address:** c/o Faber and Faber Ltd., 3 Queen Square, London WC1N 3AU, England.

PUBLICATIONS

Novels

The Barracks. London, Faber, 1963; New York, Macmillan, 1964.
The Dark. London, Faber, 1965; New York, Knopf, 1966.
The Leavetaking. London, Faber, 1974; Boston, Little Brown, 1975; revised edition, Faber, 1984.
The Pornographer. London, Faber, and New York, Harper, 1979.

Amongst Women. London, Faber, and New York, Viking, 1990.
The Power of Darkness. London, Faber, 1991.

Short Stories

Nightlines. London, Faber, 1970; Boston, Little Brown, 1971.
Getting Through. London, Faber, 1978; New York, Harper, 1980.
High Ground and Other Stories. London, Faber, 1985; New York, Viking, 1987.
The Collected Stories. New York, Knopf, and London, Faber, 1993.

Plays

Sinclair (broadcast, 1971; produced London, 1972).

Radio Play: *Sinclair,* 1971.

Television Plays: *Swallows,* 1975; *The Rockingham Shoot,* 1987.

*

Bibliography: *Brian Moore, Alasdair Gray, John McGahern: A Bibliography of Their First Editions* by David Rees, London, Colophon Press, 1991.

Critical Study: *Outstaring Nature's Eye: The Fiction of John McGahern* by Denis Sampson, Washington, D.C., Catholic University of America Press, and Dublin, Lilliput Press, 1993.

*   *   *

John McGahern's novels create a world where domesticity is dramatic and the mundane are important and where the most bland conversation is underlain with tension and emotion. McGahern's writing has an obsession with the home (both domestic and national) and the family; taken as a whole, his work is a revealing insight into the relationships between family, the individual, the state, religion, and education, especially in Ireland, where most of his novels are set.

It is in the style which he has found, or forged, for himself that McGahern's success lies. The language of his novels is terse, unflamboyant, and pared down to the essentials. But, as the protagonist of *The Pornographer* says, "The words had to be mixed with my own blood." The superficial flatness of his prose manages to create a tension suited to the themes with which the novels deal, so that descriptions of everyday tasks, washing or working in the fields, can suggest melancholy or simmering fury. What initially seems a restrictive style carries with it emotion and commitment and opens the way for a piercing and studied observation of domestic life.

McGahern's first novel, *The Barracks,* which centres on the story of a policeman's wife dying of breast cancer, was widely acclaimed for its sensitive handling both of the homelife of the barracks and, especially, of the suffering of Elizabeth, the main character. It was, however, McGahern's second novel, *The Dark,* which earned him a "reputation" (in a pejorative sense). The novel was seized by Irish Customs and banned in Ireland because it was considered indecent. *The Dark,* appropriately named, certainly goes further than *The Barracks* did in its portrayal of the violence and intense claustrophobia of family life. The father of the family, who is seen beating his son in the first chapter of the novel, is at other times sullen

or contrite, while remaining at all times the centre holding together the family. His stifling egoism, which gains its strength from the ethos of "family," is at once repulsive and compelling and is seen best in his maudlin but pathetic sentimentality when he sleeps in the same bed as his son. This part of the novel is narrated, unusually, in the second person ("What right had he to come and lie with you in bed . . . "), effectively stressing the horrified distance between the son, as narrator, and his father, and putting a safer distance beween the narrator and his past "self," to whom these events have happened.

The Leavetaking takes further McGahern's interest in "home" as an idea, and focuses more directly on Ireland and Irish institutions as a "home." An Irish schoolteacher, taking a year's leave (one of the variants on the title), finds himself in London and married to a divorced woman. The story is told within the framework of the teacher's last day at the school when he faces the inevitability of being sacked because he has married outside the laws of the Catholic church. But even here the magnetism of home is stressed; the teacher, when in London, sees a return to Ireland, despite knowing the consequences, as the only course of action, and he prolongs his stay until the last possible moment, not taking his last "leave" of the job (and the country) until he is forced to. Indeed the bulk of the novel is taken up with the long "leavetaking" (the death) of the teacher's mother, stressing the formative importance of his home and childhood. The novel ends with the teacher and his wife on the verge of leaving for England again, with the incantatory words, reminiscent of the end of Joyce's "The Dead," that stress a final "leavetaking": "I would pray for the boat of our sleep to reach its morning, and see that morning lengthen to an evening of calm weather that comes through night and sleep again to morning after morning, until we meet the first death."

What *The Leavetaking* suggests is the beginning, in McGahern's novels, of a sharper sense of detachment from, of less unquestioning commitment to, the home and childhood than has previously been the case. England offers a potentially new perspective for both the characters of the novels and McGahern as author, though it remains a perspective very much defined by being not-Ireland/home, and leads to reflection on "home" in a new way, so that Ireland, Irish childhood and family remain the central concern of the novels and short stories after *The Leavetaking.*

Evidence of this is *Amongst Women,* which came at the end of a 10-year period in which McGahern had published no novels. Again it is the family that provides the locus of the novel, a centre around which McGahern is able to explore the male-female relationships within a household. Moran, the "daddy" of the novel, an old and disillusioned Republican, places ultimate faith in the importance of his family. As the novel moves towards the death of Moran, carefully, and with exacting detail, it studies the increasingly tense father-daughter and father-son relationships, showing the various degrees of detachment attained by the children. For its understated drama, its controlled prose, and its carefully drawn central character, *Amongst Women* is the most solidly crafted of McGahern's novels.

—Colin Graham

McGRATH, Patrick

Nationality: British. **Born:** London in 1950. **Education:** The University of London, B.A. in English. **Career:** Orderly, Ontario State

Mental Hospital, Oakridge, from 1971, then teacher in Vancouver. **Agent:** Jane Gregory Agency, Riverside Studios, Crisp Road, London NW6 9RL, England.

PUBLICATIONS

Novels

The Grotesque. London, Viking, and New York, Poseidon Press, 1989.
Spider. New York, Simon and Schuster, 1990; London, Viking, 1991.
Dr. Haggard's Disease. London, Viking, and New York, Poseidon Press, 1993.

Short Stories

Blood and Water and Other Tales. London, Penguin, and New York, Poseidon Press, 1989.

Other

Editor, with Bradford Morrow, *The New Gothic: A Collection of Contemporary Gothic Fiction.* New York, Random House, 1991; London, Picador, 1992.

*   *   *

The grotesque and macabre dominate Patrick McGrath's work, as his writing seeks to explore the dimensions of the bizarre, the pathological and the neurotic. In *The Grotesque,* the main protagonist observes "that in the absence of sensory information, *the imagination always tends to the grotesque . . .* I mean when I speak of the grotesque—the fanciful, the bizarre, the absurdly incongruous." The struggle to control hypothesis by incontrovertible fact, to restrain the imagination by empirical data, structures *The Grotesque,* as well as many of the short stories in *Blood and Water.* The reader is frequently faced with the problems arising from a collapse of the distinctions between reality and illusion. McGrath's most recent novel *Spider,* a riveting suspense narrative, also explores the motives of the murderer, the insane, and the causes of psychological trauma.

McGrath's collection *Blood and Water* is a fresh approach to the Gothic genre, the deft combination of horror and comedy striving after what he terms an "elegant weirdness." With speaking boots, talking flies, blood-drinking humans, severed hands, putrefying angels, psychopathic killers, and such classic horror-story locations as the lonely country inn, the isolated mansion, the prison, and the remote English public school, these stories construct a fiction which is both compulsive and intriguing. While there are aspects of these stories which suggest a consciously stylized treatment of the supernatural, this does not detract from their originality of conception.

The Grotesque continues this fascination with murder and mystery. It is part suspense thriller, part horror story, part detective story. The narrative is related retrospectively (if somewhat improbably) by a severely physically and mentally disabled country gentleman bound to a wheelchair, Sir Hugo Crook, who reflects upon the series of bizarre events that followed the employment of Fledge the new butler. The murder of Sidney Giblet, Sir Hugo's prospec-

tive son-in-law, emerges as the first step in a devious strategy of a *coup d'état* in the Crook household, during which Fledge seduces Sir Hugo's wife, causes Sir Hugo to be severely paralysed and ultimately manages to supplant Sir Hugo as lord of the manor. Sir Hugo's gardener and longtime friend, George Lecky, is framed and wrongly convicted of the murder, despite the efforts of various characters to save him from execution.

The Grotesque frequently involves itself in philosophical speculation, pondering the nature and materiality of the "self," particularly as Sir Hugo is pronounced "ontologically dead" in the wheelchair. These existential speculations occur as the result of the attempt to establish the events to which Sir Hugo is witness, as a form of order: "Retrospection does yield order, no doubt about that, but I wonder if this order isn't perhaps achieved solely as a function of the remembering mind, which of its very nature tends to yield order." For challenge to social order and hierarchy are at the heart of the narrative. As a paleontologist, the predominant interest in Sir Hugo's life is the "birdlike" dinosaur that he discovered in Africa—*Phlegmosaurus Carbonensis*—and the prehistoric predatory behaviour of this animal increasingly becomes an analogy for the manner in which Sir Hugo is attacked and savaged by Fledge, "in this case, calculated opportunism on the part of an innately devious inferior with inflated social aspirations." The novel presents the dinosaur world of hunter and hunted, transplanted into the modern peaceful rural scenes of the "civilized" home county of Berkshire. Thus, the novel is not merely a mystery-suspense thriller, but also a sustained, wry critique and analysis of the values of the landed gentry and the relationship between master and servant, where the traditional relationship is comically, but subtly and calculatingly undermined.

Spider, also continues McGrath's preoccupation with murder and mystery, but achieves a complexity and intensity missing from his earlier work. As with *The Grotesque,* one is again presented with the perspective of a passive observer, Denis Cleg (alias Spider), who is recording in a journal, his lonely, isolated childhood in the East End of London, seeking to piece together his life by the means of narrative, "like a shattered window, in the quiet years that followed, fragment by fragment until the picture was whole." Spider's father murders his wife to make way for his new relationship with the prostitute Hilda Wilkinson, who proceeds to take over the household, and which leads to Spider's own breakdown and incarceration in a hospital for the mentally insane. The unexpected twist in the conclusion is well disguised by a complex narrative which throws out proleptic hints about its future direction, and traces the threads back to Spider's early life, as the narrative becomes a web that Spider weaves about his childhood: "And oddly, as my childhood took shape, so did I, Spider, become more coherent, firmer, stronger—I began to have substance."

The book is a study of both mental and physical cruelty, mapping the development of a schizophrenia resulting from the psychological trauma that Spider undergoes. Spider increasingly has a sense of doubleness, and erects barriers against the people he meets: "I would speak and eat and move and *to their eyes* be me, and only I knew that 'I' wasn't there . . . " The crisis of identity becomes increasingly more forceful as Spider's journal progresses, since the difficulties of language and representation become part of the preoccupation with ordering the past and protecting a self-identity, "for I am conscious always of the danger of shattering, which in turn makes me crave *control,* which is why the sensation of being formed, framed, *written* makes me so desperately afraid. For that which can write me can also destroy me."

McGrath is a novelist whose fiction interestingly explores a wide range of ideas in a condensed space, and he has breathed new and vigorous life into the well-trodden paths of the Gothic and mystery genres.

—Tim Woods

McGUANE, Thomas (Francis, III)

Nationality: American. **Born:** Wyandotte, Michigan, 11 December 1939. **Education:** The University of Michigan, Ann Arbor; Olivet College, Michigan; Michigan State University, East Lansing, 1958-62, B.A. 1962; Yale University School of Drama, New Haven, Connecticut, 1962-65, M.F.A. 1965; Stanford University, California (Stegner fellow), 1966-67. **Family:** Married 1) Portia Rebecca Crockett in 1962 (divorced 1975), one son and one daughter; 2) the actress Margot Kidder in 1976 (divorced 1977), one daughter; 3) Laurie Buffett in 1977, two daughters. **Career:** Since 1968 freelance writer and film director. **Awards:** Rosenthal Foundation award, 1972; Montana Governor's award, 1988. **Agent:** Amanda Urban, International Creative Management, 40 West 57th Street, New York, New York 10019. **Address:** P.O. Box 25, McLeod, Montana 59052, U.S.A.

PUBLICATIONS

Novels

The Sporting Club. New York, Simon and Schuster, 1968; London, Deutsch, 1969.
The Bushwhacked Piano. New York, Simon and Schuster, 1971; London, Minerva, 1989.
Ninety-Two in the Shade. New York, Farrar Straus, 1973; London, Collins, 1974.
Panama. New York, Farrar Straus, 1978.
Nobody's Angel. New York, Random House, 1982.
Something to Be Desired. New York, Random House, 1984; London, Secker and Warburg, 1985.
Keep the Change. Boston, Houghton Mifflin, 1989; London, Secker and Warburg, 1990.
Nothing But Blue Skies. Boston, Houghton Mifflin, and London, Secker and Warburg, 1992.

Short Stories

To Skin a Cat. New York, Dutton, 1986; London, Secker and Warburg, 1987.

Uncollected Short Stories

"Another Horse," in *Atlantic* (Boston), October 1974.
"The El Western," in *Writers of the Purple Sage,* edited by Russell Martin and Marc Barasch. New York, Viking, 1984.

Plays

The Missouri Breaks (screenplay). New York, Ballantine, 1976.

Screenplays: *The Bushwhacked Piano,* 1970; *Rancho Deluxe,* 1973; *The Missouri Breaks,* 1975; *Ninety-Two in the Shade,* 1975; *Tom Horn,* with Bud Shrake, 1980.

Other

An Outside Chance: Essays on Sport. New York, Farrar Straus, 1980; revised edition, Boston, Houghton Mifflin, 1990.

*

Manuscript Collections: University of Rochester, New York; Brigham Young University, Provo, Utah; Michigan State University, East Lansing.

Critical Study: *The New American Novel of Manners: The Fiction of Richard Yates, Dan Wakefield, and Thomas McGuane* by Jerome Klinkowitz, Athens, University of Georgia Press, 1986; *Thomas McGuane* by Dexter Westrum, New York, Twayne.

Theatrical Activities:
Director: **Film**—*Ninety-Two in the Shade,* 1975.

Thomas McGuane comments:

I write fiction in the hope of astounding myself. I am seldom successful, and have long ago lost interest in the rest of my audience.

*   *   *

Thomas McGuane writes a new style novel of manners, crafted for an age in which the signs of behavior have become a self-conscious medium with the name of *semiotics.* We cannot know characters until we understand the codes by which they function—Henry James established that truth in his own mastery of the novel of manners. But in McGuane's world manners have become a topic themselves, and as his characters posture in a display of cultural signs the novelist is challenged to sort out the active from the reflexive. It is the drama between these two poles which creates the energy of McGuane's fiction.

His first novel, *The Sporting Chance,* adapts the Hemingway code of sportsmanship and grace under pressure to contemporary times. There has been an apparent generational decline, as the descendants of a 100-year-old sporting club destroy themselves and the camp in an atavistic fury. Two main characters, Stanton and Quinn, emerge as the contrary tendencies within the club's tribal framework: the spokesman for order, and the shamanistic "fiend" who by exaggerating all tendencies to disorder provides the tension which holds the group intact even as it threatens to fly apart. As in all of McGuane's novels, there is "a readiness for calamity . . . in the air," and expressing this sense allows the author scope for his best writing. Stanton "thrusts" rather than "steps," and transforms the club's civil practice of sport into a primeval combat. When Quinn himself reverts to Stanton's beliefs, the cycle is nearly complete, and is rounded off when a time capsule reveals that the founders' genteel standards have been a sham all this time.

From the northern Michigan woods McGuane moves the action of his next three novels to the Florida Keys, "America's land's end" as he calls it, and within this context of intermingled exoticness and shabbiness he conducts his most thorough survey of manners. In *The Bushwhacked Piano* it is the region to which young Nicholas Payne flees with his girlfriend (who has decided to adopt "floozihood" with the ambition other girls her age would look forward to a prestigious woman's college). Payne has rejected the bland "Waring blender" world of his parents' suburbia, choosing instead to embrace the raw aspects of his country and its people with a sensuosity that infuses his prose. A motorcycle ride through a valley and out onto a beach is described with a heady sense of smell and sound; even an inventory of his girlfriend's room becomes a riot of unconnected materiality celebrated for its sense of being. "I am at large" is Payne's testimony to his role in life, and in his vision the extremes of America are created.

Ninety-Two in the Shade finds another dropout, Thomas Skelton, leaving college for a life of guide-fishing in the Keys. Here he finds two alternative models of conduct, and even though he knows one is a sure road to destruction, he embraces it with a sense of destiny. "He had long since learned that the general view was tragic, but he had simultaneously learned that the trick was to become interested in something else. Look askance and it all shines on," which is Skelton's method for feasting on the manners of Key West while his own life rushes toward its destructive end. *Panama* transforms the typical McGuane hero into a rock star whose career and sanity are on the skids. Because of his inability to control his own poetic vision, he has destroyed everything of value around him. As a performer he is "paid to sum up civilization or to act it out in a glimmer," and as his rock theatrics become more bizarre the culture rushes ahead of him. One of contemporary fiction's best insights into drug use, *Panama* shows its central character walking a tightrope between life and death. In lucid moments between the effect of drugs one can appreciate "memory," which is "the only thing which keeps us from being murderers." Yet destruction predominates. "Something about our republic makes it go armed," the narrator confesses. "I myself am happier having a piece within reach, knowing that if some goblin humps into the path, it's away with him." In this subtle rhythm of cultural malevolence lies the novel's fascination.

Key West proved to be a burnout for McGuane himself as well as for his characters, and his recent novels have been set in the harsher country of Montana, where nature conspires to enforce an isolated sense of stability and self-reliance on the characters McGuane now considers. *Nobody's Angel* finds an Army officer returning to his family's ranch, where he serves as the reflector of a narrative action whose language expresses his feelings of change and loss—from an empty water sluice which cooled milkcans before the supermarket days to a friend's Cadillac which is parked nose-up to the straw outside the barn. A devotee of lost causes, McGuane's protagonist invites danger and failure by falling in love with a married woman, largely because she is as unobtainable as the fantasy girlfriend he used to keep life at bay as a teenager. But as his barren West is peopled, he must flee it for a more pure legend of himself, living alone in Seville, Spain, from whence his old friends can concoct their own off-base fantasies of what his life is like.

With *Something to Be Desired* McGuane shows the ability to synthesize his work, using a Montana setting for the enactment of a carnival equal to any of the excesses of his previous novels. His protagonists have always gravitated toward living at the edge, and in this case Lucien Taylor withdraws from a conventional career and marriage in order to tempt fate by romancing the much wilder woman timidity kept him from years before. Yet even on the edge in Montana, where he begins an outlandish tourist resort attracting all types of crazies, he still finds that life is shrouded in a protec-

tive textuality. People relate via lines of dialogue instead of with meaningful statements, and roles are played more often than lives are lived. Yet Lucien is also a painter, and his artistic eye relates to nature better than to the thin, superficial social types around him, which gives him a higher goal.

Returning to ranch life from a life of painting motivates the plot of *Keep the Change* as well. Here protagonist Joe Starling faces several issues: the decline of his father's once grand ambitions of ranching and the consequent economic and moral decay attendant upon such lost hopes, and Joe's own attempt to recapture a style of perception from his youth which prompted his career as a painter. The key events for each center on the image of an abandoned mansion constructed in the last century by a would-be silver-rush baron and now fallen into ruin. Joe remembers how one of the few scraps of ambition and success remaining in the ruins is a picture still hanging on the wall, a painting that captures the purest essence of white. Having pursued a painter's career and now returning to save his ranch and place it in hands that will assure its future, Joe ventures back to the crumbling mansion to find that its painting, his ideal of perfect art, is not a painted canvas at all, but only an empty frame designating a blank expanse of wall. Thus even though Joe has recovered his ranch only to lose it again, it is the act of framing that remains important.

Frank Copenhaver, the protagonist of *Nothing But Blue Skies,* is a more sociologically representative Montanan. As a successful rancher and real estate developer he finds himself positioned to enjoy the fishing that is such an important element in McGuane's fiction, perhaps the most important in a major American novelist's work since Ernest Hemingway. Like the Hemingway hero, McGuane's has woman trouble, too, and having his wife leave him coincided with financial ruin and personal disarray. McGuane's genius is to play this familiar crisis against the backdrop of American popular culture (some of which is a response to Hemingway himself in equal parts adulation and parody), such as the scene where Frank and his equally distraught friend Phil listen to a radio interview with Dolly Parton where "country" equated with "family" and "You could feel her dimples come over the airways. . . . As though each man were assigned one of Dolly's big breasts, the room grew calm. They gazed off in comfortable friendship, the ghastly weeping now subsided into tolerable ungainliness. They sucked down the bourbon."

Since 1981 McGuane has published short fiction in a wide range of magazines. Collected in *To Skin a Cat,* these stories employ the same styles of quirky dialogue, behavior exquisitely mannered yet idiosyncratic to the modern American West, and metaphorical expression that have characterized his novels. Like his friend Richard Brautigan, McGuane delights at stretching the distance between tenor and vehicle as he draws similes from the most surprising places, as when a story's protagonist suffers "a spell of dullness like the two weeks that make the difference between a bad and a good haircut." Such devices remind McGuane's readers that one of his primary interests remains in language, and how the subtle turn of it can reawaken attention to matters that might otherwise remain deadeningly familiar.

McGuane's progress has been to celebrate the materiality of his fiction—the lilting song of his characters' language, especially the minor ones; the mad fandango of their behavior, especially when it counterpoints the narrator's more inquisitive action; and the special atmospheres of the regions about which he writes. Like his protagonists, these regions are always on the edge: in the northernmost woods of Michigan, at the extreme tip of Florida, and at

America's virtual disappearance into perspective in the foothills of the Rocky Mountains. Finding the right words for each makes his fiction a success of language and image, providing readers with an aural picture of life in these places and times.

—Jerome Klinkowitz

McINERNEY, Jay

Nationality: American. **Born:** Hartford, Connecticut, 13 January 1955. **Education:** Williams College, Williamstown, Massachusetts, B.A. 1976; Syracuse University, New York. **Family:** Married Merry Reymond in 1984. **Career:** Reporter, Hunterdon *Country Democrat,* Flemington, New Jersey, 1977; editor, *Time-Life,* Osaka, Japan, 1978-79; fact checker, *New Yorker,* 1980; reader, Random House, publishers, New York, 1980-81; Instructor in English, Syracuse University, 1983. Since 1983 full-time writer. Lives in New York. **Agent:** Deborah Rogers, Rogers Coleridge and White Ltd., 20 Powis Mews, London W11 1JN, England; or, International Creative Management, 40 West 57th Street, New York, New York 10019, U.S.A.

PUBLICATIONS

Novels

Bright Lights, Big City. New York, Vintage, 1984; London, Cape, 1985.
Ransom. New York, Vintage, 1985; London, Cape, 1986.
Story of My Life. London, Bloomsbury, and New York, Atlantic Monthly Press, 1988.
Brightness Falls. New York, Knopf, 1992; London, Penguin, 1993.

Uncollected Short Stories

"The Real Tad Allagash," in *Ms.* (New York), August 1985.
"It's Six a.m. Do You Know Where You Are?," in *Look Who's Talking,* edited by Bruce Weber. New York, Washington Square Press, 1986.
"Reunion," in *Esquire* (New York), March 1987.
"Smoke," in *Atlantic* (Boston), March 1987.
"She Dreams of Johnny," in *Gentlemen's Quarterly* (New York), March 1988.
"Lost and Found," in *Esquire* (New York), July 1988.

Other

Editor, *Cowboys, Indians and Commuters.* London, Viking, 1994.

*

Critical Study: "You Will Have to Learn Everything All Over Again" by Richard Sisk, in *Pacific Review,* Spring 1988.

*   *   *

Jay McInerney has been heralded as the "J.D. Salinger of the 1980s," and his first novel, *Bright Lights, Big City,* has been called

"a *Catcher in the Rye* for MBA's." It might also be accurate to call McInerney the "Fitzgerald of current fiction." In the same way that *This Side of Paradise* captured the spirit of the "Jazz Age," *Bright Lights, Big City* earned McInerney almost instant fame for its timely chronicling of New York City's club scene in the 1980s, a scene that could be found in recognizable form in almost any big city in America.

Bright Lights, Big City is the story of a disillusioned young man who is trying to deal with the impending death of his mother from cancer, the breakup of his marriage to a fashion model, his addiction to cocaine, and his pointless job in the "Department of Factual Verification" for a large magazine. (The last is McInerney's sarcastic exposure of the *New Yorker's* fact-checking department where he worked for a time). In the novel, the narrator travels from club to club in search of women and cocaine. McInerney illustrates how pointless life is for those addicted to the pursuit of sensation and the forgetfulness that accompanies that pursuit. In the end, the narrator has lost mother, wife, and job; but he has gained a sense of direction: "I was thinking that we have a responsibility to the dead— the living, I mean." The novel's final scene places the narrator on his knees, eating bread. "You will have to learn everything all over again," he says. The narrator must learn that life's true value rests in a place where hedonism is not the central altar.

McInerney's next novel follows the theme of searching for direction and meaning in life. *Ransom* is the tale of Chris Ransom, an American expatriate in Japan who is studying Goju karate and trying to come to terms with the death of his friends in Pakistan when a dope deal turns deadly. For Ransom, "the dojo, with its strange incantations and white uniforms seemed a sacramental place, an intersection of body and spirit, where power and danger were ritualized in such a way that a man could learn to understand them." This is especially important to the narrator because, "Ransom had lost his bearings spiritually, and he wanted to reclaim himself."

Ransom is also the story of the protagonists' manipulation by his Hollywood-director father and his conflict with DeVito, a fellow American and "karate-ka" who is dangerous because he is "the sort who made a personal contest out of a coin toss" and who would "stake everything on nothing." The novel moves to a climax on "a wide stretch half way between the Kitaoji and Imadegawa bridges" in Japan's ancient capital where Ransom and DeVito face off with Samurai swords.

Although Ransom's search for meaning in life ultimately is not successful, the disillusionment that motivates him continues to be McInerney's primary concern as one can see in his next novel.

Story of My Life is the hip narrative of Allison Poole who is caught in the sexual hedonism and committed shallowness of the 1980s. As Allison says, "The first year I was in New York I didn't do anything but guys and blow. Staying out all night at the Surf Club and the Zulu, waking up at five in the afternoon with plugged sinuses and sticky hair. Some kind of white stuff in every opening. Story of my life."

Story of My Life is an all-talk novel like Brett Easton Ellis's *The Rules of Attraction* or Norman Mailer's *Why Are We in Vietnam?* The novel depends upon pop idiom catchphrases. Throughout the novel, Allison asks her friends what the three biggest lies are. She remembers that one is, the check is in the mail and that two is, I won't come in your mouth. But she can't remember the third biggest lie until the book's final pages when she says, "The third lie is, I love you."

Allison is more than a representative character, "a postmodern girl," as she calls herself. She is representative of a demographic entity. She, like the narrator in *Bright Lights, Big City* and like Chris Ransom, is representative of a portion of a generation that wealth and privilege cannot protect from disillusionment and pain.

—Tom Colonnese

McMURTRY, Larry (Jeff)

Nationality: American. **Born:** Wichita Falls, Texas, 3 June 1936. **Education:** Archer City High School, Texas, graduated 1954; North Texas State College, Denton, B.A. 1958; Rice University, Houston, 1954, 1958-60, M.A. 1960; Stanford University, California (Stegner fellow), 1960-61. **Family:** Married Josephine Scott in 1959 (divorced 1966); one son. **Career:** Taught at Texas Christian University, Fort Worth, 1961-62, Rice University, 1963-64 and 1965, George Mason College, Fairfax, Virginia, 1970, and American University, Washington, D.C., 1970-71. Since 1971 owner, Booked Up Inc., antiquarian booksellers, Washington, D.C., Archer City, Texas, and Tucson, Arizona. Regular reviewer, Houston *Post,* 1960s, and Washington *Post,* 1970s; contributing editor, *American Film,* New York, 1975. President, PEN American Center, 1989. **Awards:** Guggenheim grant, 1964; Pulitzer prize, 1986. **Address:** Booked Up Inc., 2509 North Campbell Avenue, No. 95, Tucson, Arizona 85719, U.S.A.

PUBLICATIONS

Novels

Horseman, Pass By. New York, Harper, 1961; as *Hud,* New York, Popular Library, 1963; London, Sphere, 1971.
Leaving Cheyenne. New York, Harper, 1963; London, Sphere, 1972.
The Last Picture Show. New York, Dial Press, 1966; London, Sphere, 1972.
Moving On. New York, Simon and Schuster, 1970; London, Weidenfeld and Nicolson, 1971.
All My Friends Are Going to Be Strangers. New York, Simon and Schuster, 1972; London, Secker and Warburg, 1973.
Terms of Endearment. New York, Simon and Schuster, 1975; London, W.H. Allen, 1977.
Somebody's Darling. New York, Simon and Schuster, 1978.
Cadillac Jack. New York, Simon and Schuster, 1982.
The Desert Rose. New York, Simon and Schuster, 1983; London, W.H. Allen, 1985.
Lonesome Dove. New York, Simon and Schuster, 1985; London, Pan, 1986.
Texasville. New York, Simon and Schuster, and London, Sidgwick and Jackson, 1987.
Anything for Billy. New York, Simon and Schuster, 1988; London, Collins, 1989.
Some Can Whistle. New York, Simon and Schuster, 1989; London, Century, 1990.
Buffalo Girls. New York, Simon and Schuster, 1990; London, Century, 1991.
Pretty Boy Floyd, with Diana Ossana. New York, Simon and Schuster, 1994; London, Orion, 1995.
The Late Child. New York, Simon and Schuster, and London, Orion, 1995.

Uncollected Short Stories

"The Best Day Since," in *Avesta* (Denton, Texas), Fall 1956.
"Cowman," in *Avesta* (Denton, Texas), Spring 1957.
"Roll, Jordan, Roll," in *Avesta* (Denton, Texas), Fall 1957.
"A Fragment from Scarlet Ribbons," in *Coexistence Review* (Denton, Texas), vol. 1, no. 2, 1958(?).
"There Will Be Peace in Korea," in *Texas Quarterly* (Austin), Winter 1964.
"Dunlop Crashes In," in *Playboy* (Chicago), July 1975.

Play

Screenplay: *The Last Picture Show,* with Peter Bogdanovich, 1971.

Other

In a Narrow Grave: Essays on Texas. Austin, Texas, Encino Press, 1968.
It's Always We Rambled: An Essay on Rodeo. New York, Hallman, 1974.
Larry McMurtry: Unredeemed Dreams, edited by Dorey Schmidt. Edinburg, Texas, Pan American University, 1980.
Film Flam: Essays on Hollywood. New York, Simon and Schuster, 1987.

*

Manuscript Collection: University of Houston Library.

Critical Studies: *Larry McMurtry* by Thomas Landess, Austin, Texas, Steck Vaughn, 1969; *The Ghost Country: A Study of the Novels of Larry McMurtry* by Raymond L. Neinstein, Berkeley, California, Creative Arts, 1976; *Larry McMurtry* by Charles D. Peavy, Boston, Twayne, 1977; *Larry McMurtry's Texas: Evolution of a Myth* by Lera Patrick Tyler Lich, Austin, Texas, Eakin Press, 1987; *Taking Stock: A Larry McMurtry Casebook* edited by Clay Reynolds, Dallas, Southern Methodist University Press, 1989.

*   *   *

In the 1880s if a cowhand woke up one day with blood on his knife and his shirt, or if an Ohio bank teller made off with the receipts, or if a woman stared at her husband as he snored and decided she had just had enough, the territories was where they got away. In the vast rugged western portion of the United States your name was what you called yourself at that time and you could ride a horse for three or four days and not see another human being. The West took its toll, however, on those who tried to live there.

In an October 1990 *New Republic* article, "How the West Was Won or Lost," Larry McMurtry writes about the Old West and reminds his readers that in the Real West "it was too hot or too cold, too wet or too dry, the animals wouldn't behave, the Indians were scary, the distances interminable, and the pioneers were starving, sick, injured and often defeated." But despite this reality, the West was and remains a place of freedom, individuality, and opportunity. The West remains as a place of shining hope.

McMurtry's accomplishment as an author has been to restructure the western myth and to harness the vitality of the West in the form of contemporary characters.

In his first two novels McMurtry wove tales which linked the past and the present. *Horseman, Pass By* is the story of three generations of cowboys and is told from the point of view of a 17-year-old boy. The boy's grandfather, Homer Bannon, seeks to protect his neighbor's cattle from being infected from his cattle's disease, even though it means his own financial destruction. Hud, Homer's amoral stepson, desires to defy the government, sell the cattle and take control of the ranch. As the young man looks on, two Wests collide: the West of cowboys and old-time values and the New West where nothing matters except making money.

McMurtry's second novel, *Leaving Cheyenne,* is the story of two cowboys, Johnny and Gid, who compete from boyhood to old age for the love of Molly. Written in three sections with each character taking a turn as narrator, the novel illustrates that Molly loves both male characters and that this love is due, in part, to what each man represents. Each represents an historical type—the rancher who loves the land but has to convert to big ranching in order to save that land, and the cowboy who will never own much of anything but whose individualism is still attractive even though it may be almost as misplaced as his dying craft.

McMurtry's third novel, *The Last Picture Show,* depicts a past with which many readers can identify. The novel is evocative of first love and small-town America. Like the romantic world of the cinema which is about to present its last picture show, the romantic ideals of Sonny, Duane, and Jacy are dashed as they move from high school to adulthood.

McMurtry's next novel, *Moving On,* introduced characters who would take central stage in later novels. Pete and Patsy Carpenter are the primary characters of the novel and they are involved in the seemingly unconnected worlds of rodeo and graduate school. Pete and Patsy wish to move from their affluent Texan backgrounds to some form of individual achievement. Pete wishes to capture ritualized cowboy skills in a photography book on rodeo. The failure of this ambition is indicated early on when one of the rodeo stars accidentally introduces himself to Patsy by urinating on the side of her car while she waits for her husband at the darkened rodeo grounds. Pete drops his rodeo book and takes up the study of literature, soon becoming absorbed in collecting first editions of old works. The reader comes to see that the past has no meaning in the present world.

Danny Deck, who is briefly introduced in *Moving On,* becomes the main figure in *All My Friends Are Going to Be Strangers.* Deck has achieved instant fame and wealth when his first novel is produced as a movie. Deck is a symbol of the rootless young people of the 1970s and when he loses his wife and newborn daughter we realize that there is nothing which provides him with security. The book ends with Deck wading into a river to destroy his second novel and, we believe, himself.

Emma Horton is also introduced in *Moving On* and she and her mother, Aurora Greenway, are the primary characters in *Terms of Endearment.* The novel traces the relationship between mother and daughter and their relationships with men. Jill Peel is a girlfriend of Danny Deck in *All My Friends Are Going to Be Strangers. Somebody's Darling* deals with her advancement as a film artist. *Moving On, All My Friends Are Going to Be Strangers, Terms of Endearment,* and *Somebody's Darling* are all loosely tied to one another with characters that keep reappearing in one anothers' lives. McMurtry's next two novels introduced new characters and explored new issues.

Cadillac Jack is the story of a man whose job is to scout for antiques at yard sales and farm sales. McMurtry states that he be-

came introduced to the yard sale scene by an actress friend. In the novel, Jack discovers a plot to sell off priceless treasures from the Smithsonian Institution and readers are treated to a humorous portrayal of life in Washington, D.C.

The Desert Rose is the story of a Las Vegas showgirl. Harmony was known as the most beautiful showgirl in the city, but at age 39 she is being replaced by her own daughter. McMurtry deals well with the issues of exploitation of women; the novel is a testament to female strength and resilience.

McMurtry's next novel won him a Pulitzer prize and made him one of the most popular novelists in America. *Lonesome Dove* started out as a screen offering in 1971 for John Wayne, James Stewart, and Henry Fonda as a bittersweet end-of-the-West western in which no victories were won. The three actors were horrified at the thought of the West being over and with the thought of a western with no triumph, no white man holding up the scalp at the movie's end. *Lonesome Dove* is a western divested of myth and is built around the true hardships of life in the West. The novel is about a trail drive from Texas to Montana and is set in 1876, the year of the first national centennial, the battle of the Little Big Horn, and the beginning of the cowboy's heyday. However, as the characters travel north, readers are stuck by how hard the journey is and even the young characters who initially see the trip as a grand adventure learn quickly how fast the fun can run out. One is struck finally with this point: the winning of the West was in large measure an imaginative act and the spirit of the West, a place of freedom, opportunity, and imagination, is still a big part of the framework of contemporary America.

McMurtry next returned to Thalia, Texas, the site of *The Last Picture Show,* for *Texasville. Texasville* reunites the characters from the previous novel and we learn what became of Duane, Sonny, and Jacy 20 years after high school.

Anything for Billy is another western. The narrator of the novel is Ben Sippy, a writer of dime novels and a cultured Easterner who travels west to compare the real West to the West he has portrayed in fiction. He falls in with Billy the Kid, but the Billy of this novel is a runt and a terrible shot who "never killed a man who stood more than 20 feet from him. Billy was a blaster, not a marksman." McMurtry reworks the myth by having Billy die at the hands of a jealous woman and seems to be emphasizing a point he makes in the novel: "Gunfighters spent their lives in ugly towns, ate terrible food and drank a vile grade of whisky, and few managed to die gloriously in a shoot-out with a peer."

In what would seem to be a pattern, McMurtry went from a western to another novel which brings his readers up to date on earlier characters. In *Some Can Whistle,* readers learn that Danny Deck did not drown himself. Instead, he walked out of the river and created a TV sitcom called *Al and Sal* which made him $300 million. Deck is retired in an isolated mansion near Thalia, Texas and his life is fairly simple until his daughter shows up. Deck is happy at the thought of a reunion, but his daughter turns out to be a foul-mouthed, dope-smoking mother of two.

Buffalo Girls is another reworking of the western myth and is a fictionalizing of the life of Calamity Jane. Again, McMurtry deals with the hardships and violence of the American West in a realistic manner.

McMurtry's novels illustrate the power of the West and remind us that the West is still filled with contemporary characters who view America as a land of problems, but also a place of great promise.

—Tom Colonnese

McPHERSON, James A(lan)

Nationality: American. **Born:** Savannah, Georgia, 16 September 1943. **Education:** Morris Brown College, Atlanta, 1961-63, 1965, B.A. 1965; Morgan State College, Baltimore, 1963-64; Harvard University, Cambridge, Massachusetts, LL.B. 1968; University of Iowa, Iowa City, M.F.A. 1971. **Family:** Married in 1973 (divorced); one daughter. **Career:** Instructor, University of Iowa Law School, 1968-69; Lecturer in English, University of California, Santa Cruz, 1969-70; Assistant Professor of English, Morgan State University, 1975-76; Associate Professor of English, University of Virginia, Charlottesville, 1976-81. Since 1981 Professor of English, University of Iowa. Guest editor of fiction issues of *Iowa Review,* Iowa City, 1984, and *Ploughshares,* Cambridge, Massachusetts, 1985, 1990. Since 1969 contributing editor, *Atlantic Monthly,* Boston; since 1994 staff writer, *Double-Take.* **Awards:** *Atlantic* Firsts award, 1968; American Academy award, 1970; Guggenheim fellowship, 1972; Pulitzer prize, 1978; MacArthur Foundation award, 1981; award for excellence in teaching, University of Iowa, 1993. **Agent:** Brandt and Brandt, 1501 Broadway, New York, New York 10036. **Address:** 711 Rundell Street, Iowa City, Iowa 52240, U.S.A.

PUBLICATIONS

Short Stories

Hue and Cry. Boston, Little Brown, and London, Macmillan, 1969.
Elbow Room. Boston, Little Brown, 1977.

Uncollected Short Story

"There Was Once a State Called Franklin," in *Callaloo* (Lexington, Kentucky), May 1979.

Other

Railroad: Trains and Train People in American Culture, with Miller Williams. New York, Random House, 1976.

*   *   *

In two collections of brilliant short fiction, James A. McPherson has surveyed contemporary black American culture and defined its sensibility. His work, sharply realistic and dramatic, focuses on the connections and abrasions of black and white individuals in our time. The insights accumulated in the stories form a comprehensive mosaic of U.S. life as viewed by black citizens.

Hue and Cry, McPherson's first collection, revolves around the world of work and black positions in it. The stories deal with "traditional" black occupations—waiter, Pullman porter, stockboy, janitor—from the inside, where each position is a window on the white world. McPherson's controlled, incisive style offers shrewdly defined character-types almost mythic in proportion. Stories like "A Solo Song: for Doc," which describes the end of a man's lifelong career as a railroad waiter, offer important illuminations on daily life for black people in America. "Gold Coast" and "Hue and Cry," two of the best-known stories of the book, deal directly with the tensions and tragic ironies of black-white sexual relationships.

The stories in *Elbow Room* are more complex extensions of McPherson's concerns. His narrative style is often dense and subtle, but his focus is still on archetypal characters and situations. "The Story of a Dead Man," for example, is a kind of bad-man ballad contrasting a near-mythic "bad nigger" with his educated, upwardly mobile nephew. This "Railroad Bill" character is a fighting, lying wanderer whose existence embarrasses blacks aspiring to gentility in white middle-class terms. The same theme emerges in "Elbow Room," which describes the marriage of a young white draft resister to a sharp, urbane black woman. It is narrated by a black consciousness tormented with problems of definition. The young white man is obsessed with the question "What is a nigger?" He finally bursts out:

> "At *least* I tried! At *least* I'm *fighting!* And I know what a *nigger* is, too. It's what you are when you begin thinking of yourself as a work of art!" I did not turn to answer, although I heard him clearly. I am certain there was no arrogance at all left in his voice.

McPherson has used the medium of the short story to extend the intense meditations on black Americans begun by Ralph Ellison in *Invisible Man.* McPherson's stories are carefully crafted, subtle and penetrating observations of the range and variety of the contemporary black experience. His characters are vivid storytellers, too, and he captures their inflections and idioms precisely. His people—black and white—struggle to know themselves and each other, to penetrate the barriers of appearances to the central mysteries of being. As the narrator of "Just Enough for the City" expresses it:

> I think love must be the ability to suspend one's intelligence for the sake of something. At the basis of love therefore must be imagination. Instead of thinking always *"I am I,"* to love one must be able to feelingly conjugate the verb *to be.* Intuition must be part of the circuitous pathway leading ultimately to love.

This seeking for love and identity, love for self and others, the world itself, is at the center of McPherson's stories. His people become visible to others because they learn to see themselves.

—William J. Schafer

McWILLIAM, Candia

Nationality: British. **Born:** Candia Francis Juliet McWilliam in Edinburgh, Scotland, 1 July 1955. **Education:** Cambridge University, 1973-76, B.A. **Family:** Married 1) Q.G.C. Wallop in 1981 (divorced 1985), one son and one daughter; 2) F.E. Dinshaw in 1986, one son. **Career:** *Vogue* Magazine, 1976-79; Slade, Bluffix, and Bigg, 1979-81. **Awards:** *Vogue* talent contest, 1970; Betty Trask prize, 1988, Scottish Arts Council prize, 1989; *Guardian* prize for fiction, 1994. **Member:** Society of Authors, Royal Society of Literature. **Agent:** Janklow and Nesbit, 598 Madison Avenue, New York, New York 10022, U.S.A.

PUBLICATIONS

Novels

A Case of Knives. London, Bloomsbury, and New York, Beech Tree, 1988.
A Little Stranger. London, Bloomsbury, and New York, Doubleday, 1989.
Debatable Land. London, Bloomsbury, 1994.

*   *   *

Candia McWilliam's three novels have established her as one of a trio of exceptionally talented young Scottish writers (Janice Galloway and A. L. Kennedy being the other two). In her fiction style is just as seductive as the story. Her language is spare and exact, yet elegant and strangely mysterious, though not without a touch of mordant humor. Descriptions are precise but less important for what they reveal about the external world than about inner reality; quotidian facts serve as the raw material for intricate psychological musings on social, sexual, and national identity.

A Case of Knives is her highly accomplished first novel. Divided into four parts, each told by a different character and in a different style, the novel is a study in English class structure and the ways people "experiment with human flesh," both physically and psychologically. Lucas Salik, the son of Polish Jews, has transformed himself into a proper Englishman, a respected pediatric cardiologist. He is also a homosexual (a fact known only to his very closest friends) who, as the novel's ominous opening line puts it, "needs a woman," for his lover, Hal, who has decided to lead a more respectable and conventional life as a married man. The girl Lucas selects proves, however, less the helpless prey than hungry predator in need of a husband to play the part of father of her unborn child. Indeed no character is quite what he or she appears. Neither is any character nearly as much in control of his or her respective plot as he or she assumes, except for the novel's most manipulative, and therefore most monstrous character, the "vegan carnivore" Angelica Coney, whose evil nature is the by-product of upper-class privilege. Pulling a series of skeletons out of her characters' figurative closets, McWilliam crafts a story that both seduces and shocks with its succession of narratively compelling and at times morally appalling surprises.

The capacity for self-delusion and the negative, potentially tragic consequences of English class structure reappear in *A Little Stranger,* a shorter and still more intense (and more intensely secretive) novel. Rendered with all the precision of a 17th-century still life and reminiscent of Jane Austen, *Jane Eyre,* and Henry James (*The Turn of the Screw, What Maisie Knew*), this study in repression is narrated by another of McWilliam's culturally and psychologically divided characters. Raised by her Dutch father after her English mother "waltzed off to Vienna, bored by Amsterdam," the self-effacing narrator does not even mention her name until novel's end. Daisy only slowly realizes that she has lived at the very margin of her own life, "the useless but essential" wife of a wealthy landowner. She has little to do as wife and even less as mother—other than write letters to people she does not know and closely observe (though not quite understand) the latest nanny, Margaret Pride. At first the novel seems to be about Margaret, who is not the pearl of great price Daisy believes her to be. Margaret's lower-class background has led her to create a fantasy in which she patiently awaits the coming of her prince, Daisy's emotionally and often geographically distant husband. More interesting than the revelations concerning Margaret are those having to do with Daisy's failure to apprehend something amiss earlier, as the reader does (though not altogether correctly). As in *A Case of Knives,* the sudden introduction of a topical issue (AIDS then, anorexia now) seems at once relevant and intrusive. More successful is McWilliam's appending to her novels—which seem about to end so disastrously—tentatively happy endings that do not so much resolve matters as remind readers of the precariousness of the characters' lives.

The claustrophobic intensity of the first two novels is not so much lacking as differently figured in *Debatable Land,* McWilliam's third and most ambitious work, in which her interest in the shaping effects of childhood is most pronounced. Following the last leg of a sailing voyage from Tahiti to New Zealand, this modern-day *Odyssey* brings six characters together on the *Ardent Spirit.* Playing the vastness of the ocean against the confinement of the sailboat, the sense of freedom and adventure against the sense of commitment and community, the novel creates a debatable land of its own. As the *Ardent Spirit* navigates well-charted but at times treacherous seas and reef-rimmed coastal waters, *Debatable Land* narratively tacks back and forth between characters, between a variously idealized past and a disappointing present, between a postparadisiacal (and postcolonial) Pacific and a Scotland that seems less a specific place than a multiplicity of psychological meanings resulting from her Scots having been raised in quite diverse geographical and socioeconomic settings. Although more intricately structured and broad-ranging than her two earlier novels, *Debatable Land* renders the complex inner lives of its characters with the same combination of intelligence, precision, and sympathetic understanding.

—Robert A. Morace

MERTZ, Barbara

Pseudonyms: Barbara Michaels; Elizabeth Peters. **Nationality:** American. **Born:** Barbara Louise Gross Mertz in Canton, Illinois, 29 September 1927. **Education:** University of Chicago Oriental Institute, Ph.B. 1947, M.S. 1950, Ph.D. 1952. **Family:** Married Richard R. Mertz in 1950 (divorced 1968); one daughter and one son. **Career:** Egyptologist. **Awards:** Grandmaster award, Bouchercon, 1986; Agatha award for best mystery novel, 1989, and Malice Domestic Convention, 1989, both for *Naked Once More;* D.H.L.: Hood College, 1989. **Member:** American Crime Writers League, Egypt Exploration Society, American Research Council in Egypt, Society for the Study of Egyptian Antiquities, National Organization for Women. **Agent:** Dominick Abel Literary Agency, 146 West 82nd St., Suite 1B, New York, New York 10024, U.S.A.

PUBLICATIONS

Novels as Elizabeth Peters (series: Vicky Bliss; Amelia Peabody Emerson; Jacqueline Kirby)

The Jackal's Head. New York, Meredith, 1968; London, Jenkins 1969.

The Camelot Caper. New York, Meredith, 1969; London, 1976.

The Dead Sea Cipher. New York, Dodd Mead, 1970; London, Cassell, 1975.

The Night of Four Hundred Rabbits. New York, Dodd Mead, 1971; as *Shadows in the Moonlight,* London, Coronet, 1975.

The Seventh Sinner (Kirby). New York, Dodd Mead, 1972; London, Coronet, 1975.

Borrower of the Night (Bliss). New York, Dodd Mead, 1973; London, Cassell, 1974.

The Murders of Richard III (Kirby). New York, Dodd Mead, 1974; London, Piatkus, 1989.

Crocodile on the Sandbank (Emerson). New York, Dodd Mead, 1975; London, Cassell, 1976.

Legend in Green Velvet. New York, Dodd Mead, 1976; as *Ghost in Green Velvet,* London, Cassell, 1977.

Devil-May-Care. New York, Dodd Mead, 1977; London, Cassell, 1978.

Street of the Five Moons (Bliss). New York, Dodd Mead, 1978; London, Piatkus, 1988.

Summer of the Dragon. New York, Dodd Mead, 1979; London, Souvenir Press, 1980.

The Love Talker. New York, Dodd Mead, 1980; London, Souvenir Press, 1981.

The Curse of the Pharaohs (Emerson). New York, Dodd Mead, 1981; London, Souvenir Press, 1982.

The Copenhagen Connection. New York, Congdon and Lattes, 1982; London, Souvenir Press, 1983.

Silhouette in Scarlet (Bliss). New York, Congdon and Weed, 1983; London, Souvenir Press, 1984.

Die for Love (Kirby). New York, Congdon and Weed, 1984; London, Souvenir Press, 1985.

The Mummy Case (Emerson). New York, Congdon and Weed, 1985; London, Souvenir Press, 1986.

Lion in the Valley (Emerson). New York, Atheneum, 1986; London, Piatkus, 1987.

Trojan Gold (Bliss). New York, Atheneum, and London, Piatkus, 1987.

The Deeds of the Disturber (Emerson). New York, Atheneum, and London, Piatkus, 1988.

Naked Once More (Kirby). New York, Warner, 1989; London, Piatkus, 1990.

Novels as Barbara Michaels

The Master of Blacktower. New York, Appleton Century Crofts, 1966; London, Jenkins, 1967.

Sons of the Wolf. New York, Meredith, 1967; London, Jenkins, 1968.

Ammie, Come Home. New York, Meredith, 1968; London, Jenkins, 1969.

Prince of Darkness. New York, Meredith, 1969; London, Hodder and Stoughton, 1971.

The Dark on the Other Side. New York, Dodd Mead, 1970; London, Souvenir Press, 1973.

Greygallows. New York, Dodd Mead, 1972; London, Souvenir Press, 1973.

The Crying Child. New York, Dodd Mead, and London, Souvenir Press, 1973.

Witch. New York, Dodd Mead, 1973; London, Souvenir Press, 1975.

House of Many Shadows. New York, Dodd Mead, 1974; London, Souvenir Press, 1975.

The Sea King's Daughter. New York, Dodd Mead, 1975; London, Souvenir Press, 1977.

Patriot's Dream. New York, Dodd Mead, 1976; London, Souvenir Press, 1978.

Wings of the Falcon. New York, Dodd Mead, 1977; London, Souvenir Press, 1979.

Wait for What Will Come. New York, Dodd Mead, 1978; London, Souvenir Press, 1980.

The Walker in Shadows. New York, Dodd Mead, 1979; London, Souvenir Press, 1981.

The Wizard's Daughter. New York, Dodd Mead, 1980; London, Souvenir Press, 1982.

Someone in the House. New York, Dodd Mead, 1981; London, Souvenir Press, 1983.

Black Rainbow. New York, Congdon and Weed, 1982; London, Souvenir Press, 1983.

Here I Stay. New York, Congdon and Weed, 1983; London, Souvenir Press, 1985.

Dark Duet. New York, Congdon and Weed, 1983.

The Grey Beginning. New York, Congdon and Weed, 1984; London, Souvenir Press, 1986.

Be Buried in the Rain. New York, Atheneum, 1985; London, Piatkus, 1986.

Shattered Silk. New York, Atheneum, 1986; London, Piatkus, 1987.

Search the Shadows. New York, Atheneum, 1987; London, Piatkus, 1988.

Smoke and Mirrors. New York, Simon and Schuster, and London, Piatkus, 1989.

Into the Darkness. New York, Simon and Schuster, 1990.

Vanish with the Rose. New York, Simon and Schuster, 1992.

Houses of Stone. New York, Simon and Schuster, 1993.

Uncollected Short Stories

"The Locked Tomb Mystery" (as Elizabeth Peters) in *Sisters in Crime,* edited by Marilyn Wallace. New York, Berkley, 1989; London, Robinson, 1990.

"The Runaway" (as Barbara Michaels) in *Sisters in Crime,* edited by Marilyn Wallace. New York, Berkley, 1989; London, Robinson, 1990.

Other

Temples, Tombs, and Hieroglyphs: The Story of Egyptology. New York, Coward McCann, and London, Gollancz, 1964; revised edition, New York, Dodd Mead, 1978; revised edition, New York, Bedrick, 1990.

Red Land, Black Land: The World of the Ancient Egyptians. New York, Coward McCann, 1966; London, Hodder and Stoughton, 1967; revised edition, New York, Dodd Mead, 1978; revised edition, New York, Bedrick, 1990.

Two Thousand Years in Rome, with Richard Mertz. New York, Coward McCann, 1968; London, Dent, 1969.

*

Manuscript Collections: Mugar Memorial Library, Boston University; University of Wyoming, Laramie.

*　　*　　*

Barbara Mertz is a prolific writer using several pseudonyms for her forays into different types of novels. As Barbara Michaels, Mertz writes gothic romances about human and supernatural terrors. An Elizabeth Peters mystery relies on history, mythology, and archaeology to provide an erudite foundation for modern romantic suspense: a Yuma turquoise mine (*Summer of the Dragon*), the sacred Scottish Stone of Scone (*Legend in Green Velvet*), Nefertiti's lost tomb (*The Jackal's Head*), King Arthur's crown (*The Camelot Caper*), Mexico City's Walk of the Dead (*The Night of Four Hundred Rabbits*), the Schliemann treasure (*Trojan Gold*), Richard the Third (*The Murders of Richard III*), the subterranean Temple of Mithra (*The Seventh Sinner*), and so on. Typical of the genre is *The Dead Sea Cipher* wherein the American heroine searches exotic cities (Beirut, Sidon, Tyre, Damascus) to explain odd marks on torn paper from a doomed stranger; her search leads to treasure and two compelling men, an enemy and a future lover. Mertz's academic heroines (anthropologists, librarians, antiquarians, and students) become enmeshed in criminal pursuits related to historical concerns, but eventually find themselves forcibly assisted by a strong, practical, intellectually challenging male, like the irritatingly handsome, gruff, down-to-earth, unromantic young Scottish laird Jamey Erskine in *Legend in Green Velvet*.

Mertz revels in parody and satire, as in *Die for Love,* set at a convention for the Historical Romance Writers of the World, or in *Naked Once More,* in which series character Jacqueline Kirby, a middle-aged, copper-haired librarian who regularly abandons her academic boyfriends for a smart cop, is chosen to write the sequel to a blockbuster novel, a cross between *The Clan of the Cave Bear* and *Gone with the Wind.* Wry, cynical, witty, and courageous, Mertz's heroines challenge men with spirited confrontations, antagonistic love-hate responses, and sometimes role-reversals, as when series character Vicky Bliss, a tall, blonde, good-humored art historian at a Munich museum, must regularly rescue her wandering lover, Sir John Smythe, an art thief of distinction.

Mertz's finest creation in her Peters mode is Amelia Peabody-Emerson, a highly unconventional, independently wealthy Victorian bluestocking, deeply interested in Egyptology and in the hot-blooded, hot-tempered, irascible Egyptologist she eventually marries, Radcliffe Emerson. Her keen intellect, sharp tongue, curiosity, and competitiveness repeatedly place her in awkward and threatening situations. An amateur sleuth, she trusts logic, good sense, and reason but then leaps intuitively to sometimes quite erroneous conclusions. However, her resilient inductive method allows her to discard the untenable and to readily formulate new theories. The Peabody-Emerson series incorporates delightful satire of Victorian types, comic romping, tongue-in-cheek high romance, and the excitement of archaeological discovery (with all the attendant rivalries, mummy's curses, haunted pyramids, flooded tombs, dangerous pitfalls, and outrageous hoaxes); at the same time readers learn much about scholarly research and archaeological methods. Always the Emersons find rational explanations to debunk the supernatural.

Ms. Peabody-Emerson records her judiciously edited memoirs (to the "Gentle Reader") in elevated, convoluted, euphemistic Victorian prose, prides herself on her nursing skills (she must frequently deal with dagger wounds, poisons, and murderous attacks) and repeatedly effects rescues with a wickedly deft use of her umbrella. She is a sensible woman, continually frustrated by encumbering clothing decreed by fashion; in later novels she creates her own practical wardrobe, a compromise between Victorian propriety and archaeological necessity. She never meant to marry, but in Emerson she finds her match and defines marriage with him as "a balanced stalemate between equal adversaries."

Peabody-Emerson becomes a highly competent Egyptologist, finding in that field clues to modern mysteries. The romance begun in *Crocodile on the Sandbank* produces an imperious, precocious son Ramses, who, with his Egyptian cat Bastet, evokes biting, unsentimental commentaries on the tribulations of parenthood and domesticity. In *The Curse of the Pharaohs,* a mysterious death and inexplicable accidents at a "cursed" tomb point to a modern perpetrator, in *Lion in the Valley* a master criminal dealing in illegal antiquities pursues Amelia romantically, and in *The Last Camel Died at Noon* the Emersons face death on sun-scorched Nubian desert sands while pursuing a cryptic map and an enigmatic papyrus message. Mertz as Peters merges the gothic romance and the romance thriller with satiric comedy and detailed Egyptology to create a winning combination that intrigues, teaches, and delights.

Mertz's Barbara Michaels incognita is more overtly "thrilling," dealing as it does with gothic romance and the spiritually questionable. Some of these, like *Here I Stay* and *Shattered Silk,* are very convincing ghost stories, lent strength by practical, no-nonsense heroines. They draw on historical events (*Wings of the Falcon, Search the Shadows, Patriot's Dream*) and legend (*Ammie, Come Home*), involve psychic powers (*Wizard's Daughter*) and psychological trauma (*The Crying Child*), include werewolves (*Mystery on the Moors*), haunted castles (*Greygallows*) and demonic possession (*The Dark on the Other Side*), or provide interesting background on an assortment of oddities (like old roses in *Vanish with the Rose*).

Mertz's battles of the sexes are equal contests, and the verbal repartee of her main characters is lively, witty, and literate. She is a skillful storyteller, who thrills, chills, and amuses.

—Gina Macdonald

METCALF, John (Wesley)

Nationality: Canadian. **Born:** Carlisle, Cumberland, England, 12 November 1938. **Education:** Bristol University, 1957-61, B.A. (honors) in English 1960, Cert. Ed. 1961. **Family:** Married 1) Gail Courey in 1965 (marriage dissolved 1972), one daughter; 2) Myrna Teitelbaum in 1975, one stepson and two adopted children. **Career:** Taught at a secondary school and a boys' borstal, Bristol, 1961; Rosemount High School, Montreal, 1962-63; Royal Canadian Air Force Base, Cold Lake, Alberta, 1964-65; at a Catholic comprehensive school in England, 1965; and at schools and universities in Montreal, part-time, 1966-71. Writer-in-residence, University of New Brunswick, Fredericton, 1972-73, Loyola College, Montreal, 1976, University of Ottawa, 1977, Concordia University, Montreal, 1980-81, and University of Bologna, Italy, 1985. **Awards:** Canada Council award, 1968, 1969, 1971, 1974, 1976, 1978, 1980, 1983, 1986; University of Western Ontario President's medal, for short story, 1969. **Agent:** Denise Bukowski, The Bukowski Agency, 125B Dupont St., Toronto, Ontario M5R 1V4. **Address:** P.O. Box 2700, Station D, Ottawa, Ontario K1P 5W7, Canada.

PUBLICATIONS

Novels

Going Down Slow. Toronto, McClelland and Stewart, 1972.
Girl in Gingham. Ottawa, Oberon Press, 1978; as *Private Parts: A Memoir,* Scarborough, Ontario, Macmillan-New American Library of Canada, 1980.
General Ludd. Downsview, Ontario, ECW Press, 1980.

Short Stories

New Canadian Writing 1969, with C.J. Newman and D.O. Spettigue. Toronto, Clarke Irwin, 1969.
The Lady Who Sold Furniture. Toronto, Clarke Irwin, 1970.
The Teeth of My Father. Ottawa, Oberon Press, 1975.
Dreams Surround Us: Fiction and Poetry, with John Newlove. Delta, Ontario, Bastard Press, 1977.
Selected Stories. Toronto, McClelland and Stewart, 1982.
Adult Entertainment. Toronto, Macmillan, 1986; New York, St. Martin's Press, 1989.
Shooting the Stars (novellas). Erin, Ontario, Porcupine's Quill, 1993.

Other

Kicking Against the Pricks (essays). Downsview, Ontario, ECW Press, 1982.
Freedom from Culture. Vancouver, Tanks, 1987.
What Is Canadian Literature? Guelph, Ontario, Red Kite Press, 1988.
Freedom from Culture: Selected Essays 1982-1992. Toronto, ECW Press, 1994.

Editor, with others, *Wordcraft 1-5* (textbooks). Toronto, Dent, 5 vols., 1967-77.
Editor, *Razor's Edge,* by Somerset Maugham. Richmond Hill, Ontario, Irwin, 1967.
Editor, *The Flight of the Phoenix,* by Elleston Trevor. Scarborough, Ontario, Bellhaven House, 1968.
Editor, *Daughter of Time,* by Josephine Tey. Richmond Hill, Ontario, Irwin, 1968.
Editor, with Gordon Callaghan, *Rhyme and Reason.* Toronto, Ryerson Press, 1969.
Editor, with Gordon Callaghan, *Salutation.* Toronto, Ryerson Press, 1970.
Editor, *Sixteen by Twelve: Short Stories by Canadian Writers.* Toronto, Ryerson Press, and New York, McGraw Hill, 1970.
Editor, *The Narrative Voice: Short Stories and Reflections by Canadian Authors.* Toronto, McGraw Hill Ryerson, 1972.
Editor, *Kaleidoscope: Canadian Stories.* Toronto, Van Nostrand, 1972.
Editor, *The Speaking Earth: Canadian Poetry.* Toronto, Van Nostrand, 1973.
Editor, with Joan Harcourt, *76 [77]: Best Canadian Stories.* Ottawa, Oberon Press, 2 vols., 1976-77.
Editor, with Clark Blaise, *Here and Now.* Ottawa, Oberon Press, 1977.
Editor, with Clark Blaise, *78 [79, 80]: Best Canadian Stories.* Ottawa, Oberon Press, 3 vols., 1978-80.
Editor, *Stories Plus: Canadian Stories with Authors' Commentaries.* Toronto, McGraw Hill Ryerson, 1979.

Editor, *New Worlds: A Canadian Collection of Stories.* Toronto, McGraw Hill Ryerson, 1980.
Editor, *First [Second, Third] Impressions.* Ottawa, Oberon Press, 3 vols., 1980-82.
Editor, with Leon Rooke, *81 [82]: Best Canadian Stories.* Ottawa, Oberon Press, 2 vols., 1981-82.
Editor, *Making It New: Contemporary Canadian Stories.* Toronto, Methuen, 1982.
Editor, with Leon Rooke, *The New Press Anthology 1-2: Best Canadian Short Fiction.* Toronto, General, 2 vols., 1984-85.
Editor, *The Bumper Book.* Toronto, ECW Press, 1986.
Editor, with Leon Rooke, *The Macmillan Anthology 1-2.* Toronto, Macmillan, 2 vols., 1988-89.
Editor, *Carry On Bumping.* Toronto, ECW Press, 1988.
Editor, *Writers in Aspic.* Montreal, Véhicule Press, 1988.
Editor, with Kent Thompson, *The Macmillan Anthology 3.* Toronto, Macmillan, 1990.
Editor, with Sam Solecki and W.J. Keith, *Volleys* (critical essays). Erin, Ontario, Porcupine's Quill, 1990.
Editor, *The New Story Writers.* Kingston, Ontario, Quarry Press, 1992.
Editor, with J.R. Struthers, *Canadian Classics.* Toronto, Ryerson, 1993.
Editor, with J.R. Struthers, *How Stories Mean.* Erin, Ontario, Porcupine's Quill, 1993.

*

Manuscript Collections: Special Collections, University of Calgary, Alberta; University of Maine, Orono.

Critical Studies: *On the Line* by Robert Lecker, Downsview, Ontario, ECW Press, 1982; article by Douglas Rollins, in *Canadian Writers and Their Works 7* edited by Lecker, Jack David, and Ellen Quigley, ECW Press, 1985; "John Metcalf Issue" of *Malahat Review 70* (Victoria, British Columbia); *John Metcalf* by Barry Cameron, Boston, Twayne, 1986; two essays in *Feat of the Open Heart* by Constance Rooke, Toronto, Coach House, 1989.

*   *   *

When one realizes why so little commentary has been devoted to John Metcalf's fiction, one also understands the unique quality of his work: his prose is so chaste, so uncompromisingly direct, that exegesis often seems to be redundant. But to be seduced by this directness is to ignore the extraordinary narrative compression which multiplies the weight of Metcalf's words and to miss the ideas he develops through his concentration on things. As a mature writer, Metcalf advises the novice to "avoid literary criticism which moves away from the word on the printed page" and to "stick to the study of the placement of commas." Only through this study, and by knowing "the weight, color, and texture of *things*" will the writer create "the distillation of experience" that makes fiction valid.

The terminology here suggests that Metcalf is a traditionalist, and he is. He believes that a plot should be interesting, mysterious, and constructed in such a way that it will endure. He is concerned with the morality of his characters and their culture. His stories are generally realistic in their emphasis on the details of time and place. Above all, he is preoccupied with a traditional theme: the relationship between art and human experience. Consequently his stories explore the nature of the aesthetic process and the ingredients from which his own art is composed.

The Lady Who Sold Furniture contains several stories in which the nature of art and the nature of learning about art are explored through a central character who is sensitive, intelligent, and in the process of learning about himself as he learns about his world. In the title novella, Peter's encounter with Jeanne forces him to examine his own values and his responsibility as a teacher. "The Tide Line" presents a younger protagonist, but one who must also define his future—here explicitly connected with art—against the influence of his parents and the various forms of tradition their presence implies. "Keys and Watercress," one of Metcalf's most anthologized stories (along with "Early Morning Rabbits" from the same collection), again focuses on the initiation of a young boy into a world of symbols, and, by extension, into a new world that can be transformed through imagination. If the stories seem self-conscious it is because they are actually self-critical. Here, as in his later fiction, Metcalf uses the story to explore the value of storytelling itself.

This self-critical stance is certainly revealed in his first novel, *Going Down Slow*, through the character of David Appelby, a teacher who is obviously involved with the conflict between his ideals—both aesthetic and political—and those held by a provincial social order that would stifle all forms of personal expression, be they social, sexual, or cerebral. The novel's episodic form suggests that it is the first long work of a writer who really feels most at home in the short story mode. Nevertheless, it provides a strong sense of Metcalf's finicky attention to detail, and to the linguistic precision that is the hallmark of all his writing.

The Teeth of My Father, a second short story collection, revealed a much more mature writer than the earlier works. Metcalf's language is tighter than before; his attention to structure is more sophisticated and complex; and the stories are increasingly autobiographical and overtly concerned with the implications of storytelling. Five of the stories focus explicitly on art and artists, often in allegorical terms. Metcalf is most successful in "Gentle As Flowers Make the Stones," a bitter, complex, and ultimately poignant record of one day in the life of the poet Jim Haine; in "The Years in Exile," a moving record of a senescent, displaced writer's thoughts; and in the title story, in which the antiphonal structure suggests an implicit exchange between writer and critic, significant because it allows Metcalf to assume the role of self-commentator, the role his fiction seems to seek from its inception.

In *Girl in Gingham* his commentary is expressed through Peter Thornton, whom we meet after the divorce that isolates him, shakes his sense of identity, and forces him to attempt some form of personal recovery by finding a new, ideal woman. The juxtaposition of Peter's educated sensibility with the tastelessness and frequently grotesque lifestyles of successive CompuMate dates invests the novella with a sustained level of comedy that tends to mask Peter's tragic desperation. Peter's encounters with the CompuMate women provide a fertile ground for Metcalf to satirize the debased values of contemporary society. But Peter's failure in those encounters, and Anna's fate, are connected with a death of taste that Metcalf increasingly mourns. As the story develops it becomes clear that for Peter the pursuit of true art is inseparable from the pursuit of true love. Because the search for an ideal girl in gingham is part of Peter's quest for aesthetic fulfillment, he becomes more and more preoccupied with art as his relationship with Anna takes form.

This preoccupation is even more obvious in *Private Parts*, Metcalf's third published novella. Here the narrator is all-too-conscious of the aesthetic implications arising from the autobiographical fragments he presents. "Life," as T.D. Moore sees it, is "mainly lies." In short, life in *Private Parts* is private art. It comes as no surprise to discover that Moore is himself a writer dedicated to mythologizing those autobiographical fragments which constitute the private parts of memory. In him we find the qualities and frustrations that define all of Metcalf's highly articulate first-person narrators: an ability to fashion life through meaning; a rejection of contemporary taste and the threat it poses to genuine creativity; an involvement in others' art; and a consciousness of being involved in the narrative structure of his tale.

Metcalf's second novel makes his criticism of contemporary society hard to ignore. *General Ludd* takes its name from the 19th-century Luddite movement's radical opposition to so-called "progress" through technology and mechanization. Metcalf's Jim Wells is a contemporary Luddite, and a poet, who takes exception to the debased forms of communication—be they audiovisual, sartorial, or verbal—that seem ever-present in his world. No summary of this kind can do justice to the range of Metcalf's ferocious satire, or to his exposition of a host of characters through powerful vignettes, or to the continual purity of his language. Although the success of *Ludd* as a novel is still in debate, what cannot be questioned is Metcalf's dedication to his craft, or his reputation as one of Canada's most accomplished fiction writers.

—Robert Lecker

MICHAELS, Barbara. *See* **MERTZ, Barbara.**

MICHAELS, Leonard

Nationality: American. **Born:** New York City, 2 January 1933. **Education:** The High School for Music and Art, New York, graduated 1949; New York University, 1949-53, B.A. 1953; University of Michigan, Ann Arbor, M.A. 1956, Ph.D. in English 1967. **Family:** Married 1) Priscilla Older in 1966 (divorced), two sons; 2) Brenda Hillman in 1976, one daughter. **Career:** Teacher, Paterson State College, New Jersey, 1961-62; assistant professor of English, University of California, Davis, 1967-69. Since 1970 professor of English, University of California, Berkeley. Visiting professor at many universities, including Johns Hopkins University and the University of Alabama. Since 1977 editor, *University Publishing* review, Berkeley. Corresponding editor, *Partisan Review;* contributing editor, *Threepenny Review,* 1980. Contributor of short stories to numerous literary journals and popular magazines, including *Esquire, Paris Review, Evergreen Review, Partisan Review,* and *Tri-Quarterly.* **Awards:** Quill Award, *Massachusetts Review,* 1964, 1966; National Endowment for the Arts grant, 1967; *Massachusetts Review* award, 1969, 1970; Guggenheim fellowship, 1969; National Endowment for the Humanities fellow, 1970, American Academy Award in Literature, National Institute of Arts and Letters, 1971; *New York Times Book Review* Editor's Choice award,

1975. **Agent:** Lynn Nesbit, Janklow and Nesbit, 598 Madison Avenue, New York, New York 10022. **Address:** Department of English, University of California, Berkeley, California 94720, U.S.A.

PUBLICATIONS

Novel

The Men's Club. New York, Farrar Straus, and London, Cape, 1981.
Sylvia: A Fictional Memoir, illustrated by Sylvia Block. San Francisco, Mercury House, 1992.

Short Stories

Going Places. New York, Farrar Straus, 1969; London, Weidenfeld and Nicolson, 1970.
I Would Have Saved Them If I Could. New York, Farrar Straus, 1975.
Shuffle. New York, Farrar Straus, 1990; London, Cape, 1991.

Play

City Boy (produced in New York City, 1985).

Screenplay: *The Men's Club,* 1986.

Other

To Feel These Things: Essays. San Francisco, Mercury House, 1993.

Contributor, Theodore Solotaroff, editor, *American Review 26,* New York, Bantam, 1977.
Contributor, William Abrahams, editor, *Prize Stories, 1980: The O. Henry Awards,* New York, Doubleday, 1980.

Editor, with Christopher Ricks, *The State of the Language.* Berkeley, University of California Press, 1980; 1990 edition, University of California Press, and London, Faber, 1990.
Editor, with Raquel Scherr and David Reid, *West of the West: Imagining California.* Berkeley, California, North Point Press, 1990.

*

Leonard Michaels comments:

My writing tends to be terse and quick, usually about urban types and the kinds of psychological violence they inflict upon one another. I have no philosophical or political messages. My work depends on traditional beliefs.

*   *   *

Leonard Michaels's fiction is not easily described—it resists categories. It is realistic, but its dominant feature is irrationality of plot, sometimes comic, sometimes tragic, sometimes both at once. It is symbolic in its depiction of urban life, but its meanings are never reducible to messages, never allegorical. It is surreal and fragmented, but there is a consistency of viewpoint which can tie stories together and make for an overall coherence not to be found in the individual pieces. It reflects, sometimes self-consciously, the

influence of such writers as Kafka, Roth, Malamud, Barthelme, and Borges, but it is nevertheless distinctive and compelling. At their best, Michaels's stories are intense, active, and imaginative; they can also be vague and even incomprehensible.

Michaels's fiction has been published in two volumes of stories, *Going Places* and *I Would Have Saved Them If I Could;* one short novel, *The Men's Club;* a book mixing essays, autobiographical vignettes, and stories, *Shuffle;* and a "fictional memoir," *Sylvia.* The earlier pieces provide brief glimpses of contemporary urban existence, bizarre incidents suggesting the unnatural condition of city life: a naked boy is denied entrance to the subway for lack of a token; a couple maim each other in a fight and then decide to marry; a Talmudic scholar slips on an icy street and is assumed to be a drunken derelict; by never speaking in class, a professor of philosophy wins a reputation for profundity; an honors graduate preferring to make a living by driving a cab is beaten gratuitously; a boy spying on his rabbi making love falls to his death; a telephone call to a friend's apartment reaches the burglar there. Some form of intense, though often anonymous, sexual encounter begins or ends many of the stories. In all of this there is the recognition of the craziness of things and yet of their plausibility—at least so long as the setting is New York City.

The element that provides continuity in both collections is the "central intelligence" of Phillip Liebowitz. Identified in many stories, present as unnamed narrator in others, he is a self-proclaimed, streetwise "city boy." Phillip emerges as a character not in any particular story but only in the collection as a whole. His contact with others is almost entirely in a sexual context: the women in the stories are merely objects of his lust, the other men his rivals for their favors. Through sexual conquest, Phillip asserts his existence and a degree of control over the hostile urban environment.

Although novelistic in form, *The Men's Club* is strongly reminiscent of Michaels's story collections. A group of men get together to form what might be called a consciousness-raising group. They decide that each will tell the story of his life, but what we get instead are fragments of stories, not biographical data but moments of intense self-awareness. As in a group of Chaucer tales (one of the characters is named Canterbury), there is a recurring theme: the fascinating power of women over men. These husbands who come together this evening specifically to be free of women can speak of nothing but their wives and lovers, women they have lived with for many years, women they spent a few moments with many years before. The anecdotes, like all Michaels's stories, lack endings. When one character complains that he did not get the point of another's story, the narrator expresses views which apply to all Michaels's fiction:

> Doesn't matter . . . I don't get it either. I could tell other stories that have no point. This often happens to me. I start to talk, thinking there is a point, and then it never arrives. What is it, anyhow, this point? Things happen. You remember. That's all. If you take a large perspective, you'll realize there never is a point.

Sylvia, which Michaels calls "a fictional memoir" is the story of the stormy relationship between a young writer and the troubled woman he marries. Interspersed within the narrative are passages labeled as "journal" entries which are dated between 1960, the year the narrator meets Sylvia Bloch, and 1963, the year of her suicide. As in his stories, Michaels has his narrator recount anecdotes of his life with Sylvia without any attempt to convey why the characters behave as they do. Throughout his narrative, the writer refuses to explain: "My life, after all, wasn't a story. It was just moments, what happens from day to day, and it didn't mean anything, and there was no moral."

Things happen in Michaels's fiction, often strange things, but there are no explanations, no point, no moral. Readers who choose to enter Michaels's world do so on his terms.

—Robert E. Lynch

MICHENER, James A(lbert)

Nationality: American. **Born:** 1907(?); brought up by foster parents. **Education:** Doylestown High School, Pennsylvania; Swarthmore College, Pennsylvania, A.B. (summa cum laude) 1929 (Phi Beta Kappa); University of Northern Colorado, Greeley, A.M. 1935; University of St. Andrews, Fife, Scotland. **Military Service:** Served in the United States Navy, 1944-45: Lieutenant Commander. **Family:** Married 1) Patti Koon in 1935 (divorced 1948); 2) Vange Nord in 1948 (divorced 1955); 3) Mari Yoriko Sabusawa in 1955. **Career:** Master, Hill School, Pottstown, Pennsylvania, 1929-31, and George School, Newtown, Pennsylvania, 1934-36; professor, University of Northern Colorado, 1936-40; visiting professor, Harvard University, Cambridge, Massachusetts, 1940-41; associate editor, Macmillan Company, New York, 1941-49. Since 1949 freelance writer. Lives in Austin, Texas. **Awards:** Pulitzer prize, 1948; National Association of Independent Schools award, 1954, 1958; Einstein award, 1967; National Medal of Freedom, 1971. D.H.L.: Rider College, Lawrenceville, New Jersey, 1950; Swarthmore College, 1954; LL.D.: Temple University, Philadelphia, 1957; Litt.D.: Washington University, St. Louis, 1967; Yeshiva University, New York, 1974; D.Sc.: Jefferson Medical College, Philadelphia, 1979. **Member:** Advisory Committee on the Arts, United States Department of State, 1957; chair, President Kennedy's Food for Peace Program, 1961; secretary, Pennsylvania Constitution Convention, 1967-68; member of the Advisory Committee, United States Information Agency, 1970-76, and NASA, 1980-83. Since 1983 member of the Board, International Broadcasting. **Address:** 2719 Mount Laurel Lane, Austin, Texas 78703, U.S.A.

PUBLICATIONS

Novels

The Fires of Spring. New York, Random House, 1949; London, Corgi, 1960.
The Bridges at Toko-Ri. New York, Random House, and London, Secker and Warburg, 1953.
Sayonara. New York, Random House, and London, Secker and Warburg, 1954.
The Bridge at Andau. New York, Random House, and London, Secker and Warburg, 1957.
Hawaii. New York, Random House, 1959; London, Secker and Warburg, 1960.
Caravans. New York, Random House, 1963; London, Secker and Warburg, 1964.

The Source. New York, Random House, and London, Secker and Warburg, 1965.
The Drifters. New York, Random House, and London, Secker and Warburg, 1971.
Centennial. New York, Random House, and London, Secker and Warburg, 1974.
Chesapeake. New York, Random House, and London, Secker and Warburg, 1978; selections published as *The Watermen,* Random House, 1979.
The Covenant. New York, Random House, and London, Secker and Warburg, 1980.
Space. New York, Random House, and London, Secker and Warburg, 1982.
Poland. New York, Random House, 1983; London, Secker and Warburg, 1984.
Texas. New York, Random House, and London, Secker and Warburg, 1985.
Legacy. New York, Random House, and London, Secker and Warburg, 1987.
Alaska. New York, Random House, and London, Secker and Warburg, 1988.
Journey. New York, Random House, and London, Secker and Warburg, 1989.
Caribbean. New York, Random House, and London, Secker and Warburg, 1989.
The Eagle and the Raven, with drawings by Charles Shaw. Austin, Texas, State House Press, 1990; London, Secker and Warburg, 1992.
The Novel. New York, Random House, and London, Secker and Warburg, 1991.
Mexico. New York, Random House, and London, Secker and Warburg, 1992.
Recessional. New York, Random House, 1994; London, Secker and Warburg, 1995.
Miracle in Seville. New York, Random House, 1995.

Short Stories

Tales of the South Pacific. New York, Macmillan, 1947; London, Collins, 1951.
Return to Paradise. New York, Random House, and London, Secker and Warburg, 1951.
Creatures of the Kingdom: Stories of Animals and Nature, illustrated by Karen Jacobsen. New York, Random House, and London, Secker and Warburg, 1993.

Other

The Unit in the Social Studies, with Harold M. Long. Cambridge, Massachusetts, Harvard University Graduate School of Education, 1940.
The Voice of Asia. New York, Random House, 1951; as *Voices of Asia,* London, Secker and Warburg, 1952.
The Floating World (on Japanese art). New York, Random House, 1954; London, Secker and Warburg, 1955.
Rascals in Paradise, with A. Grove Day. New York, Random House, and London, Secker and Warburg, 1957.
Selected Writings. New York, Modern Library, 1957.
Japanese Prints from the Early Masters to the Modern. Rutland, Vermont, Tuttle, and London, Paterson, 1959.
Report of the County Chairman. New York, Random House, and London, Secker and Warburg, 1961.

The Modern Japanese Print: An Introduction. Rutland, Vermont, Tuttle, 1962.

Iberia: Spanish Travels and Reflections. New York, Random House, and London, Secker and Warburg, 1968.

The Subject Is Israel: A Conversation Between James A. Michener and Dore Schary. New York, Anti-Defamation League of B'nai B'rith, 1968.

Presidential Lottery: The Reckless Gamble in Our Electoral System. New York, Random House, and London, Secker and Warburg, 1969.

The Quality of Life. Philadelphia, Lippincott, 1970; London, Secker and Warburg, 1971.

Facing East: A Study of the Art of Jack Levine. New York, Random House, 1970.

Kent State: What Happened and Why. New York, Random House, and London, Secker and Warburg, 1971.

A Michener Miscellany 1950-1970, edited by Ben Hibbs. New York, Random House, 1973; London, Corgi, 1975.

About "Centennial": Some Notes on the Novel. New York, Random House, 1974.

Sports in America. New York, Random House, 1976; as *Michener on Sport,* London, Secker and Warburg, 1976.

Testimony. Honolulu, White Knight, 1983.

Collectors, Forgers—and a Writer: A Memoir. New York, Targ, 1983.

Six Days in Havana, with John Kings. Austin, University of Texas Press, 1989; London, Souvenir Press, 1990.

Pilgrimage: A Memoir of Poland and Rome. Emmaus, Pennsylvania, Rodale Press, 1990.

James A. Michener's Writer's Handbook: Explorations in Writing and Publishing. New York, Random House, 1992.

My Lost Mexico, with photographs by the author. Austin, Texas, State House Press, and London, Secker and Warburg, 1992.

The World Is My Home: A Memoir. New York, Random House, 1992.

Editor, *The Future of the Social Studies: Proposals for an Experimental Social-Studies Curriculum.* New York, National Council for the Social Studies, 1939.

Editor, *The Hokusai Sketch Books: Selections from the Manga.* Rutland, Vermont, Tuttle, 1958.

Editor, *Firstfruits: A Harvest of 25 Years of Israeli Writing.* Philadelphia, Jewish Publication Society of America, 1973.

*

Manuscript Collection: Library of Congress, Washington, D.C.

Critical Studies: *James Michener* by A. Grove Day, New York, Twayne, 1964, revised edition, 1977; *James Michener* by George J. Becker, New York, Ungar, 1983; *James A. Michener: A Biography* by John P. Hayes, Indianapolis, Bobbs Merrill, and London, W.H. Allen, 1984.

James A. Michener comments:

I had the good fortune to arrive on the scene when America was broadening its intellectual horizons to include the entire world. Millions of our men would experience the South Pacific; millions of families would live in Japan or Germany, and countries like Great Britain and Italy became commonplace adventures. Had I written as I did 20 years earlier, I doubt seriously that I would have en-joyed much of a readership. America was not only prepared for what I had to say, but apparently eager to hear it.

Also, I came along when the television set was about to command the attention of the middle American family to the exclusion of almost all else, and I made a conscious decision: "If they look at television long enough, they will grow hungry for the more substantial experience they can get only through books," and it became evident to me that instead of abandoning reading, the people I was aiming at would demand more of it, and would be prepared to accept long and difficult books, would indeed seek them out. In this judgment I was confirmed.

I am sometimes thought of, for these reasons, as an exotic writer. On the contrary, I have worked in an unusually wide spectrum of human experience, from politics to ecology to education to Asian art to the fine arts. I have also worked in these fields, having been an active politician and a connoisseur of the arts. My life has been therefore a vain attempt to keep many interests in balance, and my books have been proof of how one or the other of those interests has run away with me from time to time.

My style has always been deceptively simple, and I have worked assiduously to keep it that way. This requires not only careful writing, but endless rewriting, redrafting, rejection, and final polishing. I find that I work principally in a Latinized vocabulary, in fairly long sentences; revision consists of going back to simpler Anglo-Saxon words and shorter sentences. My ideals have been Henry James, Gustave Flaubert, and Ivan Turgenev, whom I have never tried to ape, and William Thackeray, Honoré Balzac, Leo Tolstoy, and Samuel Butler, whom I have. My influences have thus been almost exclusively European rather than American, a consequence of my education, and I have always felt this to have been a pity.

*   *   *

No one could ever justifiably accuse James A. Michener of being intellectually stagnant or lazy. Few, if any, other contemporary American writers have dared to explore the vast territories he has covered in so much depth. No period of history or topic of social concern, it would seem, has escaped Michener's pen. From the ancient Middle East to modern-day Texas, Michener has written the histories of places and their inhabitants, always with a sharp, clear eye for detail and description. His nonfiction work is perhaps even more impressive in scope and bulk; his subjects range from the Kent State killings and ensuing investigation to the world of Japanese art.

Michener began his writing career in 1947 with the publication of *Tales of the South Pacific,* a collection of loosely connected stories concerning the lives and loves of American soldiers stationed in that area during World War II. The book, an immediate success which was hailed as one of the most significant books to emerge from a wartime experience in decades, won the Pulitzer prize. Against the backdrop of the lush islands and sensuous natives, Michener places a group of American military personnel. The lives and cultures of the two disparate peoples become entwined, the first of many such juxtapositions of cultures to be found in Michener's works. (A later novel, *Sayonara,* displays even more of this clash as it chronicles the tragic love affair of an American GI and his Japanese mistress.) Although a definite flair for storytelling is evident, the author does have a tendency to go into rather too much detail, causing some of the weaker stories to fall flat.

An attempt at an autobiographical novel, *The Fires of Spring,* followed. The story of a poor boy from Pennsylvania who, through academic success and help from a Quaker family, travels to New York to try his luck at writing has all the marks of a too-autobiographical work. It comes off as hastily written and lacking in perspective.

Depending upon the reader's taste, Michener is at either his best or his worst in his long historical novels. After *Sayonara* was published in 1954, Michener allowed his love of place and history to overtake his fiction. Whereas in his earlier novels he paid careful consideration to characterization and dialogue, in his later novels, he seems to believe that the sweeping historical plots will interest his readers enough to carry them through books that even his most avid fans must find too often long and sometimes dull.

Hawaii, perhaps the most famous of the historical novels, is a panoramic book that depicts the formation, development, and settlement of the islands. While rich in historical and cultural description, the book is flawed in that the characters are not well-drawn or expanded. Still, the novel is a masterful example of the genre. *Centennial* and *Chesapeake* both rival *Hawaii* as Michener's historical masterpieces, but, again, the books suffer from length, lack of characterization, and descriptive overkill. Even less successful are *Caravans* and *The Source,* in which the background and sense of history play a larger part than do essential fictional elements.

That Michener is an important and popular novelist there is no denying. He would prove himself a more capable novelist, however, if he developed his characters more fully and kept a tighter rein on his rather unwieldy historical descriptions.

—Sally H. Bennett

MIDDLETON, O(sman) E(dward Gordon)

Nationality: New Zealander. **Born:** Christchurch, 25 March 1925. **Education:** New Plymouth Boys High School, 1939-41; Auckland University, 1946, 1948; the Sorbonne, Paris (New Zealand Government bursary), 1955-56. **Military Service:** Served in the Royal New Zealand Air Force, 1944-45. **Family:** Married Maida Edith Middleton (marriage dissolved 1970); two children. **Career:** Resident, Károlyi Memorial Foundation, Vence, France, Summer 1983; lectured at several European universities, 1983. **Awards:** New Zealand Award of Achievement, 1960, and scholarship in letters, 1965; Hubert Church Prose award, 1964; University of Otago Robert Burns fellowship, 1970; New Zealand Prose Fiction award, 1976. **Address:** 20 Clifford Street, Dunedin, New Zealand.

PUBLICATIONS

Short Stories

Short Stories. Wellington, Handcraft Press, 1954.
The Stone and Other Stories. Auckland, Pilgrim Press, 1959.
A Walk on the Beach. London, Joseph, 1964.
The Loners. Wellington, Square and Circle, 1972.
Selected Stories. Dunedin, McIndoe, 1975.
Confessions of an Ocelot, Not for a Seagull (2 novellas). Dunedin, McIndoe, 1978.

Poetry

Six Poems. Wellington, Handcraft Press, 1951.

Other

From the River to the Tide (for children). Wellington, School Publications Branch, 1964.

*

Manuscript Collections: Auckland Public Library; Hocken Library, Dunedin.

Critical Studies: *New Zealand Fiction Since 1945* by H. Winston Rhodes, Dunedin, McIndoe, 1968; "O.E. Middleton: Not Just a Realist" by Jim Williamson, in *Islands* (Auckland), Winter 1973; *O.E. Middleton: The Sympathetic Imagination and the Right Judgements,* Dunedin, Pilgrims South Press, 1980, "Out from Under My Uncle's Hat: Gaskell, Middleton and the Sargeson Tradition," in *Critical Essays on the New Zealand Short Story* edited by Cherry Hankin, Auckland, Heinemann, 1982, and *Barbed Wire and Mirrors: Essays on New Zealand Prose,* Dunedin, University of Otago Press, 1987, all by Lawrence Jones.

O.E. Middleton comments:

(1991) My published fiction comprises two novellas, several dozen short stories and a work for children. Unpublished material includes two novels and numerous stories.

It is not my wish to explain, analyze, or otherwise obscure what I have sought to render in fictional terms. I should feel that I had failed as a writer if my work did not speak for itself.

*   *   *

As a short story writer primarily devoted to the New Zealand scene, O.E. Middleton remains faithful to the tradition of unsophisticated realism. He is less interested in technical innovation than in his wide experience of people and places at home and abroad, less attracted to ironic or symbolic patterns than to the rhythms of the spoken language and the texture of the workaday world. The titles of his best-known collections, *The Stone and Other Stories* and *A Walk on the Beach,* are symptomatic of an unpretentious manner and direct approach to subject matter that is rarely remote from the commonplace, but is raised to a level of significance by its truth of substance.

Unlike some writers held in greater esteem he never adopts an authorial position from which he finds it convenient to look down on the antics of his characters with fastidious disapproval or superior sensibility. On the contrary he is always democratically at ease in the scene and among the people he has created. The narrators of "The Corporal's Story" and "The Greaser's Story" are familiar with their occupations and in harmony with their backgrounds.

Middleton populates his fictional world with laborers and seamen, farmers and city-dwellers, Europeans and Maoris, children and adolescents. They are ordinary people, generally unremarkable for subtlety of thought or emotion; and the incidents related are associated with their normal activities during work and leisure. Their understanding is limited and their conversation borders on the banal; but what must be lost in felicity of expression is gained in authenticity and restraint. "A Married Man" concludes tritely with

"'Never mind,' she said, smiling and friendly, 'It will come right in the end.'" The narrator of "A Day by Itself" observes "It had been a funny day really, and there were things about it which I still didn't understand." Even when stories are based on episodes derived from the eventful years of the writer's wanderings, both language and character become absorbed into the raw material of life.

Despite the absence of any guidelines which can be attributed to the author, a moral sensibility is distinctly present in choice of theme, development of action, and establishment of character. A particular kind of neocolonial egalitarian humanism informs every aspect of his writing and is readily detected in what he has called "sorties into the no-man's-land of inter-racial relations." The most substantial of these stories is found in the novella *Not for a Seagull*, told by a young Maori who is continually made aware that goodfellowship often masks attitudes of racial discrimination. This has recently been republished with the addition of a later and more sophisticated work, *Confessions of an Ocelot,* which relates the experiences of a human victim innocently trapped in a city-jungle. The narrator is a withdrawn and sensitive youth whose "confessions" are intended to reveal "to any who may share a like sensibility the perils that can await its flowering." With characteristic thoroughness Middleton enters into the interior world of his guideless recorder and at the same time uncovers the external world in which he moves uncomprehendingly. Yet, surprisingly enough, the didacticism latent in this and other themes does not often obtrude. Middleton is too honest a craftsman to allow strongly held opinions to falsify his representation of the life he has both experienced and observed. His characters play their parts in the diverse activities of the communities in which they find themselves, with the result that any temptation to overemphasize private perplexities is checked by the recognition of otherness, and Middleton is able both to explore his chosen terrain and disclose rather than publish his humane attitudes.

The measure of his work is to be found not in terms of quantity, for his output has not been large, but in the success he has achieved in responding to the epigraph from Dryden which he attached to his *Selected Stories*—"For the spirit of man cannot be satisfied but with truth or at least verisimility. . . ." It is also to be found in the range and variety of scene, character, and situation. He moves easily from land to sea, from the Americas to Europe and back again to New Zealand, distilling fragments of his wide experiences and activity into imaginative work that attains significance from the authenticity of its treatment. Such stories as "The Crows," "For Once in Your Life," "The Doss-House and the Duchess," and "The Collector" (all in *Selected Stories*) are characterized by the same concern with variations of the human predicament as is to be found in his more frequent New Zealand narratives.

—H. Winston Rhodes

MIDDLETON, Stanley

Nationality: British. **Born:** Bulwell, Nottingham, 1 August 1919. **Education:** High Pavement School, Nottingham; University College of Nottingham (now Nottingham University), 1938-40, 1946-47, B.A. (London) 1940; M.Ed. (Nottingham) 1952. **Military Service:** Served in the Royal Artillery and the Army Education Corps, 1940-46. **Family:** Married Margaret Shirley Welch in 1951; two daughters. **Career:** English Master, 1947-81, and head of the English Department, 1958-81, High Pavement College, Nottingham. Judith E. Wilson Visiting Fellow, Emmanuel College, Cambridge, 1982-83. **Awards:** Booker prize, 1974. M.A.: Nottingham University, 1975. **Address:** 42 Caledon Road, Sherwood, Nottingham NG5 2NG, England.

PUBLICATIONS

Novels

A Short Answer. London, Hutchinson, 1958.
Harris's Requiem. London, Hutchinson, 1960.
A Serious Woman. London, Hutchinson, 1961.
The Just Exchange. London, Hutchinson, 1962.
Two's Company. London, Hutchinson, 1963.
Him They Compelled. London, Hutchinson, 1964.
Terms of Reference. London, Hutchinson, 1966.
The Golden Evening. London, Hutchinson, 1968.
Wages of Virtue. London, Hutchinson, 1969.
Apple of the Eye. London, Hutchinson, 1970.
Brazen Prison. London, Hutchinson, 1971.
Cold Gradations. London, Hutchinson, 1972.
A Man Made of Smoke. London, Hutchinson, 1973.
Holiday. London, Hutchinson, 1974.
Distractions. London, Hutchinson, 1975.
Still Waters. London, Hutchinson, 1976.
Ends and Means. London, Hutchinson, 1977.
Two Brothers. London, Hutchinson, 1978.
In a Strange Land. London, Hutchinson, 1979.
The Other Side. London, Hutchinson, 1980.
Blind Understanding. London, Hutchinson, 1982.
Entry into Jerusalem. London, Hutchinson, 1983; New York, New Amsterdam, 1989.
The Daysman. London, Hutchinson, 1984.
Valley of Decision. London, Hutchinson, 1985; New York, New Amsterdam, 1987.
An After-Dinner's Sleep. London, Hutchinson, 1986.
After a Fashion. London, Hutchinson, 1987.
Recovery. London, Hutchinson, 1988.
Vacant Places. London, Hutchinson, 1989; New York, New Amsterdam, 1990.
Changes and Chances. London, Hutchinson, 1990.
Beginning to End. London, Hutchinson, 1991.
A Place to Stand. London, Hutchinson, 1992.
Married Past Redemption. London, Hutchinson, 1993.
Catalysts. London, Hutchinson, 1994.
Toward the Sea. London, Hutchinson, 1995.

Uncollected Short Story

"The Noise," in *Critical Quarterly* (Manchester), Winter 1987.

Plays

Radio Plays: *The Captain from Nottingham,* 1972; *Harris's Requiem,* 1972; *A Little Music at Night,* 1972; *Cold Gradations,* from his own novel, 1973.

*

Manuscript Collection: Central Library, Nottingham.

Critical Studies: "Stanley Middleton and the Provincial Novel" by John Lucas, in *Nottingham Quarterly,* 1978; article by June Sturrock, in *British Novelists Since 1960* edited by Jay L. Halio, Detroit Gale, 1983; "The Art of Stanley Middleton" by A.S. Byatt, in *Fiction Magazine* (London), 1985; "A Roaring Whisper," in *Stand* (Newcastle upon Tyne), Autumn 1988, and "Einstein in the Patent Office," in *Encounter* (London), July-August 1989, both by Philip Davis; "Master of the Unspectacular" by John Mellors, in *London Magazine,* August-September 1990.

Stanley Middleton comments:

(1972) I put down a few obvious points about my novels.

They are set mainly in the English midlands with characters drawn from the professional middle-classes (students, teachers, actors, writers, musicians, lawyers, painters, architects), though one will find laborers and factory workers as well as businessmen of real affluence.

The action usually occupies a short period of some months only (*Wages of Virtue* is an exception), and the plot deals with people in a state of crisis or perplexity caused by illness and death, or a breakdown of personal relationships, or the difficulties of creating a work of art (which may be music, *Harris's Requiem,* or poetry, *Him They Compelled,* or a novel in *Brazen Prison*). At this time of dilemmas, friends or relatives intervene, and thus learn their own inadequacies and, sometimes, strengths. No perfect characters or solutions exist; all is difficult, compromising, but a bonus of success or joy is occasionally found.

My idea is not only to tell an interesting story but to demonstrate the complexity of human character and motive. One must not only describe what has happened to people, or what they are like; one must make the characters live out what they are said to be, and this must include deviations from normality and actions "out of character." I find this most difficult, but when I am charged, sometimes, with "mere reportage," I can see no sense at all in the accusation. My novels are imaginative attempts to write down illuminating actions and talk from the lives of fictional people, and not transcriptions of tape recordings of real conversations or blow-by-blow commentaries on events which have really taken place. I am sometimes praised for the "realism" of my dialogue, and this makes me wonder if these critics, who may of course be using a "shorthand" dictated by the small space at their disposal, know how different my sort of dialogue is from that of real life.

This preoccupation leads to a choice of different levels of writing. A novel cannot always be intense; both by the shape of my work and my use of language I try constantly to interfere with the reader, to rest him as well as violently assault him. Therefore it is galling when I find critics who apparently subscribe to the notion that contemporary novels are either "well-written" (i.e. in "mandarin") or dashed down without care. Mine are usually dumped by such people in the second category. Shifts on my part from the point of view of one character to that of another also seem to pass unnoticed. I enjoy putting obstacles in my own way to find out if I can surmount them.

I am often asked if my novels are didactic. I wouldn't object to that word since the greatest work of art I know—Bach's *St. Matthew Passion*—could be so described. But unless a novel is complex, memorable, capable of holding a reader and moving him deeply, I've not much time for it.

I can't think these notes very helpful. General exegesis as opposed to critical discussion of precise points in specific books has little attraction for me as a writer. A novel should be its own defense; if it does not speak for itself to a well-equipped reader, call out echoes in him, it's not properly written.

*　　*　　*

Middle-class, middle-aged, midland dwellers provide most of the material for Stanley Middleton's novels from 1960 to the 1990s. His remarkable achievement in producing such lively work from such an unpromising source lies in his ability to make most of his characters both unlikeable and interesting at the same time. His women for the most part are tormented frigid tormentors, while his affluent men are generally mediocrities in their professions and indecisive shamblers in their personal lives, if they are not driven by an ugly and ruthless streak of ambition or obsessed by the demands of art.

He makes his readers understand that people at the end of their tether do not become heroic and loveable through their suffering, and that emotional snarl-ups render the participants selfish, irritable, and dull. The skill of Middleton's handling of dialogue is that although the first two qualities are caught, the third is avoided. The reader is held by the way the seemingly pointless remarks of the speakers can grate against each other. This is especially true when there is any attempt to bridge gaps of generation, social class, or economic status. In *Terms of Reference* the two late-middle-aged couples are perplexed and powerless when confronted by the failure of the marriage between the son of the very wealthy pair and the daughter of the academics. Yet although they can do nothing to hold their wayward children together, and are by no means certain that it would be a good thing to do so, all four are too fascinated by the situation to leave it alone.

Edward Tenby, the architect hero of *Apple of the Eye,* is not only the sole moderately creative and productive character in the novel, he is also the only man. He becomes involved with three neurotic women, each young enough to be his daughter. One of them has enough money to indulge her sickness to its limit, while the other two are poor enough to be flattered and astounded at making any contact so high in the social scale. In *Brazen Prison* Charles Stead, the ex-grammar school novelist, has to cope with the social nuances of relating to his wealthy socialite wife and the company she keeps, while at the same time involving himself with the husband and family of the local girl he had picked up in the dance hall as a youth.

Many novelists use the device of seeing their created world through the eyes of a fellow writer, and it is one that Middleton is fond of. As well as Charles Stead, there is the bestselling novelist Eric Chamberlain in *Ends and Means.* His obsession with success makes him almost insensitive to the fatal distress of his son and mistress, who both kill themselves. His detachment is matched by that of Frank, the modest, doomed, and isolated poet in *Two Brothers.*

Middleton is at his best, however, when he uses music or the visual arts to convey the excitement and compulsion of creation, and to give an added dimension to the construction of a novel. There are marvelous passages of musical analysis in *In a Strange Land,* which is an unusual Middleton novel in that the protagonist, James Murren, organist and composer, leaves the midlands to further his career in London. In *Valley of Decision,* which concerns a young music teacher married to an ambitious singer, the stages of the novel almost correspond to musical movements which are heightened by the analysis of the performances of an amateur quartet with whom the husband is invited to play.

Entry into Jerusalem explores the way a man can be driven to create a visual image. Like Middleton's novelists and musicians, John Worth, the 30-year-old painter of this novel, successfully harnesses his imagination by living a life somewhat detached from his fellows, however many disasters take place around him. His work is barely touched when his former teaching colleague has a breakdown and kills himself.

Suicides of minor characters are frequent in Middleton's later novels, throwing the main events into a sharper focus. Death is ever-present, lurking in the background of everyday life, or accepted as a concomitant of age as it is in *Blind Understanding*. That novel follows the ruminations of a retired small-town solicitor as he lives out a day between attending a funeral in the morning and hearing of the heart attack suffered by a member of his wife's bridge party in the evening.

In these later novels, Middleton makes little use of his experience as a school teacher, the main exception being his sensitive exploration in *The Daysman* of the character of John Richardson, headmaster of a comprehensive school in a middle-class area and general friend and counselor to pupils and staff alike. He is a man who lets ambition and the lure of the media gradually rot his integrity and understanding. In this he is contrasted with his practical, capable wife, and the working out of their marriage is the main point of that novel. Indeed Middleton's preoccupation with the shifting adjustment of marriages enables him to make full use of his remarkable gift for describing the minute nuances of human interaction from the merest twitchings of "body language" to full-scale emotional and physical outbursts.

The most recent novels, however, tackle a different problem: the adjustment to reality that has to be made by anyone living on their own. This is often, but not always, linked to the circumstance of aging. So, in *An After-Dinner's Sleep,* the widower Alaistair Murray, a recently retired Director of Education, struggled with his need to fill his days in a meaningful way, and with an intermittent relationship with a woman friend from a long distant past.

Job Turner in *Recovery* is also widowed, but although he is coming towards the end of his career as a headmaster, he has yet to face the empty days of retirement. Both men are influenced by their grown children, and these connections make a natural web of time into which their married years are absorbed.

Joe Harrington in *After a Fashion* and Henry Fairfax in *Vacant Places* come into a different category. They are both young and successful enough to envisage promotion in their different careers; Harrington is an academic, Fairfax a business executive. They both live alone because their marriages have failed. Yet they both still have a relationship with their ex-wives, and the reader is left feeling that they are both the sort of men who will eventually remarry.

The theme of old age comes up as a subplot in both these novels. In *After a Fashion,* Joe Harrington is confronted with the declining powers of the professor of English in the university where he lectures, as well as the more extreme senility of one of his former schoolmasters and a neighbor's father, whose reminiscences he has reluctantly agreed to read. These three characters form a constant, if shadowy, chorus to the main action. In *Vacant Places,* the reminder of old age comes in the form of a garrulous Welshman, met in a pub. It is a brief but haunting portrait.

In *Changes and Chances* the novel pivots on a really disagreeable character, and that is a rare feature in Middleton's work. Adrian

Hillier is a rich dilettante in his forties, who likes to dabble in the arts. His halfhearted attempt at marriage was doomed to failure, and the course of the novel finds him enlivening his pampered and solitary existence with bouts of sensual but loveless womanizing, embarked on from the maternal and sexual comforts provided by his housekeeper, Elsie. In this novel old age is presented in its most positive aspects in the person of the poet, Stephen Youlgrave; and the chorus is provided by an astutely observant child, Peter Fowler, who takes a Saturday job helping with the chores in Adrian's household.

In all these novels, the disciplines of music and poetry provide solace for the challenges of loneliness and the passage of time; and give meaning to the apparently trivial events through which Middleton displays and shapes his characters.

—Shirley Toulson

MILLER, Alex

Nationality: Australian (originally British, immigrated to Australia c.1952). **Born:** 1936. **Career:** Has held a variety of jobs, including cattle ranching, horse breaking, art brokering, and teaching. Currently a full-time writer. **Awards:** Miles Franklin award, 1993, and Commonwealth Writers prize, 1993, both for *The Ancestor Game.*

PUBLICATIONS

Novels

Watching the Climbers on the Mountain. Sydney, Pan, 1988.
The Tivington Nott. Ringwood, Victoria, Penguin, 1989.
The Ancestor Game. Ringwood, Victoria, Penguin, 1992; St. Paul, Minnesota, Graywolf Press, 1994.
The Sitters. N.p., 1995.

Plays

Exiles. Melbourne, Australian Nouveau Theatre, 1981.

*   *   *

Migration is a recurrent theme in Alex Miller's four novels, which vividly reveal the pressures of alienation and the need to belong. Miller's first novel, *Watching the Climbers on the Mountain* of 1988, is set in the Central Highlands of Queensland. The novel's intensity of passion in isolated situations is reminiscent of D.H. Lawrence and Molly Skinner's *The Boy in the Bush* and Randolph Stow's first novel *A Haunted Land.* Miller's landscape and climate are, however, those of north Queensland with its heat, tropical storms, and mosquitoes. When the 18-year-old English stockman Robert Crofts arrives at a remote cattle station to work, he is drawn into a series of physical and psychological struggles. Initiation occurs when he becomes the focus of the simmering discontents and desires of the family on whose station he works. His sexual relationship with the station owner's wife leads to tragedy. Anger, jealousy, madness, and revenge drive the plot, but these are counterpointed by the woman's sense of belonging to the mountainous landscape into which she was born. As in later novels, sexual ambivalence is evident and the psychological relationships of parents with children, and brothers with sisters are important elements.

Miller's second novel *The Tivington Nott,* written in 1989, returns to the English West Country setting of Somerset on the edges of Exmoor. The novel's youthful first-person narrator, a Londoner, is a newcomer to the strict class barriers of provincial England. He is perhaps incipiently Australian in refusing to call his employer "master" but settling for "boss." But his main access to power is through retreat to a private inner world: he thus identifies with the elusive wild stag (the "nott") on Exmoor, which has eluded the local hunters for years by retreating to its secret soiling pit in the woods. The novel's major action is a hunt which celebrates the call of the wild in defiance of the forces of "civilization."

The Ancestor Game of 1992 is a more finely wrought, ambitious novel than the previous two, bringing to a point of subtle imaginative development Miller's preoccupations with home, homeland, and alienation. The sentient center of this novel is an English immigrant, Steven Muir, who lives and teaches in Melbourne. Muir's struggles with his sense of identity as an English-born Australian find their imaginative correlatives in a Chinese-Australian friend, Lang Tzu, and an artist friend of German and Asian extraction, Gertrude Spiess. The Chinese-born Lang Tzu's name is made up of two characters in Mandarin signifying "the son who goes away." But Lang's ancestry is complicated by the fact that his great-grandfather Feng had come to Australia in 1848, and made his fortune on the Victorian goldfields before returning to China. Thus the "son who goes away" paradoxically returns to an ancestral dwelling-place when he migrates to Australia.

The action in *The Ancestor Game,* carried on in a series of parallel or interwoven histories, moves principally between the cities of Melbourne, Shanghai, and Hangzhou (Marco Polo's "City of Heaven"). At a thematic level, much is made of the notion of "extraterritoriality," a state of being beyond history, place, and circumstance, promoted principally by the German-born Dr. Spiess, father of Gertrude. For Dr. Spiess, life in the International Settlement in prewar Shanghai had seemed ideally "extraterritorial," but he too is drawn inexorably towards a recognition of his involvement in history. When Lang Tzu burns his maternal grandfather's book of ancestors he recognizes himself, like other protagonists in Miller's work, as "a stranger on this earth." But Dr Spiess offers the young Lang an antidote: "Long for something you can't name . . . and call it Australia." One of the novel's chief sources of appeal is that it reappraises Australia as a country of postcolonial possibility where ancestry, allegiance, and identity coalesce in an uncertain process of becoming.

Miller's fourth novel, *The Sitters,* develops a leitmotif from earlier work, namely the power of art to release human emotions and to transcend local conditions. The first-person narrator in this short novel is a late-middle-aged English-born painter living in Canberra. He lives alone, having been left some years previously by his wife and son. When he meets an Australian-born woman academic who works in England but has returned on a visiting appointment to a university in Australia, the two lives and lineages intersect. The narrator is attracted to the woman as a person and as a potential subject of his paintings. As the relationship develops, so too does his renewed desire to paint, which releases him in turn to cope with the psychological effects of his unresolved and truncated past

in England. While postcolonial theory informs aspects of *The Ancestor Game, The Sitters* draws to some extent on Roland Barthes's speculative essays on words and images. A feature of *The Sitters* is its interweaving of present circumstances with vignettes of memory. A crisis occurs when the narrator returns with his new friend to her childhood home in the Araluen Valley in New South Wales. Here, in a finely evoked poetry of place the artist achieves a consummation through art, and imagines himself for the first time in a place of belonging. Through a deft use of parallel images and intersecting motifs, Miller's fourth novel explores afresh his preoccupations with place, community, and individual identity.

—Bruce Bennett

MILLHAUSER, Steven (Lewis)

Nationality: American. **Born:** New York, 3 August 1943. **Education:** Columbia College, New York, 1961-65, B.A., Brown University, Providence, Rhode Island, 1986-1971 and 1976-77. **Family:** Married Cathy Allis in 1984, one son and one daughter. **Career:** Visiting associate professor of English, Williams College, 1986-88; associate professor of English, Skidmore College, 1988-1992. Since 1992 professor of English, Skidmore College. **Awards:** Prix Medicis Étranger, 1975; American Academy and Institute of Arts and Letters award, 1987, for literature; Lannan literary award, 1994, for fiction. **Agent:** Amanda Urban, International Creative Management, 40 West 57th St., New York, New York 10019, U.S.A.

PUBLICATIONS

Novels

Edwin Mullhouse: The Life and Death of an American Writer. New York, Knopf, 1972.
Portrait of a Romantic. New York, Knopf, 1977.
From the Realm of Morpheus. New York, Morrow, 1986.

Short Stories

In the Penny Arcade. New York, Knopf, 1986.
Little Kingdoms (novellas). New York, Simon and Schuster, 1993.

*   *   *

A short story writer and novelist who specializes in the curious relationship of childhood and creativity, Steven Millhauser is best known for his first book, *Edwin Mulhouse: The Life and Death of an American Writer, 1943-1954.* In the decades since it was published, the penchant for ever-thicker biographies has only increased, as has the satiric power of Millhauser's novel. The burden of Millhauser's subsequent career was to somehow match the brilliance of his first book. That he has not done so is at once predictable and further testament to the enduring greatness of *Edwin Mulhouse.* Few contemporary American novels have a legitimate claim to being regarded as classics, but Millhauser's elaborate account of the Boswell to Johnson relationship of a ten-year-old writer and his adoring but deeply jealous classmate is one of them.

Although reviewer-critics often mention the heavy debts that *Edwin Mulhouse* owes to Vladimir Nabokov's *Pale Fire,* a whole range of other books are more likely influences, including Thomas Mann's *Doctor Faustus* and Nabokov's *The Real Life of Sebastian Knight.* Moreover, biography itself is only part of the novel's landscape; unsentimental portraits of childhood—either as beings closer to the truth than adults are likely to realize, or as complicated characters in their own right—also matter greatly. Indeed, no contemporary American writer is more adroit or more penetrating when it comes to rendering children from the inside out.

Millhauser is also concerned with the curious relationship between art and life, or in the case of Edwin Mulhouse, between the artist and his biographer. At one point Jeffrey, the child who has escaped death's clutches to chronicle the story of a writer-friend who did not, puts it this way:

> God pity the poor novelist. Standing on his omniscient cliff, with painful ingenuity he must contrive to drop bits of important information into the swift current of his all-powerful plot, where they are swept along like so many popsicle sticks, turning and turning. He dare not delay for one second, not even for one-tenth of a second, for then the busy and impatient reader will yawn and lay aside the book and pick up the nearest newspaper, with all those slender columns that remind you of nothing so much as the sides of cereal boxes. The modest biographer, fortunately, is under no such obligation. Calmly and methodically, in one fell swoop, in a way impossible for the harried novelist who is always trying to do a hundred things at once, he can simply say what he has to say, ticking off each item with his right hand on the successively raised fingers of his left.

There is a good deal of truth in the selection, also with a perhaps even greater amount of tongue in Millhauser's cheek, for *Edwin Mulhouse* is a novel that lives or dies on the accumulative effect of its elaborate style.

Excess comes with the territory, but the argument is harder to sustain in Millhauser's subsequent work. In *Portrait of a Romantic,* Arthur Grumm, the novel's 29-year old protagonist, replaces his present situation with elaborately recalled dreams from his adolescence. As he insists, "A work of fiction is a radical act of the imagination whose sole purpose is to supplant the world." One could say similar things about the stories Millhauser has been publishing in recent years (*In the Penny Arcade, The Barnum Museum,* and *Little Kingdoms: Three Novellas*): they are often populated by characters who, in the words of Edwin Mulhouse's suicide note, "aspire to the condition of fiction." Moreover, Millhauser is a writer whose allusion-packed paragraphs never quite know when to say when.

The result is at once large swatches of dazzling verbal magic and a disturbing sense that the pyrotechnics never move beyond the status of learned exercise. Millhauser receives respectful attention whenever a new volume appears, but his work has not yet managed to step outside the long shadow that *Edwin Mulhouse* cast.

—Sanford Pinsker

MINOT, Susan (Anderson)

Nationality: American. **Born:** Boston, Massachusetts, 1956. **Education:** Brown University, Providence, Rhode Island, B.A.; Columbia University, New York, M.F.A. **Career:** Associate editor, Grand Street, New York, 1982-86; adjunct professor, Graduate Writing Program, New York University, 1987, and Columbia University, New York, 1989. **Awards:** Prix Femina Étranger, 1987. **Address:** c/o Georges Borchardt, 136 East 57th St., New York, New York 10022, U.S.A.

PUBLICATIONS

Novels

Monkeys. New York, Dutton, 1986.
Folly. Boston, Houghton Mifflin, 1992.

Short Stories

Lust and Other Stories. Boston, Houghton Mifflin, 1989.

*   *   *

A loving detailer of her region—Boston and the North Shore—and a detailed critic of love, Susan Minot weaves stories whose sadness bespeak a piercing intelligence and courageous honesty. Her contribution to the genres of short story and novel is a feminized minimalist style. Although minimalism is more often associated with male writers like Raymond Carver, Minot gives us a hybridized version. She incorporates minimalism's narrow brush strokes, while at the same time painting the emotions clearly.

Minot's protagonists, mostly women, are searching for love. The theme remains constant in different milieus: *Monkeys* is set in 1970s North Shore; *Lust* takes place in yuppie 1980s New York City; *Folly* is set on Beacon Hill from the 1920s to the 1950s. Although the language and mores of each time and place are different, the sentiments expressed by the characters are similar: in the space where love should be, there is emptiness, lack, "an overwhelming sadness, an elusive gaping worry."

Family love is the primary concern in the two novels, whereas romantic love is the aim in the short story collection, *Lust.* Although romance is harder to achieve and more transitory, family love is also elusive, unexpected, sometimes even a great surprise. In *Monkeys,* Minot creates a whole family, including seven kids, with a degree of particularity that one would expect for a smaller cast. Her portraits of troubled adolescent males are as sensitive as those of their sisters. In the chapter, "Accident," teenaged Sherman is introduced by a typically minimalist *reductio ad absurdum,* which succeeds in conveying a sufficient amount of information: "Sherman has the cat in his lap, not thinking much, sixteen years old." As if being a 16-year-old male means, *prima facie,* that you don't think too much, but you do like to feel living creatures in your lap. This story climaxes in a scene that any of us would like to have written: Sherman, dead drunk and talking like a thug, confronts his alcoholic dad with the question: "Are you my faddah? Then why don't you act like a faddah?" Predictably, Dad scurries away, leaving Sherman in an uncharacteristically expressive state. One wail escapes him; it sets his siblings in motion. Chicky, the younger brother, knows that this is not like the grief when their mother died: *that* was like seeing the Devil for a flash; *this* was the Devil swooping down, hulking in the middle of the kitchen table, and settling down to stay. In this family, as in many real-life ones, the children have been forced to take responsibility for their alcoholic father. Minot creates a recognizable family dynamic, evoking pathos without melodrama.

In *Lust,* the characters are wistful; they can't quite understand what it is they stand to gain from their sexual relationships, even though they need them like bodies need water. Women pursue and are pursued by men in a fast-whirling social environment that includes cocaine-snorting and glamorous careers in film and journalism. Minot's sure rhythms capture the hard-boiled verities of this party life. In short paragraphs, she begins with short, simple sentences, building gradually to longer ones to create the inevitable conclusion: men don't love like women do. Her logic appears in simple two- or three-liners that capture a sense of futility. After sex, boys are like this: "Their blank look tells you that the girl they were fucking is not there anymore. You seem to have disappeared." Before sex, things are much better: "He pressed close. She felt as if she were setting off for a place she'd only vaguely heard about. Her heart was going madly, knowing nothing, feeling no pain." During the affair, you learn that you can't take it: "Slowly it dawned on me this was one of those loose and easy things. Maybe I'll learn something, I thought. I did. I learned things. I learned I didn't have the stomach for it. You need an iron stomach, and nerves of steel." Do not look for a happy, mutual, heterosexual relationship in Minot. You will not find it.

Folly's title warns us that it is about another inadequate relationship, this time a marriage that begins in the 1920s. Because Lilian is more sheltered than the protagonists of *Monkey* and *Lust,* her loss of innocence is more gradual. Her life is measured by three encounters with Walter Vail that take place every dozen years. He is the kind of cad who first appears in *Lust,* but whose looks and actions are even more deceiving to a 1920s Boston girl who is not exactly a flapper. The story is a realistic account of changed feelings over time. After Walter leaves her the first time, Lilian eventually finds a man, Gilbert Finch, who is Walter's opposite in temperament: deeply sensitive, introverted, and conservative. She convinces herself that *this* is true love, not that heart-flapping sensation she had felt with Walter. She marries Gilbert and has children. But when Gilbert's sensitivity develops into clinical depression, Lilian decides that Walter is her type of man, after all. Walter haunts her Bostonian scene at decade-intervals, always aware that Lilian is still infatuated with him, and always neglectful of the consequence of his actions. In the last scene, Lilian is finally able to name his indifference for what it is: "Caring was beneath him. He could not have done a better job if someone had dared him not to care." Minot dramatizes his condition in an absurd, yet realistic gesture: he doesn't care enough to finish his sentence. He reaches for a drink instead.

Minot's titles, *Monkeys, Lust,* and *Folly,* tell us what she thinks about people seeking or running from love. Yet she is not a pessimist; rather, she accepts that life contains greater mystery than words can say.

—Jill Franks

MIRSKY, Mark (Jay)

Nationality: American. **Born:** Boston, Massachusetts, 11 August 1939. **Education:** Harvard University, Cambridge, Massachusetts, B.A. (magna cum laude) 1961 (Phi Beta Kappa); Stanford University, California (Woodrow Wilson fellow), M.A. 1962. **Military Service:** Served in the United States Air Force Reserve, 1962-68. **Family:** Married Kinger Channah Grytting in 1980; two children. **Career:** Schoolteacher, Boston, 1962; staff writer, *American Heritage,* New York, 1964; lecturer in English, Stanford University, 1966. Lecturer, 1967-70, assistant professor, 1970-74, associate professor, 1975-80, director of the M.A. program, 1978-84, and since 1980 professor of English, City College, New York. Founding member of the Board, Teachers-Writers Collaborative, 1967, and Fiction Collective, 1974, both New York; editor, *Fiction,* New York, 1972-91. **Awards:** Bread Loaf Writers Conference grant; National Endowment for the Arts award, for editing, 1980, and senior fellowship, 1981; Creative Artists Public Service grant, 1982. **Address:** 513 E. 13th St., New York, New York 10009, U.S.A.

Publications

Novels

Thou Worm, Jacob. New York, Macmillan, and London, Collier Macmillan, 1967.
Proceedings of the Rabble. Indianapolis, Bobbs Merrill, 1970.
Blue Hill Avenue. Indianapolis, Bobbs Merrill, 1972.
The Red Adam. Los Angeles, Sun and Moon Press, 1989.

Short Stories

The Secret Table. New York, Fiction Collective, 1975.

Uncollected Short Stories

"Swapping," in *Statements 1,* edited by Jonathan Baumbach. New York, Braziller, 1975.
"The Last Lecture," in *Tri-Quarterly* (Evanston, Illinois), Spring 1976.
"Last Boat to America," in *Massachusetts Review* (Amherst), Summer 1981.
"Child's Alphabet," in *Literary Review* (Madison, New Jersey), Summer 1982.

Other

My Search for the Messiah: Studies and Wanderings in Israel and America. New York, Macmillan, 1977.
The Absent Shakespeare. Rutherford, New Jersey, Fairleigh Dickinson University Press, 1994.

Editor, with David Stern, *Rabbinic Fantasies: Imaginative Narratives from Classic Hebrew Literature.* Philadelphia, Jewish Publication Society of America, 1990.

*   *   *

A catalogue of Mark Mirsky's fictional liabilities in his early work is short and bittersweet: he reworks worn material; he cannot resist dreamworld and fantasyland scenes; he is too delighted with royal-purple prose and "experimentalism"; finally he breaks himself up with broad ethnic humor that often offends. Yet he has such large talent that he skillfully turns each of these faults to advantage even when he does not transcend them.

His first volume of fiction seemed partly to be a parodic mélange of Aleichem, Singer, and Malamud. The inversions of Yiddish, the barrage of exclamation and interrogation points, the spread-finger resignation of the Jewish immigrant, all knotted and clotted the young writer's style and suggested the bar mitzvah school of cheap Catskill entertainment. Thus, the "Introduction" begins:

> "I've got the whole state of Jewish affairs right between my fingers! What? You don't understand? Take a seat. Don't worry, it won't break. A bit cracked but it's had a rest. Watch out! Watch out for that pile of books. Knock one over, my whole place is on your head. Pages, dust, dirty yarmulkes. Eh! Let it fall."

In spite of such false starts, Mirsky knows and loves his "material" and manages to move us to both laughter and pity in this collection of tales about East European immigrants struggling to remain Jews in their new homeland. The familiar figure of the schlemiel hero is brilliantly renewed in the collection's finest story, "The Shammos from Aroostook County." Five years later, Mirsky returned to the struggling Jews of the old towns near Boston with *Blue Hill Avenue.* Although he labeled his tale "vaudeville," he writes here with more control, except for an inappropriate slapstick ending. Four of the characters are superbly drawn: Rabbi Lux, who is "a little too good, too pious for much of Dorchester"; the rabbi's wife, once timid and passionate, now a loving, lunatic protectress; Simcha Tanzenn, a canny, lisping politician who collects on favors rarely delivered; and a demented Jewish mother, who uses the telephone like a mortar and wills her war-lost (and worthless) son back to safety. Mirsky's latest treatment of Jewish traditions, *The Secret Table,* is more serious in tone and, despite some obscurity of form, marks another fictional advance for the author in portraying his fierce bookish forebears. The first novella depicts the search through memory of 30-year-old Maishe for the womb-security now lacking in the decayed streets of Blue Hill Avenue: the companion novella, "Onan's Child," builds upon Genesis to explore, through Jacob, Isaac, Joseph, and Onan, the terrible contradictions of man's nature and Jewish history. In both stories, past and present, subjective and objective worlds, the Jew and the universal man, are blended into a believable, densely-textured reality.

Mirsky's second novel, *Proceedings of the Rabble,* may be his most ambitious to date. Anticipating Robert Altman's film, *Nashville,* in an urban locale, Mirsky uses the evangelical right-wing political crusade of William Starr to portray the murderous impotence moving American democracy toward rage, outrage, and self-destruction. Despite the straining interior-cinema technique employed, Mirsky's apocalyptic ending matches the final upheaval of West's *The Day of the Locust.* Indeed, in all four "novels," Mirsky renews such staple items of contemporary American fiction as violence, sexual sickness, and the Jew as representative sufferer, so that they still serve to tell us about ourselves.

—Frank Campenni

MISTRY, Rohinton

Nationality: Canadian (originally Indian; immigrated to Canada, 1975; naturalized Canadian citizen). **Born:** Bombay, India, 1952. **Education:** University of Bombay, B.S. 1975; University of Toronto, B.A. 1984. **Family:** Married Freny Elavia; two daughters. **Career:** Has worked in a bank in Toronto. Since 1985 full-time writer. **Awards:** *Canadian Fiction* annual contributor's award, 1985; Governor General's award for best fiction, 1991, Smith Books/*Books in Canada* first novels award, and Commonwealth Writers prize, 1992, all for *Such a Long Journey.* **Agent:** Lucina Vardey Agency, 297 Seaton St., Toronto, Ontario M5A 2T6, Canada.

PUBLICATIONS

Novels

Such a Long Journey. Toronto, McClelland, New York, Knopf, and London, Faber, 1991.

Short Stories

Tales from Firozsha Baag. Toronto, Penguin, 1987; London, Faber, 1992; as *Swimming Lessons, and Other Stories from Firozsha Baag,* Boston, Houghton Mifflin, 1989.

*   *   *

Rohinton Mistry's small body of fiction has received high praise, numerous honors, and been favorably, if inevitably, compared to the work of the best known and most respected contemporary Indian writers. Much of his achievement derives from the seamless way in which he has fashioned a decidedly personal style from a variety of literary precursors (Euro-American as well as Indian: Joyce, Cheever, Malamud, and Bellow most notably) perfectly suited to his Indian subject matter. Although his style lacks Rushdie's postmodern brilliance, it deftly avoids Mukherjee's melodramatic excesses and Naipaul's air of critical detachment while successfully adapting Narayan's studied naivete to more modern urban as well as immigrant experience. Mistry's achievement also derives from his willingness to devote himself to those aspects of his subject that he knows best and that most of his Western readers know not at all: the small Parsi community, both in Bombay and in Toronto.

Mistry's is an art of the bittersweet about a world more sad than tragic, where frustrations rather than defeats are the general rule. It is an art gently ironic in its depiction of the everyday lives of mainly middle-class Parsi characters either living in apartment complexes in Bombay or struggling to adapt to immigrant life in Canada. The religious strife that figures prominently in much writing about India serves as backdrop for the more pressing quotidian problems faced by Mistry's characters: straitened finances, the effect of modern ways on cultural traditions (particularly as manifested in generational conflict), ambivalence regarding immigration, and the consequences of sexual repression—all compounded by life's little inconveniences: shoddy goods, petty neighbors, government corruption, and the like. The 11 stories included in *Swimming Lessons* concern the interconnected lives of the residents of Forozsha Baag, with its "surfeit of bank clerks and bookkeepers" leavened by the occasional professor, lawyer, or chartered accountant. In these stories spanning about a decade, people grow old, spouses die, and children emigrate only to exchange the constrictiveness of home life for a new set of anxieties. The title story brings together the two worlds and generations in an especially effective manner, shuttling between two cities, two typefaces, and two sensibilities. In writing a book of stories not unlike *Swimming Lessons,* the son comes to understand the world he has left behind; in reading that book his parents come in turn to understand the son whom they feared was growing not just geographically distant but culturally distant as well.

Such a Long Journey is at once a more narrowly focused fiction (having a single protagonist and center of consciousness) and, in its depiction of life in modern India, more wide-ranging (even if temporally more circumscribed). The novel is set in 1971, during the time of Pakistan's brutal but (as the result of Indian intervention) unsuccessful attempt to suppress the uprising in its eastern wing, the future Bangladesh, and against the backdrop of India's 1965 war with Pakistan over Kashmir and the 1962 defeat by the Chinese army. It deals more specifically with Gustad Noble in his various roles: husband, father, bank clerk, resident in the block of flats called the Khodadad Building. At once petty and heroic (in a decidedly minor, middle-class key), Noble struggles on various fronts: with the threat of war, his youngest daughter's persistent illness, his wife's superstitious beliefs, his son's preferring to pursue a worthless liberal arts degree rather than study engineering, and the decline of the family's fortunes (from the bankruptcy of his grandfather's furniture business to his father's "despoiled" bookstore to Gustad's ignoble position at the bank). There are the surly bus conductors, rising prices resulting from the Refugee Relief Tax, and passersby who relieve themselves on the wall surrounding his apartment block, a wall the municipal government wants to raze in order to widen the road, and thus deprive Gustad of the little space he has to breathe the already fetid air. And there are the deaths of the building's retarded caretaker whom Gustad must himself take care of, a coworker whose antics both amuse and irritate, and the former friend and neighbor, Major Jimmy Bilimoria, whose mysterious letter makes Gustad an accomplice in crime even as it exposes him to corruption in government that leads all the way to the prime minister herself. Caught between resignation and resistance, Gustad is an essentially good man doing the best he can in troubling times and under difficult circumstances. Within his unassuming public self, one finds a depth of quiet heroism that corresponds to those moments of elegiac lyricism that arise from Mistry's artfully artless prose.

—Robert A. Morace

MITCHELL, Joseph (Quincy)

Nationality: American. **Born:** Fairmont, North Carolina, 27 July 1908. **Education:** The University of North Carolina, Chapel Hill, 1925-29. **Family:** Married Therese Dagny Jacobsen in 1931; two daughters. **Career:** Reporter, New York *World,* 1929-30, New York *Herald Tribune,* 1929-31, and New York *World Telegram* 1931-38. Since 1938 staff writer, the *New Yorker* magazine. Commissioner, New York City Landmarks Preservation Commission, 1982-

87. **Awards:** American Academy award, 1965; State of North Carolina gold medal for literature, 1983. **Member:** Vice-President, 1971, and Secretary, 1972-74, National Institute of Arts and Letters. **Address:** c/o The New Yorker, 25 West 43rd Street, New York, New York 10036, U.S.A.

PUBLICATIONS

Short Stories

McSorley's Wonderful Saloon. New York, Duell, 1943; London, Porcupine Press, 1946.
Old Mr. Flood. New York, Duell, 1948.
The Bottom of the Harbor. Boston, Little Brown, 1959; London, Chatto and Windus, 1961.
Joe Gould's Secret. New York, Viking Press, 1965.
Up in the Old Hotel and Other Stories. New York, Pantheon, 1992.

Other

My Ears Are Bent (collection of newspaper articles). New York, Sheridan House, 1938.

*

Critical Studies: "The Grammar of Facts" by Malcolm Cowley, in *New Republic* (New York), 26 July 1943; "The Art of Joseph Mitchell" by Stanley Edgar Hyman, in *New Leader* (New York), 6 December 1965; "Paragon of Reporters: Joseph Mitchell" by Noel Perrin, in *Sewanee Review* (Sewanee, Tennessee), Spring 1983.

*   *   *

Throughout his works Joseph Mitchell places himself in the tradition of the tall tale in America and reveals why he can say in *McSorley's Wonderful Saloon* to the "Gifted Child" that Mark Twain's *Life on the Mississippi* is the one book he likes above all others. He walks in wonder and records what he sees. All of his central figures emerge as larger-than-life people, yet there is almost always a quality of reflection and tone-setting that makes them believable as well as memorable.

In an author's note to *McSorley's Wonderful Saloon* Mitchell concludes with, "There are no little people in this book. They are as big as you are, whoever you are." And he then works with a fine eye, ear, and hand to give profile to such "little" people as John McSorley, president of "an organization of gluttons called the Honorable John McSorley Pickle, Beefsteak, Baseball Nine and Chowder Club"; Mazie P. Gordon, owner of, ticket seller, and bouncer at the Venice theater in the Bowery; King Cockeye Johnny Nikanov, a Russian and King of the Gypsies in New York; Lady Olga Jane Bardwell, the freak show bearded lady, with a 14-and-a-half-inch beard, mustache, and her fourth husband; and various others. His favorite setting is lower Manhattan, and his stories become urban pastorals, strongest when he focuses with care on his people: Mr. Hugh G. Flood, in *Old Mr. Flood,* and Joe Gould, in *Joe Gould's Secret,* exemplify best Mitchell's role as profilist-storyteller.

Mr. Flood, age 93 to 95, wants to live to be 115, is a "seafoodetarian," and can eat bushels of clams and consume large quantities of whiskey. From the many scenes and wild anecdotes of "Old Mr. Flood," "The Black Clams," and "Mr. Flood's Party" comes a man whom the narrator obviously loves, one who, as Mr. Mitchell says, is not one man but "several old men, who work or hang out in Fulton Fish Market." He's too big to exist, but he is nonetheless there, and the *I* of the story penetrates his moods—from extreme loneliness to convivial joy—with touching sensitivity. One feels that Mr. Flood will indeed live to age 115.

Joe Gould, on the other hand, is, as the author says in a note, "a lost soul." As Professor Sea Gull in *McSorley's Wonderful Saloon,* he is a tall-tale character too—a blithe and emaciated little man who has been a notable in the cafeterias, diners, barrooms, and dumps of Greenwich Village for a quarter of a century. A Harvard alumnus, class of 1911, he sometimes brags that he is the last of the bohemians. Of chief interest to Mitchell is Gould's *An Oral History of Our Time*—a document 11 times as long as the Bible, over 9,000,000 words in longhand and still unfinished. As a solitary nocturnal wanderer he talks much of his *Oral History* and of his ability, among other things, to translate Longfellow's "Hiawatha" into sea gull. Here he shouts to a Village waitress: "I'm Joe Gould, the poet; I'm Joe Gould, the historian; I'm Joe Gould, the wild Chippewa Indian dancer; and I'm Joe Gould, the greatest authority in the world on the language of the sea gull."

Joe Gould's secret, however, discovered by Mitchell years later, is that there is no *Oral History.* Gould has not only duped Mitchell and the people but has duped himself. He can recite it but cannot put it down. Mitchell keeps the secret until he writes it down in his story, stepping out of, as he says, "the role I had stepped into the afternoon I discovered that the *Oral History* did not exist."

My Ears Are Bent and *The Bottom of the Harbor* show Mitchell's consistency throughout his career in reporting on but also building on the people and places of his world, from Sloppy Louie's, the old Fulton Ferry Hotel, and the "Baymen" to the rats on the waterfront. When he writes of his home country in rural North Carolina he uses his same profilist's eye and feeling for his "people" to bring to life such characters as Mrs. Copenhagen Calhoun in "I Blame It All on Mama," Uncle Dockery in "Uncle Dockery and the Independent Bull" and Mr. Catfish Giddy in "The Downfall of Fascism in Black Ankle County." Mitchell is the country boy who went to the city to find his way—and found it in the *New Yorker* where he perfected the urban tall-tale pastoral.

—Frank T. Phipps

MITCHELL, (Charles) Julian (Humphrey)

Nationality: British. **Born:** Epping, Essex, 1 May 1935. **Education:** Winchester College, Hampshire, 1948-53; Wadham College, Oxford, B.A. 1958; St. Antony's College, Oxford, M.A. 1962. **Military Service:** Served in the Royal Naval Volunteer Reserve, 1953-55: Midshipman. **Career:** Member, Arts Council Literature Panel, 1966-69; formerly, Governor, Chelsea School of Art, London; chair, Welsh Arts Council Drama Committee, 1988-92. Lives in Gwent, Wales. **Awards:** Harkness fellowship, 1959; Rhys Memorial prize, 1965; Maugham award, 1966; International Critics prize, for television play, 1977; Christopher award, for television play, 1977 (U.S.A.); Florio prize, for translation, 1980; Society of West End Theatre award, 1982. **Agent:** Peters Fraser and Dunlop Group, 503-

504 The Chambers, Chelsea Harbour, Lots Road, London SW10 0XF, England.

Publications

Novels

Imaginary Toys. London, Hutchinson, 1961.
A Disturbing Influence. London, Hutchinson, 1962.
As Far as You Can Go. London, Constable, 1963.
The White Father. London, Constable, 1964; New York, Farrar Straus, 1965.
A Circle of Friends. London, Constable, 1966; New York, McGraw Hill, 1967.
The Undiscovered Country. London, Constable, 1968; New York, Grove Press, 1970.

Short Stories

Introduction, with others. London, Faber, 1960.

Plays

A Heritage and Its History, adaptation of the novel by Ivy Compton-Burnett (produced London, 1965). London, Evans, 1966.
A Family and a Fortune, adaptation of the novel by Ivy Compton-Burnett (produced Guildford, Surrey, 1966; Seattle, 1974; London, 1975). London, French, 1976.
Shadow in the Sun (televised 1971). Published in *Elizabeth R,* edited by J.C. Trewin, London, Elek, 1972.
Half-Life (produced London, 1977; New York, 1981). London, Heinemann, 1977.
Henry IV, adaptation of the play by Pirandello. London, Eyre Methuen, 1979.
The Enemy Within (produced Leatherhead, Surrey, 1980).
Another Country (produced London, 1981; New Haven, Connecticut, 1983). Ambergate, Derbyshire, Amber Lane Press, 1982; New York, Limelight, 1984.
Francis (produced London, 1983). Oxford, Amber Lane Press, 1984.
After Aida; or, Verdi's Messiah (produced London, 1986). Oxford, Amber Lane Press, 1986.
Adelina Patti, Queen of Song (produced Swansea, 1987).
The Evils of Tobacco, adaptation of a work by Chekhov, translated by Ronald Hingley (produced London, 1987).
August, adaptation of Chekhov's *Uncle Vanya* (produced Mold, 1994). Oxford, Amber Lane Press, 1993.
Falling Over England (produced London, 1994). Oxford, Amber Lane Press, 1994.

Screenplays: *Arabesque,* with Stanley Price and Pierre Marton, 1966; *Another Country,* 1984; *Vincent and Theo,* 1990.

Radio Documentary: *Life and Deaths of Dr. John Donne,* 1972.

Television Plays: *Persuasion,* from the novel by Jane Austen, 1971; *Shadow in the Sun,* 1971; *The Man Who Never Was,* 1972; *A Perfect Day,* 1972; *Fly in the Ointment,* 1972; *A Question of Degree,* 1972; *The Alien Corn,* from a story by W. Somerset Maugham, 1972; *Rust,* 1973; *Jennie,* 1974; *Abide with Me,* from the book *A Child in the Forest,* by Winifred Foley, 1976; *Staying On,* from the novel by Paul Scott, 1980; *The Good Solider,* from the novel by Ford Madox Ford, 1981; *The Weather in the Streets,* from the novel by Rosamond Lehmann, 1984; episodes for *Inspector Morse* series, 1986-93; *All the Waters of Wye* (documentary), 1990; *Survival of the Fittest,* 1990.

Other

Truth and Fiction (lecture). London, Covent Garden Press, 1972.
Jennie, Lady Randolph Churchill: A Portrait with Letters, with Peregrine Churchill. London, Collins, 1974; New York, St. Martin's Press, 1975.

Editor, with others, *Light Blue, Dark Blue: An Anthology of Recent Writing from Oxford and Cambridge Universities.* London, Macdonald, 1960.

*

Film Adaptations: *August,* 1995.

*   *   *

Julian Mitchell's books reveal a remarkably talented writer, whose work is consistently fluent, witty and ingenious. But they do leave a doubt in the mind whether his literary gifts are, in the last analysis, those of a natural novelist. He began his career precociously early, and published four novels before he was 30. The first of them, *Imaginary Toys,* is, like many other first novels, a partly sentimental, partly satirical recreation of university life. It covers a small group of young people during a few days in one summer term at Oxford; the story is of the slightest, but Mitchell uses it as the vehicle for some serious disquisitions on sexual and social problems. The novel is at its most engaging, though, in its fanciful, essay-like speculations, which make it a little reminiscent of the early Aldous Huxley. Mitchell is like Huxley, too, in his acute sense of period; *Imaginary Toys* effectively catches the feel of the late 1950s, though this responsiveness to contemporary atmosphere inevitably made the book seem dated after a few years. His next novel, *A Disturbing Influence,* was not a particularly exciting development, though it was a smoothly written narrative. It described the impact on a complacent, even sleepy Berkshire village of a strange, destructive, amoral young man, the "disturbing influence" of the title. Such types evidently have a particular fascination for Mitchell, for they tend to recur in his fiction. This book was followed by a more substantial and interesting work, *As Far as You Can Go,* in which Mitchell drew on some of his own recent experience to write the kind of novel that was to become increasingly common in England in the 1960s—the account of a peripatetic Englishman's adventures in America. Harold Barlow, the central character, is a typical Mitchell hero—intelligent, amiable, rather inept—and he conveys a tourist's eye view of life in the hipster subculture of California.

The White Father, which won Mitchell the Somerset Maugham award, was a more determinedly ambitious novel than its predecessors. The narrative is divided between London and a remote African territory, and Mitchell shows much of the action through the eyes of Hugh Shrieve, a district officer in Africa who has come to London to plead for his tribe at a conference to arrange independence for the territory. Shrieve has been out of England for years,

and he is unprepared for what he finds when he arrives: the frenetic beginnings of the "Swinging London" cult. Mitchell looks satirically though tolerantly at the world of pop music, and there is a powerful imaginative touch in his portrayal of the megalomaniac Mr. Brachs, head of a vast commercial empire catering to the youth cult, who is going steadily mad in his inaccessible penthouse on top of the London skyscraper that houses all his many enterprises. *The White Father* is one of Mitchell's best novels, which makes some sharp observations about life in a high-consumption society, as well as telling an entertaining story. The novelist and the essayist are more closely fused than is usual in his fiction. Two years later Mitchell published an extremely thin novel, *A Circle of Friends,* which moves between New York and the English Home Counties, showing how one of his characteristically weak young men gets unhappily entangled with a wealthy Anglo-American family, culminating in a wholly undeserved position as co-respondent in a divorce action.

All these novels present, at varying levels of literary achievement, some recurring characteristics: a tendency to draw fairly directly on personal experience and to use the novel as a vehicle for airing ideas, a taste for likable but weak central characters, and a generally relaxed and good-humored tone. In *The Undiscovered Country,* Mitchell's most striking fiction, all these qualities are present in a new combination. Unlike his previous novels, it is a deliberately experimental work, which plays with the conventions of fiction writing, and the relations between art and reality, in the manner of Nabokov or Borges. The first part is, on the face of it, undisguised autobiography, where Mitchell writes in his own person about his friendship with an enigmatically attractive young man, Charles Humphries, who dies at an early age. He leaves behind the fragmentary manuscript of a novel called "The New Satyricon," which Mitchell edits with introduction and commentary, and presents as the second part of *The Undiscovered Country.* Undoubtedly "Humphries" is an alter ego for "Mitchell" (whose full Christian names are Charles Julian Humphrey), though the relation between them remains teasing. *The Undiscovered Country* is a generally entertaining novel, and the second part is full of pleasant literary jokes, where Mitchell engages to the full his essayistic tendencies. It also marks his dissatisfaction with his more conventional earlier novels. Indeed, at the end of part one, before he introduces "The New Satyricon," Mitchell observes, "I think it unlikely that I shall write another book of my own for a long time, with the fact of this one before me. Charles said that all art comes from an inner need. He said that I began to write because I wanted to be a writer, and that was the wrong kind of need." Mitchell continued to write, but as a dramatist rather than a novelist. He has not published a novel since *The Undiscovered Country,* which is a pity, given the wit and liveliness of his fiction at its best. But the course of his later career suggests that for Mitchell novel-writing was a temporary early phase, where he learned how to be a writer but was never entirely at home.

—Bernard Bergonzi

MITCHELL, W(illiam) O(rmond)

Nationality: Canadian. **Born:** Weyburn, Saskatchewan, 13 March 1914. **Education:** St. Petersburg High School, Florida; University of Manitoba, Winnipeg (gold medal for philosophy, 1934), 1932-34; University of Alberta, Edmonton, 1940-42, B.A. 1942. **Family:** Married Merna Lynne Hirtle in 1942; two sons and one daughter. **Career:** Teacher and journalist in Seattle, 1934-36; teacher and high school principal, Castor and New Dayton, Alberta, 1942-44; freelance writer in High River, Alberta, 1945-68; fiction editor, *Maclean's,* Toronto, 1948-51; Director of Creative Writing, Banff School of Fine Arts, Alberta, summers 1975-86. Writer-in-residence, University of Calgary, Alberta, 1968-71, University of Alberta, 1971-73, Massey College, University of Toronto, 1973-74, York University, Downsview, Ontario, 1976-78, and University of Windsor, Ontario, 1979-87. Lives in Calgary. **Awards:** *Maclean's* award, 1953; University of Western Ontario President's medal, 1953; CCAA award, for drama, 1956; Leacock medal, 1962; Drainie award, 1968; Actra award, for drama, 1975; Chalmers award, for drama, 1976; Banff School of Fine Arts award, 1980; Canadian Authors Association award, for drama, 1983. D.Litt.: University of Ottawa, 1972; LL.D.: University of Saskatchewan, Saskatoon, 1972. Officer, Order of Canada, 1973; Honorary Member of the Queen's Privy Council, 1993. **Address:** c/o McClelland and Stewart Inc., 481 University Avenue, Suite 900, Toronto, Ontario M5G 2E9, Canada.

PUBLICATIONS

Novels

Who Has Seen the Wind. Boston, Little Brown, 1947; Edinburgh, Canongate, 1980.
The Kite. Toronto, Macmillan, 1962.
The Vanishing Point. Toronto, Macmillan, 1973.
How I Spent My Summer Holidays. Toronto, Macmillan, 1981.
Since Daisy Creek. Toronto, Macmillan, 1984; New York, Beaufort, 1985.
Ladybug Ladybug. Toronto, McClelland and Stewart, 1988.
Roses Are Difficult Here. Toronto, McClelland and Stewart, 1990.
For Art's Sake. Toronto, McClelland and Stewart, 1992.
The Black Bonspiel of Wullie MacCrimmon. Toronto, McClelland and Stewart, 1993.

Short Stories

Jake and the Kid. Toronto, Macmillan, 1961.
According to Jake and the Kid: A Collection of New Stories. Toronto, McClelland and Stewart, 1989.

Uncollected Short Stories

"But as Yesterday," in *Queen's Quarterly* (Kingston, Ontario), Summer 1942.
"Elbow Room," in *Maclean's* (Toronto), 15 September 1942.
"Gettin' Born," in *Maclean's* (Toronto), 1 May 1943.
"Something's Gotta Go," in *Maclean's* (Toronto), 1 July 1945.
"Shoparoon for Maggie," in *Maclean's* (Toronto), 15 May 1948.
"Air-Nest and the Child Harold," in *Maclean's* (Toronto), 1 August 1948.
"Air-Nest and La Belle Dame," in *Maclean's* (Toronto), 1 November 1948.
"Crocus at Coronation," in *Maclean's* (Toronto), 1 June 1953.
"The Alien" (serial), in *Maclean's* (Toronto), 15 September 1953-15 January 1954.

"Princess and the Wild Ones," in *Cavalcade of the North,* edited by George F. Nelson. New York, Doubleday, 1958.
"How Crocus Got Its Seaway," in *Maclean's* (Toronto), 20 June 1959.
"Patterns," in *Ten for Wednesday Night,* edited by Robert Weaver. Toronto, McClelland and Stewart, 1961.
"Melvin Arbuckle's First Course in Shock Therapy," in *Singing under Ice,* edited by Grace Merserau. Toronto, Macmillan, 1974.
"A Tree of Feathers," in *Globe and Mail* (Toronto), 25 December 1975.

Plays

The Devil's Instrument (broadcast 1949; produced Ottawa, 1972). Toronto, Simon and Pierre, 1973.
Royalty Is Royalty (produced Saskatoon, Saskatchewan, 1959).
The Black Bonspiel of Wullie MacCrimmon, adaptation of his own story (broadcast 1951; produced Regina, Saskatchewan, 1976). Calgary, Alberta, Frontiers Unlimited, 1965.
Ladybug, Ladybug (radio play), in *Edge 5* (Edmonton, Alberta), Fall 1966.
Centennial Play, with others (produced Lindsay, Ontario, 1967). Ottawa, Centennial Commission, 1967.
Wild Rose (produced Calgary, Alberta, 1967).
The White Christmas of Archie Nicotine (televised 1971). Published in *Prairie Performance,* edited by Diane Bessai, Edmonton, Alberta, NeWest Press, 1980.
Back to Beulah (broadcast 1974; produced Vancouver, 1976). Included in *The Dramatic W.O. Mitchell,* 1984.
The Day Jake Made 'er Rain (produced Winnipeg, 1979).
The Kite, adaptation of his own novel (produced Calgary, Alberta, 1981). Included in *The Dramatic W.O. Mitchell,* 1984.
For Those in Peril on the Sea (produced Calgary, Alberta, 1982). Included in *The Dramatic W.O. Mitchell,* 1984.
The Dramatic W.O. Mitchell (includes *The Devil's Instrument, The Black Bonspiel of Wullie MacCrimmon, The Kite, For Those in Peril on the Sea, Back to Beulah*). Toronto, Macmillan, 1984.

Screenplays (documentaries): *Face of Saskatchewan,* 1955; *Fires of Envy,* 1957; *Political Dynamite,* 1958; *Alien Thunder,* 1976.

Radio Plays: *The Devil's Instrument,* 1949; *Jake and the Kid* series, 1950-56; *The Black Bonspiel of Wullie MacCrimmon,* 1951; *Foothill Fables* series, 1963-64; *Ladybug, Ladybug; Back to Beulah,* 1974; and other plays for CBC since 1947.

Television Plays: *The Devil's Instrument,* 1956; *The White Christmas of Archie Nicotine,* 1971; and other plays for CBC.

*

Bibliography: by Sheila Latham, in *The Annotated Bibliography of Canada's Major Authors 3* edited by Robert Lecker and Jack David, Downsview, Ontario, ECW Press, 1981.

Manuscript Collection: University of Calgary Library, Alberta.

*　　*　　*

W.O. Mitchell, generally considered a "regional humorist," perhaps himself encourages such a reputation. In the guise of the homespun philosopher he finds a traditional folk identity with which to meet contemporary life and a literary format which matches his penchant for the humor of understatement, wise saws, tall tales, and home truths. But this is not to say that he spurns sophistication, progress, or the 20th century. His stories constantly ask blunt questions about reality and values, probing "sophistication" to see if it isn't hypocrisy by a different name, and reducing contemporary problems to domestic proportions in order to reveal the lineage of human foible which the present has inherited.

Most clearly illustrative of such a technique are the wry though somewhat dated stories of Jake and the Kid, which were written first as dramas and were performed on the Canadian Broadcasting Corporation as a continuing radio series in the 1940s. Set in the ranching country of the Alberta foothills which Mitchell knows well, they detail the laconic education in the vagaries of life which Jake, a hired hand, gives to the young son of his employers—and incidentally, always ironically, to himself. They seldom directly invoke contentious social issues—indeed, when Mitchell does contend head-on with such matters as race relations, as in his serialized novel *The Alien,* the result is more melodramatic than provocative. In rewritten form, *The Alien* was published as *The Vanishing Point* in 1973, but the radical structural changes do not alter its central weakness. Despite Mitchell's wit, his capacity for creating lively scenes and clever caricatures, his central characters here do not develop. Accordingly, their reflections on life seem to lack substance. More Jake stories were collected as *According to Jake and the Kid* in 1989.

One of Mitchell's most successful uses of anecdote occurs in his novel *The Kite,* when the centenarian central character, Daddy Sherry, irrepressibly individual (particularly when officialdom dictates prudence to him), accepts a flooding river as an invitation to a South Seas cruise and sails his uprooted house matter-of-factly away, at dark of night, across the American border. The wit is paramount, but incidentally Mitchell manages bemused swipes at customs regulations and bureaucratic nervousness, and builds up the engagingly exaggerated personalities of his cast. The book as a whole celebrates the virtue of living life fully, of engaging oneself in the *process* of living, of which the cruise incident is merely a genial sign.

The developing spiritual affinity between Daddy and a young boy varies the Jake-Kid relationship, and adds a Wordsworthian dimension to Mitchell's world that is more readily seen in his best book, *Who Has Seen the Wind.* In it, the young Brian O'Connal is broken out of his innocent childhood oneness with the world (into the imperfect loves and prejudices of ordinary humanity) by his increasingly adaptive encounters with death and disorder. The "sleep and forgetting" that marks his growth are accompanied by a developing social conscience, however, revealed ultimately in his "mature" child's commitment to agricultural science, and counterpointed by the novel's subplots. Their exploration of institutional hypocrisy, educational rigidity, race prejudice, and religious intemperance tends sometimes towards the maudlin, but in the characters of Saint Sammy and the Young Ben, "naturals" whose oneness with the prairie and the wind serves as a kind of true spiritual example to Brian, Mitchell has created unforgettable animated forces. With Brian's renegade Uncle Sean, they together fill the "Jake" role to Brian's "kid" and widen rather than reduce the intensity of the effect Jake was meant to exert. For a generation of radio listeners Jake was a shrewd observer of daily life; Brian's relationship with the world of the Young Ben appeals to rather more, for the imaginative experience it represents transcends place and time. Tracing

the loss of a child's self and the gain of a man's, the book probes the many dimensions of reality—raising Berkeleyan dilemmas, countering them with Wordsworthian intuitions—and covering all with the gentle humor of a man in love with life whose acute eyes remind him constantly of the failings of mankind as well as of its humane possibilities.

Mitchell's subsequent novels—*How I Spent My Summer Holidays, Since Daisy Creek, Ladybug Ladybug,* and *Roses Are Difficult Here*—probe the dark counterpoint to the young Brian's summer hopes. The world of childhood, in the first of these, ends abruptly when the central character's pretend-adventure runs into real violence instead, when the small town's geniality is discovered to be riddled with bitterness and vice. *Ladybug Ladybug,* with an artificial subplot involving Mark Twain, is essentially a violent thriller. *Since Daisy Creek* reaches for greater equanimity, but more by indirection than by grasp: the aging narrator, recovering from a grizzly attack, reflects sardonically on staid expectations and professorial criticism. The moments of tenderness are those when he admits to his own infirmities, and accepts his opportunities for love.

—W.H. New

MITCHISON, Naomi

Nationality: British. **Born:** Naomi Margaret Haldane, Edinburgh, 1 November 1897. **Education:** Lynam's School, Oxford; St. Anne's College, Oxford. **Career:** served as a volunteer nurse, 1915. **Family:** Daughter of the scientist John Scott Haldane; sister of the writer J.B.S. Haldane; married G.R. Mitchison (who became Lord Mitchison, 1964) in 1916 (died 1970); three sons and two daughters. **Career:** Labour candidate for Parliament, Scottish Universities constituency, 1935; member, Argyll County Council, 1945-66; member, Highland Panel, 1947-64, and Highlands and Islands Development Council, 1966-76. Tribal adviser, and Mmarona (Mother), to the Bakgatla of Botswana, 1963-89. **Awards:** D. Univ.: University of Stirling, Scotland, 1976; University of Dundee, Scotland, 1985; D.Litt.: University of Strathclyde, Glasgow, 1983. Honorary Fellow, St. Anne's College, 1980, and Wolfson College, 1983, both Oxford. Officer, French Academy, 1924. C.B.E. (Commander, Order of the British Empire), 1985. **Address:** Carradale House, Carradale, Campbeltown, Scotland.

PUBLICATIONS

Novels

The Conquered. London, Cape, and New York, Harcourt Brace, 1923.
Cloud Cuckoo Land. London, Cape, 1925; New York, Harcourt Brace, 1926.
The Corn King and the Spring Queen. London, Cape, and New York, Harcourt Brace, 1931; as *The Barbarian,* New York, Cameron, 1961.
The Powers of Light. London, Cape, and New York, Peter Smith, 1932.
Beyond This Limit. London, Cape, 1935.
We Have Been Warned. London, Constable, 1935; New York, Vanguard Press, 1948.

The Blood of the Martyrs. London, Constable, 1939; New York, McGraw Hill, 1948.
The Bull Calves. London, Cape, 1947.
Lobsters on the Agenda. London, Gollancz, 1952.
Travel Light. London, Faber, 1952; New York, Penguin, 1987.
To the Chapel Perilous. London, Allen and Unwin, 1955.
Behold Your King. London, Muller, 1957.
Memoirs of a Spacewoman. London, Gollancz, 1962.
When We Become Men. London, Collins, 1965.
Cleopatra's People. London, Heinemann, 1972.
Solution Three. London, Dobson, and New York, Warner, 1975.
Not by Bread Alone. London, Boyars, 1983.
The Oath Takers. Nairn, Balnain, 1991.
Sea-Green Ribbons. Nairn, Balnain, 1991.

Short Stories

When the Bough Breaks and Other Stories. London, Cape, and New York, Harcourt Brace, 1924.
Black Sparta: Greek Stories. London, Cape, and New York, Harcourt Brace, 1928.
Barbarian Stories. London, Cape, and New York, Harcourt Brace, 1929.
The Delicate Fire: Short Stories and Poems. London, Cape, and New York, Harcourt Brace, 1933.
The Fourth Pig: Stories and Verses. London, Constable, 1936.
Five Men and a Swan: Short Stories and Poems. London, Allen and Unwin, 1958.
Images of Africa. Edinburgh, Canongate, 1980.
What Do You Think Yourself? Scottish Short Stories. Edinburgh, Harris, 1982.
Beyond This Limit: Selected Shorter Fiction of Naomi Mitchison, edited by Isobel Murray. Edinburgh, Scottish Academic Press, 1986.
Early in Orcadia. Glasgow, Drew, 1987.
A Girl Must Live. Glasgow, Drew, 1990.

Plays

Nix-Nought-Nothing: Four Plays for Children (includes *My Ain Sel', Hobyah! Hobyah!, Elfen Hill*). London, Cape, 1928; New York, Harcourt Brace, 1929.
Kate Crackernuts: A Fairy Play. Oxford, Alden Press, 1931.
The Price of Freedom, with L.E. Gielgud (produced Cheltenham, 1949). London, Cape, 1931.
Full Fathom Five, with L.E. Gielgud (produced London, 1932).
An End and a Beginning and Other Plays (includes *The City and the Citizens, For This Man Is a Roman, In the Time of Constantine, Wild Men Invade the Roman Empire, Charlemagne and His Court, The Thing That Is Plain, Cortez in Mexico, Akbar, But Still It Moves, The New Calendar, American Britons*). London, Constable, 1937; as *Historical Plays for Schools,* 2 vols., 1939.
As It Was in the Beginning, with L.E. Gielgud. London, Cape, 1939.
The Corn King, music by Brian Easdale, adaptation of the novel by Mitchison (produced Glasgow, 1951). London, French, 1951.
Spindrift, with Denis Macintosh (produced Glasgow, 1951). London, French, 1951.

Poetry

The Laburnum Branch. London, Cape, 1926.
The Alban Goes Out. Harrow, Middlesex, Raven Press, 1939.

The Cleansing of the Knife and Other Poems. Edinburgh, Canongate, 1978.

Other (for children)

The Hostages and Other Stories for Boys and Girls. London, Cape, 1930; New York, Harcourt Brace, 1931.
Boys and Girls and Gods. London, Watts, 1931.
The Big House. London, Faber, 1950.
Graeme and the Dragon. London, Faber, 1954.
The Swan's Road. London, Naldrett Press, 1954.
The Land the Ravens Found. London, Collins, 1955.
Little Boxes. London, Faber, 1956.
The Far Harbour. London, Collins, 1957.
Judy and Lakshmi. London, Collins, 1959.
The Rib of the Green Umbrella. London, Collins, 1960.
The Young Alexander the Great. London, Parrish, 1960; New York, Roy, 1961.
Karensgaard: The Story of a Danish Farm. London, Collins, 1961.
The Young Alfred the Great. London, Parrish, 1962; New York, Roy, 1963.
The Fairy Who Couldn't Tell a Lie. London, Collins, 1963.
Alexander the Great. London, Longman, 1964.
Henny and Crispies. Wellington, New Zealand, Department of Education, 1964.
Ketse and the Chief. London, Nelson, 1965; New York, Nelson, 1967.
A Mochudi Family. Wellington, New Zealand, Department of Education, 1965.
Friends and Enemies. London, Collins, 1966; New York, Day, 1968.
The Big Surprise. London, Kaye and Ward, 1967.
Highland Holiday. Wellington, New Zealand, Department of Education, 1967.
African Heroes. London, Bodley Head, 1968; New York, Farrar Straus, 1969.
Don't Look Back. London, Kaye and Ward, 1969.
The Family at Ditlabeng. London, Collins, 1969; New York, Farrar Straus, 1970.
Sun and Moon. London, Bodley Head, 1970; Nashville, Nelson, 1973.
Sunrise Tomorrow. London, Collins, and New York, Farrar Straus, 1973.
The Danish Teapot. London, Kaye and Ward, 1973.
Snake! London, Collins, 1976.
The Little Sister, with works by Ian Kirby and Keetla Masogo. Cape Town, Oxford University Press, 1976.
The Wild Dogs, with works by Megan Biesele. Cape Town, Oxford University Press, 1977.
The Brave Nurse and Other Stories. Cape Town, Oxford University Press, 1977.
The Two Magicians, with Dick Mitchison. London, Dobson, 1978.
The Vegetable War. London, Hamish Hamilton, 1980.

Other

Anna Comnena. London, Howe, 1928.
Comments on Birth Control. London, Faber, 1930.
The Home and a Changing Civilisation. London, Lane, 1934.
Vienna Diary. London, Gollancz, and New York, Smith and Haas, 1934.

Socrates, with Richard Crossman. London, Hogarth Press, 1937; Harrisburg, Pennsylvania, Stackpole, 1938.

The Moral Basis of Politics. London, Constable, 1938; Port Washington, New York, Kennikat Press, 1971.

The Kingdom of Heaven. London, Heinemann, 1939.

Men and Herring: A Documentary, with Denis Macintosh. Edinburgh, Serif, 1949.

Other People's Worlds (travel). London, Secker and Warburg, 1958.

A Fishing Village on the Clyde, with G.W.L. Paterson. London, Oxford University Press, 1960.

Presenting Other People's Children. London, Hamlyn, 1961.

Return to the Fairy Hill (autobiography and sociology). London, Heinemann, and New York, Day, 1966.

The Africans: A History. London, Blond, 1970.

Small Talk: Memories of an Edwardian Childhood. London, Bodley Head, 1973.

A Life for Africa: The Story of Bram Fischer. London, Merlin Press, and Boston, Carrier Pigeon, 1973.

Oil for the Highlands? London, Fabian Society, 1974.

All Change Here: Girlhood and Marriage (autobiography). London, Bodley Head, 1975.

Sittlichkeit (lecture). London, Birkbeck College, 1975.

You May Well Ask: A Memoir 1920-1940. London, Gollancz, 1979.

Mucking Around: Five Continents over Fifty Years. London, Gollancz, 1981.

Margaret Cole 1893-1980. London, Fabian Society, 1982.

Among You, Taking Notes: The Wartime Diary of Naomi Mitchison 1939-1945, edited by Dorothy Sheridan. London, Gollancz, 1985.

Naomi Mitchison (autobiographical sketch). Edinburgh, Saltire Society, 1986.

As It Was. Glasgow, Drew, 1988.

Editor, *An Outline for Boys and Girls and Their Parents.* London, Gollancz, 1932.

Editor, with Robert Britton and George Kilgour, *Re-Educating Scotland.* Glasgow, Scoop, 1944.

Editor, *What the Human Race Is Up To.* London, Gollancz, 1962.

*

Manuscript Collections: National Library of Scotland, Edinburgh; University of Texas, Austin.

Critical Study: *Naomi Mitchison: A Century of Experiment in Life and Letters* by Jill Benton, London, Pandora Press, 1990.

Naomi Mitchison comments:

I write a number of different kinds of books, as you see. When I began writing this was possible because at that time books were written because the authors had something they wanted to say; today books are a commodity like other commodities. What is important is whether publishers think they can sell them. Most publishers have definite selling plans and if a given book does not fit into this, the author has little chance of getting it published. Today, if one wants to write about something special, one has to try and persuade a publisher that this was something he had already thought of. I like writing children's books because one has to write absolutely straight, without playing any of the stylistic or literary tricks which will take in an adult audience. I like digging out the facts of history and seeing what they will add up to. I like thinking what people do in strange situations, for instance in the past, in Africa

or India, or in imaginary but possible situations in science fiction. This may enable one—or other people—to make some contribution towards a happier world.

*   *   *

In Naomi Mitchison's historical novels and short stories, with which she established her earliest reputation, an essential theme is conflict of loyalties, whether in Gaul at the time of Caesar's conquest, as in her first novel, *The Conquered,* or among the people of a small Aegean island who are dragged willy-nilly, on one side or another, into the bitter fratricidal battle between Athens and Sparta in the 4th century B.C.—the subject of her ironically entitled *Cloud Cuckoo Land.* Her major work in this genre is *The Corn King and the Spring Queen,* a study in the realtionships between the people of three different societies—an agricultural community in the Crimea where the old fertility religion still remains strong enough to provide the folk with purposive unity; a decadent Greece where religious belief has broken down and the struggle to create a just society is conducted—and fails—on a secular basis; and an imperial Egypt where despotism has led to political apathy, disillusion, cynical hedonism, and a frantic search for religious consolation. At once a presentation of personal breakdown and reintegration, a picture of the stresses between idealism and expediency involved in the rise and fall of a revolutionary movement, and an exploration of the relationship between religious conviction and communal solidarity, between scepticism and the loosening of social cohesion, this novel is unsurpassed in 20th-century British historical fiction for range and variety of scene and characterisation, for political awareness, and for religious depth.

On Scottish subjects, Mitchison is at her best in *The Big House,* a children's fairytale which is also a tragicomedy expressing a profound understanding of the intermingled light and darkness of the human situation, a book where the natural magic of childhood, the terrible charm of the supernatural, the dark power of history, and a vision of life as at once dreadful and sublime, are all woven together. From the fairytale she has gone on to a science-fiction fantasy with *Memoirs of a Spacewoman,* where she shows—in three related chapters about a world inhabited by butterflies and their larvae—a deep imaginative comprehension of extraterrestrial modes of existence, and a compassionate reverence for life, even at its most remote and mysterious, which lift her work out of the category of the merely inventive and fanciful to give it something of the universality of legend. A poet as well as a prose writer, Mitchison has written a futuristic story about the exploration of space which is itself a myth, a concentrated symbolical expression of generations of experience.

Alongside fantasy, Mitchison has also written "documentary" novels on contemporary social experience, some with a Scottish location and some set in Africa, where she has worked in Botswana. In these, characterisation tends to be subordinated to background detail. Perhaps the finest of her contemporary studies is the title story of her collection *Five Men and a Swan,* a modern Scottish folktale which combines tenderness, brutality, humour, beauty, and sheer magic in a parable on the theme of human greed and stupidity. While the detail of this story is exactly in period, the writing has a quality of timelessness before which criticism must be silent.

—Alexander Scott

MO, Timothy

Nationality: British. **Born:** Hong Kong in 1950; brought to London in 1960. **Education:** Mill Hill School, London; St. John's College, Oxford. **Career:** Journalist, *Times Educational Supplement, New Statesman,* and *Boxing News,* all London. **Awards:** Geoffrey Faber Memorial prize, 1978; Hawthornden prize, 1982. **Address:** c/o Chatto and Windus, 20 Vauxhall Bridge Road, London SW1V 2SA, England.

PUBLICATIONS

Novels

The Monkey King. London, Deutsch, 1980; New York, Doubleday, 1980.
Sour Sweet. London, Deutsch, 1982; New York, Vintage, 1985.
An Insular Possession. New York, Chatto and Windus, 1986; New York, Random House, 1987.
The Redundancy of Courage. London, Chatto and Windus, 1991.

* * *

Mr. Nolasco, deceased father of the protagonist of *The Monkey King,* once told his son "Understand the English and you will understand the Chinese." The comment might serve as an ironic guide and humorous caveat for readers new to the works of Timothy Mo, an Anglo-Chinese novelist of great ingenuity and ambition. He is an Amis or Waugh with a global sensibility, that is to say a deeper than average disrespect for the human race and a greater than average capacity to be amused by the desperate state of the modern world. Mo's world is populated by miscreants, buffoons, sloths, dipsomaniacs, petty adventurers, opium addicts, would-be idealists enmeshed in the Opium Wars and most recently, in guerrilla warfare. His characters tend to be motivated by greed first, fear second, and altruism only after exhausting a long list of vicious motives. Their stories tend to be driven forward by forces of which they remain largely ignorant, and over which they have almost no control. They strive, but their endeavors are usually irrelevant, or swept aside by the accidental effects of the secret mechanisms of fate.

One might, like Confucius, take a disciplined ethical stance in the face of a relentless cosmos; Mo is also saying that the fiercer the machinery of circumstance the better, and the grimmer the determinism, the funnier the fate. Small wonder that Mo's first novel won the Geoffrey Faber Memorial prize in 1979, that his second got nominations for Booker and Whitbread awards and took the Hawthornden, and that his third novel was blurbed in its North American editions as "perhaps the most highly praised work of fiction published in England in 1986." In short, there is something about Mo's attitude that is familiar and comfortably bleak. More positively, Mo is no practitioner of kitchen realism, for he eschews its trivia in preference for large questions with sociopolitical significance. Yet as a satirist (out of Aristophanes, by Wu Chieng-en) Mo is a quintessential writer of two Empires, the Celestial and the British, the one defeated, the second now gone beyond decadence to dust, and he can use his art to investigate the nature of history, culture, and selfhood with the reassurance that in the long run each will be good at least for laughter.

There are signs that Mo may be growing out of his glib pessimism, and to say that his irony can become tiresome ought not obscure his considerable talent as a storyteller. *The Monkey King,* published when Mo was still in his 20s, reveals an author of mature craft. The story of how young Wallace Nolasco, a Portuguese-Chinese of almost complete naivete, comes to assume control of his father-in-law's business dealings, and, with the old Mr. Poon's death, succeeds to the position of patriarch, *The Monkey King* advances with skill and surprise. Characters are firmly conceived, swiftly and vividly created. Descriptions of decaying quarters of Hong Kong, its old mansions, the whimsical and grotesque sculpture garden, and the cemetery in which Mr. Poon is buried in a comic *tour de force* are convincing and memorable. The evocation of the cultural ethos of a peasant village in the New Territories shows a sure intelligence and insight into the effects of modernization on a traditional society. Through it all, the author keeps his distance, leaving much unsaid, and so creates a subtextual suspense that draws readers into a labyrinth of psychological tensions.

The second novel, *Sour Sweet,* is similarly conceived. Comic in its impulses, it also plays with racialist stereotypes, but it shifts the setting to England where racism is part of the inevitable background of circumstance against which its cast of immigrant Chinese struggle for security, prosperity, and a better life for the next generation. Primarily the story of Chen and his wife Lily and their efforts as small-time restaurateurs to make their way, *Sour Sweet* adds to Mo's achievements in characterization, description, plotting, and sociology. Readers cannot fail to be convinced of the veracity of his depiction of the Chen family's difficult position. The Chens must live among the constant menace of the Hung family (a Triad society, or Chinese mafia, which exploits immigrant Chinese in its drug smuggling operations), traditional obligations to family left in Hong Kong, and the inscrutable English, who can be intimidating, unpredictable, obnoxious, and astonishing. The English are particularly wonderful for their bus drivers, policemen, benign educators, welfare workers, and an agent of the Inland Revenue who prefers to initiate the Chens into the secrets of bookkeeping rather than send them before a magistrate. Significantly, the Chens choose to live on the margins of English society, and having been sagacious enough to pick a niche that no English would want—one which Mo concretely represents with a marvelously rendered old house near a petrol station—the Chens attain marginal prosperity. As immigrants, however, they are incapable of seeing the extreme tenuousness of their economic life. Indeed, for all of its shortcomings, the host country comes off quite well in *Sour Sweet.* But failure to keep full obedience to one's Chinese masters proves lethal.

Mo's third novel, *An Insular Possession,* addresses a very different audience from the one that is apt to be enchanted by the serio-comic and relatively brief *Monkey King* and *Sour Sweet.* Endowed with many voices, postmodernist in conception, and set against the historical backdrop of the Opium Wars, *An Insular Possession* is a doorstop of a novel in more ways than one. Nothing in the previous works instructs the reader in how to approach *An Insular Possession.* It is a rather static book, in part because of Mo's conscious effort to subvert the conventional narrative paradigm—especially in matters of characterization, point of view, coherence, and closure—substituting a purely linear and Western model of time with a more nearly Eastern view of time as a kind of field on which essence pre-empts event. Thus causation, whether in fiction or in life, appears to be less a matter of necessary sequence than of the arrangement of ideas and personalities on the spatial field of history. Moreover, if past and future can only be viewed from the present, space has as many vantages as one might be pleased to occupy. Mo's principal characters are peripatetic. Here they look out from the windows or balcony of the foreign factories in Canton, now from the terraced gardens of a rich merchant's house in Macao, or from the deck of the fighting steamer *Nemesis,* and later they will look down from the heights above the juvenile free port of Hong Kong. With each new perspective, the certainties of the previous position are called into question.

In short, *An Insular Possession* is a novel of multiplicities. There are, of course, the multiple perspectives of painter, photographer, journalist, soldier, merchant, and so forth, but more important are the multiplicities of technique. The novel opens with a powerful description of the estuary below Canton, choked with commerce and the bodies of discarded infant girls. So portentous is the passage, so heavy with moral freight, that one must recall Conrad and his Eastern tales of ambiguity. But the manner is soon dropped to make way for an amalgam of styles. There are letters interspersed with dramatized narrative which increasingly tends to slip into a terse present tense. There are long pieces of fictionalized reportage, ostensibly taken from the established *Canton Monitor* and its upstart antagonist *The Lin Tin Bulletin and River Bee.* Cleverly contrasting views on the issues of the Opium War, the newspaper passages could pass for real were they not obviously endowed with the personalities of fictional characters who write them. Thus Mo thoroughly baffles any effort to decide where history ends and fiction begins. Some minor characters are real—notably the honorable and hence discharged Captain Charles Elliott—for Mo is scrupulous about the details of the Opium War and the founding of Hong Kong. Yet more of this novel is fiction than meets the eye. There is, of course, a moral to this, something about the "undecidability of fictionality/historicity," or some other trendy formulation. Like Umberto Eco's *The Name of the Rose, An Insular Possession* is a very good story with an obtrusive understory centered smugly on the premise that all fiction is history and vice versa. Finally, the novel had the potentiality of reaching the breadth of significance of a Conrad novel, or might have easily entertained as splendidly as an historical novel by Antonia Fraser or George Garrett, but instead suffers the corrosive effects of Franco-American deconstruction and narratology. Readers who cannot be sufficiently rewarded by the novel's many brilliant parts, but desire instead an architecturally harmonious whole, are apt to find *An Insular Possession* a rather long, hard read.

—Mark A.R. Facknitz

MOMADAY, N(avarre) Scott

Nationality: American. **Born:** Lawton, Oklahoma, 27 February 1934. **Education:** The University of New Mexico, Albuquerque, A.B. 1958; Stanford University, California (creative writing fellow, 1959), A.M. 1960, Ph.D. 1963. **Family:** Married 1) Gaye Mangold in 1959 (divorced), three daughters; 2) Regina Heitzer in 1978, one daughter. **Career:** Assistant professor, 1963-67, and associate professor, 1967-69, University of California, Santa Barbara; professor of English and comparative literature, University of California, Berkeley, 1969-72; professor of English, Stanford University, 1972-80. Since 1980 professor of English and comparative literature, University of Arizona, Tucson. Professor, University of California Institute for the Humanities, 1970; Whittall Lecturer, Library of Congress, Washington, D.C., 1971; visiting professor, New Mexico State University, Las Cruces, 1972-73, State University of Moscow, Spring 1974, Columbia University, New York, 1979, and Princeton University, New Jersey, 1979; writer-in-residence, Southeastern University, Washington, D.C., 1985, and Aspen Writers' Conference, Colorado, 1986. Artist: has exhibited drawings and paintings. Since 1978 member of the Board of Trustees, Museum of the American Indian, New York. **Awards:** Academy of American Poets prize, 1962; Guggenheim grant, 1966; Pulitzer prize, 1969; American Academy award, 1970; Western Heritage award, 1974; Mondello prize (Italy), 1979; Western Literature Association award, 1983. D.H.L.: Central Michigan University, Mt. Pleasant, 1970; University of Massachusetts, Amherst, 1975; Yale University, New Haven, Connecticut, 1980; Hobart and William Smith Colleges, Geneva, New York, 1980; College of Santa Fe, New Mexico, 1982; D.Litt.: Lawrence University, Appleton, Wisconsin, 1971; University of Wisconsin, Milwaukee, 1976; College of Ganado, 1979; D.F.A.: Morningside College, Sioux City, Iowa, 1980. **Address:** Department of English, University of Arizona, Tucson, Arizona 85721, U.S.A.

PUBLICATIONS

Novels

House Made of Dawn. New York, Harper, 1968; London, Gollancz, 1969.
The Ancient Child. New York, Doubleday, 1989.

Poetry

Angle of Geese and Other Poems. Boston, Godine, 1974.
Before an Old Painting of the Crucifixion, Carmel Mission, June 1960. San Francisco, Valenti Angelo, 1975.
The Gourd Dancer. New York, Harper, 1976.
In the Presence of the Sun: Stories and Poems, 1961-1991, illustrated by the author. New York, St. Martin's Press, 1992.

Other

Owl in the Cedar Tree (for children). Boston, Ginn, 1965.
The Journey of Tai-me (Kiowa Indian tales). Privately printed, 1967; revised edition, as *The Way to Rainy Mountain,* Albuquerque, University of New Mexico Press, 1969.
Colorado: Summer, Fall, Winter, Spring, photographs by David Muench. Chicago, Rand McNally, 1973.
The Names: A Memoir. New York, Harper, 1976.
Circle of Wonder (for children). Santa Fe, New Mexico, Clear Light, 1994.

Editor, *The Complete Poems of Frederick Goddard Tuckerman.* New York, Oxford University Press, 1965.
Editor, *American Indian Authors.* Boston, Houghton Mifflin, 1976.
Editor, *A Coyote in the Garden,* by An Painter. Lewiston, Idaho, Confluence Press, 1988.

*

Manuscript Collection: Bancroft Library, University of California, Berkeley.

Critical Studies: *Four American Indian Literary Masters* by Alan R. Velie, Norman, University of Oklahoma Press, 1982; *N. Scott Momaday: The Cultural and Literary Background* by Matthias Schubnell, Norman, University of Oklahoma Press, 1986; *Approaches to Teaching Momaday's "The Way to Rainy Mountain"* edited by Kenneth M. Roemer, New York, Modern Language Association of America, 1988; *Ancestral Voice: Conversations with N. Scott Momaday* (includes bibliography) by Charles L. Woodard, Lincoln, University of Nebraska Press, 1989; *Landmarks of Healing: A Study of "House Made of Dawn"* by Susan Scarberry-Garcia, Albuquerque, University of New Mexico Press, 1990; *Place and Vision: The Function of Landscape in Native American Fiction* by Robert M. Nelson, New York, Lang, 1993.

                                *   *   *

In a 1971 lecture at Colorado State University, N. Scott Momaday said:

> At one time in my life I suddenly realized that my father had grown up speaking a language that I didn't grow up speaking, that my forebears on his side made a migration from Canada along with Athapaskan peoples I knew nothing about, and so I determined to find something out about these things and in the process I acquired an identity; and it is an Indian identity.

In acquiring his own Indian identity, Momaday has also created two novels which help to define identity for many Native Americans. When Momaday's first novel, *House Made of Dawn,* received the Pulitzer prize for fiction in 1969 it was the first major recognition for a work of Native American literature and a landmark for those seeking to understand "Indian identity."

House Made of Dawn is the story of Abel, a Native American caught between two worlds, the traditional world of Indian heritage and the white man's world. Momaday employs sharply drawn imagery, multiple points of view, flashbacks, journal entries and sermons, and passages in italic print to create a complex tapestry of myth and recollection. The novel begins with a one-page prologue which depicts Abel marked with ashes and running through the beautiful dawn of a New Mexico landscape. The prologue is a ritual celebration, but the novel is the tale of the path the character ran to bring him to that place.

The novel recounts Abel's return to the reservation after World War II; his affair with Angela St. John, a rich Anglo woman; and his conflict with an albino Indian named Juan Reyes Fragua, whom Abel murders. The novel goes on to depict Abel's life in Los Angeles after he is paroled from prison, his involvement with the Los Angeles Indian community, his friendship with Ben Benally, his intimate relationship with a sympathetic social worker named Milly, and his conflict with a corrupt policeman. After being badly beaten, Abel returns to the reservation and learns from his grandfather how to get beyond the pain of living. This book presents a Native American view of the world and of reality. Abel is damaged by the white man's world, but he ultimately is healed when he understands his true home rests within a place of harmony with the natural world, a "house made of dawn."

The themes of the healing force of nature and of the Indian caught between two worlds resurface in Momaday's second novel, *The Ancient Child.* The novel's primary character is Locke Setman, or Set, a Kiowa artist in San Francisco who has been raised as an Anglo. Set is a successful landscape artist but a personal crisis develops when his Indian identity begins to assert itself. As Set attempts to find his bearlike Kiowa identity he is aided by a 19-year-old medicine woman named Grey who takes him first to his Kiowa homeland and then to the Navajo reservation.

Like *House Made of Dawn, The Ancient Child* is a novel told in a complex manner. The book contains traditional Native American tales of bears and lost and transformed children, the legend of Billy the Kid, the evolution of a young Indian girl into womanhood, and lyrical descriptions of nature. At its heart, however, the novel is about the cultural crisis most Native Americans must face: how do ancient peoples whose collective memories recall a once intact and beautiful land cope with what that land and their lives have become?

Momaday's most vital message is that native cultures must endure. In the same way that Set is healed by Grey, American culture can learn to heal its shattered and broken self if respect for the land and land's people can be regained.

                                                —Tom Colonnese

MONETTE, Paul

Nationality: American. **Born:** Lawrence, Massachusetts, 1945. **Education:** Phillips Academy, Andover, Massachusetts; Yale University, New Haven, Connecticut, B.A. 1967. **Family:** Companion of 1) Roger Horwitz (died, 1986); 2) Stephen Kolzak (died, 1990); 3) Winston Wilde, since 1990. **Career:** Taught at Milton Academy and Pine Manor College. Active supporter of ACT UP (AIDS Coalition to Unleash Power). **Awards:** National Book award, 1992, for *Becoming a Man: Half a Life Story.* Honorary degree: State University of New York College at Oswego, 1992; Wesleyan University, 1993.

PUBLICATIONS

Novels

Taking Care of Mrs. Carroll. Boston, Little Brown, 1978.
The Gold Diggers. New York, Avon, 1979.
The Long Shot. New York, Avon, 1981.
Lightfall. New York, Avon, 1982.
Afterlife. New York, Crown, 1990.
Halfway Home. New York, Crown, 1991; London, GMP, 1992.

Poetry

The Carpenter at the Asylum. Boston, Little Brown, 1975.
No Witnesses, drawings by David Schorr. New York, Avon, 1981.
Love Alone: Eighteen Elegies for Rog. New York, St. Martin's Press, 1988.
West of Yesterday, East of Summer: New and Selected Poems, 1973-1993. New York, St. Martin's Press, 1994.

Other

Nosferatu: The Vampire (adaptation of screenplay by Werner Herzog). New York, Avon, and London, Pan, 1979.
Scarface (adaptation of screenplay by Oliver Stone). New York, Berkley, and London, Sphere, 1983.
Predator. New York, Berkley, 1986; London, Allen, 1987.
Borrowed Time: An AIDS Memoir. San Diego, Harcourt Brace, and London, Collins Harvill, 1988.
Havana. N.p., Ivy, and London, Arrow, 1991.
Midnight Run. New York, Berkley, 1990.
Becoming a Man: Half a Life Story. New York, Harcourt Brace, 1992; London, Abacus, 1994.
The Politics of Silence. Washington, D.C., Library of Congress, 1993.
Last Watch of the Night: Essays Too Personal and Otherwise. New York, Harcourt Brace, 1994; London, Abacus, 1995.

*

Manuscript Collections: University of California, Los Angeles Library special collections.

Critical Studies: "'The Time before the War': AIDS, Memory, and Desire" by John M. Clum, in *American Literature,* 62(2), 1990; *The Gay Novel in America* by James Levin, New York, Garland, 1991; "Paul Monette" by David Roman, in *Contemporary Gay American Novelists,* edited by Emmanuel S. Nelson, Westport, Connecticut, Greenwood Press, 1993.

*   *   *

The work of Paul Monette constitutes an exploration—in fiction, nonfiction, and poetry—of what it means to be gay in the United States after Stonewall and during the age of AIDS. His novels in particular, most of them gay love stories, explore the nature of gay identity and the gay community. The memoirs and essays trace his coming out, the loss of a lover to AIDS, and his own physical and philosophical grappling with the disease. His best-known poetry, the 1988 collection *Love Alone: Eighteen Elegies for Rog,* a series of elegies for his lover of over a decade, Roger Horwitz, is a profoundly moving chronicle of grief and loss. He has also written a number of novelizations of screenplays, such as *Scarface* and *Predator.* Inevitably Monette may be better known for his prizewinning nonfiction works than his fiction. The two autobiographical memoirs, *Borrowed Time: An AIDS Memoir* of 1988, and *Becoming a Man: Half a Life Story* of 1992, received wide critical attention. *Borrowed Time* was nominated for a National Book Award, and *Becoming a Man* won the award for nonfiction in 1992. It is the novels, however, that offer a sustained exploration of gay life and the possibilities for gay love and community in a society rendered indifferent if not hostile by religious disapprobation, closeted sexuality, and AIDS.

The earliest novels engage the idea of personal history, the stories that people tell about themselves, and the stories told about them. Monette also portrays the relationships of gay men and lesbians, and the shifting but close affectional bonds of friends, lovers, friends-become-lovers, and former-lovers-become-friends: the alternative families and communities that gay men create. Like the preceding novels, the two most recent novels, *Afterlife* and *Halfway Home,* are compelling love stories, but the trajectories of love and sex are traced in a time and a society colored by AIDS. All of Monette's novels value gay lives and sexuality, insisting that love and sex must be found and cherished, especially in the face of death.

Monette's familiarity with Hollywood entertainment culture provides a context for his novels, which are peopled with screenwriters, actors, performance artists, and television executives. Both *The Gold Diggers* and *The Long Shot* take place in Los Angeles, and the first novel, *Taking Care of Mrs. Carroll,* features at its center an aging Hollywood actress. The actress, Madeleine Cosquer, and her friend Rick, the novel's narrator, repeatedly refer to the clichéd dialogue and sentimental scripts of romantic movies, and Monette's novels repeatedly seem to rework traditional plots of melodrama, humor, and romance through a gay lens. Monette, in fact, queers a number of familiar narratives—romance, family reconciliation, murder mystery, western, celebrity exposés—in his novels, suggesting an interest in how such narratives work, how they may be altered with gay characters, and even how narratives may function in relation to identity.

In *Taking Care of Mrs. Carroll,* for example, there is a repeated focus on the relation of stories to lives. In the novel, a group of mostly gay characters connive to save Mrs. Carroll's pastoral estate from her greedy children and suburban developers. Mrs. Carroll had planned a will and her own death, writing in advance that she intended to swim out into the ocean at the end of the summer (shades of Virginia Woolf and Kate Chopin). Unfortunately, she dies before these plans can be effected. Much of the novel's suspense and humor lies in the other characters' actions to ensure that her story—and her inheritance—are enacted as planned.

Mrs. Carroll's narrative, however, isn't the only one in which truth and fiction and intent become commingled. Madeleine begins to write her memoirs, and she is concerned about the relation between the truth and the past, deciding finally to affirm the stories people have told about her rather than the boring and less legendary life she remembers. (Her name is surely a witty reference to Proust's famous "madeleine" scene.) Rick, the novel's narrator, concludes the novel affirming his life as a gay man, reaching an understanding of both his past and his sentimental fantasies: "I gave up the past I wanted to invent along with the one I spent my life burying."

Telling the stories of gay men, their pasts and futures, is Monette's literary project. He wishes to combat the closeting of gay lives, which erases or denies gay identity, and he especially wishes to tell the story of gay men living with AIDS. As Monette writes in *Becoming a Man,* "Until I was twenty-five, I was the only man I knew who had no story at all," emphasizing that the closet is an erasure and a fiction. Madeleine's obsession with the relation of truth to fiction may itself suggest an allegory for the construction of gay lives, and the ways the closet and coming out determine personal history. In *The Long Shot,* a disappointed gay screenwriter discovers that a murdered actor had a secret gay life, though Hollywood publicity and press perpetuate his seeming heterosexuality. This discovery precipitates the mystery's solution, and through it Monette indicts the homophobia of American culture, which enforces the closeting, both professional and personal, of gay men.

The denial or erasure of gay lives after AIDS seems especially troubling to Monette. "The story that endlessly eludes the decorum of the press," Monette writes in the preface to *Love Alone,* "is the death of a generation of gay men." In *Afterlife,* one character roams a cemetery, looking for "telltale signs"—unmarried men, men under 40, telling quotations on tombstones—that his lover is not alone in having died of AIDS. The man's new lover asks, "Will anyone understand what it was like?" He answers, maybe the gay men will, but both agree that even "they'll have to see through all the lies," since history is always the tale of "folks covering their ass."

Afterlife and *Halfway Home*—undoubtedly Monette's best novels by far—tell the story of gay life after AIDS. *Afterlife* follows three AIDS widowers as they move through loss into new love, religious and hedonistic escapism, and political anger. *Halfway Home* focuses on the reconciliation of a gay man suffering from AIDS with his straight brother, whose job and family are falling apart. Although the central narrative plots are, again, romantic, both novels include angry diatribes about AIDS and gay life. *Halfway Home* is suffused with a vicious anti-Catholicism, and *Afterlife* concludes with a horrifying act of political terrorism against a homophobic televangelist. Monette's novels are not exactly political, but they have become progressively more and more engaged with social issues. Of course, one could argue that Monette's positive portrayals of out gay men openly involved in sexual and romantic relationships and living in supportive communities are themselves political. The novels are concerned with the realities of living an openly gay life—of creating bonds, resisting oppression, and finding love.

This primary theme of finding love achieves real poignancy in the two AIDS novels, since both feature HIV-positive men who fall in love. In *Afterlife,* a retired man tells his positive son, "That's all there is, son. Someone to love." His son, Mark, a Hollywood executive, at first resists such "mawkish packaged sentiment," but by the end of the novel falls in love with Steven, an AIDS widower, also positive. In *Halfway Home,* dying actor Tom Shaheen simultaneously reconciles with his homophobic brother and falls in love with another man. The novel's emotional climax is an embrace among Tom, his lover, and his nephew Daniel, for whom Tom wishes: "let him not grow up among people who learned too late how to feel." During their embrace, Tom thinks, "At last, to feel everything down to the marrow. If it only lasted a moment more, it had come to me in time." Feeling deeply, and finding love "in time." Although Monette's novels are important literary examinations of gay life and gay culture, and although they may engage serious social issues, the primary theme is love—and more specifically, finding love in the flux of time and in the face of death.

—Ed Madden

MOORCOCK, Michael

Pseudonyms: Bill Barclay; Edward P. Bradbury; James Colvin; Hank Janson; Desmond Reid. **Nationality:** British. **Born:** Mitcham, Surrey, 18 December 1939. **Military Service:** Served in the Royal Air Force Training Corps. **Family:** Married 1) Hilary Bailey in 1962, two daughters and one son; 2) Jill Riches in 1978; 3) Linda Steel in 1983. **Career:** Editor, *Tarzan Adventures,* London, 1956-57, and Sexton Blake Library, Fleetway Publications, London, 1958-61; editor and writer for Liberal Party, 1962-63. Editor since 1964 and publisher since 1967, *New Worlds,* London. Since 1955 songwriter and member of various rock bands including Hawkwind, Deep Fix, and Blue Oyster Cult. **Awards:** British Science Fiction Association award, 1966; Nebula award 1967; Derleth award 1972, 1974, 1975, 1976; *Guardian* Fiction prize, 1977; Campbell Me-

morial award, 1979; World Fantasy award, 1979. Guest of Honor, World Fantasy Convention, New York, 1976. **Agent:** Anthony Sheil Associates Ltd., 43 Doughty Street, London WC1N 2LF, England.

PUBLICATIONS

Novels

Caribbean Crisis (as Desmond Reid, with James Cawthorn). London, Fleetway, 1962.
Stormbringer. London, Jenkins, 1965; New York, Lancer, 1967; revised edition, New York, DAW, 1977.
The Sundered Worlds. London, Compact, 1965; New York Paperback Library, 1966; as *The Blood Red Game,* London, Sphere, 1970.
The Fireclown. London, Compact, 1965; New York, Paperback Library, 1967; as *The Winds of Limbo,* Paperback Library, 1969.
The Twilight Man. London, Compact, 1966; New York, Berkley, 1970; as *The Shores of Death,* London, Sphere, 1970.
Printer's Devil (as Bill Barclay). London, Compact, 1966; revised edition, as *The Russian Intelligence,* as Michael Moorcock, Manchester, Savoy, 1980.
Somewhere in the Night (as Bill Barclay). London, Compact, 1966; revised edition, as *The Chinese Agent,* London, Hutchinson, and New York, Macmillan, 1970.
The Jewel in the Skull. New York, Lancer, 1967; London, Mayflower, 1969; revised edition, New York, DAW, 1977.
The Wrecks of Time. New York, Ace, 1967; revised edition, as *The Rituals of Infinity; or, The New Adventures of Doctor Faustus,* London Arrow, 1971; New York, DAW, 1978.
The Final Programme. New York, Avon, 1968; London, Allison and Busby, 1969; revised edition, London, Fontana, 1979.
Sorcerer's Amulet. New York, Lancer, 1968; as *The Mad God's Amulet,* London, Mayflower, 1969; revised edition, New York, DAW, 1977.
The Sword of the Dawn. New York, Lancer, 1968; London, Mayflower, 1969; revised edition, New York, DAW, 1977.
The Secret of the Runestaff. New York, Lancer, 1969; as *The Runestaff,* London, Mayflower, 1969; revised edition, New York, DAW, 1977.
The Ice Schooner. London, Sphere, and New York, Berkley, 1969; revised edition, London, Harrap, 1985.
Behold the Man. London, Allison and Busby, 1969; New York, Avon, 1970.
The Black Corridor, with Hilary Bailey. London, Mayflower, and New York, Ace, 1969.
The Eternal Champion. London, Mayflower, and New York, Dell, 1970; revised edition, New York, Harper, 1978.
Phoenix in Obsidian. London, Mayflower, 1970; as *The Silver Warriors,* New York, Dell, 1973.
A Cure for Cancer. London, Allison and Busby, and New York, Holt Rinehart, 1971; revised edition, London, Fontana, 1979.
The Warlord of the Air. London, New English Library, and New York, Ace, 1971.
The Swords Trilogy. New York, Berkley, 1977.
The Knight of the Swords. London, Mayflower, and New York, Berkley, 1971.
The Queen of the Swords. London, Mayflower, and New York, Berkley, 1971.
The King of the Swords. London, Mayflower, and New York, Berkley, 1971.

The Sleeping Sorceress. London, New English Library, 1971; New York, Lancer, 1972; revised edition, as *The Vanishing Tower,* New York, DAW, 1977.

Elric of Melniboné. London, Hutchinson, 1972; as *The Dreaming City,* New York, Lancer, 1972.

An Alien Heat. London, MacGibbon and Kee, and New York, Harper, 1972.

Breakfast in the Ruins: A Novel of Inhumanity. London, New English Library, 1972; New York, Random House, 1974.

The English Assassin. London, Allison and Busby, and New York, Harper, 1972; revised edition, London, Fontana, 1979.

The Chronicles of Corum. London, Grafton, 1986.

The Bull and the Spear. London Allison and Busby, and New York, Berkley, 1973.

The Oak and the Ram. London, Allison and Busby, and New York, Berkley, 1973.

The Sword and the Stallion. London, Allison and Busby, and New York, Berkley, 1974.

The Chronicles of Castle Brass. London, Granada, 1985.

Count Brass. London, Mayflower, 1973; New York, Dell, 1976.

The Champion of Garathorm. London, Mayflower, 1973.

The Quest for Tanelorn. London, Mayflower, 1975; New York, Dell, 1976.

The Land Leviathan. London, Quartet, and New York, Doubleday, 1974.

The Hollow Lands. New York, Harper, 1974; London, Hart Davis MacGibbon, 1975.

The Distant Suns, with Philip James. Llanfynydd, Dyfed, Unicorn Bookshop, 1975.

The Sailor on the Seas of Fate. London, Quartet, and New York, DAW, 1976.

The Adventures of Una Persson and Catherine Cornelius in the Twentieth Century. London, Quartet, 1976.

The End of All Songs. London, Hart Davis MacGibbon, and New York, Harper, 1976.

The Condition of Muzak. London, Allison and Busby, 1977; Boston, Gregg Press, 1978.

The Transformation of Miss Mavis Ming. London, W.H. Allen, 1977; as *Messiah at the End of Time,* New York, DAW, 1978.

The Cornelius Chronicles (omnibus). New York, Avon, 1977.

The Weird of the White Wolf. New York, DAW, 1977; London, Panther, 1984.

The Vanishing Tower. New York, DAW, 1977.

The Bane of the Black Sword. New York, DAW, 1977; London, Panther, 1984.

Gloriana; or, The Unfulfill'd Queen. London, Allison and Busby, 1978; New York, Avon, 1979.

The History of the Runestaff (collection). London, Hart Davis MacGibbon, 1979.

The Great Rock 'n' Roll Swindle. London, Virgin, 1980; revised edition as "Gold Diggers of 1977", in *Casablanca and Other Stories,* London, Gollancz, 1989.

The Golden Barge. Manchester, Savoy, and New York, DAW, 1980.

The Entropy Tango. London, New English Library, 1981.

The Steel Tsar. London, Mayflower, 1981; New York, DAW, 1982.

The War Hound and the World's Pain. New York, Timescape, 1981; London, New English Library, 1982.

Byzantium Endures. London, Secker and Warburg, 1981; New York, Random House, 1982.

The Brothel in Rösenstrasse. London, New English Library, 1982; New York, Carroll and Graf, 1987.

The Dancers at the End of Time (omnibus). London, Granada, 1983.

The Laughter of Carthage. London, Secker and Warburg, and New York, Random House, 1984.

The Crystal and the Amulet. Manchester, Savoy, 1986.

The Dragon in the Sword. New York, Ace, 1986; London, Grafton, 1987.

The City in the Autumn Stars. London, Grafton, 1986; New York, Ace, 1987.

Mother London. London, Secker and Warburg, 1988; New York, Harmony, 1989.

The Fortress of the Pearl. London, Gollancz, and New York, Ace, 1989.

The Revenge of the Rose. New York, Ace, and London, Grafton, 1991.

Novels as Edward P. Bradbury

Warrior of Mars. London, New English Library, 1981.

Warriors of Mars. London, Compact, 1965; New York, Lancer, 1966; as *The City of the Beast* (as Michael Moorcock), Lancer, 1970.

Blades of Mars. London, Compact, 1965; New York, Lancer, 1966; as *The Lord of the Spiders* (as Michael Moorcock), Lancer, 1970.

The Barbarians of Mars. London, Compact, 1965; New York, Lancer, 1966; as *The Masters of the Pit* (as Michael Moorcock), Lancer, 1970.

Short Stories

The Stealer of Souls and Other Stories. London, Spearman, 1963; New York, Lancer, 1967.

The Deep Fix (as James Colvin). London, Compact, 1966.

The Time Dweller. London, Hart Davis, 1969; New York, Berkley, 1971.

The Singing Citadel: Four Tales of Heroic Fantasy. London, Mayflower, and New York, Berkley, 1970.

The Jade Man's Eyes. Brighton, Unicorn Bookshop, 1973.

Elric: The Return to Melniboné (cartoon), illustrated by Philippe Druillet. Brighton, Unicorn Bookshop, 1973.

Moorcock's Book of Martyrs. London, Quartet, 1976; as *Dying for Tomorrow,* New York, DAW, 1978.

The Lives and Times of Jerry Cornelius. London, Allison and Busby, 1976; New York, Dale, n.d.

Legends from the End of Time. London, W.H. Allen, and New York, Harper, 1976.

My Experiences in the Third World War. Manchester, Savoy, 1980.

The Opium General and Other Stories. London, Harrap, 1984.

Elric at the End of Time: Fantasy Stories. London, New English Library, 1984; New York, DAW, 1985.

Casablanca and Other Stories. London, Gollancz, 1989.

Uncollected Short Stories

"The Girl Who Shot Sultry Kane" (as Hank Janson), in *Golden Nugget,* April 1965.

"The Museum of the Future," in *Daily Telegraph* (London), May 1990.

"The Ciarene Purse," in *Zenita,* June 1990.

"Colour," in *New Worlds* (London), 1991.

Play

Screenplay: *The Land That Time Forgot,* with James Cawthorn, 1974.

Other

Sojan (for children). Manchester, Savoy, 1977.
Epic Pooh. London, British Fantasy Society, 1978.
The Retreat from Liberty: The Erosion of Democracy in Today's Britain. London, Zomba, 1983.
Letter from Hollywood, with Michael Foreman. London, Harrap, 1986.
Wizardry and Wild Romance: A Study of Epic Fantasy. London, Gollancz, 1987.

Editor, *The Best of New Worlds.* London, Compact, 1965.
Editor, *Best SF Stories from New Worlds 1-8.* London, Panther, 8 vols., 1967-74; New York, Berkley, 6 vols., 1968-71.
Editor, *The Traps of Time.* London, Rapp and Whiting, 1968.
Editor (anonymously), *The Inner Landscape.* London, Allison and Busby, 1969.
Editor, *New Worlds Quarterly 1-5.* London, Sphere, 5 vols., 1971-73; New York, Berkley, 4 vols., 1971-72.
Editor, with Langdon Jones, *The Nature of the Catastrophe.* London, Hutchinson, 1971.
Editor, with Charles Platt, *New Worlds 6.* London, Sphere, 1973; as *New Worlds 5,* New York, Avon, 1973.
Editor, *Before Armageddon: An Anthology of Victorian and Edwardian Imaginative Fiction Published Before 1914.* London, W.H. Allen, 1975.
Editor, *England Invaded: A Collection of Fantasy Fiction.* London, W.H. Allen, and New York, Ultramarine, 1977.
Editor, *New Worlds: An Anthology.* London, Fontana, 1983.
Editor, with James Cawthorn, *Fantasy: The 100 Best Books.* London, Xanadu, and New York, Carroll and Graf, 1988.

Ghostwriter: *The LSD Dossier,* by Roger Harris. London, Compact, 1966.

*

Bibliography: *Michael Moorcock: A Bibliography* by Andrew Harper and George McAulay, T-K Graphics, 1976.

Manuscript Collections: Bodleian Library, Oxford University; Sterling Library, Texas A & M University, College Station.

Critical Study: *Speaking of Science Fiction: The Paul Walker Interviews* edited by Paul Walker, Luna, 1978; *The Entropy Exhibition: Michael Moorcock and the British "New Wave" in Science Fiction* by Colin Greenland, London, Routledge, 1983; *Michael Moorcock: A Reader's Guide* by John Davey, revised edition, London, privately printed, 1992.

Michael Moorcock comments:

My work varies so radically in type that I've no way of introducing it. I write very little science fiction, in my own view and that of most science fiction readers. My genre fiction is mostly fantasy.

Much of my work borrowed from the iconography and vocabulary of science fiction in the 1960s but I would not, for instance, classify the Jerry Cornelius tetralogy as a genre work while *The Dancers at the End of Time* though a comedy *is* generically science fiction.

Since I've worked hard to break down the classifications I'm uncomfortable with them being applied to my own stuff. In the past 10 years most of my fiction has been nongeneric.

Cross-fertilisation—internationally—is always what I aim for in an edition. My own work owes as much to German *Schelmenroman* as to the English 19th-century novel and very little, to say, pulp science fiction.

* * *

> "Invent phantoms? Fabulous beasts? Powerful Gods? Whole Cosmologies?" said the astonished traveller. "Are all these things, then unreal?"
>
> "They're real enough," Corum replied. "Reality, after all, is the easiest thing in the world to create."
>
> *(The Chronicles of Corum)*

Corum's wit is a fitting introduction to the fictional world of Michael Moorcock. The paradox, "reality is the easiest thing to create" directs us to the astonishing fertility of Moorcock's imagination: Moorcock's work does indeed contain powerful gods, whole cosmologies, and fabulous beasts. The epigram also alerts us to the peculiarly persuasive nature of Moorcock's fiction. It is not of course reality that Moorcock creates in his books. His heroes, demigods, and monsters are spectacularly unlike anything we may recognise as reality. Yet his ideas attain "reality" because we, his readers, are willing to accept them as such: Moorcock is one of the most popular as well as the most prolific of contemporary fantasy writers.

He works quickly, wasting little effort on what Tolkien termed "subcreation." Entire continents are created in the space of a paragraph; characters in a single line. Significantly, Moorcock's books do not have maps. Stories such as the Elric saga and *The History of the Runestaff* pare characterisation and setting to the bone, resulting in a fictional form which moves at breathtaking speed and consists of a series of action sequences. Such novels owe much to the art of graphic "comic strip" magazines. Our pleasure is not in the imaginative exploration of other worlds but in the imaginative experience of sensations which the fictional device of another world makes possible. Brilliant *tours de force* such as the ornithopters and beast masks of *The Jewel in the Skull* are never developed at length. The stories are simply moving too fast to allow this. Moorcock succeeds in this because he is able to draw on a wealth of conventions established by a generation of fantasy writers since Tolkien.

Many of these derive ultimately from the epic: the overall structure of protracted revenge or quest within which occurs an episodic series of adventures characterised by discovery of marvels, capture, escape, and intervention by patron gods. The influence of the epic even extends down to dialogue:

> I am Elric of Melniboné, last of a line of great sorcerer kings. This blade I wield will do more than kill you, friend demon. It will drink your soul and feed it to me. Perhaps you have heard of me by another name? . . . soul thief?

The ritualised challenge with its declaration of name and lineage, the savouring of the exotic sounds of an alien language, and the riddling around the hero's identity, all stem directly from the epic.

From the conventions of this genre Moorcock derives a number of essential principles. Firstly, the struggle of good (law) against evil (chaos). Secondly, the extension of this struggle, which is centered on earth, into other planes or dimensions. Thirdly, the movement of characters and objects of power between these dimensions, bringing "supernatural" elements into the initial conflict. Fourthly, the central importance of the hero, who is the decisive force in the battle between law and chaos.

While of crucial importance in Moorcock's world, the hero is nonetheless an ambiguous figure, at once attractive and forbidding. Like the antihero of Gothic literature many of his protagonists bear some scar or stigma which serves as an emblem of their alienation from mankind. Elric is an Albino, Corum has lost a hand and an eye, Dorian Hawkmoon has a black jewel embedded in his forehead. These scars symbolise the alienated, slightly inhuman perspective with which we enter the narratives. The prologue of *The Dancers at the End of Time* describes its protagonists: "Most of the old emotions had atrophied. . . . They had rivalry without jealously, affection without lust, malice without rage, kindness without pity."

This dark edge to Moorcock's fantasy emerges vividly in his portrayal of women: women are whores, warrior queens, demonesses or lovers. But love for Moorcock's heroes is often contaminated by bitterness, betrayal, or bereavement. Elric has to slay his wife, Zarozina, in *Stormbringer,* and Corum is slain by Medhbh, the woman he loves, in *The Sword and the Stallion.* In the unrestrained Cornelius saga, the hero's love is both incestuous and necrophilic. Moorcock, then, both embraces and subverts the conventions of 20th-century fantasy.

Among more than 60 novels, one, perhaps, can be singled out: *The City in the Autumn Stars.* The hero, Von Beck, enters the Mittelmarch, a hidden realm contiguous to Europe in which occult forces reign. Here he finds his dreams and nightmares becoming real. Driven by his search for the goddess-like Libussa, Duchess of Crete, he is unwillingly caught up in supernatural mysteries in which Lucifer struggles with God for the redemption of the earth.

Here the story is not simply one of adventure but of initiation. Symbols from ancient myth and from the unconscious are awoken and come alive: the labyrinth, the minotaur, and the hermaphrodite. Sequences of mystical and erotic union are conveyed in dream-like images and in a heightened poetic, quasi-biblical language. Moorcock creates a fantasy which takes its protagonist through spiritual struggle to eventual wholeness. The effect of this on the reader is intensified by the author's exceptional use of a first person narrator. The epigraph to the work suggests an intriguing comparison between fantasy fiction and magic. Both are arts that transform those who deal with them: "At its deepest, this magic is concerned with the creative powers of the will."

No essay on Moorcock would be complete without mention of the playfulness which affectionately undercuts all the conventions of the genre he employs. This extends from the experiments with chapter titles and typography in the Cornelius chronicles to the wry humour of his fantasy heroes: in *The Vanishing Tower* Ereköse asks, "Why cannot I—we—ever be faced with a small problem, a domestic problem? Why are we forever involved with the destiny of the universe?"

—Edmund Cusick

MOORE, Brian

Pseudonym: Michael Bryan. **Nationality:** Canadian. **Born:** Belfast, Northern Ireland, 25 August 1921; moved to Canada in 1948 and to the U.S. in 1959. **Education:** Saint Malachy's College, Belfast. **Military Service:** Served in the Belfast Fire Service, 1942-43, and with the British Ministry of War Transport, in North Africa, Italy, and France, 1943-45. **Family:** Married 1) Jacqueline Sirois in 1951; 2) Jean Denney in 1967; one son. **Career:** Served with United Nations Relief and Rehabilitation Administration (UNRRA) mission to Poland, 1946-47; reporter, Montreal *Gazette,* 1948-52; Regents' Professor, 1974-75, and professor, 1976-89, University of California, Los Angeles. **Awards:** Authors Club of Great Britain award, 1956; Beta Sigma Phi award, 1956; Quebec literary prize, 1958; Guggenheim fellowship, 1959; Governor-General's award, 1961, 1975; American Academy grant, 1961; Canada Council fellowship, 1962; W.H. Smith literary award, 1973; National Catholic book award, 1973; James Tait Black Memorial prize, 1976; Scottish Arts Council senior fellowship, 1983; Royal Society of Literature Heinemann award, 1986; *Sunday Express* Book of the Year award, 1988; Hughes Irish Fiction award, 1988. **Agent:** Curtis Brown, 10 Astor Place, New York, New York 10003. **Address:** 33958 Pacific Coast Highway, Malibu, California 90265, U.S.A.

PUBLICATIONS

Novels

The Executioners (as Michael Bryan). Toronto, Harlequin, 1951.
Wreath for a Redhead (as Michael Bryan). Toronto, Harlequin, 1951.
Judith Hearne. Toronto, Collins, and London, Deutsch, 1955; as *The Lonely Passion of Judith Hearne,* Boston, Little Brown, 1956.
Intent to Kill (as Michael Bryan). New York, Dell, and London, Eyre and Spottiswoode, 1956.
Murder in Majorca (as Michael Bryan). New York, Dell, 1957; London, Eyre and Spottiswoode, 1958.
The Feast of Lupercal. Boston, Little Brown, 1957; London, Deutsch, 1958; as *A Moment of Love,* London, Panther, 1965.
The Luck of Ginger Coffey. Boston, Little Brown, and London, Deutsch, 1960.
An Answer from Limbo. Boston, Little Brown, 1962; London, Deutsch, 1963.
The Emperor of Ice-Cream. New York, Viking Press, 1965; London, Deutsch, 1966.
I Am Mary Dunne. New York, Viking Press, and London, Cape, 1968.
Fergus. New York, Holt Rinehart, 1970; London, Cape, 1971.
Catholics. London, Cape, 1972; New York, Harcourt Brace, 1973.
The Great Victorian Collection. New York, Farrar Straus, and London, Cape, 1975.
The Doctor's Wife. New York, Farrar Straus, and London, Cape, 1976.
The Mangan Inheritance. New York, Farrar Straus, and London, Cape, 1979.
The Temptation of Eileen Hughes. New York, Farrar Straus, and London, Cape, 1981.
Cold Heaven. New York, Holt Rinehart, and London, Cape, 1983.
Black Robe. New York, Dutton, and London, Cape, 1985.
The Colour of Blood. London, Cape, and New York, Dutton, 1987.
Lies of Silence. London, Bloomsbury, and New York, Doubleday, 1990.
No Other Life. London, Bloomsbury, and New York, Doubleday, 1993.

Short Stories

Two Stories. Northridge, California, Santa Susana Press, 1978.

Plays

Catholics, adaptation of his own novel (televised 1973; produced Seattle, 1980; Belfast, 1985).

Screenplays: *The Luck of Ginger Coffey,* 1964; *Torn Curtain,* 1966; *The Slave,* 1967; *Catholics,* 1973; *The Blood of Others,* 1984; *The Sight,* 1985; *Black Robe,* 1991.

Television Play: *Catholics,* 1973.

Other

Canada, with the editors of *Life.* New York, Time, 1963; revised edition, 1968.
The Revolution Script. New York, Holt Rinehart, 1971; London, Cape, 1972.

*

Manuscript Collection: Special Collections, University of Calgary, Alberta.

Critical Studies: "The Simple Excellence of Brian Moore" by Christopher Ricks, in *New Statesman* (London), 18 February 1966; "Crisis and Ritual in Brian Moore's Belfast Novels" by John Wilson Foster, in *Eire-Ireland* (St. Paul, Minnesota), Autumn 1968; *Brian Moore,* Toronto, Copp Clark, 1969, and *Brian Moore,* Boston, Twayne, 1981, both by Hallvard Dahlie; *Odysseus Ever Returning* by George Woodcock, Toronto; McClelland and Stewart, 1970; "The Novels of Brian Moore" by Michael Paul Gallagher, S.J., in *Studies (Ireland)* (Dublin), Summer 1971; "The Crisis of Identity in the Novels of Brian Moore" by Murry Prosky, in *Eire-Ireland* (St. Paul, Minnesota), Summer 1971; *Brian Moore* by Jeanne Flood, Lewisburg, Pennsylvania, Bucknell University Press, 1974; "Brian Moore: Private Person" by Bruce Cook, in *Commonweal* (New York), 23 August 1974; "The Novels of Brian Moore: A Retrospective" by De Witt Henry, in *Ploughshares* (Cambridge, Massachusetts), Fall 1974; "Webs of Artifice" by Derek Mahon, in *New Review* (London), October 1975; "Brian Moore: Past and Present" in *Critical Quarterly* (Manchester), 1976, and *Four Contemporary Novelists,* Montreal, McGill-Queen's University Press, 1982, London, Scolar Press, 1983, both by Kerry McSweeney; "Portrait of the Artist as Emigré" by Philip French, in *Observer* (London), October 1977; "The Calligraphy of Pain" by Hubert de Santana, in *Maclean's* (Toronto), September 1979; "Brian Moore Issue" of *Irish University Review* (Dublin), Spring 1988; *Brian Moore: A Critical Study* by Jo O'Donoghue, Montreal, McGill-Queen's University Press, 1991.

*   *   *

According to Christopher Ricks (in *The New Statesman,* 19 February 1966), the most remarkable feature of Brian Moore's novels is their capacity for "abolishing brow-distinction," while at the same time avoiding condescension. Moore is certainly blessed with a clear and straightforward prose style, readable and unintrusive. But be-

cause unencumbered by complexity in authorial language, Moore's novels are often heavily dependent upon their central characters and plots in attempting to engage the reader; and thus some of the more subtle of Moore's intentions in his fiction can be lost in the machinery of the plot.

Throughout Moore's novels, central characters, both male and female, are carefully delineated, so that the notion of the psychological entity of the "self," its formation and its existence, are problems that Moore's work repeatedly turns to, often concentrating the problematic nature of the "self" by focusing on crucial events in the life of the individual. In *The Luck of Ginger Coffey* a lifetime of self-deception accumulates in Ginger's unemployment and temporary destitution, leading to a painful self-reassessment of his character. Ginger Coffey, through his inability to understand his own weaknesses, past and present, stands to lose his wife and daughter. The shock brings Coffey to a moment of self-realisation, if of a limited kind: "He would die in humble circs: it did not matter. There would be no victory for Ginger Coffey, no victory big or little. . . . Life was the victory, wasn't it?" The last rhetorical question affirms the reader's sense that the novel presents no long-lasting revelation, but rather the beginnings of self-understanding.

While Moore has become adept at economically and convincingly portraying a "self," his novels have often suffered a loss of sharpness in dealing with the wider social and political issues which they raise and which necessarily affect the "self" (for example, unemployment in the case of Ginger Coffey). The short novel *Catholics,* an exception to this criticism, succeeds largely because, in a work concerned with religious issues, it has a concision of characterisation and maintains a distance from the protagonist, Father Kinsella, a priest sent from Rome to reprimand and reform an out-of-touch Irish priory. Here the conflicts between past and present, traditionalism and modernism (issues that touch and yet also extend beyond the concerns of the Catholic church) are carefully dealt with (they are also major concerns in *The Mangan Inheritance* and *The Great Victorian Collection*).

However, in *Lies of Silence* large political issues get a blunter and less perceptive treatment than is due to them. Irish terrorism, Irish politics, and the suffering that is often a result of both, are always in danger of being either oversimplified or sensationalised. The combination of thriller-derived plot with a crisis-ridden central hero is not enough to stop *Lies of Silence* (and its prosaic displays of political anger) from being at times closer to the borderline of typical Troubles fiction—a category Moore is presumably trying to avoid. Moore may relish tracing the edge of this margin between the popular and the literary in his writing, but *Lies of Silence* is certainly unintentionally on the side of the popular.

It is, perhaps surprisingly, in his female characters that Moore best overcomes the difficulties of writing carefully about individuals in society, while at the same time writing about society (which is often an implicit intention of his novels). *I Am Mary Dunne, The Lonely Passion of Judith Hearne,* and *The Doctor's Wife* all illustrate Moore's ability to create a fictional female "self"; usually a "self" under stress or undergoing transformation. Most memorable is Eileen Hughes, in *The Temptation of Eileen Hughes,* who is never quite as engaging a character as the reader expects; thus a distance over which we can view Eileen is created. Steadfast in the face of the overzealous and eventually insane love for her of Bernard McAuley, Eileen remains true to the moral strictures of her social and religious background. The reader of *The Temptation of Eileen Hughes* can never quite come to "side" with Eileen; and as Bernard's love is revealed in all its passionate irrationality the reader's sympathies become further complicated. Moore thrives on the creation of moral dilemmas, placing his characters in unenviably difficult positions and offering them little in the way of an escape route.

Lies of Silence, shortlisted for the 1990 Booker prize, epitomises this trait in Moore's writing. Michael Dillon, manager of a hotel in Belfast, is forced by the I.R.A. to drive his car containing a bomb to the hotel in order to assassinate a Unionist luminary. Meanwhile the I.R.A. hold Dillon's wife at gunpoint, threatening to kill her if he does not carry out their orders. Dillon finds himself forced to choose between saving his wife's life or the lives of those at the hotel. (This is complicated by the contempt he feels for the object of the assassination attempt.) To further confuse the dilemma for Dillon, these events take place on the day when he intends to tell his wife that he is going to leave her to go to London with his young lover. Dillon makes his choice, and raises the alarm about the bomb; the I.R.A. have left his wife unharmed. Moore creates the maximum of tension leading up to the explosion, but when it comes, it is only halfway through the novel; in this sense Moore is at least interested in the moral and political aftermath of such events. How will Dillon's wife react to her husband having taken a decision which could have cost her her life? How will the terrorists take their revenge on someone who defies them? The denouement is as, if not more, enthralling than the tension of the unexploded bomb earlier, and although *Lies of Silence* cannot resist crude and naive political statements and a violent ending, its fascination with moral dilemmas and how they illustrate, determine, and shape the personality of the individual is typical of the best of Moore's writing. With his subsequent novel *No Other Life* Moore swung back significantly to the darker intellectualism of some of his earlier work; moving away from home seems to sharpen Moore's prose style, narrative techniques, and, ironically, the political acuteness of his fiction.

—Colin Graham

MOORE, Lorrie

Nationality: American. **Born:** Marie Lorena Moore in Glens Falls, New York, 13 January 1957. **Education:** St. Lawrence University, Canton, New York, 1974-78, B.A. (summa cum laude) 1978; Cornell University, Ithaca, New York, 1980-82, M.F.A. 1982. **Career:** Assistant professor, 1984-87, and since 1987 associate professor of English, University of Wisconsin, Madison. **Awards:** National Endowment for the Arts award, 1989; Rockefeller Foundation fellowship, 1989; Guggenheim fellowship, 1991. **Agent:** Melanie Jackson Agency, 250 West 57th Street, New York, New York 10107. **Address:** Department of English, University of Wisconsin, 600 North Park Street, Madison, Wisconsin 53706, U.S.A.

PUBLICATIONS

Novel

Anagrams. New York, Knopf, 1986; London, Faber, 1987.

Short Stories

Self-Help. New York, Knopf, and London, Faber, 1985.
Like Life. New York, Knopf, and London, Faber, 1990.
Who Will Run the Frog Hospital? New York, Knopf, and London, Faber, 1994.

Uncollected Short Stories

"Willing," in *Best American Short Stories 1991,* edited by Alice Adams and Katrina Kenison. Boston, Houghton Mifflin, 1991.
"Community Life," in *Best American Short Stories 1992.* Boston, Houghton Mifflin, 1992.
"Terrific Mother" in *Best American Short Stories 1993.* Boston, Houghton Mifflin, 1993.

*   *   *

Lorrie Moore quickly established herself as an American writer to watch with a well-received first collection of quirky short stories, which was then followed by a novel and another, more confident collection of stories. Her stories, and to a lesser extent her novel, strike a fine balance between humor and sadness, compassion and cynicism.

Moore's first book is entitled *Self-Help,* and is at times a kind of mock self-help manual. Most of the story titles emphasize this theme: "How to Be an Other Woman," "The Kid's Guide to Divorce," "How to Become a Writer," "Go Like This." Moreover, six of the nine stories are told in the peculiar second-person voice favored in self-help manuals. It is difficult to tell a story using this voice without sounding controlling and bossy. However, Moore uses second person precisely to show how much the character takes over a story, and how hard it is to remain objective. The sense of control and authority of the second-person voice is constantly subverted, as are any "truths" in the stories.

Moore has said that her use of second person was primarily a stylistic experiment. She also experiments throughout with structure and narrative. "How to Talk to Your Mother (Notes)" is made up of diary entries going backwards; in "Go Like This" the narrator has decided to commit suicide and writes her last words literally as she is dying (they trail off); several of the stories are made up of short disconnected paragraphs without an obvious story line. Wordplay, especially punning, is frequent and often very funny. In fact the stories are full of humor and compassion, even as they bite.

This experimentation can be exhausting, however. So much is undercut stylistically that it is difficult at times to take the stories seriously. Significantly, the two best stories in the collection, "What Is Seized" and "To Fill" are straightforward narratives told in first person and without a hint of self-help in their titles. "What Is Seized" begins "My mother married a cold man" and chronicles a painful marriage through the now grown-up daughter's eyes. "To Fill" is also about a failing marriage, told from the woman's point of view. Moore gracefully builds to moments of sadness and understanding, edged with a humor that clarifies rather than relieves pain.

With her second collection, *Like Life,* Moore has dropped experimentation and sounds much more assured as a result, although perhaps not as unusual, and certainly not as funny. In fact, these new stories are sadder, bleaker. Characters are older now, and their problems seem more hopeless. The plots are full of sad situations and details: a writer has the little work he has managed to produce ripped off by a television screenwriter; a mother tries to recreate her runaway son in a young houseguest and manages only to drive him away as well; a woman takes her cat to the vet and sees another family grieve over their cat's sudden death; a woman with "precancer" ("'*Precancer?*' she had repeated quietly, for she was a quiet woman. 'Isn't that . . . like *life?*'") thinks she sees her husband jump off the Brooklyn Bridge.

Above all there is a sense of despair surrounding the relations between men and women. Couples flounder, remain in unloving atmospheres, are unable to connect. "Vissi d'Arte" ends with a vivid image of the gulf between the sexes as a man goes into a sex pavilion on 42nd Street and watches a naked woman dance behind a pane of glass:

> But as he watched she seemed to lift her eyes, to spot him, to head toward his window, slow and smiling, until she was pressing her breast against his pane, his alone. He moaned, placed his mouth against the cold single rose of her nipple, against the hard smeared glass, though given time, in this, this wonderful town, he felt, it might warm beneath his labors, truly, like something real.

Two excellent stories from *Like Life*—"The Jewish Hunter" and "You're Ugly, Too"—further illustrate the impossibility of men and women understanding one another. In "The Jewish Hunter" Odette, an East Coast poet-in-residence in a small Midwestern town, begins seeing Pinky, a local man very different from her. She finds she is unable to accept her feelings for him or explain why she will not let herself love. The story is full of strange, disturbing images such as Jewish Pinky's insistence on watching videos of concentration camp survivors after he and Odette have made love; or dead deer tied to the fronts of hunters' cars; or Odette's response to Pinky's suggestion that she is falling in love with him: "she stared, disbelievingly, up at him. Sometimes she thought she was just trying to have fun in life, and other times she realized she must be terribly confused. She narrowed her eyes. Then she opened her mouth wide so that he could see the train wreck of chewed-up bagel and lox. 'I like that,' said Pinky. 'You're onto something there.'"

"You're ugly, too" is the punchline of the main character Zoë's favorite joke. She is a history professor, single, and encouraged by her sister to meet men; she has just learned she may have cancer. At her sister's Halloween party a man dressed as a naked woman (with fake breasts and steel wool glued to a body stocking) tells Zoë a similar joke with a different, sexist punchline that painfully points up the chasm between them. That he makes a pass at her almost immediately afterwards simply reinforces their mutual understanding.

Moore's novel *Anagrams,* written between the two collections, is similar to *Self-Help* in its extensive use of wordplay and sometimes confusing experimentation with narrative. The main character Benna is first introduced as a nightclub singer, but after a chapter she is portrayed as an aerobics teacher for the elderly, then an art history professor, and finally a poetry teacher at a community college. Her friends Gerard (also an ex-lover in some chapters) and Eleanor go through similar metamorphoses; in fact Eleanor finally becomes Benna's imaginary alter ego. Benna also imagines a daughter, Georgianne.

Anagrams is a chaotic, at times hilarious novel about a woman's loneliness and hesitant attempts to establish links with others. Benna's insecurity is underlined stylistically, for very little in the book can be pinned down and trusted: puns turn word meanings upside down, the narrative jumps back and forth between first and third person, and real characters keep changing circumstances, while imaginary characters play a large part in the story. In fact Georgianne and Eleanor figure so naturally and prominently in Benna's life that it is a shock to be reminded at the end of the novel that they are not real. As with the stories in *Self-Help,* this constant shifting and undercutting can be disconcerting, and at times *Anagrams* loses its focus. Sometimes the jokey style is just too flippant. But the book can be surprisingly moving too, particularly when Benna is forced to acknowledge that she has peopled her life with imaginary characters and is losing the real ones. Unfortunately the ending swings out of control, with a disturbing visit to Benna's brother that unnecessarily opens up wider issues and jars with the rest of the story.

Moore has demonstrated a fine writing talent, particularly for short stories. Unfortunately, despite their recent renaissance, short stories are not considered as significant as novels; however, if Moore can successfully transfer her assured portrayal of characters and mood to more full-length work she will be a force to be reckoned with.

—Tracy Chevalier

MOORHOUSE, Frank

Nationality: Australian. **Born:** Nowra, New South Wales, 21 December 1938. **Education:** The University of Queensland, 1959-61. **Military Service:** Served in the Australian Army and Reserves, 1957-59. **Family:** Divorced. **Career**: Journalist, Sydney *Telegraph,* 1956-59; editor, *Lockhart Review,* New South Wales, 1960, and *Australian Worker,* Sydney, 1962; assistant secretary, Workers' Educational Association, Sydney, 1963-65; union organizer, Australian Journalists' Association, 1966; editor, *City Voices,* Sydney, 1966; contributor and columnist, 1970-79, and nightclub writer, 1980, *Bulletin,* Sydney; co-founding editor, *Tabloid Story,* Sydney, 1972-74. Writer-in-residence, University of Melbourne and other Australian universities; travelled in Europe and Middle East, late 1980s; moved to France, 1991. Vice president, 1978-80, and president, 1979-82, Australian Society of Authors; chairman, Copyright Council of Australia, 1985. **Awards:** Lawson Short Story prize, 1970; National Book Council Banjo award for fiction, 1975; senior literary fellowship, 1976; *Age* Book of the Year, 1988; Australian Literature Society gold medal, 1989; South Australian Festival Award, 1993. **Member:** Order of Australia, 1985. **Address:** c/o Pan Books, 63-71 Balfour Street, Chippendale, New South Wales 2008, Australia.

PUBLICATIONS

Novel

Grand Days: A Novel. New York, Pantheon Books, and London, Picador, 1993.

Short Stories

Futility and Other Animals. Sydney, Powell, 1969.
The Americans, Baby. Sydney and London, Angus and Robertson, 1972.

The Electrical Experience. Sydney, Angus and Robertson, 1974.
Conference-ville. Sydney, Angus and Robertson, 1976.
Tales of Mystery and Romance. London, Angus and Robertson, 1977.
The Everlasting Secret Family and Other Secrets. Sydney and London, Angus and Robertson, 1980.
Selected Stories. Sydney and London, Angus and Robertson, 1982; as *The Coca Cola Kid: Selected Stories,* Sydney, Angus and Robertson, 1985.
Room Service: Comic Writings. Ringwood, Victoria, and London, Penguin, 1985; New York, Penguin, 1987.
Forty-Seventeen. Ringwood, Victoria, Penguin, and London, Faber, 1988; San Diego, Harcourt Brace, 1989.
Lateshows. Sydney, Pan, 1990.

Plays

Screenplays: *Between Wars,* 1974; *The Disappearance of Azaria Chamberlain,* 1984; *Conference-ville,* 1984; *The Coca-Cola Kid,* 1985; *The Everlasting Secret Family,* 1988

Television Plays: *Conference-ville,* 1984; *The Disappearance of Azaria Chamberlain,* 1984; *Time's Raging,* 1985.

Other

Editor, *Coast to Coast.* Sydney, Angus and Robertson, 1973.
Editor, *Days of Wine and Rage.* Ringwood, Victoria, Penguin, 1980.
Editor, *The State of the Art: The Mood of Contemporary Australia in Short Stories.* Ringwood, Victoria, Penguin, 1983.
Editor, *A Steele Rudd Selection: The Best Dad and Dave Stories, with Other Rudd Classics.* St. Lucia, University of Queensland Press, 1986.

*

Manuscript Collections: Fryer Library, University of Queensland, Brisbane; National Library of Australia, Canberra.

Critical Studies: "The Short Stories of Wilding and Moorhouse" by Carl Harrison-Ford, in *Southerly* (Sydney), vol. 33, 1974; "Frank Moorhouse's Discontinuities" by D. Anderson, in *Southerly* (Sydney), vol. 35, 1975; "Some Developments in Short Fiction 1969-80" by Bruce Clunies Ross, in *Australian Literary Studies* (Hobart, Tasmania), vol. 10, no. 2, 1981; interview in *Sideways from the Page* edited by J. Davidson, Melbourne, Fontana, 1983; "The Thinker from the Bush" by Humphrey McQueen, in *Gallipoli to Petrov,* Sydney, Hale and Iremonger, 1984; "Form and Meaning in the Short Stories of Moorhouse" by C. Kanaganayakam, in *World Literature Written in English,* vol. 25, no.1, 1985; interview in *Yacker 3: Australian Writers Talk About Their Work* by Candida Baker, 1989; "The Short Story Cycles of Moorhouse" by Gay Raines, in *Australian Literary Studies,* vol. 14, 1990.

Frank Moorhouse comments:

(1991) *Futility and Other Animals, The Americans, Baby, The Electrical Experience,* and *The Everlasting Secret Family* are described as "discontinuous narratives" and are experiments with interlocked and overlapped short stories. The individual books also overlap and characters recur.

*   *   *

Frank Moorhouse entered Australian fiction during the 1960s speaking a voice politically radical, witty, unabashedly intelligent, and—in a society engaged in widespread censorship—sexually explicit. Moorhouse and his contemporaries took on the hegemony of English culture as it was being played out in not quite postcolonial circumstances. They were a generation who, instead of sailing to London as soon as they were old enough and able, stayed in their homeland and remapped its literary space. At a time when fiction to most Australians meant social realist tales of the bush and rural life, Moorhouse wrote about his countrymen as an urban tribe changed utterly by the Americanization of its culture and by immigration which from World War II onward had altered the ethnic mix. Alert to the fracturing of social certainties, Moorhouse developed the structure he called "discontinuous narrative."

This phrase, the subtitle for his first three books, *Futility and Other Animals, The Americans, Baby,* and *The Electrical Experience,* called attention to the shape which remains characteristic of Moorhouse's fiction. His books of short stories are more cohesive than conventional collections, though their unity is never linear. Within meticulously constructed fictional locales, realistic in their surface detail, episodes are structured. Characters and incidents from one episode may reappear in other stories in the same volume, or turn up years later in some altogether different work. These repetitions are not continuities: Moorhouse's Australia is a world without underlying harmony, a world fragmented and isolating.

Reaction to the first volumes was mixed. Among Australians of Moorhouse's own generation, and those who were younger, were many admirers delighting in an audacity others found shocking and profoundly distasteful, as they did the social changes about which he wrote. In *The Americans, Baby* the milieu is a Sydney under-40 population who, hoping that being earnest or outrageous will make them feel real, are left saturated with anxiety instead. Carl, moving into the arms of the American journalist Paul Jonson, afterwards feels guilty, humiliated, trapped—though he will return. Throughout these stories dramatic tension develops between impulse, figured as sex in various combinations, and an obsessively cerebral approach to life, an approach which suffocates physicality and seems to offer nothing much more appealing than an ideologically correct dinner of baked potatoes with lemon, served in a beautiful dark wooden bowl beside a pile of coarse black bread. Refusing all social pieties, Moorhouse pushes against his audience's expectations of the territory a writer can inhabit while remaining "serious." In the title story of *The Everlasting Secret Family,* a politician who has seduced a schoolboy brings to him years later his own son for initiation into a secret and unrecognized "family." Some readers recoiled from a prose enfusing political allegory with detailed homoeroticism.

Moorhouse is undoubtedly one of Australia's best writers of the erotic; unexpectedly, he is also its most acute observer of bureaucratic forms and process. In *Conference-ville* he uses the conference as a social ritual during which people detached from their ordinary life become vulnerable. *Tales of Mystery and Romance* details the narrator's intricate relationship with a Sydney academic and affords an opportunity to chart university life. The narrator of these collections is so given to ironic detachment, self-deprecation, and world-weariness that the prose was threatened by the enervation portrayed. It is in the League Nations about which Moorhouse writes in *Grand Days* that he finds a bureaucracy and cast of characters sufficiently significant to sustain his focus on the tactics of life as played out in the workings of an organization. In this long novel, a departure in form from the earlier fiction though recognizably evolving from the discontinuous narrative, the young diplomat Edith Campbell Berry—like some American counterpart in a novel by Henry James—brings to Geneva an Australian innocence both attracted to and repelled by what she finds in Europe.

Though *Grand Days* won the South Australian Festival Award, it was judged insufficiently "Australian" to be considered for the important Miles Franklin prize, a decision hotly debated in the literary community and the newspapers. Frank Moorhouse has already won many of the country's most prestigious literary prizes, and his contribution to letters has been recognized in the national honors list by his appointment as a Member of the Order of Australia, perhaps an ironic tribute to a persistently disturbing writer.

—Lucy Frost

MORRIS, Wright (Marion)

Nationality: American. **Born:** Central City, Nebraska, 6 January 1910. **Education:** Lakeview High School, Chicago; Crane College, Chicago; Pomona College, Claremont, California, 1930-33. **Family:** Married 1) Mary Ellen Finfrock in 1934 (divorced 1961); 2) Josephine Kantor in 1961. **Career:** Lecturer at Haverford College, Pennsylvania, Sarah Lawrence College, Bronxville, New York, Swarthmore College, Pennsylvania, Princeton University, New Jersey, 1971-72, and University of Nebraska, Lincoln, 1975; professor of English, California State University, San Francisco, 1962-75. Also a photographer. **Awards:** Guggenheim fellowship, 1942, 1946, 1954; National Book award, 1967; National Endowment for the Arts senior fellowship, 1976, award, 1986; Western Literature Association award, 1979; American Book award, 1981; Commonwealth award, 1982; Whiting award, 1985. Honorary degrees: Westminster College, Fulton, Missouri, 1968; University of Nebraska, Lincoln, 1968; Pomona College, 1973. **Member:** American Academy, 1970. **Address:** c/o Harper Collins, 10 East 53rd Street, New York, New York 10022, U.S.A.

PUBLICATIONS

Novels

My Uncle Dudley. New York, Harcourt Brace, 1942.
The Man Who Was There. New York, Scribner, 1945.
The World in the Attic. New York, Scribner, 1949.
Man and Boy. New York, Knopf, 1951; London, Gollancz, 1952.
The Works of Love. New York, Knopf, 1952.
The Deep Sleep. New York, Scribner, 1953; London, Eyre and Spottiswoode, 1954.
The Huge Season. New York, Viking Press, 1954; London, Secker and Warburg, 1955.
The Field of Vision. New York, Harcourt Brace, 1956; London, Weidenfeld and Nicolson, 1957.
Love among the Cannibals. New York, Harcourt Brace, 1957; London, Weidenfeld and Nicolson, 1958.
Ceremony in Lone Tree. New York, Atheneum, 1960; London, Weidenfeld and Nicolson, 1961.
What a Way to Go. New York, Atheneum, 1962.
Cause for Wonder. New York, Atheneum, 1963.

One Day. New York, Atheneum, 1965.
In Orbit. New York, New American Library, 1967.
Fire Sermon. New York, Harper, 1971.
War Games. Los Angeles, Black Sparrow Press, 1972.
A Life. New York, Harper, 1973.
The Fork River Space Project. New York, Harper, 1977.
Plains Song: For Female Voices. New York, Harper, 1980.

Short Stories

Green Grass, Blue Sky, White House. Los Angeles, Black Sparrow Press, 1970.
Here Is Einbaum. Los Angeles, Black Sparrow Press, 1973.
The Cat's Meow. Los Angeles, Black Sparrow Press, 1975.
Real Losses, Imaginary Gains. New York, Harper, 1976.
The Origin of Sadness. University, Alabama, Parallel Editions, 1984.
Collected Stories 1948-1986. New York, Harper, 1986.

Uncollected Short Story

"Uno más," in *New Yorker,* 6 February 1989.

Other

The Inhabitants (photo-text). New York, Scribner, 1946.
The Home Place (photo-text). New York, Scribner, 1948.
The Territory Ahead (essays). New York, Harcourt Brace, 1958; London, Peter Smith, 1964.
A Bill of Rited, A Bill of Wrongs, A Bill of Goods (essays). New York, New American Library, 1968.
God's Country and My People (photo-text). New York, Harper, 1968.
Wright Morris: A Reader. New York, Harper, 1970.
Love Affair: A Venetian Journal (photo-text). New York, Harper, 1972.
About Fiction: Reverent Reflections on the Nature of Fiction with Irreverent Observations on Writers, Readers, and Other Abuses. New York, Harper, 1975.
Structure and Artifacts: Photographs 1933-1954. Lincoln, Nebraska, Sheldon Memorial Arts Gallery, 1975.
Conversations with Wright Morris: Critical Views and Responses, edited by Robert E. Knoll. Lincoln, University of Nebraska Press, 1977.
Earthly Delights, Unearthly Adornments: American Writers as Image Makers. New York, Harper, 1978.
Will's Boy: A Memoir. New York, Harper, 1981.
Wright Morris (portfolio of photographs). Roslyn Heights, New York, Witkin Berley, 1981.
Picture America, photographs by Jim Alinder. Boston, New York Graphic Society, 1982.
Wright Morris: Photographs and Words, edited by Jim Alinder. Carmel, California, Friends of Photography, 1982.
The Writing of My Uncle Dudley (address). Berkeley, California, Friends of the Bancroft Library, 1982.
Solo: An American Dreamer in Europe 1933-34. New York, Harper, 1983; London, Penquin, 1984.
Time Pieces: The Photographs and Words of Wright Morris (exhibition catalogue). Washington, D.C., Corcoran Gallery, 1983.
A Cloak of Light: Writing My Life. New York, Harper, 1985.
Time Pieces: Photography, Imagination, and Writing. New York, Aperture, 1989.

Writing My Life: An Autobiography. Santa Rosa, California, Black Sparrow Press, 1993.

Editor, *The Mississippi River Reader.* New York, Doubleday, 1962.

*

Manuscript Collection: Bancroft Library, University of California, Berkeley.

Critical Studies: *Wright Morris* by David Madden, New York, Twayne, 1965; *Wright Morris* by Leon Howard, Minneapolis, University of Minnesota Press, 1968; *The Novels of Wright Morris: A Critical Interpretation* (includes bibliography) by G.B. Crump, Lincoln, University of Nebraska Press, 1978; *Wright Morris: Memory and Imagination* by Roy K. Bird, New York, Lang, 1985.

*   *   *

No contemporary American novelist has managed to be so persistently unfashionable as Wright Morris. Despite his many books, and despite both occasional public honors and a continuous critical assent to his talents, intelligence, integrity, and seriousness, he has never commanded a general attention. His work has resisted categories and obvious affiliations, while in its uniqueness it has prevented imitation. Morris is now an undeniable literary fact, without ever having been an event.

It is in part strange that this should be the case, because no other contemporary American novelist has been so diligently or sensitively in touch with the manners, voices, and things of American civilization. Morris's knowledge has led him, however, to an effort which prohibits ideological assertion for the reason that it prevents final judgments. Narrative line in Morris's fiction is seldom forthright. Thematic development is always subject to new doubts and allurements. The prose is elliptical, allusive, punning, to so great an extent as to seem sometimes incapable of statement. Indeed, language itself seems to be for Morris one more of those mysterious objects produced by the American civilization, which is to be explored for the hint of a revelation rather than be exploited. And the individual novels are not even discrete episodes of realization. Morris borrows freely from himself from book to book, reusing not only characters and events but lengthy passages of narration and reflection. He seems to have been long engaged in thinking through a single work—consisting of fiction, photographs, and an amount of literary and cultural criticism—the end of which is not yet in sight.

He has been so engaged for some 50 years and through more than 40 books. In this time his single subject has been American nativity, and, if he has been influenced by any literary or cultural movement, it is the new nationalism which was being predicated in the 1910s and 1920s by Van Wyck Brooks, Lewis Mumford, Waldo Frank, Sherwood Anderson, the photographer Alfred Stieglitz, and others, Brooks had made a case for what he called the "usable past." More particularly, he had called upon American writers and critics to seek their own—American—literary past in such a way as to discover a cultural coherence, in which they then might participate. The invitation had itself become a part of the past by the time that Morris began to write, but he seems to have been impressed by some of the later nationalists, notably James Agee and Walker Evans. In any event, quite like those artists who participated in Brook's enterprise, Morris has made his field of endeavor the American folk past and its relationship to the American present. The subject

is the continuity of the American character, sought in its typicality and in its everydayness.

Despite the continuousness—indeed, the circularity—of effort proposed to Morris by his subject, the subject has also commanded a distinguishable progress in his thinking. He began with a commitment to discovery of the past, and he repeated that commitment without qualification, though with varying kinds of cunning, in the five books which he published in the 1940s. In the first, *My Uncle Dudley,* he composed a narrative which would ironically recapitulate the American past of the middle 19th century. The novel is set in the 1920s. Uncle Dudley and his sidekick, the boy who tells the story, do a stint of vagabondage, which secures its significance because it stimulates pioneering. In this day and age, the pursuit of the frontier must go from west to east, from Los Angeles to Chicago, and the pretense of the vagabonds to a covered wagon is an ancient touring car. They are assaulted on all sides by contemporary materialism, timidity, and restrictiveness, but they thereby are able to prove the value of the older ways and virtues. And they succeed in their pretense until, just like Huckleberry Finn before them, they are incarcerated in a small town in Missouri. In the succeeding books in this period, Morris reversed his strategy for recovery of the past. *My Uncle Dudley* accepts a conventional myth of the older America and imposes it upon the present. The next books—a volume of novellas, two photo-texts, and a novel—have protagonists who, from their vantage in the present, come upon suggestive, buried, and ambiguous mementos of the past. As is usually the case in Morris's work, the locus of the past is the rural or small-town Midwest. The protagonists of these books find a beckoning but elusive vitalism in occasional survivors from the past, and in such artifacts as peeling Mail Pouch signs on old barns, the fading pages of the old mail order catalogue, or an old and sputtering Model T. The process of apprehension is the area of Morris's concern.

This process seems finally, however, to have borne malign implications for Morris. With *The World in the Attic* he began to explore another realization, to the effect that the past was also potentially imprisoning, and the books thereafter become progressively less retrospective. The protagonists are not at home in the present, which is seen to be a spiritual wasteland, but they avoid regressive nostalgia. The intent of the books of the 1950s—novels and one volume of literary criticism—is recovery into the present not of the past but of a native American character, which is seen to be at once conservative, practical, desperate for spiritual liberation, and audacious. Salvation, if there is to be any, is in the occasional gesture on the part of the protagonists which combines past and present, transcending both.

In these books there was an implication of an astonishing persistence of the rural, frontiering American past, symbolized perhaps most aptly by a character who appeared first in *The World in the Attic* and who becomes the protagonist of *Ceremony in Lone Tree.* Tom Scanlon is the one remaining inhabitant of the town of Lone Tree, Nebraska. Lone Tree is a ghost town in which there is a life, which if solitary and ancient is yet imperative.

In likely response to a more anarchic climate in American society, in recent novels Morris has begun to explore still another realization within his general subject. That audacity which had been proposed as one of the resources of heroism in the American character, might well be criminal in this time. In *One Day* he speculates on the native American character as it emerges in the American boy who killed President Kennedy. The novel *In Orbit* speculates, not quite so harshly, on the nativity of those randomly violent American boys who are to be seen crossing the landscape on their motorcycles, in perpetual flight. In still more recent novels, stories, and photo-texts the area of discovery has again been broadened, now to include speculation on the qualities of resiliency or merely quirky defiance that may be the secret direction of seemingly feckless lives in America. In the title story of the collection *Here Is Einbaum* the protagonist survives wars and insults by the stratagem of refusing usual commitments. (In this instance the protagonist, for once, is not a Midwestern American. He is an Austrian-Jewish refugee living in New York, but he is nonetheless clearly related to Morris's usual characters, as may be indicated by the fact that a credible translation of "Einbaum" would be "Lone Tree.") In the paired novels *Fire Sermon* and *A Life,* Morris repeats the plot lineaments of his first novel, *My Uncle Dudley,* but now both the mode and the objects of the defiance which is the old man's legacy to the young boy are more complex and more desperate. Defying God, Heaven, and progress, the old man manages to be murdered by a surviving American Indian. In such seemingly topical novels as *The Fork River Space Project* and *Plains Song: For Female Voices,* which find their subject matters alternately in space landings and in the women's movement, Morris's protagonists again discover the true sources of their defiant knowledge in their inheritance of the rural American past. In the severity and loneliness of that past is the origin of the imaginative independence with which they can confront a crowded and demanding contemporary civilization.

These later novels, too, fail to make final assertions. Like all of Morris's novels, they are populated by characters who confess themselves to be frustrated and bewildered, thereby providing opportunity for other and continuous reaches of realization.

—Marcus Klein

MORRISON, Toni

Nationality: American. **Born:** Chloe Anthony Wofford, Lorain, Ohio, 18 February 1931. **Education:** Howard University, Washington, D.C., B.A. 1953; Cornell University, Ithaca, New York, M.A. 1955. **Family:** Married Harold Morrison in 1958 (divorced 1964); two sons. **Career:** Instructor in English, Texas Southern University, Houston, 1955-57, and Howard University, 1957-64; senior editor, Random House, publishers, New York, 1965-84; associate professor, State University of New York, Purchase, 1971-72; visiting lecturer, Yale University, New Haven, Connecticut, 1976-77, Rutgers University, New Brunswick, New Jersey, 1983-84, and Bard College, Annandale-on-Hudson, New York, 1986-88; Schweitzer Professor of the Humanities, State University of New York, Albany, 1984-89; Regents' Lecturer, University of California, Berkeley, 1987; Santagata Lecturer, Bowdoin College, Brunswick, Maine, 1987. Since 1989 Golheen Professor of the Humanities, Princeton University, New Jersey. **Awards:** American Academy award, 1977; National Book Critics Circle award, 1977; New York State Governor's award, 1985; Book of the Month Club award, 1986; Before Columbus Foundation award, 1988; Robert F. Kennedy award, 1988; Melcher award, 1988; Pulitzer prize, 1988; MLA Commonwealth award in literature, 1989; Nobel prize, 1993, for literature; Pearl Buck award, 1994; Condorcet medal (Paris), 1994; Rhegium Julii prize, 1994, for literature. Honorary degree:

College of Saint Rose, Albany, 1987. **Agent:** International Creative Management, 40 West 57th Street, New York, New York 10019. **Address:** Department of Creative Writing, Princeton University, Princeton, New Jersey 08544, U.S.A.

PUBLICATIONS

Novels

The Bluest Eye. New York, Holt Rinehart, 1970; London, Chatto and Windus, 1980.
Sula. New York, Knopf, and London, Allen Lane, 1974.
Song of Solomon. New York, Knopf, 1977; London, Chatto and Windus, 1978.
Tar Baby. New York, Knopf, and London, Chatto and Windus, 1981.
Beloved. New York, Knopf, and London, Chatto and Windus, 1987.
Jazz. New York, Knopf, and London, Chatto and Windus, 1992.

Play

Dreaming Emmett (produced Albany, New York, 1986).

Other

Playing in the Dark: Whiteness and the Literary Imagination. Cambridge, Massachusetts, and London, Harvard University Press, 1992.
Conversations with Toni Morrison, edited by Danille Taylor-Guthrie. Jackson, University Press of Mississippi, 1994.
Lecture and Speech of Acceptance upon the Award of the Nobel Prize for Literature. London, Chatto and Windus, 1994.

Editor, *Race-ing Justice, En-gendering Power: Essays on Anita Hill, Clarence Thomas, and the Construction of Social Reality.* New York, Pantheon, 1992; London, Chatto and Windus, 1993.

Bibliography: *Toni Morrison: An Annotated Bibliography* by David L. Middleton, New York, Garland, 1987.

Critical Studies: *New Dimensions of Spirituality: A Biracial and Bicultural Reading of the Novels of Toni Morrison* by Karla F.C. Holloway, Westport, Connecticut, Greenwood Press, 1987; *The Crime of Innocence in the Fiction of Toni Morrison* by Terry Otten, Columbia, University of Missouri Press, 1989; *Toni Morrison* by Wilfred D. Samuels and Clenora Hudson-Weems, Boston, Twayne, 1990; *Toni Morrison* edited by Harold Bloom, Chelsea House, 1990; *Fiction and Folklore: The Novels of Toni Morrison* by Trudier Harris, Knoxville, University of Tennessee Press, 1991; *Folk Roots and Mythic Wings in Sarah Orne Jewett and Toni Morrison: The Cultural Function of Narrative* by Marilyn Sanders Mobley, Baton Rouge and London, Louisiana State University Press, 1991; *Toni Morrison's Developing Class Consciousness* by Doreatha Drummond Mbalia, Selinsgrove, Susquehanna University Press, and London, Associated University Presses, 1991; *The Voices of Toni Morrison* by Barbara Hill Rigney, Columbus, Ohio State University Press, 1991; *The Novels of Toni Morrison: The Search for Self and Place Within the Community* by Patrick Bryce Bjork, New

York, Lang, 1992; *The Dilemma of "Double-Consciousness": Toni Morrison's Novels* by Denise Heinze, Athens and London, University of Georgia Press, 1993; *Toni Morrison: Critical Perspectives Past and Present* edited by Henry Louis Gates Jr. and K.A. Appiah, New York, Amistad, 1993; *Toni Morrison* by Douglas Century, New York, Chelsea House, 1994; *Bridging the Americas: The Literature of Paule Marshall, Toni Morrison, and Gayl Jones* by Stelamaris Coser, Philadelphia, Temple University Press, 1994; *A World of Difference: An Inter-Cultural Study of Toni Morrison's Novels* by Wendy Harding and Jacky Martin, Westport, Greenwood Press, 1994.

*		*		*

A comparison of Toni Morrison with Joyce and Faulkner is irresistible. One dominant aspect of her work is an exhaustive, mythical exploration of place. Another is the search for the nexus of past and present. She is to the black milieu of Lorain what Joyce and Faulkner are to Dublin and Oxford, and her Medallion is as curiously fascinating as Anderson's Winesburg. Her stories translate a multiplicity of places, often superficially tawdry, into a rich cultural matrix. Likewise, the times of her forebears and herself in Ohio are a duration, not a chronology. She thus makes the legendary altogether new, and discovers in colloquial habit and naming the altogether legendary. Legend includes not only the tales of her black folk, but the myths of world literature. She has excluded Caucasians from her fiction more than Joyce and Faulkner have excluded ethnic "others" from theirs. But her focus on personality and character (in the moral sense) is indisputably universal. Her pervasive irony and paradox are not merely adroit but ethically motivated. At times they accentuate an erosion of the dignified, reliable courtlines of ancestral blacks, the more profound because it was maintained through the grossest depredations in American history. She is able to say of her contemporaries: "We raised our children and reared our crops; we let infants grow, and property develop." It is a deep regard for craft—for verbal nuance, metaphor image, point of view—that enables Morrison not merely to discourse upon but to animate social process and existential crisis.

The Bluest Eye tells of the incestuous rape of 11-year-old Pecola Breedlove by her father. The girl's need to be loved (pushed to the extreme when she observes her mother, a "domestic," heaping upon a little white girl affections Pecola has only dreamed of) takes the doomed form of a yearning for blue eyes. The insanity of this flight from reality comes to fruition after the death of the baby, when she actually believes herself to have acquired them. With her ubiquitous metaphor of flight, Morrison sums up this personal fate and the novel's powerful theme:

> The damage was total. She spent her days . . . walking up and down, up and down, her head jerking to the beat of a drummer so distant only she could hear. Elbows bent, hands on shoulders, she flailed her arms like a bird in an eternal, grotesquely futile effort to fly. Beating the air, a winged but grounded bird, intent on the blue void it could not reach—could not even see—but which filled the valleys of the mind.

We are led to conclude that the narrator, Claudia Macteer, and her sister Frieda probably dodged this perversion by directing an ordinate malice at their Shirley Temple dolls and by being born to a family that, though rough and austere, did know how to breed love.

Sula explores equally an extraordinary consciousness and the gap between generations. Sula Mae Peace and her grandmother, Eva, share a great deal in common. Both left the same home in Medallion's "Bottom" only to return and inhabit it in willful isolation. Both shun tender expressions of love. Both have authored another's death. But in her indifference to family bonds, Sula is her grandmother's opposite. Where Eva left to save her family, Sula left to indulge her fancy. Where Eva returned for her children (though only content alone on the second floor), Sula returned from boredom and put her grandmother in a home. Where Eva, with tragic awareness, ignited her son's drug-addicted body, Sula dropped the little boy "Chicken" to his death with a weird inadvertence. And where Eva maimed herself trying to save her flaming daughter Hannah, Sula watched her mother's immolation with distant curiosity.

Yet this portrait is not simply a paean to the old ways. There is sympathy for Sula because as a child she had misconceived Hannah's remark about her, "I love her, I just don't like her," and because of her vain effort to save "Chicken." Of that the narrator remarks that it has exorcised "her one major feeling of responsibility." Moreover, her temperament blends "Eva's arrogance and Hannah's self indulgence" in an "experimental life" which itself seems a precondition for seeing and acting upon hard social truths. And finally, she seems like Pecola Breedlove, whose "guilt" mysteriously sanctified those around her. Sula performs the original Eve's purpose; as a community "witch," she provides others with a scapegoat, a model of such evil conduct that their own is actually elevated thereby.

Song of Solomon is a work of enormous breadth. Macon and Ruth Dead complete an often devastating characterization of genteel blacks begun with Geraldine and Helene in the earlier novels. Self-serving and cool, their son "Milkman" has given full life to the family name. Burdened by his parents' merciless marriage and prompted by his saintly aunt, Pilate, he sets out for Virginia and the skeletons in his family closet. But lore steadily leads and yields to more interesting truth, in the form of persons who correct his myopic view. He discovers his dead grandmother, Sing, so called because she was half Indian, Singing Bird, but also the daughter of a white Virginian named Byrd. And he discovers his great-grandfather, Solomon, who once proudly flew the coop of slavery and about whom the country black kids still sing: "O Solomon don't leave me." Song and flight make life endurable and beautiful in Morrison's world. Having discovered these true ancestors, Milkman forgets the mundane, taking his best friend Guitar's advice to heart: "[If you] wanna fly, you got to give up the shit that weighs you down." The murderous conflict that had developed between the two (Guitar is a consummate study of an extremist racial approach toward which the novel displays both sympathy and disgust) is ended: "For now [Milkman] knew what Shalimar knew: If you surrendered to the air, you could *ride* it."

The design of *Tar Baby,* so allegorical and symbolic, probably overextends the mythic note of *Song of Solomon.* Folk legend is provided by the title, but elsewhere little is quite so down to earth and the supporting realism is undercut by both the fabulous Haitian settings and Morrison's anthropomorphizing of them. The key figures are Jadine and Son. Their union and divorce embody a black man's search for an authentic, natural past and a black woman's estrangement from it. Committed to materialistic white values, she ends by fondling her sealskin coat. He ends, more unbelievably than the airborne Milkman, by entering a jungle so humanoid that it "make[s] the way easier for a certain kind of man," Morrison's archetype.

Beloved, properly, earned Morrison the Pulitzer prize. The plot entails the struggle of Sethe (Suggs), from the summer of 1873 to the spring of 1874, to bear the resurgent impact of her past, particularly the moment 18 years earlier when she had drawn a handsaw across the throat of her baby girl, named Beloved. She had done so rather than hand the child and her siblings to a vicious plantation manager who had come to Cincinnati, in the name of the "Fugitive Bill," for the family of escaped Kentucky slaves. Once again using magic realism, Morrison simply allows the child's ghost to cross back into her mother's world, in the form of a living and troubled young woman. Readers will struggle to see it otherwise, but this seems the only viable interpretation of the latter-day Beloved. The plot moves constantly between the present in a spuriously free North and an exactingly drawn past in the South before the Civil War. The detail Morrison provides here about plantation existence for slaves, chain gang existence for black convicts, and the terrors of the runaway's passage to freedom is potently authentic. But all is cast in the most lyrical of her fictions to date.

—David M. Heaton

MORTIMER, John (Clifford)

Nationality: British. **Born:** Hampstead, London, 21 April 1923. **Education:** Harrow School, Middlesex, 1937-40; Brasenose College, Oxford, 1940-42, B.A. 1947; called to the bar, 1948; Queen's Counsel, 1966; Master of the Bench, Inner Temple, 1975. **Military Service:** Served with the Crown Film Units as scriptwriter during World War II. **Family:** Married 1) Penelope Dimont (i.e., Penelope Mortimer, *q.v.*) in 1949 (divorced 1971), one son and one daughter; 2) Penny Gollop in 1972, one daughter. **Career:** drama critic, *New Statesman, Evening Standard,* and *Observer,* 1972, all London; member of the National Theatre Board, 1968-88; president, Berkshire, Buckinghamshire, and Oxford Naturalists' Trust, from 1984; chairman, League of Dramatists; chairman of the council, Royal Society of Literature for 1989; chairman, Royal Court Theatre since 1990; president, Howard League for Penal Reform since 1991; chairman, the Royal Society of Literature since 1992. Lives in Henley-on-Thames, Oxfordshire. **Awards:** Italia prize, for radio play, 1958; Screenwriters Guild award, for television play, 1970; BAFTA award, for television series, 1980; *Yorkshire Post* award, 1983. D. Litt.: Susquehanna University, Selinsgrove, Pennsylvania, 1985; University of St. Andrews, Fife, 1987; University of Nottingham, 1989; LL.D.: Exeter University, 1986. C.B.E. (Commander, Order of the British Empire), 1986. **Agent:** Peters Fraser and Dunlop, 503-504 The Chambers, Chelsea Harbour, Lots Road, London SW10 0XF, England.

PUBLICATIONS

Novels

Charade. London, Lane, 1948.
Rumming Park. London, Lane, 1948.
Answer Yes or No. London, Lane, 1950; as *The Silver Hook,* New York, Morrow, 1950.

Like Men Betrayed. London, Collins, 1953; Philadelphia, Lippincott, 1954.
The Narrowing Stream. London, Collins, 1954; New York, Viking, 1989.
Three Winters. London, Collins, 1956.
Will Shakespeare: The Untold Story. London, Hodder and Stoughton, 1977; New York, Delacorte Press, 1978.
Paradise Postponed. London and New York, Viking, 1985.
Summer's Lease. London and New York, Viking, 1988.
Titmuss Regained. London and New York, Viking, 1990.
Dunster. London and New York, Viking Penguin, 1992.

Short Stories

Rumpole. London, Allen Lane, 1980.
Rumpole of the Bailey. London, Penguin, 1978; New York, Penguin, 1980.
The Trials of Rumpole. London, Penguin, 1979; New York, Penguin, 1981.
Regina v. Rumpole. London, Allen Lane, 1981.
Rumpole's Return. London, Penguin, 1980; New York, Penguin, 1982.
Rumpole for the Defence. London, Penguin, 1982.
Rumpole and the Golden Thread. New York, Penguin, 1983.
The First Rumpole Omnibus (includes *Rumpole of the Bailey, The Trials of Rumpole, Rumpole's Return*). London, Penguin, 1983.
Rumpole's Last Case. London, Penguin, 1987; New York, Penguin, 1988.
The Second Rumpole Omnibus (includes *Rumpole for the Defence, Rumpole and the Golden Thread, Rumpole's Last Case*). London, Viking, 1987; New York, Penguin, 1988.
Rumpole and the Age of Miracles. London, Penguin, 1988; New York, Penguin, 1989.
Rumpole à la Carte. London and New York, Viking Penguin, 1990.
Rumpole on Trial. London and New York, Viking Penguin, 1992.
The Best of Rumpole. London and New York, Viking Penguin, 1993.

Plays

The Dock Brief (broadcast 1957; produced London, 1958; New York, 1961). In *Three Plays,* 1958.
I Spy (broadcast 1957; produced Salisbury, Wiltshire, and Palm Beach, Florida, 1959). In *Three Plays,* 1958.
What Shall We Tell Caroline? (produced London, 1958; New York, 1961). In *Three Plays,* 1958.
Three Plays: The Dock Brief, What Shall We Tell Caroline?, I Spy. London, Elek, 1958; New York, Grove Press, 1962.
Call Me a Liar (televised 1958; produced London, 1968). In *Lunch Hour and Other Plays,* 1960; in *The Television Playwright: Ten Plays for B.B.C. Television,* edited by Michael Barry, New York, Hill and Wang, 1960.
Sketches in *One to Another* (produced London, 1959). London, French, 1960.
The Wrong Side of the Park (produced London, 1960). London, Heinemann, 1960.
Lunch Hour (broadcast 1960; produced Salisbury, Wiltshire, 1960; London, 1961; New York, 1977). In *Lunch Hour and Other Plays* 1960; published separately, New York, French, 1961.
David and Broccoli (televised 1960). In *Lunch Hour and Other Plays,* 1960.

Lunch Hour and Other Plays (includes *Collect Your Hand Baggage, David and Broccoli, Call Me a Liar*). London, Methuen, 1960.

Collect Your Hand Baggage (produced Wuppertal, Germany, 1963). In *Lunch Hour and Other Plays,* 1960.

Sketches in *One over the Eight* (produced London, 1961).

Two Stars for Comfort (produced London, 1962). London, Methuen, 1962.

A Voyage round My Father (broadcast 1963; produced London, 1970). London, Methuen, 1971.

Sketches in *Changing Gear* (produced Nottingham, 1965).

A Flea in Her Ear, adaptation of a play by Feydeau (produced London, 1966; Tucson, Arizona, 1979). London and New York, French, 1967.

A Choice of Kings (televised 1966). In *Playbill Three,* edited by Alan Durband, London, Hutchinson, 1969.

The Judge (produced London, 1967). London, Methuen, 1967.

Desmond (televised 1968). In *The Best Short Plays 1971,* edited by Stanley Richards, Philadelphia, Chilton, 1971.

Cat Among the Pigeons, adaptation of a play by Feydeau (produced London, 1969; Milwaukee, 1971). New York, French, 1970.

Come As You Are: Four Short Plays (includes *Mill Hill, Bermondsey, Gloucester Road, Marble Arch*) (produced London, 1970). London, Methuen, 1971.

Five Plays (includes *The Dock Brief, What Shall We Tell Caroline?, I Spy, Lunch Hour, Collect Your Hand Baggage*). London, Methuen, 1970.

The Captain of Köpenick, adaptation of a play by Carl Zuckmayer (produced London, 1971). London, Methuen, 1971.

Conflicts, with others (produced London, 1971).

I, Claudius, adaptation of the novels *I, Claudius* and *Claudius the God* by Robert Graves (produced London, 1972).

Knightsbridge (televised 1972). London, French, 1973.

Collaborators (produced London, 1973). London, Eyre Methuen, 1973.

The Fear of Heaven (as *Mr. Lucy's Fear of Heaven,* broadcast 1976; as *The Fear of Heaven,* produced with *The Prince of Darkness* as *Heaven and Hell,* London, 1976). London, French, 1978.

Heaven and Hell (includes *The Fear of Heaven* and *The Prince of Darkness*) (produced London, 1976; revised version of *The Prince of Darkness,* as *The Bells of Hell* produced Richmond, Surrey, and London, 1977). *The Bells of Hell* published London, French, 1978.

The Lady from Maxim's, adaptation of a play by Feydeau (produced London, 1977). London, Heinemann, 1977.

John Mortimer's Casebook (includes *The Dock Brief, The Prince of Darkness, Interlude*) (produced London, 1982).

When That I Was (produced Ottawa, 1982).

Edwin (broadcast 1982). In *Edwin and Other Plays,* 1984.

A Little Hotel on the Side, adaptation of a play by Feydeau and Maurice Desvalliers (produced London, 1984). In *Three Boulevard Farces,* 1985.

Edwin and Other Plays (includes *Bermondsey, Marble Arch, The Fear of Heaven, The Prince of Darkness*). London, Penguin, 1984.

Three Boulevard Farces (includes *A Little Hotel on the Side, A Flea in Her Ear, The Lady from Maxim's*). London, Penguin, 1985.

Die Fledermaus, adaptation of the libretto by Henri Meihac and Ludovic Halévy, music by Johann Stauss (produced London, 1989). London, Viking, 1989.

A Christmas Carol, adaptation of the novel by Charles Dickens (produced London, 1994).

Screenplays: *Ferry to Hong Kong,* with Lewis Gilbert and Vernon Harris, 1959; *The Innocents,* with Truman Capote and William Archibald, 1961; *Guns of Darkness,* 1962; *I Thank a Fool,* with others, 1962; *Lunch Hour,* 1962; *The Running Man,* 1963; *Bunny Lake Is Missing,* with Penelope Mortimer, 1964; *A Flea in Her Ear,* 1967; *John and Mary,* 1969.

Radio Plays: *Like Men Betrayed,* 1955; *No Hero,* 1955; *The Dock Brief,* 1957; *I Spy,* 1957; *Three Winters,* 1958; *Lunch Hour,* 1960; *The Encyclopedist,* 1961; *A Voyage round My Father,* 1963; *Personality Split,* 1964; *Education of an Englishman,* 1964; *A Rare Device,* 1965; *Mr. Luby's Fear of Heaven,* 1976; *Edwin,* 1982; *Rumpole,* from his own stories, 1988; *Glasnost,* 1988.

Television Plays: *Call Me a Liar,* 1958; *David and Broccoli,* 1960; *A Choice of Kings,* 1966; *The Exploding Azalea,* 1966; *The Head Waiter,* 1966; *Hughie,* 1967; *The Other Side,* 1967; *Desmond,* 1968; *Infidelity Took Place,* 1968; *Married Alive,* 1980; *Swiss Cottage,* 1972; *Knightsbridge,* 1972; *Rumpole of the Bailey,* 1975, and series, 1978, 1979, 1987, 1988; *A Little Place off the Edgware Road, The Blue Film, The Destructors, The Case for the Defence, Chagrin in Three Parts, The Invisible Japanese Gentlemen, Special Duties,* and *Mortmain,* all from stories by Graham Greene, 1975-76; *Will Shakespeare,* 1978; *Rumpole's Return,* 1980; *Unity,* from the book by David Pryce-Jones, 1981; *Brideshead Revisited,* from the novel by Evelyn Waugh 1981; *Edwin,* 1984; *The Ebony Tower,* from the story by John Fowles, 1984; *Paradise Postponed,* from his own novel, 1986; *Summer's Lease,* from his own novel, 1989; *The Waiting Room,* 1989.

Other

No Moaning of the Bar (as Geoffrey Lincoln). London, Bles, 1957.

With Love and Lizards (travel), with Penelope Mortimer. London, Joseph, 1957.

Clinging to the Wreckage: A Part of Life (autobiography). London, Weidenfeld and Nicolson, and New Haven, Connecticut, Ticknor and Fields, 1982.

Murderers and Other Friends (autobiography). London and New York, Viking Penguin, 1994.

In Character (interviews). London, Allen Lane, 1983.

The Liberty of the Citizen (lecture), with Franklin Thomas and Lord Hunt of Tanworth. London, Granada, 1983.

Character Parts (interviews). London, Viking, 1986.

Editor, *Famous Trials,* edited by Harry Hodge and James H. Hodge. London, Viking, and New York, Penguin, 1984.

Editor, *Great Law and Order Stories.* London, Bellew, 1990.

*

Manuscript Collections: Boston University; University of California, Los Angeles.

*   *   *

John Mortimer's work as a playwright, novelist, and television scriptwriter has made him one of England's best-known living authors. The "Rumpole of the Bailey" stories, inspired by his own experience as a barrister, are enormously popular both in print and on the screen. Mortimer is also known for his autobiographical television drama, *A Voyage round My Father,* and for his adaptation of Evelyn Waugh's *Brideshead Revisited.* In recent years he has returned to the novel form with *Paradise Postponed, Summer's Lease, Titmuss Regained,* and *Dunster,* all well received and either already adapted or likely to be adapted for television. Mortimer's engaging personality, which so frequently reveals itself in the figure of Horace Rumpole, may make readers predisposed in favor of his work, for whatever the genre or medium Mortimer has been consistently praised both by the critics and the public.

In his earlier days, while still an active barrister, Mortimer wrote two novels which did not attract much attention: *Like Men Betrayed,* the story of a London solicitor whose son has misappropriated a client's investments, and *The Narrowing Stream* in which a young woman's murder disrupts the lives of an ordinary family. Both novels take a characteristically perceptive view of English life and have many of the themes Mortimer would develop to better effect in his later novels.

Inspired perhaps by Evelyn Waugh's criticism of English society, Mortimer attempted his own novel of manners in *Paradise Postponed.* Using many of the conventions of Victorian and Edwardian novels, though with telling variations, Mortimer deftly weaves throughout his story sharp observations on the state of postwar England. When the revered Rector of Rapstone Fanner, Simeon Simcox, dies leaving his entire estate to Leslie Titmuss, Conservative M.P. from Rapstone, his widow and his two sons attempt to understand their father's surprising bequest. Mortimer traces the story of the Simcox, Titmuss, and Fanner families, moving back and forth in time until at last family secrets are revealed and the inheritance explained.

Along the way, Mortimer draws on familiar features from earlier English novels, from the idealistic village Rector (reminiscent of Trollope's Septimus Harding) to any of Dickens's accounts of lower-class boys striving for acceptance in high society. In *Paradise Postponed,* however, the characters break their stereotypes. The seeming innocence of the rector is qualified at the end, and the working lad, Titmuss, at first treated sympathetically, proves to be utterly without scruple as he marries his way into the best family of the village on his climb up the ranks of the Thatcher government. Mortimer's own political leanings come through clearly. The leftists in the novel may be muddled and ineffective, but they are never as mean-spirited as their right-wing opponents.

Following the success of *Paradise Postponed* and responding to the public's interest in the character of Leslie Titmuss, Mortimer continued his story in *Titmuss Regained.* Now a conservative government minister, Titmuss purchases the very Fanner Manor where his mother had worked as a servant and which in the earlier novel had represented unattainable social preeminence. But corporate developers are determined to reconstruct the village into a real estate agent's version of English rustic life. Mortimer is at his best describing the various factions involved in promoting or opposing the enterprise: developers, environmentalists, local politicians, even the villagers themselves—all are shown to be self-serving hypocrites. While his portrait of this cluster of peripheral characters is bitingly satiric, Mortimer is somewhat easier on his hero, and in his efforts to make his second marriage a success, he even wins back a measure of the sympathy we felt for Titmuss as a child in *Paradise Postponed.*

In *Summer's Lease* Mortimer draws on themes of the English abroad he had found in *Brideshead Revisited.* The setting is Tuscany, where an English family has leased a villa for the summer. The wife, Molly Pargenter, is determined to investigate the mysterious absence of their landlord, uncovering a complex web of relationships in which her family becomes entangled. As she comes to terms with what is happening around her, she is forced as well to fight to save her own integrity and her marriage. Her father-in-law's irresponsible nonchalance beautifully contrasts Molly's determination to understand and control her life. While Mortimer's focus is still on English character types, the Italian surroundings depict those traits in sharper focus.

An incident involving English officers in Italy during World War II plays a role in Mortimer's latest book, *Dunster,* but the core of the novel is the relationship between the narrator, Philip Progmire, an accountant and amateur actor, and his old school nemesis, Richard Dunster, now a producer of television documentaries. The determined and dynamic but ruthless Dunster has accused Progmire's employer of a war crime, prompting a libel suit. Mortimer explores the comic effects of the contrast between Progmire and Dunster, though the reader may be too sympathetic to the long-suffering narrator to enjoy the humor. The conclusion of the war-crime plot, that even the best and the brightest are potential war criminals, may be too unsettling for what is essentially a comic novel.

Mortimer's view of humankind is rarely comforting, but he manages to show us our worst side without condemning us. Like his Horace Rumpole, who has no romantic illusions about the criminals he defends, Mortimer is simultaneously harsh and forgiving. The first quality gives his work its import, the latter its appeal.

—Robert E. Lynch

MORTIMER, Penelope

Nationality: British. **Born:** Penelope Ruth Fletcher, Rhyl, Flint, 19 September 1918. **Education:** Croydon High School; New School, Streatham; Blencathra, Rhyl; Garden School, London; St. Elphin's Clergy Daughters School; Central Educational Bureau for Women; University College, London. **Family:** Married 1) Charles Dimont in 1937 (divorced 1949), four daughters; 2) John Mortimer, *q.v.,* in 1949 (divorced 1971), one son and one daughter. **Career:** Freelance writer and journalist; movie critic, the *Observer,* London, 1967-70. **Awards:** Whitbread award, for nonfiction, 1979. Fellow, Royal Society of Literature. **Agent:** Sheil Land Associates, 43 Doughty Street, London WC1N 2LF, England.

PUBLICATIONS

Novels

Johanna (as Penelope Dimont). London, Secker and Warburg, 1947.
A Villa in Summer. London, Joseph, 1954; New York, Harcourt Brace, 1955.
The Bright Prison. London, Joseph, 1956; New York, Harcourt Brace, 1957.
Daddy's Gone A-Hunting. London, Joseph, 1958; as *Cave of Ice,* New York, Harcourt Brace, 1959.

The Pumpkin Eater, London, Hutchinson, 1962; New York, McGraw Hill, 1963.
My Friend Says It's Bullet-Proof. London, Hutchinson, 1967; New York, Random House, 1968.
The Home. London, Hutchinson, 1971; New York, Random House, 1972.
Long Distance. London, Allen Lane, and New York, Doubleday, 1974.
The Handyman. London, Allen Lane, 1983; New York, St. Martin's Press, 1985.

Short Stories

Saturday Lunch with the Brownings. London, Hutchinson, 1960; New York, McGraw Hill, 1961.

Uncollected Short Stories

"Philpot," in *New Yorker,* 25 August 1962.
"The Skylight," in *Tales of Unease,* edited by John Burke. London, Pan, 1966; New York, Doublday, 1969.
"Love Story," in *New Yorker,* 15 July 1974.
"Curriculum Vitae," in *New Yorker,* 26 May 1975.
"In the First Place," in *New Yorker,* 22 December 1975.
"Granger's Life So Far," in *New Yorker,* 22 December 1976.
"Diver," in *Encounter* (London), February 1978.

Plays

Screenplays: *Bunny Lake Is Missing,* with John Mortimer, 1965; *A Summer Story,* 1988.

Television Plays: *The Renegade,* from her own story, 1961; *Ain't Afraid to Dance,* 1966; *Three's One,* 1973; *Portrait of a Marriage,* from the biography by Nigel Nicolson, 1990.

Other

With Love and Lizards (travel), with John Mortimer. London, Joseph, 1957.
About Time: An Aspect of Autobiography. London, Allen Lane, and New York, Doubleday, 1979.
Queen Elizabeth: A Life of the Queen Mother. London, Viking, 1986; as *A Portrait of the Queen Mother,* New York, St. Martin's Press, 1986.
About Time Too. London, Neidenfeld and Nicolson, 1994.

*

Manuscript Collection: Mugar Memorial Library, Boston University.

Penelope Mortimer comments:

(1972) My father was a C. of E. clergyman and I was brought up in Buckinghamshire, Thornton Health, and Belper in Derbyshire. For various reasons (my father's changing theories as well as residences) I went to seven schools, ending up at a School for the Daughters of the Clergy. Did a secretarial course in London at the age of 17, hated it, went to London University, left after a year because my father said he was broke, took a job as a secretary to the Publicity Manager of Butlins Holiday Camp, decided after three weeks that marriage was preferable, married, had four children, wrote the odd piece for the *New Statesman* and *Our Time* and spent four years writing *Johanna,* which sank like a stone in 1947.

As well as the eight books and two Mortimer children, I wrote a lot for the *New Yorker,* did fiction reviews for the *Sunday Times,* wrote a Lonely Hearts column under the pseudonym of Ann Temple for the *Daily Mail,* and did a considerable amount of other journalism.

The canvas of my fiction is narrow—domestic, mainly concerned with sexual and parental relationships—but I hope makes up in depth what it lacks in breadth. So far, I am almost entirely concerned with individuals, motives (i.e., what "makes them tick") and the development of their personalities from an early age (*Pumpkin Eater* and *The Home* particularly). Rather obviously (though not necessarily) I write through the eyes and ears of a woman. My men, I think, are getting better, and maybe I will someday venture to try to put myself inside a man's head and write from there. I believe that comedy is absolutely essential to tragedy, and I hope my books are almost as funny as they are (I'm told) sad or depressing. I would like to enlarge my scope, but not if it's at the expense of depth. Once my characters are established psychologically—heredity, environment, the lot—they take over their own growth and perform their own actions; I have very little to do with it.

*   *   *

The themes of popular fiction remain what they have always been: sex and marriage, class, money, and power. What has changed is the writer's attitude towards this material. A Victorian novel in this genre ended with a wedding; nowadays the plot tends to begin with an unhappy marriage, trace the course of the more or less unhappy affairs and end where it began, in sexual stalemate.

Of the many English novelists who have explored this territory, none has more sheer ability to write than Penelope Mortimer. She catalogues the debris of failure: the repetitive rows, the broken resolutions, the betrayals which would exact revenge had they not paralyzed their victim. In each book the central relationship is destructive; only the children survive: "sitting in a patient row on the sofa . . . their eyes restless as maggots, expecting us to bring them up." This description from *The Pumpkin Eater* is an example of her writing at its best, candid and original.

A Villa in Summer is an accomplished study of corruption, a portrait of a couple who cling together out of habit as much as out of love. Emily has drifted so far from her husband that he feels "there were two species: Emily and women." Their marriage is vulnerable enough and easily shaken by a predatory pair of adulterers, teachers from the local progressive school.

Emily is the first in a string of lost innocents, heroines who are aware of the truth but unable to act on it. The central character in *Daddy's Gone A-Hunting* is shut off from potential pleasure, experiencing life in waves of guilt and pain. She cannot use her suffering to change her own situation but is able to protect her daughter against their common enemy, Rex, the unfaithful husband and callous father. Rex is typical of the men in Mortimer's fiction, drifting in and out of the story, excluded, pacified, accused. Only occasionally does the implicit violence break through into an open declaration of war. "A man has to be drunk, insane or unbalanced by talent before he'll behave like a woman," comments the heroine of *The Pumpkin Eater,* begging an awful lot of questions.

It is ironic that Mortimer has been both praised and criticized for her analysis of modern marriage. She keeps a witty and compassionate eye on that institution, it is true, but her observations do not set out to be objective. She is not a satirist, nor does her writing reflect the struggles of that old phenomenon, the new woman. Society is of secondary importance in her novels, which are intense, imaginative explorations of an inner world. It is an enclosed world, dominated by fear, in which physical experiences such as sterilization and abortion isolate her characters from their fellow beings and are metaphors for a deeper spiritual isolation. More recent work shows an intensification of this mood. *My Friend Says It's Bullet-Proof* and *The Home* are about women at the edge, held from destruction by an obsessive need to record and understand their own despair.

—Judy Cooke

MOSLEY, Nicholas

Nationality: British. **Born:** Lord Ravensdale in London, 25 June 1923; eldest son of Sir Oswald Mosley; became 3rd Baron Ravensdale, 1966; succeeded to the baronetcy of his father, 1980. **Education:** Eton College, Berkshire, 1937-42; Ballio College, Oxford, 1946-47. **Military Service:** Served in the Rifle Brigade, 1942-46; Captain; Military Cross, 1944. **Family:** Married 1) Rosemary Laura Salmond in 1947 (marriage dissolved 1974), three sons and one daughter; 2) Verity Elizabeth Bailey in 1974, one son. **Awards:** Whitbread Book of the Year award, 1990. **Address:** 2 Gloucester Cresent, London NW1 7DS, England.

PUBLICATIONS

Novels

Spaces of the Dark. London, Hart Davis, 1951.
The Rainbearers. London, Weidenfeld and Nicolson, 1955.
Corruption. London, Weidenfeld and Nicolson, 1957; Boston, Little Brown, 1958.
Meeting Place. London, Weidenfeld and Nicolson, 1962.
Accident. London, Hodder and Stoughton, 1965; New York, Coward McCann, 1966.
Assassins. London, Hodder and Stoughton, 1966; New York, Coward McCann, 1967; revised edition, London, Minerva, 1993.
Impossible Object. London, Hodder and Stoughton, and New York, Coward McCann, 1969; revised edition, London, Minerva, 1993.
Natalie Natalia. London, Hodder and Stoughton, and New York, Coward McCann, 1971.
Catastrophe Practice: Plays for Not Acting, and *Cypher: A Novel* (includes *Skylight, Landfall, Cell*). London, Secker and Warburg, 1979; Elmwood Park, Illinois, Dalkey Archive Press, 1989; revised edition, London, Minerva, 1992.
Imago Bird. London, Secker and Warburg, 1980; Elmwood Park, Illinois, Dalkey Archive Press, 1989; revised edition, London, Minerva, 1991.
Serpent. London, Secker and Warburg, 1981; Elmwood Park, Illinois, Dalkey Archive Press, 1990; revised edition, London, Minerva, 1992.

Judith. London, Secker and Warburg, 1986; Elmwood Park, Illinois, Dalkey Archive Press, 1991.
Hopeful Monsters. London, Secker and Warburg, 1990; Elmwood Park, Illinois, Dalkey Archive Press, 1991.
Efforts at Truth. London, Secker and Warburg, 1994.

Plays

Screenplays: *The Assassination of Trotsky,* with Masolini d'Amico, 1972; *Impossible Object,* 1975.

Other

Life Drawing, with John Napper. London, Studio, 1954.
African Switchback (travel). London, Weidenfeld and Nicolson, 1958.
The Life of Raymond Raynes. London, Faith Press, 1961.
Experience and Religion: A Lay Essay in Theology. London, Hodder and Stoughton, 1965; Philadelphia, United Church Press, 1967.
The Assassination of Trotsky. London, Joseph, 1972.
Julian Grenfell: His Life and the Times of His Death 1888-1915. London, Weidenfeld and Nicolson, and New York, Holt Rinehart, 1976.
Rules of the Game: Sir Oswald and Lady Cynthia Mosley 1896-1933. London, Secker and Warburg, 1982; with *Beyond the Pale,* Elmwood Park, Illinois, Dalkey Archive Press, 1991.
Beyond the Pale: Sir Oswald Mosley and Family 1933-1980. London, Secker and Warburg, 1983; with *Rules of the Game,* Elmwood Park, Illinois, Dalkey Archive Press, 1991.

Editor, *The Faith: Instructions on the Christian Faith,* by Raymond Raynes. London, Faith Press, 1961.

*

Critical Studies: "Nicholas Mosley Issue" of *Review of Contemporary Fiction* (Elmwood Park, Illinois), vol. 2, no. 2, 1982.

Nicholas Mosley comments:
   My novels are attempts to see how life works: I hope to learn from them.

*   *   *

Since 1951 Nicholas Mosley has published 13 novels as well as a miscellaneous assortment of other books, notably biographies, and although his fiction has not won widespread popularity or much academic recognition, he is acknowledged in the literary world to be one of the most individual and innovative English novelists of his generation. What is most striking about his *oeuvre* as a whole is his ability to break free from one mode of writing and to experiment with something very different in his constant quest for appropriate forms and authentic expression.

The four novels he wrote during the 1950s—the second, *A Garden of Trees,* has not been published—form a distinct group and can be considered as the first phase in his growth as a writer. The three published novels of this decade, *Spaces of the Dark, The Rainbearers,* and *Corruption,* are essentially realistic in mode, although they explore beneath the level of character and society to locate a metaphysical or spiritual malaise in modern Western civilization. All three novels are mainly set in the postwar world, although they look back both directly and indirectly to the war itself, and not surprisingly they reveal the influence of the dominant European philosophical movement of the 1940s and 1950s, existentialism. *Spaces of the Dark* (a phrase from T.S. Elliot's "Rhapsody on a Windy Night") is an ambitious attempt at a tragic novel whose protagonist, Paul Shaun, is torn apart by guilt and angst as a result of a wartime incident in which he killed a close friend and fellow officer. The past again casts its shadow on the present in *The Rainbearers,* and, although this novel lacks the tragic intensity of his first novel, the emphasis is on unrealized potential, lost possibilities, and failure. *Corruption,* in which the Venetian setting plays an important part, is structurally and stylistically more complex than *Spaces of the Dark* and *The Rainbearers,* and differs from them in being a first-person narrative. The title could be that of a medieval morality play, and the characters in this analysis of modern decadence and corruption function symbolically as well as realistically. Until its later stages, *Corruption* emanates a similar type of doom-laden fatalism and pessimism as the earlier novels, but then there is a crucial episode in which the oppression and bleakness lift to produce an unexpectedly open ending rather than a tragic denouement. This shift, marked by the adoption of a simpler idiom, may be inconsistent but it dramatizes Mosley's subversion of his own tragic pretensions as he discovers light at the end of the existential tunnel his fiction had been probing in the 1950s.

Five years separate *Corruption* from his next novel, *Meeting Place,* a transitional novel inaugurating the second phase of his development, ending with *Natalie Natalia* in 1971. Mosley now discards many of the features of his previous novels, which had been long, exhaustively analytical, densely written (Henry James and William Faulkner are important influences), and sometimes convoluted to the point of turgidity. The prose is simpler, sentences and paragraphs shorter, and the style more visually immediate, indeed cinematic. Furthermore, the narrative method is elliptical, selective, and discontinuous, and involves intercutting between the various strands of the plot with its Murdochian network of relationships. Comedy, conspicuous by its absence from the earlier novels, plays an important part in *Meeting Place,* which also features a broader range of characters than its predecessors and is remarkable for its positive conclusion, embodying Mosley's new commitment to the possibilities of renewal, growth, and creativity. With *Meeting Place* Mosley liberated himself from his preoccupations of the 1950s and therefore prepared the way for his first major achievement, *Accident,* subsequently turned into a distinguished film by Joseph Losey using a screenplay by Harold Pinter. The story in *Accident* is very simple: a version of the eternal triangle narrated by an Oxford philosophy don, Stephen Jervis, who knows the three people involved. Mosley's way of telling the story, however, is highly original because the unorthodox style enacts both the indeterminacy of reality and the inevitable tentativeness of human attempts to apprehend it. By using verbal fragments and staccato rhythms, Mosley captures the disjointed, ambiguous, even contradictory nature of experience in a way that may owe something to the French *nouveau roman* and its underlying phenomenology. Yet although *Accident* begins with a death and incorporates disintegration and severed relationships, it is not pessimistic; the end, with the birth of a baby to the narrator's wife, looks forward, not back, and emphasizes continuity, not finality.

In *Assassins* Mosley applies the methods of *Accident* to the world of public affairs and politics by narrating the attempted assassination of an Eastern bloc leader in England. The subject matter is that of the political thriller, but Mosley completely transforms and revitalizes that genre without, however, achieving such subtlety and profundity as he did in *Accident.* The most difficult of the novels

belonging to his second phase is *Impossible Object,* which at first sight seems to be a collection of short stories about love and marriage but proves to be a complex study in multiple viewpoint. By means of certain repetitions and patterns, Mosley provides his readers with a key to decode his collage of narratives and reassemble the fragments, but the reflexivity of the novel, as in *Accident,* draws attention to the impossibility of ever being able to fix or represent something as fluid and relativistic as reality. *Natalie Natalia,* one of Mosley's finest achievements, is less consciously experimental and more accessible than *Impossible Object,* but again displays his willingness to take risks with both language and narrative technique. The story line about a politician, Anthony Greville, and involving love, adultery, shame, and breakdown is unexceptional, but Mosley's way of treating familiar material is, as usual, startlingly different, and illuminates it in unexpected, mind-opening ways. The title, providing two names for the same woman, Greville's mistress, epitomizes Mosley's preoccupation with the enigmatic inconsistencies of life, because she is a living contradiction, both ravenous Natalie and angelic Natalia.

After *Natalie Natalia* Mosley published no fiction for eight years, and then in 1979 he launched by far his most ambitious project with *Catastrophe Practice,* initially intended to be the first of a group of seven novels, although he subsequently reduced the number to five. *Catastrophe Practice,* a compilation of three "plays not for acting" (with prefaces and a concluding essay) and a novella-length piece of fiction, is much more abstract than any of his other work. Catastrophe Theory is a mathematical attempt to account for discontinuities in the natural world: *Catastrophe Practice* is Mosley's attempt to create a literary form capable of encompassing and articulating the discontinuities of human experience. Superficially, the book is fragmented and dislocated, but by means of a complicated arrangement of correspondences and cross-references, including the appearance of the six principal characters in various guises in different sections, Mosley creates a form of unity out of apparent disunity and chaos. Running through *Catastrophe Practice* is a strain of polemic about the need to free consciousness, language, and art from the confines of convention, and also to rescue modern art from its devotion to versions of negativity—failure, disillusionment, pessimism, despair.

Mosley conceived the subsequent novels in the sequence to be self-contained yet interrelated books, each concentrating on one or two of the main figures in *Catastrophe Practice* itself. After the complexities of the very demanding *Catastrophe Practice, Imago Bird* is an immediately engaging and relatively straightforward novel, which presents a wide spectrum of contemporary life through the innocent eyes of its 18-year-old narrator, Bert. In trying to come to terms with the randomness of experience and to reconcile inner and outer reality, Bert apprehends the essential theatricality of adult life—how human beings allocate stereotyped parts to themselves and then proceed to act these out in a fictional illusion they mistake for reality. While believing themselves to be free, people, whether establishment politicians, media personalities, or dedicated revolutionaries, have imprisoned themselves in linguistic and behavioral conventions. *Imago Bird,* like its predecessor, is about the need to break out of the cage of false consciousness. *Serpent* is more intricate and less satisfactory than *Imago Bird.* Mosley interweaves a screenplay about the Jewish revolt against the Romans at Masada with contemporary events involving its writer, Jason, and a crisis in Israel. Parallels emerge between past and present, especially concerning the polarities of devotion and reason and of the individual and society. After *Serpent* Mosley temporarily shelved work on his large-scale project in order to write two books about his father, Sir Oswald Mosley, who died at this time leaving all his papers to his son.

Five years after publishing *Serpent,* Mosley returned to his *Catastrophe Practice* series with *Judith,* and four years later completed the quintet of novels with the large-scale *Hopeful Monsters,* which deservedly won the Whitbread award, one of Britain's most prestigious literary prizes. *Judith* is cast in the form of three letters from Judith herself to other main characters in the sequence, each letter describing a separate episode in her life. At the narrative level there is a radical discontinuity between these episodes, but at a metaphorical level the narrative leaps can be interpreted as a progression towards a new conception of unity. Judith's training as an actress makes her particularly sensitive to the constantly shifting levels of stage or in life. Brecht's influence on Mosley's novel sequence is evident in Judith's awareness of the way in which people often speak as though in quotation marks. *Judith* is very much a novel about the enigma of human consciousness, including the consciousness of consciousness. The complex biblical symbolism, especially recurring references to the Garden of Eden, the Tree of Knowledge, and the story of Judith and Holofernes, develops motifs present in the earlier novels and points forward to *Hopeful Monsters.*

In this concluding novel Mosley ambitiously attempts to pursue the main themes of the sequence in relation to the political history of the 20th century as well as to the history of science, especially the consequences of Einstein's theories. Major issues in the philosophy of language and the philosophy of science are interwoven with important historical events, as experienced by the two principal characters, Eleanor Anders and Max Ackerman, between whom the narrative alternates until the concluding section by a "correlator" (who turns out to be Jason). Eleanor's interest in anthropology and psychiatry and Max's in biology, theoretical physics, and cybernetics mean that crucial intellectual problems about the nature of matter, reality, subjectivity, and objectivity provide a way of interpreting the ideological and existential traumas of Europe, particularly between the two world wars. Mosley introduces such philosophers as Husserl, Heidegger, and Wittegenstein into the narrative as much as he introduces political figures like Rosa Luxemburg, Hitler, and Franco. Max's involvement in the Manhattan Project to develop nuclear weapons during World War II foregrounds the impossibility of an ivory-tower approach to scientific research, remote from ethical questions and political manipulation. As the culmination of the *Catastrophe Practice* sequence, *Hopeful Monsters* suggests an unorthodox way of coming to terms with the human condition in the 20th century, facing up to the worst (the Spanish Civil War, Stalin's purges, the Nazi Holocaust) while not abandoning hope in human potentialities. Despite its length, *Hopeful Monsters* is one of Mosley's most accessible novels, possessing an urgent narrative drive that makes the high intellectual content palatable rather than indigestible. It is a novel of ideas in the best sense of the term.

—Peter Lewis

MPHAHLELE, Es'kia

Nationality: South African. **Born:** Ezekiel Mphahlele in Pretoria, 17 December 1919. **Education:** St. Peter's Secondary School, Johannesburg; Adam's College, Natal, 1939-40; University of South Africa, Pretoria, 1946-49, 1953-54, 1956, B.A. (honours) 1949, M.A. in English 1956; University of Denver, 1966-68, Ph.D. in English 1968. **Family:** Married Rebecca Molchadibane in 1945; five children. **Career:** Clerk in institution for the blind, 1941-45; English and Afrikaans teacher, Orlando High School, Johannesburg, 1945-52; lecturer in English literature, University of Ibadan, Nigeria, 1957-61; director, African Programmes, International Association for Cultural Freedom, Paris, 1961-63; director, Chemchemi Creative Centre, Nairobi, Kenya, 164-65; lecturer, University College, Nairobi, 1965-66; senior lecturer in English, University of Zambia, Lusaka, 1968-70; associate professor of English, University of Pennsylvania, Philadelphia, 1974-77; Inspector of Education, Lebowa, Transvaal, 1978-79; professor of African literature, University of Witwatersrand, Johannesburg, 1979-87. Since 1987 director of a community education project in Soweto for the Council for Black Education and Research. Fiction editor, *Drum,* Johannesburg, 1955-57; editor, *Black Orpheus,* Ibadan, 1960-66, and *Journal of New African Literature and the Arts.* **Awards:** D. Litt.: University of Natal, Durban; Rhodes University, Grahamstown; L.H.D.: University of Pennsylvania. **Address:** P.O. Box 165, Pimville 1808, Johannesburg, South Africa.

PUBLICATIONS

Novels

The Wanderers. New York, Macmillan, 1971; London, Macmillan, 1972.
Chirundu. Johannesburg, Ravan Press, 1979; Walton-on-Thames, Surrey, Nelson, 1980; Westport, Connecticut, Hill, 1981.

Short Stories

Man Must Live and Other Stories. Cape Town, African Bookman, 1947.
The Living and Dead and Other Stories. Ibadan, Black Orpheus, 1961.
In Corner B and Other Stories. Nairobi, East African Publishing House, 1967.
Renewal Time. Columbia, Louisiana, and London, Readers International, 1988.

Other

Down Second Avenue (autobiography). London, Faber, 1959; New York, Doubleday, 1971.
The African Image (essays). London, Faber, and New York, Praeger, 1962; revised edition, Faber and Praeger, 1974.
The Role of Education and Culture in Developing African Countries. Tel Aviv, Afro-Asian Institute for Labor Studies and Cooperation in Israel, 1965.
A Guide to Creative Writing. Nairobi, East African Literature Bureau, 1966.
Voices in the Whirlwind and Other Essays. New York, Hill and Wang, 1972; London, Macmillan, 1973.
The Unbroken Song: Selected Writings of Es'kia Mphahlele. Johannesburg, Ravan Press, 1981.
Let's Write a Novel. Cape Town, Maskew Miller, 1981.
Bury Me at the Marketplace: Selected Letters of Es'kia Mphahlele 1943-1980, edited by N. Chanbani Manganyi. Johannesburg, Skotaville, 1984.

Father Come Home (for children). Johannesburg, Ravan Press, 1984.

Afrika My Music: An Autobiography 1957-1983. Johannesburg, Ravan Press, 1984; Athens, Ohio University Press-Swallow Press, 1986.

Let's Talk Writing: Prose [Poetry]. Johannesburg, Skotaville, 2 vols., 1986.

Poetry and Humanism: Oral Beginnings (lecture). Johannesburg, University of the Witwatersrand Press, 1986.

Mandela: Echoes of an Era, with photographs by Alf Kumalo. London, Penguin, 1990.

Editor, with Ellis Komey, *Modern African Stories.* London, Faber, 1964.

Editor, *African Writing Today.* London, Penguin, 1967.

Editor, with Michael Chapman and Colin Gardner, *Perspectives on South African English Literature.* Parklands, Donker, 1992.

*

Critical Studies: *Seven African Writers,* London, Oxford University Press, 1962, and *The Chosen Tongue,* London, Longman, 1969, both by Gerald Moore; "The South African Short Story," by Mphahlele in *Kenyon Review* (Gambier, Ohio), 1969; *Ezekiel Mphahlele* by Ursula A. Barnett, Boston, Twayne, 1976; "The Humanism of Ezekiel Mphahlele" by Samuel Omo Asein, in *Journal of commonwealth Literature,* 15(1), 1980; *Exiles and Homecomings: A Biography of Es'kia Mphahlele* by N. Chabani Manganyi, Johannesburg, Ravan Press, 1983; *Footprints Along the Way: A Tribute to Es'kia Mphahlele* edited by Peter N. Thuynsma, Johannesburg, Skotaville/Justified, 1989.

Es'kia Mphahlele comments:

(1972) I began my writing career as a short-story writer during World War II. I wrote for *Drum* magazine in Johannesburg, *Fighting Talk* and *New Age* in Johannesburg, and *Africa South* in Cape Town (the last 3 journals since banned by the South African government). My earliest stories, i.e., *Man Must Live,* were escapist stuff which came spontaneously. I moved on to vitriolic protest fiction. I left South Africa as an exile in September 1957 to teach in Nigeria, where I finished the second half of *Down Second Avenue,* my autobiography. Even in exile my fictional themes have always been South Africa. But *In Corner B,* which I wrote in Paris in 1963, has two stories set in Nigeria: "The Barber of Bariga" and "The Ballad of Oyo." The rest are set in South Africa. I wrote these Nigerian stories and "Mrs. Plum" in Paris. The rest had appeared in Johannesburg journals. "Mrs. Plum" in that volume was my first attempt at the long short-story. I have often thought of fiction as my specific commitment; when I am still composing such a work in my mind, I write critical essays—such as *The African Image* and *Voices in the Whirlwind. The Wanders* has an autobiographical outline but the incidents are fictional. I am planning a novel set in Zambia. I am trying to come to terms with the greater Africa as a setting, but I know the South African in me will accompany me to the grave.

*   *   *

Eskia Mphahlele has been one of the most versatile and influential of African authors. As literary critic, autobiographer, journalist, short story writer, novelist, dramatist, and poet, he has probably contributed more than any other individual to the growth and de-velopment of an African literature in English. Since leaving South Africa he has travelled widely, stopping to teach for a year or two in at least five different countries—Nigeria, Kenya, Zambia, France, and the United States.

In South Africa Mphahlele wrote mainly short stories about life in the urban black ghettos where he had grown up and spent most of his adult years. The events of these stories were based on his personal experiences and reflected a wide variety of responses to the people and places he knew best. There were humorous sketches and satirical vignettes as well as more serious stories about human or social problems. Later, as stringent apartheid legislation made life more difficult for urban blacks, Mphahlele began to write angry protest fiction. By the mid-1950s he felt stifled in his home country and applied for an "exit permit," a document allowing him to leave South Africa on the condition that he never return. The South African government granted his request in 1957, and he lived in exile for the next 20 years, finally returning to South Africa in 1977.

His first major piece of writing abroad was an autobiography, *Down Second Avenue,* in which he tried to work off the emotional steam and creative energy that had been building up inside him during his last years in South Africa. It is a moving story, told with candour and compassion for his people. In 1962 he published a pioneering work of literary criticism, *The African Image,* part of which he had written in South Africa as a M.A. thesis. He also brought out two collections of his short stories and produced a manual for aspiring fiction writers. His first novel, *The Wanderers,* examined the plight of the black South African intellectual in exile, a depressing tale constructed out of the debris of his own personal life. A second novel, *Chirundu,* which appears to have been inspired by his years in Zambia, dealt with postcolonial power politics in an independent African state. In 1972 he published another volume of perceptive literary criticism.

During his years in exile Mphahlele was able to arrive at the kind of emotional balance and aesthetic distance from his subject matter that he found impossible to achieve as a young man living in South Africa. But after a time he began to feel increasingly restless, angry, and politically impotent abroad, so he elected to return to his homeland, despite the hazards and frustrations he knew would confront him there. In recent years he has been extremely prolific, producing a sequel to his autobiography, a children's book, another manual for writers, and a new selection of his writings, including short stories and poems. These books have contained forthright protest, yet he has managed to get them all published in South Africa. In addition, a volume of his letters has appeared, and he has been the subject of a locally written biography. Repatriation, like exile, has obviously served as intense creative stimulus for him, releasing pent-up energies of passionate self-expression. Instead of aiming for aesthetic distance, he now seeks close emotional engagement with the people and places that serve as primary sources of his inspiration. After decades of wandering, he has rediscovered his roots as a South African writer.

—Bernth Lindfor

MUDROOROO

Also writes as Colin Johnson and Mudrooroo Narogin. **Nationality:** Australian. **Born:** East Cubbaling, Western Australia, 1938.

Education: Brought up in a Roman Catholic orphanage. **Career:** Lived in India for 6 years, three as a Buddhist monk. Holds the Chair of Aboriginal Studies at Murdech University, Perth. **Awards:** Wieckhard prize, 1979; Western Australia Literary award, 1989; WA Premier's Book award, for most outstanding entry and for poetry, 1992; Australia Council Writer's grant, 1994. **Agent:** Iarune Little. **Address:** School of Humanities, Murdoch University, Murdoch, Western Australia 6150, Australia.

PUBLICATIONS

Novels

Doin' Wildcat (as Mudrooroo Narogin). South Yarra, Victoria, Hyland House, 1988.
Master of the Ghost Dreaming. Sydney, HarperCollins, 1991.
Wildcat Screaming. Sydney, HarperCollins, 1992.
The Kwinkan. Sydney, HarperCollins, 1993.

Novels as Colin Johnson

Wild Cat Falling. Sydney and London, Angus and Robertson, 1965.
Long Live Sandawara. Melbourne, Quartet, 1979; London, Quartet, 1980.
Doctor Wooreddy's Prescription for Enduring the Ending of the World. Melbourne, Hyland House, 1983.

Poetry

Dalwurra: The Black Bittern (as Colin Johnson). Nedlands, Western Australia, Centre for Studies in Australian Literature, 1988.
The Garden of Gethsemane. Melbourne, Hyland House, 1991.

Other

Before the Invasion: Aboriginal Life to 1788 (as Colin Johnson), with Colin Bourke and Isobel White. Melbourne, Oxford University Press, 1980.
Writing from the Fringe (as Mudrooroo Narogin). South Yarra, Victoria, Hyland House, 1990.
The Mudrooroo/Mueller Project. Sydney, New South Wales University Press, 1993.
Aboriginal Mythology. London, Aquarian, 1994.

*

Critical Study: *Mudrooroo—A Critical Study* by Adam Shoemaker, Sydney, HarperCollins, 1994.

*   *   *

Colin Johnson's novels deal with the displacement of modern Aborigines and their inability either to find a place in white society or to hold to the traditional ways. His first novel was concerned with the world he knew growing up in Perth—a world of the bodgie subculture often in trouble with the law—while subsequent novels confront events from the Australian past and their implications for Aborigines today.

Wild Cat Falling portrays a cynical young Aborigine on his release after a prison sentence. One leitmotif of the novel is Beckett's *Waiting for Godot.* It is the absurdist view of a pointless world which appeals to the principal character as he moves among various groups in Perth, reticent and detached. He becomes involved in a burglary during which he shoots a policeman. Fleeing, he encounters an old Aborigine who represents both the lore of the Aboriginal and the moral center which he is seeking even while he thinks he is impervious to it. The conclusion sees him showing concern for the man he shot, and finding a glimmer of humanity even in the policeman who is arresting him.

A number of motifs in this novel reappear in the next, in particular the opposition between a directionless "modern" Aborigine and a decayed though still integral Elder. *Long Live Sandawara* is the story of a group of young Perth Aborigines whose 16-year-old leader, Alan, is keen to organize them to improve their opportunities, but his attempts to do so through the local Aboriginal leader get nowhere. Alan eventually leads the gang in a farcical raid on a bank during which all except himself are killed. Throughout the novel he has visited Noorak who as a child saw the clash between an Aboriginal resistance fighter, Sandawara, and the whites. Noorak recounts the adventures of the past, and it is in emulation of these that Alan leads his ill-fated raid. Johnson treats the freedom fighters of the past with seriousness and dignity as true spiritual products of the soil. The sort of holistic integrity in Sandawara and his fighters contrasts strongly with the rootlessness of the modern characters. This is marked by different narrative styles, a sort of biblical cadence being used for the past events, while the modern story is told in a sometimes awkward historical present using a good deal of dialogue. Johnson has attempted to render in the one novel the ethos of two quite different genres, the epic past, and the problem-drama present. In this novel, the past offers to the present a model of what may be done to correct injustice. However, Johnson argues that more than Western guerrilla resistance is required—that to make anything of their lives modern Aborigines must re-establish contact with the centers of their cultural heritage. At the conclusion of the novel Alan leads the old man, Noorak, to the airport to fly north to their tribal country where he, Alan, will undergo initiation and Noorak will die contented.

The past in this novel is a time of glorious and inspiring resistance to the whites, invariably referred to as "invaders." In Johnson's recent novel, history becomes less a source of political instruction than a crucible within which a philosophy of survival must be forged. *Doctor Wooreddy's Prescription for Enduring the Ending of the World* is concerned with the annihilation of the Tasmanian Aborigines in the first half of the 19th century. The controlling viewpoint is that of a learned man of the Bruny Island tribe who sees his land polluted by the aggressive practices of the whites. The focus of the novel is on Wooreddy's attempts to understand the processes of change where there had been no change before. Wooreddy is obsessed with the belief that he has been chosen to survive to see the imminent end of the world. This insight comes to him as a child when he sees his first sailing ship which he takes to be a floating island drawn by clouds from the domain of the evil spirit, *Ria Warawah.* Wooreddy's sense of being select enables him to avoid the worst pangs of outrage and regret as the dispossession of the Aborigines proceeds. He retreats into a fatalistic numbness which cannot be termed cowardice, for bravery and cowardice are no longer meaningful concepts.

Wooreddy's initial vision of the ship is balanced by a second vision which collapses the Manichean world-view which the Aborigines have held. In a sea cave to which he is led by a Port Phillip Aborigine he comes to see that instead of the traditional binary cosmology of a good spirit, *Great Ancestor,* and an opposing evil spirit, *Ria Warawah,* there is but one force which is primal and that all things are a manifestation of it. Johnson uses historical events and characters in this novel to investigate the state of doomed suspension in which the Aborigines found themselves after the arrival of the white man. Since there never was any chance of the Tasmanian Aborigines resisting the invaders, their world effectively ended from the appearance of the whites. From early in the novel the invading and polluting whites are seen as the embodiment of the evil spirit, *Ria Warawah,* but when the disjunction between him and the benevolent creator, *Great Ancestor,* is rejected by Wooreddy's second major vision the processes of history no longer allow the assignment of guilt. The whites are a force of history as much as a manifestation of the evil of man. Wooreddy is denied even the satisfaction of having someone to blame.

—Chris Tiffin

MUKHERJEE, Bharati

Nationality: Canadian. **Born:** Calcutta, India, 27 July 1940; became Canadian citizen, 1972. **Education:** Loreto Convent School, Calcutta; University of Calcutta, B.A. (honors) in English 1959; University of Baroda, Gujarat, M.A. 1961; University of Iowa, Iowa City, M.F.A. 1963; Ph.D. 1969. **Family:** Married Clark Blaise, *q.v.,* in 1963; two sons. **Career:** Instructor in English, Marquette University, Milwaukee, Wisconsin, 1964-65, and University of Wisconsin, Madison, 1965; lecturer, 1966-69, assistant professor, 1969-73, associate professor, 1973-78, and professor, 1978, McGill University, Montreal. Professor, Skidmore College, Saratoga Springs, New York; associate professor, Montclair State College, New Jersey, 1984-87; Queen's College, City University of New York, Flushing, 1987-89; professor, University of California, Berkeley, 1990-95. **Awards:** Canada Arts Council grant, 1973, 1977; Guggenheim Fellowship, 1977; National Book Critics Circle award, 1989. **Agent:** Timothy Seldes, Russell and Volkening, 551 Fifth Avenue, New York, New York 10017, U.S.A.

PUBLICATIONS

Novels

The Tiger's Daughter. Boston, Houghton Mifflin, 1972; London, Chatto and Windus, 1973.
Wife. Boston, Houghton Mifflin, 1975; London, Penguin, 1987.
Jasmine. New York, Grove Weidenfeld, 1989; London, Virago Press, 1990.
The Holder of the World. New York, Knopf, and Chatto and Windus, 1993.

Short Stories

Darkness. Toronto, Penguin, 1985.
The Middleman and Other Stories. New York, Grove Press, 1988; London, Virago Press, 1989.

Play

Screenplay: *Days and Nights in Calcutta,* with Clark Blaise, 1991.

Other

Kautilya's Concept of Diplomacy: A New Interpretation. Calcutta, Minerva, 1976.
Days and Nights in Calcutta, with Clark Blaise. New York, Doubleday, 1977; London, Penguin, 1986.
The Sorrow and the Terror: The Haunting Legacy of the Air India Tragedy, with Clark Blaise. Toronto, Viking, 1987.
Political Culture and Leadership in India: A Study of West Bengal. New Delhi, India, Mittal Publications, 1991.

*

Critical Study: *Bharati Mukherjee: Critical Perspectives* edited by Emmanuel S. Nelson, New York, Garland Press, 1993.

*　　*　　*

Bharati Mukherjee is a versatile writer whose *oeuvre* includes four novels, two collections of short stories, some powerful essays, and two nonfiction books which she co-authored with her husband Clark Blaise. Her early work led to her being seen as a writer firmly enclosed in the bosom of Indian writing in English. But this was an embrace that Mukherjee herself sought to avoid. With the publication of *Darkness,* her third book of fiction, she convincingly declared her desire to be seen as a North American writer. In the hard-hitting introduction to this collection of stories Mukherjee explains this shift as "a movement away from the aloofness of expatriation, to the exuberance of immigration."

Mukherjee's early novels, *The Tiger's Daughter* and *Wife,* both published in the early 1970s, are novels about the isolation of Indian expatriates. A reading of *Days and Nights in Calcutta* reveals that there is a strong autobiographical element in *A Tiger's Daughter.* Tara Banerjee, like the Bharati Mukherjee of *Days and Nights in Calcutta,* is an outsider in India because of her decision to leave India, to live in North America, and to marry an American, *mleccha* (outcaste) husband. On her return, Tara sees India through the eyes of a Western imagination rather than through her own childhood eyes. Her sense of alienation in Calcutta is symbolized by her regular visits to the Catelli-Continental Hotel, from where she views the turmoil of Calcutta from the safe heights of a tourist, cut off from the "real" India which seethes below her. Tara is no longer able to feel a part of her family, who belong to an old Bengal which is now lost to her, nor is she able to feel at ease with her old friends who, like her family, belong to a Calcutta which is rapidly fading, and who, in their different ways are as isolated as Tara from the beast beneath them. On another level, *The Tiger's Daughter* is an interesting parody of E.M. Forster's *A Passage to India.*

The theme of expatriation and isolation which is handled with such assurance in *The Tiger's Daughter* is again treated in her second novel. In *Wife,* Dimple Dasgupta is married off to a young engineer, and soon finds herself emigrating to America. She finds her new life impossible to adjust to, and her attempts to become American—to learn to speak American English by watching the television, for example—cause her to question her own cultural values, and even her own happiness. These are questions she might never have asked herself in Calcutta, and had she done so and found herself equally disillusioned, her solution, the novel suggests, would probably have been suicide. The infidelity and the murder which brings the novel to its shocking close are the alternatives with which Dimple's American experience has provided her.

Darkness is an important landmark for Mukherjee. It is in this book, her first collection of stories, that she begins to exchange the robes of an Indian expatriate writer for the new, but not borrowed, robes of a North American writer who is an immigrant. The specifically Canadian stories in this collection continue to explore the painful world of the expatriate she writes about in *Wife* —indeed the story "Visitors" is a reworking of the essential elements of that novel. Other stories, though, explore North America through the alien voices of its various immigrant cultures— Italian, Latin American, Sri Lankan, as well as Indian. With *The Middleman and Other Stories* Mukherjee's exchange of mantles is complete. In these stories, sometimes with anger, often with violence, sometimes with comedy, often with tenderness, Mukherjee gives voice to the "other" within America. The result is a broader, more detailed portrait of the North American immigrant experience than *Wife* or even the impressive stories in *Darkness* provide. "The Management of Grief," which deals with the sorrow of the bereaved relatives of the victims of the 1985 Air India disaster, is perhaps the most moving story in the collection. The horror of that tragedy is dealt with in harrowing detail in Mukherjee's second nonfiction collaboration, *The Sorrow and the Terror.*

After a gap of 14 years, Mukherjee made a welcome return to the novel form with the publication of *Jasmine,* which explores female identity through the story of an Indian peasant woman whose path takes her from the Punjab, to Florida, to New York, to Iowa, and as the novel draws to a close she is about to set off for California. With each new move the protagonist reinvents herself with a new name—Jyoti, Jasmine, Jase, Jane—and with each new name she moves closer to her dream of being an American, of belonging to the New World. Jasmine's ongoing journey is an effective device which highlights her rootless position and her search for identity. The move to California, which resonates with hope and invests her with the aspirations of America's early pioneers, suggests that Jasmine has finally found her identity in America, which, perhaps more than any other country, can contain her many identities without contradiction.

In *The Holder of the World,* her latest and most accomplished work of the 1990s, Mukherjee turns her attention to one of the founding novels of the postcolonial American canon—Nathaniel Hawthorne's *The Scarlet Letter.* Reversing the usual binary opposition between occidental and oriental texts, Mukherjee presents Hawthorne's novel as one which has been written out of a knowledge of India. And in doing this Mukherjee has written herself (as an American whose roots are in India) into her text perhaps more effectively even than in the seemingly autobiographical *The Tiger's Daughter.* The novel is also interesting for the way it very subtly parodies the Western construct of India as a nation and the perception of Indians as a homogeneous group.

Bharati Mukherjee is a writer who profitably draws on her experiences of the Old World while writing with insight about the New World to which she now belongs. Her most recent books, *The Middleman and Other Stories, Jasmine,* and particularly *The Holder of the World,* confirm that hers is an original voice at the cutting edge of American immigrant literature.

—Ralph J. Crane

MUNONYE, John (Okechukwu)

Nationality: Nigerian. **Born:** Akokwa, 28 April 1929. **Education:** Christ the King College, Onitsha, 1943-47; University College, Ibadan, 1948-52, B.A. in classics and history 1952; Institute of Education, University of London, 1952-53, Cert. Ed. 1953. **Family:** Married Regina Nwokeji in 1957; one daughter and one son. **Career:** Education Officer, 1954-57, and Provincial Education Officer and Inspector of Education, 1958-70, Nigerian Ministry of Education; Principal, Advanced Teachers College, Oweri, 1970-73; Chief Inspector of Education, East Central State, 1973-76, and Imo State, 1976-77. Columnist, *Catholic Life* magazine, Lagos, and *Nigerian Statesman,* Owerri. Member of the Board of Directors, East Central State Broadcasting Service, Enugu, 1974-76. **Member:** Order of the Niger, 1980. **Agent:** David Higham Associates, 5-8 Lower John Street, London W1R 4HA, England. **Address:** P.O. Box 436 Orlu, Imo State, Nigeria.

PUBLICATIONS

Novels

The Only Son. London, Heinemann, 1966.
Obi. London, Heinemann, 1969.
Oil Man of Obange. London, Heinemann, 1971.
A Wreath for Maidens. London, Heinemann, 1973.
A Dancer of Fortune. London, Heinemann, 1974.
Bridge to a Wedding. London, Heinemann, 1978.

Uncollected Short Stories

"Silent Child," in *Okike 4* (Amherst, Massachusetts), December 1973.
"Pack Pack Pack," in *Festac Anthology of Nigerian New Writing.* Lagos, Ministry of Information, 1977.
"Man of Wealth," in *Catholic Life* (Lagos), 1981.
"On a Sunday Morning," in *Catholic Life* (Lagos), 1982.
"Rogues," in *Catholic Life* (Lagos), 1985.

Other

Drills and Practice in English Language (textbook), with J. Cairns. Lagos, African Universities Press, 1966.

*

John Munonye comments:

(1991) All six of my novels are children of the land. Set in the Igbo area of Nigeria, they draw from the experiences of ordinary men and women, children too. The motif is the processes of change that started with the arrival of Christian missionaries some 60 years ago. Culture ("all the arts, beliefs, social institutions . . . characteristic of a community") had to shift ground. And the environment, sensitive in its own way, was transformed too. How did our ordinary men and women fare in it all? Is there anything of their authentic nature that could be said to have survived the stress? The earliest experiences, which are depicted in *The Only Son* and *Obi,* were severe and traumatic. Later, people came to live with the new state of things, and the result is *Bridge to a Wedding,* a novel of accommodation and reconciliation between traditional and modern. We do indeed need the bridge.

Oil Man of Obange is a relentless tragedy, a novel of confrontation on an individual scale. The Oil Man musters all his energy, zeal, optimism, and integrity towards improving his low social status. But did he consult the god of success? *A Wreath of Maidens* also deals with moral issues—on a wider canvas. The blood shed in the end is not, unfortunately, that of the protagonists: it is a novel of futility. *A Dancer of Fortune* proceeds on much lighter feet.

What next? The beautiful ones are not yet born—yes. But hope is one of man's sustaining gifts, a gift of the spirit. With it goes vision (without which a people perish) and commitment. Nothing shrill or didactic; no sermons; no protest.

*   *   *

Though he wrote six novels in one 12-year period, John Munonye has attracted surprisingly little critical attention. The reason is not far to seek: despite the intrinsically interesting material he works on, his craftsmanship and command of English have flagged noticeably since his earliest books. Yet, as a compassionate chronicler of the ways in which ordinary Eastern Nigerian people have been affected by historical and social change, he is a writer well worth reading. In his first and third novels, *The Only Son* and *Oil Man of Obange,* theme and treatment interlock admirably and reveal his competence at its best. Jeri, the petty trader in palm oil of *Oil Man of Obange,* pits his own elemental resources of courage, devotion, and physical strength against fate, accident, and malice to raise money for his children's schooling; Munonye subdues the narration rigorously to a stark recording of the everyday hardships of bare human existence that is still the lot of most Nigerians, indeed of the peoples of the Third World in general. With similar, though slightly less stringent, narrative austerity, *The Only Son* presents the privations of a self-reliant widow whose humble, sparse life is touched into tragic proportions by her simple courage and steadfastness: the relationship between Chiaku and her son is tenderly but unsentimentally handled, and, in their estrangement, when he seeks Western and Christian education, Munonye achieves a sympathetic insight into both sides of an irreconcilable clash of aspirations.

The Only Son is the first novel in Munonye's trilogy about the fortunes of one family, the 20th-century descendants of the legendary Udemezue of Burning Eyes in the community of Umudiobia of ten villages and two. In *Obi* the fully Christianized son and his Christian wife return to Umudiobia to re-establish his father's *obi* or homestead, but the tensions between traditional custom and their new faith culminate in their flight into exile in a distant town. *Bridge to a Wedding* introduces them as the materially prosperous parents of six children and traces the patient and successful efforts of a highly respected Umudiobian to heal the feud between them and their village kinsfolk so that his son can marry their daughter. While these two novels share the attractive unifying theme of how African custom still operates upon the lives of ordinary Nigerians, for good and for ill, Munonye's concern with this theme, especially in *Bridge to a Wedding,* leads him into an often irritating discursiveness.

The virtue of Munonye's civil-war novel, *A Wreath for the Maidens,* rests upon his intimate knowledge of how the common people are affected for the worse by large historical events, despite the public rhetoric that accompanies them. Poor characterization and a tendency to wordiness do not vitiate the somber moral concern at the heart of this book. That it could so soon be followed by *A Dancer of Fortune,* with its apparent endorsement of mere individualist opportunism, is a disturbing measure of Munonye's increasing lack of self-criticism as a writer.

—Arthur Ravenscroft

MUNRO, Alice (Anne)

Nationality: Canadian. **Born:** Alice Anne Laidlaw, Wingham, Ontario, 10 July 1931. **Education:** Wingham public schools; University of Western Ontario, London, 1949-51. **Family:** Married 1) James Armstrong Munro in 1951 (separated 1972; divorced 1976), four daughters (one deceased); 2) Gerald Fremlin in 1976. Lived in Vancouver, 1951-63, Victoria, British Columbia, 1963-71, London, Ontario, 1972-75, and Clinton, Ontario, from 1976. **Career:** Writer-in-residence, University of Western Ontario, 1974-75, and University of British Columbia, Vancouver, 1980. **Awards:** Governor-General's award, 1969, 1978, 1987; B.C. Library Association Outstanding Fiction Writer's award, 1972; Great Lakes Colleges Association award, 1974; Province of Ontario Council for the Arts award, 1974; Canada-Australia literary prize, 1977; National Magazine Awards Foundation Gold Medal award, 1977, 1982; Foundation for the Advancement of Canadian Letters and Periodical Distributors of Canada Author's award, 1980; Marian Engel award, 1986; Canada Council Molson prize, 1991; Commonwealth Writers prize (Canada and Caribbean Region), 1991; Trillium Book award, 1991; Order of Ontario medal, 1994; Canadian Booksellers Association Author of the Year award, 1995. D.Litt.: University of Western Ontario, 1976. **Address:** c/o Writers Union of Canada, 24 Ryerson Street, Toronto, Ontario M5T 2P4, Canada.

PUBLICATIONS

Novels

Lives of Girls and Women. Toronto, McGraw Hill Ryerson, 1971; New York, McGraw Hill, 1972; London, Allen Lane, 1973.

Short Stories

Dance of the Happy Shades. Toronto, Ryerson Press, 1968; New York, McGraw Hill, 1973; London, Allen Lane, 1974.
Something I've Been Meaning to Tell You: Thirteen Stories. Toronto, McGraw Hill Ryerson, and New York, McGraw Hill, 1974.
Personal Fictions, with others, edited by Michael Ondaatje. Toronto, Oxford University Press, 1977.
Who Do You Think You Are? Toronto, Macmillan, 1978; as *The Beggar Maid: Stories of Flo and Rose,* New York, Knopf, 1979; London, Allen Lane, 1980.
The Moons of Jupiter. Toronto, Macmillan, 1982; New York, Knopf, and London, Allen Lane, 1983.
The Progress of Love. Toronto, McClelland and Stewart, and New York, Knopf, 1986; London, Chatto and Windus, 1987.
Friend of My Youth. New York, Knopf, and London, Chatto and Windus, 1990.

A Wilderness Station. New York, Knopf, 1994.
Open Secrets. Toronto, McClelland & Stewart, New York, Alfred A. Knopf, and London, Chatto and Windus, 1994.

Plays

How I Met My Husband (televised 1974). Published in *The Play's the Thing,* edited by Tony Gifford, Toronto, Macmillan, 1976.

Television Plays: *A Trip to the Coast,* 1973; *Thanks for the Ride,* CBC, 1973; *How I Met My Husband,* 1974; *1847: The Irish* (*The Newcomers* series), 1978.

*

Bibliography: "Alice Munro: A Checklist (To December 31, 1974)" by D.E. Cook, in *Journal of Canadian Fiction* 16, 1976; "Some Highly Subversive Activities: A Brief Polemic and a Checklist of Works on Alice Munro" by J.R. (Tim) Struthers, in *Studies in Canadian Literature* 6, 1981; "Munro, Alice (1931-)" by Helen Hoy, in her *Modern English-Canadian Prose: A Guide to Information Sources,* Detroit, Gale Research, 1983; "Alice Munro: An Annotated Bibliography" by Robert Thacker, in *The Annotated Bibliography of Canada's Major Authors: Volume Five,* edited by Robert Lecker and Jack David, Downsview, Ontario, ECW Press, 1984; *The Alice Munro Papers First Accession: An Inventory of the Archive at The University of Calgary Libraries* compiled by Jean M. Moore and Jean F. Tener and edited by Apollonia Steele and Jean F. Tener, Calgary, University of Calgary Press, 1986; *The Alice Munro Papers Second Accession: An Inventory of the Archive at The University of Calgary Libraries* compiled by Jean M. Moore and edited by Apollonia Steele and Jean F. Tener, Calgary, University of Calgary Press, 1987; "Munro, Alice (1931-)" by Allan Weiss, in his *A Comprehensive Bibliography of English-Canadian Short Stories, 1950-1983,* Toronto, ECW Press, 1988.

Manuscript Collection: The University of Calgary Libraries, Alberta.

Critical Studies: "A Conversation with Alice Munro" in *Journal of Canadian Fiction* 1(4), 1972, and "Casting Sad Spells: Alice Munro's 'Walker Brothers Cowboy'" in *Writers in Aspic,* Montreal, Vehicule Press, 1988, both by John Metcalf; "Unconsummated Relationships: Isolation and Rejection in Alice Munro's Stories," in *World Literature Written in English,* 11(1), 1972, "The Fiction of Alice Munro," in *Ploughshares* 4(3), 1978, and *Alice Munro and Her Works,* Toronto, ECW Press, 1985, all by Hallvard Dahlie; "Alice Munro" by Graeme Gibson, in his *Eleven Canadian Novelists: Interviewed by Graeme Gibson,* Toronto, House of Anansi Press, 1973; "Alice Munro and the American South," in *Here and Now, The Canadian Novel,* edited by John Moss, vol. 1, Toronto, NC Press, 1978, and "Reality and Ordering: The Growth of a Young Artist in *Lives of Girls and Women,*" in *Modern Canadian Fiction,* Richmond, British Columbia, Open Learning Institute, 1980, both by J.R. (Tim) Struthers; "Pronouns and Propositions: Alice Munro's *Something I've Been Meaning To Tell You,*" by W.H. New, in his *Dreams of Speech and Violence: The Art of the Short Story in Canada and New Zealand,* Toronto, University of Toronto Press, 1987; "Women's Lives: Alice Munro" by Bronwen Wallace, in *The Human Elements: Critical Essays,* edited by David Helwig, Ot-

tawa, Oberon Press, 1978; "Alice Munro and James Joyce," in *Journal of Canadian Fiction,* 24, 1979, and *Alice Munro: Paradox and Parallel,* Edmonton, University of Alberta Press, 1987, both by W.R. Martin; "'Dull, Simple, Amazing and Unfathomable': Paradox and Double Vision in Alice Munro's Fiction," in *Studies in Canadian Literature* 5, 1980, and "Alice Munro: 'Unforgettable, Indigestible Messages',," in *Journal of Canadian Studies,* 26(1), 1991, and "'Rose and Janet': Alice Munro's Metafiction," in *Canadian Literature,* 121, 1989, all by Helen Hoy; "Alice Munro" by Geoff Hancock, in his *Canadian Writers at Work: Interviews with Geoff Hancock,* Toronto, Oxford University Press, 1987; *Probable Fictions: Alice Munro's Narrative Acts* edited by Louis K. MacKendrick, Downsview, Ontario, ECW Press, 1983, and *Some Other Reality: Alice Munro's "Something I've Been Meaning To Tell You"* by MacKendrick, Toronto, ECW Press, 1993; "Three Jokers: The Shape of Alice Munro's Stories," in *Centre and Labyrinth: Essays in Honour of Northrop Frye,* edited by Eleanor Cook et al, Toronto, University of Toronto Press, 1983, and *The Other Country: Patterns in the Writing of Alice Munro,* Toronto, ECW Press, 1993, both by James Carscallen; *Alice Munro* by B. Pfaus, Ottawa, Golden Dog Press, 1984; *The Art of Alice Munro: Saying the Unsayable* edited by Judith Miller, Waterloo, Ontario, University of Waterloo Press, 1984; "Connection: Alice Munro and Ontario," in *The American Review of Canadian Studies* 14, 1984, and "Conferring Munro" in *Essays on Canadian Writing* 34, 1987, "Go Ask Alice: The Progress of Munro Criticism," in *Journal of Canadian Studies,* 26(2), 1991, all by Robert Thacker; "'What Happened to Marion?': Art and Reality in *Lives of Girls and Women*" by Thomas E. Tausky, in *Studies in Canadian Literature,* 11(1), 1986; *Alice Munro* by E.D. Blodgett, Boston, Twayne/Hall, 1988; "Alice Munro" by Michelle Gadpaille, in her *The Canadian Short Story,* Toronto, Oxford University Press, 1988; "*The Other Side of Dailiness": Photography in the Works of Alice Munro, Timothy Findley, Michael Ondaatje, and Margaret Laurence* by Lorraine M. York, Toronto, ECW Press, 1988; "Alice Munro" by W.J. Keith, in his *A Sense of Style: Studies in the Art of Fiction in English-Speaking Canada,* Toronto, ECW Press, 1989; *Controlling the Uncontrollable: The Fiction of Alice Munro* by Ildiko de Papp Carrington, DeKalb, Northern Illinois University Press, 1989; *Dance of the Sexes: Art and Gender in the Fiction of Alice Munro* by Beverly J. Rasporich, Edmonton, University of Alberta Press, 1990; *Introducing Alice Munro's "Lives of Girls and Women": A Reader's Guide* by Neil K. Besner, Toronto, ECW Press, 1990; *Alice Munro: A Double Life* by Catherine Sheldrick Ross, Toronto, ECW Press, 1992; *Figuring Grief: Gallant, Munro, and the Poetics of Elegy* by Karen Smythe, Montreal, McGill-Queen's University Press, 1992; "A Hopeful Sign: The Making of Metonymic Meaning in Munro's 'Meneseteung'" by Pam Houston, in *The Kenyon Review* 14.4, 1992; *Mothers and Other Clowns: The Stories of Alice Munro* by Magdalene Redekop, London, Routledge, 1992; *How Stories Mean* edited by John Metcalf and J.R. (Tim) Struthers, Erin, Ontario, Porcupine's Quill, 1993; "Alice Munro: The Art of Fiction CXXXVII" by Jean McCulloch and Mona Simpson, in *The Paris Review* 131, 1994; *The Tumble of Reason: Alice Munro's Discourse of Absence* by Ajay Heble, Toronto, University of Toronto Press, 1994; "The Woman Out Back: Alice Munro's 'Meneseteung'" by Dermot McCarthy, in *Studies in Canadian Literature,* 19(1), 1994; "A National Treasure: An Interview with Alice Munro" by Pleuke Boyce and Ron Smith, in *O Canada 2,* edited by Cassandra Pybus, *Meanjin,* 54, 1995.

Alice Munro comments:

(1982) I did promise to talk about using reality. "Why, if Jubilee isn't Wingham, has it got a Shuter Street in it?" people want to know. Why have I described somebody's real ceramic elephant sitting on the mantelpiece? I could say I get momentum from doing things like this. The fictional room, town, world, needs a bit of starter dough from the real world. It's a device to help the writer—at least it helps me—but it arouses a certain baulked fury in the people who really do live on Shuter Street and the lady who owns the ceramic elephant. "Why do you put in something true and then go and tell lies?" they say, and anybody who has been on the receiving end of this kind of thing knows how they feel.

"I do it for the sake of my art and to make this structure which encloses the soul of my story, that I've been telling you about," says the writer. "That is more important than anything." Not to everybody it isn't.

So I can see there might be a case, once you've written the story and got the momentum, for going back and changing the elephant to a camel (though there's always a chance the lady might complain that you made a nasty camel out of a beautiful elephant), and changing Shuter Street to Blank Street. But what about the big chunks of reality, without which your story can't exist? In the story "Royal Beatings," I use a big chunk of reality: the story of the butcher, and of the young men who may have been egged on to "get" him. This is a story out of an old newspaper; it really did happen in a town I know. There is no legal difficulty about using it because it has been printed in a newspaper, and besides, the people who figure in it are all long dead. But there is a difficulty about offending people in that town who would feel that use of this story is a deliberate exposure, taunt and insult. Other people who have no connection with the real happening would say "Why write about anything so hideous?" And lest you think that such an objection could only be raised by simple folk who read nothing but Harlequin Romances, let me tell you that one of the questions most frequently asked at universities is, "Why do you write about things that are so depressing?" People can accept almost any amount of ugliness if it is contained in a familiar formula, as it is on television, but when they come closer to their own place, their own lives, they are much offended by lack of editing.

There are ways I can defend myself against such objections. I can say, "I do it in the interests of historical reality. That is what the old days were really like." Or, "I do it to show the dark side of human nature, the beast let loose, the evil we can run up against in communities and families." In certain countries I could say, "I do it to show how bad things were under the old system when there were prosperous butchers and young fellows hanging around livery stables and nobody thought about building a new society." But the fact is, the minute I say *to show* I am telling a lie. I don't do it to show anything. I put this story at the heart of my story because I need it there and it belongs there. It is the black room at the centre of the house with all other rooms leading to and away from it. That is all. A strange defence. Who told me to write this story? Who feels any need of it before it is written? I do. I do, so that I might grab off this piece of horrid reality and install it where I see fit, even if Hat Nettleton and his friends were still around to make me sorry.

*   *   *

Alice Munro is not an explicitly political or feminist writer, nor does she write autobiography. However, her stories are largely concerned with the struggle between rebellion and respectability; they dramatize the "underbelly of relationships"; and in each collection we regularly see the same small-town, rural, Canadian setting where she grew up and continues to live "because I live life here at a level of irritation which I would not achieve in a place that I knew less well."

The stories are studies in perspective. They take family structures, neighborhoods, individuals, and groups of people, and show how they shift in the memory as they appear suddenly from an unexpected angle. Her characters move through layers of time and reality, and it is the gaps between those layers that reveal the power of Munro's fiction. "There are no such things as big and little subjects," she has said. "The major things, the evils, that exist in the world have a direct relationship to the evil that exists around a dining room table when people are doing things to each other."

Her first book of stories, *Dance of the Happy Shades,* charts the adolescent discovery of love and fear. "Boys and Girls" deals with two recurring themes in Munro's stories: domestic power plays and the impossibility of the functional mother/daughter relationship. When a girl, whose mother was "plotting to get me to stay in the house more, although she knew I hated it (*because* she knew I hated it) and keep me from working for my father" cries, it is because "she's only a girl." "I didn't protest that, even in my heart. Maybe it was true." Early sexual experiences in "Postcard" and "Thanks for the Ride" provide the vehicle for exploring adult sexual deceit. Many of the stories in this collection present a recognizable physical world rendered impenetrable by the emotionally disaffected people attempting to exist in it.

Munro's only novel, *Lives of Girls and Women,* follows the life of Del Jordan, a woman struggling to avoid the obscurity made seemingly inevitable by growing up in a small town, Jubilee. As Del Jordan remembers the milestones of her emotional growth, we see her pursuing different ways of being "endangered and desired." The novel is in a sense less satisfying than Munro's short stories; the form affords Del Jordan the opportunity to "go out and take on all kinds of experiences . . . and come back proud." But it does not make her any more complex a character than those who live in the short stories.

In the next collection of stories—*Something I've Been Meaning To Tell You*—the emphasis is on remembering, rather than projecting; on making sense of the past. *Something I've Been Meaning To Tell You* is one of Munro's bleaker collections, with disarray increasing through examination, rather than being resolved. In "Winter Wind" a character believes "that we have some connections that cannot be investigated."

Where many short story writers fall into the trap of making the form shrink to fit, Munro's stories bulge with details and density and are extended by the tensions and contradictions they generate. *Who Do You Think You Are?* is as much a novel as *Lives of Girls and Women;* it has the same episodic structure and offers ten "moments" from the life of Rose, who manages to leave the confines of her small town on a university scholarship. Neither Rose nor Del Jordan is able to "shuck off" fully the things they don't want, although Del affects some kind of certainty about what she does want. Rose, however, is often trapped by what the narrator in "Simon's Luck" calls "those shifts of emphasis that throw the story line open to question, the disarrangements which demand new judgments and solutions, and throw the windows open on inappropriate unforgettable scenery."

The Moons of Jupiter focuses on the nature of relationships between characters, rather than on the nature of the isolation these connections often seem to create in Munro's stories. Again, the contradictions between different levels of reality give these stories an atmosphere of threat: beneath the seemingly benign surface of experience real danger lurks. In "The Moons of Jupiter" the narrator describes "various knowns and unknowns and horrific immensities." The connections dramatized in this collection —between cousins ("Chaddeleys and Flemings"), lovers ("Hard-Luck Stories," "Accident"), or rest home companions ("Mrs. Cross and Mrs. Kidd")—are undermined by personal deceits, or by "the gap between what she wanted and what she could get," or by the overlap of need and want. "Connection. That was what it was all about. A connection with the real, and prodigal, and dangerous world." In "The Turkey Season," about relationships between women in a turkey factory, the protagonist explains how "I got to the stage of backing off from the things I couldn't really know."

The three most recent collections of stories—*The Progress of Love, Friend of My Youth,* and *Open Secrets*—provide, perhaps, the best introduction to Munro's work. In *The Progress of Love* all the elements of her previous work combine in an orgy of dishonesty and dissatisfaction. Jesse, the teenage girl conducting an imaginary affair with an older man in "Jesse and Meribeth," concedes "I didn't at all mind the lying. Once I had taken the plunge into falsehood . . . falsehood felt wonderfully comfortable." In "Eskimo" Mary Jo is having an affair with her married boss, Dr. Streeter, a man of "incurable, calm, and decent sadness. . . . This sadness seems to come from obedience." In the title story the narrator realizes that "Moments of kindness and reconciliation are worth having, even if the parting has to come sooner or later. I wonder if those moments aren't more valued, and deliberately gone after, in the setups some people like myself have now, than they were in those old marriages, where love and grudges could be growing underground, so confused and stubborn, it must have seemed they had forever." In "Fits" the apparent murder-suicide of a local couple provides such a moment for Peg and Robert: "They needed something new to talk about. Now he felt more like going home." In these stories Munro draws the tensions between everyday dissatisfaction and its chaotic possibilities brilliantly. The characters' realizations of these consequences—and their bearing on their own existence—are always insidious, revealed in flashes of light.

In *Friend of My Youth* the stories are more personal in feeling, the writing more controlled, and the characters' lives more full of falsity. In "Wigtime" Margot is reduced to stalking her adulterous husband in a wig and leaving anonymous notes under his windscreen. Hazel in "Hold Me Fast, Don't Let Me Pass" is a widow in her 50s, taking a leave of absence, who scribbles in notebooks: "It prevents the rise of panic. . . . This sort of panic had nothing to do with money or ticket arrangements, it had to do with a falling off of purpose, and the question why am I here?" There is a note of elegy in these stories, but the changes of mood and the shifts in perspective betray the deceptive gentleness of Munro's writing. The daughter in "Oh, What Avails" reflects that her mother had formed in the children "a delicate, special regard for themselves, which made them want to go out and grasp what they wanted, whether love or money."

The eight darkly luminous stories in *Open Secrets* explore with increasing precision and wonder, with increasing graveness and love, the tensions and contradictions of the human condition. "A Wilderness Station" presents—through a group of letters and recollections by, and to, a variety of persons—the fictional biography of Annie Herron, a woman of somewhat uncertain beginning, middle, and end who reaches early adulthood and marries in the

mid-19th century and lives on into the 20th. Following the seemingly accidental death of her husband while he is out working in the bush with his younger brother, Annie temporarily seeks refuge (of sorts) in a local Southwestern Ontario gaol for criminals and the insane and only gains retribution (of sorts) more than half a century later. The deeper historical note sounded in "A Wilderness Station" is reminiscent of "Meneseteung," an overwhelmingly original fictional biography, from *Friend of My Youth,* about an invented 19th-century southwestern Ontario poetess named Almeda Joynt Roth. Like so many of Munro's later stories, but somehow more compellingly, "Meneseteung" fills and empties the reader in ways we associate with classical tragedy. This is not to say that her later stories are without comedy, for comedy represents an extremely important, and equally ritualistic, component of her work.

In "Spaceships Have Landed"—a story describing the friendship, then and now, of two country girls —imaginative play and verbal play are crucial to Munro's achievement: "And the worst thing was when Eunie launched into accounts that Rhea found both boring and infuriating, of murders and disasters and freakish events that she had heard about on the radio. Rhea was infuriated because she could not get Eunie to tell her whether these things had really happened, or even to make that distinction—as far as Rhea could tell—to herself. "Was that on the news, Eunie? Was it a story? Were there people acting it in front of a microphone or was it reporting? Eunie! Was it real or was it a play?" It was Rhea, never Eunie, who would get frazzled by these questions. Eunie would just get on her bicycle and ride away. 'Toodeley oodeley oo! See you in the zoo!'" What nonsense, we think—or is it? Might Eunie be seen to possess an understanding of the indivisibility of truth and imagination, seriousness and play, the natural and the supernatural, that surpasses Rhea's meagrely realistic, literal-minded understanding? Might Eunie be seen to represent some kind of metaphor, or an alter ego, for the artist?

In story after story, Munro reveals the exhilarating character of life itself, with all of life's surprising but inevitable interventions in the form of a death, unexpected visitors, an unusual letter, whatever. Such occurrences pervade Munro's later stories, fracturing each character's—and each reader's—expectations, rendering easy accommodations with life or art impossible. Moreover, from these interventions other actions unfailingly unfold. Increasingly in Munro's later stories, we see something of the quality that Eudora Welty (an acknowledged influence on Munro) admired in William Faulker: "veracity and accuracy about the world" that reveals both the comedy of being human and what Welty terms "that comedy's adjoining terror."

Perhaps Munro's stories should be read as a new kind of novel; not one after the other, but each allowed time to resonate in the reader's head. As Munro says: "I want the stories to keep diminishing but not to be suddenly over with, so one is left with the central mystery of the story."

—Juliette Bright, updated by J.R. (Tim) Struthers

MURDOCH, (Jean) Iris

Nationality: British. **Born:** Dublin, Ireland, 15 July 1919. **Education:** The Froebel Education Institute, London; Badminton

School, Bristol; Somerville College, Oxford, 1938-42, B.A. (first class honors) 1942; Newnham College, Cambridge (Sarah Smithson student in philosophy), 1947-48. **Family:** Married the writer John Bayley in 1956. **Career:** Assistant principal in the Treasury, London, 1942-44; administrative officer with the United Nations Relief and Rehabilitation Administration (UNRRA) in London, Belgium, and Austria, 1944-46; fellow, St. Anne's College, Oxford, and University Lecturer in philosophy, Oxford University, 1948-63; Honorary Fellow of St. Anne's College from 1963; lecturer, Royal College of Art, London, 1963-67. Lives in Oxford. **Awards:** James Tait Black Memorial prize, 1974; Whitbread award, 1974; Booker prize, 1978; Shakespeare prize (Hamburg), 1988; National Arts Club (U.S.A.) Medal of Honor, 1990. D. Litt.: Oxford University, 1987. Member, Irish Academy, 1970; honorary member, American Academy, 1975, and American Academy of Arts and Sciences, 1982; honorary fellow, Somerville College, 1977, and Newnham College, 1986. Companion of Literature, Royal Society of Literature, 1987. C.B.E. (Commander, Order of the British Empire), 1976; D.B.E. (Dame Commander, Order of the British Empire), 1987. **Agent:** Ed Victor Ltd., 162 Wardour Street, London W1V 4AT, England.

PUBLICATIONS

Novels

Under the Net. London, Chatto and Windus, and New York, Viking Press, 1954.
The Flight from the Enchanter. London, Chatto and Windus, and New York, Viking Press, 1956.
The Sandcastle. London, Chatto and Windus, and New York, Viking Press, 1957.
The Bell. London, Chatto and Windus, and New York, Viking Press, 1958.
A Severed Head. London, Chatto and Windus, and New York, Viking Press, 1961.
An Unofficial Rose. London, Chatto and Windus, and New York, Viking Press, 1962.
The Unicorn. London, Chatto and Windus, and New York, Viking Press, 1963.
The Italian Girl. London, Chatto and Windus, and New York, Viking Press, 1964.
The Red and the Green. London, Chatto and Windus, and New York, Viking Press, 1965.
The Time of the Angels. London, Chatto and Windus, and New York, Viking Press, 1966.
The Nice and the Good. London, Chatto and Windus, and New York, Viking Press, 1968.
Bruno's Dream. London, Chatto and Windus, and New York, Viking Press, 1969.
A Fairly Honourable Defeat. London, Chatto and Windus, and New York, Viking Press, 1970.
An Accidental Man. London, Chatto and Windus, 1971; New York, Viking Press, 1972.
The Black Prince. London, Chatto and Windus, and New York, Viking Press, 1973.
The Sacred and Profane Love Machine. London, Chatto and Windus, and New York, Viking Press, 1974.
A Word Child. London, Chatto and Windus, and New York, Viking Press, 1975.

Henry and Cato. London, Chatto and Windus, 1976; New York, Viking Press, 1977.
The Sea, The Sea. London, Chatto and Windus, and New York, Viking Press, 1978.
Nuns and Soldiers. London, Chatto and Windus, 1980; New York, Viking Press, 1981.
The Philosopher's Pupil. London, Chatto and Windus, and New York, Viking Press, 1983.
The Good Apprentice. London, Chatto and Windus, 1985; New York, Viking Press, 1986.
The Book and the Brotherhood. London, Chatto and Windus, 1987; New York, Viking, 1988.
The Message to the Planet. London, Chatto and Windus, 1989; New York, Viking, 1990.
The Green Knight. London, Chatto and Windus, 1993; New York, Viking, 1994.

Uncollected Short Story

"Something Special," in *Winter's Tales 3.* London, Macmillan, and New York, St. Martin's Press, 1957.

Plays

A Severed Head, with J.B. Priestley, adaptation of the novel by Murdoch (produced Bristol and London, 1963; New York, 1964). London, Chatto and Windus, 1964.
The Italian Girl, with James Saunders, adaptation of the novel by Murdoch (produced Bristol, 1967; London, 1968). London, French, 1969.
The Servants and the Snow (produced London, 1970). With *The Three Arrows,* London, Chatto and Windus, 1973; New York, Viking Press, 1974.
The Three Arrows (produced Cambridge, 1972). With *The Servants and the Snow,* London, Chatto and Windus, 1973; New York, Viking Press, 1974.
Art and Eros (produced London, 1980). Included in *Acastos,* 1986.
The Servants (opera libretto), adaptation of her play *The Servants and the Snow,* music by William Mathias (produced Cardiff, 1980).
Ascastos: Two Platonic Dialogues (includes *Art and Eros* and *Above the Gods*). London, Chatto and Windus, 1986; New York, Viking, 1987.
The Black Prince, adaptation of her own novel (produced London, 1989). Included in *Three Plays,* 1989.
Three Plays (includes *The Servants and the Snow, The Three Arrows, The Black Prince*). London, Chatto and Windus, 1989.

Radio Play: *The One Alone* (in verse), music by Gary Carpenter, 1987.

Poetry

A Year of Birds. Tisbury, Wiltshire, Compton Press, 1978.

Other

Sartre, Romantic Rationalist. Cambridge, Bowes, and New Haven, Connecticut, Yale University Press, 1953; as *Sartre, Romantic Realist,* Brighton, Harvester Press, 1980.
The Sovereignty of Good over Other Concepts (lecture). Cambridge, University Press, 1967.

The Sovereignty of Good (essays). London, Routledge, 1970; New York, Schocken, 1971.

The Fire and the Sun: Why Plato Banished the Artists. London, and New York, Oxford University Press, 1977.

Reynolds Stone (address). London, Warren, 1981.

The Existential Political Myth. Birmingham, Delos Press, 1989.

Metaphysics as a Guide to Morals. New York, Viking, 1992.

*

Bibliography: *Iris Murdoch and Muriel Spark: A Bibliography* by Thomas T. Tominaga and Wilma Schneidermeyer, Metuchen, New Jersey, Scarecrow Press, 1976; *Iris Murdoch: A Reference Guide* by Kate Begnal, Boston, Hall, 1987.

Manuscript Collection: University of Iowa, Iowa City.

Critical Studies: *Degrees of Freedom: The Novels of Iris Murdoch,* London, Chatto and Windus, and New York, Barnes and Noble, 1965, and *Iris Murdoch,* London, Longman, 1976, both by A.S. Byatt; *The Disciplined Heart: Iris Murdoch and Her Novels* by Peter Wolfe, Columbia, University of Missouri Press, 1966; *Iris Murdoch* by Rubin Rabinovitz, New York, Columbia University Press, 1968; *Iris Murdoch* by Frank Baldanza, New York, Twayne, 1974; *Iris Murdoch* by Donna Gerstenberger, Lewisburg, Pennsylvania, Bucknell University Press, 1974; *Iris Murdoch: The Shakespearian Interest,* New York, Barnes and Noble, and London, Vision Press, 1979, and *Iris Murdoch,* London, Methuen, 1984, both by Richard Todd, and *Encounters with Iris Murdoch* edited by Todd, Amsterdam, Free University Press, 1988; *Iris Murdoch: Work for the Spirit* by Elizabeth Dipple, Chicago, University of Chicago Press, 1981, London, Methuen, 1982; *Iris Murdoch's Comic Vision* by Angela Hague, Selinsgrove, Pennsylvania, Susquehanna University Press, 1984; *Iris Murdoch: The Saint and the Artist* by Peter J. Conradi, London, Macmillan, and New York, St. Martin's Press, 1986; *Iris Murdoch* edited by Harold Bloom, New York, Chelsea House, 1986; *Iris Murdoch: The Novelist as Philosopher, The Philosopher as Novelist* by Guy Backus, Bern, Switzerland, Lang, 1986; *A Character Index and Guide to the Fiction of Iris Murdoch* by Cheryl K. Bove, New York, Garland, 1986; *Iris Murdoch* by Deborah Johnson, Bloomington, Indiana University Press, and Brighton, Sussex, Harvester Press, 1987; *Iris Murdoch: Figures of Good* by Suguna Ramanathan, London, Macmillan, 1990.

*   *   *

Iris Murdoch has established a prodigious body of reflective and philosophical work, a wide-ranging, discursive, often metaphorically conveyed commentary on the contemporary world. She began with *Under the Net,* with what seems in retrospect a novel in the avant-garde mode of the 1950s, following a group of rootless characters in picaresque adventures around London as they try to develop some semblance of individual identities. Two of the characters are actresses, sisters, able to switch and create roles, although far less certain of what the self is behind the various selves they create. These and other characters manage to avoid or slip through the "Nets" of conventional or exterior definition, to preserve their independence and existential freedom by reducing their scale or function to little more than the amorphous identity of the living creature. With her second novel, *The Flight from the Enchanter,*

Murdoch began to assert more explicitly her difference from Sartrean existentialism (about which she wrote a book entitled *Sartre, Romantic Rationalist*). In *The Flight from the Enchanter* some of the characters are less free than others, conditioned to a point of incapacity to choose by circumstance, nation, psyche, or history. Even among those for whom meaningful choice is possible, Murdoch maintains a difference between those who choose to exercise power over others, to "enchant," and those who build their identities, however trivial, to preserve the creature in resistance to various contemporary "enchantments." The novels that followed, like *The Sandcastle* and *The Bell,* detailed similarly elaborate constructions of human identity, presented with striking drama in metaphors like scaling towers and dredging sunken bells from lakes, in which the creature was visible despite the impossibility of his or her project. Identities were always in flux, related in different combinations, a texture of constantly shifting relationship nowhere more visible than in *A Severed Head,* in which each of the three principal males, at some point in the novel, has an affair with each of the three principal females. The sudden and unpredictable coupling is not, however, the sign of a solipsistic world, for, through these changes, the central character learns to value relationships that depend on his risks and his wine-tasting abilities, his instincts, not those carefully calibrated by the various conventions of the "head."

Subsequent novels expanded the range of experience Murdoch treated and began to question the value of the simple creature, the sanction of unconsciousness. *An Unofficial Rose* for example, uses the cultivation of roses as a central metaphor and values "unofficial" forms that can give rich, floral, yet individual and ethical shapes to human experience. The novel is also distinguished by the careful and moving treatment of a love affair between an elderly couple. *The Unicorn* adds dimensions of mystery and myth to Murdoch's treatment of human identity, and this novel, along with *The Time of the Angels,* begins to probe the meaning and value of religious experience (religion had appeared earlier, in *The Bell,* although its complexities were more those of the religious community as social entity, less the significance of the religious experience itself). History and politics are apparent in a novel like *The Red and the Green,* transferring the issues of individual and social identity to a group of characters in Dublin just before the Easter uprising of 1916. Murdoch's England has never been insular or self-enclosed; it is always, metaphorically, an England after World War II, conscious of its good fortune in surviving and sympathetic with various displaced persons. Acute sympathy for Poles, for example, is important to novels as far apart in time and as dissimilar in theme as *The Flight from the Enchanter* and *Nuns and Soldiers.*

In the late 1960s Murdoch's fiction became more directly and coherently ethical in focus. In novels such as *The Nice and the Good, Bruno's Dream, A Fairly Honourable Defeat,* and *An Accidental Man,* the ethical framework provides a fairly consistent structure, a central debate and resolution worked through the usual Murdoch world of bizarre incident and predictably unpredictable encounters. In two of these novels, *The Nice and the Good* and *A Fairly Honourable Defeat,* the debate contrasts a false morality with a genuine one by establishing a married couple who think their relationship a model for others. In one novel, Murdoch satirizes their hollowness; in the other, she introduces an agent of evil, impelled by his own isolation and pain, who destroys them. In these novels, characters seen as false, smug, or self-righteous are articulate about their pretended virtues; they theorize and erect structures that delude themselves and others. But those posed against them, the genuinely good, are not the unconscious creatures of the earlier novels; rather, more quietly, less grandiosely, they both articulate and act out their ethics, their concern for others, and their respect for the boundaries between the self and others. The unconscious characters, in these novels, are often seen as "accidental," just following random personal impulse and living as harmful parasites. God figures, too, are not simply the deluding myths of the earlier novels, but can choose whether to involve themselves in human concerns or retain the mystery of their own power and remoteness. In these novels, too, interference in the lives of others is a complex ethical issue, reflecting all the possibilities of human connection. Sometimes interference is cruel and brutal, an immoral imposition; at other times, it is incompetent but warmhearted, leading to the ludicrous rather than to disaster. Some who theorize too much and too consistently, interfere in the wrong way at the wrong time, violate, in their inconsistent attempts at consistency, both themselves and others; some interfere only as a projection of themselves, with no recognition of the other. Yet some interference is genuinely relevant and helpful to others, as one of the characters says, in *An Accidental Man,* "separated" help is possible. In Murdoch's world, characters reveal themselves through the quality of their impositions, their deliberate and conscious connections with other people.

Murdoch also sees her fiction as itself a form of interference that engages. The bizarre plots, the elaborate structures overturned, the human pretensions made comic—all interfere with settled abstract versions of experience. In a May 1972 speech before the American Academy of Arts and Letters, Murdoch defended both this moral role of serious literature in the modern world and the moral function of language itself: "Words constitute the ultimate texture and stuff of our moral being, since they are the most refined and delicate and detailed, as well as the most universally used and understood of the symbolisms whereby we express ourselves into existence. We became spiritual animals when we became verbal animals. The *fundamental* distinctions can only be made in words. Words are spirit. Of course eloquence is no guarantee of goodness, and an inarticulate man can be virtuous. But the quality of a civilization depends upon its ability to discern and reveal truth, and this depends on the scope and the purity of its language."

Murdoch's fiction continues to suggest the range of human thought, the classically philosophical as well as the linguistic and ethical. In addition to her novels, she has published a book on ethics, *The Sovereignty of Good,* and a more recent consideration of Plato, *The Fire and the Sun.* The fiction expands and elaborates, or converts to metaphor, the abstract inquiry. *The Sacred and Profane Love Machine* explores various versions of human passion and commitment, both conscious and unconscious. *A Word Child* treats the kind of linguistic analysis common in academic philosophy since the days of the Logical Positivists; Wittgenstein, both as cultural tag and as representing questions that cannot be avoided, is a frequent reference point in a number of the novels. Often, the later fiction, like *The Sea, The Sea,* is mystical and visionary. *The Black Prince* considers possible justification for murder, as well as an entire artistic career based on imposition. Death and its effects on survivors are metaphorically central in novels like *Bruno's Dream* and *Nuns and Soldiers.* *The Good Apprentice* establishes the civilized great house in the center of the wilderness and examines both the religious and the artistic forms that emanate from the house into the wider and more chaotic world of the fiction. In all Murdoch's novels, existence is precarious and difficult: plot consists of unexpected assaults on any certainty and unexpected changes in allegiance or emotion; most characters' backgrounds, increasingly in more recent novels, include the sudden deaths or desertion of parents and the early deaths of siblings or close friends. The existence of God, of some pattern or meaning, or of faith in something beyond the knowable, is always a question, considered, debated, treated with indifference or anguish, yet never resolved. Myth and metaphor suggest a world outside the self: the generalization of particular human dilemmas into all of history, or the externalization of particular issues in a given novel, like the crucible of heat in which *The Nice and the Good* takes place or the isolating frost or dissolving rain that surrounds some of the other novels. In all these novels, the human being is tested by her or his response to or possible recovery from pain and deprivation. The forms of response are various and imaginative; as one of the characters in *Nuns and Soldiers* concludes, "We are all the judges and the judged, victims of the casual malice and fantasy of others, and ready sources of fantasy and malice in our turn." Yet, in Murdoch's world, despite all the pain of existence, most people (and all of those seen as worthy) resist the safety and stasis of the enclosures of the incompletely knowable self.

—James Gindin

MURNANE, Gerald

Nationality: Australian. **Born:** Melbourne, Victoria, in 1939. **Education:** The University of Melbourne, B.A. 1969. **Family:** Married; three sons. **Career:** Currently lecturer in creative writing, Victoria College, Melbourne. **Address:** 2 Falcon Street, Macleod, Victoria 3085, Australia.

PUBLICATIONS

Novels

Tamarisk Row. Melbourne, Heinemann, 1974.
A Lifetime on Clouds. Melbourne, Heinemann, 1976.
The Plains. Carlton, Victoria, Norstrilia Press, 1982; London, Penguin, 1984; New York, Braziller, 1985.
Landscape with Landscape. Carlton, Victoria, Norstrilia Press, 1985.
Inland. Richmond, Victoria, Heinemann, 1988; London, Faber, 1989.

Short Stories

Velvet Waters. Ringwood, Victoria, McPhee Gribble, 1990.

Other

Editor, with Jenny Lee and Phillip Mead, *Temperament of Generations: Fifty Years of Writing in Meanjin.* Carlton, Victoria, Meanjin, 1990.

*

Critical Studies: *Gerald Murnane* edited by John Hanrahan, Footscrag, Victoria, Footscrag Foundation for Australian Studies,

1987; *Gerald Murnane* by Imre Salusinszky, Melbourne and Oxford, Oxford University Press, 1993.

*   *   *

Gerald Murnane began as a writer of confessedly autobiographical fiction of a talented but fairly conventional kind but developed eventually into a writer who has been variously classified as postmodernist or fabulist and who has been described hyperbolically by at least one Australian critic as "the most original writer this country has produced." *Tamarisk Row,* for instance, is a comparatively familiar story of growing up Catholic in the Australian countryside. Clement Killeaton lives in the town of Bassett. His father is a compulsive gambler and the family live in perpetual poverty. The boy inherits his father's love of gambling but converts it into an activity of the imagination. Already, though, there are signs of the direction which Murnane's fiction will eventually lead—in the constant references to maps and calendars, in the boy's substitution for the dull reality of numbers and figures images of his own devising and in the beginnings of the hypnotic absorption in his own imaginative processes.

Murnane's second novel *A Lifetime on Clouds* remains more or less in the realm of realism. It suffers, despite the witty treatment of its material from the fact that the material is very familiar, in Australia at least—the tormented nature of adolescent sexuality for Catholic-educated youths. More specifically it concerns masturbation and, *Portnoy's Complaint* not withstanding, there has probably never been any other novel which examines, explores, concerns itself with the subject so relentlessly and in such detail. What elements of fantasy are present are employed crudely, for example with the protagonist driving in Florida with Jayne, Marilyn, and Susan—whose identities can easily be guessed.

With *The Plains,* however, Murnane more or less abandons realism altogether to move in the direction of something best described by his own term of fable. None of the characters is named; there are hardly any references to specific places, though the city of Melbourne is mentioned with abhorrence; there are no personal relationships, little or no action and scarcely any dialogue except for one long series of lateral monologues which occasionally intersect as the plainsmen converse. The plains work on the level of myth or metaphor but the problem is to decide what they are a metaphor of. The plains, the novel seems to be saying, are the "real" Australia to which residents of Outer Australia or the coast flee in relief. *Landscape with Landscape,* the second of three successive works to have titles concerning landscape, confirms the movement towards a kind of metarealism, a fiction preoccupied with a kind of infinite regression, not the representation of reality but the exploration of modes of representing reality, through modes of exploring those modes . . . etc. As the narrator of the fourth of the book's six sections puts it, "I decided to include the poem below in this story when I understood that the young man who wrote it was not myself but a character in a work of fiction and that as soon as I began to write about him I became an author of fiction. (Since the previous sentence is part of a work of fiction a certain young man and the man he might have become are doubly difficult to image any-where but in fiction. [The sentence just ended is also part of a work of fiction as is this sentence]." The concern is not merely with experience as such but with the possibility of representing experience, the substitution of language for experience, the ways in which fiction and reality merge and become conflated. The self-consciousness and the preoccupation with writing itself—the inner landscape at the expense of the outer one—come out in the long parentheses, in the intertextual references and in the narrator/writer defining himself as writer. "Now he seemed almost defined by the long shapely sentences in the pages on his desk . . . "

Inland is constructed of some dozen or so unmarked sections, linked only by the probable presence of an identical yet nevertheless anonymous narrator, which become shorter and shorter and closer to home in scope. The opening words of the novel are: "I am writing in the library of a manor-house in a village I prefer not to name, near the town of Kunmadaras, in Szolnok County." The narrator addresses and engages with the reader constantly, quickly establishing a self-conscious mode with his long, meditative, elaborate sentences; he mentions in particular his editor, Anne Kristaly Gunnarsen, who lives "in the land of America, in the state of South Dakota, in Tripp County, in the town of Ideal": America is yet another of Murnane's mythical landscapes. The landscape of Szolnok County seems to merge into that of South Dakota and then in turn to that of "Melbourne county." The autobiographical references as well as allusions to Murnane's earlier work become more frequent. There are the same key motifs: maps and atlases, calendars, colours, references to suburbs. The constant allusions to Proust are both appropriate and justified. One of the many books that the novel refers to or quotes points to Proust's achievement in making France real for people who have never been there. Murnane is much concerned with the boundaries—or blurring of boundaries—of the real and the imagined and with the role of literature in mediating between them.

Murnane's most recent book, *Velvet Waters,* is a collection of his shorter fiction dating back to 1972 and as one would expect is closely related to and refers back to his earlier writing. "Stream System" in fact is taken from an earlier version of *The Plains* but the stories in general deal with the same material and themes as the novels. Murnane's prose, in its almost ritualistically repetitive cadences and stylised simplicities, can seem like a strange combination of Proust and Calvino while the story "Precious Bane" is Borgesian in its preoccupation with a self-contained world of writing. Murnane can descend almost into self-parody at times, as in "Finger Webb" with its deliberately reiterated cadences ('The man in this story . . . The man in this story . . .') but some of the stories are among the most moving that he has ever written. "When the Mice Failed to Arrive," for instance, cuts between past and present to offer a delicate portrait of the relationship between the narrator and his father, and the former's realisation of his failure with the students he loves, while "Stream System" becomes a poignantly retrospective act of self-understanding as the narrator recognises his failure to love his retarded brother.

—Laurie Clancy

N

NAHAL, Chaman (Lal)

Nationality: Indian. **Born:** Sialkot (now in Pakistan), 2 August 1927. **Education:** The University of Delhi, M.A. in English 1948; University of Nottingham (British Council scholar), 1959-61, Ph.D. in English 1961. **Family:** Married Sudarshna Rani in 1955; two daughters. **Career:** Lecturer at universities in India, 1949-62; reader in English, Rajasthan University, Jaipur, 1962-63; reader in English, 1963-80, and professor of English, University of Delhi, 1980-92; visiting Fulbright Fellow, Princeton University, New Jersey, 1967-70; from 1971 visiting lecturer at several universities in the U.S.A., Malaysia, Japan, Singapore, Canada, and North Korea; fellow, Churchill College, Cambridge, 1991. Columnist ("Talking about Books"), *Indian Express,* New Delhi, 1966-73. **Awards:** Sahitya Academy award, 1977; Federation of Indian Publishers award, 1977, 1979. **Agent:** Margaret Hanbury, 27 Walcot Square, London SE11 4XB, England. **Address:** 2/1 Kalkaji Extension, New Delhi 110019, India.

PUBLICATIONS

Novels

My True Faces. New Delhi, Orient, 1973.
Into Another Dawn. New Delhi, Sterling, 1977.
The English Queens. New Delhi, Vision, 1979.
Sunrise in Fiji. New Delhi, Allied, 1988.
The Ghandi Quartet. New Delhi, Allied, 1993.
Azadi (Freedom). New Delhi, Arnold-Heinemann, and Boston, Houghton Mifflin, 1975; London, Deutsch, 1977.
The Crown and the Loincloth. New Delhi, Vikas, 1981.
The Salt of Life. New Delhi, Allied, 1990.
The Triumph of the Tricolour. New Delhi, Allied, 1993.

Short Stories

The Weird Dance and Other Stories. New Delhi, Arya, 1965.

Uncollected Short Stories

"Tons," in *The Statesman* (New Delhi), 12 June 1977.
"The Light on the Lake," in *Illustrated Weekly of India* (Bombay), 22 July 1984.
"The Take Over," in *Debonair* (Bombay), August 1985.

Other

Moby Dick (for children), adaptation of the novel by Melville. New Delhi, Eurasia, 1965.
A Conversation with J. Krishnamurti. New Delhi, Arya, 1965.
D.H. Lawrence: An Eastern View. South Brunswick, New Jersey, A.S. Barnes, and London, Yoseloff, 1971.
The Narrative Pattern in Ernest Hemingway's Fiction. New Delhi, Vikas, and Rutherford, New Jersey, Fairleigh Dickinson University Press, 1971.

The New Literatures in English. New Delhi, Allied, 1985.
Jawaharlal Nehru as a Man of Letters. New Delhi, Allied, 1990.

Editor, *Drugs and the Other Self: An Anthology of Spiritual Transformations.* New York, Harper, 1971.

*

Bibliography: In *The New Literatures in English,* 1985.

Critical Studies: *Commonwealth Literature in the Curriculum* edited by K.L. Goodwin, St. Lucia, University of Queensland Press, 1980; introduction by A. Komarov to *The Crown and the Loincloth,* Moscow, Raduga, 1984; *Three Contemporary Novelists: Khushwant Singh, Chaman Nahal, and Salman Rushdie* edited by R.K. Dhawan, New Delhi, Classical, 1985.

Chaman Nahal comments:

(1991) I have largely concerned myself with two themes in my novels; the individual vs. the joint family system in India, and my historical identity as an individual, as an Indian. For the latter theme I have drawn extensively on history, especially our freedom movement, 1915-47. *Azadi, The Crown and the Loincloth,* and *The Salt of Life* are part of a quartet on that theme; I'm working on the fourth volume of the quartet now. I use Gandhi as the ultimate symbol of that identity.

(1995) I am now working on a novel for children.

*   *   *

Chaman Nahal's distinction lies in writing about India without any touch of exoticism; he scrupulously avoids the stereotyped "East" of maharajahs, tigers and snakecharmers. The actual town of Delhi (in *My True Faces* and *The English Queens*) and the typical Punjabi town of Sialkot are presented vividly, and we get a good idea of middle-class life in India. *Azadi* is the best of the Indian-English novels written about the traumatic partition which accompanied Indian Independence in 1947. *The Crown and the Loincloth* and *The Salt of Life* portray Mahatma Gandhi as a complex character with human failings. *The English Queens* breaks new ground by using the comic mode to treat a problem which has concerned all Indians—the tendency of the educated elite in India to ape the West.

Nahal's first novel, *My True Faces,* adequately portrays the agony of a sensitive young man when he finds his wife and baby son missing. But the crisis seems to be too minor to warrant the heavy philosophical treatment, with the hero realizing at the end of the novel that all earthly manifestations are but faces of Krishna, and they are all his "true faces." The involved language betrays the fact that it is the work of a scholarly professor of English.

Azadi ("Freedom"), which won the award of the Sahitya Akademi (India's national academy of letters), employs an entirely different style. It is a straightforward account of a rich Hindu grain merchant and his family. The novel begins in mid-1947 with the people of Sialkot (now in Pakistan) hearing the announcement regarding partition, but they refuse to believe that they now have to move. Nahal shows how Kanshi Ram the Hindu, Barkat Ali the Mohammedan, and Teja Singh the Sikh share the same Punjabi culture and language, and consider Sialkot their homeland. Meticulous attention to details and a firsthand knowledge of the life of the characters enable Nahal to make the plight of the refugees real to the reader. The novel ends with a sadly depleted family trying to begin life anew in Delhi. *Azadi* has none of the sensationalism of other novels about India's partition, such as Khushwant Singh's *Train to Pakistan* or Manohar Malgonkar's *A Bend in the Ganges.* Nahal shows the cruelty as well as the humanity of both sides. The novel also shows the maturing of Arun, Kanshi Ram's only son, but the account of his love, first for Nur, the Muslim girl left behind in Pakistan, and then for Chandni, a low-caste girl who is abducted on the way to India, is not as gripping as the rest of the novel.

Nahal's next novel, *Into Another Dawn,* is basically an East-West love story, set chiefly in the U.S.A. Nahal's sixth novel, *Sunrise in Fiji,* is a psychological study of Harivansh, a successful architect in his forties, who finds his personal life empty and meaningless. He goes to Fiji to bid for a building contract, and uses the break from routine to do some much needed soul-searching.

The English Queens is unique in Indian-English fiction; it is a very funny but hard-hitting satire against the elitism of the English-speaking groups in India, such as the officers of the defense forces, the *nouveau riche,* the highly placed civil servants, or Indians having foreign wives. Nahal unfolds a fantastic plot hatched by Lord Mountbatten, the last British Viceroy of India, to ensure India's subjugation to Britain. On the eve of handing over political power he prepares a charter for the "safe transfer of linguistic power" by which he gives the English language to India. To "preserve, propagate and spread" English in India he appoints six women in New Delhi to "The Order of the Queens." Rekha, the daughter of one of these queens, horrifies them by wanting to marry a young man from a working-class slum; worse still, he wears Indian clothes and is an expert in Indian classical music. The novel takes a further fantastic turn when the bridegroom reveals himself as an avatar of Vishnu, who has come to destroy this pernicious second-hand English culture. He flies back to heaven with the charter, but it drops out of his hand accidentally, and comes back to continue its destructive work; perhaps even God cannot help India! Of course, Nahal is not against the English language as such; his satire is against the kind of Indian who thinks that it is shameful to know anything about his own culture. One wonders whether non-Indian readers would enjoy the book as much as Indians do, because much of the humor rests on topical allusions.

"The Gandhi Quartet," Nahal's work-in-progress, covers three decades of Indian history, from 1915 to 1947. *Azadi,* which describes the last phase of the struggle for independence, was the first to be published. *The Crown and the Loincloth* is the first of three novels with Mahatma Gandhi as central character. Nahal presents Gandhi directly as well as in terms of the effect he has on the family of Thakur Shanti Nath, a landowner in a Punjabi village. This novel is set in the period from 1915 to 1922, and deals with many historical events such as Gandhi's return to India in 1915 and the Jallianwala Bagh massacre. Sunil, the landlord's son, and Sunil's wife Kusum are followers of Mahatma Gandhi. Sunil dies in 1922 while saving the Prince of Wales from an attack by terrorists, and Kusum joins Gandhi's ashram at Sabarmati with their young son Vikram. The second novel, *The Salt of Life,* centers on Gandhi's salt satyagraha of 1930. The heroine, Kusum, leaves the ashram when she gets married to Raja Vishal Chand, the ruler of a small princely state in the Himalayas. Her son Vikram stays on with Gandhi and participates in the Dandi march. When Vishal

Chand dies, Kusum comes back to the ashram. *The Triumph of the Tricolour,* the third volume, deals with the Quit India movement of 1942. Nahal plans to join up these three novels with *Azadi* by writing an epilogue showing how Kusum's family fares in newly independent India. The narrative style of the later novels is quite complex, integrating Indian modes of storytelling with Western techniques like the stream-of-consciousness novel. But they lack the power of *Azadi,* which remains Nahal's best novel.

—Shyamala A. Narayan

NAIPAUL, (Sir) V(idiadhar) S(urajprasad)

Nationality: Trinidadian. **Born:** Trinidad, 17 August 1932; brother of the writer Shiva Naipaul. **Education:** Tranquillity Boys School, 1939-42; Queen's Royal College, Port of Spain, Trinidad, 1943-49; University College, Oxford, 1950-54, B.A. (honors) in English 1953. **Family:** Married Patricia Ann Hale in 1955. **Career:** Editor, "Caribbean Voices," BBC, London, 1954-56; fiction reviewer, *New Statesman,* London, 1957-61; contributor to *New York Review of Books, New Statesman,* and other periodicals. **Awards:** Rhys Memorial prize, 1958; Maugham award 1961; Phoenix Trust award, 1962; Hawthornden prize, 1964; W.H. Smith literary award, 1968; Arts Council grant, 1969; Booker prize, 1971; Bennett award (*Hudson Review*), 1980; Jerusalem prize, 1983; T.S. Eliot award, 1986; Trinity Cross (Trinidad), 1989. D.Litt.: University of the West Indies, Trinidad, 1975; St. Andrews University, Fife, Scotland, 1979; Columbia University, New York, 1981; Cambridge University, 1983; University of London, 1988. Honorary fellow, University College, Oxford, 1983. Knighted, 1990. **Agent:** Aitken and Stone Ltd., 29 Fernshaw Road, London SW10 0TG, England.

PUBLICATIONS

Novels

The Mystic Masseur. London, Deutsch, 1957; New York, Vanguard Press, 1959.
The Suffrage of Elvira. London, Deutsch, 1958; in *Three Novels,* New York, Knopf, 1982.
Miguel Street. London, Deutsch, 1959; New York, Vanguard Press, 1960.
A House for Mr. Biswas. London, Deutsch, 1961; New York, McGraw Hill, 1962.
Mr. Stone and the Knights Companion. London, Deutsch, 1963; New York, Macmillan, 1964.
The Mimic Men. London Deutsch, and New York, Macmillan, 1967.
In a Free State. London, Deutsch, and New York, Knopf, 1971.
Guerrillas. London, Deutsch, and New York, Knopf, 1975.
A Bend in the River. London, Deutsch, and New York, Knopf, 1979.
The Enigma of Arrival. London, Viking, and New York, Knopf, 1987.
A Way in the World. London, Heinemann, and New York, Knopf, 1994.

Short Stories

A Flag on the Island. London, Deutsch, 1967; New York, Macmillan, 1968.

Other

The Middle Passage: Impressions of Five Societies—British, French and Dutch—in the West Indies and South America. London, Deutsch, 1962; New York, Macmillan, 1963.

An Area of Darkness: An Experience of India. London, Deutsch, 1964; New York, Macmillan, 1965.

The Loss of El Dorado: A History. London, Deutsch, 1969; New York, Knopf, 1970; revised edition, London, Penguin, 1973.

The Overcrowded Barracoon and Other Articles. London, Deutsch, 1972; New York, Knopf, 1973.

India: A Wounded Civilization. London, Deutsch, and New York, Knopf, 1977.

The Return of Eva Perón, with *The Killings in Trinidad* (essays). London, Deutsch, and New York, Knopf, 1980.

A Congo Diary. Los Angeles, Sylvester and Orphanos, 1980.

Among the Believers: An Islamic Journey. London, Deutsch, and New York, Knopf, 1981.

Finding the Centre: Two Narratives. London, Deutsch, and New York, Knopf, 1984.

A Turn in the South. London, Viking, and New York, Knopf, 1989.

India: A Million Mutinies Now. London, Heinemann, 1990; New York, Viking, 1991.

*

Bibliography: *V.S. Naipaul: A Selective Bibliography with Annotations* by Kelvin Jarvis, Metuchen, New Jersey, Scarecrow Press, 1989.

Critical Studies: By David Pryce-Jones, in *London Magazine,* May 1967; Karl Miller, in *Kenyon Review* (Gambier, Ohio), November 1967; *The West Indian Novel* by Kenneth Ramchand, London, Faber, and New York, Barnes and Noble, 1970; *V.S. Naipaul: An Introduction to His Work* by Paul Theroux, London, Deutsch, and New York, Africana, 1972; *V.S. Naipaul* by Robert D. Hamner, New York, Twayne, 1973, and *Critical Perspectives on V.S. Naipaul* edited by Hamner, Washington, D.C., Three Continents, 1977, London, Heinemann, 1979; *V.S. Naipaul* by William Walsh, Edinburgh, Oliver and Boyd, and New York, Barnes and Noble, 1973; *V.S. Naipaul: A Critical Introduction* by Landeg White, London, Macmillan, and New York, Barnes and Noble, 1975; *Paradoxes of Order: Some Perspectives on the Fiction of V.S. Naipaul* by Robert K. Morris, Columbia, University of Missouri Press, 1975; *V.S. Naipaul* by Michael Thorpe, London, Longman, 1976; *Four Contemporary Novelists* by Kerry McSweeney, Montreal, McGill-Queen's University Press, 1982, London, Scolar Press, 1983; *V.S. Naipaul: A Study in Expatriate Sensibility* by Sudha Rai, New Delhi, Arnold-Heinemann, 1982; *Contrary Awareness: A Critical Study of the Novels of V.S. Naipaul* by K.I. Madhusudana Rao, Madras, Centre for Research on New International Economic Order, 1982; *V.S. Naipaul: In Quest of the Enemy* by Anthony Boxill, Fredericton, New Brunswick, York Press, 1983; "V.S. Naipaul Issue" of *Modern Fiction Studies* (West Lafayette, Indiana), Autumn 1984; *The Fiction of V.S. Naipaul* by Nonditor Mason, Calcutta, World Press, 1986; *Journey Through Darkness: The Writing of V.S. Naipaul* by Peggy Nightingale, St. Lucia, University of Queensland Press, 1987; *The Web of Tradition: Uses of Allusion in V.S. Naipaul's Fiction* by John Thieme, Mundelstrup, Denmark, Dangaroo Press, and London, Hansib, 1987; *V.S. Naipaul* by Peter Hughes, London, Routledge, 1988; *V.S. Naipaul: A Materialist*

Reading by Selwyn R. Cudjoe, Amherst, University of Massachusetts Press, 1988; *V.S. Naipaul* by Richard Kelly, New York, Continuum, 1989; *The Novels of V.S. Naipaul: A Study of Theme and Form* by Shashi Kamra, New Delhi, Prestige, 1990; *London Calling: V.S. Naipaul, Postcolonial Mandarin* by Rob Nixon, New York and Oxford, Oxford University Press, 1992; *On the Margins: The Art of Exile in V.S. Naipaul* by Timothy F. Weiss, Amherst, University of Massachusetts Press, 1992; *Irony in the Novels of R.K. Narayan and V.S. Naipaul* by K.N. Padmanabhan Nair, Trivandrum, S. India, CBH Communications, 1993; *Self and Colonial Desire: Travel Writings of V.S. Naipaul* by Wimal Dissanayake, New York, Lang, 1993; *V.S. Naipaul* by Bruce King, New York, St. Martin's Press, and Basingstoke, Macmillan, 1993.

V.S. Naipaul comments:

I feel that any statement I make about my own work would be misleading. The work is there: the reader must see what meaning, if any, the work has for him. All I would like to say is that I consider my nonfiction an integral part of my work.

*   *   *

V.S.Naipaul's central place in Caribbean, and indeed, world literature, has been hard won. His double honor in receiving a British knighthood and the Trinidad Trinity Cross are the fruits of an often painful search for identity across English and Caribbean cultures, in which fiction and autobiography constantly interact.

His work falls broadly into five phases. These are his early satirical writing, the major Trinidadian novels, work exploring a rootless existence "in a free state," the ambivalent recovery of a sense of place in *The Enigma of Arrival,* and recent exploration of global cultures. *Miguel Street* was his first-written (though third-published) novel, begun in 1955 while Naipaul was freelancing for the BBC. It offers a gallery of vivid characters from Port of Spain, Trinidad, seen through the eyes of a growing child. It is an affectionate book, investing bizarre, almost caricatured figures with humanity: B. (Black) Wordsworth who spends his life trying to write one line; Laura who has many children by different men, but drives her daughter to suicide when she follows her mother's behavior; and Man Man, the religious enthusiast who asks to be crucified but is scandalized when bystanders begin throwing stones.

Naipaul omitted the section originally intended to implicate the boy-narrator directly in the narrative, leaving *Miguel Street* as a series of impressions rather than a novel. Nevertheless, it is one of his most attractive works, pointing to his achievement in the short stories published in *A Flag for the Island* (which includes the previously omitted story, "The Enemy") and elsewhere.

The Mystic Masseur is more complex and directly satirical. The anti-hero, Pandit Ganesh Ramsummair, through the fraudulent assumption of powers as a mystic and writer, rises from humble beginnings to the position of G. Ramsay Muir, Esq., M.B.E., Member of the Legislative Council. The satire on popular superstition and the unstable roots of political power in Trinidad is sharply focused by Ramsummair himself, who tells his story both in direct narrative and in the form of a suppressed diary, significantly called The Years of Guilt. *The Suffrage of Elvira Naipaul* again turns Naipaul's mordant satire on popular politics in Trinidad.

The early work was attacked by his fellow West Indian novelist George Lamming in 1960 as "castrated satire," signaling the resentment many in the Caribbean felt against their most accomplished novelist until the late 1980s. Yet Naipaul's often scarifying account of the futility of West Indian culture grew out of an intense exploration of his own cultural roots, an ambivalence nowhere more clearly seen than in his major Caribbean novel, *A House for Mr. Biswas,* which owes much to the career of his own father, who became a journalist in Port of Spain.

The novel is mediated through the sensibility of Mohun Biswas. Born with an extra finger—at once an indicator of endemic bad luck and malnutrition—he reacts to his privations with a defensive and often self-destructive clowning. He has a genius for disaster— a childish flirtation leads to a marriage into the Tulsis, a predatory merchant family who wish to possess Biswas for the sake of his Brahmin status, and who embody all the values of vulgarity and possessive clannishness Biswas detests. Biswas, artistic by nature, can find an outlet for his talents only in sign-painting, and the creative reporting of sensational events for the island paper. Throughout the book his search for a house of his own is an attempt to find both independence and a meaning for his life, and the often hilarious account of petty island life is underpinned with a deeper sense of the essential loneliness of the human state. This is vividly intimated at the center of the book, when a hurricane blows Biswas's precarious house from around him, precipitating a moment of nervous breakdown. But by the end Biswas has his own (if heavily mortgaged) house, while the Tulsi family is disintegrating. A tender tragicomedy, the book becomes an epic of Trinidad life between the world wars.

After a comparatively unsuccessful sortie into English life with *Mr. Stone and the Knights Companion,* Naipaul returned to Caribbean themes in *The Mimic Men.* Set largely on the fictional island of Isabella, it narrates Ralph Kripalsingh's rise to power on fortunes acquired through Coca-Cola and real estate. Politics becomes a metaphor for the essential futility of the Caribbean predicament, based as Naipaul sees it on the "mimicry" of other cultures. Ralph's self-destructive career is set against the possibilities suggested by Ralph's father, who becomes a *sunyasi* ("holy man"), but Ralph comes to see this only at the end, when, in a lonely London boarding house, he seeks to shape the absurdity of his island history through the medium of writing. A rich, finely crafted novel, its final impact is lessened by its despair.

By 1967, Naipaul was a novelist of international stature, and, partly influenced by his travel and journalism, his fiction increasingly took on a world perspective. *In a Free State* is a thematically linked trio of stories, set between two diary entries of a Middle East tour. Its subjects are an Indian servant in the United States, West Indians in Britain, and an Englishman in an African state in revolution. The rich detail characteristic of the earlier books is stripped away, giving spare action and description—an image on a television set, a blank stare—momentous impact. The trauma underlying the loss of roots becomes universalized, and is conveyed with a disquieting energy.

Guerrillas, based on the factual journalism republished as *The Killings in Trinidad,* is set in a thinly disguised Trinidad on the brink of revolution. Jimmy Ahmed, Afro-Chinese, Muslim, and English-educated, attempts to organize a socialist commune, but is finally defeated by his own flawed vision and the self-defeating racial and social conflicts of the island. His tragedy is paralleled by that of Roche, a hero of the South African freedom struggle, who is tricked into confessing his moral disillusionment. Jane, an English girl, attempts to relate to both Roche and Ahmed, and is murdered. The novel reveals Naipaul at his bleakest.

Offering a richer imaginative impact, *A Bend in the River* is related to Naipaul's *A Congo Diary.* It masterfully recreates life in a contemporary central African state under a dictatorship, where race, education, and conflicting ideologies uneasily coexist with traditional African cultures. The political struggles are played out against the background of river, jungle, and forest peoples impervious to the changing cycles of history.

In 1984 Naipaul published *Finding the Centre,* two narratives, one directly about Naipaul's early experiences in London, the other a travelogue describing the African search for identity among the upheavals of the contemporary Ivory Coast. The highly individual use of travel autobiography to explore issues of culture and identity prepared the way for *The Enigma of Arrival.* Starting with Naipaul's experiences of coming to England from Trinidad with Indian ancestry, the work builds up an evocation of life in rural Wiltshire, as seen from a cottage in the grounds of an Edwardian mansion. As the narrative weaves a pattern of the seasons in the English countryside, one becomes aware of subtle links with patterns in Caribbean and Indian cultures. By coming to terms with the change, rhythms, and decay in rural England, the narrator comes to an intuitive understanding of his own predicament, an ambivalent sense that the journey in time and space is also "the enigma of arrival." Resisting précis, the work takes Naipaul's work onto a further stage of experimentation and achievement.

Enigma of Arrival confirmed Naipaul's coming to terms with the Caribbean, and it coincided with his being received of state honors in Trinidad. But he was also a writer of the world. In a series of controversial travelogues, he examined the world of Islam (*Among the Believers*), the United States (*A Turn in the South*), and India (*A Million Mutinies Now*).

After seven years, Naipaul returned to novel writing with *A Way in the World.* The theme is the European contact with the Caribbean that he had explored in his early *The Loss of El Dorado.* But now history is presented in a multilayered work of fiction and autobiography. In it, Raleigh's 16th-century expedition to Guyana and Miranda's disastrous invasion of Cuba interact with the contemporary experience of expatriates in London, and revolutionary change and brutal death in East Africa. The work shifts effortlessly between historical periods and three continents, revealing correspondences that illuminate both past and present. Starting as an alienated postcolonial, Naipaul has evolved into a writer with a world perspective, whose constantly evolving literary skill has few rivals in contemporary fiction.

—Louis James

NARAYAN, R(asipuram) K(rishnaswamy)

Nationality: Indian. **Born:** Madras, 10 October 1906. **Education:** Collegiate High School, Mysore; Maharaja's College, Mysore, graduated 1930. **Family:** Married Rajam Narayan c. 1934 (died 1939); one daughter. **Career:** Teacher, then journalist, early 1930s; owner, Indian Thought Publications, Mysore. **Awards:** Sahitya Academy award, 1961; Padma Bhushan, India, 1964; National Association of Independent Schools award (U.S.A.), 1965; English-Speaking Union award, 1975; Royal Society of Literature Benson medal, 1980. Litt.D.: University of Leeds, Yorkshire, 1967; D.Litt.: University of Delhi; Sri Venkateswara University, Tirupati; University of Mysore. Fellow, Royal Society of Literature, 1980; honorary member American Academy, 1982. **Agent:** Anthony Sheil

Associates Ltd., 43 Doughty Street, London WC1N 2LF, England.
Address: 15 Vivekananda Road, Yadavagiri, Mysore 2, India.

PUBLICATIONS

Novels

Swami and Friends: A Novel of Malgudi. London, Hamish Hamilton, 1935; with *The Bachelor of Arts,* East Lansing, Michigan State College Press, 1954.

The Bachelor of Arts. London, Nelson, 1937; with *Swami and Friends,* East Lansing, Michigan State College Press, 1954.

The Dark Room. London, Macmillan, 1938.

The English Teacher. London, Eyre and Spottiswoode, 1945; as *Grateful to Life and Death,* East Lansing, Michigan State College Press, 1953.

Mr. Sampath. London, Eyre and Spottiswoode, 1949; as *The Printer of Malgudi,* East Lansing, Michigan State University Press, 1957.

The Financial Expert. London, Methuen, 1952; East Lansing, Michigan State College Press, 1953.

Waiting for the Mahatma. London, Methuen, and East Lansing, Michigan State College Press, 1955.

The Guide. Madras, Higginbothams, London, Methuen, and New York, Viking Press, 1958.

The Man-Eater of Malgudi. New York, Viking Press, 1961; London, Heinemann, 1962.

The Vendor of Sweets. New York, Viking Press, 1967; as *The Sweet-Vendor,* London, Bodley Head, 1967.

The Painter of Signs. New York, Viking Press, 1976; London, Heinemann, 1977.

A Tiger for Malgudi. London, Heinemann, and New York, Viking Press, 1983.

Talkative Man. London, Heinemann, 1986; New York, Viking, 1987.

The World of Nagaraj. London, Heinemann, and New York, Viking, 1990.

Short Stories

Malgudi Days. Mysore, Indian Thought, 1943.

Dodu and Other Stories. Mysore, Indian Thought, 1943.

Cyclone and Other Stories. Mysore, Indian Thought, 1944.

An Astrologer's Day and Other Stories. Mysore, Indian Thought, and London, Eyre and Spottiswoode, 1947.

Lawley Road. Mysore, Indian Thought, 1956.

A Horse and Two Goats. London, Bodley Head, and New York, Viking Press, 1970.

Old and New. Mysore, Indian Thought, 1981.

Malgudi Days (not same as 1943 book). London, Heinemann, and New York, Viking Press, 1982.

Under the Banyan Tree and Other Stories. London, Heinemann, and New York, Viking, 1985.

The Grandmother's Tale, with sketches by R.K. Laxman. Madras, Indian Thought, 1992; London, Heinemann, 1993; as *The Grandmother's Tale and Other Stories,* New York, Viking, 1994.

Salt & Sawdust: Stories and Table Talk. New Delhi, Penguin, 1993.

Uncollected Short Story

"The Cobbler and the God," in *Playboy* (Chicago), 1975.

Other

Mysore. Mysore, Government Branch Press, 1939.

Next Sunday: Sketches and Essays. Mysore, Indian Thought, 1956.

My Dateless Diary: A Journal of a Trip to the United States in October 1956. Mysore, Indian Thought Publications, 1960; New York and London, Penguin, 1988.

Gods, Demons, and Others. New York, Viking Press, 1964; London, Heinemann, 1965.

The Ramayana: A Shortened Modern Prose Version of the Indian Epic. New York, Viking Press, 1972; London, Chatto and Windus, 1973.

Reluctant Guru (essays). New Delhi, Hind, 1974.

My Days: A Memoir. New York, Viking Press, 1974; London, Chatto and Windus, 1975.

The Emerald Route (includes play *The Watchman of the Lake*). Bangalore, Government of Karnataka, 1977.

The Mahabharata: A Shortened Modern Prose Version of the Indian Epic. New York, Viking Press, and London, Heinemann, 1978.

A Writer's Nightmare: Selected Essays 1958-1988. New Delhi, Penguin, 1988; New York, Penguin, 1989.

A Story-Teller's World: Stories, Essays, Sketches. New Delhi, Penguin, 1989.

*

Manuscript Collection: Mugar Memorial Library, Boston University.

Critical Studies: *R.K. Narayan: A Critical Study of His Works* by Harish Raizada, New Delhi, Young Asia, 1969; *R.K. Narayan,* London, Longman, 1971, and *R.K. Narayan: A Critical Appreciation,* London, Heinemann, and Chicago, University of Chicago Press, 1982, both by William Walsh; *The Novels of R.K. Narayan* by Lakshmi Holmstrom, Calcutta, Writers Workshop, 1973; *R.K. Narayan,* New Delhi, Arnold-Heinemann, 1973, and *R.K. Narayan as Novelist,* New Delhi, B.R., 1988, both by P.S. Sundaram; *Perspectives on R.K. Narayan* edited by Atma Ram, Ghaziabad, Vimal, 1981; *R.K. Narayan: A Critical Spectrum* edited by Bhagwat S. Goyal, Meerut, Shalabh Book House, 1983; *The Ironic Vision: A Study of the Fiction of R.K. Narayan* by M.K. Naik, New Delhi, Sterling, 1983; *R.K. Narayan: His World and His Art* by Shiv K. Gilra, Meerut, Saru, 1984; *The Novels of R.K. Narayan* by Cynthia Vanden Driesen, Nedlands, University of Western Australia Centre for South and Southeast Asian Studies, 1986; *A Critical Study of the Novels of R.K. Narayan* by J.K. Biswal, New Delhi, Nirmal, 1987; *Patterns of Myth and Reality: A Study in R.K. Narayan's Novels* by U.P. Sinha, New Delhi, Sandarbh, 1988; *The Language of Mulk Raj Anand, Raja Rao, and R.K. Narayan* by Reza Ahmad Nasimi, New Delhi, Capital, 1989; *Human Struggle in the Novels of R.K. Narayan* by Nazar Singh Sidhu, New Delhi, Bahri, 1992; *A Critical Study of the Novels of R.K. Narayan* by Nagendra nath Sharan, New Delhi, Classical, 1993; *Cultural Imperialism and the Indo-English Novel: Genre and Ideology in R.K. Narayan, Anita Desai, Kamala Markandaya, and Salman Rushdie* by Fawzia Afzal-Khan, University Park, Pennsylvania State University Press; *Indian Life and Problems in the Novels of Mulk Raj Anand, Faja Fao, and R.K. Narayan* by G.N. Agnihtri, Meerut, Shalabh Prakashan, 1993; *Irony in the Novels of R.K. Narayan and V.S. Naipaul* by K.N. Padmanabhan Nair, Trivandrum, S. India, CBH,

1993; *Major Themes in the Novels of R.K. Narayan* by R.M. Varma, New Delhi, Jainsons, 1993; *Message in Design: A Study of R.K. Narayan's Fiction* by P.S. Ramana, New Delhi, Harman, 1993; *R.K. Narayan: Contemporary Critical Perspectives* edited by Geoffrey Kain, East Lansing, Michigan State University Press, 1993; *R.K. Narayan's India: Myth and Reality* edited by Bhagwat S. Goyal, New Delhi, Sarup, 1993.

*   *   *

No other 20th-century novelist besides William Faulkner has so well succeeded in creating through a succession of novels an imagined community that microcosmically reflects the physical, intellectual, and spiritual qualities of a whole culture as has R.K. Narayan in his tales of the South Indian community of Malgudi. His stories have made a naive, highly emotional society half a world away as much a part of a reader's experience as Faulkner's novels have made the mad, decadent world of the red hills of Mississippi.

Narayan took longer than Faulkner to discover his metier, though all the Indian writer's novels have been largely set in Malgudi. With his third novel, *Sartoris* (1929), published when he was 32, Faulkner laid the cornerstone for his Yoknapatawpha saga of pride-doomed families. Narayan published four apprentice works based largely on reminiscences before producing, at the age of 43, *Mr. Sampath,* the first of the five most remarkable studies of flamboyant characters who electrified the sleepy city of Malgudi.

It is unlikely that anyone would have guessed that Narayan's first two novels were the work of a major artist. *Swami and Friends* is a kind of charming Indian *Penrod and Sam,* an episodic account of the adventures of two cricket-playing chums as they start high school. *The Bachelor of Arts* is another episodic account of a young man's graduating from college, experiencing a frustrating love affair, wandering about the country disconsolately, returning home to become an agent for a big city newspaper, and finally marrying under family auspices. His third novel, *The Dark Room,* he describes as dealing with a Hindu wife who submitted passively to an overbearing husband.

His work changed drastically with *The English Teacher,* a thinly veiled account of his own marriage and the event that most matured and shaped his character, the early death of his beloved wife. This novel begins like Narayan's earlier ones with episodic sketches of a young preparatory school teacher's relationships with his students, colleagues, and family. After the tragic death of the wife while househunting, however, the novel becomes a much deeper and more tightly unified work.

With his next novel, Narayan settled upon the kind of characters and narrative patterns that he was to employ in his five remarkable explorations of the fantastic agitations beneath the enervating surface of the life of Malgudi. Near the end of *Mr. Sampath,* Narayan observes of Srinivas, the principal character, that "he felt he had been involved in a chaos of human relationships and activities."

Nearly all of Narayan's subsequent novels involve characters and readers in such chaos. Srinivas is a rather aimless young man who has finally been driven by his family to choose a profession and who comes to Malgudi in 1938—when war clouds hang over the whole world—to found a newspaper that has "nothing special to note about any war, past or future," but is "only concerned with that war that is always going on—between man's inside and outside." He falls into the hands of a printer, Mr. Sampath, who takes a proprietary interest in the success of the paper, but who is lured from his printing trade into a film-producing venture. Even Srinivas

is briefly tempted to abandon his paper and take up script writing. Despite frantic activity and great expenditures, however, the movie-making venture collapses. Only Srinivas emerges unscathed. He finds another printer and returns to publishing his paper, reflecting on one of the men involved in the catastrophe he has witnessed:

> throughout the centuries . . . this group was always there: Ravi with his madness, his well-wishers with their panaceas and their apparatus of cure. Half the madness was his own doing, his lack of self-knowledge, his treachery to his own instincts as an artist, which had made him a battleground. Sooner or later he shook off his madness and realized his true identity—though not in one birth, at least in a series of them.

The passage is a key to understanding Narayan's major works and their relationship to Hindu philosophy; for the characters he focuses upon are those who are "mad" as a result of their lack of self-knowledge. Some must await another reincarnation; but some manage to shake off the madness and find their true identities.

One who must wait is the title character of *The Financial Expert,* Margayya, whom we meet sitting under a banyan tree assisting peasants in obtaining loans from a cooperative banking institution. The society's officers resent Margayya's activities, but his business flourishes until his spoiled young son throws into a sewer the book in which all accounts are kept. During a trip to collect a red lotus needed for a penitential ritual, Margayya meets Dr. Pal, a self-styled sociologist, who has written a pornographic manuscript based on the *Kama Sutra.* Margayya recoups his fortune by publishing it under the title *Domestic Harmony;* then, embarrassed by the source of his new wealth, he goes back into a money-lending business that is based on withholding the interest from the first installment on the loan. He becomes so successful that he achieves an honored position in the community and recruits Dr. Pal to attract investors. The scheme collapses, however, when the son, who has been gambling with Dr. Pal, demands a share in the business; Margayya assaults Dr. Pal, who in turn discredits the money-lender with his investors. When investors demand their money back, both Margayya and his son are ruined and driven back into dealings with the peasants beneath the banyan tree.

Narayan's next novel, *Waiting for the Mahatma,* is one of his most noble-minded, but least successful. It tells, in the episodic manner of his earlier books, of the misadventures of two young disciples of Mahatma Gandhi during the master's long effort to free his native land. Written after Gandhi's assassination, the book is an admirable tribute, but the fictional characters are too sketchily developed to make it of more than historical interest.

Narayan next turned to the work that has generally been recognized as his most outstanding, *The Guide,* an extremely complicated tale of a confidence man turned saint. In flashbacks, we learn of the rise of Raju from food-seller in the Malgudi railroad station to manager and apparent husband of Rose, who becomes an extremely popular dancer, and his quick fall when he is jailed for forging her signature to a package of jewels. We meet him first, however, when he has installed himself in an abandoned temple after his release from jail and has begun to play the role of spiritual advisor to a peasant community that accepts him as a Mahatma. Gradually he comes to believe in the role he has created, and to relieve a drought he feels compelled to make a 15-day fast that he has suggested as an appropriate penance. As a great crowd gathers, he gains "a peculiar strength" from, for the first time in his life, "learning the thrill of full application, outside money and love."

Despite grave peril to his health he continues to fast until he feels that the rain is falling in the hills. The ending of this novel like that of *The English Teacher* is ambiguous: does Swami Raju die? do the rains come? Narayan tells us only, "He sagged down"; but he has transcended the madness that once affected him and found a fulfillment denied the printer of Malgudi and the financial expert.

Such fulfillment is denied also Vasu, the fanatical taxidermist of *The Man-Eater of Malgudi,* Narayan's greatest picture of the madness that leads to self-destruction. After successfully flaunting his great strength about the community unchecked through a series of outrageous incidents, he finally devises a plot against Malgudi's beloved temple elephant. The beast seems doomed, but Vasu dies instead; and in one of the most spectacular conclusions to any of Narayan's works, the almost incredible but carefully foreshadowed way in which he destroyed himself is disclosed. In the complementary *The Vendor of Sweets* Narayan portrays a man who discovers his true identity. Jagan had been freed from patriarchal thralldom when he broke with his orthodox family and followed Mahatma Gandhi. His example, however, proves of no value to a son who prefers American "get-rich-quick" ideas to the self-sacrificial life Gandhi recommended. Jagan indulges the boy by selling sweetmeats to the luxury-loving community; but when the son gets into serious trouble, Jagan feels helpless. He abandons his business and retires to a decrepit garden of meditation. Having freed himself from successive bondages to parents, hero, and child, he finds a tranquillity unique to this point in Narayan's tales.

Only confusion, however, awaits the protagonist of *The Painter of Signs,* in which Narayan also deals boldly with a new India's urgent and controversial problem of population control. Raman, a highly traditional 30-year-old bachelor, who took up signboard painting because he "loved calligraphy," is cared for selflessly by his aunt until he meets Daisy, a dynamic propagandizer for birth control. When Raman induces Daisy to marry him, the aunt departs on a religious pilgrimage from which she does not expect to return. Then when Daisy discovers that she cannot give up her missionary work for marriage, Raman finds that he has destroyed his old life without creating a new one.

Reviewers accustomed to the down-to-earth manner of Narayan's ironic fictions were as disconcerted by *A Tiger for Malgudi* as the frantic villagers who are confronted by Raja, the tiger. Since Raja is the hero-narrator of the novel, Narayan seems to be abandoning reality for fantasy; but *A Tiger for Malgudi* is no traditional anthropomorphic beast fable. Drawing delicately on Hindu doctrines of reincarnation, Narayan depicts Raja as a creature with a soul, who lacks only the faculty of conversing with humans. His tale is told by those who learn to read his mind: the fictional master that saves Raja from the rest of the wryly depicted human community and the master of fiction who has conjured him up. The tale is of the overcoming of "the potential of violence," with which, Raja's master observes, "every creature is born." The seemingly whimsical history of a talking tiger thus expands into an ironic fable and prophecy about not just the recent troubled history of Narayan's own country, but of mankind generally. A wise and witty message from one who has aged serenely without missing the significance of a moment of his experiences, this novel should take its place among the most beatific visions of a century that has produced far more diabolical ones. It climaxes the achievement of the major Malgudi novels in depicting the soul's erratic progress from fanaticism toward the tranquil transcendence of the dusty streets of Malgudi.

—Warren French

NAROGIN, Mudrooroo. *See* **MUDROOROO.**

NAYLOR, Gloria

Nationality: American. **Born:** New York City, 25 January 1950. **Education:** Brooklyn College, New York, B.A. in English 1981; Yale University, New Haven, Connecticut, 1981-83, M.A. in Afro-American Studies 1983. **Career:** Missionary for the Jehovah's Witnesses, New York, North Carolina, and Florida, 1968-75; telephone operator, New York City hotels, 1975-81. Writer-in-residence, Cummington Community of the Arts, Massachusetts, Summer 1983; visiting professor, George Washington University, Washington, D.C., 1983-84, University of Pennsylvania, Philadelphia, 1986, New York University, 1986, Princeton University, New Jersey, 1986-87, and Boston University, 1987; Fannie Hurst Visiting Professor, Brandeis University, Waltham, Massachusetts, 1988; United States Information Agency Cultural Exchange Lecturer, India, Fall 1985. Columnist, *New York Times,* 1986. Since 1988 judge, Book-of-the-Month Club. **Awards:** American Book award, 1983; National Endowment for the Arts fellowship, 1985; Guggenheim fellowship, 1988. **Address:** c/o One Way Productions, 638 Second Street, Brooklyn, New York 11215, U.S.A.

PUBLICATIONS

Novels

The Women of Brewster Place: A Novel in Seven Stories. New York, Viking Press, 1982; London, Hodder and Stoughton, 1983.
Linden Hills. New York, Ticknor and Fields, and London, Hodder and Stoughton, 1985.
Mama Day. New York, Ticknor and Fields, and London, Hutchinson, 1988.
Bailey's Café. New York, Harcourt Brace, 1992; London, Minerva, 1993.

Uncollected Short Story

"Life on Beekman Place," in *Essence* (New York), March 1980.

*

Critical Study: *Gloria Naylor: Critical Perspectives Past and Present* edited by Henry Louis Gates and K.A. Appiah, New York, Amistad, 1993.

Gloria Naylor comments:

I think of *The Women of Brewster Place* as a love letter to the black women of America—a celebration of their strength and endurance. *Linden Hills* is a cautionary tale—an example of the drastic results if a people forsake their ethnocentric identity under the pressure to assimilate into a mainstream society and seek its rewards.

*   *   *

Gloria Naylor has written three original and absorbing novels, *The Women of Brewster Place: A Novel in Seven Stories* (which won the American Book award for best first writing in 1983), *Linden Hills,* and *Mama Day.* Naylor's success lies, in part, in the intensity of her presentation of such social issues as poverty, racism, discrimination against homosexuals, the unequal treatment of women, the value of a sense of community among blacks, and the failure of some upper middle-class educated blacks to address racial problems and social injustice.

The Women of Brewster Place has a simple structure. Most of the scenes take place in the decaying apartment complex, Brewster Place. The dwellers expect to go nowhere else. The brick wall that closed their street several years earlier now separates them from the rest of the city and symbolizes their psychological and spiritual isolation. In the closing pages of the novel, one woman removes a brick that she thinks is stained with the blood of a resident recently gang-raped and left to die. Impulsively, the other women join her and collectively they tear down the wall, experiencing as they do so an inner regeneration, a sense of community and solidarity, and a rebirth of hope.

The novel includes seven narratives, each focusing on a woman and illuminating her present situation while abundant flashbacks recapitulate her earlier experience. The dominant woman in one chapter appears as a less important figure in several others, so that the entire book, consisting of related though not always consecutive episodes, emerges as a novel rather than as a collection of stories only. While each of the narratives has its own climax, the book builds toward the most threatening crises faced by the Brewster Place community: Ciel's starving herself almost to death in grief for her lost child, the antagonism that builds against two lesbian tenants, and the rape-murder of Lorraine, the lesbian elementary school teacher who has tried to help Kiswana (an idealistic radical) establish a closely organized community among the tenants. Through the suffering of Ciel and that of Lorraine, the other women achieve a new understanding of one another and deepened insight into the problems that confront them individually and collectively. The work considered as a novel gains unity through Naylor's use of a single setting, her concentration upon a small number of women in each narrative, her analysis of the major threats to the community in the tragedies of Ciel and Lorraine, and her resort to rituals of healing in which the characters join each other in expressing their human concern in acts rather than in words.

In *Linden Hills* Naylor again confines her scenes to one location, but her tone and outlook are more sardonic and pessimistic. In her castigation of middle-class black society, Naylor here finds little hope for renewal of spiritual values or for a development of communal responsibility or identity among the residents. Linden Hills blacks are ambitious and selfish; the richer ones live close to the bottom of the hillside; and richest of all is Luther Nedeed. For five generations Luther Nedeed has controlled Linden Hills real estate and also been the local mortician. Next to the Nedeed home and morgue lies the cemetery. The Nedeed wives in each generation have been so deprived of affection and companionship by their "frog-eyed" husbands that they looked forward finally only to death.

Linden Hills has a far more intricate narrative structure than Naylor's first novel. Two young poets, Willie and Lester, in the six days before Christmas earn gift money doing odd jobs. Most of the action is seen through their eyes, except for flashbacks related to the past experiences of the householders who employ them. As they journey further down the hillside each day, they encounter death, suicide, hypocrisy, exploitation, and treachery. The poets ago-

nize and rage over the people who are living a meaningless, death-like existence.

An additional narrative line appears in "inserts" in the text that interrupt the narration of the experiences of Willie and Lester during this week. The lines addressed directly to the reader reveal secret horrors unknown to Willie and Lester. Luther Nedeed, dissatisfied with the light skin of his infant son, has banished his wife, Willa, and their infant to his abandoned basement morgue, and he begins lowering food and water to her only after the infant has starved to death. In her desperate isolation, Willa searches for any sign of humanity. From day to day she discovers—and furtively reads—the secret notes recorded in diaries, letters, Bibles, and recipe books by the wives of Nedeed men since 1837. Sharing their tales of abuse, she feels their presence with her and gains strength to climb the stairs on Christmas Eve, carrying her dead son, and to confront her husband. At that moment the decorated tree bursts into flame and in the inferno that follows all traces of the Nedeeds disappear. No neighbor bothers to assist them or even to sound an alarm.

Naylor uses Dante's journey through the lower world in the symbolism that gives additional coherence and depth to the multiple plots. The powerful in Linden Hills resist spiritual illumination and prefer a life in Hell to a life in Paradise. They illustrate the principle underlying Dante's vision of those who inhabit the netherworld, "Abandon hope, all ye who enter here." Naylor's work demonstrates that in hell all malefactors are concerned only with their own suffering, rather than with their guilt. Blacks in Linden Hills have the wealth and resources to attain self-awareness, love, and grace, but they are actually far less receptive to the promptings of the spirit than the poor women in Brewster Place, who are capable of spiritual illumination and conversion to a regenerate existence.

Naylor's third novel, *Mama Day,* shows a continued progression in her boldly imagined fiction. It recounts a love story of a good marriage that was sometimes far from calm, and it presents for the first time in her novels a kind, responsible, and interesting husband. Ophelia and George Andrews work in a small Manhattan engineering office and hesitantly fall in love, frequently fight, and finally learn to listen to each other by taking turns expressing themselves in long monologues. This continues even after one is in a grave and the other is sitting next to the grave. The novel speaks of the death in the early pages and what one might hear in the cemetery. The courtship and marriage are thus recounted for the reader after the marriage has been broken by death. They recall memories of the details of arguments, happy events, and of their childhood. The alternate passages in the book develop a kind of antiphonal poetry, with long questions and long answers. The love story is told in first person by the two narrators in alternating sections. Only occasionally and when another person appears in the story does the third-person omniscient narrator speak. The connected monologues begin in New York City and end in Willow Springs, a sea island where Ophelia (also called Cocoa and Baby Girl) was raised by her grandmother, Abigail, and her great-aunt, Miranda (Mama Day). George, abandoned as an infant in New York, grew up in a shelter for boys. He has learned to stress intellectuality and insist upon reason and provable facts. Cocoa values not only what she has been taught in college but also the folk wisdom of Mama Day and Abigail, their intuition, but not their connection with magic, conjure, or hexes.

The island of Willow Springs is connected by a bridge to both Georgia and South Carolina but is not a part of either state. The latter three-fourths of the novel takes place at Willow Springs. Most of the action in Willow Springs is narrated in the first-person voice of Mama Day, as are the philosophical or spiritual messages that Naylor seeks to convey. During their summer visit to the island both Cocoa and George are forced to compromise and both develop greater understanding. Cocoa, after violent confrontation and deadly illness, finds less need to insist on her own way. George, with greater difficulty, begins to acknowledge some kind of faith in Mama Day's power to heal and to respect both nature and the supernatural.

The folkways, celebrations, and eccentricities of the populace on the island provide an intriguing sequence of events, but the novel ends chaotically with a hurricane and flood that confuses intricate lines of the plots and their intersection. While the extensive symbolism leads the reader to search for mythic and universal truth in the novel, Naylor raises as many questions as answers. Although the "Candle Walk," in which the villagers march to the bridge carrying lighted candles, is impressive, no one knows why they observe it. They know that something happened to free their ancestors in 1823, but are unsure how a slave named Sapphira Wade was able to marry the slave owner, get him to sign papers freeing all his slaves on the island, and then murder him. Mama Day and Abigail recognize that Baby Girl is a descendant of Sapphira and accept her aggressive and stubborn nature as inevitable, but they are concerned that she and George will never find peace.

In making a quilt for their wedding present, they consider protecting her by not including pieces of cloth that belonged to "contrary" women—only using remnants from women who were sheltered and timid. But they decide against this, because Mama Day thinks the broad experience of life is to be treasured rather than avoided. While they include scraps of cloth from women who broke men's hearts and who never found inner peace, they also choose a quilt pattern that is composed of interlocking rings, suggesting the support one woman needs from other women. Mama Day is supported by the community in the gift-giving that follows the Candle Walk. In recognition of the old woman's healing, midwifery, and sage advice throughout the past year, the people bring her provisions of every sort to be stored to last all through the next year.

But if the Candle Walk activities suggest an idyllic black community, Naylor negates this impression with her stories of vengeance, hexes, and curses and makes clear that the people consult not only Mama Day but also her rival in advising and healing—a man who is a fraud, a bootlegger, and a card shark. Mama Day's thoughts are shadowed by grief for her mother, who drowned herself, and Mama Day is responsible late in the story for the violent murder of a jealous woman who has poisoned Cocoa. George, though drawn to the family and community, values his urban life and job and seeks to swim through the flood to return "beyond the bridge." If less carefully structured than Naylor's earlier novels, *Mama Day* is a rich and powerful novel that shows the influence of both Toni Morrison and Alice Walker in venturing beyond the natural into suggestions of the power of the supernatural and the spirit.

—Margaret B. McDowell

NDEBELE, (Nimrod) Njabulo S(imakahle)

Nationality: South African. **Born:** Ladysmith, Natal Province, South Africa, 12 October 1913. **Education:** St. Peter's High School, Resettenvelle, Johannesburg, 1929-31; Amanzimtoti (Adams') College, 1933-34, earned teaching certificate; University of Witwatersrand, A.B. in Zulu language and political science 1948. **Career:** Assistant teacher, Khaiso Secondary School, 1935-45; assistant teacher, Madibane High School, Johannesburg, 1945-53; principal, Charterston High School, Nigel, 1953-57; inspector of schools, Middleburg Circuit, from 1957. **Awards:** Esther May Bedford prize, 1937, for *UGubudele namazimuzimu.*

PUBLICATIONS

Short Stories

Fools and Other Stories. Johannesburg, Raven Press, 1983; Harlow, Longman, 1985.

Play

UGubudele namazimuzimu. Johannesburg, University of Witwatersrand Press, 1941.

Other

Rediscovery of the Ordinary: Essays on South African Literature and Culture. Johannesburg, COSAW, 1991; Manchester, Manchester University Press, 1994.
Bonolo and the Peach Tree, illustrated by Vusi Malindi (for children). Johannesburg, Raven Press, 1992.

*   *   *

The relationship between politics and art is by definition always mediated by reflection. We distinguish only between immediate action, on the one hand, and delayed action, on the other. We do not choose between politics and art: rather, we participate in the dialectic between them. To understand this is to understand the creative possibilities of both.

For Njabulo Simakahle Ndebele, the role art plays in political struggle has been central to both his artistic development and his pronouncements on South African literature. Western critics have welcomed Ndebele's finely crafted prose in *Fools and Other Stories* as a pleasant change from the didactic propagandeering of politically motivated literature. J. M. Coetzee invokes Dostoevsky and Chekhov. Certainly, Ndebele's tales, coupled with his essays, helped move South African literature beyond a stagnant "protest literature" obsessed with constructing "a totally debased people whose only reason for existence is to receive the sympathy of the world." The tales are set in a location but eschew descriptions of overt racist tensions in favor of accounts of less sensational conflicts emerging from the range of inhabitants.

However, Ndebele has not left the political arena and entered a specious "objective" aestheticism. He does resist the narrow view that politically committed writing must identify and draw moral conclusions from oppression because, as he states in "Beyond `Protest,'" it can too easily lead to "the simplification and trivialization of moral perception," thereby allowing "the rhetoric of protest" to replace "paying critical attention to the concrete social, political details of that oppression."

But rather than endorsing apoliticism, such concrete details broaden the writer's scope: "Politics is not only the seizure of state power, it can also be the seizure of a woman's burial society in the township." Ndebele focuses his storyteller's gaze on these localized, everyday instances to build a sense of the human potential for resistance and intervention in the monoliths of political power.

In *Fools,* a young boy defies his parents' middle-class, Westernized values by refusing to play the great European masters on his violin. Another boy masters the fear of getting a vial of water for his sick mother from a local sorceress. In the title novella, a Boer cracks a whip preparatory to beating the narrator, a weak and abusive man, who realizes "I knew then that his whip was all there was to him." In silently resisting, he thinks, "my silence was my salvation; the silence of years of trying to say something without much understanding. . . . This would be the first silence that would carry meaning." Such limited epiphanies power Ndebele's creative work, which explores complex political issues through their manifestation in seemingly insignificant social contexts.

Ndebele demonstrates that literature crafted with a sophisticated awareness of the only metaphorical connection between "narrative and the real world" can nonetheless create and consolidate "a subjective confidence which will enable people to have the will to go out with an inner commitment to smash the oppression that is keeping them down." Such a revitalizing of both the aesthetic and the political components of literary work imparts a significance to Ndebele's writing that resonates far beyond South Africa.

—Victoria Carchidi

NEUGEBOREN, Jay

Nationality: American. **Born:** New York City, 30 May 1938. **Education:** Columbia University, New York, B.A. 1959 (Phi Beta Kappa); Indiana University, Bloomington, M.A. 1963. **Family:** Married 1) Betsy Bendorf in 1964 (divorced 1983), three children; 2) Judy Karasik in 1985 (divorced 1987). **Career:** Junior executive trainee, General Motors Corporation, Indianapolis, 1960; English teacher, Saddle River Country Day School, New Jersey, 1961-62; teacher, New York City public high and junior high schools, 1963-66; preceptor in English, Columbia University, 1964-66; lecturer, Stanford University, California, 1966-67; assistant professor, State University of New York, Old Westbury, 1968-69. Since 1971 writer-in-residence, University of Massachusetts, Amherst. **Awards:** Bread Loaf Writers Conference De Voto fellowship, 1966; *Transatlantic Review* novella award, 1969; National Endowment for the Arts grant, 1973; Guggenheim fellowship, 1977; Massachusetts Council on the Arts fellowship, 1978; American Jewish Committee, best novel prize, 1981; Smilen-*Present Tense* award, 1982; PEN Syndicated Fiction prize, 1982-88 (6 prizes); National Endowment for the Arts fellowship, 1989. **Agent:** Richard Parks, 138 E. 16th St., New York, New York, 10003. **Address:** Department of English, University of Massachusetts, Box 30515, Amherst, Massachusetts 01003-0515, U.S.A.

PUBLICATIONS

Novels

Big Man. Boston, Houghton Mifflin, 1966.

Listen Ruben Fontanez. Boston, Houghton Mifflin, and London, Gollancz, 1968.
Sam's Legacy. New York, Holt Rinehart, 1974.
An Orphan's Tale. New York, Holt Rinehart, 1976.
The Stolen Jew. New York, Holt Rinehart, 1981.
Before My Life Began. New York, Simon and Schuster, 1985.

Short Stories

Corky's Brother and Other Stories. New York, Farrar Straus, 1969; London, Gollancz, 1970.
Penguin Modern Stories 3, with others. London, Penguin, 1970.

Uncollected Short Stories

"My Son, The Freedom Rider," in *Colorado Quarterly* (Boulder), Summer 1964.
"Connorsville, Virginia," in *Transatlantic Review* (London), Winter 1969.
"My Life and Death in the Negro American Baseball League: A Slave Narrative," in *Massachusetts Review* (Amherst), Summer 1973.
"The Place Kicking Specialists," in *Transatlantic Review* (London), Fall-Winter 1974.
"Monkeys and Cowboys," in *Present Tense* (New York), Summer 1976.
"A Worthy Cause," in *Willmore City 6-7* (Carlsbad, California), 1978.
"Uncle Nathan," in *Ploughshares* (Cambridge, Massachusetts), vol. 4, no. 4, 1978.
"His Violin," in *Atlantic* (Boston), November 1978.
"Kehilla," in *Present Tense* (New York), Winter 1978.
"Star of David," in *Tri-Quarterly* (Evanston, Illinois), Spring 1979.
"The St. Dominick's Game," in *Atlantic* (Boston), December 1979.
"Poppa's Books," in *Atlantic* (Boston), July 1980.
"Bonus Baby," in *John O'Hara Journal* (Pottsville, Pennsylvania), Fall 1980.
"Visiting Hour," in *Shenandoah* (Lexington, Virginia), Fall 1980.
"Noah's Song," in *Present Tense* (New York), Winter 1980.
"Daughter," in *Confrontation* (New York), Spring 1981.
"When the Cheering Turned to Sorrow," in *Inside Sports* (Evanston, Illinois), May 1981.
"Death and the Schoolyard," in *Boston Globe Magazine,* 3 May 1981.
"The 7th Room," in *Rendezvous* (Pocatello, Idaho) Summer 1981.
"Leaving Brooklyn," in *Literary Review* (Madison, New Jersey), Fall 1981.
"Jonathan," in *Tri-Quarterly* (Evanston, Illinois), Winter 1981.
"The Imported Man," in *Midstream* (New York), February 1982.
"The Golden Years," in *New England Review* (Hanover, New Hampshire), Spring 1982.
"Before the Camps," in *Congress Monthly* (New York), April 1982.
"Lev Kogan's Journey," in *Boston Globe Magazine,* 6 June 1982.
"The Year Between," in *Boston Review,* January 1983.
"On a Beach near Herzlia," in *The Ploughshares Reader,* edited by DeWitt Henry. Wainscott, New York, Pushcart Press, 1985.
"Cold Storage," in *Massachusetts Review* (Amherst), Spring 1985.
"Fix," in *Denver Quarterly,* Spring 1985.
"Stairs," in *Present Tense* (New York), Fall 1985.
"Abe's Room," in *Confrontation* (New York), Fall 1985.
"Drawing Home," in *San Francisco Chronicle,* 22 December 1985.

"1945," in *Floridian*, 5 September 1987.

"What Satisfaction Canst Thou Have Tonight?" in *Columbia* (New York), October 1987.

"About Men," in *American Scholar* (Washington, D.C.), Winter 1987.

"Don't Worry about the Kids," in *Prize Stories 1988*, edited by William Abrahams. New York, Doubleday, 1988.

"High Concept," in *Confrontation* (Greenvale, New York), Spring 1988.

"Tolstoy in Maine," in *New Letters* (Kansas City), Spring 1988.

"Workers to Attention Please," in *Louder than Words*, edited by William Shore. New York, Vintage, 1989.

"How I Became an Orphan in 1947," in *Willow Springs* (Cheney, Washington), Spring 1989.

"Your Child Has Been Towed," in *Gettysburg Review* (Gettysburg, Pennsylvania), Autumn 1989.

"In Memory of Jane Fojarbi," in *Tikkun*, September 1989.

"Minor 6ths, Diminished 7ths," in *Gentlemen's Quarterly* (New York), June 1990.

"Overseas," in *Michigan Quarterly Review* (Ann Arbor), Summer 1990.

"Have You Visited Israel?" in *New Letters* (Kansas City), Summer 1991.

"Dept. of Athletics," in *Conference Quarterly*, Winter 1992.

"What Is the Good Life?" in *Gettysburg Review* (Gettysburg, Pennsylvania), Autumn 1992.

"Meanwhile Back on the Word," in *The American Scholar* (Washington, D.C.), Summer 1994.

"Where Do We Live Now?" in *Tikkun*, September/October 1994.

Plays

The Edict (produced New York, 1981).

Radio Play: *The Stolen Jew*, 1980.

Television Play: *The Hollow Boy*, 1991.

Other

Parentheses: An Autobiographical Journey. New York, Dutton, 1970.

Poli: A Mexican Boy in Early Texas (for children). San Antonio, Texas, Corona, 1989.

Editor, *The Story of "Story" Magazine: A Memoir*, by Martha Foley. New York, Norton, 1980.

*

Critical Studies: Statement by Ian Watt, in *Listen Ruben Fontanez*, London, Gollancz, 1968; "Parentheses" by Charles Moran, in *Massachusetts Review* (Amherst), Fall 1970; "From Kerouac to Koch" by Michael Willis, in *Columbia College Today* (New York), Winter-Spring 1971; "A Decade of the Ethnic Fiction of Jay Neugeboren," in *Melus* (Los Angeles), Winter 1978 and article in *Twentieth-Century American-Jewish Fiction Writers* edited by Daniel Walden, Detroit, Gale, 1984, both by Cordelia Candelaria; interview with Steven Goldleaf, in *Columbia College Today* (New York), December 1979, and "A Jew Without Portfolio" by Goldleaf, in *Partisan Review* (Boston), Summer 1983; interview in *Literary Review* (Madison, New Jersey), Fall 1981; "Wonderful Lies That Tell the Truth: Neugeboren Reviewed" by Peter Spackman in *Columbia* (New York), November 1981.

*　　*　　*

It is easy, perhaps too easy, to dismiss all American-Jewish novelists as confirmed self-haters, as "know-nothings" bent on turning Jewish life into a vulgar joke. In this respect, Jack Portnoy of Philip Roth's 1969 *Portnoy's Complaint* speaks up for those who have grown impatient with their belligerent sons: "Tell me something, do you know Talmud? Do you know history? . . . Do you know a single thing about the wonderful history and heritage of the saga of your people?" And while such charges are true enough about the likes of Alexander Portnoy—and his wisecracking creator—they are no longer an accurate assessment of contemporary Jewish-American fiction. Writers like Cynthia Ozick, Arthur Cohen, and Hugh Nissenson have made mighty efforts on behalf of a Jewish aesthetic, one that would draw its sustenance from Jewish sources both wider and deeper than suburban assimilation. With *The Stolen Jew* Jay Neugeboren—a journeyman writer with a half-dozen volumes to his credit—adds himself to their number.

The Stolen Jew is a thick, complicated novel, but at bottom it is about the inextricable connections between personal memory and Jewish history, between the patterning that Art makes possible and the insistencies of Life, between an aging ex-writer named Nathan Malkin and his obligations to those, living and dead, who comprise his "family." The result is a novel-within-a-novel, as Nathan rewrites "The Stolen Jew," hoping to sell the manuscript at a high price on the Russian black market and, thus, to raise money to aid the refusniks. Whole chapters of Nathan's novel are interspersed with the Neugeboren's; each refracts upon the other. As Nathan puts it: "A true mosaic was made by shattering the original picture—and putting it together again." *The Stolen Jew* was selected as best novel of 1981 by the American Jewish Committee and, suddenly, Neugeboren became a writer to reckon with. As he himself suggests in a recent interview:

> In my early books [e.g. *Big Man* or *Listen Ruben Fontanez*], I used to pride myself on their "objective" quality. I mean, I don't think I'd ever done an autobiographical novel in a way that even anyone who knew me could feel. My books always seemed to be very much about other things. I think that was one way, in my own life, of not dealing with certain materials, potentially very rich materials, things that I do know about, but also material that I was afraid of, and felt I couldn't handle. . . . Now, with *The Stolen Jew* I've found a *subject*, a subject that comes from deep personal wells with me.

Before My Life Began is another installment in Neugeboren's continuing effect to combine aspects of traditional fiction (character, plot, naturalistic surface) with experimentation. As Neugeboren would have it, describing his new aesthetic manifesto, "I'd like to raise some of the questions some of the innovative writers are raising about the relation to art to life, but I would like to do it without losing the nineteenth-century novel—without losing character, history, story, the love of these things." In *The Stolen Jew* the result was as compelling as it was densely textured; with *Before My Life Began* one feels Neugeboren's ambition insisting too much:

Oh you are so good *inside,* David, don't you know that? You're a truly good *and* strong person, and there aren't many of your kind left. It's just so hard for me to watch you walking through the world, pulled on from so many sides, without my being able to help. I keep wanting to run in front of you—the court Jester, yes?—so I can steer you away from Evil and Hate and Anger and Cruelty and all the forces of Darkness—so I can point you to the true path—to righteousness and to light and to happiness.

For an author who can capture speech rhythms so accurately, who can reduplicate the Brooklyn streets of his doomed protagonist, David Voloshin, so well, such flights through airy abstraction may strike one as embarrassing. *Before My Life Began* is the story of a man forced by circumstances to live "two" lives—one as the David Voloshin who grows up in Brooklyn during the years immediately after World War II; the other as Aaron Levin, a civil rights activist during the mid-1960s.

The rub with Neugeboren's ever-thickening plot is that David, as a character, gets lost in the process. Somewhere, despite the rich texture and the patches of lyrical prose, there is no "David" one can grab hold of. He reappears as Aaron Levin, Freedom School teacher and civil rights activist, a man out to do dangerously good work in the Deep South. Once again, Neugeboren has an admirable feel for that time, that place, but he cannot quite resist those moments when David/Aaron speculates abstractly about his situation:

Sometimes, as now, he feels that his second life—all the years that have passed since he left Brooklyn, along with all the years to come—will only prove to be a rumination on his first life. . . . Why is it so, he wonders—that truth sometimes has the potential to destroy, while lies can save?

Given the displacement and wrenching dislocations of Neugeboren's protagonist, we are hardly surprised that he seeks pockets of respite. Unfortunately, Neugeboren protests too much about the happiness Voloshin/Levin presumably achieves. *Before My Life Began* ends in a litany of future tenses, of those movements back to a Brooklyn that will bring the novel—and David's life—full circle:

He will take his boys to his old neighborhood and show them his street and his house and the courtyards and the alleyways. He can see the four small rooms of his apartment, can see himself walking through them with his boys, room by room. The rooms are clean and white and empty, freshly painted and full of pale morning light—the way they might have been, he thinks, before his life began.

Evidently one *can* go home again, at least in the final vision of *Before My Life Began.* In *Poli: A Mexican Boy in Early Texas,* Neugeboren departs from the urban Jewish landscape of his previous fiction to tell the tale of quite another young initiate—and in the genre of the juvenile book, this one suggested for grades seven upward. But if Neugeboren's last works of fiction suggest differing views of childhood—either recaptured or imagined out of whole cloth—his growing readership is, I suspect, much more interested in the treatments of adulthood that lie in Neugeboren's novels as yet unwritten.

—Sanford Pinsker

NEWBY, P(ercy) H(oward)

Nationality: British. **Born:** Crowborough, Sussex, 25 June 1918. **Education:** Hanley Castle Grammar School, Worcester; St. Paul's College, Cheltenham, 1936-38. **Military Service:** Served in the Royal Army Medical Corps, in France and Egypt, 1939-42. **Family:** Married Joan Thompson in 1945; two daughters. **Career:** Lecturer in English language and literature, Fouad I University, Cairo, 1942-46; freelance writer and journalist, 1946-49; joined the BBC, London, 1949; producer, Talks Department, 1949-58; controller of the Third Programme, subsequently Radio 3, 1958-71; Director of Programmes, Radio, 1971-75; Managing Director of Radio, 1975-78; chair, English Stage Company, 1978-84. **Awards:** Atlantic award, 1946; Maugham award, 1958; Smith-Mundt fellowship, 1952; Booker prize, 1969. C.B.E. (Commander, Order of the British Empire), 1972. **Address:** Garsington House, Garsington, Oxfordshire OX9 9AB, England.

PUBLICATIONS

Novels

A Journey to the Interior. London, Cape, 1945; New York, Doubleday, 1946.
Agents and Witnesses. London, Cape, and New York, Doubleday, 1947.
Mariner Dances. London, Cape, 1948.
The Snow Pasture. London, Cape, 1949.
The Young May Moon. London, Cape, 1950; New York, Knopf, 1951.
A Season in England. London, Cape, 1951; New York, Knopf, 1952.
A Step to Silence. London, Cape, 1952.
The Retreat. London, Cape, and New York, Knopf, 1953.
The Picnic at Sakkara. London, Cape, and New York, Knopf, 1955.
Revolution and Roses. London, Cape, and New York, Knopf, 1957.
A Guest and His Going. London, Cape, 1959; New York, Knopf, 1960.
The Barbary Light. London, Faber, 1962; Philadelphia, Lippincott, 1964.
One of the Founders. London, Faber, and Philadelphia, Lippincott, 1965.
Something to Answer For. London, Faber, 1968; Philadelphia, Lippincott, 1969.
A Lot to Ask. London, Faber, 1973.
Kith. London, Faber, and Boston, Little Brown, 1977.
Feelings Have Changed. London, Faber, 1981.
Leaning in the Wind. London, Faber, 1986.
Coming in with the Tide. London, Hutchinson, 1991.
Something About Women. London, Deutsch, 1995.

Short Stories

Ten Miles from Anywhere and Other Stories. London, Cape, 1958.

Other

The Spirit of Jem (for children). London, Lehmann, 1947; New York, Delacorte Press, 1967.
The Loot Runners (for children). London, Lehmann, 1949.

Maria Edgeworth. London, Barker, and Denver, Swallow, 1950.
The Novel 1945-1950. London, Longman, 1951.
The Third Programme. London, BBC Publications, 1965.
The Egypt Story: Its Art, Its Monuments, Its People, photographs by Fred J. Maroon. London, Deutsch, and New York, Abbeville Press, 1979.
Warrior Pharaohs: The Rise and Fall of the Egyptian Empire. London, Faber, 1980.
Saladin in His Time. London, Faber, 1983.

Editor, *A Plain and Literal Translation of the Arabian Nights' Entertainments,* by Sir Richard Burton. London, Barker, 1950; as *Tales from the Arabian Nights,* New York, Pocket Books, 1951(?).

*

Critical Studies: "Portrait of the Artist as a Jung Man" by Lucia Dickerson, in *Kenyon Review* (Gambier, Ohio), Winter 1959; "A Novelist on His Own," in *Times Literary Supplement* (London), 6 April 1962; *The Fiction of P.H. Newby* by F.X. Mathews, Madison, University of Wisconsin Press, 1964; *Identity in Four of P.H. Newby's Novels* by M.G. St. Leger, unpublished master's thesis, American University, Beirut, 1969; *P.H. Newby* by G.S. Fraser, London, Longman, 1974; *P.H. Newby* by E.C. Bufkin, Boston, Twayne, 1975.

P.H. Newby comments:

In common with many English novelists my preoccupations have always been with what seems and what is. Many of my novels have been set in the Middle East but that is only because I spent some years there; it does not mean that I regard myself as particularly knowledgeable about that part of the world, only that I used this part of my experience to say what I would otherwise have said out of my English background—that the most interesting problem is the relationship between innocence and knowledge.

*   *   *

The lengthy series of novels by P.H. Newby can, with some justice, be assigned to two categories. There are novels which represent Newby's assessment of the contacts of two cultures; *Revolution and Roses, The Picnic at Sakkara,* and *Something to Answer For* are examples of these. And there are novels like *A Season in England, The Barbary Light,* and *One of the Founders* which abandon the fascinating game of assessing sharp cultural differences and that instead take up an analysis of a single culture: the texture of middle- and lower-class British life. The center of awareness in the novels which specialize in cultural dash is always that of some British traveler or teacher who has been thrust into an alien world, usually Arab but in one instance—*Revolution and Roses*—Greek. The center of awareness in novels that take up a specifically British theme is usually that of a fairly well-educated person who can assess the clash and diversity inherent in a society that, to the careless viewer, is or should be homogeneous.

Both varieties of subject matter have long been worked on by writers of British fiction. Alien cultural contacts experienced in the course of Britain's bearing "the white man's burden" are the stock-in-trade of writers as various as Kipling, E.M. Forster, and Joyce Cary. And novels which relate the maturing of an English hero in his own environment abound. But it is not just to Newby to suggest that he works in two traditions only loosely related to each other. For he brings to either tradition a variation that is his own. Moreover, this variation appears in almost every novel and effects a unity of tone that pervades the novels despite the variety of subject matter. That tone is the tone of farce.

It is a tone that separates the novels that represent contact with an alien culture from Forster's *A Passage to India* in which the English characters achieve some kind of understanding of the world they visit. Newby's English visitors begin in incomprehension and end there; at certain moments they indeed think they grasp the mystery of Arab or Greek temperament, but later turns of event and later deeds of the "natives" indicate that the comprehension of the English visitor rests on an insecure basis or no basis at all. Thus, in as late a novel as *Kith,* the young Englishman who becomes involved with his uncle's Coptic wife never "has a clue" when he tries to understand his aunt who is also his mistress. He has, instead, a series of encounters with her that are isolated rather than interdependent.

Newby's tone of farce also separates his novels with an English setting from the "coming of age" category they may seem to belong to. For in novels like *The Barbary Light* the characters only seem to "come of age"; new events and new potentialities within the hero's own nature give the lie to stances that had seemed final. Only in *A Season in England* and *One of the Founders* do the heroes finally transcend the texture of farce and achieve positions that are crypto-Christian. More usually, the heroes of the English novels just move through a succession of attitudes—attitudes that are related to each other only in that they flow in upon the same person. They do not come to compose a character, a fixed personality, a settled body of convictions. The attitudes simply overtake the hero, temporarily overwhelm him, and presently give way to other emotions and impressions thrust upon him by new events or by discovery of new potentialities within himself. The character lives in a society which is far from unified; this being so, how can he arrive at any consistency of gesture and aspiration? He has no more chance to arrive at a consistent view of his own motives than does the English visitor in *The Picnic at Sakkara.* He will fall in and out of love, will alter his purposes from year to year. Just as will the traveling Englishmen impose one revision after another on their impressions about "natives."

If a discrimination can indeed be made between the two groups of novels, it is this one. The farce of *The Picnic at Sakkara* and *Revolution and Roses* is overt and often violent. The farce of the British novels—which on the surface seem to be more serious—is covert. If one defines farce as existence seen under the sign of radical inconsequence, the definition is easily applied to the non-British novels, which despite the acuteness of Newby's notations on foreign customs and sensibilities are rich in the traditional pleasures of farce: the pleasures that come to us from events that are unpredictable and utterly disconcerting. A "native" who has seemed to be a friend, in *The Picnic at Sakkara,* turns into a bitter foe—and yet gives the English visitor a farewell gift. A man spits in an English woman's face (*Revolution and Roses*) and yet later turns up in London as a suitor. The pleasures of such foreign contacts are not much more predictable than entrance into a lion's cage; docility or murderous assault is equally likely. Such experience cannot be expected to yield a steady meaning; in its presence the visitor can brace himself to offer resignation and, at the worst, amused contempt. The safest course, in such farcically operating worlds, is to keep one's distance and expect very little in the way of fixed and dependable certainties.

One might expect a diminution of these farcical inconsequences when the hero of a novel is living in a world that is culturally his own. But this is not so of Newby's novels that represent the English world. The farcical texture of that world is simply more difficult to bear just because it is indeed one's own world. Gestures of kindness that ought to yield happy results beget unforeseen consequences—consequences that disconcert because of the unpredictable choices of other characters and, most painfully, because of changes in one's own wishes. For the British world of Newby is, in large part, that of Kingsley Amis's *Lucky Jim,* where farce is the product of an endemic British hypocrisy and, still worse, of a lack of any fixed values that could support social consensus. Farce experienced at one remove, in a visit to a foreign country, has become, in novels like *One of the Founders* and *The Barbary Light,* farce experienced at the very center of the culture one belongs to and, indeed, at the very center of one's own nature. Both tragedy and comedy, in varying ways, presuppose a society of shared values. Farce, instead, invites one to the fashioning of a detached, self-protective monologue that celebrates, as do the novels of Newby, the lack of consequence and coherence. It is a lack that just as strongly marks one's own culture and, if sharply inspected, one's own nature. If farce is to be left behind, this must be done by religious gesture (as in *One of the Founders*) which is private and quite incommunicable. Or by religious gesture, as in *A Lot to Ask,* that when it comes to the surface finally reveals itself as not notably unlike hopes for identity and meaning that are both commonplace and important in our time.

—Harold H. Watts

NEWMAN, (Jerry) C(oleman) J(oseph)

Nationality: Canadian. **Born:** Montreal, Quebec, 17 February 1935. **Education:** Sir George Williams University, Montreal (Woodrow Wilson fellow), 1954-59, B.A. in English 1959; University of Toronto, 1959-60; Marianopolis College, Montreal, 1967-68. **Family:** Married Frances Margaret Newman in 1962 (separated 1977); two sons and one daughter. **Career:** Lecturer, 1960-66, and assistant professor of English, 1971-72, Sir George Williams University; assistant professor, Macdonald College, McGill University, Montreal, 1966-71. Assistant professor, 1972-77, and since 1977 associate professor of creative writing, University of British Columbia, Vancouver. **Awards:** Canada Council bursary, 1966, and grant, 1968, 1969. **Address:** Department of Creative Writing, University of British Columbia, Vancouver, British Columbia V6T 1W5, Canada.

PUBLICATIONS

Novels

We Always Take Care of Our Own. Toronto, McClelland and Stewart, and London, Gollancz, 1965.
A Russian Novel. Toronto, New Press, and London, Gollancz, 1973.

Short Stories

New Canadian Writing 1969, with John Metcalf and D.O. Spettigue. Toronto, Clarke Irwin, 1969.

Uncollected Short Stories

"A Time To Heal," in *Canadian Genesis* (Toronto), 1971.
"Your Green Coast," in *Malahat Review* (Victoria, British Columbia), 1973.
"That Old David Copperfield Kind of Crap," in *Canadian Fiction* (Prince George, British Columbia), Winter 1973.
"The Best Lay I Ever Had," in *Journal of Canadian Fiction* (Fredericton, New Brunswick), vol. 3, no. 3, 1974.
"Falling in Love, Again," in *Fiddlehead* (Fredericton, New Brunswick), Fall 1974.
"The Game of Limping," in *Prairie Schooner* (Lincoln, Nebraska), Winter 1974-75.
"The Last Beginning. The Last! The Last!" in *Canadian Fiction* (Prince George, British Columbia), Winter 1975.

Plays

Radio Plays: *All the State Children Got Shoes, The Jam on Gerry's Rocks, A Work of Art, The Last Potato,* and *The Haunted House of Capuscins,* 1959-63.

Television Plays: *The Birth of a Salesman; A Bottle of Milk for Mother.*

Poetry

Sudden Proclamations. Vancouver, Cacanadada, 1994.

Other (for children)

Green Earrings or a Felt Hat. New York, Holt, 1993.

*   *   *

C.J. Newman's first novel, *We Always Take Care of Our Own,* is a *Bildungsroman* in which the protagonist Meyer Rabinovitch seeks an identity independent of the series of roles offered him by his parents, his rich relatives, and the Jewish community of Montreal as a whole. The family and the community, dedicated to the North American ideal of material success, are self-enclosing and self-absorbed. Meyer, in such an atmosphere, suffocates, but he is primarily motivated by a need to replace the deadening material conformity with values he believes to be essentially spiritual and peculiarly Jewish, values which derive from a Jewish past of suffering and humility. Hence his decision to be the only Jewish beggar in Montreal. Much of the novel is devoted to Meyer's droll and sometimes grotesque attempts to remain a beggar in face of the family's and the Jewish community's attempts to return him to a conformity more North American than Jewish; or more exactly because the Jewish community strives neurotically to be accepted, even more North American than the North Americans themselves. The simple plot is complicated by Meyer's disturbance at his father's business inability, by his socialistic uncle's approval which becomes disapproval, and his love for Rachel, the daughter of the crass *nouveau riche* Eli Echenberg. During the latter's decline and eventual death Meyer becomes indispensable to the family and almost weds the pregnant Rachel. She, however, marries into an even richer Jewish family and the abandoned and disillusioned Meyer is left at the end of the book contemplating the image of his earlier self, this time in the form of another young man who has also decided to be the only Jewish beggar in Montreal. Reflecting on the young man's triumphant hopelessness and smug humility Meyer decides that it is not enough to be Jewish, that the self-definition he seeks must lie in areas beyond the mere inversion of the acceptable patterns of the Jewish and North American community.

Newman's short stories have appeared in many Canadian and American little magazines. Only three so far have been collected, in *New Canadian Writing 1969*. The first two, "Yenteh" and "Everything Must Be Sold," are set in contemporary Montreal and the third, "An Arab Up North," though set in the Canadian Arctic is paradoxically intensely aware of the international situation in the Middle East. The first two stories have in common a strong sense of an urban setting in transition from the small, intimate, and dilapidated to the large, impersonal, and modern. These settings are important inasmuch as they emphasize Newman's apparent theme of the loss of humane warmth in face of a world increasingly materialistic, insecure, and either suspicious of, or hostile to, the idiosyncrasies of being. Mrs. Klein may well be a *yenteh,* but energetic vulgarity is preferable to the deadly gentility of the ironically named Wisemans and the dis-ease of the Schachters who trail after the Wisemans of this world. Likewise the aged owner of the store which is about to be demolished so that the neighborhood may be "renewed" arouses the malice of the two young men—a malice obscurely motivated by the rootlessness and depersonalization which such renewal seems to breed. Again in the third story it is the claims of history, race, religion, or class which blind the central characters. Arab and Jew, to the important realization that they have more in common with each other than with the rest of the men in the camp. It is because the recognition of each other's humanity is finally less important than a situation seemingly so remote from the Canadian Arctic that the story ends in death and desperate isolation.

A Russian Novel is a much more ambitious book than Newman's first one, and also a less successful one. The protagonist, David Miller, like Meyer Rabinovitch, is Jewish-Canadian and this novel too, appears to be concerned with an identity quest. Miller's mother emigrated many years ago from Russian, and after her death he decides to go there. It is only at the beginning, however, that the quest theme is emphasized. Much of the book is concerned with the love affair between Miller and the wife of the Russian novelist he is supposed to be studying, and with the political complexities surrounding Mikhali Ratin. It is especially in these areas that the novel becomes more of a tract than anything else and the didactic and documentary interests which have always been present in Newman's work usurp narrative, dramatic, and character emphases. One's final impression is of a novel which lacks both direction and linguistic vigor.

—Barrie Davies

NEWMAN, Charles (Hamilton)

Nationality: American. **Born:** St. Louis, Missouri, 27 May 1938. **Education:** North Shore Country Day School, Winnetka, Illinois, graduated 1956; Yale University, New Haven, Connecticut (editor, *Criterion* magazine), B.A. (summa cum laude) in American Studies 1960 (Phi Beta Kappa); Balliol College, Oxford (Woodrow Wilson fellow, Fulbright fellow), 1960-62. **Military Service:** Served in the United States Air Force Reserve. **Career:** Administrative assistant to Congressman Sidney R. Yates (Democrat, Illinois), 1962-63. Instructor, 1964-65, assistant professor, 1965-68, associate professor, 1968-73, and professor of English, 1974-75, Northwestern University, Evanston, Illinois; professor of English, and Chairman of the Writing Seminars, Johns Hopkins University, Baltimore, 1975-78. Since 1985 professor of English, Washington University, St. Louis. Founding editor, 1964-75, and advisory editor, 1975-80, *Tri-Quarterly,* Evanston, Illinois. Director, Coordinating Council of Literary Magazines, National Endowment for the Arts, Washington, D.C., 1968-74; member of the executive board, PEN American Center, 1977-80. **Awards:** National Endowment for the Arts grant, for editing, 1966, and fellowship, 1973; Rockefeller grant, 1967; Bread Loaf Writers Conference Atherton fellowship, 1969; Ingram Merrill Foundation grant, 1974; Guggenheim grant, 1974; American Academy Morton Dauwen Zabel award, 1975. **Agent:** Georges Borchardt Inc., 136 East 57th Street, New York, New York 10022. **Address:** Washington University, P.O. Box 1122, St. Louis, Missouri 63130, U.S.A.

PUBLICATIONS

Novels

New Axis; or, Little Ed Stories: An Exhibition. Boston, Houghton Mifflin, 1966; London, Calder and Boyars, 1968.
The Promisekeeper: A Tephromancy. New York, Simon and Schuster, 1971.
White Jazz. New York, Dial Press, 1984.

Short Stories

There Must Be More to Love Than Death: Three Short Novels. Chicago, Swallow Press, 1976.

Uncollected Short Stories

"That's the Way the American People Like to Do," in *Tri-Quarterly* (Evanston, Illinois), Spring 1964.
"The Scavengers," in *Vogue* (London), 1968.
"Eclipse, Etc." in *Chicago Review,* Spring 1971.
"Comprehensive Development Project for These United States . . . ," in *Tri-Quarterly* (Evanston, Illinois), Winter 1976.
"Age of Art," in *Paris Review,* Winter 1976.
"The Woman Who Thought Like a Man," in *The Best American Short Stories 1977,* edited by Martha Foley. Boston, Houghton Mifflin, 1977.

Other

A Child's History of America: Some Ribs and Riffs for the Sixties. Chicago, Swallow Press, 1973.
The Post-Modern Aura: The Act of Fiction in an Age of Inflation. Evanston, Illinois, Northwestern University Press, 1985.

Editor, with George Gömöri, *New Writing from East Europe.* Chicago, Quadrangle, 1968.

Editor, *The Art of Sylvia Plath: A Symposium.* Bloomington, Indiana University Press, and London, Faber, 1970.

Editor, with William A. Henkin, Jr., *Under 30: Fiction, Poetry, and Criticism of the New American Writers.* Bloomington, Indiana University Press, 1970.

Editor, *For Edward Dahlberg.* Evanston, Illinois, Northwestern University Press, 1970.

Editor, with Alfred Appel, Jr., *Nabokov: Criticism and Reminiscences, Translations and Tributes.* Evanston, Illinois, Northwestern University Press, 1970; London, Weidenfeld and Nicolson, 1971.

Editor, with George Abbott White, *Literature in Revolution.* New York, Holt Rinehart, 1972.

Editor, with Mary Kinzie, *Prose for Borges.* Evanston, Illinois, Northwestern University Press, 1974.

*   *   *

Charles Newman is one of America's better experimental writers. Writing in the tradition of Burgess, Barth, Pynchon, and Vonnegut, Newman employs his verbal pyrotechnics and Derridean deconstructions to create the fictive world of postmodern man threatened by obsolescence in a high-tech age.

From 1964 to 1975 Newman served as founding editor of *TriQuarterly* and forged the magazine in his own style, attracting the works of the best experimental writers of this continent and abroad. Later, he edited several volumes of criticism on Plath, Borges, and the literature of revolution, while 1985 saw the publication of *The Post-Modern Aura: The Act of Fiction in an Age of Inflation.* Dissecting the underlying principles of postmodern literature, he exposes a literature that is as debased as our money supply, and he dates the swings in postmodernism to coincide with the periodicity of the velocity of the money supply from 1946 when it first started rising, through the 1950s when it accelerated, to 1968 when it peaked at the height of the Great Society and the Vietnam War, on through the 1970s when it was out of control, and ending in 1981 when it subsided as one by one the myths of inflation were dismantled.

Paralleling the collapse in value of our money is the collapse of the house of fiction and its replacement with the growth of metafiction and a banal poetry which comes near to being prose or primitive speech. Newman charts the course of fiction and criticism, launching a scathing attack on the fallacy of the indeterminists, and exposing the false dichotomy created by William Gass and Donald Barthelme of the avant garde on the one hand, and Saul Bellow of the realist revival on the other. In Gass, we find the absolutist aesthetic: he takes formalism to its affirmative extreme and asserts that the novel is all technique with no mimetic obligations; it is a cultural object that transcends and transforms history. Bellow responds by insisting that mimesis and an audience be restored to art, that art and the artist recover the centrality they once held in an integrated society that privileged each, and that art seek again to find that "lost something" which once inhabited it and gave it meaning and value beyond its own literary confines. Newman's credo is to reject all binary classifications as misguided and to draw upon the methods of science, of the wave/particle theories of light, to give him direction. Refusing to partake of the formalist/realist debate, he argues that what is needed is a method that permits one to hold simultaneously irreconcilable ideas—to entertain a wave/particle theory of reality. Newman asks that the artist rededicate himself to literature's peculiar generic constitution, "its lack of an

ontology, and the consequent cross-processing which defies autonomy—a practical energy which can never be systematic, but cannot fail to be inclusive." He concludes that "Fiction, in short, is modern man's method by which antinomies can be unlearned; a process in which oppositions are neither resolved nor transcended but made reciprocally evocative. . . . And the truth of fiction is not indeterminate—only a set of facts which cannot be presumptively inferred from other facts, which is thus unlikely to find expression as a coherent theory." Newman's imaginative writing, like his books of criticism, is unpredictable, verbally adroit, and utterly committed to the task of describing minutely the consciousness industry— our society as a massive communications industry, an information system of extraordinary technical sophistication tied to a kinetic media and operating like a planetary system of "increasingly merged bodies which conform to an increasingly inexorable set of mundane laws." The artist's task is still the one Forster wrote about: "one connect," and this connection must relate art to its audience and its world. Art to survive must serve an ethical function. *White Jazz,* Newman's latest novel, travels the farthest in fulfilling the credo Newman writes about in *The Post-Modern Aura.* It is marked by his zany imagination, a fine intelligence, an inquiring mind, a genius with words, and a stubborn humanistic craving for meaning in a world where future shock threatens to reduce life to a computer game.

An examination of Newman's novels and satirical history since 1966 is usefully informed by reference to the periods of inflation that he describes in *The Post-Modern Aura.* In the period of the Great Society and the Vietnam War when the modernist idea of salvation through aesthetics seemed sorely wanting, and when fiction reveled in egalitarianism and filled its margins in a search for a new point of view, Newman wrote *New Axis* and *A Child's History of America.* In *New Axis,* Little Ed narrates a series of stories about the life of the affluent D family and their neighbors in a wealthy suburb located in middle America. Little Ed's world is one of diminished, ordinary, well-meaning affection. It is also a world of inflation and automation: Vibrolators restore the circulation and make plump, curved women slim. In *A Child's History of America* Newman recounts with colloquial ease his travels through Haight-Ashbury when the Hippies were confronting the "pigs," on to Paris during the May revolt of the students, and ending in Czechoslovakia during the Russian invasion. The margins of his book are cluttered with aptly chosen quotes from such notables as Trotsky and Marx, Bergson and Merleau-Ponty, Locke and Thoreau, and a gentleman who left graffiti on a lavatory wall. The book offers a disarming and refreshingly original portrait of the confusion of 1968.

In 1971 Newman wrote *The Promisekeeper,* his "tephromancy." Auguries of the future are found by reading the ashes of Chicago. Superelegant, suave, executive Sam Hooper climbs the ladder of success at Management Concerns. Hooper, the technocrat's dream of efficiency and success, is a promise-keeper who only pledges what he can deliver; he is only victor when he relinquishes his limited powers and lets himself be killed. Hooper's relaxation takes the form of reading the journal of Captain Fuess, a millionaire mariner who voyages around the world in ever smaller ships crafted by his own hands. The narrative, in the manner of metafiction, is interspersed with Captain Fuess's tale, relics of Sam's past, his report cards, his Christmas market analysis, and other diverse odds and ends. In *There Must Be More to Love Than Death* Newman presents three novelettes. The first tells the story of Gee Patek of the 112st Air Dispensary Unit. Never seeing active duty, Patek manages to be accused of sexual deviancy and of attacking Commander

Pompillo with a hypodermic needle filled with morphine. The story recounts the events that lie behind these accusations. The second short novel, a masque, is a "hopelessly confused affair in which everyone feels neglected." The third short novel is the narrative of a 13-year-old boy who possesses a photographic memory and perfect recall of all that he hears. He admonishes the reader to "please remember that what I'm saying is what other people said—something I've read or heard somewhere—and a lot of time I honestly don't understand myself." The story is allegorical. With the advantage of hindsight and anachronism, one could say that the story is Newman's answer to Harold Bloom's idea of the anxiety of influence. The story tells of a trip the narrator takes with his imaginary brother into the forest and back home. It is not the entrance into the forest that matters, nor the discovery that at the heart of the forest is a broken-down machine. What matters, and what is difficult to tell, is the story of how one comes out of the forest and survives. Newman's latest novel is exploring the same question but the forest is replaced by Yuppie highrises and strobe-lit discos.

White Jazz is Newman's novel of the 1980s; the myth of inflation is in ruins; the hype of the information age is bust; the protagonist's dream of discovering the Great Computer is shattered; and the protagonist's need to make human contact in an age where the consciousness industry has almost emptied man of meaning is poignantly expressed in the final pages of the novel. Newman's novel insists that we register the textures of the media age. He fashions the Nowspeak of computers and videogame; he is the architect of the urban metropolis surrounded by eight-laned Interstate highways, looping around retirement parks that face upscale young-adult communities, all built by the same architect out of the same mindless mold. His novel is lit by the artificial orb light of the expressways, or the bombarding rays of electrons projected from a television screen or computer terminal, or the hot and cool strobe lights of a jazz disco. The novel charts a week in the life of the protagonist, Sandy—Sandman to his CB-radio cronies—who probes the circuitry of his computer terminal at Human Resources by day and unwinds by night at el Cielito Lindo. His book is liberally laced with quotations from Bishop Berkeley, Albert Einstein, and the latest self-help moral inventory generated by the computer.

Newman is an accomplished writer who delights in language and its deceptions and who forges stories that force us to confront our technological age and consider what can give us meaning in this minimalist, mediocritizing world.

—Carol Simpson Stern

NGUGI wa Thiong'o

Formerly wrote as James T. Ngugi. **Nationality:** Kenyan. **Born:** Kamiriithu, near Limuru, Kiambu District, 5 January 1938. **Education:** Kamaand ra School, Limuru; Karing'a School, Maangu; Alliance High School, Kikuyu; University College, Kampala, Uganda (editor, *Penpoint*), 1959-63, B.A. 1963; Leeds University, Yorkshire, 1964-67, B.A. 1964. **Family:** Married Nyambura in 1961; five sons and three daughters. **Career:** Columnist ("As I See It"), early 1960s, and reporter, 1964, Nairobi *Daily Nation;* editor, *Zuka,* Nairobi, 1965-70; lecturer in English, University College, Nairobi, 1967-69; Fellow in Creative Writing, Makerere University, Kampala, 1969-70; visiting lecturer, Northwestern Univer-

sity, Evanston, Illinois, 1970-71; senior lecturer, associate professor, and chairman of the Department of Literature, University of Nairobi, 1972-77; imprisoned under Public Security Act, 1977-78; left Kenya, 1982; now lives in London. **Awards:** East African Literature Bureau award, 1964. **Address:** c/o Heinemann International, Halley Court, Jordan Hill, Oxford OX2 8EJ, England.

PUBLICATIONS

Novels

Weep Not, Child. London, Heinemann, 1964; New York, Collier, 1969.
The River Between. London, Heinemann, 1965.
A Grain of Wheat. London, Heinemann, 1967.
Petals of Blood. London, Heinemann, 1977; New York, Dutton, 1978.
Caitaani Mutharaba-ini (in Kikuyu). Nairobi, Heinemann, 1980; as *Devil on the Cross,* London, Heinemann, 1982.
Matigari (in Kikuyu). Nairobi, Heinemann, 1986; translated by Wangui wa Goro, London, Heinemann, 1989.

Short Stories

Secret Lives and Other Stories. London, Heinemann, and New York, Hill, 1975.

Plays

The Black Hermit (produced Kampala, Uganda, 1962; London, 1988). London, Heinemann, 1968.
This Time Tomorrow (broadcast 1967). Included in *This Time Tomorrow,* 1970.
This Time Tomorrow (includes *The Rebels* and *The Wound in the Heart*). Nairobi, East African Literature Bureau, 1970.
The Trial of Dedan Kimathi, with Micere Mugo (produced London, 1984). Nairobi, Heinemann, 1976; London, Heinemann, 1977.
Ngaahika Ndeenda (in Kikuyu), with Ngugi wa Mirii (produced Limuru, 1977). Nairobi, Heinemann, 1980; as *I Will Marry When I Want,* London, Heinemann, 1982.

Radio Play: *This Time Tomorrow,* 1967.

Other

Homecoming: Essays on African and Caribbean Literature, Culture, and Politics. London, Heinemann, 1972; New York, Hill, 1973.
The Independence of Africa and Cultural Decolonisation, with *The Poverty of African Historiography,* by A.E. Afigbo. Lagos, Afrografika, 1977.
Writers in Politics: Essays. London, Heinemann, 1981.
Detained: A Writer's Prison Diary. London, Heinemann, 1981.
Education for a National Culture. Harare, Zimbabwe Publishing House, 1981.
Barrel of a Pen: Resistance to Repression in Neo-Colonial Kenya. London, New Beacon, and Trenton, New Jersey, Africa World Press, 1983.
Decolonising the Mind: The Politics of Language in African Literature. London, Currey, 1986.

Njamba Nene and the Cruel Chief (for children). Nairobi, Heinemann, 1986.

Njamba Nene's Pistol (for children). Nairobi, Heinemann, 1986.

Writing Against Neocolonialism. London, Vita, 1986.

Walter Rodney's Influence on the African Continent. London, Friends of Bogle, 1987.

Moving the Centre: The Struggle for Cultural Freedoms. London, Currey, and Portsmouth, New Hampshire, Heinemann, 1993.

*

Bibliography: *Ngugi wa Thiong'o: A Bibliography of Primary and Secondary Sources 1957-1987* by Carol Sicherman, London, Zell, 1989.

Critical Studies: *Ngugi wa Thiong'o* by Clifford Robson, London, Macmillan, 1979, New York, St. Martin's Press, 1980; *An Introduction to the Writings of Ngugi* by G.D. Killam, London, Heinemann, 1980; *Ngugi wa Thiong'o: An Exploration of His Writings* by David Cook and Michael Okenimkpe, London, Heinemann, 1983; *East African Writing in English* by Angela Smith, London, Macmillan, 1989; *Ngugi wa Thiong'o: The Making of a Rebel: A Source Book in Kenyan Literature and Resistance* by Carol Sicherman, 1990; *The Novel as Transformation Myth: A Study of the Novels of Mongo Beti and Ngugi wa Thiong'o* by Kandioura Dram, Syracuse, New York, Syracuse University, 1990; *"Justice for the Oppressed—": The Polictical Dimension in the Language Use of Ngugi wa Thiong'o* by Herta Meyer, Essen, Verlag Die Blaue Eule, 1991; *African Independence from Francophone and Anglophone Voices: A Comparative Study of the Post-Independence Novels by Ngugi and Sembene* by Clara Tsabedze, New York, Lang, 1994.

*   *   *

Ngugi wa Thiong'o was a Kikuyu adolescent in Kenya during the Mau Mau Rebellion, and the events of those years, of the larger issues of black dispossession by white settlers, and of the history of the Kikuyu from pre-colonial times to the present, lie at the center of his novels and most of his short stories. He was the first Anglophone African writer to give in fiction a Kikuyu view of the bitter colonial war that the British called the Mau Mau Emergency—a healthy corrective to other fictional accounts, like Robert Ruark's, from a white man's point of view. Ngugi's attitudes to larger political questions are by no means unambiguous in his first two novels (hence some considerable uncertainty of craftsmanship in them) but what emerges clearly from *The River Between* (the first to be written, but the second published) is a deep sense of African deprivation and of the desire to win back a lost heritage. It is expressed in *Weep Not, Child* through Ngotho's religious attachment to the land of his ancestors taken from him by Mr. Howlands, and through his older sons' determination to fight for their lands by joining the Mau Mau. But Ngugi is also aware of another part of the African heritage diminished by white colonialism—the Kikuyu religion and tribal culture; it is this aspect of their disinheritance that figures particularly in *The River Between*.

The river is a symbol of sustenance and growth, but it also divides the christianized half of the tribe from the adherents of the traditional tribal ways, soon after the advent of colonialism. Waiyaki, the hero, is an idealistic youth, who dreams with messianic fervor of leading his people out of colonial tutelage, peacefully, by ac-

quiring the white man's education. He would also reconcile the two religiously divided villages; though associated with the traditionalists, he loves a daughter of the fanatical Christian Kikuyu pastor. But Waiyaki's enthusiasm for Western education blinds him to political methods, and he is rejected by his people. The weakness of the novel is that Ngugi romanticizes and glamorizes Waiyaki: his tribal opponents are presented as vindictive personal enemies; their different political approach is not seriously considered.

Njoroge in *Weep Not, Child* is another self-centered youth with mission-school education and messianic ambitions, whose hopes are destroyed when his brothers' involvement in Mau Mau forces him out of school, but again self-centeredness is not part of any ironic regarding of the hero by the novelist. Yet *Weep Not, Child* is a better novel, for Ngugi develops some complexity of structure. There are ironic parallels between the African devotion to ancestral lands and the white settler's love of the soil he has acquired, with the opposed characters oblivious to their common human suffering. Such ironical treatment is a great advance in Ngugi's technique, as are the convincing portraits of subsidiary characters who betray the very values they struggle to achieve, or who suffer constant frustration.

A Grain of Wheat is a novel of mature outlook and much subtler technique. Ostensibly about the Uhuru celebrations of Kenya's independence in 1963, it keeps flashing back to individual sufferings in Mau Mau days. There is no single, central hero this time, but four major characters, each guilty of betraying himself and others when sorely tried in the Rebellion. Mugo, regarded by his people as a Mau Mau hero, has messianic visions before the Rebellion, but his jealousy of the real leader led him to betray him to the British. At last Ngugi is able to treat a messianic figure with detachment, but also with humane sympathy: the years of Mugo's lonely, conscience-ridden life are movingly conveyed. Other characters who also committed acts of betrayal painfully learn, first, the depths of utter disillusion, and then, the harrowing experience of coming to terms with their own limitations. Mugo's public confession brings *him* peace of mind, and helps *them* to face the future with some hope. A great strength of this finely orchestrated novel is Ngugi's skillful use of disrupted time sequence to indicate the interrelatedness of the characters' behavior in the Rebellion and the state of their lives (and of the nation) at Independence. Ngugi's maturity appears also in his sober attitude both to the struggle for, and attainment of, Independence; there are signs of the new African politicians already betraying the ordinary people who suffered under colonialism. Though a disturbing novel, it proclaims hope for the regenerative capabilities of ordinary human nature.

In his critical essays in *Homecoming,* Ngugi argues the vital social function of literature in Africa, and the Third World generally. In *Petals of Blood* he impressively puts this belief into practice. A convincing attack, often Marxist in language, upon neocolonialism in Independent Africa is achieved fictionally by indicating powerfully and effectively how the lives of dispossessed little people are all but broken by an imported capitalist system. The four major characters, each a misfit in Independent Kenyan society, have come to the distant village of Ilmorog to seek personal peace and modest new beginnings. Long associated with heroic Kikuyu legends, Ilmorog becomes a living presence in the novel. In the grip of prolonged drought, and ignored by the M.P. who had begged their votes, the desperate villagers undertake an epic march to the capital to lay their troubles before the authorities. Subsequently religious, political, and economic exploiters swarm upon Ilmorog to "develop" it, and using such devices as foreclosed loans eventually dispossess the local inhabitants and establish New Ilmorog. The ample detail with which Ngugi conveys the ruthless stripping of already deprived ordinary people gains power from a sophisticated narrative technique that enables Kenya's history since 1963 to be felt through the consciousness of its social victims. *Petals of Blood* is an angry novel but it does affirm the potentialities of native communality for a just, humane African polity.

With greater fervor of feeling and rhetoric, Ngugi renews in *Devil on the Cross* his attack upon neocolonial exploiters of ordinary Kenyan people. The story of the economically and sexually exploited young woman, War nga, is given some of the drama of fantasy by being told by "G caand Player, Prophet of Justice," a figure drawn from the oral tradition, who uses language emotively and didactically in ways reminiscent of Armah's novel *Two Thousand Seasons* (1973). While the device allows Ngugi to employ a variety of highly charged rhetorical modes, it is questionable whether he deploys them as convincingly as he might have. Would such a narrator use not only songs, incantations, the very idiom of oral tradition, but also echoes and parodies of Bible stories and biblical English, together with Marxist analysis and denunciation of capitalism? Ngugi doesn't seem to have tried very hard to disguise his authorial voice, or perhaps it is the effect of translating from his own original Kikuyu. While in *Devil on the Cross* he combines the biblical linguistic and moral flavor of his first two novels with the acerbic political tones of *Petals of Blood,* the cost is much wordy reiteration. Nevertheless, the catastrophic effects of the Western economic stranglehold on many African nations is starkly revealed in the misery of the destitute and starving and the monstrosity of the new Kenyan affluent class.

—Arthur Ravenscroft

NISSENSON, Hugh

Nationality: American. **Born:** Brooklyn, New York, 10 March 1933. **Education:** Fieldston School, New York; Swarthmore College, Pennsylvania, B.A. 1955. **Family:** Married Marilyn Claster in 1962; two daughters. **Career:** Since 1958 full-time writer. **Awards:** Stegner fellowship, 1961; Wallant Memorial award, 1965. **Address:** 411 West End Avenue, New York, New York 10024, U.S.A.

PUBLICATIONS

Novels

My Own Ground. New York, Farrar Straus, and London, Secker and Warburg, 1972.
The Tree of Life. New York, Harper, 1985; Manchester, Carcanet, 1991.

Short Stories

A Pile of Stones. New York, Scribner, 1965.
In the Reign of Peace. New York, Farrar Straus, and London, Secker and Warburg, 1972.
The Elephant and My Jewish Problem: Selected Stories and Journals 1957-1987. New York, Harper, 1988.

Other

Notes from the Frontier. New York, Dial Press, 1968.

*

Hugh Nissenson comments:

(1995) Professor Mario Materassi, chairman of the Department of American Literature at the University of Florence, wrote in an article on December 5, 1994, in the newspaper *La Nazione* that the "work of Hugh Nissenson is totally his own, totally original."

Professor Materassi says "Nissenson feels compelled to reinvent the language and the art of narrative."

My creed as a novelist was elucidated at the beginning of this century by Ezra Pound, who said, "Make it new." As Materassi reports, I call myself "the last modernist—probably the last of my kind."

I am now working on a novel called *The Song of the Earth* which I hope will bring into fruition a fusion of prose, verse, and visual art in a new narrative form which I initiated in *The Tree of Life.*

*   *   *

In spite of having produced relatively few books, including only two novels, Hugh Nissenson has gained a reputation as an important writer of historical fiction and of fiction dealing with present-day Jews, especially in Israel. Typically, his works deal with the lives of Jews in America, especially during the latter part of the period of the Great Migration from around 1885 to 1920, in Eastern Europe during the period just before and during the Great Migration, and in Israel since shortly before the War of Independence.

His historical fiction, especially his two novels, has been praised for its fidelity to fact and for its ability to reproduce the texture of the times in which it is set. The first novel, *My Own Ground,* is set in New York City around 1912. In it Nissenson recreates the sights and sounds of everyday life on the Lower East Side. The clicking of the gas meter, the habitual motions of a presser, the details of a steam bath all give a sense of solidity to the work. The novel depicts the seamier side of Jewish life in the New York ghetto. A pimp and a revolutionary fight for control of the essentially innocent Hannah Isaacs, who ends the conflict by committing suicide. Narrated in 1965 by the mature Jacob Brody who looks back at his 15th year, the novel depicts his initiation into the darker side of life and his eventual flight to upstate New York, where he starts life anew.

Nissenson's second novel, *The Tree of Life,* is set in frontier Ohio during 1811 and 1812, with a short glance into 1845. Using diary form, Nissenson gives insight into the life of Thomas Keene, who tries to survive in a wilderness in which he is threatened by wild animals, wild men (both Native Americans and European-Americans), and sickness. It too concentrates on many of the seamier sides of life, including Keene's and his neighbors' illnesses and sexual problems. The novel explores the white man's treachery towards the Indians and the blacks as well as the Indians' treachery toward the whites. The novel does, however, provide moments of hope specifically through the character of Keene who repeatedly gives up drinking, finally with success; marries for a second time and accepts his wife's infant son as though he were his own.

Until the publication of *The Tree of Life,* Nissenson was almost exclusively known as a writer about Jews. Although several of his short stories, such as "Grace," treat nonJews only, most deal with limited aspects of Jewish life in America, Eastern Europe, and Israel. Often ending in a state of indeterminacy, these works highlight the ambiguity of life in a world often arbitrarily divided between the secular and the profane. His is a world of hard work and constant suffering in which evil people often prosper at the expense of good.

Nissenson's published journals enable readers to see how they serve as raw material from which he draws for his works of fiction, especially his works about Israel. His own experiences covering the Eichmann trial and living on a kibbutz have given him insight into nature and humanity at their worst and best; these insights have clearly become the source of some of the ambiguity that lies at the center of his works.

Although the revised version of "The Groom of Zlota Street" (in *The Elephant and My Jewish Problem*) is set in Warsaw in 1906, it and stories like it obviously draw on Nissenson's direct observations of people's ability to inflict incredible suffering on one another. The groom of Zlota Street represents hope for Yechiel: when all other ways of making money by selling carriage whips fail, he can always turn to the groom, who will buy every whip Yechiel has. Because he refuses to shave his beard or modernize his dress, Yechiel's life is one of perpetual fear, dodging the soldiers who live across from the combination shop-home where he lives with the narrator's father and his family, trying desperately to sell his whips. But the groom of Zlota Street holds a promise of great gain for Yechiel. All Yechiel has to do is allow the groom to pull his beard once for each whip the groom buys. Central to the story, however, is not Yechiel but the narrator's father, a child who is initiated by Yechiel into the horrors of life at the same time that Yechiel feels that he is introducing the boy to the blessings of a bountiful God who always provides people with a choice.

Obviously, Nissenson is not content with easy answers. His characters experience moments of great joy but also great suffering. Imperfect themselves, they live in an imperfect world and often try to discover how such things are possible if God is perfect. Many become atheists, but others, like Yechiel, retain an ecstatic faith in divine goodness in spite of apparently overwhelming reasons for despair.

—Richard Tuerk

NORFOLK, Lawrence

Nationality: British. **Born:** 1963.

PUBLICATIONS

Novels

Lemprière's Dictionary. London, Sinclair Stevenson, and New York, Harmony, 1991.

*   *   *

With a second novel, *The Pope's Rhinoceros,* yet to appear, Lawrence Norfolk's formidable reputation rests upon a single work, *Lemprière's Dictionary.* The success of this erudite, intricately de-

signed, and densely textured novel derives chiefly from its pastiche of literary forms and sensibilities even more varied than its range of geographical and temporal settings (from England to India, from 1600 to 1788). Impossible to classify (or summarize), the novel combines numerous genres—Gothic, Victorian, historical, adventure, mystery, detective, political thriller, and quest—in a decidedly postmodern (even postcolonial) way that strongly suggests the influence of writers such as Umberto Eco, Thomas Pynchon, and Peter Ackroyd.

Norfolk's protagonist is John Lemprière, a fictional version of the author of the well-known *Classical Dictionary* (1788). Building upon the relative dearth of information about the real Lemprière's life, Norfolk fashions his own version (a narrative ploy of considerable thematic import). His Lemprière is a myopic youth whose reading has addled his brain, causing him to see the myths he reads about come to life. Instead of correcting the problem, glasses only enable him to see all the better his father torn apart by his own hunting dogs, in the manner of Actaeon. Himself torn apart by guilt and the desire to solve the family mystery, Lemprière begins his exile/quest. Early in his wanderings, it is suggested that he write a dictionary as a form of therapy. Although it offers him a refuge from a series of baffling mysteries (and thus functions in much the same way the novel itself does for the similarly naive and escapist reader), the dictionary also serves a more sinister purpose. It is the "signed confession" linking its innocent author to a series of myth-inspired murders perpetrated by a shadowy Cabbala. It is this Cabbala, comprising descendants of François Lemprière's former business partners, that the hero believes he is searching out but has in fact been directing his efforts all along.

Norfolk's title recalls other, more famous dictionaries. Unlike Samuel Johnson's (1755), Norfolk's does not attempt to "fix" and "preserve" its subject. Like the *Oxford English Dictionary,* it is "based upon historical principles" that in the novel are to be understood semiotically rather than scientifically. As Norfolk explains in "Bosnian Alphabet" in the Spring 1993 issue of *Granta,* a dictionary is a very useful but also highly arbitrary means for organizing chaotic experience. It is also a way to organize a novel, as Walter Abish (*Alphabetical Africa*) and Milorad Pavic (*The Dictionary of the Khazars*) have demonstrated. And just as Pavic's novel exists in two forms, male and female, each with its own ending, so does Norfolk's: the longer, denser, more fantastic original English edition and the shorter American, with its greater "forward momentum." Appropriately, *Lemprière's Dictionary* is filled with twins, metamorphoses, mistaken identities, and deliberate disguises and pretends to be a good many things that it is not, including a historical novel (about the East India Company, England's coming-of-age as a colonial power, the events leading up to the French Revolution, and so on). Even as the details are deployed to create a Jamesian "sense of the past," they also serve as a set of facts, some real, some fictional, whose permutational possibilities allow for a seemingly endless series of rearrangement and reinterpretation, that may be understood as an instance of postmodern play or, more seriously, as Don DeLillo has said of his novel *Libra,* as a way of thinking about history, including the history of the novel).

Norfolk's novel repeatedly calls attention to the reading process: to how characters read or, more often, misread events and texts, sometimes, as in François's message to his partners still in the besieged city of La Rochelle, with disastrous consequences. The consequences for the novel and its readers are of course quite different, misinterpretation being the engine that drives them both. Reading a novel such as *Lemprière's Dictionary* becomes at times a highly self-conscious affair. What is said about characters and events often applies equally well to the novel itself. Like the Cabbala, it is "a kind of joke, a huge prank" turned serious; like the rumors of impending massacre, it is something that the reader, like the citizens of La Rochelle, perversely "want to believe." It is as well a bog, a fraud, a game of chess, a conspiracy, a simulacrum (in the Baudrillardian sense, a postmodern image having no antecedent reality). Ultimately it resembles the creation of one of Lemprière's own mythical subjects, the master artificer Daedalus, maker of automata and labyrinths.

—Robert A. Morace

NYE, Robert

Nationality: British. **Born:** London, 15 March 1939. **Education:** Dormans Land, Surrey; Hamlet Court, Westcliff, Essex; Southend High School, Essex. **Family:** Married 1) Judith Pratt in 1959 (divorced 1967), three sons; 2) Aileen Campbell in 1968, one daughter, one stepdaughter, and one stepson. **Career:** Since 1961 freelance writer: since 1967 poetry editor, the *Scotsman,* Edinburgh; since 1971 poetry critic, the *Times,* London. Writer-in-residence, University of Edinburgh, 1976-77. **Awards:** Eric Gregory award, 1963; Scottish Arts Council bursary, 1970, 1973, and publication award, 1970, 1976; James Kennaway Memorial award, 1970; *Guardian* Fiction prize, 1976; Hawthornden prize, 1977; Society of Authors' Travel scholarship, 1991. Fellow, Royal Society of Literature, 1977. **Agent:** Sheil Land Associates, 43 Doughty Street, London WC1N 2LF, England; or, Wallace Literary Agency, 177 East 70th Street, New York, New York 10021, U.S.A. **Address:** 2 Westbury Crescent, Wilton, Cork, Ireland.

PUBLICATIONS

Novels

Doubtfire. London, Calder and Boyars, 1967; New York, Hill and Wang, 1968.
Falstaff. London, Hamish Hamilton, and Boston, Little Brown, 1976.
Merlin. London, Hamish Hamilton, 1978; New York, Putnam, 1979.
Faust. London, Hamish Hamilton, 1980; New York, Putnam, 1981.
The Voyage of the Destiny. London, Hamish Hamilton, and New York, Putnam, 1982.
The Memoirs of Lord Byron. London, Hamish Hamilton, 1989.
The Life and Death of My Lord Gilles de Rais. London, Hamish Hamilton, 1990.
Mrs. Shakespeare: The Complete Works. London, Sinclair-Stevenson, 1993.

Short Stories

Tales I Told My Mother. London, Calder and Boyars, 1969; New York, Hill and Wang, 1970.
Penguin Modern Stories 6, with others. London, Penguin, 1970.
The Facts of Life and Other Fictions. London, Hamish Hamilton, 1983.

Uncollected Short Stories

Lines Review 38 (includes 4 stories, verse, and a film script) (Edinburgh), 1971.

Plays

Sawney Bean, with William Watson (produced Edinburgh, 1969; London, 1972; New York, 1982). London, Calder and Boyars, 1970.
Sisters (broadcast 1969; produced Edinburgh, 1973). Included in *Penthesilea, Fugue, and Sisters,* 1975.
Penthesilea, adaptation of the play by Heinrich von Kleist (broadcast 1971; produced London, 1983). Included in *Penthesilea, Fugue, and Sisters,* 1975.
The Seven Deadly Sins: A Mask, music by James Douglas (produced Stirling and Edinburgh, 1973). Rushden, Northamptonshire, Omphalos Press, 1974.
Mr. Poe (produced Edinburgh and London, 1974).
Penthesilea, Fugue, and Sisters. London, Calder and Boyars, 1975.

Radio Plays: *Sisters,* 1969; *A Bloody Stupit Hole,* 1970; *Reynolds, Reynolds,* 1971; *Penthesilea,* 1971; *The Devil's Jig,* music by Humphrey Searle, from a work by Thomas Mann, 1980.

Poetry

Juvenilia 1. Northwood, Middlesex, Scorpion Press, 1961.
Juvenilia 2. Lowestoft, Suffolk, Scorpion Press, 1963.
Darker Ends. London, Calder and Boyars, and New York, Hill and Wang, 1969.
Agnus Dei. Rushden, Northamptonshire, Sceptre Press, 1973.
Two Prayers. Richmond, Surrey, Keepsake Press, 1974.
Five Dreams. Rushden, Northamptonshire, Sceptre Press, 1974.
Divisions on a Ground. Manchester, Carcanet, 1976.
A Collection of Poems 1955-1988. London, Hamish Hamilton, 1989.
14 Poems. Cadognan, France, Editions Ottezec, 1994.
Henry James and Other Poems. Edgewood, Kentucky, Barth, 1995.
Collected Poems. London, Sinclair-Stevenson, 1995.

Other (for children)

Taliesin. London, Faber, 1966; New York, Hill and Wang, 1967.
March Has Horse's Ears. London, Faber, 1966; New York, Hill and Wang, 1967.
Bee Hunter: Adventures of Beowulf. London, Faber, 1968; as *Beowulf: A New Telling,* New York, Hill and Wang, 1968; as *Beowulf, The Bee Hunter,* Faber, 1972.
Wishing Gold. London, Macmillan, 1970; New York, Hill and Wang, 1971.
Poor Pumpkin. London, Macmillan, 1971; as *The Mathematical Princess and Other Stories,* New York, Hill and Wang, 1972.
Cricket: Three Stories. Indianapolis, Bobbs Merrill, 1975; as *Once upon Three Times,* London, Benn, 1978.
Out of the World and Back Again. London, Collins, 1977; as *Out of This World and Back Again,* Indianapolis, Bobbs Merrill, 1978.
The Bird of the Golden Land. London, Hamish Hamilton, 1980.
Harry Pay the Pirate. London, Hamish Hamilton, 1981.
Three Tales. London, Hamish Hamilton, 1983.
Lord Fox and Other Spine-Chilling Tales. London, Orion, 1995.

Other

Editor, *A Choice of Sir Walter Ralegh's Verse.* London, Faber, 1972.

Editor, *William Barnes: A Selection of His Poems.* Cheadle, Cheshire, Carcanet, 1972.

Editor, *A Choice of Swinburne's Verse.* London, Faber, 1973.

Editor, *The Faber Book of Sonnets.* London, Faber, 1976; as *A Book of Sonnets,* New York, Oxford University Press, 1976.

Editor, *The English Sermon 1750-1850.* Manchester, Carcanet, 1976.

Editor, *PEN New Poetry.* London, Quartet, 1986.

Editor, with Elizabeth Friedmann and Alan J. Clark, *First Awakenings: The Early Poems of Laura Riding.* Manchester, Carcanet, and New York, Persea books, 1992.

Editor, *A Selection of the Poems of Laura Riding.* Manchester, Carcanet, 1994.

*

Manuscript Collections: University of Edinburgh; University of Texas, Austin; National Library of Scotland, Edinburgh; Colgate University, Hamilton, New York.

*   *   *

A hallmark of Robert Nye's fiction has been his ability to harness the imagination to his will, to take the facts of everyday life and to transform them into fantastic happenings so that myth and reality become as one. The stories in *Tales I Told My Mother* rework the lives of literary personalities, and his first novel, *Doubtfire,* ranges in time and space between different worlds with remarkable ease and fluidity of style. Equally fantastic have been his children's novels which have followed faithfully C.S. Lewis's dictum that children's stories should be just as enjoyable to adults.

In later novels like *Falstaff, Merlin, Faust,* and *The Voyage of the Destiny,* Nye created a quartet of loosely related myths from characters, real or imaginary, who exist in our collective pasts. The worlds that they people are dream-like and fabulous, half-caught, half-forgotten by the subconscious mind. And yet their darksome existence is lightened by Nye's ability to steer away from allegory by making their worlds new again and instantly recognizable: Falstaff lives in an England that is demonstrably 14th century, Merlin's world is one of medieval chivalry, and Faust knows a Europe shared by Luther and Calvin.

Falstaff, a novel of 100 chapters, tells the story of Sir John Falstaff—his relationship to the English aristocracy and to the giant of Cerne Abbas, his conduct at the siege of Kildare, his friendship with Prince Hal, and his prowess at the Battle of Agincourt. His adventures, often unlikely and scabrous, unfold before the reader's eyes like a medieval tapestry, and by the end of the novel he has been consumed by the myth he has created for himself, the eternal John Bull, both patriot and buffoon. Myth of a different kind lies at the heart of *Merlin* whose central character is at once

the unmistakable Merlin of Sir Thomas Malory's *Le Morte D' Arthur* and at the same time an older, more cunning figure from Welsh vernacular literature and from the poetry of the 12th-century French poet Robert de Boron, who created a Merlin capable of seeing both past and future and thus able to connect the ancient history of the Grail with the court of King Arthur.

Faust is the story of Dr. Faust's final 40 days on Earth, having sold his soul to the devil, and it follows many of the themes of the previous two novels and expands on them: a delight in mixing myth with reality, an earthy eroticism, and a fast-moving dialogue that is both funny and deeply serious. Here the story is seen through the excited reaction of his servant Kit Wagner—a device which Nye was to repeat in *The Life and Death of My Lord Gilles de Rais.* The mythical strain was continued in *The Voyage of the Destiny* which tells the story of Sir Walter Raleigh, explorer, poet, adventurer, and favorite of Queen Elizabeth I. Raleigh himself is the narrator and his voice leads us through the three great voyages of his life: his return from the Americas, his journey through life, and the impending transition from life to death which gives the book its title. As in all Nye's novels the writing is crisp and lucid, a mixture of scholarly anecdotes racily told and erudite low comedy.

However well crafted and ingenious these novels undoubtedly are, they pale before Nye's most recent work, *The Life and Death of My Lord Gilles de Rais.* As with the other novels, it is based on a historical figure who has assumed mythical proportions: Gilles de Rais, one of the greatest French noblemen of the 15th century and a boon companion of Joan of Arc. Unlike *Falstaff* or *Merlin,* though, it has been stripped of literary extravagance and fine flourishes. One reason for the change of mood lies in the subject. Gilles was hanged and his body burned at Nantes in 1440 after he confessed to crimes ranging from pederasty to murder. The second reason, perhaps the more imperative of the two, is the overriding necessity to explore the nature of evil. Gilles has committed his crimes because he has allowed himself to be seduced by pride and vanity, two sins which he fails to recognize in himself. Over 140 children died at his hands, yet throughout his short life he believed that his behavior stood above the law.

All this becomes clear through the testimony of a priest called Blanchet who acts as the narrator and thereby distances the reader from the full horror of Gilles's crimes. This device also allows Blanchet to give his version of the truth, for he, too, was arraigned with Gilles but found not guilty. The other great character in the novel remains unseen: Joan of Arc, who provides Blanchet with the theme of redemption and Christian charity.

In his earlier historical novels Nye established himself as one of the most inventive and adventurous of contemporary novelists, with an imagination of Rabelaisian proportions. In *The Life and Death of My Lord Gilles de Rais* he has added to that wit and learning profound insights into the nature of evil and a deep understanding of matters Christian.

—Trevor Royle

O

OATES, Joyce Carol

Pseudonym: Rosamond Smith. **Nationality:** American. **Born:** Millersport, New York, 16 June 1938. **Education:** Syracuse University, New York, 1956-60, B.A. in English 1960 (Phi Beta Kappa); University of Wisconsin, Madison, M.A. in English 1961; Rice University, Houston, 1961. **Family:** Married Raymond J. Smith in 1961. **Career:** Instructor, 1961-65, and assistant professor of English, 1965-67, University of Detroit; member of the Department of English, University of Windsor, Ontario, 1967-78. Since 1978 writer-in-residence, and currently Roger S. Berlind Distinguished Professor, Princeton University, New Jersey. Since 1974 publisher, with Raymond J. Smith, *Ontario Review,* Windsor, later Princeton. **Awards:** National Endowment for the Arts grant, 1966, 1968; Guggenheim fellowship, 1967; O. Henry award, 1967, 1973, and Special Award for Continuing Achievement, 1970, 1986; Rosenthal award, 1968; National Book award, 1970; Rea award, for short story, 1990; Bobst Lifetime Achievement award, 1990; Heideman award, 1990, for one-act play; Walt Whitman award, 1995. **Member:** American Academy, 1978. **Agent:** John Hawkins and Associates, 71 West 23rd Street, Suite 1600, New York, New York 10010. **Address:** 185 Nassau Street, Princeton, New Jersey 08540, U.S.A.

PUBLICATIONS

Novels

With Shuddering Fall. New York, Vanguard Press, 1964; London, Cape, 1965.
A Garden of Earthly Delights. New York, Vanguard Press, 1967; London, Gollancz, 1970.
Expensive People. New York, Vanguard Press, 1968; London, Gollancz, 1969.
Them. New York, Vanguard Press, 1969; London, Gollancz, 1971.
Wonderland. New York, Vanguard Press, 1971; London, Gollancz, 1972.
Do with Me What You Will. New York, Vanguard Press, 1973; London, Gollancz, 1974.
The Assassins: A Book of Hours. New York, Vanguard Press, 1975.
Childwold. New York, Vanguard Press, 1976; London, Gollancz, 1977.
Son of the Morning. New York, Vanguard Press, 1978; London, Gollancz, 1979.
Cybele. Santa Barbara, California, Black Sparrow Press, 1979.
Unholy Loves. New York, Vanguard Press, 1979; London, Gollancz, 1980.
Bellefleur. New York, Dutton, 1980; London, Cape, 1981.
Angel of Light. New York, Dutton, and London, Cape, 1981.
A Bloodsmoor Romance. New York, Dutton, 1982; London, Cape, 1983.
Mysteries of Winterthurn. New York, Dutton, and London, Cape, 1984.
Solstice. New York, Dutton, and London, Cape, 1985.
Marya: A Life. New York, Dutton, 1986; London, Cape, 1987.
You Must Remember This. New York, Dutton, 1987; London, Macmillan, 1988.
American Appetites. New York, Dutton, and London, Macmillan, 1989.
Because It Is Bitter, and Because It Is My Heart. New York, Dutton, 1990; London, Macmillan, 1991.
I Lock My Door upon Myself. New York, Ecco Press, 1990.
The Rise of Life on Earth. New York, New Directions, 1991.
Black Water. New York, Dutton, 1992.
Foxfire: Confessions of a Girl Gang. New York, Dutton, 1993.
What I Lived For. New York, Dutton, 1994.
Zombie. New York, Dutton, 1995.

Novels as Rosamond Smith

Lives of the Twins. New York, Simon and Schuster, 1987.
Soul-Mate. New York, Dutton, 1989.
Snake Eyes. New York, Dutton, 1992.
You Can't Catch Me. New York, Dutton, 1995.

Short Stories

By the North Gate. New York, Vanguard Press, 1963.
Upon the Sweeping Flood and Other Stories. New York, Vanguard Press, 1966; London, Gollancz, 1973.
The Wheel of Love and Other Stories. New York, Vanguard Press, 1970; London, Gollancz, 1971.
Cupid and Psyche. New York, Albondocani Press, 1970.
Marriages and Infidelities. New York, Vanguard Press, 1972; London, Gollancz, 1974.
A Posthumous Sketch. Los Angeles, Black Sparrow Press, 1973.
The Girl. Cambridge, Massachusetts, Pomegranate Press, 1974.
Plagiarized Material (as Fernandes/Oates). Los Angeles, Black Sparrow Press, 1974.
The Goddess and Other Women. New York, Vanguard Press, 1974; London, Gollancz, 1975.
Where Are You Going, Where Have You Been? Stories of Young America. Greenwich, Connecticut, Fawcett, 1974.
The Hungry Ghosts: Seven Allusive Comedies. Los Angeles, Black Sparrow Press, 1974; Solihull, Warwickshire, Aquila, 1975.
The Seduction and Other Stories. Los Angeles, Black Sparrow Press, 1975.
The Poisoned Kiss and Other Stories from the Portuguese (as Fernandes/Oates). New York, Vanguard Press, 1975; London, Gollancz, 1976.
The Triumph of the Spider Monkey. Santa Barbara, California, Black Sparrow Press, 1976.
The Blessing. Santa Barbara, California, Black Sparrow Press, 1976.
Crossing the Border. New York, Vanguard Press, 1976; London, Gollancz, 1978.
Daisy. Santa Barbara, California, Black Sparrow Press, 1977.
Night-Side. New York, Vanguard Press, 1977; London, Gollancz, 1979.
A Sentimental Education. Los Angeles, Sylvester and Orphanos, 1978.
The Step-Father. Northridge, California, Lord John Press, 1978.

All the Good People I've Left Behind. Santa Barbara, California, Black Sparrow Press, 1979.

The Lamb of Abyssalia. Cambridge, Massachusetts, Pomegranate Press, 1979.

A Middle-Class Education. New York, Albondocani Press, 1980.

A Sentimental Education (collection). New York, Dutton, 1980; London, Cape, 1981.

Funland. Concord, New Hampshire, Ewert, 1983.

Last Days. New York, Dutton, 1984; London, Cape, 1985.

Wild Saturday and Other Stories. London, Dent, 1984.

Wild Nights. Athens, Ohio, Croissant, 1985.

Raven's Wing. New York, Dutton, 1986; London, Cape, 1987.

The Assignation. New York, Ecco Press, 1988.

Heat and Other Stories. New York, Dutton, 1991.

Where Is Here? Hopewell, New Jersey, Ecco, 1992.

Haunted: Tales of the Grotesque. New York, Dutton, 1994.

Plays

The Sweet Enemy (produced New York, 1965).

Sunday Dinner (produced New York, 1970).

Ontological Proof of My Existence, music by George Prideaux (produced New York, 1972). Included in *Three Plays,* 1980.

Miracle Play (produced New York, 1973). Los Angeles, Black Sparrow Press, 1974.

Daisy (produced New York, 1980).

Three Plays (includes *Ontological Proof of My Existence, Miracle Play, The Triumph of the Spider Monkey*). Windsor, Ontario Review Press, 1980.

The Triumph of the Spider Monkey, from her own story (produced Los Angeles, 1985). Included in *Three Plays,* 1980.

Presque Isle, music by Paul Shapiro (produced New York, 1982).

Lechery, in *Faustus in Hell* (produced Princeton, New Jersey, 1985).

In Darkest America (*Tone Clusters* and *The Eclipse*) (produced Louisville, Kentucky, 1990; *The Eclipse* produced New York, 1990).

American Holiday (produced Los Angeles, 1990).

I Stand Before You Naked (produced New York, 1991).

How Do You Like Your Meat? (produced New Haven, Connecticut, 1991).

Twelve Plays. New York, Dutton, 1991.

Black (produced Williamstown, 1992).

The Secret Mirror (produced Philadelphia, 1992).

The Perfectionist (produced Princeton, New Jersey, 1993). In *The Perfectionist and Other Plays,* 1995.

The Truth-Teller (produced New York, 1995).

Here She Is! (produced Philadelphia, 1995).

The Perfectionist and Other Plays. Hopewell, New Jersey, Ecco, 1995.

Poetry

Women in Love and Other Poems. New York, Albondocani Press, 1968.

Anonymous Sins and Other Poems. Baton Rouge, Louisiana State University Press, 1969.

Love and Its Derangements. Baton Rouge, Louisiana State University Press, 1970.

Woman Is the Death of the Soul. Toronto, Coach House Press, 1970.

In Case of Accidental Death. Cambridge, Massachusetts, Pomegranate Press, 1972.

Wooded Forms. New York, Albondocani Press, 1972.

Angel Fire. Baton Rouge, Louisiana State University Press, 1973.

Dreaming America and Other Poems. New York, Aloe Editions, 1973.

The Fabulous Beasts. Baton Rouge, Louisiana State University Press, 1975.

Public Outcry. Pittsburgh, Slow Loris Press, 1976.

Season of Peril. Santa Barbara, California, Black Sparrow Press, 1977.

Abandoned Airfield 1977. Northridge, California, Lord John Press, 1977.

Snowfall. Northridge, California, Lord John Press, 1978.

Women Whose Lives Are Food, Men Whose Lives Are Money. Baton Rouge, Louisiana State University Press, 1978.

The Stone Orchard. Northridge, California, Lord John Press, 1980.

Celestial Timepiece. Dallas, Pressworks, 1980.

Nightless Nights: Nine Poems. Concord, New Hampshire, Ewert, 1981.

Invisible Woman: New and Selected Poems 1970-1982. Princeton, New Jersey, Ontario Review Press, 1982.

Luxury of Sin. Northridge, California, Lord John Press, 1984.

The Time Traveller: Poems 1983-1989. New York, Dutton, 1989.

Other

The Edge of Impossibility: Tragic Forms in Literature. New York, Vanguard Press, 1972; London, Gollancz, 1976.

The Hostile Sun: The Poetry of D.H. Lawrence. Los Angeles, Black Sparrow Press, 1973; Solihull, Warwickshire, Aquila, 1975.

New Heaven, New Earth: The Visionary Experience in Literature. New York, Vanguard Press, 1974; London, Gollancz, 1976.

The Stone Orchard. Northridge, California, Lord John Press, 1980.

Contraries: Essays. New York, Oxford University Press, 1981.

The Profane Art: Essays and Reviews. New York, Dutton, 1983.

Funland. Concord, New Hampshire, Ewert, 1983.

On Boxing, photographs by John Ranard. New York, Doubleday, and London, Bloomsbury, 1987; expanded edition, Hopewell, New Jersey, Ecco, 1994.

(Woman) Writer: Occasions and Opportunities. New York, Dutton, 1988.

Conversations with Joyce Carol Oates, edited by Lee Milazzo. Jackson, University Press of Mississippi, 1989.

Editor, *Scenes from American Life: Contemporary Short Fiction.* New York, Vanguard Press, 1973.

Editor, with Shannon Ravenel, *The Best American Short Stories 1979.* Boston, Houghton Mifflin, 1979.

Editor, *Night Walks: A Bedside Companion.* Princeton, New Jersey, Ontario Review Press, 1982.

Editor *First Person Singular: Writers on Their Craft.* Princeton, New Jersey, Ontario Review Press, 1983.

Editor, with Boyd Litzinger, *Story: Fictions Past and Present.* Lexington, Massachusetts, Heath, 1985.

Editor, with Daniel Halpern, *Reading the Fights* (on boxing). New York, Holt, 1988.

*

Bibliography: *Joyce Carol Oates: An Annotated Bibliography* by Francine Lercangée, New York, Garland, 1986.

Manuscript Collection: Syracuse University, New York.

Critical Studies: *The Tragic Vision of Joyce Carol Oates* by Mary Kathryn Grant, Durham, North Carolina, Duke University Press, 1978; *Joyce Carol Oates* by Joanne V. Creighton, Boston, Twayne, 1979; *Critical Essays on Joyce Carol Oates* edited by Linda W. Wagner, Boston, Hall, 1979; *Dreaming America: Obsession and Transcendence in the Fiction of Joyce Carol Oates* by G.F. Waller, Baton Rouge, Louisiana State University Press, 1979; *Joyce Carol Oates* by Ellen G. Friedman, New York, Ungar, 1980; *Joyce Carol Oates's Short Stories: Between Tradition and Innovation* by Katherine Bastian, Bern, Switzerland, Lang, 1983; *Isolation and Contact: A Study of Character Relationships in Joyce Carol Oates's Short Stories 1963-1980* by Torborg Norman, Gothenburg, Studies in English, 1984; *The Image of the Intellectual in the Short Stories of Joyce Carol Oates* by Hermann Severin, New York, Lang, 1986; *Joyce Carol Oates: Artist in Residence* by Eileen Teper Bender, Bloomington, Indiana University Press, 1987; *Understanding Joyce Carol Oates* by Greg Johnson, Columbia, University of South Carolina Press, 1987.

*   *   *

The sheer quantity and range of Joyce Carol Oates's writing is impressive: 22 novels since her first, *With Shuddering Fall* (1964), in addition to numerous volumes of short stories, poems, plays, and criticism. She usually writes about extraordinary people whose fanatical desire to compel life to conform to their vision finally becomes all-consuming and self-destructive. In these books, she relentlessly charts the disintegration of the self. *Son of the Morning* offers perhaps her most shocking and gripping exploration of this theme. A pentecostal preacher, Nathanael Vickery, witnesses seven visitations from the Lord, each more terrifying than the last. The last shows Nathanael that God has withdrawn himself and left him to sink back into oblivion and write the book of himself. In other novels Oates has moved beyond a vision in which man can free himself only through an explosion of violence. These novels work toward quieter endings in which her central protagonists survive and transcend their nightmarish experiences to construct more stable lives, integrating themselves into the social fabric. Other books exploit the macabre. In *Blackwater,* she delves into the consciousness and the experience of drowning in an imaginative recreation of the Teddy Kennedy/Mary Jo Kopechne incident at Chippaquiddick. Most recently, in *Foxfire: Confessions of a Girl Gang,* Maddy-Monkey, the official chronicler of the gang, shares the secrets and sacred rites of the gang. She dwells on the fateful year of 1956 when their crimes led to the notorious kidnapping and ransoming of Whitney Kellogg Jr.; their leader, Legs Sadovsky, mysteriously disappeared never to be seen again, or at least the chronicler of the confessions is uncertain that a recent sighting has any validity.

Oates's appetite as a writer is as voracious as the will of her most willful protagonists. She consumes and disgorges experience, her own and that of others. She has recast the visions and stories of numerous writers, displaying her debt to such continental writers as Dostoyevsky, Flaubert, Kafka, Mann, and Balzac while remaining firmly planted in the American realistic narrative tradition. She has imaginatively entered into the lives of pentecostal preachers, children of the slums, a 19th-century detective, professors in academia, schoolteachers, artists, a drowned woman, and countless others.

Her writing is thoroughly American, after the manner of Fitzgerald and Faulkner, Dreiser and Farrell. Faulkner's Yoknapatawpha County is her fictitious Eden County, set near Millersport, New York, where she lived as a child. Farrell's Chicago is her Detroit: Studs Lonigan is made over into Jules and Maureen Wendall in *Them.* Fitzgerald's Gatsby is her Jules, a man in love with the aloofness money brings, crazily hungry for Nadine, Daisy's counterpart in *Them.* Like her American ancestors, Oates is fascinated with property and the violence it engenders in those obsessed with it. She struggles to write an American epic, built around a dynastic family, which will express the American experience.

Bellefleur is her ambitious attempt at such an epic, an attempt that eluded the grasp of writers whose talents dwarf hers—Melville and Twain, Faulkner and Bellow. *A Bloodsmoor Romance* and *Mysteries of Winterthurn* continue Oates's treatment of 19th-century and early-20th-century America. Each imitates brilliantly the genre of the Gothic saga, the romance, and the detective novel respectively.

Oates is a storyteller of considerable gifts. She is also a writer's writer. In her novels of social and psychological realism, she reveals little interest in postmodern experimental modes, avoiding the dexterous verbal play and intricate parodic structures developed by writers like John Barth, Thomas Pynchon, or Donald Barthelme. John Updike and Saul Bellow are writers more to her tastes. More recently, she has embarked on literary projects in which fabulation, invention, and intertextuality figure prominently. In these, her flair for irony and her playful reimaginings of popular 19th-century genres are evident, but the novels remain ultimately stable in their meaning. They are not true works of deconstruction or postmodernity. She generally writes with a social purpose out of concerns that are moral, psychological, and political. There are times, however, when the violence in her novels seems gratuitous and the work itself seems, finally, immoral. *Expensive People* is such a book.

Childwold and *Cybele* offer the first real evidence of Oates's shift away from naturalism, with *The Assassins* figuring as a transitional, experimental work. The assassin who stalks Andrew Petrie, the one-time state senator, is Andrew. The murderer in this book is monistic thinking, the willful fixation upon one idea, be it religious, philosophical, or literary. It severs the individual from the community of man, isolating and destroying him. The monism encases its believer in an isolation as total as that which Hugh experiences as a paralytic, breathing with the aid of an iron lung, without his sight. *Bellefleur* and *Unholy Loves*—few books could be less alike—testify to Oates's skill and range.

Bellefleur is vast, sprawling book that weirdly welds the natural and supernatural together to create a psychologically and imaginatively plausible history of six generations of the Bellefleur family from 1744 to the present. The book belongs in the tradition of American Gothic, but it has stretched the genre, bringing history into its domain. *Unholy Loves* is a tightly constructed, unified book: five chapters, five parties, it lays bare the soul of Brigit Stott, a recent divorcee, member of the English Department, and writer in a university modeled after Syracuse University, where Oates earned her B.A. *Unholy Loves* and *American Appetites* belong with Amis's *Lucky Jim* and Murdoch's *A Severed Head. Unholy Loves* contains scenes of erupting violence, but the general atmosphere is one of forced conviviality. Oates knows intimately the scandals of the university, the ambitions, bitchiness, pomposity, petty jealousy, and colossal loneliness that are endemic to modern university life.

Marya: A Life and *Solstice* each extend Oates's treatments of teachers and academics. *Marya: A Life,* in some ways an autobiographical book, treats in 11 disconnected episodes the life of a woman from her squalid origins to her rapid success as a writer. *Solstice* offers an absorbing study of an obsessive relationship between Monica Jensen, a thirtyish divorcee and teacher in a private school in the wilds of Pennsylvania, and a much older, widowed, eccentric artist, Sheila Trask, whose self-dramatization and self-destructiveness ensnare Monica, binding her in a relationship as passionate and all-consuming as any Oates has hitherto delineated.

Cybele and *Childwold* move away from the quasinaturalistic fiction that dominated Oates's early writing. The style of *Childwold* is lyrical. It is set back in Eden County, but nature is more mysterious and erotic, and, in a Faulknerian way, Oates celebrates the survivors. *Cybele* is more disturbing. Edwin Locke is the luckless victim of Cybele, the great goddess of nature who asks for nothing less than the life of this man who falls under her enchantment during his midlife crisis. She is a demanding goddess: he pays her the ultimate sacrifice when he allows himself to be consumed by his own passions. He confuses eros with love and falls. The action of *Cybele* is typical of the action in portions of *Do with Me What You Will.* However, love redeems Elena in the latter novel, whereas Edwin never experiences it. The narrative angle of *Cybele* shifts, reflecting Oates's desire to move more overtly into the realm of the demonic and the unconscious. She embraces the terrain in *Bellefleur, A Bloodsmoor Romance,* and *Mysteries of Winterthurn.*

Much has been written about Oates's obsession with violence. Rape, incest, patricide, infanticide, self-mutilation, animal mutilation, suicide, wife-beating, child abuse, murder, and drowning abound in her fiction, shocking and numbing her readers, often occasioning a shudder of recognition of the acts we want to deny. Sometimes the violence is gratuitous—too often, it is sensational—but more often than one wants to admit it demands to be confronted. Conceptions are violent in her fiction, blighting the children born of them. In *Them,* Jules is conceived in a coupling that results in the murder of his natural father by his mother's brother, leaving his mother bathed in the blood of her dead lover and hostage to the policemen whose help she seeks. The violence that marked his conception doggedly pursues him. Hopelessly drawn to Nadine, he finds himself the target of her gun after a night of lovemaking in which he could not satisfy her. Later, caught up in the chaos of the Detroit fires, he kills a man and paradoxically recovers himself.

Nathanael Vickery, the pentecostal preacher of *Son of the Morning,* is a child born of his mother's rape. Lacking a father, he grows up believing he is God's child and that his will is not his own. The initiation that rids him of this delusion, leaving him a nullity, is a terrifying one. When God withdraws from this man he has inhabited for 35 years, Nathanael is left without words or gestures. He crawls off the platform where he had been preaching before thousands, numbering himself among the damned. Stephen in *The Assassins* and Jebediah in *Bellefleur* are similarly abandoned by the god of their willful self-creation. In *Bellefleur,* Oates is not satisfied to stop with only two or three of these familiar scenes of sensational violence. Every one of the violent acts numbered above and many more plague the lives of six generations of Bellefleurs. And this violence is not enough. Germaine is one of the Bellefleurs who survives. Her father, Gideon, wreaks his vengeance on his past and his wife when he flies a plane into the Bellefleur Mansion, destroying it, and killing himself, his wife, and her numerous followers. The special child he saves is the child whose birth chills us in the opening of the book. She is born a biological freak, with the genitalia of her male twin protruding from her abdomen to be sliced off by her quick-thinking mother. (I could not read this without thinking that Judith Rossner's *Attachments* had had an unfortunate influence upon the already sufficiently grotesque imagination of Oates.)

A Bloodsmoor Romance is a 19th-century romance, narrated by a young virgin and chronicling the "ignominious" history of the five marriageable daughters of the Zinn family settled in the Bloodsmoor valley of Pennsylvania. More overtly feminist than Oates's early naturalistic writing, this book has been described as the other side of *Little Women,* the tale it did not dare to tell. The style is turgid; the tale is replete with the trademarks of the historical romance—fainting virgins, a sudden abduction, ghosts, and the unspeakable evils of drink and dissipation. An odd mingling of myth and history, *A Bloodsmoor Romance* and its successor, *Mysteries of Winterthurn,* indulge Oates's excursions into Victoriana and humor.

Mysteries of Winterthurn disguises itself as a detective story told by an orotund, male connoisseur of criminal investigations while it probes the mystery of personality and religion. The detective-hero, Xavier Kilgarvan, confronts three bizarre cases, each separated by 12 years. The first begins when he is but a 12-year-old boy, besmitten with his wayward cousin and caught up in a bizarre series of bedchamber murders, the first being the vampirish murder of a child. The second mystery, "Devil's Half-Acre; or the Mystery of the 'Cruel Suitor,'" occurs 12 years later and involves a succession of butchered factory girls. The third case, "The Bloodstained Bridal Groom," involves an outbreak of frenzy in a disbeliever resulting in the death of a clergyman, his mother, and a female parishioner. The detective finally surrenders to brain-fever and forgetfulness rather than know what Perdita, his wayward cousin, has done. The story dissolves into one of radical ambiguity in which guilt and innocence cannot be distinguished. All three of the sagas of 19th-century America are full of ghastly circumstances, authorial asides, quaint, baroque descriptions, extravagances, and morbid preoccupations. All three are pointedly feminist. All are stylistically self-indulgent.

After plumbing the depths of chaotic nightmares and nihilation of the self, Oates in the mid-1980s begins reconfiguring her tragic vision, concentrating more on a character's capacity to survive and transcend. Oates leaves behind the Gothic extravagances she has written and revisits the naturalistic landscape of her earlier fiction so brilliantly handled in *Them.* But the fiction also reveals some noteworthy differences. She continues her project of minutely depicting American cultural history in her novels, returning to the era of the Depression in flashbacks in *You Must Remember This* and fleshing out her description of America between 1944-1956, complete with the bomb shelters and civil defense drills, the adulation of Eisenhower, the Army-McCarthy hearings, and the electrocution of the Rosenbergs. In *I Lock the Door Upon Myself,* she imaginatively reenters a turn-of-the-century rural community, recounting the narrative of a willful white woman's defiant flight with a black itinerant water diviner. In *American Appetites,* the main action occurs in 1986 and it is set in Hazelton-on-Hudson, New York, at the prestigious Institute for Independent Research in the Social Sciences, yet the book also captures the flavor of the 1980s. Returning to the vein of *Unholy Loves,* Oates satirizes the petty rivalries and pretensions of illustrious members of the American research university while she unfolds a terrifying story of an eruption of domestic violence that results in the death of the wife and criminal charges against her husband, the protagonist, Ian McCullough. *Foxfire* is set in upstate New York and the episodes recalled occurred in the mid-1950s. Oates explores the sensibility and dreams of the young, impressionable, wild, bad adolescent girl that have long preoccupied her imagination. The story of the exploits of the girl gang members starts innocently enough but draws them into the world of thievery and prostitution and threatens to destroy them all when they act on their kidnapping plot.

The difference in the evolving sensibility of Oates lies in her handling of the aftermath of the violence unleashed in her novels. In *Because It Is Bitter, and Because It Is My Heart, You Must Remember This,* and *Foxfire,* the protagonists survive the brutal events that threaten to engulf them. In the first, Iris Courtney is both complicit in a black man's murder of an adolescent thug and a victim of her father's neglect and her mother's whorish, alcoholic life, and yet she endures to move beyond these events in her past. In the second, Enid, suicidal at the opening of the novel and suffering from anorexia nervosa, survives the protracted incestuous relationship with her uncle to marry and come to a forgiveness of those who hurt her. *American Appetites,* in some aspects one of the most shocking novels she has written, also emerges from its dark night of the soul, portraying an altered man, but one capable of a complex moral understanding of the events that led to his accidental killing of his wife in the midst of a marital quarrel. Madeleine Faith Wirst is expelled from the Foxfire gang, miraculously paving the way for her to return to society, have a short marriage followed by divorce, get a university degree, and pursue a career as an astronomer's assistant, probing negative light in films of identical parts of the sky.

It is difficult to know what finally to say about Oates's reliance on violence. It is integral to her vision. It rivets her action and often constellates her characters. And it does not go away. Often it seems to mar her characterization, leaving motives ill-defined or murky. The tensions unleashed by the violence threaten the boundaries of her art. But the violence is often believable and it does not let us forget. It stuns us, makes us wonder how the imagination that so clear-sightedly depicts it can remain intact. Some would say that Oates is obsessively consumed with violence, reveling in its brutishness, caught in its senseless repetitions, salaciously reveling in its psychosexual dimensions, thrilled, somehow, by the recurring theme of domination and submission, discipline and punishment.

Oates's fascination with the sport of boxing has fueled the critical response to her writing that is so often colored by references to Oates's gender and the body image of the woman herself. *Blackwater* provides Oates with an occasion to reflect on the death penalty and the five ways in which it can still be carried out in America. But it is too easy and misguided to complain that she writes too much and too easily and that she exploits the violence in her novels. She is a supreme teller of tales and her imagination never fails to startle the reader. The scene of domestic violence in *American Appetites* and the circumstances of the drowning in *Blackwater* are portrayed vividly and unforgettably. The novels are importantly about crime and punishment, remorse and forgiveness. Oates's excursions into a world of violence touch something little understood, but now that she is tunnelling behind it, letting us glimpse its mainsprings more fully, I think she may in the end justify the experience she forces us to endure. Oates is a writer who embarks on ambitious projects; her imagination is protean; her energies seemingly boundless; and throughout all her writing, the reader detects her sharp intelligence, her lively curiosity, and her zeal to tell a story.

—Carol Simpson Stern

O'BRIEN, Edna

Nationality: Irish. **Born:** Tuamgraney, County Clare, 15 December 1932. **Education:** National School, Scariff; Convent of Mercy, Loughrea; Pharmaceutical College of Dublin: licentiate, Pharmaceutical Society of Ireland. **Career:** practiced pharmacy briefly; novelist, playwright, and screenwriter. **Family:** Married Ernest Gebler in 1952 (marriage dissolved 1967); two sons. Lives in London. **Awards:** Kingsley Amis award, 1962; *Yorkshire Post* award, 1971. **Agent:** Robert Lescher, 155 East 71st St., New York, NY 10021, U.S.A. **Address:** Duncan Heath Associates, 162-170 Wardour St., London W1V 3AT, England.

PUBLICATIONS

Novels

The Country Girls. London, Hutchinson, and New York, Knopf, 1960.
The Lonely Girl. London, Cape, and New York, Random House, 1962; as *Girl with Green Eyes,* London, Penguin, 1964.
Girls in Their Married Bliss. London, Cape, 1964; New York, Simon and Schuster, 1968.
August Is a Wicked Month. London, Cape, and New York, Simon and Schuster, 1965.
Casualties of Peace. London, Cape, 1966; New York, Simon and Schuster, 1967.
A Pagan Place. London, Weidenfeld and Nicolson, and New York, Knopf, 1970.
Night. London, Weidenfeld and Nicolson, 1972; New York, Knopf, 1973.
Johnny I Hardly Knew You. London, Weidenfeld and Nicolson, 1977; as *I Hardly Knew You,* New York, Doubleday, 1978.
The Country Girls Trilogy and Epilogue. New York, Farrar Straus, 1986; London, Cape, 1987.
The High Road. London, Weidenfeld and Nicolson, and New York, Farrar Straus, 1988.
Time and Tide. New York, Farrar Straus Giroux; London, Penguin; and Toronto, HarperCollins, 1992.
An Edna O'Brien Reader (includes *August is a Wicked Month, Casualties of Peace,* and *Johnny I Hardly Knew You*). New York, Warner Books, 1994.
House of Splendid Isolation. New York, Farrar Straus Giroux, and London, Weidenfeld and Nicolson, 1994.

Short Stories

The Love Object. London, Cape, 1968; New York, Knopf, 1969.
A Scandalous Woman and Other Stories. London, Weidenfeld and Nicolson, and New York, Harcourt Brace, 1974.
Mrs. Reinhardt and Other Stories. London, Weidenfeld and Nicolson, 1978; as *A Rose in the Heart,* New York, Doubleday, 1979.
Returning. London, Weidenfeld and Nicolson, 1982.
A Fanatic Heart: Selected Stories. New York, Farrar Straus, 1984; London, Weidenfeld and Nicolson, 1985.
Lantern Slides. London, Weidenfeld and Nicolson, and New York, Farrar Straus Giroux, 1990.

Plays

A Cheap Bunch of Nice Flowers (produced London, 1962). Published in *Plays of the Year 1962-1963,* London, Elek, and New York, Ungar, 1963.

The Wedding Dress (televised 1963). Published in *Mademoiselle* (New York), November 1963.

Zee & Co. (screenplay). London, Weidenfeld and Nicolson, 1971.

A Pagan Place, adaptation of her own novel (produced London, 1972; New Haven, Connecticut, 1974). London, Faber, 1973; Port Townsend, Washington, Graywolf Press, 1984.

The Gathering (produced Dublin, 1974; New York, 1977).

The Ladies (produced London, 1975).

Virginia (produced Stratford, Ontario, 1980; London and New York, 1981). London, Hogarth Press, and New York, Harcourt Brace, 1981.

Flesh and Blood (produced Bath, 1985; New York, 1986).

Madame Bovary, adaptation of the novel by Flaubert (produced Watford, Hertfordshire, 1987).

Screenplays: *Girl with Green Eyes,* 1964; *I Was Happy Here* (*Time Lost and Time Remembered*), with Desmond Davis, 1965; *Three into Two Won't Go,* 1969; *Zee & Co.* (*X, Y, & Zee*), 1972; *The Tempter,* with others, 1975; *The Country Girls,* 1984.

Television Plays: *The Wedding Dress,* 1963; *The Keys of the Café,* 1965; *Give My Love to the Pilchards,* 1965; *Which of These Two Ladies Is He Married To?,* 1967; *Nothing's Ever Over,* 1968; *Then and Now,* 1973; *Mrs. Reinhardt,* from her own story, 1981.

Poetry

On the Bone. Warwick, Greville Press, 1989.

Other (for children)

The Dazzle. London, Hodder and Stoughton, 1981.

A Christmas Treat. London, Hodder and Stoughton, 1982.

The Rescue. London, Hodder and Stoughton, 1983.

Tales for the Telling: Irish Folk and Fairy Tales. London, Joseph, and New York, Atheneum, 1986.

Other

Mother Ireland. London, Weidenfeld and Nicolson, and New York, Harcourt Brace, 1976.

Arabian Days, photographs by Gerard Klijn. New York, Horizon Press, and London, Quartet, 1977.

The Collected Edna O'Brien (miscellany). London, Collins, 1978.

James and Nora: A Portrait of Joyce's Marriage. Northridge, California, Lord John Press, 1981.

Vanishing Ireland, photographs by Richard Fitzgerald. London, Cape, 1986; New York, Potter, 1987.

Editor, *Some Irish Loving: A Selection.* London, Weidenfeld and Nicolson, and New York, Harper, 1979.

*

Critical Study: *Edna O'Brien* by Grace Eckley, Lewisburg, Pennsylvania, Bucknell University Press, 1974.

Edna O'Brien comments:

I quote from two critics: William Trevor and John Berger.

A Pagan Place: "Constitutes a reconstruction of a childhood experience which so far as I know, is unique in the English language. In this respect, though otherwise it is different, it invites comparison with Proust; a book whose genius is memory" (Berger).

The Love Object: "Rarely has a woman protested as eloquently as Edna O'Brien. In sorrow and compassion she keens over the living. More obviously now, despair is her province" (Trevor).

My aim is to write books that in some way celebrate life and do justice to my emotions as well as form a connection with the reader, the unknown one.

*   *   *

The major theme of Edna O'Brien's fiction is the ineffable pain of loneliness, guilt, and loss. Her works record a bleak odyssey from naive optimism, through rancor, bitterness and hatred, to the scarred wisdom that comes from having wrestled with her suffering. Her insights into the conflicting dilemmas that beset women today have won her international acclaim.

Her fiction grows out of the trilogy which follows Caithleen and Baba from their initiation into life and love to their chilling disillusionment with both. At the outset, innocent and intelligent Caithleen Brady (Kate) wants every story to have a happy ending. Baba is so brazen that even her father, Mr. Brennan, prefers Kate: "Poor Caithleen, you've always been Baba's tool." *The Country Girls* and its sequel represent a woman's version of a traditionally masculine motif: that of an ego tempted by an alter ego to enjoy forbidden fruit (like Faust and Mephistopheles). The entire trilogy operates around this theme. Kate has "one mad eye," but her softness, daftness, and wantonness are not her essential nature. They come to her from an alter ego whose influence she is unable to resist. Baba promotes Kate's decisions, and the story follows their consequence: their expulsion from the convent school, an affair with Mr. Gentleman in *The Country Girls,* and an affair with Eugene Gaillard in *The Lonely Girl.* Because Kate is so influenced by her friend, she is always restless. She feels "lonely" without the weight of Eugene's body, but she cannot commit herself to him: "Before she left Eugene she had often thought of being with other men—strange distant men who would beckon to her." She recognizes that she is disloyal to anyone who is "real" for her, and that what she yearns for is a "shadow"—but she cannot stop herself. This weakness is reflected in the shift in narrative perspective. In *Girls in Their Married Bliss,* Baba, the temptress, has become the narrator and Kate, the ego, is correspondingly unable to determine her actions. She becomes increasingly introverted, afraid of giving herself: "Life was a secret with the Self. The more one gave out the less there remained for the centre." The novel ends with Baba regretting the loss of "some important region that they both knew nothing about." In the epilogue that O'Brien added when her trilogy was republished in 1986, Kate, utterly wasted by life, has committed suicide, and Baba, while waiting to meet the coffin at Waterloo Station, reflects on the conflict between her own desires and the emptiness of her own life. It is a bleak ending to what is still O'Brien's finest work.

The sense of being divided also lies at the heart of O'Brien's next novel. "This is not me, I am not doing this," thinks Ellen, the heroine of *August Is a Wicked Month.* While the "Not-I" has her "jaunt into iniquity"—a holiday in France following her separation—her son, on holiday with his father, is killed. Unable to discover an adequate reaction to the loss of part of her essential self, she returns to England, anxious only about whether she has contracted gonorrhea. Worry about the "Not-I"—which proves needless—replaces concern about the "I." This mechanism anticipates the next novel, *Casualties of Peace,* in which the insubstantial ego (Willa) is accidentally killed in place of the alter ego figure (Patsy). The motif is further explored in *Zee & Co.,* the only work in which it achieves even a tentative, though unstable, resolution.

The humor, so intrinsic to the early work, is gradually replaced by sharp and sometimes acid observations. But the most notable tendency in O'Brien's fiction is the progress from the "realism" of the trilogy to the introverted monologues, reminiscences, and reconstructions of her later work. The author has declared that her favorite is *A Pagan Place,* which tells the problems of a young girl very similar to Kate. Its second-person narrative voice is a bold but sometimes disconcerting device. *Night,* a disturbing and impressive novel, traces Mary Hooligan's reconstruction of her past. In *Johnny I Hardly Knew You,* bitterness and invective detract from its technical merits. *The High Road*'s heroine, Anna, on holiday to a Spanish island to forget an affair, is drawn into a circle of characters that includes a waitress called Catalina, who falls in love with her. When Catalina's husband discovers this, he kills her. Anna, devastated by the realization that it might have been her that Juan meant to kill, determines to return to Ireland. For all the brilliance with which the various scenes are painted, this is an angry, claustrophobic book.

All these works rest on the assumption that there is an inevitable conflict between men's and women's needs, and that the only way for a woman to come to terms with this is to learn to be independent. At the end of *Girls in Their Married Bliss,* Kate says: "What Baba doesn't know is that I'm finding my feet, and when I'm able to talk I imagine that I won't be alone." The subsequent novels represent ever bolder experiments in *talking*—that is, in narrative technique. They lean on words to ward off an increasingly desperate inner loneliness.

Her finest novel since *The Country Girls* is *Time and Tide,* which tells the story of Nell, who runs away from home to live with a man. Their marriage goes sour, he becomes brutal and tries to prevent her having custody of their two sons. As they grow from children to young men, she struggles to discover a sense of her own identity. Pared of all inessentials, each of the short episodes takes a scalpel to the shattering ironies that pass for life.

House of Splendid Isolation, which is set in contemporary Ireland, represents a new direction in O'Brien's writing. McGreevy is a Republican activist on the run: he hides for a few days in the house of an elderly woman called Josie. The partisan is made subservient to the personal; the personal, to the integrity of motivation. It is a work infused by a numbed awareness of the waste of human worth. O'Brien's short stories are among her finest work. They explore very much the same ground as her novels—the various kinds of misfortune and loneliness that beset the lives of her Irish characters—and reverberate freely in the reader's imagination. Her weakness is that her characters can often seem only vehicles for the dilemmas that confront them. Her strength is the lyricism of her language. No other contemporary novelist has better captured, and with as much poignancy, the agony brought about by confused longings.

—Terence Dawson

O'BRIEN, Tim

Nationality: American. **Born:** William Timothy O'Brien in Austin, Minnesota, 1 October 1946. **Education:** Macalaster College, St. Paul, Minnesota, B.A. in political science (summa cum laude) 1968; Harvard University, Cambridge, Massachusetts, 1970-76. **Military Service:** Served in the United States Army during the Vietnam war; discharged wounded 1970: Purple Heart. **Career:** Reporter, Washington *Post,* 1971-74. **Awards:** National Book award, 1978; National Endowment for the Arts award; Bread Loaf Writers Conference award. **Agent:** International Creative Management, 40 West 57th Street, New York, New York 10019, U.S.A.

PUBLICATIONS

Novels

Northern Lights. New York, Delacorte Press, and London, Calder and Boyars, 1975.
Going after Cacciato. New York, Delacorte Press, and London, Cape, 1978.
The Nuclear Age. Portland, Oregon, Press 22, 1981; London, Collins, 1986.
In the Lake of the Woods. Boston, Houghton Mifflin, 1994.

Short Stories

The Things They Carried. Boston, Houghton Mifflin, and London, Collins, 1990.

Uncollected Short Stories

"Keeping Watch by Night," in *Redbook* (New York), December 1976.
"Night March," in *Prize Stories of 1976,* edited by William Abrahams. New York, Doubleday, 1976.
"Fisherman," in *Esquire* (New York), October 1977.
"Calling Home," in *Redbook* (New York), December 1977.
"Speaking of Courage," in *Prize Stories of 1978,* edited by William Abrahams. New York, Doubleday, 1978.
"Civil Defense," in *Esquire* (New York), August 1980.
"The Ghost Soldiers," in *Prize Stories of 1982,* edited by William Abrahams. New York, Doubleday, 1982.
"Quantum Jumps," in *The Pushcart Prize 10,* edited by Bill Henderson. Wainscott, New York, Pushcart Press, 1985.
"Underground Tests," in *The Esquire Fiction Reader 2,* edited by Rust Hills and Tom Jenks. Green Harbor, Massachusetts, Wampeter Press, 1986.
"The Lives of the Dead," in *Esquire* (New York), January 1989.
"Sweetheart of the Song Tra Bong," in *Esquire* (New York), July 1989.
"In the Field," in *Gentlemen's Quarterly* (New York), December 1989.
"Enemies and Friends," in *Harper's* (New York), March 1990.
"Field Trip," in *McCall's* (New York), August 1990.
"Speaking of Courage," in *The Other Side of Heaven: Post-War Fiction by Vietnamese and American Writers,* edited by Wayne Karling. Williamatic, Connecticut, Curbstone Press, 1995.

Other

If I Die in a Combat Zone, Box Me Up and Ship Me Home (memoirs). New York, Delacorte Press, and London, Calder and Boyars, 1973; revised edition, Delacorte Press, 1979.
Speaking of Courage. Santa Barbara, California, Neville, 1980.

*

Critical Studies: "Imagining the Real: The Fiction of Tim O'Brien" by Daniel L. Zins, in *Hollins Critic* (Hollins College, Virginia), June 1986; "Tim O'Brien's Myth of Courage" by Milton J. Bates, in *Critique* (Washington, D.C.), Summer 1987; *Understanding Tim O'Brien* by Steven Kaplan, Columbia, University of South Carolina Press, 1994.

*   *   *

Looking back, it almost seems as if, during the 1970s and 1980s, in order to have a book acclaimed as one of the best pieces of writing to emerge from the Vietnam War, all an author needed to do was get it published. Whatever the reason for the hype, some highly commendable work was produced as a result of America's military misadventures in southeast Asia. Few writers contribute more than once to the list though, and few have really been able to forge much headway beyond their first couple of books. Tim O'Brien is the exception.

O'Brien's debut, *If I Die in a Combat Zone,* a collection of newspaper and magazine journalism supplemented by other articles, would have been enough to ensure him a lasting reputation as a gritty and reliable witness to some of the worst stupidity of the war in Vietnam. Anecdotal and sometimes jarring in its juxtaposition of Socratic dialogue and personal meditation, *If I Die in a Combat Zone* is a clear-sighted and unsensationalist account of one young enlistee's fears and aspirations. In no way does it prepare us for *Going after Cacciato,* O'Brien's intense, impressionistic, and impassioned fictionalization of the experiences of ordinary combat personnel in Vietnam. Here O'Brien's narrative stretches across Asia and Europe as the remaining members of a platoon hunt a deserter. Gradually it becomes evident that this epic chase is a graft of fantasy onto fact—Paul Berlin, the central character, and his colleagues follow their prey no further than a grassy knoll not far from their departure point. The subsequent developments are all the products of an imagination feverishly creating alternative scenarios to the horrors of a foot-soldier's daily existence. Reality becomes malleable as O'Brien weaves memorable sections of recalled events—sentry duty, ambush, patrol, and death—into the path of Cacciato's flight. Imagination is the metaphor for and means of survival—a theme that unites O'Brien's work.

Northern Lights brings together two brothers—one returned from Vietnam, the other homebound—and pitches them into a battle for life in the untamed Minnesotan Arrowhead country after a skiing trip goes disastrously wrong. In a not unexpected role reversal, Harvey, who has proved his manhood in battle, becomes utterly dependent upon Paul, who has "flown a desk" for the duration. O'Brien's portrayals of an impersonal but fiercely hostile winter wilderness and the oppressive atmosphere of a dying small town are vivid and impressive. *Northern Lights* also introduces us, somewhat ominously, to a bomb shelter dug by Harvey.

O'Brien's third novel, *The Nuclear Age,* draws that shelter out of the background and deposits it in a dominant position, in the middle (and beginning and end) of the plot. William Cowling, the narrator of this tale of paranoia and atrophied passion, has led a life determined by dread—the same interminable panic felt by O'Brien in Vietnam but modified into the more universal concept of the all-consuming terror of nuclear Armageddon. As a child he constructed a refuge in his basement out of a ping-pong table, surrounding it at one point with pencils purloined from school, in the belief that radiation from a nuclear explosion would not penetrate the "lead." At college, Cowling's personal antibomb protests are mistaken for the actions of a putative politician, and he is soon embroiled in campus revolt, orchestrated by Sarah, the childhood sweetheart he never had. The primary motive of the hero is, however, self-preservation: "She was out to change the world, I was out to survive it." As Cowling grows out of love with Sarah, so his concern with his imminent obliteration becomes more profound, and we join him, late at night, in his garden, obeying the "voice" of a hole that is telling him to dig or perish.

The Things They Carried, more short story cycle than novel, reads so much like a memoir that the author has to emphasize, in a subtitle and prefatory note, that what follows is "a work of fiction." The intensely autobiographical tone of the stories is underscored by the presence of a first person narrator named Tim O'Brien. The stories that follow all attempt to come to terms with the narrator's Vietnam experience and frequently try to account for the purpose of telling or writing stories. "How to Tell a True War Story" begins with the assertion, "This is true" and, like many of the other stories in the collection, goes on to question what truth is. Truth and reality are even fuzzier in Vietnam than elsewhere, and examining how experience is converted into meaning matters more than trying to figure out what is real. Despite the narrator's playing with the notion of truth in stories, the reader comes away from these stories with a sense of the awful truth that was Vietnam, though we share the frustrations of the various storytellers, who will never quite be able to communicate their experience.

This frustration becomes the theme of O'Brien's next novel, *In the Lake of the Woods,* the story of John Wade, who goes into exile after losing a primary election for U.S. senate, and his wife Kathy, who disappears while they are in exile. The novel comprises various testimonies of people who knew John, the local authorities who suspect foul play, neighbors who try to comfort John after the disappearance, and other "evidence" in the form of documents chronicling Wade's life. Bringing it all together is a narrator who is self-conscious about his role as a writer, and his inability to "know" anything beyond direct personal experience. "Evidence is not truth," he tells us in a footnote, "and if you require solutions, you will have to look beyond these pages." Like the rest of O'Brien's work, this novel takes on Vietnam, yet more obliquely; Wade had been involved in the My Lai incident, and his experience there becomes part of the evidence in his case. The connection is clear enough: despite all of our various attempts to make sense of the disturbing side of human existence, our capacity to understand is limited. O'Brien has certainly not left the war behind, but he has gotten beyond the war itself and begun to delve into its long-term implications. He remains the most compelling voice to emerge from the Vietnam war, but he is also developing into a master of storytelling who is aware of his craft and of the necessity for its continuation.

—Ian McMechan, updated by D. Quentin Miller

O'FAOLAIN, Julia

Nationality: Irish. **Born:** London, England, 6 June 1932; daughter of the writer Sean O'Faolain. **Education:** The Sacred Heart Convent, Dublin; University College, Dublin, B.A. in French and Italian 1952, M.A. 1953; University of Rome; the Sorbonne, Paris. **Family:** Married Lauro Martines in 1957; one son. **Career:** Translator for Council of Europe, and worked as supply teacher and cook in London, 1955-57; instructor in French, Reed College, Portland, Oregon, and taught evening classes in Italian, Portland State University, 1957-61; teacher, Scuola Interpreti, Florence, 1962-65. Lives in London. **Awards:** Arts Council of Great Britain bursary, 1981. **Agent:** Deborah Rogers, Rogers Coleridge and White Ltd., 20 Powis Mews, London, W11 1JN, England; or, International Creative Management, 40 West 57th Street, New York, New York 10019, U.S.A.

PUBLICATIONS

Novels

Godded and Codded. London, Faber, 1970; as *Three Lovers,* New York, Coward McCann, 1971.
Women in the Wall. London, Faber, and New York, Viking Press, 1975.
No Country for Young Men. London, Allen Lane, 1980; New York, Carroll and Graf, 1987.
The Obedient Wife. London, Allen Lane, 1982; New York, Carroll and Graf, 1985.
The Irish Signorina. London, Viking, 1984; Bethesda, Maryland, Adler, 1986.
The Judas Cloth. London, Sinclair Stevenson, 1992.

Short Stories

We Might See Sights! and Other Stories. London, Faber, 1968.
Man in the Cellar. London, Faber, 1974.
Melancholy Baby and Other Stories. Dublin, Poolbeg Press, 1978.
Daughters of Passion. London, Penguin, 1982.

Other

Editor, with Lauro Martines, *Not in God's Image: Women in History from the Greeks to the Victorians.* London, Temple Smith, and New York, Harper, 1973.

Translator (as Julia Martines), *Two Memoirs of Renaissance Florence: The Diaries of Buonaccorso Pitti and Gregorio Dati,* edited by Gene Brucker. New York, Harper, 1967.
Translator, *A Man of Parts,* by Piero Chiara. Boston, Little Brown, 1968.

*

Critical Studies: *Two Decades of Irish Writing* edited by Douglas Dunn, Manchester, Carcanet, and Philadelphia, Dufour, 1975; "The Irish Novel in Our Time" edited by Patrick Rafroidi and Maurice Harmon, in *Publications de l'Université de Lille 3,* 1975-76; by O'Faolain, in *Contemporary Authors Autobiography Se-*ries 2 edited by Adele Sarkissian, Detroit, Gale, 1985; *Irish Women Writers* by Ann Owens Weekes, Lexington, University Press of Kentucky, 1990; articles by Thomas R. Moore and Laura B. Van Dale, in *Colby Quarterly* (Waterville, Maine), March 1991.

Julia O'Faolain comments:

I like fiction to be a Trojan horse. It can seem to be engineering an escape from alien realities but its true aim is to slip inside them and get their measure. Sly and demystificatory, it dismantles myths. This can arouse mixed feelings, for myths, though more interesting when taken apart, are grander while intact. But then ambivalence, it seems, is the nerve of narrative. Regret plus pleasure moves more than either can alone. Moreover, having grown up in a place where myth ran rampant, my native impulse is to cut through and past it.

(1995) Recently I have gone back to writing short stories, a notoriously tricky genre which should be able to condense enough light to burn through to the essence of things. I aim for realism and particularity, then try—nervously—to achieve a lift-off to some angle of vision from which my narrative will look different. The genre is prodigal in that it compresses what a novel would spin out, and risky, since it can misfire. When it works, there's nothing like it for catching the vibrancy of the evanescent. Just now the writers who seem to me to bring this off best are nearly all American and Canadian. A response to a need? Surely. The day they seize is so protean. Living, as I do, in London's slower tempo, I may be working against the odds.

*   *   *

There is something *déjà vu* about Julia O'Faolain's first novel, *Godded and Codded,* centring on the innocent Irish Sally's further education—in several senses—in Paris, not wholly redeemed by the book's uproarious comedy. The inevitably pregnant Sally's equally inevitable Christmas visit to her parents in Ireland covers even more familiar ground, as we are shown the circumstances that have made Sally what she is—that is, what she must react against. O'Faolain's earlier story "A Pot of Soothing Herbs" encapsulated this—the archetypal Irish virginal dilemma; the later story "Lots of Ghastlies" more adroitly transplants to an English bourgeois setting the theme of a return visit to the parental home. More interesting in *Godded and Codded* than the "innocents abroad" theme is the peripheral description of the underground activities of a group of Algerian students in Paris shortly before Independence. Irish expatriates provide much of the novel's burlesque comedy.

Her first collection, *We Might See Sights!,* are divided by O'Faolain into Irish and Italian stories. The outstanding story is "Dies Irae," set in an Italian hairdresser's salon and perhaps influenced by Colette; to pacify an elderly Russian princess, the hairdresser points out signs of decay in the narrator, for whom a normally pleasant occasion becomes her *dies irae.* There is black comedy in the plight of the husband chained in the cellar by his wife, in the title story of *Man in the Cellar;* the story is told in letters and the final surprisingly affectionate letter from the decamped and mentally disturbed wife reveals how securely *invisible* chains are fastened on her. The didactic element is stronger in this later collection of stories, but is offset by these of out-of-the-way situations; "This is My Body," for instance, set in a 6th-century convent, handles the female Irish writer's stock-in-trade of convent material from a new angle, which *Women in the Wall* also exploits.

In *Women in the Wall,* set in 6th-century Gaul, O'Faolain breathes life into a group of characters who—except two—existed in history, though as the author explains in her introduction, she departed from history in plotting. The monologue of the anchoress in the convent alternates with an account of the darkening political situation, bringing barbarism to the very convent walls; the two threads finally merge in the denouement. But even behind the convent walls, the nuns' lives are shown as often far from quiet, as O'Faolain probes the stresses of celibacy, its occasional abandonment and its link to mystical experience. Her description of nature is always vivid, especially here where she relies heavily on natural imagery to avoid anachronism.

O'Faolain also interweaves different narrative threads to provide explosive connections in *No Country for Young Men:* the death of an American Republican fundraiser in Ulster in 1922 casts a long shadow as an American ex-academic arrives in Ireland in 1979 to interview survivors of the 1920s Troubles for a film and so crosses paths with an old half-insane nun through his romantic entanglement with her married great-niece. This novel, shortlisted for the Booker prize, is O'Faolain's best novel to date, enabling her to deploy all her skills of allusively connecting social, cultural, historical, and economic insights. These electric interconnections are often wittily achieved, sometimes pivoting on linguistic humour. O'Faolain's style is so exciting that the reader may overlook the fact that her characters tend to share a similar wide-ranging, ironic perception, imposed by the style.

An outstanding illustration of the disadvantage of O'Faolain's brilliant style, notwithstanding that it provides a vivid impression of whatever society she's writing about, comes in *The Obedient Wife;* Carla is endowed by the author with witty dialogue and far-ranging ironic thought that seem too dazzling for the character as otherwise presented. An Italian living in California from where her husband has returned, supposedly temporarily, to Italy, Carla despite her paganism believes in the traditional role of the wife—or has been culturally brainwashed into believing in it. Yet, she becomes emotionally involved with a Catholic priest. Carla's relationship with her teenage son is especially well drawn, with empathy for both sides.

In *The Irish Signorina,* as in earlier books, the plot is engendered by the crisscrossing of intergenerational threads. A young Irish girl is invited by the dying Italian Marchesa Cavalcanti to stay in the villa where her mother had worked for the marchesa as a girl. Against the background of the Cavalcanti family's roots in the land and modern terrorism, complex webs of personal relationships, old and new, emerge. Though a shorter novel than O'Faolain's previous novels, the economy and restraint that she here shows in dealing with her always interesting material illustrate her extraordinary stylistic development since her early writing and ensure this book is by no means slight but the work of a major novelist.

—Val Warner

OKRI, Ben

Nationality: Nigerian. **Born:** Minna, 15 March 1959. **Education:** In Nigeria; at University of Essex, Colchester, B.A. in comparative literature. **Career:** Broadcaster, "Network Africa," BBC World Service, 1984-85; poetry editor, *West Africa,* 1981-87. Full-time writer and reviewer for the *Guardian,* the *Observer,* and the *New Statesman,* all London. **Awards:** Commonwealth Prize for Africa, 1987; *Paris Review* Aga Khan prize, 1987, for fiction; Booker prize, 1991, for *The Famished Road.* **Address:** c/o Jonathan Cape, 20 Vauxhall Bridge Road, London SW1V 2SA, England.

PUBLICATIONS

Novels

Flowers and Shadows. London, Longman, 1980.
The Landscapes Within. London, Longman, 1981.
The Famished Road. London, Cape, 1991; New York, Talese, 1992.
Songs of Enchantment. London, Cape, and New York, Talese, 1993.

Short Stories

Incidents at the Shrine. London, Heinemann, 1986.
Stars of the New Curfew. London, Secker and Warburg, and New York, Viking, 1989.

Uncollected Short Stories

"The Dream-Vendor's August," in *Paris Review* (New York), Winter 1987.
"Disparities," in *Literary Review* (Madison, New Jersey), Fall 1990.

Poetry

An African Elegy. London, Cape, 1992.

*   *   *

Ben Okri's writing career began early, his first novel, *Flowers and Shadows,* was published when he was 21. The novel recounts the growth into adulthood of Jeffia Okwe, the sensitive son of a corrupt and ruthless businessman and a woman who, from being "beautiful, fresh" with "so much life and vigour," becomes a "walking tragedy" after the death of her husband. Jeffia's discovery of the nature of his father's business and his business associates is economically described and frequently the pathos of the characters—particularly Juliet, his father's former mistress—is all the more effective for its understatement. Okri is exceptionally deft at evoking moments and meetings fraught with emotion, such as Jeffia's tentative falling in love with Cynthia, a night nurse. The social context of a Nigerian town is effortlessly realised.

If *Flowers and Shadows* was a relatively conventional *Bildungsroman, The Landscapes Within,* Okri's next novel, takes a similarly conventional form and, as the title suggests, begins to stretch the imaginative properties it holds. The central character here is a solitary painter named Omovo, whose artistic vision leads him into conflict not only with his family and friends but also with the state. Social and political corruption are the condition and context of Omovo's artistic effort. If the clarity and precision of Okri's style owe something to Chinua Achebe, then his vision of social squalor and human degradation is as unflinching and as compassionate as that of Wole Soyinka. Omovo is actually described at one point, reading Soyinka's novel *The Interpreters,* whose title points up the social significance of his own artistic dedication. Omovo's tender love for Ifeyinwa, the wife of a neighbour, develops towards emotional disaster when she leaves their squalid township and wanders unwittingly to a senseless and anonymous death, shot by soldiers and dumped "into the brackish stream nearby." The novel ends with Omovo picking his way "slowly through the familiar darkness, alone."

This turning out and movement away from conventional contexts is mirrored in Okri's next two books, both collections of short stories which develop the nightmare visions of nocturnal landscapes, filling them with the bodies of spirits, living and dead. *Incidents at the Shrine* is a slim volume of eight stories, each one a strong but unemphatic marvel. The stories are set in Nigeria during the Civil War, in London among the derelicts and the dispossessed, and in dream-worlds suffused with an African sensibility and experience of Britain in the 1980s, where a ruthless Conservative government oversees urban and industrial collapse. Hidden histories reveal themselves, disparities converge and prayers go crooked in an unkempt, deregulated world. Yet the pace and procedure of Okri's prose is undaunted. He maintains a fluent attention to realistic detail. He is still observant of those moments and places of "very perceptible demarcation." *Stars of the New Curfew* opens with an epigraph by Christopher Okigbo: "We carry in our worlds that flourish our worlds that have failed." The "worlds that have failed" resurface and submerge. In the title-story, a recalcitrant salesman is forced into dispensing fake ringworm medicines which actually multiply ringworm, then finds work with a new firm called "CURES UNLIMITED." From describing the "nightmare of salesmen" Okri moves to depicting the "salesman of nightmares." In both short story collections, Okri's visions have the vividness of hallucination.

The Famished Road expands the hallucinatory medium of the stories over the length of a 500-page novel. This is Okri's most haunting, entertaining, and challenging work to date. It is as if Soyinka and Amos Tutuola had coauthored a work with the South American "magic realists" Borges and Marquez, although there is also a singularly elegant lightness of touch and a constancy of pace.

The narrator is Azaro, a "spirit-child" who is still linked with the protean spirits that lie unborn behind or underneath creation's struggling forms. His innocuous naiveté, unquenchable curiosity, and endless thirst are unchecked by his adventures. His experience is articulated within a limited but shifting constellation of characters and places: his home and his parents; the shrewd, magisterial Madame Koto and her bar; the forest that surrounds the village; and the interstellar spaces into which his wayward imagination sails. Realistic details and dream-scenarios are syncopated and run together. The result is not counterpoint but a unique blend of physical, sensual, and creatural particularities within a radically unpredictable metaphysical context. The staple diet in Madam Koto's bar is hot pepper soup and palm wine. This scalds the palate and the imagination at the same time that it sustains both. The book is populated with grotesque and wonderful characters from the compound, the forest, the world beyond the forest, and the spirit world. We encounter a two-legged dog, a photographer, hundreds of rats, various parties of politicians, the motley inhabitants of Madame Koto's bar, Azaro's Dad (who becomes a champion boxer, a political revolutionist, and a fantastic storyteller), and his Mum, who hawks her wares around the streets of the compound to pay for food and "ogogoro."

Despite the unremitting grimness of much of what Okri describes, the lasting impression of *The Famished Road* is of the regenerative power of the imagination. Medicines are found for the harshest poisons; fevers rage and die; performances take their exultant forms and shift camp once again. Nevertheless, if the imagination is a source of future hope, it is often unreliable. Azaro's naive perceptiveness, his childlike wisdom and insouciance, undercut the potential banality in his ingenuous pronouncements. He accepts, with some scepticism, his Dad's judgements: "The heart is bigger than a mountain. One human life is deeper than the ocean. Strange tribes and sea-monsters and mighty plants live in the rockbed of our spirits. The whole of human history is an undiscovered continent deep in our souls." Azaro's response brings reality into perspective: "A dream can be the highest point of a life."

—Alan Riach

OLSEN, Tillie

Nationality: American. **Born:** Tillie Lerner, Omaha, Nebraska, 14 January 1912 or 1913. **Education:** Some high school. **Family:** Married Jack Olsen in 1943 (died); four daughters. **Career:** Has worked in the service, warehouse, and food processing industries, and as an office typist. Writer-in-residence, Amherst College, Massachusetts, 1969-70; visiting professor, Stanford University, California, Spring 1971; writer-in-residence, Massachusetts Institute of Technology, Cambridge, 1973; visiting professor, University of Massachusetts, Boston, 1974; visiting lecturer, University of California, San Diego, 1978; International Visiting Scholar, Norway, 1980; Hill Professor, University of Minnesota, Minneapolis, 1986; writer-in-residence, Amherst College; writer-in-residence, Kenyon College, Gambier, Ohio, 1987; Regents' professor, University of California, Los Angeles, 1988. Creative Writing fellow, Stanford University, 1956-57; fellow, Radcliffe Institute for Independent Study, Cambridge, Massachusetts, 1962-64. **Awards:** Ford grant, 1959; O. Henry award, 1961; American Academy award, 1975; Guggenheim fellowship, 1975; Unitarian Women's Federation award, 1980; National Endowment for the Humanities grant, 1966 and 1984; Bunting Institute fellowship, 1986; Nebraska Library Association Mari Sandoz award, 1991; Rea award, for distinguished contribution to the short story, 1994. Doctor of Arts and Letters: University of Nebraska, Lincoln, 1979; D.Litt.: Knox College, Galesburg, Illinois, 1982; Albright College, Reading, Pennsylvania, 1986, Mills College, 1995; L.H.D.: Hobart and William Smith Colleges, Geneva, New York, 1984; Clark University, Worcester, Massachusetts, 1985; Wooster College, Ohio, 1991. "Tillie Olsen Day" observed in San Francisco, 1981. **Address:** 1435 Laguna, No. 6, San Francisco, California 94115, U.S.A.

PUBLICATIONS

Novel

Yonnondio: From the Thirties. New York, Delacorte Press, 1974; London, Faber, 1975.

Short Stories

Tell Me a Riddle: A Collection. Philadelphia, Lippincott, 1961; London, Faber, 1964.
Dream Vision. New York, Mother to Daughter, Daughter to Mother, n.d.

Uncollected Short Story

"Requa-I," in *The Best American Short Stories 1971,* edited by Martha Foley and David Burnett. Boston, Houghton Mifflin, 1971.

Other

Silences. New York, Delacorte Press, 1978; London, Virago Press, 1980.

Mothers and Daughters: That Special Quality: An Exploration in Photographs, with Julie Olsen-Edwards and Estelle Jussim. New York, Aperture, 1987.

Afterword, Life in the Iron Mills. Old Westbury, New York, Feminist Press, 1972.

The Word Made Flesh. Iowa City, Iowa Humanities Council, 1984.

Editor, *Mother to Daughter, Daughter to Mother: Mothers on Mothering.* Old Westbury, New York, Feminist Press, 1984; London, Virago Press, 1985.

*

Manuscript Collection: Berg Collection, New York Public Library; Stanford Library American Literature Archives, Stanford University, California.

Critical Studies: *Tillie Olsen* by Abigail Martin, Boise, Idaho, Boise State University, 1984; *Tillie Olsen and a Feminist Spiritual Vision* by Elaine Neil Orr, Jackson, University Press of Mississippi, 1987; *Tillie Olsen* by Abby Werlock and Mickey Pearlman, Boston, Twayne, 1991; *Protest and Possibility in the Writing of Tillie Olsen* by Mara Faulkner, Charlottesville and London, University Press of Virginia, 1993; *The Critical Response to Tillie Olsen* edited by Kay Hoyle Nelson and Nancy Huse, Westport, Connecticut, and London, Greenwood Press, 1994; *Listening to Silences* edited by Elaine Hedges and Shelley Fisher Fishkin, New York and Oxford, Oxford University Press, 1994; *Better Red* by Constance Coiner, New York, Oxford University Press, 1995; *Tillie Olsen: A Study of the Short Fiction* by Joanne Frye, Boston, Twayne, 1995; *Tell Me A Riddle* by Deborah Rosenfelt, Rutgers, Rutgers University Press, 1995.

*   *   *

Tillie Olsen repeatedly expresses her conviction that literature is impoverished to the degree that creativity is not nourished and sustained in women and in people of the working class. Her speeches and essays on the waste of talent and on periods of aridity in the lives of authors, her long treatise on Rebecca Harding Davis's thwarted career following marriage, and her notes and quotations of this theme—collected over a period of 15 years—constitute *Silences.* Her own artistic recognition was postponed by the exigencies of making a living for herself and her children. She "mislaid" a novel for 35 years and wrote no story she thought worthy of publication until she was 43.

Tell Me a Riddle includes the three stories and the novella published between 1956 and 1960. "Tell Me a Riddle" centers on the antagonism which arises between two Jewish immigrants after their 37 years of marriage. In this novella Olsen reflects also upon the embarrassment and bewilderment of their married children as the "gnarled roots" of this marriage split apart. The wife's slow death from cancer greatly intensifies the conflict, but also dramatizes the love that remains only because it has become a habit. The wife returns in her delirium to their 1905 revolutionary activism, as her husband sighs, "how we believed, how we belonged." Almost without plot, this novella demonstrates Olsen's artistry in characterization, dialogue, and sensory appeal, and it fully displays, as does all her fiction, her highly rhythmic and metaphorical use of language.

In the monologue "I Stand Here Ironing" a woman reviews the 19 years of her daughter's life and mourns those days which blighted the daughter's full "flowering." Most intense are the mother's memories of being torn away from her infant in order to support her after they were abandoned. In "Hey Sailor, What Ship?" Whitey, a sailor, is given to drink and to buying admiration from the children of Lennie and Helen by giving them expensive gifts. Here he endures his last visit with his adopted family, with whom he has spent San Francisco shore leaves for years. The oldest daughter, embarrassed before her friends, turns in judgment upon the man who has brought a sense of adventure and romance to the family, while they have provided him some understanding and security over the years. In the elegiac close, Whitey pauses at the top of the third of seven hills to look back through the fog to the house with "its eyes unshaded." In the story "O Yes" a 12-year-old black girl invites her white friend to her baptism. As the throb of voices and clapping and the swaying of bodies intensifies the congregation's religious fervor, the white child feels her senses assailed and faints. The next year in junior high, as rigid social patterns separate the two friends, she mourns the warmth and openness she felt momentarily at the baptism.

The novel *Yonnondio: From the Thirties,* which Olsen began at the age of 19 (when she was already a mother), she abandoned five years later, a few pages short of its close. The manuscript was found 35 years later, and in 1973, in "arduous partnership" with her younger self, Olsen selected, edited, and organized the fragments, but she could not write the ending or rewrite sections. The novel significantly adds to American fiction of the Depression years, and it provides remarkable evidence of Olsen's artistry in her early youth. Greatly impressive are the imagery, the use of smells and sounds, the rhythms which shift notably between the first two sections written from the view of the child Mazie, and the third section which emerges from the narrative consciousness of the mother, Mary Holbrook, dying gradually of exhaustion, childbearing, and malnutrition. The title of this novel is taken from Walt Whitman's "Yonnondio" and in Iroquois means a lament for the aborigines—the authors mourn the common folk who suffered greatly but left "No picture, poem, statement, passing them to the future." During the course of the novel, Jim Holbrook moves from a Wyoming mine to a North Dakota tenant farm and finally to a Chicago or Omaha meat-packing plant with his wife and family. The zestful and imaginative Mazie in the early months of their life on the farm becomes ecstatically pantheistic in the style of Whitman's nature poetry, but in the city, in section three, she has lost her aspiration and much of her sensitivity and moves into the background in her bewilderment at her mother's illness and her father's increasing bad temper and dependence on alcohol. Critics generally acclaimed the novel, but several complained that Olsen gives her readers no mercy and that her work may be too painful for sustained reading and too unrelenting in its despair to allow characters to triumph through suffering.

—Margaret B. McDowell

ONDAATJE, (Philip) Michael

Nationality: Canadian. **Born:** Colombo, Ceylon (now Sri Lanka), 12 September 1943. **Education:** St. Thomas' College, Colombo; Dulwich College, London; Bishop's University, Lennoxville, Quebec, 1962-64; University of Toronto, B.A. 1965; Queen's University, Kingston, Ontario, M.A. 1967. **Family:** Married 1) Betty Kimbark in 1963, one daughter and one son; 2) Kim Jones (separated). **Career:** Taught at the University of Western Ontario, London, 1967-71. Since 1971 member of the Department of English, most recently a full professor, Glendon College, York University, Toronto. Visiting professor, University of Hawaii, Honolulu, summer 1979. Editor, *Mongrel Broadsides.* **Awards:** Ralph Gustafson award, 1965; Epstein award, 1966; E.J. Pratt medal, 1966; President's medal, University of Western Ontario, 1967; Canada Council grant, 1968, 1977; Books in Canada First Novel award. 1977 Governor-General's Award for Poetry, 1979; Governor-General's Award for Fiction, 1971, 1980, 1992; Canada-Australia prize, 1980; Toronto Book award, 1988; Booker prize, 1992; Literary Lion award (New York Public Library), 1993. **Address:** Department of English, Glendon College, York University, 2275 Bayview Ave., Toronto, Ontario M4N 3M6, Canada.

PUBLICATIONS

Novels

Coming Through Slaughter. Toronto, Anansi, 1976; New York, Norton, 1977; London, Boyars, 1979.
In the Skin of a Lion. Toronto, McClelland and Stewart, New York, Knopf, and London, Secker and Warburg, 1987.
The English Patient. New York, Knopf, and London, Bloomsbury, 1992.

Plays

The Collected Works of Billy the Kid (produced Stratford, Ontario, 1973; New York, 1974; London, 1984).
Coming Through Slaughter, adaptation of his own novel (produced Toronto, 1980).

Poetry

The Dainty Monsters. Toronto, Coach House Press, 1967.
The Man with Seven Toes. Toronto, Coach House Press, 1969.
The Collected Works of Billy the Kid: Left Handed Poems. Toronto, Anansi, 1970; New York, Norton, 1974; London, Boyars, 1981.
Rat Jelly. Toronto, Coach House Press, 1973.
Elimination Dance. Ilderton, Ontario, Nairn Coldstream, 1978; revised edition, Ilderton, Brick, 1980.
There's a Trick with a Knife I'm Learning to Do: Poems 1963-1978. Toronto, McClelland and Stewart, and New York, Norton, 1979; as *Rat Jelly and Other Poems 1963-1978,* London, Boyars, 1980.
Secular Love. Toronto, Coach House Press, 1984; New York, Norton, 1985.
Two Poems. Milwaukee, Woodland Pattern, 1986.
The Cinnamon Peeler: Selected Poems. London, Pan, 1989; New York, Knopf, 1991.

Other

Leonard Cohen. Toronto, McClelland and Stewart, 1970.
Claude Glass. Toronto, Coach House Press, 1979.
Tin Roof. Lantzville, British Columbia, Island, 1982.
Running in the Family. Toronto, McClelland and Stewart, and New York, Norton, 1982; London, Gollancz, 1983.

Editor, *The Broken Ark* (animal verse). Toronto, Oberon Press, 1971; revised edition, as *A Book of Beasts,* 1979.
Editor, *Personal Fictions: Stories by Munro, Wiebe, Thomas, and Blaise.* Toronto, Oxford University Press, 1977.
Editor, *The Long Poem Anthology.* Toronto, Coach House Press, 1979.
Editor, with Russell Banks and David Young, *Brushes with Greatness: An Anthology of Chance Encounters with Greatness.* Toronto, Coach House Press, 1989.
Editor, with Linda Spalding, *The Brick Anthology.* Toronto, Coach House Press, 1989.
Editor, *From Ink Lake: An Anthology of Canadian Stories.* New York, Viking, 1990.
Editor, *The Faber Book of Contemporary Canadian Short Stories.* London, Faber, 1990.

*

Bibliography: By Judith Brady, in *The Annotated Bibliography of Canada's Major Authors 6* edited by Robert Lecker and Jack David, Toronto, ECW Press, 1985.

Manuscript Collection: National Archives, Ottawa; Metropolitan Toronto Library.

Critical Study: *Spider Blues: Essays on Michael Ondaatje* edited by Sam Solecki, Montreal, Véhicule Press, 1985; *Michael Ondaatje* by Douglas Barbour, New York, Twayne, 1993.

Theatrical Activities:
Director: **Films**—*Sons of Captain Poetry,* 1971; *Carry on Crime and Punishment,* 1972; *Royal Canadian Hounds,* 1973; *The Clinton Special,* 1974.

*   *   *

Michael Ondaatje wanted to call *Secular Love,* his seventh book of poetry, a novel, but of his three prose works, only *In the Skin of a Lion* can be clearly identified as a novel: Sam Solecki notes that Ondaatje once described *Coming Through Slaughter* as "a soup" (a word equally applicable to *The Collected Works of Billy the Kid*); and he identifies the autobiographical *Running in the Family* as "a portrait or 'gesture'" with a "fictional air." As a documenter of human experience, Ondaatje begins in these lyrical prose works with seeds of historical fact and renders them resonant through fictionalizing. Like *The Cricket,* Buddy Bolden's community newspaper in *Coming Through Slaughter,* he "respect[s] stray facts, manic theories, and well-told lies" as much as the seeds of historical fact.

Concerned always to focus on the human, the private, and the "real" over the theoretical and the ideological, Ondaatje examines the internal workings of characters who struggle against and burst through that which renders people passive and which renders human experience programmatic and static. To this end, his style—

for which two lines from his poem "The Linguistic War Between Men and Women" act as a perfect comment—is raw, stark, energetic: "Men never trail away./ They sweat adjective." He employs a consistent set of images for concentrated energy; for instance arrows, insects, explosions, twitching nerves and veins, coiled muscles. And he points to palpable vitality at an almost molecular level: grains of pollen and dust, seeds, are as alive as working, sweating shoulders and rainstorms; air is "fraught" and "forensic"; everywhere are "remnants of energy." Energy frequently takes the form of heat and light, with which scenes are often suffused. It is more appropriate to talk of Ondaatje's fiction as proceeding through "scenes" than through episodes or chapters: his extensive work and interest in film informs his preoccupation with matters of shaping and form.

Through Ondaatje's prose the reader is taken beyond morality into a realm of human action and interaction that is at the same time nightmarish, resonantly mythic, and truly creative. His protagonists take great risks because they cannot do otherwise: they are driven to break through the limitations of mediocrity in a personal anarchy that is often destructive to self and others. The fractured narrative *Coming Through Slaughter* traces the personal anarchy of jazz trumpet player Buddy Bolden and the perspectives on him of those who knew him best. Bolden was never recorded and "never professional in the brain," but he was hailed as a great and powerful innovator. Ondaatje molds the little-known facts of Bolden's life into a fictional yet ostensibly objective account of the years of his fame, from the moment in approximately 1900 (age 22) he walks into a New Orleans parade playing his loud, moody jazz. In a manic push beyond the order and certainty by which he was always tormented, he goes insane while playing in a parade in 1907, and is committed to an asylum where he dies in 1931.

In the Skin of a Lion draws less on historical fact than any of his previous "fictions." For the first time he uses culturally marginalized and wholly fictional central characters—except for Ambrose Small—and draws out their mythic potential rather than relying on and reshaping a preexistent cultural myth or a historical figure. In this novel, which seems indebted to John Berger's *Pig Earth,* Ondaatje explores the pulse of physical labor and the life of an immigrant neighborhood in Toronto and Southwestern Ontario from 1900 to 1940, and reveals its sense of community, solidarity, and hatred of the solipsistic idle rich. The protagonist Patrick, like Buddy Bolden, "departs from the world," but unlike Bolden, he has a private revolution that eventually takes the form of public political action.

All of Ondaatje's "fictions" have a metafictional aspect: Patrick, like the police detective Webb in *Coming Through Slaughter,* like Ondaatje himself in *Running in the Family,* is the searcher-figure, analogous to the writer, who stands to an extent outside of "lived experience" observing, rooting out facts and "truths," trying to shape a coherent history, or story. Through these figures, Ondaatje inscribes the perspective of the history-writer and sets up a tension between their observing and others' experiencing. In his novels, Ondaatje himself becomes a kind of historiographer and underscores the fact that the observer's impulse to articulate, an impulse experience almost as a physical drive, is necessary to history. And hence Nicholas Temelcoff (*In the Skin of a Lion*), the solitary, daredevil bridge builder who rescues a nun from her fall from the partially completed bridge, urges the nun out of a state of shock and silence with "Talk, you must talk," and thereby releases her into a new, active identity; and, though initially silent and secretive himself,

Nicholas later finds that Patrick "shows him the wealth in himself, how he has been sewn into history. Now he will begin to tell stories."

Ondaatje's most recent novel, *The English Patient,* might be considered a sequel to *In the Skin of a Lion.* It features characters from the previous novel—Hana (Patrick's daughter), Caravaggio the thief—and continues Ondaatje's alertness to the fundamental importance of writing history. But Ondaatje's novels are characterized so much by inner transformations of character, voice, and scene, that it would be against the tenor of his craft to presume rigid connections between them, or to read them in a sequential manner. Like the sands of the North African desert that feature so prominently, *The English Patient* is a novel about shape-shifting. Set in the final days of World War II, as the map of Europe is about to be redrawn and Hiroshima and Nagasaki are soon to be disfigured utterly, it depicts the lives of four characters in a derelict villa north of Florence. The English patient (whose Englishness is not secure) is an aircraft pilot burned beyond recognition. He is cared for by a shell-shocked Hana, a nurse in the Canadian forces. They are joined by Caravaggio and Kirpal Singh (abbreviated to Kip). Caravaggio has been tortured and suffered the removal of his thumbs. The emphasis upon the damage that each of these three characters has suffered finds its contrast in Kip, a Sikh sapper who spends his days defusing the mines that litter the vicinity of the villa. Kip symbolizes the propensity to reverse potential destruction. Ondaatje's descriptions of his work are some of the most memorable in all his prose—those passages depicting Kip defusing the complex circuitry of mines makes you tremble with relief at his eventual success.

Kip's presence at the villa helps emphasize storytelling as an form of defusing, an act that makes approachable an incendiary past. Gradually, through the act of recounting their histories, each character clears a path through their pasts that allows them to remember in safety. Their stories resemble the tattered books in the villa's library: fragmentary, full of gaps and parentheses. Indeed, the importance of rewriting is a theme that emerges in the novel's structure. There are gestures towards Hemingway and Kipling in certain of its features, and it is intertextually complex. Ondaatje builds its narrative upon the fragments of other texts, just as the English patient records his thoughts in the pages of an old copy of Herodotus that is similarly ripped and torn.

But the bombs that cannot be defused fall on Hiroshima and Nagasaki, and the novel is never far from this apocalypse. When Kip learns of the news on the radio in the novel's climactic scene, his response is to confront the English patient with a rifle, outraged at this latest "tremor of Western wisdom." This, it seems, is one historical experience that renders redundant the narratives of Western history—with their emphasis on civilization and progress. A new narrative of history is required, perhaps one the novel itself tries to fashion, that rents the fabric of existing history in its attempt to bear witness to the immensity of what has happened. Although much the novel's the emphasis is on healing, its final pages are dark.

One reviewer of *The English Patient* wondered if the novel was part of a wider project, perhaps a trilogy, that begins with *In the Skin of a Lion.* Certainly, Ondaatje's central concern with writing history has not been exhausted in his work. If so, it will be interesting to see where Ondaatje's lyrical and hypnotic prose will next focus. One of Canada's best writers, Ondaatje is fulfilling his potential as a teller of stories in prose fiction promised by his earlier work.

—Diane Watson, updated by John McLeod

OSBORNE, David. *See* **SILVERBERG, Robert.**

O'SULLIVAN, Vincent (Gerard)

Nationality: New Zealander. **Born:** Auckland, 28 September 1937.
Education: University of Auckland, M.A. 1959; Lincoln College,
Oxford, B.Litt. 1962. **Career:** Editor, *Comment,* Wellington, 1963-
66; lecturer, Victoria University of Wellington; senior lecturer,
Waikato University, Hamilton. Literary editor, *New Zealand Lis-
tener,* 1978-79. **Awards:** Commonwealth scholarship, 1960;
Macmillan Brown prize, 1961; Jessie Mackay award, 1965, for
Our Burning Time; Farmers Poetry prize, 1967. **Address:**
Pukeroro, R.D. 3, Hamilton, New Zealand.

PUBLICATIONS

Novels

Miracle: A Romance. Dunedin, McIndoe, 1976.
The Boy, the Bridge, the River. Dunedin, McIndoe, 1978.
Butcher and Co. Auckland and Oxford, Oxford University Press, 1977.
The Butcher Papers. Auckland and Oxford, Oxford University
   Press, 1982.
The Pilate Tapes. Auckland and Oxford, Oxford University Press, 1986.
Let the River Stand. Auckland and Oxford, Oxford University
   Press, n.d.

Short Stories

Dandy Edison for Lunch, and Other Stories. Dunedin, McIndoe,
   1981.
The Snow in Spain. Wellington, Allen and Unwin, 1990.
Palms and Minarets: Selected Stories. Wellington, Victoria University Press, 1992.

Poetry

Our Burning Time. N.p., Prometheus, 1965.
Revenants. N.p., Prometheus, 1969.
Bearings. Wellington and London, Oxford University Press, 1973.
From the Indian Funeral. Dunedin, McIndoe, 1976.
Brother Jonathan, Brother Kafka, with prints by John Drawbridge.
   Wellington and Oxford, Oxford University Press, 1980.
Selected Poems. Auckland, Oxford University Press, 1992.

Other

New Zealand Poetry in the Sixties. Wellington, Wellington Depart-
   ment of Education, 1973.
Katherine Mansfield's New Zealand. London, Muller, 1975.
James K. Baxter. Wellington and London, Oxford University Press,
   1977.
*Finding the Pattern, Solving the Problem: Katherine Mansfield, the
   New Zealand European.* Wellington, Victoria University Press,
   1989.

Editor, *An Anthology of Twentieth-Century New Zealand Poetry.*
   Auckland and London, Oxford University Press, 1970.
Editor, *New Zealand Short Stories: Third Series.* Wellington and
   London, Oxford University Press, 1975.
Editor, *The Aloe;* with *Prelude,* by Katherine Mansfield. Manches-
   ter, Carcanet, 1983.
Editor, with Margaret Scott, *The Collected Letters of Katherine
   Mansfield. Volume 1: 1903-1917.* Oxford, Clarendon Press, 1985.
Editor, *Collected Poems,* by Ursula Bethell. Auckland and Oxford,
   Oxford University Press, 1985.
Editor, with S.C. Harrex. *Kamala Das: A Selection with Essays
   on Her Work.* Adelaide, Centre for Research in the New Litera-
   ture in English, 1986.
Editor, with Margaret Scott, *The Collected Letters of Katherine
   Mansfield. Volume 2: 1918-1919.* Oxford, Clarendon Press, 1987.
Editor, *Katherine Mansfield: Selected Letters.* Oxford, Clarendon
   Press, 1989.
Editor, *The Poems of Katherine Mansfield.* Auckland and Oxford,
   Oxford University Press, 1990.
Editor, with Margaret Scott, *The Collected Letters of Katherine
   Mansfield. Volume 3: 1919-1920.* Oxford, Clarendon Press, 1993.

*   *   *

Vincent O'Sullivan's versatility as short story writer, poet, playwright, scholar, and editor, makes him perhaps New Zealand's most
literary "man for all seasons." Following the social satire *Miracle:
A Romance,* he has come into his own as a novelist relatively late
in life with *Let the River Stand.*

Miracle: A Romance is a satire on major political and cultural
icons of New Zealand society: its politicians, its passion for rugby.
O'Sullivan caricatures national vices through the grotesque ruler,
Mr. Sagwheel, and Stumpy Smith, a barman turned sports ambassador in South Africa. But in equating popular responses to sporting success with the phenomenal Miracle Hornbeam, who acquires
the status of a national trophy, replacing the Ranfruly Shield, due
to her renewed virginity after nightly rape, he overlaps satire with
fantasy, the improbable with the incomprehensible. O'Sullivan uses
an interlaced narrative technique in this comedy of obsession, which
gathers momentum as a decentered, bizarre vision of society. Although its macabre humor sometimes verges on the crudely simplistic, the image of New Zealanders as inward-looking and repressed reinforces national stereotypes.

Let the River Stand has been acclaimed for the sustained excellence of the writing, its perceptive characterization, and its teasing,
jigsaw structure. Ostensibly an historical, social-realist fiction of
rural New Zealand society between the 1920s and the 1950s, moving from Waikato in the Depression to Tasmania and Spain, its complex narrative structure—in which images resonate against exact
observations of events, places, and people to evoke feelings and
memories developing over time—invites a more symbolic interpretation. Through his hero, Alex McLeod, O'Sullivan revisits the masculine world of his short stories and verse, and through the mind
of Collins/Schwarz, a failed boxer turned pigraiser, he investigates
the bleakly limited world of the besieged, marginal man. Drawing
from several local literary traditions and models, but predominantly
from John Mulgan's archetypal motif of "man alone"—at one point
introducing into the narrative Mulgan's own character, Johnson—
O'Sullivan apotheosizes the fate of the outsider in Schwarz's death.
Other images of isolation reverberate throughout the novel: Alex is
a loner whose youthful idealism drives him and his cousin, Rory,

to fight in the Spanish Civil War; later he and his communist wife, Bet, are ostracized by the rural community because of their socialist beliefs.

O'Sullivan's originality, however, is in creating an erotically charged image of female purity—dangerous yet vulnerable—symbolized by the white dress that Barbara Trevaskis wears to school instead of the regulation gym tunic. When the maelstroms of repression and desire lead to tragedy, this stimulus to masculine obsessions comes to signify a displaced romanticism. Associated images of the river, sunlight, and water described in the hospital scenes, the setting of the brief passages in italics, which link the five different parts of the novel, reinforce the theme of sexual passion out of control; these represent the novel's most solitary character: the mysterious, silent accident victim.

O'Sullivan creates a discontinuous narrative of anticipation and deferral in which several stories and memories interact. By playing with readers' expectations of a linear, causal sequence, by hinting at the central tragedy while delineating contingent events sharply, he sustains dramatic tension. The meaning of some episodes emerges like a film running backward; conversely the journal entries of Alex's mother, Emily McLeod, suggest that the flux of time is irreversible. These juxtapositions of time past against time present contribute to the novel's lyrical, sensuous texture, drawing attention to the power of language to transcend chronological boundaries.

Like his forebears, Maurice Duggan and Dan Davin, O'Sullivan has flavored the predominantly puritan, Protestant ethic of New Zealand social realism with an Irish-Catholic sensibility and wit. His numerous short stories—many containing themes and techniques anticipate those of *Let the River Stand*—have an international flavor in their range across different cultures and diverse characters; yet O'Sullivan's focus on middle-class hypocrisy and his dispassionate portrayals of the underprivileged are both distinctive and convincing. Precise observation correlated to a low-key emotional register and an understated social vision bordering on the satiric are his hallmarks. Epiphanies are rare, and metaphor, when it occurs, functions as a principle of structure rather than of style. In his early stories, confrontations between his misfit heroes and the pretensions of bourgeois New Zealand society are underpinned by a recognition of loss or the hint of an alternative worldview; in his later stories he turns to social satire or black comedy. O'Sullivan's versions of emotional repression, estrangement, and betrayal usually work by implication and by insight into motive and character. But pervasive images of concealment, lying, and dissimulation, which contrast to his narrators' masks of literal-minded obtuseness, also suggest that for him storytelling is preeminently an act of performance.

—Janet Wilson

OZICK, Cynthia

Nationality: American. **Born:** New York City, 17 April 1928. **Education:** New York University, B.A. (cum laude) in English 1949 (Phi Beta Kappa); Ohio State University, Columbus, M.A. 1951. **Family:** Married Bernard Hallote in 1952; one daughter. **Career:** Instructor in English, New York University, 1964-65; Distinguished Artist-in-Residence, City University, New York, 1982; Phi Beta Kappa Orator, Harvard University, Cambridge, Massachusetts, 1985. Lives in New Rochelle, New York. **Awards:** National En-

dowment for the Arts fellowship, 1968; Wallant award, 1972; B'nai B'rith award, 1972; Jewish Book Council Epstein award, 1972, 1977; American Academy award, 1973; Hadassah Myrtle Wreath award, 1974; Lamport prize, 1980; Guggenheim fellowship, 1982; Strauss Living award, 1982-1987; Distinguished Alumnus award, New York University, 1984; Rea award, for short story, 1986; Lucy Martin Donnelly award, Bryn Mawr College, 1991-92. D.H.L.: Yeshiva University, New York, 1984; Hebrew Union College, Cincinnati, 1984; Williams College, Williamstown, Massachusetts, 1986; Hunter College, New York, 1987; Jewish Theological Seminary, New York, 1988; Adelphi University, Garden City, New York, 1988; State University of New York, 1989; Brandeis University, Waltham, Massachusetts, 1990; Bard College, Annandale-on-Hudson, New York, 1991; Skidmore College, 1992. **Agent:** Raines and Raines, 71 Park Avenue, New York, New York 10016. **Address:** c/o Knopf Inc., 201 East 50th Street, New York, New York 10022, U.S.A.

PUBLICATIONS

Novels

Trust. New York, New American Library, 1966; London, MacGibbon and Kee, 1967.
The Cannibal Galaxy. New York, Knopf, 1983; London, Secker and Warburg, 1984.
The Messiah of Stockholm. New York, Knopf, and London, Deutsch, 1987.

Short Stories

The Pagan Rabbi and Other Stories. New York, Knopf, 1971; London, Secker and Warburg, 1972.
Bloodshed and Three Novellas. New York, Knopf, and London, Secker and Warburg, 1976.
Levitation: Five Fictions. New York, Knopf, and London, Secker and Warburg, 1982.
The Shawl: A Story and a Novella. New York, Knopf, 1989.

Uncollected Short Stories

"The Sense of Europe," in *Prairie Schooner* (Lincoln, Nebraska), June 1956.
"Stone," in *Botteghe Oscure* (Rome), Autumn 1957.
"The Laughter of Akiva," in *New Yorker,* 10 November 1980.
"At Fumicaro," in *New Yorker,* 6 August 1984.
"Puttermesser Paired," in *New Yorker,* 8 October 1990.

Plays

Blue Light (produced Long Island, 1994).

Poetry

Epodes: First Poems, with woodcuts by Sidney Chafetz. N.p., 1992.

Other

Art and Ardor (essays). New York, Knopf, 1983.
Metaphor and Memory (essays). New York, Knopf, 1989.

What Henry James Knew, and Other Essays on Writers (essays). London, n.p. 1993.

*

Bibliography: "A Bibliography of Writings by Cynthia Ozick" by Susan Currier and Daniel J. Cahill, in *Texas Studies in Literature and Language* (Austin), Summer 1983.

Critical Studies: "The Art of Cynthia Ozick" by Victor Strandberg, in *Texas Studies in Literature and Language* (Austin), Summer 1983; *Cynthia Ozick, Texas Studies in Literature and Language,* edited by Catherine Rainwater and William J. Scheick, University Press of Kentucky, 1983; *Contemporary American Women Writers: Narrative Strategies,* edited by Catherine Rainwater and William J. Scheick, University Press of Kentucky, 1985; *Crisis and Covenant: The Holocaust in American Jewish Fiction,* by Alan L. Berger, State University of New York, 1985; *Cynthia Ozick* edited by Harold Bloom, New York, Chelsea House, 1986, and *Cynthia Ozick: Modern Critical Views,* by Bloom, Chelsea Publishers, 1986; *The World of Cynthia Ozick: Studies in American Jewish Literature,* edited by Daniel Walden, Kent State University Press, 1987; *Since Flannery O'Conner: Essays on the Contemporary Short Story,* by Loren Logsdon and Charles W. Mayer, Western Illinois University Press, 1987; *The Uncompromising Fictions of Cynthia Ozick* by Sanford Pinsker, Columbia, University of Missouri Press, 1987; *Cynthia Ozick* by Joseph Lowin, Boston, Twayne, 1988; *Understanding Cynthia Ozick* by Lawrence S. Friedman, University of South Carolina Press, 1991; *Cynthia Ozick: Tradition and Invention* by Elaine M. Kasuvar, Indiana University Press, 1993; *Greek Mind, Jewish Soul* by Victor Strandberg, University of Wisconsin Press, 1994; *Cynthia Ozick's Comic Art,* by Sarah Blacher Cohen, Indiana University Press, 1994.

*   *   *

Cynthia Ozick has said that she began her first novel as an American writer and ended it six-and-a-half years later as a Jewish writer. Overarching this book, *Trust,* is a third cultural presence made manifest in the seductive appeal of the pagan Earth-gods, who have maintained their potency under various names from old Greek and Canaanite times to our own. Ozick's conviction regarding this insight is attested by her view of "the issue of Hellenism-versus-Hebraism as the central quarrel of the West." Nevertheless, it was the American writer Henry James who most deeply stamped his image upon her youthful imagination. She wrote her master's thesis on parable in James's fiction, and spent seven apprentice years writing a never-published novel in the Jamesian manner, followed by almost as long a period working on the neo-Jamesian *Trust.*

Completed on the day President Kennedy was murdered, *Trust* was published in 1966 to a thin but highly favorable chorus of reviews. Its Jamesian elements are immediately evident in its style ("both mandarin and lapidary," Ozick calls it), its social milieu (a wealthy American family), its masking of greed and duplicity under an elegant surface of manners, and its international theme (half the book is set in Europe, half in America). The title itself is ironic to a Jamesian degree of complexity in that lack of trust affects every relationship from the familial (husband-wife, mother-daughter) to the theological (God's covenant having been broken in the Holocaust). What revives trust in the end is the young heroine's disavowal of her decaying cultural heritage (epitomized in her mother's

crassly misspent trust fund) in favor of the spontaneous gods of nature—which is to say, her reversion to the ancient pagan ethos. Her discovery of that ethos in her lost father (who had sired her as his "illegitimate issue" and then was succeeded by unsatisfactory Christian and Jewish father figures) makes up the central plot line of this immense and densely written novel. In the end, her father's apotheosis as a fertility god (which she witnesses) occasions one of the most vividly imagined sexual encounters in American literature—an imagistic rendering of sensation that is perhaps Ozick's finest (and most difficult) artistic achievement.

Even while she was working on *Trust,* Ozick's fascination with the Pan vs. Moses theme (as a character in *Trust* calls it) gathered such force as to promulgate her next book, the collection of stories titled *The Pagan Rabbi.* Within the title story, Pan overcomes Moses when the rabbi couples with a dryad—in another vividly imagined sexual encounter—and then hangs himself from her tree, not in guilt but in pantheistic ecstasy. "The molecules dance within all forms . . . and within the atoms dance still profounder sources of divine vitality. There is nothing that is Dead," says the rabbi's last testament. Behind this heretical hunger for the world's beauty lies the chief paradox, for Ozick, of the Jewish artist. "The single most serviceable description of a Jew—as defined 'theologically'— . . . is someone who shuns idols," she has written; yet to create literature is to put oneself "in competition, like a god, with the Creator," so that "[art] too is turned into an idol." Ozick memorably transmutes this theme into fiction in her next book, *Bloodshed,* where the artist-as-idolator appears triumphant in "Usurpation (Other People's Stories)." Here the Jewish poet, so apostate as to have published a hymn to Apollo, ascends to the Olympic rather than Jewish afterworld in the end, totally rejecting his Jewish heritage. But though the God of Israel permits him to espouse the new identity, the Gentile gods do not: "Then the taciturn little Canaanite idols call him, in the language of the spheres, kike." Flight from and coerced movement back toward Jewish identity is thus the unifying theme of the four tales in *Bloodshed,* with the Holocaust exerting the most powerful such coercive force. In "A Mercenary" a Polish Jew who survived the Holocaust tries to expunge his Jewishness by becoming United Nations ambassador for a black African nation, but he is subtly called Jew by his black aide and even by inanimate objects: his cigarette reminds him of Holocaust smoke; his "white villa on the blue coast," of the "bluish snow" and "snow-white hanging stars of Poland" during his Holocaust period. Conversely, in the title story, "Bloodshed," despair over the Holocaust prompts its Jewish protagonist to contemplate suicide, until he is rescued by a Holocaust survivor's powerful lesson that "despair must be earned."

The later stages of Ozick's career have featured two books of essays, *Art and Ardor* and *Metaphor and Memory,* which embrace a quarter-century of journal contributions. Many of these essays offer incisive insights into her imaginative writing, especially concerning the dilemmas of contemporary Jewish-American culture. Her later fiction explores those dilemmas in a transatlantic range of settings. *Levitation: Five Fictions,* set almost wholly in New York City, uses its title as a three-part pun for its opening story: levitation, levity, the priestly tribe of Levi. It portrays the Holocaust as an identity-defining event, levitating genuine Jews away from the pseudo- or de-Judaized Jews who remain below on ground level. The most expansive, ambitious, and original part of this collection is the Puttermesser-Xanthippe series, a new version of Pan vs. Moses. In this instance the Pan figure (Xanthippe) is a female golem chanted into existence by Puttermesser to save New York City, but in the end the Jewish lawgiver (Puttermesser has become mayor) must sorrowfully chant her charming friend back to a pile of mud after Xanthippe begins to inflame the whole city with illicit sexual hunger. An extensive sequel to this series, in which Puttermesser falls in love, has appeared in the *New Yorker* magazine.

The Cannibal Galaxy revives the Jamesian theme of interaction between Europe and America via a Holocaust survivor, Joseph Brill, who hopes to unite the best of both cultures in a Jewish-American educational program. Although his school, located in the Midwest, thrives financially, in the end the American culture (which may be the "cannibal galaxy") crushes out the European, in part because the high culture of Europe did not truly survive the Holocaust. *The Messiah of Stockholm,* the only Ozick novel set wholly in Europe, concerns the effort of Lars Andemening, a Swedish book reviewer, to verify his claim that Bruno Schulz (the real-life Polish Jew, murdered in 1942) is his father. Schulz's dichotomy between "Cinnamon Shops" and "The Street of Crocodiles"—his best known story titles—repeats itself in Ozick's novel, as Andemening in the end is stripped of his energizing illusions (the comforting refuge of "Cinnamon Shops") and left to cope with the cold barrenness of reality ("The Street of Crocodiles"). And finally, *The Shawl*—Ozick's little book combining the stories "The Shawl" and "Rosa"—plays off

Jewish-American and Jewish-European cultures against each other, to the discredit of both. Rosa, a Holocaust survivor from Warsaw, relies on her high-class, assimilated Polish family heritage to assert her superiority over the degraded Jewish-American culture she experiences in New York and Miami. "My Warsaw is not your Warsaw," she insists to Persky, her kindly but vulgar friend in Miami who had emigrated from the impoverished Warsaw ghetto before the war. Rosa's use of magic to invoke the spirit of her infant daughter (who had been murdered at Auschwitz) comprises yet another instance of the enticement of the pagan gods, tying Ozick's latest work to early books like *Trust* and *The Pagan Rabbi.*

Although Ozick's Jewish materials—including a sprinkling of Yiddish words on many pages—can create an initial impression of opacity, her general reading audience should not find her cultural heritage more difficult to apprehend than Faulkner's or Toni Morrison's materials. Through her greatly original and powerful expression of her Jewish ethos, Ozick contributes importantly to the larger American literary tradition.

—Victor Strandberg

P

PALEY, Grace

Nationality: American. **Born:** Grace Goodside in New York City, 11 December 1922. **Education:** Evander Childs High School, New York; Hunter College, New York, 1938-39. **Family:** Married 1) Jess Paley in 1942, one daughter and one son; 2) the playwright Robert Nichols in 1972. **Career:** Has taught at Columbia University, New York, and Syracuse University, New York. Since 1966 has taught at Sarah Lawrence College, Bronxville, New York, and since 1983 at City College, New York. New York State Author, 1986-88. **Awards:** Guggenheim grant, 1961; National Endowment for the Arts grant, 1966; American Academy award, 1970; Edith Wharton award, 1988, 1989. **Member:** American Academy, 1980. **Address:** Box 620, Thetford Hill, Vermont 05074, U.S.A.

PUBLICATIONS

Short Stories

The Little Disturbances of Man: Stories of Men and Women in Love. New York, Doubleday, 1959; London, Weidenfeld and Nicolson, 1960.
Enormous Changes at the Last Minute. New York, Farrar Straus, 1974; London, Deutsch, 1975.
Later the Same Day. New York, Farrar Straus, and London, Virago Press, 1985.

Uncollected Short Story

"Two Ways of Telling," in *Ms.* (New York), November-December 1990.

Poetry

Leaning Forward. Penobscot, Maine, Granite Press, 1985.
New and Collected Poems. Maine, Tilbury Press, 1991.

Other

365 Reasons Not to Have Another War. Philadelphia and New York, New Society Publications—War Resisters' League, 1989.
Long Walks and Intimate Talks. New York, Feminist Press, 1991.

*

Critical Studies: *Grace Paley: Illuminating the Dark Lives* by Jacqueline Taylor, Austin, University of Texas Press, 1990; *Grace Paley: A Study of the Short Fiction* by Neil Isaacs, Boston, Twayne, 1990.

*   *   *

The individuality of Grace Paley's voice—warm, comic, defensive, and without illusions—and the sophistication of her technique led to the reissue of her first collection of short stories, *The Little Disturbances of Man,* 10 years after it first appeared. Her stories, invariably set in New York and often with a Jewish background, depend especially on her ear for dialogue. Her realism, with a concision sometimes deliberately telescoped into the absurd, admits sudden surrealistic perceptions: "A Subject of Childhood" ends as the sun comes out above a woman being comforted by her child for the desertion of her lover: "Then through the short fat fingers of my son, interred forever, like a black and white barred king in Alcatraz, my heart lit up in stripes."

According to one character, who has risen above the slums of his childhood, the difficulties of a woman bringing up four children on her own in the New York slums are merely "the little disturbances of man" beside the real cataclysms of existence. All the stories in *Enormous Changes at the Last Minute* are set in these slums, but in *The Little Disturbances of Man* Paley ranges over the wider social strata, probing similar preoccupations of loneliness, lust, and escapism. "An Irrevocable Diameter" relates the forced marriage of Charles C. Charley to a rich teenager, less than half his age, who claimed to have seduced him. "The Pale Pink Roast" swings between farce and lyricism in a picture of a woman going to bed with her ex-husband immediately after her new marriage to a richer man.

Paley's concern in *The Little Disturbances of Man* with broken and shifting relationships where the women are dominant is even more important in *Enormous Changes.* For each of the unmarried or separated mothers, it is a question of whether her "capacity for survival has not been overwhelmed by her susceptibility to abuse." There is also a new sense of commitment in *Enormous Changes,* where the key story is "Faith in a Tree"; when the police break up a tiny demonstration against napalm-bombing in Vietnam, Faith's son defiantly writes up the demonstrators' slogan again. The story concludes: "And I think that is exactly when events turned me around . . . directed . . . by my children's heartfelt brains, I thought more and more and every day about the world."

Earlier in that story, Faith says of some of her neighbors, "our four family units, as people are now called, are doomed to stand culturally still as this society moves on its caterpillar treads from ordinary affluent to absolute empire." These tenants crop up in other stories, some reappearing from *The Little Disturbances of Man.* "An Interest in Life" in the earlier book is retold from another character's angle as "Distance" in the later one: "There is a long time in me between knowing and telling."

The subject of "Dreamer in a Dead Language" in *Later the Same Day,* a father-daughter relationship is important in several stories in *Enormous Changes,* where in an introductory note the author states: "Everyone in this book is imagined into life except the father. No matter what story he has to live in, he's my father. . . ." *Enormous Changes at the Last Minute* is altogether darker in tone than *The Little Disturbances of Man:* the interplay of two generations is used to show the long shadow of "the cruel history of Europe" continuing to darken second-generation immigrant lives, while the "last minute" of the title refers to the nuclear threat. As the title suggests, *Later the Same Day* picks up these concerns where *Enormous Changes at the Last Minute* left off.

These later stories are set against a backcloth of the grass roots political struggle of the peace movement, although this is never intrusive in the stories but indissolubly meshed, as it must be, with the everyday concerns of semiadult and adult children, aging parents, and the sickness and death of middle-aged friends. The "day" of *Later the Same Day* is the dangerous contemporary moment in the life of the planet as the "poor, dense, defenseless thing—rolls round and round. Living and dying are fastened to its surface and stuffed into its softer parts" and also in Paley's life as she approaches old age. A striking example of her habitual crisscrossing of perceptions is the story "Zagrowsky Tells," where the first-person narrator, an old Jew, tells Faith how his mentally handicapped daughter came to bear a black baby. Faith, the woman who continues to appear centrally in the stories, often in the first person, in this book is old enough to be "remembering babies, those round, staring, day-in day-out companions of her youth"; now, her son and his stepfather are equal companions, in "Listening." Celebrating precarious human relationships in a society, and a world, of dangerous inequalities, Grace Paley's voice is comically appalled and positive.

—Val Warner

PALLISER, Charles

Nationality: American and Irish. **Born:** the United States in December 1947. **Education:** Exeter College, Oxford, 1967-70, B.A. (honors) in English 1970; Wolfson College, Oxford, 1971-75, B.Litt. 1975. **Career:** Lecturer, Huddersfield Polytechnic, Yorkshire, 1972-74, and University of Strathclyde, Glasgow, 1974-90; visiting teacher in creative writing, Rutgers University, New Brunswick, New Jersey, 1986. **Awards:** American Academy award, 1991. **Agent:** Giles Gordon, Sheil and Associates, 43 Doughty Street, London WC2N 2LF, England; or, Diane Cleaver, Sanford J. Greenburger Associates, 55 Fifth Avenue, New York, New York 10003, U.S.A. **Address:** 78 Alkham Rd., London N16 6XF, England.

PUBLICATIONS

Novels

The Quincunx. Edinburgh, Canongate, 1989; New York, Ballantine, 1990.
The Sensationist. London, Cape, 1991.
Betrayals. New York, Ballantine, 1995.

*

Charles Palliser comments:

On the evidence of my first two novels I would suggest that what motivates me as a novelist is the idea of surprising the reader into a new perception of something. So *The Quincunx* at first appeals to the expectations the reader derives from his or her knowledge of Victorian fiction and social history, but then gradually undermines these expectations with its distinctively modernist elements—the irony, the moral neutrality, and the final impossibility of ever knowing the truth for sure. Much more straightforwardly, *The Sensationist* fragments and "defamiliarizes" the everyday experiences of living in a big modern city, using jump-cuts, elisions,

and highly metaphorical language to stress the strangeness of so much that we take for granted. In terms of subject matter, I seem to be interested in people in extreme situations—a young boy starving in the streets of London in the 1820s or a young man under pressure and at the edge of a breakdown in the 1980s.

I suppose I'm reacting against the idea of the novel as an unproblematical reflection of shared experience. Instead I see it as a tool for making discoveries—not just on the part of the reader, but also myself. For one of the strongest motives that drives me to write is out of curiosity, and I write in order to find things out. In the most obvious sense, writing lets me research things I don't know about already. (I sometimes think it's no more than an excuse to read the books and visit the places and meet the people I am already interested in.) But in another sense, writing enables me—or, rather, requires me—to find out things I already know. It's a way of forcing myself to think hard about difficult issues, to try to go beyond the evasions and half-truths that I'm satisfied with in my own life but which are ruthlessly exposed within a novel.

Writing fiction, moreover, is one of the few occupations in which you never have to repeat yourself. Every challenge is new and so the solution to it is unprecedented. And unlike most other pursuits, the challenge is the one that you've created for yourself. There's an interesting paradox there, and I often think of Houdini having himself elaborately manacled, coffined, and then dropped into a river. Like Houdini, you have to want to go on taking risks and making things difficult for yourself. Otherwise there's no point in doing it.

*   *   *

Rarely has a first novel achieved the instant acclaim and the high sales enjoyed by Charles Palliser's *The Quincunx*. A big novel in the true sense of the word—it is over 800 pages long—it lacked the modesty and restricted ambition usually found in a writer's first offering. Instead, it appeared to aspire to the loftiness and the magnitude of a novel by Dickens or Wilkie Collins, both writers who are much admired by Palliser. The comparison is not fanciful for Palliser seems deliberately to have set out to write a Victorian-style novel, or at the very least a historical novel set in the 19th century, the great age of historical fiction. Certainly, his descriptions of the London underworld and of the moneymaking and industrialization that was overtaking London in the Victorian period are as vivid as anything to be found in *Bleak House* or *The Woman in White*. And like both Dickens and Collins, Palliser has a penchant for creating an intricate, even tortuous, plot which meanders through the narrative as ceaselessly as the main characters wander through the alleyways of London in search of hidden family secrets and lost inheritances.

At the heart of the novel is young John Huffman who is found living with his mother under the assumed name of Mellamphy. The small family is in hiding, but no reason is given for this state of affairs and attempts by John to unravel the secret are met with silence or obfuscation. Into this uneasy existence a sense of danger intrudes and John and his mother are forced to flee to London where poverty soon beckons. What follows is a tale of misunderstandings, criminal folly and corruption as mother and son attempt to enforce the codicil which will bring John into his rightful inheritance. A gallery of colorful characters is introduced into their lives, some for good, others for evil, and hope follows disaster until all the disparate elements in this rambling novel are disentangled in the final chapter. Throughout the novel Palliser holds the structure together in masterly fashion and his firm command of narrative allows the plot to unfold without ever running ahead of itself, no mean feat in a such an ambitious novel. A good example of his technique can be found in the episodes where his mother dies, and in the lunatic asylum where John comes face to face with his long-lost father.

Given the novel's range and scope and the author's unself-conscious use of Victorian literary themes it was hardly surprising that some critics dismissed *The Quincunx* as mere pastiche, an enjoyable read but one which only reproduced the big Victorian novel for a modern readership. There is some truth in the accusation but Palliser's ability to recreate scenes from Victorian life and his knowing awareness of the foibles of human behavior give this novel an existence of its own. By any reckoning it is an admirable achievement.

Palliser's second novel, *The Sensationist,* also broke most of the rules about what a novel should or should not be. Spare, intensely bleak and devoid of emotion, the prose has none of the literary embellishment and color which suffuses *The Quincunx.* Indeed, the casual reader would have been forgiven for thinking that the two novels had been written by different authors. Whereas John Huffman is painfully human in his reactions to life and suffers and celebrates accordingly, David, the "sensationist" of the title, is a man without heart, seemingly devoid of any recognizable human feeling. Here is a man who does not engage in life or even experience it; instead he moves through his existence without ever touching it or even being a part of it. A university lecturer in a hideously depicted Glasgow—all overbearing buildings and wasteland parks—he proceeds through a history of casual sexual couplings, all graphically described, yet all clearly depressing and meaningless, until, suddenly, he falls in love. The unexpected choice is Lucy, a painter with a young child, who resists his advances, thereby only adding strength to his attraction to her. With the roles reversed—David has always enjoyed easy sexual conquests—he is left mystified and tormented. Ultimately the relationship ends as unexpectedly as it began and David's last words mirror the sense of emptiness and withdrawal that dominates the novel: "I don't know anything about that. You'll have to ask someone else."

The appearance of both novels in quick succession introduced Palliser as a disturbing and quirky voice in modern fiction. In *The Sensationist* in particular he shows himself to be capable of capturing the artificiality of a life without roots, in which people are disfigured by their inability to make contact with their fellow human beings. It is as if he is saying that the sensationist, for all his easy conquests and his success in the academic field, is at heart an empty vessel, devoid of emotion or even the ability to nurture them.

—Trevor Royle

PARGETER, Edith (Mary)

Pseudonyms: Ellis Peters; Peter Benedict; Jolyon Carr; John Redfern. **Nationality:** British. **Born:** Horsehay, Shropshire, 28 September 1913. **Education:** Dawley Church of England Elementary School, Shropshire; Coalbrookdale High School for Girls, Oxford School Certificate. **Military Service:** Women's Royal Navy Service, 1940-45; British Empire Medal, 1944. **Career:** Worked as a chemist's assistant, Dawley, 1933-40. **Awards:** Mystery Writers of America Edgar Allen Poe award, 1963; Czechoslovak Society for International Relations gold medal, 1968; Crime Writers Association Silver Dagger award, 1981. Fellow, International Institute of Arts and Letters, 1961. **Agent:** Deborah Owen, 78 Narrow Street, London E14 8BP, England. **Address:** Troya, 3 Lee Dingle, Madeley, Telford, Salop TF7 5TW, England.

PUBLICATIONS

Novels (series: Felse family)

Hortensius, Friend of Nero. London, Lovat Dickson, 1936; New York, Greystone Press, 1937.
Iron-Bound. London, Lovat Dickson, 1936.
Day Star (as Peter Benedict). London, Lovat Dickson, 1937.
The City Lies Foursquare. London, Heinemann, and New York, Reynal, 1939.
The Victim Needs a Nurse (as John Redfern). London, Jarrolds, 1940.
Ordinary People. London, Heinemann, 1941; as *People of My Own,* New York, Reynal, 1942.
She Goes to War. London, Heinemann, 1942.
The Eighth Champion of Christendom. London, Heinemann, 1945.
Reluctant Odyssey. London, Heinemann, 1946.
Warfare Accomplished. London, Heinemann, 1947.
The Fair Young Phoenix. London, Heinemann, 1948.
By Firelight. London, Heinemann, 1948; as *By This Strange Fire,* New York, Reynal, 1948.
Fallen into the Pit. London, Heinemann, 1951.
Lost Children. London, Heinemann, 1951.
Holiday with Violence. London, Heinemann, 1952.
This Rough Magic. London, Heinemann, 1953.
Most Loving Mere Folly. London, Heinemann, 1953.
The Soldier at the Door. London, Heinemann, 1954.
A Means of Grace. London, Heinemann, 1956.
A Bloody Field by Shrewsbury. London, Macmillan, 1972; New York, Viking Press, 1973.
Sunrise in the West. London, Macmillan, 1974.
The Dragon at Noonday. London, Macmillan, 1975.
The Hounds of Sunset. London, Macmillan, 1976.
Afterglow and Nightfall. London, Macmillan, 1977.
The Marriage of Meggotta. London, Macmillan, and New York, Viking Press, 1979.
The Heaven Tree Trilogy. New York, Warner, 1993; London, Warner, 1994.
> *The Heaven Tree.* London, Heinemann, and New York, Doubleday, 1960.
> *The Green Branch.* London, Heinemann, 1962.
> *The Scarlet Seed.* London, Heinemann, 1963.

Novels as Ellis Peters (series: Brother Cadfael; members of the Felse family—Inspector George Felse, Bunty Felse, Dominic Felse)

Death Mask. London, Collins, 1959; New York, Doubleday, 1960.
The Will and the Deed. London, Collins, 1960; as *Where There's a Will,* New York, Doubleday, 1960.
Death and the Joyful Woman (Felse). London, Collins, 1961; New York, Doubleday, 1962.
Funeral of Figaro. London, Collins, 1962; New York, Morrow, 1964.

Flight of a Witch (Felse). London, Collins, 1964.

A Nice Derangement of Epitaphs (Felse). London, Collins, 1965; as *Who Lies Here?*, New York, Morrow, 1965.

The Piper on the Mountain (Felse). London, Collins, and New York, Morrow, 1966.

Black Is the Colour of My True-Love's Heart (Felse). London, Collins, and New York, Morrow, 1967.

The Grass-Widow's Tale (Felse). London, Collins, and New York, Morrow, 1968.

The House of Green Turf (Felse). London, Collins, and New York, Morrow, 1969.

Mourning Raga (Felse). London, Macmillan, 1969; New York, Morrow, 1970.

The Knocker on Death's Door (Felse). London, Macmillan, 1970; New York, Morrow, 1971.

Death to the Landlords! (Felse). London, Macmillan, and New York, Morrow, 1972.

City of Gold and Shadows (Felse). London, Macmillan, 1973; New York, Morrow, 1974.

The Horn of Roland. London, Macmillan, and New York, Morrow, 1974.

Never Pick Up Hitch-Hikers! London, Macmillan, and New York, Morrow, 1976.

A Morbid Taste for Bones: A Mediaeval Whodunnit (Cadfael). London, Macmillan, 1977; New York, Morrow, 1978.

Rainbow's End (Felse). London, Macmillan, 1978; New York, Morrow, 1979.

One Corpse Too Many (Cadfael). London, Macmillan, 1979; New York, Morrow, 1980.

Monk's-Hood (Cadfael). London, Macmillan, 1980; New York, Morrow, 1981.

Saint Peter's Fair (Cadfael). London, Macmillan, and New York, Morrow, 1981.

The Leper of Saint Giles (Cadfael). London, Macmillan, 1981; New York, Morrow, 1982.

The Virgin in the Ice (Cadfael). London, Macmillan, 1982; New York, Morrow, 1983.

The Sanctuary Sparrow (Cadfael). London, Macmillan, and New York, Morrow, 1983.

The Devil's Novice (Cadfael). London, Macmillan, 1983; New York, Morrow, 1984.

Dead Man's Ransom (Cadfael). London, Macmillan, and New York, Morrow, 1984.

The Pilgrim of Hate (Cadfael). London, Macmillan, and New York, Morrow, 1984.

An Excellent Mystery (Cadfael). London, Macmillan, 1985; New York, Morrow, 1986.

The Raven in the Foregate (Cadfael). London, Macmillan, and New York, Morrow, 1986.

The Rose Rent (Cadfael). London, Macmillan, and New York, Morrow, 1986.

The Hermit of Eyton Forest (Cadfael). London, Headline, 1987; New York, Mysterious Press, 1988.

The Confession of Brother Haluin (Cadfael). London, Headline, 1988; New York, Mysterious Press, 1989.

The Heretic's Apprentice (Cadfael). London, Headline, 1989; New York, Mysterious Press, 1990.

The Potter's Field (Cadfael). London, Headline, 1989; New York, Mysterious Press, 1990.

The Summer of the Danes (Cadfael), with Roy Morgan. Stroud, Gloustershire, Sutton, and New York, Mysterious Press, 1991.

The Holy Thief (Cadfael). London, Headline, and New York, Mysterious Press, 1992.

Brother Cadfael's Penance. London, Headline, and New York, Mysterious Press, 1994.

Novels as Jolyon Carr

Murder in the Dispensary. London, Jenkins, 1938.

Freedom For Two. London, Jenkins, 1939.

Death Comes by Post. London, Jenkins, 1940.

Masters of the Parachute Mail. London, Jenkins, 1940.

Short Stories

The Assize of the Dying. London, Heinemann, and New York, Doubleday, 1958.

The Lily Hand and Other Stories. London, Heinemann, 1965.

A Rare Benedictine (as Ellis Peters). London, Headline, 1988; New York, Mysterious Press, 1989.

Uncollected Short Stories

"The Face of Wax," in *Good Housekeeping* (London), December 1936.

"Change of Heart," in *Argosy* (New York), January 1959.

"Starcrossed," in *Argosy* (New York), April 1964.

"The Light Boy," in *Argosy* (New York), October 1964.

"Hostile Witness," in *Argosy* (New York), May 1965.

Uncollected Short Stories as Ellis Peters

"The Chestnut Calif," in *This Week* (New York), December 1963.

"With Regrets," in *This Week* (New York), May 1965.

"Golden Girl," in *Alfred Hitchcock Presents: Stories Not for the Nervous.* New York, Random House, 1965; as "O Gold, O Girl!" (as Edith Pargeter), in *Argosy* (New York), January 1965.

"Villa for Sale," in *This Week* (New York), December 1965.

"A Grain of Mustard Seed," in *This Week* (New York), January 1966.

"Guide to Doom," in *Alfred Hitchcock Presents: Stories That Scared Even Me.* New York, Random House, 1967.

"Maiden Garland," in *Winter's Crimes 1,* edited by George Hardinge. London, Macmillan, and New York, St. Martin's Press, 1969.

"The Trinity Cat," in *Winter's Crimes 8,* edited by Hilary Watson. London, Macmillan, and New York, St. Martin's Press, 1976.

"Come to Dust," in *Winter's Crimes 16,* edited by Hilary Hale. London, Macmillan, 1984; New York, St. Martin's Press, 1985.

"Let Nothing You Dismay!," in *Winter's Crimes 21,* edited by Hilary Hale. London, Macmillan, 1989.

Other

The Coast of Bohemia. London, Heinemann, 1950.

Shropshire (as Ellis Peters), with Roy Morgan. Stroud, Gloustershire, Sutton, and New York, Mysterious Press, 1992; as *Ellis Peter's Shropshire,* London, Headline, 1994.

Strongholds and Sanctuaries: The Borderland of England and Wales (as Ellis Peters), with photographs by Roy Morgan. Stroud, Gloustershire, Sutton, 1993.

Translator, *Tales of the Little Quarter: Stories,* by Jan Neruda. London, Heinemann, 1957; New York, Greenwood Press, 1976.

Translator, *The Sorrowful and Heroic Life of John Amos Comenius,* by Frantisek Kosik. Prague, State Educational Publishing House, 1958.

Translator, *A Handful of Linden Leaves: An Anthology of Czech Poetry.* Prague, Artia, 1958.

Translator, *Don Juan,* by Josef Toman. London, Heinemann, and New York, Knopf, 1958.

Translator, *The Abortionists,* by Valja Stýblová. London, Secker and Warburg, 1961.

Translator, *Granny,* by Bozena Nemcová. Prague, Artia, 1962; New York, Greenwood Press, 1976.

Translator, with others, *The Linden Tree* (anthology). Prague, Artia, 1962.

Translator, *The Terezin Requiem,* by Josef Bor. London, Heinemann, and New York, Knopf, 1963.

Translator, *Legends of Old Bohemia,* by Alois Jirásek. London, Hamlyn, 1963.

Translator, *May,* by Karel Hynek Mácha. Prague, Artia, 1965.

Translator, *The End of the Old Times,* by Vladislav Vancura. Prague, Artia, 1965.

Translator, *A Close Watch on the Trains,* by Bohumil Hrabal. London, Cape, 1968.

Translator, *Report on My Husband,* by Josefa Slánská. London, Macmillan, 1969.

Translator, *A Ship Named Hope,* by Ivan Klima. London, Gollancz, 1970.

Translator, *Mozart in Prague,* by Jaroslav Seifert. Prague, Orbis, 1970.

Translator, *Closely Watched Trains.* London, Sphere, and Evanston, Illinois, Northwestern University Press, 1990.

*

Critical Study: *The Cadfael Companion: The World of Brother Cadfael* by Robin Whiteman, London, Macdonald, 1991.

*   *   *

Ellis Peters may seem to be two writers in one. Beginning in the mid-1930s, she had a distinguished career as a novelist and translator of Czech fiction under her birthname, Edith Mary Pargeter. (While serving with the Royal Navy during World War II she learned Czech through her friendship with Czechs attached to the Royal Air Force, and later she translated 15 works between 1957 and 1963.) Her reason for using a pen name for many of her mystery novels reflects the decency that drives the heroes of all of her books: when she began writing mysteries, she has said, she realized that "they were not very different" from her other works except that they "included the act of murder; but I acknowledged, reluctantly, that a pseudonym might after all be more, not less, honest, and that those who wanted only the one side of me had a right to some guidance as to where to find it."

Edith Pargeter has written over 70 novels (and some short fiction) since her first (*Hortensius, Friend of Nero*) in 1936. Her range of events and settings is considerable, including the ancient world, World War II, and the world of the 13th-century Welsh hero Prince Llewelyn (on whose life she based two series of historical novels). Indeed, her creative imagination seems to be most at home in medieval times in the area where the Welsh border meets Shropshire (her birthplace) at or near the English abbey town of Shrewsbury. This is the time and place, for example, of the extremely popular (and numerous, with over 20 in the series) Brother Cadfael mysteries, written under the Ellis Peters name, and of Edith Pargeter's

favorite of all her fiction, *The Heaven Tree Trilogy.* Published serially in Britain between 1960 and 1963 as *The Heaven Tree, The Green Branch,* and *The Scarlet Seed,* the work was published under the trilogy title in the United States in 1993 and may be her most representative fiction. Here she exhibits her virtuoso ability to recreate a historical milieu. Vividly represented are all of the strata of feudal society and its political intrigue, war-making, nobility of character, cruelty, love, and devotion. Pitted against each other are the hero, a courageous and self-sacrificing young stone carver named Harry Talvace—a true artist who creates the "heaven tree," a magnificently lovely stone church—and the villain, Harry's patron, Ralf Isambard, a powerful Norman baron, who is perhaps the most completely drawn, realistically complex character in the trilogy. Although Ralf can be overbearing and barbaric, he also has in him intelligence, sensitivity, and bravery—sufficient strength of character, in fact, to permit his redemption in the end.

A strong thread running through all of Edith Pargeter's work, under whichever name she is using, is her deep sense of morality. All of her fictions are, in some way, morality dramas in which the villains are, like Ralf Isambard, redeemed, or come to rue the evil they have wrought, or seem to simply pale into insignificance against the triumph of good, often in the form of love. This is true of her more than a dozen Felse-family mysteries and certainly of her Brother Cadfael novels, in which the hero-detective, an herbalist and former soldier, manages to combine a modern, worldly, and rational sensibility with medieval religious devotion as he *always* exposes even the subtlest evil and vindicates young true love.

The notion of "always" is important, for there is a sameness about the Brother Cadfael mysteries, which they share with all of her novels and which the author herself speaks of with uncommon self-insight: "Apart from treating my characters [in all my mysteries] with the same respect as in any other form of novel, I have one sacred rule about the thriller. It is, it ought to be, it must be, a morality. If it strays from the side of the angels, provokes total despair, wilfully destroys . . . the innocent and the good, takes pleasure in evil, that is the unforgivable sin." And in picking up on some criticism of her work, she has observed, "It is probably true that I am not very good at villains. The good interest me so much more." This need to write "a morality," to perhaps anachronistically assert the triumph of virtue, is both the annoying vice and the reassuring strength of the Brother Cadfael series, as it is of all of Edith Pargeter's work.

—Alan Shucard

———

PARK, Jordan. *See* **POHL, Frederik.**

———

PATTERSON, (Horace) Orlando (Lloyd)

Nationality: American. **Born:** Jamaica, 5 June 1940. **Education:** The University of the West Indies, Kingston, 1959-62 (Jamaica Government Exhibition scholar), B.Sc. in economics 1962; London School of Economics (Commonwealth scholar), 1962-65, Ph.D. in sociology 1965. **Family:** Married Nerys Wyn in 1963; two children. **Career:** Assistant lecturer in sociology, London School of Economics, 1965-67; lecturer in sociology, University of the West Indies, 1967-70. Visiting associate professor, 1970-71, Allston Burr Senior Tutor, 1971-73, and since 1971 professor of sociology, Harvard University, Cambridge, Massachusetts. Special Adviser to the Prime Minister of Jamaica, 1972-79; member of the Technical Advisory Council, Government of Jamaica, 1972-74; Visiting member, Institute for Advanced Study, Princeton University, New Jersey, 1975-76; visiting fellow, Wolfson College, Cambridge, 1978-79; Phi Beta Kappa Visiting Scholar, 1988-89. Member of the Editorial Board, *New Left Review,* London, 1965-66. **Awards:** Dakar Festival prize, 1966; National Endowment for the Humanities grant, 1973, 1978, 1981, 1983; Guggenheim fellowship, 1978; Ralph Bunche award, 1983; Harvard University Cabot fellowship, 1984; U.S. National Book award for nonfiction, for volume 1 of *Freedom,* 1991. **Member:** American Academy of Arts and Sciences. A.M.: Harvard University, 1971. **Address:** Department of Sociology, Harvard University, Cambridge, Massachusetts 02138, U.S.A.

PUBLICATIONS

Novels

The Children of Sisyphus. London, Hutchinson, 1964; Boston, Houghton Mifflin, 1965; as *Dinah,* New York, Pyramid, 1968.
An Absence of Ruins. London, Hutchinson, 1967.
Die the Long Day. New York, Morrow, 1972; London, Mayflower, 1973.

Uncollected Short Stories

"The Very Funny Man: A Tale in Two Moods" and "One for a Penny," in *Stories from the Caribbean,* edited by Andrew Salkey. London, Elek, 1965; as *Island Voices,* New York, Liveright, 1970.
"The Alien," in *New Left Review* (London), September-October 1965.
"Into the Dark," in *Jamaica Journal* (Kingston), vol. 1, no. 2, 1968.

Other

The Sociology of Slavery: An Analysis of the Origins, Development, and Structure of Negro Slave Society in Jamaica. London, MacGibbon and Kee, 1967; Rutherford, New Jersey, Fairleigh Dickinson University Press, 1969.
Ethnic Chauvinism: The Reactionary Impulse. New York, Stein and Day, 1977.
Slavery and Social Death: A Comparative Study. Cambridge, Massachusetts, Harvard University Press, 1982.
Freedom. Vol. 1: *Freedom in the Making of Western Culture.* New York, Basic Books, 1991.

*

Manuscript Collection: University of the West Indies, Kingston.

Orlando Patterson comments:

(1991) My main concern is with the theme of survival on all levels—physical, emotional, moral. Also concerned with related themes of isolation and exile.

*　　*　　*

Jamaican fiction is marked by its "realistic" examination of the local social scene. Though this reduces neither its technical range nor its emotional potency—the prose tone poems of Roger Mais, the imaginative adventures of Andrew Salkey, and the mythmaking of Vic Reid and Lindsay Barrett offer ready evidence to the contrary—it does mean that its central concern for the sociological exigencies of daily life often overcomes the urge to use words to build worlds rather than to analyze them. Of the contemporary analytic writers, three stand out as particularly shrewd observers/participators: John Hearne, whose austere novels explore the political impact of race and class; Sylvia Wynter, whose Marxist economic observations underlie her interpretation of Jamaican history; and Orlando Patterson, the sociologist, whose sense of individual potential is informed and guided always by his understanding of class structure and slave heritage.

Patterson's treatise *The Sociology of Slavery,* an analysis of the patterns of Negro slave society in Jamaica, supplies an intelligent background to his novels, considering both the subservient and the resistant responses of the slave population to white society, and the social institutions—sorcery, religion, folk song and story, and so on—that provided some way of contending with life. To Patterson's mind, those responses and institutions continue to exert their effect, and in his novels he has attempted to demonstrate the inhibition that such a history casts over the lives of people today. Freedom in such a world is a watchword and a dream, always urging individuals into open acts of defiance, and always thwarted by the dead weight of the past.

The Children of Sisyphus is set in the slum world of Kingston, and traces the attempts that the prostitute Dinah makes to break out of the Dungle, to flee her surroundings and the course of life that circumstance has forced her into, and to find happiness, order, peace. Paralleling her search is the back-to-Africa quest of the Rastafarian movement, seeking its heritage and home in Ethiopia— "the soil . . . so fertile with everything that's joy back home in Zion"—and a different dream of freedom. But just as that dream is denied by deceit within Rastafarian ranks, so inside Dinah's experience is the Dungle that she cannot altogether leave. Drawn back to it and destroyed, she is typical of not only *her* world, but in Patterson's view *the* world. The suicide that closes the novel, the "soul-consuming" mockery of the shanty surroundings and the universal void, and the attempt thus to reach paradise willfully supply an ironic perspective towards man's lot. The human ritual of striving for order appears as nothing so much as flight from uncertainty—a negative rather than a positive action—and because it is founded in emptiness and need, it lacks the self-possession that might make it anything but futile. Hence the circle back to the Dungle, like Dinah's, is closed, and absurd. For Alexander Blackman, in *An Absence of Ruins,* the discovery of such a relationship with futility voids his attempts not only to enunciate his identity but also to believe in his possession of one. Walking in London at the end, he recognizes himself only as an absence, the nothingness that a cipher concretely and phenomenally represents: "I cannot say whether I am civilized or savage, standing as I do outside of race, outside of culture, outside of history, outside of any value that could make your question meaningful. I am busy going nowhere, but I must keep up the appearance of going in order to forget that I am not." Thus the dilemma of existentiality—the conflict involved between intention, desire, history, and circumstance—is taken from Camus and given a Caribbean voice. As Patterson realized, freeing the mind from slavery is a greater task than freeing the body, for it cannot be enacted by law. When people do not even believe in their capacity to attain freedom, however, the knowledge of the absurdity of their actions offers little comfort and no cure, and becomes their only reality.

—W.H. New

PEARSON, Bill

Nationality: New Zealander. **Born:** William Harrison Pearson in Greymouth, 18 January 1922. **Education:** Greymouth Technical High School; Canterbury University College, Christchurch, 1939, 1947-48; University of Otago, Dunedin, 1940-41, B.A. in English, M.A.; King's College, London, 1949-51, Ph.D. 1952. **Military Service:** Served in the New Zealand forces, in Fiji, Egypt, Italy, and Japan, 1942-46. **Career:** Student teacher, Dunedin Teachers Training College, 1940-41; teacher, Blackball School, 1942, Oxford District High School, 1949, and in London County Council schools, 1952-53; lecturer in English, University of Auckland, 1954-66; Senior Research Fellow, Department of Pacific History, Australian National University, Canberra, 1967-69; associate professor of English, University of Auckland, 1970-86; now Honorary Research Fellow. Closely associated with Maori students at the University of Auckland, 1956-66, and was patron of their club for some of those years; internal rapporteur at several Maori Leadership Conferences, 1959-63. **Awards:** *Landfall* Readers' award, for nonfiction, 1960; Hubert Church Prose award, for nonfiction, 1975. **Address:** 49 Lawrence Street, Herne Bay, Auckland, New Zealand.

Publications

Novel

Coal Flat. Hamilton, Paul's Book Arcade, and London, Angus and Robertson, 1963; revised edition, Auckland, Longman Paul, 1970.

Short Stories

Six Stories. Wellington, Victoria University Press, 1991.

Other

Henry Lawson Among Maoris. Canberra, Australian National University Press, and Wellington, Reed, 1968.
Fretful Sleepers and Other Essays. Auckland, Heinemann, 1974.
Rifled Sanctuaries: Some Views of the Pacific Islands in Western Literature to 1900. Auckland, Auckland University Press, 1984.

Editor, *Collected Stories, 1935-63,* by Frank Sargeson. Auckland, Blackwood and Janet Paul, 1964; London, MacGibbon and Kee, 1965.

Editor, *Brown Man's Burden and Later Stories,* by Roderick Finlayson. Auckland, Auckland University Press, 1973.

*

Critical Studies: "*Coal Flat:* The Major Scale, The Fine Excess," in *Comment* (Wellington), October 1963, and "*Coal Flat* Revisited," in *Critical Essays on the New Zealand Novel* edited by Cherry Hankin, Auckland, Heinemann, 1976, both by Allen Curnow; "Conversation on a Train" by Frank Sargeson, in *Landfall* (Christchurch), December 1967.

Bill Pearson comments:

(1991) Some commentators have seen a correspondence between my aims in *Coal Flat* and my analysis of the motifs of New Zealand behavior and the implications for the artist which I wrote in 1951, "Fretful Sleepers."

While it has been said that a traditional structure, with subplots and a wide range of characters, is appropriate to a social novel set in a community whose attitudes and aspirations and social relations were rooted in 19th-century Britain, it has sometimes been a matter of objection that I chose a structure and style that appeared to take no cognizance of the developments in the form of the novel since Joyce. Yet I think that those commentators who stress the social realism or what they miscall "sociology" have been thrown off by a distaste for what they mistake for an outmoded technique, appropriate to *New Writing* reportage. The writers in the light of whose practice my aspirations as a writer developed were those that in common with young men of my time I read with sympathy and a deep respect, Lawrence, Joyce, Forster, Faulkner, Hemingway, Koestler; and I had a series of passions for the novels of Virginia Woolf and John Dos Passos and Thomas Hardy. At the time of my novel's first conception in 1946, the novelist who most excited me was Graham Greene. What I hoped to do when I was writing it (mostly in 1952 and 1953) was to devise a traditional structure that would be large enough to comprehend a community and sensitive enough to reflect the crises of feeling and conscience that might come to a man who was out of sympathy with the materialist values of the community. The plot would grow easily from the initial situation and by its own logic would reach a satisfying outcome without recourse to any of the tricks and evasions or improbabilities by which some of the 19th-century English novelists reached their answers. I had found, I thought, theoretical justification in Aristotle's conception of the plot as the probable and necessary consequence of certain initial acts and I conceived it as having the shape of the noble symmetrical curve that I saw in the plots of *Troilus and Criseyde* and *Wuthering Heights* and the great 19th-century Russian novels. This was not a scale that I pretended my ability or the comparatively pedestrian quality of New Zealand life would allow me to reach. But my concern for probability was necessary as a check against the rhetorical falsification that would be the risk of writing in the awareness of such examples, created from other communities and other times. My hope was to achieve an imaginative authenticity that my compatriots would immediately recognize as true, and which at the same time would be sufficiently clear of the accidents of parochiality to translate into human experience recognizable to readers from other societies. Whether I succeeded in this I cannot tell; but no one but an expatriate knows the pleasure of imaginatively recreating one's country in its detail, without sentimentality. It has often surprised me that some New Zealand commentators have seen sourness and "unappeased resentment" in a work that was written with love.

Since the moral meaning of the novel was to be in the sequence or consequence of events and their outcome, it was this rather than diction or characters or setting that demanded most thought. In its 13 years between conception and the last version, the novel survived a number of rethinkings and radical overhauls, by which I think it gained. The last major revision was the discarding of a superficially optimistic ending, in keeping with a broadly Marxist literary theory hardly tenable after the events of 1956.

If I am moved to write fiction again, however, it is likely to be different in treatment.

*   *   *

Bill Pearson, essayist, critic, and scholar, has edited Frank Sargeson's *Collected Stories,* written about the impact of Western society on the Polynesian as reflected in literature, investigated in *Henry Lawson Among Maoris* a little-known area of the Australian writer's life, and produced a number of short stories together with a long novel, *Coal Flat.* Novels are sometimes written with a thesis. This may be religious or sociological but, whichever it is, the thesis may too easily destroy those qualities we have a right to expect in any attempt to create a life-like representation.

Coal Flat contains a thesis but survives as a novel. In "Fretful Sleepers," described as "a sketch of New Zealand behaviour and its implications for the artist," Pearson suggested that "our job is to penetrate the torpor and out of meaninglessness make a pattern that means something." *Coal Flat,* with its depressing but significant title, became not only a demonstration of the difficulties involved in such an attempt, but also as a novel partially fulfilled the aim that had been proposed for at least some artists.

Without allowing it to turn into satire or degenerate into a sociological survey, Pearson chose a small coal mining and gold-dredging settlement on the West Coast of New Zealand in order to chart the course of family and community life; and by close attention to naturalistic detail evoked its oppressive narrowness, puritanism, and smugness. At one level the reader is introduced to a wide range of provincial characters, including the publican, parson, policeman, and visiting politicians, to miners, dredgers and their officials, to schoolteachers and children, to the doctor and priest, all firmly established in their local setting that combines natural grandeur with human inadequacy. The shriek of the dredge echoes and reechoes through the book and acts as an inhuman accompaniment to the bitter animosities, perverted affections, and destructive behavior of the people of Coal Flat. At another and perhaps more significant level these become signs and portents of a wider deterioration in the quality of life, extending well beyond its confines. Nevertheless, Coal Flat is by no means an inferno of lost souls. There are kindness, comradeship, and loyalty in abundance; there is not even a complete absence of sweetness and light; there are moments of idyllic charm and many good intentions. It is New Zealand, the world, reduced to Coal Flat.

Because its pitfalls cannot always be avoided, a close adherence to the slightly outmoded method of naturalism is liable to provoke criticism that is seldom without justification. *Coal Flat* is not a faultless novel, but it is a valuable one and especially for New Zealand. By the accumulation of detail relevant to the settlement and its inhabitants, by involving the central character, a young teacher of liberal instincts, in a mesh of conflicting loyalties, Pearson is able to dramatize the struggle between the individual conscience and the collective will, explore personal and family relationships in the broader context of the community and reveal distortions of sexual,

parental, and social love. *Coal Flat* is neither a blueprint for future novels about New Zealand, nor is it an imitation of earlier novels in the naturalistic mode; but its achievement is such that it becomes an anatomy of social and spiritual decline, an exploration of the impoverishment of life, and a melancholy comment on thwarted but confused idealism unable to make headway against the conventional attitudes and mental lethargy of the majority.

—H. Winston Rhodes

PERRY, Anne

Nationality: British. **Born:** London, 28 October 1938. **Education:** Privately educated. **Career:** Has had a variety of jobs, including airline stewardess, 1962-64; assistant buyer, Newcastle upon Tyne, 1964-66; property underwriter, Muldoon and Adams, Los Angeles. Since 1972 full-time writer. Lived in California, 1967-72. **Agent:** Meg Davis, MBA Literary Agency Ltd., 45 Fitzroy Street, London W1P 5HR, England. **Address:** 1 Seafield, Portmabomack, Rossshire IY20 IYB, Scotland.

PUBLICATIONS

Novels (series: Charlotte and Thomas Pitt in all books except as indicated)

The Cater Street Hangman. New York, St. Martin's Press and London, Hale, 1979.
Callander Square. New York, St. Martin's Press, and London, Hale, 1980.
Paragon Walk. New York, St. Martin's Press, 1981.
Resurrection Row. New York, St. Martin's Press, 1981.
Rutland Place. New York, St. Martin's Press, 1983.
Bluegate Fields. New York, St. Martin's Press, 1984; London, Souvenir Press, 1992.
Death in the Devil's Acre. New York, St. Martin's Press, 1985; London, Souvenir Press, 1991.
Cardington Crescent. New York, St. Martin's Press, 1987; London, Souvenir Press, 1990.
Silence in Hanover Close. New York, St. Martin's Press, 1988; London, Souvenir Press, 1989.
Bethlehem Road. New York, St. Martin's Press, 1990; London, Souvenir Press, 1991.
Face of a Stranger (Monk William). New York, Fawcett, 1990; London, Headline, 1993.
A Dangerous Mourning (Monk William). New York, Fawcett, 1991; London, Headline, 1994.
Highgate Rise. New York, Fawcett, 1991; London, Souvenir Press, 1992.
Belgrave Square. New York, Fawcett, 1992; London, Souvenir Press, 1993.
Defend and Betray (Monk William). New York, Fawcett, and London, Headline, 1992.
Farriers' Lane. New York, Fawcett, 1993; London, Collins Crime, 1994.
A Sudden, Fearful Death (Monk William). New York, Fawcett, and London, Headline, 1993.

The Hyde Park Headsman. New York, Fawcett, 1994.
The Sins of the Wolf (Monk William). New York, Fawcett, and London, Headline, 1994.
Traitor's Gate. New York, Fawcett, 1995.

Uncollected Short Story

"Digby's First Case," in *Alfred Hitchcock's Mystery Magazine* (New York), February 1988.

*

Manuscript Collection: Mugar Memorial Library, Boston University.

*   *   *

Beginning with *The Cater Street Hangman* in 1978, Anne Perry has supplied readers of detective novels with an annual volume in either her Thomas and Charlotte Pitt series or her more recent William Monk-Hester Latterley mysteries. Because of her love of history, her novels are set in the mid- and late 19th century—Monk and Latterley in the 1850s, the Pitts in the 1880s and early 1890s—and she does her best to reconstruct the sights, smells, menus, costumes, and concerns of each.

Concurrently with the self-contained mystery of each novel is an ongoing development of the marriage of Charlotte Ellison, an outspoken young woman who "lowers" herself by marrying a police inspector, Thomas Pitt. They meet when her sister is murdered in the first novel, marry, and have two children in subsequent books. Pitt himself is falsely charged with murder in *Silence in Hanover Close,* enabling the reader to look inside the brutalities of a Victorian prison to which his superior officer, the power-server, Ballaret, is anxious to condemn him.

Charlotte, although she becomes proficient in housewifery, assists in her husband's investigations, at times without his knowledge. Aided by her own social *savoir faire* and by elegant borrowed clothes, Charlotte meets and probes the interests of upper-middle and upper-class suspects, accessories, and innocents. Pitt, a gamekeeper's son, whose education and accent are those of a gentleman, deals with more unsavory criminal classes—brothel-keepers, money-lenders, informers—often in dirty disguises. In more recent novels, Ballaret is replaced by the gentlemanly Drummond and, eventually, by Pitt himself, who prefers street work but is now able to give Charlotte something more than a working-class home.

These events, moving through some 15 narratives of violent death, have accrued other ongoing personages: Charlotte's sister, Lady Emily, for example, whose first husband is murdered and who eventually marries Jack Radley, a successful candidate for Parliament. Emily, too, uses her social position to gather information for Pitt, especially when, bored with the seclusion demanded by widowhood, she impersonates a maid in the York household, which also allows Perry to show us the heavy demands made upon servants. Lady Vespasia, Emily's aunt by marriage, adds her aged beauty, superb gowns, and advanced social convictions to each case. Charlotte's father dies, but her mother finally loves and marries an actor; an elderly humor character, Charlotte's grandmother is repellently venomous in her brief appearances.

The mysteries these characters help to solve are identified by place-names—for example, *Rutland Place, Farrier's Lane, Paragon Walk, Traitor's Gate, The Hyde Park Headsman*—in which a group of well-born neighbors often supply a tightly knit community, secretly riddled with loves and hatreds. Few of Perry's murderers come from the working classes, and their crimes are frequently bizarre in conception, shocking in solution, or both. A mother kills two newborn children of her venereal-diseased, blackmailing husband; a man is crucified; a judge is poisoned by an opium-laden cigar at the theater; two homosexuals are found dead and naked together, a murder and suicide; a young girl has taken part in rites of black magic and is branded with a "devil's mark"; another young girl kills her brother after he persuades her to abort their incestuously conceived child; and so on. Moreover, in two novels innocent men are hanged.

Several recent works have introduced the mysterious and seemingly omnipresent Inner Circle, ostensibly a secret society for doing good but really an intricate series of groups devoted to power, including the power of death. Pitt and Jack refuse to join but the Inner Circle's influence is difficult to combat. The other concern of Perry's latest novels is "the African question," which involves the foreign office and the British-German race to colonize Africa.

By now Perry's fiction has settled into a pattern, although it still has surprises. Perhaps that is why she began the Monk-Latterley series in 1990 with a brilliantly conceived first volume, *The Face of a Stranger.* It opens with Monk's amnesia from a cab accident, requiring him to discover who and what he is while trying to solve a tenuously leftover murder. In subsequent works, he still adds flashes of memory. He is thrown into the abrasive company of a former Crimean nurse, Hester Latterley, too anxious to initiate Florence Nightingale's reforms in English hospitals to be long employable in one. They are joined by Lady Callandra Daviot, a younger, untidy variant of Aunt Vespasia, and later by the admirable barrister, Oliver Rathbone. Crimes include child abuse and abortion. Like Pitt, Monk has an intolerable superior officer, Runcorn, who drives him into resigning from the force and setting up as a private detective.

Like the Pitt series, these novels have been praised for their fullness of Victorian detail, and their dialogue is generally more realistic than the stilted conversations of the drawing rooms that Charlotte visits. Perhaps Perry should read more Victorian fiction to sharpen her ear for the way people talked. At present this is the chief weakness of her determined historicity.

—Jane W. Stedman

PERUTZ, Kathrin

Pseudonym: Johanna Kingsley. **Nationality:** American. **Born:** New York City, 1 July 1939. **Education:** Barnard College, New York, B.A. 1960; New York University, M.A. 1966. **Family:** Married Michael Studdert-Kennedy in 1966; one son. **Career:** Lived in London, 1960-64. **Address:** 16 Avalon Road, Great Neck, Long Island, New York 10021, U.S.A.

PUBLICATIONS

Novels

The Garden. London, Heinemann, and New York, Atheneum, 1962.

A House on the Sound. London, Heinemann, 1964; New York, Coward McCann, 1965.

The Ghosts. London, Heinemann, 1966.

Mother Is a Country: A Popular Fantasy. New York, Harcourt Brace, and London, Heinemann, 1968.

Reigning Passions: Leopold von Sacher-Masoch and the Hapsburg Empire. Philadelphia, Lippincott, and London, Weidenfeld and Nicolson, 1978.

Scents (as Johanna Kingsley, in colloboration). New York, Bantam, and London, Corgi, 1985.

Faces (as Johanna Kingsley, in collaboration). New York, Bantam, and London, Corgi, 1987.

Writing for Love and Money. Fayetteville, University of Arkansas Press, 1991.

Uncollected Short Story

"An American Success," in *Voices 2,* edited by Michael Ratcliffe. London, Joseph, 1965.

Other

Beyond the Looking Glass: America's Beauty Culture. New York, Morrow, 1970; as *Beyond the Looking Glass: Life in the Beauty Culture,* London, Hodder and Stoughton, 1970.

Marriage Is Hell: It's Better to Burn Than to Marry. New York, Morrow, 1972; as *The Marriage Fallacy: It's Better to Burn Than to Marry,* London, Hodder and Stoughton, 1972; as *Liberated Marriage,* New York, Pyramid, 1973.

Polly's Principles, with Polly Bergen. New York, Wyden, 1974.

I'd Love To, But What'll I Wear?, with Polly Bergen. New York, Wyden, 1977.

*

Critical Studies: *Don't Never Forget* by Brigid Brophy, London, Cape, 1966, New York, Holt Rinehart, 1967; "The Truth about Fiction" by George P. Elliott, in *Holiday* (New York), March 1966.

Kathrin Perutz comments:

(1972) The only general theme (or background) of my books is America. *Mother Is a Country* is a direct parody of certain American dreams (the acquisition of power and the desire to become a commodity); *A House on the Sound* charts the distance from reality to where rich liberals have their camp. *Beyond the Looking Glass,* a nonfiction book often fictionalized, examines preoccupation with appearance in America, where people have the hope of seeming what they have not yet become, and where self-knowledge is replaced by concern over minutiae of deception.

My first three novels also concern sub-rosa relationships, the area of self that is undeveloped or suppressed. *The Garden* presents a love affair between two girls, not lesbian (both girls are young and boy-crazy), but of an essential intensity to contradict fears of not existing. *A House on the Sound* shows different manifestations of embryonic love—homosexuality, incest, masochism—never acknowledged by the characters. The two main characters of *The Ghosts* have not reconciled themselves to the sexual roles, male and female, they are supposed to play, and often parody or pervert these roles.

But mainly, each book has been my attempt to learn more of the craft. The first was a simple diary; the second tried, in six hours,

to cut through time past and present, more similar to movie techniques than traditional flashbacks. The third book tried to give a sense of development, over the space of a year. The fourth, a satire, was deliberately "surface," a board game played over true but generalized emotions. My fifth book presented problems of journalism, in organization of material, tone, pace, and the creation of a personal, but abstracted, narrator.

(1976) My last book, *Marriage Is Hell,* is an essay on the institution of marriage as it exists today in the West, particularly in America. It deals with the anachronism of marriage, its false expectations, its imprisonment of personality and distortion of both privacy and personal liberty. The book, which is strongly opinionated, attacks marriage from many perspectives—legal, historical, anthropological, sexual—and then goes on to suggest reform and finally a turning that will make marriage possible again. I consciously tried to keep the style loose and colloquial, the better to let readers argue with me, and literary experiment is superseded in this book by political, or pragmatic, aims.

*   *   *

Kathrin Perutz has a baroque spider-web sensibility; it is as exquisite as it is tough, and permits her to explore such matters as incest, sadomasochism, homosexuality, suicide, and murder with the delicacy of an appropriate dinner wine. It is the most pervasive force in her novels and the one that diminishes the importance of whatever flaws may appear in them as a consequence of her experimentation with form and theme.

The first novel, *The Garden,* is a straightforward first-person narrative of life at a small women's college in Massachusetts. Its treatment of the urge to put aside the burden of virginity becomes tedious, and the book is marked with jejune expressions ("O.K., Pats, shoot") that may be true to dormitory life but are vexatious in a novel. Perutz handles the garden symbolism of the novel well, however; describes a memorably tender, vivacious relationship between Kath and the Blossom, the two principal characters; and, with perfect briskness of pace and lightness of tone, captures the banal essence of a party weekend at an American men's college probably better than any other writer has.

The Ghosts, Perutz's third novel, walks the maze of a love affair in which the participants—or combatants—Luke, an excessively cerebral writer, and Judith, an undercerebral but sensitive hairdresser, are haunted chiefly by Luke's dead father and an assortment of cast-off lovers. The deficiency of the volume is that there is no one with whom an audience would much care to identify. Luke is insatiably clinical toward the involvement, and he and Panda, a deep platonic love of his who befriends Judith, are sometimes mouthpieces discussing their actions and Judith's, and examining one of the immediate themes of the novel, abortion, and, of more general metaphysical interest, the nature of human action. The conception of the characters is acute; their mechanism, however, is too much exposed and not enough is left for the reader to infer. They are often pieces of an essay rather than people in a work of fiction. Judith is too pliable, too much prop for Luke, until the end, when she takes control of herself and Luke becomes more human. But that occurs too late to place the novel in balance.

Mother Is a Country is a satiric fantasy that strikes at the mass-produced, antiseptic, Saran-wrapped materialism in American life. That quality accounts for the death of the three main characters, and the most palpable reaction in the cosmically unfeeling nation is that "a mother eagle in her nest flapped powerful wings and laid another egg." Though the book has been criticized for its superficiality of characterization, it can be argued that since superficial consumerism is primarily what the satire is about, John Scudely (a hero with much of the feeling of a Bellow character, but without the profundity) and the other characters are properly shallow. *Reigning Passions,* Perutz's latest novel, has done nothing to enhance her reputation. It is a fictionalized account of the complex man who gave his name to masochism, and so flat are the nuances of his life made to seem that to get through the book it helps to have a fair dose of the affliction.

It was Perutz's second novel, *A House on the Sound,* that proved her excellence. She paints a dinner party of sham liberals on a small canvas with precise detail, probing through the word, the facial expression, the gesture, the nuance of conversation the variety of characters present and their secret relationships. In this and in her control of time through brief, illuminating flashbacks and staging of the moments of her characters, there is the clear echo—but just the echo—of Virginia Woolf. When the experimentation ends, as far as it ever does, it is to be hoped that Perutz will return to a place like the house on the Sound and give full voice to her sensibility.

—Alan R. Shucard

PETERKIEWICZ, Jerzy (Michal)

Nationality: British. **Born:** Fabianki, Poland, 29 September 1916; emigrated to England in 1940. **Education:** Dlugosz School, Wloclawek; University of Warsaw; University of St. Andrews, Scotland, M.A. in English and German 1944; King's College, London, Ph.D. 1947. **Family:** Married Christine Brooke-Rose, *q.v.,* in 1948 (divorced 1975). **Career:** Lecturer, 1950-64, reader, 1964-72, and professor of Polish language and literature, 1972-79, School of Slavonic and East European Studies, University of London. **Address:** 7 Lyndhurst Terrace, London NW3 5QA, England.

PUBLICATIONS

Novels

The Knotted Cord. London, Heinemann, 1953; New York, Roy, 1954.
Loot and Loyalty. London, Heinemann, 1955.
Future to Let. London, Heinemann, 1958; Philadelphia, Lippincott, 1959.
Isolation: A Novel in Five Acts. London, Heinemann, 1959; New York, Holt Rinehart, 1960.
The Quick and the Dead. London, Macmillan, 1961.
That Angel Burning at My Left Side. London, Macmillan, 1963.
Inner Circle. London, Macmillan, 1966.
Green Flows the Bile. London, Joseph, 1969.

Plays

Sami Swoi (produced London, 1949).
Scena ma trzy sciany. London, Wiadomosci, 1974.

Poetry

Prowincja. Warsaw, 1936.

Wiersze i poematy. Warsaw, Prosto z Mostu, 1938.
Pokarm cierpki. London, Mysl Polska, 1943.
Pity poemat. Paris, Instytut Literacki, 1950.
Poematy londynskie i wiersze przedwojenne. Paris, Kultura, 1965.
Kula magiczna (Selected Poems). Warsaw, Ludowa Spóldzielnia, 1980.
Poezje wybrane. Warsaw, Ludowa Spóldzielnia, 1986.
Modlitwy intelektu. Warsaw, Pax, 1988.

Other

Znaki na niebie. London, Mildner, 1940.
Po chlopsku: Powiesc. London, Mildner, 2 vols., 1941.
Umarli nie sa bezbronni. Glasgow, Ksiaznica, 1943.
Pogrzeb Europy. London, Mildner, 1946.
The Other Side of Silence: The Poet at the Limits of Language. London and New York, Oxford University Press, 1970.
The Third Adam. London, Oxford University Press, 1975.
Messianic Prophecy: A Case for Reappraisal. London, University of London Press, 1991.
In the Scales of Fate: An Autobiography. London, Boyars, 1993.
Literatura polska w perspektywie europejskiej (essays translated from English). Warsaw, Panstwowy Instytut, 1986.

Editor, *Polish Prose and Verse.* London, Athlone Press, 1956.
Editor and Translator, *Antologia liryki angielskiej 1300-1950.* London, Veritas, 1958.
Editor and Translator, with Burns Singer, *Five Centuries of Polish Poetry 1450-1950.* London, Secker and Warburg, 1960; Philadelphia, Dufour, 1962; revised edition, with Jon Stallworthy, as *Five Centuries of Polish Poetry 1450-1970,* London and New York, Oxford University Press, 1970.
Editor and Translator, *Easter Vigil and Other Poems,* by Karol Wojtyla. London, Hutchinson, and New York, Random House, 1979.
Editor and Translator, *Collected Poems,* by Karol Wojtyla. London, Hutchinson, and New York, Random House, 1982.
Editor and Translator, *The Place Within: The Poetry of Pope John Paul II,* New York, Random House, 1994.

*

Critical Studies: In *New Statesman* (London), 10 October 1959; *Sunday Times Magazine* (London), 10 June 1962; "Speaking of Writing" by Peterkiewicz, in *The Times* (London), 9 January 1964; *Le Monde* (Paris), 28 June 1967; *The Novel Now* by Anthony Burgess, London, Faber, and New York, Norton, 1967, revised edition, Faber, 1971; by Peterkiewicz, in *Times Literary Supplement* (London), 30 July 1971; "Three Conversations," in *New Literary History* (Charlottesville, Virginia), vol. 15, 1984.

Jerzy Peterkiewicz comments:
If titles are significant, *Isolation* and *Inner Circle* seem to be my representative novels, both structurally and thematically.

*   *   *

Three of Jerzy Peterkiewicz's last six novels are comic entertainments of a high order of literary craftsmanship; three others show a marked falling-off of standards. His first novels have little bearing on the later work. *The Knotted Cord* is a genuinely moving account of a peasant boyhood in Poland; its hero has to escape from many things, but particularly from the "cord" of the scratchy brown cassock that his pious mother has thrust him into, and from all that cord represents. The work is a "first novel" of promise, and it is a pity the Peterkiewicz has chosen not to develop or integrate into his later work a mode which might have provided a carbohydrate counterbalance to the sometimes too frothy champagne of the books which follow. *Loot and Loyalty* is a trivial and poorly constructed historical novel about a 17th-century Scots soldier of fortune exiled in Poland, and his connection with the "false Dmitri."

Future to Let, the first of the really successful books, is less "mannerist" by far than its successors. It is a very funny *roman à clef* on the tortured loves, English plots, and politics of contemporary Polish émigrés, chief among them Julian Atrament ("ink" in Polish), quite unidentifiable, of course, but almost recognizable, whose "escape to freedom" by means of his St. Bernard dog is Peterkiewicz's finest comic turn. *Isolation,* probably his best book, parodies the erotic mystifications of a modern spy story with a skill that even the suggestions of deep meanings about the mutual isolation of sexuality, etc., cannot spoil. The Powell-esque (or Waugh-like) Commander Shrimp (alias Pennyworthing), faded semi-spy and bathetic con-man, is a great comic creation. *That Angel Burning at My Left Side* has some of the virtues of *The Knotted Cord;* it is realism with a light touch, of a boy growing up through World War II and postwar refugeehood, looking for father, country, and self. The gimmick of the "angels" grows tiresome, but descriptions of place and event and the hero himself are vivid and concrete—until the hero gets to England, and everything, including him, suddenly (and apparently inadvertently on the author's part) becomes less real.

The three unsuccessful works include *The Quick and the Dead,* a spoof ghost story and fantasy of serio-comic realism, involving among other things the amorous relations of the dead in Limbo, the suffering and repentance of ghosts (a somewhat Golding-like concept), with significance, apparently, but the coy handling of its basic situation makes for heavy reading. Still harder to read, but even more significant, is *Inner Circle* in which a three-layered story of Surface (the far future), Underground (present-day sub-Firbankian London), and Sky (a version of the Eden story), is held together by repeated "circle" and "underground" image patterns, and by analogous destinies. The themes and point-of-view games again make it seem almost like a collaboration between Golding, Burgess, and Arthur C. Clarke. Peterkiewicz's most recent novel, *Green Flows the Bile* is as tastelessly affected a social satire as its title would suggest. It recounts the last journey together of two "fellow-travellers" (in all senses), the Secretary, a "political gigolo," and his employer, the "senior prophet of the age . . . the travelling peace salesman." The comic travelogue is passable in places, but the political satire is either painfully obvious or intensely private; the two pitfalls that await the topical *roman à clef* have caught Peterkiewicz this time.

Peterkiewicz's heroes are almost all coyly hollow semi-comic shadow-men, pretending to contain abysses and seeking with morose jocularity for an "identity" to which they are fundamentally indifferent. Their human relationships are sketched with equal shallowness. Even the intrigues are lower Greeneland, territory more powerfully explored by Burgess, though at times Peterkiewicz is clearly aiming for the playful, complex "meanings" of a Chesterton, or a Woolf (*Orlando*), or a Nabokov, or for the light, horrid satire of a Waugh (*Scott-King's Modern Europe*). Stage metaphors, mirrors, masks, costumes, photographs, cute but pallid versions of

Nabokovian artifices, crowd the pages of *Isolation,* in which mock-pornography and reciprocal voyeuristic spyings, slowly building up a posthumous portrait, bring to mind *Lolita* (courteously, or perhaps coincidentally, acknowledged in a parrot of that name) or *The Real Life of Sebastian Knight.* These are samples of tone, not assertions of source; but even the best of Peterkiewicz's work is marred by hearing continually whispered chords made up of the murmurs of other men's voices, almost as if he were unwilling to hear his own voice. His real talent for language and comedy is almost swamped by his need to be terribly à la mode in these six novels, and it is a pity, for, to paraphrase a comment he makes on one of his characters, "his anonymous extraterritorial aura predicts at every step a possible eruption of personality."

It may be that, for all the polished virtues and assurance of his better novels, Peterkiewicz will be remembered longest and known most widely for his critical essays and anthologies, and for his book *The Other Side of Silence,* in which he sensitively discusses some intricacies of modern literature and places Polish literature in their context. One would like, however, to have as well his views on his own Polish contemporaries, who are giving us one of the most flourishing of modern minor literatures. Perhaps in his criticism he has more truly earned the right than he has in his fiction, to the inevitable, and specious, comparison with Conrad, that other Polish man of letters who turned himself, in adult life, and not without success, into an English writer.

—Patricia Merivale

PETERS, Elizabeth. *See* **MERTZ, Barbara.**

PETERS, Ellis. *See* **PARGETER, Edith (Mary).**

PETRAKIS, Harry Mark

Nationality: American. **Born:** St. Louis, Missouri, 5 June 1923. **Education:** The University of Illinois, Urbana, 1940-41. **Family:** Married Diane Perparos in 1945; three sons. **Career:** Has worked in steelmills, and as a real estate salesman, truck driver, and sales correspondent. Since 1960 freelance writer and lecturer. Taught at the Indiana University Writers Conference, Bloomington, 1964-65, 1970, 1974; McGuffey Visiting Lecturer, Ohio University, Athens, 1971; writer-in-residence, Chicago Public Library, 1976-77, and for the Chicago Board of Education, 1978-80; taught at Illinois Wesleyan University, Bloomington, 1978-79, Ball State University, Muncie, Indiana, 1978 and 1980, University of Wisconsin, Rhinelander, 1978-80, and University of Rochester, New York, 1979-80; Nikos Kazantzakis Professor, San Francisco State University, 1992. **Awards:** *Atlantic* Firsts award, 1957; Benjamin

Franklin citation, 1957; Friends of American Writers award, 1964; Friends of Literature award, 1964; Carl Sandburg award, 1983. D.H.L.: University of Illinois, 1971; Governors State University, Park Forest South, Illinois, 1980; Hellenic College, Brookline, Massachusetts, 1984. L.H.D.: Roosevelt University, Chicago, 1987. **Address:** 80 East Road, Dune Acres, Chesterton, Indiana 46304, U.S.A.

PUBLICATIONS

Novels

Lion at My Heart. Boston, Little Brown, and London, Gollancz, 1959.
The Odyssey of Kostas Volakis. New York, McKay, 1963.
A Dream of Kings. New York, McKay, 1966; London, Barker, 1967.
In the Land of Morning. New York, McKay, 1973.
The Hour of the Bell. New York, Doubleday, 1976; London, Severn House, 1986.
Nick the Greek. New York, Doubleday, 1979; London, New English Library, 1980.
Days of Vengeance. New York, Doubleday, 1983; London, Sphere, 1985.
Ghost of the Sun. New York, St. Martin's Press, 1990.

Short Stories

Pericles on 31st Street. Chicago, Quadrangle, 1965.
The Waves of Night and Other Stories. New York, McKay, 1969.
A Petrakis Reader. New York, Doubleday, 1978.
Collected Stories. Chicago, Lake View Press, 1987.

Plays

Screenplays: *A Dream of Kings,* with Ian Hunter, 1969; *In the Land of Morning,* 1974; *Ghost of the Sun,* with John Petrakis, 1994.

Television Plays: *Pericles on 31st Street,* with Sam Peckinpah, from the story by Petrakis, and *The Judge,* with Bruce Geller (both in *Dick Powell Show*), 1961-62; *The Blue Hotel,* from the story by Stephen Crane, 1978; *Song of Songs,* with John Petrakis, from the story by Petrakis, 1994.

Other

The Founder's Touch: The Life of Paul Galvin of Motorola. New York, McGraw Hill, 1965.
Stelmark: A Family Recollection (autobiography). New York, McKay, 1970.
Reflections: A Writer's Life, A Writer's Work. Chicago, Lake View Press, 1983.

*

Critical Studies: In *Old Northwest* (Oxford, Ohio), December 1976; interview in *Chicago Review,* Winter 1977; *Hellenes and Hellions* by Alexander Karanikas, Urbana, University of Illinios Press, 1981.

Harry Mark Petrakis comments:

(1991) My task now as I reach the threshold of 70 (how swiftly a lifetime has passed) is to find that language born of the years I have lived that expresses my vision now, a language that belongs to a mature age.

What I feel now is gratefulness because from an early age I was allowed to discover what I wished to do. For all the insecurities, my vocation has never failed to provide me those moments, however rare, when I could say with a figure in an old Greek chorus, "still there surges within me a singing magic."

*   *   *

In a book of personal recollections, *Stelmark,* Harry Mark Petrakis confirms what the reader of his novels would guess: that Petrakis is the son of Greek immigrants to the United States. He is in fact a second generation man who is intent on estimating the meaning of his presence in a country that is far from the Crete of his ancestors. To the territory of South Chicago, Petrakis's father, a Greek Orthodox priest, brought the recollections of a strange and noble sort of life where poverty was the foreground of an existence lived in an awesome setting of mountains and an equally demanding texture of ancient custom and suffering. As a young man, Petrakis was impressed by the interplay of his inheritance and the sections of American culture that he came into contact with in the land of promise: the narrow opportunities of a great and indifferent city, the materialism of Midwestern life as the immigrants encountered it and the continuation of the pride and violence that crossed the Atlantic with the Greek immigrants. It is this basic contrast between America as dreamed in the Cretan valleys and America as experienced by an ethnic minority that gives Petrakis his subject.

It is a subject full of challenges to Petrakis's novelistic imagination. And that imagination is equal to the passions, the disappointments, and the envies of the newcomers among whom, as a mediator and creator, Petrakis has lived his artistic life. He has created a striking company of persons who are, as Kurt Vonnegut has observed, at least 14 feet tall. These persons are swept by passions that are awesome when they are compared with the feebler desires and lesser dignities of men and women who have had several generations to adapt to the conditions of American life. The male figures still know the Greek versions of *omertà,* the Sicilian code of honor. These men act on the basis of personal pride and have loyalties that bind them less to American society than to family and a few close acquaintances. They have a sentimental vision of the cruel and impoverished land they—or their parents—fled. There is a dual center to their lives. One center is the church, whose ministers they respect, but whose teachings they put aside as having little to do with the lives of Greeks in South Chicago. The other center, more compulsive for them, is the world of cheap restaurants, backroom gambling dens that are full of con-men and bookies, and seedy offices above grocery stores where, as in *A Dream of Kings,* palms are read and advice is given to clients who do not know where to turn in a society that has scant tolerance for new arrivals. This male world has, in large part, a cold indifference for wives and mistresses; women are tolerated because men must have sons or because sexual desires must find expression. Sincere and deep affection is known to some of the men, as in *The Odyssey of Kostas Volakis.* But even so, the hopes of women remain alien to male concerns and are seldom respected or shared.

Mention of particular novels fills out this general description. *Lion at My Heart,* Petrakis's first novel, rehearses the fortunes of an immigrant household made up of a father and two sons. The father, with pride and suspicion, watches over the education and the marriages of his two sons, esteeming the son who takes a Greek wife and repudiating the son who marries "outside." A priest, a familiar figure in the novels, intervenes to mollify the father's harshness. *The Odyssey of Kostas Volakis* tells a similar story. Kostas is a young Cretan man who married a slightly older woman for her dowry, which pays for the passage to America. The novel traces stages in Kostas's adjustment to his new land: his struggle as a restaurant owner, his overcoming of his illiteracy, and—most important—his final forgiveness of his murderer-son who has disgraced his family.

A Dream of Kings explores a slightly higher social level and tells of the life of Masoukas the palm-reader and consultant, half charlatan and half-concerned adviser, by turns a compulsive gambler and adulterer. But Masoukas's dreams are fixed on an ailing son, for whose cure everything must be sacrificed. A journey to the sacred land of Greece will restore the health of the child and, perhaps, of the father. In another novel with a Chicago setting, *In the Land of Morning,* Petrakis moves into the post-Vietnam American world where the shock of a veteran's return is gradually merged with the ongoing tumult of life in the community. All this is a passionate and sad human encounter which the reader can find elsewhere in Petrakis, as in the collections of short stories, *Pericles on 31st Street* and *The Waves of Night.* Petrakis circles back to such themes—Greeks in a strange land—in *Nick the Greek.* Here the hero, Nick Dandalos, comes to the United States in the 1920s and allows himself to be drawn into the gambling life of Chicago, all at the cost of a sound future and a happy love affair. Particularly strong are the gambling scenes which take readers back to a distant time in the Greek community.

A bit to one side is *The Hour of the Bell.* This novel is an account of the revolution that commenced in Greece in 1820 when a confused but finally successful revolt against Turkish power began. Instead of finding the usual cultural enclave in South Chicago, the reader moves back and forth over the tumultuous Greek landscape, which is seen through various eyes: those of military leaders, some savage, some resigned to years of violence; those of a priest who respects the humanity of the slaughtered Turks; and those of an educated young man who is trying to write the history of the confusion that surrounds him. With his usual power, Petrakis, as it were, adds the completing piece to the Greek-American puzzle that is his concern. *The Hour of the Bell* is the "explanation" of the pride and the harsh tauntings and the intermittent tenderness that the novels about South Chicago record.

It is a record that is made up of prose of varying textures: realistic and poetically fierce by turns. The result is an indispensable report and also an imaginative world that takes its place along with the works of fiction—Chekhov's and others—that, Petrakis tells us, used to make him weep as a youth.

—Harold H. Watts

PETRY, Ann (Lane)

Nationality: American. **Born:** Old Saybrook, Connecticut, 12 October 1908. **Education:** Connecticut College of Pharmacy (now University of Connecticut School of Pharmacy), 1928-31, Ph.G.

1931; Columbia University, New York, 1943-44. **Family:** Married George D. Petry in 1938; one daughter. **Career:** Pharmacist, James Pharmacy, Old Saybrook and Old Lyme, Connecticut, 1931-38; writer and reporter, *Amsterdam News,* New York, 1938-41; women's editor, *People's Voice,* New York, 1941-44; visiting professor of English, University of Hawaii, Honolulu, 1974-75. Secretary, Authors League of America, 1960. **Awards:** Houghton Mifflin Literary fellowship, 1946; National Endowment for the Arts grant, 1977. D.Litt.: Suffolk University, Boston, 1983; University of Connecticut, Storrs, 1988; L.H.D.: Mount Holyoke College, South Hadley, Massachusetts, 1989. **Agent:** Russell and Volkening Inc., 50 West 29th Street, New York, New York 10001. **Address:** 113 Old Boston Post Road, Old Saybrook, Connecticut 06475, U.S.A.

PUBLICATIONS

Novels

The Street. Boston, Houghton Mifflin, 1946; London, Joseph, 1947.
Country Place. Boston, Houghton Mifflin, 1947; London, Joseph, 1948.
The Narrows. Boston, Houghton Mifflin, 1951; London, Gollancz, 1954.

Short Stories

Miss Muriel and Other Stories. Boston, Houghton Mifflin, 1971.

Other (for children)

The Drugstore Cat. New York, Crowell, 1949.
Harriet Tubman, Conductor on the Underground Railroad. New York, Crowell, 1955; as *The Girl Called Moses: The Story of Harriet Tubman,* London, Methuen, 1960.
Tituba of Salem Village. New York, Crowell, 1964.
Legends of the Saints. New York, Crowell, 1970.

*

Bibliography: *Ann Petry: A Bio-Bibliography* by Hazel Arnett Ervin, New York, Hall, 1993.

Manuscript Collection: Mugar Memorial Library, Boston University.

Critical Studies: *Black on White: A Critical Study of Writing by American Negroes* by David Littlejohn, New York, Grossman, 1966; *Interviews with Black Writers* edited by John O'Brien, New York, Liveright, 1973.

Ann Petry comments:
(1991) I write short stories, novels, books for children and young people. I vary what I write, even the style, but the underlying theme deals with race relations in the U.S.A.

*   *   *

Ann Petry has written three novels for adults, *The Street, Country Place,* and *The Narrows.* Her short stories of the early 1940s in *The Crisis* and *Phylon,* as well as more recent fiction in *Redbook* and the *New Yorker,* also merit attention. "On Saturday the Siren Sounds at Noon" began her career: its reception encouraged her to write *The Street.* "Like a Winding Sheet" was chosen for *The Best American Short Stories of 1946.* "Solo on the Drums," appearing in *'47 Magazine of the Year,* has a lyrical anguish that reflects her novels in theme and style.

The Street offers more than just another example of environmental determinism overshadowed by its precursor, *Native Son.* True, it opens with "a cold November wind" on 116th Street in Harlem that "did everything it could to discourage the people walking along the street" and closes with "the grime and the garbage and the ugliness" of that street as the defeated, pretty heroine-turned-murderess flees by train. Boots Smith, unscrupulous in avoiding a return to "a life of saying 'yes sir' to every white bastard who had the price of a Pullman ticket," is an old Bigger Thomas, with cash, a luxurious car, and political connections. Authorial digressions that rationalize Lutie Johnson's fear of the street—"an evil father and a vicious mother" to black children like her Bub—replace Boris Max's 16-page courtroom speech that blames a racist environment for Bigger's dilemma. Petry's own life had verified the glum details of *The Street,* but her feminine and racial perceptions of those domestic tragedies that cluster in black slums gave psychological sharpness to passages still alive with meaning. The Connecticut middle class with its insulting generalizations about black women, the unemployed Harlem men reduced to loitering and philandering and desertion, the black man with a resentment of his oppressors "so bad and so deep that I wouldn't lift a finger to help 'em stop Germans or nobody else," the tenement radios blaring to kill the feel of unbearable misery, "carrying pain and a shrinking from pain"— all these are realistic types that advance the author's theme of entrapment and resignation. The sometimes excessive description and the rather contrived plights of Lutie and Bub are redeemed by a sympathy that humanizes even the maniacally obsessed William Jones and the repulsively scarred Mrs. Hedges.

The ugliness of a small-town New England white environment, personified early by the scandalmongering cab driver "the Weasel," permeates *Country Place.* The conflict sustained between past and present is moral in the frustrations of returning war veteran Johnnie Roane and his faithless wife Glory, and philosophical in the insistence of Mrs. Gramby that her middle-aged son Mearns uphold a gracious tradition beyond his powers and desires. Sensitive to fusions of imagery, metaphor, and symbol, the author has Johnnie struggle past storm-felled trees to reach Ed Barrell's cabin and suffer disillusion in Glory's infidelity. The long storm, like the rain in which Johnnie walks after his first doubts about his wife, is emblematic of the turbulence of climactic changes forced upon the main characters. The thematic absorption of disenchantment into thinner but stronger life is presaged in Johnnie's decision not to strangle his wife and, later not to kill her lover; it is advanced—through an equally distressing decision by Mrs. Gramby—by his opportunity to become an artist in New York. *Country Place,* marred like *The Street* by seemingly thesis-conjured death at the end, continues Petry's attack against a cash-and-carry society hostile to moral beauty.

The Narrows, titled after its setting, the black neighborhood in Monmouth, Connecticut, not only has a conscience-gripping theme, but is remarkable for its vivid array of minor characters. Sexually radiant, blues-singing Mamie Powther; the frightful amputee, Cat Jimmie, who speeds on his homemade cart to peer under the dresses of women; Cesar the Writing Man, who records his sonorous

prophecies on the sidewalk with colored chalk; and Weak Knees, with his collapsible limbs and innumerable gestures and mutterings ("Get away, Eddie, get away!") at the ghost of his best friend— these and others unforgettably enliven Dumble Street and the foggy dock of the River Wye. The novel is about love and its betrayal. Abbie Crunch lets puritanical snobbishness fatally betray her love for her husband, then lets grief betray her love for their adopted child, Link. Later, Link scarifices his love for rich, white Camilo Treadway to black pride, while she gives in to jealousy and racism. And mistakenly jealous little Malcolm Powther, having no manhood himself, betrays that of Link. "All of us," Abbie concludes, "had a hand in [Link's death], we all reacted violently . . . because he was colored and she was white." Almost every character applies to himself the author's repeated refrain: "I, executioner." *The Narrows* is attuned to the 1970s in other racial themes, and it thoughtfully views the responsibilities that attend power and artistic talent. Flashbacks are excessive, sometimes confusing; but stream of consciousness passages are skillfully written, and the leaven of humor appears.

The craftsmanship, social truth, and humanity of Petry's fiction deserve wider recognition. Her basically tragic vision, linked in some way with themes of Lorraine Hansberry and Ralph Ellison, could culminate, if she produces more, in a distinguished, comprehensive novel.

—James A. Emanuel

PHILLIPS, Caryl

Nationality: British. **Born:** St. Kitts, West Indies, 13 March 1958; brought to England in 1958. **Education:** Schools in Leeds to 1974, and in Birmingham, 1974-76; Queen's College, Oxford, 1976-79, B.A. (honors) 1979. **Career:** Founding chairman, 1978, and artistic director, 1979, *Observer* Festival of Theatre, Oxford; resident dramatist, The Factory Arts Centre, London 1981-82; writer-in-residence, Mysore, India, 1987, and Stockholm University, Sweden, 1989. Visiting lecturer, University of Ghana, 1990; visiting lecturer, University of Poznan, Poland, 1991; visiting writer, Humber College, Toronto, 1992-93; visiting professor of English, New York University, 1993; writer-in-residence, National Institute of Education, Singapore, 1994; writing instructor, Arvon Foundation, England, since 1983; visiting writer, 1990-92, writer-in-residence since 1992, Amherst College, Massachusetts. Member of the Board of Directors, Bush Theatre, London, 1985-88; member, British Film Institute Production Board, London, 1985-88; honorary senior member, the University of Kent, England, 1985; board member, *The Caribbean Writer,* St. Croix, 1989. Consulting editor, Faber, Inc., 1992-94; contributing editor, *Bomb Magazine,* New York, 1993; consultant editor, Graywolf Press, Minneapolis, 1994. Lives in London. **Awards:** Arts Council of Great Britain Bursary in Drama, 1984; British Council Fiftieth Anniversary fellowship, 1984; Malcolm X Prize for Literature, 1985; Martin Luther King Memorial prize, 1987; Guggenheim fellowship, 1992; *Sunday Times* (London) Young Writer of the Year, 1992; Rockefeller Foundation Bellagio residency, 1994; James Tait Black Memorial prize, 1994; Lannan Literary award, 1994. **Agent:** Anthony Harwood,

Curtis Brown Ltd., Haymarket House, 28/29 Haymarket, London
SW1Y 4SP, England.

PUBLICATIONS

Novels

Higher Ground. London, Viking, 1986; New York, Viking, 1989.
The Final Passage. London, Faber, 1985; New York, Penguin, 1990.
A State of Independence. London, Faber, and New York, Farrar
    Straus, 1986.
Cambridge. London, Bloomsbury, 1991; New York, Knopf, 1992.
Crossing the River. London, Bloomsbury, and New York, Knopf,
    1994.

Plays

Strange Fruit (produced Sheffield, 1980; London, 1982).
    Ambergate, Derbyshire, Amber Lane Press, 1981.
Where There Is Darkness (produced London, 1982). Ambergate,
    Derbyshire, Amber Lane Press, 1982.
The Shelter (produced London, 1983). Oxford, Amber Lane Press,
    1984; New York, Applause, 1986.
The Wasted Years (broadcast 1984). In *Best Radio Plays of 1984,*
    London, Methuen, 1985.

Screenplay: *Playing Away,* 1986.

Radio Plays: *The Wasted Years,* 1984; *Crossing the River,* 1986;
    The Prince of Africa, 1987; *Writing Fiction,* 1991.

Television Plays: *The Hope and the Glory,* 1984; *The Record,* 1984;
    Lost in Music, 1985.

Other

The European Tribe (travel). London, Faber, and New York, Farrar
    Straus, 1987.

*

Critical Studies: "Caryl Phillips Talks to Linton Kwesi Johnson"
in *The Race Today Review* (London), 1987; "Caryl Phillips: Interview" by Kay Saunders, *Kunapipi* (Denmark), vol. 9, no. 1, 1987;
"Interview with Caryl Phillips" by Frank Birbalsingh, in *Displaced
Persons* edited by Kirsten Holst Peterson and Anna Rutherford,
Denmark, Dangeroo Press, 1988; "The Slippery Bounds of Somewhere Else: Caryl Phillips's *The European Tribe*" by Socorro Suarez
in *Passage to Somewhere Else* edited by D. McDermott and S.
Ballyn, Barcelona, PPU, 1988; "Caryl Phillips" by Mario Relich
in *Contemporary Writers: The British Council,* London, 1989; "On
Dislocation and Connectedness in Caryl Phillips's Writing" by H.
Okazaki, in *The Literary Criterion* (Mysore, India), vol. 26, no. 3,
1991; "The Fictional Works of Caryl Phillips" by Charles P. Sarvan
and Hasan Marhama, in *World Literature Today,* vol. 65, no. 1,
Winter 1991; "An Interview With Caryl Phillips" by Graham Swift,
in *Kunapipi* (Denmark), vol. 13, no. 3, 1991; "Worlds Within: An
Interview with Caryl Phillips," in *Callaloo,* vol. 14, no. 3, Fall
1991; "Voyages into Otherness: Cambridge and Lucy" by Benedicte

Ledent, in *Kunapipi* (Denmark), vol. 14, no. 2, 1992; "Caryl
Phillips" by Benedicte Ledent, in *Post-War Literatures in English*
(Belgium, University of Liege), March 1993; "Historical Fiction
and Fictional History: Caryl Phillips's *Cambridge*" by Evelyn
O'Callaghan, in *Journal of Commonwealth Literature,* vol. 29, no.
2, 1993; "The Unkindness of Strangers" by Nadar Alexander
Mousavizadeh, in *Transition,* issue 61, 1994; "Caryl Phillips," in
Current Biography, vol. 55, no. 7, 1994.

Caryl Phillips comments:

My dominant theme has been cultural and social dislocation, most
commonly associated with a migratory experience.

*   *   *

Caryl Phillips writes novels of disinheritance, of rootlessness
and impotence. They are works concerned with the human cost of
inhumanity and ignorance, and in which the price is largely, but
not uniquely, paid by black men and women. Phillips returns consistently to the themes of imposed or motiveless migration, of nostalgia for a homeland which does not exist, of betrayal and emptiness. His early novels depict loveless worlds, where characters are
torn from or never know their family, where new loves and friendships stagnate, or die, or never begin. Yet, in *Crossing the River* of
1994, Phillips explores the possibility of love to redeem even the
most desolate life and marks a shift from his earlier despondency.

In Phillips's early novels, rootless and disoriented characters
search for or imagine their identities. In *The Final Passage,* the
first and bleakest novel, Leila is a mulatto living on a Caribbean
island in the 1950s. Culturally disenfranchised by mixed parentage, she imagines her parents other than they are in order to find
her own identity. She dreams of her absent white father, perceiving
him a financial benefactor and believing him real in order to discover herself. Yet Leila's mother, herself betrayed in youth by an
incestuous rape, knows not nor cares which of her "lovers" fathered Leila, discerning instead that the child "belonged to all of
them and none of them." Leila craves her mother's friendship and,
although she does not doubt her mother's love, she is in truth "not
to know that her mother had never wanted a child." The love this
mother eventually gives is begrudging, bestowed as a reward for
the direction given to her life by motherhood. It is not a love to
cherish nor one from which to build self-knowledge. Leila is eventually granted an identity in London, a dismal place where the rivers "were like dirty brown lines, full of empty bottles and cigarette
ends, cardboard boxes and greying suds of pollution." Color is her
identity and one which affords her only abuse, misuse or, at best,
condescension. It proves an unbearable alternative to her island non-
self and Leila finally allows life to dribble away.

In "Heartland," the first chapter in *Higher Ground,* the narrator
loses his identity by betraying his own people. Using his grasp of
English, he collaborates with slave traders, acting as interpreter between them and village head men who part with their human future
in exchange for a few trinkets. In his effort to evade physical bondage, he feigns assimilation with Englishness, apparently understanding English behavior better than that of his own people. He notices
"inner stillness . . . as a trait" of his native kin but not one with
which he now identifies, and announces proudly that he has "finally mastered the art of forgetting—of murdering the memory" in
order to leave his former self behind.

But his very language does not ring true. He is certainly clever,
using English as a tool for discourse and imagery. Yet it is a dis-

jointed use, clipped and unnatural. During the story's course he perceives reality. He learns that he is indeed "held captive" though his arms and legs move with deceptive freedom. Betrayed by a soldier "friend" for having a forbidden woman in his room, he is thrown into the bonds he had feared, but which ultimately release him to his brotherhood and his identity.

In Phillips's work, identity is also something which may be bestowed, changed, or taken away by the powerful. The powerless are either enticed, like Leila, from their only known home by some nebulous hope of change, or by the false promise of education (*A State of Independence*). The powerful may rip the impotent from their homes in a callous and cynical bid to perpetuate their own society and at the intentional expense of another. This is the fate of all four characters in *Higher Ground* and *Cambridge*. The loss of identity in this way is then compounded by the imposition of new names. In *Higher Ground,* Irena, an escapee from Nazism's elitist brutality, finds her name stolen by ignorance—an ignorance which is certain of its own precision: "It was now that the Irene-Irina-Irene-Irina-Irene-Irina-Irene problem would begin for English people were too lazy to bend their mouths or twist their tongues into unfamiliar shapes." This ignorance attempts to force her divorce with a past which she cannot, in fact, let go. She is a misfit, and turns in on herself, confused between past and present, and sure only that she has no future. Cambridge suffers three changes to his name. Two of these, Tom and Cambridge, are the products of a smug mid-18th century (by which time slavery has been abolished in law, but not in practice). Cambridge is twice torn from home and family, one African and one English, where he could act as an individual. His naming at these points resembles that of a dog, the single name pointedly affirming a position of inferiority which his masters intend to maintain.

In England, Cambridge finds his true identity. As David Henderson, a name bestowed without cynicism, he embraces Christianity. With a dearly loved white wife at his side, he is accepted, if begrudgingly, into society, and on an evangelical tour of England he encounters a merchant who "was commonly very pleasant to both my wife and myself, directing us with witty turns and fanciful stories, but never to the prejudice of religion or good taste." The merchant, an African trader with a retinue of servants, is surely amusing himself. But there is a glimpse that in time, David Henderson might achieve a social integration that would affirm his own confidence in this identity.

But a loving relationship which might grant security cannot last. David Henderson's wife dies in childbirth, and with her dies Henderson's tenuous credibility. Society will not allow him to perpetuate the myth of equality and, in trying to extend his mission to Africa, he is again taken captive to become the subjugated Cambridge.

Phillips's novel of 1994, *Crossing the River,* reworks these characteristic themes: slavery, identity, and desolation. But the scope is wider and more ambitious, and it offers a conclusion uncharacteristic of Phillips's previous work. *Crossing the River* concerns the selling into slavery of three children—Nash, Martha and Travis—by their father, when his crops fail and he is left with nothing. Their journey—the eponymous crossing of the river—takes them across space and time. Nash spends his slavery in America, undergoing a rigorous Christian education, and is returned to Africa by his "father," Edward Williams, under the Auspices of the American Colonisation Society, to assist in the Christian mission. Martha emerges in Virginia as a slave of the Hoffmans. When their financial difficulties make it impossible to keep her, Martha travels west-

ward in search of the daughter from whom she was separated at an auction. Travis appears as an American GI stationed "somewhere in England" during World War II. His relationship with a local girl, Joyce, results in a child that Joyce is forced to give away. Their marriage is cut short by Travis's premature death.

The anomalies in space and time between the characters suggest that Phillips uses them to bear witness to the *legacy* of slavery, the many generations whose lives were shaped by that initial crossing of the river. Nash, Martha, and Travis are individual figures through whom the experiences of many lives are inferred. Their father is the voice of 18th-century Africa, and we join him in watching how those taken from him survive the fracturing of lives by sinking "hopeful roots into difficult soil." Their legacy is one of pain and desolation, but most important in this novel is the capacity for love and survival in times of immense difficulty. Nash rejects both the values of Christianity and the American dream, but takes what is positive from his education to contend for the rights of "the coloured man" in Liberia. Martha's quest for her lost family is achieved in her mind only, as she dies freezing in a doorway, dreaming of their reunion. But on her journey she has encountered people willing to help her, and in her final moments she is received into the care of a stranger. Although Travis is killed in action, his son, Greer, is emotionally and compellingly reunited with his mother in 1963.

Crossing the River is ultimately about the pain involved in revisiting the past, but also discovering there the persistence of positive values. It searches the centuries for brief moments of altruism and love. They may be exceptional and rare, but to ignore them is to give a distorted account of history. The children's father celebrates in the novel's final sentence how Nash, Martha, and Travis "arrived on the far bank of the river, loved." Such an affirmative ending makes the novel Phillips's bravest to date, and strikes a tentative note of hope absent from *Cambridge*.

Cambridge and *Crossing the River* are Phillips's most effective novels by far. While *Higher Ground* is thematically complete, it is a collection of fragmented stories, and indeed, both *The Final Passage* and *A State of Independence* read as long short stories rather than novels. The success of *Cambridge* is ensured by Phillips's use of narrators, first the mannered daughter of an English landowner and second, Cambridge himself. *Crossing the River* extends Phillips's skill in modulating between narrative voices across time and space without sacrificing thematic sophistication or becoming unnecessarily convoluted. Also a successful playwright, Phillips writes with ease in this form and certainly to great effect.

—Pat Gordon-Smith, updated by John McLeod

PHILLIPS, Jayne Anne

Nationality: American. **Born:** Buckhannon, West Virginia, 19 July 1952. **Education:** West Virginia University, Morgantown, B.A. 1974; University of Iowa, Iowa City, M.F.A. 1978. **Family:** Married Mark Brian Stockman in 1985; one son and two stepsons. **Career:** Taught at Humboldt State University, Arcata, California, Williams College, Williamstown, Massachusetts, Boston University, from 1982, and Brandeis University, Waltham, Massachusetts, 1986-87. **Awards:** Pushcart prize, 1977, for *Sweethearts,* 1979, for short stories "Home" and Lechery," 1983, for short story "How Mickey Made It"; National Endowment for the Arts grant, 1977,

1984; Coordinating Council of Literary Magazines Fels award, 1978, for *Sweethearts;* St. Lawrence award, 1978, for *Counting;* American Academy Kaufman award, 1980, for *Black Tickets;* O. Henry award, 1980, for "Snow"; Bunting Institute fellowship, Radcliffe College, 1981. **Agent:** International Creative Management, 40 West 57th Street, New York, New York 10019, U.S.A.

PUBLICATIONS

Novel

Machine Dreams. New York, Dutton, and London, Faber, 1984.
Shelter. Boston, Houghton Mifflin, 1994; London, Faber, 1995.

Short Stories

Sweethearts. Carrboro, North Carolina, Truck Press, 1976.
Counting. New York, Vehicle, 1978.
Black Tickets. New York, Delacorte Press, 1979; London, Allen Lane, 1980.
How Mickey Made It. St. Paul, Bookslinger Press, 1981.
Fast Lanes. New York, Vehicle, 1984; London, Faber, 1987.

Uncollected Short Stories

"Something That Happened," in *The Best American Short Stories 1979,* edited by Joyce Carol Oates and Shannon Ravenel. Boston, Houghton Mifflin, 1979.
"Bess," in *Esquire* (New York), August 1984.

*   *   *

Black Tickets, Jayne Anne Phillips's first major collection of short fiction, is a curious anthology, both irritating and impressive. Many of the stories end too quickly to permit a conventional readerly engagement. Sixteen of the twenty-seven pieces are really sketches rather than stories—a few paragraphs of intensely wrought language and emphatic image. Primarily about love, alienated sexuality, and the street worlds of destitution, prostitution, and drug addiction, these are best understood as exercises in voice. They suggest a remarkable invention and a drive to articulate what is usually muted or unsaid. In places, they are truly dazzling (see, for example, "Stripper," "Cheers," and "Happy"). But too often these compositions leave us with an impression of authorial self-consciousness, grotesqueness for its own sake. Phillips's more substantial achievements lie in some of the longer stories, where she seems less anxious to be poetic and more at ease with the rhythms of the lives she explores.

The best piece in the collection is "Home," a perfectly told story of complex family relationships. This wistful but pungent tale of mother-daughter empathy and disjunction focuses on the impasse at the heart of generational difference, as experienced by a rather ordinary but perceptive protagonist. In its telling, Phillips uses language that is modest and spare, appropriate to the commonplaces of familial suffering. Relations are drawn with a subtle counterpart, as when a daughter remarks, "It upsets my mother to see me naked, she looks at me so curiously, as though she didn't recognize my body," then later observes her mother: "She is so fragile, standing there, naked, with her small shoulders. Suddenly I am horribly frightened."

In the most effective stories (in addition to "Home," see "Souvenir" and "The Heavenly Animal"), Phillips slowly draws us down into the undertow of middle-class trauma—filial sexuality, divorce, gradual psychosis. The prose succeeds as we are pulled in by something beneath its surface.

With *Machine Dreams,* a full-length family chronicle, Phillips combines depth and resonance with the interest of alternating voices. The novel develops through a succession of storytellers whose narrative choices at first seem casual and unrelated. Autobiography, letters, and omniscient narration recount major and minor events in the history of the Hampson family through two generations, from the Depression to the early 1970s. The Hampsons, who live in a small town in West Virginia, lead apparently undistinguished lives—Jean and Mitch are unhappily married and just scraping by, Danner and her brother Billy share the usual childhood adventures and the indignities of adolescence. As representatives of any lower-middle-class American family of their time, these characters are familiar and conventional. But the varying inflections and mundane details of their stories, as they accumulate, suggest human experience that is profoundly troubling. What the storytellers reveal are affiliated tragedies of powerlessness, the psychic wounds of postwar American culture.

Throughout the narrative, Phillips contrasts the promise of fulfillment with the insufficient lives of people whose most powerful experiences are in some way tied to machines. Mitch's fascination with things mechanical, with the technological possibilities of his time, leads him to open a concrete plant which the local economy cannot support. Jean realizes her dream of higher education, but her schooling is joyless, prompted by the failure of her husband's factory and the subsequent misery of their family life. Longing for connection, both Billy and Danner learn a makeshift sexuality in the cramped, confined quarters of automobiles. Cars, trucks, planes, trains, televisions, and radios punctuate the most significant events in this novel—but subtly, so that their presence signifies without disruption. Technology is a means for marking frustrated human desire: "Fuck was the word written all over basement walls of the old school; it was scrawled even on the big round pipes that were too hot to touch. Scrawled with crayon that melted and left a bright wax thickness, then a pale stain after the janitor scraped the texture off. There were ghostly fucks every few feet along the round steaming pipes; an angry, clinched word, wild." Phillips's skillful meshing of the mechanical and the human culminates in her final, devastating chapters on Vietnam, in which she shows us the shattering of both machines and dreams and the awful impotence of what survives.

Machine Dreams is not a flawless work. The first half of the book moves slowly, and one chapter repeats information unnecessarily. But the varying voices of the Hampson family, rich with what cannot be spoken, are moving and provide an effective commentary on our most destructive cultural myths. Phillips's first novel is a good one.

—Janis Butler Holm

PIERCY, Marge

Nationality: American. **Born:** Detroit, Michigan, 31 March 1936. **Education:** The University of Michigan, Ann Arbor (Hopwood award, 1956, 1957), A.B. 1957; Northwestern University, Evanston,

Illinois, M.A. 1958. **Family:** Married Ira Wood (third marriage) in 1982. **Career:** Instructor, Indiana University, Gary, 1960-62; poet-in-residence, University of Kansas, Lawrence, 1971; visiting lecturer, Thomas Jefferson College, Grand Valley State Colleges, Allendale, Michigan, 1975; visiting faculty, Women's Writers' Conference, Cazenovia College, New York, 1976, 1978, 1980; staff member, Fine Arts Work Center, Provincetown, Massachusetts, 1976-77; writer-in-residence, College of the Holy Cross, Worcester, Massachusetts, 1976; Butler Professor of Letters, State University of New York, Buffalo, 1977; Elliston Professor of Poetry, University of Cincinnati, 1986. Member of the board of directors, 1982-85, and of the advisory board since 1985, Coordinating Council of Literary Magazines; since 1988 poetry editor, *Tikkun* magazine, Oakland, California. **Awards:** Borestone Mountain award, 1968, 1974; National Endowment for the Arts grant, 1978; Rhode Island School of Design Faculty Association medal, 1985; Carolyn Kizer prize, 1986, 1990; Shaeffer Eaton-PEN New England award, 1989; New England Poetry Club Golden Rose, 1990. **Agent:** Lois Wallace, Wallace Literary Agency, 177 East 70th Street, New York, New York 10021. **Address:** Box 1473, Wellfleet, Massachusetts 02667, U.S.A.

PUBLICATIONS

Novels

Going Down Fast. New York, Simon and Schuster, 1969.
Dance the Eagle to Sleep. New York, Doubleday, 1970; London, W.H. Allen, 1971.
Small Changes. New York, Doubleday, 1973; London, Penguin, 1987.
Woman on the Edge of Time. New York, Knopf, 1976; London, Women's Press, 1979.
The High Cost of Living. New York, Harper, 1978; London, Women's Press, 1979.
Vida. New York, Summit, and London, Women's Press, 1980.
Braided Lives. New York, Summit, and London, Allen Lane, 1982.
Fly Away Home. New York, Summit, and London, Chatto and Windus, 1984.
Gone to Soldiers. New York, Summit, and London, Joseph, 1987.
Summer People. New York, Summit, and London, Joseph, 1989.
He, She and It. New York, Knopf, 1991; as *Body of Glass,* London, Joseph, 1992.
The Longings of Women. New York, Fawcett, and London, Joseph, 1994.

Uncollected Short Stories

"Crossing over Jordan," in *Transatlantic Review* (London), Fall 1966.
"Love Me Tonight, God," in *Paris Review,* Summer 1968.
"A Dynastic Encounter," in *Aphra* (New York) Spring 1970.
"And I Went into the Garden of Love," in *Off Our Backs* (Washington, D.C.), Summer 1971.
"Do You Love Me?," in *Second Wave* (Cambridge, Massachusetts), vol. 1, no. 4, 1972.
"The Happiest Day of a Woman's Life," in *Works in Progress 7* (New York), 1972.
"Somebody Who Understands You," in *Moving Out* (Detroit), vol. 2, no. 2, 1972.

"Marriage Is a Matter of Give and Take," in *Boston Phoenix,* 3 July and 10 July 1973.
"Little Sister, Cat and Mouse," in *Second Wave* (Cambridge, Massachusetts), Fall 1973.
"God's Blood," in *Anon,* no. 8, 1974.
"Like a Great Door Closing Suddenly," in *Detroit Discovery,* March-April 1974.
"The Retreat," in *Provincetown Poets* (Provincetown, Massachusetts), vol. 2, nos. 2-3, 1976.
"What Can Be Had," in *Chrysalis 4* (San Diego, California), 1977.
"The Cowbird in the Eagles' Nest," in *Maenad,* Fall 1980.
"I Will Not Describe What I Did," in *Mother Jones* (San Francisco), February-March 1982.
"Spring in the Arboretum," in *Michigan Quarterly Review* (Ann Arbor), Winter 1982.
"Of Chilblains and Rotten Rutabagas," in *Lilith* (New York), Winter-Spring 1985.

Play

The Last White Class: A Play About Neighborhood Terror, with Ira Wood (produced Northampton, Massachusetts, 1978). Trumansburg, New York, Crossing Press, 1980.

Poetry

Breaking Camp. Middletown, Connecticut, Wesleyan University Press, 1968.
Hard Loving. Middletown, Connecticut, Wesleyan University Press, 1969.
A Work of Artifice. Detroit, Red Hanrahan Press, 1970.
4-Telling, with others. Trumansburg, New York, Crossing Press, 1971.
When the Drought Broke. Santa Barbara, California, Unicorn Press, 1971.
To Be of Use. New York, Doubleday, 1973.
Living in the Open. New York, Knopf, 1976.
The Twelve-Spoked Wheel Flashing. New York, Knopf, 1978.
The Moon Is Always Female. New York, Knopf, 1980.
Circles on the Water: Selected Poems. New York, Knopf, 1982.
Stone, Paper, Knife. New York, Knopf, and London, Pandora Press, 1983.
My Mother's Body. New York, Knopf, and London, Pandora Press, 1985.
Available Light. New York, Knopf, and London, Pandora Press, 1988.
Mars and Her Children. New York, Knopf, 1992.
Eight Chambers of the Heart. London, Penguin, 1995.

Recordings: *Marge Piercy: Poems,* 1969; *Laying Down the Tower,* Black Box, 1973; *Reclaiming Ourselves,* 1973; *At the Core,* 1976; *Reading and Thoughts,* Everett Edwards, 1976; *At the Core,* Watershed, 1976.

Other

The Grand Coolie Damn. Boston, New England Free Press, 1970.
Parti-Colored Blocks for a Quilt. Ann Arbor, University of Michigan Press, 1982.
The Earth Shines Secretly: A Book of Days. Cambridge, Massachusetts, Zoland Press, 1990.

Editor, *Early Ripening: Young Women's Poetry Now.* London and New York, Pandora Press, 1987.

*

Bibliography: In *Contemporary American Women Writers: Narrative Strategies* edited by Catherine Rainwater and William J. Scheick, Lexington, University Press of Kentucky, 1985.

Manuscript Collection: Harlan Hatcher Graduate Library, University of Michigan, Ann Arbor.

Critical Studies: "Marge Piercy: A Collage" by Nancy Scholar Zee, in *Oyez Review* (Berkeley, California), vol. 9, no. 1, 1975; *Ways of Knowing: Critical Essays on Marge Piercy* edited by Sue Walker and Eugenie Hamner, Mobile, Alabama, Negative Capability Press, 1986; *The Repair of the World: The Novels of Marge Piercy* by Kerstin W. Shands, Connecticut, Greenwood, 1994.

Marge Piercy comments:

Each of my novels appears to me a different miniature world, in which the style, the language appropriate to the characters, is worked out of my understanding of them and their universe of action and discourse. My intention is always appropriateness, and when I do what is usually seen as "fine writing," I do my best to strike it out. My impulse to autobiography is given ample play in my poetry, and thus has little reason to shape my novels. My novels divide into those which are placed in the present; those which are placed in speculative time; and those which occur entirely, or largely, in the past. My interest is always centered on the results of choice through time.

I start with a theme, and then work through character. Fiction is as old a habit of our species as poetry. It goes back to telling a tale, the first perceptions of pattern, and fiction is still about pattern in human life. For me, writing fiction issues from the impulse to tell the story of people who deserve to have their lives revealed, examined, clarified, to people who deserve to read good stories. To find ourselves spoken for in art gives dignity to our pain, our anger, our lust, our losses. I have been particularly although not exclusively concerned with the choices open to—or perceived to be open to—women of various eras, races, and classes. I am one of the few contemporary American novelists consciously and constantly preoccupied with social class and the economic underpinnings of decision and consequence.

In the end, I suspect my novels find readers because they create full characters easy to enter, no matter how hard they might be for the reader to identify within actuality, and because I try to tell a good story.

*   *   *

Marge Piercy is (with Lisa Alther) one of the best known of that group of American women writers who have created popular fictions about the changing face of radical America, and, in particular, about changing perceptions of and about women. Piercy writes about, and on behalf of, radical political causes, but her main interest is in (and she is most interesting on) sexual politics. Taken together her novels offer a feminist's eye-view of American history from World War II (*Gone to Soldiers*), through the 1950s (*Braided Lives*) to the heady days of 1960s student activism and anti-Vietnam war campaigns (treated retrospectively in *Vida*), and the rais-

ing of consciousness of the women's movement of the late 1960s and 1970s (*The High Cost of Living, Small Changes,* and *Fly Away Home*). Her most recent novel, *Summer People,* is an affectionate (even self-indulgent) chronicle of a group of middle-aged people whose lives and values were shaped by the revolutions of the 1960s, and are now disturbed both by the passage of time and the more abrasive climate of the 1980s. At the very least these novels will provide the future social historian with an interesting perspective on radical chic and the countercultures of the mid-20th century. Indeed Piercy's novels are frequently quoted by feminists as documents in the history of the modern American women's movement. Among the most quoted in this context is *Small Changes,* which offers a guided tour of countercultural Boston as it charts the decline into marriage of the beautiful, clever, and independent Miriam, and the emergence of her friend Beth from an adolescent marriage into a new (consciousness-raised) sense of self.

These books are all loose baggy monsters, chunky blockbusters which mix together a variety of genres. Elements of the political thriller (*Vida*) are combined with love stories of various kinds. There are portraits of the artist at various stages of development (*Braided Lives* and *Summer People*), and stories of the late-adolescent quest for identity (*The High Cost of Living, Braided Lives,* and *Small Changes*). There are mystery, intrigue, alternative "lifestyles," and above all sex, lots of it in all sorts of combinations. Piercy is no stylist. For the most part these are chronicle novels whose formal inventiveness is restricted to the frequent use of the flashback. Her aim seems to be to recreate the world-as-it-was and to draw her readers into it. Occasionally there seems to be an ironic gap between the reader's perceptions and those of the characters about whom she is reading. This is sometimes the result of Piercy's satiric focus on the way we lived then—whether the "then" be the dark ages of the 1950s or the sexual revolution of the 1960s. Indeed some of the funniest (but also the most depressing) writing focuses on the elaborately entwined, and constantly changing, patterns of relationships in the omni-sexual post-1960s (pre-AIDS) world. Sometimes, however, the ironic distance appears to derive from the author's failure to offer a satirical or critical focus on her characters and their attitudes, which increasingly, especially in novels such as *Small Changes* and *Vida,* look dated and naive. Nevertheless, these last-mentioned novels which focus on 1960s radicalism and the women's movement, also give a very powerful sense of what it must have been like to be caught up in the excitement and confusions of those times.

There seems to be a general consensus that by far the most interesting and accomplished of Piercy's novels is one of her earliest creations, *Woman on the Edge of Time.* This book is usually grouped with other feminist utopian or dystopian fantasies such as Ursula K. Le Guin's *The Dispossessed* and *The Left Hand of Darkness,* Joanna Russ's *The Female Man,* Angela Carter's *The Passion of New Eve,* and Margaret Atwood's *The Handmaid's Tale. Woman on the Edge of Time* is the story of Connie Ramos, a 37-year-old poor, Mexican-American woman, one of the have-nots who is defeated and discarded by a society which is geared towards the needs and interests of the haves. Her lover is killed, her daughter is taken away from her "unstable" mother, and Connie is incarcerated in a bleak public mental hospital where (as the pathway to release) she is subjected to a mind-control experiment involving electronic implantations in the brain. Connie is, however, also a "catcher" who is able to mind-travel—under the guidance of her "natural" Luciente—from the confines of the "real" world of her hospital ward to the possible future world of Metapoisset, a new and better society. In Metapoisset the likenesses of Connie's lover, and her daughter Angelina live on in a new, fruitful life in a world of social and ecological harmony. The class and gender roles of Connie's America have been dissolved. These roles are simply not known in Metapoisset, where sexual relationships and the nuclear family have been replaced by a collectivism that respects and preserves the individual self. In short, Metapoisset reverses the values of the world that oppresses Connie and her kind in the present. The competitive individualism which is the creed of bourgeois America become the antivalues of Metapoisset, where notions of evil "center around power and greed—taking from other people their food, their liberty, their health, their land, their customs, their prides."

Woman on the Edge of Time finely counterpoints the utopianism of Metapoisset with the dystopian realism with which Connie's actual world is represented. Metapoisset is used to make a critique of modern America, but it is also offered as a vindication of the enabling power of fantasy. Connie's fantasy is not the infantile "womanish" regression that she herself suspects at the beginning of her period as a "catcher," but the vision of a new world of possibility which emphasizes human choice and agency. Like much contemporary feminist fantasy fiction *Woman on the Edge of Time* uses a science fiction genre to enact the vision of women overcoming oppressive social and psychological conditions by transcending both the physical and ideological constraints of patriarchal society. It is a profoundly disturbing, but also inspiriting novel.

—Lyn Pykett

PLANTE, David (Robert)

Nationality: American. **Born:** Providence, Rhode Island, 4 March 1940. **Education:** Boston College, 1957-59, 1960-61, B.A. in French 1961; University of Louvain, Belgium, 1959-60. **Career:** Teacher, English School, Rome, 1961-62; guidebook writer, New York, 1962-64; teacher, Boston School of Modern Languages, 1964-65, and St. John's Preparatory School, Massachusetts, 1965-66; moved to England in 1966. Henfield Writing Fellow, University of East Anglia, Norwich, 1977; writer-in-residence, University of Tulsa, Oklahoma, 1979-82, Adelphi University, New York, 1989, and University of Quebec, Montreal, 1990; Visiting Fellow, Cambridge University, 1984-85; lecturer, Gorky Institute of Literature, Moscow, Autumn 1990. Lives in London. **Awards:** Arts Council bursary, 1977; American Academy award, 1983; Guggenheim grant, 1983. **Address:** Altken, Stone, and Wylie, 29 Fernshaw Rd., London SW10 0TG.

PUBLICATIONS

Novels

The Ghost of Henry James. London, Macdonald, and Boston, Gambit, 1970.
Slides. London, Macdonald, and Boston, Gambit, 1971.
Relatives. London, Cape, 1972; New York, Avon, 1974.
The Darkness of the Body. London, Cape, 1974.
Figures in Bright Air. London, Gollancz, 1976.
The Francoeur Family. London, Chatto and Windus, 1984.

The Family. London, Gollancz, and New York, Farrar Straus, 1978.
The Country. London, Gollancz, and New York, Atheneum, 1981.
The Woods. London, Gollancz, and New York, Atheneum, 1982.
The Foreigner. London, Chatto and Windus, and New York, Atheneum, 1984.
The Catholic. London, Chatto and Windus, 1985; New York, Atheneum, 1986.
The Native. London, Chatto and Windus, 1987; New York, Atheneum, 1988.
The Accident. New York, Ticknor and Fields, 1991.
Annunciation. New York, Ticknor and Fields, 1994.

Short Stories

Penguin Modern Stories 1, with others. London, Penguin, 1969.
My Mother's Pearl Necklace. New York, Albondocani Press, 1987.

Uncollected Short Stories

"The Buried City," in *Transatlantic Review* (London), Spring 1967.
"The Tangled Centre," in *Modern Occasions* (Cambridge, Massachusetts), Spring 1971.
"Mr. Bonito," in *New Yorker,* 7 July 1980.
"The Student," in *Tri-Quarterly* (Evanston, Illinois), Fall 1982.
"Work," in *Prize Stories 1983: The O. Henry Awards,* edited by William Abrahams. New York, Doubleday, 1983.
"Paris, 1959," in *New Yorker,* 4 June 1984.
"The Crack," in *First Love / Last Love,* edited by Michael Denneny, Charles Ortleb, and Thomas Steele. New York, Putnam, 1985.
"A House of Women," in *New Yorker,* 28 April 1986.

Other

Difficult Women: A Memoir of Three. London, Gollancz, and New York, Atheneum, 1983.

*

Bibliography: In *American Book Collector* (New York), November-December 1984.

Manuscript Collection: University of Tulsa, Oklahoma.

David Plante comments:

One of course always writes with an intention in mind, but it is what one cannot intend that is my fascination in writing. I know, all the while I am choosing my words, making as vivid as possible my descriptions, that there is something floating beneath my words and descriptions which has a will of its own, which sometimes rises up to meet my words and most often sinks away, and one can no more intend it than one can (to borrow an image from William James) turn up a bright light to see the darkness. The best one can do is allow it to well up, to give it space.

One is or isn't in touch with this sense, and one knows one is or isn't as matter of factly, as unmysteriously, as one knows one is happy or depressed. In touch with it, one writes "Mr. Stein woke to a room of shadows," and the sentence comes to life, evokes a deep world of associations, while out of touch with it the same sentence, "Mr. Stein woke to a room of shadows," is banal, dull, dead. The difference between good and bad writing is quite as simple as that.

How does one know one is in touch or not? One knows the signs, particular enough to be recognizable. For example, walking down a street most often I am unaware of the litter that's around me, or I am aware of it only to wish it weren't there. This past afternoon, however, walking along a sidewalk, I found myself studying, on the cement, a small printed target with three or four bullet holes blown through it, a match book printed with three spades, a page torn from a magazine, a parking lot ticket, an addressed envelope, and it seemed to me that everything I saw was indicative of much more than what it was—after all, just litter—was, because of its rich suggestiveness, beyond my imaginative grasp. I wanted to *write* about that target, match book, page, ticket, letter, and I wanted to with the similarly recognizable, similarly matter of fact urge one has when one wants to sneeze, *I was in touch with something.*

One is, at various times, *aware* that one has to sneeze, one is aware that one is sexually attracted to someone, one is aware that one must work and eat and sleep, and one is aware that there is a sense, informing things yet capable of being abstracted from them, which one hopes to be the essence of one's writing, which one hopes will bring one's words and one's world to life.

Sneezing is important, and making love is important, and working and eating and sleeping are important, and something else is also important, something longed for, something which is the whole purpose of my work. William James said: "It is, the reader will see, the reinstatement of the vague and inarticulate to its proper place in our mental life which I am so anxious to press on the attention."

*   *   *

Separateness and tension distinguish the writing of David Plante, his novels containing within themselves a complex balance of ambiguities. Beneath its unremarkable surface, his fiction seethes with an inner life sensed rather than observed, the books seeming to vibrate with half-heard resonances. The outer skin of the novels, crowded as they are with a succession of apparently trivial incidents, serves merely to mask the hidden conflicts waiting to explode, whose pulses travel upward to meet the consciousness of the reader.

The Ghost of Henry James explores the group identity of a family in New England, following through a series of abrupt transitions the subtle alteration in attitudes, the shifts of understanding that bind the members one to another despite their differences, and the trauma that ensues when the central character tries to break free of the rest. Lost without the family, he finds only madness and death, but from it comes a transformation and a reordering of the other lives as his ghostly presence pervades the final scenes. Plante pays homage to the author of *The Turn of the Screw,* both in his evocation of sinister New England landscapes and in a style which distinguishes the text as a separate entity from what it describes. *Slides* pursues the same theme, the group this time consisting of adolescent friends, and the violent climax an attempted suicide. The shade of Hawthorne is summoned here, the Gothic aspect of his writings recreated as Plante hints subtly at the conflict between freedom and unity, the sexuality repressed beneath an innate puritanism, in a carefully weighted language that throbs behind the matter-of-fact conversations and weekend outings that make up the action of the book.

The Darkness of the Body and *Figures in Bright Air* reveal a deeper probing beneath the surface. In them, Plante undertakes a detailed portrayal of obsessive states of mind, presenting through the charged love-hate relationships of his characters the destructive force of physical love, the body's threat to the innerness of the beloved, the need for the personality to retain separateness and distance. Lovemaking is shown as a death-struggle, a falling into a black pit. The world itself is broken down to intensely potent fragments, individuals perceived as geometric shapes that clash against each other. Elements of air and stone are balanced in opposition, mirrors of the narrator's inward struggle where art, like life, is set the incompatible tasks of all-embracing vision and the reduction of everything to nothing. Plante's finely poised language, his matching of stillness with explosive action, invest the surface with its necessary undercurrents of tension and release. In these works in particular, he appears to be striving towards the ideal of Flaubert, and later of Robbe-Grillet, of the perfect irreducible text as a self-sufficient entity from which nothing can be removed.

In his trilogy on the Francoeur family—*The Family, The Country,* and *The Woods*—Plante's expression is less elusive than before, drawing directly from his personal experience. *The Country* especially veers close to documentary at times, representing the author's sense of himself as a native of two countries, his French-speaking birthplace in Rhode Island, and the rest of the United States. His central character, Daniel Francoeur, discovers through the contact of the last days with his dying father an affinity between them, and beyond it a kinship with the father's long-dead Indian ancestors: "My father was born, as I was, among the ghosts of a small community of people of strange blood. They were people who saw that they were born in darkness and would die in darkness, and who accepted that. They spoke, in their old French, in whispers, in the churchyard, among the gravestones, in the snow, and with them, silent, were squaws with papooses on their backs, and the woods began beyond the last row of gravestones. They were strange to me, and yet they were not strange."

Daniel's transformation, the slow change that takes place in him as he witnesses the death of his father and cares for his aging mother, is movingly and simply described. Plante builds up through meetings and casual conversation the relationship between parents and brothers, the feuds and differences that strain the underlying unity. The brooding presence of the forest permeates the novel, but *The Country* is among the clearest of its author's works. Daniel's mother above all, with her hatred of sex and childbirth, explains much of the meaning behind the "destructive love" theme in previous writings.

With *The Woods* Plante forsakes documentary techniques, returning to a third-person narrative that explores Daniel's inner world, culminating in his adolescent lovemaking, again visualized as a violation. This approach is continued with *The Foreigner* and *The Catholic.* More "fictionalized" than some of the Francoeur trilogy, these novels contain a greater degree of violence and erotic force which blasts more often to the surface. Here, as in earlier works, the core of the book lies almost out of sight beneath the text, a white-hot magma that simmers under the skin.

—Geoff Sadler

PLUNKETT, James

Nationality: Irish. **Born:** James Plunkett Kelly in Dublin, 21 May 1920. **Education:** Synge Street Christian Brothers School, Dublin;

Dublin College of Music. **Family:** Married Valerie Koblitz in 1945; one daughter and three sons. **Career:** Branch secretary, Workers Union of Ireland, 1946-55; assistant head of drama, Radio Eireann, Dublin, 1955-60; producer-director, 1961-68, head of features, 1969-71, and senior producer, 1974-85, Radio Telefis Eireann (Irish Television), Dublin. Council member, Society of Irish Playwrights, 1984-85. **Awards:** Irish Television award, 1964, 1966; *Yorkshire Post* award, 1969. **Member:** 1970, and president, 1980-82, Irish Academy of Letters; Toscaire (council member), Aosdana, 1981-85. **Agent:** Peters Fraser and Dunlop Group, 503-504 The Chambers, Chelsea Harbour, Lots Road, London SW10 0XF, England. **Address:** 29 Parnell Rd., Bray, County Wicklow, Ireland.

PUBLICATIONS

Novels

Strumpet City. London, Hutchinson, and New York, Delacorte Press, 1969.
The Gems She Wore: A Book of Irish Places. London, Hutchinson, 1972; New York, Holt Rinehart, 1973.
Farewell Companions. London, Hutchinson, 1977; New York, Coward McCann, 1978.
The Circus Animals. London, Hutchinson, 1990.

Short Stories

The Trusting and the Maimed, Other Irish Stories. New York, Devin Adair, 1955; London, Hutchinson, 1959.
Collected Short Stories. Dublin, Poolbeg Press, 1977.

Plays

Homecoming (broadcast 1954). Published in *The Bell* (Dublin), June 1954.
Big Jim (broadcast 1954). Dublin, O'Donnell, 1955.
The Risen People (produced Dublin, 1958; London, 1959; New York, 1978). Dublin, Co-op, 1978.

Radio Plays: *Dublin Fusilier,* 1952; *Mercy,* 1953; *Homecoming,* 1954; *Big Jim,* 1954; *Farewell Harper,* 1956.

Television Plays and Programs: *Memory Harbour,* 1963; *The Life and Times of Jimmy O'Dea,* 1964; *Portrait of a Poet,* 1965; *When Do You Die, Friend?,* 1966; *The Great O'Neill,* 1966; *Inis Fail,* 1971; *The State of the Nation,* 1972; *A Dash of Genius,* 1979; *That Solitary Man,* 1979; *The Wicklow Way,* 1980; *I Hear You Calling Me* (on John McCormack), 1984; *The Eagles and the Trumpets,* 1984; *One Man in His Time* (on Cyril Cusack), 1985.

Other

The Boy on the Back Wall and Other Essays. Dublin, Poolbeg Press, 1987.

*

Critical Studies: *Dublin and the Drama of Larkinism* by Godeleine Carpentier, Lille, France, Université de Lille, 1975; *Great Hatred,*

Little Room: The Irish Historical Novel by James Cahalan, Dublin, Gill and Macmillan, 1984.

*   *   *

Of his native Dublin, the city which forms the backdrop to his historical novel *Strumpet City,* James Plunkett has written: "Despite its tensions and its tragedies, Dublin was a good city to grow up in. The sea was at its feet, its Georgian buildings gave it nobility, its squares and its expanses of water made it a place of openness and light and air." Something of that affection is immediately apparent in this first novel—and, indeed, Dublin appears as a character in its own right in just about everything he has written—for unlike James Joyce Plunkett did not feel compelled to leave his native city in order to put it into perspective.

Set in the angry years leading to World War I, *Strumpet City*'s first concern is with the downtrodden working classes; in particular Plunkett deals with the attempts of the trades union movement to win better conditions for its members. Standing like a colossus above his fellow men is the figure of Barney Mulhall, a trades union leader whom Plunkett based upon Barney Conway, in real life the right-hand man of the political activist Jim Larkin. The other characters are no less firmly drawn and each is created in the likeness of men whom Plunkett, himself once a trades union official, had known in Dublin: Fitz, the idealistic foreman who joins the strike, Pat his friend and sage adviser, Keever who turns traitor, and perhaps the most colorful of them all, "Rashers" Tierney, the poorest of the poor.

Although *Strumpet City* finds its truest voice in Plunkett's vivid creation of Dublin working-class life, it does not ignore other strata of society. The middle-class world of the Bradshaws is faithfully reproduced, as is the claustrophobic life led by the priests Father Giffley and O'Connor. As each character's story draws to its conclusion, all we are left with is Plunkett's faith in the essential decency of people if only they can escape from the snare of the human condition.

In *Farewell Companions* Plunkett moves ahead in time to the inter-war years. A younger generation has arrived to come to terms with a country which has broken its shackles with Britain: they have to face up to, and come to terms with, a different set of rules. As in its predecessor, politics are never far away from the main narrative line but here the arguments are polarized between the demands of sentimental nationalism and the airier ideals of international socialism. Tim McDonagh, the novel's central character, is based loosely on Plunkett himself, and his story plots the journey from the old world occupied by his parent's generation to the hopes and fears of an independent Ireland. Once again, the description of Dublin and the delineation of Irish working-class life is faultless, equaled only by Plunkett's uncanny ability to create a gallery of vivid characters, each with a story to tell. Given such a broad tapestry it is not surprising perhaps to discover some loose threads, and for many readers the novel's ending will come as an anticlimax. Unable to come to terms with the demands of industrial life, McDonagh opts out of the real world and takes holy orders, a limp conclusion that is out of keeping with the speculative intention of the first half of the novel.

The Circus Animals follows Dublin's story into the bleak post-war years when Ireland had to face up to a new economic and political dispensation as its more tempestuous history slipped into the past. As had become standard practice in the previous two novels about Dublin, Plunkett showed himself well able to mix fact and fiction to create a riveting period picture. The action is seen through the eyes of a young couple, Frank and Margaret McDonagh as they struggle to come to terms with married life in the restricted life of a modern Ireland where the Catholic faith seems increasingly out of place. Margaret, for example, wants to practice birth control, but inevitably her conscience is troubled by the church's teachings. Plunkett is particularly good at revealing his characters' feelings and at presenting them in a plausible way. Even his priests and nuns possess a rounded humanity despite the fact that they are portrayed as basically unsympathetic characters. Inevitably, Frank, a political cartoonist, is drawn into conflict with the more conservative elements of Irish society and has to struggle to keep his sense of artistic identity, hence perhaps the use of Yeats's poem in the epigraph: "Now that my ladder's gone,/I must lie down where all the ladders start/In the foul rag and bone shop of the heart." As in the previous novels, too, the supporting characters are superbly realized, especially Lemuel Cox who acts both as mentor to Frank and interpreter of the action.

No understanding of the fictional world created by Plunkett is complete without reading his collection of short stories, *The Trusting and the Maimed,* the title story in particular giving a clue to the success of Plunkett's technique: the use of multiple voices and film-like scenes as he cuts from one character, one situation, one time, to another.

—Trevor Royle

POHL, Frederik

Pseudonyms: James MacCreigh, Ernst Mason, Edson McCann, Jordan Park, Donald Stacy. **Nationality:** American. **Born:** New York City, 26 November 1919. **Military Service:** Served in the United States Air Force, in the U.S.A. and Italy, 1943-45: Sergeant. **Family:** Married 1) Doris Baumgardt in 1940 (divorced 1944); 2) Dorothy LesTina in 1945 (divorced 1947); 3) the writer Judith Merril in 1949 (divorced 1953), one daughter; 4) Carol Metcalf Ulf in 1952 (divorced 1981), two sons (one deceased) and one daughter; 5) Elizabeth Anne Hull in 1984. **Career:** Editor, Popular Publications, New York, 1939-43; copywriter, Thwing and Altman, New York, 1946; book editor and associate circulation manager, Popular Science Publication Company, New York, 1946-49; literary agent, New York, 1949-53; features editor, later editor, *If,* New York, 1959-70; editor, Galaxy Publishing Company, New York, 1961-69; executive editor, Ace Books, New York, 1971-72; science fiction editor, Bantam Books, New York, 1973-79. Since 1976 contributing editor, *Algol,* New York. President, Science Fiction Writers of America, 1974-76; president, World SF, 1980-82 and current vice president (West); Mid-West Area Chair, Authors Guild of America. **Awards:** Edward E. Smith Memorial award, 1966; Hugo award, for editing, 1966, 1967, 1968, for fiction, 1973, 1978, 1987; *Locus* award, 1973, 1978; Nebula award, 1976, 1977; John W. Campbell Memorial award, 1978, 1985; Apollo prize (France), 1979; American Book award, 1980; Popular Culture Association award, 1986; United Nations Society of Writers award, 1989. Guest of Honor, World Science Fiction Convention, 1972; Fellow, American Association for the Advancement of Science. **Agent:** Curtis Brown, 10 Astor Place, New York, New York 10003; or Pamela Buckmaster, Carnell Literary Agency, Danes Croft,

Goose Lane, Little Hallingbury, Hertfordshire CM22 7RG, England. **Address:** 855 South Harvard Drive, Palatine, Illinois 60067, U.S.A.

PUBLICATIONS

Novels

The Space Merchants, with C.M. Kornbluth. New York, Ballantine, 1953; London, Heinemann, 1955.

Search the Sky, with C.M. Kornbluth. New York, Ballantine, 1954; London, Digit, 1960; revised (by Pohl), New York, Baen, 1985.

Preferred Risk (as Edson McCann, with Lester del Rey). New York, Simon and Schuster, 1955; London, Methuen, 1983.

Gladiator-at-Law, with C.M. Kornbluth. New York, Ballantine, 1955; London, Digit, 1958.

A Town Is Drowning, with C.M. Kornbluth. New York, Ballantine, 1955; London, Digit, 1960.

Presidential Year, with C.M. Kornbluth. New York, Ballantine, 1956.

Sorority House (as Jordan Park, with C.M. Kornbluth). New York, Lion, 1956.

The God of Channel 1 (as Donald Stacy). New York, Ballantine, 1956.

Turn the Tigers Loose, with Walter Lasly. New York, Ballantine, 1956.

Edge of the City (novelization of screenplay). New York, Ballantine, 1957.

Slave Ship. New York, Ballantine, 1957; London, Dobson, 1961.

Wolfbane, with C.M. Kornbluth. New York, Ballantine, 1959; London, Gollancz, 1961; revised by Pohl, New York, Baen, and London, Gollancz, 1986.

Drunkard's Walk. New York, Ballantine, 1960; revised edition, London, Gollancz, 1961.

The Starchild Trilogy, with Jack Williamson. New York, Doubleday, 1977; London, Penguin, 1980.

The Reefs of Space. New York, Ballantine, 1964; London, Dobson, 1965.

Starchild. New York, Ballantine, 1965; London, Dobson, 1966.

Rogue Star. New York, Ballantine, 1969; London, Dobson, 1972.

A Plague of Pythons. New York, Ballantine, 1965; London, Gollancz, 1966; revised edition, as *Demon in the Skull,* New York, DAW, 1984.

The Age of the Pussyfoot. New York, Trident Press, 1969; London, Gollancz, 1970.

Farthest Star, with Jack Williamson. New York, Ballantine, 1975; London, Pan, 1976.

Man Plus. New York, Random House, and London, Gollancz, 1976.

Gateway. New York, St. Martin's Press, and London, Gollancz, 1977.

Jem: The Making of a Utopia. New York, St. Martin's Press, and London, Gollancz, 1979.

Beyond the Blue Event Horizon. New York, Ballantine, and London, Gollancz, 1980.

The Cool War. New York, Ballantine, and London, Gollancz, 1980.

Starburst. New York, Ballantine, and London, Gollancz, 1982.

Syzygy. New York, Bantam, 1982.

Wall Around a Star, with Jack Williamson. New York, Ballantine, 1983.

Midas World. New York, St. Martin's Press, and London, Gollancz, 1983.

Heechee Rendezvous. New York, Ballantine, and London, Gollancz, 1984.

The Merchants' War. New York, St. Martin's Press, 1984; London, Gollancz, 1985.

Black Star Rising. New York, Ballantine, 1985; London, Gollancz, 1986.

The Coming of the Quantum Cats. New York, Bantam, 1986; London, Gollancz, 1987.

The Annals of the Heechee. New York, Ballantine, and London, Gollancz, 1987.

Chernobyl. New York and London, Bantam, 1987.

Narabedla Ltd. New York, Ballantine, 1988; London, Gollancz, 1990.

The Day the Martians Came. New York, St. Martin's Press, 1988; London, Gollancz, 1990.

Land's End, with Jack Williamson. New York, Tor, 1988.

Homegoing. New York, Ballantine, 1989; London, Gollancz, 1990.

The World at the End of Time. New York, Ballantine, 1990; London, Grafton, 1992.

Outnumbering the Dead. London, Century, 1991.

Mining the Oort. London, Century, 1991.

The Singers of Time, with Jack Williamson. New York, Doubleday, 1991.

Short Stories

Danger Moon (as James MacCreigh). Sydney, American Science Fiction, 1953.

Alternating Currents. New York, Ballantine, 1956; London, Penguin, 1966.

The Case Against Tomorrow. New York, Ballantine, 1957.

Tomorrow Times Seven. New York, Ballantine, 1959.

The Man Who Ate the World. New York, Ballantine, 1960; London, Panther, 1979.

Turn Left at Thursday. New York, Ballantine, 1961.

The Wonder Effect, with C.M. Kornbluth. New York, Ballantine, 1962; London, Gollancz, 1967; revised edition, as *Critical Mass,* New York, Bantam, 1977.

The Abominable Earthman. New York, Ballantine, 1963.

The Frederik Pohl Omnibus. London, Gollancz, 1966; selection, as *Survival Kit,* London, Panther, 1979.

Digits and Dastards (includes essays). New York, Ballantine, 1966; London, Dobson, 1968.

Day Million. New York, Ballantine, 1970; London, Gollancz, 1971.

The Gold at Starbow's End. New York, Ballantine, 1972; London, Gollancz, 1973.

The Best of Frederik Pohl, edited by Lester del Rey. New York, Doubleday, 1975; London, Sidgwick and Jackson, 1977.

In the Problem Pit. New York, Bantam, and London, Corgi, 1976.

The Early Pohl. New York, Doubleday, 1976; London, Dobson, 1980.

Planets Three. New York, Berkley, 1982.

The Years of the City. New York, Simon and Schuster, 1984; London, Gollancz, 1985.

Pohlstars. New York, Ballantine, 1984; London, Gollancz, 1986.

Our Best: The Best of Frederik Pohl and C.M. Kornbluth. New York, Baen, 1987.

The Gateway Trip: Tales and Vignettes of the Heechee. New York, Ballantine, 1990.

Other

Undersea Quest [Fleet, City] (for children), with Jack Williamson. New York, Gnome Press, 3 vols., 1954-58; London, Dobson, 3 vols., 1966-68.

Tiberius (biography; as Ernst Mason). New York, Ballantine, 1960.

Practical Politics 1972. New York, Ballantine, 1971.

The Way the Future Was: A Memoir. New York, Ballantine, 1978; London, Gollancz, 1979.

Science Fiction: Studies in Film, with Frederik Pohl IV. New York, Ace, 1981.

Editor, *Beyond the End of Time.* New York, Permabooks, 1952.

Editor, *Shadow of Tomorrow.* New York, Permabooks, 1953.

Editor, *Star Science Fiction Stories 1-6.* New York, Ballantine, 6 vols., 1953-59; vols. 1 and 2, London, Boardman, 1954-55.

Editor, *Assignment in Tomorrow.* New York, Hanover House, 1954.

Editor, *Star Short Novels.* New York, Ballantine, 1954.

Editor, *Star of Stars.* New York, Doubleday, 1960; as *Star Fourteen,* London, Whiting and Wheaton, 1966.

Editor, *The Expert Dreamers.* New York, Doubleday, 1962; London, Gollancz, 1963.

Editor, *Time Waits for Winthrop and Four Other Short Novels from Galaxy.* New York, Doubleday, 1962.

Editor, *The Seventh* [through *Eleventh*]*Galaxy Reader.* New York, Doubleday, 5 vols., 1964-69; *Seventh* through *Tenth,* London, Gollancz, 4 vols., 1965-68; *Eighth,* as *Final Encounter,* New York, Curtis, 1970; *Tenth,* as *Door to Anywhere,* New York, Curtis, 1970.

Editor, *The If Reader of Science Fiction.* New York, Doubleday, 1966; London, Whiting and Wheaton, 1967; 2nd volume, New York, Doubleday, 1968.

Editor, *Nightmare Age.* New York, Ballantine, 1970.

Editor, *The Best Science Fiction for 1972.* New York, Ace, 1972.

Editor, with Carol Pohl, *Science Fiction: The Great Years.* New York, Ace, 1973; London, Gollancz, 1974; 2nd volume, Ace, 1976.

Editor, with Carol Pohl, *Jupiter.* New York, Ballantine, 1973.

Editor, *The Science Fiction Roll of Honor.* New York, Random House, 1975.

Editor, with Carol Pohl, *Science Fiction Discoveries.* New York, Bantam, 1976.

Editor, *The Best of C.M. Kornbluth.* New York, Doubleday, 1976.

Editor, with Martin H. Greenberg and Joseph D. Olander, *Science Fiction of the '40s.* New York, Avon, 1978.

Editor, with Martin H. Greenberg and Joseph D. Olander, *Galaxy: Thirty Years of Innovative Science Fiction.* Chicago, Playboy Press, 1980; 2nd volume, New York, Ace, 1981.

Editor, *Nebula Winners 14.* New York, Harper, 1980; London, W.H. Allen, 1981.

Editor, with Martin H. Greenberg and Joseph D. Olander, *The Great Science Fiction Series.* New York, Harper, 1980.

Editor, *Yesterday's Tomorrows: Favorite Stories from Forty Years as a Science Fiction Editor.* New York, Berkley, 1982.

Editor, with Elizabeth Anne Hull, *Tales from the Planet Earth.* New York, St. Martin's Press, 1986.

Editor, with Martin H. Greenberg and Joseph D. Olander, *Worlds of If.* New York, Bluejay, 1986.

*

Bibliography: *Frederik Pohl: A Working Bibliography* by Phil Stephensen-Payne and Gordon Benson, Jr., Leeds, Yorkshire, and Albuquerque, New Mexico, Galactic Central, 1989.

Manuscript Collection: Syracuse University Library, New York.

Critical Studies: *New Maps of Hell* by Kingsley Amis, New York, Harcourt Brace, 1960, London, Gollancz, 1961; *Frederik Pohl* by Thomas D. Clareson, Mercer Island, Washington, Starmont House, 1987.

Frederik Pohl comments:

My principal work has been in science fiction, and within that field in the special kind of science fiction best described as cautionary literature. Now that the world has been well alerted to such problems as pollution, overpopulation, and so on—largely, in the first instance, by science-fiction stories—it is old hat to say that we must look to the long-range consequences of our society and technology. My stories have often touched on such themes long before they were fashionable.

Apart from argument, I have been interested in exploring all the possible range of alternate futures for the human race. Some of the work in which I take most pride—short stories like *Day Million,* novels like *Wolfbane*—are not at all cautionary in the sense that they call attention to dangerous current trends; instead, they attempt to show some of the stranger, but quite possible, directions the human world-line may take.

However, no writer, myself least of all, writes very attractively when he writes according to a coldblooded plan. I don't set out to write either political agitprop or think-tank scenarios; I only attempt to think out the consequences of what seem to me to be interesting developments, to set living characters in such worlds and then to let them live their lives.

*   *   *

Frederik Pohl has distinguished himself both as one of the most prolific writers of science fiction and as one of its most explicit promoters. The two distinctions seem to stem from his firm didactic concern with science fiction as a social early warning system. To write science fiction, he says "is to try to look ahead to see not only what is likely to fall upon us by way of science and technology, but to see what the side effects and the consequences and the second and third order derivatives of these things will be" (MLA Forum on Science Fiction, December 1968). In a Shavian catalogue of prefaces and postscripts, Pohl repeats and amplifies his fictional purpose "to question everything . . . in the light of what Harlow Shepley calls the 'View from a distant star.'"

The explicit didactic purpose is borne out by his fiction, which historically falls in line with that of Wells, Huxley, and Hoyle as a kind of allegorical social satire, Earth-bound rather than space-speculative. His major novels are concerned with both the special consequences of particular trends in the 20th century and the general effects of our current population expansion and waste of natural resources. Thus, *The Space Merchants* and *Gladiator-at-Law* are, respectively, biting denunciations of 20th-century commercial advertising and corporation monopoly; unrestricted expansion of advertising agencies and super-corporations permits them to become the new power blocs of the 21st century, perverting the democratic process and lowering the quality of life by pandering to society's greed for immediate physical gratification.

In *The Reefs of Space* and *Starchild* Pohl looks further ahead. The Earth is teeming with 13 billion human beings necessarily organized under an entire totalitarian, computer-directed Plan of Man which has the sole aim of keeping a balance of resources. Private liberty has vanished because previous centuries have wasted natural resources only to turn the Earth into a closed-system in which there still "isn't enough to go round." *The Age of the Pussyfoot* takes the same distant view but focuses more closely on the quality of personal life in a society so dependent on computers that it is, in fact, symbiotic with them. Instant information and immediate self-indulgence are possible, yet no attempt has been made to solve the problems of poverty, war, and cultural triviality.

Throughout Pohl's work runs the paradoxical theme that, while we progress technologically, we don't improve the quality of living, we don't remove the inequalities of material possession, and we don't improve the prospects of human creativity and fulfillment. The only answer is the choice also expounded by Hoyle: we either stay in an entirely closed, programmed system or we evolve to another level.

Although many of Pohl's novels are written with collaborators, there is no discernible difference in the quality of writing of the collaborated and independent work. What emerges is a profoundly disturbing sense of reality, truth, and honesty which is Swiftian in its impact. In Pohl's hands, science fiction is a weapon to be used vigorously in defense of humanity. As a social critic, Pohl must rank high. In addition, however, as his *Undersea* novels indicate, he is a first-rate storyteller who never lets the message wholly take over the medium.

—Frederick Bowers

POTOK, Chaim

Nationality: American. **Born:** Herman Harold Potok in the Bronx, New York, 17 February 1929. **Education:** Orthodox Jewish schools; Yeshiva University, New York, 1946-50, B.A. (summa cum laude) in English 1950; Jewish Theological Seminary, New York, 1950-54, M.H.L. and rabbinic ordination 1954; University of Pennsylvania, Philadelphia, 1959-65, Ph.D. in philosophy 1965. **Military Service:** served as a chaplain in the United States Army in Korea, 1955-56: lieutenant. **Family:** Married Adena Sara Mosevitsky in 1958; two daughters and one son. **Career:** National director of Leaders Training fellowship, Jewish Theological Seminary, 1954-55; director, Camp Ramah, Ojai, California, 1957-59; instructor, University of Judaism, Los Angeles, 1957-59; scholar-in-residence, Har Zion Temple, Philadelphia, 1959-63; member of the Teachers' Institute faculty, Jewish Theological Seminary, 1964-65; managing editor, *Conservative Judaism,* New York, 1964-65. Associate editor, 1965, editor-in-chief, 1966-74, and since 1974 special projects editor, Jewish Publication Society, Philadelphia. Contributor of short stories and articles to *Commentary, Reconstructionist, Moment, Esquire, American Judaism, Saturday Review,* and the *New York Times Book Review,* among others. Lived in Israel, 1973-77. Visiting professor of philosophy, University of Pennsylvania, 1983, and Bryn Mawr College, Pennsylvania, 1985. **Awards:** Wallant award, 1968; Athenaem award, 1969. **Addresses:** c/o Alfred Knopf Inc., 201 E. 50th St., New York, New York 10022, U.S.A., and 20 Berwick Street, Merion, Pennsylvania 19131, U.S.A.

PUBLICATIONS

Novels

The Chosen. New York, Simon and Schuster, and London, Heinemann, 1967.
The Promise. New York, Knopf, 1969; London, Heinemann, 1970.
My Name Is Asher Lev. New York, Knopf, and London, Heinemann, 1972.
In the Beginning. New York, Knopf, 1975; London, Heinemann, 1976.
The Book of Lights. New York, Knopf, 1981; London, Heinemann, 1982.
Davita's Harp. New York, Knopf, 1985.
The Gift of Asher Lev. New York, Knopf, and London, Heinemann, 1990.
I Am the Clay. New York, Knopf, and London, Heinemann, 1992.

Uncollected Short Stories

"The Dark Place Inside," in *Dimensions in American Judaism* (New York), Fall 1964.
"The Cats of 37 Alfasi Street," in *American Judaism* (New York), Fall 1966.
"Miracles for a Broken Planet," in *McCall's* (New York), December 1972.
"The Fallen," in *Hadassah* (New York), December 1973.
"Reflections on a Bronx Street," in *May My Words Feed Others,* edited by Chayym Zeldis. Cranbury, New Jersey, A.S. Barnes, 1974.
"A Tale of Two Soldiers," in *Ladies Home Journal* (New York), December 1981.
"The Gifts of Andrea," in *Seventeen* (New York), October 1982.
"Long Distance," in *American Voice* (Louisville, Kentucky), Fall 1986.
"Ghosts," in *Orim* (New Haven, Connecticut), Spring 1987.

Other

Jewish Ethics (pamphlet series). New York, Leaders Training Fellowship, 14 vols., 1964-69.
The Jew Confronts Himself in American Literature. Hales Corners, Wisconsin, Sacred Heart School of Theology, 1975.
Wanderings: Chaim Potok's History of the Jews. New York, Knopf, and London, Hutchinson, 1978.
Ethical Living for a Modern World. New York, Jewish Theological Seminary of America, 1985.
Theo Tobiasse: Artist in Exile. New York, Rizzoli, 1986.
The Tree of Here, illustrated by Tony Auth (for children). New York, Knopf, 1993.
The Sky of Now, illustrated by Tony Auth (for children). New York, Knopf, 1994.

*

Critical Studies: "Culture Confrontation in Urban America: A Writer's Beginnings" by Potok, in *Literature and the Urban Experience* edited by Michael C. Jaye and Ann C. Watts, New Brunswick, New Jersey, Rutgers University Press, 1981; article by S. Lillian Kremer, in *Twentieth-Century American-Jewish Fiction Writers* edited by Daniel Walden, Detroit, Gale, 1984; interview with Elaine M. Kauvar, in *Contemporary Literature* (Madison, Wisconsin), Fall 1986; *Chaim Potok* by Edward A. Abramson, Boston, Twayne, 1986.

*   *   *

In the crowded field of Jewish-American fiction, the novelist Chaim Potok is remarkable for his persistent, intense analysis of contemporary Jews and Judaism. The question underlying most of his work is how traditional Judaism in all its forms relates to the modern world, and each of his young male protagonists struggles to make his Jewish heritage somehow fit the reality of his own life and circumstances. In *Davita's Harp,* a young female protagonist is involved in a similar conflict.

The Chosen is his first novel and perhaps still his best. The plot charts the relationship between Reuven Malter, the teenage son of a progressive or scientific Talmudic scholar at a Brooklyn yeshiva, and Danny Saunders, the son of a Hasidic rabbi, which begins in hate and ends in close friendship. Reuven, who narrates the story, slowly comes to understand the somewhat alien Hasidic world of his friend and, in particular, the gulf of silence which has been deliberately imposed by the rabbi between himself and his son. Ironically, Danny, a remarkably gifted Talmudic scholar and heir to his father's position of *tzaddik* ("spiritual leader") to his people, eventually chooses to study psychology in a secular graduate school while Reuven, the secularist, studies to be a rabbi.

A sequel entitled *The Promise* continues with the story of Reuven's yeshiva training and further develops Potok's interest in Hasidism, as Reuven attempts to formulate his own identity as a Jew somewhere between intolerant Hasidic zealots and secular humanists such as Abraham Gordon, who treasures ritual but cannot accept theology. The plot centers on the evolving case of Gordon's son Michael, who is treated by Danny Saunders, now a clinical psychologist, and once again involves intense father-son relationships.

In *My Name Is Asher Lev* the protagonist himself is Hasidic, the son of a Brooklyn-based emissary of a Landovian Rebbe. Asher must break away from his roots in order to become an artist—whose masterpieces turn out to be two crucifixions. Potok returns to his favorite subject of theological scholarship in *In the Beginning.* David Lurie is the son of a successful real estate broker and militant Zionist leader (once again, in Brooklyn), who organizes the immigration of friends and family from Poland but who loses his fortune in the Depression. Just as the Hasidic Danny Saunders had shifted his awesome intellectual powers from the study of Talmud to the secular field of psychology, David, another child prodigy and extraordinary yeshiva student, develops an interest in "secular" Bible study. David's is an even more shocking and scandalous shift, since the field was pioneered by German gentile scholars and since he announces his intention to pursue this line when the horrors of the Holocaust (which has claimed members of his own family in Europe) are fresh on everyone's mind.

In his works, Potok continually relates Jewish sacred texts to contemporary experience in a variety of ways, and *The Book of Lights* provides the most striking example. In this novel, Gershon Loran, who grows up in the midst of family tragedy, turns from the terror of World War II to the study of the cabala, an ancient form of Jewish mysticism. His roommate turns out to be the guilt-ridden son of a Jewish physicist who helped to develop the atomic bomb. In contrasting the "light" of the cabala with that of the bomb, Potok strives to develop universal moral concerns in this most ambitious novel. Finally, the protagonist of *Davita's Harp,* the daughter of Communist parents, after considerable suffering and confusion, reclaims her Jewish heritage (but then, ironically, finds sexual discrimination in the yeshiva she attends).

Potok brings back his exiled Hasidic artist hero in *The Gift of Asher Lev.* Asher, who has been living in France, returns with his family to Brooklyn in order to attend his uncle's funeral. Once he is back in America, Asher is again caught up in the tensions between his "profane" art and the religious community which rejects it, but there are new complications, notably those involving the fate of his son Avrumel.

I Am the Clay seems to represent a significant departure for Potok in subject though not necessarily in theme. In this novel set during the Korean War, he depicts an old Korean peasant couple who discover a young man named Kim Sin Gyu dying in a roadside ditch. The woman, who had lost a son in childbirth long ago, insists that they take the boy with them as they flee from the battlefront. The simple faith of the old couple and their charge is severely tested as they struggle to survive. In spite of its exotic setting, *I Am the Clay* shares the theme of spiritual journey with the other novels, and, like Reuven Malter, Kim Sin Gyu is torn between conflicting cultures. The novel is probably a rewriting of a very early, unpublished manuscript. (Potok served as a U.S. Army chaplain during the Korean War.)

Potok's concerns are consistently philosophical (or theological) and, except for *I Am the Clay,* consistently ethnic. It is as though he has set out to analyze and explain every aspect of Judaism both to society at large and to American Jews themselves, always moving from the traditional and narrowly defined aspects of Jewish religion and culture to their broad implications for the modern world. His enormous ambition in carrying out this task is also evident in his monumental but flawed popular history of the Jews entitled *Wanderings.*

Potok's novels are generally hampered by a mediocre writing style, and they deal with a relatively narrow range of human experience. Dialogue sounds unnatural, hopelessly "academic." Plots unravel tediously. In *I Am the Clay,* Potok attempted—not too successfully—to create a flat, "mythic" style that has been called "faux-naive." In the earlier novels his "good students" sometimes seem too good to be true. For example, David Lurie (*In the Beginning*) is almost unbearably earnest and solemn, a more extreme version of the studious Reuven Malter introduced in *The Chosen.* Potok is capable of portraying interesting human relationships, as in the Reuven-Danny friendship and the parallel father-son relationships in his first novel. However, his continuing popularity with a certain dedicated readership is probably not attributable to his skill at creating characters, plots, or dialogue. Sometimes Potok creates characters that seem flat and uninteresting, but in working with ideas and cultural traditions, he confronts those ambiguities and internal conflicts that most engage the mind of the reader. The controlling consciousness in a typical Potok novel may be described as ascetic, generous, intellectually uncompromising.

Potok has been accused of presenting a sentimentalized version of Judaism in his works, but this criticism is misleading. He does not shy away from factionalism and doctrinal disputes, or from the misunderstanding and even hatred that they generate. The problem is that Potok seems fully at ease with his narrative art only when he is describing the lesson in a yeshiva classroom or a philosophical dialogue. The further he drifts away from the lesson, the less convincing he becomes, and he practically ignores some areas of human experience that have little to do with intellectual or religious

perceptions. Potok is not for everyone, but it is heartening that such a novelist can maintain a certain popularity in contemporary American fiction.

—Clinton Machann

POWELL, Anthony (Dymoke)

Nationality: British. **Born:** London, 21 December 1905. **Education:** Eton College, Berkshire; Balliol College, Oxford, M.A. **Military Service:** Served in the Welch Regiment, 1939-41, and in the Army Intelligence Corps, 1941-45: Major; Order of the White Lion, Czechoslovakia; Order of Leopold II, Belgium; Oaken Crown and Croix de Guerre, Luxembourg. **Family:** Married the writer Lady Violet Pakenham in 1934; two sons. **Career:** Staff member, Duckworth, publishers, London, 1926-35; scriptwriter for Warner Brothers of Great Britain, 1936; full-time writer from 1936; literary editor, *Punch,* London, 1953-58; reviewer for the *Daily Telegraph, Times Literary Supplement,* and other periodicals. Trustee, National Portrait Gallery, London, 1962-76. **Awards:** James Tait Black Memorial prize, 1958; W.H. Smith literary award, 1974; *Hudson Review* Bennett prize, 1984; Ingersoll Foundation Eliot award, 1984. D.Litt.: University of Sussex, Brighton, 1971; University of Leicester, 1976; University of Kent, Canterbury, 1976; Oxford University, 1980; Bristol University, 1982. Honorary Fellow, Balliol College, 1974, and Modern Language Association (U.S.A.), 1981; Honorary Member, American Academy, 1977. C.B.E. (Commander, Order of the British Empire), 1956; Companion of Honour, 1988. **Address:** The Chantry, near Frome, Somerset BA11 3LJ, England.

PUBLICATIONS

Novels

Afternoon Men. London, Duckworth, 1931; New York, Holt, 1932.
Venusberg. London, Duckworth, 1932; with *Agents and Patients,* New York, Periscope Holliday, 1952.
From a View to a Death. London, Duckworth, 1933; as *Mr. Zouch, Superman: From a View to a Death,* New York, Vanguard Press, 1934.
Agents and Patients. London, Duckworth, 1936; with *Venusberg,* New York, Periscope Holliday, 1952.
What's Become of Waring. London, Cassell, 1939; Boston, Little Brown, 1963.
A Dance to the Music of Time:
  A *Question of Upbringing.* London, Heinemann, and New York, Scribner, 1951.
  A *Buyer's Market.* London, Heinemann, 1952; New York, Scribner, 1953.
  The Acceptance World. London, Heinemann, 1955; New York, Farrar Straus, 1956.
  At Lady Molly's. London, Heinemann, 1957; Boston, Little Brown, 1958.
  Casanova's Chinese Restaurant. London, Heinemann, and Boston, Little Brown, 1960.
  The Kindly Ones. London, Heinemann, and Boston, Little Brown, 1962.

The Valley of Bones. London, Heinemann, and Boston, Little Brown, 1964.

The Soldier's Art. London, Heinemann, and Boston, Little Brown, 1966.

The Military Philosophers. London, Heinemann, 1968; Boston, Little Brown, 1969.

Books Do Furnish a Room. London, Heinemann, and Boston, Little Brown, 1971.

Temporary Kings. London, Heinemann, and Boston, Little Brown, 1973.

Hearing Secret Harmonies. London, Heinemann, 1975; Boston, Little Brown, 1976.

O, How the Wheel Becomes It! London, Heinemann, and New York, Holt Rinehart, 1983.

The Fisher King. London, Heinemann, and New York, Norton, 1986.

Uncollected Short Story

"A Reference for Mellors," in *Winter's Tales 12,* edited by A.D. Maclean. London, Macmillan, and New York, St. Martin's Press, 1966.

Plays

Two Plays: The Garden God, and The Rest I'll Whistle. London, Heinemann, 1971; Boston, Little Brown, 1972.

Poetry

Caledonia: A Fragment. Privately printed, 1934.

Other

John Aubrey and His Friends. London, Heinemann, and New York, Scribner, 1948; revised edition, Heinemann, and New York, Barnes and Noble, 1963; revised edition, London, Hogarth Press, 1988.

To Keep the Ball Rolling: The Memoirs of Anthony Powell (abridged edition). London, Penguin, 1983; New York, Penguin, 1984.

Infants of the Spring. London, Heinemann, 1976; New York, Holt Rinehart, 1977.

Messengers of Day. London, Heinemann, and New York, Holt Rinehart, 1978.

Faces in My Time. London, Heinemann, 1980; New York, Holt Rinehart, 1981.

The Strangers All Are Gone. London, Heinemann, 1982; New York, Holt Rinehart, 1983.

Miscellaneous Verdicts: Writings on Writers 1946-1989. London, Heinemann, 1990.

Journals, 1982-1986. London, Heinemann, 1995.

Editor, *Barnard Letters 1778-1884.* London, Duckworth, 1928.

Editor, *Novels of High Society from the Victorian Age.* London, Pilot Press, 1947.

Editor, *Brief Lives and Other Selected Writings of John Aubrey.* London, Cresset Press, and New York, Scribner, 1949.

*

Critical Studies: *Anthony Powell* by Bernard Bergonzi, London, Longman, 1962, revised edition, 1971; *The Novels of Anthony Powell* by Robert K. Morris, Pittsburgh, University of Pittsburgh Press, 1968; *Anthony Powell: A Quintet, Sextet, and War* by John Russell, Bloomington, Indiana University Press, 1970; "Anthony Powell Issue" of *Summary* (London), Autumn 1970; "Sisyphus Descending: Mythical Patterns in the Novels of Anthony Powell" by Frederick Karl, in *Mosaic* (Winnipeg), vol. 4, no. 3, 1971; *Anthony Powell* by Neil Brennan, New York, Twayne, 1974; *Snow upon Fire: A Dance to the Music of Time* by Dan Davin, Swansea, University College of Swansea, 1976; *The Novels of Anthony Powell* by James Tucker, London, Macmillan, and New York, Columbia University Press, 1976; *Handbook to Anthony Powell's Music of Time* by Hilary Spurling, London, Heinemann, 1977, as *Invitation to the Dance: A Guide to Anthony Powell's Dance to the Music of Time,* Boston, Little Brown, 1978; *Anthony Powell's Music of Time as a Cyclic Novel of Generations* by Rudolf Bader, Bern, Switzerland, Francke, 1980; *The Album of Anthony Powell's Dance to the Music of Time* edited by Violet Powell, London, Thames and Hudson, 1987; *Reminiscent Scrutinies: Memory in Anthony Powell's A Dance to the Music of Time* by Lucy Adams Frost, Troy, New York, Whitston, 1990; *Anthony Powell* by Neil McEwan, London, Macmillan, 1991; *Time in Anthony Powell: A Critical Study* by Robert L. Selig, Rutherford, New Jersey, Fairleigh Dickinson University Press, 1991.

*   *   *

Anthony Powell has been writing books for more than 50 years, though it is only in the last 20 that he has emerged as one of a small handful of contemporary British novelists who can reasonably be considered major. His reputation rests almost exclusively on *A Dance to the Music of Time,* a panoramic sequence of extraordinary scope and complexity. A work that has never relinquished its surface brilliance at portraying the insular, private, self-contained, snobbish world of the British upper and middle classes has more latterly become a vast canvas of all English life between the wars and afterwards, and in the profoundest way no less than a comic epic on time, history, and change.

Powell's novelistic career falls into two parts with World War II as the convenient dividing line. The five novels written in the 1930s are wittily structured and skillfully textured, still of some critical interest, but hinting only imperceptibly at the great achievement to come. *Afternoon Men* is perhaps most representative of the 1930s ethos and Powell's early style. Its atmosphere is charged with the insouciance and paralysis of "the lost generation," and resonates with echoes of Waugh and Huxley, though Waugh's bright young things have become older and tarnished, some even rusty, while Huxley's windy intellectuals and poseurs have declined into frustrated, bored, laconic, loveless drifters. Powell's nine-year tenure with Duckworth as reader and editor no doubt inspired the most skillfully plotted of the early novels, *What's Become of Waring;* it is the only one of them to use the first-person narrator that Powell was to employ with increasing complexity in *The Music of Time.* The novel tells of the attempt of a handful of persons to reconstruct the biography of a bestselling author who has remained incognito even up to his death. As the ambiguities of his character unfold, so do those of the characters charged with the quest. Nearly half a century later, Powell—a classic recycler of themes, characters and situations—was to return to Grub Street and the quasi-mystery story with *O, How the Wheel Becomes It!,* and to recapture some of the comic brilliance of the 1930s novels that had decidedly darkened with the final volume of *The Music of Time. O,*

How the Wheel Becomes It! moves back and forth between the late 1920s and the present as a dull, elderly, third-rate author and literary hack, invited to edit the diary of a deceased acquaintance, uncovers in its pages the reasons for his own failure in love and letters. If, in light of *O, How the Wheel Becomes It!*, *What's Become of Waring* has taken on a new status as perhaps the most interesting of Powell's prewar books, *From a View to a Death* still remains the best of them; retrospectively it is certainly the most important, anticipating in its several character sketches the more fully realized and rounded portraits of eccentrics in *The Music of Time,* and thematically introducing a dualism of human nature that has become peculiarly associated with Powell's artistic vision and with the thrust and core of his sequence: the opposition of the man of will and the man of imagination, the power-hungry and the sensualist.

Powell began *The Music of Time* shortly after the war, projecting it initially as six volumes, then expanding the plan to twelve. In a rare aside on his work, Powell stated in 1961 that the series "is concerned with the inter-relations of individuals, their lives and love affairs, and is intended to illustrate and bring up to date considerations of the way in which the middle and upper classes live in England." This confidence proved something of a false scent to his early critics, who tended to read the series as biography or sociology with fiction as mere overlay; nor (in all fairness to them) were its intricacies and formidable design apparent even after the first trilogy: *A Question of Upbringing,* set at Eton and Oxford during the 1920s; *A Buyer's Market,* centered in a party-going ambiance similar to that of *Afternoon Men;* and *The Acceptance World,* dealing with various gambits to make it both sexually and professionally in the London of the 1930s. Narrated unhurriedly, coolly, and at times in a way that seems maddeningly pointless by Nicholas Jenkins—the hero-narrator of the entire sequence—the first three volumes interweave his life with the lives of a growing nucleus of acquaintances, introduce almost gratuitously several amiable eccentrics, and turn potentially dramatic confrontations into low-keyed comedy of manners.

Looking back over volumes of the series, however, one realizes that Powell, from the beginning, remained consistent to his title and controlling metaphor, both inspired by the painting of Poussin in which "the seasons, hand in hand and facing outward, tread in rhythm to the notes of the lyre that the winged and naked graybeard plays." Like the Seasons, Powell's dancers step "slowly, methodically, sometimes a trifle awkwardly, in evolutions that take recognizable shape: or [break] into seemingly meaningless gyrations, while partners disappear only to reappear again, once more giving pattern to the spectacle." The world of *The Music of Time,* then, is generated through continuing change, though what Powell does with the notion is unique. By seeing all possible, shifting, interchangeable patterns, but by placing the burden of interpreting them squarely on his narrator, he makes the present the center of the novel, enlarges the most underplayed actions or contracts overblown ones, without focusing on their immediate significance, integrates individual steps of the dance into the greater flux, and charts necessarily changing sensibilities against the continuum of human history.

Such is the linear movement *in* time, but there is also the vertical movement of *time:* its qualitative rather than quantitative function, the thing-in-itself that makes one "unable . . . to control the steps of the dance." As Nick says in *The Kindly Ones,* "Time can play within its own folds tricks that emphasize the insecurity of those who trust themselves over much to that treacherous concept." The

prime mover that does not ostensibly move, does—in a sequence continually reshaping the dance—move, itself become a part of a "kaleidoscope, the colors of which are always changing, always the same." Sheer, protean, fluid, spatial, time is the backdrop for posing and transporting character, theme and plot, but also the dominating archetype embracing all of life and art and of those who would take part in them.

A dozen or more archetypal patterns throughout the sequence would confirm it as the work of a mythopoeicist rather than realist. Nevertheless, Powell has created a remarkable gallery of "real" characters: originals like Giles Jenkins, General Conyers, Lady Molly Jeavons, Lord Erridge, tinged with the harmless grotesqueries of human behavior; men of imagination like Edgar Deacon, Hugh Moreland, Captain Rowland Gwatkin, Charles Stringham and Peter Templer, romantic transplants from another age who suffer "the strain of living simultaneously in two different historical periods"; and of men of will, cold, mechanical, disciplined, controlling the times and harmonizing with them, of which Kenneth Widmerpool is the most notorious and vital. He is certainly one of the great contemporary comic villains as well. Son of a liquid manure manufacturer, and fat-boy butt of his school fellows at Eton, Widmerpool ascends with astonishing persistence and phoenix-like regularity to positions of status and power. From a highly competent businessman to army colonel and Labour M.P., from peer of the realm to university chancellor to near-divine guru, he has moved uninterruptedly and unfeelingly toward success. Yet though Widmerpool is a supercompetent, specious, insensitive, self-aggrandizing, and dangerous egomaniac, one cannot dislike him. In the dance he occupies a pivotal position; and being but one more partner in the just and harmonious evolutions of time, he, like the several hundred other characters, is treated comically, not satirically. Powell accepts Widmerpool as a phenomenon of the ethos without attempting to correct the failings of either.

More importantly, perhaps, Widmerpool becomes the perfect foil for Nick Jenkins's emergent decency, dignity, and probity. Proper, fashionable, sincere, innocent, self-reliant, Nick is the above average, upper-class all-right-guy wanting to fit in and keep from becoming defeated, excessively eccentric, too ostentatiously successful, or too scandalously simple. Nick operates through a comic stoicism that one feels is Powell's as well. He witnesses dissolution about him and charts a course between extremes—measuring the smallest signs or gestures against contemporary standards and holding fast to sensible and humane values. From his shadowy beginnings as narrator and his often obvious role as author-surrogate, he has blossomed into a full-blown hero; for above and beyond other things, he has learned how a student of history and society should confront the uses of the past and of men. It is the Nick of *At Lady Molly's* who finally understands that excess of either power or sensuality may become the principal destroyer of society; the Nick of *Casanova's Chinese Restaurant,* thrust into a world of decaying marriages, infidelity, frustration, failure, and suicide, whose faith in morals and ethics is shaken, but not annihilated; and the Nick of the war trilogy (*The Valley of Bones, The Solider's Art, The Military Philosophers*) who, above all the others, remains human in the face of impersonal and fatal dehumanizing processes. It is the Nick, too, of *Temporary Kings,* who finally grasps how *The Music of Time*'s decelerating dance of death approaches the inevitable statement to which the series has long been tending. Powell's preoccupation throughout the volumes with the artist's death, and with art in general as being representative of mutability, has been transferred to the imminent death of one work of art in particular.

Temporary Kings does not merely view the passing of friends, family, society and culture; it looks to the passing of Powell's great multilayered novel itself that comes with *Hearing Secret Harmonies,* wherein Powell's *danse macabre* and antic hay are finally "suspended in the wintry silence" in which the dance of the Seasons first began and to which (one sees at last) it was always tending. As a conclusion, the suspension is esthetically perfect; for clearly Powell never meant his sequence to "end": mourning the lost past (like Galsworthy) or (like Proust) recapturing it. The gyrations and patterns of his dancers—Poussin's painting and Powell's description of it must ever be kept in mind—though drawn from life by a master ironist and comedian, were inspired by art to be turned back into art. Thus, *The Music of Time* has proven itself to be less a fictional history about 60 years of English society than a mythical delineation of it. Powell's plan, it seems, was to create a world where life and art, time and space spiraled on synchronously and parallel, a world in which his characters "disappear" at the vanishing point, "only to reappear again."

Such is the world of myth. From the seasonal dance on page two of the first volume, Powell has gone about invoking myths of the seven deadly sins, the Furies, Childe Roland and *Orlando Furioso,* Casanova and Ezekiel—to name but a trickle of the torrent of allusions. He has used these archetypes to heighten his comedy, force ironies, and swell the dimensions of the half-dozen or so recurring characters who loom larger than life. One may have long recognized how truly important the shaping power of myth has been to the sequence, but only with *Hearing Secret Harmonies* does it become crystal-clear that the force behind Powell's mythic vision has all the while been Nietzsche: another writer who fashioned his art out of the apparently contradictory materials of myth and history. What Nietzsche ultimately does for *The Music of Time* is to give it a novelistic, as well as philosophic order. For Poussin/Powell's dancers, reappearing again and again to weave the great comic tapestry of this splendid sequence, are none other than Nietzsche's timeless actors, caught up in the myth of recurrence and eternal return. Earlier writers (Spengler for one; Toynbee for another) have chosen to treat the myth tragically; Powell goes about treating it comically, balancing life and death, reality and art, accepting them and not expecting to change them; even as Nick himself, now in his late sixties, greets the news of the death of his oldest friend-antagonist-bête noire, Kenneth Widmerpool, as merely a temporary suspension of life for those, like himself, still caught up in time's dance.

Nick, a survivor, survives, endures.

—Robert K. Morris

POWERS, J(ames) F(arl)

Nationality: American. **Born:** Jacksonville, Illinois, 8 July 1917. **Education:** Quincy College Academy, Illinois; Northwestern University, Chicago campus, 1938-40. **Family:** Married the writer Betty Wahl in 1946; three daughters and two sons. **Career:** Worked in Chicago, 1935-41; editor, Illinois Historical Records Survey, 1938; hospital orderly during World War II; teacher at St. John's University, Collegeville, Minnesota, 1947 and after 1975, Marquette University, Milwaukee, 1949-51, and University of Michigan, Ann Ar-

bor, 1956-57; writer-in-residence, Smith College, Northampton, Massachusetts, 1965-66. **Awards:** American Academy grant, 1948; Guggenheim fellowship, 1948; Rockefeller fellowship, 1954, 1957, 1967; National Book award, 1963. **Member:** American Academy. **Address:** c/o Knopf Inc., 201 East 50th Street, New York, New York 10022, U.S.A.

PUBLICATIONS

Novels

Morte d'Urban. New York, Doubleday, and London, Gollancz, 1962.
Wheat That Springeth Green. New York, Knopf, and London, Chatto and Windus, 1988.

Short Stories

Prince of Darkness and Other Stories. New York, Doubleday, 1947; London, Lehmann, 1948.
The Presence of Grace. New York, Doubleday, and London, Gollancz, 1956.
Look How the Fish Live. New York, Knopf, 1975.

Uncollected Short Stories

"Sailing Against the Wind," in *Gallery of Modern Fiction,* edited by Robie Macauley. New York, Salem Press, 1966.
"Hair Shirt," in *New Yorker,* 30 January 1978.
"Warm Sand," in *New Yorker,* 26 March 1979.

*

Critical Studies: *J.F. Powers* by John F. Hagopian, New York, Twayne, 1968; *J.F. Powers* edited by Fallon Evans, St. Louis, Herder, 1968.

*   *   *

When the stories of J.F. Powers first appeared in American literary magazines during the 1940s, they were welcomed by many readers with an enthusiasm perhaps even greater than their own merits would otherwise have generated, for here was a new writer—a Northern writer, a Midwestern writer—whose stories carried as much creative authority as did the Southern writing that had dominated American fiction for three decades. Here were the same structural finesse and verbal sensitivity, but now applied to Northern materials. And here was the same concern for ultimate value, now transplanted to a milieu in which some Southern critics had contended it could never flourish.

In short, Powers wrote about Chicago and the small towns of Illinois and Wisconsin with skills learned essentially from such writers as Caroline Gordon, Eudora Welty, Robert Penn Warren, and other Southern fictionists, and thus brought to his materials a more sensitive fictional approach than that of earlier Midwestern writers, such as Sinclair Lewis, James T. Farrell, or Nelson Algren. To put it another way, a native metaphysical storywriter, using the term perhaps somewhat loosely, had appeared in the very home of American naturalism and had taken at least some of naturalism's themes for his own, with results that were stimulating to say the least.

Powers had a remarkable ear for the dialects and idioms of Mid-western speech, and could put together pages of dialogue with perfect fluency, realism, and economy. At the same time he could construct stories of great significance from the smallest episodes, using reticence of symbol and event to suggest meaning and feeling. As a stylist, he was plain rather than fancy, with a classical instinct for concision and a lively sense of prose rhythm. In general, his early stories centered on two main areas of experience: social conflict in Chicago, especially between whites and blacks, and the lives of the Roman Catholic clergy in America. Both these themes appeared powerfully in his first book, *Prince of Darkness.*

The first, that of racial conflict and the misery of blacks in northern American cities, is best developed in the story entitled "He Don't Plant Cotton," which tells about three black jazz musicians, two men and a woman, who are fired from their job in a third-rate Chicago nightclub after a disagreement with drunken white customers. The story is memorable on several counts. For one, Powers wrote about jazz and its place in black sensibility without any of the mawkishness or plain musical stupidity that has characterized most other white and even much black writing on the subject. For another, without resorting to violence of either speech or event, he conveyed the real violence of feeling that dominates the black community's response to its predicament in America, and it is worth noting that this was done a full decade before the beginning of the modern civil rights movement. Nothing since then has surpassed Powers's story in seriousness, integrity, and artistic relevance, though much recent writing has been more turbulent.

The second theme, that of Catholic religious life in America, is perhaps best exemplified in the early story called "Lions, Harts, Leaping Does," in which Powers wrote about an elderly Franciscan friar plagued by intellectual self-doubt and spiritual anxiety. As he approaches his own death, his small shortcomings seem more and more ominous to him, until in a state of demoralization he cannot experience the least impulse toward good without questioning it and reversing his motives. Very subtly Powers contrasts this spiritual finickiness with the real crassness and brutishness of modern commercial civilization, showing the true value of spiritual discipline even in its own weakest condition.

These two stories, "Lions, Harts, Leaping Does," and "He Don't Plant Cotton," belong among the best short stories written in America during the years of mid-century.

In Powers's second book, *The Presence of Grace,* the religious theme became dominant, and the mood turned from that of spiritual anguish to something more objective and satirical. Some stories in the collection moved toward whimsy, including several narrated by a rectory cat, but though they won much popularity for Powers when they were first published in the *New Yorker,* in retrospect they seem comparatively insubstantial. Other stories dealt more toughly with subversion in the Church and with the restlessness of modern clerics who are drawn from true priestliness by ideas of status, power, and popular success; and these were the stories which culminated in Powers's third and most important book, the satirical novel entitled *Morte d'Urban.*

Father Urban is a proselytizing priest attached to the (fictional) Clementine Order. Beginning with the purest motives, a desire to bring renewed strength and spiritual influence to his Order, he moves more and more in the direction of manipulator, a spiritual wheeler-and-dealer, in the most degraded American commercial tradition. In other words, he is progressively subverted by the methods and ideals of the wealthy businessmen whom he parasitizes, and though for a time his efforts, like theirs, succeed remarkably,

in the end they lead to catastrophe. The novel is perfectly controlled, perfectly articulated in its elaboration of the levels of religious and lay sensibility. What saves it from being merely an "in" novel for Catholic intellectuals is its clear if indirect exposure of the broad social forces at work behind the dereliction of certain elements in the Church. *Morte d'Urban* is the best American satire of any kind in recent decades.

—Hayden Carruth

POWERS, Richard

Nationality: American. **Born:** 1957. **Career:** Has been a computer professional. Currently a full-time writer. **Awards:** MacArthur grant, 1990-94. **Address:** c/o William Morrow, 1350 Avenue of the Americas, New York, New York 10019, U.S.A.

PUBLICATIONS

Novels

Three Farmers on Their Way to a Dance. New York, Morrow, 1985; London, Weidenfeld and Nicolson, 1988.
Prisoner's Dilemma New York, Morrow, 1988; London, Weidenfeld and Nicolson, 1989.
Gold-Bug Variations. New York, Morrow, 1991; London, Scribner, 1992.
Operation Wandering Soul. New York, Morrow, 1993; London, Abacus, 1994.
Galatea 2.2. New York, Farrar Straus, 1995.

*   *   *

Richard Powers is the prodigy of recent American fiction. Recipient of a MacArthur "genius grant" in his mid-30s, Powers published five widely praised novels before the age of 40. Because of his historical subjects, including 20th-century wars, and his scientific orientations, including cybernetics and biology, Powers has been most frequently compared to Thomas Pynchon, prodigy of an earlier generation. In his output and accessibility, Powers is more like Don DeLillo, with whom he shares interests in neurology and cognition, media such as photography and film, and the disasters of contemporary American life. Using autobiography to examine the sources and values of fictions, Powers also resembles John Barth and his invented doubles. "Crackpot realism"—a phrase from Powers's second novel—represents his combination of these older writers' postmodern methods and materials. What distinguishes Powers's work is his imaginative earnestness, this prodigy's premodern urge to impart his knowledge to readers.

To understand the ingenious and large-hearted mind of Powers, readers should begin with his last novel and move backward. Like Barth's *Chimera* and DeLillo's *Mao II, Galatea 2.2* works close to the author's life: a novelist named Powers returns to the university where he learned to read literature and attempts to teach a computer the same skill. While exploring the nature of literary processing Powers comments on his novels, recalls his motives for writing, and remembers his first reader, his former lover. Synthesizing extremes of abstract intelligence and intimate revelation, *Galatea 2.2* is an excellent introduction to earlier generations of Powers's wordprocessing program.

Operation Wandering Soul, like Pynchon's *Vineland* and Barth's *Sabbatical,* is a moving story about recovery of health and a collection of stories about moving, the forced wandering of refugees. The novel's main characters are a resident and nurse in a Los Angeles children's ward, a collection point for the horrors of urban violence. As the doctor attempts to save bodies, the nurse comforts souls with fictions. Cut into the text are children's tales, such as the Pied Piper and Peter Pan, and anecdotes from the protagonists' childhoods. In the *Age of Abuse,* Powers asks, what stories should be told to children and what stories can the novelist tell to readers desensitized by daytime and nighttime television?

The Gold-Bug Variations is Powers's *Gravity's Rainbow* and *Ratner's Star,* an encyclopedic novel that twists together the recursive science of genetics and the recursive art of Bach. In this book about four-part variation, there are two love stories: genetics researchers in the l950s, a librarian and art historian in the 1980s. As the contemporary characters investigate the earlier lives, *Gold-Bug* becomes a Poe-like tale of detection for the characters and a treasure hunt for readers, who learn only at book's end that it, like an offspring, has been spliced from the contemporary lovers' independent narrations. The literal and conceptual center of the novel is a section called "The Natural Kingdom," which celebrates life itself as a prodigy, unlikely as genius, both artfully regular and imaginatively accidental. In its understanding of sexual combination and cognitive mutation, *The Gold-Bug Variations* is, in my opinion, the most profound novel published in America since Joseph McElroy's *Women and Men* in 1987.

In *Operation Wandering Soul,* Powers treated the war in Vietnam and in city streets. In *Prisoner's Dilemma,* members of a Midwestern family of the l980s are victims of the husband's and father's radiation exposure in World War II. Physically and perhaps mentally ill, Eddie Hobson, a high school history teacher, both imprisons and frees his four children with paradoxical mind games and an unreliable autobiography, a taped journal called "Hobstow" that mixes personal facts, Japanese internment, and Disney films. Told through the family members' six points of view, the novel authoritatively records domestic double binds and inventively recounts prewar and postwar history.

In *Prisoner's Dilemma,* Powers refers to the butterfly effect of chaos theory: "a butterfly flapping its wings in Peking . . . alter[s] tomorrow's weather in Duluth." This unpredictable relation between small and large—personal and historical, mutation and code, biography and story, book and readership—coils through all of Powers's fiction. *Three Farmers on Their Way to a Dance* imagines the lives of the Europeans shown in August Sander's photo and connects the farmers to both World War I and a young computer journalist in Boston. Although *Three Farmers* has the intellectual range and global concern of Powers's later novels, it lacks their artistic ingenuity, their formal butterfly effects. For most contemporary writers, this first novel would be an *Invisible Man* or *Catch-22.* But for Richard Powers, *Three Farmers* was just the beginning of his prodigious fiction.

—Tom LeClair

POWNALL, David

Nationality: British. **Born:** Liverpool, 19 May 1938. **Education:** Lord Wandsworth College, Long Sutton, Hampshire, 1949-56; University of Keele, Staffordshire, 1956-60, B.A. (honors) 1960. **Family:** Married 1) Glenys Elsie Jones in 1961 (divorced 1971), one son; 2) Mary Ellen Ray in 1972, one son. **Career:** Personnel officer, Ford Motor Co., Dagenham, Essex, 1960-63; personnel manager, Anglo-American, Zambia, 1963-69; resident writer, Century Theatre touring group, 1970-72, and Duke's Playhouse, Lancaster, 1972-75; founder and resident writer, Paines Plough Theatre, Coventry, 1975-80. **Awards:** John Whiting award, for drama, 1982, 1986. Fellow, Royal Society of Literature, 1976. **Agent:** Andrew Hewson, John Johnson Ltd., 45-47 Clerkenwell Green, Clerkenwell House, London EC1R 0HT, England. **Address:** 136 Cranley Gardens, London N10 3AH, England.

PUBLICATIONS

Novels

The Raining Tree War. London, Faber, 1974.
African Horse. London, Faber, 1975.
God Perkins. London, Faber, 1977.
Light on a Honeycomb. London, Faber, 1978.
Beloved Latitudes. London, Gollancz, 1981.
The White Cutter. London, Gollancz, 1988; New York, Viking, 1989.
The Gardener. London, Gollancz, 1990.
Stagg and His Mother. London, Gollancz, 1991.
The Sphinx and the Sybarites. London, Sinclair-Stevenson, 1993.

Short Stories

My Organic Uncle and Other Stories. London, Faber, 1976.

Plays

As We Lie (produced Cheltenham, 1973). Zambia, Nkana-Kitwe, 1969.
How Does the Cuckoo Learn to Fly? (produced on tour, 1970).
How to Grow a Guerrilla (produced Preston, Lancashire, 1971).
All the World Should Be Taxed (produced Lancaster, 1971).
The Last of the Wizards (for children; produced Windermere, Cumbria, and London, 1972).
Gaunt (produced Lancaster, 1973).
Lions and Lambs (produced on Lancashire tour, 1973).
The Dream of Chief Crazy Horse (for children; produced Fleetwood, Lancashire, 1973). London, Faber, 1975.
Beauty and the Beast, music by Stephen Boxer (produced Lancaster, 1973).
The Human Cartoon Show (produced Lancaster, 1974).
Crates on Barrels (produced on Lancashire tour, 1974; London, 1984).
The Pro (produced London, 1975).
Lile Jimmy Williamson (produced Lancaster, 1975).
Buck Ruxton (produced Lancaster, 1975).
Ladybird, Ladybird (produced Edinburgh and London, 1976).
Music to Murder By (produced Canterbury, 1976; Miami, 1984). London, Faber, 1978.

A Tale of Two Town Halls (produced Lancaster, 1976).

Motocar, and Richard III, Part Two, music by Stephen Boxer (produced Edinburgh and London, 1977). London, Faber, 1979.

An Audience Called Edouard (produced London, 1978). London, Faber, 1979.

Seconds at the Fight for Madrid (produced Bristol, 1978).

Livingstone and Sechele (produced Edinburgh, 1978; London, 1980; New York, 1982).

Barricade (produced on tour, 1979).

Later (produced London, 1979).

The Hot Hello (produced Edinburgh, 1981).

Beef (produced London, 1981; New York, 1986). Published in *Best Radio Plays of 1981,* London, Methuen, 1982.

Master Class (produced Leicester, 1983; London and Washington, D.C., 1984; New York, 1986). London, Faber, 1983.

Pride and Prejudice, adaptation of the novel by Jane Austen (produced Leicester, 1983; New Haven, Connecticut, 1985; London, 1986).

Ploughboy Monday (broadcast 1985). Published in *Best Radio Plays of 1985,* London, Methuen, 1986.

The Viewing (produced London, 1987).

Black Star (produced Bolton, Lancashire, 1987).

The Edge (produced London, 1987).

King John's Jewel (produced Birmingham, 1987).

Rousseau's Tale (produced London, 1991).

My Father's House (1991).

Elgar's Rondo (1993).

Dreams and Censorship (1993).

Radio Plays: *Free Ferry,* 1972; *Free House,* 1973; *A Place in the Country,* 1974; *An Old New Year,* 1974; *Fences,* 1976; *Under the Wool,* 1976; *Back Stop,* 1977; *Butterfingers,* 1981; *The Mist People,* 1981; *Flos,* 1982; *Ploughboy Monday,* 1985; *Beloved Latitudes,* from his own novel, 1986; *The Bridge at Orbigo,* 1987; *A Matter of Style,* 1988; *Plato Not Nato,* 1990; *The Glossomaniacs,* 1990; *Bringing Up Nero,* 1991.

Television Plays: *High Tides,* 1976; *Mackerel Sky,* 1976; *Return Fare,* 1978; *Follow the River Down,* 1979; *Room for an Inward Light,* 1980; *The Sack Judies,* 1981; *Love's Labour* (Maybury series), 1983; *The Great White Mountain* (Mountain Men series), 1987; *Something to Remember You By,* 1991.

Poetry

An Eagle Each: Poems of the Lakes and Elsewhere, with Jack Hill. Carlisle, Cumbria, Arena, 1972.

Another Country. Liskeard, Cornwall, Harry Chambers/Peterloo Poets, 1978.

Other

Between Ribble and Lune: Scenes from the North-West, photographs by Arthur Thompson. London, Gollancz, 1980.

The Bunch from Bananas (for children). London, Gollancz, 1980; New York, Macmillan, 1981.

Editor, with Gareth Pownall, *The Fisherman's Bedside Book.* London, Windward, 1980.

*   *   *

David Pownall's vision reveals and satirizes a world in microcosm. The favored territory for his early novels is the crammed, seething canvas peopled with grotesques, whose collective idiocy he lampoons in a style at once comic and macabre. Several of his books have African locations, and it is here—where technology rubs shoulders uneasily with tribal magic—that he appears most at home. Pownall utilizes a variety of literary techniques, subordinating them to a single individual utterance. His wit is caustic and pitiless, sparing no one, yet at times he shows glimpses of a touching faith in humanity.

The Raining Tree War depicts a power struggle between the ruthless president Mulombe and the Muntu religious cult under their prophetess Maud, an archetypal Earth-mother figure who claims to be the "Wife of God." Maud embodies the strength of older African traditions, and constitutes a challenge to Mulombe's authority. Into their gradually intensifying conflict Pownall weaves the threads of other lives, following his eccentric characters through the turmoil of a comic-opera war. The ridiculous, mock-heroic climax of the government's attack on Maud's capital in the Bengweulu swamp is a *tour de force,* Pownall expertly juxtaposing the broadest slapstick with the most stygian of humor. In the aftermath of this lethal "main event," the novel's conclusion is strangely poignant and moving. *The Raining Tree War* is an excellent work, skillfully handled in its action sequences, the thumbnail character sketches capably achieved.

African Horse uses the same location and several characters from the previous novel, but the main plot is devoted to the Englishman Hurl Halfcock and his search for an imagined animal ancestor. Hurl's odyssey through the bars, brothels, and house parties of the newly independent Zonkendavo provides a mixture of picaresque adventure and potent symbolism which Pownall continually ridicules en route. Confrontations abound, whether Hurl's battle with an Afrikaner rugby 15, or the more deeply layered duel between a power shovel operator and a crocodile in a colliery sump, while Hurl's weird metamorphosis into his "animalself," for instance, is both absurd and convincing. *African Horse* amuses, but lacks the coherence of *The Raining Tree War,* which is the more satisfying novel of the two.

More impressive is *Light on a Honeycomb,* set in a fictional English town where for centuries insane people have been settled and rehabilitated, and which is now ruled by madmen. Pownall recreates the biblical concept of an upper and lower world, the "honeycomb" of limestone caverns with its shadowy dream-population of slaves, Irish laborers, and ancestral tribes overset by its modern counterpart run by lunatic businessmen and gangsters, typified by the spray-on carpet foam they use to hide the universe beneath their feet. The "light" is cast by Kevin, inmate of the mental hospital, who invokes the dormant ancestors to overthrow the world above as its rulers succumb to death and madness. *Light on a Honeycomb* is a striking success, Pownall's skills marshalled to full effect. Characterization is sure, with contrasting and symbolic portrayals, and the blending of scenes is ably rendered. The author's keen eye for the ridiculous touches coldly on landowners and ineffectual revolutionaries alike, both being shown as deluded simpletons unaware of the reality about to burst from the ground beneath them. Pownall compels the reader's attention, drawing him or her through a complex network of scenes to the light above, where a new world waits to be made. Perhaps the most controlled of his early works, *Light on a Honeycomb* must be ranked among his best.

Beloved Latitudes marks a departure for Pownall. Outwardly the most "serious" of his books, it also has the smallest cast. Presented in the form of a spoken autobiography, the story follows the career of an overthrown African dictator, recounted in prison to his English "advisor" and friend. Central to the novel is the close, lover-like relationship between the two men, and the tension of their conflicting personalities. Touches of humor brighten the work, but for once Pownall's mood is unusually sombre. *Beloved Latitudes* is a powerful, thought-provoking novel, whose visual strength is matched by the author's careful understatement.

The later novels show a startling advance on previous writings, Pownall revealing himself as a novelist of considerable depth and maturity, a world away from the barbed, satirical humor of his earlier fiction. *The White Cutter, The Gardener, Stagg and His Mother,* and *The Sphinx and the Sybarites* are epic and memorable creations which show a major fiction writer at the height of his powers. Complex, brooding works, they present a bleak, tragic vision while at the same time compelling the reader's attention with their subtlety and strength. Just as the early novels reveal their attraction to tribal societies, so the most impressive of the recent works are those set furthest back in historical time. *The White Cutter* explores the life of the great medieval builder Hedric Herbertson and his encounters with a world which defines itself as a constant struggle between Good and Evil spiritual forces. These manifest themselves in a variety of forms, notably the powerful ruling group of "The Four", whose actions determine much of Hedric's life, and whose mirror-image is found in a particularly dark, disturbing version of Robin Hood's Sherwood. Hedric, driven to crime and renunciation, is a brilliantly tragic figure, and his fate is echoed by that of the Greek diviner Kallias, who in *The Sphinx and the Sybarites* is called on to solve an apparent malaise at the heart of the rich city of Sybaris. Foreseeing the destruction of Sybaris in a nightmare vision, Kallias finds himself enmeshed in a merciless web of politics and warfare which ends in tragedy. Pownall's characters are unwilling pawns to gods and men, cynically manipulated and deceived as they progress painfully to a tragic resolution. The doomed love of Eric and Pauline in *The Gardener* and the fraught love-hate relationship of *Stagg and His Mother,* both dissolved by death, are further examples. Pownall's vision is unremittingly bleak, but his imaginative power and the skillful use of language compels the respect of the reader. These latest works establish him as not only an accomplished, but an important writer of fiction.

—Geoff Sadler

PRATCHETT, Terry

Nationality: British. **Born:** 1948. **Education:** Wycombe Technical High School. **Career:** Journalist in Buckinghamshire, Bristol, and Bath, then press officer, Central Electricity Board Western Region, until 1987. **Awards:** British Science Fiction award, 1990. **Agent:** Colin Smythe Ltd., P.O. Box 6, Gerrards Cross, Buckinghamshire SL9 8XA, England.

PUBLICATIONS

Novels (series: Discworld; Truckers/Bromeliad)

Carpet People. Gerrards Cross, Buckinghamshire, Smythe, 1971; revised edition, London, Doubleday, 1992.

The Dark Side of the Sun. Gerrards Cross, Buckinghamshire, Smythe, 1976.
Strata. Gerrards Cross, Buckinghamshire, Smythe, and New York, St. Martin's Press, 1981.
The Colour of Magic (Discworld). Gerrards Cross, Buckinghamshire, Smythe, and New York, St. Martin's Press, 1983.
The Light Fantastic (Discworld). Gerrard's Cross, Buckinghamshire, Smythe, and New York, St. Martin's Press, 1986.
Mort (Discworld). London, Gollancz, and New York, New American Library, 1987.
Sourcery (Discworld). London, Gollancz, 1988; New York, New American Library, 1989.
Pyramids (Discworld). London, Gollancz, and New York, Penguin, 1989.
Guards! Guards! (Discworld; with Gray Jolliffe). London, Gollancz, 1989; New York, Roc, 1991.
Truckers (first of the Truckers trilogy; in the U.S. as the Bromeliad trilogy). London, Doubleday, 1989; New York, Delacorte, 1990.
Eric (Discworld). London, Gollancz, 1989.
Good Omens: The Nice and Accurate Predictions of Agnes Nutter, Witch, with Neil Gaiman. London, Gollancz, and New York, Workman, 1990.
Moving Pictures (Discworld). London, Gollancz, 1990.
Diggers (Truckers/Bromeliad). London, Doubleday, and New York, Delacorte, 1990.
Wings (Truckers/Bromeliad; with Neil Gaiman). London, Doubleday, 1990; New York, Delacorte, 1991.
Reaper Man (Discworld). London, Gollancz, 1991.
Lords and Ladies. London, Gollancz, 1992.
Only You Can Save Mankind. London, Doubleday, 1992.
Small Gods (Discworld). London, Gollancz, and New York, HarperCollins, 1992.
Men at Arms (Discworld). London, Gollancz, 1993.
Johnny and the Dead. London, Doubleday, 1993.
Interesting Times. London, Gollancz, 1994.
Soul Music (Discworld). London, Gollancz, 1994; New York, HarperPrism, 1995.
The Witches Trilogy (Discworld). London, Gollancz, 1995.
Equal Rites. London, Gollancz, 1986; New York, New American Library, 1987.
Wyrd Sisters. London, Gollancz, and New York, Penguin, 1988.
Witches Abroad. London, Gollancz, 1991.

Other

The Unadulterated Cat, with illustrations by Gray Jolliffe. London, Gollancz, 1989.
The Discworld Companion, with Stephen Briggs. London, Gollancz, 1994.

*   *   *

Terry Pratchett's texts are woven from the stuff of fantasy: wizards, witches, trolls, dwarves, gnomes, elves, demons, gods; magic spells, sudden space-and-time shifts, drastic metamorphoses. His fiction is both a hilarious parody of the fantasy genre and a genuine contribution to it, in that it creates a rich, imaginative "multiverse" that absorbs and intrigues the reader. It shares with the strongest fantasy a concern with fundamental issues such as death, and it incorporates aspects of contemporary culture such as fast food and rock music. Pratchett has a witty, inventive style that draws attention to itself in an engaging way and that often seizes on a phrase drawn from common speech or from literature and brings out a buried or alternative meaning—as when Robert Frost's line "good fences make good neighbors" is applied to living next door to a receiver of stolen goods.

Pratchett's major corpus of novels is the Discworld series. The Discworld is a flat disc, carried on the back of four giant elephants, who in turn stand on the shell of the huge turtle Great A'Tuin, swimming slowly through space. It is the ideal fantasy world for the postmodernist era, since its flatness means that its inhabitants have no truck with those "global" theories denounced by postmodernist thinkers. Its capital city is Ankh-Morpork, densely overpopulated, impossibly labyrinthine, and egregiously foul-smelling. The Discworld is full of stories that bear on our social and metaphysical concerns. In *Equal Rites,* for example, a dying wizard gives his staff of power to a baby who turns out to be a girl and grows up to become the first female wizard in the face of male prejudice and opposition. *Moving Pictures* looks at how cinema comes to the Discworld, whereas *Soul Music* charts the effects of a new and overwhelming form of rock music. In *Mort,* Death takes on an apprentice and tries to train him on the job, but the young man disturbs the order of the multiverse when he reprieves a young princess who is about to be assassinated.

Each of the Discworld novels is enjoyable and absorbing in its own right, with a strong and complex narrative structure and a range of character and incident. Taken together, these novels create an imaginative zone that is rich and strange, offering the reader both the pleasures of discovery, as new aspects are revealed, and of recognition, as familiar figures recur. Among the most notable of these are the Luggage, a traveling chest with hundreds of little legs, which follows its owner everywhere, proffering clean linen whenever he requires it and dealing ruthlessly with anyone or anything else that gets in its way; the Librarian of Unseen University who, having been inadvertently changed by magic into an orangutan, prefers to remain that way, since it simplifies life's philosophical problems and enables him to get by with only one utterance, "Oook"; and Death, a tall skeleton who always speaks in capital letters but who turns out to be lonely, troubled, and strangely human.

Among Pratchett's other novels, particular mention should be made of *Only You Can Save Mankind* and *Johnny and the Dead,* which combine fantasy and science fiction with a realistic portrayal of a group of teenagers in a rundown English city. In *Only You Can Save Mankind,* Johnny Maxwell finds himself involved in a video game in which the aliens against whom he is fighting turn out to be real; the novel invokes and echoes the blurring of the distinction between image and reality in the Gulf War. *Johnny and the Dead* engages with the issue of the loss of the sense of the past in the postmodernist era: Johnny joins a campaign to save a local cemetery from redevelopment after he has discovered that he can see and talk to the people buried there.

The eclectic mixture of elements and the crossing of cultural boundaries in Pratchett's fiction might mark it as postmodernist. But postmodernist work that has found critical acceptance tends to assume a knowing, distanced attitude toward the popular materials on which it draws, whereas Pratchett remains deeply rooted in those materials even as he parodies them; he thus challenges the postmodernist aesthetic as well as traditional cultural categories. The question now is whether he will continue to mine the same vein— the Discworld series shows no signs of exhaustion—or whether he will produce work that is either serious in a more conventional literary sense or which—in the manner of Thomas Pynchon—develops a new mode of seriousness.

—Nicolas Tredell

PRICE, (Edward) Reynolds

Nationality: American. **Born:** Macon, North Carolina, 1 February 1933. **Education:** Duke University, Durham, North Carolina, 1951-55 (Angier Duke scholar), A.B. (summa cum laude) 1955 (Phi Beta Kappa); Merton College, Oxford, 1955-58 (Rhodes scholar), B.Litt. 1958. **Career:** Member of the faculty since 1958, assistant professor, 1961-68, associate professor, 1968-72, professor of English, 1972-77, and since 1977, James B. Duke Professor, Duke University. Writer-in-residence, University of North Carolina, Chapel Hill, 1965, and Greensboro, 1971, and University of Kansas, Lawrence, 1967, 1969, 1980; Glasgow Professor, Washington and Lee University, Lexington, Virginia, 1971; member of the faculty, Salzburg Seminar on American Studies, 1977. Editor, the *Archive,* Durham, 1954-55. Since 1964 advisory editor, *Shenandoah,* Lexington, Virginia. Chair, National Endowment for the Arts Literature Advisory Panel, 1976. **Awards:** Faulkner Foundation prize, 1963; Guggenheim fellowship, 1964; National Association of Independent Schools award, 1964; National Endowment for the Arts fellowship, 1967; American Academy award, 1971; Bellamann Foundation award, 1976; Lillian Smith award, 1976; National Book Critics Circle award, 1987; Bobst award, 1988. Litt.D.: St. Andrews Presbyterian College, Laurinburg, North Carolina, 1978; Wake Forest University, Winston-Salem, North Carolina, 1979. **Agent:** Harriet Wasserman Literary Agency, 137 East 36th Street, New York, New York 10016. **Address:** 4813 Duke Station, Durham, North Carolina 27706, U.S.A.

PUBLICATIONS

Novels

A Long and Happy Life. New York, Atheneum, and London, Chatto and Windus, 1962.
A Generous Man. New York, Atheneum, 1966; London, Chatto and Windus, 1967.
Love and Work. New York, Atheneum, and London, Chatto and Windus, 1968.
The Surface of Earth. New York, Atheneum, 1975; London, Arlington, 1978.
The Source of Light. New York, Atheneum, 1981.
Mustian (2 novels and a story). New York, Atheneum, 1983.
Kate Vaiden. New York, Atheneum, 1986; London, Chatto and Windus, 1987.
Good Hearts. New York, Atheneum, 1988.
The Tongues of Angels. New York, Atheneum, 1990.
Blue Calhoun. New York, Atheneum, 1992.

Short Stories

The Names and Faces of Heroes. New York, Atheneum, and London, Chatto and Windus, 1963.

Permanent Errors. New York, Atheneum, 1970; London, Chatto and Windus, 1971.
Home Made. Rocky Mount, North Carolina Wesleyan College Press, 1990.
The Foreseeable Future: Three Long Stories. New York, Atheneum, 1991.
An Early Christmas. Rocky Mount, North Carolina Wesleyan College Press, 1992.
The Collected Stories. New York, Atheneum, 1993.

Uncollected Short Stories

"Night and Day at Panacea," in *Harper's* (New York), August 1974.
"Commencing," in *Virginia Quarterly Review* (Charlottesville), Spring 1975.
"His Final Mother," in *New Yorker,* 21 May 1990.
"Two Useful Visits," in *Virginia Quarterly Review* (Charlottesville), Summer 1990.
"Serious Need," in *Esquire* (New York), November 1990.
"Full Day," in *Harper's* (New York), January 1991.

Plays

Early Dark (produced New York, 1978). New York, Atheneum, 1977.
Private Contentment. New York, Atheneum, 1984.
New Music: A Trilogy. New York, Theatre Communications, 1990.
Full Moon and Other Plays. New York, Theatre Communications, 1993.

Poetry

Late Warning: Four Poems. New York, Albondocani Press, 1968.
Torso of an Archaic Apollo—After Rilke. New York, Albondocani Press, 1969.
Lessons Learned: Seven Poems. New York, Albondocani Press, 1977.
Christ Child's Song at the End of the Night. Privately printed, 1978.
Nine Mysteries (Four Joyful, Four Sorrowful, One Glorious). Winston-Salem, North Carolina, Palaemon Press, 1979.
Vital Provisions. New York, Atheneum, 1982.
The Laws of Ice. New York, Atheneum, 1986.
The Use of Fire. New York, Atheneum, 1990.

Other

The Thing Itself (address). Durham, North Carolina, Duke University Library, 1966.
Two Theophanies: Genesis 32 and John 21. Privately printed, 1971.
Things Themselves: Essays and Scenes. New York, Atheneum, 1972.
The Fourth Eclogue of Vergil. Privately printed, 1972.
An Apocryphal Hymn of Jesus. Privately printed, 1973.
Presence and Absence: Versions from the Bible. Bloomfield Hills, Michigan, Bruccoli Clark, 1973.
A Nativity from the Apocryphal Book of James. Privately printed, 1974.
Annuciation. Privately printed, 1975.
Conversations, with William Ray. Memphis, Memphis State University, 1976.
The Good News According to Mark. Privately printed, 1976.

Oracles: Six Versions from the Bible. Durham, North Carolina, Friends of the Duke University Library, 1977.
A Palpable God: Thirty Stories Translated from the Bible with an Essay on the Origins and Life of Narrative. New York, Atheneum, 1978.
Christ Child's Song at the End of the Night. Privately printed, 1978.
Question and Answer. Privately printed, 1979.
The Annual Heron. New York, Albondocani Press, 1980.
Country Mouse, City Mouse (essay). Rocky Mount, North Carolina, Friends of the Wesleyan College Library, 1981.
A Start (miscellany of early work). Winston-Salem, North Carolina, Palaemon Press, 1981.
A Common Room: Essays 1954-1987. New York, Atheneum, 1987.
Real Copies: Will Price, Crichton Davis, Phyllis Peacock, and More. Rocky Mount, North Carolina Wesleyan College Press, 1988.
Back Before Day. Rocky Mount, North Carolina Wesleyan College Press, 1989.
Clear Pictures: First Loves, First Guides. New York, Atheneum, 1989.
Conversations with Reynolds Price, edited by Jefferson Humphries. Jackson, University Press of Mississippi, 1991.
Michael Egerton (for children). Mankato, Minnesota, Creative Education, 1993.
A Whole New Life. New York, Atheneum, 1994.

*

Bibliography: *Reynolds Price: A Bibliography 1949-1984* by Stuart Wright and James L.W. West III, Charlottesville, University Press of Virginia, 1986.

Critical Studies: "A Conversation with Reynolds Price" by Wallace Kaufman, in *Shenandoah* (Lexington, Virginia), Summer 1966; "The Reynolds Price Who Outgrew the Southern Pastoral" by Theodore Solotaroff, in *Saturday Review* (New York), 26 September 1970; "Love (and Marriage) in *A Long and Happy Life,*" in *Twentieth Century Studies* (Los Angeles), January 1971.

*   *   *

Reynolds Price has moved from detailed examination of North Carolina rural life to an intense concern with the artist's vision of reality. Beginning with the tragicomic saga of the Mustian family (the novels *A Long and Happy Life* and *A Generous Man* and the story "A Chain of Love," now collected in *Mustian*), he has come in *Love and Work* and *Permanent Errors* to wrestle with narrative forms closer to the bone. In the preface to *Permanent Errors* Price described his work as "the attempt to isolate in a number of lives the central error of act, will, understanding which, once made, has been permanent, incurable, but whose diagnosis and palliation are the hopes of continuance."

This applies to all Price's fiction. *A Long and Happy Life* is the inside story of Rosacoke Mustian, a country girl seeking a conventional life with an unconventional young man, Wesley Beavers. Her error is that she conceives "a long and happy life" only in the clichéd terms of romance, of settled-wedded-bliss tradition. She reviews her life, her family's life, is discontent, becomes pregnant by Wesley and finally comes to see him and herself in larger terms, terms of myth, in a Christmas pageant which shows her the complete (and divine) meanings of motherhood, birth, and love.

Myth becomes the vehicle of self-understanding more overtly in *A Generous Man,* which shows the Mustian family several years earlier. It describes an allegorical search for an escaped circus python, a giant serpent named Death, and the discovery of a lost treasure. Milo Mustian describes the stifling forces of convention which circumscribe their lives: "it's what nine-tenths of the humans born since God said 'Adam!' have thought was a life, planned out for themselves—all my people, my Mama, my Daddy (it was what strangled him), Rosacoke . . ." Only by transcending the everyday, by seeing human life in larger terms, can the individual escape the slow strangulation of "permanent errors" and find direction and meaning in existence.

Good Hearts updates and completes the saga of Rosacoke Mustian and Wesley Beavers, who have reached married middle age and the wisdom of accumulated domestic experience. Wesley, after 28 years of marriage to Rosacoke, suddenly leaves home. Both Wesley and Rosacoke learn about their unique needs and natures, especially their sexual temperaments, in this separation. By the end of the story they are reunited after realizing essential truths about the evolving physical and spiritual demands of love.

Price's fiction has become increasingly abstract and complex as he has moved to a more inward vision. From the first he has used sets of images and metaphors to suggest a mysterious or magical reality beyond his pastoral settings. He has deepened this metaphorical (and psychological) interest in *Love and Work* and *Permanent Errors,* where the protagonists are no longer the eccentric pastoral figures of the Mustian clan but are closer to Price's own viewpoint. Price's fiction has always dealt with confusion of the heart and alienation of the mind, but the recent work draws its images and symbols from Price's own experience—his family, a visit to Dachau prison camp, the writer's situation. The grotesqueness and unfamiliarity of the Mustian clan are replaced by more familiar and universal facts of contemporary life.

In *The Tongues of Angels,* Price creates a memoir-like *Bildungsroman,* a story of adolescent initiation and adult epiphany, set in a Smoky Mountain summer camp. The novel explores directly the spiritual springs of art and the religious meaning of experience as an artist renders it. This is Price's most overt and effective disquisition on profound religious experience and memory as the bases of art.

In two large novels, *The Surface of Earth* and *The Source of Light,* Price is most ambitious. The narratives deal with a family saga encompassing the first half of our century and drawing from Price's own experience. The novels detail through letters, conversations, and lyrical soliloquies the Mayfield family and its cycle of birth, maturity and death as viewed by Rob Mayfield, who focuses the narratives. The family is more genteel than the Mustians, and these novels detail a world of important things and social valences. The search by Rob Mayfield for a sense of himself and for a peaceful reconciliation with his father's memory is an important mirror image of Rosacoke Mustian's growth into adulthood.

Love and death are polarities in Price's work—how to save life from death, how to prevent life from becoming deathly, stale, void of myth and magic. The theme appears most clearly in *A Generous Man,* when the Mustians set out to find and kill Death, the great serpent, and are finally told, "Death is dead." In the course of this magical hunt, Milo Mustian comes to understand what he must do to save himself from the slow death of a clichéd life; Rato Mustian, the wise fool, grapples with Death and escapes its coils through his cunning folly; Rosacoke moves from complete innocence to the dawn of maturity. In his later fiction Price has moved from symbols of external life to more internalized ones: sleep, dreams, a writer seeking a relationship between love and work, self and others, private life and shared life. Price's fiction describes the individual's perceptions of himself and of the realities around him, the uses of imagination. His characters travel on a quest for the potency of myth and the ability to transcend a closed vision of everyday reality. They move toward permanent truths through "permanent errors."

—William J. Schafer

PRITCHETT, (Sir) V(ictor) S(awdon)

Nationality: British. **Born:** Ipswich, Suffolk, 16 December 1900. **Education:** Alleyn's School, Dulwich, London. **Family:** Married Dorothy Rudge Roberts in 1936; one son and one daughter. **Career:** Worked in the leather trade in London, 1916-20, and in the shellac, glue, and photographic trade in Paris, 1920-32; correspondent in Ireland and Spain for the *Christian Science Monitor,* Boston, 1923-26; critic from 1926, permanent critic from 1937, and director, 1946-78, *New Statesman,* London; Christian Gauss Lecturer, Princeton University, New Jersey, 1953; Beckman Professor University of California, Berkeley, 1962; writer-in-residence, Smith College, Northampton, Massachusetts, 1966, 1970-72; Visiting Professor, Brandeis University, Waltham, Massachusetts, 1968; Clark Lecturer, Cambridge University, 1969; Visiting Professor, Columbia University, New York, 1972; writer-in-residence, Vanderbilt University, Nashville, 1981. President, PEN English Centre, 1970, and President of International PEN, 1974-76; President, Society of Authors, from 1977. **Awards:** Heinemann award, for nonfiction, 1969; PEN award, for nonfiction, 1974; W.H. Smith award, 1990; Silver Pen award, 1990. D.Litt.: University of Leeds, 1972; Columbia University, 1978; University of Sussex, Brighton, 1980; Harvard University, Cambridge, Massachusetts, 1985. Fellow, 1969, and Companion of Literature, 1987, Royal Society of Literature; Honorary Member, American Academy, 1971, and American Academy of Arts and Sciences, 1971. C.B.E. (Commander, Order of the British Empire), 1968. Knighted, 1975; Companion of Honour, 1994. **Address:** 12 Regent's Park Terrace, London N.W.1, England.

PUBLICATIONS

Novels

Clare Drummer. London, Benn, 1929.
Shirley Sanz. London, Gollancz, 1932; as *Elopement into Exile,* Boston, Little Brown, 1932.
Nothing like Leather. London, Chatto and Windus, and New York, Macmillan, 1935.
Dead Man Leading. London, Chatto and Windus, and New York, Macmillan, 1937.
Mr. Beluncle. London, Chatto and Windus, and New York, Harcourt Brace, 1951.

Short Stories

The Spanish Virgin and Other Stories. London, Benn, 1930.
You Make Your Own Life. London, Chatto and Windus, 1938.

It May Never Happen and Other Stories. London, Chatto and Windus, 1945; New York, Reynal, 1947.

Collected Stories. London, Chatto and Windus, 1956.

The Sailor, The Sense of Humour, and Other Stories. New York, Knopf, 1956.

When My Girl Comes Home. London, Chatto and Windus, and New York, Knopf, 1961.

The Key to My Heart. London, Chatto and Windus, 1963; New York, Random House, 1964.

The Saint and Other Stories. London, Penguin, 1966.

Blind Love and Other Stories. London, Chatto and Windus, 1969; New York, Random House, 1970.

Penguin Modern Stories 9, with others. London, Penguin, 1971.

The Camberwell Beauty and Other Stories. London, Chatto and Windus, and New York, Random House, 1974.

Selected Stories. London, Chatto and Windus, and New York, Random House, 1978.

On the Edge of the Cliff. New York, Random House, 1979; London, Chatto and Windus, 1980.

Collected Stories. New York, Random House, and London, Chatto and Windus, 1982.

More Collected Stories. New York, Random House, and London, Chatto and Windus, 1983.

A Careless Widow and Other Stories. London, Chatto and Windus, and New York, Random House, 1989.

Complete Short Stories. London, Chatto and Windus, 1990; as *Complete Collected Stories,* New York, Random House, 1991.

Plays

The Gambler (broadcast 1947). Published in *Imaginary Conversations,* edited by Rayner Heppenstall, London, Secker and Warburg, 1948.

La Bohème, adaptation of the libretto by Giuseppe Giacosa and Luigi Illica, music by Puccini. Boston, Little Brown, and London, Joseph, 1983.

Screenplays: *Essential Jobs* (documentary), 1942; *The Two Fathers,* with Anthony Asquith, 1944.

Radio Play: *The Gambler,* 1947.

Other

Marching Spain. London, Benn, 1928.

In My Good Books. London, Chatto and Windus, 1942; Port Washington, New York, Kennikat Press, 1977.

Build the Ships: The Official Story of the Shipyards in War-Time. London, His Majesty's Stationery Office, 1946.

The Living Novel. London, Chatto and Windus, 1946; New York, Reynal, 1947; revised edition, New York, Random House, 1964.

Why Do I Write: An Exchange of Views Between Elizabeth Bowen, Graham Greene, and V.S. Pritchett. London, Marshall, 1948; New York, Haskell House, 1976.

Books in General. London, Chatto and Windus, and New York, Harcourt Brace, 1953.

The Spanish Temper. London, Chatto and Windus, and New York, Knopf, 1954.

London Perceived. London, Chatto and Windus, and New York, Harcourt Brace, 1962.

Foreign Faces. London, Chatto and Windus, 1964; as *The Offensive Traveller,* New York, Knopf, 1964.

New York Proclaimed. London, Chatto and Windus, and New York, Harcourt Brace, 1965.

The Working Novelist. London, Chatto and Windus, 1965.

Dublin: A Portrait. London, Bodley Head, and New York, Harper, 1967.

A Cab at the Door: Childhood and Youth 1900-1920. London, Chatto and Windus, and New York, Random House, 1968.

George Meredith and English Comedy. London, Chatto and Windus, and New York, Random House, 1970.

Midnight Oil (autobiography). London, Chatto and Windus, 1971; New York, Random House, 1972.

Balzac: A Biography. London, Chatto and Windus, and New York, Knopf, 1973.

The Gentle Barbarian: The Life and Work of Turgenev. London, Chatto and Windus, and New York, Random House, 1977.

Autobiography (address). London, English Association, 1977.

The Myth Makers: Essays on European, Russian, and South American Novelists. London, Chatto and Windus, and New York, Random House, 1979.

The Tale Bearers: Essays on English, American, and Other Writers. London, Chatto and Windus, and New York, Random House, 1980.

The Turn of the Years, with Reynolds Stone. Salisbury, Russell, and New York, Random House, 1982.

The Other Side of a Frontier: A V.S. Pritchett Reader. London, Clark, 1984.

A Man of Letters: Selected Essays. London, Chatto and Windus, 1985; New York, Random House, 1986.

Chekhov: A Spirit Set Free. London, Chatto and Windus, and New York, Random House, 1988.

At Home and Abroad (essays). Berkeley, California, North Point Press, 1989; London, Chatto and Windus, 1990.

Lasting Impressions: Essays 1961-1987. London, Chatto and Windus, and New York, Random House, 1990.

Editor, *This England.* London, New Statesman and Nation, 1938.

Editor, *Novels and Stories,* by Robert Louis Stevenson. London, Pilot Press, 1945; New York, Duell, 1946.

Editor, *Turnstile One: A Literary Miscellany from the New Statesman.* London, Turnstile Press, 1948.

Editor, *The Oxford Book of Short Stories.* Oxford and New York, Oxford University Press, 1981.

*

Manuscript Collections: Humanities Research Center, University of Texas, Austin; Berg Collection, New York Public Library.

Critical Study: *V.S. Pritchett* by Dean R. Baldwin, Boston, Twayne, 1987.

V.S. Pritchett comments:

(1991) My chief interests have been: travel, especially Spanish; short stories, which I value most; literary criticism over the years for the *New Statesman.*

*   *   *

V.S. Pritchett is one of the most richly endowed of living men of letters and has written with equal distinction as literary critic, travel writer, autobiographer, novelist, and short story writer. In whatever field he writes the work bears his thumbprint and is marked by his unfailing curiosity about the oddities and vagaries of human nature and by his exceedingly close observation of the human scene, and these are allied to darting, idiosyncratic prose akin to brilliant talk.

If there is one subject that Pritchett has made his own and that, in one way or another, informs his writings, it is puritanism. He is, so to say, the connoisseur of puritanism in its characteristically English manifestations, which are generally lower-middle-class. As he writes in his essay on Gosse's *Father and Son:*

> Extreme puritanism gives purpose, drama and intensity to private life. . . . Outwardly, the extreme puritan appears narrow, crabbed, fanatical, gloomy and dull; but from the inside—what a series of dramatic climaxes his life is, what a fascinating casuistry beguiles him, how he is bemused by the comedies of duplicity, sharpened by the ingenious puzzles of the conscience, and carried away by the eloquence of hypocrisy.

Such a character is described in Matthew Burkle, the central figure in Pritchett's early novel, *Nothing like Leather.* As the title indicates, the novel is set against the background of the leader trade: though it may not be its main interest, Pritchett's fiction is always saturated in the actual.

Burkle is a man who, hating sex, channels his energies to making money. To the extent that one feels Pritchett to be moved in his delineation by intellectual curiosity rather than by sympathy, Burkle is still a more or less conventional representation of the puritan. This is true also of the representation of Harry Johnson in *Dead Man Leading,* an explorer who deserts the scientific expedition he is with in Brazil in order to search for his father, who has disappeared in the interior. The background—the heat, damp, and squalor of the Amazon forests—is most brilliantly rendered; and so, too, is the tortured mind of Johnson, who goes up the river "with the speechless fear of a son guiltily approaching his father."

But something appears in *Dead Man Leading* that is not present in the earlier novel. Intermittently, Pritchett displays himself as a comic writer, which is how one thinks of him, and there is, in these comic passages, a sense of liberation, of ease, a delight in human oddity for its own sake.

In Pritchett's major novel, *Mr. Beluncle,* comedy takes over completely, and comedy here is an aspect of sympathy; Beluncle is accepted totally. Beluncle, a furniture manufacturer on a small scale, during the course of life has been in turn Congregationalist, Methodist, Plymouth Brother, Baptist, Unitarian, Theosophist, Christian Scientist. All these changes are related in some way to his economic situation. When the novel begins, he is a member of an American sect called The Church of the Last Purification, Toronto, a sect that denies the objective existence of evil.

Beluncle may seem and is indeed a self-deceiver, a liar, a cheat, a hypocrite, and a domestic tyrant. But all this is not so important as the fact that he is a man who is as it were lived by a dream, the victim of a compulsive fantasy that rules his life and turns everything and everyone he meets into its accomplices, a fantasy that renders his life and those of his children who must suffer under him always dramatic. He is a character, in the tradition and even the mode of Dickens, on whom Pritchett, as literary critic, has written with such intuitive understanding. And the novel is extraordinarily faithful to and revealing of one section, which seems to be permanent, of English lower-middle-class life.

Pritchett's novels are intellectually exciting and wonderfully well-written. But they are less satisfying aesthetically. *Mr. Beluncle* for instance, is curiously static. He is there all the time but does not develop or change in his being. The same could be said of Pecksniff, but Pecksniff, great creation though he is, is, in *Martin Chuzzlewit,* only one character among many. One feels, indeed, that for all his great knowledge of it Pritchett is not wholly at home or comfortable in the novel form. In the short story, on the other hand, he is completely at home, and it is in the short story, for which he seems to have abandoned the novel, that he has done his finest work in fiction.

Settings and characters are much the same as in the novels. Very often the scene is the southeast of England, with London and the City not far away; the characters again from the lower-middle-class, clerks and commercial travelers. It is a world closely akin to Wells's in his early novels; the characters might be the children or grandchildren of Wells's. One thinks of a story like "Many Are Disappointed," with its four characters, office workers, on a cycling tour dreaming of beer in an inn and, in the end, settling for tea. At times, too, the matter is much the same, as in "The Saint," which might almost be an episode in *Mr Beluncle.* The difference, however, is that in his short stories Pritchett's touch is absolutely sure; he is the complete master of the form. There are also, of course, the qualities one takes for granted in him: the swift economical language, racy, colloquial, the Dickensian eye for detail, the unerring instinct for idiosyncrasy that reveals character. There is the sense, too, that the stories are not abstractions; one feels that behind them there is a whole actual observable world which in some mysterious way they sum up in themselves. Pritchett is not a writer easily classified; his stories are his own and like no one else's. They seem very English. But each one of them, like Joyce's in *Dubliners,* is the rendering of what Joyce called an "epiphany," an incident or a sudden glimpse of a happening in which a moment of reality is made manifest. This is indeed the modern storywriter's art, and among contemporary writers no one is a greater master of it than Pritchett.

—Walter Allen

PROFUMO, David

Nationality: British. **Born:** London, 30 October 1955. **Education:** Eton College, 1968-73; Magdalen College, Oxford, B.A. and M.A. (with honors), both 1977. **Family:** Married 1) Valerie Hobson; 2) Helen Ann Fraser in 1980, two sons. **Career:** Assistant master of English, Eton College, Windsor, 1978, and The Royal School, Shrewsbury, 1978-79; part-time lecturer of English, King's College, London, 1981-83. Deputy editor, *The Fiction Magazine,* 1982-84. **Awards:** Geoffrey Faber Memorial prize, for *Sea Music,* 1989. **Agent:** Peters Fraser & Dunlop, The Chambers, Chelea Harbour, Lots Road, London SW10. **Address:** 24 Argyll Road, London W8, England.

PUBLICATIONS

Novel

Sea Music. London, Secker and Warburg, 1988.
The Weather in Iceland. London, Picador, 1993.

Uncollected Short Story

"The Blind Man Eats Many Flies," in *Foreign Exchange,* edited by Julian Evans. London, Sphere, 1985.

Other

In Praise of Trout. London, Viking, 1989.

Editor, with Graham Swift, *The Magic Wheel: An Anthology of Fishing Literature.* London, Picador, 1985.

*   *   *

A keen and knowledgeable angler, David Profumo permeates his writing with his interest in fishing. *In Praise of Trout* is a personal account of this passion, in this case trout fishing. It details types of trout, the characteristics of their habitat, and the methods used to catch them. However, it is more than yet another treatise on trout angling for devotees, since it is related in informal and anecdotal fashion with the easy skill of a writer, as well as the fervent passion of an angler.

The advent of *The Magic Wheel: An Anthology of Fishing in Literature* edited by Profumo and Graham Swift, should therefore come as no surprise. It produces an interesting and compelling range of sources, to compile an unusual and intriguing collection of literary material on matters piscatorial. The collection goes much further than the obligatory homage to Izaak Walton, bringing together in chronological manner, such unlikely writers as Virginia Woolf, John Donne, Herodotus, George Orwell, Li Yu and John Gay among others. The introduction to the anthology provides an informative history of the representation of angling in diverse literary works from the ancient Greeks to Ted Hughes. It points out that this huge body of literary representation has a basis in the not infrequent correlations between fishing and acts of imagination as they have been conceived of by writers over the years: angling is "a mythopoeic activity, the shapes of its experience being representative of experience elsewhere." The idiosyncratic guiding principal of fishing as "a paradigm of the individual struggle," makes this anthology committed and earnest, yet equally something of a rewarding curiosity for the nonangler.

Such themes and preoccupations reemerge in Profumo's first novel *Sea Music* which appeared to general acclaim. Set on a remote western Scottish island in the early 1950s, it narrates the adventures of a public schoolboy, James Benson, on his summer holiday. His businessman father and an assortment of Tory friends have rented a hunting lodge for the summer, and they generally engage themselves in huntin'-shootin'-fishin' pursuits. The adults treat the islanders with colonial contempt and insouciance, preoccupied with their various sporting triumphs and business transactions, while passing the wine and port around the dining table. Enclosed in their conservative milieu, little attention is given to James by these people beyond a condescending pretense of interest. With his mother incarcerated in an asylum (for some action which is never entirely clear), and somewhat estranged from his distant, severe father and his father's friends, James finds himself lonely, alienated and isolated in the group.

In such circumstances, it is not surprising that James is drawn into a friendship with the lodge underkeeper Alec Campbell, one of the indigenous islanders, who takes him under his wing. He introduces James to his aunt Rachel, a woman with the reputed mystical properties of second sight, and with whom James becomes increasingly fascinated. It is Alec and Rachel who engage James's attention: with stories about the island's past; jaunts to different parts of the island; anecdotes about various natural phenomena like the blood-stone; myths and legends about the Three Sons of the North Wind, and Bride, the foster-mother of Christ. It is through Alec's friendship that James undergoes an initiation in various island rites sufficient for Alec to acknowledge "You're an island boy now," in what appears to be all but an adoption of James as a surrogate son.

Profumo's writing is understated, working more by suggestion and hint than by emphatic declaration. It uses the Scottish islands as a gentle backdrop to the boy's unfolding consciousness, and the Gaelic language which marks the speech of the native inhabitants seems somewhat too "atmospheric" at times. Nevertheless, his novel constantly brings one back to water—the rivers and lochs of the island, the surrounding sea, and its animal life. The book is punctuated with James's initial observation of and contact with sea life: the "inky, arched backs" of lobsters; the jellyfish "like an egg poaching in a pan;" the skinning of a dead seal; the tense excitement of catching a trout; the surreptitious stealth in the night expedition to poach salmon; the compelling horror of finding a rotting monkey carcass on the shoreline. Profumo subtly brings his knowledge and love of fishing into the narrative and his dialogue between the portly Doctor and James about the art of making flies for fly-fishing; the descriptions of various fish throughout the holiday; and the lore attached to various fishing pursuits. This serves to give the narrative a delicate touch of depth, in a novel which is finely balanced between sketch and full portrait. Most of the characters are no more than suggestive types, from Mr. Benson's garrulous mistress Mrs. Walker who gushes and oozes affection throughout the novel, to the obsequious gamekeeper Willie Grant, who desires to rid himself of Alec Campbell and please the squirearchy.

It comes as something of a shock when James Benson dies in the final pages of the novel. He is diagnosed as having some form of blood disease, but the causes of death are inexact and there are symbolic and structural hints of some mysterious links with the illness Rachel suffered in the final days of James's vacation on the island. In the concluding scene, Alec launches a small leaf-boat on the sea and this returns the novel back to the realms of Scottish folk-myth which so riveted James in Rachel's company. The return to the sea also completes the symbolic dimension of the novel, with its fascination for the sound of water and the music of the sea. This first foray into fiction produces a compelling drama of childhood development, which provides a sympathetic depiction of a lonely and marginalized youth, whilst simultaneously acting as an oblique indictment of the class and community values of the English postwar bourgeoisie.

—Tim Woods

PROULX, E(dna) Annie

Nationality: American. **Born:** Norwich, Connecticut, 22 August 1935. **Education:** University of Vermont, Burlington, B.A.(cum laude), 1969 (Phi Beta Kappa); Sir George Williams University, Montreal, M.A., 1973. **Family:** Married James Hamilton Lang in 1969 (divorced 1990); three children. **Awards:** Kress Fellow,

Harvard University, Boston, 1974; Vermont Council of the Arts fellowship, 1989, National Endowment for the Arts fellowship, 1991, Guggenheim Foundation fellowship, 1992; PEN/Faulkner award, 1993, for *Postcards;* National Book award, 1993, *Chicago Tribune* Heartland award, 1993, *Irish Times International* award, 1993, and Pulitzer prize, 1994, all for *The Shipping News.* D.H.L.: University of Maine, Orono, 1994. **Address:** c/o Scribners Publishing Co., 866 Third Avenue, 7th floor, New York, New York 10022, U.S.A.

PUBLICATIONS

Novels

Postcards. New York, Scribner, 1992; London, Fourth Estate, 1993.
The Shipping News. New York, Scribner,1993; London, Fourth Estate, 1994.

Short Stories

Heart Songs, and Other Stories. New York, Scribner, 1988; London, Flamingo, 1989.

Other

Sweet and Hard Cider: Making It, Using It, and Enjoying It, with Lew Nichols. Charlotte, Vermont, Garden Way, 1980.
"What'll You Take for It?": Back to Barter. Charlotte, Vermont, Garden Way, 1981.
The Complete Dairy Foods Cookbook: How to Make Everything from Cheese to Custard in Your Kitchen, with Lew Nichols. Emmaus, Pennsylvania, Rodale Press, 1982.
The Gardener's Journal and Record Book. Emmaus, Pennsylvania, Rodale Press, 1983.
Plan and Make Your Own Fences and Gates, Walkways, Walls and Drives. Emmaus, Pennsylvania, Rodale Press, 1983.
The Fine Art of Salad Gardening. Emmaus, Pennsylvania, Rodale Press, 1985.
The Gourmet Gardener: Growing Choice Fruits and Vegetables with Spectacular Results, illustrated by Robert Byrd. New York, Fawcett Columbine, 1987.

*   *   *

Arguably one of the most exciting fictionists to come along in decades, E. Annie Proulx is hardly what one might call an overnight success. For nearly two decades, she worked as freelance journalist and was a writer of "how-to" books on assignment; meanwhile, stories bubbled inside her. They finally erupted in her first collection, *Heart Songs and Other Stories.* Set in a northern New England, a landscape that can only be described as "severe," the nine stories gave evidence of greatness to follow. Their odd-sounding names and battered conditions were simultaneously a mirror of the landscape and of Proulx's own quirky humor.

Heart Songs was followed by *Postcards,* a novel that won the PEN/Faulkner Award for Fiction. In other hands Proulx's decision to launch each chapter with a postcard tied to Loyal Blood, an aimless wanderer who serves as the book's protagonist, would have been a disaster, but Proulx so integrates the furious pace of story

with the dazzle of technique that the result seems at once aesthetically coherent and entirely effortless.

Moreover, in documenting the decline-and-fall of a small American farm, one that had been in the Blood family for generations, Proulx was driving toward the very heart of America itself. Not that she preaches her message in an overt, editorializing manner; rather, her fiction dramatizes the particularities of a time and place with the fury of a gothic vision.

Shipping News is also set in an essentially hostile environment: Killick-Claw, a remote coastal village in Newfoundland. Known for its sudden storms and icy seas, the setting seems as unlikely as the postcards faithfully reproduced in Proulx's earlier novel. However, the saga of Quoyle, a hapless journalist who returns to his Newfoundland family home when his faithless wife is killed in a car wreck, serves as the springboard for an ambitious, multilayered novel.

At the center of *The Shipping News* is both the column of maritime comings-and-going that Quoyle writes for *The Gammy Bird* (Prouxl's hilarious send-up of a small town newspaper) and her protagonist's ongoing effort to pull his life together. As Proulx's delightfully quirky style makes clear, he has a long way to go:

> [He had] a great damp loaf of a body. At six he weighed eighty pounds. At sixteen he was buried under a casement of flesh. Head shaped like a crensaw, no neck, reddish hair ruched back. Features as bunched as kissed fingertips. Eyes the color of plastic. The monstrous chin, a freakish shelf jutting from the lower face.

As for *The Gammy Bird,* it specializes in car wrecks ("We run a front-page photo of a car wreck every week, whether we have a wreck or not"), sexual abuse stories garnered from the wire service, and the "shipping news," the paper's effort to spread the good news that commerce still goes on in Killick-Claw.

Quoyle digs out of his disastrous past by digging into work and the strange community he encounters through it. Even more remarkable, what might have been the unrelenting tale of his perpetual loserhood takes a sharp turn at the end toward love. Not only does Quoyle's unlikely column become an unqualified success (rather like *The Shipping News* itself, which won a Pulitzer Prize), but Quoyle finds himself "coiled" in the grasp of the community in general and of Wavey Prowse in particular. That he marries her at the end seems as magical—given Quoyle's long history of estrangement—as Newfoundland. But that may well be Proulx's point: darkness, even dark comedy, may not be the final word. Rather,

> Water may be older than light, diamonds crack in hot goat's blood, mountaintops give off cold fire, forests appear in mid-ocean, it may happen that a crab is caught with the shadow of a hand on its back, that the wind be imprisoned in a bit of knotted string. And it may be that love sometimes occurs with pain or misery.

With only three books, Annie Proulx has convinced readers that she is simply not capable of writing unengaging fiction; and they are waiting impatiently for her to prove them right.

—Sanford Pinsker

PURDY, James (Otis)

Nationality: American. **Born:** near Fremont, Ohio, 14 July 1923.
Education: The University of Chicago, 1941, 1946; University of
Pueblo, Mexico. **Career:** Worked as an interpreter in Latin America,
France, and Spain; taught at Lawrence College, Appleton, Wisconsin, 1949-53. Since 1953 full-time writer,. Visiting professor, University of Tulsa, Oklahoma, 1977. **Awards:** American Academy
award, 1958, 1993; Guggenheim fellowship, 1958, 1962; Ford fellowship, for drama, 1961. **Address:** 236 Henry Street, Brooklyn,
New York 11201, U.S.A.

PUBLICATIONS

Novels

Malcolm. New York, Farrar Straus, 1959; London, Secker and
Warburg, 1960.
The Nephew. New York, Farrar Straus, 1960; London, Secker and
Warburg, 1961.
Cabot Wright Begins. New York, Farrar Straus, 1964; London
Secker and Warburg, 1965.
Eustace Chisholm and the Works. New York, Farrar Straus, 1967;
London, Cape, 1968.
Sleepers in Moon-Crowned Valleys:
 Jeremy's Version. New York, Doubleday, 1970; London, Cape,
 1971.
 The House of the Solitary Maggot. New York, Doubleday, 1974;
 London, Owen, 1986.
I Am Elijah Thrush. New York, Doubleday, and London, Cape, 1972.
Narrow Rooms. New York, Arbor House, 1978; Godalming, Sur-
rey, Black Sheep, 1980.
Mourners Below. New York, Viking Press, 1981; London, Owen, 1984.
On Glory's Course. New York, Viking, 1984; London, Owen, 1985.
In the Hollow of His Hand. New York, Weidenfeld and Nicolson,
1986; London, Owen, 1988.
Garments the Living Wear. San Francisco, City Lights, and Lon-
don, Owen, 1989.
Out with the Stars. London, Owen, 1993.
Kitty Blue (fairy tale). Utrecht, The Netherlands, Ballroom, 1993.

Short Stories

Don't Call Me by My Right Name and Other Stories. New York,
William Frederick Press, 1956.
63: Dream Palace. New York, William Frederick Press, 1956; Lon-
don, Gollancz, 1957.
Color of Darkness: Eleven Stories and a Novella. New York, New
Directions, 1957; London, Secker and Warburg, 1961.
Children Is All (stories and plays). New York, New Directions,
1961; London, Secker and Warburg, 1963.
An Oyster Is a Wealthy Beast (story and poems). Los Angeles,
Black Sparrow Press, 1967.
Mr. Evening: A Story and Nine Poems. Los Angeles, Black Spar-
row Press, 1970.
A Day after the Fair: Collection of Play and Stories. New York,
Note of Hand, 1977.
Sleep Tight. New York, Nadja, 1979.
The Candles of Your Eyes. New York, Nadja, 1985.

The Candles of Your Eyes and Thirteen Other Stories. New York,
Weidenfeld, 1987; London, Owen, 1988.

Plays

Mr. Cough Syrup and the Phantom Sex, in *December* (Western
Springs, Illinois), vol. 8, no. 1, 1960.
Cracks (produced New York, 1963).
Wedding Finger, in *New Direction 28.* New York, New Directions,
1974.
Two Plays (includes *A Day after the Fair* and *True*). Dallas, New
London Press, 1979.
Scrap of Paper, and The Berry-Picker: Two Plays. Los Angeles,
Sylvester and Orphans, 1981.
The Berry-Picker (produced New York, 1985). With *Scrap of Pa-
per,* 1981.
Proud Flesh:Four Short Plays (includes *Strong, Clearing in the
Forest, Now, What Is It, Zach?*). Northridge, California, Lord
John Press, 1980.
Ruthanna Elder. New York, Zenith Winds, 1990.
In the Night of Time and Four Other Plays. Amsterdam, Polak and
Van Genned.

Poetry

The Running Sun. New York, Paul Waner Press, 1971.
Sunshine Is an Only Child. New York, Aloe, 1973.
I Will Arrest the Bird That Has No Light. Northridge, California,
Santa Susana Press, 1977.
Lessons and Complaints. New York, Nadja, 1978.
The Brooklyn Branding Parlors. New York, Contact II, 1986.
Collected Poems. Amsterdam, Polak and Van Genned, 1992.

*

Bibliography: By Jay Ladd, in *American Book Collector*
(Ossining, New York), September-October 1981.

Manuscript Collections: Yale University, New Haven, Connecticut; Ohio State University, Columbus.

Critical Studies: Introduction by David Daiches to *Malcolm,* 1959,
by Edith Sitwell to *Color of Darkness,* London, Secker and
Warburg, 1961, and by Tony Tanner to *Color of Darkness,* and
Malcolm, New York, Doubleday, 1974; *The Not-Right House: Es-
says on James Purdy* by Bettina Schwarzchild, Columbia, Univer-
sity of Missouri Press, 1968; *City of Words,* London, Cape, and
New York, Harper, 1971, and "Birdsong," in *Partisan Review* (New
Brunswick, New Jersey), Fall 1972, both by Tony Tanner; "James
Purdy on the Corruption of Innocents" by Frank Baldanza, in *Con-
temporary Literature* (Madison, Wisconsin), 1974; interview with
Fred Barron, in *Penthouse* (New York), July 1974; *James Purdy*
by Henry Chupack, Boston, Twayne, 1975; *James Purdy* by
Stephen D. Adams, London, Vision Press, and New York, Barnes
and Noble, 1976; "James Purdy and the Black Mask of Humanity" by Joseph T. Skerrett, Jr., in *Melus* (Los Angeles), 1979.

James Purdy comments:

 (1972) As I see it, my work is an exploration of the American
soul conveyed in a style based on the rhythms and accents of American speech. From the beginning my work has been greeted with a

persistent and even passionate hostility on the part of the New York literary establishment which tries to rule America's literary taste—and the world's. My early work was privately printed by friends. Dame Edith Sitwell read these works and persuaded Victor Gollancz to publish the book in England. Without her help I would never have been published in America and never heard of. The mediocrity of the American literary scene, as is evidenced in the *New York Times* and the creatures of the vast New York establishment, has tried to reduce me to starvation and silence. Yet as a matter of fact I believe my work is the most American of any writer writing today. My subject, as I said, is the exploration of the inside of my characters, or as John Cowper Powys put it, "under the skin." The theme of American culture, American commercial culture, that is, is that man can be adjusted, that loudness and numbers are reality, and that to be "in" is to exist. My work is the furthest from this definition of "reality." All individual thought and feeling have been silenced or "doped" in America today, and to be oneself is tantamount to non-existence. I see no difference between Russia and America; both are hideous failures, both enemies of the soul, both devourers of nature, and undisciplined disciplinarians who wallow in the unnatural. Anything in America is sacred which brings in money, and the consumers can easily be persuaded to move from their old crumbling Puritan ethic to belief in things like sexual stereotyping and coprophilia, provided and only provided these bring in money and notoriety. The one crime is to be oneself, unless it is a "self" approved and created by the commercial forces. Beneath this vast structure of madness, money, and anesthetic prostitution, is my own body of work.

I prefer not to give a biography since my biography is in my work, and I do not wish to communicate with anybody but individuals, for whom my work was written in the first place. I began writing completely in the dark, and so continue. Were I in a financial position to do so, I would never publish anything commercially, since the literary establishment can promote only lies, and the critics, newspapers, and public, having been fed on poison so long, are incapable of reading anything that is not an advertisement for their own destruction. The most applauded writers in America are those who seem to have been born in a television studio where words are hourly produced from baking tins. In New York city, where American speech is unknown, a writer such as myself is considered a foreigner. Clarity and idiomatic language are considered in fact mad, while the language of dope addicts and coprophiliacs is now standard "American," approved for use by the dowagers who make best-sellers.

*   *   *

James Purdy is fascinated by the "color of darkness." His stories and novels deal with consuming narcissism and they assume, consequently, that "normal" love is, for the most part, cruel and nightmarish.

In *Color of Darkness* he gives us many heroes who are confused, lonely, and freakish. They do not know how to love (or to be loved). They are afraid to commit themselves. We see them sitting in dark rooms or roaming city streets; we hear their silent screams. Fenton Riddleway is so tormented by love for Claire, his dying brother, in "63: Dream Palace," the most impressive story in the collection, that he must kill him. The murder is the culmination of perverse love; it is perfectly in keeping with the "not-rightness" and rot of their dream palace.

In another collection, *Children Is All*, Purdy returns to the conflicts in family relationships. Often his heroes are orphans or bach-

elors. The narrator of "Daddy Wold," for example, has seen his wife and child leave him; he turns for solace to the invisible "daddy." He calls him on the "trouble phone", he rants, confesses, and rambles. But he is, finally, alone—except for the rats which crawl near him. "Goodnight, Sweetheart," like all of the best stories, fuses the realistic (or cliché) dialogue and the fantastic incident. It begins with Pearl Miranda walking "stark naked from her class-room in the George Washington" to the house of Winston, a former pupil. Both are victims of love (or "rape"); both cannot exist in the wolfish world. Unfortunately, they cannot even live with each other. As the story ends, they "both muttered to themselves in the darkness as if they were separated by different rooms from one another." They pray for help.

Purdy's novels are more varied than his stories. (It is questionable whether they surpass the great achievement of the stories.) The hero of his first novel, *Malcolm,* searches for his father, hoping thereby to affirm his own identity and *name*. But, like Fenton Riddleway, he cannot exist as a "person"—he becomes another shadow in the rotten city. He is manipulated by others; he is never understood completely, except as a mere reflection of their selfish demands. Malcolm is, to quote his lusty wife, "a little bit of this and that," and when he dies—has he ever lived?—he apparently vanishes into thin air. *Malcolm* is a wonderfully strange mixture of comedy and pathos, and it alone asserts Purdy's impressive gifts as a novelist. Although it deals with the lack of substance in relationships—between human beings and the cosmos—it creates its own substantial texture largely as a result of Purdy's mixed, "transformational" style.

The Nephew is set in Rainbow Center, a small American town. (It is a change from the "fairy-tale" *Malcolm.*) It delights in clichés, minor scandals, and popular holidays; it is, at least superficially, a realistic picture of the middle Americans. But it represents Boyd and Alma (and Cliff, their missing nephew) in such a deceptive, complex way that "local color" changes subtly to universal darkness. When Alma discovers that she has never known Cliff (despite having lived with him for many years) and, consequently, realizes her own needs and dreams, she is depressed *and* exalted. She grasps the hard truth; she understands that we are all "missing" shadows; we live briefly and secretly. She accepts the significance of memorial days—the novel begins and ends on this holiday—and the "faint delicious perfume" of our lives before the court house clock strikes again. Thus *The Nephew,* like all of Purdy's novels, must be read closely (as Alma reads her nephew's life)—it presents two worlds and demands the recognition that only art can reconcile their differences.

Cabot Wright Begins is a savage satire on American life. It attacks the automatic, false, and empty values which make us treat people as *valuable objects.* Cabot Wright becomes a rapist because he can assert his identity only as a vital, pumping being. Later he runs away from the others—Bernie, Zoe, and Princeton—who want to trap and use his exotic past for their narcissistic ends. Cabot Wright begins to laugh and write; he rises from the "deadly monotony of the human continuity" when he lies on the ground, "weeping a little from the pain of his laughter, a thread of drivel coming down from his mouth onto his pointed dimpled chin." Despite the cluttered sermons, this novel is brilliantly effective when its says "HA!" to the boredom of our daily routines. It is Purdy's blackest comedy.

Eustace Chisholm and the Works details the various strategies of lovers who refuse to acknowledge their own potentialities. The homosexuality which colored *Malcolm, The Nephew* and *"63:*

Dream Palace" flourishes here. Daniel Haws, for example, cannot accept his love for Amos (except at the end); he flees from it into the Army. There he is "satisfied" by sadistic Captain Stadger in a powerfully detailed execution (or embrace?). These Army scenes are perhaps the most brutal ones in all of Purdy's fiction.

Eusatce Chisholm is a writer. He resembles Alma, Cabot Wright, and Bernie of *Cabot Wright Begins* in trying to solve the mysteries of love and will in the community, and, like them, he discovers that he cannot get to the heart of the matter. He *abdicates*—unlike Purdy himself—and turns instead to his wife for incredible love. He warms her with "a kind of ravening love," knowing that they will probably "consume" each other in the future. He is saved only momentarily.

Jeremy's Version is the first part of an uncompleted trilogy called *Sleepers in Moon-Crowned Valleys,* but it stands alone. Jeremy is an adolescent who writes down the sermons, tales, and histories of Matthew Lacy. He is, therefore, the familiar character we have met before, but unlike the other earlier writers, he is more open, innocent and *human* than they are. He learns as he listens and transcribes.

Jeremy moves into the past. He becomes so involved with the family conflicts of the 19th-century Fergises—he identifies especially with Jethro, another adolescent writer—that at times he becomes a free-floating *spirit*. Thus he forces us to recognize that only by giving oneself to others can we survive and create. He offers hope. His "version" is finally a mellow, full, and sunny account, which indicates some new directions for Purdy's forthcoming novels.

The House of the Solitary Maggot, the second volume of the trilogy, presents different characters—Lady Bythwaite and her illegitimate sons—but it also assumes that love is a bloody mixture. The "family" is, again, a maggot-ridden, melodramatic structure. Thus this novel, a discontinuous part of the trilogy, parallels the first, implying a mythic, disturbing, general design; it offers few solutions and little hope for American society.

—Irving Malin

PUZO, Mario

Nationality: American. **Born:** New York City, 15 October 1920. **Education:** The New School for Social Research, New York; Columbia University, New York. **Military Service:** Served in the United States Army Air Force during World War II. **Family:** Married Erika Lina Broske in 1946; three sons and two daughters. **Career:** Administrative assistant in U.S. Government offices, in New York and overseas, for 20 years; assistant editor of a magazine, late 1960s. Lives on Long Island, New York. **Awards:** Oscar, for screenplay, 1972, 1974. **Agent:** Candida Donadio and Associates, Inc., 111 West 57th St., New York, New York 10019. **Address:** c/o G.P. Putnam and Sons Inc., 200 Madison Ave., New York, New York 10022, U.S.A.

PUBLICATIONS

Novels

The Dark Arena. New York, Random House, 1955; London, Heinemann, 1971.

The Fortunate Pilgrim. New York, Atheneum, 1965; London, Heinemann, 1966.
The Godfather. New York, Putnam, and London, Heinemann, 1969.
Fools Die. New York, Putnam, and London, Heinemann, 1978.
The Sicilian. New York, Linden Press, 1984; London, Bantam Press, 1985.
The Fourth K. New York, Random House, and London, Heinemann, 1991.

Uncollected Short Stories

"Last Christmas," in *American Vanguard 1950,* edited by Charles I. Glicksberg. New York, Cambridge, 1950.
"First Sundays," in *Redbook* (New York), February 1968.

Plays

Screenplays: *The Godfather,* with Francis Ford Coppola, 1972; *The Godfather, Part 2,* with Francis Ford Coppola, 1974; *Earthquake,* with George Fox, 1974; *Superman,* with others, 1978; *Superman II,* with David Newman and Leslie Newman, 1981.

Other

The Runaway Summer of Davie Shaw (for children). New York, Platt and Munk, 1966; Kingswood, Surrey, World's Work, 1976.
The Godfather Papers and Other Confessions. New York, Putnam, and London, Heinemann, 1972.
Inside Las Vegas. New York, Grosset and Dunlap, 1977.

*

Critical Study: *The Italian-American Novel* by Rose B. Green, Fairleigh Dickinson University Press, 1974.

Manuscript Collection: Boston University.

*   *   *

Mario Puzo has developed through his novels a close examination of the social and psychological bases of power and authority in human affairs. Beginning with *The Dark Arena,* a study of law, justice, compassion, and corruption in occupied Germany, and continuing through *The Godfather* and *The Sicilian,* close studies of organized crime and its operation in Sicily and the U.S., Puzo has reiterated variations on the root idea that power corrupts.

Using his observations of Italo-American culture and a strong mythopoeic imagination, Puzo has created a saga-history of the "American dream" as it has been played out in the 20th century. In *The Dark Arena* we follow Mosca, an ex-G.I. of Italian descent, who adapts himself to the complex moral-psychological drama of Germany rising from the ashes of World War II. *The Fortunate Pilgrim* traces in a parallel fashion the adaptation of an Italian woman to America after emigration. The same theme emerges in *The Godfather* and *The Sicilian,* where we follow the Corleone clan, their family connections in Sicily and the tangled web of the Mafia and its ancient codes and rules. The collision of "official" law and the laws of the family, of honor, and of social reality forms a major focus on Puzo's imagination.

In *The Godfather* the immigrant saga is epitomized by Don Corleone, a self-named, self-made "businessman" who has become the ultimate entrepreneur-controller in New York City, a "crime boss" whose operation is a close parody of legitimate corporate

America. A profound ambivalence colors the Corleone saga, a realization by the Don, his wife, and his sons that the chivalric-baronial role they uphold operates at once for good and for evil. The novel traces the development of the Corleones as modern-day Borgias, *condottieri* who impose their code of self-interested "honor" by brutal force and terror.

The Sicilian turns from the American version of the Mafia rule to that of Sicily, where we follow the parallel careers of Michael Corleone, heir to the U.S. family empire, and Turi Giuliano, his counterpart in the Old World. Puzo dexterously reveals how the "family" structure of both empires creates a powerful, repressive society. The paralleling allows Puzo to fill in details of the Corleone saga omitted in the first large novel and to reinforce his theme of the corruption that accompanies power-by-terror.

In *Fools Die* Puzo develops some of these themes in a more complex setting—the interconnecting worlds of bigtime gambling, the film industry, and publishing. The book strains in developing the chivalric theme so natural in *The Godfather* and *The Sicilian* by following the lines of brothers Arthur and (John) Merlyn through a "New Camelot" of contemporary America. The themes of personal honor and seduction to corruption are blurred by the large cast of characters and shifting scenes and made too obvious in the allegorizing parallels with the Arthurian romances.

Puzo's strongest gifts lie with a powerful, simple, and direct naturalistic style, with a grasp on the historical experience of adaptation to 20th-century America by the dispossessed immigrant and with a matter-of-fact examination of the moral, social, and psychological issues surrounding organized crime as an important U.S. subculture. His mythmaking powers are best displayed in the Corleone story, in which a Machiavellian ethos is created by the conditions and limitations of U.S. culture, so that the Sicilian codes and mores can be transferred and amplified in the economic ferment of America. The basic questions of ethics and justice are significant ones, and Puzo shows how the bootstrap philosophy of material success can operate effectively as "crime," even when it is defined as "law." The figures he creates in the Corleone family reflect important images of the American, as self-defined.

—William J. Schafer

PYNCHON, Thomas

Nationality: American. **Born:** Glen Cove, New York, 8 May 1937. **Education:** Cornell University, Ithaca, New York, 1954-58, B.A. 1958. **Military Service:** Served in the United States Naval Reserve. **Career:** Former editorial writer, Boeing Aircraft, Seattle. **Awards:** Faulkner award, 1964; Rosenthal Memorial award, 1967; National Book award, 1974; American Academy Howells medal, 1975. **Agent:** Candida Donadio and Associates, 231 West 22nd Street, New York, New York 10011. **Address:** c/o Little Brown, 34 Beacon Street, Boston, Massachusetts 02106, U.S.A.

PUBLICATIONS

Novels

V. Philadelphia, Lippincott, and London, Cape, 1963.

The Crying of Lot 49. Philadelphia, Lippincott, 1966; London, Cape, 1967.
Gravity's Rainbow. New York, Viking Press, and London, Cape, 1973.
Vineland. Boston, Little Brown, and London, Secker and Warburg, 1990.

Short Stories

Mortality and Mercy in Vienna. London, Aloes, 1976.
Low-lands. London, Aloes, 1978.
The Secret Integration. London, Aloes, 1980.
The Small Rain. London, Aloes, 1980(?).
Slow Learner: Early Stories. Boston, Little Brown, 1984; London, Cape, 1985.

Other

A Journey into the Mind of Watts. London, Mouldwarp, 1983.
Deadly Sins, illustrations by Etienne Delessert. New York, Morrow, 1994.

*

Bibliography: *Thomas Pynchon: A Bibliography of Primary and Secondary Materials* by Clifford Mead, Elmwood Park, Illinois, Dalkey Archive Press, 1989.

Critical Studies: *Thomas Pynchon* by Joseph V. Slade, New York, Warner, 1974, and *Thomas Pynchon,* New York, Lang, 1990; *Mindful Pleasures: Essays on Thomas Pynchon* edited by George Levine and David Leverenz, Boston, Little Brown, 1976; *The Grim Phoenix: Reconstructing Thomas Pynchon* by William M. Plater, Bloomington, Indiana University Press, 1978; *Pynchon: A Collection of Critical Essays* edited by Edward Mendelson, Englewood Cliffs, New Jersey, Prentice Hall, 1978; *Pynchon: Creative Paranoia in Gravity's Rainbow* by Mark Richard Siegel, Port Washington, New York, Kennikat Press, 1978; *Thomas Pynchon: The Art of Allusion* by David Cowart, Carbondale, Southern Illinois University Press, 1980; *The Rainbow Quest of Thomas Pynchon* by Douglas A. Mackey, San Bernardino, California, Borgo Press, 1980; *Pynchon's Fictions: Thomas Pynchon and the Literature of Information* by John O. Stark, Athens, Ohio University Press, 1980; *A Reader's Guide to Gravity's Rainbow* by Douglas Fowler, Ann Arbor, Michigan, Ardis, 1980; *Critical Essays on Thomas Pynchon* edited by Richard Pearce, Boston, Hall, 1981; *Pynchon: The Voice of Ambiguity* by Thomas H. Schaub, Urbana, University of Illinois Press, 1981; *Thomas Pynchon* by Tony Tanner, London, Methuen, 1982; *Signs and Symptoms: Thomas Pynchon and the Contemporary World* by Peter L. Cooper, Berkeley, University of California Press, 1983; *Approaches to Gravity's Rainbow* edited by Charles Clerc, Columbus, Ohio State University Press, 1983; *Ideas of Order in the Novels of Thomas Pynchon* by Molly Hite, Columbus, Ohio State University Press, 1983; *The Style of Connectedness: Gravity's Rainbow and Thomas Pynchon* by Thomas Moore, Columbia, University of Missouri Press, 1987; *A Gravity's Rainbow Companion* by Steven C. Weisenburger, Athens, University of Georgia Press, 1988; *The Fictional Labyrinths of Thomas Pynchon* by David Seed, London, Macmillan, 1988; *A Hand to Turn the Time: The Menippean Satires of Thomas Pynchon* by Theodore D. Kharpertian, Rutherford, New Jersey, Fairleigh

Dickinson University Press, 1989; *Writing Pynchon: Strategies in Fictional Analysis* by Alec McHoul and David Wills, London, Macmillan, 1990; *The Gnostic Pynchon* by Dwight Eddins, Bloomington, Indiana University Press, 1990; *Thomas Pynchon: Allusive Parables of Power* by John Dugdale, London, Macmillan, and New York, St. Martin's Press, 1990; *New Essays on "The Crying of Lot 49"* edited by Patrick O'Donnell, Cambridge, Cambridge University Press, 1991; *The Postmodernist Allegories of Thomas Pynchon* by Deborah L. Madsen, New York, St. Martin's Press, and Leicester, Leicester University Press, 1991; *Marginal Forces/Cultural Centers: Tolson, Pynchon, and the Politics of the Canon* by Michael Bérubé, Ithaca, New York, Cornell University Press, 1992; *Thomas Pynchon* by Judith Chambers, New York, Twayne, 1992; *Pynchon's Poetics: Interfacing Theory and Text* by Hanjo Berressem, Urbana, University of Illinois Press, 1993; *The Vineland Papers: Critical Takes on Pynchon's Novel* edited by Geoffrey Green, Donald Greiner, and Larry McCaffery, Normal, Illinois, Dalkey Archive Press, 1994.

*   *   *

The work of Thomas Pynchon draws upon a wide range of Western experience. Reference to social, political, historical, scientific, and artistic phenomena is combined with brilliant invention to create novels and stories renowned for their opacity. Pynchon's stylistic virtuosity demonstrates that debt to Joyce common to those writers whose use of form is intended to absent the artist from the art. *Gravity's Rainbow,* Pynchon's longest and most difficult novel, for which a much needed guide to sources and contexts is now available (Steven C. Weisenburger, *A Gravity's Rainbow Companion,* 1988), has more than 400 characters located all over the world, but mainly in London during the bombing raids of World War II and in postwar Germany at the beginning of the modern age, each with a plot to unravel. The novel disturbs traditional narrative structures and defies paraphrase, but, as with the Pynchon canon as a whole, social and political trends are extrapolated from present events to form a chaotic world in which the reader becomes involved in a quest for significance amid too much undifferentiated information.

Gravity's Rainbow, however, is distinctly Pynchon's own. As in *V,* the first of Pynchon's four novels, the presence of the artist is detectable, and easily distinguished, by the exuberance of a style which becomes formal or colloquial at will, which delights in absurdly complex plots, and which takes pleasure in a vast array of literary parodies and imitations. The characters of *V* are impelled through labyrinthine plots which concern, among other things, alligator hunts in New York sewers, covert diplomacy in Africa during the last century, and a young woman's plastic surgery. Pynchon's characters struggle to make connections between events. This struggle he designates as individual paranoia.

Paranoia, or the suspicion of it, is not uncommon in the world of Pynchon's novels. Oedipa Maas, in *The Crying of Lot 49,* cannot be certain that she has discovered an alternative Postal Service in America, nor whether it has any connection with the legacy left by her rich one-time lover, nor whether there really is a group of alienated citizens in America whose lives are lived without participating in ordinary American life and its institutions. It may be mere delusion, and the reader like Oedipa, is tantalized into a quest for significance amid linguistic brilliance in which meaning is possible, but never quite confirmed, and a style which can charge any moment with significance. The reader's experience can be Oedipa's when she first views San Narciso. She is reminded of her first sight of a transistor circuit, ". . . though she knew even less about radios than about Southern Californians, there were to both outward patterns a hieroglyphic sense of concealed meaning, of an intent to communicate. There seemed no limit to what the printed circuit could have told her (if she had tried to find out)." This surfeit of form can forge a satiric metaphor, which measures the loss and decay of communication in the post-Joycean novel: it is akin to the debris and detritus which form the central metaphor for civilization in *The Crying of Lot 49.* This latter is epitomized in the novel by Mucho Maas's used car lot: ". . . he could still never accept the way each owner, each shadow, filed in only to exchange a dented, malfunctioning version of himself for another, just as futureless, automotive projection of somebody else's life. As if it were the most natural thing . . . it was horrible. Endless, convoluted incest." It is in this sense that Pynchon's allusions to popular or low culture, at least as frequent as his allusions to classical or high culture, may be best understood. His latest novel, *Vineland,* which casts a satiric eye at the television and video generation, is steeped in such allusion. The detritus clogs the attempted communication; the system disintegrates.

The disintegration of systems, both social and communicative, is the most pervasive metaphor of Pynchon's fiction. In his short story "Entropy" Meatball Mulligan's lease-breaking party is into its second day and rapidly declining into chaos. It is suffering, as do thermodynamic systems, from entropy, or the unavailability of energy as it is more and more randomly dispersed. In contrast, the fearful Callistro, who lives upstairs, has sealed himself into his apartment, hoping to combat social chaos with love, for Aubade and for a sick bird. Entropy, however, cannot be halted with stasis, so that it is Mulligan, who, faced with the choice of hiding away until everyone leaves his party or with calming his guests down one by one, elects to do the latter and does restore order to his apartment. Love and humane action will work, Pynchon seems to suggest, at least for a time—but only if it is energetic and active. Mulligan "gave wine to the sailors and separated the *morra* players; he introduced the fat government girl to Sandor Rojas, who would keep her out of trouble, he helped the girl in the shower to dry off and get into bed; he had another talk with Saul; he called a repairman for the refrigerator, which someone had discovered was on the blink. This is what he did until nightfall, when most of the revelers had passed out and the party trembled on the threshold of its third day." Like Melville's work before him, Pynchon's work encompasses that ambiguity, which, since it cannot be removed, must be accepted.

—Jan Pilditch

R

RAMPLING, Anne. *See* RICE, Anne.

————

RANDALL, Robert. *See* SILVERBERG, Robert.

————

RAO, Raja

Nationality: Indian. **Born:** Hassan, Mysore, 5 November 1908.
Education: Madarasa-e-Aliya School, Hyderabad, 1915-25; Aligarh
Muslim University, 1926-27; Nizam College, Hyderabad (University of Madras), B.A. in English 1929; University of Montpellier,
France, 1929-30; the Sorbonne, Paris, 1930-33. **Family:** Married
1) Camille Mouly in 1931; 2) Katherine Jones in 1965, one son.
Career: Editor, *Tomorrow,* Bombay, 1943-44. Lived in France for
many years; now lives half the year in India and half in Europe
and the United States. Since 1965 professor of philosophy, teaching one semester a year, University of Texas, Austin. **Awards:**
Sahitya Academy award, 1964; Padma Bhushan, India, 1969;
Neustadt International prize, 1988. **Address:** Department of Philosophy, University of Texas, Austin, Texas 78712, USA.

PUBLICATIONS

Novels

Kanthapura. London, Allen and Unwin, 1938; New York, New
Directions, 1963.
The Serpent and the Rope. London, Murray, 1960; New York, Pantheon, 1963.
The Cat and Shakespeare: A Tale of India. New York, Macmillan,
1965.
Comrade Kirillov. New Delhi, Orient, 1976.

Short Stories

The Cow of the Barricades and Other Stories. Madras and London, Oxford University Press, 1947.
The Policeman and the Rose. New Delhi and London, Oxford University Press, 1978.
On the Ganga Ghat. New Delhi, Vision, 1989.

Uncollected Short Story

"Jupiter and Mars," in *Pacific Spectator* (Stanford, California), vol.
8, no. 4, 1954.

Poetry

Alien Poems and Stories. Calcutta, Writers Workshop, 1983.

Other

The Chess Master and His Moves. New Delhi, Vision, 1978.

Editor, with Iqbal Singh, *Changing India.* London, Allen and
Unwin, 1939.
Editor, with Iqbal Singh, *Whither India?* Baroda, Padmaja, 1948.
Editor, *Soviet Russia: Some Random Sketches and Impressions,*
by Jawaharlal Nehru. Bombay, Chetana, 1949.

*

Critical Studies: *Raja Rao* by M.K. Naik, New York, Twayne,
1972; *Raja Rao: A Critical Study of His Work* (includes bibliography) by C.D. Narasimhaiah, New Delhi and London, Heinemann,
1973; *The Fiction of Raja Rao* by K.R. Rao, Aurangabad, Parimal,
1980; *Perspectives on Raja Rao* edited by K.K. Sharma, Ghaziabad,
Vimal, 1980; *Indo-Anglian Literature and the Works of Raja Rao*
by P.C. Bhattacharya, Lucknow, Atma Ram, 1983; *Raja Rao* by
Shiva Niranjan, Ghaziabad, Vimal, 1985; *Raja Rao and Cultural
Tradition* by Paul Sharrad, New Delhi, Sterling, 1987; *Raja Rao:
The Man and His Works* by Shyamala A. Narayan, New Delhi,
Sterling, 1988; *The Language of Mulk Raj Anand, Raja Rao, and
R.K. Narayan* by Reza Ahmad Nasimi, New Delhi, Capital, 1989.

Raja Rao comments:

(1972) Starting from the humanitarian and romantic perspective
of man in *Kanthapura* and *The Cow of the Barricades*—both deeply
influenced by Mahatma Gandhi's philosophy of nonviolence—I
soon came to the metaphysical novel, *The Serpent and the Rope,*
and *The Cat and Shakespeare,* based on the Vedantic conception
of illusion and reality. My main interest increasingly is in showing
the complexity of the human condition (that is, the reality of man
is beyond his person), and in showing the symbolic construct of
any human expression. All words are hierarchic symbols, almost
mathematical in precision, on and of the unknown.

*   *   *

Raja Rao has published two collections of short stories. One,
The Cow of the Barricades, reveals its author's dedication to Indian independence. The second, *The Policeman and the Rose,* contains stories from the previous volume plus three others which are
more metaphysical than the earlier ones. But Rao is best known
and most successful as a novelist. A South Indian Brahmin, he is
chiefly concerned with religion and philosophy, not only of India
but also of the West, which he has come to know through many
years of residence and study in France and, more recently, in the
United States. During his youth he was deeply influenced by Mahatma Gandhi; and his first novel, *Kanthapura,* testifies unmistakably to its author's intellectual involvement in the Gandhian drive
for national independence—to Rao as much a religious as a political movement.

E.M. Forster considered *Kanthapura* to be the best novel ever
written in English by an Indian, and indeed it has great literary
strength. Not the least of its merits is the picture it provides of life
in one of the innumerable villages that are the repositories of India's

ancient but living culture. In vivid detail, Rao describes the daily activities, the religious observances, and the social structure of the community; and he brings to life a dozen or more unforgettable individual villagers. The novel is political on a superficial level in that it chronicles a revolt against an exploitative plantation manager and the police who support him. But more profoundly it traces the origins of the revolt to an awakening of the long-dormant Indian soul rather than to the efforts of the Congress party. One of the young men of the village, while away, undergoes a mystical conversion to Satyagraha, and returns to incite his fellow villagers to civil disobedience. He arouses in them not only a sense of social wrong but, more importantly, a religious fervor which proves to be the real source of their strength against the oppressors.

Kanthapura is a novel in which the reader's interest is held mainly by its action and characters. *The Serpent and the Rope* and *The Cat and Shakespeare* are unabashedly metaphysical novels in which plot, setting, and even characters are of secondary interest. Semiautobiographical, *The Serpent and the Rope* traces the disintegration of the marriage of an Indian Brahmin and a French woman professor. The union founders on the Brahmin's conviction that "reality is my Self" and the wife's Western belief—even though she has become a Buddhist—that the evidence of the senses is based on an objective reality outside ourselves. "The world is either unreal or real—the serpent or the rope," the husband assures the wife. "There is no in-between-the-two. . . ." The intellectual demands in this novel that Rao, roaming at large through world history and among the religions, philosophies, and literatures of Europe and Asia, makes upon his readers were, at the time, unequaled in any modern novel since Thomas Mann's *The Magic Mountain,* though they are surpassed in Rao's more recent work. Quoting at length from a bewildering assortment of languages, he provides translations in the case of only one—Sanskrit. The reader is flatteringly assumed to be fluent in Latin, Provençal, Italian, Old French, and other tongues.

The Cat and Shakespeare is much shorter and lighter in tone, though scarcely less metaphysical. The subject of its probings is the problem of individual destiny, and the solution is conveyed in an odd analogy stated by a government clerk: "Learn the way of the kitten. Then you are saved. Allow the mother cat, sir, to carry you." Critics disagree as to what the mother cat symbolizes. The most likely suggestion, made by Uma Parameswaran, is that the cat is Karma, the inevitable results of our actions.

Rao's *Comrade Kirillov* was first written in the late 1940s and underwent much revision and rewriting before it was finally published, in French in 1965 and in English in 1976. Scarcely more than a novella in length, it recounts the efforts of a Westernized Indian to interpret and advance the Indian independence movement in accord with Marxist theory and practice. His efforts came to naught, because, as Rao made clear in *Kanthapura,* the movement's strength and hope of success resided in the Indian soul and the Hindu religion. Attempted infusions of alien ideologies were not only bound to fail but were irrelevant and doomed to be ignored by the Indian populace.

Rao's most recent, longest, and most concentratedly metaphysical novel is *The Chessmaster and His Moves* (not yet published in volume form), the first part of a projected trilogy. Its philosophical basis, as in Rao's earlier writings, is advaita (non-dualistic) vedanta, and it focuses on the progress of its protagonist, the Brahmin mathematician Sivarama Sastri, toward knowledge of Brahman and hence self-knowledge and through such knowledge achieving "the death of death." Sivarama does not, however, attain this knowl-

edge, which he realizes can be reached only through the help of a guru. The indispensable role of the guru is stated in the epigraph of the novel, a quotation from Rao's own guru, Sri Atmananda: "I am the light in the perception of the world." Thus the guru does not lead the way but provides the light by which his disciple can *see* the way. As one critic, R. Parthasarathy, explains, "the guru is thus the Chessmaster, and in His moves the compassion and grace that wipe away the disciples' ignorance." The action of the novel takes place in India, France, and England; and many different cultural backgrounds are represented by its characters, with some of whom Sivarama engages in philosophic dialogues.

All of Rao's writings are notable for seriousness of purpose, profundity of thought, and distinctive, vigorous, and sometimes lyrical English prose. Writing, to him, is the equivalent of prayer. "Unless word becomes mantra," he has written, "no writer is a writer, and no reader, a reader." Concerning Indian writers in the English language, he has asserted: "We cannot write like the English. We should not. We cannot write only as Indians. We have grown to look at the large world as part of us. Our method of expression therefore has to be a dialect which will some day prove to be as distinctive and colorful as the Irish or the American. Time alone will justify it." We might add that Rao's works have gone far to justify it.

—Perry D. Westbrook

RAPHAEL, Frederic (Michael)

Nationality: American. **Born:** Chicago, Illinois, 14 August 1931. **Education:** Charterhouse School, Godalming, Surrey; St. John's College, Cambridge, 1950-54 (Major Classics Scholar, 1950; Harper Wood Studentship, 1954), M.A. (honours) 1954. **Family:** Married Sylvia Betty Glatt in 1955; two sons and one daughter. **Career:** Since 1962 contributor, and fiction critic, 1962-65, *Sunday Times,* London. **Awards:** British Screen Writers award, 1965, 1966, 1967; British Academy award, 1965; Oscar, for screenplay, 1966; Royal Television Society Writer of the Year award, 1976. Fellow, Royal Society of Literature, 1964. **Agent:** Deborah Rogers, Rogers, Coleridge, and White, 20 Powis Mews, London WJ1 1JN, England.

PUBLICATIONS

Novel

Obbligato. London, Macmillan, 1956.
The Earlsdon Way. London, Cassell, 1958.
The Limits of Love. London, Cassell, 1960; Philadelphia, Lippincott, 1961.
A Wild Surmise. London, Cassell, 1961; Philadelphia, Lippincott, 1962.
The Graduate Wife. London, Cassell, 1962.
The Trouble with England. London, Cassell, 1962.
Lindmann. London, Cassell, 1963; New York, Holt Rinehart, 1964.
Darling. London, Fontana, and New York, New American Library, 1965.
Orchestra and Beginners. London, Cape, 1967; New York, Viking Press, 1968.

Like Men Betrayed. London, Cape, 1970; New York, Viking Press, 1971.
Who Were You with Last Night? London, Cape, 1971.
April, June and November. London, Cape, 1972; Indianapolis, Bobbs Merrill, 1976.
Richard's Things. London, Cape, 1973; Indianapolis, Bobbs Merrill, 1975.
California Time. London, Cape, 1975; New York, Holt Rinehart, 1976.
The Glittering Prizes. London, Allen Lane, 1976; New York, St. Martin's Press, 1978.
Heaven and Earth. London, Cape, and New York, Beaufort, 1985.
After the War. London, Collins, 1988; New York, Viking, 1989.
The Hidden I: A Myth Revised. London and New York, Thames and Hudson, 1990.
A Double Life. London, Orion, 1993.
Old Scores. London, Orion, 1995.

Short Stories

Sleeps Six. London, Cape, 1979.
Oxbridge Blues and Other Stories. London, Cape, 1980; Fayetteville, University of Arkansas Press, 1984.
Oxbridge Blues (includes *Sleeps Six* and *Oxbridge Blues and Other Stories*). London, Penguin, 1984.
Think of England. London, Cape, 1986; New York, Scribner, 1988.
The Latin Lover. London, Orion, 1994.

Plays

Lady at the Wheel, with Lucienne Hill, music and lyrics by Leslie Bricusse and Robin Beaumont (produced London, 1958).
A Man on the Bridge (produced Hornchurch, Essex, 1961).
The Island (for children), in *Eight Plays 2,* edited by Malcolm Stuart Fellows. London, Cassell, 1965.
Two for the Road (screenplay). London, Cape, and New York, Holt Rinehart, 1967.
An Early Life (produced Leicester, 1979).
The Serpent Son: Aeschylus: Oresteia, with Kenneth McLeish (televised 1979). London, Cambridge University Press, 1979.
From the Greek (produced Cambridge, 1979).

Screenplays: *Bachelor of Hearts,* with Leslie Bricusse, 1958; *Don't Bother to Knock* (*Why Bother to Knock*), with Denis Cannan and Frederic Gotfurt, 1971; *Nothing But the Best,* 1963; *Darling,* 1965; *Two for the Road,* 1967; *Far from the Madding Crowd,* 1967; *A Severed Head,* 1970; *Daisy Miller,* 1974; *Richard's Things,* 1981; *The Man in the Brooks Brothers Shirt,* 1990.

Radio Writing: *The Daedalus Dimension,* 1979; *Death in Trieste,* 1981; *The Thought of Lydia,* 1988; *The Empty Jew,* 1994.

Television Plays: *The Executioners,* 1961; *Image of a Society,* from the novel by Roy Fuller, 1963; *The Trouble with England,* from his own novel, 1964; *The Glittering Prizes,* 1976; *Rogue Male,* from the novel by Geoffrey Household, 1976; *Something's Wrong,* 1978; *The Serpent Son,* with Kenneth McLeish, 1979; *Of Mycenae and Men,* with Kenneth McLeish, 1979; *School Play,* 1979; *The Best of Friends,* 1980; *Byron: A Personal Tour* (documentary; also narrator), 1981; *Oxbridge Blues,* 1984; *After the War* series, 1989.

Other

W. Somerset Maugham and His World. London, Thames and Hudson, and New York, Scribner, 1977; revised edition, Sphere, 1989.
Cracks in the Ice: Views and Reviews. London, W.H. Allen, 1979.
A List of Books: An Imaginary Library, with Kenneth McLeish. London, Mitchell Beazley, and New York, Harmony, 1981.
Byron. London, Thames and Hudson, 1982.
Of Gods and Men, with illustrations by Sarah Raphael. London, Folio Society, 1992.
France: The Four Seasons, with photographs by Michael Busselle. London, Pavilion, 1994.

Editor, *Bookmarks.* London, Cape, 1975.

Translator, with Kenneth McLeish, *The Poems of Catullus.* London, Cape, 1978; Boston, Godine, 1979.
Translator, with Kenneth McLeish, *The Complete Plays of Aeschylus.* London, Methuen, 1991.
Translator, with Kenneth McLeish, *Medea,* by Euripides. London, Hern, 1994.

*

Critical Study: "The Varied Universe of Frederic Raphael" by Frederick P.W. McDowell in *Critique* (Minneapolis), Fall 1965.

Theatrical Activities:
Director: **Television**—*Something's Wrong,* 1978; *He'll See You Now,* 1984; **Film**—*The Man in the Brooks Brothers Shirt,* 1990.

Frederic Raphael comments:

Although in many ways I am the most marginal of Jews (I am agnostic in religion and wary of communities), I suppose it is honest to say that I would not be a novelist if it were not for the singular experiences of the Jewish people and for my sense of being, if not a direct participant, at least a witness, of them. My themes, if I have themes, are scarcely Jewish since I lack intimate knowledge of the practices and habits of those who live in so-called Jewish society. When I do come in contact with them I do not necessarily find them congenial. Yet, the Final Solution—its vulgarity no less than its brutality, its greedy malice no less than its murderous factories—lies always at the back of my mind even if I myself, as a child growing up in England, suffered nothing more than its bad breath blowing in my face from across the Channel. It may be an indulgence for anyone who did not have closer experience to claim personal acquaintance with the holocaust; it is equally frivolous to ignore it. It is too convenient a conclusion to dispose of the Jewish experience under the Germans (and the Austrians and the Poles and the Hungarians and the Ukrainians and the Russians, and the English and the Americans) as a sort of freakish explosion, a San Francisco earthquake of an event, a once-and-for-all catastrophe after which, in the comforter's cliché, one has to "go on living." And yet, of course, one does.

For me, the novelist is, above all, the historian of conscience. How does the individual conscience—in other words, how do I— go on living in a world which gives the clearest possible testimony of the cruelty and indifference of man? How does one continue to worry about the nuances of personal life, about love, friendship, taste, and responsibility when all the signs are that man is essentially rapacious, vindictive, and stupid? I have no answers to these questions, nor do I pretend they are in themselves new; they have been asked often enough and yet one does live at a particular time and, despite all the elegant suggestions to the contrary, it seems to me that our time is still linear. Certain things are beyond change, others lie ahead.

The problem is, in a sense, of language. Only in language is it possible to assimilate horrors and yet to achieve something which is both clear and, in a sense, pure. The way in which man remembers meaningfully is by not refusing sense in his language to those things which most profoundly influence or instruct him. This might be an argument for writing either history or philosophy and in a way I tried to do this, but I am not an historian or a philosopher. An obsession with a particular instance of the human character and a desire no less than a tendency—to show the futility of generalisation in the face of the fatuous and magnanimous individuality of human beings, lead me to examine the world through dramatic and emotional states rather than through a study of documents or the analysis of trends. Beyond and through the tragic comes the comic—the comic which does not explode the tragic but defines it—and this interpenetration is only one example of the sort of ambiguities in which the novelist finds himself at home. These ambiguities reveal themselves in drama and I have always found that, in spite of the attractions of both the theatre and the cinema, the drama can be worked out at its most personal and in the most piercing fashion in fiction. Truth may be stranger than fiction but fiction is truer.

How loftily one speaks in such generalising terms as these. The actual impulses which start a book are, of course, less grand. They spring as much from a sense of one's own contradictions as from any perception of human inadequacy or follies. When one begins to speak in the first person it sounds like conceit but it is more often confession, at least at my age. I am conscious above all of being equipped to be a novelist because it is only in a multiplicity of characters that I can reconcile my own ragbag personality. When people speak of a crisis of identity, I remind them that we know very well who we are, where we are having dinner and with whom we are sleeping, yet when I consider myself I am less commonsensical.

I was born in Chicago of a British father and an American mother. Beyond them, my grandparents and great-grandparents branched off across the world like an airline network. I was educated at Charterhouse which, I am told, is a great English Public School, and at Cambridge. I was readily influenced both by the ethos of the English middle class and by the intellectual habits of a classical education. Although I now regret much of what I was told and some of what I learned, I cannot shrug off the influence of these places, nor am I certain that I would wish to do so. The conflict of values reveals itself in fiction in the conflict of characters. I am conscious of being foreign in England and I find myself at home to some extent in many other places, yet I cannot sever myself entirely from the country where I live or from the language in which I write. I am sickened by xenophobia and yet in many ways I fear what lies beyond me. I believe that reason is better than unreason and that intelligence is better than instinct but I have not always been impressed by the decency of those who are most intelligent or by the capacity for affection and love of those who are most reasonable.

Within the nooks and crannies of the great edifices of generalisation and judgement, the innocently guilty and the guiltily innocent scurry about carrying nuts to their families, seeking their pleasures, snapping at their enemies, and providing, for those who

have eyes to see, the proof of the impossibility of final solutions to the human condition.

*   *   *

Frederic Raphael began with a slight novel, *Obbligato,* a satiric and mock-heroic account of the rise to fame of an improvising popsinger. Literary merit is abundant, however, in Raphael's second book, *The Earlsdon Way,* a realistic novel about the futility of British suburban life and the ineffectual revolt against its mores undertaken by Edward Keggin and his daughter Karen.

The Limits of Love gained for Raphael wide and deserved recognition. Its protagonist, Paul Riesman, is a Jew divorced by his training and inclinations from his race. Because he will not recognize what is necessity for him, his Jewishness, he becomes a selfish, life-destroying man despite his continuing efforts to achieve identity. But Paul increasingly sees that love is a defeating force if it is limited to the personal sphere and if it rejects the community; and he finds in his mother-in-law, Hannah Adler, stability that he lacks and in her daughter Julia, his wife, flexibility and depth.

In *A Wild Surmise* Raphael used a technique of montage to reveal his protagonist, Robert Carn, gradually. Carn hopes to escape British conventions in San Roque and to find genuine value through the spontaneous, impassioned, disinterested self. Ultimately, he supplements his introspective endeavors with a commitment to others in his efforts, ostensibly unsuccessful, to save some Indians from being poisoned. The novel is powerful and evocative, especially as it charts the processes of Carn's mind and the subtleties of his psychic life.

Raphael has written a number of brief novels, ironically executed, which concentrate upon a moral problem and its significance for the chief characters. *The Trouble with England* develops the moral contrasts between two vacationing couples on the French Riviera; *The Graduate Wife* focuses upon the forward development of a priggish heroine to inner stability. *Who Were You with Last Night?* has, as first-person narrator, the disenchanted Charles Hanson, who is amusing as he deflates bourgeois values (sometimes his own), recounts his satisfactions and frustrations with wife and mistress, and analyzes the delicate balance existing between love and hate in intimate relationships. *Richard's Things* is a *tour de force,* suggesting the impermanence not only of the marital relationship but of life itself, as the piquant relationship between the wife of the now dead Richard and his mistress diminishes from its first ardor to something near hatred. *The Glittering Prizes* reveals Raphael's remarkable technical expertise and depth of emotional insight as he traces the unfolding lives after their graduation, of a group of Cambridge contemporaries. The chief of these, Adam Morris, is a novelist similar in temperament to Raphael himself. He is an ironically minded but aesthetically talented Jew whose temporary foray into the world of the mass media is engaging farce, meant also to define the difficulties that the serious artist encounters in holding fast to his genuine impulses.

The peak of Raphael's achievement in writing the experimental novel is *Lindmann.* A British civil servant, James Shepherd, connived in 1942 to prevent the *SS Broda* from landing in Turkey with its Jewish refugees. Shepherd, to expiate his guilt and to achieve self-definition, assumes the identity of Jacob Lindmann, one of the two survivors from the ship who later died from exposure. A certain chastity gives Shepherd as Lindmann his moral force, since he forgoes any kind of fulfillment for himself; and he is, by his spiritual tenacity, something more than the failure he judges himself to be. Through patience and love he tries to influence others to a course of moderation, toleration, consideration, and affection.

Orchestra and Beginners, Like Men Betrayed, April, June, and November, and *California Time* are also works of considerable scope. In *Orchestra and Beginners* Raphael analyzes the ineffectual decency and the effete decay which characterized British upper-middle-class society just prior to World War II. Linda Strauss suffers from the moral paralysis of the class into which as an American she has married but is sympathetically seen, even if she fails her husband at his military enlistment because of her intensely personal reactions to experience. Leonard, in turn, is too impersonal toward Linda. Paradoxically, Linda's passion and Leonard's critical intelligence are both needed in confronting the complexities of modern life.

Like *Men Betrayed* is about Greek and, by implication, English politics, and it is remarkable for penetrating the relationships between the individual's psyche and social institutions. Three main points in time contrapuntally organize the book: the Greece of the 1930s under the Marshal's moderate dictatorship; Greece during World War II when factional jealousies are only less intense than hatred for the Italians and Germans; and postwar Greece when a power struggle develops between the corrupt royalist regime and the leftist insurgents. Artemis Theodoros defects from the Royalists when government troops fail in World War II to support the leftist General Papavastrou against the Germans. The novel is subtle and complex as it traces Artemis's endeavors to reach spiritual and political truth. As the novel opens he is fleeing north to the frontier where supposedly his forces will reach asylum. Instead, he learns that they will be betrayed. He remains faithful to his inner standards, however, despite misunderstanding, violence, betrayal, imprisonment, and exile. In Artemis a deplorable waste of genius occurs. The integrity inherent in such a heroic man, however, is the resource which we will have to learn how to use to insure a revitalized polity, Raphael would seem to be saying.

April, June, and November, California Time, and *Heaven and Earth* are also novels about talented men whose creative energies are deflected either by weakness of will or by circumstances. In *April, June, and November* the liberal and magnetic Daniel Meyer is, in fact, capable of a heroism which he can never display to any purpose in his hedonistic, effete milieu. The football field rather than the political arena claims his intelligence and genius. In *California Time* Victor England is likewise a victim, but could he have ever achieved distinction in the cutthroat and standardless world of the motion pictures studios, a world which needs his creativity but which also humiliates him to the greatest possible extent? Raphael is frankly experimental in this novel, collapsing all of Victor's experience into the ongoing present and creating doubts in him as to the reality of his perceptions of the given moment, in a milieu in which the reality and the hallucination become barely distinguishable. In *Heaven and Earth* Gideon Shand is a good man whose happiness, prosperity, and integrity seem unassailable. Underneath, the irrational forces in himself and others lead, unexpectedly to him (and to the reader), to destruction and self-destruction. Life is at once tougher and more fragile than he had at first realized; and the implicit question raised in this novel, but not decisively answered, is whether a man like Gideon can survive the violent effects of these unconscious forces. In these three novels Raphael develops the tragedy of the man who cannot actualize his good intentions and give free expression to his genius, with the same density, elusiveness, and complication that characterize his fiction as a whole.

—Frederick P.W. McDowell

RAVEN, Simon (Arthur Noël)

Nationality: British. **Born:** London, 28 December 1927. **Education:** Charterhouse, Godalming, Surrey, 1941-45; King's College, Cambridge, 1948-52, B.A. 1951, M.A. 1955. **Military Service:** Served in the British Army, 1946-48 (commissioned in India, 1947), and 1953-57 (Captain, King's Shropshire Light Infantry). **Family:** Married Susan Mandeville Kilner in 1951 (divorced 1957); one son. **Agent:** Curtis Brown, Haymarket House, 28/29, Haymarket, London SW1Y 4SP, England.

PUBLICATIONS

Novels

The Feathers of Death. London, Blond, 1959; New York, Simon and Schuster, 1960.
Brother Cain. London, Blond, 1959; New York, Simon and Schuster, 1960.
Doctors Wear Scarlet. London, Blond, 1960; New York, Simon and Schuster, 1961.
Close of Play. London, Blond, 1962.
Alms for Oblivion:
   The Rich Pay Late. London, Blond, 1964; New York, Putnam, 1965.
   Friends in Low Places. London, Blond, 1965; New York, Putnam, 1966.
   The Sabre Squadron. London, Blond, 1966; New York, Harper, 1967.
   Fielding Gray. London, Blond, 1967; New York, Beaufort, 1985.
   The Judas Boy. London, Blond, 1968.
   Places Where They Sing. London, Blond, 1970.
   Sound the Retreat. London, Blond, 1971; New York, Beaufort, 1986.
   Come like Shadows. London, Blond and Briggs, 1972.
   Bring Forth the Body. London, Blond and Briggs, 1974.
   The Survivors. London, Blond and Briggs, 1975.
The Roses of Picardie: A Romance. London, Blond and Briggs, 1980.
An Inch of Fortune. London, Blond and Briggs, 1980.
September Castle. London, Blond and Briggs, 1983.
The First-Born of Egypt:
   Morning Star. London, Muller Blond and White, 1984.
   The Face of the Waters. London, Muller Blond and White, 1985.
   Before the Cock Crow. London, Muller Blond and White, 1986.
   New Seed for Old. London, Muller, 1988.
   Blood of My Bone. London, Muller, 1989.
   In the Image of God. London, Muller, 1990.
The Troubadour. London, Hutchinson, 1992.
The Islands of Sorrow. London, Winged Lion, 1994.

Short Stories

The Fortunes of Fingel. London, Blond and Briggs, 1976.

Plays

The Scouncing Stoup (broadcast 1964). Published in *New Radio Drama,* London, BBC Publications, 1966.

Royal Foundation and Other Plays (radio and television plays: *The Move Up Country; The Doomsday School; The Scapegoat; Panther Larkin; The High King's Tomb; The Gaming Book; Sir Jocelyn, The Minister Would Like a Word*). London, Blond, 1966.
The Case of Father Brendan (produced London, 1968).

Screenplays: *On Her Majesty's Secret Service,* with Richard Maibaum, 1969; *Unman, Wittering, and Zigo,* 1971.

Radio Plays: *Loser Pays All,* 1961; *A Present from Venice,* 1961; *The Gate of Learning,* 1962; *A Friend in Need,* 1962; *The Doomsday School,* 1963; *The High King's Tomb,* 1964; *The Scouncing Stoup,* 1964; *Panther Larkin,* 1964; *The Melos Affair,* 1965; *The Last Expedition,* 1967; *The Tutor,* 1967; *The Prisoners in the Cave,* 1968; *Salvation,* 1974; *In Transit,* 1978.

Television Plays: *Royal Foundation,* 1961; *The Scapegoat,* 1964; *The Gaming Book,* 1964; *Advise and Dissent,* 1965; *Sir Jocelyn, The Minister Would Like a Word,* 1965; *A Soirée at Bossom's Hotel,* 1966; *A Pyre for Private James,* 1966; *Point Counter Point,* from the novel by Aldous Huxley, 1968; *The Way We Live Now,* from the novel by Trollope, 1969; *The Human Element,* from the novel by Somerset Maugham, 1970; *The Pallisers,* from novels by Trollope, 1974; *An Unofficial Rose,* from the novel by Iris Murdoch, 1974; *Red Sky at Night (The Brothers* series), 1976; *Edward and Mrs. Simpson,* from a work by Frances Donaldson, 1978; *Sexton Blake* series, 1978; *Love in a Cold Climate,* from the novels *Love in a Cold Climate* and *The Pursuit of Love* by Nancy Mitford, 1980; *The Search for Alexander the Great,* with George Lefferts, 1981; *The Blackheath Poisonings,* adapted from the novel by Julian Symons, 1992.

Other

The English Gentleman: An Essay in Attitudes. London, Blond, 1961; as *The Decline of the Gentlemen,* New York, Simon and Schuster, 1962.
Boys Will Be Boys and Other Essays. London, Blond, 1963.
Shadows on the Grass: Memoirs. London, Blond and Briggs, 1982.
The Old School: A Study in the Oddities of the English Public School System. London, Hamish Hamilton, 1986.
The Old Gang: A Sporting and Military Memoir. London, Hamish Hamilton, 1988.
Bird of Ill Omen. London, Hamish Hamilton, 1989.
"Is Anybody There?" Said the Traveller: Memories of a Private Nuisance. London, Muller, 1991.

Editor, *The Best of Gerald Kersh.* London, Heinemann, 1960.

*

Critical Study: "The Novels of Simon Raven" by Kerry McSweeney, in *Queen's Quarterly* (Kingston, Ontario), Spring 1971.

Simon Raven comments:
My theme is the vanity of human wishes.
My object is to make money by presenting this theme in such a way as to interest and amuse intelligent readers of the upper and middle-classes.

(1995) Out of fashion: politically incorrect and "uncompassionate" passion.

*   *   *

In over 30 years as a professional author and scriptwriter Simon Raven has produced an impressive number of novels, short stories, essays, and plays for radio and screen.

Of the novels, 10 form the *Alms for Oblivion* sequence (1964-75); 20 years after publishing the first of these he embarked on a further sequence, now half-completed, under the general title *The First-Born of Egypt.* This continues to trace the fortunes of the aging survivors of the cast of *Alms for Oblivion,* and to explore the social world and changing attitudes of their descendants and younger contemporaries.

His other novels include two outstanding specimens of the Gothic horror novel in modern guise, *The Roses of Picardie* and *September Castle,* replete with cryptic inscriptions and lost manuscripts whose scholarly decipherment and decoding uncover ancient scandals and crimes. Some of the persons, places, and institutions in the two novel sequences also appear in these fictions, in which their role is to operate the mechanisms for the unraveling of the plots. The delineation of character is accordingly slight and subordinated to this end. The same may be said of *Doctors Wear Scarlet,* Raven's neat variation on the Oxbridge murder story, in which the college and its dons are clearly the Lancaster College and its Fellows of *Alms for Oblivion,* but the central interest lies in the denouement of the crime by the logic of detection and deduction.

It is, however, on the merits of the two novel sequences that Raven will mainly be judged. The society they depict is that of the English upper and upper-middle classes since the end of World War II, the loosely (and in Raven's books often louchely) knit society of politicians and businessmen, soldiers and civil servants, journalists and dons, crooks, decent chaps, and cads whose overlapping interests and influence comprise the English establishment. In Raven's fiction even the decent men tend to become embroiled in crooked or squalid behaviour, while the nastier men and women are very nasty indeed.

Alms for Oblivion was planned by the author as a loosely linked series of novels, each of which would present an independent story and be assimilable on its own. The element which holds the series together is the fact that the principal characters are related by ties of birth, education, and professional interests. The plan allowed Raven to move backwards as well as forwards in time, the earliest novel in the fictional chronology, *Fielding Gray,* appearing as the fourth in the sequence. Here he introduced the young members of the cast as schoolboys in the process of initiation into the conflicts of adult life in which he had already portrayed them. The themes of self-advancement and self-preservation, of personal and group loyalty, of sexual adventure and emotional betrayal (both homosexual and heterosexual), examined here with the social microcosm of an English public school, recur throughout the series with different complications and in different settings.

"If there is one theme which will dominate the series," wrote the author, "it is that human effort and goodwill are persistently vulnerable to the malice of time, chance, and the rest of the human race." This sounds like a blueprint for black comedy; and farcical events, many of them blue enough, abound in his novels. But there is more to Raven than pure farce. He sets out deliberately to contrive violent and macabre accidents and incidents, drawing aside the curtain on scenes of debauchery and corruption, blackmail and double-dealing, malpractice and malversation. In particular, he beckons the reader to witness, in a kind of fictional voyeurism, extraordinary sexual practices and perversions. The aim, no doubt, is partly to titillate and thus to amuse; it is also partly to shock, especially to shock bourgeois notions of respectability. But one senses also an undertone of anger, perhaps a wish to take revenge for lost innocence or to offload a burden of guilt or regret.

Raven works brilliantly within the confines of his chosen territory. He is always entertaining; his prose is lucid and well crafted; his powers of invention are vigorous and imaginative; his stance is Rabelaisian and robust. But the territory of his *roman fleuve* is undoubtedly restricted, with the consequent danger that the reader may become bored with repeated visits to its more noisome corners, or else sated with the spicy flavours of course after course—or coarse upon coarse—of Raven's literary menu-planning. This and other dangers become apparent in *The First-Born of Egypt,* where the author aims to depict "the purposes, beliefs and ways of life of the growing young as observed, deplored, or encouraged by their elders."

One might have expected from this declaration of intent that Raven would refine his novelistic technique so as to present the action entirely through the eyes of the older generation. Not so, however. Many scenes are played by the young alone, their actions, thoughts, and speech being reported with authorial omniscience. It is apparent that the novelistic mixture is much as before—pungent, highly seasoned, and not entirely free from unpleasant flavours in the after-taste. Both matter and manner seem a little less convincing than in *Alms for Oblivion,* despite the recalibration of the permissive society's coordinates by intermittent references to Aids. The preoccupation with the mores of the upper classes also seems rather dated since the shifts in the bases of establishment power in the last decade or so.

On the other hand, the more sombre tone of these novels is relieved by the author's fluency and energetic capacity to entertain his readers with scandalously gross comic invention as well as mystery and calculated suspense. The final plan of this half-finished work is not yet clear and one can pass only provisional judgment on it. Raven's innumerable readers look forward to its completion.

—Stewart Sanderson

READ, Piers Paul

Nationality: British. **Born:** Beaconsfield, Buckinghamshire, 7 March 1941; son of the writer Herbert Read. **Education:** Gilling Castle, York, 1949-52; Ampleforth College, York, 1953-57; St. John's College, Cambridge, 1959-62, B.A. in history 1962, M.A. 1966. **Family:** Married Emily Boothby in 1967; two sons and two daughters. **Career:** sub-editor, *Times Literary Supplement,* London, 1964-65. Artist-in-residence, Ford Foundation, Berlin, 1963-64; adjunct professor of writing, Columbia University, New York, 1980. Since 1992, chair, Catholic Writers' Guild. **Awards:** Commonwealth Fund Harkness fellowship, 1967; Faber Memorial award, 1968; Hawthornden prize, 1969; Maugham award, 1970; Thomas More Association medal, 1974; Enid McLeod award, 1988; James Tait Black Memorial prize, 1988. Fellow, Royal Society of Literature, 1972. **Agent:** Aitken and Stone Ltd., 29 Fernshaw Road, London SW10 0TG. **Address:** 50 Portland Road, London W11 4LG, England.

PUBLICATIONS

Novels

Game in Heaven with Tussy Marx. London, Weidenfeld and Nicolson, and New York, McGraw Hill, 1966.
The Junkers. London, Secker and Warburg, 1968; New York, Knopf, 1969.
Monk Dawson. London, Secker and Warburg, 1969; Philadelphia, Lippincott, 1970.
The Professor's Daughter. London, Secker and Warburg-Alison Press, and Philadelphia, Lippincott, 1971.
The Upstart. London, Alison Press, and Philadelphia, Lippincott, 1973.
Polonaise. London, Alison Press, and Philadelphia, Lippincott, 1976.
A Married Man. London, Secker and Warburg, 1979; Philadelphia, Lippincott, 1980.
The Villa Golitsyn. London, Secker and Warburg, 1981; New York, Harper, 1982.
The Free Frenchman. London, Secker and Warburg, 1986; New York, Random House, 1987.
A Season in the West. London, Secker and Warburg, 1988; New York, Random House, 1989.
On the Third Day. London, Secker and Warburg, 1990; New York, Random House, 1991.

Uncollected Short Story

"Son and Heir," in *Winter's Tales 2* (new series), edited by Robin Baird-Smith. London, Constable, and New York, St. Martin's Press, 1986.

Plays

The Class War, in *Colloquialisms* (produced London, 1964).

Radio Plays: *The Family Firm,* 1970; *The House on Highbury Hill,* music by Julian Slade, 1971.

Television Plays: *Coincidence,* 1968; *The Childhood Friend,* 1974; *Margaret Clitheroe (Here I Stand* series), 1977.

Other

Alive! The Story of the Andes Survivors. London, Secker and Warburg, and Philadelphia, Lippincott, 1974.
The Train Robbers. London, Allen and Unwin-Alison Press, and Philadelphia, Lippincott, 1978.
Ablaze: The Story of Chernobyl. London, Secher and Warburg, and New York, Random House, 1993.

*

Critical Studies: Article by Philip Flynn, in *British Novelists since 1960,* edited by Jay L. Halio, Detroit, Gale, 1983; "The Novels of Piers Paul Read" by C.J. Taylor, in *Spectator,* 23 February 1990.

* * *

Piers Paul Read once observed that he was much influenced by the novels of Graham Greene, and indeed moral and political issues, ambiguity, belief, and skepticism are given considerable focus in his work. In *A Season in the West,* for example, the political decadence of Communist-ruled Czechoslovakia is contrasted with the moral decadence of the capitalist west. Even in the Communist east the right family and party connections can protect a dissident, while in England the defecting dissident discovers that the right family and class connections are also more significant than political idealism.

Like Greene, Read sets his novels in various locales besides England: Germany, France, the United States, and the Eastern bloc. Each country evinces a pronounced ambiguity to political aspirations and activism. The most altruistic theories and motives, while seemingly presenting utopian solutions, are marred by inherent human corruption and deficiencies. On the extreme is Nazism, examined by Read in *The Junkers,* which demonstrates how mankind can reach total depravity. Degeneracy and animalism with the behavior of the SS and the horrors of the Holocaust dominate in an era of unrivaled viciousness. Further, the snobbery and obsession with class differences so frequently associated with the English are in their own form characteristic of the Germans as well.

Even when the political cause is noble, as in *The Free Frenchman,* the pure goal of working for freedom from oppression is often thwarted and obfuscated by family differences, love entanglements, and human betrayals. Comrades working together in the Resistance movement cannot avoid disagreements and hostilities. In Read's fiction manifestations of Manichean conflict must always rage in every individual and situation. Read's world is one where integrity is often compromised, love and sex are ambivalent if not treacherous, and hedonism, honor, and cruelty co-exist. Quoting Pierre d'Harcourt, Read observes that "the real enemy is within." The struggle between the sinner and the saint promises endless conflict. Even though one phase is in the ascendant, the other aspect makes progress on the imaginative plane so that this mixture and conflict will produce constant turmoil, and the yearning for betterment will continue to torment. In the fiction of Read we are reminded that all too often "the devil is prince of the world . . . He has powers too."

Read reiterates this theme in numerous forms. As soon as humans involve themselves with other members of society, evil will intensify. Edward Dawson, the protagonist of one of Read's best novels, *Monk Dawson,* is a well-meaning, civilized man; but a decadent, sex-obsessed, and excessively materialistic society soon contaminates him with its folly. His ultimate decision to enter a monastery, while a symbol of personal salvation, is a scathing commentary on the hopelessness of attempting to find moral decency and stability in contemporary society. Basic kindness, integrity, and fair-minded behavior are regarded as anachronistic and naive. Read's world is a Greeneland, sometimes more flashy and dazzling than the atmosphere used by Greene, but nevertheless filled with treachery, hostility, disbelief, and despair.

Professor Henry Rutledge in *The Professor's Daughter* is trapped in a typical Read dilemma. He champions liberal and progressive ideas, yet ironically his death results from militant revolutionary activity carried out by some of his own graduate students. While politically Rutledge may be on the side of the angels, his own family is torn apart by alcoholism, prostitution, and attempted suicide. The mutual devotion between his favorite daughter and himself cannot withstand the chaos of 1960s activism. Read constantly stresses that 20th-century life has shattered family values and cohesiveness and maintains that until some stability can be returned to the family unit, the pervasiveness of evil will increase uncontrollably.

There is hope in genuine repentance and atonement as Hilary Fletcher demonstrates in *The Upstart,* but repentance is a rare occurrence in today's world, and is not even considered a workable option by most of Read's characters.

Read is a born storyteller with a cold, dispassionate style that often yields ironic overtones. He invents plots which of themselves are intriguing. In his latest novel, *On the Third Day,* Israelis on an archeological dig in Jerusalem, used as camouflage to spy on Arab rebels, discover the 2000-year-old skeleton of a crucified man which has a nail through its feet, thorn marks on the skull, and evidence of a spear having pierced the rib cage. Is this possibly the remains of Christ? Read has more than once been accused by some critics of contriving melodramatic plots based on sensational events; yet at times melodrama can be powerful and effective, and the nature of the characters, situation, and settings can justify some melodramatic aspects and treatment.

In his best novels, *Monk Dawson, The Junkers,* and *The Villa Golitsyn,* Read handles vital themes with evident talent that establishes him as an important figure in contemporary fiction.

—Paul A. Doyle

RECHY, John (Francisco)

Nationality: American. **Born:** El Paso, Texas, 10 March 1934. **Education:** Texas Western College, El Paso, B.A.; New School for Social Research, New York. **Military Service:** Served in the United States Army. **Career:** Has taught creative writing at University of California, Occidental College, and University of Southern California, all Los Angeles. Lives in Los Angeles. **Awards:** Longview Foundation prize, 1961; National Endowment for the Arts grant, 1976. **Agent:** Georges Borchardt Inc., 136 East 57th Street, New York, New York 10022, USA.

PUBLICATIONS

Novels

City of Night. New York, Grove Press, 1963; London, MacGibbon and Kee, 1964.
Numbers. New York, Grove Press, 1967.
This Day's Death. New York, Grove Press, and London, MacGibbon and Kee, 1970.
The Vampires. New York, Grove Press, 1971.
The Fourth Angel. New York, Viking Press, and London, W.H. Allen, 1972.
Rushes. New York, Grove Press, 1979.
Bodies and Souls. New York, Carroll and Graf, 1983; London, W.H. Allen, 1984.
Marilyn's Daughter. New York, Carroll and Graf, 1988.
The Miraculous Day of Amalia Gómez. Boston, Little Brown, 1991.

Plays

Momma As She Became—Not As She Was (produced New York, 1978).
Tigers Wild (produced New York, 1986).

Other

The Sexual Outlaw: A Documentary . . . of Three Days and Nights in the Sexual Underground. New York, Grove Press, 1977; London, W.H. Allen, 1978.

*

Manuscript Collection: Boston University.

John Rechy comments:

Because my first novel, *City of Night,* was greeted by two personally assaultive reviews, one in "The New York Review of Books," the other in "The New Republic," both of which shrilly attacked the novel's salient subject (homosexuality and male-hustling) while ignoring its careful literary form, much of my subsequent work is still frequently mis-viewed, especially since those two reviews have been anthologized. I consider myself a literary writer, one attentive to structure and style as essential to meaning. Employing a variety of forms, I've explored many subjects, ranging from male-hustling (*City of Night, The Sexual Outlaw*) to the power of legend over myth as epitomized by Marilyn Monroe (*Marilyn's Daughter*), to a day in the life of a Mexican-American woman (*The Miraculous Day of Amalia Gómez*) to a panoramic view of Los Angeles as a modern paradise of "lost angels" (*Bodies and Souls*). I wish that equal critical attention were paid to the literary aspects of my writing as, often—and years later—to the subject, only the subject, of my first novel.

*   *   *

John Rechy's world is the heir of Hawthorne's. His characters inhabit a moral universe whose codes are as rigorous as Calvin's and whose cops are the vigilantes of a new unmerciful Salem. The "youngmen" of *City of Night* and *Numbers* are the fallen angels of an eternally inaccessible paradise and their lives are characterized by a search for the *eros* that will at last become *agape.* That the search is frenetic is scarcely surprising; it has all the desperate urgency that characterizes the role of the sensitive American—the anguish of exile within one's own country. And although in *City of Night* Rechy never quite succeeds in conveying Francis Thompson's added sense of "dreadful," it is plain that the implication is there. New York, from the first page, is a metaphor city, a fairy city—in a sense like the London of Stevenson—where anything might happen. That is not to say that Rechy's urban fantasy has the caliber of Purdy's. It is more limited in its focus. Its world is a moral world turned upside down, where the *Deus absconditus* is Priapus. The quest for that god is a never-ending and insatiable one and one in which the tyrants of the old moral order have all the destructive vindictiveness of Diocletian against the Christians.

Having said all that, one should also say that neither *City of Night* nor *Numbers* (in spite of the deliberate "allegorical" pretensions of the former) often rises above what seem to be the masturbatory fantasies of an aging queen—bad Genet. Only with his third and by far his best novel, *This Day's Death,* does Rechy get beyond the unfortunate dualisms of his earlier novels—a catalogue of well-equipped muscleboys on the one hand and a labored novelistic artifice to contain it on the other. That is not to say that *This Day's Death* does not suffer from a somewhat contrivedly concealed central event and a time scheme that is sometimes confusing and tedious. Its *à la recherche de la virginité perdue,* however, is con-

vincing in a way that is true of neither of the earliest novels. Rechy's New Mexico, like Steinbeck's Oklahoma, is a small-town world of poverty and pain, the anguish of growth and the desire to break out. His California is the nightmare inversion of that desire—a world where the law is a monster devouring the innocents who nonetheless have a Genet-like fascination with its devious iniquities. And together these worlds, as commentaries on one another, form a larger moral universe than any Rechy has created before.

It is disenchanting then to find that in *The Vampires,* the novel that succeeds *This Day's Death,* he returns to the world of gothic fiction with an overlay of baroque Satanism—a parody of scenarios for Heliogabalus as rewritten by Albee. *The Fourth Angel* suffers less from this, being set once again in the southwest. But if its teenage characters are more "real," their problems are too much the stereotypes of the late 1960s to remain interesting, and the sentimentality of their presentation—"and so, suddenly, they're gentle children playing gentle children's games"—sounds like the worst of the Woodstock inheritance.

Rechy discovered earlier than most what Tom Wolfe drew attention to—the new reporting style of the 1960s. His first two pieces appeared in *Evergreen Review* and from one of them came *City of Night.* But journalists are as prone as anyone else to being taken over by easy "rhetoric," and the mode of confession that fascinates Rechy easily becomes trite. As Ruskin said of the first painting by Leighton, the Victorian painter, "if he does not do much better he will do worse."

—D.D.C. Chambers

REDFERN, John. *See* **PARGETER, Edith (Mary).**

REED, Eliot Reed. *See* **AMBLER, Eric.**

REED, Ishmael (Scott)

Nationality: American. **Born:** Chattanooga, Tennessee, 22 February 1938. **Education:** Buffalo Technical High School; East High School, Buffalo, graduated 1956; University of Buffalo, 1956-60. **Family:** Married 1) Priscilla Rose in 1960 (separated 1963, divorced 1970), one daughter; 2) Carla Blank-Reed in 1970, one daughter. **Career:** Staff writer, *Empire Star Weekly,* Buffalo, 1960-62; freelance writer, New York, 1962-67; co-founder, *East Village Other,* New York, and *Advance,* Newark, New Jersey, 1965; teacher, St. Mark's in the Bowery prose workshop, New York, 1966. Since 1971 chair and president, Yardbird Publishing Company, editor, *Yardbird Reader,* 1972-76, since 1973 director, Reed Cannon and Johnson Communications, and since 1981 editor and publisher, with Al Young, *Quilt* magazine, all Berkeley, California. Since 1967 lecturer, University of California, Berkeley. Lecturer, University of Washington, Seattle, 1969-70, State University of New York, Buffalo, 1975, 1979, Sitka Community Association, Summer 1982, University of Arkansas, Fayetteville, 1982, Columbia University, New York, 1983, Harvard University, Cambridge, Massachusetts, 1987, and University of California, Santa Barbara, 1988. Visiting professor, Fall 1979, and since 1983 Associate Fellow of Calhoun House, Yale University, New Haven, Connecticut; visiting professor, Dartmouth College, Hanover, New Hampshire, 1980; since 1987 Associate Fellow, Harvard University Signet Society. Since 1976 president, Before Columbus Foundation. Chair, Berkeley Arts Commission, 1980, 1981. Associate editor, *American Book Review.* **Awards:** National Endowment for the Arts grant, 1974; Rosenthal Foundation award, 1975; Guggenheim fellowship, 1975; American Academy award, 1975; Michaux award, 1978. **Agent:** Ellis J. Freedman, 415 Madison Avenue, New York, New York 10017, U.S.A.

PUBLICATIONS

Novels

The Free-Lance Pallbearers. New York, Doubleday, 1967; London, MacGibbon and Kee, 1968.
Yellow Back Radio Broke-Down. New York, Doubleday, 1969; London, Allison and Busby, 1971.
Mumbo-Jumbo. New York, Doubleday, 1972; London, Allison and Busby, 1989.
The Last Days of Louisiana Red. New York, Random House, 1974.
Flight to Canada. New York, Random House, 1976.
The Terrible Twos. New York, St. Martin's Press-Marek, 1982; London, Allison and Busby, 1990.
Reckless Eyeballing. New York, St. Martin's Press, 1986; London, Allison and Busby, 1989.
The Terrible Threes. New York, Atheneum, 1989.
Japanese by Spring. New York, Atheneum, 1993.

Poetry

Catechism of d neoamerican hoodoo church. London, Paul Breman, 1970.
Conjure: Selected Poems 1963-1970. Amherst, University of Massachusetts Press, 1972.
Chattanooga. New York, Random House, 1973.
A Secretary to the Spirits. New York, NOK, 1978.
New and Collected Poems. New York, Atheneum, 1988.

Other

The Rise, Fall and . . . ? of Adam Clayton Powell (as Emmett Coleman), with others. New York, Bee-Line, 1967.
Shrovetide in Old New Orleans (essays). New York, Doubleday, 1978.
God Made Alaska for the Indians. New York, Garland, 1982.
Cab Calloway Stands In for the Moon. Flint, Michigan, Bamberger, 1986.
Airing Dirty Laundry. Reading, Addison-Wesley, 1993.

Editor, *19 Necromancers from Now.* New York, Doubleday, 1970.
Editor, *Yardbird Reader* (annual). Berkeley, California, Yardbird, 5 vols., 1971-77.
Editor, with Al Young, *Yardbird Lives!* New York, Grove Press, 1978.

Editor, *Calafia: The California Poetry.* Berkeley, California, Yardbird, 1979.
Editor, with Al Young, *Quilt 2-3.* Berkeley, California, Reed and Young's Quilt, 2 vols., 1981-82.
Editor, *Writin' Is Fightin': Thirty-Seven Years of Boxing on Paper.* New York, Atheneum, 1988.
Editor, with Kathryn Trueblood and Shawn Wong, *The Before Columbus Foundation Fiction Anthology: Selections from the American Book Awards, 1980-1990.* New York, Norton, 1992.

*

Bibliography: "Mapping Out the Gumbo Works: An Ishmael Reed Bibliography" by Joe Weixlmann, Robert Fikes, Jr., and Ishmael Reed, in *Black American Literature Forum* (Terre Haute, Indiana), Spring 1978.

Critical Studies: "Ishmael Reed Issue" of *Review of Contemporary Fiction* (Elmwood Park, Illinois), vol. 4, no. 2, 1984; *Ishmael Reed and the New Black Aesthetic Critics* by Reginald Martin, New York, Macmillan, 1988; *Ishmael Reed* by Jay Boyer, Boise, Idaho, Boise State University, 1993.

*   *   *

In an introduction to an essay collection, *Shrovetide in Old New Orleans,* Ishmael Reed says: "Many people here called my fiction muddled, crazy, incoherent, because I've attempted in fiction the techniques and forms painters, dancers, film makers, musicians in the West have taken for granted for at least fifty years, and the artists of many other cultures, for thousands of years." Reed's strengths are enunciated here: flexible, vivid language ranging from street argot to lofty estheticism, experimentation with materials and means, and a deep awareness of the mythic roots of all cultures. Reed is an Afro-American ironist, but his gifts and insights are multicultural, multimedia.

Reed's early novels, *The Free-Lance Pallbearers* and *Yellow Back Radio Broke-Down,* are musical and mythical in conception and development. Using "hoodoo" as a system both of ideas and of language, Reed describes our world in terms of the hero and the prison of society. In *The Free-Lance Pallbearers* Bukka Doopeyduk is the epigonous hero fighting against **HARRY SAM**, which is the nation-state transformed into a monstrous personification, a dragon. In similar fashion, the Loop Garoo Kid of *Yellow Back Radio Broke-Down* is a shaman-hero (Loupe Garou=werewolf in Creole-French folklore) of a cowboy saga, in which the town of Yellow Back Radio is threatened by Drag Gibson, the stultifying force of the square world. The vaudevillian jokes, surrealism, and wordplays flow at *allegro* tempo.

In *Mumbo Jumbo* Reed concentrates on a mythic time (the 1920s) and magic places (New Orleans and Harlem) in U.S. culture. The ideas of hoodoo/voodoo and other Afro-American magic-religious cults figure in Reed's tapestry of the Jazz Age and the Harlem Renaissance. Reed describes the epic struggle between Jes Grew, the black cultural impulse, and the Atonists, i.e., the monotheistic Western tradition. In the narrative, Reed incorporates drawings, photographs, collages, and handwritten texts, along with many scholarly references.

The Last Days of Louisiana Red extends this mythology, bringing many of the same characters and ideas to Berkeley in the 1970s. "Louisiana Red" is the plague of modern technocratic-industrial culture:

Louisiana Red was the way they related to one another, oppressed one another, maimed and murdered one another, carving one another while above their heads, fifty thousand feet, billionaires flew in custom-made jet planes equipped with saunas tennis courts swimming pools discotheques and meeting rooms decorated like the Merv Griffin show set.

In *Flight to Canada* Reed moves back to the mythos of slavery and the Civil War, applying the same wild, anachronistic expressionism to the central tragedy of the black American culture. In ironic, dramatic terms, Reed answers the "cliometric" revisers of history: "Revisionists. Quantitative historians. What does a computer know? Can a computer feel? Make love? Can a computer feel passion?" Quickskill tears off his shirt. "Look at these scars. Look at them! All you see is their fruit, but their roots run deep. The roots are in my soul."

The Terrible Twos is a comic-mythological tour de force, uniting elements of our culture's Christmas story—Dicken's "A Christmas Carol," the legend of St. Nicholas, the commercial street-corner Santa Claus—into a bizarre satire on greed, racism and inhumanity. Reed chides the U.S. of the 1980s as a mindless, grasping two-year-old, an infant-giant draining the world of resources, hope, and compassion, hiding behind a phony costume of charity and concern. *The Terrible Threes* updates the sociopolitical allegory to summarize the hedonism, egocentricity, and fatuous self-satisfaction of the Reagan years. It focuses on the impact of TV evangelism, TV political advertising, paranoid militarism, and the all-pervasive role of sales pitches in contemporary America.

With *Reckless Eyeballing,* Reed returns to the elaborate mythology of racism in the idea of "reckless eyeballing" (i.e., ogling of white women by black men) as a "crime." In his usual high-energy mix of history, folkore, contemporary observation and mythopoeic imagination, Reed investigates the way sexual mores and folklore have colluded with political expediency to stifle U.S. culture.

Reed's brilliant comic vision of American history brings together the basic ingredients of black culture in a rich musical-dramatic form. His expansion of language into a radically personal style points to the richness of that culture as a storytelling source. Reed's wide interests in traditions outside the received mainstream of "Western Culture" courses, in magic, myth, and ritual, make him one of the most forceful and persuasive novelists of the past 20 years.

—William J. Schafer

———

REID, Desmond. *See* **MOORCOCK, Michael.**

———

REID, Vic(tor Stafford)

Nationality: Jamaican. **Born:** Jamaica, 1 May 1913. Educated in Jamaica. **Family:** Married Monica Jacobs in 1935; two daughters and two sons. **Career:** Reporter, editor, and foreign correspondent for various newspapers; worked in advertising; currently, manag-

ing director and chair of a printing and publishing company in Kingston, Jamaica. **Awards:** Canada Council fellowship, 1958; Guggenheim fellowship, 1959. **Address:** c/o Institute of Jamaica Publications, 2-A Suthermere Road, Kingston 10, Jamaica.

PUBLICATIONS

Novels

New Day. New York, Knopf, 1949; London, Heinemann, 1950.
The Leopard. New York, Viking Press, and London, Heinemann, 1958.

Short Stories

The Jamaicans. Kingston, Institute of Jamaica, 1976.

Other (for children)

Sixty-Five. London, Longman, 1960.
The Young Warriors. London, Longman, 1967.
Peter of Mount Ephraim. Kingston, Jamaica Publishing House, 1971.
The Sun and Juan de Bolas. Kingston, Institute of Jamaica, 1974.
Nanny-Town. Kingston, Jamaica Publishing House, 1983.

Other

Buildings in Jamaica. Kingston, Jamaica Information Service, 1970.
The Horses of the Morning: About the Right Excellent N.W. Manley, National Hero of Jamaica: An Understanding. Kingston, Caribbean Authors, 1985.

*   *   *

Vic Reid gives the impression of being a "loner," a man of few words. His literary output has not been large, but he has been an innovative and unusual novelist.

When *New Day* appeared in 1949, it proved to be innovative in two ways: in its use of a formalized Jamaican English, and in its concerns—for national growth, for the resumption and expansion of responsible government, for the role of a local family in national growth. *The Leopard,* set as it is in Kikuyu land, does not use a distinctive form of Jamaican speech, but it is structurally more interesting than *New Day,* and its concerns are not as unconnected with West Indian experience as they might seem. In fact, Reid's life as a Jamaican would have prepared him well to work out such a combination of gentleness and violence, in fact a fugue and coda, which could also be a prelude to a "new day" in Africa, and in the world.

New Day, using the flashback technique, has structural weaknesses, and from time to time its special formalized Jamaican language does not ring absolutely true. (To give two small examples: "Duppy-ghost," "congo-pea soup".) Was Reid too concerned with the fact that his Jamaican characters had to speak not only to each other, but also to a wider audience?

His historical grasp of the political and power situation in 1865 has been criticized both on ideological and historical grounds. In this connection, it should not be forgotten that Reid was very careful to say in the last paragraph of the "Author's Note" prefaced to the first edition of *New Day:* "I have not by any means attempted a history of the period from 1865 to 1944. . . . What I have attempted is to transfer to paper some of the beauty, kindness, and humor of my people . . . creating a tale that will offer as true an impression as fiction can of the way by which Jamaica and its people come to today."

There are many remarkable things in *New Day;* one notable section deals with Pastor Humphrey's sermon on "constituted authority." It starts, "Whenever we go to church . . . Naomi and me sit side-and-side . . . but when the sermon begins we close our knees tight, and then there is good space for crab-race. You know how to play crab-race?" That very Jamaican question sets the aspect of the children's presence at the service, while as Humphrey warms to his theme—"Mouth came down *snap* on authority, long neck shot out, then drew back into his cassock like iguana in stonehill"—the Stoney Gut men are about to create a groaning objection to Paul's text on obedience and the pastor's interpretation of it. The chapter ends with "'Let us pray for rain,' says Pastor Humphrey." But we know that it is blood that will soon be quenching the long drought which had intensified, and symbolized, the disillusion and deterioration in St. Thomas Parish.

Often old John Campbell (as narrator) slips delightfully into the skin of the young boy, he had been when "in media res": "Good it is to hear her laugh but when mother says *Heh!* like that, all of your manhood is gone. . . . Is funny how your breeches drop off anytime Mother says *heh!*" But the ably-used device of having a sleepless narrator recall his family's role in the dawning of the "new day" has its disadvantages. For one thing, John Campbell has to rush a few sequences to help us suspend, willingly, our disbelief, and it might well be this technical difficulty that tends to exaggerate a falsely Romantic view (even in Campbell's mouth) of the fighting years of Jamaican men.

The Leopard is in some ways, particularly in structure, even more noteworthy. The clean juxtapositioning of the few personae, the untransitioned switching from group to group of those concerned and then converging for the final point of the story—and meanwhile the leopard alone understands Kenya "for he avoids the strong and eats the wounded, and the weak is stalking the stalked"—all these build up into an image of sick, hunting and hunted man, not unlike Derek Walcott's in "A Far Cry from Africa." In the end the lieutenant ("robbed me of my first Kike") becomes the leopard, whom he has just deprecatingly, but more truthfully than he realizes, called "Brother Leopard," and the fate long since planned for that animal becomes the lieutenant's at the hands of Nebu ("one of the loyal bucks").

Reid is a flexible and varied writer, with, at times, a fist of mail beneath that gauntlet of silk. An innovator on the West Indian literary scene, he has written, besides the novels mentioned, a variety of short stories and books for young people. His work shows forth his gifts and care, and underlines our need for more from him.

—John J. Figueroa

RENDELL, Ruth (Barbara)

Pseudonym: Barbara Vine. **Nationality:** British. **Born:** Ruth Barbara Grasemann, London, 17 February 1930. **Education:** Loughton High School, Essex. **Family:** Married Donald Rendell in 1950 (divorced 1975); remarried in 1977; one son. **Career:** Reporter and sub-editor, *Express* and *Independent* newspapers, West Essex, 1948-52. **Awards:** Mystery Writers of America Edgar Allan Poe award, for short story, 1975, 1984; Crime Writers Association Silver Dagger award, 1984, and Gold Dagger award, 1976, 1986, 1987; Arts Council National Book award, 1981; Arts Council bursary, 1981; Popular Culture Association award, 1983. **Agent:** Peters Fraser and Dunlop, 503-504 The Chambers, Chelsea Harbour, Lots Road, London SW10 0XF. **Address:** Nussteads, Polstead, Colchester, Essex CO6 5DN, England.

PUBLICATIONS

Novels

From Doon with Death. London, Hutchinson, 1964; New York, Doubleday, 1965.
To Fear a Painted Devil. London, Long, and New York, Doubleday, 1965.
Vanity Dies Hard. London, Long, 1965; New York, Beagle, 1970; as *In Sickness and in Health,* New York, Doubleday, 1966.
A New Lease of Death. London, Long, and New York, Doubleday, 1967; as *Sins of the Fathers,* New York, Ballantine, 1970.
Wolf to the Slaughter. London, Long, 1967; New York, Doubleday, 1968.
The Secret House of Death. London, Long, 1968; New York, Doubleday, 1969.
The Best Man to Die. London, Long, 1969; New York, Doubleday, 1970.
A Guilty Thing Surprised. London, Hutchinson, and New York, Doubleday, 1970.
No More Dying Then. London, Hutchinson, 1971; New York, Doubleday, 1972.
One Across, Two Down. London, Hutchinson, and New York, Doubleday, 1971.
Murder Being Done Once. London, Hutchinson, and New York, Doubleday, 1972.
Some Lie and Some Die. London, Hutchinson, and New York, Doubleday, 1973.
The Face of Trespass. London, Hutchinson, and New York, Doubleday, 1974.
Shake Hands for Ever. London, Hutchinson, and New York, Doubleday, 1975.
A Demon in My View. London, Hutchinson, 1976; New York, Doubleday, 1977.
A Judgement in Stone. London, Hutchinson, 1977; New York, Doubleday, 1978.
A Sleeping Life. London, Hutchinson, and New York, Doubleday, 1978.
Make Death Love Me. London, Hutchinson, and New York, Doubleday, 1979.
The Lake of Darkness. London, Hutchinson, and New York, Doubleday, 1980.
Put On by Cunning. London, Hutchinson, 1981; as *Death Notes,* New York, Pantheon, 1981.
Master of the Moor. London, Hutchinson, and New York, Pantheon, 1982.
The Speaker of Mandarin. London, Hutchinson, and New York, Pantheon, 1983.
The Killing Doll. London, Hutchinson, and New York, Pantheon, 1984.

The Tree of Hands. London, Hutchinson, 1984; New York, Pantheon, 1985.

An Unkindness of Ravens. London, Hutchinson, and New York, Pantheon, 1985.

Live Flesh. London, Hutchinson, and New York, Pantheon, 1986.

A Warning to the Curious. London, Hutchinson, 1987.

Heartstones. London, Hutchinson, and New York, Harper, 1987.

Talking to Strange Men. London, Hutchinson, and New York, Harper, 1987.

Wexford: An Omnibus. London, Hutchinson, 1988.

The Veiled One. London, Hutchinson, and New York, Pantheon, 1988.

The Bridesmaid. London, Hutchinson, and New York, Mysterious Press, 1989.

The Fourth Wexford Omnibus. London, Hutchinson, 1990.

Going Wrong. London, Hutchinson, and New York, Mysterious Press, 1990.

The Fifth Wexford Omnibus. London, Hutchinson, 1991.

Kissing the Gunner's Daughter. London, Hutchinson, and New York, Mysterious Press, 1992.

The Crocodile Bird. London, Hutchinson, and New York, Crown, 1993.

Inspector Wexford. London, Cresset, 1993.

Simisola. London, Hutchinson, 1994.

Novels as Barbara Vine

The Dark-Adapted Eye. London, Viking, and New York, Bantam, 1986.

A Fatal Inversion. London, Viking, and New York, Bantam, 1987.

The House of Stairs. London, Viking, and New York, Crown, 1989.

Gallowglass. London, Viking, and New York, Crown, 1990.

King Solomon's Carpet. London, Viking, 1991.

Asta's Book. London, Viking, 1993.

No Night Is Too Long. London, Viking, 1994.

Short Stories

The Fallen Curtain and Other Stories. London, Hutchinson, and New York, Doubleday, 1976.

Means of Evil and Other Stories. London, Hutchinson, 1979; New York, Doubleday, 1980.

The Fever Tree and Other Stories. London, Hutchinson, and New York, Pantheon, 1982.

The New Girl Friend. London, Hutchinson, 1985; New York, Pantheon, 1986.

Collected Short Stories. London, Hutchinson, 1987; New York, Pantheon, 1988.

The Strawberry Tree (with *Flesh and Grass* by Helen Simpson). London, Pandora Press, 1990.

The Copper Peacock and Other Stories. London, Hutchinson, and New York, Mysterious Press, 1991.

Other

Ruth Rendell's Suffolk, photographs by Paul Bowden. London, Muller, 1989.

Editor, *A Warning to the Curious: The Ghost Stories of M.R. James.* London, Century Hutchinson, 1987; Boston, Godine, 1989.

Editor, with Colin Ward, *Undermining the Central Line.* London, Chatto and Windus, 1989.

* * *

Ruth Rendell has created three distinct groups of novels as well as a number of gripping short stories, earning warm praise from her peers as well as from an army of fans. Both prolific and artistically exacting, she has created a distinguished series of novels about Kingsmarkham police officers, an array of single novels which include some of her best work, and the short stories as Ruth Rendell. In the late 1980s she introduced the pseudonymous Barbara Vine, whose voice differs from the Ruth Rendell voice but whose standards of performance remain just as high.

Rendell first achieved fame with the series featuring Detective Chief Inspector Reg Wexford and his associate, Mike Burden. The interplay between the central character, Wexford—senior in years and rank, pragmatic, yet imaginative—Burden—straight-laced and somewhat inflexible—is an important attraction of these works. Their acerbic comradeship, both personally and professionally fulfilling, brings each man vividly to life, and their relationships with their families supply wide-ranging complications and subplots. The recently widowed Burden dominates the action of *No More Dying Then,* in which the mystery centers upon the second child to go missing from the area within a short time. Mike and Gemma Lawrence, single mother of the victim, both grieving profoundly, find comfort in one another's arms, despite Burden's extreme conventionality and Gemma's more "modern" life-style. A neat combination of solid detection and coincidence solves the kidnappings, and Burden's bittersweet romance is realistically resolved. *Murder Being Once Done* takes place in London, where Wexford goes to recover from a stroke. The body of a young woman found in Kenbourne Vale Cemetery lures the Chief Inspector into unofficial but intense involvement with several families whose dreams are sadly disrupted. Here, as in *No More Dying Then,* parents' attitudes toward their children are a central theme. Indeed, family interactions are a frequent theme in Rendell's work, and the Wexford and Burden families not only compare and contrast with one another but also with families of victims and criminals.

Parental influence is thematically important in a number of other Rendell novels as well. *A Demon in My View,* considers the burden of guilt and self-distrust borne by Arthur Johnson, "sold" by his mother and reared by a strict, cold aunt. A successful serial killer, Arthur constructs a narrow but safe routine which includes fanatic attention to the details of daily life—and the periodic strangulation of a shop-window mannequin he keeps at hand—until the innocent intrusion of Anthony Johnson, a neighbor, destroys Arthur's control. Rendell's trademark irony permeates the powerful conclusion.

Like Arthur Johnson, Eunice Parchman in *A Judgement in Stone* reveals effects of her upbringing throughout a disastrous adulthood. A handy dogsbody for her feckless parents, she grows up illiterate and without affection. Such extreme intellectual and emotional isolation makes Eunice profoundly suspicious of the lively, literate family for whom she keeps house and fairly easy prey for Joan Smith, amoral, mad, and dangerous. Here, Rendell compares Joan's manic religiosity with the dreamy mysticism of Giles Mont, teenaged son of Eunice's victims.

Giles, one of Rendell's most interesting characters, is a privileged youngster who exists worlds away from his mother and stepfather, even though he dwells in their household. Fascinated with language, religion, and his stepsister, Melinda Coverdale, Giles is preoccupied with his studies, his imagination, and his fantasies. Similarly, important young characters in *Talking to Strange Men* are at least theoretically close to their families but conduct wholly separate, secret lives. Mungo Cameron heads a gang of schoolboy "spies" taking part in a complex, absorbing game until John Creevy, divorced and asocial, and a traitorous gameplayer transforms fun into disenchantment. Another player, Charles Mabledene, tests his courage by tempting a pederast. This study of the loss of innocence compares adult manipulations to children's imitative games with searing effect. In *The Bridesmaid,* a young woman's self-indulgent fantasies exact a terrible toll; like John Creevy, Senta is lost in love and too immature to grasp the difference between her attitudes and those of others.

The Barbara Vine novels examine the impact of past crimes upon a complex present. In *A Dark-Adapted Eye,* Faith Severn attempts to uncover the facts of the 30-year-old murder for which her aunt was executed. After 10 years of silence and concealment, Adam Verne-Smith learns that the crime which climaxed a youthful summer adventure is under investigation; in *A Fatal Inversion,* the details of that summer and of the lives of its survivors (some of whom cling willfully to childish passions) are revealed. In *The House of Stairs,* Elizabeth Vetch exploits her widowed aunt, Cosette, and soon, a number of hangers-on invade Cosette's home, capitalizing on her desire for youth, affection, and admiration. The open ending is tantalizing yet completely satisfying.

No Night Is Too Long, which features intriguing but not very likable characters, is set partially on a rain-drenched voyage along the Alaskan coast. A speculation about the emotional impact of guilt, the novel centers upon the convoluted relationship between handsome, irresponsible Tim Cornish and the older, more learned and sophisticated Ivo Steadman. The men's commitment to one another is complicated by Tim's passion for Isabel Winwood and by her relationship with Ivo. Using such old-fashioned devices as letters and journal entries in this modern story, Rendell makes coincidence seem completely logical.

Clearly, obsessive love and an individual's failure or inability to mature are frequent motifs in the Rendell-Vine canon, always illuminated by detailed, absorbing characterization and enhanced with beautifully developed suspense.

—Jane S. Bakerman

RICE, Anne

Pseudonyms: Anne Rampling; A.N. Roquelaure. **Nationality:** American. **Born:** Howard Allen O'Brien, New Orleans, Louisiana, 4 October 1941; name changed to Anne c.1947. **Education:** Texas Women's University, Denton, Texas, 1959-60; San Francisco State College (now University), California, B.A. 1964, M.A. 1971; graduate study at University of California, Berkeley, 1969-70. **Family:** Married Stan Rice in 1961; one daughter (deceased), and one son. **Career:** Has held a variety of jobs, including waitress, cook, theater usherette, and insurance claims examiner. Currently, a full-time writer. **Awards:** Joseph Henry Jackson award honorable mention, 1970. **Address:** 1239 First St., New Orleans, Louisiana 70130, U.S.A.

PUBLICATIONS

Novels

The Feast of All Saints. New York, Simon and Schuster, 1980; Harmondsworth, Penguin, 1982.

Cry to Heaven. New York, Knopf, 1982; London, Chatto and Windus, 1990.

Exit to Eden (as Anne Rampling). New York, Arbor House, and London, Futura, 1985.

Belinda (as Anne Rampling). New York, Arbor House, 1986; London, Macdonald, 1987.

The Mummy: Or Ramses the Damned. New York, Ballantine, and London, Chatto and Windus, 1989.

Vampire Chronicles. New York, Ballantine, 1989.

   Interview with the Vampire. New York, Knopf, and London, Raven, 1976.

   The Vampire Lestat. New York, Ballantine, and London, Macdonald, 1985.

   The Queen of the Damned. New York, Knopf, 1988; London, Macdonald, 1989.

The Witching Hour. New York, Knopf, 1990; London, Chatto and Windus, 1991.

The Tale of the Body Thief. New York, Knopf, and London, Chatto and Windus, 1992.

Lasher. New York, Knopf, and London, Chatto and Windus, 1993.

Taltos: Lives of the Mayfair Witches. New York, Knopf, and London, Chatto and Windus, 1994.

Novels as A.N. Roquelaure

The Sleeping Beauty Novels. New York, New American Library/Dutton, 1991.

The Claiming of Sleeping Beauty. New York, Dutton, and London, Macdonald, 1983.

Beauty's Punishment. New York, Dutton, 1984.

Beauty's Release. New York, Dutton, 1985; London, Warner, 1994.

*

Critical Studies: *Prism of the Night: A Biography of Anne Rice* by Katherine M. Ramsland, New York, Dutton, 1991; *Anne Rice* by Bette B. Roberts, New York, Twayne, and Oxford, Maxwell Macmillan, 1994.

*   *   *

Anne Rice has achieved considerable success with her imaginative forays into the occult, especially the lore of vampires and witches, the focal concerns of her two major sagas. In these books, Rice spins complex tales that weave through both time and space and the minds of her characters in convoluted patterns that make her works fascinating but slow reading. Plot-dilating passages of introverted and tormented inner questing blanket external action, as in Louis's confessional in *Interview with the Vampire,* the first of the author's popular vampire books. Like many of Rice's succeeding works, it is a lengthy and intricate odyssey of self-discovery rather than a chronicle of sharply delineated action. Given the book's length, external events in *Interview* seem almost meager.

The narrative paths in Rice's novels are sometimes difficult to follow. They often evolve as narratives within narratives. For example, in *The Queen of the Damned,* the third vampire book, the plot weaves through the impressions of many characters. As Lestat's coven converges and the history of Akasha the Queen unfolds, the reader is taken back and forth from the modern world to the dark recesses of pre-Egyptian antiquity. Lestat is merely the nominal narrator, who both introduces the story and ends its telling from a contemporary vantage point. In between, the story evolves through a series of ever-shifting narrative perspectives.

A reader who is unsympathetic to Rice's convoluted plots, androgynous protagonists, gender-bending ideas, elaborate myth making, and the rhapsodic but cloying self-consciousness of her principal characters, can easily lose the direction of her narratives and grow impatient with her style. She is a prolix and at times very turgid writer. Yet her strengths lie precisely in that baroque style—in her sensual verbal panoply, her lush and exotic detail, her constant reference to the physicalness of her characters and their self-indulgent, fugitive, "savage-garden" existence.

As *The Mummy* reveals, without those full phantasmagoric trappings and inner focus, Rice's plots exploiting the occult may seem merely incredible, even faintly absurd. In that novel, intended or not, whimsy tempers credibility when Ramses the Damned and Cleopatra both quicken from the long dead into, respectively, an Edwardian gentleman and a roadster-driving, murderous nymphomaniac—all in the matter of a few hours. That is the stuff of a B-grade horror movie, from which the plot partially sprang.

Rice exploits the sensational without apology, whether eroticism, as in the novels written under her two pseudonyms, Anne Rampling and A.N. Roquelaure, or the occult, as in her two sagas. In fact, eroticism pervades all her work, even in her novels focusing on androgynous characters, as in *Interview with the Vampire* and *The Vampire Lestat,* where it is either transmuted or barely suppressed. There it takes the form of homoeroticism and thinly veiled incest and pedophilia. Even Rice's heterosexual, non-androgynous characters, are either sexually offbeat, caught up in the sadomasochistic bondage exploited in *Exit to Eden,* for example, or guilt ridden by taboos, as in her study of the Louisiana Creole culture in *The Feast of All Saints.* In the occult books, the erotic is often bound to the ubiquitous blood and flesh-tearing images.

Yet, despite the author's gruesome images, horror and a sense of terror both seem oddly muted in her novels. There are lurid details, but none are very memorable, except, perhaps, the distinctly grotesque, as, when, for example, Maharet devours her own eyes in *The Queen of the Damned* or Cleopatra, in *The Mummy,* tries to disguise her gaping wounds as she searches for sexual prey.

Clearly, Rice, unlike Stephen King, is less interested in chilling effects than in the minds of her dark, lost-soul characters and her evolving myths and themes. She is concerned with human liberation, sexual and otherwise, with human emotions ravaged by conflicting needs and with her recurring themes of nurturing and self-reconciliation in her pariah and androgynous protagonists. It is these elements that give her novels their dense texture, not the supernatural, even when she works out the elaborate details of the vampire myth surrounding Akasha and Enkil, "those who must be kept." In *Cry to Heaven,* which may be her best work fashioned outside her sagas, Rice reveals her considerable range in subject matter, but in using a castrato hero, Tonio, and his teacher-mentor-lover, Guido, she does not stray from the themes that underlie all her more serious fiction. The lonely outcast's quest for an acceptable identity is the epicenter of most of her novels.

—John W. Fiero

ROBBINS, Tom

Nationality: American. **Born:** Thomas Eugene Robbins in Blowing Rock, North Carolina, 22 July 1936. **Education:** High school in Warsaw, Virginia; Hargarve Military Academy; Washington and Lee University, Lexington, Virginia; Richmond Professional Institute (now Virginia Commonwealth University), graduated 1960. **Military Service:** Served in the United States Air Force in Korea. **Family:** Married Terrie Robbins (second marriage; divorced); one child. **Career:** Copy editor, Richmond *Times-Dispatch,* 1960-62, and Seattle *Times* and *Post-Intelligencer,* 1962-63; reviewer and art columnist, *Seattle Magazine,* and radio host, 1964-68. **Agent:** Phoebe Larmore, 228 Main Street, Venice, California 90291, USA.

PUBLICATIONS

Novels

Another Roadside Attraction. New York, Doubleday, 1971; London, W.H. Allen, 1973.
Even Cowgirls Get the Blues. Boston, Houghton Mifflin, 1976; London, Corgi, 1977.
Still Life with Woodpecker. New York, Bantam, and London, Sidgwick and Jackson, 1980.
Jitterbug Perfume. New York, Bantam, 1984.
Skinny Legs and All. New York, Bantam, 1990; London, Bantam, 1991.
Half Asleep in Frog Pajamas. New York, Bantam, 1994.

Uncollected Short Story

"The Chink and the Clock People," in *The Best American Short Stories 1977,* edited by Martha Foley. Boston, Houghton Mifflin, 1977.

Other

Guy Anderson. Seattle, Gear Works Press, 1965.
Guy Anderson (exhibition catalogue), with William Ivey and Wallace S. Baldinger. Seattle, Seattle Art Museum, 1977.

*

Critical Study: *Tom Robbins* by Mark Siegel, Boise, Idaho, Boise State University, 1980.

Tom Robbins comments:

I sometimes think of my serio-comic novels as cakes with files baked in them. If you choose, you can throw the file away and simply enjoy the cake. Or, you may use the file to saw through the iron bars erected by those forces in life that are forever trying to imprison us. Of course, if you aren't hip enough to know the file is there, you may end up with dental problems of an acute nature.

*   *   *

Although practically ignored by academic critics, except as an eccentric regionalist, Tom Robbins with his first two novels became the only American novelist since J.D. Salinger and Jack

Kerouac in the 1950s to become a cult hero among disaffected college undergraduates.

Like Salinger—and the even more elusive Thomas Pynchon, who has uncharacteristically publicly praised Robbins's second novel—the author lives in seclusion. He allows himself to be described only as "a student of art and religion" who "dropped out" to write fiction in a Washington State fishing village. Although Kerouac is the only author Robbins mentions in his novels, these more nearly resemble Salinger's Glass Family stories. The ostensible "author" frequently interrupts the stories; and, although the characters are more bizarre than Salinger's, they tend like his to be highly talkative, much given to self-analysis, lengthy confessions, and populist philosophical speculation.

Robbins's writing is even more bitterly anti-Establishment than Salinger's or Kerouac's; FBI and CIA violence and treachery and the conspiratorial practices of the Roman Catholic Church are his most frequent targets. Much of the action of *Another Roadside Attraction,* for example, deals with the involvement of Plucky Purcell (a regenade football player) in a secret order of monks that leads to his discovery during an earthquake of the mummified body of Jesus hidden in the Vatican catacombs. He brings his grotesque find to the "roadside attraction," a giant West Coast hot-dog stand operated by drop-out artist John Paul Ziller and his wife Amanda, an archetypal matriarchal figure. The principal movement of the story, narrated by Marx Marvelous, a skeptical scientific dropout from an East Coast think tank, is toward "light," toward a physical dissolution of the individual in his reunion with the sun, which Ziller describes to Marvelous as "the source of all biological energy, and ultimately . . . the source of you." While Plucky debates how to use Christ's corpse to expose the hoax of Christian culture, Ziller steals it and sets off with it and his pet baboon on a space balloon for the "return to sunlight," which he had said was an "inevitability" he'd been "reckoning with." "Let Amanda by your pine cone," the novel concludes as a joyous tribute to her survival.

Even Cowgirls Get the Blues is longer, talkier, and more self-consciously whimsical than its predecessor. The first half of the novel dwells upon the picaresque adventures of Sissy Hankshaw, a born hitch-hiker with monstrous thumbs. Most of the second half is dominated by the "clock people," Indian refugees from the San Francisco earthquake, who have substituted rigid individual rituals for societal rituals. The two fantasies are united by events at the Rubber Rose Ranch, a wealthy women's retreat that is seized by insurgent cowgirls. Their brush with the government culminates in the Whooping Crane war, after the cowgirls disrupt the endangered species' migration by feeding them peyote. The convoluted story, which is related by an offbeat psychiatrist curiously named Robbins, winds up with the cranes circling the globe while Sissy is envisioned as the mother of a tribe of big-thumbed people in the "postcatastrophe" world.

Whimsy predominates in Robbins's third book, the short and relatively uncomplicated *Still Life with Woodpecker,* which counterpoints such trendy topics of the early 1980s as deposed royalty, red-headed bombers, and pyramid power to ask the plaintive question, "Who knows how to make love stay?" Robbins despairs of an answer during an era of distrust between the sexes, but an almost *Aida*-like ending hints at a way out of the dilemma.

Heavy-handed whimsy turns into sheer fantasy in *Jitterbug Perfume.* The action of this fourth novel focuses on Alobar, tribal king of a tiny, barbarous medieval city-state, who escapes the customary execution of the ruler at his first sign of aging to become for a thousand years a wanderer to exotic places who has learned the

Bandaloop principles of immortal life. Interpolated into this bizarre pilgrimage are brief glimpses of life among the perfume-makers in contemporary Seattle, New Orleans, and Paris. This fable simply lays the groundwork for the climactic proclamation of Wiggs Dannyboy (a character reminiscent of Timothy Leary) a man that is on the verge of leaving behind his reptilian and mammalian consciousness to enter the phase of "floral consciousness," during which the production of sensorily stimulating perfumes will be his highest good. It is hard to tell how seriously to take this preachment; but if it isn't serious, there seems no point at all to the long stretches of Robbins's increasingly self-indulgent prose. As the title suggests, the whole production has the dated air of celebrating the culture of the flower children of the 1960s. These two later works have done little to sustain Robbins's position as guru to an underground cult.

—Warren French

ROBERTS, Michèle (Brigitte)

Nationality: British. **Born:** Bushey, Hertfordshire, 20 May 1949. **Education:** Oxford University, B.A. (with honors) 1970; University of London Library Associate, 1972. **Career:** Has worked as a librarian, cook, teacher, cleaner, pregnancy counselor, and researcher; writer-in-residence, Lambeth Borough, London, 1981-82, and Bromley Borough, London, 1983-84. Poetry editor, *Spare Rib,* 1975-77, and *City Limits,* 1981-83. **Awards:** *Gay News* Literary award, 1978, for *A Piece of the Night.* **Agent:** Caroline Dawnay, A.D. Peters, 10 Buckingham St., London W.C.2, England.

PUBLICATIONS

Novels

A Piece of the Night. London, Women's Press, 1978.
The Visitation. London, Women's Press, 1978.
The Wild Girl. London, Methuen, 1984.
The Book of Mrs. Noah. London, Methuen, 1987.
In the Red Kitchen. London, Methuen, 1990.
Psyche and the Hurricane. London, Methuen, 1991.
Daughters of the House. London, Virago, and New York, Morrow, 1992.
During Mother's Absence. London, Virago, 1993.
Flesh & Blood. London, Virago, 1994.

Short Stories

Tales I Tell My Mother, with Alison Fell. London, Journeyman Press, 1978.

Poetry

Licking the Bed Clean. N.p., 1978.
Smile, Smile, Smile, Smile. N.p., 1980.
Touch Papers, with Judith Karantris and Michelene Wandor. London, Allison and Busby, 1982.

The Mirror of the Mother: Selected Poems 1975-1985. London, Methuen, 1985.
All the Selves I Was: New and Selected Poems. London, Virago, 1995.

Other

Editor,with Michelene Wandor, *Cutlasses and Earrings.* London, Playbooks, 1976.

* * *

Michèle Roberts is one of a group of novelists who emerged from 1970s British feminism and has become recognized as an important author concerned to represent the body, particularly the female body, in writing. Using realistic and non-realistic modes, Roberts has always been concerned to recover the lost body of the mother/female experience and female art. Influenced by both Freudian and Jungian theory, her novels seek out the unconscious as a creative force and explore ways of recuperating religious experience from patriarchal structures as Roberts reinterprets her Catholic heritage. All her novels engender their own authors using Christian, classical, artistic, and maternal myths to try to free female creativity from a patriarchal culture.

A Piece Of The Night, the first novel, strongly reflects the contemporary British feminist movement. In realistic form, it charts the career of Julie, insufficiently mothered, who marries in a state of dependence, is trapped into domesticity but finds liberation in lesbian love. Later novels give more space to problematic heterosexuality. This novel also struggles with problems of representing women in a radical way and finds Julie's Catholic heritage offers only images of repression, submission, and death, leaving women to feel themselves only "a piece of the night."

The next work, *The Visitation,* begins Roberts's project of rewriting Christian myth to figure the independent woman since it uses the New Testament friendship of Elizabeth and Mary (here Beth and Helen) to privilege the relationship of two heterosexual women and represent female creativity in motherhood and in writing. Beth becomes pregnant but the Virgin birth seems to be Helen's novel, possibly *The Visitation* itself. Just as religious myths are now available to be rewritten, so is the unconscious; dreams are a sustaining force for female selfhood. These two aspects of Roberts's style are particularly prominent in her next, most controversial, text, *The Wild Girl,* purporting to be the fifth Gospel as told by Mary Magdalen. This novel is a marvellous fusing of Roberts's theme of the meaningfulness of the female body, religious experience, and female authority as religious teacher, as author. Significantly influenced by feminist Jungians, it is structured around a sexual romance between Jesus and Mary Magdalen becoming a sacred marriage, an initiation into the unconscious which is also religious. Like the earlier two novels the form resembles a romance but the intensity of *The Wild Girl* also figures as tragedy. *The Book of Mrs. Noah* tries to escape the dual structure of romance and tragedy by containing a more multifarious plot, leaving realism for myth and fantasy and adopting comedy. At one level it continues earlier works by restructuring the Old Testament story of Noah's Ark, offering an Ark devoted to female writers. This brings in the contemporary narrative as the sibyls who visit the Ark are all representatives of the peculiar struggles of the female writer in a male-dominated society. They tell stories on the Ark that rewrite Christian heritage while Mrs. Noah, the narrator, ponders the fraught issue of moth-

erhood. Much of the comedy of the Ark comes from the stowaway, the Voice of God, a male artist suffering from writer's block after his blockbuster, the Bible. This is a complex work suggesting for the first time that feminist problems cannot be solved easily but it asserts the healing power of the unconscious, here the Ark, as manifested in storytelling.

In The Red Kitchen, the fifth novel, returns to realism while investigating father-daughter bonds in a series of female histories linked by spiritualism, that female-dominated movement that preceded the birth of psychoanalysis. Based on a real case, Victorian Flora Milk has as a spirit guide Hat, an Egyptian princess who acquires power through incest with her father. Flora becomes involved with the middle-class patriarchal marriage of Minnie and William and with the mysterious death of their daughter. In turn, Flora haunts Hattie, a single woman living in her house in contemporary London who is a cookery writer because she has a vision of a giantess in a red kitchen (the repressed place of female creativity).

Perhaps Roberts most successful novel is *Daughters of the House,* which mingles autobiography with a saint's life, using the story of Saint Therese of Lisieux. An intensely poetic piece, it tells the story of two cousins, Therese and Leonie, who spend summers together in post-war France. What comes up from the Catholic and historical repressions of the period is Leonie's archetypal visions of a "red lady" connected to the villagers' suppressed worship of a goddess. This causes the discovery of a grave, the murdered remains of Jews who had been betrayed by the priest. Therese also claims to have visions, but orthodox ones, and becomes a nun. The novel again privileges female relationships but here in a political context. Roberts most recent novel is *Flesh and Blood,* an almost Gothic series of interlocking stories focusing on female sexual experience through history in France and Britain. Michele Roberts is an important contemporary explorer of female identity and creativity.

—S.A. Rowland

ROBINSON, Kim Stanley

Nationality: American. **Born:** Waukegan, Illinois, 23 March 1952. **Education:** University of California, San Diego, B.A. in literature, 1974, Ph.D. 1982; Boston University, M.A. in English 1975. **Family:** Married Lisa Howland Nowell in 1982. **Career:** Visiting lecturer, University of California, in Davis, 1982-84, 1985, and in San Diego, 1982, 1985. **Awards:** World Fantasy award, 1983; *Locus* award, 1985. **Address:** c/o Tor Books, 49 West 24th Street, 9th floor, New York, New York 10010, U.S.A.

PUBLICATIONS

Novels (series: Orange County)

The Wild Shore (Orange County). New York, Ace, 1984; London, Futura, 1985.
Icehenge. New York, Ace, 1984; London, Futura, 1985.
The Memory of Whiteness: A Scientific Romance. New York, Tor, 1985; London, Macdonald, 1986.

Green Mars, with *A Meeting with Medusa,* by Arthur C. Clarke. New York, Tor, 1988; as *Green Mars,* London, HarperCollins, 1993.

The Blind Geometer. New Castle, Virginia, Cheap Street, 1986; with *Return from Rainbow Bridge,* and *The New Atlantis,* by Ursula Le Guin, New York, Tor, 1989.

The Gold Coast (Orange County). New York, St. Martin's Press, and London, Macdonald, 1988.

Pacific Edge (Orange County). New York, Tor, and London, Unwin Hyman, 1990.

A Short, Sharp Shock. Shingletown, California, Siesing, 1990.

Down and Out in the Year 2000. London, Grafton, 1992.

Red Mars. London, HarperCollins, 1992; New York, Bantam, 1993.

Short Stories

The Planet on the Table. New York, Tor, 1986; London, Futura, 1987.

Escape from Kathmandu. Eugene, Oregon, Axolotl Press, 1987; London, Unwin Hyman, 1990.

Remaking History, and Other Stories. New York, Tor, 1991.

Other

The Novels of Philip K. Dick. Ann Arbor, Michigan, UMI Research Press, 1984.

Editor, *Future Primitive: The New Ecotopias.* New York, Tor, 1994.

*   *   *

Kim Stanley Robinson is a writer of hard science fiction, a spiritual descendant of Jules Verne, and a writer most closely aligned with such hard science fiction creators as Isaac Asimov. When Jules Verne disparaged the work of H. G. Wells by calling Wells an "inventor," he created a schism that divided science fiction writers into at least two camps: Verne considered himself to be a writer of "extrapolative" fiction, that based in known and projected fact. He considered that writers of Wells's camp "invented" material, making up whatever was necessary to create a good story. Robinson is a writer of the Verne/Asimov/hard science fiction camp, even perhaps further toward the hard science end of the spectrum than either of those two writers. Aside from the fact that all of science fiction is a branch of the larger category of fantasy, there is little that seems "fantastic" about Robinson's work. His knowledge of and use of science and technology in his fiction is impressive.

Until his most recent works, Robinson was best known among science fiction readers for a series known as his *Orange County* trilogy. Strictly speaking, the three books in the group are not a trilogy in the sense of books that are connected by a series of characters and/or themes. Instead, the books are based on three different visions of the future of Orange County, California, and are written in three science fiction traditions. *The Wild Shore,* the first of the books, is a post-nuclear holocaust novel. *The Gold Coast* is dystopian; *Pacific Edge* is utopian. The first of the books, *The Wild Shore,* is probably the weakest of the three, using as it does a rather self-conscious adolescent as its protagonist. In general, however, the books are well written and carefully researched, and as an exercise they provide a beautifully done set of answers to the implicit questions in science fiction of "What if the worst happens?" and "If we keep going this way, what becomes of us?" and, finally, "Could we do this better, and if so, how?"

However, Robinson's most recent trilogy promises to make se-

cure his reputation as a first-rate science fiction writer. His *Mars* trilogy, of which two volumes, *Red Mars* and *Green Mars,* have been published (the final volume, *Blue Mars,* is reported to be near completion), are works of considerable depth and power. Robinson's work is indeed extrapolative in terms of science and technology but also in terms of economics, politics, business, and social trends. Robinson's ability to push forward our society's inclinations in each of those areas is fascinating; much of his work reads as if it were written the day after tomorrow.

A recurrent theme in Robinson's work deals with the persistent nature of the human being. In the *Mars* books as well as in other works, such as *The Memory of Whiteness,* Robinson seems to consider that even if the human experience is moved to Mars or Jupiter or any other planet, the human being remains the human being and, as such, behaves in human, and therefore limited, ways. In the *Mars* books, factional and national differences on Earth are merely transferred to Mars; the fact of a new planet, of an interplanetary experience, does not erase them. Further, Robinson's characters are so well delineated that he can portray two characters who express virtually opposite viewpoints yet make each character likable and capable of engaging the reader's sympathies. Unlike those science fiction writers who focus on their ideas to the exclusion of in-depth character portrayal, Robinson creates strong, believable, and engaging characters whose views pull the reader into their worlds. Indeed, so adept is he at the expression of various viewpoints through the characters he creates that the reader would be very hard put to determine which of the viewpoints he might personally support.

A reader unaccustomed to the in-depth use of scientific background information may find Robinson's science textbook style difficult to handle, though fans of the genre will probably embrace his verisimilitude. More likely to be a problem for both veteran and novice science fiction readers are the fairly repetitious descriptions of the Martian landscape. Those descriptions do tend to run on at more than necessary length.

Still, those are minor quibbles. Robinson's *Mars* trilogy promises to set the standard by which interplanetary colonization novels will be judged in the future.

—June Harris

ROBINSON, Marilynne

Nationality: American. **Born:** Sandpoint, Idaho, in 1943. **Education:** Brown University, Providence, Rhode Island, B.A. in American literature; University of Washington, Seattle, M.A. and Ph.D. in English. **Family:** Married; two sons. Lives in Massachusetts. **Awards:** American Academy Rosenthal Foundation award, 1982; Hemingway Foundation award, 1982. **Address:** c/o Farrar Straus and Giroux Inc., 19 Union Square West, New York, New York 10003, USA.

PUBLICATIONS

Novel

Housekeeping. New York, Farrar Straus, 1980; London, Faber, 1981.

Uncollected Short Stories

"Orphans," in *Harper's* (New York), February 1981.
"Connie Bronson," in *Paris Review,* Summer-Fall 1986.

Other

Mother Country: Britain, The Nuclear State, and Nuclear Pollution. New York, Farrar Straus, and London, Faber, 1989.

*   *   *

Housekeeping is, for most people, a basic requirement, if only on the simplest level of maintaining shelter. Little chores become so routine that they are done without thinking: washing the dishes or clothes, sweeping, dusting, all take up time and energy that we disregard, write off. Not many of us can or would bother to total the hours spent in such minor labors, any more than we could tally up the hours spent in the bath; they are just necessary losses. Those hours are acceptably, if boringly, spent in the small acts that give our lives some structure, some normality. Changing the linens on Mondays, shopping on Thursdays, church on Sundays, accumulate to keep our lives from flapping loose out into the chaos, like a dress blown off the laundry line and clean away.

Marilynne Robinson's novel *Housekeeping* is about the collapse and abandonment of housekeeping and of the frail structure it provides. For Ruth, who tells the story, housekeeping is a phase of the past, disintegrated in a childhood of isolated women and the constant presence of a lake. Ruth and Lucille were little girls when their mother drove them to her home town on a mountain lake in Idaho. The town, with the macabre and ludicrous name of Fingerbone, is small, completely surrounded, with the lake on one side, and the mountains and forest on the others. As in all remote towns, the people know one another too well, and the closeness is oppressive: "The people of Fingerbone and its environs were very much given to murder. And it seemed that for every pitiable crime there was an appalling accident. What with the lake and the railroads, and what with blizzards and floods and barn fires and forest fires and the general availability of shotguns and bear traps and homemade liquor and dynamite, what with the prevalence of loneliness and religion and the rages and ecstasies they induce, and the closeness of families, violence was inevitable." With long, slow sentences, Ruth tells how the mountains shut out light and the rest of the world, the forest holds darkness and danger, and the lake is a bowl of death. Never once is there any mention of "natural beauty."

The lake, the reason for the town's location, sits by, always in one's awareness, passive, a relentless presence. Ruth's first experience of the lake comes when, after dropping the girls off at the house of a grandmother they had never met, her mother drives her car off the cliffs and into the lake, drowning herself. Years earlier, a train had derailed and, plunging into the lake, drowned all aboard, including Ruth's grandfather. All of the dead remain in their underwater capsules. When the lake freezes, people go ice-skating. During the summer, Ruth and her sister play by it, fish in it. Slowly and undramatically, its importance grows. One winter, the snows melt but the lake does not, leaving the water to back up and flood the town. In Ruth's house, they move upstairs, letting the water take the downstairs, soaking furniture and curtains and sloshing against the walls. The whole town sits and waits, sodden, for the ice on the lake to melt so the water can flow home. "The clashes

and groans from the lake continued unabated, dreadful at night, and the sound of the night wind in the mountains was like one long indrawn breath. Downstairs the flood bumped and fumbled like a blind man in a strange house, but outside it hissed and trickled, like the pressure of water against your eardrums, and like the sounds you hear in the moment before you faint."

There are no men in this story, no sweet romance, no subtle sexuality, and the women are quiet, solitary, odd. Ruth's mother rarely spoke to her children. After her suicide, the girls are cared for by a very old grandmother living in her memories. When the girls find her dead, two elderly aunts are summoned from Spokane, but they then track down another aunt, Sylvie, to take over. Desertions and deaths are recounted in Ruth's helpless, rarely angry tone of acceptance in the same way that she tells of a fishing trip with Lucille, or of Sylvie's strange, transient ways. Sylvie rummages in rubbish bins, eats only in the dark, saves all tins, never cleans anything, plays crazy eights during the flood. She does her best to care for the girls, but housekeeping and structure left her life long ago.

As they reach adolescence, Ruth begins to acquiesce to her fate, while Lucille begins to fight it. Lucille wants to dress cleanly, to have friends, be normal, learn housekeeping. In a final desertion, she moves in with her Home Economics teacher. Ruth is left to drift, having decided "it is better to have nothing."

Robinson's style itself is evocative of drifting and drifters' tales, with long, often poetic descriptions that suddenly snap back to the original point or deflect to a new, unrelated one. At times, Ruth's anger appears in harsher narrative: a cold realization about Lucille, snide comments about Fingerbone's church ladies, or one long tirade about Cain's betrayal of Abel, which seems slightly inappropriate in a book without men: betrayal exists among sisters as well. At times, too, the sneering is so rough as to seem more than could be felt by this bland girl who cannot tell the difference between what she has dreamed and what she has imagined. These are small flaws in a book that is so rich with thought and feeling that it compels the reader to slow down and truly read.

—Anne Morddel

ROBINSON, Peter

Nationality: Canadian. **Born:** Castleford, Yorkshire, 17 March 1950. **Education:** University of Ledds, B.A. 1974; University of Windsor, M.A. 1975; York University, Ph.D. 1983. **Family:** Married Janice Hyndman in 1984. **Awards:** Arthur Ellis award for Canadian crime novel of the year, 1992. **Address:** 30 Lawlor Ave., Toronto, Ontario M4E 3L7, Canada.

PUBLICATIONS

Novels

The Gallows View. Toronto, Viking, 1987; New York, Scribner, 1990.
A Dedicated Man. Toronto, Viking, 1988; New York, Scribner, 1991.

The Hanging Valley. Toronto, Viking, 1989; New York, Scribner, 1992.

A Necessary End. Toronto, Viking, 1990; New York, Scribner, 1992.

Caedmon's Song. Toronto, Viking, 1990.

Past Reason Hated. Toronto, Viking, 1991; New York, Scribner, 1993.

Wednesday's Child. Toronto, Viking, 1992; New York, Berkley, 1995.

Final Account. Toronto, Penguin, 1994; New York, Berkley, and London, Constable, 1995.

No Cure for Love. Toronto, Penguin, 1995.

*   *   *

Peter Robinson, who emigrated to Canada in 1974, is best known for his seven detective novels featuring Detective Chief Inspector Alan Banks of the Eastvale Criminal Investigation Department, Yorkshire, England. In addition, Robinson has published two nonseries novels, the psychological thriller *Caedmon's Song* and a police procedural set primarily in Los Angeles, *No Cure for Love.* In each case, Robinson combines what might be called "psychological realism," or a focus on character and motivation, with thoughtful cultural commentary, particularly with respect to post Thatcher England and its susceptibility to the values, tastes, and practices of urban America.

Robinson's Inspector Banks series is built around the character of Alan Banks and the quiet, methodical, and ruminative way in which he sets about solving crimes in the Yorkshire Dales with the assistance of his investigative team. Banks is relatively new to the Dales, having recently transferred from London in search of (ironically, given the number of murders that fall his way) a quieter professional life. He is married to an independent woman he genuinely enjoys and who challenges rather than acquiesces to him. A consummate family man, Banks runs miniature trains for relaxation, relishes his Sunday beef with Yorkshire pudding, and mourns his children's adolescent trajectory away from hearth and home. He enjoys a good working partnership with his superior, Detective Superintendent Gristhorpe, a gritty Yorkshireman who struggles to replicate the ancient technology of dry stone wall-building on his Dales farm. In employing cool logic, honed instinct, and sheer doggedness in pursuing his inquiries, and in avoiding violence for the most part, Inspector Banks is very much the classic police investigator—which is not surprising, given Robinson's acknowledgment of writers like Simenon, Maigret, and Christie as early influences upon his work.

Yet Banks is distinctive in the robust psychological contours that Robinson affords him. A working-class lad who had failed his "eleven plus" exams and barely escaped being shoehorned into a manual trade of little interest to him, Banks is acutely aware of his good luck but also of his lack of formal education. He hungers for knowledge and culture. He loves classical music, especially opera, and crams his home and his mind with the detritus of things he wishes he knew more about—from Dickens and winemaking to bird eggs and local geology. He has an instinct for ferreting out white-collar and class-motivated crime as a result of what Robinson calls a "working-class chip on the shoulder" and exploits what is second nature to him, that sense of cautious distrust that characterizes the perpetual outsider.

Indeed, as "incomer" to fictional Swainsdale (a composite, Robinson says, of the four main Yorkshire Dales), Banks is well positioned to see more clearly than longtime residents both its quix-

otic regional characteristics, such as the wry taciturnity of those raised in the Dales, and the simultaneous ways in which even remote Yorkshire is being invaded and eroded by the electronic juggernaut that is American popular culture. Tourism has become the main industry in Swainsdale, bringing trailer parks, campsites, snack bars, and tarted-up pubs to a town traditionally known for its ancient cross, its Norman church, and its Roman ruins. Against these relics of earlier invasions of Britain, Banks links the current importation of all things American (from the wearing of expensive hiking gear to the yuppie-style renovations of venerable Dales farmhouses) to an increase in violent crime in the Dales.

Yet the real danger that Banks points to is less the ubiquity of American popular culture and the inevitable urbanization of northern England than the habits and habits of mind that such changes signal. Swainsdale is moments by car from the cities of Leeds, Bradford, and York and no longer immune to the instant pleasures of contemporary city life, from fast food to satellite broadcasts to anonymous sex and its aftermath. Throw-away gratification is certainly an affront to traditional Yorkshire values of perseverance, deferral, and endurance. But the larger danger, Robinson suggests, is the way that electronic or "virtual" cultures increasingly blunt our capacity for thought and, especially, for separating illusion from reality.

In Robinson's novels, as in most crime fiction, it is camouflage, disguise, pretense, or masking that must be penetrated if the mystery is to be solved. The social issues change from novel to novel, and to move from *Gallows View* to *No Cure for Love* is to encounter teen crime, marital treachery, class privilege, police brutality, homophobia, child abuse, and organized crime in rapid succession. The common element, however, is the need—in the face of the many ways that the same thing or same person can be perceived—for a heightened ability to spot the illusion, the sleight-of-hand, that obscures "reality."

Robinson's is a conservative vision, as is crime fiction itself a conservative genre with its insistence upon "knowing," upon solution and closure. What Robinson's fiction offers, however, whether in the Banks series or in his nonseries novels like *Caedmon's Song,* is a certain richness of cultural commentary and moral inquiry. In the face of a contemporary culture that (from a police perspective, at any rate) valorizes glamour and surface and over-tolerates greasy deals and unfettered greed, his fiction celebrates the will to dismember illusion while retaining one's basic decency and humanity—as in the case of the redoubtable Inspector Banks. It is an interesting and challenging response to the tumbling of old certainties that marks our time.

—Marilyn Rose

ROBISON, Mary

Nationality: American. **Born:** Mary Reiss in Washington, D.C., 14 January 1949. **Education:** Johns Hopkins University, Baltimore, M.A. 1977. **Family:** Married to James N. Robison. **Career:** From 1981, member of the Department of English, Harvard University, Cambridge, Massachusetts. Visiting lecturer, Ohio University, Athens, 1979-80; writer-in-residence, University of Southern Mississippi, Hattiesburg, 1980 and 1985, University of North Carolina, Greensboro, 1980, College of William and Mary, Williamsburg, Virginia, 1981, and Bennington College, Vermont, 1984, 1985; visiting assistant professor of Writing, Oberlin College, Ohio, 1984-85. **Awards:** Yaddo fellowship, 1978; Bread Loaf Writers Conference fellowship, 1979; Authors Guild award, 1979; Guggenheim fellowship, 1980. **Address:** c/o Andrew Wylie, Wylie, Aiken and Stone, Inc., 250 West 57th St., #2106, New York, New York 10107, USA.

PUBLICATIONS

Novel

Oh! New York, Knopf, 1981.

Short Stories

Days. New York, Knopf, 1979.
An Amateur's Guide to the Night. New York, Knopf, 1983.
Believe Them. New York, Knopf, 1988.
Subtraction. New York, Knopf, 1991.

*   *   *

To date Mary Robison has published one novel and four collections of short stories. Many readers have been introduced to her writing through the appearance of her short stories in the prestigious pages of the *New Yorker.* She writes of people caught in a web of alienation and living in the trivia of contemporary suburban America. Many of her characters seem cut off from events in their lives and their own innermost feelings. For example, in her novel, *Oh!,* Maureen and Howdy, the two adult children of Mr. Cleveland (a self-made, semi-retired millionaire) still live at home, passing the time drinking, complaining, watching TV, and vaguely trying to figure out what to do with their lives. At one point Maureen says "I love this house . . . I've never lived any place else. I couldn't be comfortable or feel safe anywhere else. . . . Yet I don't want to be stuck here the rest of my life. . . . Except I'm scared of going anywhere else. Of living out my days being poor." The narrator of one short story "Smart" is an unmarried, pregnant, 36 year-old woman living alone in a seedy apartment. She spends her hours sitting, or getting up "just to change a record or twist my spine, or to nibble some of the food my neighbor, Mrs. Sally Dixon, brought me."

Robison's characters are often rootless and without ambition. They have difficulty making connections with anyone or anything. They live their lives in a holding pattern. Like Maureen and Howdy, few find anything that motivates them to improve their lives. One exception to this, however, is the 17-year-old protagonist of the title story in *An Amateur Guide to the Night.* Lindy lives with her divorced mother and her maternal grandfather. She works as a waitress, goes to school, and watches *Fright Night* with the family. But beyond that, Lindy has discovered for herself the beauty of the night sky, and armed with her star charts and telescope she explores the splendor of one of nature's most spectacular shows.

The narrative voice of Robison contains a stark, unmelodic poetry devoid of frills, usually brushing only the surface, describing rather than exploring. Although much can be learned in this way, the author's detachment from her characters has been a persistent criticism leveled at her work. A scene in a Robison story is like a snapshot. She has an eye for detail and tends to focus on mun-

dane, ordinary events. The short story "In the Woods" has this: "Evenings on the farm, Kenneth would grill steaks or chops outside and my sister and I would do the salad, sometimes corn. We'd open wine. We would cut up muskmelon. After eating, we'd sit on the long flagstone patio, with its view of yard and pond, and maybe drink a Scotch."

The author's voice throughout is cool and meticulous. The reader watches along with the author as the story unfolds, slowly at times, just the same as it does in life. Sometimes the insight gleaned from this approach is no more discerning than when we observe strangers. Often, though, we catch a clear, penetrating glimpse into a person's heart and mind. At these times, despite the distancing, something quite profound is achieved. For example, in "I Am Twenty-one" a college student struggles with an essay question on an exam, watching the time pass, unable to answer all the questions. The young narrator is obviously under severe strain, something more than worry over a test, but only later do we understand the depth of her struggle to just keep going. She describes her apartment, a spartan arrangement except for one photograph, an eight-by-ten glossy of her parents in their youth. "My folks (are) two and a half years gone," she says flatly yet meaningfully, and then talks of her visits to the scene of the accident.

Robison has a playwright's ear for dialogue. Her characters speak the way people really do, in fits and starts with half-formed thoughts and sentences. Their conversations center on common events. In "Mirror" the narrator visits her longtime friend, Lolly. The scene opens in a beauty parlor where these two are discussing the boredom of being there and problems associated with getting a permanent. At times, it might seem that these conversations go nowhere, but through these snippets of talk the essences of the characters evolve, and their values are revealed. Sometimes that revelation comes suddenly, as the meaningless chitchat abruptly becomes substantive. At one point Maureen (*Oh!*) and her seven-year-old daughter, Violet, are splashing in the child's pool. They are talking about the maid, Lola, when suddenly the conversation shifts to the topic of Maureen's mother. Maureen's resentment of her father and anguish over her mother's abandonment are poignantly revealed. She wants only to remember the good things about this woman and tells her daughter, "You just remember when your grandpa talks about your grandma, no matter what he's saying, he's making it all up. Everything about drinking or about ranting and raving? That's all rubbish."

Robison gives her readers vignettes of life that have a great deal of power in their sparseness. Her scenes begin in the middle and stop, as if a TV were being switched on and off with the program in progress. The characters are talking, dreaming, or moving about when the reader arrives, and they continue as the reader exits. It is this ability to convince us that we are observing living, breathing people who will proceed with their lives whether observed by the reader or not, that gives such strength and power to Robison's writing.

—Patricia Altner

ROOKE, Daphne (Marie)

Nationality: British and South African. **Born:** Daphne Marie Pizzey in Boksburg, Transvaal, South Africa, 6 March 1914. **Education: Durban Girls' High School. **Family:** Married Irvin Rooke in 1937; one daughter. Lived in Australia, 1946-53, and since 1965. **Awards:** Afrikaanse Pers Beperk prize, 1946. **Address:** 54 Regatta Court, Oyster Row, Cambridge CB5 8NS, England.

PUBLICATIONS

Novels

The Sea Hath Bounds. Johannesburg, A.P.B. Bookstore, 1946; as *A Grove of Fever Trees,* Boston, Houghton Mifflin, 1950; London, Cape, 1951.
Mittee. London, Gollancz, 1951; Boston, Houghton Mifflin, 1952.
Ratoons. London, Gollancz, and Boston, Houghton Mifflin, 1953.
Wizards' Country. London, Gollancz, and Boston, Houghton Mifflin, 1957.
Beti. London, Gollancz, and Boston, Houghton Mifflin, 1959.
A Lover for Estelle. London, Gollancz, and Boston, Houghton Mifflin, 1961.
The Greyling. London, Gollancz, 1962; New York, Reynal, 1963.
Diamond Jo. London, Gollancz, and New York, Reynal, 1965.
Boy on the Mountain. London, Gollancz, 1969.
Margaretha de la Porte. London, Gollancz, 1974.

Uncollected Short Stories

"The Deal," in *Woman* (Sydney), 26 June 1950.
"Emily," in *John Bull* (London), 1952.
"The Boundary Dog," in *John Bull* (London), 1957.
"The Friends," in *South African Stories,* edited by David Wright. London, Faber, and New York, Duell, 1960.
"Fikizolo," in *Over the Horizon.* London, Gollancz, 1960.
"There Lies Hidden . . . ," in *Optima* (Johannesburg), 1963.

Other (for children)

The South African Twins. London, Cape, 1953; as *Twins in South Africa,* Boston, Houghton Mifflin, 1955.
The Australian Twins. London, Cape, 1954; as *Twins in Australia,* Boston, Houghton Mifflin, 1956.
New Zealand Twins. London, Cape, 1957.
Double Ex! London, Gollancz, 1971.
A Horse of His Own. London, Gollancz, 1976.

*

Bibliography: *Daphne Rooke: Her Works and Selected Criticism: A Bibliography* by Helen Camburg, Johannesburg, University of the Witwatersrand, 1969.

Manuscript Collections: Mugar Memorial Library, Boston University; National English Literary Museum, Grahamstown, South Africa.

Critical Studies: By Orville Prescott, in *New York Times,* 1 March 1950; Dorothy Canfield Fisher, in *Book-of-the-Month News* (New York), January 1952; Sylvia Stallings, in *New York Herald Tribune,* 20 December 1953; *Illustrated London News,* 21 December 1957; *Saturday Review of Literature* (New York), 7 March 1959; *Chicago Tribune,* 26 February 1961; Paul Scott, in *Country Life* (London), 24 May 1962.

Daphne Rooke comments:

(1991) The places where I have lived have been most important to my writing. My early memories of the Transvaal are reflected in *Mittee.* *Ratoons* has for background the South Coast of Natal where I lived for many years on a sugar plantation. Zululand made a most profound impression on me: I lived there for years as a girl: *A Grove of Fever Trees, A Lover for Estelle,* and *Wizard's Country* all have Zululand for background. *Beti* is set in India and East Africa, and *Boy on the Mountain* in New Zealand. All are written in the first person.

There is a pattern of sorts in some of the South African works: the race of the narrator has an important bearing on the story. In *Mittee* the whole story hinges on the fact that the narrator Selina is a Colored girl; in *Ratoons* the narrator is an English-speaking South African girl who falls in love with an Afrikaner; in *Wizards' Country* the narrator is a Zulu; in *A Lover for Estelle* the narrator is an Afrikaans girl whose life is influenced by a sophisticated Englishwoman. I did not consciously set out to create this pattern; it was pointed out to me after I had written *Wizards' Country.*

All the stories, including those for children, are imaginative works but have a basis in fact. In *Wizards' Country* when writing about superstition I attempted to avoid the supernatural; for example, Benge is a hunchback and masquerades as a magic dwarf (the tokoloshi). In my short story for children, "Fikizolo," the ingredients of a fairytale were actually present in Zululand: the two children were called a prince and princess, there was a real old witch, and Fikizolo himself was like a fabled beast, a cross between a donkey and a zebra!

*   *   *

Though Daphne Rooke's novels were favorably reviewed in journals such as the *Times Literary Supplement* when they first appeared in the 1950s and 1960s, they did not receive the same critical attention in her home country, South Africa. Since the more recent reissue of certain of her novels, Rooke's work has begun to be reassessed—not least because a novel such as *Mittee,* in dealing with sexuality and gender relations as well as race, touches upon themes currently being explored in terms of patriarchal discourse in colonial society.

The novels are striking a new generation of readers afresh with their unmistakable flavor of "South African Gothic": a startling mixture of the ordinary and the bizarre that appears to meet white/western subliminal expectations of Africa; a galloping plot so laden with incident that others might have spun two or three books from the same material; and an overwhelming response to landscape which tends to make it (as in Hardy or Emily Brontë) the most important character in the book, leaving the human ones to become strangely strident, even melodramatic and sentimental, in their efforts to be seen and heard.

Mittee centers upon a young Boer woman and her lifelong companion and servant Selina, a "colored" girl who is like a sister to Mittee but is never allowed to forget her place in Afrikaner society. Though she is ostensibly the narrator, in a sense Selina is the "shadow" of the Boer girl, as if the two characters were really one, and the underlying aim of relating their mutual struggles was to explore women's repression—and bitter revenge—in the Afrikaner world of the late 19th century.

Both Selina and Mittee love the same man, the Afrikaner Paul, who marries Mittee while using Selina. Both women suffer at his hands, and both exact their own revenge in a drama dwarfed by the harshness of the land and by the cruel course of the Boer War which overtakes their lives. But all is not solemn. Selina tells her story with the kind of humor that illuminates Olive Schreiner's *Story of an African Farm,* and details of vanished Boer customs and manners throng the pages with intentional comic effect. There is an inimitable lilt to the language of the characters, which is written with a strongly idiomatic Afrikaans flavor. Few beside Pauline Smith and short story writer Herman Charles Bosman have so effortlessly captured the particular note of the Afrikaner world: "Mittee called and called me again, her voice pitched on a note of anger. Ag what, let her call until she is black in the face, I thought, I won't wait on their table tonight. The way she carried on now that she was married, with Paul hanging after her as though she was gold." The dialogue is exact and often extremely funny; and Mittee's hero, the cultured English doctor Basil Castledene, is throughout the book designated as "Doctor Besil" in imitation of the flat Transvaal intonation of his name. All in all, the novel has the density of tapestry, richly and delightfully filled.

If there remains a critical suspicion that *Mittee* leans towards melodrama, Rooke's first novel, *A Grove of Fever Trees* (published internationally in 1950), is undeniably open to the accusation. Its narrator Danny is evil, not merely amoral: a twisted man through whose eyes we see the whole plot as if through strangely colored glass. The lurid light cast on the story of his doomed brother Edward and ironically named girlfriend Prudence, falls on a violence of passion and incident that would destroy a lesser book. What transforms the novel is the memorable evocation of its backdrop: an arid Zululand of ghostly fever trees and deadly poisonous snakes, the whole dominated by the mysterious peak Tshaneni, among the Lebombo Mountains. Such names are repeated like a litany, chanted to a presence more powerful than any human one could ever hope to be—or so Rooke seems to imply, as she dispatches her characters.

In *Ratoons,* set in a lusher Natal of canefields, tensions between white and black, Zulu and Indian are thrown up by the stormy plot as if by chance. What we chiefly remember is the sheer force of nature: floods, devastating fires, the "charred trash and the blackened stalks of the cane" from which the green of the new shoots, the ratoons, will spring after rain. Humanity appears to be shaped by this force, and sometimes swept away; human violence appears a vain attempt to assert control, born in rage and ending in a whimper.

In *A Lover for Estelle* the drought that grips the country mirrors the gradual attrition of the Kramer family's innocence even as it brings on their economic ruin. Once again the landscape dominates, impassive in its beauty: "We love this earth for nothing: the grassy plain and mountains are for whoever passes and our suffering or joy makes no mark on them."

If the novels contain an amount of violence that even today seems shocking, history has not disproved this view of southern Africa. Neither an academic nor a political writer, Rooke is content to be a storyteller. She succeeds magnificently, leaving the echoes to do their work—for, though you may forget the details of one of her novels, the particular atmosphere of each remains indelible in the memory.

—Lynne Bryer

ROQUELAURE, A.N. *See* **RICE, Anne.**

ROSS, Leonard Q. *See* **ROSTEN, Leo.**

ROSS, (James) Sinclair

Nationality: Canadian. **Born:** Shellbrook, Saskatchewan, 22 January 1908. **Education:** Graduated from high school, 1924. **Military Service:** Served in the Canadian Army, 1942-46. **Career:** Staff member, Union Bank (now Royal Bank) of Canada, in Abbey, 1924-28, Lancer, 1929, and Arcola, 1929-33, all Saskatchewan, and in Winnipeg, 1933-42, and Montreal, 1946-68; lived in Athens, 1968-71, Barcelona, 1971-73, Málaga, Spain, 1973-80, Montreal, 1980-81, and Vancouver from 1981. **Address:** c/o Writers Union of Canada, 24 Ryerson Avenue, Toronto, Ontario M5T 2P3, Canada.

PUBLICATIONS

Novels

As for Me and My House. New York, Reynal, 1941.
The Well. Toronto, Macmillan, 1958.
Whir of Gold. Toronto, McClelland and Stewart, 1970.
Sawbones Memorial. Toronto, McClelland and Stewart, 1974.

Short Stories

The Lamp at Noon and Other Stories. Toronto, McClelland and Stewart, 1968.
The Race and Other Stories, edited by Lorraine McMullen. Ottawa, University of Ottawa Press, 1982.

Other

Just Wind and Horses (memoir). Toronto, Macmillan, 1988.

*

Bibliography: By David Latham, in *The Annotated Bibliography of Canada's Major Authors 3* edited by Robert Lecker and Jack David, Downsview, Ontario, ECW Press, 1981.

Critical Studies: Introduction by Roy Daniells to *As for Me and My House,* Toronto, McClelland and Stewart, 1957; "Wolf in the Snow" by Warren Tallman, in *A Choice of Critics* edited by George Woodcock, Toronto, Oxford University Press, 1966; introduction by Margaret Laurence to *The Lamp at Noon,* 1968; "Sinclair Ross's Ambivalent World" by W.H. New, in *Canadian Literature* (Vancouver), Spring 1969; "No Other Way: Sinclair Ross's Stories and Novels" by Sandra Djwa, in *Canadian Literature* (Vancouver), Winter 1971; *Sinclair Ross and Ernest Buckler* by Robert D. Chambers, Vancouver, Copp Clark, 1975; introduction to *Sawbones Memorial,* Toronto, McClelland and Stewart, 1978, and *Sinclair Ross,* Boston, Twayne, 1979, both by Lorraine McMullen; *Sinclair Ross: A Reader's Guide* by Ken Mitchell,

Regina, Saskatchewan, Thunder Creek, 1981; essay in *Canadian Literature* (Vancouver), Autumn 1984; *"As For Me and My House": Five Decades of Criticism* edited by David Stouck, Toronto, University of Toronto Press, 1991; *From the Heart of the Heartland: The Fiction of Sinclair Ross* by John Moss, Ottawa, University of Ottawa Press, 1992.

Sinclair Ross comments:

(1972) The little I have done has been spread over so many years that there is no outstanding or unifying theme. Man and nature, perhaps—especially in *The Lamp at Noon* and to some degree in *As for Me and My House*. *The Well* is a bad novel: an attempt, unsuccessful, to stretch a little the prairie and small town world of which I had been writing. *Whir of Gold* is, I suppose, another breakaway attempt—or stretch; better, with some fairly good things in it, but small in range.

*   *   *

Sinclair Ross is primarily a chronicler of life on the Canadian prairies, and his first novel, *As for Me and My House,* seems destined to become established as a classic of prairie realism, along with the novels of Frederick Philip Grove and Margaret Laurence. Even better than his first novel are some of his short stories, such as "The Lamp at Noon," "The Painted Door," and "One's a Heifer." Ross's later novels, *The Well* and *Whir of Gold,* have some traces of the subdued intensity which makes his early work so memorable, but as wholes they are disappointing. Ross's career seems to bear out the theory that Herbert Read advanced about Wordsworth: that as his memories of his boyhood faded, his art too lost its strength. Ross lived on the prairies as a boy and young man, but his adult life has been lived mainly in Montreal, and in his later work he was too far removed from the life he once knew to write of it with continuous conviction and accuracy.

It is, then, on the early fiction that Ross's reputation is almost certain to rest. The qualities of this early work are quite remarkable. Perhaps most remarkable of all is Ross's gift for empathy, for full identification of himself with the character he is portraying. For the boys who are the central figures of several of his short stories this is not surprising, since one is able to assume that the hero is Ross himself slightly disguised, and that he is drawing heavily upon the memories of his own boyhood. The feat is more surprising when it is applied to Philip Bentley, the clergyman and amateur artist of *As for Me and My House,* particularly since much of the tension in the novel springs from Philip's relationship with his wife: Ross is a bachelor. But what is really remarkable is that Ross is able to enter with apparently equal facility into the minds of women, as in the powerful story of a prairie dust storm, "The Lamp at Noon," and in the portrayal of Mrs. Bentley in the novel.

The special quality in the human situation which seems to attract Ross as an artist and which he treats with consummate skill is the sense of isolation and of alienation, the feeling of being trapped in a set of circumstances from which there is no apparent escape. Thus Philip Bentley finds himself trapped in a profession for which he no longer feels a vocation, in a small prairie town which seems to have no sympathy for the values he cherishes, and in a marriage which has come to be an irritant rather than an unguent. In "The Lamp at Noon" the prairie farm-wife finds herself trapped in an isolated farmhouse when she would like to be in a city, and the dust storm in which she goes mad and her baby dies becomes a symbol of the inexorable doom which is closing in upon her. Only her husband's fidelity and love stand between her and total defeat.

This use of the prairie climate and landscape both as a realistic setting and as a symbolic obbligato to the human situation is another of Ross's strengths as a writer of fiction. In words which are carefully chosen to achieve the maximum of accuracy in description, he makes vivid to us the reality of the prairie landscape with its vast distances and its overwhelming sky, and the fierce extremes of heat and cold, the long harsh winters and brief, brilliant, but often explosive summers, that mark the climate of that region. Beyond the accuracy of the descriptions, however, lie the powerful atmospheric effects which Ross achieves by relating the fluctuations of the weather to the moods and aspirations of his characters, and the way in which snow-storms and wind-storms are made to seem symbolic of the malevolence of the universe in which man finds himself a victim.

The somberness of Ross's fiction is to some extent relieved, however, by the positive way in which he records the efforts of his characters to overcome or transcend the forbidding environment in which fate has placed them. The wife in "The Lamp at Noon" is broken, but her husband perseveres until he sees the storm go down; for all the tribulations to which the Bentleys are subjected, it is their human will which finally prevails: the last words of the novel are "I want it so." Philip's art is his means of transcending the environment: by portraying the prairie in all its harsh power he reduces it to form, transforms it by the power of the human imagination, asserts his human will in the face of its vast indifference.

Ross's own art as a novelist and writer of short stories represents a similar triumph of the human imagination. By his unremitting honesty in portraying human beings living in a physical environment which presents the maximum challenge to the instinct for survival, he has produced a small but significant volume of work that will endure.

—Desmond Pacey

ROSSNER, Judith

Nationality: American. **Born:** Judith Perelman in New York City, 31 March 1935. **Education:** City College of New York, 1952-55. **Family:** Married 1) Robert Rossner in 1954 (divorced 1972), one daughter and one son; 2) Mort Persky (divorced 1983). Lives in New York City. **Address:** c/o Simon and Schuster, 1230 Avenue of the Americas, New York, New York 10020, U.S.A.

PUBLICATIONS

Novels

To the Precipice. New York, Morrow, 1966; London, Barker, 1977.
Nine Months in the Life of an Old Maid. New York, Dial Press, 1969; London, Weidenfeld and Nicolson, 1977.
Any Minute I Can Split. New York, McGraw Hill, 1972; London, Weidenfeld and Nicolson, 1977.
Looking for Mr. Goodbar. New York, Simon and Schuster, and London, Cape, 1975.
Attachments. New York, Simon and Schuster, and London, Cape, 1977.

Emmeline. New York, Simon and Schuster, and London, Cape, 1980.
August. Boston, Houghton Mifflin, and London, Cape, 1983.
His Little Women. New York, Simon and Schuster, and London, Sinclair Stevenson, 1990.
Olivia; or, The Weight of the Past. New York, Crown, 1994.

Uncollected Short Stories

"Please Think of Me as a Friend," in *Ararat* (New York), Winter 1967.
"Voyage of the Earth Maiden," in *Cosmopolitan* (New York), May 1968.
"The Unfaithful Father," in *Mademoiselle* (New York), August 1986.

Other

What Kind of Feet Does a Bear Have? (for children). Indianapolis, Bobbs Merrill, 1963.

*

Manuscript Collection: Mugar Memorial Library, Boston University.

*   *   *

Judith Rossner's novels are concerned with women and relationships. In almost all of them, starting with *To the Precipice* in 1966 and continuing through *August* in 1983, the story opens with the protagonist's admission that the choices she has made, or not made, in life have been painfully wrong. In most cases, Rossner employs a first-person narrative to chronicle her protagonist's journey to self-discovery. The self-discovery never comes easily and it usually requires hard choices. Rossner's women are often outrageously self-indulgent and needy. They take their pride in thinking of themselves as hysterical types; they bemoan their maimed childhoods; they dwell upon their dreams and daydreams; and most have woken up one day to discover that their marriage of many years is hopelessly inadequate and must be abandoned if they are ever to have a chance to live as complete women with a self of their own. In the hands of a less able and inventive writer, this theme could quickly become banal. It is Rossner's interest in character and her flair for the grotesque and extravagant that carry her narratives. Many of her novels offer a clinical dissection of America's failed marriages and of a culture that has not permitted women to have a life apart from their children and husband. Almost all her books deal with women and their children, women and their sexual hunger, and women and their men. It is difficult to read her novels without keenly appreciating the depth of the psychological disorders which plague our era. Her novels travel from the quiescence and affluence of the 1950s, through the turbulence of the sexual and political upheavals in the mid-1960s, to the more mature feminism of the 1970s and early 1980s when women began to reassess their cry for independence and judge anew another set of sacrifices they have made in the pursuit of balancing the rival claims of mate, children, and work. Even in *Emmeline,* a novel which ostensibly takes the cotton mills in Lowell, Massachusetts in the early 19th century as its subject, Rossner makes the reader feel a 20th-century feminist's outrage at the status of women and the plight of her heroine, a 14-year-old girl seduced by a mill foreman and later luckless enough to marry unwittingly her own son, the child she had given up for adoption some 19 years earlier.

Rossner is intimately knowledgeable about women's dependency and her novels examine it with an often witty and ironic lens. She is thoroughly conversant with the world of what she calls her "off-the-wall" women and details in a most convincing way the world of the commune or the New York singles bar or the 19th-century mill town. She is immensely indebted to Freud, to the point that one entire novel, *August,* devotes itself to the month when psychiatrists vacation and patients struggle with the pains of withdrawal and transference while the analysts try to resist the tugs of counter-transference. She is heavily influenced by the writing of Doris Lessing, most particularly, *The Golden Notebook* and *The Children of Violence* series, as well as by Erica Jong's ribald *Fear of Flying.* Her writing is often sexually explicit, reveling in its own creation of women's fantasies, quick to celebrate multiple orgasms, and candid in its study of impotence and sexual indifference between married couples. She is savvy about the novel and its readership, exploiting her feminist subject and catering to the tastes of the New York/California sophisticate with an insatiable appetite for novels about neurotic women, free sex, and identity. She has also capitalized on the vogue for non-fiction, drawing on Truman Capote's *In Cold Blood* in her own clinical dissection of a rapist-murderer in *Looking for Mr. Goodbar* and upon the oral telling of Nettie Mitchell, a 94-year-old woman who knew Emmeline when she herself was a child and Emmeline was an old woman. Whether she is exploring the victimization of Emmeline or Terry Dunne, the attractive, educated young schoolteacher of *Looking for Mr. Goodbar* whose sex with a stranger costs her her life, or whether she is analyzing the self-destructiveness of Ruth Kossoff in *To the Precipice,* or Nadine in *Attachments,* or Margaret in *Any Minute I Can Split,* or Dawn Henley in *August,* Rossner manages to make her reader recognize a part of themselves in her confused protagonists. Even when she is depicting with Rabelaisian humor some of the most grotesque scenes—the four-way orgy of Nadine and Dianne and the two joined Siamese twins Amos and Eddie in *Attachments,* or the scene where a 250-pound pregnant naked Margaret prances about her house, hardly raising an eyebrow among her husband's friends in *Any Minute I Can Split*—she is able to make her scene credible, illuminating, and capable of arousing our compassion. Understanding women in psychological *extremis,* Rossner can write ably about them.

In Rossner's early novels the women choose men for the wrong reasons and have their children also for wrong reasons. A goodly proportion of the novels chart the womens' bewildered emotional state in which they are afraid to leave the man they married but never loved, afraid to leave their children, and afraid to accept responsibility for the lives they have chosen and for the actions they belatedly recognized they must take. *To the Precipice* ends with the protagonist pregnant with her lover's child contemplating the difficult decisions she is going to have to confront when she finally acknowledges to her husband that this new child is not his. Knowing she may risk losing custody of her other children, knowing that she has already lost any chance of marrying her childhood lover, knowing that in all probability she might be simply a single mother, she has come to know that no matter what the pain and suffering she fears, she must not slip back into the depression-unto-death that she has previously succumbed to, but rather must face the difficulties ahead. Margaret, in *Any Minute I Can Split,* also learns self-respect. This woman, who flees her husband when she is nine months pregnant at the opening of the book and bears his children in a commune where he does not bother to visit her for many months, and who flirts with the notion of loving either the young hippie who has befriended her on the road, or the married guru of the commune, finally comes to terms with herself, her father, and her husband. Again, the novel leaves us uncertain whether Margaret will, in fact, remain with her husband. He, like the male protagonist in most of Rossner's novels, knows himself most imperfectly, but Margaret has come to recognize some of her own delusions and is herself determined to grow up even if her husband cannot. In *Attachments,* Nadine's needs and capacity for anomie are seemingly without limits. Marrying one of the freakish Siamese twins, and coercing her friend to marry the other so that the two women can remain together, Nadine lives in the circus atmosphere of her own making for more than 13 years—through the birth of several children, the operation which separates the twins, the trials of her adolescent daughter, to her final decision to leave Amos and accept the guilt of knowing she had neither loved him when he was a freak, nor when he becomes normal. She has to go because she has now learned limits and it has become intolerable to live with the image of her own twisted, hopelessly vulnerable adolescent self. But in this novel, unlike the other two, the reader feels a terrible pity for the male protagonist and much more ambivalent about Nadine's decision.

Emmeline is a poignant book. It is written simply, capturing life in the industrial city of Lowell, and making us see how Emmeline's deprivations and innocence lead to her ruin. There is a sentimentality in the tale, but it is also simple and affecting. When the incest theme completes itself, there is a darkness reminiscent of Edith Wharton's *Ethan Frome.*

In *August* Rossner offers a full portrait of a divorced psychiatrist's life with her children and her lovers, not to mention her patients. In the other novels we see much of the moral confusion of broken households and much of the weight of despair alternating with boredom of the household which remain intact. *August,* although it traces the torturous childhood of Lulu Shinefeld's patient, Dawn, is a more compassionate and healing novel than any of the others. Dawn's life has more than its share of aberrations—after the tragic death of her parents, she has been raised by two lesbians, her surrogate parents, whose "divorce" when the novel opens drives Dawn into the arms of the analyst and many lovers. Nonetheless, despite the lurid details of Dawn's past which are recounted upon the analyst's couch as Dawn tries to recover her past, the novel itself is full of comic and affecting moments and the subplot about Dr. Shinefeld's private life is handled with humor and warmth. Ultimately, in this novel, both women mend, and, in the case of Dr. Shinefeld, we witness how life feels after she has mended and what life without a husband and with a career and children is actually like. The more affirmative character of this novel marks a greater maturity in its author.

His Little Women, Rossner's most recent novel, offers a feminist revisionist's response to Louisa May Alcott's *Little Women.* It counters the Victorian ideals of family, mother and sisterhood with its scathing examination of the broken family of the late 20th century and its progeny. This new book is replete with divorces, rivalries between half-sisters and wives, and lurid accounts of the breakdown of the family. It offers a late 20th-century critique of Alcott's novel. In *His Little Women,* the modern counterpart for Marmie is three different women, all connected by the fact that they have been married to the same man, Sam Pearlstein, the Papa March of this postmodern world. One of the Marmie figures is a neurasthenic, narcissistic movie star who coyly plays mistress to her husband, a Hollywood producer with four daughters from three wives. The bookish Jo March from Alcott's *Little Women* is transformed in *His Little Women* into Louisa, an ambitious woman, scarred by her father's neglect. Leaving her own family in order to be joined again

with her natural father and ushered into his Hollywood world, Louisa becomes a best-selling novelist, penning a so-called "libelous" novel at the expense of her father and his extended family. It is probably no accident that this figure bears the first name of Alcott, thus commenting upon Alcott's relationship to her subject at the same time as it comments upon one of the characters in Alcott's book. It is difficult to tell who are Meg and Amy in Rossner's rereading of Alcott's novel and certainly Sam Pearlstein, the charismatic, Don Juan father is an unexpected counterpart to Mr. March. There is much in the novel that is more the stuff of pulp fiction and *Princess Daisy* than the work of a serious writer working in the literary traditions that gave rise to the much loved *Little Women.* Too much of Rossner's novel is preoccupied with the role of the writer, the license a writer can take with fact, and the personal costs of writing when the author is a woman, and a mother at that. Nonetheless, the book is funny in places. Its portrait of the Hollywood era of the big stars, producers, and paternalistic studio has a certain authentic ring to it. And like *August,* it is written heavily under the spell of Freud while simultaneously attacking him.

Rossner is an accomplished writer. She can spin a good tale; she can write a chilling, taut novel of suspense and murder or a raucous, bawdy tale of attachments. She writes mostly about women and her writing has further broken the silence that has shrouded so much of women's lives. Her accounts of pregnancy, sex with a stranger, the introduction of a man into a single-parent household, and women's needs explore areas of experience that have traditionally been ignored in the novel.

—Carol Simpson Stern

ROSTEN, Leo (Calvin)

Nationality: American. **Born:** Lodz, Poland, 11 April 1908; emigrated to the United States in 1910. **Education:** The University of Chicago, Ph.B. 1930 (Phi Beta Kappa), Ph.D. 1937 (research assistant, Political Science Department, 1933-35; fellow, Social Science Research Council, 1934-36); London School of Economics, 1934. **Family:** Married 1) Priscilla Ann Mead in 1935 (died), one son and two daughters; 2) Gertrude Zimmerman in 1970. **Career:** English teacher in Chicago, 1930-32; motion picture writer, 1937-38; special consultant to the National Defense Commission, 1939-40; director, Motion Picture Research Project (Carnegie Foundation grant), 1939-41; chief, Motion Picture Division, Office of Facts and Figures, Washington, D.C., 1941-42; deputy director, Office of War Information, Washington, 1942-43; special consultant to the United States Secretary of War, 1945 (Colonel, United States Army, 1945); member, Senior Staff, RAND Corporation, Santa Monica, California, 1947-49; editorial adviser, *Look* magazine, New York, 1949-71. Since 1955 lecturer, Columbia University, New York. Ford Visiting Professor of Political Science, University of California, Berkeley, 1960-61. Member of the National Board of the Authors League of America. **Awards:** Rockefeller grant, 1940; George Polk Memorial award, 1955; Freedoms Foundation award, 1955; Professional Achievement award, University of Chicago, 1969. D.H.L.: University of Rochester, New York, 1973; Hebrew Union College, Cincinnati, 1980. **Member:** Honorary Fellow, London School of Economics, 1975; American Academy of Arts and Science. **Address:** 36 Sutton Place South, New York, New York 10022, USA.

PUBLICATIONS

Novels

The Education of Hyman Kaplan (as Leonard Q. Ross). New York, Harcourt Brace, and London, Constable, 1937.
Dateline: Europe (as Leonard Ross). New York, Harcourt Brace, 1939; as *Balkan Express,* London, Heinemann, 1939.
Adventure in Washington (as Leonard Ross). New York, Harcourt Brace, 1940.
The Dark Corner. New York, Century, 1945; London, Edward, 1946.
Sleep, My Love. New York, Triangle, 1946.
The Return of Hyman Kaplan. New York, Harper, and London, Gollancz, 1959.
Captain Newman, M.D. London, Gollancz, 1961; New York, Harper, 1962.
A Most Private Intrigue. New York, Atheneum, and London, Gollancz, 1967.
Dear "Herm"—With a Cast of Dozens. New York, McGraw Hill, 1974; London, W.H. Allen, 1975.
O Kaplan! My Kaplan! New York, Harper, 1976; London, Constable, 1979.
Silky: A Detective Story. New York, Harper, 1979.
King Silky! New York, Harper, 1980.

Uncollected Short Stories

"Happy Was the Soldier!," in *Saturday Evening Post Stories 1956.* New York, Random House, 1956.
"Medal in the Sky," in *Atlantic* (Boston), February 1956.
"Lonely Pursuit," in *Cosmopolitan* (New York), September 1956.
"The Guy in Ward 4," in *The Best American Short Stories 1959,* edited by Martha Foley and David Burnett. Boston, Houghton Mifflin, 1959.
"The 'P' Party," "The Chaos Club," "The Happiest Couple in the World," "Freud and Monte O.," "I, The Count of Monte Cristo," and "The Cigar: A Fervent Footnote to History," in *Saturday Review/World* (New York), 1973-74.

Plays

Screenplays: *All Through the Night,* with Leonard Spigelgass and Edward Gilbert, 1942; *The Conspirators,* with Vladimir Pozner and Jack Moffitt, 1944; *Lured,* 1947; *Sleep, My Love,* with others, 1947; *The Velvet Touch,* with others, 1948; *Where Danger Lives,* with Charles Bennett, 1950; *Whistle at Eaton Falls,* with others, 1951; *Double Dynamite,* with Mel Shavelson and Harry Crane, 1952; *Walk East on Beacon,* with others, 1952.

Other

The Washington Correspondents. New York, Harcourt Brace, 1937.
The Strangest Places (as Leonard Ross). New York, Harcourt Brace, and London, Constable, 1939.
Hollywood: The Movie Colony, The Movie Makers. New York, Harcourt Brace, 1941.
112 Gripes about the French. Washington, D.C., United States War Department, 1944.
The Story Behind the Painting. New York, Doubleday-Cowles, 1962.
The Many Worlds of Leo Rosten. New York, Harper, 1964; as *The Leo Rosten Bedside Book,* London, Gollancz, 1965.

The Joys of Yiddish. New York, McGraw Hill, 1968; London, W.H. Allen, 1970.
A Trumpet for Reason. New York, Doubleday, 1970; London, W.H. Allen, 1971.
People I Have Loved, Known, or Admired. New York, McGraw Hill, 1970; London, W.H. Allen, 1971.
Rome Wasn't Burned in a Day: The Mischief of Language. New York, Doubleday, 1972; London, W.H. Allen, 1973.
Leo Rosten's Treasury of Jewish Quotations. New York, McGraw Hill, 1972; London, W.H. Allen, 1973.
The 3:10 to Anywhere. New York, McGraw Hill, 1976.
The Power of Positive Nonsense. New York, McGraw Hill, 1977.
Passions and Prejudices; or, Some of My Best Friends Are People. New York, McGraw Hill, 1978.
Hooray for Yiddish: A Book about English. New York, Simon and Schuster, 1982; London, Elm Tree, 1983.
Leo Rosten's Giant Book of Laughter. New York, Crown, 1985; as *Leo Rosten's Book of Laughter,* London, Elm Tree, 1986.
The Joys of Yinglish. New York, McGraw Hill, 1989.
Leo Rosten's Carnival of Wit and Wisdom: Plus Wisecracks, Ad-Libs, Malaprops, Puns, One-Liners, Quips, Epigrams, Boo-Boos, Dazzling Ironies . . . from Aristotle to Groucho Marx. New York, Dutton, 1994.

Editor, *A Guide to the Religions of America.* New York, Simon and Schuster, 1955; as *Religions of America,* London, Heinemann, 1957; revised edition, as *Religions in America,* Simon and Schuster, 1963, 1975.
Editor, *The "Look" Book.* New York, Abrams, 1975.
Editor, *Infinite Riches: Gems from a Lifetime of Reading.* New York, McGraw Hill, 1979.

*

Manuscript Collection: Brandeis University, Waltham, Massachusetts.

Leo Rosten comments:

I write as my interests guide and seduce me: see the preface to *The Many Worlds of Leo Rosten.* My work ranges from political analysis to humor, from social comment to art to movie screenplays, from inquiries about science and theology to biographical vignettes of Churchill, Freud, Groucho Marx, Adam Smith—and a juicy assortment of wits, half-wits, sages, psychiatrists, and trailblazers.

People I Have Loved, Known, or Admired suggests the range of my susceptibilities—and the varieties of techniques to which I resort. I write melodrama for pleasure, as some men play chess or go fishing. The titles of my works indicate the range of the nets I have cast into the sea of my fancies. I find writing an indescribably complex, difficult, frustrating, challenging, exhilarating, unyielding, exciting, depressing, and joyous calling, to which I commit the resources of the self. I also enjoy the play and elusiveness of my fantasies.

The only reason for being a professional writer is that you just can't help it.

*   *   *

Leo Rosten earned a permanent place (as Leonard Q. Ross) on the rolls of ethnic-humorists with the publication in 1937 of *The Education of Hyman Kaplan.* The title is a parody of the autobiographical "study of failure" of the patrician Henry Adams; Rosten's collection of his *New Yorker* short stories chronicles the sharply contrasting efforts of European immigrants to learn "good English" in night school and thereby succeed in America. The brash hero of these episodes is the determined, cagey and warmly likable Kaplan, who signs his name in red crayon capitals, outlined in blue and punctuated with green stars. Kaplan innocently torments his fusspot teacher, Mr. Parkhill, with bold syntax, dazzling malapropisms, and creative mispronunciations, whereby the plural of "sandwich" is "delicatessen" and the Chinese premier becomes "Shanghai Jack." In 1959, Rosten offered a revival of the popular Kaplan-Parkhill duels, complete with familiar minor characters, but critics agreed that Rosten was too distant from the early years when he had actually taught garment workers in a Chicago night school.

Although his reputation rests on Kaplan's eager shoulders, Rosten's work has been varied, as suggested by one anthology, *The Many Worlds of Leo Rosten.* His Ph.D thesis in sociology at the University of Chicago became *The Washington Correspondents,* followed by a Carnegie Foundation-supported study entitled *Hollywood: The Movie Colony, The Movie Makers.* Both studies are methodically sound, thorough and readable. Among his potboilers, his best is *A Most Private Intrigue,* an old-fashioned spy thriller which eschews James Bond-like violence, sex, and technology in favor of romance, plot twists, and breath-holding escapes.

Rosten's bestselling novel *Captain Newman, M.D.,* illustrates his major strengths and weaknesses. As chief of the mental ward of an Air Force base in wartime, psychiatrist Newman is superhumanly insightful, while the ranking officers are as predictably arrogant as the G.I.'s are cute in their shenanigans. If the comic ethnic stereotypes in the Hyman Kaplan stories seemed embarrassing upon re-issue, Rosten nevertheless repeats them all here: the simple-minded Negro private is lovable and humble, the Italian P.O.W.'s roll their eyes and mutter "Mama Mia," the Jewish Laibowitz schemes shrewdly and parries questions with questions. The author skillfully alternates chapters of situation comedy and melodrama to suggest emotional range, but all sequences are as neatly rounded out as in television series.

Rosten handles many genres with professional competence and intelligence but clearly prefers a light, superficial touch. *The Joys of Yiddish* displayed Rosten's impressive knowledge of the impact of English and Yiddish upon each other, as well as his familiarity with Jewish humor and history. *People I Have Loved, Known, or Admired* offers facile interpretations of public figures but is deeply moving in the author's splendid portrait of his own father. *A Trumpet for Reason* resonantly sounds off on contemporary militancy, but the author seems much more attuned to the status quo than he cares to admit. At his best, Rosten writes smooth, witty prose and wears his layers of learning with grace. At worst, he succumbs to the easy appeal of the stock character or belief and reveals the slick writer's affinity for the heart-warming cliché.

—Frank Campenni

ROTH, Henry

Nationality: American. **Born:** Tysmenica, Austria-Hungary, 8 February 1906; brought to New York City, 1908. **Education:** DeWitt Clinton High School, New York, graduated 1924; City College,

New York, B.S. 1928. **Family:** Married Muriel Parker in 1939; two sons. **Career:** Worked for the Works Progress Administration (WPA), 1939; teacher, Roosevelt High School, New York, 1939-41; precision metal grinder in New York, Providence, Rhode Island, and Boston, 1941-46; teacher in Montville, Maine, 1947-48; attendant, Maine State Hospital, 1949-53; waterfowl farmer, 1953-62; private tutor, 1956-65. **Awards:** American Academy grant, 1965; City College of New York Townsend Harris medal, 1965; University of New Mexico D.H. Lawrence fellowship, 1968. **Agent:** Roslyn Targ Literary Agency, 105 West 13th Street, New York, New York 10011. **Address:** 2600 New York Avenue N.W., Albuquerque, New Mexico 87104, U.S.A.

PUBLICATIONS

Novel

Call It Sleep. New York, Ballou, 1934; London, Joseph, 1963.
Mercy of a Rude Stream. New York, St. Martin's Press, 1994; London, Weidenfeld and Nickolson, 1994.

Uncollected Short Stories

"Broker," in *New Yorker,* 18 November 1938.
"Somebody Always Grabs the Purple," in *New Yorker,* 23 March 1940.
"Petey and Yorsee and Mario," in *New Yorker,* 14 July 1956.
"At Times in Flight," in *Commentary* (New York), July 1959.
"The Dun Dakotas," in *Commentary* (New York), August 1960.
"The Surveyor," in *The Best American Short Stories 1967,* edited by Martha Foley and David Burnett. Boston, Houghton Mifflin, 1967.
"Final Dwarf," in *Atlantic* (Boston), July 1969.

Other

Nature's First Green (memoir). New York, Targ, 1979.
Shifting Landscape: A Composite 1925-1987, edited by Mario Materassi. Philadelphia, Jewish Publication Society, 1987.

*

Manuscript Collections: Mugar Memorial Library, Boston University; New York Public Library.

Critical Studies: *Bilingual Markers of a Culture in Translation* by Frances Kleederman, unpublished dissertation, New York University, 1974; *World of Our Fathers* by Irving Howe, New York, Harcourt Brace, 1976, as *The Immigrant Jews of New York 1881 to the Present,* London, Routledge, 1976; *Henry Roth* by Bonnie Lyons, New York, Cooper Square, 1977; "Weekends in New York: A Memoir" by Roth, in *Commentary* (New York), September 1984; *Between Mother Tongue and Native Language: Multilingualism in Henry Roth's Call It Sleep* by Hana Wirth-Nesher, Baltimore, Johns Hopkins University Press, 1990; foreword by Alfred Kazin to *Call It Sleep,* New York, Farrar Straus, 1991.

Henry Roth comments:

(1972) The writing of the novel, I feel, was too long ago for me to have anything cogent to say about it now, which is not to imply that I ever did have a clear notion of what I was doing. I recall the ambience and the sensation—the affect—of the writing more than I do the "ideas" connected with it. However, one of these does persist in the memory, a kind of guide or credo: That I had no thesis whatever to advance (that I was aware of), only to convey what it felt to be alive, in my time.

I have a strong suspicion that the reason I wrote no more than I did was that I failed of maturity, lost the will to force the next stage in development at the opportune moment.

(1986) As afterthought, I would add that separation from source, or the abandonment of the parochial in favor of the cosmopolitan, could also serve to explain my failure, as well as that of others, to develop and mature as a writer. The separation, which gives the writer a vantage point at first, opposes return—if anything is left to return to—and leaves him stranded in the new world with nothing like the same degree of imaginative and emotional certainty he felt in the old.

*　　*　　*

Although Henry Roth's only novel, *Call It Sleep,* received favorable reviews and sold tolerably well when it first appeared in 1934, it was known to relatively few readers until its republication in 1960. Its first paperback reprinting in 1964 was a turn in the public reception of the book. *Call It Sleep* is now recognized as one of the finest American novels of this century, perhaps the best novel about childhood ever written by an American, rivalling Dickens's and Dostoevsky's sense of the pathos of childhood.

The popularity of *Call It Sleep* during the 1960s can be explained on a number of levels. The interest in Jewish writers and the rediscovery of "ethnic identity," along with increasing curiosity about the life of the Jews in the lower East Side of New York around the turn of the century, are some of the explanations for the book's increasing readership. Also, the concern for urban experience and a renewed interest in the writers of the 1930s contributed toward a rediscovery of Roth's novel.

The vitality of the novel can be felt in the fact that it relates to and yet escapes convenient literary and social categories. A product of the 1930s, and a reflection of some of that decade's concerns, the book can hardly be categorized as a proletarian novel. A description of a Jewish family in New York City during the years preceding World War I, the book cannot be fixed by the term "Jewish novel." A keen portrayal of the mind of a boy, the book cannot quite be called a psychological novel. Yet all of these elements are vibrantly part of the novel.

Call It Sleep begins with the child David Schearl slightly less than two years old and continues to the time he is eight, concentrating on his life in the family and in the streets from his sixth to eighth year. His troubled relationships with his mother and father are keenly portrayed by Roth who describes an oedipal situation with the force of actual life and with no factitious clinical details. The novel resembles D.H. Lawrence's *Sons and Lovers* in its ability to evoke that conflict as a literary and not just a clinical event.

The image of the morose, physically powerful, and stern father is counterpointed by the characterization of the sympathetic, loving mother. The child is torn between his affection for his mother (his only security in the novel) and his secret desire to emulate and challenge the powerful and threatening stance of his father.

The scenes both in the apartment and in the street, among the family and among other children, are overwhelming experiences for David. He struggles to gain some kind of foothold by means of which he can withstand the onslaught of both his father and the

gangs and friends of the street. The terrors of the family life eventually relate to the terrors and the testing of experience outside the family.

There are three levels of language in the book which Roth sometimes interweaves. First of all there is the language of narration; then there is the Yiddish spoken at home, rendered through an intelligible and confident English, unlike the broken and noisy English of the street, the third level. There is even a fourth level of language in one scene when Roth also brings into play the Hebrew of the Bible during a Hebrew class the boy attends. In that scene (in chapter IV of Book III). Roth intersperses the Biblical-ritual Hebrew of the rabbi-teacher; the angry Yiddish of that teacher as he curses his recalcitrant pupils; the puzzled, exploratory thoughts of David; and the whining, aggressive remarks of the children. It is a passage that shows to good effect Roth's absorption of Joyce and Eliot.

In an effort to match the power of his father, to meet the frustrations of his family life, to escape the puzzlements of street life, and to emulate the rabbi's description of Isaiah and the burning coal that purified his soul and burned away his sins, as well as to recover a vision he once had when staring into the light of the East River, David slips a metal milk ladle into a slot of a third rail from a trolley car line. He causes a blinding flash (the light of salvation and of authority that he longs for). He is also knocked unconscious and causes a temporary power failure in the neighborhood. In an unsuccessful effort to bring together many persons from different backgrounds in response to that power failure. Roth is forced to leave the consciousness of the child for the first time in the book and tries an unsuccessful collage of "proletarian voices" around the unconscious child in his search for light. Roth's poetic prose becomes forced at this point but regains its regular force when the novel returns to the now awakened boy who back home thinks of rest and self-possession before he falls again into sleep.

Henry Roth has not written prolifically since *Call It Sleep.* A few stories have appeared over the years as Roth destroyed a second novel, imperfectly started a third, and went on to hold a number of jobs, finally becoming a raiser of waterfowl in Maine. Probably the best of those stories are "At Times in Flight" and "The Dun Dakotas." Both tales reflect Roth's difficulty in returning to writing. But whether or not Roth will be able to write again at the level of *Call It Sleep,* he has accomplished in that novel one of the finest works of imagination by an American novelist in this century.

—Richard J. Fein

ROTH, Philip (Milton)

Nationality: American. **Born:** Newark, New Jersey, 19 March 1933. **Education:** Weequahic High School, New Jersey; Newark College, Rutgers University, 1950-51; Bucknell University, Lewisburg, Pennsylvania, 1951-54; A.B. 1954 (Phi Beta Kappa); University of Chicago, 1954-55, M.A. 1955. **Military Service:** Served in the United States Army, 1955-56. **Family:** Married 1) Margaret Martinson in 1959 (separated 1962; died 1968); 2) the actress Claire Bloom in 1990. **Career:** Instructor in English, University of Chicago, 1956-58; visiting writer, University of Iowa, Iowa City, 1960-62; writer-in-residence, Princeton University, New

Jersey, 1962-64; visiting writer, State University of New York, Stony Brook, 1966, 1967, and University of Pennsylvania, Philadelphia, 1967-80. Since 1988 Distinguished Professor, Hunter College, New York. General editor, Writers from the Other Europe series, Penguin, publishers, London, 1975-80. Member of the Corporation of Yaddo, Saratoga Springs, New York. **Awards:** Houghton Mifflin literary fellowship, 1959; Guggenheim fellowship, 1959; National Book award, 1960; Daroff award, 1960; American Academy grant, 1960; O Henry award, 1960; Ford Foundation grant, for drama, 1965; Rockefeller fellowship, 1966; National Book Critics Circle award, 1988, for *The Counterlife,* 1992, for *Patrimony;* National Jewish Book award, 1988; PEN-Faulkner award, 1993, for *Operation Shylock.* Honorary degrees: Bucknell University, 1979; Bard College, Annandale-on-Hudson, New York, 1985; Rutgers University, New Brunswick, New Jersey, 1987; Columbia University, New York, 1987. **Member:** American Academy, 1970. **Address:** c/o Simon and Schuster, 1230 Avenue of the Americas, New York, New York 10020, U.S.A.

PUBLICATIONS

Novels

Letting Go. New York, Random House, and London, Deutsch, 1962.
When She Was Good. New York, Random House, and London, Cape, 1967.
Portnoy's Complaint. New York, Random House, and London, Cape, 1969.
Our Gang (Starring Tricky and His Friends). New York, Random House, and London, Cape, 1971.
The Breast. New York, Holt Rinehart, 1972; London, Cape, 1973; revised edition in *A Philip Roth Reader,* 1980.
The Great American Novel. New York, Holt Rinehart, and London, Cape, 1973.
My Life as a Man. New York, Holt Rinehart, and London, Cape, 1974.
The Professor of Desire. New York, Farrar Straus, 1977; London, Cape, 1978.
Zuckerman Bound (includes *The Prague Orgy).* New York, Farrar Straus, 1985.
The Ghost Writer. New York, Farrar Straus, and London, Cape, 1979.
Zuckerman Unbound. New York, Farrar Straus, and London, Cape, 1981.
The Anatomy Lesson. New York, Farrar Straus, 1983; London, Cape, 1984.
The Prague Orgy. London, Cape, 1985.
The Counterlife. New York, Farrar Straus, and London, Cape, 1987.
Deception. New York, Simon and Schuster, and London, Cape, 1990.
Operation Shylock: A Confession. New York, Simon and Schuster, and London, Cape, 1993.

Short Stories

Goodbye, Columbus, and Five Short Stories. Boston, Houghton Mifflin, and London, Deutsch, 1959.
Penguin Modern Stories 3, with others. London, Penguin, 1969.
Novotny's Pain. Los Angeles, Sylvester and Orphanos, 1980.

Uncollected Short Stories

"Philosophy, or Something Like That" May 1952, "The Box of Truths" October 1952, "The Fence" May 1953, "Armando and the Frauds" October 1953, and "The Final Delivery of Mr. Thorn" May 1954, all in *Et Cetera* (Lewisburg, Pennsylvania).
"The Day It Snowed," in *Chicago Review,* Fall 1954.
"The Contest for Aaron Gold," in *Epoch* (Ithaca, New York), Fall 1955.
"Heard Melodies Are Sweeter," in *Esquire* (New York), August 1958.
"Expect the Vandals," in *Esquire* (New York), December 1958.
"The Love Vessel," in *Dial* (New York), Fall 1959.
"Good Girl," in *Cosmopolitan* (New York), May 1960.
"The Mistaken," in *American Judaism* (New York), Fall 1960.
"Psychoanalytic Special," in *Esquire* (New York), November 1963.
"On the Air," in *New American Review 10,* edited by Theodore Solotaroff. New York, New American Library, 1970.
"Smart Money," in *New Yorker,* 2 February 1981.
"His Mistress's Voice," in *Partisan Review* (Boston), vol. 53, no. 2, 1986.

Play

Television Play: *The Ghost Writer,* with Tristram Powell, from the novel by Roth, 1983.

Other

Reading Myself and Others. New York, Farrar Straus, and London, Cape, 1975; revised edition, London, Penguin, 1985.
A Philip Roth Reader. New York, Farrar Straus, 1980; London, Cape, 1981.
The Facts: A Novelist's Autobiography. New York, Farrar Straus, 1988; London, Cape, 1989.
Patrimony: A True Story. New York, Simon and Schuster, and London, Cape, 1991.
Conversations with Philip Roth, edited by George J. Searles. Jackson, University Press of Mississippi, 1992.
The Conversion of the Jews (for children). Mankato, Minnesota, Creative Education, 1993.
A Philip Roth Reader. London, Vintage, 1993.

*

Bibliography: *Philip Roth: A Bibliography* by Bernard F. Rodgers, Jr., Metuchen, New Jersey, Scarecrow Press, 1974; revised edition, 1984.

Manuscript Collection: Library of Congress, Washington, D.C.

Critical Studies: *Bernard Malamud and Philip Roth: A Critical Essay* by Glenn Meeter, Grand Rapids, Michigan, Eerdmans, 1968; "The Journey of Philip Roth" by Theodore Solotaroff, in *The Red Hot Vacuum,* New York, Atheneum, 1970; *The Fiction of Philip Roth* by John N. McDaniel, Haddonfield, New Jersey, Haddonfield House, 1974; *The Comedy That "Hoits": An Essay on the Fiction of Philip Roth* by Sanford Pinsker, Columbia, University of Missouri Press, 1975, and *Critical Essays on Philip Roth* edited by Pinsker, Boston, Twayne, 1982; *Philip Roth* by Bernard F. Rodgers, Jr., Boston, Twayne, 1978; "Jewish Writers" by Mark Shechner, in *The Harvard Guide to Contemporary American Writing* edited by Daniel Hoffman, Cambridge, Massachusetts, Harvard University Press, 1979; introduction by Martin Green to *A Philip Roth Reader,* New York, Farrar Straus, 1980, London, Cape, 1981; *Philip Roth* by Judith Paterson Jones and Guinevera A. Nance, New York, Ungar, 1981; *Philip Roth* by Hermione Lee, London, Methuen, 1982; *Reading Philip Roth* edited by A.Z. Milbauer and D.G. Watson, London, Macmillan, 1988; *Understanding Philip Roth* by Murray Baumgarten and Barbara Gottfried, Columbia, University of South Carolina Press, 1990; *Philip Roth Revisited* by Jay L. Halio, New York, Twayne, 1992; *Comic Sense: Reading Robert Coover, Stanley Elkin, Philip Roth* by Thomas Pughe, Basel, Birkhäuser, 1994.

*   *   *

In the title of one of the best essays on Philip Roth, Alfred Kazin used the word "toughminded." This quality pervades his novels, stories, and essays. Roth's unsparing portraits of Jews too adept at scheming and compromise have upset rabbis and Jewish organizations. His frank acknowledgment of such unmentionables as abortion, masturbation, and sexual calisthenics has alarmed the bluenoses. These irate—usually unliterary—responses have fortunately failed to unsettle him.

Until now Roth has seemed most at ease with Jewish characters and settings. His ear is especially sensitive to the verbal rhythm and pulse beat of the second-generation American Jew who has recently abandoned the inner city for the suburbs. The stories in Roth's first book, *Goodbye, Columbus,* are almost all concerned with confrontations between Jews of radically different persuasions and temperaments. Thus Neil Klugman, in the title story, confronts the Jewish society of Short Hills, as represented by Brenda Patimkin and her family, where "fruit grew in their refrigerator and sporting goods dropped from their trees!" Neil's wrong-side-of-the-track Judaism fails to make the proper concessions and adjustments. In "Eli, The Fanatic" the assimilated Jews of another suburban community, Woodenton, employ the lawyer Eli Peck to force a Yeshivah to move elsewhere or at least to "modernize." We see a skillful confrontation between the Talmudic logic of the Yeshivah's headmaster and the more worldly logic of Eli. Eli ends by donning the Hasidic garb of one of the Yeshivah instructors—which suggests to his fellow Jews of Woodenton the return of an earlier nervous breakdown. Jew is also pitted against Jew in "The Conversion of the Jews," This time the questioning Jewish schoolboy Ozzie Freedman forces embarrassing ideological concessions from Rabbi Binder and the Jewish establishment when he threatens to jump from the roof of the synagogue. The stories in *Goodbye, Columbus* are brilliantly irreverent.

Roth's heterodoxy continues into his first novel, *Letting Go,* He enlarges the focus here to include not only the idiosyncrasies of the Jewish community but also of university faculties, charlatan abortionists, and ill-suited love relationships. Very little is left out. Gabe Wallach's "I" controls the early parts of the novel; then it recedes into a kind of background first-person and finally turns into a more respectably detached third-person. Wallach is the intruder who keeps moving in and out of delicate situations—always avoiding complete involvement—and so this changing of narrative focus is especially apt. He defines his position early in the novel: "It was beginning to seem that toward those for whom I felt no strong sentiment, I gravitated; where sentiment existed, I ran." Wallach's years as a graduate student at the University of Iowa and

as an instructor at the University of Chicago offer a rejection of his eastern seaboard Jewish background (born in New York, educated at Harvard). The first words of the novel are the deathbed letter of Gabe Wallach's mother. This letter, inadvertently tucked between the pages of his copy of James's *Portrait of a Lady,* starts Gabe off on the midwestern pilgrimage which involves the series of precarious relationships with Libby and Paul Herz and with Martha Reganhart. The terribly flawed Herz marriage somehow survives Gabe's "meddling"; in fact, it is strengthened by the adoption of a child and by a spirited assertion of Judaism. Gabe Wallach's love affair with Martha Reganhart fares less well. Gabe speaks of himself in a final letter to Libby as an "indecisive man" who had had but "one decisive moment."

Roth also places his next novel, *When She Was Good,* in the midwest—this time a midwest without Jews. The texture of his writing changes markedly; it seems to flatten out, to become, as Theodore Solotaroff suggests, "a language of scrupulous banality." The midwestern Protestantism which underlies the novel is threatened only by an adolescent flirtation with the Catholic Church by the heroine Lucy Nelson; this is lightly dismissed as "all that Catholic hocus-pocus." Lucy's intolerance and uncomfortable moral provincialism manage to get in the way of her own marriage and that of her parents. She cannot put up with her husband's rather puerile brashness and incompetence or with her father's alcoholism.

Just as Roth was able to capture the special quality of the conversation of both first and second generation American Jews in *Goodbye, Columbus* and *Letting Go,* so in *When She Was Good* he manages handsomely with the cliché-ridden language of Main Street.

Portnoy's Complaint is a return, with a vengeance, to Roth's earlier manner. It seems to come out of the best pages of *Goodbye, Columbus* and *Letting Go.* Roth has settled here on all the things he knows how to do best, especially in his creation of the urban Jewish family with the mother at its moral center. *Portnoy's Complaint* is the staccato confession of Alexander Portnoy to his psychiatrist Dr. Spielvogel (who makes another appearance in *My Life As a Man*) in heavily free associative prose.

The novel begins with a section entitled "The Most Unforgettable Character I've Met"; the reference is to Sophie Portnoy who dominates not only the family but also the "confessions" of her son. (She is in part anticipated by Aunt Gladys in "Goodbye, Columbus" and Paul Herz's mother in *Letting Go.*) She characteristically pushes to the background her perpetually constipated and henpecked husband and her pathetically unendowed daughter. The confrontation is between mother and son. The fiercely aggressive, domineering mother seems to win out since it is the son who does the confessing from the analyst's couch. Alex, however, gains some measure of revenge through sieges of masturbation in his youth and through affairs with gentiles (*shiksas*) in his more mature years. He masterfully uncovers chinks in his Jewish mother's armor by taunting her with his conquest of Christian girls and by abusing the family rabbi, but always at the expense of his own too active feelings of guilt. Everything in this novel, it would seem, "can be traced to the bonds obtaining in the mother-child relationship." Jewish mothers, in the past few years, have presented a challenge to some of the best American Jewish novelists, like Wallace Markfield, Bruce Jay Friedman, and Herbert Gold. Probably the most realized and convincing of all is Sophie Portnoy.

Roth's versatility is very much in evidence in *Our Gang (Starring Tricky and His Friends),* he seems able to manage the rhetoric of political corruption quite as easily as the language of the Jewish urban dweller who has recently retreated to the suburbs. In *Our Gang* Roth takes on a formidable adversary, the Nixon administration: he carried a certain Trick E. Dixon from a press conference, an underground meeting with his "coaches;" an address to his "fellow Americans," to an election speech—following his assassination—to his "fellow Fallen" in Hell. This speech ends with the revealing sentence: "And let there be no mistake about it: if I am elected Devil, I intend to see Evil triumph in the end; I intend to see that our children, and our children's children, need never know the terrible scourge of Righteousness and Peace." Passages from Swift and Orwell appropriately serve as epigraphs for this novel.

The Breast, in certain ways, marks a return to *Portnoy's Complaint.* One might think of this novella—with its college professor narrator, David Alan Kepesh, who turns into a female breast—as a working out of certain fantasies suggested by *Portnoy* with some help from Kafka, Gogol, and Swift. The bookish hero cannot resist likening his peculiar condition to that of Kafka's Gregor Samsa who awakens to discover that he has turned into a huge bug or to that of Gogol's Kovalyov who awakens to find that he is missing his nose; he makes reference also to Swift's "self-satisfied Houyhnhnms" and to "Gulliver among the Brobdingnags," in which country "the king's maidservants had him walk out on their nipples for the fun of it."

The Great American Novel seems to have little in common with the previous fiction. This baseball novel is Roth's contributions to a genre that has already attracted several other American Jewish writers, including Bernard Malamud and Mark Harris. It is filled with oblique references to a wide variety of literary works. Thus it begins with the sentence, "Call me Smitty." A sensational pitcher goes under the name Gil Gamesh. American literature and baseball are occasionally brought together in uneasy confrontation; they make for strange bedfellows. This mock-heroic tone reinforces the sense of caricature and pastiche which runs through the novel. Roth holds up the myth of the Great American Novel to the same ridicule as the myth of the Great American Pastime.

My Life As a Man fits snugly into place in the main line of Philip Roth's development. The Jewish ingredients are less pronounced here than in *Goodbye, Columbus, Letting Go,* and *Portnoy's Complaint,* yet the ambience is unmistakably the same. The writer-hero of the novel, Peter Tarnopol, has much in common with Gabe Wallach, Alexander Portnoy, and David Alan Kepesh. Indeed he has the same bookish tendencies as Kepesh. Roth offers a clever variation on the novel-within-the-novel device as he prefaces the main part of his work, "My True Story" (Tarnopol's sustained confessional), with two of his protagonist's short stories. The "useful fictions," as Roth calls these stories, have a great deal to do with Tarnopol's "true story"; truth and fiction, it would seem, are ultimately interchangeable. *My Life As a Man* reveals Roth in his dual roles as novelist and critic. The narrative strategy allows for a good deal of theorizing about the nature of novel-writing and a certain amount of literary criticism.

The Professor of Desire and *The Ghost Writer,* both first-person novels, borrow as narrators characters who appeared in the earlier fiction. *The Professor of Desire,* like *The Breast,* is told by David Kepesh while Nathan Zuckerman, the central presence in the "Useful Fictions" section of *My Life As a Man,* narrates *The Ghost Writer. The Professor of Desire* offers an elaborate unfolding of Kepesh's *wanderjahre* in the years preceding his metamorphosis. The restless narrative starts and ends in the Catskills—the Jewish still point of the novel. The itinerary is dotted with literary and amorous "excavations." Since his graduate school days at Stanford, Kepesh has been working intermittently on a book about romantic disillusionment in Chekhov's stories. A real and imagined Kafka occupies a central position in the Prague interlude. The amorous is even more in evidence than the literary, as Kepesh makes his way from a succession of girl friends, to a marriage and divorce, finally to a rather idyllic relationship with Claire Ovington.

The literary and the amorous are also strongly in evidence in *The Ghost Writer.* The novel turns about an odd triangular relationship, involving the narrator, Zuckerman, the renowned writer E.I. Lonoff, and a young lady who has served a kind of apprenticeship (literary and perhaps also sexual) at Lonoff's feet, Amy Bellette. Zuckerman, a youthful author, arrives at Lonoff's house at the beginning of this short novel, in retreat from his cloying Jewish parents and his Newark childhood. He is an onlooker, in much the same way as Styron's narrator in *Sophie's Choice,* as he tries to unravel the complications of a situation that couples the erotic with the literary. With some help from Henry James's *The Middle Years* and other literary texts, Zuckerman weaves a complex mosaic which turns Amy Bellette into the author of *The Diary of Anne Frank.* The mythological machinery he invents here is in a sense his work of art: the gesture which will make him worthy of becoming Lonoff's "spiritual son" and perhaps eventually Amy's sexual partner. In *The Ghost Writer* Roth seems to have moved his familiar literary baggage to a new setting, rural New England; with the change has come a minimizing of the ethnically Jewish world of the early fiction in favor of a broader Judaeo-Christian canvas.

The Ghost Writer can probably be read, as several reviewers have suggested, as being something of a *roman à clef:* with Zuckerman taking on many aspects of the young Roth, halfway through his first book, *Goodbye, Columbus,* looking for a Jewish literary patron and finding him in Lonoff, who is probably a composite figure with a heady dose of Bernard Malamud and a suspicion of Isaac Bashevis Singer and Isaac Babel. One can continue this kind of reading with *Zuckerman Unbound,* which takes place in 1969, 13 years after the events of *The Ghost Writer.* Nathan Zuckerman, who has abdicated his role as narrator in this third-person novel, has just published a controversial best-seller, *Carnovsky,* which bears an uncanny resemblance to Roth's 1969 *Portnoy's Complaint.* (This title may offer an oblique reminder of I.J. Singer's *The Family Carnovsky* which, in its translation from the Yiddish, also appeared in 1969).

Zuckerman Unbound concerns the aftermath of this event as Zuckerman spends much of his time coping with the bittersweet smell of post-*Carnovsky* success, disentangling himself from his creature Gilbert Carnovsky, picking up the pieces of his most recent broken marriage. We see him during a variety of encounters: with his agent, his answering service, a beautiful Irish actress, members of his family, and a curious interloper named Alvin Pepler (who takes on the role of his "double" or "secret sharer"). If the novel has an epiphany it occurs toward the end when Zuckerman flies to Miami to witness the death of his father, only to hear him pronounce, as his dying word, "bastard"—unmistakably directed at his author son. Nathan's desperate litany in the final paragraph sums up the futility: "You are no longer any man's son, you are no longer some good woman's husband, you are no longer your brother's brother, and you don't come from anywhere anymore, either."

The Anatomy Lesson sounds an even more wrenching note of despair. Zuckerman, now 40 years old, is unable to write and is forced to wear an orthopedic collar to support his neck; psychic pain combines with physical pain to make his life unbearable. The only reprieve is offered by the visits of four women who "exercise" (also exorcise) him on a "playmat." The central text in *The Anatomy Lesson* is probably Mann's *The Magic Mountain,* which one of the woman reads to him; it serves something of the same purpose as *The Middle Years* did in *The Ghost Writer.* Alvin Pepler was a haunting presence throughout *Zuckerman Unbound,* but nothing quite as terrifying and obsessive as the literary critic Milton Appel proves to be here. (In another flirtation with the possibilities of *roman à clef,* Roth has modeled Appel after Irving Howe who had singularly harsh things to say about his work, including the devastating comment, in a December 1972 *Commentary* article, "Philip Roth Reconsidered," that the cruelest thing would be to read *Portnoy's Complaint* twice.)

Zuckerman finally decides to renegotiate the circumstances of his life, as he leaves New York for Chicago: "By nightfall his career as a writer would be officially over and the future as a physician underway." The closest he gets to a medical career is a long stay at a university hospital, first as patient, then as patient accompanying interns on their monotonous rounds.

Zuckerman Bound contains the three Zuckerman novels, now declared to be a trilogy, and an epilogue, the novella-length *The Prague Orgy.* This postlude offers segments from Zuckerman's notebooks, one from New York, dated 11 January 1976, the other two from Prague, dated February 4 and 5 of the same year. A seemingly revitalized Zuckerman leaves New York for Prague to recover the unpublished Yiddish stories of a certain Sisovsky, the father of a Czech writer he meets in New York; we are told that "this is not the Yiddish of Sholem Aleichem. This is the Yiddish of Flaubert," Zuckerman does finally gain possession of this material only to have it confiscated before he leaves Prague. This failed mission seems to be linked to Kafka at every turn. The author of "The Metamorphosis," for example, makes an intriguing appearance: "*As Nathan Zuckerman awoke one morning from uneasy dreams he found himself transformed in his bed into a sweeper of floors in a railway café*" (Roth's italics). This is not only the 20th-century Prague of Kafka revisited but also perhaps the 16th-century Prague of the golem—the creation of the Maharal, Rabbi Jehuda Loew— who was to save the Jews from Czech atrocities. One can agree with Harold Bloom who sees *The Prague Orgy* as something of a summa, "a kind of coda to all his [Roth's] fiction so far."

Roth's Zuckermania continues into *The Counterlife,* which critics were quick to characterize as Roth's first serious flirtation with metafiction. David Denby expressed this as well as anybody when he spoke of Roth's having "abandoned narrative solidity altogether, reviving characters supposedly dead, allowing characters to review their fictional representation, folding fictions within fictions, becoming, in fact, an earnest writer of 'metafiction.'" Nathan Zuckerman and his brother Henry dominate the narrative which restlessly moves across the globe, with stops in New Jersey, Israel, and England. Among other unlikely occurrences, we see both Henry and Nathan returning from the dead after unsuccessful encounters with open-heart surgery. Toward the end of the novel, Nathan receives a long letter from his beloved Maria, which begins: "I'm leaving. I've left. I'm leaving you and I'm leaving the book . . . I know characters rebelling against their author has been done before . . ."

The Facts completes the task started by *The Counterlife* and emphatically brings Roth onto the postmodern scene, especially in the sense that distinctions between fact and fiction no longer apply. Roth brackets the memoir part of his narrative—five chapters and a prologue of seeming "factual" autobiography—with epistolary exchanges between himself and Nathan Zuckerman. Zuckerman's 35-page letter, which concludes *The Facts,* is filled with the rebelliousness of the character turning on the author, a more realized example of the species than Maria's letter in *The Counterlife.* Nathan questions the nature of Roth's enterprise in postmodern language: "With autobiography there's always another text, a countertext, if you will, to the one presented. It's probably the most manipulative of all literary forms." In *The Facts,* fact and fiction seem to rub up against each other, blurring distinctions between the two.

Deception relies entirely on dialogue, dialogue rendered through quotation marks rather than Joycean dashes. We listen in on a babel of voices—often recycling material from the earlier novels— which allow the erotic to mingle freely with the aesthetic. One of the unnumbered, untitled chapters begins: "'This is the situation. Zuckerman, my character, dies. His young biographer is having lunch with somebody, and he's talking about his difficulties getting started with the book.'" The biographer's craft is discussed for several pages as fact and fiction once again seem to be on a collision course: "The Lonoff book turned out to be a critical biography, *Between Worlds, The Life of E.I. Lonoff.* The tentative title of the Zuckerman book is *Improvisations on a Self . . .*"

Deception seems to thrive on *trompe l'oeil* effects. The author himself enters the frame of his novel and makes a number of revealing statements, such as "'I write fiction and I'm told it's autobiography, I write autobiography and I'm told it's fiction . . .'" Or this metafictional insertion: "'I have been imagining myself, outside of my novel, having a love affair with a character inside my novel.'"

The Counterlife, The Facts, and *Deception* form a curious trilogy of artistic dissent. The presence of Nathan Zuckerman in all three makes one feel that he has emphatically replaced all those earlier literary alter egos, such as Gabe Wallach, Peter Tarnopol, and David Alan Kepesh.

—Melvin J. Friedman

RUBENS, Bernice (Ruth)

Nationality: British. **Born:** Cardiff, Wales, 26 July 1928. **Education:** Cardiff High School for Girls; University College of South Wales and Monmouthshire, Cardiff, 1944-47, B.A. (honours) in English 1947. **Family:** Married Rudi Nassauer in 1947; two daughters. **Career:** English teacher, Handsworth Grammar School for Boys, Birmingham, 1948-49. Since 1950 documentary film writer and director, for the United Nations and others. **Awards:** American Blue Ribbon Award, for filmmaking, 1968; Booker prize, 1970; Welsh Arts Council award, 1976. Fellow, University of Wales, Cardiff, 1982. **Address:** 16-A Belsize Park Gardens, London NW3 4LD, England.

PUBLICATIONS

Novels

Set on Edge. London, Eyre and Spottiswoode, 1960.
Madame Sousatzka. London, Eyre and Spottiswoode, 1962.
Mate in Three. London, Eyre and Spottiswoode, 1965.

The Elected Member. London, Eyre and Spottiswoode, 1969; as *Chosen People,* New York, Atheneum, 1969.

Sunday Best. London, Eyre and Spottiswoode, 1971; New York, Summit, 1980.

Go Tell the Lemming. London, Cape, 1973; New York, Washington Square Press, 1984.

I Sent a Letter to My Love. London, W.H. Allen, 1975; New York, St. Martin's Press, 1978.

The Ponsonby Post. London, W.H. Allen, 1977; New York, St. Martin's Press, 1978.

A Five Year Sentence. London, W.H. Allen, 1978; as *Favours,* New York, Summit, 1979.

Spring Sonata. London, W.H. Allen, 1979; New York, Warner, 1986.

Birds of Passage. London, Hamish Hamilton, 1981; New York, Summit, 1982.

Brothers. London, Hamish Hamilton, 1983; New York, Delacorte Press, 1984.

Mr. Wakefield's Crusade. London, Hamish Hamilton, and New York, Delacorte Press, 1985.

Our Father. London, Hamish Hamilton, and New York, Delacorte Press, 1987.

Kingdom Come. London, Hamish Hamilton, 1990.

A Solitary Grief. London, Sinclair Stevenson, 1991.

Mother Russia. London, Chapmans, 1992.

Autobiopsy. London, Sinclair Stevenson, 1993.

Plays

I Sent a Letter to My Love, adaptation of her own novel (produced New Haven, Connecticut, 1978; London, 1979).

Hijack. New York and London, French, 1993.

Screenplays (documentaries; also director) : *One of the Family,* 1964; *Call Us By Name,* 1968; *Out of the Mouths,* 1970.

Television Play: *Third Party,* 1972.

*

Bernice Rubens comments:

(1972) I am never consciously aware of the actual matter of my work and never think about it unless the question is directly raised. There seems to be a terrible finality about assessing one's own work, because such an assessment might bind you to that evaluation forever. I am open to the most radical changes in my thinking and outlook. I hope it will be reflected in my work. My first four novels were essentially on Jewish themes in a Jewish environment, for in that environment I felt secure. My fifth novel, *Sunday Best,* was an attempt to challenge myself to step outside that familiarity. I noticed that my radical change of location did not involve as radical a change of style, which seems to remain simple, direct, always empty of what in school is called "descriptive passages," for these frighten me. As to the matter of what I write about, I can only be general. I am concerned with the communication, or non-communication as is more often the case, between people and families. A general enough statement, and in this general sense my books will always be about that theme.

*   *   *

The salient feature of Bernice Ruben's writing is her maddening refusal to fit neatly into any single category, while proffering the same unchanging, unmistakably individual vision of humanity. Some of her novels approach sheer slapstick (*Set on Edge*), others a Hitchcockian murder story (*Mr. Wakefield's Crusade, Sunday Best*), others a case study of the strains of family life (*The Elected Member, Set on Edge, Spring Sonata, Brothers*), others again a comedy of manners (the expatriate set in *The Ponsonby Post,* a cruise in *Birds of Passage,* eccentric lodgers in *Madame Sousatzka*). The variety is considerable, but they all present the same picture of human misery, miscomprehension, of loneliness slipping into madness.

Her earlier novels pillory the claustrophobic closeness of Jewish family life, pointing an accusing finger at the Jewish matriarch with her devouring, ambitious mother love. Her first novel, *Set on Edge,* takes its title from the words of the prophet Ezekiel ("The fathers have eaten sour grapes, and the children's teeth are set on edge") which ought to hang as a motto over any analyst's couch. Mrs. Sperber burdens her daughter Gladys with guilt, and at the close of the novel we watch Gladys taking over her mother's role as the accuser as well as the provider. Mrs. Crominski in *Madame Sousatzka,* Mrs Zweck in *The Elected Member,* Sheila's mother and grandmother in *Spring Sonata* all provide good Laingian material, parading their maternal guilt. Indeed Bernice Rubens shows her *romans* to be very much *à thèse* here, particularly in her Booker prize winner, *The Elected Member,* with its epigraph from R.D. Laing himself ("If patients are *disturbed,* their families are *disturbing*").

Her novelist's imagination, however, refuses to be circumscribed, and she turns away from the familiarity of Jewish life in North London to find the same tragicomedies of emotional crippling played out against a gentile background. The transvestite George Verrey Smith in *Sunday Best,* the lonely spinster Jean Hawkins in *A Five Year Sentence,* the sad homosexual Luke in *Mr. Wakefield's Crusade* are all walking wounded on the battlefield of life, maimed by a loveless childhood, free of guilt because they are the victims, the sinned against rather than the sinning.

Faces with such unspeakable misery, Rubens chooses to laugh, and her echoing laughter is truly shocking. She is a witty writer, with a brilliant sense of comedy: Jenny's client in *Madame Sousatzka,* in his shirtsleeves, masquerading as a carpenter; Mrs. Sperber in *Set on Edge* taking her rolled-up corset to bed with her like a child with a teddy bear; the parade of too many Hitlers at the fancy dress party in *Birds of Passage* (like "the Hall of Mirrors in Berchtesgaden"), all these are very funny set pieces. There are many such moments of high comedy in Rubens's novels, but she is equally skilled in the use of sly verbal wit (Luke's comment on the "posh deaths" in *The Times,* Betty Knox in *Birds of Passage* asking her husband how many people had witnessed her humiliation "as if he were responsible for the gate"). In her recent novel *Kingdom Come* Rubens returns to the Jewish theme but with a difference, telling the tale of Sabbotai Zvi, the founder of a 17th-century Middle Eastern messianic sect. The comic scenes, the flip echoes of the New Testament, oddly enhance the underlying terror of her story.

Like all witty writers she uses language with great care—if a single right word (like "gate" in the quotation above) is enough to make a reader laugh then words must be treated with proper respect. Her writing is spare, as befits the bleak landscape of her vision. Her sombre, plain sentences can be very moving (the chilling prayer that closes *The Elected Member,* "Dear God, look after us cold and chosen ones," has such power). There is a striking absence of description. Although she provides those recognisable authentic touches that mark present-day novels—Alice's silk dungarees in *Birds of Passage,* the shuffling post office queue in *Mr. Wakefield's Crusade*—her characters move against a blank background, almost faceless themselves. This technique, particularly remarkable in *Birds of Passage* where full descriptions are provided of the supporting cast and yet we never see the two protagonists, Ellen and Alice, is obviously deliberate. By blurring the faces she is calling our attention to the turmoil behind. It is the human mind and the human heart that interest her, and if her interest strikes us at times as chillingly clinical (as, again in *Birds of Passage,* in the description of the two women's reaction to rape: "The women were reacting in diametrically opposed fashion to exactly the same agent, though neither knew of the other's connection") then our shocked reaction is exactly what the author intended. Her purpose is to shock, as well as to amuse, and to achieve this dual purpose she will stop at nothing. Such deliberate excesses (as the episode of Betty Knox's soiled skirt in *Birds of Passage*) are of course all the more startling in a writer so much in control of her material.

To dwell only on her attention to her craft, however, is to present a false picture, for she is a writer of imagination, with a penchant for the bizarre, the grotesque. The foetus which refuses to be born, playing the fiddle and writing his diary in his mother's womb (*Spring Sonata*), is the product of no ordinary imagination, and comparisons with Gogol's *Nose* are not entirely out of place. The same rich imagination is at work on the plot of *Mr. Wakefield's Crusade* (over which the plump shadow of Alfred Hitchcock seems to hover) and on the domesticated madness of *A Five Year Sentence.* These are excesses of imagination, shocking and frightening as they are fully intended to be, for they are a part of Bernice Rubens's world in which the dullness of pain can only be broken by a loud laugh or a scream of terror.

With two epic novels, *Brothers* and *Mother Russia,* Bernice Rubens marked what was be a complete change in her subject matter and treatment of her characters. Rubens has put aside her cynical observations on society, but she has not lost her acute powers of analysis. Instead she projects compassion directly, rather than through accidents of farce or the comic. *Brothers* and *Mother Russia* particularly embody her new style and also show her gift in sustaining, very ably, the threads of extremely long narratives. Both have similarities in that they trace the progress of families and their paths of destiny. In *Brothers,* the Bindel family, who are Russian Jews, survive through each generation of various persecutions, from 1825 to the 1970s, because they learn the message that is passed on, that "There is no cause on earth worth dying for. . . . Only in the name of love is Death worthy!" The panorama is vast, taking in the Odessa, Wales, and Buchenwald. If at times the Bindel's accident of fate seems rather contrived to fit "real" historical events they are involved in, the cumulative effect of *Brothers* is a sensitive account of Jewish oppression.

Mother Russia, which opens in the year 1900 and ends in 1985, is both the history of two families and a 20th century history of Russia, the USSR, and the second Revolution of Gorbachev. Although extremely long, the appalling trials of Anna Larionov, formerly an aristocrat, and her peasant husband Sasha Volynin, who becomes a writer, are profoundly moving. Both born on the first day of the new century, on the Larionov estate, they are inseparable, even through family betrayal, Stalinism, and Siberia, until they return to die at the place they were born,. "All that matters" Rubens writes, "is the loving. Without it there is no beginning. And without a beginning there is little reason to reach for the end," emphasising her philosophy of *Brothers.*

A Solitary Grief is a tragedy about Doris, a Down's Syndrome baby, and the inability of her father, Dr Crown, to look on her face. "Physician heal thyself" might be the hidden motto for this novel, for the father is a psychiatrist who has no ability to analyse himself. Both he and his daughter are victims, common enough Rubens characters, but Doris functions more "normally" than her father, until he murders her for complex reasons, involving the betrayal and death of a man society judged to be hideous because of excessive body hair. The details are grotesque, but instead of evoking a response of humour, as it would had it appeared in her earlier work, Rubens now rouses deep compassion. Less convincing because it moves in the realms of fantasy is *Autobiopsy,* where the brain of a dead world-famous novelist is kept in a freezer, and his hitherto past secret life, is syphoned off by a friend who plans to turn it into a book. The improbability of the plot perhaps strains the imagination, although if the book is a failure, it is a quite brilliant one.

—Hana Sambrook, updated by Geoffrey Elborn

RULE, Jane (Vance)

Nationality: Canadian. **Born:** Plainfield, New Jersey, United States, 28 March 1931. **Education:** Palo Alto High School, California; Mills College, Oakland, California (Ardella Mills award, 1952), 1948-52, B.A. in English 1952 (Phi Beta Kappa); University College, London, 1952-53; Stanford University, California, 1953. **Career:** Teacher of English and biology, Concord Academy, Massachusetts, 1954-56; assistant director of International House, 1958-59, intermittent lecturer in English, 1959-72, and guest lecturer in creative writing, 1972-73, University of British Columbia, Vancouver. Since 1974 full-time writer. **Awards:** Canada Council award, 1969, 1970; Canadian Authors Association prize, for short story, 1978, for novel, 1978; Gay Academic Union (USA.) award, 1978; Fund for Human Dignity (USA.) award, 1983. D.H.L., University of British Columbia, 1994. **Agent:** Georges Borchardt Inc., 136 East 57th Street, New York, New York 10022, USA. **Address:** The Fork, Route 1 S.19 C17, Galiano, British Columbia V0N 1P0, Canada.

PUBLICATIONS

Novels

Desert of the Heart. Toronto, Macmillan, and London, Secker and Warburg, 1964; Cleveland, World, 1965.
This Is Not for You. New York, McCall, 1970; London, Pandora Press, 1987.
Against the Season. New York, McCall, 1971; London, Davies, 1972.
The Young in One Another's Arms. New York, Doubleday, 1977; London, Pandora Press, 1990.
Contract with the World. New York, Harcourt Brace, 1980; London, Pandora Press, 1990.
Memory Board. Tallahassee, Florida, Naiad Press, and London, Pandora Press, 1987.
After the Fire. Tallahassee, Florida, Naiad Press, and London, Pandora Press, 1989.

Short Stories

Theme for Diverse Instruments. Vancouver, Talonbooks, 1975; Tallahassee, Florida, Naiad Press, 1990.
Outlander (includes essays). Tallahassee, Florida, Naiad Press, 1981.
Inland Passage and Other Stories. Tallahassee, Florida, Naiad Press, 1985.

Uncollected Short Stories

"Your Father and I," in *Housewife* (London), vol. 23, no. 8, 1961.
"No More Bargains," in *Redbook* (New York), September 1963.
"Three Letters to a Poet," in *Ladder* (Reno, Nevada), May-June 1968.
"Moving On," in *Redbook* (New York), June 1968.
"Houseguest," in *Ladder* (Reno, Nevada), January 1969.
"The List," in *Chatelaine* (Toronto), April 1969.
"Not an Ordinary Wife," in *Redbook* (New York), August 1969.
"Anyone Will Do," in *Redbook* (New York), October 1969.
"The Secretary Bird," in *Chatelaine* (Toronto), August 1972.
"The Bosom of the Family," in *75: New Canadian Stories,* edited by David Helwig and Joan Harcourt. Ottawa, Oberon Press, 1975.
"This Gathering," in *Canadian Fiction* (Vancouver) Autumn 1976.
"Pictures," in *Body Politic* (Toronto), December 1976-January 1977.
"The Sandwich Generation," in *Small Wonders,* edited by Robert Weaver. Toronto, CBC, 1982.
"Ashes, Ashes," in *New: West Coast Fiction.* Vancouver, Pulp Press, 1984.
"Blessed Are the Dead," in *The Vancouver Fiction Book,* edited by David Watmough. Winlaw, British Columbia, Polestar Press, 1985.

Other

Lesbian Images (history and criticism). New York, Doubleday, 1975; London, Davies, 1976.
A Hot-Eyed Moderate. Tallahassee, Florida, Naiad Press, 1985.

*

Manuscript Collection: University of British Columbia, Vancouver.

Critical Studies: "Jane Rule and the Reviewers" by Judith Niemi, in *Margins* (Milwaukee), vol. 8, no. 23, 1975; "Jane Rule Issue" of *Canadian Fiction* (Vancouver), Autumn 1976; interview with Michele Kort, in *rara avis* (Los Angeles), Summer-Fall 1981.

*   *   *

Jane Rule's writing is best known for its open exploration of unconventional human relationships, particularly lesbianism. Her first two novels contrast two different types of relations between women. *Desert of the Heart* traces, in alternating chapters, the lives of two women, widely separated by age and background, as they overcome their initial fear and prejudice and risk living together. *This Is Not for You,* the only one of Rule's novels to be narrated from a single perspective (it takes the form of an unmailed letter) follows the development of two women, friends from their Cali-

fornia college days, who fail to break free of convention, so that their love for each other remains unfulfilled.

Rule's third novel branches out to embrace a larger cross-section of the human community. Set in a small American town, *Against the Season* explores the intersecting lives of a wider range of female and male characters, including a lame 72-year-old spinster, two pregnant teenage girls from a home for "unwed mothers," and a lesbian businesswoman of Greek descent. Although kinship, habit, and professional functions link some of the townspeople, Rule highlights the element of free choice in their social interactions, and her work extends the usual boundaries of romantic love to include the longings and desires of the elderly.

The tyranny of conventional morality, which marginalizes the handicapped and nonconforming, set against a more generous and innovative concept of community, which values human differences, is explored further in Rule's fourth and fifth novels, where multiple points of view again are used to reflect a non-hierarchical vision of society. *The Young in One Another's Arms* describes how the residents of a Vancouver boarding house—slated for demolition in a program of urban renewal—regroup around the owner, a crippled 50-year-old woman, to form a voluntary four-generation "family," related by bonds of affection rather than by legal or blood titles. They seek shelter from urban politics and an intrusive social order by working together to establish a restaurant as an experiment in communal living. *Contract with the World* describes the life and work of six different Vancouver artists or art dealers, all friends, who must confront philistinism, prejudice, and failure, and who suffer existential crises over their sexual and artistic identities, being homosexuals in a homophobic culture or artists in a barbarous climate.

Rule's short stories, collected in three books—*Theme for Diverse Instruments, Outlander,* and *Inland Passage*—present a similar diversity of emotional and sexual relationships. Again, despite her primary interest in female sexuality and identity, especially lesbianism, Rule does not ignore male and heterosexual perspectives. The characters' attempts at self-definition are sometimes frustrated, resulting in feelings of weakness, vulnerability, alienation, and even madness. However, most of the characters, in the end, manage to discover some means of integrating personal and social realities. The stories are set variously in England, the U.S., and West Coast Canada; but more significant than geographic location are the smaller domestic spaces or psychic "houses" which the characters inhabit, construct, or deconstruct. Arguably her best stories, "Themes for Diverse Instruments" and "Outlander" celebrate women's vitality and emphasize a recurring theme—that tolerance for a variety of lifestyles engenders a sense of community, thereby extending the creative potential of the group and of each of its members.

Rule's essays, many written for her column in the controversial paper *The Body Politic,* deal with various aspects of sexuality, morality, and literature, and are particularly valuable on the subject of lesbianism. Twelve essays appear alongside the short stories in *Outlander;* others have been collected in *Lesbian Images* and *A Hot-Eyed Moderate.* The former begins with an essay surveying attitudes to female sexuality over the centuries, condemning the prejudices fostered by churchmen and psychologists, and it contains searching studies of individual women writers such as Radclyffe Hall, May Sarton, and Vita Sackville-West, and of the veiled forms through which they projected their love for other women. The latter is a collection of Rule's reflections, courageously honest and deeply personal, on her own life as a lesbian and a writer; in addition there are miscellaneous reviews and articles on topics such as pornography, censorship, morality in literature, homosexuals and children, and caring for the elderly.

In all her writing, Rule says, she has tried "to speak the truth as I saw it," to present lesbians and homosexuals as "not heroic or saintly but *real.*" Refusing the strategies of evasion of many earlier women's texts, but equally resisting the separatist and utopian tendencies of some contemporary lesbian literature, Rule has been criticized recently by the gay community for not being political enough; she maintains, however, that "literature is the citadel of the individual spirit which inspires rather than serves the body politic."

—Wendy Robbins Keitner

RUMAKER, Michael

Nationality: American. **Born:** Philadelphia, Pennsylvania, 5 March 1932. **Education:** Rider College, Trenton, New Jersey; Black Mountain College, North Carolina, graduated 1955; Columbia University, New York, M.F.A. 1970. **Career:** Visiting writer-in-residence, State University of New York, Buffalo, 1967; Lecturer in Creative Writing, New School for Social Research, New York, 1967-71; writer-in-residence and Lecturer, City College of New York, 1969-71, 1985. **Awards:** Dell Publishing Foundation award, 1970. **Agent:** Harold Ober Associates, 425 Madison Avenue, New York, New York 10017. **Address:** 139 South Broadway, South Nyack, New York 10960, USA.

PUBLICATIONS

Novels

The Butterfly. New York, Scribner, 1962; London, Macdonald, 1968.
A Day and a Night at the Baths. Bolinas, California, Grey Fox Press, 1979.
My First Satyrnalia. San Francisco, Grey Fox Press, 1981.
To Kill a Cardinal. Rocky Mount, North Carolina, Mann Kaye, 1992.

Short Stories

The Bar. San Francisco, Four Seasons, 1964.
Exit 3 and Other Stories. London, Penguin, 1966; as *Gringos and Other Stories,* New York, Grove Press, 1967; as *Gringos and Other Stories: A New Edition,* Rocky Mount, North Carolina, Mann Kaye, 1991.

Play

Schwul (Queers), translated by Wylf Teichmann and Dirk Mülder. Frankfurt, März, 1970.

Other

Prose 1, with Ed Dorn and Warren Tallman. San Francisco, Four Seasons, 1964.

*

Bibliography: By George F. Butterick, in *Athanor 6* (Clarkson, New York), Spring 1975.

Manuscript Collection: University of Connecticut, Storrs.

Critical Studies: "The Use of the Unconscious in Writing" by Rumaker, in *New American Story* edited by Donald Allen and Robert Creeley, New York, Grove Press, 1965; article by George F. Butterick, in *The Beats* edited by Ann Charters, Detroit, Gale, 1983.

Michael Rumaker comments:

Story can be, obliquely, a map of the unconscious, its terrain and peopling. The intense preoccupation with the physical, with the self and with story, sets up an involitional force which is the unconscious, its contents moving parallel with the known contents as the narrative progresses. A rhythm, as car gears meshing, grabbing and jibing, each causing the other to move, to prompt and to yield the substance and power of each—an absolute rhythm of movement, instantaneous, going . . .

* * *

Michael Rumaker's coterie reputation rests upon an astonishingly small output, none of it very recent. Yet he demonstrates virtuosity, versatility, and sophistication, all traits which normally suggest the maturity of experience. Rumaker must be counted among the new breed of writers who deliberately call attention to the artifice of their writing: with these fellow-writers he achieves his effects mostly through style, especially in the brilliantly clear rendering of the world of objects, his created milieu regressing to primal states of being and manifestations of the unconscious. What sets him off from his counterparts is his willingness to work within the apparent constraints of traditional fiction, so that his stories may be mass-read (and perhaps misread) as easily as those of Stephen Crane or Mark Twain.

Rumaker is best within the short story form, particularly when writing of "natural" men in raw settings. His three best stories, "Gringos," "The Pipe," and "The Desert," depict intuitive men—misfits, cast-offs, wanderers—who create temporary "societies" with each other which threaten imminently to explode. They fight, lust, drink, and sometimes kill each other, yet at their most bizarre or violent they remain intensely human, and, for that reason, are interesting, even likeable, though grotesque. In "Gringos" a young American named Jim teams up with a friendly, blustering sailor in a small Mexican town. Jim agrees to share the sailor's room and hospitality; they saunter through the streets, dodge the aggressive prostitutes, drink, turn down a young male prostitute and finally "purchase" a girl (sailor's treat). At the night's end, they are attacked by Mexicans with knives, but they beat them off and return home. Simply as experience, this account is brilliantly realized, but from the start the mutual hostility of the intruding Americans and the impoverished Mexicans, the sink-hole quality of the squalid town, the oppressive atmosphere of cripples, pornography, exploitation, and homosexuality all point a descent into the hells of our own making. "The Pipe" is even more vividly a landscape of the unconscious, projecting myth and symbol without obtruding upon the bare narrative. Five men wait by the mouth of a huge pipe. A dredgeboat anchored in mid-river will soon blow submerged waste into their midst; these scavengers will then extract the pig-iron and other "valuables" in which they trade for a livelihood. Waiting, they tease and brag, swap stories, talk sex; the idiot-boy Billy amuses his companions with an elaborate re-enactment of finding an infant's legless corpse within the muck. The "blow" comes, the men scramble among tons of oozy waste and Sam and Alex (who had found the dead baby) quarrel over a disputed find. A sudden burst of violence and Sam is dead. Bunk, who was earlier denied a drink from the common bottle because of mouth-sores, brushes the swirling flies from Sam's wound and covers his head with a sack. As the men leave, the circling chicken hawks land near the pipe and strut among the slime toward the body. Two other impressive stories, entirely different in locale and plot, deal with a group of young thieves in Camden, and suggest an incipient novel which never materialized.

In *The Butterfly,* a 28-year-old man (emotionally, a 17-year-old boy) fearfully re-enters society after two years in a mental institution. Different again from Rumaker's other fiction, the novel's cloistered atmosphere and simple story line hazard the risk on each page of descending from pathos to bathos yet rarely do so. Jim moves from the loving protection of a sensitive doctor to his love affair with a Japanese girl; the love affair fails, but only because Eiko, too, is disturbed and, unlike Jim, is fearful of loving someone. His courage in risking further disappointment is rewarded when he meets Aice and their love develops without mishap. There are perhaps too many significant, detailed dream-sequences, and the novel abounds with symbols—yellow balloons rising to the sun, birds hunted by thoughtless boys, flat rocks skipping across streams—but the sensitivity of the protagonist and the aptness of the imagery sustain a novel as delicate as haiku. Rumaker here avoids dramatizing a subject intrinsically pregnant with drama and, as with his stories, invents the form and language necessary to his ends.

—Frank Campenni

RUSHDIE, (Ahmed) Salman

Nationality: British. **Born:** Bombay, India, 19 June 1947. **Education:** Cathedral School, Bombay; Rugby School, Warwickshire, 1961-65; King's College, Cambridge, 1965-68, M.A. (honours) in history 1968. **Family:** Married 1) Clarissa Luard in 1976 (divorced 1987), one son; 2) the writer Marianne Wiggins in 1988. **Career:** Worked in television in Pakistan and as actor in London, 1968-69; freelance advertising copywriter, London, 1970-81; council member, Institute of Contemporary Arts, London, from 1985. Sentenced to death for *The Satanic Verses* in a religious decree (*fatwa*) by Ayatollah Khomeini, and forced to go into hiding, February 1989. **Awards:** Arts Council bursary; Booker prize, 1981; English-Speaking Union award, 1981; James Tait Black Memorial prize, 1982; Foreign Book prize (France), 1985; Whitbread prize, 1988. Fellow, Royal Society of Literature, 1983. **Agent:** Viking Penguin, 27 Wright's Lane, London W8 5TZ, England.

Publications

Novels

Grimus. London, Gollancz, 1975; New York, Overlook Press, 1979.
Midnight's Children. London, Cape, and New York, Knopf, 1981.
Shame. London, Cape, and New York, Knopf, 1983.

The Satanic Verses. London, Viking, 1988; New York, Viking, 1989.

Short Stories

East, West: Stories. New York, Pantheon, 1994.

Uncollected Short Stories

"The Free Radio," in *Firebird 1,* edited by T.J. Binding. London, Penguin, 1982.
"The Prophet's Hair," in *The Penguin Book of Modern British Short Stories,* edited by Malcolm Bradbury. London, Viking, 1987; New York, Viking, 1988.
"Good Advice Is Rarer than Rubies," in *New Yorker,* 22 June 1987.
"Untime of the Imam," in *Harper's* (New York), December 1988.

Fiction (for children)

Haroun and the Sea of Stories. London, Granta, 1990; New York, Viking, 1991.

Plays

Television Writing: *The Painter and the Pest,* 1985; *The Riddle of Midnight,* 1988.

Other

The Jaguar Smile: A Nicaraguan Journey. London, Pan, and New York, Viking, 1987.
Is Nothing Sacred? (lecture). London, Granta, 1990.
Imaginary Homelands: Essays and Criticism 1981-1991. London, Granta, and New York, Viking, 1991.
The Wizard of Oz. London, BFI, 1992.

*

Critical Studies: *Three Contemporary Novelists: Khushwant Singh, Chaman Nahal, and Salman Rushdie* edited by R.K. Dhawan, New Delhi, Classical, 1985; *The Perforated Sheet: Essays on Salman Rushdie's Art* by Uma Parameswaran, New Delhi, Affiliated East West Press, 1988; *The Rushdie File* edited by Lisa Appignanesi and Sara Maitland, London, Fourth Estate, 1989, Syracuse, New York, Syracuse University Press, 1990; *Salman Rushdie and the Third World: Myths of the Nation* by Timothy Brennan, London, Macmillan, 1989; *A Satanic Affair: Salman Rushdie and the Rage of Islam* by Malise Ruthven, London, Chatto and Windus, 1990; *The Rushdie Affair: The Novel, The Ayatollah, and the West* by Daniel Pipes, New York, Birch Lane Press, 1990; *Salman Rushdie: Sentenced to Death* by W.J. Weatherby, New York, Carroll and Graf, 1990; *Distorted Imagination: Lessons from the Rushdie Affair* by Ziauddin Sardar and Merryl Wyn Davies, London, Grey Seal, 1990; *The Novels of Salman Rushdie* edited by G.R. Tanefa and R.K. Dhawan, New Delhi, Indian Society for Commonwealth Studies, 1992; *Salman Rushdie* by James Harrison, New York, Twayne, 1992; *Salman Rushdie's Fiction: A Study* by Madhusudhana Rao, New Delhi, Sterling, 1992; *For Rushdie: A Collection of Essays by 100 Arabic and Muslim Writers,* New York, Braziller, 1994.

*   *   *

Salman Rushdie is a provocative writer. Among the targets for his satire have been Indira Gandhi, Zulfikar Ali Bhutto, Zia ul-Haq, Margaret Thatcher, and Prophet Mohammed. A migrant in England, he has exploited the advantages of his position and triumphed over its difficulties. His fiction partakes of the non-realist European tradition, beginning with Rabelais and Cervantes, through Sterne and Gogol, to Joyce and Gunter Grass; as well as of the Indian tradition of storytelling, allegory and myth. He combines both to produce his brand of magic realism.

Grimus is Rushdie's only novel which originates in another book—a 12th-century Sufi narrative poem, Farid Ud-din Attar's *The Conference of Birds;* an allegory clever but cerebral, a failure mainly because it corresponds to abstract thought rather than reality.

Midnight's Children placed Rushdie on the literary map. It is a *tour de force*. The main subject of the novel is nothing less than India itself and its destiny. Crucial events are incorporated into the text as vivid reportage, particularly from the Partition of 1947 to the "Emergency" of 1975. The presentation of events shows the Indian leaders as having failed to fulfil the expectations of the people and guide them, while the presentation of society shows it as deeply divided and undeveloped. As they grow up, the children of midnight (born in the hour before Independence, midnight on 15 August 1947), the younger generation, take over "the prejudices and world-views of adults." Their final destruction is not just the work of the Widow (Indira Gandhi) but made possible by one of their own number, appropriately, Shiva, the hero Saleem's alter ego, the other baby with whom he had been switched in his cradle, the dispossessed who grows up in the gutter, who is the voice of expediency and self-interest and ultimately sells out to the world of power. The crushing of what India might have been deepens the disillusionment despite the novel's comic gusto. Yet the final impression is not totally pessimistic: Saleem's foster-child, born of Shiva and Parvati, offers a hint of hope.

Rushdie's presentation of Pakistan in *Shame* is bleaker. The political plot turns largely on the feud between Iskander Harappa and Raza Hyder, characters freely modelled on Zulfikar Ali Bhutto and Zia ul-Haq, and Rushdie's scalding satire exposes both civilian and military rule as horrors. The female plot, equally important, exposes the repression of women, particularly acute in Islamic society. Rani Harappa resists only passively and does not break with her socially ordained role. Rushdie is critical of conventional views of womanhood, but is unable to transcend them. Too close to actual events, the political allegory and fable remaining disparate, *Shame* is less successful, though more compact, than *Midnight's Children.*

Like V.S. Naipaul, Rushdie writes non-fiction in between novels. *The Jaguar Smile: A Nicaraguan Journey* is a fluent but superficial account of Nicaragua. Rushdie is fond of taking a left-wing or revolutionary stance in his non-fiction and in public, but his touchstone in *Midnight's Children, Shame* and *Haroun* is western liberal democracy. In *The Satanic Verses,* however, he exposes its ugly aspects, particularly in its treatment of immigrants.

This novel which aroused the fury of Muslims and prompted Ayatollah Khomeini to call for Rushdie's murder, includes a brief, thinly veiled attack on the Ayatollah himself, depicting him as a despot no better than the Shah he deposed. However, it is Rushdie's presentation of the founding of Islam that has outraged the Muslims. His spirit is signalled in the very choice of a satanic name for Prophet Mohammed—Mahound. It serves to introduce Rushdie's chief philosophic point—that good and evil are two sides of the same coin, not contraries in the usual way.

But *The Satanic Verses* is, in the main, a tragicomic immigrants' saga, set for the most part in Britain. Salahuddin Chamchawala transforms himself into Saladin Chamcha, a "good and proper Englishman," yet, after his miraculous escape from an air crash, he is again metamorphosed, into a fantastic caricature of qualities detested by the British. He acquires horns, goat hooves, and an enlarged, erect phallus, exhibiting uncleanliness, sexuality and lust, and displaying features of the devil. The tragedies of denationalization are brought out through less important characters as well. *The Satanic Verses* is Rushdie's most ambitious, capacious, and brilliant novel.

In exile from this planet, Rushdie produced *Haroun and the Sea of Stories,* which probably stems from his own situation. It is an effervescent story for children which a play of ideas regarding the artist and creativity renders interesting to adults.

The Wizard of Oz, an appreciation of the classic film, gives a clue to Rushdie's imaginative sources and process of creation. *East, West: Stories* is Rushdie in the miniature mode, uneven, yet the comma in the title is important: the hyphen signalled the earlier version of Rushdie's hybridity, the comma signifies a change in perspective, an understanding of separate but connected worlds.

Rushdie has proved his mettle as an innovative novelist and made an important contribution towards internationalizing the tradition of English literature.

—D.C.R.A. Goonetilleke

RUSS, Joanna

Nationality: American. **Born:** New York City, 22 February 1937. **Education:** Cornell University, Ithaca, New York, B.A. 1957; Yale University School of Drama, New Haven, Connecticut, M.F.A. 1960. **Family:** Married Albert Amateau in 1963 (divorced 1967). **Career:** Lecturer in Speech, Queensborough Community College, New York, 1966-67; instructor, 1967-70, and assistant professor of English, 1970-72, Cornell University; assistant professor of English, State University of New York, Binghamton, 1972-73, 1974-75, and University of Colorado, Boulder, 1975-77. Associate professor, 1977-84, and professor of English, 1984-94, University of Washington, Seattle. Occasional book reviewer, *Fantasy and Science Fiction,* 1966-79, *The Village Voice, The Washington Post Book World, The Feminist Review of Books,* and others. Also essayist for *Science-Fiction Studies, Extrapolation, The Village Voice, Ms.,* and others. **Awards:** Nebula award, 1972, 1983; O. Henry award, 1977; National Endowment for the Humanities fellowship, 1974; Hugo award, 1983; *Locus* award, 1983; *Science Fiction Chronicle* award, 1983. **Agent:** Ellen Levine Literary Agency, 432 Park Avenue South, New York, New York 10016. **Address:** 8961 E. Lester St., Tucson, Arizona 85715, U.S.A.

PUBLICATIONS

Novels

Picnic on Paradise. New York, Ace, 1968; London, Macdonald, 1969.
And Chaos Died. New York, Ace, 1970.
The Female Man. New York, Bantam, 1975; London, Star, 1977.
We Who Are About to. . . . New York, Dell, 1977; London, Women's Press, 1987.

The Two of Them. New York, Berkley, 1978; London, Women's Press, 1986.
Kittatinny: A Tale of Magic. New York, Daughters, 1978.
On Strike Against God. New York, Out and Out, 1980; London, Women's Press, 1987.
Extra(Ordinary) People. New York, St. Martin's Press, 1984; London, Women's Press, 1985.

Short Stories

Alyx. Boston, Gregg Press, 1976.
The Adventures of Alyx. New York, Pocket Books, 1983; London, Women's Press, 1985.
The Zanzibar Cat. Sauk City, Wisconsin, Arkham House, 1983.
The Hidden Side of the Moon. New York, St. Martin's Press, 1987; London, Women's Press, 1989.

Play

Window Dressing, in *The New Women's Theatre,* edited by Honor Moore. New York, Random House, 1977.

Other

How to Suppress Women's Writing. Austin, University of Texas Press, 1983; London, Women's Press, 1984.
Magic Mommas, Trembling Sisters, Puritans and Perverts: Feminist Essays. Trumansburg, New York, Crossing Press, 1985.

*

Critical Studies: Article by Marilyn Hacker, in *Chrysalis,* 4, 1977; article by Samuel Delany, in *Science-Fiction Studies,* 19, 3 November 1979; *In the Chinks of the World Machine: Feminism and Science Fiction* by Sarah Lefanu, London, Women's Press, 1988; *Feminist Utopias* by Frances Bartkowski, Lincoln, University of Nebraska, 1989.

*   *   *

The work of Joanna Russ is thematically unified and formally, generically, and stylistically diverse. She has written six fine novels that fall under the rubric of speculative fiction; she has written brilliant short stories; she has written what's called mainstream fiction (*On Strike Against God*). She has written in the genre of thematically related tales such as Mary McCarthy's *The Company She Keeps* and John Horne Burns's *The Gallery (Extra[Ordinary] People*); she has written a fantasy, verging on lush fairy tale (*Kittatinny: A Tale of Magic*); she has written a closely reasoned and scholarly book, *How to Suppress Women's Writing,* and the very personal, peppery, and opinionated essays of *Magical Mommas, Trembling Sisters, Puritans and Perverts: Feminist Essays.*

Her underlying theme in all these works is empowerment: empowerment and powerlessness; aggression and negation. Other concerns that run through the body of her work include survival, alienation, loneliness, community, violence, sex roles, the nature of oppression both external and internal, the necessity and the nature of further civilization and what is gained and what is lost by its progress.

One advantage of working in a genre is that the plot must move along, and that discipline keeps Russ's springy intelligence an-

chored. If she resembles another writer, it is Swift. She is as angry, as disgusted, as playful, as often didactic, as airy at times and at times as crude, as intellectual. Appreciating the quality of outraged, clear-sighted pained intelligence at once incandescent and exacerbated, is one of the major experiences in reading her work. Her critical essays are often witty and savage. She has started frequent controversies with her criticism, partly because of her habit of saying what others may think but will not dare publish.

Russ gives a sense of speed in her narration. She is a master of pacing and often eliminates intermediate steps and decisions. She has the habit of starting *in medias res* and in a place and time the reader will simply have to deduce, whether we are on earth or elsewhere and what essentially is going on among all these articulate people. Sometimes she uses a jazzy style that gives a feeling of clever and controlled improvisation. I am in no way suggesting that the novels are, in fact, improvisations, for they are put together intricately in all their parts.

Another characteristic of her style is the combination of serious, even dark concerns with wit. *The Female Man,* is studded with jokes, vaudeville routines, addresses to the reader, instructive vignettes, catalogues. Her short piece "Useful Phrases for the Tourist" is a stand-up comic routine. At the core of her humor is the perception of incongruity, absurdity.

She is precise in her characterization. In a sense, the four protagonists of *The Female Man,* Jeannine, Joanna, Jael, and Janet, are the same woman in four social contexts. Jeannine lives in a New York City where World War II never happened and which is only slowly emerging from a generations-long depression. Joanna lives here and now. Janet lives in Whileaway, an all-female society far in the future after a plague has carried off the men. Jael is an agent and assassin from the near future, part of the "plague" that gives birth to bucolic Whileaway. They are all "the same woman," yet each (with the exception of Joanna) is sharply flavored and unmistakable in habits of thought, words, and movement. Alyx, a Greek thief from Alexandrian times, is the heroine of *Picnic on Paradise* and a number of short stories, extremely sharply etched. From the sexually ambiguous Victorian traveller of *Extra(Ordinary) People* to the brave and pragmatic young girl of *Kittatinny: A Tale of Magic,* Russ's works present a gallery of fully fleshed-out women of great diversity.

Russ is one of our best novelists of ideas because she possesses the traditional fictional virtues. She creates characters full of quirks, odd memories, hot little sexual nodes that make them believable. She embodies ideas in a fast-moving arc of action. Finally, she has wide emotional range, from savage indignation to broad humor, from the bleak to the lush, from extreme alienation (as in *We Who Are About to . . . ,* where the protagonist fights and kills for the right to die) to a warm and powerful projection of community (as in "Nobody's Home").

What Russ does not create is a world where love conquers all, certainly not her women. The push toward freedom, appetite, curiosity both intellectual and sensual, the desire to control and expand their own existence, figure far more importantly in the lives of her female characters than does traditional romance. In *The Two of Them* her protagonist Irene enjoys a long and satisfying emotional and sexual bond with her mentor Ernst. However Ernst, besides being Irene's lover, is her limiting factor. As their goals diverge, he begins to use his power not to free but to confine her. Ultimately in order to save a young girl she has rescued and to preserve her own ability to act in accordance with her own values, she kills Ernst. A theme that Russ identifies in her own work and that of other contemporary feminist writers is the quest for the lost daughter, or the quest to save the daughter or young woman who will be true posterity.

One aspect of Russ's work that sometimes shocks is the place that violence holds in her fiction, particularly violence not against women—a commonplace of our fiction as of our society—but violence by women. Russ is concerned with what price freedom and autonomy may exact. In her works violence is never glorified and never without consequence, but neither is it for long absent. Her women are as apt as her men to consider the full range of alternatives open to them in carrying out their will or their duty as they see it. Certainly nobody saves them unless they save themselves, which is often not possible. Hers are worlds in which there is frequently a wide range of nasty consequence to action, as to inaction.

Russ is a writer equally serious and entertaining. Although themes recur, she never repeats herself. Each book represents a new intellectual and literary voyage into darkness and light.

Her most recent book is a new collection of stories, *The Hidden Side of the Moon,* only a couple (such as one about a unique solution to overpopulation and retirement) of them falling under the category of science fiction, although time is quite elastic and variable. Many of them are fantasies on themes of family history and identity. A woman picks up a strange dirty little girl at the supermarket who turns out to be her own childhood; a woman tries to talk her mother out of marrying and giving birth to her, and rocks the same mother to sleep in an infant's body. George Sand encounters her literary destiny; Oscar Wilde rejects a second chance at respectability (long life as a nonentity). These stories from three decades are rich, varied and an excellent introduction to a fascinating talent.

—Marge Piercy

S

SAHGAL, Nayantara (Pandit)

Nationality: Indian. **Born:** Allahabad, 10 May 1927. **Education:** Wellesley College, Massachusetts, 1943-47, B.A. in history 1947. **Family:** Married 1) Gautam Sahgal in 1949 (divorced 1967), three children; 2) E.N. Mangat Rai in 1979. **Career:** Scholar-in-residence, Southern Methodist University, Dallas, 1973, 1977; research scholar, Radcliffe Institute, Cambridge, Massachusetts, 1976; lecturer, University of Colorado semester-at-sea, 1979; fellow, Woodrow Wilson International Center, Washington, D.C., 1981, and National Humanities Center, North Carolina, 1983. Political journalist for Indian, American, and British newspapers; columnist, *Sunday Observer,* New Delhi. **Awards:** Sinclair prize, 1985; Sahitya Akademi award, 1987; Commonwealth Writers prize, 1987. Foreign honorary member, American Academy of Arts and Sciences, 1990. **Member:** United Nations Indian Delegation, New York, 1978. **Address:** 181-B Rajpur Road, Dehra Dun 248 009, Uttar Pradesh, India.

PUBLICATIONS

Novels

A Time to Be Happy. New York, Knopf, and London, Gollancz, 1958.

This Time of Morning. London, Gollancz, 1965; New York, Norton, 1966.

Storm in Chandigarh. New York, Norton, and London, Chatto and Windus, 1969.

The Day in Shadow. New Delhi, Vikas, 1971; New York, Norton, 1972; London, London Magazine Editions, 1975.

A Situation in New Delhi. London, London Magazine Editions, 1977.

Rich Like Us. London, Heinemann, 1985; New York, Norton, 1986.

Plans for Departure. New York, Norton, 1985; London, Heinemann, 1986.

Mistaken Identity. London, Heinemann, 1988; New York, New Directions, 1989.

Uncollected Short Stories

"The Promising Young Woman," in *Illustrated Weekly of India* (Bombay), January 1959.

"The Golden Afternoon," in *Illustrated Weekly of India* (Bombay), February 1959.

"The Trials of Siru," in *Triveni* (Madras), January 1967.

"The Girl in the Bookshop," in *Cosmopolitan* (London), September, 1973.

"Martand," in *London Magazine,* August-September 1974.

"Crucify Me," in *Indian Horizons* (New Delhi), October 1979.

"Earthy Love," in *Trafika* (Prague), Autumn 1993.

Other

Prison and Chocolate Cake (autobiography). New York, Knopf, and London, Gollancz, 1954.

From Fear Set Free (autobiography). London, Gollancz, 1962; New York, Norton, 1963.

The Freedom Movement in India. New Delhi, National Council of Educational Research and Training, 1970.

Sunlight Surround You, with Chandralekha Mehta and Rita Dar. Privately printed, 1970.

A Voice for Freedom. New Delhi, Hind, 1977.

Indira Gandhi's Emergence and Style. New Delhi, Vikas and Durham, North Carolina, Academic Press, 1978.

Indira Gandhi: Her Road to Power. New York, Ungar, 1982; London, Macdonald, 1983.

*

Bibliography: *Bibliography of Indian Writing in English 2* by Hilda Pontes, New Delhi, Concept, 1985.

Critical Studies: *Bridges of Literature* by M.L. Malhotra, Ajmer, Sunanda, 1971; essay by Sahgal, in *Adam* (London), August 1971; *Nayantara Sahgal and the Craft of Fiction* by Suresh Kohli, New Delhi, Vikas, 1972; *Nayantara Sahgal: A Study of Her Fiction and Non-Fiction 1954-1974* by A.V. Krishna Rao, Madras, Seshachalam, 1976; *Nayantara Sahgal* by Jasbir Jain, New Delhi, Arnold-Heinemann, 1978; interview with Nergis Dalal, in *Times of India Sunday Review* (New Delhi), 30 June 1985; "Naryantara Sahgal's *Rich Like Us*" by Shirley Chew, and "The Search for Freedom in Indian Women's Writing" by Ranjana Ash, both in *Motherlands,* edited by Susheil Nasta, London, Women's Press, 1992; "The Crisis of Contemporary India and Nayantara Sahgal's Fiction" by Makarnd Paranjape, in *World Literature Today,* Spring 1994.

Nayantara Sahgal comments:

I am a novelist and a political journalist. My novels have a political background or political ambiance. I didn't plan it that way—I was dealing with people and situations—but looking back, each one seems to reflect the hopes and fears the political scene held out to us at the time.

I have a very strong emotional as well as intellectual attachment to my roots . . . I have certainly been plagued with wondering from time to time why I was born and what I'm doing here and why I haven't had to worry about my next meal when millions live lives of anxiety and drudgery. And then there is the problem of evil and pain. At times all that abstract conjecture has become very personal, with the need to atone for the terrible things people do to each other. Some of these matters fell into place for me when I gave up the struggle to be an atheist. Atheism—or agnosticism—is my general family background, but I am a believer to the marrow of my bones, and much has become clearer to me since I faced the fact.

I see myself as both novelist and journalist. In the course of a lifetime one is many things, fiction is my abiding love, but I need to express myself on vital political issues. Political and social forces shape our lives. How can we be unaware of them? I believe there is a "poetics of engagement" where commitment and aesthetics meet and give each other beauty and power.

*   *   *

Most of Nayantara Sahgal's characters belong to the affluent upper class of Indian society. Sahgal sticks scrupulously to the people she knows intimately; she does not try to write about the caste-ridden middle class or the poor Indian villager just to conform with the accepted image of India. Her range of characters simplifies her technique; she does not have to struggle to present Indian conversation in English (a problem which bedevils many other Indian novelists writing in English) as most of her characters are the kind of people who would talk and think in English in real life.

Sahgal has a first-hand knowledge of politics and political figures in India, for she spent most of her childhood in Anand Bhawan, the ancestral home of the Nehrus in Allahabad. One could say that politics is in her blood—Jawaharlal Nehru was her mother's brother, while her father died because of an illness he suffered in prison when he was jailed for participating in India's freedom struggle. An important political event forms the background for each of her novels. Her first novel, *A Time to Be Happy,* presents the dawn of Indian independence. *This Time of Morning* comes later, when the initial euphoria has worn off, and things no longer look rosy. *Storm in Chandigarh* deals with the partition of the Punjab on linguistic lines just when the state had recovered from the trauma of the 1947 partition. *A Situation in New Delhi* presents the Indian capital faced with the After-Nehru-Who question; established politicians have given up all moral values, and the frustrated youth are becoming Naxalites (Communist extremists). But sometimes this political consciousness is not transmuted fully in artistic terms. Some of her characters are easily recognizable public figures: Kailash Sinha (Krishna Menon) in *This Time of Morning* or Shivraj (Jawaharlal Nehru) in *A Situation in New Delhi* are two examples. Her autobiographies, *Prison and Chocolate Cake* and *From Fear Set Free* are more satisfying than her earlier novels. An outstanding novel is *The Day in Shadow;* here personal concerns take precedence over politics. The heroine, Simrit Raman, a writer, is a divorcée (like Sahgal herself), and the novel shows the prejudice she faces in male-dominated Indian society. She grows close to Raj, an idealistic Member of Parliament, who shares her values, unlike her husband, who believes in money-making above all. Sahgal gives an authentic picture of high-level politicians and bureaucrats, wrapped up in their cocktail parties, worried more about themselves than about the problems which face the country. The mutual attraction between Simrit and Raj is not primarily sexual. As in her other novels, Sahgal suggests that marriage is not just a sexual relationship, it means companionship on equal terms. She pleads for a basic honesty in human relationships, whether they are between man and woman or the ruler and the ruled.

Because of her birth and upbringing, Sahgal makes an ideal spokesman for the western-educated Indian who finds it difficult to come to terms with India. As her character Sanad in *A Time to Be Happy* confesses, "I don't belong entirely to India. I can't. My education, my upbringing, and my sense of values have all combined to make me unIndian. . . . Of course there can be no question of my belonging to any other country." Jawaharlal Nehru, too, had articulated the same problem when he wrote in his autobiography, "I have become a queer mixture of the East and the West, out of place everywhere, at home nowhere. Perhaps my thoughts and approach to life are more akin to what is called Western than Eastern, but India clings to me as she does to all her children, in innumerable ways." This realization leads to a passionate concern with the Indian heritage and its meaning in the modern age; all of Sahgal's novels are concerned with the present decadence of India, and how creative use can be made of its past. It is this concern

with the country which led her to protest against the Emergency imposed by her cousin Indira Gandhi when the majority of Indian writers preferred to keep silent. Her political acumen had led her to anticipate Mrs. Gandhi's action, and she had cautioned against it in her weekly newspaper column.

Rich Like Us, which won the Sinclair prize for fiction, is probably her best novel. Sahgal's searching look at India during the Emergency reveals that democracy and spirituality are only skin-deep. The murder of the narrator Sonali's great-grandmother in the name of *suttee,* the mutilation of the sharecropper because he asks for his due, the rape of the village women by the police because their menfolk dare to resist the landlord, and the murder of Rose, the large-hearted Englishwoman in New Delhi just because her frank talk is an embarrassment to her stepson Dev, are all described in an entirely credible manner. The narrative technique is interesting; the narrator is Sonali, but alternate chapters deal (in the third person) with her father Keshav's friend Ram, a businessman who loves Rose, so we get a dual perspective on events. The novel ends on a note of hope; in the midst of sycophancy, there are persons like Kishori Lal, a petty shopkeeper, who have the courage to protest against tyranny.

Sahgal's latest novels go back to the past. *Plans for Departure* has been hailed as a "novel of ideas," though a less sympathetic reviewer has labelled it a "backdated *Jewel in the Crown.*" The usual Raj characters are present in the imaginary hill station of Himapur—the sympathetic British administrator, the missionary, the racist white woman out to uphold Imperialistic glory, the nationalist Indian leader etc. The heroine is Anna Hansen, a Danish woman on a visit to India, who makes her plans for departure when the shadows of World War I fall over Europe. She goes back to marry Nicholas Wyatt, the scion of an old English family. Anna's Indian experiences reach a kind of consummation when their son marries an Indian girl who is a political activist. The India of the early decades of this century is evoked more vividly in Sahgal's eighth novel, *Mistaken Identity,* which has a male narrator, just like her first novel, *A Time to Be Happy.* Bhushan Singh, the playboy son of the Raja of Vijaygarh, is on his way home from college in America in 1929 when he is arrested on a mistaken charge of sedition. He has to spend almost three years in jail, where his companions are idealistic followers of Mahatma Gandhi and militant trade union leaders, both trying to win freedom in their own ways; the hero's interaction with them is at times quite comic. These two latest novels show Sahgal's continued preoccupation with India, though they lack the social commitment and contemporary relevance of *Rich Like Us.*

—Shyamala A. Narayan

SALINGER, J(erome) D(avid)

Nationality: American. **Born:** New York City, 1 January 1919. **Education:** McBurney School, New York, 1932-34; Valley Forge Military Academy, Pennsylvania (editor, *Crossed Sabres*), 1934-36; New York University, 1937; Ursinus College, Collegetown, Pennsylvania, 1938; Columbia University, New York, 1939. **Military Service:** Served in the 4th Infantry Division of the United States Army, 1942-45: Staff Sergeant. **Family:** Married 1) Sylvia Salinger in 1945 (divorced 1946); 2) Claire Douglas in 1955 (divorced 1967), one daughter and one son. Has lived in New Hampshire since 1953. **Agent:** Dorothy Olding, Harold Ober Associates, 425 Madison Avenue, New York, New York 10017, U.S.A.

PUBLICATIONS

Novel

The Catcher in the Rye. Boston, Little Brown, and London, Hamish Hamilton, 1951.

Short Stories

Nine Stories. Boston, Little Brown, 1953; as *For Esmé—With Love and Squalor and Other Stories,* London, Hamish Hamilton, 1953.
Franny and Zooey. Boston, Little Brown, 1961; London, Heinemann, 1962.
Raise High the Roof Beam, Carpenters, and Seymour: An Introduction. Boston, Little Brown, and London, Heinemann, 1963.

Uncollected Short Stories

"The Young Folks," in *Story* (New York), March-April 1940.
"The Hang of It," in *Collier's* (Springfield, Ohio), 12 July 1941.
"The Heart of a Broken Story," in *Esquire* (New York), September 1941.
"Personal Notes on an Infantryman," in *Collier's* (Springfield, Ohio), 12 December 1942.
"The Varioni Brothers," in *Saturday Evening Post* (Philadelphia), 17 July 1943.
"Both Parties Concerned," in *Saturday Evening Post* (Philadelphia), 26 February 1944.
"Soft-Boiled Sergeant," in *Saturday Evening Post* (Philadelphia), 15 April 1944.
"Last Day of the Last Furlough," in *Saturday Evening Post* (Philadelphia), 15 July 1944.
"Once a Week Won't Kill You," in *Story* (New York), November-December 1944.
"A Boy in France," in *The Saturday Evening Post Stories 1942-45,* edited by Ben Hibbs. New York, Random House, 1945.
"Elaine," in *Story* (New York), March-April 1945.
"The Stranger," in *Collier's* (Springfield, Ohio), 1 December 1945.
"I'm Crazy," in *Collier's* (Springfield, Ohio), 22 December 1945.
"Slight Rebellion Off Madison," in *New Yorker,* 21 December 1946.
"A Young Girl in 1941 with No Waist at All," in *Mademoiselle* (New York), May 1947.
"The Inverted Forest," in *Cosmopolitan* (New York), December 1947.
"Blue Melody," in *Cosmopolitan* (New York), September 1948.
"The Long Debut of Lois Taggett," in *Story: The Fiction of the Forties,* edited by Whit and Hallie Burnett. New York, Dutton, 1949.
"A Girl I Knew," in *The Best American Short Stories 1949,* edited by Martha Foley. Boston, Houghton Mifflin, 1949.
"This Sandwich Has No Mayonnaise," in *The Armchair Esquire,* edited by Arnold Gingrich and L. Rust Hills. New York, Putnam, 1958.
"Hapworth 16, 1924," in *New Yorker,* 19 June 1965.
"Go See Eddie," in *Fiction: Form and Experience,* edited by William M. Jones. Lexington, Massachusetts, Heath, 1969.

*

Bibliography: *J.D. Salinger: A Thirty Year Bibliography 1938-1968* by Kenneth Starosciak, privately printed, 1971; *J.D. Salinger: An Annotated Bibliography 1938-1981* by Jack R. Sublette, New York, Garland, 1984.

Critical Studies (selection): *The Fiction of J.D. Salinger* by Frederick L. Gwynn and Joseph L. Blotner, Pittsburgh, University of Pittsburgh Press, 1958, London, Spearman, 1960; *Salinger: A Critical and Personal Portrait* edited by Henry Anatole Grunwald, New York, Harper, 1962, London, Owen, 1964; *J.D. Salinger and the Critics* edited by William F. Belcher and James W. Lee, Belmont, California, Wadsworth, 1962; *J.D. Salinger* by Warren French, New York, Twayne, 1963, revised edition, 1976, revised edition, as *J.D. Salinger Revisited,* 1988; *Studies in J.D. Salinger* edited by Marvin Laser and Norman Fruman, New York, Odyssey Press, 1963; *J.D. Salinger* by James E. Miller, Jr., Minneapolis, University of Minnesota Press, 1965; *J.D. Salinger: A Critical Essay* by Kenneth Hamilton, Grand Rapids, Michigan, Eerdmans, 1967; *Zen in the Art of J.D. Salinger* by Gerald Rosen, Berkeley, California, Creative Arts, 1977; *J.D. Salinger* by James Lundquist, New York, Ungar, 1979; *Salinger's Glass Stories as a Composite Novel* by Eberhard Alsen, Troy, New York, Whitston, 1984; *In Search of J.D. Salinger* by Ian Hamilton, London, Heinemann, and New York, Random House, 1988; *Brodie's Notes on J.D. Salinger's The Catcher in the Rye,* by Catherine Madinaveitia, London, Pan, 1987; *Critical Essays on Salinger's The Catcher in the Rye* edited by Joel Salzberg, Boston, Hall, 1990; *Holden Caulfield* edited by Harold Bloom, New York, Chelsea House, 1990; *Alienation in the Fiction of Carson McCullers, J.D. Salinger, and James Purdy* by Anil Kumar, Amritsar, Guru Nanak Dev University Press, 1991; *J.D. Salinger: A Study of the Short Fiction* by John Wenke, Boston, Twayne, 1991; *New Essays on The Catcher in the Rye* by Jack Salzman, Cambridge, Cambridge University Press, 1991; *The Catcher in the Rye: Innocence Under Pressure* by Sanford Pinsker, New York, Twayne, 1993.

*   *   *

In terms of subject matter, the fiction of J.D. Salinger falls into two groups. His most celebrated work, *The Catcher in the Rye,* tells of several days in the life of a young man, Holden Caulfield, after he has left the school from which he has been expelled; he wanders around New York City in a late-adolescent pursuit of contacts that will have meaning for him. The novel itself is Holden's meditation on these days some months later when he is confined to a West Coast clinic. The rest of Salinger's work, with the exception of some of the stories in *Nine Stories,* has for its subject elements drawn from the experience of the Glass family who live in New York. The parents, Les and Bessie, are retired vaudeville dancers; Les is Jewish in origin, Bessie Catholic—a fact that announces the merging of religious traditions effected in the lives of their children. The children, begotten over a considerable period of time, are seven in number. They are Seymour, a gifted poet; Buddy, a writer; Walker and Wake, twins—one killed in war, the other finally a priest; Boo Boo, a happily married daughter; and two much younger children, Franny and Zooey.

The diverse subject matter of Salinger's fiction tends, in retrospect, to coalesce. Holden Caulfield's parents, less loving and concerned than the Glass couple, have also begotten several children. But in Holden's case, there is only one child—a 10-year-old girl—to whom Holden can turn in his desperation.

But it is not just the mirror-image of subject matter that binds the Caulfield narrative together with the tales of the Glass family. There is a unity of tone and a prevailing interest that inform all of Salinger's narratives and that have made them appeal deeply to readers for decades. The tone and interest combine to produce a sad, often ironic meditation on the plight of young persons who are coming to maturity in a society where precise and guiding values are absent. This recurrent meditation, concealed in wrappings that are usually grotesque and farcical, has drawn readers to Salinger. His characters move through a "world they never made;" they address questions to that world and receive, for the most part, only a "dusty answer." Casual social contacts so nauseate Holden Caulfield, for example, that he is frequently at the point of vomiting. His quest for love is harassed by the sexual basis of love, and he is repelled. The only good relation in his life rests on the affection he feels for his younger sister; she is the one light in a wilderness of adult hypocrisy, lust, and perversion. In contrast, affection takes in a larger area in the Glass family chronicles; mutual esteem and concern bind the family together and somewhat offset the dreary vision of human relations in *The Catcher in the Rye.*

Perhaps one reason for this contrast is that, in *The Catcher in the Rye,* the narrative is presented from the point of view of Holden, a malleable, only half-conscious person. He moves in many directions, but none leads him toward the goals he aspires to. His teachers are "phonies;" the one in whom he puts some trust turns out to be a homosexual. His encounter with a prostitute gives him nothing, and his relations with girls of his class do not offer him the gift of comprehension. His parents are as deceived as he is about the proper use of the gift of life. As indicated, only his younger sister can offer him the love he needs, and she is too immature to counterbalance the panorama of insincerity that unfolds before Holden's eyes. So for Holden, all is in suspense—an effect that appealed strongly to Salinger's readers.

But for members of the Glass family, all is not fully in suspense. That gifted group of young people has indeed been badly shaken by the suicide of Seymour, their most gifted sibling. Thus, the central "mystery" which they must come to terms with is not Holden's general panorama of hypocrisy; the death and even more the remembered life of Seymour contain a secret that they are haunted by. The actual death of Seymour is briefly narrated in the story, "A Perfect Day for Bananafish," in *Nine Stories.* Later work, told from various points of view, relates the efforts of members of the Glass family to grasp and apply the eclectic religious truths that the memory of Seymour reminds them of. In none of these tales is there an effort to explain the suicide; this is a fact which the brothers and sisters accept rather than assess. What they do assess, in terms of their own later experience, is the teaching presence of Seymour as they recall it. In the two sections of *Franny and Zooey,* the two youngest members of the family reach out in directions that Seymour, in effect, has already pointed out. In "Franny" the heroine is obsessed by the "Jesus prayer" which she has come across in the memoirs of a Russian monk; she does not know how to pray the prayer and is only aware that, until she does, all her other relations will be without meaning. In "Zooey" her charming brother helps her and himself to come to a grasp of what Seymour's existence had announced: repetition of the Jesus prayer transforms life that is contemptible into a constant act of love and reveals that a "fat lady" is indeed Christ—the "fat lady" and every other human being one encounters. In "Raise High the Roof Beam, Carpenters"—told from the point of view of Buddy, the writing brother—the ridiculous circumstances of Seymour's wedding day are related:

Seymour and his fiancée finally elope rather than endure an elaborate and empty wedding ceremony. Finally, in "Seymour: An Introduction"—also told from the point of view of Buddy—all that can be recalled of Seymour is put down. Recalled are his mastery of the allusive oriental haiku and his even more important mastery of the process of extorting the greatest significance from trivial events (e.g., a game of marbles becomes a vehicle of Zen instruction).

It is undoubtedly the merging of Eastern and Western religious wisdom—the solution of the "mystery" of existence—that gives the work of Salinger its particular élan. In pursuit of what might be called the Seymour effect, the other Glasses consume innumerable packs of cigarettes and break out into perspiration when they find themselves in blind alleys. But the alleys occasionally open up, and fleeting vistas of human unity flash before the eyes. One can but hope that Holden Caulfield, in his later years, will meet one of the younger Glasses whose personal destinies swell to the proportions of regulative myth.

—Harold H. Watts

SALKEY, (Felix) Andrew (Alexander)

Nationality: Jamaican. **Born:** Colon, Panama, 30 January 1928. **Education:** St. George's College, Kingston, Jamaica; Munro College, St. Elizabeth, Jamaica; University of London (Thomas Helmore Poetry prize, 1955), B.A. (honors) in English 1955. **Family:** Married Patricia Verden in 1957; two sons. **Career:** Freelance interviewer and scriptwriter, BBC External Services (Radio), London, 1952-76; English teacher, London, 1957-59; private instructor in Latin and Greek, 1959-64. Since 1976 professor of creative writing, Hampshire College, Amherst, Massachusetts. **Awards:** Guggenheim fellowship, 1960; Sri Chinmoy Poetry award, 1977; Casa de las Américas Poetry prize, 1979. **Address:** Flat 8, Windsor Court, Moscow Road, London W.2., England; or, School of Humanities and Arts, Hampshire College, Amherst, Massachusetts 01002, USA.

PUBLICATIONS

Novels

A Quality of Violence. London, Hutchinson, 1959; New York, Beacon, 1978.
Escape to an Autumn Pavement. London, Hutchinson, 1960.
The Late Emancipation of Jerry Stover. London, Hutchinson, 1968.
The Adventures of Catullus Kelly. London, Hutchinson, 1969.
Come Home, Malcolm Heartland. London, Hutchinson, 1976.

Short Stories

Anancy's Score. London, Bogle L'Ouverture, 1973.
The One (single story). London, Bogle L'Ouverture, 1985.
Anancy, Traveller. London, Bogle L'Ouverture, 1988.
In the Border Country and Other Stories. London, Bogle L'Ouverture, 1995.

Fiction (for children)

Hurricane. London, Oxford University Press, 1964; New York, Oxford University Press, 1979.

Earthquake. London, Oxford University Press, 1965; New York, Roy, 1969.

Drought. London, Oxford University Press, 1966.

Riot. London, Oxford University Press, 1967.

Jonah Simpson. London, Oxford University Press, 1969; New York, Roy, 1970.

Joey Tyson. London, Bogle L'Ouverture, 1974.

The River That Disappeared. London, Bogle L'Ouverture, 1980.

Danny Jones. London, Bogle L'Ouverture, 1980.

Brother Anancy and Other Stories. London, Longman Education International, 1994.

Poetry

Jamaica. London, Hutchinson, 1973.

In the Hills Where Her Dreams Live: Poems for Chile 1973-1978. Havana, Casa de la Américas, 1979; Sausalito, California, Black Scholar Press, 1981.

Away. London, Allison and Busby, 1980.

Other

The Shark Hunters (school reader). London, Nelson, 1966.

Havana Journal. London, Penguin, 1971.

Georgetown Journal: A Caribbean Writer's Journey from London via Port of Spain to Georgetown, Guyana, 1970. London, New Beacon, 1972.

Editor, *West Indian Stories.* London, Faber, 1960.

Editor, *Stories from the Caribbean.* London, Elek, 1965; as *Island Voices: Stories from the West Indies,* New York, Liveright, 1970.

Editor, Caribbean Section, *Young Commonwealth Poets '65.* London, Heinemann, 1965.

Editor, *Caribbean Prose: An Anthology for Secondary Schools.* London, Evans, 1967.

Editor, *Breaklight: An Anthology of Caribbean Poetry.* London, Hamish Hamilton, 1971; as *Breaklight: The Poetry of the Caribbean,* New York, Doubleday, 1972.

Editor, with others, *Savacou 3-4.* Kingston, Jamaica, and London, Caribbean Artists Movement, 2 vols., 1972.

Editor, *Caribbean Essays.* London, Evans, 1973.

Editor, *Writing in Cuba since the Revolution: An Anthology.* London, Bogle L'Ouverture, 1977.

Editor, *Caribbean Folk Tales and Legends.* London, Bogle L'Ouverture, 1980.

*

Theatrical Activities:

Actor: **Film**—*Reggae* (narrator), 1978.

*   *   *

Andrew Salkey's novels deal with the situation of the brown-skinned Jamaican, a man whose social origins lie between the black masses and the white elite, whose tongue is divided between standard and dialect, who is driven towards exile and then caught by "a double lock-out," who has missed his role in history and is caught between attraction to women and flight from the "tender snare." There is a yet bigger ambivalence in the novels which subsumes all these, between the hope that the Salkey hero can hold these divisions in complementary creative tension, and the fear that they will destroy him.

A Quality of Violence, set in 1900 in a remote rural parish in Jamaica during a drought which is driving the villagers off the land, explores the antagonisms between the wealthier brown-skinned planters and the black villagers. Both groups are divided in their response to the drought, the brown families, the Marshalls and the Parkins, between the rational solution of emigration and the millenarian hope of divine providence, and the blacks between incipient class consciousness and lingering African beliefs in the redemptive power of ritual sacrifice. Salkey's response to the vestiges of Africa in the pocomania cult is ambivalent. He describes the rites dismissively, emphasizing their "primitive," exotic features, and the fact that Dada Johnson, the leader, abuses the credulity of the villagers to enrich himself. And yet, what Johnson represents cannot be dismissed. The culture he keeps alive is one of the few things that actually belongs to the people, and when he and his chief acolyte flog each other to death as a sacrifice to end the drought, the image of shallow confidence trickster is undermined. After Johnson's death, Brother Parkin, the archetypal Salkey figure, a "man who always finding himself in the middle of things," tries to bridge the gulf between the Marshalls with their view of pocomania as savage nastiness and Mother Johnson's persuasive plea for holding onto Africa in the heart. Parkin fears that if his class does not assert leadership and stand for the "slow, thoughtful process of salvation and decency," that once the dreams of Africa turn sour, all that will be left will be nihilistic rage. At the end of the novel Mother Johnson has sacrificed herself to keep the African dream alive, an ugly nihilism has surfaced, and the brown group begins its journey away.

That flight is continued by Johny Sobart in *Escape to an Autumn Pavement,* a "rather white-washed nig with lots of coolth" as he describes himself. Johny has escaped from middle-class Jamaica, and from the "slave-class skeletons-in-the-cupboard," but only to wondering what "happened to me between African bondage and British hypocrisy" and trying on and rejecting various roles. His most serious bid is to find the human beneath the skin, but he discovers that he can't shed his history and relationships can't be separated from issues of race and identity. However, *Escape to an Autumn Pavement* is not a pessimistic novel; it is often very funny, though Johny's relentless, self-protective wise-cracking sometimes becomes wearisome. At the end, nothing has been resolved, but Sobart has learned that the choices he must make require patience, courage, and the honesty to "learn the truth about myself."

In *The Late Emancipation of Jerry Stover* Salkey returns to the Jamaica of his early adulthood to portray the middle class from which Jerry Stover will at some point flee into exile. It is a novel full of energy and despair, memories of a "halcyon time" of sybaritic youth and the painful recognition of the waste and futility which the hell-raising of the Termites cannot disguise. The Termites are Jerry's civil service friends, a group with vitality, ritual loyalty, and an illusion of freedom but no sense of creative responsibility. They see themselves gnawing away at the fabric of hypocritical middle-class Jamaica, but Jerry comes to recognize that they are part of the problem, merely shadow-boxing. He makes the gesture of leaving his comfortable home and going to live amongst the Rastafarians of the Dung'll, teaching them and fighting for their cause like a

Felix Holt among the unwashed Victoria working class. In his relationship with the Rastas, the children of Dada Johnson, Jerry plays a Brother Parkin role. He is skeptical of their mystical beliefs and hostile to their dream of returning to Africa, seeing them mainly as the foot soldiers for his idea of protest politics. The Dung'll gives Jerry a confessional where he can pour out his middle-class guilt, but his political gestures are naive failures and he is forced to recognize that he is what his mother says, a do-gooder without a plan, playing at social reform. All that is left for Jerry is either burial on the island, as the other Termites are literally buried under a landslide, or flight. The only other force for change in the island are the Blood and Thunder Brethren who despise gentle mysticism and promise the fire next time. They are the descendants of the ganga addicts in *A Quality of Violence,* who lead the attack on both Brother Parkin and Mother Johnson. Jerry's emancipation from his illusions is both belated and too late. What is left is an honest examination of the reasons for failure.

Both *The Adventures of Catullus Kelly* and *Come Home, Malcolm Heartland* deal with the position of the exiled middle-class Jamaican contemplating return. Neither, in their different ways, is a very satisfactory novel. *The Adventures of Catullus Kelly* uses the form of a Voltairian innocent's journey through London. Much of the writing is entertaining, particularly its exploration of Catullus's "two-way Weltanschauung: his Kingston dialect mood, and his Standard English mood," but the emphasis on language and satirical social vignettes makes it a rather wordy and static novel. Underlying the satire is a black comedy whose seriousness is not fully integrated into the novel as a whole. Catullus's experiences of racism in London make him "blacker an' blacker wit' the days," and he begins to lose his ability to celebrate his "split allegiance, schizophrenic delight, synthesis through analysis and fracture." As a result he decides to return to Jamaica but fails to grasp that exile has changed his heart. Back home, the schizophrenic delight becomes real schizophrenia, and Catullus is incarcerated when having first appeared as Churchill's representative on the island, and then as a matted-haired rasta, he then sheds these false skins and parades himself naked.

In *Come Home, Malcolm Heartland,* Salkey's least successful novel, the hero never reaches home. Its theme is once more the inability of the middle-class Caribbean man to make commitments, in this instance either to the British "Black Power" movement or to home. Return to Jamaica is no more than another escape, from racism and from the guilt he feels over his casual and exploitative use of relationships. However, just before his return, Heartland becomes involved with an absurd but dangerously paranoid group of conspiratorial pseudo-revolutionaries, whom, unfortunately, Salkey fails to bring alive as characters. Finally, the nihilistic retribution which Salkey has warned of in his earlier novels is exacted on Malcolm as a punishment for the sins of his class, when Clovis, a Jamaican migrant, "ravaged by Kingston poverty" and "spiritual desolation," stabs him to death on the order of the conspirators.

One suspects that Salkey's novels have reached a point of exhaustion. However, his collections of short stories, *Anancy's Score* and *Anancy, Traveller,* reworkings of the traditional tales of the trickster spider which explore their contemporary social and political resonances, suggests that he has found a form more appropriate to the kind of preaching he is tempted into in the later novels. Here the use of a poetic, literary Creolese and the form of the fable provides an engaging and serious vehicle for Salkey's perceptiveness, honesty, and aphoristic wit.

—Jeremy Poynting

SARTON, (Eleanor) May

Nationality: American. **Born:** Wondelgem, Belgium, 3 May 1912, daughter of the historian of science George Sarton; brought to the United States in 1916; became citizen, 1924. **Education:** The Institut Belge de Culture Française, Brussels, 1924-25; Shady Hill School and the High and Latin School, both in Cambridge, Massachusetts. **Career:** Apprentice, then member, and director of the Apprentice Group, Eva Le Gallienne's Civic Repertory Theatre, New York, 1930-33; founder and director, Apprentice Theatre, New York, and Associated Actors Inc., Hartford, Connecticut, 1933-36; teacher of creative writing and choral speech, Stuart School, Boston, 1937-40; documentary scriptwriter, Office of War Information, 1944-45; poet-in-residence, Southern Illinois University, Carbondale, Summer 1946; Briggs-Copeland Instructor in English composition, Harvard University, Cambridge, Massachusetts, 1950-53; lecturer, Bread Loaf Writers Conference, Middlebury, Vermont, 1951, 1953, Boulder Writers Conference, Colorado, 1955, 1956, and Radcliffe College, Cambridge, Massachusetts, 1956-58; Phi Beta Kappa Visiting Scholar, 1959-60; Danforth Lecturer, 1960-61; lecturer in creative writing, Wellesley College, Massachusetts, 1960-64; poet-in-residence, Lindenwood College, St. Charles, Missouri, 1964, 1965; visiting lecturer, Agnes Scott College, Decatur, Georgia, Spring 1972. **Awards:** New England Poetry Club Golden Rose, 1945; Bland Memorial prize, 1945 (*Poetry,* Chicago); American Poetry Society Reynolds prize, 1953; Bryn Mawr College Lucy Martin Donnelly fellowship, 1953; Guggenheim fellowship, 1954; Johns Hopkins University Poetry Festival award, 1961; National Endowment for the Arts grant, 1967; Sarah Josepha Hale award, 1972; College of St. Catherine Alexandrine medal, 1975; Before Columbus Foundation award, for prose, 1985. Litt.D.: Russell Sage College, Troy, New York, 1959; New England College, Henniker, New Hampshire, 1971; Clark University, Worcester, Massachusetts, 1975; Bates College, Lewiston, Maine, 1976; Colby College, Waterville, Maine, 1976; University of New Hampshire, Durham, 1976; King School of the Ministry, Berkeley, California, 1976; Nasson College, Springvale, Maine, 1980; University of Maine, Orono, 1981; Bowdoin College, Brunswick, Maine, 1983; Union College, Schenectady, New York, 1984; Bucknell University, Lewisburg, Pennsylvania, 1985; Rhode Island College, Providence, 1989; Centenary College, Hackettstown, New Jersey, 1990. Fellow, American Academy of Arts and Sciences. **Agent:** Russell and Volkening Inc., 50 West 29th Street, New York, New York 10001. **Address:** Box 99, York, Maine 03909, U.S.A.

PUBLICATIONS

Novels

The Single Hound. Boston, Houghton Mifflin, and London, Cresset Press, 1938.
The Bridge of Years. New York, Doubleday, 1946.
Shadow of a Man. New York, Rinehart, 1950; London, Cresset Press, 1952.
A Shower of Summer Days. New York, Rinehart, 1952; London, Hutchinson, 1954.
Faithful Are the Wounds. New York, Rinehart, and London, Gollancz, 1955.

The Birth of a Grandfather. New York, Rinehart, 1957; London, Gollancz, 1958.

The Small Room. New York, Norton, 1961; London, Gollancz, 1962.

Joanna and Ulysses. New York, Norton, 1963; London, Murray, 1964.

Mrs. Stevens Hears the Mermaids Singing. New York, Norton, 1965; London, Owen, 1966.

Miss Pickthorn and Mr. Hare: A Fable. New York, Norton, 1966; London, Dent, 1968.

The Poet and the Donkey. New York, Norton, 1969.

Kinds of Love. New York, Norton, 1970; London, Norton, 1980.

As We Are Now. New York, Norton, 1973; London, Gollancz, 1974.

Crucial Conversations. New York, Norton, 1975; London, Gollancz, 1976.

A Reckoning. New York, Norton, 1978; London, Gollancz, 1980.

Anger. New York, Norton, 1982.

The Magnificent Spinster. New York, Norton, 1985; London, Women's Press, 1986.

The Education of Harriet Hatfield. New York, Norton, 1989; London, Women's Press, 1990.

Uncollected Short Stories

"Old-Fashioned Snow," in *Collier's* (Springfield, Ohio), 23 March 1946.

"The Return of Corporal Greene," in *American Mercury* (New York), June 1946.

"The Contest Winner," in *Liberty* (New York), 10 August 1946.

"Mrs. Christiansen's Harvest," in *Ladies Home Journal* (New York), March 1947.

"The Town Will Talk," in *Ladies Home Journal* (New York), June 1947.

"The Miracle in the Museum," in *Church and Home* (London), March 1948.

"The Paris Hat," in *Cosmopolitan* (New York), March 1948.

"Mr. Pomeroy's Battle," in *Better Homes and Gardens* (Des Moines, Iowa), November 1948.

"If This Isn't Love," in *Woman's Home Companion* (Springfield, Ohio), April 1949.

"The Little Purse," in *Redbook* (New York), June 1949.

"Alyosha and His Horse," in *World Review* (London), September 1949-February 1950.

"The Last Gardener," in *Woman's Day* (New York), April 1953.

"The Screen," in *Harper's Bazaar* (New York), October 1953.

"Aunt Emily and Me," in *Woman's Day* (New York), April 1960.

Plays

The Underground River. New York, Play Club, 1947.

Screenplays (documentaries): *Valley of the Tennessee,* 1945; *A Better Tomorrow,* with Irving Jacoby, 1945; *The Hymn of the Nation,* 1946.

Poetry

Encounter in April. Boston, Houghton Mifflin, 1937.

Inner Landscape. Boston, Houghton Mifflin, 1939; with a selection from *Encounter in April,* London, Cresset Press, 1939.

The Lion and the Rose. New York, Rinehart, 1948.

The Leaves of the Tree. Mount Vernon, Iowa, Cornell College, 1950.

Land of Silence and Other Poems. New York, Rinehart, 1953.

In Time like Air. New York, Rinehart, 1957.

Cloud, Stone, Sun, Vine: Poems, Selected and New. New York, Norton, 1961.

A Private Mythology: New Poems. New York, Norton, 1966.

As Does New Hampshire and Other Poems. Peterborough, New Hampshire, Richard R. Smith, 1967.

A Grain of Mustard Seed: New Poems. New York, Norton, 1971.

A Durable Fire: New Poems. New York, Norton, 1972.

Collected Poems 1930-1973. New York, Norton, 1974.

Selected Poems, edited by Serena Sue Hilsinger and Lois Brynes. New York, Norton, 1978.

Halfway to Silence: New Poems. New York, Norton, 1980; London, Women's Press, 1993.

A Winter Garland. Concord, New Hampshire, Ewert, 1982.

Letters from Maine: New Poems. New York, Norton, 1984.

The Phoenix Again: New Poems. Concord, New Hampshire, Ewert, 1987.

The Silence Now: New and Uncollected Earlier Poems. New York, Norton, 1988.

Coming into Eighty: New Poems. New York, Norton, 1994.

Recording: *My Sisters, O My Sisters,* Watershed, 1984.

Other

In Memoriam (memoir). Brussels, Godenne, 1957.

The Fur Person: The Story of a Cat. New York, Rinehart, 1957; London, Muller, 1958.

I Knew a Phoenix: Sketches for an Autobiography. New York, Holt Rinehart, 1959; London, Owen, 1963.

Plant Dreaming Deep (autobiography). New York, Norton, 1968.

Journal of a Solitude. New York, Norton, 1973; London, Women's Press, 1985.

Punch's Secret (for children). New York, Harper, 1974.

A World of Light: Portraits and Celebrations. New York, Norton, 1976.

A Walk Through the Woods (for children). New York, Harper, 1976.

The House by the Sea: A Journal. New York, Norton, 1977; London, Prior, 1978.

Recovering: A Journal 1978-1979. New York, Norton, 1980.

Writings on Writing. Orono, Maine, Puckerbrush Press, 1980.

At Seventy: A Journal. New York, Norton, 1984; London, Norton, 1987.

A Self-Portrait (includes verse), edited by Marita Simpson and Martha Wheelock. New York, Norton, 1986.

After the Stroke: A Journal. New York, Norton, and London, Women's Press, 1988.

Honey in the Hive: Judith Matlack 1898-1982. Boston, Warren, 1988.

Sarton Selected: An Anthology of Novels, Journals, and Poetry, edited by Bradford Dudley Daziel. New York, Norton, 1991.

Endgame: A Journal of the Seventy-Ninth Year. New York, Norton, 1992; London, Women's Press, 1993.

Encore: A Journal of the Eightieth Year. New York, Norton, and London, Women's Press, 1993.

May Sarton: Among the Usual Days: A Portrait: Unpublished Poems, Letters, Journals, and Photographs, selected and edited by Susan Sherman. New York, Norton, 1993.

Editor, *Letters to May,* by Eleanor Mabel Sarton. Orono, Maine, Puckerbrush Press, 1986.

*

Bibliography: *May Sarton: A Bibliography* by Lenora P. Blouin, Metuchen, New Jersey, Scarecrow Press, 1978.

Manuscript Collections: Berg Collection, New York Public Library; Houghton Library, Harvard University, Cambridge, Massachusetts; Amherst College, Massachusetts (letters); Westbrook College, Maine.

Critical Studies: *May Sarton* by Agnes Sibley, New York, Twayne, 1972; *May Sarton: Woman and Poet* edited by Constance Hunting, Orono, Maine, National Poetry Foundation, 1982; *World of Light: A Portrait of May Sarton,* New York, Two Lip Art, 1982; interview with Karen Saum, in *Paris Review,* October 1983; *May Sarton Revisited* by Elizabeth Evans, Boston, Twayne, 1989; *That Great Sanity: Critical Essays on May Sarton* edited by Susan Swartzlander and Marilyn R. Mumford, Ann Arbor, University of Michigan Press, 1992.

May Sarton comments:

The novelists of the moderate human voice, from Trollope through Tchekov and Forster, are not in fashion, but I like to believe that I am in their line of descent, for what has interested me always is ordinary human relations, the heroism, despair, and rich complex fibre of day to day living among the middle class. European as I am by birth, it was natural that my first four novels should be laid in Europe, Belgium and England—my father was Belgian and my mother English—though the important thing has never been the setting but the intimate relationships explored. Five of the novels are centered in a marriage, from the coming of age through marriage of a young man (*Shadow of a Man*), to a marriage in its middle years (*The Bridge of Years*), to late middle age (*The Birth of a Grandfather*), and old age (*Kinds of Love*). The other major theme of my novels has been how the singular man or woman may find his identity and/or fulfillment through an art or profession. In two cases the protagonist is homosexual, a male professor in *Faithful Are the Wounds,* and a female poet in *Mrs. Stevens Hears the Mermaids Singing.* The former is a relentless exploration of the effect of a suicide (a political suicide) on the protagonist's colleagues at Harvard University. The latter is a study of the woman as artist. And the theme of the value of the single woman to society is touched on again in a novel, *The Small Room,* laid in a woman's college. Finally there is a group of slighter short novels, humorous or poetic accounts of how solitary individuals—a woman painter, a male poet—have dealt with kinds of deprivation, and triumphed.

It is my hope that all the novels, the books of poems, and the autobiographical works may come to be seen as a whole, the communication of a vision of life that is unsentimental, humorous, passionate, and, in the end, timeless. We can bear any Hell if we can "break through" to each other and come to understand ourselves.

*   *   *

May Sarton (also a poet and memoirist) is particularly skillful at character development and the examination of the pleasures and difficulties of important human relationships, steadily analyzing her characters' simultaneous needs for independence from and union with others.

She is also very able in the evocation of place, and setting is often central to her novels. The physical and intellectual milieu of Boston and Harvard in *Faithful Are the Wounds,* for example, symbolizes the characters' habits of introspection and self-analysis which generate the action. *Kinds of Love* is set in Willard, New Hampshire, during its bicentennial, and several characters have important responsibilities for the celebration. Their researches into the village's changes and consistencies parallel their serious consideration of the stable and the unstable patterns of their own lives, resulting in a splendid unification of action and theme. *Kinds of Love* is also a sound portrait of modern New England village life, and, when contrasted with the equally vivid European settings of such earlier works as *The Single Hound, The Bridge of Years,* and *A Shower of Summer Days,* reveals Sarton's deep love for her adopted homeland as well as her appreciation of her European heritage and roots. *Joanna and Ulysses* is set on Santorini. The Aegean island's well-rendered atmosphere, its isolation, and its distance from Joanna's home all dramatize her growing understanding of her obligations to herself as opposed to her obligations to her father. This wedding of theme and setting is one of Sarton's greatest strengths.

One of the author's most significant themes is her protagonists' professional commitment. *Mrs. Stevens Hears the Mermaids Singing* is a portrait of an elderly writer, based on Sarton herself, reflecting upon her life and work. She reconfirms the worth of her writing, recognizing and accepting the fact that professional dedication often impinges upon love and friendship. In contrast, Lucy Winter, protagonist of *The Small Room,* is depicted at the outset of her career as a professor. Having undertaken her job almost accidentally, Lucy falls in love with her work even as she achieves a realistic understanding of it. The demands of original research are delineated in the portrayal of a highly revered senior professor, and those of the classroom are conveyed through the characterization of a brilliant but deeply troubled student. *The Small Room* offers a remarkably fair and moving analysis of the joys as well as the responsibilities of academe.

Like *Mrs. Stevens Hears the Mermaids Singing* and *Joanna and Ulysses, The Small Room,* presents useful insights into modes of balancing human relationships against professional drive, always stressing the fact that honorable commitment to one's talent demands sacrifice and self-discipline. Sarton's belief that this level of dedication is particularly taxing for women is clearly evident in these three important works.

Some novels explore major social problems. The powerful *Faithful Are the Wounds* depicts anti-communist witch hunts while it examines the effect of Edward Cavan's suicide upon his circle of friends. *Crucial Conversations,* a somewhat weaker novel, incorporates insights about the Vietnam War and the Watergate scandal into the account of Poppy Whitelaw's late decision to abandon marriage to attempt a career as a sculptor. The brilliant *As We Are Now* denounces substandard care for the infirm through Caro Spencer's struggle to control her own destiny as well as to preserve her very sense of self within the debasing atmosphere of the "home" into which she has been remanded. Plot and social commentary are always firmly united, translating sweeping issues into human terms.

With Keats, Sarton believes that the fruitful life is a continuing process of "soul-making"; this theme, particularly well conveyed in *The Birth of a Grandfather,* which recounts Sprig Wyeth's development as husband, father, and friend, is almost invariably present in the author's work. Used as a positive motivation in that novel and in *A Reckoning,* the effective story of Laura Spelman's responses to cancer and approaching death, it also lends biting irony to *As We Are Now.*

In *Anger,* the author offers a more intimate view of relationships by exploring the emancipating and imprisoning aspects of anger. Taking as her text Rilke's phrase, "Perhaps everything terrible in us is in its deepest being something helpless that needs help," Sarton delineates neatly the imbedded rages and hard-to-relinquish prejudices that undermine human relationships.

The Magnificent Spinster again concerns itself chiefly with relationships, this time through the celebration of a single, unconventionally heroic life. Alternating between personal biography and fictional retelling, the narrator Cam, a history professor, captures the life of a woman who possessed none of the typical hallmarks of success—career, marriage, and family—but who enhanced life through a rich, balanced existence and an inexhaustible responsiveness to people and the world around her. As with previous novels, Sarton stresses relationships of permanence rather than passion, explores with great understanding the various stages of grief, and does much to validate the lives of older women.

Sarton's most recent novel, *The Education of Harriet Hatfield,* is a slightly old-fashioned yet nonetheless refreshing account of an elderly woman's discovery of a second life after the death of a long-time companion. Opening up a women's bookstore in a blue-collar Boston neighborhood broadens Harriet's world and, as might be expected, exposes her to new and unexpected dangers. Although awkward dialogue and implausible circumstances occasionally create a strained intimacy among the characters, the author does present the rare point of view of an older lesbian woman who for most of her life lived under the protective canopy of wealth, and who now both literally and figuratively comes out to bravely face and remake a new world.

Willing to confront challenging issues and basic human problems, Sarton has also experimented with form; her works range from the panoramic *Kinds of Love* through the slender, delicate *Joanna and Ulysses* to *As We Are Now,* spare and incisive. She has won deserved respect and wide popularity.

—Jane S. Bakerman, updated by Lynda Schrecengost

SAVAGE, Thomas

Nationality: American. **Born:** Salt Lake City, Utah, 25 April 1915. **Education:** Colby College, B.A. 1940, M.A. 1955. **Family:** Married, 1939; two sons, one daughter. **Career:** Faculty member, Suffolk University, Boston, 1947-48; assistant professor, Brandeis University, 1949-55. **Awards:** Guggenheim fellowship, 1980; Northwest Booksellers award, 1989. **Agent:** Blanche Gregory, 2 Tudor City Place, New York, New York 10017, U.S.A.

PUBLICATIONS

Novels

The Pass. New York, Doubleday, 1944.
Lona Hanson. New York, Simon and Schuster, 1948.
A Bargain with God. New York, Simon and Schuster, 1953.
Trust in Chariots. New York, Random House, 1961.

The Power of the Dog. New York, Little Brown, and London, Chatto and Windus, 1967.
The Liar. New York, Little Brown, 1967.
Daddy's Girl. New York, Little Brown, 1970.
A Strange God. New York, Little Brown, 1974.
Midnight Line. New York, Little Brown, 1976.
I Heard My Sister Speak My Name. New York, Little Brown, 1977.
Her Side of It. New York, Little Brown, 1981.
For Mary with Love. New York, Little Brown, 1983.
The Corner of Rife and Pacific. New York, Morrow, 1988.

*

Thomas Savage comments:

Mrs. Bridge, by Evan S. Connell, is one of the best novels I ever read. I was influenced by John Steinbeck, Robert Benchley, and Dorothy Parker. I was a history major, read little fiction, chiefly biography and history. I read S.J. Perelman.

I believe all organized religion is based on myths and is responsible for most of the horror in the world now and in the past. I think nothing will change much because of continuing, probably atavistic, superstition, ignorance, and greed. It's frightening that human beings continue to need scapegoats in order to justify themselves. I once made a speech somewhere and said, " The more education you have, the less money you need." I still believe this. And if you don't have much education you'd damned well better have money.

*   *   *

Despite having spent most of his life on the Atlantic and Pacific coastlines, "within sight of water," he says, Thomas Savage returns to the Montana valley of his youth as the setting for over half of his 14 novels, the latest of which he completed in May of 1995, two weeks after celebrating his eightieth birthday.

The people who settled and live in the geographic center of Savage's West (southwestern Montana and Idaho's Lemhi Valley) face hard work, harsh weather conditions, isolation, and rugged terrain. Against such a backdrop, Savage's western characters struggle to attain, maintain, or retain their individuality, family pride, love, success—and sometimes the land itself. One might expect people tested by such landscape to toughen themselves, both physically and emotionally, in order to survive; and though such characters do appear in Savage's work, he tends to focus most often on the more vulnerable citizens of his western ranching communities— the young and sensitive "outsider," the woman who cannot cope with her circumstances, the man who fails himself and everyone else in his life through what Savage identifies as "an inability to face unpleasantness."

Although Savage says he writes fiction and not autobiography, he acknowledges the role that memory plays in his western fiction. As a youngster, Savage "boarded out" in Dillon, the town closest to the family ranch, while he attended school. In several novels, Dillon is transformed into Herndon or Grayling, and the experiences of the protagonists mirror those of the creator. There are also some "stock" fixtures in Savage's fictional household and domestic arrangements, such as the grandfather's clock that is ceremoniously wound once a week by the proprietor of the ranch or the home; the large cars (a Rolls-Royce; a Roamer) that Savage's businessmen and ranchers drive; the rings that wives of successful husbands wear as symbols of the family prosperity.

Several themes also resurface in many of Savage's novels, including that of the "unsolicited kindness" that is rewarded (sometimes years after the fact) at a time when the characters are most in need of the financial or emotional boost that is offered. Many of his female characters, be they located in the West or the East, lament the changes taking place in their lives or their surroundings; "nothing's the same," Norma Reed says in *A Strange God* (1974), an eastern-setting novel. Her comment echoes the sentiments of a woman speaking her mind in Savage's first novel, *The Pass,* published 30 years earlier: "All the new things, all the new ways, spoiled something." That "something " is the quality, the texture of life enjoyed by the characters before changes—what Martin Levin called "the accidents of success and the accidents of failure" in his *New York Times* review of *A Strange God* (25 August 1974)—occur. These changes can also sometimes be counted as losses, and loss is another familiar element in Savage's novels. Redemption or restoration is also possible for Savage's characters, however, and most of his novels do end on an optimistic note.

Savage identifies *Her Side of It,* the novel he wrote as a Guggenheim recipient in 1980, as his best work to date. (Ironically, his most commercially successful books, *Lona Hanson,* set in the West, and *A Bargain with God,* which takes place in Boston, are the two he feels least positive about in terms of artistic achievement.) The main character in *Her Side of It,* Liz Phillips, is a novelist, and Savage's narrator is able to comment on both the working life of a writer and on the achievement possible in that field of endeavor. In words that critics might apply to Savage's own work, he says that Phillips's novels "promote a reader to search for answers . . . and to find them. The search makes of life a sharper pleasure."

—Sue Hart

SCHAEFFER, Susan Fromberg

Nationality: American. **Born:** Brooklyn, New York, 25 March 1941. **Education:** Simmons College, Boston; University of Chicago, 1958-66, B.A. 1961, M.A. 1963, Ph.D. 1966. **Family:** Married Neil J. Schaeffer in 1970; one son and one daughter. **Career:** Instructor in English, Wright Junior College, Chicago, 1964-65; instructor, 1965-66, and assistant professor of English, 1966-67, Illinois Institute of Technology, Chicago. Assistant Professor, 1967-71, associate professor, 1972-74, since 1974 professor of English, and since 1985 Broeklundian Professor, Brooklyn College. **Awards:** Wallant award, 1975; O. Henry award, 1980; St. Lawrence award, 1984; Guggenheim fellowship, 1984; *Centennial Review* award, for poetry, 1985. **Agent:** Virginia Barber, 101 Fifth Ave., New York, New York 10003. **Address:** Department of English, Brooklyn College, Brooklyn, New York 11210, U.S.A.

PUBLICATIONS

Novels

Falling. New York, Macmillan, 1973.
Anya. New York, Macmillan, 1974; London, Cassell, 1976.
Time in Its Flight. New York, Doubleday, 1978.

Love. New York, Dutton, 1981.
First Nights. New York, Knopf, and London, Hamish Hamilton, 1983.
The Madness of a Seduced Woman. New York, Dutton, 1983; London, Hamish Hamilton, 1984.
Mainland. New York, Simon and Schuster, and London, Hamish Hamilton, 1985.
The Injured Party. New York, St. Martin's Press, and London, Hamish Hamilton, 1986.
Buffalo Afternoon. New York, Knopf, and London, Hamish Hamilton, 1989.

Short Stories

The Queen of Egypt. New York, Dutton, 1980.

Uncollected Short Stories

"In the Hospital and Elsewhere," in *Prairie Schooner* (Lincoln, Nebraska), Winter 1981-82.
"Virginia; or, A Single Girl," in *Prairie Schooner* (Lincoln, Nebraska), Fall 1983.

Poetry

The Witch and the Weather Report. New York, Seven Woods Press, 1972.
Granite Lady. New York, Macmillan, 1974.
The Rhymes and Runes of the Toad. New York, Macmillan, 1975.
Alphabet for the Lost Years. San Francisco, Gallimaufry, 1976.
The Red, White, and Blue Poem. Denver, The Ally, 1977.
The Bible of the Beasts of the Little Field. New York, Dutton, 1980.

Fiction (for children)

The Dragons of North Chittendon. New York, Simon and Schuster, 1986.
The Four Hoods and Great Dog. New York, St. Martin's Press, 1988.

*

Critical Study: *Jewish American Women Writers* by Dorothy Bilik, Westport, Connecticut, Greenwood Press, 1995.

*   *   *

Susan Fromberg Schaeffer's novels, spanning 16 years, are basically mainstream fictions that employ stream of consciousness, radical time shifts, and other modernist techniques, but only incidentally. Apparently she believes that the traditional form is adequate to her purposes, and she is right in so thinking. Schaeffer is mainly interested in exploring and illuminating the shapes of her characters' lives through presentation of the mundane details of their existences. Although she sometimes has her characters move through the larger contexts of historical times, and although she often offers elaborate explanations for behavior, her main strengths as a novelist are her ability to evoke the real quality of quotidian life and the particularities of emotional states.

Falling, Schaeffer's first novel, contains all her strengths and weaknesses as a writer. It is the story of Elizabeth Kamen, a graduate-school Jewish intellectual who suffers several near mental breakdowns, who has unfailingly bad judgment about the men in her life, and whose life is largely determined by her family background. In this and subsequent novels, the lives of characters are traced through their often harrowing childhoods which permanently stamp their personalities. As a child, Elizabeth had stolen a quarter to buy a doll, which her mother and grandmother demolished then hung on the wall to remind Elizabeth of her "crime." This and other accounts, including events from her present life, are woven together in sessions with her psychiatrist. The aim is to arrest her falling and to get control of her life which, like others characters' lives, suffers from various kinds of slippage. But the human condition is to fall because, as Elizabeth's mother says in Elizabeth's dream. "There is no bottom, there is only this falling," only motion and journey, as opposed to stasis and goal. Elizabeth's mother also asks, "Can you swim, Elizabeth?" "Yes, Mother, if you hold, I'll kick,"

However, as a narrative *Falling* suffers from a peculiar stasis. The story is a series of vignettes or anecdotes that do not make up a single, satisfying narrative framework. This is not principally due to Schaeffer's abandoning traditional narrative technique; rather, the episodes are disjointed and without flow. As in other novels, characters are introduced only to show up later, after the reader has forgotten them; adding to the diffuseness that characterizes the entire novel. Yet the strengths of *Falling* remain. Schaeffer's skill as a poet saves many of the scenes; vivid images and descriptions help give the novel a heightened sense of life.

In *Anya* Schaeffer again concentrates on the incidental, even minute aspects of dailiness that are presented with the quality of a personal diary. The novel chronicles the life of Anya, a young Jewish woman in Poland, from the mid-1930s up to the present. Though the novel is partly set during the holocaust years, it is not really about the holocaust (descriptions of life before the Hitler years are among the most compelling in the novel), but about Anya whose life intersects, but is not principally affected by, social events of the time. Schaeffer almost always selects family history as more determinative of character and personality than culture or history. Again, life is the accretion of small things. Anya says, "If you are going to learn a person's life, then, like learning a language, you must start with the little things, the little pictures, the tiny, square images, like rooms, that will grow into a film." To this must be added all of Anya's personal history, from naive, happy student to tough survivor in contemporary America. And Anya always draws on her former lives for strength, so the reader—more so than in *Falling*—experiences a more multi-dimensional character. It should be added that at the time Schaeffer was writing *Anya*, American-born Jewish novelists were more concerned with American social history than with the formation of a "Jewishness" as a response to the death camps and the World War II years. One thinks immediately of Bellow, say, as opposed to a writer like Cynthia Ozick. Now, of course, the holocaust has become an almost fashionable subject.

Love again details the potent, permanent effects of family and married lives, as opposed to culture and history. Esheal Luria is abandoned at the age of 10 by his widowed mother after he has been rejected by his stepfather. He is rescued by a mysterious "zenshima" (witch) whose memory haunts him through adulthood and is in part responsible for his wanting, from childhood, "to find an American woman and take care of her." Despite the fact that the novel is a saga of two Jewish immigrant families, the ultimate determinant is, as Luria's wife Emily puts it, the fact that we are "only a new step in the continuing dance . . . of the genes." Resembling

at times an Isaac Bashevis Singer tale, *Anya* gains its strength through evocative detail, even the oddities of life lived away from the sweep of events. Emily's mother speaks for Schaeffer: "I remember all those things, but now I don't like to save odd things. They take you over, all those books, cards, litter and pictures. They keep accumulating and it becomes a chore to sort them out and they pile up until they overwhelm you and then you get rid of them all."

As though trying to escape the influence of Emily's mother's words, *The Madness of a Seduced Woman* is Schaeffer's attempt to understand a single life as compounded of personal history, woman's biology, psychiatry, and community standards. The novel is based on an actual murder trial in Vermont early in the century in which Agnes Dempster is tried for the murder of her rival and pronounced insane, largely on psychiatric testimony that Agnes's insanity resulted from "the madness of a seduced woman." However, Schaeffer does not accept this judgment and painstakingly examines her motives (reminiscent of Joyce Carol Oates) as seen through the speculations of lawyers, friends, and her father. No firm conclusions are reached, except that no life may be understood exclusively by objective or subjective means. This process of examination is often numbing, especially since Agnes's life is more complicated than understood. Schaeffer, in this novel, does not allow the character's life to speak for itself; analyses and comment are often substituted for dramatization and the tale itself as an adequate vehicle for meaning.

Mainland, is in many ways a return to her more lighthearted first novel and to a less complex tale, whose theme is maturity. Eleanor, the main character, is a famous writer and professor, basically happy but almost obsessed by the moralistic voices of her dead grandmother and mother. The novel, comically delightful, avoids the diffuseness of much of her earlier work. The theme is expertly handled and the characterization fully realized. Before the novel's end Elizabeth realizes that her adulterous affair was necessary, so she forgives herself, realizing along the way that the dialogues in her head are only carry-overs from childhood and that "maturity" is a false ideal. Schaeffer demonstrates here that a less ambitious theme does not necessarily preclude a higher art.

—Peter Desy

SCHULBERG, Budd (Wilson)

Nationality: American. **Born:** New York City, 27 March 1914; son of the Hollywood film pioneer, B.P. Schulberg. **Education:** Los Angeles High School, 1928-31; Deerfield Academy, 1931-32; Dartmouth College, Hanover, New Hampshire, 1932-36, A.B. (cum laude) 1936 (Phi Beta Kappa). **Military Service:** Served in the United States Navy, 1943-46: Lieutenant. **Family:** Married 1) Virginia Ray in 1936 (divorced 1942), one daughter; 2) Victoria Anderson in 1943 (divorced 1964), two sons; 3) the actress Geraldine Brooks in 1964 (died 1977); 4) Betsy Anne Langman in 1979, one son and one daughter. **Career:** Screenwriter, Hollywood, 1936-39; in charge of photographic evidence for the Nuremberg trials; boxing editor, *Sports Illustrated,* New York, 1954. Has taught writing at Columbia University, New York, Phoenixville Veterans Hospital, University of the Streets, New York, Southampton College, New York, Darmouth College, and Hofstra University, Hempstead, New York; founder, Watts Writers Workshop, Los Angeles, 1965.

Since 1958 president, Schulberg Productions, New York; since 1970 founding chair, Frederick Douglass Creative Arts Center, New York. Member of the New York Council, Authors' Guild, 1958-60; since 1983 council member, Writers Guild. Lives in Westhampton Beach, New York. **Awards:** American Library Association award, New York Critics award, Foreign Correspondents award, Screen Writers Guild award, and Oscar, all for screenplay, 1955; Christopher award, 1956; German Film Critics award, for screenplay, 1958. D.Litt.: Dartmouth College, 1960; Long Island University, Greenvale, New York, 1983; Hofstra University, 1985. **Address:** c/o Random House Inc., 201 East 50th Street, New York, New York 10022, U.S.A.

PUBLICATIONS

Novels

What Makes Sammy Run? New York, Random House, and London, Jarrolds, 1941.
The Harder They Fall. New York, Random House, and London, Lane, 1947.
The Disenchanted. New York, Random House, 1950; London, Lane, 1951.
Waterfront. New York, Random House, 1955; London, Lane, 1956; as *On the Waterfront,* London, Corgi, 1959.
Sanctuary V. Cleveland, World, 1969; London, W.H. Allen, 1970.
Everything That Moves. New York, Doubleday, 1980; London, Robson, 1981.

Short Stories

Some Faces in the Crowd. New York, Random House, 1953; London, Lane, 1954.
Love, Action, Laughter, and Other Sad Tales. New York, Random House, 1989; London, Allison and Busby, 1992.

Plays

Hollywood Doctor (broadcast 1941). Published in *The Writer's Radio Theatre,* edited by Norman Weiser, New York, Harper, 1941.
Tomorrow, with Jerome Lawrence (radio play), in *Free World Theatre,* edited by Arch Oboler and Stephen Longstreet. New York, Random House, 1944.
The Pharmacist's Mate, in *The Best Television Plays 1950-1951,* edited by William I. Kauffman. New York, Merlin Press, 1952.
A Face in the Crowd: A Play for the Screen. New York, Random House, 1957.
Across the Everglades: A Play for the Screen. New York, Random House, 1958.
The Disenchanted, with Harvey Breit, adaptation of the novel by Schulberg (produced New York, 1958). New York, Random House, 1959.
What Makes Sammy Run?, with Stuart Schulberg, music by Ervin Drake, adaptation of the novel by Budd Schulberg (produced New York, 1964).
On the Waterfront: Original Story and Screenplay, edited by Matthew J. Bruccoli. Carbondale, Southern Illinois University Press, 1980.

Screenplays: *Little Orphan Annie,* with Samuel Ornitz and Endre Bohem, 1938; *Winter Carnival,* with Maurice Rapf and Lester Cole, 1939; *Weekend for Three,* with Dorothy Parker and Alan Campbell, 1941; *Government Girl,* with Dudley Nichols, 1943; *City Without Men,* with Martin Berkeley and W.L. River, 1943; *On the Waterfront,* 1954; *A Face in the Crowd,* 1957; *Wind Across the Everglades,* 1958; *Joe Louis—For All Time,* 1984.

Radio Play: *Hollywood Doctor,* 1941.

Television Play: *A Question of Honor,* 1982.

Other

Loser and Still Champion: Muhammad Ali. New York, Doubleday, and London, New English Library, 1972.
The Four Seasons of Success. New York, Doubleday, 1972; London, Robson, 1974; revised edition, as *Writers in America,* New York, Stein and Day, 1983.
Swan Watch, photographs by Geraldine Brooks. New York, Delacorte Press, and London, Robson, 1975.
Moving Pictures: Memories of a Hollywood Prince. New York, Stein and Day, 1981; London, Souvenir Press, 1982.

Editor, *From the Ashes: The Voices of Watts.* New York, New American Library, 1967.

*

Manuscript Collections: Princeton University, New Jersey; Dartmouth College, Hanover, New Hampshire.

Critical Study: interview in *Cineaste* (New York), 1981.

Budd Schulberg comments:
(1972) I was raised in Hollywood, in the middle of the film capital, and had an early education in the vicissitudes of success and failure. I became convinced, before I was out of high school, that the dynamics of success and failure were of earthquake proportions in American, and that Hollywood was only an exaggerated version of the American success drive. Undoubtedly this influenced my first novel, *What Makes Sammy Run?*, as it did *The Harder They Fall, The Disenchanted,* and many other things I have tried to write. I believe it is the prime American theme, prompting my essays on Sinclair Lewis, Scott Fitzgerald, William Saroyan, Nathanael West, Thomas Heggen, and John Steinbeck, all writers I knew well. I believe that the seasons of success and failure are more violent in America than anywhere else on earth. Witness only Herman Melville and Jack London, to name two of the victims.

I have been influenced by Mark Twain, by Frank Norris, Jack London, Upton Sinclair, John Steinbeck, and the social novelists. I believe in art, but I don't believe in art for art's sake; while despising the Soviet official societal writing, I believe in art for people's sake. I believe the novelist should be an artist cum sociologist. I think he should see his characters in social perspective. I think that is one of his obligations. At the same time, I think he also has an obligation to entertain. I think the novel should run on a double track. I am proud of the fact that *Uncle Tom's Cabin* and *The Jungle* and *The Grapes of Wrath* helped to change or at least alarm society. I am proud of the fact that books of mine, *Sammy,* or *On the*

Waterfront, caught the public attention but also made it more aware of social sores, the corruption that springs from the original Adam Smith ideal of individuality. I think Ayn Rand tries to apply 18th-century ideals to 20th-century problems—and I'm not sure they worked that well then. My flags are down: I believe in neither Smith nor Marx, in neither Nixon nor Mao nor the Soviet bureaucrats who persecute my fellow writers. There was a time when I was young when I sang the "International." Who would have guessed that the "International" would result in the two largest countries in the world, both "Socialist," brandishing lethal weapons at each other? As long as we can wonder and remember, speculate and (perhaps vainly) hope, we are not dead. The non- or anti-communist humanist writer of novels may be slightly out of style, but there are miles and decades and many books to go before he sleeps.

* * *

Budd Schulberg earned fame with his first and best novel, *What Makes Sammy Run?,* published in 1941 on the author's 27th birthday. This narrative of an obnoxious office boy's quick rise to head of a major motion picture studio threatened to become the author's type story for all his novels. *The Harder They Fall* told the pathetic story of the rise of Toro Molina to heavy-weight boxing champion, although "El Toro" is actually the victim of an ambitious, unscrupulous fight promoter named Nick Latka. Schulberg's *The Disenchanted* traced the doomed comeback attempt of Manley Halliday, a novelist and culture-hero of the 1920s now reduced to writing movie scenarios when sober. In these three early novels and many of the collected short stories of *Some Faces in the Crowd,* Schulberg is absorbed with the theme of rapid success and the psychic losses of public winners: compromise with self, betrayal by or of others, doubt, guilt, isolation, and fear haunt and shame his restless characters.

Schulberg's plots have frequently reflected the author's background as screenwriter and son of a Hollywood producer. Not surprisingly, many of his novels have been produced as movies, but his fourth novel, *Waterfront,* was a successful movie first, with the novel version a distinct improvement over the author's own scenario. After a 15 year lapse, Schulberg returned to the novel with *Sanctuary V,* a melodramatic study of a failed revolution and the ruinous effects of sudden power. In this least successful novel, Justo Suarez, the provisional president of what is obviously Cuba, has fled from the corrupted revolutionary Angel Bello to take sanctuary in a corrupt embassy among corrupt or perverted refugees and jailer-hosts.

Not only is Angel Bello clearly Fidel Castro, earlier novels just as recognizably modeled their protagonists on real-life counterparts: the hapless, peasant-fighter Toro Molina is Primo Carnera, while Manley Halliday is Scott Fitzgerald, with whom Schulberg ("Shep" in the book) had once worked on a Dartmouth winter carnival scenario. When Schulberg is not "exposing" Hollywood through memories of real-life counterparts or composites, he utilizes journalistic skill and thorough research for fictional exposés of the fight game (*Harder They Fall*) and the brutal life around New York harbor (*Waterfront*). Like most exposés, the novels exploit the most sensational elements, though Schulberg reveals an un-Hollywoodian preference for the seamy over the sexy. He does commit many other major "Hollywood" faults, employing gimmicks, stereotyped characters, sentimentality, and mechanical, reflex responses to life-situations in place of serious ideas or a personal vision.

With *Sammy,* however, even the faults seem appropriate. The snappy repartee and artificial dialogue brilliantly sum up the brittle, superficial world of 1930s Hollywood. The novel's fast pace, the picaresque audacity of the almost likable, conscienceless heel-hero, the predictable ending of the betrayer betrayed (and, implicitly, of the hunter about to be hunted) still add up, after 50 years, to one of the best Hollywood novels ever written. Like many other commercial writers, Schulberg knows that first-person is the easiest way to tell a story; he uses this form often and well, and in *What Makes Sammy Run?* he created a minor classic of this form and the Hollywood sub-genre.

—Frank Campenni

SEALY, I(rwin) Allan

Nationality: Indian. **Born:** Allahabad, India, 31 March 1951. **Education:** La Martiniere College; Delhi University, B.A. (with honors) in English 1971; Western Michigan University, B.A. (with honors) in English 1972, M.A. 1974. **Family:** Married Cushla Fitzsimmons, 1985. **Career:** Writer. **Award:** Commonwealth Writers' prize for best first book, 1989, for *The Trotter-Nama.* **Agent:** A.P. Watt, 20 John St., London WC1N 2DR, England. **Address:** D-101 Race Course, Dehra Dun, U.P.248001, India.

PUBLICATIONS

Novels

The Trotter-Nama: A Chronicle. New York, Knopf, and London, Viking, 1988.
Hero: A Fable. New Delhi, Viking, 1990; London, Secker and Warburg, 1991.

Other

From Yukon to Yukaton: A Western Journey. London, Secker and Warburg, 1994.

* * *

Although I. Allan Sealy divides his time between India and New Zealand, he writes out of India rather than the Indian diaspora. Both his novels to date, *The Trotter-Nama: A Chronicle* and *Hero: A Hero,* bring something distinctly Indian to what is, after all, a European literary form (written in English). In *The Trotter-Nama,* Sealy adapts the Indian epic *nama* form (a form once used to flatter emperors and ideally suited to Sealy's expansive and digressive style), whereas in *Hero* he transfers the formulaic "masala movie" of India's popular and prodigious film industry from celluloid to paper. What clearly links these two novels is Sealy's gift for storytelling.

In *The Trotter-Nama,* Sealy presents a history of India unreliably narrated by Eugene, the Seventh Trotter, a painter, and a chronicler of his Anglo-Indian family history, from its founding by the Great

Trotter (a French mercenary soldier) in the 18th century through to the present day. Significantly, Eugene paints in a mock-Mughal style—a style in which perspective is often distorted, reflected in his role as historian. His story (and history) is centered on the predictably named Trotter family seat of Sans Souci near Nakhlau (another name for Lucknow and, notably, the one used by Kipling in *Kim*); but as the Trotter family branches out across India and the world Sealy is able to introduce the postcolonial concerns of identity, exile, and the diaspora into his fiction. Eugene Trotter's riotous chronicle, which recalls the work of both Sterne and Rabelais as well as recent postmodernist fictions, playfully flexes the boundaries of the novel to encompasses maps, a family tree, and numerous digressions, interpolations, sections of verse, letters, recipes, household bills, authorial intrusions, and, on the cover, a miniaturist painting that portrays all the major events of the novel.

In his second novel, *Hero,* Sealy moves away from the expansive style of *The Trotter-Nama* and directs his narrowed lens on India's pop-culture film world in an attempt to interpret the subcontinent through the unlikely, but surprisingly common, Indian mix of politics and the cinema. Indeed, the novel borrows its structure from the masala movie mix—which is clearly outlined on the contents page. Again Sealy's interest in postmodernist games is evident from the outset. There is, for example, a skilled parody of structuralist theory in the opening section of the novel, which challenges theory as another tool of colonization. Literary allusions abound, as in the opening line of the novel: "He stood six feet tall but it was his slouch that made him a hero," which clearly echoes the opening sentence of Joseph Conrad's *Lord Jim;* authorial intrusions are legion, and the many instructions that direct the gaze of the camera once more test the boundaries of the genre. Via the trope of the Bombay cinema, Sealy explores the nature of image, the portrayal of "real life" through image, and the relationship between "reality" and "fiction." The novel is also a penetrating discourse on the nature of power and an exposé of the corruption that has dogged recent Indian politics. All this is achieved through the story of Hero, a film superstar-cum-prime minister, whose story in many ways resembles that of Tamil Nadu's superstar of the popular cinema and erstwhile chief minister, M. G. Ramachandran. Hero's tale is told by his longtime sidekick, Zero, a Bombay scriptwriter and, later, Hero's political speechwriter, whose presence (among other things) challenges any notion about the death of the author. In fact, Sealy himself appears in the "ENTRANCE," "INTERMISSION," and "EXIT" sections of the novel, where he instructs the reader on how to read this fabulous (the novel is subtitled *A Fable*) novel.

Sealy's most recent book, *From Yukon to Yucatan: A Western Journey,* is a work of nonfiction that recounts his journey across the North American continent following in the footsteps of its first people—from their landing place on the shores of the Arctic Sea down to the Gulf of Mexico. Of particular interest is his focus on the displaced people he meets along the way—Spaniards, Malaysians, and more.

Sealy is a writer to watch. His first two novels show that he is a writer who likes to challenge the borders of his preferred genre, and though his literary games may at times be distracting, for the most part he carries them off with consummate skill.

—Ralph J. Crane

SEE, Carolyn

Pseudonym: Monica Highland (with Lisa See and John Espey). **Nationality:** American. **Born:** Carolyn Penelope Laws, Pasadena, California, 13 January 1934. **Education:** Los Angeles City College, A.A.; California State University, Los Angeles, M.A., Ph.D. **Family:** 1) married Richard See, 1954 (divorced 1959), one daughter; 2) married Tom Sturak, 1961 (divorced 1969), one daughter; 3) lives with John Espey, since 1974. **Career:** Waitress, 1950s; teaching assistant, 1960s; professor of English, Loyola Marymount University, 1970-85; visiting professor of English, 1986-89, and adjunct professor of English, both University of California, Los Angeles. Book reviewer, *Los Angeles Times,* 1981-93; *New York Newsday,* 1990-92; and since 1993 *Washington Post.* President, PEN West International, 1990-91. **Awards:** Vesta award, 1989, for writing; Guggenheim fellowship in fiction, 1990-91; Lila Wallace teaching grant, 1992-93; Women's Care Cottage Apple award, 1991; *Los Angeles Times* Robert Kirsch body of work award, 1993. **Member:** National Book Critics Circle; Writers Guild of America. **Agent:** Anne Sibbold, Janklow Nesbit Agency, 589 Madison Ave., New York, New York 10022, U.S.A.

PUBLICATIONS

Novels

The Rest Is Done with Mirrors. New York, Little Brown, 1970.
Mothers, Daughters. New York, Coward McCann Geoghegan, 1977.
Rhine Maidens. New York, Coward McCann Geoghegan, 1980; Harmondsworth, Middlesex, Penguin, 1981.
Golden Days. New York, McGraw Hill, 1986; London, Century, 1987.
Making History. New York, Houghton Mifflin, 1991.
Dreaming: Hard Luck and Good Times in America. New York, Random House, 1995.

Novels as Monica Highland (with Lisa See and John Espey)

Lotus Land. New York, McGraw Hill, 1983.
110 Shanghai Road. New York, McGraw Hill, 1986.
Greeting from Southern California. New York, McGraw Hill, 1988.

Others

Blue Money: Pornography and the Pornographers. New York, Rawson, 1973.
Two Schools of Thought, with John Espey. Santa Barbara, California, Daniel, 1991.

*

Manuscript Collection: Special Collections, University of California, Los Angeles.

Carolyn See comments:

When I started to write I was relatively old, and lived in California. So I was the wrong sex, wrong age, wrong coast. Luckily I was too ignorant to know it. I've always had to write to make a living, and have a solid background in journalism from my father. My formal education more or less rolled off my back, critical theory means nothing to me, less than nothing.

I try to write about the larger world—nuclear war, the random nature of the universe, the oppression of the American underclass through drugs and drink. I've only written one "lady" novel, *Mothers, Daughters,* and I'm embarrassed for it. But I'm proud of the rest of my work.

* * *

Carolyn See's novels explore women's lives, broken relationships, and all things Californian. See has tackled the usual gamut of male-female romance, but she has also taken on the subjects of mothers, daughters, and aging in *Rhine Maidens;* female friendship, religious evangelism, and nuclear war in *Golden Days;* and international business, stepfamilies, and grieving in *Making History.* See uses strong first-person narration in her best work, some of which is rendered in diary form.

The Rest is Done With Mirrors, See's first novel (and generally not thought to be her best work), tells of two UCLA graduate students and troubled relationships. Much of See's early work appears to be loosely biographical and deals with marital breakups. Her second novel, *Mothers, Daughters,* follows a divorced TV reporter, Ruth, as she negotiates a blossoming romance with Marc, the former beau of two of her female friends. Both the third-person narration and the plot are highly formulaic and plodding. See includes many cavalier references to her characters' acid trips and a great deal of humor, however, thus preventing the novel's easy categorization as mass-market romance.

With *Rhine Maidens,* See's masterful characterizations and clever dialogue emerge more fully formed. The story of the neurotic, stubborn Grace, left by several husbands and facing retirement alone, is coupled with that of her daughter, Garnet, a "useless" wealthy housewife who is into est and interior decorating. Garnet's story is presented as her assigned journal from the freshman composition class she has enrolled in to improve herself. Grace's narration is given as a would-be dialogue with the dead friend of her youth, Pearl. Both women unwillingly take stock of their failing and failed relationships with husbands and children.

The "Rhine maidens" of the title refers to a cruise on the Rhine River that Grace begrudgingly takes with the aging (and similarly alone) Edna. At novel's end, Grace, forever unable to have a good time, may in fact be letting go of her worries, and Garnet is poised to leave her rich housewife days behind her. The novel masterfully explores what happens when mothers and daughters not only don't get along but don't even like each other. Class conflicts and colliding generational values add further color.

Golden Days's title is taken from John Milton's *Paradise Lost,* and See's novel verges on religious allegory. It is no less gripping a tale for this feature. Readers follow gemologist Edith as she negotiates single parenting and teaches classes to prepare wealthy married women for their husbands' desertions by stockpiling jewels. Edith's reestablished friendship with Lorna, a caged housewife turned healer and evangelist, provides one of the most interesting story lines.

Women's friendships rarely receive short shrift from See. She writes:

> There was a basic inequality in the country I grew up and lived in. One man, one story. For women, it generally

took two or even three to make one story. . . . This is partly the story of Lorna Villanelle and me; two ladies absolutely crazed with the secret thought that they were something special.

Everyone's "specialness" is seemingly leveled with the dropping of a nuclear bomb. See's novel, however, is one of hope and survival rather than mere despair—an ode to the sustenance of storytelling.

See's past efforts made use of "miracles," but *Making History* is the first to delve so deeply into the supernatural and into life after death. This novel deals with the functional yet vapid marriage of Jerry and Wynn and their family: Whitney (Wynn's teenage daughter by a first marriage), Tina, and Josh. Jerry's frequent business trips to Asia involve visits to prostitutes, written of as inconsequential infidelities. Wynn involves herself in the second-rate prep school her children attend and congratulates herself for having gotten out of a bad first marriage and into relative comfort. As Wynn remembers her father saying, however, "Life has a way of kicking the shit out of you." The novel involves fatal car accidents, friendships broken by grief, and marriages strained to the breaking point. As in *Golden Days,* however, See manages to hone the resilience in her characters while showing us the fragility of the order in our daily lives.

See is also a memoirist. With her partner, John Espey, she published *Two Schools of Thought: Some Tales of Learning and Romance,* reflections on Oxford (his) and UCLA (hers). Most recently, she's written an account of generations of her family's alcoholism, *Dreaming: Hard Luck and Good Times in America.* Espey, See's daughter Lisa See Kimball, and See have also joined forces to create the novels of Monica Highland, *Lotus Land* and *110 Shanghai Road.*

—Devoney Looser

SELBY, Hubert, Jr.

Nationality: American. **Born:** Brooklyn, New York, 23 July 1928. Educated in New York City public schools, including Peter Stuyvesant High School. **Military Service:** Served in the United States Merchant Marine, 1944-46. **Family:** Married 1) Inez Taylor in 1953 (divorced 1960), one daughter and one son; 2) Judith Lumino in 1964; 3) Suzanne Shaw in 1969, one daughter and one son. **Career:** Hospital patient, with tuberculosis, 1946-50; held various jobs, including seaman and insurance clerk, 1950-64. Lives in Los Angeles. **Member:** Writer's Guild of America, and Authors Guild. **Address:** c/o Grove Weidenfeld, 841 Broadway, New York, New York 10003-4793, U.S.A.

PUBLICATIONS

Novels

Last Exit to Brooklyn. New York, Grove Press, 1964; London, Calder and Boyars, 1966.
The Room. New York, Grove Press, 1971; London, Calder and Boyars, 1972.

The Demon. New York, Playboy Press, 1976; London, Boyars, 1977.

Requiem for a Dream. New York, Playboy Press, 1978; London, Boyars, 1979.

Short Stories

Song of the Silent Snow. New York, Grove Press, and London, Boyars, 1986.

Uncollected Short Stories

"Home for Christmas," in *Neon 2* (New York), 1956.

"Love/s Labour/s Lost," in *Black Mountain Review* (Black Mountain, North Carolina), Autumn 1957.

"Double Feature," in *Neon 4* (New York), 1959.

"Another Day, Another Dollar," in *New Directions 17.* New York, New Directions, 1961.

"A Penny for Your Thoughts," in *The Moderns,* edited by LeRoi Jones. New York, Corinth, 1963; London, MacGibbon and Kee, 1965.

"And Baby Makes Three," in *New American Story,* edited by Robert Creeley and Donald Allen. New York, Grove Press, 1965.

"Fat Phil's Day," in *Evergreen Review* (New York), August 1967.

"Happy Birthday," in *Evergreen Review* (New York), August 1969.

Plays

Screenplays: *Day and Night,* 1985; *Soldier of Fortune,* 1990.

*

Critical Studies: "Hubert Selby Issue" of *Review of Contemporary Fiction* (Elmwood Park, Illinois), vol. 1, no. 2, 1981.

Hubert Selby, Jr., comments:

(1991) I write by ear. Music of line important. Want to put reader through emotional experience.

*   *   *

If *Last Exit to Brooklyn* and its ludicrous obscenity trial hadn't exhausted moralistic disgust, Hubert Selby, Jr.'s work could probably stand at the bench in perpetuity. The Seventh Circle of the Violent in Dante's *Inferno;* Gulliver upon the cancerous Brobdignagian breast; Genet's onanist reveries. These suggest Selby's fictive world. He is our eye-witness on the dead-ends of the daily. Stuck in the sick gut of the city, his camera fixes the disaffected masses and completes a picture begun with Crane's *Maggie.* On the other hand, his biblical epigraphs are both ironically and straightforwardly applicable. He is, then, at once a determinist and a moralist whose narratives are naturalistic fables. Consequently, his psychological landscape is more than social realism or a Hogarth satire could accommodate. It is a Bosch and Francis Bacon triptych. As the witness for the damned, Selby *is* mired in America's slime. But given a populace which could nod off on the Vietnam War, his ability to shock may be remarkable, even morally so.

The title of his first novel is taken from an expressway sign that overlooks a cemetery of solid concrete. The work thematically connects six tales of hopeless human isolation. Its people delude themselves with faith in family and ideal dreams of profound sexual communion. But Abraham's infidelity, angry remoteness, and, finally, sleep are domesticity. Tralala's rape is heterosexuality. "Georgette's" and Vinnie's bestiality is homosexuality. Casual and sadistic, the violent are little Eichmanns and Mengeles. In the background Selby works with a timeless symbology of darkness overwhelming light. This is conveyed to us by depth associations with *Ecclesiastes,* Poe's *Raven,* and our own disillusioned black "Bird," Charlie Parker. It is only by viewing Selby in this context that we can grasp his preoccupation with drugs. He knows unequivocally the life-renouncing and futile lie at the heart of "kind nepenthe."

The Room shifts our focus from the sick social to the sick individual organism. Its sole province is the mind of a nameless paranoid schizophrenic, though Selby might resist terminology. The "room" is both a cell and the disconnected consciousness of the single character. Locked within each, he constructs antithetically lofty and brutal fantasies, but always out of a single-minded hatred of authority. Thus his imaginary revenges include delusions of magnanimity in which he self-sacrificially fights social injustice with the help of liberal lawyers. Conversely, they include totally dehumanizing tortures of police officers, sadistic acts which reduce his adversaries to canines. These are rendered with nauseating detail. Selby seems unwilling to attribute this state of mind to a sick society, an indifferent family, or a bad character. It is simply a *donnée,* and Selby's forte is neither sociological nor psychological reductionism but graphic presentation. The novel's unsavory force and its interest are considerably enhanced by the author's tactic of gliding constantly between an omniscient and a first person perspective.

The "demon" of Selby's third novel is sexual obsession and its mutations. It begins as womanizing so unalleviated that Harry White can sustain no connection, except tenuously to his career, with any other activity. (He cannot last out a softball game with friends or a party for his grandparents.) It ends with his murdering, on Palm Sunday, a Christlike Cardinal and his subsequent suicide. So the demoniacal obsession is larger than carnality, passing through debauchery and theft toward this ultimately exciting destructiveness which seems proof for Selby that "The wages of sin is death." The novel's complementary epigraph is from *James* 1:15. At all times, whether White is fornicating or thieving, the demon exists as a physical tension so great that Harry hates whatever stands between himself and a feeling of exhausting gratification. But all respite from enslavement, including his marriage to Linda (the healthiest person Selby has drawn), is stop-gap. Only death does the job. As a study of the connection between sex and violence in the obsessive person, the book has merit. But the conclusion is unfortunately mystical in part, especially because the only psychological perspective is provided by an arrogant neo-Freudian simpleton. This straw man certainly doesn't exhaust more modestly agnostic interpretations of the events.

Requiem for a Dream is about hope ruined by narcotic habit. It sees America in terms of a pervasive dependence upon metaphorical and literal drugs. The widow Sara Goldfarb eats compulsively and lives a stuporously vicarious life through soap operas and TV game shows. Thinking she has a chance to appear in one and wanting to be appropriately svelte, she sees a physician who addicts her to Dexedrine. She ends up a skeletal and slavering schizoid in a mental hospital. Concurrently, her son Harry, his friend Tyrone Love, and Harry's lover, Marion, plot their own dreams' fulfillment's. All are sad clichés—and the trio are heroin addicts. From drug profits, Harry will build a coffeehouse for sensitive artists and writers where Marion's drawings will be admired; the black Tyrone will buy into the bliss of a modest suburb. But their endeavors only increase their addiction. Marion winds up in a sort of bisexual freak show working for her portion of bliss. Harry loses his arm from an infection and sinks into oblivion in a Miami hospital. Having gone south with Harry for a big pay-off, Tyrone gets to be brutalized by rednecks and thrown in prison. By now we have to ask if Selby Jr. has anything more to tell us along these lines.

—David M. Heaton

SELF, Will(iam)

Nationality: British. **Born:** London. **Family:** Married; two children. **Awards:** Geoffrey Faber Memorial prize, 1993, for *The Quantity Theory of Insanity.*

PUBLICATIONS

Novels

The Quantity Theory of Insanity: Together with Five Supporting Propositions. London, Bloomsbury, 1991; New York, Atlantic Monthly Press, 1995.
My Idea of Fun: A Cautionary Tale. London, Bloomsbury, 1993; New York, Atlantic Monthly Press, 1994.
Junk Male. London, Bloomsbury, 1995.

Short Stories

Cock and Bull (novellas). London, Bloomsbury, 1992; New York, Atlantic Monthly Press, 1993.
Grey Area, and Other Stories. London, Bloomsbury, 1994.

*   *   *

Will Self is a satirist on the order of Swift and Voltaire writing in the England of Malcolm Bradbury, David Lodge, and Martin Amis. Drawing on his experience as a heroin addict, a philosophy student at Oxford, and a cartoonist, he has crafted a style perfectly suited to his time and place. He pillories the absurdities of modern England and possesses a special genius for making the ridiculous appear credible. Passages of grotesque realism, horrific humor, and absurdist fantasy are delivered in an unnerving deadpan that manages to be at once sinister and slangy, erudite and wildly funny.

The stories in *The Quantity Theory of Insanity: With Five Supporting Propositions* introduce his chief targets. His English bear a curious resemblance to the Ur-Bororo, a "relentlessly banal" tribe bent upon "boring one another still further." (As for Londoners, "When you're dead," one narrator's dead mother explains, "you move to another part of London, that's all there is to it.") On Ward Nine for the "metamad," therapists and patients exchange places according to Dr. Zack Busman's latest "cost-effective" theory. Busman, who reappears in several stories here and in *Grey Area,* serves as one of several representatives of pseudoscientific theories and Thatcherite economics that attract the author's special ire. The Quantitative Theory of Insanity, for example, proposes "a fixed

proportion of sanity available in any given society at any given time." In a brave new world where sanity is available on the time-share plan and (in "Mono-Cellular") plankton farmers sit down with Child Bankers to discuss investment opportunities in the adoption market, people have clearly lost the ability to think critically, to distinguish the genuine from the bogus, the important from the trivial, the morally monstrous from the financially feasible. They have (in *Grey Area*) lost a sense of "Scale"; they are addicted to Inclusion, an antidepressant drug that makes them perfectly passive consumers indiscriminately interested in anything and everything.

The absurdity is even wilder in *Cock & Bull.* In the first of these two complementary stories, a submissive Carol discovers the joy of sex via masturbation, grows a penis, and sodomizes her husband to death, thus avenging past wrongs by becoming a grotesque version of masculinity at its very worst. In Self's daisy chain of dominance-submission plots, husband Dan is not the only one being diddled. The narrator finds himself first trapped and then raped on a train by a donnish gay-bashing anti-Semitic ancient mariner-like companion who turns out to be the fully metamorphosed Carol. The reader will undoubtedly empathize with the male narrator's feeling of female helplessness and complicity after having sat there "like a prat, listening to a load of cock . . . and bull." Unlike "Cock: A Novelette," "Bull: A Farce" begins in Kafkaesque fashion with the manly Bull waking up one morning to discover a vagina growing behind his left knee. His physician takes a more than clinical interest in the suddenly helpless Bull, who, busy discovering his female nature, is quickly seduced and soon abandoned. Foregoing suicide, he ends up a single parent in Wales, as complaisant now as Carol once was.

Sex is given an economic twist in *My Idea of Fun: A Cautionary Tale.* Self's novel takes its title from I. B. Singer and its underlying subject from Freud: the channeling of the sexual drive into primitive sadistic fantasies and postindustrial business ventures. With his split, "borderline" personality, the narrator-protagonist (first as *I* then as *he*) in effect resembles both Carol and Bull. However, unlike *Cock & Bull, My Idea of Fun: A Cautionary Tale* is polymorphously perverse, its satire more diffuse, its metamorphoses more numerous. The son of an absent father and an overprotective, class-conscious mother, Ian Wharton is an "eidetiker" who learns to use his psychological gift (or curse) for his own benefit as a marketeer under the tutelage of The Fat Controller. Either a real, if endlessly, metamorphosing person or a figment of Ian's disturbed imagination, The Fat Controller is most obviously a sinister version of the character in a series of children's books subsequently turned into a commercially successful TV series (with its own set of spin-off products) in Britain and America. Serving as Ian's "personified id," The Fat Controller acts as the perfect guide for an age in which "people had begun to feel less awkward about being greedy and of wanting more than their fair share." In this "cautionary tale," eidetiking allows Ian and his tutor to indulge in their murderous fantasies without needing to act them out. In a Thatcherite world of relentless marketeering and postmodern simulacrum, of virtual reality and virtual money, all differences between the real and the imaginary may seem beside the point. It is, however, very much to the point of a writer whose display of stylistic effects and range of literary reference (from De Quincey and Dostoyevsky to Maurice Sendak and Thomas the Tank Engine) do not so much distract from as lend weight to the social consciousness that is at the heart of Will Self's pyrotechnic art.

—Robert A. Morace

SENIOR, Olive (Marjorie)

Nationality: Jamaican (immigrated to Canada in 1991). **Born:** Jamaica, 23 December 1944. **Education:** Carleton University, Ottawa, 1963-67, B.S. 1967. **Career:** Reporter and sub-editor, *Daily Gleaner* newspaper, Jamaica; information officer, Jamaica Information Service, 1967-69; public relations officer, Jamaica Chamber of Commerce and editor, *JCC Journal,* 1969-71; publications editor, Institute of Social and Economic Research, University of the West Indies, Jamaica, and editor, *Social and Economic Studies,* 1972-77; freelance writer and researcher, part-time teacher in communications, publishing consultant, and speech writer, Jamaica, 1977-82; managing editor, Institute of Jamaica Publications, and editor, *Jamaica Journal,* 1982-89; freelance teacher, writer, lecturer, internationally, 1989-94; visiting lecturer/writer-in-residence, University of the West Indies, Cave Hill, Barbados, 1990. Director of Fiction Workshop, Caribbean Writers Summer Institute, University of Miami, Florida, 1994, 1995. Dana Visiting Professor of creative writing, St. Lawrence University, Canton, New York, 1994-95. **Awards:** Commonwealth Writers' prize, 1967; Gold, Silver, and Bronze medals for poetry and fiction, Jamaica Festival Literary Competitions, 1968-70; Winner in two categories, Longman International Year of the Child Short Story Competition, 1978; Institute of Jamaica Centenary medal for creative writing, 1979; UNESCO award for study in the Philippines, 1987; Jamaica Press Association award for editorial excellence, 1987; United States Information Service, International Visitor award, 1988; Institute of Jamaica, Silver Musgrave medal for literature, 1989; F.G. Bressani Literary prize for poetry, 1994, for Gardening in the Tropics. Hawthornden fellow, Scotland, 1990; International Writer-in-Residence, Arts Council of England, 1991. **Agent:** Nicole Aragi, Watkins/Loomis Agency, 133 East 35th Street, Suite 1, New York, New York 10016, U.S.A.

PUBLICATIONS

Short Stories

Summer Lightning and Other Stories. London, Longman, 1987.
Arrival of the Snake-Woman. London, Longman, 1989.
Quartet, with others. London, Longman, 1994.
Discerner of Hearts. Toronto, McClelland and Stewart, 1995.

Poetry

Talking of Trees. Kingston, Calabash, 1986.
Gardening in the Tropics. Toronto, McClelland and Stewart, 1994.

Other

The Message Is Change. Kingston, Jamaica, Kingston, 1972.
Pop Story Gi Mi (four booklets on Jamaican heritage for schools). Kingston, Ministry of Education, 1973.
A-Z of Jamaican Heritage. Kingston, Heinemann Educational, 1983.
Working Miracles: Women's Lives in the English-Speaking Caribbean. London, James Currey, and Bloomington, Indiana University Press, 1991.

*

Critical Studies: Olive Senior issue of *Callalloo* (Baltimore), 11(3), Summer 1988; in *Critical Strategies* by Malcolm Kinnery and Michael Rose, Boston, Bedford Books/St. Martin's Press, 1989; in *Out of the Kumbla: Caribbean Women and Literature,* edited by Carole Boyce Davies and Elaine Savory Fido, New York, Africa World Press, 1990; in *Caribbean Women Writers,* edited by Selwyn Cudje, Wellesley, Massachusetts, Calaloux Publications, 1990; in *Motherlands. Black Women's Writing from Africa, the Caribbean and South Asia,* edited by Susheila Nasta, London, The Women's Press, 1991; in *Come Back to Me My Language: Poetry and the West Indies* by J.E. Chamberlin, Champaign, University of Illinois Press, 1993; in *Woman Version: Theoretical Approaches to West Indian Fiction by Women* by Evelyn O'Callaghan, London, Macmillan, 1993; "The Fiction of Olive Senior" by Richard F. Patteson, in *Ariel, A Review of International English Literature* (Calgary, Alberta), 24(1), January 1993.

*   *   *

Olive Senior is a leading Jamaican short story writer and poet. Her publications to date include the poetry collection *Talking of Trees* and the prose collections *Summer Lightning,* which won the Commonwealth Writers Prize, and *The Arrival of the Snake Woman.*

She was born in 1943 in rural Jamaica, and at the heart of her writing is her childhood experience of growing up in an isolated village. There she was caught between two cultures. On the one hand there was the financially poor, but culturally rich, life of her parents' community; and on the other, the society of the "landed gentry" enjoyed by her mother's relatives, whom she visited from the age of four. In an interview that appeared in *Kunapipi,* she declared that she "ended up feeling quite alienated from both backgrounds because it was very difficult for me to make the adjustments between the two worlds." Although not directly autobiographical, much of her writing was a way of coming to terms with tensions in her own divided background.

These are directly addressed in "The Two Grandmothers" (in *The Arrival of the Snake Woman and Other Stories*). The developing consciousness of the young first-person narrator is reflected through successive monologues in which she moves alternately between Grandma Dell, who lives a simple country existence, and Grandma Elaine, upwardly mobile in the society of a small town, with television and all the luxuries of modern living. Within a small compass Senior explores many aspects of changing Jamaican life while sensitively evoking the individual consciousness of the young narrator, who by the end has come, through her experiences, to make her own choice of a racial and social identity.

Senior typically uses a child's vision as a focus for her stories, often that of a girl. Within this she explores a wide range of subjects and themes, from religious and racial issues in the community (as in "Do Angels Wear Brassieres?" and "Ballad" and "The Coming of the Snake Woman"), to the closeness, violence, and isolation she sees as characteristic of Jamaican family life ("The Boy Who Loved Ice Cream" and "Ascot").

Yet if island life provides the rich basis for her work—its imaginative center is always the search for individual identity—and she has spoken of the need to "create self-identity out of a chaotic personal and social history." Characteristically the persona at the center of her stories ends by achieving independent selfhood. Thus in "Confirmation Day" (in *Summer Lightning*), the desolation experienced in the church ritual paradoxically ends with exultation, as the girl protagonist realizes she no longer needs to be bound within her stifling background.

The variety and complexity of her stories owe much to her skill in re-creating the rhythms and nuances of Jamaican speech. Her stories range from "standard" English to densely creolized dialect, from descriptive narrative to poetic evocation. Although best known for her short stories, her poetry shows the same profound consciousness of Jamaican place and people, expressed through a style intimately in touch with the speech rhythms of her island people. Previously editor of the *Jamaican Journal* and director of the Institute of Jamaica Publications, increasing recognition of her own writing has given her financial freedom and opportunities for international travel. Always an innovative writer, she may well direct her skills into still new avenues.

—Louis James

SETH, Vikram

Nationality: Indian. **Born:** Calcutta, India, 20 June 1952. **Education:** Doon School, India; Corups Christi College, Oxford, B.A. 1975; Stanford University, M.A. in economics 1979; Nanjing University, 1982. **Career:** Senior editor, Stanford University Press, 1985-86. **Awards:** Thomas Cook travel book award, 1983, for *From Heaven Lake;* Ingram Merrill fellowship, 1985-86; Commonwealth poetry prize, 1986; Guggenheim fellowship, 1986-87; Sahitya Akademi award, 1988. **Address:** c/o HarperCollins, 10 East 53rd St., New York, New York 10022-5299, U.S.A.

PUBLICATIONS

Novels

The Golden Gate: A Novel in Verse. New York, Random House, and London, Faber, 1986.
A Suitable Boy. New York, HarperCollins, and London, Phoenix, 1993.

Poetry

Mappings. Calcutta, Writers Workshop, 1981; London, Viking, 1994.
The Humble Administrator's Garden. Manchester, Carcanet, 1985.
All You Who Sleep Tonight (verse play). New York, Knopf, and London, Faber, 1990.
Beastly Tales from Here to There, illustrated by Ravi Shankar. New Delhi, Viking, 1992; New York, HarperCollins, 1994.

Other

From Heaven Lake: Travels Through Sinkiang and Tibet. London, Chatto and Windus, 1983; Boston, Faber, 1986.
Arion and the Dolphin (for children), illustrated by Jane Ray. London, Orion Children's Books, 1994; New York, Dutton Children's Books, 1995.

Translator, *Three Chinese Poets: Translations of Poems by Wang Wei, Li Bai, and Du Fu.* New Delhi, Viking, and New York, HarperPerennial, 1992.

Vikram Seth is a poet, travel writer, playwright, writer of fables, translator, and librettist, but it is as a novelist that he has been most highly acclaimed. His two novels, one in verse (*The Golden Gate*) and the other in prose (*A Suitable Boy*) form a curious pair and a curious achievement.

A novel in verse is not a long narrative poem but one that deals with characters and human relationships in a social milieu as a novel does but in the medium of verse. The form is rare; Seth's only precursors are Byron's *Don Juan* and Pushkin's *Eugene Onegin,* which in its English translation by Charles Johnston was the book's original stimulus. *The Golden Gate* is about American society; when Seth, an Indian, was asked why he writes about it, his reply was: "One can't quarrel with inspiration." The novel deals with personal relations, love, loss, and mortality with an acuteness and delicacy of perception, a humorous yet compassionate and very robust understanding of human beings—particularly the difference in generations—not conflicts but just stances, desires. Seth deals with two sorts—the older, modern kind of living, feeling, and thinking; and the sometimes crippling freedom of the postmodern period, where the old monogamous loves between sexes are now a part of a rosy past. It is different from Restoration comedy, which is essentially mechanical and heartless. *The Golden Gate* is witty—but it is all heart.

The influence of Pushkin is exceedingly strong as regards the meticulous reflection of the social fabric, individual characters, interaction, and, above all, the pervasive irony, directed often (as Alexander Pope's is not) against the author himself. Seth himself is like Goldmith's Chinaman, a poised, amused outsider who considers this society from the inside, is critical, but (like Pushkin) never sets himself to be a judge, only a wry commentator. He shows us how balled-up their loves, their art, and publicity are—but *he* is Kim Tarvesh in anagram, the alcoholic, thesis-bedeviled foreigner on the fringe. Tarvesh is like Chaucer the pilgrim, narrower and more naive than the omniscient Vikram Seth. The unbroken use of the Pushkin stanza form, the tetrameter sonnet, enhances rather than impedes the poised style, the sophistication of diction and the effortless yet persuasive rhythm.

A Suitable Boy made a literary lion of Seth. The media dwelt on its 700,000 words and 1,349 pages—the longest novel published in England since Richardson's *Clarissa* (1747-1748) and longer than Tolstoy's *War and Peace*—and on Seth's advance of more than $2 million. More relevant are the artistic comparisons made to Jane Austen, George Eliot, Tolstoy, and Dickens.

A Suitable Boy is set wholly in India, where Seth now resides. The main plotline, like that of *The Golden Gate,* centers on the question of finding a suitable partner, and here it assumes an Austenean form. Will the heroine, Lata, submit to Mrs. Rupa Mehra's arrangements or will she follow her own spirit, even if that means defying not only her mother but barriers of caste and religion? Three candidates present themselves: Kabir, a cricketer, dashing but a Muslim; Amit Chatterji, a Bengali poet and novelist, sophisticated, rich, and a Brahmin; and Harish, a brisk young man determined to make a career for himself in the shoe manufacturing industry. Lata finally settles for Harish, not implausible because unromantic, an index of Seth's own pragmatism and of the direction in which India is, probably, heading.

Affinities to *Middlemarch* also exist. Just as George Eliot examined the great political and social changes in an earlier England, so Seth writing in the 1990s recreates the period of transition (1951-1952) after independence (1947)—but without Eliot's rigorous critical dimension. In addition to the Mehras, three other families are important: the Kapoors, the Khans, and the Chatterjis. Their fates are intertwined. Really, a multitude of characters and events throng the novel; the setting moves back and forth between the cities of Brahmpur (which is fictional) and Calcutta, with excursions to New Delhi, Kanpur, and Lucknow and to a remote village where Maan Kapoor spends a month in exile. Seth offers a huge, thick, and multilayered slice of Indian life that, in its veracity, serves to counter the widespread false views of India and improve the world's understanding of his country.

The historical scale of Seth's novel invites comparison with *War and Peace*. Like Tolstoy, Seth writes the history of the recent past from the point of view of individuals whose lives are affected by the great historical events of the time and also crosses the boundary between the invented and the historical. Nehru is his equivalent of Napoleon.

In contrast to the fierce "magic realism" of Salman Rushdie, Seth writes in a 19th-century realist mode with a vein of 18th-century sentiment, flat at times but generally eminently readable and engaging (but not quite equaling his great predecessors or the sparkle of *The Golden Gate*). Seth's novels show that it is wrong to privilege modernist or postmodernist modes or innovation; tradition endures, sustains, and can provide for major achievement.

—D.C.R.A. Goonetilleke

SETTLE, Mary Lee

Nationality: American. **Born:** Charleston, West Virginia, 29 July 1918. **Education:** Sweet Briar College, 1936-38. **Military Service:** Women's Auxiliary, R.A.F., 1942-43. **Family:** Married William Littleton Tazewell, 1978; has one son. **Career:** Editor, *Harper's Bazaar,* 1945; English correspondant, *Flair,* 1950-51; associate professor, Bard College, New York, 1956-76. Visiting lecturer, University of Virginia, 1978. **Awards:** Guggenheim fellow, 1958, 1960; Merrill Foundation award, 1975; National Book award, 1978, for *Blood Ties;* Janet Heidinger Kafka prize, 1983, for fiction. **Address:** c/o Farrar Straus & Giroux, 19 Union Sq. W., New York, New York 10003-3304, U.S.A.

PUBLICATIONS

Novels

The Love Eaters. New York, Harper, and London, Heinemann, 1954.
The Kiss of Kin. New York, Harper, and London, Heinemann, 1955.
Beulah Quintet:
　O Beulah Land. New York, Viking, and London, Heinemann, 1956.
　Know Nothing. New York, Viking, 1960; London, Heinemann, 1961.
　Prisons. New York, Putnam, 1973; as *The Long Road to Paradise,* London, Constable, 1974.
　The Scapegoat. New York, Random House, 1980.
　The Killing Ground. New York, Farrar Straus, 1982.
Fight Night on a Sweet Saturday (originally part of the Beulah Quintet). New York, Viking, 1964; London, Heinemann, 1965.
The Clam Shell. New York, Delacorte Press, and London, Bodley Head, 1971.
Blood Tie. Boston, Houghton Mifflin, 1977.

Celebration, illustrated by John Collier. New York, Farrar Straus, and London, Hutchinson, 1986.
Charley Bland. Franklin Center, Pennsylania, Franklin Library, 1989.
Choices. New York, Talese/Doubleday, 1995.

Uncollected Short Stories

"Congress Burney," in *Paris Review,* 7, 1954-55.
"The Old Wives' Tale," in *Harper's Magazine,* September 1955.
"Paragraph Eleven," in *The Girl in the Black Raincoat,* edited by George Garrett. New York, Duell, 1966.
"Coalburg, Virginia: One of the Lucky Ones," in *While Someone Else Is Eating,* edited by Earl Shorris. Garden City, Doubleday, 1984.

Other

All the Brave Promises: The Memories of Aircraft Woman 2nd Class 2146391. New York, Delacorte, and London, Heinemann, 1966.
The Story of Flight (for children), illustrated by George Evans. New York, Random House, 1967.
The Scopes Trial: The State of Tennessee v. John Thomas Scopes. New York, Watts, 1972.
Water World (for children). New York, Dutton, 1984.
Turkish Reflections: A Biography of a Place. New York, Prentice Hall, and London, Grafton, 1991.

*

Critical Studies: "The Searching Voice and Vision of Mary Lee Settle" by Peggy Bach, in *The Southern Review,* 20(4), October 1984; "Mary Lee Settle and the Tradition of Historical Fiction," in *The South Atlantic Quarterly,* 86(3), Summer 1987, and "Mary Lee Settle and the Critics" in *Virginia Quarterly Review,* 65(3), Summer 1989, both by Brian Rosenberg; *Understanding Mary Lee Settle* by George Garrett, Columbia, University of South Carolina Press, 1988; "Mary Lee Settle: 'Ambiguity of Steel'" by Jane Gentry Vance, in *American Women Writing Fiction: Memory, Identity, Family, Space,* edited by Mickey Pearlman, The University Press of Kentucky, 1989; *Mary Lee Settle's Beulah Quintet: The Price of Freedom* by Brian Rosenberg, Baton Rouge, Louisiana State University Press, 1991.

*   *   *

"First you're an unknown," Martin Myers once observed, "then you write one book and you move up to obscurity." After more than a dozen books spread over four decades, Mary Lee Settle, one of the most large-minded of American novelists, still languishes in relative obscurity, and the fault lies with the prejudices of contemporary criticism.

Out of reviewers' compulsion to impose order by corralling art within the convenience of labels, Settle, like equally undervalued southerners Elizabeth Spencer and George Garrett, has been shoved under the blanket of "southern writer," where she fails to meet imposed expectations. Why, critics demand, can't she be more baroque, like Faulkner, or tender, like Carson McCullers? Or, since her best-known work, the Beulah Quintet, is historical fiction, why can't Settle whisk us into the gothic romantic world of Margaret Mitchell?

Yet, Settle's fascination with the past, far from the exotic escapism of genre historical fiction, embodies nothing less than the quest to define the American character through a minute exploration of how it came to be formed. The picture that to this point emerges is a braided paradox: A national character shaped on the one side by hope and on the other by memory, each looking, Janus-like, in opposite directions, each guided by its own myth. On the one hand, Settle's America is founded by protean souls looking forward, to freedom, for a better life, willing to mortgage their past for a happier future. Simultaneously, its oedipal side wishes desperately to know who it is, which can only be discovered by learning where it came from.

The origins of the Beulah Quintet, which chronicles the saga of the Lacey, Catlett, and McKarkle families from the 1640s to 1980s, lie in the hero of the fourth-written of the quintet, *Promises.* Jonathan Church, fired by democratic passion for freedom, had rallied to Oliver Cromwell's rebellion against the Stuart monarchy. However, when he, like those later romantics who would at first cheer the French Revolution, grows disenchanted with Cromwell's own arrogance and refuses to bow before him, 20-year-old Church is executed in 1649.

Church's illegitimate son (by Church's aunt) emigrates to that part of the Ohio River Valley in Virginia that would later become part of West Virginia. In *O Beulah Land,* set in the years preceding the American Revolution, Church's descendant, Jonathan Lacey, settles at Beulah and achieves for a time the vision of freedom of his English ancestor. Over ensuing decades, the Laceys blend into the melting pot Beulah had become, and Settle picks up their story next in *Know Nothing,* in which Johnny Catlett, master of Beulah Plantation, under family pressure fights for the Confederacy. The next Beulah novel, *The Scapegoat,* focusing on less than one day's time in 1912, provides a wealth of richly refracted inner experience in lives caught up in the early days of labor organizing at the Lacey family's Seven Stars Coal Mine. The final piece of the quintet, *The Killing Ground* (which expands upon and is meant to replace the earlier *Fight Night on a Sweet Saturday*), clarifies the pattern evolving over the whole as descendent/novelist Hannah McKarkle, whose books bear the same titles as Settle's, comes home to Canona, West Virginia (near Beulah and strikingly like Charleston) to investigate her brother Johnny's death and, while there, explain her novels.

Whereas Settle's first two novels, *Kiss of Kin* and *The Love Eaters,* were also set in Canona and contain characters who appear in the Beulah Quintet, her *Blood Tie,* winner of the 1978 National Book Award, is set in Turkey. Yet it, as well as the weaker *Celebration* (1986), shares the quintet's attention to the need to grasp the past, even the ancient past. So too do Settle's two most recent novels, quite possibly her best: *Charley Bland* and *Choices.* The outward shape of these novels could not be more different, the former being a close-up focusing on one small, ill-fated love affair, the latter a panoramic sweep over a long and remarkable life.

We know from the first pages of *Charley Bland* that the love affair between the unnamed narrator and Charley is doomed. The lovers are enmeshed in an inviolable triangle, where character lacks strength and compassion enough to permit love to survive. "He won't marry you, you know, he never does," a woman calls out to the narrator. She'd known it from the start. In 1960, 16 years after she'd run off with a British airman and become almost immediately widowed, the narrator returns to West Virginia.

Waiting there is the dissolute Charley Bland, the town's 45-year-old ladies' man. Two decades earlier, he had been the romanticized focus of her dreams. Back then it seemed "all the wild roads led to Charley Bland. . . . He acted out our dreams of what we could hope to do when we grew up, if we only had the nerve." To her teenaged eyes, the ironically named Bland was so idealized that when he leapt into a pool "his dive was so clean there was only a parting, not a splash."

Though at 35 her eyes have matured, they gaze longingly on a past she had thus far rejected. She had cut herself off from her roots and feels desperate to return to them through Charley. He woos her ("Being with you is like being alone"). Knowing that Bland "hated and used women," the narrator nevertheless yields both body and heart to him. But then there's Mrs. Bland, Charley's mother, the third corner of this most familiar of triangles. "It is," the narrator says, "the stuff of jokes, and comic strips, and suicides. It is the mother, and the son, and the woman, whether she is holy, whore, or wife."

Mrs. Bland uses her "charm like a blunt instrument," knowing this woman too will pass and become another autographed photo in the Bland attic, leaving herself at almost 80 to hold her middle-aged son as securely as any mother with her toddler on a leash. He must return to the mother who trained him in charm rather than character, a cripple caring for a cripple until her death.

Why, then, does the narrator remain in this hopeless love affair? She tells us, "It is when the ordinary becomes luminous that we are transformed." Both Charley and Mrs. Bland are, to her adult vision, ordinary. Even their triangle is ordinary, if heartbreaking. Yet, she allows both the love affair and its tragic course to attain the quixotic luminosity her girlhood eyes would have given them because she feels a desperate need for transformation.

"I am a Southerner," she says, "and there is bred in us, as carefully as if we were prize hounds, a sense of betrayal in leaving our roots." Charley Bland, the hero of her childhood, offers the hope of atonement. He "made the past shine; what he promised without saying a word was neither of our real lives but some mutual hope. The part of me I had not let live was no longer rejected." Faced with a doomed love affair, she is nevertheless in a position where she can scarcely lose. She either fulfills her past with Charley or she gets betrayed, one betrayal atoning for another, and can put her past at peace.

The past of Melinda Kregg Dunston in Settle's *Choices* (1995), hardly needs to be put at peace, for hers has been an extraordinary and heroic life, which she recollects as spring dawns in 1993 and Melinda, 82, lies dying on the Italian coast. In 1930 Richmond, Virginia, Melinda was a bright and lovely debutante in a world that doesn't reward belles for questioning too closely the established order. Surrounded by beaus who say things like "don't worry about [exploited laborers]. Leave that to ugly women. You're much too beautiful to be high-minded," Melinda began as the naive product of a land where a mind is a terrible thing to waste on a girl.

Her father's suicide changes that. Hoping to leave his family safely rich with his insurance money, he instead turns Melinda away from safety and points her toward service, danger, and a lifetime of championing the oppressed. As she leaves Richmond, her Aunt Boodie extracts a promise that Melinda will keep: "Do *everything,*" Boodie urges.

First, Melinda becomes a Red Cross volunteer and crosses the Kentucky border to feed the starving families of coal miners. Trying to unionize, miners are starved, blacklisted, evicted, jailed, and shot by hired thugs. Melinda sees emaciated girls of 20 bent like old women and signs reading "YOUR DOGS EAT BETTER THAN OUR KIDS," and she herself lands in jail for feeding the hungry. She has lost her innocence. And she has heard from a Kentucky widow another piece of life-defining advice: "My husband used to say you can argy all day long, but when you wake up at three o'clock in the mornin a thing is either wrong or it's right, and either you take a drink or do something about it."

That advice contains the key to the empathy that guides not only Melinda's life but the moral foundation of all of Settle's fiction. Melinda may be, in fact, the personification of all Settle most powerfully believes. The coal mines provide just the first of the battlefields Melinda enters to "do something about it." In 1937, she sails for Spain to wage battle against Franco's fascism, a young woman who can speak Spanish, type, and drive ambulance trucks.

But even Kentucky's gunfire hadn't prepared her for the massive carnage she sees in Spain. Settle shows Melinda stepping over piles of corpses, working to exhaustion beside nuns with the hearts of Madonna and the mouths of sailors, rushing "to take blood from the newly dead and pump it into the veins of the dying"—all in apparent futility, as Franco is copiously supplied by Hitler and Mussolini while the democracies stand idly by. But the British physician she marries reminds her what makes even a losing battle for justice essential: "Tye said *anyway*. You do it anyway."

Her remaining battles take on more muted, autumnal tones. But she fights them with every bit as much conviction. In London, Melinda comforts victims of V-2 bombings and supports her husband's efforts to launch the National Health Service. Melinda's last active battle fittingly takes place in her native south, in 1965 Mississippi, where she heads into the Deep South as a spy in her own country to find a missing cousin who'd been working for civil rights: "I can go in disguise. . . . I'll be a white lady with a white mind and white gloves in a black Buick." The scene has changed, and it is now a woman in late middle age fighting, but the battle has always been the same, for the faces of hate, of fear at not being able to hold one's advantage, of rage at being blocked from the pursuit of happiness, are the same wherever she's been.

Though *Choices* is an eyewitness sojourn through the history of our century, the book's artistic magic, typically of Settle, lies in its details, how vividly she gives that history local habitations and names. More than that, though, we grow enrapt by Settle's richly human tapestry woven of wisdom, experience, and compassion around a woman whose heart seems to beat in constant sympathy with the hearts of others: "The day her heart refused to creak and break a little," Melinda thinks, "was the day she wanted to be dead."

So, the study of the past has brought Settle to an understanding of the present as a place where the ongoing struggle for freedom and justice must always be fought because in that fight, even when it appears futile or even suicidal, lies the key to love and the meaning of life within the human community. In one way or another, all of Settle's most realized characters have sensed that. And the best of them, like Melinda Kregg Dunston, base their lives on it.

—Andy Solomon

SHADBOLT, Maurice (Francis Richard)

Nationality: New Zealander. **Born:** Auckland, 4 June 1932. **Education:** Te Kuiti High School; Avondale College; University of Auckland. **Family:** Married 1) Gillian Heming in 1953, three sons and two daughters; 2) Barbara Magner in 1971; 3) Bridget Armstrong in 1978. **Career:** Journalist for various New Zealand publications, 1952-54; documentary scriptwriter and director for the New Zealand National Film Unit, 1954-57; full-time writer from 1957; lived in London and Spain, 1957-60, then returned to New Zealand. **Awards:** New Zealand Scholarship in Letters, 1959, 1970, 1982; Hubert Church Prose award, 1960; Katherine Mansfield award, 1963, 1967; University of Otago Robert Burns fellowship, 1963; National Association of Independent Schools award (U.S.A.), 1966; Freda Buckland award, 1969; Pacific Area Travel Association award, for non-fiction, 1971; James Wattie award, 1973, 1981, 1987; New Zealand Book award, 1981; Literary Fund travel bursary, 1988. C.B.E. (Commander, Order of the British Empire), 1989. **Agent:** Curtis Brown, 162-168 Regent Street, London W1R 5TA, England. **Address:** Box 60028, Titirangi, Auckland 7, New Zealand.

PUBLICATIONS

Novels

Among the Cinders. London, Eyre and Spottiswoode, and New York, Atheneum, 1965; revised edition, Auckland, Hodder and Stoughton, 1984.
This Summer's Dolphin. London, Cassell, and New York, Atheneum, 1969.
An Ear of the Dragon. London, Cassell, 1971.
Strangers and Journeys. London, Hodder and Stoughton, and New York, St. Martin's Press, 1972.
A Touch of Clay. London, Hodder and Stoughton, 1974.
Danger Zone. Auckland, Hodder and Stoughton, 1975; London, Hodder and Stoughton, 1976.
The Lovelock Version. Auckland and London, Hodder and Stoughton, 1980; New York, St. Martin's Press, 1981.
Season of the Jew. London, Hodder and Stoughton, 1986; New York, Norton, 1987.
Monday's Warriors. London, Hodder and Stoughton, 1990; Boston, Godine, 1992.
The House of Strife. London, Bloomsbury, 1993.

Short Stories

The New Zealanders: A Sequence of Stories. Christchurch, Whitcombe and Tombs, and London, Gollancz, 1959; New York, Atheneum, 1961.
Summer Fires and Winter Country. London, Eyre and Spottiswoode, 1963; New York, Atheneum, 1966.
The Presence of Music: Three Novellas. London, Cassell, 1967.
Figures in Light: Selected Stories. London, Hodder and Stoughton, 1979.

Play

Once on Chunuk Bair. Auckland, Hodder and Stoughton, 1982.

Other

New Zealand: Gift of the Sea, photographs by Brian Brake. Christchurch, Whitcombe and Tombs, 1963; revised edition, 1973; London, Hodder and Stoughton, 1991.

The Shell Guide to New Zealand. Christchurch, Whitcombe and Tombs, 1968; London, Joseph, 1969; revised edition, Whitcombe and Tombs, 1973; Joseph, 1976.

Isles of the South Pacific, with Olaf Ruhen. Washington, D.C., National Geographic Society, 1968.

Love and Legend: Some Twentieth Century New Zealanders. Auckland, Hodder and Stoughton, 1976.

Voices of Gallipoli. Auckland and London, Hodder and Stoughton, 1988.

Reader's Digest Guide to New Zealand, photographs by Brian Brake. Sydney, Reader's Digest, 1988.

*

Bibliography: "A Bibliography of Maurice Shadbolt 1956-1984" by Murray Gadd, in *Journal of New Zealand Literature* (Dunedin), no. 2, 1984.

Critical Study: by the author, in *Islands* (Auckland), June 1981.

Theatrical Activities:
Actor: **Film**—*Among the Cinders,* 1983.

Maurice Shadbolt comments:

I should like to say only that, as a man of my time and place, I have simply tried to make sense of both, in the course of a journey which allows no satisfying destination; my books might thus be seen as bottled messages tossed out at points along that journey. I know I might have been otherwise: I am frequently unsure why I write at all. But then I look from my study window out upon a bruised Eden, my country, and I begin again; there is no escape. My equivocal feeling for the country in which I happened to be born admits of no easy release in either a physical or literary sense. So I make, in diverse shapes, in stories and novels, my not always unhappy best of it. As a New Zealander, resident at the ragged edge of Western civilization, upon the last land of substance to be claimed by mankind, I often feel my involvement with the rest of the human race rather peripheral—as if upon a lonely floating raft. Yet fires lit upon the periphery may still illuminate the central and abiding concerns of man—the fires, I mean, which everywhere the human spirit ignites, and which everywhere shape the artist. So I make no apology. I might envy a Russian or an American—a Solzhenitsyn or a Mailer—his capacity to approach the giant themes of the 20th century. But I would not wish, really, to be otherwise. For I have tried, beyond the particularities of time and place, to observe and examine those hungers and thirsts which remain constant in man; those hungers and thirsts which, in my peripheral position, may sometimes be more evident than elsewhere.

*   *   *

Maurice Shadbolt is one of New Zealand's most prolific and popular writers of fiction. His first book, the collection of stories boldly entitled *The New Zealanders: A Sequence of Stories,* brought him almost immediate recognition. With their emphasis on the often uneasy relationship of New Zealanders in the first half of this century with their environment, these first stories foreshadow the themes of Shadbolt's subsequent writing.

A personal identification with the landscape has continued to inform his fiction. The exploration of New Zealand in terms of its history, its topographical characteristics, and its people is not, how-

ever, a mere exercise in nationalism: it exemplifies the imaginative writer's search, in a rapidly changing world, for the inner permanence afforded by conscious recognition and acceptance of one's roots.

For Shadbolt, these roots derive chiefly from a near-emotional involvement with the land. If this preoccupation with the "spirit of place" has been remarked upon frequently, it is because the visually intense depiction of his characters' relationships with their physical surroundings is one of his major strengths. There is a suggestion, in this "painterly" approach to writing, of an affinity with New Zealand's school of landscape artists and with the similar concern of the Australian novelist Patrick White to delineate in words the actual appearance as well as the feeling of life in his own country.

Following *The Presence of Music: Three Novellas,* where he used the form of the novella to examine in three complementary pieces the position of the artist in New Zealand society, Shadbolt wrote his first novel, *Among the Cinders.* Structurally loose and with a somewhat contrived ending, this light-hearted account of a run-away boy's adventures with his unconventional grandfather has been one of his most popular books.

The most typical characters in Shadbolt's earlier fiction are aimless young adults. Torn between a desire for escape from binding commitment on the one hand and for emotional security on the other, they seek but rarely find solace in personal relationships. In *This Summer's Dolphin* a variety of narrative techniques is used to investigate the troubled inner lives of several such isolated individuals. Unifying their essentially separate stories is the novel's island setting and the appearance of a friendly dolphin who, through his temporary transcendence of the characters' self-absorption, becomes a symbol with Christlike overtones.

The incorporation of easily traceable biographical material in *An Ear of the Dragon* aroused some local criticism. Nevertheless, the skilful manipulation of flashbacks to illuminate the link between an immigrant writer's adolescent experiences in wartime Italy and his difficult adjustment to New Zealand life and people make this a compelling narrative.

Strangers and Journeys, written over a period of 10 years, is a long and ambitious book. Gathering together many of the themes and characters of his previous fiction, Shadbolt details in a complex pattern of social realism the contrasting lives and aspirations of two generations of fathers and sons. There is an epic sweep to the first part of the novel with its masterly evocation of the two separate working men who, in an economically harsh era, pitted themselves against their environment and survived. This is not sustained, partly because Shadbolt himself is too close to the sons. For them, external battle against the land has given way to an even more debilitating, internal struggle to find meaning in the city.

Two shorter novels, *A Touch of Clay* and *Danger Zone,* chronicle aspects of New Zealand society in the 1970s. The former, centering on the unsatisfactory relationship between an ex-lawyer turned potter and a drug-addicted girl from a neighboring hippy commune, is emotionally unconvincing. *Danger Zone* takes as its subject New Zealand's opposition to French nuclear testing in the Pacific. The work derives its force from Shadbolt's exploration of the differing motives and attitudes of the four men who crew a small protest yacht into the Mururoa danger zone.

In *The Lovelock Version,* Shadbolt's focus turns away from contemporary society to the colonial history of New Zealand. Set amid the rugged conditions of life in 19th-century New Zealand, this is an exuberant, near-epic saga of three pioneering brothers, their families, lovers, friends and enemies. In terms of time, place, events, and people, the scope of the narrative is vast while its form is innovative. The reader is presented with an exciting, if sometimes outrageous, mixture of realism and melodrama, fact and fantasy, history and myth. Narrated in the present tense, the work is sustained by a detached, ironic style that balances the tragedies of human existence with the comedies.

Season of the Jew opens a new vein of historical writing for Shadbolt, that dealing with the Maori wars of the 1860s and the events following the escape of the formidable chief, Te Kooti, from the Chatham Islands. Thoroughly researched, the story of Te Kooti and the land wars is told from the viewpoint of one George Fairweather, a British regular in the Waikato war but also a landscape painter whose sympathies lie more with the Maori than the colonists. A carefully patterned book in which Fairweather and Te Kooti are linked by the symmetry of counterbalancing incidents, *Season of the Jew* is probably the best New Zealand historical novel yet written and Shadbolt's major work to date.

The subject of *Monday's Warriors* is again the New Zealand land wars of the 1860s. Here, the central character is Kimbal Bent, an American who, having blundered into the British army, is driven by its sadistic discipline to desert in the wilds of New Zealand. Eventually adopted as the "grandson" of the Maori chief, Titoko, Bent takes a Maori wife and fights with his adopted Taranaki tribe against his former tormentors and the land-hungry colonists. A racy adventure story marked stylistically by the use of 20th-century slang, *Monday's Warriors* is emotionally engaging but less powerful than *The Season of the Jew.* Together, these novels comprise the first two volumes of a projected trilogy.

—Cherry A. Hankin

SHARPE, Tom

Nationality: British. **Born:** Thomas Ridley Sharpe in London, 30 March 1928. **Education:** Lancing College, Sussex, 1942-46; Pembroke College, Cambridge, 1948-51, M.A.; teacher's training, Cambridge University, 1962-63, P.C.G.E. 1963. **Military Service:** Served in the Royal Marines, 1946-48. **Family:** Married Nancy Anne Looper in 1969; three daughters. **Career:** Social worker, 1951-52, and teacher, 1952-56, Natal, South Africa; photographer, Pietermaritzburg, South Africa, 1956-61; deported from South Africa on political grounds, 1961; teacher, Aylesbury Secondary Modern School, Buckinghamshire, 1961; Lecturer in History, Cambridge College of Arts and Technology, 1963-71. Since 1971, full-time writer. **Agent:** Anthony Sheil Associates, 43 Doughty Street, London, WC1N 2LF. **Address:** 38 Tunwells Lane, Great Shelford, Cambridgeshire CB2 5LJ, England.

PUBLICATIONS

Novels

Riotous Assembly. London, Secker and Warburg, 1971; New York, Viking Press, 1972.
Indecent Exposure. London, Secker and Warburg, 1973; New York, Atlantic Monthly Press, 1987.

Porterhouse Blue. London, Secker and Warburg, and Englewood Cliffs, New Jersey, Prentice Hall, 1974.
Blott on the Landscape. London, Secker and Warburg, 1975; New York, Vintage, 1984.
Wilt. London, Secker and Warburg, 1976; New York, Vintage, 1984.
The Great Pursuit. London, Secker and Warburg, 1977; New York, Harper, 1984.
The Throwback. London, Secker and Warburg, 1978; New York, Vintage, 1984.
The Wilt Alternative. London, Secker and Warburg, 1979; New York, St. Martin's Press, 1981(?).
Ancestral Vices. London, Secker and Warburg, 1980.
Vintage Stuff. London, Secker and Warburg, 1982; New York, Vintage, 1984.
Wilt on High. London, Secker and Warburg, 1984; New York, Random House, 1985.

Plays

The South African (produced London, 1961).

Television Play: *She Fell among Thieves,* from the novel by Dornford Yates, 1978.

*　　*　　*

Tom Sharpe's comic vision was formed under the pressure of state persecution strong enough to infuriate but not crush him. His initial satires on South Africa set the pattern for all his subsequent fiction. These early works draw their energy from the seditious author's deportation from South Africa in 1961.

Sharpe's first published novel, *Riotous Assembly,* is as funny as anything he has written. It has as its hero the tormented Anglophile policeman Kommandant Van Heerden. Van Heerden's feud with his scheming subordinate Verkramp (a fanatic Boer) and the murderous blunderings of Konstabel Els are one source of black merriment. Another is the degenerate world of the upper-class English colonials. Bungling authoritarian institutions and the English ruling class reappear as black beasts in all Sharpe's later novels. *Indecent Exposure* is a straight sequel, with the same principal characters as *Riotous Assembly* and the same "Piemburg" setting. Its comedy, however, is even broader. (At one point in the narrative the whole of Van Heerden's police force is subjected to electric shock therapy and converted to rampant homosexuality.)

After this novel, Sharpe evidently felt his South African vein was exhausted. *Porterhouse Blue* is set in a Cambridge college. Most of the plot revolves around the maneuverings of a reform and a reactionary faction. There is the usual play with comic ruthlessness and sexual perversions. (One comic climax has the quad full of inflated condoms.) In the largest sense, *Porterhouse Blue* can be read as a satire on English life, and its resistance to change. *Blott on the Landscape* is more straightforwardly funny. The central joke of the narrative is the modernization of Handyman Hall from stately home to theme park. The vivaciously homicidal lady of the house, Maude Lynchwood, is particularly well done.

With his next novel, *Wilt,* Sharpe created his most durable hero. The first in the series presents Henry Wilt as a henpecked and downtrodden lecturer at "Fenland College" (based transparently on the polytechnic where Sharpe himself taught). There is some effective incidental comedy on Wilt's futile attempts to educate a day release class of butchers ("Meat One"). But the main plot concerns

Henry's involvement in suspected murder, following his witnessed disposal of a life-size sex doll which he accidentally came by. This leads to an epic struggle of will with the long-suffering Inspector Flint. Flint and Wilt reappear in *The Wilt Alternative,* which embroils the hero with international terrorists who mount a siege in his house. Wilt's murderously maternal wife Eva makes a notable comic appearance in this novel. *Wilt on High* (which brings in Greenham Common-style peace protesters) suggests that a whole saga may evolve around the misadventures of Sharpe's most likeable hero.

The Great Pursuit returns to the high Cambridge of *Porterhouse Blue.* The title plays on the titles of Cambridge critic F.R. Leavis's best known works. And Sharpe's novel is a jaundiced burlesque on the Leavisite disdain for merely popular literature. The story has a female don of austere critical rectitude who clandestinely writes pulp romance. An ingenuous acolyte, Peter Piper, is manipulated into fronting for her and undertakes an American promotional tour. Cantabrigian snobbishness and transatlantic vulgarity are comically opposed, with the usual fiendish plot complications.

The Throwback is a routine Sharpe comedy on the British rural gentry, and their inextinguishable capacity for survival even among the persecutions of a democratic age and modern world. *Ancestral Vices* has much the same theme. Walden Yapp, an American professor of demotic historiography, is hired to write the family history of the Petrefacts. In their native Vale of Bushampton, he discovers unspeakable sexual horrors underlying their prosperity. *Ancestral Vices* is probably the nastiest of Sharpe's novels, with some incredibly tasteless comedy on the subject of dwarves. But the rule of his fiction is that the more offensive to common decency, the funnier it is. *Vintage Stuff* finds Sharpe in the territory of the English public school. The novel climaxes in a chase across France, and a chateau siege. (Chases and sieges recur in many of Sharpe's narratives.) Again, the novel comically testifies to the indestructibility and the simultaneous awfulness of England's upper classes.

The main influence on Sharpe's fiction is clearly early Evelyn Waugh. Unlike the mature Waugh, Sharpe seems still to be waiting for something to believe in, to ballast the otherwise increasingly brittle negativities of his fiction. But for his admirers (they remain almost exclusively cis-Atlantic, incidentally) it is probably enough that he is consistently the most amusing novelist writing.

—John Sutherland

SHEED, Wilfrid (John Joseph)

Nationality: American. **Born:** London, England, 27 December 1930; emigrated to the United States in 1940. **Education:** Downside Academy, Bath; Lincoln College, Oxford, B.A. 1954, M.A. 1957. **Family:** Married Miriam Ungerer; three children. **Career:** Film critic, 1957-61, and associate editor, 1959-66, *Jubilee* magazine, New York; drama critic and book editor, *Commonweal* magazine, New York, 1964-67; film critic, *Esquire* magazine, New York, 1967-69; Visiting Lecturer in Creative Arts, Princeton University, New Jersey, 1970-71; columnist, *New York Times Book Review,* 1971-75. Judge, Book-of-the-Month Club, 1972-88. **Agent:** International Creative Management, 40 West 57th Street, New York, New York 10019. **Address:** Rysam and High Streets, Sag Harbor, New York 11963, U.S.A.

PUBLICATIONS

Novels

A Middle Class Education. Boston, Houghton Mifflin, 1960; London, Cassell, 1961.
The Hack. New York, Macmillan, and London, Cassell, 1963.
Square's Progress. New York, Farrar Straus, and London, Cassell, 1965.
Office Politics. New York, Farrar Straus, 1966; London, Cassell, 1967.
Max Jamison. New York, Farrar Straus, 1970; as *The Critic,* London, Weidenfeld and Nicolson, 1970.
People Will Always Be Kind. New York, Farrar Straus, 1973; London, Weidenfeld and Nicolson, 1974.
Transatlantic Blues. New York, Dutton, 1978; London, Sidgwick and Jackson, 1979.
The Boys of Winter. New York, Knopf, 1987.

Short Stories

The Blacking Factory, and Pennsylvania Gothic: A Short Novel and a Long Story. New York, Farrar Straus, 1968; London, Weidenfeld and Nicolson, 1969.

Other

Joseph. New York, Sheed and Ward, 1958.
The Morning After (essays). New York, Farrar Straus, 1971.
Three Mobs: Labor, Church and Mafia. New York, Sheed and Ward, 1974.
Muhammad Ali. New York, Crowell, and London, Weidenfeld and Nicolson, 1975.
The Good Word and Other Words (essays). New York, Dutton, 1978; London, Sidgwick and Jackson, 1979.
Clare Boothe Luce. New York, Dutton, and London, Weidenfeld and Nicolson, 1982.
Frank and Maisie: A Memoir with Parents. New York, Simon and Schuster, 1985; London, Chatto and Windus, 1986.
The Kennedy Legacy: A Generation Later, photographs by Jacques Lowe. New York and London, Viking, 1988.
Essays in Disguise. New York, Knopf, 1990.
Baseball and Lesser Sports. New York, HarperCollins, 1991.
My Life as a Fan. New York, Simon and Schuster, 1993.

Editor, *Essays and Poems,* by G.K. Chesterton. London, Penguin, 1958.
Editor, *Sixteen Short Novels.* New York, Dutton, 1985.

*   *   *

Wilfrid Sheed is an acute cultural historian, critic, and satirist who has mapped out a special province of Anglo-American life as his own. His novels are polished comedies of manners on highly serious topics: the degeneracy of the "communications industry" in all its forms, the anxiety of Roman Catholics in a secularized society, the profound alienation of individuals who find themselves trapped between two cultures.

Beginning with *A Middle Class Education,* Sheed deals with the failure of both schooling and learning, especially the vaunted British public school and university system, a major target of satire recurring in *The Blacking Factory* and *Transatlantic Blues*. In *The Hack* Sheed combines two favorite subjects—the failure of the Roman Catholic church in the modern world and the variegated follies of modern communications media. The story tracks hapless Bert Flax, a freelance writer grinding out theological pulp for popular religious magazines. *Office Politics* focuses half of this theme on Gilbert Twining, a writer for a struggling popular magazine, in an extended study of self-deception in life and literature.

Behind the vaudevillian comic turns Sheed constructs are serious investigations of alienated, self-divided individuals in a world with little solace or aid. Fred and Alison Cope (who, of course, *can't* cope) in *Square's Progress* try to flee the confines of their middle-class educations and marriage for beat-bohemian-hippy freedoms, only to find the hip life as empty and sharp-cornered as suburbia. *Max Jamison* charts another hack writer's attempts to understand his own unravelling life. Max, a magazine critic, finds himself unable to reconcile his vocation with his desires, although writing criticism has been his life's goal: "The difference between a critic and a reviewer is, I forget . . . I've always wanted to be a critic. Yes, really. Like wanting to be a dentist or an undertaker. Some kids are funny that way. No, ma'am, I have never wanted to write creatively. I was an unnatural little boy in many ways. The rumor that I used to torture flies probably contains some truth. I did write a poem once, in alexandrines, but I didn't much care for it. Yes, it's in my wallet now."

People Will Always Be Kind observes the anomalies and aberrations of American politics in the early 1970s through a journalistic point of view, a mock-biography of an Irish Catholic presidential candidate feeling profound conflicts between religious, moral, and political realities. The novel is divided between a view of Brian Casey's personal and political life and the ruminations of a political hack writer, Sam Perkins, so Sheed again analyzes the failure of journalism, of writing, to capture the subtleties of life.

In *Transatlantic Blues* Sheed pulls together many early satiric themes. In some ways, the novel inverts and expands the brilliant short novel *The Blacking Factory*, detailing the schizophrenic development of Pendrid "Monty" Chatworth, a TV talk-show host educated in Britain and working in the U.S. Chatworth, a Roman Catholic, dictates the novel in the form of a sprawling mock-confession, a litany of the sins and disasters of his life. The conflicts between a British identity (Pendrid) and an American one (Monty), between high British culture (Oxford) and U.S. popular culture (TV ratings), between Catholicism and secular fame, make the novel painful as well as comic. Pendrid is another version of the "hack writer," the "office politician," the Anglo-American accepted in neither world, the Catholic who finds no solace in the church and who is rejected by the secular-Protestant culture in which he is immersed.

In *The Boys of Winter,* Sheed constructs a clever intellectual comedy based on analogies between writing, publishing, sexual pursuit, and sandlot softball. Set in a Long Island writer's haven, it chronicles a "hot stove league" of hack writers and their editor, Jonathan Oglethorpe, who organizes and coaches them to compete against a visiting Hollywood film crew. The skein of satire involves parallels between macho gamesmanship and schlock-merchandizing, a theme which provokes Sheed to some of his most penetrating analysis of American literary culture.

Sheed's acute ear for both British and American speech (and thought), his ability to parody popular idioms in journalism, his serious questions about education, the content of popular culture, the role of the Roman Catholic church in a secularized society all make him one of the most penetrating satirists of our day. His specific view of the world in which rootlessness, divorce, and flamboyant failure are imposed against the old values of work, stability, marriage, and modest success gives his novels a sharp edge and clarity, the bite of classic satire.

—William J. Schafer

SHIELDS, Carol

Nationality: Canadian and American. **Born:** Carol Warner, Oak Park, Illinois, 2 June 1935. **Education:** Hanover College, Indiana, 1953-57, A.B.; University of Ottawa, 1969-75, M.A. **Family:** Married Donald Shields, 1957; four daughters, one son. **Career:** Editorial assistant, *Canadian Slavonic Papers,* 1972-74; faculty member, University of Ottawa, 1976-77, and University of British Columbia, 1978-79. Since 1980, faculty member, University of Manitoba. **Awards:** Canada Council grant, 1972, 1974, 1976; Canadian Authors Association prize, 1976, for *Small Ceremonies;* Governor General's award for fiction, 1993; National Book Critics Circle award, 1994; Pulitzer prize for fiction, 1995. Honorary doctorate: University of Ottawa, 1995. **Agent:** Bella Pomer, 22 Shallmar Blvd., Toronto, Ontario M5N 2Z8, Canada. **Address:** 701-237 Wellington Cr., Winnipeg, Manitoba R3M 0A1, Canada.

Publications

Novels

Small Ceremonies. Toronto, McGraw Hill Ryerson, 1976; London, Fourth Estate, 1995.
The Box Garden. Toronto, McGraw Hill Ryerson, 1977; London, Fourth Estate, 1995.
Happenstance. Toronto, McGraw Hill Ryerson, 1980; with *A Fairly Conventional Woman,* London, Fourth Estate, 1993, New York, Viking, 1994.
A Fairly Conventional Woman. Toronto, Macmillan Canada, 1982; with *Happenstance,* London, Fourth Estate, 1993, New York, Viking, 1994.
Swann: A Mystery. Don Mills, Ontario, Stoddart, 1987; New York, Viking, 1989; London, Fourth Estate, 1992.
A Celibate Season, with Blanche Howard. N.p., Coteau, 1991.
The Republic of Love. Toronto, Random House Canada, New York, Viking, and London, Fourth Estate, 1992.
The Stone Diaries. Toronto, Random House Canada, and London, Fourth Estate, 1993; New York, Viking, 1994.

Short Stories

Various Miracles. Don Mills, Ontario, Stoddart, 1985; New York, Viking, 1989; London, Fourth Estate, 1994.
The Orange Fish. Toronto, Random House Canada, 1989; New York, Viking, 1990.

Plays

Arrivals and Departures. N.p., Blizzard, 1990.
Thirteen Hands. N.p., Blizzard, 1993.

Poetry

Others. Ottawa, Borealis Press, 1972.
Intersect. Ottawa, Borealis Press, 1974.
Coming to Canada. N.p., Carleton University Press, 1992.

Other

Susanna Moodie: Voice and Vision. Ottawa, Borealis Press, 1976.

*

Manuscript Collection: National Library of Canada.

Carol Shields comments:

My novels have centred on half a dozen concerns: the lives of women, notions of gender, the force of time, the genesis of art, synchronicity, the relationship of fiction and biography.

*   *   *

Carol Shields adds something to a traditional theme of contemporary women writers: the difficulty of negotiating the gender gap. She explores this territory with signature-style humor and optimism. She does not perceive the problem with any less acuity for her funniness; she only gives her characters a likable resilience. Her writing uses a form of black humor that incites a giggle just because it so categorically refuses to romanticize the situation. Absurdity, satire, paradox, and mistaken identity are also the source of much pleasure.

Small Ceremonies and *The Box Garden* are twin novels, much in the vein of another famous Canadian writer, Margaret Laurence. In fact, some of the characters of the Shields novels overlap with Laurence's: for instance, the martyring, fussbudgety, stingy, widowed, emotional-blackmailing, and wickedly funny mother of two grown daughters; and the two daughters themselves, one married with kids and living a life that looks full and enviable to her single sister—one out west in Vancouver, the other back home near mom in Manitoba. One novel per sister. Although the married sister doesn't often think of the single one, the single sister's envy is palpable. Thus Shields is very derivative of Margaret Laurence's *A Jest of God* and *The Fire-Dwellers*. The trick is that once you have read the narrative of the lucky, married sister, you know her jealous sister's vision is skewed. The marriage isn't so rosy, communication isn't so flourishing, and romance isn't so hot as the sister thought.

This intertextuality makes good suspense and enriches the plot for one who reads both novels. Shields does not hide her derivativeness but rather makes the derivative nature of writing theme and plot the subject of many jokes throughout her canon. Her main characters are all writers of some description, and each one commits a fraud, an infringement, a plagiarism, or a distortion in the course of plying a trade. According to one of her characters, who has stolen the plot of his best-seller from a novel written by his graduate student (who in turn ripped it off from her former landlord), there are only seven plots in the world, so you might as well make use of them. The resemblance of *The Box Garden* and *Small Ceremonies* in plot and character to Laurence's early work affected this reader—a Canadianist—in a pleasurable, comforting way, somewhat like the feeling of the scholar when encountering the repetition of facts already familiar to her: the sense that she is beginning to know the field.

In the 1980s, Shields tried a new genre: mystery. With this shift in direction, her writing gained individuality and force. *Swann: A Mystery* is a hilarious send-up of academics, biographers, critics, archivists, book collectors, and conferenciers. Each of the four main characters has an interest in deceased poet Mary Swann. Each one's literary interest is adulterated by his or her own ambitions. But someone is stealing, buying, and destroying all of the remaining Swann manuscripts and artifacts, making it difficult for the others to carry on the international Swann conference with dignity. Perhaps Shields's criminal is not as difficult for the reader to identify as those in the best of Sherlock Holmes or Agatha Christie, but what Shields provides is a romp through the corruptions of the book business and an exposé of the average psyche: the small lies that normal people tell, the little corners that they cut, and their rationalizations that help make their behavior seem acceptable in the context of the lonely, bookish lives they lead. "Who would ever know?" is the question, not "Is this right or wrong?"

Although *The Stone Diaries* won the Pulitzer Prize and the Governor General's Award, it is not her best novel. In the attempt to tell the stories of too many uneventful lives from too many points of view, much of Shields's native irony, twisty plots, and light-hearted sarcasm disappears. Perhaps the historical or genealogical epic is not her genre.

Shields's skills as a short story writer are strong, yet she seems to have peaked in 1985, with the publication of *Various Miracles,* and faltered by the time *The Orange Fish* was published in 1989. The first volume contains several gems. The subject about which Shields writes best is mother-daughter relationships that are full of ambivalence yet founded on unshakable love and understanding. The mother-daughter bond is so much more profound or real than the man-woman connection that the latter is nearly always a source of jest. Nor is the preference meant to show favoritism of the female; rather it honors the bonding of women and of motherhood while questioning the strength of most romantic female-male ties. Shields shows her characters, especially the "sensitive one of the family," relating to, identifying with, and rebelling against their mothers but always returning later to seek them out, to question, to support, to respect, and to understand.

Shields's themes are typical of postmodern fiction: mother-daughter symbiosis; husband-wife estrangement; the inventiveness of the writer; the pretentiousness of the academy; loneliness and our anger at our aloneness; the role that chance plays in all encounters and happenings, good or bad. Her writer-protagonists are so literary that, in the end, they see their own selves as characters in a book. Successful feminist critic Sarah Maloney suddenly chooses marriage because she wants to live a good metaphor. Anatomizing her psyche, she says of "the irrepressible Sarah," her academic self, "Her awful energy seems to require too much of me, and I wonder: Where is her core? Does she even have a core? I want to live for a time without irony, without rhetoric, in a cool, solid metaphor. A conch shell, that would be nice."

Shields herself cannot live without irony, a fact for which her readers should be grateful.

—Andy Solomon

SIDHWA, Bapsi

Nationality: American (Pakistani exile, emigrated to United States, 1984). **Born:** Bapsi Bhandara, Karachi, Pakistan, 11 August 1938.

Education: Kinnaird College for Women, B.A. 1956. **Family:** Married 1) Gustad Kermani, 1957 (died); 2) Noshir R. Sidhwa, 1963; has three children. **Career:** Conducted novel writing workshops, Rice University, 1984-86; assistant professor of creative writing, University of Houston, 1985. President, International Women's Club of Lahore, 1975-77. Pakistan's delegate to Asian Women's Congress, 1975. **Agent:** Elizabeth Grossman, Sterling Lord Literary Agency Inc., 1 Madison Ave, New York, New York 10021, U.S.A. **Address:** 1600 Massachusetts Ave., #603, Cambridge, Massachusetts 02138, U.S.A.

PUBLICATIONS

Novels

The Crow Eaters. Lahore, Pakistan, Imani Press, 1978; London, Cape, 1980; New York, St. Martin's Press, 1983.
The Bride. New York, St. Martin's Press, and London, Cape, 1983.
Ice-Candy-Man. London, Heinemann, 1988; as *Cracking India,* Minneapolis, Milkweed Editions, 1991.
An American Brat. Minneapolis, Milkweed Editions, 1993; London, Penguin, 1994.

*   *   *

With the publication of her third novel, *Ice-Candy-Man* (or *Cracking India*), Bapsi Sidhwa established herself as Pakistan's leading English-language novelist. Pakistan is the location of Sidhwa's first three novels, and in each there is a strong sense of place and community which she uses to examine the post-colonial Pakistani identity. In her novel *The American Brat* she shifts the predominant locale of her fiction from Lahore and Pakistan to various cities across America as she explores the Parsi/Pakistani diaspora. Multiple alternative voices are heard in Sidhwa's fiction through her choice of narrators and characters from Pakistan's minority communities—members of the Parsi religion, Kohistanis from Pakistan's Tribal Territories, and, perhaps most importantly, women.

Sidhwa's first three novels, although very different from one another, share what Anita Desai has described as "a passion for history and for truth telling." And in each her desire to understand the terrible events of the Partition of the Indian sub-continent in 1947 and the subsequent birth of Pakistan as a nation is evident. Her first-published novel, *The Crow Eaters,* is a delightfully rambunctious comedy in which Faredoon Junglewalla tells the story of his life and times from the turn of the century to the eve of Partition. In common with such a writer as Salman Rushdie, Sidhwa believes that in order to understand any single event it is necessary to consider the many events which led up to it. Like the author herself, Faredoon is a Parsi and his story takes the reader to the heart of that minority community. The focus on the Parsis, their rites, and customs, not only provides a rich subject in itself, but also an ideal vehicle for observing the history of India, and in particular the events played out between Hindus, Sikhs, and Muslims, from a detached yet intimate insider/outsider perspective. Through the contact Faredoon and his family have with other groups in India (including the British) a picture of the whole is skillfully created. But always, behind her panoramic canvas, history ticks away and moves the reader gradually but inexorably towards 1947.

Whereas *The Crow Eaters* ends with the horrors of Partition still to come, *The Bride* (or *The Pakistani Bride,* her second published

novel, but actually written before *The Crow Eaters*) uses those horrors as its starting point, and thus focuses on the first chapter of Pakistan's history as an independent nation. In this novel Sidhwa again makes use of a detached and marginalized character from one of Pakistan's minority groups. She uses Qasim, a Kohistani tribesman, as her window onto the period of history she treats. After witnessing a brutal attack on a train of refugees (a common Partition motif), Qasim adopts a young girl left orphaned by the massacre. When, years later, he takes Zaitoon to his ancestral village to be married, Sidhwa demonstrates the extent of the cultural divisions which exist within the newly drawn political boundaries of Pakistan, and in doing so raises questions about the construction of national identity. Her focus on the relationship between dominant and minority communities in Pakistan is extended specifically to include gender relations, which indeed is a strong theme in all her fiction.

In both *The Crow Eaters* and *The Bride,* Partition is a significant event without being the main subject of either novel. But in *Ice-Candy-Man*—which is revisionist history of Partition from a Pakistani perspective, and major contribution to the growing list of novels which treat Partition—Sidhwa meets that terrible event head-on. Here Sidhwa returns to the Parsi community and chooses Lenny, a young Parsi girl with polio, as her narrator. The political and historical consciousness of her previous novels reaches a pinnacle in this novel, and the young narrator, naive, innocent, and free of the various prejudices an older narrator would be subject to, proves to be an ideal means of exposing the complexities of the period. The frequent intertextual referencing in *Ice-Candy-Man* is testament to Sidhwa's dual literary heritage, but more significantly, her use of Eugene O'Neill's play *The Iceman Cometh,* which provides both the title and the framework for *Ice-Candy-Man,* insists on the importance of fiction as a shaping force of history, and lends one more twist to Sidhwa's exploration of the nature of truth.

In her richly comic novel *An American Brat,* Sidhwa chronicles the departure of Feroza Ginwalla—a member of the Junglewalla clan first encountered in *The Crow Eaters*—from an increasingly fundamentalist Pakistan of the late 1970s and her subsequent exposure to American culture. More than simply the tale of a young girl coming of age, it shows Feroza coming to terms with her identity in the increasingly diasporic climate of the late 20th century. Sidhwa convincingly handles the personal growth of her central character and the difficulties that arise when two cultures come into contact. This novel, with its focus on diaspora, is a logical extension of the interest in displacement and the clashes between communities which is present in all her previous three novels.

—Ralph J. Crane

SIGAL, Clancy

Nationality: American. **Born:** Chicago, Illinois, 6 September 1926. **Education:** The University of California, Los Angeles, B.A. in English 1950. Staff Sergeant in the United States Army Infantry, 1944-46. **Career:** Assistant to the Wage Coordinator, United Auto Workers, Detroit, 1946-47; story analyst, Columbia Pictures, Hollywood, 1952-54; agent, Jaffe Agency, Los Angeles, 1954-56. Member, Citizens Committee to Defend American Freedoms, Los Angeles, 1953-56, and Group 68, Americans in Britain Against the Indo-China War. Has lived in England since 1957. **Awards:** Houghton Mifflin Literary fellowship, 1962. **Agent:** Elaine Greene Ltd., 37 Goldhawk Road, London W12 8QQ. **Address:** 58 Willes Road, London N.W.5, England.

PUBLICATIONS

Novels

Weekend in Dinlock. Boston, Houghton Mifflin, and London, Secker and Warburg, 1960.
Going Away: A Report, A Memoir. Boston, Houghton Mifflin, 1962; London, Cape, 1963.
Zone of the Interior. New York, Crowell, 1976.
The Secret Defector. New York, HarperCollins, 1992.

Uncollected Short Story

"Doctor Marfa," in *Paris Review 35,* Fall 1965.

Play

Radio Play: *A Visit with Rose,* 1983.

*   *   *

Two documentary novels, *Weekend in Dinlock* and *Going Away,* have given Clancy Sigal a large reputation. These novels, imaginative fusions of autobiography, social history and fiction, convey a strong sense of time and place, a powerful feeling of reality.

Going Away (Sigal's first novel, though revised and published after *Weekend in Dinlock*) is subtitled "A Report, A Memoir." It is a compendium of significant social and political observations, an "American Studies" novel answering the question, "*What's it like in America these days?*" The time is 1956, the opening days of the Hungarian Revolt, and the autobiographical narrator drives from Los Angeles to New York with the manuscript of a confessional novel, experiencing a nervous breakdown as he passes through America and reviews his past. It is an "on-the-road" novel, a pursuit of lost time, a gathering of the narrator's experiences and a diagnosis of America's spiritual and political malaise: "For years, possibly since adolescence, I have dryly and studiously examined the indications of my own life as a clue to the country at large, as though reading a psychic thermometer."

The narrator is half-Irish, half-Jewish, a radical ex-union-organizer, an ex-Hollywood-agent, an ex-soldier in Occupied Germany; by age 29 he has led half a dozen full, complex lives and reached the end of his road in America. He realizes he must leave America in order to find it. He visits old friends and enemies, sees them in despair and collapse, so he flees his dead past encapsulated in an America of brutalizing forces—billboards, highways, movies, the blank, alienating face of capitalist culture.

Once in England, where he finished *Going Away,* Sigal also wrote a much smaller but beautifully articulated study of Yorkshire mines and miners, *Weekend in Dinlock.* A documentary study of a composite mining village in the midlands, the book compares favorably with George Orwell's classic *The Road to Wigan Pier.* It chronicles the miner's life in the nationalized mines and draws almost the same conclusion Orwell made a generation earlier—that mining is an atrocity, a deadening, dehumanizing torment on which all industrial civilization rests. The novel is also the story of Davie, a Lawrence-like young man who is both a gifted painter and a miner, caught between the need to paint, to escape Dinlock, and the powerful *machismo* ethic of the miners which demands that he stay on the job and prove himself at the coal face. Finally, the narrator leaves Davie wrestling with his irresolvable conflict, still trapped by Dinlock.

This brilliant small study is a logical extension of *Going Away.* The narrator has fled America and found in England's coal country yet another world of dehumanizing technology and alienated individuals. The wide-open feeling of crossing America (the loneliness of the land itself) is replaced by the paranoid claustrophobia of the mine shaft and the paranoid closed society of the provincial village. Both novels chronicle the pressures of modern life on the individual, both reflect Sigal's own history: "I was a member, in good standing, of the Double Feature Generation: nothing new was startling to me." Sigal, in *Going Away,* gives the intense, confessional view of the 1950s in the backwash of McCarthyism, the collapse of the old left, and draws conclusions about his own sense of self: "I see no salvation in personal relationships, in political action, or in any job I might undertake in society. Everything in me cries out that we are meaningless pieces of paste; everything in me hopes this is not the end of the story."

Zone of the Interior carries forward Sigal's odyssey into the 1960s, exploring a subculture of artists and dropouts. An R.D. Laing-like protagonist observes the disintegration of culture and personality in British society of the time. The world has gone thoroughly mad, and the personal experience of insanity, first encountered in *Going Away,* seems less scarifying against a background of general disillusionment, drugs, and the cornucopia of therapeutic theories that promise personal salvation in the face of apocalypse.

—William J. Schafer

SILKO, Leslie Marmon

Nationality: American. **Born:** 1948. **Education:** Board of Indian Affairs schools, Laguna, New Mexico, and a Catholic school in Albuquerque; University of New Mexico, Albuquerque, B.A. (summa cum laude) in English 1969; studied law briefly. **Family:** Has two sons. **Career:** Taught for 2 years at Navajo Community College, Tsaile, Arizona; lived in Ketchikan, Alaska, for 2 years; taught at University of New Mexico. Since 1978 professor of English, University of Arizona, Tucson. **Awards:** National Endowment for the Arts award, 1974; *Chicago Review* award, 1974; Pushcart prize, 1977; MacArthur Foundation grant, 1983. **Address:** Department of English, University of Arizona, Tucson, Arizona 85721, U.S.A.

PUBLICATIONS

Novel

Ceremony. New York, Viking Press, 1977.
Almanac of the Dead. New York, Simon and Schuster, 1991.

Uncollected Short Stories

"Bravura" and "Humaweepi, the Warrior Priest," in *The Man to Send Rain Clouds: Contemporary Stories by American Indians,* edited by Kenneth Rosen. New York, Viking Press, 1974.
"Laughing and Loving," in *Come to Power,* edited by Dick Lourie. Trumansburg, New York, Crossing Press, 1974.
"Private Property," in *Earth Power Coming,* edited by Simon J. Ortiz. Tsaile, Arizona, Navajo Community College Press, 1983.

Play

Lullaby, with Frank Chin, adaptation of the story by Silko (produced San Francisco, 1976).

Poetry

Laguna Woman. Greenfield Center, New York, Greenfield Review Press, 1974.
Storyteller (includes short stories). New York, Seaver, 1981.

Other

The Delicacy and Strength of Lace: Letters Between Leslie Marmon Silko and James A. Wright, edited by Anne Wright. St. Paul, Minnesota, Graywolf Press, 1986.
Yellow Woman, edited by Melody Graulich. New Brunswick, New Jersey, Rutgers University Press, 1993.

*

Manuscript Collection: University of Arizona, Tucson.

Critical Studies: *Leslie Marmon Silko* by Per Seyersted, Boise, Idaho, Boise State University, 1980; *Four American Indian Literary Masters* by Alan R. Velie, Norman, University of Oklahoma Press, 1982.

*   *   *

Through her works Leslie Marmon Silko has defined herself as a Native American writer, concentrating on ethnic themes, motifs, and genres. She had already established a minor reputation as a short story writer when she published her novel *Ceremony,* which, along with N. Scott Momaday's *House Made of Dawn,* is one of the two most important novels in modern Native American literature.

Like the earlier novel, *Ceremony* focuses on a young American Indian who, under somewhat similar circumstances, struggles to realign himself with traditional Indian culture and reservation life after having been torn away. Tayo, Silko's half-Laguna, half-Anglo protagonist, returns to his New Mexico reservation just after World War II. The horrors of the war against the Japanese in the Philippine jungles have led him to the brink of insanity and the mental ward of a veterans' hospital. Back home, he is in constant danger of succumbing to mental illness as he faces a sad, apparently hopeless life. His half-breed status among his own people and the legacy of shame from his promiscuous mother, now dead, exacerbate the pain of living among a dispossessed people who are constantly reminded of their lost heritage. He associates with fellow veterans who fill their meaningless lives with alcohol and anecdotes about

their sexual exploits among white women during the war, and he observes Indian prostitutes and winos in scenes of skid-row squalor that remind him of his own ruined mother. Guided by Betonie, an old medicine man, Tayo finds a helpmeet in a sort of Indian earth-goddess figure and gradually proceeds through the series of mystical ceremonies and rituals that will make him whole again, and in the process he outwits the witchcraft of his evil antagonist Emo.

Storyteller, an anthology of tribal folk tales, short stories, family anecdotes, photographs, and poems, demonstrated Silko's continuing fascination with narrative, but fourteen years passed before she published her second novel, *Almanac of the Dead.* The reason for the interlude is obvious: *Almanac* is massive and ambitious. This apocalyptic novel, set in the unspecified present, describes the collapse of white European-American civilization and the resurgence of Native American peoples. It is divided into six sections: "The United States of America," "Mexico," "Africa," "The Americas," "The Fifth World", and "One World, Many Tribes." The main action begins at a heavily fortified ranch near Tucson, Arizona, and focuses on the characters Lecha and Zeta, 60-year-old twin sisters of Mexican extraction and grand-daughters of Yoeme, a Yaqui woman who escaped a death sentence for sedition in 1918. Lecha is a psychic with visionary powers. Zeta, with Lecha's estranged son Ferro, directs an operation for smuggling drugs, illegal immigrants, and arms. The sisters inherit from Yoeme an ancient, fragmentary almanac of tribal narratives which, Yoeme believed, contains a mysterious power "that would bring all the tribal people of the Americas together to retake the land." The working out of this prophecy generates the novel's plot as a whole, and at the open-ended conclusion, a series of bombings and murders in Tucson coincides with a gathering of shamans and would-be revolutionaries while in Mexico an army of disfranchised Indians begins to march north. But in developing this overall scheme, Silko weaves together multiple interrelated tales and anecdotes, employing about 70 characters and a wide range of settings. The overall movement toward the destruction of decadent Western culture in North America is associated with the rapid decline of late capitalism predicted by Marx.

As a Native American writer, Silko deals with the usual dichotomies: white culture is cruel, artificial, dead, cut off from nature, based on greed; traditional Indian culture is holistic, natural, communal. However, Silko is by no means simple-minded in working within this framework of values, and she is a close observer of both nature and human nature.

Like many contemporary writers, Silko experiments with the narrative line, weaving in and out of chronological time as she explores the consciousness of her characters. However, her habitual use of what she takes to be the Indian concept of reality—or at least one's experience of reality—as narrative (or myth) enables her to avoid the morbid extremes of self-consciousness that can result from an analysis of the narrative process. She begins *Ceremony* with a description of Thought-Woman, the spider, "sitting in her room/thinking of a story now/I'm telling you the story she is thinking." In *Almanac of the Dead* the visionary or mystical mode of storytelling is represented by the almanac itself, as well as by the visionary Lecha and by a character named Tacho, who offers prophecies about "The Reign of the Fire-Eye Macaw" (the present era).

The success of *Ceremony* was largely due to Silko's ability to deal convincingly with Indian traditions and myth while recognizing the demands of psychological realism and exercising a strict control over her narrative art. *Almanac of the Dead* is extremely ambitious but uneven and finally unsatisfying as a work of fiction:

narrative control seems to break down toward the end of the novel as realism is sacrificed to apocalyptic vision.

Silko, of Laguna Pueblo, Mexican, and Anglo descent, has become more than a personal, tribal, or even regional writer: she is an important figure in Native American literature. As such, she writes for two audiences: the small group of readers who identify with her ethnic background and share her Indian sensibilities and the general readers who, regardless of their sympathy for Indian problems and concerns, find her works somewhat exotic. Indeed, this exotic quality provides a large part of their appeal. Silko herself reveals insights into her art of storytelling in the series of letters she exchanged with James Wright prior to that writer's death in 1980, published as *Delicacy and Strength of Lace*. Since the image of the Indian has always been problematic in American culture—with strong tendencies toward the mythic, either "Devil" or "Noble Savage"—Silko, like other writers in her position, must be wary of appealing to easy sentimentality or other conventional responses.

One interesting development in literary criticism in recent years has been to place Silko and other Native American writers in the context of postcolonial, postmodern literature. Silko is said to be searching in her fiction for an alternative to both traditional Western, humanist discourse and the postmodern critique of that discourse (which denies the autonomous subject). From this point of view her project as a Native American writer has been to model a "dynamic" identity and redefine multiple possibilities of the subject. On the one hand, Silko obviously offers a powerful critique of the Western, "imperial" self that has worked toward the dominance and destruction of nature and native peoples. On the other hand, Silko has expressed biting criticism of fellow Native American novelist Louise Erdrich for her "postmodern, so-called experimental influences." Silko remains committed to the referential dimension of literary language and to the shared, communal experience that she associates with Native American oral tradition.

—Clinton Machann

SILLITOE, Alan

Nationality: British. **Born:** Nottingham, 4 March 1928. Educated in Nottingham schools until 1942. **Military Service:** Served as a wireless operator in the Royal Air Force, 1946-49. **Family:** Married the writer Ruth Fainlight in 1959; one son and one daughter. **Career:** Factory worker, 1942-45; air control assistant, Langar Aerodrome, Nottinghamshire, 1945-46; lived in France and Spain, 1952-58. **Awards:** Authors Club prize, 1958; Hawthornden prize, for fiction, 1960. Fellow, Royal Geographical Society, 1975; Honorary Fellow, Manchester Polytechnic, 1977. **Agent:** Tessa Sayle Agency, 11 Jubilee Place, London SW3 3TE. **Address:** 21 The Street, Wittersham, Kent, England.

PUBLICATIONS

Novels

Saturday Night and Sunday Morning. London, W.H. Allen, 1958; New York, Knopf, 1959.

The General. London, W.H. Allen, 1960; New York, Knopf, 1962; as *Counterpoint,* New York, Avon, 1968.
Key to the Door. London, W.H. Allen, 1961; New York, Knopf, 1962.
The Death of William Posters. London, W.H. Allen, and New York, Knopf, 1965.
A Tree on Fire. London, Macmillan, 1967; New York, Doubleday, 1968.
A Start in Life. London, W.H. Allen, 1970; New York, Scribner, 1971.
Travels in Nihilon. London, W.H. Allen, 1971; New York, Scribner, 1972.
Raw Material. London, W.H. Allen, 1972; New York, Scribner, 1973; revised edition, W.H. Allen, 1979.
The Flame of Life. London, W.H. Allen, 1974.
The Widower's Son. London, W.H. Allen, and New York, Harper, 1976.
The Storyteller. London, W.H. Allen, and New York, Simon and Schuster, 1979.
Her Victory. London, Granada, and New York, Watts, 1982.
The Lost Flying Boat. London, Granada, and Boston, Little Brown, 1983.
Down from the Hill. London, Granada, 1984.
Life Goes On. London, Grafton, 1985.
Out of the Whirlpool (novella). London, Hutchinson, 1987; New York, Harper, 1988.
The Open Door. London, Grafton, 1989.
Last Loves. London, Grafton, 1990.
Leonard's War. London, HarperCollins, 1991.
Snowstop. London, HarperCollins, 1993.

Short Stories

The Loneliness of the Long-Distance Runner. London, W.H. Allen, 1959; New York, Knopf, 1960.
The Ragman's Daughter. London, W.H. Allen, 1963; New York, Knopf, 1964.
A Sillitoe Selection, edited by Michael Marland. London, Longman, 1968.
Guzman Go Home. London, Macmillan, 1968; New York, Doubleday, 1969.
Men, Women, and Children. London, W.H. Allen, 1973; New York, Scribner, 1974.
Down to the Bone (selection). Exeter, Wheaton, 1976.
The Second Chance and Other Stories. London, Cape, and New York, Simon and Schuster, 1981.
The Far Side of the Street. London, W.H. Allen, 1988.

Plays

The Ragman's Daughter (produced Felixstowe, Suffolk, 1966).
All Citizens Are Soldiers, with Ruth Fainlight, adaptation of a play by Lope de Vega (produced Stratford upon Avon and London, 1967). London, Macmillan, 1969; Chester Springs, Pennsylvania, Dufour, 1970.
The Slot Machine (as *This Foreign Field,* produced London, 1970). Included in *Three Plays,* 1978.
Pit Strike (televised 1977). Included in *Three Plays,* 1978.
The Interview (produced London, 1978). Included in *Three Plays,* 1978.
Three Plays. London, W.H. Allen, 1978.

Screenplays: *Saturday Night and Sunday Morning,* 1960; *The Lone-liness of the Long Distance Runner,* 1961; *Counterpoint,* adaptation of his novel *The General,* 1968; *Che Guevara,* 1968; *The Ragman's Daughter,* 1972.

Radio Play: *The General,* from his own novel, 1984.

Television Play: *Pit Strike,* 1977.

Poetry

Without Beer or Bread. London, Outposts, 1957.
The Rats and Other Poems. London, W.H. Allen, 1960.
A Falling Out of Love and Other Poems. London, W.H. Allen, 1964.
Love in the Environs of Voronezh and Other Poems. London, Macmillan, 1968; New York, Doubleday, 1969.
Shaman and Other Poems. London, Turret, 1968.
Poems, with Ted Hughes and Ruth Fainlight. London, Rainbow Press, 1971.
Canto Two of the Rats. Privately printed, 1973.
Barbarians and Other Poems. London, Turret, 1973.
Storm: New Poems. London, W.H. Allen, 1974.
Words Broadsheet 19, with Ruth Fainlight. Bramley, Surrey, Words Press, 1975.
Day-Dream Communiqué. Knotting, Bedfordshire, Sceptre Press, 1977.
From "Snow on the North Side of Lucifer." Knotting, Bedfordshire, Sceptre Press, 1979.
Snow on the North Side of Lucifer. London, W.H. Allen, 1979.
More Lucifer. Knotting, Bedfordshire, Booth, 1980.
Israel. London, Steam Press, 1981.
Sun Before Departure: Poems 1974 to 1982. London, Granada, 1984.
Tides and Stone Walls, photographs by Victor Bowley. London, Grafton, 1986.
Three Poems. Child Okeford, Dorset, Words Press, 1988.
Collected Poems. London, HarperCollins, 1993.

Other

Road to Volgograd (travel). London, W.H. Allen, and New York, Knopf, 1964.
The City Adventures of Marmalade Jim (for children). London, Macmillan, 1967; revised edition, London, Robson, 1977.
Mountains and Caverns: Selected Essays. London, W.H. Allen, 1975.
Big John and the Stars (for children). London, Robson, 1977.
The Incredible Fencing Fleas (for children). London, Robson, 1978.
Marmalade Jim at the Farm (for children). London, Robson, 1980.
The Saxon Shore Way: From Gravesend to Rye, photographs by Fay Godwin. London, Hutchinson, 1983.
Marmalade Jim and the Fox (for children). London, Robson, 1984.
Alan Sillitoe's Nottinghamshire, photographs by David Sillitoe. London, Grafton, 1987.
Every Day of the Week: An Alan Sillitoe Reader. London, W.H. Allen, 1987.

Editor, *Poems for Shakespeare 7.* London, Bear Gardens Museum and Arts Centre, 1979.

Translator, *Chopin's Winter in Majorca 1838-1839,* by Luis Ripoll. Palma de Majorca, Sivrell, 1955.

Translator, *Chopin's Pianos: The Pleyel in Majorca,* by Luis Ripoll. Palma de Majorca, Messen Alcover Press, 1958.

*

Bibliography: *Alan Sillitoe: A Bibliography* by David E. Gerard, London, Mansell, 1988.

Critical Studies: *Alan Sillitoe* edited by Michael Marland, London, Times Authors Series, 1970; *Alan Sillitoe* by Allen Richard Penner, New York, Twayne, 1972; *Commitment as Art: A Marxist Critique of a Selection of Alan Sillitoe's Political Fiction* by R.D. Vaverka, Stockholm, Almqvist & Wiksell, 1978; *Alan Sillitoe: A Critical Assessment* by Stanley S. Atherton, London, W.H. Allen, 1979; *Working-Class Fiction in Theory and Practice: A Reading of Alan Sillitoe* by Peter Hitchcock, Ann Arbor, Michigan, UMI Research Press, 1989; *Brodie's Notes on Alan Sillitoe's Selected Fiction: Saturday Night and Sunday Morning, The Loneliness of the Long-distance Runner, and A Sillitoe Selection* by Andrew Copping, London, Pan, 1991.

Alan Sillitoe comments:

As one gets older there is less to say about why one writes, but at the same time there is more to write. The writing also gets more difficult, which is as it should be.

*   *   *

As Alan Sillitoe's fiction developed beyond the self-contained and brilliantly presented world of *Saturday Night and Sunday Morning,* the point of view changed from that of Arthur Seaton, the energetic, unsentimental, and superficially satisfied protagonist of the first novel, to that of his elder brother, Brian, the central figure of *Key to the Door.* Arthur, grateful for the luck involved in the contrast between his current well-paid job at the capstan lathe and his father's life on the dole before World War II, is relatively content so long as he can find a plentiful supply of beer and women. Sillitoe, emphasizing his perceptive intransigence in a world that is both hypocritical and hostile, makes him an attractive force. Brian, however, is more intellectual, a man who questions and feels strongly, who, like Frank Dawley, the Midlands working-man in a later trilogy, searches for a more complete life he cannot easily find. Brian is given more background, more development from childhood, than Arthur was, seen in incidents like that in which he saves pennies to buy a copy of *The Count of Monte Cristo,* his impoverished parents furious that he could waste his hard-scrounged money on a book. Part of the difference in these points of view is apparent in the treatment of politics. For Arthur, all political systems are fraudulent rhetoric to cheat the working-man, although he has some sympathy with the Communists because, in England in the 1950s, they are so universally despised or ignored. Brian is interested in Communism as an idea, a possible transformation of the society of privilege. When conscripted after the war and sent to Malaya, Brian considers helping a Communist revolution against the establishment he now inadvertently represents. Frank Dawley, in *The Death of William Posters* and *A Tree on Fire,* running guns to the FLN in Algeria, aids the Communists directly by ideological choice, although back in England in *The Flame of Life,* the final novel of the trilogy, concerning the death of a comrade in Algeria, he questions the value of his revolutionary commitment.

Although these presentations of the working-class intellectual developing against strong pressures of class and society are more vulnerable to sentimentality or rhetorical rant than is Arthur Seaton's tightly controlled perspective, they are deeper both intellectually and emotionally. Sillitoe's interest in abstract ideas has been evident since his early novel, *The General,* in which the symbols of music (in the form of a symphony orchestra) and mathematics (in the form of the general's focus on precise maps) contrast contradictory attitudes toward the best way of controlling the "primeval slime" of men involved in war. Many later novels are similarly constructed around an idea: *Travels in Nihilon* recounts the adventures of five travelers who go into the corrupt world of nihilism to write a guidebook; *A Start in Life,* in which the metaphors are more literary, follows the picaresque account of a contemporary bastard looking for a social locus; a later novel, *The Lost Flying Boat,* chronicles the disastrous journey of eight former military crewmen to retrieve treasure from the island of Kerguelen in the Indian Ocean near the Antarctic, a metaphor for the actions of a small group of the dedicated and accomplished defeated by the larger, greedier, more amorphous social forces outside. Sillitoe is not always at his best in the novels totally dependent on a single idea or metaphor. *Travels in Nihilon* degenerates into a kind of farcical violence, as if characters from a Marx brothers film are suddenly caught in a James Bond world taken seriously, and *A Start in Life* blends the comic and picaresque techniques of the early John Wain with those of Henry Fielding, without the sense of humor of either. Rather, Sillitoe is most probing and effective in fiction, like *Key to the Door, The Death of William Posters, The Flame of Life, The Widower's Son,* and *Her Victory,* in which the struggle to become intelligent and independent is part of a developing perspective and the ideas part of the attitude toward experience.

In *Key to the Door* Sillitoe depicts effectively the lives of Brian's parents: his mother's childhood as the daughter of a rural blacksmith, his father as the draftsman who slowly decays in an economy of continuous slump between the two World Wars, and the origins of the constant emotional violence and alternations between love and hatred. The background is close to that which Sillitoe gives himself in *Raw Material,* a volume of memoirs that he calls fiction designed to get at the truth since "everything written is fiction." *Raw Material* details his family background, the contrast between the simple, explosive blacksmiths, "the poetry," the Burtons, his mother's family, and the dark, sallow, complex, politically rebellious Sillitoes, "the force that pushes" the poetry. Accounts of the personal past are interspersed with and connected to an argument that the social fabric of England was destroyed by the disaster of World War I, the needless struggle in which the upper classes sent millions to their deaths in order to preserve their own mindless kind of privilege: "Before 1914 a unity could have been possible, and the men might then have tried it. Joining up to fight was, in a sense, their way of saying yes, but the old men used this affirmation to try and finish them off." This view of history provides a combination of intensity and a social dimension that are consistent and cogently argued in all Sillitoe's fiction. This sense of a social past, behind descriptions like that of the Nottingham Goose Fair in *Saturday Night and Sunday Morning,* the grubby night lights and Nottingham music hall in the 1920s in *Key to the Door,* the 1972 miners' strike in "Pit Strike" (as well as descriptions in "Before Snow Comes" and "The Chiker," other stories published in *Men, Women, and Children*), and the rural Lincolnshire where Albert Handley, Frank Dawley's friend, the proletarian painter, begins, gives Sillitoe's prose a violent energy, a hard explosive quality. His

speculations about the complicated nature of fiction are also dramatized in *The Storyteller,* a novel in which a poor Nottingham boy escapes schoolyard beatings by telling stories, an art he develops into a career as storyteller in pubs. As his stories increasingly mix with his own life, the art of fiction is seen reflexively as both destroying and creating its maker.

In all Sillitoe's fiction, the world is seen as a jungle. Yet the nature of the jungle changes. In the earliest fiction, like *Saturday Night and Sunday Morning* and "The Loneliness of the Long Distance Runner," society and the exterior world are jungles in which the protagonist, himself neutral, must survive through a combination of luck and shrewd skill. But, starting with *Key to the Door,* the jungle is both the exterior worlds of Nottingham and Malaya and the questions, uncertainties, false starts, and violence within the protagonist himself. Brian has internalized all the casual violence in his background, and, unlike Arthur, cannot relegate it to a cheerful acceptance of a Saturday night punch-up. Brian begins the recognition that brutality, although endemic, can be overcome, that violence is not the "key to the door," a recognition developed further in the character of Frank Dawley through the three novels of the trilogy. In *The Death of William Posters,* chronicling Frank's movement away from his stifling Nottingham world, William Posters is the fictional image of the working-class man, defiant, persecuted, always hounded by society but never finally caught, using violence against others and himself indiscriminately and self-destructively. Frank derives his name from the notices that read "Bill posters will be prosecuted." As Frank tries to move out of Nottingham, then out of England, directing his sense of violence appropriately outward and politically, he attempts to exorcise the image of Posters, leaving it moribund in Nottingham. Yet, in Sillitoe's world, Posters is never finally exorcised. Appearing as a casualty in World War I and as a figure who casually beats his wife or his children, he is even reincarnated in *The Flame of Life* as an itinerant, pot-smoking youth of the 1970s, Dean William Posters, who runs off with Albert Handley's wife, just one of the gestures of irrationality and violence that destroys the community Albert and Frank Dawley have tried to establish. The theme of brutality, in Sillitoe's world, is also treated in its rationalized and institutionalized version, the military. Although many of the working-class characters deride the military and none is patriotic, Sillitoe demonstrates, particularly in an excellent novel, *The Widower's Son,* the use of the military career as the conscious focus for working out all the stresses of the individual and social jungles within modern man. Although unable finally to justify his interest in gunnery or the parallel war of his marriage to a general's daughter, the career soldier, heroic back at Dunkerque, an analogue for an attempted assimilation of class in England, is treated with complexity and sympathy. In the best and most comprehensive of the later novels, *Her Victory,* a Nottingham woman, after 20 years of marriage, leaves her crass, newly successful husband and his three brutal, parasitic brothers. Alone in London, she attempts suicide and is rescued by a former naval man who lives by maps, routines, and carefully calibrated assertions against the jungle and chaos of human emotions. Although their ensuing relationship is stormy, even violent, and is not seen as conclusive or permanent (she is also strongly attracted to a bisexual woman who lives with them), he teaches her some capacity to give her life conscious direction and control while she helps him discover a hitherto unknown partial Jewish identity that leads him to Israel. The military and cartographic are partial measures of human and civilized control.

Although his most effectively articulated details are often those of geography and class, Sillitoe has always felt that the majority of any class is unintelligent and unresponsive. In all his fiction, he frequently refers to "rats," a term that in his long poem called "The Rats" he uses to refer to all the agents of organized religious, political, or industrial society, a category that includes most people. Increasingly in the later fiction, he concentrates attention on the non-rat, the special person (even, as in *The Widower's Son*, the special person within an institution of "rats"), the man who attempts to challenge experience, to achieve something more than might have been expected. The special person is devoted to work, to human dignity, and to exorcising his own brutality and that of others. Yet contemporary society rewards futile, parasitic, or soul-destroying work; England remains, for the most part, the land of William Posters, or that of the greedy capitalist or advertising agency. The special person is always posed against the society, burns with energy, and has roots in a meaningful past. He is, imagistically, "a tree on fire" or "the flame of life," needing to test his specialness in some kind of vital connection with the modern world (the terms of that connection were more political in the 1960s than later). The similarity between Sillitoe's fiction and that of D.H. Lawrence goes deeper than a common origin in the working-classes in and near Nottingham, a capacity to describe the area physically and acutely, and possible imitation in a particular novel, as *The Death of William Posters* particularly resembles *Aaron's Rod*. As Sillitoe's concerns have widened, he has, with similar themes and attitudes, developed an authentically Lawrentian perspective of his own. The two writers are alike in their representation of the complexity of working-class characters (Albert Handley, for example, had a portrait of the Queen in his front hall when he was poor and replaced it with one of Mao Tse-tung when he became rich), in their insistence on the need to recognize violence and brutality in human experience, in their incipient romanticism, in their essays about work, in their constantly restless thoughtfulness, in their slow recognition of the need for the special person to get away from England (although this is never, finally, a panacea), and even in their occasional reduction of and lack of sympathy for middle-class characters. Sillitoe lacks Lawrence's ease with theoretical and metaphysical argument, for which he is likely to substitute charts, calibrations, and equations. But both writers share a restless energy, probing and serious, as well as a social and historical range, that make possible the creation of unique and effective fiction.

Sillitoe returns to the impoverished landscape of working-class Nottingham as the setting of his novella, *Out of the Whirlpool*. Like Frank Dawley in *The Death of William Posters*, the young protagonist, eighteen-year-old Peter Granby, attempts to rise above the dungheap of his existence and find meaning in a hostile world. It seems to Peter, an inarticulate factory worker, that fate intervenes in the form of an old woman whom he aids after she falls in the street and her wealthy daughter, Eileen Farnsfield, who rewards his goodness to her mother. Although he resists her help at first, Peter eventually becomes Eileen Farnsfield's handyman, and it seems fate has again intervened. His outlook on life brightens and his future looks better, the dungheap dimmer in the background. However, Peter's attempts to become something more than life has prescribed for him seem doomed to end tragically. In this poetic tale, Peter Granby pays a bitter price for his encounter with Sillitoe's "rats," and his destiny as a non-rat or special person comes to a heartbreaking but inevitable end.

—James Gindin, updated by Sandra Ray

SILVERBERG, Robert

Pseudonyms: Walker Chapman; Ivar Jorgenson; Calvin M. Knox; David Osborne; Robert Randall; Lee Sebastian. **Nationality:** American. **Born:** New York City, 15 January 1935. **Education:** Columbia University, New York, A.B. 1956. **Family:** Married Barbara H. Brown in 1956. **Career:** Full-time writer: associate editor, *Amazing*, January 1969 issue, and associate editor, *Fantastic*, February-April 1969 issues. President, Science Fiction Writers of America, 1967-68. **Awards:** Hugo award, 1956, 1969; Nebula award, for story, 1969, 1971, 1974, for novel, 1971, for novella, 1985; Jupiter award, 1973; Prix Apollo, 1976; *Locus* award, 1981. Guest of Honor, 28th World Science Fiction Convention, 1970. **Agent:** Ralph Vicinanza, 432 Park Avenue South, Room 1205, New York, New York 10016, U.S.A.

PUBLICATIONS

Novels (series: Majipoor; Nidor)

The 13th Immortal. New York, Ace, 1957.
Master of Life and Death. New York, Ace, 1957; London, Sidgwick and Jackson, 1977.
The Shrouded Planet (Nidor; as Robert Randall, with Randall Garrett). New York, Gnome Press, 1957; London, Mayflower, 1964.
Invaders from Earth. New York, Ace, 1958; London, Sidgwick and Jackson, 1977.
Invincible Barriers (as David Osborne). New York, Avalon, 1958.
Stepsons of Terra. New York, Ace, 1958.
Aliens from Space (as David Osborne). New York, Avalon, 1958.
Starhaven (as Ivar Jorgenson). New York, Avalon, 1958.
The Dawning Light (Nidor; as Robert Randall, with Randall Garrett). New York, Gnome Press, 1959; London, Mayflower, 1964.
The Planet Killers. New York, Ace, 1959.
Collision Course. New York, Avalon, 1961.
The Seed of Earth. New York, Ace, 1962; London, Hamlyn, 1978.
Recalled to Life. New York, Lancer, 1962; revised edition, New York, Doubleday, 1972; London Gollancz, 1974.
The Silent Invaders. New York, Ace, 1963; London, Dobson, 1975.
Regan's Planet. New York, Pyramid, 1964.
A Pair from Space. New York, Belmont, 1965.
To Open the Sky. New York, Ballantine, 1967; London, Sphere, 1970.
Thorns. New York, Ballantine, 1967; London, Rapp and Whiting, 1969.
Those Who Watch. New York, New American Library, 1967; London, New English Library, 1977.
The Time-Hoppers. New York, Doubleday, 1967; London, Sidgwick and Jackson, 1968.
Planet of Death. New York, Holt Rinehart, 1967.
Hawksbill Station. New York, Doubleday, 1968; as *The Anvil of Time*, London, Sidgwick and Jackson, 1969.
The Masks of Time. New York, Ballantine, 1968; as *Vornan-19*, London, Sidgwick and Jackson, 1970.
Up the Line. New York, Ballantine, 1969; London, Gollancz, 1987.
Nightwings. New York, Avon, 1969; London, Sidgwick and Jackson, 1972.

To Live Again. New York, Doubleday, 1969; London, Sidgwick and Jackson, 1975.

Downward to the Earth. New York, Doubleday, 1970; London, Gollancz, 1977.

Tower of Glass. New York, Scribner, 1970; London, Panther, 1976.

A Robert Silverberg Omnibus. London, Sidgwick and Jackson, 1970.

The World Inside. New York, Doubleday, 1971; London, Millington, 1976.

A Time of Changes. New York, Doubleday, 1971; London, Gollancz, 1973.

Son of Man. New York, Ballantine, 1971; London, Panther, 1979.

The Book of Skulls. New York, Scribner, 1971; London, Gollancz, 1978.

Dying Inside. New York, Scribner, 1972; London, Sidgwick and Jackson, 1974.

The Second Trip. New York, Doubleday, 1972; London, Gollancz, 1979.

The Stochastic Man. New York, Harper, 1975; London, Gollancz, 1976.

Shadrach in the Furnace. Indianapolis, Bobbs Merrill, 1976; London, Gollancz, 1977.

Lord Valentine's Castle (Majipoor). New York, Harper, and London, Gollancz, 1980.

The Desert of Stolen Dreams. Columbia, Pennsylvania, Underwood Miller, 1981.

A Robert Silverberg Omnibus. New York, Harper, 1981.

Majipoor Chronicles. New York, Arbor House, and London, Gollancz, 1982.

Valentine Pontifex. New York, Arbor House, 1983; London, Gollancz, 1984.

Lord of Darkness. New York, Arbor House, and London, Gollancz, 1983.

The Conglomeroid Cocktail Party. New York, Arbor House, 1984; London, Gollancz, 1985.

Gilgamesh the King. New York, Arbor House, 1984; London, Gollancz, 1985.

Tom O'Bedlam. New York, Fine, 1985; London, Gollancz, 1986.

Sailing to Byzantium. Columbia, Pennsylvania, Underwood Miller, 1985.

Star of the Gypsies. New York, Fine, 1986; London, Gollancz, 1987.

At Winter's End. New York, Warner, and London, Gollancz, 1988.

The Secret Sharer (novella). Los Angeles, California, Underwood Miller, 1988.

The Mutant Season, with Karen Haber. New York, Doubleday, 1989.

Time Gate, with Bill Fawcett. New York, Baen, 1989.

To the Land of the Living. London, Gollancz, 1989; Norwalk, Connecticut, Easton Press, 1990.

The Queen of Springtime. London, Gollancz, 1989.

The New Springtime. New York, Warner, 1990.

Nightfall, with Isaac Asimov. New York, Doubleday, and London, Gollancz, 1990.

The Man in the Maze. London, Gollancz, 1990.

In Another Country, with *Vintage Season* by C.L. Moore. New York, Tor, 1990.

Child of Time, with Isaac Asimov. London, Gollancz, 1991.

The Face of the Waters. New York, Bantam, and London, Grafton, 1991.

The Ugly Little Boy, with Isaac Asimov. New York, Doubleday, 1992.

Thebes of the Hundred Gates. London, HarperCollins, 1993.

The Positronic Man, with Isaac Asimov. London, Gollancz, 1992; New York, Doubleday, 1993.

Kingdoms of the Wall. London, HarperCollins, 1992; New York, Bantam, 1993.

Hot Sky at Midnight. New York, Bantam, and London, HarperCollings, 1994.

The Mountains of Majipoor. New York, Bantam, and London, Macmillan, 1995.

Novels as Calvin M. Knox

Lest We Forget Thee, Earth. New York, Ace, 1958.

The Plot Against Earth. New York, Ace, 1959.

One of Our Asteroids Is Missing. New York, Ace, 1964.

Short Stories

Next Stop the Stars. New York, Ace, 1962; London, Dobson, 1979.

Godling, Go Home! New York, Belmont, 1964.

To Worlds Beyond. Philadelphia, Chilton, 1965; London, Sphere, 1969.

Needle in a Timestack. New York, Ballantine, 1966; London, Sphere, 1967; revised edition, Sphere, 1979.

To Open the Sky. New York, Ballantine, 1967.

Dimension Thirteen. New York, Ballantine, 1969.

Parsecs and Parables. New York, Doubleday, 1970; London, Hale, 1973.

The Cube Root of Uncertainty. New York, Macmillan, 1970.

Moonferns and Starsongs. New York, Ballantine, 1971.

The Reality Trip and Other Implausibilities. New York, Ballantine, 1972.

Valley Beyond Time. New York, Dell, 1973.

Unfamiliar Territory. New York, Scribner, 1973; London, Gollancz, 1975.

Earth's Other Shadow. New York, New American Library, 1973; London, Millington, 1977.

Born with the Dead (three novellas). New York, Random House, 1974; London, Gollancz, 1975.

Sundance and Other Science Fiction Stories. Nashville, Nelson, 1974; London, Abelard Schuman, 1975.

The Feast of St. Dionysus. New York, Scribner, 1975; London, Gollancz, 1976.

The Shores of Tomorrow. Nashville, Nelson, 1976.

The Best of Robert Silverberg. New York, Pocket Books, 1976; London, Sidgwick and Jackson, 1977.

Capricorn Games. New York, Random House, 1976; London, Gollancz, 1978.

The Songs of Summer and Other Stories. London, Gollancz, 1979.

World of a Thousand Colors. New York, Arbor House, 1982.

Beyond the Safe Zone: Collected Short Fiction. New York, Fine, 1986.

Fiction (for children)

Revolt on Alpha C. New York, Crowell, 1955.

Starman's Quest. New York, Gnome Press, 1959.

Lost Race of Mars. Philadelphia, Winston, 1960.

Time of the Great Freeze. New York, Holt Rinehart, 1964.

Conquerors from the Darkness. New York, Holt Rinehart, 1965.

The Calibrated Alligator. New York, Holt Rinehart, 1969.

The Gate of Worlds. New York, Holt Rinehart, 1967; London, Gollancz, 1978.

Across a Billion Years. New York, Dial Press, 1969; London, Gollancz, 1977.

The Man in the Maze. New York, Avon, and London, Sidgwick and Jackson, 1969.

Three Survived. New York, Holt Rinehart, 1969.

World's Fair 1992. Chicago, Follett, 1970.

Sunrise on Mercury. Nashville, Nelson, 1975; London, Gollancz, 1983.

Project Pendulum. New York, Walker, 1987; London, Hutchinson, 1989.

Letters from Atlantis. New York, Atheneum, 1990.

Other (for children)

Treasures Beneath the Sea. Racine, Wisconsin, Whitman, 1960.

Lost Cities and Vanished Civilizations. Philadelphia, Chilton, 1962.

Sunken History: The Story of Underwater Archaeology. Philadelphia, Chilton, 1963.

Home of the Red Man: Indian North America Before Columbus. Greenwich, Connecticut, New York Graphic Society, 1963.

The Great Doctors. New York, Putnam, 1964.

The Man Who Found Nineveh: The Story of Austen Henry Layard. New York, Holt Rinehart, 1964; Kingswood, Surrey, World's Work, 1968.

The World of Coral. New York, Duell, 1965.

The Mask of Akhnaten. New York, Macmillan, 1965.

Socrates. New York, Putnam, 1965.

Niels Bohr, the Man Who Mapped the Atom. Philadelphia, Macrae Smith, 1965.

Forgotten by Time: A Book of Living Fossils. New York, Crowell, 1966.

Kublai Kahn, Lord of Xanadu (as Walker Chapman). Indianapolis, Bobbs Merrill, 1966.

Rivers (as Lee Sebastian). New York, Holt Rinehart, 1966.

To the Rock of Darius: The Story of Henry Rawlinson. New York, Holt Rinehart, 1966.

Four Men Who Changed the Universe. New York, Putnam, 1968.

The South Pole (as Lee Sebastian). New York, Holt Rinehart, 1968.

Bruce of the Blue Nile. New York, Holt Rinehart, 1969.

Other

First American into Space. Derby, Connecticut, Monarch, 1961.

The Fabulous Rockefellers. Derby, Connecticut, Monarch, 1963.

15 Battles That Changed the World. New York, Putnam, 1963.

Empires in the Dust. Philadelphia, Chilton, 1963.

Akhnaten, The Rebel Pharaoh. Philadelphia, Chilton, 1964.

Man Before Adam. Philadelphia, Macrae Smith, 1964.

The Loneliest Continent (as Walker Chapman). Greenwich, Connecticut, New York Graphic Society, 1965; London, Jarrolds, 1967.

Scientists and Scoundrels: A Book of Hoaxes. New York, Crowell, 1965.

The Old Ones: Indians of the American Southwest. Greenwich, Connecticut, New York Graphic Society, 1965.

Men Who Mastered the Atom. New York, Putnam, 1965.

The Great Wall of China. Philadelphia, Chilton, 1965.

Frontiers of Archaeology. Philadelphia, Chilton, 1966.

The Long Rampart: The Story of the Great Wall of China. Philadelphia, Chilton, 1966.

Bridges. Philadelphia, Macrae Smith, 1966.

The Dawn of Medicine. New York, Putnam, 1967.

The Adventures of Nat Palmer, Antarctic Explorer. New York, McGraw Hill, 1967.

The Auk, the Dodo, and the Oryx. New York, Crowell, 1967; Kingswood, Surrey, World's Work, 1969.

The Golden Dream: Seekers of El Dorado. Indianapolis, Bobbs Merrill, 1967.

Men Against Time: Salvage Archaeology in the United States. New York, Macmillan, 1967.

The Morning of Mankind. Greenwich, Connecticut, New York Graphic Society, 1967; Kingswood, Surrey, World's Work, 1970.

The World of the Rain Forest. New York, Meredith Press, 1967.

Light for the World: Edison and the Power Industry. Princeton, New Jersey, Van Nostrand, 1967.

Ghost Towns of the American West. New York, Crowell, 1968.

Mound Builders of Ancient America. Greenwich, Connecticut, New York Graphic Society, 1968.

Stormy Voyager: The Story of Charles Wilkes. Philadelphia, Lippincott, 1968.

The World of the Ocean Depths. New York, Meredith Press, 1968; Kingswood, Surrey, World's Work, 1970.

The Challenge of Climate: Man and His Environment. New York, Meredith Press, 1969; Kingswood, Surrey, World's Work, 1971.

Vanishing Giants: The Story of the Sequoias. New York, Simon and Schuster, 1969.

Wonders of Ancient Chinese Science. New York, Hawthorn, 1969.

The World of Space. New York, Meredith Press, 1969.

If I Forget Thee, O Jerusalem: American Jews and the State of Israel. New York, Morrow, 1970.

Mammoths, Mastodons, and Man. New York, McGraw Hill, 1970; Kingswood, Surrey, World's Work, 1972.

The Pueblo Revolt. New York, Weybright and Talley, 1970.

The Seven Wonders of the Ancient World (for children). New York, Crowell Collier, 1970.

Before the Sphinx. New York, Nelson, 1971.

Clocks for the Ages: How Scientists Date the Past. New York, Macmillan, 1971.

To the Western Shore: Growth of the United States 1776-1853. New York, Doubleday, 1971.

Into Space, with Arthur C. Clarke. New York, Harper, 1971.

John Muir: Prophet among the Glaciers. New York, Putnam, 1972.

The Longest Voyage: Circumnavigation in the Age of Discovery. Indianapolis, Bobbs Merrill, 1972.

The Realm of Prester John. New York, Doubleday, 1972.

The World Within the Ocean Wave. New York, Weybright and Talley, 1972.

The World Within the Tide Pool. New York, Weybright and Talley, 1972.

Drug Themes in Science Fiction. Rockville, Maryland, National Institute on Drug Abuse, 1974.

The Ultimate Dinosaur, with Byron Preiss, edited by Peter Dodson. New York, Bantam, 1992.

Editor, *Great Adventures in Archaeology.* New York, Dial Press, 1964; London, Hale, 1966.

Editor, *Earthmen and Strangers.* New York, Duell, 1966.

Editor (as Walker Chapman), *Antarctic Conquest.* Indianapolis, Bobbs Merrill, 1966.

Editor, *Voyagers in Time.* New York, Meredith Press, 1967.

Editor, *Men and Machines.* New York, Meredith Press, 1968.

Editor, *Mind to Mind.* New York, Meredith Press, 1968.

Editor, *Tomorrow's Worlds.* New York, Meredith Press, 1969.

Editor, *Dark Stars.* New York, Ballantine, 1969; London, Ballantine, 1971.

Editor, *Three for Tomorrow.* New York, Meredith Press, 1969; London, Gollancz, 1970.

Editor, *The Mirror of Infinity: A Critics' Anthology of Science Fiction.* New York, Harper, 1970; London, Sidgwick and Jackson, 1971.

Editor, *Science Fiction Hall of Fame 1.* New York, Doubleday, 1970; London, Gollancz, 1971.

Editor, *The Ends of Time.* New York, Hawthorn, 1970.

Editor, *Great Short Novels of Science Fiction.* New York, Ballantine, 1970; London, Pan, 1971.

Editor, *Worlds of Maybe.* New York, Nelson, 1970.

Editor, *Alpha 1-9.* New York, Ballantine, 5 vols., 1970-74; New York, Berkley, 4 vols., 1975-78.

Editor, *Four Futures.* New York, Hawthorn, 1971.

Editor, *The Science Fiction Bestiary.* New York, Nelson, 1971.

Editor, *To the Stars.* New York, Hawthorn, 1971.

Editor, *New Dimensions 1-12* (vols. 11 and 12 edited with Marta Randall). New York, Doubleday, 3 vols., 1971-73; New York, New American Library, 1 vol., 1974; New York, Harper, 6 vols., 1975-80; New York, Pocket Books, 2 vols., 1980-81; *5-7* published London, Gollancz, 3 vols., 1976-77.

Editor, *The Day the Sun Stood Still.* Nashville, Nelson, 1972.

Editor, *Invaders from Space.* New York, Hawthorn, 1972.

Editor, *Beyond Control.* Nashville, Nelson, 1972; London, Sidgwick and Jackson, 1973.

Editor, *Deep Space.* Nashville, Nelson, 1973; London, Abelard Schuman, 1976.

Editor, *Chains of the Sea.* Nashville, Nelson, 1973.

Editor, *No Mind of Man.* New York, Hawthorn, 1973.

Editor, *Other Dimensions.* New York, Hawthorn, 1973.

Editor, *Three Trips in Time and Space.* New York, Hawthorn, 1973.

Editor, *Mutants.* Nashville, Nelson, 1974; London, Abelard Schuman, 1976.

Editor, *Threads of Time.* Nashville, Nelson, 1974; London, Millington, 1975.

Editor, *Infinite Jests.* Radnor, Pennsylvania, Chilton, 1974.

Editor, *Windows into Tomorrow.* New York, Hawthorn, 1974.

Editor, with Roger Elwood, *Epoch.* New York, Berkley, 1975.

Editor, *Explorers of Space.* Nashville, Nelson, 1975.

Editor, *The New Atlantis.* New York, Hawthorn, 1975.

Editor, *Strange Gifts.* Nashville, Nelson, 1975.

Editor, *The Aliens.* Nashville, Nelson, 1976.

Editor, *The Crystal Ship.* Nashville, Nelson, 1976; London, Millington, 1980.

Editor, *Triax.* Los Angeles, Pinnacle, 1977; London, Fontana, 1979.

Editor, *Trips in Time.* Nashville, Nelson, 1977; London, Hale, 1979.

Editor, *Earth Is the Strangest Planet.* Nashville, Nelson, 1977.

Editor, *Galactic Dreamers.* New York, Random House, 1977.

Editor, *The Infinite Web.* New York, Dial Press, 1977.

Editor, *The Androids Are Coming.* New York, Elsevier Nelson, 1979.

Editor, *Lost Worlds, Unknown Horizons.* New York, Elsevier Nelson, 1979.

Editor, *The Edge of Space.* New York, Elsevier Nelson, 1979.

Editor, with Martin H. Greenberg and Joseph D. Olander, *Car Sinister.* New York, Avon, 1979.

Editor, with Martin H. Greenberg and Joseph D. Olander, *Dawn of Time: Prehistory Through Science Fiction.* New York, Elsevier Nelson, 1979.

Editor, *The Best of New Dimensions.* New York, Simon and Schuster, 1979.

Editor, with Martin H. Greenberg, *The Arbor House Treasury of Modern Science Fiction.* New York, Arbor House, 1980; as *Great Science Fiction of the 20th Century,* New York, Avenel, 1987.

Editor, with Martin H. Greenberg, *The Arbor House Treasury of Great Science Fiction Short Novels.* New York, Arbor House, 1980; as *Worlds Imagined,* New York, Avenel, 1989.

Editor, with Martin H. Greenberg and Charles G. Waugh, *The Science Fictional Dinosaur.* New York, Avon, 1982.

Editor, *The Best of Randall Garrett.* New York, Pocket Books, 1982.

Editor, with Martin H. Greenberg, *The Arbor House Treasury of Science Fiction Masterpieces.* New York, Arbor House, 1983; as *Great Tales of Science Fiction,* New York, Galahad, 1985.

Editor, with Martin H. Greenberg, *Fantasy Hall of Fame.* New York, Arbor House, 1983; as *The Mammoth Book of Fantasy All-Time Greats,* London, Robinson, 1988.

Editor, *The Nebula Awards 18.* New York, Arbor House, 1983.

Editor, with Martin H. Greenberg, *The Time Travelers: A Science Fiction Quartet.* New York, Fine, 1985.

Editor, with Martin H. Greenberg and Charles G. Waugh, *Neanderthals.* New York, New American Library, 1987.

Editor, *Robert Silverberg's Worlds of Wonder.* New York, Warner, 1987; London, Gollancz, 1988.

Editor, with Karen Haber, *Universe 1.* New York, Doubleday, 1990.

Editor, with Martin H. Greenberg, *The Horror Hall of Fame.* New York, Carroll and Graf, 1991.

Editor, *Murasaki: A Novel in Six Parts,* by Poul Anderson. New York, Bantam, 1992; London, Grafton, 1993.

*

Bibliography: In *Fantasy and Science Fiction* (New York), April 1974.

Manuscript Collection: Syracuse University, New York.

Critical Studies: "Robert Silverberg Issue" of *SF Commentary* (Melbourne), March 1977; *Robert Silverberg* by Thomas D. Clareson, Mercer Island, Washington, Starmont House, 1983; *Robert Silverberg's Many Trapdoors: Critical Essays on His Science Fiction* edited by Charles L. Elkins and Martin Harry Greenberg, Westport, Connecticut, Greenwood Press, 1992.

*   *   *

Robert Silverberg is a masterly science fiction writer who has demonstrated the capacity of the genre to encompass and enrich the themes of the traditional realistic novel. He quickly developed the qualities that made him a very successful purveyor of commercial science fiction: the ability to grasp a reader's attention with his opening sentences, to sustain a compelling narrative, to evoke character and setting vividly and swiftly, to generate and elaborate fascinating ideas. He has carried these qualities into his later work, and they have been complemented, in his best novels and short stories, by characterization in depth and by a prose style that is rhythmically resourceful and rich in allusion and imagery.

Silverberg is especially concerned with time and death; with journeys to, and visions of, past and future; and with attempts to avoid or overcome mortality. For instance, *Recalled to Life,* by means of imaginative extrapolations from American society in the second half of the 20th century, vividly dramatizes the social, political, and ethical consequences of the discovery of a scientific means of resurrecting the newly dead. *To Live Again* evokes a world that offers the wealthy not physical immortality but the survival, in recorded form, of a persona that can be transplanted into the mind of a living individual: The individual chooses the persona that will best complement her or him, but there is always the risk that the persona may take over. By means of a science fiction hypothesis, *To Live Again* recasts and extends the traditional theme of the divided self.

The Book of Skulls may be Silverberg's most powerful dramatization of the quest for immortality. Four American students—one Jewish, one gay, one a WASP, and one an upwardly mobile Kansas farmer's boy—set out on a journey to Arizona to find a sect they believe can grant them immortality. There is one drawback: Only two students will be eligible; they must kill the third student, and the fourth must kill himself. They do not know, however, who is to die and who is to be saved. The novel is a compelling combination of a science fiction story and a thriller, the suspense of which is increased by a narrative technique that alternates between first-person accounts by each student. This technique also enables Silverberg to offer complex psychological portrayals of each of his four protagonists.

The combination of complex psychological characterization with science fiction achieves possibly its greatest success in *Dying Inside,* a novel about a middle-aged Jewish telepath, David Selig, who is losing his powers. The novel combines memories of Selig's unhappy childhood and youth with an evocation of his present life, in which he ekes out a living by ghostwriting essays for students. Selig laments the loss of his gift, even though it has been more of a curse than a blessing, isolating him from his fellows and thwarting his hopes of forming enduring relationships. At times we might be reading a realistic novel; but the science fiction element adds an extra dimension, Selig's telepathic power serving as a metaphor for intensity of emotion and for a faculty of perception that makes one special but sets one apart.

Silverberg's fiction grew less intense in the 1970s, when he produced novels and short stories about the fantasy world of Majipoor and historical novels like *Lord of Darkness.* As he entered the 1990s, he could still produce very effective work, such as *Thebes of the Hundred Gates,* which combines elements of a science fiction story and an historical novel in its tale of a time traveler returning to ancient Thebes in search of two other travelers who have gone missing. Silverberg vividly evokes the sights, sounds, and smells of ancient Egypt, but the novel is more than a skillful rhetorical construction. It poses, once again, a question often raised in his previous work: whether to choose the past or the future. Some of his most notable earlier fiction, despite its pessimistic projections, ended on a progressive note: The choice was made for the future, despite all its perils. The choice made in *Thebes of the Hundred Gates* may mark a change of emphasis for Silverberg.

Although he has been highly praised, Silverberg has not won promotion to the ranks of a significant contemporary novelist as quickly and easily as some other science fiction writers, such as Philip K. Dick or William Gibson. His overwhelming productivity, as well as his continued willingness to publish fiction that is highly competent but not ostentatiously literary, may have inhibited the growth of his serious reputation. In the 1990s, however, it is possible to take stock of his work and to see that it comprises a substantial, and sometimes outstanding, contribution to modern fiction.

—Nicolas Tredell

SIMPSON, Mona

Nationality: American. **Born:** Green Bay, Wisconsin, 14 June 1957. **Education:** University of California, Berkeley, B.A. 1979; Columbia University, M.F.A. 1983. **Awards:** Whiting Writers' award, 1986; National Endowment for the Arts grant, 1986; Guggenheim fellowship, 1988, Hodder fellowship, 1988. **Agent:** Amanda Urban, International Creative Management, 40 West 57th St., New York, New York 10019, U.S.A.

PUBLICATIONS

Novels

Anywhere but Here. New York, Knopf, and London, Bloomsbury, 1986.
The Lost Father. New York, Knopf, and London, Faber, 1992.

*   *   *

In *Anywhere but Here* and *The Lost Father,* Mona Simpson has created characters who are oddly likable, benignly to profoundly troubled, and eerily familiar, though rarely predictable. Simpson fashions powerful, simple prose and tackles awkward subjects with straightforward grace. Her settings—though ranging from California to Egypt to New York—capture the manners and mores of the American Midwest, particularly exploring how "heartland" sensibilities mix with those of either coast. Her novels center on Wisconsin small-town life and the inhabitants who fled, searching for glamour and opportunity, as well as those who stayed in all of their mediocre and eccentric glory.

The primary narrator of *Anywhere But Here,* Ann Stevenson, lives out an adolescent tug-of-war with her unstable and needy mother, Adele. The novel's opening sentence, "We fought," only scratches the surface of their bizarre rapport. Adele, abandoned by her husband, spends much of her adulthood chasing living beyond her means and emotionally abusing her daughter. The word "abuse" is never used in the novel, though Adele's habit of dropping Ann on the side of the highway and driving away (only to return in search of her an hour later) should qualify. It is often difficult to determine who is parenting whom.

Ann recognizes Adele's emotional and financial immaturity. But Adele sometimes becomes the more sympathetic character, as when we see her difficulties as a single mother, trying to provide her daughter with a cosmopolitan, advantaged life in California rather than an ordinary one in Racine. There are moments when it becomes difficult to approve of Ann as well. Readers are not left with an easy identification or an easy hatred.

Adele ostensibly leaves her kindly, aging mother's home to allow Ann to pursue a Hollywood acting career. In the process, she leaves a stale marriage with a washed-up figure skater in search of glamour in Beverly Hills. The title's lament of "anywhere but here" signals not only Adele's restlessness but Ann's, too. Adele and Ann's understanding of what it means to be "have-nots" among the "haves"—and their attempts to pretend otherwise—provide many painful and humorous episodes. The novel is rightly acclaimed for its complex treatment of familial relationships and its keen rendering of mother-daughter bonds.

Simpson's second novel, *The Lost Father,* although still exploring the same modern family, shifts focus to a father-daughter relationship. This time Ann Stevenson is transformed into Mayan Amneh Atassi—her birthname, reflecting her Egyptian heritage. We hear very little from Adele during the course of the novel; she is primarily a reflection of Mayan's often self-destructive and fruitless quest for "Joh" Atassi, a washed up college professor, gambler, swindler, and ladies' man. Again, we follow Mayan's journey, this time from medical school to near madness, as she shuffles her loyalties and her priorities in search of lost origins.

This adult "An" is every bit as savvy and wise as the child. Her desire for the father she never had becomes the focal point for all of the other problems in her life. She questions her search for and wish for a father, but each time she gives it up the desire returns to consume her, poison her romantic relationships, and prevent her from feeling "normal." Mayan's wish for her father is never naive, however. She recognizes that finding her father may be "beside the point"—that she may not want him after all. We follow her hiring detectives, badgering distant relatives, and making friends with telephone operators. Mayan ruminates over her fear of being abandoned by men, her fragmented cultural heritage, and her status as a contemporary American middle-class white woman. She is obsessed with her beauty and weight, her ambition, and her intelligence, never sure precisely how each talent might be put to use or downplayed in the name of her desire to be "like anybody else."

Simpson's novels are remarkable for their unsentimental versions of contemporary womanhood. Her female narrators are strong characters but not invincible heroines; they are victimized but not merely victims. Simpson's prose is insightful but not preachy, eccentric but not outlandish, and entertaining but not simply comedic. Simpson's novels read much more like memoir, providing readers with intricate and painful windows into her characters' psyches.

—Devoney Looser

SINCLAIR, Andrew (Annandale)

Nationality: British. **Born:** Oxford, 21 January 1935. **Education:** The Dragon School, Oxford; Eton College, Berkshire (King's scholar), 1948-53; Trinity College, Cambridge, 1955-58, B.A. (double 1st) in history, 1958; Churchill College, Cambridge, Ph.D. in American history 1962. **Military Service:** Served in the Coldstream Guards, 1953-55: Ensign. **Family:** Married 1) Marianne Alexandre in 1960 (divorced), one son; 2) Miranda Seymour in 1972 (divorced 1984), one son; 3) Sonia Lady Melchett in 1984. **Career:** Harkness fellow, Harvard University, Cambridge, Massachusetts, and Columbia University, New York, 1959-61; fellow and director of Historical Studies, Churchill College, Cambridge, 1961-63; fellow, American Council of Learned Societies, 1963-64; lecturer in American History, University College, London, 1965-67; managing director, Lorrimer Publishing Ltd., London, 1967-84, and Timon Films, 1969-95. **Awards:** Maugham award, 1967. Fellow, Royal Society of Literature, 1973; Fellow, Society of American Historians, 1974. **Address:** 16 Tite Street, London SW3 4HZ, England.

PUBLICATIONS

Novels

The Breaking of Bumbo. London, Faber, and New York, Simon and Schuster, 1959.
My Friend Judas. London, Faber, 1959; New York, Simon and Schuster, 1961.
The Project. London, Faber, and New York, Simon and Schuster, 1960.
The Hallelujah Bum. London, Faber, 1963; as *The Paradise Bum,* New York, Atheneum, 1963.
The Raker. London, Cape, and New York, Atheneum, 1964.
Gog. London, Weidenfeld and Nicolson, and New York, Macmillan, 1967.
Magog. London, Weidenfeld and Nicolson, and New York, Harper, 1972.
The Surrey Cat. London, Joseph, 1976; as *Cat,* London, Sphere, 1977.
A Patriot for Hire. London, Joseph, 1978.
The Facts in the Case of E.A. Poe. London, Weidenfeld and Nicolson, 1979; New York, Holt Rinehart, 1980.
Beau Bumbo. London, Weidenfeld and Nicolson, 1985.
King Ludd. London, Hodder and Stoughton, 1988.
The Far Corners of the Earth. London, Hodder and Stoughton, 1991.
The Strength of the Hills. London, Hodder and Stoughton, 1992.

Uncollected Short Stories

"To Kill a Loris," in *Texas Quarterly* (Austin), Autumn 1961.
"A Head for Monsieur Dimanche," in *Atlantic* (Boston), September 1962.
"The Atomic Band," in *Transatlantic Review 21* (London), Summer 1966.
"Twin," in *The Best of Granta.* London, Secker and Warburg, 1967.

Plays

My Friend Judas (produced London, 1959).
Adventures in the Skin Trade, adaptation of the work by Dylan Thomas (produced London, 1966; Washington, D.C., 1970). London, Dent, 1967; New York, New Directions, 1968.
Under Milk Wood (screenplay). London, Lorrimer, and New York, Simon and Schuster, 1972.
The Blue Angel, adaptation of the screenplay by Josef von Sternberg, music by Jeremy Sams (produced Liverpool, 1983).

Screenplays: *Before Winter Comes,* 1969; *The Breaking of Bumbo,* 1970; *Under Milk Wood,* 1972; *Blue Blood,* 1974; *Malachi's Grove (The Seaweed Children),* 1977.

Television Plays: *The Chocolate Tree,* 1963; *Old Soldiers,* 1964; *Martin Eden,* from the novel by Jack London, 1980.

Other

Prohibition: The Era of Excess. London, Faber, and Boston, Little Brown, 1962; as *Era of Excess,* New York, Harper, 1964.
The Available Man: The Life Behind the Masks of Warren Gamaliel Harding. New York, Macmillan, 1965.

The Better Half: The Emancipation of the American Woman. New York, Harper, 1965; London, Cape, 1966.

A Concise History of the United States. London, Thames and Hudson, and New York, Viking Press, 1967; revised edition, Thames and Hudson, 1970; London, Lorrimer, 1984.

The Last of the Best: The Aristocracy of Europe in the Twentieth Century. London, Weidenfeld and Nicolson, and New York, Macmillan, 1969.

Guevara. London, Fontana, and New York, Viking Press, 1970.

Dylan Thomas: Poet of His People. London, Joseph, 1975; as *Dylan Thomas: No Man More Magical,* New York, Holt Rinehart, 1975.

Inkydoo, The Wild Boy (for children). London, Abelard Schuman, 1976; as *Carina and the Wild Boy,* London, Beaver, 1977.

Jack: A Biography of Jack London. New York, Harper, 1977; London, Weidenfeld and Nicolson, 1978.

The Savage: A History of Misunderstanding. London, Weidenfeld and Nicolson, 1977.

John Ford: A Biography. London, Allen and Unwin, and New York, Dial Press, 1979.

Corsair: The Life of J. Pierpont Morgan. London, Weidenfeld and Nicolson, and Boston, Little Brown, 1981.

The Other Victoria: The Princess Royal and the Great Game of Europe. London, Weidenfeld and Nicolson, 1981; as *Royal Web,* New York, McGraw Hill, 1982.

Sir Walter Raleigh and the Age of Discovery. London, Penguin, 1984.

The Red and the Blue: Intelligence, Treason and the Universities. London, Weidenfeld and Nicolson, 1986; Boston, Little Brown, 1987.

Spiegel: The Man Behind the Pictures. London, Weidenfeld and Nicolson, 1987; Boston, Little Brown, 1988.

War Like a Wasp: The Lost Decade of the Forties. London, Hamish Hamilton, 1989; New York, Viking Hamilton, 1990.

The Need to Give: The Patrons and the Arts. London, Sinclair Stevenson, 1990.

The Naked Savage. London, Sinclair Stevenson, 1991.

The Sword and the Grail. New York, Crown, 1992; London, Century, 1993.

Francis Bacon: His Life and Violent Times. London, Sinclair Stevenson, 1993; New York, Crown, 1994.

In Love and Anger: A View of the 'Sixties. London, Sinclair Stevenson, 1994.

Arts and Cultures: The History of the 50 Years of the Arts Council of Great Britain. London, Sinclair Stevenson, 1995.

Editor, *GWTW* [Gone with the Wind]: *The Screenplay,* by Sidney Howard. London, Lorrimer, 1979.

Editor, *The Call of the Wild, White Fang, and Other Stories,* by Jack London. London, Penguin, 1981.

Editor, *The War Decade: An Anthology of the 1940s.* London, Hamish Hamilton, 1989.

Translator, *Selections from the Greek Anthology.* London, Weidenfeld and Nicolson, 1967; New York, Macmillan, 1968.

Translator, with Carlos P. Hansen, *Bolivian Diary: Ernesto "Che" Guevara.* London, Lorrimer, 1968.

Translator, with Marianne Alexandre, *La Grande Illusion* (scenario), by Jean Renoir. London, Lorrimer, 1968.

*

Critical Study: *Old Lines, New Forces* edited by Robert K. Morris, Rutherford, New Jersey, Fairleigh Dickinson University Press, 1976.

Theatrical Activities:
Director: **Films**—*The Breaking of Bumbo,* 1970; *Under Milk Wood,* 1972; *Blue Blood,* 1974.

Andrew Sinclair comments:

I work between fact and fiction: history and biography, the novel and film. The one informs the other without confusion, I hope. Aging, I find myself admiring professionals, not philosophers. Like the Victorians I have found liberty in writing and in not working for wages. Freedom is having four jobs—and only on hire. Yet age is a stimulus to write only what I want to write, given the tick of time.

*   *   *

From the beginning Andrew Sinclair established himself as a writer of extraordinary fluency and copiousness, whether in fiction or in American social history. His early novels were light-hearted attempts to capture significant moments in the life of the 1950s: the misadventures of a young National Service officer in the Brigade of Guards in *The Breaking of Bumbo* (later adventures are recounted in *Beau Bumbo*), or life in Cambridge when traditional academic forms were coming apart at the seams in *My Friend Judas.* Sinclair's awareness of social nuance and his ready ear for changing forms of speech made him an effective observer, though at the cost of making these novels soon seem dated. *The Project* was a deliberate attempt to move to new ground—the moral fable and apocalyptic science fiction—but the result was wooden and contrived. In *The Hallelujah Bum* Sinclair returned to Ben Birt, the cheerfully iconoclastic hero of *My Friend Judas,* and thrust him into a thin but fast-moving narrative about driving across the United States in a stolen car. The book was partly a loving evocation of American landscape, and partly an example of a new fictional genre that emerged in the 1960s which showed the impact of America on a visiting Englishman.

Sinclair's next novel, *The Raker,* was a fresh endeavour to get away from the fictional recreation of personal experience, though it was still a projection of a personal obsession, in this case what Sinclair has described as a preoccupation with death. *The Raker* is, if anything, too nakedly allegorical, with a strong flavour of Gothic fantasy about it. But it brings together the separate vision of the novelist and the historian, and it is most powerful in its superimposition of the plague-ridden London of the 17th century on the modern metropolis. The preoccupation with history and myth in *The Raker* was fully worked out in *Gog,* which is Sinclair's one outstanding contribution so far to contemporary fiction, compared with which he dismisses his previous five novels as no more than "experiments in style." "Gog" is a legendary giant of British mythology, personified in the novel by an enormous naked man washed up on the Scottish coast in the summer of 1945. The book is essentially a long picaresque account of his walk to London to claim his inheritance as a representative of the British people. On the way he has many fantastic adventures, some comic, some cruel, but all reflecting Sinclair's extraordinary imaginative exuberance. The journey takes him to many sacred places, such as York Minster, Glastonbury, and Stonehenge, and on one level the story is an exploration of the multi-layered past of England, almost like the excavation of an archaeological site. The richness of content is matched by a great variety of formal device: *Gog* draws on the techniques of the comic strip and the cinema, as well as those of the novel. It may, though, be an isolated achievement. *Magog,* its sequel, which describes the life and times of Gog's villainous brother in post-war England, is much less interesting. Although an intelligent, inventive and entertaining piece of social satire, it has little of *Gog's* mythic power.

—Bernard Bergonzi

SINGH, Khushwant

Nationality: Indian. **Born:** Hadali, India (now Pakistan) 2 February 1915. **Education:** The Modern School, New Delhi; St. Stephen's College, New Delhi; Government College, Lahore, B.A. 1934; King's College, London, LL.B. 1938; called to the bar, Inner Temple, London, 1938. **Family:** Married Kaval Malik in 1939; one son and one daughter. **Career:** Practicing lawyer, High Court, Lahore, 1939-47; press attaché, Indian Foreign Service, in London and Ottawa, 1947-51; staff member, Department of Mass Communications, Unesco, Paris, 1954-56; editor, *Yejna,* an Indian government publication, New Delhi, 1956-58; visiting lecturer, Oxford University, 1965, University of Rochester, New York, 1965, Princeton University, New Jersey, 1967, University of Hawaii, Honolulu, 1967, and Swarthmore College, Pennsylvania, 1969; editor, *Illustrated Weekly of India,* Bombay, 1969-78; editor-in-chief, *National Herald,* New Delhi, 1978-79; chief editor, *New Delhi,* 1979-80; editor-in-chief, *Hindustan Times* and *Contour,* both New Delhi, 1980-83. Since 1980 member of the Indian Parliament. Head of the Indian Delegation, Manila Writers Conference, 1965. **Awards:** Rockefeller grant, 1966; Punjab Government grant, 1970; Mohan Singh award, Padma Bhushan, India, 1974. **Address:** 49-E Sujan Singh Park, New Delhi 110 003, Delhi, India.

PUBLICATIONS

Novels

Train to Pakistan. London, Chatto and Windus, 1956; New York, Grove Press, 1961; as *Mano Majra,* Grove Press, 1956.
I Shall Not Hear the Nightingale. New York, Grove Press, 1959; London, Calder, 1961.

Short Stories

The Mark of Vishnu and Other Stories. London, Saturn Press, 1950.
The Voice of God and Other Stories. Bombay, Jaico, 1957.
A Bride for the Sahib and Other Stories. New Delhi, Hind, 1967.
Black Jasmine. Bombay, Jaico, 1971.
The Collected Stories. N.p., Ravi Dayal, 1989.

Play

Television Documentary: *Third World—Free Press* (also presenter; *Third Eye* series), 1982 (UK).

Other

The Sikhs. London, Allen and Unwin, and New York, Macmillan, 1953.
The Unending Trail. New Delhi, Rajkamal, 1957.
The Sikhs Today: Their Religion, History, Culture, Customs, and Way of Life. Bombay, Orient Longman, 1959; revised edition, 1964; revised edition, New Delhi, Sangam, 1976, 1985.
Fall of the Kingdom of the Punjab. Bombay, Orient Longman, 1962.
A History of the Sikhs 1469-1964. Princeton, New Jersey, Princeton University Press, and London, Oxford University Press, 2 vols., 1963-66.
Ranjit Singh: Maharajah of the Punjab 1780-1839. London, Allen and Unwin, 1963.
Not Wanted in Pakistan. New Delhi, Rajkamal, 1965.
Ghadar, 1915: India's First Armed Revolution, with Satindra Singh. New Delhi, R and K, 1966.
Homage to Guru Gobind Singh, with Suneet Veer Singh. Bombay, Jaico, 1966.
Shri Ram: A Biography, with Arun Joshi. London, Asia Publishing, 1968.
Religion of the Sikhs (lecture). Madras, University of Madras, 1968.
Khushwant Singh's India: A Mirror for Its Monsters and Monstrosities. Bombay, India Book House, 1969.
Khushwant Singh's View of India (lectures), edited by Rahul Singh. Bombay, India Book House, 1974.
Khushwant Singh on War and Peace in India, Pakistan, and Bangladesh, edited by Mala Singh. New Delhi, Hind, 1976.
Good People, Bad People, edited by Rahul Singh. New Delhi, Orient, 1977.
Khushwant Singh's India Without Humbug, edited by Rahul Singh. Bombay, India Book House, 1977.
Around the World with Khushwant Singh, edited by Rahul Singh. New Delhi, Orient, 1978.
Indira Gandhi Returns. New Delhi, Vision, 1979.
Editor's Page, edited by Rahul Singh. Bombay, India Book House, 1981.
We Indians. New Delhi, Orient, 1982.
Delhi: A Portrait. New Delhi and Oxford, Oxford University Press, 1983.
The Sikhs, photographs by Raghu Rai. Benares, Lustre Press, 1984.
Tragedy of the Punjab: Operation Bluestar and After, with Kuldip Nayar. New Delhi, Vision, 1984.
Many Faces of Communalism. Chandigarh, Centre for Research in Rural and Urban Development, 1985.
My Bleeding Punjab. New Delhi and London, UBSPD, 1992.

Editor, with Peter Russell, *A Note . . . on G.V. Desani's "All about H. Hatterr" and "Hali."* London and Amsterdam, Szeben, 1952.
Editor, with Jaya Thadani, *Land of the Five Rivers: Stories of the Punjab.* Bombay, Jaico, 1965.
Editor, *Sunset of the Sikh Empire,* by Sita Ram Kohli. Bombay, Orient Longman, 1967.
Editor, *I Believe.* New Delhi, Hind, 1971.
Editor, *Love and Friendship.* New Delhi, Sterling, 1974.
Editor, with Qurratulain Hyder, *Stories from India.* New Delhi, Sterling, 1974.
Editor, *Gurus, Godmen, and Good People.* Bombay, Orient Longman, 1975.
Editor, with Shobha Dé, *Uncertain Liaisons: Sex, Strife and Togetherness in Urban India,* New Delhi and London, Viking, 1993.

Translator, *Jupji: The Sikh Morning Prayer.* London, Probsthain, 1959.

Translator, with M.A. Husain, *Umrao Jan Ada: Courtesan of Lucknow,* by Mohammed Ruswa. Bombay, Orient Longman, 1961.

Translator, *The Skeleton and Other Writings,* by Amrita Pritam. Bombay, Jaico, 1964.

Translator, *I Take This Woman,* by Rajinder Singh Bedi. New Delhi, Hind, 1967.

Translator, *Hymns of Guru Nanak.* Bombay, Orient Longman, 1969.

Translator, *Dreams in Debris: A Collection of Punjabi Short Stories,* by Satindra Singh. Bombay, Jaico, 1972.

Translator, with others, *Sacred Writings of the Sikhs.* London, Allen and Unwin, 1974.

Translator, with others, *Come Back, My Master, and Other Stories,* by K.S. Duggal. New Delhi, Bell, 1978.

Translator, *Shikwa and Jawab-i-Shikwa/Complaint and Answer: Iqbal's Dialogue with Allah.* New Delhi and Oxford, Oxford University Press, 1981.

Translator, *Amrita Pritam: Selected Poems.* New Delhi, Bharatiya Jnanpith, 1982.

Translator, *The Skeleton and That Man,* by Amrita Pritam. London, Oriental University Press, 1987.

*

Critical Studies: *Khushwant Singh* by V.A. Shahane, New York, Twayne, 1972; *Three Contemporary Novelists: Khushwant Singh, Chaman Nahal, and Salman Rushdie* by R.K. Dhawan, New Delhi, Classical, 1985.

*   *   *

Although Khushwant Singh is a distinguished Sikh historian, his reputation as a fiction writer rests solely upon *Train to Pakistan,* a harrowing tale of events along the borders of the newly divided nations of India and Pakistan in the summer of 1947.

The atrocities that accompanied the division of these nations had an enormously depressing effect on a world that had just fought a long, bitter war to defeat practitioners of genocide. The somewhat artificial division of the subcontinent (the boundaries remain in dispute) had been strictly along religious lines: Pakistan was to be a nation of Moslems; India, of Hindus, Sikhs, and what Singh calls "pseudo Christians." There were, however, colonies of non-coreligionists left within each nation. Rather than settle down to peaceful coexistence or permit a passive exchange of populations, partisans on both sides set out on a violent campaign of annihilating the communities that were trapped on their ancestral lands beyond friendly borders.

Train to Pakistan is set against a background of this ruthless and senseless mass destruction. This powerful novel derives its title from a squalid border town, where a rail line crosses from India to Pakistan. At first this mixed community of Sikhs and Moslems is undisturbed by the violence that is breaking out elsewhere on the frontier, but inevitably it, too, is caught up in the mass hysteria as ominous "ghost trains" of slain Sikhs begin to arrive in town from across the border. Agitation for reprisals follows when the Moslems of the town are at last rounded up and fanatics urge the Sikhs of the community to kill their former neighbors as the train carrying them to Pakistan passes through town.

Singh's story contrasts the ineffectualness of the educated and ruling classes with the power of the violent and irrational peasants.

Early in the story the town's only educated citizen, a Hindu moneylender, is gruesomely murdered by a band of Dacoity (professional bandits). Juggut Singh, a passionate Sikh farmer with a bad record, is suspected of the crime—though he played no part in it—and imprisoned; at the same time, an educated young former Sikh, Iqbal, comes to the community to agitate for a radical cause and is also imprisoned on suspicion of being a Moslem League agent. While these two are off the scene, the unlighted trains with their cargoes of dead begin to roll into town, and the agitation for reprisals begins. Both the young radical and a government commissioner, Hukum Chand, are unable to prevent the vicious plot against the fleeing Moslems from being carried out, and collapse emotionally; but in an extraordinary gesture of self-sacrifice, Juggut Singh—who had been in love with a Moslem girl—foils the plotters and allows the train to roll over his body "on to Pakistan."

Singh's terse fable suggests a profound disillusionment with the power of law, reason, and intellect in the face of elemental human passions. The philosophy that sparked his tale seems to be expressed through the thoughts of Iqbal, the young radical, as he realizes his helplessness and drifts off into a drugged sleep the night of the climactic incident of the train's passing: "If you look at things as they are . . . there does not seem to be a code either of man or God on which one can pattern one's conduct. . . . In such circumstances what can you do but cultivate an utter indifference to all values? Nothing matters." The same disillusioned tone characterizes Singh's second novel, *I Shall Not Hear the Nightingale,* but the rather wooden tale is almost overwhelmed by heavy-handed ironies. The action occurs about five years before that of the earlier novel, at a time when the British are expressing a willingness to get out of India once the Axis nations have been defeated in World War II. Sher Singh, the ambitious but lazy son of a Sikh senior magistrate, cannot decide between two worlds, "the one of security provided by his father . . . and the other full of applause that would come to him as the heroic leader of a band of terrorists." His dabblings in terrorism—actually abetted by a cynical young British civil servant—end in the pointless killing of a village leader, who has also been a political spy. Sher is suspected of the murder and imprisoned, but on the advice of his mother (when his father will not speak to him) he refuses to betray his companions. The British release him for lack of evidence, and he is honored as a kind of local hero—seemingly his political future is assured. His father is even honored by the British.

The novel takes a much dimmer view of the human capacity for compassion and self-sacrifice than *Train to Pakistan* (at one point Sher Singh reflects that "for him loyalties were not as important as the ability to get away with the impression of having them"), so that the novel ends not with the kind of thrilling gesture that its predecessor did, but with the obsequious magistrate, Sher Singh's father, sitting in the Britisher's garden observing, "As a famous English poet has said, 'All's well that ends well.'" The title of the book comes from Sher Singh's reply to his mother when she asks, "What will you get if the English leave this country?" He replies lyrically, "Spring will come to our barren land once more . . . once more the nightingales will sing." Khushwant Singh evidently thinks not, if the land is to fall into such self-serving hands as Sher Singh's.

His ironic short stories resemble Angus Wilson's and express a similar disillusionment about man's rationality. Singh is a brilliant, sardonic observer of a world undergoing convulsive changes; and his novels provide a unique insight into one of the major political catastrophes of this century. His difficulties in fusing his editorial comments with the action in his stories, however, cause his novels to remain principally dramatized essays.

—Warren French

SIONIL JOSE, F(rancisco)

Nationality: Filipino. **Born:** Rosales, Pangasinan, 3 December 1924. **Education:** The University of Santo Tomas, Manila, Litt.B. 1949. **Family:** Married Teresita G. Jovellanos in 1949; five sons and two daughters. **Career:** Staff member, *Commonweal,* Manila, 1947-48; assistant editor, United States Information Agency, U.S. Embassy, Manila, 1948-49; associate editor, 1949-57, and managing editor, 1957-60, Manila *Times Sunday* magazine, and editor of Manila *Times* annual *Progress,* 1958-60; editor, *Comment* quarterly, Manila, 1956-62; managing editor, *Asia* magazine, Hong Kong, 1961-62; information officer, Colombo Plan Headquarters, Ceylon, 1962-64; correspondent, *Economist,* London, 1968-69. Since 1965 publisher, Solidaridad Publishing House, and general manager, Solidaridad Bookshop, since 1966 publisher and editor, *Solidarity* magazine, and since 1967 manager, Solidaridad Galleries, all Manila. Lecturer, Arellano University, 1962, University of the East graduate school, 1968, and De La Salle University, 1984-86, all Manila; writer-in-residence, National University of Singapore, 1987; visiting research scholar, Center for Southeast Asian Studies, Kyoto University, Japan, 1988. Consultant, Department of Agrarian Reform, 1968-79. Founder and national secretary, PEN Philippine Center, 1958. **Awards:** U.S. Department of State Smith-Mundt grant, 1955; Asia Foundation grant, 1960; National Press Club award, for journalism, 3 times; British Council grant, 1967; Palanca award, for journalism, 3 times, and for novel, 1981; ASPAC fellowship, 1971; Rockefeller Foundation Bellagio award, 1979; Cultural Center of the Philippines award, 1979; City of Manila award, 1979; Magsaysay award, 1980; East-West Center fellowship (Honolulu), 1981; International House of Japan fellowship, 1983; Outstanding Fulbrighters award, 1988, for literature; Cultural Center of the Philippines award, 1989, for literature. **Address:** Solidaridad Publishing House, 531 Padre Faura, Ermita P.O. Box 3959, Manila, Philippines.

PUBLICATIONS

Novels

The Pretenders. Manila, Solidaridad, 1962.
Tree. Manila, Solidaridad, 1978.
My Brother, My Executioner. Manila, New Day, 1979.
Mass. Amsterdam, Wereldvenster, 1982; London, Allen and Unwin, 1984; as *Mis,* Manila, Solidaridad, 1983.
Po-on. Manila, Solidaridad, 1985.
Ermita. Manila, Solidaridad, 1988.
Spiderman. Manila, Solidaridad, 1991.
Sin. Manila, Solidaridad, 1994.

Short Stories

The Pretenders and Eight Short Stories. Manila, Regal, 1962.

The God Stealer and Other Stories. Manila, Solidaridad, 1968.
Waywaya and Other Short Stories from the Philippines. Hong Kong, Heinemann, 1980.
Two Filipino Women (novellas). Manila, New Day, 1982.
Platinum and Other Stories. Manila, Solidaridad, 1983.
Olvidon and Other Stories. Manila, Solidaridad, 1988.
Three Filipino Women (novellas). New York, Random House, 1992.

Uncollected Short Stories

"The Chief Mourner" (serial), in *Women's Weekly* (Manila), 11 May-10 July 1953.
"The Balete Tree" (serial), in *Women's Weekly* (Manila), 4 March 1954-6 July 1956.

Poetry

Questions. Manila, Solidaridad, 1988.

Other

(Selected Works). Moscow, 1977.
A Filipino Agenda for the 21st Century. Manila, Solidaridad, 1987.
Conversations with F. Sionil Jose, edited by Miguel Bernad. Manila, Vera-Reyes, 1991.

Editor, *Equinox 1.* Manila, Solidaridad, 1965.
Editor, *Asian PEN Anthology 1.* Manila, Solidaridad, 1966; New York, Taplinger, 1967.

*

Critical Study: *F. Sionil Jose and His Fiction* edited by Alfredo T. Morales, Manila, Vera-Reyes, 1990.

*   *   *

F. Sionil Jose holds two distinctions in Philippine writing in English, indeed in Philippine writing in general. He is the only writer who has produced a series of novels that constitute an epic imaginative creation of a century of Philippine life, and he is perhaps the most widely known abroad, his writings having been translated into more foreign languages than those of any other Filipino writer.

We are introduced to the early world of Sionil Jose in *Po-on.* The earliest novel in terms of chronology, it is set in the later decades of the 19th century during the decaying years of the Spanish Empire, which still retained some struggling remnants of its colonial civil services, including some manorial lords in the plains of Central Luzon, descendants of the Basque and Spanish-Catalan settlers, served by immigrants from the deep Ilocano country up north. In one scene a Basque grandee comes to the town of Rosales, when the settlement is still unorganized, and designates the limits of his domain with his whip.

After the Philippine revolution, which saw the change of colonial masters from Spanish to American, no significant change occurred in the feudal relations of the agrarian economy. In fact, free trade was instituted between the Philippines and the United States, benefiting the native landowners and their hirelings and the leaders of industry and their subalterns while impoverishing the tenants of the land and the laborers in small-scale industries. Such relationships are examined in *Tree.* Despite all the injustices they suffered during the American colonial regime, when war came in December 1941, the tenants and their leaders decided to fight the Japanese invaders as guerrillas, hoping that at the end of the war they would be afforded improved living conditions.

My Brother, My Executioner occurs at this point in Sionil Jose's epic narrative. It deals with the activities of two half-brothers, one a dispossessed guerrilla. With more than enough property to keep his family in comfort, the bourgeois half-brother can afford to entertain liberal ideas and even consider embracing progressive ways, but his dispossessed half-brother avenges himself by destroying the more fortunate.

The master-servant, lord-slave relationship may also be found in the industrial world in Manila. One specific case is Antonio Samson in *The Pretenders*. Overcoming the disadvantages of rural birth, Samson manages to earn a doctorate at a prestigious New England university, afterwards planning to return to his hometown sweetheart whom he had impregnated. Instead, he is snatched away by a powerful agro-industrial baron and married off to his socialite daughter. Samson is now made to move in elevated social circles and do work he had not prepared himself to do. He has frequent spats with his wife who, he discovers to his dismay, has been conducting affairs. Determined to end his shame, Samson throws himself under a train.

We are afforded a rich composite picture of events of the contemporary Philippines in the last novel, *Mass,* covering the years before and after the proclamation of martial rule. A few of the old names reappear, but new characters emerge—student activists, women's liberation movement followers, drug addicts, intellectuals. The major character is the bastard son of Antonio Samson, Pepe Samson, now living in the slums of Tondo. He is a faithful follower of a former anti-Japanese Huk commander now devoted to local affairs, and a student leader at a university in Manila. A reform movement that started with protest at the increase in oil prices becomes a struggle for human rights, student rights, tenant's rights, women's liberation, and eventually a heterogeneous mass of protests manipulated by fraudulent leaders. After the failure of the intended uprising, one of the dedicated characters decides to return to Central Luzon to seek his roots and build anew.

The Philippines has been under colonial rule for some four centuries, one fourth of which has been portrayed in this epic. We are shown all kinds of people, from the moral cowards to the fiercely heroic, from the ferociously greedy to the selflessly philanthropic. In the face of all the tragic events in their lives, many of the people in Sionil Jose's epic are still able to say "We shall overcome."

—Leopoldo Y. Yabes

SLAUGHTER, Carolyn

Nationality: British. **Born:** New Delhi, India, 7 January 1946. Educated in Botswana and England. **Family:** Married 1) Denis Pack-Beresford (divorced); 2) Daniel Cromer (divorced), one daughter and one son; 3) Kemp Battle, one daughter and one son. **Career:** Advertising copywriter, Garland Compton Ltd., 1966-68, Norman Craig and Kummel, 1969-71, Collett Dickenson and Pearce, 1971-72, Nadler Larimer and Cromer, 1972-74, all London. Freelance writer, 1974-85. **Awards:** Geoffrey Faber Memorial prize, 1977. **Address:** 2805 Main Street, Lawrenceville, New Jersey 08648, U.S.A.

PUBLICATIONS

Novels

The Story of the Weasel. London, Hart Davis, 1976; as *Relations,* New York, Mason Charter, 1977.
Columba. London, Hart Davis, 1977; New York, Panther House, 1979.
Magdalene. London, Hart Davis, 1978; New York, Evans, 1979.
Dreams of the Kalahari. London, Granada, 1981; New York, Scribner, 1987.
Heart of the River. London, Granada, 1982; New York, St. Martin's Press, 1983.
The Banquet. London, Allen Lane, 1983; New Haven, Connecticut, Ticknor and Fields, 1984.
A Perfect Woman. London, Allen Lane, 1984; New York, Ticknor and Fields, 1985.
The Innocents. London, Viking, and New York, Scribner, 1986.
The Widow. London, Heinemann, 1989.

*   *   *

> She decided she'd read more than enough of those well-balanced, neatly clipped English parochial novels where the greatest excitement was reading the last page and being done with the damn thing.
>
> *(Heart of the River)*

With this resolution, Constance, Caroline Slaughter's heroine, throws her paperback "with a flabby flop" into the swimming pool. It is not hard to see the author behind the character. Slaughter herself first grasps and then rejects the English paperback, casting off the norms of the genre, transmuting it with her own fierce emotional vitality. Her art sheds, easily but with far reaching consequences, the conventions of romantic fiction, creating novels which are characterized by a naked honesty which is at times almost confessional in its intimacy. While her themes are those of paperback romances—love, relationships, and the family—her quest for psychological reality leaves the art of idealization and euphemism far behind. Her art shatters the convenient collusion between romance writer and reader as to what human beings feel.

Slaughter portrays the dark knots of bitterness and vulnerability, pain and need, which lie within the individual psyche. Her vision strikes dramatic contrasts to fictional norms. One example of this is an unusual frankness in her treatment of sex. Another fictional taboo to be broken is that of monogamous love. Constance in *Heart of the River* (as Humphrey in *A Perfect Woman*) is torn by love for more than one person. The violence of our needs and our own inner contradictions destroy the easy assumptions about the consequences of falling in love.

The thirst for psychological honesty—and Slaughter is acutely psychologically aware—draws her work deeper and deeper into the inner wounds from which our compulsive emotions spring: the traumas of childhood and early sexual experience, the relationship with the mother, the secrets passed from one generation to another within the family. The epigraph to *Heart of the River,* from Eliot, is appropriate to all her work:

> We shall not cease from exploration
> And the end of all our exploring
> Will be to arrive where we started
> And know the place for the first time.

While not making explicit use of psychoanalysis, there is an impulse within Slaughter's work which parallels that of the analyst: the search for inner knowledge, for discovery of, and confrontation with, the secrets hidden within the self. Her plots are driven not only by the momentum of unfolding action, but by that of unfolding knowledge. As in classical tragedy, there is a pattern of concealment and revelation leading to eventual denouement and catharsis. At the climax of her novels are realizations: both in the sense of comprehension, and in the sense of fulfillment of what has long lain hidden. At the same time as characters approach the crisis of their lives they (and the reader) approach understanding of the seeds of that crisis, often sown far in the past. In *Heart of the River* Slaughter quotes Shiva Naipaul, "To rediscover a lost past is to rediscover an essential part of the self." Such rediscovery however, as in *The Innocents* and *The Banquet,* can be destructive as well as enlightening.

As the analyst's sensitivity and acuteness are brought to bear on individuals, so Slaughter also scrutinizes tensions between people, particularly between lovers. *The Banquet* and *A Perfect Woman* show how our deepest needs become focused on the objects of erotic attraction; *The Widow* and *Heart of the River* demonstrate the violent battles which take place within relationships. We feel, too, the rage of the lover against those parts of the beloved which cannot be contained by a relationship. Such tension and mutual incomprehension are cleverly illustrated by Slaughter's technique of split narratives, where each of the protagonists tells a segment of story in turn.

The psychological conflicts which fascinate Slaughter find logical extension in the split personality of Bella in *The Widow*. Similarly, the psychological violence Slaughter records is writ large in the act of homicide; in men who kill women (Harold in *The Banquet*) and in women who kill men (Rebecca in *The Widow,* Zelda in *The Innocents*). The characters who commit these acts are not incomprehensible monsters: they are themselves the heroes and heroines, and their stories are recounted from within, and in their own words. They are acted upon by the same compulsions and passions which drive us all.

Slaughter's novels are at the same time love stories and dispatches from a war between women and men, a war for the goals of fulfillment and the satisfaction of emotional need. This war spills over into sexual politics. *The Widow* shows the dissociation between two personalities: Rebecca, an earthy, home-loving woman in floral dresses, and Bella, a severe, cerebral career-minded surgeon. The war is however primarily fought out between lovers. Constance's weary acknowledgment of "the sadomasochistic cycle" of her relationship highlights an underlying connection between love and pain. We, the readers, are implicated in this war, and are brought to identify with the characters who take it to its most violent extreme. In *The Banquet* Slaughter teases the reader with sensuous prose which anticipates the fulfillment of exquisite fantasies:

> Then she opened her lips and the red fruit disappeared into the wet dome of her mouth; he watched with intensity, as though at any moment he expected the pink flesh to cry out . . . the seductive breath of the warm strawberries pierced him with longing; the juices ran into the corners of her lips and it was agonizing not to kiss her.

The sheer eroticism of Harold's descriptions, and his sensitivity, draw us into his disturbed mind. Similarly in *The Widow*, Bella succeeds in showing that Joseph, the psychiatrist, is as incomplete

and as broken as she is: that all face the same inner search and struggle for wholeness.

Slaughter's power to portray a particular place and culture is considerable, whether it be rich suburban life in Britain of the 1980s, or the heat and brutality of Africa in revolution. It is however in setting new standards of emotional veracity that her greatest achievement lies.

—Edmund Cusick

SMILEY, Jane

Nationality: American. **Born:** Los Angeles, 26 September 1949. **Education:** Vassar College, B.A. in English 1971; University of Iowa, M.A. 1975, M.F.A. 1976, Ph.D. 1978. **Family:** Married 1) John Whiston, 1970 (divorced 1975); 2) William Silag, 1978 (divorced), two daughters; 3) Stephen Mark Mortensen, 1987. **Career:** Assistant professor, 1981-84, associate professor, 1984-89, professor, 1989-90, and since 1992, Distinguished Professor, all Iowa State University. Visiting assistant professor, University of Iowa, 1981, 1987. **Awards:** Fulbright grant, 1976-77; Pushcart prize, 1977, for "Jeffrey, Believe Me"; O. Henry award, 1982, for "The Pleasure of Her Company," 1985, for "Lily," and 1988; NEA grant, 1978, 1987; Friends of American Writers prize, 1981; Pulitzer prize, 1992, and National Book Critics Circle award, 1992, both for *A Thousand Acres;* Midland Author's award, 1992; Heartland prize, 1992; **Address:** Department of English, Iowa State University, 201 Ross, Ames, Iowa 50011-1401, U.S.A.

PUBLICATIONS

Novels

Barn Blind. New York, Harper and Row, 1980; London, Flamingo, 1994.
At Paradise Gate. New York, Simon and Schuster, 1981.
Duplicate Keys. New York, Knopf, and London, Cape 1984.
Greenlanders. New York, Knopf, and London, Collins, 1988.
A Thousand Acres. New York, Knopf, and London, Flamingo, 1991.
Moo. New York, Knopf, and London, Flamingo, 1995.

Short Stories

The Age of Grief. New York, Knopf, 1987; London, Collins, 1988.
Ordinary Love and Good Will (novellas). New York, Knopf, 1989; London, Collins, 1990.
The Life of the Body, with linoleum cuts by Susan Nees. Minneapolis, Minnisota, Coffee House Press, 1990.

Other

Catskill Crafts: Artisans of the Catskill Mountains. New York, Crown, 1988.

*   *   *

Jane Smiley's congenial turf is the dailiness of daily life, as its domestic rhythms play themselves out in a variety of settings and circumstances. She writes, in short, about families—a subject that once occupied literature's very center but now seems ignored. That Smiley came to wide critical attention with *A Thousand Acres,* a novel that won her both a Pulitzer Prize and a National Circle Critics Award, is true enough, but it is even truer that earlier collections (*The Age of Grief* and *Ordinary Love & Good Will*) amply demonstrated that she could write beautifully about family members.

As a tale of a tyrannical father who resolves to divide his thousand-acre Iowa farm among his three daughters, only to slip into madness, curse his offspring, and venture out alone into a fearsome storm, Smiley's novel is filled with correlations to *King Lear*—not only in terms of allusion and plot but also in its inevitable arc toward tragedy. Generally speaking, reviewer-critics praised Smiley's large ambitions and infectious style, but some worried that the novel's schema was a bit *too* schematic. However, there are at least as many reasons to think of Dreiser's *Sister Carrie* or Arthur Miller's *The Death of a Salesman* as one turns the pages of Smiley's altogether engrossing novel.

Moreover, *King Lear* represents only a fraction of Smiley's concerns; others include farming as it has evolved into big business, dysfunctional families, and even dashes of feminist theory. Perhaps Smiley tried to pack too many disparate concerns between the covers of a single novel (a criticism that might also be made of *Moo,* her effort to squeeze a large land-grant university under the novelist's microscope), but it is clear that *A Thousand Acres* is a brava performance in ways that *Barn Blind, At Paradise Gate,* or even *The Greenlanders* are not. For in *A Thousand Acres,* the slow gathering of quotidian detail means to tackle large, existential questions: Not only what it means to be a true daughter but also, as Ron Carlson points out, "what is the price to be paid for trying one's whole life to please a proud father who slenderly knows himself—who coveted his land the way he loved his daughters, not wisely but too well?"

By contrast, *Moo* asks what kind of institution is the American university in the 1990s, and it sets about making its estimates by focusing not so much on individual characters (several administrators, a handful of colorful professors, and a slice of students) within an academic setting as on the setting itself. "What is a university?" one of her characters asks, and the answer seems hazy at best. Indeed, the novel's main character is not a human being at all but rather a pig named Earl Butz. Like most of those feeding from the university's deep trough, Smiley's pig lives only to eat and then to eat some more. He is, in short, the deep secret hidden in the bowels of Moo University. As Provost Harstad puts it:

> Over the years . . . everyone around the university had given free reign to his or her desires, and the institution had, with a fine, trembling responsiveness, answered, "Why not?" It had become, more than anything, a vast network of interlocking wishes.

No doubt there will be those who resist Smiley's portrait of the university as hog heaven ("Unfair! Unfair!" I can hear them muttering), just as there must have been those Iowa farmers who did not see their lives on the land accurately reflected in *A Thousand Acres.* But a novelist has other allegiances, and Smiley's commitment to the dictums of art has produced reams of extraordinary prose already and promises even more in the future.

—Sanford Pinsker

SMITH, Emma

Nationality: British. **Born:** Newquay, Cornwall, 21 August 1923. **Family:** Married R.L. Stewart-Jones in 1951 (died 1957); one son and one daughter. **Awards:** Atlantic award, 1947; Rhys Memorial prize, 1949; James Tait Black Memorial prize for *The Far Cry,* 1950. **Agent:** Curtis Brown, 162-68 Regent Street, London W1R 5TB, England.

PUBLICATIONS

Novels

Maidens' Trip. London, Putnam, 1948.
The Far Cry. London, MacGibbon and Kee, 1949; New York, Random House, 1950.
The Opportunity of a Lifetime. London, Hamish Hamilton, 1978; New York, Doubleday, 1980.

Uncollected Short Stories

"A Surplus of Lettuces," in *The Real Thing,* edited by Peggy Woodford. London, Bodley Head, 1977.
"Mackerel," in *Misfits,* edited by Peggy Woodford. London, Bodley Head, 1984.

Fiction (for children)

Emily: The Story of a Traveller. London, Nelson, 1959; as *Emily: The Travelling Guinea Pig,* New York, McDowell Obolensky, 1959.
Out of Hand. London, Macmillan, 1963; New York, Harcourt Brace, 1964.
Emily's Voyage. London, Macmillan, and New York, Harcourt Brace, 1966.
No Way of Telling. London, Bodley Head, and New York, Atheneum, 1972.

Other

Village Children: A Soviet Experience. Moscow, Progress, 1982.

*

Emma Smith comments:

(1991) What one writes for children is quite as important as what one writes for adults, and I'm not at all sure it isn't more important; because what children read can color their feelings, and affect their behavior, for the rest of their lives. If they are sufficiently impressed, what they read is absorbed into themselves and becomes part of their own experience to an extent that can't be so after they've grown up. Consequently, everything I write for children is really full of secret messages and exhortations and warnings of what I think the whole of life, which lies ahead waiting for them, is all about, and what I think they're going to need in the way of equipment.

*   *   *

Emma Smith has published three novels and several books designed for the young. In all her work there are a precise creation of character, a sensitive response to setting, and a careful attention to detail.

Her first book, *Maidens' Trip,* set in England during World War II, is the story of three girls, Emma, Charity, and Nanette, who, during the manpower shortage, become "boaters" and guide their motorboat *Venus* and its "butty" *Adrane* over the network of locks and canals running through the heartland of the English countryside. Their adventures, observations, and problems make up the substance of the story as, without formal plot or characterizations, Smith manages to create a forward-moving, frequently suspenseful narrative. The adventures become misadventures as awkwardly at first, and later with more skill, the girls make the trip for supplies from London to Birmingham and back again. There are the physical hardships of rain and cold, blistered hands and aching backs; the hazards of machinery broken down, accidents with other boats, mud that sticks and locks that refuse to open. Charity is the housewife; Nanette, the coquette; Emma, the steady "professional" who directs the whole operation. The reality of the constant rain and cold with the contrasted coziness of the little cabin on the *Venus,* the ubiquitous steaming cups of tea, the hearty flavor of the cooking stew, and the sights and sounds of the loading docks form a background for the most memorable feature of the book—the characterization of the girls and their realization of the world of the "boaters," a world completely apart from that of a great nation at war. Even the brief appearance of a young soldier on leave is no more than a vague reminder of the danger and death in the world beyond. The other notable feature of the book is Smith's understanding of the three young girls forced by circumstances to deal with people and situations totally foreign to them. Each is a real person; not one of the three a stereotype of the adolescent. Each, however, at the same time is realized as young and immature.

Smith's second book, *The Far Cry,* is even more distinguished than *Maidens' Trip.* It is the story of an eccentric schoolmaster, Mr. Digby, who flees with his 14-year-old daughter, Teresa, to India and the sanctuary of his elder daughter, Ruth, to escape his estranged second wife, Teresa's mother. Their departure and trip across the ocean make up the first two sections of the book; the trip across India by train, the third. The fourth section is Ruth's as the reader discovers that she and her husband Edwin have not succeeded in resolving all the differences of their marriage. The last section is a kind of summary for Teresa when, confronted by the sudden horror of her father's death from a heart attack and Ruth's accidental death in Calcutta, she is obliged to become more mature than seems possible for her to be. Even at the end she "had yet to learn that the relationships of people are never established, are ever mutable. . . ." All the principal characters are skillfully drawn: Mr. Digby, a failure as husband, father, and schoolmaster; Ruth, an exotic beauty without confidence in herself or her role as wife; Teresa, sensitive and perceptive, escaping from the repression of her unimaginative Aunt May; and Edwin, the young English tea planter who understands India and his tea workers far more than he does his beautiful wife Ruth.

The journey from England to India, the introduction of India itself, and the daily life of the tea plantation make up the chronology of the story. There is hardly a plot in the conventional definition of the term since there is little doubt from the beginning that Teresa and her father will escape her American mother. The real focus of the novel is on Teresa and her varying responses to the people she meets and the constantly shifting scenery she observes. Smith is especially good in realizing the detail of setting—the crowded life on board ship; the arresting picture of camels and their drivers at Port Suez, a kind of point in time for Teresa; the arrival at Bombay and the acquisition of their bearer, Sam; the long uncertain train trip in dirty cramped quarters; the English way of life Ruth has created in the midst of a tea plantation. The book is as full of the multitude of details as is reality itself, but each so skillfully chosen that it seems precisely right for the observation of the characters to whom it is assigned. *The Far Cry* is a beautifully sensitive novel of time, place, and character.

The Opportunity of a Lifetime was Smith's first adult novel for almost 30 years. It again centers on a young girl. In this case the heroine is a 15-year-old on a summer holiday in Cornwall in 1937. And again there are many finely wrought characters, a nice sense of time and place, and moving contrasts between innocence and betrayal. If Smith has chosen a rather limited range, her virtue is that she has done well what she set out to do, and her work shows an unusual sensitivity to people and a real artist's eye for detail.

—Annibel Jenkins

SMITH, Iain Crichton

Nationality: British. **Born:** Iain Mac A'Ghobhainn in Glasgow, Scotland, 1 January 1928. **Education:** The University of Aberdeen, M.A. (honours) in English 1949. **Military Service:** Served in the British Army Education Corps, 1950-52: Sergeant. **Family:** Married in 1977. **Career:** Secondary school teacher, Clydebank, 1952-55; teacher of English, Oban High School, 1955-77. Since 1982 member of Literature Committee, Scottish Arts Council. **Awards:** Scottish Arts Council award, 1966, 1968, 1974, 1978, and prize, 1968; BBC award, for television play, 1970; Book Council award, 1970; Silver Pen award, 1971; Queen's Silver Jubilee medal, 1978, Commonwealth Poetry prize, 1986; Society of Authors Travelling scholarship, 1987; Saltire award, 1992; Forward prize for best poem, 1994. LL.D.: Dundee University, 1983; D.Litt.: University of Aberdeen, 1968; Glasgow University, 1984. Fellow, Royal Society of Literature. O.B.E. (Officer, Order of the British Empire), 1980. **Address:** Tigh na Fuaran, Taynuilt, Argyll PA35 1JW, Scotland.

PUBLICATIONS

Novels

Consider the Lilies. London, Gollancz, 1968; as *The Alien Light,* Boston, Houghton Mifflin, 1969.
The Last Summer. London, Gollancz, 1969.
My Last Duchess. London, Gollancz, 1971.
Goodbye, Mr. Dixon. London, Gollancz, 1974.
An t-Aonaran (The Hermit). Glasgow, University of Glasgow Celtic Department, 1976.
An End to Autumn. London, Gollancz, 1978.
On the Island. London, Gollancz, 1979.
A Field Full of Folk. London, Gollancz, 1982.
The Search. London, Gollancz, 1983.
The Tenement. London, Gollancz, 1985.

In the Middle of the Wood. London, Gollancz, 1987.
The Dream. London, Macmillan, 1990.
An Honourable Death. London, Macmillan, 1992.

Short Stories

Burn is Aran (Bread and Water; includes verse). Glasgow, Gairm, 1960.
An Dubh is an Gorm (The Black and the Blue). Aberdeen, Aberdeen University, 1963.
Maighstirean is Ministearan (Schoolmasters and Ministers). Inverness, Club Leabhar, 1970.
Survival Without Error and Other Stories. London, Gollancz, 1970.
The Black and the Red. London, Gollancz, 1973.
An t-Adhar Ameireagenach (The American Sky). Inverness, Club Leabhar, 1973.
The Village. Inverness, Club Leabhar, 1976.
The Hermit and Other Stories. London, Gollancz, 1977.
Murdo and Other Stories. London, Gollancz, 1981.
Mr. Trill in Hades and Other Stories. London, Gollancz, 1984.
Selected Stories. Manchester, Carcaret, 1990.

Plays

An Coileach (The Cockerel; produced Glasgow, 1966). Glasgow, An Comunn Gaidhealach, 1966.
A'Chuirt (The Trial; produced Glasgow, 1966). Glasgow, An Comunn Gaidhealach, 1966.
A Kind of Play (produced Mull, 1975).
Two by the Sea (produced Mull, 1975).
The Happily Family: Married Couple (produced Mull, 1977).

Radio Plays: *Goodman and Death Mahoney,* 1980; *Mr. Trill,* 1988; *The Visitor,* 1988.

Poetry

The Long River. Edinburgh, M. Macdonald, 1955.
New Poets 1959, with Karen Gershon and Christopher Levenson. London, Eyre and Spottiswoode, 1959.
Deer on the High Hills: A Poem. Edinburgh, Giles Gordon, 1960.
Thistles and Roses. London, Eyre and Spottiswoode, 1961.
The Law and the Grace. London, Eyre and Spottiswoode, 1965.
Biobuill is Sanasan Reice (Bibles and Advertisements). Glasgow, Gairm, 1965.
Three Regional Voices, with Michael Longley and Barry Tebb. London, Poet and Printer, 1968.
At Helensburgh. Belfast, Festival, 1968.
From Bourgeois Land. London, Gollancz, 1969.
Selected Poems. London, Gollancz, and Chester Springs, Pennsylvania, Dufour, 1970.
Penguin Modern Poets 21, with George Mackay Brown and Norman MacCaig. London, Penguin, 1972.
Love Poems and Elegies. London, Gollancz, 1972.
Hamlet in Autumn. Edinburgh, M. Macdonald, 1972.
Rabhdan is rudan (Verses and Things). Glasgow, Gairm, 1973.
Eadar Fealla-dhà is Glaschu (Between Comedy and Glasgow). Glasgow, University of Glasgow Celtic Department, 1974.
Orpheus and Other Poems. Preston, Lancashire, Akros, 1974.
Poems for Donalda. Belfast, Ulsterman, 1974.
The Permanent Island: Gaelic Poems, translated by the author. Edinburgh, M. Macdonald, 1975.

The Notebooks of Robinson Crusoe and Other Poems. London, Gollancz, 1975.
In the Middle—. London, Gollancz, 1977.
Selected Poems 1955-1980, edited by Robin Fulton. Edinburgh, M. Macdonald, 1982.
Na h-Eilthirich. Glasgow, Glasgow University, 1983.
The Exiles. Manchester, Carcanet, 1984.
Selected Poems. Manchester, Carcanet, 1985.
A Life. Manchester, Carcanet, 1986.
An t-Eilean is an Canain. Glasgow, Glasgow University, 1987.
The Village and Other Poems. Manchester, Carcanet, 1989.
Collected Poems. Manchester, Carcanet, 1992.
Ends and Beginnings. Manchester, Carcanet, 1994.

Other

The Golden Lyric: An Essay on the Poetry of Hugh MacDiarmid. Preston, Lancashire, Akros, 1967.
Iain Am Measg nan Reultan (Iain among the Stars; for children). Glasgow, Gairm, 1970.
River, River: Poems for Children. Edinburgh, M. Macdonald, 1978.
Na h-Ainmhidhean (The Animals; verse for children). Aberfeldy, Perthshire, Clo Chailleann, 1979.
Towards the Human: Selected Essays. Edinburgh, M. Macdonald, 1986.
On the Island (for children). Glasgow, Drew, 1988.
George Douglas Brown's The House with Green Shutters. Aberdeen, Association for Scottish Literary Studies, 1988.

Editor, *Scottish Highland Tales.* London, Ward Lock, 1982.
Editor, with Charles King, *Twelve More Scottish Poets.* London, Hodder and Stoughton, 1986.
Editor, *Moments in the Glasshouse: Poetry and Prose by 5 New Scottish Writers.* Aberdeen, Thistle, 1987.

Translator, *Ben Dorain,* by Duncan Ban Macintyre. Preston, Lancashire, Akros, 1969.
Translator, *Poems to Eimhir,* by Sorley Maclean. London and Newcastle upon Tyne, Gollancz-Northern House, 1971.

*

Bibliography: in *Lines Review 29* (Edinburgh), 1969.

Critical Studies: interview in *Scottish International* (Edinburgh), 1971; *Iain Crichton Smith,* Glasgow, National Book League, 1979; *Literature of the North* edited by David Hewitt and M.R.G. Spiller, Aberdeen, Aberdeen University Press, 1983; *New Edinburgh Review,* Summer 1984; Douglas Gifford, in *Chapman* (Blackford, Perthshire), 34; Carol Godwin, in *Cencrastus* (Edinburgh), 35; *A Biography of Iain Crichton Smith* by Grant F. Wilson, Aberdgen University Press, 1990; *Iain Crichton Smith: New Critical Essays* edited by Colin Nicholson, Edinburgh, Edinburgh University Press, 1991; *Mirror and Marble* by Carol Sow, Edinburgh, Saltirg, 1992.

Iain Crichton Smith comments:

(1972) There is no real connection between my first two novels: one is about old age, the other about youth. However, I would like to write novels which have imagist content, like poetry, but not "poetic" novels. I like them if possible to be generated from some kind of image or "given" imaginative fact.

*   *   *

One of Iain Crichton Smith's greatest virtues as a writer of fiction is his sustained exploration of the insular worlds inhabited by his main characters. His work might be timeless or rooted in history as in *Consider the Lilies,* his first novel, but it is difficult not to believe that environmental factors have also played a part in his literary development. He was brought up in the Hebridean island of Lewis and he writes in English and in his native Gaelic; both have affected his work.

Consider the Lilies is a tautly written evocation of the period of 19th-century Scottish history known as the Clearances, when the people of the Highlands were evicted from their land to make way for sheep. One of the greater losses of that period was the steady degradation of Gaelic, and Smith is intensely aware of the recession in his native Gaelic culture and of the threat to the language's well-being; originally these fears were expressed in poems like *Deer on the High Hills* and "Shall Gaelic Die?" but the concept has also left a mark on his fiction. In *Consider the Lilies* the world is seen through the eyes of an old woman, Mrs. Scott, whose own life has been wasted by the devastation of the Clearances which broke up the community in which she lived. A later novel, *The Dream,* takes the idea a stage further by relating Gaelic's slow death to the failure of a dislocated relationship in modern Glasgow. Martin, a lecturer in Gaelic, dreams of returning to the island of Raws where he can teach Gaelic to a living community, but his wife Jean, also a native of Raws, detests Gaelic and dreams instead of a brave new world of foreign travel. As a result of their disagreement they stop communicating and fail to bring their dreams to "the bare negotiating table of reality."

Another typical Smith hero-narrator who acts as a cipher for our better understanding of a cultural or social problem is Mark Simmons, the diffident Scottish intellectual of *My Last Duchess* who loses his faith in literature and in the ability of human beings to communicate. His detachment from the modern world and all its ills leaves him with little chance of survival until he comes to the realization that life can be made more acceptable when coarser and more worldly values are taken for granted instead of being despised.

Mental torment and a failure to connect with others is a typical failing in Smith's characters. Ralph Simmons, the central character of *In the Middle of the Wood,* a novel in three parts, is a West Highland writer living on the verge of a nervous breakdown. Significantly, he believes that his wife wants to destroy his work and then murder him and as a result of his fears he moves to Glasgow where his behavior becomes more ridiculous and absurd. A holiday abroad to recuperate only damages his confidence further and it is only when he is forced to come face to face with himself in a mental institution that his paranoia eventually breaks down. This is a bravely told novel about mental illness; shocking, profound, and sad.

A key to a better understanding of Smith's characters can be found in the schoolmaster Mr. Trill, the eponymous hero of *Mr. Trill in Hades.* As he lies dying Mr. Trill imagines that he descends into Hades and meets the classical figures who fueled his imagination while he was a schoolmaster. What he sees and hears of his heroes and heroines is deeply disillusioning: Agamemnon and Achilles, "those marvelous heroes," are revealed as simple boasters; Hector has no nobility and only lusts after Helen; Ulysses is treacher-

ous and false. After discovering their duplicity, Mr. Trill recovers, returns to life as a seller of newspapers and eschews academe. Beneath his character's ironic stance Smith seems to be questioning traditional values: intellectual ability and delight in the imagination are naught in comparison to the triumph of the senses.

Mr. Trill is a fictional cousin to the Reverend Donald Black of Smith's short story "The Missionary" (from *Murdo and Other Stories*). Black is a Christian minister who goes to Africa to convert the heathen but is overpowered by the strange and hostile environment in which he has to live. Gradually, though, he is drawn into the life of the tribe, but when his well-meant Christian interference results in the massacre of a family he begins to crack. Suddenly he realizes how thin is the dividing line between naked aggression and the ability to live in harmony, and it is only a new-found grace which gives him the humanity to survive his personal crisis. As with Mr. Trill, Smith is at his most convincing when he deals with the intellectual torment undergone by the missionary and with his eventual salvation.

In recent years Smith has shown himself to be an accomplished writer of short fiction and the publication of his *Selected Stories* demonstrates the range of his literary concerns. There is a poetic quality and linguistic intensity in his work that shows him to be well capable of embracing a wide range of human experience within the span of a few thousand well-chosen words.

—Trevor Royle

———

SMITH, Rosamond. *See* **OATES, Joyce Carol.**

———

SOMERS, Jane. *See* **LESSING, Doris (May).**

———

SONTAG, Susan

Nationality: American. **Born:** New York City, 16 January 1933. **Education:** The University of California, Berkeley, 1948-49; University of Chicago, 1949-51, B.A. 1951; Harvard University, Cambridge, Massachusetts, 1954-57, M.A. 1955; St. Anne's College, Oxford, 1957. **Family:** Has one son. **Career:** Instructor in English, University of Connecticut, Storrs, 1953-54; Teaching Fellow in Philosophy, Harvard University, 1955-57; editor, *Commentary,* New York, 1959; Lecturer in Philosophy, City College of New York, and Sarah Lawrence College, Bronxville, New York, 1959-60; Instructor in Religion, Columbia University, New York, 1960-64; writer-in-residence, Rutgers University, New Brunswick, New Jersey, 1964-65. President, PEN American Center, 1987-89.

Lives in New York City. **Awards:** American Association of University Women fellowship, 1957; Rockefeller fellowship, 1965, 1974; Guggenheim fellowship, 1966, 1975; American Academy award, 1976; Brandeis University Creative Arts award, 1976; Ingram Merrill Foundation award, 1976; National Book Critics Circle award, 1977; Academy of Sciences and Literature award (Mainz, Germany), 1979; MacArthur Foundation fellowship, 1990-95; Premio Malaparte award (Italy), 1992. **Member:** American Academy, 1979; Officer, Order of Arts and Letters (France), 1984. **Address:** c/o Wylie, Aitken & Stone, 250 West 57th Street, New York, New York 10107, U.S.A.

PUBLICATIONS

Novels

The Benefactor. New York, Farrar Straus, 1963; London, Eyre and Spottiswoode, 1964.
Death Kit. New York, Farrar Straus, 1967; London, Secker and Warburg, 1968.
The Volcano Lover. New York, Farrar Straus, and London, Cape, 1992.

Short Stories

I, etcetera. New York, Farrar Straus, 1978; London, Gollancz, 1979.
The Way We Live Now, illustrated by Howard Hodgkin. New York, Farrar Straus, and London, Cape, 1991.

Uncollected Short Stories

"Man with a Pain," in *Harper's* (New York), April 1964.
"Description (of a Description)," in *Antaeus* (New York), Autumn 1984.
"The Letter Scene," in *The New Yorker,* 18 August 1986.
"Pilgrimage," in *The New Yorker,* 21 December 1987.

Plays

Duet for Cannibals (screenplay). New York, Farrar Straus, 1970; London, Allen Lane, 1974.
Brother Carl (screenplay). New York, Farrar Straus, 1974.
Alice in Bed. New York, Farrar Straus, 1993.

Screenplays: *Duet for Cannibals,* 1969; *Brother Carl,* 1971.

Other

Against Interpretation and Other Essays. New York, Farrar Straus, 1966; London, Eyre and Spottiswoode, 1967.
Trip to Hanoi. New York, Farrar Straus, and London, Panther, 1969.
Styles of Radical Will (essays). New York, Farrar Straus, and London, Secker and Warburg, 1969.
On Photography. New York, Farrar Straus, 1977; London, Allen Lane, 1978.
Illness as Metaphor. New York, Farrar Straus, 1978; London, Allen Lane, 1979.
Under the Sign of Saturn (essays). New York, Farrar Straus, 1980; London, Writers and Readers, 1983.
A Susan Sontag Reader. New York, Farrar Straus, 1982; London, Penguin, 1983.

Aids and Its Metaphors. New York, Farrar Straus, and London, Allen Lane, 1989.

Editor, *Selected Writings of Artaud,* translated by Helen Weaver. New York, Farrar Straus, 1976.
Editor, *A Barthes Reader.* New York, Hill and Wang, and London, Cape, 1982; as *Barthes: Selected Writings,* London, Fontana, 1983.
Editor, *Best American Essays: 1992.* New York, Ticknor and Fields, 1992.
Editor, with Danilo Kis, *Homo Poeticus.* New York, Farrar Straus, 1995.

*

Critical Study: *Susan Sontag: The Elegiac Modernist* by Sohnya Sayres, New York, Routledge Chapman and Hall, 1989; London, Routledge, 1990.

Theatrical Activities:
Director: **Plays**—*As You Desire Me* by Pirandello, Turin and Italian tour, 1979-80; *Jacques and His Master* by Milan Kundera, Cambridge, Massachusetts, 1985; *Waiting for Godot* by Samuel Beckett, Sarajevo, 1993-94. **Films**—*Duet for Cannibals,* 1969; *Brother Carl,* 1971; *Promised Lands* (documentary), 1974; *Unguided Tour,* 1983.

* * *

Traditionally readers have approached works of fiction as verbal structures which reveal and generally make statements about a pre-existing "real" subject. The writer may represent his subject directly, "imitating" in accordance with conventional understandings about the probable behavior of the human and the natural order; or he may render his subject indirectly by presenting a metaphor which stands for and usually implies a generalization about the same reality. Thus traditional criticism was designed to judge the verisimilitude of fiction and to provide a way of understanding metaphor, allegory, and parable as symbolic statements. It is impossible, however, to discuss the fiction of Susan Sontag in critical terms derived from this essentially naturalistic tradition, just as Sontag herself has attempted to construct a new critical approach to do justice to those works of *avant-garde* artists whose rendering of the modern world she finds significant.

The tough, polemical essays collected in *Against Interpretation* and *Styles of Radical Will* are more impressive than Sontag's fiction thus far, which too often seems contrived to illustrate a doctrine. For Sontag, the final "most liberating value of art" is "transparency," which means experiencing "the luminousness of the thing in itself, of things being what they are." Interpretation, which seeks to replace the work with something else—usually historical, ethical or psychological paraphrase—is essentially "revenge which the intellect takes upon art." To interpret is "to impoverish, to deplete." Sontag's chief interest as a critic is the work of artists (especially film makers) whose work is misunderstood because it resists "being reduced to a story." Thus Sontag observes that in his film *Persona* Bergman presents not a story, but "something that is, in one sense, cruder, and, in another, more abstract: a body of material, a subject. The function of the subject or material may be as much its opacity, its multiplicity, as the ease with which it yields itself to being incarnated by a determinate plot or action." Deliberately frustrating any conventional attempt to determine "what happens," the new novels and films are able, she maintains, to involve the audience "more directly in other matters, for instance in the very processes of seeing and knowing. . . . The material presented can then be treated as a thematic resource, from which different (and perhaps concurrent) narrative structures can be derived as variations." The artist intends his work to remain "partly encoded": the truly modern consciousness challenges the supremacy of naturalism and univocal symbolism.

While vestiges of naturalistic situations remain in Sontag's fiction (her story "The Will and the Way," for example, seems to be an allegory concerning the image of women in modern life), "interpretation" is by definition more or less irrelevant. *The Benefactor* is in its general outline a dream novel; its "thematic resource" is the problem of attaining selfhood and genuine freedom. Just as Sontag sees Montaigne's essays as "dispassionate, varied explorations of the innumerable ways of being a self," the hero of *The Benefactor* uses his dreams as a means of achieving freedom. "It seemed to me," Hippolyte concludes, "all my life had been converging on the state of mind . . . in which I would finally be reconciled to myself—myself as I really am, the self of my dreams. That reconciliation is what I take to be freedom." The device which keeps the reader from treating the novel as paraphrasable allegory is the deliberate ambiguity of the narrative frame: we are left to decide whether the narrative is an account of what happened or an account which is at least in part the construction of a mad Hippolyte whose dreams are symbolic transformations, in the usual Freudian sense, of "what happened." Sontag owes a good deal to Sartre and Camus, but even more to the *auteurs* of *Last Year at Marienbad* and *L'Avventura*. *Death Kit* has as its concern the failure of a man who has no true self. "Diddy, not really alive, had a life. Not really the same. Some people are their lives. Others, like Diddy, merely inhabit their lives." Diddy commits a murder, or thinks he commits a murder; there is no way of determining this, but what matters is how Diddy handles the possibility that he is a murderer, and how he tries to appropriate the self of a blind girl whom he selfishly "loves." Out of the materials of his life Diddy assembles his death; out of his failure the reader may assemble an understanding of vanity, inauthenticity, and death. Wholly successful or not, *The Benefactor* and *Death Kit* are haunting works, effective to the degree to which the reader can accept Sontag's powerful arguments elsewhere about the exhaustion of the naturalistic tradition. As the American critic E.D. Hirsch puts it, "Knowledge of ambiguity is not necessarily ambiguous knowledge."

—Elmer Borklund

SORRENTINO, Gilbert

Nationality: American. **Born:** Brooklyn, New York, 27 April 1929. Educated in New York public schools; Brooklyn College, 1950-51, 1955-57. **Military Service:** Served in the United States Army Medical Corps, 1951-53. **Family:** Married 1) Elsene Wiessner (divorced); 2) Vivian Victoria Ortiz; two sons and one daughter. **Career:** Re-insurance clerk, Fidelity and Casualty Company, New York, 1947-48; messenger, American Houses Inc., 1948-49; freight checker, Ace Assembly Agency, New York, 1954-56; packer, Bennett Brothers, New York, 1956-57; shipping room supervisor,

Thermo-fax Sales, 1957-60. Editor, *Neon* magazine, 1956-60, and Grove Press, 1965-70, both New York; book editor, *Kulchur,* New York, 1961-63; taught at Columbia University, New York, 1965; Aspen Writers Workshop, Colorado, 1967; Sarah Lawrence College, Bronxville, New York, 1971-72; New School for Social Research, New York, 1976-79, 1980-82; Edwin S. Quain Professor of Literature, University of Scranton, Pennsylvania, 1979. Since 1982 professor of English, Stanford University, California. **Awards:** Guggenheim fellowship, 1973, 1987; National Endowment for the Arts grant, 1974, 1978; Fels award, 1975; Ariadne Foundation grant, 1975; Creative Artists Public Service grant, 1975; John Dos Passos prize, 1981; American Academy award, 1985; Lannan Literary award for fiction, 1992. **Agent:** Mel Berger, William Morris Agency, 1350 Avenue of the Americas, New York, New York 10019, U.S.A. **Address:** Department of English, Stanford University, Stanford, California 94305, U.S.A.

PUBLICATIONS

Novels

The Sky Changes. New York, Hill and Wang, 1966.
Steelwork. New York, Pantheon, 1970.
Imaginative Qualities of Actual Things. New York, Pantheon, 1971.
Splendide-Hôtel. New York, New Directions, 1973.
Mulligan Stew. New York, Grove Press, 1979; London, Boyars, 1980.
Aberration of Starlight. New York, Random House, 1980; London, Boyars, 1981.
Crystal Vision. Berkeley, California, North Point Press, 1981; London, Boyars, 1982.
Blue Pastoral. Berkeley, California, North Point Press, 1983; London, Boyars, 1985.
Odd Number. Berkeley, California, North Point Press, 1985.
Rose Theatre. Elmwood Park, Illinois, Dalkey Archive, 1987.
Misterioso. Elmwood Park, Illinois, Dalkey Archive, 1989.
Under the Shadow. Elmwood Park, Illinois, Dalkey Archive, 1991.
Red the Fiend. New York, Fromm International, 1995.

Short Story

A Beehive Arranged on Human Principles (novella). New York, Grenfell Press, 1986.

Uncollected Short Stories

"The Moon in Its Flight," in *New American Review 13,* edited by Theodore Solotaroff. New York, Simon and Schuster, 1971.
"Land of Cotton," in *Harper's* (New York), November 1977.
"Decades," in *The Best American Short Stories 1978,* edited by Theodore Solotaroff and Shannon Ravenel. Boston, Houghton Mifflin, 1978.
"Chats with the Real McCoy," in *Atlantic* (Boston), March 1979.
"The Gala Cocktail Party," in *The Pushcart Prize 9,* edited by Bill Henderson. Wainscott, New York, Pushcart Press, 1984.

Play

Flawless Play Restored: The Masque of Fungo. Los Angeles, Black Sparrow Press, 1974.

Poetry

The Darkness Surrounds Us. Highlands, North Carolina, Jargon, 1960.
Black and White. New York, Totem, 1964.
The Perfect Fiction. New York, Norton, 1968.
Corrosive Sublimate. Los Angeles, Black Sparrow Press, 1971.
A Dozen Oranges. Santa Barbara, California, Black Sparrow Press, 1976.
White Sail. Santa Barbara, California, Black Sparrow Press, 1977.
The Orangery. Austin, University of Texas Press, 1978.
Selected Poems 1958-1980. Santa Barbara, California, Black Sparrow Press, 1981.

Other

Something Said (essays). Berkeley, California, North Point Press, 1984.

Translator, *Sulpiciae Elegidia/Elegiacs of Sulpicia.* Mount Horeb, Wisconsin, Perishable Press, 1977.

*

Bibliography: *Gilbert Sorrentino: A Descriptive Bibliography* by William McPheron, Elmwood Park, Illinois, Dalkey Archive, 1991.

Manuscript Collection: University of Delaware, Newark.

Critical Studies: "Gilbert Sorrentino Issue" of *Vort* (Silver Spring, Maryland), Fall 1974, and *Review of Contemporary Fiction* (Elmwood Park, Illinois), Fall 1981.

Gilbert Sorrentino comments:
My writing is the act of solving self-imposed problems.

*   *   *

Gilbert Sorrentino's novels are dedicated to several anti-traditional propositions: that space, rather than time, is the most revealing principle for narrative structure; that the physical texture of language, rather than its semantic properties, is the key to communication between a novelist and the reader; and that an awareness of the author's act of writing, rather than the willing suspension of disbelief, yields the greatest pleasure in experiencing a novel.

The Sky Changes and *Steelwork,* Sorrentino's earliest novels (from the days when he was still best known as a poet), are demonstrations of spatial order. The first is the record (told in block sections of separate narrative) of a protagonist's dissolving marriage, framed by an auto trip across the United States. Both the relationship and the journey would seem to imply a temporal order; but at several points Sorrentino self-consciously violates that order to show that the human imagination transcends simple chronology—the trip's emotional resolution comes as early as two-thirds through the cross-country journey. *Steelwork* is the spatial portrait of a Brooklyn neighborhood over two decades of human experience. On one street-corner, for example, the events of several years' distance are imaginatively rehearsed; and characters' lives are studied in a simultaneity of presence, although by the clock they have lived through much of their lives. Because space—the neighborhood—is the organizing principle, the chronology is deliberately

scrambled, so that we move back and forth from 1951 to 1942 to 1949. As a result, the reader experiences the neighborhood as the spatial whole it would be for anyone who lived there all those years. Emotions and the imagination outstrip time.

Imaginative Qualities of Actual Things is Sorrentino's wildly comic exercise of his most self-apparent writing techniques. Ostensibly a *roman à clef* exposing the petty jealousies and seductions of the 1950s and 1960s New York art world, the book is in fact a demonstration of Sorrentino's pleasure in writing a novel. Characters' statements are undercut by rudely sarcastic footnotes; midway through a piece of exposition the author will stop and berate the reader for making him supply such petty details; and when the author hates a character, ludicrous scenes are devised for the unfortunate soul's humiliation and punishment. Throughout, the reader is aware that the real subject of this novel is not its mimicry of a projected real world, but instead the process of its own composition, which the reader witnesses firsthand.

Making fiction its own subject—not a representation of an illusionary world but instead its own artifice as added to the world, an aesthetic Sorrentino learned from his mentor, William Carlos Williams—is the achievement of *Splendide-Hôtel.* Its brief chapters are named after the successive letters of the alphabet, which provide the topics for composition—the capital letter A's on the page looking like flies on a wall, breeding in decay; the letter K reminding Sorrentino of the baseball score-card symbol for strike-out, and of a headline which spoke volumes just by saying "K-K-K-Koufax!!!!"

In his fifth and most commercially successful work of fiction, *Mulligan Stew,* Sorrentino offers a full display of novelistic talents at work. Indeed, he wishes to surpass his previous efforts by showing all aspects of fiction writing, from the novelist's act of composition to his notebooks, letters, and even the personal thoughts of his characters. Borrowing his structure from Flann O'Brien's novel *At Swim-Two-Birds* (1939), Sorrentino invents an imaginary novelist named Anthony Lamont who is struggling to shore up a sagging career with an experimental novel, a piece of "surfiction" (Sorrentino despises the term) titled *Guinea Red.* A murder mystery, it features unabashedly miserable writing; Lamont keeps losing the murdered body and forgetting where he's placed the fatal wound, and the prose itself is dreadfully overwritten in a parody of low-brow style. The reader is also given access to Lamont's letters, notebooks, and journal entries. Midway through, his characters mutiny and seek ways to escape Lamont's leaden narrative and find work in a more promising repertoire. A massive novel which by its very bulk and meticulous range of styles immerses the reader in its own subject, *Mulligan Stew* is Sorrentino's fullest repertoire of writing talent.

Mulligan Stew exhausts the innovative techniques of 1960s fiction, and also clears the way for a new lyricism in Sorrentino's work. Whereas his earlier novels turned to poetic devices as a way of eclipsing the quotidian *Aberration of Starlight, Crystal Vision,* and *Blue Pastoral* are able to confront both experience and the act of writing directly.

Aberration of Starlight explains experience as a matter of point of view, fragmenting a summer's experience at a New Jersey vacation lodge into four narratives, much in the manner of William Faulkner's *The Sound and the Fury.* Sorrentino uses these distinct modes of vision in order to highlight language, especially how essentially stupid world views are, in the manner of Flaubert's *Dictionnaire des idées reçues,* created by and not just expressed through banalities of language. *Crystal Vision* embraces language directly, transcribing streetcorner conversations from the verbally rich Brooklyn of Sorrentino's youth, as the characters of his earlier *Steelwork* re-emerge from their "world of light" to speak directly. Their language expands the author's previous vision, showing how they have the vitality to survive on their own in fiction, without narrative's customary supporting devices. *Blue Pastoral* celebrates the stylistics of Blue Serge Gavotte as he creates a pastoral accompanying his journey from New York to San Francisco (a less lyrical trip once made west by the protagonist of *The Sky Changes*). Sorrentino takes the occasion to parody pastoral forms and satirize stock characters; much of his play consists in delighting with obviously bad writing. But with all conventions demolished by his earlier works, and with unconventionality itself made a sham by the achievement of *Mulligan Stew*, there seems little else for Sorrentino to do with the novel than continue to write it, even poorly.

Sorrentino's inward turn of narrative is confirmed by his practice in *Odd Number*, a brief (159-page) reinvestigation of how his earlier novel, *Imaginative Qualities of Actual Things*, might have been assembled. In the earlier work Sorrentino had used the well-established formal device of the *roman à clef* to structure his narrative; his use of footnotes and intrusively parenthetical remarks indicates that the form is barely able to contain his rage against some of these characters drawn from a lifestyle he was now rejecting. *Odd Number* transposes this volatility to the novel's form itself. Like *Aberration of Starlight*, the tale is told several times, but here the emphasis is even more on the uncertainty of events. The first time through the reader is given a question-and-answer dialogue, as in detective fashion the voice of the novel interrogates its own resources to discover exactly what has happened. This section's awkward and uncertain rhythm yields to a more fluently conversational account of the book's events—all of which originally transpired in *Imaginative Qualities of Actual Things*, now supplemented with coy references to Sorrentino's other novels. But the authority of part two yields to a cross examination of the documents themselves: the contents of dresser drawers, photographs, and other possessions which contradict certain assertions of both previous sections, virtually unmaking the novel which has been read. The novel, therefore, is no more reliable a report on the world than the self-conscious rage of Sorrentino's earlier version, a reminder that truth, if one cares for it, must be found beyond the fiction writer's practice no matter how it might be structured.

That the matters of *Imaginative Qualities* can be extended infinitely across time and space is evident from Sorrentino's success with *Rose Theatre*, in which the female characters attempt to correct apparent misinformation from *Odd Number*, data now considered errant not because of any mistakes in that particular work but because the questions which generated it excluded certain possibilities of discourse. The very attempt to stabilize reality, however, adds a new dimension to its nature, which invites further uncertainties—a reminder of the continuously evolving nature of fiction, which in its struggles to provide a persuasive account of reality only confounds its unverifiable nature.

Sorrentino's trilogy of responses to *Imaginative Qualities* concludes with *Misterioso*. Here the narrative aspires toward the encyclopedic as a strategy for both inclusiveness and authority. Yet because previous facts can only be clarified by the introduction of new materials, verifiability still remains in dispute. That the novel is set in a supermarket implies both its structure and utility: there is no firm basis for its narrative, but rather a wide variety of materials from which to select, a treasury of stories one can choose according to fancy. Yet no one would ever try to draw conclusive substance from everything; there can even be narratives that threaten to distract by their intrusion, the resistance to which constitutes a sub-theme in itself. Simply to comprehend all that is possible remains the novel's goal, an activity reflecting on Sorrentino's activity in writing the initial work, a novel that can expand infinitely with each reconsideration.

—Jerome Klinkowitz

SOUTHERN, Terry

Pseudonym: Maxwell Kenton. **Nationality:** American. **Born:** Alvarado, Texas, 1 May 1924. **Education:** Southern Methodist University, Dallas; University of Chicago; Northwestern University, Evanston, Illinois, B.A. 1948; the Sorbonne, Paris, 1948-50. **Military Service:** Served in the United States Army, 1943-45. **Family:** Married Carol Kauffman in 1956; one son. **Awards:** British Screen Writers award, 1965; Writers Guild of America West award, 1965. **Address:** R. F. D., East Canaan, Connecticut 06024, U.S.A.

PUBLICATIONS

Novels

Flash and Filigree. London, Deutsch, and New York, Coward McCann, 1958.
Candy (as Maxwell Kenton, with Mason Hoffenberg). Paris, Olympia Press, 1958; as Terry Southern and Mason Hoffenberg, New York, Putnam, 1964; London, Geis, 1968.
The Magic Christian. London, Deutsch, 1959; New York, Random House, 1960.
Lollipop (as Maxwell Kenton). Paris, Olympia Press, 1962.
Blue Movie. Cleveland, World, 1970; London, Calder and Boyars, 1973.
Texas Summer. New York, Arcade, 1991.

Short Stories

Red-Dirt Marijuana and Other Tastes. New York, New American Library, 1967; London, Cape, 1971.

Uncollected Short Story

"Heavey Put-Away," in *Paris Review*, Spring 1981.

Plays

Easy Rider (screenplay), with Peter Fonda and Dennis Hopper. New York, New American Library, 1969.

Screenplays: *Candy Kisses*, with David Burnett, 1955; *Dr. Strangelove*, with Stanley Kubrick and Peter George, 1963; *The Loved One*, with Christopher Isherwood, 1965; *The Cincinnati Kid*, with Ring Lardner, Jr., 1965; *Casino Royale* (uncredited), with others, 1967; *Barbarella*, with others, 1968; *Easy Rider*, with Peter Fonda and Dennis Hopper, 1969; *The End of the Road*, with Aram Avakian, 1969; *The Magic Christian*, with others, 1969; *Meetings with Remarkable Men*, 1979.

Television Play: *The Emperor Jones,* from the play by Eugene O'Neill, 1958 (U.K.).

Other

The Journal of "The Loved One": The Production Log of a Motion Picture. New York, Random House, 1965.
The Rolling Stones on Tour. New York, Dragon's Dream, 1978.
The Early Stones: Legendary Photographs of a Band in the Making 1963-1973, with photographs by Michael Cooper. New York, Hyperion, 1992; London, Secker and Warburg, 1993.

Editor, with Richard Seaver and Alexander Trocchi, *Writers in Revolt.* New York, Fell, 1963.

*   *   *

Terry Southern has baffled American reviewers and annoyed critics since the appearance in 1958 of *Flash and Filigree,* which had been well received in England. This novel and subsequent efforts have variously been labeled "pointless," "pornographic," and "sick" for their thematic content or apparent lack of it. The form of Southern's fiction similarly defies easy classification: part put-on, part satire, part parody, with occasional stretches of "straight," well-written prose. Plotting is rarely conventional: *Flash and Filigree* is really two completely separate plots, while *The Magic Christian* and *Candy* are disjointedly picaresque. *Blue Movie* is straightforwardly told, but conventional style and plotting seem strange indeed when used to chronicle (in living detail) the filming, and subsequent seizure by a Vatican Army, of a Hollywood-produced stag movie.

The main plot in *Flash and Filigree* centers on a dermatologist sports-car buff named Dr. Frederick Eichner, who is haunted by a prank-playing transvestite named Felix Treevly. Eichner kills his weird nemesis and is tried for murder and acquitted. Dr. Eichner is too aloofly repulsive to sustain interest, but the heroine of the subplot, Nurse Babs of Eichner's clinic, is just "darling," Southern's satirical tip-off word about the pretty, puerile, American Dream Girl he loves to parody. Objects of satire also include television shows ("What's My Disease?"), the medical profession, law courts, the drug scene, the American mania for gadgetry and technical data, and the crazy-culture of California. But the best scene is the seduction in a taxicab of "darling" Babs the button-nosed beauty.

Candy (co-authored with Mason Hoffenberg) was originally published pseudonymously in Paris in 1958, then published in America in 1964, by which time its shocking pornography had lost some sting. The titular heroine, a female, saccharine Candide, is reminiscent also of De Sade's Justine, Harold Gray's Little Orphan Annie, and Southern's own Nurse Babs. The book may be read equally as a satire on cherished American institutions and current delusions, or as a geography of pornography; in Southern's mind the two areas obviously blend, perhaps in their common language of cant and cliché. Candy encounters faddists and fakes in the stronghold of western culture: in academia, the mad bi-sexual Professor Mephisto; in science, the mother-ridden Irving Krankheit, author of *Masturbation Now!;* in religion, Guru Grindle, who convinces Candy of matter's unreality even as he enjoys her body. The most successful scene evolves as a psychotic, witless hunchback—whom sentimental Candy re-names Derek—copulates with the heroine ("he needs me") while he struggles to keep his half-mind on his real goal—money.

Whatever social targets the earlier works neglected, *The Magic Christian* shoots for. Guy Grand, a rich practical joker, spends 10 million a year "making it hot for them": he builds superlong autos that jam up intersections; publishes a newspaper cluttered with foreign language phrases; enters a cannibalistic panther in a dog show; and goes on safari with a 75 mm. howitzer. He also inserts short pornographic scenes into film classics; in *The Best Years of Our Lives,* the war hero's hook-hands grapple under his sweetheart's skirt. Guy also opens grocery stores with preposterously low prices—then closes them the same night, to re-locate in mysterious places.

Southern's collected short stories, *Red-Dirt Marijuana and Other Tastes,* revealed greater range and sympathy than the novels. Southern writes well of boys and men, of poor southern whites, of razor fights between Negro brothers, of an American in Paris who is "too hip," and of a surrealistic auto trip through Mexico. The writing is uneven and Southern's questionable taste prevails, but style and mood in the successful stories are superbly lyrical. *Blue Movie* explores sexual boundaries never visited by Candy, but boredom is defeated only by Southern's fine ear for trade talk and some brilliantly awful Hollywood types. Southern is familiar with movie argot and technique, having written scenarios for *Dr. Strangelove, The Loved One,* and *Barbarella.* In his movies he employed the same shock therapy by indecency and dehumanization which dominates his novelistic black comedies.

—Frank Campenni

SOYINKA, Wole

Nationality: Nigerian. **Born:** Akinwande Oluwole Soyinka, in Abeokuta, 13 July 1934. **Education:** St. Peter's School, Ake, Abeokuta, 1938-43; Abeokuta Grammar School, 1944-45; Government College, Ibadan, 1946-50; University College, Ibadan (now University of Ibadan), 1952-54; University of Leeds, Yorkshire, 1954-57, B.A. (honors) in English. **Family:** Married; has children. **Career:** Play reader, Royal Court Theatre, London, 1957-59; Rockefeller Research Fellow in drama, University of Ibadan, 1961-62; lecturer in English, University of Ife, Ile-Ife, 1963-64; senior lecturer in English, University of Lagos, 1965-67; head of the department of theater arts, University of Ibadan, 1969-72 (appointment made in 1967); professor of comparative literature, and head of the department of dramatic arts, University of Ife, 1975-85. Visiting fellow, Churchill College, Cambridge, 1973-74; visiting professor, University of Ghana, Legon, 1973-74, University of Sheffield, 1974, Yale University, New Haven, Connecticut, 1979-80, and Cornell University, Ithaca, New York, 1986. Founding director, 1960 Masks Theatre, 1960, and Orisun Theatre, 1964, Lagos and Ibadan, and Unife Guerilla Theatre, Ile-Ife, 1978; co-editor, *Black Orpheus,* 1961-64; editor, *Transition* (later *Ch'indaba*) magazine, Accra, Ghana, 1975-77. Secretary-General, Union of Writers of the African Peoples, 1975. Tried and acquitted of armed robbery, 1965; political prisoner, detained by the Federal Military Government, Lagos and Kaduna, 1967-69. **Awards:** Dakar Festival award, 1966; John Whiting award, 1967; Jock Campbell award *(New Statesman),* for fiction, 1968; Nobel Prize for Literature, 1986; Benson Medal, 1990; Premio Letterario Internazionalle Mondello, 1990. D.Litt: University of Leeds, 1973, Yale University, University of Montpellier, France, University of Lagos, and University of Bayreuth, 1989. Fellow, Royal Society of Literature (U.K.); member, American Academy, and Academy of Arts and Letters of the German Democratic Republic. Named Commander, Federal Republic of Nigeria, 1986, Order of La Legion d'Honneur, France, 1989, and Order of the Republic of Italy, 1990; Akogun of Isara, 1989; Akinlatun of Egbaland, 1990. **Agent:** Morton Leavy, Leavy Rosensweig and Hyman, 11 East 44th Street, New York, New York 10017; or Triharty (Nig.) Ltd. Agency Division, 4, Ola-ayeni Street, Ikeja, Lagos, Nigeria. (U.K. Correspondent: Cognix Ltd., Media Suite, 3 Tyers Gate, London SE1 3HX). **Address:** P.O. Box 935, Abeokuta, Nigeria.

PUBLICATIONS

Novels

The Interpreters. London, Deutsch, 1965; New York, Macmillan, 1970.
Season of Anomy. London, Collings, 1973; New York, Third Press, 1974.

Plays

The Swamp Dwellers (produced London, 1958; New York, 1968). Included in *Three Plays,* 1963; in *Five Plays,* 1964.
The Lion and the Jewel (produced Ibadan, 1959; London, 1966). Ibadan, London, and New York, Oxford University Press, 1963.
The Invention (produced London, 1959).
A Dance of the Forests (produced Lagos, 1960). Ibadan, London, and New York, Oxford University Press, 1963.
The Trials of Brother Jero (produced Ibadan, 1960; Cambridge, 1965; London, 1966; New York, 1967). Included in *Three Plays,* 1963; in *Five Plays,* 1964.
Camwood on the Leaves (broadcast 1960). London, Eyre Methuen, 1973; in *Camwood on the Leaves, and Before the Blackout,* 1974.
The Republican and The New Republican (satirical revues; produced Lagos, 1963).
Three Plays. Ibadan, Mbari, 1963; as *Three Short Plays,* London, Oxford University Press, 1969.
The Strong Breed (produced Ibadan, 1964; London, 1966; New York, 1967). Included in *Three Plays,* 1963; in *Five Plays,* 1964.
Childe Internationale (produced Ibadan, 1964). Ibadan, Fountain, 1987.
Kongi's Harvest (produced Ibadan, 1964; New York, 1968). Ibadan, London, and New York, Oxford University Press, 1967.
Five Plays: A Dance of the Forests, The Lion and the Jewel, The Swamp Dwellers, The Trials of Brother Jero, The Strong Breed. Ibadan, London, and New York, Oxford University Press, 1964.
Before the Blackout (produced Ibadan, 1965; Leeds, 1981). Ibadan, Orisun, 1971; in *Camwood on the Leaves, and Before the Blackout,* 1974.
The Road (produced London, 1965; also director: produced Chicago, 1984). Ibadan, London, and New York, Oxford University Press, 1965.
Rites of the Harmattan Solstice (produced Lagos, 1966).
Madmen and Specialists (produced Waterford, Connecticut, and New York, 1970; revised version, also director: produced Ibadan, 1971). London, Methuen, 1971; New York, Hill and Wang, 1972.
The Jero Plays: The Trials of Brother Jero, and Jero's Metamorphosis. London, Eyre Methuen, 1973.

Jero's Metamorphosis (produced Lagos, 1975). Included in *The Jero Plays,* 1973.
The Bacchae: A Communion Rite, adaptation of the play by Euripides (produced London, 1973). London, Eyre Methuen, 1973; New York, Norton, 1974.
Collected Plays: A Dance of the Forests, The Swamp Dwellers, The Strong Breed, The Road, The Bacchae. London and New York, Oxford University Press, 1973.
Collected Plays:The Lion and the Jewel, Kongi's Harvest, The Trials of Brother Jero, Jero's Metamorphosis, Madmen and Specialists. London and New York, Oxford University Press, 1974.
Camwood on the Leaves, and Before the Blackout: Two Short Plays. New York, Third Press, 1974.
Death and the King's Horseman (also director: produced Ile-Ife, 1976; Chicago, 1979; also director: produced New York, 1987). London, Eyre Methuen, 1975; New York, Norton, 1976.
Opera Wonyosi, adaptation of *The Threepenny Opera* by Brecht (also director: produced Ile-Ife, 1977). Bloomington, Indiana University Press, and London, Collings, 1981.
Golden Accord (produced Louisville, 1980).
Priority Projects (revue; produced on Nigeria tour, 1982).
Requiem for a Futurologist (also director: produced Ile-Ife, 1983). London, Collings, 1985.
A Play of Giants (also director: produced New Haven, Connecticut, 1984). London, Methuen, 1984.
Six Plays (includes *The Trials of Brother Jero, Jero's Metamorphosis, Camwood on the Leaves, Death and the King's Horseman, Madmen and Specialists, Opera Wonyosi*). London, Methuen. 1984.
From Zia with Love. London, Methuen, 1992

Screenplay: *Kongi's Harvest,* 1970.

Radio Plays: *Camwood on the Leaves,* 1960; *The Detainee,* 1965; *Die Still, Dr. Godspeak,* 1981; *A Scourge of Hyacinths,* 1990; *Nineteen Ninety-Four,* 1993.

Television Plays: *Joshua: A Nigerian Portrait,* 1962 (Canada); *Culture in Transition,* 1963 (USA).

Poetry

Idanre and Other Poems. London, Methuen, 1967; New York, Hill and Wang, 1968.
Poems from Prison. London, Collings, 1969.
A Shuttle in the Crypt. London, Eyre Methuen-Collings, and New York, Hill and Wang, 1972.
Ogun Abibimañ. London, Collings, 1976.
Mandela's Earth and Other Poems. New York, Random House, 1988; London, Deutsch, 1989.

Other

The Man Died: Prison Notes. London, Eyre Methuen-Collings, and New York, Harper, 1972.
In Person: Achebe, Awoonor, and Soyinka at the University of Washington. Seattle, University of Washington African Studies Program, 1975.
Myth, Literature, and the African World. London, Cambridge University Press, 1976.

Aké: The Years of Childhood (autobiography). London, Collings, 1981; New York, Vintage, 1983.
The Critic and Society (essay). Ile-Ife, University of Ife Press, 1981.
The Past Must Address Its Present (lecture). N.p., Nobel Foundation, 1986; as *This Past Must Address Its Present,* New York, Anson Phelps Institute, 1988.
Art, Dialogue and Outrage: Essays on Literature and Culture. Ibadan, New Horn, 1988.
Isara: A Voyage Around "Essay." New York, Random House, 1989; London, Methuen, 1990.
Ibadan—The Penkelemes Years. London, Methuen, 1994.

Editor, *Poems of Black Africa.* London, Secker and Warburg, and New York, Hill and Wang, 1975.

Translator, *The Forest of a Thousand Daemons: A Hunter's Saga,* by D.O. Fagunwa. London, Nelson, 1968; New York, Humanities Press, 1969.

*

Bibliography: *Wole Soyinka: A Bibliography* by B. Okpu, Lagos, Libriservice, 1984.

Critical Studies: *Wole Soyinka* by Gerald Moore, London, Evans, and New York, Africana, 1971, revised edition, Evans, 1978; *The Writing of Wole Soyinka* by Eldred D. Jones, London, Heinemann, 1973, revised edition, 1983, 2nd revised edition, London, Curry, 1988; *Three Nigerian Poets: A Critical Study of the Poetry of Soyinka, Clark, and Okigbo* by Nyong J. Udoeyop, Ibadan, Ibadan University Press, 1973; *Critical Perspectives on Wole Soyinka* edited by James Gibbs, Washington, D.C., Three Continents Press, 1980, London, Heinemann, 1981, and *Wole Soyinka* by Gibbs, London, Macmillan, and New York, Grove Press, 1986; *A Writer and His Gods: A Study of the Importance of Yoruba Myths and Religious Ideas in the Writing of Wole Soyinka* by Stephan Larsen, Stockholm, University of Stockholm, 1983; *Wole Soyinka: An Introduction to His Writing* by Obi Maduakar, London, Garland, 1986; *Before Our Very Eyes: Tribute to Wole Soyinka* edited by Dapo Adelugba, Ibadan, Spectrum, 1987; *Index of Subjects, Proverbs and Themes in the Writings of Wole Soyinka* by Greta M.K. Coger, New York, Greenwood, 1988.

Theatrical Activities:
Director: **Plays**—by Brecht, Chekhov, Clark, Easmon, Eseoghene, Ogunyemi, Shakespeare, Synge, and his own works; *L'Espace et la Magie,* Paris, 1972; *The Biko Inquest* by Jon Blair and Norman Fenton, Ile-Ife, 1978, and New York, 1980.
Actor: **Plays**—Igwezu in *The Swamp Dwellers,* London, 1958; Obaneji and Forest Father in *A Dance of the Forests,* Lagos and Ibadan, 1960; Dauda Touray in *Dear Parent and Ogre* by R. Sarif Easmon, Ibadan, 1961; in *The Republican,* Lagos, 1963; **Film**—*Kongi's Harvest,* 1970; **Radio**—Konu in *The Detainee,* 1965.

*   *   *

Early in his career, Wole Soyinka produced two novels which distil several of the Nobel laureate's key themes. Both *The Interpreters* and *Season of Anomy* focus on the tensions and contradictions of post-colonial Nigerian society. They explore the social and political consequences of the uncomfortable coexistence of African and Western European values within a single cultural framework. Soyinka's characters try to affect various temporary (and often unsatisfying) resolutions in their lives, and to reconcile past to present, tradition to modernity, local life to global economies.

Soyinka's writing style has been criticized as overly erudite and unnecessarily allusive; in both his dialogue and his narration, he tends to blend references to Yoruba traditions (which would be inaccessible to Western readers and which require him to include a glossary in *The Interpreters*) and to European art and philosophy (which would be largely foreign, his critics have suggested, to his Nigerian readership). Soyinka's cultural politics push him to discover and to recover a distinctively African form of literary self-expression; however, his thought and writing have also been indelibly informed by Western traditions. The difficult, abstract textures of his prose emerge from a fluctuating position he establishes between these two cultural systems, as he attempts to negotiate his own uneasy compromise. In fact, that lack of ease or stability gives his writing its energy and its vital interest.

The Interpreters opens with a complex nightclub scene which sets the tone for the rest of the novel. Six friends, who represent various functions in contemporary Nigerian society (such as journalist, engineer, artist, and teacher), get drunk and discuss their lives. The dialogue, in keeping with their situation, is highly fluid, restless, and ironic. The time frame shifts from present to past, establishing resonances but also suggesting the interconnectedness of memory and action. Soyinka's narrative remains somewhat nonlinear throughout the book, preferring to follow multiple threads of event and history. Various voices and perspectives interpenetrate, creating a verbal web rather than a monolithic, disciplined plot. Like his character Egbo, who cannot reconcile the demands of his native heritage with contemporary life, Soyinka tends to float between worlds, exploring the manifestations and consequences of that medial state without necessarily resolving his dilemma. The novel is often bitterly satiric, particularly through the character of Sagoe, whose pseudo-philosophy of "voidancy" (a scatology run amuck, not unlike that of Jonathan Swift) offers an ongoing misanthropic commentary on the corruption and absurdity of Nigerian society. Little escapes the novel's incisive harshness. Sekoni, the one idealist, is killed at the novel's midpoint, and the second half of the text finds no alternatives for social recovery or happiness. Symbolically, a schoolgirl whom Egbo has made pregnant offers some hope for new life, but she remains nameless and lost to Egbo himself. *The Interpreters* traces the dissolution and despair often brought about by post-colonial states of cultural hybridity and uncertainty.

While *Season of Anomy* also remains uncertain at its conclusion, it takes up the duplicitous situations of post-colonial life and attempts to suggest tentative social, political, and imaginative resolutions. The title refers both to the anarchy that comes with the violent political upheavals in the novel and to the yearly cycles of death and rebirth in nature. The narrative follows the attempts by Ofeyi, a marketing genius who works for a nameless cartel controlling the government, to subvert his employers' social and economic power by introducing a counter-philosophy he discovers at the agricultural community of Aiyéró, which is collectivist, peaceful, native, and benign. The five parts of the novel trace the slow vegetal spread of the indigenous "way of life" of Aiyéró, which leads to violence as ideologies of greed and corruption collide with grassroots philosophy. The revolution appears to fail, although Soyinka also suggests that "spores" have been released among the people and that the possibility of betterment remains. The figure of Suberu, the prison guard who has thoughtlessly served the interests of corruption but later chooses to follow Ofeyi, represents such potential conversions. Iriyise, Ofeyi's kidnapped lover whom he sees as intimately and symbolically tied to the land and to Aiyéró, becomes sick and then lapses into a coma from which she has not emerged at the novel's close; her eventual rescue represents the possible healing of Africa in the wake of terrifying social upheavals, while her lack of consciousness suggests that all is not yet well. Soyinka's novel has been criticized for over-simplifying the political conflicts in post-colonial Nigeria, but he aims, at least, to advocate in his fiction a positive, forceful change for African society.

—Kevin McNeilly

SPARK, Muriel (Sarah)

Nationality: British. **Born:** Muriel Sarah Camberg in Edinburgh, 1 February 1918. **Education:** James Gillespie's School for Girls and Heriot Watt College, both Edinburgh. **Family:** Married S.O. Spark in 1937 (marriage dissolved by 1944); one son. **Career:** Worked in the Foreign Office Political Intelligence Department during World War II. General secretary, Poetry Society, and editor, *Poetry Review,* London, 1947-49. Lives in Rome. **Awards:** *Observer* story prize, 1951; Italia prize, for radio play, 1962; James Tait Black Memorial prize, for fiction, 1966; F.N.A.C. prize (France), 1987; Bram Stoker award, 1988; Royal Bank of Scotland—Saltire Society award, 1988; Ingersoll T.S. Eliot award, 1992. D.Litt.: University of Strathclyde, Glasgow, 1971; University of Edinburgh, 1989. Fellow, Royal Society of Literature, 1963; Honorary member: American Academy, 1978. O.B.E. (Officer, Order of the British Empire), 1967; Officer, Order of Arts and Letters (France), 1988. **Agent:** David Higham Associates, 5-8 Lower John Street, London W1R 4HA, England.

PUBLICATIONS

Novels

The Comforters. London, Macmillan, and Philadelphia, Lippincott, 1957.
Robinson. London, Macmillan, and Philadelphia, Lippincott, 1958.
Memento Mori. London, Macmillan, and Philadelphia, Lippincott, 1959.
The Ballad of Peckham Rye. London, Macmillan, and Philadelphia, Lippincott, 1960.
The Bachelors. London, Macmillan, 1960; Philadelphia, Lippincott, 1961.
The Prime of Miss Jean Brodie. London, Macmillan, 1961; Philadelphia, Lippincott, 1962.
The Girls of Slender Means. London, Macmillan, and New York, Knopf, 1963.
The Mandelbaum Gate. London, Macmillan, and New York, Knopf, 1965.
The Public Image. London, Macmillan, and New York, Knopf, 1968.
The Driver's Seat. London, Macmillan, and New York, Knopf, 1970.

Not to Disturb. London, Macmillan, 1971; New York, Viking Press, 1972.
The Hothouse by the East River. London, Macmillan, and New York, Viking Press, 1973.
The Abbess of Crewe. London, Macmillan, and New York, Viking Press, 1974.
The Takeover. London, Macmillan, and New York, Viking Press, 1976.
Territorial Rights. London, Macmillan, and New York, Coward McCann, 1979.
Loitering with Intent. London, Bodley Head, and New York, Coward McCann, 1981.
The Only Problem. London, Bodley Head, and New York, Coward McCann, 1984.
A Far Cry from Kensington. London, Constable, and Boston, Houghton Mifflin, 1988.
Symposium. London, Constable, and Boston, Houghton Mifflin, 1990.
Omnibus I. London, Constable, 1993.
Omnibus II. London, Constable, 1994.

Short Stories

The Go-Away Bird and Other Stories. London, Macmillan, 1958; Philadelphia, Lippincott, 1960.
Voices at Play (includes the radio plays *The Party Through the Wall, The Interview, The Dry River Bed, Danger Zone*). London, Macmillan, 1961; Philadelphia, Lippincott, 1962.
Collected Stories I. London, Macmillan, 1967; New York, Knopf, 1968.
Bang-Bang You're Dead and Other Stories. London, Granada, 1982.
The Stories of Muriel Spark. New York, Dutton, 1985; London, Bodley Head, 1987.

Plays

Doctors of Philosophy (produced London, 1962). London, Macmillan, 1963; New York, Knopf, 1966.

Radio Plays: *The Party Through the Wall,* 1957; *The Interview,* 1958; *The Dry River Bed,* 1959; *The Ballad of Peckham Rye,* 1960; *Danger Zone,* 1961.

Poetry

The Fanfarlo and Other Verse. Aldington, Kent, Hand and Flower Press, 1952.
Collected Poems I. London, Macmillan, 1967; New York, Knopf, 1968.
Going Up to Sotheby's and Other Poems. London, Granada, 1982.

Other

Child of Light: A Reassessment of Mary Wollstonecraft Shelley. London, Tower Bridge, 1951; revised edition, as *Mary Shelley: A Biography,* New York, Dutton, 1987; London, Constable, 1988.
Emily Brontë: Her Life and Work, with Derek Stanford. London, Owen, 1953.
John Masefield. London, Nevill, 1953; revised edition, London, Hutchinson, 1991.
The Very Fine Clock (for children). New York, Knopf, 1968; London, Macmillan, 1969.

The French Window and the Small Telephone (for children). London, Colophon, 1993.
The Essence of the Brontës. London, Owen, 1993.
Curriculum Vitae. London, Constable, and Boston, Houghton Mifflin, 1993.

Editor, with David Stanford, *Tribute to Wordsworth.* London, Wingate, 1950.
Editor, *A Selection of Poems,* by Emily Brontë. London, Grey Walls Press, 1952.
Editor, with David Stanford, *My Best Mary: The Letters of Mary Shelley.* London, Wingate, 1953.
Editor, *The Brontë Letters.* London, Nevill, 1954; as *The Letters of the Brontës: A Selection,* Norman, University of Oklahoma Press, 1954.
Editor, with David Stanford, *Letters of John Henry Newman.* London, Owen, 1957.

*

Bibliography: *Iris Murdoch and Muriel Spark: A Bibliography* by Thomas T. Tominaga and Wilma Schneidermeyer, Metuchen, New Jersey, Scarecrow Press, 1976.

Critical Studies: *Muriel Spark: A Biographical and Critical Study* by Derek Stanford, Fontwell, Sussex, Centaur Press, 1963; *Muriel Spark* by Karl Malkoff, New York, Columbia University Press, 1968; *Muriel Spark* by Patricia Stubbs, London, Longman, 1973; *Muriel Spark* by Peter Kemp, London, Elek, 1974, New York, Barnes and Noble, 1975; *Muriel Spark* by Allan Massie, Edinburgh, Ramsay Head Press, 1979; *The Faith and Fiction of Muriel Spark* by Ruth Whittaker, London, Macmillan, 1982, New York, St. Martin's Press, 1983; *Comedy and the Woman Writer: Woolf, Spark, and Feminism* by Judy Little, Lincoln, University of Nebraska Press, 1983; *Muriel Spark: An Odd Capacity for Vision* edited by Alan Bold, London, Vision Press, and New York, Barnes and Noble, 1984, and *Muriel Spark* by Bold, London, Methuen, 1986; *Muriel Spark* by Velma Bourgeois Richmond, New York, Ungar, 1984; *The Art of the Real: Muriel Spark's Novels* by Joseph Hynes, Rutherford, New Jersey, Fairleigh Dickinson University Press, 1988; *Muriel Spark* by Norman Page, London, Macmillan, 1990; *Vocation and Identity in the Fiction of Muriel Spark* by Rodney Stenning Edgecombe, Columbia, University of Missouri Press, 1990.

* * *

"Her prose is like a bird, darting from place to place, palpitating with nervous energy; but a bird with a bright beady eye and a sharp beak as well." Francis Hope's description crystallizes one important aspect of Muriel Spark's highly idiosyncratic talent. A late starter in the field of fiction, she had until early middle age published only conventional criticism and verse which gave little hint of her real gifts and future development. These were triumphantly released with the publication of *The Comforters* in 1957, and the spate of creative activity which followed, speedily establishing her reputation as a genuine original with a style and slant on life uniquely her own.

Spark spoke in an interview of her mind "crowded with ideas, all teeming in disorder." In 1954 she had become a convert to Roman Catholicism; and she regards her religion primarily as a disci-

pline for this prodigal fertility—"something to measure from," as she says, rather than a direct source of its inspiration. Yet her Catholicism pervasively colours a vision of life seen, in her own phrase, "from a slight angle to the universe." For all her inventive energy, verve and panache, and glittering malice, this writer is profoundly preoccupied with metaphysical questions of good and evil. Like Angus Wilson, she is a moral fabulist of the contemporary scene who works through the medium of comedy; and like him, she is often most in earnest when at her most entertaining.

Her novels abound in Catholic characters, but these are by no means always on the side of the angels. In *The Comforters* they teeter on the brink of delusion, retreating from orthodoxy into eccentric extremes of quasi-religious experience satirized with the wicked acuteness with which she later pillories spiritualism in *The Bachelors,* focussing upon the trial of a medium for fraud. Religious hypocrites such as the self-consciously progressive couple in "The Black Madonna" are quite as likely to be her targets as rationalist unbelievers. Her awareness of the powers of darkness as a palpable force at work in the world is most effectively embodied in her study of Satanism in the suburbs, *The Ballad of Peckham Rye,* in the diabolic person and activities of an industrial welfare worker born with horns on his head.

Such manifestations of the supernatural in the midst of prosaic actuality are a central element in Spark's novels. Her fantasy, earthed in the everyday, is presented as not illusion but natural extension of the material scene: the product of "that sort of mental squint," as she calls it, which perceives the credible co-existence of the uncanny with the most rational aspects of experience. Those who attempt to ignore or reject its reality—like the cynics staging their tawdry Nativity play and confounded by the avenging intervention of a real angel in "The Seraph and the Zambesi," or the sceptical George trying to explain away the flying saucer of "Miss Pinkerton's Apocalypse"—do so at their peril. Another short story, "The Portobello Road," is narrated by the ghost of a girl who materializes to her murderer in the Saturday morning street market; while *Memento Mori,* in which a number of old people are the victims of a sinister anonymous telephone caller, is a mordant exercise in the macabre. It is subtly suggested that these events might well, for those who choose to believe so, have a straightforward psychological explanation. The ghostly visitant need be no more than an externalization of the murderer's guilty conscience belatedly returned to plague him; the grim practical joker of *Memento* (never finally traced by the police) may embody the insistent reminder of imminent mortality already present within each aged subconscious mind.

Spark's work was highly praised by Evelyn Waugh, whose influence is detectable in the quickfire satirical wit of what one critic called her "machine-gun dialogue." The savage grotesqueries of early Waugh comedy are strongly recalled, too, by the chilling vein of heartlessness, even cruelty, in the violent ends to which so many Spark characters are remorselessly doomed: Needle, smothered in a haystack; the octogenarian Dame Letty, battered in her bed; Joanna Childe, bizarrely chanting passages from the Anglican liturgy as she burns to death; and the bored and loveless office worker of *The Driver's Seat* obsessively resolved to get herself killed in the most brutal fashion possible.

Yet if disaster and death haunt the pages of Spark's novels, her piquant humours are still more abundant. Although *The Girls of Slender Means* ends in tragedy, its portrayal of the impoverished inmates of a war-time hostel for young women of good family is as delectably funny as the depiction, in *The Bachelors,* of their gossipy male counterparts in London bedsitterland; or as the intrigues among nuns at a convent besieged by the media avid for ecclesiastical scandal in *The Abbess of Crewe.* Perhaps Spark's greatest comic triumph is her creation of the exuberant Edinburgh schoolmistress Jean Brodie, grooming her girls for living through an educationally unorthodox but headily exhilarating curriculum ranging from her heroes, Franco and Mussolini, to the love-lives of remarkable women of history, including her own.

Spark's narrative expertise is best exemplified in shorter forms, where her stylistic economy so often achieves a riveting intensity of impact. By contrast a longer, more ambitious book like *The Mandelbaum Gate,* about the adventures of a half-Jewish Catholic convert caught up in the divisions of warring Jerusalem, seems laboured and diffuse. Two novels, *The Takeover,* set during the 1970s but rooted in classical mythology, and *Territorial Rights,* have the Italian background which the author clearly finds a fruitful imaginative climate for exploring such themes as the exploitation of bogus religion and excessive wealth.

Loitering with Intent returns to her earlier London scene, and a time just after World War II. The composition of a struggling author's first novel is skilfully interwoven with her experiences in the employ of a bizarre society of pseudo-writers, whose grotesque fantasies, deceptions, and intrigues entertainingly reveal the possibilities of confusion between life and art. In *The Only Problem* the central character is a hapless scholar vainly seeking peace and seclusion in order to wrestle with interpreting the Book of Job. The daily problems of his own life increasingly impinge upon this task—not least the procession of modern counterparts of his biblical subject's comforters, or persecutors.

All these works wryly illustrate those characteristic qualities of sly, deadly wit in observing human oddity and weakness, the ingenious fusion of fact with fantasy and unpredictable surprise, and the underlying moral seriousness, which make Spark one of our most stimulating and quirkily individual novelists.

—Margaret Willy

SPENCE, Alan

Nationality: British. **Born:** Glasgow, 5 December 1947. **Education:** Glasgow University, 1966-69, and 1973-74. **Career:** Writer-in-residence, Glasgow University, 1975-77, Traverse Theatre, Edinburgh, 1982, Edinburgh District Council, 1986-87, and since 1990 Edinburgh University. **Address:** c/o Canongate Publishing, 16 Frederick Street, Edinburgh EH2 2HB, Scotland.

PUBLICATIONS

Novels

The Magic Flute. Edinburgh, Canongate, 1990.

Short Stories

Its Colours They Are Fine. London, Collins, 1977.

Uncollected Short Stories

"Sailmaker," in *Modern Scottish Short Stories,* edited by Fred Urquhart and Giles Gordon. London, Hamish Hamilton, 1978; revised edition, London, Faber, 1982.
"The Rain Dance" and "Tinsel," in *Street of Stone,* edited by Moira Burgess and Hamish Whyte. Edinburgh, Salamander Press, 1985.

Plays

Sailmaker. Edinburgh, Salamander Press, 1982.
Space Invaders. Edinburgh, Salamander Press, 1983.
Change Days. London, Hodder and Stoughton, 1991.

Poetry

Plop! 15 Haiku. Glasgow, No Name Press, 1970.
Glasgow Zen. Glasgow, Print Studio Press, 1981.

Other

Crab and Lobster Fishing. N.p., Fishing News, 1989.

*   *   *

Alan Spence's current reputation as a novelist and writer of short stories is much stronger in his native Scotland than elsewhere, and he deserves to be brought into greater prominence. His published output so far is not extensive—only two substantial books have appeared—but his work as a writer-in-residence at the universities of Glasgow and Edinburgh and at the Traverse Theatre in Edinburgh has given him a much wider following than that for more prolific authors.

His first book, *Its Colours They Are Fine,* is a very intense and carefully crafted collection of short stories. Dealing powerfully with childhood and early adulthood in Glasgow through the 1950s and 1960s, it is a volume on which the author's own formative experiences seem to exert creative pressure. Its central concerns are made local by the emphasis on male, Protestant, working-class characters, but Spence's work is always illuminated and broadened by his perception of the spiritual dimension to everyday experience. To talk of influences may inevitably be belittling, but Spence in this book seems very much in the tradition of James Joyce, looking for the magical revealing moments in the lives of ordinary urban citizens. However, where the lives of Joyce's Dubliners are full of disappointment and disillusion, the lives of Spence's creations are more richly nuanced. In "Tinsel," for example, a boy's excitement at putting up Christmas decorations is turned into a glimpse of a mysterious world of beauty and light which seems to overlap with the more mundane surroundings of a tenement flat in Govan. In "Sheaves," the tensions between boyish rough and tumble and a dimly intuited holiness are worked out without pretention. The collection is consistently impressive for its willingness to take on a reverent mystical suggestiveness, influenced no doubt by the author's developed interest in the Indian spiritual teacher Sri Chinmoy. The recurring theme in the book is that at moments of ceremony, however local or fleeting, we may gain insight into greater cosmic forces. The best story is without any doubt "The Rain Dance," which gives a beautifully modulated account of a Glasgow registry office wedding and all its attendant festivities, at once culturally specific and universal. Other stories deal with the lives of dispossessed and lonely characters, but Spence cannot manage the controlled outrage and vehemence of James Kelman, and occasionally his humane tolerance falls into sentimentality. Nonetheless, there are some truly exceptional pieces in this volume, and its sensibility is invigoratingly dignified and humane.

After an interval of 13 years, in which Spence concentrated mostly on poetry and occasional radio pieces, his first novel, *The Magic Flute,* appeared. It returns to the concern with childhood which distinguished the earlier short stories, and revisits some of the episodes to construct a complex tale of the different paths various people take through their lives. It follows four Glasgow boys through more than 20 years, from the late 1950s to the early 1980s, and to some extent it could be seen alongside the more popular saga novels of, say, Margaret Drabble. But that would be a distortion of the book's main enterprise, as well as of its unmistakable seriousness of purpose. Spence is highly ambitious and intricate in this work, as he tries to weave a very elaborate pattern of divergence and convergence around his characters. Each one is taken to represent a plausible journey through difficult times, conducted with different degrees of sensitivity, integrity, and success. The narrative is sustained by a deft allusiveness, touching upon identifiable cultural and historical references, and encompassing other literary archetypes, like Mozart's opera and a wide range of "quest" stories. The novel is certainly a very impressive piece of design, its architecture skillfully created and maintained. Furthermore, it contains wonderfully evocative sketches of times and places, which readers of a certain age will find acute and haunting. However, it is unevenly imagined, with much greater care being taken in the presentation of the more sensitive figures of Tam and Brian, and rather less in the sketching of the violent Eddie and the spiritless George. And it has to be said that Spence's female characters remain too lifeless. Overall, *The Magic Flute* is an intermittently powerful and searching book, serious and humane in its treatment of its participants, with a high sense of purpose and intelligence, which also sprawls and drifts too much.

Spence is a writer whose continuing development should be closely followed. If he can find a way of integrating his exceptional perceptiveness and reverence for experience in a compelling extended narrative, he could be one of the most interesting and individual novelists in Britain.

—Ian A. Bell

SPENCER, Colin

Nationality: British. **Born:** London, 17 July 1933. **Education:** Brighton Grammar School, Selhurst; Brighton College of Art. **Military Service:** Served in the Royal Army Medical Corps, 1950-52. **Family:** Married Gillian Chapman in 1959 (divorced 1969); one son. **Career:** Paintings exhibited in Cambridge and London; costume designer. Chair, Writers Guild of Great Britain, 1982-83. **Agent:** Richard Scott Simon, Anthony Sheil Associates, 43 Doughty Street, London WC1N 2LF, England.

PUBLICATIONS

Novels

An Absurd Affair. London, Longman, 1961.

Generation:
  Anarchists in Love. London, Eyre and Spottiswoode, 1963; as
     The Anarchy of Love, New York, Weybright and Talley, 1967.
  The Tyranny of Love. London, Blond, and New York, Weybright
     and Talley, 1967.
  Lovers in War. London, Blond, 1969.
  The Victims of Love. London, Quartet, 1978.
Asylum. London, Blond, 1966.
Poppy, Mandragora, and the New Sex. London, Blond, 1966.
Panic. London, Secker and Warburg, 1971.
How the Greeks Kidnapped Mrs. Nixon. London, Quartet, 1974.

Uncollected Short Stories

"Nightworkers," in *London Magazine,* vol. 2, no. 12, 1955.
"An Alien World," in *London Magazine,* vol. 3, no. 6, 1956.
"Nymph and Shepherd," in *London Magazine,* vol. 6, no. 8, 1959.
"It's Anemones for Mabel," in *Transatlantic Review* (London),
     Spring 1963.
"The Room," in *Transatlantic Review* (London), Summer 1966.
"Carpaccio's Dream," in *Harpers and Queen* (London), December
     1985.

Plays

The Ballad of the False Barman, music by Clifton Parker (produced London, 1966).
Spitting Image (produced London, 1968; New York, 1969). Published in *Plays and Players* (London), September 1968.
The Trial of St. George (produced London, 1972).
The Sphinx Mother (produced Salzburg, Austria, 1972).
Why Mrs. Neustadter Always Loses (produced London, 1972).
Keep It in the Family (produced London, 1978).
Lilith (produced Vienna, 1979).

Television Plays: *Flossie,* 1975; *Vandal Rule OK?* (documentary), 1977.

Other

Gourmet Cooking for Vegetarians. London, Deutsch, 1978.
Good and Healthy: A Vegetarian and Wholefood Cookbook. London, Robson, 1983; as *Vegetarian Wholefood Cookbook,* London, Panther, 1985.
Reports from Behind, with Chris Barlas, illustrated by Spencer. London, Enigma, 1984.
Cordon Vert: 52 Vegetarian Gourmet Dinner Party Menus. Wellingborough, Northamptonshire, Thorsons, 1985; Chicago, Contemporary, 1987.
Mediterranean Vegetarian Cooking. Wellingborough, Northamptonshire, Thorsons, 1986.
The New Vegetarian: The Ultimate Guide to Gourmet Cooking and Healthy Living. London, Elm Tree, 1986.
The Vegetarian's Healthy Diet Book, with Tom Sanders. London, Dunitz, 1986; as *The Vegetarian's Kitchen,* Tucson, Arizona, Body Press, 1986.
One-Course Feasts. London, Conran Octopus, 1986.
Feast for Health: A Gourmet Guide to Good Food. London, Dorling Kindersley, 1987.
Al Fresco: A Feast of Outdoor Entertaining. Wellingborough, Northamptonshire, Thorsons, 1987.

The Romantic Vegetarian. Wellingborough, Northamptonshire, Thorsons, 1988.
The Adventurous Vegetarian. London, Cassell, 1989.
Which of Us Two? The Story of a Love Affair. London, Viking, 1990.
The Heretic's Feast: A History of Vegetarianism. Pullisle, Fourth Estate, and New England University Press, 1992.

Editor, *Green Cuisine: The Guardian's Selection of the Best Vegetarian Recipes.* Wellingborough, Northamptonshire, Thorsons, 1986.

*

Critical Study: Interview with Peter Burton, in *Transatlantic Review 35* (London), 1970.

Theatrical Activities:
Director: **Play**—*Keep It in the Family,* London, 1978.

Colin Spencer comments:

I have the impression that my work taken as a whole can be confusing to a critic or a reader. Both the novels and the plays appear to be written in too many various styles; if this is true I make no apologies but will attempt an explanation. The main core of my work as a writer is found in the four volumes of the unfinished sequence of novels: *Generation.* This, in its simplest form is nothing but fictionalised autobiography—the line where fiction begins and reality ends is a philosophical enigma that continually fascinates me. The volumes are sagas of various families, their children and grandchildren, their marriages and relationships; their social context is firmly middle-class though in later volumes some of the characters move into the upper-middle stratas while others remain socially rootless. I have struggled in these books to make the characters and their backgrounds as true to what I have observed and experienced as my perception and recollection allow. For I believe that the novel form is unique in being as exact a mirror to our experience as is afforded in the whole range of art forms. For not only can the novel communicate the great obsessive passions, frustrations, and longings of individuals, but it can also conjure up a picture of all the myriad details—quite trivial in themselves—which at certain times affect major actions. In form I based these interrelating novels on the 19th-century tradition (it is a complicated story with many characters) but I have allowed myself within that framework to use all the literary experiments forged in the first half of this century. The characters that I have created from my experience and observation are not puppets; I cannot control and guide them into some preconceived aesthetic pattern, for they exist in life and in the narration I have to pursue and relate as truthfully as possible their own tragic mistakes, their comic failures and triumphs, their self-deceit and affirmation of life.

But in my plays there is no direct autobiographical experience: they are, like some of the other novels, satires on social problems that oppress individuals. I like to entertain in the theatre, to make an audience laugh but at the same time debate at the core of the work a serious and unresolved problem. The novels *Poppy, Mandragora, and the New Sex* and *How the Greeks Kidnapped Mrs. Nixon* also use comedy to expose gross injustice. *Panic* treats another subject, that of child assault, on the surface as a murder mystery, yet its main intention was to induce the reader to understand the psychological nature of the killer. I would dismiss my first novel,

An Absurd Affair, as merely a public rehearsal in the craft of fiction. But there is one novel that falls outside any of the above categories—*Asylum.* The Oedipus myth has always fascinated me. (The play *The Sphinx Mother* is a contemporary account of the Jocasta figure refusing to commit suicide and struggling for final and complete possession of her son/husband.) Another myth, the Fall of Man, with its pervasive sense of original sin corroding free will seems for me with the Oedipus myth to have influenced the compulsive aspirations in Western culture for over two thousand years. In *Asylum* I created a plot, loosely based on a 19th-century American scandal, where I united both myths in the same family and set it in a hierarchic social commune, almost a science-fiction Asylum. I then tried to imply how our religious and judicial structure worked through arbitrary indifference and cruel repression. I might add that for large passages of the book I allowed myself the indulgence of writing in a style akin to poetic prose.

If I may sum up I would say that I feel my job as a writer is to state the truth in as vivid a manner as is possible and to involve the reader in a celebration of life, while uncovering the injustices that as individuals and as society we impose upon each other.

* * *

Colin Spencer's novels revel in the eccentric, the bizarre, and the grotesque while tending toward social commentary. His event-filled books treat of human relationships buffeted by sexual antagonisms of various, extreme types. In depicting his frequently polymorphously perverse characters, Spencer plays a recurrent theme of protest against conventional mores and morality, although, perhaps unintentionally, the alternatives he presents hardly seem more satisfactory. With casts of almost Dickensian proportions and curiosity, he runs the gamut of sexual expression, particularly homosexual. Sympathetic understanding, graphic detail, and a fine talent for low comedy do not often, however, extend his narratives beyond the superficial or raise them from mere sensationalism to genuine significance. Nor does his tendency to have protagonist-spokesmen speechify make his arguments more appealing.

In *An Absurd Affair* Spencer sketches some telling scenes of marital dependence and oppression, but soon gives way to improbable melodrama. Conceited, petty, and dull, James dominates his immature, thoughtless child-wife, Sarah. Though he is undereducated and boring, James finds his wife inferior and her love of art beyond his comprehension. By accident, Sarah finds the negative of a "dirty" picture, and, to the prudish James's shock, she is fascinated. Undue influence by this "art," along with romantic infatuation and huge amounts of alcohol, leads the insecure woman into a ludicrous pursuit of a sadistic schoolteacher and finally into a delusory affair with a Sicilian gigolo. Though James rescues her, she finds she no longer loves him and declares her independence. For all Spencer's obvious and overdrawn psychologizing, both characters remain rather implausible caricatures in what is, indeed, an absurd affair, unredeemed by the crude poetic justice—or ladies' magazine moralizing—of its pat ending.

Of considerably more merit and interest are the volumes of the series *Generation,* a sizeable contribution to the large corpus of English novels examining life in reaction to post-World War II conditions, in this case a sprawling saga of the Simpson family from World War I through the 1960s. Shifting back and forth over the years, Spencer draws vivid, well-rounded portraits of several characteristic types, some of which develop into unique personalities; the ever more complicated alliances and misalliances of the heterogeneous Simpsons reveal a fascinating panorama of several social milieus. While realistic scenes are well-executed, the more emotional confrontations take on the unfortunate tone of a soap opera. And though characters occasionally mention and blame the War for their uncertain, disjointed worlds, its significance for their individual struggles is implied more than clearly stated.

Weaving in and out of the separate stories of the factional family members, friends, and lovers, Eddy Simpson's raunchy career, depicted in short, often raucous vignettes, becomes a central focus for understanding the wayward, amusing, and sometimes pathetic journeys in the novels. Crude and conscious only of his own desires, paterfamilias Eddy jokes, drinks, and womanizes. His Rabelaisian zest for life can be hilarious, but it is also ruinous for the rest of the Simpsons. Long-suffering wife Hester turns to religion, whose comforts are of little use to her artistic and volatile children Sundy and Matthew. The major portions of the novels are devoted to their painful growing up and tortured adulthood.

Hetero-, homo-, and bi-sexual roles are played out in several combinations; in the convoluted course of the interconnected plots there is more changing of partners than in a country square dance. Sundy is most original. After dallying with lesbianism, she is caught briefly in an incestuous bond. She takes up with Reg, a handsome liar, self-proclaimed anarchist, and sometime rent-boy, aborts their illegitimate child, and finally, confusedly, marries him. After losing Reg to her brother Matthew, she leads a bohemian life with an unreliable publisher. Through tumultuous years, Matthews's reactions to his father's boorishness and cruelty alternate between dejection and desire for revenge, religious fanaticism and self-hatred. His homosexuality comes slowly to consciousness but not acceptance, and his ambivalence ends in a disastrous and mutually destructive marriage to a priggish, unstable shrew.

Along the way Spencer portrays lower-, middle-, and upper-class life, as well as the more baroque aspects of the homosexual world, with deftness and insight. Sometimes his prose sags, but generally Spencer's humor, irony, and use of contrast are skillful, allowing his themes to reveal themselves by inference. Perhaps his strongest points are made by the self-inflicted wounds of the "anarchists" whose intellectual poses ineffectually mask their adolescent, mixed-up libertinism.

Constructed in a fantastic mode, *Asylum* displays Spencer's penchant for the macabre. The patients in the ultra-modern insane asylum are prompted to act out their twisted pasts and perverse imaginings by the equally but scientifically demented psychiatrists (who are, in turn, directed by monstrous computers), before they are hunted and left to die. Spencer's surrealistic vision combines and curiously reworks *Oedipus* and the Book of Genesis through phantasmagoric permutations. In the confused dimension of illusion-reality, Cleo-Jocasta tries to work her incestuous vindictive will upon her priest-husband Max (Addams) through their dark-skinned son Carl, but Carl prefers the charms of his fair-skinned brother Angelo. While the inversions and embroidery of the Greek and Judaic myths are imaginative, their point is often as obscure as Cleo's mad history.

Perhaps Spencer's most mature work is his probing analysis of the mentality of the child molester in *Panic*. With the seamy Brighton underworld as a backdrop, the novel unfolds the wretched life of Woody and his mother Saffron May and their increasingly perverted relationship, culminating in the tragic child-murders. Spencer tells the gripping story through the voices of the major characters, carefully controlling the tensions to the last climactic moments. What was once used largely for shock value in earlier books, is

now integral to theme and structure. Both killer and victims are revealed with sympathy from the inside, and even the freakish characters of the lesbian burglar Trigger and the wretched dwarf Jumbo emerge as strange but human beings.

—Joseph Parisi

SPENCER, Elizabeth

Nationality: American. **Born:** Carrollton, Mississippi, 19 July 1921. **Education:** Belhaven College, Jackson, Mississippi, 1938-42, A.B. 1942; Vanderbilt University, Nashville, 1942-43, M.A. 1943. **Family:** Married John Rusher in 1956. **Career:** Instructor, Northwest Mississippi Junior College, Senatobia, 1943-44, and Ward-Belmont College, Nashville, 1944-45; reporter, Nashville *Tennessean,* 1945-46; instructor, 1948-49, and instructor in creative writing, 1949-51, 1952-53, University of Mississippi, Oxford; Donnelly Fellow, Bryn Mawr College, Pennsylvania, 1962; creative writing fellow, University of North Carolina, Chapel Hill, 1969; writer-in-residence, Hollins College, Virginia, 1973. Member of the creative writing faculty, 1976-81, adjunct professor, 1981-86, Concordia University, Montreal; visiting professor, University of North Carolina, Chapel Hill, 1986-92. Charter member, 1987, vice-chancellor, 1993, Fellowship of Southern Writers. **Awards:** American Academy Recognition award, 1952, Rosenthal award, 1957, and Award of Merit Medal, 1983; Guggenheim fellowship, 1953; *Kenyon Review* fellowship, 1957; McGraw-Hill fiction award, 1960; Bellaman award, 1968; National Endowment for the Arts grant, 1982, and award, 1988; Salem award, 1992, for literature; Dos Passos award, 1992, for fiction; North Carolina Governor's award, 1994, for literature. D.L.: Southwestern (now Rhodes) University, Memphis, 1968; LL.D.: Concordia University, Montreal, 1988; Litt.D.: University of the South, Sewanee, Tennessee. **Member:** American Academy, 1985. **Agent:** Virginia Barber, 353 West 21st Street, New York, New York 10011, U.S.A. **Address:** 402 Longleaf Drive, Chapel Hill, North Carolina 27514, U.S.A.

PUBLICATIONS

Novels

Fire in the Morning. New York, Dodd Mead, 1948.
This Crooked Way. New York, Dodd Mead, and London, Gollancz, 1952.
The Voice at the Back Door. New York, McGraw Hill, 1956; London, Gollancz, 1957.
The Light in the Piazza. New York, McGraw Hill, 1960; London, Heinemann, 1961.
Knights and Dragons. New York, McGraw Hill, 1965; London, Heinemann, 1966.
No Place for an Angel. New York, McGraw Hill, 1967; London, Weidenfeld and Nicolson, 1968.
The Snare. New York, McGraw Hill, 1972.
The Salt Line. New York, Doubleday, 1984; London, Penguin, 1985.
The Night Travellers. New York, Viking, 1991.

Short Stories

Ship Island and Other Stories. New York, McGraw Hill, 1968;
London, Weidenfeld and Nicolson, 1969.
The Stories of Elizabeth Spencer. New York, Doubleday, 1981; London, Penguin, 1983.
Marilee: Three Stories. Jackson, University Press of Mississippi,
1981.
The Mules. Winston-Salem, North Carolina, Palaemon Press,
1982.
Jack of Diamonds and Other Stories. New York, Viking, 1988.
On the Gulf. Jackson, University Press of Mississippi, 1991.

Uncollected Short Stories

"To the Watchers While Walking Home," in *Ontario Review*
(Princeton, New Jersey), 1982.
"Madonna" and "Puzzle Poem," in *Hudson Review* (New York),
Summer 1983.
"Up the Gatineau," in *Boulevard* (Philadelphia), Spring 1989.
"The Weekend Travellers," in *Story* (Cincinnati), Winter 1994.
"The Runaways," in *Antaeus* (Hopewell, New Jersey), Spring
1994.
"The Master of Shongalo," in *Southern Review* (Baton Rouge, Louisiana), Winter 1995.

Play

For Lease or Sale, in *Mississippi Writers 4: Reflection of Childhood and Youth,* edited by Dorothy Abbott. Jackson, University
Press of Mississippi, 1991.

Other

Conversations with Elizabeth Spencer, edited by Peggy Whitman
Prenshaw. Jackson, University Press of Mississippi, 1991.

*

Bibliography: By Laura Barge, 1976, and by C.E. Lewis, 1994,
both in *Mississippi Quarterly* (Starkville).

Manuscript Collections: National Library of Canada, Ottawa;
University of Kentucky, Lexington.

Critical Studies: *Elizabeth Spencer* by Peggy Whitman Prenshaw,
Boston, Twayne, 1985; *Self and Community in the Fiction of Elizabeth Spencer* by Terry Roberts, Baton Rouge, Louisiana State University Press, 1994.

Elizabeth Spencer comments:

I began writing down stories as soon as I learned how to write;
that is, at about age six; before that, I made them up anyway and
told them to anybody who was handy and would listen. Being a
rural Southerner, a Mississippian, had a lot to do with it, I have
been told, with this impulse and with the peculiar mystique, importance, which attached itself naturally thereto and enhanced it. We
had been brought up on stories, those about local people, living
and dead, and Bible narratives, believed also to be literally true, so
that other stories read aloud—the Greek myths, for instance—while
indicated as "just" stories, were only one slight remove from the

"real" stories of the local scene and the Bible. So it was with history, for local event spilled into the history of the textbooks; my
grandfather could remember the close of the Civil War, and my
elder brother's nurse had been a slave. The whole world, then, was
either entirely in the nature of stories or partook so deeply of stories as to be at every point inseparable from them. Even the novels
we came later to read were mainly English 19th-century works
which dealt with a culture similar to our own—we learned with no
surprise that we had sprung from it.

Though I left the South in 1953, I still see the world and its
primal motions as story, since story charts in time the heart's assertions and gives central place to the great human relationships.
My first three novels, written or projected before I left the South,
deal with people in that society who must as the true measure of
themselves either alter it or come to terms with it. Years I spent in
Italy and more recently in Canada have made me see the world in
other than this fixed geography. The challenge to wring its stories
from it became to me more difficult at the same time that it became
more urgent that I and other writers should do so. A story may not
be the only wrench one can hurl into the giant machine that seems
bent on devouring us all, but is one of them. A story which has
been tooled, shaped, and slicked up is neither real nor true—we
know its nature and its straw insides. Only the real creature can
satisfy, the one that is touchy and alive, dangerous to fool with.
The search for such as these goes on with me continually, and I
think for all real writers as well.

(1995) I returned to the South in 1986 and have found a not
altogether different world, for the South can maintain its continuity
better perhaps than most other areas. But the media and the electronic age are doing their work of restructuring, and enduring as a
separate, recognizable region of the United States tests and will
continue to test the considerable talents of southern writers. We
remain, however, what we have always been—storytellers, some
of the world's best.

*   *   *

Elizabeth Spencer's first three novels portray the upper middle
class of her native Mississippi trapped between the decadent planter
aristocrats and politically ambitious "redneck" bigots who were William Faulkner's special province. *Five in the Morning* (titled from
Djuna Barnes's *Nightwood*) grimly depicts the effectiveness of petty
greed in stifling a small community's vitality. The Gerrard family
moved into Tarsus in the wake of Civil War disruptions and made
themselves leading citizens through perjury and blackmail. Their
machinations result, however, only in the destruction of almost everyone involved except one Gerrard son and a former schoolmate,
son of one of the family's principal victims. These young men
achieve a reconciliation when the Gerrard follows the many other
people driven from the community and the other, Kinloch
Armstrong, learns that his strength is the very "strangeness" he
has always felt that allows him to transcend the squalor that engulfs the others. *This Crooked Way* is a less complex and more
cynical tale about an opportunist who comes down from the hills
to become a Delta planter. Amos Dudley has always dreamed of
seeing a ladder of angels, but his inability to face reality results
only in the wreckage of the lives of his family and most of those
around him.

Spencer's most powerful novel, *The Voice at the Back Door,*
bares the history of a well-educated and inherently decent young
lawyer, Kerney Woolbright, who must sacrifice his integrity to win

political preferment in his community. The novel contrasts Kerney's lying about his knowledge of an explosive situation involving a Negro in order to assure his victory at the polls with the behavior of Duncan Harper, a truculently honest athlete—once idol of the community—who sacrifices a comfortable career to protect the Negro from ignorant bigotry.

After this chilling revelation of the corruption of competence and the persecution of decency, Spencer abandoned Mississippi for Italy, which inspired two brief novels about women who escape abroad to victory. *The Light in the Piazza,* source of an unusually tasteful and subtle film, tensely relates an American mother's risky effort to marry her mentally retarded daughter to an attractive young Florentine despite her husband's misgivings and the Italian family's efforts to profit by the match. *Knights and Dragons* studies an American woman who has fled to Rome after her marriage collapse and who finds at last that human love demands too much of the individual to be worth the struggle, so that she frees herself— like Federico Fellini's Juliet of the Spirits—to become "a companion to cloud and sky."

After these short, intense international novels, Spencer returned by stages to the United States and, at last, Mississippi. *No Place for an Angel* chronicles against an international background (Washington-Florida, Rome-Sicily and elsewhere) the intricate interrelationships of two married couples and their sprawling families and a young American sculptor, who dreams like Amos Dudley of angels. One wife says of her husband, "Jerry had to be great, and he almost made it." The novel is a mature, unsentimental account of characters that almost make it, only to find—as one put it—that "life keeps turning into a vacuum," though the author tempers the bleakness by suggesting that these people's children may find happiness by wanting less. *The Snare* concentrates on a woman who does at last "make it" by never seeking greatness. Julia Garrett's life in a New Orleans that the novelist pictures with special skill has been a search on "a many-branched road" for an identity from the time that her aimless father abandons her in the arms of better-placed relatives. Frustrated in efforts to achieve mature relationships, Julia realizes herself at last not through the vision of an angel, but the person of her own very real child.

After a long period during which she experimented with a variety of short stories, Spencer returned to Mississippi's Gulf Coast in *The Salt Line;* but the region is no longer Faulkner's gothic south nor the transitory plastic America that materialized after World War II. *The Salt Line* occurs after Hurricane Camille, which in 1969 devastated the modernizing region. We witness efforts to rebuild principally through three survivors—two of whom were former friends as college professors, the other a petty gangster—through whose own lives hurricanes have passed. While they blame "bad luck," they are what Scott Fitzgerald called "careless people." Just as residents of the hurricane-prone areas return to waiting out seasons nervously, these leading characters return to their old ways. At the end of the novel, Spencer holds out the possibility of "the bright redemption of love"; but the vision illuminating the novel is that love helps people endure, but not prevail. As Peggy Prenshaw points out, the Byronic central figure of *The Salt Line* faces the future asking the same question as Robert Frost's oven-bird—what to make of "a diminished thing."

—Warren French

ST. AUBIN de TERAN, Lisa

Nationality: British. **Born:** Lisa Rynveld, London, 2 October 1953. **Education:** Attended school in London. **Family:** Married 1) Jaime Teran, 1981 (divorced 1981), one daughter; 2) George MacBeth, 1981 (divorced 1986), one son; 3) Robbie Duff-Scott, 1989, one daughter. **Career:** Farmer of sugar cane, avocados, pears, and sheep, Venezuela, 1972-78. Since 1972, writer. **Awards:** Somerset Maugham award, 1983, for *The Long Way Home;* John Llewellyn Rhys memorial prize, 1983, for *Slow Train to Milan;* Eric Gregory award, 1983, for poetry. **Agent:** A.M. Heath, 79 St. Martins Lane, London WC2N 4AA, England. **Address:** 5437 Castello, Venesia, Italy; and 7 Canynge Aquare, Clifton, Bristol, England.

PUBLICATIONS

Novels

Keepers of the House. London, Cape, 1982; as *The Long Way Home,* New York, Harper and Row, and London, Cape, 1983.
The Slow Train to Milan. London, Cape, and New York, Harper and Row, 1983.
The Tiger. London, Cape, 1984.
The Bay of Silence. London, Cape, 1986.
Black Idol. London, Cape, 1987.
Joanna. London, Virago, 1990; New York, Carroll and Graf, 1991.
Nocturne. London, Hamilton, 1992; New York, St. Martin's Press, 1993.

Short Stories

The Marble Mountain and Other Stories. London, Cape, 1989.

Poetry

The Streak. Knotting, Martin Booth, 1980.
The High Place. London, Cape, 1985.

Other

Off the Rails: Memoirs of a Train Addict. London, Bloomsbury, 1989.
Landscape in Italy, with photographs by John Ferro Sims. London, Pavilion, 1989.
Venice: The Four Seasons, with photographs by Mick Lindberg. London, Pavilion, and New York, Clarkson Potter, 1992.
A Valley in Italy: Confessions of a House Addict. London, Hamilton, 1994.

Editor, *Indiscreet Journeys: Stories of Women on the Road.* London, Virago, 1989; Boston, Faber, 1990.

*   *   *

Much of Lisa St. Aubin de Teran's early work was autobiographical, and chronologically the fictionalized events of *Keepers of the House,* although published first, followed her second novel, *The Slow Train to Milan.* St. Aubin de Teran is unusual for an English writer in setting her fiction abroad, often in Italy and South America.

Her extraordinary sense of place, perhaps more obviously than her characterization, has made her work distinguished and memorable.

Little happens in *Keepers of the House,* which concerns the final decay of an old farmhouse, La Bebella, near Venezuela. The second last survivor of the Beltrán family, Diego, has married Lydia, an Englishwoman. They return to La Bebella, where years of drought and disease have gradually driven the servants away. Previously uncommunicative by nature, Diego slips into a deep depression and becomes a hermit-like recluse. Lydia has to manage the dilapidated farm and the uncertain avocado and sugar crops, despite being nearly defeated by the effect of the death of her newborn son. Lydia is sustained by Benito, an old retainer who relates to her two centuries of Beltrán family history. These exotic legends of this once powerful family are a rare imaginative achievement, and such writing has earned St. Aubin de Teran the accolade of the English Márquez. One learns little of Lydia or Diego, who is eventually paralyzed by a stroke; as in much of St. Aubin de Teran's writing, the past matters more than the present. The carefully detailed descriptive passages evoke a sympathy for the long-dead characters and their struggles. When the barren lands yield nothing more, Lydia abandons La Bebella when Benito dies, carrying her invalid husband to a jeep, to escape to a place of safety. Lydia, once again pregnant, has inherited a knowledge she can pass to her child. Only Diego's cousin, Christebal Beltrán, aged about 112, remains as a sentinel watching over the deserted valley.

The Slow Train to Milan has no plot, only a series of rather fantastic episodes about political exiles from South America on the run in Europe. The tone of the novel is casual, from the rapid marriage of Lisaveta, the 16-year-old narrator, to César, an amiable if self-centered eccentric. He and his exiled friends, Otto and Elias, are mysterious figures who shuffle aimlessly with Lisaveta between cities living in borrowed accommodations, pawning valuables for survival when their money runs outs, and fluctuating between the extremes of poverty and luxury. The uncomplaining, adventurous Lisaveta, though curious about her husband's past and his friends, rarely questions them and is content to be part of their unsettled existence, much of it spent on "the slow train to Milan." The novel depends on the atmosphere of the innumerable contrasting places the travelers visit and people they encounter and the tension created by the constant fear that these exiles will be caught. The narrator identifies herself at least partly with St. Aubin de Teran and Lydia, remarking that she later grew avocados with her husband in the Andes.

The autobiographical element is less marked in *Tiger,* where the dominating character is Misia Schmutter, a murderous despot and head of her family, and her grandson, Lucien, whose course of life she influences even from beyond the grave. *Nocturne* is, perhaps, more plausible; it is a triumph of characterization and evocation of place. The setting is mainly in San Severino, a peasant village in Italy in the first decade of this century; this is where Alessandro Mezzanotte is born and lives until he dies. From the age of 15, Mezzanotte is obsessively in love with Valentina, a young gypsy who is part of a traveling fair. For some years he is compelled to travel from San Severino to be wherever the fair is, although his love is scorned by both families. Forced to be in Mussolini's army, Mezzanotte, previously handsome, is blinded and facially scarred and loses an arm when hit by a shell; he is pensioned off. His name, translating as "Midnight," suggests his fate is preordained. However, his solitary life for the next 50 years is endurable because of his unshakable belief that Valentina will come to him, even in old age. Near the end of his life, Mezzanotte is looked after by a young army conscript, Stefano, whose own troubled life and character are deeply affected by the old man, who unburdens his secrets on the soldier. When Mezzanotte dies, Stefano finds Valentina's last letters, which the blind man could not read. To save his sanity, Mezzanotte had been told the reverse of Valentina's intentions. Unable to cope with his appearance, she had, in fact, finally written to say she had discarded Mezzanotte for someone else. *Nocturne* is poignant and haunting and is a further indication that St. Aubin de Teran has still much to say as a distinctive writer.

—Geoffrey Elborn

ST. OMER, Garth

Nationality: St. Lucian. **Born:** Castries, St. Lucia. **Education:** The University of the West Indies, Kingston, Jamaica, degree in French. **Career:** Has lived in France, Ghana, and England. **Address:** c/o Faber and Faber Ltd., 3 Queen Sq., London WC1N 3AU, England.

PUBLICATIONS

Novels

A Room on the Hill. London, Faber, 1968.
Nor Any Country. London, Faber, 1969.
J—, Black Bam and the Masqueraders. London, Faber, 1972.

Short Stories

Shades of Grey. London, Faber, 1968.

Uncollected Short Story

"Syrop," in *Introduction 2.* London, Faber, 1968.

*   *   *

Garth St. Omer creates in his fiction characters filled with an unrest which they themselves cannot define or explain. It is a *malaise* of the islands which makes them hesitate even before opportunities which are apparently dazzling, which makes them hurt and abandon those they love, or turn aside from courses of action they have embarked on with every sign of conviction. The immediacy of his writing springs from the fact that he is so involved himself with this unrest that he is not yet able to distance or judge his heroes. The passion and the pain of these young island lives are fully conveyed, but it is perhaps this very lack of distance that makes his writing ideally suited to the novella form. His reputation was first made with "Syrop," and the fact that he followed his first novel with a volume comprising two more novellas demonstrates his addiction to the form.

"Syrop" is a harsh, tragic story of a family blighted by inexplicable misfortune, as well as by the poverty they share with their neighbors. Syrop, the young hero, differs from other St. Omer protagonists in that he doesn't live to carry his anguish and restlessness into adult life. He is smashed by a ship's propellers, diving for pennies on the very day he has been chosen to join the fishing crews, and on the eve of his much-loved brother's return from prison. John Lestrade, in St. Omer's first novel, *A Room on the Hill,* is older and tougher, but still haunted by intimate misfortunes and early deaths in his little island circle of relatives, friends and lovers. This book ends with a hard gesture towards departure, for it is increasingly obvious that all who stay in the island are doomed or lost, and Lestrade is determined to survive and transmute grief into action.

Of the two stories in *Shades of Grey* the first, "The Lights on the Hill," is the more tightly organized. It starts at a moment of crisis in the hero's relationship with Thea, the beautiful and original girl whom he has long desired and who now loves him. Neither can explain the nature of this crisis and it can only cause pain to them both, yet Stephenson knows in his being that he must now leave her. The madman's cry from the asylum which punctuates this realization begins and ends the story. In between these cries (or are they the same?) St. Omer cross-cuts a number of short scenes from the hero's past in Jamaica and in his native St. Lucia. We see him charcoal-burning with his father and his illiterate brother Carl in the mountains, or seeking refuge with his mother in the empty barracks on the Morne after the Castries fire of 1948, or drifting into corruption, trial and dismissal as a petty official in the Civil Service. And we see the other affairs, some furtive and bourgeois, others casual and earthy, which have preceded all the phases of his rich relationship with Thea. Through it all we are conscious of the two lovers sitting on the hillside, smoking and talking in the darkness, numbed by their awareness that some force within him is sweeping them apart. The writing is full of sharp, perfectly registered dialogue. His narrative and descriptive passages are rendered throughout in short, rather spiky paragraphs and staccato sentences, which carry the same burden of unease as the lives they describe. The effect can occasionally be irritating for the reader who longs for a deeper and more measured breath. Again, it is a style for the novella rather than the novel, but it perfectly fits the peculiar and sustained tension of this story in which jobs, lives and love affairs are all snapped off before fruition.

The second story, "Another Place Another Time," adopts a more chronological approach to a short period in the boyhood of its hero, Derek Charles. It lacks the originality and power of the first, but is full of a distinctive pain of its own. This pain stems largely from the sheer unlikeableness of this boy. He is priggish, snobbish, and jumpy, difficult to reach. He behaves brutally to Berthe, the simple girl whom he seduces and throws over. Yet we see in this society of few and roving males, of unfathered children, abortions, poverty and abandonment, how difficult it is for the growing child to find models by which to climb to maturity. It is as though leaving the island were an indispensable part of growing up, a *rite de passage* from which most of the initiates never return. The story is a cry from the forest of exile, a cry to which St. Omer fits the words of Shakespeare: "How like a winter has my absence been/From thee."

St. Omer is particularly good at rendering the speech of those who, though educated elsewhere, are still very close to the islands and unable to relate their living satisfactorily to any other place. The uncertainty of their position is registered in the groping movement of the sentences with which they seek to explain their lives. The handling of dialogue is less successful where it derives from the *patois* of St. Lucia, a dialect largely of French derivation for which St. Omer tries to find an English dialect equivalent. The shape and rhythm of this dialect are necessarily very different from those of *patois,* and the effect, despite an occasional "oui" or "non" at the end of a sentence, is vaguely West Indian rather than specifi-

cally St. Lucian. Yet it is hard to think of any more faithful alternative which would not leave most readers struggling.

To Peter Breville in *Nor Any Country,* as to all St. Omer's heroes, the memories of St. Lucia are the sore tooth which mars his enjoyment of more exotic pleasures and experiences. That nagging pain draws him at last to revisit the island in which he has left for eight years a scarcely-known wife, married only because of her pregnancy. Yet the return, which perhaps he hoped would be purgative, leads to a partial acceptance of what he is and has ever been. Phyllis is still there, still young, still open to his love and still able to awaken his lust. Peter's long-standing resentment of her existence is modified by what he sees of other lives forgotten during his absence. His brother Paul, who likewise impregnated a local girl, has become a special kind of island failure because of his refusal to marry her. The girl herself has committed suicide but her neglected son Michael has survived, whereas Peter's marriage has produced the mirror image of twins born and dead in his absence but a neglected wife who survives to challenge his egotism by her presence. At the end of his week-long visit Peter knows that he must take both Phyllis and Michael with him now. By this single gesture he will attempt to redeem the past. *Nor Any Country* thus ends on a more positive note than any of St. Omer's earlier writing. It stints nothing of the narrow fate attending those who stay in the islands. The failures lie steeped in rum and self-pity, while the few successes grow flashy and Americanized in their loud insecurity. Yet, when all this is said, it was the long-postponed return to the island which brought Peter Breville to his late maturity. For the last *rite de passage* is the reunification with one's origins, without which the cycle of exile can never be complete.

J—, Black Bam and the Masqueraders is a return to the themes and situations of *Nor Any Country,* with the same actors. The approach in this short novel is less naturalistic, intermingling long epistles from Paul (in St. Lucia) to Peter (in Europe), with snatches from the life of Peter in exile. There is far less memorable descriptive writing than in any of St. Omer's earlier work. The anguish of personal failure is as strong as ever, but this book gives off a powerful odor of decay. The actions, motives, and lost possibilities of the past are being raked over and examined yet again, but the novelist himself impresses us as a talent desperately in need of an entirely new subject.

—Gerald Moore

STACY, Donald. *See* **POHL, Frederik.**

STEAD, C(hristian) K(arlson)

Nationality: New Zealander. **Born:** Auckland, 17 October 1932. **Education:** Balmoral Intermediate School; Mount Albert Grammar School; Auckland University, B.A. 1954, M.A. (honors) 1955;

Bristol University (Michael Hiatt Baker Scholar), Ph.D. 1961. **Family:** Married Kathleen Elizabeth Roberts in 1955; two daughters and one son. **Career:** Lecturer in English, University of New England, New South Wales, 1956-57; lecturer, 1960-61, senior lecturer, 1962-64, associate professor, 1964-67, and professor of English, 1967-86, University of Auckland. Chair, New Zealand Literary Fund, 1972-75, and 1988-90, New Zealand Authors Fund. **Awards:** Poetry Awards Incorporated prize (U.S.A.), 1955; Readers award (*Landfall*), 1959; Katherine Mansfield award, for fiction and for essay, 1961, and fellowship, 1972; Nuffield traveling fellowship, 1965; Jessie Mackay poetry award, 1973; New Zealand Book award, for poetry, 1976, for fiction, 1986; New Zealand Arts Council scholarship, 1987, 1992; Queen's Medal, 1990. D.Litt.: University of Auckland, 1981. C.B.E. (Commander, Order of the British Empire), 1985. **Address:** 37 Tohunga Crescent, Parnell, Auckland 1, New Zealand.

PUBLICATIONS

Novels

Smith's Dream. Auckland, Longman Paul, 1971; revised edition, 1973.
All Visitors Ashore. Auckland, Collins, and London, Harvill Press, 1984.
The Death of the Body. London, Collins, 1986.
Sister Hollywood. London, Collins, 1989; New York, St. Martin's Press, 1990.
The End of the Century at the End of the World. London, Harvill Press, 1992.
The Singing Whakapapa. Auckland, Penguin Books, 1994.

Short Stories

Five for the Symbol. Auckland, Longman Paul, 1981.

Uncollected Short Stories

"Concerning Alban Ashtree," in *London Magazine,* December 1983-January 1984.
"Ludwig and Jack," in *Rambling Jack 2,* August 1986.
"The Last Life of Clarry," in *Vital Writing: New Zealand Poems and Stories 1989-90,* edited by Andrew Mason. N.p., Godwit Press, 1990.
"A Short History of New Zealand," *Sport* (Wellington), May 1992.
"Sex in America," *Sport* (Wellington), March 1994.
"Of Angels and Oystercatchers," in *The Inward Sun,* edited by Elizabeth Alley. Wellington, Daphne Brasell Press, 1994.

Poetry

Whether the Will Is Free: Poems 1954-62. Auckland, Paul's Book Arcade, 1964.
Crossing the Bar. Auckland, Auckland University Press-Oxford University Press, 1972.
Quesada: Poems 1972-74. Auckland, The Shed, 1975.
Walking Westward. Auckland, The Shed, 1979.
Geographies. Auckland, Auckland University Press-Oxford University Press, 1982.
Poems of a Decade. Dunedin, Pilgrims South Press, 1983.

Paris. Auckland, Auckland University Press-Oxford University Press, 1984.
Between. Auckland, Auckland University Press, 1988.
Voices. Wellington, Government Printing Office, 1990.

Other

The New Poetic: Yeats to Eliot. London, Hutchinson, 1964; New York, Harper, 1966.
In the Glass Case: Essays on New Zealand Literature. Auckland, Auckland University Press-Oxford University Press, 1981.
Pound, Yeats, Eliot and the Modernist Movement. London, Macmillan, and New Brunswick, New Jersey, Rutgers University Press, 1986.
Answering to the Language: Essays on Modern Writers. Auckland, Auckland University Press, 1989.

Editor, *New Zealand Short Stories: Second Series.* London, Oxford University Press, 1966.
Editor, *Measure for Measure: A Casebook.* London, Macmillan, 1971.
Editor, *The Letters and Journals of Katherine Mansfield: A Selection.* London, Allen Lane, 1977.
Editor, *Collected Stories,* by Maurice Duggan. Auckland, Auckland University Press-Oxford University Press, 1981.
Editor, with Elizabeth Smither and Kendrick Smithyman, *The New Gramophone Room: Poetry and Fiction.* Auckland, University of Auckland, 1985.
Editor, *The Faber Book of Contemporary South Pacific Stories.* London, Faber and Faber, 1994.

*

Manuscript Collection: Alexander Turnbull Library, Wellington.

Critical Studies: Ken Arvidson, in *Journal of New Zealand Literature 1,* 1983; interview with Michael Harlow, in *Landfall 132* (Christchurch), 1983; "A Deckchair of Words" in *Landfall 159* (Christchurch), September 1986, and "Stead's Dream" in *Landfall 163* (Christchurch), September 1987, both by Reginald Berry; "Modernist Making and Self-Making" by A. Walton Litz, in *Times Literary Supplement* (London), 10 October 1986; interview in *Talking About Ourselves,* edited by Harry Ricketts, Wellington, Mallinson Rendel, 1986; *Barbed Wire and Mirrors: Essays on New Zealand Prose* by Lawrence Jones, Dunedin, Otago University Press, 1987; *The Writer Written* by Jean-Pierre Durix, New York, Greenwood Press, 1987; *Leaving the Highway: Six Contemporary New Zealand Novelists* by Mark Williams, Auckland, Auckland University Press, 1990; *The Penguin History of New Zealand Literature* edited by Patrick Evans, Auckland, Penguin, 1990; *The Oxford History of New Zealand Literature* edited by Terry Stern, Oxford, 1991.

C.K. Stead comments:

For a good part of my writing life in New Zealand I have been known as a poet and critic who occasionally ventures into short stories; but in my own mind, since I began writing at the age of 14, I have thought of myself as a *writer.* It has never seemed to me that one had to choose between poetry and fiction (and there are honorable precedents—Goldsmith, for example, who also wrote plays; Thomas Hardy; and D.H. Lawrence). But novels require time;

and until 1986, when I gave up my position as professor of English at the University of Auckland, my time was limited. As an academic I made poetry, in particular 20th-century poetry, my special field with the consequence that I could see my own work as a poet on a broad historical map. As a fiction writer I possess no such map and have proceeded more by instinct, or intuition, with the possible consequence that in fiction I may have been more original, or individual, or peculiar, than I have been as a poet.

Of my first two significant experiments in fiction, one "A Race Apart," is a Mandarin comedy set in rural England, and the other, "A Fitting Tribute," is a New Zealand fantasy and social satire about a man who achieves engineless flight and vanishes. Both have female first-person narrators. Both were published outside New Zealand, the first in England, the second in America (and the latter was almost at once translated into Spanish and Hungarian). These stories indicate, I think, an early preoccupation with the question of narrative voice and "point of view." I was troubled (without knowing that this was a current preoccupation of theorists of fiction) about the question of the authority of the information fiction offers. Not its authenticity, or its truth; but rather the question, Who is supposed to be giving us this supposed information; what is its provenance? I was not much interested in current British and American fiction; but I read, for example, in translation, everything by the Italian Alberto Moravia and the Argentinian Jorge Luis Borges, writers whose approach to fiction seemed clever enough to overcome this problem of authority—Moravia by his intense clarity of "seeing" (in the sense both of visualizing and understanding) through the eyes of a single character, and Borges by signalling in various ways that fiction was a game with rules, an agreement between writer and reader to pretend that the story was true. These were sophistications I had already found in Fielding, Sterne, Emily Brontë, and Dickens, but which modern fiction writers in English (or those I tried to read in the 1950s and 1960s) had largely forgotten.

But it would be wrong to say that I thought clearly and historically about all this. I can now see, though I would not have seen it at the time, that what I wanted to do was to make the voice which gave the story its authority a part of the fiction; and the simplest—though certainly not the only, or always the best—way to do this, was first person narration. This is a problem which grows larger as the fiction expands in size, because it involves consistency of tone, of persona, of style, of manner; and a mercurial, or anyway protean temperament, such as suits the writer of lyric poems, must be damped down and made dependable and consistent in the writer of novels.

My other strong impulse in fiction has been the simple one towards narrative. I enjoy telling stories, and hearing stories well told, and admire narrative management, especially in places (such as Wordsworth's poems in The Lyrical Ballads) where it does its work largely unnoticed. The difference between Borges and his many recent imitators is that most of them acquire something of his sophistication without possessing any of his native skill as a storyteller.

I offer these remarks only as background, which the reader may find ways of applying to my novels and stories.

*   *   *

Since 1959 C.K. Stead has intermittently published a small number of shorter fictions in journals and magazines. Five of these have been gathered in Five for the Symbol while the rest remain uncollected. Read in concert with the first four novels, these shorter works can be seen not only as freestanding stories but also as an experimental body of knowledge, about narrative technique and political and literary relations with other formative cultures, which makes the achievement in these novels possible. Post-1990, these experiments have been confidently absorbed into Stead's mature style, in which he investigates a second body of knowledge, that concerning memory, death, and human understanding. An intense awareness of the New Zealand scene is paramount in these forms of knowledge, and is central to all of Stead's works.

Stead's 1965 story, "A Fitting Tribute", although urban in setting, is predictive of the political fantasy which characterizes his first novel, Smith's Dream. The novel is the most strongly political of Stead's works because it responds so directly to the perceived menace of American influence on New Zealand politics during the Vietnam War. This response, however, is disguised by the absence of any crudely direct references to that situation and by Stead's intertextual skills. What first appears as a counterculture-culture escape story with the main character, Smith, retreating from an unhappy marriage, becomes an eidetic fable combining elements of Orwell's 1984 and the archetypal New Zealand novel, John Mulgan's Man Alone. Stead's Smith inadvertently becomes involved with a guerilla group violently resisting the military intervention of the United States in New Zealand to pacify the citizenry for a puppet ruler. The allegorical parallel with the then-contemporary American involvement in Vietnam is thus perfectly clear, but Stead leavens this by developing the character relations outside the allegory and by landscaping the setting in the Coromandel bush, east of Auckland. As if in preparation for his later novels he also begins to experiment with narrative position here, defining the narrative subject as plural ("we"), representative of the many average New Zealanders victimized by a government reliant on American military control.

"The Town," "A New Zealand Elegy," and "Concerning Alban Ashtree" are autobiographical fictions; as such they are related to Stead's most radical novel, All Visitors Ashore. Here Stead creates Curl Skidmore, who can be read as a fictional ur-version of the real C.K. Stead, and the Auckland literary scene (circa 1951), under the tutelage of one Melior Farbro, who can be read as if he were the real New Zealand writer Frank Sargeson. The novel as a whole is a virtuoso display of postmodern narrative games; centrally, the unbalanced narrative simultaneously encourages us to read the novel as Stead's own autobiography yet also refuses that possibility. This is evident in the relationship between Skidmore and his lover, Patagonia Aorewa deThierry Bennett. While his youthful career is typical of the Bildungsroman her name suggests how the novel also departs from those categories, by incorporating in one New Zealand woman Maori, British, European, and other colonial and historical resonances. Thus the subject of the novel is "the matter of New Zealand," at a crucial time in its intellectual and cultural development. As in Smith's Dream this scene is also crossed with a political crisis, the 1951 Waterfront strike, which alters the course of New Zealand society.

In The Death of the Body the politics are miniaturized to the level of feminist activism within the University of Auckland Philosophy Department, where Harry Butler, the professor, is also struggling with his second wife Claire's interest in Sufism and with the mind/body conundrum. Although it lacks the high postmodern game-playing of his previous novel, Stead's accomplishment here is more serious. This is reflected throughout in the obsessive reflection on death and extinction, and also in the relation of the narrative structure to the philosophical debate conducted within it. In "The Town" (in Five for the Symbol), as in much of Stead's fiction, there is an "artist [or writer] trapped inside his design." Here, just as Harry Butler is trapped inside the philosophical design and inside two complicated sexual relationships with designing women, so the writer-narrator is trapped inside the narrative of the mind/body problem. The question is, how can one get inside a story to design it without (as may be the case in *All Visitors Ashore*) physically entering it? The solution in this novel is for the writer-narrator openly to cede responsibility to the bodiless voice of the story and let it control the subsequent events, so exemplifying perfectly one answer to the mind/body problem. The result is another version of the autobiographical fiction.

Much of the action of *The Death of the Body* occurs in Auckland and the North, but everything is filtered through a narrative consciousness located in England and Europe. Such a division suggests (as predicted in "A Race Apart" in *Five for the Symbol*) what is for Stead a second strand of his fiction, the "matter of Europe," which New Zealand has inherited and cannot ignore. A third strand, implicit in his fiction since *Smith's Dream* and also in much of his critical writing, is the "matter of America." This surfaces most strongly in *Sister Hollywood,* a novel which recreates the American life of Bill Harper's long-lost memory-sister, Edie, who has fled family violence and Auckland at the end of the World War II to surface as the bit-player and then screen-writer Arlene Tamworth in the capital of film culture. Harper's search for his exiled sister (hinted at in the minor character of Ellie in "A New Zealand Elegy") is not only a search for her identity but also for his. Thus the scene alternates between Edie's continuing American present and the remembered New Zealand past. Throughout, the American influence on New Zealand—cinematically, culturally, and politically—is constantly brought up. In the process, Stead creates another version of the autobiographical fiction about the process of becoming a writer, a familiar trope in all of his fiction. Arlene Tamworth is not the only writer in the process. So subtly does Stead have Harper decenter the narrative towards his sister's life that we neglect to see that he is ghostwriting her life for her. At the same time he is constructing a partial autobiography of himself and of the New Zealand mind under the influence of the American empire.

1990 marked the sesquicentennial of the signing of the Treaty of Waitangi (under which the Maori became subjects of the British Crown) and the culmination of the massive economic and political changes in New Zealand in the 1980s. The importance of these changes is implied in the mock-apocalyptic title of Stead's fifth novel, *The End of the Century at the End of the World* and in the historical and personal rewriting of the Maori/*pakeha* interface in *The Singing Whakapapa.* Like the earlier novels both are doubly encoded, signifying a specific insider knowledge related to contemporary New Zealand events and persons (including Stead himself and his status as cultural commentator) and also an engrossing complex of narrative elements. Like Maurice Shadbolt's *The House of Strife,* Ian Wedde's *Symmes Hole,* Witi Ihimaera's *The Matriarch* or Stead's own *Sister Hollywood,* both extend recent New Zealand fiction's formative trope of writer/researcher/narrator in new ways.

The End of the Century at the End of the World gives us the life of a woman writer-to-be researching the life of a minor New Zealand writer-who-was which is crossed by a contradictory account of the same life by her politician-lover of the past; this same politician, the nephew of the writer-who-was, is also the inheritor of family mysteries which the life-writing does and does not solve. The academic setting (the University of Auckland again) and the political milieu allow for a complex interrelation of fiction, New Zealand literary history and current cultural issues. On top of this literary-

biographical detective fiction, *The Singing Whakapapa* imposes the structure of the family saga to create Stead's most profound achievement. Certainly Stead continues to engage local issues mischievously, to create familiar characters out of bits of real antecedents (including himself), and to object to political revisionism. But these are secondary to the masterful creation of the saga's *whakapapa* or genealogy, in which the *pakeha* historian Hugo Wolf (hence the "Singing") Grady and his assistant researcher excavate the hidden life of his ancestor, the early New Zealand missionary-settler John Flatt.

In fiction, lives are about the inevitability of unexpected connections, and Grady unveils the unexpected parallels of his own life to Flatt's in a way which connects him, inevitably, to his young research assistant; she is the fulfillment of his history and of his genealogy. The act of writing in this novel, as in so much of Stead's work, is to confront the death of the body, to control memory, to understand memory's gifts and stories, and to deflect and subvert its pains and aggressions by reinventing them in (auto)biographical fictions.

—Reginald Berry

STEFFLER, John (Earl)

Nationality: Canadian. **Born:** Toronto, Ontario, 13 November 1947. **Education:** University of Toronto, Ontario, 1967-71, B.A. in English 1971; University of Guelph, Ontario, 1972-74, M.A. in English 1974. **Family:** Married Shawn O'Hagan, 1970; one daughter and one son. **Career:** Since 1975 professor of English, Sir Wilfred Grenfell College, Memorial University of Newfoundland. **Awards:** Canada Council Arts grant, 1988, 1993; Newfoundland Arts Council Artist of the Year award, 1992; Smith Books/*Books in Canada* First Novel award, 1993; Thomas Raddall Atlantic Fiction award, 1993; Joseph S. Stauffer prize, 1993. **Member:** League of Canadian Poets. **Agent:** Susan Schulman Literary Agency, 454 West 44th St., New York, New York 10036, USA. **Address:** Department of English, Sir Wilfred Grenfell College, Corner Brook, Newfoundland A2H 6P9, Canada.

PUBLICATIONS

Novels

The Afterlife of George Cartwright. Toronto, McClelland and Stewart, 1992; New York, Holt, 1993.

Poetry

An Explanation of Yellow. Ottawa, Borealis Press, 1980.
The Grey Islands. Toronto, McClelland and Stewart, 1985.
The Wreckage of Play. Toronto, McClelland and Stewart, 1988.

Other

Flights of Magic (for children). Victoria, Press Porcepic, 1987.

*

Critical Study: "The Writings of John Steffler" by James Harrison, *Brick*, 45, Winter 1993.

John Steffler comments:

I am essentially a poet. All my writing begins with immediate experience, the stuff of time and space. Without planning to, I find myself writing about the interaction of people and nature, people and landscape, the character of place. In the same way, I'm interested in how the past influences the present, how we live in a flow of time, a choir of ghosts. I am not interested in obeying the restrictions of traditional genres. My novel is part history, part fantasy, part poetry. We should feel free inside a work of literature. I like the pull of "What happens next?" in a story. I also like the pull of invention and surprise in the way a work is constructed.

*   *   *

John Steffler's first novel, *The Afterlife of George Cartwright*, comes out of the directions mapped by his considerable achievements in poetry and *The Grey Islands*, a diary mixture of poetry and prose describing a summer spent alone on a tiny island off the northeast shore of Newfoundland. In his early work, he demonstrated a mixture of preoccupation with the search for the inner self, a quiet center, and considerations of the effects of place on strangers, largely his own migration from Ontario to rugged Newfoundland. Quietly brilliant, *The Afterlife of George Cartwright* emerges from his reading of the real George Cartwright's 1792 journal and interleaves Steffler's fascination with Newfoundland-Labrador—the land and its history—with his concerns about personal destiny.

Cartwright, part of whose life was spent in the British army in Germany and India, wrote a journal of fact until December 1779 and then made up the later entries (which cover time when he was not actually in the Labrador he is describing) while barracks master of the Nottingham militia. Steffler is equally free with fact, mixing entries from the journal with entries of his own making and surrounding the journal with a richly imagined world of the Cartwright family and Britain, Germany, India, and Labrador. The whole is framed by the device of imagining Cartwright living on after his death, alone except for his hunting hawk and his horse as he wanders the English countryside and sometimes lets wandering omnibuses drive right through his hearty ghost (a ghost who enjoys decent cooking). The most extensive portion of the novel deals with Cartwright's creation of several settlements in Labrador and his sorrow when his Inuit mistress and her party die of smallpox after he has taken them to England. Cartwright was ever eager to learn in Labrador, survived the extreme challenges of that bleak yet sensational coast, and was among the first to befriend the native peoples. But his methods were often brutal, and through Mrs. Selby, Cartwright's housekeeper-mistress, Steffler introduces ideas about the blind rapacity of the colonial enterprise.

Besides the richly pictured 18th-century world of city and wilderness colony, the true center of this novel is the paradoxes surrounding Cartwright. Steffler pictures a man frozen in the amber of his era, unable to grasp the implications of fault in the greedy struggle for furs and timber. He is the imperfect traveler who brings all his values with him to impose upon an alien world and who freely treats its people as exhibits when he brings them to England. There is a wonderful heady mixture of distaste and admiration for Cartwright, and to make the mixture even more potent the George Cartwright of the Afterlife is no more aware of the paradoxes than the living one was.

The Afterlife of George Cartwright is a first novel of both promise and distinctive achievement. Like fellow poets Michael Ondaajte and Jane Urquhart before him, Steffler has chosen fiction to anatomize the Canadian past, which makes it luminous and at the same time raises paradoxes of power and personal morality that reflect sharply on the present.

—Peter Brigg

STEPHENS, Michael (Gregory)

Nationality: American. **Born:** Washington, D.C., 4 March 1946. **Education:** City College of New York, B.A. and M.A. 1976; Yale University, M.F.A. in drama 1979. **Family:** Married Okhee Stephens, 1974; one daughter. **Career:** Assistant professor of communications, Fordham University, 1979-85; lecturer, Columbia University, 1977-91; lecturer, Princeton University, 1987-91; lecturer, New York University, 1989-91, 1994-95; Gertz Professor of Writing, Alfred University, 1991. Public relations specialist, The Asia Society, 1992-93; Comptroller's Office, Audit Bureau of the City of New York, 1992. Since 1994 editor, *Flatiron News*. **Awards:** Fletcher Pratt Prose fellowship, Breadloaf Writers Conference, 1971; New York State Arts award, 1976; Associated Writing Programs award in creative nonfiction, 1993, for *Green Dreams*. **Address:** 520 West 110th St., #5C, New York, New York 10025, USA.

PUBLICATIONS

Novels

Season at Coole. New York, Dutton, 1972.
Still Life (novella). New York, Kroesen, 1978.
Shipping Out (novella). Cambridge, Massachusetts, Apple Wood, 1979.
The Brooklyn Book of the Dead. Normal, Illinois, Dalkey Archive, 1994.

Short Stories

Paragraphs. New York, Mulch Press, 1974.

Uncollected Short Stories

"Red Black and Whitey Greene," in *Provincetown Review*, 1968.
"The Hare Apparent," in *Evergreen Review*, February 1971.
"Prospecting," in *Evergreen Review*, May 1971.
"The Last Poetry Reading," in *Tri-Quarterly*, (26), 1973.
"Meat Lust," in *Broadway Boogie*, (2), 1974.
"Two Stories: 'Hemingway in Paris' and 'Mooney's Bartleby,'" in *Mulch*, (5), 1974.
"In Praise of Earwigs," in *The Falcon*, (13) Fall 1983.
"The Thug," in *North American Review*," 268(1), March 1983.
"In Memory," in *Kairos*, 1(3), 1984.
"MASH Bureau," in *Exquisite Corpse*, 3(9-10), September-October 1985.
Walking Papers," in *Other Voices*, 1(1), 1985.
"Eight Ruins," in *Exquisite Corpse*, 4(5-8), May-August 1986.

"The Fights," in *Ontario Review,* (25), Fall-Winter 1986-87.

"Bronx Fighter," in *Ontario Review,* (28), Spring-Summer 1988.

"Everlast," in *The Equator Hot Type Anthology.* New York, Scribner, 1988.

"Travels in Mexico," in *Hanging Loose,"* (55), Fall 1989.

"The Sixth Man," in *Witness,* Spring 1989.

"Still Life with Anjou Pears," in *Fiction International,* 1990.

"Scrambled," in *Writ* (Toronto), Spring 1990.

"Tomato Cans," in *Writ* (Toronto), Summer 1991.

"Revenge," in *Manoa,* 3(2), Fall 1991.

"Five Jack Cool," in *The Black Pig, Imagining America,* edited by Wesley Brown and Amy Ling. New York, Persea, 1991.

Plays

Off-Season Rates (produced New Haven, Connecticut, 1978).

Cloud-Dream (produced New Haven, Connecticut, 1979).

Our Father (produced New York, 1984; London, 1985). In *Our Father and Other Plays,* 1995.

Circles End (produced Cambridge, Massachusetts, 1985).

R & R (produced New York, 1985).

Horse (produced New York, 1986). In *Kairos Magazine* (New York), 2(2), 1988.

Adam's Curse (produced New York, 1987).

Walking Papers (produced New York, 1987).

Cracow (produced New York, 1988).

Our Father and Other Plays. New York, Spuyten Duyvil, 1995.

Radio Plays: *Paragraphs,* 1978.

Poetry

Alcohol Poems. Binghamton, Loose Change Press, 1973.

Tangun Legend. Iowa City, Iowa, Seamark Press, 1978.

Circles End (includes prose). New York, Spuyten Duyvil, 1982.

Translations. New York, Red Hanrahan, 1984.

Jigs and Reels. New York, Hanging Loose Press, 1992.

After Asia. New York, Spuyten Duyvil, 1993.

Other

The Dramaturgy of Style: Voice in Short Fiction. Carbondale, Southern Illinois University Press, 1986.

Lost in Seoul and Other Discoveries on the Korean Peninsula. New York, Random House, 1990.

Green Dreams: Essays Under the Influence of the Irish. Athens, University of Georgia Press, 1994.

*

Critical Studies: "Interview with Michael Stephens" by Jerome Klinkowitz, in *Tri-Quarterly,* 1975; "Michael Stephens," by Klinkowitz, in his *The Life of Fiction,* Urbana, University of Illinois Press, 1977; by John O'Brien, in *Adrift,* Winter 1983-84.

Michael Stephens comments:

I am a writer comfortable with writing in many different genres of writing, but I always perceive of poetry being the essence of all my work. By that I don't mean a vague impressionism informing, say, my prose, but rather the rigorous linguistic pursuit of *le mot juste,* as Flaubert called it; and also being concise, emotionally

charged in the language, seeing that every experience has its own unique rhythms, that there are no ideas but in things, as Dr. Williams wrote, and like Olson, that writing is about breath and syllable, even prose and playwriting. What else? Writing is a love affair, sometimes amorously beautiful, though often a dogged curse, just the way love is, its face always changing. As Yeats wrote, I see writing being cold and passionate, at once, and forever.

*   *   *

An Irish lyricism contesting with the harsher features of lower-middle-class American life has distinguished Michael Stephens's work from inception through maturity. As the child and grandchild of immigrants from Counties Clare and Mayo and raised in a large family where Irish-Americanism was both cultural treasure and battle flag, Stephens crafts a verbal song that contends with and eventually transforms the sordid details of dysfunctional social life into a magic realism that is ultimately redeeming of the creative self.

Season at Coole details just such a family. Gathering together for Christmas eve, its forces are at once centrifugal and centripetal, and from these contrary energies Stephens derives a structure that allows both descriptive coverage and exuberance of language. The circumstance at hand is so volatile that similes mix and collide in attempts to express it, particularly the enmity between the alcoholic father and his schizophrenic eldest son, "for this Christmas he and the old man had decided to go off the edge of the planet like a brace of ducks in orange sauce together, a duet for father and son." Following an initial chapter that introduces the family and details the father's boozy, inept, and disconcerting violence, the novel continues with a chapter for each of the grown siblings, followed by briefer looks at the mother and the three youngest children off in their own world in attic rooms above. Each family member is seeking escape, pursuing it in such ways as madness, drugs, alcohol, crime, sex, art, alcohol-induced religious visions, physical training, prepubescent love, and sports. Matters are resolved when the mother and her children stand up to the father's attempt to functionalize them in their roles, divesting him of "his excuses"—a technique with validity in therapy as well as in art.

Stephens followed this compactly written but large-scale first novel with an exercise in exquisite miniaturization, the novella *Still Life.* Beckettian in concept and slapstick in execution, it focuses its 90 spare pages on the attempt of a Buster Keaton-like protagonist, Buster Shigh ("pronounced 'Shee,' like the good people"), to shimmy up the drainpipe when drunk and locked out of his room. Rendered like a painted still life, there is little action other than this self-contained flurry that gets absolutely nowhere. Yet in the process Stephens's comic protagonist is all liveliness, proving that "still, life goes on," an echo of Samuel Beckett's epigraph cited in *Season at Coole* that "all is not then yet quite irrevocably lost." A second novella, *Shipping Out,* extends this Irish lyricism by mixing it with another element, the Hispanic, which the author had absorbed in his adopted upper West side Manhattan neighborhood. Here he creates a character named Rico O'Reilly, who, in working as a dishwasher on a trans-Atlantic liner, experiences the exotic life among ship hands beneath decks.

Even shorter prose works offer clues to Stephens's method, such as the physical sensuosity of language in *Paragraphs* and competing definitions of time in *Circles End.* Language as a body and one's body itself as a grammar of experience motivate the vignettes of *Jigs and Reels.* These concerns are studied in *The Dramaturgy of Style: Voice in Short Fiction,* a critical meditation on the role of voice in fiction. Autobiographically, *Lost in Seoul and Other Discoveries on the Korean Peninsula* characterizes the author's marriage into a happy Korean family as *Season at Coole* virtually inside out and upside down, whereas *Green Dreams: Essays Under the Influence of the Irish* reclaims his parents' heritage as well as his own, particularly its artistically linguistic features. "I found the song of the savage and the antisocial, of the outlaw and even the misfit as tuneful as anything from the world of reason and responsibility and intelligence," Stephens writes.

> Even if my father did not write and could not sing and had not been in a battle for many years, I think perhaps there was more than a touch of that ancient, maniac Celt in him, and when he drank I knew he discovered that the sound of English was ridiculous and barbarian, that the only way to quell the thirst for the ancient words he no longer remembered—was to drink.

In *The Brooklyn Book of the Dead,* Michael Stephens draws on over two decades of work to produce what critics consider his masterpiece. In subject matter it is a sequel to *Season at Coole,* for 25 years afterwards the family is being once more reunited, this time for the father's wake and burial. This time chapters focus on the children's responses to the father's influence on what has become their lives; to some extent each can now appreciate how his crazed tyranny has forced them into a style of art in order to survive. Yet it is the innocent, hopeful second-youngest brother of the first novel, Terry, who is seen as the most desolate at the end of this narrative. Almost literally stripped naked and propelled not to an intended future but confusedly into the past, he is left crying piteously for the mother circumstances have denied him.

—Jerome Klinkowitz

STERN, Daniel

Nationality: American. **Born:** New York, 18 January 1928. **Education:** Columbia University, The New School for Social Research, Julliard School of Music. **Military Service:** United States Army Infantry, 1946-47: staff sergeant. **Family:** Married 1963; one son. **Career:** Senior vice-president, managing director, McCann-Erickson, Advertising, 1964-69; vice-president advertising and publicity, Warner Bros. Motion Pictures, 1969-71; vice-president east coast, CBS Entertainment, 1979-86; director of humanities, 92nd Street Y, New York, 1986-88; president, Entertainment Division, McCaffrey & McCall, Advertising, 1989; professor of English, University of Houston, 1992-93. Since 1993 Cullen Distinguished Professor of English, University of Houston. Fellow, 1969, Boynton Professor in Creative Writing, 1975, visiting professor in letters and English, 1976-78, all Wesleyan University; visiting professor of creative writing, New York University Film School, 1981; Dyson Memorial Lecturer in the Humanities, Pace University, 1982 and 1984; literary director, Institute for Advanced Theatre Training and American Repertory Theatre, Harvard University, 1992. **Awards:** International Prix du Souvenir, 1978, for *Who Shall Live, Who Shall Die;* O'Henry prize, 1987, for "The Interpretation of Dreams by Sigmund Freud"; *Paris Review* John Train Humor award, 1990, for "The Psychopathology of Everyday Life by Sigmund

Freud"; American Academy of Arts and Letters Rosenthal award, 1990, for *Twice Told Tales;* O'Henry prize, 1993, and Pushcart prize, 1993, both for "A Hunger Artist by Franz Kafka"; City of Houston Recognition award for academic and literary distinction, 1993. **Agent:** Borchardt Agency, 136 E. 57th St., New York, New York 10022, U.S.A.

PUBLICATIONS

Novels

The Girl with the Glass Heart. New York, Bobbs Merrill, 1957.
The Guests of Fame. New York, Ballantine, 1958.
Miss America. New York, Random House, 1959.
Who Shall Live, Who Shall Die. New York, Crown, 1963.
After the War. New York, Putnam, 1965.
The Suicide Academy. New York, McGraw Hill, and London, Allen, 1968.
The Rose Rabbi. New York, McGraw Hill, 1971.
Final Cut. New York, Viking, 1975.
An Urban Affair. New York, Simon and Schuster, 1980.

Short Stories

Twice Told Tales. N.p., Paris Review Editions, 1989.
Twice Upon a Time. New York, Norton, 1992.

Uncollected Short Stories

"The Oven Bird by Robert Frost: A Story," in *Paris Review,* Spring 1995.
"Grievances and Griefs by Robert Frost: A Story," in *Boulevard,* Spring 1995.
"Comfort," in *American Short Fiction,* Spring 1995.

Play

The Television Waiting Room. In *Playwrights Horizons,* 1987.

*   *   *

"All men are artists. After all, they have their lives." In just this way Daniel Stern opens his novel *The Rose Rabbi,* with an epigram that also serves as the story's thematic center, a terse, cryptic anchorhold that alone will finally make sense of the swirl of events that come to occupy Wolf Walker in the course of a day. Yet the epigram as thematic center is characteristic throughout Stern's fiction, revealing a central thesis at work in his aesthetic, whatever the story: life is always a problem in art. Whether it be art as the cinema (*Final Cut*), or the more practical sphere of urban planning (*An Urban Affair*), or art as theater (*Who Shall Live, Who Shall Die*), or art as language (*After the War, The Suicide Academy,* and *The Rose Rabbi*), for Daniel Stern art as form is elemental, imposed on a world otherwise chaotic without it, a form that molds and makes sense finally of lives and predicaments, and renders what is the ultimate concern of all Stern's fiction: redemption.

Fundamental to Stern's narrative approach in shaping the crises of his characters—crises that demand answers if life is to be lived at all in a world otherwise irrational and chaotic—is his concern with memory, and its function in time as a paradoxical force of both continuity and discontinuity. The paradox is detailed as a push and pull of what is past, impossible except as memory, and what is the present, equally impossible without some meaning rendered it by the past. We see this in *After the War* with especial clarity, where the protagonist, Richard Stone, back in New York after service in World War II, tries to live a life entirely in the present, a life of what he calls "disconnectedness," trying to escape memory, yet unable to escape the reality of a father who deserted him as a child. He tries to make sense of what happened to his close friend Jake, blown apart on the Italian front, the "brute fact," the "thingness" of Jake's dismembered body, evoking as it does the disconnectedness of Stone's present life as also "brute fact." The crisis that overcomes Richard Stone is thus life as aftermath, and how to live it.

Echoing the resolution finally achieved in *After the War*, Stern follows with two novels in the surrealist vein that take the matter further by illustrating the idea we can even create in the present the memory needed for just the necessary sense of making life as aftermath something purposeful. Thus the Wolf Walker of *The Rose Rabbi* can say on the occasion of his fortieth birthday, an occasion that propels the novel into action, that he was "eager to escape backward again, to be off to invent a past for the present." And he adds: "First, to invent myself, and then a locale." And in *The Suicide Academy* it is a dream of the other Wolf Walker which opens and propels that novel into action, of his former wife Jewel singing "Aprés un rève" by Fauré, and in particular the repetition of her singing "*reviens, reviens.*" It is a matter addressed still further, and in an entirely fresh way, by Stern's more recent venture into short fiction: *Twice Told Tales* and *Twice Upon a Time*. The magic and tension of "twice" designates every story a return, a mirror in aftermath of the story behind it and recreating it.

Yet nowhere does Stern achieve this vision more dramatically than in the dark, haunted pages of *Who Shall Live, Who Shall Die*. Nowhere is aftermath a more profound and oppressive entity, yet also an ultimate ground for choice, than in this story of two men, Judah Kramer and Carl Walkowitz, protagonist and antagonist, who survive the Holocaust and meet years later, becoming colleagues and yet at odds in the preparation of a Broadway play, *At the Gates*, directed by Kramer and set in a Nazi death camp much like that which the two men had known. But Kramer, to save his own family, had been responsible for the death of Walkowitz's family in that camp. It is evidence of the particularly close ties between this novel and the one that follows, *After the War*, that, as different as they are in many respects, the signal question which defines and drives the narrative of *After the War*, "Who will tell us how to lead our lives?," is the essential question of the earlier novel. And that the solution each man seeks to realize is finally enacted on a stage, with all the props of a concentration camp in place, and with all that is memory of the real camp years earlier impinging upon the moment as these two men face off, is a tour de force, and elevates *Who Shall Live, Who Shall Die* to a rare achievement in American letters.

—Eric Muirhead

STERN, Richard G(ustave)

Nationality: American. **Born:** New York City, 25 February 1928. **Education:** Stuyvesant High School; University of North Caro-
lina, Chapel Hill, B.A. 1947 (Phi Beta Kappa); Harvard University, Cambridge, Massachusetts, M.A. 1949; University of Iowa, Iowa City, Ph.D. 1954. **Military Service:** Served as an educational adviser, United States Army, 1951-52. **Family:** Married 1) Gay Clark in 1950 (divorced 1972), three sons and one daughter; 2) Alane Rollings in 1985. **Career:** Lecturer, Jules Ferry College, Versailles, France, 1949-50; Lektor, University of Heidelberg, 1950-51; instructor, Connecticut College, New London, 1954-55. Assistant professor, 1956-61, associate professor, 1962-64, professor of English, 1965-91, and since 1991, Helen Regenstein Professor of English, University of Chicago. Visiting Lecturer, University of Venice, 1962-63; University of California, Santa Barbara, 1964; State University of New York, Buffalo, 1966; Harvard University, 1969; University of Nice, 1970; University of Urbino, 1977. **Awards:** Longwood fellowship, 1960; Friends of Literature award, 1963; Rockefeller fellowship, 1965; American Academy grant, 1968, and Award of Merit for the Novel Medal, 1985; National Endowment for the Arts grant, 1969; Guggenheim fellowship, 1977; Sandburg award, 1979; Chicago *Sun-Times* Book of the Year award, 1990. **Address:** Department of English, University of Chicago, 1050 East 59th Street, Chicago, Illinois 60637, U.S.A.

PUBLICATIONS

Novels

Golk. New York, Criterion, and London, MacGibbon and Kee, 1960.
Europe; or, Up and Down with Schreiber and Baggish. New York, McGraw Hill, 1961; as *Europe; or, Up and Down with Baggish and Schreiber*, London, MacGibbon and Kee, 1962.
In Any Case. New York, McGraw Hill, 1962; London, MacGibbon and Kee, 1963; as *The Chaleur Network*, Sagaponack, New York, Second Chance Press, and London, Sidgwick and Jackson, 1981.
Stitch. New York, Harper, 1965; London, Hodder and Stoughton, 1967.
Other Men's Daughters. New York, Dutton, 1973; London, Hamish Hamilton, 1974.
Natural Shocks. New York, Coward McCann, and London, Sidgwick and Jackson, 1978.
A Father's Words. New York, Arbor House, 1986.
Shares and Other Fictions. New York, Delphinium Books, 1992.

Short Stories

Teeth, Dying, and Other Matters, and The Gamesman's Island: A Play. New York, Harper, and London, MacGibbon and Kee, 1964.
1968: A Short Novel, An Urban Idyll, Five Stories, and Two Trade Notes. New York, Holt Rinehart, 1970; London, Gollancz, 1971.
Packages. New York, Coward McCann, and London, Sidgwick and Jackson, 1980.
Noble Rot: Stories 1949-1988. New York, Grove Press, 1989.

Other

The Books in Fred Hampton's Apartment (essays). New York, Dutton, 1973; London, Hamish Hamilton, 1974.
The Invention of the Real. Athens, University of Georgia Press, 1982.

The Position of the Body (essays). Evanston, Illinois, Northwestern University Press, 1986.
One Person and Another: On Writers and Writing. Dallas, Baskerville, 1993.
A Sistermony. New York, Fine, 1995.

Editor, *Honey and Wax: Pleasures and Powers of Narrative: An Anthology.* Chicago, University of Chicago Press, 1966.

*

Manuscript Collection: Regenstein Library, University of Chicago.

Critical Studies: By Marcus Klein, in *Reporter* (Washington, D.C.), 1966; article by Hugh Kenner and interview with Robert Raeder, in *Chicago Review,* Summer 1966; "Conversation with Richard Stern" by Elliott Anderson and Milton Rosenberg, in *Chicago Review,* Winter 1980; "On Richard Stern's Fiction" by G. Murray and Mary Anne Tapp, in *Story Quarterly* (Northbrook, Illinois), Winter 1980; M. Harris, in *New Republic* (Washington, D.C.), March 1981; David Kubal, in *Hudson Review* (New York), Summer 1981; John Blades, in *Washington Post Book World,* November 1982; J. Spencer, in *Chicago Tribune,* 25 April 1985; James Schiffer, in *Dictionary of Literary Biography Yearbook: 1987,* Detroit, Gale, 1988; *Richard Stern* by James Schiffer, Boston, Twayne, 1993.

*   *   *

In a time when serious American fiction has tended towards extreme personal assertion and extravagance of manner, Richard G. Stern has been composing a body of work which is notable for its detailed craftsmanship, its intricacy, and its reticences. His novels and stories are neither lyrically confessional nor abstractly experimental. They are processes quite in the mode of an older tradition, in which character and event discover theme. In one and another incidental observation within his fiction, Stern has rejected both the idea of the novel as "a roller coaster of distress and sympathy, love and desire," and the idea of the novel as a deliberate attack on formal expectations (*Europe*); he has addressed qualification to the view that a story is fully autonomous (see the sketch called "Introductory" in *1968*), but he has also rejected the idea of the author as solipsist (see "Story-Making" in *1968*). His own fiction accepts no extremities of technique and form. Its characteristic tone as well as its strategy of development is created by ironic modulations.

The tone and the technique are, moreover, exact functions of Stern's characteristic subject. The broad theme is the adjustment of private lives with public events. Typically, Stern's protagonist has been a passive, sensitive fellow, who is a little too old for adventuring, or a little too fat, or a little too fine-grained, but nonetheless possessing romantic inclinations. His latent disposition is tested when public event of one sort and another seeks him out. He is now forced to regard his own actions and the actions of others as moral events. And, typically, this protagonist has found himself engaged in a drama of betrayals, which have the effect of chastening his new ambitions as a public man. The end is his rather baffled, nonetheless scrupulous assessment of personal adventure. Between the beginning and the end, his motives are subjected to more and more contingencies. He has been lured from his innocent privacy into life, defined as public action which by its nature is dangerous and ambiguous. At the end he has sacrificed the self-protectedness with which he began, and he has also failed to discover an easy

ground of general participation in life. His modest success is that he has become potentially moral.

Stern's first novel, *Golk,* is somewhat more spare and blatant in its actions than the fictions which follow, but it is otherwise exemplary. The hero is a 37-year-old boy, Herbert Hondorp, who lives with his widowed father in New York City. As he has done for most of the days of his life, he now spends his days wandering in and near Central Park, until on an occasion, abruptly, he is snared into public view and public occupation. The agent is a television program—"Golk"—which is created, precisely, by making public revelation of privacy. Ordinary, unwary people are caught by the television camera in prearranged, embarrassing situations. Stern's hero discovers that he likes not only the being caught, as do most of the Golk victims, but he also likes the catching. He takes a job with the television program, and not fortuitously at the same time he secures his first romance. Within this new situation there are moral implications, of course, but both "Golk" and Hondorp's romance are tentative and jesting. The novel then proceeds to raise the stakes of involvement: the program is transformed by its ambitious director into a device for political exposé, and Hondorp's romance becomes a marriage. This newer situation beckons and perhaps necessitates treacheries, which make it morally imperative that public involvement be terminated. Hondorp betrays the director of the program, in order to save the program—so he believes—from the fury of the political powers, and he thereby reduces it to vapidity. In a consequent narrative movement, his wife leaves him. Hondorp goes home at the end, "all trace of his ambition, and all desire for change gone absolutely and forever."

In his subsequent fictions, Stern has avoided such metaphorical ingenuity as the television program in *Golk,* and the lure to public action has been carefully limited to a matter of background or accident, but the area of his concerns has remained constant. In *Europe; or, Up and Down with Schreiber and Baggish,* the two protagonists are American civil employees in post-war occupied Germany. The pattern of their adventuring—despite the comic suggestion in the title of the novel—allows nothing implausible, and there are no sudden reversals. Realization is to be achieved, rather, through implied contrasts and comparisons. Schreiber is an aging sensitive gentleman who tries for intimate understanding of the ancient, bitter, guilty, and conquered people. Baggish is a shrewd young opportunist, who exploits the populace. Baggish succeeds, and Schreiber fails. *In Any Case* is the story of another aging American in post-war Europe, who is innocent for the reason that he has never sufficiently risked anything, his affections included. His testing comes when he is told that his son, dead in the war, was a traitor. In a belated and ironic act of love, he tries to prove that his son was really innocent, and he discovers that treachery is a vital ingredient of all social living. Although his son was indeed not guilty in the way supposed, everyone is a double agent.

His acceptance of that discovery provides the hero with the possibility of a modest participation in other people's lives. In his more recent fiction, Stern has apparently wanted to make that possibility more emphatic, by bringing historical and aesthetic confirmations to it. *Stitch* is in large part a *roman à clef* about one of the great modern traitors, Ezra Pound. The would-be disciple in the novel receives from the aged master, Stitch, lessons in the fusion of personality with civilization, and the consequence of expression in art. The background of the novel is Venice, which, from the muck of its history, raises its beauties. In the short novel Veni, Vidi . . . Wendt (included in *1968*), the protagonist is a composer who is writing an opera about modern love. The opera will extend backwards to include great love affairs of the past, which are founded on adulteries. The composer himself, meanwhile, realizes both his composition and his domestic love for wife and children only after experiments in romantic duplicity. The chief adventurer in *Other Men's Daughters* is a middle-aged professor of biology at Harvard. His life heretofore has been completely defined by such seeming ineluctabilities as filial ties, domestic habits, and the concretion of compromises, and the stern decencies of his New England ancestry. He betrays everything when he falls in love with a girl not much older than the eldest of his own children, and hopefully discovers, in nature, the justification for this treachery to nurture. In *Natural Shocks* Stern writes about a talented and successful journalist, which in this case is to say a man who with all decent goodwill has made a career of transforming private lives into public knowledge. The protagonist is now forced to confront the fact of death, alternately as a subject for journalism and as a domestic event, and he is thereby invited to learn the necessary treachery that is involved in his calling and also its ethical insufficiency. A true participation in life will require more strenuous sympathies, which he may or may not achieve.

The endings of Stern's fictions record an acquiescence at the most, and always something less than the assertion of a principle. The kind of realization that is in the novels makes it necessary that they be probationary and open-ended. They are by that, as well as by their detailed, persistent, and moderate account of human motives, in the great tradition of moral realism.

—Marcus Klein

STONE, Robert (Anthony)

Nationality: American. **Born:** Brooklyn, New York, 21 August 1937. **Education:** New York University, 1958-59; Stanford University, California (Stegner fellow, 1962). **Military Service:** Served in the United States Navy, 1955-58. **Family:** Married Janice G. Burr in 1959; one daughter and one son. **Career:** Editorial assistant, New York *Daily News,* 1958-60; writer-in-residence, Princeton University, New Jersey, 1971-72; taught at Amherst College, Massachusetts, 1972-75, 1977-78, Stanford University, 1979, University of Hawaii, Manoa, 1979-80, Harvard University, Cambridge, Massachusetts, 1981, University of California, Irvine, 1982, and San Diego, 1985, New York University, 1983, Princeton University, 1985; Johns Hopkins University, 1993-94; and since 1994, Yale University. **Awards:** Houghton Mifflin Literary fellowship, 1967; Faulkner Foundation award, 1967; Guggenheim grant, 1968; National Book award, 1975; Dos Passos prize, 1982; American Academy award, 1982; National Endowment for the Arts fellowship, 1983; Strauss Living award, 1987. **Agent:** Donadio and Ashworth, 121 West 27th Street, New York, New York 10001, U.S.A.

PUBLICATIONS

Novels

A Hall of Mirrors. Boston, Houghton Mifflin, 1967; London, Bodley Head, 1968.

Dog Soldiers. Boston, Houghton Mifflin, 1974; London, Secker and Warburg, 1975.
A Flag for Sunrise. New York, Knopf, and London, Secker and Warburg, 1981.
Children of Light. New York, Knopf, and London, Deutsch, 1986.
Outerbridge Reach. New York, Ticknor and Fields, and London, Deutsch, 1992.

Uncollected Short Stories

"Geraldine," in *Twenty Years of Stanford Short Stories,* edited by Wallace Stegner and Richard Scowcroft. Stanford, California, Stanford University Press, 1966.
"Farley the Sailor," in *Saturday Evening Post* (Philadelphia), 14 January 1967.
"Thunderbolts in Red, White, and Blue," in *Saturday Evening Post* (Philadelphia), 28 January 1967.
"Porque no tiene, porq le falta," in *The Best American Short Stories 1970,* edited by Martha Foley and David Burnett. Boston, Houghton Mifflin, 1970.
"Aquarius Observed," in *American Review 22,* edited by Theodore Solotaroff. New York, Bantam, 1975.
"A Hunter in the Morning," in *American Review 26,* edited by Theodore Solotaroff. New York, Bantam, 1977.
"WUSA," in *On the Job,* edited by William O'Rourke. New York, Vintage, 1977.
"War Stories," in *Harper's* (New York), May 1977.
"Absence of Mercy," in *Harper's* (New York), November 1987.
"Helping," in *The Best American Short Stories 1988,* edited by Mark Helprin and Shannon Ravenel. Boston, Houghton Mifflin, 1988.
"Not Scared of You," in *Gentlemen's Quarterly* (New York), March 1989.

Plays

Screenplays: *WUSA,* 1970; *Who'll Stop the Rain,* with Judith Rascoe, 1978.

Other

Images of War, edited by Julene Fischer. Boston, Boston Publishing Company, 1986.

* * *

Robert Stone combines old-fashioned concerns—the morality of human behavior, the responsibility of choice, the relationship between the individual and history—with topical interests—racism in the U.S., the war in Vietnam, American involvement in Latin-American revolutions—to produce fiction that is both emotionally engaging and thought provoking.

A Hall of Mirrors, Stone's first novel, tells the story of three rootless drifters whose paths converge in New Orleans: Rheinhardt, an alcoholic ex-musician; Geraldine, a battered woman; and Morgan Rainey, an idealistic social worker. Victims both of circumstance and of their own self-destructiveness, the trio is eventually caught up in an orgy of violence touched off by a patriotic rally sponsored by the owner of right-wing radio station WUSA, where Rheinhardt works. The final third of the novel is devoted to a nightmarish description of the rally and the ensuing riot (portrayed in almost hallucinatory language), which leaves 19 persons dead. The apocalyptic conclusion is reminiscent of the movie premiere riot that ends Nathaniel West's *The Day of the Locust,* but Stone's version of Armageddon has its roots not so much in the unrealized longings of the alienated outsider as in the racism and fanatical right-wing extremism he sees poisoning American society in the 1960s.

Dog Soldiers centers on the desperate flight of Ray Hicks, an ex-marine, and Marge Converse, wife of Hicks's friend John Converse, a journalist on assignment in Vietnam, to escape the narcotics agents who are after the three kilos of heroin Hicks smuggled into California from Vietnam. Exciting as the narrative is, *Dog Soldiers* is much more than an adventure thriller, for by showing that the action is set in motion by events which have their origin in Vietnam where the novel begins, Stone links the madness of the war depicted in the early sections with the tragic fallout it has at home.

The novel begins with a quotation from Joseph Conrad's *Heart of Darkness,* a work which has strongly influenced *Dog Soldiers.* Like Conrad, who saw in Kurtz's ivory a symbol of man's "rapacious and pitiless folly," Stone uses heroin as a symbol of his characters' obsessions and of the war's tragic cost. In Vietnam Converse finds himself, as Kurtz did in the African jungle, torn loose from all the conventional supports of civilized society. Afloat emotionally and morally, he turns to heroin as a way of asserting himself ("This is the first real thing I ever did in my life," he declares), but his decision will soon prove to have costly consequences as the heroin's deadly poison begins to spread.

Like *A Hall of Mirrors, Dog Soldiers* concludes with an apocalyptic finale, a shootout between Hicks and the federal agents pursuing him, the action punctuated by the recorded sounds of combat amplified over loudspeakers set up around the mountain compound where the scene occurs. By reminding the reader of the actual battle taking place in Vietnam, Stone underscores the relationship between the war in Asia and its consequences at home. Also, he makes the point that here, as in Vietnam, it is difficult to tell the good guys from the bad buys: Antheil, the government agent who ends up with the heroin at the end, decides to keep it and use it for his own profit. In Stone's view, there are no victors; everyone is corrupted by the poison.

A Flag for Sunrise is Stone's most ambitious and successful novel to date. Set in the fictional Central American country of Tecan, it features the stories of three Americans, each with his own reason for coming to the country: Sister Justin Feeney, a devoted young Roman Catholic nun who runs a local mission; Frank Holliwell, an anthropologist who declines the request of a CIA buddy to look into the situation at the mission, but whose curiosity compels him to go anyway; and Pablo Tabor, a paranoid, pill-popping soldier of fortune whose thirst for excitement leads to his involvement in the dangerous business of gun-running to the Tecanecan revolutionaries. Inexorably, the fates of all three Americans become intertwined, just as, Stone suggests, America itself has gotten itself involved in the fate of this ravaged little country.

The novel represents Stone's most effective attempt at incorporating political issues—here the economic, military, political, and cultural roles the U.S. is playing in Latin American countries—and personal ones—individual commitment and responsibility for one's actions. By examining a variety of motives ranging from the simple purity of Sr. Justin's desire to help the poor, a commitment for which she is willing to die, to Holliwell's feckless drifting, to the combination of "circumstance, coincidence, impulse, and urging" that has driven a host of other characters (e.g., whiskey priests, journalists, CIA agents, resort developers, soldiers of fortune) to Tecan, Stone exposes the reasons which have led the U.S. itself to

an active involvement in the affairs of undeveloped countries like Tecan.

Children of Light, a satirical novel about Hollywood and filmmaking, fails to measure up to the best of that genre (i.e. novels like *Day of the Locust* or *Play It as It Lays*), nor does it measure up to Stone's previous books. The novel features some brilliant flashes of satire at Hollywood's expense, and Stone's ear for absurd dialogue among the film types is well-tuned. In actress Lu Anne Verger, Stone also paints an affecting portrait of a schizophrenic whose tormented psyche finally overwhelms her during the filming of Kate Chopin's *The Awakening* on location in Mexico. But talk largely replaces action in this novel and *Children of Light* lacks the dramatic intensity and moral dimension that characterizes Stone's best work.

Stone returns to familiar philosophical and moral territory in *Outerbridge Reach* as he continues to explore such weighty issues as truth, honesty, self-knowledge, and betrayal. Owen Browne is a fortyish copywriter and commercial spokesman for a pleasure boat manufacturer. He is unexpectedly presented with an opportunity for the kind of adventure he sees as an antidote to his mid-life restlessness when his company names him to sail their entry in a solo around-the-world race. Alone at sea, he encounters, like Kurtz in Conrad's *Heart of Darkness,* the awesome challenge of isolation. In the process he discovers hidden truths about himself that have dire consequences for him and profound repercussions for the two other principals in the novel: his wife Anne and Ron Strickland, a filmmaker shooting a documentary about Browne's adventure. As in all his best work, Stone's sure control over language, character, and narrative produces dramatic and ambitious fiction of the highest order.

—David Geherin

STOREY, David (Malcolm)

Nationality: British. **Born:** Wakefield, Yorkshire, 13 July 1933; brother of the writer Anthony Storey. **Education:** Queen Elizabeth Grammar School, Wakefield, 1943-51; Wakefield College of Art, 1951-53; Slade School of Fine Art, London, 1953-56, diploma in fine arts 1956. **Family:** Married Barbara Rudd Hamilton in 1956; two sons and two daughters. **Career:** Played professionally for the Leeds Rugby League Club, 1952-56. Associate artistic director, Royal Court Theatre, London, 1972-74. Lives in London. **Awards:** Rhys Memorial award, for fiction, 1961; Maugham award, for fiction, 1963; *Evening Standard* award, for drama, 1967, 1970; New York Drama Critics Circle award, 1971, 1973, 1974; Faber Memorial prize, 1973; Obie award, for drama, 1974; Booker prize, 1976. Fellow, University College, London, 1974. **Address:** c/o Jonathan Cape Ltd., 20 Vauxhall Bridge Road, London SW1V 2SA, England.

PUBLICATIONS

Novels

This Sporting Life. London, Longman, and New York, Macmillan, 1960.

Flight into Camden. London, Longman, 1960; New York, Macmillan, 1961.

Radcliffe. London, Longman, 1963; New York, Coward McCann, 1964.

Pasmore. London, Longman, 1972; New York, Dutton, 1974.

A Temporary Life. London, Allen Lane, 1973; New York, Dutton, 1974.

Saville. London, Cape, 1976; New York, Harper, 1977.

A Prodigal Child. London, Cape, 1982; New York, Dutton, 1983.

Present Times. London, Cape, 1984.

Plays

The Restoration of Arnold Middleton (produced Edinburgh, 1966; London, 1967). London, Cape, 1967; New York, French, 1968.

In Celebration (produced London, 1969; Los Angeles, 1973; New York, 1984). London, Cape, 1969; New York, Grove Press, 1975.

The Contractor (produced London, 1969; New Haven, Connecticut, 1970; New York, 1973). London, Cape, 1970; New York, Random House, 1971.

Home (produced London and New York, 1970). London, Cape, 1970; New York, Random House, 1971.

The Changing Room (produced London, 1971; New Haven, Connecticut, 1972; New York, 1973). London, Cape, and New York, Random House, 1972.

The Farm (produced London, 1973; Washington, D.C., 1974; New York, 1976). London, Cape, 1973; New York, French, 1974.

Cromwell (produced London, 1973; Sarasota, Florida, 1977; New York, 1978). London, Cape, 1973.

Life Class (produced London, 1974; New York, 1975). London, Cape, 1975.

Mother's Day (produced London, 1976). London, Cape, 1977.

Sisters (produced Manchester, 1978; London, 1989). Included in *Early Days, Sisters, Life Class,* 1980.

Early Days (produced Brighton and London, 1980). Included in *Early Days, Sisters, Life Class,* 1980.

Early Days, Sisters, Life Class. London, Penguin, 1980.

Phoenix (produced London, 1984). Woodstock, Dramatic, 1993.

The March on Russia (produced London, 1989). London, French, 1989.

Screenplays: *This Sporting Life,* 1963; *In Celebration,* 1976.

Television Play: *Grace,* from the story by James Joyce, 1974.

Poetry

Storey's Lives: Poems 1951-1991. London, Cape, 1992.

Other

Writers on Themselves, with others. London, BBC Publications, 1964.

Edward, drawings by Donald Parker. London, Allen Lane, 1973.

*

Manuscript Collection: Boston University.

Critical Studies: *David Storey* by John Russell Taylor, London, Longman, 1974; *David Storey: A Casebook* edited by William Hutchings, New York, Garland, 1992.

Theatrical Activities:
Director: **Television**—*Portrait of Margaret Evans,* 1963; *Death of My Mother* (D.H. Lawrence documentary), 1963.

*   *   *

David Storey's first three novels were organized around a concept. In *This Sporting Life,* he attempted to show the world of the body, the atmosphere of physicality in both players and spectators, in the account of a young man from the lower middle classes who plays professional rugby. His second novel, *Flight into Camden,* is the novel depicting soul, the description of the hard spiritual independence of a miner's daughter who defies family to live with her married lover in London. *Radcliffe,* the third and most ambitious novel, portraying the troubled and violent relationship between Leonard Radcliffe, the sensitive descendant of impoverished gentility and aestheticism, and Victor Tolson, the powerful representative of the working classes, demonstrates the incompatibility of body and soul. In all the religious discussions and images in the novel, as well as in the epigraph from Yeats's "Vacillation VII," this irreconcilability between body and soul is regarded as original sin. A projected fourth novel in which body and soul were to be reconciled, never appeared after the 1963 publication of *Radcliffe,* and more recent novels are not dependent on the concept.

Explicitly apparent in *Radcliffe,* the body-soul conflict is reflected in the conflict between the working classes and the remnants of the aristocracy in northern English society. Beaumont, the place where Leonard's family lives, his father as caretaker and restorer, represents an aesthetically and historically valuable past that cannot survive in current industrial society without special and privileged attention. Similarly, Leonard himself needs the vital and sexual connection to Tolson's physicality in order to feel "whole." Storey combines the religious, social, and personal dimensions of the body-soul controversy, keeps his metaphors consistent, and presents the issues with a fierce emotional intensity, but he also pushes his characters to the point where the intense, narrow focus and the representational quality explodes into melodrama. Leonard kills Tolson and soon dies himself; another central character, a buffoon who also wanted Tolson, kills his family and himself. The melodrama simplifies the questions of class and religion presented, yet the power of the presentation itself, the intensity, invites the melodrama.

In spite of the limitations implicit in working out his concept, Storey's early fiction has considerable power, especially in dramatic scenes that come to life apart from their function as demonstrations of an idea. Characters in revolt from working-class origins, like Arthur Machin in *This Sporting Life* and Margaret Thorpe and her brother in *Flight into Camden,* are seen with a strong sympathy and complexity, described as partially entering a new world alien to their backgrounds and partially tied to the values and attitudes of their parents. Relationships between parents and children, the unique combinations of love and hatred bred in tidy, self-contained working-class kitchens, are particularly well done. The children, like Margaret Thorpe and her brother, or like Colin, the college teacher who deserts his wife and children in *Pasmore,* or another Colin who is a central figure in *Saville,* have been educated because of their parents' self-sacrifice, yet the process of education has moved them further from their parents, produced a difficult combination of independence, stubborn freedom, and guilt. For the parents, educating children had seemed the passport to the good life, a release from the grinding physicality of survival in the pits, and the parents, like those in *Pasmore* or the baffled mother of

Yvonne, a young wife whose incapacity to handle the strains of her life and education cause mental breakdown in *A Temporary Life,* cannot understand the complications of their educated childrens' lives. The children, too, like almost all Storey's characters, are characterized by a defensive intensity, an inability to release themselves into the flux of contemporary classless experience, and still carry something of the working-man's bitter intransigence and self-protective isolation. Women, like the defensively unyielding Mrs. Hammond in *This Sporting Life* or the remote and incommunicative mistress of the central characters in both *Pasmore* and *A Temporary Life,* sometimes display this intransigence more fully than men do in Storey's world; as the author comments on a character in *Pasmore,* the woman reveals "a determination, in effect, not to deny herself the pleasure as well as the security which came from holding herself apart." Relationship, in Storey's world, is difficult and dangerous, likely to lead to breakdown or dissolution, and this quality is seen as part of a social and historical inheritance. This inheritance is still manifest in *Present Times,* in which Attercliffe, a former rugby professional, demonstrates Job-like endurance under the assaults of his wife leaving him, his five children immured in one form or another of contemporary inanity, his lost job, and his best friend's death.

In a nine-year gap between novels, Storey turned toward drama, writing highly praised and effective plays. Often, characters and situations in the plays are similar, sometimes even identical, to those in the novels. Both *In Celebration* and *The Farm* reveal the highly charged familial emotions involved when educated children return to visit their parents in the mining or the farming village where they grew up. The parents are reminiscent of those in *Pasmore* or the Thorpes in *Flight into Camden. The Contractor* divides attention between the workmen setting up a large tent for a wedding and the family of the tenting company's owner, also the father of the bride. Again family and class issues dominate the play. A similar group of workmen setting up tents is detailed in *Radcliffe,* although the dramatic version is more comic; even the name of the company's owner—Ewbank—is the same. *Life Class* depicts a simplified version of some of the events, those centering around the life model in a class in a northern art school, of *A Temporary Life,* although a full characterization of the teacher, his background, and his connection to other characters, is omitted in the play. Generally, the dramatic version of each character or incident is simpler and more immediately communicable than is the novelistic version. Yet Storey's parallel working of themes, incidents, and characters has also given his novelistic treatments an immediacy and force, perhaps contributed by his work in drama, that make his later novels, especially *Pasmore* and *A Prodigal Child,* particularly effective and compelling.

Storey is also trained and talented in drawing and painting. His writing has always been characterized by an acute sense of visual imagery, apparent in descriptions of the industrial town or the rugby crowd in *This Sporting Life.* The later fiction, particularly *A Temporary Life,* in which the first-person narrator is a painter and a teacher of painting, and *A Prodigal Child,* which describes the development of the artist, exploits this sense of visual imagery even more effectively, creating descriptions that are precisely detailed and representative of the character's or observer's state of mind or emotion simultaneously. Color, shape, and landscape become terse yet complex metaphors. Later novels also use sharply observed short dramatic scenes to portray changing psychological patterns within characters. *Pasmore* depicts a dissolving marriage, the changes from dependence to almost comatose shock and neglect to a nervous,

tenuous independence in the deserted wife, as well as changes between concerned indifference, an artificial sense of jolly control, passivity, guilt, jealousy, explosive fury, and, finally, near breakdown before ultimate recovery, in the erring husband. Yvonne's breakdown in *A Temporary Life* is also carefully portrayed, the alternations between withdrawal and the desperate efforts to make life and relationships around her seem "whole." *Saville,* although like its principal character evolving more slowly, carefully constructs the miner's environment and complicates the pressures of differing representations of parents, brothers, and potential wives from which Colin emerges as educated, sensitive, and finally independent. In *A Prodigal Child,* Storey's most deeply and convincingly realized fiction, the background through and against which the artist gains consciousness is agricultural as well as industrial, sophisticated as well as simple, middle-class as well as working-class, and destructively as well as creatively sexual. Here, as in the other fiction, breakdown, loss of control, is always at the edge of Storey's fictional world.

All the novels since 1972 show little of the generalized concept about experience that restricted the earlier fiction, particularly *Radcliffe.* Rather, the reliance on theories about life is satirized in the treatment of theories about art in *A Temporary Life.* Both the radical art students, who refuse to learn technique and justify work that is both slovenly and unimaginative in the name of free expression and an "empirical" point of view, and the principal of the art school, who spends his time campaigning against smoking, madly collecting excreta in his locked bathroom, and painting pseudo-realistic advertising posters that proclaim the "old values," are made ludicrous. Teachers and their theories, variously made brutal, self-preening, or insensitive, are more often than not barriers to genuine education in *Saville* and *A Prodigal Child.* The human being, isolated, attempting to unify the world around him, searches for his own intellectual and emotional forms of control. The fiction expresses this with a packed, potentially explosive prose, a form that dramatically conveys the pressure of experience. At its best, the fiction itself, steadily gaining range as Storey continues to develop, is a strong and intensely human achievement, a bastion, just on the edge of chaos.

—James Gindin

STOW, (Julian) Randolph

Nationality: Australian. **Born:** Geraldton, Western Australia, 28 November 1935. **Education:** Geraldton Primary School, 1941-47; Geraldton High School, 1948-49; Guildford Church of England Grammar School, Perth, 1950-52; St. George's College, University of Western Australia, Perth, 1953-56, B.A. in French and English 1956, further study, 1961; University of Sydney, 1958. **Career:** Storeman at an Anglican mission, Wyndham, Western Australia, 1957; tutor in English, University of Adelaide, 1957; anthropological assistant, Papua New Guinea, 1959; lecturer in English, University of Leeds, Yorkshire, 1961-62, and University of Western Australia, 1963-64; Harkness Fellow, U.S.A., 1964-66; lived in New Mexico, Maine and Alaska and studied Indonesian language, Yale University; returned to England, 1966; lecturer in English and Fellow in commonwealth Literature, University of Leeds, 1968-69; lived in East Bergholt, Suffolk, 1969-81, and Harwich,

Essex, from 1981. **Awards:** Australian Literature Society gold medal, 1957, 1958; Miles Franklin award, 1959; Harkness traveling fellowship, 1964-66; Britannica—Australia award, 1966; Grace Leven prize, 1969; Commonwealth Literary Fund grant, 1974; Patrick White award, 1979. **Agent:** Richard Scott Simon, Anthony Sheil Associates, 43 Doughty Street, London WC1N 2LF, England.

PUBLICATIONS

Novels

A Haunted Land. London, Macdonald, 1956; New York, Macmillan, 1957.
The Bystander. London, Macdonald, 1957.
To the Islands. London, Macdonald, 1958; Boston, Little Brown, 1959; revised edition, Sydney, Angus and Robertson, 1981; London, Secker and Warburg, and New York, Taplinger, 1982.
Tourmaline. London, Macdonald, 1963; New York, Taplinger, 1983.
The Merry-Go-Round in the Sea. London, Macdonald, 1965; New York, Morrow, 1966.
Visitants. London, Secker and Warburg, 1979; New York, Taplinger, 1981.
The Girl Green as Elderflower. London, Secker and Warburg, and New York, Viking Press, 1980.
The Suburbs of Hell. London, Secker and Warburg, and New York, Taplinger, 1984.

Plays (opera librettos, music by Sir Peter Maxwell Davies)

Eight Songs for a Mad King (produced London, 1969). London, Boosey and Hawkes, 1971.
Miss Donnithorne's Maggot (produced Adelaide, 1974). London, Boosey and Hawkes, 1977.

Poetry

Act One. London, Macdonald, 1957.
Outrider: Poems 1956-1962. London, Macdonald, 1962.
A Counterfeit Silence: Selected Poems. Sydney and London, Angus and Robertson, 1969.
Poetry from Australia: Pergamon Poets 6, with Judith Wright and William Hart-Smith, edited by Howard Sergeant. Oxford, Pergamon Press, 1969.

Recording: *Poets on Record 11,* University of Queensland, 1974.

Other

Midnite: The Story of a Wild Colonial Boy (for children). Melbourne, Cheshire, and London, Macdonald, 1967; Englewood Cliffs, New Jersey, Prentice Hall, 1968.
Visitants, Episodes from Other Novels, Poems, Stories, Interviews, and Essays, edited by Anthony J. Hassall. St. Lucia, University of Queensland Press, 1990.

Editor, *Australian Poetry 1964.* Sydney, Angus and Robertson, 1964.

*

Bibliography: *Randolph Stow: A Bibliography* by P.A. O'Brien, Adelaide, Libraries Board of South Australia, 1968; "A Randolph Stow Bibliography" by Rose Marie Beston, in *Literary Half-Yearly* (Mysore), July 1975.

Manuscript Collection: National Library of Australia, Canberra.

Critical Studies: "Raw Material" by Stow, in *Westerly* (Nedlands, Western Australia), 1961; "The Quest for Permanence" by Geoffrey Dutton, in *Journal of Commonwealth Literature* (Leeds, Yorkshire), September 1965; "Outsider Looking Out" by W.H. New, in *Critique* (Minneapolis), vol. 9, no. 1, 1967; "Waste Places, Dry Souls" by Jennifer Wightman, in *Meanjin* (Melbourne), June 1969; "Voyager from Eden" by Brandon Conron, in *Ariel (Canada)* (Calgary, Alberta), October 1970; *The Merry-Go-Round in the Sea* by Edriss Noall, Sydney, Scoutline, 1971; "The Family Background and Literary Career of Randolph Stow" by John B. Beston, in *Literary Half-Yearly* (Mysore), July 1975; *Randolph Stow* by Ray Willbanks, Boston, Twayne, 1978; "Randolph Stow's *Visitants,*" in *Australian Literary Studies* (Brisbane), October 1980, and *Strange Country: A Study of Randolph Stow,* St. Lucia, University of Queensland Press, 1986, both by Anthony J. Hassall.

*   *   *

The contrast between *The Merry-Go-Round in the Sea,* with its local "realism," and *Tourmaline,* which makes a symbolic landscape out of Randolph Stow's native land, indicates the initial range of his fiction. *The Merry-Go-Round* by no means eschews symbolic patterns, but it emerges more directly from Australian national sensibilities. Stow's novel links the isolating impact that World War II had on the country with the older traditions of convict settlement and South Pacific paradise. (Stow is careful to debunk the easy myths which see convict and bushranger mateyness as the *sole* generative character trait *throughout* Australia; his comic children's book *Midnite: The Story of a Wild Colonial Boy,* about the triumphant adventures of a native bushranger and his gang—a cockatoo and a cat—delightfully overturns assorted local archetypes. Yet with linguistic playfulness it celebrates the spirit of the country as well, which serves as a reminder of the ambivalent blend of prison and paradise which has always provoked the Australian imagination.) For Rick Maplestead, in *The Merry-Go-Round,* imprisoned in Changi and then freed only to discover his bonds to history, family, mates, and mediocrity, there is no escape but flight. But as he and his young cousin Rob Coram (whose offshore vision gives the book its title) know, glimpses of paradise are illusory and attempts to inhabit them fraught with disappointment.

By focusing ultimately on the quests of the mind, the book recapitulates many of Stow's earlier themes. His first books, full of mad characters and melodramatic incidents, are the Gothic attempts of a young novelist to record his knowledge of power and passion, of the relation between man and landscape and the impact of belief on action. Not till these sensibilities were controlled by Stow's anthropological and historical commitments did they exert a powerful literary effect. *To the Islands* reduced the reliance on incident and traced instead the wanderings of a man through the desert of his belief, in search of the afterworld islands of aboriginal dream order. His soul, he discovers, "is a strange country"—which seems at first to be no advance on what he began by knowing. Increasingly, however, that very state of suspended apprehension becomes the world that Stow tries to explore. *Tourmaline,* about a wasteland of that name, which welcomes a stranger as a water-diviner (who begins to clothe himself in such a role), only to be desolated and turn to another authority when he fails, provides an even more archetypal canvas. Consciously symbolic and heavily mannered in style, the book tries to evoke the world of symbol, the fleeting perceptions that symbols try to convey, rather than the realities of everyday event. The reiteration on the part of the Law, the narrator, that to describe a heritage as "bitter" is "not to condemn it," urges readers also to consider what it is that he does not say, what it is that he cannot say.

Tarot, Tao, and Jungian commentary become means to fathom the deep intuitive communications of silence, but wordless understandings present problems for a writer to communicate. Later novels pursue the imaginative reaches of the reflective mind. *Visitants* explores Melanesian tribal life and traces its impact on Australians of different sensibilities; the novel is cast as a series of depositions at a legal inquiry, which prove unable entirely to explain the cultural other-worldliness. *The Girl Green as Elderflower* turns imaginative threat—the pressures of tropical disease and a foreign tongue upon a sensitive young man—into imaginative renewal; the young man, in Suffolk, reconciles himself with his heritage and his experience, and in a series of fables he writes out his recognition of the ways in which the unusual has always permeated the everyday. To admit to such flights of mind, he discovers, is to admit to a kind of health and a kind of love, and to win a "paradise" of a different, more fluid, perhaps freer, certainly more comic nature.

But in *The Suburbs of Hell* Stow's vision is once again more problematic. The novel tells of a series of murders among both insiders and outsiders in an isolated East Anglia village. Who is the culprit? Adapting the forms of popular fiction, the narrative contrives to suggest a number of possibilities—but settles on none. The novelist here is interested more in the nature of motive and interpretive response than he is in simply bringing a story to a conclusion. He probes what the pressure of fear and uncertainty does to an apparently stable society—an interest not without its sociological import. But he fastens particularly on the power of narrative, and on the sometimes insidious capacity that the impulse to create narrative has on the way people (readers included) encode and therefore enclose all human behavior around them.

—W.H. New

STUART, (Henry) Francis (Montgomery)

Nationality: Irish. **Born:** Townsville, Queensland, Australia, 29 April 1902. **Education:** Rugby School, Warwickshire. **Family:** Married 1) Iseult Gonne in 1920 (died), one son and one daughter; 2) Gertrude Meiszner in 1954; 3) Finola Graham in 1987. **Career:** Fought on the side of the Irish Nationalists in the Civil War; imprisoned by the British, 1922. Lecturer in English and Irish Literature, University of Berlin, 1940. Imprisoned by the Allied forces, 1945-46. Founding member, Irish Academy of Letters. **Awards:** Young Poet's prize (*Poetry,* Chicago), 1921; Royal Irish Academy award, 1924; Northern Ireland Arts Council bursary, 1974. **Address:** 2 Highfield Park, Dublin 14, Ireland.

PUBLICATIONS

Novels

Women and God. London, Cape, 1931.
Pigeon Irish. London, Gollancz, and New York, Macmillan, 1932.
The Coloured Dome. London, Gollancz, 1932; New York, Macmillan, 1933.
Try the Sky. London, Gollancz, and New York, Macmillan, 1933.
Glory. London, Gollancz, and New York, Macmillan, 1933.
In Search of Love. London, Collins, and New York, Macmillan, 1935.
The Angel of Pity. London, Grayson, 1935.
The White Hare. London, Collins, and New York, Macmillan, 1936.
The Bridge. London, Collins, 1937.
Julie. New York, Knopf, and London, Collins, 1938.
The Great Squire. London, Collins, 1939.
The Pillar of Cloud. London, Gollancz, 1948.
Redemption. London, Gollancz, 1949; New York, Devin Adair, 1950.
The Flowering Cross. London, Gollancz, 1950.
Good Friday's Daughter. London, Gollancz, 1952.
The Chariot. London, Gollancz, 1953.
The Pilgrimage. London, Gollancz, 1955.
Victors and Vanquished. London, Gollancz, 1958; Cleveland, Pennington Press, 1959.
Angels of Providence. London, Gollancz, 1959.
Black List, Section H. Carbondale, Southern Illinois University Press, 1971; London, Martin Brian and O'Keeffe, 1975.
Memorial. London, Martin Brian and O'Keeffe, 1973.
A Hole in the Head. London, Martin Brian and O'Keeffe, and Nantucket, Massachusetts, Longship Press, 1977.
The High Consistory. London, Martin Brian and O'Keeffe, 1981.
Faillandia. Dublin, Raven Arts Press, 1985.
A Compendium of Lovers. Dublin, Raven Arts Press, 1990.

Uncollected Short Stories

"Relativity," in *Lovat Dickson's Magazine* (London), November 1934.
"Isles of the Blest," in *English Review* (London), December 1934.
"Bandit," in *Cornhill* (London), February 1938.
"The Stormy Petrel," in *Paddy No More,* edited by William Vorm. Nantucket, Massachusetts, Longship Press, 1978.
"The Heart That Melted," in *Irish Times* (Dublin), August 1985.

Plays

Men Crowd Me Round (produced Dublin, 1933).
Glory, adaptation of his own novel (produced London, 1936).
Strange Guest (produced Dublin, 1940).
Flynn's Last Dive (produced Croydon, Surrey, 1962).
Who Fears to Speak? (produced Dublin, 1970).

Poetry

We Have Kept the Faith (as H. Stuart). Dublin, Oak Leaf Press, 1923.
Night Pilot. Dublin, Raven Arts Press, 1989.

Other

Nationality and Culture (lecture). Dublin, Sinn Fein Ardchomahairle, 1924.

Mystics and Mysticism. Dublin, Catholic Truth Society of Ireland, 1929.

Things to Live For: Notes for an Autobiography. London, Cape, 1934; New York, Macmillan, 1935.

Racing for Pleasure and Profit in Ireland and Elsewhere. Dublin, Talbot Press, 1937.

Der Fall Casement: Das Leben Sir Roger Casement und der Verleumdungsfeldzug des Secret Service, translated by Ruth Weiland. Hamburg, Hanseatische, 1940.

States of Mind: Selected Short Prose 1936-1983. Dublin, Raven Arts Press, and London, Martin Brian and O'Keeffe, 1984.

Translator, *The Captive Dreamer,* by Christian de La Mazière. New York, Saturday Review Press, 1974; as *Ashes of Honour,* London, Wingate, 1975.

*

Manuscript Collections: Southern Illinois University Library, Carbondale; National Library of Ireland, Dublin; University of Ulster, Coleraine.

Critical Studies: *A Festschrift for Francis Stuart on His Seventieth Birthday 29 April 1972,* Dublin, Dolmen Press, 1972 (includes bibliography); *Francis Stuart* by J.H. Natterstad, Lewisburg, Pennsylvania, Bucknell University Press, 1974; *Francis Stuart: A Life* by Geoffrey Elborn, Dublin, Raven Arts, 1990.

Francis Stuart comments:

(1976) I consider myself a dissident writer, someone who is keeping flowing a countercurrent to many of the assumptions and attitudes of contemporary society. For this reason I have been called a Ghetto novelist, and several of my books have been black-listed not only in Ireland but elsewhere. For instance, *Black List, Section H.* has taken five years since its appearance in America to considerable acclaim (Lawrence Durrell in *The New York Times,* etc.) to find a publisher in England.

*   *   *

High praise has come Francis Stuart's way on a number of occasions—from W.B. Yeats, for example, who engineered a prize from the Royal Irish Academy for his early book of poems *(We Have Kept the Faith)* and lauded several of the early novels, especially *The Coloured Dome;* from Compton MacKenzie, whose enthusiasm extended as far as *Try the Sky* (generally regarded as one of Stuart's weakest efforts); and from Lawrence Durrell, who called *Black List, Section H* "a book of the finest imaginative distinction" and presumably assisted the slow and cautious recognition that it has had from the academic establishment.

Yet Stuart's reputation does not seem to have grown greater than the sum of such individual plaudits. Even *Black List, Section H* tends to be admired on extrinsic rather than intrinsic grounds—for the frankness of its discussion of various Irish notables, including Maud and Iseult Gonne (who was Stuart's first wife), Yeats, and Liam O'Flaherty, and for its unusual and (given Stuart's contribution to broadcasts of Nazi propaganda) even scandalous account of the Second World War from the German side.

Since Stuart was an Irish national and most of his broadcasts from Germany were directed to Ireland (which remained neutral during the war) the question of whether or not he should be regarded as a collaborator is a moot one. His German venture is much easier to explain on aesthetic grounds; it represents a putting into effect of the conviction that seized him at the very beginning of his creative life that "a poet must be a countercurrent to the flow around him," must explore "the dark deep flow beneath the surface [of life], subtle, crude, beautiful, terrible".

In his early novels Stuart's notion of "a countercurrent" is one that many late Romantics—especially the pioneers of the Irish Renaissance—would have felt relatively comfortable with. Like Yeats, he insisted that creativity involved "liberating himself from outward existence and gaining another level of consciousness." This juxtaposition of outwardness and inwardness, the physical and the spiritual, positivism and mysticism became the central theme of his work.

Many of the motifs used on both sides of the scale in these early novels are conventional enough. Yeats no doubt approved the withering portrait of bourgeois values in novels like *The Coloured Dome* and *The White Hare,* for example. And he must have rejoiced in the extravagant symbolism with which Stuart embellished the obverse of this latter-day Gradgrindism. *The White Hare* also uses the common Irish topos of "the big house" as a repository of traditional spiritual values. So does a later novel, *The Great Squire.* In addition, the traditional idea of Ireland itself as "the island of the saints," whose integrity offsets a general spiritual decline elsewhere, lies behind several of the novels—notably the futuristic *Pigeon Irish,* the most remarkable of his early works. (*The Bridge,* however, proves that Stuart was not blind to the drabness and puritanism of provincial Ireland.) More frequent (and more traditional) than all of these topoi is the crucifixion motif; again and again in Stuart's novels characters sacrifice themselves or their well-being for the sake of others and discover deeper levels of consciousness as a result.

Stuart himself once observed that he always wrote best "at the start of a creative phase," and certainly one senses a falling off in intensity during the latter part of the 1930s. He himself felt that at this time he was becoming "too mental," "turning to the world" (e.g. *In Search of Love,* a satirical account of the film industry, lacks Stuart's usual spiritual counterpoise).

The war revitalized his work. He undertook a lecture tour to Germany in April 1939 and returned to take up a position at Berlin University early in 1940. As early as 1942 he could write that "what has happened to me is like a second conversion. The first conversion was at Ballycoyle in 1926 [where he read Underhill's *Mysticism*] but it was an illumination of the mind." He stayed in Germany until July 1946, experiencing the postwar shambles and even suffering some months of imprisonment at the hands of the French. From 1941 he had as his constant companion a former student and colleague at Deutscher Kurzwellensender, Gertrud Meissner, whom he subsequently married after Iseult's death in 1954.

Stuart's harrowing wartime experiences (and his love for Gertrud Meissner) are reflected not only in *Black List, Section H* (which he has called "a memoir in fictional form") but also, more obliquely, in the two fine novels that he wrote straight after the war, *The Pillar of Cloud* and *Redemption. The Pillar of Cloud,* an intense, slow-moving book, gives emphatic expression to Stuart's conviction that "a new peace and justice" would come not from the Allied victory, not "through the fighting" nor even through "organising, calculating, planning" of any kind; rather "it was out of pain and suffering that, if there was to be a new peace, it would be shaped." The milieu of Ireland and "the big house"—represented in the book by the home of the protagonist's Uncle Egan—begins to look like an escapist dream. It is replaced by a vision of selfless "fraternity" among the down-and-out—a vision based to some extent on the example of a demythologized Christ, as well as on the precedent of various modern writers (including Beaudelaire, Poe, Keats, Melville, Emily Brontë, Dostoevsky, Proust, Kafka and Lawrence), who because of alcoholism, sexual excess, tuberculosis, venereal disease, rejected love, condemnation , and banishment, as well as even more extreme isolating factors unnamed and unknown, acting on ultra-responsive neurological systems, had been driven beyond the place where the old assumptions are still acceptable.

The emphasis on fraternity recurs in almost all of Stuart's postwar work, most memorably, perhaps, in *Redemption,* whose unusually arresting plot makes it arguably his best book. In the other novels of the 1950s there is a noticeable falling off in intensity and in the quality of the prose. Even his indispensable portrait of the artist, *Black List, Section H,* which broke a twelve-year drought in 1971, is flat and clumsy in parts.

Black List, Section H seems to have had some sort of cathartic effect on the author, however, and ushered in a new "creative phase"; the subsequent novels, though they break little new ground in respect of theme, display some interesting formal innovations. The first part of *A Hole in the Head,* for example, features a mentally disturbed narrator who holds imaginary conversations with his "muse," Emily Brontë. And the plot of *The High Consistory* moves backwards and forwards in time, ostensibly because the narrator's manuscript was "lightly shuffled" in an aeroplane crash. Thanks to these technical experiments, Stuart has remained a remarkably challenging and contemporary writer even in old age.

—Harry T. Moore, updated by Richard Corballis

STYRON, William

Nationality: American. **Born:** Newport News, Virginia, 11 June 1925. **Education:** Christchurch School, Virginia; Davidson College, North Carolina, 1942-43; Duke University, Durham, North Carolina, 1943-44, 1946-47, B.A. 1947 (Phi Beta Kappa). **Military Service:** Served in the United States Marine Corps, 1944-45, 1951: 1st Lieutenant. **Family:** Married Rose Burgunder in 1953; three daughters and one son. **Career:** Associate editor, McGraw Hill, publishers, New York, 1947. Since 1952 advisory editor, *Paris Review,* Paris and New York; member of the editorial board, *American Scholar,* Washington, D.C., 1970-76. Since 1964 fellow, Silliman College, Yale University, New Haven, Connecticut. **Awards:** American Academy Prix de Rome, 1952; Pulitzer prize, 1968; Howells Medal, 1970; American Book award, 1980; Connecticut Arts award, 1984; Cino del Duca prize, 1985; MacDowell Medal, 1988; Bobst award, 1989; National Magazine award, 1990; National Medal of Arts, 1993; National Arts Club Medal of Honor, 1995. Litt.D.: Duke University, 1968; Davidson College, Davidson, North Carolina, 1986. **Member:** American Academy, American Academy of Arts and Sciences, and American Academy of Arts and Letters; Commander, Order of Arts and Letters (France), and Legion of Honor (France). **Address:** 12 Rucum Road, Roxbury, Connecticut 06783, U.S.A.

Novels

Lie Down in Darkness. Indianapolis, Bobbs Merrill, 1951; London, Hamish Hamilton, 1952.
The Long March. New York, Random House, 1956; London, Hamish Hamilton, 1962.
Set This House on Fire. New York, Random House, 1960; London, Hamish Hamilton, 1961.
The Confessions of Nat Turner. New York, Random House, 1967; London, Cape, 1968.
Sophie's Choice. New York, Random House, and London, Cape, 1979.

Short Story

Shadrach. Los Angeles, Sylvester and Orphanos, 1979.

Uncollected Short Stories

"Autumn," and "Long Dark Road," in *One and Twenty,* edited by W.M. Blackburn. Durham, North Carolina, Duke University Press, 1945.
"Moments in Trieste," in *American Vanguard 1948,* edited by Charles I. Glicksburg. New York, Cambridge, 1948.
"The Enormous Window," in *American Vanguard 1950,* edited by Charles I. Glicksburg. New York, Cambridge, 1950.
"The McCabes," in *Paris Review 22,* Autumn-Winter 1959-60.
"Pie in the Sky," in *The Vintage Anthology of Science Fantasy,* edited by Christopher Cerf. New York, Random House, 1966.

Play

In the Clap Shack (produced New Haven, Connecticut, 1972). New York, Random House, 1973.

Other

The Four Seasons, illustrated by Harold Altman. University Park, Pennsylvania State University Press, 1965.
Admiral Robert Penn Warren and the Snows of Winter: A Tribute. Winston-Salem, North Carolina, Palaemon Press, 1978.
The Message of Auschwitz. Blacksburg, Virginia, Press de la Warr, 1979.
Against Fear. Winston-Salem, North Carolina, Palaemon Press, 1981.
As He Lay Dead, A Bitter Grief (on William Faulkner). New York, Albondocani Press, 1981.
This Quiet Dust and Other Writings. New York, Random House, 1982; London, Cape, 1983.
Conversations with William Styron (interviews), edited by James L.W. West III. Jackson, University Press of Mississippi, 1985.
Darkness Visible (memoirs). New York, Random House, 1990; London, Cape, 1991.
A Tidewater Morning (Three Tales from Youth). Helsinki, Eurographica, 1991; New York, Random House, 1993; London, Cape, 1994.

Editor, *Best Short Stories from the Paris Review.* New York, Dutton, 1959.

*

Bibliography: *William Styron: A Descriptive Bibliography* by James L.W. West III, Boston, Hall, 1977; *William Styron: A Reference Guide* by Jackson R. Bryer and Mary B. Hatem, Boston, Hall, 1978; *William Styron: An Annotated Bibliography of Criticism* by Philip W. Leon, Westport, Connecticut, Greenwood Press, 1978.

Manuscript Collections: Library of Congress, Washington, D.C.; Duke University, Durham, North Carolina.

Critical Studies: *William Styron* by Robert H. Fossum, Grand Rapids, Michigan, Eerdmans, 1968; *William Styron* by Cooper R. Mackin, Austin, Texas, Steck Vaughn, 1969; *William Styron* by Richard Pearce, Minneapolis, University of Minnesota Press, 1971; *William Styron* by Marc L. Ratner, New York, Twayne, 1972; *William Styron* by Melvin J. Friedman, Bowling Green, Ohio, Popular Press, 1974; *The Achievement of William Styron* edited by Irving Malin and Robert K. Morris, Athens, University of Georgia Press, 1975, revised edition, 1981; *Critical Essays on William Styron* edited by Arthur D. Casciato and James L.W. West III, Boston, Hall, 1982; *The Root of All Evil: The Thematic Unity of William Styron's Fiction* by John K. Crane, Columbia, University of South Carolina Press, 1985; *William Styron* by Judith Ruderman, New York, Ungar, 1989; *The Novels of William Styron* by Gavin Cologne-Brookes, Baton Rouge, Louisiana State University Press, 1995.

*   *   *

Of the American novelists who have come onto the literary scene since the end of World War II, William Styron would seem to have worked most directly in the traditional ways of story-telling. As a writer from the American South, he was heir to a mode of fiction writing most notably developed by William Faulkner and practiced to striking effect by such fellow southerners as Robert Penn Warren, Thomas Wolfe, Eudora Welty, and Katherine Anne Porter. It involved—as the mode of Hemingway did not involve—a reliance upon the resources of a sounding rhetoric rather than upon understatement, a dependence upon the old religious universals ("love and honor and pity and pride and compassion and sacrifice," as Faulkner once termed them) rather than a suspicion of all such external moral formulations, and a profound belief in the reality of the past as importantly affecting present behavior—an "historical sense," as contrasted with the dismissal of history as irrelevant and meaningless.

His first novel, *Lie Down in Darkness,* was strongly indebted to the example of Faulkner; Styron began it, he said, after reading Faulkner night and day for several weeks. Yet though Styron portrayed a young southern woman, Peyton Loftis, as she battled for love and sanity in a dreary family situation, doomed to defeat by her father's weak, self-pitying ineffectuality and her mother's hypocrisy and sadistic jealousy, and though the setting was a tidewater Virginia city among an effete upper-class society, what resulted was not finally Faulknerian. At bottom the causes of Styron's tragedy were familial, not dynastic; the deficiencies of Milton and Helen Loftis were not importantly those of decadent aristocracy whose concept of honor and pride has become empty posturing and self-indulgence, as they would have been for a writer such as Faulkner, but rather personal and psychological. When Peyton flees Virginia for New York City, there is little sense of her plight as representing isolation from the order and definition of a time and place that are no longer available. Instead, hers was a break for freedom, and the failure to make good the break is the result of the

crippling conflict within her mind and heart imposed by the example of her parents, and which symbolizes the hatreds engendered by a society that does not know how to love. The suicide of Peyton Loftis represents a plunge into the moral abyss of a self-destructive modern world. Styron, in other words, wrote out of a tradition that taught him to measure his people and their society against the traditional values, and to see the absence of those values in their lives as tragic; but he did not depict that absence as a falling away from a more honorable, more ordered Southern historical past.

The success of *Lie Down in Darkness* was considerable, perhaps in part because a novel that could depict the modern situation as tragic, rather than merely pathetic, and could thus make use of the High Style of language to chronicle it, was all too rare. Styron followed it with *The Long March,* a novella set in a Marine Corps camp during the Korean War (Styron himself was briefly recalled to active duty in 1951). Depicting the irrationality of war and the military mentality, it demonstrates the dignity, and also the absurdity, of an individual's effort to achieve nobility amid chaos.

Eight years elapsed before Styron's second full-length novel, *Set This House on Fire.* The story of a Southern-born artist, Cass Kinsolving, who is unable to paint, and is married and living in Europe, it involved a man in spiritual bondage, undergoing a terrifying stay in the lower depths before winning his way back to sanity and creativity. In Paris, Rome, and the Italian town of Sambucco, Cass Kinsolving lives in an alcoholic daze, tortured by his inability to create, wandering about, drinking, pitying himself, doing everything except confronting his talent. The struggle is on existential terms. Kinsolving has sought to find a form for his art outside of himself, looking to the society and the people surrounding him for what could only be located within himself: the remorseless requirement of discovering how to love and be loved, and so to create.

Set This House on Fire encountered a generally hostile critical reception, to some extent because it was sprawling and untidy, occasionally overwritten, and therefore so very different from his well-made first novel. It seemed, too, even further removed than *Lie Down in Darkness* from the customary Southern milieu: not only were there no decaying families, no faithful black retainers, no blood-guilt, and no oversexed Southern matrons, but we are told very little about the protagonist's past, either familial or personal, that might explain how he got the way he was. Yet there *was* a past; but Styron gives it to a friend of Kinsolving's, Peter Leverett, who tells the story. The fact is that Leverett's failure to find definition in his Southern origins is what really accounts for Kinsolving's present-day plight. Styron apparently could not avoid grounding his tragedy in history one way or the other. And after Kinsolving has fought his way back to personal responsibility and creativity, he leaves Europe and returns to the South. There is thus a kind of circular movement involved in the first two novels. Peyton Loftis finds the Southern community impossible to live within and love within, and she goes to New York. Cass Kinsolving, equally at loose ends, goes abroad and conducts his struggle for identity and definition there, and then comes home to the South. He has had in effect to ratify the individual and social worth of his attitudes and values away from the place and the institutions of their origins, and make them his own, not something merely bequeathed automatically to him.

If so, it was not surprising that Styron's next and most controversial novel, *The Confessions of Nat Turner,* once again was set in the South—in Southside Virginia, no more than an hour's automobile drive from Port Warwick where Peyton Loftis grew up and

Newport News, Virginia, where Styron was born and raised—and that it concerned itself squarely with the southern past, as exemplified in the presence and the role of the black man. For though *The Confessions of Nat Turner* is based upon a famous slave insurrection that took place in 1831, its implications involve race and racism, integration and separatism, and the use of violent means in order to achieve political and social ends. Styron's strategy, for what he termed his "meditation upon history," was to tell his story from the viewpoint of the slave leader Nat Turner, of whose actual life almost nothing is known. Rather than restrict his protagonist's language, however, to that which a plantation slave in the early 19th-century might be expected to have used, Styron decided that the range and complexity of such a man's mind could not be adequately represented in any such primitive fashion, and he cast Nat Turner's reflections in the rich, allusive, polysyllabic mode of the early Victorian novel. Styron was thus able to have his slave leader utilize the resources of a sounding rhetoric in order to look beyond his immediate circumstance into the moral and ethical implications of his actions.

The initial critical verdict on *The Confessions of Nat Turner* was highly favorable, with such critics as Alfred Kazin, Philip Rahv, C. Vann Woodward, and others declaring it an impressive contribution both to contemporary American fiction and to the knowledge of slavery. Almost immediately, however, the book became embroiled in a controversy, not so much literary as sociological, which made both novel and novelist into a *cause célèbre*. For in presuming, as a white man, to portray the consciousness of a black revolutionist of a century-and-a-half ago, Styron came into collision with the impetus of the black separatist movement. His novel appeared at a time when the black American was straining as never before to assert his identity and his independence of white paternalism, and the result was that numerous black critics, together with some white sympathizers, began heaping abuse on Styron for his alleged racism, his alleged unwarranted liberties with historical "fact," and his alleged projection of "white liberal neuroses" onto a revolutionary black leader's personality. A host of reviews and essays and even a book appeared in denunciation of Styron. Other critics rose to the rebuttal, and historians joined in to certify the authenticity of Styron's historical portrayal. The outcome has been a voluminous literature of controversy that may well interest future social historians almost as much as the Nat Turner insurrection itself.

In 1979 Styron entered the lists again with a lengthy novel on another controversial subject. *Sophie's Choice* involved the confrontation of a young and very autobiographically clued Virginian with a Polish refugee who has undergone the horrors of concentration camp existence, and her lover, a young New York Jew who is a brilliant conversationalist but turns out to be quite mad. Written very much in the mode of Thomas Wolfe's fiction of encounter with the metropolis, Styron's novel records the growing helplessness of a youthful American in the face of a developing acquaintance with the enormity of human evil and irrationality. The novel drew much criticism for its excesses of rhetoric and the apparent irrelevance of much of its sexual material; in effect it would seem to imitate the author's own difficulties in coming to terms with the subject matter described. Yet it contains powerful sequences, and as always represents Styron's unwillingness to seek easy ways out or avoid central human problems.

—Louis D. Rubin, Jr.

SUKENICK, Ronald

Nationality: American. **Born:** Brooklyn, New York, 14 July 1932. **Education:** Cornell University, Ithaca, New York, B.A. 1955; Brandeis University, Waltham, Massachusetts, M.A. 1957, Ph.D. in English 1962. **Family:** Married Lynn Luria in 1961 (divorced). **Career:** Lecturer, Brandeis University, 1956-57, and Hofstra University, Hempstead, New York, 1961-62; part-time teacher, 1963-66; assistant professor of English, City College, New York, 1966-67, and Sarah Lawrence College, Bronxville, New York, 1968-69; writer-in-residence, Cornell University, 1969-70, and University of California, Irvine, 1970-72. Since 1975 professor of English, and director of the Publications Center, University of Colorado, Boulder. Taught at Université Paul Valéry, Montpellier, France, Fall 1979; Butler Professor of English, State University of New York, Buffalo, Spring 1981. Contributing editor, *Fiction International,* Canton, New York, 1970-84; chairman, Coordinating Council of Literary Magazines, 1975-77. Since 1974 founding member and co-director, Fiction Collective, New York; since 1977 founding publisher, *American Book Review,* New York; since 1989 editor, *Black Ice,* New York. **Awards:** Fulbright fellowship, 1958, 1984; Guggenheim fellowship, 1977; National Endowment for the Arts fellowship, 1980, Faculty fellowship, 1982; Coordinating Council of Literary Magazines award, for editing, 1985; Before Columbus Foundation award, 1988. **Address:** Department of English, University of Colorado, Boulder, Colorado 80309, U.S.A.

PUBLICATIONS

Novels

Up. New York, Dial Press, 1968.
Out. Chicago, Swallow Press, 1973.
98.6. New York, Fiction Collective, 1975.
Long Talking Bad Conditions Blues. New York, Fiction Collective, 1979.
Blown Away. Los Angeles, Sun and Moon Press, 1986.
Doggy Bag. Boulder, Colorado, Black Ice, 1994.

Short Stories

The Death of the Novel and Other Stories. New York, Dial Press, 1969.
A Postcard from "The Endless Short Story" (single story). Austin, Texas, Cold Mountain Press, 1974.
The Endless Short Story. New York, Fiction Collective, 1986.

Uncollected Short Stories

"One Every Minute," in *Carolina Quarterly* (Chapel Hill, North Carolina), Spring 1961.
"A Long Way from Nowhere," in *Epoch* (Ithaca, New York), Fall 1964.
"Extract from *The Fortune Teller,*" in *Trema* (Paris), no. 2, 1977.

Other

Wallace Stevens: Musing the Obscure. New York, New York University Press, 1967.

In Form: Digressions Towards a Study of Composition.
Carbondale, Southern Illinois University Press, 1985.
Down and In: Life in the Underground. New York, Morrow, 1987.

*

Critical Studies: "Getting Real: Making It (Up) with Ronald Sukenick," in *Chicago Review,* Winter 1972, and "Persuasive Account: Working It Out with Ronald Sukenick," in *Seeing Castaneda,* edited by Daniel Noel, New York, Putnam, 1976, both by Jerome Klinkowitz; "Reading *Out*" by Melvin J. Friedman, in *Fiction International 1* (Canton, New York), Fall 1973; "Imagination and Perception" (interview), in *The New Fiction: Interviews with Innovative American Writers* by Joe David Bellamy, Urbana, University of Illinois Press, 1974; "Tales of Fictive Power: Dreaming and Imagining in Ronald Sukenick's Postmodern Fiction" by Daniel Noel, in *Boundary 2* (Binghamton, New York), Fall 1976; "Obscuring the Muse: The Mock-Autobiographies of Ronald Sukenick" by Timothy Dow Adams, in *Critique* (Atlanta), vol. 20, no. 1, 1978; "Way Out West: The Exploratory Fiction of Ronald Sukenick" by Alan Cheuse, in *Itinerary Criticism 7* edited by Charles Crow, Bowling Green, Ohio, Bowling Green State University Press, 1978; *The Novel as Performance: The Fiction of Ronald Sukenick and Raymond Federman* by Jerzy Kutnik, Carbondale, Southern Illinois University Press, 1986.

Ronald Sukenick comments:
(1991) My fiction is not "experimental."

*   *   *

As the most representative example of the innovative writers who contributed to the transformation of both American fiction and its supporting culture, Ronald Sukenick has remained active for over three decades, not so much adapting to conditions as challenging and in some cases changing the literary, publishing, and academic worlds about him. As such, he suggests the activist role of his artistic generation; not content to be, like Ken Kesey, a seismograph of cultural shock and a barometer of radical change, Sukenick has undertaken a revolution himself, leading developments that have reformed the culture in and of which Americans write.

Like several key figures of the 1960s group of innovators, Sukenick earned a doctorate (in English from Brandeis University) and undertook a career as a university professor. His first book was a revision of his dissertation on the poet Wallace Stevens, and while not directly related to any theory or style of narrative does demonstrate Sukenick's affinity for writing that exercises imaginative control. Aware of how Stevens believed that "a fiction is not an ideological formulation of belief but a statement of a favorable rapport with reality," Sukenick began his own efforts as a writer by following this code for ordering reality: "not by imposing ideas on it but by discovering significant relations with it." The most significant section of *Wallace Stevens: Musing the Obscure* is collected in Sukenick's book of essays, *In Form: Digressions Towards a Study of Composition,* where it complements an aesthetic underlying the fictive art of an era.

Sukenick's first novel, *Up,* activates this imagination as the generating force for narrative. As a gesture toward suspending the suspension of disbelief, Sukenick names his narrator/protagonist "Ronald Sukenick" and has him doing many of the same things Sukenick did at the time: struggling to study and teach free of the inhibitions that had smothered academic life in the preceding age, working to complete a novel (titled *Up*), and trying to establish a rapport with the reality around him—a reality that includes the just-developing countercultural world of the New York's Lower East Side and the community of artists and hustlers who are his friends. Fantasy merits the same treatment as experience, and at one point Sukenick's protagonist teaches a lesson from Wallace Stevens to his class: that art is "the invention of reality" that seeks "a vital connection with the world that, to stay alive, must be constantly reinvented to correspond with our truest feelings." *Up* is a *Bildungsroman* of just such a struggle, and by the end, when the artist has come to maturity, the point is not to celebrate this status but to appreciate how it is achieved.

The Death of the Novel and Other Stories collects a novella (from which the volume takes its title) and five short stories, all of which suggest various strategies for such imaginative connection with the world. "The Death of the Novel" is famous for its opening paragraph, a statement that not only sums up critically the eclipse of realistic fiction but, as the protagonist's lecture notes, propels him into a narrative experience that proves each point. Equally significant are "Momentum" and "The Birds," two stories that propound Sukenick's belief, stated later in *In Form,* that fiction "is not about experience but is more experience." The test of such work, which another essay from *In Form* compares to the anthropological tales of Carlos Castaneda, is the degree to which the teller can present "a persuasive account." In league with how anthropologists understand the world, Sukenick argues that there is not one reality but only various accounts of it, the most convincing of which succeeds as the culture's model.

A cultural model for the revolutionary America of the late 1960s and early 1970s is provided in Sukenick's second novel, *Out.* Its structure draws on the vernacular American format of a cross-country journey with characters being formed and reshaped by their experiences along the way. Its East to West movement expresses both the historical settling of the Continent and the rhythm of increasing speed and opening up of space that the geography implies. To replicate this experience for the reader, Sukenick numbers his chapters backwards, starting with 10 and proceeding in the manner of a rocket-launch countdown; at the same time, each chapter reads more quickly, with chapter 10 offering 10-line blocks of print, chapter nine introducing a line of blank space for each nine lines of print, chapter eight adjusting the ratio to eight-to-two, and so forth until chapter one is rushing by with only one line of narrative for every nine of open space. Yet the novel, which has by now progressed to the near-vacancy of California, the virtual opposite of New York City's cluttered accumulation, has one more chapter: chapter zero, whose 10 lines of space and no lines of print at all send the reader spinning off into emptiness, much like the drag-racing cars in the James Dean film, *Rebel Without a Cause,* that speed out over the cliff into the nothingness beyond.

From the mid-1970s onwards Sukenick has devoted much of his energy to organizational causes, a commitment that has both biographical and artistic consequences. As a full professor at the University of Colorado, he attracted several key writers as faculty, including Clarence Major and Steve Katz. For a time he directed the Coordinating Council of Literary Magazines, working for grant support of alternative publishing venues; at the same time he became one of the founders of The Fiction Collective, a collaborative venture in which writers would fund their books' publication and therefore retain control of all phases of production, distribution, and sales. Working for equal reform in the profession of English,

Sukenick became a member of the executive council of the Modern Language Association. His greatest impact, however, has been as publisher of *The American Book Review,* a tabloid dedicated to covering books neglected by the commercial reviews. He also began editing the magazine *Black Ice.*

His own novels began reflecting this increased social awareness and offered models for both resisting control by others and initiating personal reform. *98.6,* published in 1975, offers three models for society: an initial section which interpolates dreams interfacing ancient and postmodern worlds, a central narrative detailing the attempts of countercultural revolutionaries to establish a commune, and a third part devoted to a utopian venture in psychic consciousness called, with pun intended, "the state of Israel." One of the author's most comically exuberant novels, *98.6* nevertheless answers critics' objections that innovative fiction was ignoring social and moral issues. Though ending in an exceedingly up-beat manner, its central indictment of the 1960s generation for failing to produce an enduring model is compelling (the title refers to the body temperature being monitored as a woman from the commune miscarries the child meant to be this world's future).

Sukenick's most recent work plays with elements from realistic fiction in the service of just such social commentary, but always in ways that reaffirm the primacy of the imagination as the creative force in any world. *Long Talking Bad Conditions Blues* takes its form from a blues/jazz narrative, the style of composition Sukenick favors as proceeding by improvisation and being fueled by its own compositional energy. Set in Paris, where Sukenick owns an apartment and lives for a portion of each year, it is reminiscent of *Up* in that its world is created by not just a community but a central intelligence coming to terms with the experience of its being. *Blown Away* draws similar energy from the Colorado-California life the author has lived in the decades since leaving New York. Here the focus is on how Hollywood seeks to produce the country's imagination, a power based on the willing suspension of disbelief Sukenick scorns as the undoing of art. If audiences yield control of their imaginations, he argues, others will do their imagining for them—which means they will have no effective experience of life. *Blown Away* creates a culture suffering from just such imaginative stasis. Antidotes are found in the author's second collection of short stories, a book that bears the optimistic title *The Endless Short Story*—endless because the model is that of creation itself, on the order of Simon Rodia and his Watts Towers, an assemblage whose essence consists in a state of continual building from the detritus of an otherwise dead culture. Such rebuildings take the form of what Sukenick calls "hyperfictions" in the novel *Doggy Bag.* Here scenes from the global culture of European travel and international terrorism are played out within a cleverly comic language in which imaginatively dead citizens are not only called "Zombies" but are said to suffer from an unstoppable mind control plague called Zombie Immune Tolerance Syndrome, or "ZITS." Thus life becomes atomized, everyone mounting his or her own private revolution in isolation from others, a condition the author calls "the privatization of revolution." The counterforce to such stasis is to avoid rigidity by "getting your mojo working," something the hyperfiction of *Doggy Bag* enacts. Though clearly recognizable as a satire of contemporary life, Sukenick's writing moves a step further by creating its own typologies, taxonomies, grammars, and eventually a language itself in which to comment on present conditions.

Respect for the genius of creation and a curiosity about the ways in which it functions motivated Sukenick's writing of *In Form: Digressions Toward a Study of Composition,* his commentary on the nature of postmodern narrative art, and *Down and In: Life in the Underground,* an autobiographical account of Sukenick's fascination with the transformative styles of literary art initiated in Greenwich Village and the East Village during the 1950s and early 1960s. Behind both studies is the example of Henry Miller, who in Paris a quarter-century before had learned how to deny "official experience" and shape both his life and art according to a more imaginative model. Such has been the imperative for all of Sukenick's work, in literature and in the professions of English and publishing alike.

—Jerome Klinkowitz

SWIFT, Graham

Nationality: British. **Born:** London, 4 May 1949. **Education:** Dulwich College, 1960-67; Queens' College, Cambridge, 1967-70, B.A., M.A.; York University, 1970-73. Lives in London. **Awards:** Geoffrey Faber Memorial prize, 1983; *Guardian* Fiction prize, 1983; Royal Society of Literature Winifred Holtby award, 1984; Premio Grinzane Cavour (Italy), 1987; Prix du meilleur livre étranger (France), 1994. Fellow, Royal Society of Literature, 1984. **Agent:** A.P. Watt Ltd., 20 John Street, London WC1N 2DR, England.

PUBLICATIONS

Novels

The Sweet Shop Owner. London, Allen Lane, 1980; New York, Washington Square Press, 1985.
Shuttlecock. London, Allen Lane, 1981; New York, Washington Square Press, 1984.
Waterland. London, Heinemann, 1983; New York, Poseidon Press, 1984.
Out of This World. London, Viking, and New York, Poseidon Press, 1988.
Ever After. London, Picador, and New York, Knopf, 1992.

Short Stories

Learning to Swim and Other Stories. London, London Magazine Editions, 1982; New York, Poseidon Press, 1985.

Other

Editor, with David Profumo, *The Magic Wheel: An Anthology of Fishing in Literature.* London, Picador, 1985.

*

Critical Study: "History and the 'Here and Now': The Novels of Graham Swift" by Del Ivan Janik, in *Twentieth Century Literature* (Hempstead, New York) vol. 35, No. 1, 1989.

*   *   *

A schoolboy gazes out the classroom window at the playground while a teacher rambles on about Henry VIII. The boy in question is Willy Chapman, the mild-mannered proprietor in Graham Swift's *The Sweet Shop Owner,* and the contrast between the gray asphalt of ordinary life and the colorful costume-drama of history is an important one in Swift's work. In his first novel, it is conveyed in the counterpointing of Willy's courtship and marriage to Irene against the backdrop of World War II. Willy is stationed as quartermaster at Carbury Camp in Hampshire, where he issues helmets and sidepacks to troops who will face combat overseas, and so misses his appointment with the larger forces of history. But the normal routine returns, "Wars pass but sweet shops remain." Unfortunately, many years later (after his wife has died and his daughter Dorry no longer visits him), the sweet shop is all that remains, and Willy determines to commit suicide by straining his weak heart.

Shuttlecock adopts a lighter tone, but features a somewhat darker figure, Prentis, who also looked out of the window at primary school during natural history lessons as his teacher drew toadstools on the blackboard, and wondered what nature had to do with him. A hamster was brought into the classroom one day, and he pestered his parents for a pet of his own. Once in his possession, he tortured the poor animal. This sadistic streak surfaces later in his married life, and he treats his wife as if she were little more than a blow-up doll, and prohibits his children from watching television if they neglect to say hello to him when he returns from work. A tyrant at home, he feels tyrannized outside it. Henry James described Maisie as a "little feathered shuttlecock" flying between her divorced parents, and Prentis is also volleyed between two rackets: Quinn, his boss, who steals files from the police archives office where they both work; and his father, who remains mute during his son's weekly visits to the mental hospital. His father wrote about his undercover activities prior to D-Day with the French Resistance in his book *Shuttlecock: The Story of a Secret Agent,* which Prentis rereads to see if he can understand his current silence. The official line is that his father was imprisoned and tortured at a Chateau near Caen, but outwitted his German captors in a spectacular escape. Quinn leads Prentis to reconsider whether or not his father squealed under pressure.

These first two novels are competent studies of a man and his past, but lack that mysterious ingredient which transforms *Waterland* into something more than standard fare. The central protagonist, Tom Crick, is not the passive schoolboy who doesn't pay attention, but the frustrated history teacher who tries to bring the past to life in the classroom. He has been goaded into early retirement after his wife Mary's nervous breakdown, and struggles to persuade jaded sixth-formers of the importance of the French Revo-

lution: "Before you a balding quinquagenarian who gabbles about the Ancien Régime, Rousseau, Diderot and the insolvency of the French Crown; behind you, beyond the window, gray winter light, an empty playground, forlorn and misty tower blocks . . ." To come to grips with the past himself, he entertains the class with episodes from his own personal history, which turn out to be almost as colorful as those of 1789. Three deaths resulted from Tom and Mary's teenage romance in East Anglia during the war: his friend Freddie Parr, his backward brother Dick, and Mary's aborted child which triggered Freddie's murder and Dick's suicide. More indirectly, this period later caused Mary to kidnap a baby from outside a supermarket, a scandal which has cost Crick his job. But this tale, tangled though it is, still does not explain the present. So Crick lectures his class on more remote topics concerned with the history of the Fens (the rise of the Atkinson brewery, the sex-life of the eel) which have contributed in some way, however convoluted, to his own personal drama. Ultimately Crick fails to make a pact between the here-and-now and the past (unlike Chapman and Prentis), but his investigations demonstrate the complex interrelatedness of the three types of history referred to in the book's epigraph: "1. inquiry, investigation, learning. 2. a) a narrative of past events, history. b) any kind of narrative: account, tale, story."

This conflict between individual biography and the grand narratives of history is expressed succinctly in *Out of This World,* where it is stated that small worlds can blot out big worlds, just as the moon sometimes eclipses the sun. It is April 1982 and Harry Beech (a news photographer) recalls the night man first walked on the moon, when he had an important discussion with his father Robert (an arms manufacturer). It was an occasion when the lunar landscape itself was blotted out, as Harry's suspicions about his father's act of heroism during World War I (which led to the loss of his arm) were confirmed. Throughout the book the point-of-view alternates between Harry and his daughter, Sophie. Harry's cold detachment from the many atrocities he has witnessed is emphasized, while his daughter unburdens her pent-up fury to an American psychiatrist called Dr. K. She cannot forgive her father for instinctively reaching for his camera when Robert was killed by terrorists in 1972, and is resentful about his forthcoming wedding to a girl less than half her age. The horrors of history are glimpsed more fully here, but Swift's goal is essentially that of Harry's when he photographs the Nazis at the Nuremburg trials: "It is this ordinariness I must capture."

—Barry Lewis

T

TAN, Amy (Ruth)

Nationality: American. **Born:** Oakland, California, 19 February 1952. **Education:** San Jose State University, California, B.A. in linguistics and English, 1973, M.A. in linguistics, 1974; University of California, Berkley, 1974-76. **Family:** Married Louis M. DeMattei in 1974. **Career:** Specialist in language development, Alameda County Association for Mentally Retarded, Oakland, 1976-80; project director, MORE Project, San Francisco, 1980-81; reporter, managing editor, and associate publisher, *Emergency Room Reports*, 1981-83; technical writer, 1983-87. **Awards:** Commonwealth Club gold award, 1989, and Bay Area Book Reviewers award, 1990, both for *The Joy Luck Club;* Best American Essays award, 1991. Honorary D.H.L.: Dominican College, San Rafael, 1991. **Address:** c/o Random House, Inc., Publicity, 201 E. 50th St., 22nd Floor, New York, New York 10022, U.S.A.

PUBLICATIONS

Novels

The Joy Luck Club. New York, Putnam, and London, Heinemann, 1989.
The Kitchen God's Wife. New York, Putnam, and London, Collins, 1991.

Play

Screenplay: *The Joy Luck Club,* 1993.

Other

The Moon Lady (for children). New York, Macmillan, 1992.
The Chinese Siamese Cat, illustrated by Gretchen Shields (for children). New York, Macmillan, and London, Hamilton, 1994.

*

Film Adaptation: *The Joy Luck Club,* 1993.

*   *   *

When Amy Tan's first novel *The Joy Luck Club* appeared in 1989, there had been a long interval since the publication of any work on Chinese-American identity, a thematic briefly and convincingly worked upon by Maxine Hong Kingston in *The Woman Warrior* and *China Men* in the previous decade. Both of Tan's novels, *The Joy Luck Club* and *The Kitchen God's Wife* use the framing device of mother-daughter relationships which manages to locate the Chinese-American not as the other of dominant American identity, but rather as the same because of the long exploration of this particular theme in works of American novelists such as Alice Walker, Toni Morrison, Edith Wharton, and Anzia Yezierska to name just a few.

In this way Tan draws upon a familiar and comforting tradition for the Western reader. Strategically too this theme is central to Western women in that it explores the twin poles of the daughter's desire for individuation, wherein she demands an identity as separate from her mother, which clashes with her intense and fierce attachment to and sense of continuum with her mother's life. In this, Tan's pursuit of mother-daughter relationships, rather than father-son ones, reinscribes the woman in the interrogation of origins, a theme only explored via sons who are the "legitimate" heirs to any notion of origins.

Marianne Hirsch points out in *The Mother-Daughter Plot* of 1989, that the mother-daughter narrative varies from the traditional father-son relationship in that the former is marked with opposition and contradiction. She argues that the Western narrative of mother-daughter relationships is located in the Demeter-Persephone myth which enacts the daughter's unbreakable attachment to her mother which is constantly interrupted by her relationship to her husband. To this extent, the daughters in Tan's novels, Jing-Mei Woo (along with a host of others) in *The Joy Luck Club* and Pearl in *The Kitchen God's Wife* indicate the tremendous difficulties of individuation and the loss of the maternal.

In Tan's two novels, mother-daughter dyads ultimately become a metaphor for the relationship between China and the U.S. In the early part of this century Anzia Yezierska had written immigrant novels where the mother and daughter embody the old country and the new world respectively and it is within this framework that Tan too explores the Chinese part of a Chinese-American identity. Thus mother-daughter relationships as well as its intersection with the inscription of the old country get played out in the overarching theme of identity. As first-generation Americans, Jing-Mei Woo and Pearl signify the assimilation that America requires whereas their mothers, as immigrants, embody a severe sense of displacement. Jing-Mei and Pearl's desire for individuation thus goes beyond a break from the mother. Their lives also mirror the ambiguous relationship that Chinese-Americans have with the two mother-countries, the U.S. and China. In a further turn of the screw, Tan shows Pearl's mother, Winnie, as a daughter, in China. This repetition of mothers as daughters prefigures in the characters of Ying-Ying St. Clair and An-Mei Hsu in *The Joy Luck Club*. In this foregrounding of mothers as daughters, Tan reveals her ploy, wherein she wrests this particular theme from the Western tradition and locates it squarely within China. The oriental other who functions as the object of inquiry of the West is revealed to be the maternal progenitor of a Western tradition.

Ultimately, the issues that Tan's novels raise are: Can one really assimilate? Does assimilation bring about equality or is the Chinese-American always in an inferior position within dominant American identity? Can one emphasize difference while maintaining equality? There is no resolution to these questions but rather conclusions that always end in the mother-country, China.

In addition to her two novels, Tan has written two works of children's fiction, *The Moon Lady* (an excerpt from *The Joy Luck Club*), and *The Chinese Siamese Cat,* both of which deal with clever daughters.

—Radhika Mohanram

TENNANT, Emma (Christina)

Nationality: British. **Born:** London, 20 October 1937. **Education:** St. Paul's Girls' School, London. **Family:** Has one son and two daughters. **Career:** Travel correspondent, *Queen,* London, 1963; features editor, *Vogue,* London, 1966; editor, *Bananas,* London, 1975-78. Since 1982 general editor, *In Verse,* London; since 1985 editor, Lives of Modern Women series, Viking, publishers, London. Fellow, Royal Society of Literature, 1982. **Address:** 141 Elgin Crescent, London W.11, England.

PUBLICATIONS

Novels

The Colour of Rain (as Catherine Aydy). London, Weidenfeld and Nicolson, 1964.
The Time of the Crack. London, Cape, 1973; as *The Crack,* London, Penguin, 1978.
The Last of the Country House Murders. London, Cape, 1974; New York, Nelson, 1976.
Hotel de Dream. London, Gollancz, 1976.
The Bad Sister. London, Gollancz, and New York, Coward McCann, 1978.
Wild Nights. London, Cape, 1979; New York, Harcourt Brace, 1980.
Alice Fell. London, Cape, 1980.
Queen of Stones. London, Cape, 1982.
Woman Beware Woman. London, Cape, 1983; as *The Half-Mother,* Boston, Little Brown, 1985.
Black Marina. London, Faber, 1985.
The Adventures of Robina, by Herself. London, Faber, 1986; New York, Persea, 1987.
The Cycle of the Sun:
The House of Hospitalities. London, Viking, 1987.
A Wedding of Cousins. London, Viking, 1988.
The Magic Drum. London, Viking, 1989.
Two Women of London: The Strange Case of Ms. Jekyll and Mrs. Hyde. London, Faber, 1989.
Sisters and Strangers. London, Grafton, 1990.
Faustine. London, Faber, 1991.
Pemberley; or, Pride and Prejudice Continued. New York, St. Martin's Press, 1993; as *Pemberley: A Sequel to Pride and Prejudice,* London, Hodder and Stoughton, 1993.
Tess. London, HarperCollins, 1993.
An Unequal Marriage; or, Pride and Prejudice Twenty Years Later. London, Sceptre, and New York, St. Martin's Press, 1994.

Uncollected Short Stories

"Mrs. Ragley," in *Listener* (London), 1973.
"Mrs. Barratt's Ghost," in *New Statesman* (London), 28 December 1973.
"Philomela," in *Bananas,* edited by Tennant. London, Quartet-Blond and Briggs, 1977.
"The Bed That Mick Built," in *New Stories 2,* edited by Derwent May and Alexis Lykiard. London, Arts Council, 1977.
"Cupboard Love," in *New Stories 4,* edited by Elaine Feinstein and Fay Weldon. London, Hutchinson, 1979.
"Tortoise-Shell Endpapers," in *Time Out* (London), 21 December 1979.

"The Frog Prints," in *London Tales,* edited by Julian Evans. London, Hamish Hamilton, 1983.
"The German in the Wood," in *London Review of Books,* 1984.

Play

Television Script: *Frankenstein's Baby,* 1990.

Other (for children)

The Boggart. London, Granada, 1980.
The Search for Treasure Island. London, Penguin, 1981.
The Ghost Child. London, Heinemann, 1984.
Dave's Secret Diary. London, Longman, 1991.

Other

The ABC of Writing. London, Faber, 1992.

Editor, *Bananas.* London, Quartet-Blond and Briggs, 1977.
Editor, *Saturday Night Reader.* London, W.H. Allen, 1979.

*

Manuscript Collection: National Library of Scotland, Edinburgh.

Critical Study: "Emma Tennant, Hyper-Novelist" by Gary Indiana, in *Village Voice Literary Supplement* (New York), May 1991.

*   *   *

Since the early 1970s, when she was in her mid-thirties, Emma Tennant has been a prolific novelist and has established herself as one of the leading British exponents of "new fiction." This does not mean that she is an imitator of either the French *nouveaux romanciers* or the American post-modernists, although her work reveals an indebtedness to the methods and preoccupations of some of the latter. Like them, she employs parody and rewriting, is interested in the fictiveness of fiction, appropriates some science-fiction conventions, and exploits the possibilities of generic dislocation and mutation, especially the blending of realism and fantasy. Yet, although parallels can be cited and influences suggested, her work is strongly individual, the product of an intensely personal, even idiosyncratic, attempt to create an original type of highly imaginative fiction.

The first novel she published under her own name is *The Time of the Crack.* This futuristic fable about an ever-widening crack in the riverbed of the Thames is a fusion of black farce, wide-ranging satire, and apocalyptic vision. One reviewer described it as "Lewis Carroll technique applied to H.G. Wells material," but other names suggest themselves even more strongly, notably Orwell and Waugh. Like *Nineteen Eighty-Four, The Time of the Crack* is, in its bizarre way, a "condition of England" novel, projecting onto the immediate future current obsessions with decline and fall, and literalizing the metaphor of national disintegration. Stylistically, the book is characterized by a satirical panache recalling Waugh's early period, as Tennant mercilessly caricatures many aspects of contemporary society.

Her next novel, *The Last of the Country House Murders,* is also set in the near future—Britain after the Revolution—and in its oblique way is another "condition of England" novel. Again like

Orwell, Tennant extrapolates from the present a possible picture of the future, but what makes this novel so different from other dystopias is her ingenious fusion of the novel of pessimistic prophecy with an amusing parodistic re-working of the country-house brand of detective fiction. Indeed, the book increasingly focuses on the small group of peculiar, virtually caricature figures who arrive at Woodiscombe Manor to participate in the murder mystery planned by the government as a tourist attraction; the wider social and national issues become more marginal than in *The Time of the Crack.* The result is bizarre comedy, replete with the eccentricities, foibles, and oddities that recur throughout her *oeuvre.*

Eccentricity also pervades the small hotel that provides the setting for *Hotel de Dream,* in which the dreams and fantasies of the few residents, one of whom is a romantic novelist, play a much more important part than the framework of waking reality. Reality itself dissolves into fantasy and vice versa, and the various dreams and fictions merge with one another to create a super-reality of the collective unconscious, in which the dreamers acquire new identities and the romantic novelist's imaginary characters become as real as their creator. While the book is certainly not lacking in the weird humour of her two previous books, and actually abounds in the grotesque, there is a shift away from satirical comedy in favour of psychological fantasy, from a broad perspective to a closed world. Even so, Tennant still provides a tangentially symbolic comment on the "condition of England" issue through her characters and their dream-selves.

In both *The Last of the Country House Murders* and *Hotel de Dream,* Tennant plays self-consciously with novelistic conventions, but in *The Bad Sister* she attempts something much more daring and ambitious—some would say foolhardy. She models the entire book very closely on a literary masterpiece, Hogg's *Confessions of a Justified Sinner.* While setting her novel in the present and locating only part of it in Scotland, she adheres to Hogg's highly original structure, adopts some of the main features of his plot, and retains his embodiment of the Devil, Gil-Martin, though in a peripheral role. However, she does alter the sex of the main characters, the equivalent of the Justified Sinner being Jane Wild and her evil genius being Meg rather than Gil-Martin. This change allows Tennant to introduce the subject of feminism and the contemporary phenomenon of female urban guerrillas, but the main focus is not social or political but psychological—the split personality of Jane under the influence of the obsessional Meg. Like Hogg, Tennant is concerned with human duality, fanaticism, the subjectivity of reality, and the possibility of possession, but she interprets these in a contemporary context, developing the theme of the schizoid nature of modern woman.

If *The Bad Sister* is imaginatively claustrophobic, her two subsequent novels, *Wild Nights* and *Alice Fell,* are even more so, the dividing line between reality and fantasy being increasingly blurred and ambiguous. In *Wild Nights,* for example, the child-narrator presents a vision of the world controlled by the imagination rather than reason, in which magic and enchantment are an integral part of nature. Seasonal symbolism and archetypal images play a vital part, and the action seems timeless and placeless despite being located in postwar Scotland and England. For the most part, the relatively few characters in this closed world are strange, eccentric beings, more mythical than social. *Alice Fell* is strikingly similar to *Wild Nights* in a number of these respects, despite the differences that arise from it being a third-person narration. Tennant sustains the obsessive visionary quality of both novels by brilliant and evocative writing, but she does so at a price. In moving so far from

The Time of the Crack, she sacrifices some of her most attractive qualities as a novelist. Nevertheless, *Alice Fell,* a reworking of the myth of Persephone in terms of contemporary British society in a state of upheaval, is a most ambitious imaginative feat, even if the symbolism and archetypal characterization tend to be too intrusive.

Queen of Stones represents a move away from the cul-de-sac of poetic fiction into which Tennant was in danger of becoming trapped. After *The Time of the Crack,* Tennant's fiction in the 1970s had gradually become more intense, more introspective, and narrower in focus. There was a gain in the sheer virtuosity of her writing, but there was also a loss of the comedy and satire of *The Time of the Crack,* together with its panoramic sweep. Like *The Bad Sister,* *Queen of Stones* has a specific literary model, *Lord of the Flies* (itself an antidote to Ballantyne's *The Coral Island*), but Tennant does not provide such close parallels to Golding's novel as she does to Hogg's in her earlier book.

The most striking resemblance between *Queen of Stones* and *The Bad Sister* is Tennant's use of sex-reversal, substituting females for their male equivalents in her sources. A sponsored walk in Dorset goes terribly wrong when a group of girls are lost in appalling fog; cut off from their normal everyday surroundings and the adult world, like Golding's schoolboys, they create their own imaginative reality involving ritual and sacrifice. Tennant arrives at a conclusion not dissimilar from Golding's. In her next novel, *Woman Beware Woman,* Tennant again investigates the deeper mythic reality behind the appearances of social reality, the subconscious drives that shape reality itself, especially as they manifest themselves in women and their behaviour. The literary roots of *Woman Beware Woman* are less obvious than in *The Bad Sister* and *Queen of Stones,* but the close similarity to the title of Middleton's Jacobean revenge tragedy *Women Beware Women* suggests that Tennant is creating her own highly imaginative equivalent of a drama of thwarted love, resentment, suppressed passion, hatred and revenge as various people assemble in a quiet part of Ireland following the death of a distinguished literary man.

Political undercurrents are present in a number of Tennant's novels, but *Black Marina* is the most explicitly political. The setting is the imaginary island of St. James, adjacent to Grenada in the Caribbean; the time, Christmas Eve 1983, not long after the murderous real-life coup against Maurice Bishop's government in Grenada which precipitated American military intervention. During the day in which the novel is set St. James is expected to be the target of a similar Marxist-Leninist coup by a group of those involved in the attempt to seize power in Grenada. The subject-matter is topical and journalistic, but Tennant's handling of it is characteristically complex and far removed from orthodox social realism. The principal narrator, Holly Baker, an English woman who came to the island in the 1960s and stayed, gradually unfolds in piecemeal fashion the network of human relationships in St. James and England that has eventually precipitated the happenings of Christmas Eve 1983. As usual in Tennant's fiction, mythic elements lie just beneath the contemporary surface, and the title itself, alluding to Shakespeare's *Pericles* (Marina is the King's long-lost daughter) and Eliot's related Ariel poem "Marina," points towards the most important of these, a daughter's quest for her father. Even so, *Black Marina* is something of a new departure for Tennant in setting and theme, and it confirms her ability to go on regenerating herself as a novelist.

The Adventures of Robina, by Herself is a lighter work in picaresque vein, but stylistically it is one of Tennant's most bravura performances, a brilliant display of sustained literary pastiche.

Throughout she imitates the idiom Defoe adopts for his female narrators while wryly adapting it to accommodate her 20th-century concerns. After this "imitation" of Defoe, Tennant began work on something different again, a sequence of novels with the overall title *The Cycle of the Sun* that is intended to explore aspects of aristocratic and bohemian life in England from the 1950s to the 1980s, reflecting the major changes in the country's international role during these decades. So far two of these novels have appeared. In the first, *The House of Hospitalities,* Tennant introduces her central character Jenny going through a crisis of adolescence, while the second, *A Wedding of Cousins,* continues Jenny's confused life story four years later. Although Tennant's approach is essentially comic and satirical, there are elements of sadness and confusion at both social and individual levels. Despite the underlying realism of the sequence, Jenny's frequent inability to distinguish between reality and fantasy gives the novels a pervasive ambiguity typical of Tennant.

In 1989 Tennant published two novels outside the *The Cycle of the Sun* sequence, *Two Women of London: The Strange Case of Ms. Jerkyll and Mrs. Hyde* and *The Magic Drum,* both being crime stories of a characteristically eccentric and gothic kind. The subtitle of *Two Women of London, The Strange Case of Ms. Jekyll and Mrs. Hyde,* indicates that this is another of Tennant's reworkings of famous literary texts. Cast in fabular rather than realistic form, Tennant's tale of rape and murder in West London is a timely feminist adaptation of Robert Louis Stevenson's seminal exploration of the divided self, in which she examines the enormous pressure experienced by women in a violent, competitive society. The divided self she portrays reflects the divisions in a society where poverty and deprivation co-exist with conspicuous consumption and a "loadsamoney" philosophy. The subtext of the novel is highly political. By refurbishing an important Victorian work of fiction, Tennant radically subverts the "Victorian values" advocated by free-market and self-help politicians in the 1980s.

The Magic Drum is set in an isolated country house, Cressley Grange, the home of the cult feminist poet Muriel Cole before her suicide at the age of 32 (the same age as Sylvia Plath, to whom there are parallels and even references). Since Cole's death, her husband, also a famous poet, has turned the house into a shrine to her memory and a place of literary pilgrimage. The Grange has the potential for the kind of closed-world crime story favoured by such Golden Age authors as Agatha Christie, and there is certainly a mystery at the heart of the novel—a murder, too, if the main narrator, Catherine Treger, is to be believed. Yet the status of Catherine's diary entries for her five days of detective work at the Grange is uncertain. Do they provide a reliable, factual account or are they the imaginative outpourings of a disturbed mind? Is she observing reality or creating a "reality" of her own out of the materials of crime and gothic fiction? The ambiguous conclusion does not provide a clear answer. *The Magic Drum* is a teasingly enigmatic book in which Tennant remodels elements of crime fiction to examine the posthumous power exerted by the real-life equivalents of Cole, and to undermine commonsense assumptions about the meaning of "reality."

After *Two Women of London: The Strange Case of Ms. Jekyll and Mrs. Hyde* and *The Magic Drum,* Tennant did not return immediately to *The Cycle of the Sun* but published *Sisters and Strangers,* perhaps her most ambitious attempt to provide a comprehensive survey of the life-lies, contradictions and hypocrisies central to women's lives, both past and present. Although couched in the form of an a historical fable or *A Moral Tale,* as the subtitle puts it,

Sisters and Strangers is, paradoxically, a history of woman. Within a fairy-tale format, Tennant retells the story of Eve in an imaginatively exuberant as well as incisively sardonic manner. The Genesis story is blended with 20th-century reality in a freewheeling, synchronic way that incorporates myth, legend, and fantasy as the narrative surveys the recurring roles offered to women, such as Harlot, Madonna, Courtesan, Bluestocking, and Witch (titles of some of the sections). For all its wit and inventiveness, *Sisters and Strangers* is a disturbing post-feminist analysis of the deceptions and self-deceptions, especially concerning love and romance, by which women are virtually forced to live if they are to survive at all.

—Peter Lewis

THAROOR, Shashi

Nationality: British. **Born:** London, 1956. **Education:** Delhi University, B.A. (with honors) 1975; Tufts University, M.A. 1976; M.A.L.D. 1977; Ph.D. 1978. **Career:** Assistant to the director of external affairs, 1978-79, public information officer, 1980-81, head of Singapore office, 1981-84, senior external affairs officer, 1985-87, executive assistant to the deputy high commissioner, 1987-89, all United Nations High Commissioner for Refugees. Since 1989 special assistant to the undersecretary general for peacekeeping operations, United Nations. **Awards:** Rajika Kripalani Young Journalist award, 1976; Federation of Indian Publishers and *Hindustan Times* Best Book of the Year, 1990, and Commonwealth Writers prize (Eurasian region), 1990, both for *The Great Indian Novel.*

PUBLICATIONS

Novels

The Great Indian Novel. New Delhi, Penguin, London, Viking, and New York, Arcade, 1989.
Show Business. New Delhi, Viking, 1991; New York, Arcade, 1992; London, Picador, 1994.

Short Stories

The Five-Dollar Smile: Fourteen Early Stories and a Farce in Two Acts. New Delhi, Viking, 1990; as *The Five-Dollar Smile and Other Stories,* New York, Arcade, 1993.

Other

Reasons of State: Political Development and India's Foreign Policy Under Indira Ghandi, 1966-1977. New Delhi, Vikas Publishing House, 1982.

*   *   *

Despite living and working overseas (in Switzerland and the United States) for much of his adult life, Shashi Tharoor's writing shares few of the concerns (identity, place, and displacement) that have become the stock-in-trade of writers of the Indian diaspora. His two novels, *The Great Indian Novel* and *Show Business,* and a collection of early stories, *The Five-Dollar Smile: Fourteen Early Stories and a Farce in Two Acts* (published in response to the success of *The Great Indian Novel*), have in common Tharoor's postmodernist interest in playing games with his readers. Indeed his taste for often awful puns and his delight in elaborate wordplay is evident even in the early stories.

The title of Tharoor's first novel, *The Great Indian Novel,* immediately signposts his interest in language games. The title is at once a play on the elusive "great American novel" and a reference to the work which provides the framework of Tharoor's novel, India's greatest epic the *Mahabharata* (which roughly translated means "great India"). In his retelling of modern Indian history and politics, Tharoor explores ground similar to that covered by Salman Rushdie in *Midnight's Children.* Yet though Tharoor's voice is evidently of the post-Rushdie generation of Indian writing in English, it remains distinct. In the novel, figures from the *Mahabharata* are recreated as characters who in turn represent figures from recent Indian history. Thus Bhishma from the *Mahabharata* becomes Ganga Datta (who is also a fictional representation of Mahatma Gandhi) in Tharoor's version of the epic. Similarly, Karna becomes Muhammad Ali Karna in the novel, and a figure who parallels Jinnah from history. And just as all the major figures from recent Indian history are included in Tharoor's novel, so all the major events are recorded too, though at times two or three historical events are condensed into a single fictional one.

But perhaps of even greater importance than the history and politics in this novel is Tharoor's interest in language. Through his many linguistic and literary games—such as the novel's self-reflexivity and the frequent spot-the-allusion games—Tharoor exposes the power of language as a tool of the colonial process while at the same time pointing the reader back to literature. History and politics, the novel seems to suggest, are best understood via literature (the *Mahabharata,* for example). This is a neat conceit which also privileges Tharoor's own text.

In *Show Business,* his second novel, Tharoor casts his satirical eye over Bollywood, India's popular, Bombay-based cinema industry. The novel closely follows the career of Ashok Banjara, an Indian film hero (who despite the mandatory disclaimers is clearly based on India's superstar of the screen, Amitabh Bacchan)—his rise to fame, his marriage to an up-and-coming young heroine, his many affairs, his vast wealth, his flirtation with politics, and so on. Interspersed with Ashok Banjara's own story and ultimately indistinguishable from it are the plots of the various films in which he stars. The novel is at once a comic tale about the Indian film industry, a homily on greed and ambition, and a highly entertaining look at the boundaries between fiction and reality (which in the celluloid world of Bollywood is surely all illusion anyway).

Tharoor's early stories—some of which he wrote as a teenager for Indian mass-circulation periodicals—and a two-act play have been published in *The Five-Dollar Smile.* The stories, which treat such issues as racism ("The Boutique"), hypocrisy ("The Temple Thief"), and gender stereotyping ("City Girl, Village Girl"), show signs of the language skills which Tharoor exploits to such great effect in *The Great Indian Novel.* "Twenty-Two Months in the Life of a Dog" is a short play about abuses of power during Indira Gandhi's Emergency which lacks the satirical and political bite of a novel like Nayantara Sahgal's *Rich Like Us,* which covers the same territory. Tharoor has also written a work of non-fiction, *Reasons of State: Political Development and India's Foreign Policy Under Indira Gandi, 1966-1977,* which examines the making of Indian foreign policy.

While Tharoor's work has so far received scant critical attention, *The Great Indian Novel* alone suggests that he deserves to be considered among the major Indian writers of recent decades.

—Ralph J. Crane

THEROUX, Alexander (Louis)

Nationality: American. **Born:** Medford, Massachusetts, 17 August 1939; brother of Paul Theroux, *q.v.* **Education:** St. Joseph's Seminary, 1960-62; St. Francis College, Biddeford, Maine, B.A. 1964; University of Virginia, Charlottesville (Woodrow Wilson fellow), M.A. 1965, Ph.D. 1968; Brasenose College, Oxford. **Career:** Instructor, University of Virginia, 1968; Fulbright lecturer, University of London, 1968-69; instructor, Longwood College, Farmville, Virginia, 1969-73, and Harvard University, Cambridge, Massachusetts, 1973-78; writer-in-residence, Phillips Academy, Andover, Massachusetts, 1978-83; visiting artist, Massachusetts Institute of Technology, Cambridge, from 1983. Currently member of the Department of English, Yale University, New Haven, Connecticut. **Awards:** National Endowment for the Arts grant, 1966; Academy of American Poets award, 1966; Encyclopaedia Britannica award, 1973; Guggenheim fellowship, 1974. **Address:** Department of English, Yale University, P.O. Box 3545, New Haven, Connecticut 06520, U.S.A.

PUBLICATIONS

Novels

Darconville's Cat. New York, Doubleday, 1981; London, Hamish Hamilton, 1983.
An Adultery. New York, Simon and Schuster, 1987; London, Hamish Hamilton, 1988.

Short Stories

Three Wogs. Boston, Gambit, 1972; London, Chatto and Windus-Wildwood House, 1973.

Uncollected Short Stories

"Fark Pooks," in *Esquire* (New York), August 1973.
"Scugnizzo's Pasta Co.," in *Encounter* (London), September 1974.
"Lynda Van Cats," in *The Pushcart Prize 1,* edited by Bill Henderson. Yonkers, New York, Pushcart Press, 1976.
"Finocchio; or, The Tale of a Man with a Long Nose," in *Massachusetts Review* (Amherst), Summer 1976.

Plays

Christmas Eve at the Gordon Crumms, in *Rapier,* Spring 1968.
The Sweethearts and Chagrin of Roland McGuffey, in *Rapier,* Winter 1968.
The Master's Oral (produced Cambridge, Massachusetts, 1974).
The Confessions of Mrs. Motherwell, in *Rapier,* Autumn 1976.

Poetry

The Lollopop Trollops and Other Poems. Normal, Illinois, Dalkey Archive Press.

Other (for children)

The Great Wheadle Tragedy. Boston, Godine, 1975.
The Schinocephalic Waif. Boston, Godine, 1975.
Master Snickup's Cloak. New York, Harper, and Limpsfield, Surrey, Dragon's World, 1979.

Other

The Primary Colors: Three Essays. New York, Holt. 1994.
Theroux Metaphrastes: An Essay on Literature. Boston, Godine, 1975.

*

Critical Studies: "Alexander Theroux/Paul West Issue" of *Review of Contemporary Fiction* (Elmwood Park, Illinois), Spring 1991.

*   *   *

Unlike his prolific brother Paul, whose travel books and novels supply readers the here and now with journalistic directness, Alexander Theroux is the soul of anachronism, a backwards literary history: unconcerned with modern markets, romantic in sensibility, neo-classical in aesthetic judgments, renaissance in learning and style, medieval in spirit. His line of descent recedes from game-playing Nabokov to the late-Victorian romance writer Baron Corvo, satirists Swift and Sterne, and encyclopedist Thomas Browne. For Theroux, observation of the present, whether the London of *Three Wogs* or the American eastern seaboard of *Darconville's Cat,* is the occasion for, not the purpose of, writing, an activity generated by a long memory of other writing. And yet, despite or, perhaps, because of his hyperliteracy—his esoteric allusions, archaic lexicon, elegant inversions, and orotund voice—the here and now are somehow defamiliarized, his artificial characters made curiously human, by his hermetic eccentricities.

Theroux's first book, *Three Wogs,* collects three long stories, each featuring an immigrant from the Empire clashing with a representative 1960s Londoner. In "Mrs. Proby Gets Hers" a widowed middle-class matron develops a paranoid and ultimately killing fear of an old shopkeeper from Hong Kong. "Childe Roland" exercises a stupid laborer's hatred for an educated Indian student. In "The Wife of God" an epicene Anglican priest selfishly attempts to stop his African choirmaster's marriage. The Britishers' pride and racism mask feelings of inferiority to and envy of the more energetic and even better-mannered "wogs." While Theroux has innocent fun with his foreigners' malapropisms and misinformation, the English are savaged by their own smugly expressed pretensions and by the ironic punishments Theroux gives them at stories' ends. Wholly appropriate for the dilettante Reverend Which Therefore (sic) of "The Wife of God," Theroux's stylistic contrivances sometimes overwhelm their satiric targets in the first two stories, manufacturing sentence to sentence wit but risking a reversal of sympathies for his characters from the present "Age of Shoddy."

Three Wogs was a startling debut, sufficiently noticed to be read by a character in *Darconville's Cat;* but it's this later book that earns Theroux prominent shelfspace in the Library of Literary Ex-

travagance, the "A" range of alphabetical amusements, anomalies, anatomies, and artificial autobiographies. Theroux's predilections struggled within the constraints of the short story; here they are freed to create a 704-page, densely printed story of courtly love gone sour. A crazed character named Crucifer slightly scrambles the novel's strategy and achievement: "Nothing exceeds like excess."

According to an essay on the Theroux family by James Atlas (*New York Times Magazine,* 30 April 1978), Alexander was once engaged to and then jilted by one of his students at Longwood College. He vowed literary revenge, and she said "Do your worst." *Darconville's Cat* is his best and worst, a very funny send-up of young love and a compendium of misogyny in which, says Atlas, Theroux doesn't change the name of the girl who disappointed him. The novel's writer-protagonist, Alaric Darconville, was, like Theroux, in and out of monasteries as a youth and taught at Harvard and a Virginia college for women. But as the very simple plot inches from first meeting through courtship to betrayal and bitterness, the parallels between life and art increasingly feel like literary hoaxing, a way to draw life-minded readers into worlds made of words. Once again, Crucifer seems to speak for Theroux, "Love was the invention of the Provençal knight-poets to justify their verse."

What's best about *Darconville's Cat* is the advantage Theroux takes of the tradition of The Book, the large storehouse of knowledge such as The Bible, *Gargantua,* or *Moby-Dick.* Elaboration is all. The reader who doesn't care for a chapter on college girls' late-night rap sessions or the dialogue in verse between Alaric and his beloved Isabel or a classical oration by Crucifer can skip ahead or back without losing essential continuity. There are learned disquisitions on love, hate, and the human ear; wonderful odd-lot lists; Shandyian japes such as a one-word chapter and a page of asterisks; and Swiftian renderings of small-town southern life, ranting religionists, academic foolery, and much more. The parts are all related but don't disappear into a whole, into an illusion of reality.

Darconville's Cat is boring and brilliant, both puerile and profound, self-indulgent and often cruel. Theroux lacks Thomas Pynchon's interest in this century and the popular humor of Gilbert Sorrentino's *Mulligan Stew,* the novel Theroux's most closely resembles. "Madness," Darconville says of a book very like the one in which he is a character. But like that excessive anomaly of the 1950s, William Gaddis's *The Recognitions, Darconville's Cat* should find a dedicated following, readers with an appetite for ambition and literary aberration, for a prodigal art that, in Darconville's world, "declassifies."

—Thomas LeClair

THEROUX, Paul (Edward)

Nationality: American. **Born:** Medford, Massachusetts, 10 April 1941; brother of Alexander Theroux, *q.v.* **Education:** Medford High School; University of Maine, Orono, 1959-60; University of Massachusetts, Amherst, B.A. in English 1963. **Family:** Married Anne Castle in 1967; two sons. **Career:** Lecturer, University of Urbino, Italy, 1963; Peace Corps lecturer, Soche Hill College, Limbe, Malawi, 1963-65; lecturer, Makerere University, Kampala, Uganda, 1965-68, and University of Singapore, 1968-71; writer-in-residence, University of Virginia, Charlottesville, 1972. **Awards:** *Playboy* award, 1971, 1977, 1979; American Academy award, 1977;

Whitbread award, 1978; *Yorkshire Post* award, 1982; James Tait Black Memorial prize, 1982; Thomas Cook award, for travel book, 1989. D. Litt.: Tufts University, Medford, Massachusetts, 1980; Trinity College, Washington, D.C., 1980; University of Massachusetts, 1988. Fellow, Royal Society of Literature, and Royal Geographical Society. **Member:** American Academy, 1984. **Address:** c/o Hamish Hamilton Ltd., 27 Wright's Lane, London W8 5TZ, England.

PUBLICATIONS

Novels

Waldo. Boston, Houghton Mifflin, 1967; London, Bodley Head, 1968.

Fong and the Indians. Boston, Houghton Mifflin, 1968; London, Hamish Hamilton, 1976.

Girls at Play. Boston, Houghton Mifflin, and London, Bodley Head, 1969.

Murder in Mount Holly. London, Ross, 1969.

Jungle Lovers. Boston, Houghton Mifflin, and London, Bodley Head, 1971.

Saint Jack. London, Bodley Head, and Boston, Houghton Mifflin, 1973.

The Black House. London, Hamish Hamilton, and Boston, Houghton Mifflin, 1974.

The Family Arsenal. London, Hamish Hamilton, and Boston, Houghton Mifflin, 1976.

Picture Palace. London, Hamish Hamilton, and Boston, Houghton Mifflin, 1978.

The Mosquito Coast. London, Hamish Hamilton, 1981; Boston, Houghton Mifflin, 1982.

Doctor Slaughter. London, Hamish Hamilton, 1984.

Half Moon Street: Two Short Novels (includes *Doctor Slaughter* and *Doctor DeMarr*). Boston, Houghton Mifflin, 1984.

O-Zone. London, Hamish Hamilton, and New York, Putnam, 1986.

My Secret History. London, Hamish Hamilton, and New York, Putnam, 1989.

Doctor DeMarr. London, Hutchinson, 1990.

Chicago Loop. London, Hamish Hamilton, 1990; New York, Random House, 1991.

Millroy the Magician. London, Hamish Hamilton, 1993; New York, Random House, 1994.

Short Stories

Sinning with Annie and Other Stories. Boston, Houghton Mifflin, 1972; London, Hamish Hamilton, 1975.

The Consul's File. London, Hamish Hamilton, and Boston, Houghton Mifflin, 1977.

World's End and Other Stories. London, Hamish Hamilton, and Boston, Houghton Mifflin, 1980.

The London Embassy. London, Hamish Hamilton, 1982; Boston, Houghton Mifflin, 1983.

Plays

The Autumn Dog (produced New York, 1981).
The White Man's Burden. London, Hamish Hamilton, 1987.

Screenplay: *Saint Jack,* with Peter Bogdanovich and Howard Sackler, 1979.

Television Play: *The London Embassy,* from his own story, 1987.

Other

V.S. Naipaul: An Introduction to His Work. London, Deutsch, and New York, Africana, 1972.

The Great Railway Bazaar: By Train Through Asia. London, Hamish Hamilton, and Boston, Houghton Mifflin, 1975.

A Christmas Card (for children). London, Hamish Hamilton, and Boston, Houghton Mifflin, 1978.

The Old Patagonian Express: By Train Through the Americas. London, Hamish Hamilton, and Boston, Houghton Mifflin, 1979.

London Snow (for children). Salisbury, Wiltshire, Russell, 1979; Boston, Houghton Mifflin, 1980.

Sailing Through China. Salisbury, Wiltshire, Russell, 1983; Boston, Houghton Mifflin, 1984.

The Kingdom by the Sea: A Journey Around the Coast of Great Britain. London, Hamish Hamilton, and Boston, Houghton Mifflin, 1983.

Sunrise with Seamonsters: Travels and Discoveries 1964-1984. London, Hamish Hamilton, and Boston, Houghton Mifflin, 1985.

The Imperial Way: Making Tracks from Peshawar to Chittagong, photographs by Steve McCurry. London, Hamish Hamilton, and Boston, Houghton Mifflin, 1985.

Patagonia Revisited, with Bruce Chatwin. Salisbury, Wiltshire, Russell, 1985; Boston, Houghton Mifflin, 1986.

The Shortest Day of the Year: A Christmas Fantasy. Leamington, Warwickshire, Sixth Chamber Press, 1986.

Riding the Iron Rooster: By Train Through China. London, Hamish Hamilton, and New York, Putnam, 1988.

Travelling the World. London, Sinclair Stevenson, 1990.

The Happy Isles of Oceania: Paddling the Pacific. London, Hamish Hamilton, and New York, Putnam, 1992.

*

Paul Theroux comments:

(1986) Both in my fiction and non-fiction I have tried to write about the times in which I have lived. Although I have been resident in various countries for the past 25 years, and these countries have been the settings for my books, I consider myself an American writer. I have a strong homing instinct.

*   *   *

Paul Theroux has emerged as a major writer of novels, short fiction, and travel reportage. His fiction ranges over England, America, and many foreign settings, and it focuses on complex relationships between people and places. His travel books (*The Great Railway Bazaar, The Old Patagonia Express, Riding the Iron Rooster*) are vivid, minutely detailed, and ironically elegant. Theroux's fiction reflects the same qualities.

Some of the novels echo Joseph Conrad and V.S. Naipaul, centering on Westerners caught in remote and alien settings—*Girls at Play, Jungle Lovers, Saint Jack,* and the short stories in *The Consul's File.* An important theme is the stranger who can discover himself only in the strangeness of alien society. This appears also in *Fong and the Indians* but is most elaborately developed in

Saint Jack. It recurs in the macabre *The Black House,* in which an Englishman must come home to discover a ghostly "foreigner." It appears in transmuted form in *The Family Arsenal,* in which IRA terrorists (led by an American) are the strangers, and London is the "foreign land." If Jack in *Saint Jack* is a Dostoevskian hoodlum-saint, a pander peddling material salvation, the bombers of *The Family Arsenal* are a parody of close community, offering not love and comfort but violence and death to the unsaved world of London.

Theroux has mastered the art of exact observation and cultivated his memory for sights, voices, and sensations. As Maude Coffin Pratt, the central character in *Picture Palace,* says of her photography: "art should require no instrument but memory, the pleasurable fear of hunching in a dark room and feeling the day's hot beauty lingering in the house." The drama in Theroux's fiction often arises in the complexity of his characters' sensibilities and in the sexual and spiritual desires they are driven to express.

Theroux's novels often revolve around physical violence—revolutions or civil wars in Africa or Asia, terrorism, casual assault—but also involve the violence of suppressed, warped, or mistaken desires. Frustrated desires lead to sadism, which leads inexorably to masochism. The colonialist who beats his servant keeps a closetful of chains and whips to be used on himself. Theroux opens these closets in England and America as well as in Malaysia. Maude Coffin Pratt of *Picture Palace* prepares for a 50-year retrospective photography show and reveals the single image that has warped her life—her thwarted incestuous desire for her brother, who preferred their sister. Alfred Munday of *The Black House* returns from haunted Africa to find a succubus in an English country house.

The Mosquito Coast is a large and important novel on the theme of American ideals and energies, echoing Melville and Twain. It details the suicidal odyssey of a brilliant but crazed inventor, Allie Fox, and his family, who flee an imagined nuclear holocaust to set up an ideal community in the jungles of Honduras. It is a complex meditation on technology, belief, and the values of the 1980s and an arresting study of the basic American character.

In *Half Moon Street* Theroux combines two novellas on the theme of double identity, *Doctor Slaughter* (set in England) and *Doctor DeMarr* (set in the U.S.). The complementary tales recall Poe's "William Wilson" or Conrad's "The Secret Sharer" and other tales of the *doppelgänger* or magic double. Theroux develops the mystery of identity in contrasting ways but shows how self-deception and delusion erode character and lead to final dissolution of the true self.

The characters Theroux depicts most sharply are complexly folded. His fiction shows us the disguises and distractions which shield them from the world. Hood, the sharply observant, ironic American terrorist of *The Family Arsenal,* sees his world turn alien:

> For every one who used the city as an occasion to perform, a thousand chose it as a place of concealment. In its depths bombs were stifled. His own was local, personal, a family matter; it had not been heard here. . . . He had thought the world was his to move in, an extension of his own world. But he had seen it grow unfamiliar, and smaller, and he was not moving at will.

O-Zone is a dystopian complement to *The Mosquito Coast*—a view of North America following environmental apocalypse. It describes an excursion of effete New Yorkers into the proscribed U.S. interior—the Ozarks or "O-Zone"—contaminated by radioactive waste. This world is divided between the heartless, decadent wealthy ("owners") and the suffering poor ("aliens"). The owners live inside hermetic suits and travel over the contaminated wastelands by "rotor." Theroux invents a harsh language, echoing Anthony Burgess's *A Clockwork Orange,* to convey the desperation of his characters. Yet in the end, Fisher (or "Fizzy"), the adolescent genius at the heart of the tale, discovers he is "the new breed, an O-Zonian, a sort of indestructible alien—stronger than any owner."

In *My Secret History,* Theroux constructs a *David Copperfield* for the late 20th century—a fiction that parallels and mirrors Theroux's own life and career but that is still separate and mythical in import. Like Philip Roth's late novels, the work explores paradoxes of autobiography, fiction, art, reporting. It gives him a more personal and immediate voice than in any but his very earliest novels but maintains the distance and objectivity of his fantasies and sociopolitical fictions.

Chicago Loop is a Dostoevskian study in sexual obsession and violence. It harks back to earlier Theroux themes; the idea of photographs as sexual icons in *Picture Palace* and the idea of sexual possession in *The Black House.* However, *Chicago Loop* is highly original, tracing the mental and spiritual disintegration of Parker Jagoda, a highly successful entrepreneur who turns sexual serial killer and ultimately victim of the same crime. The story summarizes the greed, egocentrism and anomie of the 1980s in a parable of the circular logic of greed and disorder.

Theroux's novels are urbane, paradoxical, and often comic. They also probe tragic fractures in the modern world and sensibility, in brightly evocative snapshots of foreign places—at home and abroad.

—William J. Schafer

THOMAS, Audrey (Grace)

Nationality: Canadian citizen. **Born:** Audrey Callahan in Binghamton, New York, 17 November 1935. **Education:** Smith College, Northampton, Massachusetts, B.A. 1957; University of British Columbia, Vancouver, M.A. in English 1963. **Family:** Married Ian Thomas in 1958 (divorced); three daughters. Moved to Canada, 1959; lived in Kumasi, Ghana, 1964-66. **Career:** Since 1990 visiting professor, Concordia University, Montreal. Scottish-Canadian Exchange Fellow, Edinburgh, 1985-86; writer-in-residence, University of Victoria, British Columbia, University of British Columbia, Vancouver, Simon Fraser University, Burnaby, British Columbia, and David Thompson University Centre, Nelson, British Columbia. **Awards:** Atlantic Firsts award, 1965; Canada Council grant, 1969, 1971, 1972, 1974, and Senior Arts grant, 1974, 1977, 1979, 1987, 1991, 1994. Honorary doctorate: Simon Fraser University, 1994; University of British Columbia, 1994. **Address:** R.R. 2, Galiano, British Columbia V0N 1P0, Canada.

PUBLICATIONS

Novels

Mrs. Blood. Indianapolis, Bobbs Merrill, 1967.
Munchmeyer, and Prospero on the Island. Indianapolis, Bobbs Merrill, 1972.
Songs My Mother Taught Me. Indianapolis, Bobbs Merrill, 1973.

Blown Figures. Vancouver, Talonbooks, 1974; New York, Knopf, 1975.

Latakia. Vancouver, Talonbooks, 1979.

Intertidal Life. Toronto, Stoddart, 1984; New York, Beaufort, 1985.

Graven Images. Toronto, Penguin Canada, 1993.

Short Stories

Ten Green Bottles. Indianapolis, Bobbs Merrill, 1967.

Ladies and Escorts. Ottawa, Oberon Press, 1977.

Personal Fictions, with others, edited by Michael Ondaatje. Toronto, Oxford University Press, 1977.

Real Mothers. Vancouver, Talonbooks, 1981.

Two in the Bush and Other Stories. Toronto, McClelland and Stewart, 1981.

Goodbye Harold, Good Luck. Toronto, New York, and London, Viking, 1986.

The Wild Blue Yonder. Toronto, Viking, 1990.

Plays

Radio Plays: *Once Your Submarine Cable Is Gone . . . ,* 1973; *Mrs. Blood,* from her own novel, 1975.

*

Manuscript Collection: National Library of Canada, Ottawa, Ontario.

Critical Studies: "Audrey Thomas Issue" of *Room of One's Own* (Vancouver), vol. 10, no. 3-4, 1986.

Audrey Thomas comments:

I write primarily about women—modern women with their particular dreams, delights, despairs. Also how these women relate to men and the terrible things we do to one another in the name of love. I am also interested in what happens to a person set down in a strange city or country, without a familiar environment, friends, or job to define him, when he must ask serious questions. Madness, too, interests me, and the delicate balance between sanity and madness.

I like to tell a good tale, and at the same time I like to make the reader work. I assume my readers will want to run a bit for their money.

*   *   *

Audrey Thomas has demonstrated in her quasi-autobiographical fictions how small the territory of incident need be for the writer to create a continent of psychological complexity. Such categories as novel, novella, and short story are not easily applied to Thomas's work, for continuities are always present, within and between works. The short stories that form her first book, *Ten Green Bottles,* for example, are very closely inter-related; all of them are told by an unhappy female persona, so in the end the book takes on in one's mind the character of a sequence of psychologically linked incidents. More loosely, the later collections—*Ladies and Escorts, Real Mothers* and *Goodbye Harold, Good Luck*—appear as true organic unities in their representation respectively of the pain and sadness in sexual relations and the reality of generational links.

Similarly, the two novellas published in a single volume, *Munchmeyer* and *Prospero on the Island,* are not in reality separate works. They are linked by the fact that *Munchmeyer* (itself a kind of mirror work in which it is hard to tell what is meant as plot and what is the novelist-hero's fantasizing) is presented as the novel that had been written by Miranda, the narrator in *Prospero on the Island,* and is being discussed by her with "Prospero," an elderly painter friend who lives on the same British Columbian island. And the novels—*Mrs. Blood, Songs My Mother Taught Me, Latakia* and *Intertidal Life*—are in turn constructed within loose frameworks, so that structurally there are considerable resemblances between the groups of inter-related stories and the highly episodic novels.

It soon becomes evident that the structural principle of Thomas's fictions is one in which the psychological patterns take precedence over the aesthetic or self-consciously formal. The experience in them is, in merely physical terms, limited and largely repetitious; it also runs fairly closely parallel to Thomas's own life. She was born and brought up in upstate New York, spent time in England and Ghana, travelled in the Levant and in recent years has been dividing her life between Vancouver and the nearby islands of the Gulf of Georgia, with their mixed population of ageing English expatriates, writers and artists.

In fictional terms it is equally interesting to observe that the central persona of the books appears to be the same, yet treated unchronologically. For example, a middle period book, *Songs My Mother Taught Me,* deals in a rather shapelessly flowing narrative with the childhood memories that already find their place as fleeting recollections in earlier stories. *Mrs. Blood,* which harrowingly evokes a somewhat perilous pregnancy in West Africa, also incorporates the persona's sentimental journeys in England. In the novella *Prospero on the Island* creation and memory meld together with the persona-now-turned novelist reflecting on the creative present to which all these pasts contribute. As in the case of even the novella, *Munchmeyer* (the one item presented as totally fictitious), it is hard to tell when the actuality of the author's life merges into the invented narrative.

An added complication arises from Thomas's acute sense of place, whose expression she has developed from book to book, so that in her more recent novels, *Latakia* and *Intertidal Life,* the evocations of the Levantine background and of the Pacific coast, respectively, become almost as important as the always frustrated and pathetic relationships between human beings.

Perhaps Thomas has been more successful, more *herself* as a writer, in her novellas and stories than in the large fictions, where the intimate facet views she handles so well in her stories tend to resist co-ordination, so that the structure often seems precarious. A recent volume of stories, *The Wild Blue Yonder* presents an interesting view of Thomas at what we must presumably regard as her literary prime. It shows her as having settled down into a rather comfortable pattern, absorbing the postmodernist experimentalism of her earlier days and offering, instead of the unexpected, the reassurance of her unerring sense of style, now splendidly mature.

The stories in *The Wild Blue Yonder,* falling into three categories, provide a kind of anthology of Thomas's fictional preoccupations. Some go back to the old transatlantic pattern so splendidly launched by Henry James, of North American women setting off to find themselves in Europe and discovering something different. Other stories are concerned with the incongruity in a contemporary setting of behaviour patterns left over from the 1960s and the alternate culture. Yet others involve another fringe area of society as ordinary respectable women are forced by circumstances to deal with criminal lodgers and intrusive alcoholic neighbours. The final story, "The Wild Blue Yonder," with its recollection of an American family whose father, mentally damaged by his war experiences, is finally grotesquely killed by the inmates of the lunatic asylum where he takes up work, has strange echoes of Thomas's haunting semi-autobiographical novel, *Songs My Mother Taught Me.* This is a relatively elaborate story, but mostly, Thomas is dealing with simple motifs, small encounters, passing moods, the true fragile material of short fiction.

Constant in Thomas's fiction is the fact of suffering, and an acute awareness of suffering's psychological results—its power to distort our perceptions and our memories. A recurrent situation takes us to the appalling borderland between sanity and madness; on that knife edge of mental anguish appears the terror that haunts all Thomas's fiction. Yet the essential quality of her work does not lie in the nightmare that shadows her psychologically complex characters and loosens their grasp of experience, but rather in the precarious equilibrium between the fear and joy of existence which so intermittently they achieve.

—George Woodcock

THOMAS, D(onald) M(ichael)

Nationality: British. **Born:** Redruth, Cornwall, 27 January 1935. **Education:** Redruth Grammar School; University High School, Melbourne; New College, Oxford, B.A. (honours) in English 1958, M.A. 1961. **Military Service:** Served in the British Army (national service), 1953-54. **Family:** Married twice; two sons and one daughter. **Career:** Teacher, Teignmouth Grammar School, Devon, 1959-63; senior lecturer in English, Hereford College of Education, 1964-78, visiting lecturer in English, Hamline University, St. Paul, Minnesota, 1967; lecturer in Creative Writing, American University, Washington, D.C., 1982. **Awards:** Richard Hillary Memorial prize, 1960; Arts Council award, for translation, 1975, Cholmondeley award, for poetry, 1978; *Guardian*—Gollancz Fantasy Novel prize, 1979; *Los Angeles Times* prize, for novel, 1980; Cheltenham prize, 1981; Silver Pen award, 1982. **Address:** The Coach House, Rashleigh Vale, Truro, Cornwall TR1 1TJ, England.

PUBLICATIONS

Novels

The Flute-Player. London, Gollancz, and New York, Dutton, 1979.
Birthstone. London, Gollancz, 1980.
The White Hotel. London, Gollancz, and New York, Viking Press, 1981.
Russian Nights:
Ararat. London, Gollancz, and New York, Viking Press, 1983.
Swallow. London, Gollancz, and New York, Viking, 1984.
Sphinx. London, Gollancz, 1986; New York, Viking, 1987.
Summit. London, Gollancz, 1987; New York, Viking, 1988.
Lying Together. London, Gollancz, and New York, Viking, 1990.
Flying in to Love. London, Bloomsbury, 1991.
Pictures at an Exhibition. London, Bloomsbury, 1993.
Eating Pavlova. London, Bloomsbury, 1994.

Uncollected Short Stories

"Seeking a Suitable Donor," in *The New SF,* edited by Langdon Jones. London, Hutchinson, 1969.
"Labyrinth," in *New Worlds* (London), April 1969.

Plays

The White Hotel, adaptation of his own novel (produced Edinburgh, 1984).
Boris Godunov, adaptation of the play by Pushkin (broadcast 1984). Leamington, Warwickshire, Sixth Chamber Press, 1985.

Radio Plays: *You Will Hear Thunder,* 1981; *Boris Godunov,* 1984.

Poetry

Personal and Possessive. London, Outposts, 1964.
Penguin Modern Poets 11, with D.M. Black and Peter Redgrove. London, Penguin, 1968.
Two Voices. London, Cape Goliard Press, and New York, Grossman, 1968.
The Lover's Horoscope: Kinetic Poem. Laramie, Wyoming, Purple Sage, 1970.
Logan Stone. London, Cape Goliard Press, and New York, Grossman, 1971.
The Shaft. Gillingham, Kent, Arc, 1973.
Lilith-Prints. Cardiff, Second Aeon, 1974.
Symphony in Moscow. Richmond, Surrey, Keepsake Press, 1974.
Love and Other Deaths. London, Elek, 1975.
The Rock. Knotting, Bedfordshire, Sceptre Press, 1975.
Orpheus in Hell. Knotting, Bedfordshire, Sceptre Press, 1977.
The Honeymoon Voyage. London, Secker and Warburg, 1978.
Protest: A Poem after a Medieval Armenian Poem by Frik. Privately printed, 1980.
Dreaming in Bronze. London, Secker and Warburg, 1981.
Selected Poems. London, Secker and Warburg, and New York, Viking Press, 1983.
News from the Front, with Sylvia Kantaris. Todmorden, Lancashire, Arc, 1983.
The Puberty Tree, New & Selected Poems. Newcastle upon Tyne, Bloodaxe, 1992.

Other

The Devil and the Floral Dance (for children). London, Robson, 1978.
Memories and Hallucinations: An Autobiographical Excursion. London, Gollancz, and New York, Viking, 1988.

Editor, *The Granite Kingdom: Poems of Cornwall.* Truro, Cornwall, Barton, 1970.
Editor, *Poetry in Crosslight.* London, Longman, 1975.
Editor, *Songs from the Earth: Selected Poems of John Harris, Cornish Miner, 1820-84.* Padstow, Cornwall, Lodenek Press, 1977.

Translator, *Requiem, and Poem Without a Hero,* by Anna Akhmatova. London, Elek, and Athens, Ohio University Press, 1979.
Translator, *Way of All the Earth,* by Anna Akhmatova. London, Secker and Warburg, and Athens, Ohio University Press, 1979.

Translator, *Invisible Threads,* by Evtushenko. New York, Macmillan, 1981.

Translator, *The Bronze Horseman and Other Poems,* by Pushkin. London, Secker and Warburg, and New York, Viking Press, 1982.

Translator, *A Dove in Santiago,* by Evtushenko. London, Secker and Warburg, 1982; New York, Viking Press, 1983.

Translator, *You Will Hear Thunder: Poems,* by Anna Akhmatova. London, Secker and Warburg, and Athens, Ohio University Press-Swallow Press, 1985; as *Selected Poems,* London, Penguin, 1988.

*

Manuscript Collection: University of Michigan, Ann Arbor.

*   *   *

D.M. Thomas began his writing career as a poet, and his early work in this medium was notable for the way it ranged across the heights of the fantasy worlds of science fiction and the stocking-topped suspender-belt of sensuality. Both of these clearly demonstrated Thomas's obvious narrative ability and his gifts for imaginative fantasy which have been developed and extended in his novels, and it is not surprising that eventually the poet and the novelist came together in his later writing.

Thomas's first novel, *The Flute-Player,* is set in an unnamed city of chaos. There are strong suggestions it is in Russia, and the dedication of the book to the Russian poets Mandlestam, Pasternak, Akhmatova, and Tsvetayeva tends to underline this, as do the glimpses of Leningrad which appear from time to time. But the city is deliberately undefined and left mysteriously so. Indeed, it would not be out of place in one of Thomas's science-fiction narratives. It is an amalgam of cities which Thomas populates with his own imagined phantasmagoria, the chief of which is Elena, the flute-player, who embodies the persecuted creative spirit which is endangered and threatened with destruction by the city's totalitarian regime. The purport of the dedication can now be seen. But in a sense Thomas is too successful in depicting the chaos of the city with its plethora of characters, fast-moving incidents, and changes of mood, in that the theme of the novel itself becomes obscured while Thomas's fecund imagination is always in danger of going over the top. It is as if the engine of Thomas's powerful imagination has not quite engaged with the vehicle it is to drive, as if it is running de-clutched and that all the time Thomas is searching for a theme with which his creative energies can mesh. He found this theme in *The White Hotel.*

The terrain of *The White Hotel* is that of hysteria. On the title page Thomas quotes from W.B. Yeats's "Meditations in Time of Civil War": "We have fed the heart on fantasies," which could be a description of Thomas's earlier novels; now the fantasies were to be the theme of the novel itself. It was a daring enough enterprise to enter the world of hysteria; to begin the novel with an extended poem, "Don Giovanni," in which Lisa Erdman, an imagined patient of Sigmund Freud, expresses her hysterical sexual fantasies in all their exaggerated and crudely masochistic sensuality was daring indeed: "Am I too sexual? I sometimes think/I am obsessed by it, — ." Had Thomas gone over the top this time in a self-indulgent orgy of sexual fantasy? It could well have daunted and proved an initial obstacle to anyone coming to Thomas's writing for the first time. But the poem is followed by Thomas at his narrative best,

with brilliant displays of his remarkable skills in pastiche when he catches convincingly the tenor and style of Freud's case studies. For sheer skill in writing the book is remarkable in itself; but there are a human warmth and concern informing *The White Hotel* which distinguish it from the earlier novels. In those it was as if Thomas's penchant for fantasy had distanced him from his characters. In *The White Hotel,* because he is writing of the fantasies of others, he is able to empathize the better with his characters.

This is evident especially in the Babi Yar sequence towards the end of *The White Hotel,* which while relying heavily on Anatoli Kuznetsov's book of that name for the factual information, is informed by Thomas's own imaginative response: "The soul of man is a far country, which cannot be approached or explored. Most of the dead were poor and illiterate. But every single one of them had dreamed dreams, seen visions and had amazing experiences. — If a Sigmund Freud had been listening and taking notes from the time of Adam, he would still not fully have explored even a single group, even a single person." And it is to the horrors of Babi Yar to which the novel relentlessly progresses, and it is its theme. The hysteria of Lisa Erdman, with its perverted masochistic brutality, is paralleled by the perverted mass hysteria of a world in which a Babi Yar can take place. Thus *The White Hotel* moves from a particular to the general in a convincing, overwhelmingly forceful way.

Following *The White Hotel* Thomas published *Ararat* and *Swallow,* which return to his imagined world of free-wheeling fantasy. In both novels there are involved a number of "improvisatores." In *Swallow* there is an actual Olympiad of these extempore storytellers whose rhyming narratives take up a large proportion of the novel: so we see Thomas the poet and Thomas the novelist. All the improvisatores' stories in *Swallow* are paralleled in their own lives and those of the people they encounter. So the reader is never quite sure, nor is meant to be sure, where the frontiers of reality and fantasy lie, if indeed there are any frontiers. Which comes first, the fiction or the actuality? Or are they, in fact, both fictions where we cannot be sure if life is imitating art or vice versa. It is all brilliantly done and there are some fine narrative passages; but it tends towards an abstract juggling and juxtapositioning of ideas and themes which distances itself from the direct and telling humanity we encounter in *The White Hotel.* This is emphasised when in *Swallow* Thomas includes episodes from his own childhood; while they are ingeniously interlaced with adapted passages from *King Solomon's Mines,* the episodes themselves stand out from the rest of the novel because of their warmth and human feeling. It is as if Thomas's remarkable gifts are beginning to mesh again and that he could be working towards another novel as humanly relevant as *The White Hotel.*

But the feeling engendered by the novels that have followed *Ararat* and *Swallow* is that Thomas's novels seem to be feeding off themselves, that they are breeding novels, that we are witnessing some sort of literary binary fission, or what follows is an extension of what has gone before. They are so much part of each other, sharing characters, plots and the theme of the "improvisatores." *Sphinx* was followed by *Summit,* which seemed to be a break away from all this. *Summit* is, we are told, in the ancient tradition of a serious trilogy being succeeded by a farcical or satirical coda. So in the antics of a thinly disguised President O'Rielly and a Russian Grobichov we have a couple of lampooning caricatures on the "Spitting Image" level. The novel is in fact an extended joke based mainly on O'Rielly's mental difficulties such as a delayed ratiocination that finds him answering a question at least one before the question actually being asked. It is amusing, but wears a bit thin as it goes on. Extended jokes are always very difficult to sustain.

Then having rounded off his trilogy/quartet in such a traditional manner, we find Thomas follows it with *Lying Together,* and the quartet becomes a quintet! The characters of the earlier books meet up at a writers' conference and they take up their roles as "improvisatories" once again. *Lying Together* has been described as "pure satire/poetic fantasy/autobiography and dirty book" all in one. Certainly there is difficulty in deciding what it is. For it is a book in which even more than in its predecessors it is difficult to sort reality from fantasy. Thomas himself is again a character in the book, so we must assume him as true, and we are aware from time to time that what we are reading are the improvisations of the other characters in the book, though often the improvisations sound more "realistic" than the characters who invent them. When one of the main "actual" characters is a lustful menstruating blind film producer who spends a deal of time groping about on the carpet for lost tampons she has removed to accommodate her lover, the frontier between reality and fantasy begins to melt before our eyes. If the purpose of the book is to demonstrate that madness in which reality and fantasy are confused, well one could say it succeeds. Though it leaves one with a sneaking feeling that it is a shade self indulgent, a lubricious going over the top.

—John Cotton

THUBRON, Colin (Gerald Dryden)

Nationality: British. **Born:** London, 14 June 1939. **Education:** Eton College, Berkshire, 1953-57. **Career:** Editorial assistant, Hutchinson, publishers, London, 1959-62; production editor, Macmillan, publishers, New York, 1964-65; since 1965 freelance documentary filmmaker and writer. **Awards:** PEN award, 1985; Thomas Cook award, for travel book, 1988; Hawthornden prize, 1989. **Agent:** Gillon Aitken and Stone, 29 Fernshaw Road, London SW10 0TG. **Address:** Garden Cottage, 27 St. Ann's Villas, London W11 4RT, England.

PUBLICATIONS

Novels

The God in the Mountain. London, Heinemann, and New York, Norton, 1977.
Emperor. London, Heinemann, 1978.
A Cruel Madness. London, Heinemann, 1984; New York, Atlantic Monthly Press, 1985.
Falling. London, Heinemann, 1989; New York, Atlantic Monthly Press, 1990.
Turning Back the Sun. London, Heinemann, 1991.

Uncollected Short Stories

"Nothing Has Changed," in *Firebird 4,* edited by R. Robertson. London, Penguin, 1985.
"The Ear," in *Foreign Exchange,* edited by Julian Evans. London, Sphere, 1985.

Plays

Radio Plays: *Emperor,* from his own novel, 1989; *A Cruel Madness,* from his own novel, 1991.

Other

Mirror to Damascus. London, Heinemann, 1967; Boston, Little Brown, 1968.
The Hills of Adonis: A Quest in Lebanon. London, Heinemann, 1968; Boston, Little Brown, 1969.
Jerusalem, photographs by Alistair Duncan. London, Heinemann, and Boston, Little Brown, 1969.
Journey into Cyprus. London, Heinemann, 1975.
Istanbul, with others. Amsterdam, Time-Life, 1978.
The Venetians, with others. Alexandria, Virginia, Time-Life, 1980.
The Ancient Mariners, with others. Alexandria, Virginia, Time-Life, 1981.
The Royal Opera House Covent Garden, photographs by Clive Boursnell. London, Hamish Hamilton, 1982.
Among the Russians. London, Heinemann, 1983; as *Where the Nights Are Longest: Travels by Car Through Western Russia.* New York, Random House, 1984.
Behind the Wall: A Journey Through China. London, Heinemann, 1987; New York, Atlantic Monthly Press, 1988.
The Silk Road China: Beyond the Celestial Kingdom. London, Pyramid, 1989.
The Lost Heart of Asia. London, Heinemann, and New York, HarperCollins, 1994.

*

Colin Thubron comments:

My work as a novelist arises less from a fascination with plot or even character, than with the exploration of areas of experience which are distressing or (to me) unresolved. Hence the novels revolve around loss of religious faith, pain of love, enigma of memory; the gulf between ideal and reality.

*   *   *

Colin Thubron is well known as a travel writer but enjoys a growing reputation as a novelist. Thubron himself has stressed the distinction between his travel books, which focus away from himself on exterior landscapes, and the novels, which explore the strange interior landscape of the self. However, the novels are also intense love stories mainly ending in death. In three of them, the male protagonist kills the woman he loves most, though in widely differing circumstances. Part of the movement of the second novel, *Emperor* (it is set on a journey) is the Empress Fausta's realization that her husband will kill her and we are told in a postscript that this eventually happens. In *A Cruel Madness,* the man kills literally to touch his lover's heart, and *Falling* meditates about the mercy killing of a paralysed trapeze artist, Clara, by her lover, Mark.

Thubron claims retarded adolescence for his passive male heroes. The most deranged of the three, Daniel of *A Cruel Madness,* says he gives "a plausible imitation of masculinity," and even Constantine, the *Emperor,* conquers while feeling unable to control his wife, his emotions, and his religion. This so called "immaturity" is Thubron's Romanticism, predominant in both his fiction and travel writing—a quest for something he says he knows intellectually is not there.

In the novels, the quest is contained within a love affair, pursuing a woman who tends to be idealized and who has an inaccessible part: a region the male hero cannot enter. The resulting frustration is most evidently dangerous in *A Cruel Madness,* set in a mental hospital. We become increasingly aware of the narrator's fantasy world, blamed on the shadowy Sophia, who closed herself to him. The same motif occurs in a simpler form in *The God in the Mountain:* Julian missed the early passionate surrender of Ekaterina because he was too immature to give himself to their relationship. Returning after many years, he finds her unhappily married, with that part of her closed to him, and unable to give herself fully now that he is ready. Fausta, in *Emperor,* is remote and cannot love her husband, perhaps through damage in childhood. A profound and continuing dependence is demonstrated between them, even though she realizes it will end in her death. *Falling* is a study in loving two women, and Mark the narrator finds parts of both unreachable. He comes to need most the most independent Clara, who is culturally furthest from him (in the circus) and who chooses to leave him (in death): "She acknowledged a human separateness which I never deeply accepted."

Thubron's novels exhibit a tension between an intellectual unbeliever and a romantic quest for perfect fulfillment in love or in God. This duality influences the novel's structure as the plots increase the tension to a moment of tragic action (Julian goes to the mountain, Clara falls, Daniel strikes, Constantine has a vision) and then a release at the end, usually in death, where Romantic and "realist" are resolved. Thubron experiments with narrative forms, notably in *Emperor* with multiple narration from the journals, diaries, and letters of the major characters. Some accounts are omitted, ostensibly "lost," "damaged by rain" etc., so what we have is an artful selection by the author disguised as historical chance.

This carefully arranged yet apparently wandering text is reinterpreted in *A Cruel Madness* and *Falling.* The former is narrated by a wandering mind but the novel is effectively organised to release significant information to the reader. *Falling* is similar, except that Mark is not mad but remembering in prison, and there is also the governing metaphor of the Fall. Clara, the swallow, falls literally, and disastrously because she won't use a safety net. Katherine makes a stained glass window of the Fall from heaven and all three fall in love, unsafely. *Turning Back The Sun* may offer hope in the romantic quest in sexual terms if not in the encounter with other cultures. Set in an unnamed colonial country, Rayner, a doctor, is exiled to a frontier town where "savages" roam, dangerous but also vulnerable. Romantically longing for his childhood home, "the Capital," he loves Zoe, another of Thubron's heroines desired for their separateness, their intense selves. Rayner, unusually, avoids tragedy when he treats the demonized savages but cannot cure a mysterious skin disease blackening the white colonists. After repression and torture, a massacre of savages is averted when Rayner's army patrol witness their religious attempt to "turn back the sun" to restore an Eden before sin and death. Rayner is able to stay with Zoe but the novel's colonial themes are tentatively mapped rather than thoroughly explored. Yet this novel is characteristic of Thubron's work in its longing for intensity, beyond the well-trodden margins of safety.

—S. A. Rowland

TINDALL, Gillian (Elizabeth)

Nationality: British. **Born:** London, 4 May 1938. **Education:** Lady Margaret Hall, Oxford, B.A. (honours) in English, M.A. 1959. **Family:** Married Richard G. Lansdown in 1963; one son. **Career:** Freelance journalist since 1960. **Awards:** Mary Elgin prize, 1970; Maugham award, 1972. **Agent:** Curtis Brown, 28-29 Haymarket, London SW1Y 4SP, England.

PUBLICATIONS

Novels

No Name in the Street. London, Cassell, 1959; as *When We Had Other Names,* New York, Morrow, 1960.
The Water and the Sound. London, Cassell, 1961; New York, Morrow, 1962.
The Edge of the Paper. London, Cassell, 1963.
The Youngest. London, Secker and Warburg, 1967; New York, Walker, 1968.
Someone Else. London, Hodder and Stoughton, and New York, Walker, 1969.
Fly Away Home. London, Hodder and Stoughton, and New York, Walker, 1971.
The Traveller and His Child. London, Hodder and Stoughton, 1975.
The Intruder. London, Hodder and Stoughton, 1979.
Looking Forward. London, Hodder and Stoughton, 1983; New York, Arbor House, 1985.
To the City. London, Hutchinson, 1987.
Give Them All My Love. London, Hutchinson, 1989.
Spirit Weddings. London, Hutchinson, 1992.

Short Stories

Dances of Death: Short Stories on a Theme. London, Hodder and Stoughton, and New York, Walker, 1973.
The China Egg and Other Stories. London, Hodder and Stoughton, 1981.
Journey of a Lifetime and Other Stories. London, Hutchinson, 1990.

Play

Radio Play: *A Little Touch of Death,* 1985.

Other

A Handbook on Witches. London, Barker, 1965; New York, Atheneum, 1966.
The Born: Exile: George Gissing. London, Temple Smith, and New York, Harcourt Brace, 1974.
The Fields Beneath: The History of One London Village. London, Temple Smith, 1977.
City of Gold: A Biography of Bombay. London, Temple Smith, 1982; New York, Penguin, 1992.
Rosamond Lehmann: An Appreciation. London, Chatto and Windus, 1985.
Countries of the Mind: The Meaning of Place to Writers. London, Hogarth Press, 1991.

Célestine: Voices from a French Village. London, Sinclair Stevenson, 1995.

*   *   *

Gillian Tindall's first novel, *No Name in the Street,* was published soon after she graduated from Oxford, and its heroine, Jane, is 19 years old. However, it was not just another autobiographical first novel about teenagers, jazz, and ennui. Though concerned with bohemian life on the Left Bank in Paris, it is written in a lucid and formal prose, and the novel is straightforward, if unexpected in its movement and denouement.

Jane is a half-French visitor from England who falls in love with Vincent Lebert, a painter much older than herself. She lives happily with him till she discovers that Vincent is having a homosexual affair with an English boy, and finds herself pregnant. Up to this point, the novel is merely pleasant, chiefly because of its somewhat naive, but innocent and thorough, romanticism; from this point on, it develops a dramatic power which Tindall handles with striking maturity and dexterity. The contrast between the everyday materials she chooses to use, and the depth of the uses to which she puts them, marks all of Tindall's most successful work.

Her second novel, *The Water and the Sound,* is also about a young girl, Nadia, and about Bohemian life in Paris. Nadia hopes to find out the truth about her parents, both of whom died young. She has been told that her father was a poetic genius, wild in his private life; and that her mother had misguidedly attempted to save him from himself, having loved him so much that she had committed suicide the day after he died. Nadia interviews every person she can find who had known her parents: friends, enemies, literary critics, servants, doctors, gossips, all. Tindall's sketches of these people are memorable, and her allusive descriptions bring the atmosphere of Paris, with its night clubs and trendies, to vivid life. There is nothing notable about the story itself: it is interesting because of Tindall's delineation of her characters, her compassionate insight into their psychology. She masters her wealth of material by the sheer quality of her writing, welding together the similar but historically separate worlds of Nadia and her parents with unhurried aplomb.

The Youngest, too, is a kind of psychological detective story of the soul. Elizabeth, intelligent, sensitive, educated, articulate, gives birth to a deformed baby, whom she smothers. Tindall's novel explores the question of what sort of woman Elizabeth is. Increasingly disturbed, Elizabeth undergoes a hard journey of self-discovery, realizing that her response to her deformed baby has typified her response to life as a whole: she has consistently rejected her responsibility towards others in her absorption with herself and her towering effort to become "independent," and she has, without earlier realizing it or putting it in these terms, actually sacrificed her mother, sister, and husband to her own views and desires. Written in the mid-1960s, this implicit condemnation of the attitudes of the "me-generation" was highly unusual in the fiction of the time, and remains unusual in contemporary fiction. Possibly for this reason, the virtues of this novel were not as widely appreciated as they might have been. Tindall has always been keen to use symbolism, but it had not been wholly integrated into her earlier novels; here, however, the deformed baby provides a powerful symbol of Elizabeth herself, with her own character and actions triggering her self-discovery. The book was variously received; some people perceived it as a complex and insightful work, her best book so far; others thought of it as "intelligent but limited," as failing to subjugate a social problem to the art of fiction, and as a fictionalised documentary rather than a novel.

In *Fly Away Home* Antonia is a fairly sensitive, but not particularly intelligent woman nearing 30 and going through an emotional crisis. She is married to Marc, a well-to-do and thoroughly assimilated Parisian Jew; her two daughters are growing up and needing her less than they did. We share Antonia's journey of self-discovery through the diary she keeps from 1966 to 1968. This diary is one of Tindall's best achievements, revealing the pattern of Antonia's life with something of the surprising-but-inevitable quality of reality. Events that are outwardly dramatic (deaths, births, violent quarrels) rub shoulders with more internal, emotional dramas "which prepare themselves for years and then are abruptly revealed." Antonia is excited by the Israeli victories, and she cannot understand why Marc remains unelated, putting it down to his Jewish fear of involvement. However, when students take over the Sorbonne, Marc's youthful revolutionary romanticism is stirred and he does become enthusiastically involved; Antonia, on the other hand, finds herself unmoved by the excitement of the times, perceiving the events as obscure and senseless. Such moments come rarely in fiction, moments in which people who think they know each other discover, by their unexpected reactions to events, how little they know each other in reality. Such moments occur repeatedly in this novel — for example, in the different way that people regard Marc's brother Jean-Luc after his accidental death in Israel; or in Antonia's deepening understanding of her mother whom she had earlier regarded as a typical do-gooder, always rushing after the latest thing which might be considered progressive, without her activities actually making much positive impact; or in the change in Marc's attitude to his parents, from dutiful politeness to anger when they condemn the students as gangsters or, worse, as anarchists. Like all of Tindall's best novels, this is moving and tender in its portrayal of human relationships, exquisitely written, and packed with insights. These qualities are even more in evidence in the short stories in *Dances of Death: Short Stories on a Theme* and *The China Egg and Other Stories.*

The Traveller and His Child concerns the unusual theme of the paternal instinct. Robert, divorced by his appalling American wife for his inability to adjust to her orgasmic sexuality, finds that he misses his son Robbie terribly; so much, in fact, that he decides to kidnap another boy, the seven-year-old son of old friends. This is apparently done on impulse, though Tindall shows how his character and situation have been leading up to this moment through the years of his miserable childhood and unfortunate marriage. Robert's longing for his own son, now in America, and the way in which that unexpressed love and longing are focused on the boy, Pip, are convincingly narrated. In showing us Robert's heart, Tindall is showing us too the heart of the woman who steals someone else's baby from a pram. Robert is selfish as much as he is self-deceived but, on a desperate journey through France with the boy, he experiences fear and shame, and slowly gains insight. He realizes that he has caused overwhelming anguish, and that he has caused this anguish to people who have trusted him and for whom he cares. He sees that his action is unforgivable. Yet, miraculously, he is forgiven, by the child, by his friends, and — it is hinted — by himself.

In *Looking Forward* Tindall's protagonist is a childless gynaecologist concerned with finding ways of overcoming infertility; and the book typifies the qualities of Tindall's less successful novels. The infertility is emblematic of the book itself: good intentions struggle against creative deficiency. Earnest, professional, and well researched, it lacks the germ of imaginative vitality which might be warmed to life by Tindall's brooding. This is partly due to an over-concern with formal cleverness. The characters — families and friends whose careers are charted through the first seven decades of this century — are relatively inert, but arranged in tableaux characteristic of the various periods in which the narrative is set.

What really interests Tindall and brings her characters to life are the emotional cores of people. Where she is content to let her heart lead her, Tindall's work comes alive; where she allows her considerable intellectual gifts too much play, she has not yet shown that she can embody her strong and subtle moral sense to produce impressive fictional work. This is not to deride her intellectual gifts, which are best evidenced by her non-fictional books. In all her books she has a highly accomplished style, and her fictional examination of current shibboleths is cool and penetrating. Unpretentious and unusual, she has an impeccable sense of the nuances of life.

—Prabhu S. Guptara

TINNISWOOD, Peter

Nationality: British. **Born:** Liverpool, 21 December 1936. **Education:** Sale County Grammar School, 1947-54; University of Manchester, 1954-57, B.A. 1957. **Family:** Married 1) in 1966, three children; 2) Liz Goulding, 1980. **Career:** Insurance clerk, Vienna, 1957; journalist, Sheffield *Star,* 1958-63, Thomson newspapers, London, 1964-65, Cardiff *Western Mail,* 1966-69, and Liverpool *Echo,* 1967. **Awards:** Authors Club award, 1969; Winifred Holtby prize, 1974; Welsh Arts Council bursary, 1974, and prize, 1975; Sony Radio award, 1988, for play; Writers' Guild Best Radio Comedy of the Year, 1991. Fellow, Royal Society of Literature, 1974. **Agent:** Jonathan Clowes Ltd., Iron Bridge House, Bridge Approach, London NW1 8BD, England.

PUBLICATIONS

Novels

A Touch of Daniel. London, Hodder and Stoughton, and New York, Doubleday, 1969.
Mog. London, Hodder and Stoughton, 1970.
I Didn't Know You Cared. London, Hodder and Stoughton, 1973.
Except You're a Bird. London, Hodder and Stoughton, 1974.
The Stirk of Stirk. London, Macmillan, 1974.
Shemerelda. London, Hodder and Stoughton, 1981.
The Home Front (novelization of TV series). London, Granada, 1982.
The Brigadier Down Under. London, Macmillan, 1983.
The Brigadier in Season. London, Macmillan, 1984.
The Brigadier's Brief Lives. London, Pan, 1984.
Call It a Canary. London, Macmillan, 1985.
The Brigadier's Tour. London, Pan, 1985.
Uncle Mort's North Country. London, Pavilion-Joseph, 1986.
Hayballs. London, Hutchinson, 1989.
Uncle Mort's South Country. London, Arrow, 1990.
Winston. London, Hutchinson, 1991.

Short Stories

Collected Tales from a Long Room. London, Hutchinson, 1982.
    Tales from a Long Room. London, Arrow, 1981.
    More Tales from a Long Room. London, Arrow, 1982.
Tales from Witney Scrotum. London, Pavilion-Joseph, 1987.

Uncollected Short Story

"Summer, New York, 1978—That's All," in *The After Midnight Ghost Book,* edited by James Hale. London, Hutchinson, 1980; New York, Watts, 1981.

Plays

The Investiture (produced Bristol, 1971).
Wilfred (produced London, 1979).
The Day the War Broke Out (produced London, 1981).
You Should See Us Now (produced Scarborough, 1981; London, 1983). London, French, 1983.
Steafel Variations (songs and sketches), with Keith Waterhouse and Dick Vosburgh (produced London, 1982).
At the End of the Day (produced Scarborough, 1984).
The Village Fete (broadcast 1987; produced Scarborough, 1991).
Napoli Milionaria, adaptation of the play by Eduardo De Filippo (produced London, 1991).

Radio Plays and Features: *Hardluck Hall* series, with David Nobbs, 1964; *Sam's Wedding,* 1973; *The Bargeman's Comfort,* 1977; *A Touch of Daniel,* from his own novel, 1977; *The Umpire's Thoughts Regarding a Certain Murder,* 1979; *Jake and Myself,* 1979; *The Siege,* 1979; *A Gifted Child,* 1980; *Home Again* series, 1980; *An Occasional Day,* 1981; *Crossing the Frontier,* 1985; *The Village Fete,* 1987; *M.C.C.: The Fully Harmonious and Totally Unauthorised History,* 1987; *Winston* series, 1989-91; *A Small Union,* 1989; *Call It a Canary,* 1989; *The Sitters,* 1990; *I Always Take Long Walks,* 1991; *Two into Two,* 1992; *The Governor's Consory,* 1993; *Tales from the Brigadoon,* 1993; *Uncle Mot's Celtic Fringe,* 1994.

Television Plays and Features: scripts for *That Was the Week That Was* and *Not So Much a Programme* series, with David Nobbs; *Lance at Large* series, with David Nobbs, 1964; *The Signal Box of Grandpa Hudson,* with David Nobbs, 1966; *Never Say Die* series, 1970; *The Rule Book,* 1971; *The Diaries of Stoker Leishman,* 1972; *I Didn't Know You Cared,* 4 series, 1975-79; *Tales from a Long Room* series, 1980; *More Tales from a Long Room* series, 1982; *A Gifted Adult* and *At the Grammar* (*The Home Front* series), 1983; *South of the Border,* 1985; *Tinniswood's North Country,* 1987; *Uncle Mort's North Country* series, 1987-88; *Can You Hear Me, Mother?,* 1988; *Tinniswood Country,* 1989.

*

Critical Study: In *New Review* (London), November 1974.

Peter Tinniswood comments:
    I write very short sentences.
    And very short paragraphs.
    I try to make people laugh. I am a very serious writer, who has a gloomily optimistic outlook on life.

My books about the Brandon family contain all the above qualities.

* * *

Peter Tinniswood is a journalist, a television-script writer, and the author of a large number of popular novels and short stories. He is predominantly a highly skilled craftsman and his style reflects both his professional background and his own self-confessed northern English temperament. His works tend to be set in the north of England, thematically dependent on the northern ethos, informed by the happy morbidity of the stock comic conventions of the north, and filled with stock northern characters. Tinniswood is a great creator of the memorable character.

Many of Tinniswood's novels are continuations of the same characters. The Brigadier is the acerbic narrator of *Collected Tales from a Long Room, Tales from Witney Scrotum,* and all of those works bearing his name. He leaps from the pages bristling with the kind of prejudice which can only stem from a military background coupled with the thoroughly English belief that the game of cricket is the only proper foundation for all social, sexual, moral, and intellectual judgments. Since the ultimate test for such a mind lies not with the conquering of the Antarctic, with war, with art, nor yet with Margaret Thatcher's Britain, but takes place between Lancashire and Yorkshire every summer, a comic perspective is created for what might otherwise be considered serious. Similarly, in Tinniswood's work, the more working-class prejudices of the Brandon family form a comic filter through which the changing face of the north of England in recent decades can be viewed.

A Touch of Daniel, I Didn't Know You Cared and *Except You're a Bird,* all novels which feature the Brandon family, are potentially the most seriously comic of Tinniswood's novels and perhaps the most intrinsically northern. Les and Annie, Uncle Mort, who is Annie's brother, Carter, Les and Annie's son, and Pat, Carter's girlfriend and later his wife are all stock northern characters. The women feed the men on Yorkshire puddings, treacle tart, and porridge with brown sugar. They keep their blood clear with sulfur tablets, their bowels free with Gregory powder, their complexions clear with bile beans, and colds at bay with daily doses of halibut oil, wheat germ oil, cod-liver oil and Virol. The men wait for the women to serve their food and grumble. "Isn't it rum the way women think catering's the way to a man's heart?" says Uncle Mort. "I don't like these onions" says Les, "They make me sweat." Carter, of the second generation, flirts with the idea of running away and freedom, as he flirts with the idea of sexuality with the voluptuous Linda Preston, but ultimately he wants neither: ". . . I don't want to run away. I want to stay here. I want things to be simple and clear-cut like what they used to be. I want it to be like when I was a nipper. I didn't have to make no decisions then." The pathetic exploration of entrapment and futility is eschewed by Tinniswood in favor of the comic. Carter retreats into characteristically passive disobedience before his wife and his moments of introspection and self-knowledge are confined to conversations with Daniel, his much younger cousin who dies of pneumonia when Carter takes him out in the rain. Pat, who hopes by carefully rationing her sexuality to achieve her dream of a new house, a "young executive" lifestyle, and the attention she craves, is also disappointed. Even her pregnancy is offset by other events; a silver wedding, her mother's courtship, Uncle Mort and Olive Furnival, or Carter's football team. "It's not fair" says Pat, "Well what about me and baby? Why can't we have the field clear for ourselves? Why can't we have all the lime-

light?" The Brandons are, as they would say in the north, set in their ways.

The blighted lives of the Brandon family are played out against the slow erosion of a way of life. This is epitomized in the novels by the new housing estate on which Carter and Pat live, and by Uncle Mort's trenchant refusal to sell off his allotment to developers. The emphasis is placed not on the intrinsic seriousness of stunted lives and stunted relationships, but on imaginative verbal flights informed by the cheerful misery of stock northern humor. "Life's not worth living is it?" reflects Les. "No" agrees Uncle Mort, "I wish there were summat else you could do with it". Tinniswood is at his best when tossing words and logic about without reference to the actual living of life. In this sense his novels are not realistic, but rather full blown caricatures of northern life. It is a sense of humor not always easily exported however, and drove one New York Times book reviewer to declare that Tinniswood's work should be read when "ready for a good chuckle at the expense of old age, deformity, sickness and death . . ." Death is as sudden, frequent, and funny in Tinniswood's work, as sex is serious, infrequent and if possible to be avoided altogether.

The treatment of elementals in Tinniswood's work is entirely blasé. The form and style of his work allows their discussion to take place with all of the intensity normally accorded to the need for a nice cup of tea. When Uncle Mort says that Olive Furnival has been fatally injured falling off a bus, as was his wife, he is driven to consider that he "never did have much luck with public transport," "'Is your bust tender?' asks Mrs. Partington of the pregnant Pat. 'Yes' she replies. 'Well don't let Carter play with it.'" It is a style which will not ultimately cope with seriousness, not even that demanded by the good parody and satire. Thus *Shemerelda,* a satire on beautiful and spoilt American womanhood, fails insofar as it is unable to emulate and parody the form of the brief dialogue that has been perfected by those working in the tradition of Twain and Hemingway. *The Stirk of Stirk,* an attempt to parody the epic fable loses humor in the telling of a straight narrative, while the characters remain stereotypical and superficial. When seriousness is attempted in the Brandon novels, usually via Carter's moments of introspection, it allows the misogyny latent in stock northern humor, and therefore in most of Tinniswood's writing, to break through and reveal its unfortunate aspect. For the most part however the accent remains strictly on the comic. It is no accident that the Brandon household, when transferred to the timeless medium of the television situation comedy where neither change nor resolution are to be expected, have become something of a television classic. It is this medium which allows Tinniswood to excel.

—Jan Pilditch

TLALI, Miriam (Masoli)

Nationality: South African. **Born:** Doornfontein, Transvaal. **Education:** University of the Witwatersrand, Johannesburg. **Career:** Co-founder, *Staffrider* magazine; board member, Skotaville Press. **Address:** c/o Pandora Press, 77-85 Fulham Palace Road, London W6 8JB, England.

PUBLICATIONS

Novels

Muriel at Metropolitan. Johannesburg, Ravan Press, 1975; London, Longman, 1979.
Amandla. Johannesburg, Ravan Press, 1980.

Short Stories

Mihloti. Johannesburg, Skotaville, 1984.
Footprints in the Quag: Stories and Dialogues from Soweto. Cape Town, Philip, 1989; as *Soweto Stories,* London, Pandora Press, 1989.

*   *   *

Miriam Tlali was brought up in Sophiatown, that legendary community within Johannesburg which was razed because it was the sole area where Africans were permitted to take permanent title to land. She successfully completed high school and entered Witwatersrand University. A series of practical difficulties forced her to seek employment as a book-keeper/typist. This background makes it the more remarkable that she is one of the few black South African women who have been able to express their experiences and concerns in print. Her first publication, *Muriel at the Metropolitan,* seems largely autobiographical, the events deriving predominantly from her office experience. In spite of being so personal this is not pure autobiography, the events are embellished with considerable skill and the sequence of incidents is controlled by a deliberate, artistic structuring.

Metropolitan Radio is a shop that provides radios and furniture to Africans on tempting but greedy hire-purchase terms. The staff becomes a microcosm of the society and the characters are designed to become representative of the racial elements which make up this complex country. The owner, Mr. Bloch, is a Jew who displays all the traditional expectations of sharp dealing to make a barely legal extra profit. There are two white female cashiers; an overtly racist Afrikaaner Mrs. Stein and an English-speaking liberal Mrs. Kuhn, whose racism is more subtle but ultimately similar. Then there are the "coloured" mechanics, and below them, a variety of African drivers and attendants. They work together not very harmoniously, and from time to time, all express antagonistic inter-racial prejudice.

If one took this work too seriously, the people would become mere symbols. In particular the underlying anti-Semitism would be cruelly evident. Mr. Bloch would become a modern Shylock, always eager to make a rand/ducat at the expense of the ignorant and unfortunate Africans. But the entire work is based upon an attitude of extraordinary tolerance and amiability. Muriel enjoys her work. She likes her involvement with the business. Generally she even likes Mr. Bloch. Since she is employed as an office worker, a status usually reserved for Whites, and manages her duties every bit as efficiently as they do, she is inevitably treated disrespectfully and often blamed for errors the White staff have made. She is used and abused; and given the task, beneath White dignity, of coping with a series of very legitimate African complaints. Sometimes she helps, by explaining the dangerous results of compound interest and is accused of disloyalty to the company. Sometimes she finds herself unavoidably becoming a tool of Mr. Bloch's calculated exploitation. The surprising thing about this book is its tone. It is

occasionally defiant as Muriel stands up to false accusations with articulate denials. But there is a strange tolerance and humor, a genuine acceptance that sees the racist extremes as absurd as they are threatening. She can laugh at the comic illiteracy of the African clients' letters without unkindness. She beautifully rises above the political and racial status that has been imposed on her by saying, "I am just myself, just a person." It is this tolerant vein which sustains this work.

Eventually Miriam is offered the chance of a much better job. Government inspectors come and determine that the struggling immigrant employer cannot afford to build an "African woman" toilet. It is illegal for Muriel to share either African male or White women's facilities, therefore she cannot be employed. Although Muriel is denied her promotion, the explanation exposes the madness of the divisions imposed upon South African society. They are as ludicrous as wicked. Indicatively this book itself was immediately and even more absurdly "banned" by the government censors.

After *Muriel at Metropolitan* Tlali wrote a collection of short stories, *Mihloti,* some plays and essays. Her major work is a lengthy novel, *Amandla.* The title is chanted at public demonstrations and means power. This novel is very different from *Muriel* and displays no tolerance, rather, it takes a strongly committed and activist posture. The events take place in 1976 and such actual plot as there is, consists of a review of the circumstances of the Soweto rebellion against the imposition of Afrikaans in the African schools—the children's uprising. There is a single coherent aspect, violence imposed by the police, by troops, and by Africans against each other. Blood and shootings are a constant backdrop. There are various minimal sub-plots; a youthful love affair between the student leader Pholoso and his girlfriend Felleng which is aborted by his being driven to political activism by governmental persecution. There is an adulterous love relationship between the wife of the police sergeant and his subordinate. There is loving old Gramsy who contemplates the horrendous present from the warm sentiment of the past. There are other characters, too numerous to recall individually, who play their cameo roles but are forgotten against the main sweep of the story, which is political challenge against the existing regime. Many of such small incidents are portrayed with conviction. The language is colloquial and realistic, their concerns, though briefly detailed, connect to the local events at the true level of human consequence, the personal conflicts and miseries that are suffered. Unhappily these painful and tender circumstances are not the focal point of this novel in which the prime purpose is to make bitter political complaint about the appalling injustice of the South African system. In itself, this intention is legitimate enough. Hardly anyone would offer a defense of apartheid. But the writer of fiction must create a conviction in the reader by inventing realistic individuals who, by their acts, expose the social issues, and engage our imaginative sympathies. Richard Rive successfully acheived this with *Emergency.* Here Tlali prefers argument. Many will approve of her denunciations of this regime but the rhetoric in which it is conducted is full of improbably pompous speech and palpable jargon. The young students enforcing the trade boycott speak with an extreme formality before they pour the unacceptably purchased quarts of paint on the head of an unhappy man who sought only to renovate the walls of his house, and so politely explain why they must burn the new clothes an affectionate mother has bought for her children. One long section consists of nothing more than a debate between two characters, which is meant to educate the reader by making reference to the entire history of South

African oppressive legislation detailing all the parliamentary enactments with their dates. Perhaps this has to be told. Many political scientists have expressed it more academically, but the inventor of fiction should give it life. Without that humanity the novel is stultified unless its admirers determine that its contents are of such supervening importance that the normal practices of fiction no longer apply. This is less novel than diatribe. At the same time it includes many enticing elements that show that Tlali is still a uniquely sensitive observer of the intolerably grotesque society in which she lives. When free from her perceived obligation to convince through denunciation and the political clichés which voice that stance, she still has all the qualities which will allow her to express with loving accuracy the human feelings of her people.

—John Povey

TRAPIDO, Barbara

Nationality: British (emigrated from South Africa, 1963; granted British citizenship, 1968). **Born:** Barbara Schuddeboom, Capetown, South Africa, 5 November 1941. **Education:** University of Natal, South Africa, B.A. 1963; University of London, diploma in education, 1967. **Family:** Married Stanley Trapido, 1963; one daughter and one son. **Career:** English teacher, Greenwich Park School, London, 1964-67, and Sunderland College of Further Education, 1967-70. Since 1970, full-time writer. **Awards:** Whitbread Special prize for fiction, 1982, for *Brother of the More Famous Jack*. **Agent:** Felicity Bryan, 2A North Prade, Oxford OX2 6PE, England.

PUBLICATIONS

Novels

Brother of the More Famous Jack. London, Gollancz, and New York, Viking, 1982.
Noah's Ark. London, Gollancz, 1984; and New York, Watts, 1985.
Temples of Delight. London, Michael Joseph, 1990; New York, Grove Weidenfeld, 1991.
Juggling. London, Hamish Hamilton, 1994; New York, Penguin, 1995.

*

Barbara Trapido comments:
Funny/warm/satirical/slightly highbrow but accessible.

* * *

Barbara Trapido was born in South Africa in 1941, the daughter of dissident academic parents. She emigrated to England in 1963 and has lived in Oxford since 1971. Her first novel won a special prize in the Whitbread Awards in 1982 and was widely praised.

All Trapido's novels feature a dominating, unconventional older man. In the first three books he causes the heroine to fall in love with him or with the freedom from convention he represents; in the last he has something like the opposite effect. *In Brother of the More Famous Jack,* Katherine's friendship with her urbane phi-

losophy teacher, Jacob Goldman, and his family gives her, living in suburban rectitude with her mother "at the far reaches of the Northern line," an entrée into a world in which passions are visibly displayed and strong views are essential. Katherine falls in love with a series of unsuitable men, but the uxorious Jacob is the real hero of the novel. A shaggy Jew from the East End, he is sexy, uninhibited, and refreshingly trenchant; when Katherine eventually finds a man worthy of her, it is with the most Jacob-like of his sons.

The eponymous Noah Glazer, in *Noah's Ark,* is an American. He is as uxorious and bossy and cocksure as Jacob but with a different accent and somewhat less charm. Effortlessly, he rescues vague Ali from a dreary existence as a single parent still under the thumb of her awful ex and marries her. But such dazzling rescues bring their own problems. Compliant Ali hasn't ever got over her first love. As she slowly comes to terms with him, with the country of her birth, South Africa, and also her talent for painting, her marriage almost founders. Noah, like Jacob, isn't a man to relish coming second. Ali is ultimately forgiven, though Noah has been softened by an inconvenient summer spent apart from her. Forgiveness, like marital happiness, is fragile.

By the third novel we know that the typical Trapido heroine is young, demure, clever, and ripe to be rescued by someone vivid and powerful by virtue of their subversive plain-speaking. In *Temples of Delight,* it is Jem, neither male nor Jewish nor even adult but nonetheless poised, Catholic, and well-read, who first rescues Alice. She is tall, scruffy, unconventional, given to flights of fancy (to disguise her humble origins), and believes in passion. Alice adores her and uses her as a touchstone—it is passion and not materialism that makes life worth living.

In *Temples of Delight,* Trapido uses attitudes toward food as an index of class and religion. Alice's friend Flora's appalling parents are so stingy that Flora is brought up to eat lumps of gristle and wear an overcoat indoors. Alice's mother treats Flora's family to a celebration meal in a restaurant. It is an episode of high comedy: Alice's builder father chats about bricks, Flora's father gropes Alice's mother and promptly dies of an unsuspected allergy to mussels, and the incontinent old grandmother piddles on the floor.

Though *Temples of Delight* uses the conventions of a school story, it includes elements of satire, melodrama (with some elements drawn from Mozart's *Magic Flute*), and comedy. The glue that sticks it together is psychological realism. Alice is fully drawn, though other characters, apart from Joe, the dominating male (this time Catholic and Italian-American), are lightly sketched. But when Joe arrives late in the novel—literally at Jem's deathbed—Alice, like Ali and Katherine before her, is ready to be swept off her feet.

Juggling is a sequel to *Temples of Delight* (though there are some inconsistencies with dates). It is more complex, full of unexpected twists and contrivances, and the women characters are its glory. Pamina is Jem's daughter, born by cesarean section while Jem lay dying. Christina was born early in Alice's marriage to Joe. But time moves on. Alice is less impressed by Joe than hitherto. As a teenager, Christina is filled with the need to rebel—both to quell Joe and to make her way in the world without his help. Abandoning her beloved sister, she finds a black, working-class replacement in the ebullient, capable Dulce. Alice also rebels, and there is an intricate, careful patterning of joinings-together and splittings-apart, of mistaken identities and disappearances, that mirrors the patterning of a Shakespearean comedy.

An undergraduate at Cambridge, Christina develops strong views on the Comedies. She has also learned more than the basics on relations between the sexes. "In the conflict of gender, the women win the war of words, but the men will win the battle." Katherine, and Alice before her, clever though they were, spent their youth without discovering as much. The book's ending, "frozen in a moment of precarious, brilliant symmetry," promises much for the future.

—Anne French

TREMAIN, Rose

Nationality: British. **Born:** Rose Thomson in London, 2 August 1943. **Education:** Frances Holland School, 1949-54; Crofton Grange School, 1954-60; the Sorbonne, Paris, 1960-61, diploma in literature 1962; University of East Anglia, Norwich, 1964-67, B.A. (honors) in English 1967. **Family:** Married 1) Jon Tremain in 1971 (divorced 1978), one daughter; 2) Jonathan Dudley in 1982 (divorced 1991). **Career:** Teacher, Lynhurst House School, London, 1968-70; assistant editor, British Printing Corporation, London, 1970-72; part-time research jobs, 1972-79; creative writing fellow, University of Essex, Wivenhoe, 1979-80. Since 1980 full-time writer and part-time lecturer in creative writing, University of East Anglia. **Awards:** Dylan Thomas prize, for short story, 1984; Giles Cooper award, for radio play, 1985; Angel Literary award, 1985, 1989; *Sunday Express* Book of the Year award, 1989; James Tait Black Memorial prize, 1993; Prix Femina étranger (France), 1994. Fellow, Royal Society of Literature, 1983. **Agent:** Richard Scott Simon, 43 Doughty Street, London WC1N 2LF. **Address:** 2 High House, South Avenue, Thorpe St. Andrew, Norwich NR7 0EZ, England.

PUBLICATIONS

Novels

Sadler's Birthday. London, Macdonald, 1976; New York, St. Martin's Press, 1977.
Letter to Sister Benedicta. London, Macdonald, 1978; New York, St. Martin's Press, 1979.
The Cupboard. London, Macdonald, 1981; New York, St. Martin's Press, 1982.
The Swimming Pool Season. London, Hamish Hamilton, and New York, Summit, 1985.
Restoration. London, Hamish Hamilton, 1989; New York, Viking, 1990.
Sacred Country. London, Sinclair Stevenson, 1993; New York, Atheneum, 1994.

Short Stories

The Colonel's Daughter and Other Stories. London, Hamish Hamilton, and New York, Summit, 1984.
The Garden of the Villa Mollini and Other Stories. London, Hamish Hamilton, 1987.
Evangelista's Fan. London, Sinclair Stevenson, 1994.

Plays

Mother's Day (produced London, 1980).

Yoga Class (produced Liverpool, 1981).
Temporary Shelter (broadcast 1984). Published in *Best Radio Plays of 1984*, Methuen, 1985.

Radio Plays: *The Wisest Fool,* 1976; *Dark Green,* 1977; *Blossom,* 1977; *Don't Be Cruel,* 1978; *Leavings,* 1978; *Down the Hill,* 1979; *Half Time,* 1980; *Hell and McLafferty,* 1982; *Temporary Shelter,* 1984; *The Birdcage,* 1984; *Will and Lou's Boy,* 1986; *The Kite Flyer,* 1987.

Television Plays: *Halleluiah, Mary Plum,* 1978; *Findings on a Late Afternoon,* 1980; *A Room for the Winter,* 1981; *Moving on the Edge,* 1983; *Daylight Robbery,* 1986.

Other

The Fight for Freedom for Women. New York, Ballantine, 1973.
Stalin: An Illustrated Biography. New York, Ballantine, 1975.
Journey to the Volcano (for children). London, Hamish Hamilton, 1985.

*

Rose Tremain comments:

Most interesting to me is my attempt to communicate ideas through many different forms of writing; this is allied to my belief that a writer who stays working in one form only risks becoming repetitive and stale. Hence, the large output of plays for radio and the three collections of short stories and children's novels.

I have strenuously resisted categorisation as a "woman's writer" and the notion that women should address themselves only to women's problems, as this strikes me as limiting and inhibiting, a kind of literary sexism in itself.

Themes that recur in my work are: dispossession, the effect of religious and exclusive "clubs" of all kinds on the individual's compassion, class antagonisms, solitariness, sexual bereavement, emotional bravery, and, above all, love.

*   *   *

The writings of Rose Tremain reveal an author with a hard, unsentimental vision. Her novels probe the essence of the human tragedy in studies of loneliness, old age, and failure, an exploration of lives that touch but cannot fit together. Adroit, often poignantly sad, these works avoid mawkishness and self-pity, the author's skill enlivening the procession of tragic events with deft touches of humor, and memorable dialogue and characterization.

Sadler's Birthday, her first novel, is perhaps the most stark of her portrayals, depicting as it does the bleak desert of old age. Sadler, a former butler living in the stately home willed to him by the gentry he once served, moves alone and friendless through the maze of empty rooms. A decrepit old man, betrayed by his body and its humiliations, he looks back over the existence that has shaped him for a life apart. In a carefully mustered sequence which mingles recollections with the routine visits of the day—the vicar, the cleaning lady, a prying estate agent—the reader is acquainted with the course of Sadler's past life. Parted from his mother as a boy, finding love only to have it taken from him, Sadler has spent the years imprisoned in the strait-jacket of domestic service, his feelings hidden behind a polite, dehumanizing reserve. His unacknowledged emotions, the longings of a lonely man for love and friendship, move by their presentation, which is shorn of all sentiment. As a first novel, *Sadler's Birthday* is a remarkably accomplished work. Characters and conversations have the ring of authenticity, and the blend of incidents is capably achieved.

Letter to Sister Benedicta centers on the struggle of the heroine, Ruby Constad, to survive the crises of those about her. Fat and unattractive, a middle-aged woman passed over by life, Ruby exists in the shadow of her successful lawyer husband and their beautiful children. When her husband succumbs to a stroke, and her son and daughter embark upon an incestuous relationship, Ruby's character is tested to the utmost. Her battle for self-preservation, written in the form of a letter to the nun who raised her at a convent school in India, reveals her personality gradually and subtly, showing not only her inner turmoil but her innate warmth, strength, and self-deprecating humor. Ruby's emergence from the family traumas to begin living her own life is ably portrayed, the interest sustained through a succession of quiet, perfectly constructed scenes.

The Cupboard is more ambitious in scope, embodying as it does one woman's vision of the 20th century and its two world wars. At the novel's core is the life of Erica March, a major but neglected novelist, now old and nearing death. The work is balanced between the polar characters of Erica herself and Ralph, the failed hack journalist, who is sent to interview her. Erica's past and her innermost feelings unfold slowly in a series of conversations, interspersed with quotations from her books. A forerunner of the modern radical feminists, she has managed with difficulty to shape her existence to her own desires. Her ability to act for herself is contrasted with the impotence of Ralph, who mirrors the modern age in his willingness to conform to the rules imposed upon him. Tired of being the faceless member of a team, Ralph seizes on the interview as an act of rebellion, hoping to draw from Erica's life some meaning that will infuse his own. Erica, meanwhile, knows her time is running out and prepares for death. A powerful, complex, and intriguing novel, *The Cupboard* is perhaps the least accessible of Tremain's works, but the richness of its content rewards a careful reading.

With the stories of *The Colonel's Daughter* and the novel *The Swimming Pool Season* Tremain broadens her vision still further, moving beyond single central characters to encompass a network of lives. The title story and the novel have strong similarities. Written in a firm, direct present tense, they build to climax through a series of brief, sharply visualized incidents, showing the differing perceptions, the unforeseen ways in which lives touch and affect one another. Whether the criminal act of "The Colonel's Daughter," or the ill-fated venture to build a swimming pool in a remote French village, the plot of each serves as a focus around which the author connects the interwoven lives of her characters, the events unfolding almost imperceptibly and with deceptive stillness, as crisis and tragedy reveal themselves.

Tremain's versatility, her eagerness to explore the many different forms of writing, is fully evidenced in her radio plays, her children's story *Journey to the Volcano,* and in her short story collections for adults, *The Colonel's Daughter* and *The Garden at the Villa Mollini and Other Stories.* This appetite for other modes of expression is matched by the continuing experimentation and variety of her novels. *Restoration,* perhaps her most ambitious venture in this field, marks a radical departure from previous work by being a historical rather than a contemporary novel, but shares with *The Swimming Pool Season* the sense of interconnected lives, the gradual workings of fate foreshadowed by a series of crucial incidents which act as epiphanies.

Robert Merivel, the narrator and unlikely hero of *Restoration,* confesses his helplessness to the reader, admitting in the opening pages that: "I am also in the middle of a story which might have a variety of endings, some of them not entirely to my liking." Set against the background of the early reign of Charles II, taking in the twin catastrophes of the Great Plague and Great Fire of London, the novel examines Merivel's checkered career as King's Fool and cuckold husband, his ennoblement and downfall as favor is withdrawn, and his final efforts at reintegration. Tremain varies her style skillfully, alternating past tense in the main body of the story with a sharper present-tense immediacy as the crucial events are recalled in flashback. She explores the many complexities of her ugly, good-natured hero—the intemperance and lechery, the knowledge of anatomy that brings only a fear of death, above all his obsessive and unrequited love for Celia, his wife, for his Quaker friend Pearce, and for the adored but ruthless King, who "moves like God in our world." Merivel mirrors his age in his early excess and later, flawed efforts at renunciation of the flesh. His story forms the core of an epic and fascinating narrative which abounds in sudden revelations and shifts of focus, and whose strands reach out to enmesh a diverse cast of characters from lunatics, Quakers, and failed portrait painters to the King himself. *Restoration,* whose title refers not only to the time but to Merivel's own re-ordering of his broken world, is a deep, many-layered work, and at all levels the author's touch is firm and assured. Tremain brings the age alive with her words, evokes a talismanic quality from a caged bird or a set of surgeon's instruments, takes the reader with Merivel as he encounters the King in the royal apartments, to a background of chiming clocks whose strokes foretell the relentless march of time. *Restoration* is the most challenging novel Tremain has produced; it is also her greatest achievement as a writer.

Sacred Country, however, runs a very close second. Set mainly in rural Norfolk in the period 1952-80, it centers on the search by a farmer's daughter, Mary Ward, to discover her true self, not as a girl, but as a man. Her slow and painful odyssey to personal fulfillment as Martin Ward is paralleled by the lives of her bitter, lonely father Sonny and mentally unstable mother Estelle, and by the linked experiences of the Simmonds and Loomis families with whom their lives intertwine. Tremain once more creates a rich, multi-layered, and fascinating text, studded with evocative symbols and talismans. The essence of passing decades is captured in remembered songs and incidents, places and times brought to life in superb dialogue and description, ranging from East Anglia to Tennessee, from the England World Cup win to Grand Ole Opry, Nashville. It is a striking, memorable achievement. Tremain's continued mastery of the shorter fictional forms is evidenced in the recent collection *Evangelista's Fan,* whose themes extend over the thoughts of a French herald before Agincourt, and the subtle musings on the nature of time in the title story. Tremain presents the psychology and responses of her characters with brevity and assurance, her skillful prose compressing a variety of experience into a handful of pages.

—Geoff Sadler

TREVOR, William

Nationality: Irish. **Born:** Mitchelstown, County Cork, 24 May 1928. **Education:** St. Columba's College, Dublin, 1942-46; Trinity College, Dublin, B.A. 1950. **Family:** Married Jane Ryan in 1952; two sons. **Career:** History teacher, Armagh, Northern Ireland, 1951-53; art teacher, Rugby, England, 1953-55; sculptor in Somerset, 1955-60; advertising copywriter, Notley's, London, 1960-64. Lives in Devon, England. **Awards:** *Transatlantic Review* prize, for fiction, 1964; Hawthornden prize, for fiction, 1965; Society of Authors travelling fellowship, 1972; Allied Irish Banks prize, for fiction, 1976; Heinemann award, for fiction, 1976; Whitbread Award, 1976, 1983, Book of the Year, 1994; Irish Community prize, 1979; BAFTA award, for television play, 1983; *Sunday Express* Book of the Year, 1994. D.Litt.: University of Exeter, 1984; Trinity College, Dublin, 1986; D.Litt.: Queen's University, Belfast, 1989; National University, Cork, 1990. **Member:** Irish Academy of Letters. C.B.E. (Commander, Order of the British Empire), 1977. **Agent:** Peters Fraser and Dunlop Group, 503-504 The Chambers, Chelsea Harbour, Lots Road, London SW10 0FX, England; or, Sterling Lord Literistic Inc., 1 Madison Avenue, New York, New York 10010, U.S.A.

PUBLICATIONS

Novels

A Standard of Behaviour. London, Hutchinson, 1958.
The Old Boys. London, Bodley Head, and New York, Viking Press, 1964.
The Boarding-House. London, Bodley Head, and New York, Viking Press, 1965.
The Love Department. London, Bodley Head, 1966; New York, Viking Press, 1967.
Mrs. Eckdorf in O'Neill's Hotel. London, Bodley Head, 1969; New York, Viking Press, 1970.
Miss Gomez and the Brethren. London, Bodley Head, 1971.
Elizabeth Alone. London, Bodley Head, 1973; New York, Viking Press, 1974.
The Children of Dynmouth. London, Bodley Head, 1976; New York, Viking Press, 1977.
Other People's Worlds. London, Bodley Head, 1980; New York, Viking Press, 1981.
Fools of Fortune. London, Bodley Head, and New York, Viking Press, 1983.
The Silence in the Garden. London, Bodley Head, and New York, Viking, 1988.
Two Lives (includes *Reading Turgenev* and *My House in Umbria*). London and New York, Viking, 1991.
Felicia's Journey. London and New York, Viking, 1995.

Short Stories

The Day We Got Drunk on Cake and Other Stories. London, Bodley Head, 1967; New York, Viking Press, 1968.
Penguin Modern Stories 8, with others. London, Penguin, 1971.
The Ballroom of Romance and Other Stories. London, Bodley Head, and New York, Viking Press, 1972.
The Last Lunch of the Season. London, Covent Garden Press, 1973.
Angels at the Ritz and Other Stories. London, Bodley Head, 1975; New York, Viking Press, 1976.
Lovers of Their Time and Other Stories. London, Bodley Head, 1978; New York, Viking Press, 1979.

The Distant Past and Other Stories. Dublin, Poolbeg Press, 1979.
Beyond the Pale and Other Stories. London, Bodley Head, 1981; New York, Viking Press, 1982.
The Stories of William Trevor. London and New York, Penguin, 1983.
The News from Ireland and Other Stories. London, Bodley Head, and New York, Viking, 1986.
Nights at the Alexandra (novella). London, Century Hutchinson, and New York, Harper, 1987.
Family Sins and Other Stories. London, Bodley Head, and New York, Viking, 1990.

Plays

The Elephant's Foot (produced Nottingham, 1965).
The Girl (televised 1967; produced London, 1968). London, French, 1968.
A Night with Mrs. da Tanka (televised 1968; produced London, 1972). London, French, 1972.
Going Home (broadcast 1970; produced London, 1972). London, French, 1972.
The Old Boys, adaptation of his own novel (produced London, 1971). London, Davis Poynter, 1971.
A Perfect Relationship (broadcast 1973; produced London, 1973). London, Burnham House, 1976.
The 57th Saturday (produced London, 1973).
Marriages (produced London, 1973). London, French, 1973.
Scenes from an Album (broadcast 1975; produced Dublin, 1981). Dublin, Co-op, 1981.
Beyond the Pale (broadcast 1980). Published in *Best Radio Plays of 1980,* London, Eyre Methuen, 1981.
Autumn Sunshine adaptation of his own story (televised 1981; broadcast 1982). Published in *Best Radio Plays of 1982,* London, Methuen, 1983.

Radio Plays: *The Penthouse Apartment,* 1968; *Going Home,* 1970; *The Boarding House,* from his own novel, 1971; *A Perfect Relationship,* 1973; *Scenes from an Album,* 1975; *Attracta,* 1977; *Beyond the Pale,* 1980; *The Blue Dress,* 1981; *Travellers,* 1982; *Autumn Sunshine,* 1982; *The News from Ireland,* from his own story, 1986; *Events at Drimaghleen,* 1988; *Running Away,* 1988.

Television Plays: *The Baby-Sitter,* 1965; *Walk's End,* 1966; *The Girl,* 1967; *A Night with Mrs. da Tanka,* 1968; *The Mark-2 Wife,* 1969; *The Italian Table,* 1970; *The Grass Widows,* 1971; *O Fat White Woman,* 1972; *The Schoolroom,* 1972; *Access to the Children,* 1973; *The General's Day,* 1973; *Miss Fanshawe's Story,* 1973; *An Imaginative Woman,* from a story by Thomas Hardy, 1973; *Love Affair,* 1974; *Eleanor,* 1974; *Mrs. Acland's Ghosts,* 1975; *The Statue and the Rose,* 1975; *Two Gentle People,* from a story by Graham Greene, 1975; *The Nicest Man in the World,* 1976; *Afternoon Dancing,* 1976; *The Love of a Good Woman,* from his own story, 1976; *The Girl Who Saw a Tiger,* 1976; *Last Wishes,* 1978; *Another Weekend,* 1978; *Memories,* 1978; *Matilda's England,* 1979; *The Old Curiosity Shop,* from the novel by Dickens, 1979; *Secret Orchards,* from works by J.R. Ackerley and Diana Petre, 1980; *The Happy Autumn Fields,* from a story by Elizabeth Bowen, 1980; *Elizabeth Alone,* from his own novel, 1981; *Autumn Sunshine,* from his own story, 1981; *The Ballroom of Romance,* from his own story, 1982; *Mrs. Silly (All for Love* series), 1983; *One of Ourselves,* 1983; *Broken*

Homes, from his own story, 1985; *The Children of Dynmouth,* from his own novel, 1987; *August Saturday,* from his own novel, 1990; *Events at Drimaleen,* from his own story, 1992.

Other

Old School Ties (miscellany). London, Lemon Tree Press, 1976.
A Writer's Ireland: Landscape in Literature. London, Thames and Hudson, and New York, Viking, 1984.
Excursions in the Real World. London, Hutchinson, and New York, Knopf, 1994.

Editor, *The Oxford Book of Irish Short Stories.* Oxford and New York, Oxford University Press, 1989.

*

Manuscript Collection: University of Tulsa, Oklahoma.

Critical Studies: "William Trevor's System of Correspondences," in *Massachusetts Review* (Amherst), Autumn 1987, and *William Trevor,* New York, Twayne, 1993, both by Kristin Morrison; *William Trevor: A Study of His Fiction* by Gregory A. Schirmer, London, Routledge, 1990; *William Trevor: A Study of Short Fiction* by Suzanne Morrow Paulson, New York, Twayne, 1993.

*   *   *

Readers of William Trevor's early novels, *The Old Boys* and *The Boarding-House,* will at once understand why some critics refer to his fiction as "Dickensian." Filled with colorful characters drawn from London life, they display not only a fascination with eccentricity but, more profoundly, the motives that set characters against one another in wicked and often comical fashion. The comedy, in fact, tends to overlay and thus disguise the kinds of evil that ultimately show through and that Trevor becomes more concerned with in his later fiction. Mr. Jaraby's ambition to become president of the Old Boys Association of his school is hardly diabolical, and the extent to which he is willing to go to insure his election is as funny as it is outlandish. But as we learn more and more about him and his ambition, aspects of his private life—particularly his attitude towards his wife and son—reveal a sinister side to his nature that even his worst enemy, Mr. Nox, does not suspect. At the end, defeated in ways he had not anticipated, Mr. Jaraby is left alone with his wife who, though she counsels hope, rightly questions, "Has hell begun, is that it?" and urges, "Come now, how shall we prove we are not dead?"

William Wagner Bird's death at the beginning of *The Boarding-House* provides one answer to Mrs. Jaraby's question. He leaves a will that bequeaths his boarding-house, occupied by an odd assortment of individuals of both sexes, to two of its most vigorous enemies, Studdy and Nurse Clock, both of them senior residents. Studdy is a petty con artist whose success in stealing one of Nurse Clock's elderly patients away from her has heightened the rivalry and ugliness between the pair. The specific condition of the bequest—that they make no changes in the residents or staff—puts them in an awkward position, but not for long. Like many of Trevor's less reputable characters, they are extremely acquisitive and quickly see that they have more to gain by working together than by working against each other. Unholy alliance though it may be, it seems to be succeeding, as they systematically try to rid them-

selves of those strange and solitary inmates in whose hearts Mr. Bird believed he had kindled some comfort by bringing them together in his "great institution in the south-western suburbs of London." Studdy and Nurse Clock intend to convert the boarding-house into a home for old folks, easy targets for their different skills. But they have not reckoned sufficiently with the nature of those already within the premises, about whom Mr. Bird had much greater understanding, as his "Notes on Residents" show. By attempting to disrupt the careful arrangement Bird had created and cultivated, they finally destroy everything else, as from his grave Mr. Bird takes his revenge—in the person of a deranged and dispossessed resident who believes he is taking revenge on *him.*

Timothy Gedge in *The Children of Dynmouth* is a younger version of Mr. Studdy, and, being younger, displays the causes of his behavior more clearly. An unwanted child, neglected at home by his working mother and sister and abandoned by his father, Gedge finds in others' lives not so much vicarious pleasures as sources of information and feelings that feed his diseased imagination. These help him to blackmail various townspeople, even those once kindly disposed towards him. While his demands are seemingly innocuous—a wedding dress, a dog's-tooth suit, a discarded tin bath—his means to secure those ends are entirely vicious, masked by a false heartiness and cheer that belie his true feelings. Ironically—and Trevor is a master of irony—what he invents to piece out his knowledge often comes close to the truth, close enough in any case to cause considerable anguish and hurt, for example, to Commander and Mrs. Abigail, who for years—ever since they first got married—have been living a lie; or to Stephen and Kate, whose parents—Stephen's father and Kate's mother—have just been married and are off on a honeymoon, leaving their children to begin a difficult adjustment to a new family life. In these and other relationships, Gedge pretends to a friendship that none of the others feels, and that tends to drive him into greater fantasies—and greater invasions of their privacy. His worse invasions, however, are those of the human heart—until he is stopped by someone who recognizes what he is doing and whose wife, through understanding Gedge's plight, puts away her own discontents and concerns herself more fully with her family's future—and his, too.

This somewhat upbeat ending should not be overemphasized, for though subsequent novels also show an effort to overcome despair and pathos, optimism is always very qualified in Trevor's fiction and very hard-won, as his many short stories also reveal. *Other People's Worlds* and *Fools of Fortune,* give a good idea of just how high the costs can be. Francis Tyte, another descendant of Studdy in Trevor's own rogue's gallery, is a very attractive young man who works as an actor in bit parts and in making commercials. Even more than Timothy Gedge, he has been victimized in his youth by a male boarder in his parents' home, a debt-collector who draws Francis into what one of his later benefactors aptly describes as a "bitter world." Since that time, Francis has also turned into a debt-collector of sorts, like Studdy and Gedge reaping from others what he regards as his due. Already married to an elderly dressmaker in Folkestone who has thrown him out, he later meets Julia, 14 years his senior, who becomes infatuated with him and agrees to marry him and give him her jewelry. Their Italian honeymoon lasts a single day, during which Francis tells Julia everything, including the daughter he has fathered with Doris Smith, a poor shopgirl in Fulham, 12 years earlier. He absconds with the jewels and is not heard from again. But Julia is drawn into Dorrie Smith's world as well as Francis's other circles, including that of the aged parents he has long since abandoned in a retirement home.

Despite the humiliation and despondency she naturally suffers because of her folly, Julia becomes more and more deeply involved in the shambles of others' lives Francis has left behind him. Once a devout Catholic, she nearly loses her faith altogether. But Francis's and Dorrie's joy in more than one sense finally becomes her own, as Gedge becomes Lavinia Featherston's. Drawn into other people's worlds and the messes they contain, she learns to value more her own, but not with smugness. The pain she has experienced has made her invulnerable to that and more truly compassionate than she had ever been before.

Fools of Fortune deepens the focus and the tone displayed in all of these novels, as Trevor resorts to first-person narrative and tells a story of revenge and retribution from several points of view. His eccentrics are still present, but here subordinated to their proper functions in a novel that spans the present century and deals with the perennial conflict between the Irish and their erstwhile British masters. Actually, the narrative goes back to the 19th century, when Irish Protestant William Quinton married English Anna Woodcombe and brought her to live in Kilneagh, County Cork. Two generations later, when for the third time a Quinton had taken a Woodcombe for his bride, Kilneagh is burned down by Black and Tans under the leadership of a Liverpool sergeant named Rudnick. Young Willie and his widowed mother survive the ordeal, but when years afterward Eve Quinton commits suicide—an alcoholic, she has never recovered from the disaster—Willie decides to exact his revenge upon Rudnick. Just before he does so, he falls in love with yet another Woodcombe, Marianne, and fathers a child. But he is forced to spend most of the rest of his life in lonely exile, while Marianne and their daughter Imelda are taken in by Willie's aging aunts at what is left of Kilneagh.

Anglo-Irish himself, Trevor has for many years lived in England and only occasionally attempted to treat the people and the landscapes of his native land in his fiction. In his short story "Attracta," about an elderly Protestant schoolteacher in a village near Cork, he sketched out some of the same themes he developed more fully in *Fools of Fortune.* But in "Matilda's England" he shows how the atrocities of the past and their impact upon the present are by no means limited to a single time or place or series of events.

Two more recent works, *The Silence in the Garden,* and his novella, *Nights at the Alexandra,* tend to bear out this trend. Both are set in Ireland, where Trevor grew up, and both reflect the elegiac tone that has grown more pronounced in his later work. *Nights at the Alexandra* looks back to the boyhood of a 58-year-old bachelor and the strange infatuation he felt for a beautiful and rather mysterious woman, Frau Messinger, an Englishwoman married to a German and brought to live in Ireland as World War II began. Isolated from the rest of the townsfolk in their home, Cloverhill, Frau Messinger befriends Harry, the narrator, who quickly falls under her spell. To provide some entertainment for his wife as well as for the townsfolk, Herr Messinger decides to establish a cinema, but it takes a long time to build, and meanwhile Frau Messinger falls ill. She dies shortly after the cinema opens and Harry is employed by her husband to help run it. Eventually he inherits the movie house, which at first was extremely popular. As the customers gradually stop coming, he closes it, just as Cloverhill is closed up when Herr Messinger leaves after his wife's death, and Harry is left to look after the boarded windows and her grave. At the end, he refuses to take a good offer for the place from a business partnership that would turn it into a furniture store.

The Silence in the Garden is a more complex and fully developed novel that uses several narrative techniques, including flashbacks and diary entries. Futile and misdirected love are part of the story, but so are senseless violence, superstition, family pride, and war. The novel is related from several viewpoints: the spinster Sarah Pollexfen's, a poor relation who comes to work at Carriglas, first as a governess, later as a companion to family duenna, old Mrs. Rolleston; Tom, son of the parlormaid (later cook) Brigid, whose intended husband, the butler Linchy, was killed in a Black and Tan ambush intended for the Rolleston men, Lionel and John James; Villana, granddaughter of Mrs. Rolleston, whose engagement to Sarah's brother, Hugh, is suddenly and mysteriously broken off shortly after Linchy's murder. Other Rollestons and townsfolk populate the novel; for example, Colonel Rolleston, Mrs. Rolleston's son and Villana's father, killed at Passchendaele; his sons, Lionel and John James; Finnamore Balt, the pedantic and elderly lawyer who eventually marries Villana; Mrs. Moledy, a widow who runs a boarding house, where she carries on a long liaison with John James, her "king," and who puts in an uninvited and comical appearance at Villana and Finnamore's wedding at Carriglas.

But the real protagonist of the novel is Ireland and her long unhappy history of Protestant landowners and Catholic servants and tenant farmers. If during the Great Famine an earlier generation of Rollestons had taken pity and forgiven rents, the later generation is still largely despised. As an example, when a bridge is proposed and built between the mainland and the island on which Carriglas is situated, it is named after Cornelius Dowley, the man responsible for Linchy's death but otherwise regarded as a hero of the struggle against the British. Over the course of the present century, Carriglas falls into disuse and disrepair, as one by one the Rollestons die out or leave, and only Tom is left. He inherits what is left of the estate, the old house whose value lies mainly in the valuable lead of its roof, and a little land—too little to make farming profitable. Although his would-be fiancée, Esmeralda Coyne, thinks it would make a good resort hotel, Tom shows little interest in her or her idea, and the novel ends, like *Nights at the Alexandra,* with Tom likely to remain a bachelor and the old house steadily disintegrating.

Trevor's growth and development as a novelist are stronger than ever, and he is an heir along with Iris Murdoch to the Anglo-Irish tradition in fiction that has given us the superb novelist and short-story writer Elizabeth Bowen.

—Jay L. Halio

TRICKETT, (Mabel) Rachel

Nationality: British. **Born:** Lathom, Lancashire, 20 December 1923. **Education:** The High School for Girls, Wigan, Lancashire; Lady Margaret Hall, Oxford, 1942-45, B.A. (honors) in English 1945, M.A. 1947. **Career:** Assistant to the curator, Manchester City Art Galleries, 1945-46; assistant lecturer, 1946-49, and lecturer, 1950-54, University College of Hull, Yorkshire; fellow and tutor, 1954-73, and principal, 1973-91, St. Hugh's College, Oxford. Visiting lecturer, 1962-63, and Drew Professor, 1971, Smith College, Northampton, Massachusetts; lecturer, Bread Loaf School of English, Middlebury, Vermont, 1967, 1969. **Awards:** Commonwealth Fund fellowship, 1949; Rhys Memorial prize, 1953. Honorary Fellow, Lady Margaret Hall, 1978. **Address:** Flat 4, 18 Norham Gardens, Oxford OX2 6QB, England.

PUBLICATIONS

Novels

The Return Home. London, Constable, 1952.
The Course of Love. London, Constable, 1954.
Point of Honour. London, Constable, 1958.
A Changing Place. London, Constable, 1962.
The Elders. London, Constable, 1966.
The Visit to Timon. London, Constable, 1970.

Uncollected Short Story

"The Schoolmasters," in *Cornhill* (London), Summer 1965.

Plays

Antigone, music by John Joubert (broadcast 1954). London, Novello, 1954.
Silas Marner, music by John Joubert (produced Cape Town and London, 1960). London, Novello, 1960.

Radio Play: *Antigone,* 1954.

Other

The Honest Muse: A Study in Augustan Verse. Oxford, Clarendon Press, 1967.
Browning's Lyricism (lecture). London, Oxford University Press, 1971.
Tennyson's Craft. Lincoln, Tennyson Society, 1981.

*

Rachel Trickett comments:

I have always been particularly interested in my novels in the relationships between people, and between people and their environment. Place plays an important part in all my books. I have also grown increasingly interested in the essential solitude and uniqueness of my characters. This is not the same as the popular idea of alienation or isolation; it is rather the individual differentiating principle which identifies character and is most obviously exhibited in love where so often those who love each other are, consciously or not, learning to recognize their differences, their separateness. The passing of time has become an important element in my novels from *A Changing Place* to *A Visit to Timon.* My works are often retrospective in tone and mood as I am particularly interested in the way in which the imagination plays over the past and relates it to the present.

*   *   *

In one of Rachel Trickett's novels, *The Elders,* a character is asked, "And what is your contribution to the war effort?" to which she replies quite simply, "Literature." The ironic implications of this exchange are best understood in the context of the novel, but we see here one of the rare moments in this writer's work where the relation between the inner and outer worlds is given direct critical presentation. Her chosen territory appears to be the private world of personal relationships, often among highly cultivated people. Nevertheless her presentation of it is such that her work reflects very clearly the changing public world of her time. A tough searching out of the responses of individual sensibilities to private experience, given in language of unfailing clarity, inevitably leads to an accurate recording of how the inner world is affected by the outer. In *A Changing Place* a working-class hero's attachment to a girl from the upper middle class follows a course in which private emotions are seen as subtly bound up with the wider social circumstances of pre-war hardship, the war, and the disorientating effects of the war on people's private lives. *A Visit to Timon* shows a different reaction to experience on the part of a man whose retreat from public life is complicated by his relationship with a friend who works in television. Similarly, Trickett's ability to evoke a sense of place and of time passing is partly a matter of vividly realized landscape and a rare gift for the delineation of nostalgia, but also rests in a strong sense of the community, a recognition of the relations and tensions in a social structure. This may range in different novels from the non-conformist community of a small town in Yorkshire, to the life of industrial quarry workers in Lancashire, and again to the quite different structures of life in Oxford University.

A common theme is the confrontation between worlds, the invasion of one set of values by another. Often the clash is between spontaneity of feeling and the more sophisticated attitude to experience cultivated by certain artistic, literary, and academic circles. In *The Return Home* the simple and passionate young innocent, Christiana, becomes the victim of more sophisticated beings, but in *The Elders* there is a comic reversal of this theme when the return from abroad of a spontaneous, romantic poet disturbs the existing pattern of relationships in an academic community and causes a reassessment of values by both old and young alike. These confrontations, too, are subject to the processes of time, and one of Rachel Trickett's gifts as a moralist is the careful account she takes of change and the complexity of the moral life in relation to it. Do civilized rituals of friendship really preserve love, or do they cause it to become atrophied, or do they perhaps simply come to disguise a lack of true commitment? In her work, this is a question that becomes increasingly important. It would be difficult to show by quotation the way in which she uses small acts, remarks, and gestures to build gradually a strong sense of the distinctive atmosphere peculiar to a relationship; but this extract from *A Changing Place,* in which she describes the refusal to envisage love, shows another important gift, the ability to describe emotional states with both elegance and accuracy:

> Love of the kind Sarah no longer envisaged is rare after all, because it is so seldom wanted. It seems dangerous in the dependence it creates, and some would rather have less than be threatened with the demand for this surrender. As they grow older the urge to protect themselves from it grows stronger and appears disguised as a sort of wisdom and settled maturity that can afford to smile at excesses of the heart and the imagination. But it is not emotion as such they fear; it is commitment, the loss of any part of themselves. The desire to conserve what remains of the self becomes so strong with age that it grows harder to believe that only he who loses his life shall save it. Superficially we become more generous with time and with new acquaintances and new responsibilities, all those things which have a touch of virtue in them and so often cover up for the lack of any real surrender of the self. It is like a religion that consists entirely of thinking and doing, of the

theological arguments and pious duties and refuses to take into account feeling, because it is dangerous.

—Bridget O'Toole

TUCCI, Niccolò

Nationality: American. **Born:** Lugano, Switzerland, 1 May 1908; emigrated to the United States, 1938; became citizen, 1953. Educated in Florence, Italy, Dr. in law and political sciences 1933. **Family:** Married Laura Rusconi in 1936; two children. **Career:** Writes in Italian and English. Correspondent, *Politics Magazine,* New York, 1943-46; co-founder, 1955, and columnist ("The Press of Freedom"), *Village Voice,* New York; columnist ("Offhand"), *Saturday Review,* New York, 1961-62. Writer-in-residence, Columbia University, New York, 1965-66. Co-founder, Wide Embrace theater company, New York, 1973. **Awards:** Viareggio prize, 1956; Ford grant, 1959; Bagutta prize, 1969. **Address:** c/o New Directions, 80 Eighth Avenue, New York, New York 10011, U.S.A.

PUBLICATIONS

Novels

Il Segreto. Milan, Garzanti, 1956.
Those of the Lost Continent (in Italian: *Gli Atlantici*):
Before My Time. New York, Simon and Schuster, 1962; London, Cape, 1963.
Unfinished Funeral. New York, Simon and Schuster, 1964; London, Cape, 1965.
Gli Atlantici. Milan, Garzanti, 1968.
Confessioni involontarie. Milan, Mondadori, 1975.
The Sun and the Moon. New York, Knopf, 1977; London, Allen Lane, 1979.

Short Stories

The Rain Came Last and Other Stories. New York, New Directions, 1990.

Play

Posterity for Sale (produced New York, 1967).

*

Niccolò Tucci comments:

The reason I have never allowed anyone to translate me from one of my two present languages into the other is that I consider myself alive, and these two languages are the two parts of me into which my experiences were split, so that my daily effort is to weld them together again. Perhaps I am another Humpty-Dumpty who sees himself as a new Lazarus. I don't know but I see no great danger of self-delusion in this: Lazarus was not a great man and certainly not a writer, he was a poor guinea-pig, and we have never been told how he climbed back into life after his place was taken by his Absence. I only know that no one in the world is worth his

absence, and *as a writer,* I feel this very intensely, for I associate with words more than with people. I still don't know how to write a good thank-you letter in English, French, or German, even in my native Italian, but the *word-population* of all languages is still at my orders for nonsense, fairy tales, plays, stories, polemical articles and even love letters, in spite of my venerable age. In fact I find it hard to limit myself to English and Italian, and none of the king's jet-planes and supermen, let alone his horses and men, could put me together again as well as I do every time I jump back into Italian or into English from that terrible wall. In the process of doing this almost daily repair-work I have learned a great deal about languages, and I know how to avoid the Temptations of the Writing Devil, namely hot-water and wind in the place of blood and soul to fill your characters with. It is an interesting life, but it dooms me to poverty as long as it lasts, because I can't let anyone bury me under *his* words while I am away from one of my two homes. But then this arrangement has its advantages too: the temptations of Success are far more sinister than those of habit, laziness or fatigue, in fact they are the *real* tools of the Devil.

*   *   *

The privileged deserve their literary investigators, as much as do the disadvantaged. Niccolò Tucci has devoted generous attention to an interesting minority group, the continental aristocracy and their heirs. Time and democracy have reduced their numbers and influence, but their fascination remains, less because of what they are than what they represent: the confluence of wealth, education, tradition, power, and social *élan* evidenced in a lifestyle where eccentricity and self-will are not fatal flaws but the identifying stripes of their breed.

Like jet travel or new money, the clash of conflicting moral or social values is not Tucci's ostensible concern. Yet it is there, under the Tucci characters' public show of conservatism and propriety. A young Spanish woman in *Unfinished Funeral,* the author's second novel in English, is reminded that she is "a girl of 26" and that her honor may have to be avenged, not because she may or may not have been compromised by an elderly gentleman met on a train, but because all will assume she has been. "The defense of your honor is my business, not yours," her brother insists. To liberate woman is to deprive man of his protector image, and, always, appearances count. Yet paradoxically, the strongest characters in Tucci's English novels are women—not the equals of men, but their proven superiors in the art of tyranny.

Tucci's reputation as a short story writer was already established before his first English novel, *Before My Time,* appeared in 1962. The long novel, in part an autobiographical nod to the author's own Russian-Italian parentage, is not merely dominated, but overwhelmed, by the idiosyncratic widow, Mamachen. A rich Russian matriarch at the turn of the century, she plays czarina to the large, elegant, and slavish family entourage she pilots from Italy to Switzerland to France to Germany—and to despair at times. Yet there is no family revolution, least of all by the daughter, Mary, who verges on treason by falling in love with a humble Italian doctor, and then in turn makes him a family thrall. The possible rebels are really defectors, the daughter Ludmilla and the son Pierre, who find lives of their own elsewhere. Mamachen's eventual death, with tragicomic dividing of the spoils by her heirs, changes nothing, but merely hands on the matriarchal torch to Mary. Aristocracy persists, Tucci suggests, because its leaders are equal to those they succeed. And why not? They have been handpicked and rigorously trained.

Unfinished Funeral is another investigation of tyranny, this time very compressed in length and told in symbols (largely Freudian) so obvious that they themselves invite questions. Ermelinda, the widowed Duchess of Combon de Triton, is "the acrobat of pain" who has survived 36 major operations and innumerable heart attacks, having found that physical crises are the handles by which she can grasp and hold power. Her funeral cortege is always on call, yet she never dies—and so her son, Bernandrasse, and daughter, Eloise, never really live. The book states and restates a proposition rather than treating a question; hence those who seek ready answers are doomed to disappointment.

In all of Tucci's work the style is witty, clever, polished—appropriate to the worldly figures he illuminates but never dissects.

—Marian Pehowski

TUOHY, Frank

Nationality: British. **Born:** John Francis Tuohy in Uckfield, Sussex, 2 May 1925. **Education:** Stowe School, Buckinghamshire; King's College, Cambridge, 1943-46, B.A. (honours) 1946. **Career:** Lecturer, Turku University, Finland, 1947-48; professor of English language and literature, University of São Paulo, Brazil, 1950-56; contract professor, Jagiellonian University, Krakow, Poland, 1958-60; visiting professor, Waseda University, Tokyo, 1964-67; visiting professor and writer-in-residence, Purdue University, Lafayette, Indiana, 1970-71, 1976, 1980; visiting professor, Rikkyo University, Tokyo, 1983-89. **Awards:** Katherine Mansfield-Menton prize, 1959; Society of Authors Travelling fellowship, 1963; James Tait Black Memorial prize, 1965; Faber Memorial prize, 1965; E.M. Forster award (U.S.A.), 1972; Heinemann award, 1979, for *Live Bait.* D.Litt.: Purdue University 1987. Fellow, Royal Society of Literature, 1965. **Agent:** Peters Fraser and Dunlop, 503-504 The Chambers, Chelsea Harbour, Lots Road, London SW10 0XF. **Address:** Shatwell Cottage, Yarlington, near Wincanton, Somerset BA9 8DL, England.

Publications

Novels

The Animal Game. London, Macmillan, and New York, Scribner, 1957.
The Warm Nights of January. London, Macmillan, 1960.
The Ice Saints. London, Macmillan, and New York, Scribner, 1964.

Short Stories

The Admiral and the Nuns with Other Stories. London, Macmillan, 1962; New York, Scribner, 1963.
Fingers in the Door. London, Macmillan, and New York, Scribner, 1970.
Live Bait and Other Stories. London, Macmillan, 1978; New York, Holt Rinehart, 1979.
The Collected Stories. London, Macmillan, and New York, Holt Rinehart, 1984.

Play

Television Play: *The Japanese Student,* 1973.

Other

Portugal. London, Thames and Hudson, and New York, Viking Press, 1970.
Yeats (biography). London, Macmillan, and New York, Macmillan, 1976; as *Yeats: An Illustrated Biography,* London, Herbert Press, 1991.

*

Critical Study: "Foreign Bodies: The Fiction of Frank Tuohy" by John Millors, in *London Magazine,* n.s.18, February 1979.

Frank Tuohy comments:

Most of what I write seems to start off with the interaction between two cultures, modes of behaviour, ways of living, etc. Sometimes this confrontation is between a foreigner and an alien environment, sometimes between groups in that environment itself. For me, the sense of displacement, loss, anxiety which happens to people derives from the world outside them, in their relationships with that world. If I thought of it as starting inside, as being a part of the Self, I probably would not write at all.

*   *   *

The novels and short stories of Frank Tuohy are marked by a strong sense of social reality. They are set in various places—England, Brazil, Poland—and give one a vivid sense of the physical place: the climate, landscape, local customs. Against the backdrop of special place, the drama of the characters' lives unfolds. In the short stories interest focuses usually on intense personal encounters in which the protagonist is made to face some unpleasant decision or harsh truth about himself or people close to him. These stories, sharply etched and intensely though quietly dramatic, have no apparent underlying theme. It is the revelation itself, the exquisitely rendered but "painful bite down on the rotten tooth of fact," to borrow a phrase from Tuohy, that one is meant to savor.

In his novels and longer stories there are the same sharp awareness of external reality and savoring of unpleasant fact, but there is also clearly a discernible moral structure. The writer's sympathies are with those who suffer and respond, who are capable of loyalty and self-abnegation. His dislike is for characters who, protected by money, indulge their appetites at the expense of those socially or culturally inferior or morally more sensitive.

The protagonist of Tuohy's first novel, *The Animal Game,* is Robin Morris, a young Englishman working in São Paulo, who encounters the beautiful corrupt daughter of a Brazilian aristocrat. Morris is attracted to this woman but is saved at the end of the novel from a relationship which, one sees, would have been sterile, self-indulgent, and ultimately destructive. Tuohy's moral sense is even more fully involved in his second novel about Brazil, *The Warm Nights of January,* which also deals with self-indulgence and sexual corruption. *The Ice Saints* takes place in Poland, some time after the Stalinist "thaw." Here the protagonist, an attractive, pleasant, but inexperienced and pampered young English woman visits her married sister and Polish brother-in-law with the idea of rescuing their son from what she regards as a grim and depressing existence, and taking him back to England to live. Although we are at first allowed to identify with the young woman's point of view (the horrors of Polish life are vividly presented), we are made to see, finally, the moral superiority of the Polish brother-in-law whose human qualities outweigh his lack of polish and urbanity.

Tuohy's stories and novels are written in a style that is compressed and economical yet remarkably evocative. One has the immediate sense of a physical world vividly and objectively presented and yet one also feels, but unobtrusively, the authorial presence choosing and arranging for judgmental effect.

—W.J. Stuckey

TURNER, George (Reginald)

Nationality: Australian. **Born:** Melbourne, Victoria, 8 October 1916. **Education:** Educated in Victoria state schools; at University High School, Melbourne. **Military Service:** Served in the Australian Imperial Forces, 1939-45. **Career:** Employment officer, Commonwealth Employment Service, Melbourne, 1945-49, and Wangaratta, Victoria, 1949-50; textile technician, Bruck Mills, Wangaratta, 1951-64; senior employment officer, Volkswagen Limited, Melbourne, 1964-67; beer transferer, Carlton and United Breweries, Melbourne, 1970-77. Fiction and non-fiction reviewer, Melbourne *Age,* 1970-89. **Awards:** Miles Franklin award, 1963; Commonwealth Literary Fund award 1968; Ditmar award, 1984 and 1989; Arthur C. Clarke award, 1988; Commonwealth Literary prize, 1988. **Agent:** Cherry Weiner, 28 Kipling Way, Manalapan, New Jersey 07726, U.S.A. **Address:** 16/207 Bell Street, Ballarat, Victoria 3350, Australia.

PUBLICATIONS

Novels

Young Man of Talent. London, Cassell, 1959; as *Scobie,* New York, Simon and Schuster, 1959.
A Stranger and Afraid. London, Cassell, 1961.
The Cupboard under the Stairs. London, Cassell, 1962.
A Waste of Shame. Melbourne and London, Cassell, 1965.
The Lame Dog Man. Melbourne, Cassell, 1967; London, Cassell, 1968.
Beloved Son. London, Faber, 1978; New York, Pocket Books, 1979.
Transit of Cassidy. Melbourne, Nelson, 1978; London, Hamish Hamilton, 1979.
Vaneglory. London, Faber, 1981.
Yesterday's Men. London, Faber, 1983.
The Sea and Summer. London, Faber, 1987; as *Drowning Towers,* New York, Arbor House, 1988.
Brain Child. New York, Morrow, 1991.
The Destiny Makers. New York, Avon/Nova Morrow, 1993.
Genetic Soldier. New York, Avon/Nova Morrow, 1994.

Short Stories

A Pursuit of Miracles: Eight Stories. Adelaide, Aphelion Press, 1988.

Uncollected Short Stories

"I Still Call Australia Home," in *Aurealis* (Melbourne), 1990.
"Worlds," in *Eidolon* (Perth, Western Australia), 1991.
"Flowering Mandrake," in *Alien Shores* (Adelaide, South Australia), 1994.

Other

In the Heart or in the Head (autobiography). Melbourne, Norstrilia Press, 1984.
Off-Cuts (memoirs). Perth, Western Australia, Swanco, 1986.

Editor, *View from the Edge.* Melbourne, Norstrilia Press, 1977.

*

George Turner comments:

I make few specific statements in my novels, and don't consider it my business to do so since the themes are usually such as bedevil the experts as much as they do the man in the street—insanity, alcoholism, the urge to meddle, the habit of making moral judgments and so on. I try to examine these themes under reasonably familiar circumstances, with no more of the exotic than is to be found in an average life, in the hope that some useful insight or recognition will emerge. The intention is that the reader will be able to identify with the problem as well as the characters.

To eliminate personal point of view as much as possible, I do not plan a novel in detail in advance of writing it. I select my general theme on no better ground than that I find it interesting and challenging, conceive a few characters who could reasonably become involved in such a matter, and set them in motion. Since plot is very literally character in action, something useful usually emerges in 20 or 30 thousand words, and I know in which direction I am going.

Only at this point do I begin to shape the work as a whole (and it generally means scrapping everything so far written) but rarely have more than a generalized idea of what the climax and resolution will be. These must be decided by the interactions of the characters: authorial manipulation is restricted to the minimum necessary to give shape and balance to the work.

One personally useful by-product of this method is that I find that such concentration on a problem for many months often changes my original points of view about it, and the outcome is commonly rather far from what I had in mind during the shaping phase.

I am sufficiently old-fashioned to prefer a story with a beginning, a development, and a resolution (though not to the point of tying up every loose end in sight) but sufficiently of my time to avoid moral or ethical attitudes. Those of my characters who display them are apt to come to grief as the theme tests and retests them.

For this reason I have been termed "existentialist," which is probably true, and have also been said to have no moral or ethical views at all, which is not. I merely condemn rigidity of attitude and I suppose that in the final summation that is what my novels so far have been about.

When I took up writing science fiction with *Beloved Son* in 1978 I found it necessary to modify my method of composition, since in sf the futuristic setting and background must to some degree determine the types of people who inhabit it, if the strange setting is to be justified. At first this was an inhibiting problem which I did not feel I solved until *Drowning Towers,* in which I managed a fully character-based novel with a fully eloborated "future" background, and now I feel much easier with the form.

*   *   *

George Turner is unusual, even perhaps unique, among Australian novelists in having achieved success in the two very different genres of realist fiction and science fiction. His first and arguably best novel, *Young Man of Talent,* is set in New Guinea in 1943, with the Japanese in retreat and is a grim and graphic account of war, even though as both author and publisher rush to assure us, it is not a war novel. Then he wrote four novels set in the fictitious Victorian country town of Treelake, 120 miles north of Melbourne, followed by a straightforward novel about a teenage boy's search for his ex-boxer father, *Transit of Cassidy.* This was actually written before *Beloved Son* but was published after it and marked the beginning of Turner's career as a writer of speculative fiction. It is the first part of a trilogy dealing with the earth in respectively AD 2032, 2037 and 2087. In retrospect it can be seen that Turner's concerns—psychological, moral, often didactic—are the same in both genres and that the two sequences of books are linked by much more than their habit of employing the same characters, locales and situations, viewed from a multitude of different perspectives.

Turner is concerned first of all with the outsider, the misfit, such as Payne in *Young Man of Talent* or Ted Johnson in *The Lame Dog Man* or the eponymous Cassidy. Where Patrick White, however, would celebrate the special insight or wisdom of the societal reject, Turner sees him as a man usually driven by obsessions of a destructive and anti-social kind. The misfit frequently suffers from some form of delusion. Sometimes it is symbolized in alcoholism, a disease which, Turner's frank and fascinating autobiography *In the Heart or the Head* makes clear, was not unknown to him. In *A Waste of Shame,* for instance, Joe Bryen's refusal to acknowledge his own alcoholism (and his loyal but self-deluded wife's support of him) results eventually in his own destruction as well as that of a man he befriends.

But Turner deals not only with the misfit but with the person who takes it upon himself to assist him, out of an ambiguous mixture of reasons. In *Young Man of Talent,* for instance, Andrew Payne is a man demonstrably unsuited to the army, or anywhere else for that matter. His commanding officer Peter Scobie is warned against him but in his boredom finds the challenge irresistible and sets out to convert the man into a creature of his own making. What seems on the face of it to be an altruistic gesture is slowly shown to proceed out of a kind of corruption, out of a vanity and egotism in Scobie that delights in the brilliance of his own exploitation of the brute. Something like the same thing happens with Jimmy Carlyon, the "lame dog man," and his protegé Ted Johnson. Although Turner is not as harsh in his judgment of Carlyon, other characters in the novel point constantly to the elements of vanity in the assistance he feels obliged to provide to characters weaker than himself.

In the later novels, the qualities of unruliness and disorderliness of personality have not merely personal but cosmic consequences. Turner sees man's impulse to order as inherently fragile and only barely preserved and maintained. Even the leaders in *Yesterday's Men,* for instance, are as driven by doubtful personal motivations as the enemies they affect to despise. Their leader Albert Raft, the offspring of two famous but neglectful parents, is a man who seems increasingly incapable of love and prone to intense bitterness. As in much of Turner's fiction he is depicted as suffering from a deeply-rooted Oedipal complex. In the novel Turner is critical of both the "old," contemporary world, with its violence, nationalistic rivalry and technological and environmental despoilation and the extended processes of controlling and conditioning of the "new" (future) one, by drugs, ultra-sophisticated bugging devices of various kinds and use of hypnosis.

Again in *Vaneglory* he suggests that the people of the 21st century are merely repeating the mistakes of their predecessors of the 20th, who they so much despise, by substituting biological violence for the physical violence of the "Gone-Time" people in the last book of the trilogy. *Yesterday's Men* returns the novelist to New Guinea, where he began, but in vastly different circumstances. The leaders of the planet in the 21st century have decided to conduct a complex experiment to recreate and record on film the conditions of 1942-43 New Guinea (now Niugini) in order to try and understand their own nature by investigating its origins. Turner's basic conclusion in this and throughout his fiction generally is summed up by his most sympathetic character Dunbar, ". . . man's basic nature doesn't change with circumstances."

Turner's recent novel *The Sea and Summer* again tackles the future but in a much more directly didactic way. As the postscript suggests, Turner was moved to write it by his concern for problems of the immediate future (and therefore the present) which few people seem to be planning for. He lists them as population, food, employment, finance, nuclear war, and the greenhouse effect. The novel employs a framing device of someone well into the future attempting to write a play about the past but the majority of the novel consists of a manuscript, also titled *The Sea and Summer,* which is, in fact, set in our not so distant future—AD 2041 to 2061. This novel is set in a Melbourne that has been overtaken by tidal wives, is divided into the Old and New City, and in which the population is divided into the Swills and the Sweets. The former live in appalling conditions with no hope of ever escaping them, though later it emerges that they are actually healthier than the Sweets, the minority with jobs. The financial system collapses during the course of the novel and we also learn that there is a plan to sterilize the Swills without their knowledge. This is one of Turner's strongest narratives with some memorable characters, such as the Swill leader Billy Kovacs who proves unexpectedly to be a man of conscience and even idealism.

A firm although by no means rigid or uncharitable moralist, Turner believes that human beings must always seek to explore and examine the motives of their own behavior as rigorously as they do that of others. Most of his work is marked by a tone of almost Conradian pessimism and skepticism.

—Laurie Clancy

TUTUOLA, Amos

Nationality: Nigerian. **Born:** Abeokuta, Western Nigeria, in June 1920. **Education:** The Salvation Army School and the Anglican Central School, Abeokuta. **Military Service:** Served as a blacksmith in the Royal Air Force, Lagos, 1943-46. **Family:** Married Victoria Alake in 1947; four sons and four daughters. From 1956 stores officer, Nigerian (later Federal) Broadcasting Corporation,

Ibadan; now retired. Visiting Research Fellow, University of Ife, 1979. Founder, Mbari Club of Nigerian Writers. **Address:** Box 2251, Ibadan, Nigeria.

PUBLICATIONS

Novels

The Palm-Wine Drinkard and His Dead Palm-Wine Tapster in the Deads' Town. London, Faber, 1952; New York, Grove Press, 1953.
My Life in the Bush of Ghosts. London, Faber, and New York, Grove Press, 1954.
Simbi and the Satyr of the Dark Jungle. London, Faber, 1955; New York, Grove Press, 1962.
The Brave African Huntress. London, Faber, and New York, Grove Press, 1958.
Feather Woman of the Jungle. London, Faber, 1962; San Francisco, City Lights, 1988.
Ajaiyi and His Inherited Poverty. London, Faber, 1967.
The Witch-Herbalist of the Remote Town. London, Faber, 1981.
The Wild Hunter in the Bush of the Ghosts, edited by Bernth Lindfors. Washington, D.C., Three Continents, 1982.
Pauper, Brawler, and Slanderer. London, Faber, 1987.

Short Stories

Yoruba Folktales. Ibadan, Ibadan University Press, 1986.
The Village Witchdoctor and Other Stories. London, Faber, 1990.

Play

The Palm-Wine Drinkard, with Professor Collis, adaptation of the novel by Tutuola (produced Ibadan, 1962).

Other

Editor, with Jomo Kenyatta and Chinua Achebe, *Winds of Change: Modern Stories from Black Africa.* London, Longman, 1977.

*

Manuscript Collection: Humanities Research Center, University of Texas, Austin.

Critical Studies: *Amos Tutuola* by Harold R. Collins, New York, Twayne, 1969; *Critical Perspectives on Amos Tutuola* edited by Bernth Lindfors, Washington, D.C., Three Continents, 1975, London, Heinemann, 1980; *The Orality of Prose: A Comparatist Look at the Works of Rabelais, Joyce, and Tutuola* by Femi Osofisan, Ife-Ife, Nigeria, Ife Monographs on African Literature, 1986.

Amos Tutuola comments:

My stories reveal how the Yoruba people of the past lived in their days.

*   *   *

Amos Tutuola's 11 books follow the same basic narrative pattern. A hero (or heroine) with supernatural powers or access to supernatural assistance sets out on a journey in quest of something important and suffers incredible hardships before successfully ac-

complishing his mission. He ventures into unearthly realms, performs arduous tasks, fights with fearsome monsters, endures cruel tortures, and narrowly escapes death. Sometimes he is accompanied by a relative or by loyal companions; sometimes he wanders alone. But he always survives his ordeals, attains his objective, and usually emerges from his nightmarish experiences a wiser, wealthier man. The cycle of his adventures — involving a Departure, Initiation, and Return — resembles that found in myths and folktales the world over.

Tutuola's first and most famous book, *The Palm-Wine Drinkard and His Dead Palm-Wine Tapster in the Deads' Town,* which describes a hero's descent into an African underworld in search of a dead companion, was greatly influenced by oral tradition. Tutuola made use of common Yoruba tales and motifs, stringing them together like a fireside raconteur. As a consequence, the book's neat cyclical narrative pattern rests on a very loosely coordinated inner structure. The hero is involved in one adventure after another but these adventures are not well integrated. Like boxcars on a freight train, they are independent units joined with a minimum of apparatus and set in a seemingly random and interchangeable order. There is no foreshadowing of events, no dramatic irony, no evidence of any kind that the sequence of events was carefully thought out. Tutuola appears to be improvising as he goes along and employing the techniques and materials of oral narrative art in his improvisations. This is true of his other writings too, especially *The Wild Hunter in the Bush of the Ghosts,* a manuscript that antedates *The Palm-Wine Drinkard.* All these fantastic tales have been inspired and shaped by indigenous storytelling traditions. In two of his latest books, *Yoruba Folktales* and *The Village Witch Doctor and Other Stories* the oral influence is even more transparent, for Tutuola simply tells his stories as separate narratives, abandoning any attempt to link them together into one synoptic adventure. He appears to have returned to his roots.

However, research has shown that none of Tutuola's works is entirely innocent of literary influence either. He clearly owes his greatest debt to D.O. Fagunwa, who began to publish folkloric "novels" in Yoruba in 1938. In his earliest fiction Tutuola tried to imitate Fagunwa's method of weaving a number of old stories into an elastic narrative pattern that could be stretched into a book. Both Fagunwa and Tutuola appear to have been stimulated by John Bunyan's *The Pilgrim's Progress* and *The Arabian Nights,* which were widely used in Nigerian elementary schools. Later Tutuola turned to other foreign sources of inspiration; Edith Hamilton's *Mythology* may have been responsible for the nymphs, satyrs, myrmidons, and phoenixes which started to infiltrate his African jungles. Goblins, imps, and gnomes also turned up regularly. Tutuola, like a great syncretic sponge, easily obsorbed these alien creatures into his exotic imaginative universe.

This is not to say, of course, that all his writing is derivative or that it lacks originality or accomplishment. In descriptive ability and sheer visionary power Tutuola far surpasses most of his contemporaries. His fertile imagination, never fettered by reason or common sense, constantly begets the surprising, the unorthodox, the incongruous, the bizarre. Events are recounted with a hallucinatory energy that swiftly transports the reader into realms of fantasy. Characters are painted in the most vivid and memorable colors. Whatever Tutuola borrows from oral or literary tradition he immediately makes his own, enlarging it with details of his own invention. He is a master storyteller.

Tutuola's most conspicuous idiosyncrasy as a writer, and perhaps his most controversial, is his style, which Dylan Thomas once termed "naive English." Because he grew up speaking Yoruba and had only six years of formal schooling, Tutuola tends to make spectacular grammatical and spelling blunders on every page he writes. Some critics hold that this fractured idiom is one of his greatest assets for it adds extra tang to the primitive flavor of his works; his language is just as weird and unpredictable as the adventures he describes. Others argue that it is an unfortunate liability for it quickly tires the average reader who is not conditioned to jumping unfamiliar linguistic hurdles. It is unlikely that this critical debate will have any appreciable effect on Tutuola's writing, for he is not a conscious stylist experimenting with language. He is simply trying to do the best he can in a foreign tongue he has not adequately mastered.

The initial reaction to Tutuola's first books was mixed. Readers in Europe and America were enthusiastic for they had never seen anything quite like them before, and they were convinced that Tutuola was a marvellous "original," a diamond in the rough with rich and dazzling creative powers. Reviewers hailed him as an uncouth genius unspoiled by civilization, a mute, inglorious Milton who had suddenly found his voice, albeit a curiously cracked one. Many educated Nigerians, however, were extremely angry that such an unschooled author should receive so much praise and publicity abroad, for they recognized his borrowings, disapproved of his bad grammar, and suspected he was being lionized by condescending racists who had a clear political motive for choosing to continue to regard Africans as backward and childlike primitives. Since Nigeria was struggling to free itself from colonial rule at the time, Tutuola was more than merely an embarrassment; he was a disgrace, a setback, a national calamity. Later, after Nigeria had achieved its independence, Tutuola was no longer an explosive literary or political issue, and his works began to receive more intelligent critical attention. Today his reputation is secure both at home and abroad, for he has come to be accepted as a unique phenomenon in world literature, a writer who bridges two narrative traditions and two cultures by translating oral art into literary art.

—Bernth Lindfors

TYLER, Anne

Nationality: American. **Born:** Minneapolis, Minnesota, 25 October 1941. **Education:** Duke University, Durham, North Carolina, 1958-61, B.A. 1961; Columbia University, New York, 1961-62. **Family:** Married Taghi Modarressi in 1963; two daughters. **Career:** Russian bibliographer, Duke University Library, 1962-63; assistant to the librarian, McGill University Law Library, Montreal, 1964-65. **Awards:** American Academy award, 1977; Janet Kafka prize, 1981; PEN Faulkner award, 1983; National Book Critics Circle award, 1986; Pulitzer prize, 1989. **Agent:** Russell and Volkening Inc., 50 West 29th Street, New York, New York 10001. **Address:** 222 Tunbridge Road, Baltimore, Maryland 21212, U.S.A.

PUBLICATIONS

Novels

If Morning Ever Comes. New York, Knopf, 1964; London, Chatto and Windus, 1965.

The Tin Can Tree. New York, Knopf, 1965; London, Macmillan, 1966.
A Slipping-Down Life. New York, Knopf, 1970; London, Severn House, 1983.
The Clock Winder. New York, Knopf, 1972; London, Chatto and Windus, 1973.
Celestial Navigation. New York, Knopf, 1974; London, Chatto and Windus, 1975.
Searching for Caleb. New York, Knopf, and London, Chatto and Windus, 1976.
Earthly Possessions. New York, Knopf, and London, Chatto and Windus, 1977.
Morgan's Passing. New York, Knopf, and London, Chatto and Windus, 1980.
Dinner at the Homesick Restaurant. New York, Knopf, and London, Chatto and Windus, 1982.
The Accidental Tourist. New York, Knopf, and London, Chatto and Windus, 1985.
Breathing Lessons. New York, Knopf, 1988; London, Chatto and Windus, 1989.
Saint Maybe. New York, Knopf, and London, Chatto and Windus, 1991.
Ladder of Years. New York, Knopf, 1995.

Uncollected Short Stories

"I Play Kings," in *Seventeen* (New York), August 1963.
"Street of Bugles," in *Saturday Evening Post* (Philadelphia), 30 November 1963.
"Nobody Answers the Door," in *Antioch Review* (Yellow Springs, Ohio), Fall 1964.
"I'm Not Going to Ask You Again," in *Harper's* (New York), September 1965.
"Everything But Roses," in *Reporter* (New York), 23 September 1965.
"As the Earth Gets Old," in *New Yorker,* 29 October 1966.
"Feather Behind the Rock," in *New Yorker,* 12 August 1967.
"Flaw in the Crust of the Earth," in *Reporter* (New York), 2 November 1967.
"Common Courtesies," in *McCall's* (New York), June 1968.
"With All Flags Flying," in *Redbook* (New York), June 1971.
"Bride in the Boatyard," in *McCall's* (New York), June 1972.
"Respect," in *Mademoiselle* (New York), June 1972.
"Misstep of the Mind," in *Seventeen* (New York), October 1972.
"Knack for Languages," in *New Yorker,* 13 January 1975.
"Some Sign That I Ever Made You Happy," in *McCall's* (New York), October 1975.
"Your Place Is Empty," in *New Yorker,* 22 November 1976.
"Holding Things Together," in *New Yorker,* 24 January 1977.
"Average Waves in Unprotected Waters," in *New Yorker,* 28 February 1977.
"Foot-Footing On," in *Mademoiselle* (New York), November 1977.
"The Geologist's Maid," in *Stories of the Modern South,* edited by Ben Forkner and Patrick Samway. New York, Penguin, 1981.
"Laps," in *Parents' Magazine* (New York), August 1981.
"The Country Cook," in *Harper's* (New York), March 1982.
"Teenage Wasteland," in *The Editors' Choice 1,* edited by George E. Murphy, Jr. New York, Bantam, 1985.
"Rerun," in *New Yorker,* 4 July 1988.
"A Street of Bugles," in *Saturday Evening Post* (Indianapolis), July-August 1989.

"A Woman Like a Fieldstone House," in *Louder than Words,* edited by William Shore. New York, Vintage, 1989.

Other

Tumble Tower (for children). New York, Orchard, 1993.

Editor, with Shannon Ravenel, *The Best American Short Stories 1983.* Boston, Houghton Mifflin, 1983; as *The Year's Best American Short Stories,* London, Severn House, 1984.

*

Critical Studies: *Art and the Accidental in Anne Tyler* by Joseph C. Voelker, Jackson, University Press of Mississippi, 1989; *The Temporal Horizon: A Study of the Theme of Time in Anne Tyler's Major Novels* by Karin Linton, Uppsala, Sweden, Studia Anglistica, 1989; *The Fiction of Anne Tyler* edited by C. Ralph Stephens, Jackson, University Press of Mississippi, 1990; *Understanding Anne Tyler* by Alice Hall Petty, Columbia, University of South Carolina Press, 1990.

*   *   *

When Anne Tyler won the Pulitzer prize in 1989 for her novel *Breathing Lessons,* she perhaps should have won it for her work as a whole. While *Breathing Lessons* is assuredly written, it does not necessarily stand superior to any of Tyler's mature novels (from *Morgan's Passing* in 1980 onwards). It bears all the hallmarks of her work: a Baltimore setting, neighborhoods that remain neighborhoods, gentle, bemused characters who seem permanently lodged in the early 1960s no matter the year, peculiar, offhand family relationships, and a world held at bay by persistent obliquity.

Although she was born in Minnesota, Tyler grew up in the South, and much has been made of her allegiance to the southern school of American writing. However, rather like her beloved Baltimore, she is not so easily categorized. (Baltimore, Maryland has that slightly schizophrenic feel of being not quite northern, not quite southern; during the American Civil War Maryland was one of the only states in the Union to uphold slavery.) To its benefit, Tyler's writing does not hold to recognized borders; she sets her own.

Characters' relationships to their families and spouses are at the crux of all of Tyler's novels—from her first, *If Morning Ever Comes,* in which a young man travels back to North Carolina to come to terms with the expectations and the realities of his family, to her latest, *Saint Maybe,* in which a young man spends 20 years doing much the same thing. Tyler families are peculiar, spiky things—to be taken for granted and yet terribly fragile and easily hurt. Members forever vacillate between remaining individuals and conforming to the collective family character. Tyler often describes family get-togethers, whether sitting down to a Thanksgiving dinner or just an ordinary meal, as a series of stops and starts, misunderstandings, stepped-on toes, misalliances and realliances, all underpinned by a tacit familiarity and similarity. If one of Tyler's characters is an oddball, you can be sure his or her family is as well. And yet the families endure; simply their existence is their great strength.

And if they do not endure, new ones are engendered. Tyler is constantly taking a broken family and trying to fix it, no matter if the cracks show. Both *The Clock Winder* and *Celestial Navigations* begin with losses in families (husband and mother respectively) which are quickly filled by odd, competent women; both novels are the story of their fitting in and of the families fitting around them. *Dinner at the Homesick Restaurant* takes its title from one of the character's idea to run a restaurant more in the style of a family home, a place where the waiters mother you a bit and suggest what you should have, where you can eat food you are homesick for. Ezra is from a family whose father deserted them and whose mother seems distant and hard-hearted. By creating new (if temporary) families at his restaurant, he can vicariously fulfill his own family needs. In *Breathing Lessons* Maggie tries to patch up her son's broken marriage, with disastrous results. *Saint Maybe* is based around Ian's attempt, which backfires tragically, to inform his brother Danny of a flaw in the latter's marriage. Only when Ian is able to forgive himself his error of judgement, and his brother and sister-in-law for having revealed their weaknesses—only then can he live a whole, real life, symbolized at the end of the book by his marrying and making a family of his own.

Possibly Tyler's finest novel, *The Accidental Tourist,* also explores the power of family and of love, and their limitations. Macon Leary and his wife separate a year after their 12-year-old son is murdered. Macon is a cautious, orderly man. For a living he writes travel books for business people who want "to take trips without a jolt." He instructs accidental tourists—people who would rather not be travelling—on how to get through awkward, alien terrain with the least amount of disturbance to their normal routines. (In Paris he eats at Burger King, in London at Yankee Delight.) He applies these techniques to alien emotional terrain as well, and with some success until Sarah leaves him. At first he copes with her departure by trying to perfect daily life so that he can get through it with the least amount of hassle and energy—a kind of accidental tourist at home. (For instance, he starts washing his clothes by treading on them when he takes his daily shower.) Then, when he breaks his leg as a result of one of these energy-saving systems, he goes back to live with his sister and two brothers. The Learys are all accidental tourists of a sort, with systems for doing things and a studied vagueness about the world outside of their home. Macon fits right in as if he had never left.

All this changes, however, when Macon gets involved with Muriel Pritchett, a loopy woman who trains Macon's dog Edward. (Unlike Macon, Edward does not navigate phlegmatically through unsettling events; he is a very emotional dog.) Muriel is spunky, neurotic, needy, vocal—completely the opposite to the Learys. She also has a seven-year-old son Alexander (the father has left them), a sad, sickly boy who, in some of the book's best scenes, blossoms under Macon's offhand nurturing.

Eventually Macon leaves Muriel and reunites with his wife, but what he has learned from Muriel has penetrated his accidental tourist cocoon, and finally he has to choose between old ways and new. And he discovers "that people could, in fact, be used up—could use each other up, could be of no further help to each other and maybe even do harm to each other. He began to think that who you are when you're with somebody may matter more than whether you love her." In the end, family may not be the most important mainstay; you have the ability to choose other people and other ways.

The Accidental Tourist gracefully charts Macon's transformation from (in Sarah's words) a "dried-up kernal of a man that nothing really penetrates" to a man who "had never been suspected of narrowness, never been accused of chilliness; in fact, was mocked for his soft heart. And was anything but orderly." Tyler makes clear that such a choice and change is not without its price, however—there is always someone left behind, "used-up."

The Accidental Tourist should silence critics who have said
Tyler's characters tend to end up where they started from without
developing. *Saint Maybe* also makes such a progression, but without quite the same affection and interest. There are signs, in fact,
that since *The Accidental Tourist* Tyler is slipping into a comfortable pattern of novels that do not probe so accurately. If so, it is to
our great loss, for few writers explore the oddities and ambivalence of family life so wisely and so well.

—Tracy Chevalier

U

UNSWORTH, Barry (Forster)

Nationality: British. **Born:** Durham, England, 10 August 1930. **Education:** University of Manchester, B.A. (with honors in English) 1951. **Military Service:** British Army, Royal Corps of Signals, 1951-53: second lieutenant. **Family:** 1) married Valerie Moor, 1959 (marriage dissolved, 1991) three daughters; 2) Aira Pohjanvaara-Buffa, 1992. **Career:** Lecturer in English, Norwood Technical College, 1960 and 1963-65; lecturer in English for British Council, University of Athens, Greece, 1960-63. Since 1965 lecturer in English for British Council, University of Istanbul, Turkey. **Awards:** Royal Society of Literature-Heinemann award for literature, 1974, for *Mooncranker's Gift;* Booker prize, 1992, for *Sacred Hunger.* **Address:** c/o Hamish Hamilton, 22 Wright's Lane, London W8 5TZ, England.

PUBLICATIONS

Novels

The Partnership. London, Hutchinson, 1966.
The Greeks Have a Word for It. London, Hutchinson, 1967.
The Hide. London, Gollancz, 1970.
Mooncranker's Gift. London, Allen, 1973; New York, Houghton Mifflin, 1974.
The Big Day. London, Michael Joseph, 1976; New York, Mason/Charter, 1977.
Pascali's Island. London, Michael Joseph; as *The Idol Hunter,* New York, Simon and Schuster, 1980.
The Rage of the Vulture. London, Granada, 1982; New York, Houghton Mifflin, 1983.
Stone Virgin. London, Hamilton, 1985; New York, Houghton Mifflin, 1986.
Sugar and Rum. London, Hamilton, 1988.
Sacred Hunger. London, Hamilton, and New York, Doubleday, 1992.

Other

The Student's Book of English: A Complete Coursebook and Grammar to Advanced Intermediate Level, with John Lennox Cook and Amorey Gethin. Oxford, Blackwell, 1981.
Novels and Novelists in the 1990's. London, Random House, 1993.

*   *   *

Barry Unsworth's fiction offers powerful and closely observed explorations of human relationships in which desire is entangled with exploitation and with potential, sometimes actual, violence. In *The Partnership,* for example, the association of two business partners is complicated and eventually destroyed by the repressed homoerotic attraction that one of them has for the other, and in *The Hide,* a semiarticulate gardener is pressured by his dominating friend into arranging the rape of a young woman. Both of these early novels are set in England in modern times, and their close focus on the relationships they portray largely excludes explicit engagement with wider concerns; but in Unsworth's most characteristic work, such relationships are placed in broader geographical, political, and historical contexts. *Pascali's Island* and *The Rage of the Vulture,* for instance, go back to the last throes of the Ottoman Empire in 1908; *Stone Virgin* takes place in Venice, partly in the 15th century, partly in the 18th century, and partly in the later 20th century; and *Sacred Hunger,* set in the 18th century, moves from the British port of Liverpool to a slave ship, the Guinea Coast, and Florida.

A recurrent concern of Unsworth's novels is the link between the relationships of his characters and the artifacts that they make, display, observe, exchange, or desire. In *The Partnership,* for example, the pixies turned out by one of the partners, Foley, provide the staple of the business, whereas the seraphs and cherubs he also makes represent his desire for independence and finally become the object of his partner's violence. *Pascali's Island* sets up a complex relationship between a marble head of a woman that is fraudulently claimed to have been found on an archaeological site, a bronze male statue, which is actually buried on the site and provokes a fatal attempt at theft, and a wax model of a saint that topples down during the ceremony of his Assumption. The central motif of *Stone Virgin* is a carved Venetian Madonna that is first fashioned by Girolamo, a Piedmontese stonecutter; is subsequently discovered after three hundred years by a rake called Ziani; and finally, in 1972, falls into the hands of an English conservation expert, Simon Raikes. The ambiguity of the artifact—as both a product and a denial of mortality—is forcefully encapsulated in *Mooncranker's Gift,* where the "gift" of the title is a bandaged effigy of the crucified Christ that is in fact made of sausage meat and turns rotten and stinking. Artifacts take on a range of symbolic functions in Unsworth's novels, and they link up with his other concerns, such as voyeurism, in *The Hide,* or the commodification of human beings, in *Sacred Hunger.*

At his best, Unsworth has a precise, nuanced, and rhythmically accomplished style that enables him to register psychological complexity and to evocatively render time and place. Some of his novels, such as *The Greeks Have a Word For It,* employ an omniscient narrator, and Unsworth avails himself freely of the opportunities that this technique offers to move between the minds of different characters for dramatic effect; in other novels, for instance *Pascali's Island,* the story is told in the first person, whereas *Stone Virgin* combines third person with some first-person narration. The novels are skillfully structured to maintain narrative interest and to provide a range of perspectives on their themes and symbols.

Unsworth's fiction has stayed largely within the realist mode, although *Sugar and Rum,* which portrays a novelist who wants to write a novel about the Liverpool slave trade but is suffering from writer's block, provides a kind of metafictional commentary on the book that follows it, *Sacred Hunger.* His earlier novels proved him to be a skilled practitioner of realism, and his more recent work has shown his readiness to use those skills to tackle large themes—most notably in *Sacred Hunger,* which confronts an area of Britain's imperial past, its involvement with the slave trade, which is a deeply repressed but still potent subtext in contemporary British debates about immigration and national identity. In postwar British culture, realistic fiction has sometimes been identified with a restriction of the novelist's scope; Unsworth has demonstrated the continuing capacity of realism to roam widely in time and space and to engage vigorously and resourcefully with crucial issues.

—Nicolas Tredell

UPDIKE, John (Hoyer)

Nationality: American. **Born:** Shillington, Pennsylvania, 18 March 1932. **Education:** Public schools in Shillington; Harvard University, Cambridge, Massachusetts, A.B. (summa cum laude) 1954; Ruskin School of Drawing and Fine Arts, Oxford (Knox fellow), 1954-55. **Family:** Married 1) Mary Pennington in 1953 (marriage dissolved), two daughters and two sons; 2) Martha Bernhard in 1977. **Career:** staff reporter, *New Yorker,* 1955-57. **Awards:** Guggenheim fellowship, 1959; Rosenthal award, 1960; National Book award, 1964; O. Henry award, 1966; Foreign Book prize (France), 1966; New England Poetry Club Golden Rose, 1979, MacDowell medal, 1981; Pulitzer prize, 1982, 1991; American Book award, 1982; National Book Critics Circle award, for fiction, 1982, 1991, for criticism, 1982; Union League Club Abraham Lincoln award, 1982; National Arts Club Medal of Honor, 1984; National Medal of the Arts, 1989. **Member:** American Academy, 1976. **Address:** 675 Hale Street, Beverly Farms, Massachusetts 01915, U.S.A.

PUBLICATIONS

Novels

The Poorhouse Fair. New York, Knopf, and London, Gollancz, 1959.
Rabbit, Run. New York, Knopf, 1960; London, Deutsch, 1961
The Centaur. New York, Knopf, and London, Deutsch, 1963.
Of the Farm. New York, Knopf, 1965.
Couples. New York, Knopf, and London, Deutsch, 1968
Rabbit Redux. New York, Knopf, 1971; London, Deutsch, 1972.
A Month of Sundays. New York, Knopf, and London, Deutsch, 1975.
Marry Me: A Romance. New York, Knopf, 1976; London, Deutsch, 1977.
The Coup. New York, Knopf, 1978; London, Deutsch, 1979.
Rabbit Is Rich. New York, Knopf, 1981; London, Deutsch, 1982.
The Witches of Eastwick. New York, Knopf, and London, Deutsch, 1984.
Roger's Version. New York, Knopf, and London, Deutsch, 1986.
S. New York, Knopf, and London Deutsch, 1988.
Rabbit at Rest. New York, Knopf, 1990; London, Deutsch, 1991.
Memories of the Ford Administration. New York, Knopf, 1992; London, Hamish Hamilton, 1993.
Brazil. New York, Knopf, and London, Hamish Hamilton, 1994.

Short Stories

The Same Door. New York, Knopf, 1959; London, Deutsch, 1962.
Pigeon Feathers and Other Stories. New York, Knopf, and London, Deutsch, 1962.
Olinger Stories: A Selection. New York, Knopf, 1964.
The Music School. New York, Knopf, 1966; London, Deutsch, 1967.
Penguin Modern Stories 2, with others. London, Penguin, 1969.
Bech: A Book. New York, Knopf, and London, Deutsch, 1970.
The Indian. Marvin, South Dakota, Blue Cloud Abbey, 1971.
Museums and Women and Other Stories. New York, Knopf, 1972; London, Deutsch, 1973.
Warm Wine: An Idyll. New York, Albondocani Press, 1973.
Couples: A Short Story. Cambridge, Massachusetts, Halty Ferguson, 1976.
Too Far to Go: The Maples Stories. New York, Knopf, 1979; London, Deutsch, 1980.
Three Illuminations in the Life of an American Author. New York, Targ, 1979.
The Chaste Planet. Worcester, Massachusetts, Metacom Press, 1980.
The Beloved. Nothridge, California, Lord John Press, 1982.

Bech Is Back. New York, Knopf, 1982; London, Deutsch, 1982.
Getting Older. Helsinki, Eurographica, 1985.
Going Abroad. Helsinki, Eurographica, 1987
Trust Me. New York, Knopf, and London, Deutsch, 1987.
The Afterlife. Leamington, Warwickshire, Sixth Chamber Press, 1987.
Baby's First Step. Huntington Beach, California, Cahill, 1993.
The Afterlife and Other Stories. New York, Knopf, and London, Hamish Hamilton, 1994.

Uncollected Short Stories

"Morocco," in *Atlantic* (Boston), November 1979.

Plays

Three Tests from Early Ipswich: A Pageant. Ipswich, Massachusetts, 17th Century Day Committee, 1968.
Buchanan Dying. New York, Knopf, and London, Deutsch, 1974.

Verse

The Carpentered Hen and Other Tame Creatures. New York, Harper, 1958; as *Hoping for a Hoopoe,* London, Gollancz, 1959.
Telephone Poles and Other Poems. New York, Knopf, and London, Deutsch, 1963.
Verse. New York, Fawcett, 1965.
Dogs Death. Cambridge, Massachusetts, Lowell House, 1965.
The Angels. Pensacola, Florida, King and Queen Press, 1968.
Bath after Sailing. Monroe, Connecticut, Pendulum Press, 1968.
Midpoint and Other Poems. New York, Knopf, and London, Deutsch, 1969.
Seventy Poems. London, Penguin, 1972.
Six Poems. New York, Aloe, 1973.
Query. New York, Albondocani Press, 1974.
Cunts (Upon Receiving the Swingers Life Club Memberships Solicitation). New York, Hallman, 1974.
Tossing and Turning. New York, Knopf, and London, Deutsch, 1977.
Sixteen Sonnets. Cambridge, Massachusetts, Halty Ferguson, 1979.
An Oddly Lovely Day Alone. Richmond, Virginia, Waves Press, 1979.
Five Poems. Cleveland Bits Press, 1980.
Spring Trio. Winston-Salem, North Carolina, Palaemon Press, 1982.
Jester's Dozen. Northridge, California, Lord John Press, 1984.
Facing Nature. New York, Knopf, 1985; London, Deutsch, 1986.
A Pear Like a Potato. Northridge, California, Santa Susana Press, 1986.
Two Sonnets. Austin, Texas, Wind River Press, 1987.
Collected Poems, 1953-1993. New York, Knopf, and London, Hamish Hamilton, 1993.

Other

The Magic Flute (for children), with Warren Chappell. New York, Knopf, 1962.
The Ring (for children), with Warren Chappell. New York, Knopf, 1964.
Assorted Prose. New York, Knopf, and London, Deutsch, 1965.
A Child's Calendar. New York, Knopf, 1965.
On Meeting Authors. Newburyport, Massachusetts, Wickford Press, 1968.
Bottom's Dream: Adapted from William Shakespeare's "A Midsummer Nights Dream" (for children). New York, Knopf, 1969.
A Good Place. New York, Aloe, 1973.
Picked-Up Pieces. New York, Knopf, 1975; London, Deutsch, 1976.
Hub Fans Bid Kid Adieu. Northridge, California, Lord John Press, 1977.
Talk from the Fifties. Northridge, California, Lord John Press, 1979.
Ego and Art in Walt Whitman. New York, Targ, 1980.

People One Knows: Interviews with Insufficiently Famous Americans. Northridge, California, Lord John Press, 1980.

Invasion of the Book Envelopes. Concord, New Hampshire, Ewert, 1981.

Hawthorne's Creed. New York, Targ, 1981.

Hugging the Shore: Essays and Criticism. New York, Knopf, 1983; London, Deutsch, 1984.

Confessions of a Wild Bore (essay). Newton, Iowa, Tamazunchale Press, 1984.

Emersonianism (lecture). Cleveland, Bits Press, 1984.

The Art of Adding and the Art of Taking Away: Selections from John Updike's Manuscripts, edited by Elizabeth A. Falsey. Cambridge, Massachusetts, Harvard College Library, 1987.

Self-Consciousness: Memoirs. New York, Knopf, and London, Deutsch, 1989.

Just Looking: Essays on Art. New York, Knopf, and London, Deutsch, 1989.

Odd Jobs: Essays and Criticism. New York, Knopf, and London, Deutsch, 1991.

Concerts at Castle Hill. Northridge, California, Lord John Press, 1993.

The Twelve Terrors of Christmas. New York, Gotham Book Mart, 1993.

Editor, *Pens and Needles,* by David Levine. Boston, Gambit, 1970.

Editor, with Shannon Ravenel, *The Best American Short Stories 1984.* Boston, Houghton Mifflin, 1984; as *The Year's Best American Short Stories,* London, Severn House, 1985.

*

Bibliography: *John Updike: A Bibliography* by C. Clarke Taylor, Kent, Ohio, Kent State University Press, 1968; *An Annotated Bibliography of John Updike Criticism 1967-1973, and a Checklist of His Works* by Michael A. Olivas, New York, Garland, 1975; *John Updike: A Comprehensive Bibliography with Selected Annotations* by Elizabeth A. Gearhart, Norwood, Pennsylvania, Norwood Editions, 1978.

Manuscript Collection: Harvard University, Cambridge, Massachusetts

Critical Studies: Interviews in *Life* (New York), 4 November 1966, *Paris Review,* Winter 1968, and *New York Times Book Review,* 10 April 1977; *John Updike* by Charles T. Samuels, Minneapolis, University of Minnesota Press, 1969; *The Elements of John Updike* by Alice and Kenneth Hamilton, Grand Rapids, Michigan, Eerdmans, 1970; *Pastoral and Anti-Pastoral Elements in John Updike's Fiction* by Larry E. Taylor, Carbondale, Southern Illinois University Press, 1971; *John Updike: Yea Sayings* by Rachael C. Burchard, Carbondale, Southern Illinois University Press, 1971; *John Updike* by Robert Detweiler, New York, Twayne, 1972, revised edition, 1984; *Rainstorms and Fire: Ritual in the Novels of John Updike* by Edward P. Vargo, Port Washington, New York, Kennikat Press, 1973; *Fighters and Lovers: Theme in the Novels of John Updike* by Joyce B. Markle, New York, New York University Press, 1973; *John Updike: A Collection of Critical Essays* by Suzanne H. Uphaus, New York, Ungar, 1980; *The Other John Updike: Poems/Short Stories/Prose/Play,* 1981, and *John Updike's Novels,* 1984, both by Donald J. Greiner, Athens, Ohio University Press; *John Updike's Images of America* by Philip H. Vaughan, Reseda, California, Mojave, 1981; *Married Men and Magic Tricks: John Updike's Erotic Heroes* by Elizabeth Tallent, Berkeley, California, Creative Arts, 1982; *Critical Essays on John Updike* edited by William R. Macnaughton, Boston, Hall, 1982; *John Updike* by Judie Newman, London, Macmillan, 1988; *Conversations with John Updike* edited by James Plath, Jackson, Mississippi, University Press, 1994.

John Updike comments:

In over thirty years as a professional writer I have tried to give my experience of life imaginative embodiment in novels, short stories, and poems. Art is, as I understand it, reality passed through a human mind, and this secondary creation remains for me unfailingly interesting and challenging.

*   *   *

The novelist John Updike, briefly a staff member of the *New Yorker* and a frequent contributor throughout his writing career, has also published poetry, several collections of short stories, some of the most perceptive and readable literary criticism to appear in that journal's discriminating pages, and an engaging autobiography, *Self-Consciousness.*

This is the record of a wholly professional dedication to the art of letters. Intelligence, imagination, and impeccable craftsmanship are the hallmarks of his versatile work. The novels seem as freshly minted today as when they were first issued; but while they gleam with a surface polish of urbanity and wit, their structure and design are of solid metal. They are deeply serious in theme but never solemn in manner.

Updike is, in short, a moralist. The mores he examines are typically those of small-town New England/Pennsylvania WASPS. His characters are adrift amid the materialistic flotsam of modern American life. Uncertain of their bearings and bewildered by the assorted mess that surrounds them, they struggle to make headway in the hope of sighting some beacon which will guide them to safety. Bereft of religious and moral certainties they nonetheless strive to discern a meaningful pattern in their apparently haphazard existence; as Harry Angstrom inarticulately puts it in *Rabbit, Run,* "there's something out there that wants me to find it."

Though the series of Rabbit novels constitutes the crux for the decipherment of Updike's moral intimations, the essentials of his fictional tactics are disclosed in his first and other early novels. These are firmly underpinned by structures of myth, ritual, biblical reference, and metaphor, whose resonances reverberate beneath the ground plan of the stories.

In *Poorhouse Fair* we witness the collision of two mythologies inadequate to their purpose. The setting is a poorhouse in which a handful of old people are waiting to die. The poorhouse master is a self-proclaimed humanitarian and idealist, the oldest of the inmates is a professed Christian. The clash between them eventually erupts in the stoning of the master, in a martyrdom as futile as St. Stephen's and as grim as the inmates' faltering lives. *The Centaur* also uses myth as metaphor in an extension of the field of inquiry beyond the urgency of sex. The protagonists are a school-teacher father and his son, the former threatened by cancer. Centaur-like he holds his head high though his body is low and sinking. Reflecting on his life, he detects a linking pattern between his own career and his father's as a clergyman. The son, overwhelmed by his father's potential death and his own sexual compulsions, discovers that sexual escapades and human love are not coterminous. Love is transcendental; art, his chosen career, is potentially a means towards the ordering of human experience. Priest, teacher and artist, Updike seems to assert, are the possible purveyors of human salvation.

Updike's fullest affirmation of man's need for myth, as a way of ordering perceived chaos, is to be found in *Couples,* which explores the live of the inhabitants of Tarbox, Massachusetts. They have abandoned the imperatives of responsibility, duty, and the work ethic, replacing them with the self-indulgence of "having fun" in what is a moral vacuum. The permutations of ritualistic formulae, taboos, and developing adulteries are polarized in Freddy Thorne, the town dentist (dentists deal in decay), and Piet Hanema, carpenter and Calvinistic determinist (Christ was a carpenter) who, when his church is destroyed by a thunderbolt, departs from Tarbox (or Sodom) to start a new life. Rich in allusion and metaphorical undertones, this is one of Updike's most brilliantly handled novels.

The Coup adventured into new territory with its study of a military dictator in an emergent African country caught up in the cold war between the superpowers; with *The Witches of Eastwick* Updike returned to New England and a witty tale of magic and fantasy in which his gift for comedy is given full play.

The Rabbit novels, however, can be seen as the matrix of his work. Occupying 30 years of his writing life, this tetralogy was completed after a long pause, a necessary strategy since the last volume was to conclude a life cycle in which Harry "Rabbit" Angstrom's death occurs when his son is of much the same age as Rabbit when we first meet him, and in his own set of predicaments.

In *Rabbit, Run* we are introduced to Harry, a hero to the basketball playing kids in his neighborhood and a villain in the eyes of his wife, Janice, her family and their children. Backed into a corner by his inadequacies, Rabbit makes a bolt for freedom from his family and mistress, driving dead south but paradoxically pointlessly to an unknown destination. With every dash that Rabbit makes from the snares that beset him, he becomes more entangled in the meshes spread across his pathways. In *Rabbit Redux* he is back with his collapsing job; in *Rabbit Is Rich* he shares in the prosperity of the boom when what's good for General Motors is also good for his wife's family's Toyota dealership. But America is beginning to run out of gas in the energy crunch; Rabbit also, overweight, jogging, breathless but still hopefully seeking illumination, the "something that wants me to find it."

Rabbit at Rest shows us Angstrom on the run again, heading south for his retirement condominium in Florida only to be recalled to Pennsylvania, where his cocaine-addicted son has ruined the business and destroyed his own family. Rabbit, succumbing to thrombosis, reckons that the "something" has now found him "and is working him over". This bleak conclusion is reinforced by images of national decline in the years of Reaganomics. Rabbit and his country are at one. But there is a moment of grace at the end. Rabbit the basket-ball hero runs and leaps to pitch a final perfect ball, and finds peace in cardiac arrest. The moral is uncompromising, the conclusion pitiful; but Updike also conveys a message of compassion.

—Stewart Sanderson

UPWARD, Edward (Falaise)

Nationality: British. **Born:** Romford, Essex, 9 September 1903. **Education:** Repton School, Derby, 1917-21; Corpus Christi College, Cambridge (Chancellors's medal for English verse), 1922-24, M.A. 1925. **Family:** Married to Hilda Maude Percival; one son and one daughter. **Career:** Schoolmaster, 1928-62; Member of the Editorial Board, the *Ploughshare,* London, 1936-39. Lives in Sandown, Isle of Wight. **Address:** c/o Heinemann Ltd., 81 Fulham Road, London SW3 6RB, England.

PUBLICATIONS

Novels

Journey to the Border. London, Hogarth Press, 1938; revised edition, London, Enitharmon Press, 1994.
The Spiral Ascent (includes *No Home But the Struggle*). London, Heinemann, 1977.
   In the Thirties. London, Heinemann, 1962.
   The Rotten Elements. London, Heinemann, 1969.

Short Stories

The Railway Accident and Other Stories. London, Heinemann, 1969.
The Night and Other Stories. London, Heinemann, 1987.

Uncollected Short Stories

"The Scenic Railway," in *Best Short Stories 1989,* edited by Giles Gordon and David Hughes. London, Heinemann, 1989; as *The Best English Short Stories,* New York, Norton, 1989.
"The Theft," in *Colours of a New Day: Writing for South Africa,* edited by Sarah Lefnau and Stephen Hayward. London, Lawrence and Wishart, and New York, Pantheon, 1990.
"Investigation after Midnight," in *London Magazine,* April-May 1990.

Poetry

Buddha. London, Cambridge University Press, 1924.

*

Manuscript Collection: British Library, London.

Critical Studies: *The Destructive Element: A Study of Modern Writers and Beliefs* by Stephen Spender, London, Cape, 1935, Boston, Houghton Mifflin, 1936; introduction by W.H.Sellers to *The Railway Accident and Other Stories,* 1969; article by Upward, in *London Magazine,* June 1969; *Leben und Werk von Edward Upward* by Dieter Mensen, unpublished thesis, Berlin, Free University, 1976; *Aestheticism and Political Commitment in the Works of Edward Upward* by Clarke Thayer, unpublished thesis, Tulsa, Oklahoma, University of Tulsa, 1981; *History and Value* by Frank Kermode, Oxford, Oxford University Press, 1988.

*   *   *

Edward Upward as a young writer in the 1930s achieved a great reputation, was indeed something of a legend, among a number of writers of his own age and younger. Christopher Isherwood told in *Lions and Shadows* how he and Upward (called Chalmers in Isherwood's book) at Cambridge invented a fantasy world they called Mortmere which paralleled and parodied the world about them. Mortmere seems to have been at once sinister and comic, partly surrealist and partly Gothic. That it had affinities with Auden's early poetry, influenced as it was by Freud, seems clear, and something of it seems to merge in the plays Isherwood wrote in collaboration with Auden, notably *The Dog Beneath the Skin.* Upward, however, overtly pursued the vein of fantasy in his fiction, but was even then politically committed in the cause of Marxism. The central character of *Journey to the Border* is a middle-class young man employed as a tutor in the house of a rich man; he is constantly struggling against the implications and ignominies of his position but is unable to resolve them. He is persuaded against his will to accompany his employer to a race-meeting. On the way, and while there, he experiences a series of hallucinations that mount in intensity and are the counterparts of the debate going on in his mind. By the end of the novel he is forced to realize that the only solution to this problem, the only way to reality, is for him to identify himself with the working-class struggle.

When the novel was first published, reviewers read the influence of Kafka into it. This is not much apparent now, if it ever existed. Upward's novel is much less complex than those in simple allegory. Nevertheless, the voltage of imaginative work is admirably sustained. It remains a brilliant experimental novel of a very unusual kind.

Upward published nothing for 25 years, and then in 1962 published *In the Thirties* (followed by *The Rotten Elements* and, as a complete trilogy incorporating *No Home But the Struggle, The Spiral Ascent*). These novels are based, it is impossible not to think, on the author's own life. *In the Thirties* describes the stages by which a young middle-class man comes to Communism. In a sense, the theme is that of *Journey to the Border,* but the treatment is entirely different. Fantasy has been replaced by literal realism, which is also the vein of later volumes of the trilogy. In *The Rotten Elements* the hero of the earlier novel, a school teacher now married, finds himself compelled in the years immediately after the war to leave the Communist Party, not because he has lost his political faith but because for him and his wife the British Communist Party, under the influence of Moscow, has deviated from Marxism-Leninism. *No Home But the Struggle* shows them recommitted to the campaign for nuclear disarmament. The trilogy lacks the literary interest of *Journey to the Border,* but it has an anguish of its own and a documentary quality which suggests that, though it may not be read in the future for its artistic value, it will be essential reading for scholars concerned with the role of the Communist party in Britain.

—Walter Allen

URIS, Leon (Marcus)

Nationality: American. **Born:** Baltimore, Maryland, 3 August 1924. **Education:** Schools in Baltimore. **Military Service:** Served in the United States Marine Corp, 1942-45. **Family:** Married 1) Betty Beck in 1945 (divorced 1965); 2) Margery Edwards in 1968 (died 1969); 3) Jill Peabody in 1970; three children. **Career:** Newspaper driver for the San Francisco *Call-Bulletin,* late 1940s. Full-time writer since 1950. Lives in Aspen, Colorado. **Awards:** Daroff Memorial award, 1959; American Academy grant, 1959. **Address:** c/o Doubleday, 666 Fifth Avenue, New York, New York 10103, U.S.A.

PUBLICATIONS

Novels

Battle Cry. New York, Putnam, and London, Wingate, 1953.
The Angry Hills. New York, Random House, 1955; London, Wingate, 1956.
Exodus. New York, Doubleday, 1958; London, Wingate, 1959.
Mila 18. New York, Doubleday, and London, Heinemann, 1961.
Armageddon: A Novel of Berlin. New York, Doubleday, and London, Kimber, 1964.

Topaz. New York, McGraw Hill, 1967; London, Kimber, 1971.
Q.B. VII. New York, Doubleday, 1970; London, Kimber, 1971.
Trinity. New York, Doubleday, and London, Deutsch, 1976.
The Haj. New York, Doubleday, and London, Deutsch, 1984.
Mitla Pass. New York, Doubleday, 1988; London, Doubleday, 1989.

Plays

Ari, music by Walt Smith and William Fisher, adaptation of his own novel *Exodus* (produced New York, 1971).

Screenplays: *Battle Cry,* 1955; *Gunfight at the OK Corral,* 1957; *Israel* (documentary), 1959.

Other

Exodus Revisted. New York, Doubleday, 1960; as *In the Steps of Exodus,* London, Heinemann, 1962.
The Third Temple, with *Strike Zion,* by William Stevenson. New York, Bantam, 1967.
Ireland, A Terrible Beauty: The Story of Ireland Today, with Jill Uris. New York, Doubleday, 1975; London, Deutsch, 1976.
Jerusalem: Song of Songs, with Jill Uris. New York, Doubleday, and London, Deutsch, 1981.

*   *   *

Leon Uris is an extremely popular novelist. Most of his books make bestseller lists. He served in the United States Marine Corps in the Pacific during World War II, and he draws heavily upon his wartime experiences in several of his novels, especially *Battle Cry,* which became an extremely popular movie.

His most successful novel, *Exodus,* traces the history of the State of Israel from before World War II through the War of Independence. He has written several other novels primarily on Jewish themes, including *Mila 18, Q.B.VII,* and *Mila Pass. Mitla 18* is about the heroic resistance in the Warsaw Ghetto during the Nazi Occupation. *Q.B. VII* is about the trial of an American author in Queen's Bench 7 for supposedly libeling a Polish surgeon by saying that he performed sterilizations on Jews in a Nazi concentration camp. *Mitla Pass* focuses on the Sinai Campaign of 1956, which Uris covered as a journalist.

Uris has also written several novels on non-Jewish themes. For example, *The Angry Hills* treats British and Greek underground actions in Greece during World War II, *Topaz* concerns a Soviet espionage network in France, and *Trinity* deals with problems in the history of Ireland. In addition, *The Haj* treats Palestinian Arab life in and around Israel. Although Jews are prominent in the novel, its focus is the life of the title character, so-named because he has made a pilgrimage to Mecca. He tries to lead his people from the days before Israeli statehood through the Israeli War of Independence and the Sinai Campaign. Unable to lead them successfully largely because of the treachery of Arab leaders and his own relatives, he ends up a refugee, unable to keep his people together. He eventually gets killed by one of his sons. Incidentally, in this book a true friendship develops between the Haj and Jewish Israeli, but the Haj is unable openly to acknowledge that friendship.

Obviously, a great deal of research lies behind Uris's historical novels. In fact, some of them have been labeled non-fiction novels because of his fidelity to his historical sources. In *The Angry Hills* Uris draws heavily, he says, on the diary of one of his uncles for "background and historical events." Still, the book reads like a wartime thriller, full of far-fetched coincidences. Nonetheless, Uris often succeeds to a certain extent to capture the texture of the times he treats, especially in his novels about Jewish life in and out of Israel. In spite of its blatant sentimentality, *Exodus* brings to life Palestine before the United Nations' mandate, recreates the texture of the lives of the illegals as they tried to enter Palestine, and recreates Israel's early struggle for existence. *Q.B. VII* brings to life, especially during the trial scenes, experiences from the Nazi death camps and from the lives of survivors of the death camps in Europe, England, and Israel after the war. And *Mitla Pass* gives a feeling for life in Israel shortly before and during the Sinai Campaign.

Few critics consider Uris a serious novelist. The great popularity of *Exodus* and of the movie based on it has been attributed in part to what one critic calls its "positive, heroic Jewish types." However, like most of Uris's books, *Exodus* is blatantly sentimental, and from that sentimentality grows some of its popularity. It develops what was to become one of Uris's stock figures in his books that center on Jews as well as in *The Haj:* the Jewish superman. This character is larger than life. Although he may feel fear, he acts as though he is fearless, and in moments of extremely severe stress, his fear leaves him. Consequently, he is able to perform heroic feats both in and out of battle. His many weaknesses, often involving lack of fidelity in love, only serve to make his successes and strengths all the more remarkable.

Uris has been criticized for careless use of grammar and sentence structure, shallow characterization, superficiality of theme, lack of attention to details of plot, using cliché-ridden language, and injecting gratuitous sexual scenes into his work. In fact, reviews of his works sometimes degenerate into lists of his many faults. One critic even went so far as to say about Uris: "He has for the first time brought off genuine trash about Jews." Obviously, these words are an exaggeration. Still, Uris's strong story lines help his works stay extremely popular. To put it simply, his works are fun to read; readers want to find out what happens next.

Apparently completely untouched by postmodernism, Uris uses straightforward chronological narrative along with numerous flashbacks to keep his stories moving rapidly. Reviewers often note his use of cinematic techniques such as fade-ins and fade-outs and theorize that he has movie versions in mind as he writes his books. His tales demand that his readers willingly suspend their disbelief as they get caught up in the adventures of his central figures. His novels tend to be fast paced, full of action, and extremely exciting. Consequently, he will probably continue to be extremely popular at the same time that he will continue to be scorned by literary critics.

—Richard Tuerk

URQUHART, Fred(erick Burrows)

Nationality: British. **Born:** Edinburgh, 12 July 1912. **Education:** Village schools in Scotland; Stranraer High School, Wigtownshire; Broughton Secondary School, Edinburgh. **Career:** Worked in an Edinburgh bookshop, 1927-34; reader for a London literary agency, 1947-51, and for MGM, 1951-54; London scout for Walt Disney Productions, 1959-60; reader for Cassell and Company, publishers, London, 1951-74, and for J.M. Dent and Sons, publishers, 1967-71. **Awards:** Tom Gallon Trust award, 1951; Arts Council of Great Britain grant, 1966, bursary, 1978, 1985; Scottish Arts Council grant, 1975. **Address:** 5-A Victoria Terrace, Musselburgh, Lothian EH21 7LW, Scotland.

PUBLICATIONS

Novels

Time Will Knit. London, Duckworth, 1938.
The Ferret Was Abraham's Daughter. London, Methuen, 1949.
Jezebel's Dust. London, Methuen, 1951.
Palace of Green Days. London, Quartet, 1979.

Short Stories

I Fell for a Sailor and Other Stories. London, Duckworth, 1940.
The Clouds Are Big with Mercy. Glasgow, Maclellan, 1946.
Selected Stories. Dublin, Fridberg, 1946.
The Last GI Bride Wore Tartan: A Novella and Some Short Stories. Edinburgh, Serif, 1948.
The Year of the Short Corn and Other Stories. London, Methuen, 1949.
The Last Sister and Other Stories. London, Methuen, 1950.
The Laundry Girl and the Pole: Selected Stories. London, Arco, 1955.
The Dying Stallion and Other Stories. London, Hart Davis, 1967.
The Ploughing Match and Other Stories. London, Hart Davis, 1968.
Proud Lady in a Cage: Six Historical Stories. Edinburgh, Harris, 1980.
A Driver in China Seas. London, Quartet, 1980.
Seven Ghosts in Search. London, Kimber, 1983.
Full Score: Short Stories. Aberdeen, Aberdeen University Press, 1989.

Other

Scotland In Colour. London, Batsford, and New York, Viking Press, 1961.

Editor, with Maurice Lindsay, *No Scottish Twilight: New Scottish Stories.* Glasgow, Maclellan, 1947.
Editor, *W.S.C.: A Cartoon Biography* (on Winston Churchill). London, Cassell, 1955.
Editor, *Great True War Adventures.* London, Arco, 1956; New York, Arco, 1957.
Editor, *Scottish Short Stories.* London, Faber, 1957.
Editor, *Men at War: The Best War Stories of All Time.* London, Arco, 1957.
Editor, *Great True Escape Stories.* London, Arco. 1958.
Editor, *The Cassell Miscellany 1848-1958.* London, Cassell, 1958.
Editor, *Everyman's Dictionary of Fictional Characters,* by William Freeman, revised edition. London, Dent, and New York, Dutton, 1973.
Editor, with Giles Gordon, *Modern Scottish Short Stories.* London, Hamish Hamilton, 1978; revised edition, London, Faber, 1982.
Editor, *The Book of Horses: The Horse Through the Ages in Art and Literature.* London, Secker and Warburg, and New York, Morrow, 1981.

*

Manuscript Collection: National Library of Scotland, Edinburgh; University of Texas Library, Austin; Edinburgh University Library.

Critical Studies: Alexander Reid, in *Scotland's Magazine* (Edinburgh), February 1958; Iain Crichton Smith in *The Spectator* (London), 24 May 1968; *History of Scottish Literature* by Maurice Lindsay, London, Hale, 1977; *A Companion to Scottish Culture* edited by David Daiches, London, Arnold, 1981; "Fred Urquhart: Lad for Lassies" by Graeme Roberts, in *Scottish Review* (Edinburgh) May 1982; *Modern Scottish Literature* by Alan Bold, London, Longman, 1983; *The Macmillan Companion to Scottish Literature* by Trevore Royle, London, Macmillan, 1983, as *Com-*

panion to Scottish Literature, Detroit, Gale, 1983; *Guide to Modern World Literature* by Martin Seymour-Smith, London, Macmillan, and New York, Bedrick, 1985.

Fred Urquhart comments:

I never talk to people about my work. When I'm writing a story or novel I don't want anybody to see it or know anything about it until it is completely finished and it satisfies me. I can't understand the habit of some authors of reading their work aloud to their friends as the work progresses. It is only after I've written a story that I show it to friends, inviting criticism.

*　*　*

Fred Urquhart is a wonderful listener. He gets the exact lilt of Clydeside or the Mearns or Leith or Scots dialect modified by the army or navy. He seems to be fascinated by the corruption of language; how Glasgow speech adds an embroidering diminutive "ie"—flashie, steamie—but is itself a corrupted English from what was the Clyde ditch into which the fleeing Gaelic speakers piled themselves hoping for a puckle siller and a wee housie or roomie to live and love in. Those are his backgrounds. But his tongue or maybe his pen is as skilled as his deeply interested ear. He gets it all down, often with a minimal plot but with such liveliness and such involvement of characters that the story line hardly matters. Indeed there are times when he has a good heart-throb ending but he usually gets away with it because of the way it is told. This is why his work is so successful on radio.

These writings of his are too artful and delicate to be in fact the kind of stories which have been told into the unsympathetic ear of a tape recorder. Thus always another human but invisible listener may be asking the odd question that stirs the story up and this invisible other is infinitely aware of the fine points of dialogue and the hidden feelings of the characters, which only appear between the lines, making tensions which are never underlined. Oddly enough Urquhart is best with his women characters, his schoolmistresses and farmers' wives or daughters; his Glasgow lassies on the make or his dirty old wifies. He really gets into the skin of the "Last G.I. Bride." Why? Maybe he finds the toughness of the average male Scot a bit of a bore—as so many women also find it! But he is sensitive to other second class citizens, for instance the Italian prisoners working on a lowland farm in one of his World War II stories.

He is not a quick writer. Perhaps that is why his novels are really longer short stories, though *Palace of Green Days* is the kind of long novel that takes us right into the lowland heartland. On the whole he spends little time on the background unless it is farm detail, and here he is often away back to the days of splendid Clydeside mares and comparatively unhygienic byres and dairies. Most comes through conversation or the fleeting thoughts which are near to speech. He is also very much interested in what other writers are doing, especially in Scotland. He must often have been sorely tempted to do a bit of quick slick writing for the "popular" family magazines. But he believes that writers have a certain duty to tell the truth, even when it is displeasing to the audience they would most like—their own folk. This audience of course is what all writers want but few if any get, because of the thick mud layer pushed under our noses.

It is hard luck to have to wait till you are dead before you are appreciated. One hopes this won't have to happen to Fred Urquhart.

—Naomi Mitchison

V

van der POST, (Sir) Laurens (Jan)

Nationality: South African. **Born:** Philippolis, 13 December 1906. **Education:** Grey College, Bloemfontein. **Military Service:** Served in the British Army, in the Western Desert and the Far East, in World War II; prisoner of war in Java, 1943-45; military attaché to the British Minister, Batavia, 1945-47: C.B.E. (Commander, Order of the British Empire), 1947. **Family:** Married 1) Marjorie Wendt in 1929 (divorced 1947), one son (deceased) and one daughter; 2) the writer Ingaret Giffard in 1949. **Career:** Reporter, *Natal Advertiser,* Durban, 1925-26; leader writer, *Cape Times,* Cape Town, 1930; editor, *Natal Daily News,* Durban, 1948; farmer in the Orange Free State, South Africa, 1948-65. Explorer: several missions in Africa for the Colonial Development Corporation and the British Government, including a mission to Kalahari, 1952. Since 1974 trustee, World Wilderness Fund. Lives in London and Aldeburgh, Suffolk. **Awards:** Anisfield-Wolf award, 1951; National Association of Independent Schools award (U.S.A.), 1959; CNA award, 1964, 1968. D.Litt.: University of Natal, Pietermaritzburg, 1964; University of Liverpool, 1976; Rhodes University, Grahamstown, 1978; St. Andrews University, Scotland, 1980; D. Univ.: University of Surrey, Guildford, 1971. Fellow, Royal Society of Literature, 1955. Knighted, 1981. **Address:** c/o Viking, 27 Wrights Lane, London W8 5TZ, England.

PUBLICATIONS

Novels

In a Province. London, Hogarth Press, 1934; New York, Coward McCann, 1935.
The Face Beside the Fire. London, Hogarth Press, and New York, Morrow, 1953.
A Bar of Shadow. London, Hogarth Press, 1954; New York, Morrow, 1956.
Flamingo Feather. London, Hogarth Press, and New York, Morrow, 1955.
The Seed and the Sower (includes *A Bar of Shadow* and *The Sword and the Doll*). London, Hogarth Press, and New York, Morrow, 1963.
The Hunter and the Whale: A Tale of Africa. London, Hogarth Press, and New York, Morrow, 1967.
A Story like the Wind. London, Hogarth Press, and New York, Morrow, 1972.
A Far-Off Place. London, Hogarth Press, and New York, Morrow, 1974.
A Mantis Carol. London, Hogarth Press, 1975; New York, Morrow, 1976.
About Blady: A Pattern Out of Time. London, Chatto and Windus, 1991.

Plays

Screenplays: *The Lost World of the Kalahari,* 1956; *A Region of Shadow,* 1971; *The Story of Carl Gustav Jung,* 1971; *All Africa Within Us,* 1975; *Zulu Wilderness: Black Umfolozi Rediscovered,* 1979.

Other

Venture to the Interior. New York, Morrow, 1951; London, Hogarth Press, 1952.
The Dark Eye in Africa. London, Hogarth Press, and New York, Morrow, 1955.
Race Prejudice as Self-Rejection. New York, Workshop for Cultural Democracy, 1957.
The Lost World of the Kalahari. London, Hogarth Press, and New York, Morrow, 1958; reprinted with *The Great and Little Memory: A New Epilogue,* London, Chatto and Windus, 1988.
The Heart of the Hunter. London, Hogarth Press, and New York, Morrow, 1961.
Patterns of Renewal. Wallingford, Pennsylvania, Pendle Hill, 1962.
Intuition, Intellect, and the Racial Question. New York, Myrin Institute, 1964.
Journey into Russia. London, Hogarth Press, 1964; as *A View of All the Russias,* New York, Morrow, 1964.
A Portrait of All the Russias. London, Hogarth Press, and New York, Morrow, 1967.
A Portrait of Japan. London, Hogarth Press, and New York, Morrow, 1968.
The Night of the New Moon: August 6, 1945 . . . Hiroshima. London, Hogarth Press, 1970; as *The Prisoner and the Bomb,* New York, Morrow, 1971.
African Cooking, with the editors of Time-Life. New York, Time, 1970.
Man and the Shadow. London, South Place Ethical Society, 1971.
Jung and the Story of Our Time: A Personal Experience. New York, Pantheon, 1975; London, Hogarth Press, 1976.
First Catch Your Eland: A Taste of Africa. London, Hogarth Press, 1977; New York, Morrow, 1978.
Yet Being Someone Other. London, Hogarth Press, 1982; New York, Morrow, 1983.
Testament to the Bushmen, with Jane Taylor. London, Viking, 1984; New York, Viking, 1985.
A Walk with a White Bushman: Conversations with Jean-Marc Pottiez. London, Chatto and Windus, 1986; New York, Morrow, 1987.
The Voice of the Thunder. London, Chatto and Windus, 1993.
Feather Fall: An Anthology, edited by Jean-Marc Pottiez. London, Chatto and Windus, 1994.

*

Critical Study: *Laurens van der Post* by Frederic I. Carpenter, New York, Twayne, 1969.

*   *   *

All the novels of Laurens van der Post have dealt, at least in part, with the life and problems of his native South Africa. All draw upon the author's actual life, which his most famous books of nonfiction (such as *Venture to the Interior*) have described autobiographically. All are distinguished by vivid descriptions of the natural scene, and by psychological depth. But each has been written from a different point of view, and has used a different technique.

In a Province is narrated in the first person by a young, white South African whose black friend runs afoul of the law. Both become involved with a communist agitator, and are finally killed by a posse of self-appointed commandos. The novel is realistic in technique, and is distinguished both by its wealth of incidents involving race relations, and by its balance between the theme of racial injustice on the one hand, and communist exploitation on the other. Although the author has opposed apartheid all his life, he has equally opposed communist subversion.

19 years elapsed between the author's first and second novels—years including his move to England and his distinguished service in World War II, ending with his capture and imprisonment by the Japanese. *The Face Beside the Fire* deals with the problems of an expatriate South African artist in London. Narrated by a life-long friend of the hero, the novel covers a period of many years, and moves from Africa to England and back. Its many episodes find unity in the psychological theme of alienation. Its technique is that of the psychological novel pioneered by Thomas Mann.

Flamingo Feather is a fast-paced tale of mystery and adventure set in war-time South Africa. Narrated in the first person by a young anthropologist, the plot concerns a communist attempt to subvert a native tribe in the interior. The action includes a vividly narrated trek through tropical jungles. A mystery-melodrama, the novel is distinguished both by its fast action and its vivid description of the wild country of Africa.

The Seed and the Sower consists of three "novellas" describing warfare in Africa and Asia, but focusing on the life of the prisoner-of-war. The first novella, *A Bar of Shadow* (published separately in 1954), centers upon the narrator's attempt to understand his Japanese captors. The second (and longest) returns to South Africa to narrate the early experiences of another officer, and ends with his capture and execution by the Japanese. The third narrates a brief wartime romance. All focus upon the author's experiences as prisoner-of-war, which also shadow much of his autobiographical writing.

The Hunter and the Whale, subtitled *A Tale of Africa,* is narrated by a 17-year-old boy who serves as lookout on a whaling ship working out of Durban. The novel is richer and more complex than the others, and combines realistic with symbolic techniques. Its unusual subject matter and unusual techniques both suggest comparison with Melville's *Moby Dick,* and help to explain both the fascination and the occasional difficulty of the novel.

A Story like the Wind narrates the adventures of a white boy whose ancestral farm in the interior of South Africa is attacked and captured by communist-led guerrillas, and of his escape with the help of a Bushman friend of his own age. *A Far-Off Place* is a continuation of *A Story like the Wind,* though self-contained. The second novel tells of the long journey of these two across the southwest African desert to the coast, and their rescue. Both novels are fastpaced, and filled with adventure and the lore of the Africa which the author knows so well.

—Frederic I. Carpenter

VANSITTART, Peter

Nationality: British. **Born:** Bedford, 27 August 1920. **Education:** Marlborough House School; Haileybury College, Hertford; Worces-

ter College, Oxford (major scholar in modern history). **Career:** Director, Burgess School, London, 1947-59; formerly, publisher, Park Editions, London. **Awards:** Society of Authors travelling scholarship, 1969; Arts Council bursary, 1981, 1984. Fellow, Royal Society of Literature, 1985. **Agent:** Sheil and Associates Ltd., 43 Doughty Street, London WC1N 2LF. **Address:** 9 Upper Park Road, London N.W.3; or, Little Manor, Kersey, Ipswich, Suffolk, England.

PUBLICATIONS

Novels

I Am the World. London, Chatto and Windus, 1942.
Enemies. London, Chapman and Hall, 1947.
The Overseer. London, Chapman and Hall, 1949.
Broken Canes. London, Lane, 1950.
A Verdict of Treason. London, Lane, 1952.
A Little Madness. London, Lane, 1953.
The Game and the Ground. London, Reinhardt, 1956; New York, Abelard Schuman, 1957.
Orders of Chivalry. London, Bodley Head, 1958; New York, Abelard Schuman, 1959.
The Tournament. London, Bodley Head, 1959; New York, Walker, 1961.
A Sort of Forgetting. London, Bodley Head, 1960.
Carolina. London, New English Library, 1961.
Sources of Unrest. London, Bodley Head, 1962.
The Friends of God. London, Macmillan, 1963; as *The Siege,* New York, Walker, 1963.
The Lost Lands. London, Macmillan, and New York, Walker, 1964.
The Story Teller. London, Owen, 1968.
Pastimes of a Red Summer. London, Owen, 1969.
Landlord. London, Owen, 1970.
Quintet. London, Owen, 1976.
Lancelot. London, Owen, 1978.
The Death of Robin Hood. London, Owen, 1981.
Harry. London, Park, 1981.
Three Six Seven. London, Owen, 1983.
Aspects of Feeling. London, Owen, 1986.
Parsifal. London, Owen, 1988; Chester Springs, Pennsylvania, Dufour, 1989.
The Wall. London, Owen, 1990.
A Choice of Murder. London, Owen, 1992.
A Safe Conduct. London, Owen, 1995.

Other

The Dark Tower: Tales from the Past (for children). London, Macdonald, 1965; New York, Crowell, 1969.
The Shadow Land: More Stories from the Past (for children). London, Macdonald, 1967.
Green Knights, Black Angels: The Mosaic of History (for children). London, Macmillan, 1969.
Vladivostok (essay). London, Covent Garden Press, 1972.
Dictators. London, Studio Vista, 1973.
Worlds and Underworlds: Anglo-European History Through the Centuries. London, Owen, 1974.
Flakes of History. London, Park, 1978.
The Ancient Mariner and the Old Sailor: Delights and Uses of Words. London, Centre for Policy Studies, 1985.

Paths from a White Horse: A Writer's Memoir. London, Quartet, 1985.
London: A Literary Companion. London, Murray, 1992.
In the Fifties. London, Murray, 1995.

Editor, *Voices from the Great War.* London, Cape, 1981; New York, Watts, 1984.
Editor, *Voices: 1870-1914.* London, Cape, 1984; New York, Watts, 1985.
Editor, *John Masefield's Letters from the Front 1915-1917.* London, Constable, 1984; New York, Watts, 1985.
Editor, *Happy and Gorious! An Anthology of Royalty.* London, Collins, 1988.
Editor, *Voices of the Revolution.* London, Collins, 1989.
Editor, *Kipps,* by H.G. Wells. London, Everyman, 1993.

*

Peter Vansittart comments:

Though I have published non-fiction, novels alone excite my ambitions; not plays, short stories, poems, manifestos, sermons. My novels have been appreciated, if not always enjoyed, more by critics than the reading public, which shows no sign of enjoying them at all. This must be partly due to my obsession with language and speculation at the expense of narrative, however much I relish narrative in others. Today I take narrative more seriously, though still relying, perhaps over-relying, on descriptive colour, unexpected imagery, the bizarre and curious, no formula for popular success. *The Game and the Ground, The Tournament, Lancelot,* and *Quintet,* have succeeded the most in expressing initial vision and valid situation in fairly accessible terms. Others—*A Verdict of Treason, A Sort of Forgetting*—had interesting and provocative material, clumsily handled. *The Story Teller,* my own favourite, failed through excess of ambition, *A Little Madness* and *Sources of Unrest,* through too little.

My novels range in time from the 2nd millennium BC, to AD 1986. They share the effect of time, and the apparently forgotten or exterminated on the present, time transmuting, distorting, travestying, ridiculing facts and ideas, loves and hates, generous institutions and renowned reputations. I was long impressed by the woeful distinction between the historical Macbeth and Shakespeare's: by the swift transformation of E.M. Forster's very English Mrs. Moore into an Indian goddess. Such phenomena relate very immediately to my own work, in which myth can be all too real, and the real degenerate into fantasy.

*   *   *

In his memoirs, *Paths from a White Horse,* Peter Vansittart comments enlighteningly on the genre with which he is most closely associated, the historical novel. He knows that it has come to be disdained by many readers because of its long tradition of crude sentimentality and easy picturesqueness, with language that is either over-spiced with random archaism in vocabulary and syntax or else bled white for the sake of coining a supposedly timeless idiom. Worst of all, the desire to present the "facts" is too often allowed to come between the novelist and his primary duty of creating significant fictions. Though Vansittart is uncommonly well informed about history, it has never been his intention to attempt to rehabilitate the historical novel by basing his work on a sounder foundation of scholarship. Instead, appreciating that the objects and methods of history and fiction are distinct, for all that the starting

point in both enterprises is a serious contemplation of the past, he is content to leave research and verification to the historians and claims for novelists the right to speculate over the facts that are available. He argues that he is entitled to let his imagination brood over events, situations, and characters, discovering by poetic insight mythic continuities that could be too daring for academic minds. This can happen in especially interesting ways when the past is reflected through the personalities of highly individualised characters whose outlook necessarily colours every interpretation of what is related. For Vansittart, the historical novel is, moreover, not exclusively concerned with the depiction of the past. Far more excitingly, he always presents past and present as a continuity, and while relishing the otherness of remote ages and of the people who lived through them, he makes his historical fiction a vehicle for an alert commentary on our present discontents.

The Death of Robin Hood, for instance, is an ambitious attempt to unify experiences by portraying a huge tract of time, with fantasy and realism mingled to create myth. First comes a spell-binding evocation of the forest in primal times when strange rites are already seen as failing to arrest the processes of change and decay. The second part of the novel, "John in the Castle," depicts the paranoid terrors of a tyrant who cowers behind stone walls, dreading the prospect of conflict with the unruly bands that have taken refuge in the forest. Here there is fine descriptive writing, but it is John's state of mind that is the centre of attention. Next, not pausing to make the linkage explicit, Vansittart moves on to the Luddite riots of 1811 when Nottinghamshire workers rose up and smashed the new machines that were taking away their livelihood and then, as the forces of repression gathered, ran off in droves into the forest. Finally, reverting to the environment he had portrayed with satiric verve in *Broken Canes,* Vansittart shows the old values under attack in the closed world of an independent school just before the outbreak of World War II. With its abrupt transitions, *The Death of Robin Hood* can be puzzling, but the immediacy of the emotions and the vividness of the scenes carry the reader along. *Lancelot* is more straightforward. It takes as its starting point Field-Marshal Wavell's observation that "Arthur was probably a grim figure in a grim, un-romantic struggle in a dark period of history," and, once again, it presents within a framework of exciting events an enquiry into the meaning of change and apparent decay. *Three Six Seven* is set in A.D. 367, a year of cataclysm for Roman Britain.

Parsifal is a novel that has some affinities with *The Death of Robin Hood.* The cryptic first chapter makes an explicit reference to Richard Wagner, but then the narrative doubles back to the present in chronological sequence a series of portrayals of the Arthurian quasi-hero through the ages, from a curiously indeterminate prehistorical era to the fall of the Nazis. With his precise choice of vocabulary and tight-lipped style, Vansittart, without here trying very often for pictorial effects, creates compelling fiction. It evokes a world sadly out of joint, with legendary and literary elements curiously combined and with the extraordinary blend of reinterpreted myth and remorseless psychological realism which is the hallmark of Vansittart's historical novels.

Vansittart is by no means only a historical novelist, and his gift for description and his disabused insight into human motivations are equally well revealed in the portrayal of the life of the bourgeoisie in modern times in such novels as *Quintet.* The first of its five parts is set in Africa in the immediate post-war era when Britain was shedding its colonial responsibilities, and institutional decay is generally the framework within which flawed human beings pursue their complex ways.

As well as presenting a personal vision of man's lot and exploring the possibilities of narrative technique in challenging fashion, Vansittart possesses a most distinguished prose style. Provided every thought of complacent exuberance and lush imagery is banished, it might well be called poetic, for here there is a rare regard for the communicative power of the exact word in precisely the right place. Nouns in particular he values, not cluttering them with adjectives but letting them stand stark and unmodified to convey meaning. This gives an impression of elemental vigour which is apt in *Lancelot,* for example, and the tight-lipped statements suggest pressures that can be held in check only with difficulty just as dark hints leave us to draw dire conclusions for ourselves. In *The Death of Robin Hood* the prose, which is very stylised at first, becomes more and more relaxed as we move towards modern times, though Vansittart continues to use words with scrupulous care for their effect. In his novels there is humour too, but usually the laughter is uneasy, in situations that are becoming uncomfortable. Quite a prolific novelist, Vansittart has kept a voice that is distinctively his own.

—Christopher Smith

VASSANJI, M(oyez) G.

Nationality: Canadian (originally Kenyan, emigrated to United State, 1970; emigrated to Canada, 1978). **Born:** Nairobi, Kenya, 30 May 1950. **Education:** Massachusetts Institute of Technology, B.S. 1974; University of Pennsylvania, Ph.D. 1978. **Family:** Married Nurjehan Aziz; one child. **Career:** Affiliated with Atomic Energy of Canada at Chalk River power station, 1978-80; research associate and lecturer in physics, 1980-89. Since 1989 full-time writer. **Agent:** Peter Livingston Associates, Inc., 89 Collier St., Toronto, Ontario M4W 1M2, Canada.

PUBLICATIONS

Novels

The Gunny Sack. Oxford, Heinemann International, 1989.
No New Land. Toronto, McClelland and Stewart, 1991.
The Book of Secrets. N.p., n.d.

Short Stories

Uhuru Street. Heinemann International, 1991.

Other

A Meeting of Streams: South Asian Canadian Literature. Toronto, TSAR, 1985.

*   *   *

As a storyteller, M.G. Vassanji is fascinated with the often elliptical forms that stories can take and with the vestiges of experience (tangible and otherwise) that connect us to them. And, as is often the case, it is this willingness to explore continually the potentiali-

ties of form that is at once the principal strength and weakness of his fiction.

Illustrative of this tension is *The Gunny Sack,* an episodic generational novel set, like most of Vassanji's fiction, in and against the multicultural panorama of East Africa. Engaging a form which reflects the randomness of reaching into a bag of treasures, he organizes this narrative around the artifacts that his narrator, Salim, recovers from an almost mythical repository passed to him by a great-aunt. Forever being ordered and reordered by the holder of the bag, each wisp of memory elicits any number of stories about one extended family's arrival and existence in East Africa. Considered individually, these episodes take many forms—fables of community, lyrical remembrances of family, and recollections of political events. Considered cumulatively, they intermingle, though not always smoothly, to form a lush polyphony, an exploration of place and character which avoids flat archetypes and the subsumption of individual voices in any grand pattern of history or myth. Indeed, at times the genealogical details that accumulate with each subsequent episode threaten to become frustratingly labyrinthine.

This occasional awkwardness dissipates when Vassanji shifts form for his only short fiction collection, *Uhuru Street,* the 16 linked stories that share a number of characters and episodes with *The Gunny Sack.* More modernist in style than his longer fiction, these are economical, but nonetheless vivid, evocations of the anxious movement of East Africa from the final days of colonial rule to the harsh realities of newfound independence. In the strongest inclusions, "All Worlds Are Possible Now," in which a man endeavors to reclaim a sense of place and self during a trip "home," and the bittersweet remembrances of "the London-returned," Vassanji's control of the story format creates fiction that moves almost seamlessly across the frontiers of geography and history to speak of stories at once individual and collective, singular and diverse.

Moving from the fluidity of *The Gunny Sack* and the interdependence that characterizes linked stories, Vassanji finds the form for *The Book of Secrets,* his most accomplished work of fiction, in a more fixed trace of the past: the 1913 diary of a colonial administrator which is discovered hidden in a shopkeeper's backroom in modern Dar es Salaam. Lent to Pius Fernandes, a retired teacher whose own notebook entries also become part of the novel, the diary becomes the centerpiece in a quest to (re)construct the enigmatic family history believed to be concealed in its pages. Although the dual presence of diary and notebook suggests a certain precision to the notation and relationship of the times, places, and events that shape this story, Vassanji reveals both to be versions of the titular book of secrets, necessarily incomplete records of experiences that have no witnesses and of questions that remain unanswered—and perhaps unanswerable.

An intriguing palimpsest of vernacular, historical, and cultural discourses, *The Book of Secrets* also foregrounds the *ideas* that recur in Vassanji's fiction: notions of history and memory; questions about how much one can (and dare) know about the past; the ideas of home and community as they extend across time and space; and the insidious legacies of colonialism, war, race prejudice, and religious intolerance. And although these books suggest that a relatively harmonious coexistence of peoples and cultures is at least possible, and at best vital, in the modern world, the potential for conflict is omnipresent. Institutional hypocrisy and racism, family feuds, petty jealousies, and sexual exploitation are never far from the surface of Vassanji's narratives.

At times, this undercurrent of discord erupts in viciousness, notably in the violence of the Kurtz-like Maynard (*The Book of Se-*

crets), in the frequent convergence of commerce and sexual exploitation ("For a Shilling"), and in the racially motivated murder that symbolizes the changing times in "What Good Times We Had." Indeed, it is the image that ends this story, a tableau of death in which the brutalized victim hangs by her feet from a tree branch, that resonates in a number of subsequent stories in the *Uhuru* cycle.

More often, Vassanji opts for subtlety. With the possible exception of *No New Land,* a less satisfying and more traditionally structured novel which sacrifices some nuances of character and story in favor of an ironic look at the experiences of a Tanzan-Asian family upon immigration to Canada, he explores contentious issues through understated instances of ambiguity, incidents which reveal struggles more emotional and spiritual than physical. Moreover, throughout *The Book of Secrets* and in stories like "The Beggar" and "Alzira," the threat of confrontation is replaced or diffused by sudden and unexpected acts of kindness, allowing questions of dignity, humanity, and love to be invoked as optimistic counterpoints to the darker shadows that ripple through the lives of his characters and the stories they tell.

—Klay Dyer

VIDAL, Gore

Pseudonym: Edgar Box. **Nationality:** American. **Born:** Eugene Luther Gore Vidal, Jr. in West Point, New York, 3 October 1925. **Education:** Los Alamos School, New Mexico, 1939-40; Phillips Exeter Academy, New Hampshire, 1940-43. **Military Service:** Served in the United States Army, 1943-46: Warrant Officer. **Career:** Editor, E.P. Dutton, publishers, New York, 1946. Lived in Antigua, Guatemala, 1947-49, and Italy, 1967-76; member, advisory board, *Partisan Review,* New Brunswick, New Jersey, 1960-71; Democratic-Liberal candidate for Congress, New York, 1960; member, President's Advisory Committee on the Arts, 1961-63; co-chairman, New Party, 1968-71. **Awards:** Mystery Writers of America award, for television play, 1954; Cannes Film Critics award, for screenplay, 1964; National Book Critics Circle award, for criticism, 1983. **Address:** La Rondinaia, Ravello, Salerno, Italy; or c/o Random House Inc., 201 East 50th Street, New York, New York 10022, U.S.A.

PUBLICATIONS

Novels

Williwaw. New York, Dutton, 1946; London, Panther, 1965.
In a Yellow Wood. New York, Dutton, 1947; London, New English Library, 1967.
The City and the Pillar. New York, Dutton, 1948; London, Lehmann, 1949; revised edition, Dutton, and London, Heinemann, 1965.
The Season of Comfort. New York, Dutton, 1949.
Dark Green, Bright Red. New York, Dutton, and London, Lehmann, 1950.
A Search for the King: A Twelfth Century Legend. New York, Dutton, 1950; London, New English Library, 1967.
The Judgment of Paris. New York, Dutton, 1952; London, Heinemann, 1953; revised edition, Boston, Little Brown, 1965; Heinemann, 1966.

Messiah. New York, Dutton, 1954; London, Heinemann, 1955; revised edition, Boston, Little Brown, 1965; Heinemann, 1968.
Three: Williwaw, A Thirsty Evil, Julian the Apostate. New York, New American Library, 1962.
Julian. Boston, Little Brown, and London, Heinemann, 1964.
Washington, D.C. Boston, Little Brown, and London, Heinemann, 1967.
Myra Breckinridge. Boston, Little Brown, and London, Blond, 1968.
Two Sisters: A Memoir in the Form of a Novel. Boston, Little Brown, and London, Heinemann, 1970.
Burr. New York, Random House, 1973; London, Heinemann, 1974.
Myron. New York, Random House, 1974; London, Heinemann, 1975.
1876. New York, Random House, and London, Heinemann, 1976.
Kalki. New York, Random House, and London, Heinemann, 1978.
Creation. New York, Random House, and London, Heinemann, 1981.
Duluth. New York, Random House, and London, Heinemann, 1983.
Lincoln. New York, Random House, and London, Heinemann, 1984.
Empire. New York, Random House, and London, Deutsch, 1987.
Hollywood. New York, Random House, and London, Deutsch, 1990.
Live from Golgotha. New York, Random House, 1992.

Novels as Edgar Box

Death in the Fifth Position. New York, Dutton, 1952; London, Heinemann, 1954.
Death Before Bedtime. New York, Dutton, 1953; London, Heinemann, 1954.
Death Likes It Hot. New York, Dutton, 1954; London, Heinemann, 1955.

Short Stories

A Thirsty Evil: Seven Short Stories. New York, Zero Press, 1956; London, Heinemann, 1958.

Plays

Visit to a Small Planet (televised 1955). Included in *Visit to a Small Planet and Other Television Plays,* 1956; revised version (produced New York, 1957; London, 1960), Boston, Little Brown, 1957; in *Three Plays,* 1962.
Honor (televised 1956). Published in *Television Plays for Writers: Eight Television Plays,* edited by A.S. Burack, Boston, The Writer, 1957; revised version as *On the March to the Sea: A Southron Comedy* (produced Bonn, Germany, 1961), in *Three Plays,* 1962.
Visit to a Small Planet and Other Television Plays (includes *Barn Burning, Dark Possession, The Death of Billy the Kid, A Sense of Justice, Smoke, Summer Pavilion, The Turn of the Screw*). Boston, Little Brown, 1956.
The Best Man: A Play about Politics (produced New York, 1960). Boston, Little Brown, 1960; in *Three Plays,* 1962.
Three Plays (includes *Visit to a Small Planet, The Best Man, On the March to the Sea*). London, Heinemann, 1962.
Romulus: A New Comedy, adaptation of a play by Friedrich Dürrenmatt (produced New York, 1962). New York, Dramatists Play Service, 1962.
Weekend (produced New York, 1968). New York, Dramatists Play Service, 1968.

An Evening with Richard Nixon and . . . (produced New York, 1972). New York, Random House, 1972.

Screenplays: *The Catered Affair,* 1956; *I Accuse,* 1958; *The Scapegoat,* with Robert Hamer, 1959; *Suddenly, Last Summer,* with Tennessee Williams, 1959; *The Best Man,* 1964; *Is Paris Burning?,* with Francis Ford Coppola, 1966; *Last of the Mobile Hot-Shots,* 1970; *The Sicilian,* 1970; *Gore Vidal's Billy the Kid,* 1989.

Television Plays: *Barn Burning,* from the story by Faulkner, 1954; *Dark Possession,* 1954; *Smoke,* from the story by Faulkner, 1954; *Visit to a Small Planet,* 1955; *The Death of Billy the Kid,* 1955; *A Sense of Justice,* 1955; *Summer Pavillion,* 1955; *The Turn of the Screw,* from the story by Henry James, 1955; *Honor,* 1956; *The Indestructible Mr. Gore,* 1960; *Vidal in Venice* (documentary), 1985; *Dress Gray,* from the novel by Lucian K. Truscott IV, 1986.

Other

Rocking the Boat (essays). Boston, Little Brown, 1962; London, Heinemann, 1963.
Sex, Death, and Money (essays). New York, Bantam, 1968.
Reflections upon a Sinking Ship (essays). Boston, Little Brown, and London, Heinemann, 1969.
Homage to Daniel Shays: Collected Essays 1952-1972. New York, Random House, 1972; as *Collected Essays 1952-1972,* London, Heinemann, 1974.
Matters of Fact and of Fiction: Essays 1973-1976. New York, Random House, and London, Heinemann, 1977.
Sex Is Politics and Vice Versa (essay). Los Angeles, Sylvester and Orphanos, 1979.
Views from a Window: Conversations with Gore Vidal, with Robert J. Stanton. Secaucus, New Jersey, Lyle Stuart, 1980.
The Second American Revolution and Other Essays 1976-1982. New York, Random House, 1982; as *Pink Triangle and Yellow Star and Other Essays,* London, Heinemann, 1982.
Vidal in Venice, edited by George Armstrong, photographs by Tore Gill. New York, Summit, and London, Weidenfeld and Nicolson, 1985.
Armegeddon? Essays 1983-1987. London, Deutsch, 1987; as *At Home,* New York, Random House, 1988.
A View from the Diners Club. London, Deutsch, 1991.
The Decline and Fall of the American Empire. Berkeley, California, Odonian Press, 1992.
Screening History. Cambridge, Harvard University Press, and London, Deutsch, 1992.
United States: Essays, 1952-1992. New York, Random House, and London, Deutsch, 1993.

Editor, *Best Television Plays.* New York, Ballantine, 1956.

*

Bibliography: *Gore Vidal: A Primary and Secondary Bibliography* by Robert J. Stanton, Boston, Hall, and London, Prior, 1978.

Manuscript Collection: University of Wisconsin, Madison.

Critical Studies: *Gore Vidal* by Ray Lewis White, New York, Twayne, 1968; *The Apostate Angel: A Critical Study of Gore Vidal* by Bernard F. Dick, New York, Random House, 1974; *Gore Vidal* by Robert F. Kiernan, New York, Ungar, 1982; *Gore Vidal: Writer Against the Grain* edited by Jay Parini, New York, Columbia University Press, and London, Deutsch, 1992.

*   *   *

Although a prolific author with recognizable stances, Gore Vidal is among the most versatile of contemporary American writers. In scholarly novels about ancient-world potentates, in doomsday fictions, in a playfully pornographic diptych of novels, in an American politics trilogy, and in a pseudonymous series of detective stories, he has played a dazzling variety of autorial roles. No American writer of comparable stature has proven less predictable in his choice of subjects.

Vidal's first novel was *Williwaw,* set on an army transport vessel laying a course among the Aleutian Islands during World War II. In an obvious imitation of the terse, Hemingway style, Vidal tells a story of seven self-absorbed men whose enforced closeness, results finally in a homicide half-accidental, half-murder, about which no one really cares. The novel is remarkable for its proficiency if one considers that Vidal was 19 years old when he wrote it. Of more lasting interest among the early novels, however, is *The City and the Pillar,* in which Vidal employs the Hemingway manner to tell the story of a young man's gradual discovery that he is homosexual. Because the protagonist is stereotypically all-American, the novel was a *succès de scandale* in its day. Its obvious distinction now is in having charted the young man's discovery without resort to sentiment or sermon.

The Hemingway style that served Vidal well in *The City and the Pillar* served him less well in *In a Yellow Wood,* the story of an unimaginative clerk who is afforded a glimpse of the Manhattan demimonde, and in *Dark Green, Bright Red,* a novel of revolution and Weltschmerz in the tropics. With equally limited success, Vidal abandoned the Hemingway manner in *The Season of Comfort* to write an archly overripe tale of incest and generational conflicts in a genteel Southern family. More successful than these fumbled experiments in tone is *A Search for the King: A Twelfth Century Legend,* the first of Vidal's historical novels. Set in the 12th century and recounting the search for Richard Couer de Lion by the troubadour Blondel De Néel, *A Search for the King: A Twelfth Century Legend* is noteworthy among early Vidal fictions for its lucid characterizations, witty contrivances, and general charm. Its experiments bore fruit in two subsequent novels of equally liberated technique: *The Judgment of Paris,* a camp updating of a Greek myth, and *Messiah,* a savagely apocalyptic novel about merchandizing a savior.

Vidal's first major novel is *Julian,* which purports to be the Emperor Julian's autobiographical memoir and private journal, as intemperately annotated 17 years after the emperor's death by the philosophers Priscus of Athens and Libanius of Antioch. In scenes complexly imagined and impressively researched, Vidal recreates Julian's path from Christianity to Mithraism and from philosophy to military science. The novel is rewarding for its rich historicity, but also for the interplay of Julian's elevated discourse with the witty phrase-making of Priscus and the pedantry of Libanius. Its loose, self-indulgent mode of narration proves hospitable to Vidal's sudden flashes of wit and his serendipitous interest in ideas. Indeed, its ventriloquistic mode of narration has proved the formula of Vidal's most accomplished fiction.

If *Julian* earned Vidal the reputation of a serious novelist, an atemporal trilogy of novels about public life in America confirmed the reputation. *Washington, D.C.,* the first novel of this sequence, is a wry comedy of political manners that focuses on two Washington families, one headed by a newspaper magnate, the other by a senator. As national events from Pearl Harbor to Korea stage themselves in the background, the characters indulge a common taste for histrionics, and through a careful interweaving of the characters with affairs of state, Vidal suggests that an overwrought national life takes its keynote from such personal theatrics. Hollywood melodrama, he implies, *is* the national style. Even more sardonic in tone is the third novel in the sequence, *1876,* in which an old man named Charlie Schuyler returns from Europe to New York for the first time since 1837 and travels about the country in the service of a newspaper. Everywhere he sees violence and mendacity lurking behind the patriotic scrim of the nation's centenary—particularly in the scandals of the Grant Administration and the bitterly contested Hayes-Tilden presidential election.

The centerpiece of the trilogy and one of Vidal's best novels is *Burr,* an account of Aaron Burr's last days as written by the young Charlie Schuyler, whom Vidal imagines Burr employing and befriending. Schuyler's interest in Burr's life encourages the older man to give his written account of the early days of the republic—a compelling, gossipy account in which the Founding Fathers are little more than despoilers of infant America. The alternation of Burr's own narrative with Schuyler's worshipful memoir results in a composite portrait of Burr as both an unregenerate adventurer and an elegant arbiter of political style. It also shows Vidal at his best: iconoclastic, anecdotal, intellectually and stylistically agile.

In a duo of confections entitled *Myra Breckinridge* and *Myron* Vidal indulges freely the taste for camp extravagance evident in his work as early as *The Season of Comfort. Myra Breckinridge* takes the form of a journal that the eponymous Myra begins when she arrives in Hollywood after a sex-change operation. Firm in her belief that film is the only art and militant in her devotion to Hollywood's Golden Age, she is no less imperious in her determination to realign the sexes—a determination rooted in her former life as Myron. The results are gaudily offensive, climaxing in her rape of a chauvinistic young man and ending (to her chagrin) in her accidental reversion into Myron. *Myron* picks up the story five years later when Myron falls into his television and discovers himself on a Hollywood set in 1948. As the novel progresses, Myra and Myron alternately commandeer the Breckinridge psyche, Myra bent on saving Hollywood from television, Myron on defeating Myra's revisionist imperative. Although not to everyone's taste, the books are enormously rich—a comedic feast of styles and sexualities, invention and invective. Their charm is considerable.

Vidal's greatest success in recent years has been in the historical mode. In *Creation* his central character and narrator is a fictional diplomat named Cyrus Spitama (a grandson of Zoroaster), who cuts a broad swath through the Persian-Greek wars and recounts fascinating meetings with the Buddha, Master Li, Confucius, and a host of kindred figures. Revisionist speculations and tantalizing "what ifs" energize what amounts to a Cook's Tour of the fifth century. If *Lincoln* overshadows *Creation,* it overshadows very nearly everything else in Vidal's oeuvre. A compelling, thoughtful, and well-researched portrait of America's 16th president, it renders his tragic Civil War years through candid viewpoints of his family, his political rivals, and even his future assassins. The result is a rare fusion of monumentality and intimacy, quite distinct from the idealized portraits created by romantic nationalism.

Although the historical novel seems increasingly Vidal's métier, he continues to write in a variety of modes. *Kalki* is a mordant

doomsday novel, narrated with odd restraint by a bisexual aviatrix, the personal pilot of a Vietnam veteran who exterminates the human race in a belief that he is the last avatar of Vishnu. Because of its emotional coolness, the story fails to engage us except in scattered passages, as does the story in *Duluth,* a broad parody of law-and-order thinking in middle America. More interesting than these novels is the undervalued *Two Sisters: A Memoir in the Form of a Novel,* a Chinese box of narrations in which each narrative replicates a single story-line encapsulated in a screenplay at the heart of the novel.

The greatness of Vidal's fiction lies not only with its extraordinary range but with its small-scale effects: witty, autobiographical indiscretions; aphoristic nuggets, firm and toothsome; a fine interplay of the demonic and the mannered. Indeed, he must be regarded as one of the most important stylists of contemporary American prose. His ear for cadence and his touch with syntax are sure, and few can equal his ability to layer a sentence with wit and to temper it with intelligence.

—Robert F. Kiernan

VIRTUE, Noel

Nationality: New Zealander. **Born:** 1947. **Career:** Formerly a zookeeper. Since 1987 a writer. **Address:** David Bolt Associates, 12 Heath Drive, Send, Surrey GU23 7ED, England.

PUBLICATIONS

Novels

The Redemption of Elsdon Bird. London, Owen, and New York, Grove Press, 1987.
Then upon the Evil Season. London, Owen, 1988.
In the Country of Salvation. Auckland, Random Century, and London, Hutchinson, 1990.
Always the Islands of Memory. London, Hutchinson, 1991.
The Eye of the Everlasting Angel. London, Owen, 1992.
Sandspit Crossing. London, Owen, 1993.

Other

Among the Animals: A Zookeeper's Story. London, Owen, 1988.

*   *   *

A latecomer to novel writing (he was a zoo keeper for many years) Noel Virtue has made a small but definite name for himself in contemporary New Zealand fiction. Conservative in style and form, his novels are, at their best, powerful, even disturbing—a quality that comes, to a great extent from the very peculiar family life he portrays in his books.

The Redemption of Elsdon Bird, Virtue's first work, is to my mind his most successful. In libraries it is often classed as teenage fiction, but this designation is misleading, as the emotions and themes it deals with (religious mania and violence against children) are distinctly adult. Written in a spare, vivid style, it tells the story of a lonely youngster whose upbringing at the hands of "holy roller" parents is strange and nightmarish. Isolated by his family's religious convictions, Elsdon is the subject of constant physical abuse; systematically deprived of everyone and everything he loves, by the end of the book he faces life alone. As a story it would be almost unbearable were it not for the protagonist's poignantly cheerful character—one has the feeling that somehow he will survive. Especially noteworthy is Virtue's skilled use of New Zealand slang, which, in Elsdon's innocent mouth, is both comic and touching.

Then Upon the Evil Season continues the themes of violence and religious mania. As in the earlier novel the focus is on a child (or teenager) Lubin, who must cope with his parent's fundamentalist belief and the persecution they invite. Mixed in with this there is a murder, and two unusual animals (an ostrich and a dolphin) whose natural goodness serves to highlight man's cruelty and greed. More ambitious than *The Redemption of Elsdon Bird* (there is a larger cast of characters and a more complex plot) *Then Upon the Evil Season* succeeds less well, for it lacks the former's intensity, and the characters (animal as well as human) are somewhat stereotyped. This perhaps really *is* teenage fiction.

With *In the Country of Salvation* Virtue has attempted to write a properly adult novel, one moreover that deals with several different lives over a long period of time. The main focus, once again, is on a lonely child, Billy, whose upbringing at the hands of religiously obsessed parents causes him such unhappiness and even drives him to attempt suicide. Billy, as it happens, has a double cross to bear (he is homosexual) but all the family members in fact suffer in their own way till, in the end, they arrive at a kind of forgiveness. It is an ambitious plot, and the first half of the book works well; during the second part, however, the writing sags and the narrative becomes patchy. To some extent the problem lies with the characters themselves: lacking Elsdon's touching optimism their unhappiness is more gruelling than affecting. Another problem is that the focus of the novel is too diffuse—the stories of Colin and Seddon, Billy's older brothers, though interesting, tend to distract the reader from Billy's agony. Virtue, would appear to have bitten off more than he could chew with this plot—which is not to say that *In the Country of Salvation* does not have its moments.

All Virtue's fictional works so far deal with religious mania and the suffering it inflicts on children. It has been a fruitful theme (especially in *The Redemption of Elsdon Bird*)—one is curious, though, to discover if Virtue's undoubted talent can express itself in future in other, different stories.

—John O'Leary

VONNEGUT, Kurt, Jr.

Nationality: American. **Born:** Indianapolis, Indiana, 11 November 1922. **Education:** Shortridge High School, Indianapolis, 1936-40; Cornell University, Ithaca, New York, 1940-42; Carnegie Institute, Pittsburgh, 1943; University of Chicago, 1945-47. **Military Service:** Served in the United States Army Infantry, 1942-45: Purple Heart. **Family:** Married 1) Jane Marie Cox in 1945 (divorced 1979), one son and two daughters, and three adopted sons; 2) the photographer Jill Krementz in 1979, one daughter. **Career:** Police reporter, Chicago City News Bureau, 1946; worked in public relations for the General Electric Company, Schenectady, New York,

1947-50. Since 1950 freelance writer. After 1965, teacher, Hopefield School, Sandwich, Massachusetts. Visiting lecturer, Writers Workshop, University of Iowa, Iowa City, 1965-67, and Harvard University, Cambridge, Massachusetts, 1970-71; visiting professor, City University of New York, 1973-74. **Awards:** Guggenheim fellowship, 1967; American Academy grant, 1970. M.A.: University of Chicago, 1971; D.Litt.: Hobart and William Smith Colleges, Geneva, New York, 1974. **Member:** American Academy, 1973. Lives in New York City. **Address:** c/o Donald C. Farber, Tanner Gilbert Propp and Sterner, 99 Park Avenue, 25th Floor, New York, New York 10016, U.S.A.

PUBLICATIONS

Novels

Player Piano. New York, Scribner, 1952; London, Macmillan, 1953; as *Utopia 14,* New York, Bantam, 1954.
The Sirens of Titan. New York, Dell, 1959; London, Gollancz, 1962.
Mother Night. New York, Fawcett, 1962; London, Cape, 1968.
Cat's Cradle. New York, Holt Rinehart, and London, Gollancz, 1963.
God Bless You, Mr. Rosewater; or, Pearls Before Swine. New York, Holt Rinehart, and London, Cape, 1965.
Slaughterhouse-Five; or, The Children's Crusade. New York, Delacorte Press, 1969; London, Cape, 1970.
Breakfast of Champions; or, Goodbye, Blue Monday. New York, Delacorte Press, and London, Cape, 1973.
Slapstick; or, Lonesome No More! New York, Delacorte Press, and London, Cape, 1976.
Jailbird. New York, Delacorte Press, and London, Cape, 1979.
Deadeye Dick. New York, Delacorte Press, 1982; London, Cape, 1983.
Galápagos. New York, Delacorte Press, and London, Cape, 1985.
Bluebeard. New York, Delacorte Press, 1987; London, Cape, 1988.
Hocus Pocus; or, What's the Hurry, Son? New York, Putnam, and London, Cape, 1990.

Short Stories

Canary in a Cat House. New York, Fawcett, 1961.
Welcome to the Monkey House: A Collection of Short Works. New York, Delacorte Press, 1968; London, Cape, 1969.

Uncollected Short Stories

"2BR02B," in *If* (New York), January 1962.
"The Big Space Fuck," in *Again, Dangerous Visions,* edited by Harlan Ellison. New York, Doubleday, 1972; London, Millington, 1976.
"The Dream of the Future (Not Excluding Lobsters)," in *The Esquire Fiction Reader 2,* edited by Rust Hills and Tom Jenks. Green Harbor, Massachusetts, Wampeter Press, 1986.
"The Boy Who Hated Girls," in *Saturday Evening Post* (Indianapolis), September 1988.

Plays

Happy Birthday, Wanda June (as *Penelope,* produced Cape Cod, Massachusetts, 1960; revised version, as *Happy Birthday, Wanda June,* produced New York, 1970; London, 1977). New York, Delacorte Press, 1970; London, Cape, 1973.

The Very First Christmas Morning, in *Better Homes and Gardens* (Des Moines, Iowa), December 1962.
Between Time and Timbuktu; or, Prometheus-5: A Space Fantasy (televised 1972; produced New York, 1976). New York, Delacorte Press, 1972; London, Panther, 1975.
Fortitude, in *Wampeters, Foma, and Granfalloons,* 1974.
Timesteps (produced Edinburgh, 1979).
God Bless You, Mr. Rosewater, adaptation of his own novel (produced New York, 1979).

Television Plays: *Auf Wiedersehen,* with Valentine Davies, 1958; *Between Time and Timbuktu,* 1972.

Other

Wampeters, Foma, and Granfalloons: Opinions. New York, Delacorte Press, 1974; London Cape, 1975.
Sun Moon Star. New York, Harper, and London, Hutchinson, 1980.
Palm Sunday: An Autobiographical Collage. New York, Delacorte Press, and London, Cape, 1981.
Fates Worse Than Death. Nottingham, Spokesman, 1982(?).
Nothing Is Lost Save Honor: Two Essays. Jackson, Mississippi, Nouveau Press, 1984.
Conversations with Kurt Vonnegut, edited by William Rodney Allen. Jackson, University Press of Mississippi, 1988.
Fates Worth than Death: An Autobiographical Collage of the 1980s. New York, Putnam, 1991.

*

Bibliography: *Kurt Vonnegut: A Comprehensive Bibliography* by Asa B. Pieratt, Jr., Julie Huffman-Klinkowitz, and Jerome Klinkowitz, Hamden, Connecticut, Archon, 1987.

Critical Studies: *Kurt Vonnegut, Jr.,* by Peter J. Reed, New York, Warner, 1972; *Kurt Vonnegut: Fantasist of Fire and Ice* by David H. Goldsmith, Bowling Green, Ohio, Popular Press, 1972; *The Vonnegut Statement* edited by Jerome Klinkowitz and John Somer, New York, Delacorte Press, 1973, London, Panther, 1975, *Vonnegut in America: An Introduction to the Life and Work of Kurt Vonnegut* edited by Klinkowitz and Donald L. Lawler, New York, Delacorte Press, 1977, *Kurt Vonnegut,* London, Methuen, 1982 and *Slaughterhouse Five: Reforming the Novel and the World,* Boston, Twayne, 1990, both by Klinkowitz; *Kurt Vonnegut, Jr.* by Stanley Schatt, Boston, Twayne, 1976; *Kurt Vonnegut* by James Lundquist, New York, Ungar, 1977; *Vonnegut: A Preface to His Novels* by Richard Giannone, Port Washington, New York, Kennikat Press, 1977; *Kurt Vonnegut: The Gospel from Outer Space* by Clark Mayo, San Bernardino, California, Borgo Press, 1977; *Vonnegut's Duty-Dance with Death: Theme and Structure in Slaughterhouse-Five* by Monica Loeb, Ume[ao], Sweden, Ume[ao] Studies in the Humanities, 1979; *Critical Essays on Kurt Vonnegut* edited by Robert Merrill, Boston, Hall, 1990; *Forever Pursuing Genesis: The Myth of Eden in the Novels of Kurt Vonnegut* by Leonard Mustazza, Lewisburg, Pennsylvania, Bucknell University Press, 1990; *Understanding Kurt Vonnegut* by William Rodney Allen, Columbia, University of South Carolina Press, 1991; *Kurt Vonnegut* by Donald E. Morse, San Bernardino, California, Borgo Press, 1992; *Critical Response to Kurt Vonnegut* edited by Leonard Mustazza, Westport, Connecticut, Greenwood Press, 1994.

*   *   *

During the 1960s Kurt Vonnegut emerged as one of the most influential and provocative writers of fiction in America. His writing, indeed, constitutes an unremitting protest against horrors (as he sees them) of our century—the disastrous wars, the deterioration of the environment, and the dehumanization of the individual in a society dominated by science and technology. Such protest is by no means new in literature. The peculiar force of Vonnegut's voice may be traced to its complete contemporaneity. Fantasy (usually of the science variety), black humor, a keen sense of the absurd are the ingredients of his novels and stories.

Vonnegut has described himself as "a total pessimist." And indeed his writing offers little except wry laughter to counteract despair. This is certainly true of his first novel, *Player Piano.* The time of the story is the not-too-distant future and the place is an industrial city, Ilium, New York, which serves as the setting for much of Vonnegut's fiction and which resembles Schenectady, New York, where Vonnegut once worked in public relations. In the novel not only the local industry but industries throughout the nation have been completely mechanized. Machines supplant human workers because machines make fewer errors. All national policy is determined by huge computers located in Mammoth Cave. A small elite of scientists are in charge of all production. The masses, who are provided with all material necessities and comforts, including an impressive array of gadgetry, serve in either military or work battalions. Acutely aware of their dehumanization and worthlessness except as consumers of the huge output of the machines, the common people revolt under the leadership of a preacher and several renegade scientists. Though the revolt in Ilium, at least, is successful and many of the objectionable machines are destroyed, Vonnegut denies his readers any sense of satisfaction. He records that the rebels destroyed not only obnoxious machinery but also useful and necessary technological devices such as sewage disposal plants. Also, they soon began to tinker with the unneeded machines with a view to making them operative again. In the face of such inveterate stupidity the leaders suicidally surrender to the government forces.

An obvious question arises: Why should Vonnegut or his readers concern themselves with the dehumanization of apparent morons? What, indeed, is there to be dehumanized? An answer is not readily forthcoming, but perhaps Vonnegut believes that there is some value in trying to save humanity from its own stupidity. In each novel there is at least one person who is aware of human folly, and thus is living proof that intellectual blindness is not universal. More frequently than not, these discerning individuals are reformers, as in *Player Piano,* who make self-sacrificing efforts to improve the lot of their fellow beings. Thus *The Sirens of Titan,* which in plot is a rather conventional example of science fiction with an interplanetary setting, has as its reformer a man who, having been rendered immortal, omniscient, and virtually omnipotent by entrapment in a "chrono-synclastic-infundibulum," sets about uniting all nations of the world in bonds of brotherhood by staging an abortive attack against the earth by Martians. The latter are earthlings abducted to Mars and converted to automatons by the insertion in their skulls of radio antennae through which orders are transmitted from a central directorate. These unfortunates are thus subjected to ruthless dehumanization and exploitation, but for a worthwhile end. The scheme is successful; the earth becomes united after the defeat of the Martians and the unity is cemented by the establishment of a new religion—the Church of God the Utterly Indifferent. The happy outcome is somewhat clouded, however, by the revelation that all human history has been determined by the trivial needs of the inhabitants of the planet Tralfamadore in one of the more remote galaxies.

Cat's Cradle and *God Bless You, Mr. Rosewater; or, Pearls Before Swine* also focus upon the efforts of altruistic individuals to alleviate misery. *Cat's Cradle* presents an entirely new religion, Bokonism, (named for its founder, Bokonon), much of the doctrine of which is written in Calypso verse. According to Bokonism religion *should* be an opiate; its function is to deceive and, by deceiving, make people happy. It teaches that God directs human destinies and that humankind is sacred, and it promotes an ethic of love, which believers manifest by pressing the soles of their feet against those of fellow believers. Bokonism was founded and flourished on a Caribbean island oppressed by a Duvalier-type dictator. It flourished because it was outlawed, for, according to *Cat's Cradle* at least, a religion functions most vigorously when opposed to the existing social order. There can be no doubt that Bokonism brings relief to the wretched islanders, the final horror of whose existence is that of being congealed, along with the rest of the world, by ice-nine, a discovery of an Ilium scientist. *God Bless You, Mr. Rosewater; or, Goodbye, Blue Monday* recounts the efforts of an enormously wealthy man to alleviate human misery through the more or less random disbursement of the Rosewater Foundation's almost limitless funds.

Two other novels, *Mother Night* and *Slaughterhouse-Five; or, The Children's Crysade,* both of which focus on World War II, contain no such reformers or philanthropists. In these the protagonists are never really in a position to be altruistic, even though they wish to be. In *Mother Night* Howard W. Campbell, Jr., serves schizophrenically as the Nazis' chief English-language radio propagandist at the same time that he is one of the allies' most effective spies. Years after the war he finds himself in an Israeli prison awaiting trial along with Adolf Eichmann. Here he commits suicide, even though a bizarre turn of events has ensured his acquittal. He realizes that one who has played his dual roles has betrayed beyond recovery his own humanity—a realization achieved by few Vonnegut characters in analogous situations.

Slaughterhouse-Five; or, The Children's Crusade, perhaps Vonnegut's most impressive novel, presents two characters who can see beneath the surface to the tragic realities of human history but make no attempt to bring about a change. These are the author himself, who is a frequent commentator, and the protagonist, Billy Pilgrim. The central event is the fire-bombing of Dresden—a catastrophe that Vonnegut had witnessed as a prisoner of war. Billy Pilgrim's liberating insights are the outgrowth of his being freed from the prison of time and, as a result, seeing the past, present and future as one and coexistent. One consequent realization is that death is an illusion. Though his periods of release from time occur on earth, their significance is explained to him by inhabitants of the distant planet Tralfamadore, to which he is transported on a Tralfamadorian spaceship. Though Billy finds no way to improve the tragically absurd condition of humanity, he does arrive at an understanding of it and a resultant deepening of compassion.

Four novels after *Slaughterhouse-Five—Breakfast of Champions; or, Goodbye, Blue Monday, Slapstick; or, Lonesome No More!,*

Jailbird, and *Deadeye Dick*—continue to satirize human folly in its contemporary manifestations, still relying on fantasy, black humor, and the absurd as tools of satire. Yet their tone differs from that of the earlier fiction. The seriousness of theme and, above all, the compassion implicit in such books as *Cat's Cradle* and *Slaughterhouse-Five* are all but absent. *Slapstick; or, Lonesome No More!,* indeed, would be appropriate as a title for any of the four. Fun and wit and laughs aplenty are not lacking, but thought is in short supply. The clown has shoved aside the thinker. But in the novel following these four, *Galápagos,* Vonnegut achieves a more subtle and more effective irony. For an epigraph he quotes from Anne Frank's *Diary:* "In spite of everything, I still believe people are really good at heart." Though Vonnegut, or the narrator, declares that he agrees with this statement, the characters and events in the novel provide overwhelming evidence that most people are evil at heart. According to the novel, human beings have used their "big brains"—evolution's prized gift—to destroy themselves and the world they live in. But when, by a fantastic series of events that only Vonnegut could dream up, the human species is reduced to only 10 individuals marooned on the Galápagos Islands, a reverse process of evolution sets in, the "big brains" disappear, and after a million years the human species is transformed into a gentle, seal-like mammal which actually is "good at heart."

In *Galápagos* there is a haunting quality that is not sustained in Vonnegut's two most recent novels—*Bluebeard* and *Hocus Pocus; or, What's the Hurry, Son?* The protagonist in *Bluebeard* is an artist, one of the founders of the abstract expressionist school of painting but later a fanatical representationalist. His great opus, which he keeps locked in a potato barn on Long Island, is an eight-by-sixty-four foot depiction of a World War II scene, presenting each object and every one of innumerable men and women in the minutest detail. Most of the satire, which is gentler than in most of Vonnegut's work, is directed against artists and writers, though peripherally other matters such as war and genocide are dealt with. *Hocus Pocus; or, What's the Hurray, Son?* roams over a wider field of ills: the deterioration of American education, the "buying of America" by the Japanese, the Vietnam war, the prison system, and racism.

The narrator of *Hocus Pocus* remarks: "All I ever wanted to overthrow was ignorance and self-serving fantasies." Later he asserts: "The truth can be very funny in an awful way, especially as it relates to greed and hypocrisy." These two statements admirably sum up Vonnegut's intention and tone in most of his fiction. To achieve his purposes (and perhaps to carry along readers with short attention spans) he employs a technique, especially in his later novels, of breaking his narratives into brief sections of no more than a paragraph, in which he recounts an anecdote that more often than not ends with a punch line. The effect somewhat resembles the performance of a stage or television comedian, though with Vonnegut there is an underlying seriousness.

—Perry D. Westbrook

WAGONER, David (Russell)

Nationality: American. **Born:** Massillon, Ohio, 5 June 1926. **Education:** Pennsylvania State University, University Park, B.A. 1947; Indiana University, Bloomington, M.A. in English 1949. **Military Service:** Served in the United States Navy, 1944-46. **Family:** Married 1) Patricia Parrot in 1961 (divorced 1982); 2) Robin Heather Seyfried in 1982. **Career:** Instructor, DePauw University, Greencastle, Indiana, 1949-50, and Pennsylvania State University, 1950-53; assistant professor, 1954-57, associate professor, 1958-66, and since 1966 professor of English, University of Washington, Seattle. Elliston Professor of Poetry, University of Cincinnati, 1968; editor, Princeton University Press Contemporary Poetry Series, 1977-81. Since 1966 editor, *Poetry Northwest,* Seattle; since 1983 poetry editor, University of Missouri Press, Columbia. **Awards:** Guggenheim fellowship, 1956; Ford fellowship, for drama, 1964; American Academy grant, 1967; Morton Dauwen Zabel prize, 1967, Oscar Blumenthal prize, 1974, Eunice Tietjens Memorial prize, 1977, and English-Speaking Union prize, 1980 (*Poetry,* Chicago); National Endowment for the Arts grant, 1969; Fels prize, 1975; Sherwood Anderson award, 1980. Chancellor, Academy of American Poets, 1978. **Address:** English Department, University of Washington, Seattle, Washington 98195, U.S.A; or 5416 154th Place, S.W., Edmonds, Washington 98026, U.S.A.

PUBLICATIONS

Novels

The Man in the Middle. New York, Harcourt Brace, 1954; London, Gollancz, 1955.
Money, Money, Money. New York, Harcourt Brace, 1955.
Rock. New York, Viking Press, 1958.
The Escape Artist. New York, Farrar Straus, and London, Gollancz, 1965.
Baby, Come On Inside. New York, Farrar Straus, 1968.
Where Is My Wandering Boy Tonight? New York, Farrar Straus, 1970.
The Road to Many a Wonder. New York, Farrar Straus, 1974.
Tracker. Boston, Little Brown, 1975.
Whole Hog. Boston, Little Brown, 1976.
The Hanging Garden. Boston, Little Brown, 1980; London, Hale, 1982.

Uncollected Short Stories

"Afternoon on the Ground," in *Prairie Schooner* (Lincoln, Nebraska), Fall 1978.
"Mr. Wallender's Romance," in *Hudson Review* (New York), Spring 1979.
"Cornet Solo," in *Boston Globe Magazine,* 20 May 1979.
"The Water Strider," in *Boston Globe Magazine,* 14 October 1979.
"Fly Boy," in *Ohio Review 25* (Athens), 1980.
"The Bird Watcher," in *Georgia Review* (Athens), Spring 1980.
"Snake Hunt," in *Western Humanities Review* (Salt Lake City), Winter 1980.
"Magic Night at the Reformatory," in *Shenandoah* (Lexington, Virginia), vol. 34, no. 4, 1981.

"The Sparrow," in *Epoch* (Ithaca, New York), Spring 1981.
"Mermaid," in *Western Humanities Review* (Salt Lake City), Summer 1981.
"Wild Goose Chase," in *Necessary Fictions,* edited by Stanley W. Lindberg and Stephen Corey. Athens, University of Georgia Press, 1986.
"The Land of the Dead," in *Georgia Review* (Athens), Summer 1987.
"The Riding Lesson," in *Southwest Review* (Dallas), Autumn 1987.

Plays

Any Eye for an Eye for an Eye (produced Seattle, 1973).

Screenplay: *The Escape Artist,* 1981.

Poetry

Dry Sun, Dry Wind. Bloomington, Indiana University Press, 1953.
A Place to Stand. Bloomington, Indiana University Press, 1958.
Poems. Portland, Oregon, Portland Art Museum, 1959.
The Nesting Ground. Bloomington, Indiana University Press, 1963.
Five Poets of the Pacific Northwest, with others, edited by Robin Skelton. Seattle, University of Washington Press, 1964.
Staying Alive. Bloomington, Indiana University Press, 1966.
New and Selected Poems. Bloomington, Indiana University Press, 1969.
Working Against Time. London, Rapp and Whiting, 1970.
Riverbed. Bloomington, Indiana University Press, 1972.
Sleeping in the Woods. Bloomington, Indiana University Press, 1974.
A Guide to Dungeness Spit. Port Townsend, Washington, Graywolf Press, 1975.
Travelling Light. Port Townsend, Washington, Graywolf Press, 1976.
Collected Poems 1956-1976. Bloomington, Indiana University Press, 1976.
Who Shall Be the Sun? Poems Based on the Lore, Legends, and Myths of Northwest Coast and Plateau Indians. Bloomington, Indiana University Press, 1978.
In Broken Country. Boston, Little Brown, 1979.
Landfall. Boston, Little Brown, 1981.
First Light. Boston, Little Brown, 1983.
Through the Forest: New and Selected Poems 1977-1987. New York, Atlantic Monthly Press, 1987.

Other

Editor, *Straw for the Fire: From the Notebooks of Theodore Roethke 1943-1963.* New York, Doubleday, 1972.

*

Manuscript Collections: Olin Library, Washington University, St. Louis; University of Washington, Seattle.

Critical Studies: "David Wagoner's Fiction: In the Mills of Satan" by William J. Schafer in *Critique* (Minneapolis), vol. 9, no. 1, 1965; "It Dawns on Us That We Must Come Apart," in *Alone with America* by Richard Howard, New York, Atheneum, 1969, London, Thames and Hudson, 1970, revised edition, Atheneum, 1980; "An Interview with David Wagoner," in *Crazy Horse 12* (Marshall, Minnesota), 1972; "A Conversation with David Wagoner," in *Yes* (Avoca, New York), vol. 4, no. 1, 1973; "On David Wagoner," in *Salmagundi* (Saratoga Springs, New York), Spring-Summer 1973, and "Pelting Dark Windows," in *Parnassus* (New York), Spring-Summer 1977, both by Sanford Pinsker; *David Wagoner* by Ron McFarland, Boise, Idaho, Boise State University, 1989.

David Wagoner comments:

It is almost impossible for me to comment coherently on my own fiction, except to say that I began writing poetry first and received early encouragement as a writer of fiction from Edward J. Nicols at Penn State and Peter Taylor at Indiana University, and later from Malcolm Cowley at Viking Press and Catherine Carver who was then at Harcourt Brace. I seem to have a penchant for what might be called serious farce, but whether farce can stand the serious strains I put on it, I must leave to others to say. I also recognize my tendency to write what I believe critics call "initiation" novels. I tend to dramatize or write in scenes rather than to be discursive. One clear theme would seem to be the would-be innocent protagonist *vs.* the corrupt city, perhaps a result of my having grown up between Chicago and Gary, Indiana, where the most sophisticated and effective forms of pollution were first perfected.

*   *   *

In his novels, David Wagoner has pursued the themes of innocence and corruption, of the connections between past, present and future, of the individual trapped in a violent society. The novels depict individuals corrupted by modern urban life, protagonists essentially innocent and helpless damaged by the pressures of family and further maimed by society. Wagoner skillfully uses Dickensian comedy and drama to create a tragic myth of man stripped and abandoned by his parents and his fellows yet struggling to survive and to remain intact.

The Man in the Middle and *Money, Money, Money* describe helpless, childlike adults caught up in criminal machinations. *The Escape Artist* and *Where Is My Wandering Boy Tonight?* treat the same theme from the viewpoint of juvenile protagonists. Each novel involves criminals and corrupt politicians who pursue and persecute an innocent victim. There is a strong element of picaresque comedy in this drama of innocence adapting to a wicked world. The later novels also develop a complex sexual theme revolving around an Oedipal relationship—a child confronted and fascinated by a destructive mother figure. Each of the protagonists must overcome this infantile sexual bondage before he is free to live wholly, just as each must learn the depth of the world's wickedness before he can shed his infantile social innocence.

The Road to Many a Wonder continues Wagoner's comedy of 19th-century America (begun in *Where Is My Wandering Boy Tonight?*) and his parable of innocence and the frontier. In it a gold-seeker, Isaac Bender, succeeds by the most improbable means, his questing innocence overcoming the money-corruption of the gold rush and the Hobbesian savagery of the raw West. The novel is marked by a comic sweetness and light that offsets the bleak portraiture of venal American character-types.

Tracker and *Whole Hog* extend Wagoner's story of the frontier and the wild west by focusing on the uncertainties of the pioneer spirit, the fragility of familial and social relations and the ultimate triumph of intelligent virtue over mindless evil. Both tales revolve around juvenile protagonists (Wagoner's type of innocence) who learn by painful experience to outwit a lawless adult world.

In *Rock* and *Baby, Come On Inside* Wagoner deals with the destructiveness of family life and the crippling effects of the past. Both stories concentrate on the conflict between leaving home and returning home: "You can't go home again" vs. "You *must* go home again." In each novel, the protagonist tries to recapture his past, to find a home place, but ends in confusion and further exile.

A recurrent pattern in Wagoner's novels is that of pursuit and flight, a nightmarish sense of implacable evil, and a recurrent scene is a metaphorical return to the womb, to primordial shelter. Charlie Bell in *The Man in the Middle* spends a night in a railway coin locker. Willy Grier is left in a garbage can in *Money, Money, Money*. Danny Masters in *The Escape Artist* hides out in a Goodwill Industries collection box and a US mailbox. The pattern of flight and hiding, a fragile individual pursued by a terrifying nemesis, occurs in a comic context—cynical wit and slapstick farce—for the dream-like or mythic dimension of Wagoner's novels derives from their mixed tone. The stories encompass suspense, adventure, comedy, pathos, and a strong sense of the social and political life of midwestern cities.

In *The Hanging Garden* Wagoner returns to a detective-story format of homicidal insanity defeated by a man who is basically good but worn from personal and political struggle. Returning to nature (a holiday cottage), the protagonist is confronted with "natural evil" in the form of a sadistic killer. The tale becomes a description of survival of the intelligent, cultured man faced with the most primitive forces of the human psyche.

Wagoner's tragicomedies of violence achieve effects somewhat like François Truffaut's *Shoot the Piano Player*. The mixture of naiveté, tough-guy dialogue, violence, thriller action, and insight into complex states of mind creates a fantasy world as an accurate analog for contemporary urban life. Danny Masters, in *The Escape Artist,* muses on violence and trickery and how to escape them:

> Danny felt his own life shut inside him, keeping as quiet as it could, shying away. Nobody should be able to break anybody open like a nut and clean out the insides, but some people did it, and he would never let them come close. That was why getting away was important, getting out, getting loose, because they had to make you sit still long enough so they could crack you open, otherwise it spoiled their aim. They were no good with moving targets, no good if you weren't where they thought you were. They knew a lot of tricks, and that was why you had to keep ahead of them, and then if you got a big enough lead, you could afford to let them know who you were, taunting them from a distance yet always ready to change shape to fool them.

Wagoner's novels reflect society's torments and traps and also explore the paths to freedom—self-understanding, imagination, and the uses of experience. While they detail corruption and destruction, they also reflect innocence and virtue. The possibilities in this world are tragic and comic, and the inevitable price of survival is loss of innocence.

—William J. Schafer

WAKEFIELD, Dan

Nationality: American. **Born:** Indianapolis, Indiana, 21 May 1932.
Education: Shortridge High School, Indianapolis, graduated 1950;
Indiana University, Bloomington, 1950-51; Columbia University,
New York, 1951-55, B.A. (honors) in English 1955. **Career:**
News editor, *Princeton Packet,* New Jersey, 1955; research assis-
tant to C. Wright Mills, Columbia University, 1955; staff writer,
the *Nation,* New York, 1956-61; contributing editor, *Atlantic
Monthly,* Boston, 1968-82; since 1992 contributing writer, *GQ
Magazine.* Since 1983 co-chairperson of religious education, King's
Chapel, Boston. Visiting lecturer, University of Massachusetts, Bos-
ton, 1965-67, 1981, Bread Loaf Writers Conference, Middlebury,
Vermont, 1966, 1968, 1970, University of Illinois, Urbana, 1968,
University of Iowa, Iowa City, 1972, and Emerson College, Bos-
ton, 1982-83. Distinguished visiting writer, Florida International
University, 1995. Creator and story consultant, *James at 15* series,
NBC Television, 1977-78. Since 1994, Board of Directors, Na-
tional Writers Union. **Awards:** Bread Loaf Writers Conference De
Voto fellowship, 1957; Nieman Foundation fellowship, for jour-
nalism, Harvard University, 1963; Rockefeller grant, 1968; National
Endowment for the Arts award, for "A Visit from Granny," 1966,
for unknown, 1968; Golden Eagle award, for screenplay, 1983.
Address: King's Chapel, 64 Beacon Street, Boston, Massachusetts 02108, U.S.A.

PUBLICATIONS

Novels

Going All the Way. New York, Delacorte Press, 1970; London,
    Weidenfeld and Nicholson, 1971.
Starting Over. New York, Delacorte Press, 1973; London, Hart
    Davis MacGibbon, 1974.
Home Free. New York, Delacorte Press, and London, Hart Davis
    MacGibbon, 1977.
Under the Apple Tree. New York, Delacorte Press, 1982.
Selling Out. Boston, Little Brown, 1985.

Uncollected Short Stories

"The Rich Girl," in *Playboy,* September 1965.
"Autumn Full of Apples," in *The Best American Short Stories 1966,*
    edited by Martha Foley and David Burnett. Boston, Houghton
    Mifflin, 1966.
"A Visit from Granny," in *American Literary Anthology #2,* 1966.
"Full Moon in Sagittarius," in *Atlantic,* Boston, January 1973.

Plays

Television Films: *James at 15,* 1977; *The Seduction of Miss Leona,*
    1980; *The Innocents Abroad,* from the novel by Mark Twain,
    1983.

Other

Island in the City: The World of Spanish Harlem. Boston,
    Houghton Mifflin, 1959.
Revolt in the South. New York, Grove Press, 1961.

*Between the Lines: A Reporter's Personal Journey Through Pub-
    lic Events.* New York, New American Library, 1965.
Supernation at Peace and War. Boston, Little Brown, 1968.
All Her Children: The Making of a Soap Opera. New York,
    Doubleday, 1976.
Returning: A Spiritual Journey. New York, Doubleday, 1988.
The Story of Your Life: Writing a Spiritual Autobiography. Bos-
    ton, Beacon Press, 1990.
New York in the Fifties. Boston, Houghton Mifflin, 1991.
Expect a Miracle. San Francisco, HarperSanFrancisco, 1995.

Editor, *The Addict: An Anthology.* New York, Fawcett, 1963.

*

Manuscript Collection: Mugar Memorial Library, Boston University.

Critical Study: *The New American Novel of Manners: The Fiction of Richard Yates, Dan Wakefield, and Thomas McGuane* by
Jerome Klinkowitz, Athens, University of Georgia Press, 1986;
"Remembering the '50s": Three Spiritual Mentors" by James Wall,
in *The Christian Century,* 109(19), 3-10 June 1992.

Dan Wakefield comments:

I believe in the novel as story, entertainment, and communication—as if those elements could be separated! One of my college
English professors defined the novel as "how it was with a group
of people." I believe it is that and more. I want my novels to convey interior as well as social truth. I want them to enable readers to
appreciate how other people felt, to make connections among human beings in all their diversity and in their alikeness as well. I
love it when readers recognize some aspect of themselves in one
of my characters and thus feel "I am not the only one!" who experienced some particular type of pain or joy. I try to write the way
my characters think, the way they would express themselves, and I
fear this attempt to be "plain" and open is sometimes misconstrued
as an inability to write in a more self-consciously "literary" style.
So be it. My aim is to convey the perception of the people I write
about. I write about people I love, and in so doing I wish to honor
them and celebrate our common humanity.

*   *   *

Dan Wakefield had already established himself as a feature journalist a decade before writing his first novel, but the unique style
of his journalistic writing would lay the groundwork for his fiction. *Island in the City: The World of Spanish Harlem, Revolt in
the South, Between the Lines,* and *Supernation at Peace and War,*
were pioneering efforts in a field which became known as "The
New Journalism." Sacrificing the distance and objectivity of conventional journalism, Wakefield found the best way to write about
an issue was to immerse himself within it and then write about
himself. Thus he lived inside the poverty of New York City's Spanish Harlem, experienced firsthand the civil rights movements in the
American south, and travelled from coast to coast talking with common citizens about the state of their nation. Moreover, the New
Journalism used the techniques of realistic fiction, including characterization, narrative development, imagery, and symbolism to tell
its story—conventions which had recently been discarded by the
innovative novelists who wished their fiction to practice no such

structuring illusions. As a result, by 1970 Wakefield was prepared to write a new American novel of manners, using the traditional form of fiction to express the new semiotics of culture he had experienced firsthand as a New Journalist.

A strong sense of how the signs of culture operate pervades Wakefield's fiction, and his novels provide an excellent cross-section of the development of American manners since World War II. *Going All the Way* shows two young men returning to their homes in Indianapolis after serving in the Korean War. Anxious for their own lives to begin, they face the obstacles of being fettered by their parent's obsolescent manners and by the confusions, sexual and otherwise, being wrought by their exuberant young manhood. The times are changing as well, and within this kaleidoscope of radically different values Sonny and Gunner attempt to sort out new trends in dress, music, and social conduct. That matters do not improve with age is shown in *Starting Over,* in which a recently divorced advertising executive refashions his life in a new city, with a new profession and friends. An entirely new system of manners takes over, with innovations such as the single-person's lonely Sunday and holidays providing difficult tests of adjustment. His protagonist's mind, however, proves to be a *tabula rasa* upon which any suggestion can be planted. Therefore, readers can find an index to the manners of the times (the late 1960s and early 1970s in America) simply by watching the hero's reactions. The novel closes with him drifting into another marriage, with everyone telling him how lucky he is, as he stares wistfully after a young woman on the beach.

In Wakefield's first two novels his characters are richly imprinted by their social environment. That the radically changing times may have exhausted themselves and become as blank as the tablets of his characters is suggested by Wakefield's third novel, *Home Free.* Change has its rhythms and dynamics, and in this case the author shows how he can employ periods of lull and regression just as effectively. The protagonist begins college but is swept away by the countercultural movement of the times. When this movement fizzles out to its entropic end, he is cast adrift on a sea of nothingness. His stimuli have been ethereal—often just the suggestive lyrics of popular music—and when faced with reality, he has little ability to respond. He crosses America, but in a parody of Jack Kerouac's *On the Road,* for instead of energy Wakefield's hero draws on ennui. He winds up at the extreme edge of America, on the beach outside Los Angeles, where he lives in a situation as blank as a movie screen:

> His life.
> He'd walked into it like walking up the aisle of a movie and melting into the screen and becoming part of the picture, the story, finding out what happened as you went along, knowing from the beginning how it would end but not when. Then he'd be standing on the stage feeling silly and strange with the screen dark and the houselights on. Bright. He'd be blinking, trying to find his way out. In the meantime this was his life.

Under the Apple Tree and *Selling Out* are much fuller works because Wakefield again builds his fiction from the materials of popular culture, rather than from their lack. The first, set in a small Illinois town during the years of World War II, traces the maturation of a young boy as his older brother goes off to fight and the home community responds with a semiotic riot of patriotic support. The novel's action is a study of reading habits, as the war's far-off action is translated to the "home front" by means of advertisements, promotional campaigns, and instructive attitudes. Their signal nature is perfectly matched to the boy's innocence, and as he grows up so do popular notions toward the conflict. His own understanding of sexuality and human relations parallels this cultural development as his own ability to read his brother's and future sister-in-law's emotions rises from the comic-book level to the sophisticated.

Selling Out shows Wakefield's semiotic method in high relief, because the novel constitutes a test of it. His central character is a short-story writer named Perry Moss, who experiments with a new medium (film writing) in a new environment (Hollywood). Wakefield is judicially precise in his contrast of the bi-coastal and intermedia realities, as Perry finds the jet ride from Boston to Los Angeles has taken him into an entirely different world. The contrasts are shown to good purpose, not simply for their own value but for what they contribute to an understanding of Perry's fatal attempt at change. Yet his true allegiances remain to the printed word and life in New England, and when he returns to them at the end it is with a heightened sense of appreciation which his west coast adventures have made so obvious.

Based as it is upon self-evidently autobiographical materials, *Selling Out* paves the way for Wakefield's subsequent work in what he calls "spiritual autobiography." *Returning: A Spiritual Journey* documents his commercial success in Hollywood and chronicles his physical breakdown from the stress it entailed. To this point the book parallels *Selling Out.* Yet where *Selling Out* ends, with the protagonist's return to New England, *Returning* begins its major work, that of detailing the restorative powers Wakefield found in a spiritual understanding of himself. It is the employment of theological and not just intellectual elements that makes such a "return" possible, and in *The Story of Your Life* Wakefield presents a workable program for combining narrative activity with spiritual understanding as a way of constructing one's life as a meaningful work. Such patterns appear in his own canon, as *New York in the Fifties* not only summarizes his own involvement with the writers and thinkers of that era but investigates his own artistic growth; as such, it serves as the legwork for a novel in progress, set in the same time and region.

Wakefield knows that man is the sign-making animal, and his appreciation of the semiosis by which human life is conducted makes him ably qualified to describe how life is lived in America today.

—Jerome Klinkowitz

WALKER, Alice (Malsenior)

Nationality: American. **Born:** Eatonton, Georgia, 9 February 1944. **Education:** Spelman College, Atlanta, 1961-63; Sarah Lawrence College, Bronxville, New York, 1963-65, B.A. 1965. **Family:** Married Melvyn R. Leventhal in 1967 (divorced 1976); one daughter. **Career:** Voter registration and Head Start program worker, Mississippi, and with New York City Department of Welfare, mid-1960s; teacher, Jackson State College, 1968-69, and Tougaloo College, 1970-71, both Mississippi; lecturer, Wellesley College, Cambridge, Massachusetts, 1972-73, and University of Massachusetts,

Boston, 1972-73; associate professor of English, Yale University, New Haven, Connecticut, after 1977. Distinguished Writer, University of California, Berkeley, Spring 1982; Fannie Hurst Professor, Brandeis University, Waltham, Massachusetts, Fall 1982. Co-founder and publisher, Wild Trees Press, Navarro, California, 1984-88. **Awards:** Bread Loaf Writers Conference scholarship, 1966; *American Scholar* prize, for essay, 1967; Merrill fellowship, 1967; MacDowell fellowship, 1967, 1977; Radcliffe Institute fellowship, 1971; Lillian Smith award, for poetry, 1973; American Academy Rosenthal award, 1974; National Endowment for the Arts grant, 1977; Guggenheim grant, 1978; American Book award, 1983; Pulitzer prize, 1983; O. Henry award, 1986. Ph.D.: Russell Sage College, Troy, New York, 1972; D.H.L.: University of Massachusetts, Amherst, 1983. Lives in San Francisco. **Address:** c/o Harcourt Brace Jovanovich Inc., 1250 Sixth Avenue, San Diego, California 92101, U.S.A.

PUBLICATIONS

Novels

The Third Life of Grange Copeland. New York, Harcourt Brace, 1970; London, Women's Press, 1985.
Meridian. New York, Harcourt Brace, and London, Deutsch, 1976.
The Color Purple. New York, Harcourt Brace, 1982; London, Women's Press, 1983.
The Temple of My Familiar. San Diego, Harcourt Brace, and London, Women's Press, 1989.
Possessing the Secret of Joy. New York, Harcourt Brace, and London, Cape, 1992.

Short Stories

In Love and Trouble: Stories of Black Women. New York, Harcourt Brace, 1973; London, Women's Press, 1984.
You Can't Keep a Good Woman Down. New York, Harcourt Brace, 1981; London, Women's Press, 1982.
Complete Short Stories, London, Women's Press, n.d.
Everyday Use, edited by Barbara T. Christian. New Brunswick, Rutgers University Press, 1994.

Uncollected Short Stories

"Cuddling," in *Essence* (New York), July 1985.
"Kindred Spirits," in *Prize Stories 1986,* edited by William Abrahams. New York, Doubleday, 1986.

Poetry

Once. New York, Harcourt Brace, 1968; London, Women's Press, 1986.
Five Poems. Detroit, Broadside Press, 1972.
Revolutionary Petunias and Other Poems. New York, Harcourt Brace, 1973; London, Women's Press, 1988.
Good Night, Willie Lee, I'll See You in the Morning. New York, Dial Press, 1979; London, Women's Press, 1987.
Horses Make a Landscape Look More Beautiful. New York, Harcourt Brace, 1984; London, Women's Press, 1985.
Her Blue Body Everything We Know: Earthling Poems 1965-1990. San Diego, Harcourt Brace, and London, Women's Press, 1991.

Other (for children)

Langston Hughes, American Poet (biography). New York, Crowell, 1974.
To Hell with Dying. San Diego, Harcourt Brace, and London, Hodder and Stoughton, 1988.
Finding the Green Stone. San Diego, Harcourt Brace, and London, Hodder and Stoughton, 1991.

Other

In Search of Our Mothers' Gardens: Womanist Prose. New York, Harcourt Brace, 1983; London, Women's Press, 1984.
Living by the Word: Selected Writings 1973-1987. San Diego, Harcourt Brace, and London, Women's Press, 1988.
Warrior Marks: Female Genital Mutilation and the Sexual Blinding of Women, with Pratibha Parmar. New York, Harcourt Brace, 1993.

Editor, *I Love Myself When I Am Laughing . . . and Then Again When I Am Looking Mean and Impressive: A Zora Neale Hurston Reader.* Old Westbury, New York, Feminist Press, 1979.

*

Bibliography: *Alice Malsenior Walker: An Annotated Bibliography 1968-1986* by Louis H. Pratt and Darnell D. Pratt, Westport, Connecticut, Meckler, 1988; *Alice Walker: An Annotated Bibliography 1968-1986* by Erma Davis Banks and Keith Byerman, London, Garland, 1989.

Critical Studies: *Brodie's Notes on Alice Walker's "The Color Purple"* by Marion Picton, London, Pan, 1991; *Alice Walker* by Conna Histy Winchell, New York, Twayne, 1992; *Alice Walker* by Tony Gentry, New York, Chelsea, 1993; *Alice Walker and Zora Neale Hurston: The Common Bond* edited by Lillie P. Howard, Westport, Connecticut, and London, Greedwood Press, 1993; *Alice Walker: Critical Perspectives Past and Present* edited by Henry Louis Gates and K.A. Appiah, New York, Amistad, 1993;

*   *   *

The era of the so-called Harlem Renaissance drew together a number of gifted black American writers who gave voice to the black experience. Some used traditional poetic forms and metaphors to describe the black condition, but others like Jean Toomer and Zora Neale Hurston worked to establish a black voice in American literature. They drew on the rich Afro-American oral culture with its store of stories, songs, narrative incidents, phrase, and metaphor, and translated the lived experience, with its idiomatic language, onto the printed page. Alice Walker, as a contemporary black writer from the American south, stands well within this tradition. Her themes are generally revolutionary and confront the contemporary experience of black Americans, particularly black American women, via their cultural, social, and political history. *Meridian,* an early work, integrates many of Walker's preoccupations. It chronicles, in episodic form, the life of Meridian, a young black woman from the south who rejects the simple options available to black women, such as marriage, children, and religion, in favor of, at first, the civil rights movement and education in the north. Finally she realizes that her struggle must take place among her own people and, since so few of them understand, must take place alone. Afro-American oral culture merges effortlessly in this work with the history of slavery, exploitation, poverty, southern decay, the black vote, civil rights, black is beautiful, and feminism, via Walker's "womanist" prose style.

"Womanist" Walker identifies as being from the black folk expression of mothers to female children: "You acting womanish". It usually refers to "outrageous, audacious, courageous or willful behavior," and is interchangeable with another black folk expression "You trying to be grown" that is "responsible, in charge, serious". She further defines the word as entailing a commitment to the survival of whole people, male and female. The word is useful to describe Walker's activities as a writer in terms of both theme and style. Thematically she is preoccupied by the question raised in her now famous essay *In Search of Our Mothers' Gardens,* that is "How was the creativity of the black woman kept alive?" Her characters move through painful black experiences towards perhaps an understanding of responsible, adult, and serious action that will allow the imaginative living of a life. The emphasis however is as much on living as on the artistic imagination. Thus Dee in "Everyday Use," from the short story collection *In Love and Trouble,* does not get her Grandmother's hand-stitched quilts to hang on the wall. They go to Maggie who, in Dee's terms, can't appreciate them, and probably will "be backward enough to put them to everyday use." This story also provides the title of her latest collection of stories, *Everyday Use,* and its governing metaphor of quilt-making.

In terms of style Walker seems committed to creating works that attempt to fuse form and content into a seamless whole. When writing of her own creative process in *Living by the Word,* she describes the importance of letting characters relate their experiences in their own language, such as Celie in *The Color Purple* speaking the language of an illiterate black child. It is, Walker says, "language more than anything else that reveals and validates one's existence, and if the language we actually speak is denied us, then it is inevitable that the form we are permitted to assume historically will be one of caricature, reflecting someone else's literary or social fantasy." Celie's story in *The Color Purple* is told in her own voice and begins with the rape perpetrated by her father: "When that hurt, I cry . . . I don't never git used to it. And now I feels sick every time I be the one to cook." Walker's fidelity to the idiom of her characters testifies to the power and viability of that language as a vehicle for the imaginative recreation of black experience.

The importance placed by Walker on language leads to an interesting fusion of genre within her work. She writes fiction, poetry, and essays that range from the brief autobiographical episode to critical works. All her work is invested with the kind of poetry that stems from an ever-ready capacity to tell a tale. An acute and critical assessment of Zora Neale Hurston's work is delightfully disrupted by a story of Walker's own family's reaction to Hurston, who inspired them to relish "the pleasure of each other's loquacious and bodacious company." *The Color Purple* also has its narrative sequence disrupted by the manner of its telling. Celie's story, that of a poor, black, and ugly women, depicts her struggle against first incest, then marital cruelty and exploitation, through to a slow and painful realization of her own worth, which comes via her love for a woman, Shug Avery. The story is told in the letters Celie writes, to God and to her beloved sister Nettie. The result is fragmented and episodic, but precisely related to the slow growth of an individual stunted by economic, social, intellectual, and emotional deprivation. The letters begin deprived of language itself, but gain in richness and depth of expression as Celie's impoverishment is replaced by love, friendship, and finally a recognition of her own worth.

Both of Walker's novels since *The Color Purple* attempt to voice the experience of the silent in the form of disrupted and fragmentary narratives, and both novels are directly linked to *The Color Purple* through the reappearance of characters from that book. Instead of the two narrative voices of *The Color Purple,* however (Celie's and her sister Nettie's), multiple narrators put together a patchwork of histories going back into dream and antiquity, reflecting the shift in Walker's interests back toward Africa and the idea of an originary matriarch. This is perhaps more successful in *Possessing the Secret of Joy* than in its predecessor, *The Temple of My Familiar;* in the latter Walker's ability to find for each character the appropriate and distinctive language seems to be submerged by a more didactic urgency, and this history of human life over several millennia becomes somehow undifferentiated and over-ambitious. *Possessing the Secret of Joy,* with its more clearly defined focus on the issue of female circumcision, is more persuasive, and displays again Walker's gift for the expression of suffering; the complex and painful experiences and motives of Tashi, the central character, give an immediate force to the wider message.

Walker's heroines end their days in the way perhaps best expressed by Walker's own poem in her collection *Revolutionary Petunias:*

> Rebellious Living
> Against the Elemental Crush.
> A Song of Color
> Blooming
> For deserving eyes.
> Blooming Gloriously
> For its Self.

Walker's own work similarly offers a fusion of experience and art which usurps traditional artistic and critical response. If her fiction is at times marred by a tendency toward sentimentality, and her critical writing is opinionated and idiosyncratic, the experience of Walker's work is nonetheless valuable. The nature of this flower may be indeed to bloom.

—Jan Pilditch

WALKER, Margaret (Abigail)

Nationality: American. **Born:** Birmingham, Alabama, 7 July 1915. **Education:** Northwestern University, Evanston, Illinois, B.A. 1935; University of Iowa, Iowa City, M.A. 1940, Ph.D. 1965; Yale University, New Haven, Connecticut (Ford fellow), 1954. **Family:** Married Firnist James Alexander in 1943 (died); two daughters and two sons. **Career:** Has worked as social worker, reporter, and magazine editor; taught at Livingstone College, Salisbury, North Carolina, 1941-42, 1945-46, and West Virginia State College, Institute, 1942-43. From 1949 professor of English, and from 1968 director of the Institute for the Study of the History, Life and Culture of Black Peoples, Jackson State College, Mississippi. **Awards:** Yale Series of Younger Poets award, 1942; Rosenwald fellowship, 1944; Houghton Mifflin Literary fellowship, 1966; Fulbright fellowship, 1971; National Endowment for the Arts grant, 1972. D.Litt: Northwestern University, 1974; Rust College, Holly Springs, Mississippi, 1974; D.F.A.: Denison University, Granville, Ohio, 1974;

D.H.L.: Morgan State University, Baltimore, 1976. **Address:** 2205 Guynes Street, Jackson, Mississippi 39213, U.S.A.

PUBLICATIONS

Novels

Come Down from Yonder Mountain. Toronto, Longman, 1962.
Jubilee. Boston, Houghton Mifflin, 1966.

Poetry

For My People. New Haven, Connecticut, Yale University Press, 1942.
Ballad of the Free. Detroit, Broadside Press, 1966.
Prophets for a New Day. Detroit, Broadside Press, 1970.
October Journey. Detroit, Broadside Press, 1973.

Recording: *The Poetry of Margaret Walker,* Folkways, 1975.

Other

How I Wrote Jubilee. Chicago, Third World Press, 1972.
A Poetic Equation: Conversations Between Margaret Walker and Nikki Giovanni. Washington, D.C., Howard University Press, 1974.
The Daemonic Genius of Richard Wright. Washington, D.C., Howard University Press, 1982; as *Richard Wright, Daemonic Genius,* New York, Warner, 1988.
How I Wrote Jubilee and Other Essays on Life and Literature, edited by Maryemma Graham. New York, Feminist Press, 1990.
For My People, photographs by Roland L. Freeman. Jackson and London, University Press of Mississippi, 1992.

*

Critical Study: *Margaret Walker's For My People,* by Roland L. Freeman, Jackson and London, University Press of Mississippi, 1992.

*   *   *

Authenticating her facts by extensive research, Margaret Walker enlarged the experiences of her great-grandmother during and after slavery into the epic novel *Jubilee.* The heroine, Vyry, is two years old when she enters the story at the childbed death of her 29-year-old mother, who has borne 15 slave children in rural Georgia for her master, John Dutton. The 58 chapters are divided into three sections subtitled "The Ante-Bellum Years," "The Civil War Years," and "Reconstruction and Reaction." The first section, beginning in 1837, introduces 10 major characters, half of whom are removed by tragedy before the middle of the novel. The cook, Aunt Sally, irritably singing "mad-mood" songs, is sold. John Dutton, "yelling and cursing in the night," is dispatched by gangrene; and his "ni-gra"-hating wife, Big Missy Salina, dies ignominiously of a stroke. Young West Pointer Johnny Dutton and his pacifist brother-in-law, Kevin MacDougall, exit heroically but pitifully as war casualties. Old Brother Zeke, the slave preacher who secretly works for the Underground Railroad, succumbs later while a Union Army spy. Three other characters embody vigorous criticism of slavery and war: Lillian, Vyry's gentle white sister, who goes insane after the death of her Kevin and an assault by one of Sheridan's "bummers";

Ed Grimes, the brutal overseer, who lives to exploit his betters; and Randall Ware, proud blacksmith and freeman from birth, whose love for his wife Vyry "just got caught in the times" during his war service.

Of sections II and III, the former, replete with historical and military details, closely reflects the author's research. It introduces Innis Brown, who slowly convinces Vyry to end her seven-year wait for her husband. The title of the Reconstruction section, "Forty Years in the Wilderness," suits the ruinous adventures of Vyry, Innis, and the children building homes in Alabama. Flooded out, exploited in sharecropping, profoundly stricken when burned out by the Ku Klux Klan, Vyry becomes almost pathologically averse to building again. But by innate acts of humanity and racial dignity in Greenville, she inspires whites to help build the family's final home. An amicable understanding ensues between Innis and Randall Ware, who pays a visit with ideas like W.E.B. Du Bois's, and with money to educate the children.

The authors' Dedication could have addressed her novel "to all the members of my race [not just 'family'] with all my love." The ancestry of almost every Black reader contains its own Vyry, thus revered in Chapter 57:

> She was only a living sign and mark of all the best that any human being could hope to become. In her obvious capacity for love, redemptive and forgiving love, she was alive and standing on the highest peaks of her time and human personality. Peasant and slave, unlettered and untutored, she was nevertheless the best true example of the motherhood of her race, an ever present assurance that nothing could destroy a people whose sons had come from her loins.

Vyry's actions, always credible, deserve that praise.

Jubilee is rich with history. Numerous details of slaves' medical and culinary arts, clothing, shelter, and marriages are given. Their legally enforced illiteracy, the planned destruction of their normal affections for one another, their physical oppressions (ranging from the Black Codes to savage plantation punishments and Confederate murders at Andersonville) are depicted. Over a dozen episodes and circumstances reveal the slaves' aggressive feelings: repressed hatreds, aid to abolitionists, revolts, and escapes after 1861 (including all 46 Dutton field slaves) to take up either guns or tools for the Union Army. Matters transcending their focus in the slavocracy come to the fore: political events, the birth of the Confederacy, the specie crisis, 1863 analyzed as a turning point in the war, the Freedmen's Bureau, and the maneuvered return of White Home Rule.

The author aims at a realistically balanced treatment. The "good whites" are represented by Lillian and Kevin, Doc, the Shackelfords, and nameless abolitionists—Lillian centralizing the tragedy of war and the psychopathy constantly threatening decent slave-holders. Vicious Grimes has no Black counterpart, and the slave-holders perform no noble deeds like Jim's bringing Johnny home to die. Regional balance is implicit in use of the New York draft riots and the indefensible destructiveness of Union soldiers after the end of the fighting.

Jubilee is history explicit in the prototypal experience of one slave woman, issuing contemporaneously in what Innis Brown saw a "a wisdom and a touching humility," and ultimately in what the author's speech in 1968 at the National Urban League Conference in New Orleans expresses as follows: "We are still a [Black] people of spirit and soul. We are still fighting in the midst of white American Racism for the overwhelming truth of the primacy of human personality and the spiritual destiny of all mankind."

—James A. Emanuel

WALKER, Mildred

Also writes as Mildred Walker Schemm. **Nationality:** American. **Born:** Philadelphia, Pennsylvania, 2 May 1905. **Education:** Wells College, B.A. 1926; University of Michigan, M.A. 1934. **Family:** Married Ferdinand Ripley Schemm, 1927 (died 1955); one daughter and two sons. **Career:** Advertising copy writer, John Wanamaker Co., 1926-27; professor of English literature, Wells College, Aurora, New York, 1955-68. Fulbright Lecturer, Kyoto, Japan, 1959-60. **Awards:** Avery Hopwood award, for *Fireweed*. **Agent:** James Brown Associates, 25 W. 43rd St., New York, New York 10036, U.S.A.

PUBLICATIONS

Novels

Fireweed. New York, Harcourt Brace, 1934; London, University of Nebraska Press, 1994.
Light from the Arcturus. New York, Harcourt Brace, 1935; London, University of Nebraska Press, 1994.
Dr. Norton's Wife. New York, Harcourt Brace, 1938.
The Brewers' Big Horses. New York, Harcourt Brace, 1940.
Unless the Wind Turns. New York, Harcourt Brace, 1941.
Winter Wheat. New York, Harcourt Brace, 1944; London, University of Nebraska Press, 1994.
The Quarry. New York, Harcourt Brace, 1947.
Medical Meeting. New York, Harcourt Brace, 1949.
The Southwest Corner. New York, Harcourt Brace, 1951; London, University of Nebraska Press, 1994.
The Curlew's Cry. New York, Harcourt Brace, 1955; London, University of Nebraska Press, 1994.
The Body of a Young Man. New York, Harcourt Brace, 1960.
If a Lion Could Talk. New York, Harcourt Brace, 1970.
A Piece of the World. New York, Atheneum, 1972.

*   *   *

All of Mildred Walker's 13 novels had their beginning in "one observation that started her thinking," according to Walker's daughter, Ripley Schemm Hugo, the widow of poet Richard Hugo. That observation often centered on a feature of the landscape, either natural or manmade, that suggested something of the lives of the people in the area. Grain elevators rising on the horizon to signal the presence of a rural Montana community, much as church steeples marked the small New England towns she knew in her youth, served as partial inspiration for *Winter Wheat,* her novel of a young woman's life on an isolated wheat ranch.

Walker admits that she often began work on a novel with only "a vague idea," but once her imagination was engaged, she says she would "scribble jottings" for whatever novel was in progress on a pad of yellow legal paper. Her "jottings" for *Winter Wheat* included descriptions of grain elevators, rural schoolhouses, and a ranch house she spotted in a coulee as well as notes made during grain market broadcasts.

"Place," Ripley Hugo notes, "gives rise to the story" in Walker's work, whether the story is set in an established New England village (*The Southwest Corner; The Quarry*), a Montana community (*Winter Wheat; The Curlew's Cry; Unless the Wind Turns; If a Lion Could Talk*), or a Michigan logging town (*Fireweed,* her first published novel and winner of the Avery Hopwood Award). Still, Walker cautions, "environment in a story should only be as important to the author as it is to the character."

Oftentimes the main importance of a story's setting is in how those surroundings shape or affect the characters whose actions comprise the plot. This is a major strength in Walker's writing; readers can see the land or the community become a character, can understand its influences on the human characters, can feel its power in the working out of the story. Walker has said that she agreed with critic Mark Schoer's comment that "writing is discovery," and her skill in evoking so many—and such diverse—settings suggests that she was always open to discovering all that she could about her own surroundings.

She also felt that she needed to know a territory before she used it in a story. She had lived in Michigan several years before she set *Fireweed* in its Upper Peninsula; she told her daughter that she "hadn't dared write a novel set in Montana until [she] had lived there for a number of years"—and, in fact, in *Unless the Wind Turns,* her first novel set in that state, she is still cautious enough to introduce vacationing easterners as her characters.

In *Winter Wheat,* however, she brings both her power of observation and her imaginative understanding of Ellen Webb's love-hate relationship with the Montana landscape and her parents to what poet-novelist James Welch calls "a classic novel of the American West." Some of the power of this novel may have come from experiences she shared with her husband, a physician, who often took her with him on calls in the country surrounding their Great Falls, Montana, home. While she waited in ranch kitchens for him to see his patient, she not only had the opportunity to look and listen, and thus gather material and details for her writing, but, Ripley Hugo believes, Dr. Schemm's "joy in his work in Montana" fired the same kind of enthusiasm in Walker for her Montana stories.

Walker has commented that "at some point in writing a novel—early on in the process—there has to come a certain excitement that gives momentum to the work." Part of that momentum comes no doubt from the discovery the author is making about her characters and their situations and surroundings. "Writing's not the most comfortable occupation in the world," Walker has said, "but it is exciting." In fact, writing never lost its excitement, mystery, or frustration for her in her years as an active author.

That Walker is able to convey that excitement to her readers is borne out in the recent reissuing of nine of her thirteen novels half a century after their first publications. Her careful depiction of person as well as place, her attention to informative details, and the universality and substance of her work not only accounts for its early popularity, but assures Walker's place in the American literary canon.

—Sue Hart

WARNER, Marina

Nationality: British. **Born:** London, 9 November 1946. **Education:** Lady Margaret Hall, Oxford, B.A. in modern languages 1963, M.A. 1964. **Family:** Married 1) William Shawcross in 1972 (marriage dissolved 1981), one son; 2) John Dewe Mathews in 1981. **Career:** Getty Scholar, 1987-88; Tinbergen Professor, Erasmus University, Rotterdam, the Netherlands, 1991. Visiting professor, University of Ulster, 1994-95; Queen Mary and Westfield College, University of London, 1994. **Awards:** PEN award, 1988; Commonwealth Writers prize, 1989. Since 1985, Fellown Royal Society of Literature. **Agent:** Rogers, Coleridge, and White, 20 Powis Mews, London W11 1NJ, England.

PUBLICATIONS

Novels

In a Dark Wood. London, Weidenfeld and Nicolson, and New York, Knopf, 1977.
The Skating Party. London, Weidenfeld and Nicolson, 1982; New York, Atheneum, 1984.
The Lost Father. London, Chatto and Windus, 1988; New York, Simon and Schuster, 1989.
Indigo. London, Chatto and Windus, 1992; New York, Simon and Schuster, 1993.

Short Stories

The Mermaids in the Basement. London, Chatto and Windus, 1993.

Plays

The Legs of the Queen of Sheba (libretto), music by Julian Grant (produced London, 1991).

Television Play: *Tell Me More,* 1991.

Other

The Dragon Empress: The Life and Times of Tz-u-hsi, 1835-1908, Empress Dowager of China. London, Weidenfeld and Nicolson, and New York, Macmillan, 1972.
Alone of All Her Sex: The Myth and Cult of the Virgin Mary. London, Weidenfeld and Nicolson, 1976; New York, Vintage, 1983.
Queen Victoria's Sketchbook. London, Macmillan, and New York, Crown 1979.
The Crack in the Teacup: Britain in the 20th Century (for children). London, Deutsch, and New York, Clarion, 1979.
Joan of Arc: The Image of Female Heroism. London, Weidenfeld and Nicolson, and New York, Knopf, 1981.
The Impossible Day [Night, Bath, Rocket] (for children). London, Methuen, 4 vols., 1981-82.
The Wobbly Tooth (for children). London, Deutsch, 1984.
Monuments and Maidens: The Allegory of the Female Form. London, Weidenfeld and Nicolson, and New York, Atheneum, 1985.
Into the Dangerous World (pamphlet). London, Chatto and Windus, 1989.
From the Beast to the Blonde: On Fairy Tales and Their Tellers. London, Chatto and Windus, 1994; New York, Farrar Straus, 1995.
Managing Monsters: Six Myths of Our Time. London, Vintage, 1994; New York, Vintage, 1995.

Editor, *Wonder Tales.* London, Chatto and Windus, 1994.

*　　*　　*

Marina Warner is a historian and author of several studies of mythology. Historical events—real or imaginary—and mythological symbols pervade the worlds in which her novels take place, literally as well as subliminally.

In Warner's first novel, *In a Dark Wood,* Gabriel Namier, a Jesuit priest, is studying and writing an account of the life of another Jesuit Father who was involved in a mission to China in the 17th century. The two men's worlds, separated by three centuries, converge, both in outer circumstance—Gabriel, too, has lived in China, and the Catholic church of his time, like that of the 17th century, is internally divided—and on a more personal level. Gabriel's subject was accused by his rivals of homosexuality and in the course of the novel Gabriel himself develops an obsession, albeit not overtly homosexual, with a young man.

In *The Skating Party,* it is not the distant past that provides a point of reference, although one central motif of the book—a cycle of frescoes discovered in a secret room in the Vatican—does provide a symbol of the patterns of male-female relationship which are enacted by Warner's characters. The story within this story is instead a more recent event, a witch-hunting ritual to which the central characters of the novel were personal witnesses, and the distance is provided not by time but by the fact that it took place in a very different country and culture.

Warner's novel *The Lost Father* is similar to *In a Dark Wood,* in that past and present are linked in the form of a historical account, a story within a story; here the narrator is writing a novel set in southern Italy, based on her own family's history, and the external and the internal narratives are shared by several characters. Warner uses the device to make a point about the fallacious nature of history—or the historical novel—itself. The narrator's imagination is captured by one dimly-remembered and ill-documented episode of family legend. When this is thrown into doubt, the reader is reminded that the narrator's portrayal of the family and its characters, however vivid and convincing, is nothing more than fiction.

More often, however, comparison between the past and the present only serves to show that human nature is a constant that transcends time and cultural differences. The dominant subject of Warner's novels is the family, and other characters are almost always seen in the context of their relationship to the family's members. *In a Dark Wood* shows the barriers that exist between different members of the same family. In *The Skating Party,* father and son are distanced, initially by lack of mutual interests and later by sexual rivalry, and the novel shows how wide the generation gap really is. The Pittagora family, the subject of *The Lost Father,* is closely knit and the relationships between mother and daughter and between sisters are warm and compassionate, but this emphasizes all the more strongly the absence of the "lost father" of the title. In all three novels, these barriers and gaps are aggravated, if not created, by an intruder. However, the relationships between Warner's characters are seldom straightforward and unambiguous; by the end of *In a Dark Wood,* Oliver is no longer Gabriel's object of temptation but is seen in the more positive role of Gabriel's niece's lover. Viola, of *The Skating Party,* whose husband is obsessed with Katy, sees the girl not only as a threat but also as someone deserving compassion.

In *The Lost Father,* with its Southern Italian setting, Warner is aided by the fact that her often highly poetic language does not jar with 20th-century English vernacular in the way that it does in her first two novels, and does not give the impression of a gratuitous display of erudition, as it occasionally does in *In a Dark Wood.* Her meticulous description of detail, too, is at its best in this novel, where it brings to life the Italy of the last century and makes it as vivid and immediate as present-day London. Moreover, the intrusive and occasionally condescending voice of the author as omniscient narrator, which throughout the first novel breaks in to reveal and explain the characters' thoughts and motives rather than revealing them through their own words and actions, in the latest novel has been replaced by the voice of a fictional narrator, through whom both the world in which she lives, as well as the world about which she writes, are seen, and whose humour and understanding of her characters contribute much to the success of the novel.

This increasing complexity of narrative structure and density of descriptive detail is seen still more clearly in her latest novel. *Indigo* draws together many of the motifs of Warner's earlier work in an impressively rich and complex book, in which the distancing effect of other times and other cultures once again both establishes and undermines parallels. Starting from the mythical Caribbean island of Shakespeare's *Tempest,* the novel is a meditation on colonialism and its consequences, and a story of displacement and the silencing of the dispossessed. Warner recreates the story of Sycorac, Caliban, and Ariel in the 16th century, whose place in the island is usurped by the coming of Europeans intent on profit; in the 20th century, the Everard family, descendants of those earlier settlers who have dominated the island's culture through the intervening centuries, are themselves suffering the dislocation and exile of those whose place in the world and understanding of themselves has been fundamentally disrupted. Conflict invades the family, which, a microcosm of the processes of imperialism, can no longer displace its own internal contradictions onto the colonized world: husband and wife, parent and child, master/mistress and servant, all exist in tension and instability.

This novel perhaps most successfully unites Warner's intellectual and imaginative languages, drawing on fantasy and romance as well as on realism, in an intricately elaborate and sensuous prose. Myth and history, and the relations between them, are fundamental: the myths people live by, colonists and others, are placed alongside alternative and unacknowledged versions of truth. Warner's recent non-fiction too has been closely concerned with myths and monsters; her collected short stories, *The Mermaids in the Basement,* reiterates these preoccupations. Many of these tales are retellings of familiar myths and histories, set in the contemporary world or in dialogue with it. "The Legs of the Queen of Sheba," for instance, moves between a woman trying to be one of the boys at a conference in Jerusalem, and the Queen of Sheba trying to hold her own in conversation with Solomon: two women struggling for their own speech in a man's world and a man's language. Several are inspired by paintings, reinforcing the powerfully visual quality of Warner's writing. Once again, too, the intense bonds of family life are crucial, as the book's sections make plain: "Mothers & Sisters," "Husbands & Lovers," and "Fathers & Daughters." These are clearly tales of women's perspectives (however variously), written mostly in the first person; here Warner is occasionally less persuasive, and her attempts to occupy more distant identities not always successful. Nonetheless, hers is a voice of increasing assurance and power in contemporary British fiction.

—Jessica Griffin, updated by Katharine Hodgkin

WATERHOUSE, Keith (Spencer)

Nationality: British. **Born:** Leeds, Yorkshire, 6 February 1929. **Education:** Osmondthorpe Council Schools, Leeds. **Military Service:** Served in the Royal Air Force. **Family:** Married 1) Joan Foster in 1951 (divorced 1968), one son and two daughters; 2) Stella Bingham (divorced 1989). **Career:** Since 1950 freelance journalist and writer in Leeds and London; columnist, *Daily Mirror,* 1970-86, and *Daily Mail* since 1986, both London. **Awards:** (for journalism): Granada award, 1970, and special award, 1982, IPC award, 1970, 1973, British Press award, 1978; *Evening Standard* award, for play, 1991. Honorary Fellow, Leeds Polytechnic. Fellow, Royal Society of Literature. **Member:** Kingman Committee on Teaching of English Language, 1987-88. **Agent:** David Higham Associates, 5-8 Lower John Street, London W1; (theatrical) London Management Ltd., 235-241 Regent Street, London W1. **Address:** 29 Kenway Road, London SW5 ORP, England.

PUBLICATIONS

Novels

There Is a Happy Land. London, Joseph, 1957.
Billy Liar. London, Joseph, 1959; New York, Norton, 1960.
Jubb. London, Joseph, 1963; New York, Putnam, 1964.
The Bucket Shop. London, Joseph, 1968; as *Everything Must Go,* New York, Putnam, 1969.
Billy Liar on the Moon. London, Joseph, 1975; New York, Putnam, 1976.
Office Life. London, Joseph, 1978.
Maggie Muggins; or, Spring in Earl's Court. London, Joseph, 1981.
In the Mood. London, Joseph, 1983.
Thinks. London, Joseph, 1984.
Our Song. London, Hodder and Stoughton, 1988.
Bimbo. London, Hodder and Stoughton, 1990.
Unsweet Charity. London, Hodder and Stoughton, 1992.
City Lights: A Street Life. London, Hodder and Stoughton, 1994.

Plays

Billy Liar, with Willis Hall, adaptation of the novel by Waterhouse (produced London, 1960; Los Angeles and New York, 1963). London, Joseph, 1960; New York, Norton, 1961.
Celebration: The Wedding and The Funeral, with Willis Hall (produced Nottingham and London, 1961). London, Joseph, 1961.
England, Our England, with Willis Hall, music by Dudley Moore (produced London, 1962). London, Evans, 1964.
Squat Betty, with Willis Hall (produced London, 1962; New York, 1964). Included in *The Sponge Room, and Squat Betty,* 1963.
The Sponge Room, with Willis Hall (produced Nottingham and London, 1962; New York, 1964). Included in *The Sponge Room, and Squat Betty,* 1963; in *Modern Short Plays from Broadway and London,* edited by Stanley Richards, New York, Random House, 1969.
All Things Bright and Beautiful, with Willis Hall (produced Bristol and London, 1962). London, Joseph, 1963.
The Sponge Room, and Squat Betty, with Willis Hall. London, Evans, 1963.

Come Laughing Home, with Willis Hall (as *They Called the Bastard Stephen,* produced Bristol, 1964; as *Come Laughing Home,* produced Wimbledon, 1965). London, Evans, 1965.

Say Who You Are, with Willis Hall (produced Guildford, Surrey, and London, 1965). London, Evans, 1966; as *Help Stamp Out Marriage* (produced New York, 1966), New York, French, 1966.

Joey, Joey, with Willis Hall, music by Ron Moody (produced Manchester and London, 1966).

Whoops-a-Daisy, with Willis Hall (produced Nottingham, 1968). London, French, 1978.

Children's Day, with Willis Hall (produced Edinburgh and London, 1969). London, French, 1975.

Who's Who, with Willis Hall (produced Coventry, 1971; London, 1973). London, French, 1974.

Saturday, Sunday, Monday, with Willis Hall, adaptation of a play by Eduardo De Filippo (produced London, 1973; New York, 1974). London, Heinemann, 1974.

The Card, with Willis Hall, music and lyrics by Tony Hatch and Jackie Trent, adaptation of the novel by Arnold Bennett (produced Bristol and London, 1973).

Filumena, with Willis Hall, adaptation of a play by Eduardo De Filippo (produced London, 1977; New York, 1980). London, Heinemann, 1978.

Worzel Gummidge (for children), with Willis Hall, music by Denis King, adaptation of stories by Barbara Euphan Todd (produced Birmingham, 1980; London, 1981). London, French 1984.

Steafel Variations (songs and sketches), with Peter Tinniswood and Dick Vosburgh (produced London, 1982).

Lost Empires, with Willis Hall, music by Denis King, adaptation of the novel by J.B. Priestley (produced Darlington, County Durham, 1985).

Mr. and Mrs. Nobody, adaptation of *The Diary of a Nobody* by George and Weedon Grossmith (produced London, 1986).

Budgie, with Willis Hall, music by Mort Shuman, lyrics by Don Black (produced London, 1988).

Jeffrey Bernard Is Unwell (produced Brighton and London, 1989). London and New York, French, 1991.

Bookends, adaptation of *The Marsh Marlowe Letters* by Craig Brown (produced London, 1990).

Jeffrey Bernard Is Unwell, with *Mr and Mrs Nobody* and *Bookends.* London, Penguin, 1992.

Our Song, adaptation of his own novel. London, French, 1993.

Screenplays, with Willis Hall: *Whistle Down the Wind,* 1961; *The Valiant,* 1962; *A Kind of Loving,* 1963; *Billy Liar,* 1963; *West Eleven,* 1963; *Man in the Middle,* 1963; *Pretty Polly* (*A Matter of Innocence*), 1967; *Lock Up Your Daughters,* 1969.

Radio Plays: *The Town That Wouldn't Vote,* 1951; *There Is a Happy Land,* 1962; *The Woolen Bank Forgeries,* 1964; *The Last Phone-In,* 1976; *The Big Broadcast of 1922,* 1979.

Television Plays: *The Warmonger,* 1970; *The Upchat Line* series, 1977; *The Upchat Connection* series, 1978; *Charlie Muffin,* from novels by Brian Freemantle, 1979; *West End Tales* series, 1981; *The Happy Apple* series, from play by Jack Pulman, 1983; *This Office Life,* from his own novel, 1984; *Charters and Caldicott,* 1985; *The Great Paper Chase,* from the book *Slip Up* by Anthony Delaro, 1988; *Andy Capp* series, 1988; with Willis Hall— *Happy Moorings,* 1963; *How Many Angels,* 1964; *Inside George Webley* series, 1968; *Queenie's Castle* series, 1970; *Budgie* se-

ries, 1971-72; *The Upper Crusts* series, 1973; *Three's Company* series, 1973; *By Endeavour Alone,* 1973; *Briefer Encounter,* 1977; *Public Lives,* 1979; *Worzel Gummidge* series, from stories by Barbara Euphan Todd, 1979.

Other

The Café Royal: Ninety Years of Bohemia, with Guy Deghy. London, Hutchinson, 1955.

How to Avoid Matrimony: The Layman's Guide to the Laywoman, with Guy Deghy (as Herald Froy). London, Muller, 1957.

Britain's Voice Abroad, with Paul Cave. London, Daily Mirror Newspapers, 1957.

The Future of Television. London, Daily Mirror Newspapers, 1958.

How to Survive Matrimony, with Guy Deghy (as Herald Froy). London, Muller, 1958.

The Joneses: How to Keep Up with Them, with Guy Deghy (as Lee Gibb). London, Muller, 1959.

Can This Be Love?, with Guy Deghy (as Herald Froy). London, Muller, 1960.

Maybe You're Just Inferior: Head-Shrinking for Fun and Profit, with Guy Deghy (as Herald Froy). London, Muller, 1961.

The Higher Jones, with Guy Deghy (as Lee Gibb). London, Muller, 1961.

O Mistress Mine: or, How to Go Roaming, with Guy Deghy (as Herald Froy). London, Barker, 1962.

The Passing of the Third-Floor Buck (*Punch* sketches). London, Joseph, 1974.

Mondays, Thursdays (*Daily Mirror* columns). London, Joseph, 1976.

Rhubard, Rhubard, and Other Noises (*Daily Mirror* columns). London, Joseph, 1979.

The Television Adventures [and *More Television Adventures*] of *Worzel Gummidge* (for children), with Willis Hall. London, Penguin, 2 vols., 1979; complete edition, as *Worzel Gummidge's Television Adventures,* London, Kestrel, 1981.

Worzel Gummidge at the Fair (for children), with Willis Hall. London, Penguin, 1980.

Worzel Gummidge Goes to the Seaside (for children), with Willis Hall. London, Penguin, 1980.

The Trials of Worzel Gummidge (for children), with Willis Hall. London, Penguin, 1980.

Worzel's Birthday (for children), with Willis Hall. London, Penguin, 1981.

New Television Adventures of Worzel Gummidge and Aunt Sally (for children), with Willis Hall. London, Sparrow, 1981.

Daily Mirror Style. London, Mirror Books, 1981; revised, edition as *Waterhouse on Newspaper Style,* London, Viking, 1989.

Fanny Peculiar (*Punch* columns). London, Joseph, 1983.

Mrs. Pooter's Diary. London, Joseph, 1983.

The Irish Adventures of Worzel Gummidge (for children), with Willis Hall. London, Severn House, 1984.

Waterhouse at Large (journalism). London, Joseph, 1985.

The Collected Letters of a Nobody (Including Mr. Pooter's Advice to His Son). London, Joseph, 1986.

The Theory and Practice of Lunch. London, Joseph, 1986.

Worzel Gummidge Down Under (for children), with Willis Hall. London, Collins, 1987.

The Theory and Practice of Travel. London, Hodder and Stoughton, 1989.

English Our English (and How to Sing It). London, Viking, 1991.

Sharon & Tracy & the Rest: The Best of Keith Waterhouse in the Daily Mail. London, Hodder and Stoughton, 1992.

Editor, with Willis Hall, *Writers' Theatre.* London, Heinemann, 1967.

* * *

Keith Waterhouse's fiction is distinguished by a sharp comic sense, a facility that works on closely polished verbal, imagistic, and logical incongruities. For example, in the well-known *Billy Liar,* a character who is one of the two owners of the funeral establishment where Billy works, a man who keeps a copy of Evelyn Waugh's *The Loved One* on his desk in order to get new ideas and who looks forward to the day when all coffins will be made of fiberglass, is introduced: "He was, for a start, only about twenty-five years old, although grown old with quick experience, like forced rhubarb," In *Billy Liar on the Moon,* a sequel to *Billy Liar* that both takes place and was written about 15 years after the original, and which moves Billy from his Yorkshire locale of the late 1950s to a carefully designed community of shopping malls, motels, and perplexing one-way streets that lead only to motorways, a new housing estate is a "suburb of the moon" with "a Legoland of crescents and culs-de-sac with green Lego roofs and red Lego chimney stacks." In *The Bucket Shop* Waterhouse depicts the bumbling, self-deceptive owner of a tatty antique shop, unsuccessful alike in his business, his adulteries, and his efforts to make his wife and his nine-year-old daughter, Melisande, fit his trendy definitions of "interesting" people. After a long passage developing Melisande's fantasies about herself, Waterhouse adds, "She had William's gift for candid self-assessment." That kind of reductive comment, like the discordant contemporary images, the play with clichés, and the exploitation of grammatical incongruities, suggest comparisons with the comic prose of Evelyn Waugh.

Waterhouse builds his verbal texture on plots that often begin with a kind of adolescent humor. Billy, in *Billy Liar,* invents highly improbable and inconsistent stories, weaving a net of public and fantastic lies that is bound to be discovered by parents, bosses, and the three girlfriends to whom he is simultaneously engaged. He is full of elaborate compulsions: if he can suck a mint without breaking it or if he walks in certain complex patterns he feels he will escape the consequences of his stories. He is also a powerful leader in his fantasy land of Ambrosia. The point of view of the young boy in Waterhouse's first novel, *There Is a Happy Land,* is even more childlike. The boy plays at being blind, drunk, or maimed, mimics all his elders and delights in calling out cheeky statements that annoy or embarrass adults. Neither child nor adolescent, the central character in *Jubb,* a rent-collector and youth-club leader in a planned "New Town," is also full of grandiose schemes that others always see through and mimics others' accepted pieties. All these characters, inventive, iconoclastic, and living almost wholly within their disordered imaginations, assault an adult world that pretends it's stable.

Underneath the texture of mimicry and iconoclasm, Waterhouse sometimes gradually shows a world far more sinister than the one suggested by the escapades of adolescent humor. As *There is a Happy Land* develops, the tone shifts and the boy recognizes the sexuality, perversion, evil, and violence (including the murder of a young girl) in the abandoned quarries and behind the picture-windows of the lower-middle-class housing estate. The character of Jubb himself is gradually revealed as psychotic. Behind his fanta-

sies and comic compulsions is the sexual impotence that has led him to become a peeping Tom, a pyromaniac, and a murderer. In *The Bucket Shop* William's incompetent management of money and women, as well as his incapacity to deal with the consequences of his fantasies, leads to the suicide of a dependent actress. Sometimes, as the humor fades from Waterhouse's novels, it leaves a melodramatic revelation of perverse and horrible humanity.

More recent novels, generally set in the anonymous world of London, focus satire or an understated pathos on more restricted treatments of contemporary life. *Office Life* centers on a worker made redundant who is absorbed into the modern corporation where everyone is sustained in a network of gossip, affairs, and shuffling papers, and nothing is produced or accomplished. *Maggie Muggins: or, Spring in Earl's Court* chronicles a day in the life of Maggie, born Margaret Moon, a promiscuous and alcoholic drifter in London for the past 10 years in revolt from a square, stable Doncaster family. During the day, she learns of a close friend's suicide, her father's decision to marry and start a new family, and the fact that the father of her aborted baby could have married her, yet the clever prose, satirizing the social services and any pretense to reform, finally and tersely establishes her ratchety integrity and capacity to survive. *Thinks* is more experimental technically. Concentrating, as a deliberate fictional device, on the anxieties and fantasies in the mind of the central character, without reporting what he says, the novel charts the pressures on the last, long day of Edgar Bapty's life. Through train journeys, a visit to his doctor, a job interview he only dimly realizes he has fumbled, thoughts of his three former wives, numerous heavy meals, a visit to a prostitute, and several recognition's of his own sexual incapacity, Bapty's thoughts and fears build to "a magnificent Hallelujah chorus of sustained and bellowing rage" before his fatal heart attack. The compressed focus and the sharp writing give these novels immediacy and vitality.

The two novels concerning Billy Liar are lighter than Waterhouse's other fiction, although the persona of Billy represents Waterhouse's only perspective that attempts to alter circumstance. Billy lies less to cover horror or perversion than "to relieve the monotony of living on the moon," where the moon is his arid contemporary civic and domestic life. Both novels, as satire, also ridicule the parochial: in *Billy Liar* the target is, equally, romanticizing an old, rugged Yorkshire tradition and the "new" world of coffee bars, record shops, and the winner of the Miss Stradhoughton contest who delivers "whole sentences ready-packed in disposable tin-foil wrapper"; in *Billy Liar on the Moon* the target is civic pride, all the contemporary designs and shapes applied to experience and undermined both by their implicit fatuity and old-fashioned corruption. In both novels, Billy, the comic, the spinner of fantasies, uses the vision of "London" as his potential escape from provincial dullness ineptitude, and self-seeking. That any "real London" is no answer for Waterhouse is clear from other novels such as *The Bucket Shop, Office Life,* and *Maggie Muggins.* Yet the point in both books about Billy Liar is that he cannot, more than momentarily in the second book, manage the break to London, cannot do more than mimic, scoff, and invent within the limited world he is dependent on. Both as satire and as a potential means of revealing some deeply thought or felt version of experience, Waterhouse's comedy is thin, a covering for the sense of horror in experience in *Jubb* or *Thinks,* in which the latent pain seems unmanageable and unchangeable. All the novels seem staged (and Waterhouse, in conjunction with Willis Hall, has written a number of plays characterized by sharply witty dialogue and clever invention). As Billy himself says, in *Billy Liar on the Moon,* he is still only a "juvenile lead" in a "comedy," not the central character in a "tragedy" he imagines, not equipped for any part in a drama of "real life." At the end of the novel, he returns to Ambrosia. Whatever the incapacities of his characters to alter or transcend experience, Waterhouse is invariably an excellent mimic, often cogent and terse, and has created a comic prose and a sense of the involuted logic of systematic fantasy that are strikingly effective and enjoyable.

—James Gindin

WATMOUGH, David

Nationality: Canadian. **Born:** London, England, 17 August 1926; became Canadian citizen in 1963. **Education:** Coopers' Company School, London, 1937-43; King's College, University of London, 1945-49, degree in theology. **Military Service:** Served in the Royal Navy, 1944-45. **Career:** Reporter, *Cornish Guardian,* Bodmin, Cornwall, 1943-44; editor, Holy Cross Press, New York, 1953-54; talks producer, BBC Third Programme, London, 1955; editor, Ace Books, London, 1956; feature writer and critic, San Francisco *Examiner,* 1957-60; arts and theater critic, Vancouver *Sun,* 1964-67; host of *Artslib,* weekly television show, 1979-80. Since 1991 arts columnist, *Step* magazine, Vancouver; since 1993 book reviewer and columnist for *Xtra West,* Vancouver, British Columbia. **Awards:** Canada Council senior arts grant, 1976, 1986; Providence of British Columbia Arts award, for creative writing, 1994-95. **Agent:** Robert Drake, 1218 Saint Paul Street, Baltimore, Maryland 21202, U.S.A. **Address:** 3358 West First Avenue, Vancouver, British Columbia V6R 1G4, Canada.

PUBLICATIONS

Novels

No More into the Garden. New York, Doubleday, 1978.
The Year of Fears. Toronto, Mosaic Press, 1988.
Families. Stamford, Connecticut, Knights Press, 1990.
Thy Mother's Glass. Toronto and New York, HarperCollins, 1992.
The Time of the Kingfishers. Vancouver, Arsenal Pulp, 1994.

Short Stories

Ashes for Easter and Other Monodramas. Vancouver, Talonbooks, 1972.
Love and the Waiting Game: Eleven Stories. Ottawa, Oberon Press, 1975.
From a Cornish Landscape. Padstow, Cornwall, Lodenek Press, 1975.
The Connecticut Countess. Trumansburg, New York, Crossing Press, 1984.
Fury. Ottawa, Oberon Press, 1984.
Vibrations in Time. Toronto, Mosaic Press, 1986.

Uncollected Short Stories

"The Wounded Christmas Choirboy," in *Canadian Short Stories.* Kingston, Ontario, Quarry Press, 1990.

"Eurydice, May I Kiss the Cop?," in *Certain Voices.* Boston, Alyson, 1991.
"Thank You Siegfried Sassoon," in *Indivisible.* New York, New American Library, 1991.
"Wedding Dress for a Greek Groom," in *Queeries.* Vancouver, 1993.
"Cool Cats on the Internet," in *Modern Words.* San Francisco, 1994.
"Maiden Voyage," in *Sayme.* Boston, 1994.
"Leonard," in *Church Wellesley Review.* Toronto, 1994.
"Secrets of Diomedes," in the *Gay Review.* Toronto, 1995.

Plays

Friedhof (produced Vancouver, 1966). Included in *Names for the Numbered Years,* 1967.
Do You Remember One September Afternoon? (produced Vancouver, 1966). Included in *Names for the Numbered Years,* 1967.
Names for the Numbered Years: Three Plays (includes *Do You Remember One September Afternoon?, Friedhof, My Mother's House Has Too Many Rooms*). Vancouver, Bau-Xi Gallery, 1967.

Other

A Church Renascent: A Study of Modern French Catholicism. London, SPCK, 1951.
The Unlikely Pioneer: Building Opera from the Pacific Through the Prairies. Toronto, Mosaic Press, 1986.

Editor, *Vancouver Fiction.* Winlaw, British Columbia, Polestar Press, 1985.

*

Critical Studies: "The Novel That Never Ends: David Watmough's Reminiscent Fictions," in *The World of Canadian Writing* by George Woodcock, Vancouver, Douglas and McIntyre, and Seattle, University of Washington Press, 1980; in *The Oxford Companion to Canadian Literature* edited by William Toye, Toronto, Oxford, and New York, Oxford University Press, 1983; article by Jerry Wasserman, in *Canadian Writers since 1960* 1st series, edited by W.H. New, Detroit, Gale, 1986; "The Human Whole" by Kate Sirluck, in *Canadian Literature* (Vancouver), Winter 1990.

David Watmough comments:

In a very real sense I regard each successive volume of my fiction as part of an ongoing "novel" that will not be complete until I can no longer write. My work is an attempt to chronicle the private history of one man of Cornish ancestry living as a Canadian through the 20th century. My fictional protagonist, Davey Bryant, is depicted in childhood, adolescence, maturity, and, currently, middle age. If the work finally succeeds then it will be because I have been able to muster the kind of candor and honesty that such a confessional narrative demands. Another feature of the work is the depiction of private history—including the most intimate sexual and psychological detail—against the backdrop of public events.

(1995) Although I continue to write through my protagonist, Davey Bryant, I have recently branched out and in my current stories have him tell of experiences inspired by Greek myth and classical legend but refashioned and shown on the Internet via his P.C. monitor. The eventual collection of connected fictions will be entitled *Odysseys on the Internet.*

*   *   *

The name of Proust often comes up when the Canadian fiction writer David Watmough is discussed, and though Watmough is no imitator of Proust, the affinities between the two are clear. Both are concerned with memory and its transforming power, and both tend to transmute their own memories into the stuff of fiction. Watmough has written several volumes of short stories, notably *Ashes for Easter* (his first), *Love and the Waiting Game,* and *The Connecticut Countess,* and also a trio of open-ended novels, (*No More into the Garden, The Year of Fears,* and *Families).*

Watmough's claim is that for the past two decades he has really been engaged in writing a single novel that will take a lifetime to complete. It is a claim that must be taken seriously, for the same central character, Davey Bryant, appears in almost all the fiction Watmough writes, whether it is short stories, novels, or the spoken and semi-dramatic fictions he calls monodramas.

Though this is no exact sense fictionalized autobiography, Davey Bryant does in many ways resemble Watmough in the same way as some of his experiences parallel his creator's. Yet the character stands apart, observed with irony and candour. But the observation is from within as well as without, and each story, each chapter of a novel, is a confession of ambivalent acts, ambivalent motives, for the screen between the straight and the gay world constantly wavers and dissolves and forms again.

In a way the saga of Davey Bryant is in the classic tradition of modernist fiction—a portrait of the artist as a young but aging man or dog. We follow him from his boyhood to—in the most recent novel—his middle forties. But real life—from which so much undoubtedly comes—is modified by memory and changed by art, and Watmough's fictions walk a variety of tightropes, between actuality and truth, between the oral and the written mode.

These fictions are all essentially ironic, with the initial nostalgia of the vision always underlaid by the nagging memory, the jarring truth that provokes the nostalgia. Some of the most telling stories are those that evoke moments of folly or unworthiness which stir similar recollections in the reader to those the writer experiences, or, alternatively, make him uneasy because of the perilous closeness of the predicaments—frequently homosexual—that are delineated by the possibilities of his own life.

In the novels, especially, Davey Bryant is shown as both the victim of ludicrous circumstances and the perpetrator of petty moral atrocities. The victim is always seen to be seeking victory, and most personal relationships are marred by a cruelty that degrades one or other of the participants.

The recurrent themes are united on another level by a pervading elegiac consciousness; in the novel *No More into the Garden,* for example, the longed-for garden that is never re-entered is in one sense the Cornwall of childhood happiness, and in another the state of collective innocence that all men seek to recover. The garden, however, can become "a harvest of threats." By the novel's end the fullness of life is balanced by ever-present death, for as the mind expands in consciousness the physical possibilities narrow. Here, for Watmough, is the irony and also the elegy. But the garden survives in the Proustian reality, and even in a fairly recent collection of stories, *Fury,* there is a return to the world of childhood with all its innocence and brutality.

Later novels have taken the narrating hero through the successive lustra of inner development and outward adventure as Davey metamorphoses from the boy of the original stories to the middle-aged man of *Families. The Year of Fears,* for example, concerns the period of the Vietnam war when Davey lives in the pre-AIDS gay culture of California. When we come to *Families* he is settled in Vancouver, a city which not only has a considerable gay world, but also a good deal of friendly and mutually tolerant intercourse between the gay and the straight communities. And here Davey seems at least to have found his special role, not only as a chronicler-participant of the gay world, but also as a kind of mediator among his friends, as if, like the celibacy of a priest, his different sexual role has given him a privileged position as a kind of emotional middle man in what turns out to be a multisexual world. The problems he encounters, and often dabbles in, give a serious cast to the novel, but the threat of solemnity is dispelled by an ironic, self-depecrating manner, in which gossip is used, rather as Proust used it, for revelation as much as diversion. Watmough has—and I say this approvingly rather than pejoratively—a talent for the trivial. He knows how to use it for the maximum ironic effect, and how to temper the dynamics of structure by beginning and ending his novel, as it were, in mid-thought. *Families* ends with two friends, a heterosexual woman and a homosexual man, in a semi-rural park:

> There, where the gravel at the lake's edge gave way to a grass bank, we sat down in the October sun and stretched our legs. This time we saw no kingfishers.

It looks like an anti-climax; in fact it is continuity, tying in a cord from the past, yet paradoxically opening to an as yet unrevealed but perhaps already lived future.

—George Woodcock

WEDDE, Ian

Nationality: New Zealander. **Born:** Blenheim, 17 October 1946. **Education:** Auckland University, M.A. (honours) 1968. **Family:** Married Rosemary Beauchamp in 1967; three sons. **Career:** Formerly forester, factory worker, gardener, and postman. British Council teacher, Jordan, 1969-70; poetry reviewer, *London Magazine* 1970-71; broadcasting editor, New Zealand Broadcasting Corporation, 1972; writer-in-residence, Victoria University, Wellington, 1984; art critic, Wellington, *Evening Post,* 1983-90. **Awards:** Robert Burns fellowship, University of Otago, 1972; Arts Council bursary, 1974, and travel award, 1983; New Zealand Book award, for fiction, 1977, and for verse, 1978; Victoria University writing fellowship, 1984. **Address:** 118-A Maidavale Road, Roseneath, Wellington 1, New Zealand.

Publications

Novels

Dick Seddon's Great Dive. Auckland, Islands, 1976.
Symmes Hole. Auckland, Penguin, and London, Faber, 1986.
Survival Arts. Auckland, Penguin, and London, Faber, 1988.

Short Stories

The Shirt Factory and Other Stories. Wellington, Victoria University Press, 1981.

Plays

Eyeball Eyeball (produced Packakariki, 1983).
Double or Quit: The Life and Times of Percy Topliss (produced on tour, England, 1984).

Radio Plays: *Stations,* music by Jack Body, 1969; *Pukeko,* music by John Rimmer, 1972.

Poetry

Homage to Matisse. London, Amphedesma Press, 1971.
Made Over. Auckland, Stephen Chan, 1974.
Pathway to the Sea. Christchurch, Hawk Press, 1974.
Earthly: Sonnets for Carlos. Akaroa, New Zealand, Amphedesma Press, 1975.
Don't Listen. Christchurch, Hawk Press, 1977.
Spells for Coming Out. Auckland, Auckland University Press, 1977.
Castaly and Other Poems. Auckland, Auckland University Press-Oxford University Press, 1980; Oxford, Oxford University Press, 1981.
Tales of Gotham City. Auckland, Auckland University Press-Oxford University Press, 1984.
Georgicon. Wellington, Victoria University Press, 1984.
Driving into the Storm: Selected Poems. Auckland, Oxford University Press, 1987.
Tendering. Auckland, Auckland University Press, 1988.

Other

Editor, with Harvey McQueen, *The Penguin Book of Contemporary New Zealand Verse.* Auckland, Penguin, 1985; revised edition, with McQueen and Miriama Evans, 1989.
Editor, with Gregory Burke, *Now See Hear! Art, Language, and Translation.* Wellington, Victoria University Press, 1990.

Translator, with Fawwas Tuqan, *Selected Poems,* by Mahmud Darwish. Cheadle, Cheshire, Carcanet, 1974.

* * *

"If I get to know the material well enough, I've kept thinking, then some sort of order will emerge. But that's been a kind of half lie." These are Kate's words, in Ian Wedde's first short novel *Dick Seddon's Great Dive.* They describe Wedde's practice as a novelist as accurately as they reflect Kate's hesitant reconstruction of her love affair with the recalcitrant anti-hero Chink, in the New Zealand of the 1970s, which forms the quirky structure of Wedde's first book. Kate's recollections of her life with Chink, before his suicidal death by drowning and her own breakdown, are prompts to passages of third-person narrative which depict the relationship from oblique angles, refusing the option of a single, secure point of reference. Moreover, Wedde's prose pays attention to the ways in which language represents changing states of consciousness, whether induced by the retarding effects of opiates or the visionary disruption of hallucinogens, or brought about by the sudden, unexpected charge of love, or the tough sense of an enduring loneli-

ness. It is not just Kate, the character, who is attempting to "get to know 'the material' well enough" but Wedde, the novelist, who is trying out his skills in this early work.

Dick Seddon's Great Dive was republished in *The Shirt Factory and Other Stories,* a collection from which Wedde proceeded to draw material for more expansive prose treatments. One story, "Snake," is an early model version of Wedde's next novel, *Symmes Hole,* where the McDonalds hamburger franchise is seen as a contemporary equivalent of the capitalist expansion of the 19th-century whaling industry, each motivated by a kind of global greed.

Symmes Hole is Wedde's major achievement to date in prose fiction, though he has also made important contributions to New Zealand literature as a poet, anthologist, and critic. In the novel, two narratives counterpoint each other in a series of episodes structured through the careers of two Ishmael-like figures, one from the early 19th-century and one from the 1980s.

James Heberley, a seaman shipped as a whaler in the 1820s, is depicted in a number of vivid scenes, his senses assaulted by the conditions of his immediate environment, and his career and life dictated by the economics of his world. Heberley was an actual person whose journal—which Wedde has drawn upon—exists in Wellington's Turnbull library, and whose descendants still live in New Zealand. In a process more dependent on chance than choice he finds himself a home, wife, and family with the Maori before the arrival of the approved settlers and colonizers. He jumps ship and drifts into a tribal family, while the established authorities continue mapping and charting the exploitable potential of New Zealand and the world. He abandons the latitudes and longitudes of his northern origins and comes to take his bearings from the co-ordinates he finds around him. If Heberley is like Herman Melville's Ishmael in *Moby Dick* by being cast-out, an *isolato* (just as the Biblical Ishamel was a "man alone"), he also resembles Melville's Ishmael in his pliant resilience, his adaptability and his durable sufferance of changing conditions.

However, *Symmes Hole* is also the story of a writer in the 1980s obsessed with Melville and increasingly drawn into an extended historical inquiry. He *loses* his home, wife, family and even his name, counterpointing Heberley's story. The spasmic and disjointed structure of the novel suggests therefore a complex reflection of the historical inquiry engaged in by its author, and Wedde's writing itself veers from the wonderfully lucid to the clotted, dense and opaque. He mixes modes of discourse with a mischievous humor and serious intent. When his publishers requested a scholarly introduction to the book, Wedde provided one by a certain "Dr. Keehua Roa" of the "University of West Hawaii". This is apocryphal but "Dr. Keehua Roa" translates back into English as "Dr. Long Ghost," a character in the book who, along with the Maori Benbo Byrne, has arrived by way of Melville's *Omoo.* Like Heberley, the "Long Ghost" was an actual historical character, a subversive Scots doctor and friend of Melville named John Troy.

Wedde is concerned in *Symmes Hole* not simply with telling the untold story, but with penetrating the thickly layered structures of history's myths and values. A dark gallery of half-lit fantastics from the undergut of Pacific history orbit the novel's two main characters, and though Wedde's novel is occasionally abrasive, packed with recondite allusions, he presents us with a deep historical vision linking those shady figures to the world of the 1980s with President Reagan in the White House. In *Symmes Hole,* Wedde has "got to know 'the material' well enough" so that "some sort of order" has emerged. If the novel he has produced is "a kind of half lie", it is also a sort of half truth.

Wedde's third novel, *Survival Arts,* returns to Wellington in the 1980s and re-introduces the character of Kate, from *Dick Seddon's Great Dive.* She and her lesbian partner B.J. are planning to start an All-Blacks sperm bank in a secondhand freezer, while a Vietnam veteran is driving a secondhand tank around Wellington, three characters are at work in an auction market and a beautiful woman is engaged in strange behavior with her Polynesian lover in a car wash. The book is a comedy of unconnected anti-spectacles and non-incidents, recounting the misadventures of four separate groups of people. What they have in common, though, is significant: they practice the arts of survival which give the novel its title. These are the fictional descendants of "riffraff" like Heberley, the "flotsam and jetsam of empire," who, finding themselves where they are, make of their world what they will.

—Alan Riach

WELCH, James

Nationality: American. **Born:** Browning, Montana, in 1940. **Education:** The University of Montana, Missoula, B.A.; Northern Montana College, Harve. **Awards:** National Endowment for the Arts grant, 1969; Los Angeles *Times* prize, for *Fools Crow,* 1987. **Address:** Roseacres Farm, Route 6, Missoula, Montana 59801, U.S.A.

PUBLICATIONS

Novels

Winter in the Blood. New York, Harper, 1974.
The Death of Jim Loney. New York, Harper, 1979; London, Gollancz, 1980.
Fools Crow. New York, Viking, 1986.
The Indian Lawyer. New York, Norton, 1990.
Killing Custer, with Paul Stekler. New York, Norton, 1994.

Poetry

Riding the Earthboy 40. Cleveland, World, 1971; revised edition, New York, Harper, 1975.

Other

Editor, with Ripley S. Hugg and Lois M. Welch, *The Real West Marginal Way: A Poet's Autobiography,* by Richard Hugo. New York, Norton, 1986.

*

Critical Studies: *Four American Indian Literary Masters* by Alan R. Velie, Norman, University of Oklahoma Press, 1982; *James Welch* by Peter Wild, Boise, Idaho, Boise State University 1983; "Beyond Myth: Welch's *Winter in the Blood*" by Jack Brenner, in *Under the Sun: Myth and Realism in Western American Literature* edited by Barbara Howard Meldrum, Troy, New York, Whitston, 1985; "Beyond Assimilation: James Welch and the Indian Dilemma"

by David M. Craig, in *North Dakota Quarterly* (Grand Forks), Spring 1985; "Variations on a Theme: Traditions and Temporal Structure in the Novels of James Welch" by Roberta Orlandini, in *South Dakota Review* (Vermillion), Autumn 1988; *Place and Vision: The Function of Landscape in Native American Fiction* by Robert M. Nelson, New York, Lang, 1993.

*   *   *

James Welch has described himself as both an "Indian writer" and "an Indian who writes." This double vision of American Indian experience as unique and yet representative is at the heart of his four novels, all set in or around reservation Montana and all revolving around protagonists, like Welch himself, of Blackfeet ancestry. Perhaps this is no more than saying that, like any good writer, Welch arrives at the universal through the particular. But the particular—the stresses and strains of Native American culture in uneasy contact with the culture that nearly destroyed it—has not much figured as a theme in serious American fiction. Welch has helped to change that, and he has done so without resort to sentimentality or preachiness.

Winter in the Blood, his first novel, takes up a week or so in the life of its unnamed narrator, a 32-year-old Blackfeet man suffering from a malaise he can neither understand nor escape from. There is no plot to speak of; the novel simply follows the narrator as he works for a few days as a farm-hand on his step-father's property, quizzes his strong-willed mother about the past, pursues an ex-girlfriend he does not really want to find into the bars and streets of small-town Montana, gets into a minor brawl, and sleeps with a couple of white women. If there is any hope in this grim depiction of aimlessness and anomie it occurs toward the end, when the narrator recognizes a dignified, blind, and ancient Blackfeet man named Yellow Calf as his grandfather and the savior of his family line. But this "opening onto light" that Reynolds Price thought the emotional climax of the novel is closed up in the equally emblematic scene that follows, in which the narrator fails to rescue a cow from a suffocating death in a mudhole. Indeed, a powerful sense of alienation seems to grip Welch as much as his narrator; in the conjunction of the personal and the cultural that might explain such desolation, Welch leans a little too heavily on the latter, and a faintly deterministic air clings to the narrator's stoic despair. Welch's taut prose, dark humor, and sharp, laconic dialogue, so much admired by the book's critics, do not finally save *Winter in the Blood* from a congealment of its own.

The alienation of the principal character is taken to its logical conclusion in *The Death of Jim Loney* with his suicide. Actually, Loney's death is a sort of ritualistic murder that he wills upon himself, but that this death is the only form of affirmation available to him suggests the impasse that Welch had worked himself into. Moreover, the novel suffers from some surprisingly clumsy dialogue and unfinished characterization, notably in the two women in Loney's life, his girlfriend Rhea, a white school teacher from Texas, and his sister Kate, a successful education official in Washington, D.C. Loney himself seems like a slightly older, more depressed version of the narrator of *Winter in the Blood.* A half-breed at home neither in the White nor in the Indian world, he knows that there is "no real love in his life; that somehow, at some time, everything had gone dreadfully wrong." Since the second novel is almost as plotless as the first, there is little for Loney to do but drink and brood and watch passively as his girlfriend and sister try, but fail, to rescue his spirit.

If *The Death of Jim Loney* was an impasse, *Fools Crow* was one way out. This long, historical novel concerning a tribe of Blackfeet (Pikuni) in northern Montana in the terrible years after the Civil War, was a major departure for Welch and an unusual instance of a story told entirely from within the Indians' point of view. In *Fools Crow* Whites (Napikwans) are at most a marginal, though threatening, presence and the interpenetration of myth, religion, and daily life takes place with perfect matter-of-factness. For example the young warrior Fools Crow is guided on a solitary trip to the mountains by Raven, at once an ordinary bird and a trickster spirit. Such scenes effectively dispense with traditional notions of verisimilitude and involve the reader in a different kind of imaginative re-creation.

Welch's protagonist, though a brave warrior and a loving husband and provider, is not immune to the self-doubt and spiritual agony that afflict his two predecessors. But the existential uncertainty experienced by Fools Crow is motivated as much by forces from without as from within. In the course of the novel the Blackfeet are plagued by internal dissension, hunger, small pox, renegade tribespeople, and finally a massacre by white soldiers. Fools Crow's struggle for self knowledge enables him to withstand these shocks to his psyche and to take upon himself as much of the burden of his people as he can. This ethical awareness, new to Welch's fiction, impresses at least as much as his always vivid sense of the Montana landscape and his use of the Blackfeet's animistic speech patterns to describe it. If he does not always succeed in transcribing the Indians' metaphoric language into an unforced, conversational English, the somewhat wooden dialogue is a small price to pay for a novel that dares to forgo irony and narrative detachment in order to represent the harsh and beautiful traditions of the plains Indians at the moment those traditions began to unravel.

In its use of deliberately commercial formulas, *The Indian Lawyer* was a further departure for Welch. It reads fast, has a suspenseful plot, and even includes a few modest sex scenes. Far from representing a compromised artistry, however, *The Indian Lawyer* shows how well Welch can use commercial formulas to crest an entertainment of a very serious kind. The Indian lawyer is Sylvester Yellow Calf, who, at 35, has risen above a childhood of deprivation and segregation to become the most promising member of an important law firm in Helena and the leading Democratic candidate for a vacant Congressional seat. Suspense is generated by a blackmail attempt against Sylvester engineered by a vengeful prison inmate whose request for parole Sylvester, as a member of the State Board of Pardons, had denied. In fact, the blackmail threat, involving Sylvester's affair with the wife of the inmate, is hard to take seriously; even in conservative Montana unmarried candidates for political office do not generally loose elections for having a sex life. But Welch arranges the mechanics of the blackmailing skillfully and Sylvester's affair with the lonely, unsophisticated Patti Ann is more than touching; here the more typical polarities of racial power are reversed, but the blue-collar white woman and the worldly, successful Indian share an experience of exclusion that allows them to transcend, if only with each other, constraints of race and class. Perhaps the novel's greatest strength is the characterization of Sylvester himself: a full-blooded Blackfeet both proud of and uncomfortable with his heritage, a liberal and idealist whose decision to run for Congress is, as he well knows, exactly as selfish as it is selfless. The novel's ambiguous ending seems far more just than Jim Loney's weirdly affirmative death wish. Sylvester opts out of the race and commits himself to pro bono work for Indian water rights, but he is still competing fiercely against himself. Whether he has reconciled his own spiritual needs with the exigencies of social and moral responsibility is a question Welch does not attempt to answer. Impressive as his first novel is, it is not a question Welch would have thought to ask of the intense and intensely self-absorbed narrator of *Winter in the Blood*.

—Stephen Akey

WELDON, Fay

Nationality: British. **Born:** Fay Birkinshaw in Alvechurch, Worcestershire, 22 September 1931; grew up in New Zealand. **Education:** Girls' High School, Christchurch; Hampstead Girls' High School, London; University of St. Andrews, Fife, 1949-52, M.A. in economics and psychology 1952. D. Litt, University of Bath, 1988, University of St. Andrews, 1992. **Family:** Married Ron Weldon in 1960; four sons. **Career:** writer for the Foreign Office and *Daily Mirror,* both London, late 1950s; later worked in advertising. **Awards:** Writers Guild award, for radio play, 1973; Giles Cooper award, for radio play, 1978; Society of Authors traveling scholarship, 1981; Los Angeles *Times* award, for fiction, 1989. Lives in London. **Agent:** Ed Victor, 6 Bayley St., London WC1B 3HB; Casarotto Company, National House, 62-66 Wardour Street, London W1V 3HP, England.

PUBLICATIONS

Novels

The Fat Woman's Joke. London, MacGibbon and Kee, 1967; as *. . . and the Wife Ran Away,* New York, McKay, 1968.

Down among the Women. London, Heinemann, 1971; New York, St. Martin's Press, 1972.

Female Friends. London, Heinemann, and New York, St. Martin's Press, 1975.

Remember Me. London, Hodder and Stoughton, and New York, Random House, 1976.

Words of Advice. New York, Random House, 1977; as *Little Sisters,* London, Hodder and Stoughton, 1978.

Praxis. London, Hodder and Stoughton, and New York, Summit, 1978.

Puffball. London, Hodder and Stoughton, and New York, Summit, 1980.

The President's Child. London, Hodder and Stoughton, 1982; New York, Doubleday, 1983.

The Life and Loves of a She-Devil. London, Hodder and Stoughton, 1983; New York, Pantheon, 1984.

The Shrapnel Academy. London, Hodder and Stoughton, 1986; New York, Viking, 1987.

The Heart of the Country. London, Hutchinson, 1987; New York, Viking, 1988.

The Hearts and Lives of Men. London, Heinemann, 1987; New York, Viking, 1988.

Leader of the Band. London, Hodder and Stoughton, 1988; New York, Viking, 1989.

The Cloning of Joanna May. London, Collins, 1989; New York, Viking, 1990.

Darcy's Utopia. London, Collins, 1990; New York, Viking, 1991.
Life Force. London, Collins, and New York, Viking, 1992
Affliction. London, Collins, 1994; as *Trouble,* New York, Viking, 1994.
Splitting: A Novel. N.p., Grove Atlantic, 1994.

Short Stories

Watching Me, Watching You. London, Hodder and Stoughton, and New York, Summit, 1981.
Polaris and Other Stories. London, Hodder and Stoughton, 1985; New York, Penguin, 1989.
The Rules of Life (novella). London, Hutchinson, and New York, Harper, 1987.
Moon over Minneapolis. London, Harper Collins, 1991.

Uncollected Short Story

"Ind Aff; or, Out of Love in Sarajevo," in *Best Short Stories 1989,* edited by Giles Gordon and David Hughes. London, Heinemann, 1989; as *The Best English Short Stories 1989,* New York, Norton, 1989.

Plays

Permanence, in *We Who Are about to . . . ,* later called *Mixed Doubles* (produced London, 1969). London, Methuen, 1970.
Time Hurries On, in *Scene Scripts,* edited by Michael Marland. London, Longman, 1972.
Words of Advice (produced London, 1974). London, French, 1974.
Friends (produced Richmond, Surrey, 1975).
Moving House (produced Farnham, Surrey, 1976).
Mr. Director (produced Richmond, Surrey, 1978).
Polaris (broadcast 1978). Published in *Best Radio Plays of 1978,* London, Eyre Methuen, 1979.
Action Replay (produced Birmingham, 1978; as *Love Among the Women,* produced Vancouver, 1982). London, French, 1980.
I Love My Love (broadcast 1981; produced Richmond, Surrey, 1982). London, French, 1984.
After the Prize (produced New York, 1981; as *Word Worm,* produced Newbury, Berkshire, 1984).
Jane Eyre, adaptation of the novel by Charlotte Brontë (produced Birmingham, 1986).
The Hole in the Top of the World (produced Richmond, Surrey, 1987).
Someone Like You, music by Petula Clark and Dee Shipman (produced London, 1990).

Radio Plays: *Spider,* 1973; *Housebreaker,* 1973; *Mr. Fox and Mr. First,* 1974; *The Doctor's Wife,* 1975; *Polaris,* 1978; *Weekend,* 1979; *All the Bells of Paradise,* 1979; *I Love My Love,* 1981; *The Hole in the Top of the World,* 1993.

Television Plays: *Wife in a Blonde Wig,* 1966; *A Catching Complaint,* 1966; *The Fat Woman's Tale,* 1966; *What About Me,* 1967; *Dr. De Waldon's Therapy,* 1967; *Goodnight Mrs. Dill,* 1967; *The 45th Unmarried Mother,* 1967; *Fall of the Goat,* 1967; *Ruined Houses,* 1968; *Venus Rising,* 1968; *The Three Wives of Felix Hull,* 1968; *Hippy Hippy Who Cares,* 1968; *£13083,* 1968; *The Loophole,* 1969; *Smokescreen,* 1969; *Poor Mother,* 1970; *Office Party,* 1970; *On Trial (Upstairs, Downstairs,* series), 1971; *Old*

Man's Hat, 1972; *A Splinter of Ice,* 1972; *Hands,* 1972; *The Lament of an Unmarried Father,* 1972; *A Nice Rest,* 1972; *Comfortable Words,* 1973; *Desirous of Change,* 1973; *In Memoriam,* 1974; *Poor Baby,* 1975; *The Terrible Tale of Timothy Bagshott,* 1975; *Aunt Tatty,* from the story by Elizabeth Bowen, 1975; *Act of Rape,* 1977; *Married Love (Six Women* series), 1977; *Act of Hypocrisy (Jubilee* series), 1977; *Chickabiddy (Send in the Girls* series), 1978; *Pride and Prejudice,* from the novel by Jane Austen, 1980; *Honey Ann,* 1980; *Life for Christine,* 1980; *Watching Me, Watching You (Leap in the Dark* series), 1980; *Little Mrs. Perkins,* from a story by Penelope Mortimer, 1982; *Redundant! or, The Wife's Revenge,* 1983; *Out of the Undertow,* 1984; *Bright Smiles (Time for Murder* series), 1985; *Zoe's Fever (Ladies in Charge* series), 1986; *A Dangerous Kind of Love (Mountain Men* series), 1986; *Heart of the Country* serial, 1987.

Other

Simple Steps to Public Life, with Pamela Anderson and Mary Stott. London, Virago Press, 1980.
Letters to Alice: On First Reading Jane Austen. London, Joseph, 1984; New York, Taplinger, 1985.
Rebecca West. London and New York, Viking, 1985.
Wolf the Mechanical Dog (for children). London, Collins, 1988.
Sacred Cows. London, Chatto and Windus, 1989.
Party Puddle (for children). London, Collins, 1989.

Editor, with Elaine Feinstein, *New Stories 4.* London, Hutchinson, 1979.

*　　　*　　　*

Fay Weldon's concern began as personal relationships in contemporary society, focusing on women, especially as mothers, and thus widening to take in relationships between the generations: "By our children, you shall know us." She amusingly traces long chains of cause and effect, inexorable as Greek tragedy, stemming from both conscious and unconscious motivation, and from chance circumstances. She looks at society with devastating clearsightedness, showing how good may spring from selfishness, evil from altruism.

Weldon's unique narrative style highlights the contradiction between free will which her characters, like us, assume and the conditioning which we know we undergo. Her characters are continually referred to by their names, where English style would normally use a pronoun, and addressed directly in the second person by the author and assessed by her—"Lucky Lily" the author appraises a leading character in *Remember Me,* where she also "translates" passages of the characters' dialogue into what they *mean,* rather than say. In *The Hearts and Lives of Men* the author continually buttonholes "Reader." Weldon's apparently disingenuous surface, with her own paragraphing lay-out, is underpinned by a whole battery of ironic devices, indicating the limitations on her characters'—and our—autonomy from cradle to grave. In *Puffball* this process is pushed back before the cradle, with sections "Inside Liffey" about the growth of the fetus and its conditioning via the circumstances of the mother's life.

The Fat Woman's Joke, Weldon's first novel, follows a greedy couple on a diet: this novel originated as a television play, and Weldon hadn't fully developed her unique style. Her characteristic plangent note, that the worst can happen and does, is accompanied by a muted optimism, especially in her novels' endings: gradual progress occurs, at least for the majority if not for the unfortunate individual. *Down among the Women* concludes "We are the last of the women"—that is, the half of the population defined earlier as living "at floor level, washing and wiping."

Weldon's feminism colors all her work, and is powerful when she doesn't shrink from detailing the faults of individual women, or the way women exploit what advantages the system yields them. Men are the exploiting sex because the system favors them, and they take for granted the *status quo*. In *Female Friends,* focusing on three women friends and their mothers, Grace is shown as worthless, until perhaps the end, while Oliver and Patrick take what the system offers—and more.

The machinery of plot in *Remember Me* is ostensibly supernatural, as a dead divorced wife haunts her ex-husband's second *ménage*. Weldon's apparent reliance on the supernatural may seem unsatisfactory both here and in *Puffball,* where pregnant Liffey is "overlooked" by the local witch. But in both novels the psychology suggests something of Marjorie's realization about her "haunted" home in *Female Friends:* "it was me haunting myself, sending myself messages."

In *Little Sisters* (*Words of Advice* in the U.S.) Weldon turned to the very rich. This black comedy centers melodramatically on the wheelchair-bound Gemma, narrator of the story within a story. Weldon also uses this device in *The Fat Woman's Joke, Praxis, The President's Child,* and *Darcy's Utopia.* The story-within-a-story device enables her to run different time-sequences simultaneously, emphasizing the interlocking of cause and effect between the generations, and also to highlight our imperfect understanding and information, through each individual's partial perception.

Praxis charts the life of a woman who served a prison sentence for killing "a poor little half-witted" baby, as we learn from one of the first-person chapters alternating at the start of the novel with the third-person chapters that subsequently take over. *Puffball,* about Liffey's pregnancy in Somerset while her husband remains working in London, is as strongly feminist, incorporating much information about female physiology and pregnancy. In *The President's Child* Isabel, the mother of an American presidential candidate's illegitimate child, is ruthlessly hunted in a parody of a thriller. *The Life and Loves of a She-Devil* describes Ruth's remorseless revenge on the bestseller writer who "stole" her husband.

Weldon's two collections of short stories, *Watching Me, Watching You* and *Polaris and Other Stories,* are mainly concerned with men exploiting women in different domestic settings: an exception, the title story of the latter, is the best. Its anti-war theme is continued in *The Shrapnel Academy:* over the snowbound weekend of the Academy's prestigious Wellington Lecture, the contemporary "servant problem" with a largely Third World staff escalates into a "local" nuclear explosion. Chapters of military history, describing warfare's "development," break up the story.

The Hearts and Lives of Men, set against the 1960s swinging London art market, more frothily charts the marriages—mainly to each other—of a trendy pair and the fraught childhood of their kidnapped daughter. In *The Heart of the Country* Sonia, now in a psychiatric hospital, explains her attempts to help Natalie, suddenly abandoned by her husband. Weldon parades the countryside's problems, from pesticides to the withdrawal of buses.

As one of the dead able to "re-wind" their life-stories, Gabriella reviews her lovers in the novella *The Rules of Life* set in 2004. In *Leader of the Band* "Starlady Sandra," incidentally the result of a genetic experiment, abandons astronomy, TV program, and hus-

band to accompany "mad Jack the trumpet-player" and his jazz band on tour in France.

The Cloning of Joanne May, set in the present day, shows Joanna secretly cloned by her husband, so that she has four sisters, young enough to be her daughters—all brought together by the plot. *Darcy's Utopia* is structured by the device of two journalists interviewing the notorious Mrs. Darcy, wife of an imprisoned government economic adviser; the journalists also have an affair. Despite much space, Darcy's ideas for a money-less and permissive society remain arbitrary and contradictory.

Although Weldon has widened her range, and has always used techniques of "alienation" to encourage the reader to think as well as feel, her characterization latterly has become very thin. She increasingly relies on her unique narrative techniques, with her often deliberately intrusive authorial voice, to sustain each novel.

—Val Warner

WELTY, Eudora (Alice)

Nationality: American. **Born:** Jackson, Mississippi, 13 April 1909. **Education:** Mississippi State College for Women, Columbus, 1925-27; University of Wisconsin, Madison, B.A. 1929; Columbia University School for Advertising, New York, 1930-31. **Career:** Part-time journalist, 1931-32; publicity agent, Works Progress Administration (WPA), 1933-36; staff member, *New York Times Book Review,* during World War II. Honorary Consultant in American Letters, Library of Congress, Washington, D.C., 1958. **Awards:** Bread Loaf Writers Conference fellowship, 1940; O. Henry award, 1942, 1943, 1968; Guggenheim fellowship, 1942, 1948; American Academy grant, 1944, Howells Medal, 1955, and gold medal, 1972; Ford fellowship, for drama; Brandeis University Creative Arts award, 1965; Edward MacDowell medal 1970; Pulitzer prize, 1973; National Medal for Literature, 1980; Presidential Medal of Freedom, 1980; American Book award, for paperback, 1983; Bobst award, 1984; Common Wealth award, 1984; Mystery Writers of America award, 1985; National Medal of Arts, 1987; National Endowment for the Arts Award, 1989; National Book Foundation Medal, 1991; Charles Frankel prize, 1992. D.Litt.: Denison University, Granville, Ohio, 1971; Smith College, Northampton, Massachusetts; University of Wisconsin, Madison; University of the South, Sewanee, Tennessee; Washington and Lee University, Lexington, Virginia. **Member:** American Academy, 1971; Chevalier, Order of Arts and Letters (France), 1987. **Address:** 1119 Pinehurst Street, Jackson, Mississippi 39202, U.S.A.

Publications

Novels

The Robber Bridegroom. New York, Doubleday, 1942; London, Lane, 1944.
Delta Wedding. New York, Harcourt Brace, 1946; London, Lane, 1947.
The Ponder Heart. New York, Harcourt Brace, and London, Hamish Hamilton, 1954.
Losing Battles. New York, Random House, 1970; London, Virago Press, 1982.

The Optimist's Daughter. New York, Random House, 1972; London, Deutsch, 1973.

Short Stories

A Curtain of Green. New York, Doubleday, 1941; London, Lane, 1943.
The Wide Net and Other Stories. New York, Harcourt Brace, 1943; London, Lane, 1945.
Music from Spain. Greenville, Mississippi, Levee Press, 1948.
The Golden Apples. New York, Harcourt Brace, 1949; London, Lane, 1950.
Selected Stories. New York, Modern Library, 1954.
The Bride of Innisfallen and Other Stories. New York, Harcourt Brace, and London, Hamish Hamilton, 1955.
Thirteen Stories, edited by Ruth M. Vande Kieft. New York, Harcourt Brace, 1965.
The Collected Stories of Eudora Welty. New York, Harcourt Brace, 1980; London, Boyars, 1981.
Moon Lake and Other Stories. Franklin Center, Pennsylvania, Franklin Library 1980.
Retreat. Jackson, Mississippi, Palaemon Press, 1981.

Poetry

A Flock of Guinea Hens Seen from a Car. New York, Albondocani Press, 1970.

Other

Short Stories (essay). New York, Harcourt Brace, 1949.
Place in Fiction. New York, House of Books, 1957.
Three Papers on Fiction. Northampton, Massachusetts, Smith College, 1962.
The Shoe Bird (for children). New York, Harcourt Brace, 1964.
A Sweet Devouring (on children's literature). New York, Albondocani Press, 1969.
One Time, One Place: Mississippi in the Depression: A Snapshot Album. New York, Random House, 1971.
A Pageant of Birds. New York, Albondocani Press, 1975.
Fairy Tale of the Natchez Trace. Jackson, Mississippi Historical Society, 1975.
The Eye of the Story: Selected Essays and Reviews. New York, Random House, 1978; London, Virago Press, 1987.
Ida M'Toy (memoir). Urbana, University of Illinois Press, 1979.
Miracles of Perception: The Art of Willa Cather, with Alfred Knopf and Yehudi Menuhin. Charlottesville, Virginia, Alderman Library, 1980.
Conversations with Eudora Welty, edited by Peggy Whitman Prenshaw. Jackson, University Press of Mississippi, 1984.
One Writer's Beginnings. Cambridge, Massachusetts, Harvard University Press, 1984; London, Faber, 1985.
Photographs. Jackson, University Press of Mississippi, 1989.
A Worn Path (for children). Mankato, Minnesota, Creative Education, 1991.
A Writer's Eye: Collected Book Reviews, edited by Pearl Amelia McHaney. Jackson, University Press of Mississippi, 1994.

Editor, with Ronald A. Sharp, *The Norton Book of Friendship.* New York, Norton, 1991.

*

Bibliography: In *Mississippi Quarterly* (Mississippi State), Fall 1973, and *Eudora Welty—A Bibliography of Her Work,* Jackson, University Press of Mississippi, 1994, both by Noel Polk; *Eudora Welty: A Reference Guide* by Victor H. Thompson, Boston, Hall, 1976; *Eudora Welty: A Critical Bibliography* by Bethany C. Swearingen, Jackson, University Press of Mississippi, 1984; *The Welty Collection: A Guide to the Eudora Welty Manuscripts and Documents at the Mississippi Department of Archives and History* by Suzanne Marrs, Jackson, University Press of Mississippi, 1988.

Manuscript Collection: Mississippi Department of Archives and History, Jackson.

Critical Studies (selection): *Eudora Welty* by Ruth M. Vande Kieft, New York, Twayne, 1962, revised edition, 1986; *A Season of Dreams: The Fiction of Eudora Welty* by Alfred Appel, Jr., Baton Rouge, Louisiana State University Press, 1965; *Eudora Welty* by Joseph A. Bryant, Jr., Minneapolis, University of Minnesota Press, 1968; *The Rhetoric of Eudora Welty's Short Stories* by Zelma Turner Howard, Jackson, University Press of Mississippi, 1973; *A Still Moment: Essays on the Art of Eudora Welty* edited by John F. Desmond, Metuchen, New Jersey, Scarecrow Press, 1978; *Eudora Welty: Critical Essays* edited by Peggy Whitman Prenshaw, Jackson, University Press of Mississippi, 1979; *Eudora Welty: A Form of Thanks* edited by Ann J. Abadie and Louis D. Dollarhide, Jackson, University Press of Mississippi, 1979; *Eudora Welty's Achievement of Order* by Michael Kreyling, Baton Rouge, Louisiana State University Press, 1980; *Eudora Welty* by Elizabeth Evans, New York, Ungar, 1981; *Tissue of Lies: Eudora Welty and the Southern Romance* by Jennifer L. Randisi, Boston, University Press of America, 1982; *Eudora Welty's Chronicle: A Story of Mississippi Life* by Albert J. Devlin, Jackson, University Press of Mississippi, 1983, and *Welty: A Life in Literature* edited by Devlin, University Press of Mississippi, 1988; *With Ears Opening Like Morning Glories: Eudora Welty and the Love of Storytelling* by Carol S. Manning, Westport, Connecticut, Greenwood Press, 1985; *Eudora Welty* by Louise Westling, London, Macmillan, 1989; *Eudora Welty: Eye of the Storyteller* edited by Dawn Trouard, Kent, Ohio, Kent State University Press, 1989; *Eudora Welty: Seeing Black and White* by Robert MacNeil, Jackson, University Press of Mississippi, 1990; *Serious Daring from Within: Female Narrative Strategies in Eudora Welty's Novels* by Franziska Gygax, New York, Greenwood, 1990; *Eudora Welty: Seeing Black and White* by Robert MacNeil, Jackson, University Press of Mississippi, 1990; *The Heart of the Story: Eudora Welty's Short Fiction* by Peter Schmidt, Jackson, University Press of Mississippi, 1991; *The Critical Response to Eudora Welty's Fiction* by Laurie Champion, Westport, Connecticut, Greenwood Press, 1994; *Daughter of the Swan: Love and Knowledge in Eudora Welty's Fiction* by Gail Mortimer (Gail Linda), Athens, University of Georgia Press, 1994; *The Dragon's Blood: Feminist Intertextuality in Eudora Welty's "The Golden Apples"* by Rebecca Mark, Jackson, University Press of Mississippi, 1994; *Eudora Welty's Aesthetics of Place* by Jan Nordby Gretlund, Newark, University of Delaware Press, 1994; *The Still Moment* by Paul Binding, London, Virago, 1994.

*   *   *

For Peggy Whitman Prenshaw's collection of tributes, I described Eudora Welty as a rare phenomenon in American letters, "a civilized writer." To explain my meaning, I must turn to Ruth M. Vande Kieft's introduction to the revised version of her *Eudora Welty*. Though Vande Kieft does not employ my term, she explains that as an artist Welty "does not seem to have felt any deep personal alienation from her culture, made no strong protests about the encroachment of industrialism or passing of the old order." Unlike the modernists, she is a writer who has accepted, as the price of civilization, its discontents.

This acceptance finds form in her still too much neglected first novel, *The Robber Bridegroom*, which comes as close as any American fiction to providing a myth of the nation's maturing as, with the passing of the frontier, the wilderness gives way to the mercantile state. "All things are double," planter Clement Musgrove observes ruefully as his own pastoral world that has replaced the Indian wild gives way in its turn to urban society. As for Jamie Lockhart, the two-faced hero of this serio-comic fantasy, Welty notes that "the outward transfer from bandit to merchant had been almost too easy to count it a change at all." The transformation is only cosmetic; merchants use the same gifts as bandits to operate legally in polite society.

Even in her first published story, "Death of a Traveling Salesman," Welty had subtly countered the Wastelanders of the 1920s and 1930s by counterpointing the death of the titular figure (that Arthur Miller would later confirm as emblematic of the dying world) with a Promethean bringer of fire as head of a family just emerging from barbarism to give promise of civilization's renewal.

The kind of memorable stories collected in Welty's first book, *A Curtain of Green*—"Why I Live at the P.O.," "Petrified Man," "A Visit of Charity," and the lilting jazz text "Powerhouse"—had been enthusiastically received by Cleanth Brook's and Robert Penn Warren's *Southern Review*, house organ of the New Criticism that flourished on ironic portrayals of the differences between people's expectations and their fulfillment. Unlike other writers, however, Welty was able to expand her vision with changing times. With two stories in her next collection, *The Wide Net*, employing such historical figures as Aaron Burr ("First Love") and the bandit Murrell, the Man of God Lorenzo Dow, and the naturalist Audubon in "A Still Moment," Welty seemed embarked (as in *The Robber Bridegroom*) on creating a mythology that earlier aspirants had failed to produce for the emerging nation. In "A Still Moment" she had indeed captured as tellingly as Melville in *Billy Budd* the awful cost of civilization in the destruction of beauty as the quiet naturalist-artist horrifies the two wild men into whose company he has fallen by his cool shooting of a beautiful heron to use as a model for a painting.

Welty did not linger in the distant past, but returned with her next novel, *Delta Wedding*, to the world where she best found her voice (as she describes the climactic step in her development in the autobiographical *One Writer's Beginnings*), the Mississippi of her own lifetime where outsiders were beginning to challenge the rule of imperiously aristocratic family-clans that had dominated the society. Against the most tranquil background that Welty could summon up, she depicts the struggle of an uncle's bride and a niece's groom from what the Fairchilds regard as an inferior class to claim their spouses from a deeply loving but overprotective and tradition-ridden family.

Family dominates also *The Golden Apples*. Welty includes this work in her *Collected Stories*, but it is really what Forrest Ingram calls "a short-story cycle," a novel composed of tales that can be read individually but that gain additional meaning when considered in relationship to each other. Welty explains in *One Writer's Be-*

ginnings how stories that she had originally written about various characters "under different names, at different periods in their lives, in situations not yet interlocking but ready for it," grew into "a shadowing of Greek mythological figures, gods and heroes that wander in various guises, at various times, in and out, emblems of the characters' heady dreams." Focused on "one location already evoked," the portentously named town of Morgana, Mississippi, the meandering tales demonstrate how these provincial versions of universal types, though some wander afar and some stay at home, all return at last to their origins.

Despite the principle of the eternal return seemingly underlying this story-sequence, Welty over the next decade began casting about to evoke what she regards as supremely important in fiction, "a sense of place," about somewhere beyond contemporary Mississippi—the Civil War in "The Burning," the Mississippi delta beyond New Orleans in "No Place for You, My Love," and dreamlike regions as far afield as Italy and Cork, Ireland, in "Going to Naples" and "The Bride of Innisfallen," in the stories collected in the volume named for the last mentioned. None of these experiments, however, had quite the authenticity of a story included with them, "Ladies in Spring," and the separately published novelette *The Ponder Heart*, both of which take place in the rural Mississippi to which Welty returned, like her characters in *The Golden Apples*, after wandering.

The Ponder Heart, which went on to become a successful play after first being published in its entirety in one issue of the *New Yorker*, exemplifies the narrative form Welty handles with the most consummate skill, the first-person monologue of a figure with whom she by no means identifies, but whose mind she can read and whose words she can capture with the skill of the mockingbird, mimicking the sounds of its Southern "place." This tale, told by a busy-body small-town hotel-keeper about the surprising outcome of the trial of her elderly uncle Daniel Ponder for literally tickling his teen-aged bride to death, appropriately won the William Dean Howells award of the American Academy of Arts and Letters for the most distinguished work of American fiction for the years 1950 to 1955; for it was Howells who had in *The Rise of Silas Lapham* laid down the challenge to American writers to which Welty's work has become the major response, ". . . it is certain that our manners and customs go for more in life than our qualities. The price that we pay for civilization is the fine yet impassable differentiation of these. Perhaps we pay too much." Whatever Welty's views of Howell's last speculation, after her triumphs with *The Ponder Heart*, she settled down to working in the same vein for 15 years as she was preoccupied with her longest and most complex novel, *Losing Battles*, the chronicle in many voices (that she reads aloud magically) of the reunion of an immense clan of subsistence farmers in one of the poorest backwoods regions of the northeast Mississippi hills. In part *Losing Battles* returns (as does later *The Optimist's Daughter*) to the story of an outside bride's attempts to rescue (as she sees it) the husband for whom she has given up her own ambitions to improve her place in the world from the clutches of his dependent family. As the story takes shape, however, Julia Mortimer, the kind of schoolteacher whom Welty admits in *One Writer's Beginnings* she has most often written about, although she dies beyond the principal scenes of the novel during the day and a half of its action, takes over as the focal figure. She is the embodiment of the enlightened disciplinarian who, though constantly losing battles, has never surrendered in the war to share her illumination with her charges in the waste land at the margin of civilization. A marvelous mixture of comedy and pathos, the long folk-like tale is a remarkable tribute to the indomitability of the human spirit, especially the female spirit in the role that Howells celebrated as the poised guardian of civilized culture.

The writing of the novel was interrupted by two of Welty's most powerful stories that did not appear in book form until her stories were collected in 1980. "Where Is the Voice Coming From?," written in a single night after the shooting of Civil Rights leader Medgar Evers, is the internal monologue of his killer, for which, Welty explains in *One Writer's Beginnings,* she entered "into the mind and inside the skin of a character who could hardly have been more alien or repugnant to me." "The Demonstrators" is an almost equally harrowing account of a small community's white doctor's involvement in some sordid affairs of the blacks during the years of the Civil Rights crises that he perceives necessitate the transformation of his traditional community. Most remarkable about the two stories is their revelation of the intensity that the most crucial experiences of her "place" can evoke from her.

Perhaps under the impact of such recent events, even Welty's good humor and civilized virtues have been sorely tried, as is suggested by her most recent novel, *The Optimist's Daughter,* in which she reverts to the ironic mode of her earliest stories to depict the plight of a woman who has lost her beloved husband, her mother, and her father as she is deprived of her inheritance and driven out of her home place by her father's young second wife, a redneck (never Welty's term) from Texas (envisioned here as beyond the edge of civilization). Despite all the honors that Welty has justifiably received and despite her avowal in *One Writer's Beginnings* that "Of all my strong emotions, anger is the one least responsible for my work," the ironically titled *The Optimist's Daughter* seems an acknowledgment that like Julia Mortimer, she and her society have been fighting losing battles, although the struggle has been worthwhile in honoring what she describes as her reverence for "the holiness of life."

—Warren French

WENDT, Albert

Nationality: Samoan. **Born:** Apia, Western Samoa, 27 October 1939; member of the Aiga Sa-Tuala. **Education:** New Plymouth Boys High School, New Zealand, graduated 1957; Ardmore Teacher's College, diploma in teaching, 1959; Victoria University, Wellington, 1960-64, M.A. (honours) in history 1964. **Family:** Married Jennifer Elizabeth Whyte in 1964; two daughters and one son. **Career:** Teacher, 1964-69, and principal, 1969-73, Samoa College, Apia; senior lecturer, 1974-75, assistant director of Extension Services, 1976-77, and professor of pacific literature, 1982-87, University of the South Pacific, Suva, Fiji. Since 1988 professor of English, University of Auckland. Director, University of the South Pacific Centre, Apia, Western Samoa, after 1978. Editor, *Bulletin,* now *Samoa Times,* Apia, 1966, and Mana Publications, Suva, Fiji, 1974-80. Coordinator, Unesco Program on Oceanic Cultures, 1975-79. **Awards:** *Landfall* prize, 1963; Wattie award, 1980. **Agent:** Tim Curnow, Curtis Brown (Australia) Pty. Ltd., 27 Union Street, Paddington, New South Wales 2021, Australia. **Address:** Department of English, University of Auckland, Private Bag 92019, Auckland 1, New Zealand.

Novels

Sons for the Return Home. Auckland, Longman Paul, 1973; London, Penguin, 1987.
Pouliuli. Auckland, Longman Paul, 1977; Honolulu, University Press of Hawaii, 1980; London, Penguin, 1987.
Leaves of the Banyan Tree. Auckland, Longman Paul, 1979; London, Allen Lane, 1980; as *The Banyan,* New York, Doubleday, 1984.
Ola. Auckland, Penguin, 1990.
Black Rainbow. Auckland, Penguin, 1991.

Short Stories

Flying-Fox in a Freedom Tree. Auckland, Longman Paul, 1974.
The Birth and Death of the Miracle Man. London and New York, Viking, 1986.

Plays

Comes the Revolution (produced Suva, Fiji, 1972).
The Contract (produced Apia, Western Samoa, 1972).

Poetry

Inside Us the Dead: Poems 1961 to 1974. Auckland, Longman Paul, 1976.
Shaman of Visions. Auckland, Auckland University Press, 1984; Oxford, Oxford University Press, 1985.

Other

Editor, *Some Modern Poetry from Fiji* [Western Samoa, *the New Hebrides, the Solomon Islands, Vanuatu*]. Suva, Fiji, Mana, 5 vols., 1974-75.
Editor, *Lali: A Pacific Anthology.* Auckland, Longman Paul, 1980.
Editor, *Nuanua: A Pacific Anthology.* Auckland, Auckland University Press, 1995.

*

Critical Studies: "Towards a New Oceania" by Wendt, in *Mana Review* (Suva, Fiji), January 1976; chapter on Wendt in *South Pacific Literature: From Myth to Fabulation* by Subramani, Suya, Fiji, University of the South Pacific, 1985.

*   *   *

As the Samoan novelist, short story writer, and poet Albert Wendt has said, he "belongs to two worlds in almost every way." For more than a decade after his early teens he experienced the difficulties of adapting himself to an alien culture in New Zealand, and his return to Samoa gave rise to a process of readjustment both to his ancestral past and to the post-independence present of his country. His writing stems in some measure from this bi-cultural predicament. It is a return to and a quest for the roots of his being. Significantly enough, *Inside Us the Dead* is the title of his volume of poems.

If his novels and short stories are the work of a self-acknowledged literary pioneer, they are much more than a welcome indication that a Polynesian literature is developing in the southwest Pacific. However difficult it may be to assess the ultimate value of productions for which in many important ways no firm basis for comparison exists, it is nonetheless clear that they achieve distinction as explorations of human relations and a way of life that have almost escaped the attention of romantic or racist outlanders.

Sons for the Return Home, Wendt's first novel, was published many years after his own return to Western Samoa. The simplicity of its plot and language is in marked contrast to the ambiguities and ironies of the pursuit of selfhood that, interwoven with a Samoan myth, provides the theme and gives substance and meaning to the narrative. Because it is mainly concerned with a Samoan family living in New Zealand, the fa'a Samoa or the Samoan way of life becomes an integral part of the novel's structure and not an intrusive element requiring unnecessary explanation. The doubts and difficulties implicit in the theme are developed in terms of incident and human relationship, and the disillusion experienced after "the return home" becomes the novel's climax, which offers no easy solution to the personal problems arising from cultural shock.

Wendt's later publications are centred on the extended families in the villages of Samoa, but they contain little to suggest that they are guidebooks to an exotic and romantic island-world. In the short stories of *Flying-Fox in a Freedom Tree,* in *Pouliuli,* and in the three parts of *Leaves of the Banyan Tree* the quest for identity, the attempt to discover the true self caught between the claims of contending cultures, and the search for a precarious freedom from the dictates of competing orthodoxies are raised to a higher level. They are not merely the consequences of racial disharmony, but originate in the basic conditions of human existence. The flying-fox hangs upside-down in the freedom tree. The powerful head of an extended family rejects his past, repudiates his present, and in advanced old age seeks freedom in Pouliuli, in darkness. The rise and fall of another titled head of an aiga in *Leaves of the Banyan Tree,* with his lust for power and his imitation of Papalagi (European) ways, may be related to the social pollution of the islands but have their source in a deeper corruption.

This long and powerful novel explores in myth and legend, in traditional social structure, and in the changing post-independence present not only what has happened to the fa'a Samoa, but what has happened to human beings. The comedy and the tragedy, the violence, the horror and the glory of human life, together with man's desperate search for the meaning of existence, are localised in a village setting populated by an extraordinary variety of characters. The middle section of an expanded version of *Flying-Fox in a Freedom Tree,* the novella that gives its title to the earlier volume of short stories, becomes an essential and thoroughly coordinated part of the whole book, linking the first section, "God, Money, and Success," to the third, "Funerals and Heirs," of this saga of a Samoan village.

The Birth and Death of the Miracle Man is a divergence from Wendt's earlier writings. Where in previous works Wendt's protagonists struggled to find a place for themselves in a society that suppressed individualism, in *Birth and Death* communal values, parent-child relationships, and a strong familial structure are emphasized. Particularly prevalent are the relationships between fathers and sons. "A Talent," "Elena's Son," and "The Balloonfish and the Armadillo" deal with fathers who have failed in their obligations and sons who are held hostage by unreasonable expectations, both of their fathers and of themselves. Occasionally a story like "Hamlet" verges on the sentimental, but most of the tales in this collection leave the reader with an affecting, memorable impression, entirely in keeping with Wendt's belief that the fa'a Samoa is best presented by Samoans themselves.

Ola, a novel, delves into issues concerning the creative process. A Samoan word that functions as both noun and verb, Ola means "life" and "to create life." It is these two merging concepts that the author tinkers with in the novel. When a biographer begins to rearrange Olamaiileoti Farou Monroe's letters, diaries, and poems, he finds that he has begun to reconstruct an entirely singular existence. Particularly effective is the chapter "Crocodile," which captures the conflict between public fictions and private realities. The schoolgirl Ola gets a glimpse of this conflict after sharing a moment of empathy with a middle-aged schoolteacher who had been previously shrouded in myth and innuendo.

Black Rainbow, Wendt's next novel, adopts the devices of science fiction to advocate cultural differentness. Set in a futuristic New Zealand, ala Orwell's *1984, Black Rainbow* addresses the relationship between postcolonialism and postmodernism, contending that the creation of a national literature is a kind of colonialization itself—the imposition of a criteria on something that should be fluid. Through humor and a willful mixing of Anglo and Samoan popular culture, Wendt challenges the idea of a "pure culture," untainted by the outside world. Culture is not immutable, the novel suggests, but constantly in flux—modified and enhanced by outside influences. Taking as its subtext a lithograph by Maori artist Ralph Hotere, which protests nuclear testing in the South Pacific, the novel explores also the legacy of cultural imperialism and the effects of progress on the Polynesian Garden of Eden.

As a Polynesian writer Wendt has not been satisfied to produce fiction that has entertainment value alone or to exploit the fa'a Samoa for the benefit of the foreign tourist. His aim has been far more ambitious, and he has taken greater risks. If at times he lays himself open to adverse critical comment and his intentions have not always been realised, his achievement is nonetheless impressive. He has set a standard that augurs well for the future.

—H. Winston Rhodes, updated by Lynda Schrecengost

WESLEY, Mary

Nationality: British. **Born:** Mary Farmar in Englefield Green, Berkshire, 24 June 1912. **Education:** Queen's College, London, 1928-39; London School of Economics, 1931-32. **Family:** Married 1) Lord Swinfen in 1937 (divorced 1944), two sons; 2) Eric Siepmann in 1951, one son. **Career:** Staff member, War Office, London, 1939-41. C.B.E. (Commander, Order of the British Empire), 1995. **Address:** c/o Bantam Press, 61-63 Uxbridge Road, London W5 5SA, England.

PUBLICATIONS

Novels

The Sixth Seal. London, Macdonald, 1969; New York, Stein and Day, 1971.
Jumping the Queue. London, Macmillan, 1983; New York, Penguin, 1988.
Haphazard House. London, Dent, 1983.

The Camomile Lawn. London, Macmillan, 1984; New York, Summit, 1985.

Harnessing Peacocks. London, Macmillan, 1985; New York, Scribner, 1986.

The Vacillations of Poppy Carew. London, Macmillan, 1986; New York, Penguin, 1988.

Not That Sort of Girl. London, Macmillan, 1987; New York, Viking, 1988.

Second Fiddle. London, Macmillan, 1988; New York, Viking, 1989.

A Sensible Life. London, Bantam, and New York, Viking, 1990.

A Dubious Legacy. London, Bantam, 1992; New York, Viking, 1993.

An Imaginative Experience. London, Bantam, 1994; New York, Viking, 1995.

Other (for children)

Speaking Terms. London, Faber, 1969; Boston, Gambit, 1971.

*   *   *

Mary Wesley's popularity can be traced in part to the humor, sensitivity, and wit with which she handles her characters and plots. Depicting quintessentially British middle-class life she creates fast moving, tightly constructed scenarios written in simple yet evocative language. The frankness with which she deals with her subject matter has led one critic to comment that Wesley ". . . has reached an age when she can say dangerous or naughty things without shocking." All seven of her novels deal with seemingly taboo subjects such as incest, matricide, suicide, and prostitution; love, sex, and death are dominant themes throughout.

The female protagonists of her books are misfits—eccentric, for the most part independent women who live on the periphery of the middle-class world so often described. Matilda Poliport the central figure in Wesley's first novel *Jumping the Queue* begins this trend of characterization. Matilda comes from a comparatively privileged world, she resides in the South West of England (a favorite setting for Wesley's books) and she is alone. Recently widowed at the opening of the book Matilda meticulously plans her suicide only to be thwarted by the entrance of Hugh, a fugitive from the police. Also contemplating suicide Hugh is instead taken home by Matilda and life begins again for them both.

Jumping the Queue is original and often maliciously witty. In common with Wesley's later novels the plot contains a series of sub-plots, farcical scenes, and bitter twists. We find for example that Tom, Matilda's much idolized husband, was in reality having an incestuous relationship with his daughter and was also involved in drug smuggling and espionage. Perhaps most shocking of all is the discovery that Matilda is aware of some if not all of these occurrences. Although the novel is filled with black humor it also possesses moments of extreme sadness and poignancy the most surprising of which is Matilda's successful suicide at the end of the book. In this respect the novel differs from the author's other works which have somewhat happier endings. Even in *Second Fiddle* which ends with the protagonist Laura walking away from the men who love her there is some semblance of hope as the reader knows that Laura is a capable and strong woman, a survivor. However Matilda dies completely disillusioned, having lost everything she ever cared for, even her dignity in death.

The Camomile Lawn introduces the colorful Calypso Grant who reappears in four of the later works. Set initially during World Ward II the book follows the fortunes and relationships of five cousins,

Oliver, Polly, Calypso, Walter and Sophie over a period of 40 years. Sex is a dominant theme and the war becomes the liberating factor in allowing the female characters in particular the freedom to experiment with their own sexuality. Hence we find Polly enjoying a relationship with two twin brothers, one or both of whom father her children and Calypso and Sophie embark on a series of affairs. Sophie is the misfit child (a common character in Wesley's books) who at the beginning of the book is hopelessly in love with Oliver, a love which endures and which is finally consummated four decades later.

The theme of a lasting love that finally wins through is a favored one in Wesley's work occurring in *Harnessing Peacocks, Not That Sort of Girl,* and *A Sensible Life.* In *Not That Sort of Girl* the central figure Rose rejects her beloved yet impoverished Mylo Cooper for the staid and rich Ned Peel. Over the next 40 years she remains faithful to both men; Ned, her husband, and Mylo her lover. When Ned dies, Rose and Mylo finally marry, their love having survived marriages, births, and deaths. Similarly in *Harnessing Peacocks* Hebe falls pregnant at the beginning of the book then rediscovers and falls in love with the father of her son some 17 years later. Hebe is probably one of the most likable of Wesley's female characters. Running away from her grandparents who plan to force her to have an abortion, Hebe instead becomes first a cook and then a prostitute who sells her favors for vast amounts of money in order to school her son Silas. Hebe is independent, pragmatic, and very much in control of the men who pass through her life.

Laura, the protagonist in *Second Fiddle,* shares with Hebe her attraction for men. Both women are mysterious and unattainable, Hebe because of the nature of her work and Laura because of her avoidance of entanglement. Although Wesley never actually states it, through suggestion and innuendo the reader concludes that Laura is the product of an incestuous relationship between her mother and uncle, the twins Emily and Nicholas Thornby. To complicate matters further we find that Laura has also been sexually abused by Nicholas, who if not her father is certainly her uncle. Laura is a strange character who the reader never really knows. Combining strength with surprising vulnerability she embarks on a relationship with a 23-year-old would-be writer and inevitably falls in love with him. Choosing to be alone she ends the relationship and rejects the two men who love her.

Poppy Carew in *The Vacillations of Poppy Carew* advocates pleasure over commitment. Left a great deal of money by her milkman father (also an inveterate but successful gambler) Poppy is suddenly thrust into a completely new world. Moving from North Africa to the South West of England the novel is crammed with charming and vital characters, sub-plots and petty intrigues. Although Poppy, like Laura, rejects the man who loves her (the pig farmer Willie Guthrie) she finally realizes that she can have both pleasure and commitment with him. Thus, unlike Laura, Poppy decides to take the risk.

Flora, the pivotal character in Wesley's most recent book *A Sensible Life,* combines the independence of Laura and Hebe with the awkwardness of the young Sophie. Sojourning with her parents in Dinard in 1926 the 10-year-old Flora meets and falls in love with three young men, Cosmo, Hubert, and Felix. Rejected by her parents who consider her a misfit in the same way that Laura, Sophie, and Hebe are considered strange by their parents, guardians and grandparents, Flora turns instead to the three men for love and attention. Over a period of 40 years (a popular time span in Wesley's books) she explores her feelings for all of them and ends up with Cosmo.

In addition to these novels Wesley has also written three other books: *The Sixth Seal* an apocalyptic and frightening vision of the world; *Haphazard House* which focuses on an eccentric painter and his family who go to live in an old and haunted house in the country, (this book differs from Wesley's other works in that the reader receives a much more personal account of events as seen through the eyes of the narrator Lisa) and finally a children's book called *Speaking Terms* in which a group of children learn to understand and speak to the animals through a bullfinch named Mr. Bull. Charmingly written and illustrated the message of the book is essentially conservationist. *The Sixth Seal, Haphazard House,* and *Speaking Terms* are different from Wesley's other works. Stylistically Wesley's use of language is still concise and simple yet her sentence structure is shorter in these books and her use of dialogue more extensive. Thematically several of the topics tackled in the later novels such as love, death, and age also occur in these books and her characters retain their sense of individuality, humor, and eccentricity.

Wesley's books show a great understanding of human nature. Young and old alike are depicted with sensitivity, perception, and wit. The combination of a frank style, rich and complex plots, and a concise and simple use of language create extremely charming and readable books.

—Aruna Vasudevan

WEST, Anthony C(athcart Muir)

Nationality: Irish. **Born:** County Down, Northern Ireland, 1 July 1910. **Military Service:** Served in the Royal Air Force Pathfinder Force during World War II: air observer and navigator bomber. **Family:** Married Olive Mary Burr in 1940; 11 children. **Awards:** Atlantic award, 1946. **Address:** c/o Midland Bank Ltd., Castle St., Beaumaris, Anglesey, Gwynedd LL58 8AR, Wales.

PUBLICATIONS

Novels

The Native Moment. New York, McDowell Obolensky, 1959; London, MacGibbon and Kee, 1961.
Rebel to Judgment. New York, Obolensky, 1962.
The Ferret Fancier. London, MacGibbon and Kee, 1963; New York, Simon and Schuster, 1965.
As Towns with Fire. London, MacGibbon and Kee, 1968; New York, Knopf, 1970.

Short Stories

River's End and Other Stories. New York, McDowell Obolensky, 1958; London, MacGibbon and Kee, 1960.
All the King's Horses and Other Stories. Dublin, Poolbeg Press, 1981.

*

Critical Studies: *Forces and Themes in Ulster Fiction* by John Wilson Foster, Dublin, Gill and Macmillan, 1974; *Celtic, Christian, Socialist: The Novels of Anthony C. West* by Audrey S. Eyler, Rutherford, New Jersey, Fairleigh Dickinson University Press, 1993.

Anthony C. West comments:

I have a creative and an a-political interest in the human condition, wherever and however it may be found, with the incorrigible hope for social harmony and world tolerance.

*   *   *

The fiction of Anthony C. West is filled with poignant and great tenderness, yet it is not just lyric. The main characters of his novels are all very much attuned to nature, yet *in* the world if not entirely *of* it. He handles scenes of childhood well, yet his children grow up. *As Towns with Fire,* his latest novel, creates a focus, almost a culmination, for *The Native Moment* and *The Ferret Fancier.*

As Towns with Fire is the portrait of a man and a war. Beginning New Year's Eve, 1939, it traces the experiences of Christopher MacMannan, an Irishman who has settled in London to train himself as a writer, to the day of his discharge from the R.A.F. after the war has ended. During this time he has done odd jobs and worked with the A.R.P., married, had two children, gone to Belfast where he suffered employment, unemployment, and air raids, joined the Air Force, and flown many missions as observer in Mosquitoes.

There is almost too much in this book, but all of it is good. The war scenes are vivid and suspenseful. There is a charming lyric episode when MacMannan camps out in the hills of Northern Ireland. There is mystery in that, although a long flashback traces his childhood in detail, his history stops when he leaves school; however, references throughout the story imply that between then and the beginning of the story proper, he had traveled widely and saved enough money for a free year in London, at the same time maturing without losing the sensitivity he had as a child. He refuses to submit his poetry for publication until it reaches some form of perfection known only to him. There is some sort of symbolism in his efforts to protect little ducks from the cruelty of thoughtless children.

A similar affinity with nature is in *The Native Moment,* an account of the day Simon Green goes to Dublin with a live eel in a pail; because London sales have dropped off, he is seeking an Irish market for the eels that abound in the northern lakes. He gets drunk, sleeps with a prostitute, is disappointed in a meeting with an old friend, and resolves to marry a girl made pregnant by her uncle. Yet so long as he can keep the eel alive, changing its water regularly he survives his crises. *The Ferret Fancier* is a pastoral in which the same kind of sensitive character is given a ferret as a pet when a child.

West has been compared with Joyce and Beckett, and if one does not seek word play or the broadly comic, it is possible to see the comparison. But in his feeling for nature, for the persons and places of the Irish countryside, he adds another ingredient. For all of their accomplishments this century, Irish writers have tended to be parochially Irish, or write mainly of urban settings or rural settings, but rarely both. West has broken through this barrier.

—William Bittner

WEST, Morris (Langlo)

Nationality: Australian. **Born:** Melbourne, Victoria, 26 April 1916. **Education:** St. Mary's College, St. Kilda, Victoria; University of Melbourne, B.A. 1937; University of Tasmania, Hobart. **Military Service:** Served in the Australian Imperial Forces Corps of Signals, in the South Pacific, 1939-43: Lieutenant. **Family:** Married Joyce Lawford in 1953; three sons and one daughter. **Career:** For several years member of the Christian Brothers Order, and taught in New South Wales and Tasmania, 1933 until he left the order before taking final vows, 1939; secretary to William Morris Hughes, former Prime Minister of Australia, 1943; publicity manager, Radio Station 3 DB, Melbourne, 1944-45; founder, later managing director, Australian Radio Productions Pty Ltd., Melbourne, 1945-54; after 1954, film and dramatic writer for the Shell Company and the Australian Broadcasting Network, and freelance commentator and feature writer. Lived in England, 1956-58. **Awards:** National Conference of Christians and Jews Brotherhood award, 1960; James Tait Black Memorial prize, 1960; Royal Society of Literature Heinemann award, 1960; Dag Hammarskjöld prize, 1978; *Universe* prize, 1981. D.Litt.: University of California, Santa Clara, 1969; Mercy College, New York, 1982; University of Western Sydney, Australia, 1993. Fellow, Royal Society of Literature, 1960, and World Academy of Arts and Sciences, 1964; **Member:** Order of Australia, 1985. **Address:** P.O. Box 102, Avalon, New South Wales 2107, Australia.

Publications

Novels

Moon in My Pocket (as Julian Morris). Sydney, Australasian Publishing Company, 1945.

Gallows on the Sand. Sydney, Angus and Robertson, 1956; London, Angus and Robertson, 1958.

Kundu. Sydney and London, Angus and Robertson, and New York, Dell, 1957.

The Big Story. London, Heinemann, 1957; as *The Crooked Road,* New York, Morrow, 1957.

The Second Victory. London, Heinemann, 1958; as *Backlash,* New York, Morrow, 1958.

McCreary Moves In (as Michael East). London, Heinemann, 1958; as *The Concubine,* as Morris West, London, New English Library, 1973; New York, New American Library, 1975.

The Devil's Advocate. London, and New York, Morrow, 1959.

The Naked Country (as Michael East). London, Heinemann, 1960; New York, Dell, 1961.

Daughter of Silence. London, Heinemann, and New York, Morrow, 1961.

The Shoes of the Fisherman. London, Heinemann, and New York, Morrow, 1963.

The Ambassador. London, Heinemann, and New York, Morrow, 1965.

The Tower of Babel. London, Heinemann, and New York, Morrow, 1968.

Summer of the Red Wolf. London, Heinemann, and New York, Morrow, 1971.

The Salamander. London, Heinemann, and New York, Morrow, 1973.

Harlequin. London, Collins, and New York, Morrow, 1974.

The Navigator. London, Collins, and New York, Morrow, 1976.

Proteus. London, Collins, and New York, Morrow, 1979.

The Clowns of God. London, Hodder and Stoughton, and New York, Morrow, 1981.

The World Is Made of Glass. London, Hodder and Stoughton, and New York, Morrow, 1983.

Cassidy. New York, Doubleday, 1986; London, Hodder and Stoughton, 1987.

Masterclass. London, Hutchinson, 1988; New York, St. Martin's Press, 1991.

Lazarus. London, Heinemann, and New York, St. Martin's Press, 1990.

The Ringmaster. London, Heinemann, 1991.

The Lovers. London, Heinemann, and New York, Fine, 1993.

Plays

Daughter of Silence (produced New York, 1961). New York, Morrow, 1962.

The Heretic (produced London, 1970). New York, Morrow, 1969; London, Heinemann, 1970.

The World Is Made of Glass (produced New York, 1982).

Screenplays: *The Devil's Advocate,* 1977; *The Second Victory,* 1984.

Television Plays: *Vendetta,* 1958 (UK).

Other

Children of the Sun. London, Heinemann, 1957; as *Children of the Shadows: The True Story of the Street Urchins of Naples,* New York, Doubleday, 1957.

Scandal in the Assembly: A Bill of Complaints and a Proposal for Reform on the Matrimonial Laws and Tribunals of the Roman Catholic Church, with Robert Francis. London, Heinemann, 1970.

*   *   *

Coming from an unhappy and deprived home, Morris West gained all the training that the Christian Brothers could give him, but turned his back on them just before taking his final vows: a period and a journey that resulted in his first book, *Moon in My Pocket,* notable chiefly for revealing few signs of promise. However, the two novels which followed, *Gallows on the Sand* and *Kundu,* are quite readable, though his first successful book was the non-fictional *Children of the Sun.* This documents the shocking conditions of the lives of Neapolitan slum children, and the selfless work of Father Borelli in attempting to help them.

The Second Victory deals with the ambiguities of administration in Allied-occupied Austria, a country that West came to know well in his search for cheap living as he set about the arduous task of writing while supporting a family. The novel's chief merit, as indeed of all of West's best work, is its pace; it weaknesses are also typical: the characters are not fully realized, the human relationships are unconvincing, and West relies rather heavily on coincidences for his denouement. *The Devil's Advocate* grew out of West's research for *Children of the Sun,* drawing together his interest in Italy and his interest in Catholicism. Over-ambitious, the novel suffers from West's penchant for philosophizing, as he tries to encompass too much material, though the novel's hero-victim is powerfully moving.

At this point in his career, worried about being labeled a Roman Catholic novelist, West commenced writing consciously for a non-Catholic and non-Christian readership. *Daughter of Silence* involves an exploration of the classic dilemma of the law: is it an instrument of public order, or is it an instrument for dispensing absolute justice? *The Shoes of the Fisherman* starts with the death of a Pope, and was launched just a week before the death of Pope John XXIII. Unexpected media and public interest in the novel followed, and, apparently as a result of having tasted the fruits of topicality, West seems to have consistently, from this time on, researched and written stories that had some chance of hitting the headlines. *The Ambassador* is set in South Vietnam before, during, and after the overthrow of President Diem, clearly identifiable in the novel as President Cung; the US Ambassador, Amberley, is fictional. Amberley has recently taken to Zen which makes him vulnerable to self-questioning, a state of being not suited to dealing with the moral crisis in which he finds himself: whether or not to set in motion a series of actions which will lead to Cung's downfall and death. Convinced that the war against the Vietcong cannot be won as long as Cung is in control, Amberley feels he has to decide against Cung, but he is shattered by the decision, and retires to a monastery to try to find peace and wholeness again. The novel was criticized for being flashy and pseudo-profound, and the Ambassador's soul-searching seems to indicate a character a little less robust than most countries would require of their diplomats, but the book renders the Vietnamese scene beautifully, conveying the feel of Saigon and the countryside after 20 years of battering, the war-weariness of the Vietnamese, and the impossibility of the American task.

Summer of the Red Wolf is a deceptively simple and under-estimated novel of a journey to the Western Isles by a man who desires only some peace and quiet, but finds no escape from love and jealousy. Though this novel too has the occasional purple passage, it is written on the whole in a controlled and evocative style, quite superior to the sorts of clichés in which West often indulges—for example in *The Salamander*. This book was remarkable in that it represented West's first (and not very successful) attempt to use symbolism. In *Harlequin* the symbolism begins to be more effective though the book has a strange set of moral notions. Basil Yanko, a self-made computer man, is determined to ruin his aristocratic rival George Harlequin, a merchant banker, by selling him false programs and then accusing him of fraud. The struggle is clearly between culture and California: culture soon draws a circle of journalists, financiers, and terrorists who start murdering people to further its interests. Yanko confesses under torture, and Harlequin (in a gesture no doubt intended to be read as magnanimous) burns the confession—though not the check that came with it! *Proteus* too has an outrageous plot concerning the idealistic and heroic John Spada, head of an international business concern, who leads an underground movement, snatching prisoners of conscience from all over the world. Unfolding at a cracking pace, the novel offers an entertaining and wish-fulfilling fantasy that appeals to the adolescent in all of us.

With the exception of a few specifically Roman Catholic novels, such as *The Shoes of the Fisherman*, West has been secularizing his fiction increasingly over the years. Though there are wider moral and spiritual issues even in the most secular of his work, *The Clowns of God* is his first novel to tackle a specifically religious subject in such a way as to interest those who do not take to Church matters. The Pope has a vision of the end of the world and is given

the task of telling the faithful to prepare for the terrible disasters that presage the Second Coming. Since such a message would destroy teetering public confidence in social and political structures, the awesome bureaucracy of the Vatican moves swiftly to silence the Pope's proposed encyclical, and he is given the choice of abdicating or being certified insane. The novel explores his reasons for abdicating and his struggles and successes in spreading the message. His deep spirituality is rendered beautifully, though West's eschatology and theology seem surprisingly unorthodox.

With admirable consistency West has extended his range, moving from romantic and adventure stories to documentary, faction, history, and what might be called prophecy. His popularity as a novelist has been established for decades. However, with *The World Is Made of Glass* West finally made a bid for recognition as a major literary writer. The book is beautifully written, down to the tiny Europeanisations of style at the appropriate places. The story concerns Jung and Magda, who represent the two poles of modern Western values: one embodies knowledge; the other has outlived the wildest dreams of wealth and sensual variety, and discovered them wanting. This is a many-layered book, which generously repays careful reading.

—Prabhu S. Guptara

WEST, Paul (Noden)

Nationality: American. **Born:** Eckington, Derbyshire, England, 23 February 1930; moved to the United States, 1961; became citizen, 1971. **Education:** The University of Birmingham, 1947-50, B.A. (1st class honours) 1950; Oxford University, 1950-52; Columbia University, New York, M.A. 1953. **Military Service:** Served in the Royal Air Force, 1954-57: flight lieutenant. **Career:** Assistant professor, 1957-58, and associate professor of English, 1959-62, Memorial University of Newfoundland, St. John's. Associate professor, 1962-68, professor of English and comparative literature, and senior fellow, 1968-94, and since 1994, emeritus professor of English, Institute for the Arts and Humanistic Studies, Pennsylvania State University, University Park. Visiting professor of comparative literature, University of Wisconsin, Madison, 1965-66; Pratt Lecturer, Memorial University of Newfoundland, 1970; Crawshaw Professor of Literature, Colgate University, Hamilton, New York, Fall 1972; Virginia Woolf Lecturer, University of Tulsa, Oklahoma, 1973; Melvin Hill Visiting Professor, Hobart and William Smith Colleges, Geneva, New York, Fall 1974; writer-in-residence, Wichita State University, Kansas, 1982, and University of Arizona, Tucson, 1984; visiting professor, Cornell University, Ithaca, New York, 1986. Contributor to *New Statesman,* London, 1954-62. Since 1962 regular contributor to *New York Times Book Review* and *Washington Post Book World.* **Awards:** Canada Council Senior fellowship, 1960; Guggenheim fellowship, 1962; Aga Khan prize (*Paris Review*), 1974; National Endowment for the Arts fellowship, 1980, 1985; Hazlett Memorial award, 1981; American Academy award, 1985; Pushcart prize, 1987; New York Public Library Literary Lion award, 1987; Grand Prix Halpérine-Kaminsky for Best Foreign Book, 1992; Lannan prize, for fiction, 1993; Distinguished Teaching award, Joint Graduate Schools of the Northeast, 1993. **Agent:** Elaine Markson, 44 Greenwich Avenue, New York, New York 10011, U.S.A.

PUBLICATIONS

Novels

A Quality of Mercy. London, Chatto and Windus, 1961.
Tenement of Clay. London, Hutchinson, 1965.
Alley Jaggers. London, Hutchinson, and New York, Harper, 1966.
I'm Expecting to Live Quite Soon. New York, Harper, 1970; London, Gollancz, 1971.
Caliban's Filibuster. New York, Doubleday, 1971.
Bela Lugosi's White Christmas. London, Gollancz, and New York, Harper, 1972.
Colonel Mint. New York, Dutton, 1972; London, Calder and Boyars, 1973.
Gala. New York, Harper, 1976.
The Very Rich Hours of Count von Stauffenberg. New York, Harper, 1980.
Rat Man of Paris. New York, Doubleday, 1986; London, Paladin, 1988.
The Place in Flowers Where Pollen Rests. New York, Doubleday, 1988.
Lord Byron's Daughter. New York, Doubleday, 1989.
The Women of Whitechapel and Jack the Ripper. New York, Random House, 1991.
Love's Mansion. New York, Random House, 1992.
The Tent of Orange Mist. New York, Scribner, 1995.

Short Stories

The Universe and Other Fictions. New York, Overlook Press, 1988.

Uncollected Short Stories

"The Man Who Ate the Zeitgeist," in *London Magazine,* April-May 1971.
"Invitation to a Vasectomy," in *Words* (Boston), Summer 1973.
"The Wet-God's Macho," in *Remington Review* (Elizabeth, New Jersey), Spring 1974.
"The Monocycle," in *Carleton Miscellany* (Northfield, Minnesota), Spring 1975.
"Gustav Holst Composes Himself," in *New Directions 33.* New York, New Directions, 1976.
"Field Day for a Boy Soldier," in *Iowa Review* (Iowa City), Spring 1979.
"Dewey Canyon," in *Conjunctions* (New York), Spring 1982.
"The Destroyer of Delight," in *Paris Review,* Spring 1983.
"He Who Wears the Pee of the Tiger," in *Tri-Quarterly* (Evanston, Illinois), Spring 1984.
"Hopi," in *Kenyon Review* (Gambier, Ohio), Fall 1986.

Poetry

(Poems). Oxford, Fantasy Press, 1952.
The Spellbound Horses. Toronto, Ryerson Press, 1960.
The Snow Leopard. London, Hutchinson, 1964; New York, Harcourt Brace, 1965.

Other

The Fossils of Piety: Literary Humanism in Decline. New York, Vantage Press, 1959.

The Growth of the Novel. Toronto, Canadian Broadcasting Corporation, 1959.
Byron and the Spoiler's Art. London, Chatto and Windus, and New York, St. Martin's Press, 1960.
The Modern Novel. London, Hutchinson, 1963; New York, Hillary House, 1965.
I, Said the Sparrow (autobiography). London, Hutchinson, 1963.
Robert Penn Warren. Minneapolis, University of Minnesota Press, 1964; London, Oxford University Press, 1965.
The Wine of Absurdity: Essays in Literature and Consolation. University Park, Pennsylvania State University Press, 1966.
Words for a Deaf Daughter. London, Gollancz, 1969; New York, Harper, 1970.
Doubt and Dylan Thomas (lecture). St. John's, Newfoundland, Memorial University, 1970.
Out of My Depths: A Swimmer in the Universe. New York, Doubleday, 1983.
Sheer Fiction. New Paltz, New York, McPherson, 1987; *Sheer Fiction II,* 1991; *Sheer Fiction III,* 1994.
Portable People. New York, Paris Review Editions, 1991.
A Stroke of Genius. New York, Viking, 1995.

*

Manuscript Collection: Pattee Library, Pennsylvania State University, University Park.

Critical Studies: By John W. Aldridge, in *Kenyon Review* (Gambier, Ohio), September 1966; *New Literary History* (Charlottesville, Virginia), Spring 1970 and Spring 1976: "The Writer's Situation II" in *New American Review 10,* New York, New American Library, 1970, and "In Defense of Purple Prose," in *New York Times,* 15 December 1985, both by West; interview with George Plimpton, in *Caliban's Filibuster,* 1971; article by Brian McLaughlin, in *British Novelists since 1960* edited by Jay L. Halio, Detroit, Gale, 1983; "Alexander Theroux / Paul West Issue" of *Review of Contemporary Fiction* (Elmwood Park, Illinois), Spring 1991; *Understanding Paul West* by David Madden, Columbia, University of South Carolina Press, 1994.

Paul West comments:

Looking back, I see myself as a late starter who, between thirty and forty, in a sustained and intensive spell of application, set down half a lifetime's pondering and moved from a restless contentment with criticism and fairly orthodox fiction to an almost Fellini-like point of view.

Imagination, as I see it, is an alembic in limbo; it invents, and what it invents has to be added to the sum of Creation—even though nothing imagination invents is wholly its own. I think the realistic novel has served its turn. Fiction has to reclaim some of its ancient privileges, which writers like Lucian and Nashe and Rabelais and Grimmelshausen exploited to the full. I think that only the plasticity of a free-ranging imagination can do justice to late-20th-century man who, as incomplete as man ever was, keeps on arming himself with increasing amounts of data which, as ever, mean nothing at all.

My own fiction I have come to see as—I want it to be—a kind of linear mosaic, which is what my second novel, *Tenement of Clay,* was in a rudimentary form and which two others—*The Very Rich Hours of Count von Stauffenberg* and *Rat Man of Paris*—are in a much more advanced and demanding way. Actually, since both vo-

cabulary and syntax are themselves fictive I don't regard my autobiographical writing as essentially different from my fiction: they're
both part of the mosaic I invent.

*   *   *

For excellent reasons, Camden, the central character in Paul
West's uneven, faintly gothic first novel, *A Quality of Mercy*, feels
that "what was wrong was not that life was too much but that it
was just too many. There was powder in the wind when there should
have been crystals immune from every wind. . . . Life was an unknown and unknowable quantity." Although now, more than 25
years later, West's fiction has grown so rich and apparently diverse
that good readers will be suspicious of generalizations, it is still
possible to see him as an artist working out unexpected variations
on the theme Camden hints at indirectly, the problem of contingency. The final human tragedy, Santayana coolly observes, lies in
our awareness that everything might just as well have been otherwise, in our consciousness that we are accidental creatures gratuitously existing in random places and forms. We might have been
Caesar or we might have been a victim of the Holocaust; and in
times when few can go on believing that angels were destined to
be angels and stones stones, this can be a devastating insight. There
are writers—Sartre, for example—who are in fact appalled by the
idea; there are writers like Wallace Stevens and Iris Murdoch who
are often exhilarated by the inexplicable variety of being; and there
are also a few writers, like Nabokov and West, who veer back and
forth eloquently but uneasily between delight and disgust.

A good many of West's characters live condemned to this awareness of contingency, and to make matters worse, condemned to
exist in exotic and unlovely forms. The archetypal figure is Caliban,
an artist of sorts, howling for justice or at least freedom. In *A Quality of Mercy* there is Camden; in *Tenement of Clay* there are Lazarus,
the defiant dwarf, and his mentor, Papa Nick, failed saint and keeper
of a flophouse whose inmates he tries to reconcile to "the truth of
life," and in helping them to swallow that truth to learn, himself,
the proper "angle of drinking." In *Caliban's Filibuster*, there is Cal,
the failed writer, and in West's finest novel Count von Stauffenberg,
who must go on suffering beyond the grave for his failures. But
clearest of all there is Alley Jaggers. At the start of that novel, Alley, longing for some dimly perceived beauty, is "enclosed and embattled but not closed up and defeated," but by the end he is both
defeated and literally locked away. In *Bela Lugosi's White Christmas* Alley provides what is probably West's bitterest cry of rage:

> I never applied for admission to your so-called universe.
> I was kidnapped into it from a better place . . . where it is
> more *optional* than it is here and now, about the time old
> God Almighty was in a poxdoctoring dither, not sure which
> day was which, and wondering why the bejesus he got
> involved with the whole thing in the first place. . . . My
> own feeling is this, in case you care, want it for your little
> black book: if only He'd kept at it all through the seventh
> day and maybe for all of the next week, we'd all of us be
> better off. It's just the same as saying the world—your so-
> called universe—is just a wee bit carelessly put together,
> fundamentally, firmamentally, fucked up, there being whole
> armies of folks with club feet, hare lips, folks with spines
> open to the fresh air and brains blown up as big as
> hunchback's humps, not to mention the deaf and the blind
> and the straightforward deformed, the slobberers and

slaverers, the daft and St. Vitus dancers, the monkey-faced
and the Siamese twins, folks whose hands grow out from
their shoulders and folks with no especial sex at all. Don't
tell me that twenty sets of quints can make up for all that.
Why, it's like asking a pharmacist for an aspirin and getting
gunpowder instead. Better to scrap it in the first place if he
couldn't get it right or couldn't make up his mind . . .
Whatever blueprint there was, well, it was just a bit
smudged. There ought to be laws against great minds
bringing universes into being just for fun. There: that's AJ's
first book of the bible; I could have done better myself once
I'd gotten the sun to co-operate.

"Blow it all up then?" asks Alley's equally failed analyst, to which
Alley replies, "*I* would, except I'd be loth to give your old universe a helping hand with a dead hand of my own." It is natural
enough to wonder where this view of things comes from, and
tempting to conclude that it grew from West's experiences with his
own deaf, brain-damaged daughter, Mandy. In such cases a parent's
first response is often to ignore the handicap, to make it "go away"—
or to make it go away by making the child go away. But there is
another possible response: to see the handicap as a special kind of
gift, and while trying to eliminate it still to "learn its nature by heart,
as a caution." *Words for a Deaf Daughter* is the astonishing account of West's infinitely patient attempts to understand the world
in which Mandy is enclosed but not, if he can help it, defeated; to
grasp, by imaginative participation, the "super-sensitivity" which
such children often possess. The "caution," that is, the lesson, turns
out to be an awareness of just how arbitrary our definitions of sense
and madness can be. The world West and his readers learn to look
at through Mandy's eyes is a world in which things are seen with
cleansed perception.

Words for a Deaf Daughter is "fact"; *Gala* is "fiction," or, as
West puts it, "the scenario of a wish-fulfillment," in which an adolescent Mandy comes to visit her father in America and finally
speaks to him. The importance of this wish-fulfillment is central to
West's fiction and makes it imperative to remember that something
like Alley's cry of rage is not really West's own cry. For all of the
pain which these characters must endure, West sees that act of expression, of imaginative creation, as an act of defiance and achievement, a substantial addition to the sum of existing things. In a 1971
interview he remarked:

> What a gratuitous universe it is, anyway; what a bloody
> surd . . . what with such defectives as waltzing mice,
> axolotls that should become salamanders but don't, children
> born without one of the human senses. Not that I'm harping
> on the universe's lapses rather than its norms; no, what
> impresses me finally is the scope for error within the
> constancy of the general set-up contrasted with the power
> to imagine things as otherwise—to rectify, to deform. What
> is man? He's the creature imaginative enough to ask that
> question. And although I know that the imagination had
> always to start with something not its own—hasn't
> *complete* underivedness—it can generate much pearl from
> little grit.

In *The Wine of Absurdity* he states even more emphatically that
the imagination is "the only restorative each man has that is entirely his own . . . Imagination, trite and presumptuous as it may
seem to express the fact, is the only source of meaning our lives

can have." Thus imagining Mandy's visit and making her speak is a triumphant act; and having so imagined, West reports that "I can begin sentences with an *I* again, not so much glad or proud as astounded to be here on this planet as myself and not as a peppermint starfish, a thistle, an emu, a bit of quartz. Or a doorknob." It is the artist's imagination, then, which can turn Camden's irritating powder into crystals—if, of course, the artist has anything like West's drive and dazzling verbal resources.

—Elmer Borklund

WHARTON, William

Name is a pseudonym. **Nationality:** American. **Born:** Phildalphia, Pennsylvania, 7 November 1925. **Education:** The University of California, Los Angeles. **Military Service:** Served in the United States Army Infantry, 1943-47. **Family:** Married; four children (one deceased). **Career:** Teacher, 1950-60; since 1960, full-time painter and writer. **Awards:** American Book award, 1980. **Address:** B.P. 18 Port Marly 78, France.

PUBLICATIONS

Novels

Birdy. New York, Knopf, and London, Cape, 1979.
Dad. New York, Knopf, and London, Cape, 1981.
A Midnight Clear. New York, Knopf, and London, Cape, 1982.
Scumbler. New York, Knopf, and London, Cape, 1984.
Pride. New York, Knopf, 1985; London, Cape, 1986.
Tidings. New York, Holt, 1987; London, Cape, 1988.
Franky Furbo. New York, Holt, and London, Cape, 1989.
Last Lovers. New York, Farrar Straus, and London, Granta, 1991.
Wrongful Deaths. London, Granta, 1995.

*

William Wharton comments:

Fantasy and intimacy are two main thrusts of my work. I usually write in the first person, continuous present to eliminate the artificial barrier of time and teller. One, too often, finds fiction told in the third person, past. It is a remnant from the "presidium" of the theatre, separating players, participants, from audience. I want to, as much as possible, dissolve that barrier from my work.

I use multiple print faces whenever possible to minimize referrals (He said, she said, Harry said), or narrative actions inserted merely to establish speaker.

I work from idea, to create stimulating, challenging dialogue with the reader, not merely to entertain. I write only about things I know, so there is often an aura of autobiography in the work. Actually the reader should be seduced to the material, so, in a sense, it is biography.

(1995) I think we are living in the age of the literate illiterate, that is, they have been taught to read, but don't. Probably the responsibility can be placed on schools, TV, and films. The wonder of creating a personal world from words in a dialogue with the writer is being lost. Too bad.

*   *   *

In *Birdy,* William Wharton's first novel, the title character longs to fly. But this is only part of his larger goal. Birdy seeks a way to "know" his life without "knowledge," to move toward a free and unselfconscious life more in tune with the rhythms of the world and nature than the life offered him as a human male. Much of *Birdy* is taken up with meticulous descriptions of the life cycles of pigeons and canaries. It is from living as closely as possible with these birds that Birdy hopes to learn how to live his ideal life. Set in contrast to Birdy is his friend Alfonso, a wrestler who is looking to "pin" the world any way he can to gain revenge or some advantage. Both Birdy and Alfonso are drawn into World War II, and the horror of the war drives Birdy out of his human self. He begins imitating a baby bird waiting to be fed. It is Alfonso, himself damaged—physically, where it can most harm his image of himself—who tries to "feed" Birdy what he needs to know to be willing to become human again, though Alfonso is in no hurry to rejoin the race, either. So much of *Birdy* is taken up with the minute particulars of the lives of the birds that Alfonso's story is only sketchily told and this asymmetry of bird life over human life makes for tedious reading at times.

Birdy's greatest happiness during his time of involvement with his birds comes not from his attempts to fly, but during the nesting time when he helps the young birds survive and learn to fly. Birdy's involvement with the canaries is centered on the female he calls "Birdie." (He names her dark, violent mate "Alfonso.") Birdy identifies strongly with the bird's nurturing side, envies her her female role. This is a thread that is part of several other Wharton characters, most notably the title character in *Scumbler.* Scum, as he calls himself, is an aging American painter living with his family in Paris. Scum at times wishes he were a woman, even telling one young woman to teach him how to love her "as a woman would." Scum rents out a string of apartments, rooms, and shelters he has fixed up. He calls these his "nests." (He also thinks of his paintings as "nests" or "hideouts.") Scum, like Birdy, attempts to recreate his own existence: "I'm always trying to design my life . . . it has to be lived on purpose with purpose." His purpose in life is as much nesting and nurturing (though his own children hardly figure in the novel at all) as it is painting. Like *Birdy, Scumbler* is episodic, almost Quixotic, and relies on a string of epiphanies rather than on any plot resolution for its effect. Both novels end abruptly, with visions of the title characters' personal Utopias.

Dad is Wharton's most conventional novel, the story of three generations of men in a family. The oldest man is dying even while enjoying a period of restored youth; his son watches and thinks of himself as "next in line," while the third, not yet out of his teens, is impatient to get on with his life out from under the cautionary umbrella of his father's wishes for him. The grandfather is a grand character, full of life and honest surprise, but the others are little more than place holders, stock figures used to illustrate the contrasts Wharton wants to establish. *Dad* is Wharton's longest novel, but brings little new insight to the generational conflict.

Set at the beginning of the Battle of the Bulge, *A Midnight Clear* is at once Wharton's most direct and believable novel and that which most clearly illustrates the absurdity of human conflict. Two groups of soldiers, one American, one German, are holed up in a mountain valley. Using a snowman, a scarecrow, and a Christmas tree the two sides communicate their desire for peace with one another. Against all their best efforts death and war descend on the scene. Wharton's always meticulous prose takes on a hardboiled sound in *A Midnight Clear:* "My being squad leader is also another story. It's another story the way *Peter Rabbit* is another story from *Crime and Punishment.*"

In *Pride* Wharton's efforts at using a nonhuman way of life to throw light on human moral questions is much more successful than in *Birdy*. The novel is set in 1938, as the Depression is easing up and unions are working their way into more industries. The young narrator's father is being threatened by union-breakers. The family travels to the sea shore while the father sorts out his thoughts. While they are there a lion escapes from a boardwalk sideshow and kills a man who has tortured him. The double meaning of the word "pride"—honor and the family group—is manipulated by Wharton to parallel the lion's condition with that of the father. The lion, whose pride(s) has been destroyed, goes to his death because he has nowhere else to go. The father gathers his pride(s) and sets off on a course of self-reliance.

—William C. Bamberger

WHITE, Edmund (Valentine III)

Nationality: American. **Born:** Cincinnati, Ohio, 13 January 1940. **Education:** The University of Michigan, Ann Arbor (Hopwood award, 1961, 1962), B.A. 1962. **Career:** Staff writer, *Time*, 1962-79, and editor, *Saturday Review*, 1972-73, both New York; assistant professor, Johns Hopkins University, Baltimore, 1977-79; adjunct professor, Columbia University, New York, 1981-83, and instructor in creative writing, Yale University, New Haven, Connecticut. Executive director, Institute for the Humanities, New York 1981-82. **Awards:** Ingram Merrill grant, 1973, 1978; Guggenheim fellowship, 1983; American Academy award, 1983. **Agent:** Maxine Groffsky, 2 Fifth Avenue, New York, New York 10011, U.S.A.

PUBLICATIONS

Novels

Forgetting Elena. New York, Random House, 1973.
Nocturnes for the King of Naples. New York, St. Martin's Press, 1978; London, Deutsch, 1980.
A Boy's Own Story. New York, Dutton, 1982; London, Picador, 1983.
Caracole. New York, Dutton, 1985; London, Pan, 1986.
The Beautiful Room Is Empty. New York, Knopf, and London, Picador, 1988.

Short Stories

The Darker Proof: Stories from a Crisis, with Adam Mars-Jones. London, Faber, 1987.
Skinned Alive. London, Chatto and Windus, 1995.

Other

When Zeppelins Flew, with Peter Wood. New York, Time/Life, 1969.
The First Man, with Dale Browne. New York, Time/Life, 1973.
States of Desire: Travels in Gay America. New York, Dutton, and London, Deutsch, 1980.
Genet: A Biography. New York, Knopf, and London, Chatto and Windus, 1993.

The Burning Library, edited by David Bergman. New York, Knopf, 1994.
Sketches from Memory: People and Places in the Heart of Our Paris, illustrated by Hubert Sorin. London, Chatto and Windus, 1994.

Editor, with Charles Silverstein, *The Joy of Gay Sex: An Intimate Guide for Gay Men to the Pleasures of a Gay Lifestyle.* New York, Crown, 1977.
Editor, *The Faber Book of Gay Short Fiction.* London, Faber, 1991; Boston, Faber, 1992.
Editor, *The Selected Writings of Jean Genet.* Hopewell, New Jersey, Ecco, 1993.

*   *   *

Edmund White is generally regarded within the gay literary community as one of its premier writers. Along with James Baldwin, Gore Vidal, Andrew Holleran, and Paul Monette, he is one of America's most successful openly gay authors. His voice, like their's, has eloquently articulated the gay community's trajectory from oppression and indecisiveness through self-definition and, finally, toward liberation. His work has often crossed over into the mainstream, winning praise from both critics and readers alike. His reputation is as a highly literate, almost *belletristic,* writer as his fiction seems to move effortlessly between prose and poetry.

White is a prolific writer. His numerous non-fictional works include *States of Desire: Travels in Gay America* and *The Joy of Gay Sex* (co-authored with Dr. Charles Silverstein). Several essays (in particular, "The Artist and AIDS") and magazine pieces have established his reputation as that of an urbane and insightful commentator on contemporary social and political issues.

His five novels, as well as a co-written collection of short stories about AIDS, reveal a love of poetic language. His writing has an erotic, sensuous quality and his images, like his phrases, are extravagant and memorable. An ethos of homoeroticism permeates almost every aspect of his fictional art; it informs his diction and gives shape to his plots. In the opening paragraphs of *Nocturnes for the King of Naples,* for example, images of water and darkness swirl rapturously around images of violence and unrequited love:

> A young man leans with one shoulder against the wall, and his slender body remains motionless against the huge open slab of night sky and night water behind him . . . On the other side of the water, lights trace senseless paths up across hills, lash-marks left by an amateur whip. He turns toward me a look of hope tempered by discretion . . . I have failed to interest him. He turns back to his river as though it were the masterpiece and I the retreating guard.

A central theme in White's work is that of sexual maturation, either individual, as in the case of his male protagonists who must break away from the repressive confines of their bourgeois families in order to express their own sexuality; or collective, as in the case of the American gay community which had to break away from various regimes of oppression in order to find a geographical and linguistic terrain in which to explore its desires. This concern with personal and communal histories informs his two most successful novels to date: *A Boy's Own Story* and its sequel *The Beautiful Room Is Empty* (a third novel in this series is forthcoming). Together these novels, as a sort of homosexual *Bildungsroman,* describe the progression of a young unnamed male narrator from a state of confusion and immaturity to an acceptance of his homosexual identity on the very night that the Stonewall riots rocked the heterosexual establishment in New York City in 1969, thus ushering in the contemporary gay liberation movement. On the night of the riots, White's narrator, finds himself proudly anticipating the day "gays might someday constitute a community rather than a diagnosis."

Because of White's personal concern with the social and political dynamics of the gay community, his novels frequently have an autobiographical element to them. They are usually written in the first-person and parallel personal events in his own life, such as fraught relationships with fathers and male lovers, a desire to have a literary career, and a sardonic outlook on the foibles of middle-class America. His narrators frequently find solace from their own self-internalized condemnation of homosexuality in their writing, as, for example, does the unnamed narrator in *The Beautiful Room Is Empty:* "there was another reason to write: to redeem the sin of my life by turning it into the virtue of art." Many of White's novels are artistic parables and they describe an individual's exploration of his literary and sexual identities.

In White's fiction, art and reality are frequently inseparable. His novels celebrate the polymorphous potentiality of contemporary gay relationships and lifestyles with their capacity to move between friendships and love relationships; and they explore the creative energy found in a minority group's ability to invent its own personal and erotic language and identity amidst overwhelming social and literary oppression.

Because nearly every story in White's collection *Skinned Alive* addresses the topic of AIDS, there is a new tenderness in the relationships, a closeness between the couples involved, and a quiet acceptance of life, threatened as it may be. The raunchy details of sex, which was a constant and vital factor in White's writing, is still present, but muted, and the celebration he writes of most often is the joy of being alive.

—Thomas Hastings, updated by Geoffrey Elborn

WIDEMAN, John Edgar

Nationality: American. **Born:** Washington, D.C., 14 June 1941.
Education: Schools in Pittsburgh; University of Pennsylvania, Philadelphia (Franklin scholar), B.A. 1963 (Phi Beta Kappa); New College, Oxford (Rhodes scholar, 1963; Thouron fellow, 1963-66), B.Phil. 1966; University of Iowa, Iowa City (Kent fellow), 1966-67. **Family:** Married Judith Ann Goldman in 1965; two sons and one daughter. **Career:** Member of the Department of English, Howard University, Washington, D.C., 1965; instructor to associate professor of English, 1966-74, assistant basketball coach, 1968-72, and director of the Afro-American Studies Program, 1971-73, University of Pennsylvania; professor of English, University of Wyoming, Laramie, 1974-85. Since 1986 professor of English, University of Massachusetts, Amherst. Phi Beta Kappa Lecturer, 1976. **Awards:** PEN Faulkner award, 1984; MacArthur fellowship, 1993. D.Litt.: University of Pennsylvania, 1985. **Agent:** Wylie Aitken and Stone Inc., 250 West 57th Street, Suite 2106, New York, New York 10107. **Address:** Department of English, University of Massachusetts, Amherst, Massachusetts 01003, U.S.A.

PUBLICATIONS

Novels

A Glance Away. New York, Harcourt Brace, 1967; London, Allison and Busby, 1986.
Hurry Home. New York, Harcourt Brace, 1970.
The Lynchers. New York, Harcourt Brace, 1973.
Reuben. New York, Holt, 1987; London, Viking, 1988.
Philadelphia Fire. New York, Holt, 1990; London, Viking, 1991.
The Homewood Books. Pittsburgh, University of Pittsburgh Press, 1992.
Damballah. New York, Avon, 1981; London, Allison and Busby, 1984.
Hiding Place. New York, Avon, 1981; London, Allison and Busby, 1984.
Sent for You Yesterday. New York, Avon, 1983; London, Allison and Busby, 1984.

Short Stories

Fever: Twelve Stories. New York, Holt, 1989.
The Stories of John Edgar Wideman. New York, Pantheon, 1992; as *All Stories Are True,* London, Picador, and New York, Vintage, 1993.

Uncollected Short Story

"Concert," in *Georgia Review* (Athens), Fall 1989.

Other

Brothers and Keepers (memoirs). New York, Holt Rinehart, 1984; London, Allison and Busby, 1985.
Fatheralong: A Meditation on Fathers and Sons, Race and Society. New York, Pantheon, 1994.

*

Critical Study: *Blackness and Modernism: The Literary Career of John Edgar Wideman* by James W. Coleman, Jackson, University Press of Mississippi, 1989.

*   *   *

John Edgar Wideman is one of the few novelists who emerged in the Black Power era without sacrificing the demands of art to the persuasions of radical militancy. Possibly as a result of his commitment to craft, his sizeable fictional production has attracted increasing attention and he is now considered as one of the best American writers of the younger generation.

A Glance Away retraces one day in the life of an ex-drug addict. As Eddie Lawson comes back home on Easter Sunday to be reunited with his mother, sister, and girlfriend, he realizes that his possible rebirth is hampered by confrontation with other people's expectations of him: his paralyzed mother, who crushes her daughter under her demanding will, wants Eddie to act as the responsible "man in the family"; and Alice, his lover, refuses to forgive him for his affair with a white girl. In this conflict-ridden and cruel world, Eddie's only stable friendship turns out to be with Brother Small, an albino who is having a homosexual relationship with

Robert Thurley, a professor. Eddie discusses his problems with Thurley, who also suffers from a broken marriage and a castrating mother. Both men try to find their own identity and preserve their dignity in an absurd social environment. Thurley's friendship finally persuades Eddie not to cop out and, at least for the present, not to return to drugs.

Hurry Home has a similar structure, in a narrative that focuses on the consciousness of Cecil Braithwaite, a black law student who works as a janitor. Out of a sense of duty and guilt, he has married the girl who supported him but he has left her on their wedding night. He is befriended and taken to Europe by an artist, Webb, who wants to assuage his own conscience for failing to acknowledge his son by his black mistress. Observing the museums and monuments of Spain and Italy, Cecil admires Western civilization, but he remains torn between two worlds; just as Webb cannot accept his past, Cecil finds it difficult to come to terms with his history and he ends up in Africa, on the threshold of a new discovery. "Home" stands for that yet undefined cultural spring which will welcome him as he comes out of a spiritual no-man's-land. The form of the narrative is appropriately fragmented: memories, relived scenes, diary-like jottings, Esther's letters to Cecil, her attempts to write her autobiography from A to Z with the help of a dictionary make the novel a crisscrossing of events and relationships. The style is one of remarkable sophistication, a poetic texture of echoes, repetitions, and prolonged metaphors.

The Lynchers, unlike *Hurry Home,* is not a reverie. A novel in four voices, it unites a quartet of utterly dissimilar blacks who conspire in a violent attempt to attack the racial oppression in Philadelphia. "Littleman," the crippled activist, sets out, with the help of Saunder Rice and Orin Wilkerson, to murder a white policeman and his black concubine. The plot fails when, angry at being manipulated (or so he feels), Rick kills Wilkerson who had begun to crack. Although the novel is not a work of social realism, the world of the ghetto plays an important role; the street corner solidarity of the males is exemplified by the love which Sweetman feels for Orin, his son. Black history looms large in the background: there is a long account of the practice of lynching in America. But individual destinies are more important, although presented fragmentarily, as the novel forcefully explores the feeling of remorse and guilt in characters who bear similarities to those in Dostoevsky's *The Possessed.*

Damballah is a collection of stories set in the working-class black community of Homewood, in Pittsburgh. The stories focus on Lizabeth, whose faith vacillates as she pays regular visits to her son in jail, on her dignified, affectionate father in "Across the Wide Missouri," and on other descendants of the nearly mythical Sybela Owens (the family genealogy is worked out in "The Beginning of Homewood" and by means of "Begat charts"). From the 1840s to the 1960s, a long line of women carry the tradition. The title of the volume derives from the name of the good serpent through voodoo and at the notion of gathering up the family.

Hiding Place tells the story of Tommy who, having bungled an attempt to hold up a local shopkeeper, is wrongly charged with the murder of his accomplice and flees to Brunston Hill where his grandmother, Bess, lives as a recluse. Their initial diffidence becomes mutual trust and love; authentic dialogue reveals the deep bond established between them, but Tommy is caught and shot by the police before he can return to this haven. Again the theme is the necessity to achieve one's identity by coming to terms with one's heritage, represented by family and community. Unlike Wideman's earlier male characters, all split and lost, Tommy achieves wholeness

at the last moment. The form here is again experimental, but less explicitly so, as the stream-of-consciousness of the "Clement" section is outweighed by the voice of Mother Bess, the repository of oral tradition.

Sent for You Yesterday goes on exploring the Homewood circle and the weight of the past: "Past lives in us, through us. Each of us harbors the spirit of people who walked the earth before we did, and those spirits depend on us for continuing existence just as we depend on their presence to live our lives to the fullest." Black musician Albert Wilkes, back in Homewood after seven years, realizes that the community he once entertained is now fast disappearing. After he is shot by the police, Lucy and Carl, lovers at 13, preserve his stories, rituals and magic, and the community legends, with the help of Brother Tate, a mysterious albino character who plays the dead man's songs on the piano. The main narrative is framed by a "Prologue in heaven" with Brother Tate. Wideman makes more extensive use than ever of the speech cadences, the rhythms and the songs, the idiom and customs of the black community. All his books are steeped in the folk tradition, but *Sent for You Yesterday* is in that respect a major achievement. The narrative is handled perfectly, whether in dream or memory. Voices, tones, inflections are attuned to the nuances of feeling; Afro-American life is celebrated in a sustained, convincing way without any obtrusive message.

A novelist potentially of the same stature as Ernest Gaines, Ishmael Reed, and Toni Morrison, Wideman is also a perceptive literary and social critic. *Brothers and Keepers* is a moving account of the social pressures and individual reactions that have led John Edgar Wideman to the path of success and his brother Robert to jail for murder. The two men appear as the two sides of a coin, the former more restrained and capable of playing the game and using standard English, the latter street-wise and fully absorbed in the vivid parlance and mores of the ghetto. The book reveals also the world of prisons, of brutal, underpaid guards suspicious of any black person, of their utter lack of concern for human qualities in the convicts. Finally, it is a soul-searching reflection on the writer's own distance from the black community and his debt towards it. A mixture of fact and fiction, biography and memoir, it blends social history and the confessional mode. This plea for Robert's parole does not try, says Ishmael Reed, "to reach the nation's conscience but to reach out to his brother to salvage him from grief and waste."

—Michel Fabre

WIEBE, Rudy (Henry)

Nationality: Canadian. **Born:** Fairholme, Saskatchewan, 4 October 1934. **Education:** Alberta Mennonite High School; University of Alberta, Edmonton, 1953-56, 1958-60 (International Nickel graduate fellow, 1958-59; Queen Elizabeth graduate fellow, 1959-60), B.A. 1956, M.A. 1960; University of Tübingen, Germany (Rotary fellow), 1957-58; University of Manitoba, Winnipeg, 1961; University of Iowa, Iowa City, 1964. **Family:** Married Tena F. Isaak in 1958; one daughter and two sons. **Career:** Research officer, Glenbow Foundation, Calgary, 1956; foreign service officer, Ottawa, 1960; high school teacher, Selkirk, Manitoba, 1961; editor, Mennonite Brethren *Herald,* Winnipeg, 1962-63; assistant professor of English, Goshen College, Indiana, 1963-67. Assistant professor, 1967-70, associate professor, 1970-77, and since 1977 professor of English, University of Alberta. **Awards:** Canada Council arts scholarship, 1964, award, 1971, grant, 1977; Lorne Pierce medal, 1987. D.Litt.: University of Winnipeg, Manitoba, 1986. **Member:** Royal Society of Canada, 1987. **Address:** 5315-143 St., Edmonton, Alberta T6H 4E3, Canada.

PUBLICATIONS

Novels

Peace Shall Destroy Many. Toronto, McClelland and Stewart, 1962; Grand Rapids, Michigan, Eerdmans, 1964.
First and Vital Candle. Toronto, McClelland and Stewart, and Grand Rapids, Michigan, Eerdmans, 1966.
The Blue Mountains of China. Toronto, McClelland and Stewart, and Grand Rapids, Michigan, Eerdmans, 1970.
The Temptations of Big Bear. Toronto, McClelland and Stewart, 1973.
The Scorched-Wood People. Toronto, McClelland and Stewart, 1977.
The Mad Trapper. Toronto, McClelland and Stewart, 1977.
My Lovely Enemy. Toronto, McClelland and Stewart, 1983.

Short Stories

Where Is the Voice Coming From? Toronto, McClelland and Stewart, 1974.
Personal Fictions, with others, edited by Michael Ondaatje. Toronto, Oxford University Press, 1977.
Alberta: A Celebration, edited by Tom Radford. Edmonton, Alberta, Hurtig, 1979.
The Angel of the Tar Sands and Other Stories. Toronto, McClelland and Stewart, 1982.

Play

Far as the Eye Can See, with Theatre Passe Muraille. Edmonton, Alberta, NeWest Press, 1977.

Other

A Voice in the Land: Essays by and about Rudy Wiebe, edited by W.J. Keith. Edmonton, Alberta, NeWest Press, 1981.
Playing Dead: A Contemplation Concerning the Arctic. Edmonton, Alberta, NeWest Press, 1989.
Silence: The Word and the Sacred (essays). Waterloo, Ontario, Wilfrid Laurier University Press, 1989.

Editor, *The Story-Makers: A Selection of Modern Short Stories.* Toronto, Macmillan, 1970.
Editor, *Stories from Western Canada: A Selection.* Toronto, Macmillan, 1972.
Editor, with Andreas Schroeder, *Stories from Pacific and Arctic Canada: A Selection.* Toronto, Macmillan, 1974.
Editor, *Double Vision: An Anthology of Twentieth-Century Stories in English.* Toronto, Macmillan, 1976.
Editor, *Getting Here: Stories.* Edmonton, Alberta, NeWest Press, 1977.
Editor, with Aritha van Herk, *More Stories from Western Canada.* Toronto, Macmillan, 1980.

Editor, with Aritha van Herk and Leah Flater, *West of Fiction.* Edmonton, Alberton, NeWest Press, 1982.
Editor, with Bob Beal, *War in the West: Voices of the 1885 Rebellion.* Toronto, McClelland and Stewart, 1985.

*

Manuscript Collection: University of Calgary Library, Alberta.

Critical Studies: *The Comedians: Hugh Hood and Rudy Wiebe* by Patricia A. Morley, Toronto, Clarke Irwin, 1977; *Epic Fiction: The Art of Rudy Wiebe* by W.J. Keith, Edmonton, University of Alberta Press, 1981; articles in *A Voice in the Land,* 1981, and *Journal of Commonwealth Literature* (Edinburgh), 19(1), 1984.

Rudy Wiebe comments:

I believe that the worlds of fiction—story—should provide pleasure of as many kinds as possible to the reader; I believe fiction must be precisely, peculiarly rooted in a particular place, in particular people; I believe writing fiction is as serious, as responsible an activity as I can ever perform. Therefore in my fiction I try to explore the world that I know: the land and people of western Canada; from my particular world view: a radical Jesus-oriented Christianity.

*   *   *

Canada's foremost Mennonite writer, and one of the most innovative writers of historical fiction today, Rudy Wiebe has consistently addressed far-reaching moral, social, and spiritual questions through narratives that focus on specific, rigorously researched, historical moments. Of his seven major novels to date, three—*Peace Shall Destroy Many, The Blue Mountains of China,* and *My Lovely Enemy*—focus directly on Mennonite communities in Canada and elsewhere; the remaining four—*First and Vital Candle, The Temptations of Big Bear, The Scorched-Wood People, A Discovery of Strangers* (and to some extent, *My Lovely Enemy*)—examine the encroachments of white society on traditional Native American, Métis, and Inuit ways of life.

Irrespective of their differences, Wiebe's works are all thematically informed by his radical Mennonite faith, and his plots are all set on motion by what, in the title of his latest work, he calls "a discovery of strangers." Wiebe emphasises the extent to which traditional indigenous and Mennonite communities were separated from the rest of humanity by barriers of space, language, culture, and, most important, religious belief. Day-to-day life in these communities was organised in accordance with religious and moral certainties, which, having solidified into fixed codes of conduct, remained for many years unquestioned. But in each of Wiebe's novels, the boundaries of a closed community are broken open. Traditional cultural practices and religious certainties are either directly challenged from without or are exposed, as a result of external pressures, to threats that were latent within. In either case, a period of spiritual and moral disorientation ensues, in which the protagonist's most fundamental beliefs and values are tested.

Wiebe subjects his readers also to forces of disorientation. As his career progresses, he departs more and more from the conventions of narrative realism. *The Blue Mountains of China, The Temptations of Big Bear, My Lovely Enemy,* and (to a lesser extent) *A Discovery of Strangers* are fragmented, multi-voiced, stylistically heterogenous narratives in which Wiebe "re-writes" existing historical documents and religious texts by inserting them into new verbal contexts. Perhaps because he is so acutely aware that meanings are intertextually generated, Wiebe continually tests the textual foundations of historical and religious certainty.

At times, Wiebe's Mennonite rhetoric intrudes awkwardly into his narratives, as in *First and Vital Candle* or in the end of *The Blue Mountains of China.* But Wiebe in fact addresses this very problem in *First and Vital Candle* and *My Lovely Enemy,* where he dramatises the unsavoury politics of Christian proselytising. Mindful that his readership is not a congregation to be browbeaten, but a diverse community to be drawn into active dialogue with his texts, Wiebe has developed various intricate modes of indirect address. In his middle and later works, his authorial intentions, if evident at all, are refracted in complex ways through the voices and texts of others. These indirect techniques free readers to act consciously as co-creators, rather than as passive recipients or consumers, of the meanings they discover in Wiebe's texts.

Those of Wiebe's novels that are concerned with Canada's indigenous peoples are readable as post-colonial historical metafictions. They dramatize the power of communications technologies—writing, print, photography, telegraphy, film, computers, and other electronic media—as instruments of colonial and neo-imperial domination. Yet in the process of recounting history from various indigenous perspectives, Wiebe also articulates Mennonite religious, social, and ecological values. In so doing, he has attracted accusations of cultural appropriation.

Throughout his writing career, Wiebe has been concerned to explore the mystery and variety of love. After touching rather awkwardly on love and divine grace in *First and Vital Candle,* Wiebe's exploration of love becomes at once more philosophical and more physically explicit, a quality that has provoked objections to his manner of representing women and female sexuality. In *My Lovely Enemy,* passionate sexual love works as a metaphor through which Wiebe revivifies the familiar Christian abstraction of God's redemptive love for humanity. In *A Discovery of Strangers,* Wiebe develops an extended metaphor of woman-as-colonised: as the first Franklin expedition advances across the far northern landscape, the beautiful face of Birdseye, a Tetsot'ine woman of great prophetic wisdom, is progressively corroded by disease. Birdseye's fifteen-year-old daughter, Greenstockings, an object of almost universal male desire, embodies the virgin territory men struggle to possess. Miraculously, given the structural imbalance of power that exists between them, two strangers—the Tetsot'ine woman Greenstockings and the English midshipman Robert Hood—come momentarily together as lovers by free mutual agreement. Although Wiebe does not openly articulate his Mennonite beliefs in *A Discovery of Strangers,* they hover behind his representation of Tetsot'ine understandings of life as a divine gift, and of human beings as spiritually connected with each other and with all living things by sacred ties of mutual physical dependence.

—Penny van Toorn

WILDING, Michael

Nationality: British. **Born:** Worcester, 5 January 1942. **Education:** Royal Grammar School, Worcester, 1950-59; Lincoln College, Oxford (editor, *Isis,* 1962), B.A. 1963, M.A. 1968. **Career:**

Primary school teacher, Spetchley, Worcestershire, 1960; lecturer in English, University of Sydney, 1963-66; assistant lecturer, 1967-68, and lecturer in English, 1968, University of Birmingham. Senior lecturer, 1969-72, reader in English, 1972-93, and since 1993 professor in English and Australian literature, University of Sydney. Visiting professor, University of California, Santa Barbara, 1987; George Watson Visiting Fellow, University of Queensland, St. Lucia, 1989. Editor, *Balcony,* Sydney, 1965-69, and *Tabloid Story,* Sydney, 1972-76; general editor, Asian and Pacific Writing series, University of Queensland Press, 1972-82; director, Wild and Woolley, publishers, Sydney, 1974-79; editor, *Post-Modern Writing,* Sydney, 1979-81; currently Australian editor, *Stand Magazine,* U.K. Since 1971 Australian editor, *Stand,* Newcastle-upon-Tyne. Fellow, Australian Academy of Humanities, 1988. **Awards:** Australia Council senior fellowship, 1978. **Address:** Department of English, University of Sydney, Sydney, New South Wales 2006, Australia.

PUBLICATIONS

Novels

Living Together. St. Lucia, University of Queensland Press, 1974.
The Short Story Embassy. Sydney, Wild and Woolley, 1975.
Pacific Highway. Sydney, Hale and Iremonger, 1982.
The Paraguayan Experiment. Ringwood, Victoria, and London, Penguin, 1985.
This Is for You. Sydney, Angus and Rotokun, 1994.
Book of the Reading. Sydney, Pope, 1994.

Short Stories

Aspects of the Dying Process. St. Lucia, University of Queensland Press, 1972.
The West Midland Underground. St. Lucia, University of Queensland Press, 1975.
Scenic Drive. Sydney, Wild and Woolley, 1976.
The Phallic Forest. Sydney, Wild and Woolley, 1978.
Reading the Signs. Sydney, Hale and Iremonger, 1984.
The Man of Slow Feeling: Selected Short Stories. Ringwood, Victoria, Penguin, 1985.
Under Saturn: Four Stories. Moorebank, New South Wales, Black Swan, 1988.
Great Climate. London, Faber, 1990; as *Her Most Bizarre Sexual Experience,* New York, Norton, 1991.

Plays

Screenplay: *The Phallic Forest,* 1972.

Television Play: *Reading the Signs,* 1988.

Other

Milton's Paradise Lost. Sydney, Sydney University Press, 1969.
Cultural Policy in Great Britain, with Michael Green. Paris, Unesco, 1970.
Marcus Clarke. Melbourne and London, Oxford University Press, 1977.
Political Fictions. London, Routledge, 1980.
Dragons Teeth: Literature and Politics in the English Revolution. Oxford, Clarendon Press, 1987.

The Radical Tradition: Lawson, Furphy, Stead. Townsville, Foundation for Australian Literary Studies, 1993.

Social Visions. Sydney, Sydney Studies in Society and Culture, 1993.

Editor, with Charles Higham, *Australians Abroad: An Anthology.* Melbourne, Cheshire, 1967.

Editor, *Three Tales,* by Henry James. Sydney, Hicks Smith, 1967.

Editor, *Marvell: Modern Judgements.* London, Macmillan, 1969; Nashville, Aurora, 1970.

Editor, with others, *We Took Their Orders and Are Dead: An Anti-War Anthology.* Sydney, Ure Smith, 1971.

Editor, *The Portable Marcus Clarke.* St. Lucia, University of Queensland Press, 1976.

Editor, with Stephen Knight, *The Radical Reader.* Sydney, Wild and Woolley, 1977.

Editor, *The Tabloid Story Pocket Book.* Sydney, Wild and Woolley, 1978.

Editor, *The Workingman's Paradise,* by William Lane. Sydney, Sydney University Press, 1980.

Editor, *Stories,* by Marcus Clarke. Sydney, Hale and Iremonger, 1983.

Editor, with Rudi Krausmann, *Air Mail from Down Under.* Vienna, Gangan, 1990.

Editor, *The Oxford Book of Australian Short Stories.* Melbourne, Oxford University Press, 1994; New York, Oxton, 1995.

*

Critical Studies: "The Short Stories of Wilding and Moorhouse" by Carl Harrison-Ford, in *Southerly* (Sydney), 33, 1973; interviews with Rudi Krausmann, in *Aspect,* 1, 1975, David Albahari, in *Australian Literary Studies* (Hobart, Tasmania), 9, 1980, Kevin Brophy and Myron Lysenko, in *Going Down Swinging,* 3, 1982, Giulia Giuffre, in *Southerly* (Sydney), 46, 1986, and Peter Lewis, in *Stand* (Newcastle-upon-Tyne), 32, 1991; "Recent Developments in Australian Writing, with Particular Reference to Short Fiction" by Brian Kiernan, in *Caliban* (Toulouse), 14, 1977; "The New Novel" by Leon Cantrell, in *Studies in the Recent Australian Novel* edited by K.G. Hamilton, St. Lucia, University of Queensland Press, 1978; "Uncertainty and Subversion in the Australian Novel," in *Pacific Moana Quarterly* (Hamilton, New Zealand), 4, 1979, and "Character and Environment in Some Recent Australian Fiction," in *Waves* (Downsview, Ontario), 7, 1979, both by Ken Gelder; "Laszlo's Testament, or Structuring the Past and Sketching the Present in Contemporary Short Fiction," in *Kunapipi 1* (Aarhus, Denmark), 1979, "A New Version of Pastoral," in *Australian Literary Studies* (Hobart, Tasmania), 11, 1983, and "Paradise, Politics, and Fiction: The Writing of Michael Wilding," in *Meanjin* (Melbourne), 45, 1986, all by Bruce Clunies Ross; "The New Writing, Whodunnit?" by G.M. Gillard, in *Meanjin* (Melbourne), 40, 1981; "Michael Wilding: Post-Modernism and the Australian Literary Heritage" by Hans Hauge, in *Overland* (Melbourne), 96, 1984; "Lost and Found: Narrative and Description in Michael Wilding's 'What It Was Like, Sometimes'" by Simone Vauthier, in *Journal of the Short Story in English* (Angers, France), 12, 1989; *The New Diversity: Australian Fiction 1970-1988* by Ken Gelder and Paul Salzman, Fitzroy, Victoria, McPhee Gribble, 1989; "Koka Kola Kulture" by Don Graham in *Southwest Review* (Dallas, Texas), 78, Spring 1993; "Frank Moorhouse and Michael Wilding and Internationalism" by Frank Parigi, in *Antipodes* (Austin, Texas) 8, June 1994; "Talking with

Michael Wilding" by Nadezda Obradovic, in *Antipodes* (Austin, Texas) 8, June 1994.

*   *   *

Michael Wilding is one of a "new generation" of writers in Australia who began publishing in the early 1970s. Impelled to political action by Australia's involvement in the Vietnam war, Wilding has also protested in his writings against censorship, conservative social values, and a subservience to American cultural imperialism.

In the first of his collections of stories *Aspects of the Dying Process,* an English persona is attracted and bemused in several stories by the hedonistic Sydney youth culture which he encounters. The title suggests the "dying" as an immigrant changes color with his new culture and extinguishes to some degree the old, and is a pun also on his sexual initiation rites. D.H. Lawrence and Henry James have left their mark on the writer's early style, in its rendering of the impulses and withdrawals of an observer who is not yet a participant in the new life. *The West Midland Underground,* Wilding's second volume of stories, has a free-wheeling variety of narrative modes and settings which include England, Greece, the United States, and Australia. In "Canal Run" a boy's claustrophobic world is evident in images of the English industrial midlands; at the center of frustration is a thwarted sexuality: "Thinking back it is hard to see exactly when one's consciousness of sex began and became a desire for, a whole youth's looking for, fulfillment. Then, though, there was only a strong sense of sin and shame and dirt; no lyricism, and none of the hatred. It was wrong and furtive and C stream; which was another way of saying lower class." Most stories in *The Phallic Forest* energetically flout "normal" sexual and social mores, or celebrate alternatives; and in a later collection, *Reading the Signs,* a more reflective consciousness draws on a background of class awareness for sharp and penetrating observations of appearance and behavior. In Wilding's later work the term "Midlander" connotes the circumscribed spirit, against which all his writings rebel.

Wilding's first novel, *Living Together,* relates the exploits, and fantasies, of young men and women cohabiting in inner suburban Sydney. The traumas of Martin, Paul, and Ann (second names are unimportant) are related with wit and verve as they paint and decorate their house and have sex, joints, or drink with neighbors and visitors. (In a later novel, a character comments that the Pill introduced "a whole new anthropology" for the writer.) The strongest character is the irenic Ann, who, after leaving her outrageously chauvinist partner Martin half way through the novel, returns at the end to give his life some shape and order. The men are weaker and more ambivalent. Paul, the author's alter ego, has taken his sexual apprenticeship, but is unsure of his future directions. Martin's scenario of the house as a sort of "cultural center" is never realized; its most memorable visits are two female grotesques, the ever-ready next-door neighbor Mrs. Bilham, and Gretel Mann, of "cavernous appetite," who helps Paul out of his innocence. Late in the novel Paul has decided that "Change is the only aphrodisiac." The literary progenitor of this urban comedy of the 1970s is perhaps Thomas Love Peacock, whose miscellaneous parties of odd characters in English country houses also mix satire and romance, but where the treatment of sex is much more circumspect.

Wilding's second novel, *The Short Story Embassy,* and his third, *Pacific Highway,* contain insights into the literary process. The "Embassy," situated "halfway to the north" on Australia's east coast, approximates to the "cultural center" envisaged by Martin in *Liv-*

ing Together. The juxtaposition of culture and nature is a source of comedy, as in this version of "pot pastoral": "The people traveling up from the south rested there and stripped off and got their bodies brown before going on to the full north. They lay around by creeks and wove garlands of bush flowers around each other. They made daisy-chains around their necks and twined poppies in their pubic hairs. The cows came and gazed on them and licked them and they licked each other".

Here, as elsewhere, Wilding is both lyrical and amused; he celebrates the new freedoms and is affectionately ironic about them. While whimsy sometimes predominates, a sharper irony is evident in observations about characters' literary outlooks and values. The middle-aged Laszlo, for instance, possessively jealous of his lover, Valda, puzzles over his generation of radicals, who read Tom Paine, while hers has been "turned on" to astrology. To Valda, Laszio seems to use books as "leaning posts." *The Short Story Embassy* quizzically examines the "new" experimental literature of process and locates its enemy as the Thought Police. But this is Kafka without the menace. The visitor, Tichborne, who mysteriously leaves the Embassy, may be one of the enemy (his name is a reminder of the famous Tichborne impersonation case), but his departure lacks consequence. There is paranoia aplenty in this novel but "plot" in the conventional sense is missing.

The pastoral element is paramount in *Pacific Highway.* In some respects it is a 1980s version of Vance Palmer's *The Passage* (1930), in which a rural holiday retreat on the Pacific Ocean is destroyed by "progress" and "development." But the tone and style of the two novels differ markedly. In *Pacific Highway* the attempt by the narrator and his girlfriend, Lily, to recreate an idyllic world of innocence among friends who will live off the land, re-cycling their waste, is confronted by a censorious, authoritarian regime. This household (two young women and a man), is differentiated from other "hippies" by being middle-class and theoretical: escapees from the midlands. Confrontations with the wider society are often presented as wry comedy: for instance, how does a household with idealistic communist notions rationalize its employment of a cleaning woman? Another dimension is the love story—of the narrator and Lily—which contains some fine lyrical passages.

A search for utopia, implicit elsewhere, is the explicit theme of Wilding's fourth novel, *The Paraguayan Experiment.* The novel is a new departure for Wilding, who uses historical documents in his firm narration of the story of the New Australia movement. Disillusioned with the economic depression and social repression in Australia in the 1890s, William Lane led a group of 400 men, women, and children to found a New Australia in Paraguay. Using letters (especially Lane's), memos, and official documents, Wilding builds a lively account of this historic precursor to the idealistic communalists of the 1970s. Anachronisms in dialogue and commentary are evident, but these seem deliberate: in certain respects, which Wilding does not wish to conceal, this was a parable for the 1980s. Hence many of the issues which have obsessed this writer—the creation of alternative human settlements, the clash between individual and group needs, sexual politics, the use of drugs—are evident in this tale of a previous era in Australian history. In form and style, this novel shows Wilding's continuing interest in literary experimentation and is rich in humor, fantasy, and sharp social observation.

—Bruce Bennett

WILLIAMS, John A(lfred)

Nationality: American. **Born:** Jackson, Mississippi, 5 December 1925. **Education:** Central High School, Syracuse, New York; Syracuse University, A.B. 1950. **Military Service:** Served in the United States Navy, 1943-46. **Family:** Married 1) Carolyn Clopton in 1947 (divorced), two sons; 2) Lorrain Isaac in 1965, one son. **Career:** Member of the public relations department, Doug Johnson Associates, Syracuse, 1952-54, and Arthur P. Jacobs Company; staff member, CBS, Hollywood and New York, 1954-55; publicity director, Comet Press Books, New York, 1955-56; publisher and editor, *Negro Market Newsletter,* New York, 1956-57; assistant to the editor, Abelard-Schuman, publishers, New York, 1957-58; director of information, American Committee on Africa, New York, 1958; European correspondent, *Ebony* and *Jet* magazines, 1958-59; announcer, WOV Radio, New York, 1959; Africa correspondent, *Newsweek,* New York, 1964-65. Regents' Lecturer, University of California, Santa Barbara, 1972; Distinguished Professor of English, LaGuardia Community College, City University of New York, 1973-78; visiting professor, University of Hawaii, Honolulu, Summer 1974, Boston University, 1978-79, and New York University, 1986-87. Professor of English, 1979-90, Paul Robeson Professor of English, 1990-94, and since 1994 professor emeritus, Rutgers University, Newark, New Jersey. Bard Center Fellow, Bard College, 1994-95. Member of the Editorial Board, *Audience,* Boston, 1970-72; contributing editor, *American Journal,* New York, 1972. **Awards:** American Academy grant, 1962; Syracuse University Outstanding Achievement award, 1970; National Endowment for the Arts grant, 1977; Rutgers University Lindback award, 1982; Before Columbus Foundation award, 1983. Litt.D.: Southeastern Massachusetts University, North Dartmouth, 1978. **Agent:** Barbara Hogenson Agency, 19 W. 44th St., New York, New York 10036. **Address:** 693 Forest Avenue, Teaneck, New Jersey 07666, U.S.A.

PUBLICATIONS

Novels

The Angry Ones. New York, Ace, 1960; as *One for New York,* Chatham, New Jersey, Chatham Bookseller, 1975.
Night Song. New York, Farrar Straus, 1961; London, Collins, 1962.
Sissie. New York, Farrar Straus, 1963; as *Journey Out of Anger,* London, Eyre and Spottiswoode, 1968.
The Man Who Cried I Am. Boston, Little Brown, 1967; London, Eyre and Spottiswoode, 1968.
Sons of Darkness, Sons of Light. Boston, Little Brown, 1969; London, Eyre and Spottiswoode, 1970.
Captain Blackman. New York, Doubleday, 1975.
Mothersill and the Foxes. New York, Doubleday, 1975.
The Junior Bachelor Society. New York, Doubleday, 1976.
! Click Song. Boston, Houghton Mifflin, 1982.
The Berhama Account. Far Hills, New Jersey, New Horizon Press, 1985.
Jacob's Ladder. New York, Thunder's Mouth Press, 1987.

Other

Africa: Her History, Lands, and People. New York, Cooper Square, 1962.

The Protectors (on narcotics agents; as J. Dennis Gregory), with Harry J. Anslinger. New York, Farrar Straus, 1964.

This Is My Country, Too. New York, New American Library, 1965; London, New English Library, 1966.

The Most Native of Sons: A Biography of Richard Wright. New York, Doubleday, 1970.

The King God Didn't Save: Reflections on the Life and Death of Martin Luther King, Jr. New York, Coward McCann, 1970; London, Eyre and Spottiswoode, 1971.

Flashbacks: A Twenty-Year Diary of Article Writing. New York, Doubleday, 1973.

Minorities in the City. New York, Harper, 1975.

If I Stop I'll Die: The Comedy and Tragedy of Richard Pryor, with Dennis A. Williams. New York, Thunder's Mouth Press, 1991.

Flashbacks 2: A Diary of Article Writing. Westport, Connecticut, Orange Ball Press, 1991.

Editor, *The Angry Black.* New York, Lancer, 1962.

Editor, *Beyond the Angry Black.* New York, Cooper Square, 1967.

Editor with Charles F. Harries, *Amistad I* and *II.* New York, Knopf, 2 vols., 1970-71.

Editor, with Gilbert H. Muller, *The McGraw Hill Introduction to Literature.* New York, McGraw Hill, 1985.

Editor, with Gilbert H. Muller, *Bridges: Literature Across Cultures.* New York, McGraw Hill, 1994.

Editor, *Ways In: Approaches to Reading and Writing about Literature.* New York, McGraw Hill, 1994.

Editor, *Introduction to Literature 2/e.* New York, McGraw Hill, 1995.

*

Manuscript Collections: Syracuse University, New York; Rochester University, New York.

Critical Studies: *America as Seen by a Black Man* by Robert T. Haley, unpublished thesis, San Jose State College, California, 1971; "The Art of John A. Williams" by John O'Brien, in *American Scholar* (Washington, D.C.), Summer 1973; *The Evolution of a Black Writer: John A. Williams* by Earl Cash, New York, Third Press, 1974; *American Fictions 1940-1980* by Frederick R. Karl, New York, Harper, 1983; *John A. Williams* by Gilbert H. Muller, Boston, Twayne, 1984; article by James L. de Jongh, in *Afro-American Fiction Writers after 1955* edited by Thadious M. Davis and Trudier Harris, Detroit, Gale, 1984.

John A. Williams comments:

I think art has always been political and has served political ends more graciously than those of the muses. I consider myself to be a political novelist and writer to the extent that I am always aware of the social insufficiencies which are a result of political manipulation. The greatest art has always been social-political, and in that sense I could be considered striving along traditional paths.

*   *   *

James Baldwin was to remind us of the descent one must make to excavate history in *Just above My Head*. And it is similar to the theme the critic Addison Gayle deals with in *The Way of the New World:* "It is to history that one looks for the best example of modern black men; there that the falsity of the old images, stereotypes, and

metaphors can be seen. History, then, rewritten and corrected, holds the key to success in the war against the imagists." Within the framework of this critical thinking John A. Williams wages war against the imagists, merging history into fiction to create new dimensions for the writings of Black novelists and fresh images for Black readers to digest.

Throwing off the image of the black protagonist struggling for confirmation of his self-worth, Williams creates, in *The Man Who Cried I Am,* Max Reddick, a black man who becomes a "success" in the white world who asks himself "was it worth what it cost?" Reddick's final confirmation of "self" comes not from the white world, but from himself, "All you ever want to do is remind me that I am black. But, goddamn it, I also am," he says.

The need for this new direction in black writing has been documented; however, few writers have matched Williams in destroying illusions of the black man as a victim subjugated by the pressures of racial injustice in the Western world. It is without uncertainty that Williams's protagonists know history, and understand its function. In *Sons of Darkness, Sons of Light* Eugene Browning mulls over the advantages of knowing his past: "Remember when we began to discover Negro history—twenty years old and blam there it was, and it was sort of like peeling an onion, one thing leading to another, translucent, slippery, thin . . . one morning I woke up and the enormity of what's been done to us was resting like a ball of badly digested lead in my stomach, but it got down, it went down, and I couldn't pretend anymore that it had meaning for me. Not only for me but for all the Negroes out there." But it is with reason and without anger, that Browning, after coming to the conclusion that civil rights and freedom marches would not bring justice to blacks, employs Mafia tactics in the assassination of a policeman guilty of killing a 16-year-old black boy. "You could work . . . with all your heart and what was left of your soul, but you also had to know finally . . . that you had to obtain your goals by the same means as Chuck."

Williams's themes are the heightened level of group consciousness, self-resolve, and resourcefulness needed by blacks to eliminate racial injustices, through as Browning states, "Secrecy, apparent non-involvement, selected acts. That was the only answer." Williams leads us to the doorway of creating new values for the good of the group while unraveling black people from a web of images, and stereotypes. "It is most imperative," Williams writes, "that the Negro be seen and seen as he is; the morality of the situation will then resolve itself, and truth, which is what we all presumably are after, will then be served." Williams does this well in leading us to the descent.

—Brenda R. Ferguson

WILLIS, Connie

Nationality: American. **Born:** Constance Elaine, Denver, Colorado, 31 December 1945. **Education:** University of Northern Colorado, B.A. in English and elementary education. **Family:** Married Courtney Wayne Willis, 1967; one daughter. **Career:** Elementary school teacher, 1967-68, and junior high teacher, 1968-69, Branford, Connecticut, public schools. **Awards:** Nebula award, 1982, and Hugo award, 1982, both for *Fire Watch;* 1982 for "A Letter from the Clearys"; Nebula award, 1988, and Hugo award, 1988, both for *The Last of the Winnebagos; Campbell Memorial award for best science fiction novel, 1988, for Lincoln's Dreams;* Nebula award, 1989 for "At the Rialto," Nebula award, 1992, Locus award, 1992, and Hugo award, 1993, both for "Even the Queen"; Nebula award, 1992, Locus award, 1992, and Hugo award, 1993, both for *Doomsday Book;* Locus award, 1993, for *Impossible Things,* 1993, for "Close Encounter"; Hugo award, 1994, for "Death on the Nile." **Agent:** Ralph Vicinanza, 111 Eighth Ave., Suite 1501, New York, New York 10011, U.S.A. **Address:** 1716 Thirteenth Ave., Greeley, Colorado 80631, U.S.A.

Publications

Novels

Water Witch, with Cynthia Felice. New York, Ace Berkeley, 1980.
Lincoln's Dreams. New York, Bantam, 1986.
Light Raid, with Cynthia Felice. New York, Ace Berkeley, 1988.
Doomsday Book. New York, Bantam, and Hodder and Stoughton, 1992.
Impossible Things. New York, Bantam, 1994.
Uncharted Territory. New York, Bantam, and Hodder and Stoughton, 1994.
Remake. New York, Bantam, 1995.

Short Stories

Fire Watch. New York, Bluejay, 1985.

*

Connie Willis comments:

I first fell in love with science fiction at age thirteen, when I read Robert A. Heinlein's *Have Space Suit, Will Travel.* That's not unusual. Science fiction and adolescence have a lot in common: love of adventure, love of ideas, boundless enthusiasm for the universe. For many readers, it's only an infatuation, but for me it has turned into a lifelong love affair, I think because the medium of science fiction is ideal for the stories I want to tell and the themes I want to write about.

I find that looking at things obliquely, through the disguise of other places, other times, cuts through not only the reader's prejudices and defenses but my own and makes it possible to look clearly at our own world, our own faces. And the conventions of science fiction—Martians, time travel, robots—carry within them the themes that matter most to me. Time travel, especially, with its built-in resonances of grief and loss and regret, I could write about forever. After all these years, I still come to science fiction with that same shock of joy and recognition that I did at thirteen.

*   *   *

Widely recognized by her peers and fans alike as an excellent short story writer, Connie Willis, a Hugo and Nebula winner, is also an innovative novelist. Some of her recent novels merge other literary forms into a science-fiction framework with considerable success. Indeed, much of Willis's mature work falls into that rare and narrow range between excellent and brilliant.

A 1989 story, "At the Rialto," speculates about physics theories and is a good example of effective humor, a device Willis uses consistently and that rises here from a certain skepticism about academic conferences. When Dr. Ruth Baringer, determined to make the most of the annual meeting of the International Congress of Quantum Physicists, checks into Hollywood's Rialto Hotel, she discovers that she might as well be in a parallel universe. The hotel's staff as well as its equipment malfunctions constantly; no academic session seems to be located in its assigned room; prominent speakers fail to appear; and conference-goers persist in slipping off to see various Tinsel Town sights, which are, like the hotel, disorganized, confusing, and chaotic. Having tried hard to be a conscientious conference-goer, Ruth Baringer finally joins colleagues in escapism, Hollywood-style: They go to the movies.

Connie Willis's earliest novels, *Water Witch* and *Light Raid,* were written with Cynthia Felice. But *Lincoln's Dreams,* written without a collaborator, moved Willis—who points out in the foreword that the Civil War continues to haunt America's dreams and will do so until its true meaning is perceived—into altogether different territory. Here, she combines speculation about the nature of time and the quest motif with elements of the historical novel. Jeff Johnson, who does research about the Civil War for a famous historical novelist, becomes fascinated with Annie, a young woman who dreams vividly and accurately about events in the War Between the States, about which she has no conscious knowledge. Together, the two travel to various wartime sites, hoping that understanding will bring Annie some peace. Willis's quiet, matter-of-fact tone supports the novel's violence-filled superstructure very well and also lends veracity to the strong bond between Jeff and Annie and the historical characters who so affect their lives. Jeff's affection for Annie is particularly well depicted and is one of the most important elements that allow the reader to accept the deeply touching yet unsentimental conclusion.

Doomsday Book, which combines science fiction with the historical novel, is perhaps Willis's finest novel to date. In its dual story lines, a group of 21st-century academic researchers is compared to the inhabitants of a small 14th-century English village. As each community deals with terrifying crises, Willis vividly demonstrates that many basic human concerns are equally compelling at any time in history. The stories of the two groups are united by the adventures of Kirvin, a student who travels through time into the Middle Ages in order to pursue on-site historical research. Despite all the research team's careful calculations, one small slip sends her into the Plague Year. Ironically, Kirvin's real-time contemporaries are also beset by a deadly epidemic. Willis generates enormous suspense, not only about the possibility of Kirvin's return to her own era but also about the fates of many other wonderfully realized characters. Readers are absolutely convinced of Kirvin's growing attachment to the villagers, and her complex relationship with the local priest is especially interesting, as is the growing affectionate respect between an elderly researcher, Dunworthy, and an adolescent visitor, Colin, who team up for a knightly quest. Willis's exploration of various loving, committed friendships as well as her depictions of the quiet heroism displayed by many 14th- and 21st-century characters creates a hopeful tone despite the grim realism of the plague scenes. This novel is a major achievement.

Though less powerful than either *Lincoln's Dreams* or *Doomsday Book,* both *Uncharted Territory* and *Remake* are sound novelettes. Set in the indeterminate future, *Uncharted Territory* transports some elements of the western genre to another planet and is an interesting exploration of comradeship and sexuality. *Remake* is set in a Hollywood rife with bribery, drugs, and corruptive power struggles. It takes place during a future time when heavily censored films have been purged of almost all interest and impact in order to "protect" the populace, and it raises serious questions of honor, personal responsibility, and devotion to one's craft. Film editing and tap dancing are the surprisingly effective metaphors Willis uses to make her points.

Never sacrificing pace or tension, never belaboring her themes, Connie Willis nevertheless makes acute observations about the human condition, challenging the thoughtful reader even as she entertains her.

—Jane S. Bakerman

WILSON, A(ndrew) N(orman)

Nationality: British. **Born:** Stone, Staffordshire, 27 October 1950. **Education:** Rugby School, Warwickshire, 1964-69; New College, Oxford (Chancellor's Essay prize, 1971; Ellerton Theological prize, 1975), 1969-72, M.A.; studied for priesthood, 1973-74. **Family:** Married 1) Katherine Duncan-Jones in 1971 (divorced 1990), two daughters; 2) Ruth Guilding. **Career:** Assistant master, Merchant Taylors' School, London, 1975-76; lecturer, St. Hugh's College, Oxford, 1976-82, and New College, 1977-80; literary editor, the *Spectator,* London, 1981-83. Presenter, *Eminent Victorians* television series, 1989. **Awards:** Rhys Memorial prize, for fiction, 1978, for biography, 1981; Maugham award, 1981; Arts Council National Book award, 1981; Southern Arts prize, 1981; W.H. Smith Literary award, 1983; Whitbread prize, for biography, 1988. Fellow, Royal Society of Literature, 1981. **Agent:** Peters Fraser and Dunlop, 503-504 The Chambers, Chelsea Harbour, Lots Road, London SW10 0XF. **Address:** 21 Arlington Rd., London NW1 7ER, England.

PUBLICATIONS

Novels

The Sweets of Pimlico. London, Secker and Warburg, 1977; New York, Penguin, 1989.
Unguarded Hours. London, Secker and Warburg, 1978.
Kindly Light. London, Secker and Warburg, 1979.
The Healing Art. London, Secker and Warburg, 1980; New York, Penguin, 1988.
Who Was Oswald Fish? London, Secker and Warburg, 1981; New York, Penguin, 1988.
Wise Virgin. London, Secker and Warburg, 1982; New York, Viking Press, 1983.
Scandal; or, Priscilla's Kindness. London, Hamish Hamilton, 1983; New York, Viking, 1984.
Gentlemen in England: A Vision. London, Hamish Hamilton, 1985; New York, Viking, 1986.
Love Unknown. London, Hamish Hamilton, 1986; New York, Viking, 1987.
Incline Our Hearts. London, Hamish Hamilton, 1988; New York, Viking, 1989.
A Bottle in the Smoke. London, Sinclair Stevenson, 1989; New York, Viking, 1990.
Daughters of Albion. London, Sinclair Stevenson, 1991; New York, Viking, 1992.

The Vicar of Sorrows. London, Sinclair Stevenson, 1993; New York, Norton, 1994.

Poetry

Lilibet: An Account in Verse of the Early Years of the Queen until the Time of Her Accession. London, Blond and Briggs, 1984.

Other (for children)

Stray. London, Walker Books, 1987; New York, Orchard, 1989.
The Tabitha Stories. London, Walker Books, 1988; as *Tabitha,* New York, Orchard, 1989.
Hazel the Guinea-Pig. London, Walker Books, 1989; Cambridge, Massachusetts, Candlewick Press, 1992.

Other

The Laird of Abbotsford: A View of Sir Walter Scott. Oxford and New York, Oxford University Press, 1980.
The Life of John Milton. Oxford and New York, Oxford University Press, 1983.
Hilaire Belloc. London, Hamish Hamilton, and New York, Atheneum, 1984.
How Can We Know? An Essay on the Christian Religion. London, Hamish Hamilton, and New York, Atheneum, 1985.
The Church in Crisis, with Charles Moore and Gavin Stamp. London, Hodder and Stoughton, 1986.
Landscape in France, photographs by Charlie Waite. London, Elm Tree, 1987; New York, St. Martin's Press, 1988.
Penfriends from Porlock: Essay and Reviews 1977-1986. London, Hamish Hamilton, 1988; New York, Norton, 1989.
Tolstoy: A Biography. London, Hamish Hamilton, and New York, Norton, 1988.
Eminent Victorians. London, BBC Publications, 1989; New York, Norton, 1990.
C.S. Lewis: A Biography. London, Collins, and New York, Norton, 1990.
Against Religion. London, Chatto and Windus, 1990.
Jesus. London, Sinclair Stevenson, 1992.
The Rise and Fall of the House of Windsor. London, Sinclair Stevenson, and New York, Norton, 1993.

Editor, *Ivanhoe,* by Scott. London, Penguin, 1982.
Editor, *Dracula,* by Bram Stoker. Oxford, Oxford University Press, 1983.
Editor, *Essays by Divers Hand 44.* Woodbridge, Suffolk, Boydell and Brewer, 1986.
Editor, *The Lion and the Honeycomb: The Religious Writings of Tolstoy.* London, Collins, and New York, Harper, 1987.
Editor, *John Henry Newman: Prayers, Poems, and Meditations.* London, SPCK, 1989; New York, Crossroad, 1990.
Editor, *The Faber Book of Church and Clergy.* London, Faber, 1992.
Editor, *The Faber Book of London.* London, Faber, 1994.

*   *   *

Two of A.N. Wilson's novels, *Wise Virgin* and *The Healing Art,* rise above the level of farcical satire, often badly written (from *Scandal:* "Derek could be *heard* implanting a slobbery kiss on a *powdered* cheek" [italics mine]) in the facile style of the clever public schoolboy who is afraid of showing emotion and being accused of sentimentality, and must therefore at all costs be flippant about what most preoccupies him. Although *Scandal* is the worst, *The Sweets of Pimlico, Unguarded Hours,* and *Kindly Light* are scant improvements, and *Who Was Oswald Fish?* is only a little better. The author suffers from the cultivation of a not-so-keen "satirical vein . . . in place of a sense of humour." What saves him from dismissal is the undoubted intelligence at work and the flashes, even in the 4th-rate novels, of genuine insight into the acerbic personality. All is not lost if a reader can come across illuminating phrases such as the above from *Wise Virgin.*

More than any other recent writer, Wilson seems actually to be trying to overcome that aspect of his personality which has been soured by an innately English and painfully inane upbringing within the public school system and the institution of the Church of England, a system and an institution undoubtedly deserving of satire. But satire only works powerfully after the satirist has seen clearly his position vis-à-vis what he is satirising, and Wilson does not always see it because he is too much part of it. He is trapped by the traditions he purports to satirise, and as a result the satire has an unpleasant hysterical edge to it as well as the archness of a teenager who dares not look anyone in the eye and say, I believe . . . in God, in love, in laughter, in life, in people . . . in the necessity for a moral scheme of things. And yet that is what Wilson wants to do, he wants to take a moral stand. When he does, as in *Wise Virgin* and *The Healing Art,* the satire is transformed into humour and we have a sympathetic comic writer confronting and exploring themes novelists have always explored: the effect of one personality on another, the strangeness of religious belief, the need for morality, the almost imperceptible way in which love can effect the largest and most fundamental changes, the nature of that love, the action of grace in a world that no longer believes in the existence of grace.

Wilson's particular talent is to capture the moment of kindness. That people can and, given a chance, will be simply kind to one another is for Wilson miraculous, and when he allows his characters and his readers to stand in front of kindness and remain in awe of it without fidgeting or snickering, he achieves some moving writing that remains funny. In *Wise Virgin,* for example, Giles, the blind father of Tibba and lover of his research assistant Louise Agar, is constantly battling against tetchiness, snobbism, acerbity. Louise and Giles have a growing complex relationship in which what one may wish to call, cautiously, love and a mutual need and desire for companionship are inextricably bound. At the end of the novel Louise and her mother come to Giles for tea on Christmas Day, thanks to the machinations of Tibba, the wise virgin who acts not only out of the sourness of the clever adolescent but also out of a selfishness that is necessary for her to free herself from her father's dependence on her and her own dependence on him. This is the first meeting between Giles and Louise's mother, whom Tibba would have called "vulgar." When they meet, the mother thinks Giles is a pansy, makes snide comments to herself about the absence of a "nice settee," does not want to linger and miss "Christmas Night with the Stars": she has her own nastiness. And yet from the proprieties between strangers and the gratuitous kindness of the mother emerge moments that restore in Giles the ability to be happy and make him, finally, propose to Louise. Those pages are funny, well controlled, and serious, though neither solemn nor pompous. This is Wilson at his best.

In *The Healing Art* Wilson explores the possibility that kindness may be the best realisation for the theological virtue of caritas, as he shows the changes wrought in Pamela by her belief that she has only a few months to live. Her story is contrasted to the story of Dorothy who really is dying, though she does not know it. Dorothy is of the same class as Mrs. Agar in *Wise Virgin,* and her kindness, and the kindness of those who surround her, are used as a constant counterpoint to Pamela's search for a way of life that is not so imbued with selfishness as hers has been. She finds this life with Hereward, one of those "touchy bigoted figures whose hard affected tones proclaimed the mysteries with such radiance and which concealed an ocean of kindness so effectively that almost no one would have guessed it was there," but the reader is led to the conclusion that it is in some mysterious way through Dorothy that Pamela is enabled to find it, that in some way Dorothy gives up her life for Pamela: Pamela is left a china lady by Dorothy in her will, "for all its hideous, cheapened, glossy unnecessary vulgarity: a *lady;* a crinoline *lady* . . . Nothing before had emphasised to Pamela so strongly that Dorothy was dead, dead . . . in her place. The figurine would follow her about now like a tutelary idol, an emblem of deliverance." She has been delivered into kindness, inescapably through the miraculous existence of Dorothy who, through all her suffering, took time to remember Pamela when "it would never have crossed her mind to remember poor Dorothy in this way." And thanks to her and to Hereward Pamela has put away childish things, "archness, intolerance, brittleness," and learned how to be happy.

Perhaps Wilson sees himself as too old to take risks in his fiction, but he is unable or unwilling to leave the very English world of London intellectuals à la Hampstead, old ladies, and the Church of England. His characters often seem wooden, and it is difficult to tell whether Wilson intends the Vicar in *Love Unknown,* Bartle Longworth, to be such a cliché, indicating his unworldliness with untidy piles of newspapers and Ovaltine tins scattered about with the lids left off. However, Wilson beautifully and sincerely describes the decline into madness of a previously powerful figure, Madge Curwen. And his humour, often a little like that of Barbara Pym, is in *Love Unknown* gentle without the savagery of previous novels.

The trilogy, referred to collectively as "The Lampitt Paper," is riddled with irritating references and allusions too closely based on a factual literary period to convince. The narrator, Julian Ramsay, is introduced to the history of the Lampitt family as a schoolboy by his uncle, who is vicar of Timplingham, the rural village where some of this multi-talented family have lived. The vicar's obsession with the Lampitt's, and especially James Petworth Lampitt, a writer, stands out as a fine study of someone who can only live through other's lives. The jokes are recognisable when one is familiar with the original, as when the family listens to a radio series called "The Mulberry's," a pastiche of the famous "The Archers," an almost daily serial about an English farming community, but which may be meaningless beyond Britain.

The continuation of the trilogy, *A Bottle in the Smoke,* attacks the rather pseudo-artistic life of Soho, London, in the 1950s, with scathing portraits of vain authors and their drinking holes. The tittle-tattling world of gossip wears very thin, and the literary allusions can only be known to a few, since Wilson refers to real writers as well as his fictitious one. The final part of the trilogy, *Daughters of Albion,* sees the last of the colourless Julian Ramsay, and any interest in the Lampitts, their biographers, and their hangers-on has vanished for the reader. Even the exploits and eventual downfall of Rice Robey, an unpleasant malicious gossip, do not carry the novel through. Wilson's recent fiction is perfectly competent, but the formula writing is maddening, given that Wilson's fiction at his best is extremely good.

—M.J. Fitzgerald, updated by Geoffrey Elborn

WILSON, Colin (Henry)

Nationality: British. **Born:** Leicester, 26 June 1931. **Education:** Gateway Secondary Technical School, Leicester, 1942-47. **Military Service:** Served in the Royal Air Force, 1949-50. **Family:** Married 1) Dorothy Betty Troop in 1951 (divorced 1952), one son; 2) Pamela Joy Stewart in 1973, two sons and one daughter. **Career:** Laboratory assistant, Gateway School, 1948-49; tax collector in Leicester and Rugby, 1949-50; laborer and hospital porter in London, 1951-53; salesman for the magazines *Paris Review* and *Merlin,* Paris, 1953. Since 1954 full-time writer. British Council lecturer in Germany, 1957; writer-in-residence, Hollins College, Virginia, 1966-67; visiting professor, University of Washington, Seattle, 1968; professor, Institute of the Mediterranean (Dowling College, New York), Majorca, 1969; visiting professor, Rutgers University, New Brunswick, New Jersey, 1974. **Agent:** David Bolt Associates, 12 Heath Drive, Send, Surrey GU23 7EP; or, Al Zuckerman, Writers House Inc., 21 West 26th Street, New York, New York 10010, U.S.A. **Address:** Tetherdown, Trewallock Lane, Gorran Haven, Cornwall, England.

PUBLICATIONS

Novels

Ritual in the Dark. London, Gollancz, and Boston, Houghton Mifflin, 1960.
Adrift in Soho. London, Gollancz, and Boston, Houghton Mifflin, 1961.
The World of Violence. London, Gollancz, 1963; as *The Violent World of Hugh Greene,* Boston, Houghton Mifflin, 1963.
Man Without a Shadow: The Diary of an Existentialist. London, Barker, 1963; as *The Sex Diary of Gerard Sorme,* New York, Dial Press, 1963; as *The Sex Diary of a Metaphysician,* Berkeley, California, Ronin, 1989.
Necessary Doubt. London, Barker, and New York, Simon and Schuster, 1964.
The Glass Cage. London, Barker, 1966; New York, Random House, 1967.
The Mind Parasites. London, Barker, and Sauk City, Wisconsin, Arkham House, 1967.
The Philosopher's Stone. London, Barker, 1969; New York, Crown, 1971.
The Killer. London, New English Library, 1970; as *Lingard,* New York, Crown, 1970.
The God of the Labyrinth. London, Hart Davis, 1970; as *The Hedonists,* New York, New American Library, 1971.
The Black Room. London, Weidenfeld and Nicolson, 1971; New York, Pyramid, 1975.
The Schoolgirl Murder Case. London, Hart Davis MacGibbon, and New York, Crown, 1974.
The Space Vampires. London, Hart Davis MacGibbon, and New York, Random House, 1976.

The Janus Murder Case. London, Granada, 1984.
The Personality Surgeon. London, New English Library, 1985; San Francisco, Mercury House, 1986.
Spider World:
The Tower. London, Grafton, 1987; as *The Desert,* New York, Ace, 1988.
The Delta. London, Grafton, 1987; New York, Ace, 1990.
The Magician from Siberia. London, Hale, 1988.
The Magician. London, HarperCollins, 1992.

Short Story

The Return of the Lloigor. London, Village Press, 1974.

Uncollected Short Story

"Timeslip," in *Aries 1,* edited by John Grant. Newton Abbot, Devon, David and Charles, 1979.

Plays

The Metal Flower Blossom (produced Southend-on-Sea, Essex, 1960). In *The Metal Flower Blossom and Other Plays,* 1993.
Viennese Interlude (produced Scarborough, Yorkshire, and London, 1960).
Strindberg (as *Pictures in a Bath of Acid,* produced Leeds, Yorkshire, 1971; as *Strindberg: A Psychological Portrait,* produced New York, 1974; as *Strindberg: A Fool's Decision,* produced London, 1975). London, Calder and Boyars, 1970; New York, Random House, 1972.
Mysteries (produced Cardiff, 1979).
Mozart's Journey to Prague. Nottingham, Paupers' Press Press, 1992.
The Metal Flower Blossom and Other Plays. San Bernardino, California, Borgo Press, 1993.

Other

The Outsider. London, Gollancz, and Boston, Houghton Mifflin, 1956.
Religion and the Rebel. London, Gollancz, and Boston, Houghton Mifflin, 1957.
The Age of Defeat. London, Gollancz, 1959; as *The Stature of Man,* Boston, Houghton Mifflin, 1959.
Encyclopaedia of Murder, with Patricia Pitman. London, Barker, 1961; New York, Putnam, 1962.
The Strength to Dream: Literature and the Imagination. London, Gollancz, and Boston, Houghton Mifflin, 1962.
Origins of the Sexual Impulse. London, Barker, and New York, Putnam, 1963.
Rasputin and the Fall of the Romanovs. London, Barker, and New York, Farrar Straus, 1964.
Brandy of the Damned: Discoveries of a Musical Eclectic. London, Baker, 1964; as *Chords and Discords: Purely Personal Opinions on Music,* New York, Crown, 1966; augmented edition, as *Colin Wilson on Music,* London, Pan, 1967.
Beyond the Outsider: The Philosophy of the Future. London, Barker, and Boston, Houghton Mifflin, 1965.
Eagle and Earwig (essays). London, Baker, 1965.
Introduction to the New Existentialism. London, Hutchinson, 1966; Boston, Houghton Mifflin, 1967; as *The New Existentialism,* London, Wildwood House, 1980.

Sex and the Intelligent Teenager. London, Arrow, 1966; New York, Pyramid, 1968.

Voyage to a Beginning (autobiography). London, Cecil and Amelia Woolf, 1969; New York, Crown, 1969.

Bernard Shaw: A Reassessment. London, Hutchinson, and New York, Atheneum, 1969.

A Casebook of Murder. London, Frewin, 1969; New York, Cowles, 1970.

Poetry and Mysticism. San Francisco, City Lights, 1969; London, Hutchinson, 1970.

The Strange Genius of David Lindsay, with E.H. Visiak and J.B. Pick. London, Baker, 1970; as *The Haunted Man,* San Bernardino, California, Borgo Press, 1979.

The Occult. New York, Random House, and London, Hodder and Stoughton, 1971.

New Pathways in Psychology: Maslow and the Post-Freudian Revolution. New York, Taplinger, and London, Gollancz, 1972.

Order of Assassins: The Psychology of Murder. London, Hart Davis, 1972.

L'Amour: The Ways of Love, photographs by Piero Rimaldi. New York, Crown, 1972.

Strange Powers. London, Latimer New Dimensions, 1973; New York, Random House, 1975.

Tree by Tolkien. London, Covent Garden Press-Inca, 1973; Santa Barbara, California, Capra Press, 1974.

Hermann Hesse. London, Village Press, and Philadelphia, Leaves of Grass Press, 1974.

Wilhelm Reich. London, Village Press, and Philadelphia, Leaves of Grass Press, 1974.

Jorge Luis Borges. London, Village Press, and Philadelphia, Leaves of Grass Press, 1974.

A Book of Booze. London, Gollancz, 1974.

Ken Russell: A Director in Search of a Hero. London, Intergroup, 1974.

The Unexplained. Lake Oswego, Oregon, Lost Pleiade Press, 1975.

Mysterious Powers. London, Aldus, and Danbury, Connecticut, Danbury Press, 1975; as *They Had Strange Powers,* New York, Doubleday, 1975; revised edition, as *Mysteries of the Mind,* with Stuart Holroyd, Aldus, 1978.

The Craft of the Novel. London, Gollancz, 1975; Salem, New Hampshire, Salem House, 1986.

Enigmas and Mysteries. Danbury, Connecticut, Danbury Press, and London, Aldus, 1976.

The Geller Phenomenon. London, Aldus, 1976.

Mysteries: An Investigation into the Occult, The Paranormal, and the Supernatural. London, Hodder and Stoughton, 1978; New York, Putnam, 1980.

Science Fiction as Existentialism. Hayes, Middlesex, Bran's Head, 1978.

The Search for the Real Arthur, with *King Arthur Country in Cornwall,* by Brenda Duxbury and Michael Williams. Bodmin, Cornwall, Bossiney, 1979.

Starseekers. London, Hodder and Stoughton, and New York, Doubleday, 1980.

The War Against Sleep: The Philosophy of Gurdjieff. Wellingborough, Northamptonshire, Aquarian Press, and York Beach, Maine, Weiser, 1980; revised edition, as *Gurdjieff: The War Against Sleep,* Aquarian Press, and San Bernardino, California, Borgo Press, 1986.

Frankenstein's Castle. Sevenoaks, Kent, Ashgrove Press, 1980; Salem, New Hampshire, Salem House, 1982.

Anti-Sartre, with an Essay on Camus. San Bernardino, California, Borgo Press, 1981.

The Directory of Possibilites, with John Grant. London, Webb and Bower, 1981; as *Mysteries: A Guide to the Unknown,* London, Chancellor, 1994.

The Quest for Wilhelm Reich. London, Granada, and New York, Doubleday, 1981.

Witches. Limpsfield, Surrey, Dragon's World, 1981; New York, A and W, 1982.

Poltergeist! A Study in Destructive Haunting. London, New English Library, 1981; New York, Putnam, 1982.

Access to Inner Worlds: The Story of Brad Absetz. London, Rider, 1983.

Encyclopaedia of Modern Murder 1962-1982, with Donald Seaman. London, Barker, 1983; New York, Putnam, 1984.

Psychic Detectives: The Story of Psychometry and the Paranormal in Crime Detection. London, Pan, 1984; San Francisco, Mercury House, 1985.

A Criminal History of Mankind. London, Granada, and New York, Putnam, 1984.

Lord of the Underworld: Jung and the Twentieth Century. Wellingborough, Northamptonshire, Aquarian Press, 1984; as *C.G. Jung, Lord of the Underworld.* Aquarian Press, and San Bernardino, California, Borgo Press, 1988.

The Essential Colin Wilson. London, Harrap, 1985; Berkeley, California, Celestial Arts, 1987.

The Bicameral Critic, edited by Howard F. Dossor. Bath, Avon, Ashgrove Press, and Salem, New Hampshire, Salem House, 1985.

Rudolf Steiner: The Man and His Vision. Wellingborough, Northamptonshire, Aquarian Press, 1985.

West Country Mysteries. Bodmin, Cornwall, Bossiney, 1985.

Afterlife: An Investigation of the Evidence for Life after Death. London, Harrap, 1985; New York, Doubleday, 1987.

Scandal! An Encyclopaedia, with Donald Seaman. London, Weidenfeld and Nicolson, and New York, Stein and Day, 1986; as *An Encyclopaedia of Scandal,* London, Grafton, 1987.

Poetry and Mysticism. San Francisco, City Lights, 1986.

An Essay on the "New" Existentialism. Nottingham, Pauper's Press, 1986; San Bernardino, California, Borgo Press, 1988.

The Laurel and Hardy Theory of Consciousness. Mill Valley, California, Briggs, 1986.

The Encyclopedia of Unsolved Mysteries, with Damon Wilson. London, Harrap, 1987; Chicago, Contemporary Books, 1988.

Jack the Ripper: Summing Up and Verdict, with Robin Odell, edited by J.H.H. Gaute. London, Bantam, 1987.

Aleister Crowley: The Nature of the Beast. Wellingborough, Northamptonshire, Aquarian Press, 1987; San Bernardino, California, Borgo Press, 1989.

The Musician as "Outsider". Nottingham, Pauper's Press, 1987; San Bernardino, California, Borgo Press, 1989.

The Misfits: A Study of Sexual Outsiders. London, Grafton, 1988; New York, Carroll and Graf, 1989.

Beyond the Occult. London, Bantam, 1988; New York, Carroll and Graf, 1989.

Autobiographical Reflections. Nottingham, Pauper's Press, 1988.

Written in Blood: A History of Forensic Detection. London, Equation, 1989; New York, Warner, 1991.

Existentially Speaking: Essays on the Philosophy of Literature. San Bernardino, California, Borgo Press, 1989.

The Untethered Mind (essays), edited by Howard F. Dossor. Bath, Avon, Ashgrove Press, 1989.

The Decline and Fall of Leftism. Nottingham, Pauper's Press, 1989.

The Serial Killers: A Study in the Psychology of Violence, with Donald Seaman. London, W.H. Allen, 1990; revised edition, London, True Crime, 1992.

Music, Nature and the Romantic Outsider. Nottingham, Paupers' Press Press, 1990.

Unsolved Mysteries Past and Present, with Damon Wilson. Chicago, Contemporary Books, 1992; London, Headline, 1993.

The Strange Life of P.D. Ouspensky. London, Aquarian/Thorsons, 1993.

World Famous Murders, with Damon and Rowan Wilson. London, Robinson, 1993.

World Famous Crimes of Passion. London, Magpie, 1992.

World Famous Gaslight Murders. London, Magpie, 1992.

World Famous Serial Killers. London, Magpie, 1992.

World Famous Unsolved Crimes. London, Magpie, 1992.

Editor, *Colin Wilson's Men of Mystery.* London, W.H. Allen, 1977; as *Dark Dimensions: A Celebration of the Occult,* New York, Everest House, 1977.

Editor, with John Grant, *The Book of Time.* Newton Abbot, Devon, David and Charles, 1980.

Editor, with John Grant, *The Directory of Possibilities.* Exeter, Webb and Bower, and New York, Rutledge Press, 1981.

Editor, *The Book of Great Mysteries,* with Christopher Evans. London, Robinson, 1986.

Editor, with Ronald Duncan, *Marx Refuted: The Verdict of History.* Bath, Avon, Ashgrove Press, 1987.

Editor, *The Mammoth Book of True Crime 1-2.* London, Robinson, and New York, Carroll and Graf, 2 vols., 1988-90.

Editor, *Colin Wilson's True Crime File: Murder in the 1930s.* London, Robinson, 1992.

Editor, with Damon Wilson, *Murder in the 1940s.* London, Robinson, 1993.

*

Bibliography: *The Work of Colin Wilson: An Annotated Bibliography and Guide* by Colin Stanley, San Bernardino, California, Borgo Press, 1989.

Manuscript Collection: University of Texas, Austin.

Critical Studies: *The Angry Decade* by Kenneth Allsop, London, Owen, 1958; *The World of Colin Wilson* by Sidney Campion, London, Muller, 1963; "The Novels of Colin Wilson" by R.H.W. Dillard, in *Hollins Critic* (Hollins College, Virginia), October 1967; *Colin Wilson* by John A. Weigel, New York, Twayne, 1975; *Colin Wilson: The Outsider and Beyond* by Clifford P. Bendau, San Bernardino, California, Borgo Press, 1979; *The Novels of Colin Wilson* by Nicolas Tredell, London, Vision Press, 1982; *An Odyssey of Freedom: Four Themes in Colin Wilson's Novels* by K. Gunnar Bergström, Uppsala, Sweden, University of Uppsala, 1983; *Colin Wilson: The Man and His Mind* by Howard F. Dossor, London, Element, 1990; *Colin Wilson: The Positive Approach* by Michael Trowell, Nottingham, Paupers' Press, 1990; *The Guerilla Philosopher: Colin Wilson and Existentialism* by Tim Dalgleish, Nottingham, Paupers' Press, 1993; *Two Essays on Colin Wilson: World Rejection and Criminal Romantics, and, From Outsider to Post-Tragic Man* by Gary Lachman, Nottingham, Pauper's Press, 1994.

Colin Wilson comments:

I am unashamedly a writer of ideas, in the tradition of Shaw, Wells, or Sartre; I see myself as part of a European rather than English literary tradition. My novels are based firmly upon the "new existentialism" expressed in the six volumes of the "Outsider Cycle" (1956-66) and *Introduction to the New Existentialism.* Although I count myself an existential phenomenologist, I am in fundamental disagreement with the pessimistic European tradition of Heidegger, Jaspers, Sartre, and Camus, and my philosophical work has been an attempt to show that their pessimism is the outcome of certain serious misunderstandings of Husserlian phenomenology, notably of the intentionality of consciousness. The foundation of my position could be expressed in the form of a contradiction of Sartre: Consciousness *does* have an "inside." Sartre's position is fundamentally Humeian: he believes the mind *adds* meaning to the chaotic and fragmented world as you might add milk to a bowl of cornflakes; I hold, with Whitehead, that meaning is an objective reality, and that the problem is the curious narrowness and inefficiency of human consciousness.

My novels are basically preoccupied with the problem of meaning, with what Pierce called the problem of "values in a universe of chance." In the first, *Ritual in the Dark,* this takes the form of an exploration of "the great mystery of human boredom." The hero has always wanted freedom and hated being tied down to an office job; yet when a small legacy gives him "a room of his own," he finds himself bewildered, bored, directionless. His meeting with a man who, he comes to suspect, is a mass-murderer of women produces a powerful sense of meaning and direction, but he feels that this is inauthentic—that he should have been capable of *doing it himself*—finding freedom *without help from outside.* This problem of freedom is at the core of all my novels. Man experiences his freedom both positively and negatively: positively in moments of intensity and ecstasy (sex, for example), negatively in the face of crisis or a threat to his existence. Both experiences reveal that the main trouble with everyday consciousness is its narrowness, its obsessive preoccupation with trivialities. There is something fundamentally wrong with human consciousness, a form of short-sightedness amounting almost to blindness. This is, in a sense, a "religious" vision—closely akin to that of T.E. Hulme, who preferred to call it "original sin." The main influences on my fiction, in my late teens and early twenties, were Joyce and Faulkner, and I felt strongly that the novel had advanced as far as possible in the direction of experimentalism, attempting, so to speak, to approximate to the condition of music. The solution I chose was based upon the notion of Brecht's "alienation effect." In the theater, Brecht invites his audiences to acknowledge that they are watching actors in a play, not reality; it seemed to me that the novel could back out of the Joycean *cul de sac* by choosing to be on one level, entertainment within a conventional framework; using the conventions of the *roman policier,* the *Bildungsroman,* science fiction, the spy novel, as a kind of symbolic form (in Cassirer's sense) which is freely acknowledged *not* to correspond to its content. This I saw as the only reasonable escape from the Joycean-Faulknerian dilemma of trying to distort the form to *correspond* to an increasingly complex content. Hence in my fiction, I have used the form of the detective story, science fiction, spy story, etc. as the "persona" or mask of the book. This also offers one enormous advantage. The Joyce disciples, in their attempt to "render" their precise meaning once and for all, robbed themselves of the possibility of free expansion and development. By treating the form as a kind of carnival mask, I am able to re-explore the same meaning or inner-conflict from different angles, so to speak. For example, the same basic meanings are explored, in *The Killer* (in the United States, *Lingard*) and *The God of the Labyrinth* (*The Hedonists*), although the first is a clinically precise study of a sexually motivated killer, and the second a literary "detective story" with more than a touch of Thorne Smith farce.

The central statement in my work occurs near the beginning of *Man Without a Shadow:* "Human beings are grandfather clocks driven by watch-springs." This is why consciousness *appears* to have no "inside." All human beings suffer, more or less, from the complaint of Sartre's café proprietor in *Nausea:* "When his café empties, his head empties too." Our sense of values, which ought to be absolute, appears to depend completely upon stimuli from the environment. This problem is explored most exhaustively in my "spy novel" *The Black Room,* in which I pose the question: How could a spy be trained to withstand total sensory deprivation in a black room? If such a method could be found, it would also be a method for creating supermen.

It is this Carlylean-Nietzschean preoccupation with the potentialities of man—and his present unsatisfactoriness—that has led certain critics to accuse me of fascism, a curious accusation since, although my cast of mind is naturally conservative, I regard my work as wholly non-political.

* * *

Colin Wilson's many novels, which include psychological thrillers, mysteries, science-fiction fantasies, diary-confessions, and one of the first "beat" stories, are integral parts of an ambitious project which began in 1956 with the publication of *The Outsider,* that precocious "seminal book on the alienation of man." Although more like a collection of quotations and ideas from a youthful autodidact's notebooks than a coherently developed thesis, *The Outsider* impressed serious critics as well as journalists, who immediately exploited the colorful personality of the author and made the book a sensational best seller. Although Wilson still sees his first work as the most important book of its generation—and he may be right—the thoughtless enthusiasm for Wilson's erudition inevitably yielded to a more thoughtful skepticism. But the cruel change in mood toward his early success fortunately did not destroy the young man, who soon went to work again—less with a vengeance than a solemn determination to prove his significance.

Some 35 years and at least as many books later, Wilson can no longer be dismissed as an amateur with only one lucky strike to his credit. Aware that he will eventually be judged as a philosopher, as the champion of a *new* existentialism which rejects the inevitability of despair, Wilson has neatly justified his fiction. "If I were to prescribe a rule," he wrote in 1958, "that all future philosophers would have to obey, it would be this: that no idea shall be expressed that cannot be expressed in terms of human beings in a novel—and perfectly ordinary human beings at that—not Peacockian brain-boxes. If an idea cannot be expressed in terms of people, it is a sure sign it is irrelevant to the real problems of life" (*Declaration,* p. 58).

As a matter of fact none of Wilson's prose has that kind of finesse which awes literary critics not interested in ideas, yet it is adequate to its purpose. The fairest way to approach Wilson's novels is to cooperate with his objectives. His apparent preoccupation with violence, sexuality, and criminality is thematically related to his concern with the outsider syndrome. Furthermore, his methodology always participates in his urgency. In a hurry to clear away

debris and passionately committed to his position, he is neither a Naturalist nor a Romantic weaving word-spells. He says that he has endorsed "the Brechtian alienation effect" in his fiction, and that he has *intended* that his novels announce their forms and make no claim to reality. In that sense they may be read as parodies of the genres they represent. Whether he has succeeded, however, is still debatable.

Since Wilson hopes to live almost forever, there is plenty of time to abide with his project. Recent experiments are currently validating his dreams of freeing humanity from the pessimism that correlates with determinism and traditional existentialism—at least as Wilson sees them. He is continuing his research into the sources of human energy, and there is certainly more to come from this indefatigable worker who says that even now he is just beginning. In 1966 in *Voyage to a Beginning* Wilson evaluated himself with characteristic candor. After modestly estimating that his first twenty years of work had not taken him far he added a firm *but:* "I know that I have come further than any of my contemporaries. I would be a fool if I didn't know it, and a coward if I was afraid to say so."

—John A. Weigel

WILSON, Sloan

Nationality: American. **Born:** Norwalk, Connecticut, 8 May 1920. **Education:** Florida Adirondack School, graduated 1938; Harvard University, Cambridge, Massachusetts, A.B. 1942. **Military Service:** Served in the United States Coast Guard, 1942-46: Lieutenant. **Family:** Married 1) Elise Pickhardt in 1941 (divorced), two daughters and one son; 2) Betty Stephens in 1963, one daughter. **Career:** Reporter, Providence *Journal,* Rhode Island, 1946-47; writer, Time Inc., New York, 1947-49; assistant director, National Citizens Commission for the Public Schools, New York, 1949-52; director of information services and Assistant Professor of English, University of Buffalo, New York, 1952-55; assistant director, White House Conference on Education, Washington, D.C., 1956; education editor, New York, *Herald-Tribune* and *Parents' Magazine,* New York, 1956-58. Writer-in-residence, Rollins College, Winter Park, Florida, 1980-82; director, Winter Park Artists Workshop, Florida, 1982-85; lecturer, Virginia Commonwealth University, Richmond, 1990. D.H.L.: Rollins College, 1982. **Agent:** Ray E. Nugent, 170 Tenth Street, Naples, Florida 33940. **Address:** c/o Jessica Green, Route 1, Box 1188, King George, Virginia 22485, U.S.A.

PUBLICATIONS

Novels

Voyage to Somewhere. New York, Wyn, 1946.
The Man in the Gray Flannel Suit. New York, Simon and Schuster, 1955; London, Cassell, 1956.
A Summer Place. New York, Simon and Schuster, and London, Cassell, 1958.
A Sense of Values. New York, Harper, 1960; London, Cassell, 1961.
Georgie Winthrop. New York, Harper, and London, Cassell, 1963.
Janus Island. Boston, Little Brown, and London, Cassell, 1967.

All the Best People. New York, Putnam, 1970; London, Cassell, 1971.
Small Town. New York, Arbor House, 1978.
Ice Brothers. New York, Arbor House, 1979; London, Sphere, 1982.
The Greatest Crime. New York, Arbor House, 1980.
Pacific Interlude. New York, Arbor House, 1982.
The Man in the Gray Flannel Suit II. New York, Arbor House, 1984.

Uncollected Short Stories

"The Arrival of the Mail," in *New Yorker,* 18 August 1945.
"Party for the Veterans," in *New Yorker,* 20 April 1946.
"We've Got to Do Something," in *New Yorker,* 11 May 1946.
"The Best and Most Powerful Machines," in *Harper's* (New York), June 1946.
"Housewarming," in *New Yorker,* 3 May 1947.
"Drunk on the Train," in *New Yorker,* 3 January 1948.
"Reunion," in *New Yorker,* 6 March 1948.
"Bygones," in *New Yorker,* 18 June 1949.
"Hunt," in *Yale Review* (New Haven, Connecticut), March 1950.
"Alarm Clock," in *New Yorker,* 24 February 1951.
"Black Mollies," in *Harper's* (New York), December 1951.
"A Letter of Admonition," in *New Yorker,* 29 December 1951.
"Regatta," in *New Yorker,* 28 June 1952.
"School Days," in *The Best Short Stories of World War II,* edited by C.A. Fenton. New York, Viking Press, 1957.

Other

Away from It All. New York, Putnam, 1969; London, Cassell, 1970.
What Shall We Wear to This Party? The Man in the Gray Flannel Suit Twenty Years Before and After (autobiography). New York, Arbor House, 1976.

*

Manuscript Collection: Boston University.

Sloan Wilson comments:

(1972) My work consists of a running commentary on the world as I have seen it from 1944 to the present. Both my strength and my limitation derive from my determination to confine myself to firsthand experiences and observations. World War II is in my books because I fought through it. The worries and frustrations of business are on my pages because I suffered them for many years before I became a full-time writer. The joys, angers, desperation, and contentment which are part of many marriages are in my novels, because I have been married twice. Children appear in my books because I have four of them. The writing in my books is rather simple and straightforward because I have a story to tell and I want to get on with it. The English language, I believe, can be used for many purposes—to make the music of poetry, to give military orders, or to give the illusion of meaning without any meaning, as most politicians employ it. I use it to give my readers the thoughts and, most of all, the emotions which I have experienced. I want the readers to be deeply moved without becoming aware of the language which is transmitting the feelings of others to them. That's why I avoid "fancy writing"—it makes readers think about words instead of about human triumph or despair.

The men, women, and children in my books are concerned with bed-rock issues, such as how to stay alive in time of war without being a coward, how to make a good living in time of war without being a coward, how to make a good living in time of peace without selling one's soul cut-rate, and, most of all, how to understand and enjoy the mysteries of love without guilt and without hurting other people. Human beings in my books get tired, cross, and discouraged sometimes, but they doggedly pursue happiness and cling to a rather old-fashioned sense of honor to the best of their ability, which sometimes is not enough. Critics often believe my books are an over-simplification of life or a naive interpretation of it, but a few million readers tell me that for them my pages are mirrors.

(1991) I have reached an age (71) where I am more proud of my four children and eight grandchildren than of my books. As a novelist I suffer the handicap of personal happiness. It's hard for me to produce the gloom and doom which fashion requires. I know the world is in terrible shape, but when was it better? And isn't a little *joie de vivre* permissible? I feel I must apologize for being a happy old man.

*   *   *

The dust jacket of the American edition of Sloan Wilson's fifth novel, *Georgie Winthrop,* describes the book in these rather sensational terms: "The story of the man who lives next door to The Man in the Gray Flannel Suit—forty-five, intelligent, modest, decent, and catapulted by an extraordinary love into trying to grow up inside." Sloan Wilson has long been the victim of this kind of cliché-ridden, high-pressure advertising, of this nod toward a low-brow readership. If he enters literary history at all it will be as the creator of the man-in-the-gray-flannel-suit metaphor.

The typical Sloan Wilson protagonist is acutely aware of his Puritan ancestry, of his New England background, and tries desperately to "live in the present." Thus Ben Powers, in *Janus Island* and George Winthrop, both 45-year-old family men, enter into relationships with younger women (in George's case a 17 year old) in vain attempts to ignore past commitments and future responsibilities. Tom Rath, before the present events of *The Man in the Gray Flannel Suit,* had a wartime love affair with an Italian girl in another futile effort to freeze the present moment. Rath has a kind of Faulknerian obsession with time, which often expresses itself lyrically: "Time was given us like jewels to spend, and it's the ultimate sacrilege to wish it away." Wilson called one of his novels *All the Best People,* a title which would serve handsomely for almost any of his books. Despite the intended irony of the phrase, there is always a certain respect in evidence in his fiction for the established eastern seaboard families, with their yachts, their islands, and their prep school and Harvard-Yale backgrounds. Dana, the main character in *All the Best People,* at one point defiantly remarks to his wife: "Of course! They call people like us WASPS, Caroline, white Anglo-Saxon Protestants." Later on, Caroline asserts formidably and characteristically: "my parents said I had to learn how to like Jews and Negros, but they never said I had to like Middle Westerners."

Wilson has proved to be a skilled chronicler of social and historical events, from the Depression years through the aftermath of World War II. *All the Best People,* his most historical novel, shows the eroding effect of various upheavals in American life on a group of families who own property at Paradise Point, near Lake George, New York. *A Sense of Values* and *All the Best People* have long sequences devoted to the military experiences of the principle male characters. World War II, if somewhat obliquely, figures crucially also in *The Man in the Gray Flannel Suit* and *A Summer Place*. *Janus Island,* which describes more recent events than most of the other novels, is concerned, in passing, with the disruptive presence of Vietnam.

There is no mistaking the richness and vitality of Wilson's fiction. Still, as certain reviewers have remarked, there is a sense of *déjà vu* for anyone who reads through all of his work. Events, characters, and symbols have a way of being reused. Thus the war experiences of Nathan in *A Sense of Values* and those of Dana in *All the Best People* are more than passingly similar. There are crotchety caretakers, all cast from the same mold, in *The Man in the Gray Flannel Suit, A Summer Place,* and *Janus Island*. Magicians serve rather similar symbolical functions in *All the Best People* and *A Sense of Values*. Sylvia's "fake mink coat over her bathing suit" in *A Summer Place* reappears in the form of Caroline's "mink-dyed muskrat coat" in *All the Best People*. Both Nort in *Janus Island* and Nathan in *A Sense of Values* have the nervous habit of clenching and unclenching their hands. Dana, at the end of *All the Best People,* comes uncannily, to resemble Hopkins in *The Man in the Gray Flannel Suit,* and Annabelle, in *A Sense of Values,* is a female—and somewhat more aggressive—Hopkins.

Critics have objected to the untidiness of Wilson's novels; their structures tend to be indecisively open-ended. Most of them are unduly episodic. They are as far removed as possible from the tautness of the best post-World War II fiction. Wilson obviously prefers a more leisurely, digressive pace. There is, however, a certain appropriateness about the rather old-fashioned open form of these novels; they deal, after all, with a world which holds on to the old pieties and stubbornly resists change. The underplayed, somewhat symbolic final remark of George Winthrop—which ends the only novel in the Wilson canon with a university setting—reveals how important traditional values are: "No, thank you very much, but I have to be getting home. I have a long drive ahead."

—Melvin J. Friedman

WINTERSON, Jeanette

Nationality: British. **Born:** Lancashire in 1959. **Education:** St. Catherine's College, Oxford. **Awards:** Whitbread award, 1985; John Llewellyn Rhys Memorial prize, 1987. **Address:** c/o Bloomsbury, 2 Soho Square, London W1V 5DE, England.

PUBLICATIONS

Novels

Oranges Are Not the Only Fruit. London, Pandora Press, 1985; New York, Atlantic Monthly Press, 1987.
Boating for Beginners. London, Methuen, 1985.
The Passion. London, Bloomsbury, 1987; New York, Atlantic Monthly Press, 1988.
Sexing the Cherry. London, Bloomsbury, and New York, Atlantic Monthly Press, 1989.
Written on the Body. London, Cape, 1992; New York, Knopf, 1993.
Art and Lies. London, Cape, 1994; New York, Knopf, 1995.

Uncollected Short Stories

"Orion," in *Winter's Tales 4* (new series), edited by Robin Baird-Smith. London, Constable, and New York, St. Martin's Press, 1988.
"The Green Man," in *The New Yorker,* 26 June-3 July 1995.

Play

Radio Play: *Static,* 1988.

Television Play: *Oranges Are Not the Only Fruit* (series), from her own novel, 1990.

Other

Fit for the Future: The Guide for Women Who Want to Live Well. London, Pandora Press, 1986.
Art Objects: Critical Essays. London, Cape, and New York, Knopf, 1995.

Editor, *Passion Fruit: Romantic Fiction with a Twist*. London, Pandora Press, 1986.

*　　*　　*

Jeanette Winterson is widely regarded as one of the most unusual and promising young talents in English fiction today. Her growing reputation rests on six novels, all conceptually dense and imaginatively rich. Successive works have been received with increasing enthusiasm by the critics, and the extremely successful 1990 television adaptation of her first novel, *Oranges Are Not the Only Fruit* has brought this exuberant talent to the attention of a much wider audience than such an experimental writer usually commands.

Winterson began her career with a *tour de force* of a first novel. *Oranges Are Not the Only Fruit* is a brilliant comic-satiric novel that combines a passionately angry, yet warm depiction of a close-knit, mutually suspicious Lancashire community; a satiric treatment of a hilarious gallery of larger-than-life (but all too believable) members of an Evangelical sect; a *Bildungsroman* of the adolescent heroine's struggle to establish her own identity in the world of distorted certainties inhabited by her mother; and the bittersweet story of her love for and betrayal by her lover Melanie and her mother. On one level this is a classic narrative of the struggle between the mother and the daughter, an Oedipal drama which the father merely spectates from the sidelines: "My father liked to watch the wrestling, my mother liked to wrestle; it didn't matter what. She was in the white corner and that was that . . . she had never heard of mixed feelings." Jeanette's mother with her passionate convictions, and indeed the daughter who wrestles with her, stand at the head of Winterton's pantheon of (varying combinations of) mad, bad, strong, and passionate women, such as the web-footed Villanelle in *The Passion,* the Rabelaisian Dog Woman in *Sexing the Cherry,* and the young artist who names herself "Picasso" in *Art and Lies*.

Oranges Are Not the Only Fruit is Winterson's "Portrait of an Artist" as a young woman. It is the history of the formation of the consciousness by which it was produced, a poignant tale of cognitive dissonance in the world of a young woman growing up adopted, lesbian, and evangelical—identities that do not easily resolve themselves. It is also the story of how "I learned to interpret the signs and wonders that the unbeliever might never understand," a process that produced a "tendency towards the exotic [which] has brought me many problems, just as it did to Blake." Like Blake, Winterson is an angry visionary and writer of paradoxical proverbs (especially about the nature of lies and truth). *Oranges,* like much postmodernist fiction, and all of Winterson's fiction to date, is also a story about history, and a story about the very conditions and possibility of narrative. In the short chapter "Deuteronomy: The last book of the law" Winterson sets out the quarrel with conventional history which drives her later fictions. Winterson's novels take issue with that version of history that in its effort to "squeeze this oozing world between two boards and typeset" denies the past by refusing to recognise its integrity—or its heterogeneity. On the contrary, "History should be a hammock for swinging and a game for playing, the way cats play, Claw it, chew it, rearrange it."

The Passion certainly sets the hammock of history swinging with great vigour as it weaves together the stories of Henri, a young French peasant, chicken chef to Napoleon to whom he is passionately devoted, and Villanelle, an androgynous Venetian girl, born with the webbed feet that properly belong to the boy-children of the Venetian fishing community to which she belongs. It is, as the title suggests, a story about passion—its grandeur and inspiring power, and also its obsessiveness and its tendency to delusion. It is a story about hero-worship and the failure of heroes, about passionate love and the betrayals that those who love passionately must inevitably suffer: passion is a form of time travel to unknown territories, "and the way there is sudden and the way back is worse."

Sexing the Cherry also deals in time travel. Like *The Passion* this is a historical novel (the setting is England around the time of the Civil War), but the two main 17th-century characters—the sailor Jordan, and his adoptive mother the Dog Woman, who lives in a hut beside the Thames—mutate into a 20th-century schoolboy obsessed by wooden sailing boats and his adult self (in the navy), and a "female chemist" with a good degree encamped beside the Thames protesting against environmental pollution. Pollution (of various kinds) and resistance are major themes of this fantasia, which is a vigorous affirmation of the physical life and of the power of fantasy. In some ways perhaps the most self-consciously literary of Winterson's works, *Sexing the Cherry* mixes Ben Jonson's *Bartholomew Fair* with Angela Carter's rewriting of folk and fairy tales.

As in all of Winterson's fictions the freewheeling narrative is repeatedly interrupted by interludes and digressions. In *Sexing the Cherry* one of the most prominent of these is the Carteresque rewriting of the story of 12 dancing princesses. Jordan, who shares the narration with the Dog Woman, not only travels in his shop to exotic places (where he also discovers that oranges are not the only fruit—he brings back a pineapple), but he also travels in his mind. On one of his mind-voyages he visits the home of the 12 dancing princesses who tell him the story of how they didn't live happily ever after. Winterson's rewriting of this fairy story, like Carter's rewriting of fairy tales, is designed to expose its coercive power, and to replace the homogenizing tendencies of romance (and of romantic love) with the narrative and sexual variety which they exclude.

Similarly, *Written on the Body* explores the nature of romance, contrasting the sloppy, diluted, and comfortable language of love—that "saggy armchair of clichés"—with the varieties of love as it is experienced in the multiple configurations of lust and loss, commitment and containment. The narrator, ungendered (though most critics imagine the voice as female) tells of an overwhelming pas-

sion for a married woman, a woman who is ready to leave her husband, a cancer-researcher, but who is also possibly dying of leukemia. The narrator interrupts her tale of obsession with anecdotes about various boyfriends and girlfriends, and the center of the novel is a beautiful and lyrical ode to the beloved's body, structured around quotations from an anatomy textbook—a bizarre but compelling juxtaposition of the dry discourse of medicine with a lover's obsessive, metaphorical explorations. This interlude, like that of the dancing princesses in *Sexing the Cherry* or the brief discourse on history in *Oranges,* accomplishes in microcosm what Winterson's fiction achieves on a larger scale: It demonstrates the disabling powers of narrative and fantasy, while at the same time reclaiming narrative and fantasy as areas in which the individual may resist the constraining myths and stories of her or his own culture.

Art and Lies is Winterson's most inventive and lyrical novel to date. Like the previous novels, it examines the nature of history and narrative and of sexuality and love, and it contrasts the reductive nature of clichéd forms (loveless marriages, gender stereotypes, journalistic prose, dead language) with the creative possibilities of love, sex, art, lyricism, and fantasy. *Art and Lies* is a baroque novel, filled with madwomen, castrati, doctors, and priests; laced with philosophical discourses on progress, art, human nature, and love; comprising a foundling tale, a dystopian fantasy of London in the year 2000, a comic piece of 18th-century pornography (which itself seems a bawdy rewrite of Woolf's *Orlando*), a lesbian romance; an allegory of how to read the works of Sappho; and, at the end, a nine-page reproduction of the trio from Richard Strauss's opera *Der Rosenkavalier.* The novel itself is a kind of trio, told in the three voices of Handel, an ex-priest turned breast surgeon; Picasso, a young artist fleeing her repressive family and a history of sexual and emotional abuse; and Sappho, the famous poet of antiquity, inexplicably alive—as both text and persona. In places the novel turns into a potentially elitist jeremiad on the value of high culture, even perhaps an attack on those critics who wish Winterson would return to the more realistic narratives of her first novel, the "journalists and novelists [who] would have me believe, to write without artifice is to write honestly—as if to speak badly is to speak truly." Art is more than confession or autobiography, more than therapeutic (though Picasso finds art a means of both escape and revenge), more than information or plot. It is a realm of invention, recognition, and contemplation. More than anything else, the novel is about the value of art as artifice, an art that does not simply reflect life, but asks life to remold itself to its fantastic and salvationary possibilities.

—Lyn Pykett, updated by Ed Madden

WINTON, Tim

Nationality: Australian. **Born:** Karrinyup, Western Australia, 1960. **Education:** Western Australian Institute of Technology. **Awards:** *Australian*/Vogel award, 1981, for *An Open Swimmer;* Miles Franklin award, 1984, for *Shallows;* Deo Gloria award, 1991, WA Premiers award, 1991, National Book Council's Banjo award, 1992, and Miles Franklin award, 1992, all for *Cloudstreet.* **Address:** c/o Pan Macmillan, Level 18, St. Martin's Tower, 31 Market St., Sydney, New South Wales 2000, Australia.

PUBLICATIONS

Novels

An Open Swimmer. Sydney, Allen and Unwin, 1982.
Shallows. Sydney, Unwin, 1985; London, Weidenfeld and Nicolson, and New York, Atheneum, 1986.
That Eye, the Sky. Melbourne, McPhee Gribble, New York, Atheneum, and London, Weidenfeld and Nicolson, 1986.
In the Winter Dark. Melbourne, McPhee Gribble, 1988; London, Weidenfeld and Nicolson, 1989.
Cloudstreet. London, Picador, 1991; Saint Paul, Minnisota, Graywolf Press, 1992.
The Riders. New York, Scribner, and London, Picador, 1995.

Short Stories

Scission. Fitzroy, Victoria, McPhee Gribble, 1985; as *Scission and Other Stories,* London, Weidenfeld and Nicolson, 1987.
Minimum of Two. Fitzroy, Victoria, McPhee Gribble, 1987; New York, Atheneum, and London, Weidenfeld and Nicolson, 1988.
Blood and Water. London, Picador, 1993.

Other

Jesse (for children). N.p., 1989.
Lockie Leonard, Human Torpedo (for children). N.p., Bodley Head, 1990; Boston, Little Brown, 1991.
Local Colour: Travels in Australia, with Bill Bachman. London, Allen and Unwin, 1994.

* * *

Tim Winton is probably the most precocious and prolific novelist Australia has yet produced. Born in 1960, he published his first novel, *An Open Swimmer,* at the age of 22 and has subsequently gone on to publish 13 books of fiction in all, including several for children. *An Open Swimmer* seems, like much of Winton's early fiction, to have been influenced by Hemingway, though Winton denies this and says he owes far more to fellow western Australian writer Randolph Stow. Its protagonist Jerra, short for Jeremiah, is a former admirer of *The Old Man and the Sea,* to which there are two references, and the novel takes laconicism almost to the point of silence. At one point the author even acknowledges this: "It was apathetic conversation, even for them." Not just Jerra and his mate Sean but all of the handful of characters in the novel speak in monosyllables, sparingly dished out, and the laconicism is carried over into the narrative voice of the novel as well. The spare, unadorned factuality of the writing is fleshed out with a few pervasive metaphors, the most important of which is the pearl that can sometimes be found in a kingfisher's head when it is cut open, but the theme of the novel is unclear, unless it is Jerra's sexual traumas, perhaps unwillingness to embrace the world of adulthood generally. As with much of Winton's work, the most interesting element is the preoccupation with landscape and especially seascape.

Set in the town of Angelus in the southern part of western Australia, Winton's second novel, *Shallows* (which won the Miles Franklin Award for best Australian novel of the year), deals with the conflict between whalers and a band of environmentalists who set out to disrupt the already dying industry. As *The Old Man and the Sea* provided a kind of reference point for the earlier novel, so

Moby-Dick does for this. The novel cuts deliberately from character to character, as *Shallows* alternated between past and present. There are the young couple, Cleveland and Queenie Cookson, Queenie's father Daniel Coupar, the egregious Des Pustling and his reluctant girlfriend Marion Lowell, and the aged Presbyterian clergyman William Pell. There is a prologue set in 1831, and Winton also makes use of the diary of Daniel Coupart's grandfather, Nathaniel, which has been given to Cleve. The central conflict is between Cleve and Queenie but it springs up almost too quickly for plausibility and is dissolved at the end in a similarly peremptory manner. In the course of the narrative Queenie becomes steadily stronger while Cleve deteriorates morally, so that their final upbeat reunion, with Queenie pregnant by him, seems to have an imposed quality. The vision of life the novel offers is perhaps best summed up by Daniel Coupar: "It's having the choices that kills a man. It's the best and the worst. You get to choose and you get to regret. Almost guaranteed to bugger it up. And sometimes not."

Jerra reappears in *Scission,* Winton's first collection of short stories. The epigraphs, this time coming from *The Book of Job* and *East Coker,* suggest the increasing importance of Christian belief in Winton's work. Again the style is spare, restrained, attempting to suggest or imply unstated significances; most of the stories are very short. Domesticity—of a young couple, of father and son—and especially its fragility is often the main concern. In the final, title story, the preoccupation with "scissions" of various kinds is taken even into the writing itself, its style and structure acting out the sense of a mind incapable of ordering its experience. The rather awkward title of *That Eye, the Sky* refers to those who have aspiration or faith. The sky or its absence is constantly referred to throughout the novel: "I go out and look at the sky but it's blank; no stars, nothing," the novel's 12-year-old narrator, Morton ("Ort") Flack, says despairingly at one point near the end. No matter. This is the most explicitly Christian of Winton's works to date, the culmination of the movement that led to the affirmations in many of the stories in *Scission.* There is literally a *deus ex machina* in the unlikely person of Henry Warburton, former poet and hippy and now evangelist and car thief as well as the seducer of Ort's renegade sister, Tegwyn, with whom he flees at the end of the novel. When Henry finally runs away for the second time and the family discovers that the car he brought back has been stolen, all would seem to be lost, but it is then that Ort experiences his epiphany. He sees his stricken father: "His eyes are open and they're on me and smiling as I come in shouting 'God! God! God!' His face is shining. I'm shaking all over. 'God! God! God!'"

The title of *Minimum of Two,* Winton's second collection of stories, refers to the sentence a rapist receives in the title story—"five years with a minimum before parole of two." Although one of the longest, at 15 pages, it is also one of the weakest stories in this rather undernourished collection, the strongest point of which is its continuity with Winton's earlier fiction. In "Laps," for instance, we meet Queenie Cookson and her husband seven years after the events narrated in *Shallows.* More commonly, the protagonists are Jerra and, by implication, in "A Measure of Eloquence," his wife Rachel, their son Sam, and friends Ann and Philip. The story "Gravity" refers directly to when the honeymooning couple stayed in Jerra's shack. Jerra himself is now something of a mess. After trying to make it as a musician he seems burned-out, living off the dole, resentful of his parents and full of self-pity. The final story takes us back in time to the agonizingly painful birth of Sam. "Blood and Water" reminds us of the dedication of the book to Winton's wife and child in its graphic, impressionist account of childbirth.

Elsewhere, though, the prose takes on the familiar cadences of Hemingway, as in this passage from "Forest Winter": "He had been broken once before, years back, when he was still half a boy, and he knew that when you were beaten properly, you didn't get up; you had to wait for some obscure grace to put you together, and there was no guarantee it would come by a second time." That "obscure grace" is the key to Winton's vision.

In the Winter Dark is unusual among Winton's fiction, a short, barely novella-length account by an old man of a series of horrifying events that took place almost a year ago. Of the four people involved, two are now dead, the narrator Maurice Stubbs is tortured by incessant nightmares, and Murray Jaccob, his neighbor in the isolated valley known as the Sink, is drinking himself to death. Something or someone, we slowly learn, has been killing and disemboweling the animals in the area, but when Maurice and his wife, Jaccob, and a pregnant young woman named Ronnie collaborate to hunt it down they are unsuccessful, as their own private fears and guilts from the past take over. The novel is a skillful study in suspense.

Cloudstreet is Winton's most impressive and substantial novel to date and won him a second Miles Franklin Award. It is the most ambitious of his novels, not only in terms of its length and in the time it covers (roughly 1943 to 1964), but also in its extraordinary gallery of characters and in the stylistic experiments that are new to Winton's fiction and seem to move him almost into the realms of magic realism. The novel is the story of two families named Lamb and Pickles (Winton has a lot of fun with names in this novel), who move into a huge house at no. 1 Cloud Street and bicker and love their way through two decades of Australian history. Lester and Oriel Lamb are God-fearing people who give thanks to the Lord when their son Fish comes back from drowning—except that not all of Fish Lamb has come back, his brain having been left behind in the sea. Sam and Dolly Pickles, on the other hand, are a feckless couple who fail to prosper. Sam loses most of the fingers of one hand in an episode of violence characteristic of this novel and takes to gambling; Dolly is an alcoholic. Winton covers the history of both sets of parents and their numerous offspring in numerous short episodes, some comic, others near tragic.

The style of the novel varies. There are sections written in the present tense, sudden bursts of lyricism, passages of interior monologue, and a great deal of slightly heightened Australian vernacular. Winton is also fond of bizarre and incongruous juxtapositions, often of a comically macabre kind: "His mother came in to find him stuffing the old boy's dentures in. He stopped rigid, they exchanged looks, and it appeared with the upper plate the way it was, that the old man had died eating a small piano." There are also ventures into fabulism: the house in which they live gives out sighs, a pig speaks in Pentecostal tongues, a woman sets up house in a tent in the backyard. If there is a sustaining theme running through the novel it is the various views of chance and the contingent that the two families hold. For Sam Pickles, luck is "the shifty shadow of God," which "you do your best to stay out of the way of." Whereas with the Lambs, there is "making luck, the hardest . . . yacker there is."

Winton's most recent novel, *The Riders,* is his most baffling, though it is also quite exhilarating to read. A young Australian man named Scully labors in the novel's first section to restore a house in Ireland that he has bought on the whim of his wife. He is sustained in his labor by the thought of her imminent arrival as well as that of their seven-year-old daughter, Billie, but when he finally gets to the airport only his daughter is there, too traumatized to explain what has happened. The rest of the novel is concerned with Scully's demented chase all over Europe—Greece, Italy, France, Holland, England—in search of his missing wife, a search that is finally left unresolved.

Winton's account of Scully's quest is as electrifying as it is implausible. Scully himself may embody all the possibilities, play all the roles that his creator suggests—"working-class boofhead with a wife who married beneath herself," "hairy bohemian with a beautiful family," "mongrel expat with the homesick twang and ambitious missus," "poor decent-hearted bastard who couldn't see the roof coming down on his head." It is not possible to decide who or what he is because his behavior and personality change from moment to moment as he is violently propelled through the next series of dramatic events. Whatever he is, he behaves with a quite exceptional stupidity that, like much else in this novel, remains as mysterious as the imagery of the night riders that runs through the novel.

The motif of the quest or the odyssey is present in most of Winton's fiction, especially the quest in search of the self. Also central is the tension between a sense of the importance of chance and the contingent in life and the wavering faith in some kind of force that imposes order upon the universe. Perhaps this is what Winton's protagonist senses in the riders he glimpses again at the end of the novel: "He knew them now and he saw that they would be here every night seen and unseen, patient, dogged faithful in all weathers and all worlds, waiting for something promised, something that was plainly their due, but he knew that as surely as he felt Billie tugging on him, curling her fingers in his and pulling them easily away, that he would not be among them and must never be, in life or death."

—Laurie Clancy

WOIWODE, Larry (Alfred)

Nationality: American. **Born:** Carrington, North Dakota, 30 October 1941. **Education:** University of Illinois, Urbana, 1959-64, A.A. 1964. **Family:** Married Carole Ann Peterson in 1965; four children. **Career:** Actor in Miami and New York, 1964-65; writer-in-residence, University of Wisconsin, Madison, 1973-74; visiting professor, Wheaton College, Illinois, summers 1981 and 1984; visiting professor, 1983-84, professor of English, 1984-88, director of the Writing Program, 1985-88, and co-director of the semester in London program, Spring 1988, State University of New York, Binghamton. Since 1988 professor of English, Beth-El Institute for the Arts and Sciences, Carson, North Dakota. Since 1978 farmer-rancher in western North Dakota, raising grains, sheep, and quarter horses. **Awards:** MacDowell fellowship, 1965; Faulkner Foundation award, 1969; Guggenheim fellowship, 1971; American Academy award, 1980; *Southern Review* award, for *The Neumiller Stories,* 1990; Aga Khan prize (*Paris Review*), 1990; John Dos Passos prize, for a literary body of work, 1991. D.Litt.: North Dakota State University, Fargo, 1977. **Agent:** Candida Donadio and Associates, 231 West 22nd Street, New York, New York 10011, U.S.A. **Address:** Route 1, Box 57, Mott, North Dakota, 57646, U.S.A.

PUBLICATIONS

Novels

What I'm Going to Do, I Think. New York, Farrar Straus, 1969;
  London, Weidenfeld and Nicholson, 1970.
Beyond the Bedroom Wall: A Family Album. New York, Farrar
  Straus, 1975.
Poppa John. New York, Farrar Straus, 1981.
Born Brothers. New York, Farrar Straus, 1988.
Indian Affairs. New York, Atheneum/Macmillan, 1991.

Short Stories

The Neumiller Stories. New York, Farrar Straus, 1989.
Silent Passengers. New York, Atheneum/Macmillan, 1993.

Uncollected Short Story

"Summer Storms," in *Paris Review,* Spring 1990.

Poetry

Poetry North: Five North Dakota Poets, with others. Fargo, North
  Dakota Institute for Regional Studies, 1970.
Even Tide. New York, Farrar Straus, 1977.

Other

Acts. San Francisco, HarperSanFrancisco, 1993.

*

Manuscript Collection: Allen Memorial Library, Valley City State
University, North Dakota.

Larry Woiwode comments:

(1981) I believe that prose should be set down so that the readers sees through it to the book's essential action: a fireplace screen behind which the blaze burns, as I've expressed it elsewhere. yet I work in my books to make the prose do as much as it is able, in realms of rhythm, imagery, and underlying sound. If this seems a paradox, it perhaps is; it sometimes feels so as I work. But I believe that our language, and its heritage, is too rich to be relegated to the utilitarian. Besides trying to keep up on contemporaries and present trends, I like to read in the century of our language's flowering, in the Elizabethans and metaphysical poets, for instance, and all of the early novelists and novels, such as *Pilgrim's Progress.* Its structure is still valid and its language full of sparks.

In my books I try to convey the contours and textures of life as it's lived. Each book is a separate entity with its special demands, since each is lived by a different character, or series of them. The rhythm of every sentence of the six-hundred-and-some pages of *Beyond the Bedroom Wall* is modulated to fit the voice that speaks it. Or there was a conscious attempt to make this so. What I want to do in my fiction, with the help of the prose I work at, is to keep all of the reader's senses informed on every moment that he lives within a certain character's skin. This world we breathe. I expect a reader to emerge from my work affected, if not with a change of heart.

*   *   *

Larry Woiwode's second novel, *Beyond the Bedroom Wall,* is sure to be ranked as one of the great achievements of American fiction of the 1970s. It is a midwestern novel, an American novel, a universal novel. It spans four generations, and could be set in almost any century. The book's significant events emerge out of the natural histories of human beings. It is about births and deaths, love and courtship, joy and grief, motherhood and fatherhood, childhood, adolescence, old age. It is about strength of character, spoiled character, redeemed character. It is about hardship and work, competence and incompetence, faith and distrust. It is about provincial bigotry and the lot of a Catholic family in a town of Methodists. It is about enduring.

Otto Neumiller emigrated from Germany in 1881. He went all the way to the Dakota plain, where he prospered and then lost most of what he had gained. In his old age, he is lonely and envied and unloved by his neighbors. His son Charles returns to the homestead to attend him at his death. In one of the book's finest chapters, Woiwode shows Charles at work making his father's coffin, lovingly washing and dressing his father's body, burying him in the unhallowed ground of the farm he loved. Like his father, Charles Neumiller has been a devout Catholic all his life; and so is Charles's son Martin. Most of the novel is the story of Martin, his wife Alpha, who dies at 34, and their six children. The older children, the fourth generation, are off on their own in the 1970s.

The great strength of this novel is in Woiwode's rendering of the commonplace. The Neumiller family may be a bit more intelligent and may perhaps possess more fortitude than the average family, but they are not particularly special. In addition to the virtues, there certainly are waywardness, carelessness, and ill-considered, impulsive behavior among them. Indeed, one of the beautiful ironies in the novel is that it is the ill-considered decision of Martin, usually so steady and prudent, to move his family from North Dakota to Illinois that brings disaster to the family, including ultimately his beloved wife's death. But the fabric of the novel is made of such scenes as the father's telling stories to his children, the father's being overcome with frustration and kicking one of his sons viciously, the acting out of guilt feelings brought on by the nearly fatal illness of a child. An important motif running through the novel is the family's emotional involvement with each of the various houses in which they live.

The marriage of Martin and Alpha is old-fashioned and ordinary. Except for what is done by acts of nature, it is a marriage that is not susceptible to disruption. This man and this woman become totally entangled with each other, and regardless of what befalls them they cannot imagine themselves married to anyone else. To Martin and Alpha, marriage is for better or for worse, forever.

Even in bulk Woiwode's first novel, *What I'm Going to Do, I Think,* is not half the novel that *Beyond the Bedroom Wall* is. It has a small cast of characters, with the focus rarely leaving Chris or Ellen; it does not range over generations, but is concerned with only a few seasons in the lives of its young couple. It is lyrical and symbolic; unfortunately it is also murky. Its central situation is commonplace: the young woman is pregnant and the couple marry. They take an extended honeymoon at an isolated lodge up in northern Michigan. Only then does the nature of the commitment he has made become real to Chris. He is not single anymore; he must take account of another person. He is uncertain about which emotions to share and which to conceal. He experiences much anger, resentment, and frustration, but he does not know what to do with such feelings in the new context. Their physical relationship is different under the blanket of marriage; expectation, disappointment, jealously, and fulfillment have a new texture. Neither Chris nor Ellen has had an appropriate model for the roles of husband and wife; Chris, especially, suffers as a result.

Both had unusual childhoods. Ellen's parents were killed in an accident, and she has been raised by four grandparents. Chris's alienation from his parents is so severe that he hardly ever thinks of them; he does not invite them to his wedding, and he does not attend his mother's funeral. It is the quality of Chris's earlier life that is suggested by the title of the novel. The words are part of a remark made by his father when Chris has hurt himself being clumsy at a chore. What his father thinks he is going to do is get himself a new kid.

The child Ellen is carrying is born dead. When Ellen calls her grandmother for consolation, she is told that this is the "wages of sin." Chris and Ellen do not have another child. The novel ends with the suggestion that Chris always will be a troubled man and that the marriage will not bring fulfillment or much joy to husband or wife. The lives of Chris and Ellen will never have the richness of the lives of Martin and Alpha. Standing by itself, the earlier novel does not have a meaning that clearly emerges from the interaction of character and plot. When it is put beside *Beyond the Bedroom Wall*, its theme is quite clear: without firm familial commitments, modern life will exact constant feelings of despair and loss.

In *Indian Affairs,* Woiwode picks up where he left off in his very first novel. It is seven years later, and Chris and Ellen are having normal marital problems. The general plot is interesting, but the many subplots are distracting and unnecessary. Woiwode's collection of stories *Silent Passengers* deals, once again, with midwestern family stories. Readers can see many threads of father-son relationships and how they influence other family members.

At his best, Woiwode renders the commonplace with such emotional and psychological truth that all the reader's capacity for empathy and compassion is tapped. Woiwode often demonstrates marvelous descriptive power; at his best, his readers see and feel and learn with him, making easy transfers of their fictional experience to their own lives.

—Paul Marx, updated by Loretta Cobb

WOLFE, Tom

Nationality: American. **Born:** Thomas Kennerly Wolfe, Jr. in Richmond, Virginia, 2 March 1930. **Education:** Washington and Lee University, Lexington, Virginia, A.B. (cum laude) 1951; Yale University, New Haven, Connecticut, Ph.D. 1957. **Family:** Married Sheila Berger Wolfe in 1978; one daughter and one son. **Career:** Reporter, Springfield *Union,* Massachusetts, 1956-59, Washington *Post,* 1959-62, and New York, *Herald Tribune,* 1962-66; writer, New York *World Journal Tribune,* 1966-67. **Awards:** American Book award, 1980; Columbia award, for journalism, 1980. D.Litt.: Washington and Lee University, 1974. **Agent:** Lynn Nesbit, Janklow and Nesbit, 598 Madison Avenue, New York, New York 10022, U.S.A.

PUBLICATIONS

Novel

The Bonfire of the Vanities. New York, Farrar Straus, 1987; London, Cape, 1988.

Uncollected Short Stories

"The Commercial," in *Esquire* (New York), October 1975.
"2020 A.D.," in *Esquire* (New York), January 1985.

Other

The Kandy-Kolored Tangerine Flake Streamline Baby (essays). New York, Farrar Straus, 1965; London, Cape, 1966.
The Electric Kool-Aid Acid Test. New York, Farrar Straus, and London, Weidenfeld and Nicolson, 1968.
The Pump House Gang (essays). New York, Farrar Straus, 1968; as *The Mid-Atlantic Man and Other New Breeds in England and America,* London, Weidenfeld and Nicolson, 1969.
Radical Chic and Mau-Mauing the Flak Catchers. New York, Farrar Straus, 1970; London, Joseph, 1971.
The Painted Word. New York, Farrar Straus, 1975.
Mauve Gloves and Madmen, Clutter and Vine, and Other Stories (essays). New York, Farrar Straus, 1976.
The Right Stuff. New York, Farrar Straus, and London, Cape, 1979.
In Our Time (essays). New York, Farrar Straus, 1980.
From Bauhaus to Our House. New York, Farrar Straus, 1981; London, Cape, 1982.

Editor, with E.W. Johnson, *The New Journalism.* New York, Harper, 1973; London, Pan, 1975.

*

Critical Study: "Tom Wolfe's Vanities" by Joseph Epstein, in *New Criterion* (New York), February 1988.

*   *   *

"The Hell with it . . . let chaos reign . . . louder music, more wine . . . All the old traditions are exhausted, and no new one is yet established—" wrote Tom Wolfe in typically demonstrative fashion at the close of his 1973 introductory essay to *The New Journalism,* the anthology he co-edited with E.W. Johnson. In so forcibly reacting to the critical response to the bastard literary genre with which he has ever since been associated, Wolfe also directly challenged the eminence in America's prosaic culture of "The Novel."

Fourteen years later, Wolfe made his own debut on the "big fiction" circuit with *The Bonfire of the Vanities,* a work every bit as wide in scope and weighty in content as some of the heavy-wrought productions against which he had once railed. *The Bonfire of the Vanities* though, represents more an exploitation of the novel form than a homage to it, and, in it's hurtling Technicolor progress through a world in which the horrible maxim is "All for one and one for all and lots for oneself!" settled a few unanswered questions about the nature of Wolfe's output.

The Electric Kool-Aid Acid Test, upon which his original reputation rested, was not so much reportage as mutant mind-lab biographical improvisation. While it relied more heavily on historical fact than most novels, and was every jumpy inch as distorted and disjointed as the hallucinogenically-induced experiences it sought to describe, ultimately, Wolfe's first novel-length outing was utterly dependent on his own imaginative vibrancy. Valuable not only as an insight into the addled consciousness of fellow experimentalist Ken Kesey, Wolfe's tract remains, in all its fragmentary, speeding glory, the outstanding document of 1960s counter-culture; an exploration not only of the wild lifestyle of Kesey's Merry Pranksters, but a catalogue of the pressures which caused the embryonic hippie movement to self-combust.

This thick, rich stew of style and content followed one collection of pieces drawn from his journalistic career and emerged simultaneously with another. Through 37 articles, essays and musings, the reader is invited to trace the growth of Wolfe's technique and the development of a highly intuitive perceptive gift—catch him eyeing California's junior surf bums as they chill out on the extra-good vibe of being independent at 14 and living in low-rent garages: "they have this life all of their own; it's like a glass-bottom boat and it floats over the 'real' world . . .''; journey through America's car-customizing shops and small-town racetracks; crest the adrenal wave of being very young and hip in swinging London; meet Phil Spector, Cassius Clay, Marshall McLuhan, the list goes on.

During the 1970s, Wolfe's inquisitive ardor seems to have diminished somewhat. Fixing his attention on other areas of criticism, Wolfe turned in some surprisingly flat period pieces. In *Mauve Gloves and Madmen, Clutter and Vine*, however, he enjoyed a renaissance. Kicking off with a ritual dismemberment of a major author, and ending with a prophetic tale about the selfishness and ruthlessness of Manhattan cab-hailers, Wolfe roamed, among other things, through a dissertation on one woman's hemorrhoids, the story of a Navy pilot risking his life on a daily basis over North Vietnam and a genuinely funny piece of short fiction concerning one black athlete's efforts to make a conscionable perfume commercial.

In 1979, entering yet another brain-warping space, Wolfe produced an effortless and enthralling, warts and all history of America's launch into astronautical flight. *The Right Stuff*, borne out of Wolfe's "ordinary curiosity" remains his best-written and most complete book, consummately encapsulating, in all seriousness, the adventurous spirit of the age, while, as in previous works, functioning on the intimate level of fraternity tale—Tom, the clever brother, spectates, while the rest of the gang go off running and jumping into all manner of colorful and phenomenal dangers; in this case, sitting atop a huge stick of dynamite, waiting "for someone to light the fuse." A must for vicarious thrill seekers everywhere (although not as appealing, probably to animal rights activists), *The Right Stuff* is Wolfe's second absolutely indispensable book—as vital to the social historian as the reader with only the most limited interest in space flight.

The Bonfire of the Vanities, like everything Wolfe has done, seeks to hold up a mirror to contemporary life and shout "There! That's what its' like." Sherman McCoy's noisy descent from a fulgent cloud of privilege and wealth, into the purgatorial nether-world of New York's criminal justice system, is fitting reward for his participation in "the greed storm" of the consumerist 1980s. Wolfe's incisive political awareness, his desire to penetrate the "thickening democratic facade" is equally as urgent as in his earlier denunciation of White liberal angst *Radical Chic* (further, his understanding of what makes the underclasses tick is as piercing as in it's accompanying piece *Mau-Mauing The Flak Catchers*). McCoy, a cartoon-like central character is pitched on a spiraling express-ride into the deepest, most decrepit tunnels of urban deprivation, becoming the victim of the startling contrast between what he is capable of possessing and what others cannot hope to touch. McCoy's culpability matters little: it is significant only that he is suitably placed to become a totemic sacrifice in a political game—for this fact alone,

Wolfe finally offers him a ragged salvation whilst damning almost everyone else.

Wolfe has held tenure as amanuensis, arbiter of style, master of the idiom, observer and interpreter of signs, symbols, and portents for quarter of a century. That he always wanted somehow to be a novelist, albeit of a unique kind is self-evident. That whatever he next presents will be as innovative and stirring as what has gone before is equally so. What the subject will be, no one is likely to guess, for Wolfe has a magpie's approach and is capable of alighting on any glittering thing. Certainly, no-one will be bored.

—Ian McMechan

WOLFF, Tobias (Jonathan Ansell)

Nationality: American. **Born:** Birmingham, Alabama, 19 June 1945. **Education:** Hill School, 1964; Oxford University, B.A. 1972, M.A. 1975; Stanford University, California, M.A. 1977. **Military Service:** Served in the United States Army, 1964-68: Lieutenant. **Family:** Married Catherine Dolores Spohn in 1975; two sons and one daughter. **Career:** Jones Lecturer in creative writing, Stanford University, (Stegner fellow), 1975-78; since 1980 Peck Professor of English, Syracuse University, New York. **Awards:** National Endowment fellowship, 1978, 1985; Rinehart grant, 1979; O. Henry award, for short story, 1980, 1981, 1985; St. Lawrence award, 1981; Guggenheim fellowship, 1982; PEN/Faulkner award, 1985; Rea award, for short story, 1989; Whiting Foundation award, 1990; Lila Wallace-Reader's Digest award, 1994; Lyndhurst Foundation award, 1994; Esquire-Volvo-Waterstone's award, 1994. **Agent:** Amanda Urban, International Creative Management, 40 West 57th Street, New York, New York 10019.

PUBLICATIONS

Novel

The Barracks Thief. New York, Ecco Press, 1984; London, Cape, 1987.

Short Stories

In the Garden of the North American Martyrs. New York, Ecco Press, 1981; as *Hunters in the Snow,* London, Cape, 1982.
Back in the World. Boston, Houghton Mifflin, 1985.

Uncollected Short Stories

"The Other Miller," in *The Best American Short Stories 1987,* edited by Ann Beattie and Shannon Ravenel. Boston, Houghton Mifflin, 1987.
"Smorgasbord," in *The Best American Short Stories 1988,* edited by Mark Helprin and Shannon Ravenel. Boston, Houghton Mifflin, 1988.
"Migraine," in *Antaeus* (New York), Spring-Autumn, 1990.
"Sanity," in *Atlantic* (Boston), December 1990.

Other

Ugly Rumours. London, Allen and Unwin, 1975.

This Boy's Life: A Memoir. New York, Atlantic Monthly Press, and London, Bloomsbury, 1989.
In Pharaoh's Army: Memories of the Lost War. New York, Knopf, and London, Bloomsbury, 1994.

Editor, *Matters of Life and Death: New American Short Stories.* Green Harbor, Massachusetts, Wampeter Press, 1983.
Editor, *The Short Stories of Anton Chekhov.* New York, Bantam, 1987.
Editor, *Best American Short Stories, 1994.* New York, Houghton Mifflin, 1994.
Editor, *The Vintage Book of Contemporary American Short Stories.* New York, Vintage, 1994.

*

Tobias Wolff comments:
Writers are the worst interpreters of their own work. If their fiction is any good, it should be saying things they weren't aware of.

* * *

Tobias Wolff writes with a sparsity and clarity typical of the voices of the best writers of his generation, realists of the ilk of Raymond Carver, Richard Ford, William Kittredge, Jayne Anne Phillips, Mary Robison, and Stephanie Vaughan, all of whom are represented in *Matters of Life and Death,* an anthology of contemporary American short stories which Wolff put together in the early 1980s. In explaining his choices, Wolff wrote that in the stories "I heard something that I couldn't ignore, some notes of menace or hope or warning or appeal or awe; and in the matter of the stories themselves, the people who inhabit them and what they do, I saw something that I couldn't look away from."

The same should be said of Wolff's work. Every story, the novella *The Barracks Thief,* and the memoir *This Boy's Life* go right to the heart. Nowhere is there a slack page; Wolff writes as if each work were the only one he will every publish. He has admitted in interviews to being a relentless reviser. *The Barracks Thief,* scarcely a novella, was once a manuscript of several hundred pages. In the stories collected in *In the Garden of the North American Martyrs* and *Back in the World,* character development is quick and vivid, background material rare, as if Wolff has always kept clear in his mind Hemingway's axiom that stories get their energy from what is left unsaid. The result is a rather modest output. After 15 years of publishing, all of Wolff's work could easily be contained in a single volume of 600 pages. But this hypothetical volume would say as much if not more than any other conceivable work about the generation of American men born in the decade after World War II.

The men in Wolff's stories have fathers and uncles who fought and won in the good war; their own war is a squalid and ambiguous affair that went on and on in a very hot place, and the themes of these fictions are deceit, betrayal, failure, and self-loathing, and the queer persistence of fellow-feeling in spite of all of these. Wolff was himself a member of the Special Forces and had a tour of duty in Vietnam. Yet nowhere has he written—not yet, anyway—of combat or his service in Southeast Asia. Instead the war is insinuated, providing the future with menace, or the past with ambivalence and depth. In other words, unconfronted, unobtruded, the Vietnam war remains in Wolff's fiction what it is for most men of his age, non-combatants as well as soldiers, the great shaping force that can never quite be understood, much less expunged. Consequently, many of

Wolff's characters seemed surprised who they have become, survivors of a catastrophe who have become dependent on safety. As the narrator of *The Barracks Thief* puts it:

> I didn't set out to be what I am . . . I'm a conscientious man, a responsible man, maybe even what you'd call a good man—I hope so. But I'm also a careful man, addicted to comfort, with an eye for the safe course. My neighbors appreciate me because they know I will never give my lawn over to the cultivation of marijuana, or send my wife weeping to their doorsteps at three o'clock in the morning, or expect them to be my friends. I am content with my life most of the time.

Comfort, however, scarcely describes the experience of reading Wolff's fiction. Instead, the reader is made uneasy by characters whose actions, often for the best of motives, lead them into error and excess. In "Hunters in the Snow" Tub and Frank rediscover their friendship while Kenny, bleeding or freezing to death, lies neglected in the back of the pick-up truck. In "Coming Attractions," a sister risks her life trying to get a bicycle out of the deep end of a swimming pool. In "Dessert Breakdown, 1968" a man nearly abandons his wife and children on a whim. And in "The Rich Brother," a man leaves his ineffectual younger brother by the side of a highway in the cold and an almost absolute darkness. Driving all of Wolff's fiction is the dynamism derived from the irreconcilable difference between who we might like to be and who our actions reveal us to be.

In *This Boy's Life,* an autobiography of his adolescence, Wolff writes "It takes a childish or corrupt imagination to make symbols of other people," and the comment affords an important insight into Wolff's aesthetic and ethical aims. For all of their economy, Wolff's works are never glib or shallow. They are never didactic, and the characters who inhabit them speak and act on their own in settings that are precisely and efficiently conceived. The plots move quickly, and since characters are never arrested and made to stand for something, reading Wolff is a headlong sort of business, wholly free of the artificial and emphatic closures of more ponderous writing. Invariably Wolff leaves the fate of his characters open. This can be exhilarating; however oblique the strike, we feel that we have made contact with the honest sufferings and joys of real people.

—Mark A.R. Facknitz

WOUK, Herman

Nationality: American. **Born:** New York City, 27 May 1915. **Education:** Townsend Harris Hall, New York, 1927-30; Columbia University, New York (Fox prize, 1934), 1930-34, A.B. 1934. **Military Service:** Served in the United States Naval Reserve, 1942-46: Lieutenant. **Family:** Married Betty Sarah Brown in 1945; three sons (one deceased). **Career:** Radio writer, 1935; scriptwriter for the comedian Fred Allen, 1936-41; consultant, United States Treasury Department, 1941. Since 1946 full-time writer. Visiting professor of English, Yeshiva University, New York, 1952-58; scholar-in-residence, Aspen Institute, Colorado, 1973-74. Trustee, College of the Virgin Islands, 1961-69; member of the Board of Directors, Washington National Symphony, 1969-71, and Kennedy Center

Productions, 1974-75. **Awards:** Pulitzer prize, 1952; Columbia University Medal of Excellence, 1952, and Hamilton medal, 1980; *Washingtonian* award, 1986; American Academy of Achievement Golden Plate award, 1986; U.S. Navy Memorial Foundation award, 1987; Kazetnik award, 1990. L.H.D.: Yeshiva University, 1955; LL.D.: Clark University, Worcester, Massachusetts, 1960; D.Lit.: American International College, Springfield, Massachusetts, 1979; Honorary Ph.D.: Bar-Ilan University, Ramat-Gan, Israel, 1990. Lives in Washington, D.C. **Agent:** BSW Literary Agency, 3255 N Street N.W., Washington, D.C. 20007, U.S.A.

PUBLICATIONS

Novels

Aurora Dawn. New York, Simon and Schuster, and London, Barrie, 1947.
The City Boy. New York, Simon and Schuster, 1948; London, Cape, 1956.
The Caine Mutiny. New York, Doubleday, and London, Cape, 1951.
Marjorie Morningstar. New York, Doubleday, and London, Cape, 1955.
Slattery's Hurricane. New York, Permabooks, 1956; London, New English Library, 1965.
Youngblood Hawke. New York, Doubleday, and London, Collins, 1962.
Don't Stop the Carnival. New York, Doubleday, and London, Collins, 1965.
The Lomokome Papers. New York, Pocket Books, 1968.
The Winds of War. Boston, Little Brown, and London, Collins, 1971.
War and Remembrance. Boston, Little Brown, and London, Collins, 1978.
Inside, Outside. Boston, Little Brown, and London, Collins, 1985.
The Hope. Boston, Little Brown, and London, Hodder and Stoughton, 1993.
The Glory. Boston, Little Brown, and London, Hodder and Stoughton, 1994.

Uncollected Short Stories

"Herbie Solves a Mystery," in *Feast of Leviathan,* edited by L.W. Schwarz. New York, Rinehart, 1956.
"Old Flame," in *Good Housekeeping* (New York), May 1956.
"Irresistible Force," in *Fireside Treasury of Modern Humor,* edited by Scott Meredith. New York, Simon and Schuster, 1963.

Plays

The Traitor (produced New York, 1949). New York, French, 1949.
Modern Primitive (produced Hartford, Connecticut, 1951).
The Caine Mutiny Court-Martial (produced Santa Barbara, California, 1953; New York, 1954; London, 1956). New York, Doubleday, 1954; London, Cape, 1956.
Nature's Way (produced New York, 1957). New York, Doubleday, 1958.

Television Series: *The Winds of War,* 1983, and *War and Remembrance,* 1986, from his own novels.

Other

The Man in the Trench Coat. New York, National Jewish Welfare Board, 1941.
This Is My God: The Jewish Way of Life. New York, Doubleday, 1959; London, 1960; revised edition, London, Collins, 1973.

*

Manuscript Collection: Columbia University Library Special Collections, New York.

Critical Studies: "You, Me and the Novel" by Wouk, in *Saturday Review-World* (New York), 29 June 1974; *Herman Wouk: The Novelist as Social Historian* by Arnold Beichman, New Brunswick, New Jersey, Transaction, 1984; *Herman Wouk* by Laurence W. Mazzeno, New York, Twayne, 1994.

Herman Wouk comments:

No author should be trusted to discuss his own work in an encyclopedia or a compendium until he has been dead thirty or forty years. Then, if anyone still cares, and if he can be raised at a séance, his opinion might be sufficiently detached to be worth something.

*   *   *

Herman Wouk continues to enjoy wide readership and to suffer critical attack for essentially the same reasons. He has a strong commitment to established values, which he champions only after energetic and attractive presentation of the Devil's case. Often, he plays Devil's advocate so well that the book's concluding reversal to affirmation of the status quo suggests mere pandering to popular prejudice. When the book is done, the rebels emerge as villains and the evils rebelled against as blemishes on the face of a healthy world.

Thus *Aurora Dawn* is an attack on vulgarity and dishonesty in advertising, not on advertising itself, and the bullying boss is only a witless product of nepotism, not a true portrait of capitalism's face. Andrew Reale, who chases money at the price of his soul, finds salvation when his discarded fiancée inherits money and takes him back—after her millionaire husband gallantly releases her from a marriage made on the rebound. Thus, Andrew is saved from money-grubbing's debasements through a millionaire's generosity and an heiress' forgiveness.

In *The Caine Mutiny,* Wouk's Pulitzer-prize novel of World War II, a strong case is made out for mutiny aboard an American destroyer during a Pacific storm, when the paranoiac Captain Queeg breaks under pressure. When all is done, however, only the legal verdict goes to the rebels; morally, Lieutenant Keefer and his followers are guilty of deserting a military system which, despite its resident fascists, has protected American freedom against foreign fascism. *Marjorie Morningstar* chronicles the false emancipation of Marjorie Morgenstern from the values and authority of her hardworking Jewish parents to the glitter of the theater and bohemian "freedom." Then, renouncing her renunciation, the beautiful, intelligent Marjorie readily accepts her suburban destiny as lawyer's wife, mother of two and community servant. Interestingly, in both novels the "intellectual" (Lt. Keefer and writer Noel Airman) is unmasked as an insubstantial fraud, while the philistine, even when vicious and insane like Queeg, is sincere and somewhat heroic. In both novels, the protagonists, Princetonian Willie Keith and

Bronxite Marjorie, must learn that the old ways are the best ways: obedience, chastity before marriage, the faith of one's fathers, hard work and money, all sound dull but ring true. In form and style, Wouk is equally traditionalist, his early works ranging from parody of Fielding (*Aurora Dawn*) and Booth Tarkington (*The City Boy*) to Victorian-sized melodramas (*Marjorie Morningstar*) bursting with incident and character.

His two next novels, *Youngblood Hawke* and *Don't Stop the Carnival,* also abound in plot and character but are below his best work. Wouk's gargantuan Arthur Youngblood was obviously modeled on Thomas Wolfe, then grated onto a melodramatic plot of the artist turned businessman, with his talent destroyed by greed and scheming women. But Wouk does not succeed in portraying Wolfe-Hawke as a dedicated artist; instead, it is Wouk and Hawke who seem to blend in the intensity of "their" business interests and speculative shenanigans, so that the money parts of the book command more authority than the literary parts. In *Don't Stop the Carnival* Wouk returned to comedy with his middle-aged cardiac victim, Norman Paperman, who exchanges a Broadway press agent's life for ownership of a Caribbean hotel. Alas, on his island paradise, life proves even more frantic as foundation walls burst, typhoons rage, and mad employees decapitate others—but Norman copes. When all is under control, Paperman unaccountably sells out cheap (as Wouk seems to do) and returns to ulcer-ridden Broadway. But the novel does display the same comedic flair for oddball characters, clever dialogue, fast intercutting, and imaginative slapstick as had *Aurora Dawn, The City Boy* (about a Jewish Penrod) and even *Marjorie Morningstar.*

Possibly, light comedy and fond satire are Wouk's forte, since his serious views seem uninspired and inhibited. But his two-volume series *The Winds of War* and *War and Remembrance* is surely his most ambitious work. The two books trace the lives of Navy Commander, later Admiral Victor Henry, and his family from 1939 through World War II, and the end of his marriage. The size and broad aims of the volumes suggest Tolstoy's *War and Peace,* but the quality of the writing is closer to Upton Sinclair's Lanny Budd series.

—Frank Campenni

WRIGHT, Charles (Stevenson)

Nationality: American. **Born:** New Franklin, Missouri, 4 June 1932. Educated in public schools in New Franklin and Sedalia, Missouri. **Military Service:** Served in the United States Army, in Korea, 1952-54. **Career:** Stockboy in St. Louis, late 1950s; then freelance writer: columnist ("Wright's World"), *Village Voice,* New York. Lives in New York City. **Address:** c/o Farrar, Straus and Giroux, 19 Union Square West, New York, New York 10003, U.S.A.

PUBLICATIONS

Novels

The Messenger. New York, Farrar Straus, 1963; London, Souvenir Press, 1964.

The Wig: A Mirror Image. New York, Farrar Straus, 1966; London, Souvenir Press, 1967.
Absolutely Nothing to Get Alarmed About. New York, Farrar Straus, 1973.

Uncollected Short Stories

"A New Day," in *The Best Short Stories by Negro Writers,* edited by Langston Hughes. Boston, Little Brown, 1967.
"Sonny and the Sailor," in *Negro Digest* (Chicago), August 1968.
"Mr. Stein," in *Black American Literature Forum* (Terre Haute, Indiana), Summer 1989.

*

Charles Wright comments:

(1972) Numbers. One number has always walked through the front door of my mind. But when I was writing my first book, *The Messenger,* I did not think of numbers. I was very bitter at the time. *The Messenger* was simply a money roof. I was amused at its success. Mini-popular first published thing. A pleasant dream with the frame of reality.

The Wig was my life. And as I write this on a night of the last week in April of 1971—I have no regrets. Let me explain: A year after the publication of *The Messenger* I was thinking of that folkloric, second novel, and began a rough draft of a novel about a group of Black men, very much like the Black Panthers. But, in 1963, America was not ready for *that* type of novel, nor were they ready for *The Wig.* Ah! That is the first horror hors d'oeuvre. My agent, Candida Donadio, said: "This is a novel. Write it." I will tell you quite simply . . . that I was afraid that I could not sustain the thing for say . . . fifty pages.

Now it was another year, another country (Morocco). Frightened, I returned to the states and rewrote *The Wig* in twenty-nine days . . . the best days of my life. The basic plot was the same but most of it was new. Thinking, working, like seven and, yes, sometimes fourteen hours a day. It took me less than three hours to make the final changes before the publishers accepted. I was *hot* . . . hot for *National Desire* . . . a short N. West-type of novel very much like *The Wig,* although *Race* would not have been the theme.

And.

And. Many things have happened to me and to my country since then. The country has always been like this, I suppose. I only know that something left me. As a result . . . I haven't written a novel in six years. I remember Langston Hughes saying: "Write another nice, little book like *The Messenger.* White folks don't like to know that Negros can write books like that." Ah, yes . . . dear, dead Friend. Then. Yes. Another *Messenger.* And, what follows? Something that I've always wanted to do, something different . . . say an action packed Hemingway novel and then say . . . a Sackville-West novel. All I've ever wanted was a home by the sea and to be a good writer.

*   *   *

The literary output of Charles Wright has been slight in volume and promising, but not always effective, in practice. Wright's three small "novels" are each the size of Nathanael West novels, and they reflect the same mordant wit, yearning despair, and surrealistic lunacy of vintage West. Wright's world, however, is essentially a race-twisted society of black grotesques, of crippled lovers and dishwasher poets whose lives of wine, whores, and junkie-songs spell slow murder in white America.

The Messenger, The Wig, and *Absolutely Nothing to Get Alarmed About* portray an Inferno-world of sexual deviates: prostitutes (male and female), pimps, transvestites, poseurs, flower-children, sadistic cops. We meet not only lovers but pretenders, false black friends who set you up, genteel female perverts, white liberals whose children suddenly snarl "nigger," beloved black musicians who betray their heritage to gain white favor. Each novel centers around the efforts of a young protagonist ("Charles Stevenson" in the first and "Charles Wright" in the third novel) to cope with city life, where literally and metaphorically the protagonists prostitute themselves to survive. Each must dissemble, disguise, and sell himself; each finds the gimmicks and the humbling tricks to hustle an existence.

In *The Messenger,* which is heavily autobiographical, a young writer, Charles Stevenson (Wright's full name is Charles Stevenson Wright), stumbles to find himself, moving from the South to the army to New York. As a writer, he knows he must feel and record; his literal job as messenger is unimportant compared to his literary obligation to spread the word about life. As a black, however, he is torn between his compassion for outcast blacks and his emotional shield compounded of numbness, indifference, and cynicism. Although the writing occasionally slips into clichés or strained metaphor, style is the novel's chief attraction and is marvelously wedded to content. The writing is terse, the narrator-hero's manner laconic and usually guarded. Most episodes are deliberately inconclusive and undeveloped, sketchy vignettes that affect the narrator more than he acknowledges. Deeply touching are the few pages in which the spiritually exhausted young veteran is united with his warm, righteous grandmother, while his athletic command performance in a southern police station is outrageously comic and brilliantly symbolic of racial debasement.

If *The Messenger* seems like a patch-quilt of styles and moods, *The Wig* is more consistent in tone and mood, but regrettably so. For Wright's second novel goes all-out as black comedy, but despite its wildness it is more black, or malicious, than comic. There is a similar gallery of transvestites and other disguise-wearing freaks in quest of identity without guilt, failure, or self-hatred, but they are portrayed without hope or compassion. The hero, Lester Jefferson, is, like all the other blacks, on the make: he has conked and curled his Afro hair into a beautiful white "wig" that will open the doors to the Great (White) Society. Alas, he doesn't make it but we are not even sorry, for neither he nor the author reaches Ellison's solution that "visibility" begins with confronting and accepting one's truly created self. There are two or three successful comic achievements: Jimmy Wishbone, who once "kept 100 million colored people contented for years" as a Stepin Fetchit type in movies and who now wants to sue white society and redeem his lost fleet of Cadillacs; and Lester himself, crawling the streets in a feathery chicken-suit as employee of the Southern Fried Chicken King.

The last exchange of dialogue in *The Messenger* goes: "'Charles, what's wrong?' 'Nothing,' I said. 'Absolutely nothing.'" Wright's latest novelistic autobiography, *Absolutely Nothing to Get Alarmed About,* picks up from its predecessor's conclusion, although the locale has moved from mid-Manhattan to the Lower East Side. The mood if more uniformly despairing, with only a few attempts at the pathos and yearning of *The Messenger* or the caustic hilarity of *The Wig.* In place of the homosexual-junkie nightmare world of *The Messenger,* Wright's metaphor of our foundering American culture is here the yellow-black-white world of the Bowery. Appropriate to their original publication in New York's *Village Voice,* many chapters echo the vivid tone and the felt immediacy of "new journalism" prose.

—Frank Campenni

WURLITZER, Rudolph

Nationality: American. **Born:** 1937. **Awards:** *Atlantic* Firsts award, 1966. **Address:** c/o Knopf Inc., 201 East 50th Street, New York, New York 10022, U.S.A.

PUBLICATIONS

Novels

Nog. New York, Random House, 1969; as *The Octopus,* London, Weidenfeld and Nicolson, 1969.
Flats. New York, Dutton, 1970; London, Gollancz, 1971.
Quake. New York, Dutton, 1972; London, Pan, 1985.
Slow Fade. New York, Knopf, 1984; London, Pan, 1985.
Walker (novelization of screenplay). New York, Perennial Library, 1987.

Uncollected Short Story

"Boiler Room," in *Atlantic* (Boston), March 1966.

Plays

Two-Lane Blacktop (screenplay), with Will Corry. New York, Award, 1971.

Screenplays: *Two-Lane Blacktop,* with Will Corry, 1971; *Glen and Randa,* with Lorenzo Mans and Jim McBride, 1971; *Pat Garrett and Billy the Kid,* 1973; *Walker,* 1989; *Voyager,* 1991.

Other

Hard Travel to Sacred Places. Boston, Shambhala, 1994.

*

Theatrical Activities:
Actor: **Films**—*Two-Lane Blacktop,* 1971; *Pat Garrett and Billy the Kid,* 1973.

Critical Studies: *Rudolph Wurlitzer, American Novelist and Screenwriter* by David Seed, Lewiston, New York, Mellen Press, 1991.

*   *   *

Rudolph Wurlitzer's novels represent a determined attempt to escape the materials of narrative. Unwilling to suspend disbelief and create a representative world of people, places, and ideals, he discards the conventions of mimetic storytelling in favor of a flat-out style of direct address which in his later novels slowly modulates into a more naturalized manner, yet never one that attempts to counterfeit a world. Instead, Wurlitzer's later work draws upon certain artifices of conduct which by virtue of long use have a structure which appears to be naturally made. In either case, the novelist is excused from proposing an enabling structure for his work; from first to last, Wurlitzer's novels speak with their own sense of authority, pretending to be nothing other than they are.

Nog and *Flats* are alternately diverse and spare works which rely upon the narrator's direct address for their substance and direction. Mirror-images of the same artistic vision, these novels contrast wild geographic narrative with a Beckett-like stasis of character, mood, and location, yet each ending with the same sense of voice alone. Even coherent character yields to this presence of mere voice, since in the first work Wurlitzer's narrator sometimes talks about Nog as a distinct person ("Nog, he was apparently of Finnish extraction, was one of those semi-religious lunatics you see wandering around the Sierras on bread and tea, or gulping down peyote in Nevada with the Indians") and other times speaks as Nog himself, while the narrator of *Flats* proposes a similar exchange of identities with a person he has met and has been describing. The effect of such shimmering exchanges is to efface any sense of represented identity, establishing the narrative voice as a pure speaking sound which draws its sense of character from what is being described. In *Nog* this iridescence becomes geographical, as the narrator's voice yields to the on-running panorama of place, from the desert American southwest, through the Pacific and the Panama Canal, to the eastern seaboard and New York City. *Flats* presents the precise opposite of this range, but not of this tendency: the narrator sits within a small square of wasteland, vocally defending his space against all interlopers. He and they are named by their apparent home towns—"Call me Memphis," he introduces himself—but in their little square of desert they are motionless and without any identities all the same. All that exists is their voice, which is the text of Wurlitzer's novel.

Thematically, Wurlitzer argues against representation as well. Nog prizes silence and is proud not to divulge information to other characters (and therefore to the reader): "No history," he remarks, "therefore no bondage." Rather than act, he makes lists, because "Lists don't need direction." *Flats* elevates this theme to phenomenological proportion, refusing to grasp events lest their surface take shape. "I don't care to look around, having disappeared in all directions," the narrator admits, refusing any identity at all. "There is only my momentum," which is the text's own movement. And even this is reductive: "I want to say the same words over and over. I want just the sound. I want to fill up what space I am with one note . . . I want a sound that is not involved with beginning or ending." Wurlitzer's subsequent novels, *Quake* and *Slow Fade,* maintain their author's spare sense of prose, but now a textually self-conscious situation relieves the burden of flat narration. In *Quake* it is an earth tremor which by devastating the landscape erases any sense of conventional continuity; as the artifices of normal behavior crumble, the narrator is free to establish his own voice as the sole reality of his story. "The words around us blurred and carried no definition," and so his voice is the only anchor of authority. Yet the unreality unleashed by the earthquake is only a destruction of conventional-

ity; what is now revealed is that "this day has given expression to what has always been latent within us." By the novel's end the narrator is reduced to guttural sounds, his own ability to articulate having been destroyed with the world around him. Yet even before this it has proven to be a talent whose time has been eclipsed.

Slow Fade is ostensibly Wurlitzer's most conventional work, as it is set securely within a recognizable world and is peopled by characters whose consistency of motive and behavior qualifies them for the most realistic fiction. But as with *Quake,* the author's choice of circumstance allows for purely self-conscious narrative, since here the action involves scriptwriting and filming, two undertakings which lend a textual self-appearance to the novel. As the stories of film director Wesley Hardin, his children, and his intrusive entrepreneur evolve, the narrative becomes less a document of their lives than a series of filters and indirect analyses, as events are perceived not as themselves but with references to scenes in films. This sense of intertextuality is enhanced by Wes's desire to learn the fate of his daughter, which he pursues by paying his son to write a film script which fictionalizes the details yet encodes the answer to his question. Yet as his son writes the script, he pauses to question his father about their relationship and to sort out the memory of his own wife's life and death. Soon so many layers of textuality have been sedimented upon the basic story that only text (and not any representations) remain. The climax of this layering occurs when Wes Hardin aborts his own film project and becomes the subject of a *cinema-verité* work encompassing his own breakdown as occasioned by his daughter's loss. In this respect the role of the entrepreneur A.D. Ballou, becomes instrumental. What happens in the world, Wurlitzer concludes, is due to direct action but by the manipulation of texts. As A.D. Ballou produces Hardin's autobiographical movie, so too does the reader produce the narrators' texts. Without either act, nothing would happen, and therefore Wurlitzer's novels place as little as possible in the way of this readerly action.

With *Walker,* Wurlitzer combines his novelist's role with his screenwriting activities to produce a work far different from the usual novelization of a film. The story itself is based on history, evoking the colorful career of the mid-19th-century American adventurer William Walker as a way of providing not just a colorful narrative about Nicaragua during those years but a metaphoric commentary on American involvement in that country during the 1980s. Walker was a freebooting entrepreneur who made use of the business interests of Cornelius Vanderbilt in installing himself as President of Nicaragua, a position he held from 1855 through 1857. That his empire fell and he was eventually executed by a Honduran firing squad does not detract from his sense of ambition and idealism, tempered by the current reader's appreciation that such motives have often led to disasters in American foreign policy and the most unconscionable exploitation of foreign lands. In presenting this work Wurlitzer provides a fictive narrative, but supplements it with both historical and Walker's autobiographical accounts; these are then framed with shooting notes, production journals, and interviews with the filmmakers.

—Jerome Klinkowitz

Y-Z

YAFFE, James

Nationality: American. **Born:** Chicago, Illinois, 31 March 1927.
Education: Fieldston School, graduated 1944; Yale University, New
Haven, Connecticut, 1944-48, B.A. (summa cum laude) 1948 (Phi
Beta Kappa). **Military Service:** Served in the United States Navy,
1945-46. **Family:** Married Elaine Gordon in 1964; two daughters
and one son. **Career:** Since 1968 member of the Department of
English, currently professor of English, and since 1981 Director
of General Studies, Colorado College, Colorado Springs. **Awards:**
National Endowment for the Arts award, for drama, 1968. **Address:**
1215 North Cascade Avenue, Colorado Springs, Colorado 80903,
U.S.A.

PUBLICATIONS

Novels

The Good-for-Nothing. Boston, Little Brown, and London, Constable, 1953.
What's the Big Hurry? Boston, Little Brown, 1954; as *Angry Uncle Dan,* London, Constable, 1955.
Nothing But the Night. Boston, Little Brown, 1957; London, Cape, 1958.
Mister Margolies. New York, Random House, 1962.
Nobody Does You Any Favors. New York, Putnam, 1966.
The Voyage of the Franz Joseph. New York, Putnam, 1970.
Saul and Morris, Worlds Apart. New York, Holt Rinehart, 1982.
A Nice Murder for Mom. New York, St. Martin's Press, 1988.
Mom Meets Her Maker. New York, St. Martin's Press, 1990.
Mom Doth Murder Sleep. New York, St. Martin's Press, 1991.
Mom Among the Liars. New York, St. Martin's Press, 1993.

Short Stories

Poor Cousin Evelyn. Boston, Little Brown, 1951; London, Constable, 1952.

Uncollected Short Stories

"Mom Knows Best," in *The Queen's Awards 7,* edited by Ellery
Queen. Boston, Little Brown, and London, Gollancz, 1952.
"On the Brink," in *The Queen's Awards 8,* edited by Ellery Queen.
Boston, Little Brown, and London, Gollancz, 1953.
"Mom Makes a Bet," in *Best Detective Stories of the Year 1953,*
edited by David Coxe Cooke. New York, Dutton, 1953.
"Mom in the Spring," in *The Queen's Awards 9,* edited by Ellery
Queen. Boston, Little Brown, and London, Gollancz, 1954.
"Mom Makes a Wish," in *The Queen's Awards 10,* edited by Ellery
Queen. Boston, Little Brown, and London, Gollancz, 1955.
"Mom Sheds a Tear," in *Best Detective Stories of the Year 1955,*
edited by David Coxe Cooke. New York, Dutton, 1955.
"One of the Family," in *The Queen's Awards 11,* edited by Ellery
Queen. New York, Simon and Schuster, and London, Collins,
1956.

"Mom Sings an Aria," in *All-Star Lineup,* edited by Ellery Queen.
New York, New American Library, 1966; London, Gollancz,
1968.
"Mom and the Haunted Mink," in *Mystery Parade,* edited by Ellery
Queen. New York, New American Library, 1969.
"The Problem of the Emperor's Mushrooms," in *All But Impossible!,* edited by Edward D. Hoch. New Haven, Connecticut,
Ticknor and Fields, 1981; London, Hale, 1983.
"D.I.C. (Department of Impossible Crimes)," in *Ellery Queen's
Book of First Appearances,* edited by Ellery Queen and Eleanor
Sullivan. New York, Dial Press, 1982.

Plays

The Deadly Game, adaptation of a novel by Friedrich Dürrenmatt
(produced New York, 1960; London, 1967). New York, Dramatists Play Service, 1960.
This Year's Genie (for children), in *Eight Plays 2,* edited by Malcolm
Stuart Fellows. London, Cassell, 1965.
Ivory Tower, with Jerome Weidman (produced Ann Arbor, Michigan, 1968). New York, Dramatists Play Service, 1969.
Cliffhanger (as *Immorality Play,* produced Atlanta, 1983; as
Cliffhanger, produced New York, 1985). New York, Dramatists
Play Service, 1985.

Television Plays: For *U.S. Steel Hour, Studio One, G.E. Theater,
Frontiers of Faith, The Defenders, Breaking Point, Alfred
Hitchcock Presents, The Doctors and the Nurses,* and other series, 1953-67.

Other

The American Jews. New York, Random House, 1968.
So Sue Me! The Story of a Community Court. New York, Saturday Review Press, 1972.

*

James Yaffe comments:

(1991) For me, to write novels has been to create characters and
to combine and juxtapose those characters, involve them in confrontations, place them in situations which challenge them,
strengthen them, destroy them, transform them, test their mettle—
and out of a variety of such characters, to build a world. Where do
I get the raw material for my characters? From my own experience, of course—mostly from my experience of the world I was
born and brought up in, the world of middle-class, second- and
third-generation Jews living in New York, Chicago, Los Angeles,
I have chosen to write about this world because I know it instinctively and subliminally, because it was part of me before I was old
enough to doubt my perceptions.

But I have always tried to treat this experience not analytically
or sociologically or philosophically but novelistically—that is, by
imagining, and trying to re-create, the world as seen through each
character's eyes. The greatest novelists, it seems to me, are those
who succeed in merging their personalities with the lives and feelings of their people. This is the special ability shared by writers as

different as Tolstoy and Jane Austen, Trollope and Joyce (to mention a few of my favorites). The attempt to follow their example may be presumptuous and doomed to failure, but it is also inevitable for anybody who wants to write novels.

*   *   *

James Yaffe is considered a leading novelist of middle-class Jewish life in America. His early collection of short stories (*Poor Cousin Evelyn*) and his first novel (*The Good-for-Nothing*) are essentially drawing room comedies set in New York. As in the novels of Jane Austen, whom Yaffe admits a special fondness for, small conflicts are closely scrutinized within a closed society—in Yaffe's case, the Jewish family, with all its attendant social hierarchies, its patriarchs, its strong-men and its failures, its pressures of shame and guilt applied by loved ones to safeguard conformity and tradition. In these earlier works, characters are simply drawn and situations directly presented, largely through dialogue.

A recurring Yaffe theme involves the "dreamer," an impractical or artistically oriented individual confronted with pressures to survive in a competitive business world of the shady deals and opportunism. In *The Good-for-Nothing* this conflict is represented by two brothers, apparently very different from each other, yet mutually dependent. The one is college-educated and totally ineffectual in the business world, a charming sycophant. The other, a Certified Public Accountant, supports him, but in so doing restricts his own life. As they interact, it becomes unclear which is the "good for nothing," which the success or the failure: in different ways, both are unwilling to face responsibilities or the possibility of failure. Self-righteousness and self-indulgence, like sentimentality, are both forms of escape, excuses for not taking risks.

In a later novel, *Mister Margolies,* this pattern of self-deception is advanced to the point where the manipulation of reality becomes a life-style. Stanley Margolies, defeated in his early attempt to become a concert pianist, yet unable to give up totally his dreams of a poetic life, withdraws into a world of fantasies. The reality of business and competition crashes in on this, and he withdraws deeper, erecting more elaborate defenses. Yaffe's "dreamers" create worlds which are both sad and poetic, but they are not the demonic Rose-gardens of the totally mad. They are the tiny fantasies of little men, dreams reinforced by sympathetic and condescending friends with whom they still retain some form of contact.

Yaffe avoids several stereotypes popular in much contemporary Jewish literature: the dominant Jewish Mother, and the Jew-Gentile confrontation, particularly in matters sexual, as an expression of, or as a means of resolving feelings of inferiority. In general, he maintains a comic narrative tone—some of the scenes are funny—and though his characters are forever lecturing each other, their messages are frequently as confused as they are. The novels themselves preach little other than a deep compassion for the small man and his hopes.

The theme of the dreamer in search of his vision makes a terrifying appearance in *Nothing But the Night,* which is based on the Nathan Leopold-Richard Loeb murder case of 1924, and the celebrated defense by Clarence Darrow. The case history is seen through the eyes of one of the young men, not as an investigation of the criminal mind, but as a study of a lonely and creative child. As in Chekhov, Yaffe's characters take their emotions very seriously and ponder them deeply. They are often trapped by their own visions and the pressures to succeed imposed from outside. In their struggle to hold on to their dreams, they are destroyed, transformed,

and occasionally liberated. An example of the latter is presented in *Nobody Does You Any Favors,* which despite its 1940s cinemasounding title is perhaps his best novel. As opposed to the earlier New York novels which suggest short stories in their structural focus on a single event, *Nobody Does You Any Favors* with its time span of roughly 40 years allows for an extended development and growth in character. The confrontation between father and son is drawn with an understanding and passion valid beyond a scene of very special terror and insight. Certainly this novel is a significant contribution to American literature of the 20th century.

The Voyage of the Franz Joseph represented an epic departure from his usual drawing room style. Like *Nothing But the Night,* it is based on an historical event, the sailing of the German liner *St. Louis* in 1939 with a thousand Jewish refugees searching for a homeland.

—Paul Seiko Chihara

YGLESIAS, Helen

Nationality: American. **Born:** Helen Bassine in New York City, 29 March 1915. **Family:** Married 1) Bernard Cole in 1938 (divorced 1950), one son and one daughter; 2) Jose Yglesias, *q.v.,* in 1950, one son. **Career:** Literary editor, the *Nation,* New York, 1965-69; Visiting Professor, Columbia University School of the Arts, New York, 1973, and University of Iowa Writers Workshop, Iowa City, 1980. **Awards:** Houghton Mifflin Literary fellowship, 1972. **Address:** North Brooklin, Maine 04616, U.S.A.

PUBLICATIONS

Novels

How She Died. Boston, Houghton Mifflin, 1972; London, Heinemann, 1973.
Family Feeling. New York, Dial Press, 1976; London, Hodder and Stoughton, 1977.
Sweetsir. New York, Simon and Schuster, and London, Hodder and Stoughton, 1981.
The Saviors. Boston, Houghton Mifflin, 1987.

Uncollected Short Stories

"Semi-Private," in *New Yorker,* 5 February 1972.
"Kaddish and Other Matters," in *New Yorker,* 6 May 1974.
"Liar, Liar," in *Seventeen* (New York), February 1976.

Other

Starting: Early, Anew, Over, and Late. New York, Rawson Wade, 1978.
Isabel Bishop. New York, Rizzoli, 1989.

*   *   *

The novels of Helen Yglesias were written from her 54th year onwards. As she notes in her book of meditations, *Starting: Early, Anew, Over, and Late,* she had already had an active career of book reviewing and editorial work; she was for a time the literary editor of the *Nation*. Yglesias's account of her career and of the careers of other men and women in *Starting* shows that a recurrent pattern in her novels is an expression of her own sense of what a proper career for a person is. Each person has, as the many conversations with others in *Starting* shows, the opportunity to discover his or her "true self" and initiate actions that allow that self to unfold. Or, alternately, to turn aside and spend the years in conformity to the expectations of a group and thus court defeat and stultification. As Yglesias asks in the Introduction to *Starting:* "Is there 'a true self'? Does it indeed exist and does its existence matter? Is there measurable damage in human and social terms when an impostor inhabits the corner of space and time reserved for a unique self—whatever that is? To do what one has always wanted to do—to be what one has always wanted to be—what does that mean?"

In the body of her book Yglesias devotes space to her own life as a young Jewish intellectual bucking the waves of indifference she met in the 1930s; it is a story that is repeated in her second novel, *Family Feeling*. She also relates the "starting" of her son, the novelist Rafael Yglesias, who, in his mid-teens, withdrew from society to realize *his* artistic destiny. And Yglesias moves on to many others whose diverse destinies are marked by the urgent questioning she directed at her own life. With a sort of modesty she remarks of herself: "I admit to a vast general ignorance of things physical, technological, mythical, religious, and political-social." Such remarks indicate the drive behind the novels, and they also suggest the areas that are left for other novelists to handle. The Yglesias novels are tales of struggle: chiefly female struggle in a society that imposes on such struggle a terminology invented by males. Yglesias is a connoisseur of the successes and failures that women like her heroines—and one supposes, herself—meet. These struggles are often well realized and convince not so much by their general truth as by the mass of detail that is clustering at center-stage. This gives the novels an effect of conviction that cannot be overlooked. Occasionally Yglesias abandons this area for theoretical speculation; she endows a heroine with her own former or present political loyalties and her own esthetic preferences, and the novels become temporarily less vivid. But the textures that are impelling are soon re-established.

Family Feeling is the novel that is a rough equivalent (and a successful one) to the story Yglesias tells in the opening section of *Starting*. *Sweetsir* is a negative version of the successful struggles in *Family Feeling;* the efforts of the heroine of *Sweetsir* commence and recommence but never move very far from the point where the repeated departures take place: the heroine's desire to be something, to realize in the relations of love some amorphous inner power that the heroine senses but cannot express. In contrast, the heroine of *Family Feeling* has an abundance of words to apply to each twist and turn of *her* journey. Yglesias's first novel, *How She Died,* is an account of a woman whose "starting" and its consequences lie somewhere between the distinct success and the grim failures related in the other two novels. The heroine of *How She Died,* Jean, devotes herself to a dying woman, has a love-affair with the woman's husband, neglects her own children, and realizes that her political ardor has brought her little reason for pride.

The other two novels, as suggested, are more decisive in their impact. *Family Feeling* reproduces the complex history of an immigrant Jewish family: a family that starts in poverty and that ends—for some of the members at least—in considerable prosperity and personal satisfaction. Barry Goddard is a son who ends as the owner of vast enterprises *and* an apartment that overlooks Central Park. Anne, whose intelligence is usually (but not always) the cen-

ter of the story, follows a different course, one which leads her through social protest, literary projects that occasionally distract the reader, and finally to several years of a happy marriage with a WASP magazine editor who finds the Jewishness of Anne's family a constant diversion. The main concern of the moving narrative is not the social and personal goods that various characters grasp; it is the panorama of endless struggle—of "starting" and then achieving a continuation that is sometimes wasteful and sometimes admirable.

Such continuations do not appear in *Sweetsir*. This long and minutely executed novel, in which many pages are devoted to the details of legal procedures, begins with a domestic battle between Sally and Morgan Sweetsir, a battle that ends when Sally pushes a knife into the body of her brutal husband. Attention thus engages, the reader is conducted through the considerable number of years that brought Sally Sweetsir to her fatal confrontation. If one chooses to wonder why Sally's many "startings" go nowhere in particular, answers arise again and again. Sally comes from a lower-class milieu where there is no such tradition of struggle and survival as that which gave strength to Anne Goddard in *Family Feeling*. Sally has almost no words to put to her desires, the desires that take her through two marriages and into the law courts. And she lacks the intelligence to direct the sexuality and the ambition that come and go in her. And quite beyond her control are the crudity and insensitivity of the two males in her life. It is no surprise that in Sally's "world" (as assembled by Yglesias) Sally does not have to pay a social penalty for her "crime." Her long list of failures to "start" constitutes a sufficient punishment.

Yglesias describes her novel writing as "a happiness I could only liken to the happiness of love." Such happiness is open to the reader in long stretches of *Family Feeling*. And its absence is keenly felt elsewhere in the work of Yglesias.

—Harold H. Watts

YGLESIAS, Jose

Nationality: American. **Born:** Tampa, Florida, 29 November 1919. **Education:** Black Mountain College, North Carolina, 1946-47. **Military Service:** Served in the United States Navy, 1942-45: Presidential Citation. **Family:** Married Helen Bassine (i.e., Helen Yglesias, *q.v.*) in 1950; one son and two stepchildren. **Career:** Dishwasher, bus boy, stock clerk; film critic, *Daily Worker,* New York, 1948-50; assistant to the vice-president, Merch Sharp and Dohme International, 1953-63; Regents' Lecturer, University of California, Santa Barbara, 1973. **Awards:** Guggenheim fellowship, 1970, 1976; National Endowment for the Arts grant, 1974. **Agent:** Wallace Literary Agency, 177 East 70th Street, New York, New York 10021. **Address:** c/o Simon and Schuster, 1230 Avenue of the Americas, New York, New York 10020, U.S.A.

PUBLICATIONS

Novels

A Wake in Ybor City. New York, Holt Rinehart, 1963.
An Orderly Life. New York, Pantheon, 1967; London, Hutchinson, 1968.

The Truth about Them. Cleveland, World, 1971.
Double, Double. New York, Viking Press, 1974.
The Kill Price. Indianapolis, Bobbs Merrill, 1976.
Home Again. New York, Arbor House, 1987.
Tristan and the Hispanics. New York, Simon and Schuster, 1989.

Uncollected Short Stories

"The Guns in the Closet," in *The Best American Short Stories 1972,* edited by Martha Foley. Boston, Houghton Mifflin, 1972.
"In the Bronx," in *American Review 19,* edited by Theodore Solotaroff. New York, Bantam, 1974.
"The American Sickness," in *The Best American Short Stories 1975,* edited by Martha Foley. Boston, Houghton Mifflin, 1975.

Other

The Goodbye Land. New York, Pantheon, 1967; London, Hutchinson, 1968.
In the Fist of the Revolution: Life in a Cuban Country Town. New York, Pantheon, 1968; as *In the Fist of the Revolution: Life in Castro's Cuba,* London, Allen Lane, 1968.
Down There (on Latin America). Cleveland, World, 1970.
The Franco Years: The Untold Human Story of Life under Spanish Fascism. Indianapolis, Bobbs Merrill, 1977.
The Raptors and Other Birds, drawings by Leonard Baskin. New York, Pantheon, 1985.

Translator, *Island of Women,* by Juan Goytisolo. New York, Knopf, 1962; as *Sands of Torremolinos,* London, Cape, 1962.
Translator, *Villa Milo,* by Xavier Domingo. New York, Braziller, 1962.
Translator, *The Party's Over,* by Juan Goytisolo. New York, Grove Press, and London, Weidenfeld and Nicolson, 1966.

*

Manuscript Collection: Boston University.

Jose Yglesias comments:

(1991) I write to have my say. There are feelings and ideas that conversations and speeches and articles and reviews will not accommodate: these are the things that fiction, always so undiscriminating, finds room for. I thank God for the novel form.

*   *   *

A primary focus in all of Jose Yglesias's novels is the bearing of Hispanic heritage upon increasingly Americanized Cuban expatriates. Most especially it is the old extended family and Spanish "republican" predilections which he probes for contemporary life signs. His work always entails some marriage of these two concerns, which gives them a compelling blend of the personal and the socio-political. Moreover, he unfailingly discovers, happily or unhappily for his characters, analogical moral crises between the generations. This aspect of his work reaches its finest, albeit pessimistic, fruition in his fourth and least ethnic novel, *Double, Double.*

Yglesias is gifted at delineating the conflicting claims of private, even mercantile, aspirations as against social and altruistic ones. The former include not only a regard for capital and personal luxury

(the narrator of his third novel remarks "a shame-faced admiration for gentility"), but particularly for the wonders of sexual gratification and familial warmth. The latter include a regard for the democratic struggle in Spain, the egalitarian yearnings of Tampa's cigar workers (often mere "cafe revolutionaries"), the fight for Cuban independence, and, increasingly after the first novel, the hopes of all minorities, including student radicals. None of this is rendered at the expense of psychological or existential curiosity or verisimilitude.

Set in Tampa's Cuban ghetto in 1958, *A Wake in Ybor City* involves action ironically heightened by the reader's knowledge of the then incipiently successful Castro revolution. The major conflict concerns an affluent Cuban woman and her penurious family. She attempts to abort the wake the others are planning for her nephew, contemptuously labeling it "barbaric." And in asserting that the affair would kill her mother she misses the obvious, for eschewing the ancient custom is precisely what would do that. The foils to this figure are a political activist, Estaban, and Robert Moran, a Cuban-American artist. Robert is reluctantly won over to Estaban's commitment and in helping to deliver weapons to Cuban freedom fighters he is the first of Yglesias's protagonists to experience the ramifications of ideology. But in this first novel, the family and the morality of its tenacious affections are the focal points.

The least overtly political of the novels, *An Orderly Life* is still laced with socio-political motifs, which touch subtly upon the protagonist Rafe's curiously successful pursuit of a structured existence. Rafe's sense of order is not rigid, but "a kind of listening to music, a response to its swells, lulls and rhythms." To this end he strikes a balance between numerous but counterpointed forces. Free enterprise, sex as an end in itself, and marital love determine Rafe in half of his nature. In the other half he is directed by the influences of three very different friends. From Jerry comes his Marxist bent, sullied in Jerry's own life by his guilt-ridden capitulation with the Bitch Goddess; from Josh, a black radical gone homosexual, comes a gift for leavening too pure motives with pragmatic choices; from Mr. Sealy, a veritable "Southern Gentleman," comes aristocratic decorum, "the vision of order itself."

The pronoun in *The Truth about Them* is finely ambiguous. "They" are Spanish Americans; their truth is the integrity of their passional lives. "They" are also their myriad antagonists. The novel builds itself upon the narrator Pini's effort to elaborate and validate his familial past and to pass on to his son Ralph the "elegiac mood" it inspires in him. This mood is intensified by Pini's realization that his "*background* . . . [is] the agony of others." Yet he has also known, shamefully, ethnic embarrassment and, anxiously, the fear "that in another generation his ambiance might at best only linger like a scent after a beautiful woman has left the room." Expelled from Columbia after the student strike, Ralph sees Ybor City too narrowly, as only "a pacified village in Vietnam." But the past and present are fused happily when his grandmother gently wins him with a lesson in the survival instincts of his ancestors.

Four well-realized aspects of *Double, Double* make it Yglesias's best work. The plot is the primary masterstroke. From this emanates an astute psychological rendering of Seth Evergood's character, a brilliant unfolding of how the limitations (if not the sins) of the father are visited upon the son, and a lucid vision of the deadly serious ramifications of political dissent in contemporary America. The old thematic interests remain but are assimilated by broader ones. The novel exposes, often comically and pathetically, the disturbing relationships of sub-cultures and right-wing police power, as it depicts the bumbling attempts of an intellectual to act out his social consciousness. One wants to compare this work with "The Short Happy Life of Francis Macomber," but Evergood is deprived of Macomber's relatively luxurious moment of self-realization because—from the rear as it were—he is exploded into oblivion. It only remains for the good-hearted but dim hippie to misevaluate totally what has transpired.

—David M. Heaton

YOUNG, Al(bert James)

Nationality: American. **Born:** Ocean Springs, Mississippi, 31 May 1939. **Education:** The University of Michigan, Ann Arbor (co-editor, *Generation* magazine), 1957-61; Stanford University, California (Stegner Creative Writing fellow), 1966-67; University of California, Berkeley, A.B. in Spanish 1969. **Family:** Married Arline June Belch in 1963; one son. **Career:** Freelance musician, 1958-64; disc jockey, KJAZ-FM, Alameda, California, 1961-65; instructor and linguistic consultant, San Francisco Neighborhood Youth Corps Writing Workshop, 1968-69; writing instructor, San Francisco Museum of Art Teenage Workshop, 1968-69; Jones Lecturer in creative writing, Stanford University, 1969-74; screenwriter, Laser Films, New York, 1972, Stigwood Corporation, London and New York, 1972, Verdon Productions, Hollywood, 1976, First Artists Ltd., Burbank, California, 1976-77, and Universal, Hollywood, 1979; writer-in-residence, University of Washington, Seattle, 1981-82. Since 1979 director, Associated Writing Programs. Founding editor, *Loveletter,* San Francisco, 1966-68. Since 1972 co-editor, *Yardbird Reader,* Berkeley, California; contributing editor, since 1972, *Changes,* New York, and since 1973, *Umoja,* New Mexico; since 1981 editor and publisher, with Ishmael Reed, *Quilt* magazine, Berkeley; vice-president, Yardbird Publishing Cooperative. **Awards:** National Endowment for the Arts grant, 1968, 1969, 1974; San Francisco Foundation Joseph Henry Jackson award, 1969; Guggenheim fellowship, 1974; Pushcart prize, 1980; Before Columbus Foundation award, 1982. **Agent:** International Creative Management, 40 West 57th Street, New York, New York 10019. **Address:** 514 Bryant St., Palo Alto, California 94301, U.S.A.

PUBLICATIONS

Novels

Snakes. New York, Holt Rinehart, 1970; London, Sidgwick and Jackson, 1971.
Who Is Angelina? New York, Holt Rinehart, 1975; London, Sidgwick and Jackson, 1978.
Sitting Pretty. New York, Holt Rinehart, 1976.
Ask Me Now. New York, McGraw Hill, and London, Sidgwick and Jackson, 1980.
Seduction by Light. New York, Delta, 1988; London, Mandarin, 1989.

Uncollected Short Stories

"My Old Buddy Shakes, Alas, and Grandmama Claude," in *Nexus* (San Francisco), May-June 1965.

"The Question Man and Why I Dropped Out," in *Nexus* (San Francisco), November-December 1965.
"Chicken Hawk's Dream," in *Stanford Short Stories 1968,* edited by Wallace Stegner and Richard Scowcroft. Stanford, California, Stanford University Press, 1968.
"Moon Watching by Lake Chapala," in *Aldebaran Review 3* (Berkeley, California), 1968.

Plays

Screenplays: *Nigger,* 1972; *Sparkle,* 1972.

Poetry

Dancing. New York, Corinth, 1969.
The Song Turning Back into Itself. New York, Holt Rinehart, 1971.
Some Recent Fiction. San Francisco, San Francisco Book Company, 1974.
Geography of the Near Past. New York, Holt Rinehart, 1976.
The Blues Don't Change: New and Selected Poems. Baton Rouge, Louisiana State University Press, 1982.
Heaven: Collected Poems 1958-1988. Berkeley, California, Creative Arts, 1989.
Heaven: Collected Poems 1956-1990. Berkeley, California, Creative Arts, 1992.

Recording: *By Heart and by Ear,* Watershed, 1986.

Other

Bodies and Soul: Musical Memoirs. Berkeley, California, Creative Arts, 1981.
Kinds of Blue: Musical Memoirs. Berkeley, California, Creative Arts, 1984.
Things Ain't What They Used to Be: Musical Memoirs. Berkeley, California, Creative Arts, 1987.
Mingus/Mingus: Two Memoirs, with Janet Coleman. Berkeley, California, Creative Arts, 1989.

Editor, with Ishmael Reed, *Yardbird Lives!* New York, Grove Press, 1978.
Editor, with Ishmael Reed, *Quilt 2-3.* Berkeley, California, Reed and Young's Quilt, 2 vols., 1981-82.

*   *   *

In his story "Chicken Hawk's Dream" Al Young tells of a young man who believes that as magically as in a dream he might become a jazz artist. Failing to bring even a sound out of a borrowed horn, Chicken Hawk retreats into dope and alcohol, but his delusion persists so that when the narrator meets him later on a Detroit street corner Chicken Hawk says that he is off to New York to cut a record—just as soon as he gets his instrument out of the pawnshop. The dream of Chicken Hawk with its refusal of discipline and lack of nerve represents a version of what Young terms "art as hustle." It is not titillation, he says in a "Statement on Aesthetics, Poetics, Kinetics" (in *New Black Voices,* 1972), but the touching of human beings so that both toucher and touched are changed that matters most in art as in life. Touch may be magical but before all else it is the sign of willingness to engage actual life.

Through the metaphor of touch and repudiation of attitudinizing Young explains most of his literary practice. His novels gain much of their force from his ability to limn the texture of experience. Precise detailing of speech demonstrates how individuals play roles uniquely significant to those with whom they have personal relationships, including readers; and ways of seeing, talking, becoming, in short, ways of expressing the feel of life's touch, engender the books' movement.

In his first novel, *Snakes,* Young infuses the traditional narrative of adolescent growth with a principle of fluidity affecting every aspect of structure, style, and theme. MC, whose journey to maturity is the story's subject, gets turned on to modern jazz, an art of process which illustrates that personality itself may derive from music. Stylistically the book is largely constructed out of raps, oral performances by MC's friends, and reminiscences of his grandmother. The first concur with the performance of improvisational music to convey the importance of expressive response; the latter carry process into biographical temporality where memory of past events maintains influence in the present. Style and structure together support Young's theme of the struggle to be free, outlined in MC's thoughts on a bus to New York where he, unlike Chicken Hawk, will cut a record: "For the first time in my life I don't feel trapped; I don't feel free either but I don't feel trapped and I'm going to try and make this feeling last for as long as I can."

Who Is Angelina? picks up Young's theme in the story of a young woman who must regain the sense of not being trapped. In one answer to the question posed by the title, Angelina finds herself, in the words of a Pepsi-drinking fortune teller, poised between freedom to choose what she wishes and weaknesses which hold her back. A return to roots among family and neighborhood renews a sense of love for origins in Angelina but also demonstrates that she has no choice but to accept her distinct individuality; and to make the best of it, she must learn to move with awareness through her own becoming. Young allows Angelina to try transcendental meditation as a means of renewal, but her crucial realization of self occurs as it must, in the context of mundane experience. In a tussle with a purse snatcher she impulsively ventilates feelings of outrage that offend the liberal sentiments of friends and bystanders. Thereby she wipes out, for herself, the illusions one gains by living second-hand.

A year in the life of Sidney J. Prettymon, known as Sitting Pretty or sometimes plain Sit, provides the story line for Young's third novel. Sit's literary cousin is Langston Hughes's Jesse B. Semple, a.k.a. Simple. By the world's reckoning both Sit and Simple are ordinary men, but each has a philosophy and style that raises him above the average. In Sit's case the philosophy involves getting by without harming others and without succumbing to the values that will compromise integrity or happiness; thus, living is an improvisational performance. Rendered in the voice of Sit the novel *Sitting Pretty* works as the prose equivalent of an Afro-American musical composition alternatively echoing the situations of blues and celebratory riffs that are unique to the character's expressive style. Sit, jogging through the streets of Palo Alto, putting his two cents worth in on a radio talk show, caring deeply for his former wife in her time of trouble and his children when they don't even know they have problems, is a triumphant creation who deserves a place in the popular imagination right alongside Simple and probably, as Wallace Stegner suggested, Huckleberry Finn too.

Like Ishmael Reed, his colleague in *Yardbird* enterprises, Young is impatient with expectations that black writers should show their ethnicity in some predictable or stereotypical way. O.O. Gabugah

the militant poet was Young's satirical treatment of such message writing, and O.O. makes an appearance in *Sitting Pretty* also. Usually, though, Young makes his point, as in *Ask Me Now,* by unselfconscious narrative of the human trials of his characters. What makes the books black is that the people, such as Woody Knight, the retired basketball player of his most recent novel, are granted a broad range of experience in which they talk and touch others in the style of black culture. That style permits comedy right along with tribulation, the sort of love that yields happy endings and the losses that create frustration and anger. Reviewers loaded with prescriptions for the ethnic author and critics who want the message straight can be displeased, but Young's art will persist as a loving treatment of the versions of human process that are its source and subject.

—John M. Reilly

YOUNG, Marguerite (Vivian)

Nationality: American. **Born:** Indianapolis, Indiana, in 1909. **Education:** Indiana University, Bloomington; Butler University, Indianapolis, B.A. 1930; University of Chicago, M.A. 1936; University of Iowa, Iowa City. **Career:** Taught at Indiana University, 1942, University of Iowa, 1955-57, Columbia University, New York, 1958, New School for Social Research, New York, 1958-67, Fairleigh Dickinson University, Rutherford, New Jersey, 1960-62, and Fordham University, Bronx, New York, 1966 and 1967. **Awards:** American Association of University Women grant, 1943; American Academy grant, 1945; Guggenheim fellowship, 1948; Newberry Library fellowship, 1951; Rockefeller fellowship, 1954. **Address:** 375 Bleecker Street, New York, New York 10014, U.S.A.

PUBLICATIONS

Novel

Miss MacIntosh, My Darling. New York, Scribner, 1965; London, Owen, 1966.

Poetry

Prismatic Ground. New York, Macmillan, 1937.
Moderate Fable. New York, Reynal, 1944.

Other

Where Is There Another? A Memorial to Paul Y. Anderson, with others. Norman, Oklahoma, Cooperative Books, 1939.
Angel in the Forest: A Fairy Tale of Two Utopias (on the New Harmony community). New York, Reynal, 1945; London, Owen, 1967.
Inviting the Muses: Stories, Essays, Reviews. Normal, Illinois, Dalkey Archive Press, 1994.

*

Critical Study: *Marguerite Young, Our Darling: Tributes and Essays* edited by Miriam Fuchs, Normal, Illinois, Dalkey Archive Press, 1994.

* * *

Marguerite Young's titanic novel, *Miss MacIntosh, My Darling* (1,198 pages), was in slow generation for more than 17 years. It is a mammoth epic, a massive fable, a picaresque journey, a Faustian question, and a work of stunning magnitude and beauty. Her only published fiction to date, it is her masterwork. Its style is one of musicalizations, rhapsodies, symbolizations that repetitively roll and resound and double back upon themselves in an oceanic tumult. Its force is cumulative; its method is clarification through amassment, as in the great styles of Joyce or Hermann Broch or Faulkner. The major passages of the work are fluent and seminal and are grounded on four beings: Miss MacIntosh, once nursemaid to the voyager-narrator; Catherine Cartwheel, the narrator's "poor dreaming mother"; Mr. Spitzer, loyal companion to Catherine Cartwheel, composer of unheard, unwritten music and twin brother to a dead gambler with whose identity he is confounded; and Esther Longtree, a voluptuous waitress in a Wabash Valley cafe (the town of the novel is What Cheer, Iowa), who is cursed by an "everlasting, lonely pregnancy." These grand sections are procreative and fertile, spurting forth richly expressive and exhaustingly revealing passages of radiant prose. The minor sub-sections explore the submerged lives of several vivid and haunting personages. In these sections, the humor is folk, slapstick, Chaplinesque, melodramatic, and Satanic. *Miss MacIntosh, My Darling* is as often mischievously funny and devilishly humorous as it is incantatory and operatic. And, finally, the novel involves and depends on the basic and traditional American literary themes: small town, childhood memory, homesickness, nostalgia, quest.

—William Goyen

YURICK, Sol

Nationality: American. **Born:** New York City, 18 January 1925. **Education:** New York University, A.B. 1950; Brooklyn College, New York, M.A. 1961. **Military Service:** Served in the United States Army, 1944-45. **Family:** Married Adrienne Lash in 1958; one daughter. **Career:** Librarian, New York University, 1945-53; social investigator, New York City Department of Welfare, 1954-59. Since 1959 fulltime writer. Lives in Brooklyn, New York. **Awards:** Guggenheim fellowship, 1972. **Agent:** Georges Borchardt Inc., 136 East 57th Street, New York, New York 10022, U.S.A. **Address:** c/o Morrow, 105 Madison Ave., New York, New York 10016, U.S.A.

PUBLICATIONS

Novels

The Warriors. New York, Holt Rinehart, 1965; London, W.H. Allen, 1966.
Fertig. New York, Simon and Schuster, and London, W.H. Allen, 1966.

The Bag. New York, Simon and Schuster, 1968; London, Gollancz, 1970.
An Island Death. New York, Harper, 1975.
Richard A. New York, Arbor House, and London, Methuen, 1982.

Short Stories

Someone Just Like You. New York, Harper, 1972; London, Gollancz, 1973.

Other

Editor, *Voices of Brooklyn: An Anthology.* Chicago, American Library Association, 1973.

*

Manuscript Collection: Tanument Library, New York University.

* * *

Taken singly, each of Sol Yurick's works constitutes a substantial contribution to the growing body of contemporary fiction that depicts the American megalopolis in perpetual crisis. Taken together, his novels make up the most compelling vision available to us (in fiction or in non-fiction) of the most nightmarish megalopolis of all: New York now. Yurick is (as surely befits someone who was involved for several years in attempting to construct a sound theoretical and practical base for action on the American left) not interested in formal experimentation in the novel for the novel's own sake. Yet neither is he a polemicist with little sense of artistic form. He is an extreme rarity: a social critic with broad theoretical and "street level" experience. Yet, he is at the same time an erudite novelist with solid historical knowledge of the genre and great skill in handling the form. In a deliberate and obviously self-conscious way, he consistently attempts to close the gap between the biblical and classical Greek world so often alluded to in his works and the world of welfare, of murder, and of political power plays, the three major elements in his portrait of New York today.

The Warriors is a novel about a decimated New York teenage gang whom we first met on hostile "turf" on their way back to their "homeland" after a gang conference which has just ended in attempted murder. The opening scene is prefaced by an epigraph drawn from Xenophon: "My friends, these people whom you see are the last obstacle which stops us from being where we have so long struggled to be. We ought, if we could, to eat them up alive." The anabasis of Hinton (the gang artist), Lunkface, Bimbo, The Junior, and Hector is filled with memories of Ismael, leader of the Delancey Thrones, organizer of the citywide gang conference, and victim of the violence with which the conference had come to an abrupt close. "Ismael," we are told, "had the impassive face of a Spanish grandee, the purple-black color of an uncontaminated African, and the dreams of an Alexander, a Cyrus, a Napolean." He will return in *The Bag* as a saturnine figure (now with only one eye), a dope pusher, rent collector for a slum landlord (Faust), and stockpiler of rifles, waiting for that moment when the downtrodden of the city will rise up and use these arms to kill their ancient oppressors. Ismael is not alone in his reappearance. Though seemingly selfcontained when read singly, the novels (much like those of Faulkner) shade from one into another. The gang artist, Hinton in *The Warriors,* reappears, for instance, as a major figure in *The*

Bag. Hinton's mother, Minnie (permanently on welfare and having a new "lover"), and his brother the addict, Alonso, minor figures at the end of Hinton's anabasis, also return but now as full-fledged characters in *The Bag.*

In contrast to the lower depths of *The Warriors* and part of *The Bag, Fertig* appears at first to be an exploration of a strictly middle-class New York Jewish milieu. But the death of Fertig's son as a result of indifference on the part of the staff of a New York hospital triggers such a paroxysm of grief that Fertig cold-bloodedly murders some seven people involved however tenuously in his son's death. As mass murderer, Fertig is then thrust into the company of the criminals, madmen, and junkies who populate Yurick's other two novels. We are also given our first view of the political elite of this mythical New York: Judge Mabel Crossland whose thighs have encompassed every prominent jurist in New York in her climb to the judgeship; Fertig's lawyer, Royboy, the small but handsome sexual athlete, with multiple obligations to his female admirers (including Mabel Crossland) on his way to becoming Senator Roy, a character whom we then meet in *The Bag;* and Irving Hockstaff, king-maker, the man who indirectly runs the whole political apparatus of the city. A pawn in the political games of the mighty. Fertig and Fertig's trial are painfully reminiscent of *An American Tragedy.*

The evocation in *Fertig* of another classic work of literature is an integral part of Yurick's aesthetic and political methodology. The book is shaped as a contemporary replay of a recurrent phenomenon; the destruction of "the little man" by the power elite. Fertig's name comments ironically on a phenomenon that never ends. Likewise Ismael and Faust in *The Bag* are conscious restatements on a theme as old as poverty. Minnie (referred to by Yurick as a black Cybele and as the Wyf of Bath) loves Alpha (Fertig or Omega's opposite?) who has left his wife, Helen. They share the world with Faust (a figure drawn not only from Goethe but from Kosinski's *The Painted Bird*), with Faust's daughter, the lesbian Eve, and with Faust's ambitious urban renewal project: Rebirth. Finally, Rebirth and all the little men and women are crushed as the ghetto detonates despite the best efforts of the man from Agape (love, affection), the master of the government's counter-insurgency game plan. We know with Yurick at the end of *The Bag* (though it is never explicitly stated) that the future of this city that is all cities lies not with the Ismael's and others who seek social improvement but with the Royboys and the Hockstaffs. It is they who seem to believe: "It didn't matter how many people you killed so long as you contained it [the revolution] and cooled it and co-opted it and made it run smoothly." So it has always been says Yurick and so it will be: Alpha and Agape are Omega and Fertig. The end of Ismael in *The Bag* returns us not only to Ismael at the beginning of *The Warriors* but to the ancient admonition drawn from the *Anabasis.* The "homeland" lies permanently within sight but beyond reach. There is some doubt that, all his aesthetic skill and political acumen notwithstanding, Yurick will ever get us any closer, but his portrayal of anabasis itself is worthy of comparison with its ancient counterpart.

—John Fuegi

ZELAZNY, Roger

Nationality: American. **Born:** Cleveland, Ohio, 13 May 1937. **Education:** Case Western Reserve University, Cleveland (Foster Po-

etry award, 1957, 1959), 1955-59, B.A. in English 1959; Columbia University, New York, M.A. 1962. **Military Service:** Ohio National Guard, 1960-63; United States Army Reserve, 1963-66. **Family:** Married 1) Sharon Steberl in 1964 (divorced 1966); 2) Judith Callahan in 1966, two sons and one daughter. **Career:** Claims representative, Social Security Administration, Cleveland, Ohio, 1962-65; claims policy specialist, Social Security Administration, Baltimore, Maryland, 1965-69. Since 1969 full-time writer. Secretary-treasurer, Science Fiction Wriers of America, 1967-68. Currently member, advisory board, PEN New Mexico; *Writer's Digest* advisory board; editorial board, *Journal of the Fantastic in Literature.* **Awards:** Nebula award, 1966, for "The Doors of His Face, the Lamps of His Mouth" and 1966, for "He Who Shapes"; Hugo award, 1966, for *. . . And Call Me Conrad,* and 1968, for *Lord of Light;* Prix Apollo, 1972, for *Isle of the Dead;* Hugo award, 1976, and Nebula award, 1976, both for "Home Is the Hangman"; Balrog award, 1980, for "The Last Defender of Camelot"; Hugo award, 1982, Daicon award (Japan), 1984, and Balrog award, 1984, all for *Unicorn Variation;* Hugo award, 1986, for "24 Views of Mt. Fuji, by Hokusai," and 1987, for "Permafrost"; Locus award for best fantasy novel, 1986, for *Trumps of Doom;* United Nations society of Writers award, 1989; First Stage Lensman award, 1992; Inkpot award for outstanding achievement in science fiction and fantasy, 1993; Forry award for lifetime achievement in science fiction, 1993. Guest of honor, 1974 World Science Fiction Convention; 1978 Australian National Science Fiction Convention; 1984 European Science Fiction Convention; 1993 World Fantasy Convention. **Agent:** Kirby McCauley, The Pimlico Agency, Inc., Box 20447, 1539 First Ave., New York, New York 10028, U.S.A.

PUBLICATIONS

Novels (series: Amber)

This Immortal. New York, Ace, 1966; London, Hart Davis, 1967.
The Dream Master. New York, Ace, 1966; London, Hart Davis, 1968.
Four for Tomorrow. New York, Ace, 1967.
Lord of Light. New York, Doubleday, 1967; London, Faber, 1968.
Isle of the Dead. New York, Ace, 1969; London, Rapp and Whiting, 1970.
Creatures of Light and Darkness. New York, Doubleday, 1969; London, Faber, 1970.
Damnation Alley. New York, Putnam, 1969; London, Faber, 1971.
Nine Princes in Amber. New York, Doubleday, 1970; London, Faber, 1972.
Jack of Shadows. New York, Walker, 1971; London, Faber, 1973.
The Guns of Avalon (Amber). New York, Doubleday, 1972; London, Faber, 1974.
Today We Choose Faces. New York, Signet, 1973; London, Millington, 1974.
To Die in Italbar. New York, Doubleday, and London, Faber, 1975.
Sign of the Unicorn (Amber). New York, Doubleday, 1975; London, Faber, 1977.
Doorways in the Sand. New York, Harper and Row, 1975; London, Allen, 1977.
My Name Is Legion. New York, Ballantine, 1976.
The Hand of Oberon (Amber). New York, Doubleday, 1976; London, Faber, 1978.

Bridge of Ashes. New York, Signet, 1976.

Deus Irae, with Philip K. Dick. New York, Doubleday, 1976; London, Gollancz, 1977.

The Courts of Chaos (Amber). New York, Doubleday, 1978; London, Faber, 1980.

The Chronicles of Amber (omnibus). New York, Doubleday, 2 vols., 1979.

The Bells of Shoredan. Columbia, Pennsylvania, Underwood Miller, 1979.

Roadmarks. New York, Ballantine, 1979; London, Futura, 1981.

For a Breath I Tarry. Columbia, Pennsylvania, Underwood Miller, 1980.

Changeling. New York, Ace, 1980.

The Changing Land. Columbia, Pennsylvania, Underwood Miller, 1981.

Madwand. Huntingon Woods, Michigan, Phantasia Press, 1981.

A Rhapsody in Amber. N.p., Cheap Street, 1981.

Coils, with Fred Saberhagen. New York, Simon and Schuster, 1982; London, Penguin, 1984.

Eye of Cat. New York, Simon and Schuster, 1982; London, Sphere, 1984.

Dilvish, the Damned. New York, Ballantine, 1982.

Trumps of Doom (Amber). Columbia, Pennsylvania, Underwood Miller, 1985; London, Sphere, 1986.

Blood of Amber. Columbia, Pennsylvania, Underwood Miller, 1986; London, Sphere, 1987.

Sign of Chaos (Amber). New York, Arbor House, 1987; London, Sphere, 1988.

Knight of Shadows (Amber). New York, Morrow, 1989.

The Black Throne, with Fred Saberhagen. New York, Baen, 1990.

The Mask of Loki, with Thomas T. Thomas. New York, Baen, 1990.

Bring Me the Head of Prince Charming, with Robert Sheckley. New York, Bantam, 1991.

Prince of Chaos. New York, Morrow, 1991.

Flare, with Thomas T. Thomas. N.p., Baen, 1992.

If at Faust You Don't Succeed, with Robert Sheckley. New York, Bantam, 1993.

A Night in the Lonesome October. New York, Morrow, 1993.

Wilderness, with Gerald Hausman. New York, Tor, 1994.

Short Stories

Four for Tomorrow. New York, Ace, 1967; as *A Rose for Ecclesiastes,* London, Hart Davis, 1969.

The Doors of His Face, The Lamps of His Mouth, and Other Stories. New York, Doubleday, 1971; London, Faber, 1973.

My Name Is Legion. New York, Ballantine, 1976; London, Faber, 1979.

The Last Defender of Camelot. New York, Underwood Miller, 1980.

Unicorn Variations. New York, Simon and Schuster, 1983.

Frost and Fire. New York, Morrow, 1989.

Poetry

When Pussywillows Last in the Catyard Bloomed. Carlton, Australia, Norstrilia Press, 1980.

To Spin Is Miracle Cat. Columbia, Pennsylvania, Underwood Miller, 1981.

Other (for children)

A Dark Traveling. New York, Walker, 1987; London, Hutchinson, 1989.

Way Up High. N.p., Grant, 1992.

Here There Be Dragons. N.p., Grant, 1992.

Other

The Illustrated Roger Zelazny, illustrated by Gray Morrow. New York, Baronet, 1978.

Roger Zelazny's Visual Guide to Castle Amber, with Neil Randall. New York, Avon, 1988.

*

Bibliography: *Roger Zelazny: A Primary and Secondary Bibliography* by Joseph L. Sanders, Boston, Hall, 1980; *Amber Dreams: A Roger Zelazny Bibliography* by Daniel J.H. Levack, Columbia, Pennsylvania, Underwood Miller, 1983.

Film Adaptations: *Damnation Alley,* 1977.

Manuscript Collections: George Arendts Research Library, Syracuse University; Special Collections, University of Maryland Library.

Critical Studies: *A Reader's Guide to Roger Zelazny* by Carl B. Yoke, West Linn, Oregon, Starmont House, 1979; *Roger Zelazny* by Theodore Krulik, New York, Unger, 1986.

*   *   *

Roger Zelazny's achievements lie mainly in the field of science fiction (his work is associated with the New Wave movement), though the corpus of his work includes a good proportion of fantasy. Classification of his work into sub-genres, however, serves little purpose, as the two frameworks (science and fantasy) only signify insofar as they serve to make available a set of tropes through which concept and theme may find formal and stylized expression. The terms are in any case, fluid; science and fantasy shift into each other in a Moebius-strip-like continuum of cause and effect. This may be observed in the Hugo-winning novels *Lord of Light* and *This Immortal*. In the latter, the age of myth, originally displaced by the age of reason/science, begins again in the spaces created by nuclear disaster, and is in fact (re)generated from science: the satyrs, for example, spawned in the still-radioactive "hot-spots," are at once the effect of science (genetic mutation) and the stuff of myth.

Zelazny's work is informed by a complex blend of romantic anxiety and scientific and philosophic curiosity about the world; interestingly, these lines of difference converge and find common expression in themes pertaining to the nature of time and its correlates: immortality, history, and myth. His fiction asks questions about what, ultimately, is objective and real, knowable, and meaningful. The anxiety is manifested in an often dystopian vision of society that threatens the individual, and is also implicit in the dwarfing infinitudes of time, space, and possibility encountered in his work, which his protagonists are constantly seeking to order and control. Many of his characters erupt into fictive life in states of forgetting and non-knowledge, needing to know who, where, and what they are (and usually find the answers to be a good deal stranger and more terrifying than might have been anticipated). The two most obvious examples of this are Corwin, of his "Amber" series and "Wakim" of *Creatures of Light and Darkness*. Reality is *not* objective and is unstable, as his metaphoric title *The Changing Land* indicates and the Amber novels demonstrate at length: Corwin thinks there is an ultimate Amber, an immutable center, of which all else is a shadow. It transpires that even this is a myth: the center is where you place it, and reality what you make of it.

The obsession with the past, peculiar perhaps in a writer of science fiction, (a futuristic literature) invades much of the writing. If science fiction may be considered a literature of the alien, the undiscovered, and the future, then myth, as a species of eternal pattern, provides a template from which the future may at once be extrapolated and made inhabitable and resonant. Zelazny constantly writes the figure of the "immortal" into his work; this may point to an intense desire to understand, a desire perhaps only fulfillable through constant return and review, where patterns of knowledge may emerge through fierce scrutiny.

In the worlds portrayed in Zelazny's fiction, the line between being and annihilation is thin, as the immensely poetic *The Dream Master* illustrates: Charles Render, the psychologist, is possibly lost for all time within someone else's version of reality. The frailty of identity thus has to be strengthened by engagement, action, and choice; as Corwin says in *The Courts of Chaos*, "I see desire as hidden identity, and striving as its growth." In *Eye of Cat,* society threatens to reduce sentient to thing, and Billy Blackhorse Singer flees civilization and the predator, Cat. Forced to engage with the physical terrain, the past, and his internal wilderness, Singer seeks himself among the shapes of Navajo mythology. The narrator of *My Name is Legion* paradoxically renounces name and legal being in order to evade the system that would take freedom and individuality from him.

Zelazny, a Romantic out of his proper time, becomes himself one of the "last defenders of Camelot," dedicated to the preservation of the ideal, the poetical, and the mythic in a prosaic, materialist age. Many of his works (e.g., "A Rose for Ecclesiastes" and *This Immortal*) deal with the post-holocaust idea, but what is interesting in his treatment of a common theme in science fiction is the way in which the value of these intangibles is reinscribed onto the palimpsest of the shattered, phenomenal world. Often, the intangible is all that is left to ease passage and also all that makes renewal possible. In "A Rose for Ecclesiastes," only the art of dance remains for dying Mars to which the narrator-poet comes; the dancer and the poet between them breed new meaning and possibility for the planet.

—Susan Ang

NATIONALITY INDEX

Below is the list of entrants divided by nationality. The nationalities were chosen largely from information supplied by the entrants. A small number of entrants submitted two nationalities (e.g., American and British) and thus are listed under both. It should be noted that "British" was used for all English entrants and for any other British entrant who chose that designation over a more specific one, such as "Scottish."

AMERICAN

Walter Abish
Kathy Acker
Alice Adams
Renata Adler
Lisa Alther
Rudolfo A. Anaya
Louis Auchincloss
Paul Auster
Elliott Baker
Nicholson Baker
Russell Banks
John Barth
Frederick Barthelme
Jonathan Baumbach
Ann Beattie
Stephen Becker
Barry Beckham
Madison Smartt Bell
Saul Bellow
Thomas Berger
Doris Betts
Burt Blechman
Vance Bourjaily
Paul Bowles
T. Coraghessan Boyle
Ray Bradbury
David Bradley
John Ed Bradley
Harold Brodkey
E.M. Broner
Rita Mae Brown
Rosellen Brown
Frederick Buechner
James Lee Burke
William S. Burroughs
Janet Burroway
Frederick Busch
Hortense Calisher
R.V. Cassill
Fred Chappell
Jerome Charyn
Alan Cheuse
Eleanor Clark
William Cobb
Cyrus Colter
Richard Condon
Evan S. Connell, Jr.
Robert Coover
Harry Crews
Michael Crichton
Moira Crone
Guy Davenport
Samuel R. Delany

Don DeLillo
Boman Desai
G.V. Desani
Joan Didion
Stephen Dixon
E.L. Doctorow
Ellen Douglas
Allen Drury
Andre Dubus
Elaine Dundy
John Gregory Dunne
William Eastlake
Stanley Elkin
Bret Easton Ellis
James Ellroy
David Ely
Louise Erdrich
Howard Fast
Irvin Faust
Raymond Federman
Leslie A. Fiedler
Thomas Flanagan
Shelby Foote
Jesse Hill Ford
Richard Ford
Leon Forrest
Marilyn French
Bruce Jay Friedman
William Gaddis
Ernest J. Gaines
Kenneth Gangemi
George Garrett
William H. Gass
Martha Gellhorn
William Gibson
Ellen Gilchrist
Brendan Gill
Gail Godwin
Herbert Gold
William Goldman
Mary Gordon
Robert Gover
Shirley Ann Grau
Joanne Greenberg
John Grisham
Doris Grumbach
Albert Guerard
Allan Gurganis
James B. Hall
Barry Hannah
Ron Hansen
Elizabeth Hardwick
Mark Harris
Jim Harrison

Jon Hassler
Marianne Hauser
John Hawkes
Shirley Hazzard
Robert Hellenga
Joseph Heller
George V. Higgins
Carol Hill
Edward Hoagland
Russell Hoban
Alice Hoffman
Maureen Howard
William Humphrey
Evan Hunter
Kristin Hunter
John Irving
Tama Janowitz
Ruth Prawer Jhabvala
Charles Johnson
Denis Johnson
Diane Johnson
Gayl Jones
Madison Jones
Erica Jong
Ward Just
Johanna Kaplan
Steve Katz
William Melvin Kelley
William Kennedy
Ken Kesey
Jamaica Kincaid
Maxine Hong Kingston
John Knowles
Richard Kostelanetz
Ursula K. Le Guin
Alan Lelchuk
Elmore Leonard
Ira Levin
Janet Lewis
Alison Lurie
Andrew Lytle
Robie Macauley
David Madden
Norman Mailer
Clarence Major
Jerre Mangione
Wallace Markfield
David Markson
Paule Marshall
Bobbie Ann Mason
Hilary Masters
Harry Mathews
Jack Matthews
Peter Matthiessen
William Maxwell
Cormac McCarthy
Joseph McElroy
Thomas McGuane
Jay McInerney
Larry McMurtry
James A. McPherson

Barbara Mertz
Leonard Michaels
James A. Michener
Steven Millhauser
Susan Minot
Mark Mirsky
Joseph Mitchell
N. Scott Momaday
Paul Monette
Lorrie Moore
Wright Morris
Toni Morrison
Gloria Naylor
Jay Neugeboren
Charles Newman
Hugh Nissenson
Joyce Carol Oates
Tim O'Brien
Tillie Olsen
Cynthia Ozick
Grace Paley
Charles Palliser
Orlando Patterson
Kathrin Perutz
Harry Mark Petrakis
Ann Petry
Jayne Anne Phillips
Marge Piercy
David Plante
Frederik Pohl
Chaim Potok
J.F. Powers
Richard Powers
Reynolds Price
E. Annie Proulx
James Purdy
Mario Puzo
Thomas Pynchon
Frederic Raphael
John Rechy
Ishmael Reed
Anne Rice
Tom Robbins
Kim Stanley Robinson
Marilynne Robinson
Mary Robison
Judith Rossner
Leo Rosten
Henry Roth
Philip Roth
Michael Rumaker
Joanna Russ
J.D. Salinger
May Sarton
Thomas Savage
Susan Fromberg Schaeffer
Budd Schulberg
Carolyn See
Hubert Selby, Jr.
Mary Lee Settle
Wilfrid Sheed

Carol Shields
Bapsi Sidhwa
Clancy Sigal
Leslie Marmon Silko
Robert Silverberg
Mona Simpson
Jane Smiley
Susan Sontag
Gilbert Sorrentino
Terry Southern
Elizabeth Spencer
Michael Stephens
Daniel Stern
Richard G. Stern
Robert Stone
William Styron
Ronald Sukenick
Amy Tan
Alexander Theroux
Paul Theroux
Niccolò Tucci
Anne Tyler
John Updike
Leon Uris
Gore Vidal
Kurt Vonnegut, Jr.
David Wagoner
Dan Wakefield
Alice Walker
Margaret Walker
Mildred Walker
James Welch
Eudora Welty
Paul West
William Wharton
Edmund White
John Edgar Wideman
John A. Williams
Connie Willis
Sloan Wilson
Larry Woiwode
Tom Wolfe
Tobias Wolff
Herman Wouk
Charles Wright
Rudolph Wurlitzer
James Yaffe
Helen Yglesias
Jose Yglesias
Al Young
Marguerite Young
Sol Yurick
Roger Zelazny

AUSTRALIAN
Glenda Adams
James Aldridge
Jessica Anderson
Thea Astley
Murray Bail
Marion Campbell

Peter Carey
Brian Castro
Jon Cleary
Peter Cowan
Blanche d'Alpuget
Liam Davison
Ralph de Boissière
Robert Drewe
Geoffrey Dutton
Beverley Farmer
David Foster
Helen Garner
Rodney Hall
Marion Halligan
Frank Hardy
Elizabeth Harrower
Nicholas Hasluck
Janette Turner Hospital
David Ireland
Elizabeth Jolley
Thomas Keneally
C.J. Koch
Morris Lurie
David Malouf
Peter Mathers
Alex Miller
Frank Moorhouse
Mudrooroo
Gerald Murnane
Randolph Stow
George Turner
Morris West
Tim Winton

BARBADIAN
Austin C. Clarke
George Lamming

BRITISH
Peter Ackroyd
Richard Adams
Brian Aldiss
A. Alvarez
Eric Ambler
Kingsley Amis
Martin Amis
Paul Bailey
Beryl Bainbridge
J.G. Ballard
Lynne Reid Banks
A.L. Barker
Pat Barker
Julian Barnes
Stan Barstow
Nina Bawden
Sybille Bedford
David Benedictus
John Berger
Chaim Bermant
Rachel Billington
Caroline Blackwood

John Bowen
William Boyd
Malcolm Bradbury
Melvyn Bragg
Sasthi Brata
Christine Brooke-Rose
Anita Brookner
Brigid Brophy
George Mackay Brown
Alan Burns
A.S. Byatt
Philip Callow
David Caute
Gerda Charles
Arthur C. Clarke
Jonathan Coe
Barry Cole
Isabel Colegate
David Cook
Lettice Cooper
William Cooper
Jim Crace
David Dabydeen
O.R. Dathorne
Lionel Davidson
Jennifer Dawson
Louis de Bernières
Len Deighton
Margaret Drabble
C.J. Driver
Maureen Duffy
Nell Dunn
Dorothy Dunnett
Janice Elliott
Alice Thomas Ellis
Buchi Emecheta
Isobel English
Zoë Fairbairns
Sebastian Faulks
Elaine Feinstein
Eva Figes
Tibor Fischer
Penelope Fitzgerald
Margaret Forster
Frederick Forsyth
John Fowles
Ronald Frame
Dick Francis
Michael Frayn
Nicolas Freeling
Gillian Freeman
Maggie Gee
Zulfikar Ghose
Brian Glanville
Julian Gloag
Rumer Godden
Giles Gordon
Winston Graham
Romesh Gunesekera
Arthur Hailey
Hammond Innes

Clifford Hanley
Wilson Harris
Susan Hill
Thomas Hinde
Barry Hines
Alan Hollinghurst
Elizabeth Jane Howard
David Hughes
Emyr Humphreys
Kazuo Ishiguro
Dan Jacobson
Howard Jacobson
P.D. James
Robin Jenkins
Glyn Jones
Gwyn Jones
Mervyn Jones
Gabriel Josipovici
Victor Kelleher
Francis King
Bernard Kops
Hanif Kureishi
John le Carré
Doris Lessing
Emanuel Litvinoff
Penelope Lively
David Lodge
Wolf Mankowitz
Hilary Mantel
Adam Mars-Jones
Allan Massie
Elizabeth Mavor
Ian McEwan
Patrick McGrath
Candia McWilliam
Stanley Middleton
Julian Mitchell
Naomi Mitchison
Timothy Mo
Michael Moorcock
John Mortimer
Penelope Mortimer
Nicholas Mosley
Iris Murdoch
P.H. Newby
Lawrence Norfolk
Robert Nye
Edith Pargeter
Anne Perry
Jerzy Peterkiewicz
Caryl Phillips
Anthony Powell
David Pownall
Terry Pratchett
V.S. Pritchett
David Profumo
Simon Raven
Piers Paul Read
Ruth Rendell
Michèle Roberts
Daphne Rooke

Bernice Rubens
Salman Rushdie
Lisa St. Aubin de Teran
Will Self
Tom Sharpe
Alan Sillitoe
Andrew Sinclair
Carolyn Slaughter
Emma Smith
Iain Crichton Smith
Muriel Spark
Alan Spence
Colin Spencer
David Storey
Graham Swift
Emma Tennant
Shashi Tharoor
D.M. Thomas
Colin Thubron
Gillian Tindall
Peter Tinniswood
Barbara Trapido
Rose Tremain
Rachel Trickett
Frank Tuohy
Barry Unsworth
Edward Upward
Fred Urquhart
Peter Vansittart
Marina Warner
Keith Waterhouse
Fay Weldon
Mary Wesley
Michael Wilding
A.N. Wilson
Colin Wilson
Jeanette Winterson

CANADIAN

Jeannette Armstrong
Margaret Atwood
Neil Bissoondath
Clark Blaise
Fred Bodsworth
Leonard Cohen
Matt Cohen
Robertson Davies
Timothy Findley
Mavis Gallant
Graeme Gibson
Douglas Glover
Dave Godfrey
Arthur Hailey
David Helwig
Jack Hodgins
Hugh Hood
Michael Ignatieff
M.T. Kelly
Thomas King
W.P. Kinsella
Joy Kogawa

Robert Kroetsch
SKY Lee
Norman Levine
Jack Ludwig
Daphne Marlatt
John Metcalf
Rohinton Mistry
W.O. Mitchell
Brian Moore
Bharati Mukherjee
Alice Munro
C.J. Newman
Michael Ondaatje
Peter Robinson
Sinclair Ross
Jane Rule
Carol Shields
John Steffler
Audrey Thomas
M.G. Vassanji
David Watmough
Rudy Wiebe

FILIPINO

F. Sionil Jose

GHANAIAN

Ama Ata Aidoo
Ayi Kwei Armah

GUYANIAN

David Dabydeen
Roy A.K. Heath

INDIAN

Ahmad Abbas
Mulk Raj Anand
Upamanyu Chatterjee
Anita Desai
Shashi Deshpande
Ahmed Essop
Amitav Ghosh
Arun Joshi
Manohar Malgonkar
Kamala Markandaya
Chaman Nahal
R.K. Narayan
Raja Rao
Nayantara Sahgal
I. Allan Sealy
Vikram Seth
Khushwant Singh

IRISH

John Banville
Maeve Binchy
Clare Boylan
J.P. Donleavy
Roddy Doyle
Aidan Higgins
Desmond Hogan

Jennifer Johnston
Neil Jordan
Molly Keane
Benedict Kiely
Mary Lavin
Bernard MacLaverty
Patrick McCabe
John McGahern
Edna O'Brien
Julia O'Faolain
Charles Palliser
James Plunkett
Francis Stuart
William Trevor
Anthony C. West

JAMAICAN
Erna Brodber
Vic Reid
Andrew Salkey
Olive Senior

KENYAN
Ngugi wa Thiong'o

NEW ZEALANDER
Barbara Anderson
Graham Billing
Errol Brathwaite
Ian Cross
Marilyn Duckworth
Alan Duff
Stevan Eldred-Grigg
Janet Frame
Maurice Gee
Patricia Grace
Russell Haley
Noel Hilliard
Keri Hulme
Witi Ihimaera
Fiona Kidman
Elizabeth Knox
Owen Marshall
Sue McCauley
O.E. Middleton
Vincent O'Sullivan
Bill Pearson
Maurice Shadbolt
C.K. Stead
Noel Virtue
Ian Wedde

NIGERIAN
Chinua Achebe

T.M. Aluko
Elechi Amadi
I.N.C. Aniebo
Cyprian Ekwensi
Festus Iyayi
John Munonye
Ben Okri
Wole Soyinka
Amos Tutuola

SAMOAN
Albert Wendt

SCOTTISH
Janice Galloway
Alasdair Gray
James Kelman
A.L. Kennedy

SINGAPOREAN
Catherine Lim

SOMALI
Nuruddin Farah

SOUTH AFRICAN
Peter Abrahams
André Brink
J.M. Coetzee
Jack Cope
Nadine Gordimer
Stephen Richard Gray
Christopher Hope
Es'kia Mphahlele
Njabulo S. Ndebele
Daphne Rooke
Miriam Tlali
Laurens van der Post

ST. LUCIAN
Garth St. Omer

TONGAN
Epeli Hau'ofa

TRINIDADIAN
Michael Anthony
Kelvin Christopher James
Marion Patrick Jones
Earl Lovelace
V.S. Naipaul

ZIMBABWEAN
Shimmer Chinodya

TITLE INDEX

The following list includes the titles of all books listed in the Novels and Short Stories (designated "s") sections of the entries in the book. The name in parenthesis is meant to direct the user to the appropriate entry, where full publication information is given.

Abandoned Woman (Condon), 1977
Abbess of Crewe (Spark), 1974
Aberration of Starlight (Sorrentino), 1980
Abominable Earthman (s Pohl), 1963
About a Marriage (G. Gordon), 1972
About Blady (van der Post), 1991
About Harry Towns (Friedman), 1974
Above Ground (Ludwig), 1968
Abracadabra! (Mankowitz), 1980
Absence of Ruins (Patterson), 1967
Absent Friends (s Busch), 1989
Absolute Hero (Humphreys), 1986
Absolutely Nothing to Get Alarmed About (Wright), 1973
Absurd Affair (C. Spencer), 1961
Abundant Dreamer (s Brodkey), 1989
Acceptance World (Powell), 1955
Accident (Mosley), 1965
Accident (Plante), 1991
Accidental Man (Murdoch), 1971
Accidental Tourist (Tyler), 1985
Accidental Woman (Coe), 1987
According to Jake and the Kid (s W.O. Mitchell), 1989
According to Mark (Lively), 1984
Accounting (s Kostelanetz), 1972
Ace of Diamonds Gang (s O. Marshall), 1993
Acolyte (Astley), 1972
Across the Black Waters (Anand), 1940
Across the Bridge (s Gallant), 1993
Across the Sea of Stars (Arthur C. Clarke), 1959
Across the Sea Wall (Koch), 1965
Act of Darkness (F. King), 1983
Act of Terror (Brink), 1991
Action (F. King), 1978
Ad Infinitum (s Kostelanetz), 1973
Adah's Story (Emecheta), 1983
Adaptable Man (J. Frame), 1965
Admiral and the Nuns (s Tuohy), 1962
Adrift in Soho (C. Wilson), 1961
Adult Entertainment (s Metcalf), 1986
Adult Life of Toulouse Lautrec (Acker), 1978
Adultery (A. Theroux), 1987
Adultery and Other Choices (s Dubus), 1977
Adventure in Washington (Rosten, as Ross), 1940
Adventures in the Alaskan Skin Trade (Hawkes), 1985
Adventures of Alyx (s Russ), 1983
Adventures of Augie March (Bellow), 1953
Adventures of Catullus Kelly (Salkey), 1969
Adventures of Christian Rosy Cross (Foster), 1986
Adventures of God in His Search for the Black Girl (Brophy), 1973
Adventures of Robina, by Herself (Tennant), 1986
Adventures of Una Persson and Catherine Cornelius (Moorcock), 1976
Advertisements for Myself (s Mailer), 1959

Advise and Consent (Drury), 1959
Aesop's Forest (s Coover), 1986
Affair of Men (Brathwaite), 1961
Affair to Remember (Cassill), 1957
Affliction (R. Banks), 1989
Affliction (Weldon), 1994
Africa and After (s Kelleher), 1983
African Horse (Pownall), 1975
African Trilogy (Achebe), 1988
After a Fashion (S. Middleton), 1987
After Anzac Day (Cross), 1961
After China (Castro), 1992
After-Dinner's Sleep (S. Middleton), 1986
After Goliath (Cassill), 1985
After Julius (E. Howard), 1965
After Lazarus (s Coover), 1980
After Rome, Africa (Glanville), 1959
After the Act (Graham), 1965
After the Fire (Rule), 1989
After the Rain (Bowen), 1958
After the War (Raphael), 1988
After the War (D. Stern), 1965
After You've Gone (s A. Adams), 1989
After Z-Hour (Knox), 1987
Afterglow and Nightfall (Pargeter), 1977
Afterlife (Monette), 1990
Afterlife of George Cartwright (Steffler), 1992
Afternoon Men (Powell), 1931
Afternoon of a Good Woman (Bawden), 1976
Against a Darkening Sky (Lewis), 1943
Against Entropy (Frayn), 1967
Against the Fall of Night (Arthur C. Clarke), 1953
Against the Season (Rule), 1971
Agatha (Colegate), 1973
Age (Aldiss), 1967
Age (Calisher), 1987
Age of Consent (Greenberg), 1987
Age of Grief (s Smiley), 1987
Age of Iron (Coetzee), 1990
Age of the Pussyfoot (Pohl), 1969
Age of the Rainmakers (s W. Harris), 1971
Agent (Hinde), 1974
Agents and Patients (Powell), 1936
Agents and Witnesses (Newby), 1947
Agrippa's Daughter (Fast), 1964
Air and Angels (S. Hill), 1991
Air Bridge (Hammond Innes), 1951
Air Disaster (Hammond Innes), 1937
Air That Kills (F. King), 1948
Air We Breathe (Josipovici), 1981
Airport (Hailey), 1968
Airs of Earth (s Aldiss), 1963
Airships (s Hannah), 1978
Ajaiyi and His Inherited Poverty (Tutuola), 1967

Backward Place (Jhabvala), 1965
Backward Sex (Cross), 1960
Backward Shadow (L. Banks), 1970
Bad Lot (s Glanville), 1977
Bad Man (Elkin), 1967
Bad Man from Bodie (Doctorow), 1961
Bad Music (McCauley), 1990
Bad Sister (Tennant), 1978
Bad Streak (s Glanville), 1961
Badlands (Kroetsch), 1975
Bag (Yurick), 1968
Bailey's Café (Naylor), 1992
Balcony of Europe (A. Higgins), 1972
Baldur's Gate (Clark), 1970
Balkan Express (Rosten), 1939
Ball of Malt and Madame Butterfly (s Kiely), 1973
Ballad of Beta-2 (Delany), 1965
Ballad of Beta-2, and Empire Star (Delany), 1977
Ballad of Dingus Magee (Markson), 1966
Ballad of Peckham Rye (Spark), 1960
Ballad of the Public Trustee (s Kinsella), 1982
Ballroom of Romance (s Trevor), 1972
Bamboo Bed (Eastlake), 1969
Bandicoot (Condon), 1978
Bandicoot Run (Malgonkar), 1982
Bandits (Leonard), 1987
Bane of the Black Sword (Moorcock), 1977
Bang-Bang You're Dead (s Spark), 1982
Bang the Drum Slowly (M. Harris), 1956
Banker (Francis), 1982
Bankrupts (Glanville), 1958
Banquet (Slaughter), 1983
Banyan (Wendt), 1984
Bar (s Rumaker), 1964
Bar of Shadow (van der Post), 1954
Barbarian (Mitchison), 1961
Barbarian Stories (s Mitchison), 1929
Barbarians of Mars (Moorcock, as Bradbury), 1965
Barbarous Tongue (Duff), 1963
Barbary Light (Newby), 1962
Barbary Shore (Mailer), 1951
Barber's Trade Union (s Anand), 1944
Barclay Family Theatre (s Hodgins), 1981
Barefoot in the Head (Aldiss), 1969
Bargain with God (Savage), 1953
Barking Man (s Bell), 1990
Barn Blind (Smiley), 1980
Barracks (McGahern), 1963
Barracks Thief (Wolff), 1984
Barrytown Trilogy (Doyle), 1992
Bats Out of Hell (s Hannah), 1993
Battle Cry (Uris), 1953
Battle for Christabel (Forster), 1991
Battle of the Villa Fiorita (Godden), 1963
Baumgartner's Bombay (A. Desai), 1988
Bay of Contented Man (s Drewe), 1989
Bay of Noon (Hazzard), 1970
Bay of Silence (St. Aubin de Teran), 1986
Be Buried in the Rain (Mertz, as Michaels), 1985
Be Sure to Close Your Eyes (Hood), 1993
Beach Umbrella (s Colter), 1970

Beachmasters (Astley), 1985
Beast of Heaven (Kelleher), 1984
Beastly Beatitudes of Balthazar B (Donleavy), 1968
Beasts of the Southern Wild (s Betts), 1973
Beau Bumbo (Sinclair), 1985
Beaufort Sisters (Cleary), 1979
Beautiful (Billington), 1974
Beautiful Empire (Ghose), 1975
Beautiful Feathers (Ekwensi), 1963
Beautiful Girl (s A. Adams), 1979
Beautiful Greed (Madden), 1961
Beautiful Losers (L. Cohen), 1966
Beautiful Room Is Empty (White), 1988
Beautiful Visit (E. Howard), 1950
Beautiful Words (Mervyn Jones), 1979
Beauty's Punishment (Rice, as Roquelaure), 1984
Beauty's Release (Rice, as Roquelaure), 1985
Beautyful Ones Are Not Yet Born (Armah), 1968
Because It Is Bitter, and Because It Is My Heart (Oates), 1990
Because of the Cats (Freeling), 1963
Because the Night (Ellroy), 1984
Becker Wives (s Lavin), 1946
Becket Factor (Anthony), 1990
Bedrock (Alther), 1990
Beehive Arranged on Human Principles (s Sorrentino), 1986
Beet Queen (Erdrich), 1986
Beetle Leg (Hawkes), 1951
Before and After (Rosellen Brown), 1992
Before My Life Began (Neugeboren), 1985
Before My Time (M. Howard), 1975
Before My Time (Tucci), 1962
Before She Met Me (Barnes), 1982
Before the Cock Crow (Raven), 1986
Beggar Maid (s Munro), 1979
Beggar My Neighbour (s D. Jacobson), 1964
Beginners (D. Jacobson), 1966
Beginning of Spring (Fitzgerald), 1988
Beginning to End (S. Middleton), 1991
Beginnings (s Hodgins), 1983
Behold the Man (Moorcock), 1969
Behold Your King (Mitchison), 1957
Being Invisible (T. Berger), 1987
Bela Lugosi's White Christmas (P. West), 1972
Beleaguered City (Foote), 1995
Belgrave Square (Perry), 1992
Believe Them (s Robison), 1988
Belinda (Rice, as Rampling), 1986
Bell (Murdoch), 1958
Bellarmine Jug (Hasluck), 1984
Bellarosa Connection (s Bellow), 1989
Bellefleur (Oates), 1980
Bells of Shoredan (Zelazny), 1979
Bellydancer (Lee), 1994
Beloved (Helwig), 1992
Beloved (Morrison), 1987
Beloved Latitudes (Pownall), 1981
Beloved Son (Turner), 1978
Ben Preserve Us (Bermant), 1965
Bend in the Ganges (Malgonkar), 1964
Bend in the River (Naipaul), 1979
Benefactor (Sontag), 1963

Blessed Assurance (s Gurganis), 1990
Blessings (s Dubus), 1987
Blind Geometer (K. Robinson), 1986
Blind Love (s Pritchett), 1969
Blind Understanding (S. Middleton), 1982
Blinder (Hines), 1966
Bliss (Carey), 1981
Bliss Body (Callow), 1969
Bliss, Vicky; series (Mertz, as Peters), from 1973
Bloch and Bradbury (s R. Bradbury), 1969
Blood (s Galloway), 1991
Blood and Guts in High School (Acker), 1984
Blood and Guts in High School Plus Two (Acker), 1984
Blood and Stones (Abbas), 1947
Blood and Water (s McGrath), 1989
Blood and Water (s Winton), 1993
Blood for Blood (Gloag), 1985
Blood Meridian (McCarthy), 1985
Blood of Amber (Zelazny), 1986
Blood of My Bone (Raven), 1989
Blood of the Martyrs (Mitchison), 1939
Blood on the Moon (Ellroy), 1984
Blood on the Snow (Litvinoff), 1975
Blood Oranges (Hawkes), 1971
Blood Red Game (Moorcock), 1970
Blood Red, Sister Rose (Keneally), 1974
Blood Sport (Francis), 1967
Blood, Tears & Folly (Deighton), 1993
Blood Tie (Settle), 1977
Bloodline (s Gaines), 1968
Bloodshed and Three Novellas (s Ozick), 1976
Bloodsmoor Romance (Oates), 1982
Bloodworth Orphans (Forrest), 1977
Bloody Field by Shrewsbury (Pargeter), 1972
Blosseville File (Hasluck), 1992
Blott on the Landscape (Sharpe), 1975
Blow Your House Down (P. Barker), 1984
Blown Away (Sukenick), 1986
Blown Figures (A. Thomas), 1974
Blue Afternoon (Boyd), 1993
Blue Arabian Nights (s Mankowitz), 1973
Blue Bed (s Glyn Jones), 1937
Blue Calhoun (Price), 1992
Blue-Eyed Buddhist (s Gilchrist), 1990
Blue-Eyed Shan (Becker), 1982
Blue Eyes (Charyn), 1975
Blue Guitar (Hasluck), 1980
Blue Hill Avenue (Mirsky), 1972
Blue Ice (Hammond Innes), 1948
Blue Mountains of China (Wiebe), 1970
Blue Movie (Southern), 1970
Blue Pastoral (Sorrentino), 1983
Bluebeard (Vonnegut), 1987
Bluebeard's Egg (s Atwood), 1983
Bluegate Fields (Perry), 1984
Bluejay's Dance (Erdrich), 1995
Blues in the Night (Beckham), 1974
Bluest Eye (Morrison), 1970
Bluette (R. Frame), 1990
Boarding-House (Trevor), 1965
Boat Load of Home Folk (Astley), 1968

Boating for Beginners (Winterson), 1985
Bobby (Abbas), 1973
Bobby-Soxer (Calisher), 1986
Bodies and Souls (Rechy), 1983
Bodily Harm (Atwood), 1981
Bodily Harm (Billington), 1993
Body (Crews), 1990
Body of a Young Man (Mildred Walker), 1960
Body of Glass (Piercy), 1992
Body of Water (s Farmer), 1990
Bodysurfers (s Drewe), 1983
Bogeyman (Forster), 1965
Bohemians (Cheuse), 1982
Boka Lives (Hanley, as Calvin), 1969
Bolt (Francis), 1986
Bombay Beware (s Malgonkar), 1975
Bomber (Deighton), 1970
Bomber's Law (G. Higgins), 1993
Bonds of Attachment (Humphreys), 1991
Bone People (Hulme), 1983
Bonecrack (Francis), 1971
Bonfire of the Vanities (Wolfe), 1987
Book and the Brotherhood (Murdoch), 1987
Book Class (Auchincloss), 1984
Book of Bebb (Buechner), 1979
Book of Brian Aldiss (s Aldiss), 1972
Book of Common Prayer (Didion), 1977
Book of Daniel (Doctorow), 1971
Book of Evidence (Banville), 1989
Book of Jamaica (R. Banks), 1980
Book of Knowledge (Grumbach), 1995
Book of Lights (Potok), 1981
Book of Mrs. Noah (Roberts), 1987
Book of Secrets (Vassanji), n.d.
Book of Skulls (Silverberg), 1971
Book of the Reading (Wilding), 1994
Books Do Furnish a Room (Powell), 1971
Bookseller (M. Cohen), 1993
Bookshop (Fitzgerald), 1978
Boomerang (Hannah), 1989
Border (Feinstein), 1984
Borderline (Hospital), 1985
Born Brothers (Woiwode), 1988
Born Indian (s Kinsella), 1981
Born of Man (S. Gray), 1989
Bornholm Night-Ferry (A. Higgins), 1983
Borrower of the Night (Mertz, as Peters), 1973
Boswell (Elkin), 1964
Bottle Factory Outing (Bainbridge), 1974
Bottle in the Smoke (A.N. Wilson), 1989
Bottom of the Harbor (s Joseph Mitchell), 1959
Bounty Hunters (Leonard), 1953
Bow Down to Nul (Aldiss), 1960
Bowmen of Shu (s Davidson), 1983
Box Garden (Shields), 1977
Box Socials (Kinsella), 1991
Boy Meets Girl (Abbas), 1973
Boy on the Mountain (Rooke), 1969
Boy, the Bridge, the River (O'Sullivan), 1978
Boy's Own Story (White), 1982
Boys and Girls Together (Goldman), 1964

Boys from Brazil (Levin), 1976
Boys in the Island (Koch), 1958
Boys of Winter (Sheed), 1987
Braided Lives (Piercy), 1982
Brain Child (Turner), 1991
Brave African Huntress (Tutuola), 1958
Brazen Prison (S. Middleton), 1971
Brazzaville Beach (Boyd), 1990
Break In (Francis), 1986
Breakfast in the Ruins (Moorcock), 1972
Breakfast of Champions (Vonnegut), 1973
Breakfast with the Nikolides (Godden), 1942
Breaking of Bumbo (Sinclair), 1959
Breast (P. Roth), 1972
Breath Dances Between Them (s Kelly), 1991
Breath of Air (Godden), 1950
Breathing Lessons (Tyler), 1988
Breathing Trouble (s Busch), 1974
Breed of Women (Kidman), 1979
Brendan (Buechner), 1987
Brewers' Big Horses (Mildred Walker), 1940
Bride (Sidhwa), 1983
Bride for the Sahib (s Singh), 1967
Bride of Innisfallen (s Welty), 1955
Bride of Lowther Fell (Forster), 1980
Bride Price (Emecheta), 1976
Bridesmaid (Rendell), 1989
Bridge (Stuart), 1937
Bridge at Andau (Michener), 1957
Bridge of Ashes (Zelazny), 1976
Bridge of Lost Desire (Delany), 1987
Bridge of Years (Sarton), 1946
Bridge to a Wedding (Munonye), 1978
Bridge to Vengeance (Graham), 1957
Bridgeport Bus (M. Howard), 1965
Bridges at Toko-Ri (Michener), 1953
Brief Conversation (s Lovelace), 1988
Brief Lives (Brookner), 1990
Briefing for a Descent into Hell (Lessing), 1971
Brigadier Down Under (Tinniswood), 1983
Brigadier in Season (Tinniswood), 1984
Brigadier's Brief Lives (Tinniswood), 1984
Brigadier's Tour (Tinniswood), 1985
Bright Center of Heaven (Maxwell), 1934
Bright Lights, Big City (McInerney), 1984
Bright Prison (P. Mortimer), 1956
Bright Road to El Dorado (Anthony), 1982
Brighten the Corner Where You Are (Chappell), 1989
Brightfount Diaries (Aldiss), 1955
Brightness Falls (McInerney), 1992
Brighton Belle (s F. King), 1968
Brill among the Ruins (Bourjaily), 1970
Bring Forth the Body (Raven), 1974
Bring Larks and Heroes (Keneally), 1967
Bring Me the Head of Prince Charming (Zelazny), 1991
Bring Me the Head of Rona Barrett (s Gover), 1981
British Museum Is Falling Down (Lodge), 1965
Broken Canes (Vansittart), 1950
Bronc People (Eastlake), 1958
Brooklyn Book of the Dead (Stephens), 1994
Brooklyn Boy (Lelchuk), 1989

Brothel in Rösenstrasse (Moorcock), 1982
Brother Cadfael series (Pargeter, as Peters), from 1977
Brother Cadfael's Penance (Pargeter, as Peters), 1994
Brother Cain (Raven), 1959
Brother of the More Famous Jack (Trapido), 1982
Brother's Tale (Barstow), 1980
Brothers (Barthelme), 1993
Brothers (Goldman), 1986
Brothers (Rubens), 1983
Brothers in Confidence (Madden), 1972
Brothers of the Head (Aldiss), 1977
Brothers of the Head, and Where the Lines Converge (Aldiss), 1979
Brown Girl, Brownstones (P. Marshall), 1959
Brown's Requiem (Ellroy), 1981
Bruno's Dream (Murdoch), 1969
Bubble (Anand), 1987
Buccaneer (Cassill), 1958
Bucket Shop (Waterhouse), 1968
Buddha of Suburbia (Kureishi), 1990
Budding Prospects (Boyle), 1984
Buddwing (E. Hunter), 1964
Buffalo Afternoon (Schaeffer), 1989
Buffalo Gals and Other Animal Presences (s Le Guin), 1987
Buffalo Gals, Won't You Come Out Tonight (Le Guin), 1994
Buffalo Girls (McMurtry), 1990
Bugles Blowing (Freeling), 1976
Bull and the Spear (Moorcock), 1973
Bull Calves (Mitchison), 1947
Burger's Daughter (Gordimer), 1979
Buried Land (Madison Jones), 1963
Burn (s Kelman), 1991
Burn is Aran (s I. Smith), 1960
Burning (Diane Johnson), 1971
Burning Angel (Burke), 1995
Burning Book (Maggie Gee), 1983
Burning Boy (Maurice Gee), 1990
Burning Grass (Ekwensi), 1962
Burning House (s Beattie), 1982
Burning World (Ballard), 1964
Burr (Vidal), 1973
Busconductor Hines (Kelman), 1984
Bushwhacked Piano (McGuane), 1971
Buster (Burns), 1972
But for Bunter (Hughes), 1985
But the Dead Are Many (Hardy), 1975
But We Are Exiles (Kroetsch), 1965
Butcher and Co (O'Sullivan), 1977
Butcher Boy (McCabe), 1992
Butcher Papers (O'Sullivan), 1982
Buttercup Chain (Elliott), 1967
Buttercup Field (s Gwyn Jones), 1945
Butterfly (Rumaker), 1962
Butterfly Plague (Findley), 1969
Buyer's Market (Powell), 1952
Buzzards (Burroway), 1969
By Firelight (Pargeter), 1948
By the Line (Keneally), 1989
By the Waters of Whitechapel (Kops), 1969
By This Strange Fire (Pargeter), 1948
Bye-Bye, Blackbird (A. Desai), 1971
Bystander (Guerard), 1958

Bystander (Stow), 1957
Byzantium Endures (Moorcock), 1981

Cabin Fever (Jolley), 1990
Cabot Wright Begins (Purdy), 1964
Cactus Country (Malgonkar), 1991
Cadillac Jack (McMurtry), 1982
Caedmon's Song (P. Robinson), 1990
Caesar (Massie), 1993
Café le dog (s M. Cohen), 1983
Cage (Hinde), 1962
Cages of Freedom (s Abbas), 1952
Caine Mutiny (Wouk), 1951
Caitaani Mutharaba-ini (Ngugi), 1980
Cal (MacLaverty), 1983
Calendar of Love (s G. Brown), 1967
Caliban's Filibuster (P. West), 1971
California Time (Raphael), 1975
Call at Corazón (s Bowles), 1988
Call for a Miracle (Kiely), 1950
Call for the Dead (le Carré), 1961
Call It a Canary (Tinniswood), 1985
Call It Sleep (H. Roth), 1934
Call of Fife and Drum (Fast), 1987
Callander Square (Perry), 1980
Caltrop's Desire (S. Gray), 1980
Camberwell Beauty (s Pritchett), 1974
Cambridge (C. Phillips), 1991
Camelot Caper (Mertz, as Peters), 1969
Cameo (Graham), 1988
Camera Always Lies (Hood), 1967
Camomile Lawn (Wesley), 1984
Campaign (Freeman), 1963
Campbell's Kingdom (Hammond Innes), 1952
Camping Out (Clark), 1986
Can't Quit You, Baby (Douglas), 1988
Canary in a Cat House (s Vonnegut), 1961
Candace (s Cheuse), 1980
Candle for St. Jude (Godden), 1948
Candles of Your Eyes (s Purdy), 1985
Candy (Southern, as Kenton), 1958
Cannibal (Hawkes), 1949
Cannibal Galaxy (Ozick), 1983
Cannibal in Manhattan (Janowitz), 1987
Canopus in Argos: Archives (Lessing), from 1979
Canopy of Time (s Aldiss), 1959
Capable of Honor (Drury), 1966
Capital (Duffy), 1975
Captain Blackman (Williams), 1975
Captain Corelli's Mandolin (de Bernières), 1994
Captain Maximus (s Hannah), 1985
Captain Newman, M.D. (Rosten), 1961
Captain with the Whiskers (Kiely), 1960
Captains and the Kings (Johnston), 1972
Captive in the Land (Aldridge), 1962
Captives of the Flame (Delany), 1963
Captivity Captive (R. Hall), 1988
Car (Crews), 1972
Caracole (White), 1985
Caravans (Michener), 1963
Card of Time (Ambler), 1981

Cardington Crescent (Perry), 1987
Cards of the Gambler (Kiely), 1953
Careless Love (A. Adams), 1966
Careless Widow (s Pritchett), 1989
Caribbean (Michener), 1989
Caribbean Crisis (Moorcock, as Reid), 1962
Carn (McCabe), 1989
Carnival (W. Harris), 1985
Carnival Trilogy (W. Harris), 1993
Carolina (Vansittart), 1961
Caroline's Daughters (A. Adams), 1991
Carpathians (J. Frame), 1988
Carpenter's Gothic (Gaddis), 1985
Carpet People (Pratchett), 1971
Casablanca (Moorcock), 1989
Casanova's Chinese Restaurant (Powell), 1960
Case Against Tomorrow (s Pohl), 1957
Case Examined (A.L. Barker), 1965
Case of Knives (McWilliam), 1988
Case of Need (Crichton, as Hudson), 1968
Case of the Angry Actress (Fast, as Cunningham), 1984
Case of the Kidnapped Angel (Fast, as Cunningham), 1982
Case of the Murdered Mackenzie (Fast, as Cunningham), 1984
Case of the One-Penny Orange (Fast, as Cunningham), 1977
Case of the Poisoned Eclairs (Fast, as Cunningham), 1979
Case of the Russian Diplomat (Fast, as Cunningham), 1978
Case of the Sliding Pool (Fast, as Cunningham), 1981
Cassandra Singing (Madden), 1969
Cassidy (M. West), 1986
Castang's City (Freeling), 1980
Castle Keep (Eastlake), 1965
Casual Acquaintance (s Barstow), 1976
Casual Brutality (Bissoondath), 1988
Casualties (L. Banks), 1986
Casualties of Peace (E. O'Brien), 1966
Cat (Sinclair), 1977
Cat and Shakespeare (Rao), 1965
Cat and the King (Auchincloss), 1981
Cat Chaser (Leonard), 1982
Cat Man (Hoagland), 1956
Cat's Cradle (Vonnegut), 1963
Cat's Eye (Atwood), 1988
Cat's Meow (s Morris), 1975
Catacomb (Glanville), 1988
Catalysts (S. Middleton), 1994
Catastrophe Practice (Mosley), 1979
Catch-22 (Heller), 1961
Catch a Falling Spy (Deighton), 1976
Catcher in the Rye (Salinger), 1951
Cater Street Hangman (Perry), 1979
Catfish Man (Charyn), 1980
Catherine Carmier (Gaines), 1964
Catherine Wheel (Harrower), 1960
Catholic (Plante), 1985
Catholics (B. Moore), 1972
Cause for Alarm (Ambler), 1938
Cause for Wonder (Morris), 1963
Cave of Ice (P. Mortimer), 1959
Cave with Echoes (Elliott), 1962
Caverns (Kesey), 1990
Celebration (Settle), 1986

Men and Women (s Abbas), 1977
Men at Arms (Pratchett), 1993
Men, Women, and Children (s Sillitoe), 1973
Men's Club (Michaels), 1981
Mendelman Fire (s Mankowitz), 1957
Menorah Men (Davidson), 1966
Mera Naam, Joker (Abbas), 1970
Merchants' War (Pohl), 1984
Merciless Ladies (Graham), 1944
Mercy of a Rude Stream (H. Roth), 1994
Mercy, Pity, Peace and Love (s Godden), 1990
Meridian (A. Walker), 1976
Merle (s P. Marshall), 1985
Merlin (Nye), 1978
Mermaids in the Basement (s Warner), 1993
Merry-Go-Round in the Sea (Stow), 1965
Message from a Spy (Helwig), 1975
Message from Harpo (Duff), 1989
Message to the Planet (Murdoch), 1989
Messenger (Wright), 1963
Messengers Will Come No More (Fiedler), 1974
Messiah (Vidal), 1954
Messiah at the End of Time (Moorcock), 1978
Messiah of Stockholm (Ozick), 1987
Messiah of the Last Days (Driver), 1974
Metroland (Barnes), 1980
Mexico (Michener), 1992
Mexico Set (Deighton), 1984
Mezzanine (N. Baker), 1988
Micky Darlin' (Kelleher), 1992
Microcosm (Duffy), 1966
Midas World (Pohl), 1983
Middle Class Education (Sheed), 1960
Middle Ground (Drabble), 1980
Middle Passage (C. Johnson), 1990
Middleman (s Mukherjee), 1988
Middlemen (Brooke-Rose), 1961
Middling (A.L. Barker), 1967
Midnight Clear (Wharton), 1982
Midnight Line (Savage), 1976
Midnight Mass (s Bowles), 1981
Midnight Turning Gray (s Matthiessen), 1984
Midnight's Children (Rushdie), 1981
Migrations (Josipovici), 1977
Miguel Street (Naipaul), 1959
Mihloti (s Tlali), 1984
Mila 18 (Uris), 1961
Mile High (Condon), 1969
Military Philosophers (Powell), 1968
Milk (s Farmer), 1983
Milk and Honey (Jolley), 1984
Miller's Dance (Graham), 1982
Millie (Fast, as Cunningham), 1973
Millroy the Magician (P. Theroux), 1993
Millstone (Drabble), 1965
Mimic Men (Naipaul), 1967
Mind Parasites (C. Wilson), 1967
Mind to Murder (P.D. James), 1963
Minds Meet (s Abish), 1975
Mine Boy (Abrahams), 1946
Minimum of Two (s Winton), 1987

Mining the Oort (Pohl), 1991
Miracle (s Deshpande), 1986
Miracle (O'Sullivan), 1976
Miracle in Seville (Michener), 1995
Miraculous Day of Amalia Gómez (Rechy), 1991
Mirage (Fast), 1965
Miranda Must Die (Hanley, as Calvin), 1968
Miriam at Thirty-four (Lelchuk), 1974
Miriam in Her Forties (Lelchuk), 1985
Mis (Sionil Jose), 1983
Misalliance (Brookner), 1986
Miscellany Two (s Humphreys), 1981
Miss America (D. Stern), 1959
Miss Doll, Go Home (Markson), 1965
Miss Gomez and the Brethren (Trevor), 1971
Miss Hobbema Pageant (s Kinsella), 1989
Miss MacIntosh, My Darling (M. Young), 1965
Miss Muriel (s Petry), 1971
Miss Owen-Owen (Forster), 1969
Miss Owen-Owen Is at Home (Forster), 1969
Miss Peabody's Inheritance (Jolley), 1983
Miss Pickthorn and Mr. Hare (Sarton), 1966
Mrs Dixon and Friend (s Kidman), 1982
Mrs. Blood (A. Thomas), 1967
Mrs. Bridge (Connell), 1958
Mrs. de Winter (S. Hill), 1993
Mrs. Eckdorf in O'Neill's Hotel (Trevor), 1969
Mrs. Reinhardt (s E. O'Brien), 1978
Mrs. Shakespeare (Nye), 1993
Mrs. Stevens Hears the Mermaids Singing (Sarton), 1965
Missing Person (Grumbach), 1981
Missing Persons (Cook), 1986
Missionaries (Jenkins), 1957
Mist in the Mirror (S. Hill), 1993
Mistaken Identity (Sahgal), 1988
Mr. Armitage Isn't Back Yet (Mervyn Jones), 1971
Mr. Barrett's Secret (s K. Amis), 1993
Mr. Bedford and the Muses (s Godwin), 1983
Mr. Beluncle (Pritchett), 1951
Mr. Bone's Retreat (Forster), 1971
Mr. Bridge (Connell), 1969
Mr. Evening (s Purdy), 1970
Mr. Majestyk (Leonard), 1974
Mister Margolies (Yaffe), 1962
Mr. Nicholas (Ely), 1974
Mr. Nicholas (Hinde), 1952
Mr. Sammler's Planet (Bellow), 1970
Mr. Sampath (Narayan), 1949
Mr. Scobie's Riddle (Jolley), 1983
Mr. Stone and the Knights Companion (Naipaul), 1963
Mr. Trill in Hades (s I. Smith), 1984
Mr. Vertigo (Auster), 1994
Mr. Wakefield's Crusade (Rubens), 1985
Mister White Eyes (Gold), 1984
Mr. Wrong (s E. Howard), 1975
Mr. Zouch, Superman (Powell), 1934
Misterioso (Sorrentino), 1989
Mitla Pass (Uris), 1988
Mittee (Rooke), 1951
Mixture of Frailties (Davies), 1958
Mobiles (s Cowan), 1979

Something I've Been Meaning to Tell You (s Munro), 1974
Something in Disguise (E. Howard), 1969
Something Leather (A. Gray), 1990
Something Out There (s Gordimer), 1984
Something to Answer For (Newby), 1968
Something to Be Desired (McGuane), 1984
Something to Remember Me By (s Bellow), 1991
Something Wicked This Way Comes (R. Bradbury), 1962
Sometimes a Great Notion (Kesey), 1964
Sometimes I Live in the Country (Busch), 1986
Somewhere East of Life (Aldiss), 1994
Somewhere in the Night (Moorcock, as Barclay), 1966
Somnambulists (Elliott), 1964
Son of Laughter (Buechner), 1993
Son of Man (Silverberg), 1971
Son of the Morning (Oates), 1978
Song of Solomon (Morrison), 1977
Song of the City (Abrahams), 1945
Song of the Silent Snow (s Selby), 1986
Songs My Mother Taught Me (A. Thomas), 1973
Songs of Distant Earth (Arthur C. Clarke), 1986
Songs of Enchantment (Okri), 1993
Sons (E. Hunter), 1969
Sons for the Return Home (Wendt), 1973
Sons of Darkness, Sons of Light (Williams), 1969
Sons of the Wolf (Mertz, as Michaels), 1967
Sophie's Choice (Styron), 1979
Sorcerer's Amulet (Moorcock), 1968
Sorcerer's Apprentice (s C. Johnson), 1986
Sorority House (Pohl, as Park), 1956
Sort of Forgetting (Vansittart), 1960
Sot-Weed Factor (Barth), 1960
Soul Clap Hands and Sing (s P. Marshall), 1961
Soul-Mate (Oates, as Smith), 1989
Soul Music (Pratchett), 1994
Souls and Bodies (Lodge), 1982
Souls Raised from the Dead (Betts), 1994
Sound Like Laughter (Helwig), 1983
Sound of Lightning (Cleary), 1976
Sound the Retreat (Raven), 1971
Soundings (Davison), 1993
Sour Sweet (Mo), 1982
Source (Michener), 1965
Source of Embarrassment (A.L. Barker), 1974
Source of Light (Price), 1981
Sourcery (Pratchett), 1988
Sources of Unrest (Vansittart), 1962
South Street (D. Bradley), 1975
South Will Rise at Noon (Glover), 1988
Southern Discomfort (Rita Mae Brown), 1982
Southern Family (Godwin), 1987
Southpaw (M. Harris), 1953
Southwest Corner (Mildred Walker), 1951
Soweto Stories (s Tlali), 1989
Space (Michener), 1982
Space Dreamers (Arthur C. Clarke), 1969
Space Merchants (Pohl), 1953
Space, Time, and Nathaniel (s Aldiss), 1957
Space Vampires (C. Wilson), 1976
Spaces of the Dark (Mosley), 1951
Spanish Doctor (M. Cohen), 1984

Spanish Virgin (s Pritchett), 1930
Spanking the Maid (Coover), 1982
Sparrow's Fall (Bodsworth), 1967
Spartacus (Fast), 1951
Speaker of Mandarin (Rendell), 1983
Spearfield's Daughter (Cleary), 1982
Special Flower (Maurice Gee), 1965
Speed (M. Harris), 1990
Speedboat (Adler), 1976
Spence + Lila (Mason), 1988
Sphere (Crichton), 1987
Sphinx (D.M. Thomas), 1986
Sphinx and the Sybarites (Pownall), 1993
Spider (McGrath), 1990
Spider Cup (Halligan), 1990
Spider World (C. Wilson), from 1987
Spider's House (Bowles), 1955
Spiderman (Sionil Jose), 1991
Spiked Heel (E. Hunter, as Marsten), 1956
Spiral Ascent (Upward), 1977
Spirit Weddings (Tindall), 1992
Spit Delaney's Island (s Hodgins), 1976
Splendide-Hôtel (Sorrentino), 1973
Split Images (Leonard), 1982
Splitting (Weldon), 1994
Spoils of Flowers (Grumbach), 1962
Sport of Nature (Gordimer), 1987
Sporting Club (McGuane), 1968
Sporting Proposition (Aldridge), 1973
Sportswriter (R. Ford), 1986
Spreading Fires (Knowles), 1974
Spring of the Ram (Dunnett), 1987
Spring Sonata (Rubens), 1979
Springer's Progress (Markson), 1977
Spy Hook (Deighton), 1988
Spy Line (Deighton), 1989
Spy Sinker (Deighton), 1990
Spy Story (Deighton), 1974
Spy Who Came In from the Cold (le Carré), 1963
Square's Progress (Sheed), 1965
Squeak (Bowen), 1983
Squeeze Play (Auster, as Benjamin), 1982
Squire of Bor Shachor (Bermant), 1977
SS-GB (Deighton), 1978
St. Augustine's Pigeon (s Connell), 1980
Stagg and His Mother (Pownall), 1991
Staggerford (Hassler), 1977
Stained White Radiance (Burke), 1992
Stand on the Saber (Leonard), 1960
Stand We at Last (Fairbairns), 1983
Standard Dreaming (Calisher), 1972
Standard of Behaviour (Trevor), 1958
Stanley and the Women (K. Amis), 1984
Star in the Family (Faust), 1975
Star of the Gypsies (Silverberg), 1986
Star-Spangled Crunch (Condon), 1974
Starburst (Pohl), 1982
Starcarbon (Gilchrist), 1994
Starchild (Pohl), 1965
Starchild Trilogy (Pohl), 1977
Starhaven (Silverberg, as Jorgenson), 1958

Sula (Morrison), 1974
Summer (Cowan), 1964
Summer Before the Dark (Lessing), 1973
Summer Bird-Cage (Drabble), 1962
Summer Fires and Winter Country (s Shadbolt), 1963
Summer Lightning (s Senior), 1987
Summer of the Danes (Pargeter, as Peters), 1991
Summer of the Dragon (Mertz, as Peters), 1979
Summer of the Red Wolf (M. West), 1971
Summer of the Royal Visit (Colegate), 1991
Summer People (Elliott), 1980
Summer People (Piercy), 1989
Summer Place (S. Wilson), 1958
Summer's Lease (J. Mortimer), 1988
Summerhouse Trilogy (A. Ellis), 1991
Summering (s Greenberg), 1966
Summit (D.M. Thomas), 1987
Sun and the Moon (Tucci), 1977
Sun Between Their Feet (s Lessing), 1973
Sun Chemist (Davidson), 1976
Sun on the Wall (s R. Frame), 1994
Sun's Net (s G. Brown), 1976
Sunday Best (Rubens), 1971
Sundered Worlds (Moorcock), 1965
Sundog (Harrison), 1984
Sundowners (Cleary), 1952
Sunrise in Fiji (Nahal), 1988
Sunrise in the West (Pargeter), 1974
Sunrise with Sea Monster (Jordan), 1994
Sunrising (Cook), 1984
Superior Women (A. Adams), 1984
Supper Waltz Wilson (s O. Marshall), 1979
Surface of Earth (Price), 1975
Surfacing (Atwood), 1972
Surrey Cat (Sinclair), 1976
Survival Arts (Wedde), 1988
Survival Kit (s Pohl), 1979
Survival Without Error (s I. Smith), 1970
Survive the Peace (Ekwensi), 1976
Survivor (Mervyn Jones), 1968
Survivor (s Joshi), 1975
Survivor (Keneally), 1969
Survivors (Feinstein), 1982
Survivors (K. Hunter), 1975
Survivors (Hammond Innes), 1950
Survivors (Raven), 1975
Survivors of the Crossing (Austin C. Clarke), 1964
Suttree (McCarthy), 1979
Swag (Leonard), 1976
Swallow (D.M. Thomas), 1984
Swami and Friends (Narayan), 1935
Swann (Shields), 1987
Swans and Turtles (s Godden), 1968
Sweet and Sour Milk (Farah), 1979
Sweet Dreams (Frayn), 1973
Sweet Hereafter (R. Banks), 1991
Sweet Second Summer of Kitty Malone (M. Cohen), 1979
Sweet Shop Owner (Swift), 1980
Sweet-Vendor (Narayan), 1967
Sweet William (Bainbridge), 1975
Sweet William (Hawkes), 1993

Sweethearts (s J. Phillips), 1976
Sweets of Pimlico (A.N. Wilson), 1977
Sweetsir (H. Yglesias), 1981
Swiftie the Magician (Gold), 1974
Swimming Lessons (s Mistry), 1989
Swimming-Pool Library (Hollinghurst), 1988
Swimming Pool Season (Tremain), 1985
Swing in the Garden (Hood), 1975
Swinging in the Rain (Bermant), 1967
Switch (Leonard), 1978
Sword and the Sickle (Anand), 1942
Sword and the Stallion (Moorcock), 1974
Sword of the Dawn (Moorcock), 1968
Swords Trilogy (Moorcock), 1977
Sybil (Auchincloss), 1951
Sycamore Tree (Brooke-Rose), 1958
Sylvia (Fast, as Cunningham), 1960
Sylvia (Michaels), 1992
Symmes Hole (Wedde), 1986
Symposium (Spark), 1990
System (Hanley, as Calvin), 1962
Syzygy (Pohl), 1982

t-Adhar Ameireagenach (s I. Smith), 1973
t-Aonaran (I. Smith), 1976
Table of Green Fields (s Davidson), 1994
Tabula Rasa (Kostelanetz), 1978
Take a Fax to the Kasbah (Dunnett), 1992
Take a Girl Like You (K. Amis), 1960
Take It or Leave It (Federman), 1976
Take My Life (Graham), 1947
Take This Man (Busch), 1981
Take Three Tenses (Godden), 1945
Take Two Popes (Hanley, as Calvin), 1972
Takeover (Spark), 1976
Taking Care of Mrs. Carroll (Monette), 1978
Taking Chances (s Kelleher, as Farrell), 1929
Taking Shelter (J. Anderson), 1990
Tale for the Mirror (s Calisher), 1962
Tale Maker (M. Harris), 1994
Tale of Asa Bean (Matthews), 1971
Tale of the Body Thief (Rice), 1992
Talent for Loving (Condon), 1961
Tales from a Long Room (s Tinniswood), 1981
Tales from Bective Bridge (s Lavin), 1942
Tales from Firozsha Baag (s Mistry), 1987
Tales from Planet Earth (s Arthur C. Clarke), 1989
Tales from the White Hart (s Arthur C. Clarke), 1957
Tales from Witney Scrotum (s Tinniswood), 1987
Tales I Tell My Mother (s Roberts), 1978
Tales I Tell My Mother (s Fairbairns), 1978
Tales I Told My Mother (s Nye), 1969
Tales of Manhattan (s Auchincloss), 1967
Tales of Mystery and Romance (s Moorhouse), 1977
Tales of Nevèrÿon (s Delany), 1979
Tales of Ten Worlds (s Arthur C. Clarke), 1962
Tales of the Ohio Land (s Matthews), 1978
Tales of the South Pacific (s Michener), 1947
Tales of the Tikongs (s Hau'ofa), 1983
Tales of the Trickster Boy (s Cope), 1990
Tales of Yesteryear (Auchincloss), 1994

Talkative Man (Narayan), 1986
Talking It Over (Barnes), 1991
Talking Room (Hauser), 1976
Talking to Strange Men (Rendell), 1987
Tall Houses in Winter (Betts), 1954
Tall Hunter (Fast), 1942
Taltos (Rice), 1994
Tamara (Dutton), 1970
Tamarisk Row (Murnane), 1974
Tame Ox (s Cope), 1960
Tar Baby (Charyn), 1973
Tar Baby (Morrison), 1981
Target Antarctica (Hammond Innes), 1993
Taste for Death (P.D. James), 1986
Taste of Sin (Cassill), 1955
Taste of Too Much (Hanley), 1960
Tatlin! (s Davidson), 1974
Tax Inspector (Carey), 1992
Tea on Sunday (L. Cooper), 1973
Teach Me to Fly, Skyfighter! (s Lee), 1983
Tear His Head Off His Shoulders (Dunn), 1974
Teeth, Dying, and Other Matters (s R. Stern), 1964
Teeth of My Father (s Metcalf), 1975
Tehanu (Le Guin), 1990
Teitlebaum's Window (Markfield), 1970
Tell Me a Riddle (s Olsen), 1961
Telling of Lies (Findley), 1986
Tempest (Cassill), 1959
Tempest-Tost (Davies), 1951
Temple of Flora (s Maxwell), 1961
Temple of Gold (Goldman), 1957
Temple of My Familiar (A. Walker), 1989
Temples of Delight (Trapido), 1990
Temporary Kings (Powell), 1973
Temporary Life (Storey), 1973
Temporary Shelter (s M. Gordon), 1987
Temptation of Eileen Hughes (B. Moore), 1981
Temptation of Jack Orfkney (s Lessing), 1972
Temptations of Big Bear (Wiebe), 1973
Ten Green Bottles (s A. Thomas), 1967
Ten Miles from Anywhere (s Newby), 1958
Ten Tales Tall and True (s A. Gray), 1993
Tenancy (Figes), 1993
Tenants (Cowan), 1994
Tenants of Time (Flanagan), 1988
Tender Mercies (Rosellen Brown), 1978
Tender to Danger (Ambler, as Reed), 1951
Tender to Moonlight (Ambler, as Reed), 1952
Tenement (I. Smith), 1985
Tenement of Clay (P. West), 1965
Tennessee Waltz (s Cheuse), 1990
Tennis Handsome (Hannah), 1983
Tent of Orange Mist (P. West), 1995
Terminal Beach (s Ballard), 1964
Terminal Man (Crichton), 1972
Termination Rock (Freeman), 1989
Terms of Endearment (McMurtry), 1975
Terms of Reference (S. Middleton), 1966
Terrible Threes (Reed), 1989
Terrible Twos (Reed), 1982
Territorial Rights (Spark), 1979

Tess (Tennant), 1993
Testostero (Foster), 1987
Texas (Michener), 1985
Texas Inheritance (Ghose, as Strang), 1980
Texas Summer (Southern), 1991
Texasville (McMurtry), 1987
Textermination (Brooke-Rose), 1991
Textures of Life (Calisher), 1963
Thank You All Very Much (Drabble), 1969
That Angel Burning at My Left Side (Peterkiewicz), 1963
That Bad Woman (s Boylan), 1995
That Darcy, That Dancer, That Gentleman (Donleavy), 1990
That Eye, the Sky (Winton), 1986
That Long Silence (Deshpande), 1988
That Summer (Drury), 1965
That Uncertain Feeling (K. Amis), 1955
That Year in Paris (Mervyn Jones), 1988
That's How It Was (Duffy), 1962
The Year of the Tempest (Matthiessen), 1957
Thebes of the Hundred Gates (Silverberg), 1993
Theft (s Bellow), 1989
Them (Oates), 1969
Theme for Diverse Instruments (s Rule), 1975
Then Again (McCauley), 1986
Then upon the Evil Season (Virtue), 1988
Theo and Matilda (Billington), 1990
Therapy (Lodge), 1995
There Are No Elders (s Austin C. Clarke), 1994
There Is a Happy Land (Waterhouse), 1957
There Is a Tree More Ancient Than Eden (Forrest), 1973
There Must Be More to Love Than Death (s Charles Newman), 1976
There Was an Ancient House (Kiely), 1955
Therefore Be Bold (Gold), 1960
These Enchanted Woods (Massie), 1993
These Small Glories (s Cleary), 1946
They Came like Swallows (Maxwell), 1937
They Do Return (s Lim), 1983
They Fly at Ciron (Delany), 1993
Thin Ice (s Levine), 1980
Thing He Loves (s Glanville), 1973
Thing of It Is. . . (Goldman), 1967
Things Fall Apart (Achebe), 1958
Things Gone and Things Still Here (s Bowles), 1977
Things They Carried (s T. O'Brien), 1990
Think of England (s Raphael), 1986
Thinks (Waterhouse), 1984
Third Life of Grange Copeland (A. Walker), 1970
13th Immortal (Silverberg), 1957
Thirteenth Victim (s Abbas), 1986
This Animal Is Mischievous (Benedictus), 1965
This Crooked Way (E. Spencer), 1952
This Day's Death (Rechy), 1970
This Immortal (Zelazny), 1966
This Is for You (Wilding), 1994
This Is Not for You (Rule), 1970
This Is the Castle (Freeling), 1968
This Island Now (Abrahams), 1966
This Perfect Day (Levin), 1970
This Rough Magic (Pargeter), 1953
This Sporting Life (Storey), 1960

Without a Hero (s Boyle), 1994
Without Motive (Graham), 1936
Wittgenstein's Mistress (Markson), 1988
Wizard of Earthsea (Le Guin), 1968
Wizard's Daughter (Mertz, as Michaels), 1980
Wizard's Tide (Buechner), 1990
Wizards' Country (Rooke), 1957
Wolf (Harrison), 1971
Wolf to the Slaughter (Rendell), 1967
Wolfbane (Pohl), 1959
Wolfnight (Freeling), 1982
Woman Beware Woman (Tennant), 1983
Woman in a Lampshade (s Jolley), 1983
Woman in Black (S. Hill), 1983
Woman in the Mirror (Graham), 1975
Woman Lit by Fireflies (Harrison), 1990
Woman of Character (Gloag), 1973
Woman of Her Age (Ludwig), 1973
Woman of Judah (R. Frame), 1987
Woman of My Age (Bawden), 1967
Woman of the Inner Sea (Keneally), 1992
Woman on the Edge of Time (Piercy), 1976
Woman Who Talked to Herself (A.L. Barker), 1989
Woman Who Was God (F. King), 1988
Woman with a Poet (s Callow), 1983
Woman's Age (Billington), 1979
Woman's Book of Superlatives (s Lim), 1993
Women and Angels (s Brodkey), 1985
Women and Ghosts (s A. Lurie), 1994
Women and God (Stuart), 1931
Women and Men (McElroy), 1987
Women in the Wall (O'Faolain), 1975
Women of Brewster Place (Naylor), 1982
Women of Whitechapel and Jack the Ripper (P. West), 1991
Women's Hour (Caute), 1991
Women's Room (French), 1977
Wonder Effect (s Pohl), 1962
Wonder-Worker (D. Jacobson), 1973
Wonderful Years, Wonderful Years (G. Higgins), 1988
Wonderland (Oates), 1971
Wooden Hunters (M. Cohen), 1975
Woods (Plante), 1982
Word Child (Murdoch), 1975
Word for World Is Forest (Le Guin), 1976
Words (Josipovici), 1971
Words of Advice (Weldon), 1977
Words of My Roaring (Kroetsch), 1966
Work (Dixon), 1977
Works of Love (Morris), 1952
World at the End of Time (Pohl), 1990
World Elsewhere (Bowen), 1965
World in the Attic (Morris), 1949
World Inside (Silverberg), 1971
World Is Made of Glass (M. West), 1983
World Is My Village (Abbas), 1983
World of Nagaraj (Narayan), 1990
World of Profit (Auchincloss), 1968
World of Strangers (Gordimer), 1958
World of Violence (C. Wilson), 1963
World of Windows (Benedictus), 1971
World of Wonders (Davies), 1975

World's End (Boyle), 1987
World's End (s P. Theroux), 1980
World's Fair (Doctorow), 1985
Worry Box (s Halligan), 1993
Wort Papers (Mathers), 1972
Would-Be Saint (Jenkins), 1978
Wound of Love (Cassill), 1956
Wounds (Duffy), 1969
Wreath for a Redhead (B. Moore, as Bryan), 1951
Wreath for Garibaldi (s Garrett), 1969
Wreath for Maidens (Munonye), 1973
Wreath for Udomo (Abrahams), 1956
Wreck of the Grey Cat (Graham), 1958
Wreck of the Mary Deare (Hammond Innes), 1956
Wreckers Must Breathe (Hammond Innes), 1940
Wrecks of Time (Moorcock), 1967
Writing for Love and Money (Perutz), 1991
Written on the Body (Winterson), 1992
Wrong Ones in the Dock (Aluko), 1982
Wrongful Deaths (Wharton), 1995
Wyrd Sisters (Pratchett), 1988

Xorandor (Brooke-Rose), 1986
XPD (Deighton), 1981

Y Tri Llais (Humphreys), 1958
Yarns of Billy Borker (s Hardy), 1965
Year Before Yesterday (Aldiss), 1987
Year in San Fernando (Anthony), 1965
Year of Fears (Watmough), 1988
Year of Living Dangerously (Koch), 1978
Year of Silence (Bell), 1987
Year of the French (Flanagan), 1979
Year of the Hot Jock (s Faust), 1985
Year of the Short Corn (s Urquhart), 1949
Year or So with Edgar (G. Higgins), 1979
Years of the City (s Pohl), 1984
Yellow Back Radio Broke-Down (Reed), 1969
Yellow Flowers in the Antipodean Room (J. Frame), 1969
Yes from No-Man's Land (Kops), 1965
Yesterday's Men (Turner), 1983
Yesterday's Spy (Deighton), 1975
Yonnondio (Olsen), 1974
Yoruba Folktales (s Tutuola), 1986
You Are Now Entering the Human Heart (s J. Frame), 1983
You Can't Catch Me (Oates, as Smith), 1995
You Can't Do Both (K. Amis), 1994
You Can't Get There from Here (Hood), 1972
You Can't Keep a Good Woman Down (s A. Walker), 1981
You Can't See Round Corners (Cleary), 1947
You Could Live If They Let You (Markfield), 1974
You Make Your Own Life (s Pritchett), 1938
You Must Remember This (Oates), 1987
You Want the Right Frame of Reference (W. Cooper), 1971
You Who Know (Freeling), 1993
You'll Catch Your Death (s Hood), 1992
You're a Big Boy Now (Benedictus), 1963
You're Not Alone (W. Cooper), 1976
Young Adolf (Bainbridge), 1978
Young Doctors (Hailey), 1962
Young Entry (s Kelleher, as Farrell), 1928

NOTES ON
ADVISERS AND CONTRIBUTORS

AKEY, Stephen. Freelance writer. **Essays:** Paul Auster; James Welch.

ALLEN, Walter. See his own entry. **Essays:** V.S. Pritchett; Edward Upward.

ALTNER, Patricia. Librarian, Department of Defense, Washington, D.C. Reviewer of historical fiction for *Library Journal;* associate editor of *This Year's Scholarship in Science Fiction, Fantasy, and Horror.* **Essays:** Carol Hill; Mary Robison.

ANDERSEN, Richard. James Thurber writer-in-residence, Ohio State University, Columbus. Author of critical studies of William Goldman and Robert Coover, and four novels—*Muckaluck, Straight Cut Ditch, On the Run,* and *The Reluctant Hero.* **Essay:** William Goldman.

ANG, Susan. Faculty member, Department of English Language and Literature, National University of Singapore. **Essays:** Catherine Lim; Roger Zelazny.

AUBERT, Alvin. Professor Emeritus of English, Wayne State University, Detroit; founding editor of *Obsidian* magazine, now *Obsidian II.* Author of five books of poetry—*Against the Blues,* 1972; *Feeling Through,* 1975; *South Louisiana,* 1985; *If Winter Come,* 1994; and *Harlem Wrestler,* 1995. **Essay:** Ernest J. Gaines.

BAKERMAN, Jane S. Professor of English Emerita, Indiana State University, Terre Haute. Author of numerous critical essays, interviews, and reviews; adviser and contributor, *American Women Writers 1-4;* and *Twentieth-Century Crime and Mystery Writers,* 1991. Co-author of *The Adolescent in the Novel After 1960.* Editor of *Adolescent Female Portraits in the American Novel 1961-1981* (with Mary Jean DeMarr), 1983; and *And Then There Were Nine: More Women of Mystery,* 1984. **Essays:** Lisa Alther; Connie Willis; Ruth Rendell; May Sarton.

BALL, John Clement. Assistant professor of English, University of New Brunswick, Fredericton. Author of articles on Dionne Brand, Austin Clarke, Janet Frame, Robert Kroetsch, and Derek Walcott. **Essay:** Amitav Ghosh.

BAMBERGER, William C. Editor and publisher of Bamberger Books, Flint, Michigan. Author of *A Jealousy for Aesop,* 1988; *William Eastlake: High Desert Interlocutor* (forthcoming); criticism in *Review of Contemporary Fiction;* and fiction in *CoEvolution, Ascent,* and other periodicals. **Essays:** Samuel R. Delany; Barry Hannah; Alice Hoffman; Diane Johnson; Steve Katz; David Madden; William Wharton.

BARNES, John. Reader in English, La Trobe University, Bundoora, Victoria; editor of *Meridian.* Author of *Henry Kingsley and Colonial Fiction,* 1971; and articles on Hal Porter and Patrick White. **Essay:** Peter Cowan.

BELL, Ian A. Professor of English, University of Wales, Swansea. Author of *Defoe's Fiction,* 1985; and *Literature and Crime in Augustan England,* 1991. Editor, with Graham Daldry, *Watching the Detectives: Essays in Crime Fiction,* 1990; and *Henry Fielding,* 1994. **Essays:** George V. Higgins; James Kelman; Bernard MacLaverty; Alan Spence.

BELLMAN, Samuel I. Professor of English, California State University; freelance writer and critic. **Essay:** Alan Cheuse.

BENNETT, Bruce. Professor of English, University College, University of New South Wales, Australian Defense Force Academy, Canberra. Formerly editor of *Westerly: A Quarterly Review,* and director of the Center for Studies in Australian Literature, University of Western Australia. Author of *Place, Region and Community,* 1985; and *An Australian Compass,* 1991. Editor of *European Relations,* 1985; *A Sense of Exile,* 1988; *Myths, Heroes and Anti-Heroes,* 1992; books of critical essays on Australian authors; and anthologies of Australian and post-colonial literatures. **Essay:** Alex Miller; Michael Wilding.

BENNETT, Sally H. Freelance writer. **Essays:** Richard Condon; James A. Michener.

BERGONZI, Bernard. Emeritus professor of English, University of Warwick, Coventry. Author of a novel, *The Roman Persuasion,* 1981; and several books on modern literature and criticism, of which the most recent are *Exploding English,* 1990; *Wartime and Aftermath,* 1993; and *David Lodge,* 1995. **Essays:** David Lodge; Julian Mitchell; Andrew Sinclair.

BERRY, Reginald. Senior lecturer in English, University of Toronto; president of the Association for Canadian Studies in Australia and New Zealand, 1988-90. Author of *Regionalism and National Identity,* 1985; and *A Pope Chronology,* 1988. **Essay:** C.K. Stead.

BEST, Marshall A. Editor, 1925-34, general manager 1935-55, and editorial vice-president, 1956-68, Viking Press, New York. Poems, reviews, and translations published in *Atlantic Monthly, Saturday Review,* and other magazines. Translator of *Avarice House* by Julien Green, 1926. Died 1982. **Essays:** Rumer Godden; Manohar Malgonkar.

BIRNEY, Earle. Formerly Regents Professor in creative writing, University of California, Irvine; past editor of *Canadian Forum, Canadian Poetry Magazine, Prism International,* and *New American and Canadian Poetry.* Author of more than 20 books of poetry (most recently *Copernican Fix,* 1985); two novels (*Turvey: A Military Picaresque,* 1949 (revised 1977) and *Down the Long Table,* 1955); short stories (*Big Bird in the Bush: Selected Stories and Sketches,* 1978); plays for stage and radio, and critical studies on creative writing. Editor of selections of poetry by Canadian writers.

BITTNER, William. Late professor of English, Acadia University, Wolfville, Nova Scotia. Author of *Poe: A Biography, The Novels of Waldo Frank;* and articles in *Atlantic Monthly, The Nation, Saturday Review, New York Post,* and other periodicals. Died 1977. **Essay:** Anthony C. West.

BORDEN, William. Chester Fritz Distinguished Professor of English, University of North Dakota, Grand Forks. Author of the novel *Superstoe,* 1968; and plays, including *The Last Prostitute,* 1982; and *Loon Dance,* 1983. **Essay:** William Melvin Kelley.

BORKLUND, Elmer. Professor of English, Pennsylvania State University, University Park. Former associate editor of *Chicago*

Review. Author of *Contemporary Literary Critics,* 1977 (2nd edition 1982); and of articles in *Modern Philology, Commentary, New York Herald-Tribune Book Week,* and *Journal of General Education.* **Essays:** Brigid Brophy; Mavis Gallant; Susan Sontag; Paul West.

BOWERS, Frederick. Associate professor of English, University of British Columbia, Vancouver. Author of articles on Arthur Hugh Clough, Gabriel Fielding, syntax, and semantics, in *Renascence, Studies in English Literature, Orbis, Journal of Linguistics,* and other journals. **Essay:** Frederik Pohl.

BRADBURY, Malcolm. See his own entry. **Essay:** William Cooper

BRADFORD, M.E. Professor of English and American Studies, University of Dallas; member of the editorial board of *Modern Age.* Author of *Rumours of Mortality: An Introduction to Allen Tate,* 1967; *A Better Guide Than Reason,* 1980; *Generations of the Faithful Heart: On the Literature of the South,* 1982; *A Worthy Company: Brief Lives of the Framers of the Constitution,* 1982; *Remembering Who We Are: Observations of a Southern Conservative,* 1985; *The Reactionary Imperative: Essays Literary and Political,* 1989; and of articles in *Bear, Man, and God,* 1971; *Allen Tate and His Work,* 1971; and *Sewanee Review, National Review, Southern Review,* and other periodicals. Editor of *The Form Discovered: Essays on the Achievement of Andrew Lytle,* 1973. **Essays:** Madison Jones; Andrew Lytle.

BRIGG, Peter. Associate professor of English, University of Guelph, Ontario. Author of works on Ursula K. Le Guin, Arthur C. Clarke, and Robertson Davies, and articles in several books and periodicals. **Essays:** Michael Ignatieff; John Steffler.

BRIGHT, Juliette. Freelance writer and journalist. **Essay:** Alice Munro.

BROUGHTON, W.S. Senior lecturer in English, Massey University, Palmerston North, New Zealand; member of New Zealand Literary Fund Advisory Committee, 1985-90. **Essay:** Owen Marshall.

BROWN, Lloyd W. Member of the Department of Comparative Literature, University of Southern California, Los Angeles. Author of *West Indian Poetry,* 1978 (revised 1984); *Amiri Baraka,* 1980; and *Women Writers in Black Africa,* 1981. Editor of *The Black Writer in Africa and the Americas,* 1973. **Essays:** Austin C. Clarke; Roy A.K. Heath; Marion Patrick Jones.

BROWN, Richard. Senior lecturer in English, University of Leeds; co-editor of *James Joyce Broadsheet.* Author of *James Joyce,* 1992; and *James Joyce and Sexuality,* 1985. **Essays:** Martin Amis; Julian Barnes.

BRYER, Lynne. Publisher, Chameleon Press, Cape Town; former critic and journalist; responsible for rediscovering and reissuing Daphne Rooke's South African novels in that country. Author of *The British Settlers of 1820,* 1986. **Essay:** Daphne Rooke.

BUCKNALL, Harry. English language teacher and freelance writer. **Essay:** Charles Johnson.

BURGESS, Anthony. See his own entry.

BURKE, Herbert C. Formerly William Morley Tweedie Professor of English, Mount Allison University, Sackville, New Brunswick; now retired. Author of articles on modern fiction and reviews in journals, and contributor of poetry and visual art to little magazines. **Essay:** Jack Ludwig.

BUXTON, Jackie. Doctoral candidate, York University, Toronto. Author of an article about postmodernism in *English Studies in Canada.* **Essays:** Margaret Atwood; Witi Ihimaera.

CADOGAN, Mary. Secretary of an educational trust, governor of an international school, and freelance writer. Author of three books on popular literature with Patricia Craig—*You're a Brick, Angela!,* 1976; *Women and Children First,* 1978; and *The Lady Investigates,* 1981—three volumes of *The Charles Hamilton Companion* (with John Wernham), 1976-82; *The Morcove Companion* (with Tommy Keen), 1981; *From Wharton Lodge to Linton Hall: The Charles Hamilton Christmas Companion* (with Tommy Keen), 1984; *Richmal Crompton: The Woman Behind William,* 1986; *Frank Richards: The Chap Behind the Chums,* 1988; and *The William Companion,* 1990. **Essay:** Gillian Freeman.

CAMPENNI, Frank. Associate professor of English, University of Wisconsin, Milwaukee. Author of articles and reviews in periodicals. **Essays:** Barry Beckham; Howard Fast; Irvin Faust; Mark Mirsky; Leo Rosten; Michael Rumaker; Budd Schulberg; Terry Southern; Herman Wouk; Charles Wright.

CARAMELLO, Charles. Associate professor of English, University of Maryland, College Park. Author of *Silverless Mirrors: Book, Self and Postmodern American Fiction,* 1983; and some 25 articles and reviews. Co-editor of *Performance in Popular Culture,* 1977. **Essay:** Richard Kostelanetz.

CARCHIDI, Victoria. Lecturer in English, Massey University, Palmerston North, New Zealand. Author of articles on cultural studies, film, T.E. Lawrence, and post-colonialism. **Essays:** Shimmer Chinodya; Njabulo Ndebele.

CARPENTER, Frederic I. Author of *Emerson and Asia,* 1930; *Emerson Handbook,* 1953; *American Literature and the Dream,* 1955; *Robinson Jeffers,* 1962; *Eugene O'Neill,* 1964 (revised 1979); and *Laurens van der Post,* 1969. Taught at the University of Chicago, Harvard University, and the University of California, Berkeley. Died. **Essay:** Laurens van der Post.

CARRUTH, Hayden. Professor of English, Syracuse University, New York; member of the editorial board, *Hudson Review;* former poetry editor of *Harper's.* Author of several books of poetry, most recently *Asphalt Georgics,* 1985; *Appendix A* (novel), 1963; a book on Camus; and three collections of essays, *Working Papers,* 1982; *Effluences from the Sacred Caves,* 1983; and *Sitting In: Selected Writings on Jazz, Blues, and Related Topics,* 1986. **Essay:** J.F. Powers.

CHAMBERS, D.D.C. Associate professor of English, Trinity College, Toronto. Editor of two book of poetry by Thomas Traherne, and *A Few Friends: Poems for Thom Gunn's 60th Birthday,* 1989. **Essay:** John Rechy.

CHARLES, Gerda. See her own entry. **Essays:** Chaim Bermant; Penelope Fitzgerald.

CHARTERS, Ann. Professor of English, University of Connecticut, Storrs. Author of *A Bibliography of Jack Kerouac,* 1967 (revised 1975); *Scenes Along the Road: Photographs of the Desolation Angels,* 1970 (2nd edition 1985); *Nobody: The Story of Bert Williams,* 1970; *Kerouac: A Biography,* 1973; *I Love: The Story of Vladimir Mayakovsky and Lili Brik,* with Samuel Charters, 1979; and *Beats and Company,* 1986. Editor of *The Beats: Literary Bohemians in Postwar America,* 2 vols., 1983; and *The Story and Its Writer,* 1983. **Essay:** William S. Burroughs.

CHEVALIER, Tracy. Editor and freelance writer. **Essays:** Bobbie Ann Mason; Lorrie Moore; Anne Tyler.

CHEW, Shirley. Lecturer in English, University of Leeds. Editor of *Selected Poems: Arthur Hugh Clough,* 1987. **Essay:** Patricia Grace.

CHIHARA, Paul Seiko. Associate professor of Music, University of California, Los Angeles. Composer of numerous works, including *Driftwood* (string quartet), 1969; *Forest Music for Orchestra,* 1970; and music for ballets and films. Author of "Revolution and Music," 1970; and other essays. **Essay:** James Yaffe.

CLANCY, Laurie. Reader in English, La Trobe University, Bundoora, Victoria. Author of three novels (*A Collapsible Man,* 1975; *Perfect Love,* 1983; and *The Wild Life Reserve,* 1994); two collections of short stories (*The Wife Specialist,* 1978; and *City to City,* 1988); and critical works on Christina Stead, Xavier Herbert, and Vladimir Nabokov, as well as *A Reader's Guide to Australian Fiction,* 1992. **Essays:** Glenda Adams; Murray Bail; Brian Castro; Jon Cleary; Blanche d'Alpuget; Beverley Farmer; David Foster; Rodney Hall; Shirley Hazzard; Elizabeth Jolley; Victor Kelleher; C.J. Koch; Peter Mathers; Gerald Murnane; George Turner; Tim Winton.

CLARK, Anderson. Associate professor of English and director of the International English Institute, Belmont College, Nashville. **Essays:** Shelby Foote; Jesse Hill Ford.

COALE, Sam. Professor of English, Wheaton College, Norton, Massachusetts. Author of *Hawthorne's Shadow: American Romance from Melville to Miller,* 1985; and *William Styron Revisited,* 1991. **Essay:** James Lee Burke.

COBB, Loretta. Director Emeritus of the Harbert Writing Center, University of Montevallo, freelance writer and editor, and columnist for *The Birmingham News.* **Essays:** Barry Hannah; Joseph Heller; Ward Just; W.P. Kinsella; Larry Woiwode.

COLONNESE, Tom. Teacher at Northern Arizona University, Flagstaff; program director for Native Americans for Community Action, and Native American Social Service Agency. Author of *American Indian Novelists: An Annotated Critical Bibliography* (with Louis Owens), 1985; and *Dictionary of American Indian Novelists* (forthcoming). **Essays:** Jim Harrison; Jay McInerney; Larry McMurtry; N. Scott Momaday.

COOKE, Judy. Freelance writer and editor, London. Editor of

The Best of Fiction Magazine (with Elizabeth Bunster), 1986; and *Passions and Reflections: A Collection of 20th-Century Women's Fiction,* 1991. **Essays:** A.L. Barker; Jennifer Dawson; Maureen Duffy; Neil Jordan; Wolf Mankowitz; Penelope Mortimer.

CORBALLIS, Richard. Senior lecturer in English, Massey University, Palmerston North, New Zealand. Author of *Stoppard: The Mystery and the Clockwork,* 1984; and *Introducing Witi Ihimaera* (with Simon Garrett), 1984. Editor of *George Chapman's Minor Translations: A Critical Edition of His Renderings of Musaeus, Hesiod and Juvenal,* 1984. **Essays:** Graham Billing; Alan Duff; Patricia Grace; Stevan Eldred-Grigg; Keri Hulme; Francis Stuart.

COTTON, John. Authur of many books of poetry—collections include *Old Movies and Other Poems,* 1971; *The Day Book,* 1983; *The Storyville Portraits,* 1984; *The Poetry File,* 1988; and *Here's Looking at You Kid,* 1990—and of *British Poetry since 1965,* 1973. **Essays:** Brian Aldiss; Maggie Gee; D.M. Thomas.

CRANE, Ralph J. Lecturer in English, University of Waikato, Hamilton, New Zealand. Author of *Inventing India: A History of English-Language Fiction,* 1992; *Ruth Prawer Jhabvala,* 1992; and numerous articles on post-colonial literature. Editor of *Passages to Ruth Prawer Jhabvala,* 1991; and *Ending the Silences: Critical Essays on the Works of Maurice Shadbolt,* 1995. Co-editor of *Span,* the journal of the South Pacific Association for Commonwealth Literature and Language Studies. **Essays:** Ruth Prawer Jhabvala; Bharati Mukherjee; I. Allan Sealy; Bapsi Sidhwa; Shashi Tharoor.

CUSICK, Edmund. Lecturer in English, Liverpool Polytechnic; formerly assistant editor of *Shorter Oxford English Dictionary.* Author of "Macdonald and Jung," in *The Gold Thread,* 1991. **Essays:** Michael Moorcock; Carolyn Slaughter.

DAHLIE, Hallvard. Emeritus professor of English, University of Calgary, Alberta. Author of *Brian Moore,* 1969 and 1981; *Alice Munro and Her Works,* 1985; *Varieties of Exile: The Canadian Experience,* 1986; and *Introducing Frederick Philip Grove's Settler of the Marsh* (forthcoming). Editor of *Literary Haly-Yearly* (special Canadian issue), 1972; *The New Land: Studies in a Literary Theme* (with Richard Chadbourne), 1978; and *Ariel* (Exile issue), 1982. **Essay:** Robert Kroetsch.

DANIEL, Helen. Freelance critic and reviewer. Author of *Double Agent: David Ireland and His Work,* 1982; and *Liars: Australian New Novelists,* 1988. Editor of *Australian Book Review,* and the books *Expressway,* 1989; *The Good Reading Guide: Australian Fiction 1968-1988,* 1989; and *Millennium,* 1991. **Essays:** Marion Campbell; Janette Turner Hospital.

DAVIES, Barrie. Professor of English, University of New Brunswick, Fredericton. Editor of *The Selected Prose of Archibald Lampman.* **Essays:** Matt Cohen; David Helwig; C.J. Newman.

DAWSON, Terence. Lecturer in English, National University of Singapore. Author of numerous articles on both English and French literature. **Essay:** Edna O'Brien.

D'CRUZ, Doreen. Lecturer in English, Massey University, Palmerston North, New Zealand. **Essay:** Barbara Anderson.

de KOCK, Leon. Lecturer in English, University of South Africa, Pretoria. **Essays:** André Brink; Nadine Gordimer; Christopher Hope.

DESY, Peter. Member of the Department of English, Ohio University, Lancaster. Author of fiction and poetry in many journals and anthologies. **Essays:** Russell Banks; Denis Johnson; W.P. Kinsella; Susan Fromberg Schaeffer.

deVILLE, Susie. Production editor and freelance writer. Contributor to *Travelers' Quarterly.* **Essay:** Festus Iyayi.

DICKINSON, Peter. Doctoral candidate in English, University of British Columbia. Author of articles on Sally Morgan and other contemporary writers. **Essay:** Stephan Richard Gray.

DILLARD, R.H.W. Professor of English and Chairman of the Graduate Program in Contemporary Literature and Creative Writing, Hollins College, Virginia; editor of *Hollins Critic.* Author of four books of poetry (most recently *The Greeting: New and Selected Poems,* 1981); two novels (*The Book of Chances,* 1974; and *The First Man on the Sun,* 1983); a screenplay; and of *Horror Films,* 1976; and *Understanding George Garrett,* 1988. Editor of two collections of essays. **Essay:** George Garrett.

DOEPKE, Dale K. Freelance writer; author of essays on 19th-century American literature. **Essay:** Eleanor Clark.

DOWLING, David. Chair of the English Programme, University of Northern British Columbia, Prince George. Author of *Bloomsbury Aesthetics and the Novels of Forster and Woolf,* 1985; *Fictions of Nuclear Disaster,* 1986; *William Faulkner,* 1989; *Mrs. Dalloway,* 1990; and articles on Hoban, Federman, and Foster. Editor of *Novelists on Novelists,* 1983; *Every Kind of Weather: The Writings of Bruce Mason,* 1986; *Katherine Mansfield: Dramatic Sketches,* 1988. **Essay:** Nicholson Baker.

DOYLE, Paul A. Professor of English, Nassau Community College, State University of New York, Garden City; editor, *Evelyn Waugh Newsletter and Studies* and *Nassau Review.* Author of *Sean O'Faolain,* 1968; *Introduction to Paul Vincent Carroll,* 1971; *Liam O'Flaherty,* 1971; *Guide to Basic Information Sources in English Literature,* 1976; *Pearl S. Buck,* 1980; *A Reader's Companion to the Novels and Short Stories of Evelyn Waugh,* 1988; of bibliographies of O'Flaherty and Waugh; and *A Concordance to the Collected Poems of James Joyce,* 1966; co-author of *Early American Trains,* 1993. Editor of *Alexander Pope's Iliad: An Examination,* 1960. **Essays:** John Ed Bradley; Moira Crone; Thomas Flanagan; Piers Paul Read.

DRABBLE, Margaret. See her own entry.

DRIVER, Dorothy. Senior lecturer in English, University of Cape Town, South Africa; South African correspondent to the *Journal of Commonwealth Literature.* Author of *Pauline Smith and the Crisis of Daughterhood* (forthcoming) and of numerous articles on writing by South African women. Editor of *The Little Karoo* by Pauline Smith, 1983.

DUCKWORTH, Deborah. Formerly instructor in English and English as a Second Language, Louisiana State University, Baton

Rouge. **Essay:** Elaine Dundy.

DYER, Klay. Doctoral candidate, University of Ottawa, currently completing a dissertation on 19th-century Canadian parody. **Essay:** M.G. Vassanji.

EDMANDS, Ursula. Former lecturer in English, Leeds Polytechnic; now with Sheffield City Council. **Essays:** Jack Cope; C.J. Driver: Dan Jacobson.

EISINGER, Chester E. Former Professor of English, Purdue University, Lafayette, Indiana; now retired. Author of *Fiction of the Forties,* 1963; and articles in *Proletarian Writers of the Thirties,* 1968; and *Saturday Review.* Editor of *The 1940's: Profile of a Nation in Crisis,* 1969. **Essays:** Louis Auchincloss; Saul Bellow; Robert Coover; William H. Gass; Shirley Ann Grau.

ELBORN, Geoffrey. Freelance writer and critic. **Essays:** Peter Ackroyd; John Banville; Pat Barker; William Boyd; Sebastian Faulks; Rumer Godden; Alan Hollinghurst; Wolf Mankowitz; Bernice Rubens; Lisa St. Aubin de Teran; William Trevor; Edmund White; A.N. Wilson.

EMANUEL, James A. Professor of English, City College of New York; general editor of the Critics Series, Broadside Press, Detroit. Author of six books of poetry including, most recently, *Deadly James and Other Poems,* 1987; and of *Langston Hughes,* 1967; and *How I Write 2* (with others), 1972. Editor, with Theodore L. Gross, of *Dark Symphony: Negro Literature in America,* 1968. **Essays:** Ann Petry; Margaret Walker.

FABRE, Michel. Professor, University of Paris III. Author of *The Unfinished Quest of Richard Wright,* 1983; *La Rive Noire: de Harlem à la Seine,* 1985; *The World of Richard Wright,* 1985; and *Richard Wright: Books and Writers,* 1990. **Essays:** Leon Forrest; John Edgar Wideman.

FACKNITZ, Mark A.R. Lecturer in English, James Madison University, Harrisonburg, Virginia. **Essays:** Andre Dubus; Timothy Mo; Tobias Wolff.

FEIN, Richard J. Professor of English, State University College at New Paltz, New York. Author of *Robert Lowell,* 1970 (revised 1979); *The Dance of Leah,* 1985; and articles on Thoreau, modern poetry, and the Jewish story. Editor and translator of *The Selected Poems of Yankev Glatshteyn,* 1986. **Essay:** Henry Roth.

FERGUSON, Brenda R. Freelance writer. **Essay:** John A. Williams.

FERRAN, Peter. Professor, Rochester Institute of Technology. **Essay:** James Ellroy.

FIEDLER, Leslie A. See his own entry.

FIERO, John W. Professor of English, University of Southwestern Louisiana, Lafayette; Director of Creative Writing and the Deep South Writers Conference. Author of several plays and articles on Bertolt Brecht, Anton Chehkov, Max Frisch, Ernest Gaines, A.R. Gurney, Jr., Bret Harte, Preston Jones, Ben Jonson, Franz Kafka, Terrence McNally, William Saroyan, and Kurt Vonnegut,

Jr. **Essays:** Michael Crichton; Anne Rice.

FIGUEROA, John J. Honorary Fellow, Centre for Caribbean Studies, University of Warwick, Coventry; formerly Professor of education and English. Author of three books of poetry (including *Ignoring Hurts,* 1979); two books on Caribbean education, and *West Indies in England: The Great Post-War Tours,* 1991; and of many critical articles on Caribbean literature. Editor of *Caribbean Writers* (reference books), 1979; and anthologies of African and Caribbean writing. **Essays:** Earl Lovelace; Vic Reid.

FITZGERALD, M.J. Freelance writer. Author of *Rope-Dancer* (short fiction), 1986; and *A Summer Ghost* (television play), 1987. Translator of *Searching for the Emperor* by Roberto Pazzi, 1989. **Essay:** A.N. Wilson.

FOSTER, Ruel E. Benedum Professor of American Literature, West Virginia University, Morgantown. Author of *Work in Progress,* 1948; *William Faulkner: A Critical Appraisal,* 1951; *Elizabeth Madox Roberts, American Novelist* (with Harry Modean Campbell), 1956; and *Jesse Stuart,* 1968. **Essay:** John Knowles.

FRANKS, Jill. Faculty member, Department of English, University of British Columbia; freelance writer and critic. **Essays:** Ama Ata Aidoo; Rosellen Brown; Susan Minot; Carol Shields.

FRENCH, Anne. Managing editor, Museum of New Zealand, Wellington. Author of four books of poetry—*All Cretans Are Liars,* 1987; *The Male as Evader,* 1988; *Cabin Fever,* 1990; and *Seven Days on Mykonos,* 1993. Contributor to *The Oxford Companion to Contemporary Poetry, The Oxford Companion to New Zealand Literature,* and *The Routledge Encyclopaedia of Commonwealth Literature.* **Essay:** Elizabeth Knox; Barbara Trapido.

FRENCH, Warren. Professor of English and Director of the Centre for American Studies, Indiana University-Purdue University, Indianapolis, retired 1986; member of the editorial board, *American Literature* and *Twentieth-Century Literature;* editor of the American Authors series for Twayne publishers. Author of *John Steinbeck,* 1961; *Frank Norris,* 1962; *J.D. Salinger,* 1963 (revised 1976); *A Companion to "The Grapes of Wrath,"* 1963; *The Social Novel at the End of an Era,* 1966; *The South in Film,* 1981; *Jack Kerouac,* 1986; and a series on American literature: *The Thirties,* 1967; *The Forties,* 1968; *The Fifties,* 1971; and *The Twenties,* 1975. **Essays:** Evan S. Connell; Jr.; R.K. Narayan; Tom Robbins; Khushwant Singh; Elizabeth Spencer; Eudora Welty.

FRIEDMAN, Melvin J. Professor of Comparative Literature, University of Wisconsin, Milwaukee; advisory editor of *Journal of Popular Culture, Studies in the Novel, Renascence, Journal of American Culture, Studies in American Fiction, Fer de Lance, Contemporary Literature, Journal of Beckett Studies, International Fiction Review, Arete, Yiddish, Journal of Modern Literature,* and *Studies in American Jewish Literature.* Author of *Stream of Consciousness: A Study in Literary Method,* 1955. Author or editor of works about Beckett, Flannery O'Connor, Styron, Ezra Pound, Catholic novelists, and Ionesco. **Essays:** Raymond Federman; Robie Macauley; Wallace Markfield; Philip Roth; Sloan Wilson.

FROST, Lucy. Senior lecturer in English, La Trobe University, Bundoora, Victoria. Author of *No Place for a Nervous Lady: Voices from the Australian Bush,* 1984; *A Face in the Glass: The Journal and Life of Annie Baxter Dawbin,* 1992; and articles on 19th- and 20th-century literature and culture. **Essay:** Marion Halligan; Frank Moorhouse.

FUEGI, John. Professor and Director of the Comparative Literature Program, University of Maryland, College Park; managing editor, *Brecht Yearbook.* Author of *The Wall* (documentary film), 1961; *The Essential Brecht,* 1972; and *Bertolt Brecht: Chaos According to Plan.* Editor of *Brecht Today,* 3 vols., 1972-74. **Essay:** Sol Yurick.

FULLER, Roy. See his own entry.

GALLOWAY, David. Chair of American Studies, University of the Ruhr, Bochum, West Germany. Author of *The Absurd Hero in American Fiction,* 1966 (revised 1970 and 1981); *Henry James,* 1967; *Edward Lewis Wallant,* 1979; and four novels—the most recent being *Tamsen,* 1983. Editor of *The Selected Writings of Edgar Allan Poe,* 1967; *Ten Modern American Short Stories,* 1968; *Calamus,* 1982; and *The Other Poe: Comedies and Satires,* 1983. **Essay:** Evan Hunter.

GEHERIN, David. Professor of English, Eastern Michigan University, Ypsilanti. Author of *Sons of Sam Spade: The Private Eye Novel in the 70s,* 1980; *John D. MacDonald,* 1982; *The American Private Eye: The Image in Fiction,* 1985; and *Elmore Leonard,* 1989. **Essays:** Frederick Barthelme; Arthur Hailey; Elmore Leonard; Robert Stone.

GINDIN, James. Late Professor of English, University of Michigan, Ann Arbor. Author of *Postwar British Fiction,* 1962; *Harvest of a Quiet Eye: The Novel of Compassion,* 1971; *The English Climate: An Excursion into a Biography of John Gals Worthy,* 1979; *John Galsworthy's Life and Art: An Alien's Fortress,* 1986; and *William Golding,* 1988. Editor of *The Return of the Native,* by Hardy, 1969. Died. **Essays:** Kingsley Amis; John Bowen; Malcolm Bradbury; David Cook; Lionel Davidson; Margaret Drabble; John Fowles; Thomas Hinde; Elizabeth Jane Howard; Norman Mailer; Iris Murdoch; Alan Sillitoe; David Storey; Keith Waterhouse.

GOONETILLEKE, D.C.R.A. Senior Professor and Department Head of English, University of Kelaniya, Sri Lanka; World Chair, Association for Commonwealth Literature and Language Studies; Vice-Chair, International Federation for Modern Languages and Literatures. Author of *Developing Countries in British Fiction,* 1977; *Between Culture: Essays on Literature, Language and Education,* 1987; *Images of the Raj: South Asia in the Literature of the Empire,* 1988; and *Joseph Conrad: Beyond Culture and Background,* 1990. Editor of *Heart of Darkness* by Joseph Conrad, 1995; and of anthologies of Sri Lankan poetry, fiction, and drama. **Essays:** Romesh Gunesekera; Salman Rushdie; Vikram Seth.

GORDON, Lois. Professor of English and Comparative Literature, Fairleigh Dickinson University, Teaneck, New Jersey. Author of Stratagems to *Uncover Nakedness: The Dramas of Harold Pinter,* 1969; *Donald Barthelme,* 1981; *Robert Coover: The Universal Fictionmaking Process,* 1983; *American Chronicle: Six Decades in American Life, 1920-1979,* 1987; *Harold Pinter: A Casebook,* 1990; *American Chronicle: Seven Decades in American Life, 1920-1989,* 1990; *The Columbia Chronicles of American Life, 1910-1995,* 1995; and articles on Faulkner, T.S. Eliot, Beckett,

Philip Roth, Arthur Miller, and other writers. **Essays:** Ann Beattie; William Gaddis; Erica Jong.

GORDON-SMITH, Pat. Commissioning editor and freelance writer. **Essay:** Caryl Phillips.

GOYEN, William. Author of five novels, *The House of Breath,* 1950; *In a Farther Country,* 1955; *The Fair Sister,* 1962; *Come, The Restorer,* 1974; and *Arcadio,* 1983; several collections of short fiction, *The Collected Stories,* 1975; *Had I a Hundred Mouths: New and Selected Stories,* 1985; plays; poetry; and non-fiction, *Selected Writings,* 1974. Died 1983. **Essay:** Marguerite Young.

GRACIAS, Marian. Doctoral candidate, University of British Columbia, Vancouver, specializing in gender studies and postcolonialism. **Essay:** David Dabydeen.

GRAHAM, Colin. Lecturer in English Literature, University of Huddersfield. Author of articles on postcolonial theory and Irish studies. Editor of poetry of Robert Browning and Elizabeth Barrett Browning. **Essays:** Roddy Doyle; Hanif Kureishi; John McGahern; Brian Moore.

GREGORY, Sinda. Associate Professor of English and Comparative Literature, San Diego State University. Author of numerous books and essays about contemporary fiction, including *Private Investigations: The Work of Dashiell Hammett* and *Alive and Writing: Interviews with American Authors of the 1980s* (with Larry McCaffery). Contributed an interview with Marianne Hauser to *Some Other Frequency: Interviews with Contemporary American Innovative Fiction Writers* by McCaffery, 1995. **Essay:** Marianne Hauser.

GRELLA, George. Associate Professor of English, Rochester University, New York. Author of studies of Ian Fleming, Ross Macdonald, and John le Carré in *New Republic;* and articles on the detective novel, film, and popular culture. **Essays:** Len Deighton; J.P. Donleavy; John Gregory Dunne; John Irving.

GRIFFIN, Jessica. Editor and freelance writer. **Essay:** Marina Warner.

GUERARD, Albert. See his own entry. **Essays:** John Hawkes; Janet Lewis.

GUPTARA, Prabhu S. Freelance writer, lecturer, and broadcaster. Author of *Indian Spirituality,* 1984; and *Black British Literature: An Annotated Bibliography,* 1986. Editor of *Third Eye: The Prospects of Third World Film,* 1986; and *The Lotus: An Anthology of Contemporary Indian Religious Poetry in English,* 1988. **Essays:** Ahmad Abbas; Lynne Reid Banks; Gillian Tindall; Morris West.

GUTTENBERG, Laurie Schwartz. Faculty member, Nassau Community College, Suffolk Community College, S.U.N.Y. College at Farmingdale, Syosset Central Schools. **Essay:** Joanne Greenberg.

HALIO, Jay L. Professor of English, University of Delaware, Newark; chair of the editorial board, University of Delaware Press. Author of *Angus Wilson,* 1964; and *Understanding Shakespeare's Plays in Performance,* 1988. Editor of *British Novelists since 1960,*

1983; *Critical Essays on Angus Wilson,* 1985; and *As You Like It: An Annotated Bibliography 1940-1980* (with Barbara C. Millard). **Essay:** William Trevor.

HALL, James B. See his own entry. **Essays:** R.V. Cassill; William Eastlake.

HALL, Joan Wylie. Instructor in English, University of Mississippi, Jackson. Author of *Shirley Jackson: A Study of the Short Fiction* (forthcoming); and articles on Francis Bacon, William Faulkner, and Willa Cather. **Essay:** Marilyn French.

HANKIN, Cherry A. Reader in English, University of Canterbury, Christchurch, New Zealand. Author of *Katherine Mansfield and Her Confessional Stories,* 1983; and the introduction to the 1974 edition of Maurice Shadbolt's *The New Zealanders.* Editor of *Critical Essays on the New Zealand Novel,* 1976; *It Was So Late and Other Stories* by John Reece Cole, 1978; *Life in a Young Colony: Selections from Early New Zealand Writing,* 1981; *Critical Essays on the New Zealand Short Story,* 1982; *The Letters of John Middleton Murry to Katherine Mansfield,* 1983; and *Letters Between Katherine Mansfield and John Middleton Murray,* 1988. **Essay:** Maurice Shadbolt.

HANRAHAN, John. Freelance writer and critic. **Essay:** Liam Davison.

HARRIS, June. Associate professor of English, East Texas State University, Commerce. Author of one novel and works of short fiction, and of essays and reviews in *ALAN Review, Masterplots II: Young Adult Biography,* and *Magill's Guide to Science Fiction and Fantasy Literature.* **Essays:** Kim Stanley Robinson; John Grisham.

HART, James A. Late Emeritus Professor of English, University of British Columbia, Vancouver; former member of the Editorial Board, *Canadian Review of American Studies* and *English Studies in Canada.* Author of articles on Alan Seeger, Allen Tate, George Sylvester Viereck, and Joyce Kilmer in *Dictionary of Literary Biography,* vols. 45 and 54, 1986, 1987. Died. **Essays:** Allen Drury; Edward Hoagland.

HART, Sue. Professor of English, Montana State University, Billings. Author of *Thomas and Elizabeth Savage,* chapters in *Women in Western American Literature, Visions of War,* and *Willa Cather: Family and Community,* and of numerous critical essays and reviews. **Essays:** Thomas Savage; Mildred Walker.

HASTINGS, Thomas. Doctoral candidate, Department of English, York University, Toronto. **Essays:** Alan Hollinghurst; Edmund White.

HAWKES, John. See his own entry.

HAYES, Heather. Freelance writer and editor. Author of numerous articles for periodicals and newspapers, including the *Washington Post.* **Essay:** Robert Hellenga.

HEATON, David M. Associate professor of English, and University Ombudsman, Ohio University, Athens. Author of poetry; poetry translations; and articles on Ted Hughes, Alan Sillitoe,

Stanley Plumly, Alan Stephens, Ben Belitt, Marvin Bell, Jon Anderson, and George P. Elliott. **Essays:** Frederick Busch; Joan Didion; Toni Morrison; Hubert Selby, Jr.; Jose Yglesias.

HERBERT, John. Freelance writer. **Essay:** E.L. Doctorow.

HERGENHAN, Laurie. Reader in English, University of Queensland, Brisbane; editor of *Australian Literary Studies.* Author of *Unnatural Lives,* 1983. Editor of *The Australian Short Story,* 1986.

HILL, Susan. See her own entry.

HODGKIN, Katharine. Faculty member, Department of English, University of Wales, Swansea. Author of articles on contemporary women writers, including Janet Frame. **Essays:** Alice Walker; Marina Warner.

HOLM, Janis Butler. Associate professor of English, Ohio University, Athens. Author of articles on cultural theory and Tudor conduct books. Editor of *The Mirrhor of Modesty* by Giovanni Bruto, 1987. **Essays:** Gayl Jones; Jayne Anne Phillips.

HUDZIAK, Craig. Doctoral candidate, Department of English, University of Wisconsin, Milwaukee. **Essay:** William Humphrey.

IKIN, Van. Lecturer in English, University of Western Australia, Nedlands. Editor of the journal *Science Fiction: A Review of Speculative Literature;* and the books *Australian Science Fiction,* 1982; and *Glass Reptile Breakout and Other Australian Speculative Stories,* 1990. **Essays:** Peter Carey; Robert Drewe; Frank Hardy; David Ireland.

JAMES, Louis. Professor of English and American Literature. Keynes College, University of Kent, Canterbury. Author of *The Islands in Between,* 1968; *Fiction for the Working Man 1830-50,* 1974; *Jean Rhys,* 1978; and *Writers from the Caribbean,* 1990. Editor of *Print and the People 1819-1851,* 1976; and *Performance and Politics in Popular Drama: Aspects of Popular Entertainment in Theatre, Film and Television* (with others), 1980. **Essays:** O.R. Dathorne; Nicholas Hasluck; V.S. Naipaul; Olive Senior.

JEFFARES, A. Norman. Professor Emeritus of English Studies, University of Stirling, Scotland; general editor of the Macmillan Histories of Literature series and the York Classics series; co-editor of the Macmillan anthologies of English Literature; past editor of *A Review of English Studies* and *Ariel.* Author of *Yeats: Man and Poet,* 1949 (revised 1962); *Seven Centuries of Poetry,* 1956; *Oliver Goldsmith,* 1959; *Gogarty,* 1961; *George Moore,* 1965; *A Critical Commentary on She Stoops to Conquer,* 1966; *A Commentary on the Collected Poems* (1968) and *Collected Plays* (1975, with A.S. Knowland) of *Yeats, Anglo-Irish Literature,* 1982; *A New Commentary on the Poems of W. B. Yeats,* 1984; and *W. B. Yeats: A New Biography,* 1988. Editor of *Scott's Mind and Art,* 1969; *Restoration Comedy,* 1974; *Yeats: The Critical Heritage,* 1977; *Poems of W.B. Yeats: A New Selection,* 1984; *Yeats's Poems,* 1989; *Yeats the European,* 1989; *Yeats's Vision,* 1990; *Swift: The Selected Poems,* 1992; *Ireland's Women* (with Brendan Kennelly and Katie Donovan), 1994; and *Images of Imaginations,* 1995. Formerly chair of the Literature Section of the Scottish Arts Council for the Study of Anglo-Irish Literature. **Essays:** Eric Ambler; Nicolas

Freeling; Mary Lavin; John le Carré.

JEFFREY, David K. Professor and Head of the English Department, James Madison University, Harrisonburg, Virginia; formerly co-editor of *Southern Humanities Review.* Editor of *Grit's Triumph: Essays on the Works of Harry Crews,* 1983. Author of numerous articles on Harry Crews, Edgar Allan Poe, Tobias Smollett, Alexander Pope, Herman Melville, and contemporary mystery writers. **Essay:** Ellen Douglas.

JENKINS, Annibel. Associate professor of English, Georgia Institute of Technology, Atlanta. Author of *Nicholas Rowe,* 1977. **Essay:** Emma Smith.

JENKINS, Ron. Lecturer in English, University of British Columbia. Author of articles on Graeme Gibson, Paul Theroux, Thomas Pynchon, Laurence Sterne, and George Peele. **Essay:** Graeme Gibson; Joy Kogawa.

KEATING, H.R.F. Crime novelist and critic. Author of the Inspector Ghote series including, most recently, *The Body in the Billiard Room,* 1987; *Dead on Time,* 1988; *Inspector Ghote, His Life and Crimes,* 1989; and *Doing Wrong,* 1994; of three novels as Evelyn Hervey: *The Governess,* 1984; *The Man of Gold,* 1985; and *Into the Valley of Death,* 1986; and of critical works including *Writing Crime Fiction,* 1986; *Crime and Mystery: The 100 Best Books,* 1987; and *The Bedside Companion to Crime,* 1989. Editor of *Agatha Christie: First Lady of Crime,* 1977; *Whodunit? A Guide to Crime, Suspense, and Spy Fiction,* 1982; and *The Best of Father Brown,* 1987. **Essay:** Dick Francis; Arun Joshi.

KEITH, Margaret. Freelance writer and researcher; also an actress and director. **Essays:** Hugh Hood; Norman Levine.

KEITNER, Wendy Robbins. Associate Professor of English, University of New Brunswick, Frederiction. **Essay:** Jane Rule.

KEMP, Sandra. Lecturer in English literature, University of Glasgow. Author of *Kipling's Hidden Narratives,* 1988. Editor of *Selected Stories,* 1987; and *Debits and Credits,* 1988, both by Kipling. **Essay:** Eva Figes.

KENDLE, Burton. Professor of English, Roosevelt University, Chicago. Author of articles on D.H. Lawrence, John Cheever, William March, Tennessee Williams, and others, and on screenwriting. **Essays:** Burt Blechman; Paul Bowles; Isabel Colegate; Brendan Gill; Alan Lelchuk.

KENNEDY, Liam. Lecturer in history, Department of American and Canadian Studies, University of Birmingham. Editor of *Economic Theory of Co-operative Enterprises: Selected Readings,* 1983; and *An Economic History of Ulster, 1820-1940* (with Philip Ollerenshaw), 1985. **Essay:** William Kennedy.

KIERNAN, Robert F. Associate professor of English, Manhattan College, Bronx, New York. Former associate editor of *Literary Research Newsletter.* Author of *Katherine Anne Porter and Carson McCullers: A Reference Guide,* 1976; *Gore Vidal,* 1982; *American Writing since 1945: A Critical Survey,* 1983; *Noel Coward,* 1986; and *Frivolity Unbound: Six Masters of the Camp Novel,* 1990. **Essay:** Gore Vidal.

KING, Bruce.   Albert S. Johnston professor of English, University of North Alabama, Florence; co-editor of Macmillan Modern Dramatists series. Author of *Dryden's Major Plays*, 1966; *Marvell's Allegorical Poetry*, 1977; *New English Literatures: Cultural Nationalism in a Changing World*, 1980; *A History of Seventeenth-Century English Literature*, 1982; *Modern Indian Poetry in English*, 1987; and *Three Indian Poets: Ezekiel, Ramanujan and Moraes*, 1990. Editor of *Introduction to Nigerian Literature*, 1971; *Literatures of the World in English*, 1974; *A Celebration of Black and African Writing*, 1976; and *West Indian Literature*, 1979. **Essays:** Anita Desai; Epeli Hau'ofa.

KING, Nicola.   Faculty member, English Department, LSU College of Higher Education, Southampton; freelance writer and critic. **Essay:** Ian McEwan.

KLAUS, H. Gustav.   Part-time professor of English, University of Osnabrück, and visiting professor, University of Halle, both Germany. Author of *Caudwell im Kontext*, 1978; and *The Literature of Labour: Two Hundred Years of Working-Class Writing*, 1985. Editor of *Gulliver: German-English Yearbook*, 1976-82; *The Socialist Novel in Britain: Towards the Recovery of a Tradition*, 1982; and *The Rise of Socialist Fiction 1880-1914*, 1987. **Essay:** Barry Hines.

KLEIN, Marcus.   Professor of English, State University of New York, Buffalo. Author of *After Alienation: American Novels at Mid-Century*, 1964; and *Foreigners: The Making of American Literature 1900-1940*, 1981. Editor of *The American Novel since World War II*, 1969; and, with Robert Pack, of *Literature for Composition on the Theme of Innocence and Experience*, 1966; and *Short Stories: Classic, Modern, Contemporary*, 1967. **Essays:** Wright Morris; Richard G. Stern.

KLINKOWITZ, Jerome.   Professor of English, University of Northern Iowa, Cedar Falls. Author of *Kurt Vonnegut Jr.: A Descriptive Bibliography* (with Asa B. Pieratt, Jr.), 1974; *Literary Disruptions*, 1975 (revised 1980); *Donald Barthelme: A Comprehensive Bibliography* (with others), 1977; *The Life of Fiction*, 1977; *Kurt Vonnegut*, 1980; *The Practice of Fiction in America*, 1980; *The American 1960's*, 1980; *Peter Handke and the Postmodern Transformation* (with James Knowlton), 1983; *The Self-Apparent Word*, 1984; *Literary Subversions*, 1985; *The New American Novel of Manners*, 1986; *Kurt Vonnegut: A Comprehensive Bibliography* (with Judie Huffman-Klinkowitz), 1987; *A Short Season and Other Stories* (as Jerry Klinkowitz), 1988; *Rosenberg, Barthes, Hassan: The Postmodern Habit of Thought*, 1988; *Their Finest Hours: Narratives of the RAF and Luftwaffe in World War II*, 1989; *Slaughterhouse-Five: Reforming the Novel and the World*, 1990; *Listen, Gerry Mulligan: An Aural Narrative in Jazz*, 1991; *Donald Barthelme: An Exhibition*, 1991; *Structuring the Voice*, 1992; and *Basepaths* (as Jerry Klinkowitz), 1995. Editor of *Innovative Fiction*, 1972; *The Vonnegut Statement*, 1973; and *Writing under Fire: Stories of the Vietnam War*, 1978 (all with John Somers); *Vonnegut in America* (with Donald L. Lawler), 1977; *The Diaries of Willard Motley*, 1979; *Nathaniel Hawthorne*, 1984; and *Writing Baseball*, 1991. **Essays:** Walter Abish; Jonathan Baumbach; Guy Davenport; Stephen Dixon; Kenneth Gangemi; Clarence Major; Thomas McGuane; Gilbert Sorrentino; Michael Stephens; Ronald Sukenick; Dan Wakefield; Rudolph Wurlitzer.

KOHL, Judith C.   Professor of English and Humanities, Dutchess Community College. Author of reviews and biographical essays for encyclopedias of women writers. **Essay:** Hilary Masters.

KORGES, James.   Freelance writer. Editor of *Critique: Studies in Modern Fiction*, 1962-70. Author of *Erskine Caldwell*, 1969. Died 1975.

KOSTELANETZ, Richard.   See his own entry. **Essay:** Leslie A. Fiedler.

LAY , Mary M.   Associate professor of Liberal Studies, Clarkson University, Potsdam, New York. Author of *Strategies for Technical Writing: A Rhetoric with Readings*, 1982; and articles on Margaret Drabble and Henry James. **Essays:** Gail Godwin; Maureen Howard.

LECKER, Robert.   Associate professor of English, McGill University, Montreal; editor of the journal *Essays on Canadian Writing*. Author of *On the Line: Readings in the Short Fiction of Clark Blaise, John Metcalf and Hugh Hood*, 1982; *Robert Kroetsch*, 1986; and *Another I: The Fictions of Clark Blaise*, 1988. Editor of *The New Canadian Anthology: Poetry and Short Fiction in English* (with Jack David), 1988; and several works on Canadian literature; coeditor of the series *The Annotated Bibliography of Canada's Major Authors* and *Canadian Writers and Their Works*. **Essays:** Clark Blaise; Dave Godfrey; John Metcalf.

LeCLAIR, Thomas.   Professor of English, University of Cincinnati. Author of *In the Loop*, 1987; *The Art of Excess: Mastery in Contemporary American Fiction*, 1989; and of articles on contemporary fiction in *Tri-Quarterly, Contemporary Literature*, and other journals; and reviews in *New York Times Book Review, New Republic, Washington Post*, and other periodicals. Editor, with Larry McCaffery, *Anything Can Happen: Interviews with Contemporary American Novelists*, 1983. **Essays:** Don DeLillo; Stanley Elkin; Joseph McElroy; Richard Powers; Alexander Theroux.

LEE, Hermione.   Lecturer in English, University of York. Presenter, Book Four television programme, 1982-85. Author of *The Novels of Virginia Woolf*, 1977; *Elizabeth Bowen: An Estimation*, 1981; *Philip Roth*, 1982; *Willa Cather: A Life Saved Up*, 1989; and introductions to works by Flannery O'Connor, Edith Oliver, Antonia White, Bowen, Woolf, and Cather. Editor of *Stevie Smith: A Selection*, 1983; *The Duke's Children* by Trollope, 1983; *The Secret Self: Short Stories by Women*, 2 vols., 1985-87; *The Mulberry Tree: Writings of Elizabeth Bowen*, 1986; and *The Short Stories of Willa Cather*, 1989.

LEHMANN, John.   Founding editor of *New Writing, Daylight, Penguin New Writing, The London Magazine* and the BBC's *New Soundings*. Author of poetry, including *The Reader at Night*, 1974; fiction, including *In the Purely Pagan Sense*, 1976; and *In My Own Time: Memoirs of a Literary Life, Thrown to the Woolfs: Leonard and Virginia Woolf and the Hogarth Press*, 1978; *Rupert Brooke: His Life and His Legend*, 1981; *The English Poets of the First World War*, 1981; *Three Literary Friendships: Byron and Shelley, Rimbaud and Verlaine, Robert Frost and Edward Thomas*, 1983; and *Christopher Isherwood: A Personal Memoir*, 1987. Editor of *The Penguin New Writing 1940-50* (with John Fuller), 1985; and *Vienna: A Travellers' Companion* (with Richard Bassett), 1988. Died 1987.

LEIGH, Chris. Freelance writer. Author of numerous articles about American literature, Henry James, and Robert Penn Warren. **Essay:** William Cobb.

LEVIN, Harry. Irving Babbitt professor of Comparative Literature, Harvard University, Cambridge, Massachusetts. Author of many critical books, including *The Myth of the Golden Age in the Renaissance, Grounds for Comparison, Shakespeare and the Revolution of the Times,* 1976; *Memories of the Moderns,* 1981; and *Playboys and Killjoys: An Essay on the Theory and Practice of Comedy,* 1987.

LEWIS, Barry. Research assistant, Sunderland Polytechnic. Author of articles in *Bete Noir, Over Here,* and *Review of Contemporary Fiction.* **Essays:** David Markson; Graham Swift.

LEWIS, Peter. Reader in English, University of Durham. Author of *John Gay: The Beggar's Opera,* 1976; *Orwell: The Road to 1984,* 1981; *John le Carré,* 1984; *Fielding's Burlesque Drama,* 1987; *Eric Ambler,* 1990; and *The National: A Dream Made Concrete,* 1990. Editor of *The Beggar's Opera* by John Gay, 1973; *Poems '74* (anthology of Anglo-Welsh poetry), 1974; *Papers of the Radio Literature Conference 1977,* 1978; *Radio Drama,* 1981; and *John Gay and the Scriblerians* (with Nigel Wood), 1988. **Essays:** Peter Ackroyd; Paul Bailey; A.S. Byatt; Maurice Gee; Ian McEwan; Nicholas Mosley; Emma Tennant.

LINDBERG, Stanley W. Editor of *The Georgia Review* and professor of English, University of Georgia, Athens. Author of *The Annotated McGuffey,* 1976; *Van Nostrand's Plain English Handbook* (with others), 1980; and co-author of *The Nature of Copyright,* 1991. Editor of *The Plays of Frederick Reynolds,* 3 vols., 1983; *Keener Sounds: Selected Poems from the Georgia Review* (with Stephen Corey), 1986; and *The Legacy of Erskine Caldwell,* 1989. **Essay:** Jack Matthews.

LINDFORS, Bernth. Professor of African and English Literature, University of Texas, Austin; founding editor, *Research in African Literatures.* Author of *Folklore in Nigerian Literature, Early Nigerian Literature, Critical Perspectives on Nigerian Literatures, Black African Literature in English,* 1982-86; *Popular Literatures in Africa, Comparative Approaches to African Literatures, Long Drums and Canons: Teaching and Reserching African Literatures;* and many articles on African literature, including essays on Richard Rive, Chinua Achebe, Cyprian Ekwensi, Amos Tutuola, and D.O. Fagunwa. **Essays:** Peter Abrahams; Es'kia Mphahlele; Amos Tutuola.

LINDSAY, Jack. Author of more than 100 books, including fiction, verse, and plays, and critical studies of William Blake, Mulk Raj Anand, Charles Dickens, George Meredith, William Morris, and others; also editor of works by Robert Herrick, Morris, J.M.W. Turner, and anthologies of poetry, and translator of Greek and Roman texts. Died 1990. **Essay:** James Aldridge.

LIVETT, Jennifer. Lecturer in English, University of Tasmania. **Essay:** Russell Hoban.

LODGE, David. See his own entry.

LOOSER, Devoney. Assistant professor of English and Women's Studies, Indiana State University. Author of numerous articles on women's literature and feminist theory. Editor, *Jane Austen and Discourses of Feminism,* 1995. **Essays:** Carolyn See; Mona Simpson.

LUCAS, John. Professor and Head of the Department of English and Drama, Loughborough University, Leicestershire; advisory editor, *Victorian Studies, Literature and History,* and *Journal of European Studies.* Author of *Tradition and Tolerance in 19th-Century Fiction,* 1966; *The Melancholy Man: A Study of Dickens's Novels,* 1970; *Arnold Bennett,* 1975; *Egitssaga: The Poems,* 1975; *The Literature of Change: Studies in the Nineteenth-Century Provincial Novel,* 1977; *The 1930's: Challenge to Orthodoxy,* 1978; *Romantic to Moderns: Literature: Essays and Ideas of Culture, 1750-1900,* 1982; *Moderns and Contemporaries: Novelists, Poets, Critics,* 1985; *Modern English Poetry from Hardy to Hughes,* 1986; *Studying Grosz on the Bus,* 1989; and *England and Englishness,* 1990. Editor of *Literature and Politics in the Nineteenth-Century,* 1971; and of works by George Crabbe and Jane Austen. **Essays:** David Caute; Barry Cole; Martha Gellhorn.

LYNCH, Robert E. Professor of English, New Jersey Institute of Technology, Newark. Author of *Professional Writing,* 1993; and articles in *The Reader's Enryclopedia of Shakespeare,* 1966; and *The Reader's Encyclopedia of World Drama,* 1969. Editor of *The Example of Science: An Approach to College Composition,* 1981. **Essays:** Frederick Forsyth; Thomas Keneally; Leonard Michaels; John Mortimer.

MACDONALD, Gina. Assistant professor, Loyola University, New Orleans. Author of *Howard Fast* (forthcoming) and *James Clavell* (forthcoming), and articles on southwestern writers, modern novelists and playwrights, science fiction, and popular culture. **Essay:** Barbara Mertz.

MACHANN, Clinton. Associate professor of English, Texas A & M University, College Station. Author of *Krásná Amerika: A Study of the Texas Czechs 1851-1939,* 1983; *Jason Jackson* (a novel), 1993; *The Essential Matthew Arnold,* 1993; *The Genre of Autobiography in Victorian Literature,* 1994; and numerous articles on British and American literature. Editor of *Matthew Arnold in His Time and Ours* (with Forrest D. Burt), 1988; *Katherine Anne Porter and Texas: An Uneasy Relationship,* 1990; *Czech Voices: Stories from the Amerikan narodní kalendár,* 1991; and *Selected Letters of Matthew Arnold* (with Forrest D. Burt), 1993. **Essays:** Chaim Potok; Leslie Marmon Silko.

MADDEN, David. See his own entry.

MADDEN, Ed. Assistant professor of English, University of South Carolina, Columbia, and poet. Author of articles on 20th-century poetry, the AIDS elegies of Paul Monette and Thom Gunn, Radclyffe Hall, Djuna Barnes, and computer pedagogy. **Essays:** Paul Monette; Jeanette Winterson.

MAKOWSKY, Veronica. Professor of English, University of Connecticut. Author of *Caroline Gordon: A Biography,* 1989; *Susan Glaspell's Century of American Women,* 1993; and articles on southern and other American writers. **Essay:** Doris Betts.

MALIN, Irving. Professor of English, City College of the City

University of New York. Author of *William Faulkner: An Interpretation,* 1957; *New American Gothic,* 1962; *Jews and Americans,* 1965; *Saul Bellow's Fiction,* 1969; *Nathanael West's Novels,* 1972; and *Isaac Bashevis Singer,* 1972. Editor of casebooks and collections of essays on Bellow, Capote, Styron, Singer, and McCullers, and of *Psychoanalysis and American Fiction* and *Contemporary American-Jewish Literature.* **Essay:** James Purdy.

MARX, Paul. Professor of English, University of New Haven, Connecticut. Editor of *12 Short Story Writers,* 1970. **Essays:** Richard Ford; Larry Woiwode.

MATHIAS, Roland. Poet and critic; former editor of *Anglo-Welsh Review,* and former chairman of the Welsh Arts Council Literature Committee. Author of seven books of poetry (most recently *Burning Brambles: Selected Poems 1944-1979,* 1983); a collection of short stories; and studies of Vernon Watkins, John Cowper Powys, and Anglo-Welsh literature. Editor of *Anglo-Welsh Poetry 1480-1980* (with Raymond Garlick), 1984; works by Welsh authors; and a collection of essays on David Jones. **Essay:** Emyr Humphreys.

MATTHEWS, Brian E. Personal Chair in English, Flinders University of South Australia, Bedford Park; professor of Australian Studies and Head, Robert Menzies Centre for Australian Studies, University of London. Author of *The Receding Wave: A Study of Henry Lawson's Prose,* 1972; *Louisa: A Diary, A Life* (biographical study of Louisa Lawson), 1986; and *Romantics and Mavericks: The Australian Short Story,* 1987; *Quickening and Other Stories,* 1989; *Oval Dreams: Larrikin Essays on Sport and Low Culture,* 1991. Editor of *Henry Lawson Selected Stories,* 1972; *Henry Lawson Selected Poems,* 1991; and co-editor of *New Literary History of Australia,* 1988. **Essay:** Thea Astley.

McCORMICK, John. Emeritus professor of Comparative Literature, Rutgers University, New Brunswick, New Jersey. Author of *Catastrophe and Imagination* (on the modern novel), 1957; *The Complete Aficionada,* 1967; *American Literature 1919-1932: A Comparative History,* 1971; *Fiction as Knowledge,* 1975; *George Santayana: A Biography,* 1987; and *Wolfe, Malraux, Hesse: A Study in Creative Vitality,* 1987. **Essay:** Sybille Bedford.

McDOWELL, Frederick P.W. Professor of English, University of Iowa, Iowa City. Author of *Ellen Glasgow and the Ironic Art of Fiction,* 1960; *Elizabeth Madox Roberts,* 1963; *Caroline Gordon,* 1966; *Forster: An Annotated Bibliography of Writings about Him,* 1976; *E.M. Forster,* 1982; and articles on Shaw and Robert Penn Warren. **Essays:** Melvyn Bragg; Gerda Charles; Frederic Raphael.

McDOWELL, Margaret B. Professor of Rhetoric and Women's Studies, University of Iowa, Iowa City. Author of *Edith Wharton,* 1975 (revised 1990); and *Carson McCullers,* 1980. **Essays:** Ellen Gilchrist; Jamaica Kincaid; Gloria Naylor; Tillie Olsen.

McLEOD, John. Lecturer in English, LSU College of Higher Education, Southampton. **Essays:** Michael Ondaatje; Caryl Phillips.

McMECHAN, Ian. Freelance writer. Author of articles on contemporary crime fiction. **Essays:** Madison Smartt Bell; Tama Janowitz; Tim O'Brien; Tom Wolfe.

McNEILLY, Kevin. Faculty member, Department of English, University of British Columbia; freelance writer and critic. **Essays:** Jeannette Armstrong; Thomas King; Wole Soyinka.

MEPHAM, John. Freelance writer and teacher of philosophy and literature, Bennington College, Vermont. Co-author of *Issues in Marxist Philosophy,* 4 vols., 1979; author of *To the Lighthouse by Virginia Woolf* (study guide), 1987; *Virginia Woolf: A Literary Life,* 1991; and *Virginia Woolf: State of the Art,* 1991; and of many articles on philosophy and literature. **Essays:** Gabriel Josipovici; David Malouf.

MERIVALE, Patricia. Professor of English, University of British Columbia, Vancouver. Author of *Pan the Goat-God: His Myth in Modern Times;* and of articles in *Harvard Studies in Comparative Literature* and other periodicals. **Essay:** Jerzy Peterkiewicz.

MIELKE, Robert E. Assistant Professor of English, Northeast Missouri State University, Kirksville. Author of *The Riddle of the Painful Earth: Suffering and Society in W.D. Howells's Major Writings of the Early 1890's;* and articles in *Northwest Review, Paintbrush,* and other journals. **Essay:** J.G. Ballard.

MILLER, D. Quentin. Freelance writer; creative writing instructor and doctoral candidate in English, University of Connecticut, Storrs. **Essays:** Cormac McCarthy; Tim O'Brien.

MILNES, Stephen. Doctoral candidate, University of British Columbia. **Essays:** Erna Brodber; SKY Lee.

MITCHISON, Naomi. See her own entry. **Essay:** Fred Urquhart.

MOHANRAM, Radhika. Lecturer, Department of Women's Studies, University of Waikato, New Zealand. Author of articles on New Zealand postcolonial feminism. Co-editor of *Postcolonial Discourse and Changing Cultural Contexts* (forthcoming), and *English Postcoloniality: Literatures from around the World* (forthcoming). **Essay:** Upamanyu Chatterjee; Amy Tan.

MONTROSE, David. Freelance writer. Regular reviewer for the *Times Literary Supplement.* **Essay:** William Boyd.

MOORE, Gerald. Editor of the Modern African Writers series. Former Professor of English, University of Jos, Nigeria. Author of *The Chosen Tongue,* 1969; *Wole Soyinka,* 1971 (revised 1978); and *Twelve African Writers,* 1980. Editor, with Ulli Beier, of *The Penguin Book of Modern African Poetry,* 1984. **Essays:** Elechi Amadi; George Lamming; Garth St. Omer.

MOORE, Harry T. Research Professor of English Emeritus, Southern Illinois University, Carbondale; editor of the Crosscurrents/Modern Critiques series. Author and editor of many books, including studies of Lawrence, Steinbeck, Forster, Rilke, Durrell, and James. Died 1981. **Essay:** Francis Stuart.

MORACE, Robert A. Associate professor of English, Daemen College, Amherst, New York; lecturer on American Literature, University of Warsaw, 1985-87. Author of *John Gardner: An Annotated Secondary Bibliography,* 1984; *The Dialogic Novels of Malcolm Bradbury and David Lodge,* 1989; and essays on contemporary fiction and literary realism in anthologies and journals.

Editor, with Kathryn Van-Spanckeren, of *John Gardner: Critical Perspectives,* 1982. **Essay:** Renata Adler; Malcolm Bradbury; Tibor Fischer; Janice Galloway; Candia McWilliam; Rohinton Mistry; Lawrence Norfolk; Will Self.

MORDDEL, Anne. Freelance writer. **Essays:** Mervyn Jones; Marilynne Robinson.

MORPURGO, J.E. Emeritus Professor of American Literature, University of Leeds. Author and editor of many books, including *The Pelican History of the United States,* 1955 (third edition 1970); *Master of None: An Autobiography,* 1990; and volumes on Cooper, Lamb, Trelawny, Cobbett, Barnes Wallis, Margery Allingham, the publisher Allen Lane, and on Athens, Venice, and rugby football.

MORRIS, Robert K. Professor of English, City College of the City University of New York. Author of *The Novels of Anthony Powell,* 1968; *The Consolations of Ambiguity: An Essay on the Novels of Anthony Burgess,* 1971; *Continuance and Change: The Contemporary British Novel Sequence,* 1972; and *Paradoxes of Order: Some Perspectives on the Fiction of V.S. Naipaul,* 1975. Editor of *The Achievement of William Styron* (with Irving Malin), 1975 (revised 1981); and *Old Lines, New Forces: Essays on the Contemporary British Novel 1960-1970,* 1976. **Essay:** Anthony Powell.

MUIRHEAD, Eric. Member of the English faculty and Director of Creative Writing, San Jacinto College, Pasadena, Texas. Author of poetry and short stories in journals and anthologies. **Essay:** Daniel Stern.

MURRAY, Heather. Researcher, New Zealand Cultural Studies Centre, University of Otago; co-editor of *Journal of New Zealand Literature;* reviewer and freelance writer. Author of *Double Lives: Women in the Stories of Katherine Mansfield,* 1990. Co-editor of *From the Mainland: An Anthology of South Island Writing,* 1995. **Essay:** Marilyn Duckworth.

MURRAY-SMITH, Stephen. Reader in Education, University of Melbourne. Founding editor of *Overland,* and former editor of *Melbourne Studies in Education.* Author of *Henry Lawson,* 1962 (2nd edition 1975); *Mission to the Islands,* 1979; and *Indirections,* 1981. Editor of *The Tracks We Travel,* 1953; *An Overland Muster,* 1965; *His Natural Life* by Marcus Clarke, 1970; *Classic Australian Short Stories* (with Judah Waten), 1974; and *The Dictionary of Australian Quotations,* 1984.

NARAYAN, Shyamala A. Lecturer in English, Ranchi Women's College, India. Author of *Sudhin N. Ghose,* 1973; *Raja Rao: The Man and His Work,* 1988; and studies of Nissim Ezekiel, Amitav Ghosh, Salman Rushdie, Shashi Tharoor, and other Indian writers; and reviews in *Indian Literature, The Hindu, Journal of Indian Writing in English,* and other periodicals. Compiler of the Indian section of "The Bibliography of Commonwealth Literature" published annually in *Journal of Commonwealth Literature.* **Essays:** Mulk Raj Anand; Sasthi Brata; Shashi Deshpande; Chaman Nahal; Nayantara Sahgal.

NEW, W.H. Professor of English, University of British Columbia, Vancouver; editor of *Canadian Literature.* Author of *Malcolm Lowry,* 1971; *Articulating West,* 1972; *Among Worlds,* 1975;

Malcolm Lowry: A Reference Guide, 1978; *Dreams of Speech and Violence: The Art of the Short Story in Canada and New Zealand,* 1987; and other books and articles. Editor of *A 20th Century Anthology* (with W.E. Messenger), 1984; *Canadian Writers in 1984: The 25th Anniversary of Canadian Life,* 1984; *Canadian Short Fiction,* 1986; *A History of Canadian Literature,* 1989; and general editor of *Literary History of Canada,* vol. 4, 1990. **Essays:** Janet Frame; Zulfikar Ghose; W.O. Mitchell: Orlando Patterson; Randolph Stow; Rudy Wiebe.

NEWMAN, Judie. Lecturer in English, University of Newcastle upon Tyne. Author of *Saul Bellow and History,* 1984; *John Updike,* 1988; and *Nadine Gordimer,* 1988. Editor of *Gred: A Tale of the Great Dismal Swamp* by Harriet Beecher Stowe, 1992. **Essay:** Mary Gordon.

NORRIS, Leslie. Poet and lecturer. Christensen Fellow in the Humanities, Brigham Young University, Salt Lake City. Author of several books of poetry including *Walking the White Fields,* 1980; *Sliding and Other Stories,* 1976; *The Girl from Cardigan: Sixteen Stories,* 1989; and a study of Glyn Jones. Editor of a translation of *The Mabinogion* and of books on Vernon Watkins and Andrew Young; and translator of *The Sonnets of Orpheus* by Rilke (with Alan Keele), 1989. **Essay:** Glyn Jones.

NOWAK, Maril. Lecturer in English, Rochester Institute of Technology and Hobart and William Smith Colleges. **Essay:** Doris Grumbach.

NYE, Robert. See his own entry. **Essay:** Alan Burns.

O'BRIEN, Liam. Freelance writer. **Essay:** Howard Jacobson.

O'HEARN, D.J. Sub-Dean, Faculty of Arts, University of Melbourne. Author of articles on Australian literature; regular fiction reviewer for Melbourne *Age* and Sydney *Australian.* Died 1993. **Essay:** Morris Lurie.

O'LEARY, John. Freelance writer. **Essays:** Ron Hansen; Noel Virtue.

O'TOOLE, Bridget. Teacher and freelance writer. Contributor to *Across a Roaring Hill: The Protestant Imagination in Modern Ireland* edited by Gerald Dawe and Edna Longley, 1985. **Essay:** Rachel Trickett.

OZICK, Cynthia. See her own entry.

PACEY, Desmond. Late Vice-President (Academic), University of New Brunswick, Fredericton. Author of *Frederick Philip Grove,* 1945; *Creative Writing in Canada,* 1952 (revised 1962); *The Picnic and Other Stories,* 1958; *Our Literary Heritage,* 1968; and *Essays in Canadian Criticism,* 1969. Editor of *A Book of Canadian Stories,* 1947; and *Ten Canadian Poets,* 1958. Died 1975. **Essay:** Sinclair Ross.

PAGE, Malcolm. Professor of English, Simon Fraser University, Burnaby, British Columbia. Author of *John Arden,* 1984; *Richard II,* 1987; *Howard's End,* 1993. Editor of the volumes in the Writers on File series on John Arden, Alan Ayckbourn, David Edgar,

Michael Frayn, David Hare, John Osborne, Harold Pinter, Peter Shaffer, and Tom Stoppard. **Essay:** Michael Frayn.

PARISI, Joseph. Editor-in-chief of *Poetry* magazine, Chicago. Author of *Viewers' Guide to "Voices and Visions,"* 1987; and *Marianne Moore: The Art of a Modernist,* 1990. Editor of *The "Poetry" Anthology 1912-1977* (with Daryl Hine), 1978. **Essays:** Janet Burroway; Colin Spencer.

PEHOWSKI, Marian. Freelance writer and critic. Has taught comparative literature or journalism at five universities. **Essays:** Harold Brodkey; Hortense Calisher; Niccoló Tucci.

PERKINS. Barbara M. Managing editor, *Journal of Narrative Technique,* Eastern Michigan University, Ypsilanti. Author of articles in *Harper Handbook to Literature, American Literary Magazines; The Eighteenth and Nineteenth Centuries, The World Book Encyclopedia,* and other books and journals. Editor of *Contemporary American Literature* (with George Perkins); and *Reader's Encyclopedia of American Literature* (with George Perkins and Phil Leininger), 1991. **Essay:** Jerre Mangione.

PERKINS, George. Professor of English, Eastern Michigan University, Ypsilanti. Author or editor of *Writing Clear Prose,* 1964; *Varieties of Prose,* 1966; *The Theory of the American Novel,* 1970; *Realistic American Short Fiction,* 1972; *American Poetic Theory,* 1972; *The Harper Handbook to Literature* (with others), 1985; *The Practical Imagination* (with others), 1987; *Contemporary American Literature* (with Barbara Perkins), 1988; *The American Tradition in Literature* (with others), seventh edition, 1990; and *Reader's Encyclopedia of American Literature* (with Barbara Perkins and Phil Leininger), 1991. **Essay:** Robert Gover.

PHIPPS, Frank T. Former chair of the Department of English, University of Akron, Ohio. **Essay:** Joseph Mitchell.

PIERCY, Marge. See her own entry. **Essays:** E.M. Broner; Joanna Russ.

PILDITCH, Jan. Lecturer in English, University of Waikato, Hamilton, New Zealand. **Essays:** Thomas Pynchon; Peter Tinniswood; Alice Walker.

PINSKER, Sanford. Shadek Humanities Professor, Franklin and Marshall College, Lancaster, Pennsylvania. Author of *The Schlemiel as Metaphor: Studies in the Yiddish and American-Jewish Novel,* 1971; *The Comedy That "Hoits": An Essay on the Fiction of Philip Roth,* 1975; *Still Life and Other Poems,* 1975; *The Languages of Joseph Conrad,* 1978; *Between Two Worlds: The American Novel in the 1960's,* 1978; *Memory Breaks Off and Other Poems,* 1984; *Conversations with Contemporary American Writers,* 1985; *The Uncompromising Fictions of Cynthia Ozick,* 1987; *Bearing the Bad News: Contemporary American Literature and Culture,* 1990; *Jewish-American Fiction, 1917-1987,* 1992; *The Catcher in the Rye: Innocence Under Pressure,* 1993; and many articles on contemporary fiction. Editor of *Critical Essays on Philip Roth,* 1982; and *America and the Holocaust* (with Jack Fischel), 1984. **Essays:** T. Coraghessan Boyle; David Bradley; Bruce Jay Friedman; Johanna Kaplan; Maxine Hong Kingston; Steven Millhauser; Jay Neugeboren; E. Annie Proulx, Jane Smiley.

PORTALES, Marco. Associate Professor of Literature, University of Houston, Clear Lake; associate editor of *MELUS.* Author of *Youth and Age in American Literature,* 1989; and articles on Virginia Woolf, Henry James, Twain, Kate Chopin, Sarah Orne Jewett, Chicano and Native American writers, and other subjects. **Essay:** Rudolfo A. Anaya.

PORTER, Hal. Fiction writer, poet, and playwright. Author of three novels (*A Handful of Pennies, The Tilted Cross, The Right Thing*); several collections of short stories (*Selected Stories,* 1971); four plays; three books of poetry; three volumes of autobiography; and other non-fiction; a general selection, *Hal Porter,* was published in 1980. Died 1984.

POVEY, John. Teacher of English as a second language and applied linguistics, Los Angeles, California. Editor of *A Sociolinguistic Profile of Urban Centers in Cameroon* (with others), 1983. **Essays:** Chinua Achebe; Cyprian Ekwensi; Miriam Tlali.

POWELL, Anthony. See his own entry.

POYNTING, Jeremy. Lecturer, Thomas Danby College, Leeds. Author of articles in *Journal of Commonwealth Literature, Journal of South Asian Literature, World Literature Written in English, Kyk-over-Al,* and other periodicals. **Essays:** Michael Anthony; Ralph de Boissière; Andrew Salkey.

PRICE, Joanna. Lecturer, Liverpool John Moores University. **Essay:** Bret Easton Ellis; A.L. Kennedy.

PYKETT, Lyn. Senior lecturer in English, University College of Wales, Aberystwyth. Author of *Emily Brontë,* 1989; and of articles on contemporary fiction in *Critical Quarterly, New Welsh Review,* and *Watching the Detectives* edited by Ian A. Bell and Graham Daldry, 1990. **Essays:** Anita Brookner; Penelope Lively; Marge Piercy; Jeanette Winterson.

QUIGLY, Isabel. Freelance writer and critic. Author of the novel *The Eye of Heaven,* 1955; *The Heirs of Tom Brown: The English School Story,* 1982; a book on Charlie Chaplin; and many articles and reviews in *The Times, The Guardian,* and other periodicals. Editor, with Susan Hill, of *New Stories 5,* 1980. Translator of works of European fiction and non-fiction. **Essays:** Lettice Cooper; Winston Graham.

RAVENSCROFT, Arthur. Late Senior Lecturer in English, University of Leeds; founding editor, *Journal of Commonwealth Literature,* 1965-79. Author of *Chinua Achebe,* 1969 (revised 1977); *Nigerian Writers and the African Past,* 1978; *A Guide to Twentieth-Century English, Irish and Commonwealth Literature* (with Harry Blamires and Peter Quartermain), 1983; and "Teaching Words" in *African Literature,* 1986. Translator, with C.K. Johnman, of *Journal of Jan van Riebeeck,* vol. 3, 1958. Died 1989. **Essays:** T.M. Aluko; I.N.C. Aniebo; Ahmed Essop; John Munonye; Ngugi wa Thiong'o.

RAY, Sandra. Novelist and freelance writer. **Essays:** Louis Auchincloss; Alice Hoffman; Alan Sillitoe.

REID, J.C. Late professor of English, University of Auckland. Author of *The Mind and Art of Coventry Patmore,* 1957; *Francis*

Thompson, Man and Poet, 1959; *Thomas Hood,* 1963; and *Bucks and Bruisers: Pierce Egan and Regency England,* 1971. Died 1972. **Essay:** Errol Brathwaite.

REILLY, John M. Professor of English, State University of New York, Albany. Author of many articles on African-American literature, popular crime writing, and social fiction, and bibliographical essays in *Black American Writers,* 1978; and *American Literary Scholarship.* Editor of *Richard Wright: The Critical Reception,* 1978; and the reference book *Twentieth-Century Crime and Mystery Writers,* 1980 (2nd edition 1985). **Essays:** Cyrus Colter; Kristin Hunter; Paule Marshall; Peter Matthiessen; Al Young.

REXROTH, Kenneth. Poet and critic; lecturer at the University of California, Santa Barbara. Author of many books of verse (including *The Morning Star,* 1979); plays (*Beyond the Mountains,* 1951); and non-fiction (including *The Elastic Retort,* 1973; and *Communalism,* 1975). Editor of several collections of poetry and translator of works by Asian, European, and classical authors. Died 1982.

RHODES, H. Winston. Late professor of English, University of Canterbury, Christchurch, New Zealand. Co-founder of *Tomorrow* and *New Zealand Monthly Review.* Author of *New Zealand Fiction since 1945,* 1968; *Frank Surgeson,* 1969; *New Zealand Novels,* 1969; *Frederick Sinclaire: A Memoir,* 1984; and other books. Editor of six volumes of Rewi Alley's prose and poetry and *I Saw in My Dream* by Sargeson, 1976. Died 1987. **Essays:** Noel Hilliard; Witi Ihimaera; O.E. Middleton; Bill Pearson; Albert Wendt.

RIACH, Alan. Senior lecturer in English, University of Waikato, Hamilton, New Zealand. Author of three collections of poetry (*The Folding Map,* 1990; *An Open Return,* 1991); and *Hugh MacDiarmid's Epic Poetry,* 1991. Editor of *The Radical Imagination: Lectures and Talks* by Wilson Harris; *Selected Poems* and *Selected Prose* by Hugh MacDiarmid; and general editor of *Collected Works* by Hugh MacDiarmid. **Essays:** Wilson Harris; Ben Okri; Ian Wedde.

ROBERTSON, Karen. Visiting assistant professor of English, Vassar College, Poughkeepsie, New York. Author of articles on Renaissance revenge tragedy. Editor of the forthcoming books *Sexuality and Politics in Renaissance Drama* (with Carole Levin) and John Pikeryng's *Horestes* (with Jodi George). **Essay:** Maeve Binchy.

ROSE, Marilyn. Associate professor, Department of English, and Director, Canadian Studies Program, Brock University, St. Catharines, Ontario. Author of various articles, papers, and encyclopedia entries on Canadian fiction and poetry, as well as a number of papers on Canadian detective fiction. **Essay:** Peter Robinson.

ROSS, Alan. Editor of *London Magazine* and managing director of London Magazine Editions. Author of several books of poetry, including *Death Valley,* 1980; and of critical works, travel books, and books for children. Editor of works by John Gay and Lawrence Durrell and of several anthologies. Translator of four French works.

ROSSET, Barney. Former President of Grove Press, Inc. Editor of *Evergreen Review Reader 1 and 2,* 1979.

ROWLAND, S.A. Freelance writer. **Essays:** Robertson Davies; Michèle Roberts; Colin Thubron.

ROYLE, Trevor. Freelance writer and broadcaster; literary editor of *Scotland on Sunday.* Author of *We'll Support You Ever More: The Impertinent Saga of Scottish Fitba',* with Ian Archer, 1976; *Jock Tamson's Bairns: Essays on a Scots Childhood,* 1977; *Precipitous City: The Story of Literary Edinburgh,* 1980; *Death Before Dishonour: The True Story of Fighting Mac,* 1982; *The Macmillan Companion to Scottish Literature,* 1983; *James and Jim: The Biography of James Kennaway,* 1983; *The Kitchener Enigma,* 1985; *The Best Years of Their Lives: The National Service Experience 1945- 63,* 1986; *War Report: The War Correspondent's View of Battle from the Crimea to the Falklands,* 1987; *The Last Days of the Raj,* 1989; *Anatomy of a Regiment,* 1990; and *In Flanders Fields: Scottish Poetry and Prose of the First World War,* 1991; and many articles in journals. Editor of *A Dictionary of Military Quotations,* 1990. **Essays:** Richard Adams; Stan Barstow; Nina Bawden; George Mackay Brown; Jonathan Coe; Ronald Frame; Brian Glanville; Giles Gordon; Alasdair Gray; Clifford Haney; Hammond Innes; Robin Jenkins; Benedict Kiely; Allan Massie; Robert Nye; Charles Palliser; James Plunkett; Iain Crichton Smith.

RUBIN, Louis D., Jr. Professor of English, University of North Carolina, Chapel Hill; general editor, Southern Literary Studies series; co-editor, *Southern Literary Journal.* Author and editor of many books, including the novel *The Golden Weather,* 1961; and *William Elliott Shoots a Bear,* 1975; *The Wary Fugitives: Four Poets and the South,* 1978; *The American South: Portrait of a Culture,* 1979; *The Even-Tempered Angler,* 1983; *A Gallery of Southerners,* 1984; *The Literary South,* 1986; *An Apple for My Teacher,* 1987; and *The Edge of the Swamp,* 1989. **Essay:** William Styron.

SADLER, Geoff. Assistant Librarian, Local Studies, Chesterfield. Derbyshire. Author of western novels (as Jeff Sadler), including, most recently *Hangrope Journey,* 1994; and (as Wes Calhoun) *Sierra Trail,* 1993; the *Justus* trilogy of planation novels (as Geoffrey Sadler), 1982; a 5-volume history of Chesterfield librarians 1879-1944; *Around Shirebrook,* 1994; and *Journey to Freedom* (with Antoni Snarski), 1990. Editor of the reference book *Twentieth-Century Western Writers,* 2nd edition, 1991. **Essays:** Rachel Billington; Clare Boylan; Desmond Hogan; David Plante; David Pownall; Rose Tremain.

SAMBROOK, Hana. Freelance editor and writer. Author of study guides to *The Tenant of Wildfell Hall, Lark Rise to Candleford, Victory, My Family and Other Animals,* and *Sylvia Plath: Selected Works.* **Essays:** Janice Elliott; Margaret Forster; Hilary Mantel; Bernice Rubens.

SANDERS, David. Emeritus professor of English, Harvey Mudd College, Claremont, California. Author of *John Hersey,* 1967; *John Dos Passos: A Comprehensive Bibliography,* 1987; *John Hersey, Revisited,* 1990. **Essays:** Vance Bourjaily; Joseph Heller.

SANDERSON, Stewart. Honorary Harold Orton Fellow, University of Leeds, now retired; former chair of the Literature Committee, Scottish Arts Council. Author of *Ernest Hemingway,* 1961 (revised 1970); and of many articles on British and comparative folklore and ethnology, and on modern literature. Editor of *The Se-*

cret Common-Wealth by Robert Kirk, 1976; *The Linguistic Atlas of England* (with others), 1978; *Studies in Linguistic Geography,* 1985; and *World Maps: A Dialect Atlas of England,* 1987. **Essays:** Dorothy Dunnett; Gerald Hanley; Simon Raven; John Updike.

SCHAFER, William J. Professor of English, Berea College, Kentucky. Author of articles on David Wagoner, Mark Harris, and Ralph Ellison in *Critique* and *Satire Newsletter.* Editor of *The William Nelson Reader,* 1989. **Essays:** Elliott Baker; Stephen Becker; David Benedictus; Thomas Berger; Harry Crews; Nell Dunn; David Ely; Mark Harris; James A. McPherson; Reynolds Price; Mario Puzo; Ishmael Reed; Wilfrid Sheed; Clancy Sigal; Paul Theroux; David Wagoner.

SCHORER, Mark. Late professor of English, University of California, Berkeley. Author of three novels, three collections of short stories, and several critical works, including studies of Blake, Lawrence, and Sinclair Lewis. Editor of anthologies of fiction and literary criticism and of works by Capote and Lawrence. Died 1977.

SCHRECENGOST, Lynda D. Freelance writer and editor. **Essays:** Boman Desai; Kelvin Christopher James; Ursula K. Le Guin; May Sarton; Albert Wendt.

SCOTT, Alexander. Formerly reader in Scottish literature, University of Glasgow. Author of many books of verse, including *Poems in Scots,* 1978; plays; a biography of William Soutar; and *The MacDiarmid Makars 1923-1972,* 1972. Editor of works by William Jeffrey, Alexander Scott (1530-1584), and Soutar, and of anthologies of Scottish poetry. **Essay:** Naomi Mitchison.

SEMMLER, Clement. Consulting editor, *Poetry Australia;* formerly director-general Australian Broadcasting Corporation. Author or editor of *For the Uncanny Man: Essays,* 1963; *The Banjo in the Bush,* 1966; *Twentieth-Century Australian Literary Criticism,* 1967; *Douglas Stewart,* 1974; *The ABC—Aunt Sahv and Sacred Cow,* 1981; *The War Diaries of Kenneth Slessor,* 1985; and *Pictures on the Margin: Memoria,* 1991. **Essay:** Geoffrey Dutton.

SEMPLE, Linda. Writer, and owner of Silver Moon Women's Bookshop, London. Author of *A Suitable Job for a Woman: Women Mystery Writers,* 1990; and many articles and reviews on women writers. **Essay:** Rita Mae Brown.

SHUCARD, Alan R. Professor of English, University of Wisconsin-Parkside, Kenosha. General editor of the English Section of Twayne's Critical History of Poetry series. Author of three books on poetry, a study of Countee Cullen, 1984; *American Poetry: The Puritans Through Walt Whitman,* 1988; and *Modern American Poetry, 1865-1950* (with Fred Moramarco and William Sullivan), 1989; as well as numerous articles on American poetry and fiction. **Essays:** Edith Pargeter; Kathrin Perutz.

SHUTTLETON, David. Lecturer in English, University College of Wales, Aberystwyth. **Essay:** Molly Keane.

SMALLMAN, Victoria A. Doctoral candidate at McMaster University, Hamilton, Ontario. **Essay:** Patrick McCabe.

SMITH, Angela. Director, Centre of Commonwealth Studies, University of Stirling, Scotland. Author of *East African Writing in*

English, 1989; the chapter on writing in Mauritius in *The Writing of East and Central Africa* edited by G.D. Killam, 1985; and of study guides to *Wuthering Heights, Persuasion,* and *Voss.* **Essays:** Ayi Kwei Armah; Nuruddin Farah.

SMITH, Christopher. Senior Lecturer, School of Modern Languages and European History, University of East Anglia, Norwich; editor of *Seventeenth-Century French Studies.* Author of *Alabaster, Bikinis and Calvados: An ABC of Toponymous Words,* 1985; *Jean Anouilh: Life, Work, Criticism,* 1985; and many articles and reviews of the performing arts. Editor of works by Antoine de Montchrestien, Jean de la Taille, and Pierre Matthieu. **Essays:** Buchi Emecheta; Julian Gloag; Peter Vansittart.

SMITH, Curtis C. Professor of Humanities, University of Houston, Clear Lake. Author of *Olaf Stapledon: A Bibliography* (with Harvey J. Satty), 1984. Editor of the reference book *Twentieth-Century Science-Fiction Writers,* 1981 (2nd edition, 1986). **Essays:** Arthur C. Clarke; Ursula K. LeGuin.

SOLOMON, Andy. Professor of English, University of Tampa.; fiction editor of *The Tampa Review;* regular book critic for the *New York Times, Washington Post, Chicago Tribune, Boston Globe, Los Angeles Times, San Francisco Chronicle, Miami Herald,* and *St. Petersburg Times*; book commentator and essayist on National Public Radio. Author of fiction, poetry, and articles in the *Atlantic, Boulevard,* and *New Orleans Review.* **Essays:** Madison Smartt Bell; Mary Lee Settle.

SOLOMON, Eric. Professor of English, San Francisco State University. Author of *Stephen Crane in England,* 1963; *Stephen Crane: From Parody to Realism,* 1966; and many articles on 19th- and 20th-century British and American fiction. Editor of *The Faded Banners,* 1960; and *The Critic Agonistes,* 1985. **Essay:** Albert Guerard.

STEDMAN, Jane W. Emeritus professor of English, Roosevelt University, Chicago. Author of *W.S. Gilbert: A Classic Victorian and His Theatre,* 1995; and poems, articles, and reviews in anthologies of Victorian studies, scholarly journals, literary periodicals, and *Opera News.* Editor of *Gilbert Before Sullivan: Six Comic Plays,* 1967. **Essays:** P.D. James; Ira Levin; Anne Perry.

STEEMSON, Caroline. Tutor in women's studies and women's history, University of Waikato, Hamilton, New Zealand. **Essay:** Sue McCauley.

STERN, Carol Simpson. Dean of the Graduate School and Professor in the Department of Performance Studies, Northwestern University, Evanston, Illinois. Author of *Performance: Text and Contexts* (with Bruce Henderson), 1993; a chapter in *New Directions in Higher Education,* 1995; and of articles, book reviews, and critical essays on contemporary writers for reference works. **Essays:** A. Alvarez; Elizabeth Hardwick; Doris Lessing; Charles Newman; Joyce Carol Oates; Judith Rossner.

STEVENS, James R. Master, Confederation College, Thunder Bay, Ontario. Author of *Sacred Legends of the Sandy Lake Cree,* 1971; *Paddy Wilson's Gold Fever,* 1976; *Legends from the Forest,* 1985; and *Killing the Shamen,* 1985. **Essay:** Fred Bodsworth.

STEVENS, Joan. Professor of English, Victoria University,

Wellington; now retired. Author of *The New Zealand Novel 1860-1965*, 1966; *New Zealand Short Stories: A Survey*, 1968; and articles on the Brontës, Thackeray, and Dickens. Editor of *Mary Taylor, Friend of Charlotte Brontë: Letters from New Zealand and Elsewhere*, 1972; and *The London Journal of Edward Jermingham Wakefield 1845-46*, 1972. Died. **Essay:** Ian Cross.

STONEHILL, Brian. Associate professor of English, Pomona College, Claremont, California; formerly fiction editor for the Chicago *Review*. Author of *The Self-Conscious Novel: Artifice in Fiction from Joyce to Pynchon*, 1988; and articles and reviews for the Los Angeles *Times* and the *Washington Post*. **Essays:** Jim Crace; Harry Mathews; Joseph McElroy.

STRANDBERG, Victor. Professor of English, Duke University, Durham, North Carolina. Author of *A Colder Fire: The Poetry of Robert Penn Warren*, 1965; *The Poetic Vision of Robert Penn Warren*, 1977; *A Faulkner Overview: Six Perspectives*, 1981; *Religious Psychology in American Literature: A Study in the Relevance of William James*, 1981; and "The Art of Cynthia Ozick" in *Texas Studies in Literature and Language*, Summer 1983. **Essay:** Cynthia Ozick.

STRUTHERS, J.R. Faculty member, Department of English, University of Guelph. Author of numerous articles in books and periodicals, including essays, interviews, and bibliographies of Hugh Hood and Alice Munro. Editor of *Before the Flood: Our Exagmination round His Factification for Incamination of Hugh Hood's Work in Progress*, 1979; *The Montreal Story Tellers*, 1985; *Origins*, 1985; *New Directions from Old*, 1991; *The Possibilities of Story*, 2 vols., 1992; *Canadian Classics* (with John Metcalf), 1993; and *How Stories Mean* (with John Metcalf), 1993. **Essays:** Jack Hodgins; Hugh Hood; Alice Munro.

STUCKEY, W.J. Professor of English, Purdue University, Lafayette, Indiana; founding editor of *Minnesota Review*, acting editor of *Modern Fiction Studies*, and associate editor of *Journal of Narrative Technique*. Author of *Pulitzer Prize Novels*, 1966 (revised 1980); and *Caroline Gordon*, 1972. **Essay:** Frank Tuohy.

SULLIVAN, Maggi R. Lecturer in English, Finger Lakes Community College, Canandaigua, New York; freelance writer. Editor of a two-volume series on local history. **Essay:** Allan Gurganis.

SUMMERS, Judith. Freelance writer. Author of two novels (*Dear Sister*, 1985; and *I, Gloria Gold*, 1988); and of *Soho: A History of London's Most Colourful Neighbourhood*, 1989. **Essay:** Zoë Fairbairns.

SUTHERLAND, Fraser. Freelance writer; managing editor of *Books in Canada* magazine. Author of several books, including *The Style of Innocence: A Study of Hemingway and Callaghan*, 1972; *Madwomen* (poetry), 1978; *John Glassco: An Essay and Bibliography*, 1984; *Whitefaces* (poetry), 1986; *The History of Canadian Magazines*, 1988; and of fiction, poetry, and criticism in journals and anthologies. **Essays:** Douglas Glover; M.T. Kelly.

SUTHERLAND, John. Professor of English, California Institute of Technology, Pasadena. Author of *Fiction and the Fiction Industry*, 1978; *Bestsellers: Popular Fiction of the 1970's*, 1980; *Offensive Literature: Decensorship in Britain*, 1982; *The Longman*

Companion to Victorian Fiction, 1988 (as *The Sanford Companion to Victorian Fiction*, 1989); and *Mrs. Humphry Ward: Eminent Victorian, Pre-eminent Edwardian*, 1990. Editor of works by Jack London, Thackeray, and Trollope. **Essay:** Tom Sharpe.

SYKES, Arlene. Senior Lecturer in English, University of Queensland, Brisbane. Formerly editor in the Drama Department, Australian Broadcasting Commission. Author of *Harold Pinter*, 1970; and of articles on modern drama and Australian fiction. Editor of *Five Plays for Radio* and four other anthologies of Australian plays. **Essay:** Jessica Anderson.

TANNER, Tony. Reader in English, King's College, Cambridge. Author of books on Conrad and Bellow and of *The Reign of Wonder: Naivety and Reality in American Literature*, 1965; *City of Words: American Fiction 1950-1970*, 1971; *Adultery in the Novel*, 1980; *Thomas Pynchon*, 1982; *Henry James: The Writer and His Work*, 1985; *Jane Austen*, 1986; and *Scenes of Nature, Signs of Men*, 1987. Editor of works by Jane Austen, Henry James, and Herman Melville, and of a collection of essays on James.

TAYLOR, Anna-Marie. Lecturer in drama, University of Wales, Swansea; freelance theatre critic. Author of numerous articles on contemporary literature and European drama. **Essays:** Kazuo Ishiguro; Alison Lurie.

THOMAS, Roy. Lecturer in Education, University College of Swansea, Wales; now retired. Author of *How to Read a Poem*, 1961; and *The Ruby Wine Man* (as Roy Heath), 1964. **Essay:** Gwyn Jones.

TIFFIN, Chris. Senior Lecturer in English, University of Queensland, Brisbane. Author of articles on Australian and Pacific literatures. Editor of *South Pacific Images*, 1978; *South Pacific Stories* (with H.M. Tiffin), 1980; and *Rosa Praed, 1851-1935: A Bibliography*, 1989. **Essays:** Helen Garner; Colin Johnson.

TIFFIN, H.M. Professor of English, University of Queensland, Brisbane. Author of *The Empire Writes Back: Theory and Practice in Post-Colonial Literatures* (with Bill Ashcroft and Gareth Griffiths), 1989; and *De-Colonixing Fictions* (with Diane Brydon), 1993; and articles on Australian and post-colonial literatures. Editor of *After Europe: Critical Teory and Post-Colonial Writing* (with Stephen Slemon), 1989; *Past the Last Post: Theorizing Post-Colonialism and Post-Modernism* (with Ian Adam), 1991; and *Re-Siting Queen's English: Text and Tradition in Post-Colonial Literatures* (with Gillian Whitlock), 1992. **Essay:** J.M. Coetzee.

TOOMEY, Philippa. Staff member, *The Times*, London. Regular reviewer for *The Times, The Tablet, Home and Country*, and other periodicals. **Essay:** Alice Thomas Ellis.

TOULSON, Shirley. Poet and freelance writer. Author of several books of poems, and of guidebooks and studies of rural history, regional folklore, and Celtic history, most recently *The Celtic Alternative*, 1987; *Walking Round Wales*, 1988; and *The Companion Guide to Devon*, 1991. **Essays:** Christine Brooke-Rose; David Hughes; Bernard Kops; Stanley Middleton.

TREDELL, Nicolas. Author of *The Novels of Colin Wilson*, 1982; *Uncancelled Challenge: The Work of Raymond Williams*, 1990; *The*

Critical Decade: Culture in Crisis, 1993; *Conversations with Critics,* 1994; *Caute's Confrontations: The Novels of David Caute,* 1994; and numerous critical essays in books and periodicals. **Essays:** Louis de Bernières; David Caute; Terry Pratchett; Robert Silverberg; Barry Unsworth.

TRUESDALE, C.W. Poet, short story writer, and essayist; founding editor and publisher of *New Rivers Press.* **Essay:** Jon Hassler.

TUERK, Richard. Professor of Literature and Languages, East Texas State University, Commerce. Author of *Central Still: Circle and Sphere in Thoreau's Prose,* 1975; and essays on Jewish-American literature, Emerson, Jacob Riis, and Twain. **Essays:** John Barth; Hugh Nissenson; Leon Uris.

TURNER, Roland. Freelance writer; former editor of the reference book *The Grants Register.* **Essay:** Emanuel Litvinoff.

UNDERWOOD, Susan O'Dell. Instructor of Appalachian and American literature, Carson-Newman College, Jefferson City, Tennessee. Author of several works of poetry, fiction, and literary criticism. **Essay:** Fred Chappell.

van de KAMP, Peter G.W. Lecturer in English, University College, Dublin. Author of *Flann O'Brien: An Illustrated Biography* (with Peter Costello), 1987; and articles on Anglo-Irish literature in *The Crane Bag* and *Yeats Annual.* **Essays:** John Banville; Aidan Higgins.

van TOORN, Penny. Postdoctoral research fellow, Department of English, University of Sydney. Author of *Rudy Wiebe and the Historicity of the Word,* 1995; and articles on postcolonial literatures and theory. Co-editor of *Speaking Positions: Aboriginality, Gender and Ethnicity in Australian Cultural Studies,* 1995. **Essay:** Neil Bissoondath; Rudy Wiebe.

VASUDEVAN, Aruna. Freelance writer. **Essay:** Mary Wesley.

VOGLER, Thomas A. Professor of English and Comparative Literature, and Chair of the Humanities Institute, University of California, Santa Cruz. Author of *Preludes to Vision,* 1970; *Unnam'd Forms: Blake and Textuality* (with Nelson Hilton), 1986; and numerous essays on poetry and fiction of the 18th to 20th centuries. **Essays:** Kathy Acker; William Gibson; Ken Kesey.

WALSH, William. Emeritus Professor of Commonwealth literature, University of Leeds. Author of *The Use of Imagination: Educational Thought and the Literary Mind,* 1959; *A Human Idiom: Literature and Humanity,* 1964; *Coleridge: The Work and the Relevance,* 1967; *A Manifold Voice: Studies in Commonwealth Literature,* 1970; *R. K. Narayan,* 1971; *Commonwealth Literature,* 1973; *V.S. Naipaul,* 1973; *D.J. Enright: Poet of Humanism,* 1974; *Patrick White's Fiction,* 1977; *F.R. Leavis,* 1980; *R.K. Narayan: A Critical Appreciation,* 1982; and *Indian Literature in English,* 1990. Editor of *Readings in Commonwealth Literature,* 1974. **Essay:** Kamala Markandaya.

WARNER, Val. Freelance writer. Author of two books of poetry (*Under the Penthouse,* 1973; and *Before Lunch,* 1986); and short stories, articles, and reviews in periodicals. Editor of *Charlotte Mew: Collected Poems and Prose,* 1981. Translator of *Centenary*

Corbière, 1974. **Essays:** Beryl Bainbridge; Caroline Blackwood; Philip Callow; Isobel English; Elaine Feinstein; Francis King; Adam Mars-Jones; Elizabeth Mavor; Julia O'Faolain; Grace Paley; Fay Weldon.

WATSON, Diane. Lecturer in English, University of British Columbia, Vancouver. **Essays:** John Berger; Louise Erdrich; Michael Ondaatje.

WATTS, Harold H. Emeritus professor of English, Purdue University, West Lafayette, Indiana. Author of *The Modern Reader's Guide to the Bible,* 1949; *Ezra Pound and the Cantos,* 1951; *Hound and Quarry,* 1953; *The Modern Reader's Guide to Religions,* 1964; and *Aldous Huxley,* 1969. **Essays:** Alice Adams; Frederick Buechner; Herbert Gold; William Maxwell; P.H. Newby; Harry Mark Petrakis; J.D. Salinger; Helen Yglesias.

WEIGEL, John A. Professor of English, Miami University, Oxford, Ohio. Author of *Lawrence Durrell,* 1965 (revised 1989); *Colin Wilson,* 1975; *B.F. Skinner,* 1977; and *Patrick White,* 1984. **Essay:** Colin Wilson.

WELDON, Fay. See her own entry.

WESTBROOK, Perry D., Emeritus Professor of English, State University of New York, Albany. Author of *Acres of Flint: Writers of Rural New England,* 1951; *Biography of an Island,* 1958; *The Greatness of Man: An Essay on Dostoevsky and Whitman,* 1961; *Mary Ellen Chase,* 1966; *Mary Wilkins Freeman,* 1967; *John Burroughs,* 1974; *William Bradford,* 1978. *Free Will and Determinism in American Literature,* 1979; *The New England Town in Fact and Fiction,* 1982; and *A Literary History of New England,* 1988. **Essays:** G.V. Desani; Raja Rao; Kurt Vonnegut, Jr.

WILLIAMS, Mark. Lecturer in English, University of Waikato, Hamilton, New Zealand. Editor of *New Zealand Poetry 1972-86,* 1987.

WILLY, Margaret. Lecturer for the British Council, and at the City Literary Institute and Morley College, London. Author of two books of poetry (*The Invisible Sun,* 1946; and *Every Star a Tongue,* 1951); and several critical books, including studies of Chaucer, Traherne, Fielding, Browning, Crashaw, Vaughan, Emily Brontë, and English diarists. Editor of two anthologies and of plays by Goldsmith. **Essays:** Susan Hill; Muriel Spark.

WILSON, Janet. Faculty member, Department of English, University of Otago. **Essays:** Russell Haley; Fiona Kidman; Vincent O'Sullivan.

WITHERUP, Bill. Freelance book reviewer and critic. Author of two collections of poetry (*Black Ash, Orange Fire* and *Men at Work*). Contributing editor to *Atomic Ghosts: Poets Respond to the Nuclear Age,* 1995. **Essay:** James B. Hall.

WOOD, Michael. Professor of English, University of Exeter, Devon. Author of *Stendhal,* 1971; and *America in the Movies,* 1975; and articles in *New York Review of Books, London Review of Books,* and other periodicals.

WOODCOCK, George. Freelance writer, lecturer, and editor. Author of poetry (*Collected Poems,* 1983); plays; travel books; biographies; autobiographies (*Letter to the Past,* 1982; and *Beyond the Blue Mountains,* 1987); and works on history and politics; critical works include *William Godwin,* 1946; *The Incomparable Aphra,* 1948; *The Paradox of Oscar Wilde,* 1949; *The Crystal Spirit* (on Orwell), 1966; *Hugh MacLennan,* 1969; *Odysseus Ever Returning: Canadian Writers and Writing,* 1970; *Mordecai Richler,* 1970; *Dawn and the Darkest Hour* (on Aldous Huxley), 1972; *Herbert Read,* 1972; *Thomas Merton,* 1978; *The World of Canadian Writers,* 1980; *Northern Spring: The Flowering of Canadian Literature,* 1987; *A Social History of Canada,* 1988; and *The Century That Made Us: Canada 1814-1914,* 1989. Editor of anthologies and of works by Charles Lamb, Malcolm Lowry, Wyndham Lewis, Hardy, Meredith, and others. Died 1995. **Essays:** Leonard Cohen; Timothy Findley; Jack Hodgins; Mordecai Richler; Audrey Thomas; David Watmough.

WOODS, Tim. Lecturer in English, University College of Wales, Aberystwyth. **Essays:** Patrick McGrath; David Profumo.

WOOLF, Michael. Director of the Council on International Education Exchange, London. Author of "Exploding the Genre: The Crime Fiction of Jerome Charyn," in *American Crime Fiction,* 1988. **Essay:** Jerome Charyn.

YABES, Leopoldo Y. Late professor Emeritus of Literature and Philippine Studies, University of the Philippines, Quezon City. Author of more than 20 books and numerous essays and articles; books include *The University and the Fear of Ideas,* 1956; *Philippine Literature in English,* 1958; *The Filipino Struggle for Intellectual Freedon,* 1959; *Jose Rizal on His Centenary,* 1963; *The Ordeal of a Man of Academe,* 1967; and *Graduate Education at the University of the Philippines,* 1975. Editor of many books, including *Philippine Short Stories,* 2 vols., 1975-81. Former editor of *Philippine Social Sciences and Humanities Review.* Died 1988. **Essay:** F. Sionil Jose.

ZWICKER, Heather. Faculty member, Department of English, University of Alberta, Edmonton. **Essay:** Daphne Marlatt.

ISBN 1-55862-189-X